PRENTICE-HALL'S
GREAT INTERNATIONAL ATLAS

Prentice-Hall's
GREAT

INTERNATIONAL ATLAS

PRENTICE-HALL, INC.
ENGLEWOOD CLIFFS, NEW JERSEY

CARTOGRAPHIC CONSULTANTS

Harold M. Mayer, Ph.D.
Professor of Geography,
University of Wisconsin — Milwaukee
Roman Drazniowsky, Ph.D.
Curator, American Geographical Society Collection,
University of Wisconsin — Milwaukee
James John Flannery, Ph.D.
Associate Professor of Geography,
University of Wisconsin — Milwaukee
Donald G. Temple, M.S.
Chief Cartographer,
University of Wisconsin — Milwaukee
Harold Fullard, M.Sc.
London, England

Library of Congress Number: 81-81362
ISBN 0-13-695-833-8
1234567890 8584838281
Printed and bound in the United States of America

Trade edition published by Prentice-Hall, Inc., 1981

TABLE OF CONTENTS

OVERVIEW

x-xvi Climate and Population Statistics
xvii-xxxii How To Use an Atlas
1-96 World Reference Information
1-144 Physical and Political Maps
145-160 Thematic Maps
161-176 Economic Statistics by Country
Index

WORLD REFERENCE INFORMATION

1 The Beginnings of Civilization
2-3 The Growth of Civilization
4-5 Mesopotamia
6-7 Ancient Egypt
8-9 The Fertile Crescent and the Mediterranean
10-11 The Fertile Crescent and the Middle East
12 Minoan Crete
13 Mycenaean Greece
14-15 The Rise of Greece
16 Alexander the Great
17 The Etruscans
18-19 The Roman Empire
20 The Indus Valley
21 India
22-23 China
24 Pre-Columbian America
25 The World As Known to the Ancients
26-27 Expanding Knowledge of the World
28-29 Expansion From the Ancient World
30 The Norsemen
31 Travelers in Asia
32-33 The Great Age of Discovery I
34-35 The Great Age of Discovery II
36-37 The Great Age of Discovery III
38 The Great Age of Discovery IV
39 Expansion in Northeast Asia and South America
40-41 North America
42 The Pacific
43 Australia and New Zealand
44-45 Africa
46 Scientific Exploration in South America and Asia
47 Polar Exploration
48 High Mountains, Ocean Depths and Space
49 Chart of the Stars
50-51 The Solar System
52 The Earth
53 The Moon
54-55 Time
56-57 The Atmosphere and Clouds
58-59 Climate and Weather
60-61 The Earth from Space
62-63 The Evolution of the Continents
64-65 The Unstable Earth
66-67 The Making of Landscape
68-69 The Earth: Physical Dimensions
70-71 Distances
72-73 Water Resources and Vegetation
74-75 Population
76 Language
77 Religion
78-79 The Growth of Cities
80-81 Food Resources: Vegetable
82 Food Resources: Animal
83 Nutrition
84-85 Mineral Resources I
86-87 Mineral Resources II
88-89 Fuel and Energy
90 Occupations
91 Industry
92-93 Transport
94-95 Trade
96 Wealth

MAPS

The World

1 **Map Key**

2-3 **The World: Physical 1:80 Million**

4-5 **The World: Political 1:64M**

Europe

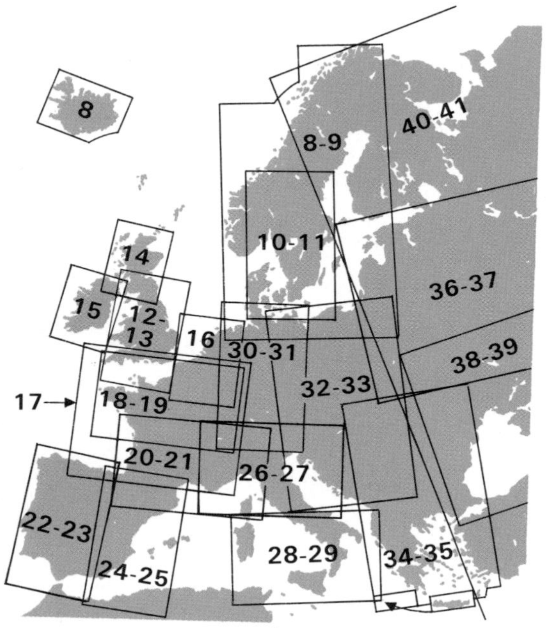

8
8-9
40-41
10-11
14
15
12-13
16
30-31
36-37
38-39
17
18-19
32-33
20-21
26-27
22-23
24-25
28-29
34-35

6 **Europe: Physical 1:16M**

7 **Europe: Political 1:16M**

8-9 **Scandinavia and the Baltic Lands 1:4M**
***Iceland* 1:4M**

10-11 **Denmark and Southern Sweden 1:2M**

12-13 **England and Wales 1:1.6M**
***Scilly Isles* 1:1.6M**

14 **Scotland 1:1.6M**
***Orkney Is.* and *Shetland Is.* 1:1.6M**

15 **Ireland 1:1.6M**

16 **The Netherlands, Belgium and Luxembourg 1:2M**

17 **France: Departments 1:4M**
***Paris Region* 1:2M**

18-19 **Northern France 1:2M**

20-21 **Southern France 1:2M**

22-23 **Western Spain and Portugal 1:2M**

24-25 **Eastern Spain 1:2M**

26-27 **Northern Italy and Western Yugoslavia 1:2M**

28-29 **Southern Italy 1:2M**

30-31 **Germany and Switzerland 1:2M**

32-33 **Central Europe 1:2.8M**

34-35 **The Balkans 1:2.8M**

36-37 **European Russia — Central 1:4M**

38-39 **European Russia — South 1:4M**

40-41 **Union of Soviet Socialist Republics 1:16M**

Asia

42 Asia: Physical 1:40M

43 Asia: Political 1:40M

44 Israel and West Jordan 1:8M

45 Arabia and the Horn of Africa 1:12M

46-47 The Near and Middle East 1:8M

48-49 Indo-Gangetic Plain 1:4.8M
Jammu and Kashmir 1:4.8M

50-51 Southern India and Sri Lanka 1:4.8M

52 Bangladesh, North-East India and Burma 1:4.8M

53 The Indian Ocean 1:40M

54-55 Mainland South-East Asia 1:4.8M

56-57 The East Indies 1:10M
Java and Madura 1:6M

58-59 Southern China 1:4.8M

60-61 Northern China and Korea 1:4.8M

62 China 1:16M

63 Japan 1:6M
Ryukyu Islands 1:6M

64-65 Southern Japan 1:2M

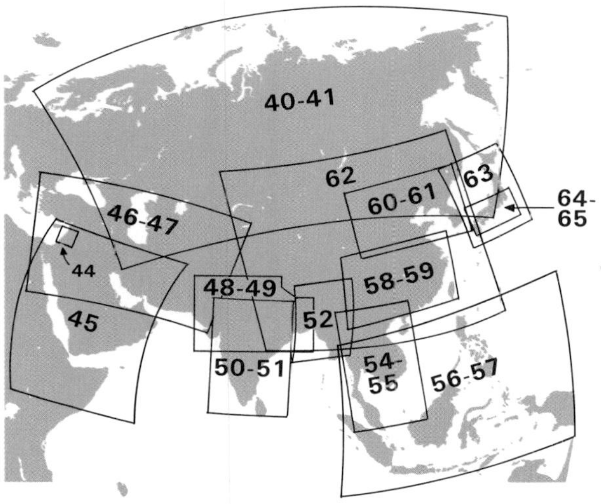

40-41
62
60-61
63
64-
65
46-47
44
48-49
58-59
52
45
50-51
54-
55
56-57

Australia

66-67 The Pacific Ocean 1:43M

68 Islands of the South-West Pacific 1:4M

69 Papua New Guinea 1:5.2M

70-71 Australia 1:11.2M

72-73 Eastern Australia 1:6.4M

74-75 Victoria 1:2M

76 New South Wales — East 1:2M

77 Northern Rivers 1:2M

78-79 Western Australia 1:6.4M

80 New Zealand — North Island 1:2.8M

81 New Zealand — South Island 1:2.8M

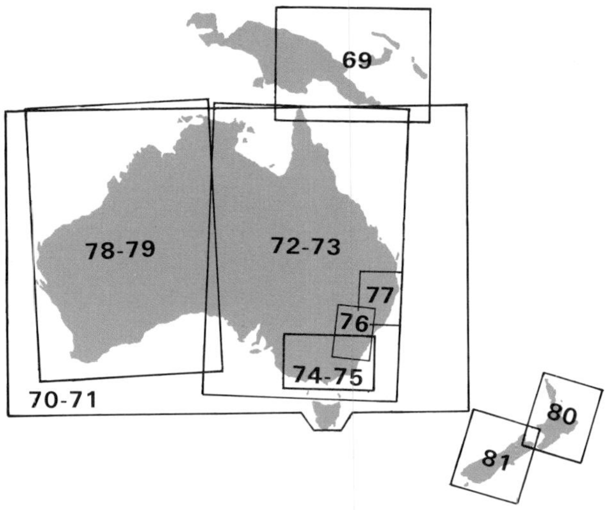

69
78-79
72-73
77
76
74-75
70-71
80
81

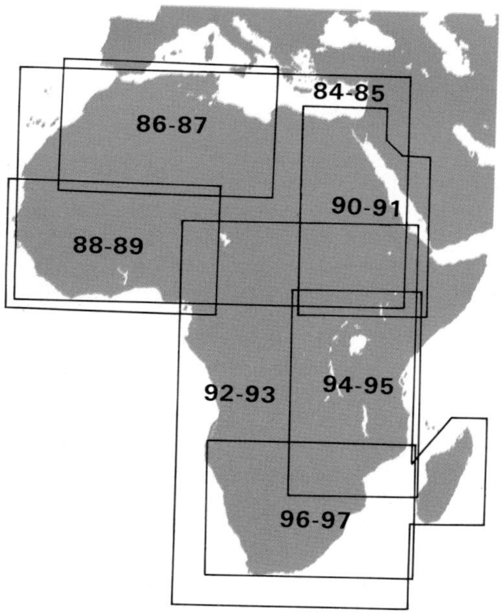
84-85
86-87
88-89
90-91
92-93
94-95
96-97

Africa

82 **Africa: Physical 1:32M**

83 **Africa: Political 1:32M**

84-85 **Northern Africa 1:12M**

86-87 **North-West Africa 1:6.4M**

88-89 **West Africa 1:6.4M**
***N.E. Nigeria* 1:6.4M**

90-91 **The Nile Valley 1:6.4M**
***The Nile Delta* 1:3.2M**

92-93 **Central and South Africa 1:12M**

94-95 **East Africa 1:6.4M**

96-97 **Southern Africa 1:6.4M**
***Madagascar* 1:6.4M**

North America

98-99 **North America: Physical 1:24M**
Political 1:56M

100-101 **Canada 1:12M**
***Alaska* 1:24M**

102-103 **Eastern Canada 1:5.6M**

104-105 **Quebec — South 1:2M**

106-107 **Ontario — South 1:2M**

108-109 **Western Canada 1:5.6M**

110-111 **United States 1:9.6M**
***Hawaii* 1:8M**

112-113 **Eastern United States 1:4.8M**

114-115 **Northeastern United States 1:2M**

116-117 **Chicago and the Midwest 1:2M**

118-119 **Middle United States 1:4.8M**

120-121 **Western United States 1:4.8M**

122-123 **Central and South California and Washington 1:2M**
***Seattle-Portland Region* 1:2M**

124-125 **Mexico 1:6.4M**

126-127 **Central America and the Antilles 1:6.4M**

128-129 **The Atlantic Ocean 1:36M**

South America

130 South America: Physical 1:24M

131 South America — South 1:12.8M

132-133 South America — North 1:12.8M
Political 1:64M

134-135 South America — North West 1:6.4M

136-137 South America — West 1:6.4M

138-139 South America — East 1:6.4M

140-141 Central South America 1:6.4M

142 Southern Chile and Argentina 1:6.4M

143 South Polar Regions 1:28M

144 North Polar Regions 1:28M

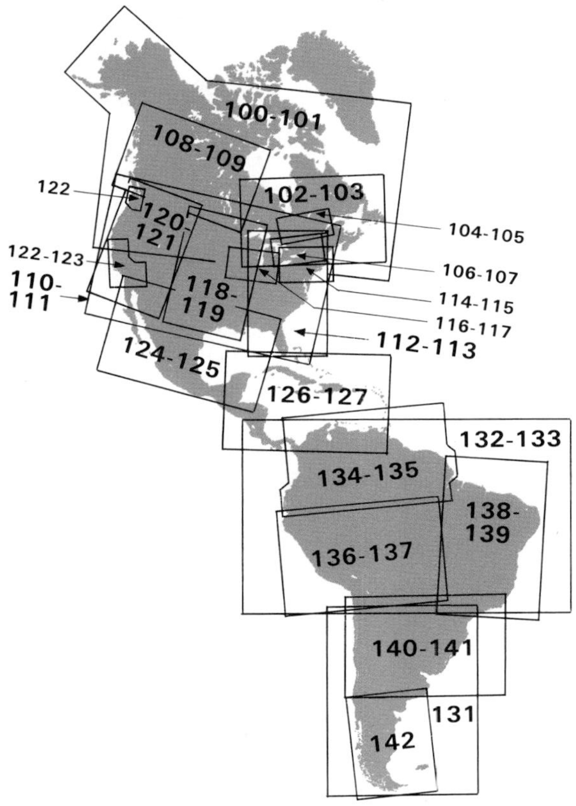

100-101
108-109
122
102-103
120-121
104-105
122-123
110-111
106-107
118-119
114-115
116-117
112-113
124-125
126-127
132-133
134-135
138-139
136-137
140-141
131
142

Thematic Maps

145 The World: Communications and Time Zones

146 The World: Wheat, Oats, Rice and Spices

147 The World: Rye, Barley, Rubber, Tea and Coffee

148 The World: Corn, Sago, Potatoes and Millets

149 The World: Vine, Cacao, Date Plums, Cane and Beet Sugar

150 The World: Wine, Beer, Spirits and Fruits

151 The World: Silk, Hemp, Jute, Sisal and Tobacco

152 The World: Cotton, Flax, Oil Seeds and Vegetable Oils

153 The World: Sheep and Hogs

154 The World: Cattle and Dairy Products

155 The World: Fertilizers and Fisheries

156 The World: Timber

157 The World: Coal, Oil, Natural Gas, Water Power and Uranium

158 The World: Iron, Manganese and other Ferro-Alloys

159 The World: Copper, Lead, Tin, Zinc, Bauxite, Antimony, Mercury and Mica

160 The World: Gold, Silver, Platinum and Precious Stones

ECONOMIC SECTION 161-176

INDEX

CLIMATIC STATISTICS

Pages X-XIII give temperature and precipitation statistics for more than 80 cities. They are arranged by continent, and within each continent, the cities are in alphabetical order. Below each city name, its elevation above mean sea level is given in feet. The average monthly precipitation is given in inches; the average monthly temperature is given in degrees Fahrenheit. The last column is the annual temperature range (the difference between the warmest and the coldest months). The next to last column gives the total yearly precipitation (top figure) and the average yearly temperature (bottom figure).

		Jan.	*Feb.*	*Mar.*	*Apr.*	*May*	*June*	*July*	*Aug.*	*Sept.*	*Oct.*	*Nov.*	*Dec.*	*Year*	*Annual Range*
AFRICA															
Addis Ababa, Ethiopia															
8 036 feet	*Precipitation*	7.91	8.11	9.41	4.02	1.1	<.12	0	<.12	.12	.98	5.32	8.39	46	
	Temperature	66	68	68	68	66	64	64	66	70	72	70	68	68	6
Cairo, Egypt															
380	*Precipitation*	.2	.2	.2	.12	.12	.12	0	0	.12	.12	.12	.2	1.5	
	Temperature	55	59	64	70	77	82	82	82	79	75	68	59	71	27
Cape Town, South Africa															
56	*Precipitation*	.59	.32	.71	1.89	3.11	3.31	3.5	2.6	1.69	1.22	.71	.39	20	
	Temperature	70	70	68	63	57	55	54	55	57	61	64	66	62	16
Casablanca, Morocco															
164	*Precipitation*	2.09	1.89	2.21	1.42	.91	.2	0	<.12	.32	1.5	2.6	2.8	16	
	Temperature	55	55	57	61	64	68	72	73	72	66	61	55	63	18
Johannesburg, South Africa															
5 461	*Precipitation*	4.49	4.29	3.50	1.5	.98	.32	.32	.32	.91	2.21	4.21	4.92	28	
	Temperature	68	68	64	61	55	50	52	55	61	64	66	68	61	18
Khartoum, Sudan															
1 279	*Precipitation*	<.12	<.12	<.12	<.12	.12	.31	2.09	2.8	.71	.2	<.12	0	6.8	
	Temperature	75	77	82	88	91	93	90	88	90	90	82	77	85	18
Kinshasa, Zaire															
1 066	*Precipitation*	5.31	5.71	7.72	7.72	6.22	.31	.12	.12	1.22	4.69	8.7	5.59	53	
	Temperature	79	79	81	81	79	75	73	75	77	79	79	79	78	8
Lagos, Nigeria															
10	*Precipitation*	1.1	1.81	4.02	5.91	10.59	18.11	10.98	2.52	5.51	8.11	2.72	.98	72	
	Temperature	80	82	84	82	82	78	78	77	78	78	82	82	80	7
Lusaka, Zambia															
4 189	*Precipitation*	9.09	7.52	5.59	.71	.12	<.12	<.12	0	<.12	.39	3.58	5.91	33	
	Temperature	70	72	70	70	66	61	61	64	72	75	73	72	69	14
Monrovia, Liberia															
75	*Precipitation*	1.22	2.2	3.82	8.5	20.31	38.31	39.21	14.69	29.29	30.39	9.29	5.12	202	
	Temperature	79	79	81	81	79	77	75	77	77	77	79	79	78	6
Nairobi, Kenya															
5 970	*Precipitation*	1.5	2.52	4.92	8.31	6.22	1.81	.59	.91	1.22	2.09	4.29	3.39	38	
	Temperature	66	66	66	66	64	61	61	61	64	66	64	64	64	5
Tananarive, Madagascar															
4 500	*Precipitation*	11.81	10.98	7.01	2.09	.71	.31	.31	.39	.71	2.4	5.31	11.3	53	
	Temperature	70	70	70	66	64	59	57	59	63	66	70	70	65	13
Timbuktu, Mali															
987	*Precipitation*	<.12	<.12	.12	<.12	.2	.91	3.11	3.19	1.5	.12	<.12	<.12	9.8	
	Temperature	72	75	82	90	93	95	90	86	90	88	82	73	85	23
Tunis, Tunisia															
216	*Precipitation*	2.52	2.01	1.61	1.42	.71	.31	.12	.31	1.3	2.01	1.89	2.4	17	
	Temperature	50	52	55	61	66	73	79	81	77	68	61	52	65	31
Walvis Bay, South Africa															
23	*Precipitation*	<.12	.2	.31	.12	.12	<.12	<.12	.12	<.12	<.12	<.12	<.12	1.7	
	Temperature	66	66	66	64	63	61	59	57	57	59	63	64	62	9
NORTH AMERICA															
Anchorage, Alaska, U.S.A.															
131	*Precipitation*	.79	.71	.59	.39	.51	.71	1.61	2.6	2.6	2.2	.98	.91	15	
	Temperature	12	18	23	36	45	54	57	55	48	36	23	12	35	45
Cheyenne, Wyo., U.S.A.															
6 137	*Precipitation*	.39	.59	.98	1.89	2.4	1.61	2.09	1.61	1.22	.98	.51	.51	15	
	Temperature	25	27	34	41	50	61	66	66	57	45	34	28	45	41
Chicago, Ill., U.S.A.															
823	*Precipitation*	2.01	2.01	2.6	2.8	3.39	3.5	3.31	3.19	3.11	2.6	2.4	2.01	33	
	Temperature	25	27	36	48	57	68	73	72	66	54	41	30	50	48
Churchill, Man., Canada															
43	*Precipitation*	.51	.59	.91	.91	.91	1.89	2.2	2.72	2.28	1.42	1.1	.71	16	
	Temperature	−18	−17	−6	14	30	43	54	52	41	27	5	−11	18	72

			Jan.	Feb.	Mar.	Apr.	May	June	July	Aug.	Sept.	Oct.	Nov.	Dec.	Year	Annual Range
Edmonton, Alta., Canada																
	3 217	*Precipitation*	.91	.59	.79	.91	1.81	3.07	3.31	2.28	1.3	.71	.71	.79	17	
		Temperature	5	12	23	39	52	57	61	59	50	41	25	12	36	56
Honolulu, Hawaii, U.S.A.																
	39	*Precipitation*	4.09	2.6	3.11	1.89	.98	.71	.91	1.1	1.42	1.89	2.52	4.09	25	
		Temperature	73	64	66	68	72	75	77	79	79	75	72	66	72	15
Houston, Tex., U.S.A.																
	39	*Precipitation*	3.5	2.99	3.31	3.58	4.69	4.61	3.9	3.9	4.09	3.7	3.5	4.29	46	
		Temperature	54	55	63	70	75	81	82	84	79	72	61	54	69	30
Kingston, Jamaica																
	112	*Precipitation*	.91	.59	.91	1.22	4.02	3.5	1.5	3.58	3.9	7.09	2.91	1.42	32	
		Temperature	77	77	77	79	79	82	82	82	81	81	79	79	80	5
Los Angeles, Calif., U.S.A.																
	312	*Precipitation*	3.11	2.99	2.8	.98	.39	.12	<.12	<.12	.2	.59	1.22	2.6	15	
		Temperature	55	57	57	61	63	66	70	72	70	64	61	57	63	17
Mexico City, Mexico																
	7 574	*Precipitation*	.51	.2	.39	.79	2.09	4.69	6.69	5.98	5.12	2.01	.71	.31	30	
		Temperature	54	55	61	64	66	66	63	64	64	61	57	55	61	12
Miami, Fla., U.S.A.																
	26	*Precipitation*	2.8	2.09	2.52	3.19	6.81	7.01	6.1	6.3	7.99	9.21	2.8	2.01	59	
		Temperature	68	68	72	73	77	81	82	82	81	77	72	70	75	14
Montreal, Que., Canada																
	187	*Precipitation*	3.82	2.99	3.5	2.6	3.11	3.39	3.7	3.5	3.7	3.39	3.5	3.58	41	
		Temperature	14	16	27	41	55	66	70	66	59	46	34	19	43	56
New York, N.Y., U.S.A.																
	315	*Precipitation*	3.7	3.82	3.58	3.19	3.19	3.31	4.21	4.29	3.39	3.5	2.99	3.58	43	
		Temperature	30	30	37	50	61	68	73	73	70	59	45	36	53	43
St. Louis, Mo., U.S.A.																
	567	*Precipitation*	2.28	2.52	3.5	3.82	4.49	4.49	3.5	3.39	3.19	2.91	2.8	2.52	39	
		Temperature	32	34	45	55	66	75	79	79	72	59	46	36	57	47
San Francisco, Calif., U.S.A.																
	52	*Precipitation*	4.69	3.82	3.11	1.5	.71	.12	<.12	<.12	.31	.98	2.52	4.41	22	
		Temperature	50	54	55	55	57	59	59	59	63	61	57	52	57	13
San José, Costa Rica																
	3 759	*Precipitation*	.59	.2	.79	1.81	9.02	9.49	8.31	9.49	12.01	11.81	5.71	1.61	71	
		Temperature	66	66	70	70	72	70	70	70	70	68	68	66	69	6
Vancouver, B.C., Canada																
	46	*Precipitation*	8.58	5.79	5	3.31	2.8	2.52	1.22	1.69	3.58	5.79	8.31	8.82	57	
		Temperature	37	39	43	48	55	61	64	64	57	50	43	39	50	27
Washington, D.C., U.S.A.																
	72	*Precipitation*	3.39	2.99	3.58	3.31	3.7	3.9	4.41	4.29	3.7	2.91	2.6	3.11	42	
		Temperature	34	36	45	54	64	73	77	75	68	57	46	37	56	43

SOUTH AMERICA

			Jan.	Feb.	Mar.	Apr.	May	June	July	Aug.	Sept.	Oct.	Nov.	Dec.	Year	Annual Range
Antofagasta, Chile																
	308	*Precipitation*	0	0	0	<.12	<.12	.12	.2	.12	<.12	.12	<.12	0	1.02	
		Temperature	70	70	68	64	61	59	57	57	59	61	64	66	63	13
Buenos Aires, Argentina																
	89	*Precipitation*	3.11	2.8	4.29	3.5	2.99	2.4	2.2	2.4	3.11	3.39	3.31	3.9	37	
		Temperature	73	73	70	63	55	48	50	52	55	59	66	72	61	25
Caracas, Venezuela																
	3 418	*Precipitation*	.91	.39	.59	1.3	3.11	4.02	4.29	4.29	4.21	4.29	3.7	1.81	33	
		Temperature	66	66	68	70	72	70	70	70	70	70	68	68	69	6
Lima, Peru																
	394	*Precipitation*	.12	<.12	<.12	<.12	.2	.2	.31	.31	.31	.12	.12	<.12	2.17	
		Temperature	73	75	75	72	66	63	63	61	63	64	66	70	68	14
Manaus, Brazil																
	144	*Precipitation*	9.8	9.09	10.31	8.7	6.69	3.31	2.28	1.5	1.81	4.21	5.59	7.99	71	
		Temperature	82	82	82	81	82	82	82	82	84	84	84	82	82	3
Paraná, Brazil																
	853	*Precipitation*	11.3	9.29	9.41	4.02	.51	<.12	.12	.2	1.1	5	9.09	12.2	62	
		Temperature	73	73	73	73	73	70	70	72	75	75	75	73	73	5
Quito, Ecuador																
	9 443	*Precipitation*	3.9	4.41	5.59	6.89	5.39	1.69	.79	1.22	2.72	4.41	3.82	3.11	44	
		Temperature	59	59	59	59	59	57	57	59	59	59	59	59	59	2
Rio de Janeiro, Brazil																
	200	*Precipitation*	4.92	4.8	5.12	4.21	3.11	2.09	1.61	1.69	2.6	3.11	4.09	5.39	43	
		Temperature	79	79	77	75	72	70	70	70	70	72	73	77	74	9
Santiago, Chile																
	1 706	*Precipitation*	.12	.12	.2	.51	2.52	3.31	2.99	2.2	1.22	.59	.31	.2	14	
		Temperature	70	68	64	59	54	48	48	50	54	59	63	66	59	22

ASIA

			Jan.	Feb.	Mar.	Apr.	May	June	July	Aug.	Sept.	Oct.	Nov.	Dec.	Year	Annual Range
Bahrain	16	*Precipitation*	.31	.71	.51	.31	<.12	0	0	0	0	0	.71	.71	3	
		Temperature	63	64	70	77	84	90	91	93	88	82	75	66	79	30
Bangkok, Thailand	7	*Precipitation*	.31	.79	1.42	2.28	7.8	6.3	6.3	6.89	12.01	8.11	2.6	.2	55	
		Temperature	79	82	84	86	84	84	82	82	82	82	79	77	82	9
Beirut, Lebanon	112	*Precipitation*	7.52	6.22	3.9	2.09	.71	.12	<.12	<.12	.2	2.01	5.2	7.28	35	
		Temperature	57	57	61	64	72	75	81	82	79	75	66	61	69	25
Bombay, India	36	*Precipitation*	.12	.12	.12	<.12	.71	19.09	24.29	13.39	10.39	2.52	.51	.12	72	
		Temperature	75	75	79	82	86	84	81	81	81	82	81	79	81	11
Calcutta, India	20	*Precipitation*	.39	1.22	1.42	1.69	5.51	11.69	12.8	12.91	9.92	4.49	.79	.2	63	
		Temperature	68	72	81	86	86	86	84	84	84	82	73	66	79	20
Colombo, Sri Lanka	23	*Precipitation*	3.5	2.72	5.79	9.09	14.61	8.82	5.31	4.29	6.3	13.7	12.4	5.79	92	
		Temperature	79	79	81	82	82	81	81	81	81	81	79	79	81	3
Harbin, China	525	*Precipitation*	.2	.2	.39	.91	1.69	3.7	4.41	4.09	1.81	1.3	.31	.2	19	
		Temperature	0	5	23	43	55	66	72	70	57	39	21	3	38	72
Ho Chi Minh City, Vietnam	30	*Precipitation*	.59	.12	.51	1.69	8.7	12.99	12.4	10.59	13.19	10.59	4.49	2.2	78	
		Temperature	79	81	84	86	84	82	82	82	81	81	81	79	82	7
Jakarta, Indonesia	26	*Precipitation*	11.81	11.81	8.31	5.79	4.49	3.82	2.52	1.69	2.6	4.41	5.59	7.99	71	
		Temperature	79	79	81	81	81	81	81	81	81	81	81	79	81	2
Hong Kong	108	*Precipitation*	1.3	1.81	2.91	5.39	11.5	15.51	15	14.21	10.12	4.49	1.69	1.22	85	
		Temperature	61	59	64	72	79	82	82	82	81	77	70	64	73	23
Kabul, Afghanistan	5 953	*Precipitation*	1.22	1.42	3.7	4.02	.79	.2	.12	.12	<.12	.59	.79	.39	14	
		Temperature	27	30	43	55	64	72	77	75	68	57	45	37	54	50
Karachi, Pakistan	13	*Precipitation*	.51	.39	.31	.12	.12	.71	3.19	1.61	.51	<.12	.12	.2	8	
		Temperature	66	68	75	82	86	88	86	84	82	82	75	68	79	22
New Delhi, India	715	*Precipitation*	.91	.71	.51	.31	.51	2.91	7.09	6.77	4.61	.39	.12	.39	25	
		Temperature	57	63	73	82	91	93	88	86	84	79	68	59	77	36
Shanghai, China	23	*Precipitation*	1.89	2.28	3.31	3.7	3.7	7.09	5.79	5.59	5.12	2.8	2.01	1.42	45	
		Temperature	39	41	48	57	68	75	82	82	73	66	54	45	61	43
Singapore	33	*Precipitation*	9.92	6.81	7.6	7.4	6.81	6.81	6.69	7.72	7.01	8.19	10	10.12	95	
		Temperature	79	81	82	82	82	82	82	81	81	81	81	81	81	3
Tehran, Iran	4 002	*Precipitation*	1.81	1.5	1.81	1.42	.51	.12	.12	.12	.12	.31	.79	1.22	10	
		Temperature	36	41	48	61	70	79	86	84	77	64	54	43	62	50
Tokyo, Japan	20	*Precipitation*	1.89	2.91	4.21	5.31	5.79	6.5	5.59	5.98	9.21	8.19	3.82	2.2	72	
		Temperature	37	39	45	55	63	70	77	79	73	63	52	43	58	42
Ulan Bator, Mongolia	4 346	*Precipitation*	<.12	<.12	.12	.2	.39	1.1	2.99	2.01	.91	.2	.2	.12	9	
		Temperature	−15	−6	9	30	43	57	61	57	46	30	9	−8	26	76

AUSTRALIA, NEW ZEALAND and ANTARCTICA

			Jan.	Feb.	Mar.	Apr.	May	June	July	Aug.	Sept.	Oct.	Nov.	Dec.	Year	Annual Range
Alice Springs, Australia	1 899	*Precipitation*	1.69	1.3	1.1	.39	.59	.51	.31	.31	.31	.71	1.22	1.5	10	
		Temperature	84	82	77	68	59	54	54	57	64	73	79	82	69	30
Christchurch, New Zealand	33	*Precipitation*	2.2	1.69	1.89	1.89	2.6	2.6	2.72	1.89	1.81	1.69	1.89	2.2	25	
		Temperature	61	61	57	54	48	43	43	45	48	54	57	61	53	18
Darwin, Australia	98	*Precipitation*	15.2	12.28	10	3.82	.59	.12	<.12	.12	.51	2.01	4.69	9.41	59	
		Temperature	84	84	84	84	82	79	77	79	82	84	86	84	82	9
Mawson, Antarctica	46	*Precipitation*	.43	1.18	.79	.39	1.73	7.09	.16	1.57	.12	.79	0	0	14	
		Temperature	32	23	14	7	5	3	0	0	−2	9	23	30	12	34

			Jan.	Feb.	Mar.	Apr.	May	June	July	Aug.	Sept.	Oct	Nov.	Dec.	Year	Annual Range
Melbourne, Australia																
	115	*Precipitation*	1.89	1.81	2.2	2.28	2.09	2.09	1.89	1.89	2.28	2.6	2.28	2.28	26	
		Temperature	68	68	64	59	55	50	48	52	55	57	61	64	58	20
Perth, Australia																
	197	*Precipitation*	.31	.39	.79	1.69	5.12	7.09	6.69	5.87	3.39	2.2	.79	.51	35	
		Temperature	73	73	72	66	61	57	55	55	59	61	66	72	64	18
Sydney, Australia																
	138	*Precipitation*	3.5	4.02	5	5.31	5	4.61	4.61	2.99	2.87	2.8	2.87	2.87	47	
		Temperature	72	72	70	64	59	55	54	55	59	64	66	70	63	18

EUROPE and U.S.S.R.

			Jan.	Feb.	Mar.	Apr.	May	June	July	Aug.	Sept.	Oct	Nov.	Dec.	Year	Annual Range
Archangel, U.S.S.R.																
	43	*Precipitation*	1.22	.75	.98	1.14	1.65	2.05	2.44	2.2	2.48	2.48	1.85	1.61	21	
		Temperature	3	7	16	32	45	54	59	57	46	36	25	12	33	56
Athens, Greece																
	351	*Precipitation*	2.44	1.46	1.46	.91	.91	.55	.24	.28	.59	2.01	2.2	2.8	16	
		Temperature	50	50	54	61	68	77	82	82	75	68	59	52	65	32
Berlin, Germany																
	180	*Precipitation*	1.81	1.57	1.3	1.65	1.93	2.56	2.87	2.72	1.89	1.93	1.81	1.69	24	
		Temperature	30	32	39	48	57	63	66	64	59	48	41	34	48	36
Istanbul, Turkey																
	374	*Precipitation*	4.29	3.62	2.83	1.81	1.5	1.34	1.34	1.18	2.28	3.19	4.06	4.69	32	
		Temperature	41	43	45	52	61	68	73	73	68	61	54	46	57	32
Kazalinsk, U.S.S.R.																
	207	*Precipitation*	.39	.39	.51	.51	.59	.2	.2	.31	.31	.39	.51	.59	5	
		Temperature	10	12	27	43	64	73	77	73	61	46	30	19	45	67
Lisbon, Portugal																
	253	*Precipitation*	4.37	2.99	4.29	2.13	1.73	.63	.12	.16	1.3	2.44	3.66	4.06	28	
		Temperature	52	54	57	61	63	68	72	73	70	64	57	54	62	21
London, U.K.																
	16	*Precipitation*	2.13	1.57	1.46	1.46	1.81	1.77	2.24	2.32	1.93	2.24	2.52	1.89	23	
		Temperature	39	41	45	48	54	61	64	63	59	52	46	41	51	25
Málaga, Spain																
	108	*Precipitation*	2.4	2.01	2.44	1.81	1.02	.2	.04	.12	1.14	2.52	2.52	2.44	19	
		Temperature	54	55	59	63	66	84	77	79	73	68	61	55	66	30
Moscow, U.S.S.R.																
	512	*Precipitation*	1.54	1.5	1.42	1.46	2.09	2.28	3.46	2.8	2.28	1.77	1.85	2.13	25	
		Temperature	9	14	25	43	55	61	64	63	54	43	30	19	40	55
Odessa, U.S.S.R.																
	210	*Precipitation*	2.24	2.44	1.18	.83	1.34	1.34	1.65	1.46	1.46	.51	1.38	2.8	20	
		Temperature	27	30	36	48	59	68	72	72	64	54	48	34	51	45
Omsk, U.S.S.R.																
	279	*Precipitation*	.59	.31	.31	.51	1.22	2.01	2.01	2.01	1.1	.98	.71	.79	13	
		Temperature	−8	−2	10	30	50	61	64	61	50	34	12	0	30	72
Palma de Mallorca, Spain																
	33	*Precipitation*	1.54	1.34	2.01	1.26	1.14	.67	.12	.98	2.17	3.03	1.85	1.57	18	
		Temperature	50	52	54	59	63	70	75	77	73	64	57	52	62	27
Paris, France																
	246	*Precipitation*	2.2	1.81	1.38	1.65	2.24	2.13	2.32	2.52	2.17	1.97	2.01	1.97	24	
		Temperature	37	39	46	52	59	64	68	66	63	54	45	39	53	31
Rome, Italy																
	56	*Precipitation*	2.8	2.44	2.24	2.01	1.81	1.46	.59	.83	2.48	3.9	5.08	3.66	29	
		Temperature	46	48	52	57	64	72	77	77	72	63	55	50	61	31
Shannon, Irish Republic																
	7	*Precipitation*	3.7	2.64	2.2	2.09	2.4	2.24	3.03	3.11	3.39	3.39	3.78	4.61	37	
		Temperature	41	41	45	48	54	57	61	61	57	52	46	43	51	20
Stavanger, Norway																
	279	*Precipitation*	3.66	2.2	1.77	2.76	1.93	3.31	3.66	4.65	5.59	5.08	4.92	4.96	45	
		Temperature	34	34	37	43	50	55	59	59	55	48	43	37	46	25
Stockholm, Sweden																
	144	*Precipitation*	1.69	1.18	.98	1.22	1.34	1.77	2.4	2.99	2.36	1.89	2.09	1.89	22	
		Temperature	27	27	30	41	50	59	64	63	54	45	37	32	44	37
Verkhoyansk, U.S.S.R.																
	328	*Precipitation*	.2	.2	.12	.2	.31	.91	1.1	.98	.51	.31	.31	.2	5	
		Temperature	−58	−49	−26	5	32	54	57	48	36	5	−36	−54	1	115
Warsaw, Poland																
	361	*Precipitation*	1.06	1.26	1.06	1.46	1.81	2.72	3.78	2.56	1.69	1.5	1.22	1.73	22	
		Temperature	27	27	36	45	57	63	66	64	57	48	37	32	47	39

POPULATION OF CITIES

The population figures used are from censuses or more recent estimates and are given in thousands for towns and cities over 200 000 (over 500 000 in China and 250 000 in Japan and U.S.S.R.). Where possible the population of the metropolitan areas is given e.g. Greater London, Greater New York, etc.

AFRICA

ALGERIA (1974)

Algiers 1 503
Oran 485
Constantine 350
Annaba 313
Tizi-Ouzou 224

ANGOLA (1970)

Luanda 475

CAMEROON (1976)

Douala 458
Yaoundé 314

CANARY ISLANDS (1974)

Las Palmas 328

CONGO (1975)

Brazzaville 290

EGYPT (1976)

Cairo 5 084
Alexandria 2 319
El Giza 1 247
Shubra el Kheima 394
El Mahalla el Kubra 293
Tanta 285
Port Said 263
El Mansura 258
Asyut 214
Zagazig 203

ETHIOPIA (1978)

Addis Abeba 1 196
Asmera 294

GABON (1976)

Libreville 186

GHANA (1970)

Accra 738
Kumasi 345

GUINEA (1972)

Conakry 526

IVORY COAST (1976)

Abidjan 850
Bouaké 318

KENYA (1979)

Nairobi 835
Mombasa 312

LIBYA (1973)

Tripoli 551
Benghazi 282

MADAGASCAR (1971)

Antananarivo 378

MALAWI (1977)

Blantyre 229

MALI (1976)

Bamako 404

MOROCCO (1973)

Casablanca 1 753
Rabat-Salé 596
Marrakesh 436
Fès 426
Meknès 403
Oujda 349
Kénitra 341
Tétouan 308
Safi 215
Tanger 208

MOZAMBIQUE (1970)

Maputo 384

NIGERIA (1975)

Lagos 1 477
Ibadan 847
Ogbomosho 432
Kano 399
Oshogbo 282
Ilorin 282
Abeokuta 253
Port Harcourt 242
Zaria 224
Ilesha 224
Onitsha 220
Iwo 214
Ado-Ekiti 213
Kaduna 202

SENEGAL (1976)

Dakar 799

SIERRA LEONE (1974)

Freetown 214

SOMALI REP. (1972)

Mogadishu 230

SOUTH AFRICA (1970)

Johannesburg 1 433
Cape Town 1 097
Durban 843
Pretoria 562
Port Elizabeth 469
Germiston 281

SUDAN (1973)

Khartoum 334

TANZANIA (1978)

Dar-es-Salaam 757

TUNISIA (1976)

Tunis 944
Sfax 475
Sousse 255

UGANDA (1975)

Kampala 331

ZAIRE (1974)

Kinshasa 2 008
Kananga 601
Lubumbashi 404
Mbuji Mayi 337
Kisangani 311

ZAMBIA (1974)

Lusaka 559
Kitwe 310
Ndola 291

ZIMBABWE (1978)

Salisbury 616
Bulawayo 357

ASIA

AFGHANISTAN (1976)

Kabul 588

BANGLADESH (1974)

Dacca 1 730
Chittagong 890
Khulna 437

BURMA (1977)

Rangoon 2 276
Mandalay 458

CAMBODIA (1973)

Phnom Penh 2 000

CHINA (1970)

Shanghai 10 820
Beijing 7 570
Tianjin 4 280
Shenyang 2 800
Wuhan 2 560
Kuangchou 2 500
Chongqing 2 400
Nanjing 1 750
Haerbin 1 670
Dalien 1 650
Xian 1 600
Lanzhou 1 450
Taiyuan 1 350
Qingtou 1 300
Chengdu 1 250
Changchun 1 200
Kunming 1 100
Qinan 1 100
Fushun 1 080
Anshan 1 050
Zhengzhou 1 050
Hangzhou 960
Tangshan 950
Baotou 920
Zibo 850
Changsha 825
Shijiazhuang 800
Qiqihaer 760
Suzhou 730
Jilin 720
Xuzhou 700
Fuzhou 680
Nanzhang 675
Guiyang 660
Wuxi 650
Hefei 630
Huainan 600
Benqi 600
Luoyang 580
Nanning 550
Huhehaote 530
Xining 500
Wulumuqi 500

HONG KONG (1971)

Kowloon 2 195
Victoria 849
Tsuen Wan 272

INDIA (1971)

Calcutta 7 031
Bombay 5 971
Delhi 3 647
Madras 3 170
Hyderabad 1 796
Ahmedabad 1 742
Bangalore 1 654
Kanpur 1 275
Pune 1 135
Nagpur 930
Lucknow 749
Jaipur 615
Agra 592
Varanasi 584
Madurai 549
Indore 543
Allahabad 491
Patna 473
Surat 472
Vadodara 467
Cochin 439
Jabalpur 426
Tivandrum 410
Amritsar 408
Srinagar 403
Ludhiana 398
Sholapur 398
Gwalior 385
Hubli-Dharwar 379
Jamshedpur 357
Coimbatore 356
Mysore 356
Visakhapatnam 353
Calicut 334
Jodhpur 318
Vijaywada 317
Salem 309
Tiruchurapalli 307
Rajkot 301
Bhopal 298
Bareilly 296
Jullundur 296
Meerut 271
Guntur 270
Ajmer 263
Kolhapur 259
Algarh 252
Gorakhpur 231
Bhavnagar 225
Saharanpur 225
Chandigarh 219
Kota 213
Warangul 208
Durgapur 207
Ujjain 203
Jamnagar 200

INDONESIA (1971)

Jakarta 4 576
Surabaya 1 556
Bandung 1 202
Semarang 647
Medan 636
Palembang 583
Ujung Pandang 435
Malang 422
Surakarta 414
Yogyakarta 342
Banjarmasin 282
Pontianak 218

IRAN (1976)

Tehran 4 496
Esfahan 672
Mashhad 670
Tabriz 599
Shiraz 416
Ahvaz 329
Abadan 296
Kermanshah 291
Qom 247

IRAQ (1970)

Baghdad 2 969
Basra 371
Mosul 293
Kirkuk 208

ISRAEL (1977)

Tel Aviv-Jaffa 1 220
Jerusalem 376
Haifa 367

JAPAN (1977)

Tokyo 11 695
Osaka 2 724
Yokohama 2 695
Nagoya 2 084
Kyoto 1 465
Kobe 1 366
Sapporo 1 308
Kitakyushu 1 068
Fukuoka 1 039
Kawasaki 1 033
Hiroshima 852
Sakai 773
Chiba 694
Sendai 619
Amagasaki 532
Okayama 530
Higashiosaka 501
Kumamoto 490
Kagoshima 481
Hamamatsu 480
Shizuoka 454
Nagasaki 447
Himeji 440
Funabashi 437
Niigata 432
Gifu 409
Yokosuka 404
Kurashiku 400
Sagamihara 399
Kanazawa 398
Wakayama 396
Nishinomiya 392
Toyonaka 390
Matsuyama 386
Matsudo 365
Utsunomiya 357
Kawaguchi 353
Hachiōji 344
Urawa 343
Omiya 342
Iwaki 341
Fukuyama 339
Takatsuki 337
Asahikawa 336
Ichikawa 333
Oita 332
Hirakata 321
Hakodate 314
Nagano 314
Takamatsu 306
Suita 305
Naha 303
Toyama 294
Toyohashi 291
Kōchi 289
Fujisawa 279
Aomori 277
Akita 273
Kōriyama 271
Nara 271
Machida 270
Shimonoseki 264
Toyota 260
Yao 260
Maebashi 257
Neyagawa 256
Sasebo 255
Fukushima 254
Yokkaichi 250

JORDAN (1977)

Amman 712
Az Zarqa 263

KOREA, NORTH (1967-70)

Pyongyang 1 500
Chongjin 265

KOREA, SOUTH (1975)

Seoul 6 879
Pusan 2 450
Taegu 1 309
Inchon 797
Kwangju 606
Taejon 506
Masan 372
Chonju 311
Seongnam 272
Utsan 253
Suweon 224

KUWAIT (1975)

Kuwait 775

LEBANON (1971)

Beirut 702

MACAU (1975)

Macau 260

MALAYSIA (1970)

Kuala Lumpur 452
Georgetown 270
Ipoh 248

MONGOLIA (1977)

Ulan Bator 400

NEPAL (1971)

Katmandu 210

PAKISTAN (1972)

Karachi 3 499
Lahore 2 165
Lyallpur 822
Hyderabad 628
Rawalpindi 615
Multan 542
Gujranwala 360
Peshawar 268
Sialkot 204
Sargodha 201

PHILIPPINES (1975)

Manila 1 438
Quezon City 995
Davao 516
Cebu 419
Caloocan 364
Iloilo 248
Pasay 241
Zamboanga 240

SAUDI ARABIA (1974)

Riyadh 667
Jedda 561
Mecca 367
Taif 205

SINGAPORE (1977)

Singapore 2 308

SRI LANKA (1976)

Colombo 607

SYRIA (1978)

Damascus 1 142
Aleppo 878
Homs 306
Latakia 204

TAIWAN (1973)

Taipei 3 050
Kaohsiung 1 115
Tainan 513
Taichung 497
Chilung 341
Sanchung 260
Chiai 247
Hsinchu 205

THAILAND (1977)

Bangkok 4 702

TURKEY (1975)

Istanbul 2 547
Ankara 1 701
Izmir 637
Abana 475
Bursa 346
Gaziantep 301
Ekisehir 260
Konya 247
Kayseri 207

UNITED ARAB EMIRATES (1976)

Abu Dhabi 236
Dubai 207

VIETNAM (1973-79)

Ho Chi Minh City 3 420
Hanoi 2 571
Haiphong 1 279
Da-Nang 492
Nha-Trang 216
Qui-Nhon 214
Hue 209

YEMEN, SOUTH (1977)

Aden 285

AUSTRALASIA

AUSTRALIA (1976)

Sydney 3 021
Melbourne 2 604
Brisbane 958
Adelaide 900
Perth 805
Newcastle 363
Canberra 215
Wollongong 211

NEW ZEALAND (1978)

Auckland 749
Wellington 328
Christchurch 297

EUROPE

AUSTRIA (1977)

Vienna 1 597
Graz 249
Linz 208

BELGIUM (1976)

Brussels 1 042
Antwerp 662
Liège 433
Gent 219
Charleroi 210

BULGARIA (1978)

Sofia 1 032
Plovdiv 333
Varna 279

CZECHOSLOVAKIA (1977)

Prague 1 176
Brno 363
Bratislava 350
Ostrava 317

DENMARK (1977)

Copenhagen 1 251
Århus 246

FINLAND (1976)

Helsinki 825
Tampere 271
Turku 240

FRANCE (1975)

Paris 9 863
Lyon 1 152
Marseille 1 004
Lille 929
Bordeaux 591
Toulouse 495
Nantes 438
Nice 433
Rouen 389
Grenoble 389
Toulon 379
Strasbourg 355
St-Etienne 335
Lens 313
Nancy 279
Le Havre 264
Grasse-Cannes 255
Tours 235
Clermont-Ferrand 225
Valenciennes 224
Mulhouse 219
Rennes 213
Montpellier 205
Orléans 205
Dijon 203
Douai 203

GERMANY, EAST (1977)

East Berlin 1 111
Leipzig 565
Dresden 511
Karl-Marx-Stadt 309
Magdeburg 281
Halle 233
Rostock 219
Erfurt 206

GERMANY, WEST (1977)

West Berlin 1 927
Hamburg 1 680
München 1 314
Cologne 977
Essen 664
Frankfurt am Main 633
Dortmund 618
Düsseldorf 608
Stuttgart 585
Duisburg 572
Bremen 563
Hannover 542
Nürnberg 489
Bochum 409
Wuppertal 399
Bielefeld 313
Gelsenkirchen 313
Mannheim 306
Bonn 284
Karlsruhe 276
Wiesbaden 270
Münster 267
Braunschweig 265
Mönchengladbach 259
Kiel 257
Augsburg 244
Aachen 243
Oberhausen 233
Lübeck 227
Hagen 225
Krefeld 224

GREECE (1971)

Athens 2 101
Thessaloniki 557
Piraeus 439

HUNGARY (1977)

Budapest 2 082
Miskolc 203

IRISH REPUBLIC (1979)
Dublin 545

ITALY (1977)
Rome 2 898
Milano 1 706
Napoli 1 225
Torino 1 182
Genova 795
Palermo 679
Bologna 481
Firenze 464
Catánia 400
Bari 387
Venézia 360
Verona 271
Messina 267
Trieste 265
Táranto 245
Cágliari 242
Padova 242
Bréscia 215

NETHERLANDS (1978)
Rotterdam 1 017
Amsterdam 965
s'Gravenhage 673
Utrecht 472
Eindhoven 363
Arnhem 284
Heerlen-Kerkrade 266
Enschede-Hengelo 241
Haarlem 229
Nijmegen 216
Tiburg 212
Groningen 200

NORWAY (1977)
Oslo 645
Bergen 212

POLAND (1977)
Warsaw 1 474
Lódz 815
Kraków 707
Wroclaw 589
Poznań 532
Gdańsk 439
Szczecin 380
Katowice 350
Bydgoszcz 333
Lublin 286
Bytom 236
Gdynia 227
Częstochowa 225
Zabrze 205
Bialystok 204
Sosnowiec 201
Gliwice 200

PORTUGAL (1975)
Lisbon 1 612
Oporto 1 315

ROMANIA (1977)
Bucharest 1 934
Timişoara 269
Iaşi 265
Cluj 262
Braşov 257
Constanţa 257
Galaţi 239
Craiova 222

SPAIN (1974)
Madrid 3 520
Barcelona 1 810
Valencia 713
Sevilla 569
Zaragoza 547
Bilbao 458
Malaga 403
Valladolid 275
Palma de Mallorca 267
Córdoba 250
Hospitalet 242
Murcia 241
Alicante 213
Granada 203

SWEDEN (1977)
Stockholm 1 375
Göteborg 693
Malmö 454

SWITZERLAND (1978)
Zürich 708
Basel 367
Genève 323
Berne 284
Lausanne 227

U.S.S.R. (1979)
Moscow 8 011
Leningrad 4 588
Kiyev 2 144
Tashkent 1 779
Baku 1 550
Kharkov 1 444
Gorkiy 1 344
Novosibirsk 1 312
Minsk 1 276
Kuybyshev 1 218
Sverdlovsk 1 211
Dnepropetrovsk 1 066
Tbilisi 1 066
Odessa 1 046
Chelyabinsk 1 031
Donetsk 1 021
Yerevan 1 019
Omsk 1 014
Perm 999
Kazan 993
Ufa 969
Rostov 934
Volgograd 929
Alma-Ata 910
Saratov 856
Riga 835
Krasnoyarsk 796
Voronezh 783
Zaporozhye 781
Lvov 667
Krivoy Rog 650
Yaroslavl 597
Karaganda 572
Krasnodar 560
Irkutsk 550
Vladivostok 550
Izhevsk 549
Novokuznetsk 541
Barnaul 533
Frunze 533
Khabarovsk 528
Tula 514
Kishinev 503
Zhdanov 503
Togliatti 502
Dushanbe 493
Penza 483
Vilnius 481
Samarkand 476
Kemerovo 471
Ivanovo 465
Ulyanovsk 464
Voroshilovgrad 463
Astrakhan 461
Orenburg 459
Ryazan 453
Nikolayev 441
Makeyevka 436
Tallinn 430
Tomsk 421
Kalinin 412
Magnitogorsk 406
Nizhniy Tagil 398
Lipetsk 396
Bryansk 394
Kirov 390
Arkhangelsk 385
Gomel 383
Murmansk 381
Groznyy 375
Kursk 375
Kaunas 370
Tyumen 359
Kaliningrad 355
Gorlovka 337
Chimkent 321
Kherson 319
Vinnitsa 313
Ashkhabad 312
Kurgan 310
Cheboksary 308
Orel 305
Chita 302
Simferopol 302
Naberezhnyye Chelny 301
Sevastopol 301
Ulan Ude 300
Vitebsk 297
Vladimir 296
Mogilev 290
Sochi 287
Semipalatinsk 283
Ordzhonikidze 279
Poltava 279
Taganrog 277
Smolensk 276
Ust-Kamenogorsk 274
Pavlodar 273
Tambov 270
Cherepovets 266
Prokopyevsk 266
Kaluga 265
Dzhambul 264
Komsomolsk-na-Amur 264
Saransk 263
Stavropol 258
Dzerzhinsk 257
Kostroma 255
Dneprodzerzhinsk 250
Makhachkala 250

UNITED KINGDOM (1974-79)
London 6 877
Birmingham 1 034
Glasgow 810
Sheffield 544
Liverpool 520
Leeds 499
Manchester 479
Edinburgh 457
Bristol 408
Teesside 387
Belfast 354
Coventry 339
Bradford 290
Cardiff 282
Nottingham 279
Leicester 277
Hull 275
Wolverhampton 258
Stoke-on-Trent 257
Plymouth 256
Derby 216
Sunderland 213
Aberdeen 209
Newcastle-upon-Tyne 209
Southampton 208

YUGOSLAVIA (1971)
Belgrade 775
Zagreb 602
Skopje 388
Sarajevo 271
Ljubljana 213

NORTH AMERICA

CANADA (1976)
Toronto 2 803
Montréal 2 802
Vancouver 1 166
Ottawa 693
Winnipeg 578
Edmonton 554
Québec 542
Hamilton 529
Calgary 470
St. Catharines 302
Kitchener 272
London 270
Halifax 268
Windsor 248
Victoria 218

COSTA RICA (1977)
San José 395

CUBA (1975)
Havana 1 861
Santiago de Cuba 316
Camagüey 222

DOMINICAN REPUBLIC (1970)
Santo Domingo 818
Santiago de los Caballeros 245

EL SALVADOR (1974)
San Salvador 366

GUATEMALA (1973)
Guatemala City 717

HAITI (1978)
Port-au-Prince 746

HONDURAS (1974)
Tegucigalpa 274

JAMAICA (1971)
Kingston 573

MEXICO (1978)
Mexico City 13 994
Guadalajara 2 343
Netzahualcóyotl 2 068
Monterrey 1 923
Puebla de Zaragoza 678
Ciudad Juárez 597
León de los Aldamas 590
Acapulco 421
Torreón 397
Tampico 375
Chihuahua 370
Mexicali 338
San Luis Potosi 315
Culiacán 302
Hermosillo 300
Veracruz Llave 295
Mérida 253
Aguascalientes 248
Saltillo 246
Morelia 239
Cuernavaca 227
Toluca 223
Durango 219
Reynosa 219
Nuevo Laredo 214

NICARAGUA (1974)
Managua 500

PANAMA (1978)
Panama 440

PUERTO RICO (1976)
San Juan 515
Bayamón 204

UNITED STATES (1977)
New York 16 479
Los Angeles 10 607
Chicago 7 664
Philadelphia 5 625
San Francisco 4 688
Detroit 4 663
Boston 3 522
Washington 3 021
Cleveland 2 872
Houston 2 697
Dallas 2 660
St. Louis 2 387
Miami 2 308
Pittsburgh 2 299
Baltimore 2 145
Minneapolis-St. Paul 2 049
Seattle 1 862
Atlanta 1 831
San Diego 1 676
Cincinnati 1 625
Milwaukee 1 600
Denver 1 466
Tampa 1 380
Buffalo 1 315
Kansas City 1 297
Phoenix 1 289
Indianapolis 1 148
New Orleans 1 132
Portland 1 126
Columbus 1 084
San Antonio 1 018
Rochester 971
Sacramento 929
Providence 904
Louisville 885
Memphis 883
Dayton 834
Salt Lake City 797
Birmingham 808
Norfolk 794
Toledo 776
Greensboro 774
Nashville 772
Oklahoma City 772
Hartford 729
Honolulu 718
Jacksonville 695
Syracuse 651
Scranton 630
Allentown 625
Tulsa 613
Richmond 604
Charlotte 596
Orlando 595
Omaha 579
Grand Rapids 576
Springfield 540
Youngstown 540
Greenville 535
Flint 517
Raleigh 485
West Palm Beach 477
Austin 476
Fresno 472
Tucson 455
Lansing 454
Knoxville 449
Baton Rouge 437
El Paso 437
Harrisburg 428
Mobile 424
New Haven 412
Johnson City 408
Albuquerque 402
Canton 402
Chattanooga 402
Bridgeport 396
Wichita 394
Charleston (S.C.) 383
Columbia 375
Worcester 375
Davenport 374
Fort Wayne 373
Little Rock 370
Bakersfield 363
Beaumont 363
Las Vegas 361
Newport News 360
Peoria 360
Shreveport 355
York 352
Lancaster 348
Des Moines 334
Utica 329
Madison 312
Spokane 312
Stockton 312
Binghampton 306
Reading 304
Corpus Christi 302
Huntington 297
Jackson 295
Lexington-Fayette 295
Colorado Springs 292
Evansville 291
Huntsville 290
Appleton 288
Santa Barbara 287
Augusta 284
Lakeland 277
South Bend 277
Pensacola 275
Salinas 275
Erie 274
Duluth 269
Kalamazoo 269
Johnstown 268
Rockford 268
Santa Rosa 263
Charleston (W. Va.) 260
New London 255
Montgomery 254
Eugene 249
Macon 241
Modesto 236
McAllen 235
Melbourne 234
Poughkeepsie 232
Fayetteville 231
Columbus 229
Saginaw 227
Waterbury 227
Salem 219
Savannah 217
Daytona Beach 214
Roanoke 213
Lima 210
Killeen 207
Lubbock 200

SOUTH AMERICA

ARGENTINA (1975)
Buenos Aires 8 436
Rosario 807
Córdoba 791
La Plata 479
Mendoza 471
San Miguel de Tucuman 366
Mar del Plata 300
Santa Fé 245
San Juan 218

BOLIVIA (1976)
La Paz 655
Santa Cruz 237

BRAZIL (1975)
São Paulo 7 199
Rio de Janeiro 4 858
Belo Horizonte 1 557
Recife 1 250
Salvador 1 237
Fortaleza 1 110
Pôrto Alegre 1 044
Nova Iguaçu 932
Belém 772
Curitiba 765
Brasilia 763
Duque de Caxias 537
São Gançalo 534
Goiania 518
Santo André 515
Campinas 473
Santos 396
Manaus 389
Osasco 377
Niterói 376
São João de Meriti 366
Natal 344
Campos 337
São Luiz 330
Maceió 324
Guarulhos 311
Teresina 290
João Pessoa 288
Juiz de Fora 284
Londrina 284
São Bernardo do Campo 267
Jaboatao 259
Ribeirão Preto 259
Olinda 251
Campina Grande 236
Pelotas 232
Feira de Santana 227
Aracaju 226
Petrópolis 217
Sorocaba 208
Jundiaí 205

CHILE (1978)
Santiago 3 692
Valparaiso 620
Concepción 519
Viña del Mar 262
Talcahuano 204

COLOMBIA (1973)
Bogotá 2 855
Medellin 1 159
Cali 990
Barranquilla 692
Cartagena 355
Bucaramanga 323
Cucuta 279
Manizales 232
Pereira 227
Ibagué 223

ECUADOR (1978)
Guayaquil 1 022
Quito 743

PARAGUAY (1974)
Asunción 565

PERU (1972)
Lima 3 303
Arequipa 302
Callao 297
Trujillo 240

URUGUAY (1975)
Montevideo 1 230

VENEZUELA (1976)
Caracas 2 576
Maracaibo 792
Valencia 439
Barquisimeto 430
Maracay 301
Barcelona-Puerto La Cruz 242
San Cristóbal 241

POPULATION OF COUNTRIES

Country	Area in thousands of square km	Population in thousands	Density of population per sq. km	Capital Population in thousands
Afghanistan	647	15 108	23	Kabul (588)
Albania	29	2 608	90	Tiranë (192)
Algeria	2 382	18 515	8	Algiers (1 503)
Angola	1 247	6 732	5	Luanda (475)
Argentina	2 767	26 393	10	Buenos Aires (8 436)
Australia	7 687	14 249	2	Canberra (215)
Austria	84	7 508	89	Vienna (1 590)
Bangladesh	144	84 655	588	Dacca (1 730)
Belgium	31	9 840	317	Brussels (1 042)
Belize	23	153	7	Belmopan (4)
Benin	113	3 377	30	Porto-Novo (104)
Bhutan	47	1 240	26	Thimphu (60)
Bolivia	1 099	5 137	5	Sucre (63) La Paz (655)
Botswana	600	726	1	Gaborone (37)
Brazil	8 512	115 397	14	Brasilia (763)
Brunei	6	201	35	Bandar Seri Begawan (37)
Bulgaria	111	8 814	79	Sofia (1 032)
Burma	677	32 205	48	Rangoon (2 276)
Burundi	28	4 256	152	Bujumbura (157)
Cambodia	181	8 574	47	Phnom Penh (2 000)
Cameroon	475	8 058	17	Yaoundé (314)
Canada	9 976	23 499	2	Ottawa (693)
Central Africa Rep.	623	2 370	4	Bangui (187)
Chad	1 284	4 309	3	Ndjamena (179)
Chile	757	10 857	14	Santiago (3 692)
China	9 597	975 230	102	Beijing (7 570)
Colombia	1 139	25 645	23	Bogota (2 855)
Congo	342	1 459	4	Brazzaville (290)
Costa Rica	51	2 111	41	San José (395)
Cuba	115	9 728	85	Havana (1 861)
Cyprus	9	616	66	Nicosia (147)
Czechoslovakia	128	15 138	118	Prague (1 176)
Denmark	43	5 104	119	Copenhagen (1 251)
Djibouti	22	113	5	Djibouti (62)
Dominican Republic	49	5 124	104	Santo Domingo (818)
Ecuador	284	7 814	28	Quito (743)
Egypt	1 001	41 000	41	Cairo (5 084)
El Salvador	21	4 365	208	San Salvador (366)
Equatorial Guinea	28	346	12	Rey Malabo (37)
Ethiopia	1 222	29 705	24	Addis Abeba (1 196)
Fiji	18	607	34	Suva (118)
Finland	337	4 752	14	Helsinki (825)
France	547	53 278	97	Paris (9 863)
French Guiana	91	60	1	Cayenne (25)
Gabon	268	538	2	Libréville (186)
Gambia	11	569	52	Banjul (48)
Germany, East	108	16 756	155	East Berlin (1 111)
Germany, West	249	61 310	246	Bonn (284)
Ghana	239	10 969	46	Accra (738)
Greece	132	9 360	71	Athens (2 101)
Greenland	2 176	51	0.02	Godthåb (9)
Guatemala	109	6 621	61	Guatemala (717)
Guinea	246	4 763	19	Conakry (526)
Guinea-Bissau	36	777	22	Bissau (109)
Guyana	215	820	4	Georgetown (187)
Haiti	28	4 833	173	Port-au-Prince (746)
Honduras	112	3 439	31	Tegucigalpa (274)
Hong Kong	1	4 606	4 386	Victoria (849)
Hungary	93	10 699	115	Budapest (2 082)
Iceland	103	224	2	Reykjavik (83)
India	3 288	638 388	194	Delhi (3 647)
Indonesia	2 027	145 100	72	Jakarta (4 576)
Iran	1 648	35 213	21	Tehran (4 496)
Iraq	435	12 327	28	Baghdad (2 969)
Irish Republic	70	3 365	48	Dublin (545)
Israel	21	3 689	177	Jerusalem (376)
Italy	301	56 697	188	Rome (2 898)
Ivory Coast	322	7 613	24	Abidjan (850)
Jamaica	11	2 133	194	Kingston (573)
Japan	372	114 898	309	Tokyo (11 695)
Jordan	98	2 984	30	Amman (712)
Kenya	583	14 856	26	Nairobi (835)
Korea, North	121	17 072	141	Pyongyang (1 500)
Korea, South	98	37 019	378	Seoul (6 879)
Kuwait	18	1 199	67	Kuwait (775)
Laos	237	3 546	15	Vientiane (177)
Lebanon	10	3 012	301	Beirut (702)
Lesotho	30	1 214	40	Maseru (29)
Liberia	111	1 742	16	Monrovia (172)
Libya	1 760	2 748	2	Tripoli (551)
Luxembourg	3	356	137	Luxembourg (78)
Madagascar	587	8 289	14	Antananarivo (378)
Malawi	118	5 669	48	Lilongwe (103)
Malaysia	330	12 960	39	Kuala Lumpur (452)
Mali	1 240	6 290	5	Bamako (404)
Malta	0.3	340	1 062	Valletta (14)
Mauritania	1 031	1 544	2	Nouakchott (135)
Mauritius	2	924	462	Port Louis (141)
Mexico	1 973	66 944	34	Mexico (13 994)
Mongolia	1 565	1 576	1	Ulan Bator (400)
Morocco	447	18 906	42	Rabat (596)
Mozambique	783	11 756	15	Maputo (384)
Namibia	824	852	1	Windhoek (61)
Nepal	141	13 421	95	Katmandu (210)
Netherlands	41	13 986	341	Amsterdam (965)
New Zealand	269	3 107	12	Wellington (328)
Nicaragua	130	2 395	18	Managua (500)
Niger	1 267	4 994	4	Niamey (130)
Nigeria	924	77 217	78	Lagos (1 477)
Norway	324	4 059	13	Oslo (645)
Oman	212	839	4	Muscat (25)
Pakistan	804	76 770	95	Islamabad (77)
Panama	76	1 826	24	Panama (440)
Papua New Guinea	462	3 000	6	Port Moresby (113)
Paraguay	407	2 888	7	Asunción (565)
Peru	1 285	16 819	13	Lima (3 303)
Philippines	300	46 351	154	Manila (1 438)
Poland	313	35 010	112	Warsaw (1 474)
Portugal	92	9 798	107	Lisbon (1 612)
Puerto Rico	9	3 317	372	San Juan (515)
Romania	238	21 855	92	Bucharest (1 934)
Rwanda	26	4 508	173	Kigali (90)
Saudi Arabia	2 150	7 866	4	Riyadh (667)
Senegal	196	5 381	27	Dakar (799)
Sierra Leone	72	3 292	45	Freetown (214)
Singapore	0.6	2 334	4 024	Singapore (2 308)
Somali Republic	638	3 443	5	Mogadishu (230)
South Africa	1 221	27 700	23	Pretoria (562) Cape Town (1 097)
Spain	505	37 109	74	Madrid (3 520)
Sri Lanka	66	14 346	217	Colombo (607)
Sudan	2 506	17 376	7	Khartoum (334)
Surinam	163	374	2	Paramaribo (151)
Swaziland	17	544	32	Mbabane (24)
Sweden	450	8 278	18	Stockholm (1 375)
Switzerland	41	6 337	155	Berne (284)
Syria	185	8 088	44	Damascus (1 142)
Taiwan	36	15 500	431	Taipei (3 050)
Tanzania	945	16 553	18	Dar-es-Salaam (757)
Thailand	514	45 100	88	Bangkok (4 702)
Togo	56	2 409	43	Lomé (135)
Trinidad and Tobago	5	1 133	222	Port of Spain (63)
Tunisia	164	6 077	37	Tunis (944)
Turkey	781	43 210	54	Ankara (1 701)
Uganda	236	12 780	54	Kampala (331)
United Arab Emirates	84	711	9	Abu Dhabi (236)
U.S.S.R.	22 402	263 400	12	Moscow (8 011)
United Kingdom	245	55 836	228	London (6 877)
United States	9 363	218 059	23	Washington (3 021)
Upper Volta	274	6 554	24	Ouagadougou (169)
Uruguay	178	2 864	16	Montevideo (1 230)
Venezuela	912	13 122	14	Caracas (2 576)
Vietnam	330	49 890	151	Hanoi (2 571)
Western Samoa	3	151	53	Apia (32)
Yemen (Sana)	195	5 642	29	Sana (448)
Yemen (South)	288	1 853	6	Aden (285)
Yugoslavia	256	21 914	86	Belgrade (775)
Zaire	2 345	27 745	12	Kinshasa (2 008)
Zambia	753	5 649	8	Lusaka (559)
Zimbabwe	391	6 930	18	Salisbury (616)

HOW TO USE AN ATLAS

HAROLD M. MAYER
JAMES JOHN FLANNERY
DONALD G. TEMPLE

UNDERSTANDING MAPS Maps offer a wealth of information to the reader who knows how to use them. By understanding a few simple principles and conventions of mapmaking, the reader can more easily extract the considerable amount of information appearing on a map. Basically, all maps are a balance between the limitations imposed by legibility (the amount of detail a map can contain) and the distortions that inevitably arise in attempting to depict the three-dimensional surface of the earth on a two-dimensional page of an atlas.

The oldest known maps were produced in the Middle East approximately 5,000 years ago. Maps have been in use ever since, and their utility is well established. They are among the most effective forms of communication for describing the physical appearance of an area, or the distribution of some specific phenomenon within an area (e.g., the population density of North America).

But a map cannot show everything about an area. To do so, it would need to be an exact, same-size duplicate of the area it depicts. In the planning and drafting of a map, only the necessary data are included. In order to understand what a specific map displays and how accurate it is, one needs to know why certain data are selected.

While space does not permit a full description of mapmaking and its fascinating history, the reader will be led from an understanding of the mapmaking process to an appreciation of an art and science that merge beauty and utility in objects of everyday use such as this atlas.

What Is an Atlas? An atlas is simply a collection of maps in bound or looseleaf form. The word *atlas* is derived from the titan Atlas, who, according to Greek mythology, supported the heavens and earth on his back. In the late sixteenth century, mapmaker Gerhardus Mercator used a drawing of Atlas as a frontispiece in a bound volume of maps representing the earth as it was known at that time. Since then, the term *atlas* has come into general use as a name for any systematic collection of maps.

There are many kinds of atlases. Some — such as economic, physical, and climatological atlases — are concerned with a single topic. Others contain maps showing a series of relationships — such as the distribution of races, religions, incomes, languages, diseases, etc. — within a particular area. Historical atlases graphically portray human activity and change over a period of time. The *Great International Atlas* has a multipurpose format. It includes a variety of maps and other reference materials that display information about the physical, political, cultural, economic, and scientific characteristics of the world.

MEXICANA
AFRICA
GERARDI MERCATORIS
EVROPA
ASIA
ATLAS
SIVE
COSMOGRAPHICÆ
MEDITATIONES
DE
FABRICA MVNDI ET
FABRICATI FIGVRA.
EXCUSUM SUB CANE VIGILANTI
QVARTA

The drawing of Atlas that appeared in Mercator's 16th century atlas.

The varied subject matter of a general purpose atlas allows the reader to see more than just the size and spatial relationships of the various land masses and bodies of water. Many different characteristics or attributes of an area are represented on various maps, thus providing a considerable amount of data and allowing for comparisons of data. For example, by comparing a climatic map and a vegetation map of the same area, the reader can identify relationships among precipitation, temperature, and different types of plant growth. Then, by comparing these two maps to a physical map of the same area, one can establish more complex interrelationships. One might discover, for example, that the highest elevation in the area has the lowest average temperature, and that much of the precipitation is in the form of snow. As a result, the vegetation at this altitude is very specialized and different from the vegetation appearing at a much lower elevation.

By comparing information on different maps, the reader can study the relationships among the features of the physical or natural environment as well as the interrelationships of such human aspects as the distribution of population, disease, and economic activity. This is one of the major informative functions of an atlas that eludes the inexperienced reader. To someone who has the ability to interpret accurately a single map, the relationships that can be inferred by comparing different maps of the same area become obvious. As you progress through this introduction, you will find out how to extract a considerable amount of data from a single map. You will then see how you can extend this ability to using atlas maps in combination.

What Is a Map? A map is a representation of a selected characteristic or set of characteristics of an area. Nearly anything that can be conceived of can be mapped directly or by inference. The subject can be tangible, like hills and valleys, or intangible, like the distribution of languages. Any attribute chosen to be represented on a map, however, must be non-ubiquitous. That is, it must vary in kind or intensity from one place to another in the mapped area. This concept can be easily understood by considering a physical relief map, which shows differences in elevation among various points in a mapped area. Similarly, a population density map displays the variation in the number of people living in different areas depicted on the map.

The elements of the environment depicted on maps may be a combination of natural and human characteristics. A map that displays a variety of these characteristics is called a *general purpose map*. The map of the United States on pages 110-111 is a good example of a general purpose map. It shows relief, rivers and streams, lakes, political boundaries, place names, railways, and highways. A map that shows only one or just a few aspects of the natural or human characteristics of an area is called a special purpose, or *thematic*, map. The map on page 158 depicting the production of iron, manganese, and other ferro-alloys is a good example of a thematic map.

As stated earlier, a map cannot depict everything about an area. Maps, therefore, are samples of reality. The number of features that can be depicted and their representation are limited by the type of projection used, by the scale of the map, and by the symbolization employed. How these factors impact on map display is dealt with below. Because the subject of map projections is somewhat complex, it is treated at greater length under Understanding Mapmaking.

Location — The Earth's Grid Maps are usually oriented with north at the top, which is purely by convention. This convention dates to classical times, when little was known of the southern hemisphere. All of the maps in this atlas follow this convention. In certain cases, because of the size or shape of the area depicted, maps are printed so that the book must be turned on its side in order to read the place names. When the book is held so that the place names can be read correctly, north will be at the top of the page.

Most maps contain a grid of lines to use in determining locations. Lines representing distances north and south of the equator are called *parallels*. They indicate the *latitude* north and south from 0° at the equator to 90° north at the North Pole and 90° south at the South Pole. Lines of latitude are called parallels because they are parallel to one another. The relative distance between parallels is nearly equal. Except for small differences due to the slight flattening of the earth near the poles, each degree of latitude is equal to every other. The actual distance between each degree is approximately 69 miles (111 km).

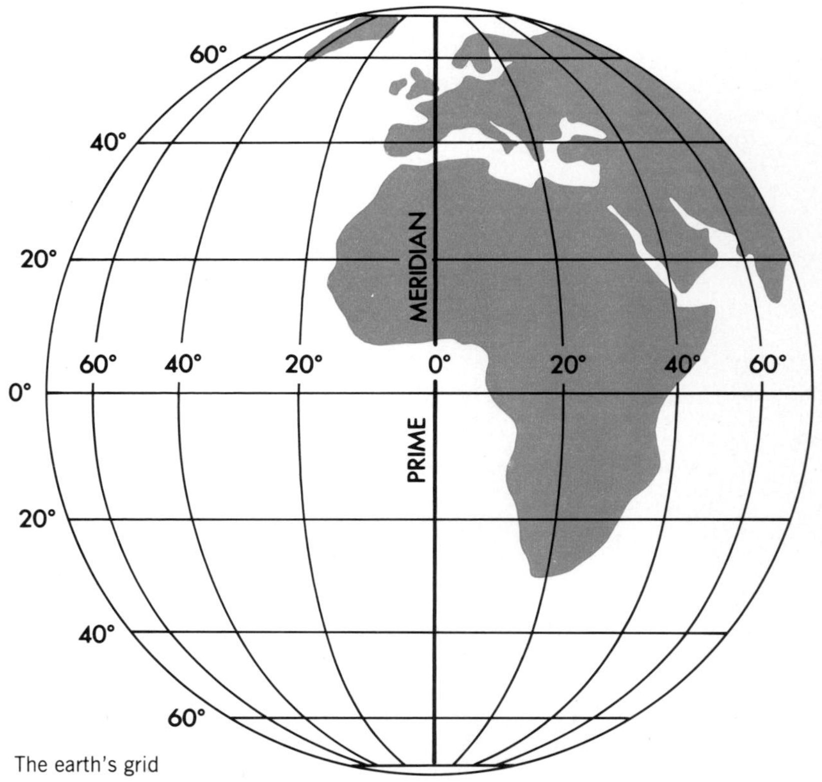
60°
40°
20°
0°
20°
40°
60°
60° 40° 20° 0° 20° 40° 60°
PRIME MERIDIAN
The earth's grid

The lines that represent east and west distances are called *meridians*. They are measured in degrees of longitude to 180° east and 180° west of the prime meridian. The prime meridian is the arbitrary line of 0° longitude established at the site of an observatory in the London borough of Greenwich. The prime meridian is often referred to as the Greenwich meridian to distinguish it from other prime meridians that may be found on some foreign maps. (The USSR, for example, places the prime meridian at Moscow.) On the other side of the earth, exactly opposite the prime meridian, is the International Date Line, which is both 180° east and 180° west longitude — except for some deviations due to international boundaries.

Unlike the lines of latitude, which are parallel, the meridians of longitude converge as they extend toward the North and South poles. At the equator (0° latitude), the distance between each meridian, or degree of latitude, is approximately 69 miles (111 km). As the earth curves toward the poles, this distance gradually lessens. At 30° north or south latitude, the distance is 60 miles (96.5 km). By 60° north or south latitude, a degree of longitude represents only 34.5 miles (55.5 km).

To enable more precision in locating a given point on the earth's surface, degrees of latitude and longitude are subdivided into minutes and seconds. There are 60 minutes within each degree and 60 seconds within each minute. One second of latitude (or of longitude near the equator) accounts for a distance of only about 101 feet (31 m). It becomes obvious, then, that by expressing latitude and longitude in degrees, minutes, and seconds, one can achieve a very high degree of accuracy in location. On most maps, including those in this atlas, an expression of latitude and longitude in degrees and minutes is sufficient to locate any point on a map.

Following the map section of this atlas is an alphabetical index of place names. Each index entry includes a series of numeric notations. The first, in **bold** print, identifies the specific page of the map upon which the place can be found. Following that are the specific latitude and longitude notations that are a guide to its location on the map. The index entry for New York City, for example, is **115** 40 45N 74 0W. This indicates that New York City may be found on the map on page 115 at or near the intersection of 40 degrees, 45 minutes north latitude and 74 degrees, zero minutes west longitude.

Turning to the map on page 115, the reader will notice that a grid is superimposed over the map, with latitude and longitude numbers appearing along the map margins. The grid on each map has the latitude numbers at the side and the longitude numbers at the top or the bottom. The margin numbers are in increments of degrees, but a position in degrees and minutes may be easily approximated by remembering that there are 60 minutes in each degree. Thus, 40 degrees, 45 minutes north latitude would be closer to 41 degrees north than to 40.

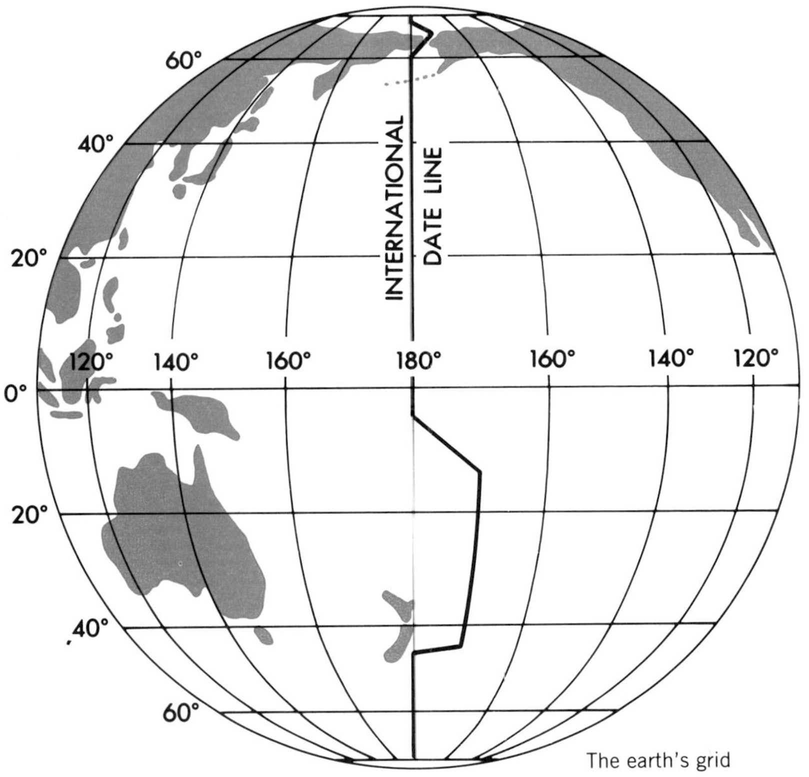

60°
40°
20°
0°
20°
40°
60°
INTERNATIONAL
DATE LINE
120°
140°
160°
180°
160°
140°
120°

The earth's grid

Time Time is related to longitude. Since it takes 24 hours for the earth to make one revolution, the time difference between places on the globe is one hour for every 15° of longitude (1/24 of 360°). Thus, clock time is one hour earlier for every 15° westward and one hour later for every 15° eastward. By convention, time is measured from the prime meridian at Greenwich and is known as Greenwich Mean Time (GMT). Standard time zones have been adopted, generally differing by one hour for each 15° of longitude.

In order to prevent the confusion that would arise if one political unit, such as a city or state, were in two time zones, the boundaries of the zones have been adjusted in many instances. In addition, a few political entities have chosen to adjust their time by increments of less than a full hour. As you can see from the world time map on pages 54 and 55 of the World Reference Information section, time zone boundaries and differences have become quite irregular.

Scale The term *scale* refers to the ratio between the distances on a map and the distances on the area of the earth that the map represents. Maps are reductions of reality. In order for the reduction to be consistent, so that the spacial relationships among various points on the earth's surface are correctly depicted on the map, the map must be drawn to one scale. The scale selected will determine the amount of information that can appear on a map. The relationship between scale and legibility can easily be visualized by imagining a map of the entire United States drawn on a 6″ x 9″ sheet of paper. It would be impossible to include the name of every community with a population of 500 or more on such a map and still maintain its legibility. Therefore, the scale of the map requires that the cartographer make decisions about what and how much information shall appear on it.

Since different maps cover different areas, the scale may vary from map to map. In this atlas, the scale of each map is given in the margin at the top of the page. It is given in two forms: a numeric ratio and a bar scale. The numeric ratio shows the relationship between distance on the map and distance on the actual area of the earth depicted. A ratio of 1:1,000,000 (one to one million), for example, means that one unit on the map represents one million units on the earth's surface. A unit of measure is not given with the numeric ratio, since the ratio holds true whether the unit is inches, centimeters, feet, etc. (That is, one inch on the map equals 1,000,000 inches on the earth, just as one centimeter on the map equals 1,000,000 centimeters on the earth.)

Bar scales in this atlas are shown in both miles and kilometers. For most readers, bar scales tend to be more meaningful and useful than numeric ratios. Using a ruler, the edge of a sheet of paper, or some other straight-edged tool, the reader can measure the distance between two points on the map and compare that distance with the bar scale, thus arriving at the approximate number of miles or kilometers between the two points.

The terms *large scale* and *small scale* sometimes cause confusion and need to be clarified. A map at a scale of 1:50,000 is larger in scale than one drawn at a scale of 1:300,000. At a scale of 1:50,000 a length of one mile of the earth's surface will be about 1.25 inches (3 cm) on the map. At a scale of 1:300,000 one mile is about 0.2 inch (0.5 cm). The smaller the figure following the colon in the numeric ratio, the larger the scale.

On a map of a given area of the earth's surface, the larger the scale is, the more detail can be included on it. Given two maps of the same size, the map with the larger scale will depict a smaller area of the earth's surface and will include more detail than the one with the smaller scale. Also, as the map scale approaches 1:1, the larger the map will be in relation to the area mapped. Thus, at a scale of 1:1, a map of one square mile of the earth's surface would need to be one square mile in size.

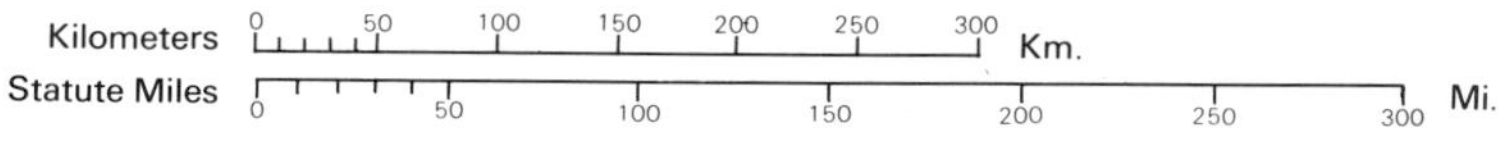
Kilometers
0 50 100 150 200 250 300 Km.
Statute Miles
0 50 100 150 200 250 300 Mi.

Numeric ratio and bar scale

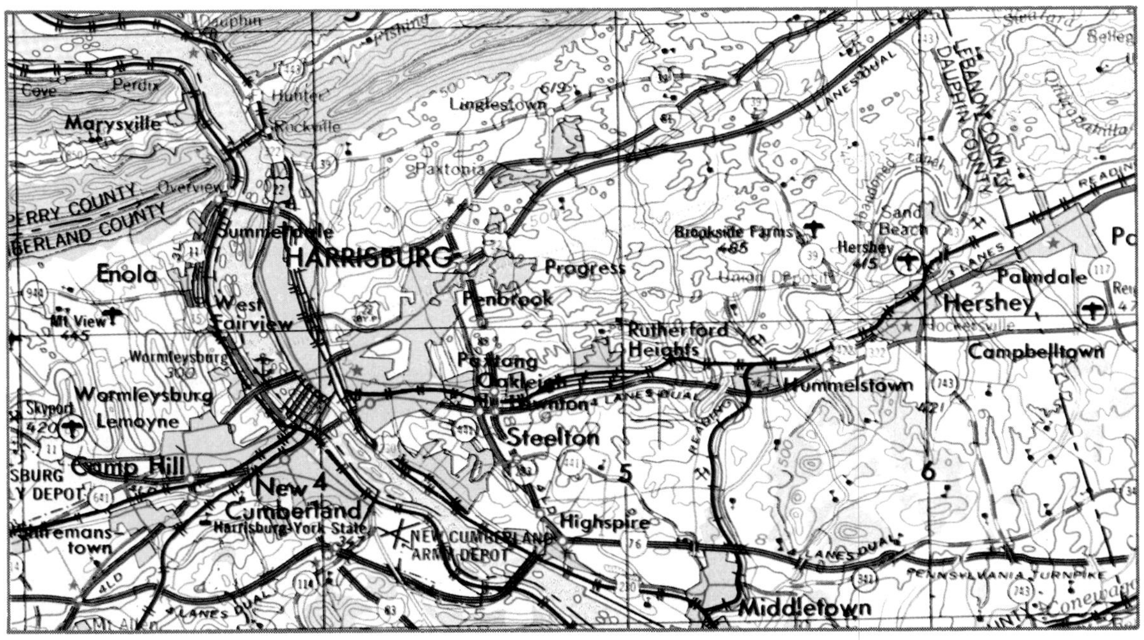
Marysville
Linglestown
Paxtonia
PERRY COUNTY
CUMBERLAND COUNTY
Summerdale
HARRISBURG
Progress
Enola
West Fairview
Penbrook
Rutherford Heights
Paxtang
Oakleigh
Wormleysburg
Lemoyne
Steelton
Camp Hill
New Cumberland
Highspire
Middletown
Hummelstown
Hershey
Palmdale
Campbelltown
Brookside Farms
Sand Beach
NEW CUMBERLAND ARMY DEPOT
LEBANON COUNTY
DAUPHIN COUNTY
PENNSYLVANIA TURNPIKE
Harrisburg, Pennsylvania, at a scale of 1:250,000

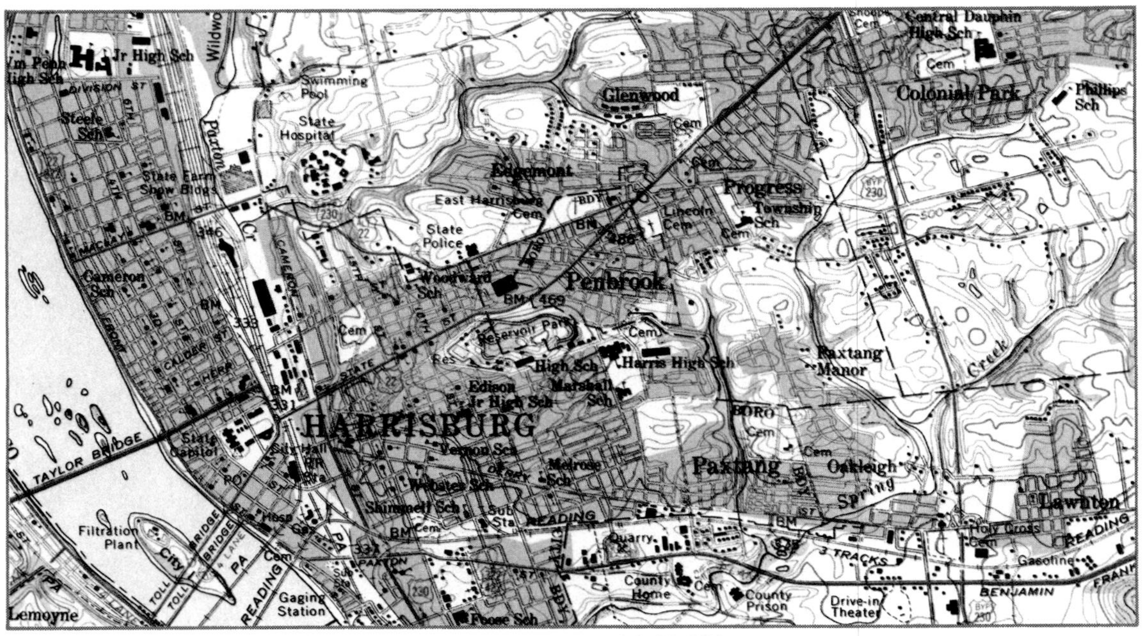
Central Dauphin High Sch
Colonial Park
Glenwood
State Hospital
Edgemont
East Harrisburg Cem
Progress
Lincoln Cem
State Police
Penbrook
Paxtang Manor
HARRISBURG
Harris High Sch
Edison Jr High Sch
Paxtang
Oakleigh
Lawnton
TAYLOR BRIDGE
State Capitol
Filtration Plant
County Home
County Prison
Drive-in Theater
Gaging Station
Lemoyne
Harrisburg at a scale of 1:62,500

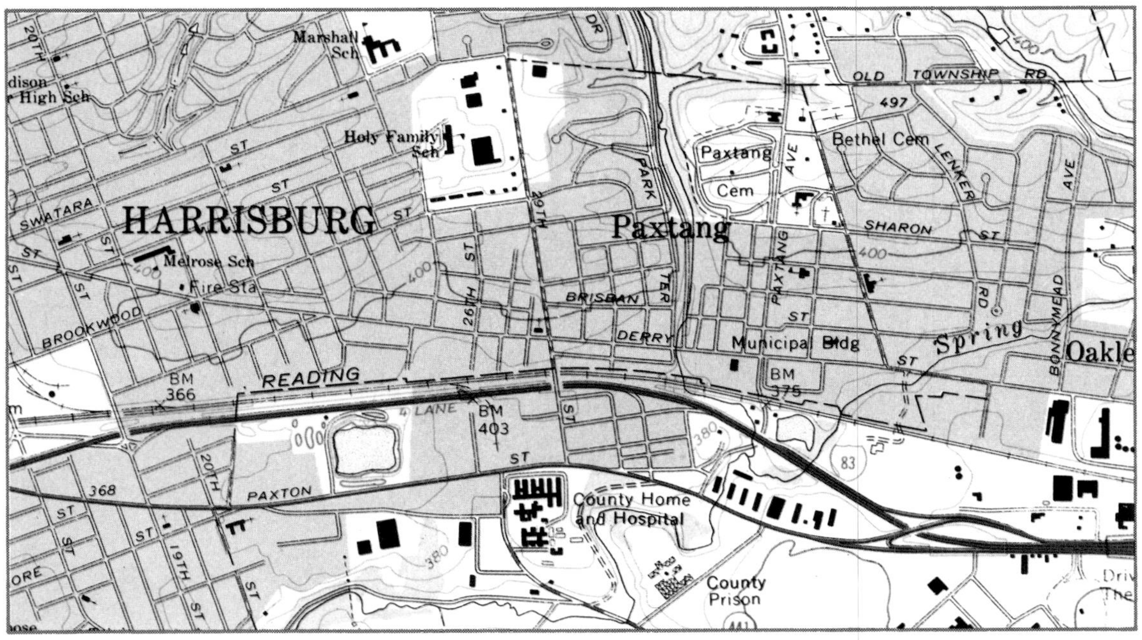
Marshall Sch
OLD TOWNSHIP RD
Holy Family Sch
Bethel Cem
Paxtang Cem
HARRISBURG
Paxtang
SHARON ST
Melrose Sch
Fire Sta
BRISBAN
DERRY
Municipal Bldg
Spring
BROOKWOOD
READING
PAXTON
County Home and Hospital
County Prison
Harrisburg at a scale of 1:24,000

Symbols The symbols used on maps influence the kinds of data that can be included and the effectiveness with which those data are presented. Basically, maps employ three general types of symbols: *point, line,* and *area*. These symbols may appear in black or in color. In fact, color itself may be used as a map symbol — to show differences in elevation for example.

Almost everyone is familiar with certain point and line symbols used on maps. Cities are frequently represented by dots or, if scale permits, by circles or squares. These may be hollow or filled, and they may be of different sizes to represent cities of various populations. Line symbols may consist of connected lines, broken lines, dotted lines, or various combinations of these forms. Symbols that are common to many or most maps in an atlas are generally identified in a key. This atlas contains such a key on page 1 of the map section. Symbols that are used on a single map are identified in a key accompanying that map.

Map symbols may be abstract — such as dots, lines, or various geometrical point symbols or patterns — or pictorial. *Pictorial symbols* are often used to indicate some special characteristic of an area, such as a particular industry. Pictorial symbols are most often used on thematic maps.

The size of a symbol is seldom proportional to the area occupied by the place or feature indicated. On all but very large-scale maps, a compromise must be made between true scale and effective visual presentation. In order to be legible, the symbol often covers a proportionately larger area on the map than the area it refers to covers on the actual landscape.

This exaggeration applies to line symbols, such as those referring to roads, railways, or rivers, as well as to point symbols. This is neither error nor poor cartography but a generalization permitted by the rules of mapmaking and necessary to assure legibility.

The principle of generalization relates to all aspects of cartography. Only a small number of all the possible features of any given area can be represented on maps of the scales used in most atlases. In order to maintain legibility, the editor or cartographer must limit the number of features to be

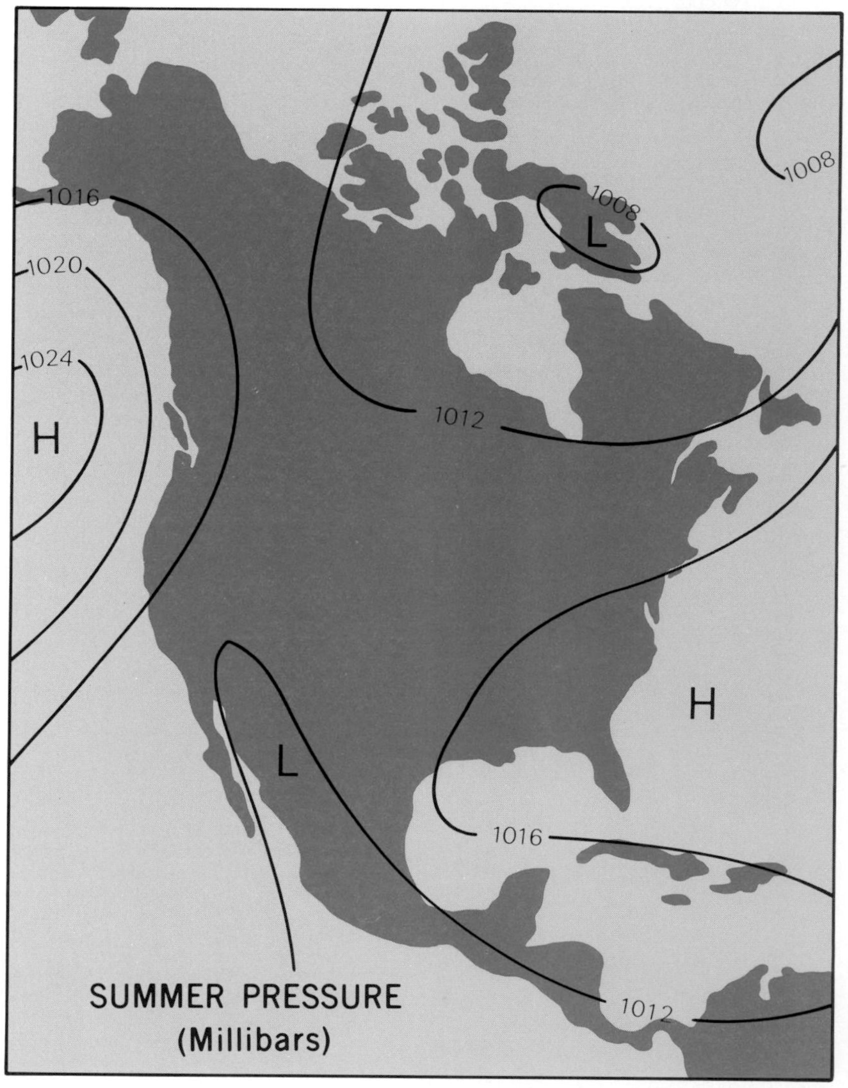
1016
1020
1024
H
1012
1008
L
1008
H
L
1016
1012
SUMMER PRESSURE
(Millibars)

A weather map showing isobars

represented. What will or will not be included depends on the purpose of the map and the significance of the various features.

As noted in the discussion of scale, a map of the United States drawn on a 6″ x 9″ sheet of paper could not show every community with a population of 500 or more. By establishing a level of significance for cities, an editor determines the minimum population size that qualifies a city for inclusion on the map. Because the space available is limited, the level of significance may be quite high, with perhaps only cities of 250,000 or more people being identified. A level of significance for nearly every characteristic of an area being mapped must be specified and applied consistently in compiling and drafting a map.

Line symbols other than boundaries, rivers, roads, etc., may also appear on maps. One type of line symbol is used to show variations in quantity or amount of things in movement. These flow-line symbols vary in width to show the movement of such things as manufactured goods, raw materials, and traffic. A series of thematic maps on pages 145-160 depict the flow of a wide variety of materials between various countries around the world.

Another group of quantitative line symbols used on maps are *isograms*, or lines of equal measure or value. One type of isogram is the contour line. A contour line connects all points of equal elevation on a map. In this atlas, contour lines are used on relief maps, where they serve as boundary lines for the different colors used to show a range of elevations.

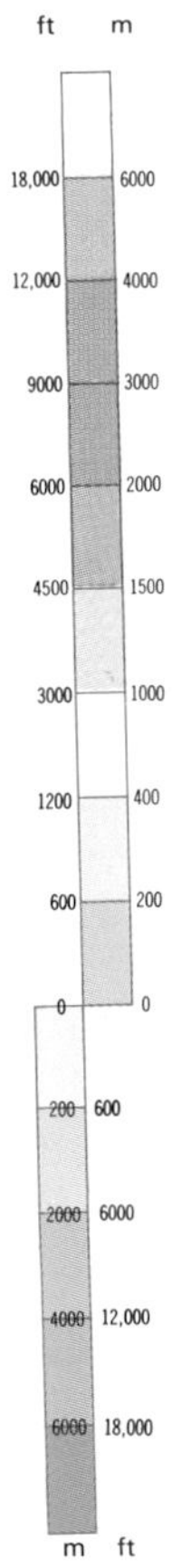
ft
m
18,000
6000
12,000
4000
9000
3000
6000
2000
4500
1500
3000
1000
1200
400
600
200
0
0
200
600
2000
6000
4000
12,000
6000
18,000
m
ft
Color bar

Isograms are also used to indicate temperature distribution and water depth. Weather maps make use of a type of isogram called an *isobar*, a line of equal atmospheric pressure.

In this atlas, isograms are used mainly as boundaries for area symbols. When patterns, tones, or colors are used over an area on a map, they are referred to as area symbols. Area symbols are used in color relief maps to indicate differences in elevation. They are also used on thematic maps, where they indicate such characteristics as the distribution of rainfall, income, temperature, and population. The most common use of area symbols in this atlas is on physical maps. In the margin of each physical map is a *color bar*, or relief scale, similar to the one shown here. The color bar correlates the various colors on a particular map with the land elevations and water depths they represent. The color bars show elevations and depths in both feet and meters.

Point, line, and area symbols all have proper roles to play in good map design. Good map design means that the proper symbol has been chosen to represent the data depicted on the map. If the data to be symbolized are discrete, such as cities, then point symbols are most appropriate. If the data concern continuous distribution over a large area, such as precipitation or land use, then area symbols are best. The use of line symbols is best seen in those cases where there is need to show boundaries, highways, rivers, railroads, or other linear features.

A final system of symbolic notation, and the most familiar, is *lettering*. Lettering identifies the place names and other features of a mapped area. Variations in both type size and typeface have symbolic significance. The relative size of population centers, for example, is indicated by the size of type used for cities. The key on page 1 of the map section shows the relationship between type size and population. An *italic* typeface is generally used to distinguish natural physical features — such as rivers or mountains — from human or cultural features — such as cities, states, or countries.

UNDERSTANDING MAPMAKING Most maps, like those in this atlas, are begun by using other maps as sources. This method of mapmaking is called *compilation* (as opposed to *survey*, which involves gathering data directly from the earth). Maps that show climatic data, economic data, and the like, use statistical sources of a non-map type, but the outlines of land areas, political boundaries, and other features on which the statistical data are displayed are taken from survey maps. The source, or survey map, used is generally at the same scale or a larger scale than the compilation map — since an enlargement of a smaller-scale map would only magnify certain errors present in all maps. Maps published by government agencies, such as the United States Geological Survey (U.S.G.S.), provide the largest source of survey maps. Firms that have been publishing atlases for generations, such as the publisher of this atlas, have their own library of source maps.

Topographic Maps The original source, or base, of all compilation maps is the *topographic map*. A topographic map is a large-scale, general purpose map of a relatively small portion of the earth's surface. It contains a variety of detailed information about the human and natural landscape features of the area covered. A key element in a topographic map is that it shows not only the correct planimetric (horizontal) relationships of all features in an area, but the hypsometric (vertical) characteristics as well. Contour lines, lines connecting points of equal elevation above sea level, are used to symbolize relief.

Before a series of topographic maps can be made, certain data must be assembled to make sure that the drawing will be as accurate as possible. It is important to know what the curvature of the earth's surface is in the area to be mapped. The earth is not a perfect sphere. As you can see from the diagram, the earth is slightly flattened at the poles and slightly bulged at the equator. A mathematical model of this shape, called an ellipsoid, is used to determine the rate of curvature of the earth's surface at various latitudes. The departure from true sphericity must be known if maps drawn to a large scale are to be accurate. If the maps are to be drawn at a small scale, the earth can be considered a perfect sphere.

A second step in creating a topographical map is the selection of a map projection. The earth is a curving, three-dimensional surface; yet maps are drawn and printed on flat sheets of paper. The relationships that exist on a curved surface, or sphere, cannot be transferred without qualification (or without some degree of error) onto a flat two-dimensional surface. There can be no absolutely true representation of the earth on a flat surface.

If you remove the skin of a sphere-like object — such as an orange — and then try to flatten it, you find that the skin stretches in some places and compresses in others. That is, some distances are increased and

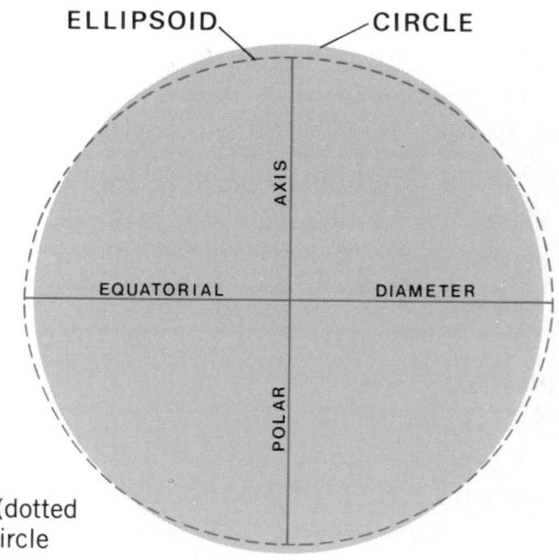

ELLIPSOID
CIRCLE
AXIS
EQUATORIAL
DIAMETER
POLAR

The earth's surface (dotted line) and a perfect circle

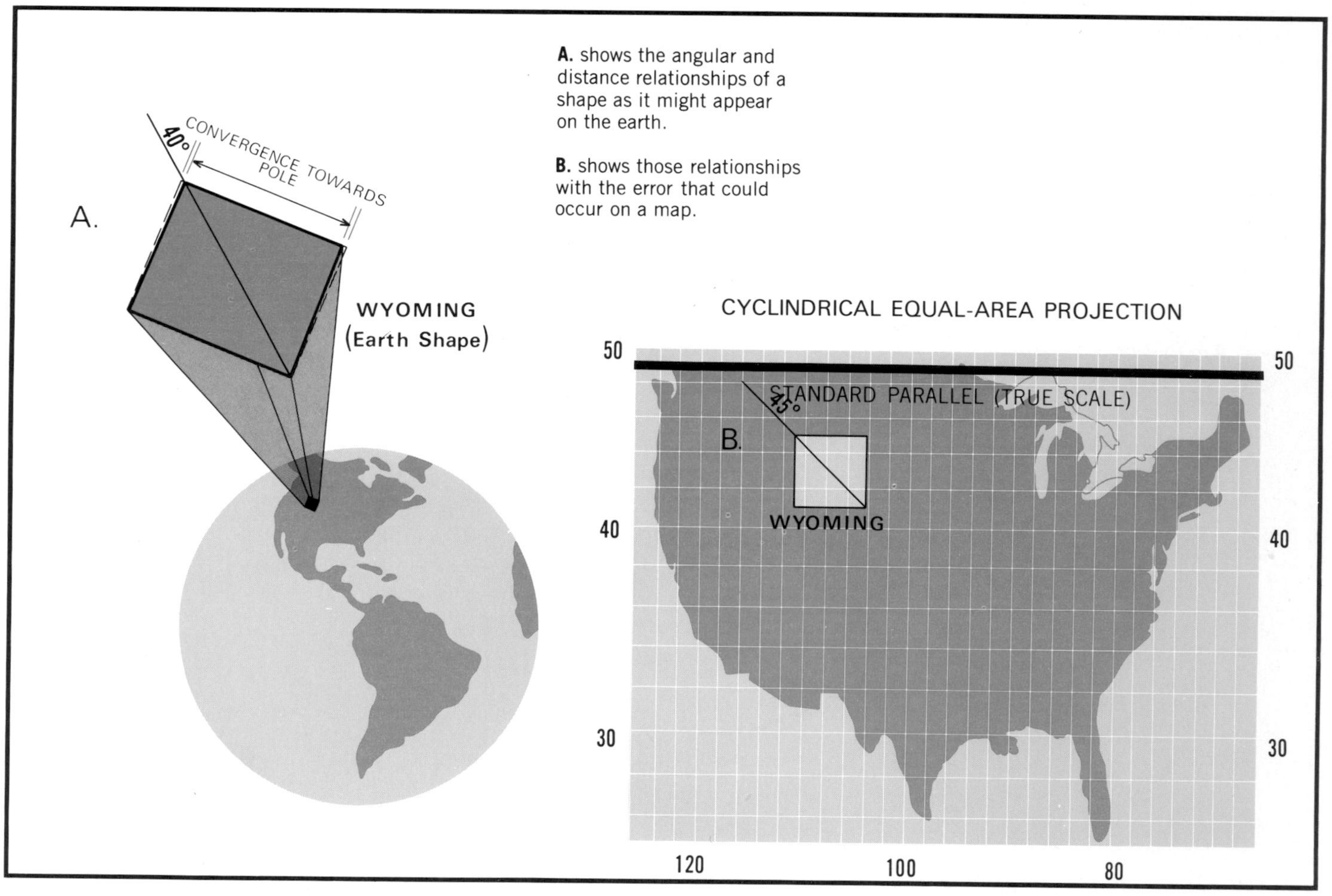

A.
40°
CONVERGENCE TOWARDS POLE
WYOMING
(Earth Shape)
CYCLINDRICAL EQUAL-AREA PROJECTION
50
STANDARD PARALLEL (TRUE SCALE)
45°
B.
WYOMING
40
30
120
100
80
50
40
30

A. shows the angular and distance relationships of a shape as it might appear on the earth.

B. shows those relationships with the error that could occur on a map.

others are decreased. The same kind of thing happens when mapmakers transfer distances from the earth's curved surface to a flat sheet of paper. And those alterations in distances result in the basic error of all maps. The larger the area of the earth covered by the map, the greater the distance alteration. In theory, even very large-scale maps (those covering small areas of the earth) tell lies about distance. But on a large-scale map the lies are so small that they can be ignored. What the basic error means is that the scale of a map is perfectly accurate only along one or two parallels or meridians.

A consequence of the basic error in distance is that locations of places on a map may not have the same angular relationships as they do on the earth's surface (or on a globe). A point on a map that seems to be exactly northwest of another point may, in fact, be one or more degrees off true northwest. Angular error, like distance error, is persistent. It cannot be completely eliminated from maps, but it can be controlled and modified.

A third potential type of error is in the depiction of the relative sizes of areas. Areas such as continents, for example, may be shown as larger or smaller in relation to one another than they really are. On some maps, for example, Greenland appears to be much larger than Australia. But in fact, Australia is about three and one-half times larger than Greenland. This exaggeration or diminution of areas can be completely corrected. It is therefore possible to have a world map on which all continents are shown in their true size relationship.

But in order to achieve this accuracy in relative size, the mapmaker must make a fourth error of mapping: shape distortion. It is not possible, on the same map, to show all areas in their true size and their true shape. This concept can be understood by again considering the orange. The orange skin can be flattened, and it will still be the same size as it was on the orange. However, the flattening process will distort its shape.

Distance, direction, size (or area), and shape — all are subject to error on flat maps. Each of these factors may be corrected, either totally or to a great extent. But all of them cannot be corrected on the same map. Therefore, any flat map will contain errors in one or more of these factors. In general, the smaller the scale, the greater the potential for error. In selecting a projection, the cartographer must decide which distortions are acceptable for the purpose of the map. These illustrations show six methods of mapping the same area. By comparing the six methods, you can see how errors in all four factors actually show themselves on maps.

The same area of the earth mapped in six different projections

Lambert's Equivalent Azimuthal

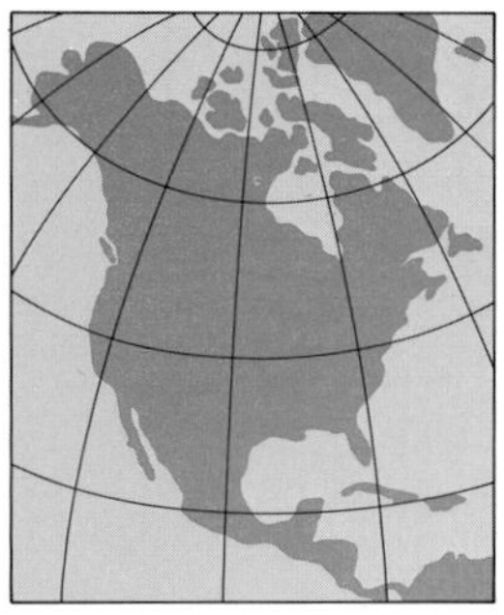

Mercator

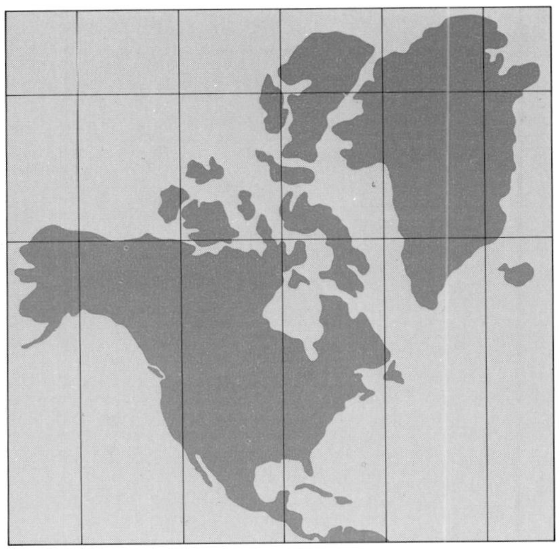

Sinusoidal

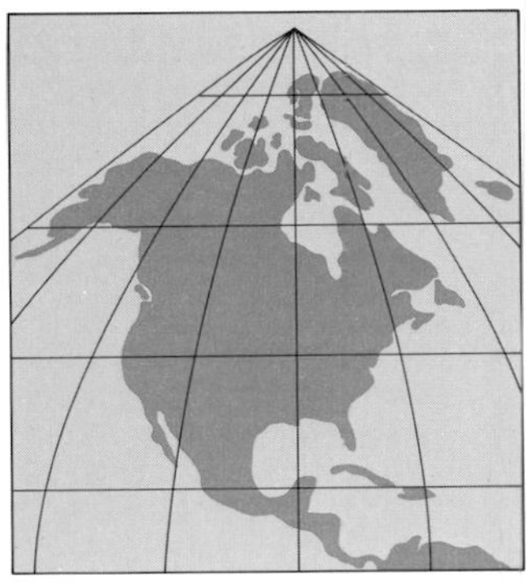

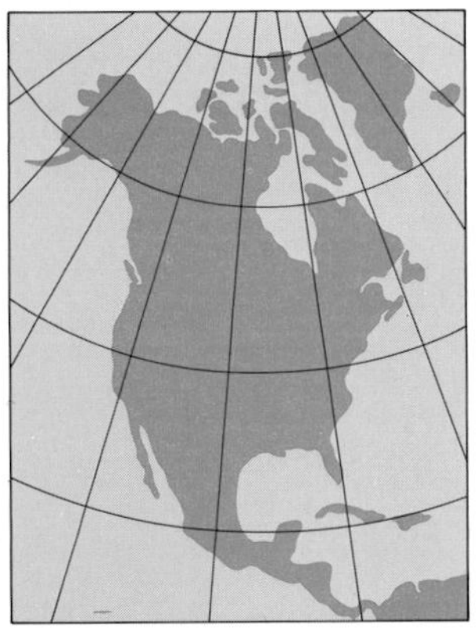

Albers Conical Equal Area

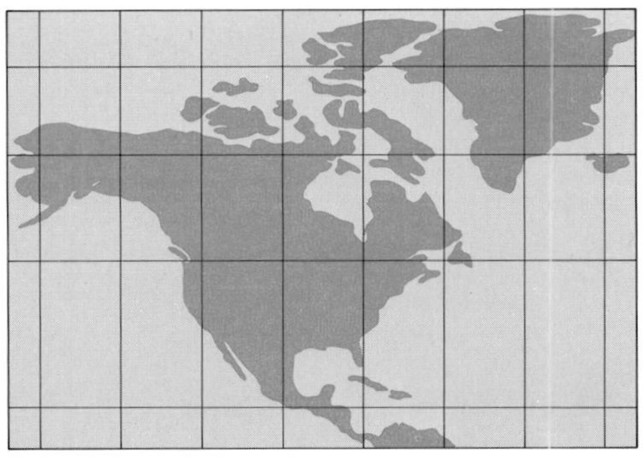

Miller

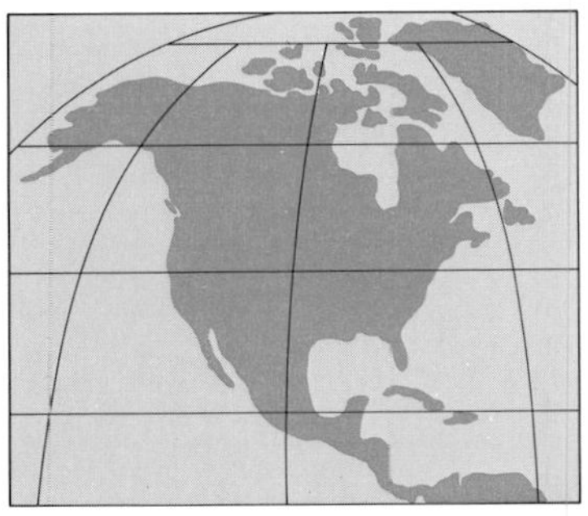

Mollweide Interrupted Homolographic

Projections *Projections* are the mechanisms that provide the cartographer with ways to control distortion. They are the means by which the features of a curved, sphere-shaped earth are transferred to a flat sheet of paper. A simple definition of a map projection is "an orderly arrangement of the earth's grid of latitude and longitude on a flat surface." By this definition, a sheet of graph paper with the horizontal lines identified as latitudes (parallels) and the vertical lines as longitudes (meridians) qualifies as a projection. And such a projection actually exists. The French call it a *plat carre;* in English, it is called a plane chart.

A projection is a kind of transformation, a transformation of the earth's grid from a sphere to a flat surface in a way that attempts to minimize the distortion of the grid. Imagine a transparent globe on which the earth's grid is drawn. Inside the globe is a light that can project the grid onto a sheet of paper. That sheet of paper could be flat and touching the globe at only one point. The sheet could be rolled into a cylinder and wrapped completely around the globe. Or the sheet could be shaped into a cone and placed over the globe like a hat. The earth's grid would look different on each sheet. The way the grid is projected in each of these methods is actually three different map projections: planar (or azimuthal), cylindrical, and conic.

Each of these three types of projections — and there are variations within each type — has advantages and disadvantages. Each produces some sort of distortion of distance, direction, area, or shape. Using mathematical formulas, cartographers can make corrections to minimize these distortions.

It is also possible to forget about the projection of the earth's grid onto a plane, cylinder, or cone and simply plot the grid on a sheet of paper by using a mathematical formula. This is the way the founder of modern cartography, Gerhardus Mercator, developed the projection that bears his name. All of the oval class of projections, so popular for world maps, have been developed without the intermediate projection onto the surface of a plane, cone, or cylinder. The accuracy of the map prepared is directly proportional to the sophistication of the mathematical formula used. In earlier times, the formula used was fairly simple, and considerable distortion occurred in the highest and lowest latitudes of maps — that is, in the latitudes nearest the North and South poles. The Mercator projection suffers from this distortion.

In developing the formulas for projections, it is possible to preserve true area (size) relationships among land masses over an entire area. These are called equal-area, or *equivalent* projections. Most of the

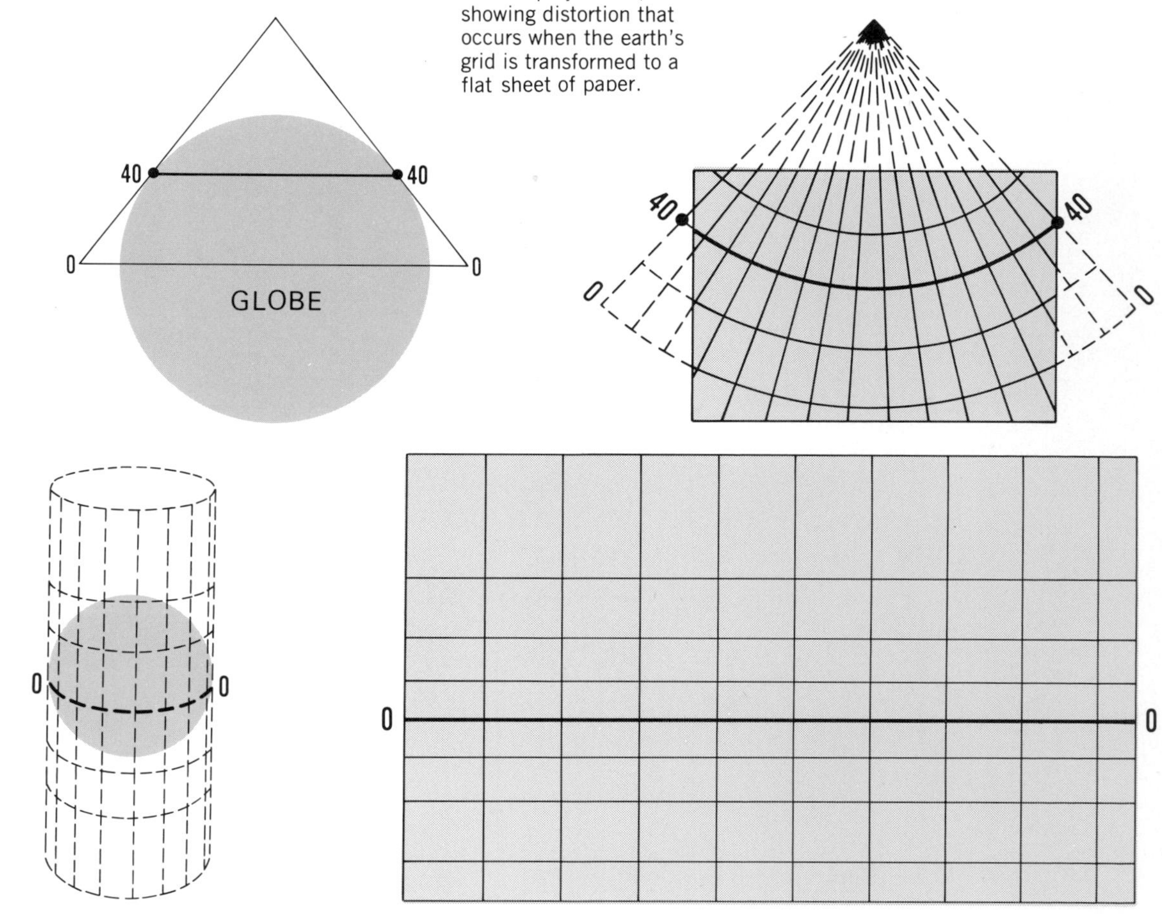

40
40
0
0
GLOBE
40
40
0
0
0
0
0
0

Various projections, showing distortion that occurs when the earth's grid is transformed to a flat sheet of paper.

projections used in this atlas are equivalent projections. There are also projections that attempt to preserve true angular relationships between points. These are *azimuthal* projections. An equivalent projection can eliminate all distortion of area, but an azimuthal projection can eliminate distortion of direction in only a limited way. Another type of projection is the *conformal*. It is another way to preserve angular relationships between points on a map, and one that is often more accurate than an azimuthal projection.

There are literally hundreds of potential projections, all of which are variations of the categories mentioned. However, only about twenty to twenty-five are in common use. This atlas uses eleven different projections. As stated earlier, most are equivalent projections, which preserve the relative sizes of the various land masses.

As you can readily see from examining different maps, the shape of an area may vary from projection to projection. But shapes can also vary on different maps using the same projection, depending on the *standard point* or *line* chosen by the cartographer. A standard point or line is a location on the map where the scale of the map is completely accurate. This concept can be better understood by referring to the illustrations of standard parallels. The necessity of scale accuracy is particularly important when a map is used for navigational purposes, since it will affect the calculation of distances between various points. Special projections have been developed to preserve true area size and also give true distances insofar as possible.

CYCLINDRICAL EQUAL-AREA PROJECTION
STANDARD PARALLEL 39°

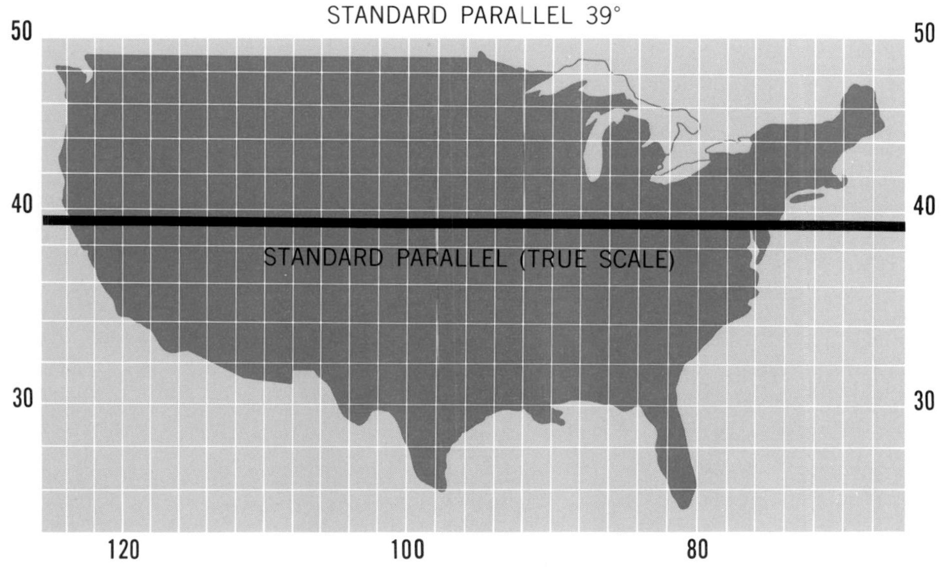

50
50
40
40
STANDARD PARALLEL (TRUE SCALE)
30
30
120
100
80

CYCLINDRICAL EQUAL-AREA PROJECTION
STANDARD PARALLEL 49°

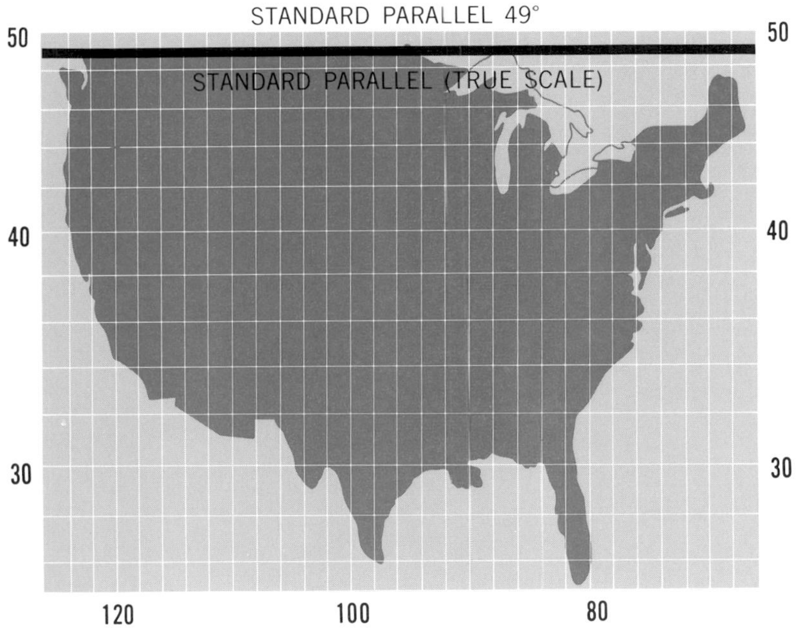

50
50
STANDARD PARALLEL (TRUE SCALE)
40
40
30
30
120
100
80

The same projection, showing shape distortion that results from using different standard lines.

Compiling Data After a projection has been selected for mapping purposes, the data to appear on the map must be compiled. If no source map of the area exists, a topographic map is usually prepared first.

Ground control is essential to topographic mapping. This control is established by surveying crews, whose responsibility is to locate the precise latitude and longitude of a series of points in the area. These points are then tied into a control network. The elevations of the points are compared to the mean sea level. Also, the distances between each point are verified by comparing them to the North American Datum. The North American Datum is a control station located at Meades Ranch in north central Kansas; it has a point for which the precise latitude and longitude are known. This point serves as a control for all mapping of North America.

Additional control can be established through aerial photography. When an area is mapped topographically for the first time, vertical aerial photographs provide not only horizontal control, but also the elevation and other detailed data that go on the map. A series of overlapping photographs that have been taken from slightly different angles can be viewed through very accurate instruments to obtain a three-dimensional, or stereoscopic, image of the earth. A skilled operator can use a device attached to the instrument to draw contour lines connecting points of equal elevation on the map. Using this method, the United States Geological Survey produces topographic maps of a high degree of accuracy.

In recent years, the U.S.G.S. has been using aerial *orthophotographs* in making topographic maps. In most aerial photographs, only a single point directly beneath the lens can be photographed straight-on; all other points are at varying angles. Orthophotographs are processed with special instruments so that all points on the photograph appear as if they are directly under the lens, thus eliminating angular distortion. Another advantage of the

Swamp
HICKORY
GROVE
ROAD
Irvin Hill Ch
Cem
Cem
GEORGIA
SOUTHERN
AND
FLORIDA
Substation
Loch
Laurel
Dasher
An orthophotograph of a section of Georgia

orthophoto is that it has a colored texture background, which makes the drawing of contour lines much easier.

Another recent development that has been of great use to cartographers is the availability of satellite imagery. Weather satellites provide cloud and temperature data for weather mapping. Sometimes, the satellite images themselves serve as maps. Since the early 1970s, Landsat satellites (originally ERTS — Earth Resources Technology Satellite) have provided a massive amount of data in the form of images of the earth's land masses. Circling the earth in polar (north to south) orbits, these satellites transmit a continuous stream of overlapping images of the land, each covering an area approximately 115 miles (185 km) square. Its orbit takes a Landsat satellite over every part of a continent every eighteen days. Landsat imagery may be used as a data source or as a base map on which place names and other information can be overprinted.

Whenever maps are compiled, *generalization* takes place. Crowded maps are difficult to use. What is included on a map is determined by its scale, its purpose, its graphic character (for example, the colors used), and the quality of the source data. When the source map is at a much larger scale than the new map being compiled (which is usually the case), much less detail can be transferred. If the purpose of the map is thematic, such as a map depicting population density, the cartographer will be more selective and avoid the inclusion of such characteristics as relief features, waterways, or highways — which would clutter the map and obscure its theme.

Generalization is an art. The amount of information to be included — the details of coastline configuration, for example — and the generalization implicit in all symbolization must be considered by the cartographer, who must always keep in mind the major purpose of the map. The compilation of high-quality general purpose maps such as those found in this atlas is an extremely time-consuming process; and, because human and physical data change with time, maps need to be updated regularly.

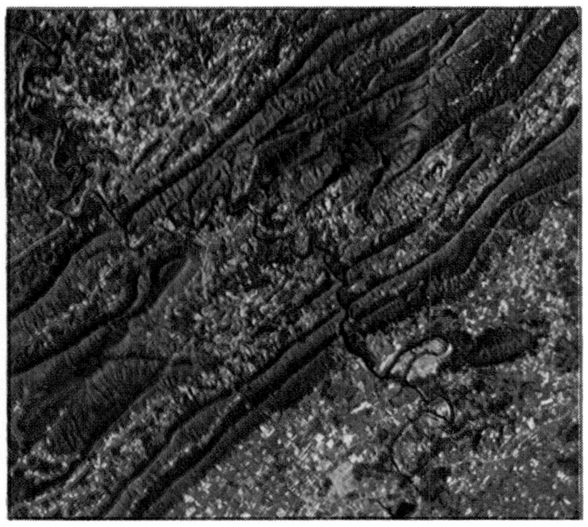

A section of a Landsat photograph

Drafting Maps Once a map has been compiled, it must be drafted. Until recent decades, maps were drafted in ink. Drafting maps in ink requires considerable skill, and it takes a number of years to train someone to reach that high level of skill. Even then, the quality of the ink-drafted map is affected by variations in paper or film surfaces, changes in humidity, and even the daily mood of the cartographer, to name only a few complications.

The time required to train a professional cartographic drafter and the time required to draft a map in ink posed some serious problems for large governmental and private mapping facilities in the United States in the 1950s. The U.S.G.S., for example, had a large backlog of compiled maps that were waiting to be drafted. New processes, such as photogrammetry, had expedited the compilation process, but drafting was still being done in the time-consuming traditional manner. As a result, a method — called *negative scribing* — was developed that proved to be a successful means of speeding up the drafting process.

In negative scribing, the drafting is done on sheets of coated plastic. Sharp tools called scribers are used to scrape off the coating, leaving translucent lines that allow light to pass through. The scribed map can be used as a photographic negative in making the printing plate.

Scribing is much faster than drafting in ink. The line work is sharper and can be reproduced without the photographic reduction necessary with ink drafting of even the highest quality. Corrections can easily be made by painting out the errors, recoating the clear plastic, and rescribing. Scribing points and blades of various widths and design give the cartographic drafter as much flexibility as pen and ink. Moreover, a skilled scriber can be trained in about one-tenth of the time it takes to train a skilled ink drafter.

Negative scribing can be used for more than just the line work on a map. It is used to create the color separations for color maps. An example is the blue used on maps to represent oceans and other large bodies of water. A material similar to the plastic used in line scribing allows the cartographer to cut out and peel off areas of an opaque coating, thus exposing an area of translucent plastic. As with line scribing, the resulting sheet may be used as a negative in making a printing plate.

Nearly all maps printed in color are drafted as color separation drawings. It is rare for an original map to be drawn in color. In color separation, a separate drawing is prepared for each color to be printed. (Most ''full-color'' printing is the result of combining four basic colors: black, blue, yellow, and red. There is a separate printing plate for each color, and each plate prints one of those colors in the printing process.) Color separation drawings require a great deal of skill and precision. The drawings must be perfectly aligned so that the resulting printing plates are perfectly aligned and, finally, so that each color will print in precisely the right place on the page. Tolerances are measured in hundredths of an inch. In this atlas, the maps in the world map section are printed with a unique six-color printing process. The process creates an additional subtlety in the coloring and shading that is not possible with conventional four-color printing. The results are maps that are more legible and more pleasing to the eye.

The only part of a map that cannot be conveniently scribed is the lettering. Today, lettering is not done by hand but is set in type on sheets. Pieces of lettering (such as place names) are then cut from the sheet and put on an overlay which is then positioned with the other colors. The lettering is generally kept on a separate drawing so that alterations (for example, additions, deletions, or changes in place names) can be easily made without interfering with other information (such as border lines or shading) on the map. Most lettering is printed in black to increase legibility.

The purpose of this introductory material has been to enlighten readers so that they can begin to use the extraordinary amount of information that appears on maps. As was stated earlier, nearly anything can be mapped, and phenomena that directly affect our daily lives can be displayed in a simple visual form that has more impact than any written description. This atlas is a remarkably comprehensive and informative tool. It takes the reader from the earliest recorded history to the present and places the present in perspective so that everyday life can be related to the world at large in a meaningful way.

The map below is printed in four colors. The illustrations that follow represent the four color-separation drawings that must be made for each color.

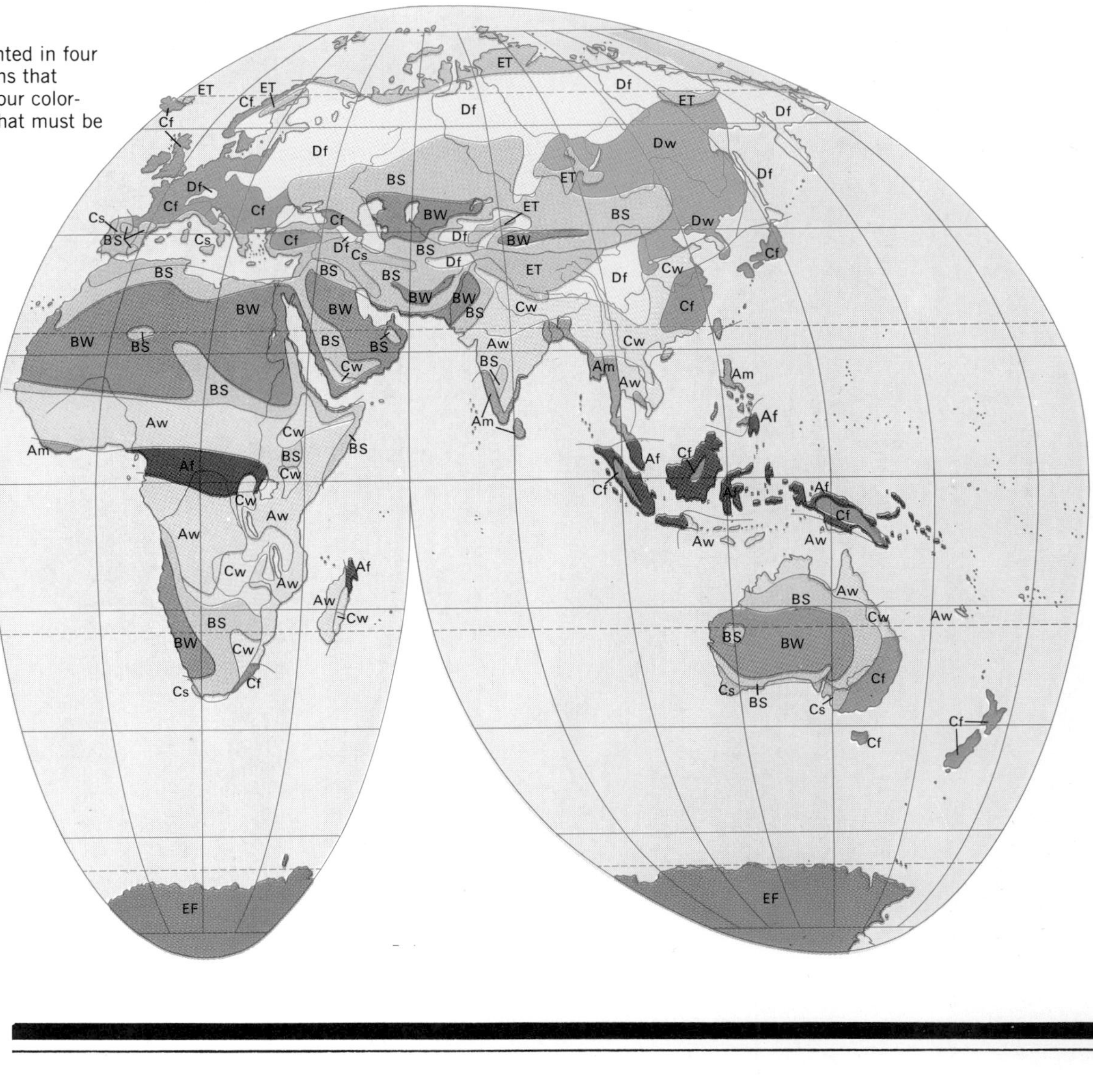
ET
Cf
Df
Dw
BS
BW
Cs
Cw
Aw
Am
Af
EF

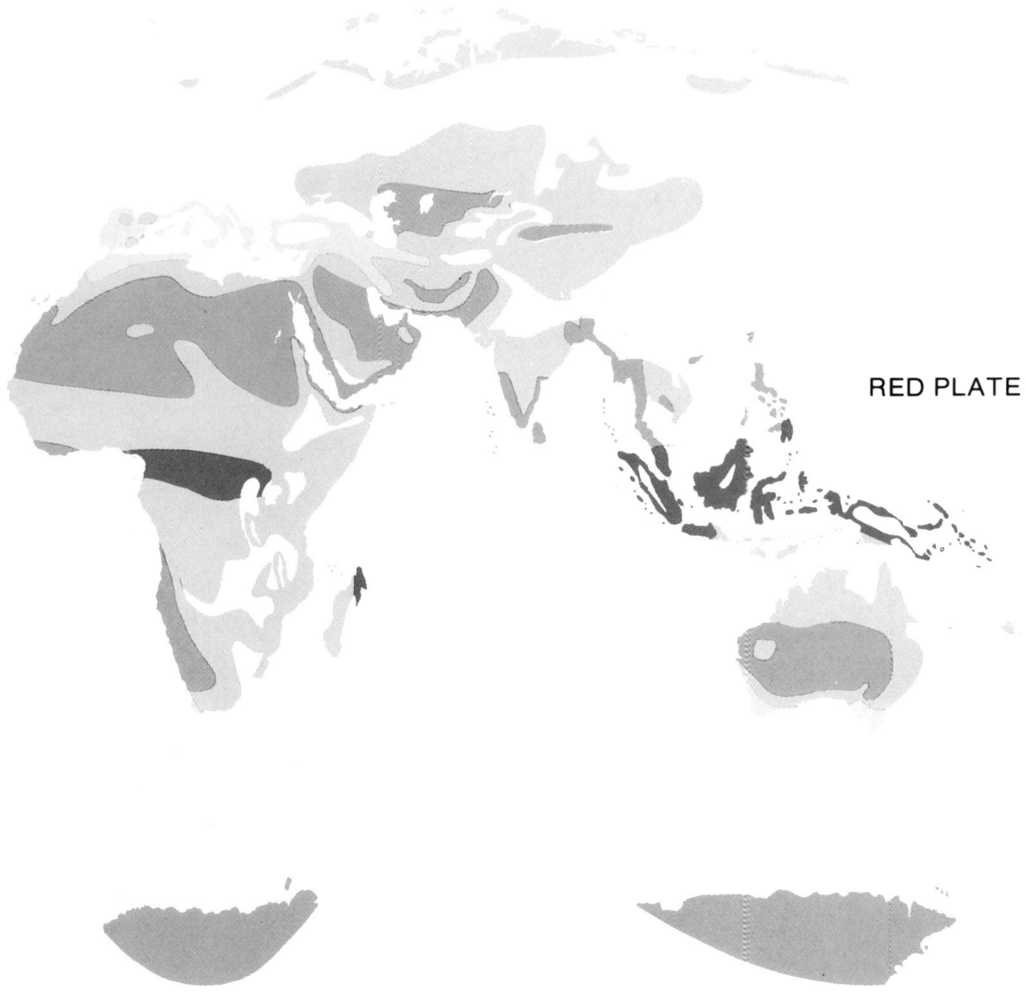

RED PLATE ONLY

YELLOW PLATE ONLY

BLUE PLATE ONLY

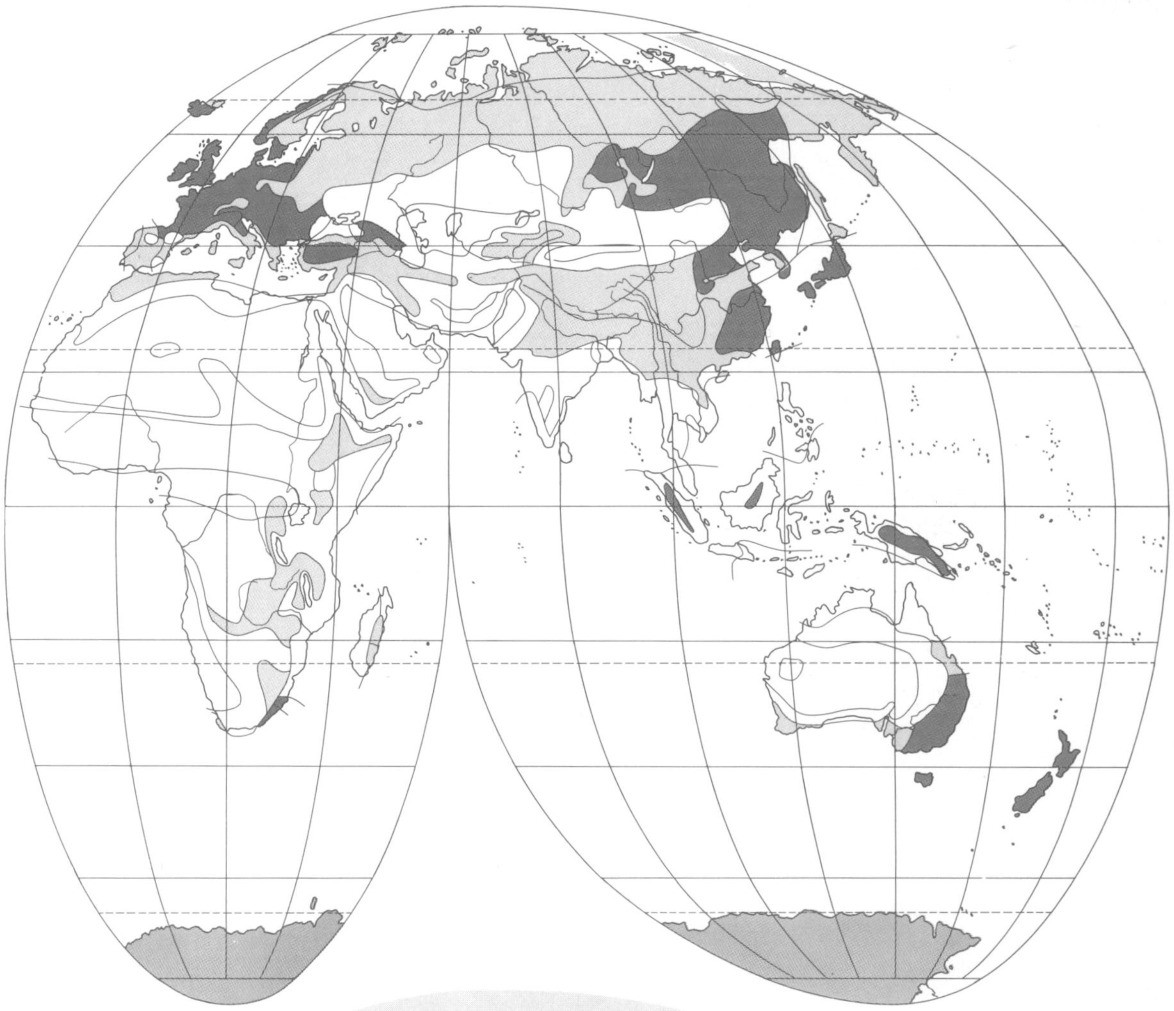

BLACK PLATE ONLY

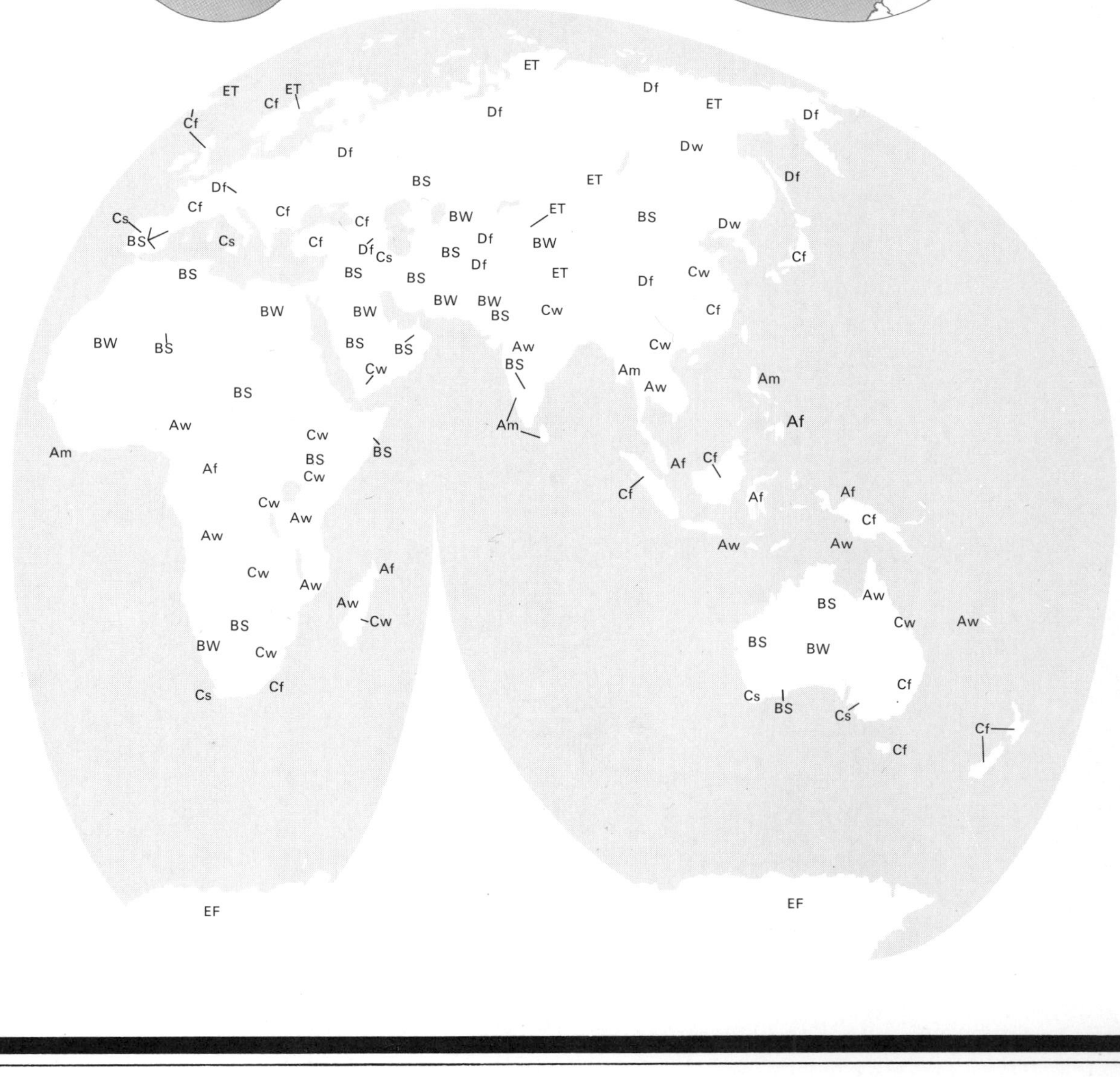
ET
Df
ET
Df
Cf
ET
Cf
Df
Dw
Df
Df
BS
ET
Df
Cs
BS
Cf
Cf
Cf
BW
ET
BS
Dw
Cs
Cf
Df
Cs
BS
Df
BW
Cf
BS
BS
Df
ET
Df
Cw
BW
BW
BW
BS
Cw
Cf
BW
BS
BS
BS
Aw
BS
Cw
Am
Aw
Am
BS
Aw
Af
Am
Cw
BS
BS
Cw
Af
Af
Cf
Cf
Cw
Aw
Af
Af
Cf
Aw
Aw
Aw
Cw
Af
Aw
Aw
BS
Aw
Cw
Aw
BS
BS
BW
Cw
BW
Cs
Cf
Cs
BS
Cf
Cs
Cf
Cf
EF
EF

THE BEGINNINGS OF CIVILIZATION

The earliest traces of humanity were found in China and Africa, far from the icebound northern world. However, before the ice receded, these early hunters were living up to the limit of glaciation of **the last ice age** across the whole of Europe. The ice began its final retreat about 10,000 years ago, leaving a land of scattered rocks and tundra.

As the ice retreated, the climate became warmer, **natural vegetation** emerged, and a new race of hunters and fishers developed around sea and lake shores. The rain belts moved away from north Africa and southwest Asia, leaving vast desert areas. Thorn forests, adapted to a drier climate, grew around the Mediterranean. To the north, where it was wetter, broadleaved trees covered the land. Coniferous forests grew in the far north and on mountain slopes, and short grass and shrubs fringed the deserts. It was in these regions that the earliest societies took the next step in their evolution. They began to gather ancestral barley and wheat and to domesticate animals in what is now southern Turkey, Syria, Jordan, and Iraq/Iran. Later, these early people cultivated crops, which led to the settlement of communities based on a mixed economy of farming, hunting, fishing, and crafts of pottery, basketry, and weaving. Jericho, the oldest town in the world, dating back to about 7800 B.C., was one such community.

In their struggle for survival, the people of this ancient world displayed considerable skill and ingenuity. They lived in caves, in tents made of animal skins, or in wooden houses made from trees, which they cut down with tools they made. In warmer areas, they made mud bricks and used them to build walls with a coating of mud plaster. They made and decorated clay pots and figurines. They developed herds of animals and learned how to maintain them. They discovered metal smelting around 6000 B.C. and later applied this technology to high-standard craftsmanship. And they invented the wheel as a means of transport.

Civilization first dawned in **Mesopotamia**, in the fertile valleys of the Tigris and Euphrates rivers. Watered by these flooding rivers, the land produced abundant crops. Fish and wildfowl were plentiful. Nomad hunters settled here, the population multiplied, and villages grew into towns and cities. The desert on either side of the valleys gave protection, and for a thousand years the cities of Sumer flourished as separate city-kingdoms such as Ur, Erech, and Nippur.

The **Nile valley**, the second great cradle of civilization, had the same physical advantages as did Mesopotamia. Annual flood waters left a rich layer of silt bounded by protective desert on each side. Unlike Mesopotamia, however, the Nile communities joined in political union. By about 3400 B.C., they had grown into two principal kingdoms — Upper and Lower Egypt. The two Egypts were united in 3200 B.C. by King Narmer.

The **Indus valley** was the third area where conditions favored civilization. From 4000 B.C. on, farming communities settled in the valley. Eventually, they grew into a number of wealthy cities such as Mohenjodaro and Harappa, which were carefully planned around a grid pattern of streets and with water and sanitation systems.

As civilized life became more complex, specialists developed. Potters and smiths had long plied their crafts, but now the growth of cities required stonemasons and carpenters as well. Increased trade called for wheelwrights and shipbuilders. And, after the invention of writing, scribes assumed an important place in society. All of these specialists were supported by the farmers, who produced a surplus of food. The land was still the source of prosperity in all the early civilizations.

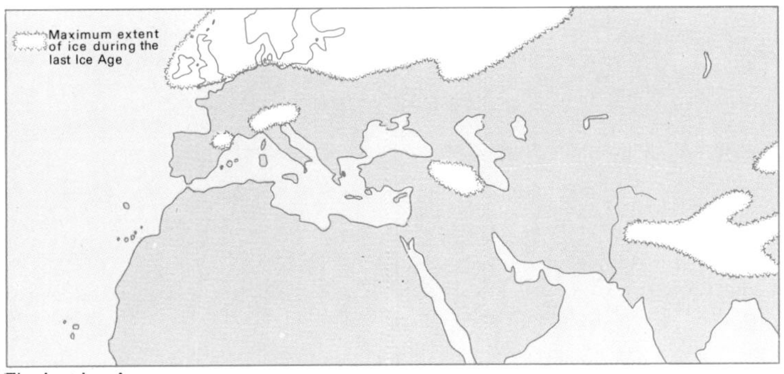
Maximum extent of ice during the last Ice Age
The last Ice Age

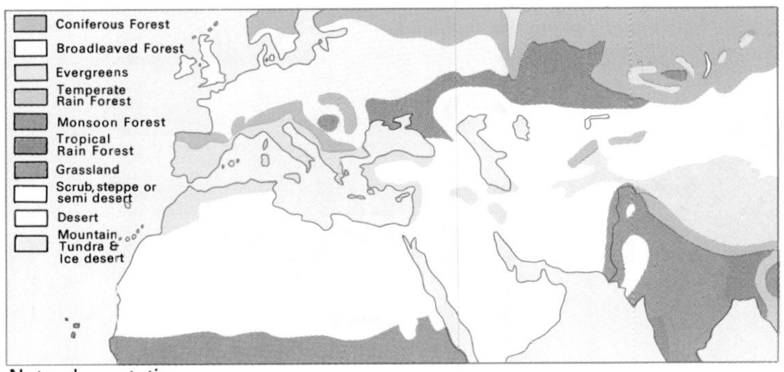
Coniferous Forest
Broadleaved Forest
Evergreens
Temperate Rain Forest
Monsoon Forest
Tropical Rain Forest
Grassland
Scrub, steppe or semi desert
Desert
Mountain, Tundra & Ice desert
Natural vegetation

Mud bricks were used for building in the warmer areas, where they could be baked hard in the sun.
Goats were among the first animals to be herded, together with cattle, pigs and sheep.
The wheel was used by some early communities and not others. The first were simple and of solid wood.
Simple, gaily decorated pottery was usually made by women in the early settlements.
Early smelting was done on an open fire using molds cut out of stone.
The first boats, for fishing and crossing rivers, were made of hollowed tree trunks or woven reeds.

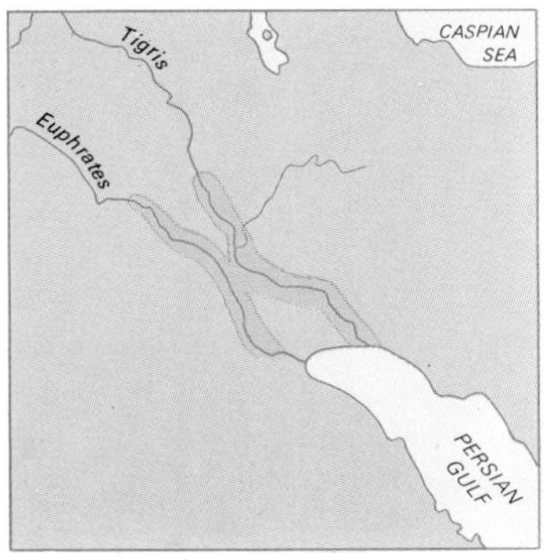
Tigris
Euphrates
CASPIAN SEA
PERSIAN GULF
Mesopotamia

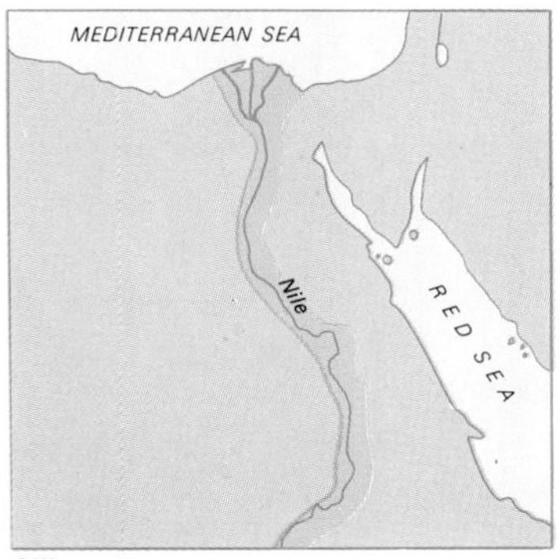
MEDITERRANEAN SEA
Nile
RED SEA
Nile valley

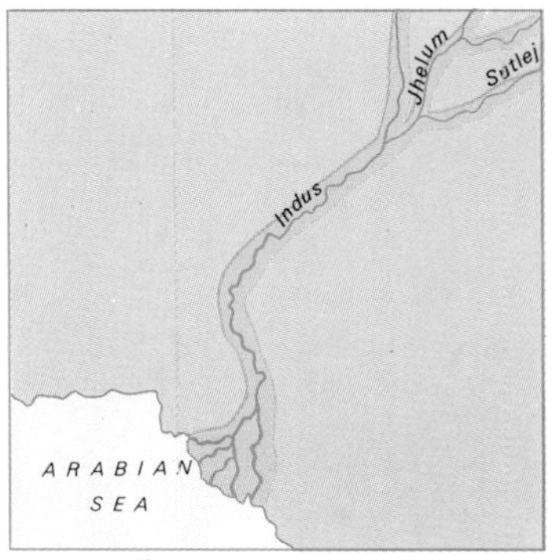
Jhelum
Sutlej
Indus
ARABIAN SEA
Indus valley

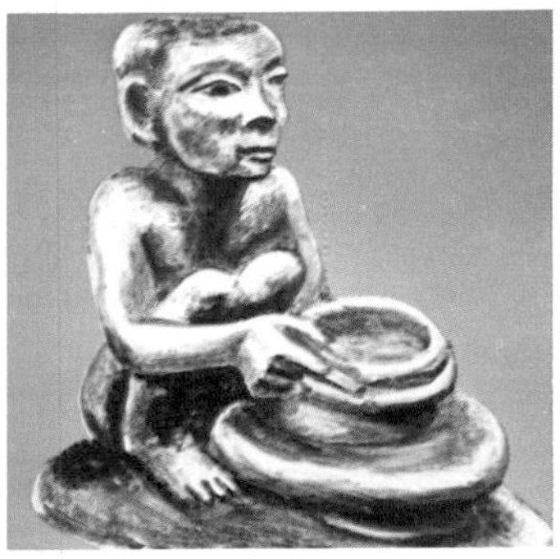

THE GROWTH OF CIVILIZATION

The growth of early civilizations is shown on the maps. These peoples did not exist in isolation, for there was frequent contact between different societies. They had a strong instinct for trade and exploration, and nomadic hunters maintained their way of life in most areas. But civilization brought increased skill in waging war, and great empires rose and fell.

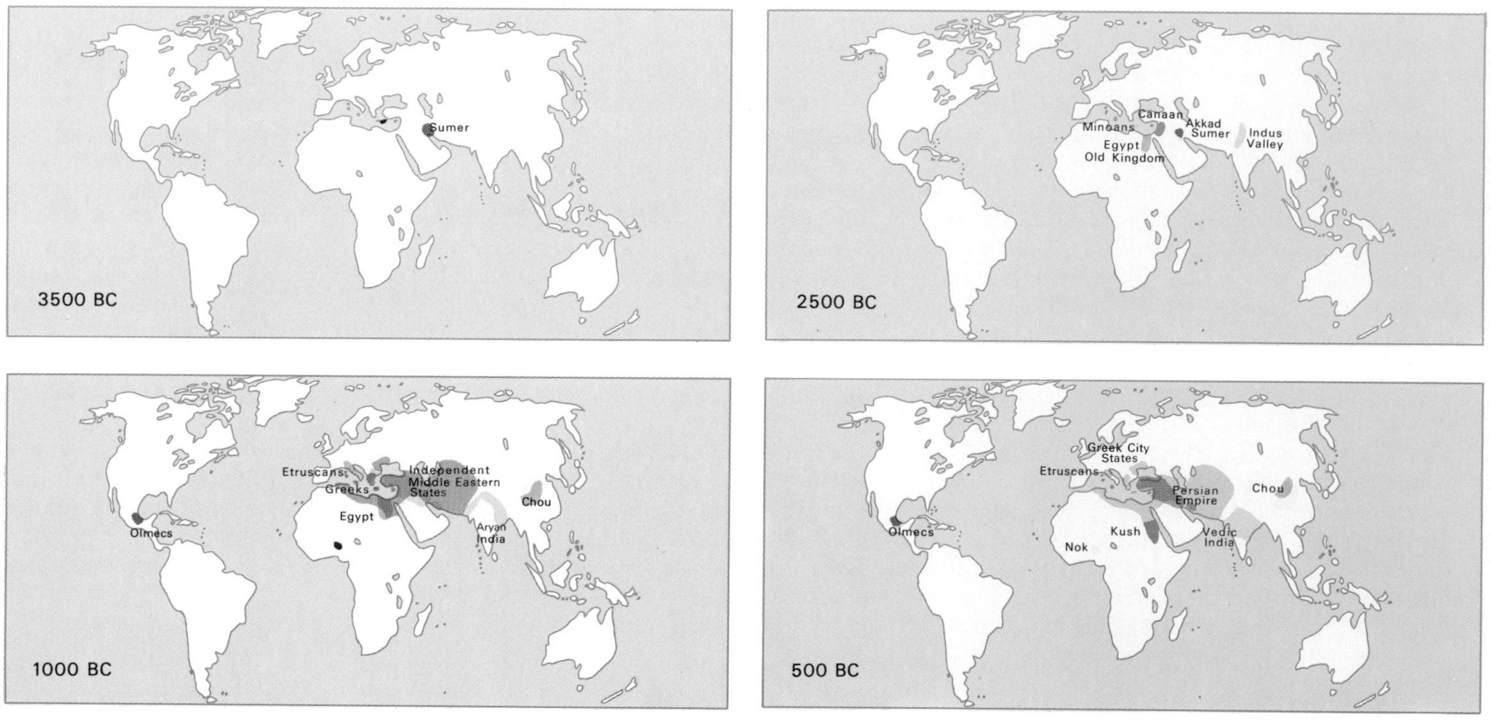

Sumer
3500 BC
Canaan
Minoans
Akkad
Sumer
Indus Valley
Egypt Old Kingdom
2500 BC
Etruscans
Greeks
Independent Middle Eastern States
Chou
Egypt
Aryan India
Olmecs
1000 BC
Greek City States
Etruscans
Persian Empire
Chou
Olmecs
Kush
Nok
Vedic India
500 BC

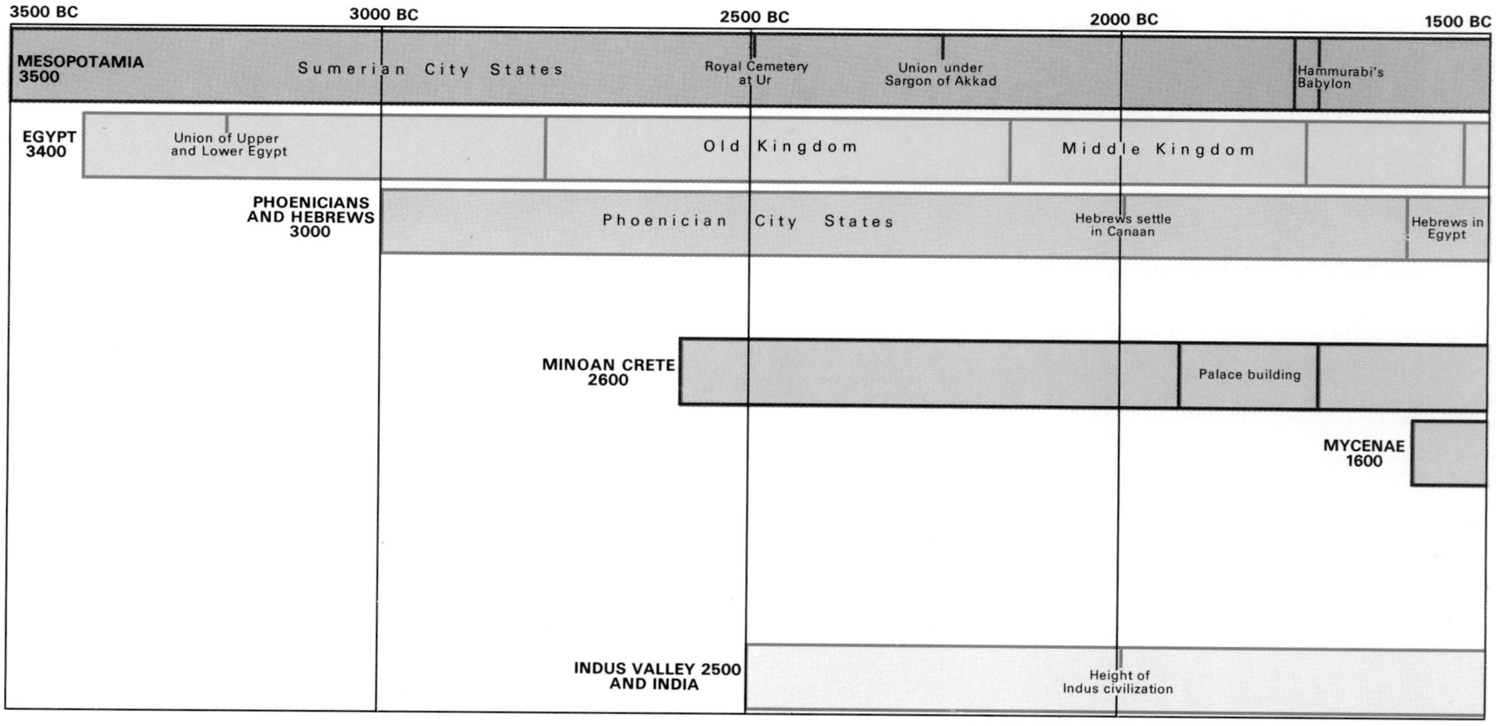

3500 BC
3000 BC
2500 BC
2000 BC
1500 BC
MESOPOTAMIA 3500
Sumerian City States
Royal Cemetery at Ur
Union under Sargon of Akkad
Hammurabi's Babylon
EGYPT 3400
Union of Upper and Lower Egypt
Old Kingdom
Middle Kingdom
PHOENICIANS AND HEBREWS 3000
Phoenician City States
Hebrews settle in Canaan
Hebrews in Egypt
MINOAN CRETE 2600
Palace building
MYCENAE 1600
INDUS VALLEY 2500 AND INDIA
Height of Indus civilization

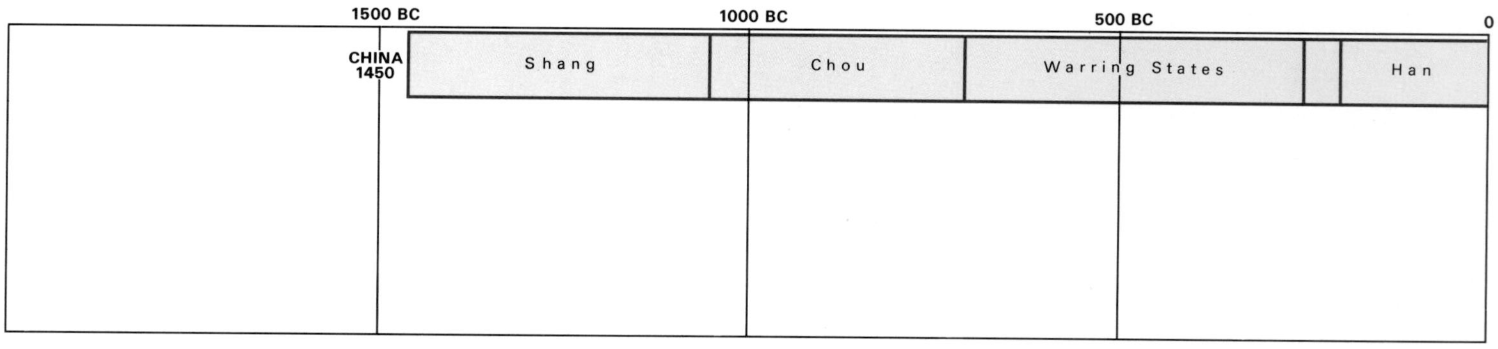

1500 BC
1000 BC
500 BC
0
CHINA 1450
Shang
Chou
Warring States
Han

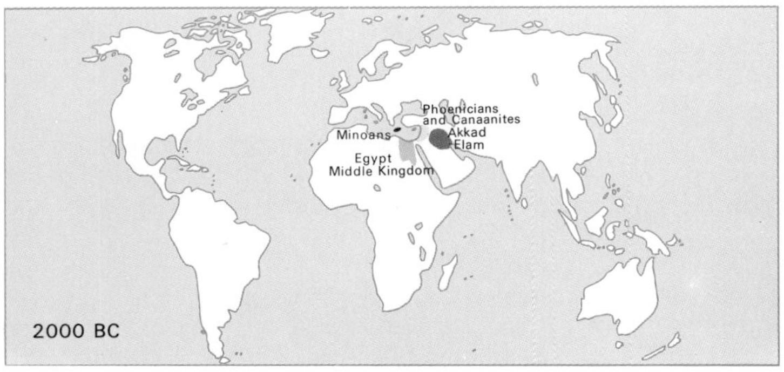

Phoenicians
and Canaanites
Minoans
Akkad
Elam
Egypt
Middle Kingdom
2000 BC

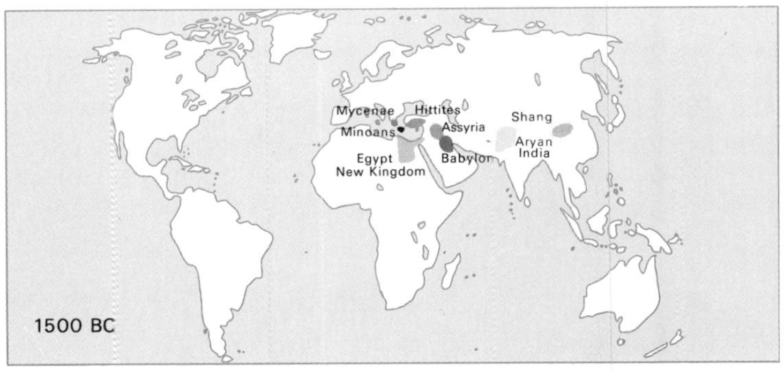

Mycenae
Hittites
Minoans
Assyria
Shang
Aryan
India
Egypt
New Kingdom
Babylon
1500 BC

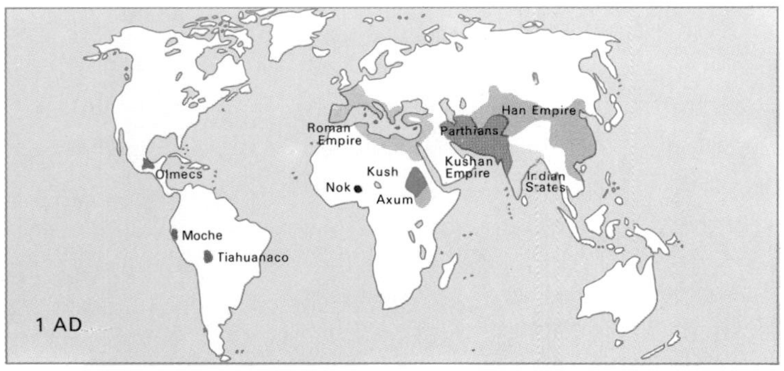

Han Empire
Roman
Empire
Parthians
Kushan
Empire
Olmecs
Kush
Nok
Axum
Indian
States
Moche
Tiahuanaco
1 AD

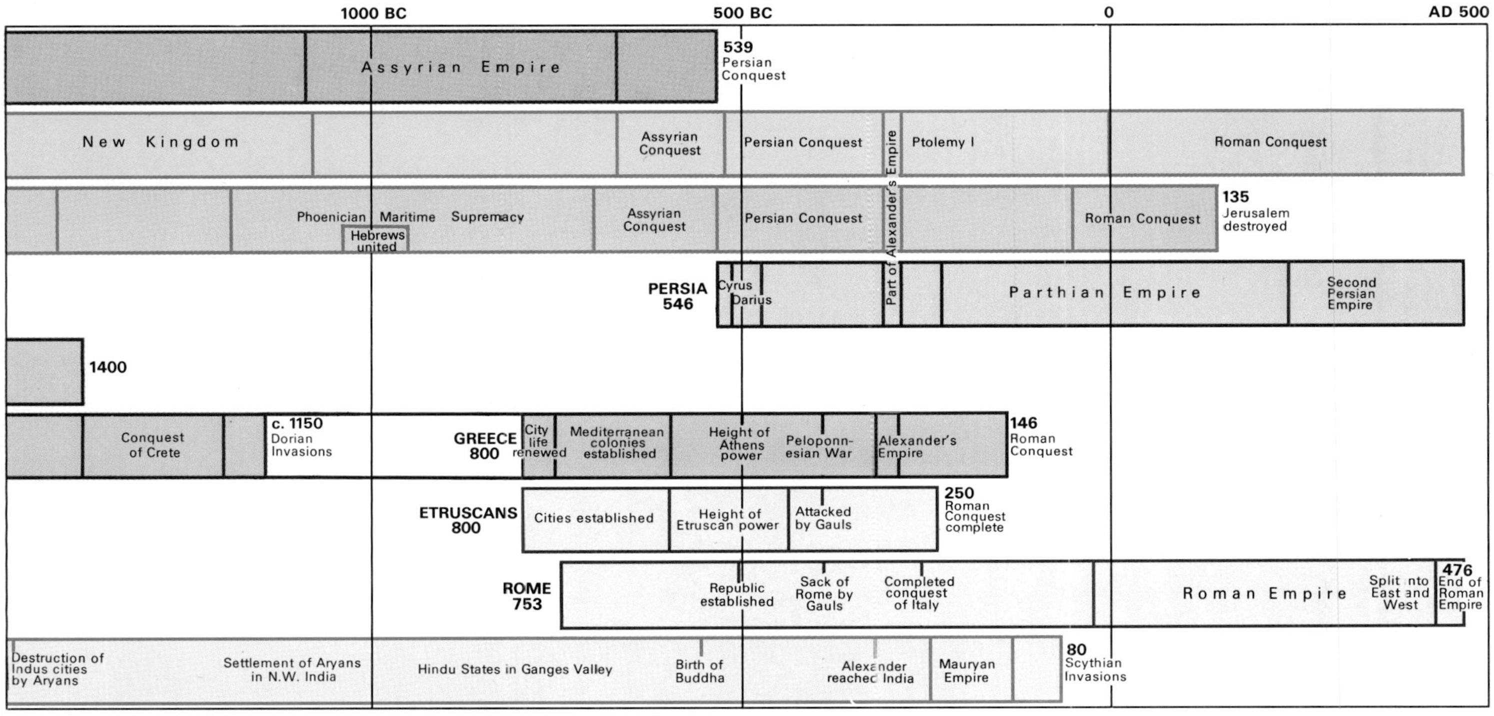

1000 BC
500 BC
0
AD 500
Assyrian Empire
539
Persian
Conquest
New Kingdom
Assyrian
Conquest
Persian Conquest
Ptolemy I
Roman Conquest
Phoenician Maritime Supremacy
Hebrews
united
Assyrian
Conquest
Persian Conquest
Part of Alexander's Empire
Roman Conquest
135
Jerusalem
destroyed
PERSIA
546
Cyrus
Darius
Parthian Empire
Second
Persian
Empire
1400
Conquest
of Crete
c. 1150
Dorian
Invasions
GREECE
800
City
life
renewed
Mediterranean
colonies
established
Height of
Athens
power
Peloponn-
esian War
Alexander's
Empire
146
Roman
Conquest
ETRUSCANS
800
Cities established
Height of
Etruscan power
Attacked
by Gauls
250
Roman
Conquest
complete
ROME
753
Republic
established
Sack of
Rome by
Gauls
Completed
conquest
of Italy
Roman Empire
Split into
East and
West
476
End of
Roman
Empire
Destruction of
Indus cities
by Aryans
Settlement of Aryans
in N.W. India
Hindu States in Ganges Valley
Birth of
Buddha
Alexander
reached India
Mauryan
Empire
80
Scythian
Invasions

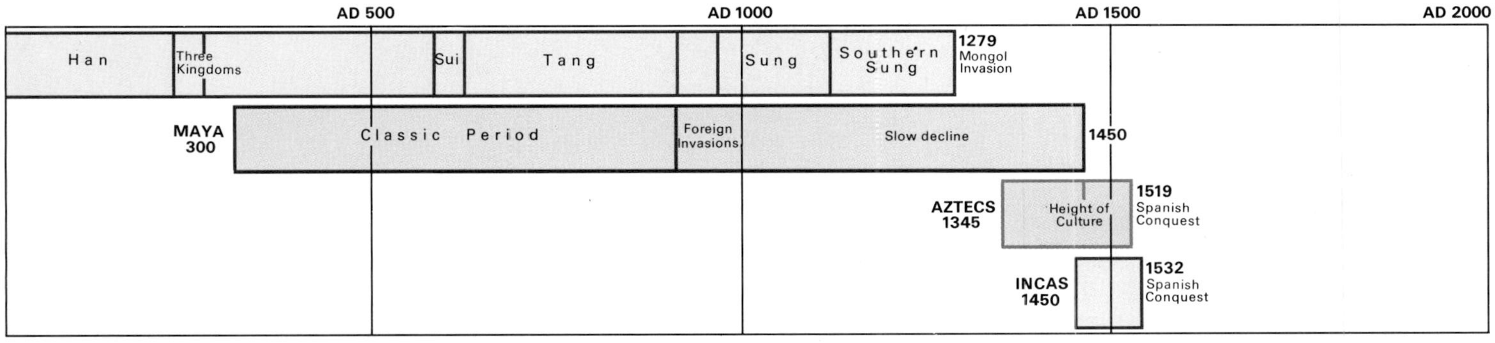

AD 500
AD 1000
AD 1500
AD 2000
Han
Three
Kingdoms
Sui
Tang
Sung
Southern
Sung
1279
Mongol
Invasion
MAYA
300
Classic Period
Foreign
Invasions
Slow decline
1450
AZTECS
1345
Height of
Culture
1519
Spanish
Conquest
INCAS
1450
1532
Spanish
Conquest

MESOPOTAMIA

As this map of **Mesopotamia** indicates, civilization progressed rapidly in the city states, which by 3500 B.C. were fully developed. The cities were walled and surrounded by irrigated fields. The dominant building, situated on an artificial hill, was the **Ziggurat**, or temple, such as this one in the **Royal Cemetery at Ur**.

Rivalry between cities led to war. Around 2350 B.C., Sargon — the first imperial conqueror — came downriver from Akkad and declared himself ruler over Sumer and Akkad. But King Sargon's empire collapsed after his death, and the city of Ur rose to prominence as Sumerian power revived. Ur was destroyed when the Amorites and Elamites invaded it around 2025 B.C. and established city states of their own. These cities warred among themselves, but in 1792 B.C. Hammurabi ascended the throne of Babylon and made this city the dominant power in Mesopotamia. After Hammurabi's death, Babylon was conquered by the Assyrians.

Part of the history of Babylon is given on this **boundary stone**, which records the grant of land to one Hasardu by Melisihu, who was king of Babylon from about 1188 to 1174 B.C. The document is square and has figures of gods carved at the top. Stones such as this demonstrated the importance of legal rights at the time. They also show us the kind of gods that were worshiped by the Babylonians, and they provide excellent examples of cuneiform writing.

In ancient Mesopotamia, ownership of personal property was signified by the use of seals. One such, a **cylinder seal**, is shown

Boundary stone

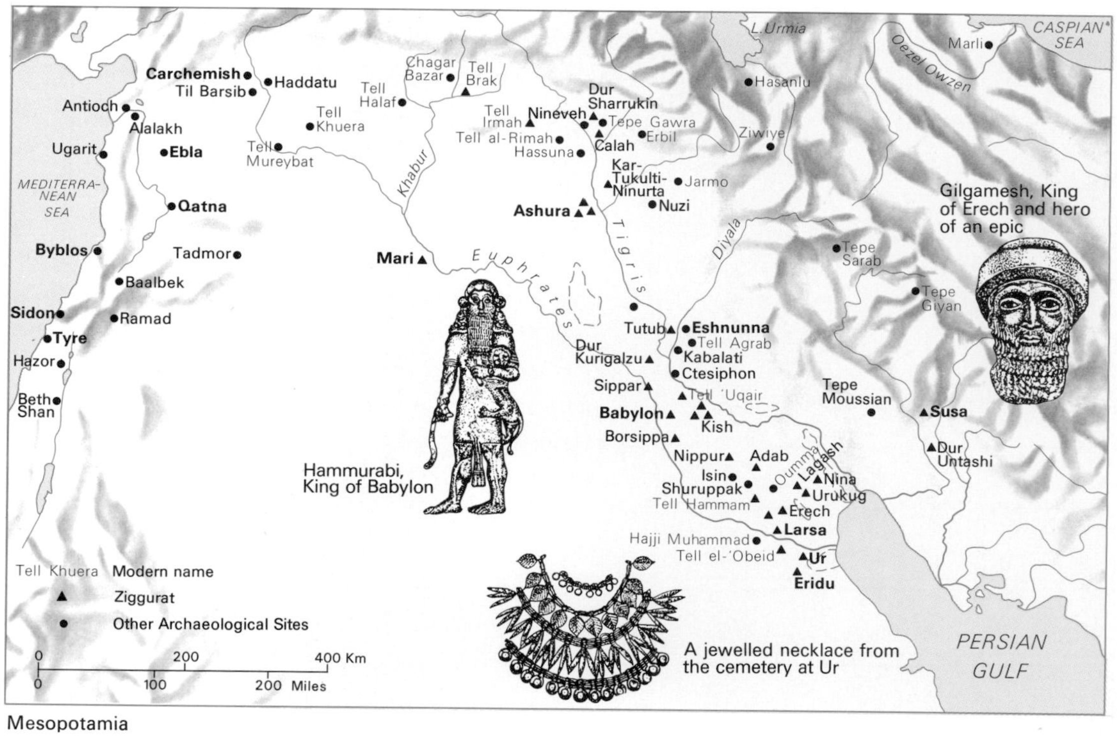

L. Urmia
CASPIAN SEA
Marli
Oezel Owzen
Hasanlu
Carchemish
Til Barsib
Haddatu
Tell Halaf
Chagar Bazar
Tell Brak
Antioch
Alalakh
Tell Khuera
Ugarit
Ebla
Tell Mureybat
Dur Sharrukin
Tell Irmah
Nineveh
Tepe Gawra
Erbil
Tell al-Rimah
Hassuna
Calah
Ziwiye
Kar-Tukulti-Ninurta
Jarmo
Nuzi
Ashura
MEDITERRANEAN SEA
Qatna
Khabur
Byblos
Tadmor
Mari
Euphrates
Tigris
Diyala
Gilgamesh, King of Erech and hero of an epic
Tepe Sarab
Tepe Giyan
Baalbek
Sidon
Ramad
Tyre
Hazor
Beth Shan
Tutub
Eshnunna
Tell Agrab
Dur Kurigalzu
Kabalati
Ctesiphon
Sippar
Tell 'Uqair
Tepe Moussian
Babylon
Kish
Susa
Borsippa
Nippur
Adab
Oumma
Lagash
Dur Untashi
Isin
Shuruppak
Nina
Urukug
Tell Hammam
Erech
Larsa
Hajji Muhammad
Tell el-'Obeid
Ur
Eridu
Hammurabi, King of Babylon
Tell Khuera Modern name
Ziggurat
Other Archaeological Sites
0 200 400 Km
0 100 200 Miles
A jewelled necklace from the cemetery at Ur
PERSIAN GULF

Mesopotamia

Ur — Royal Cemetery and Ziggurat

below along with its impression on clay. Thousands of these stone seals have been found. Their delicate carvings often depict religious and mythical scenes. The owner used the seal for identifying various kinds of property and for sealing documents. The cylinder could be rolled over damp clay covering the fastener of a basket or jar. No one could open such sealed containers without breaking the seal. The Sumerian seal shown dates from about 2500 B.C.

One of the magnificent achievements of Sumerian culture was the **Ziggurat of Ur**, shown reconstructed below at the right. Built around 2100 B.C., this temple was dedicated to Su'en, the moon god. A triple staircase led 80 feet upward to the sanctuary at the top.

The shell and stone mosaic panel of charging chariots shown below is a detail from one side of a wooden box known as the **Standard of Ur**. The box was found in the Royal Cemetery at Ur and dates from about 2500 B.C. The three-tiered panel from which the detail was taken is shown at the left beneath the enlargement. In the upper row of the panel, a king is reviewing prisoners of war. In the middle row, soldiers carrying short spears escort prisoners.

The tip of the **stele of Hammurabi**, shown at the bottom left, depicts Hammurabi receiving his code of law from Shamash, the Babylonian sun god and patron of justice. The code of law is inscribed in cuneiform script on the lower part of the stele. To the right of the stele below is a famous sample of **cuneiform writing**, a description of the Flood on the eleventh tablet of the Epic of Gilgamesh.

Cylinder seal

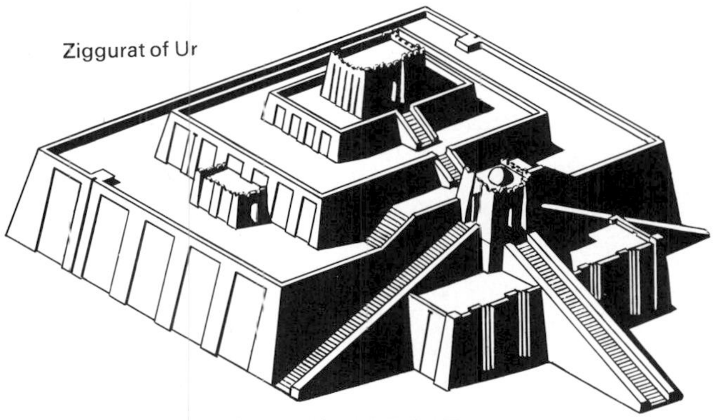

Ziggurat of Ur

Standard of Ur

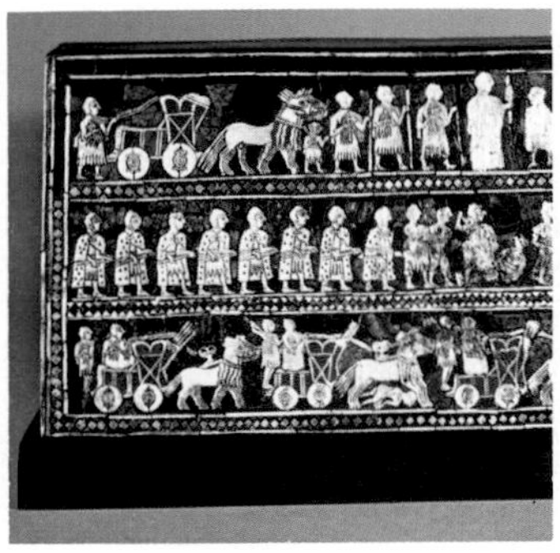

Cuneiform writing

Stele of Hammurabi

ANCIENT EGYPT

In Egypt, the establishment of central government in the Old Kingdom, 2780–2180 B.C., brought the first great phase of achievement. This phase included the pyramids, magnificent sculptures, and works of art in many materials. After a period of decline, a second period of greatness came to the Middle Kingdom, dating from 2080 to 1785 B.C. A period of imperial expansion came in the New Kingdom, 1570–1075 B.C.

The first pyramid was built at Saqqara as a tomb for King Zoser. But the **pyramids at Giza**, which include the largest — that of Cheops — are the most famous. The pyramid of Chephren and the Sphinx are shown in the photograph. These structures were built in the same reign. The diagram depicting **pyramid construction** gives some idea of the immensity of the task. Burial chambers were deep, often in solid rock below ground level, and were reached by a passage. The huge blocks of limestone had to be dragged up ramps, which were built up from the corners.

Magnificently decorated tombs were not just for the pharaohs. Private tombs also had carvings and paintings depicting the everyday life of the people. One such is the painted scene of **fowling in the marshes**. It came from the tomb of Nebamun, a scribe and counter of grain at Thebes. Burials sometimes included painted funerary scenes on papyrus, such as the one of **wailing women** shown below. The **mummified head** dates to about 1250 B.C.

Pyramids at Giza

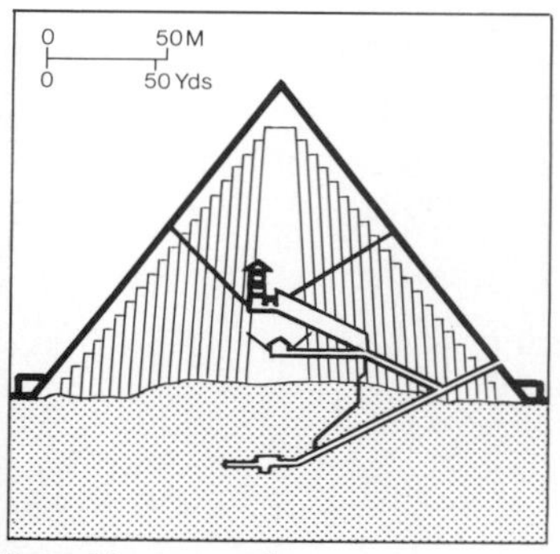
0
50M
0
50 Yds
Pyramid construction

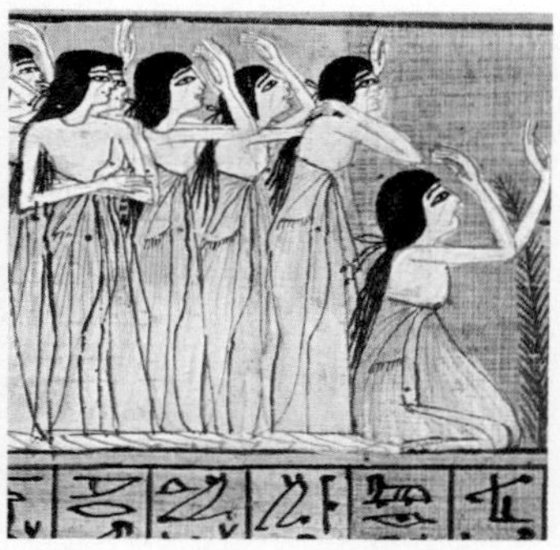
Wailing women

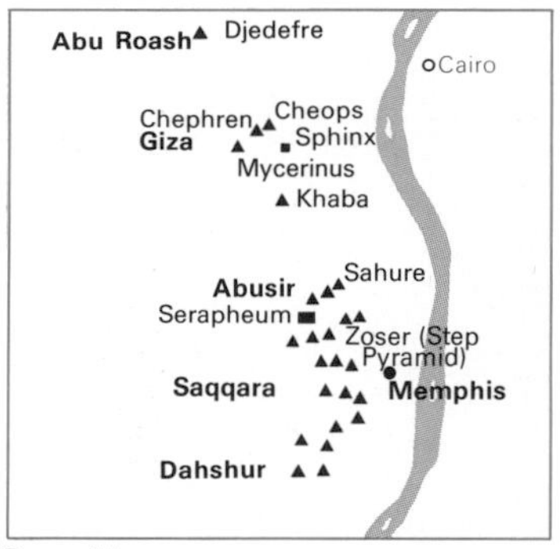
Abu Roash
Djedefre
Cairo
Chephren
Cheops
Giza
Sphinx
Mycerinus
Khaba
Abusir
Sahure
Serapheum
Zoser (Step Pyramid)
Saqqara
Memphis
Dahshur
Pyramids

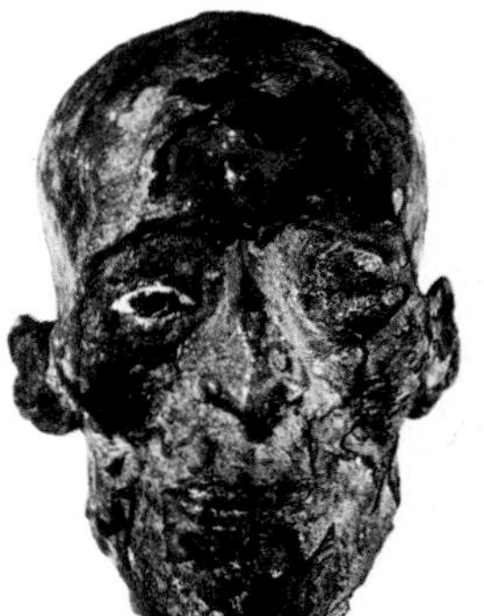
Mummified head

Fowling in the marshes

The conquest that characterized the New Kingdom brought new wealth to **ancient Egypt**, the extent of which in this period is shown on the large map below. Many temples were built during the New Kingdom. The various **temple sites** are shown on the small map. At Karnak, the great **Temple of Amun**, shown in the plan below, was started by Tuthmosis I and made even more magnificent by successive pharaohs. Other temples included the great temple at Luxor, Queen Hatshepsut's temple at Deir el Bahari, and Madinet Habu. The rock-cut temple of Abu Simbel, farther to the south, also was built at this time.

Archaeological digs have yielded carvings and paintings that tell much about the people and their culture. For example, the **stele of Kahu** shown here contains prayers to Osiris, god of the dead, on behalf of one Kahu. Osiris and the jackal-headed Anubis, whose function was to lead the dead to judgment, are depicted at the top of this stone tablet. Below them, Kahu and his wife are receiving offerings from their children.

The **papyrus of Hunefer** at the bottom of the page is from the *Book of the Dead* of the scribe Hunefer, dating at about 1300 B.C. The painting depicts the opening of the mouth ritual that took place before burial, reanimating the mummy of the deceased. The body was then placed in the tomb, together with objects the deceased would take with him into the next life.

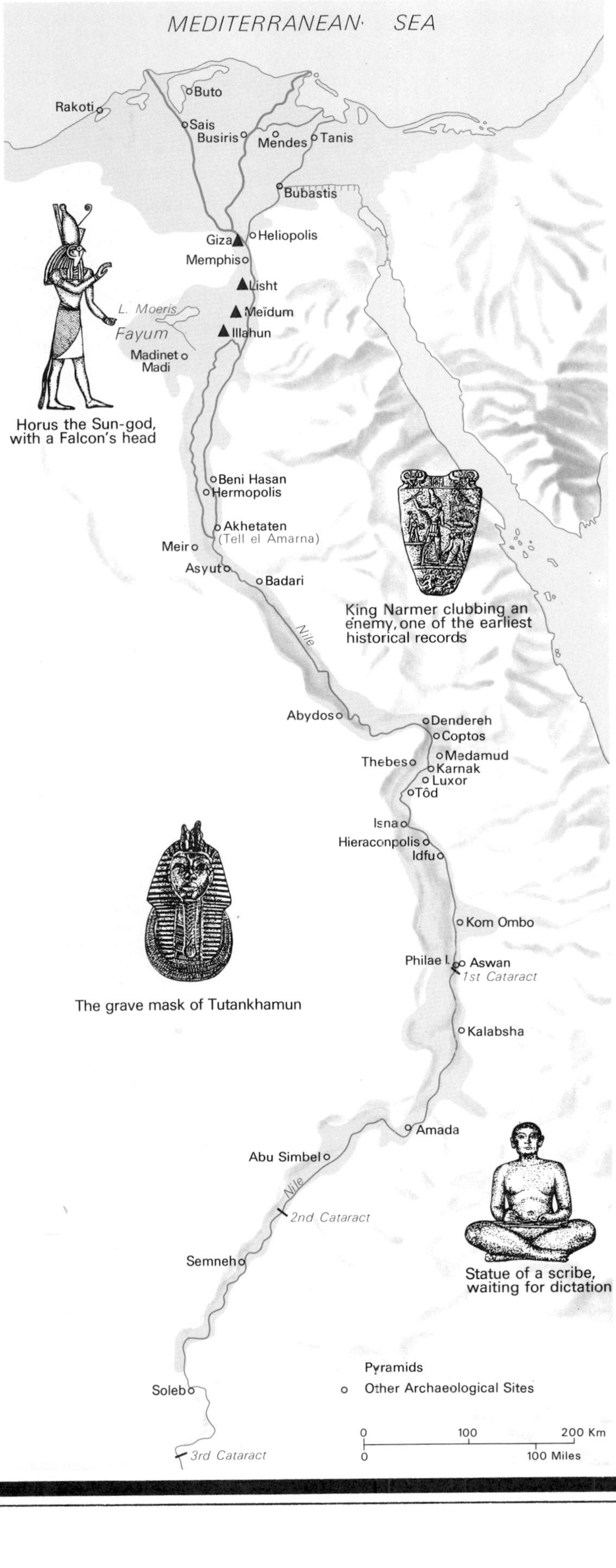

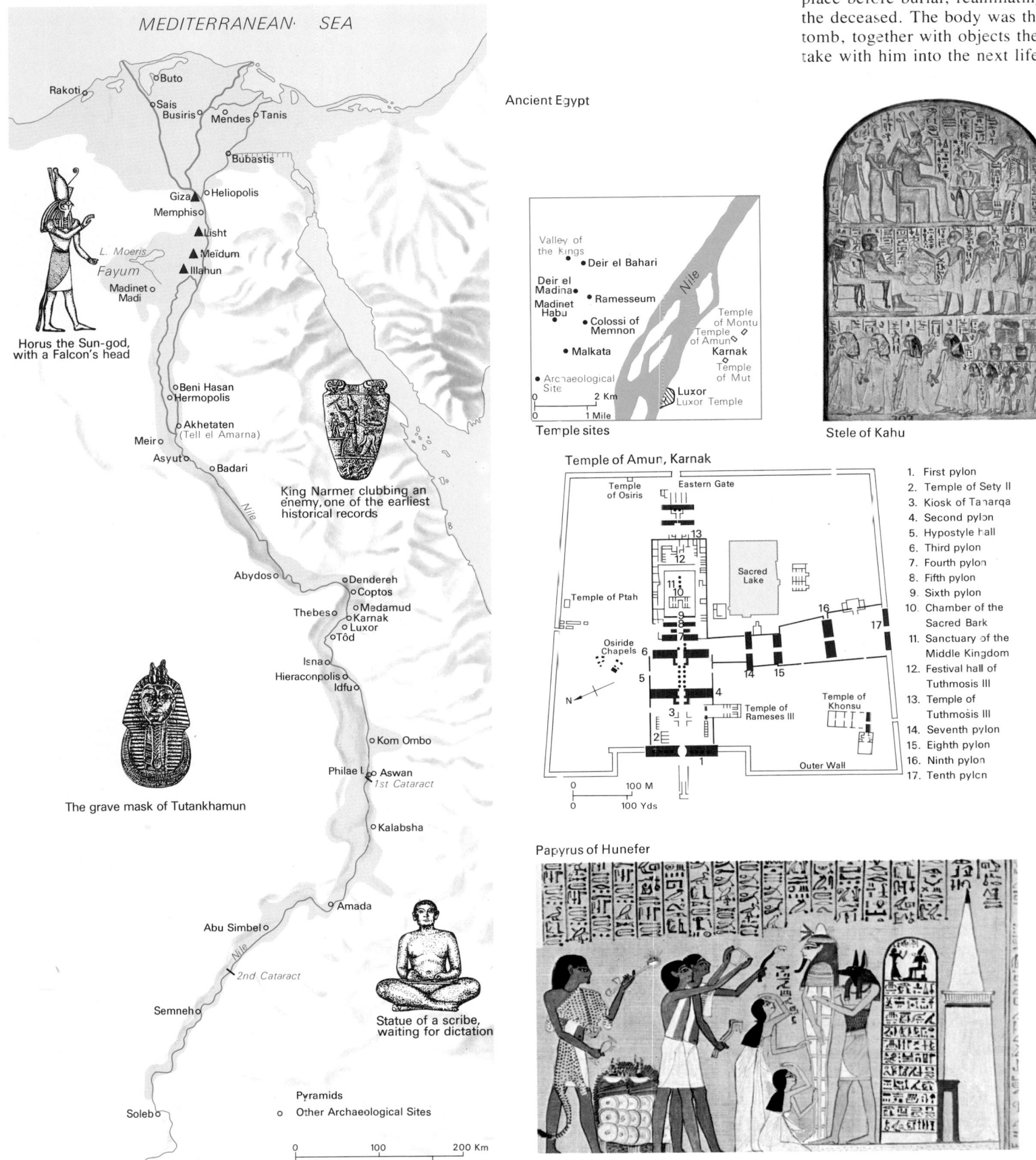

MEDITERRANEAN SEA
Rakoti
Buto
Sais
Busiris
Mendes
Tanis
Bubastis
Giza
Heliopolis
Memphis
Lisht
Meidum
Illahun
L. Moeris
Fayum
Madinet Madi
Horus the Sun-god, with a Falcon's head
Beni Hasan
Hermopolis
Akhetaten (Tell el Amarna)
Meir
Asyut
Badari
King Narmer clubbing an enemy, one of the earliest historical records
Nile
Abydos
Dendereh
Coptos
Thebes
Madamud
Karnak
Luxor
Tōd
Isna
Hieraconpolis
Idfu
The grave mask of Tutankhamun
Kom Ombo
Philae
Aswan
1st Cataract
Kalabsha
Amada
Abu Simbel
2nd Cataract
Statue of a scribe, waiting for dictation
Semneh
Soleb
3rd Cataract
Pyramids
Other Archaeological Sites
0 100 200 Km
0 100 Miles

Ancient Egypt

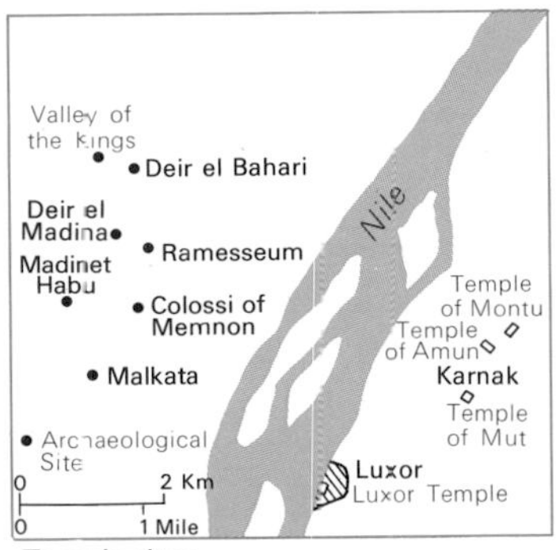

Valley of the Kings
Deir el Bahari
Deir el Madina
Ramesseum
Madinet Habu
Colossi of Memnon
Nile
Temple of Montu
Temple of Amun
Karnak
Malkata
Temple of Mut
Archaeological Site
0 2 Km
0 1 Mile
Luxor
Luxor Temple

Temple sites

Stele of Kahu

Temple of Amun, Karnak

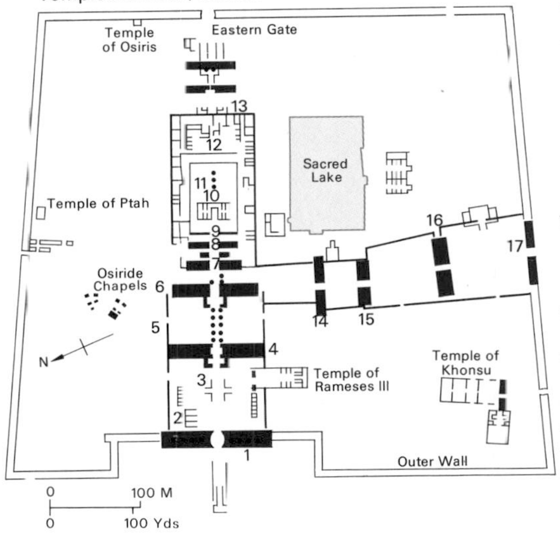

Temple of Osiris
Eastern Gate
Sacred Lake
Temple of Ptah
Osiride Chapels
N
Temple of Rameses III
Temple of Khonsu
Outer Wall
0 100 M
0 100 Yds

1. First pylon
2. Temple of Sety II
3. Kiosk of Taharqa
4. Second pylon
5. Hypostyle hall
6. Third pylon
7. Fourth pylon
8. Fifth pylon
9. Sixth pylon
10. Chamber of the Sacred Bark
11. Sanctuary of the Middle Kingdom
12. Festival hall of Tuthmosis III
13. Temple of Tuthmosis III
14. Seventh pylon
15. Eighth pylon
16. Ninth pylon
17. Tenth pylon

Papyrus of Hunefer

THE FERTILE CRESCENT AND THE MEDITERRANEAN

Between 3000 and 2000 B.C., the Phoenicians were organized in city states such as Tyre, Sidon, and Byblos. They built ships from their abundant timber and took to trading very early. Their expansion westward across the Mediterranean Sea established **Phoenician colonies** on its islands and along its southern and western perimeter, as shown on the top map. By the 6th century B.C., **Phoenician trade and exploration routes** are reputed to have circumnavigated Africa.

Trading and exploration seem to have come naturally to the Phoenicians. Their geographic position, a decline in Egypt's importance, and pressure from the Assyrians from the east led them to spread and settle in many natural and easily defended harbors. They exported manufactured goods, using raw materials that they brought back from their colonies, and even farther afield. Foreign contacts influenced their art, which developed to a high degree. At the left below is a **silver bowl** found at Cyprus. This, together with the **ivory carving**, found at Nimrud, and the **textile of stone** depicting the embroidered clothing of an Assyrian king, exemplify the advanced art of these people.

Although different forms of writing were used previously, the Phoenicians invented the alphabet before 1500 B.C. The Phoenician alphabet reached Greece soon after 1000 B.C. and was later adopted by the Etruscans, eventually becoming the base for classical Latin.

Phoenician colonies

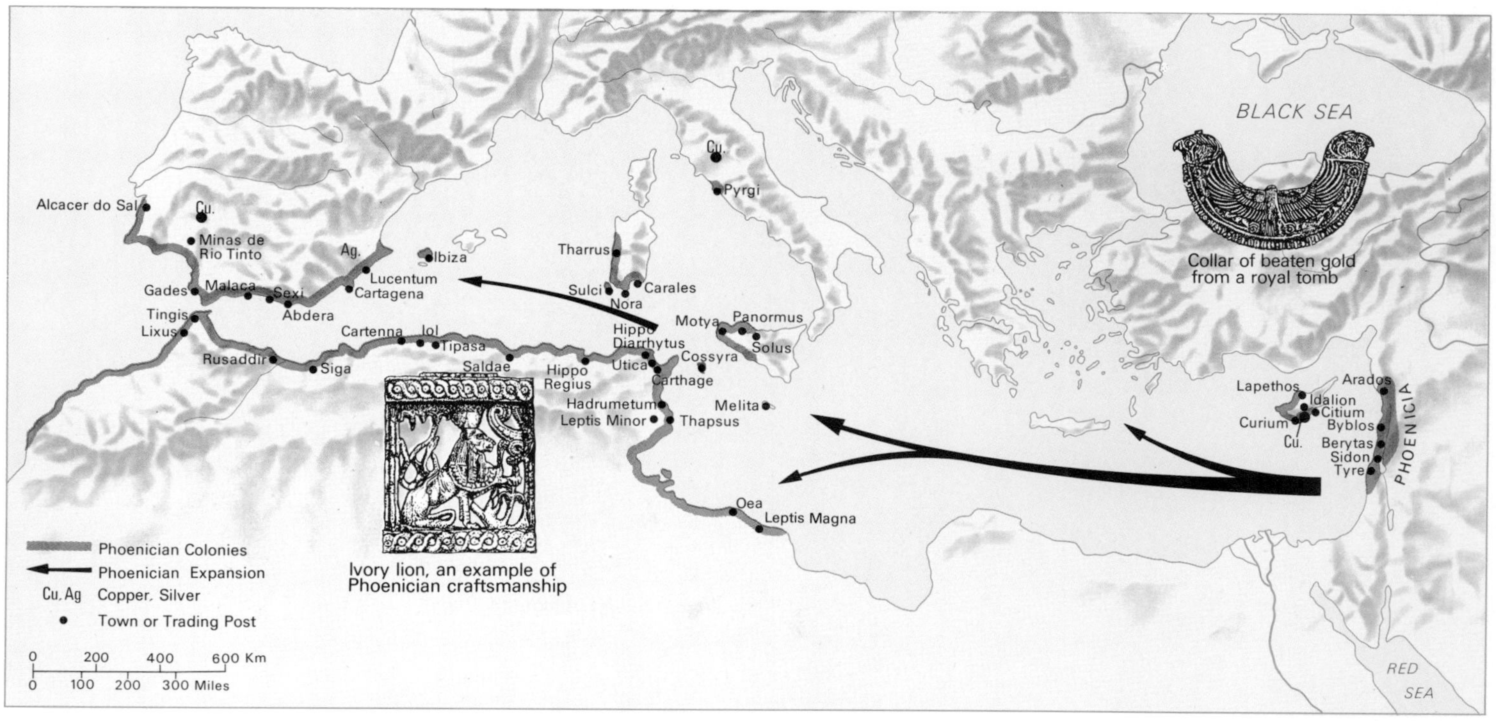

BLACK SEA
Collar of beaten gold from a royal tomb
Alcacer do Sal
Cu.
Minas de Rio Tinto
Gades
Malaca
Sexi
Abdera
Ag.
Lucentum
Cartagena
Ibiza
Tingis
Lixus
Rusaddir
Siga
Cartenna
Iol
Tipasa
Saldae
Hippo Regius
Tharrus
Sulci
Nora
Carales
Cu.
Pyrgi
Hippo Diarrhytus
Utica
Carthage
Motya
Panormus
Solus
Cossyra
Hadrumetum
Leptis Minor
Thapsus
Melita
Oea
Leptis Magna
Lapethos
Idalion
Citium
Curium
Cu.
Arados
Byblos
Berytas
Sidon
Tyre
PHOENICIA
RED SEA
Ivory lion, an example of Phoenician craftsmanship
Phoenician Colonies
Phoenician Expansion
Cu. Ag Copper. Silver
Town or Trading Post
0 200 400 600 Km
0 100 200 300 Miles

Silver bowl

Phoenician trade and exploration

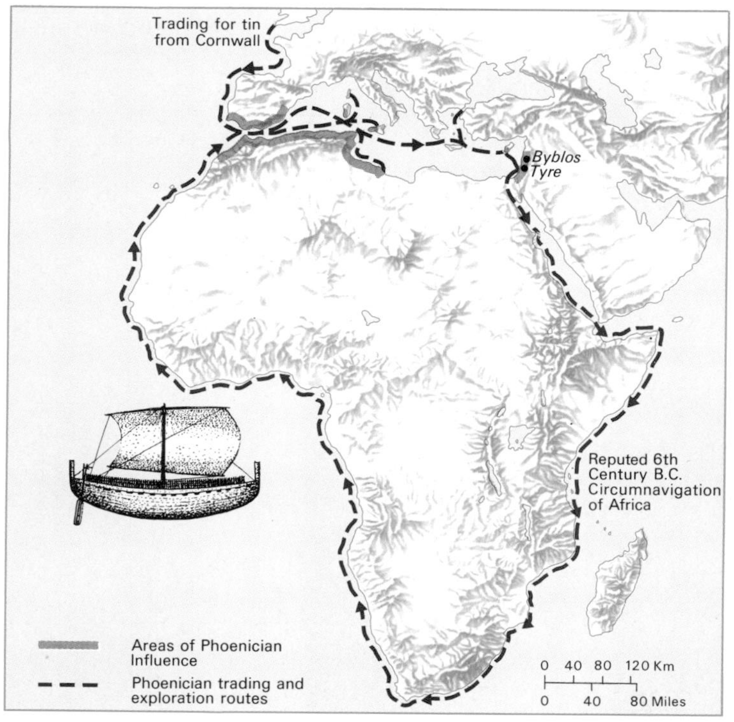

Trading for tin from Cornwall
Byblos
Tyre
Reputed 6th Century B.C. Circumnavigation of Africa
Areas of Phoenician Influence
Phoenician trading and exploration routes
0 40 80 120 Km
0 40 80 Miles

Phoenician	Classical Greek	Etruscan	Classical Latin	
𐤀	A	𐌀	A	a
𐤁	B	𐌁	B	b
𐤂	Γ	𐌂	C	c
𐤄	E	𐌄	E	e
𐤌	M	𐌌	M	m
𐤔	Σ	𐌔	S	s

Ivory carving

Textile of stone

The fertile crescent, shown in green on the map below, was the cradle of early development. Mesopotamian development was inland, along the rivers. But the Phoenicians and other early inhabitants of the Mediterranean shore took advantage of the bounty of the sea as well as of the land. The Phoenicians found ample material for their ships in the forest that covered the hills bordering the Mediterranean.

The **cedars of Lebanon**, shown below, were famous throughout the ancient world. They were used in building Solomon's temple in Jerusalem and for the palaces of Khorsabad and Nineveh in Assyria. The Egyptians used cedars to make the boats that carried the pharaohs to their tombs. The stone relief shown below the picture of the cedars of Lebanon depicts the **transport of wood** for the palace at Nineveh.

The photograph below the map shows the Temple Obelisks at **Byblos**, one of the oldest continuously inhabited towns in the world. Trading activities brought Egyptian influences to Byblos, and around 2000 B.C. magnificent underground tombs were built. At the bottom right is a photograph of a **Dead Sea scroll**, one of a number found in caves near the Dead Sea. The scrolls were primarily copies of Bible manuscripts, but they also included information on life in the Essene community at Qumran.

The Fertile Crescent

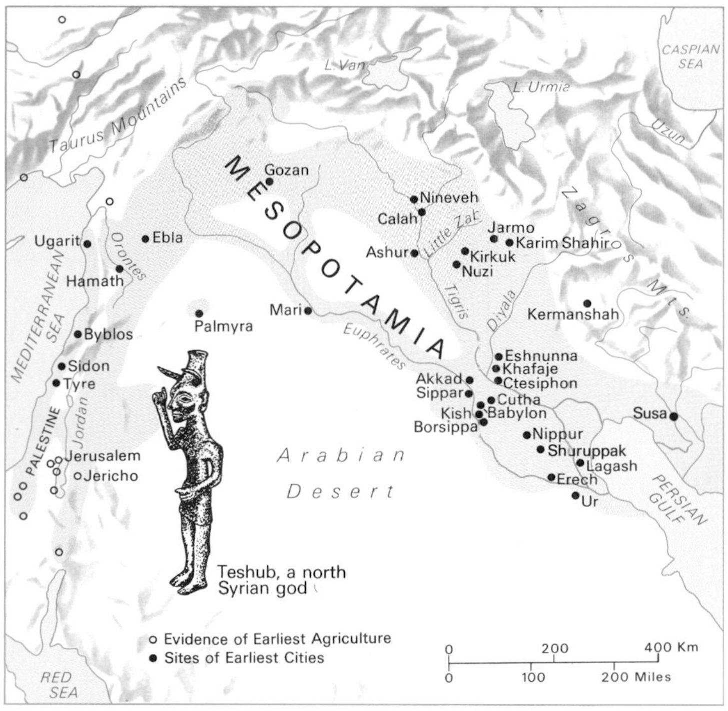
CASPIAN SEA
L. Van
L. Urmia
Taurus Mountains
MESOPOTAMIA
Gozan
Nineveh
Calah
Little Zab
Jarmo
Karim Shahir
Ashur
Kirkuk
Nuzi
Zagros Mts.
Ugarit
Ebla
Orontes
Hamath
MEDITERRANEAN SEA
Byblos
Palmyra
Mari
Tigris
Diyala
Kermanshah
Euphrates
Sidon
Tyre
Eshnunna
Khafaje
Ctesiphon
Akkad
Sippar
Cutha
Kish
Babylon
Borsippa
Susa
PALESTINE
Jordan
Jerusalem
Jericho
Arabian Desert
Nippur
Shuruppak
Lagash
Erech
Ur
PERSIAN GULF
Teshub, a north Syrian god
o Evidence of Earliest Agriculture
• Sites of Earliest Cities
0 200 400 Km
0 100 200 Miles
RED SEA

Cedars of Lebanon

Byblos

Transport of wood

Dead Sea Scroll

THE FERTILE CRESCENT AND THE MIDDLE EAST

The first **Persian Empire** reached its peak by 525 B.C. This was made possible by the military genius of Cyrus the Great (550–530 B.C.), during whose reign the far-reaching Empire was built up, as shown on the large map. King Darius (522–486 B.C.), an excellent administrator, added Egypt and northwest India to the Empire. It flourished until the 4th century B.C., when it was destroyed by Alexander the Great. The first Median Empire, as shown on the small **location map**, dated from about the 7th century B.C. In 553 B.C., Cyrus the Great defeated the Median king Astyages, annexing his empire in 549 B.C. The **gold drinking cup** shown was found at Ecbatana, the Median capital.

The location of the Kingdom of Lydia between Greece and the eastern states made it a wealthy trading nation. Coin money, such as the **silver coin** shown below, was invented in Lydia and minted at Ephesus. But expansion brought Lydia into conflict with the Medes and Persians, and Lydia was annexed by Cyrus in 546 B.C.

The **city of Babylon** had reached its height under Nebuchadnezzar, about 600 B.C., just before its capture by Persia. Among the city's splendid buildings were the Ziggurat, or Tower of Babel, and the terraced hanging gardens, shown below in reconstruction. Great works of art, such as the pictured **Babylonian lion** from the city's wall and the lion of 2200 B.C. shown below it, further attest to the cultural achievements of the Babylonians.

BLACK SEA
CASPIAN SEA
LYDIA
Ephesus
MEDIA
Ecbatana
MEDITERRANEAN SEA
Babylon
BABYLONIA
PERSIAN GULF
RED SEA
0 500 Km
0 300 Miles

Location map

Gold drinking cup

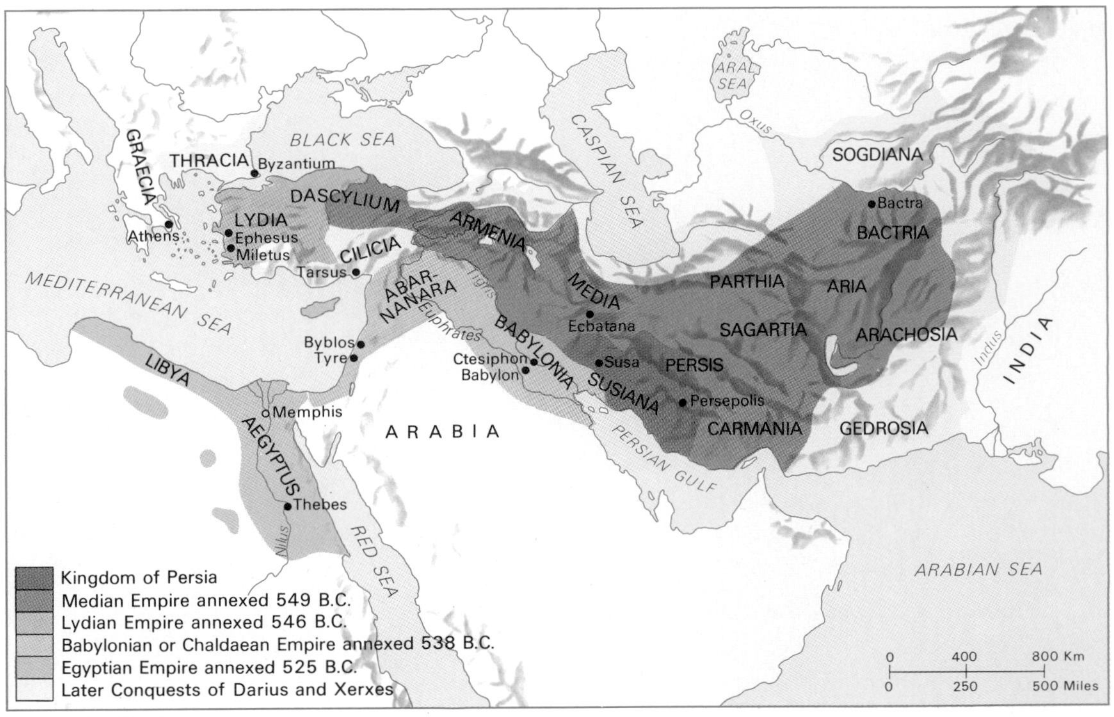

ARAL SEA
Oxus
BLACK SEA
CASPIAN SEA
SOGDIANA
GRAECIA
THRACIA
Byzantium
DASCYLIUM
Bactra
BACTRIA
ARMENIA
LYDIA
Athens
Ephesus
Miletus
CILICIA
Tarsus
MEDITERRANEAN SEA
ABAR-NANARA
Tigris
Euphrates
MEDIA
Ecbatana
PARTHIA
ARIA
SAGARTIA
ARACHOSIA
Indus
INDIA
Byblos
Tyre
Ctesiphon
Babylon
BABYLONIA
Susa
SUSIANA
PERSIS
Persepolis
CARMANIA
GEDROSIA
LIBYA
Memphis
ARABIA
AEGYPTUS
Thebes
Nilus
RED SEA
PERSIAN GULF
ARABIAN SEA
Kingdom of Persia
Median Empire annexed 549 B.C.
Lydian Empire annexed 546 B.C.
Babylonian or Chaldaean Empire annexed 538 B.C.
Egyptian Empire annexed 525 B.C.
Later Conquests of Darius and Xerxes
0 400 800 Km
0 250 500 Miles

The Persian Empire

City of Babylon

Babylon lion

Silver coin

Susa was the capital of ancient Susiana, or Elam. Its remains indicate advanced achievement at an early date, but its greatest period was from 1165 B.C. onward. Its importance began to decline with the reign of Nebuchadnezzar in Babylon. Susa became part of the Persian Empire under the reign of Cyrus the Great. It was a rich and splendid city, as the photograph of the rendering of the **Susa archer** — one of the Persian royal guard who helped Darius extend the Empire — implies.

It was customary for lesser rulers to pay tribute to powerful kings, sometimes as payment for peace and protection, as shown in the carving of **tribute bearers** at the left below. King Jehu of Israel is paying tribute to the Assyrian king Shalmaneser III. **King Darius** also received tribute, as shown in the sculpture of vassal tribute bearers at the right. Darius had Susa rebuilt, established an efficient communications network in the Empire, and was responsible for building **Persepolis**, the capital of Persia. The building of Persepolis was continued by later kings. As its extensive remains attest, the city had stood on a huge platform made of limestone blocks. It had walls of mud bricks and an imposing stairway leading to the main gate. Its many halls were supported by tall pillars topped by animal figures. Persepolis was sacked by Alexander in 330 B.C.

Tribute bearers

King Darius

Tribute bearers

Susa archer

MINOAN CRETE

A brilliant Bronze Age civilization flourished on Crete from 2600–1400 B.C., a fact which was first brought to light by Sir Arthur Evans, who called it "Minoan" after the legendary King Minos. **Minoan Crete**, which enjoyed maritime supremacy, had also attained a high cultural level.

The Minoans left **Knossos Palace** as a monument to their artistic achievements. A portion of the palace is shown below. The **plan of Knossos Palace** gives some idea of its architectural complexity. The famous **snake goddess** and **libation jug** shown here are from palace shrines. Minoans worshiped in caves, from the walls of which the **bull-leaping fresco** came. They considered the bull to be a very sacred animal.

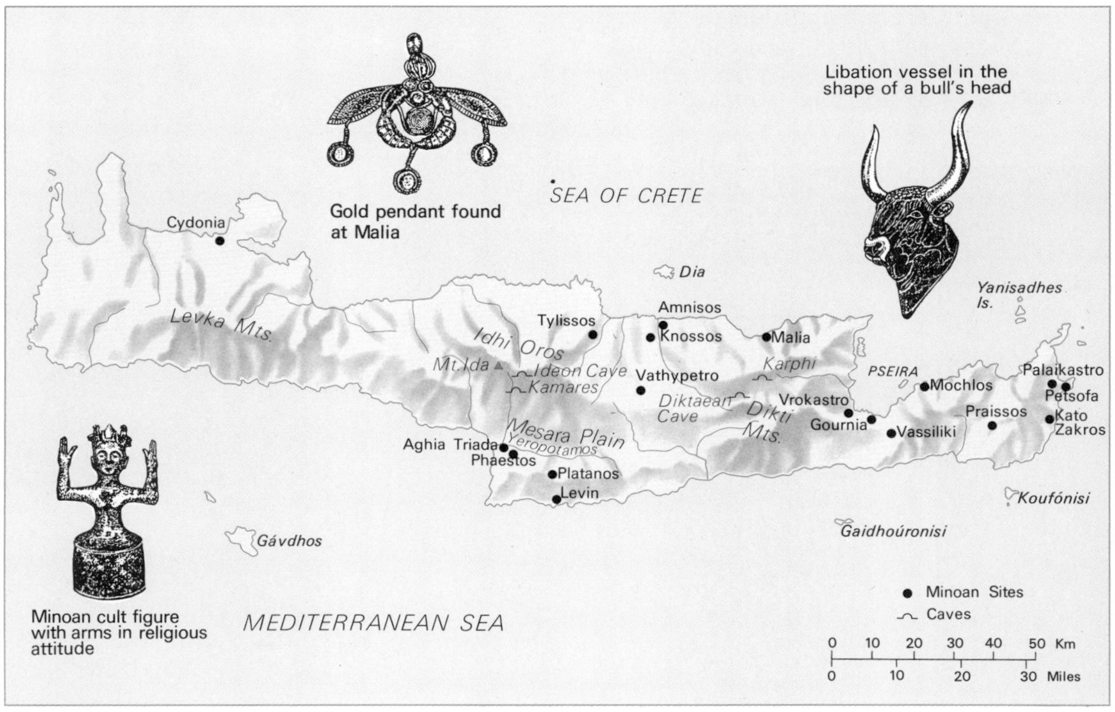

Libation vessel in the shape of a bull's head
Gold pendant found at Malia
SEA OF CRETE
Cydonia
Dia
Yanisadhes Is.
Levka Mts.
Tylissos
Amnisos
Knossos
Malia
Idhi Oros
Mt. Ida
Ideon Cave
Kamares
Vathypetro
Karphi
PSEIRA
Mochlos
Palaikastro
Petsofa
Diktaean Cave
Dikti Mts.
Vrokastro
Gournia
Vassiliki
Praissos
Kato Zakros
Mesara Plain
Yeropotamos
Aghia Triada
Phaestos
Platanos
Levin
Koufónisi
Gávdhos
Gaidhoúronisi
Minoan cult figure with arms in religious attitude
MEDITERRANEAN SEA
Minoan Sites
Caves
0 10 20 30 40 50 Km
0 10 20 30 Miles

Minoan Crete

Snake Goddess

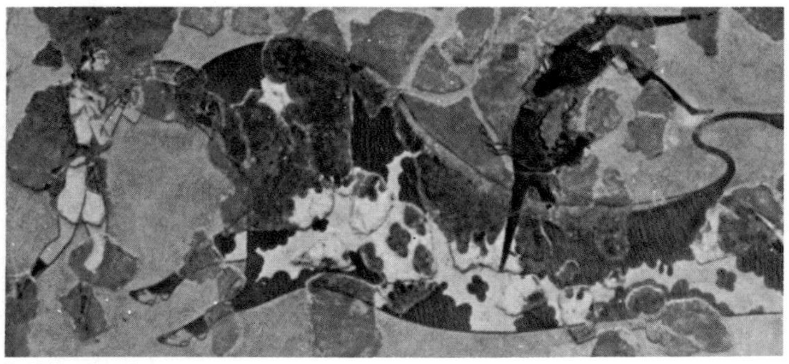

Bull-leaping fresco

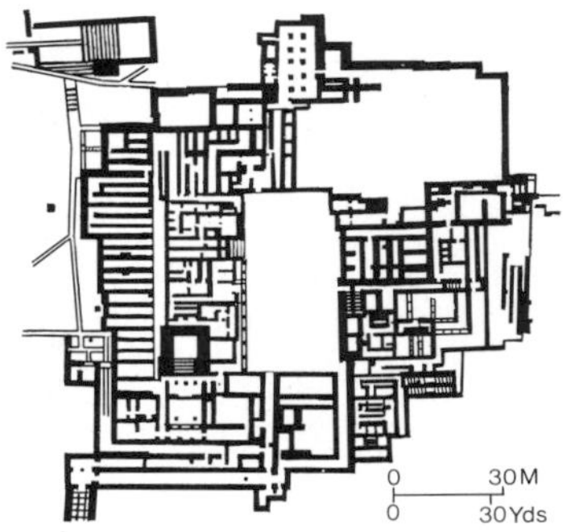

0 30M
0 30Yds

Plan of Knossos Palace

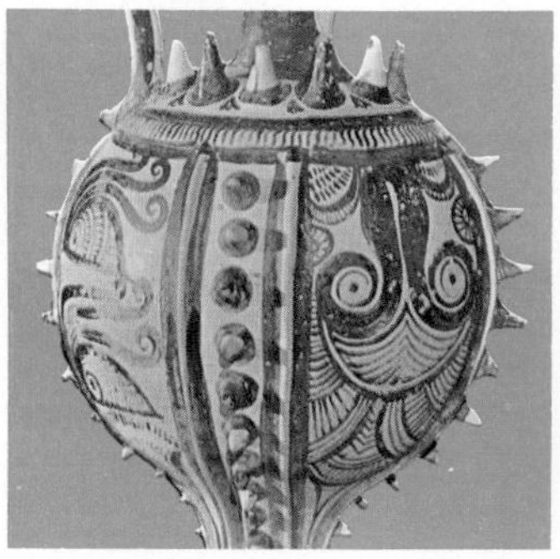

Libation jug

Knossos Palace

MYCENAEAN GREECE

The Mycenaean civilization appears to have emerged on mainland Greece about 1600 B.C. Feudal warrior leaders ruled their districts from hilltop fortresses, the principal fort being Mycenae itself. Minoan Crete exercised a strong influence in these early times; but, as **Mycenaean Greece** gradually acquired knowledge of the sea, power shifted in its favor. Feared as warriors, large mercenary detachments fought for Crete and Egypt, among other states.

The height of **Mycenaean expansion** and power was reached between 1500 and 1300 B.C. Eventually Crete, the Cyclades, Rhodes, and Cyprus were annexed, and vigorous trade was established throughout the Mediterranean, even with the tribes of north and west Europe. Weakened by internal strife and wars in Asia Minor, Mycenae was overrun by invaders from central Asia toward the end of the 12th century B.C.

The sculpture atop of the famous **lion gate at Mycenae**, the **gold death mask**, the **gold disk** from the Ladies' Grave, and the **bronze dagger** with gold and silver inlay all are indicative of the great cultural level attained by Mycenaean Greece. The citadel of Mycenae was enclosed by great walls, the entrance of which was the lion gate. Obviously, the death mask, superbly worked in gold, was made for a chieftain of great wealth and power.

Mycenaean Greece

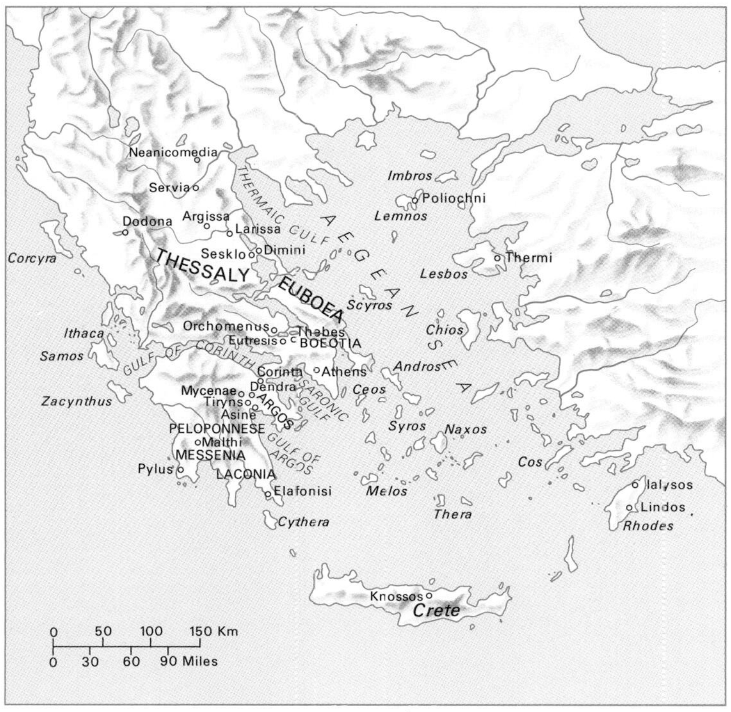

Neanicomedia
Servia
Dodona
Argissa
Larissa
Sesklo
Dimini
THESSALY
THERMAIC GULF
AEGEAN SEA
EUBOEA
Corcyra
Ithaca
Samos
Zacynthus
Orchomenus
Thebes
Eutresis
BOEOTIA
GULF OF CORINTH
Corinth
Athens
Mycenae
Dendra
Tiryns
Asine
ARGOS
SARONIC GULF
PELOPONNESE
Malthi
MESSENIA
GULF OF ARGOS
Pylus
LACONIA
Elafonisi
Cythera
Imbros
Poliochni
Lemnos
Thermi
Lesbos
Scyros
Chios
Andros
Ceos
Syros
Naxos
Cos
Melos
Thera
Ialysos
Lindos
Rhodes
Knossos
Crete
0 50 100 150 Km
0 30 60 90 Miles

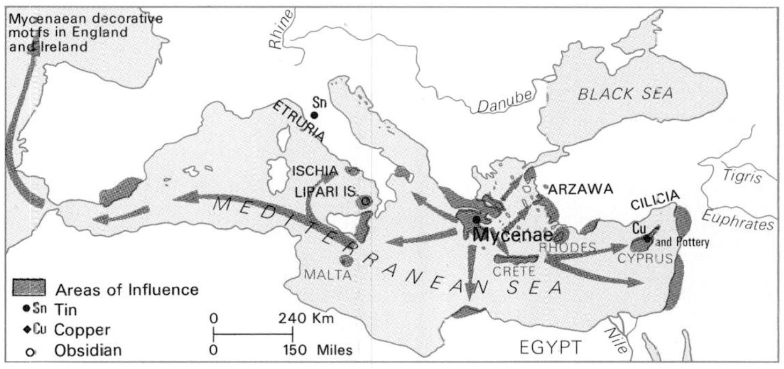

Mycenaean decorative motifs in England and Ireland
Rhine
Danube
BLACK SEA
Sn
ETRURIA
ISCHIA
LIPARI IS.
ARZAWA
CILICIA
Tigris
Euphrates
Mycenae
RHODES
Cu
and Pottery
CYPRUS
MALTA
CRETE
MEDITERRANEAN SEA
Areas of Influence
Sn Tin
Cu Copper
Obsidian
0 240 Km
0 150 Miles
EGYPT
Nile

Mycenaean expansion

Gold death mask

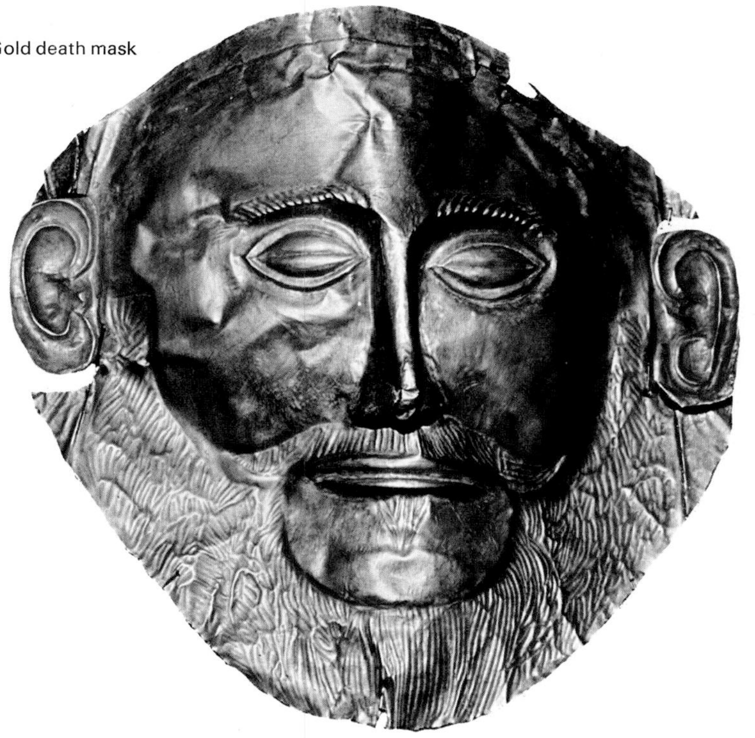

Lion Gate, Mycenae

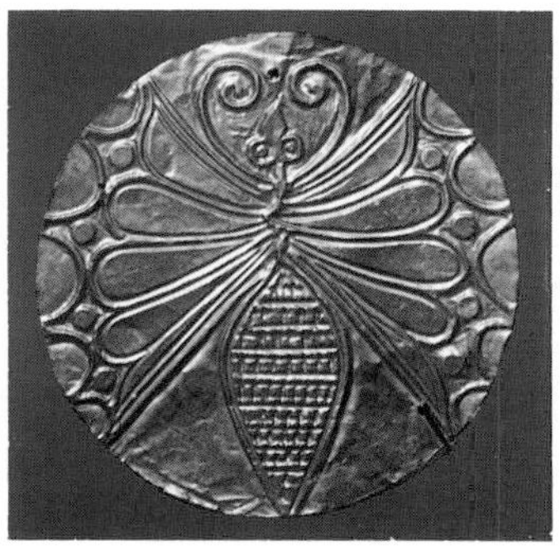

Gold disc

Bronze dagger

THE RISE OF GREECE

After the Mycenaean period, Greece was invaded by Indo-European tribes from the north, as shown on the top map. This distribution of peoples in **Greece before the city states** made for little unity, but they all took part in the Olympic Games. **Greek colonies** were established along much of the perimeter of the Mediterranean and the Black Sea, and Athens became the leading state after the Persian advance was halted in the 5th century B.C.

The **temple of Apollo** at Delphi, shown below in ruins, was one of the most magnificent in Greece. It was built over a crack in the rock from which oracular power was said to come. The god Apollo, the ideal of male beauty, was believed to preside over the oracle and was regarded as the source of wisdom.

The Greeks created modern drama in the 5th century B.C. It really started with festivals honoring Dionysus or Bacchus, gods of fertility and wine. Then contests were held in comedy and tragedy. They were performed at theaters such as the **Theatre of Epidaurus**, shown below the temple. The circular area, known as the orchestra, was where the chorus performed. Great sculptures were produced in this period, and even utilitarian objects, such as the geometric-style vase shown at the bottom of the page, were exquisitely conceived.

Temple of Apollo

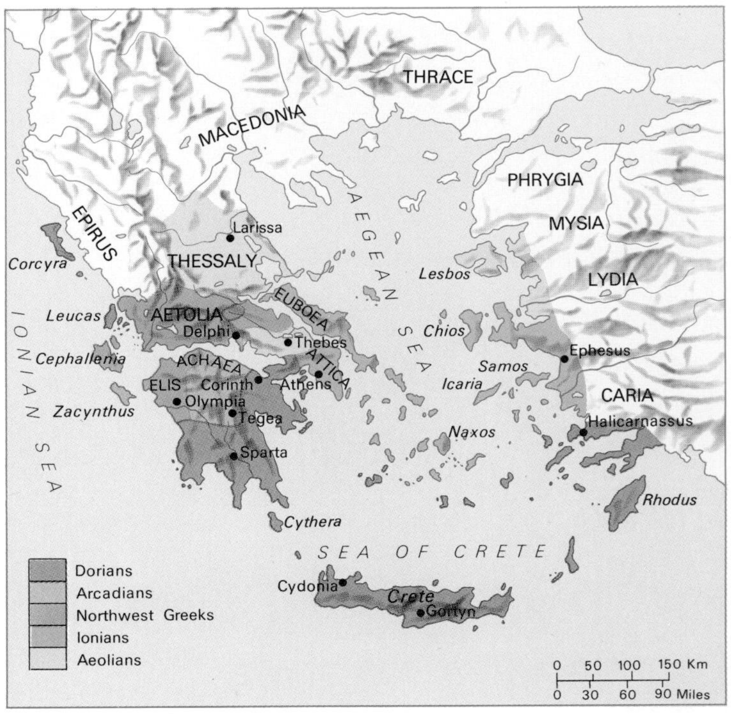
THRACE
MACEDONIA
PHRYGIA
EPIRUS
Larissa
MYSIA
Corcyra
THESSALY
AEGEAN SEA
Lesbos
LYDIA
Leucas
AETOLIA
Delphi
EUBOEA
Thebes
IONIAN SEA
Chios
Cephallenia
ACHAEA
ATTICA
Ephesus
ELIS
Corinth
Athens
Samos
Icaria
Olympia
CARIA
Zacynthus
Tegea
Halicarnassus
Naxos
Sparta
Rhodus
Cythera
SEA OF CRETE
Cydonia
Crete
Gortyn
Dorians
Arcadians
Northwest Greeks
Ionians
Aeolians
0 50 100 150 Km
0 30 60 90 Miles

Greece before the City States

Theatre at Epidaurus

0 200 400 600 Km
0 100 200 300 Miles
Agathe
Massalia
Nicaea
Emporiae
Alalia
Neapolis
Tarente
Metapontum
Elea
Croton
Hemeroscopion
Himera
Naxos
Mainake
MEDITERRANEAN SEA
Agragas
Syracuse
Tanais
Olbia
Tyras
Phanagoria
Panticapaeum
Chersonesus
Dioscurias
BLACK SEA
Mesembria
Sinope
Epidamnus
Trapezus
Heraclea
Byzantium
Chalcedon
Corcyra
Chalcis
Phocaea
Megarus
Eretria
Clazomenae
Corinth
Samos
Sparta
Andros
Miletus
Paros
Side
Phaselis
Thera
Rhodes
MEDITERRANEAN SEA
Cyrene
Apollonia
Euhesperides
Dorian Colonies
Ionian Colonies
Achaean Colonies
Areas under Greek Control
Miletus Mother Cities

Greek colonies

Greek vase

Fifth-century Greece was dominated by the Athenians, as the map at the left shows. The Acropolis was the ancient hilltop citadel of Athens, and its ruin still dominates the city today. Its buildings were constructed in the second half of the 5th century B.C. The greatest was the Parthenon, the temple dedicated to the goddess Athena. Shown below the map are the **Caryatids**, the draped female figures that support the north porch of the Erechtheum, a small temple named for King Erechtheus.

The map of **Greece after the Peloponnesian War, 404 B.C.**, shows what happened to the power of Athens at the hands of Sparta, one of the city states. Sparta had military ambitions and a well-trained professional army. Athens and Sparta fought together against Persian attacks, but afterwards became rivals. In the long Peloponnesian War (431–404 B.C.), Athens was defeated by Sparta, and the Athenian Empire was destroyed. The sculpture of the **Spartan warrior** and paintings such as the **chariot race** and the **athletes** shown here, reflect the major activities of 5th century Greece. The early Olympic Games, held every four years, consisted of foot races only.

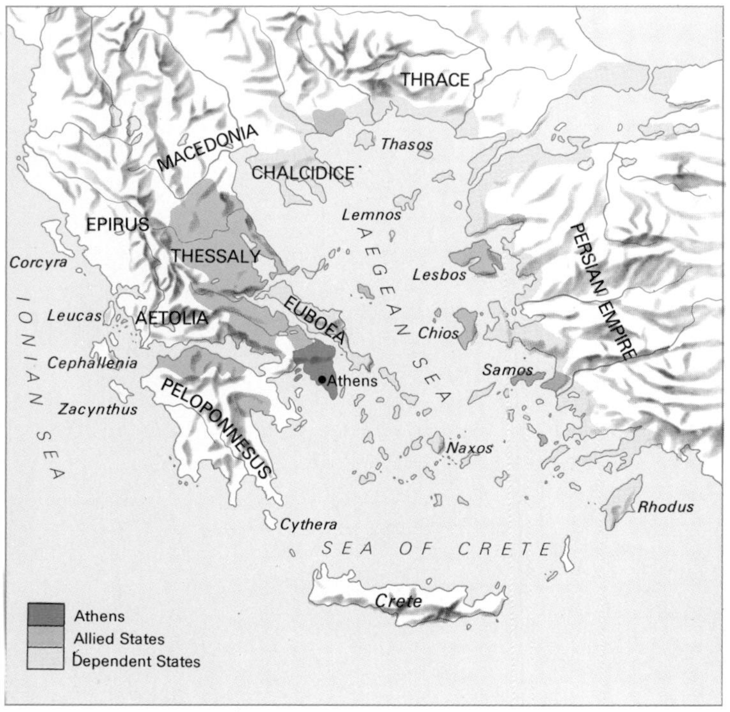
THRACE
MACEDONIA
Thasos
CHALCIDICE
EPIRUS
Lemnos
Corcyra
THESSALY
AEGEAN SEA
Lesbos
PERSIAN EMPIRE
IONIAN SEA
Leucas
AETOLIA
EUBOEA
Chios
Cephallenia
Samos
Athens
Zacynthus
PELOPONNESUS
Naxos
Rhodus
Cythera
SEA OF CRETE
Crete
Athens
Allied States
Dependent States

Fifth century Greece

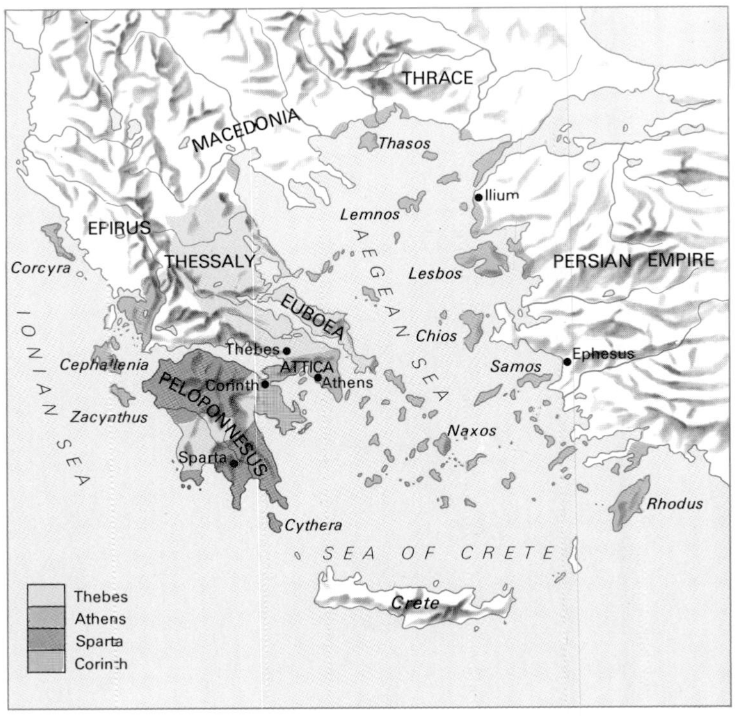
THRACE
MACEDONIA
Thasos
Ilium
Lemnos
EPIRUS
Corcyra
THESSALY
AEGEAN SEA
Lesbos
PERSIAN EMPIRE
IONIAN SEA
EUBOEA
Chios
Thebes
ATTICA
Cephallenia
Samos
Ephesus
Corinth
Athens
PELOPONNESUS
Zacynthus
Naxos
Sparta
Rhodus
Cythera
SEA OF CRETE
Crete
Thebes
Athens
Sparta
Corinth

Greece after the Peloponnesian War, 404 BC

Caryatids, Athens

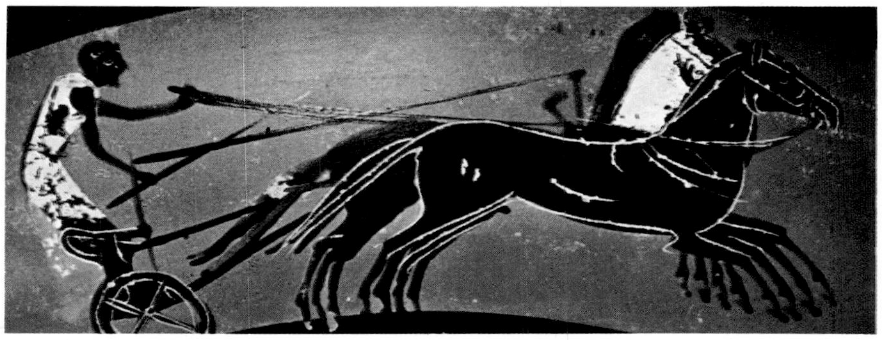

Chariot race

Spartan warrior

Athletes

ALEXANDER THE GREAT

Alexander was born in 356 B.C., the son of King Philip of Macedonia. Philip had united Greece and had intended to free the Asiatic Greeks from Persian control. He also coveted the riches of the Persian Empire to pay for his professional army. At Philip's death, Alexander first quelled rebellions in Greece and then crossed the Dardenelles to start, at the age of 22, his 2800-mile journey into Asia. The outcome of this successful venture is shown on this map of **Alexander's Empire.** His routes are also shown.

During his Asian campaigns, Alexander founded or refounded many cities to administer the conquered territories. The greatest of these was Alexandria in Egypt. From these cities, in territories later ruled by Alexander's successors, Greek culture spread and for the next three centuries was dominant throughout much of the Middle East, as shown on the map of **hellenization in Asia**. This hellenization process lasted until the spread of Roman power in the 2nd century B.C. It all stemmed from the brief career of one man, who died at the age of 32.

The photograph at the bottom left is a bronze statuette of **Alexander and Bucephalas**, the horse Alexander mastered when just eight years old, and which bore him into almost every battle he fought. The marble sculpture of the **head of Alexander** shown below was made after his death but was based on an original made in his lifetime. The **coin** shown below portrays Alexander as the god Heracles, with a lion's mane headdress. Alexander's family claimed their descent from Heracles, the son of Zeus.

Alexander's Empire

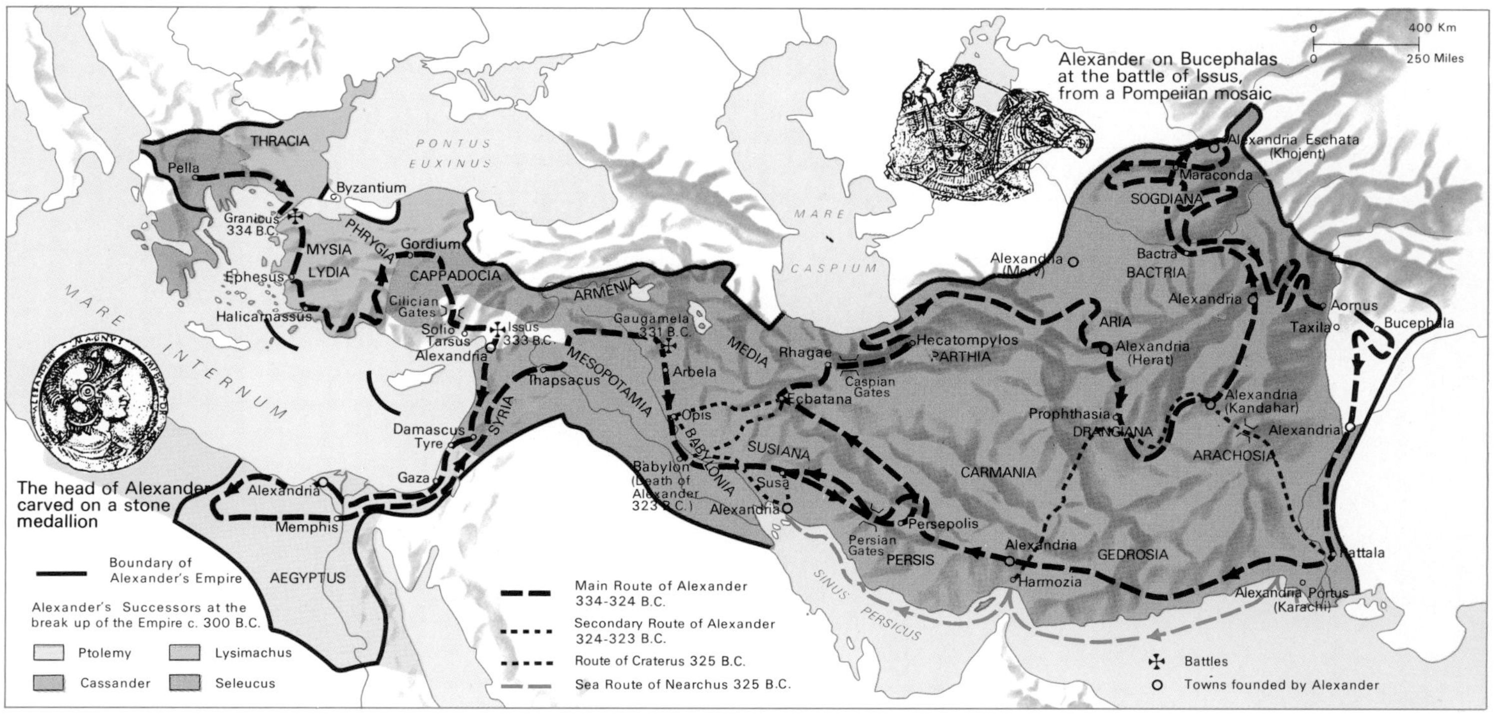
Alexander on Bucephalas at the battle of Issus, from a Pompeiian mosaic
0 400 Km
0 250 Miles
THRACIA
PONTUS EUXINUS
Pella
Byzantium
Granicus 334 B.C.
MYSIA
PHRYGIA
Gordium
Ephesus
LYDIA
CAPPADOCIA
Halicarnassus
Cilician Gates
Soli
Tarsus
Issus 333 B.C.
Alexandria
ARMENIA
Gaugamela 331 B.C.
Arbela
MESOPOTAMIA
Thapsacus
SYRIA
Damascus
Tyre
Gaza
MARE INTERNUM
MARE CASPIUM
MEDIA
Rhagae
Caspian Gates
Ecbatana
Opis
BABYLONIA
Babylon (Death of Alexander 323 B.C.)
SUSIANA
Susa
Alexandria
Persepolis
Persian Gates
PERSIS
CARMANIA
Hecatompylos
PARTHIA
Alexandria (Merv)
ARIA
Alexandria (Herat)
Prophthasia
DRANGIANA
Alexandria (Kandahar)
ARACHOSIA
Alexandria
Alexandria Eschata (Khojent)
Maraconda
SOGDIANA
Bactra
BACTRIA
Aornus
Taxila
Bucephala
Pattala
GEDROSIA
Alexandria
Harmozia
Alexandria Portus (Karachi)
SINUS PERSICUS
The head of Alexander carved on a stone medallion
Memphis
AEGYPTUS
Boundary of Alexander's Empire
Alexander's Successors at the break up of the Empire c. 300 B.C.
Ptolemy
Lysimachus
Cassander
Seleucus
Main Route of Alexander 334-324 B.C.
Secondary Route of Alexander 324-323 B.C.
Route of Craterus 325 B.C.
Sea Route of Nearchus 325 B.C.
Battles
Towns founded by Alexander

Alexander and Bucephalas

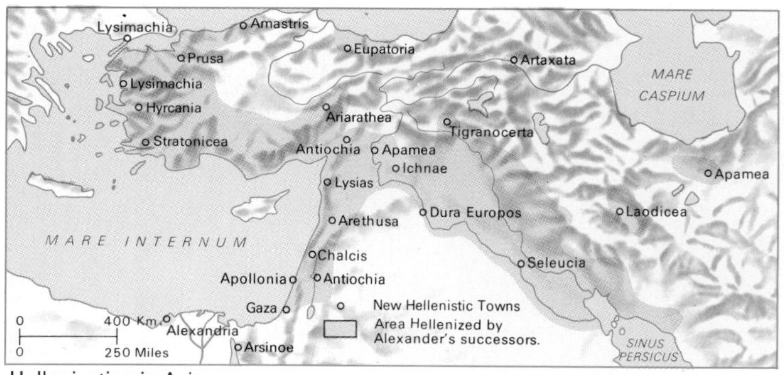
Lysimachia
Amastris
Prusa
Eupatoria
Artaxata
MARE CASPIUM
Lysimachia
Hyrcania
Ariarathea
Tigranocerta
Stratonicea
Antiochia
Apamea
Ichnae
Apamea
Lysias
Laodicea
Arethusa
Dura Europos
MARE INTERNUM
Chalcis
Seleucia
Apollonia
Antiochia
Gaza
Alexandria
Arsinoe
0 400 Km
0 250 Miles
New Hellenistic Towns
Area Hellenized by Alexander's successors.
SINUS PERSICUS

Hellenization in Asia

Head of Alexander

A coin

THE ETRUSCANS

Etruscan Italy in the 6th and 5th centuries B.C. consisted, as the map indicates, of that part of Italy that lies north of the Tiber River. The Etruscans probably came from the East. They established self-governing city states and traded widely. They were interested in sports and hunting. Their self-reliant towns were weak against aggressors, and they eventually lost their independence to Rome.

Skilled in working bronze, iron, and gold, Etruscan artists reflected Greek influences. Their tombs were richly decorated, and paintings in them tell much of everyday life. An example is the **chariot race** detail from an Etruscan vase, shown in the top photograph below. Beneath this photograph is a beautifully wrought **gold fibula**, or clasp, dating to about 650 B.C. The **gold earring** is another example of high Etruscan craftsmanship, as is the bronze of the **wrestlers**.

The **tomb painting** at the bottom of the page is a terracotta slab from a small Etruscan tomb. The painting depicts the judgment of Paris, when he had to decide who should receive the golden apple as the most beautiful goddess — Aphrodite, Athena, or Hera. He awarded it to Aphrodite, incurring the hatred of Athena and Hera.

Chariot race

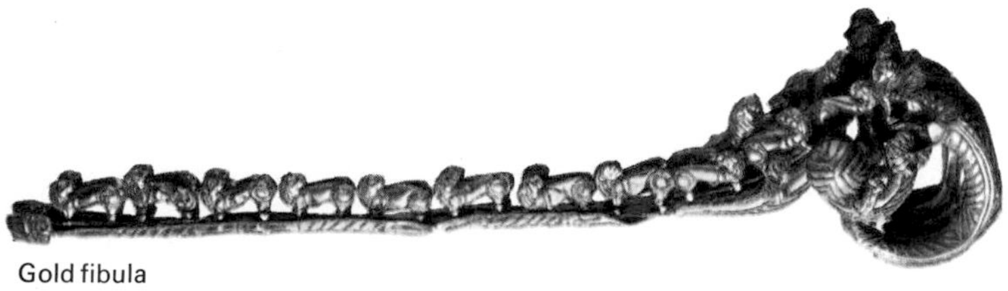
Gold fibula

Gold earring

Wrestlers

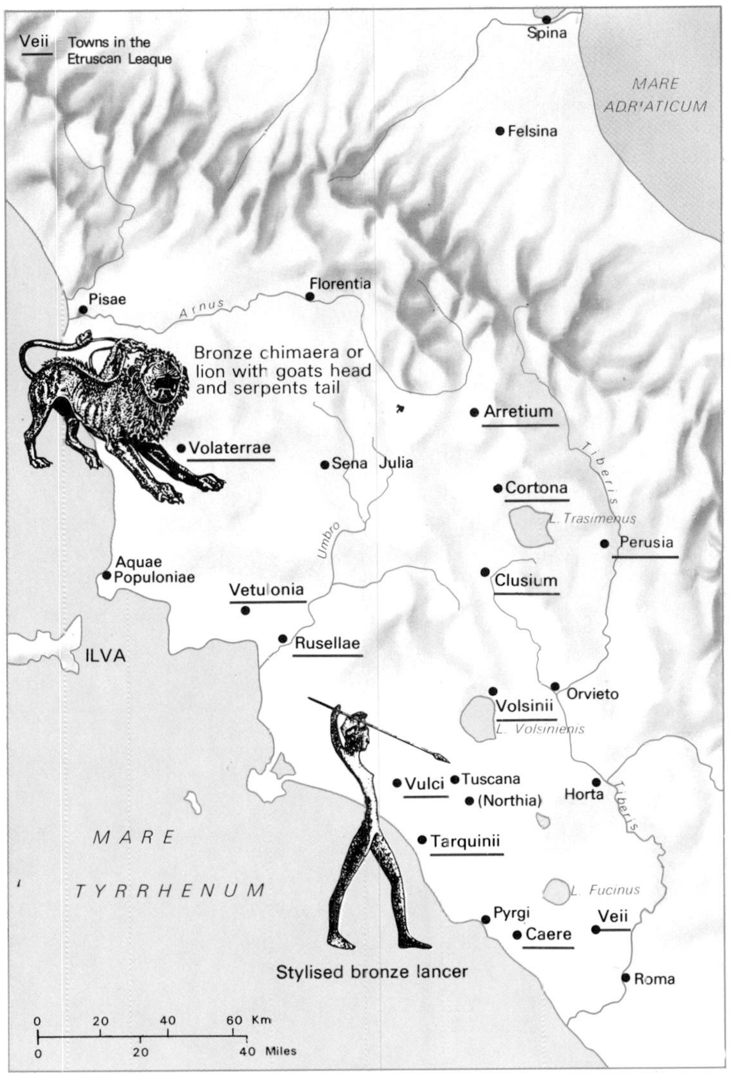
Veii Towns in the Etruscan Leaque
Spina
MARE ADRIATICUM
Felsina
Florentia
Pisae
Arnus
Bronze chimaera or lion with goats head and serpents tail
Arretium
Volaterrae
Sena Julia
Cortona
L. Trasimenus
Perusia
Umbro
Aquae Populoniae
Vetulonia
Clusium
Rusellae
ILVA
Orvieto
Volsinii
L. Volsiniensis
Vulci
Tuscana
(Northia)
Horta
Tiberis
Tarquinii
MARE TYRRHENUM
L. Fucinus
Pyrgi
Caere
Veii
Stylised bronze lancer
Roma
0 20 40 60 Km
0 20 40 Miles
Etruscan Italy

Tomb painting

THE ROMAN EMPIRE

The Roman Republic was established in the 5th century, and by 275 B.C., Rome had conquered all of Italy. After conflict with Carthage in the Punic War, Roman sea power was supreme, giving Rome control of the Mediterranean and surrounding lands. Augustus proclaimed the Empire in 30 B.C., and Rome rose to the height of its power. The gradual extension of the Empire is shown in the maps.

Under the Empire, whose borders were protected by a ring of many army legions, life proceeded in peace. Rome was rebuilt, towns were established, and trade was encouraged. Every city had its public buildings — the forum or market place, the bathhouse with complex plumbing and heating, the amphitheater, the circus or race course, and the theater. Literature and art flourished. All roads did lead to **imperial Rome**, as the map below indicates. Among the many attractions was the **chariot race**, a highly favored sport widely depicted in various different art forms — on the walls of buildings, in paintings, and as colorful decoration on pottery and other objects. As with other cultures, Roman artists and craftsmen reflected the major interests and activities of the period.

264 BC
OCEANUS ATLANTICUS
ITALIA
PONTUS EUXINUS
MARE CASPIUM
MARE INTERNUM
0 640 Km
0 400 Miles

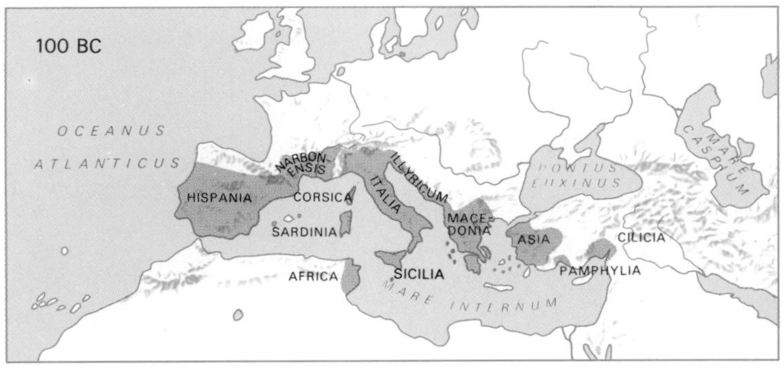

100 BC
OCEANUS ATLANTICUS
NARBONENSIS
ILLYRICUM
ITALIA
HISPANIA
CORSICA
SARDINIA
MACEDONIA
ASIA
CILICIA
PAMPHYLIA
AFRICA
SICILIA
MARE INTERNUM
PONTUS EUXINUS
MARE CASPIUM

14 AD
OCEANUS ATLANTICUS
GALLIA
HISPANIA
CORSICA
SARDINIA
ILLYRICUM
ITALIA
ASIA
SICILIA
CRETA
CYPRUS
AFRICA
AEGYPTUM
MARE INTERNUM
PONTUS EUXINUS
MARE CASPIUM

117 AD
BRITANNIA
OCEANUS ATLANTICUS
GALLIA
DACIA
HISPANIA
CORSICA
SARDINIA
ILLYRICUM
ITALIA
ASIA
MAURETANIA
SICILIA
CRETA
CYPRUS
AFRICA
AEGYPTUM
PONTUS EUXINUS
MARE CASPIUM
Temporary Acquisitions

ANNIAE
ARESCVSA

Chariot race

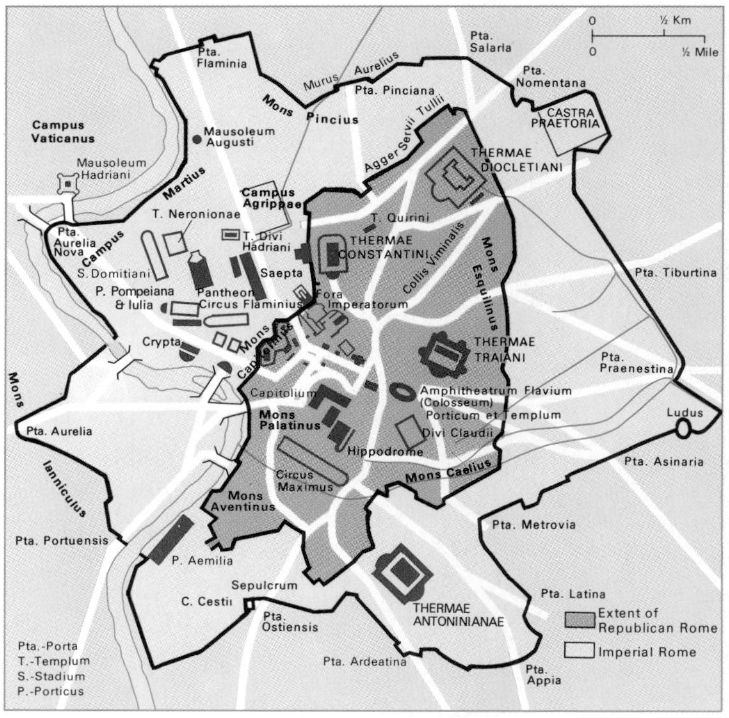

0 ½ Km
0 ½ Mile
Pta. Salaria
Pta. Flaminia
Murus Aurelius
Pta. Pinciana
Pta. Nomentana
CASTRA PRAETORIA
Mons Pincius
Agger Servii Tullii
Campus Vaticanus
Mausoleum Augusti
Mausoleum Hadriani
THERMAE DIOCLETIANI
Campus Martius
Campus Agrippae
T. Neronionae
T. Quirini
Pta. Aurelia Nova
Campus
T. Divi Hadriani
THERMAE CONSTANTINI
Collis Viminalis
Mons Esquilinus
Pta. Tiburtina
S. Domitiani
Saepta
P. Pompeiana & Iulia
Pantheon
Circus Flaminius
Fora Imperatorum
Crypta
Mons Capitolinus
THERMAE TRAIANI
Pta. Praenestina
Capitolium
Amphitheatrum Flavium (Colosseum)
Porticum et Templum Divi Claudii
Mons Palatinus
Mons
Pta. Aurelia
Ludus
Hippodrome
Pta. Asinaria
Ianiculus
Circus Maximus
Mons Caelius
Mons Aventinus
Pta. Metrovia
Pta. Portuensis
P. Aemilia
Sepulcrum C. Cestii
Pta. Latina
Pta. Ostiensis
THERMAE ANTONINIANAE
Extent of Republican Rome
Imperial Rome
Pta.-Porta
T.-Templum
S.-Stadium
P.-Porticus
Pta. Ardeatina
Pta. Appia

Imperial Rome

Augustus, depicted in sculpture at the lower right, was the first Roman emperor. He was elevated by proclamation after he had proved himself supreme among the generals. He was an able administrator who improved the organization of the Empire and created an atmosphere of security. He encouraged the arts, especially a national literature, to which writers such as Livy, Horace, and Virgil contributed.

The Empire maintained a comprehensive network of roads for several reasons — to permit fast travel to borders, to facilitate trade, to encourage the spread of culture. **Routes of the Roman Empire** are shown on the map below. These routes were usually straight, avoiding large natural obstacles. Roman engineering has stood the test of time, and many roads built then are still in use.

There is much evidence that the arts flourished in the Roman Empire. The bronze **household god** and the **gladiator** detail from a North African mosaic are typical examples. Architectural achievements were enormous, as attested by the vast **amphitheater at Arles** and the **theater at Dougga**. Other examples are the bas reliefs of **Trajan's Column** and the sculptured **Wolf with Romulus and Remus**.

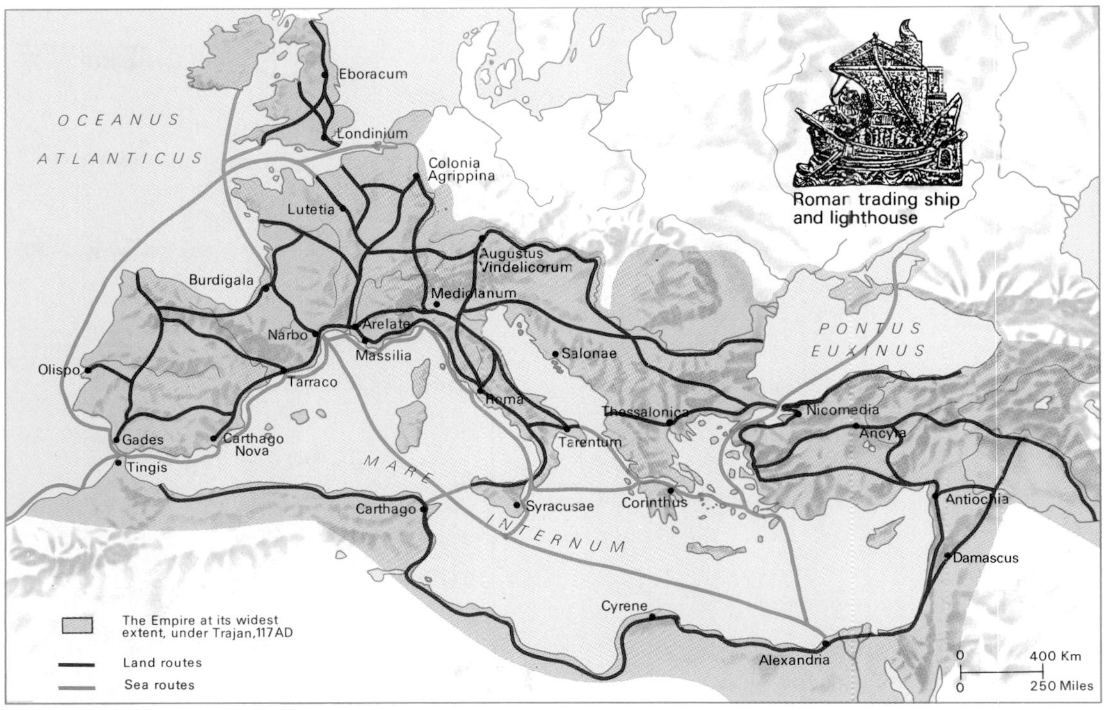
OCEANUS
ATLANTICUS
Eboracum
Londinium
Colonia Agrippina
Lutetia
Roman trading ship and lighthouse
Augustus Vindelicorum
Burdigala
Mediolanum
Narbo
Arelate
Massilia
PONTUS EUXINUS
Salonae
Olispo
Tarraco
Roma
Thessalonica
Nicomedia
Ancyra
Gades
Carthago Nova
Tarentum
Tingis
MARE INTERNUM
Syracusae
Corinthus
Antiochia
Carthago
Damascus
Cyrene
Alexandria
The Empire at its widest extent, under Trajan, 117AD
Land routes
Sea routes
0 400 Km
0 250 Miles

Routes of the Roman Empire

Household god

Gladiator

Amphitheatre at Arles

Theatre at Dougga

Part of Trajan's Column

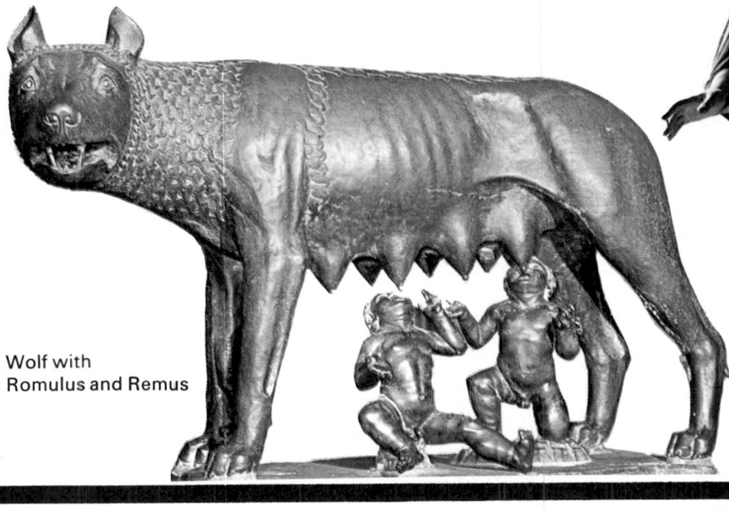

Wolf with Romulus and Remus

Augustus

THE INDUS VALLEY

In **the Indus valley**, city states developed about 2500 B.C., covering a wide area, as indicated on the map. Mohenjo-Daro was one of the largest of these states, with between 20,000 and 50,000 people. They lived comfortably in a well-planned city with wide streets and rectangular blocks of houses. At the right is a **household well**, left standing when excavated through several layers. A raised platform dominated the city and included, among other buildings, a vast granary and the large **ritual bath** shown below, left.

The **bronze dancer** at the right is an example of the best artwork from the Indus civilization. Generally their products seem to be restrained and severe. Few stone sculptures, but many terracotta figurines, were found. Their **jewelry**, as shown here, was mostly steatite or soapstone and glazed clay — but with semi-precious stones such as agate, jasper, and jade — and gold beads.

The **Indus seal** shown below is typical of many that were found, some far from the Indus valley. Many small objects, such as the **toy cart** and the **stone monkey** shown below, were also found. They are remnants of a civilization that lasted about 1000 years before Aryan invaders took over.

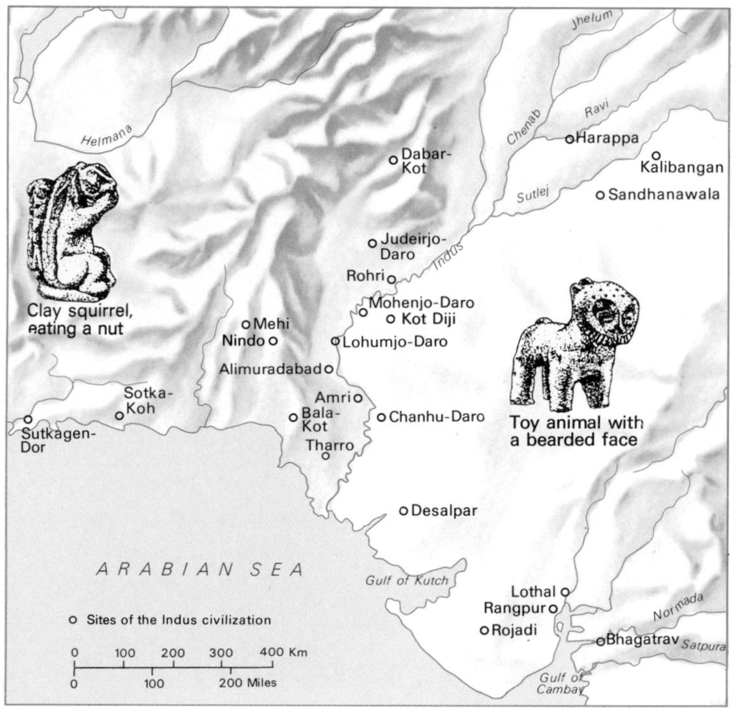

Jhelum
Helmand
Chenab
Ravi
Harappa
Kalibangan
Sutlej
Sandhanawala
Dabar-Kot
Judeirjo-Daro
Indus
Rohri
Mohenjo-Daro
Kot Diji
Clay squirrel, eating a nut
Mehi
Nindo
Lohumjo-Daro
Alimuradabad
Sotka-Koh
Amri
Bala-Kot
Chanhu-Daro
Toy animal with a bearded face
Sutkagen-Dor
Tharro
Desalpar
ARABIAN SEA
Gulf of Kutch
Lothal
Rangpur
Rojadi
Narmada
Bhagatrav
Satpura
Gulf of Cambay
Sites of the Indus civilization
0 100 200 300 400 Km
0 100 200 Miles

The Indus valley

Household well

Bronze dancer

Ritual bath

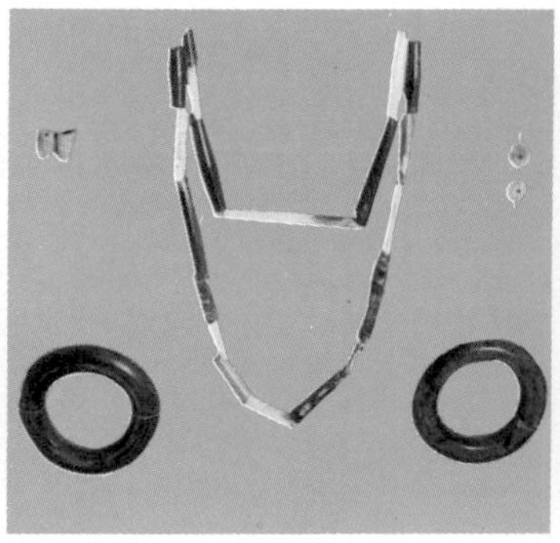
Jewelery

Indus seal

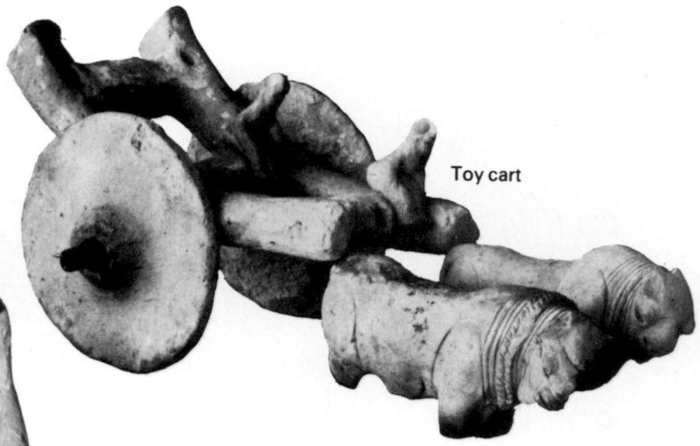
Toy cart

Stone monkey

INDIA

India has had a very turbulent history. The Aryan invaders who overwhelmed the Indus people drove on to the Ganges valley and settled there between 1000 and 500 B.C. They adopted Hinduism, and the caste system was introduced. In the 6th century, the rival religion of Buddhism was founded. The Mauryan Empire spread over most of northern and central India in the 3rd century B.C. Asoka, the third emperor, was converted to Buddhism, and his thoughts on the right way of life were engraved on pillars and rocks throughout the Empire. A map of **Asoka's Empire** and a **pillar of Asoka** are shown below.

Sanskrit, an example of which is shown at the bottom of the page, originated in the language of the early Aryan invaders. It became the language of Hinduism, which is based on the teachings set out in the Vedas, the Hindu sacred writings. Hindu temples, such as the **temple at Bhubaneswar**, are used for elaborate rituals. The photograph of the **Hindu temple** at Mahabalipuram has a roof parapet made up of sacred cows. The small map at the center below shows the **spread of Hinduism**. The map just below it shows the **spread of Buddhism**. Statues such as the **Buddha from Lahore** and the **Buddha at Patan** embody the Buddhist ideals of serenity and harmony. The **Stupa at Amaravati** shows the period's architecture.

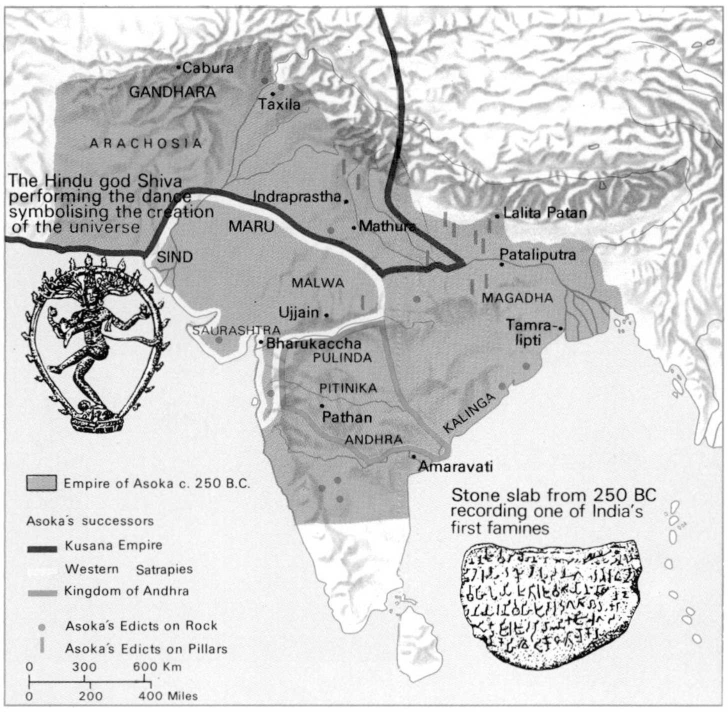

Cabura
GANDHARA
Taxila
ARACHOSIA
The Hindu god Shiva performing the dance symbolising the creation of the universe
Indraprastha
MARU
Mathura
Lalita Patan
SIND
Pataliputra
MALWA
MAGADHA
Ujjain
SAURASHTRA
Tamra-lipti
Bharukaccha
PULINDA
PITINIKA
Pathan
ANDHRA
KALINGA
Amaravati
Empire of Asoka c. 250 B.C.
Asoka's successors
Kusana Empire
Western Satrapies
Kingdom of Andhra
Asoka's Edicts on Rock
Asoka's Edicts on Pillars
0 300 600 Km
0 200 400 Miles
Stone slab from 250 BC recording one of India's first famines

Asoka's Empire

Pillar of Asoka

Buddha, Patan

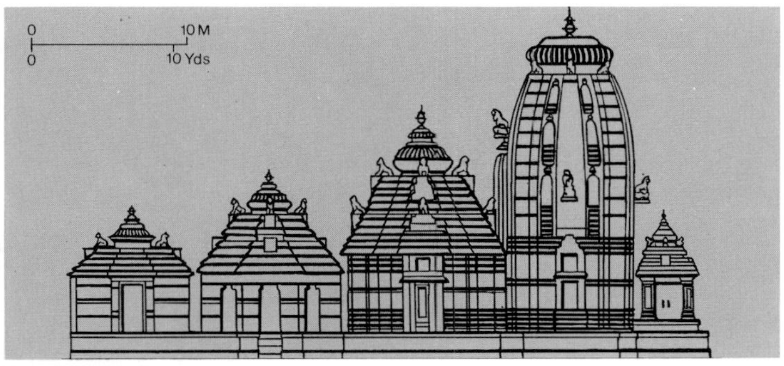

0 10M
0 10 Yds

Temple at Bhubaneswar

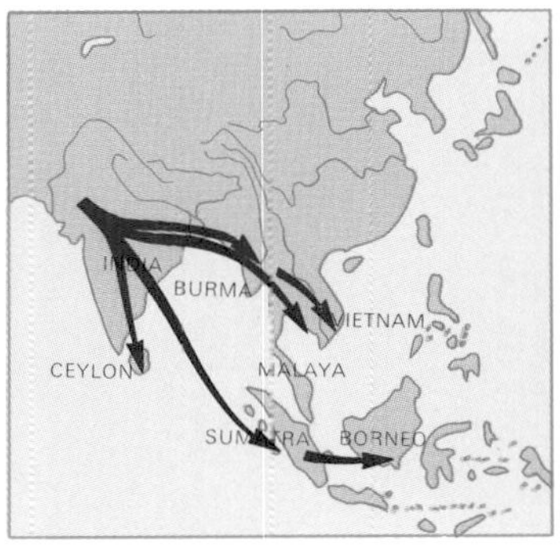

INDIA
BURMA
VIETNAM
CEYLON
MALAYA
SUMATRA
BORNEO

Spread of Hinduism

Buddha, Lahore

Hindu temple

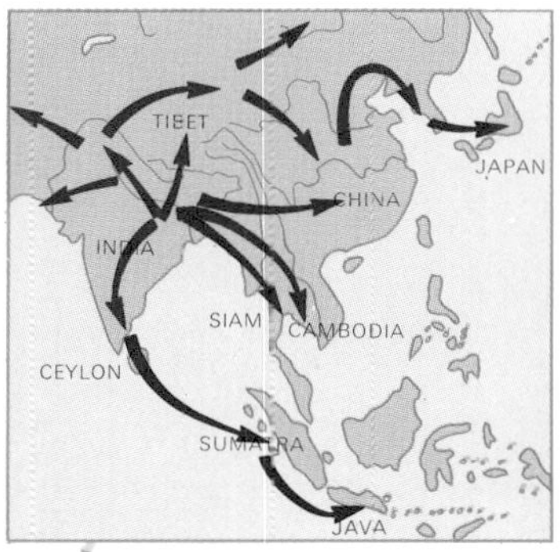

TIBET
JAPAN
CHINA
INDIA
SIAM
CAMBODIA
CEYLON
SUMATRA
JAVA

Spread of Buddhism

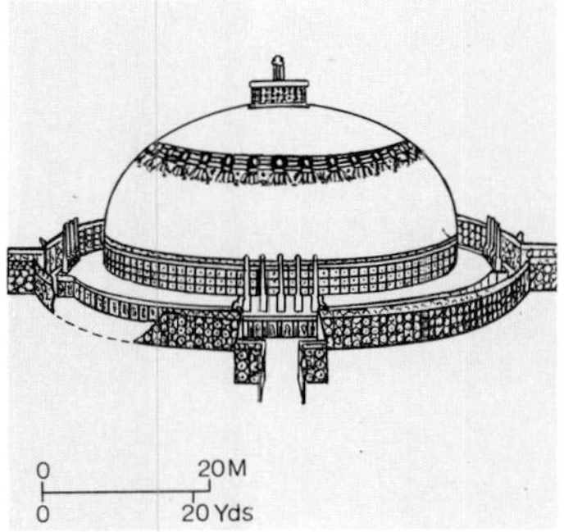

0 20M
0 20 Yds

Stupa at Amaravati

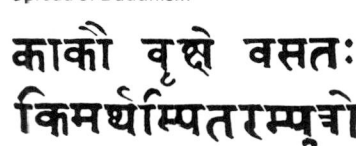

काकौ वृक्षे वसतः
किमर्थम्पितरम्पृचो

CHINA

As this series of maps indicates, recorded civilization in China dates back many centuries, starting with the Shang dynasty. This dynasty lasted from about 1450 to 1054 B.C., the period in which the **wine vessel** shown at the right was made. The Shang were conquered about 1054 B.C. by the Chou, a nomadic people from the West, under whom a feudal system developed, and local chieftains ruled small independent kingdoms. The Chin finally took over, but there was only one Chin emperor. The Han dynasty came to power in 206 B.C.

As the large map shows, Chinese rule was greatly extended under the Han. Later, the empire was split into three kingdoms — Wei, Shu, and Wu — and then into 16 warring states. Unity was achieved in A.D. 581 under the Sui dynasty and later under Tang. (A diagram of **Chang'an**, the **Tang capital**, is shown below beside a Tang **ceramic figure**.) The Tang dynasty was ended by an invasion from Manchuria and internal rebellions. After five short-lived dynasties, the Sung dynasty gained a measure of control until the Mongol invasion under Genghis Khan, and the birth of **the Mongol Empire** in 1279 under Kublai Khan.

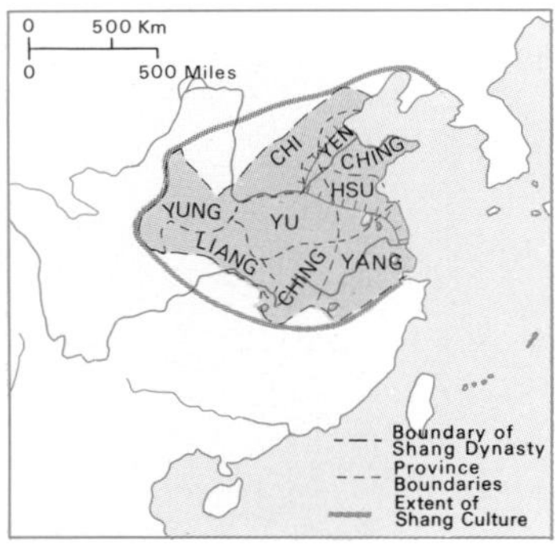

0 500 Km
0 500 Miles
YUNG
YU
HSU
YANG
Boundary of Shang Dynasty
Province Boundaries
Extent of Shang Culture

c.1054 BC

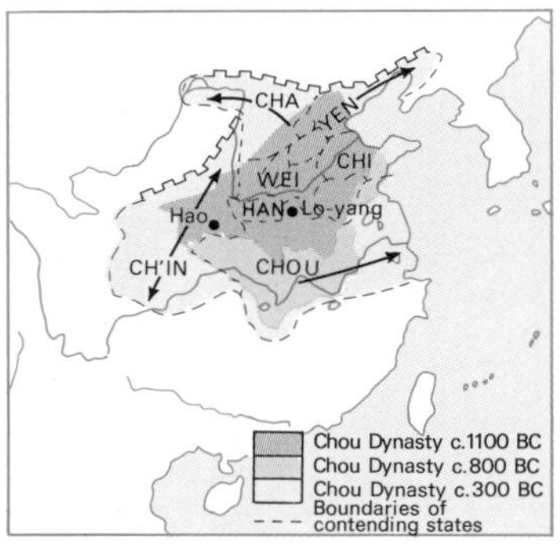

CHA
WEI
HAN
Lo-yang
Hao
CH'IN
CHOU
Chou Dynasty c.1100 BC
Chou Dynasty c.800 BC
Chou Dynasty c.300 BC
Boundaries of contending states

1054-300 BC

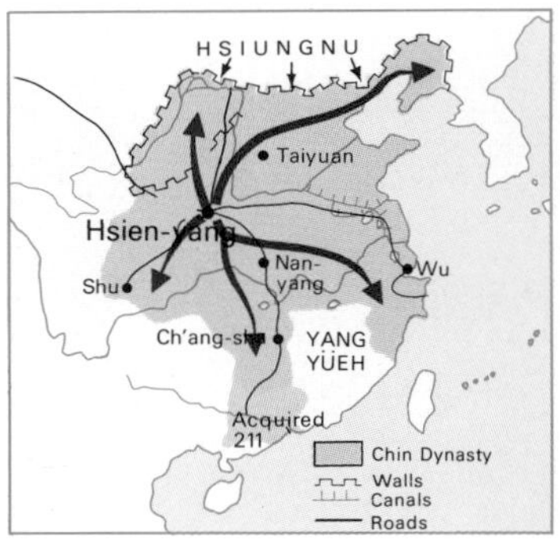

HSIUNGNU
Taiyuan
Shu
Nan-yang
Wu
Ch'ang-sha
YANG YÜEH
Acquired 211
Chin Dynasty
Walls
Canals
Roads

255-206 BC

Wine vessel — Shang

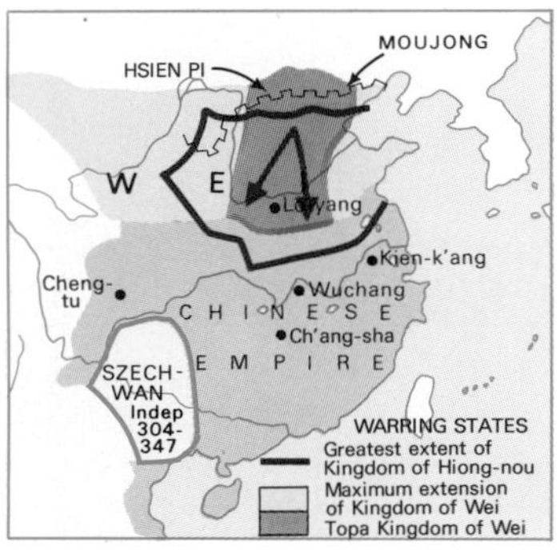

MOUJONG
HSIEN PI
W
E
Kien-k'ang
Cheng-tu
Wuchang
C H I N E S E
Ch'ang-sha
E M P I R E
SZECH-WAN Indep 304-347
WARRING STATES
Greatest extent of Kingdom of Hiong-nou
Maximum extension of Kingdom of Wei
Topa Kingdom of Wei

4th-6th centuries

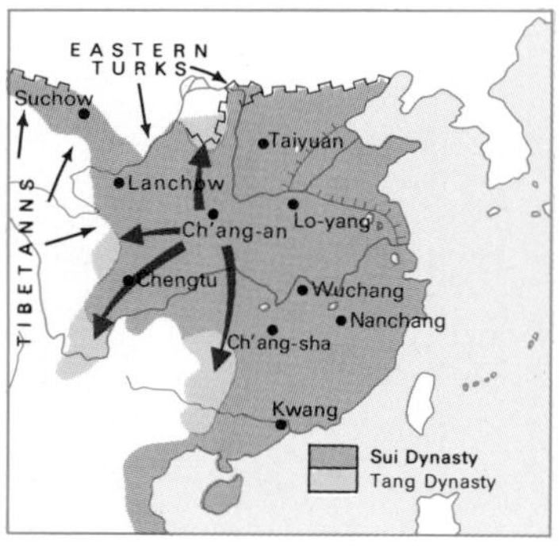

EASTERN TURKS
Suchow
Taiyuan
Lanchow
Lo-yang
Ch'ang-an
TIBETANS
Chengtu
Wuchang
Nanchang
Ch'ang-sha
Kwang
Sui Dynasty
Tang Dynasty

581-906

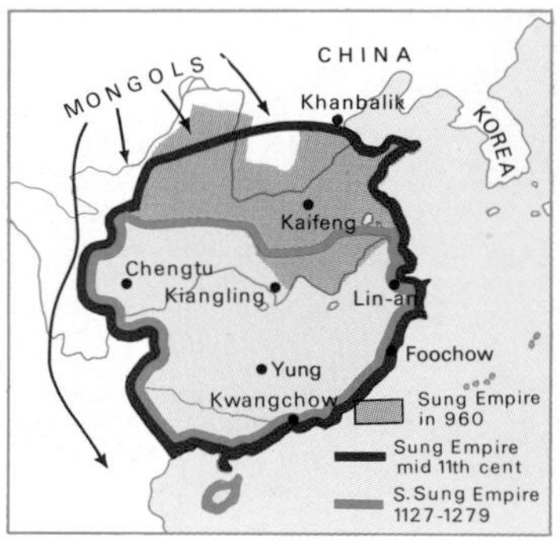

CHINA
MONGOLS
Khanbalik
KOREA
Kaifeng
Chengtu
Kiangling
Foochow
Yung
Kwangchow
Sung Empire in 960
Sung Empire mid 11th cent
S.Sung Empire 1127-1279

960-1279

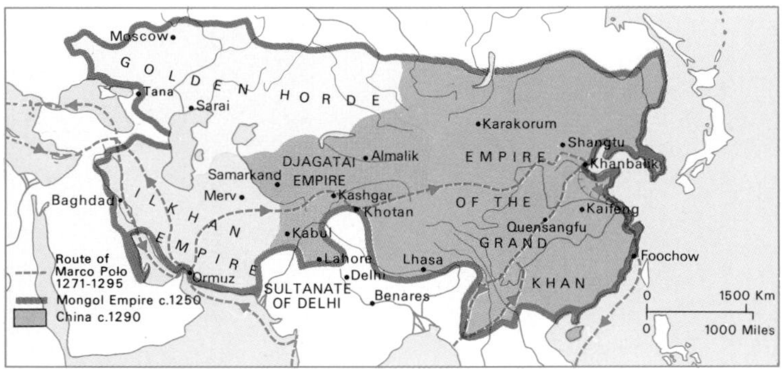

Moscow
GOLDEN HORDE
Tana
Sarai
Karakorum
Shangtu
Khanbalik
DJAGATAI EMPIRE
Almalik
Samarkand
Merv
Kashgar
Khotan
Baghdad
ILKHAN EMPIRE
Kabul
Lahore
Delhi
Lhasa
Ormuz
SULTANATE OF DELHI
Benares
EMPIRE OF THE GRAND KHAN
Kaifeng
Quensangfu
Foochow
Route of Marco Polo 1271-1295
Mongol Empire c.1250
China c.1290
0 1500 Km
0 1000 Miles

The Mongol Empire

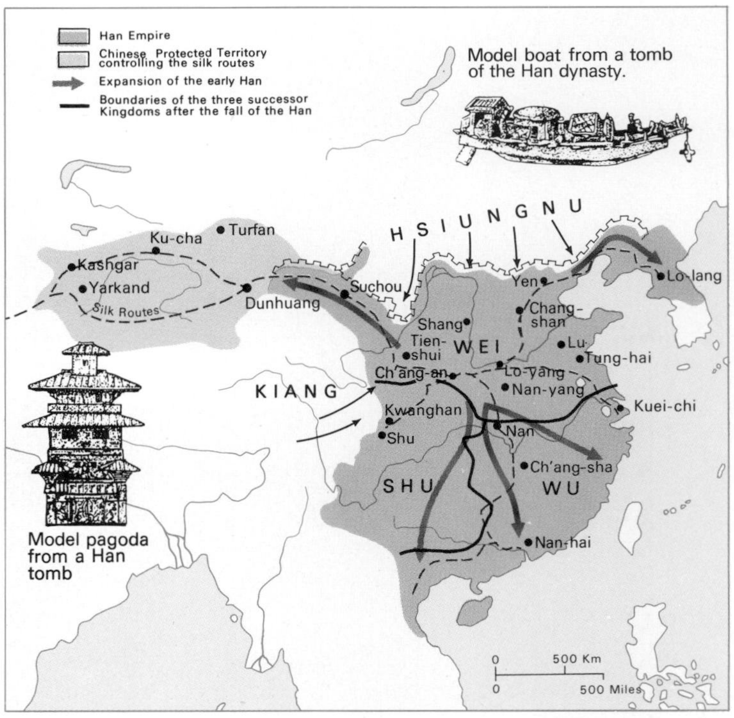

Han Empire
Chinese Protected Territory controlling the silk routes
Expansion of the early Han
Boundaries of the three successor Kingdoms after the fall of the Han
Model boat from a tomb of the Han dynasty.
HSIUNGNU
Ku-cha
Turfan
Kashgar
Yarkand
Silk Routes
Dunhuang
Suchou
Yen
Lo-lang
Chang-shan
Shang
Tien-shui
WEI
Lu
Tung-hai
Ch'ang-an
Lo-yang
Nan-yang
KIANG
Kwanghan
Shu
Kuei-chi
Nan
Ch'ang-sha
SHU
WU
Nan-hai
Model pagoda from a Han tomb
0 500 Km
0 500 Miles

202 BC — AD 265

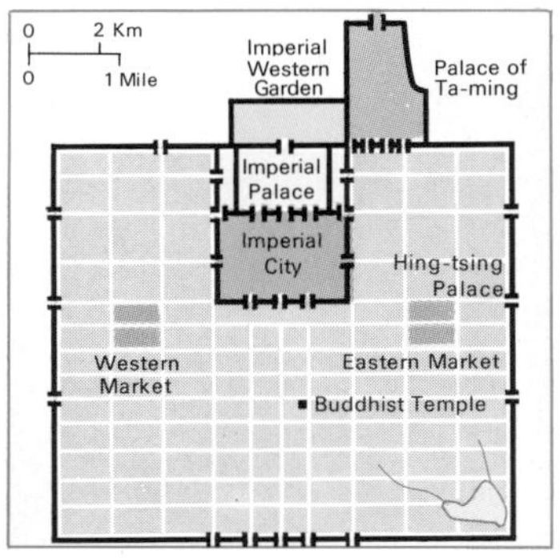

0 2 Km
0 1 Mile
Imperial Western Garden
Palace of Ta-ming
Imperial Palace
Imperial City
Hing-tsing Palace
Western Market
Eastern Market
Buddhist Temple

Ch'ang-an — Tang Capital 618-906

Ceramic figure — Tang

The Great Wall of China, shown below, was started by the Chin emperors to repel invaders from the north and was gradually extended to 1500 miles. It is 20–30 feet high and tapers in width from 25 feet at the base to 15 feet at the top. The other photographs on this page present typical examples, such as the **jade pendant** from the Chou dynasty, of the art for which China has long been famous. Pottery, jade, and bronze were used far more in China than in the West. During the Han period, silk weaving and lacquer work became important. The **ceramic vase** at the right below and the bronze **ritual vessels** and bronze **rhinoceros** of the Shang/Chou era exemplify the artistic skill and advanced culture of these people.

Many of the art objects found were either tomb or altar figures. The **jade princess**, Princess Tow Wan, is shown in the bottom photograph at the left in her burial suit, made of 2,156 pieces of jade fastened together with gold thread. The princess was the daughter-in-law of the Han emperor Ching, who ruled from 157 to 141 B.C. Jade was almost indestructible and therefore assured continual protection. Both art and literature flourished under the Han.

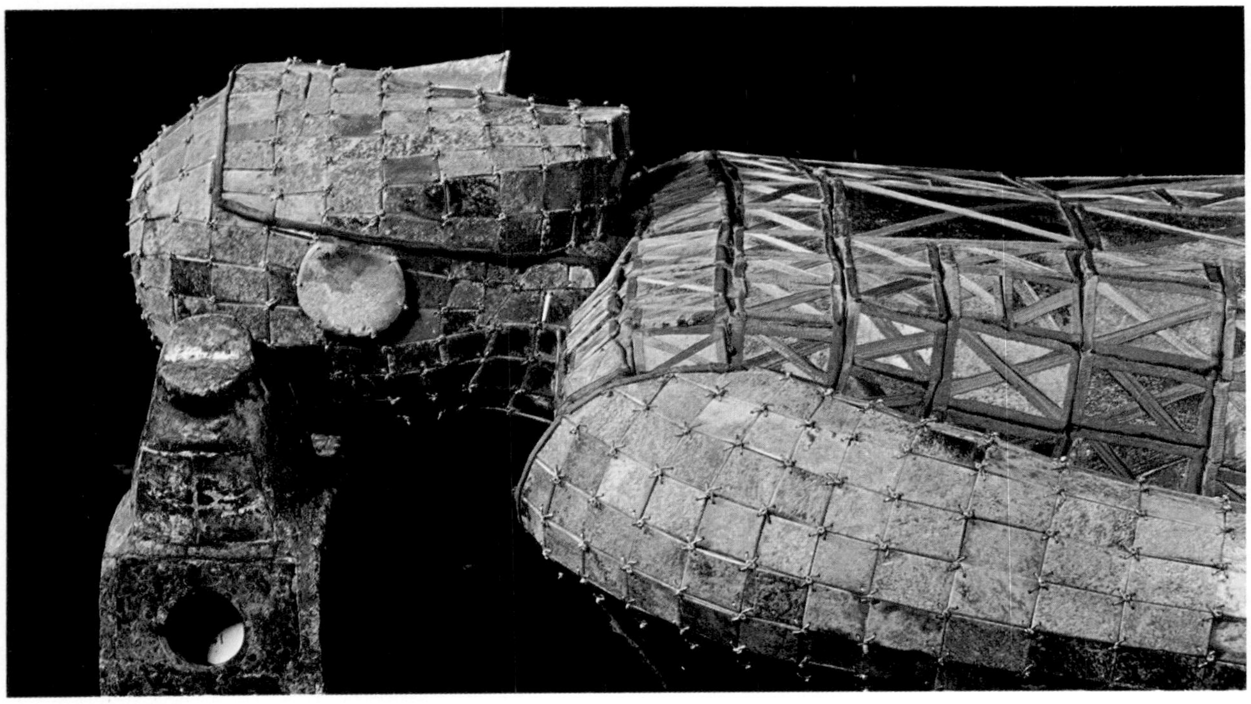
Jade Princess

Jade pendant — Chou

Ceramic vase

The Great Wall of China

Ritual vessel — Shang/Chou

Ritual vessel — Shang/Chou

Rhinoceros — Chou

PRE-COLUMBIAN AMERICA

The Mayan civilization lasted from about A.D. 300 to 900. It used no metal, nor the wheel in any form, yet was advanced in other ways — picture writing, a numbering system based on 20, and a calendar. The first map shows the extent of the **Maya** Empire. After an invasion from Mexico in the 10th century, Mayan civilization declined. It had attained a high level in the arts. Its buildings, such as the **Mayan temple** at Palenque shown below, used neither arches nor domes. The **Mayan painting** shown here is from a book made of bark.

The **Incas** settled in western South America, growing from a small state in the Cuzco valley in 1440 to a vast empire by 1530. This benevolently despotic empire produced fine metalwork, buildings of immense stone blocks, and extensive roads. Ruins of **Machu Picchu**, at the right below, were found in 1911.

The **Aztecs** were a warlike tribe whose origins are unknown. They settled in Mexico in 1345. Their culture reached its peak around 1450. Their state had a rigid class system, and their religion practiced human sacrifice. The **Aztec jade statuette** shown here, the **Aztec calendar stone** at the lower left, and the **Aztec temple** typify the Aztec culture.

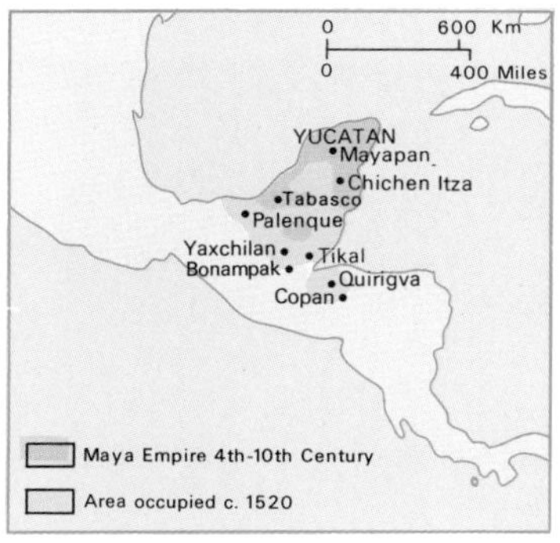
0
600 Km
0
400 Miles
YUCATAN
Mayapan
Chichen Itza
Tabasco
Palenque
Yaxchilan
Bonampak
Tikal
Quirigva
Copan
Maya Empire 4th-10th Century
Area occupied c. 1520

Maya

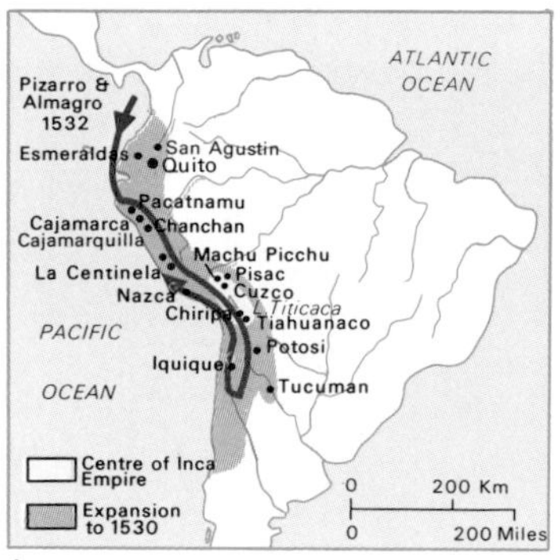
ATLANTIC OCEAN
Pizarro & Almagro 1532
Esmeraldas
San Agustin
Quito
Pacatnamu
Cajamarca
Cajamarquilla
Chanchan
Machu Picchu
La Centinela
Pisac
Nazca
Cuzco
L. Titicaca
Chiripa
Tiahuanaco
PACIFIC OCEAN
Potosi
Iquique
Tucuman
Centre of Inca Empire
Expansion to 1530
0
200 Km
0
200 Miles

Incas

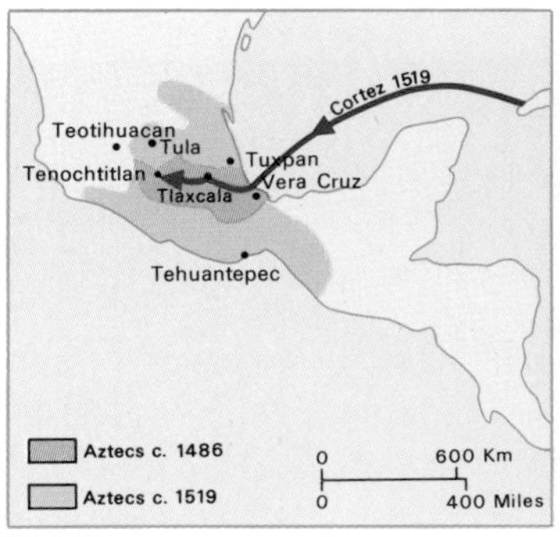
Cortez 1519
Teotihuacan
Tula
Tuxpan
Tenochtitlan
Vera Cruz
Tlaxcala
Tehuantepec
Aztecs c. 1486
Aztecs c. 1519
0
600 Km
0
400 Miles

Aztecs

Aztec jade statuette

Mayan temple

Aztec temple

Aztec calendar stone

Mayan painting

Machu Picchu

THE WORLD AS KNOWN TO THE ANCIENTS

Map makers throughout history have recorded the extent of knowledge of the world of their time. The earliest maps show good awareness of the Mediterranean Sea. The existence of India was known, but not its shape. By Ptolemy's time, knowledge of the East had increased, and China was indicated, though India's shape was still unknown, and the Indian Ocean was shown as an inland sea.

The **Babylon world map, 5th century B.C.**, shown at the base of this page, is engraved on a clay tablet. It shows a round earth with Babylon as the center and the Euphrates River flowing from the mountains to the Persian Gulf, joining an encircling ocean. The map of **Hecateus, c. 500 B.C.** depicts the world as a curving disk with the Mediterranean at the center.

Herodotus, c. 450 B.C. believed that certain places were in a north-south line — the Nile and the mouth of the Danube (Ister), for example — and that certain aspects of the world were symmetrical. **Eratosthenes, c. 200 B.C.**, is famous for his near-accurate measurement of the size of the earth. **Ptolemy, c. A.D. 150**, introduced latitude and longitude and added greatly to the world map, but he was not above invention where details were uncertain!

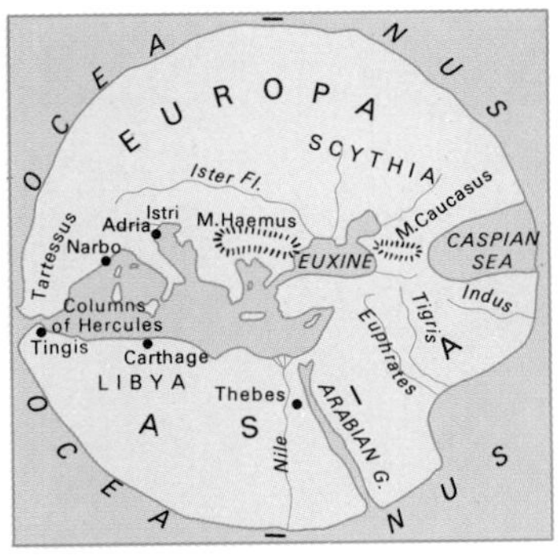
OCEANUS
EUROPA
SCYTHIA
Ister Fl.
M.Caucasus
Adria
Istri
M.Haemus
Narbo
EUXINE
CASPIAN SEA
Tartessus
Indus
Columns of Hercules
Tigris
Tingis
Carthage
Euphrates
LIBYA
Thebes
ASIA
Nile
ARABIAN G.

Hecateus c.500 BC

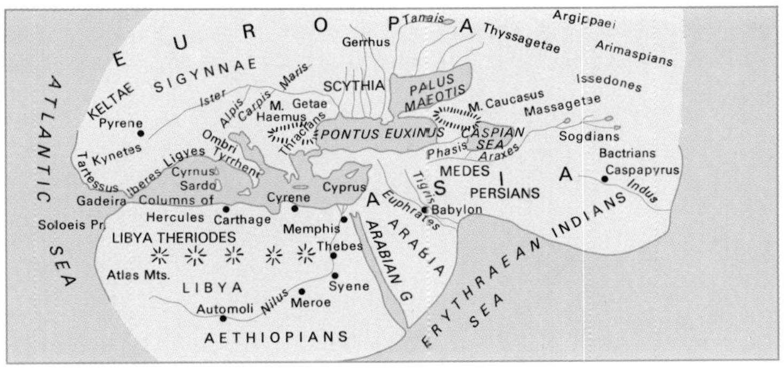
EUROPA
Tanais
Argippaei
Gerrhus
Thyssagetae
Arimaspians
KELTAE
SIGYNNAE
Issedones
ATLANTIC SEA
SCYTHIA
PALUS MAEOTIS
M. Caucasus
Massagetae
Pyrene
M. Getae
Haemus
Kynetes
PONTUS EUXINUS
CASPIAN SEA
Sogdians
Phasis
Araxes
Bactrians
Cyrnus
Sardo
MEDES
Caspapyrus
Cyprus
PERSIANS
Gadeira
Columns of Hercules
Cyrene
Babylon
Soloeis Pr.
Carthage
INDIANS
Memphis
LIBYA THERIODES
Thebes
ARABIAN G.
ARABIA
Atlas Mts.
LIBYA
Syene
Automoli
Meroe
ERYTHRAEAN SEA
AETHIOPIANS

Herodotus c.450 BC

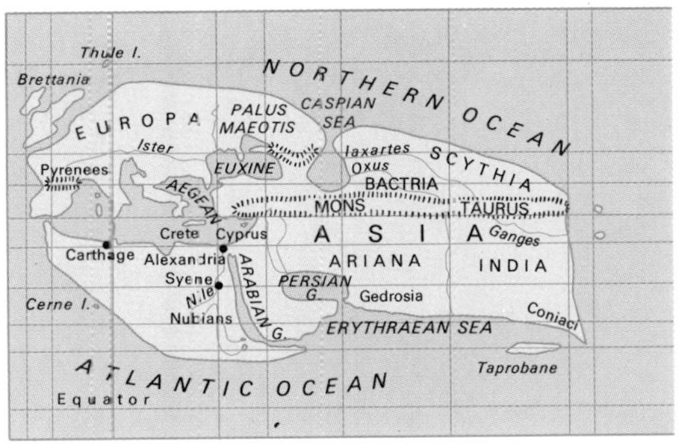
Thule I.
Brettania
NORTHERN OCEAN
PALUS MAEOTIS
CASPIAN SEA
EUROPA
Ister
Pyrenees
EUXINE
Iaxartes
Oxus
SCYTHIA
BACTRIA
AEGEAN
MONS
TAURUS
Crete
Cyprus
ASIA
Ganges
Carthage
Alexandria
ARIANA
INDIA
Syene
Nile
ARABIAN G.
PERSIAN G.
Gedrosia
Cerne I.
Nubians
ERYTHRAEAN SEA
Coniaci
ATLANTIC OCEAN
Taprobane
Equator

Eratosthenes c.200 BC

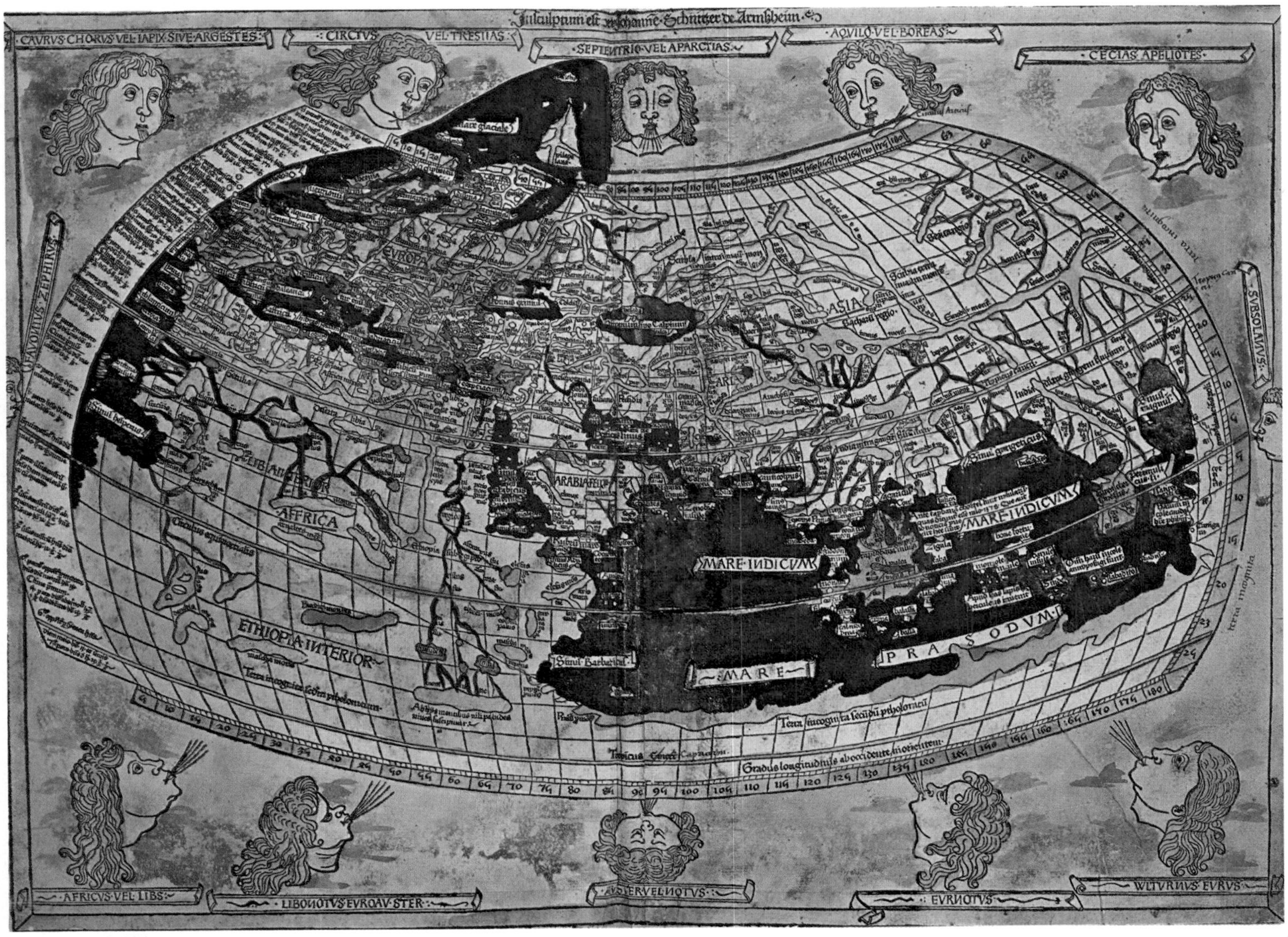
CAVRVS·CHORVS·VEL·IAPIX·SIVE·ARGESTES
CIRCIVS VEL TRESTIAS
SEPTENTRIO·VEL·APARCTIAS
AQVILO·VEL·BOREAS
CECIAS·APELIOTES
AFFRICA
MARE·INDICVM
PRASODVM
MARE
AFRICVS·VEL·LIBS

Ptolemy c.AD 150

Babylon World Map, 5th century BC

EXPANDING KNOWLEDGE OF THE WORLD

The extent of the world known to the West at about the time of the birth of Christ, **c. A.D. 1**, is shown on the map at the left. The Romans had invaded Britain, and their Empire extended along the North African coast eastward to the Persian Gulf. Explorers were not attracted to northern Europe. But in the East, travelers such as Alexander the Great sent back reports of the existence of India and Ceylon, and Egyptian sailors explored part of the Somali and Arabian coasts.

By **A.D. 500**, knowledge of the world — mostly of Asia — had increased. Considerable trade took place with China through India and Persia, and news of the East reached the West through the merchants. After the collapse of the Roman Empire, Angles and Saxons settled in England, and tribes of northern Europe and Scandinavia began to trade with the barbarians who settled around the Mediterranean. By **A.D. 1000**, the Vikings had considerably extended the known world to the west. They first reached the Faeroes, islands off Denmark, then Iceland, Greenland, and America (c. A.D. 968).

Mohammedanism had spread across Asia to India, and Arabs traveled widely in this area and beyond to the East Indies, China, and Madagascar. The Chinese also visited the east coast of Africa at this time. By **A.D. 1500**, the frontiers of the known world had advanced greatly. In the 1400s, the Portuguese had explored the west coast of Africa, trying to establish an eastern route to the Indies. The goal was finally achieved by Vasco da Gama, who reached India in 1498. Meanwhile, in 1492 Christopher Columbus, having chosen to sail westward, had discovered the West Indies.

c. **A.D.** 500

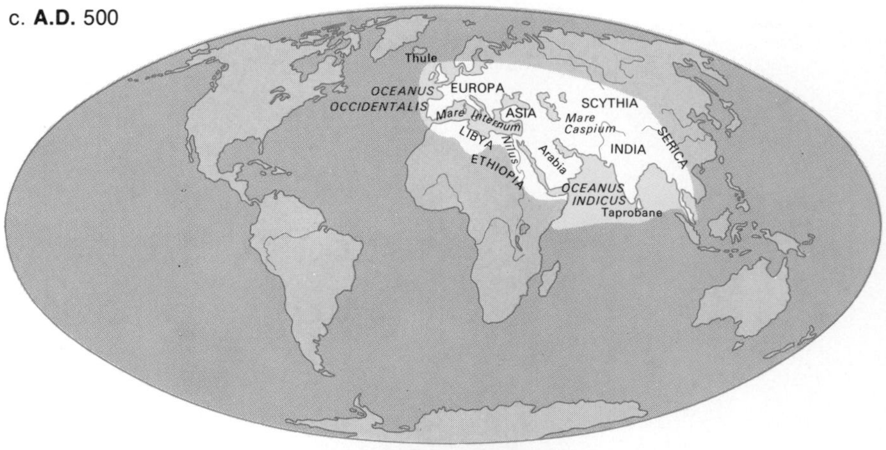
Thule
OCEANUS
OCCIDENTALIS
EUROPA
Mare Internum
ASIA
SCYTHIA
Mare
Caspium
LIBYA
Nilus
ETHIOPIA
Arabia
INDIA
SERICA
OCEANUS
INDICUS
Taprobane

c. **A.D.** 1

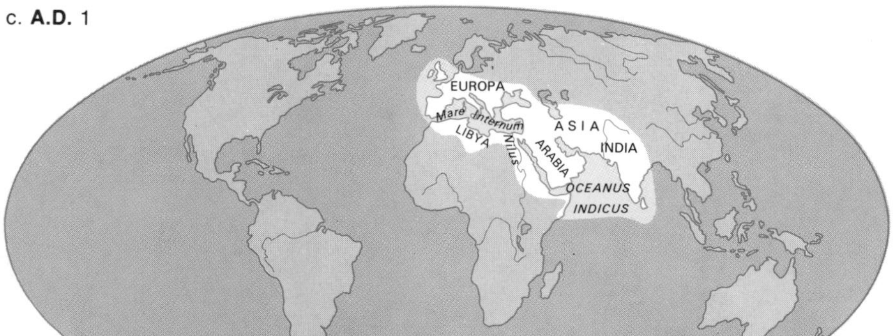
EUROPA
Mare Internum
ASIA
LIBYA
Nilus
ARABIA
INDIA
OCEANUS
INDICUS

c. **A.D.** 1000

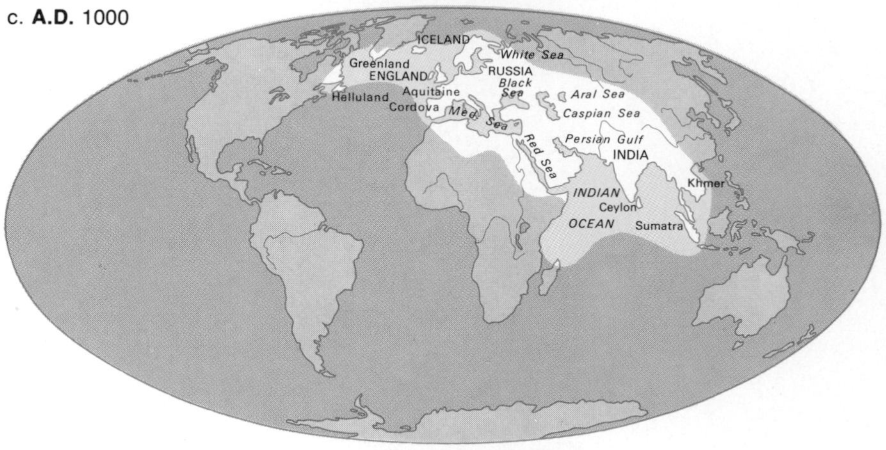
ICELAND
Greenland
ENGLAND
White Sea
RUSSIA
Black Sea
Helluland
Aquitaine
Cordova
Med. Sea
Aral Sea
Caspian Sea
Persian Gulf
Red Sea
INDIA
Khmer
INDIAN
Ceylon
OCEAN
Sumatra

c. **A.D.** 1500

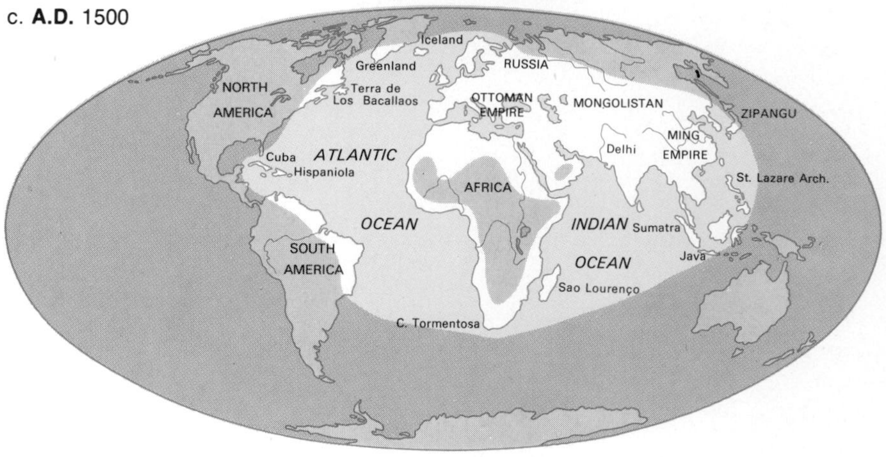
Iceland
Greenland
RUSSIA
NORTH
AMERICA
Terra de
Los Bacallaos
OTTOMAN
EMPIRE
MONGOLISTAN
ZIPANGU
MING
EMPIRE
Delhi
Cuba
ATLANTIC
Hispaniola
AFRICA
St. Lazare Arch.
OCEAN
INDIAN
Sumatra
SOUTH
AMERICA
OCEAN
Java
Sao Lourenço
C. Tormentosa

The century ending at **A.D.1600** was indeed an age of discovery. Corte Real followed Cabot to North America and Cabral discovered Brazil. Magellan found a route around the tip of America, and the Spanish explored much of the same continent. The Portuguese went on from India to the East Indies, and Cartier opened up a northern route into the interior of North America. Arctic exploration in search of northwest and northeast passages also took place. And the Dutch were playing a leading role in exploration by **c. A.D. 1700**.

The Dutch quickly displaced the Portuguese from the Cape of Good Hope and the East Indies, exploring much of the Australian coast and discovering New Zealand. During the 17th century, French fur traders were active in Canada, and La Salle explored the Great Lakes and the Mississippi valley. More detailed exploration was carried out **c. A.D. 1800** in areas known only generally before. Russian soldiers and surveyors continued their penetration eastward, begun in the previous century, while in Canada Mackenzie and others pushed westward. Cook explored the Pacific thoroughly, and Bass and Flinders filled in the details of the Australian coast. A start was made on the internal exploration of Africa.

By **c. A.D. 1900**, world exploration was virtually completed, apart from the polar regions. Africa and Australia were major areas of activity, but the search for a northwest passage was also renewed and coastal exploration of Antarctica begun. Several scientific explorations of South America were made. Arabia and central Asia were examined more thoroughly, and the west was opened up in the United States of America.

c. **A.D.** 1600

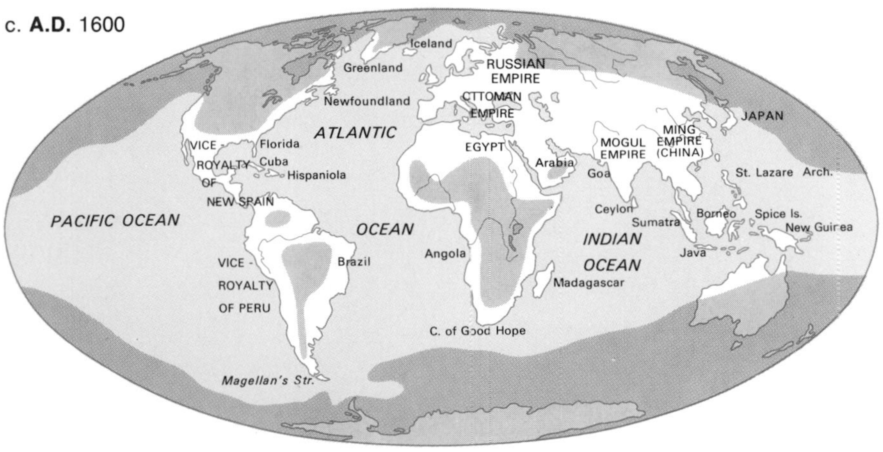

Iceland
Greenland
RUSSIAN EMPIRE
Newfoundland
OTTOMAN EMPIRE
JAPAN
ATLANTIC
VICE-ROYALTY OF NEW SPAIN
Florida
Cuba
Hispaniola
EGYPT
Arabia
MOGUL EMPIRE
MING EMPIRE (CHINA)
Goa
St. Lazare Arch.
PACIFIC OCEAN
OCEAN
Ceylon
Sumatra
Borneo
Spice Is.
New Guinea
INDIAN
OCEAN
VICE-ROYALTY OF PERU
Brazil
Angola
Java
Madagascar
C. of Good Hope
Magellan's Str.

c. **A.D.** 1700

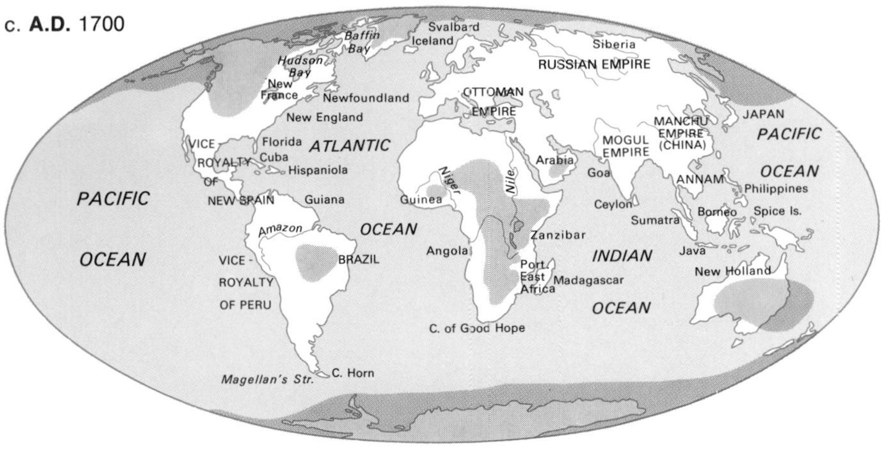

Svalbard
Baffin Bay
Iceland
Hudson Bay
Siberia
RUSSIAN EMPIRE
New France
Newfoundland
New England
OTTOMAN EMPIRE
JAPAN
ATLANTIC
MANCHU EMPIRE (CHINA)
PACIFIC
VICE-ROYALTY OF NEW SPAIN
Florida
Cuba
Hispaniola
MOGUL EMPIRE
Arabia
Goa
OCEAN
PACIFIC
Guiana
Guinea
Niger
Nile
ANNAM
Philippines
Ceylon
Borneo
Spice Is.
Amazon
OCEAN
Sumatra
Zanzibar
OCEAN
VICE-ROYALTY OF PERU
BRAZIL
Angola
INDIAN
Java
Port. East Africa
New Holland
Madagascar
OCEAN
C. of Good Hope
Magellan's Str.
C. Horn

c. **A.D.** 1800

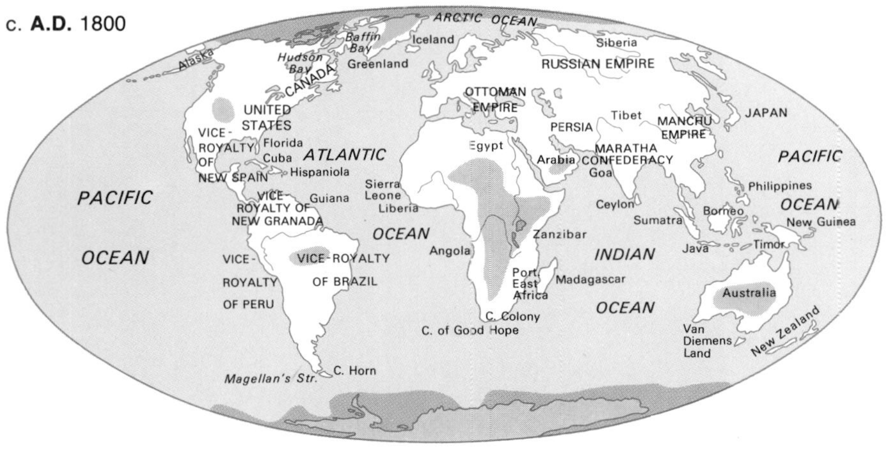

ARCTIC OCEAN
Alaska
Baffin Bay
Iceland
Hudson Bay
CANADA
Greenland
Siberia
RUSSIAN EMPIRE
OTTOMAN EMPIRE
UNITED STATES
Tibet
MANCHU EMPIRE
JAPAN
PERSIA
VICE-ROYALTY OF NEW SPAIN
Florida
Cuba
ATLANTIC
Hispaniola
Egypt
Arabia
MARATHA CONFEDERACY
Goa
PACIFIC
PACIFIC
Sierra Leone
Liberia
VICE-ROYALTY OF NEW GRANADA
Guiana
Philippines
Ceylon
Borneo
OCEAN
Sumatra
New Guinea
OCEAN
OCEAN
Zanzibar
Angola
INDIAN
Java
Timor
VICE-ROYALTY OF PERU
VICE-ROYALTY OF BRAZIL
Port. East Africa
Madagascar
Australia
OCEAN
C. Colony
C. of Good Hope
Van Diemens Land
New Zealand
Magellan's Str.
C. Horn

c. **A.D.** 1900

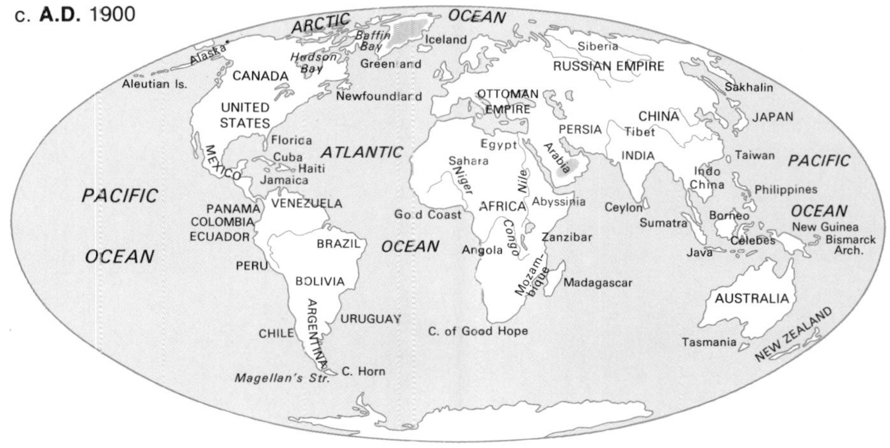

ARCTIC OCEAN
Alaska
Baffin Bay
Iceland
Hudson Bay
Siberia
CANADA
Greenland
RUSSIAN EMPIRE
Aleutian Is.
Newfoundland
Sakhalin
UNITED STATES
OTTOMAN EMPIRE
CHINA
JAPAN
PERSIA
Tibet
Florida
Egypt
MEXICO
Cuba
ATLANTIC
Sahara
Arabia
INDIA
Taiwan
PACIFIC
Haiti
Jamaica
Niger
Nile
Indo China
PACIFIC
Philippines
PANAMA
VENEZUELA
AFRICA
Abyssinia
Ceylon
COLOMBIA
Gold Coast
Sumatra
Borneo
OCEAN
ECUADOR
Congo
Zanzibar
Celebes
New Guinea
Bismarck Arch.
BRAZIL
OCEAN
Angola
Java
OCEAN
PERU
Mozambique
Madagascar
BOLIVIA
AUSTRALIA
ARGENTINA
URUGUAY
CHILE
C. of Good Hope
Tasmania
NEW ZEALAND
Magellan's Str.
C. Horn

EXPANSION FROM THE ANCIENT WORLD

The earliest recorded explorers were Egyptians who, from about 2500 B.C., made journeys **southward from Egypt**, as shown on the small map at the left below, to the fabled land of Punt. The land of Punt was reputedly rich in gold, ivory and incense brought in, perhaps, along **Arab trade routes** such as those shown on the other small map below. The Egyptians' boats were built on the Red Sea coast. As indicated by the photograph of a **model boat from an Egyptian tomb, 1800 B.C.**, these early boats had flat bottoms with projecting bow and stern. The single mast supported one sail, and standing oarsmen provided additional power. The Minoans, whose civilization flourished in Crete from 3000–1400 B.C., also developed sea power early.

Minoan ships were not large, but they traded regularly with Egypt, Cyprus, Sicily, and the lands of the eastern Mediterranean. When the Minoan civilization collapsed, the Phoenicians became the leading maritime power, moving **westward from the Mediterranean** as shown on the map at the left below. Their confined homeland, backed by mountains, forced the Phoenicians to look seaward. The **Phoenician trading ship** depicted in the drawing below at the right was a sturdy structure able to withstand voyages to the far ends of the Mediterranean and beyond. The development of sea power enabled the Phoenicians to establish many coastal colonies. When the Assyrians overran the Phoenician cities in Lebanon around 700 B.C., many of their inhabitants fled to these Mediterranean colonies. One of these, Carthage, grew and established its own empire.

The Greeks succeeded the Phoenicians in the East, and from 800–500 B.C. spread over the whole of the Mediterranean and the Black Sea. Alexander's epic journey through Persia to India in the 4th century B.C. greatly increased world knowledge, for he took surveyors along and recorded the countries **eastward from Greece** through which he passed. (See the map at the right below.) Greek art of the period, shown at the base of this page, reflected these activities: the **head of Alexander** and the painting of **Alexander in Persia destroying idols**.

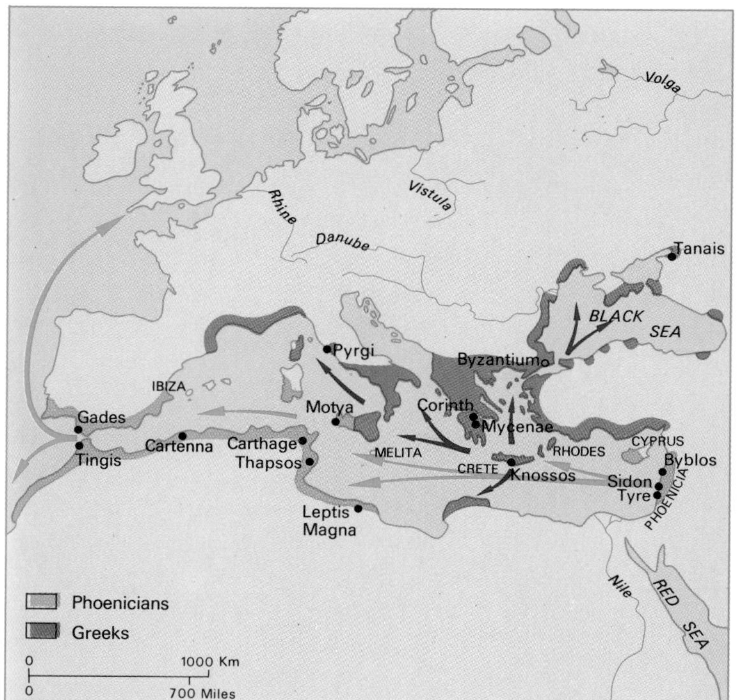
Volga
Vistula
Rhine
Danube
Tanais
BLACK SEA
Byzantium
Pyrgi
IBIZA
Gades
Tingis
Cartenna
Carthage
Thapsos
Motya
Corinth
Mycenae
MELITA
CRETE
Knossos
RHODES
CYPRUS
Byblos
Sidon
Tyre
PHOENICIA
Leptis Magna
Nile
RED SEA
Phoenicians
Greeks
0 1000 Km
0 700 Miles
Westward from the Mediterranean

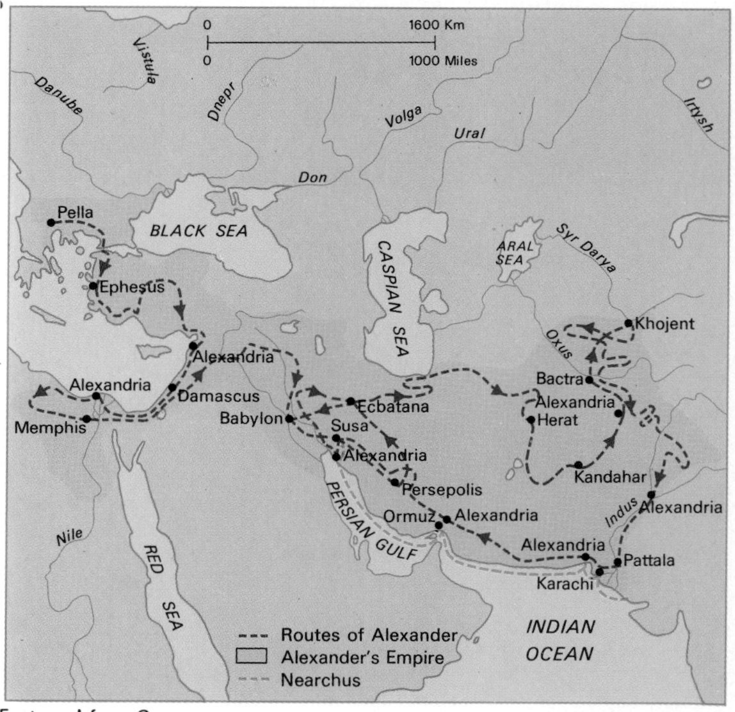
0 1600 Km
0 1000 Miles
Danube
Vistula
Dnepr
Volga
Ural
Irtysh
Don
Pella
BLACK SEA
CASPIAN SEA
ARAL SEA
Syr Darya
Ephesus
Khojent
Oxus
Alexandria
Alexandria
Damascus
Memphis
Babylon
Ecbatana
Susa
Bactra
Alexandria
Herat
Alexandria
Persepolis
Kandahar
Indus
Alexandria
Ormuz
Alexandria
PERSIAN GULF
Alexandria
Pattala
Karachi
Nile
RED SEA
Routes of Alexander
Alexander's Empire
Nearchus
INDIAN OCEAN
Eastward from Greece

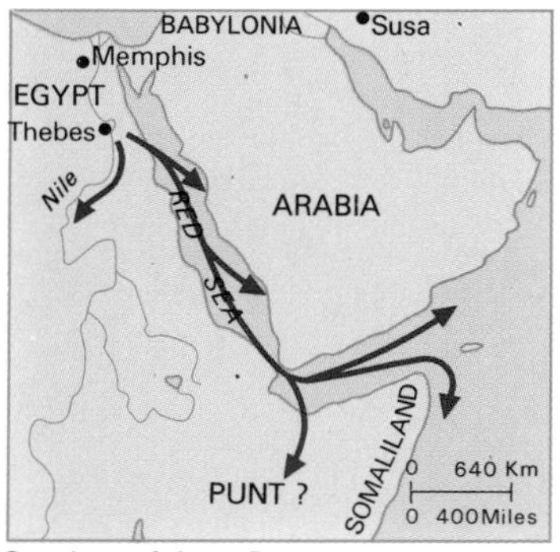
BABYLONIA
Susa
Memphis
EGYPT
Thebes
Nile
RED SEA
ARABIA
SOMALILAND
PUNT ?
0 640 Km
0 400Miles
Southward from Egypt

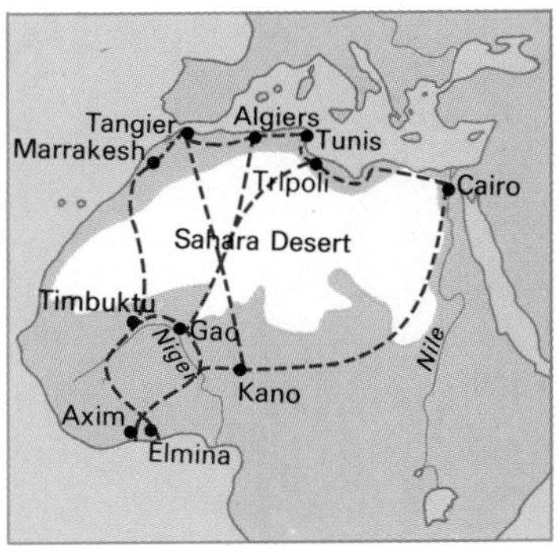
Tangier
Algiers
Marrakesh
Tunis
Tripoli
Cairo
Sahara Desert
Timbuktu
Gao
Niger
Nile
Kano
Axim
Elmina
Arab Trade Routes

Phoenician trading ship

Model boat from an Egyptian tomb, 1800 BC

Head of Alexander

Alexander in Persia destroying idols

In the East under the Han emperors, the Chinese ambassadors traveled widely in search of trade and allies. The best known one was Chang Ch'ien, who in 137 B.C. crossed the Gobi Desert and the Pamirs to reach Peshawar. His travels paved the way for the caravans that carried food, silks, and spices from China to India and thence to Europe. These products were much prized by the Romans, and trade continued until the break-up of the Roman Empire. In the 6th century, some silk-moth eggs were smuggled out of China, and the Chinese monopoly in silk was broken. Buddhism had reached China via **the silk routes**, shown on the map at the left, and from the 4th century on Chinese Buddhist monks made long and eventful journeys to India.

The spread of Mohammedanism and Arab political influence enabled **Arab traders**, depicted at the left below, to journey from the Atlantic to the Pacific and into Africa. The routes of these **Arab travelers** is shown on the map at the right below. The reports they brought back were used by the Arab geographers to write descriptive books and for such maps as **Idrisi's world map** drawn in 1154 with the south at the top, shown at the right below. Il Idrisi thought the world was flat, 22,900 miles around the edge, and surrounded by water. Also depicted at the bottom of this page at the right are **Arab sailors**, who made the journey around the Indian Ocean many times. They contributed to Arab skill in navigation. Arab merchants also led caravans of camels — the ships of the desert — laden with their precious cargoes.

Mohammedanism was the last of the great religions based on the concept of a single god, Mohammed's principle being "There is no God but Allah, and Mohammed is his prophet." The **spread of Mohammedanism** is shown on the lower map at the right. Mohammedans are required to pray five times a day, to fast, to give alms, and to make the pilgrimage to Mecca, the chief shrine of Islam. The religion inspired the Arab conquests of the 7th and 8th centuries, which spread Mohammedanism to Spain and India.

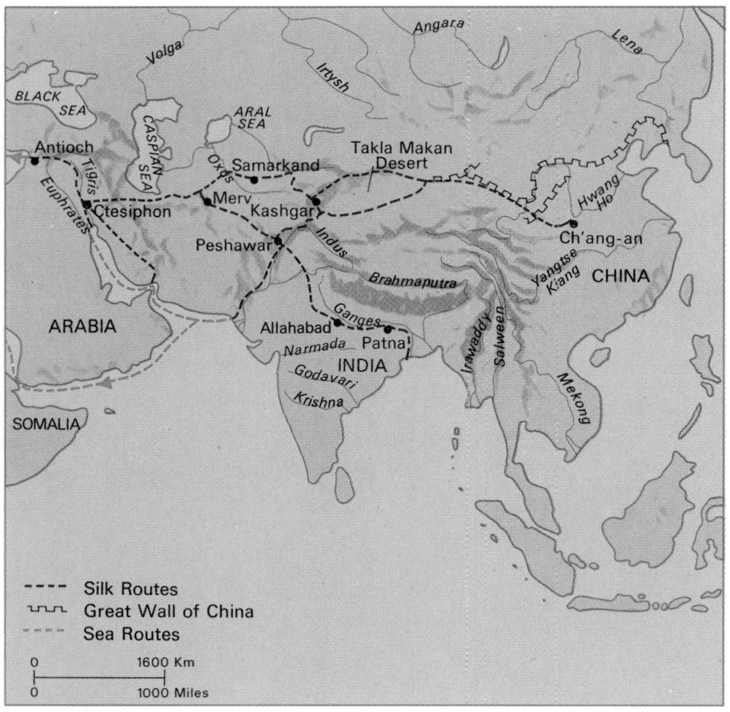
Angara
Volga
Lena
Irtysh
BLACK SEA
ARAL SEA
CASPIAN SEA
Antioch
Samarkand
Takla Makan Desert
Oxus
Tigris
Euphrates
Ctesiphon
Merv
Kashgar
Hwang Ho
Peshawar
Indus
Ch'ang-an
Brahmaputra
Yangtse Kiang
CHINA
ARABIA
Ganges
Allahabad
Patna
Narmada
INDIA
Godavari
Krishna
Irawaddy
Salween
Mekong
SOMALIA
Silk Routes
Great Wall of China
Sea Routes
0 1600 Km
0 1000 Miles
The Silk Routes

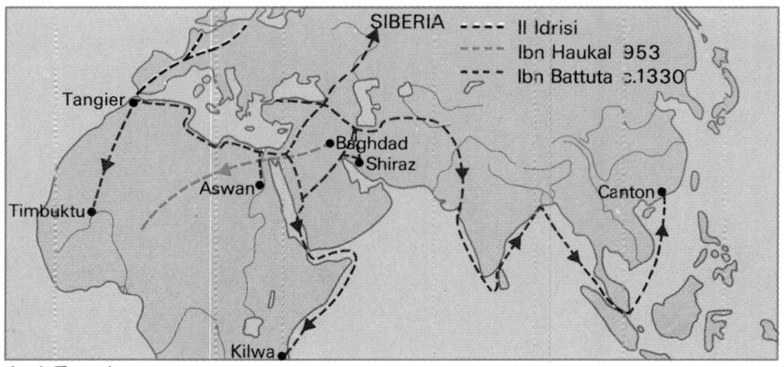
SIBERIA
Il Idrisi
Ibn Haukal 953
Ibn Battuta c.1330
Tangier
Baghdad
Shiraz
Aswan
Timbuktu
Canton
Kilwa
Arab Travelers

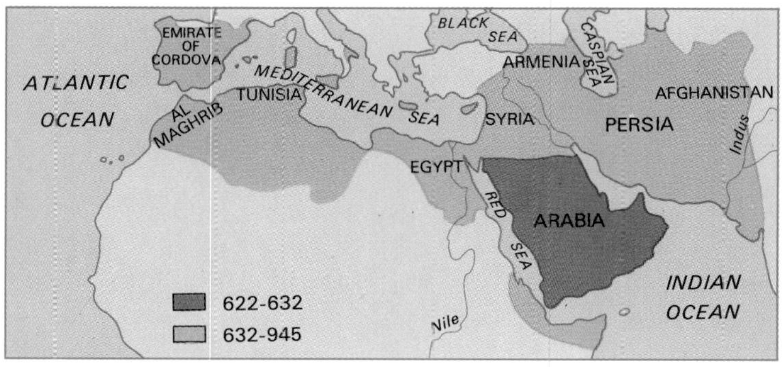
EMIRATE OF CORDOVA
BLACK SEA
CASPIAN SEA
ARMENIA
ATLANTIC OCEAN
MEDITERRANEAN SEA
TUNISIA
AL MAGHRIB
AFGHANISTAN
SYRIA
PERSIA
Indus
EGYPT
RED SEA
ARABIA
Nile
INDIAN OCEAN
622-632
632-945
Spread of Mohammedanism

Arab Traders

Idrisi's World Map 1154

Arab Sailors

THE NORSEMEN

The Vikings, as the Northmen or Norsemen were known, came from Scandinavia and gained a reputation for terrorizing and pillaging when they made lightning raids on established settlements along the coasts of northwest Europe. The lack of land in their mountain home forced them to look elsewhere for food and eventually for new land to colonize. They visited the Orkney, Shetland, and Faeroe islands, and by 860 reached Iceland. The photograph at the left below shows a **ship used for exploration**, and the map at the right depicts the **voyages of the Norsemen**.

As the map indicates, Norsemen in the east made their way up the major rivers from the sea. They carried their boats over the watersheds, through eastern Europe and Russia. They realized the potential of the rivers as trade routes and established trade centers at Novgorod, Smolensk, and Kiev. They traded with Baghdad and central Asia. Other Norsemen went south and reached Constantinople in 860. From there they sailed through the Mediterranean and eventually back home. The **8th century stone carving from Gotland** gives some idea of what the boats of this period looked like.

The photograph at the lower left shows the **remains of a Viking settlement at Brattahild in Greenland**, home of Erik the Red. His Norsemen first arrived in Greenland in 978, founding three settlements on the southwest coast, where there was rich pastureland, for the climate was warmer then and the coast was free of ice. These settlements lasted until about 1500, dying out because of increasing cold, Eskimo attacks, and lack of outside support. Leif Erikson, son of Erik, visited America in 986, naming Helluland, Markland, and Vinland. A Viking **oak stern post c. A.D. 800** is shown at the base of the page.

Ship used for exploration

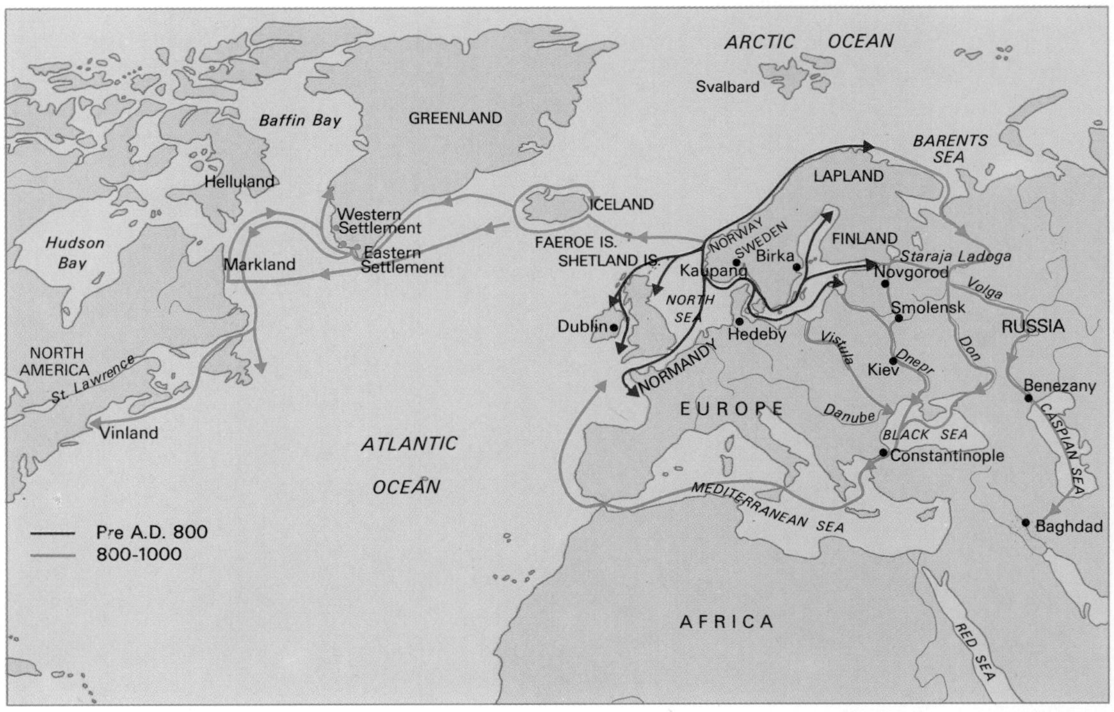

ARCTIC OCEAN
Svalbard
Baffin Bay
GREENLAND
BARENTS SEA
LAPLAND
Helluland
ICELAND
Western Settlement
Eastern Settlement
Hudson Bay
Markland
FAEROE IS.
SHETLAND IS.
NORWAY
SWEDEN
FINLAND
Kaupang
Birka
Staraja Ladoga
Novgorod
Volga
NORTH SEA
Smolensk
Dublin
Hedeby
RUSSIA
NORTH AMERICA
St. Lawrence
NORMANDY
Vistula
Dnepr
Kiev
Don
Benezany
EUROPE
Danube
CASPIAN SEA
Vinland
ATLANTIC OCEAN
BLACK SEA
Constantinople
MEDITERRANEAN SEA
Pre A.D. 800
800-1000
Baghdad
AFRICA
RED SEA

Voyages of the Norsemen

Remains of Viking settlement at Brattahlid in Greenland, home of Erik the Red

8th century stone carving from Gotland

Oak stern post c. AD 800

TRAVELERS IN ASIA

The spread of Mohammedanism encouraged Arab travelers but limited western travelers, for Islam and Christianity were bitterly opposed. In the mid-13th century, Arab domination was broken by the Mongols, who first terrorized Christendom and then turned against the Arabs. With the Moslem hold broken, the way was laid open for a century of trade and exploration. The large map shows the routes of **travelers in Asia**.

The first westerners to meet the Great Khan were Carpini and Rubruquis, Franciscan friars. Two Venetian merchants, the **Polo brothers** (center, left), reached Khanbalik in 1264. They received a golden seal from **Kublai Khan** (below, right), staying in China 15 years. Later, they went back to China, taking young **Marco Polo** with them. His powers of observation impressed Kublai Khan, who had Marco travel all over the empire in his service.

The small map, center, shows the extent of the Mongol **empire of Genghis Khan** and Kublai Khan. After the Mongols lost power, a Chinese admiral, Cheng Ho, led seven great coastal voyages between 1405 and 1431. These **Chinese voyages** are shown on the small map, center, right. At the center below is a 1375 map detail showing **part of China**; and, to its left, a **Chinese junk under sail** is represented.

Marco Polo in Mongolian style dress

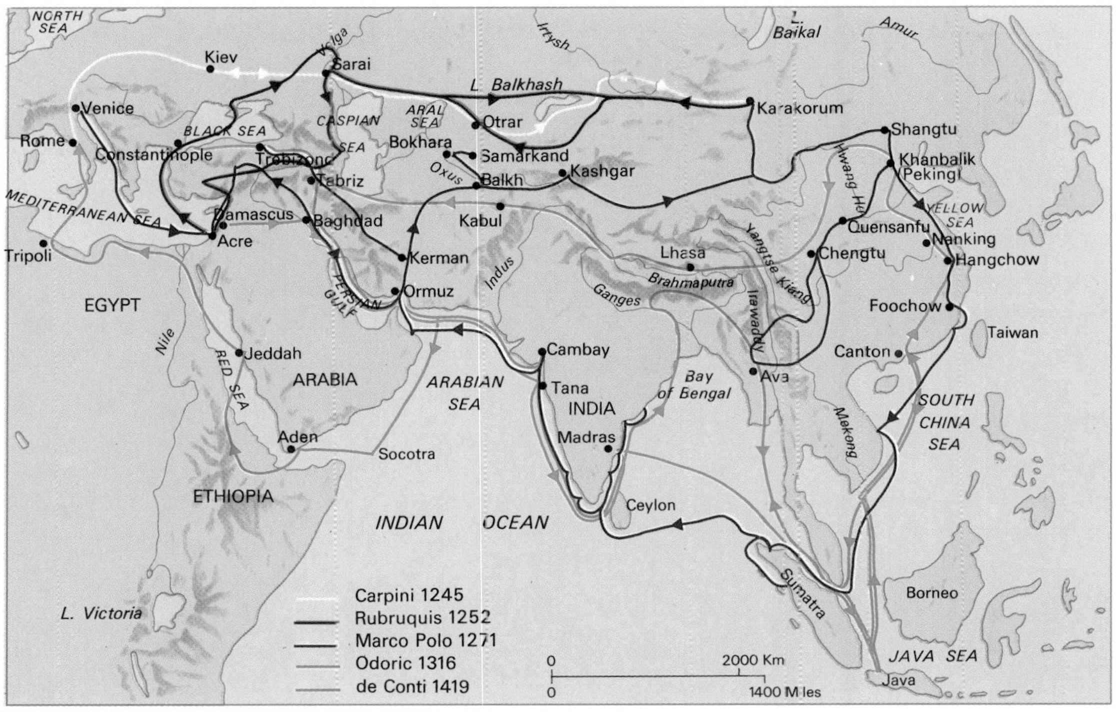

NORTH SEA
Kiev
Volga
Sarai
Irtysh
Baikal
Amur
L. Balkhash
Karakorum
Venice
Rome
BLACK SEA
CASPIAN SEA
ARAL SEA
Otrar
Bokhara
Samarkand
Constantinople
Trebizond
Tabriz
Oxus
Balkh
Kashgar
Shangtu
Khanbalik (Peking)
Hwang Ho
MEDITERRANEAN SEA
Damascus
Acre
Baghdad
Kabul
YELLOW SEA
Quensanfu
Nanking
Hangchow
Tripoli
Kerman
Lhasa
Chengtu
Brahmaputra
Yangtse Kiang
Indus
Ganges
EGYPT
Ormuz
Irrawaddy
Foochow
Nile
Taiwan
Jeddah
RED SEA
Cambay
Canton
ARABIA
ARABIAN SEA
Bay of Bengal
Ava
Tana
INDIA
SOUTH CHINA SEA
Mekong
Aden
Madras
Socotra
ETHIOPIA
Ceylon
INDIAN OCEAN
Sumatra
Borneo
L. Victoria
Carpini 1245
Rubruquis 1252
Marco Polo 1271
Odoric 1316
de Conti 1419
0 2000 Km
0 1400 Miles
JAVA SEA
Java

Travelers in Asia

Polo brothers traveling by camel caravan

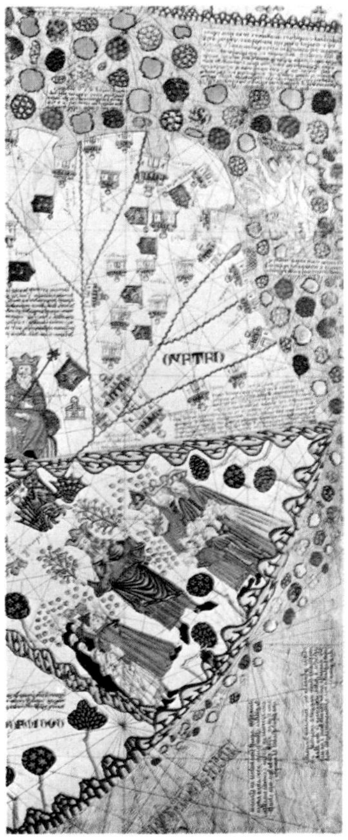

Part of China from the Catalan Atlas 1375

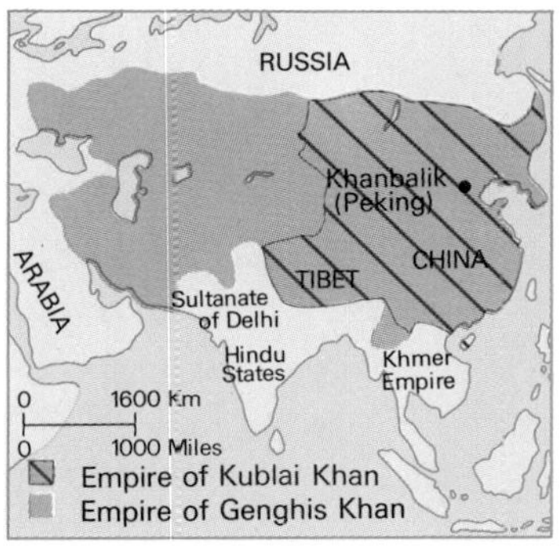

RUSSIA
Khanbalik (Peking)
CHINA
TIBET
ARABIA
Sultanate of Delhi
Hindu States
Khmer Empire
0 1600 Km
0 1000 Miles
Empire of Kublai Khan
Empire of Genghis Khan

Empire of Genghis Khan

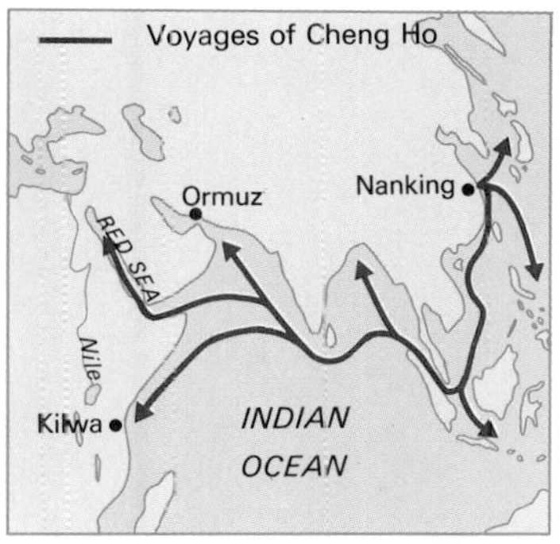

Voyages of Cheng Ho
Ormuz
Nanking
RED SEA
Nile
Kilwa
INDIAN OCEAN

Chinese Voyages

Chinese junk under sail

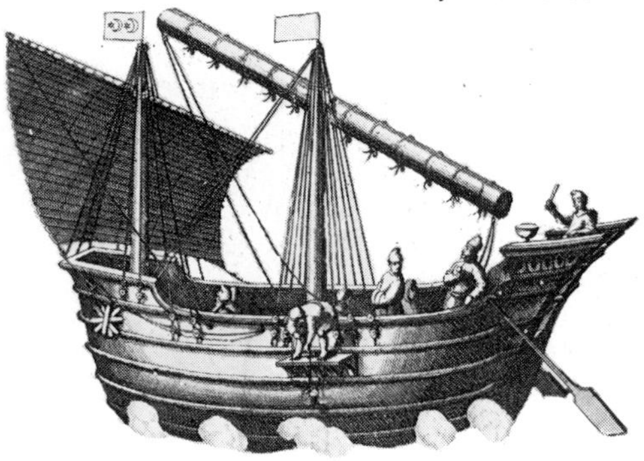

Kublai Khan handing a golden seal to the Polo brothers

THE GREAT AGE OF DISCOVERY I

The closing of the land routes to the East gave impetus to discovering a sea route. Much of Europe was occupied with internal affairs, but Portugal, poised on the edge of the continent, had a moving force for exploration in Prince Henry, the king's younger son. Henry founded a school of navigation and pilotage. Little is known about it because strict secrecy was practiced. But Portuguese sailors probably carried a compass and probably used an astrolabe to measure sun and star altitudes.

Henry also promoted a Portuguese school of cartography. He brought Catalan cartographers from Majorca, and charts were drawn that included information gained from exploration of the African coast. By early 16th century, a number of trading settlements were established along the coasts of India and Ceylon. (See small maps below.) **The Portuguese map c. 1558** shown below was drawn by Bastian Lopez. It is decorated with flags and shows a mountain range, a castle, and Portuguese horsemen chasing Moors.

Prince Henry died in 1460, and by then the Portuguese had explored as far as Sierra Leone. (See small maps below.) In 1488, Bartholomew Diaz rounded the Cape of Good Hope, determined to find a route to the East. Vasco da Gama set out in July 1497 with four ships and about 170 men. He rounded the Cape, called at several east-coast African ports, then crossed to India with a pilot. They arrived at Calicut in May 1498. This route and the relationship of **the Cape and India** are shown on the map below at the right.

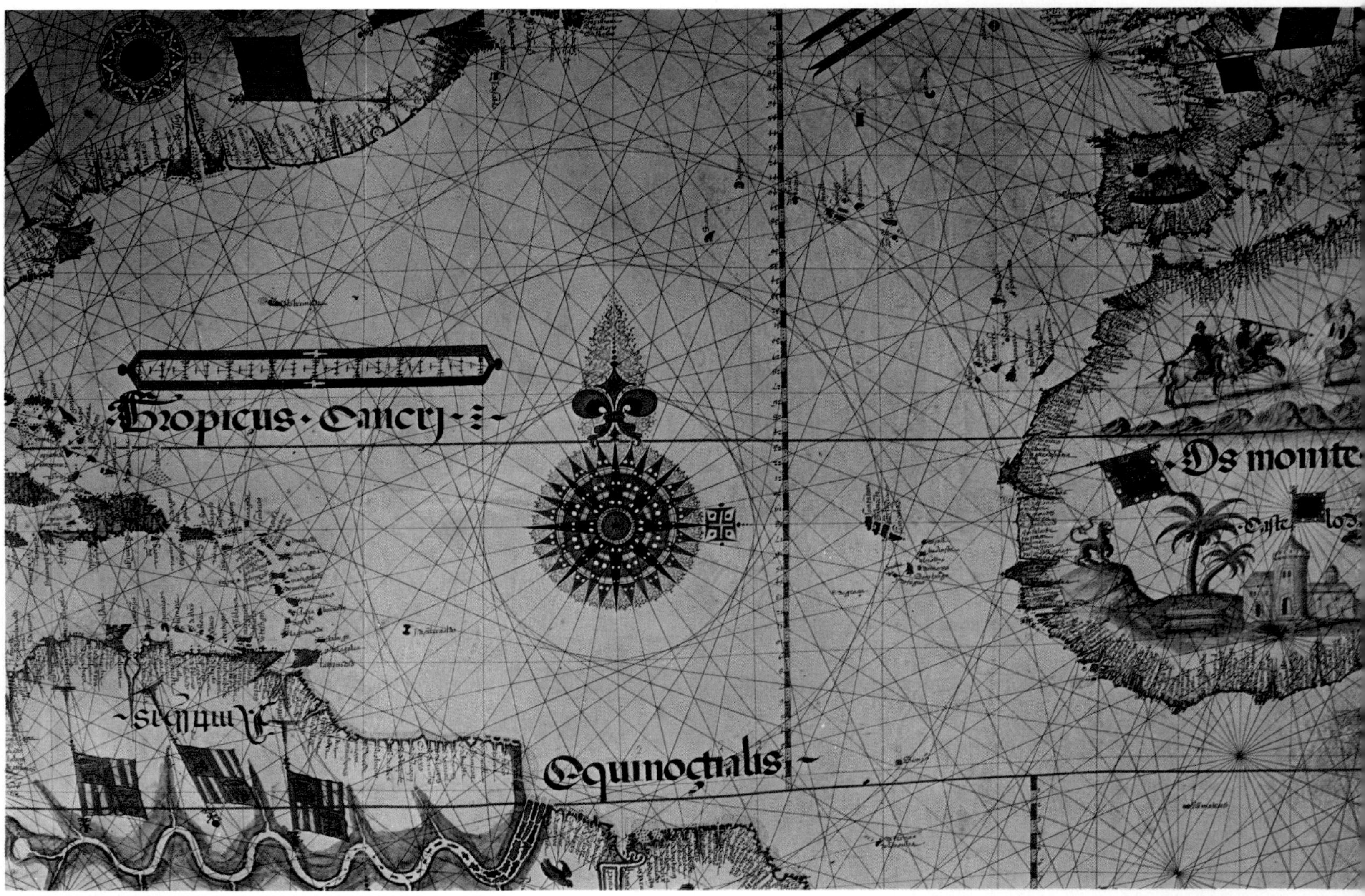

Portuguese map c.1558

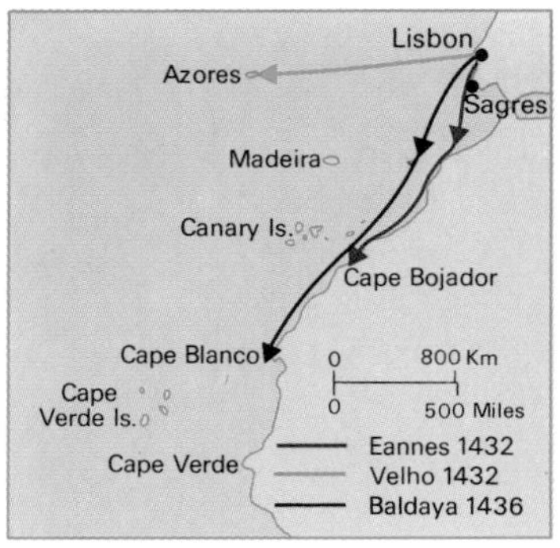
Lisbon
Azores
Sagres
Madeira
Canary Is.
Cape Bojador
Cape Blanco
Cape Verde Is.
Cape Verde
0 800 Km
0 500 Miles
Eannes 1432
Velho 1432
Baldaya 1436

Portugal to Cape Blanco

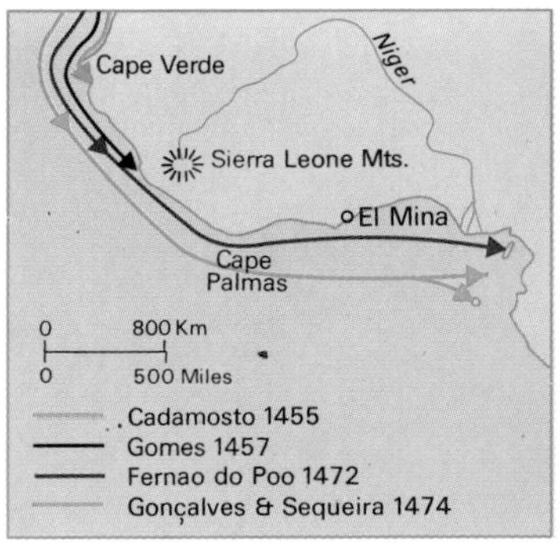
Cape Verde
Niger
Sierra Leone Mts.
El Mina
Cape Palmas
0 800 Km
0 500 Miles
Cadamosto 1455
Gomes 1457
Fernao do Poo 1472
Gonçalves & Sequeira 1474

Cape Verde to Fernando Poo

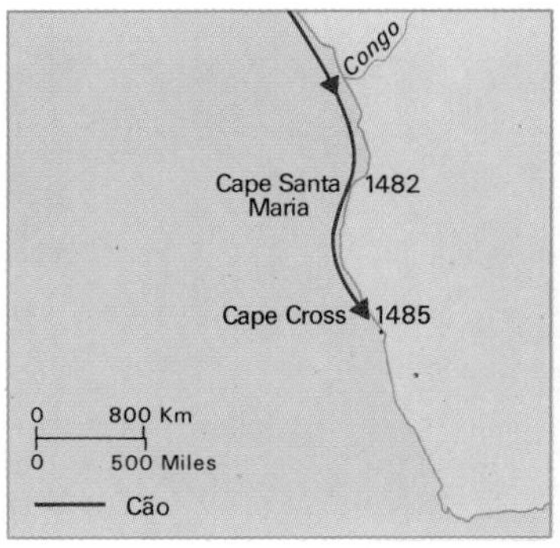
Congo
Cape Santa Maria
1482
Cape Cross
1485
0 800 Km
0 500 Miles
Cão

South to Cape Cross

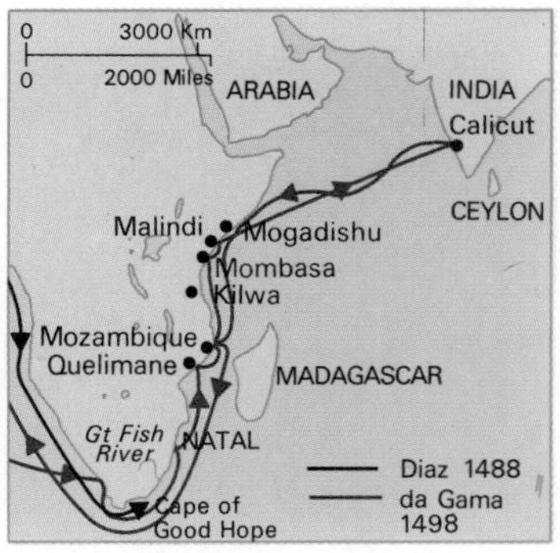
0 3000 Km
0 2000 Miles
ARABIA
INDIA
Calicut
CEYLON
Malindi
Mogadishu
Mombasa
Kilwa
Mozambique
Quelimane
MADAGASCAR
Gt Fish River
NATAL
Cape of Good Hope
Diaz 1488
da Gama 1498

The Cape and India

The Portuguese designed special ships for their journeys of exploration, using knowledge acquired over centuries of building fishing boats. The early journeys used the caravel, a broad-beamed ship that could carry ample supplies of water and provisions. It was lateen-rigged with triangular sails on tilted masts. It was rather slow but good for inshore work. Later journeys used the carrack. **Portuguese carracks**, as shown below, were square-rigged and more useful in the strong winds of the open ocean.

The map at the left below shows the **routes to the East** taken by the Portuguese who established the way to India. It was no easy task, as is indicated by the time taken, though delay occurred also because the captains scuttled or captured any Moslem ships they met. They also landed to seize slaves. After da Gama had reached India, many Portuguese followed; of these Pedro Cabral, by accident or design, touched upon Brazil, thus gaining Portugal a foothold in South America.

Portuguese merchants in India, depicted below at the right, were cruel taskmasters but did not remain aloof from wealthy Indian social circles. They eventually lost most of their Indian holdings to the Dutch in the 17th century. The arts and technology of the period centered around the major preoccupation of the nation; namely, exploration. Shown below are portraits of **Henry the Navigator** and **Vasco da Gama**, along with a **mariner's compass** and a print showing **a ship on the drawing board**.

Portuguese Carracks

Henry the Navigator

Mariner's compass, 16th century

Portuguese merchant in India

Vasco da Gama

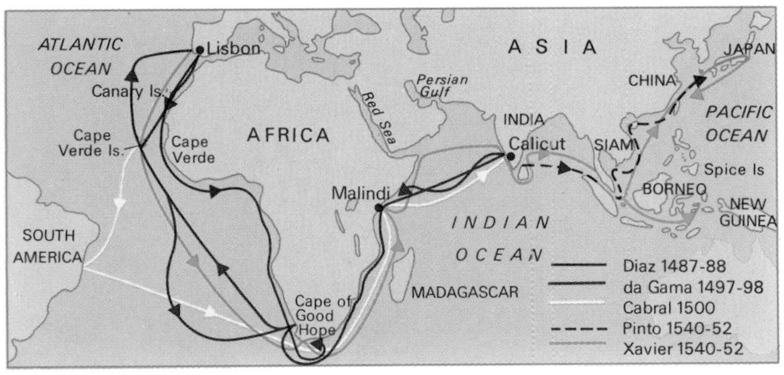
ATLANTIC OCEAN
Lisbon
ASIA
JAPAN
Canary Is.
Persian Gulf
Red Sea
CHINA
PACIFIC OCEAN
Cape Verde Is.
Cape Verde
AFRICA
INDIA
Calicut
SIAM
Spice Is
Malindi
BORNEO
NEW GUINEA
SOUTH AMERICA
INDIAN OCEAN
MADAGASCAR
Cape of Good Hope
Diaz 1487-88
da Gama 1497-98
Cabral 1500
Pinto 1540-52
Xavier 1540-52

Routes to the East

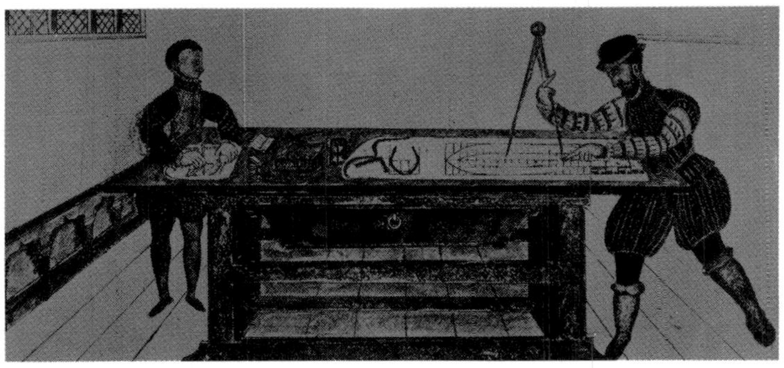

A ship on the drawing-board

THE GREAT AGE OF DISCOVERY II

Christopher Columbus was convinced that he could reach Asia by sailing westward. He was misled by maps that showed the Atlantic scattered with islands and by the writings of Marco Polo, which led him to think that Asia was much larger than it turned out to be. He tried to win support from Genoa, England, and Portugal before finally persuading Ferdinand and Isabella of Spain to finance his voyage. He sailed in August 1492 and, aided by the **prevailing winds in the Atlantic**, reached San Salvador in October. He called the natives Indians, so sure was he that he was in Asia. He sailed on to his Japan (Cuba) and then to Hispaniola, returning to Spain in March 1493.

In all, Columbus made four voyages, but he died a disillusioned man in 1506. The **voyages of Columbus** are shown on the map beneath his portrait, below. The top map at the right compares Columbus' first voyage to those of other **explorers of Central America**, the earliest of which was Amerigo Vespucci, a Florentine merchant, in 1499. He explored part of the northeast coast of South America. Balboa sailed to the New World as a colonist but led an expedition to Panama, where he discovered the Pacific.

Hernando Cortes, depicted below, center, beside a photograph of **Montezuma's headdress**, was one of the great Spanish **conquistadores**. Sent to explore Yucatan in 1519, he first founded a colony with himself as governor. He was received in friendship, but Spanish greed led to fighting. Smallpox overwhelmed the Aztecs, and Cortes took their capital in 1521. Later Spanish expeditions to North America are shown on the map at the lower right. De Soto, after conquering Peru, explored Florida. Coronado searched for the fabled "Seven Cities of Cibola," and De Vaca crossed Mexico to the Pacific Ocean. At the bottom left, is **part of a world map of 1496**.

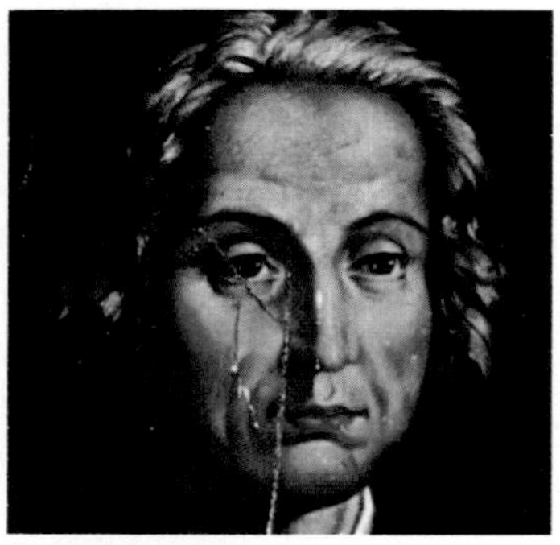
Christopher Columbus

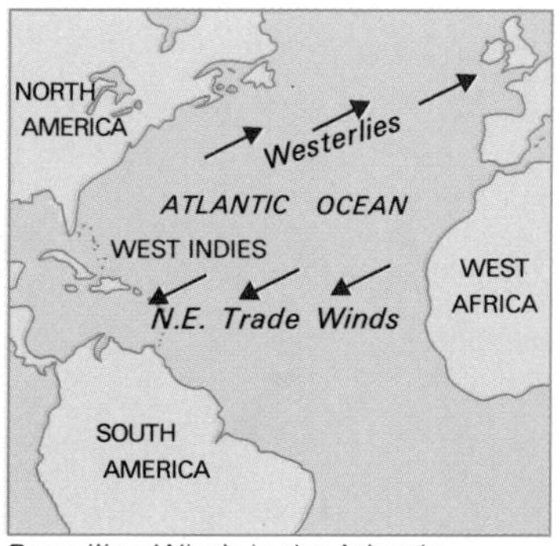

NORTH AMERICA
Westerlies
ATLANTIC OCEAN
WEST INDIES
WEST AFRICA
N.E. Trade Winds
SOUTH AMERICA

Prevailing Winds in the Atlantic

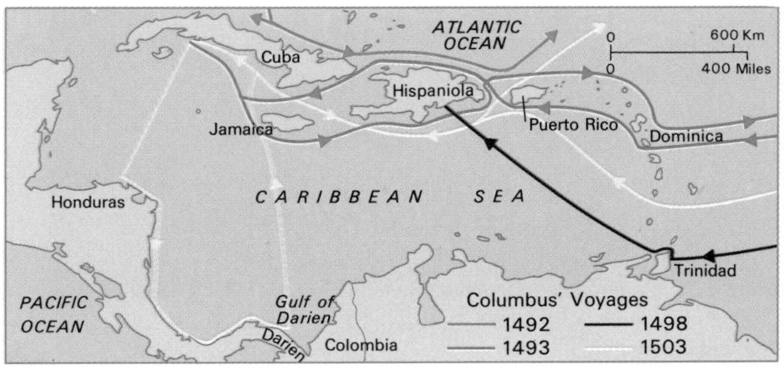

ATLANTIC OCEAN
0 600 Km
0 400 Miles
Cuba
Hispaniola
Jamaica
Puerto Rico
Dominica
Honduras
CARIBBEAN SEA
Trinidad
PACIFIC OCEAN
Gulf of Darien
Darien
Colombia
Columbus' Voyages
1492
1493
1498
1503

Voyages of Columbus

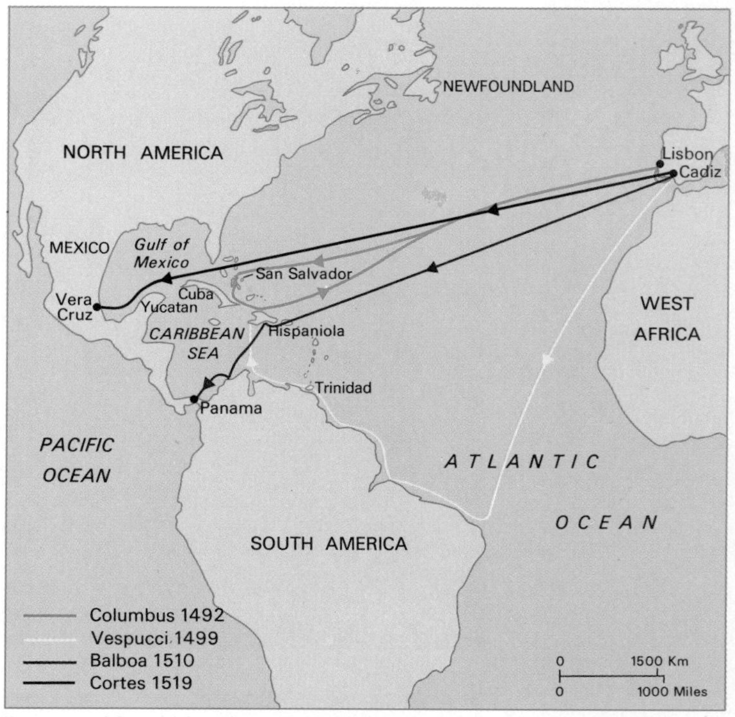

NEWFOUNDLAND
NORTH AMERICA
Lisbon
Cadiz
MEXICO
Gulf of Mexico
San Salvador
Vera Cruz
Cuba
Yucatan
CARIBBEAN SEA
Hispaniola
WEST AFRICA
Trinidad
Panama
PACIFIC OCEAN
ATLANTIC OCEAN
SOUTH AMERICA
Columbus 1492
Vespucci 1499
Balboa 1510
Cortes 1519
0 1500 Km
0 1000 Miles

Explorers of Central America

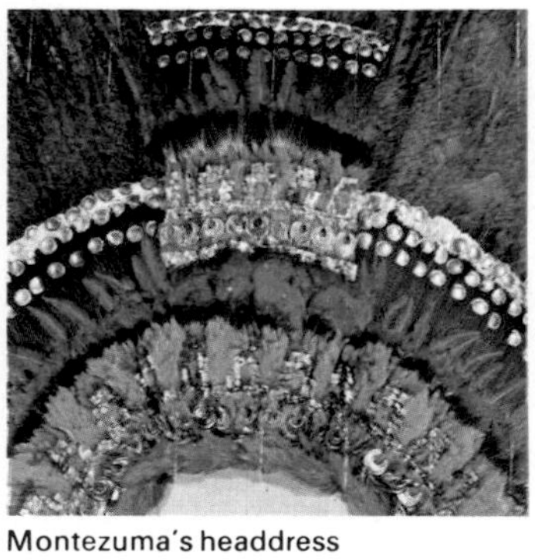
Montezuma's headdress

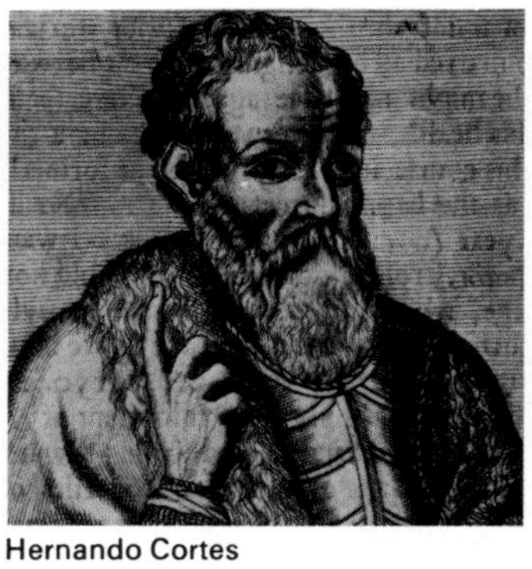
Hernando Cortes

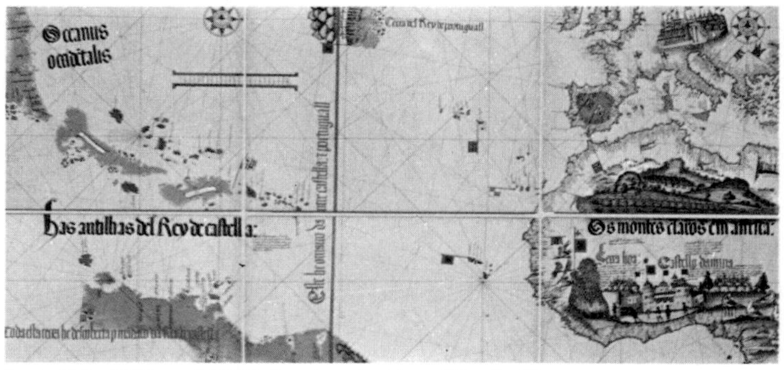
Part of World Map of 1496 showing the Line of Tordesillas

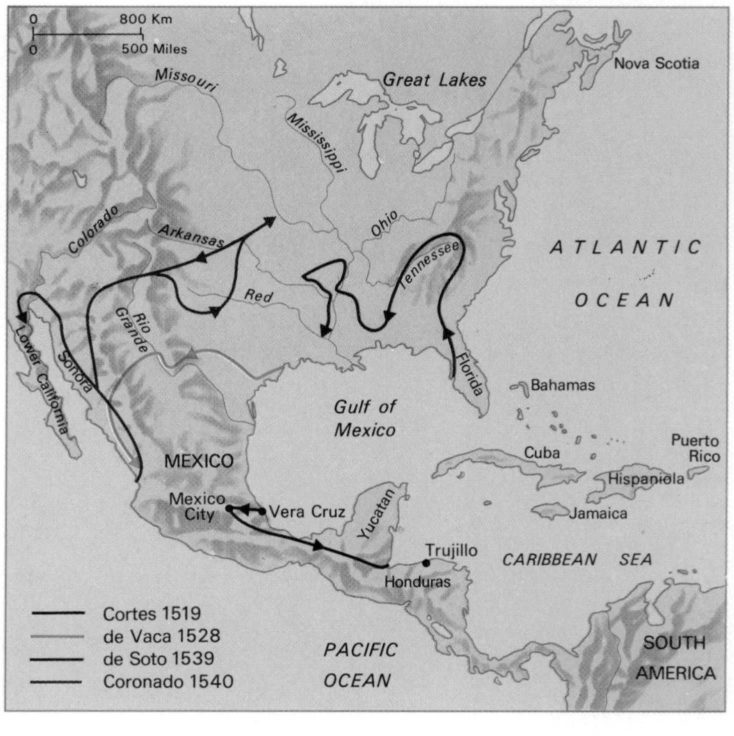

0 800 Km
0 500 Miles
Missouri
Great Lakes
Nova Scotia
Mississippi
Colorado
Arkansas
Ohio
Tennessee
ATLANTIC OCEAN
Red
Rio Grande
Lower California
Sonora
Florida
Bahamas
Gulf of Mexico
MEXICO
Cuba
Puerto Rico
Hispaniola
Jamaica
Mexico City
Vera Cruz
Yucatan
Trujillo
Honduras
CARIBBEAN SEA
Cortes 1519
de Vaca 1528
de Soto 1539
Coronado 1540
PACIFIC OCEAN
SOUTH AMERICA

Ferdinand Magellan, a minor Portuguese nobleman, was convinced that the Indies could be reached via the south of America. Portugal refused to finance him, so he offered his services to Spain. He left with five ships, but his Spanish captains mutinied, and he lost one ship. Then, halfway through the Magellan Strait, the supply ship returned home. The rest crossed the Pacific, but many died from hunger. **Magellan's voyage** is shown on the map at the left below. In the Philippines, Magellan was killed in a skirmish with natives. Del Cano completed the voyage, returning one ship to Spain around the Cape of Good Hope.

Francisco Pizarro made two expeditions south with another Spaniard, de Almagro, and discovered and explored the Inca Empire. (See the map of **exploration in the Andes** at the lower left.) Pizarro returned there in 1531 to find the Empire in a state of civil war. Taking advantage of this, the Spanish took control and killed the Inca. Later, they explored farther south and also east of the Andes. At first they followed the eternal quest for gold, but they soon realized that to retain their conquests they had to settle the area. Meanwhile, there was much activity going on along the northern coast of South America.

As the map at the lower right indicates, many Spanish explorers were interested in **the Amazon and the north** part of South America. Orellana joined Gonzales Pizarro on an expedition to explore east of the Andes. From Quito, they crossed the mountains, many of their men dying from exposure. They reached the Napo River, built a boat, and Orellana sailed in search of food. He reached a larger river and decided to continue down it, abandoning the rest of the party. He was thus the first explorer to navigate the length of the Amazon. The drawing at the center, right is **the Santa Maria**, the largest of Columbus' ships.

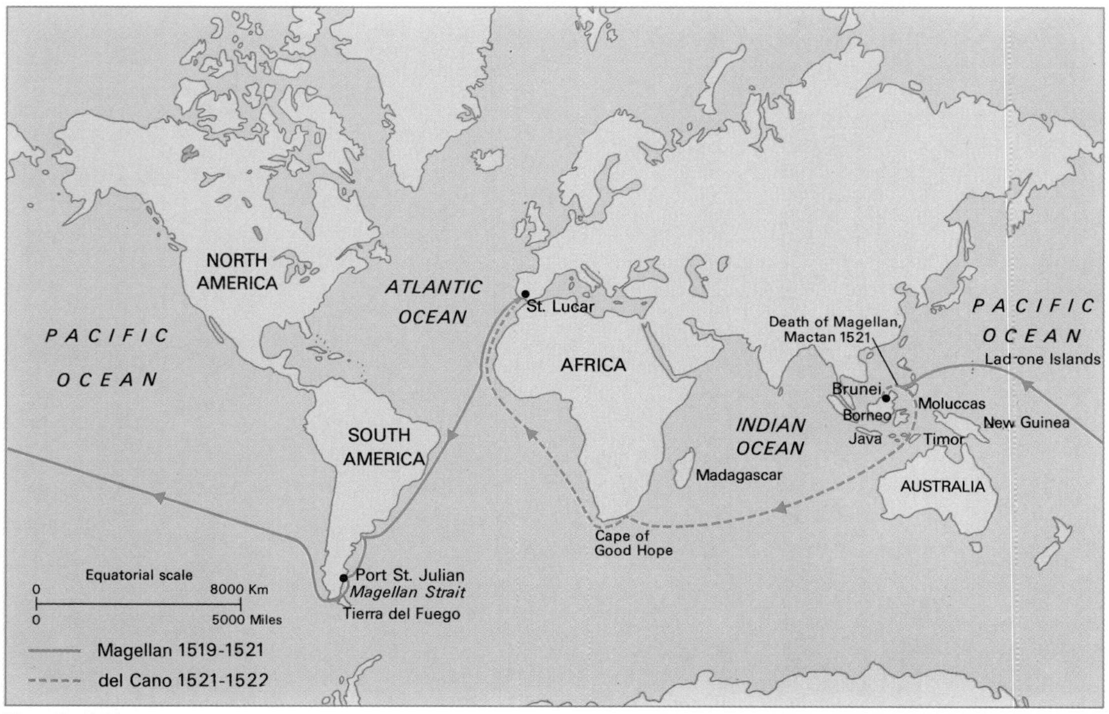

NORTH AMERICA
ATLANTIC OCEAN
PACIFIC OCEAN
St. Lucar
AFRICA
Death of Magellan, Mactan 1521
PACIFIC OCEAN
Ladrone Islands
Brunei
Borneo
Moluccas
New Guinea
Java
Timor
INDIAN OCEAN
Madagascar
SOUTH AMERICA
AUSTRALIA
Cape of Good Hope
Equatorial scale
0
8000 Km
0
5000 Miles
Port St. Julian
Magellan Strait
Tierra del Fuego
Magellan 1519-1521
del Cano 1521-1522

Magellan's Voyage

Ferdinand Magellan

The Santa Maria

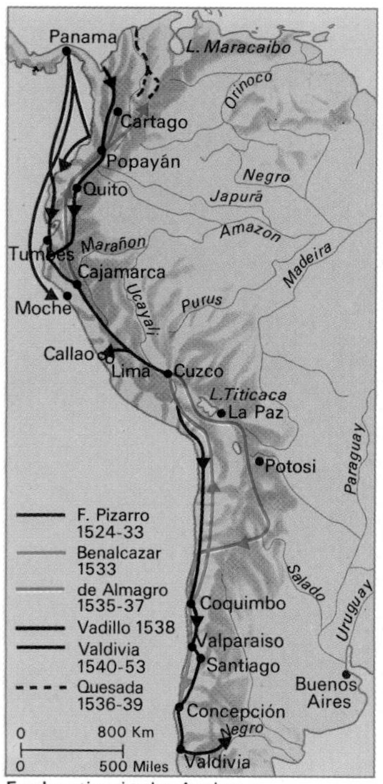

Panama
L. Maracaibo
Orinoco
Cartago
Popayán
Negro
Quito
Japurá
Amazon
Tumbes
Marañon
Madeira
Cajamarca
Ucayali
Moche
Purus
Callao
Lima
Cuzco
L.Titicaca
La Paz
Potosi
Paraguay
F. Pizarro 1524-33
Benalcazar 1533
de Almagro 1535-37
Vadillo 1538
Valdivia 1540-53
Quesada 1536-39
Salado
Uruguay
Coquimbo
Valparaiso
Santiago
Buenos Aires
Concepción
Negro
0
800 Km
0
500 Miles
Valdivia

Exploration in the Andes

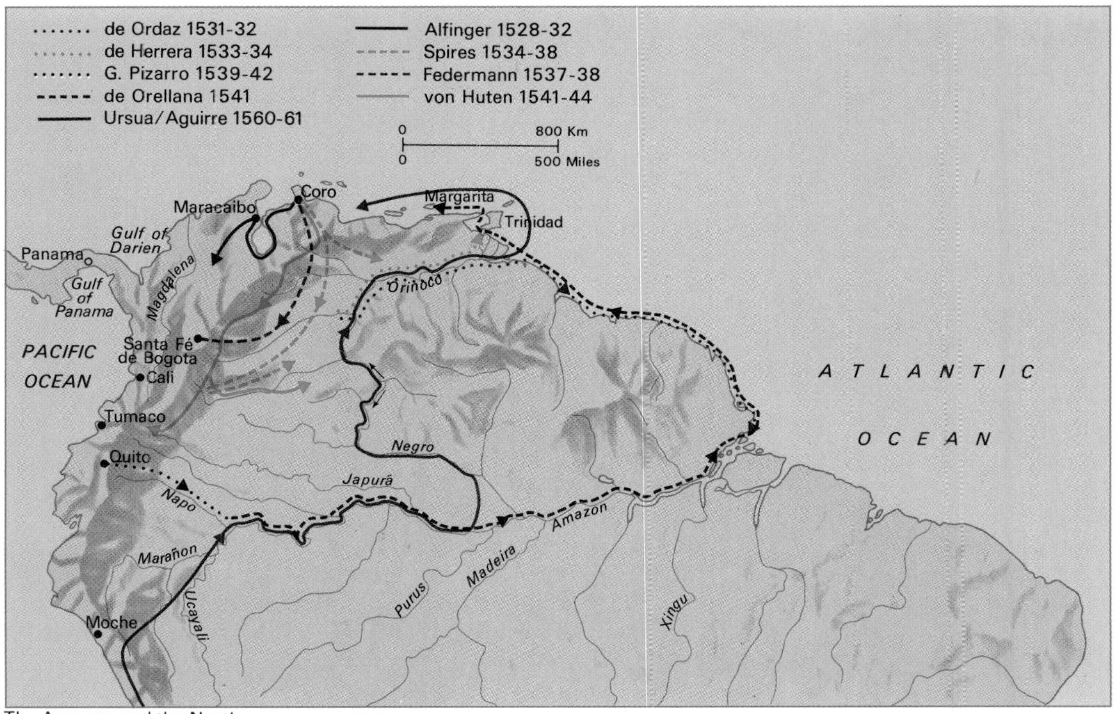

de Ordaz 1531-32
de Herrera 1533-34
G. Pizarro 1539-42
de Orellana 1541
Ursua/Aguirre 1560-61
Alfinger 1528-32
Spires 1534-38
Federmann 1537-38
von Huten 1541-44
0
800 Km
0
500 Miles
Coro
Margarita
Maracaibo
Trinidad
Gulf of Darien
Panama
Gulf of Panama
Magdalena
Orinoco
Santa Fé de Bogota
PACIFIC OCEAN
Cali
ATLANTIC OCEAN
Tumaco
Negro
Quito
Japurá
Napo
Amazon
Marañon
Madeira
Purus
Xingu
Moche
Ucayali

The Amazon and the North

THE GREAT AGE OF DISCOVERY III

While the Spanish searched for a route to the East via Central America, other explorers were looking for it farther north. Cabot, the Venetian navigator in the service of England, was the first to make **the search for the northwest passage**. Cabot made two voyages, as shown below on the top map, for Henry VII in 1497 and 1498. He was convinced that he had reached Asia north of Japan. He was soon followed in 1500-1501 by the Portuguese Corte Real and the Italian Giovanni da Verrazano in 1524. The rich fishing grounds of the Great Banks east and south of Newfoundland were appreciated, but for a while the search for a northwest passage was abandoned, to be resumed about 75 years later.

From 1576 on, a succession of English explorers searched for the northwest passage. In that year, **Sir Martin Frobisher** (below, center) sailed into Frobisher Bay, and a decade later Davis reached 73° N. **A Davis quadrant** is shown at the left below. Hudson and Button expected to find the passage through the Hudson Strait. Baffin took the right direction, but he turned south at 78° N and passed the entrances to Jones and Lancaster sounds, both of which lead west. He considered these waters to be too narrow and icy for a practical trade route, and thus attention was next turned to the continent itself. The small map at the bottom, right, represents the exploration of the **English on the east coast** of North America. Dutch explorers, seeking an alternative to the northwest passage by going eastward around northern Europe, fared no better than the English. Depicted below at the center is **the expedition of Willem Barents, 1596**, trying to hack a path through the ice for their ship.

At the time the English were searching for the northwest passage, the Spanish were occupied in Central and South America, the Portuguese in the Far East, and the French in the interior of North America. The French explorers hoped to find a route to the Pacific Ocean across the continent. **Jacques Cartier**, bottom left, established that the St. Lawrence was a river, not a strait. This superb route was not followed immediately, but from about 1600 on, starting with the voyage of **Samuel de Champlain** (center, left) Frenchmen made a series of journeys into the interior and around the Great Lakes. The map at the base of the page, center, shows the exploration routes of **the French in northeast America** from 1534–1680. To the left of the map is a representation of **Cartier's ship at Stadacona (Quebec)**.

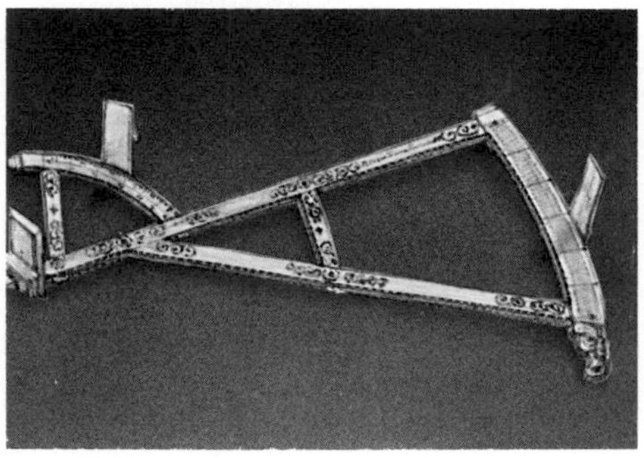

A Davis quadrant

Sir Martin Frobisher

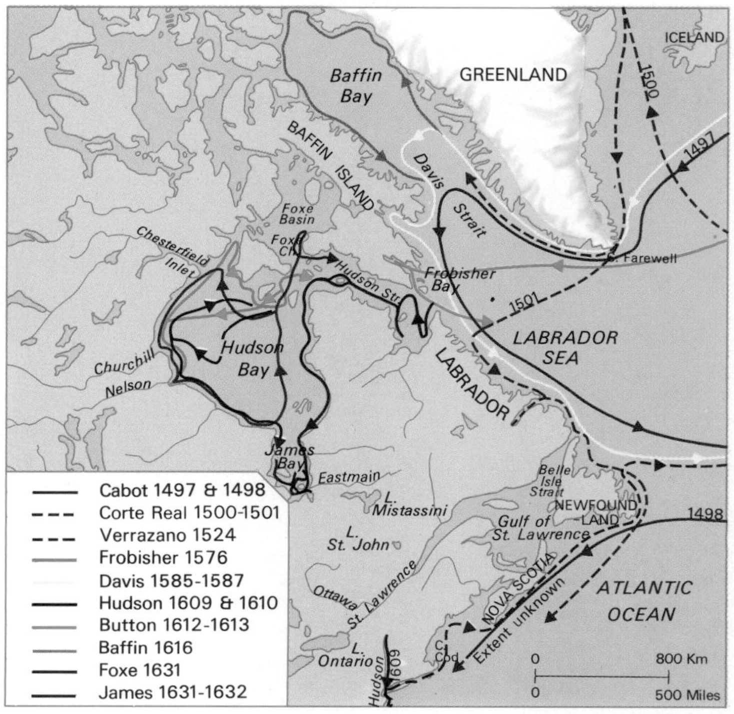
ICELAND
GREENLAND
Baffin Bay
BAFFIN ISLAND
Davis Strait
Foxe Basin
Chesterfield Inlet
Hudson Str.
Frobisher Bay
Farewell
1501
1500
1497
1498
LABRADOR SEA
LABRADOR
Hudson Bay
Churchill
Nelson
James Bay
Eastmain
L. Mistassini
Belle Isle Strait
NEWFOUNDLAND
Gulf of St. Lawrence
L. St. John
St. Lawrence
Ottawa
NOVA SCOTIA
Extent unknown
ATLANTIC OCEAN
L. Ontario
C. Cod
Hudson 1609
Cabot 1497 & 1498
Corte Real 1500-1501
Verrazano 1524
Frobisher 1576
Davis 1585-1587
Hudson 1609 & 1610
Button 1612-1613
Baffin 1616
Foxe 1631
James 1631-1632
0 800 Km
0 500 Miles

The search for the northwest passage

Samuel de Champlain

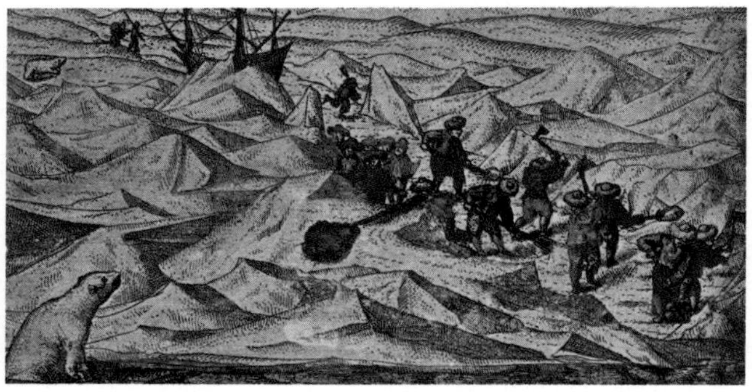

The expedition of Willem Barents, 1596

Jacques Cartier

Cartier's ship at Stadacona (Quebec)

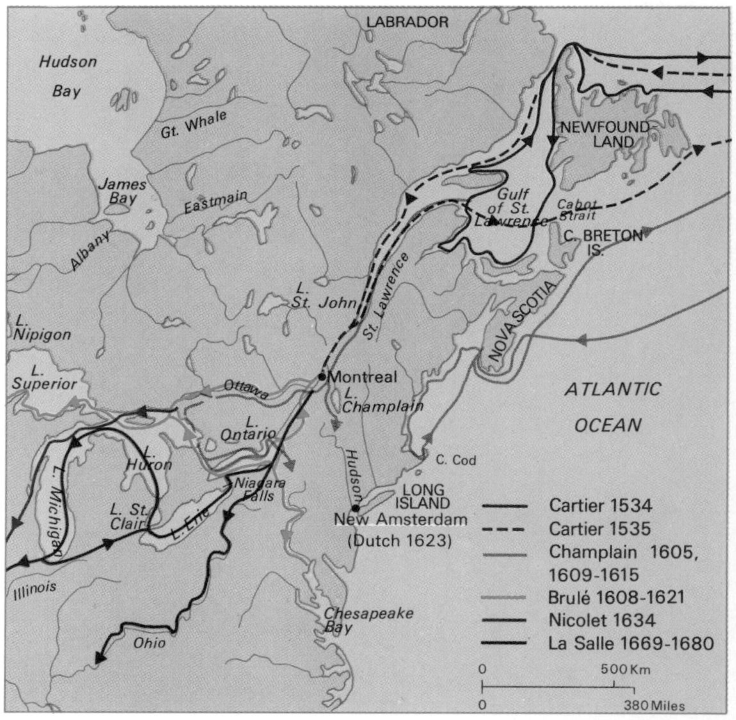
LABRADOR
Hudson Bay
Gt. Whale
James Bay
Eastmain
Albany
NEWFOUNDLAND
Gulf of St. Lawrence
Cabot Strait
C. BRETON IS.
L. St. John
St. Lawrence
NOVA SCOTIA
L. Nipigon
L. Superior
Ottawa
Montreal
L. Champlain
L. Ontario
L. Huron
L. Michigan
L. St. Clair
L. Erie
Niagara Falls
Hudson
C. Cod
LONG ISLAND
New Amsterdam (Dutch 1623)
ATLANTIC OCEAN
Illinois
Ohio
Chesapeake Bay
Cartier 1534
Cartier 1535
Champlain 1605, 1609-1615
Brulé 1608-1621
Nicolet 1634
La Salle 1669-1680
0 500 Km
0 380 Miles

The French in N.E. America

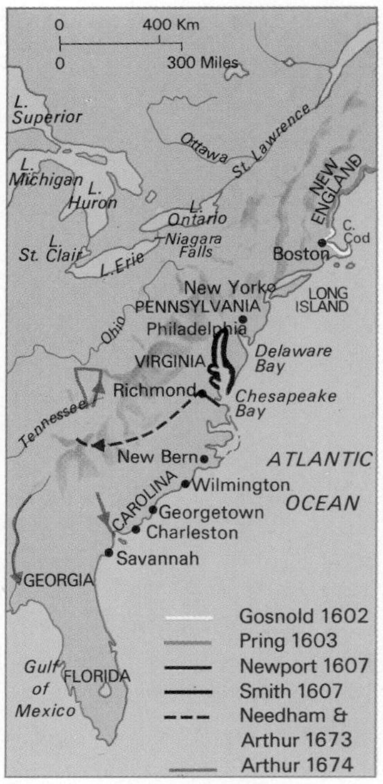
0 400 Km
0 300 Miles
L. Superior
L. Michigan
L. Huron
Ottawa
St. Lawrence
NEW ENGLAND
L. Ontario
Niagara Falls
C. Cod
St. Clair
L. Erie
Boston
New York
LONG ISLAND
PENNSYLVANIA
Ohio
Philadelphia
Delaware Bay
VIRGINIA
Richmond
Chesapeake Bay
Tennessee
New Bern
ATLANTIC OCEAN
CAROLINA
Wilmington
Georgetown
Charleston
Savannah
GEORGIA
Gulf of Mexico
FLORIDA
Gosnold 1602
Pring 1603
Newport 1607
Smith 1607
Needham & Arthur 1673
Arthur 1674

English on the east coast

Several explorers sought an alternative to the northwest passage by trying to go eastward around northern Europe and Asia. In 1553, Chancellor reached Archangel by sea and then traveled overland with his expedition to Moscow. Four decades later, Barents made his final voyage around Scandinavia and across the Barents Sea to Kara Sea, where he died in 1597. The map at the left, below, depicts **the search for the northeast passage**, showing the routes of Barents, Chancellor, and Hudson. To the right of this map is a picture of a **map by Barents from an atlas of 1596**.

Sir Francis Drake was a privateer when Queen Elizabeth commissioned him in 1577 to journey to the Pacific to look for Terra Australis. En route, Drake raided Spanish ships and settlements on the west coast of South America. Approaching the Magellan Strait, a storm blew Drake's ship, *The Golden Hind*, south to Tierra del Fuego. He realized this was an island and not part of an Antarctic continent. He sailed north along the west coast of the Americas, crossed the Pacific Ocean to the Moluccas, and returned to England via the Cape of Good Hope. He was the first Englishman to sail around the world. For this three-year feat, Queen Elizabeth knighted him.

Drake's voyages are shown on the map, left, at the bottom of the page. The illustration at the center, right, shows **The Golden Hind capturing a Spanish treasure ship**.

The second half of the 16th century, while the English and French were discovering that to cross or go around North America was no easy task, the Spanish were establishing routes across the Pacific. Mendana sailed from Peru in 1568 in search of the great continent believed to exist in the south Pacific. He reached the Solomon Islands, then sailed north and east to California, and back to Mexico. In 1595, he again sailed from Peru to the Marquesas Islands and to Santa Cruz, where he died. Quiros, his pilot, then took command.

Quiros sailed on to Manila. Many died on the way. In 1605, Quiros sailed with Torres from Peru, but they became separated, and Quiros turned back. Torres went on, discovered the Louisiade Archipelago, and sailed through the strait, which now bears his name, between Australia and New Guinea. He thus proved New Guinea to be an island. He arrived in Manila in 1607, having lost only one man on the voyage. The map at the bottom right shows the **Spanish exploration of the Pacific**.

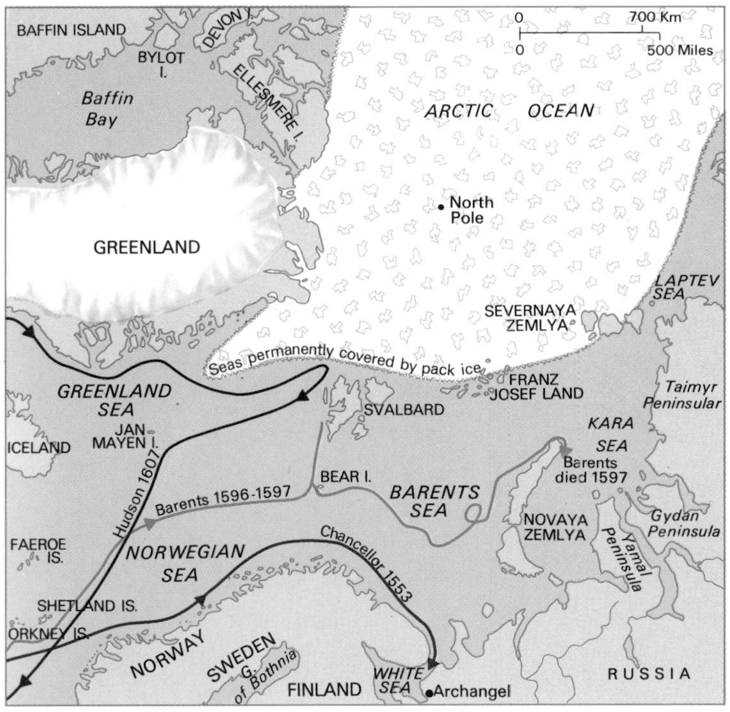

0 700 Km
0 500 Miles
BAFFIN ISLAND
BYLOT I.
DEVON I.
ELLESMERE I.
Baffin Bay
ARCTIC OCEAN
North Pole
GREENLAND
LAPTEV SEA
SEVERNAYA ZEMLYA
Seas permanently covered by pack ice
FRANZ JOSEF LAND
Taimyr Peninsular
GREENLAND SEA
SVALBARD
KARA SEA
JAN MAYEN I.
ICELAND
Hudson 1607
Barents died 1597
BEAR I.
Barents 1596-1597
BARENTS SEA
FAEROE IS.
NOVAYA ZEMLYA
Yamal Peninsula
Gydan Peninsula
NORWEGIAN SEA
Chancellor 1553
SHETLAND IS.
ORKNEY IS.
NORWAY
SWEDEN
G. of Bothnia
FINLAND
WHITE SEA
Archangel
RUSSIA

The search for the northeast passage

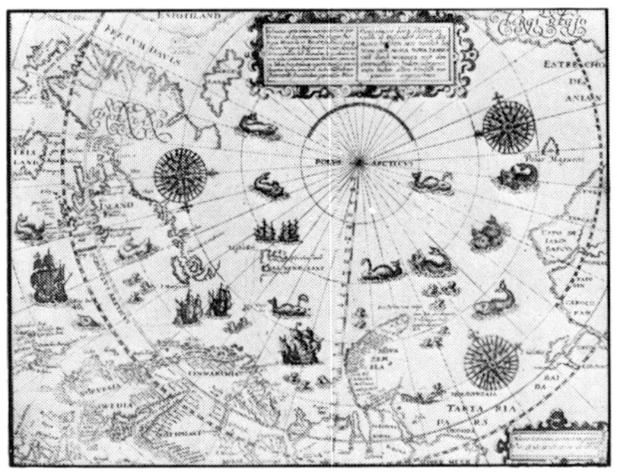
Map by Barents from an atlas of 1596

Sir Francis Drake

The Golden Hind capturing a Spanish treasure ship

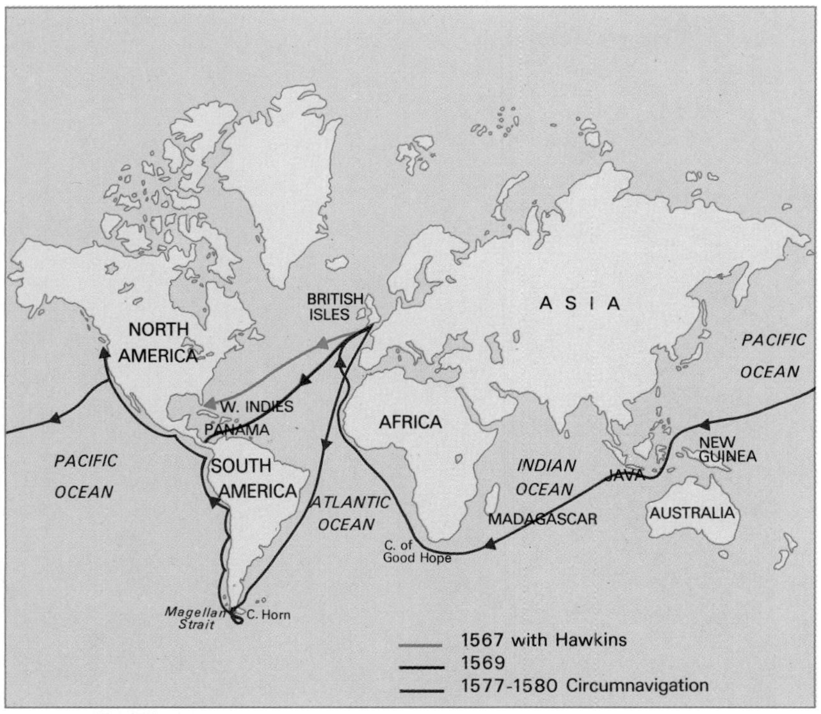

BRITISH ISLES
ASIA
NORTH AMERICA
PACIFIC OCEAN
W. INDIES
PANAMA
AFRICA
NEW GUINEA
PACIFIC OCEAN
SOUTH AMERICA
INDIAN OCEAN
JAVA
ATLANTIC OCEAN
MADAGASCAR
AUSTRALIA
C. of Good Hope
Magellan Strait
C. Horn
1567 with Hawkins
1569
1577-1580 Circumnavigation

Drake's voyages

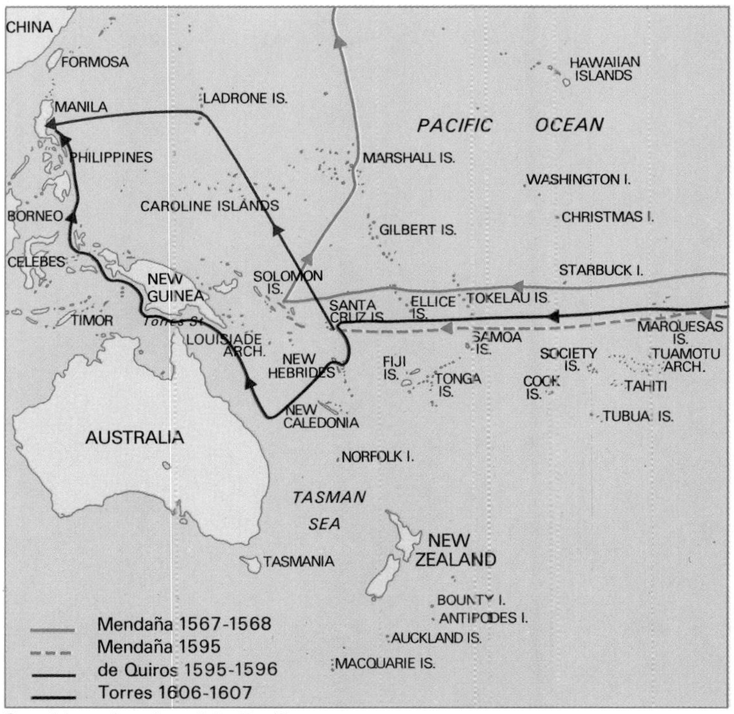

CHINA
FORMOSA
HAWAIIAN ISLANDS
MANILA
LADRONE IS.
PACIFIC OCEAN
PHILIPPINES
MARSHALL IS.
WASHINGTON I.
BORNEO
CAROLINE ISLANDS
CHRISTMAS I.
GILBERT IS.
CELEBES
STARBUCK I.
NEW GUINEA
SOLOMON IS.
SANTA CRUZ IS.
ELLICE IS.
TOKELAU IS.
TIMOR
Torres St.
MARQUESAS IS.
LOUISIADE ARCH.
SAMOA IS.
NEW HEBRIDES
FIJI IS.
SOCIETY IS.
TUAMOTU ARCH.
TONGA IS.
COOK IS.
TAHITI
NEW CALEDONIA
TUBUAI IS.
AUSTRALIA
NORFOLK I.
TASMAN SEA
NEW ZEALAND
TASMANIA
BOUNTY I.
ANTIPODES I.
AUCKLAND IS.
MACQUARIE IS.
Mendaña 1567-1568
Mendaña 1595
de Quiros 1595-1596
Torres 1606-1607

Spanish exploration of the Pacific

THE GREAT AGE OF DISCOVERY IV

After the Dutch declared their independence from Spanish control, the Spanish and Portuguese ports were closed to them. Thus, the Dutch had to make their own way to the Spice Islands. The Dutch East India Company, formed in 1602, encouraged its captains to sail south after rounding the Cape of Good Hope to let the prevailing winds carry them to the coast of Australia, which they explored piecemeal. The map below shows the routes of the **explorers in southeast Asia and Australasia**.

In 1642, **Abel Tasman**, below left, was sent to determine whether or not Australia was an island. He discovered Tasmania and New Zealand and returned to the Indies via Tonga and New Guinea. **William Dampier**, below center, explored the north New Guinea coast and western Australia. At the bottom right is **part of Coronelli's globe, 1688**.

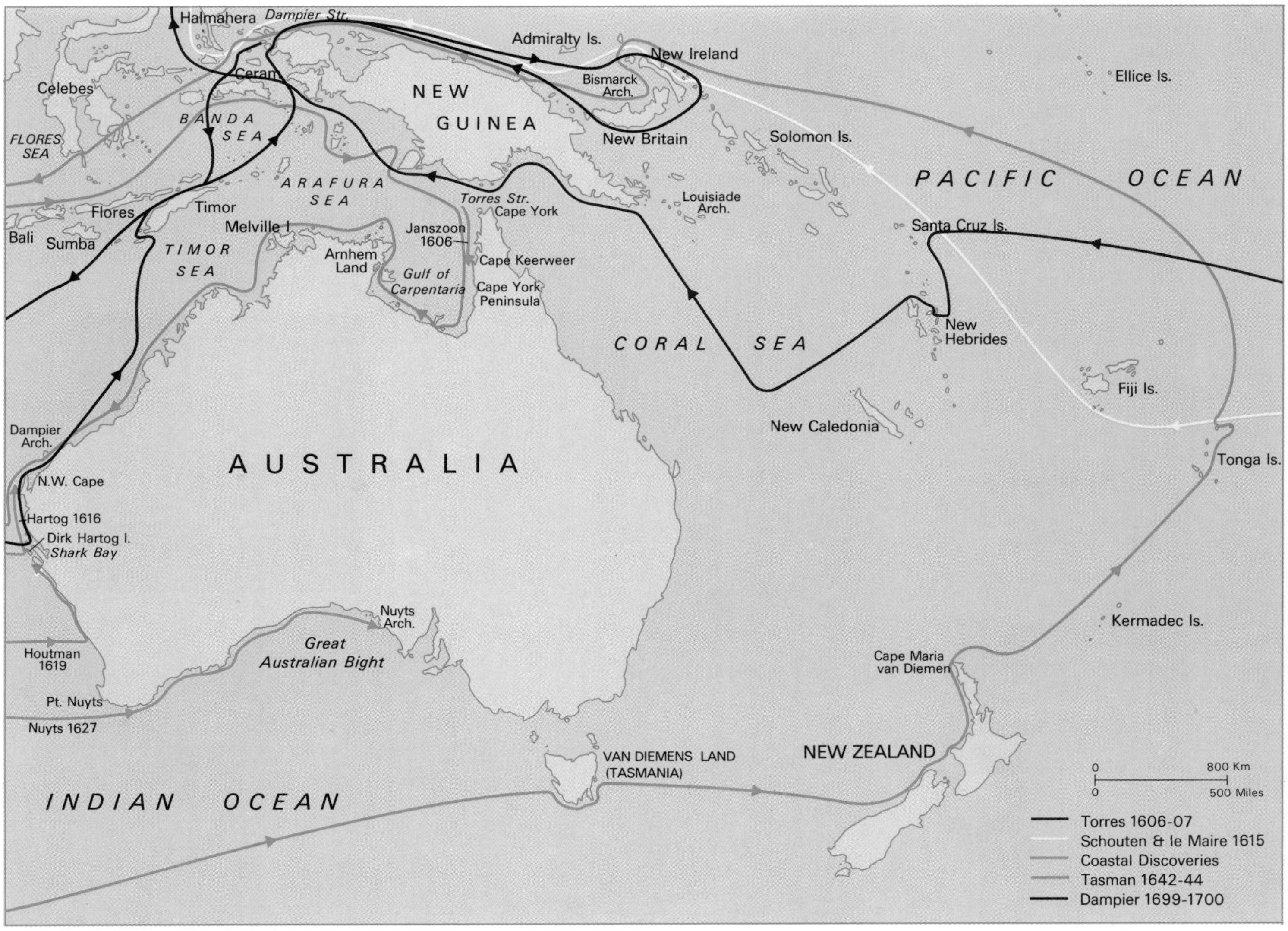
Halmahera
Dampier Str.
Admiralty Is.
New Ireland
Celebes
Ceram
Bismarck Arch.
NEW GUINEA
Ellice Is.
BANDA SEA
FLORES SEA
New Britain
Solomon Is.
PACIFIC OCEAN
ARAFURA SEA
Louisiade Arch.
Torres Str.
Cape York
Flores
Timor
Bali
Sumba
Melville I.
Janszoon 1606
Santa Cruz Is.
TIMOR SEA
Arnhem Land
Cape Keerweer
Gulf of Carpentaria
Cape York Peninsula
New Hebrides
CORAL SEA
Fiji Is.
New Caledonia
Dampier Arch.
AUSTRALIA
Tonga Is.
N.W. Cape
Hartog 1616
Dirk Hartog I.
Shark Bay
Nuyts Arch.
Kermadec Is.
Great Australian Bight
Houtman 1619
Cape Maria van Diemen
Pt. Nuyts
Nuyts 1627
VAN DIEMENS LAND (TASMANIA)
NEW ZEALAND
0
800 Km
0
500 Miles
INDIAN OCEAN
Torres 1606-07
Schouten & le Maire 1615
Coastal Discoveries
Tasman 1642-44
Dampier 1699-1700

Explorers in S.E. Asia and Australasia

Abel Tasman

William Dampier

CELEBES
MOLUCCHE
FLORES
ARCIPELAGO DE PAPOUS
NUOVA
LANTCHIDOL
HET NIEW HOLLANDT
Terra di Concordia
scoperta l'anno 1618.
Het Landt van Endracht
NUOVA HOLLANDA
Della Giaua Minore

Part of Coronelli's Globe, 1688

EXPANSION IN NORTHEAST ASIA AND SOUTH AMERICA

In the mid-13th century, western Russia was overrun by the Mongols, led by the successors of **Genghis Khan**. Principalities developed, of which Moscow was the strongest, and by the end of the 15th century, Moscow had rejected Mongol power. From the 16th to the 18th centuries, Moscow expanded and consolidated her empire in the East. Cossack soldiers and traders opened up Siberia, gradually penetrating the desolate and difficult areas and founding cities. The pattern of **Russian expansion and early travelers in Asia** are shown below on the top map. Jenkinson, the first Englishman to travel through Asia, reached Moscow in 1558 from the White Sea. He then set out to find an overland route to China. He was prevented from going farther east than Bukhara by local wars, but he gathered much useful information. He made a second journey to Persia in 1562.

Two Jesuit missionaries, Grueber and d'Orville, were the first westerners to visit Lhasa in Tibet on a journey from Peking to Europe in 1661. At the bottom left, is **a German Jesuit missionary in China**.

Considerable settlement had taken place in **South America c. 1650**, as the map below shows. This effort was partly an attempt to repel the raids by buccaneers who made hit and run attacks from the sea on isolated settlements and who could easily claim possession. These **South American buccaneers** are depicted at the left below. Spanish settlements predominated, but Portugal enforced her claim on Brazil.

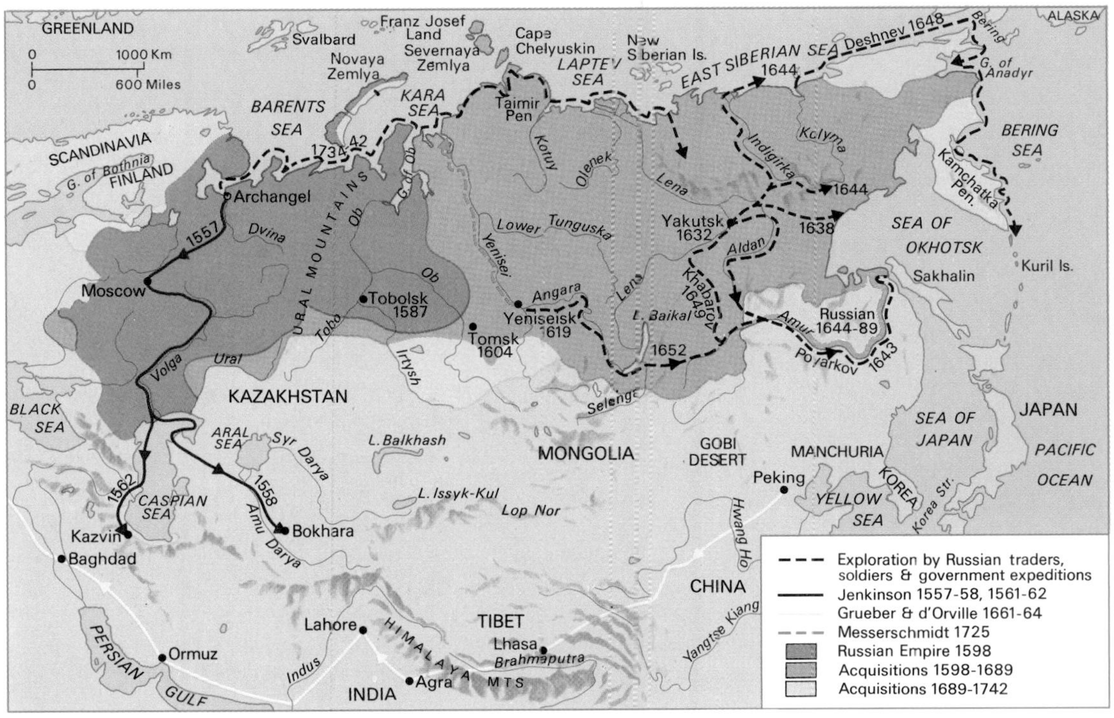

GREENLAND
0 1000 Km
0 600 Miles
Svalbard
Franz Josef Land
Novaya Zemlya
Severnaya Zemlya
Cape Chelyuskin
New Siberian Is.
LAPTEV SEA
EAST SIBERIAN SEA
Deshnev 1648
ALASKA
Bering
G. of Anadyr
BARENTS SEA
KARA SEA
Taimir Pen
1644
SCANDINAVIA
G. of Bothnia
FINLAND
1734-42
Archangel
Dvina
URAL MOUNTAINS
Ob
G. of Ob
Kotuy
Olenek
Lena
Indigirka
Kolyma
BERING SEA
Kamchatka Pen.
1644
Lower Tunguska
Yakutsk 1632
Aldan
1638
SEA OF OKHOTSK
Kuril Is.
Sakhalin
Moscow
1557
Tobolsk 1587
Tobol
Yenisei
Angara
Yeniseisk 1619
L. Baikal
Khabarov 1649
Russian 1644-89
Amur
Poyarkov 1643
Tomsk 1604
1652
Ural
Irtysh
Volga
KAZAKHSTAN
Selenga
BLACK SEA
ARAL SEA
Syr Darya
L. Balkhash
MONGOLIA
GOBI DESERT
MANCHURIA
SEA OF JAPAN
JAPAN
PACIFIC OCEAN
KOREA
Korea Str.
Peking
YELLOW SEA
1562
1558
CASPIAN SEA
Amu Darya
L. Issyk-Kul
Lop Nor
Kazvin
Bokhara
Baghdad
Hwang Ho
CHINA
PERSIAN GULF
Ormuz
Lahore
HIMALAYA MTS
TIBET
Lhasa
Brahmaputra
Indus
INDIA
Agra
Yangtse Kiang
Exploration by Russian traders, soldiers & government expeditions
Jenkinson 1557-58, 1561-62
Grueber & d'Orville 1661-64
Messerschmidt 1725
Russian Empire 1598
Acquisitions 1598-1689
Acquisitions 1689-1742

Russian Expansion and early travellers in Asia

Genghis Khan

South American buccaneers

A German Jesuit missionary in China

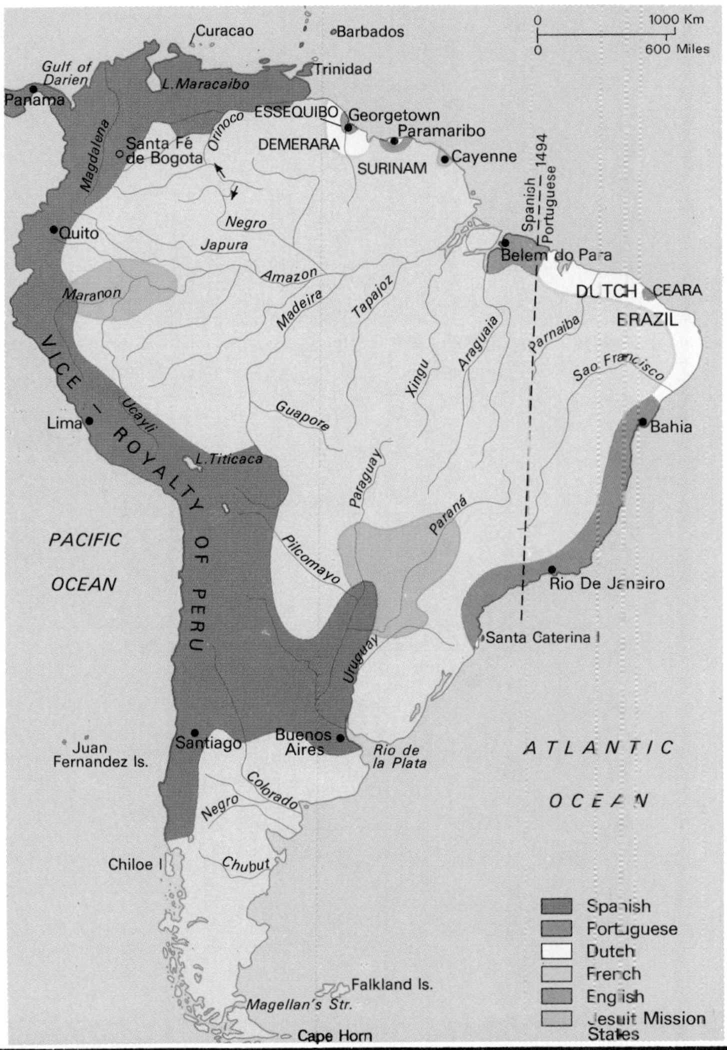

Curacao
Barbados
0 1000 Km
0 600 Miles
Gulf of Darien
Panama
L. Maracaibo
Trinidad
ESSEQUIBO
Georgetown
DEMERARA
Paramaribo
SURINAM
Cayenne
Santa Fé de Bogota
Orinoco
Magdalena
Spanish
Portuguese
1494
Quito
Negro
Japura
Amazon
Belem do Para
DUTCH
CEARA
BRAZIL
Maranon
Madeira
Tapajoz
Araguaia
Parnaiba
Xingu
Sao Francisco
VICE – ROYALTY OF PERU
Ucayli
Guapore
Bahia
Lima
L. Titicaca
Paraguay
PACIFIC
OCEAN
Pilcomayo
Paraná
Rio De Janeiro
Santa Caterina I
Uruguay
Juan Fernandez Is.
Santiago
Buenos Aires
Rio de la Plata
ATLANTIC
OCEAN
Colorado
Negro
Chiloe I
Chubut
Spanish
Portuguese
Dutch
French
English
Jesuit Mission States
Falkland Is.
Magellan's Str.
Cape Horn

South America c.1650

NORTH AMERICA

North America was mostly explored by the Spanish, the French, and the British and followed up by settlement. This **exploration** is shown in the series of three maps below. French activity was concerned mostly with fur trade, whereas the Spanish advance was made largely by Jesuit missionaries. And the British had secured a firm hold on the eastern seaboard. Intense rivalry developed as interests clashed.

The architecture of the land reflected the three cultures, as shown in the photographs below: **Spanish — Monastery, Mexico; English — Drayton Hall, South Carolina; French — Seminary in old Quebec**. Also shown are drawings of the **Niagara Falls (after Hennepin)** and **Pioneer Trappers**.

The Seven Years' War, 1756–1763, affected North America. **The Treaty of Paris, 1763** divided French holdings between Britain and Spain, as shown on the map at the lower right. The British had difficulty governing their colonies, however. The small map at the bottom center shows late 18th century **exploration in the northeast Pacific**.

Exploration

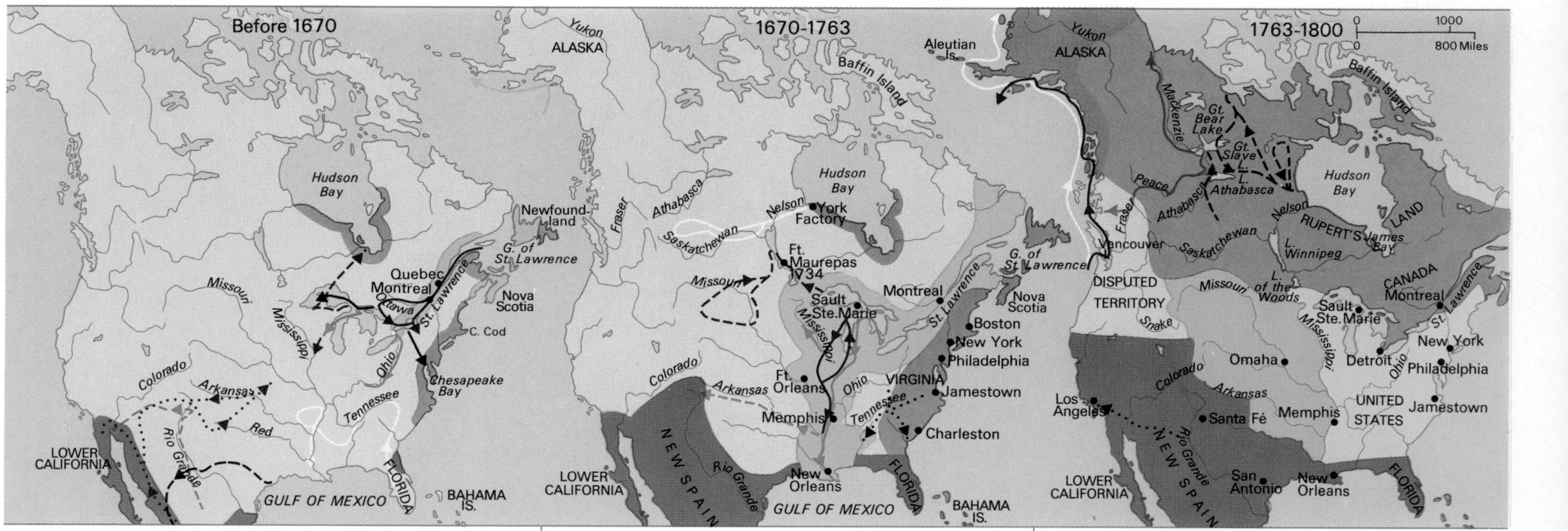

Before 1670
1670-1763
1763-1800
1000
800 Miles
Hudson Bay
Newfoundland
Quebec
Montreal
St. Lawrence
G. of St. Lawrence
Nova Scotia
C. Cod
Chesapeake Bay
Missouri
Mississippi
Ohio
Tennessee
Colorado
Arkansas
Red
Rio Grande
LOWER CALIFORNIA
GULF OF MEXICO
FLORIDA
BAHAMA IS.
ALASKA
Yukon
Aleutian Is.
Baffin Island
York Factory
Nelson
Saskatchewan
Athabasca
Fraser
Ft. Maurepas 1734
Sault Ste. Marie
Boston
New York
Philadelphia
VIRGINIA
Jamestown
Charleston
Ft. Orleans
Memphis
New Orleans
NEW SPAIN
Mackenzie
Gt. Bear Lake
Gt. Slave L.
Peace
RUPERT'S LAND
James Bay
Winnipeg
Vancouver
DISPUTED TERRITORY
Snake
L. of the Woods
CANADA
Omaha
Detroit
Los Angeles
Santa Fé
San Antonio
UNITED STATES

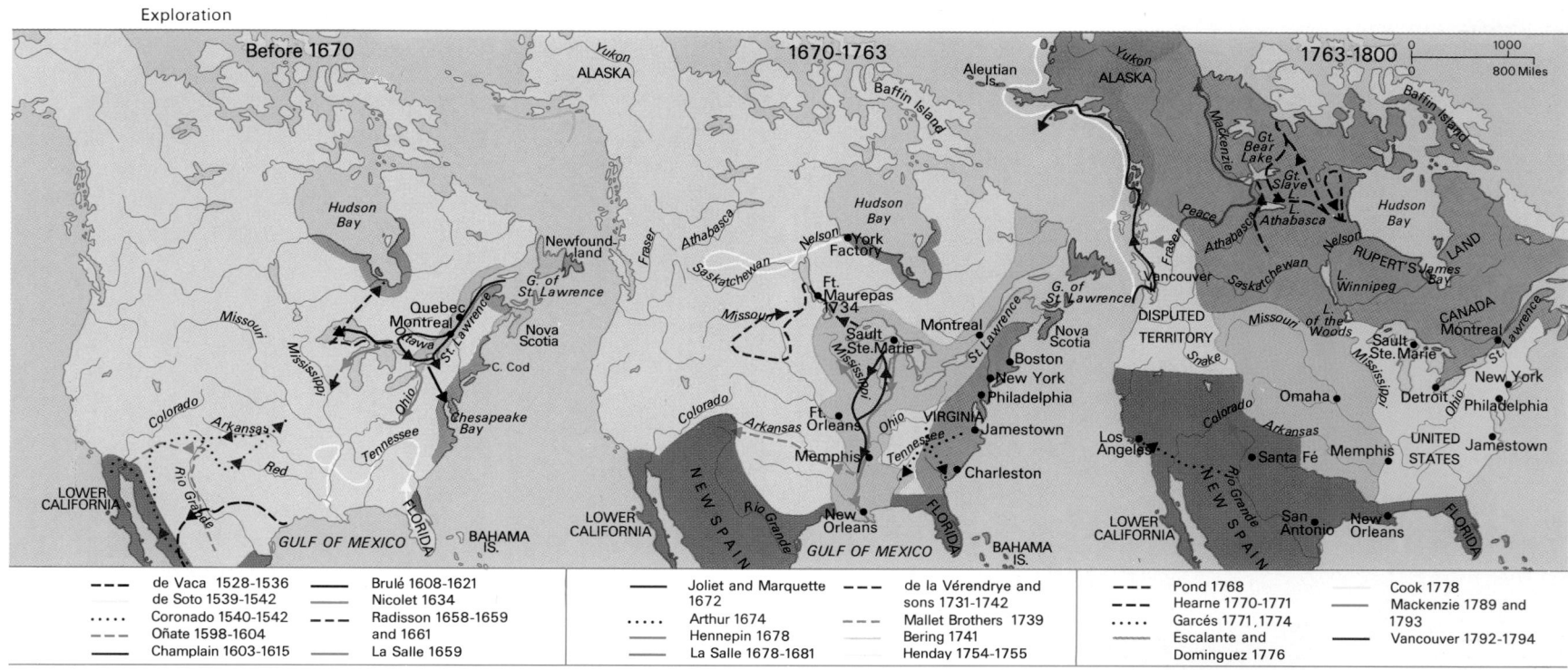

de Vaca 1528-1536	Brulé 1608-1621	Joliet and Marquette 1672	de la Vérendrye and sons 1731-1742
de Soto 1539-1542	Nicolet 1634	Arthur 1674	Mallet Brothers 1739
Coronado 1540-1542	Radisson 1658-1659 and 1661	Hennepin 1678	Bering 1741
Oñate 1598-1604	La Salle 1659	La Salle 1678-1681	Henday 1754-1755
Champlain 1603-1615			

Pond 1768	Cook 1778
Hearne 1770-1771	Mackenzie 1789 and 1793
Garcés 1771,1774	Vancouver 1792-1794
Escalante and Dominguez 1776	

Spanish — Monastery, Mexico

English — Drayton Hall, S. Carolina

Pioneer trappers

French — Seminary in old Quebec

Niagara Falls (after Hennepin)

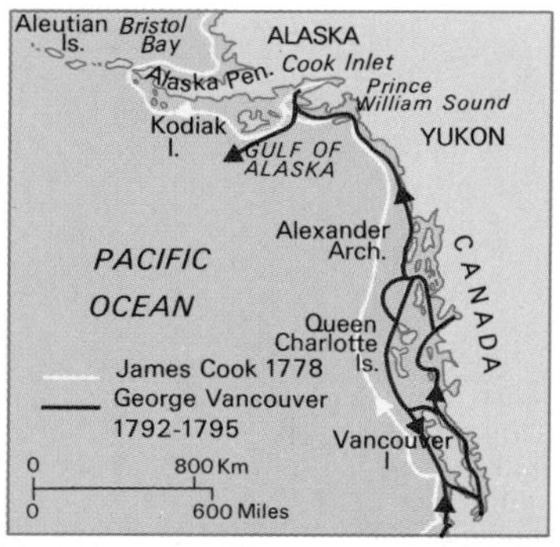

Aleutian Is.
Bristol Bay
ALASKA
Alaska Pen.
Cook Inlet
Prince William Sound
Kodiak I.
GULF OF ALASKA
YUKON
Alexander Arch.
PACIFIC OCEAN
CANADA
Queen Charlotte Is.
James Cook 1778
George Vancouver 1792-1795
800 Km
600 Miles
Vancouver I.

Exploration in the N.E. Pacific

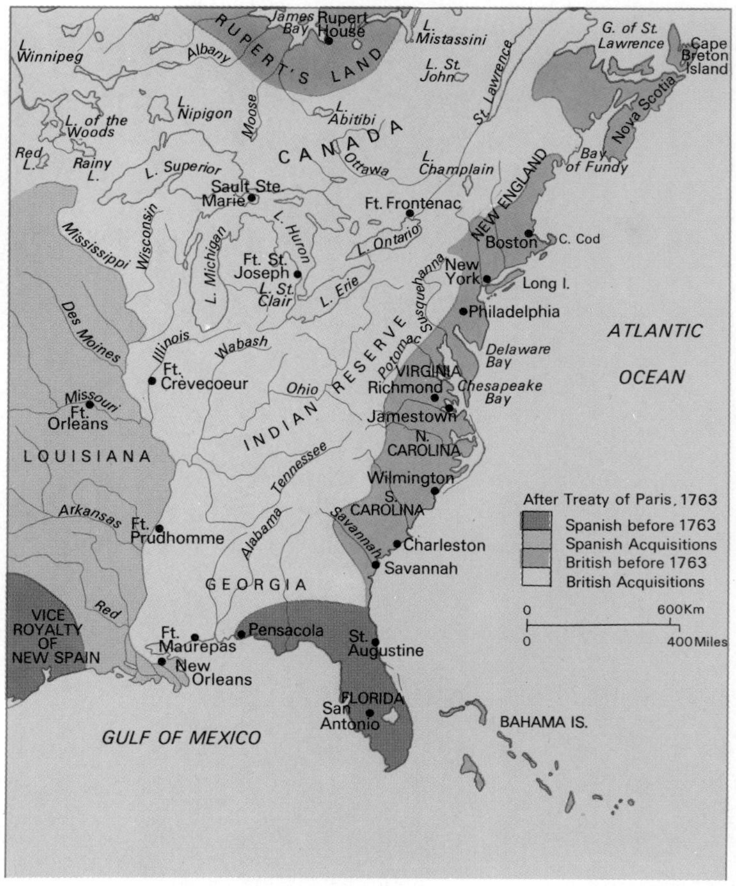

Winnipeg
Albany
James Bay
Rupert House
RUPERT'S LAND
L. Mistassini
L. St. John
St. Lawrence
G. of St. Lawrence
Cape Breton Island
L. Nipigon
Moose
Abitibi
L. of the Woods
Rainy L.
Red L.
CANADA
Ottawa
L. Champlain
Nova Scotia
Bay of Fundy
L. Superior
Sault Ste. Marie
Ft. Frontenac
NEW ENGLAND
Mississippi
Wisconsin
L. Huron
L. Ontario
Boston
C. Cod
L. Michigan
Ft. St. Joseph
L. St. Clair
L. Erie
New York
Long I.
Philadelphia
Des Moines
Illinois
Wabash
Potomac
Susquehanna
Delaware Bay
ATLANTIC OCEAN
Ft. Crèvecoeur
Ohio
INDIAN RESERVE
VIRGINIA
Richmond
Chesapeake Bay
Missouri
Ft. Orleans
Jamestown
N. CAROLINA
LOUISIANA
Tennessee
Wilmington
S. CAROLINA
Arkansas
Ft. Prudhomme
Alabama
Savannah
Charleston
Savannah
GEORGIA
Red
VICE ROYALTY OF NEW SPAIN
Ft. Maurepas
New Orleans
Pensacola
St. Augustine
FLORIDA
San Antonio
GULF OF MEXICO
BAHAMA IS.
After Treaty of Paris, 1763
Spanish before 1763
Spanish Acquisitions
British before 1763
British Acquisitions
600Km
400Miles

After the Treaty of Paris, 1763

In the 18th and 19th centuries, much of north and west Canada was explored and surveyed, mostly either by individual fur traders or by employees of the Hudson's Bay or North West companies. Activity increased after 1763 and was intensified with the news of Russian incursions from the northwest. **Sir Alexander Mackenzie** was the first to cross from coast to coast in 1793. Other expeditions attempted **the exploration of the north and west** (top map) seeking again the northwest passage. They were defeated by ice, though Parry and Franklin were close. After 1803, when the United States purchased Louisiana, surveyors explored, mapped, and also laid claim to territories. The lower map shows this **exploration of western U.S.A.** Lewis and Clark explored the headwaters of the Missouri and reached the Pacific coast. Pike explored the Mississippi headwaters. The Astorians, Pattie, and Smith were all fur traders. Long and Frémont were army surveyors. As the west became known, expansion from the east began. Traders, merchants, missionaries, and settlers — some spurred by **the Gold Rush in California, 1848–1859** — moved westward. Shown at the bottom, **emigrants to the west**.

Sir Alexander Mackenzie

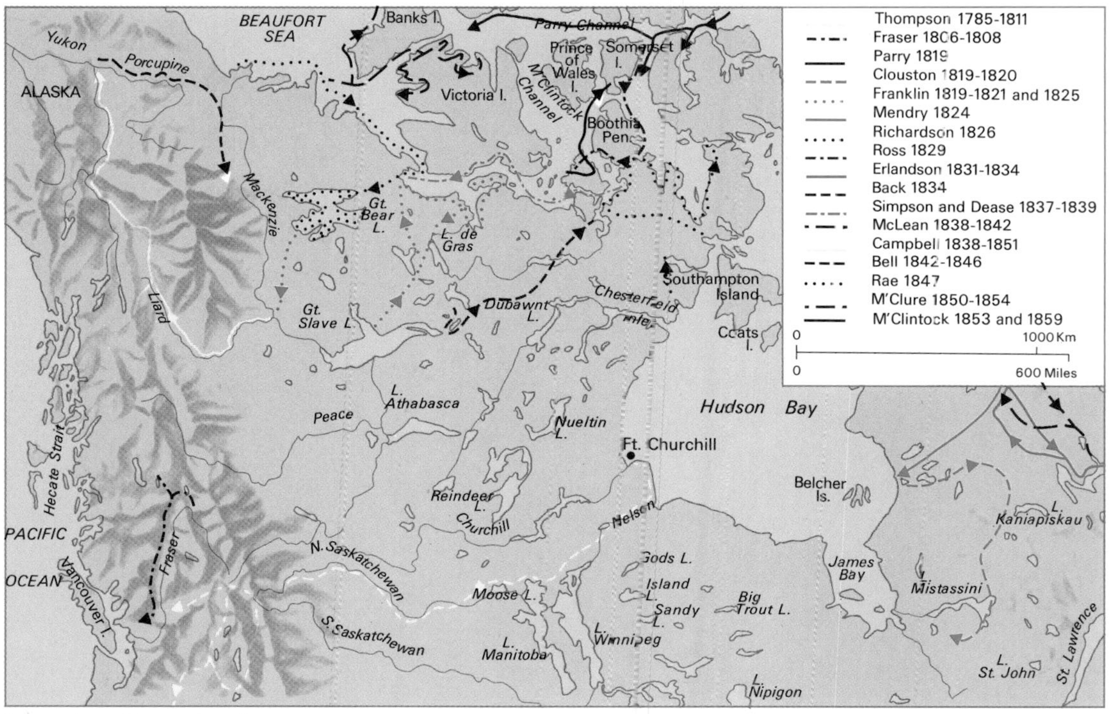

Thompson 1785-1811
Fraser 1806-1808
Parry 1819
Clouston 1819-1820
Franklin 1819-1821 and 1825
Mendry 1824
Richardson 1826
Ross 1829
Erlandson 1831-1834
Back 1834
Simpson and Dease 1837-1839
McLean 1838-1842
Campbell 1838-1851
Bell 1842-1846
Rae 1847
M'Clure 1850-1854
M'Clintock 1853 and 1859
0
1000Km
0
600 Miles
BEAUFORT SEA
Banks I.
Victoria I.
ALASKA
Yukon
Porcupine
Mackenzie
Gt. Bear L.
L. de Gras
Gt. Slave L.
Liard
Peace
L. Athabasca
Hudson Bay
Ft. Churchill
Southampton Island
Coats I.
Belcher Is.
James Bay
Mistassini
PACIFIC OCEAN
Fraser
N. Saskatchewan
S. Saskatchewan
Moose L.
L. Manitoba
Winnipeg
Nelson
Gods L.
Island
Sandy L.
Big Trout L.
Nipigon
Boothia Pen.
Reindeer L.
Churchill
Nueltin L.
Dubawnt L.
L. St. John
St. Lawrence

Exploration of the north and west

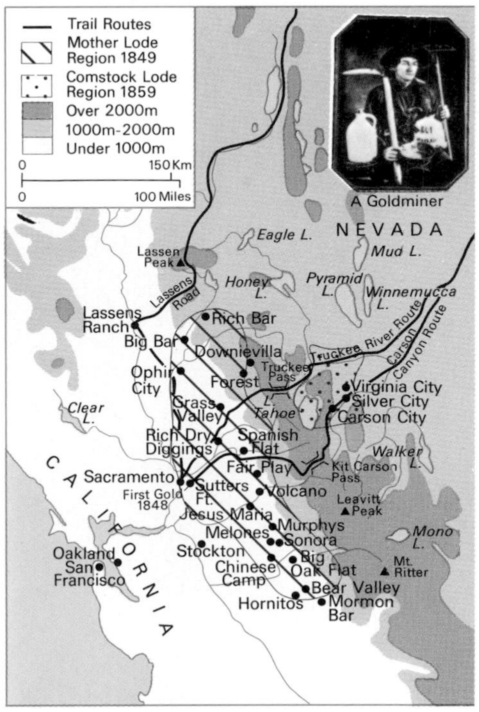

Trail Routes
Mother Lode Region 1849
Comstock Lode Region 1859
Over 2000m
1000m-2000m
Under 1000m
0
150Km
0
100 Miles
A Goldminer
NEVADA
Eagle L.
Mud L.
Honey L.
Pyramid L.
Winnemucca L.
Lassen Peak
Lassens Ranch
Rich Bar
Big Bar
Downieville
Ophir City
Forest
Grass Valley
Virginia City
Silver City
Carson City
Tahoe
Rich Dry Diggings
Spanish Flat
Walker L.
Sacramento
Fair Play
Volcano
Jesus Maria
Murphys
Melones
Sonora
Stockton
Chinese Camp
Big Oak Flat
Bear Valley
Hornitos
Mormon Bar
Oakland
San Francisco
Mono L.
Mt. Ritter
CALIFORNIA

The Gold Rush in California, 1848-59

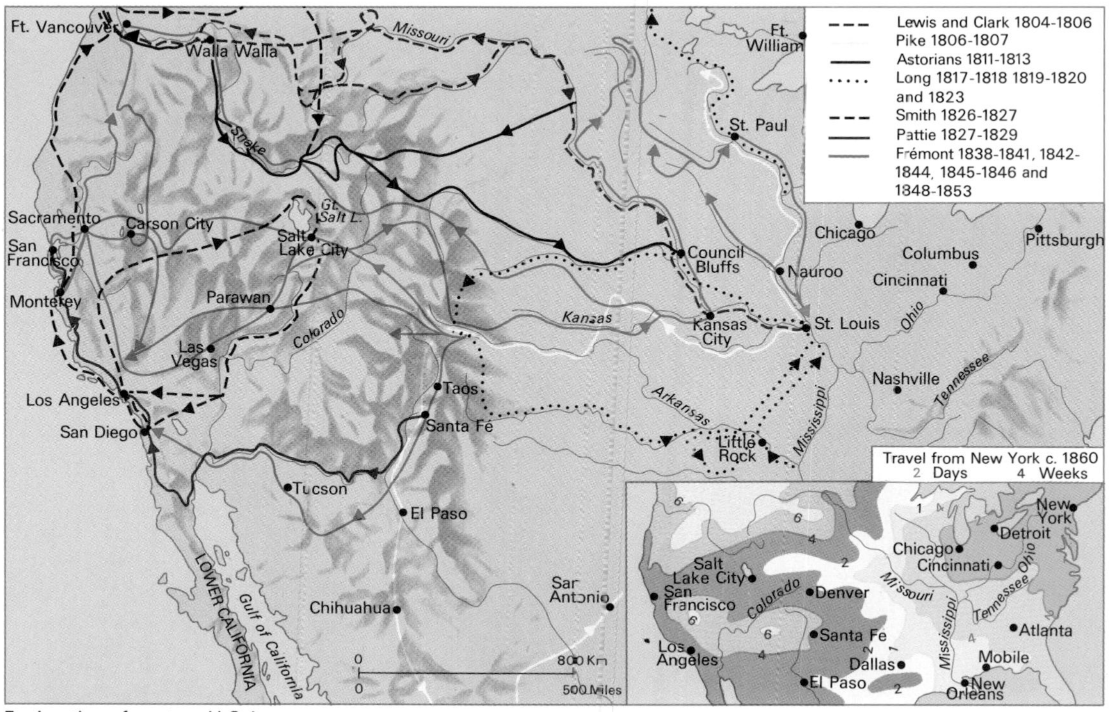

Lewis and Clark 1804-1806
Pike 1806-1807
Astorians 1811-1813
Long 1817-1818 1819-1820 and 1823
Smith 1826-1827
Pattie 1827-1829
Frémont 1838-1841, 1842-1844, 1845-1846 and 1848-1853
Ft. Vancouver
Walla Walla
Missouri
Ft. William
St. Paul
Snake
Sacramento
Carson City
Gt. Salt L.
Salt Lake City
San Francisco
Monterey
Parawan
Colorado
Las Vegas
Los Angeles
San Diego
Council Bluffs
Nauroo
Kansas
Kansas City
St. Louis
Chicago
Columbus
Pittsburgh
Cincinnati
Nashville
Taos
Santa Fe
Arkansas
Little Rock
Tucson
El Paso
Chihuahua
San Antonio
LOWER CALIFORNIA
Gulf of California
800Km
500Miles
Travel from New York c. 1860
2 Days
4 Weeks
New York
Detroit
Chicago
Cincinnati
Salt Lake City
San Francisco
Denver
Los Angeles
Santa Fe
Dallas
El Paso
Atlanta
Mobile
New Orleans

Exploration of western U.S.A.

Emigrants to the west

THE PACIFIC

By the mid-18th century, much of the world had been explored, advances in science having made the task easier. (See photographs of **a quadrant** and **chronometer used by Cook**.) But the Pacific still offered a challenge. Carteret managed to traverse this ocean in 1765 despite having a very poor ship. Two years later, Bougainville followed the same route, becoming the first Frenchman to sail around the world. Most notable of the **explorers of the Pacific** was **Captain James Cook**, an Englishman who led three expeditions, the last of which ended in his death in Hawaii. (See painting, **Death of Cook**, below.) Cook had landed on the east coast of Australia in 1770, and **Bass and Flinders** continued the exploration of this continent some 30 years later. The smallest map below shows its **New South Wales** region.

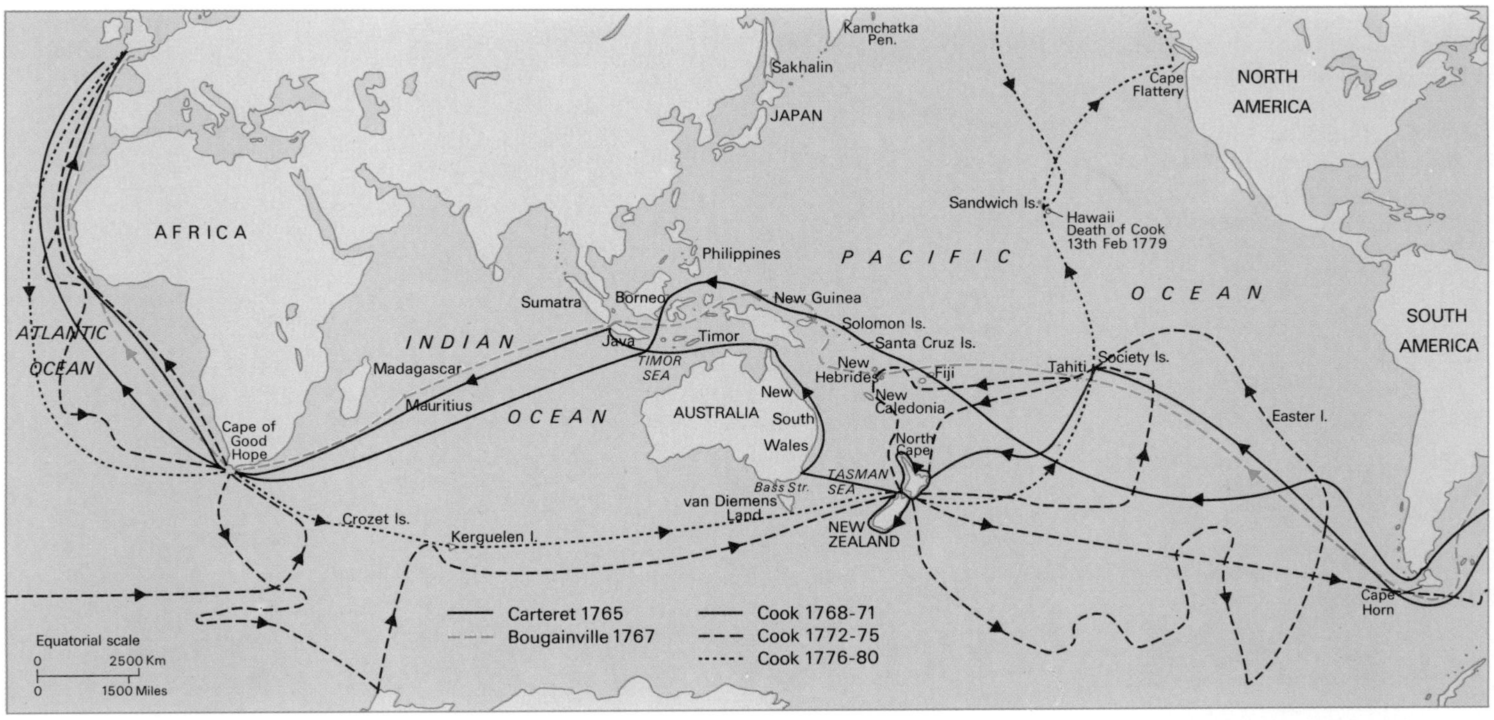

Kamchatka Pen.
Sakhalin
JAPAN
Cape Flattery
NORTH AMERICA
Sandwich Is.
Hawaii
Death of Cook
13th Feb 1779
AFRICA
Philippines
P A C I F I C
O C E A N
SOUTH AMERICA
Sumatra
Borneo
New Guinea
Solomon Is.
Santa Cruz Is.
ATLANTIC OCEAN
I N D I A N
O C E A N
Java
Timor
TIMOR SEA
Madagascar
Mauritius
New Hebrides
Fiji
Tahiti
Society Is.
New Caledonia
Easter I.
AUSTRALIA
New South Wales
Cape of Good Hope
North Cape
TASMAN SEA
Bass Str.
van Diemens Land
NEW ZEALAND
Crozet Is.
Kerguelen I.
Cape Horn
Carteret 1765
Bougainville 1767
Cook 1768-71
Cook 1772-75
Cook 1776-80
Equatorial scale
0 2500 Km
0 1500 Miles

Explorers of the Pacific

Chronometer used by Cook

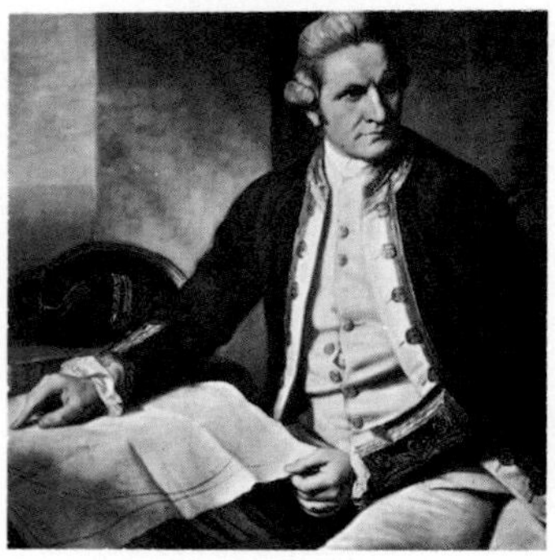
Captain James Cook

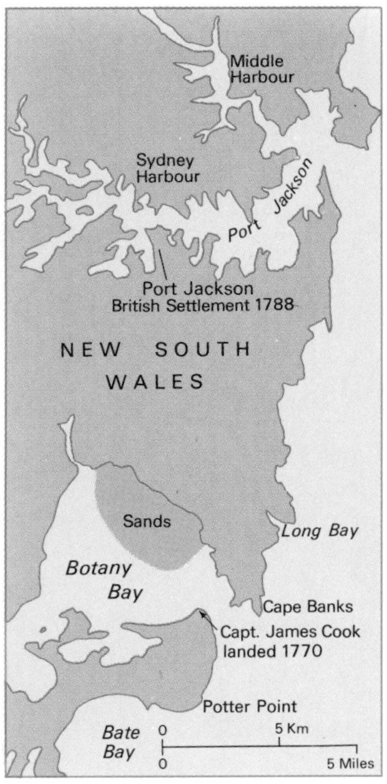

Middle Harbour
Sydney Harbour
Port Jackson
Port Jackson
British Settlement 1788
NEW SOUTH WALES
Sands
Long Bay
Botany Bay
Cape Banks
Capt. James Cook landed 1770
Potter Point
Bate Bay
0 5 Km
0 5 Miles

New South Wales

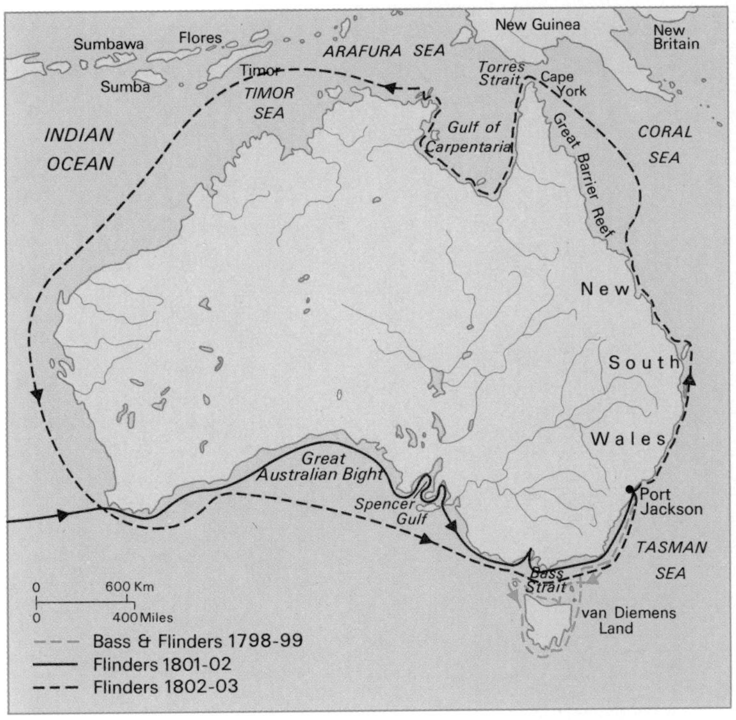

Sumbawa
Flores
ARAFURA SEA
New Guinea
New Britain
Sumba
Timor
TIMOR SEA
Torres Strait
Cape York
INDIAN OCEAN
Gulf of Carpentaria
Great Barrier Reef
CORAL SEA
New South Wales
Great Australian Bight
Spencer Gulf
Port Jackson
TASMAN SEA
Bass Strait
van Diemens Land
0 600 Km
0 400 Miles
Bass & Flinders 1798-99
Flinders 1801-02
Flinders 1802-03

Bass and Flinders

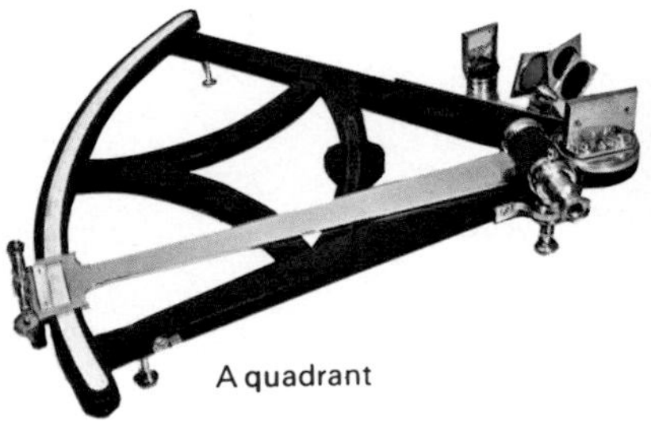
A quadrant

Death of Cook

AUSTRALIA AND NEW ZEALAND

During the 19th century, many travelers were involved in the exploration of Australia. The Blue Mountains were a formidable barrier. **A journey through the Blue Mountains** by Evans, one of the first to cross them, is shown on the map below. The main obstacles to exploration were lack of food and water. This is reflected on the map below showing the **exploration of Australia and New Zealand**.

The **aborigines**, the original inhabitants of Australia, probably came from Asia when there was a land bridge. The Maoris, natives of New Zealand, are Polynesians. They were divided into tribes, each with its own lands and chief. At the bottom left is **a Maori**.

The picture at the center below shows workers in an expedition **carrying supplies through the Blue Mountains**. The small map to the right of it, **Macquarie's Australia, 1820**, shows what was known of the continent at the time. At the bottom of the page, a painting of **Warburton's expedition, 1873**. All but two of the 17 camels taken had to be eaten before this party reached the west coast.

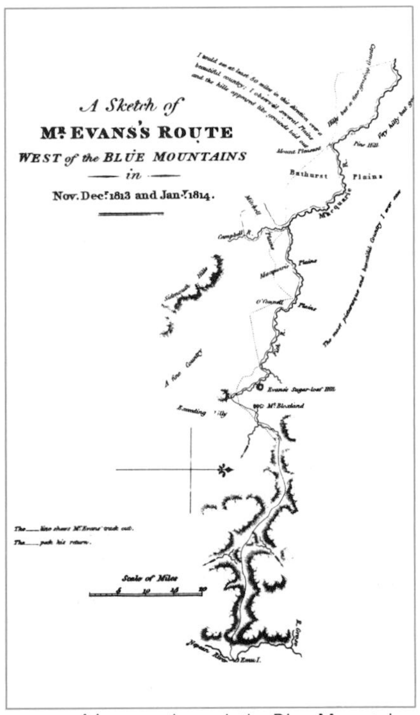
A Sketch of
Mr. EVANS'S ROUTE
WEST of the BLUE MOUNTAINS
in
Nov. Decr. 1813 and Jan. 1814.
Bathurst
Plains
A journey through the Blue Mountains

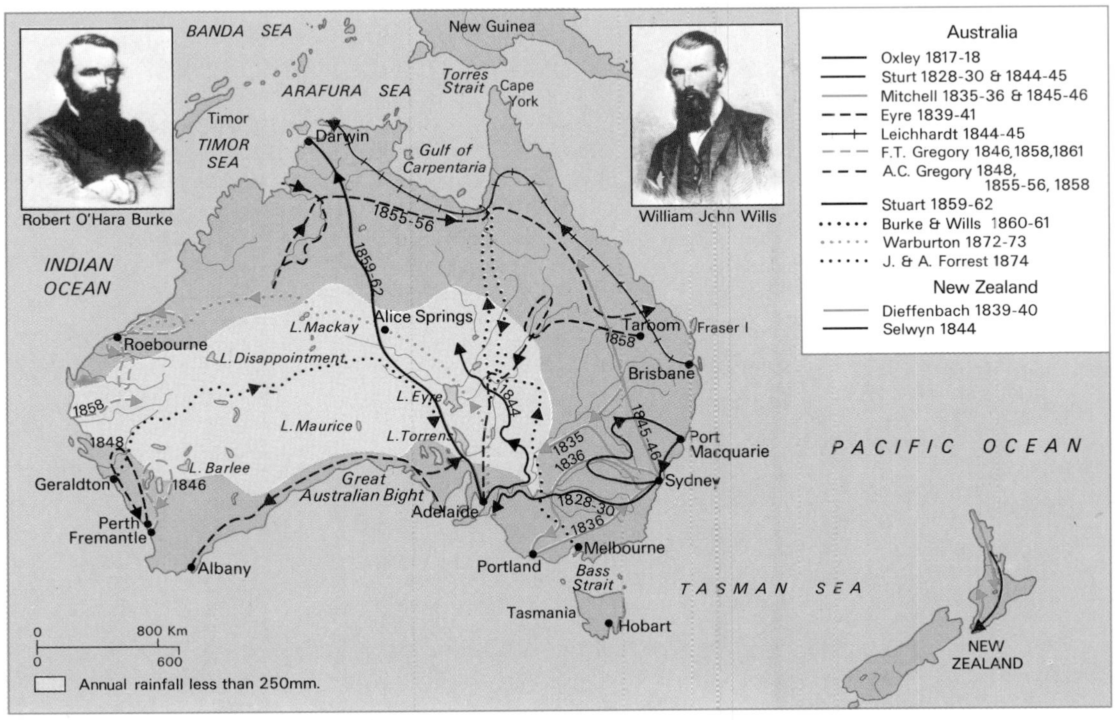
BANDA SEA
New Guinea
ARAFURA SEA
Torres Strait
Cape York
Timor
TIMOR SEA
Darwin
Gulf of Carpentaria
Robert O'Hara Burke
William John Wills
INDIAN OCEAN
1855-56
1859-62
Alice Springs
L. Mackay
Taroom
Fraser I
Roebourne
L. Disappointment
Brisbane
1858
L. Eyre
L. Maurice
L. Torrens
Port Macquarie
1848
L. Barlee
1846
Geraldton
Great Australian Bight
Adelaide
Sydney
PACIFIC OCEAN
Perth
Fremantle
Albany
Portland
Melbourne
Bass Strait
TASMAN SEA
Tasmania
Hobart
NEW ZEALAND
0 800 Km
0 600
Annual rainfall less than 250mm.
Australia
Oxley 1817-18
Sturt 1828-30 & 1844-45
Mitchell 1835-36 & 1845-46
Eyre 1839-41
Leichhardt 1844-45
F.T. Gregory 1846,1858,1861
A.C. Gregory 1848, 1855-56, 1858
Stuart 1859-62
Burke & Wills 1860-61
Warburton 1872-73
J. & A. Forrest 1874
New Zealand
Dieffenbach 1839-40
Selwyn 1844
Exploration of Australia and New Zealand

Aborigines

Carrying supplies through the Blue Mountains

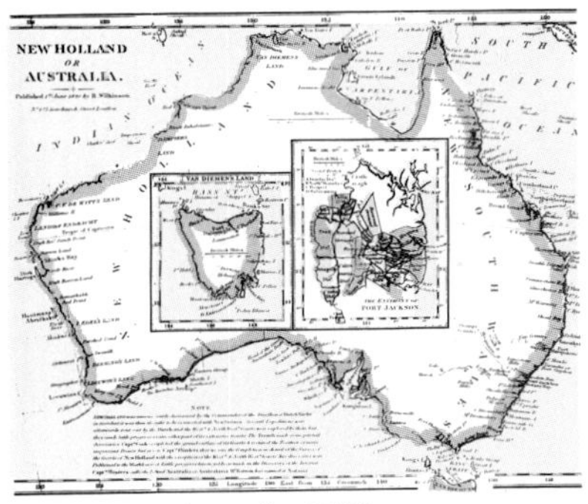
NEW HOLLAND
AUSTRALIA
Macquarie's Australia, 1820

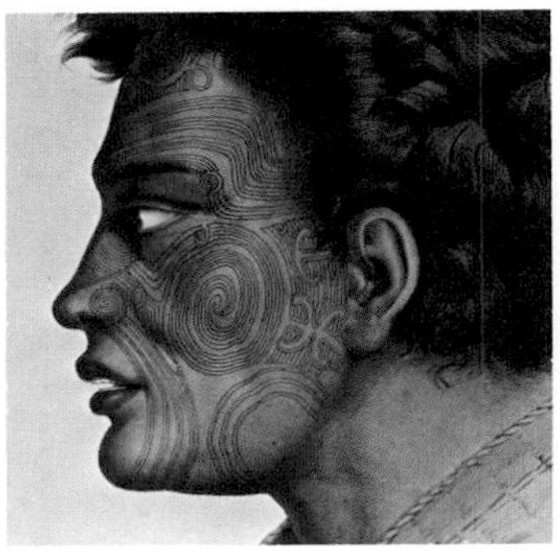
A Maori

Warburton's expedition, 1873

AFRICA

The narrow coastal belt of North Africa had close connections with Europe throughout history. The rest of Africa, however, remained unknown to Europeans until relatively recent years. This was partly because the Arabs and Moors had a firm hold on North and West Africa from about 800 on and partly because it was physically uninviting. Land near the coast was often either desert or swamp, and the few major river mouths did not offer easy access to the interior. The top map below, showing **colonial possessions to 1830**, tells the story.

The Portuguese explored the coast of West Africa in the 15th century but did not venture far inland. The slave trade had developed by this time, but as coastal tribes acted as agents, little was learned of inland Africa. **Mungo Park**, a Scot, was the first serious explorer in western Africa. Sent by the African Association to trace the source of the Niger, Park reached the river on his first journey in 1795. Ten years later, he canoed down the Niger for 1,000 miles, but was then drowned.

The photograph of the **Sahara Desert near Douz, Tunisia** and the painting showing **Mungo Park chased by a lion** give some idea of the hazards of the **exploration of West Africa**, depicted on the bottom map. The routes of Park are shown, as are those of Denham, Clapperton, and Oudney, who also sought the source of the Niger but from the north. Laing was sent via Timbuktu but was killed there by Tuareg nomads. Caillié was the first European to visit Timbuktu and leave it alive. He journeyed north from Guinea disguised as an Egyptian, traveling with caravans when possible. Lander and Clapperton approached the Niger from the Guinea coast, and later Lander discovered the Benue River and followed the Niger to its mouth.

The **exploration of south and central Africa**, as shown on the lower map on the opposite page, is dominated by one name — that of **David Livingstone**, whose portrait is shown at the right below along with that of **Sir Henry Morton Stanley**. Livingstone made extensive journeys as a missionary and sought to abolish the slave trade and to open other trade routes. In the course of his work, he explored the Zambesi River and searched for the sources of the Nile and Congo.

Mungo Park

Sahara Desert near Douz, Tunisia

Mungo Park chased by a lion

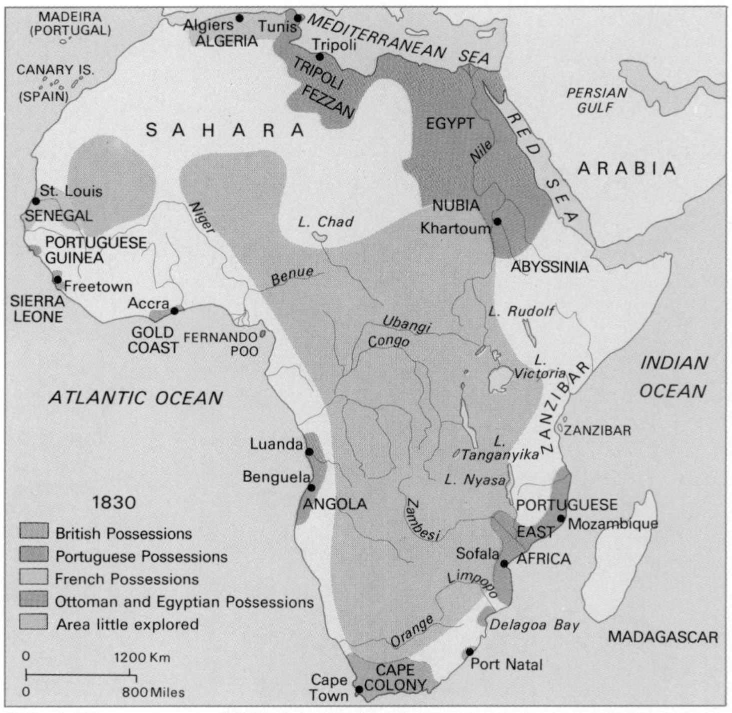

MADEIRA (PORTUGAL)
CANARY IS. (SPAIN)
Algiers
ALGERIA
Tunis
Tripoli
MEDITERRANEAN SEA
TRIPOLI
FEZZAN
SAHARA
EGYPT
RED SEA
PERSIAN GULF
ARABIA
St. Louis
SENEGAL
PORTUGUESE GUINEA
Freetown
SIERRA LEONE
Accra
GOLD COAST
FERNANDO POO
Niger
L. Chad
Benue
NUBIA
Khartoum
Nile
ABYSSINIA
L. Rudolf
Ubangi
Congo
L. Victoria
INDIAN OCEAN
ZANZIBAR
ATLANTIC OCEAN
Luanda
Benguela
ANGOLA
L. Tanganyika
L. Nyasa
Zambesi
PORTUGUESE EAST AFRICA
Mozambique
Sofala
Limpopo
Delagoa Bay
MADAGASCAR
Orange
Port Natal
Cape Town
CAPE COLONY
1830
British Possessions
Portuguese Possessions
French Possessions
Ottoman and Egyptian Possessions
Area little explored
0 1200 Km
0 800 Miles

Colonial Possessions to 1830

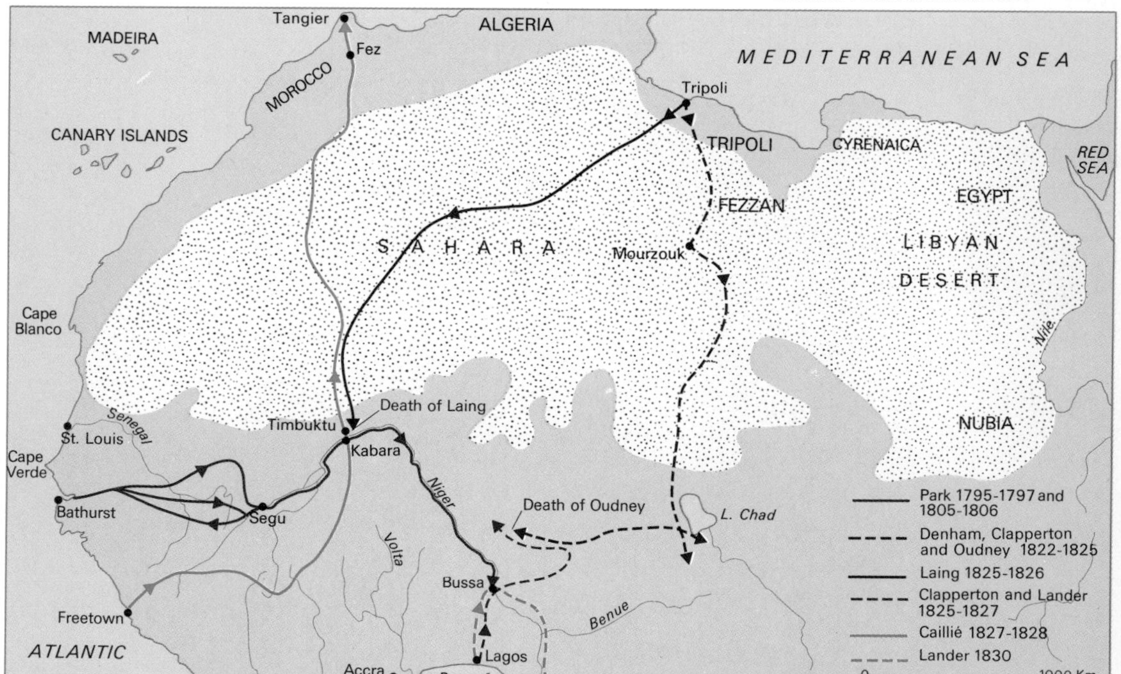

MADEIRA
Tangier
Fez
MOROCCO
ALGERIA
MEDITERRANEAN SEA
Tripoli
TRIPOLI
CYRENAICA
RED SEA
CANARY ISLANDS
FEZZAN
EGYPT
SAHARA
Mourzouk
LIBYAN DESERT
Nile
Cape Blanco
Senegal
St. Louis
Timbuktu
Death of Laing
Kabara
NUBIA
Cape Verde
Bathurst
Segu
Niger
Death of Oudney
L. Chad
Volta
Bussa
Benue
Freetown
ATLANTIC OCEAN
Accra
Lagos
Bay of Benin
Park 1795-1797 and 1805-1806
Denham, Clapperton and Oudney 1822-1825
Laing 1825-1826
Clapperton and Lander 1825-1827
Caillié 1827-1828
Lander 1830
0 1000 Km
0 600 Miles

Exploration of West Africa

David Livingstone

Sir Henry Morton Stanley

After **the historic meeting of Stanley and Livingstone at Ujiji** (shown below at the right), Stanley explored widely, mostly in the Congo. His routes are shown on the map below at the left. Others, less well known, also played a considerable part in the exploration of central Africa. The map shows the routes of Monteiro, Andersson, Porto, Cameron, and Thomson. Their travels spanned the period from 1831 to 1883.

The **search for the source of the Nile**, as shown on the map at the right, was one of the major chapters in 19th century exploration. Bruce sought the Nile through Ethiopia, and his was the first fully recorded exploration of the Blue Nile. **Sir Richard Burton** and **John Hanning Speke**, both shown below, traveled overland to Lake Tanganyika. Speke then visited Lake Victoria; which he assumed to be the source of the Nile. On a second visit with Grant, Speke followed the Nile downstream. He met **Sir Samuel Baker**, shown below, who subsequently discovered Lake Albert and the Murchison Falls.

Livingstone discovered and named **Victoria Falls** in 1855 when he was exploring the possibilities of the Zambesi as a trade route. In 1858, he was sent by the British government to lead an official exploration of the Zambesi and to investigate the possibilities for settlement and cotton cultivation. The painting at the bottom right depicts a scene on a tributary, the Shire River, with Livingstone's boat, the **Ma Robert, firing at a bull elephant**.

The Boers began **the Great Trek** in southern Africa when British rule displaced Dutch rule in the Cape area. The Boers were descendants of the original Dutch who had settled the Cape in the 17th century. They set off in search of freedom and cheap land. Like the American migrants moving westward, the Boers traveled as whole families and communities. They opened up many areas previously unknown to Europeans. However, they had to face and fight other claimants to the land, the Matabele and the Zulu. Many bloody battles took place, as shown on the small map at the center below.

John Hanning Speke meeting a Chief

Sir Richard Burton

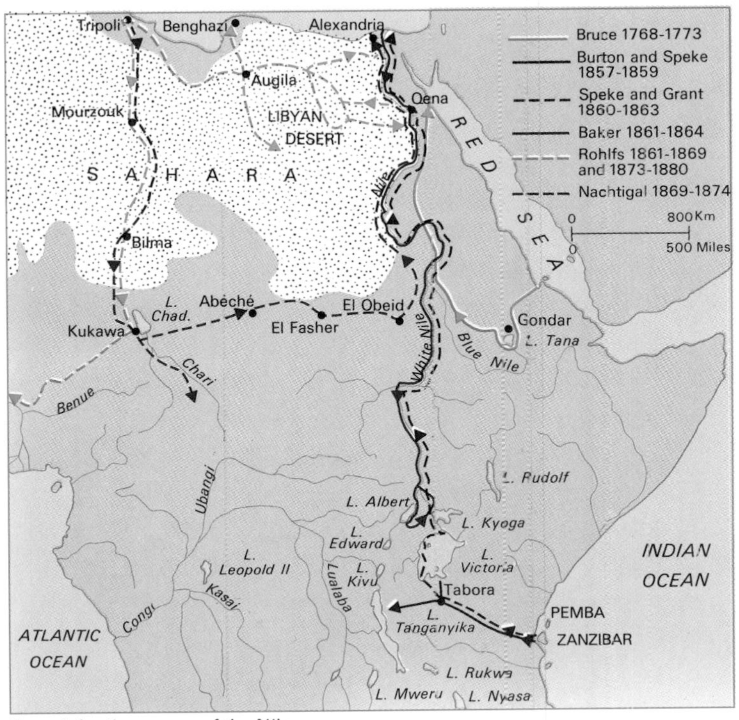

Tripoli
Benghazi
Alexandria
Augila
Mourzouk
LIBYAN DESERT
Qena
SAHARA
RED SEA
Nile
Bilma
L. Chad
Abéché
El Obeid
El Fasher
Kukawa
Gondar
L. Tana
Blue Nile
White Nile
Chari
Benue
Ubangi
L. Rudolf
L. Albert
L. Kyoga
L. Edward
L. Leopold II
L. Kivu
Lualaba
L. Victoria
Tabora
Kasai
Congo
L. Tanganyika
PEMBA
ZANZIBAR
L. Rukwa
L. Mweru
L. Nyasa
ATLANTIC OCEAN
INDIAN OCEAN
Bruce 1768-1773
Burton and Speke 1857-1859
Speke and Grant 1860-1863
Baker 1861-1864
Rohlfs 1861-1869 and 1873-1880
Nachtigal 1869-1874
0 800 Km
0 500 Miles

Search for the source of the Nile

Sir Samuel Baker

Victoria Falls

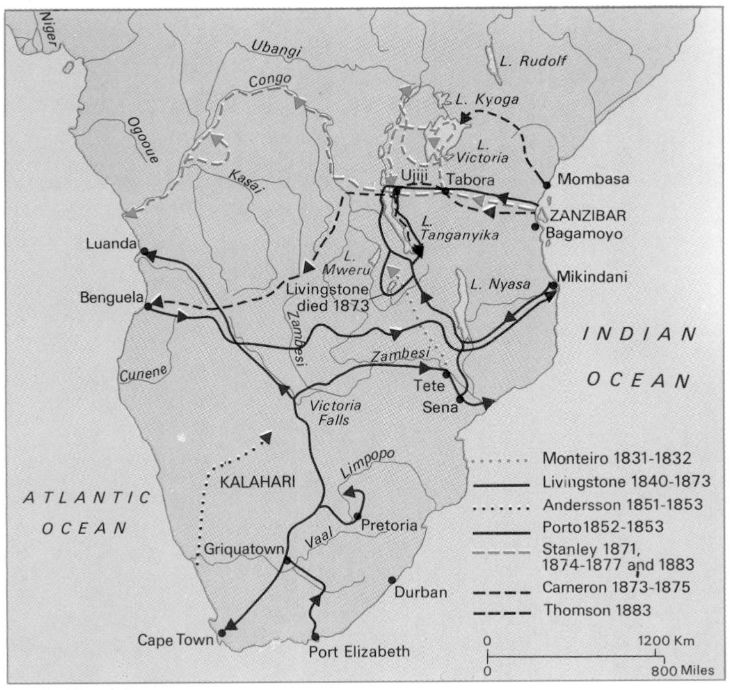

Niger
Ubangi
L. Rudolf
Congo
L. Kyoga
Ogooue
L. Victoria
Kasai
Ujiji
Tabora
Mombasa
ZANZIBAR
Bagamoyo
Luanda
L. Tanganyika
L. Mweru
Livingstone died 1873
L. Nyasa
Mikindani
Benguela
Zambesi
Cunene
Tete
Sena
Victoria Falls
INDIAN OCEAN
Limpopo
KALAHARI
ATLANTIC OCEAN
Pretoria
Griquatown
Vaal
Durban
Cape Town
Port Elizabeth
Monteiro 1831-1832
Livingstone 1840-1873
Andersson 1851-1853
Porto1852-1853
Stanley 1871, 1874-1877 and 1883
Cameron 1873-1875
Thomson 1883
0 1200 Km
0 800 Miles

Exploration of South and Central Africa

The historic meeting of Stanley and Livingstone at Ujiji

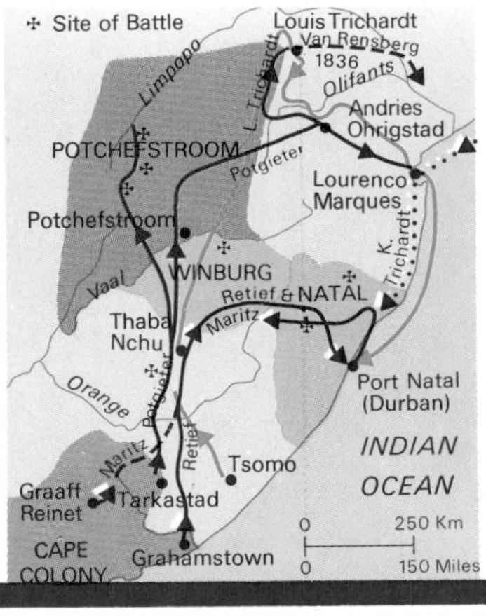

✣ Site of Battle
Louis Trichardt
Van Rensberg 1836
Limpopo
Olifants
Andries Ohrigstad
POTCHEFSTROOM
Potgieter
Lourenco Marques
Potchefstroom
Vaal
WINBURG
Retief & NATAL
Maritz
Thaba Nchu
Orange
Port Natal (Durban)
Tsomo
INDIAN OCEAN
Graaff Reinet
Tarkastad
CAPE COLONY
Grahamstown
0 250 Km
0 150 Miles

The Great Trek

The 'Ma Robert' on the Shire river firing at bull elephant

SCIENTIFIC EXPLORATION IN SOUTH AMERICA AND ASIA

Exploration continued in South America after the period of the conquistadores, much of it being done by the Jesuits. In the 18th century, scientific exploration began. Some expeditions surveyed the coasts, large tracts of Brazil, and the south. Others described or collected specimens of the rich plant life and animal. These expeditions paved the way for two giants of South American exploration, **Alexander von Humboldt** and **Charles Darwin**, portraits of whom are shown below. The top map at the right describes the **exploration of northern South America** by Humboldt and the explorers who followed him. Darwin explored the southeast coast, various islands, Chile, and Argentina.

Humboldt set out for Venezuela in 1799 and explored the Orinoco, confirming the link between the Orinoco and Negro rivers. In 1801, he journeyed up the Magdalena into Ecuador and the Andes, where he climbed to the top of **Mt. Chimborazo**.

Darwin sailed with **the Beagle**, shown below at the left, as its naturalist. In Patagonia, Darwin found the bones of many extinct animals and fossilized shells in the Chilean Andes at altitudes of more than 4,000 meters. The *Beagle* proceeded **to the Galápagos Islands** (see small map below), where he made his famous study of finches and other animals.

European exploration of Arabia came very late. Would-be explorers had to travel in disguise and speak perfect Arabic. The map at the bottom left shows the routes traveled by European **explorers in Arabia**. The map at the bottom right shows the routes of European **explorers in central Asia**. Tibet was difficult to penetrate, but Huc, Przhevalsky, and Younghusband traveled there in disguise. Between the maps, at the right are: **desert near Rifaa, Bahrain** and **Mongol camp in the Steppes c. 1800**.

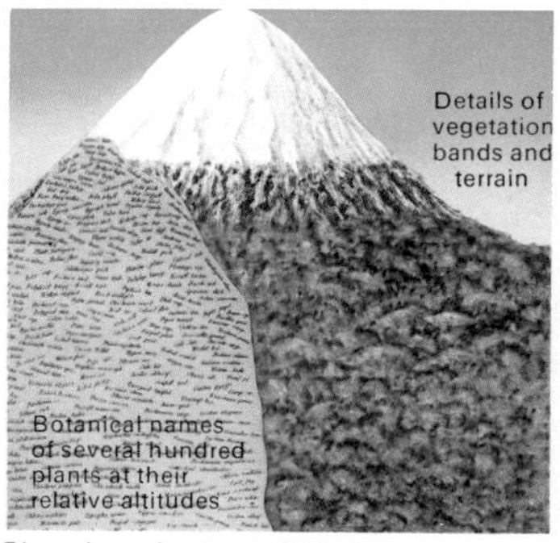
Details of vegetation bands and terrain
Botanical names of several hundred plants at their relative altitudes
Showing plants on Chimborazo

Alexander von Humboldt

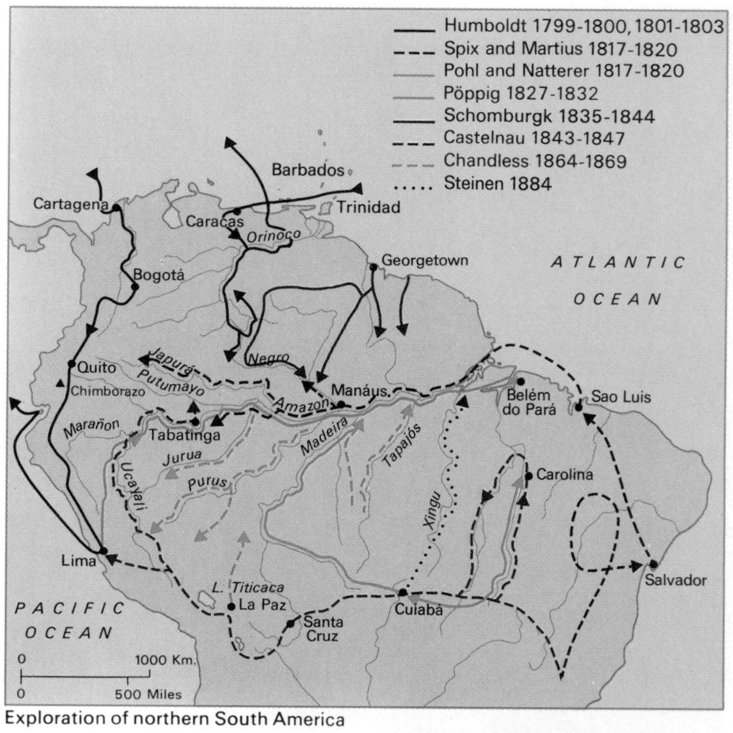
Humboldt 1799-1800, 1801-1803
Spix and Martius 1817-1820
Pohl and Natterer 1817-1820
Pöppig 1827-1832
Schomburgk 1835-1844
Castelnau 1843-1847
Chandless 1864-1869
Steinen 1884
Barbados
Trinidad
Cartagena
Caracas
Orinoco
Georgetown
ATLANTIC OCEAN
Bogotá
Quito
Chimborazo
Japurá
Putumayo
Negro
Manáus
Amazon
Belém do Pará
Sao Luis
Marañon
Tabatinga
Jurua
Madeira
Tapajós
Purus
Ucayali
Xingu
Carolina
Lima
Salvador
L. Titicaca
La Paz
Santa Cruz
Cuiabá
PACIFIC OCEAN
1000 Km.
500 Miles
Exploration of northern South America

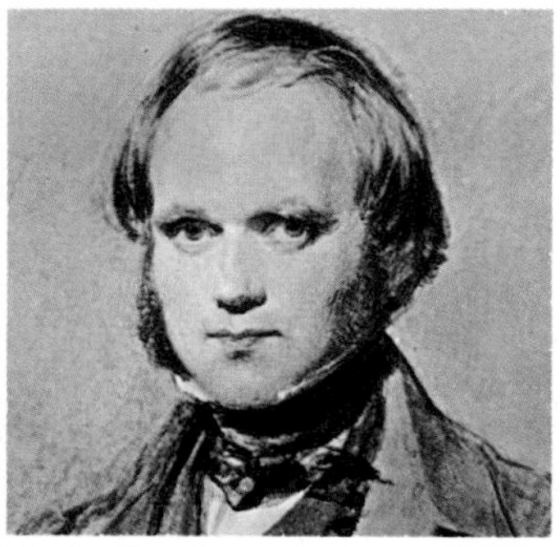
Charles Darwin

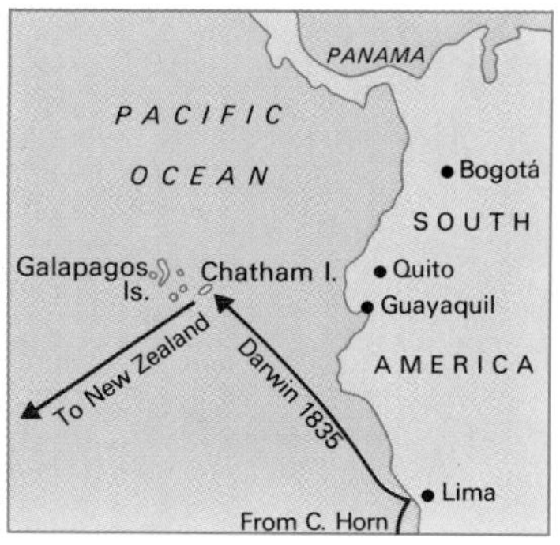
PANAMA
PACIFIC OCEAN
Bogotá
SOUTH
AMERICA
Galapagos Is.
Chatham I.
Quito
Guayaquil
To New Zealand
Darwin 1835
Lima
From C. Horn
To the Galapagos Islands

The 'Beagle' laid ashore in Patagonia

Desert near Rifaa, Bahrain

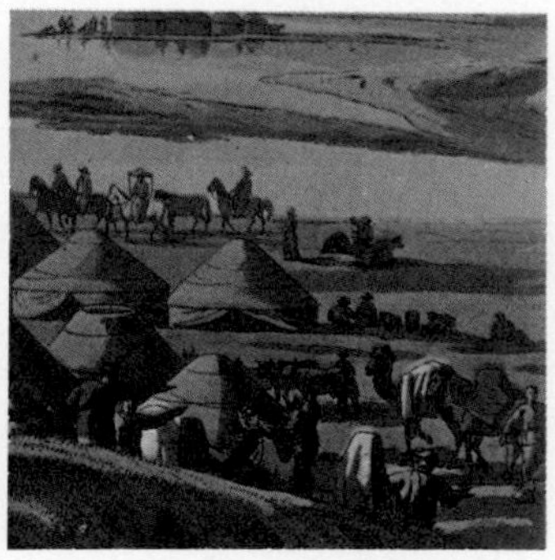
Mongol Camp in the Steppes c.1800

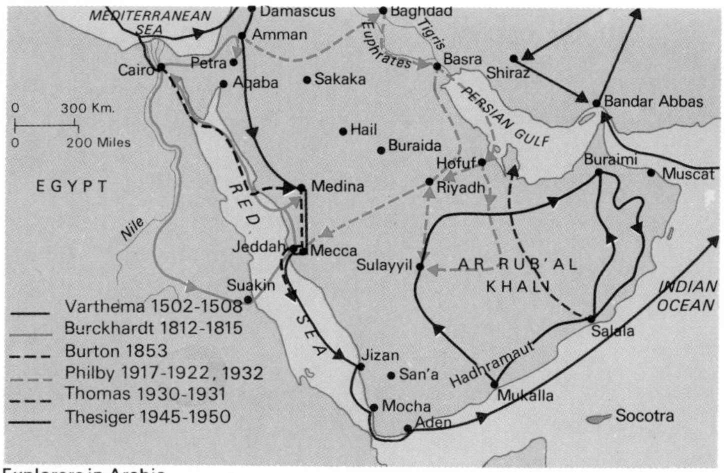
MEDITERRANEAN SEA
Damascus
Baghdad
Amman
Euphrates
Tigris
Cairo
Petra
Basra
Shiraz
Aqaba
Sakaka
PERSIAN GULF
Bandar Abbas
300 Km.
200 Miles
Hail
Buraida
Hofuf
Buraimi
Muscat
EGYPT
RED SEA
Medina
Riyadh
Nile
Jeddah
Mecca
Sulayyil
AR RUB'AL KHALI
INDIAN OCEAN
Suakin
Varthema 1502-1508
Burckhardt 1812-1815
Burton 1853
Philby 1917-1922, 1932
Thomas 1930-1931
Thesiger 1945-1950
Jizan
San'a
Hadhramaut
Salala
Mocha
Aden
Mukalla
Socotra
Explorers in Arabia

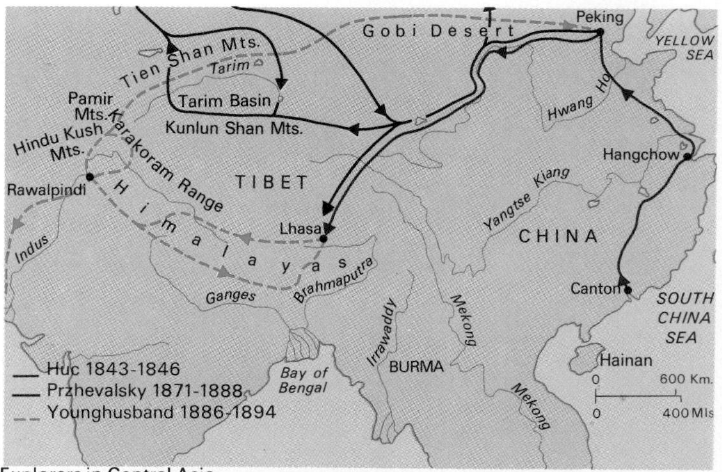
Peking
Gobi Desert
YELLOW SEA
Tien Shan Mts.
Tarim
Tarim Basin
Pamir Mts.
Hindu Kush Mts.
Karakoram Range
Kunlun Shan Mts.
Hwang Ho
Hangchow
Rawalpindi
TIBET
Himalayas
Yangtse Kiang
Indus
Lhasa
CHINA
Ganges
Brahmaputra
Canton
SOUTH CHINA SEA
Huc 1843-1846
Przhevalsky 1871-1888
Younghusband 1886-1894
Bay of Bengal
Irrawaddy
BURMA
Mekong
Hainan
600 Km.
400 Mls
Explorers in Central Asia

POLAR EXPLORATION

Interest in **Arctic exploration** revived in the 19th century. Then several English explorers — Parry, Ross, and Franklin — renewed the search for the northwest passage. In 1879, a Swede named Nordenskjöld found the northwest passage. In 1893, a Norwegian named Nansen built **the Fram** specially to withstand ice pressure. He thought it would drift with the ice, which it did (see below), but not toward the Pole. **Roald Amundsen** penetrated the northwest passage in 1903, and in 1909 **Admiral Robert Peary**, an American, reached the Pole. The painting at the right below depicts **Peary's race to the North Pole**.

The first person to fly over the North Pole was U.S. Navy Commander Richard Byrd, in 1926. A few days later, Amundsen and Nobile flew over the Pole in the airship *Norge*. Amundsen died in 1928 while searching for Nobile, who had crashed near the Pole in another airship. The first attempt to travel under the Pole was in 1931. This was unsuccessful; but, in 1958, the American nuclear submarine *Nautilus* achieved this goal.

Antarctic exploration started in 1773 when Cook crossed the Antarctic Circle. Later explorers established that Antarctica is a land mass and not a frozen sea like the Arctic. During the 19th century, many nations sent scientific expeditions to Antarctica, after which came the race to the South Pole. **Sir Ernest Shackleton** almost reached the Pole in 1908, and then **Captain Robert Falcon Scott** set out for it in 1910. Amundsen joined the race and reached the Pole in December 1911, one month before Scott arrived. The British Commonwealth Transantarctic Expedition of 1955-58 crossed from the Weddell Sea to the Ross Sea using vehicles such as the one shown in the photograph below: the **Sno-cat on Transantarctic Expedition**. After the end of World War I, many conflicting claims to sovereignty in Antarctica were made. But in 1961, a thirty-year treaty was signed, and the continent was left free for scientific work.

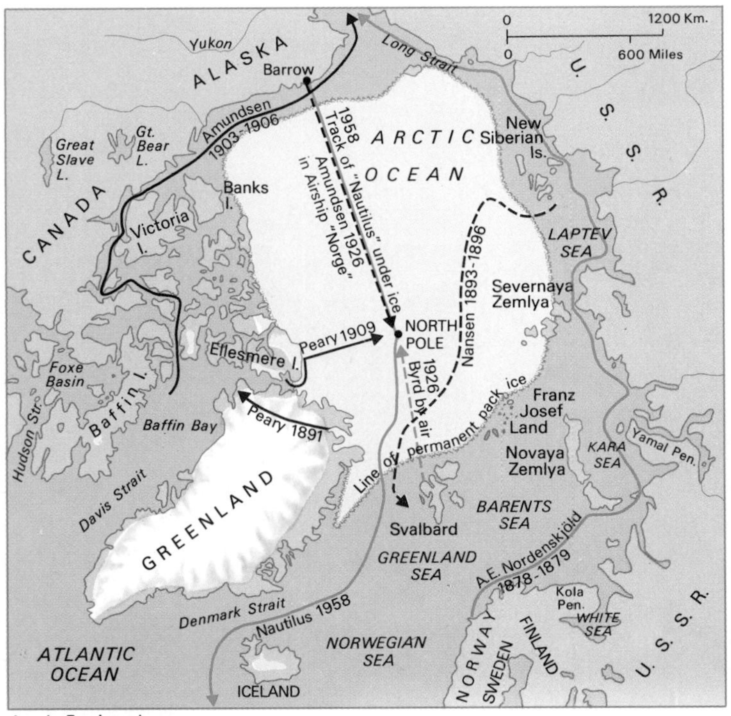

0
1200 Km.
0
600 Miles
Yukon
ALASKA
Barrow
Long Strait
U. S. S. R.
Amundsen 1903-1906
Great Slave L.
Gt. Bear L.
CANADA
1958 Track of "Nautilus" under ice
Amundsen 1926 in Airship "Norge"
ARCTIC OCEAN
New Siberian Is.
Banks I.
Victoria I.
LAPTEV SEA
Nansen 1893-1896
Severnaya Zemlya
Peary 1909
NORTH POLE
Ellesmere I.
Byrd by air 1926
Foxe Basin
Baffin I.
Baffin Bay
Peary 1891
Line of permanent pack ice
Franz Josef Land
Novaya Zemlya
Yamal Pen.
KARA SEA
Hudson Str.
Davis Strait
GREENLAND
BARENTS SEA
Svalbard
GREENLAND SEA
A.E. Nordenskjöld 1878-1879
Kola Pen.
WHITE SEA
Denmark Strait
Nautilus 1958
NORWEGIAN SEA
ATLANTIC OCEAN
ICELAND
NORWAY
SWEDEN
FINLAND

Arctic Exploration

The 'Fram' drifting with the polar ice

Admiral Robert Peary

Sir Ernest Shackleton

Sno-cat on Trans-Antarctic Expedition

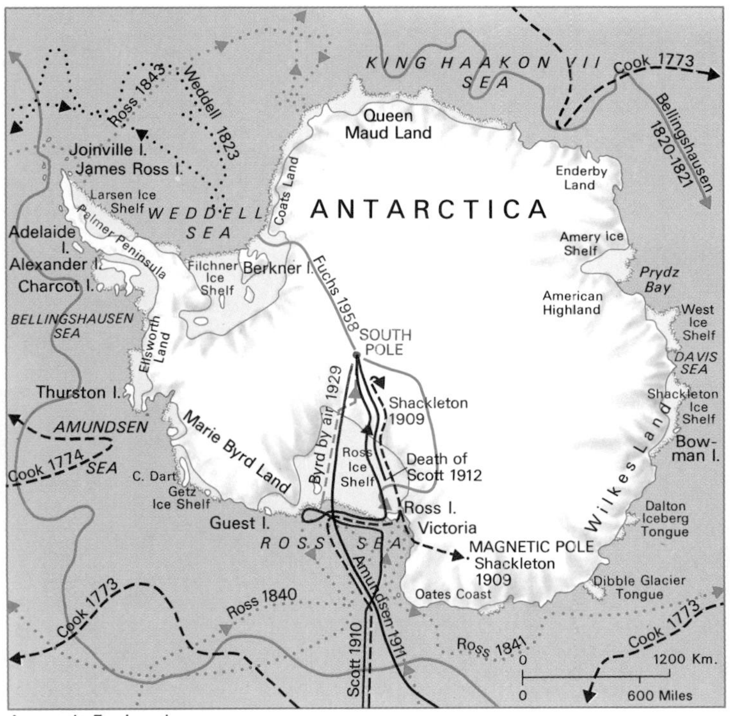

KING HAAKON VII SEA
Cook 1773
Ross 1843
Weddell 1823
Bellingshausen 1820-1821
Queen Maud Land
Joinville I.
James Ross I.
Enderby Land
Larsen Ice Shelf
WEDDELL SEA
Coats Land
ANTARCTICA
Adelaide I.
Palmer Peninsula
Amery Ice Shelf
Alexander I.
Filchner Ice Shelf
Berkner I.
Prydz Bay
Charcot I.
Fuchs 1958
American Highland
BELLINGSHAUSEN SEA
Ellsworth Land
SOUTH POLE
West Ice Shelf
DAVIS SEA
Thurston I.
Byrd by air 1929
Shackleton 1909
Shackleton Ice Shelf
AMUNDSEN SEA
Marie Byrd Land
Ross Ice Shelf
Death of Scott 1912
Bowman I.
Cook 1774
C. Dart
Getz Ice Shelf
Wilkes Land
Ross I.
Dalton Iceberg Tongue
Guest I.
Victoria
ROSS SEA
MAGNETIC POLE Shackleton 1909
Amundsen 1911
Cook 1773
Ross 1840
Oates Coast
Dibble Glacier Tongue
Scott 1910
Ross 1841
Cook 1773
0
1200 Km.
0
600 Miles

Antarctic Exploration

Peary's race to the North Pole

Roald Amundsen

Captain Robert Falcon Scott

HIGH MOUNTAINS, OCEAN DEPTHS AND SPACE

Mountains were first climbed for scientific interest — as when Humboldt made the ascent of Mt. Chimborazo. Climbing for pleasure started about 1850 and was at first mostly a British activity. By 1880, all the major Alpine peaks had been scaled. Many attempts were made on **Mt. Everest** before the success of Hillary and Tensing in 1953. The top map in the center column shows the **highest mountains and greatest ocean depths**.

Exploration of **continental shelves**, bottom map, and the deep depended on the invention of special apparatus. Diving bells were used early but, because of pressure problems, were restricted to shallow water. Rubber diving suits were invented in the 19th century; later, metal ones were found to be better in greater depths. The bathysphere was first used in 1930. It was superseded in 1960 by the **Piccards' bathyscaphe Trieste**.

Space exploration first utilized the forerunners of the **Apollo 11 space rocket**, bottom left. Russia's Yuri Gagarin was first to orbit the earth, in 1961, soon followed by John Glenn of the United States. A Russian also was first to take a **walk in space**, bottom right. But the Americans won the race to the moon when **Neil Armstrong**, top right, set foot on it in 1969. At bottom center are **earth rise seen from the moon** and **a satellite in orbit**.

Mount Everest

The Piccards' bathyscaphe 'Trieste'

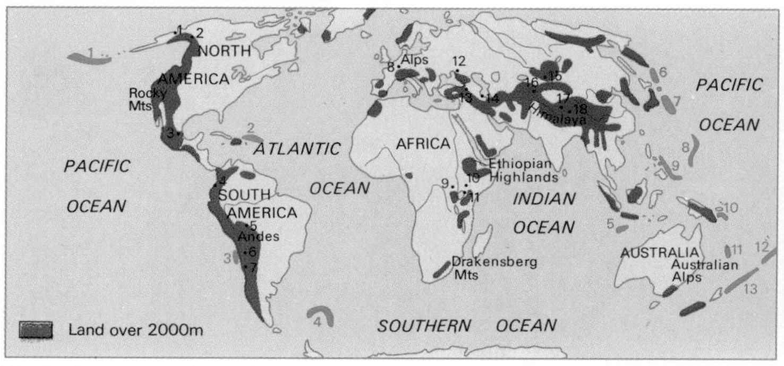
NORTH
AMERICA
Rocky
Mts
Alps
PACIFIC
OCEAN
ATLANTIC
OCEAN
AFRICA
Ethiopian
Highlands
SOUTH
AMERICA
Andes
INDIAN
OCEAN
AUSTRALIA
Australian
Alps
Drakensberg
Mts
SOUTHERN OCEAN
Land over 2000m

The highest mountains and greatest depths

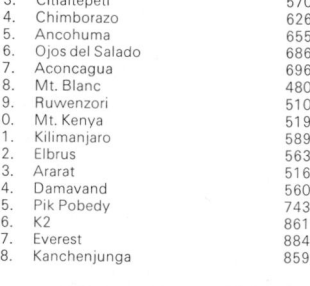

Mountain heights in metres

1.	Mt. McKinley	6194
2.	Mt. Logan	6050
3.	Citlaltepetl	5700
4.	Chimborazo	6267
5.	Ancohuma	6550
6.	Ojos del Salado	6863
7.	Aconcagua	6960
8.	Mt. Blanc	4807
9.	Ruwenzori	5109
10.	Mt. Kenya	5199
11.	Kilimanjaro	5895
12.	Elbrus	5633
13.	Ararat	5165
14.	Damavand	5604
15.	Pik Pobedy	7439
16.	K2	8611
17.	Everest	8848
18.	Kanchenjunga	8598

Satellite

The Apollo 11 rocket

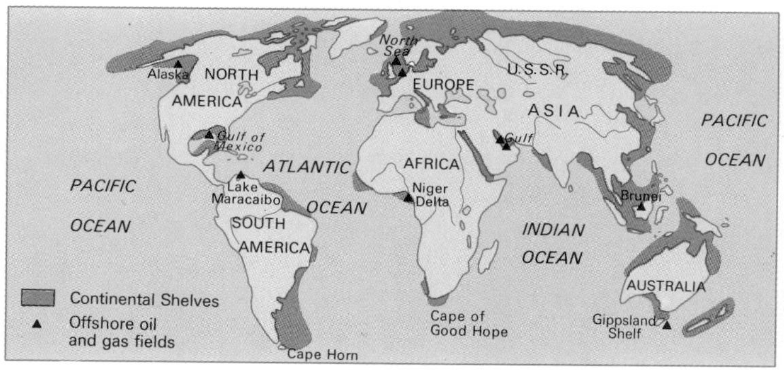
Alaska
NORTH
AMERICA
North
Sea
EUROPE
U.S.S.R.
ASIA
Gulf of
Mexico
Gulf
PACIFIC
OCEAN
ATLANTIC
OCEAN
AFRICA
Lake
Maracaibo
Niger
Delta
SOUTH
AMERICA
INDIAN
OCEAN
Brunei
AUSTRALIA
Continental Shelves
Offshore oil
and gas fields
Cape of
Good Hope
Gippsland
Shelf
Cape Horn

Neil Armstrong

Earth rising above the moon's horizon

The weightlessness of walking in space

Ocean depths in metres

1.	Aleutian Trench	7822
2.	Puerto Rico Trough	9200
3.	Bartholomew Deep	8055
4.	South Sandwich Trench	8428
5.	Java Trench	7450
6.	Kuril Trench	10,542
7.	Japan Trench	10,554
8.	Mariana Trench	11,022
9.	Mindanao Trench	10,497
10.	Planet Deep	9140
11.	New Hebrides Trench	7570
12.	Tonga Trench	10,822
13.	Kermadec Trench	10,047

CHART OF THE STARS

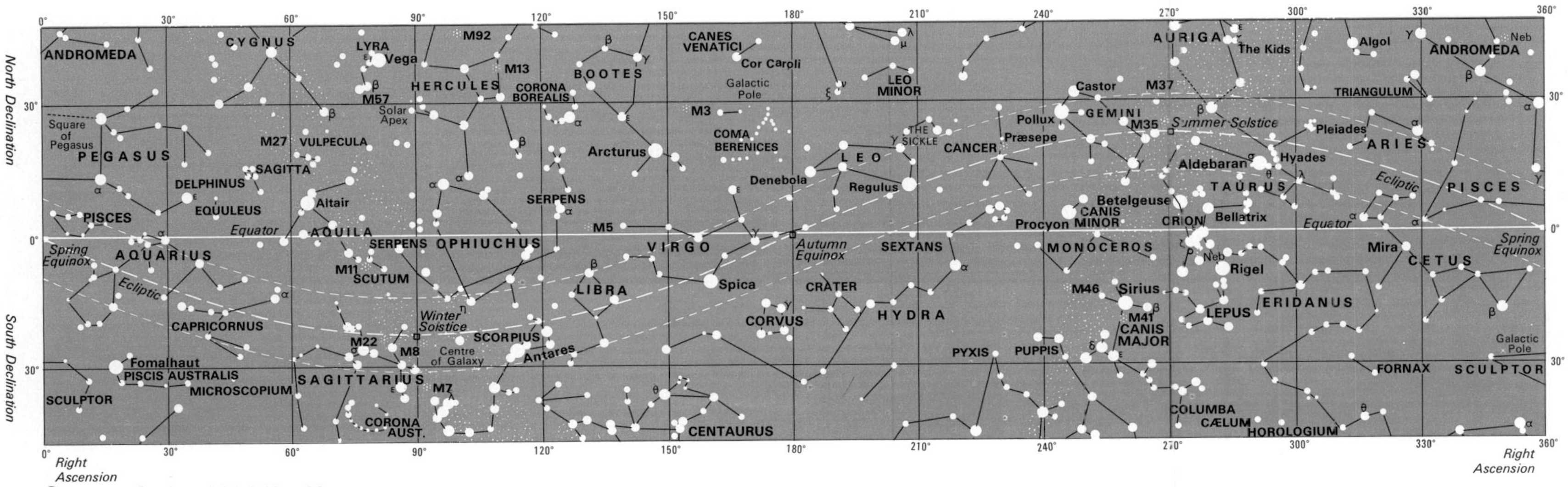
North Declination
South Declination
Right Ascension
Equator
Ecliptic
ANDROMEDA
CYGNUS
LYRA
Vega
M92
M13
HERCULES
M57
Solar Apex
CORONA BOREALIS
BOOTES
CANES VENATICI
Cor Caroli
Galactic Pole
M3
COMA BERENICES
Arcturus
LEO MINOR
THE SICKLE
CANCER
Præsepe
Pollux
Castor
GEMINI
M35
M37
AURIGA
The Kids
Algol
TRIANGULUM
Summer Solstice
Pleiades
ARIES
Hyades
Aldebaran
TAURUS
PISCES
Square of Pegasus
PEGASUS
M27
VULPECULA
SAGITTA
DELPHINUS
EQUULEUS
Altair
AQUILA
SERPENS
OPHIUCHUS
M5
VIRGO
Autumn Equinox
LEO
Regulus
Denebola
SEXTANS
Betelgeuse
CANIS MINOR
Procyon
ORION
Bellatrix
MONOCEROS
Rigel
Mira
CETUS
Spring Equinox
AQUARIUS
M11
SCUTUM
LIBRA
Spica
CRATER
CORVUS
HYDRA
M46
Sirius
M41
CANIS MAJOR
LEPUS
ERIDANUS
CAPRICORNUS
Winter Solstice
M22
M8
Centre of Galaxy
SCORPIUS
Antares
PYXIS
PUPPIS
FORNAX
SCULPTOR
Galactic Pole
Fomalhaut
PISCIS AUSTRALIS
MICROSCOPIUM
SAGITTARIUS
M7
CORONA AUST.
CENTAURUS
COLUMBA
CÆLUM
HOROLOGIUM

Stars of the Middle Heavens

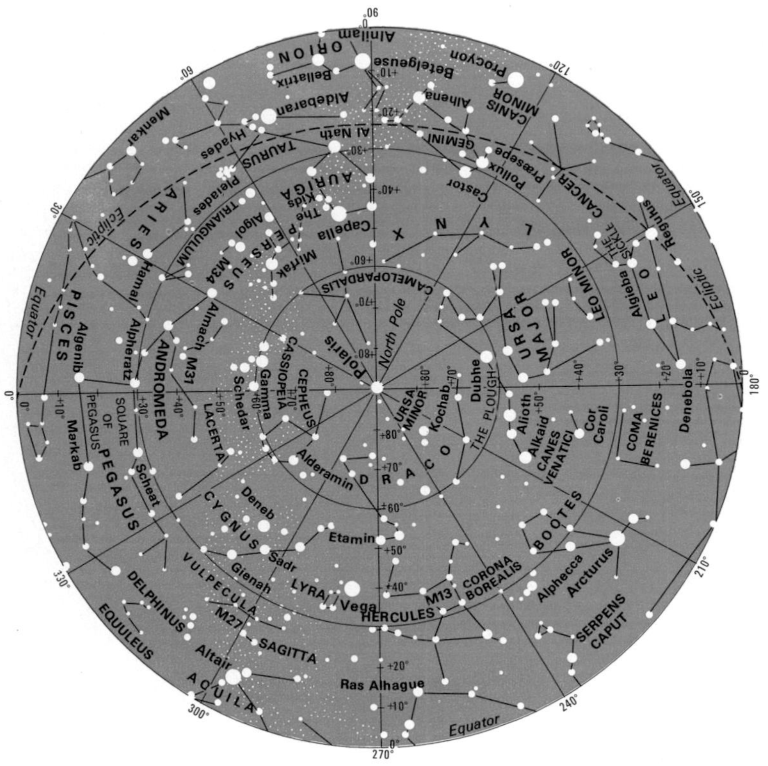
ORION
Betelgeuse
Bellatrix
Aldebaran
Procyon
CANIS MINOR
GEMINI
Hyades
TAURUS
Pleiades
ARIES
TRIANGULUM
AURIGA
Capella
The Kids
Castor
Pollux
Præsepe
CANCER
LYNX
Algol
PERSEUS
Mirfak
CAMELOPARDALIS
LEO MINOR
Regulus
LEO
PISCES
Hamal
Alpheratz
ANDROMEDA
M31
Almach
CASSIOPEIA
Polaris
North Pole
URSA MINOR
Kochab
Dubhe
THE PLOUGH
URSA MAJOR
Alioth
Alkaid
CANES VENATICI
Cor Caroli
COMA BERENICES
Denebola
SQUARE OF PEGASUS
PEGASUS
Markab
Scheat
LACERTA
CEPHEUS
Alderamin
DRACO
Schedar
Deneb
CYGNUS
Sadr
Etamin
LYRA
Vega
M13
HERCULES
CORONA BOREALIS
BOOTES
Alphecca
Arcturus
SERPENS CAPUT
DELPHINUS
VULPECULA
M27
SAGITTA
EQUULEUS
Altair
AQUILA
Ras Alhague
Equator
Ecliptic

Northern Stars

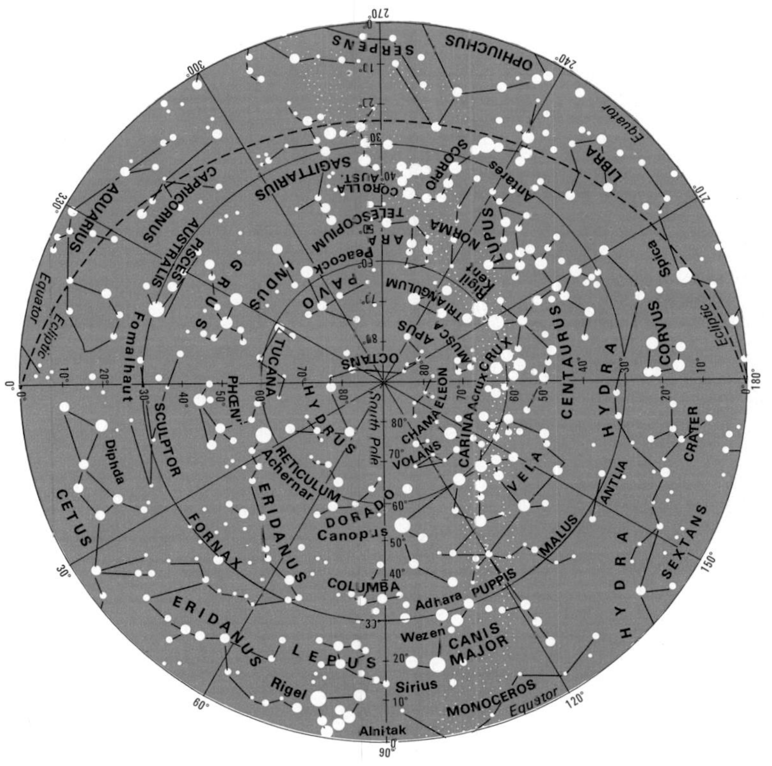
OPHIUCHUS
SERPENS
LIBRA
Equator
SCORPIO
Antares
SAGITTARIUS
CAPRICORNUS
AQUARIUS
CORONA AUST.
TELESCOPIUM
NORMA
LUPUS
ARA
PAVO
Peacock
TRIANGULUM
PISCIS AUSTRALIS
Fomalhaut
GRUS
INDUS
APUS
MUSCA
CRUX
CENTAURUS
Spica
CORVUS
OCTANS
TUCANA
PHOENIX
HYDRUS
South Pole
CHAMÆLEON
CARINA
VOLANS
HYDRA
CRATER
SCULPTOR
Diphda
CETUS
RETICULUM
Achernar
ERIDANUS
DORADO
Canopus
VELA
ANTLIA
SEXTANS
FORNAX
COLUMBA
Adhara
PUPPIS
MALUS
Wezen
CANIS MAJOR
LEPUS
Sirius
Rigel
Alnitak
MONOCEROS
Ecliptic

Southern Stars

THE SOLAR SYSTEM

The solar system is a minute part of one of the billions of galaxies that make up the universe. **Our galaxy** is represented in the top drawing at the right, with our **solar system** (S) lying 27,000 light years from its center. The system consists of a central sun with planets, moons, asteroids, comets, meteors, meteorites, dust, and gases in orbit around it. It is at least 4,700 million years old. As depicted at the bottom right, the sun's diameter is 109 times that of the earth.

S
Our galaxy

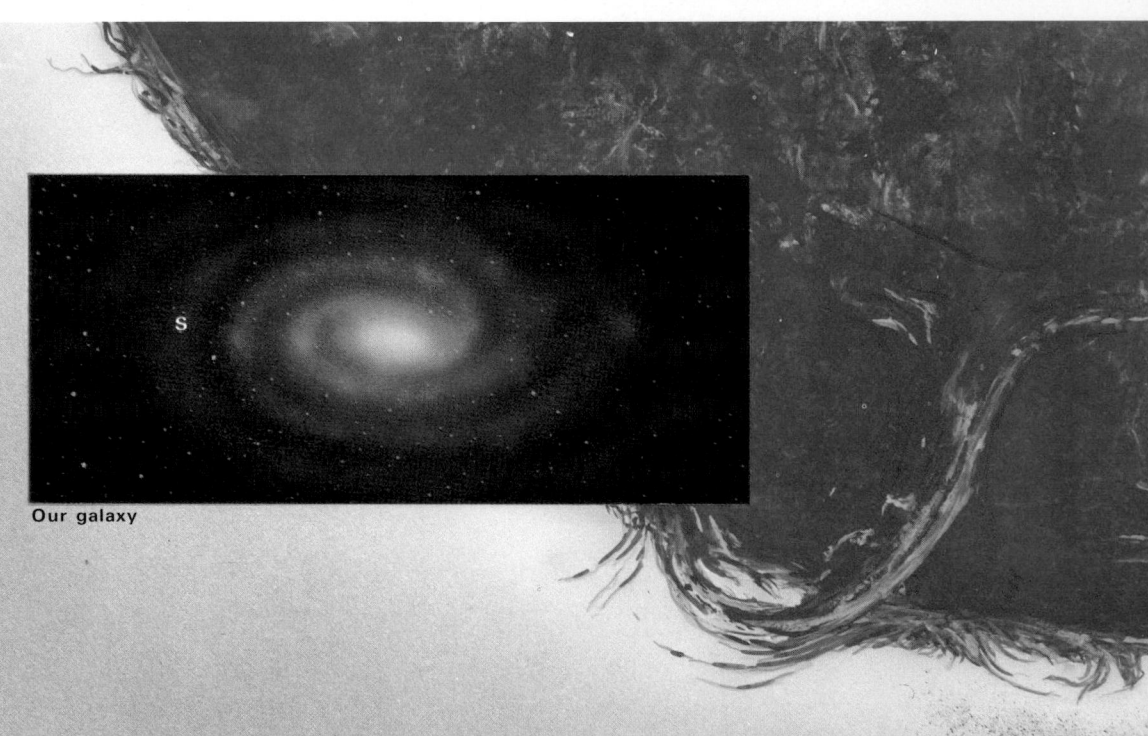

We can consider the solar system as having two parts: the **inner region planets** and the **outer region planets**. The inner planets are (from the sun outward): Mercury, Venus, Earth, and Mars. The outer ones are: Jupiter, Saturn, Uranus, Neptune, and Pluto.

Inner region planets

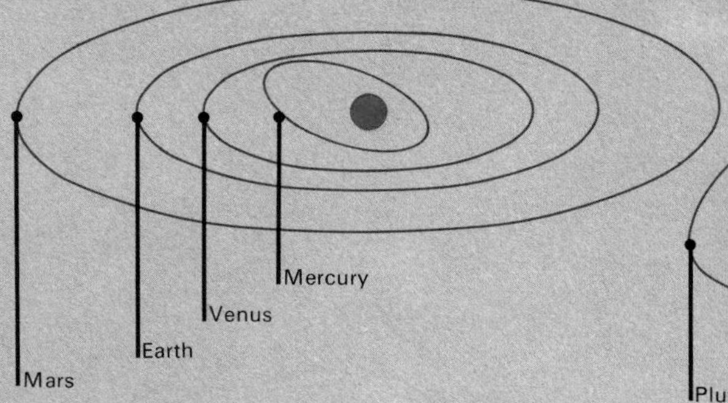
Mercury
Venus
Earth
Mars

Outer region planets

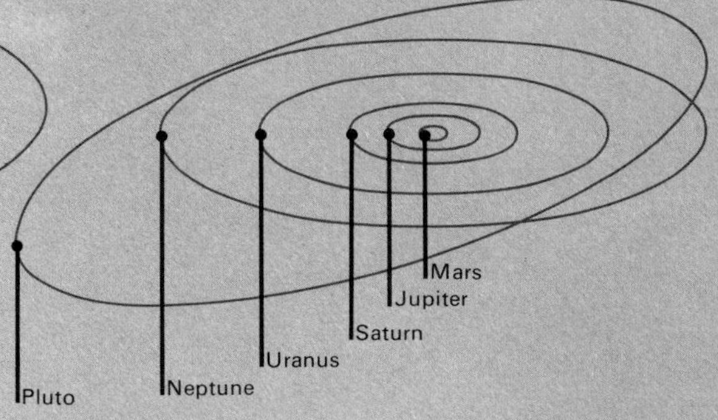
Mars
Jupiter
Saturn
Uranus
Neptune
Pluto

All the planets revolve around the sun in the same direction, and mostly in the same plane. The diagrams at the left show the planets' orbits; their paths are not perfectly circular.

The table below summarizes their dimensions and movements.

The interior of the sun has a temperature of about 15 million degrees Celsius, brought about by continuous thermonuclear fusion of hydrogen to helium. This immense energy is transferred by radiation to the surrounding layers of gas, the outer surface of which is called the chromosphere. Solar prominences, or flares, leap from the chromosphere, forming a diffuse corona. The corona can best be seen at times of **total solar eclipse**, as shown in the top photograph. The temperature of the sun's surface is calculated to be about 6,000°C. The bottom photograph shows the **surface of the sun** with sunspots prominent. Sunspots are sites of great disturbance.

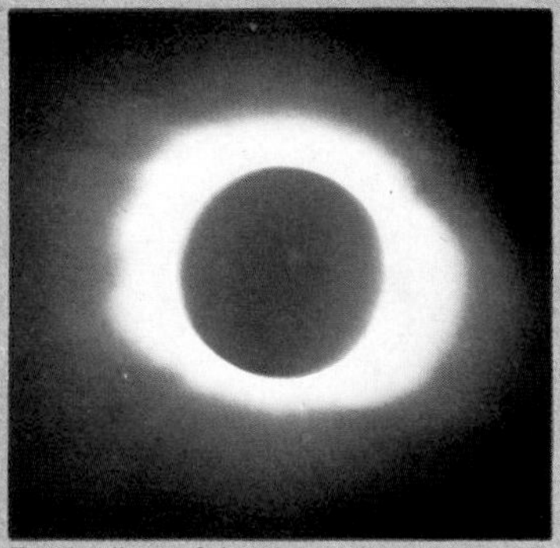
Total eclipse of the sun

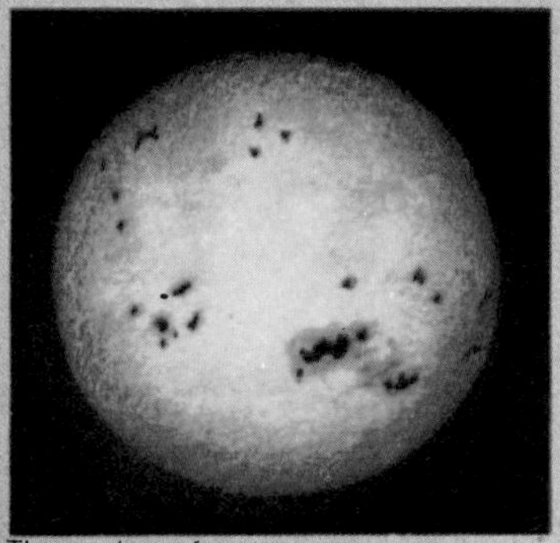
The sun's surface

	Equatorial diameter in km	Mass (earth=1)	Mean distance from sun in millions km	Mean radii of orbit (earth=1)	Orbital inclination	Mean sidereal period (days)	Mean period of rotation on axis (days)	Number of satellites
Sun	1 392 000	332 946	—	—	—	—	25·38	—
Mercury	4 878	0·05	57·9	0·38	7°	87·9	58·6	0
Venus	12 104	0·81	108·2	0·72	3°23'	224·7	243	0
Earth	12 756	1·00	149·6	1·00	—	365·2	0·99	1
Mars	6 794	0·10	227·9	1·52	1°50'	686·9	1·02	2
Jupiter	142 800	317·9	778·3	5·20	1°18'	4332·5	0·41	14 ?
Saturn	120 000	95·1	1 427	9·53	2°29'	10759·2	0·42	11
Uranus	52 000	14·5	2 869	19·17	0°46'	30684·8	0·45	5
Neptune	48 400	17·2	4 496	30·05	1°46'	60190·5	0·67	2
Pluto	3 000 ?	0·001	5 900	39·43	17°1'	91628·6	6·38	1 ?

The Sun's diameter is 109 times greater than that of the Earth.

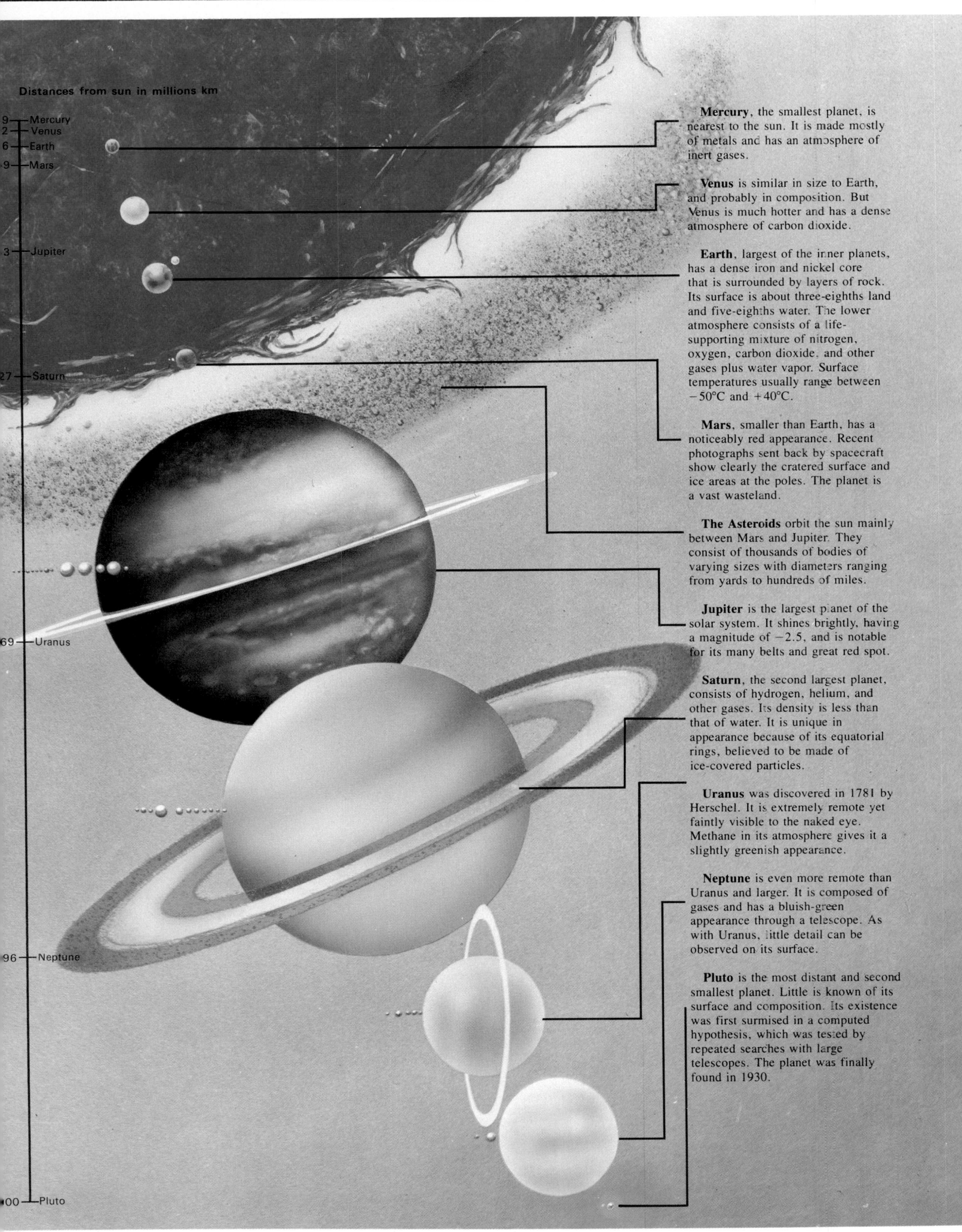

Distances from sun in millions km
9 Mercury
2 Venus
6 Earth
9 Mars
3 Jupiter
27 Saturn
69 Uranus
96 Neptune
00 Pluto

Mercury, the smallest planet, is nearest to the sun. It is made mostly of metals and has an atmosphere of inert gases.

Venus is similar in size to Earth, and probably in composition. But Venus is much hotter and has a dense atmosphere of carbon dioxide.

Earth, largest of the inner planets, has a dense iron and nickel core that is surrounded by layers of rock. Its surface is about three-eighths land and five-eighths water. The lower atmosphere consists of a life-supporting mixture of nitrogen, oxygen, carbon dioxide, and other gases plus water vapor. Surface temperatures usually range between −50°C and +40°C.

Mars, smaller than Earth, has a noticeably red appearance. Recent photographs sent back by spacecraft show clearly the cratered surface and ice areas at the poles. The planet is a vast wasteland.

The Asteroids orbit the sun mainly between Mars and Jupiter. They consist of thousands of bodies of varying sizes with diameters ranging from yards to hundreds of miles.

Jupiter is the largest planet of the solar system. It shines brightly, having a magnitude of −2.5, and is notable for its many belts and great red spot.

Saturn, the second largest planet, consists of hydrogen, helium, and other gases. Its density is less than that of water. It is unique in appearance because of its equatorial rings, believed to be made of ice-covered particles.

Uranus was discovered in 1781 by Herschel. It is extremely remote yet faintly visible to the naked eye. Methane in its atmosphere gives it a slightly greenish appearance.

Neptune is even more remote than Uranus and larger. It is composed of gases and has a bluish-green appearance through a telescope. As with Uranus, little detail can be observed on its surface.

Pluto is the most distant and second smallest planet. Little is known of its surface and composition. Its existence was first surmised in a computed hypothesis, which was tested by repeated searches with large telescopes. The planet was finally found in 1930.

THE EARTH

The **seasons, solstices, and equinoxes** are shown in the top drawing. The earth revolves around the sun once a year, rotating once daily on its axis. Its axis is inclined at 66.5° to the orbital plane and always points into space in the same direction. In summer, the North Pole (N) points toward the sun; in winter, it points away from the sun. At the spring and autumn equinoxes, day and night are of equal length.

The second drawing below compares the **length of day and night** in the northern and southern hemispheres. At the summer solstice in the northern hemisphere, the Arctic has total daylight, and the Antarctic total darkness. The opposite occurs at the winter solstice. At the equator, the length of day and night are almost equal all the year. At 30° latitude, the length of the day varies from about 14 to 10 hours and at 50°, from about 16 to 8 hours.

The diagrams in the third and fourth rows on the page show the **apparent path of the sun** at various latitudes in different seasons. In diagram A, at the equator; B, in mid-latitudes; C, at the Arctic Circle; and D, at the North Pole. At the North Pole, there is a six-month period of continuous daylight followed by six months of continuous darkness.

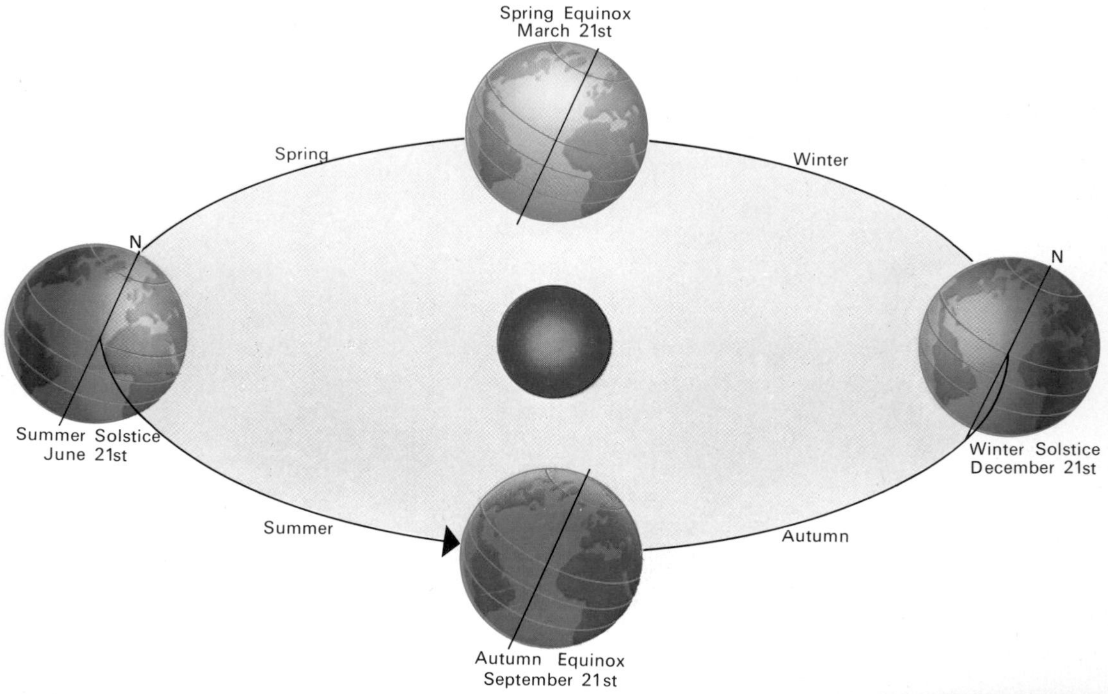

Spring Equinox
March 21st
Spring
Winter
N
N
Summer Solstice
June 21st
Winter Solstice
December 21st
Summer
Autumn
Autumn Equinox
September 21st

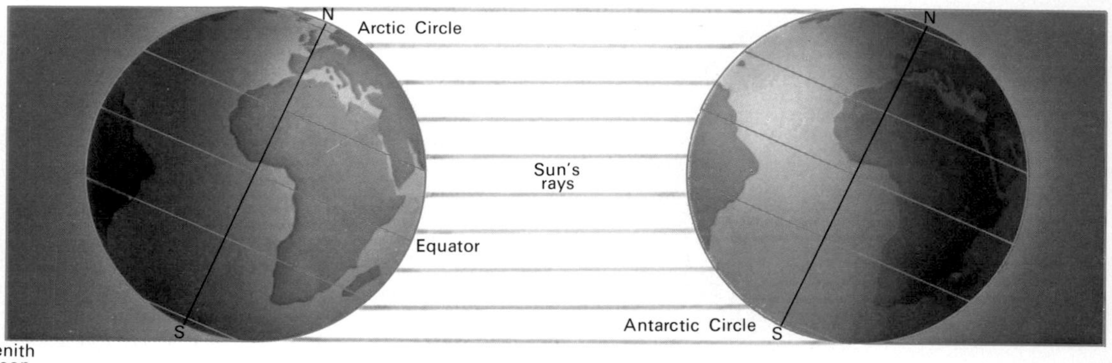

N
Arctic Circle
N
Sun's
rays
Equator
S
Antarctic Circle
S

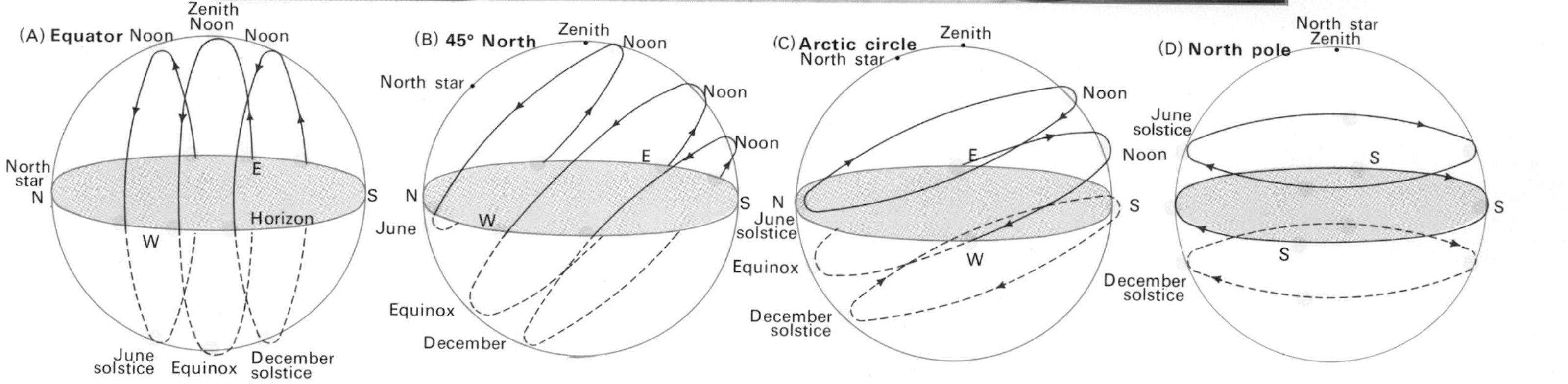

(A) Equator
Zenith
Noon
Noon
Noon
North
star
N
E
S
Horizon
W
June
solstice
Equinox
December
solstice
(B) 45° North
Zenith
Noon
North star
Noon
Noon
E
N
S
June
W
Equinox
December
(C) Arctic circle
Zenith
North star
Noon
E
Noon
N
June
solstice
S
Equinox
W
December
solstice
December
solstice
(D) North pole
North star
Zenith
June
solstice
Noon
S
S
S

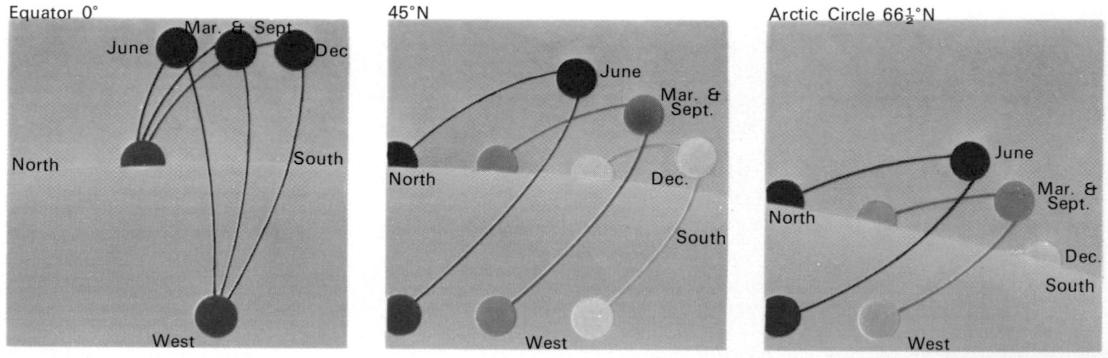

Equator 0°
June
Mar. & Sept.
Dec
North
South
West
45°N
June
Mar. &
Sept.
North
Dec.
South
West
Arctic Circle 66½°N
June
Mar. &
Sept.
North
Dec.
South
West

THE MOON

The moon rotates slowly, making one complete turn on its axis in just over 27 days. This rotation period corresponds to one **revolution of the moon around the earth** (top diagram). Thus, the moon always presents to us the same hemisphere or face. We never see the far side of the moon. The composite photograph beneath the diagram shows the **phases of the moon**, which are numbered to match the diagram. The interval between one full moon and the next is about 29½ days. The apparent changes in the shape of the moon arise from its changing position in relation to the earth.

The bottom drawing at the right depicts the relative **size of the moon and the earth**. The illustration above it shows the **landing sites of U. S. Apollo missions** 11 (Sea of Tranquility, 1969), 12 (Ocean of Storms, 1969), 14 (Fra Mauro, 1971), 15 (Hadley Rill, 1971), 16 (Descartes, 1972), 17 (Sea of Serenity, 1972). The astronauts had to cope with an environment devoid of water and atmosphere and temperatures approximating +200°C. The moon's mean diameter is 3,473 km. Its mass approximates 1/81 that of the earth. Its distance from the earth varies from 356,410 to 406,685 km.

The top diagram on the lower half of the page depicts **eclipses of the sun and moon**. When the moon passes between the sun and the earth, it causes a partial eclipse (1) of the sun if the earth passes through the moon's outer shadow (P). It causes a total eclipse (2) if the inner cone shadow crosses the earth's surface. In a lunar eclipse, the earth's shadow crosses the moon and gives either a total or partial eclipse.

The bottom diagram shows **the moon's effect on tides**. When solar and lunar gravitational forces pull together near new and full moon, high spring tides result. At the quarters, neap tides occur.

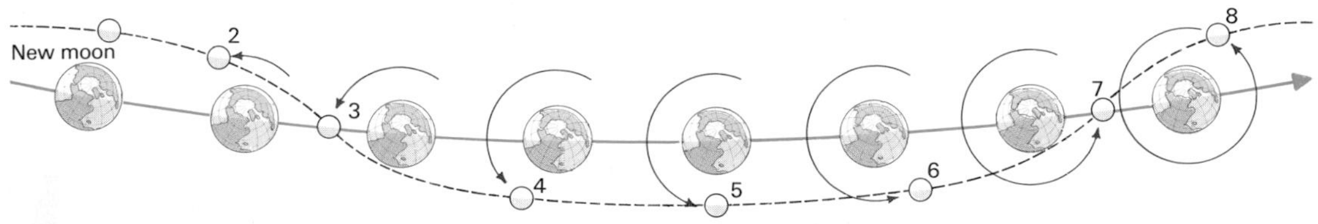
New moon
2
3
4
5
6
7
8

15
17
12
14
16
11

Landings on the Moon

Apollo 11 Sea of Tranquility (1°N 23°E) 1969
Apollo 12 Ocean of Storms (3°S 24°W) 1969
Apollo 14 Fra Mauro (4°S 17°W) 1971
Apollo 15 Hadley Rill (25°N 4°E) 1971
Apollo 16 Descartes (9°S 15°E) 1972
Apollo 17 Sea of Serenity (20°N 31°E) 1972

Crescent moon (2)
Half moon, first quarter (3)
Gibbous moon (4)
Full moon (5)
The waning moon (6)
Half moon, last quarter (7)
The old moon (8)

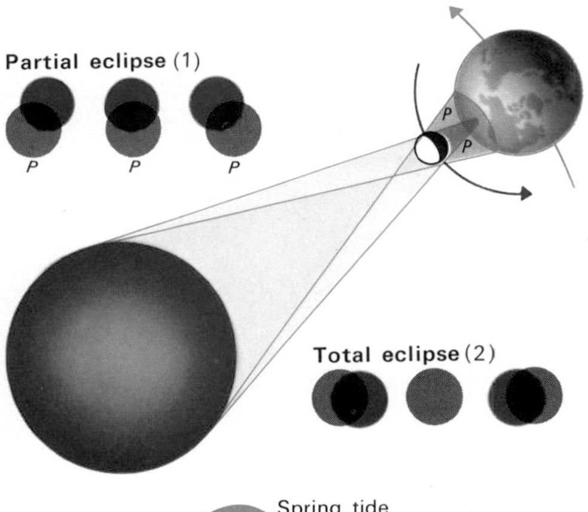
Partial eclipse (1)
P
P
P
P
P
Total eclipse (2)

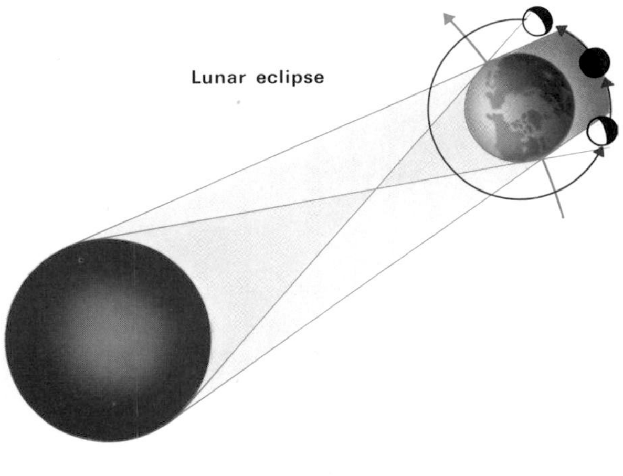
Lunar eclipse

Moon data

Distance from Earth 356 410 km to 406 685 km
Mean diameter 3 473 km
Mass approx. $\frac{1}{81}$ of that of Earth
Surface gravity $\frac{1}{6}$ of that of Earth
Atmosphere - none, hence no clouds, no weather, no sound.
Diurnal range of temperature at the Equator +200°C

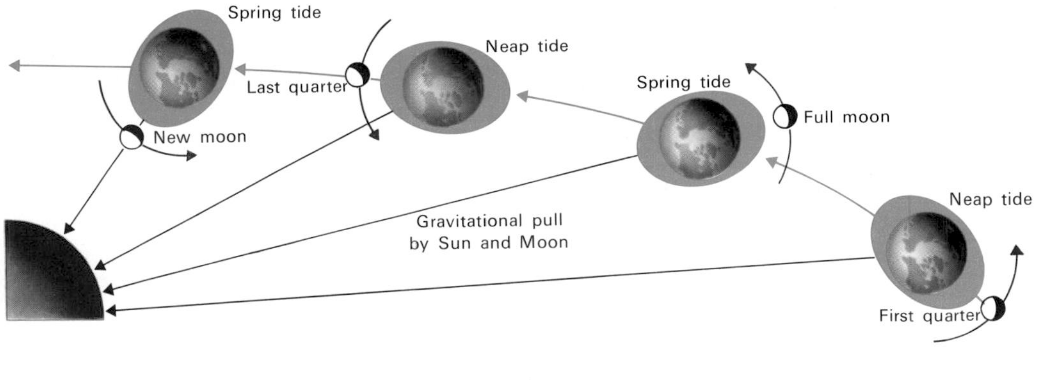
Spring tide
Last quarter
New moon
Neap tide
Spring tide
Full moon
Gravitational pull by Sun and Moon
Neap tide
First quarter

TIME

The basic unit of time measurement is the day, one **rotation of the earth** on its axis, as depicted immediately below. The subdivision of the day into hours and minutes is arbitrary and simply for our convenience. Our present calendar is based on the solar year of 365.25 days, the time taken by the earth to orbit the sun. As the earth rotates from west to east, the sun appears to rise in the east and set in the west. When the sun is setting in Shanghai, on the directly opposite side of the earth New York is just emerging into sunlight. Noon, when the sun is directly overhead, is coincident at all places on the same meridian, with shadows pointing directly toward the poles, as shown in the second diagram of the earth below.

Astronomers distinguish between **solar time** (see diagram at bottom, left) and **sidereal time** (bottom, right). Solar time has to do with the time taken by the earth to rotate on its axis. One rotation defines a solar day. But the speed of the earth along its orbit around the sun is inconstant. The length of day, or "apparent solar day," as defined by the apparent successive transits of the sun is irregular because the earth must complete more than one rotation before the sun returns to the same meridian. The constant sidereal day is defined as the interval between two successive apparent transits of a star, or the first point of Aries, across the same meridian. If the sun is at the equinox and overhead at a meridian one day, then the next day the sun will be to the east by approximately 1°. Thus, the sun will not cross the meridian until about 4 minutes after the sidereal noon.

Photographs: left, top, **Greenwich Observatory**; bottom, **Prime Meridian**; right, top, **astronomical clock at Delhi**; bottom, **Kendall's chronometer**.

Rotation of the Earth

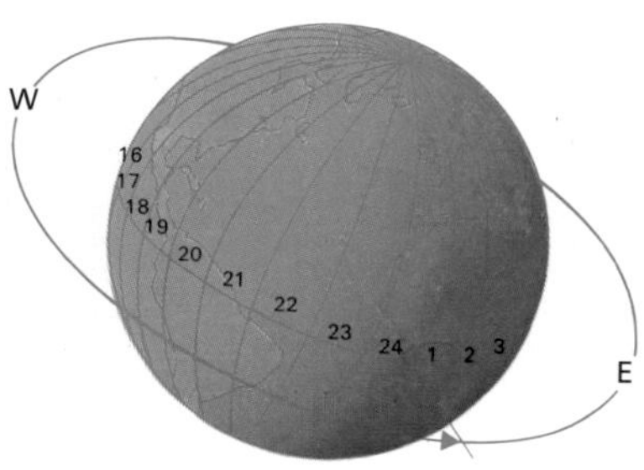
W
E
16
17
18
19
20
21
22
23
24
1
2
3

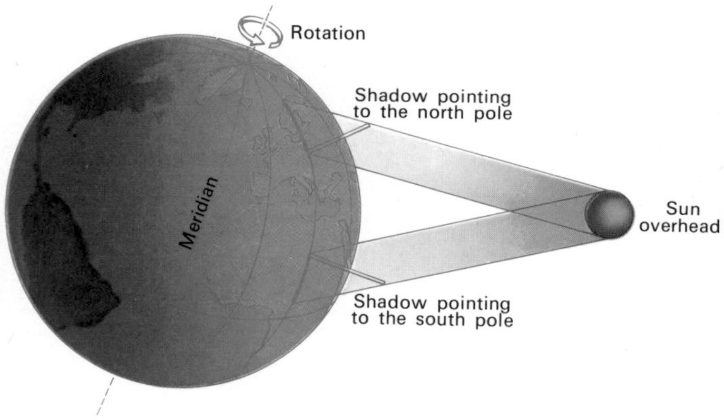
Rotation
Shadow pointing to the north pole
Meridian
Sun overhead
Shadow pointing to the south pole

Greenwich Observatory

Astronomical clock, Delhi

Prime Meridian

Kendall's chronometer

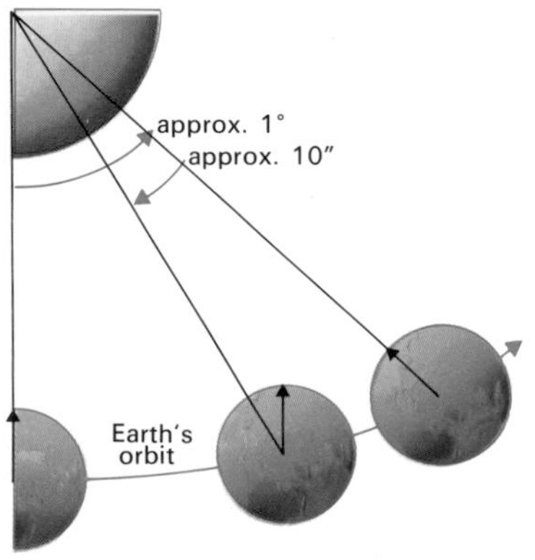
approx. 1°
approx. 10"
Earth's orbit

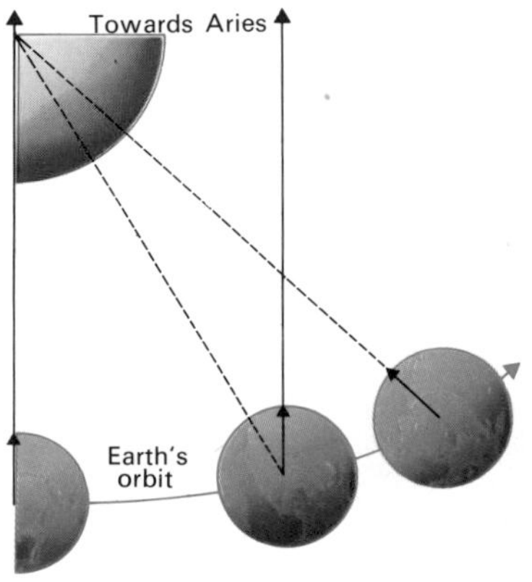
Towards Aries
Earth's orbit

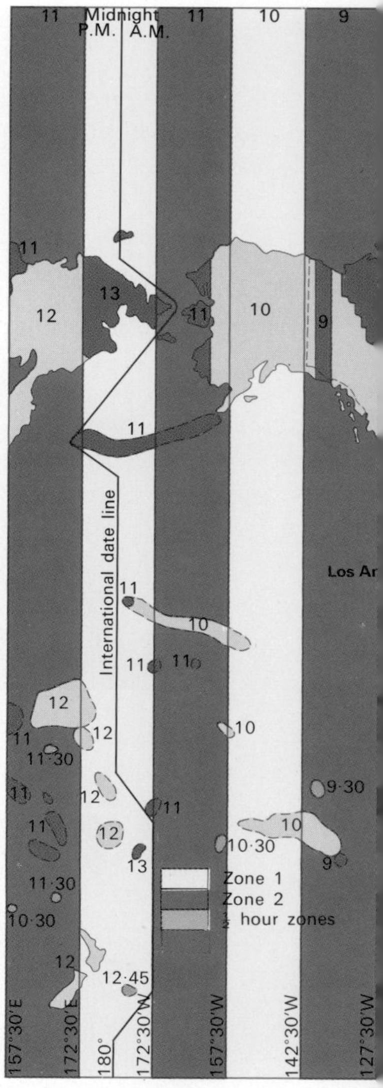
Midnight
P.M.
A.M.
International date line
Los Ar
Zone 1
Zone 2
½ hour zones
157°30'E
172°30'E
180°
172°30'W
157°30'W
142°30'W
127°30'W

International date line

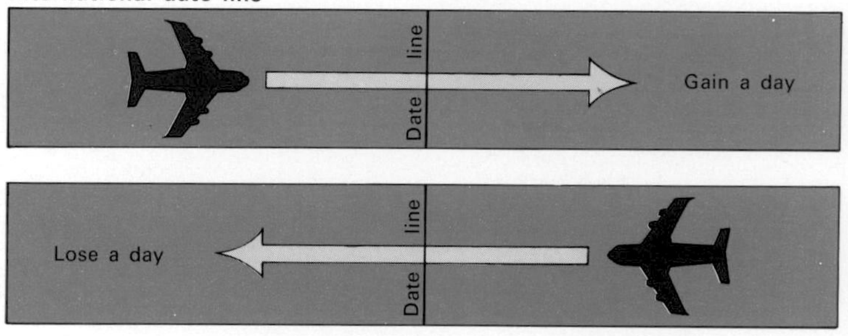
Date line
Gain a day
Lose a day

As shown on the map below, the world is divided into 24 **time zones**. Each zone is centered at 15° intervals, the longitudinal distance the sun appears to travel every hour. The meridian running through Greenwich Observatory in England passes through the middle of the first zone. At 0° longitude, it is called the Prime Meridian. Successive zones to the east of the Greenwich zone are ahead of Greenwich time by one hour for every 15° of longitude, whereas zones to the west are behind by one hour.

When it is noon at the Greenwich meridian, at a point 180° east it is midnight of the same day, and at 180° west the day is only just beginning. To overcome this discrepancy, the **International Dateline** (see map) was established, approximately following the 180° meridian. Thus, for example, traveling eastward from Japan (140 east) to Samoa (170 west), one would pass from Sunday night into Sunday morning. A plane or ship crossing the dateline from west to east gains a day; crossing in the opposite direction, it would lose a day. The chart at the right below shows **time differences when traveling by air**.

The graph at the left below shows the **progress of the accuracy of timekeepers** over the past 700 years. Inventive genius replaced the sundial with a variety of devices, including the chronometer and chronograph of the 18th and 19th centuries, topping them all with the 20th century atomic clocks. The quartz crystal clock, for example, can measure small units of time and radio frequencies. The connection between quartz clocks and the natural vibrations of atoms and molecules means that the unchanging frequencies emitted by atoms can be used to control the quartz clock. The diagram at the center below depicts the **vibration of a quartz ring**. A recent version of an atomic clock is accurate to one second in 300 years.

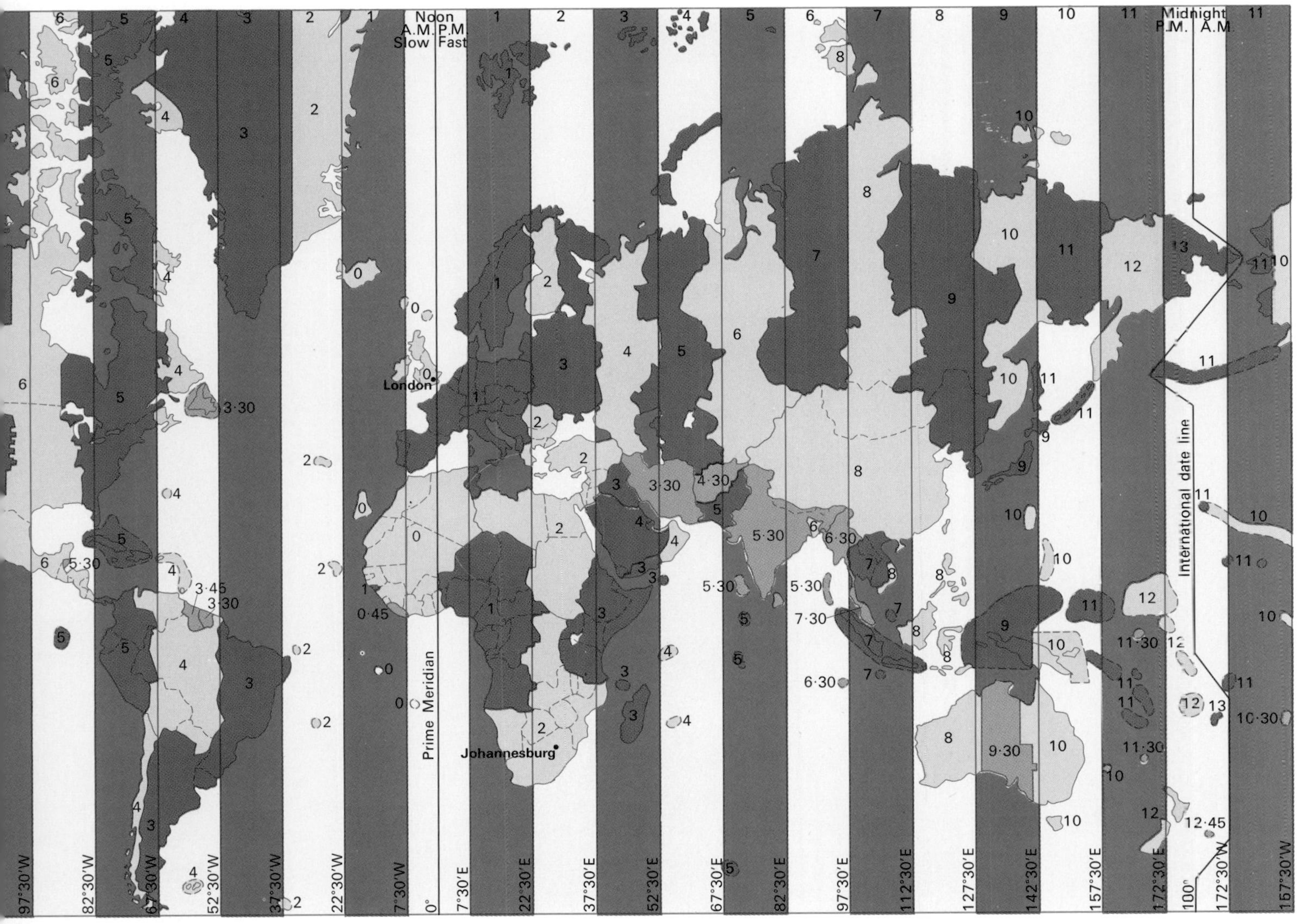
Noon
A.M. P.M.
Slow Fast
Midnight
P.M. A.M.
London
Johannesburg
Prime Meridian
International date line
97°30'W
82°30'W
67°30'W
52°30'W
37°30'W
22°30'W
7°30'W
0°
7°30'E
22°30'E
37°30'E
52°30'E
67°30'E
82°30'E
97°30'E
112°30'E
127°30'E
142°30'E
157°30'E
172°30'E
180°
172°30'W
157°30'W

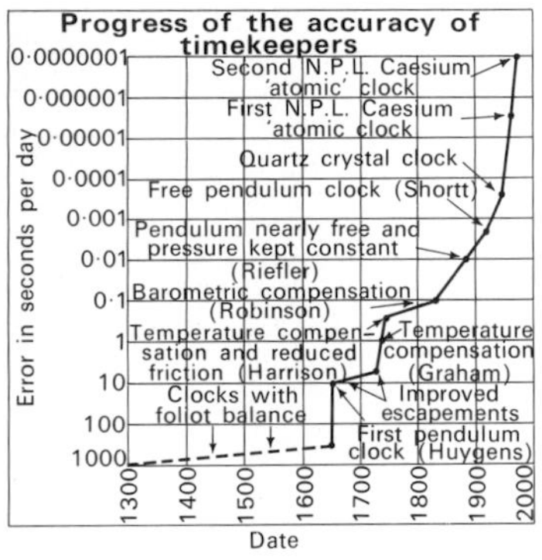
Progress of the accuracy of timekeepers
Error in seconds per day
Date
Second N.P.L. Caesium 'atomic' clock
First N.P.L. Caesium 'atomic clock
Quartz crystal clock
Free pendulum clock (Shortt)
Pendulum nearly free and pressure kept constant (Riefler)
Barometric compensation (Robinson)
Temperature compensation and reduced friction (Harrison)
Temperature compensation (Graham)
Clocks with foliot balance
Improved escapements
First pendulum clock (Huygens)

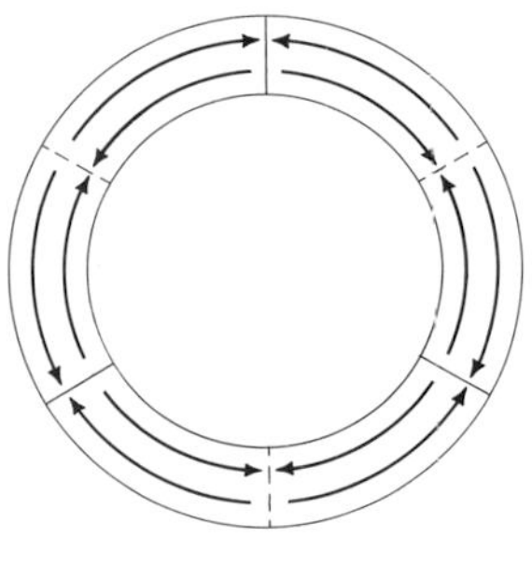
Vibration of quartz ring

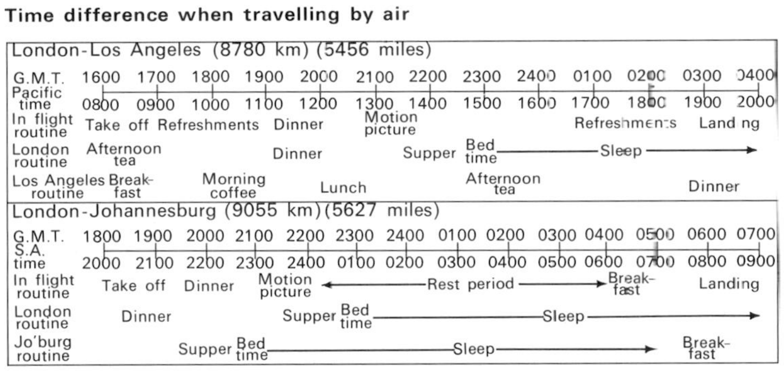
Time difference when travelling by air
London-Los Angeles (8780 km) (5456 miles)
G.M.T. 1600 1700 1800 1900 2000 2100 2200 2300 2400 0100 0200 0300 0400
Pacific time 0800 0900 1000 1100 1200 1300 1400 1500 1600 1700 1800 1900 2000
In flight routine Take off Refreshments Dinner Motion picture Refreshments Landing
London routine Afternoon tea Dinner Supper Bed time Sleep
Los Angeles routine Break-fast Morning coffee Lunch Afternoon tea Dinner
London-Johannesburg (9055 km) (5627 miles)
G.M.T. 1800 1900 2000 2100 2200 2300 2400 0100 0200 0300 0400 0500 0600 0700
S.A. time 2000 2100 2200 2300 2400 0100 0200 0300 0400 0500 0600 0700 0800 0900
In flight routine Take off Dinner Motion picture Rest period Break-fast Landing
London routine Dinner Supper Bed time Sleep
Jo'burg routine Supper Bed time Sleep Break-fast

THE ATMOSPHERE AND CLOUDS

Earth's atmosphere is a blanket of protective gases, as shown below at the left, that provide insulation against otherwise extreme alternations in temperature. The earth's gravitational pull increases the density of the atmosphere near the earth's surface so that five-sixths of the atmospheric mass is in the first 15 km. This blanket of air is a very thin layer compared with the earth's diameter of 12,680 km. The **physical and chemical structure of the atmosphere** are illustrated at the center and right below.

Four main layers comprise the atmosphere: **exosphere**, **ionosphere**, **stratosphere**, and **troposphere**. The highest layer, exosphere, merges with the interplanetary medium. Although there is no definite boundary with the next layer, the ionosphere, the exosphere starts at a height of about 600 km. Its rarefied air consists mainly of a small amount of atomic oxygen and equal proportions of hydrogen and helium at the 600-km level, but with hydrogen predominating above 2,400 km. Air particles of the ionosphere are electrically charged by the sun's radiation and congregate in four main layers — D, E, F-1, and F-2 — which can reflect radio waves. Auroras, caused by charged particles deflected toward the poles of the earth's magnetic field, are a phenomenon of the ionosphere. It is in the lower ionosphere that meteors from outer space burn up as they meet increased air resistance.

The stratosphere contains a thin layer of ozone which absorbs ultra-violet light, giving off heat. This warmer region of the stratosphere, just above the ozone layer, is called the **mesosphere**. These layers are separated from the troposphere by the **tropopause**.

Cloud formation is a major characteristic of

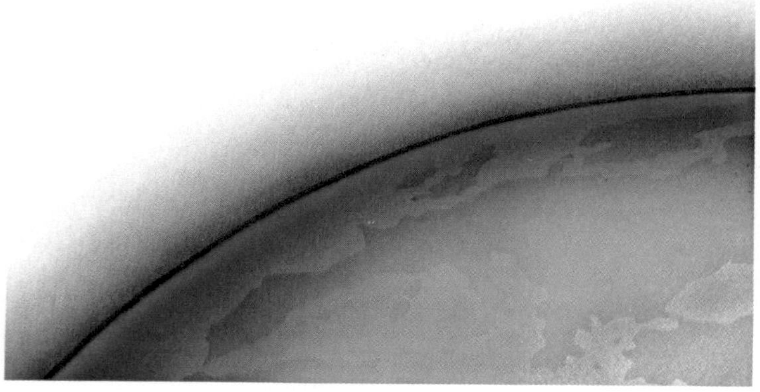

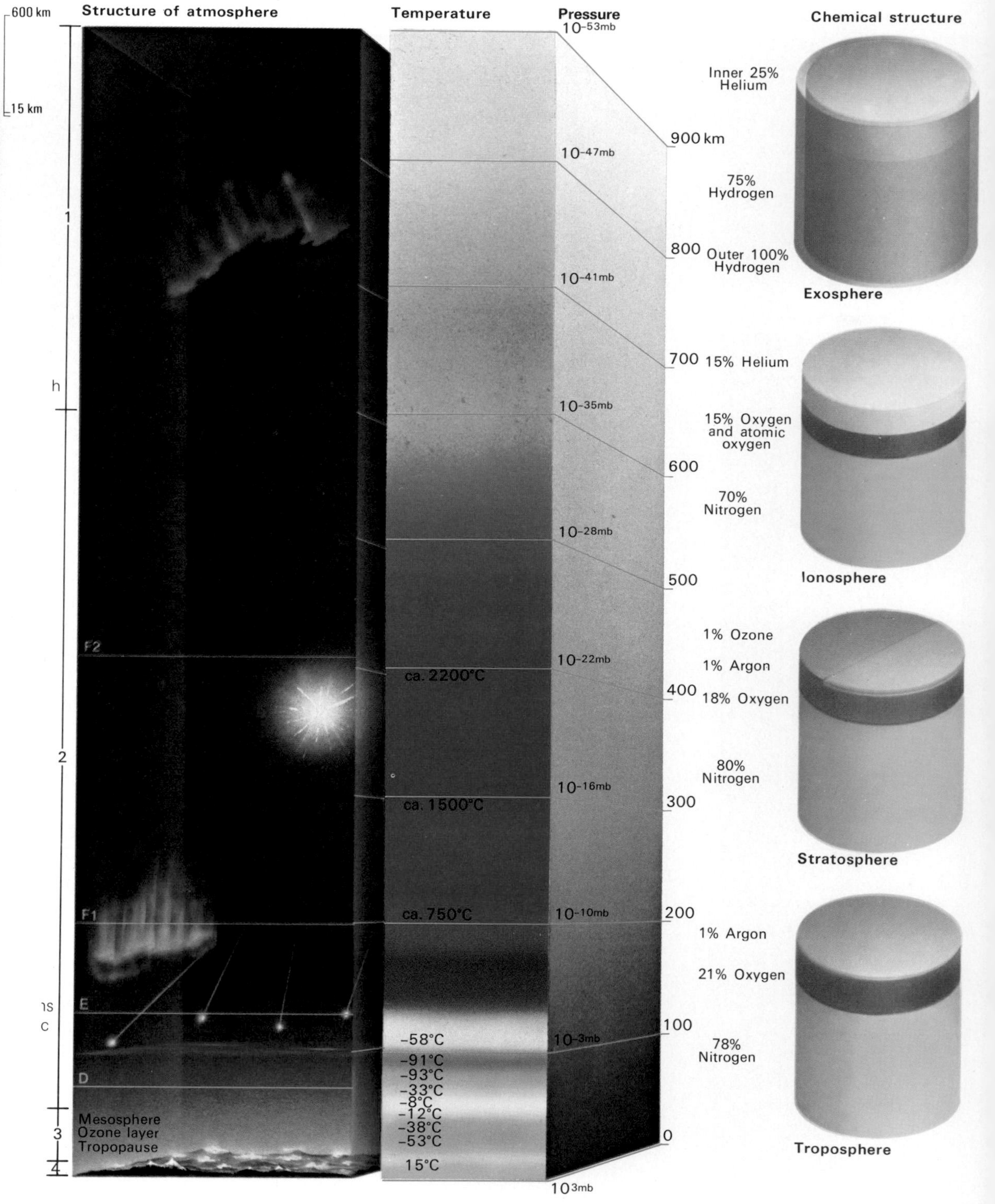
600 km
15 km
Structure of atmosphere
Temperature
Pressure
Chemical structure
10^{-53}mb
10^{-47}mb
10^{-41}mb
10^{-35}mb
10^{-28}mb
10^{-22}mb
10^{-16}mb
10^{-10}mb
10^{-3}mb
10^{3}mb
900 km
800
700
600
500
400
300
200
100
0
1
h
2
3
4
F2
F1
E
D
Mesosphere
Ozone layer
Tropopause
ca. 2200°C
ca. 1500°C
ca. 750°C
-58°C
-91°C
-93°C
-33°C
-8°C
-12°C
-38°C
-53°C
15°C
Inner 25% Helium
75% Hydrogen
Outer 100% Hydrogen
Exosphere
15% Helium
15% Oxygen and atomic oxygen
70% Nitrogen
Ionosphere
1% Ozone
1% Argon
18% Oxygen
80% Nitrogen
Stratosphere
1% Argon
21% Oxygen
78% Nitrogen
Troposphere

the troposphere. The two photographs at the lower left show the paths of prevailing winds in **cloud patterns over the Pacific Ocean**. The origin of these winds is shown in the two drawings beneath the photographs. The drawing on the left shows the **circulation of the air** set up by the high temperatures of the equatorial regions of the earth. Hot air expands and rises, producing a low pressure belt. As the air cools at high altitudes, it loses moisture, spreads out, and sinks, thus forming high pressure belts. The **interaction of high and low pressure belts** to produce prevailing winds is shown in the diagram at the bottom right.

Clouds form when damp, usually rising, air is cooled. Thus, they form when a wind rises to cross hills or mountains; when a mass of air rises over, or is pushed up by, another mass of denser air; or when local heating of the ground causes convection currents. The nine **types of clouds** are classified according to altitude as high, middle, or low. The high ones are **cirrus** (1), **cirrostratus** (2), and **cirrocumulus** (3). These clouds are made up of ice crystals. The middle clouds are **altostratus** (4), a gray or bluish striated, fibrous, or uniform sheet producing light drizzle, and **altocumulus** (5), a thicker and fluffier version of cirrocumulus. The low clouds include **nimbostratus** (6), a dark gray layer that brings almost continuous rain or snow; **cumulus** (7), a detached heap — brilliant white in sunlight but dark and flat at the base; **stratus** (8), which forms dull, overcast skies at low altitudes; and **cumulonimbus** (9), associated with storms and rain, heavy and dense with flat base and a high, fluffy outline.

1 Cirrus

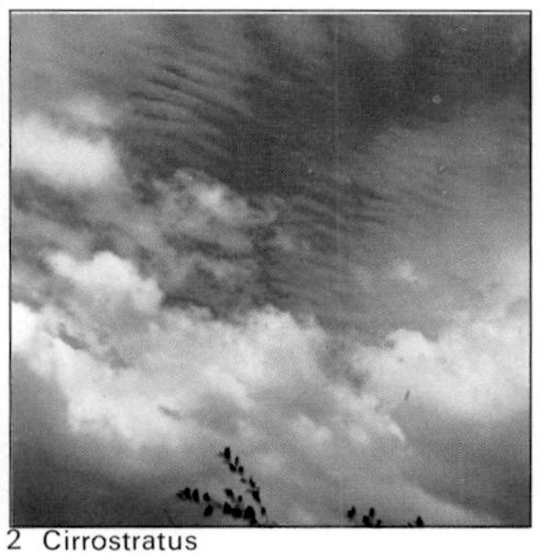
2 Cirrostratus

3 Cirrocumulus

4 Altostratus

5 Altocumulus

6 Nimbostratus

7 Cumulus

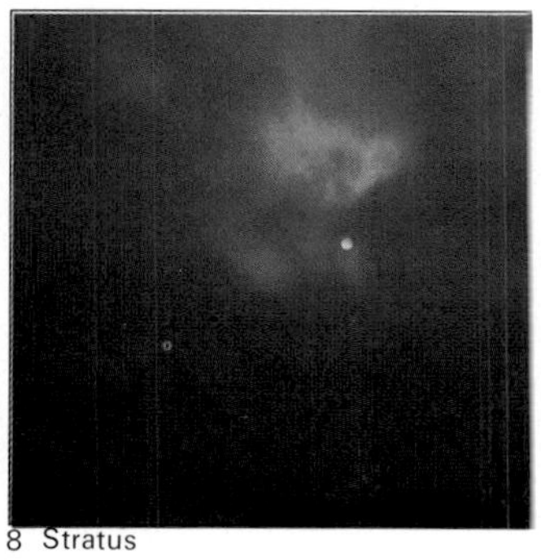
8 Stratus

9 Cumulonimbus

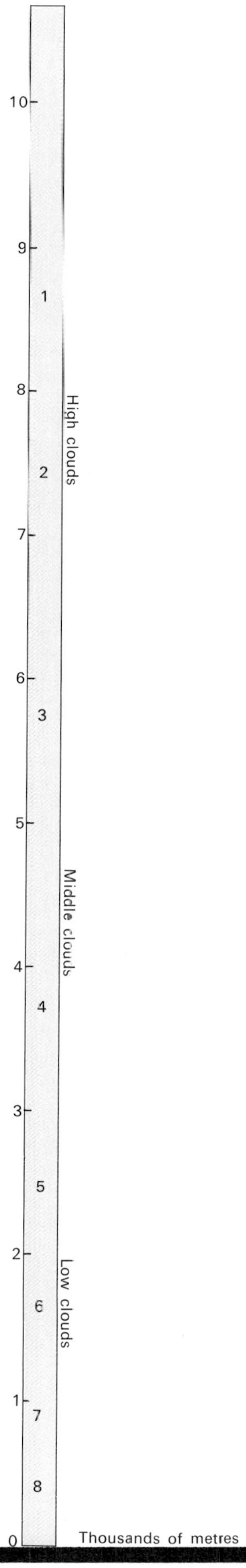

10
9
1
8
High clouds
2
7
6
3
5
Middle clouds
4
4
3
5
2
Low clouds
6
1
7
8
0
Thousands of metres

Pacific Ocean
Cloud patterns over the Pacific show the paths of prevailing winds.

Circulation of the air

30°N
Equator
30°S

CLIMATE AND WEATHER

Weather has been defined as the condition of the atmosphere at any place at a specific time with respect to various elements: temperature, precipitation, pressure, winds, and so on. Climate is the average of weather elements over previous months and years. Each of the **climate graphs** below typifies the kind of climatic conditions one would experience in the region to which the graph is related by color on the **world climate map** at the right. The scale refers to degrees Celsius for temperature and millimeters for rainfall, shown by bars.

The small map at the right below shows **tropical storm tracks**. A tropical cyclone, or storm, has winds of gale force (60 kph) but less than hurricane force (120 kph). It is a homogeneous air mass with upward spiralling currents around a windless center, or eye.

The diagrams labeled (i) through (iv) at the lower left show the **development of a depression**, or low-pressure center. In an equilibrium front (i), a wave of disturbance develops as cold air undercuts warm air (ii). Cyclone circulation is created (iii). Occlusion occurs as the warm air is pinched out (iv). **Kinds of precipitation** are shown at the bottom of the page, left to right: rain, hail, frost, snow.

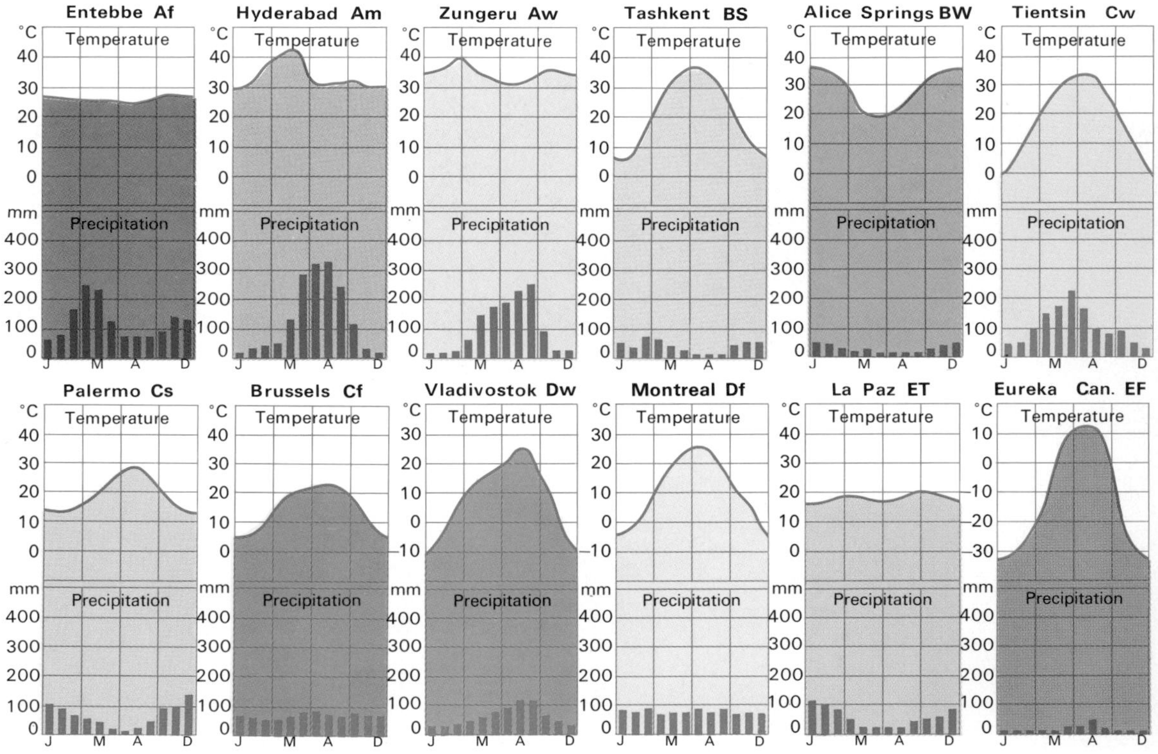

Entebbe Af
Hyderabad Am
Zungeru Aw
Tashkent BS
Alice Springs BW
Tientsin Cw
Palermo Cs
Brussels Cf
Vladivostok Dw
Montreal Df
La Paz ET
Eureka Can. EF
°C
Temperature
mm
Precipitation
J M A D

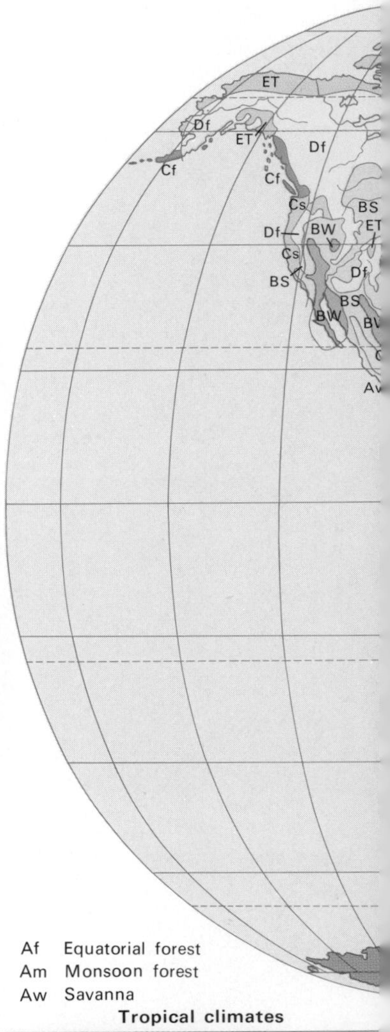

ET
Df
Cf
Cs
BS
BW

Af Equatorial forest
Am Monsoon forest
Aw Savanna
Tropical climates

Af	Am	Aw

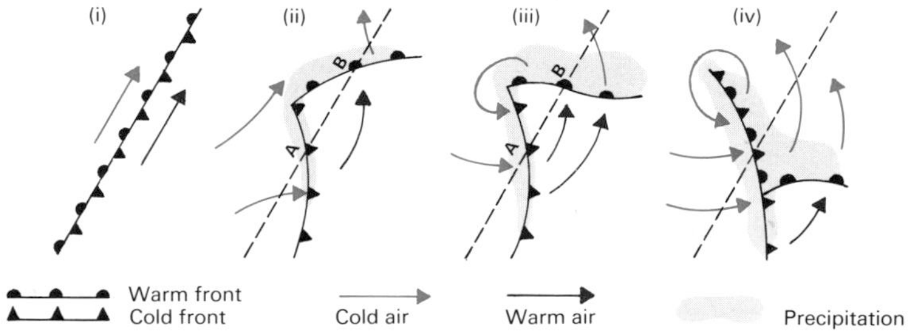

(i)
(ii)
(iii)
(iv)
A
B
Warm front
Cold front
Cold air
Warm air
Precipitation

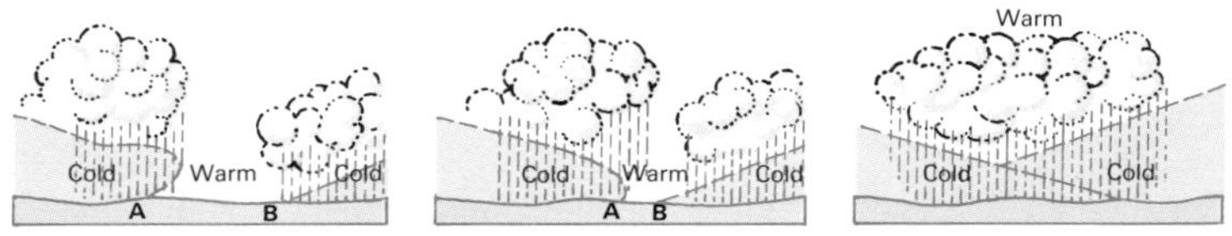

Cold
Warm
Cold
A
B
Warm

Frontal cloud
Precipitation

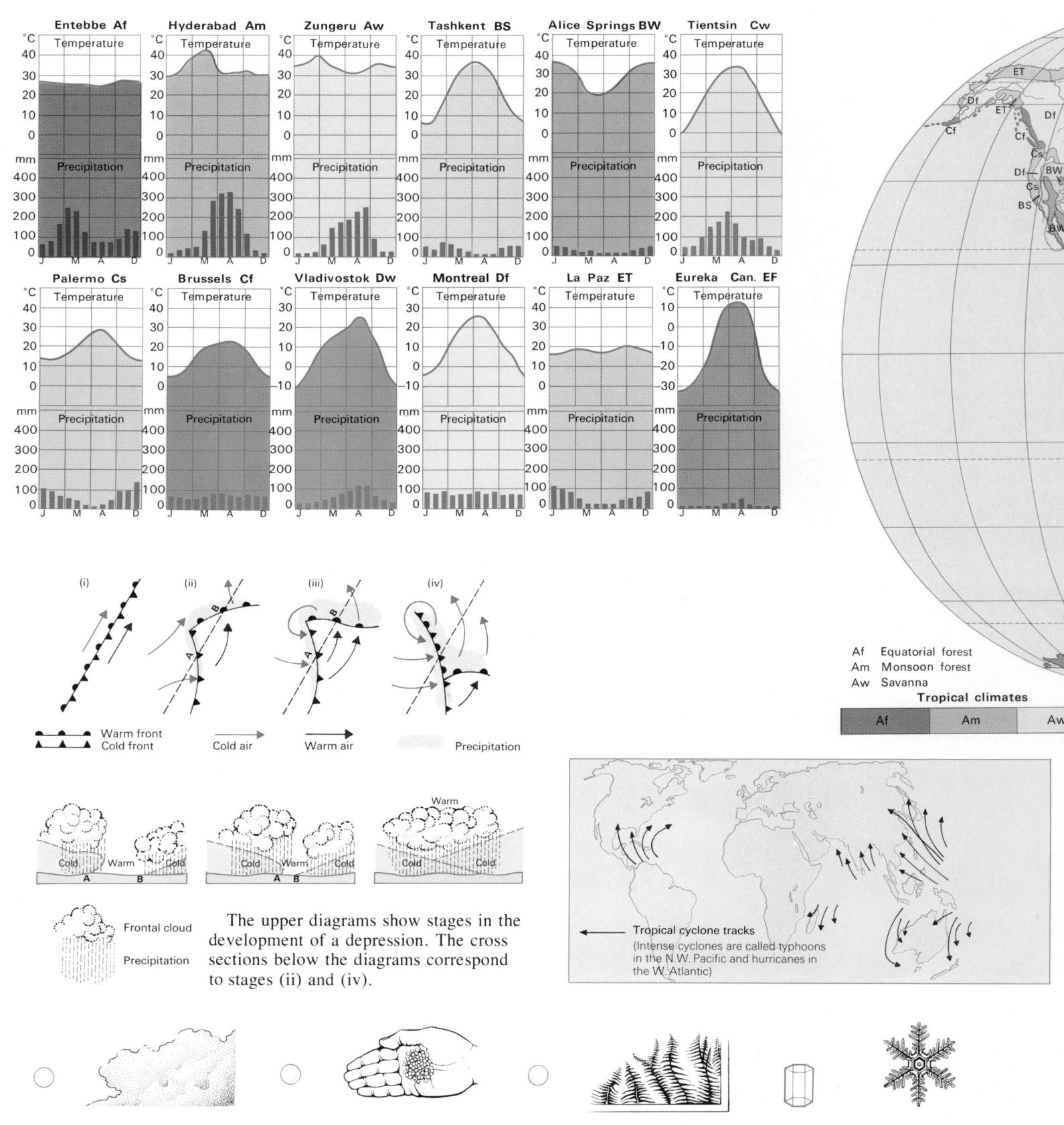

The upper diagrams show stages in the development of a depression. The cross sections below the diagrams correspond to stages (ii) and (iv).

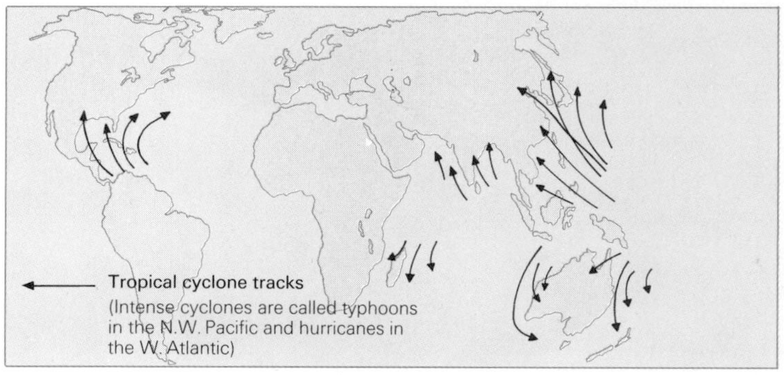

Tropical cyclone tracks
(Intense cyclones are called typhoons in the N.W. Pacific and hurricanes in the W. Atlantic)

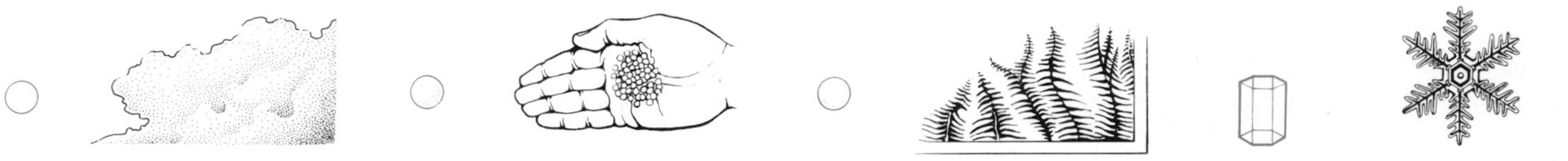

The water vapor contained in the atmosphere returns to earth as various forms of precipitation. It condenses on microscopic particles of dust, sulfur, soot, or ice to form water particles. These combine until they are heavy enough to fall as **rain**. Water particles carried to a great height freeze into ice particles that fall and become coated with fresh moisture. They are swept upward and refrozen repeatedly until heavy enough to fall as **hail**. Hoar, the most common type of **frost**, is precipitated instead of dew when water vapor changes directly to ice crystals on the surface of objects that have cooled below freezing point. **Snow** is the precipitate of ice directly from water vapor in the form of flakes, or clusters, of basically hexagonal ice crystals.

The four photographs below relate to the **extremes of weather and climate**: left to right, **hurricane devastation**; **hot desert**; **tornado**; **Arctic dwellings**. Tropical high temperatures and polar low temperatures combined with wind systems, altitude, and unequal rainfall distribution result in the extremes of climate. If these causative factors fluctuate sharply, catastrophic heat waves, floods, frosts, or storms could occur.

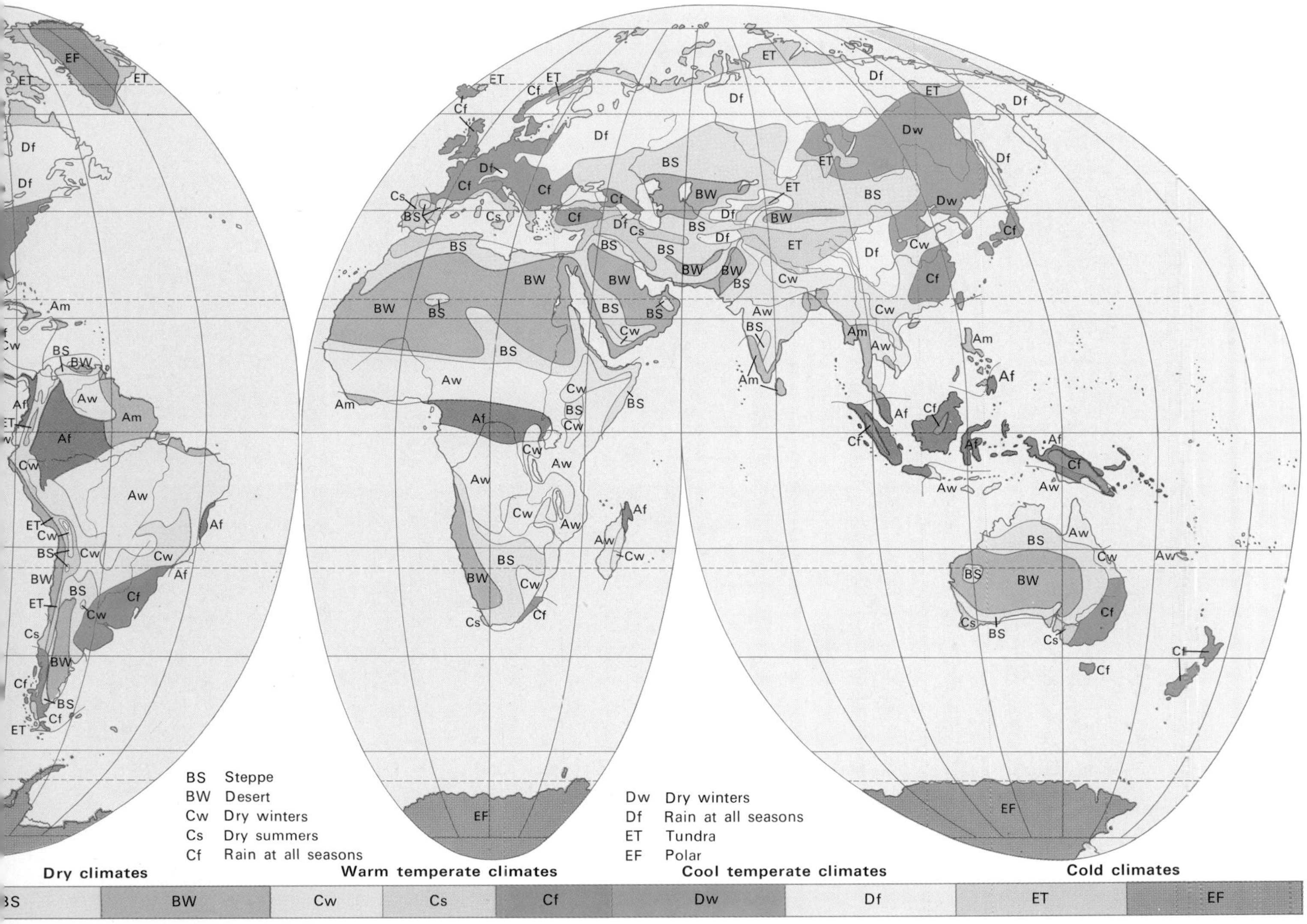
BS Steppe
BW Desert
Cw Dry winters
Cs Dry summers
Cf Rain at all seasons
Dw Dry winters
Df Rain at all seasons
ET Tundra
EF Polar
Dry climates
Warm temperate climates
Cool temperate climates
Cold climates
BS
BW
Cw
Cs
Cf
Dw
Df
ET
EF

Hurricane devastation

Hot desert

Tornado

Arctic dwellings

THE EARTH FROM SPACE

Photographs taken with cameras mounted in U. S. spacecraft have provided detailed views of the earth's topography. The top row, left to right, shows the **River Brahmaputra**, **India**, looking westward with the Himalayas on the right and the Khasi Hills of Assam to the left; the River Tachin in the mountainous region of **Szechwan**, **China**; infra-red photograph of the western end of Long Island, **New York** and the entrance to the Hudson River. The gray area is metropolitan New York; the red shows vegetation. Middle row, left: a view from Apollo IX of the **eastern Himalayas**, **Asia**; right, infra-red view of **Mount Etna**, **Sicily** at the top of the photograph with the Mediterranean to the right. Bottom row, left: **map of Sicily** locating Mount Etna; right, **Hawaii**, the largest of the Hawaiian Islands, in the central Pacific Ocean.

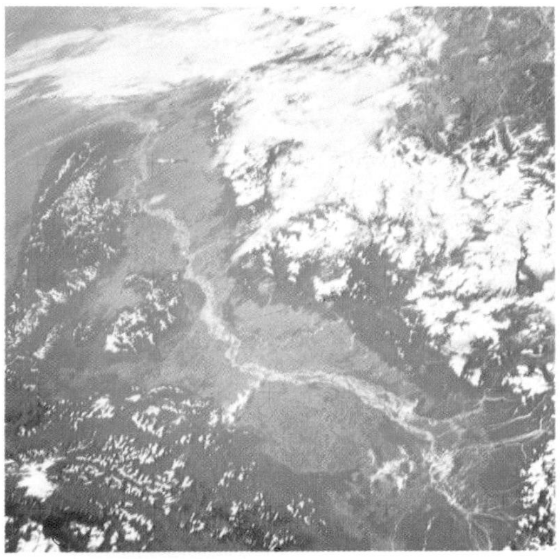
River Brahmaputra, India

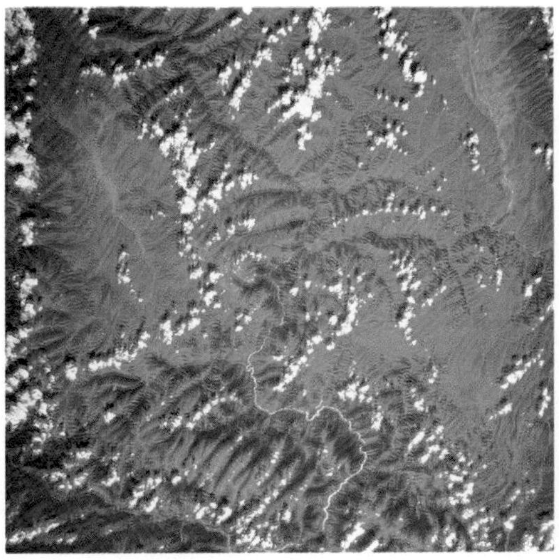
Szechwan, China

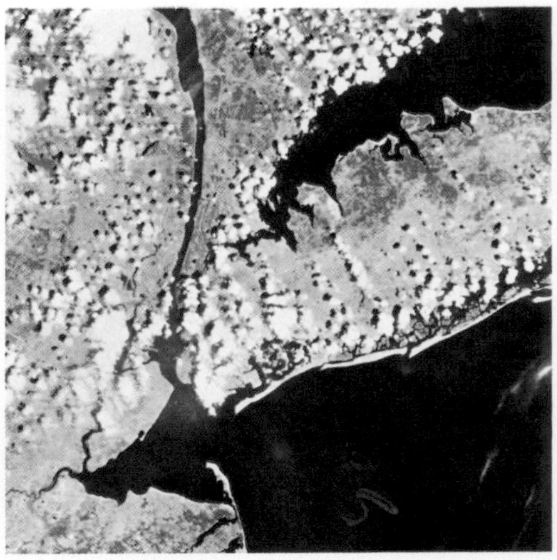
New York, U.S.A.

Eastern Himalayas, Asia

Mount Etna, Sicily

Giarre
Mount Etna
3340
Mediterranean
Sea
Bronte
Acireale
Belpasso
Catánia
Adrano
Paterno
Golfo
di Catánia
Dittáino
Simeto
Gornalunga
Augusta
N
SICILY
Piazza
Armerina

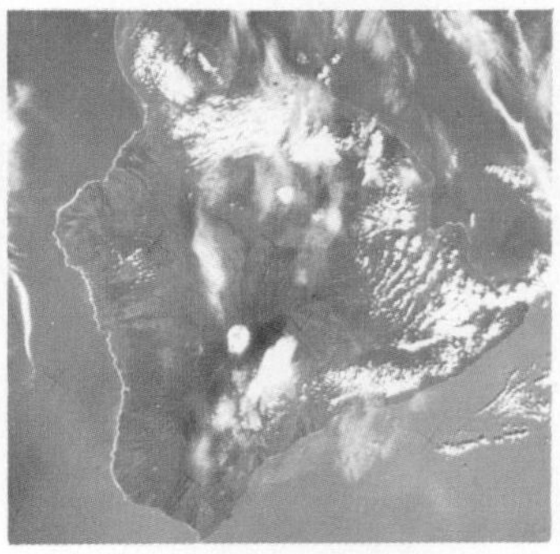
Hawaii, Pacific Ocean

Below, left, the top photograph is of the **Great Barrier Reef of Australia** and the Queensland coast from Cape Melville to Cape Flattery. Smoke from a number of forest fires can be seen in the lower center of the photograph. Left, bottom, the **Atacama Desert, Chile**. This view looks eastward from the Pacific over the Mejillones peninsula with the Andes in the background. The city of Antofagasta can be seen in the bay at the lower center of the picture.

The Alps of Europe are shown in the top photograph at the right. A location **map of the Alps** is beneath the photograph. The photograph shows the snow-covered mountains and glaciers of the Alps along the Swiss-Italian-French border. Mont Blanc and the Matterhorn are shown, and, in the north, the Valley of the Rhone can be seen making its sharp right-hand bend near Martigny. Lac d'Annecy is at the upper left.

The Great Barrier Reef, Australia

Atacama Desert, Chile

The Alps, Europe

Annecy
Lac d'Annecy
Rhône
Sion
Martigny
Valais
Chamonix
SWITZERLAND
Albertville
Mont Blanc
4807
Alpes Pennines
FRANCE
Matterhorn
4478
Isère
Moûtiers
Aosta
Dora Baltea
Valle d'Aosta
N
Arc
ITALY
Modane

THE EVOLUTION OF THE CONTINENTS

The origin of the earth is still open to much conjecture, although the most widely accepted theory is that it was formed from a solar cloud consisting mainly of hydrogen. Under gravitation, the cloud condensed and shrank to form our planets orbiting around the sun. Gravitation forced the lighter elements to the surface of the earth, where they cooled to form a crust while the inner material remained hot and molten. Earth's first rocks formed over 3,500 million years ago. Since then the surface has been constantly altered.

Until comparatively recently, the view that the primary units of the earth had remained essentially fixed throughout geological time was regarded as common sense. However, the concept of moving continents has been traced back to references in the Bible of breakup of the land after Noah's flood. The continental drift theory was first developed by Antonio Snider in 1858, but probably the most important single advocate was Alfred Wegener who, in 1915, published evidence from geology, climatology, and biology. His conclusions are very similar to those reached by current research, although he was wrong about the speed of breakup.

The measurement of fossil magnetism found in rocks has probably proved the most influential evidence. Whereas originally these drift theories were openly mocked, they are now considered to be standard doctrine. As knowledge of the shape and structure of the earth's surface grew, several of the early geographers noted a relationship in the shape of the coasts bordering the Atlantic. For example, the east coast of South America would fit the contour of the west coast of Africa, as shown in the small center drawing below. It was this remarkable coincidence that led to the first detailed geological and structural comparisons. Even more accurate fits can be made by placing the edges of the continental shelves in juxtaposition.

The four maps below show the progression of the splitting of the original single land mass into continents. Top left, **180 million years ago**, the original Pangaea land mass had split into two major continental groups. The southern group, Gondwanaland, had itself started to break up, isolating India and Antarctica-Australia. The rift had begun to appear between South America and Africa; and, in the east, Africa was closing up the Tethys Sea. Top right, **135 million years** ago, both Gondwanaland and Laurasia, the northern group, continued to drift northward, but the widening rifts in the North Atlantic and Indian Oceans persisted. The South Atlantic continued to lengthen, and a further perpendicular rift appeared, which would eventually separate Greenland from North America. India continued heading northward toward Asia. Bottom left, **65 million years ago**, South America moved quickly north and westward. Madagascar broke free from Africa, but there was no sign of the Red Sea rift that was to split Africa from the Arabian Peninsula. The Mediterranean Sea was already forming. Australia was still connected to Antarctica. Bottom right, **today**, India had moved northward and collided with Asia, crumpling up the sediments to form the Himalayas. South America had moved westward to connect with North America, and Australia had separated from Antarctica.

180 million years ago.

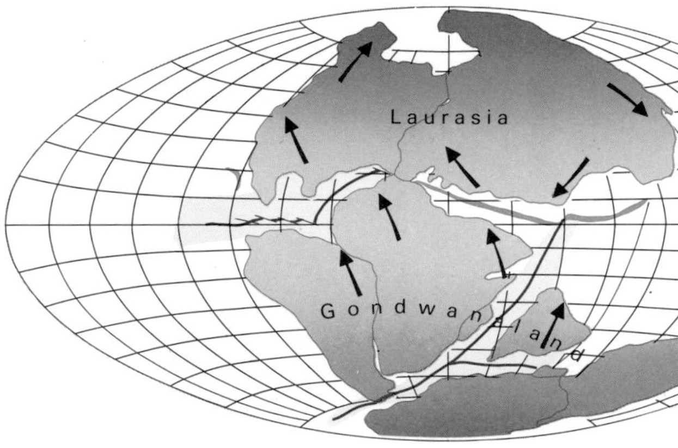
Laurasia
Gondwanaland

135 million years ago.

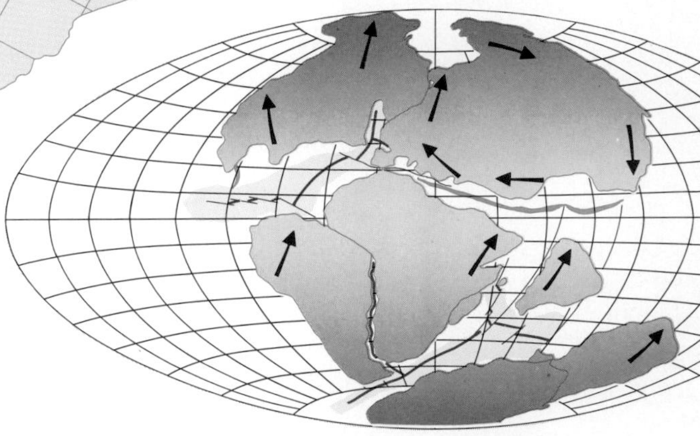

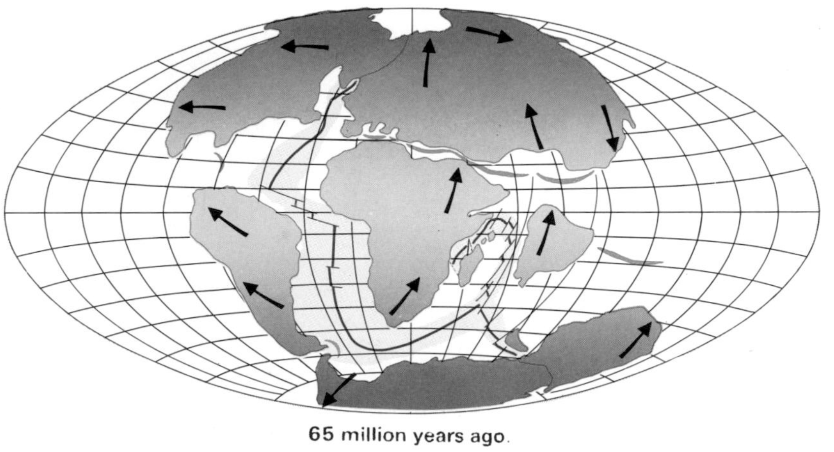

65 million years ago.

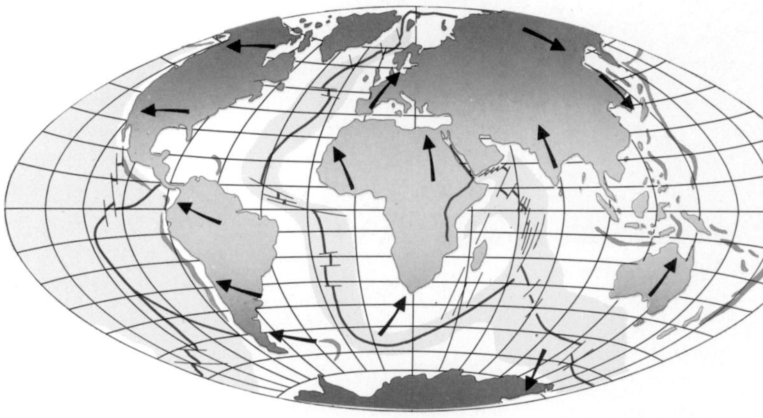

Today.

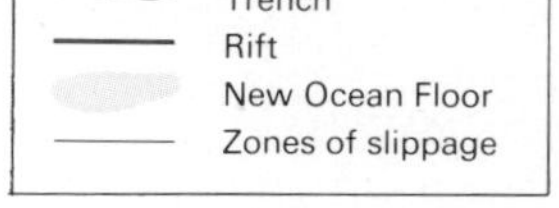
Trench
Rift
New Ocean Floor
Zones of slippage

The original debate about continental drift was only a prelude to a more radical idea: **plate tectonics**. (See distribution of tectonic plates represented on the world map below.) The basic theory here is that the earth's crust is made up of a series of rigid plates that float on a soft layer of the mantle and are moved about by convection currents in the earth's interior. These plates converge and diverge along margins marked by earthquakes, volcanoes, and other seismic activity. Plates diverge from mid-ocean ridges where molten lava pushes upward and forces the plates apart at a rate of about 30 mm a year. Converging plates form either a trench, where the oceanic plate sinks below the lighter continental rock, or mountain ranges where two continents collide. This explains the paradox that whereas there have always been oceans, none of the present oceans contains sediments more than 150 million years old.

The present explanation for the comparative youth of the ocean floors is that where an ocean and a continent meet, the ocean plate dips under the less dense continental plate at an angle of 45°. All previous crust is then ingested at the **trench boundary**, top left below, by downward convection currents. In the Japanese trench, this occurs at a rate of 120 mm a year.

The recent identification of the **transform, or transverse fault**, second left below, proved to be one of the crucial preliminaries to the investigation of plate tectonics. Such faults occur when two plates slip alongside each other without parting or approaching to any great extent. They complete the outline of the plates delineated by the ridges and trenches and demonstrate large-scale movements of parts of the earth's surface.

The third diagram at the left below illustrates a **ridge boundary**. One plate can ease itself away from another; and, when that happens, hot molten rock rises from below to fill in the incipient rift and form a ridge. These ridges trace a line almost exactly through the center of the major oceans. The bottom drawing on the left shows the **destruction of ocean plates**. As the ocean plate sinks below the continental plate, some of the sediment on its surface is scraped off and piled up on the landward side. The sediment is later incorporated in a folded mountain range, which usually appears on the edge of the continent, such as the Andes. Similarly, if two continents collide, the sediments are squeezed up into new mountains.

The map at the lower right illustrates **sea floor spreading**. Reversals in the earth's magnetic field have occurred throughout history. As new rock emerges at the ocean ridges, it cools and is magnetized in the direction of the prevailing magnetic field. By mapping the magnetic patterns on either side of the ridge, a symmetrical striped pattern of alternating fields can be observed (see inset area in map). As the dates for the last few reversals are known, the rate of spreading can be calculated.

Trench boundary

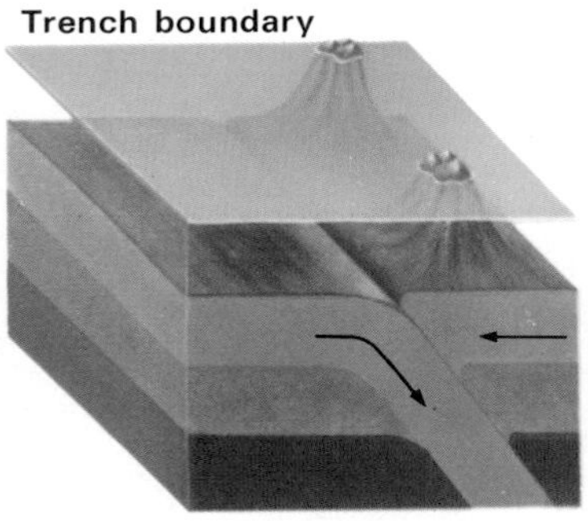

Transform fault

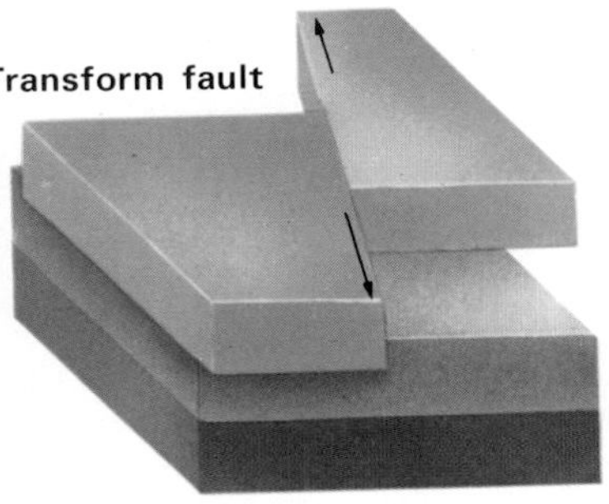

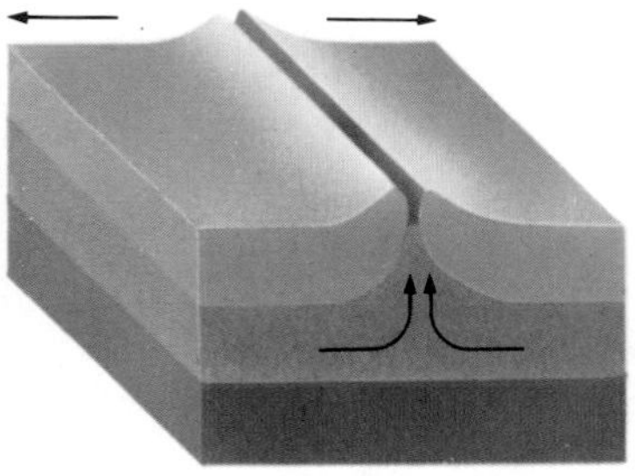

Ridge boundary

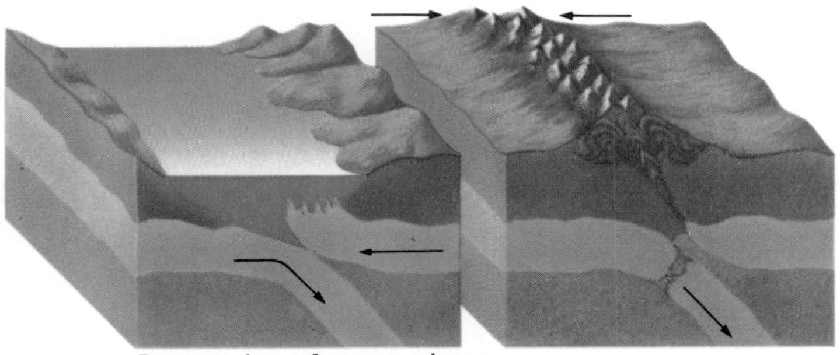

Destruction of ocean plates.

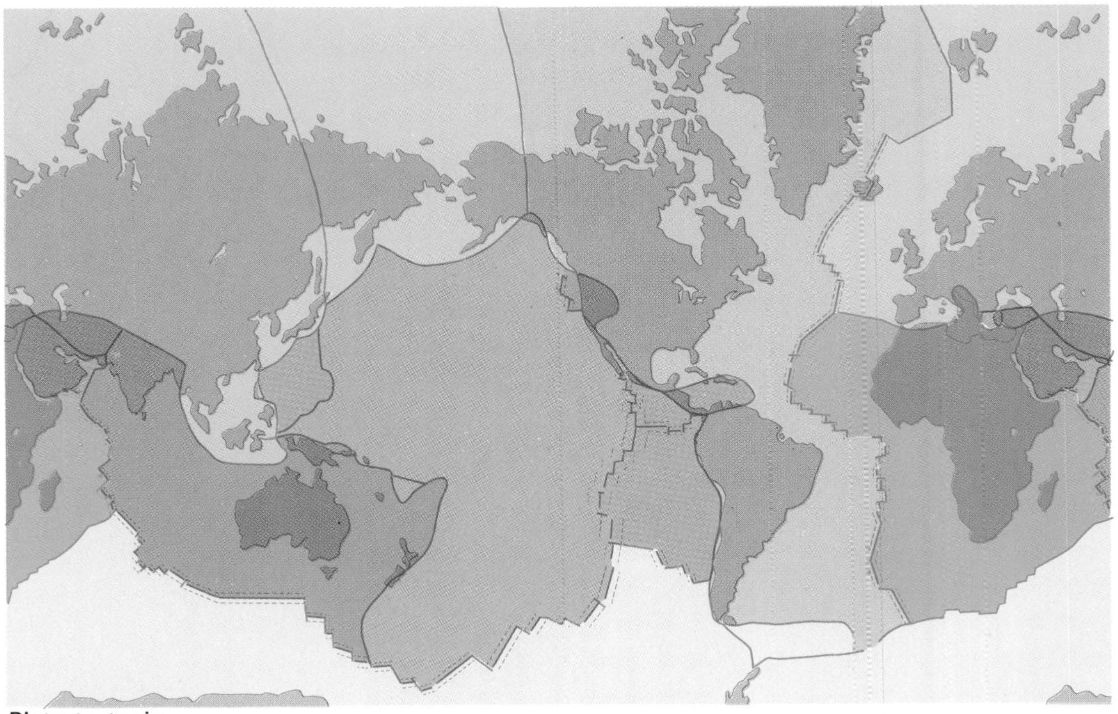

Plate tectonics

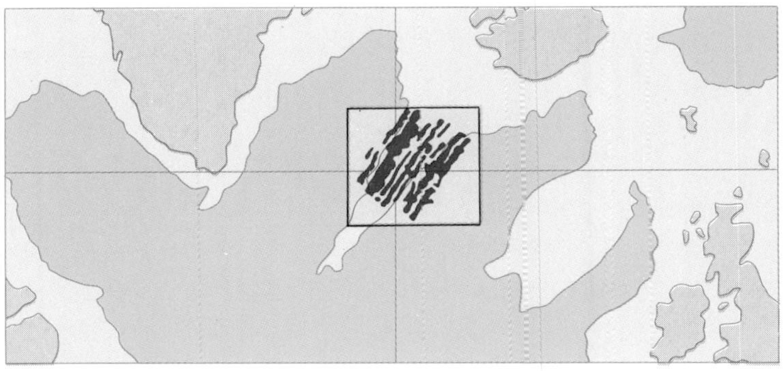

Sea floor spreading

THE UNSTABLE EARTH

The earth's surface is slowly but continually being rearranged. Some changes, such as erosion and deposition, are extremely slow, but they upset the balance, which causes other more abrupt changes that often originate deep within the earth's interior. The constant movements vary in intensity, often with stresses building up to a climax — such as a particularly violent volcanic eruption or earthquake.

The earth's crust, shown below in cross section (left) and in the cutaway sphere (right), consists of a comparatively low density, brittle material varying from 5 km to 50 km deep beneath the continents. Under the crust is a layer of rock consisting predominately of silica and aluminum; hence, it is called "sial." Extending under the ocean floors and below the sial is a basaltic layer known as "sima," since it consists mainly of silica and magnesium.

In the earth's **mantle**, the rock layer immediately below the crust shows a distinct change in density and chemical properties. The mantle is made up of iron and magnesium silicates and has temperatures that reach 1600°C. The rigid upper mantle extends down to a depth of about 1,000 km, below which is the more viscous lower mantle, which is about 1,900 km thick. The **core** of the earth consists of two layers. The outer core, approximately 2,100 km thick, is made up of molten iron and nickel at 2000°C to 5000°C. About 5,000 km below the surface there is a liquid transition zone, just above the solid inner core. The inner core is a sphere 2,740 km in diameter. It is three times as dense as the crust.

A **volcano** occurs when hot liquefied rock moves to the earth's surface, pouring out as lava. Ash and cinders form a cone around the volcano's vent. (See center photograph.) The map at the bottom shows the **world distribution of volcanoes**. The diagrams beside the map show, top to bottom, five types of volcano: **shield**, **composite**, **cinder-cone**, **hornit-cone**, and **caldera**. The caldera forms when a violent eruption blows off the top of an existing cone.

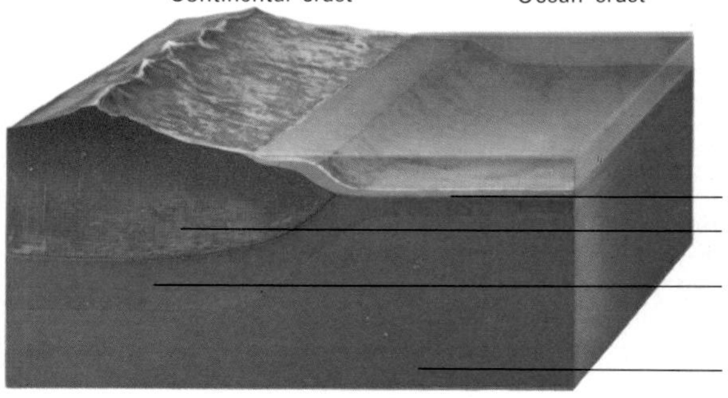
Continental crust
Ocean crust
Sediment
Granite rock (sial)
Basaltic layer (sima)
Mantle

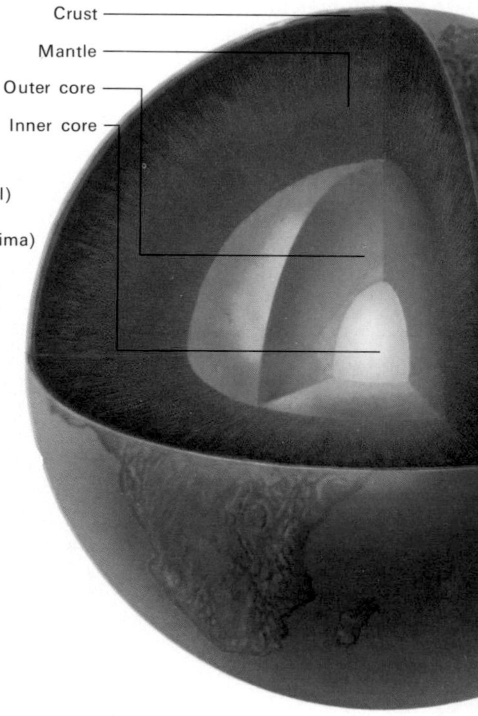
Crust
Mantle
Outer core
Inner core

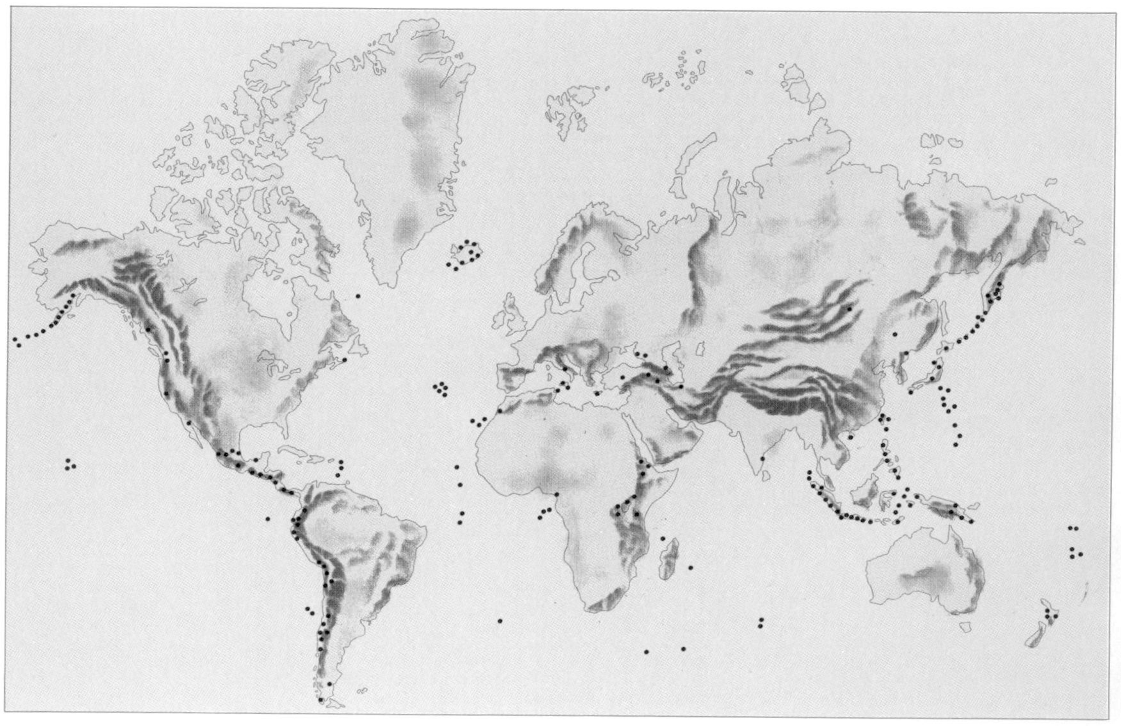

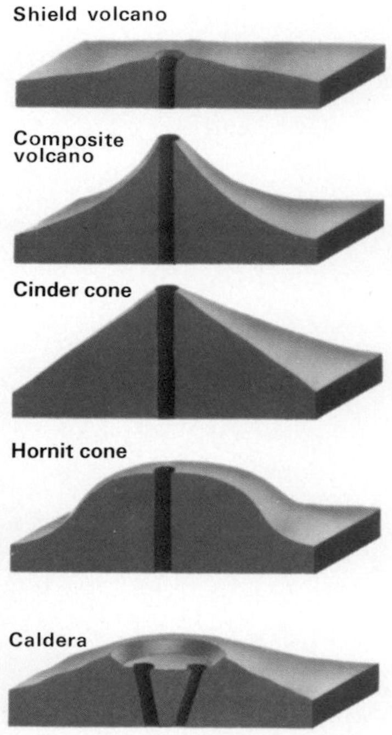
Shield volcano
Composite volcano
Cinder cone
Hornit cone
Caldera

The large map below shows the **world distribution of earthquakes** and their foci. The chart to the right of the map lists major earthquakes and their toll of human lives. An earthquake is a series of rapid vibrations originating (at an epicenter) from the slipping or faulting of parts of the earth's crust when stresses within build up to breaking point. The diagram at the left center below shows **how shock waves travel** through the earth.

Severe earthquakes may cause extensive damage destroying structures and severing communications, as in the **Alaska quake of 1964** (bottom left). Most loss of life occurs as a result of secondary causes — falling masonry, fires, or tsunami waves. The small map at the bottom of the page shows how **tsunami waves** travel from the epicenter of an earthquake. A sudden slump in the ocean bed during an earthquake forms a trough, followed by a crest and smaller waves. A more marked change in the level of the sea can start forming a tsunami crest that travels up to 60 kph with waves up to 60 m high. **Seismographic detectors**, diagramed below at the right, continuously record earthquake shocks and warn of the tsunami waves. As shown, P waves cause the first tremors, S the second, and L waves the main shock.

The two diagrams at the center right show how **seismic waves** spread through the earth. The shock waves sent out from the epicenter are of three main kinds. Primary (P) waves are compressional waves that can be transmitted through both solids and liquids and therefore will pass through the earth's liquid core. Secondary (S) waves are shear waves and pass only through solids. They are reflected at the liquid core-mantle boundary, taking a concave course back to the surface. But the surface refracts the P waves. The net result is the formation of a shadow zone that is free from P and S waves at a certain distance from the epicenter. The third main kind of wave is a long (L) wave, which travels slowly along the earth's surface, either vertically or horizontally.

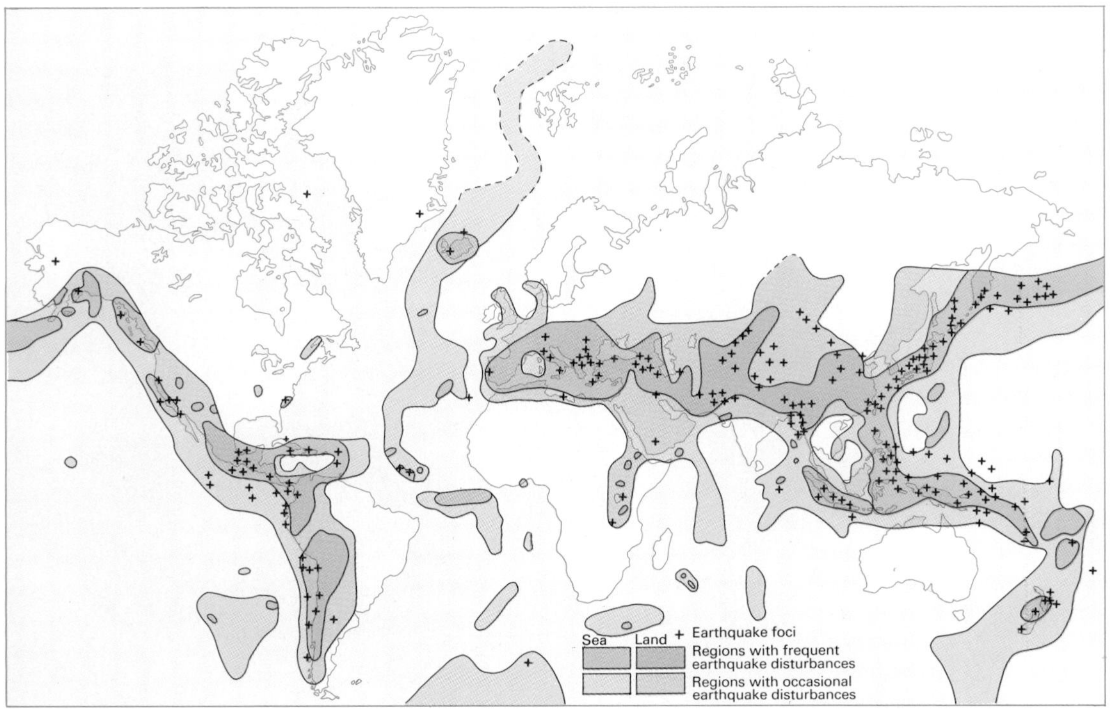
Sea
Land
+ Earthquake foci
Regions with frequent earthquake disturbances
Regions with occasional earthquake disturbances

Major earthquakes in the last 100 years	numbers killed
1896 Japan (tsunami)	22 000
1906 San Francisco	destroyed
1906 Chile, Valparaiso	22 000
1908 Italy, Messina	77 000
1915 Italy, Avezzano	30 000
1920 China, Kansu	180 000
1923 Japan, Tokyo	143 000
1927 China, Nan-Shan	200 000
1931 Nicaragua, Managua	destroyed
1932 China, Kansu	70 000
1934 India, Bihar-Nepal	10 700
1935 India, Quetta	60 000
1939 Chile, Chillan	20 000
1939/40 Turkey, Erzincan	30 000
1960 Morocco, Agadir	12 000
1962 N.W. Iran	10 000
1966 U.S.S.R., Tashkent	destroyed
1968 Northeastern Iran	12 000
1970 N. Peru	66 800
1972 Nicaragua, Managua	7 000
1974 N. Pakistan	10 000
1976 Guatemala	22 778
1976 China, Taugshan	650 000
1976 Philippines, Mindanao	8 000
1977 Rumania, Bucharest	1 500
1978 Iran, Tabas, etc.	26 000

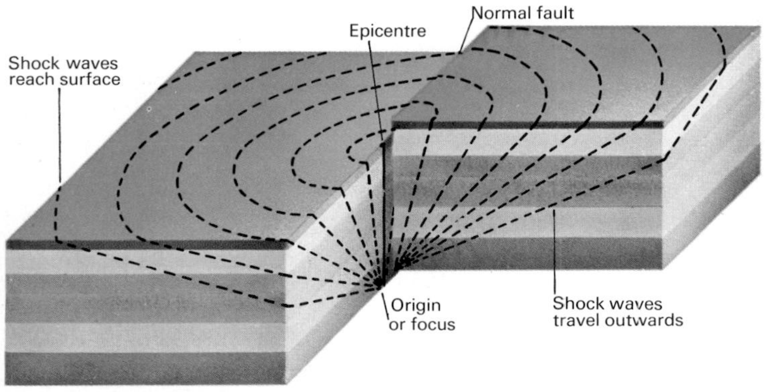
Normal fault
Epicentre
Shock waves reach surface
Origin or focus
Shock waves travel outwards

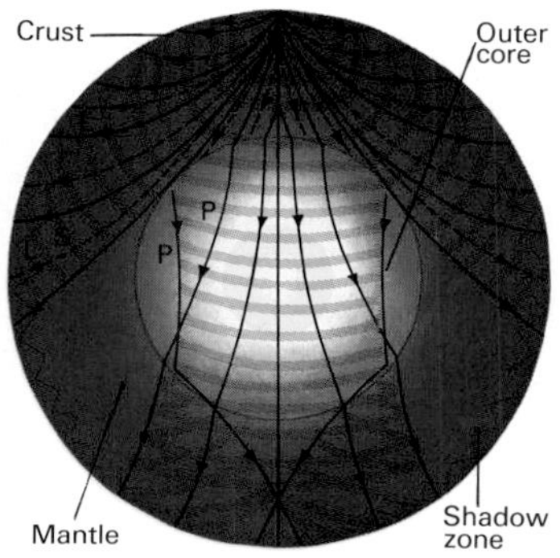
Crust
Outer core
P
P
Mantle
Shadow zone

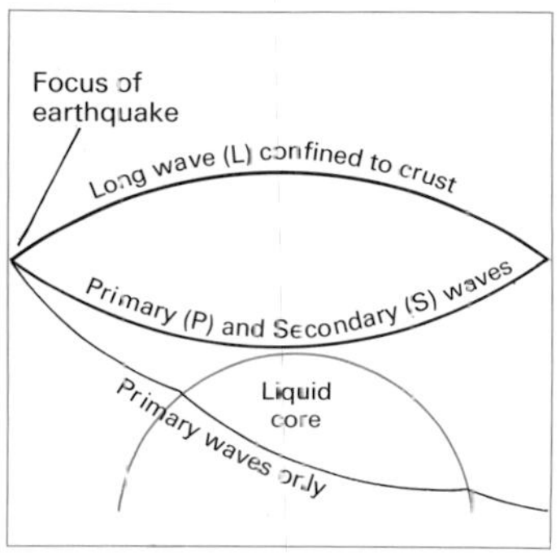
Focus of earthquake
Long wave (L) confined to crust
Primary (P) and Secondary (S) waves
Liquid core
Primary waves only

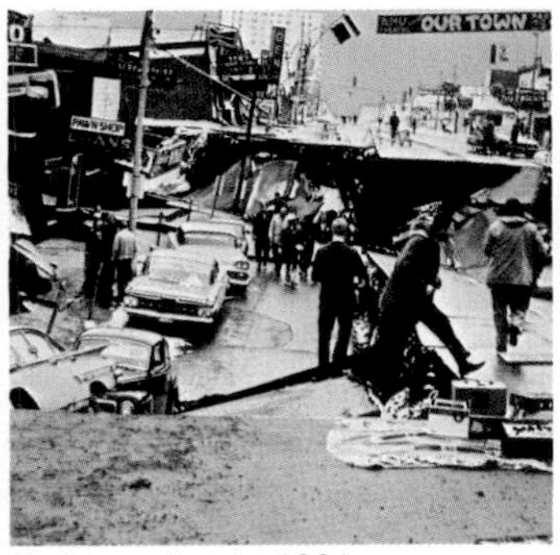
OUR TOWN
Alaskan earthquake, 1964

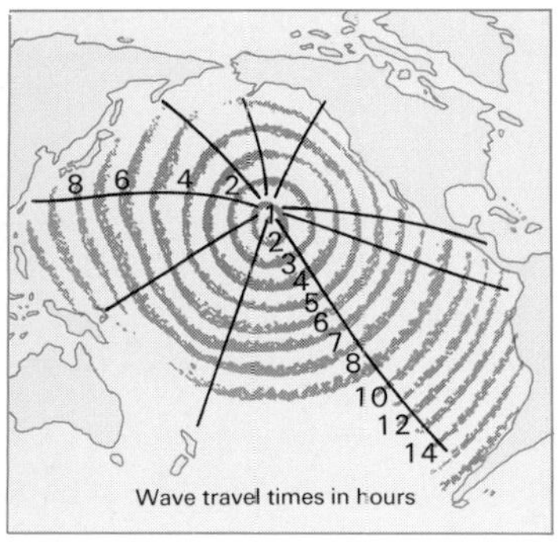
8
6
4
2
2
3
4
5
6
8
10
12
14
Wave travel times in hours

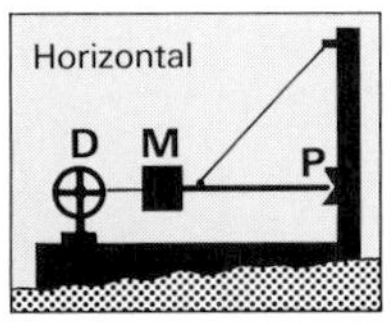
Horizontal
D
M
P

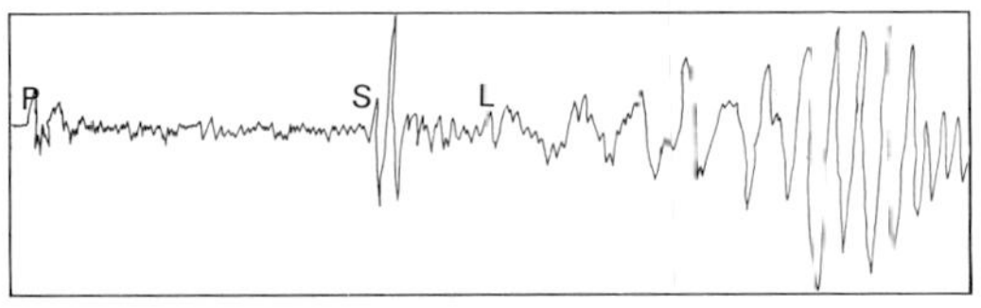
P
S
L

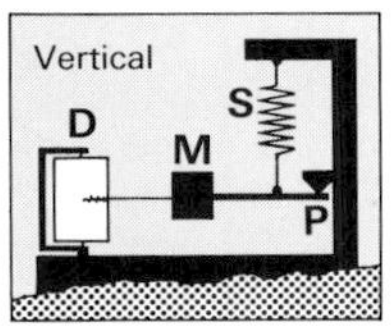
Vertical
D
M
S
P

Principles of seismographs (left)
M = Mass
D = Drum
P = Pivot
S = Spring

THE MAKING OF LANDSCAPE

The major forces that shape our land act very slowly in comparison with the average human life-span; but in geological terms the erosion of rock is, in fact, very fast. Land goes through a **cycle of transformation**. It is broken up by earthquakes and other earth movements, temperature changes, and the action of water, wind, and ice. Rock debris is then transported by water, wind, and glaciers and deposited on lowlands and on the sea floor (top left below). Here it builds up and by pressure of its own weight is converted into new rock strata (second left below). These in turn can be uplifted, either gently as plains or plateaus or more irregularly to form mountains. In either case, the new higher land is eroded as the cycle begins again. (Top right, a peneplain; second right, an uplifted peneplain.)

Rivers shape the land by three basic processes: erosion, transportation, and deposition. The three **stages in the life of a river** are shown in the three-part drawing at the right center below. Left to right: a youthful river flows fast, eroding downward to form a narrow valley; as it matures, it deposits some debris and erodes laterally to widen the valley; finally, it meanders across a wide, flat flood plain, depositing fine particles of alluvium.

The drawing at the bottom right explains the storage of **underground water**. Water enters porous and permeable rocks from the surface, moving downward until it reaches a layer of impermeable rock. Joints in the underground rock, such as limestone, are eroded to form underground caves and caverns. When the roof of a cave collapses, a gorge is formed. The illustrations at the center and bottom left show the effect of wind on the surface of the earth. **Wind erosion** (bottom left) caused by blasting of rock wastes against rock strata, can produce weird shapes. Wind also builds barchan sand dunes which slowly travel forward, horns first.

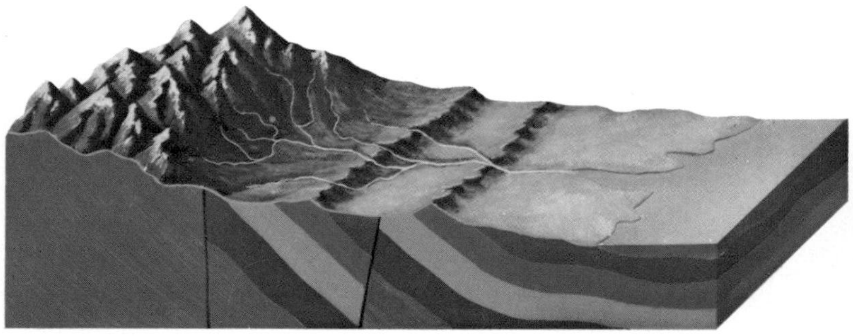

A Peneplain

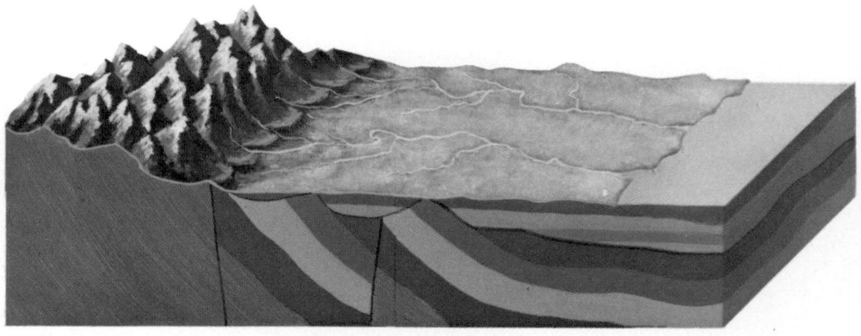

Uplifted peneplain

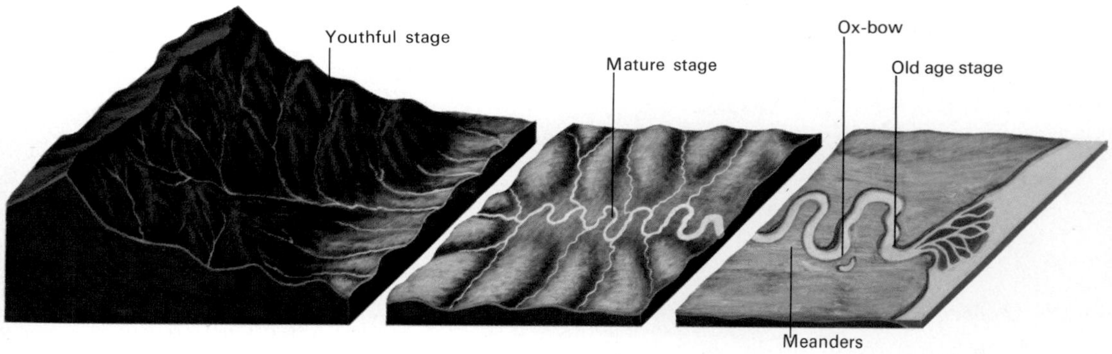
Youthful stage
Mature stage
Ox-bow
Old age stage
Meanders

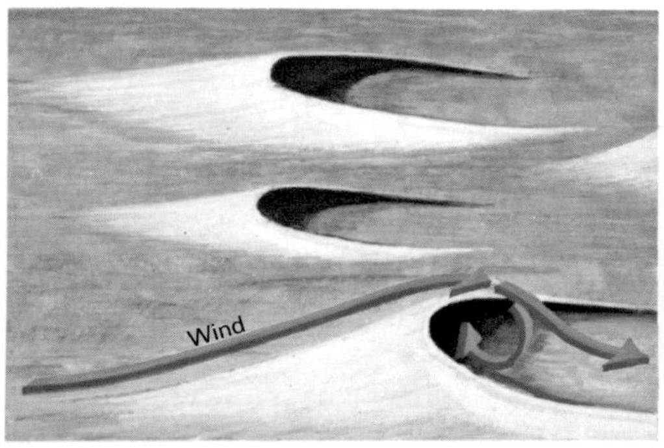
Wind

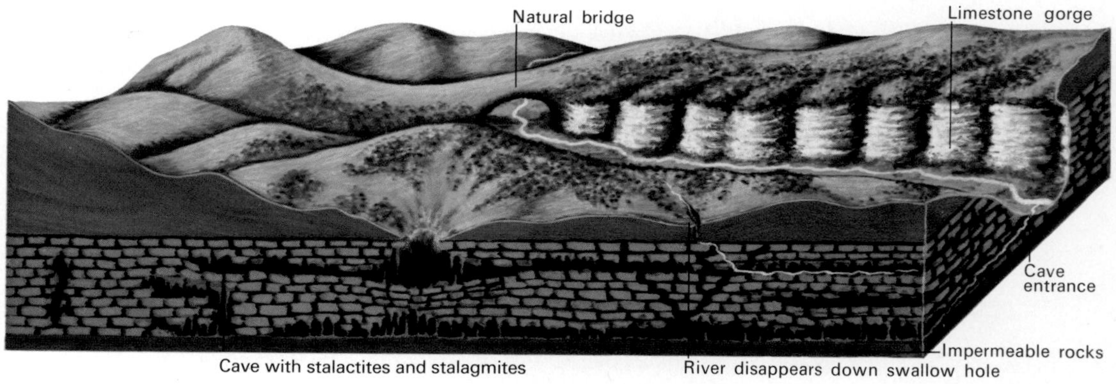
Natural bridge
Limestone gorge
Cave entrance
Impermeable rocks
Cave with stalactites and stalagmites
River disappears down swallow hole

The earth's landscape can be altered greatly by **volcanic activity**, top left, below. When pressure on rocks beneath the earth's crust is released, the normally semi-solid hot rock becomes liquid magma. The magma forces its way into cracks in the crust and may either reach the surface to form a volcano, or collect in the crust as sills, dikes, or laccoliths. When magma reaches the surface, it cools to form lava.

Mountainous landscapes may result from **folding and faulting**, below, top right. A vertical displacement in the earth's crust is called a **normal fault** or a **reverse fault**, a lateral displacement is a **tear fault**. An uplifted block is called a **horst**, the reverse of which is a **rift valley**. Compressed horizontal layers of sedimentary rock fold to form mountains. The layers that bend up form an **anticline**; those bending down form a **syncline**. Continued pressure forms an **overfold anticline**, an **overfold syncline**, and an **overthrust fold**.

The two drawings in the second row below show how **waves change the landscape**. Some coasts retreat under wave erosion; others advance with wave deposition. Steep cliffs and wave-cut platforms develop, and eroded debris deposits as terraces. Wave action also creates **odd features** such as those at the right. The next two drawings below show how **ice changes the landscape**, forming a glaciated valley. As the glacier deepens, it straightens and widens the valley. Intervalley divides are frost shattered to form sharp aretes and pyramidal peaks. Hanging valleys mark the entry of tributary rivers, and eroded rocks form moraines.

The bottom drawing depicts **subsidence and uplift**. As the land surface is eroded, it may eventually become a level plain — a peneplain, broken only by low hills that are remnants of previous mountains. In turn, this peneplain may be uplifted to form a plateau with steep edges. At the coast, a coastal plain may form.

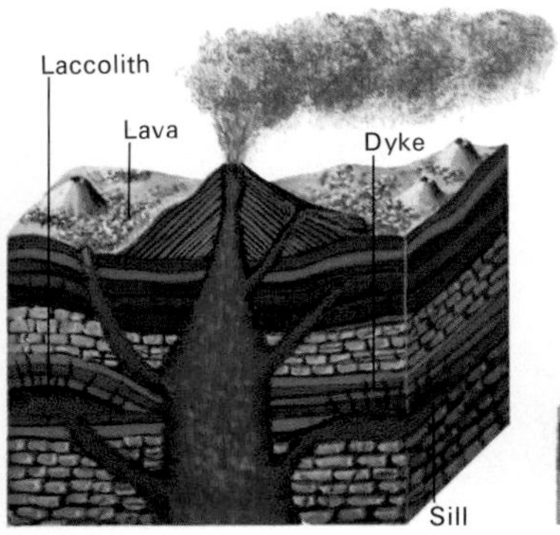
Laccolith
Lava
Dyke
Sill

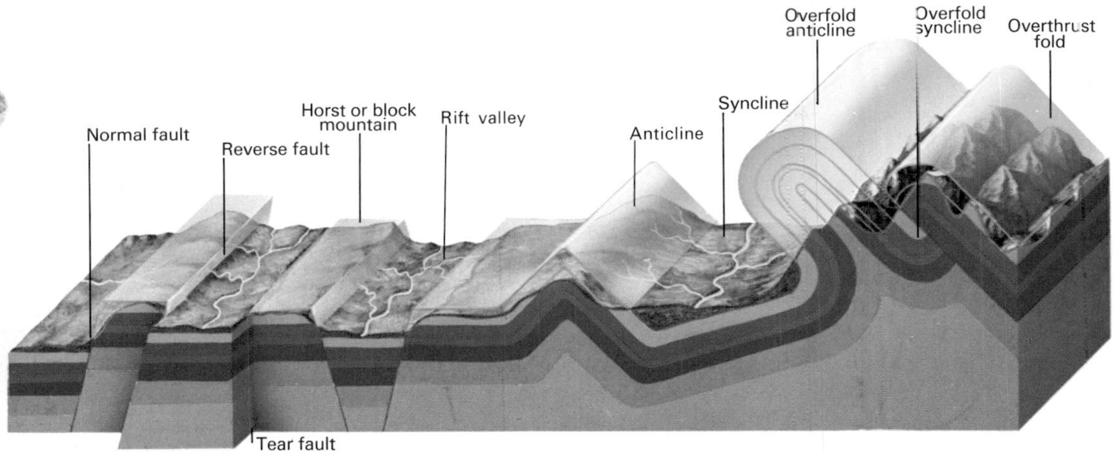
Normal fault
Reverse fault
Horst or block mountain
Rift valley
Anticline
Syncline
Overfold anticline
Overfold syncline
Overthrust fold
Tear fault

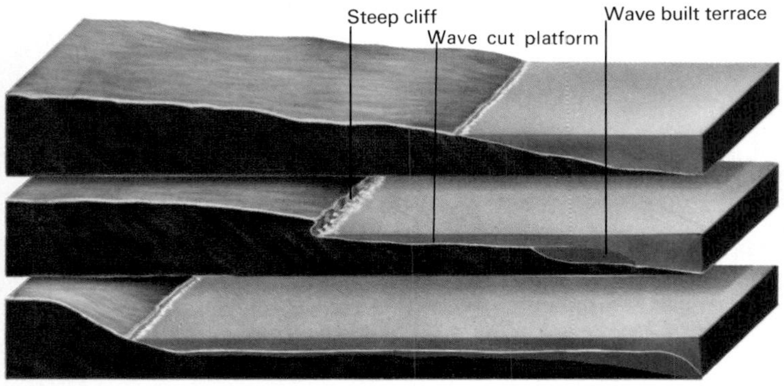
Steep cliff
Wave cut platform
Wave built terrace

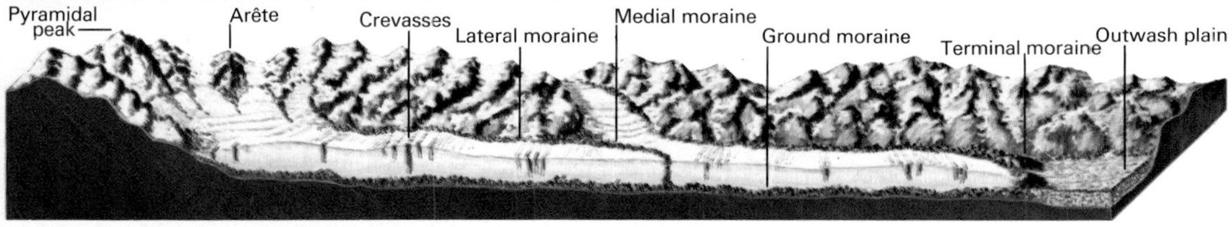
Pyramidal peak
Arête
Crevasses
Lateral moraine
Medial moraine
Ground moraine
Terminal moraine
Outwash plain

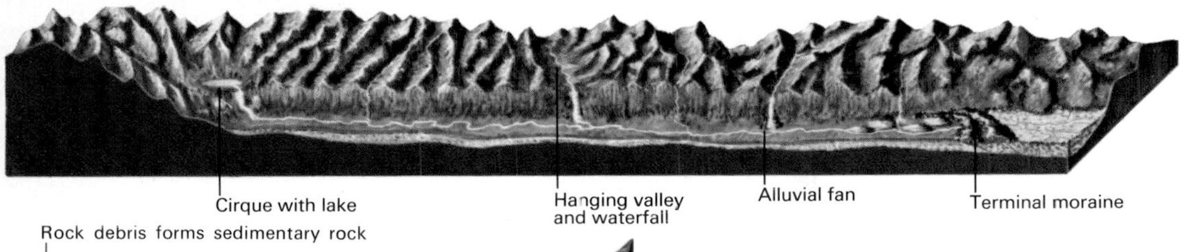
Cirque with lake
Hanging valley and waterfall
Alluvial fan
Terminal moraine

Rock debris forms sedimentary rock

THE EARTH: PHYSICAL DIMENSIONS

The figure of the earth can be expressed as a geoid, an imaginary sea-level surface, everywhere at right angles to the direction of gravity. By measuring at different places the angles from plumb lines to a fixed star, scientists found the geoid to be an oblate spheroid. Observations from satellites have now provided even more accurate data. Below, **land and sea hemispheres** are shown. About 85% of the land is contained in the hemisphere centered on a point between Paris and Brussels.

The two maps at the right below present the major **oceans and seas** (top map) and the major **lakes and inland seas** (bottom map). The accompanying data give the areas of these water bodies in 1000 km². Other **long rivers** not shown below are: Mekong, Asia; Niger, Africa; Mackenzie, N. America; Ob, Asia; and Yenisei, Asia.

High mountains and ocean depths are fascinating physical features of the earth's

Its surface

Highest point on the earth's surface: Mt. Everest, Tibet - Nepal boundary	8 848 m
Lowest point on the earth's surface: The Dead Sea, Jordan below sea level	395 m
Greatest ocean depth.: Challenger Deep, Mariana Trench	11 022 m
Average height of land	840 m
Average depth of seas and oceans	3 808 m

Dimensions

Superficial area	510 000 000 km²
Land surface	149 000 000 km²
Land surface as % of total area	29·2 %
Water surface	361 000 000 km²
Water surface as % of total area	70·8 %
Equatorial circumference	40 077 km
Meridional circumference	40 009 km
Equatorial diameter	12 756·8 km
Polar diameter	12 713·8 km
Equatorial radius	6 378·4 km
Polar radius	6 356·9 km
Volume of the Earth	1 083 230 x 10^6 km³
Mass of the Earth	5·9 x 10^{21} tonnes

Oceans and Seas
Area in 1000 km²

Pacific Ocean	165 721
Atlantic Ocean	81 660
Indian Ocean	73 442
Arctic Ocean	14 351
Mediterranean Sea	2 966
Bering Sea	2 274
Caribbean Sea	1 942
Mexico, Gulf of	1 813
Okhotsk, Sea of	1 528
East China Sea	1 248
Hudson Bay	1 230
Japan, Sea of	1 049
North Sea	575
Black Sea	448
Red Sea	440
Baltic Sea	422
Persian Gulf	238
St. Lawrence, Gulf of	236
English Channel & Irish Sea	179
California, Gulf of	161

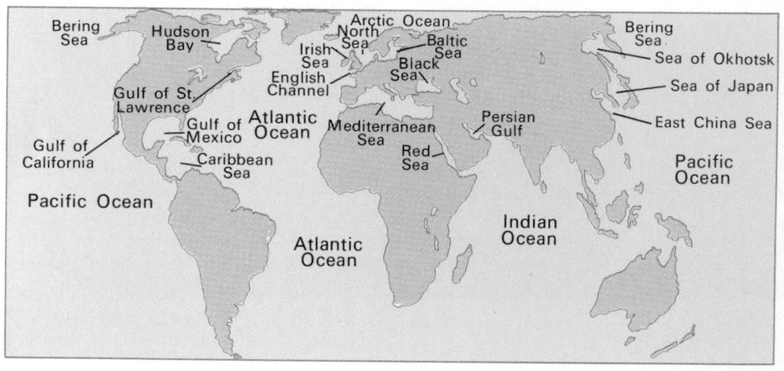
Bering Sea
Hudson Bay
Arctic Ocean
North Sea
Baltic Sea
Irish Sea
English Channel
Black Sea
Bering Sea
Sea of Okhotsk
Sea of Japan
Gulf of St. Lawrence
Gulf of Mexico
Atlantic Ocean
Mediterranean Sea
Persian Gulf
East China Sea
Gulf of California
Caribbean Sea
Red Sea
Pacific Ocean
Pacific Ocean
Atlantic Ocean
Indian Ocean

Lakes and Inland Seas
Areas in 1000 km²

Caspian Sea, Asia	424·2
Lake Superior, N.America	82·4
Lake Victoria, Africa	69·5
Aral Sea (Salt), Asia	63·8
Lake Huron, N.America	59·6
Lake Michigan, N.America	58·0
Lake Tanganyika, Africa	32·9
Lake Baikal, Asia	31·5
Great Bear Lake, N.America	31·1
Great Slave Lake, N.America	28·9
Lake Nyasa, Africa	28·5
Lake Erie, N.America	25·7
Lake Winnipeg, N.America	24·3
Lake Chad, Africa	20·7
Lake Ontario, N.America	19·5
Lake Ladoga, Europe	18·4
Lake Balkhash, Asia	17·3
Lake Maracaibo, S.America	16·3
Lake Onega, Europe	9·8
Lake Eyre (Salt), Australia	9·6
Lake Turkana (Salt), Africa	9·1
Lake Titicaca, S.America	8·3
Lake Nicaragua, C.America	8·0
Lake Athabasca, N.America	7·9
Reindeer Lake, N.America	6·3
Issyk-Kul, Asia	6·2
Lake Torrens (Salt), Australia	6·1
Koko Nor (Salt), Asia	6·0
Lake Urmia, Asia	6·0
Vänern, Europe	5·6

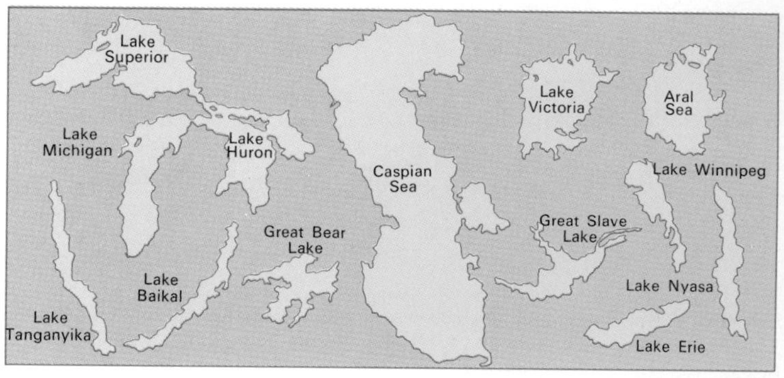
Lake Superior
Lake Michigan
Lake Huron
Caspian Sea
Lake Victoria
Aral Sea
Lake Winnipeg
Great Bear Lake
Great Slave Lake
Lake Baikal
Lake Nyasa
Lake Tanganyika
Lake Erie

Longest rivers

	km.
Nile, Africa	6 690
Amazon, S.America	6 280
Mississipi - Missouri,N.America	6 270
Yangtze, Asia	4 990
Zaïre, Africa	4 670
Amur, Asia	4 410
Hwang Ho (Yellow), Asia	4 350
Lena, Asia	4 260
Mekong, Asia	4 180
Niger, Africa	4 180
Mackenzie, N.America	4 040
Ob, Asia	4 000
Yenisei, Asia	3 800

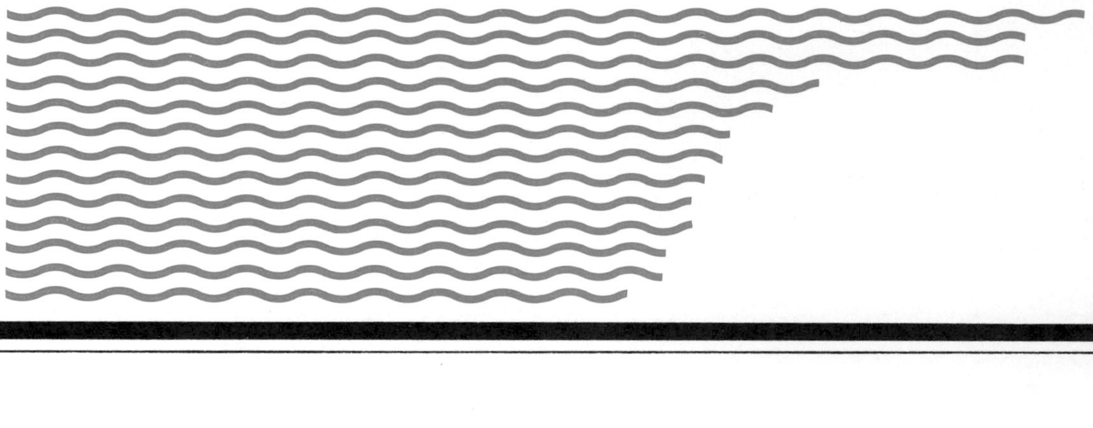

surface. **Mountain heights** (in meters) are shown below in the top chart. Trenches represent less than 2% of the total area of the sea-bed, but they are of great interest as lines of structural weakness in the earth's crust and as areas of frequent earthquakes. The greatest ocean trenches are the Puerto Rico deep (9,200 m), the Tonga (10,822 m), Mindanao (10,497 m), and Mariana (11,022 m) trenches. These **ocean depths** are shown at the right below in the second row. To the left of the chart is the **Bathyscaphe**, the vessel that made exploration of the greatest depths possible. The remaining photographs show a **waterfall** and a **dam**, natural and man-made physical features of the earth. The map at the bottom locates the mountains and trenches represented in the charts.

High mountains

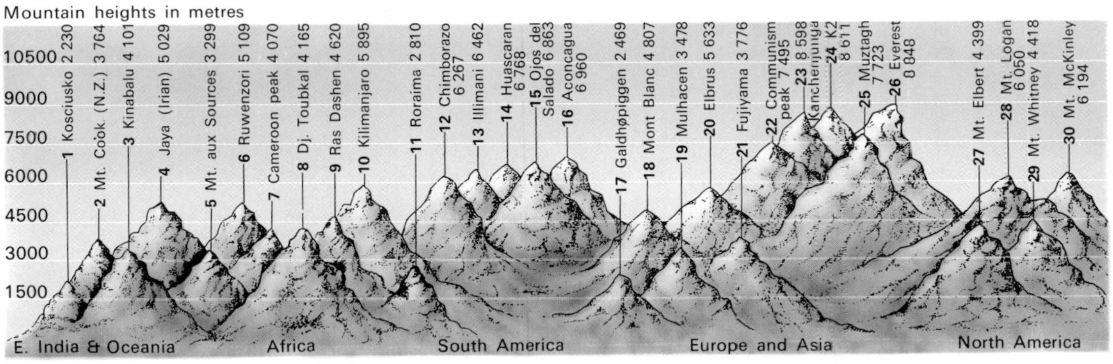

Mountain heights in metres
10500
9000
7500
6000
4500
3000
1500
1 Kosciusko 2 230
2 Mt. Cook (N.Z.) 3 764
3 Kinabalu 4 101
4 Jaya (Irian) 5 029
5 Mt. aux Sources 3 299
6 Ruwenzori 5 109
7 Cameroon peak 4 070
8 Dj. Toubkal 4 165
9 Ras Dashen 4 620
10 Kilimanjaro 5 895
11 Roraima 2 810
12 Chimborazo 6 267
13 Illimani 6 462
14 Huascaran 6 768
15 Ojos del Salado 6 863
16 Aconcagua 6 960
17 Galdhøpiggen 2 469
18 Mont Blanc 4 807
19 Mulhacen 3 478
20 Elbrus 5 633
21 Fujiyama 3 776
22 Communism peak 7 495
23 Kanchenjunga 8 598
24 K2 8 611
25 Muztagh 7 723
26 Everest 8 848
27 Mt. Elbert 4 399
28 Mt. Logan 6 050
29 Mt. Whitney 4 418
30 Mt. McKinley 6 194
E. India & Oceania
Africa
South America
Europe and Asia
North America

Bathyscaphe

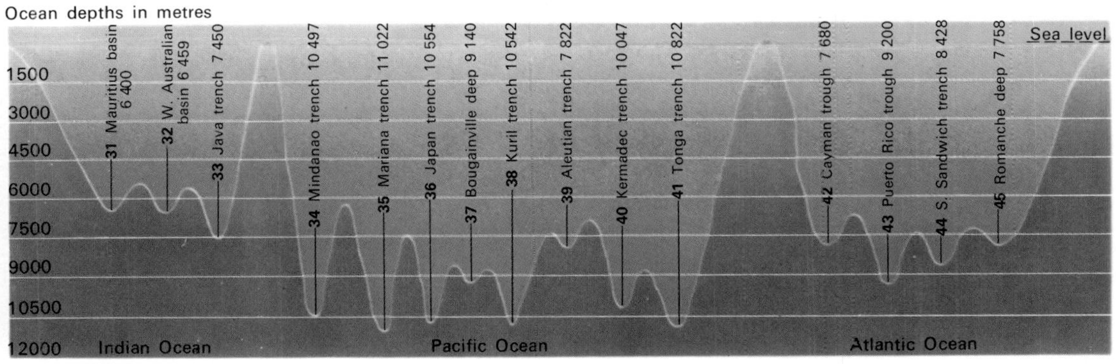

Ocean depths in metres
Sea level
1500
3000
4500
6000
7500
9000
10500
12000
31 Mauritius basin 6 400
32 W. Australian basin 6 459
33 Java trench 7 450
34 Mindanao trench 10 497
35 Mariana trench 11 022
36 Japan trench 10 554
37 Bougainville deep 9 140
38 Kuril trench 10 542
39 Aleutian trench 7 822
40 Kermadec trench 10 047
41 Tonga trench 10 822
42 Cayman trough 7 680
43 Puerto Rico trough 9 200
44 S. Sandwich trench 8 428
45 Romanche deep 7 758
Indian Ocean
Pacific Ocean
Atlantic Ocean

Waterfall

Notable Waterfalls heights in metres

Angel, Venezuela	980
Tugela, S. Africa	853
Mongefossen, Norway	774
Yosemite, California	738
Mardalsfossen, Norway	655
Cuquenan, Venezuela	610
Sutherland, N.Z.	579
Reichenbach, Switzerland	548
Wollomombi, Australia	518
Ribbon, California	491
Gavarnie, France	422
Tyssefallene, Norway	414
Krimml, Austria	370
King George VI, Guyana	366
Silver Strand, California	356
Geissbach, Switzerland	350
Staubbach, Switzerland	299
Trümmelbach, Switzerland	290
Chirombo, Zambia	268
Livingstone, Zaïre	259
King Edward VIII, Guyana	256
Gersoppa, India	253
Vettifossen Norway	250
Kalambo, Zambia	240
Kaieteur, Guyana	226
Maletsunyane, Lesotho	192
Terui, Italy	180
Murchison, Uganda	122
Victoria, Rhodesia-Zambia	107
Cauvery, India	97
Stanley, Zaïre	61
Niagara, N.America	51
Schaffhausen, Switzerland	30

Dam

Notable Dams heights in metres

Africa	
Cabora Bassa, Zambezi R.	168
Akosombo Main Dam, Volta R.	141
Kariba, Zambezi R.	128
Aswan High Dam, Nile R.	110
Asia	
Nurek, Vakhsh R., U.S.S.R.	317
Bhakra, Sutlej R., India	226
Kurobegawa, Kurobe R. , Jap.	186
Charvak, Chirchik R., U.S.S.R.	168
Okutadami, Tadami R., Jap.	157
Bhumiphol, Ping R., Thai.	154
Australasia	
Warragamba, N.S.W., Australia	137
Eucumbene, N.S.W., Australia	116
Europe	
Grande Dixence, Switz.	284
Vajont, Vajont, R., Italy	261
Mauvoisin, Drance R., Switz.	237
Contra, Verzasca R., Switz.	230
Luzzone, Brenno R., Switz.	208
Tignes, Isère R., France	180
Amir Kabir, Karadj R., U.S.S.R.	180
Vidraru, Arges R., Rum.	165
Kremasta, Acheloos R., Greece	165
North America	
Oroville, Feather R.,	235
Hoover, Colorado R.,	221
Glen Canyon, Colorado R.,	216
Daniel Johnson, Can.	214
New Bullards Bar, N. Yuba R.	194
Mossyrock, Cowlitz R.,	184
Shasta, Sacramento R.,	183
W.A.C. Bennett, Canada.	183
Don Pedro, Tuolumne R.,	178
Hungry Horse, Flathead R.	172
Grand Coulee, Columbia R.,	168
Central and South America	
Guri, Caroni R., Venezuela.	106

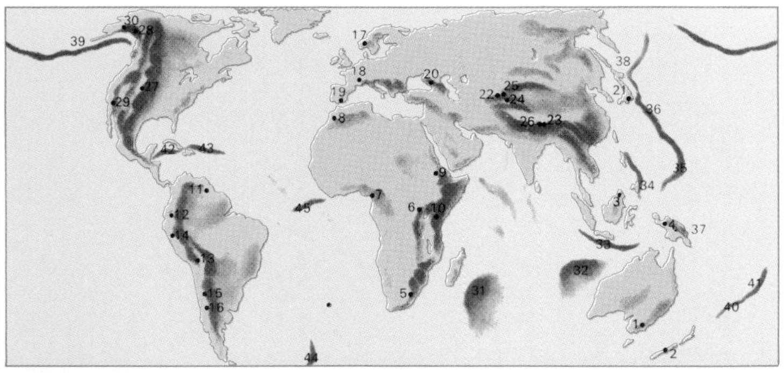

DISTANCES

Kms	Berlin	Bombay	Buenos Aires	Cairo	Calcutta	Caracas	Chicago	Copenhagen	Darwin	Hong Kong	Honolulu	Johannesburg	Lagos	Lisbon	
Berlin		3907	7400	1795	4370	5241	4402	222	8044	5440	7310	5511	3230	1436	4
Bombay	6288		9275	2706	1034	9024	8048	3990	4510	2683	8024	4334	4730	4982	4
Buenos Aires	11909	14925		7341	10268	3167	5599	7498	9130	11481	7558	5025	4919	5964	6
Cairo	2890	4355	11814		3541	6340	6127	1992	7216	5064	8838	3894	2432	2358	2
Calcutta	7033	1664	16524	5699		9609	7978	4395	3758	1653	7048	5256	5727	5639	4
Caracas	8435	14522	5096	10203	15464		2502	5215	11221	10166	6009	6847	4810	4044	4
Chicago	7084	12953	9011	3206	12839	4027		4250	9361	7783	4247	8689	5973	3992	3
Copenhagen	357	6422	12067	9860	7072	8392	6840		8017	5388	7088	5732	3436	1540	
Darwin	12946	7257	14693	11612	6047	18059	15065	12903		2654	5369	6611	8837	9391	8
Hong Kong	8754	4317	18478	8150	2659	16360	12526	8671	4271		5543	6669	7360	6853	5
Honolulu	11764	12914	12164	14223	11343	9670	6836	11407	8640	8921		11934	10133	7821	7
Johannesburg	8870	6974	8088	6267	8459	11019	13984	9225	10639	10732	19206		2799	5089	5
Lagos	5198	7612	7916	3915	9216	7741	9612	5530	14222	11845	16308	4505		2360	3
Lisbon	2311	8018	9600	3794	9075	6501	6424	2478	15114	11028	12587	8191	3799		
London	928	7190	11131	3508	7961	7507	6356	952	13848	9623	11632	9071	5017	1588	
Los Angeles	9311	14000	9852	12200	13120	5812	2804	9003	12695	11639	4117	16676	12414	9122	8
Mexico City	9732	15656	7389	12372	15280	3586	2726	9514	14631	14122	6085	14585	11071	8676	8
Moscow	1610	5031	13477	2902	5534	9938	8000	1561	11350	7144	11323	9161	6254	3906	2
Nairobi	6370	4532	10402	3536	6179	11544	12883	6706	10415	8776	17282	2927	3807	6461	6
New York	6385	12541	8526	9020	12747	3430	1145	6188	16047	12950	7980	12841	8477	5422	5
Paris	876	7010	11051	3210	7858	7625	6650	1026	13812	9630	11968	8732	4714	1454	
Peking	7822	4757	19268	7544	3269	14399	10603	7202	6011	1963	8160	11710	11457	9668	8
Reykjavik	2385	8335	11437	5266	8687	6915	4757	2103	13892	9681	9787	10938	6718	2948	1
Rio de Janeiro	10025	13409	1953	9896	15073	4546	8547	10211	16011	17704	13342	7113	6035	7734	9
Rome	1180	6175	11151	2133	7219	8363	7739	1531	13265	9284	12916	7743	4039	1861	1
Singapore	9944	3914	15879	8267	2897	18359	15078	9969	3349	2599	10816	8660	11145	11886	10
Sydney	16096	10160	11800	14418	9138	15343	14875	16042	3150	7374	8168	11040	15519	18178	16
Tokyo	8924	6742	18362	9571	5141	14164	10137	8696	5431	2874	6202	13547	13480	11149	9
Toronto	6497	12488	9093	9233	12561	3873	700	6265	15498	12569	7465	13374	8948	5737	5
Wellington	18140	12370	9981	16524	11354	13122	13451	17961	5325	9427	7513	11761	16050	19575	18

Los Angeles	Mexico City	Moscow	Nairobi	New York	Paris	Peking	Reykjavik	Rio de Janeiro	Rome	Singapore	Sydney	Tokyo	Toronto	Wellington	
85	6047	1000	3958	3967	545	4860	1482	6230	734	6179	10002	5545	4037	11272	Berlin
00	9728	3126	2816	7793	4356	2956	5179	8332	3837	2432	6313	4189	7760	7686	Bombay
22	4591	8374	6463	5298	6867	11972	7106	1214	6929	9867	7332	11410	5650	6202	Buenos Aires
80	7687	1803	2197	5605	1994	4688	3272	6149	1325	5137	8959	5947	5737	10268	Cairo
52	9494	3438	3839	7921	4883	2031	5398	9366	4486	1800	5678	3195	7805	7055	Calcutta
12	2228	6175	7173	2131	4738	8947	4297	2825	5196	11407	9534	8801	2406	8154	Caracas
42	1694	4971	8005	711	4132	6588	2956	5311	4809	9369	9243	6299	435	8358	Chicago
94	5912	970	4167	3845	638	4475	1306	6345	951	6195	9968	5403	3892	11160	Copenhagen
88	9091	7053	6472	9971	8582	3735	8632	9948	8243	2081	1957	3375	9630	3309	Darwin
32	8775	4439	5453	8047	5984	1220	6015	11001	5769	1615	4582	1786	7810	5857	Hong Kong
58	3781	7036	10739	4958	7437	5070	6081	8290	8026	6721	5075	3854	4638	4669	Honolulu
62	9063	5692	1818	7979	5426	7276	6797	4420	4811	5381	6860	8418	8310	7308	Johannesburg
13	6879	3886	2366	5268	2929	7119	4175	3750	2510	6925	9643	8376	5560	9973	Lagos
68	5391	2427	4015	3369	903	6007	1832	4805	1157	7385	11295	6928	3565	12163	Lisbon
42	5552	1552	4237	3463	212	5057	1172	5778	889	6743	10558	5942	3545	11691	London
	1549	6070	9659	2446	5645	6251	4310	6310	6331	8776	7502	5475	2170	6719	Los Angeles
		6664	9207	2090	5717	7742	4635	4780	6365	10321	8058	7024	2018	6897	Mexico City
			3942	4666	1545	3600	2053	7184	1477	5237	9008	4651	4637	10283	Moscow
				7358	4029	5727	5395	5548	3350	4635	7552	6996	7570	8490	Nairobi
					3626	6828	2613	4832	4280	9531	9935	6741	356	8951	New York
93						5106	1384	5708	687	6671	10539	6038	3738	11798	Paris
69	10724						4897	10773	5049	2783	5561	1304	6557	6700	Peking
44	14818	6344						6135	2048	7155	10325	5469	2600	10725	Reykjavik
36	3364	7510	11842						5725	9763	8389	11551	5180	7367	Rio de Janeiro
85	9200	2486	6485	5836						6229	10143	6127	4399	11523	Rome
60	12460	5794	9216	10988	8217						3915	3306	9350	5298	Singapore
36	7460	3304	8683	4206	2228	7882						4861	9800	1383	Sydney
55	7693	11562	8928	7777	9187	17338	9874						6410	5762	Tokyo
88	10243	2376	5391	6888	1105	8126	3297	9214						8820	Toronto
23	16610	8428	7460	15339	10737	4478	11514	15712	10025						Wellington
73	12969	14497	12153	15989	16962	8949	16617	13501	16324	6300					Miles
11	11304	7485	11260	10849	9718	2099	8802	18589	9861	5321	7823				
92	3247	7462	12183	574	6015	10552	4184	8336	7080	15047	15772	10316			
14	11100	16549	13664	14405	18987	10782	17260	11855	18545	8526	2226	9273	14194		

WATER RESOURCES AND VEGETATION

Fresh water is essential for life, and in some parts of the world it is a most precious commodity. Since it is easy for industrialized states to take water's existence for granted, our increasing demands may yet require the desalination of the earth's 1,250 million cubic kilometers of water. The drawing at the left below shows the global **distribution of water**. The drawing at the upper right depicts the **hydrologic cycle**, in which water is continually absorbed into the atmosphere as vapor, which in turn condenses or freezes and falls as rain, hail, or snow. As shown, vegetation plays an important part in this cycle.

The map and photographs on the opposite page show the earth's natural vegetation by climate. The photographs show: (1) tundra, (2) coniferous forest, (3) broad-leaved forest, (4) tropical rain forest, (5) monsoon forest, (6) Mediterranean scrub, (7) grassland, (8) savanna, (9) steppe, and (10) desert.

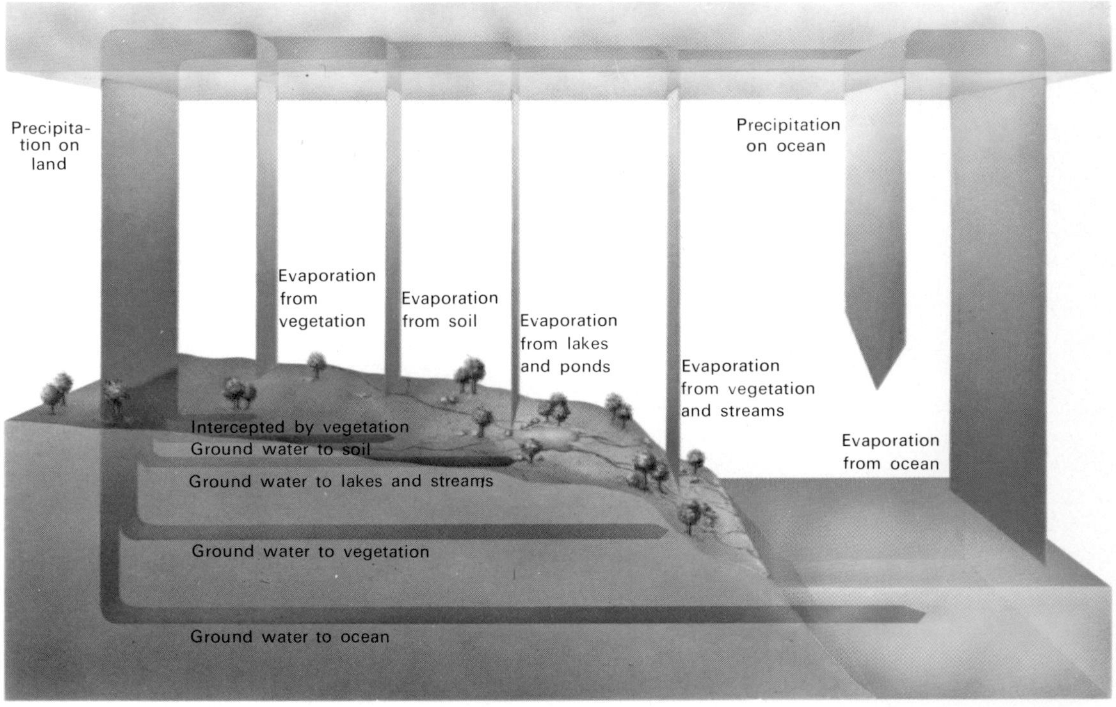
Precipita-
tion on
land
Precipitation
on ocean
Evaporation
from
vegetation
Evaporation
from soil
Evaporation
from lakes
and ponds
Evaporation
from vegetation
and streams
Evaporation
from ocean
Intercepted by vegetation
Ground water to soil
Ground water to lakes and streams
Ground water to vegetation
Ground water to ocean

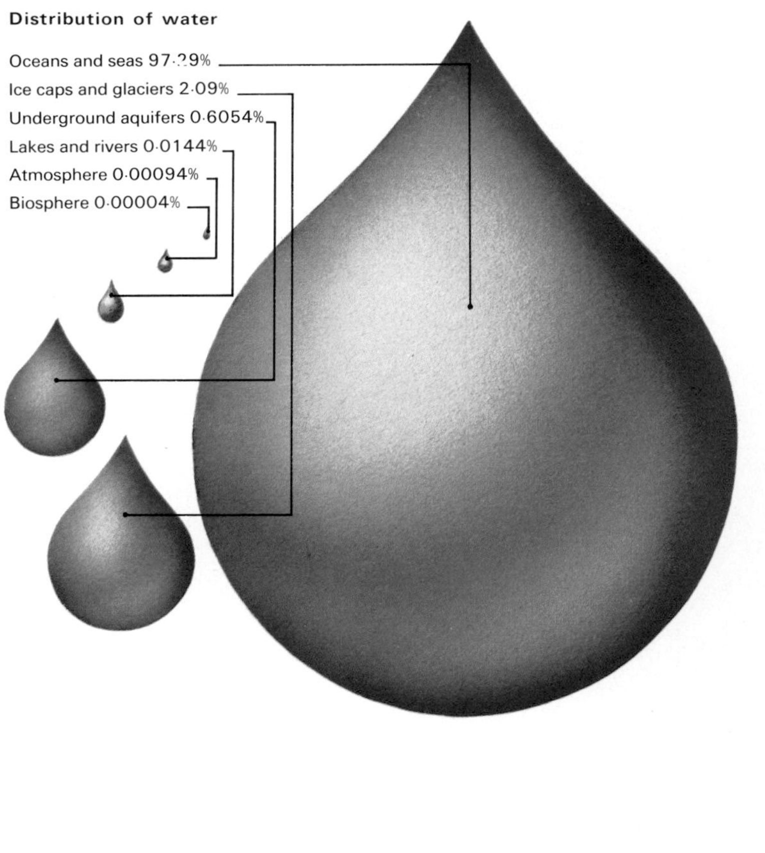
Distribution of water
Oceans and seas 97·29%
Ice caps and glaciers 2·09%
Underground aquifers 0·6054%
Lakes and rivers 0·0144%
Atmosphere 0·00094%
Biosphere 0·00004%

Tundra

Coniferous forest

Broad-leaved forest

Tropical rain forest

Monsoon forest

Mediterranean scrub

Grassland

Savanna

Semidesert

Desert

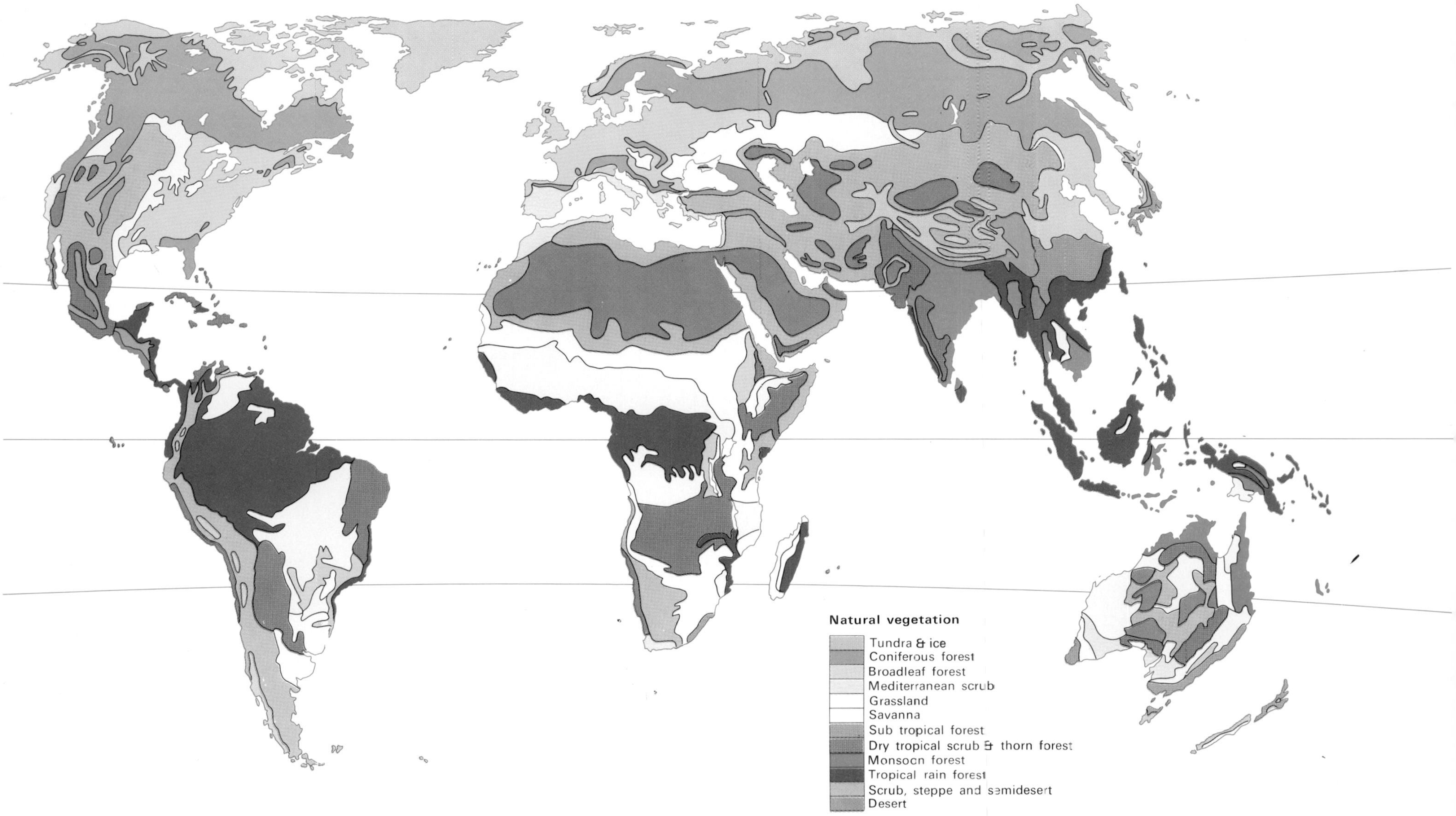
Natural vegetation
Tundra & ice
Coniferous forest
Broadleaf forest
Mediterranean scrub
Grassland
Savanna
Sub tropical forest
Dry tropical scrub & thorn forest
Monsoon forest
Tropical rain forest
Scrub, steppe and semidesert
Desert

POPULATION

World population distribution is shown on the maps at the right and on the chart below the map at the far right. The most densely populated regions are in India, China, and Europe where the average density is between 100 and 200 per square kilometer, although there are pockets of extremely high density elsewhere. In contrast, Australia has only 1.5 people per square kilometer. The countries have been drawn on the chart to make their areas proportional to their populations.

The graphs at the left below present **age distribution** for six countries in the early 1970s. France shows many demographic characteristics of European countries where birth and death rates have declined, with moderate population growth and nearly as many old as young. Note the high birth and death rates of India and Ghana.

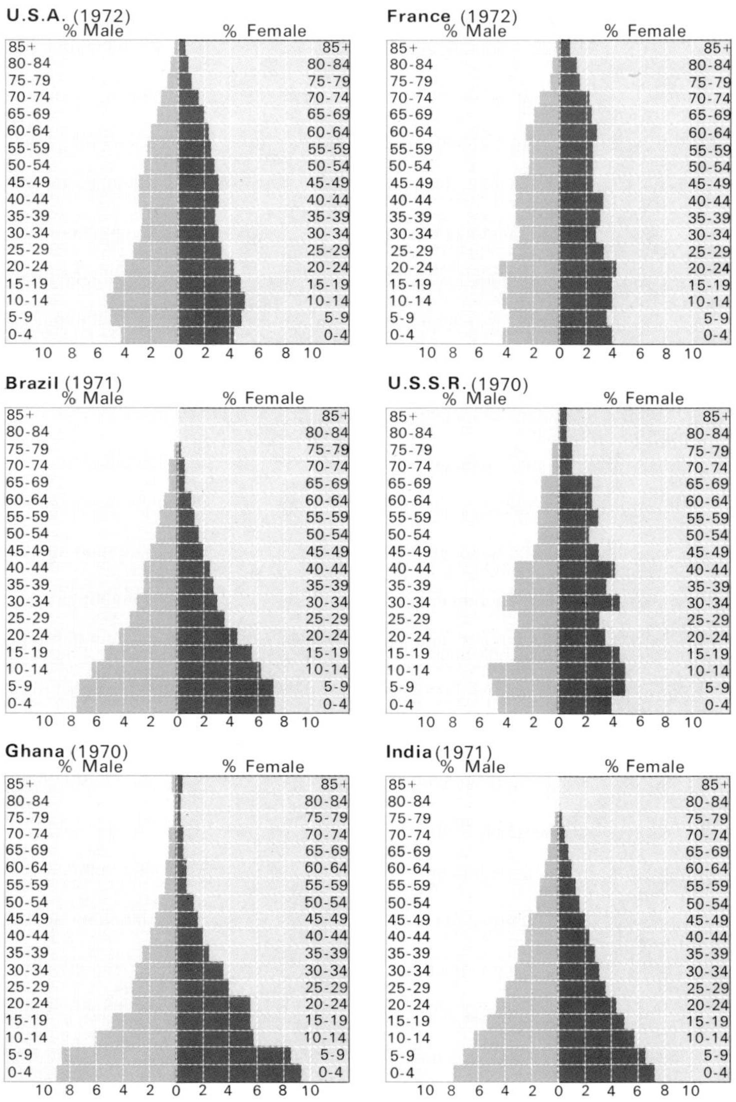
U.S.A. (1972)
France (1972)
Brazil (1971)
U.S.S.R. (1970)
Ghana (1970)
India (1971)
% Male
% Female
85+
80-84
75-79
70-74
65-69
60-64
55-59
50-54
45-49
40-44
35-39
30-34
25-29
20-24
15-19
10-14
5-9
0-4
10 8 6 4 2 0 2 4 6 8 10

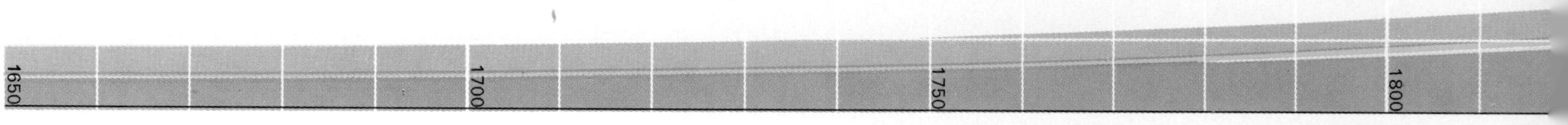
1650
1700
1750
1800

People have always been unevenly distributed in the world. Europe has for centuries contained nearly 20% of the world's population; but, after the 16–19th century explorations and consequent migrations, this proportion was rapidly reduced. In 1750, the Americas had 2% of the world's total; by A.D. 2000, they will contain 16%. This increase is reflected in the graph at the bottom of the page, on which population is given as millions. As shown on the graph, until recently there was little increase in world population. About 6000 B.C. there were probably about 200 million people in all. This level increased just over 100 million in the next 7,000 years. By the 1800s, there were about 1,000 million people. At present, world population is approximating 4,000 million. It is expected that this figure will approach 7,000 million by the year 2000.

World population distribution

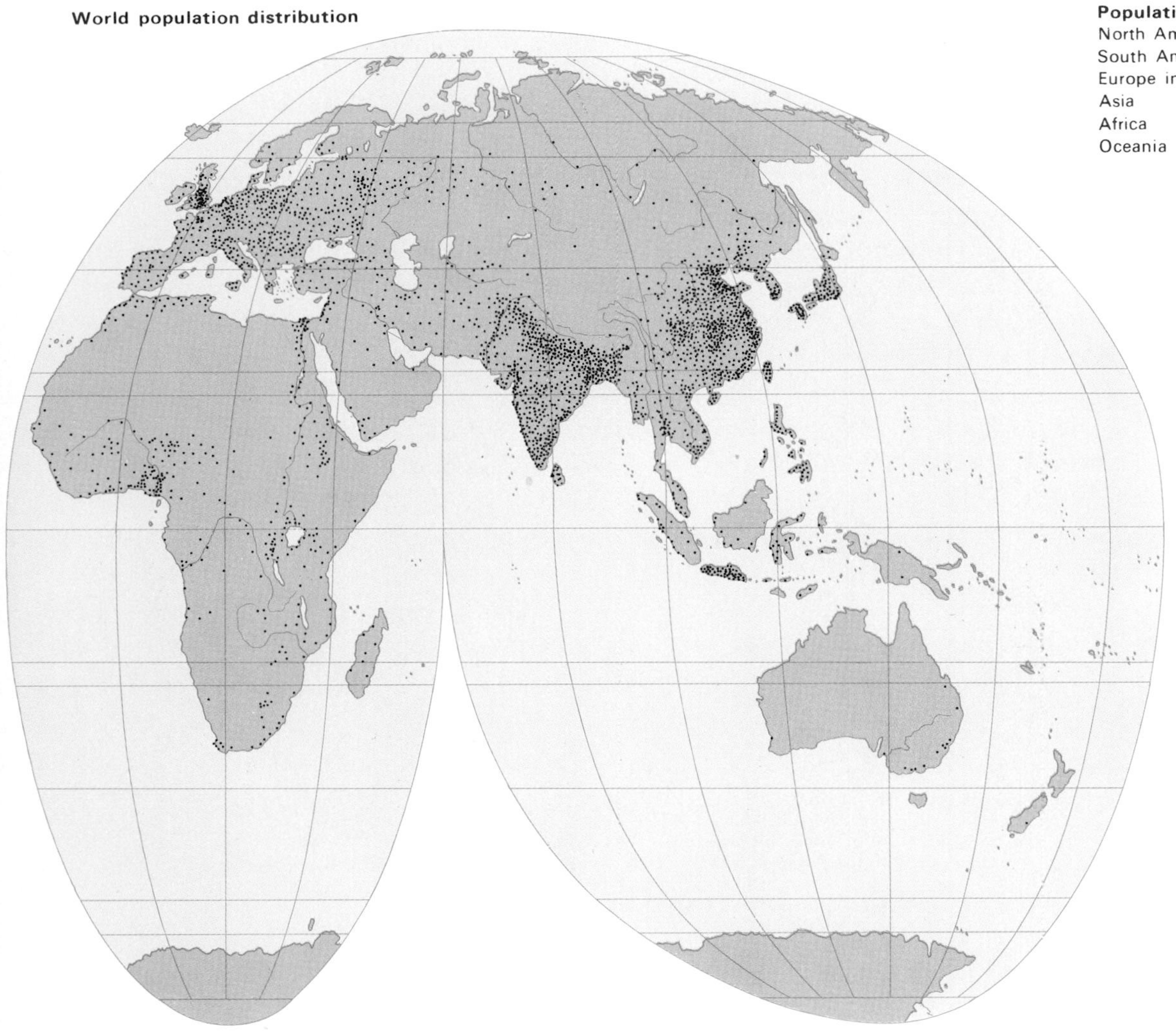

Population in 2000AD

North America	296 000 000
South America	625 000 000
Europe inc. USSR	861 000 000
Asia	3 757 000 000
Africa	834 000 000
Oceania	33 000 000

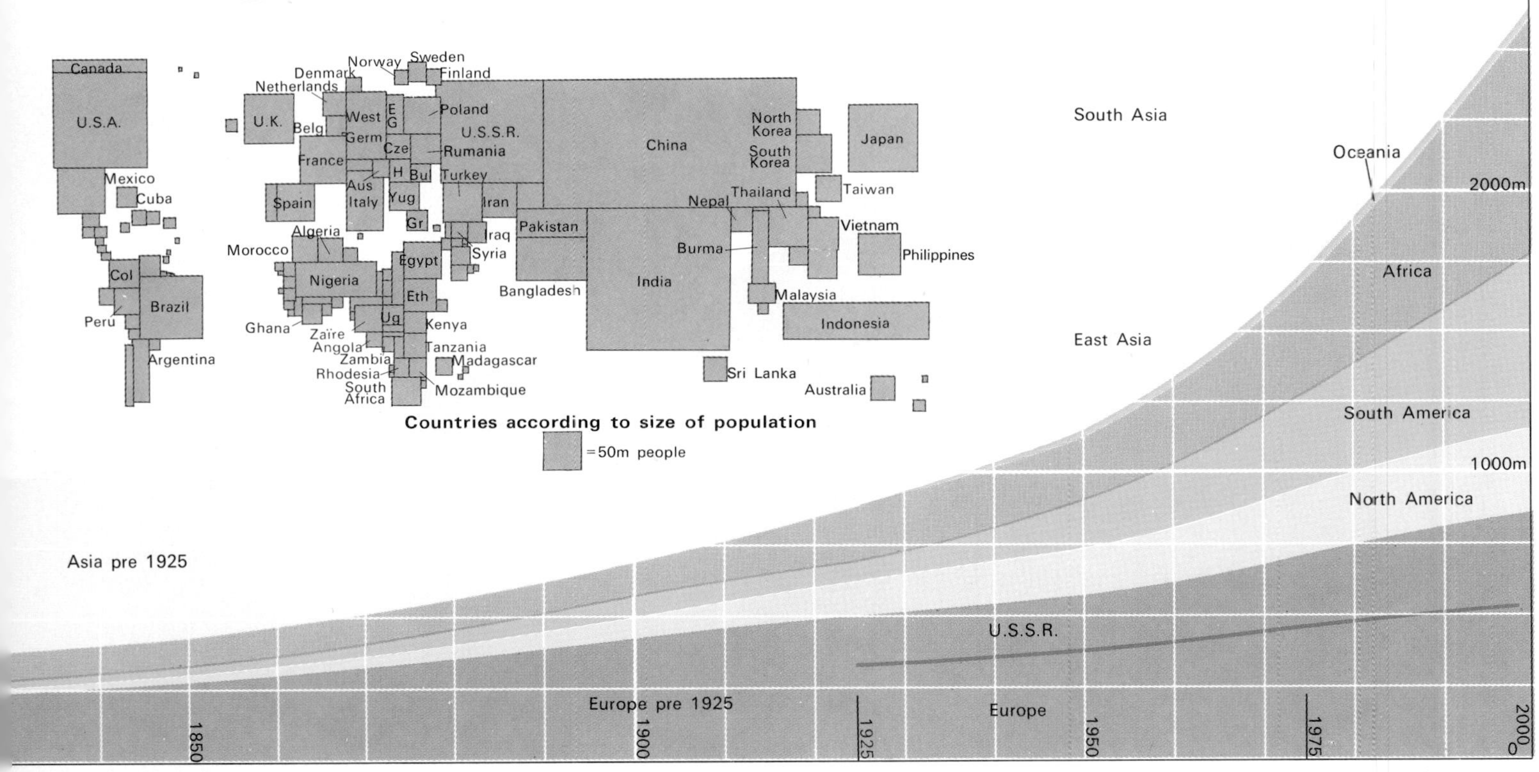
Canada
U.S.A.
Mexico
Cuba
Col
Brazil
Peru
Argentina
Norway
Sweden
Finland
Denmark
Netherlands
U.K.
Belg
West Germ
E G
Poland
U.S.S.R.
Cze
Rumania
France
Aus
H
Bu
Turkey
Spain
Italy
Yug
Gr
Iran
Iraq
Syria
Algeria
Morocco
Egypt
Nigeria
Eth
Ghana
Ug
Kenya
Zaïre
Angola
Tanzania
Zambia
Madagascar
Rhodesia
South Africa
Mozambique
Pakistan
Bangladesh
India
China
North Korea
South Korea
Japan
Taiwan
Nepal
Thailand
Burma
Vietnam
Philippines
Malaysia
Indonesia
Sri Lanka
Australia
=50m people

Countries according to size of population

6000m
5000m
4000m
3000m
2000m
1000m
0
South Asia
Oceania
Africa
East Asia
South America
North America
Asia pre 1925
U.S.S.R.
Europe pre 1925
Europe
1850
1900
1925
1950
1975
2000

LANGUAGE

To a degree, language differences may be blamed for the division and lack of understanding between nations. Whereas a common language binds countries, it also isolates them from other countries and groups. Thus beliefs, inventions, and ideas remain exclusive to these groups and different cultures develop.

The map below shows the **worldwide distribution of language**. As a result of colonization and the spread of internationally accepted languages, many countries have superimposed a language completely unrelated to their own in order to combine isolated national groups and to facilitate international understanding. Examples are the use of Spanish in South America and English in India. Certain languages that show marked similarities are thought to have developed from a common parent language, such as Latin. After the retreat of the Roman Empire, Latin remained as the released nation's new language wherever it had been firmly established. Where there was no unifying center, divergent development took place, and Latin evolved into a new language.

Written language (see chart below) originated with a series of pictures which gradually changed in style, influenced by the writing tools used. Carved alphabets tended to be angular; painted ones tended to be curved.

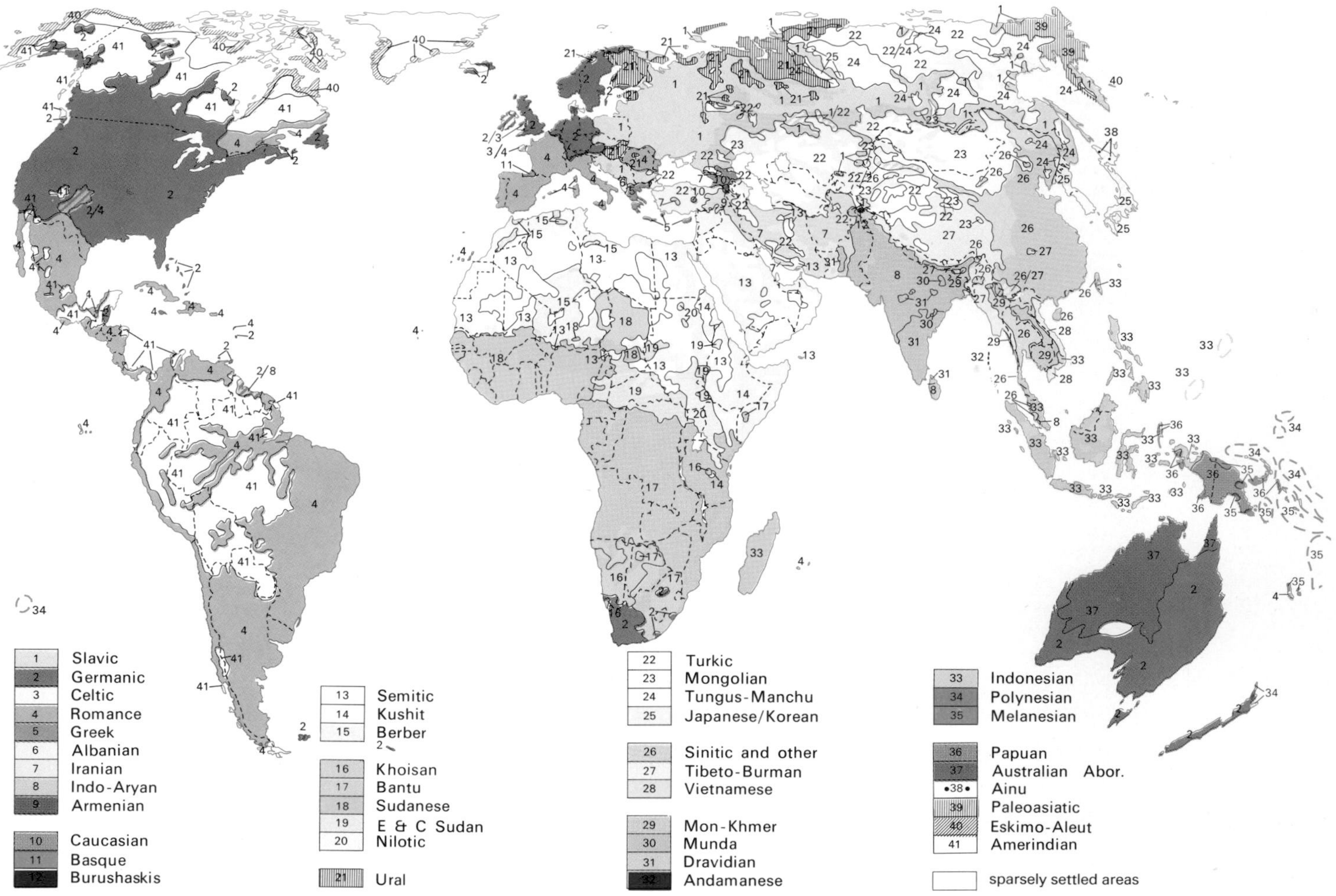

1 Slavic
2 Germanic
3 Celtic
4 Romance
5 Greek
6 Albanian
7 Iranian
8 Indo-Aryan
9 Armenian
10 Caucasian
11 Basque
12 Burushaskis
13 Semitic
14 Kushit
15 Berber
16 Khoisan
17 Bantu
18 Sudanese
19 E & C Sudan
20 Nilotic
21 Ural
22 Turkic
23 Mongolian
24 Tungus-Manchu
25 Japanese/Korean
26 Sinitic and other
27 Tibeto-Burman
28 Vietnamese
29 Mon-Khmer
30 Munda
31 Dravidian
32 Andamanese
33 Indonesian
34 Polynesian
35 Melanesian
36 Papuan
37 Australian Abor.
38 Ainu
39 Paleoasiatic
40 Eskimo-Aleut
41 Amerindian
sparsely settled areas

Assyrian (carved)
Ancient Hebrew (painted)
Egyptian hieroglyphic (painted)
Some modern non-latin type faces
Greek
ΑΒΓΔΕΖΗΘΙΚΛΜΝΞΟΠΡΣΤΥΦΧΨΩς
Cyrillic
АБВГДЕЖЗИЙІКЛМНОПРСТУФХЦЧШ
Arabic
في عام ١٨٩٧ وصل إلى إنجلترا أ نموذج
Bengali
১৮৯৭ খ্রীস্টাব্দে আধুনিক মডেলের একটি
Telugu
Japanese
国土の位置と地形
Chinese
父獨子出有之限地位司,能
司在提印芬刷奥業司上有

RELIGION

Throughout history, people have held belief in supernatural powers based on the forces of nature. They expressed this belief by worshipping a supreme being or several gods. **Hinduism**, for example, honors many gods and goddesses, all manifestations of the one Spirit, Brahma. This religion incorporates the doctrine of reincarnation and espouses the caste system. **Buddhism**, founded in northeast India by Gautama Buddha (563-483 B.C.), teaches that spiritual and moral discipline are essential to the achievement of supreme peace. **Confucianism**, a mixture of Buddhism and Confucius' teachings, provided a moral basis for the political structure of Imperial China and supported existing forms of ancestor worship. **Judaism**, which dates back many centuries, recognized but one God. Expelled from the Holy Land in A.D. 70, its adherents (Jews) were reinstated there as the state of Israel in 1948. **Islam**, founded in Mecca by Muhammad (A.D. 570-632), spread across Asia and Africa, where it still thrives. **Christianity** was founded almost 2,000 years ago. Photographs below: **Christian monastery, Jewish holy place, Hindu temple, Mohammedan mosque, Buddhist temple.**

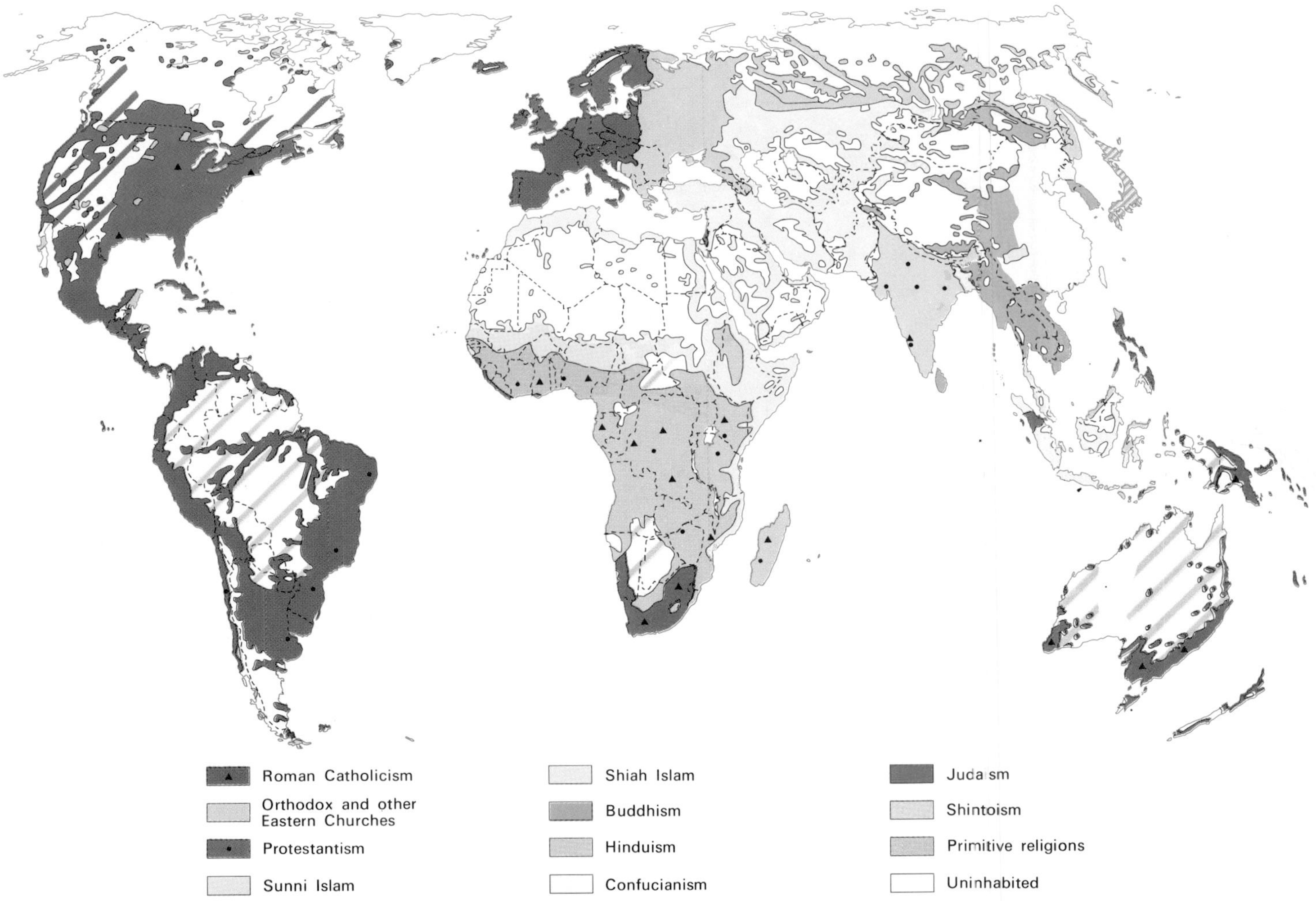

Roman Catholicism
Orthodox and other Eastern Churches
Protestantism
Sunni Islam
Shiah Islam
Buddhism
Hinduism
Confucianism
Judaism
Shintoism
Primitive religions
Uninhabited

Christian monastery

Jewish holy place

Hindu temple

Mohammedan mosque

Buddhist temple

THE GROWTH OF CITIES

The evolution of the semi-permanent Neolithic settlement into a city took 15 centuries (from 5000 to 3500 B.C.). Efficient communications and exchange systems were developed as population densities rose as high as 30,000 to 50,000 per square kilometer by 2000 B.C. in Egypt and Babylonia. New York City today has a density of 10,000 per square kilometer. The series of maps below shows the shift in location of the largest city in the world and in the distribution of the 25 largest cities between 200 B.C. and A.D. 1900. The graph at the left immediately below depicts the **increase in urbanization** from 1920 to 1970.

The increase in urbanization resulted primarily from better sanitation and health, which fostered population growth, and from the movement of people off the land into industry and service occupations in the cities. Generally, the most highly developed industrial nations are the most urbanized, although Switzerland and Norway are exceptions. The graph at the right shows the total **population of the ten largest cities** of the world in the 1970s. Modern cities have a large metropolitan area of many communities linked to the central city.

The large illustrated map at the right shows the **distribution of the major cities** of today's world. The concentration of population in temperate regions is clearly shown. Normally, these major cities are not only major centers of population and wealth; they are also centers of political power and trade. Today, they are the sites of international airports and characteristically are great ports through which imported and exported goods can flow. These goods move along roads and railways that focus on the city. The staple trades and industries of these cities are varied and flexible.

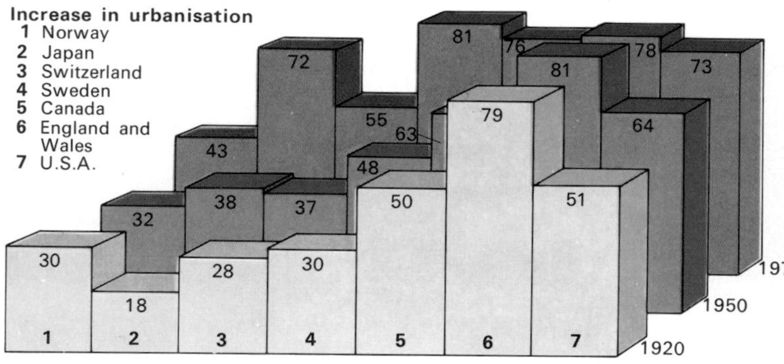
Increase in urbanisation
1 Norway
2 Japan
3 Switzerland
4 Sweden
5 Canada
6 England and Wales
7 U.S.A.
30 18 28 30 50 79 51
32 38 37 48 63
43 72 55 81 76 81 64
78 73
1 2 3 4 5 6 7
1920
1950
1970

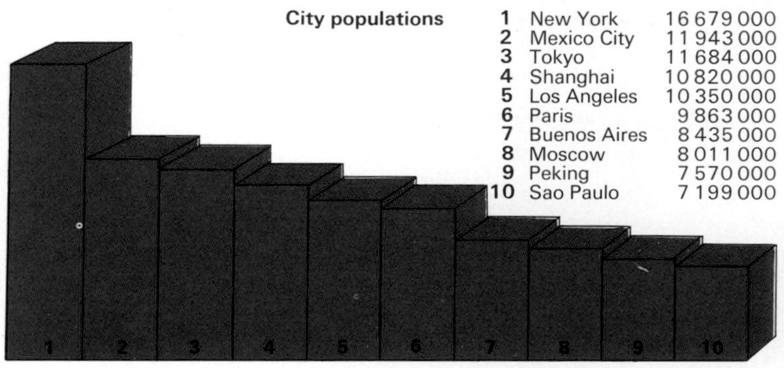
City populations
1 New York 16 679 000
2 Mexico City 11 943 000
3 Tokyo 11 684 000
4 Shanghai 10 820 000
5 Los Angeles 10 350 000
6 Paris 9 863 000
7 Buenos Aires 8 435 000
8 Moscow 8 011 000
9 Peking 7 570 000
10 Sao Paulo 7 199 000
1 2 3 4 5 6 7 8 9 10

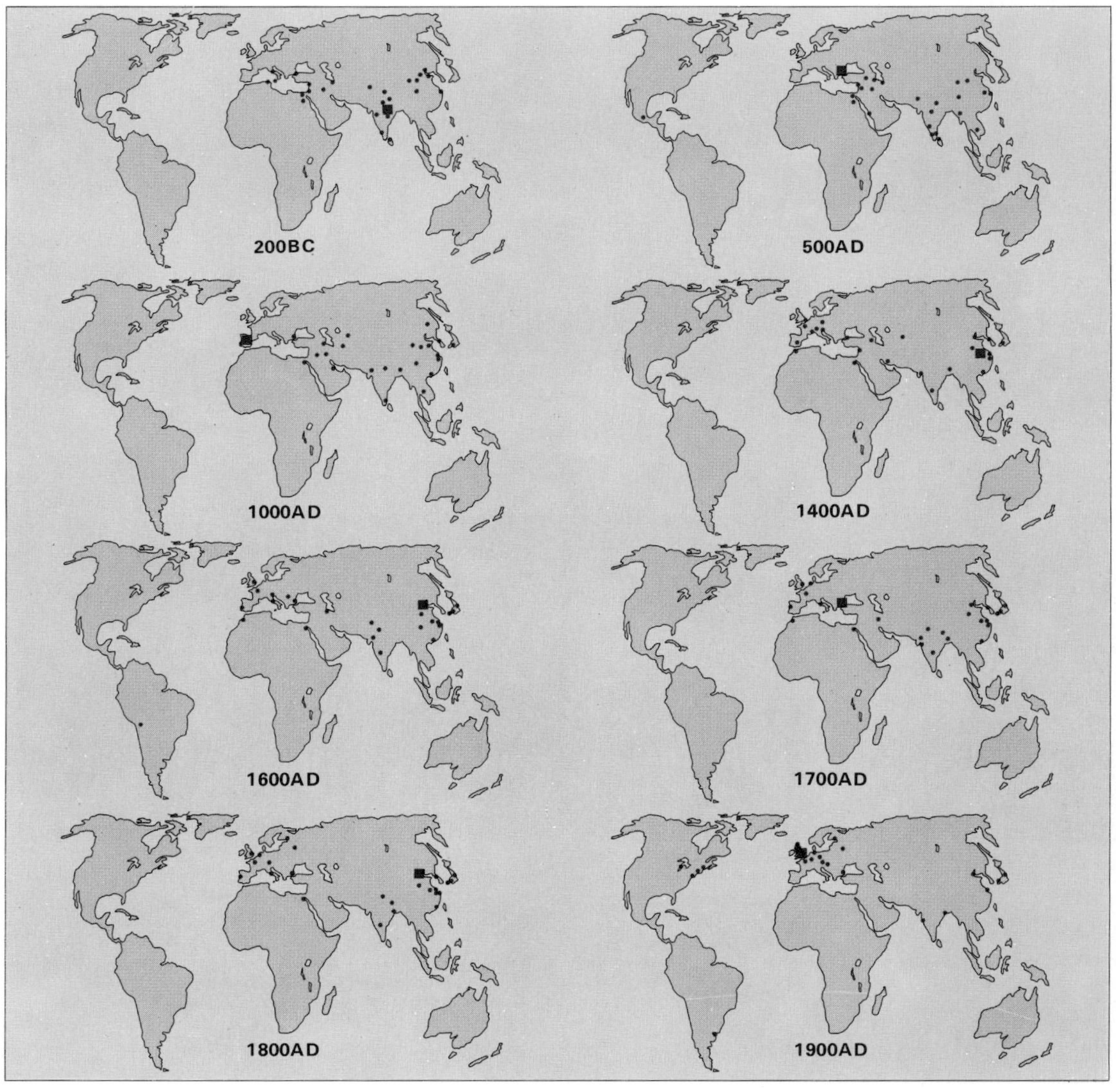
200BC
500AD
1000AD
1400AD
1600AD
1700AD
1800AD
1900AD

New York
Sydney
Moscow
Tokyo
Sao Paulo
Hong Kong
Bombay
London
Cairo
Rio de Janeiro
Rome
Cities over 5 000 000 inhabitants
2 000 000-5 000 000 inhabitants
1 000 000-2 000 000 inhabitants
250 000-1 000 000 inhabitants

FOOD RESOURCES: VEGETABLE

The vegetable kingdom has always been of prime importance to the food supply of the world. All parts of the plant contribute to this supply, but perhaps none is as important as the seed, from which all our cereals are derived and our food oils extracted. Fruits and the wines made from them also contribute to the overall food supply. The first graph at the right below shows **world production of fruits**. The second graph shows the **production of wine**. Over 80% of the grapes grown are made into wine. The maps on the opposite page indicate the major production sites of various vegetable resources other than fruits.

Tropical and sub-tropical crops such as cocoa, tea, and coffee are grown mostly for export. Another tropical crop, cane sugar, accounts for the bulk of the sugar entering the international trade. Beet sugar, which requires a temperate climate, is produced primarily for domestic consumption. Vegetable oils extracted from soya beans, peanuts (ground nuts), and rape and sunflower seeds are used widely, as shown on the maps. Cereals and potatoes are the principal sources of food for modern civilizations.

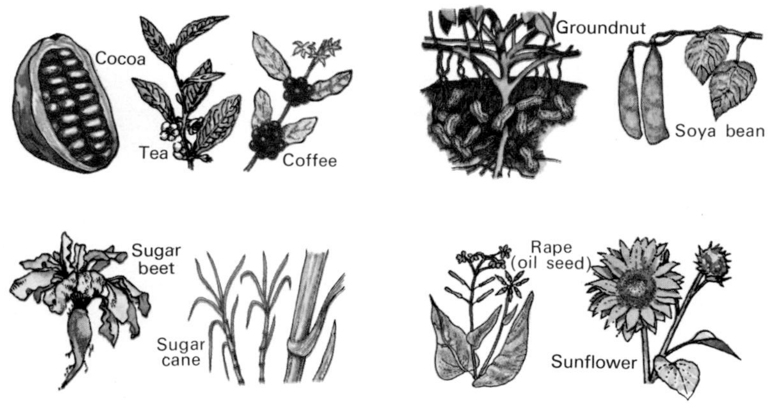

Cocoa
Tea
Coffee
Groundnut
Soya bean
Sugar beet
Sugar cane
Rape (oil seed)
Sunflower

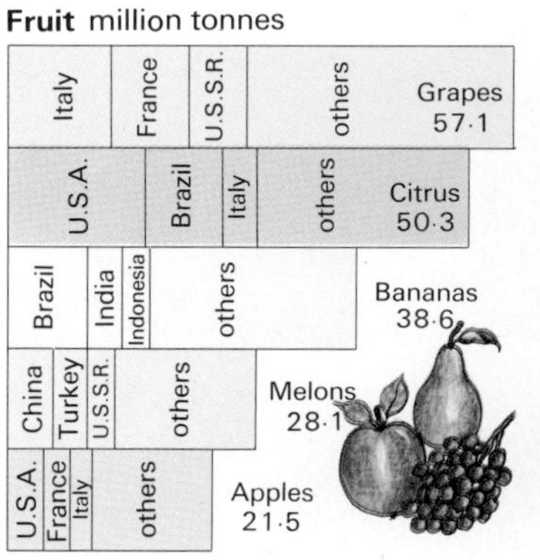

Fruit million tonnes
Italy
France
U.S.S.R.
others
Grapes 57·1
U.S.A.
Brazil
Italy
others
Citrus 50·3
Brazil
India
Indonesia
others
Bananas 38·6
China
Turkey
U.S.S.R.
others
Melons 28·1
U.S.A.
France
Italy
others
Apples 21·5

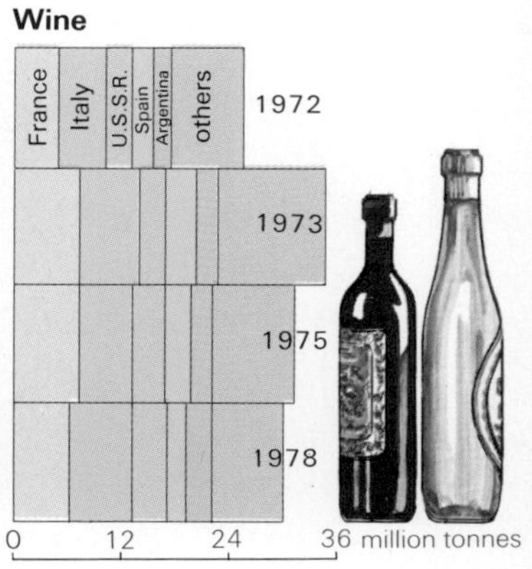

Wine
France
Italy
U.S.S.R.
Spain
Argentina
others
1972
1973
1975
1978
0
12
24
36 million tonnes

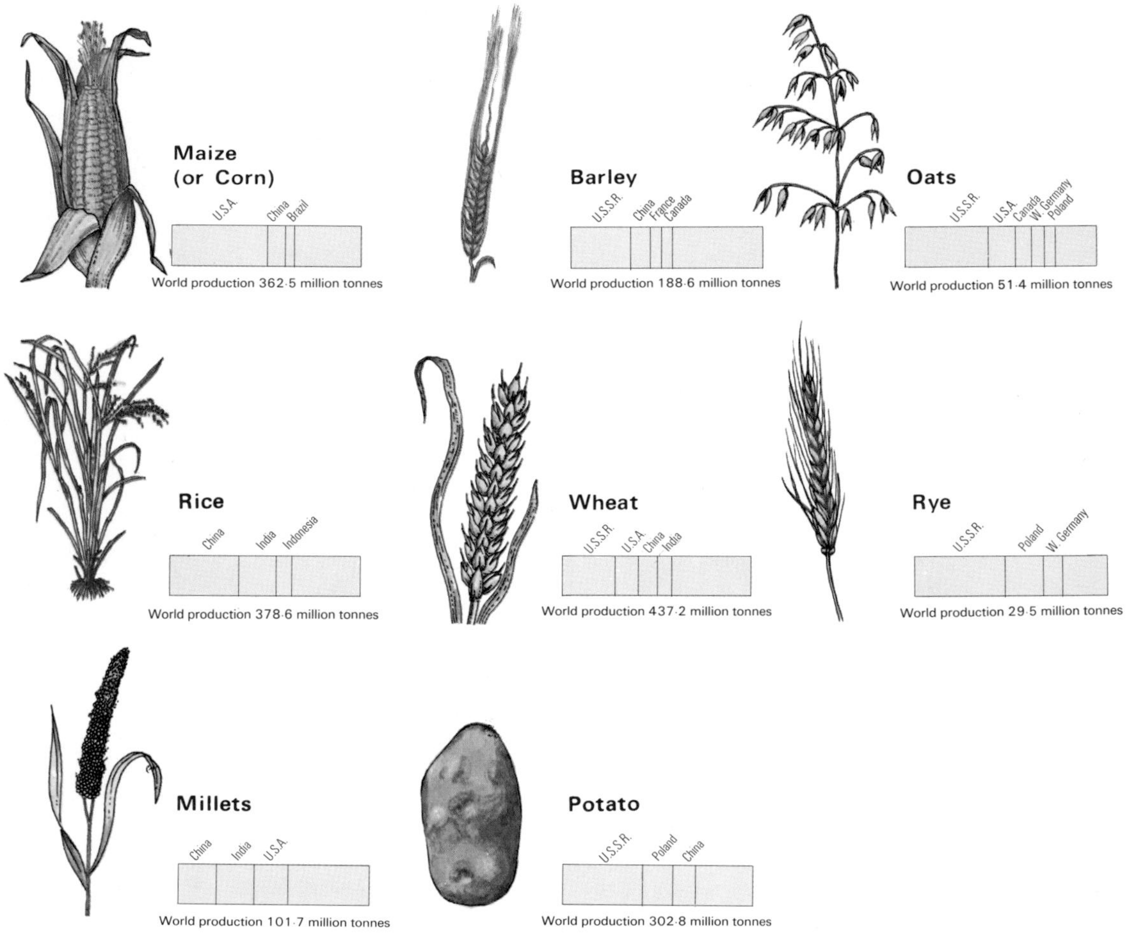

Maize (or Corn)
U.S.A.
China
Brazil
World production 362·5 million tonnes
Barley
U.S.S.R.
China
France
Canada
World production 188·6 million tonnes
Oats
U.S.S.R.
U.S.A.
Canada
W. Germany
Poland
World production 51·4 million tonnes
Rice
China
India
Indonesia
World production 378·6 million tonnes
Wheat
U.S.S.R.
U.S.A.
China
India
World production 437·2 million tonnes
Rye
U.S.S.R.
Poland
W. Germany
World production 29·5 million tonnes
Millets
China
India
U.S.A.
World production 101·7 million tonnes
Potato
U.S.S.R.
Poland
China
World production 302·8 million tonnes

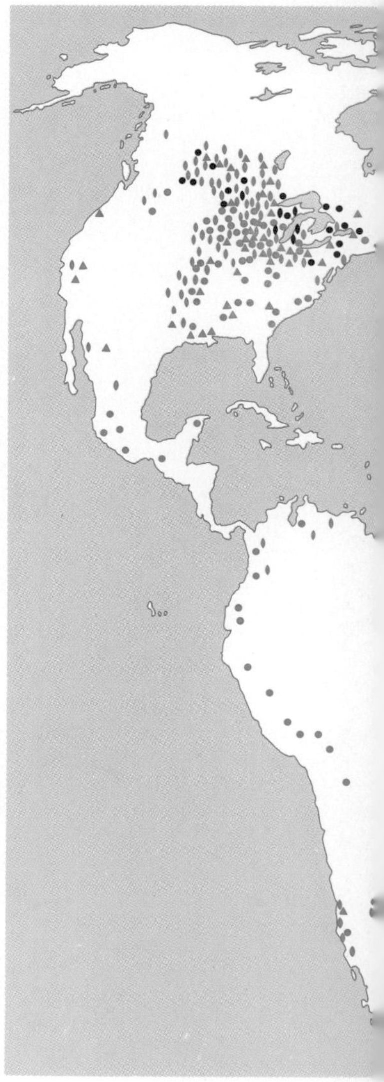

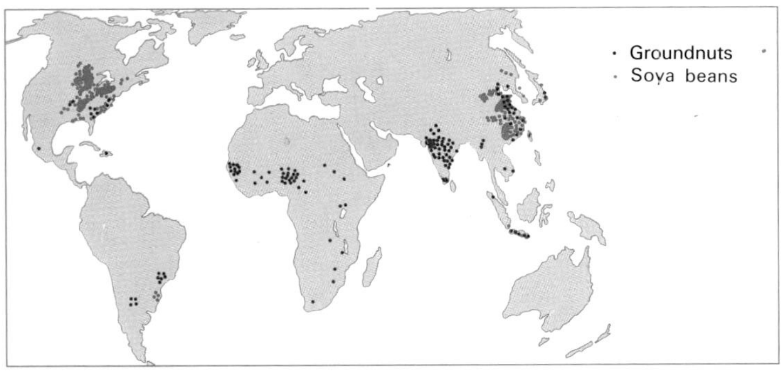
Groundnuts
Soya beans

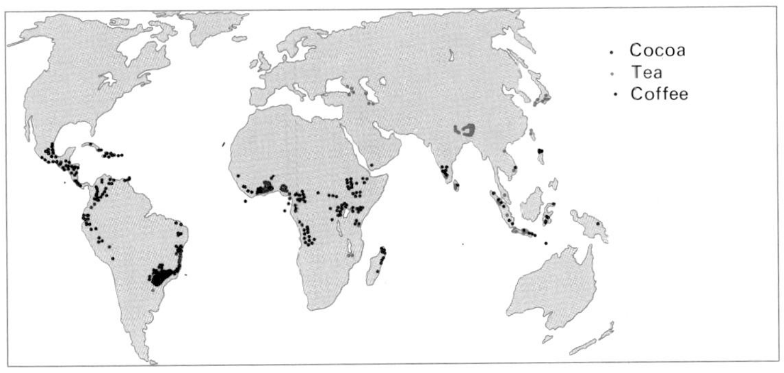
Cocoa
Tea
Coffee

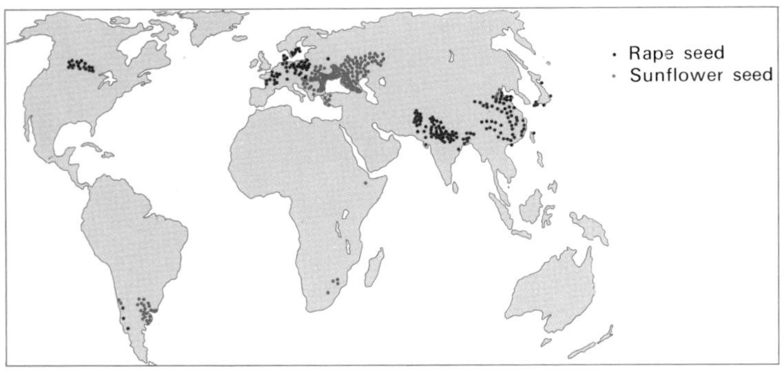
Rape seed
Sunflower seed

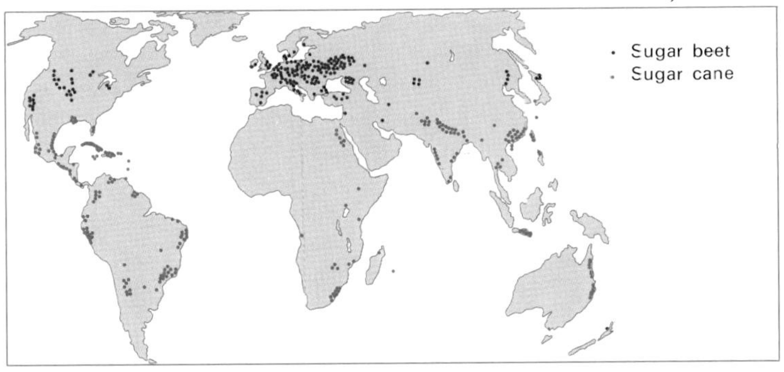
Sugar beet
Sugar cane

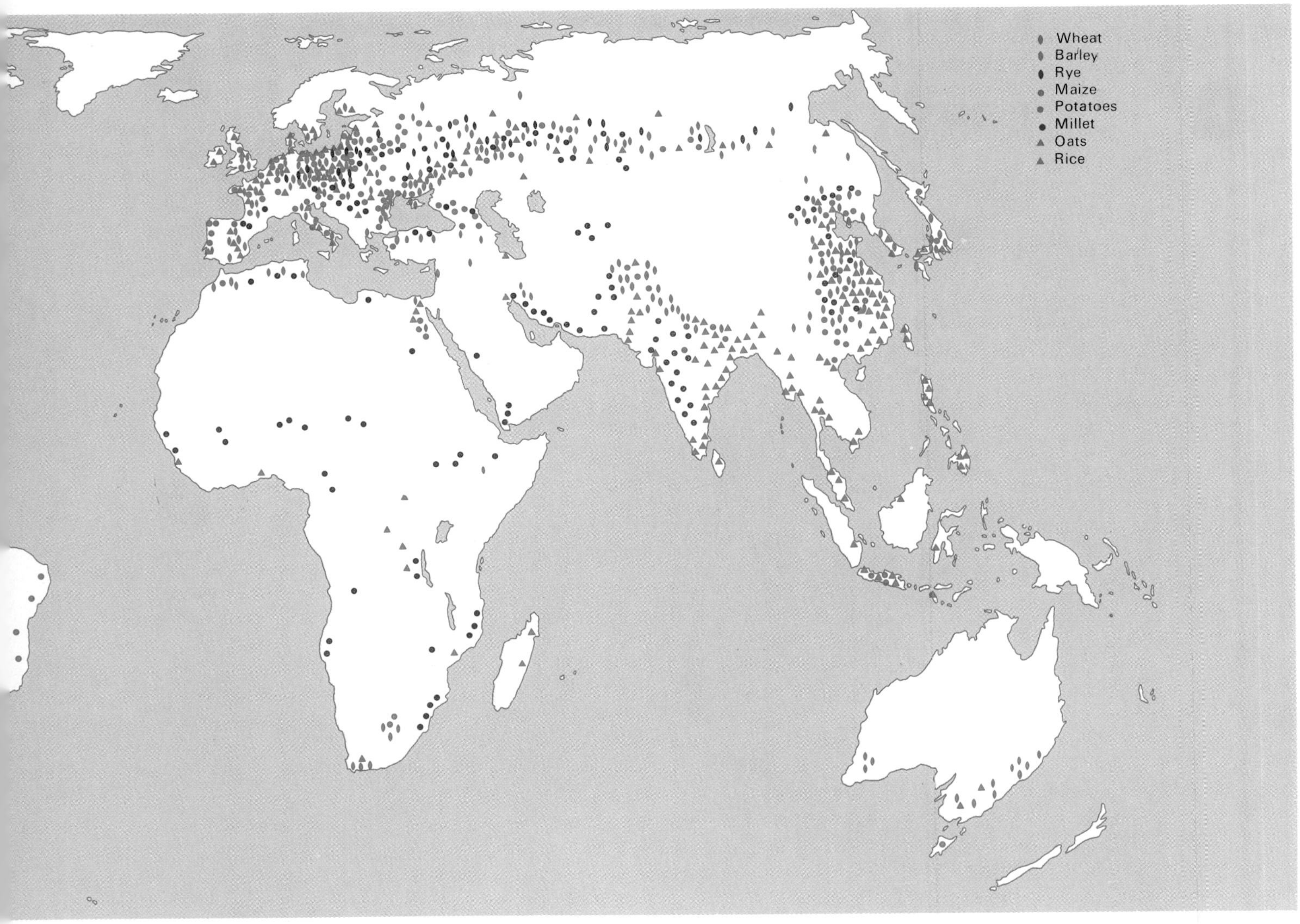
Wheat
Barley
Rye
Maize
Potatoes
Millet
Oats
Rice

FOOD RESOURCES: ANIMAL

Meat, milk, and allied foods are prime protein providers as well as sources of vitamins. Meat is mainly a product of continental and savanna grasslands and of the cool west coasts, particularly in Europe. (See map below.) Milk, cheese, eggs, and fish — though found in some quantity throughout the world — are primarily products of the temperate zones. Commercial fishing requires large shoals of fish of one species within reach of markets. The graphs below show **world production of major animal food resources**. Top row, left to right: sheep, beef cattle, dairy cattle, cheese; second row, pigs, fish, and butter.

Australia, New Zealand, and Argentina provide the major part of international beef exports, whereas western U.S.A. and Europe produce much beef for their high local demand. Dairying, which requires a rich diet for the herd as well as nearby markets for its products, is carried on in densely populated areas of the temperate zones — U.S.A., N.W. Europe, New Zealand, and S.E. Australia. As shown on the map, production of sheep is worldwide. They are raised mostly for wool and meat. The merino yields a fine wool, but crossbreds are best for meat. The skins of sheep and the cheese made from sheep's milk are important products in some countries. World production of all kinds of cheese is well over ten million tons annually, the principal producers being U.S.A., India, W. Europe, and U.S.S.R. The chief exporters are the Netherlands, New Zealand, Denmark, and France.

As indicated on the map, pigs can be reared in most climates, from monsoon to cool temperate. They are abundant in China, in the corn belt of the U.S.A., northwest and central Europe, Brazil, and in the U.S.S.R. Fish raised on fish farms as well as those caught in the wild are becoming an increasingly valuable source of protein. In addition to marine fishing, which is a worldwide enterprise, freshwater fishing is also important commercially. Long an important food source, butter still ranks high as a provider of calories and vitamin A. The biggest butter producers are U.S.S.R., W. Europe, U.S.A., New Zealand, and Australia.

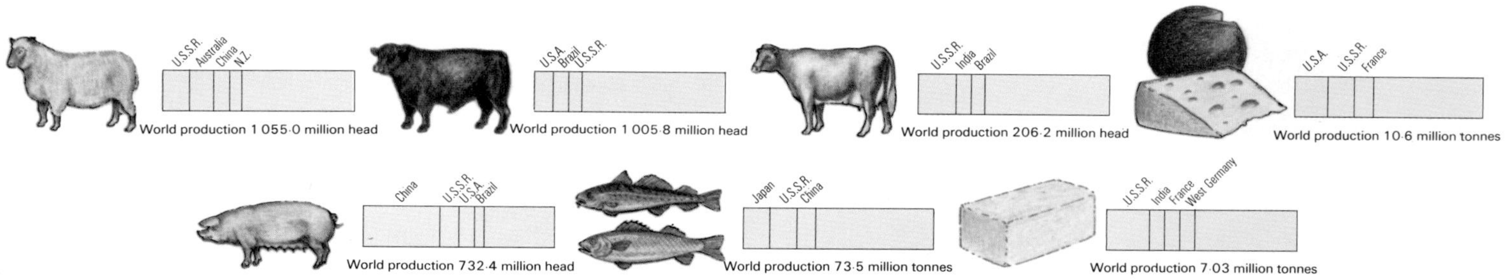
U.S.S.R.
Australia
China
N.Z.
World production 1 055·0 million head
U.S.A.
Brazil
U.S.S.R.
World production 1 005·8 million head
U.S.S.R.
India
Brazil
World production 206·2 million head
U.S.A.
U.S.S.R.
France
World production 10·6 million tonnes
China
U.S.S.R.
U.S.A.
Brazil
World production 732·4 million head
Japan
U.S.S.R.
China
World production 73·5 million tonnes
U.S.S.R.
India
France
West Germany
World production 7·03 million tonnes

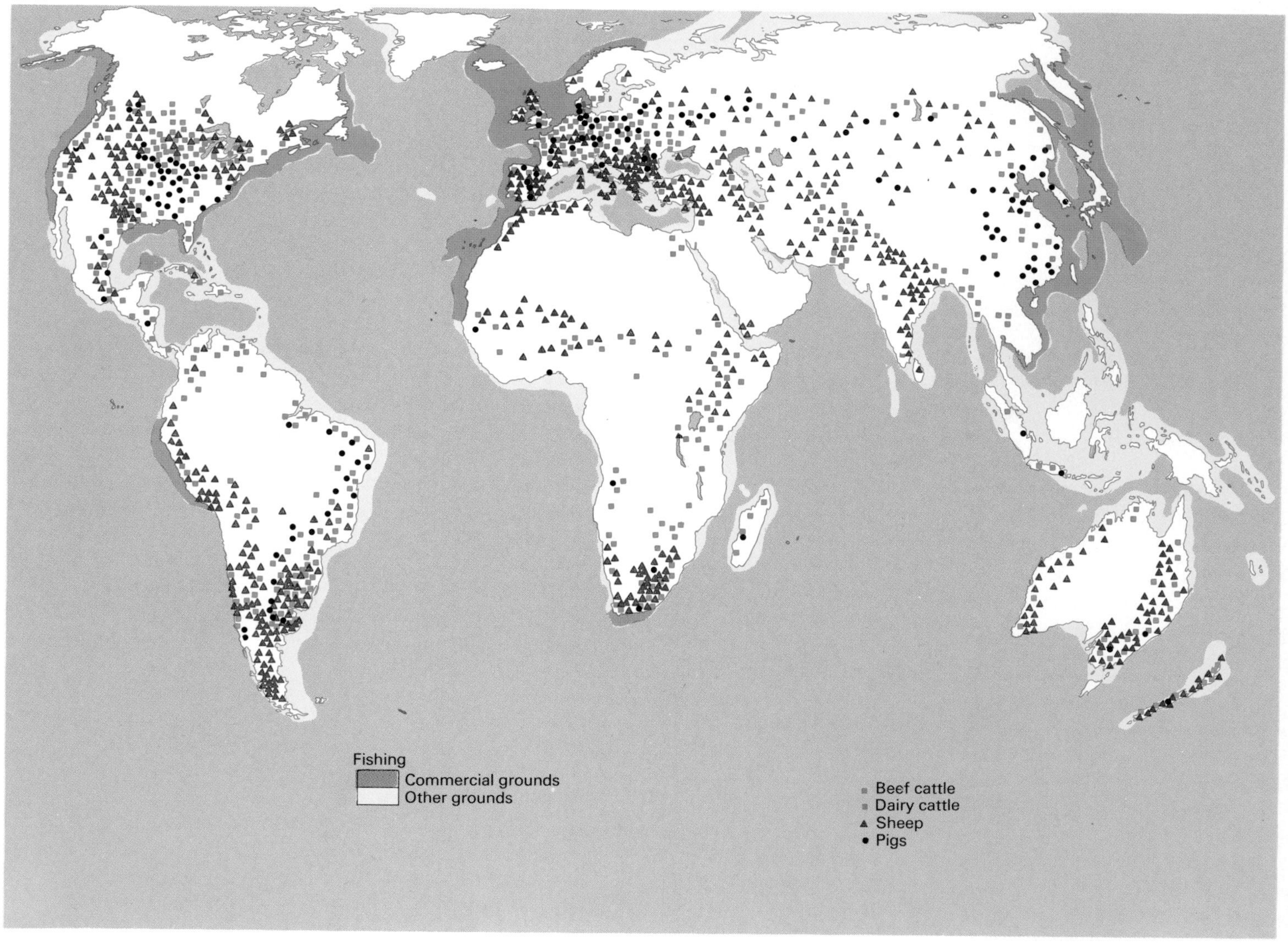
Fishing
Commercial grounds
Other grounds
Beef cattle
Dairy cattle
Sheep
Pigs

NUTRITION

Nutritionally, foods fall into four major groups — providers of energy, protein, minerals, and vitamins. Cereals and oil-seeds provide energy. Milk, milk products, fish, and meat provide energy, protein, minerals, and vitamins; fruits and vegetables provide vitamins, minerals, and some energy. The small map at the left below locates **vitamin deficiencies** in the East; the chart to the right of it, the number of **people and tractors engaged in agriculture**; the pie charts, the **proportions of calories consumed** in various countries; the bar graphs at the center right, **a comparison of daily diets**, supplies versus requirements; the world map, **calorie and protein consumption**.

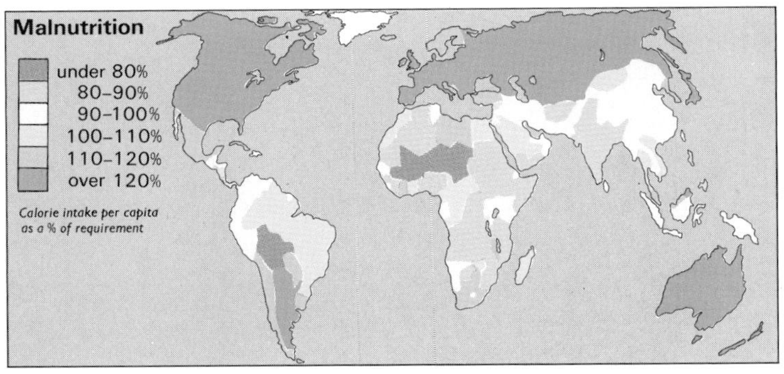
Malnutrition
under 80%
80–90%
90–100%
100–110%
110–120%
over 120%
Calorie intake per capita as a % of requirement

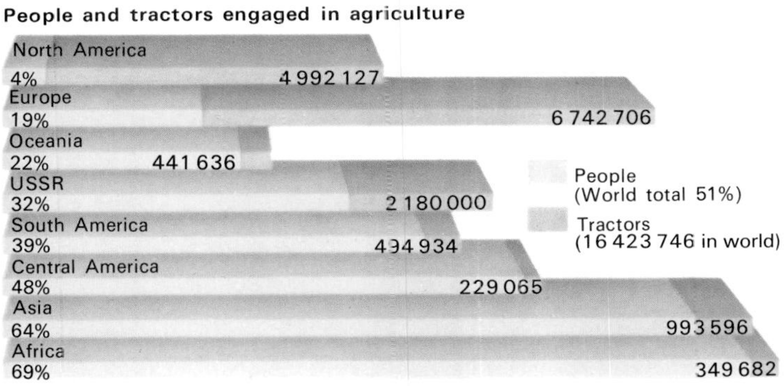
People and tractors engaged in agriculture
North America 4% 4 992 127
Europe 19% 6 742 706
Oceania 22% 441 636
USSR 32% 2 180 000
South America 39% 434 934
Central America 48% 229 065
Asia 64% 993 596
Africa 69% 349 682
People (World total 51%)
Tractors (16 423 746 in world)

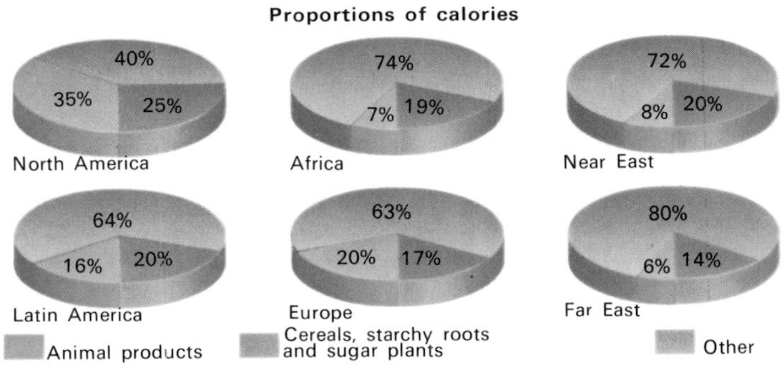
Proportions of calories
North America 40% 35% 25%
Africa 74% 7% 19%
Near East 72% 8% 20%
Latin America 64% 16% 20%
Europe 63% 20% 17%
Far East 80% 6% 14%
Animal products
Cereals, starchy roots and sugar plants
Other

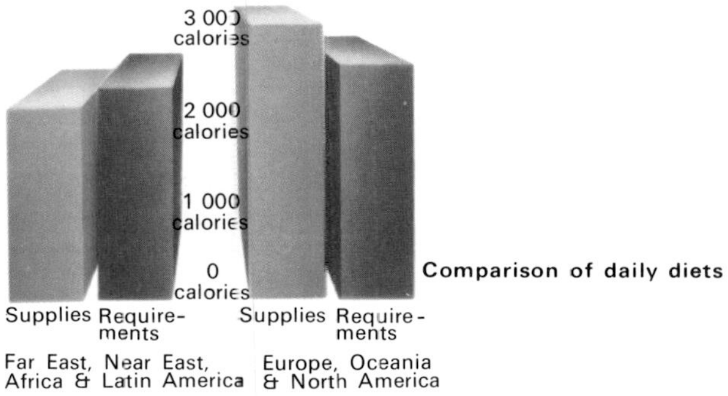
3 000 calories
2 000 calories
1 000 calories
0 calories
Supplies Require-ments
Supplies Require-ments
Far East, Near East, Africa & Latin America
Europe, Oceania & North America
Comparison of daily diets

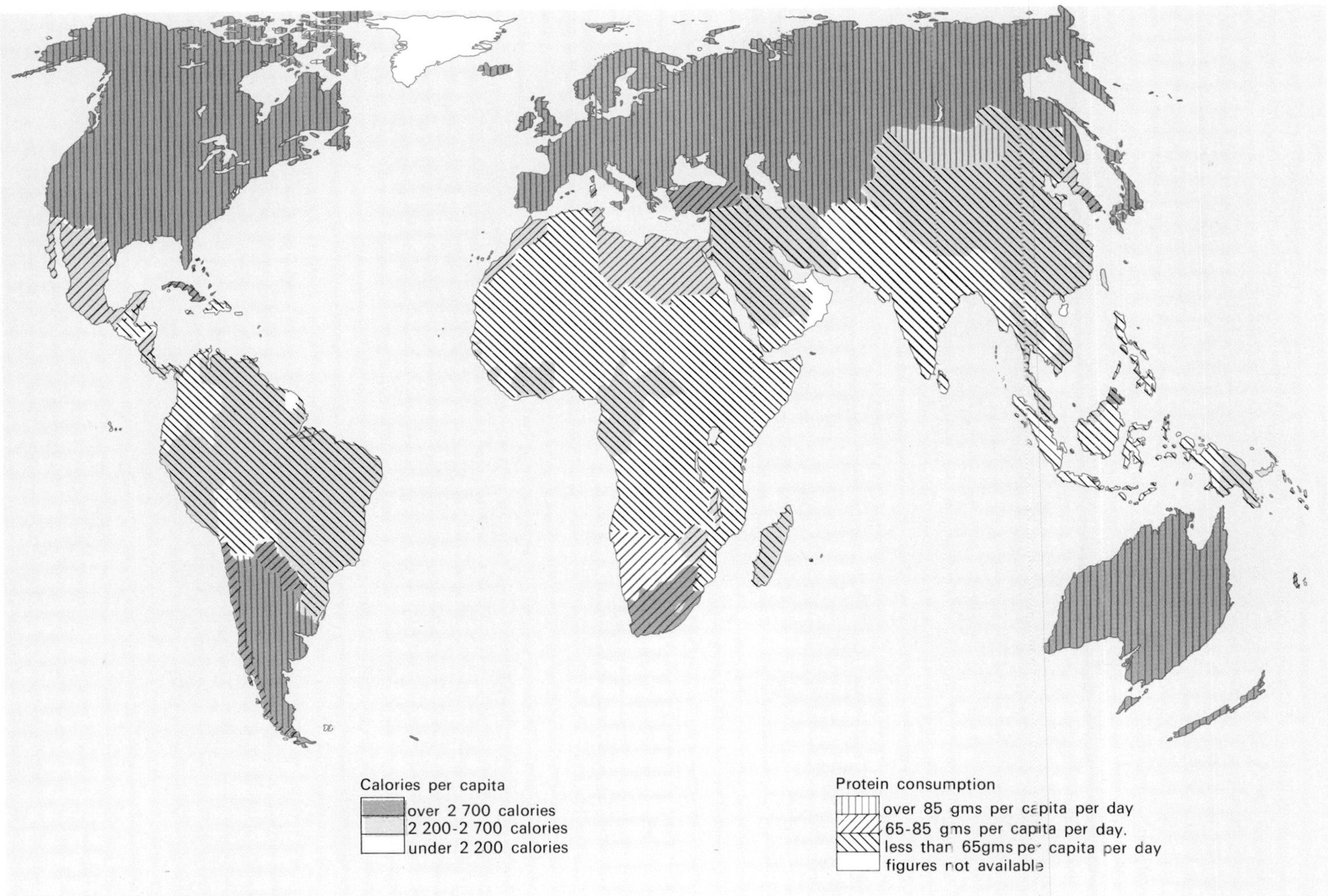
Calories per capita
over 2 700 calories
2 200-2 700 calories
under 2 200 calories
Protein consumption
over 85 gms per capita per day
65-85 gms per capita per day
less than 65gms per capita per day
figures not available

MINERAL RESOURCES I

Primitive people first used iron for tools and vessels. But with the coming of the Industrial Revolution in the late 18th century, modern people made iron, and then steel, the backbone of civilization. Much of the iron ore mined today is converted to steel, which is refined iron plus ferro-alloys, minerals that give steel special properties. The graphs at the top right show **world production of ferro-alloy metals**.

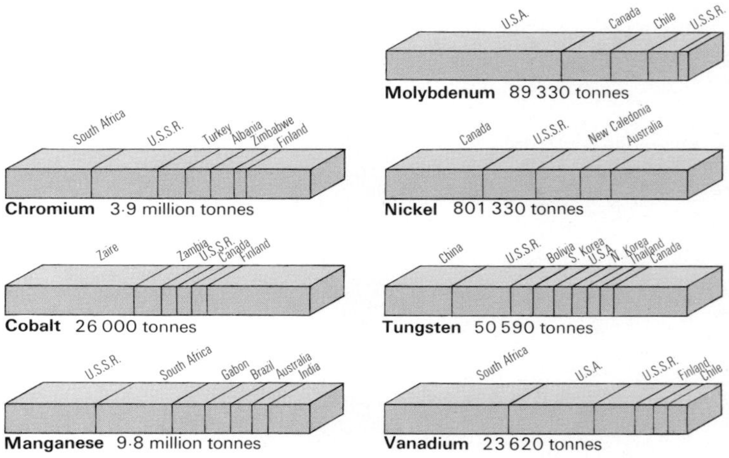

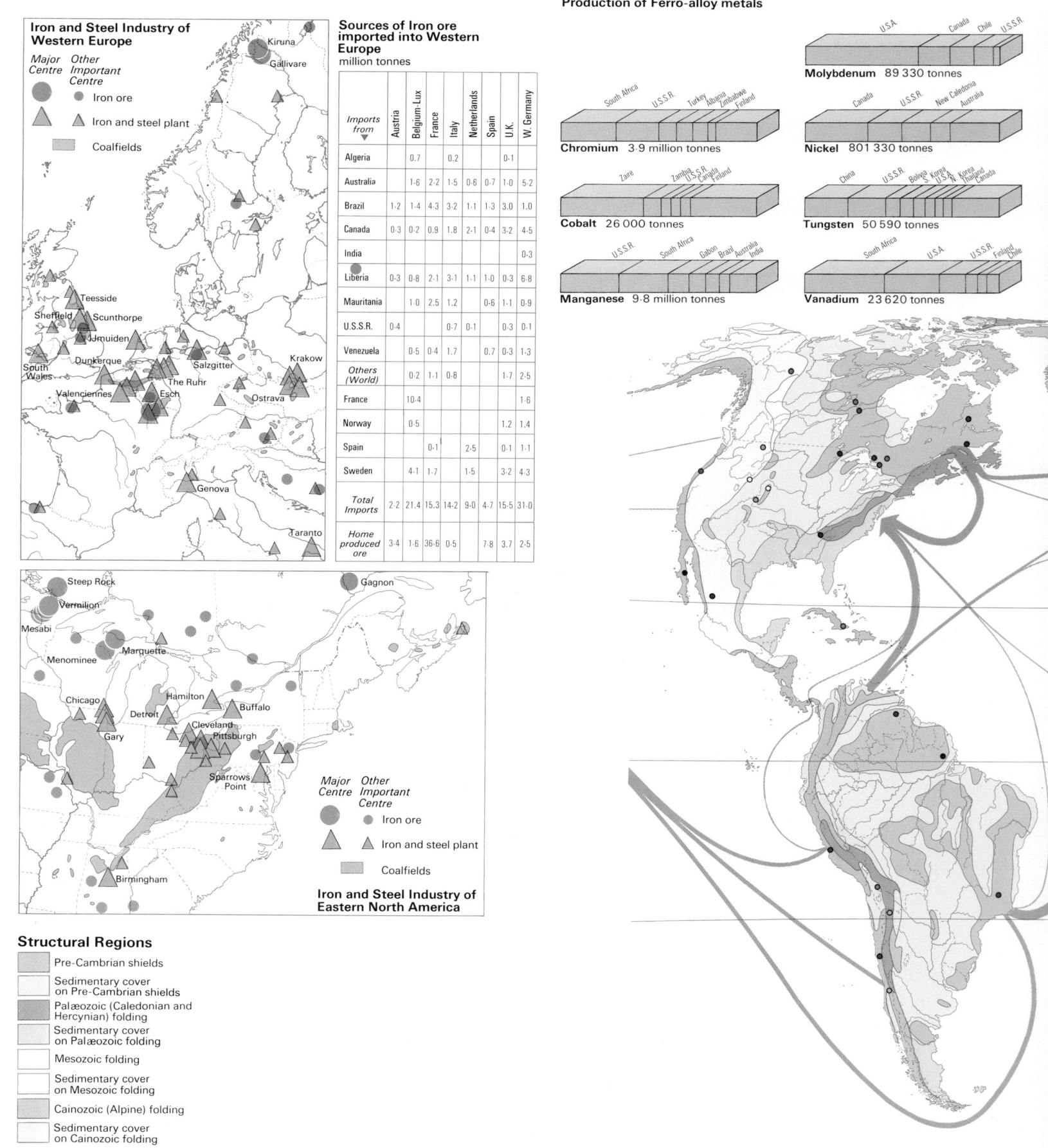

Production of Ferro-alloy metals
Molybdenum 89 330 tonnes
U.S.A.
Canada
Chile
U.S.S.R.
Chromium 3·9 million tonnes
South Africa
U.S.S.R.
Turkey
Albania
Zimbabwe
Finland
Nickel 801 330 tonnes
Canada
U.S.S.R.
New Caledonia
Australia
Cobalt 26 000 tonnes
Zaire
Zambia
U.S.S.R.
Canada
Finland
Tungsten 50 590 tonnes
China
U.S.S.R.
Bolivia
S. Korea
U.S.A.
N. Korea
Thailand
Canada
Manganese 9·8 million tonnes
U.S.S.R.
South Africa
Gabon
Brazil
Australia
India
Vanadium 23 620 tonnes
South Africa
U.S.A.
U.S.S.R.
Finland
Chile

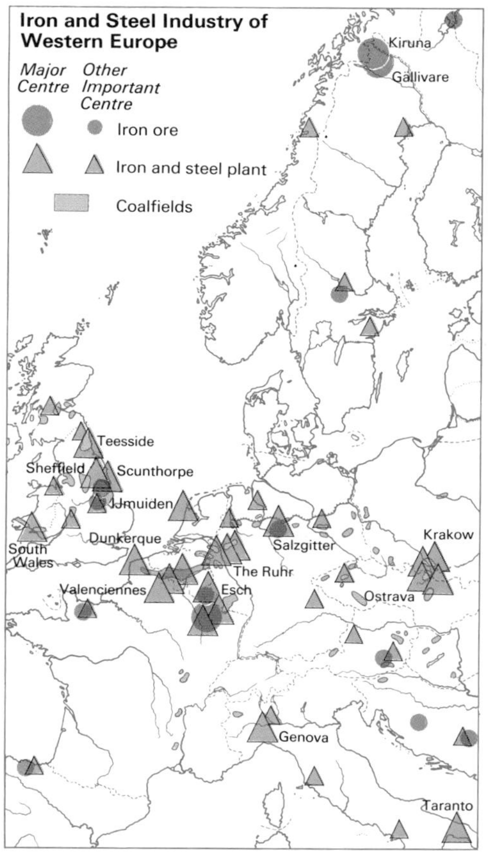

Iron and Steel Industry of Western Europe
Major Centre
Other Important Centre
Iron ore
Iron and steel plant
Coalfields
Kiruna
Gällivare
Teesside
Sheffield
Scunthorpe
IJmuiden
South Wales
Dunkerque
Salzgitter
The Ruhr
Valenciennes
Esch
Krakow
Ostrava
Genova
Taranto

Sources of Iron ore imported into Western Europe
million tonnes

Imports from ▼	Austria	Belgium-Lux	France	Italy	Netherlands	Spain	U.K.	W. Germany
Algeria		0.7		0.2			0·1	
Australia		1·6	2·2	1·5	0·6	0·7	1·0	5·2
Brazil	1·2	1·4	4·3	3·2	1·1	1·3	3.0	1.0
Canada	0·3	0·2	0.9	1.8	2·1	0·4	3·2	4·5
India								0·3
Liberia	0·3	0·8	2·1	3·1	1·1	1·0	0·3	6·8
Mauritania		1·0	2.5	1.2		0·6	1·1	0·9
U.S.S.R.	0·4			0·7	0·1		0·3	0·1
Venezuela		0·5	0·4	1.7		0.7	0·3	1·3
Others (World)		0·2	1·1	0·8			1·7	2·5
France		10·4						1·6
Norway		0·5					1.2	1.4
Spain			0·1		2·5		0·1	1·1
Sweden		4·1	1·7		1·5		3·2	4·3
Total Imports	2·2	21.4	15.3	14·2	9·0	4·7	15·5	31·0
Home produced ore	3·4	1·6	36·6	0·5		7·8	3.7	2·5

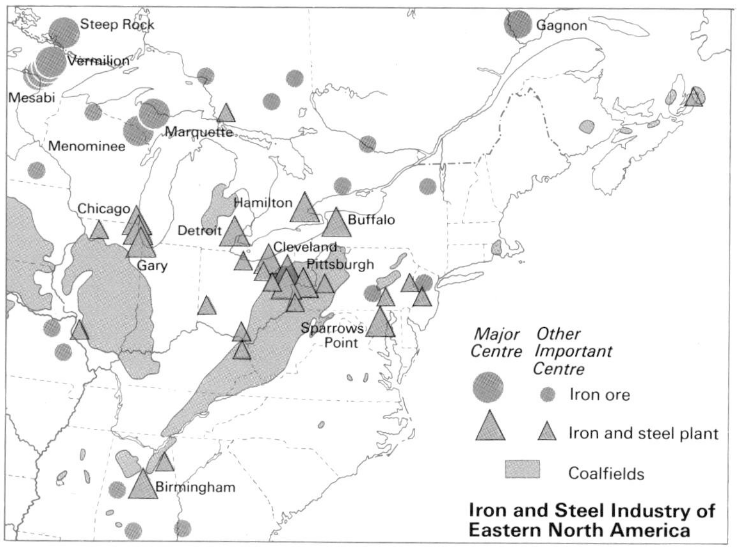

Steep Rock
Vermilion
Mesabi
Gagnon
Menominee
Marquette
Chicago
Gary
Detroit
Hamilton
Buffalo
Cleveland
Pittsburgh
Sparrows Point
Birmingham
Major Centre
Other Important Centre
Iron ore
Iron and steel plant
Coalfields
Iron and Steel Industry of Eastern North America

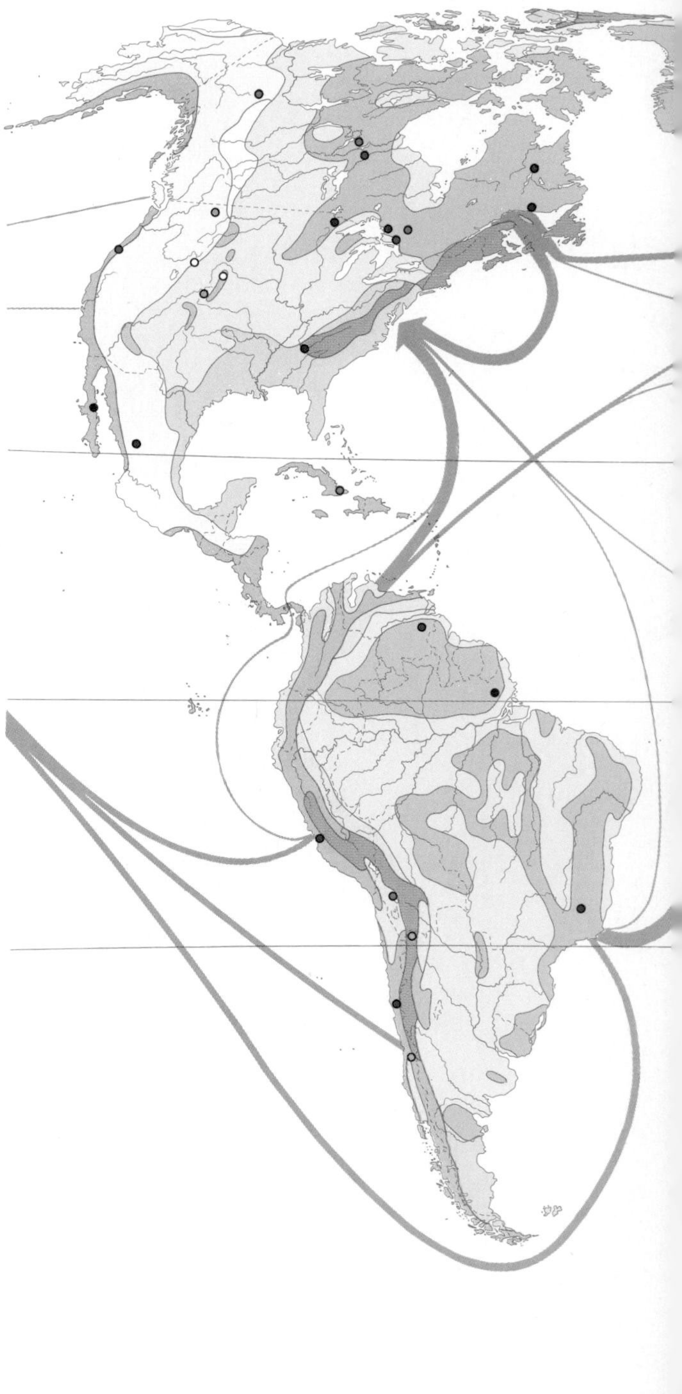

Structural Regions

- Pre-Cambrian shields
- Sedimentary cover on Pre-Cambrian shields
- Palæozoic (Caledonian and Hercynian) folding
- Sedimentary cover on Palæozoic folding
- Mesozoic folding
- Sedimentary cover on Mesozoic folding
- Cainozoic (Alpine) folding
- Sedimentary cover on Cainozoic folding

The pie chart at the left shows the **production of pig (crude) iron and ferro-alloys**. The graph at the top center shows the growth of this production through time. The map and graph, top right, compare the **iron ore output of different countries** in 1973. The large map below shows the geologic **structural regions** that are the **principal sources of iron ore and ferro-alloys**. It also shows the ore trade flow.

World production of Pig iron and Ferro-alloys
Total World production 504 million tonnes

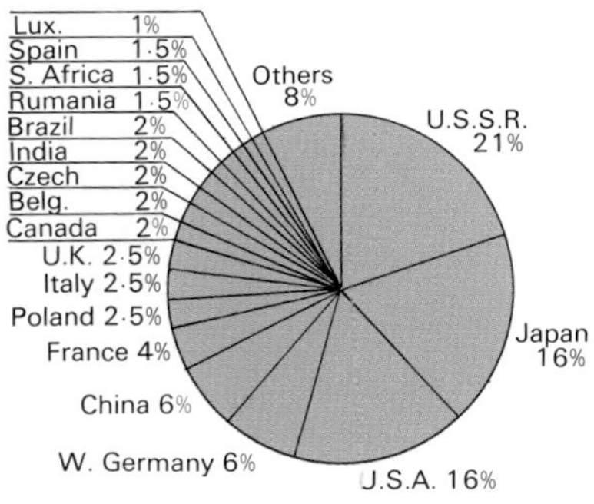
Lux. 1%
Spain 1·5%
S. Africa 1·5%
Rumania 1·5%
Brazil 2%
India 2%
Czech 2%
Belg. 2%
Canada 2%
U.K. 2·5%
Italy 2·5%
Poland 2·5%
France 4%
China 6%
W. Germany 6%
Others 8%
U.S.S.R. 21%
Japan 16%
U.S.A. 16%

Growth of World production of Pig iron and Ferro-alloys

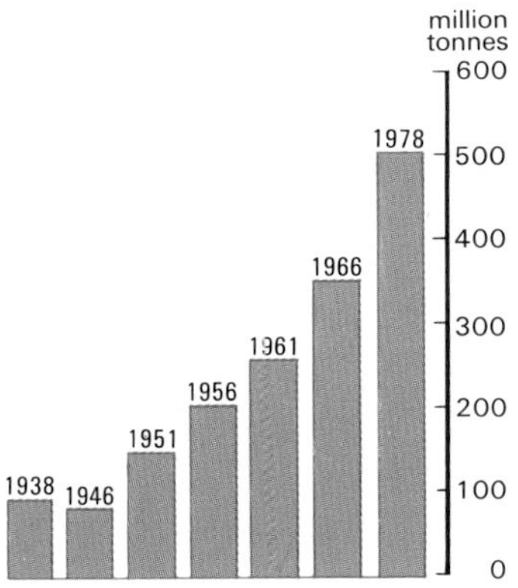
million tonnes
600
500
400
300
200
100
0
1938
1946
1951
1956
1961
1966
1978

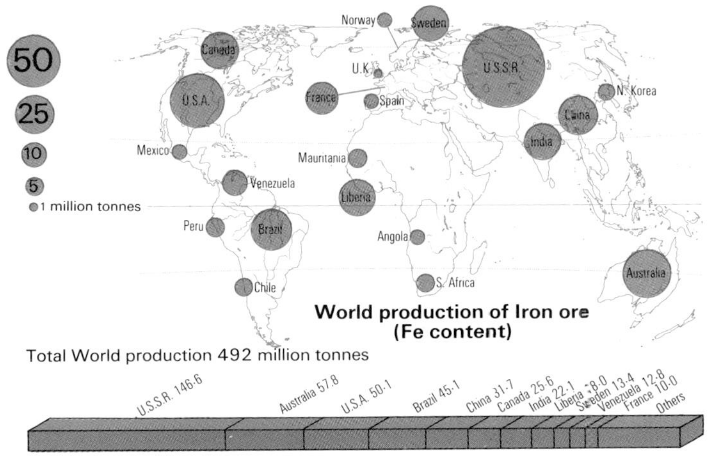
50
25
10
5
1 million tonnes
Norway
Sweden
Canada
U.K.
U.S.S.R.
N. Korea
U.S.A.
France
Spain
China
India
Mexico
Mauritania
Venezuela
Liberia
Peru
Brazil
Angola
Australia
Chile
S. Africa
World production of Iron ore
(Fe content)
Total World production 492 million tonnes
U.S.S.R. 146·6
Australia 57·8
U.S.A. 50·1
Brazil 45·1
China 31·7
Canada 25·6
India 22·1
Liberia 18·0
Sweden 13·4
Venezuela 12·8
France 10·0
Others

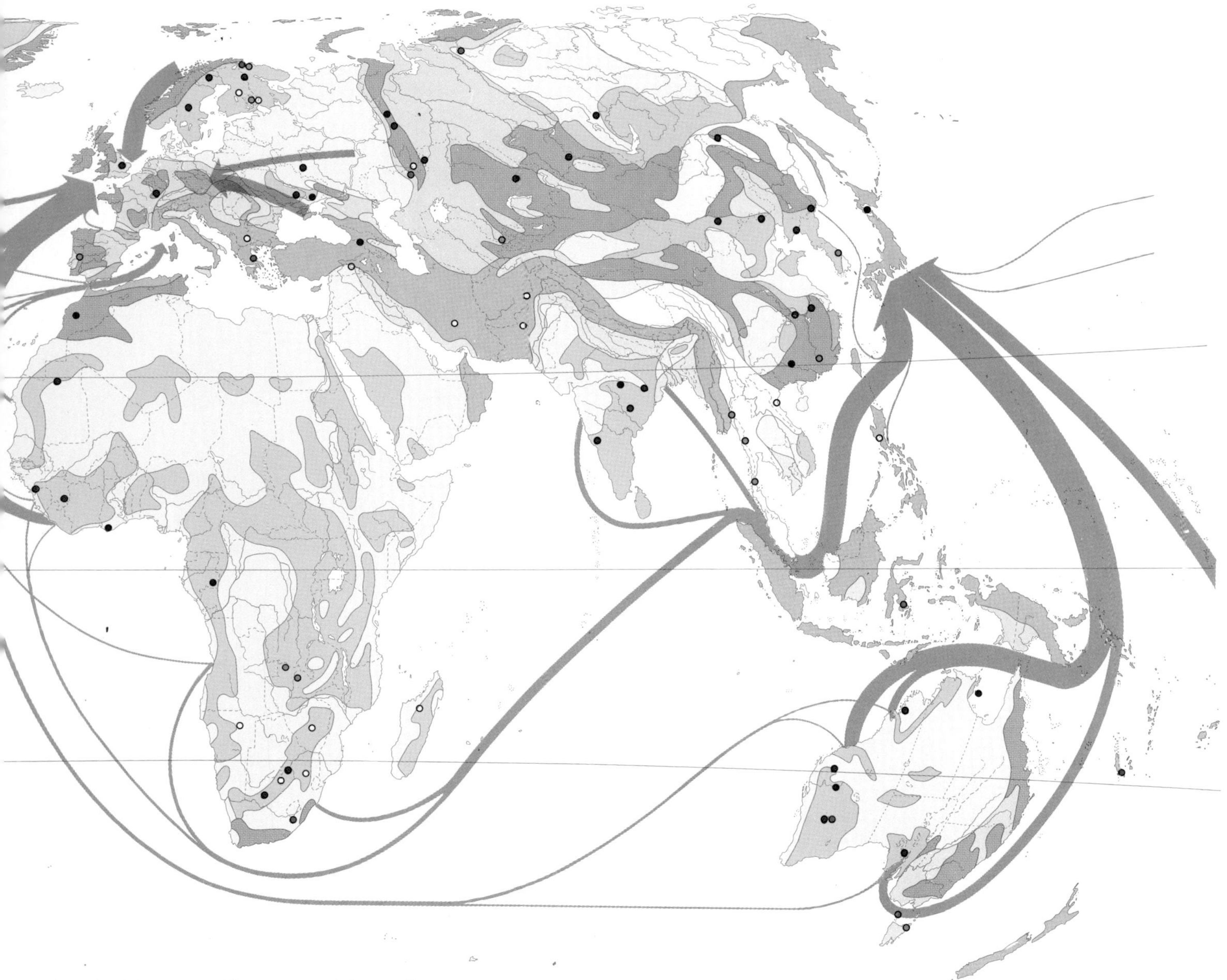

Principal Sources of Iron ore and ferro-alloys

- Iron
- Chrome
- Cobalt
- Manganese
- Molybdenum
- Nickel
- Tungsten
- Vanadium
- Iron ore trade flow

MINERAL RESOURCES II

Antimony — imparts hardness when alloyed to other metals, especially lead. Uses: type metal, pigments (paints, glass, enamels), fireproofing textiles.

World production 69 163 tonnes

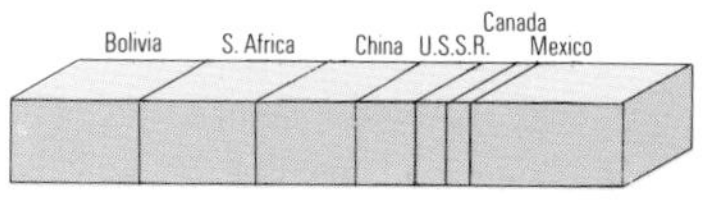
Bolivia
S. Africa
China
U.S.S.R.
Canada
Mexico

Copper — excellent conductor of electricity and heat, durable, strong, ductile, resistant to corrosion. Uses: wire, tubing, making brass and bronze.

World production 8·03 million tonnes

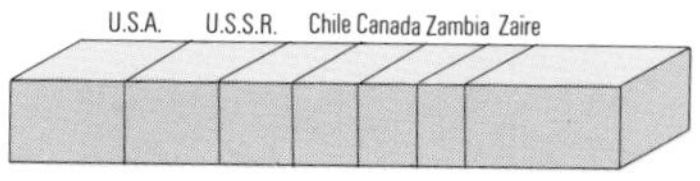
U.S.A.
U.S.S.R.
Chile
Canada
Zambia
Zaire

Lead — heavy, soft, malleable, acid-resistant. Uses: storage batteries, sheeting and piping, cable covering, ammunition, type metal, weights, gasoline additive.

World production 3·59 million tonnes

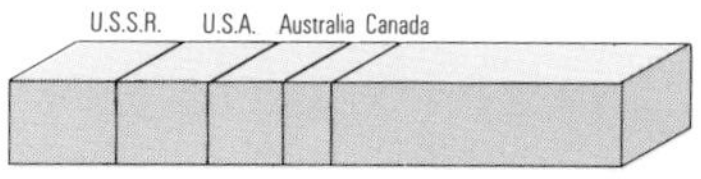
U.S.S.R.
U.S.A.
Australia
Canada

Mercury — liquid metal, excellent conductor. Uses: thermometers, drugs, pigments, in dentistry, electrical industry, gold and silver extraction.

World production 7 111 tonnes

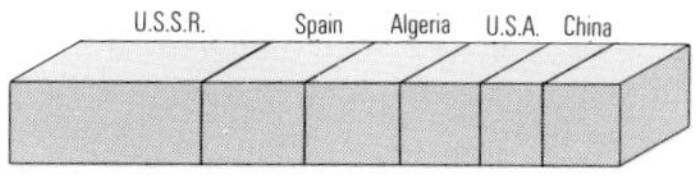
U.S.S.R.
Spain
Algeria
U.S.A.
China

Tin — resistant to organic acids, malleable. Uses: canning containers, foils, as an alloy in bronze and brass.

World production 224 600 tonnes

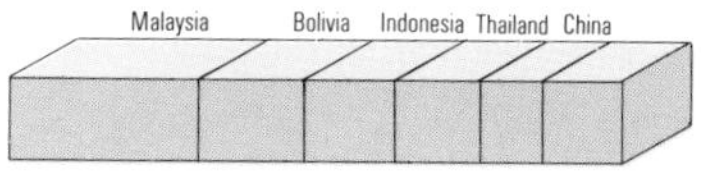
Malaysia
Bolivia
Indonesia
Thailand
China

Zinc — hard metal, low corrosion factor. Uses: brass making, galvanizing, die-casting; in medicines, paints, and dyes.

World production 6·29 million tonnes

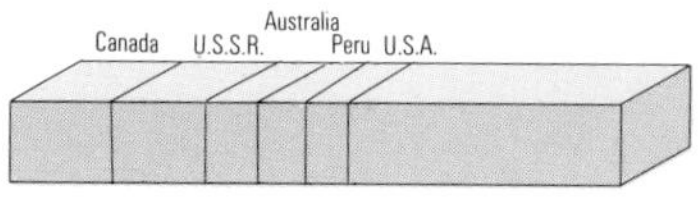
Canada
U.S.S.R.
Australia
Peru
U.S.A.

Aluminum — lightweight, resistant to corrosion, good conductor. Uses: aircraft, road and rail vehicles, utensils, cables, light and strong alloys.

World production 85·0 million tonnes (of Bauxite)

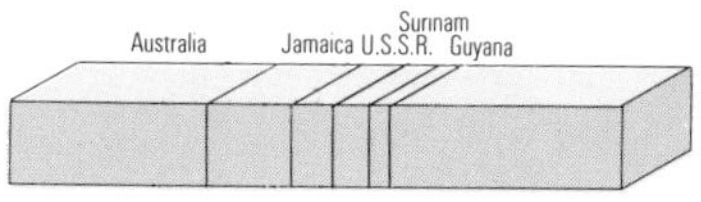
Australia
Jamaica
U.S.S.R.
Surinam
Guyana

Diamonds — very hard and resistant to chemical attack; high luster; very rare. Uses: jewelry; cutting and abrading.

World production 39·8 million carats

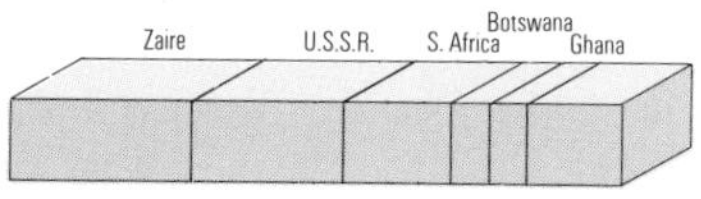
Zaire
U.S.S.R.
S. Africa
Botswana
Ghana

Gold — untarnishable and resistant to corrosion, highly ductile and malleable, good conductor. So soft it must be alloyed to harden it. Uses: bullion, coins, jewelry.

World production 1 411 tonnes

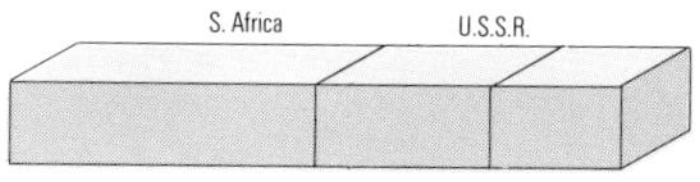
S. Africa
U.S.S.R.

Silver — ductile and malleable; soft (must be alloyed in coins). Uses: coins, jewelry, photography, electronics, medicines.

World production 10 550 tonnes

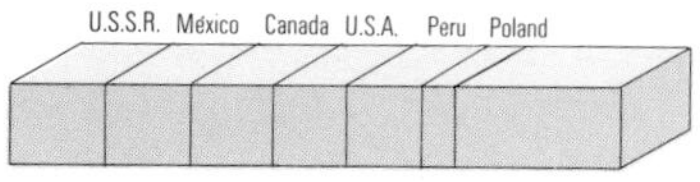
U.S.S.R.
México
Canada
U.S.A.
Peru
Poland

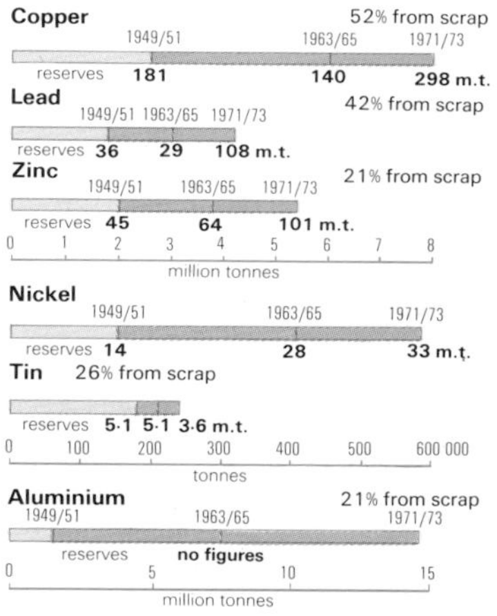
Copper
52% from scrap
1949/51
1963/65
1971/73
reserves
181
140
298 m.t.
Lead
42% from scrap
1949/51
1963/65
1971/73
reserves
36
29
108 m.t.
Zinc
21% from scrap
1949/51
1963/65
1971/73
reserves
45
64
101 m.t.
0 1 2 3 4 5 6 7 8
million tonnes
Nickel
1949/51
1963/65
1971/73
reserves
14
28
33 m.t.
Tin
26% from scrap
reserves
5·1
5·1
3·6 m.t.
0 100 200 300 400 500 600 000
tonnes
Aluminium
21% from scrap
1949/51
1963/65
1971/73
reserves
no figures
0 5 10 15
million tonnes

Non-ferrous metal consumption — The diagrams at the left show the average world consumption of certain refined metals for 1949/51, 1963/65, and 1971/73. The figures beneath each diagram show estimates made in 1950, 1964, and 1973 of reserves in the western world. The large map below and to the right shows the **structural regions** that are the **principal sources of non-ferrous metals and other minerals**. The small maps at the right show the **principal producers and users of fertilizers**.

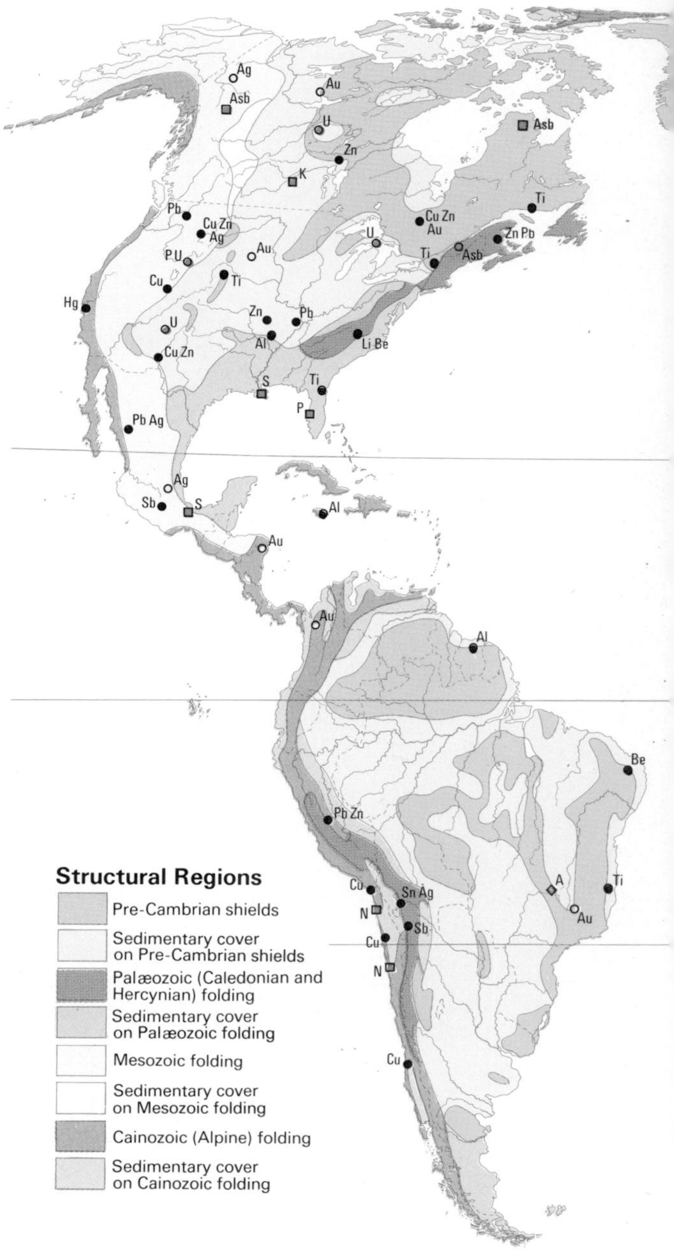
Structural Regions
Pre-Cambrian shields
Sedimentary cover on Pre-Cambrian shields
Palæozoic (Caledonian and Hercynian) folding
Sedimentary cover on Palæozoic folding
Mesozoic folding
Sedimentary cover on Mesozoic folding
Cainozoic (Alpine) folding
Sedimentary cover on Cainozoic folding

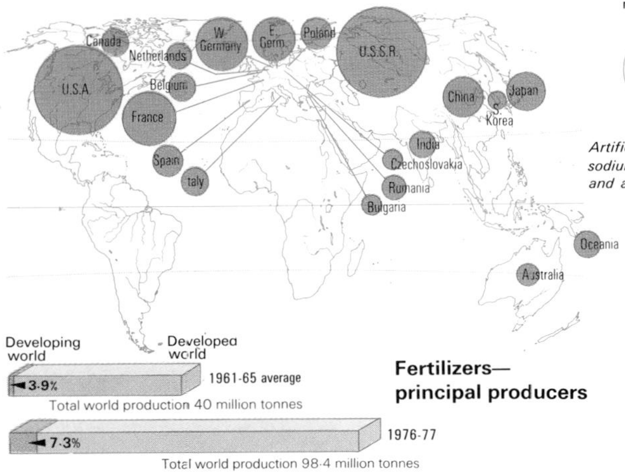

Canada
U.S.A.
Netherlands
Belgium
W. Germany
E. Germ.
Poland
U.S.S.R.
France
Spain
Italy
China
Japan
Korea
India
Czechoslovakia
Rumania
Bulgaria
Oceania
Australia
Developing world
Developed world
3·9%
1961-65 average
Total world production 40 million tonnes
7·3%
1976-77
Total world production 98·4 million tonnes

Fertilizers—principal producers

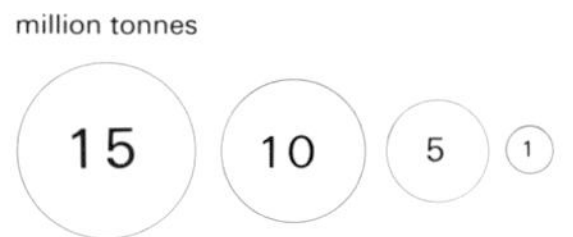

million tonnes
15
10
5
1

Artificial Fertilizers are produced from the minerals sodium nitrate, potassium, salt, phosphate and potash, and as by-products of other industries.

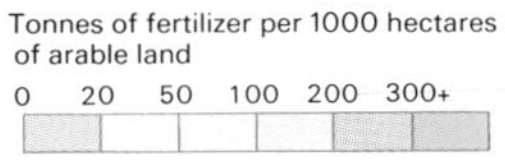

Tonnes of fertilizer per 1000 hectares of arable land
0
20
50
100
200
300+

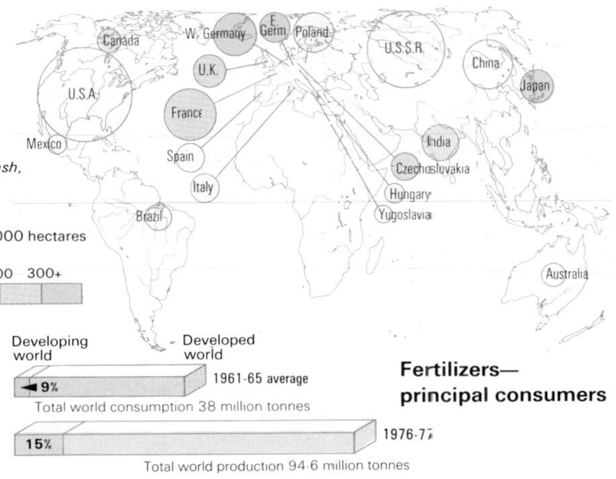

Canada
U.S.A.
Mexico
W. Germany
E. Germ.
Poland
U.K.
France
Spain
Italy
U.S.S.R.
China
Japan
India
Czechoslovakia
Hungary
Yugoslavia
Brazil
Australia
Developing world
Developed world
9%
1961-65 average
Total world consumption 38 million tonnes
15%
1976-77
Total world production 94·6 million tonnes

Fertilizers—principal consumers

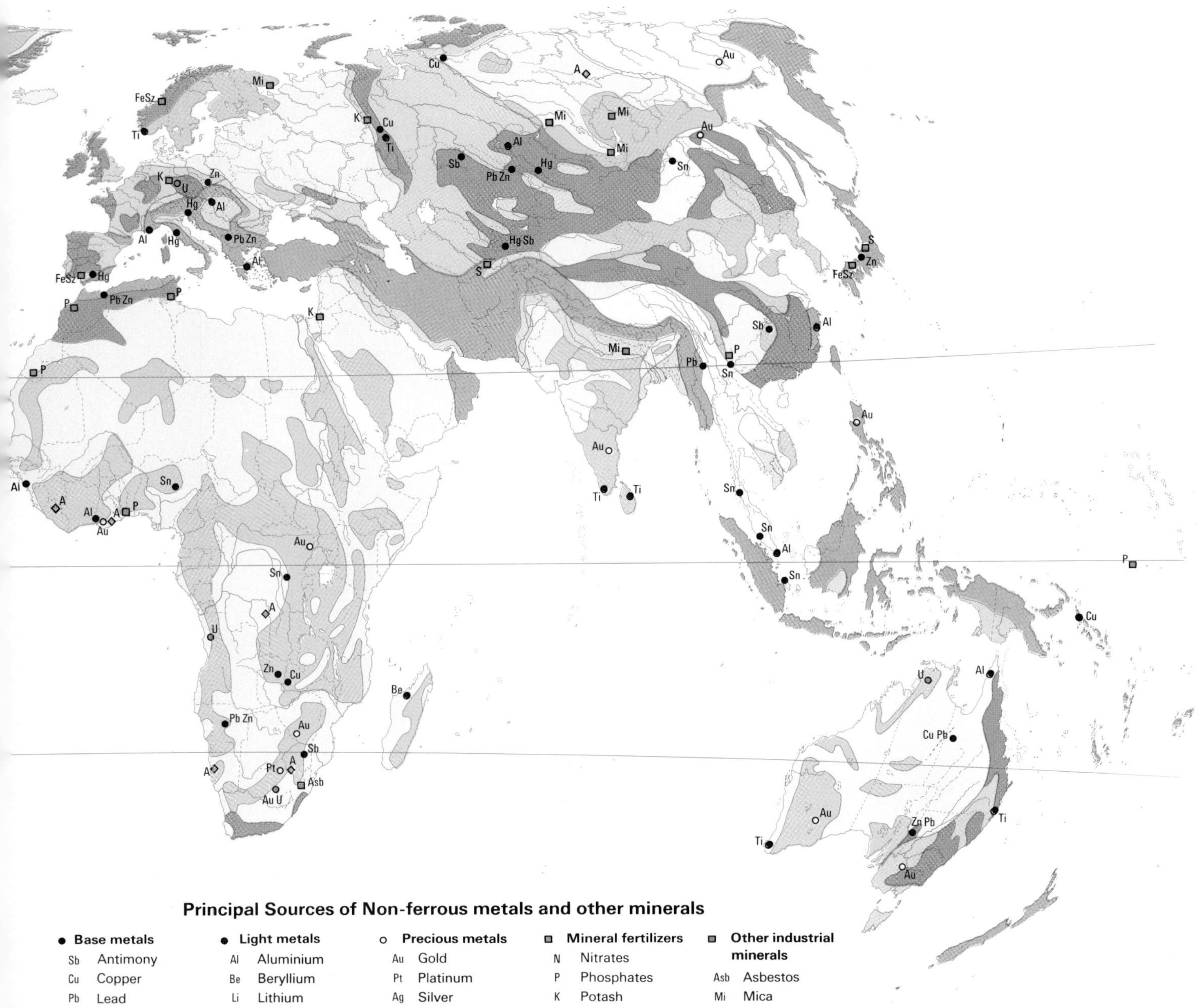

Principal Sources of Non-ferrous metals and other minerals

● Base metals
- Sb Antimony
- Cu Copper
- Pb Lead
- Hg Mercury
- Sn Tin
- Zn Zinc

● Light metals
- Al Aluminium
- Be Beryllium
- Li Lithium
- Ti Titanium

● Rare metals
- U Uranium

○ Precious metals
- Au Gold
- Pt Platinum
- Ag Silver

◇ Precious stones
- A Diamonds

▣ Mineral fertilizers
- N Nitrates
- P Phosphates
- K Potash
- S Sulphur
- FeSz Pyrites

▣ Other industrial minerals
- Asb Asbestos
- Mi Mica

FUEL AND ENERGY

Coal is the result of the accumulation of vegetation over millions of years. Under pressure from overlying sediments, it hardened through four stages: peat, lignite, bituminous coal, and finally anthracite. The map at the top lists the major coal producers and shows world distribution of coal production. The photograph at the far right, a coal mine. Coal is important in the production of electricity, plastics, and many chemicals. **Oil**, which is derived from the remains of marine animals and plants, has replaced coal as an energy source in many areas. Oil is a complex mixture of hydrocarbons, which are refined to extract various constituents such as gasoline, kerosene, and heavy fuel oils. Photograph at the far right, an oil derrick.

Natural gas, or methane, has become one of the largest sources of energy. By liquefaction, its volume can be reduced to 1/600 of that of gas and hence be easily transported. At the far right, a North Sea gas rig. **Hydro-electric power** stations use moving water to drive turbines that generate electricity. The ideal site for such a station is one in which a consistently large volume of water falls a considerable height, as in mountainous areas. At the far right, a hydro-electric power station. Potential sources of hydro-electricity using ocean waves or tides are yet to be exploited widely.

The map at the bottom of the page shows world production of **nuclear energy**. A nuclear power station is shown in the photograph to the right of the map. Here energy is obtained from heat generated by splitting atoms of certain elements, of which uranium and plutonium are the most important. Although the installation costs are high, actual running costs are low because of the slow consumption of fuel.

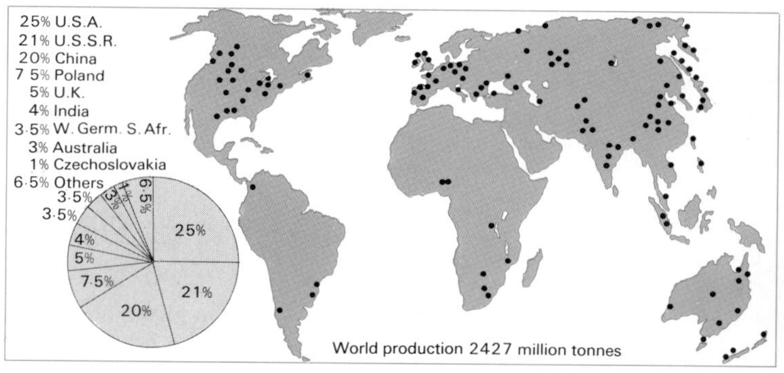
25% U.S.A.
21% U.S.S.R.
20% China
7.5% Poland
5% U.K.
4% India
3.5% W. Germ. S. Afr.
3% Australia
1% Czechoslovakia
6.5% Others
World production 2427 million tonnes

Coal mine

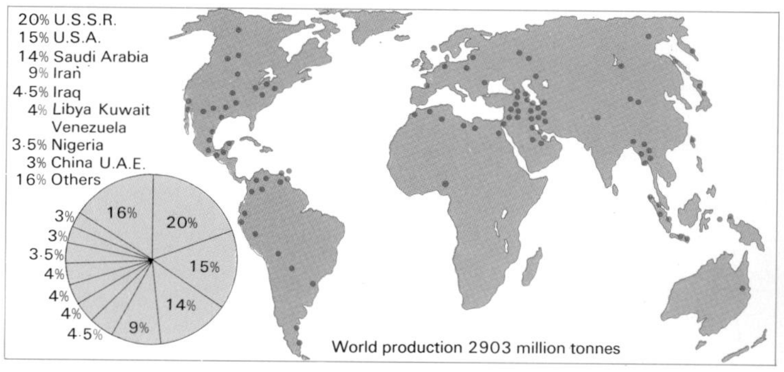
20% U.S.S.R.
15% U.S.A.
14% Saudi Arabia
9% Iran
4.5% Iraq
4% Libya Kuwait Venezuela
3.5% Nigeria
3% China U.A.E.
16% Others
World production 2903 million tonnes

Oil derrick

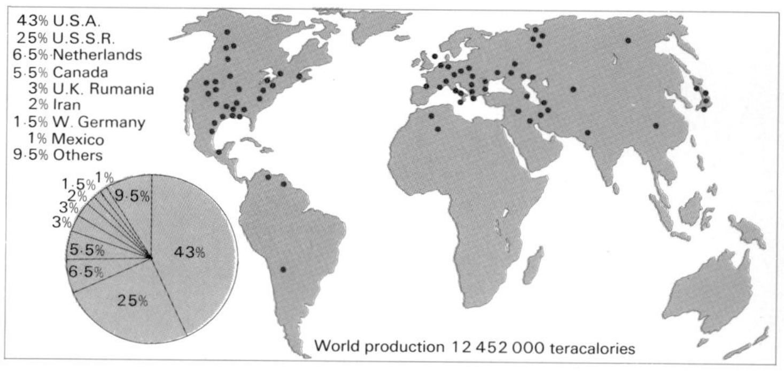
43% U.S.A.
25% U.S.S.R.
6.5% Netherlands
5.5% Canada
3% U.K. Rumania
2% Iran
1.5% W. Germany
1% Mexico
9.5% Others
World production 12 452 000 teracalories

North sea gas rig

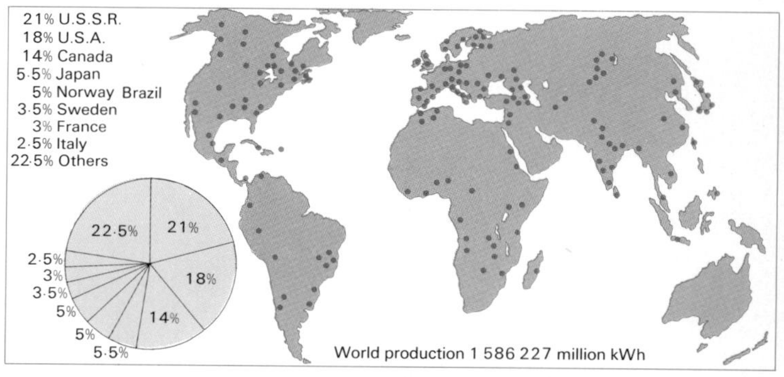
21% U.S.S.R.
18% U.S.A.
14% Canada
5.5% Japan
5% Norway Brazil
3.5% Sweden
3% France
2.5% Italy
22.5% Others
World production 1 586 227 million kWh

Water power

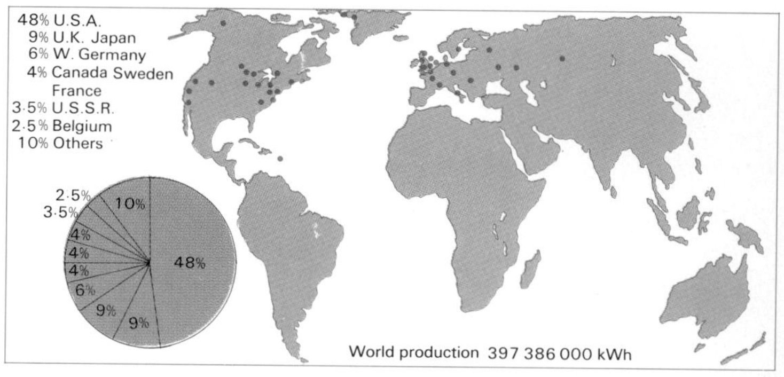
48% U.S.A.
9% U.K. Japan
6% W. Germany
4% Canada Sweden France
3.5% U.S.S.R.
2.5% Belgium
10% Others
World production 397 386 000 kWh

Nuclear power station

The diagrams below show the status of oil production and consumption in 1973. When, as shown here, countries are scaled according to their production and consumption of oil, they take on new dimensions. Large supplies of oil are concentrated in only a few countries. The Middle East, with 55% of the world's reserves, produces 37% of the world's supply but consumes less than 3% of that supply. The U.S.A., despite its great production, has a deficiency of about 300 million tons a year, consuming 30% of the world's total. Western Europe consumes 27% of that total. Japan, the largest importer of crude oil, showed an increase in consumption of 440% from 1963-73. Only the oil-rich nations have a positive energy balance, as shown on the small map at the bottom of the page.

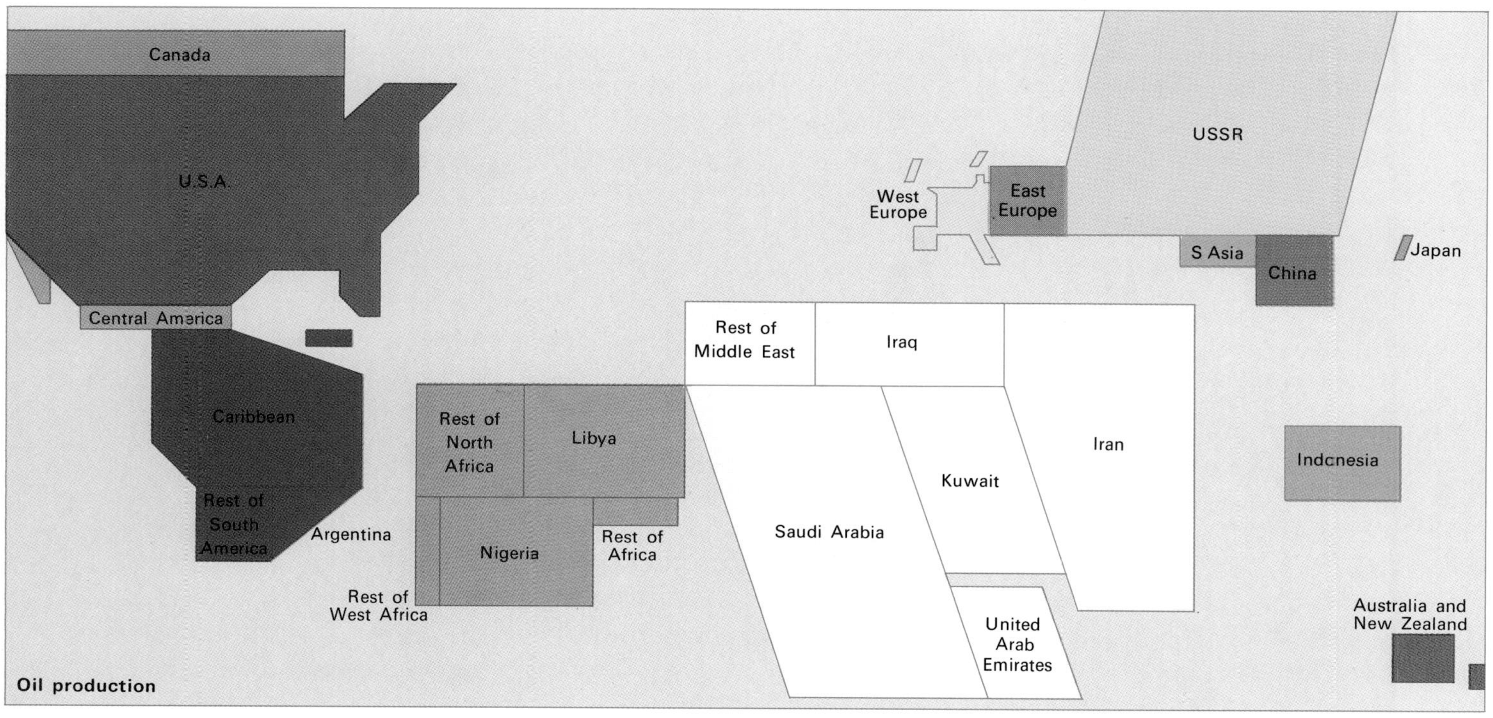
Canada
U.S.A.
Central America
Caribbean
Rest of South America
Argentina
Rest of North Africa
Libya
Nigeria
Rest of Africa
Rest of West Africa
West Europe
East Europe
USSR
S Asia
China
Japan
Rest of Middle East
Iraq
Iran
Saudi Arabia
Kuwait
United Arab Emirates
Indonesia
Australia and New Zealand
Oil production

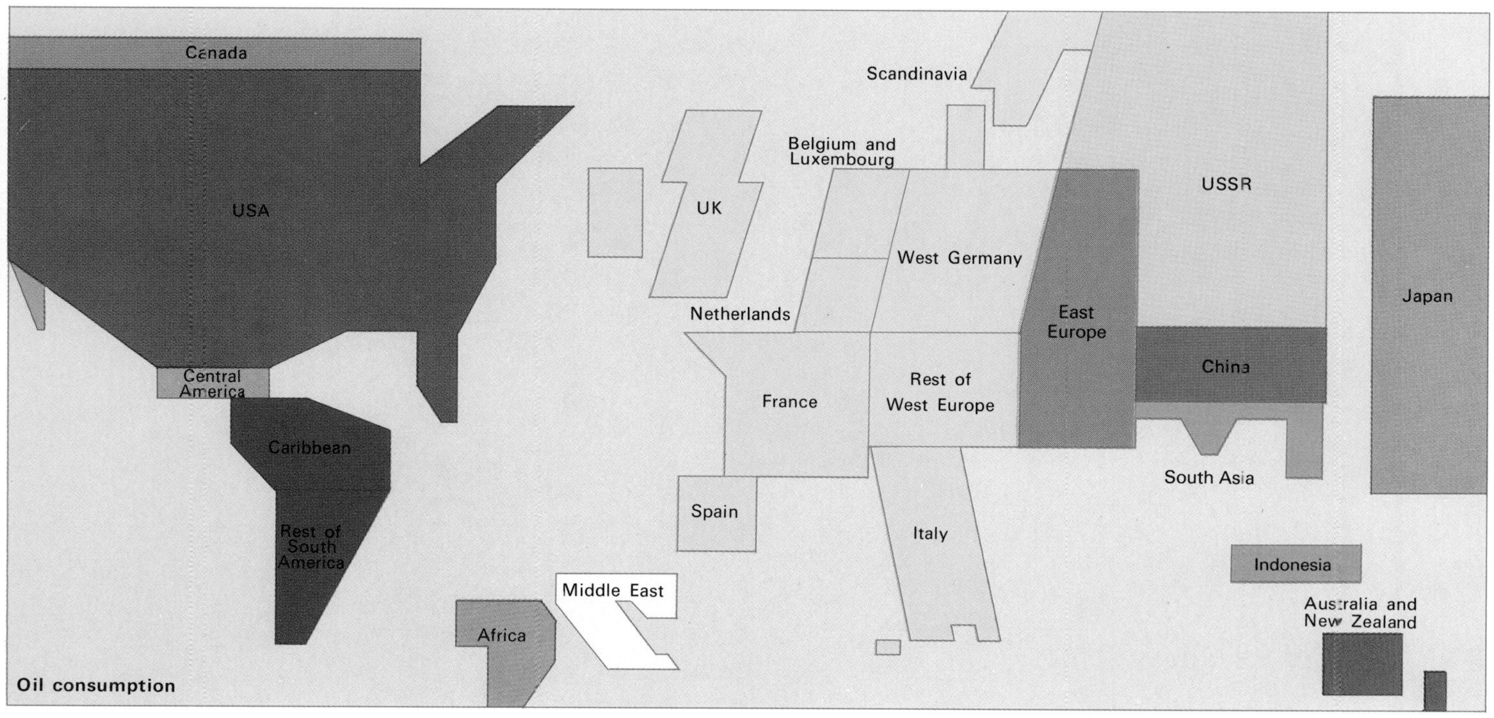
Canada
USA
Central America
Caribbean
Rest of South America
Africa
Middle East
Scandinavia
Belgium and Luxembourg
UK
West Germany
Netherlands
France
Rest of West Europe
Spain
Italy
East Europe
USSR
China
South Asia
Japan
Indonesia
Australia and New Zealand
Oil consumption

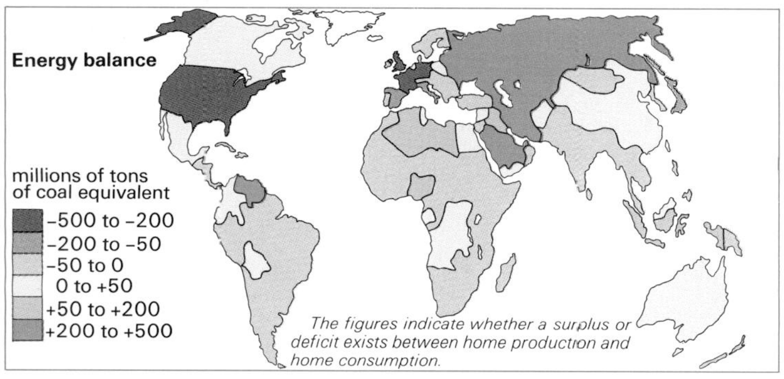
Energy balance
millions of tons of coal equivalent
-500 to -200
-200 to -50
-50 to 0
0 to +50
+50 to +200
+200 to +500
The figures indicate whether a surplus or deficit exists between home production and home consumption.

OCCUPATIONS

Proportion employed in

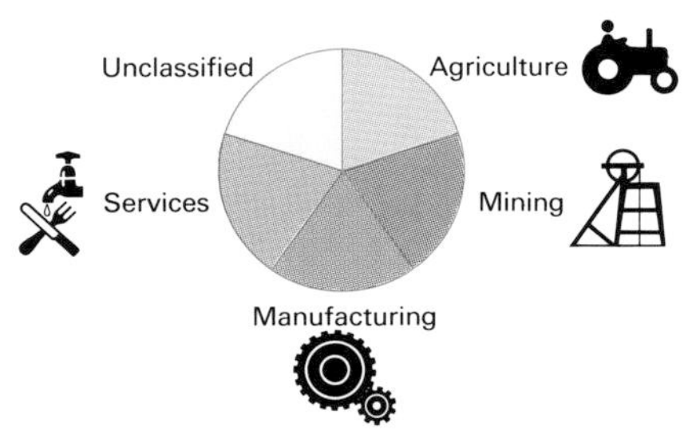
Unclassified
Agriculture
Services
Mining
Manufacturing

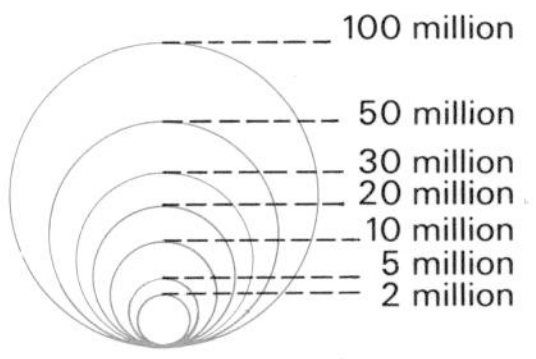
100 million
50 million
30 million
20 million
10 million
5 million
2 million

The area of the circle is in proportion to the total working population of a country.

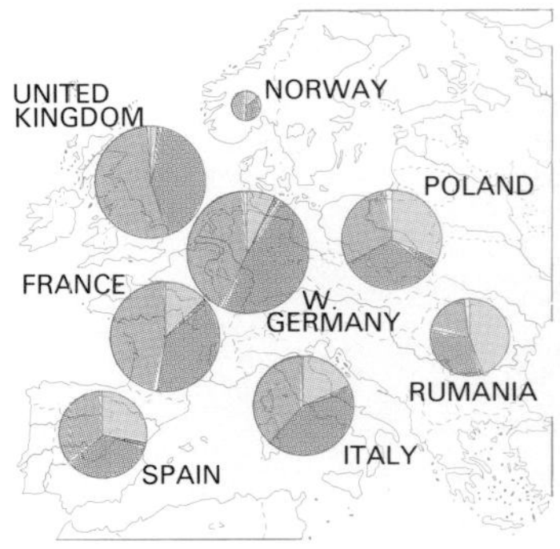
UNITED KINGDOM
NORWAY
POLAND
FRANCE
W. GERMANY
RUMANIA
SPAIN
ITALY

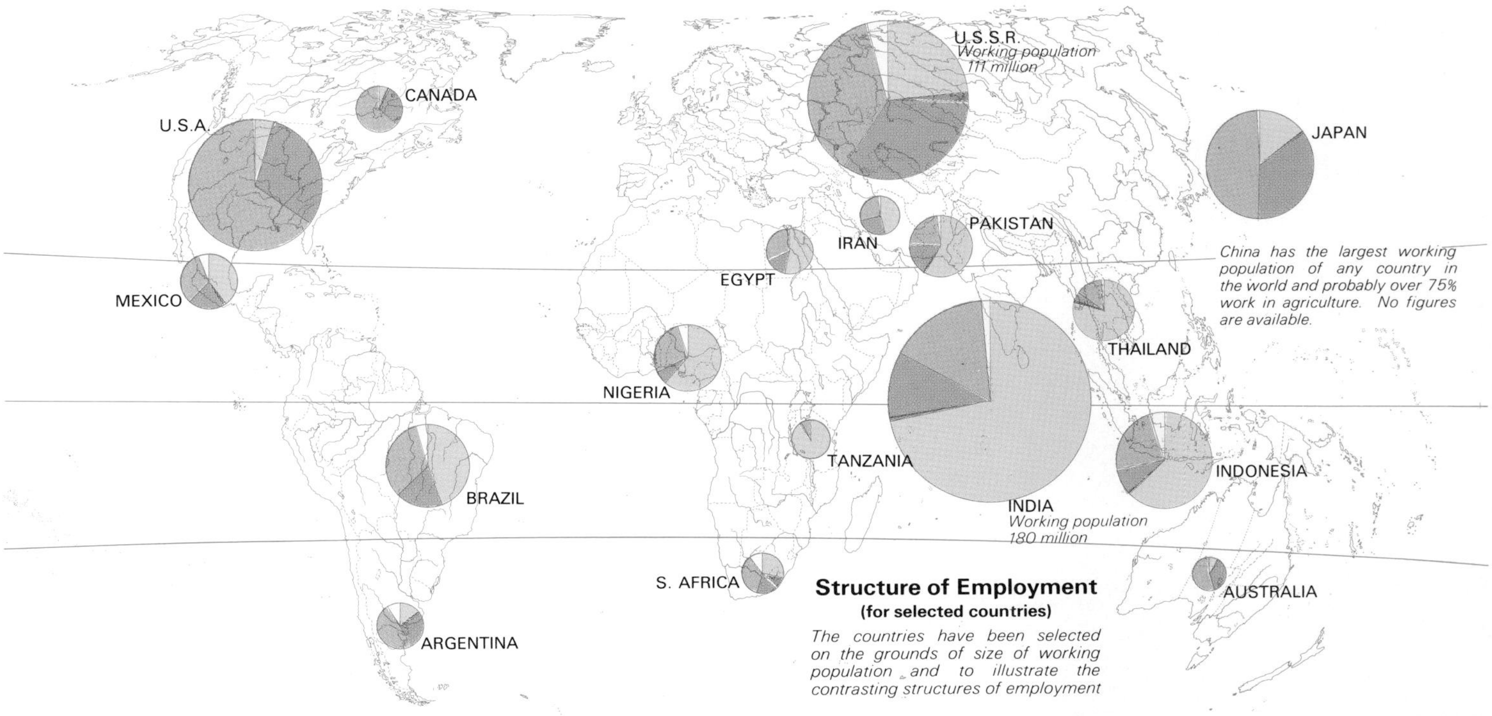
U.S.S.R.
Working population 111 million
CANADA
U.S.A.
JAPAN
PAKISTAN
IRAN
EGYPT
MEXICO
THAILAND
NIGERIA
TANZANIA
INDONESIA
BRAZIL
INDIA
Working population 180 million
S. AFRICA
AUSTRALIA
ARGENTINA

China has the largest working population of any country in the world and probably over 75% work in agriculture. No figures are available.

Structure of Employment
(for selected countries)

The countries have been selected on the grounds of size of working population and to illustrate the contrasting structures of employment

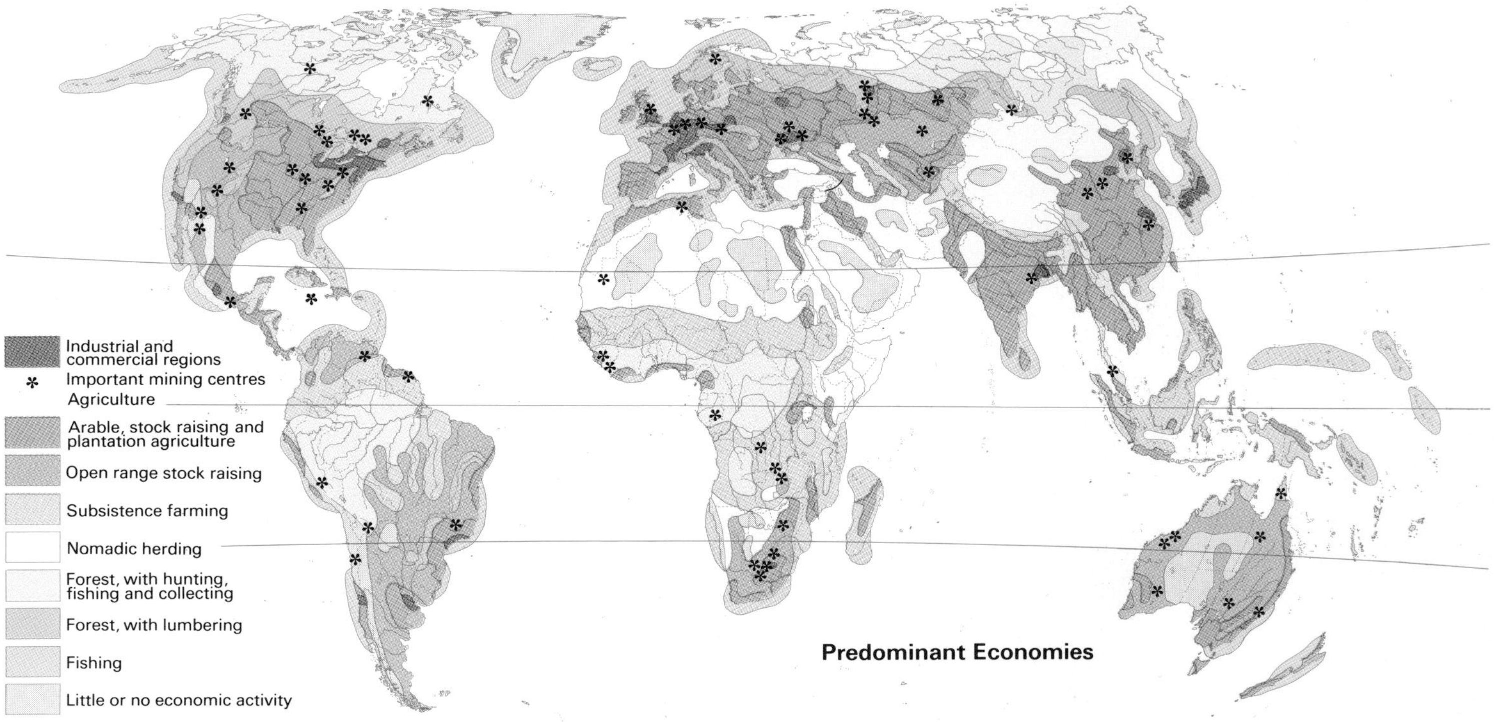
Industrial and commercial regions
* Important mining centres
Agriculture
Arable, stock raising and plantation agriculture
Open range stock raising
Subsistence farming
Nomadic herding
Forest, with hunting, fishing and collecting
Forest, with lumbering
Fishing
Little or no economic activity

Predominant Economies

Casting steel ingots

World Steel production

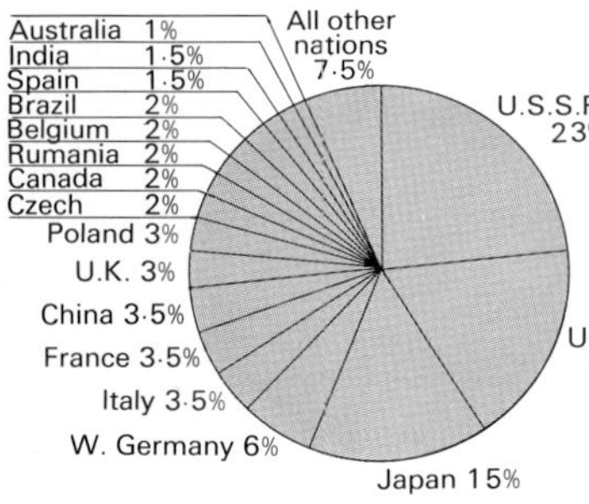

Australia 1%
India 1·5%
Spain 1·5%
Brazil 2%
Belgium 2%
Rumania 2%
Canada 2%
Czech 2%
Poland 3%
U.K. 3%
China 3·5%
France 3·5%
Italy 3·5%
W. Germany 6%
Japan 15%
U.S.A. 18%
U.S.S.R. 23%
All other nations 7·5%

Growth of World Steel production

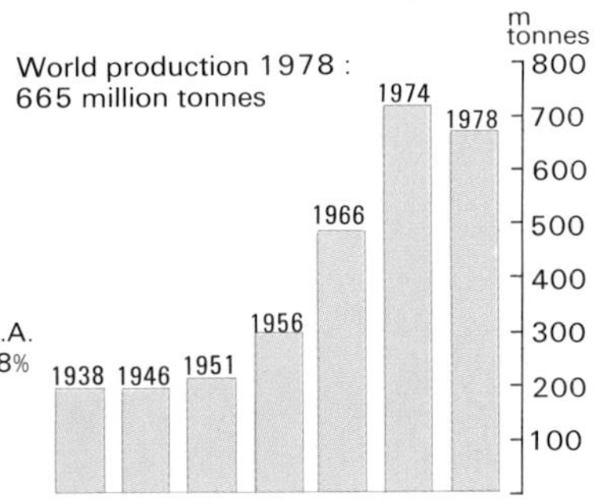

World production 1978 : 665 million tonnes
m tonnes
800
700
600
500
400
300
200
100
1938
1946
1951
1956
1966
1974
1978

World Steel production per capita

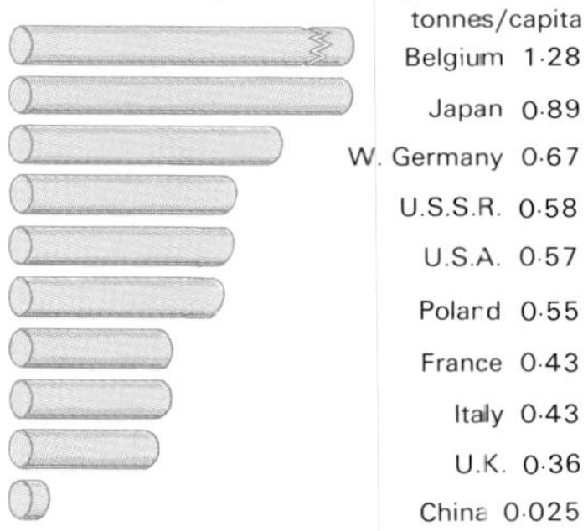

tonnes/capita
Belgium 1·28
Japan 0·89
W. Germany 0·67
U.S.S.R. 0·58
U.S.A. 0·57
Poland 0·55
France 0·43
Italy 0·43
U.K. 0·36
China 0·025

Steel production in Europe
Steel production, by country
only principal producers shown
150 million tonnes
100 million tonnes
50 million tonnes
25 million tonnes
10 million tonnes
5 million tonnes
1 million tonnes
Principal production centre

Steel production

Manufacturing industry in Europe
Principal manufacturing centres
Heavy engineering
Non-ferrous smelting
Chemicals
Cement
Textiles
Timber and paper

Manufacturing industry

TRANSPORT

Shipyards

Japan	4801
Sweden	1305
U.S.A.	913
U.K.	814
Poland	679
France	644
Spain	643
W. Germ.	599
S. Korea	402
Denmark	399
Finland	293
Belgium	266

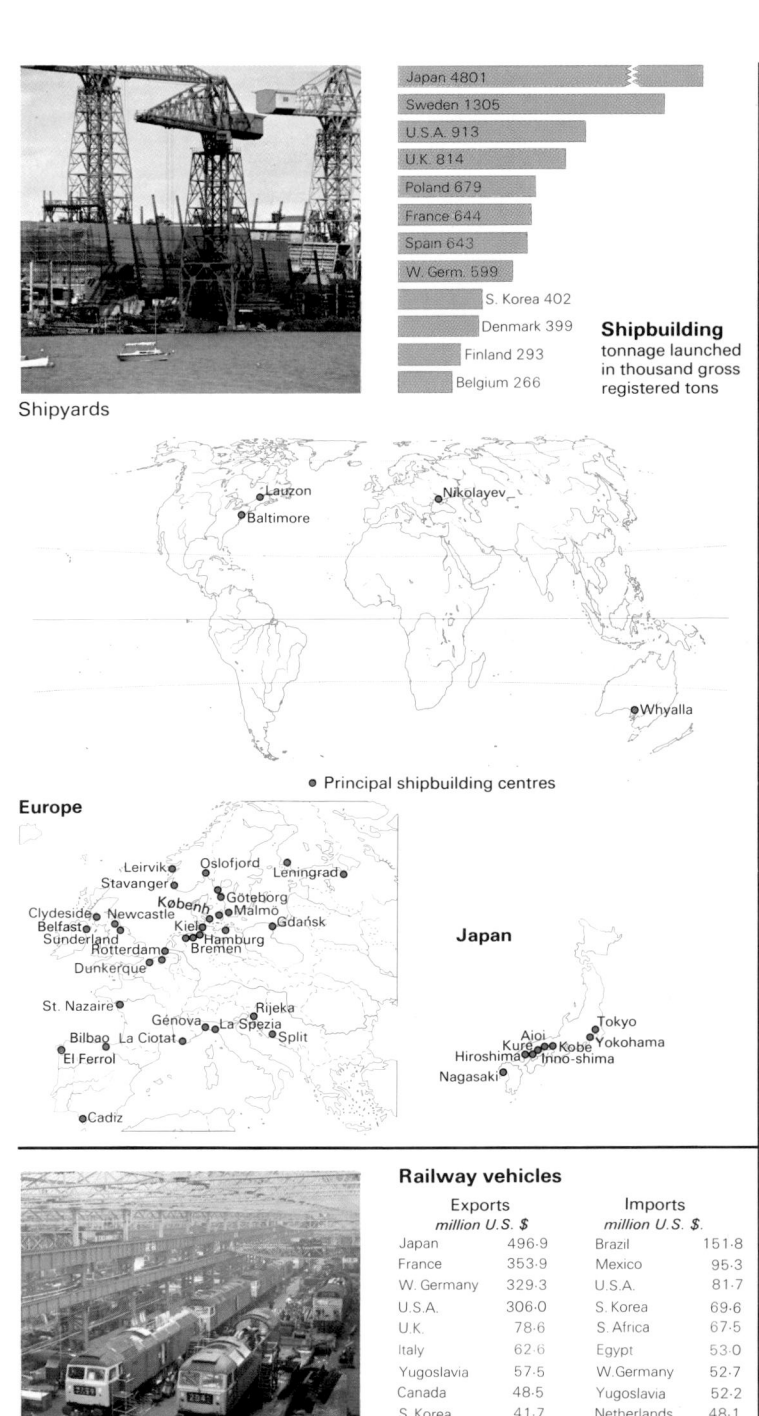

Shipbuilding
tonnage launched in thousand gross registered tons

Lauzon
Baltimore
Nikolayev
Whyalla

● Principal shipbuilding centres

Europe

Leirvik
Stavanger
Oslofjord
Leningrad
Göteborg
København
Malmö
Clydeside
Belfast
Sunderland
Newcastle
Kiel
Hamburg
Gdańsk
Rotterdam
Bremen
Dunkerque
St. Nazaire
Rijeka
Genova
La Spezia
Split
Bilbao
La Ciotat
El Ferrol
Cadiz

Japan

Tokyo
Yokohama
Aioi
Kure
Kobe
Hiroshima
Inno-shima
Nagasaki

Concorde and Boeing 747

Aircraft Industry
In 1975 there were approximately 10 000 civil passenger airliners in service. This diagram shows where they were built.

U.S.A. 53% | U.S.S.R. 33% | U.K. 6% | Netherlands 3% | France 2%

Trade in Aircraft and Aircraft Engines
million U.S. $

Exports	Aircraft	Engines	Imports	Aircraft	Engines
U.S.A.	4143	714	U.S.A.	563	218
U.K.	605	591	Canada	438	108
France	360	150	France	400	250
Canada	325	132	U.K.	389	393
W. Germ.	200		Australia	342	20
Neth.	192	89	W. Germ.	279	
Italy	137		Japan	236	107

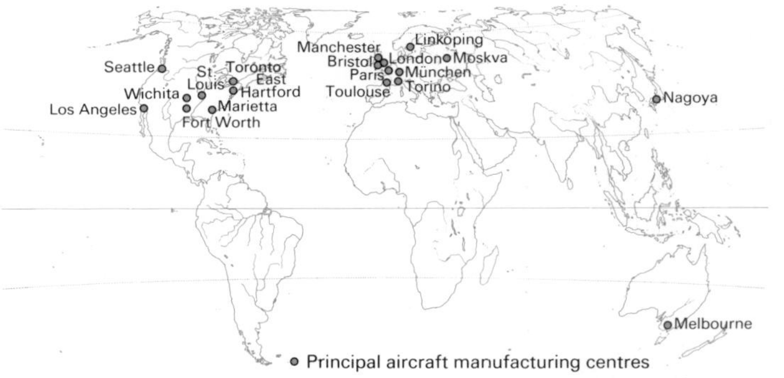

Seattle
Wichita
St. Louis
Toronto
East Hartford
Marietta
Fort Worth
Los Angeles
Manchester
Bristol
London
Paris
Toulouse
Linköping
Moskva
München
Torino
Nagoya
Melbourne

● Principal aircraft manufacturing centres

Motor vehicles

	Production *thousand units*	Exports *million U.S. $*	Imports *million U.S. $*
U.S.A.	12840	11916	17529
Japan	9240	14291	360
W. Germ.	4200	16567	5109
France	4152	7728	3846
U.S.S.R.	2066		
Canada	1907	8817	9598
Italy	1658	3928	2465
U.K.	1608	4667	3637
Spain	1139	897	389

Locomotive works

Railway vehicles

Exports *million U.S. $*		Imports *million U.S. $*	
Japan	496·9	Brazil	151·8
France	353·9	Mexico	95·3
W. Germany	329·3	U.S.A.	81·7
U.S.A.	306·0	S. Korea	69·6
U.K.	78·6	S. Africa	67·5
Italy	62·6	Egypt	53·0
Yugoslavia	57·5	W.Germany	52·7
Canada	48·5	Yugoslavia	52·2
S. Korea	41·7	Netherlands	48·1
Sweden	37·7	Sweden	44·4
Belg-Lux.	27·8	U.K.	40·5
Switzerland	37·5	Belg.-Lux.	33·6
Spain	18·5	France	30·3
		Italy	30·0

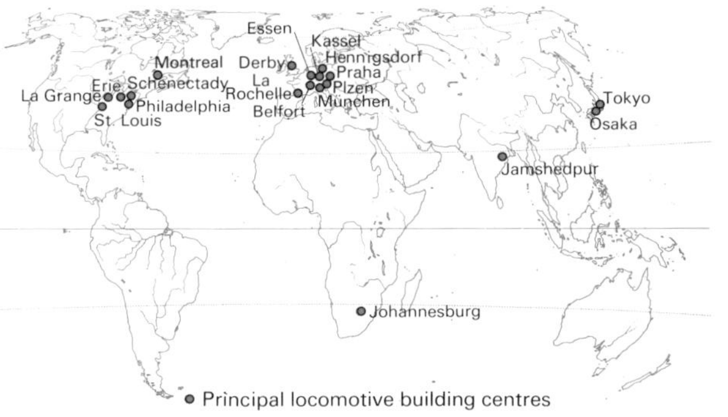

Essen
Kassel
Montreal
Derby
Henningsdorf
Praha
La Grange
Erie
Schenectady
La Rochelle
Plzen
Philadelphia
München
St. Louis
Belfort
Tokyo
Osaka
Jamshedpur
Johannesburg

● Principal locomotive building centres

Car assembly line

Europe

Trollhattan
Göteborg
Riga
Minsk
Liverpool
Coventry
Luton
Wolfsburg
Warszawa
Dusseldorf
Valenciennes
Praha
Lvov
Paris
Stuttgart
Rennes
Graz
La Rochelle
Lyon
Milano
Torino
Beograd
Barcelona
Napoli
Madrid
Lisboa

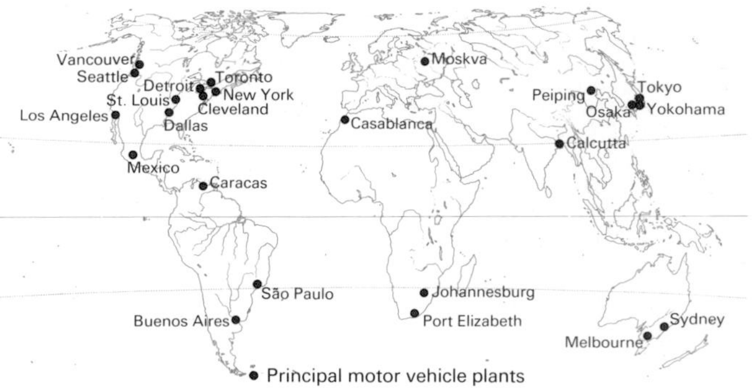

Vancouver
Seattle
Detroit
Toronto
St. Louis
New York
Cleveland
Los Angeles
Dallas
Mexico
Caracas
Moskva
Casablanca
Peiping
Tokyo
Osaka
Yokohama
Calcutta
São Paulo
Buenos Aires
Johannesburg
Port Elizabeth
Sydney
Melbourne

● Principal motor vehicle plants

Merchant Shipping

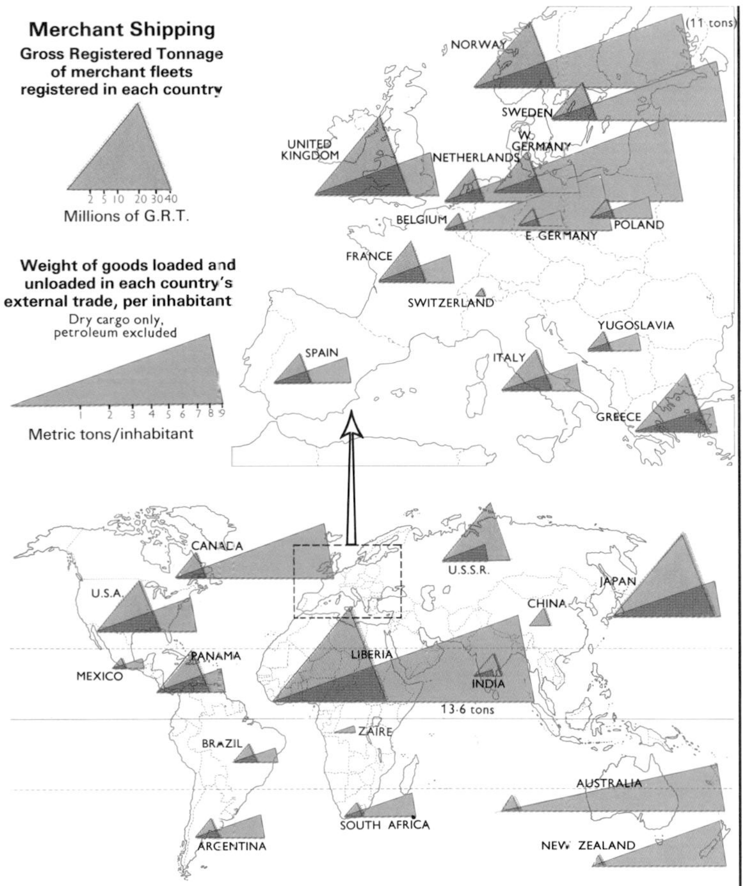

Gross Registered Tonnage of merchant fleets registered in each country
2 5 10 20 30 40
Millions of G.R.T.
Weight of goods loaded and unloaded in each country's external trade, per inhabitant
Dry cargo only, petroleum excluded
1 2 3 4 5 6 7 8 9
Metric tons/inhabitant
(11 tons)
NORWAY
SWEDEN
UNITED KINGDOM
W. GERMANY
NETHERLANDS
BELGIUM
E. GERMANY
POLAND
FRANCE
SWITZERLAND
YUGOSLAVIA
SPAIN
ITALY
GREECE
CANADA
U.S.S.R.
U.S.A.
JAPAN
CHINA
PANAMA
LIBERIA
MEXICO
INDIA
13·6 tons
BRAZIL
ZAIRE
AUSTRALIA
SOUTH AFRICA
ARGENTINA
NEW ZEALAND

Density of Transport Networks

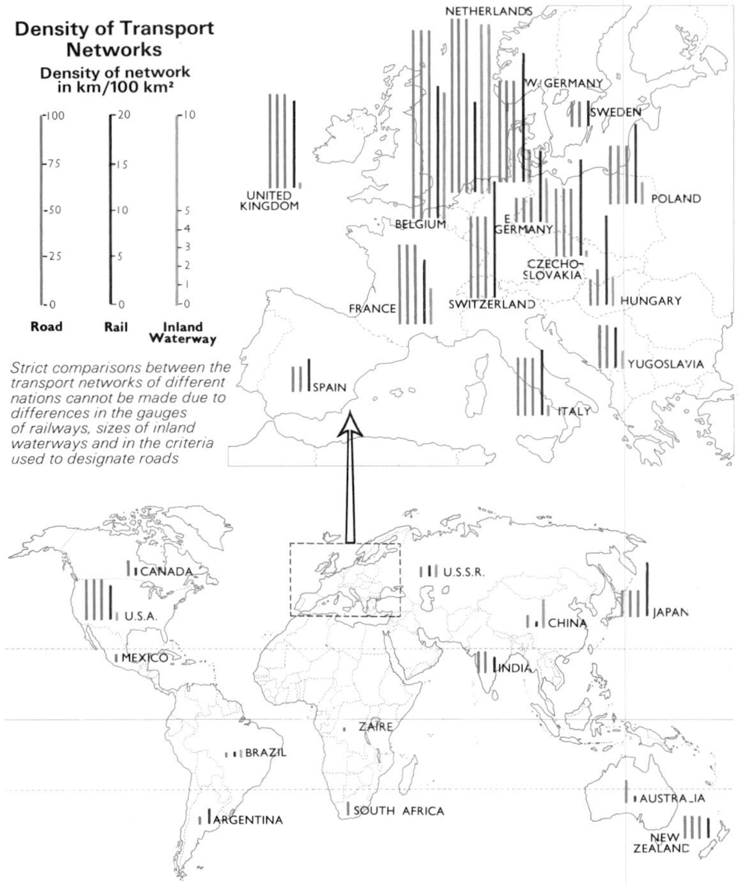

Density of network in km/100 km²
100 75 50 25 0
20 15 10 5 0
10 5 4 3 2 1 0
Road
Rail
Inland Waterway
Strict comparisons between the transport networks of different nations cannot be made due to differences in the gauges of railways, sizes of inland waterways and in the criteria used to designate roads
NETHERLANDS
W. GERMANY
SWEDEN
UNITED KINGDOM
POLAND
BELGIUM
E. GERMANY
CZECHO-SLOVAKIA
FRANCE
SWITZERLAND
HUNGARY
YUGOSLAVIA
SPAIN
ITALY
CANADA
U.S.S.R.
U.S.A.
CHINA
JAPAN
MEXICO
INDIA
ZAIRE
BRAZIL
ARGENTINA
SOUTH AFRICA
AUSTRALIA
NEW ZEALAND

Motor Vehicles and Passenger Transport

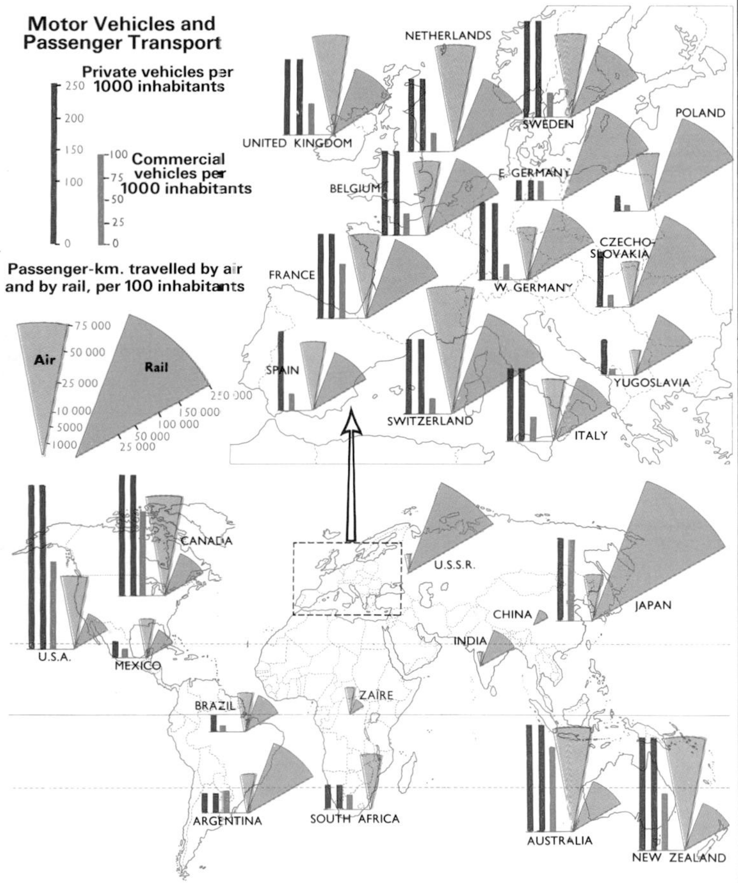

Private vehicles per 1000 inhabitants
250 200 150 100 0
Commercial vehicles per 1000 inhabitants
100 75 50 25 0
Passenger-km. travelled by air and by rail, per 100 inhabitants
Air
Rail
75 000
50 000
25 000
10 000
5000
1000
250 000
150 000
100 000
50 000
25 000
NETHERLANDS
UNITED KINGDOM
SWEDEN
POLAND
BELGIUM
E. GERMANY
CZECHOSLOVAKIA
FRANCE
W. GERMANY
SPAIN
YUGOSLAVIA
SWITZERLAND
ITALY
CANADA
U.S.S.R.
U.S.A.
MEXICO
CHINA
JAPAN
INDIA
ZAIRE
BRAZIL
ARGENTINA
SOUTH AFRICA
AUSTRALIA
NEW ZEALAND

Freight Carried

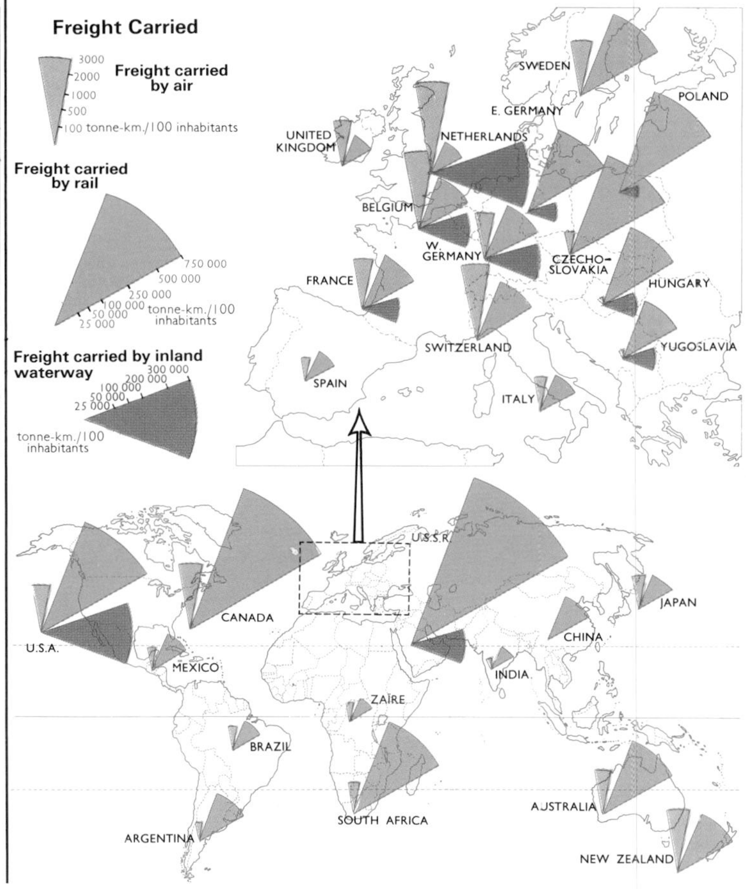

Freight carried by air
3000
2000
1000
500
100 tonne-km./100 inhabitants
Freight carried by rail
750 000
500 000
250 000
100 000
50 000
25 000
tonne-km./100 inhabitants
Freight carried by inland waterway
300 000
200 000
100 000
50 000
25 000
tonne-km./100 inhabitants
SWEDEN
E. GERMANY
POLAND
UNITED KINGDOM
NETHERLANDS
BELGIUM
W. GERMANY
CZECHO-SLOVAKIA
FRANCE
HUNGARY
SWITZERLAND
YUGOSLAVIA
SPAIN
ITALY
U.S.S.R.
JAPAN
CANADA
U.S.A.
CHINA
MEXICO
INDIA
ZAIRE
BRAZIL
AUSTRALIA
SOUTH AFRICA
ARGENTINA
NEW ZEALAND

TRADE

SCANIA

Road container lorry.

Oil tanker.

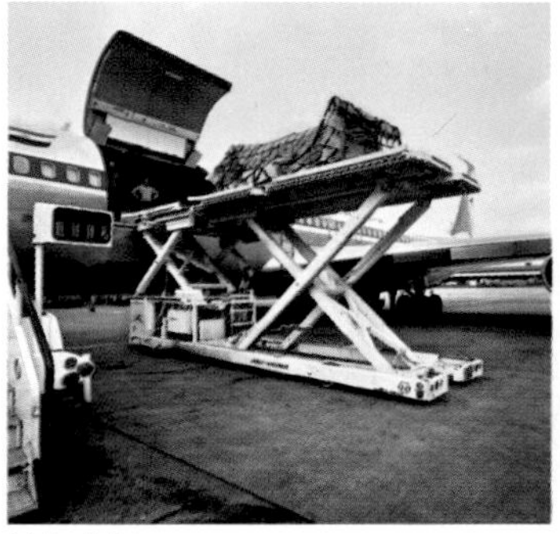

Airfreight.

Road/rail container depot.

The Trade of Europe

The semi-circles on this map are at the same scale as those on the World map below. See the legend to the latter.

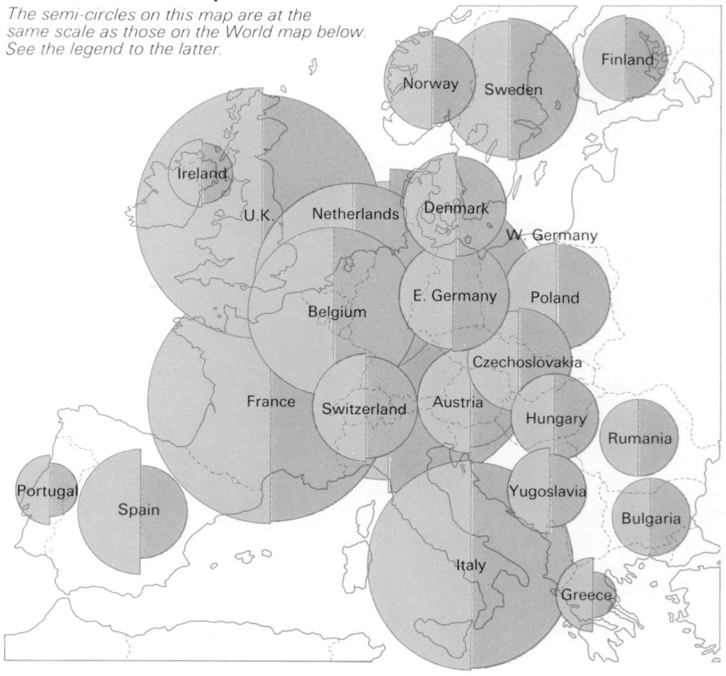

Norway
Sweden
Finland
Ireland
U.K.
Netherlands
Denmark
W. Germany
Belgium
E. Germany
Poland
Czechoslovakia
France
Switzerland
Austria
Hungary
Rumania
Portugal
Spain
Yugoslavia
Bulgaria
Italy
Greece

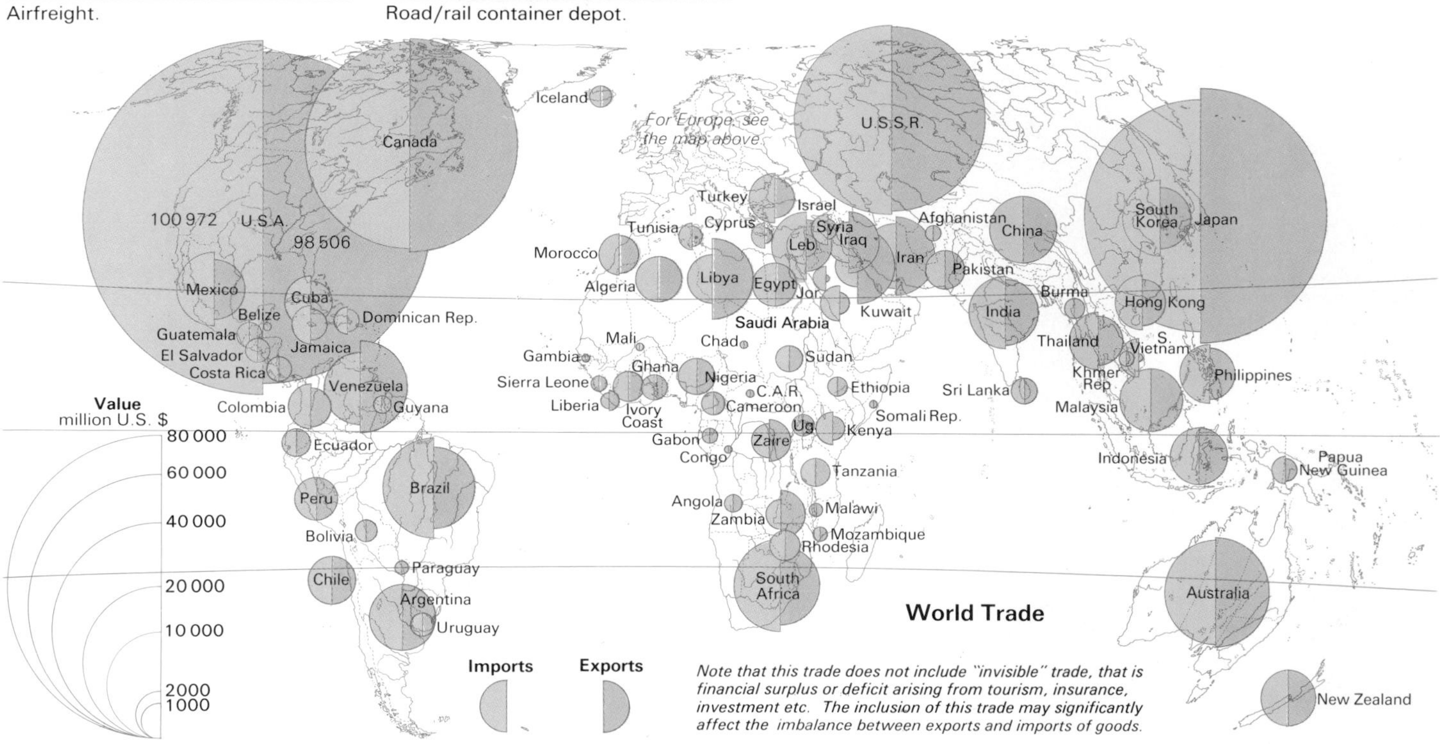

Iceland
For Europe, see the map above
U.S.S.R.
Canada
100 972
U.S.A.
98 506
Mexico
Cuba
Belize
Dominican Rep.
Guatemala
Jamaica
El Salvador
Costa Rica
Venezuela
Colombia
Guyana
Ecuador
Peru
Brazil
Bolivia
Paraguay
Chile
Argentina
Uruguay
Turkey
Israel
Tunisia
Cyprus
Syria
Iraq
Afghanistan
China
South Korea
Japan
Morocco
Leb
Iran
Pakistan
Algeria
Libya
Egypt
Jor
Kuwait
Saudi Arabia
India
Burma
Hong Kong
Mali
Chad
Sudan
Thailand
S. Vietnam
Gambia
Ghana
Nigeria
Ethiopia
Sri Lanka
Khmer Rep.
Philippines
Sierra Leone
C.A.R.
Liberia
Ivory Coast
Cameroon
Somali Rep.
Malaysia
Gabon
Zaire
Ug.
Kenya
Congo
Indonesia
Papua New Guinea
Tanzania
Angola
Malawi
Zambia
Mozambique
Rhodesia
South Africa
Australia
New Zealand
World Trade
Value
million U.S. $
80 000
60 000
40 000
20 000
10 000
2000
1000
Imports
Exports
Note that this trade does not include "invisible" trade, that is financial surplus or deficit arising from tourism, insurance, investment etc. The inclusion of this trade may significantly affect the imbalance between exports and imports of goods.

These diagrams show the destination of exports from each of the regions of the World.

= 20 000 million U.S. $

The total exports are in million U.S. $

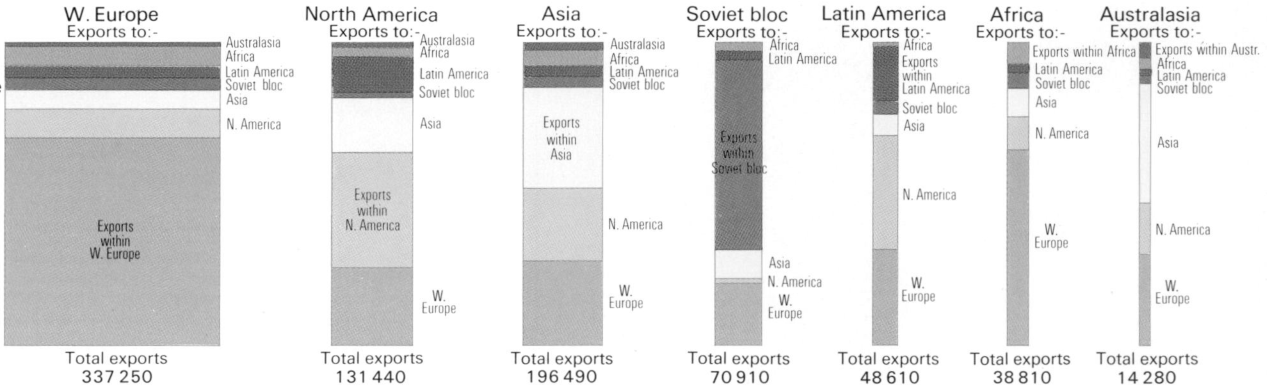

W. Europe
Exports to:-
Australasia
Africa
Latin America
Soviet bloc
Asia
N. America
Exports within W. Europe
Total exports 337 250
North America
Exports to:-
Australasia
Africa
Latin America
Soviet bloc
Asia
Exports within N. America
W. Europe
Total exports 131 440
Asia
Exports to:-
Australasia
Africa
Latin America
Soviet bloc
Exports within Asia
N. America
W. Europe
Total exports 196 490
Soviet bloc
Exports to:-
Africa
Latin America
Exports within Soviet bloc
Asia
N. America
W. Europe
Total exports 70 910
Latin America
Exports to:-
Africa
Exports within Latin America
Soviet bloc
Asia
N. America
W. Europe
Total exports 48 610
Africa
Exports to:-
Exports within Africa
Latin America
Soviet bloc
Asia
N. America
W. Europe
Total exports 38 810
Australasia
Exports to:-
Exports within Austr.
Africa
Latin America
Soviet bloc
Asia
N. America
W. Europe
Total exports 14 280

Imports

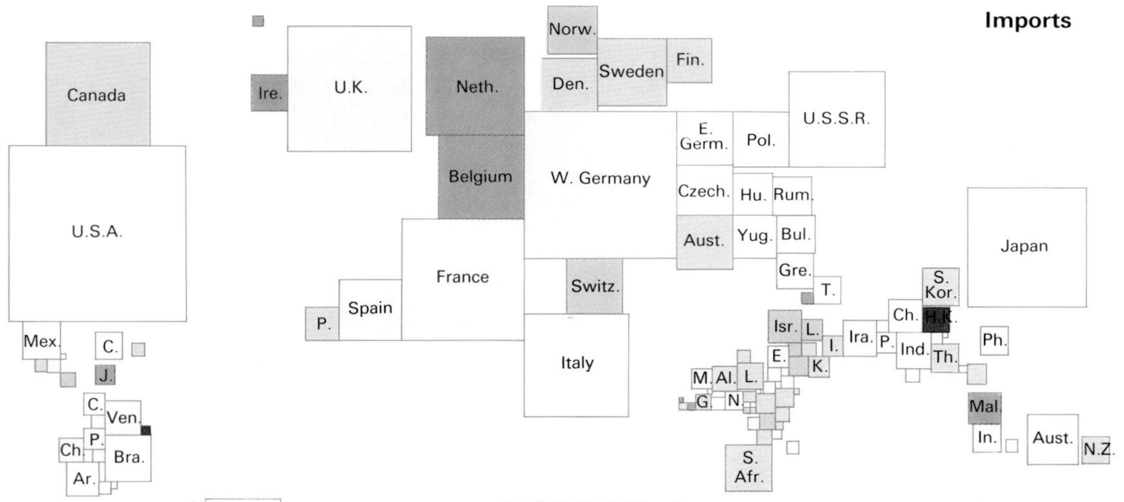
Canada
U.S.A.
Mex.
C.
J.
C.
Ven.
P.
Ch.
Bra.
Ar.
Ire.
U.K.
Neth.
Belgium
France
Spain
P.
Norw.
Den.
Sweden
Fin.
W. Germany
E. Germ.
Pol.
U.S.S.R.
Czech.
Hu.
Rum.
Aust.
Yug.
Bul.
Switz.
Gre.
T.
Italy
Isr.
L.
E.
I.
K.
Ira.
P.
Ind.
Ch.
H.K.
S. Kor.
Th.
M.
Al.
L.
G.
N.
S. Afr.
Japan
Ph.
Mal.
In.
Aust.
N.Z.

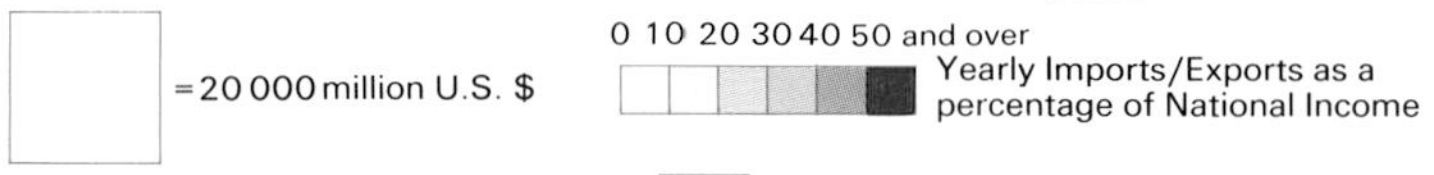
=20 000 million U.S. $
0 10 20 30 40 50 and over
Yearly Imports/Exports as a percentage of National Income

Exports

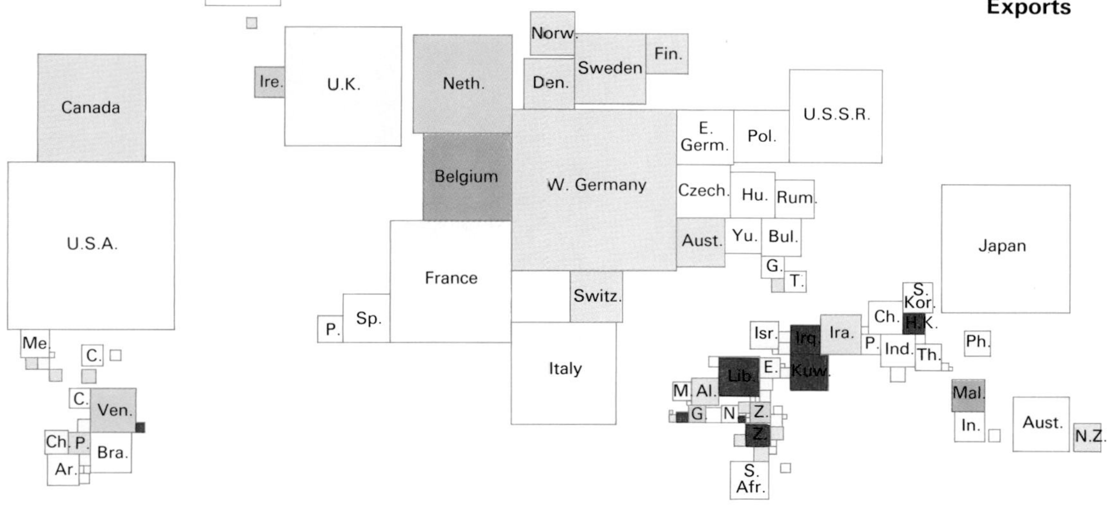
Canada
U.S.A.
Me.
C.
C.
Ven.
Ch.
P.
Bra.
Ar.
Ire.
U.K.
Neth.
Belgium
France
Sp.
P.
Norw.
Den.
Sweden
Fin.
W. Germany
E. Germ.
Pol.
U.S.S.R.
Czech.
Hu.
Rum.
Aust.
Yu.
Bul.
G.
T.
Switz.
Italy
Isr.
Irq.
Ira.
E.
Kuw.
Lib.
M.
Al.
G.
N.
Z.
Z.
S. Afr.
P.
Ind.
Ch.
H.K.
S. Kor.
Th.
Japan
Ph.
Mal.
In.
Aust.
N.Z.

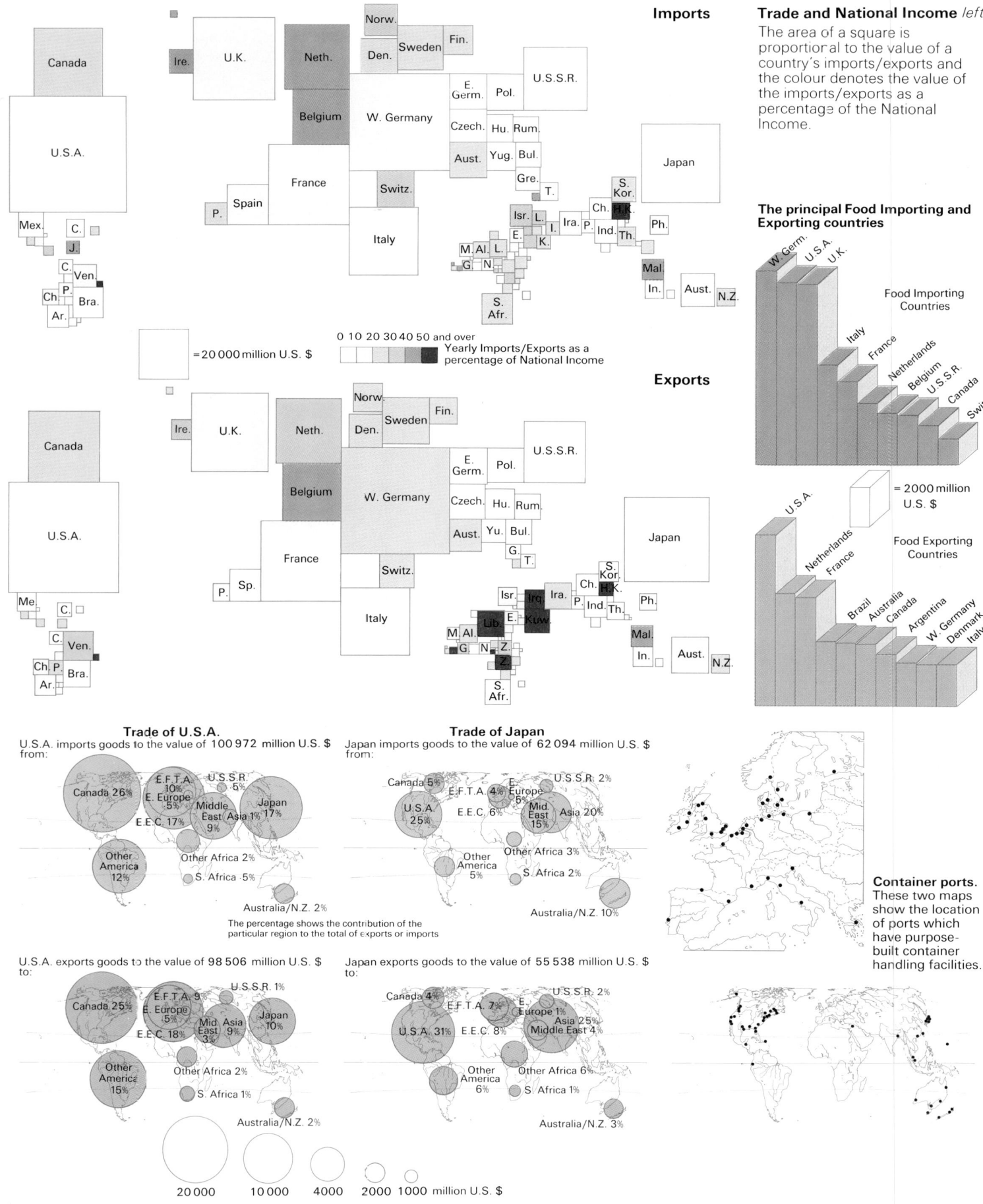

Trade and National Income *left*
The area of a square is proportional to the value of a country's imports/exports and the colour denotes the value of the imports/exports as a percentage of the National Income.

The principal Food Importing and Exporting countries

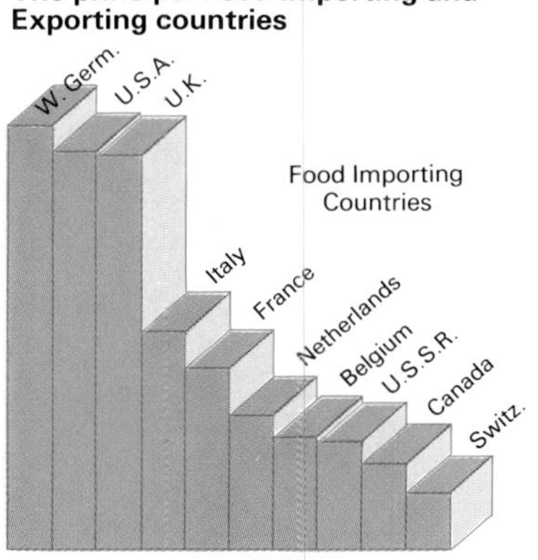
W. Germ.
U.S.A.
U.K.
Food Importing Countries
Italy
France
Netherlands
Belgium
U.S.S.R.
Canada
Switz.

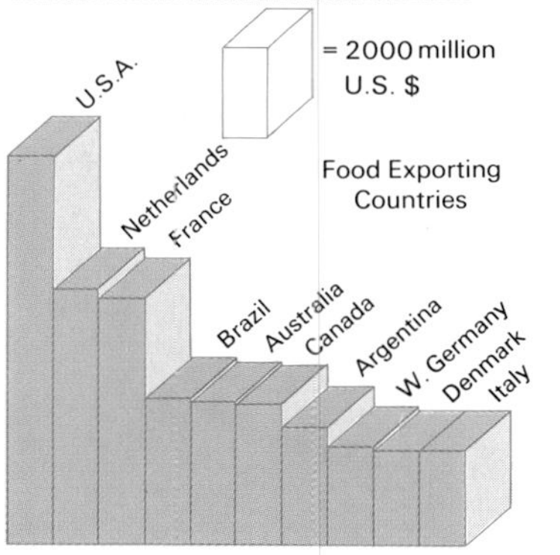
= 2000 million U.S. $
U.S.A.
Food Exporting Countries
Netherlands
France
Brazil
Australia
Canada
Argentina
W. Germany
Denmark
Italy

Trade of U.S.A.

U.S.A. imports goods to the value of 100 972 million U.S. $ from:

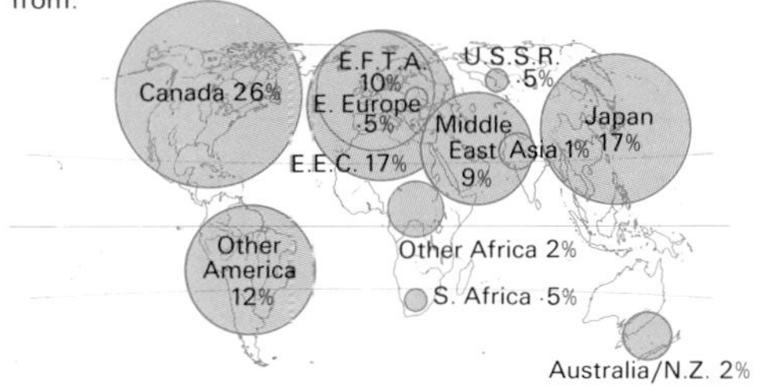
Canada 26%
E.F.T.A. 10%
E. Europe 5%
U.S.S.R. 5%
Middle East 9%
Asia 1%
Japan 17%
E.E.C. 17%
Other America 12%
Other Africa 2%
S. Africa 5%
Australia/N.Z. 2%

The percentage shows the contribution of the particular region to the total of exports or imports

U.S.A. exports goods to the value of 98 506 million U.S. $ to:

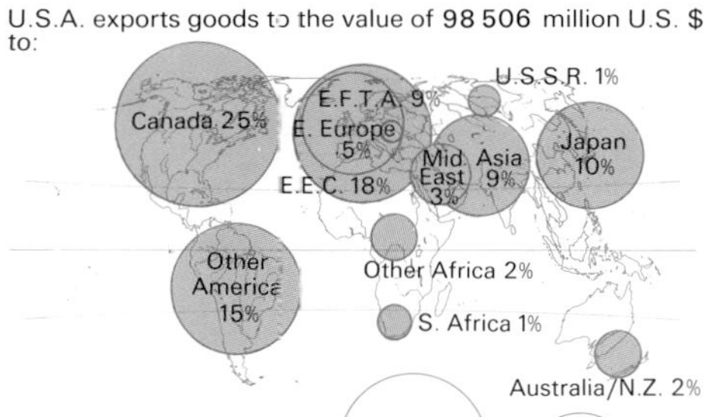
Canada 25%
E.F.T.A. 9%
E. Europe 5%
U.S.S.R. 1%
Mid. East 3%
Asia 9%
Japan 10%
E.E.C. 18%
Other America 15%
Other Africa 2%
S. Africa 1%
Australia/N.Z. 2%

Trade of Japan

Japan imports goods to the value of 62 094 million U.S. $ from:

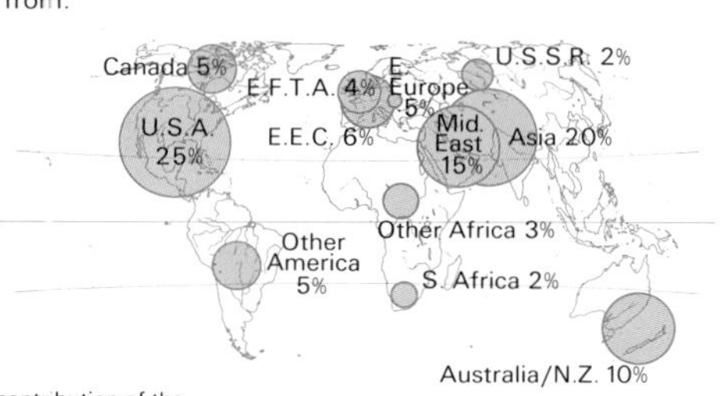
Canada 5%
E.F.T.A. 4%
E. Europe 5%
U.S.S.R. 2%
U.S.A. 25%
E.E.C. 6%
Mid East 15%
Asia 20%
Other America 5%
Other Africa 3%
S. Africa 2%
Australia/N.Z. 10%

Japan exports goods to the value of 55 538 million U.S. $ to:

Canada 4%
E.F.T.A. 7%
E. Europe 1%
U.S.S.R. 2%
U.S.A. 31%
E.E.C. 8%
Asia 25%
Middle East 4%
Other America 6%
Other Africa 6%
S. Africa 1%
Australia/N.Z. 3%

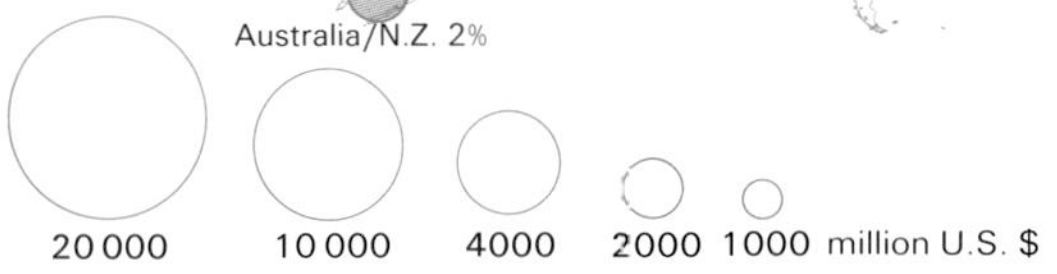
20 000
10 000
4000
2000
1000 million U.S. $

Container ports. These two maps show the location of ports which have purpose-built container handling facilities.

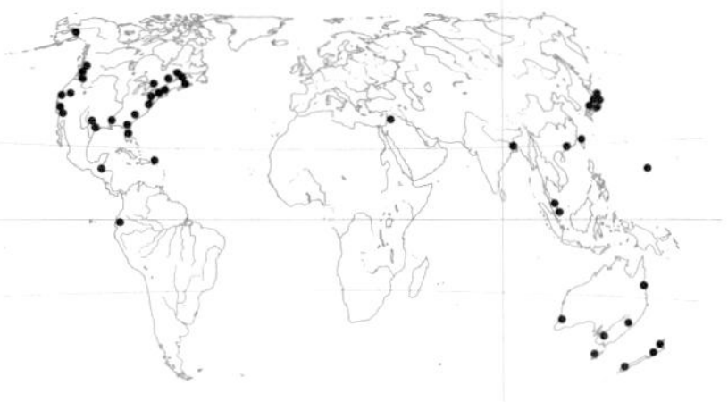

WEALTH

The living standard of a few highly developed, urbanized, industrialized countries is a complete contrast to the conditions existing in the vast majority of economically underdeveloped agrarian states. It is this contrast that divides humanity into rich and poor, well-fed and hungry. The developing world is still an overwhelmingly agricultural world. Over 70% of its people live off the land; yet, the output from that land remains very low. Many Africans, South Americans, and Asians struggle with the soil, but the bad years occur all too frequently, giving rise to a need for foreign capital. The map below, top right, shows the extent of **U.S. aid to developing countries**. The chart below, top left, gives a **comparison of national incomes**, expressed in U.S. dollars per capita, in developing and developed nations. In 1938, the per capita incomes in the United States and India were in proportions of 1:15; now that ratio is about 1:35.

The provision of foreign aid, defined as assistance on concessional terms for promoting development, is today an accepted though controversial aspect of the economic policies of most advanced countries toward less developed countries. The most important international aid committee set up after World War II was that of the United Nations. Practically all aid, however, has been given bilaterally direct from an industrialized country to an underdeveloped nation. The **distribution of wealth** throughout the world, in terms of domestic products, is shown on the large map below.

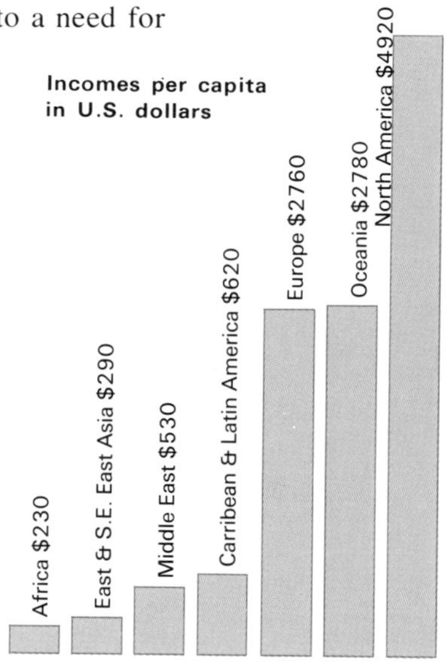

Incomes per capita in U.S. dollars
Africa $230
East & S.E. East Asia $290
Middle East $530
Carribean & Latin America $620
Europe $2760
Oceania $2780
North America $4920

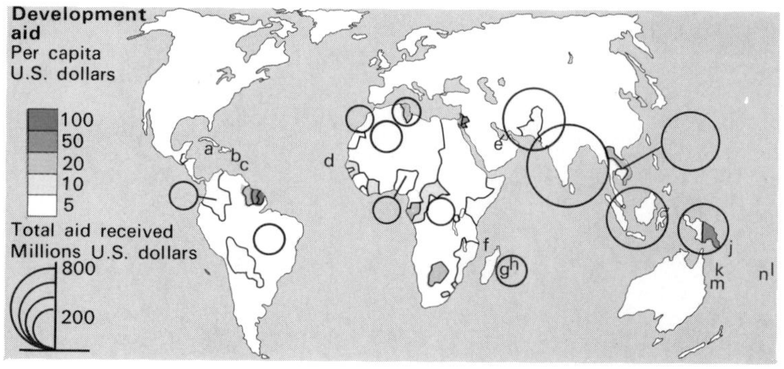

Development aid
Per capita
U.S. dollars
100
50
20
10
5
Total aid received
Millions U.S. dollars
800
200

Islands
a Antilles
b Martinique
c Barbados
d Cape Verde
e Bahrain
f Comoro
g Reunion
h Mauritius
j Solomon
k New Hebrides
l Fiji
m New Caledonia
n Tonga

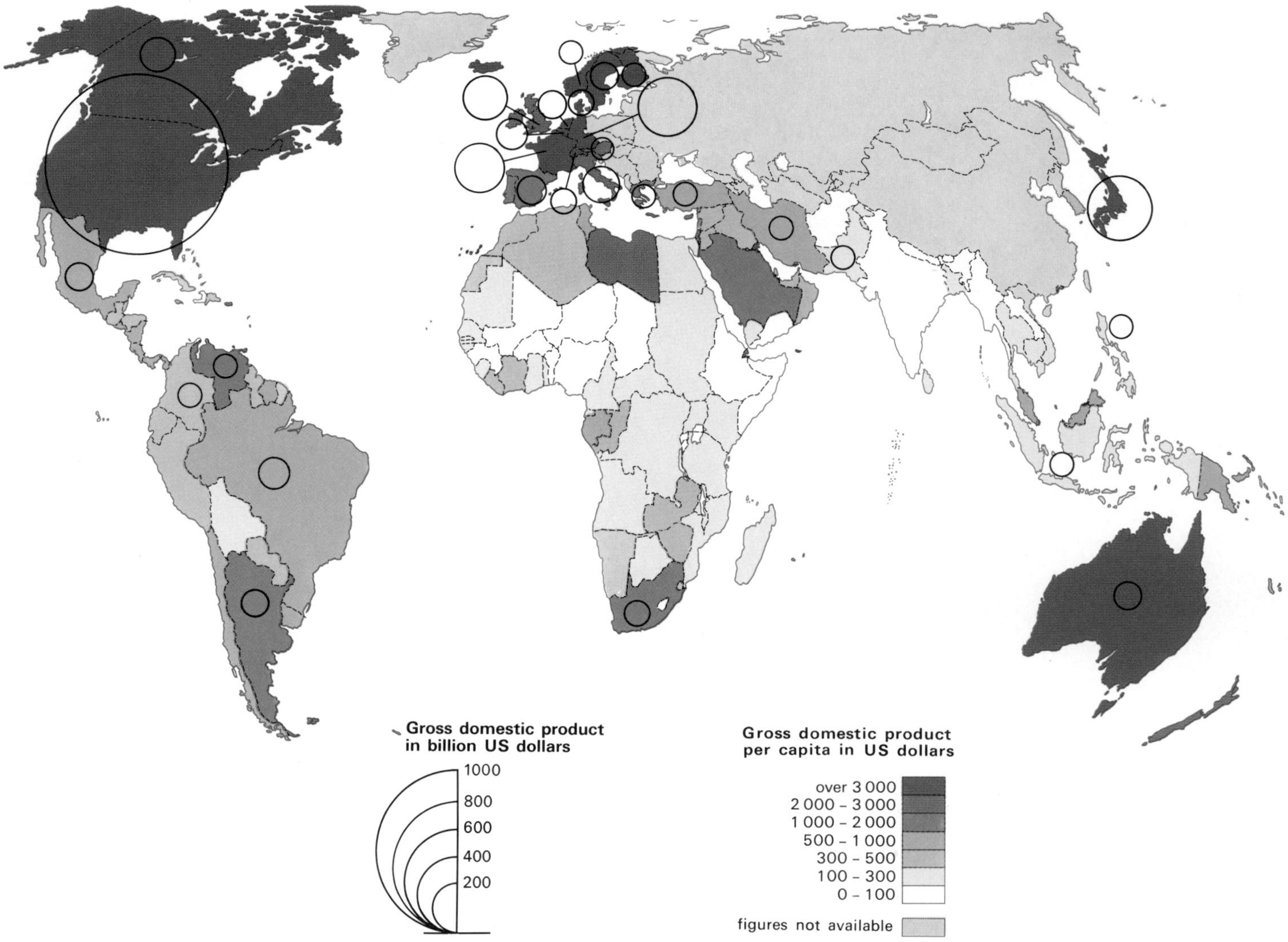

Gross domestic product in billion US dollars
1000
800
600
400
200
Gross domestic product per capita in US dollars
over 3 000
2 000 - 3 000
1 000 - 2 000
500 - 1 000
300 - 500
100 - 300
0 - 100
figures not available

SETTLEMENTS

Settlement symbols in order of size

NEW YORK   ■ Minsk   ◉ Katmandu   ◎ Prince Rupert   ◎ Bayt Lahm   ○ *Penzance*   ○ *Monte-Carlo*

Settlement symbols and type styles vary according to the scale of each map and indicate the importance of towns on the map rather than specific population figures

∴ Sites of Archæological or Historical importance

BOUNDARIES

- International Boundaries
- International Boundaries (Undemarcated or Undefined)
- Internal Boundaries

International boundaries show the *de facto* situation where there are rival claims to territory

- National and Provincial Parks

COMMUNICATIONS

- Freeways
- Freeways under construction
- Trans-Canada Highway
- Principal Roads
- Other Roads
- Trails and Seasonal Roads
- Principal Railroads
- Other Railroads
- Railroads under construction
- Railroad Tunnels
- Highway Tunnels
- Principal Canals
- Principal Oil Pipelines
- 3386 Principal Shipping Routes (Distances in Nautical Miles)
- Passes
- Airports

PHYSICAL FEATURES

- Perennial Streams
- Seasonal Streams
- ▲ 8848 Spot Height in meters
- Seasonal Lakes, Salt Flats
- Swamps, Marshes
- ▼ 8050 Sea Depths in meters
- Permanent Ice
- Wells in Desert
- *1134* Height of Lake Surface Above Sea Level, in meters

Height of Land Above Sea Level, in meters and feet

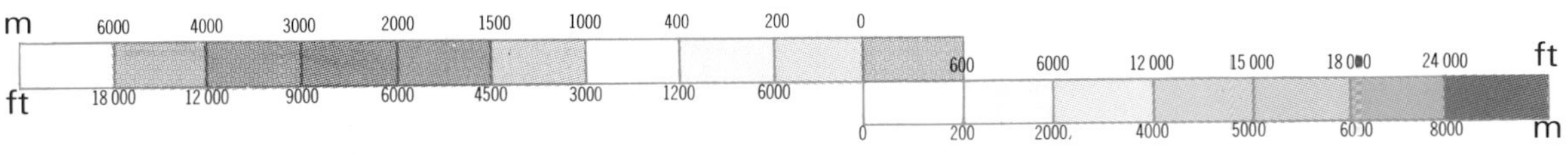
m
6000
4000
3000
2000
1500
1000
400
200
0
ft
18 000
12 000
9000
6000
4500
3000
1200
6000
600
6000
12 000
15 000
18 000
24 000
ft
0
200
2000
4000
5000
6000
8000
m

Depth of Sea in meters and feet

Some of the maps have different contours to highlight and clarify the principal relief features

Abbreviations of measures used   ft Feet   m Meters   Mi. Miles   Km Kilometers

ARCTIC OCEAN
BEAUFORT SEA
ELLESMERE I.
QUEEN ELIZABETH IS.
PARRY IS.
DEVON I.
BANKS I.
VICTORIA I.
Greenland
BAFFIN BAY
DAVIS STR.
SVALBARD
Great Bear L.
Great Slave L.
HUDSON BAY
C. Farewell
ICELAND
ALEXANDER ARCH.
NORTH AMERICA
L. Winnipeg
Labrador
British Isles
NORTH SEA
GREAT BRITAIN
IRELAND
VANCOUVER I.
L. Superior
NEWFOUNDLAND
C. Race
L. Huron
L. Michigan
L. Erie
Missouri
Great Plains
AZORES
BERMUDA
MADEIRA
CANARY IS.
GULF OF MEXICO
BAHAMAS
ATLANTIC
Tropic of Cancer
HAWAIIAN IS.
CUBA
West Indies
9200
HISPANIOLA
JAMAICA
LEEWARD IS.
C. VERDE IS.
CARIBBEAN SEA
WINDWARD IS.
PACIFIC
CHRISTMAS I.
Equator
GULF OF GUINEA
GALAPAGOS IS.
OCEAN
Selvas
SOUTH AMERICA
Mato Grosso
ASCENSION
MARQUESAS IS.
ST. HELENA
SOCIETY IS.
TUAMOTU ARCH.
COOK IS.
Tropic of Capricorn
8050
TUBUAI IS.
Gran Chaco
OCEAN
Pampas
Rio de la Plata
TRISTAN DA CUNHA
FALKLAND IS.
TIERRA DEL FUEGO
S. GEORGIA
C. Horn
SOUTH
165
150
135
120
105
90
75
60
45
30
15
0
Projection: Gall's Stereographic
West from Greenwich
East from

Equatorial Scale 1: 80 000 000

ARCTIC OCEAN
FRANZ JOSEPH LAND
SEVERNAYA ZEMLYA
BARENTS SEA
NOVAYA ZEMLYA
KARA SEA
LAPTEV SEA
NEW SIBERIAN IS.
Taimyr Pen.
WRANGEL I.
BERING STR.
North C.
WHITE SEA
L. Ladoga
Russia
ROPE
Steppe
Siberia
SEA OF OKHOTSK
BERING SEA
ALEUTIAN IS
SAKHALIN
KURIL IS.
HOKKAIDŌ
L. Balkhash
ARAL SEA
CASPIAN SEA
BLACK SEA
Danube
Volga
ASIA
Gobi
SEA OF JAPAN
HONSHŪ
KYŪSHŪ
YELLOW SEA
RYŪKYŪ IS.
0554
MIDWAY IS.
Tropic of Cancer
ANEAN SEA
Mesopotamia
PERSIAN GULF
RED SEA
Arabia
India
ARABIAN SEA
BAY OF BENGAL
TAIWAN
SOUTH CHINA SEA
LUZON
MARIANA IS.
GUAM
PACIFIC
Philippines
10497
11022
MINDANAO
CAROLINE IS.
MARSHALL IS.
Ras Asir
LACCADIVE IS.
ANDAMAN IS.
CEYLON
Malay Pen.
MALDIVES
INDIAN
Congo Basin
Chad
MOLUCCAS
GILBERT IS.
Equator
SUMATRA
East Indies
CELEBES
BISMARK ARCH.
OCEAN
ZANZIBAR
SEYCHELLES
CHAGOS ARCH.
L. Tanganyika
JAVA
SUNDA
TIMOR
SOLOMON IS.
MOZAMBIQUE CHANNEL
COCOS OR KEELING IS.
TIMOR SEA
CORAL SEA
SAMOA
OCEAN
MADAGASCAR
NEW HEBRIDES
FIJI
MAURITIUS
REUNION
NEW CALEDONIA
TONGA
Tropic of Capricorn
AUSTRALIA
10822
Kalahari
L. Eyre
NORTH I.
2230
TASMAN SEA
TASMANIA
New Zealand
3764
SOUTH I.
CROZET IS.
KERGUELEN
N OCEAN
MACQUARIE IS.
180
30
45
60
75
90
105
120
135
150
165

GREENLAND
Queen Elizabeth Is.
Ellesmere I.
Beaufort Sea
Baffin Bay
Hudson Bay
Hudson Str.
Foxe Basin
Davis Strait
Denmark Strait
ICELAND
ALASKA
Gulf of Alaska
Bering Str.
Aleutian Islands
Bristol Bay
CANADA
Newfoundland
G. of St. Lawrence
UNITED STATES
Seattle
Vancouver
Portland
San Francisco
Los Angeles
San Diego
Chicago
Detroit
Toronto
Montréal
Boston
New York
Philadelphia
Washington
Houston
New Orleans
Miami
Gulf of Mexico
MEXICO
México
Guadalajara
La Habana
West Indies
Caribbean Sea
BAHAMAS
Hispaniola
Bermuda
Azores (Port.)
Madeira (Port.)
Canary Is. (Span.)
MOROCCO
MAURITANIA
ATLANTIC OCEAN
PACIFIC OCEAN
Hawaiian Islands (U.S.)
Honolulu
Hawaii
Midway I.
Tropic of Cancer
Equator
Tropic of Capricorn
International Date Line
Galapagos Is. (Ecuador)
VENEZUELA
Caracas
COLOMBIA
Bogotá
ECUADOR
Quito
PERU
Lima
BOLIVIA
La Paz
BRAZIL
Amazon
Belém
Recife
Salvador
Belo Horizonte
Rio de Janeiro
São Paulo
PARAGUAY
Asunción
ARGENTINA
Córdoba
Buenos Aires
URUGUAY
Montevideo
Santiago
Valparaíso
Patagonia
Falkland Is. (Br.)
Tierra del Fuego
C. Horn
Magellan's Str.
S. Georgia
Scotia Sea
FALKLAND IS. DEPENDENCIES
Drake Passage
South Shetland Is.
South Orkney Is.
Antarctic Peninsula
Graham Land
Weddell Sea
Bellingshausen Sea
Amundsen Sea
Antarctic Circle
BRITISH ANTARCTIC TERRITORY
ROSS DEPENDENCY
Byrd Land
Ellsworth Land
Marquesas Is. (Fr.)
Tuamotu Archipelago (Fr.)
Society Is. (Fr.)
Tahiti
Tonga Is. (Friendly Is.)
W. Samoa
Tokelau Is.
Phoenix Is.
Cook Is.
Tubuai Is. (Fr.)
Pitcairn I. (Br.)
Easter I. (Chile)
Chatham Is. (N.Z.)
Kermadec Is. (N.Z.)
Clipperton I. (Fr.)
Cocos I. (Costa Rica)
Ascension (Br.)
St. Helena (Br.)
Tristan da Cunha (Br.)
Gough I. (Br.)
Fernando de Noronha (Brazil)
West from Greenwich

Projection: *Hammer Equal Area*

ARCTIC OCEAN
Franz Joseph Ld.
Severnaya Zemlya
Novaya Zemlya
Barents Sea
Kara Sea
Taymyr Pen.
Laptev Sea
New Siberian Is.
East Siberian Sea
Arctic Circle
UNION OF SOVIET SOCIALIST REPUBLICS
RUSSIAN SOVIET FEDERAL SOCIALIST REPUBLIC
Siberia
Bering Sea
Sea of Okhotsk
Kamchatka
Sakhalin
Kuril Islands
Leningrad
Moskva
Gorkiy
Kazan
Sverdlovsk
Novosibirsk
Omsk
Tomsk
Krasnoyarsk
Novokuznetsk
Irkutsk
L. Baykal
Ulan Ude
Chita
Khabarovsk
Vladivostok
Murmansk
Arkhangelsk
Stockholm
Helsinki
Warszawa
Berlin
Praha
Wien
Budapest
Kiyev
Kharkov
Odessa
Volgograd
Saratov
Kuybyshev
Ufa
Orenburg
Magnitogorsk
Chelyabinsk
Karaganda
KAZAKHSTAN
L. Balkhash
Caspian Sea
Black Sea
Bucuresti
Beograd
Sofiya
Istanbul
Ankara
Athinai
Roma
Napoli
Tunis
Mediterranean Sea
Crete
CYPRUS
TURKEY
Tbilisi
Yerevan
Baku
Tabriz
Tehran
IRAN (PERSIA)
Esfahan
Shiraz
Baghdad
IRAQ
Al Mawsil
SYRIA
Dimashq
Bayrut
Amman
Tel Aviv-Yafo
Iskandariya
El Qahira
Bur Said
EGYPT
Asyut
Aswan
Libyan Desert
LIBYA
Banghazi
Tarabulus
Sahara
NIGER
CHAD
SUDAN
Omdurman
El Khartum
Atbara
El Obeid
Red Sea
Makkah
SAUDI ARABIA
Nejd
Ar Riyad
KUWAIT
QATAR
Persian Gulf
OMAN
SOUTH YEMEN
YEMEN
G. of Aden
Adan
Djibouti
ETHIOPIA
Addis Abeba
SOMALI REP.
Mogadishu
KENYA
Nairobi
UGANDA
Kampala
Lake Victoria
TANZANIA
Dar es Salaam
Zanzibar
Mombasa
ZAIRE (CONGO)
Kinshasa
Kisangani
CENTRAL AFRICA
CAMEROON
NIGERIA
Kano
Ibadan
GABON
CONGO
Brazzaville
Cabinda
Luanda
ANGOLA
Benguela
ZAMBIA
Lusaka
L. Malawi
MOZAMBIQUE
Mozambique Chan.
ZIMBABWE
Salisbury
Bulawayo
Beira
BOTSWANA
NAMIBIA (SOUTH WEST AFRICA)
Windhoek
Walvis Bay
Kalahari
Pretoria
Johannesburg
Maputo (Lourenço Marques)
Durban
SOUTH AFRICA
Cape Town
C. of Good Hope
C. Agulhas
Port Elizabeth
East London
MADAGASCAR
Tananarive
Tamatave
Comoro Is.
Aldabra
Seychelles
Amirante Is.
Mauritius
Réunion (Fr.)
Rodriguez
Cargados Garajos
Chagos Arch. (Br.)
Diego Garcia (Br.)
Maldive Is.
INDIAN OCEAN
Equator
Tropic of Capricorn
Socotra (South Yemen)
Ras Asir
Kuria Muria Is.
Arabian Sea
Karachi
Masqat
PAKISTAN
Kabul
AFGHANISTAN
Rawalpindi
Quetta
Lahore
Srinagar
KASHMIR
Delhi
Agra
Kanpur
Lucknow
Varanasi
NEPAL
BHUTAN
BANGLADESH
Dacca
INDIA
Ahmadabad
Bombay
Pune
Nagpur
Calcutta
Hyderabad
Bay of Bengal
Madras
Bangalore
Tiruchchirappalli
Lakshadweep Is. (India)
SRI LANKA (CEYLON)
Colombo
Dondra Hd.
Andaman Is. (India)
Nicobar Is. (India)
TURKMENISTAN
UZBEKISTAN
KIRGIZIA
Tashkent
Alma Ata
Samarkand
Dushanbe
Urumqi
Tarim He
CHINA
Xizang (Tibet)
Lhasa
Brahmaputra
MONGOLIA
Ulaanbaatar
Hovd
Qiqihar
Harbin
Changchun
Shenyang
Beijing
Tianjin
Taiyuan
Jinan
Qingdao
Lüda
Xi'an
Lanzhou
Chengdu
Chongqing
Wuhan
Nanjing
Shanghai
Changsha
Kunming
Guangzhou
Hong Kong
Fuzhou
Taibei
TAIWAN
Hainan
East China Sea
South China Sea
Pyongyang
Soul
Pusan
Sea of Japan
JAPAN
Tokyo
Yokohama
Nagoya
Osaka
Kobe
Kyoto
Kitakyushu
Sendai
Sapporo
Hakodate
Ryukyu Is.
BURMA
Rangoon
THAILAND (SIAM)
Bangkok
G. of Siam
Vientiane
Hanoi
VIET-NAM
Hue
KAMPUCHEA
Phnom Penh
Phanh Bho Ho Chi Minh (Saigon)
PHILIPPINES
Manila
Quezon City
Cebu
MALAYSIA
Kuala Lumpur
George Town
Medan
Singapore
SABAH
SARAWAK
Kuching
BRUNEI
Borneo
Sumatra
Palembang
Jakarta
Bandung
Surabaya
Java
INDONESIA
Sulawesi
Ujung Pandang
Moluccas
Sunda Islands
Irian Jaya
New Guinea
PAPUA NEW GUINEA
Port Moresby
Timor
Timor Sea
Arafura Sea
Torres Str.
C. York
Christmas I. (Australia)
Cocos (Keeling) Is. (Australia)
Darwin
NORTHERN TERRITORY
QUEENSLAND
WESTERN AUSTRALIA
SOUTH AUSTRALIA
AUSTRALIA
NEW SOUTH WALES
VICTORIA
TASMANIA
Cairns
Townsville
Mt. Isa
Alice Springs
Rockhampton
Brisbane
Meekatharra
Geraldton
Perth
Fremantle
Kalgoorlie
C. Leeuwin
Albany
Great Australian Bight
Adelaide
L. Eyre
Darling
Murray
Newcastle
Sydney
Canberra
Melbourne
Bass Str.
Hobart
Tasman Sea
North West C.
NEW ZEALAND
Auckland
North I.
Wellington
South I.
Christchurch
Dunedin
Stewart I.
Lord Howe I. (Australia)
Norfolk I. (Australia)
New Caledonia (Fr.)
Nouméa
New Hebrides (Br.-Fr.)
Fiji Is.
Tuvalu (Ellice Is.)
Solomon Is.
New Britain
New Ireland
Bismarck Arch.
Admiralty Is.
Nauru
Kiribati
PACIFIC OCEAN
Tropic of Cancer
Mariana or Ladrone Is.
Guam (U.S.)
Caroline Is.
(U.S. Trust Territory)
Marshall Is.
Wake I. (U.S.)
Yap
Palau Is.
Truk
Ponape
Jaluit
Ogasawara-guntō
Amsterdam (Fr.)
St. Paul (Fr.)
Pr. Edward Is (South Africa)
Crozet Is. (Fr.)
Kerguelen (Fr.)
McDonald I. (Australia)
Heard I. (Australia)
Macquarie I. (Australia)
Campbell I. (N.Z.)
Auckland I. (N.Z.)
Antipodes Is. (N.Z.)
Bounty Is.
SOUTHERN OCEAN
Kong Haakon VII Sea
Antarctic Circle
Enderby Land
AUSTRALIAN DEPENDENCY
TERRE ADELIE
Wilkes Land
S. Magnetic Pole 1976
Balleny Is.
Ross Sea
East from Greenwich

EUROPE : Physical

Kilometers 0 200 400 600 800 Km.

Statute Miles 0 200 400 600 800 Mi.

1:16 000 000

One centimeter represents 160 kilometers
One inch represents approximately 250 miles

Ural Mountains
Tundra
Pechora
Obshchiy Syrt
Volga Uplands
Volga
Ural
CASPIAN SEA
-28
Caucasus
Elbrus 5633
Kura
Terek
Armenia
Kurdistan
Euphrates
Tigris
Aras
Rion
Kuban
Manych
Don
Tsimlyansk Res.
Sea of Azov
Str. of Kerch
Crimea
BLACK SEA
2211
Bosporus
S. of Marmara
Anatolia
Taurus
Kizil Irmak
L. Tuz
Cyprus
1951
Central Russian Uplands
Ukraine
Dnepr (Dnieper)
Bug
Prut
Danube
Pripyat Marshes
Pripyat (Pripet)
Dnestr (Dniester)
Oka
Rybinsk Res.
Mezen
N. Dvina
Onega
L. Onega
Kanin Peninsula
Kola Peninsula
White Sea
L. Ladoga
Neva
L. Chudskoye
Finland
Lapland
E. Inari
Nordkinn
North Cape
Torne
Kebnekaise
2123
G. of Finland
G. of Riga
G. of Bothnia
BALTIC SEA
Gotland
Mälaren
Vättern
Vänern
Kattegat
Skagerrak
Jutland
Lindesnes
Galdhøpiggen
2469
Scandinavia
Lofoten
Vesterålen
Ume
Indals
Niemen
Wisła (Vistula)
Odra (Oder)
Elbe
Weser
Harz
1142
Erz Geb.
Sudetes
Moravian Heights
Bohemian For.
North European Plain
Carpathians
Tatra
2655
Transylvanian Alps
Wallachia
Plain of Hungary
Mureș
Tisza
Bakony For.
Danube
Drava
Sava
Morava
Balkan Peninsula
Balkans
Rhodope
Pindus
Morea
C. Matapan
5121
Crete
Aegean Sea
Ionian Sea
Str. of Otranto
Dinaric Alps
ADRIATIC SEA
Apennines
Gran Sasso 2914
Vesuvius 1277
Etna 3263
Calabria
Str. of Messina
Sicily
Malta
C. Bon
Tyrrhenian Sea
Tiber
Str. of Bonifacio
Corsica
Sardinia
Ligurian Sea
C. Blanco
MEDITERRANEAN SEA
Po
Alps
Mt. Blanc 4807
Jura
Vosges
Black For.
Rhine
Inn
Hunsrück
Taunus
Westerwald
Eifel
Ardennes
Meuse
Netherlands
Heligoland
NORTH SEA
Dogger Bank
Seine
Thames
Rhône
G. of Lions
Central Massif
Mt. Dore 1886
Cevennes
Pyrenees
Pico de Aneto 3404
Garonne
Gironde
Loire
Brittany
English Channel
Land's End
Bay of Biscay
4861
Great Britain
Ben Nevis 1343
Snowdon 1085
Irish Sea
Ireland
C. Clear
Valentia I.
British Isles
Hebrides
Orkney Is.
Shetland Is.
Faroe Is.
Fisher Bank
Rockall
Iceland
Öraefa Jökull 2119
Hekla 1491
Arctic Circle
NORWEGIAN SEA
3734
ATLANTIC OCEAN
C. Finisterre
Cantabrian Mts.
Old Castile
New Castile
Iberian Peninsula
Sa. da Guadarrama
Sa. da Estrela
Douro
Tagus
C. da Roca
C. St. Vincent
Sierra Morena
Guadalquivir
Andalusia
Sa. Nevada
Mulhacén 3478
C. Trafalgar
C. Spartel
Str. of Gibraltar
Balearic Is.
Er Rif
Maritime Atlas
Plateau of the Shotts
COPYRIGHT. GEORGE PHILIP & SON, LTD.
Projection: Bonne   West from Greenwich 0 East from Greenwich

m	4000	2000	1000	400	200	0	200	2000	4000	m
ft	12 000	6000	3000	1200	600	0	600	6000	12 000	ft

Kilometers 0 200 400 600 800 Km.

Statute Miles 0 200 400 600 800 Mi.

1:16 000 000

One centimeter represents 160 kilometers
One inch represents approximately 250 miles

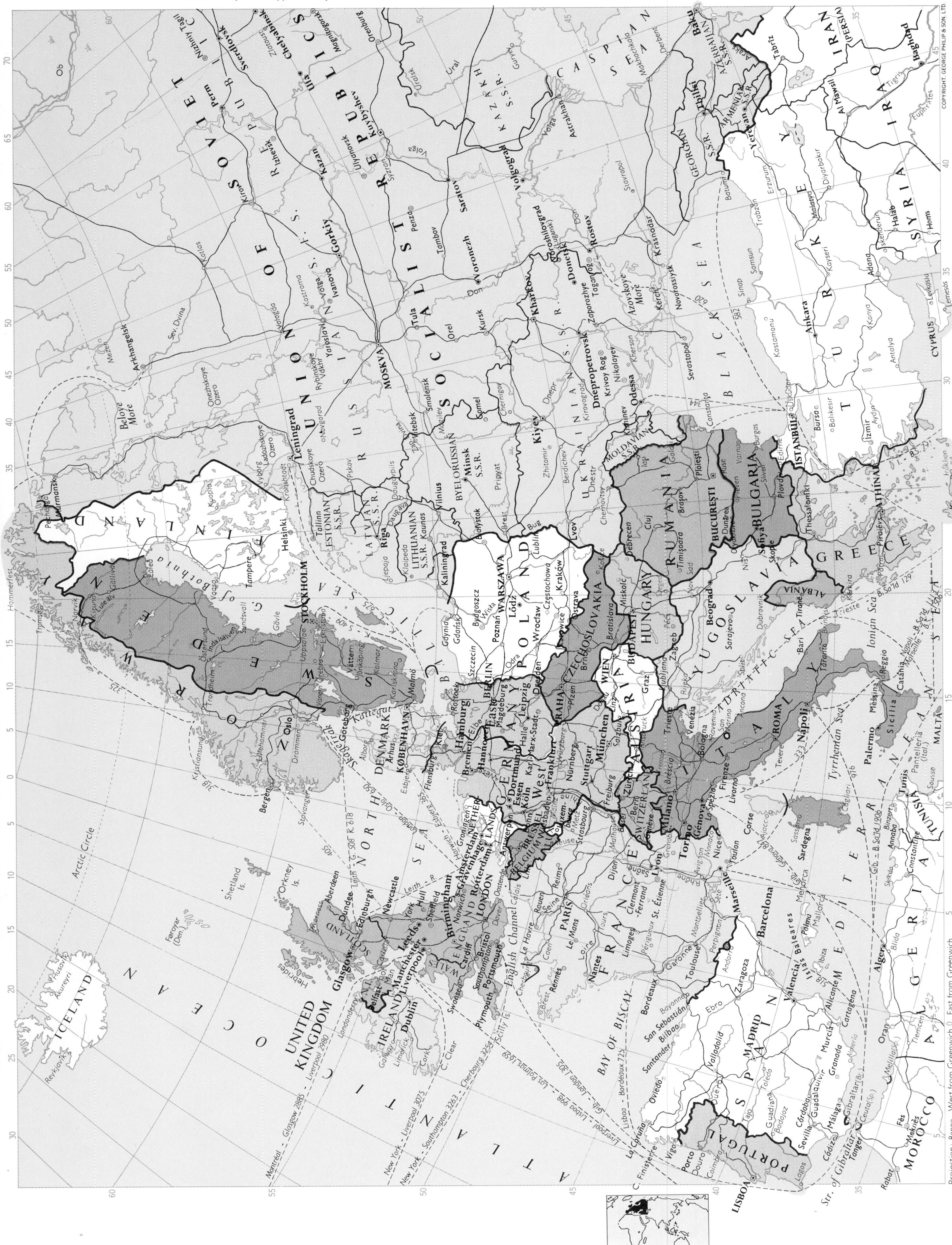
UNION OF SOVIET SOCIALIST REPUBLICS
RUSSIAN S.F.S.R.
UKRAINIAN S.S.R.
BYELORUSSIAN S.S.R.
LITHUANIAN S.S.R.
LATVIAN S.S.R.
ESTONIAN S.S.R.
MOLDAVIAN S.S.R.
GEORGIAN S.S.R.
ARMENIAN S.S.R.
AZERBAIJAN S.S.R.
KAZAKH S.S.R.
MOSKVA
Leningrad
Kiyev
FINLAND
Helsinki
SWEDEN
STOCKHOLM
NORWAY
Oslo
DENMARK
KØBENHAVN
POLAND
WARSZAWA
GERMANY
BERLIN
CZECHOSLOVAKIA
PRAHA
AUSTRIA
WIEN
HUNGARY
BUDAPEST
RUMANIA
BUCUREŞTI
BULGARIA
Sofiya
YUGOSLAVIA
Beograd
ALBANIA
Tiranë
GREECE
ATHINAI
TURKEY
Ankara
İSTANBUL
CYPRUS
SYRIA
IRAQ
IRAN (PERSIA)
ITALY
ROMA
SWITZERLAND
FRANCE
PARIS
BELGIUM
BRUXELLES
NETHERLANDS
LUX.
UNITED KINGDOM
LONDON
IRELAND
Dublin
ICELAND
Reykjavik
SPAIN
MADRID
PORTUGAL
LISBOA
MOROCCO
ALGERIA
TUNISIA
MALTA
ATLANTIC OCEAN
NORTH SEA
BALTIC SEA
BLACK SEA
CASPIAN SEA
MEDITERRANEAN SEA
ADRIATIC SEA
Tyrrhenian Sea
Ionian Sea
BAY OF BISCAY
English Channel
Gulf of Bothnia
Arctic Circle
COPYRIGHT, GEORGE PHILIP & SON, LTD.
Projection: Bonne West from Greenwich 0 East from Greenwich

NORWEGIAN SEA
ICELAND
on the same scale as general map
West from Greenwich
Arctic Circle
Vatnajökull
Reykjavík
Keflavík
Akranes
Akureyri
Húsavík
Siglufjörður
Ísafjörður
Hekla
Lofoten
Vesterålen
Narvik
Tromsø
Hammerfest
Vadsø
Kiruna
Gällivare
Luleå
Boden
Piteå
Skellefteå
Umeå
Östersund
Härnösand
Trondheim
Namsos
Kristiansund
Molde
Ålesund
Bodø
Haparanda
Tornio
Kemi
Rovaniemi
Oulu
Kajaani
Kuopio
Jyväskylä
Vaasa
Kokkola
Jakobstad
Inari
Kebnekaise
Torneträsk

Kilometers 0 40 80 120 160 200 Km.

0 40 80 120 160 200 Mi.

1:4 000 000

One centimeter represents 40 kilometers
One inch represents approximately 64 miles

COPYRIGHT, GEORGE PHILIP & SON, LTD.
Projection: Conical with two standard parallels
East from Greenwich
HELSINKI (Helsingfors)
Tampere
Turku (Åbo)
Pori
Rauma
Lahti
Kotka
Tallinn
Pärnu
Riga
Rigas Jūras Līcis (Gulf of Riga)
Liepaja
Ventspils
Klaipėda
Kaunas
Vilnius
Kaliningrad
Sovetsk
Gdańsk
Gdynia
Zatoka Gdańska
Toruń
Bydgoszcz
Szczecin (Stettin)
STOCKHOLM
Uppsala
Gävle
Västerås
Örebro
Norrköping
Linköping
Jönköping
Göteborg
Malmö
Karlskrona
Kalmar
Öland
Gotland
Visby
Bornholm
Rønne
KØBENHAVN (Copenhagen)
Helsingør
Helsingborg
Odense
Århus
Aalborg
Esbjerg
Sjælland
Fyn
Kattegat
Skagerrak
The Sound
OSLO
Drammen
Bergen
Stavanger
Kristiansand
Hamburg
Kiel
Lübeck
Rostock
Bremen
Bremerhaven
Wilhelmshaven
Groningen
Åland
Mariehamn
m ft
2000 6000
1500 4500
1000 3000
400 1200
200 600
0 0
200 600

Gulf of Bothnia
STOCKHOLM
Uppsala
Gävle
Sundsvall
Härnösand
Örnsköldsvik
Östersund
Trondheim
Lillehammer
Hamar
Oslo
Drammen
Skien
Porsgrunn
Fredrikstad
Halden
Karlstad
Örebro
Västerås
Eskilstuna
Falun
Borlänge
Mora
JÄMTLANDS LÄN
VÄSTERNORRLANDS LÄN
GÄVLEBORGS LÄN
KOPPARBERGS LÄN
UPPSALA LÄN
VÄSTMANLANDS LÄN
VÄRMLANDS LÄN
ÖREBRO LÄN
SÖDERMANLANDS LÄN
STOCKHOLMS LÄN
HEDMARK
OPPLAND FYLKE
BUSKERUD
TELEMARK
SØR TRØNDELAG FYLKE
MØRE OG ROMSDAL FYLKE
ØSTFOLD
VESTFOLD
AKERSHUS FYLKE
Jotunheimen
Dovrefjell
Transtrands-fjällen
Rotälven
Siljan

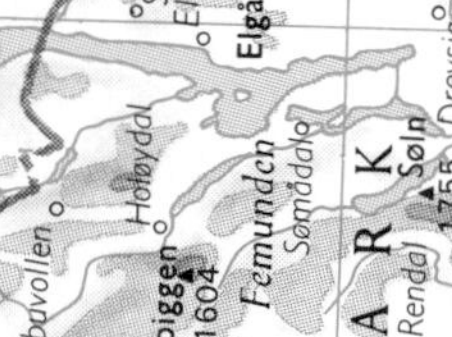

Kilometers 0 20 40 60 80 100 Km.
Statute Miles 0 20 40 60 80 100 Mi.

1:2 000 000

One centimeter represents 20 kilometers
One inch represents approximately 32 miles

BALTIC SEA
Kattegat
Skagerrak
Jammerbugt
Ålborg Bugt
Store Bælt
Femer Bælt
Kieler Bucht
Bornholmsgattet
Hanöbukten
GERMANY
POLAND
DENMARK
Gotland
Öland
Bornholm
Sjælland
Fyn
Lolland
Falster
Rügen
Anholt
Læsø
Göteborg
Malmö
Helsingborg
Lund
Trelleborg
Ystad
Kristianstad
Karlskrona
Kalmar
Växjö
Jönköping
Linköping
Norrköping
Nyköping
Visby
Halmstad
Borås
Uddevalla
Trollhättan
København (Copenhagen)
Roskilde
Helsingør
Odense
Århus
Ålborg
Randers
Esbjerg
Kolding
Vejle
Fredericia
Horsens
Viborg
Herning
Frederikshavn
Hjørring
Skagen
Rønne
Flensburg
Kiel
Rendsburg
Schleswig
Husum
Słupsk
Łebork
Sassnitz
Arkona
Stralsund
Gedser
Nykøbing
Nakskov
Svendborg
Slagelse
Næstved
Arendal
Risør
Tvedestrand
Holmsland Klit
ft m
6000 2000
4500 1500
3000 1000
1200 400
600 200
0 0
200 600
Projection: Conical with two standard parallels
East from Greenwich

NORTH SEA
IRISH SEA
North Channel
Firth of Clyde
Solway Firth
The Wash
SCOTLAND
Southern Uplands
Cheviot Hills
Pennines
NORTHUMBERLAND
TYNE & WEAR
DURHAM
CLEVELAND
CUMBRIA
NORTH YORKSHIRE
HUMBERSIDE
LANCASHIRE
W. YORKSHIRE
SOUTH YORKSHIRE
GREATER MANCHESTER
MERSEYSIDE
CHESHIRE
DERBY
NOTTS
LINCOLN
STAFFORD
CLWYD
GWYNEDD
ISLE OF MAN
Edinburgh
Glasgow
Newcastle
Sunderland
Middlesbrough
Carlisle
Leeds
Bradford
Manchester
Liverpool
Sheffield
Hull
York
Belfast
Cumbrian Mts.
N. York Moors
Lincoln Wolds
Anglesey
Douglas

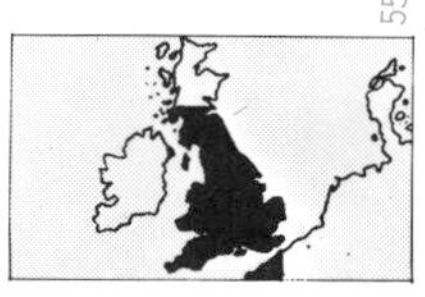

Kilometers 0 20 40 60 80 100 Km.

Statute Miles 0 20 40 60 80 100 Mi.

1:1 600 000

One centimeter represents 16 kilometers
One inch represents approximately 25 miles

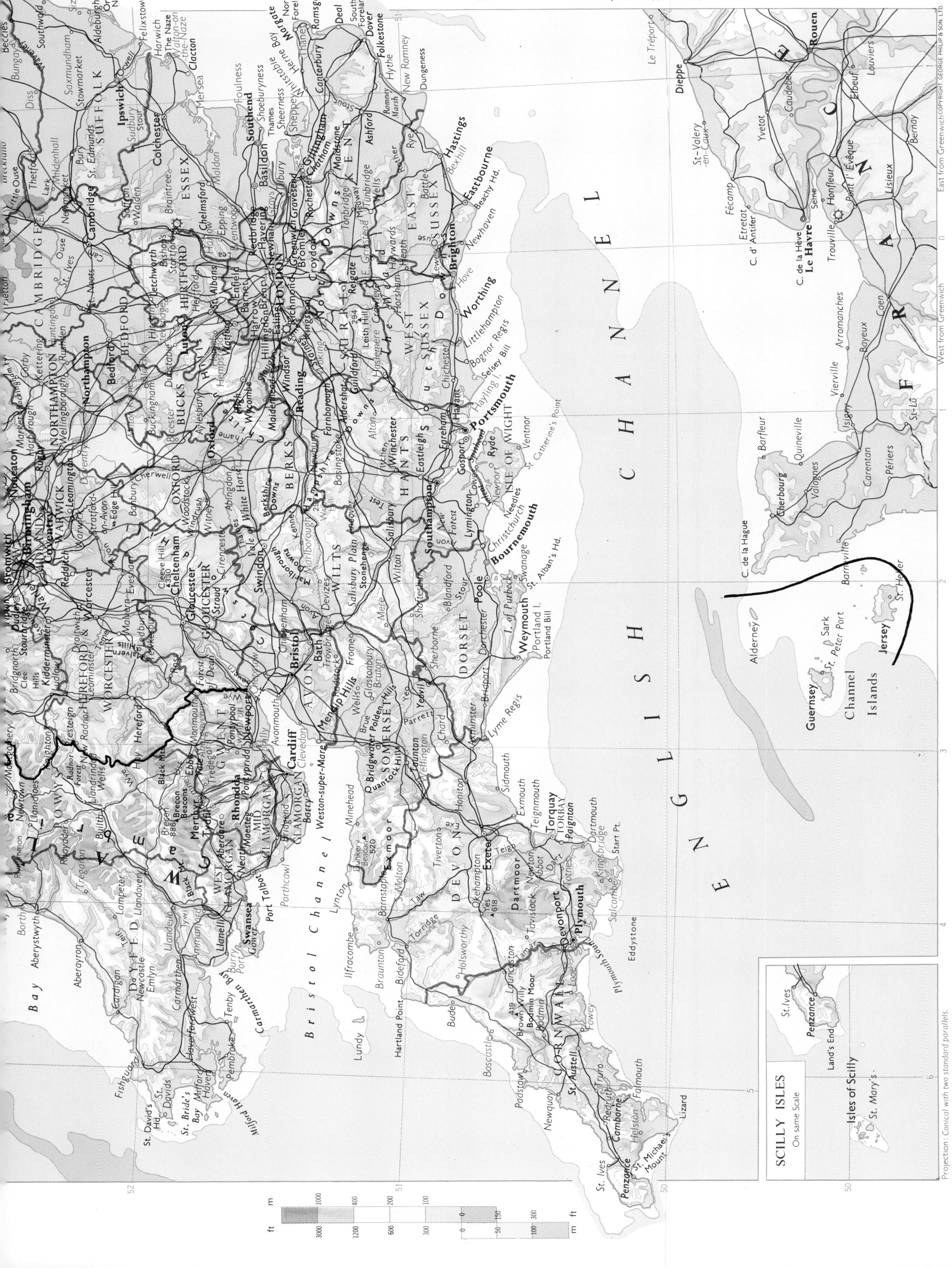
ENGLISH CHANNEL
FRANCE
Bristol Channel
LONDON
Birmingham
Coventry
Cambridge
Oxford
Reading
Southampton
Portsmouth
Bournemouth
Brighton
Hastings
Eastbourne
Dover
Folkestone
Canterbury
Margate
Ramsgate
Ipswich
Colchester
Southend
Chelmsford
Bedford
Northampton
Luton
Swindon
Gloucester
Cheltenham
Worcester
Hereford
Bristol
Bath
Cardiff
Newport
Swansea
Llanelli
Carmarthen
Exeter
Plymouth
Torquay
Taunton
Weymouth
Penzance
St. Austell
CORNWALL
DEVON
DORSET
SOMERSET
AVON
WILTS
HANTS
BERKS
SURREY
KENT
ESSEX
SUFFOLK
OXFORD
GLOUCESTER
WORCESTER
HEREFORD
WARWICK
NORTHAMPTON
BEDFORD
BUCKS
HERTFORD
CAMBRIDGE
EAST SUSSEX
WEST SUSSEX
ISLE OF WIGHT
GWENT
DYFED
POWYS
WEST GLAMORGAN
MID GLAMORGAN
SOUTH GLAMORGAN
Dieppe
Rouen
Le Havre
Cherbourg
Caen
Bayeux
Lisieux
Guernsey
Jersey
Alderney
Sark
Channel Islands
SCILLY ISLES
On same Scale
Isles of Scilly
St. Mary's
Land's End
Projection: Conical with two standard parallels.
East from Greenwich
West from Greenwich
COPYRIGHT, GEORGE PHILIP & SON, LTD.
ft 3000 1200 600 300 0
m 1000 400 200 100 0
m 50 150
ft 100 300

Kilometers 0 20 40 60 80 100 Km.
Statute Miles 0 20 40 60 80 100 Mi.

1:1 600 000

One centimeter represents 16 kilometers
One inch represents approximately 25 miles

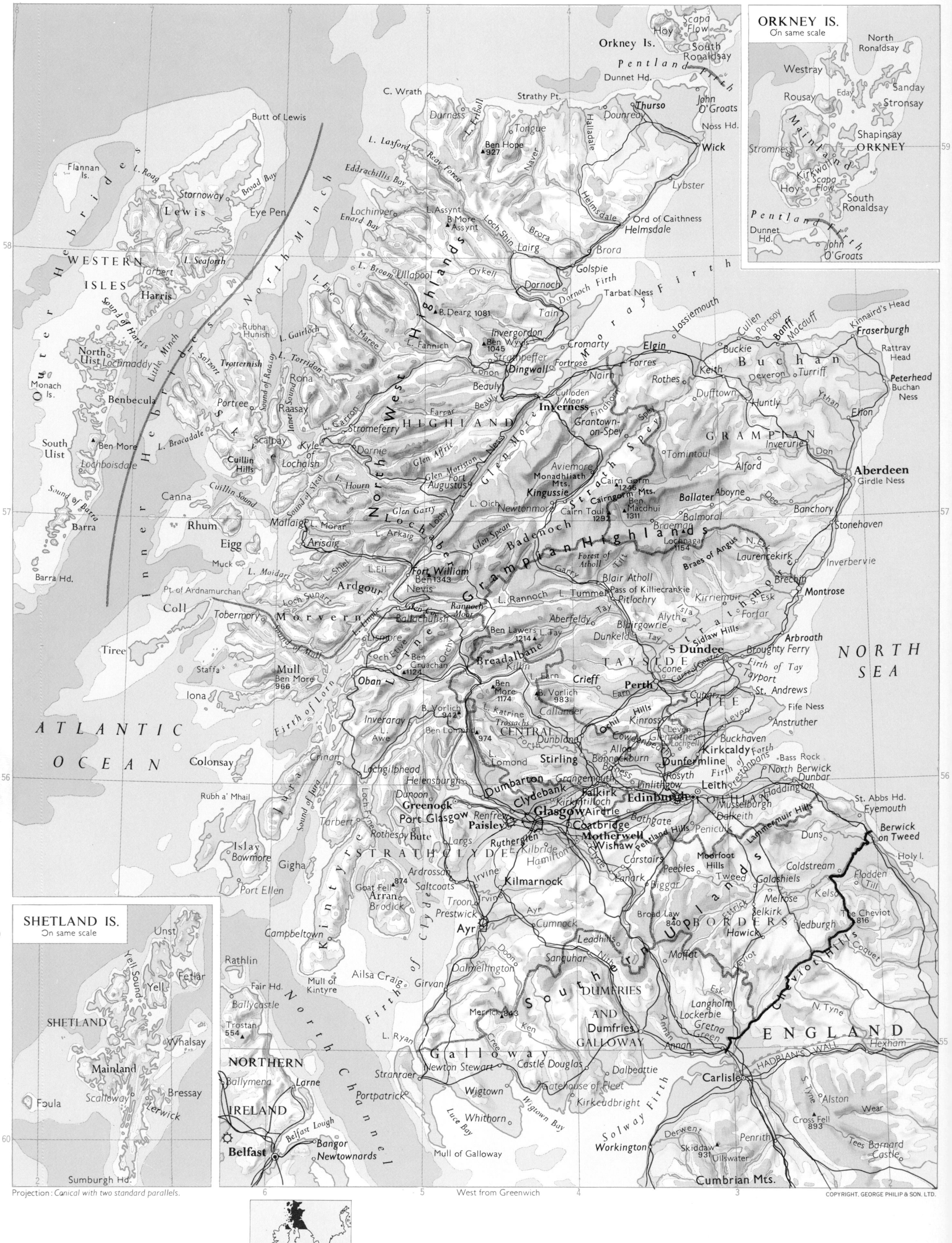
ORKNEY IS.
On same scale
North Ronaldsay
Westray
Rousay
Eday
Sanday
Stronsay
Shapinsay
ORKNEY
Mainland
Stromness
Kirkwall
Hoy
Scapa Flow
South Ronaldsay
Pentland Firth
Dunnet Hd.
John O'Groats
SHETLAND IS.
On same scale
Unst
Yell Sound
Yell
Fetlar
SHETLAND
Whalsay
Mainland
Foula
Scalloway
Bressay
Lerwick
Sumburgh Hd.
ft m
3000 1000
1200 400
600 200
300 100
0 0
50 150
100 300
m ft
Orkney Is.
Pentland Firth
Dunnet Hd.
Thurso
John O'Groats
Noss Hd.
Wick
C. Wrath
Strathy Pt.
Durness
Tongue
Ben Hope 927
Dounreay
Halladale
Naver
L. Laxford
Reay Forest
Eddrachillis Bay
Lybster
Lochinver
Enard Bay
L. Assynt
B. More Assynt
Loch Shin
Lairg
Brora
Helmsdale
Ord of Caithness
Golspie
Dornoch
Dornoch Firth
Tarbat Ness
Moray Firth
Tain
Oykell
Ullapool
L. Broom
L. Ewe
B. Dearg 1081
Invergordon
Ben Wyvis 1045
L. Fannich
L. Maree
L. Gairloch
L. Torridon
Cromarty
Strathpeffer
Dingwall
Fortrose
Conon
Beauly
Inverness
Culloden Moor
Nairn
Forres
Elgin
Lossiemouth
Cullen
Portsoy
Banff
Macduff
Kinnaird's Head
Fraserburgh
Rattray Head
Buckie
Keith
Buchan
Deveron
Turriff
Peterhead
Buchan Ness
Rothes
Dufftown
Huntly
Ythan
Ellon
GRAMPIAN
Inverurie
Don
Aberdeen
Girdle Ness
Alford
Tomintoul
Grantown-on-Spey
Spey
Findhorn
Aviemore
Monadhliath Mts.
Kingussie
Cairn Gorm 1245
Cairngorm Mts.
Ben Macdhui 1311
Cairn Toul 1292
Ballater
Aboyne
Dee
Banchory
Stonehaven
Balmoral
Braemar
Lochnagar 1154
Newtonmore
Badenoch
Grampian Highlands
Forest of Atholl
Garry
Tilt
Braes of Angus
N. Esk
Laurencekirk
Inverbervie
Brechin
Montrose
Blair Atholl
Pass of Killiecrankie
Pitlochry
Kirriemuir
S. Esk
L. Rannoch
L. Tummel
Aberfeldy
Tay
Blairgowrie
Alyth
Isla
Forfar
Arbroath
Strathmore
Sidlaw Hills
Dunkeld
Ben Lawers 1214
L. Tay
Dundee
Broughty Ferry
Firth of Tay
Tayport
TAYSIDE
Scone
Carse of Gowrie
Perth
Crieff
Earn
Cupar
St. Andrews
FIFE
Fife Ness
Anstruther
Breadalbane
Killin
L. Earn
Ben More 1174
B. Vorlich 983
Callander
Trossachs
L. Katrine
B. Vorlich 942
Ben Lomond 974
CENTRAL
Ochil Hills
Kinross
Leven
Glenrothes
Lochgelly
Cowdenbeath
Dunblane
Alloa
Bannockburn
Stirling
Kirkcaldy
Buckhaven
Dunfermline
Rosyth
Firth of Forth
Bass Rock
North Berwick
Dunbar
Grangemouth
Falkirk
Linlithgow
Leith
Edinburgh
LOTHIAN
Haddington
Musselburgh
Dalkeith
Lammermuir Hills
St. Abbs Hd.
Eyemouth
Berwick on Tweed
L. Lomond
Dumbarton
Clydebank
Kirkintilloch
Glasgow
Airdrie
Coatbridge
Bathgate
Pentland Hills
Penicuik
Motherwell
Wishaw
Carstairs
Peebles
Moorfoot Hills
Duns
Holy I.
Coldstream
Helensburgh
Dunoon
Greenock
Port Glasgow
Renfrew
Paisley
Rutherglen
E. Kilbride
Hamilton
Clyde
Lanark
Biggar
Tweed
Galashiels
Melrose
Kelso
Flodden
Till
Rothesay
Bute
Largs
STRATHCLYDE
Ardrossan
Irvine
Kilmarnock
Saltcoats
Troon
Prestwick
Ayr
Cumnock
Goat Fell 874
Arran
Brodick
Broad Law 840
Ettrick
Selkirk
Jedburgh
The Cheviot 816
Coquet
BORDERS
Hawick
Moffat
Teviot
Cheviot Hills
Southern Uplands
Leadhills
Sanquhar
Nith
Doon
Dalmellington
Girvan
Ailsa Craig
Firth of Clyde
DUMFRIES AND GALLOWAY
Merrick 843
Ken
Dumfries
Esk
Langholm
Lockerbie
Gretna Green
Annan
N. Tyne
ENGLAND
Hexham
HADRIAN'S WALL
Galloway
Newton Stewart
Castle Douglas
Dalbeattie
Gatehouse of Fleet
Kirkcudbright
Cree
Wigtown
Wigtown Bay
Whithorn
Luce Bay
Mull of Galloway
Solway Firth
Stranraer
Portpatrick
L. Ryan
North Channel
Carlisle
S. Tyne
Alston
Wear
Cross Fell 893
Tees
Barnard Castle
Penrith
Derwent
Skiddaw 931
Ullswater
Workington
Cumbrian Mts.
NORTHERN IRELAND
Ballymena
Larne
Belfast Lough
Belfast
Bangor
Newtownards
Fair Hd.
Ballycastle
Rathlin
Trostan 554
Mull of Kintyre
Campbeltown
Kintyre
Gigha
Islay
Bowmore
Port Ellen
Rubh a' Mhail
Sound of Jura
Jura
Tarbert
Loch Fyne
Lochgilphead
Crinan
Colonsay
Inveraray
L. Awe
Firth of Lorn
Oban
Loch Etive
Ben Cruachan 1124
Orchy
Loch Linnhe
Lismore
Mull
Ben More 966
Staffa
Iona
Tiree
Coll
Tobermory
Sound of Mull
Morvern
Loch Sunart
Ballachulish
Glen Coe
Rannoch Moor
Pt. of Ardnamurchan
Ardgour
Fort William
Ben Nevis 1343
L. Eil
L. Shiel
L. Moidart
Muck
Eigg
Rhum
Arisaig
Mallaig
L. Morar
L. Arkaig
Glen Garry
Lochy
Lochaber
Glen Spean
L. Oich
Fort Augustus
Glen Moriston
Glen Affric
Glen More
Ness
L. Hourn
Sound of Sleat
Kyle of Lochalsh
Dornie
Stromeferry
L. Carron
HIGHLAND
North West Highlands
Farrar
Canna
Cuillin Sound
Cuillin Hills
Scalpay
Raasay
Rona
Sound of Raasay
Inner Sound
Portree
Trotternish
L. Snizort
Skye
L. Bracadale
Rubha Hunish
Little Minch
Inner Hebrides
North Minch
Sound of Barra
Barra
Barra Hd.
South Uist
Ben More
Lochboisdale
Benbecula
Monach Is.
North Uist
Lochmaddy
Sound of Harris
Harris
Tarbert
WESTERN ISLES
L. Seaforth
Lewis
Stornoway
Broad Bay
Eye Pen.
L. Roag
Flannan Is.
Butt of Lewis
Outer Hebrides
ATLANTIC OCEAN
NORTH SEA
Projection: Conical with two standard parallels.
West from Greenwich
COPYRIGHT, GEORGE PHILIP & SON, LTD.

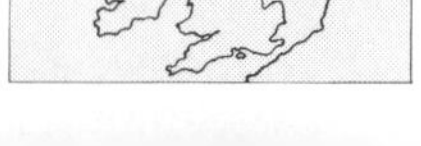

Kilometers 0 20 40 60 80 100 Km.
Statute Miles 0 20 40 60 80 100 Mi.

1:1 600 000

One centimeter represents 16 kilometers
One inch represents approximately 25 miles

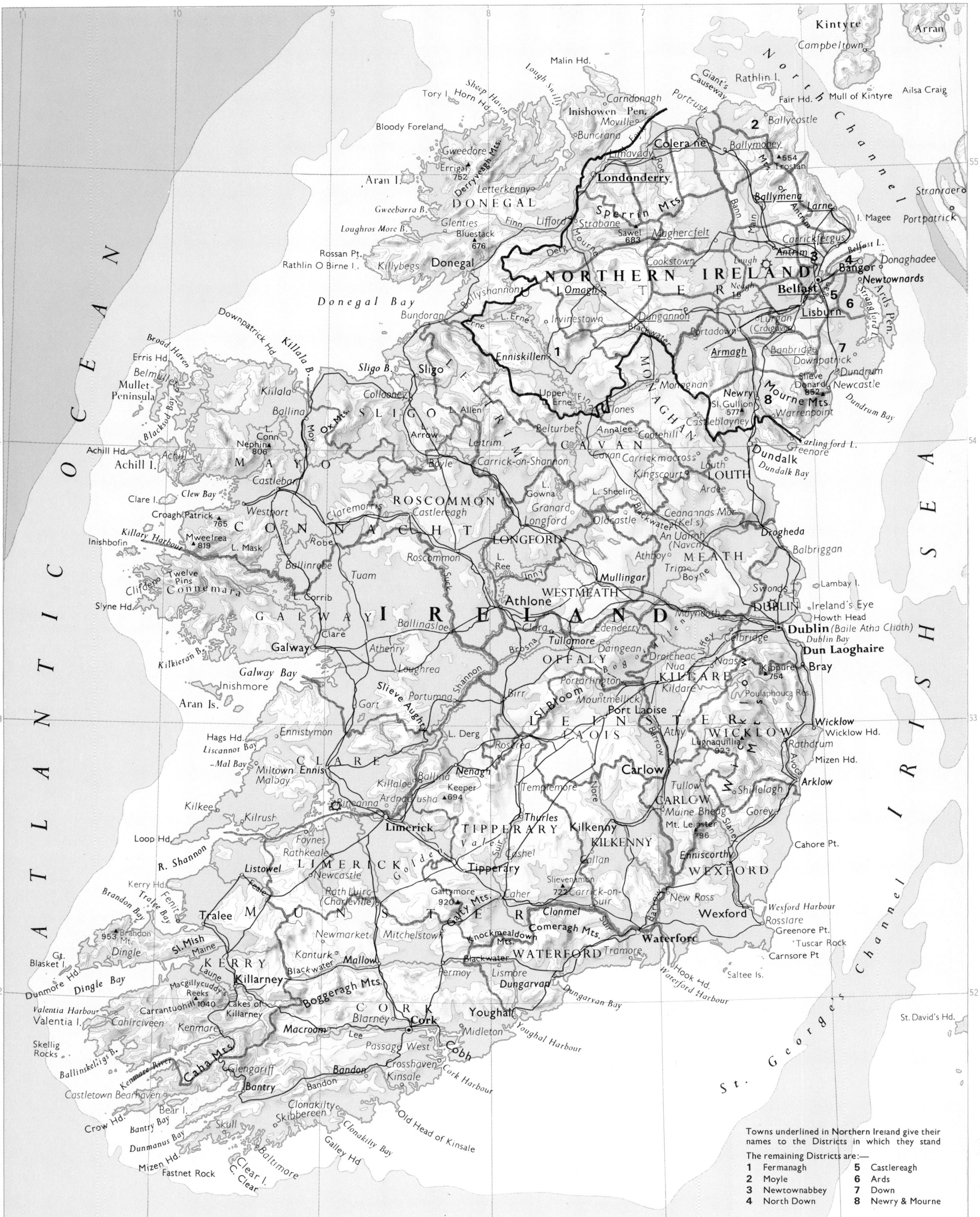
ATLANTIC OCEAN
IRISH SEA
St. George's Channel
North Channel
NORTHERN IRELAND
IRELAND
ULSTER
CONNACHT
LEINSTER
MUNSTER
DONEGAL
SLIGO
LEITRIM
MAYO
ROSCOMMON
LONGFORD
CAVAN
MONAGHAN
LOUTH
MEATH
WESTMEATH
GALWAY
OFFALY
KILDARE
LAOIS
WICKLOW
CARLOW
CLARE
TIPPERARY
KILKENNY
WEXFORD
LIMERICK
WATERFORD
KERRY
CORK
Dublin (Baile Atha Cliath)
Belfast
Londonderry
Coleraine
Ballymoney
Ballymena
Larne
Carrickfergus
Antrim
Bangor
Newtownards
Lisburn
Lurgan (Craigavon)
Portadown
Armagh
Banbridge
Downpatrick
Newry
Dungannon
Cookstown
Magherafelt
Omagh
Strabane
Limavady
Enniskillen
Donegal
Sligo
Castlebar
Westport
Galway
Athlone
Mullingar
Drogheda
Dundalk
Dun Laoghaire
Bray
Wicklow
Arklow
Carlow
Kilkenny
Port Laoise
Tullamore
Limerick
Ennis
Tipperary
Clonmel
Waterford
Wexford
Tralee
Killarney
Cork
Youghal
Dungarvan
Bantry
Macroom
Mallow
Cobh
Kinsale
Lough Neagh
Sperrin Mts.
Mourne Mts.
Galty Mts.
Comeragh Mts.
Knockmealdown Mts.
Boggeragh Mts.
Caha Mts.
Slieve Aughty
Sl. Bloom
Wicklow Mts.
Carrauntoohill 1040
Galtymore 920
Lugnaquillia 923
Kippure 754
Errigal 752
Nephin 806
Mweelrea 819
Croagh Patrick 765
Slieve Donard 852
Trostan 554
Sawel 683
Bluestack 676
Keeper 694
Slievenamon 722
Mt. Leinster 796
Slieve Gullion 577
R. Shannon
Donegal Bay
Galway Bay
Dingle Bay
Bantry Bay
Clew Bay
Malin Hd.
Mizen Hd.
C. Clear
Achill I.
Aran Is.
Valentia I.
Rathlin I.
Kintyre
Arran
Campbeltown
Mull of Kintyre
Ailsa Craig
Stranraer
Portpatrick
St. David's Hd.
West from Greenwich

Towns underlined in Northern Ireland give their names to the Districts in which they stand

The remaining Districts are:—

1	Fermanagh	5	Castlereagh
2	Moyle	6	Ards
3	Newtownabbey	7	Down
4	North Down	8	Newry & Mourne

Projection: *Conical with two standard parallels.*

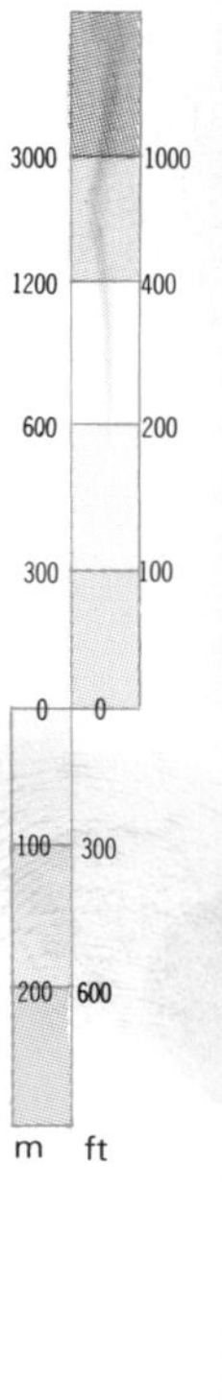
ft m
3000 1000
1200 400
600 200
300 100
0 0
100 300
200 600
m ft

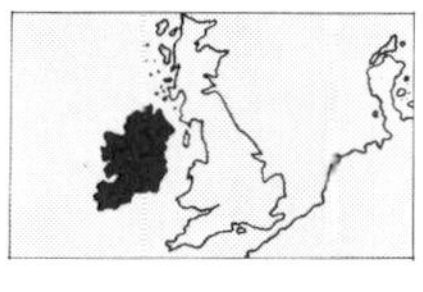

THE NETHERLANDS, BELGIUM AND LUXEMBOURG

Kilometers 0 20 40 60 80 100 Km.
Statute Miles 0 20 40 60 80 100 Mi.

1:2 000 000

One centimeter represents 20 kilometers
One inch represents approximately 32 miles

NORTH SEA
ENGLAND
NEDERLAND
BELGIUM
FRANCE
LUXEMBOURG
WADDENEILANDEN
Waddenzee
IJsselmeer
Noordoost Polder
Texel
Vlieland
Terschelling
Ameland
Schiermonnikoog
OSTFRIESISCHE INSELN
Borkum
Juist
Norderney
Baltrum
Langeoog
Spiekeroog
Wangerooge
Dollart
Groningen
Leeuwarden
Emden
Wilhelmshaven
Bremerhaven
Oldenburg
Den Helder
Alkmaar
Haarlem
AMSTERDAM
Hilversum
Utrecht
Amersfoort
Apeldoorn
Zwolle
Deventer
Enschede
Hengelo
Almelo
Arnhem
Nijmegen
's-GRAVENHAGE (The Hague)
Hoek van Holland
ROTTERDAM
Dordrecht
Breda
Tilburg
Eindhoven
's-Hertogenbosch
Venlo
Roermond
Maastricht
Heerlen
Walcheren
Vlissingen
Middelburg
Oosterschelde
Westerschelde
Oostende
Brugge
Gent
Antwerpen
Mechelen
BRUSSEL (Bruxelles)
Leuven
Liège
Namur
Charleroi
Mons
Tournai
Kortrijk
Hasselt
Verviers
Aachen
Köln
Düsseldorf
Duisburg
Essen
Dortmund
Münster
Osnabrück
Bonn
Koblenz
Trier
Luxembourg
Saarbrücken
Metz
Nancy
Strasbourg
Reims
Lille
Calais
Dover
Dunkerque
Boulogne-sur-Mer
Amiens
Abbeville
St-Quentin
Cambrai
Arras
Laon
Soissons
Beauvais
Compiègne
PARIS
Versailles
St-Denis
Châlons-sur-Marne
Épernay
Verdun
Charleville-Mézières
Sedan
Thionville
ARDENNES
Great Yarmouth
Lowestoft
Wiesbaden
Mainz
Kaiserslautern
SAARLAND
Maas
Rhein
Mosel
Meuse
Moselle
Marne
Aisne
Oise
Somme
Schelde
Ems
Weser

Projection: *Conical with two standard parallels*   East from Greenwich

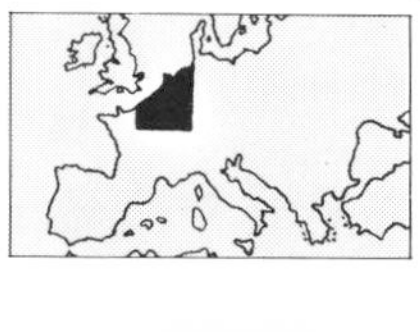

Kilometers 0 40 80 120 160 200 Km.
Statute Miles 0 40 80 120 160 200 Mi.

1:4 000 000

One centimeter represents 40 kilometers
One inch represents approximately 64 miles

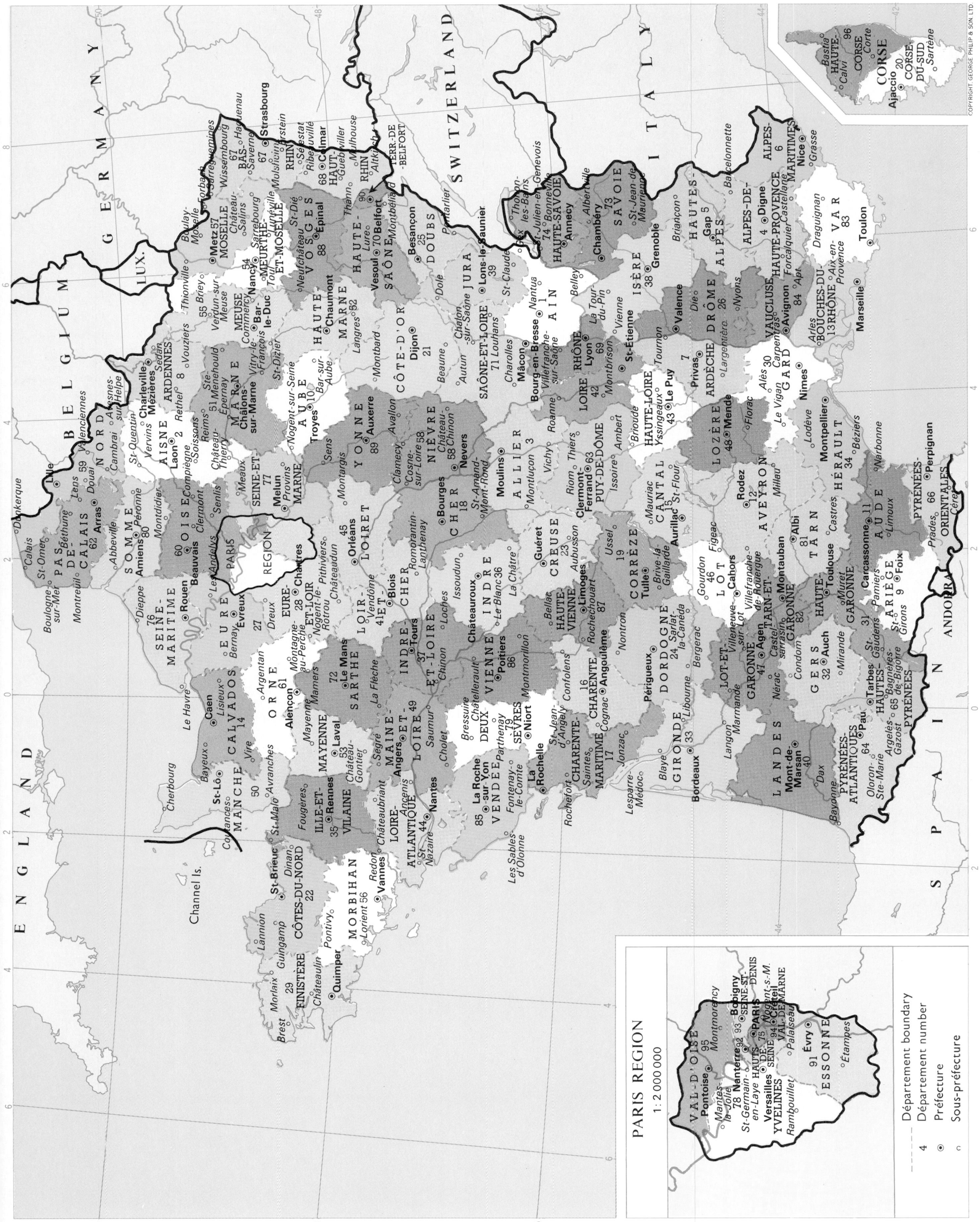
ENGLAND
BELGIUM
GERMANY
LUX.
SWITZERLAND
ITALY
SPAIN
ANDORRA
Channel Is.
PARIS REGION
1: 2 000 000
Département boundary
4 Département number
Préfecture
Sous-préfecture
COPYRIGHT, GEORGE PHILIP & SON, LTD

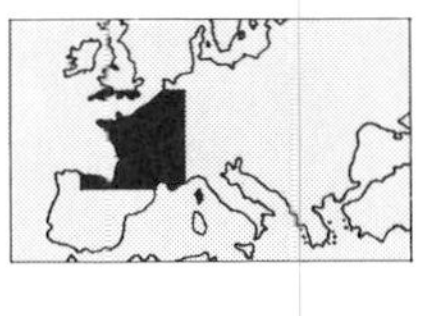

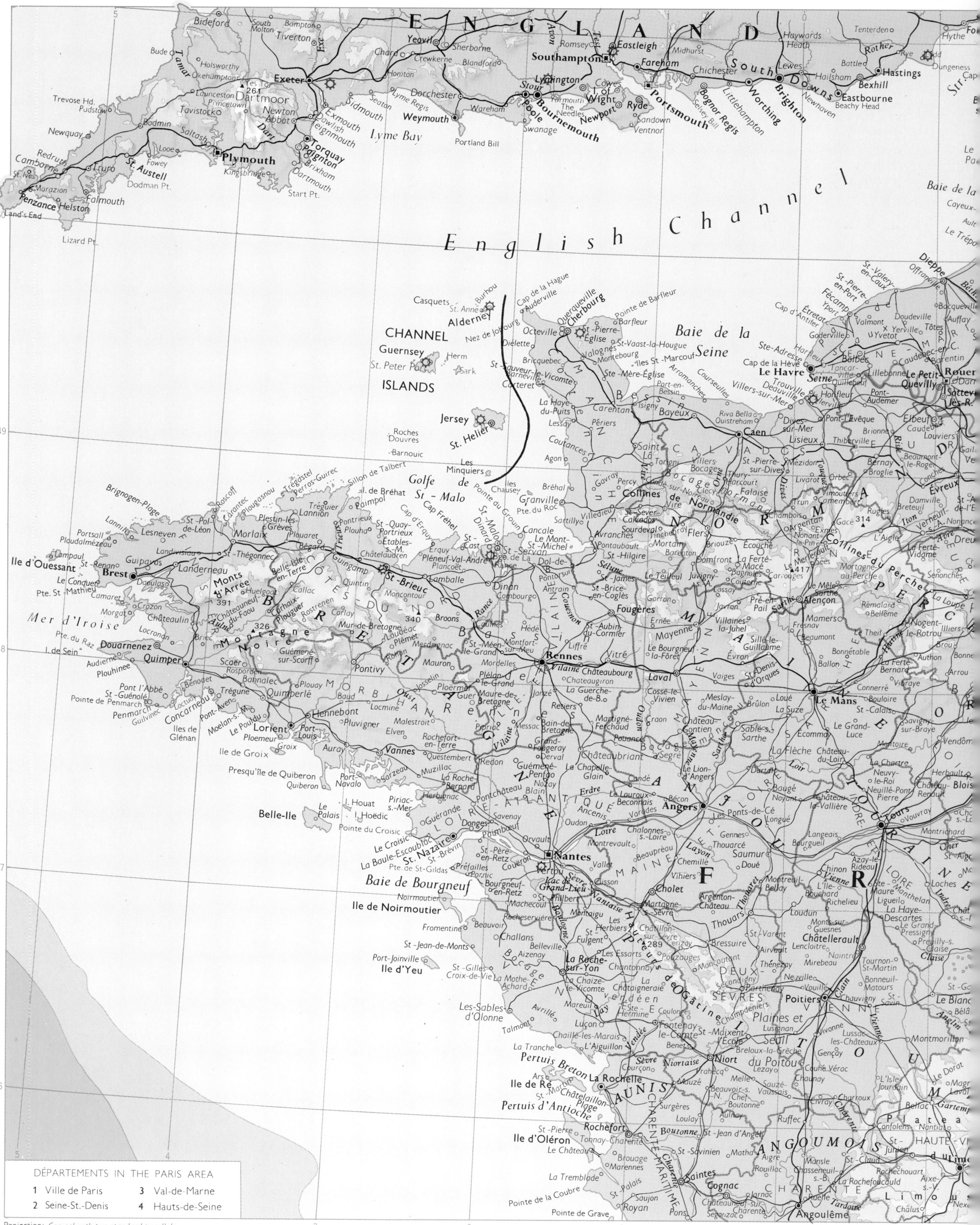
ENGLAND
English Channel
Exeter
Dartmoor
Plymouth
Torquay
Paignton
Lyme Bay
Weymouth
Southampton
Bournemouth
Poole
I. of Wight
Portsmouth
Brighton
South Downs
Eastbourne
Hastings
Penzance
Land's End
Lizard Pt.
CHANNEL ISLANDS
Alderney
Guernsey
Jersey
St. Helier
Cherbourg
Baie de la Seine
Le Havre
Dieppe
Caen
Golfe de St-Malo
St-Malo
St-Brieuc
Brest
Ile d'Ouessant
Mer d'Iroise
Quimper
Lorient
Vannes
Belle-Ile
Rennes
Laval
Le Mans
Alençon
Angers
Nantes
Tours
Saumur
Cholet
Poitiers
Niort
La Rochelle
Ile de Ré
Ile d'Oléron
Rochefort
Saintes
Cognac
Angoulême
Royan
Baie de Bourgneuf
Ile de Noirmoutier
Ile d'Yeu
La Roche-sur-Yon
Les-Sables-d'Olonne
Pertuis Breton
Pertuis d'Antioche
NORMANDIE
BRETAGNE
ANJOU
POITOU
AUNIS
ANGOUMOIS
FRANCE
Collines de Normandie
Monts d'Arrée
Montagne Noire
Seuil du Poitou
Plaines et
ft m
12 000 4000
9000 3000
6000 2000
4500 1500
3000 1000
1200 400
600 200
0 0
200 600
2000 6000
m ft
DÉPARTEMENTS IN THE PARIS AREA
1 Ville de Paris
2 Seine-St.-Denis
3 Val-de-Marne
4 Hauts-de-Seine
Projection: Conical with two standard parallels
West from Greenwich
East from Greenwich

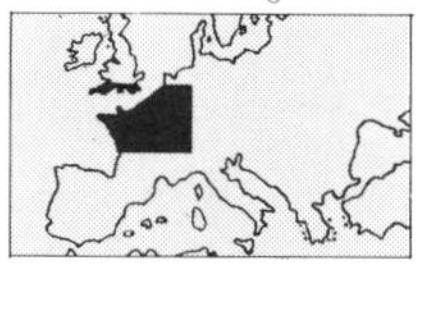

Kilometers 0 20 40 60 80 100 Km.
Statute Miles 0 20 40 60 80 100 Mi.

1:2 000 000

One centimeter represents 20 kilometers
One inch represents approximately 32 miles

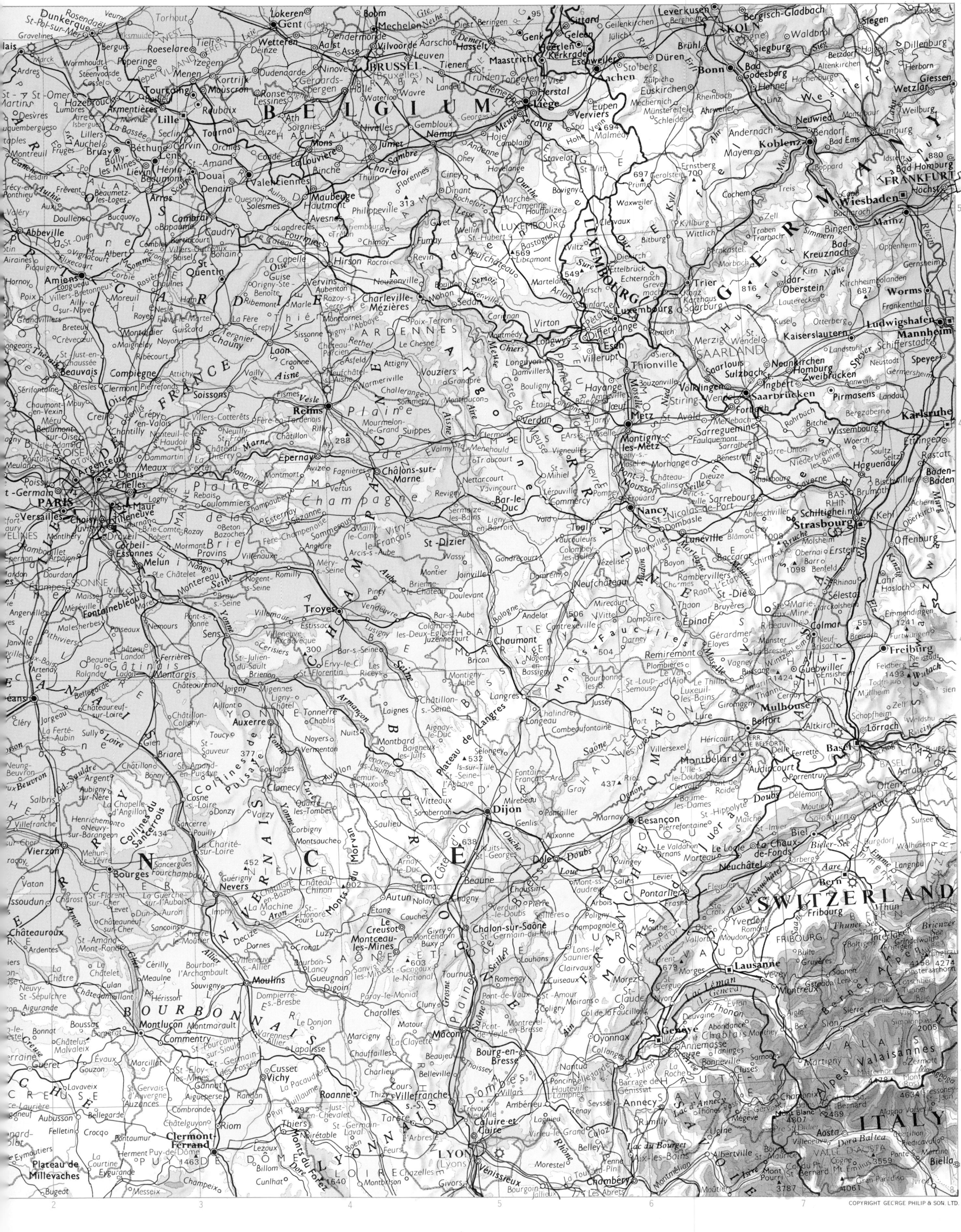
BELGIUM
LUXEMBOURG
GERMANY
FRANCE
SWITZERLAND
ITALY
PARIS
BRUSSEL (Bruxelles)
Luxembourg
FRANKFURT
KÖLN
Bonn
Lille
Reims
Nancy
Metz
Strasbourg
Dijon
Besançon
Lyon (Lyons)
Genève
Lausanne
Basel
Bern
Mulhouse
Troyes
Orléans
Clermont-Ferrand
Saarbrücken
Mannheim
Karlsruhe
Freiburg
Koblenz
Wiesbaden
Mainz
Liège
Namur
Charleroi
Gent
Aachen
Amiens
Champagne
ARDENNES
LORRAINE
SAARLAND
BOURBONNAIS
Plateau de Langres
Plateau de Millevaches
Monts du Morvan
Lac Léman (L. Genève)
Alpes Valaisannes
Berner Alpen
Mont Blanc 4807
Lac du Bourget
Lac d'Annecy
Rhône
Saône
Loire
Seine
Marne
Meuse
Moselle
Rhein
Aisne
Oise
Yonne
Doubs
Sambre
Hunsrück
Westerwald
Taunus
Eifel

2 3 4 5 6 7

ATLANTIC OCEAN
Golfe de Gascogne
Ile de Noirmoutier
Ile d'Yeu
Ile de Ré
Ile d'Oléron
Pertuis Breton
Pertuis d'Antioche
Bassin d'Arcachon
Étang d'Hourtin et de Carcans
Étang de Lacanau
Étang de Cazaux
Etang de Biscarrosse
Pointe de la Coubre
Pointe de Grave
Cholet
Bressuire
Thouars
La Roche-sur-Yon
Les Sables-d'Olonne
Luçon
Fontenay-le-Comte
Niort
Poitiers
Châtellerault
Loudun
Parthenay
La Rochelle
Rochefort
Saintes
Cognac
Angoulême
Royan
Limoges
Châteauroux
Issoudun
Bourges
Nevers
Moulins
Montluçon
Commentry
Vichy
Clermont-Ferrand
Thiers
Guéret
Aubusson
Tulle
Brive-la-Gaillarde
Aurillac
Périgueux
Bergerac
Libourne
Bordeaux
Bègles
Le Bouscat
Arcachon
La Teste
Marmande
Agen
Villeneuve-sur-Lot
Cahors
Figeac
Decazeville
Rodez
Millau
Montauban
Albi
Castres
Mazamet
Toulouse
Auch
Tarbes
Pau
Lourdes
Bayonne
Biarritz
Anglet
Dax
Mont-de-Marsan
Carcassonne
Narbonne
Béziers
Perpignan
Pamiers
Foix
Limoux
AUNIS
SAINTONGE
ANGOUMOIS
LIMOUSIN
BERRY
BOURBONNAIS
NIVERNAIS
AUVERGNE
GUYENNE
GASCOGNE
LANGUEDOC
ROUSSILLON
BÉARN
NAVARRE
ARAGON
CATALUÑA
ANDORRA
Plateau de Millevaches
Puy de Sancy 1886
Puy de Dôme 1463
Monts Dore
Plomb du Cantal 1858
Mts d'Aubrac
Mts de Lacaune
Causse Méjean
Pic de Vignemale 3303
Pic de Aneto 3404
Pic d'Estats 3141
Pic de Montcalm 3080
Carlitte 2921
Sierra de la Peña
Sierra de Guara 2077
Sierra del Cadí 2557
Pamplona
Huesca
Zaragoza
Lérida
Manresa
Gerona
Figueras
San Sebastián
Tudela
Cabo Creus
Garonne
Dordogne
Lot
Tarn
Adour
Gironde
Charente
Vienne
Creuse
Allier
Aude
Projection: Conical with two standard parallels
West from Greenwich
East from Greenwich
ft m
12,000 4000
9000 3000
6000 2000
4500 1500
3000 1000
1200 400
600 200
0 0
200 600
2000 6000
m ft

Kilometers 0 20 40 60 80 100 Km.
Statute Miles 0 20 40 60 80 100 Mi.

1:2 000 000

One centimeter represents 20 kilometers
One inch represents approximately 32 miles

SWITZERLAND
ITALY
FRANCE
CORSICA
LIGURIAN SEA
MEDITERRANEAN SEA
Golfo di Génova
Lion
LYON
Genève
Lausanne
Bern
Luzern
Grenoble
Chambéry
Annecy
TORINO
MILANO
GENOVA
Marseille
Toulon
Nice
MONACO
Cannes
Avignon
Aix-en-Provence
Bastia
Ajaccio
Livorno
Brescia
Bergamo
Parma
La Spezia
Savona
San Remo
Valence
St-Étienne
Mont Blanc
ALPES-DE-HAUTE-PROVENCE
ALPES MARITIMES
VAUCLUSE
SAVOIE
HAUTE-SAVOIE
ISÈRE
DRÔME
HAUTE CORSE
CORSE DU SUD
ILES D'HYÈRES
Elba

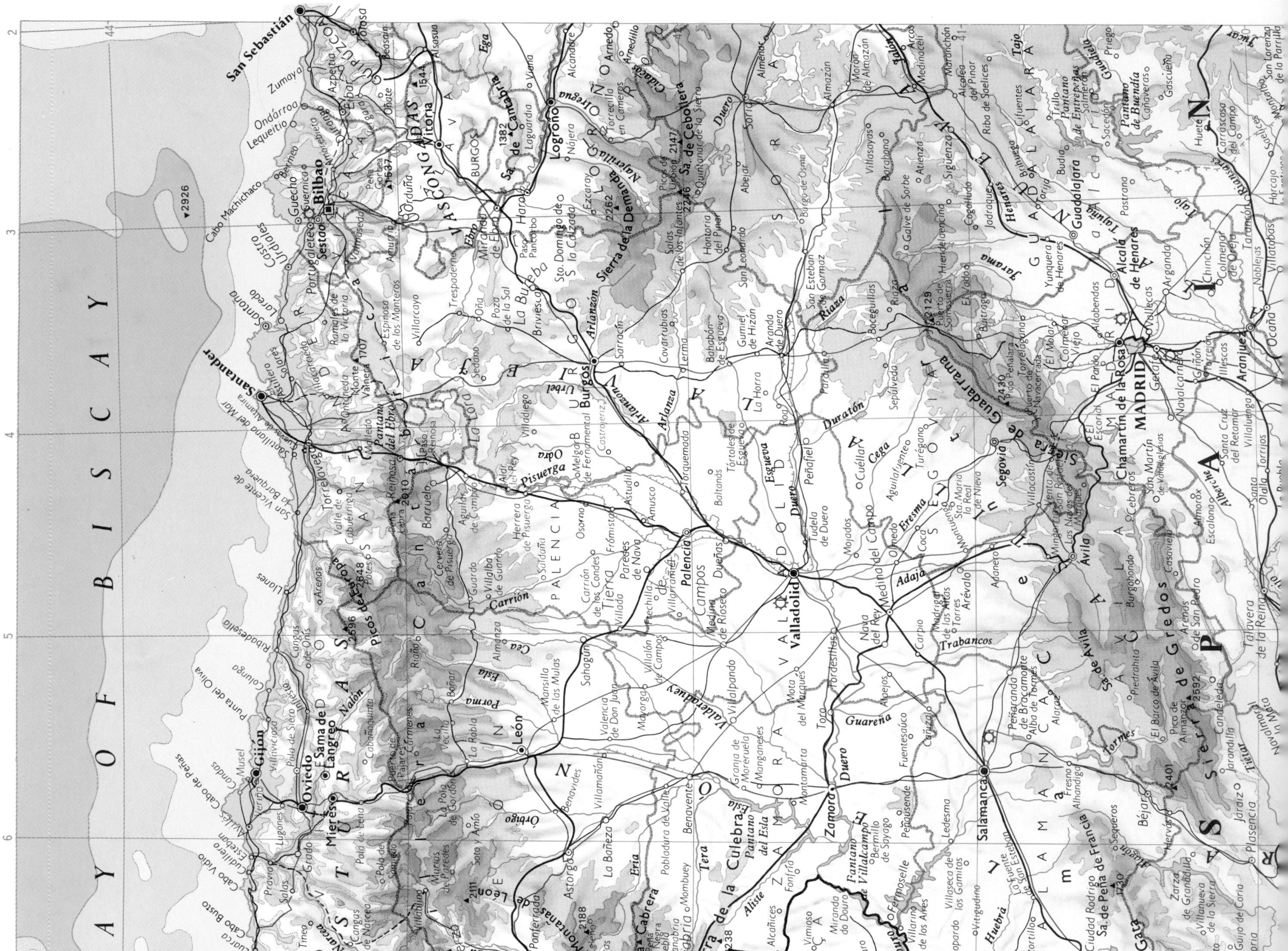
BAY OF BISCAY
ATLANTIC OCEAN
San Sebastián
Bilbao
Santander
Oviedo
Gijón
León
Burgos
Logroño
Vitoria
Palencia
Valladolid
Salamanca
Zamora
Segovia
Avila
MADRID
Guadalajara
Alcalá de Henares
Lugo
Orense
Vigo
Santiago de Compostela
La Coruña
El Ferrol
Porto (Oporto)
Vila Nova de Gaia
Matosinhos
Coimbra
Aveiro
Figueira da Foz
Bragança
Viseu
Guarda
Lamego
Chaves
Braga
Picos de Europa
Sierra de Guadarrama
Sierra de Gredos
Sierra de la Demanda
Sierra de Gata
Duero
Douro
Ebro
Tajo
Miño
Sil
Esla
Pisuerga
Tormes
Cabo Finisterre
Cabo Ortegal
Cabo Peñas
Cabo Mondego
Ría de Arosa
Ría de Vigo
Ría de Pontevedra
2926
5000

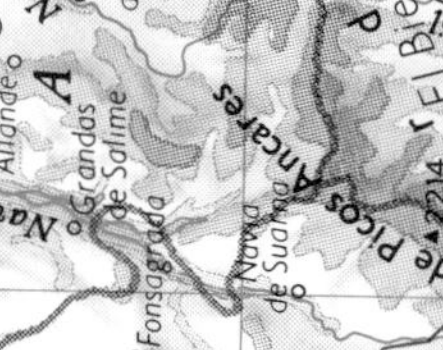

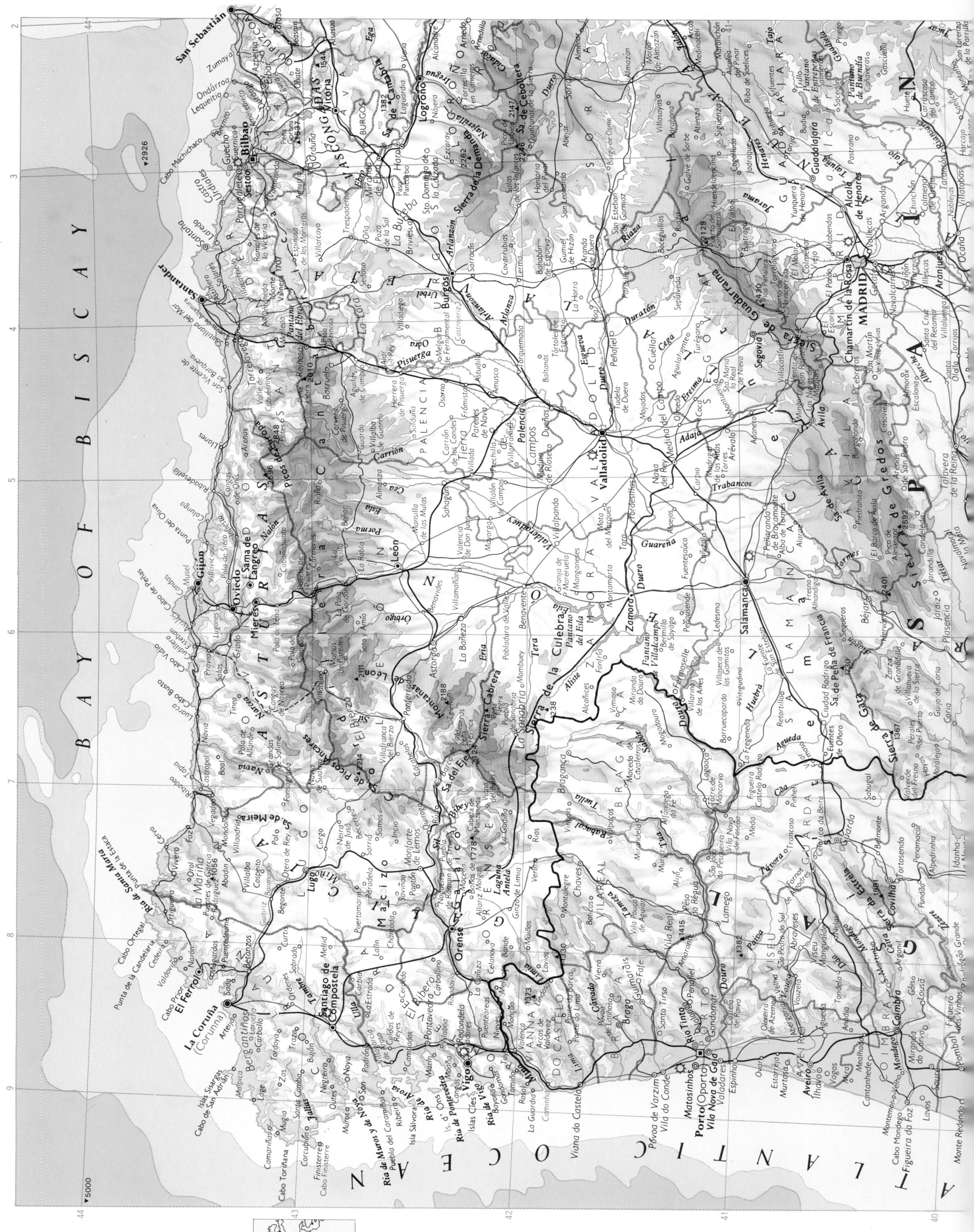

Kilometers 0 20 40 60 80 100 Km.

Statute Miles 0 20 40 60 80 100 Mi.

1:2 000 000

One centimeter represents 20 kilometers
One inch represents approximately 32 miles

MEDITERRANEAN SEA
MOROCCO
Strait of Gibraltar
Golfo de Cádiz
Golfo de Almería
Sierra Nevada
Sierra Morena
Montes de Toledo
Sierra de Alcaraz
Sierra de Cazorla
Sierra de Segura
Sierra Madrona
Sierra de Aracena
Campo de Gibraltar
Costa del Sol
Algarve
Baía de Setúbal
LISBOA (LISBON)
Setúbal
Évora
Badajoz
Mérida
Cáceres
Ciudad Real
Puertollano
Valdepeñas
Linares
Jaén
Úbeda
Córdoba
Granada
Málaga
Almería
Sevilla (Seville)
Huelva
Cádiz
Jerez de la Frontera
Algeciras
Gibraltar (Br.)
La Línea de la Concepción
Ceuta (Sp.)
Tetouan
Tanger (Tangier)
Larache
Melilla (Sp.)
Al-Hoceima
Alborán (Sp.)
Faro
Lagos
Portimão
Tavira
Beja
Playa de Castilla
Guadiana
Guadalquivir
Cabo de São Vicente
Cabo de Sines
Cabo Espichel
Cabo da Roca
West from Greenwich
Projection: Conical with two standard parallels
COPYRIGHT GEORGE PHILIP & SON LTD.
m 3000 2000 1500 1000 400 200 0
ft 9000 6000 4500 3000 1200 600 0
m 200 600 2000 6000
ft 600 2000 6000

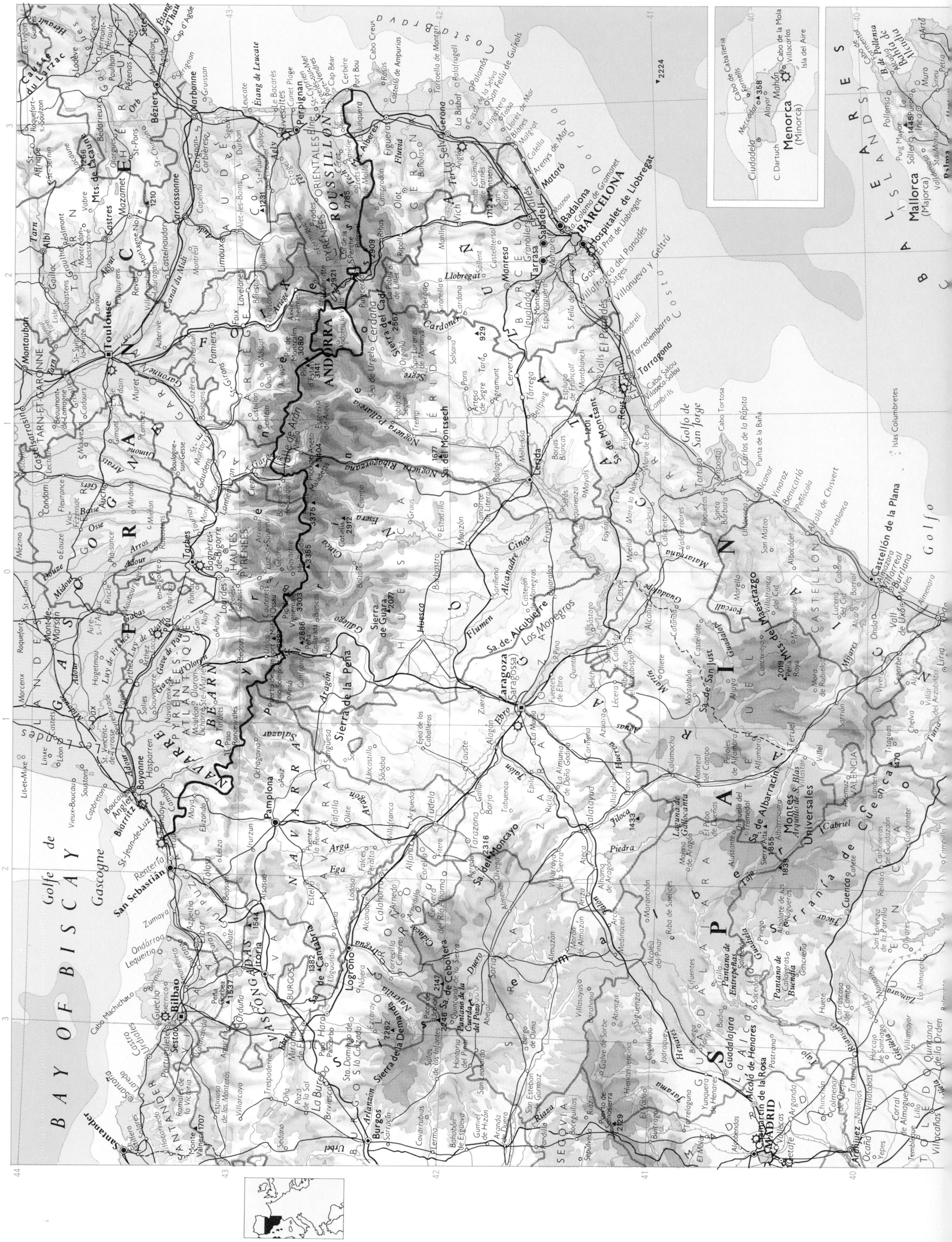
BAY OF BISCAY
Golfe de Gascogne
FRANCE
SPAIN
ANDORRA
ROUSSILLON
PYRÉNÉES ORIENTALES
HAUTES PYRÉNÉES
PYRÉNÉES ATLANTIQUES
NAVARRE
BÉARN
NAVARRA
ARAGÓN
VASCONGADAS
LÉRIDA
GERONA
BARCELONA
TARRAGONA
ZARAGOZA
HUESCA
TERUEL
CASTELLÓN
VALENCIA
CUENCA
GUADALAJARA
SORIA
BURGOS
LOGROÑO
MADRID
SEGOVIA
ISLAS BALEARES
Mallorca (Majorca)
Menorca (Minorca)
Bilbao
San Sebastián
Pamplona
Zaragoza (Saragossa)
Lérida
Barcelona
Hospitalet de Llobregat
Badalona
Sabadell
Tarrasa
Manresa
Mataró
Tarragona
Reus
Castellón de la Plana
Teruel
Huesca
Logroño
Burgos
Vitoria
Santander
Soria
Cuenca
Guadalajara
Alcalá de Henares
Toulouse
Perpignan
Carcassonne
Tarbes
Pau
Bayonne
Biarritz
Béziers
Narbonne
Montauban
Albi
Castres
Sierra de la Peña
Sa. del Moncayo
Montes Universales
Sa. de Albarracín
Mts. del Maestrazgo
Sierra de la Demanda
Sa. de Cebollera
Sa. del Montsech
Sa. de Montsant
Sierra de Guara
Sa. de Alcubierre
Los Monegros
Sa. de Cantabria
Golfo de San Jorge
Ebro
Duero
Tajo
Júcar
Segre
Cinca
Garonne
Adour
Aragón
Jalón
Jiloca
Serranía de Cuenca
Costa Brava

Kilometers 0 20 40 60 80 100 Km.
Statute Miles 0 20 40 60 80 100 Mi.

1:2 000 000

One centimeter represents 20 kilometers
One inch represents approximately 32 miles

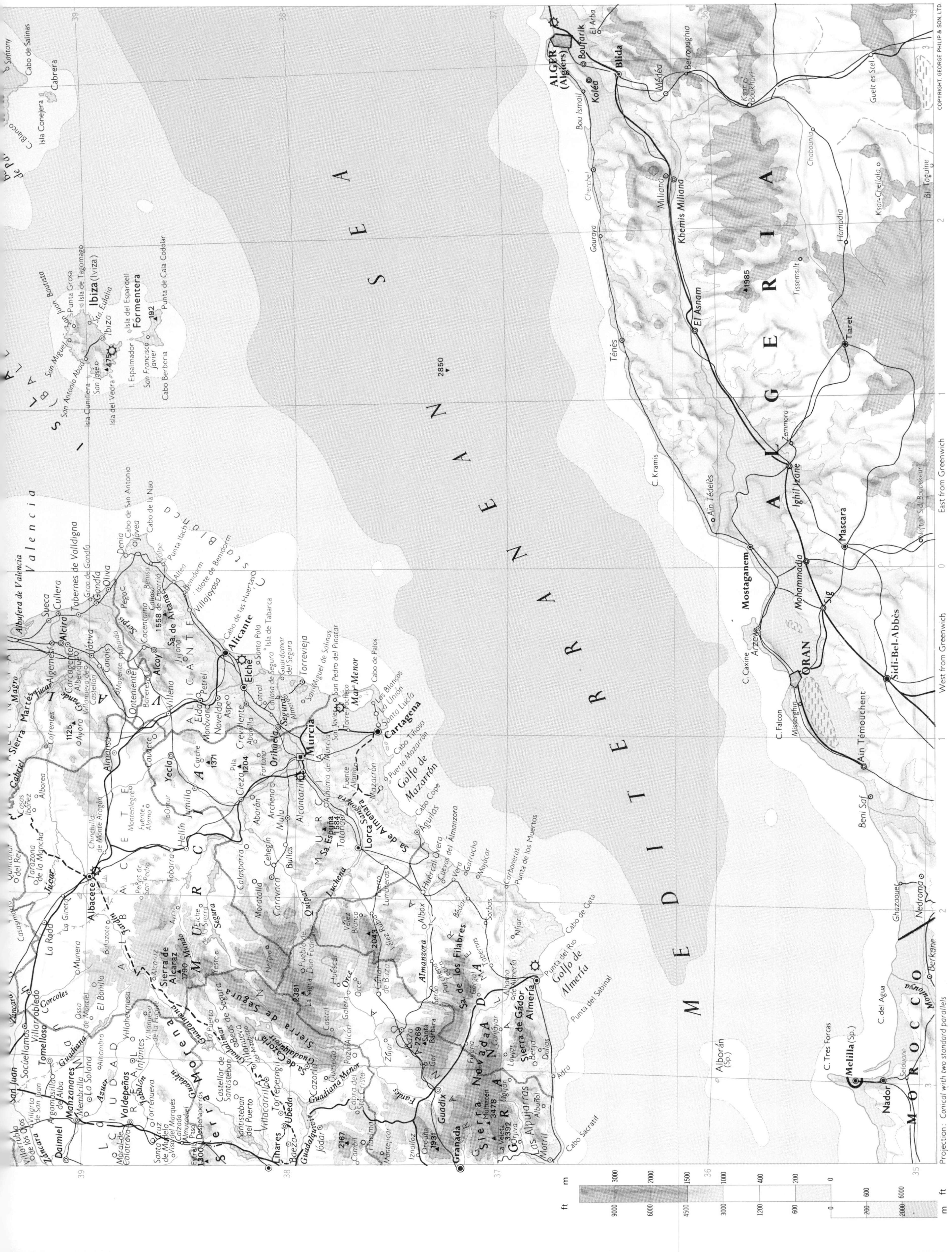
MEDITERRANEAN SEA
ALGERIA
MOROCCO
ALGER (Algiers)
Blida
Boufarik
Koléa
Médéa
Miliana
Khemis Miliana
El Asnam
Ténès
Tiaret
Mostaganem
Mascara
Mohammadia
Sig
ORAN
Arzew
Sidi-Bel-Abbès
Aïn Témouchent
Beni Saf
Nedroma
Ghazaouet
Melilla (Sp.)
Nador
Alborán (Sp.)
Ibiza (Iviza)
Formentera
Cabrera
Valencia
Alicante
Elche
Murcia
Cartagena
Lorca
Almería
Granada
Guadix
Albacete
Sierra Nevada
Sierra de Segura
Sierra Morena
Sierra de Alcaraz
Golfo de Almería
Golfo de Mazarrón
Mar Menor
Cabo de Gata
Cabo de Palos
Cabo de la Nao
Yecla
Jumilla
Hellín
Cieza
Orihuela
Linares
Úbeda
Baeza
Valdepeñas
Manzanares
Daimiel
Tomelloso
2850
East from Greenwich
West from Greenwich
ft m
9000 3000
6000 2000
4500 1500
3000 1000
1200 400
600 200
0 0
200 600
2000 6000
m ft

Projection: Conical with two standard parallels

SWITZERLAND
FRANCE
FRANCHE-COMTÉ
BOURGOGNE
RHÔNE-ALPES
PROVENCE
ALPES-DE-HAUTE-PROVENCE
ALPES-MARITIMES
VAUCLUSE
DRÔME
ISÈRE
SAVOIE
HAUTE-SAVOIE
HAUTES-ALPES
BOUCHES-DU-RHÔNE
VAR
PIEMONTE
LOMBARDIA
LIGURIA
VALLE D'AOSTA
VALAIS
TICINO
GRAUBÜNDEN
LIGURIAN SEA
Golfo di Génova
Côte d'Azur
CORSE
(CORSICA)
HAUTE-CORSE
CORSE-DU-SUD
ILES D'HYERES
Arcipelago
Toscano
Lac Léman
(L. Genève)
Lago Maggiore
L. di Como
L. di Lugano
L. d'Orta
Lago di Garda
Lac du Bourget
Lac d'Annecy
Alpi Orobie
Lyon
(Lyons)
Grenoble
Genève
(Geneva)
Lausanne
Bern
(BERNE)
Luzern
Fribourg
Annecy
Chambéry
Valence
Avignon
Arles
MARSEILLE
(Marseilles)
Toulon
Aix-en-Provence
Nice
MONACO
Monte-Carlo
Cannes
Grasse
Antibes
TORINO
(Turin)
MILANO
(Milan)
GENOVA
(Genoa)
Savona
San Remo
Impéria
Cúneo
Asti
Alessándria
Novara
Vercelli
Pavia
Piacenza
Parma
Bergamo
Bréscia
Cremona
Como
Lugano
Locarno
La Spezia
Carrara
Massa
Lucca
Pisa
Livorno
(Leghorn)
Bastia
Ajaccio
Elba
Capraia
Gorgona
Pianosa
Montecristo
Giglio
Mont Blanc
4807
Matterhorn
4478
Massif du Pelvoux
Mt. Viso
3841
Gran Paradiso
4061
Mt. Cinto
2710
2650
Projection: Conical with two standard parallels
East from Greenwich
ft
m
12,000
4000
9000
3000
6000
2000
4500
1500
3000
1000
1200
400
600
200
0
0
200
600
2000
6000
m
ft

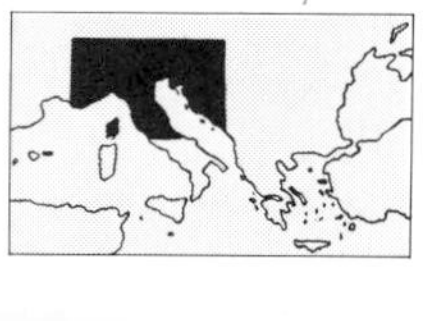

Kilometers 0 20 40 60 80 100 Km.

Statute Miles 0 20 40 60 80 100 Mi.

1:2 000 000

One centimeter represents 20 kilometers

One inch represents approximately 32 miles

HUNGARY
Golfo di Venézia
ADRIATIC SEA
Innsbruck
Graz
Klagenfurt
Maribor
Ljubljana
Zagreb
Trieste
Rijeka (Fiume)
Karlovac
Banja Luka
Zadar
Split
Venézia (Venice)
Pádova
Ferrara
Ravenna
Rímini
SAN MARINO
Ancona
Pescara
ROMA (ROME)
Perúgia
Arezzo
Udine
Bolzano
Vicenza
Treviso
Pesaro
Áscoli Piceno
Térmoli
Vasto
Vieste
Lastovo
Mljet
Pelješac
Dugi Otok
Palagruža
Tremiti
Pianosa

CORSE
CORSICA
CORSE-DU-SUD
G.d'Ajaccio
G. de Valinco
Bonifacio
Bouches de Bonifacio
Maddalena
Caprera
Costa Smeralda
Asinara
Golfo dell' Asinara
Sássari
Alghero
Porto Tórres
Tempio Pausania
Olbia
G. di Olbia
Tavolara
Posada
Nuoro
Macomer
SARDEGNA
SARDINIA
L. del Tirso
Monti del Gennargentu
1834
Golfo di Orosei
Golfo di Oristano
Oristano
Arbatax
Lanusei
Iglésias
Carbonia
San Pietro
Sant' Antíoco
G. di Pálmas
Cágliari
Golfo di Cágliari
C. Spartivento
C. Carbonara
C. Ferrato
ROMA
(Rome)
Tívoli
Frosinone
Latina
Terracina
Golfo di Gaeta
Gaeta
Ísole Ponziane
Ponza
Ventotene
Íschia
TYRRHENIAN SEA
3719
3589
Ustica
PALERMO
Bagheria
Trápani
Érice
Alcamo
Ísole Égadi
Marsala
Castelvetrano
Mazara del Vallo
Sciacca
Agrigento
Sicilian Channel
Pantelleria
836
1319
Iles de la Galite
Bizerte
(Binzert)
Menzel-Bourguiba
Golfe de Tunis
TUNIS
Halq el Oued
(La Goulette)
C. Bon
Kelibia
Menzel Temime
Nabeul
Hammamet
Zaghouan
Tabarka
El Kala
ALGERIA
Béja
Medjerda
TUNISIA
MEDITE
ft
m
9000
6000
4500
3000
1200
600
0
3000
2000
1500
1000
400
200
37
200
2000
4000
600
6000
12,000
Projection: Conical with two standard parallels
East from Greenwich

Kilometers 0 20 40 60 80 100 Km.
Statute Miles 0 20 40 60 80 100 Mi.

1:2 000 000

One centimeter represents 20 kilometers
One inch represents approximately 32 miles

ADRIATIC SEA
IONIAN SEA
Strait of Otranto
G. di Manfredónia
Golfo di Táranto
G. di Salerno
G. di Policastro
Golfo di Sant'Eufémia
Golfo di Squillace
Str. di Messina
Isole Eólie o Lípari (Æolian Is.)
Strómboli
Salina
Lípari
Vulcano
Filicudi
Alicudi
Panarea
BASILICATA
CALABRIA
Monte Sant'Ángelo
Manfredónia
Fóggia
Lucera
Campobasso
Barletta
Trani
Bisceglie
Molfetta
Bari
Monopoli
Fasano
Brindisi
Lecce
Otranto
Gallipoli
C. Santa Maria di Leuca
Táranto
Matera
Altamura
Gravina di Púglia
Potenza
Salerno
Benevento
Avellino
Caserta
Cerignola
Canosa di Púglia
Andria
Melfi
Sorrento
Capri
Sala Consilina
Lagonegro
M. Sirino 2005
Monte Pollino 2271
Castrovillari
Rossano
Corigliano Cálabro
Cosenza
La Sila 1929
Crotone
C. delle Colonne
Catanzaro
Vibo Valéntia
Tropea
Capo Vaticano
Pizzo
Palmi
Réggio di Calábria
Messina
Aspromonte 1956
C. Spartivento
Milazzo
Barcellona
Monti Nebrodi 1847
Etna 3340
Catánia
Acireale
Taormina
Augusta
Siracusa
Ragusa
Módica
Noto
Pachino
C. Passero
Caltagirone
Gela
Vittória
Enna
Piazza Armerina
Lentini
Kérkira (Corfu)
Vlora
Durrësi (Durazzo)
Tirana
Berati
Shkumbini
Drini
Laguna e Nartës
Karaburuni
3065
4116
COPYRIGHT. GEORGE PHILIP & SON. LTD

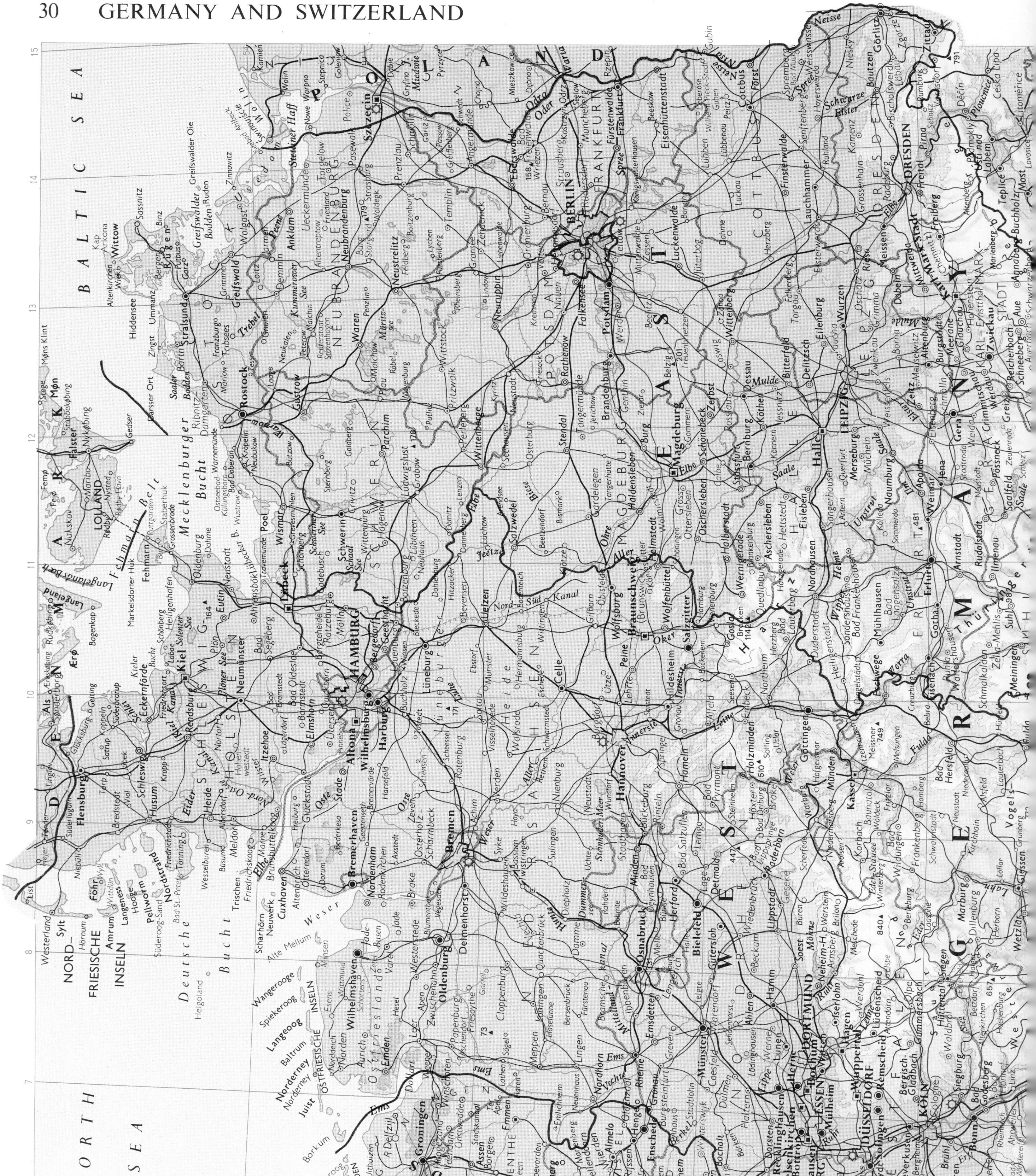

BALTIC SEA
NORTH SEA
DENMARK
POLAND
GERMANY
NORDFRIESISCHE INSELN
OSTFRIESISCHE INSELN
Deutsche Bucht
Mecklenburger Bucht
BERLIN
HAMBURG
Bremen
Hannover
Kiel
Rostock
Lübeck
Magdeburg
LEIPZIG
DRESDEN
Halle
DORTMUND
ESSEN
DÜSSELDORF
KÖLN
Bonn
Münster
Osnabrück
Bielefeld
Kassel
Erfurt
Braunschweig
Schwerin
Stettin
Szczecin
Potsdam
Groningen
Elbe
Weser
Ems
Oder
Rhein

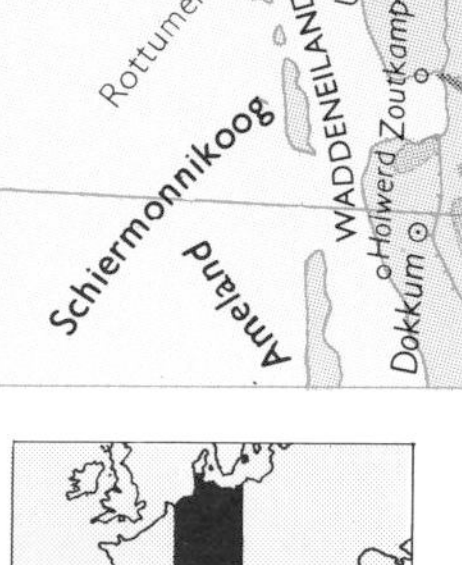

Kilometers 0 20 40 60 80 100 Km.

Statute Miles 0 20 40 60 100 Mi.

1:2 000 000

One centimeter represents 20 kilometers
One inch represents approximately 32 miles

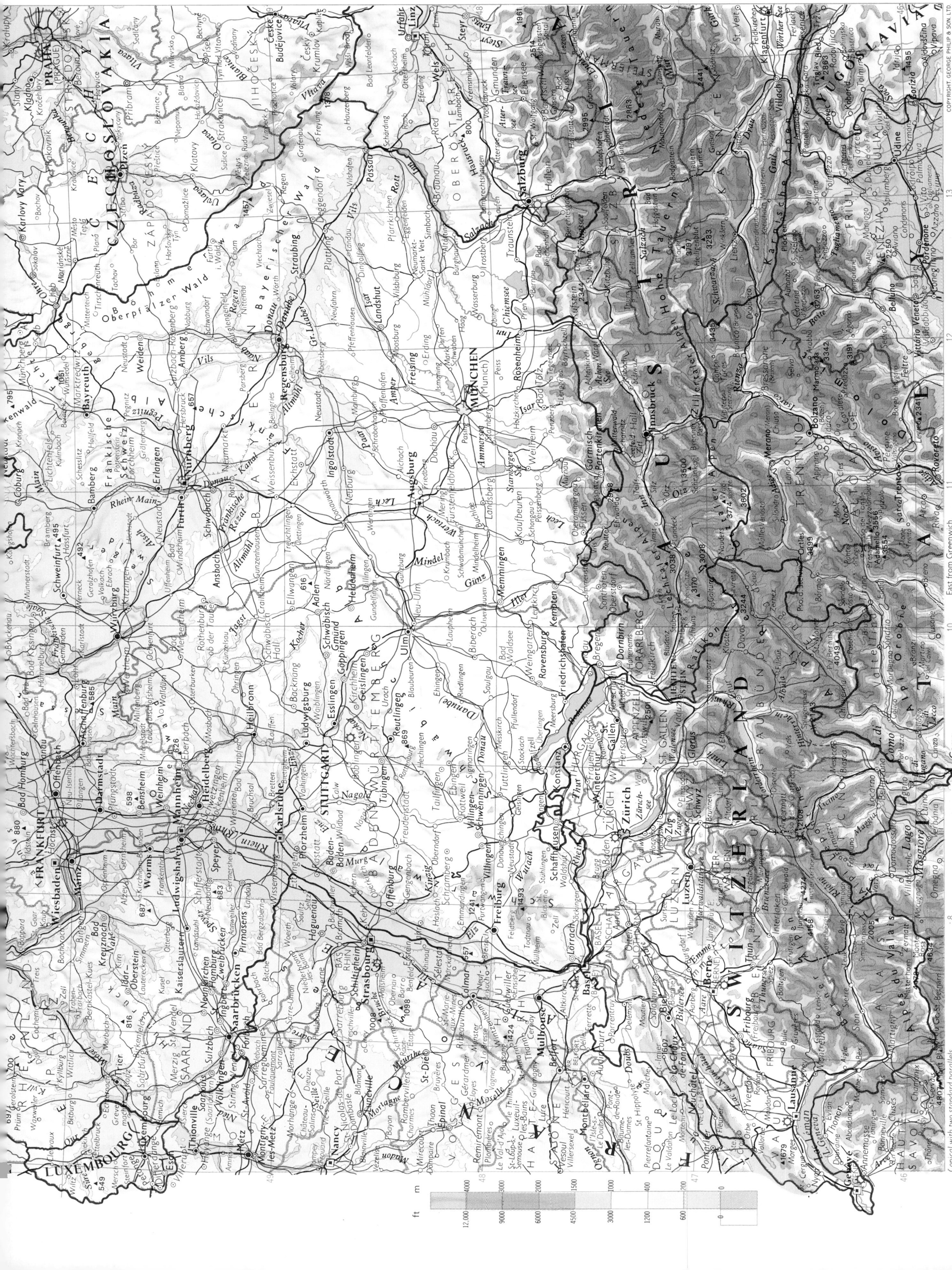

CZECHOSLOVAKIA
PRAHA (PRAGUE)
Plzeň
Linz
Salzburg
München (Munich)
Nürnberg
Regensburg
Augsburg
Ulm
Stuttgart
Frankfurt
Mannheim
Heidelberg
Karlsruhe
Strasbourg
Saarbrücken
Luxembourg
Metz
Nancy
Basel
Zürich
Bern
Lausanne
Genève
Innsbruck
Bolzano
Udine
Como
SWITZERLAND
AUSTRIA
YUGOSLAVIA
ITALY
FRANCE
Conical with two standard parallels
East from Greenwich
COPYRIGHT GEORGE PHILIP & SON, LTD
m 4000 3000 2000 1500 1000 400 200 0
ft 12,000 9000 6000 4500 3000 1200 600 0

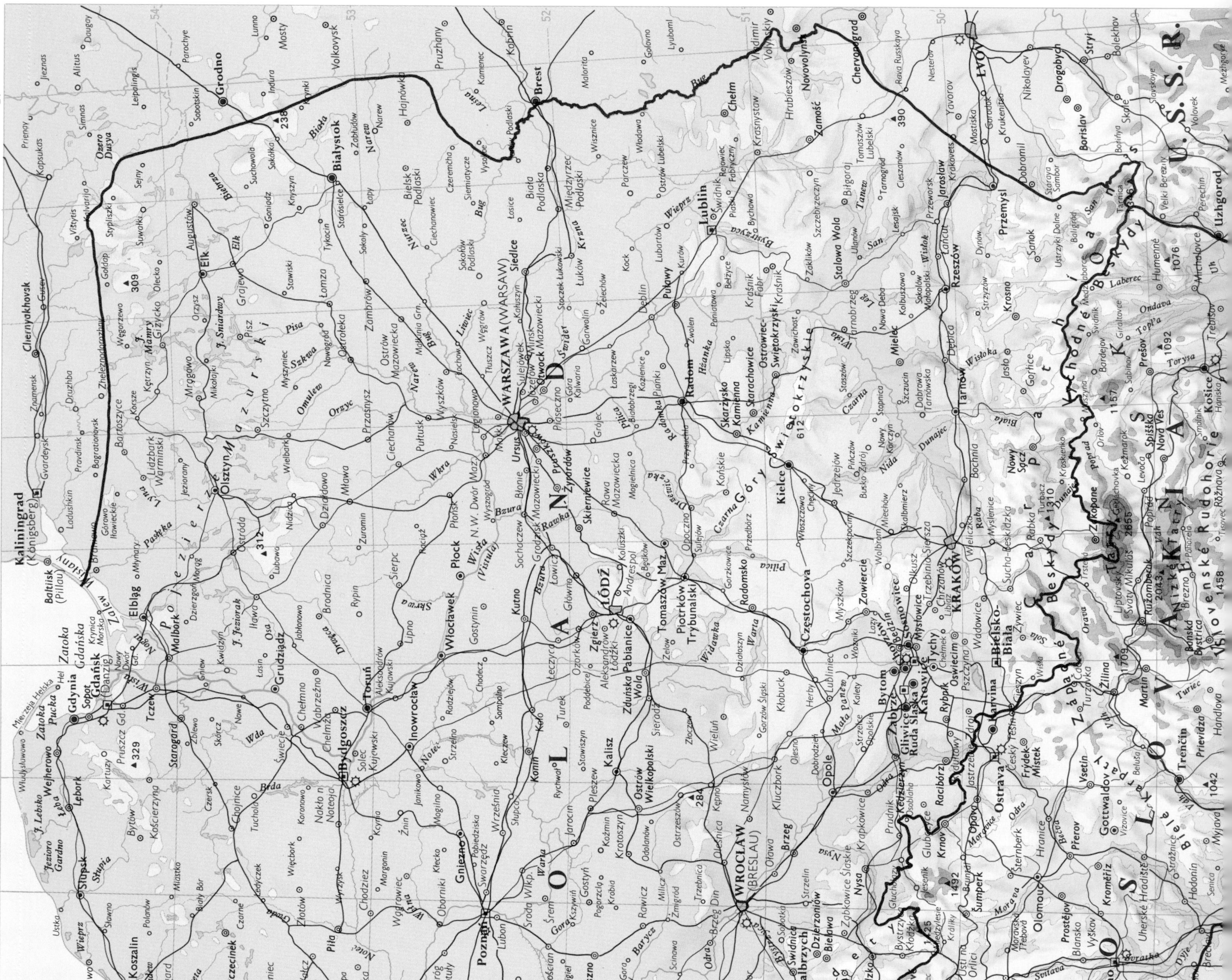
BALTIC SEA
POLAND
EAST GERMANY
CZECHOSLOVAKIA
U.S.S.R.
WEST GERMANY
Kaliningrad (Königsberg)
Gdańsk (Danzig)
Gdynia
Szczecin (Stettin)
Bydgoszcz
Toruń
Poznań
Łódź
WARSZAWA (WARSAW)
Białystok
Brest
Grodno
Lublin
Kraków
Katowice
Wrocław (BRESLAU)
Częstochowa
Kielce
Radom
Lvov
BERLIN
Potsdam
Frankfurt
Rostock
Stralsund
DRESDEN
LEIPZIG
Karl-Marx-Stadt (Chemnitz)
PRAHA (PRAGUE)
Plzeň
Brno
Ostrava
Olomouc
Košice
Uzhgorod
Wisła (Vistula)
Odra
Warta
Bug
Labe (Elbe)
Vltava
Sudety
Karpaty
Vysoké Tatry
Nízke Tatry
Bayerischer Wald

Kilometers 0 40 80 120 160 200 Km.

Statute Miles 0 40 80 120 160 200 Mi.

1:2 800 000

One centimeter represents 28 kilometers
One inch represents approximately 45 miles

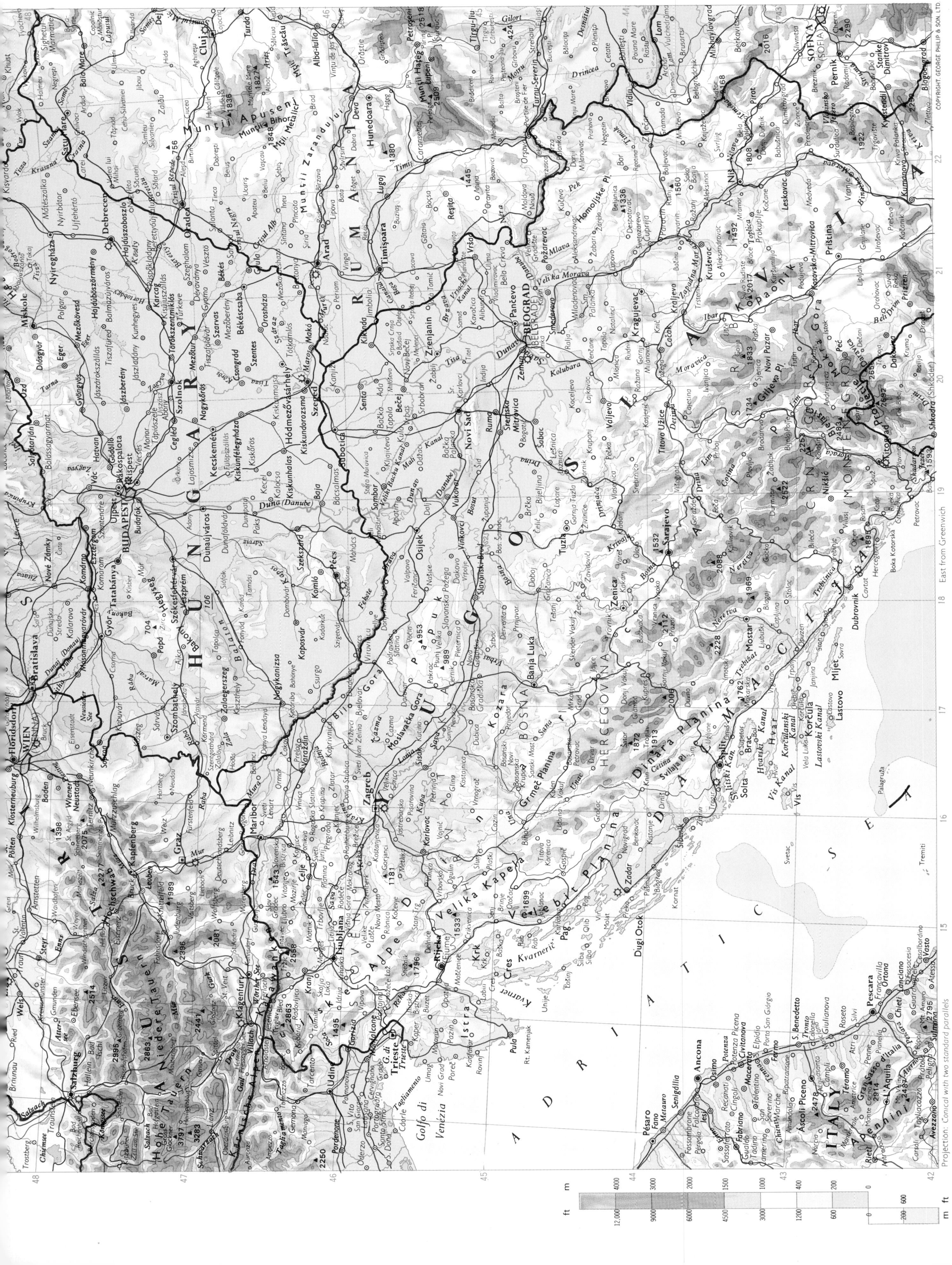
HUNGARY
RUMANIA
YUGOSLAVIA
ITALY
AUSTRIA
ADRIATIC SEA
BUDAPEST
BEOGRAD (BELGRADE)
SOFIA (SOFIJA)
WIEN (VIENNA)
Bratislava
Zagreb
Sarajevo
Ljubljana
Trieste
Debrecen
Szeged
Cluj
Timişoara
Arad
Oradea
Novi Sad
Niš
Skopje
Split
Rijeka
Dubrovnik
Mostar
Banja Luka
Graz
Klagenfurt
Salzburg
Ancona
Pescara
Duna (Danube)
Balaton
Dinara Planina
Velika Kapela
Munţii Apuseni
East from Greenwich
Projection: Conical with two standard parallels
COPYRIGHT, GEORGE PHILIP & SON, LTD.
m ft
4000 12,000
3000 9000
2000 6000
1500 4500
1000 3000
400 1200
200 600
0 0
200 600

UKRAINIAN S.S.R.
MOLDAVIAN S.S.R.
U.S.S.R.
BESSARABIYA
MOLDOVA
TRANSILVANIA
VALAHIA
DOBRUJA
ROMANIA
HUNGARY
BULGARIA
YUGOSLAVIA
SRBIJA
CRNA GORA (MONTENEGRO)
BLACK SEA
Carpaţii Meridionali (Transylvanian Alps)
Munţii Apuseni
Stara Planina
Sredna Gora
BUDAPEST
BUCUREŞTI (BUCHAREST)
BEOGRAD (BELGRADE)
SOFIYA (SOFIA)
Kishinev
Cluj
Iaşi
Constanţa
Varna
Burgas
Craiova
Timişoara
Braşov
Galaţi
Brăila
Ploieşti
Debrecen
Szeged
Novi Sad
Niš
Ruse
Pleven
Dunărea (Danube)
Duna (Danube)
Dunav
Tisa
Prut
Siret
Olt
Mureş

Kilometers 0 40 80 120 160 200 Km.

Statute Miles 0 40 80 120 160 200 Mi.

1:2 800 000

One centimeter represents 28 kilometers
One inch represents approximately 45 miles

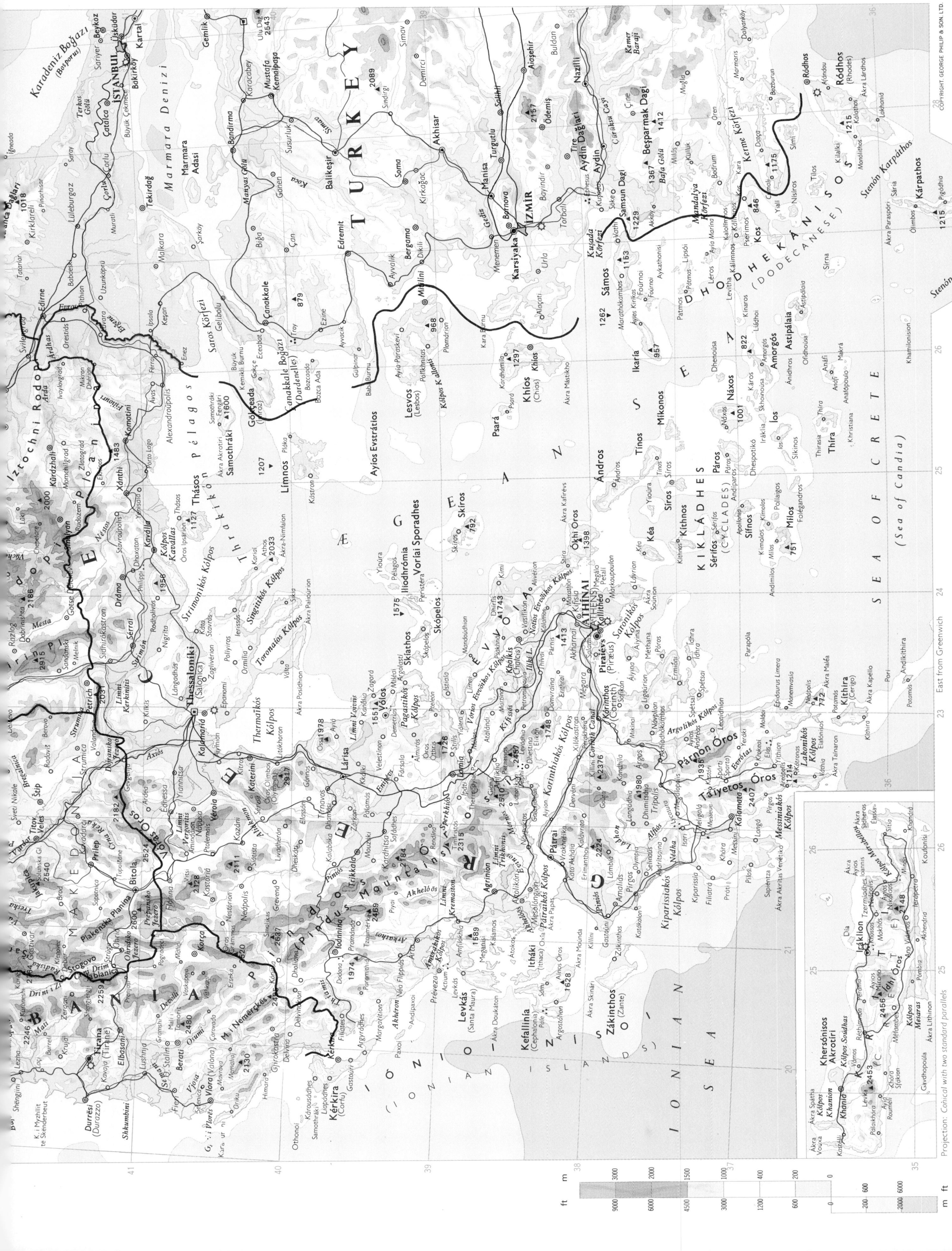
TURKEY
ISTANBUL
Marmara Denizi
Karadeniz Boğazı (Bosporus)
Çanakkale Boğazı (Dardanelles)
IZMIR
Balıkesir
Edirne
Lesvos (Lesbos)
Khíos (Chios)
Sámos
Ikaría
Límnos
Samothráki
Thásos
Thessaloníki (Salonica)
ATHÍNAI (ATHENS)
Piraiévs (Piraeus)
Pátrai
Kérkira (Corfu)
Levkás (Santa Maura)
Kefallinía (Cephalonia)
Itháki (Ithaca)
Zákinthos (Zante)
Kíthira (Cerigo)
Ródhos (Rhodes)
Kárpathos
Kásos
Kos
Náxos
Páros
Mílos
Thíra
Ándros
Tínos
Síros
Mikonos
Amorgós
Astipálaia
Skíros
Skíathos
Skópelos
Vorioi Sporadhes
Évvoia
Lárisa
Vólos
Lamía
Tiranë (Tirana)
Durrësi (Durazzo)
Vlorë (Valona)
Korçë
Elbasani
Bitola
Prilep
Veles
Kavalla
Komotiní
Xánthi
Alexandroúpolis
Tekirdağ
Gelibolu
Bandırma
Akhisar
Manisa
Aydın
ALBANIA
MAKEDONIJA
GREECE
KIKLÁDHES (CYCLADES)
DHODHEKÁNISOS (DODECANESE)
AEGEAN SEA
IONIAN SEA
SEA OF CRETE (Sea of Candia)
Thrakikón Pélagos
Khaniá
Iráklion
KRÍTI
East from Greenwich
Projection: Conical with two standard parallels
m ft
3000 9000
2000 6000
1500 4500
1000 3000
400 1200
200 600
0 0
200 600
2000 6000

G. of Finland
BALTIC SEA
ESTONIAN S.S.R.
LATVIAN S.S.R.
LITHUANIAN S.S.R.
BYELORUSSIAN S.S.R.
(WHITE RUSSIA)
RUSSIAN SOVIET
UKRAINIAN S.S.R.
POLAND
CZECHOSLOVAKIA
R.S.F.S.R.
Carpathians
LENINGRAD
Kronshtadt
Tallinn
Hiiumaa (Khiuma)
Saaremaa (Sarema)
Gotland
Gotska Sandön
Kingisepp (Kuressaare)
Parnu
Tartu
Narva
Kohtla Jarve
Chudskoye Ozero
Pskov
Luga
Novgorod
Oz. Ilmen
Staraya Russa
Valdayskaya Vozvyshennost
Bologoye
Vyshniy Volochek
Torzhok
Rzhev
Vyazma
Rizhskiy Zaliv (Gulf of Riga)
Ruhnu
Ventspils
Riga
Liepaja
Jelgava
Valga
Rezekne
Daugavpils
Velikiye Luki
Nevel
Klaipeda
Siauliai
Panevezys
Kaunas
Kaliningrad
Chernyakhovsk
Vilnius
Molodechno
Polotsk
Novopolotsk
Vitebsk
Orsha
Smolensk
Minsk
Borisov
Mogilev
Grodno
Bialystok
WARSZAWA (Warsaw)
Siedlce
Brest
Baranovichi
Bobruysk
Zhlobin
Gomel
Krichev
Roslavl
Bryansk
Sukhinichi
Kirov
Pinsk
Luninets
Kalinkovichi
Mozyr
Polesye (Pripet Marshes)
Pripyat (Pripet)
Kovel
Lublin
Radom
Lutsk
Rovno
Chernigov
Konotop
Korosten
Zhitomir
KIYEV (Kiev)
Berdichev
Belaya Tserkov
Lvov
Przemysl
Drogobych
Ternopol
Khmelnitskiy
Vinnitsa
Ivano-Frankovsk (Stanislav)
Uzhgorod
Kamenets-Podolskiy
Cherkassy
Kremenchug
Poltava
Sumy
Priluki
Nezhin
Shostka
Dnepr
Desna
Kiyevskoye Vdkhr.
Kremenchugskoye Vdkhr.
ft m
3000 1000
1200 400
600 200
0 0
200 600
m ft
20
22
24
26
28
30
32
34
58
56
54
52
50
East from Greenwich

Projection: Conical with two standard parallels

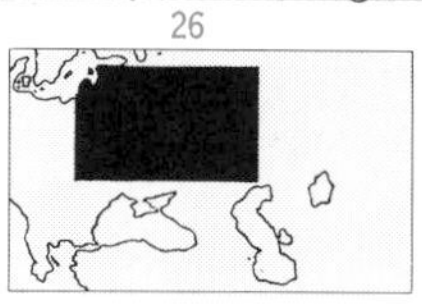

Kilometers 0 40 80 120 160 200 Km.
Statute Miles 0 40 80 120 160 200 Mi.

1:4 000 000

One centimeter represents 40 kilometers
One inch represents approximately 64 miles

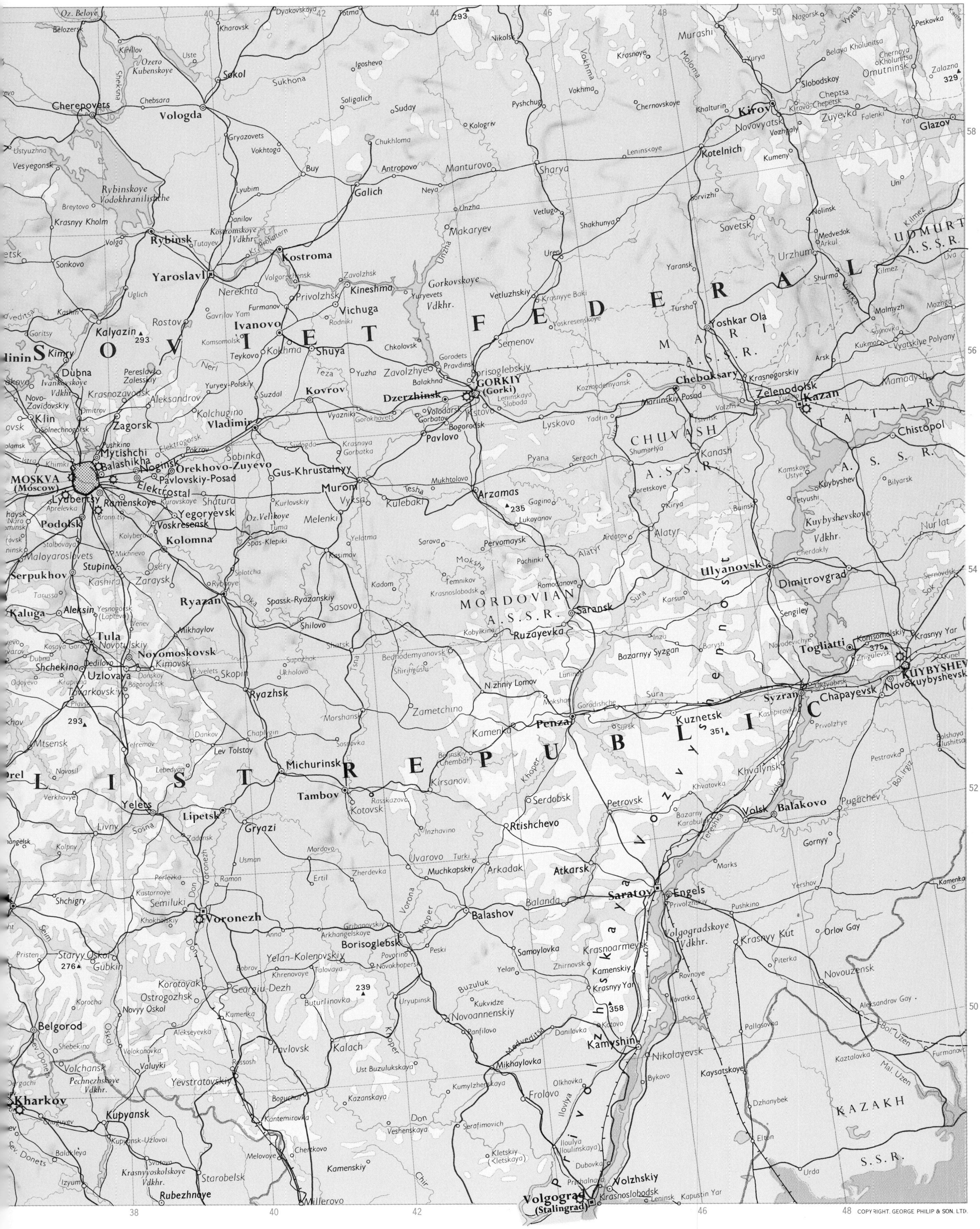

SOVIET FEDERAL SOCIALIST REPUBLIC
MOSKVA (Moscow)
Vologda
Cherepovets
Rybinskoye Vodokhranilishche
Rybinsk
Yaroslavl
Kostroma
Ivanovo
Vladimir
Galich
Sharya
Kotelnich
Kirov
Glazov
Gorkovskoye Vdkhr.
GORKIY (Gorki)
Dzerzhinsk
Kovrov
Murom
Arzamas
Cheboksary
CHUVASH A.S.S.R.
MARI A.S.S.R.
Yoshkar Ola
Kazan
TATAR A.S.S.R.
UDMURT A.S.S.R.
Chistopol
Kuybyshevskoye Vdkhr.
Ulyanovsk
Dimitrovgrad
Togliatti
KUYBYSHEV
Novokuybyshevsk
Syzran
Chapayevsk
Penza
Kuznetsk
Saransk
MORDOVIAN A.S.S.R.
Ruzayevka
Ryazan
Kolomna
Serpukhov
Kaluga
Tula
Novomoskovsk
Uzlovaya
Michurinsk
Tambov
Lipetsk
Yelets
Voronezh
Borisoglebsk
Balashov
Rtishchevo
Atkarsk
Saratov
Engels
Volgogradskoye Vdkhr.
Volsk
Balakovo
Kamyshin
Volgograd (Stalingrad)
Volzhskiy
Belgorod
Kharkov
Kupyansk
Starobelsk
Rubezhnoye
Millerovo
KAZAKH S.S.R.
Privolzhskaya Vozvyshennost

Rovno
Dubno
Lvov
Zhitomir
KIYEV (Kiev)
Nezhin
Bakhmach
Sumy
Belgorod
Kharkov
Priluki
Berdichev
Belaya Tserkov
Khmelnitskiy
Vinnitsa
Ivano-Frankovsk (Stanislav)
Chernovtsy
Kamenets-Podolskiy
Uman
Cherkassy
Kremenchugskoye Vdkhr.
Poltava
Kremenchug
Kirovograd
Dneprodzerzhinsk
Dnepropetrovsk
Pavlograd
Zaporozhye
Krivoy Rog
Nikopol
Donetsk (Stalino)
Makeyevka
Gorlovka
Zhdanov
Melitopol
Berdyansk
Nikolayev
Kherson
Odessa
Kishinev
Beltsy
Tiraspol
Bendery
U K R A I N I A N S. S. R.
M O L D A V I A N S. S. R.
R U M A N I A
Iasi
Bacău
Galaţi
Braila
Ploieşti
BUCUREŞTI (Bucharest)
Constanţa
Ismail
Ruse (Rusčuk)
Varna
Burgas
B U L G A R I A
Kirklareli
Edirne
İstanbul
Üsküdar
İzmit
Adapazari
Bursa
MARMARA DENIZI (Sea of Marmara)
Karadeniz Boğazi (Bosporus)
Zonguldak
Kastamonu
Samsun
Sinop
Amasya
Tokat
Ankara
T U R K
Kuzey Anadolu
Karkinitskiy Zaliv
Krymskiy P.-ov (Crimea)
Dzhankoi
Yevpatoriya
Simferopol
Sevastopol
Yalta
Feodosiya
Kerch
Kerchenskiy Proliv
Anapa
Novorossiysk
AZOVSKOYE MORE (Sea of Azov)
B L A C K S E A
2135
2211

Projection: Conical with two standard parallels

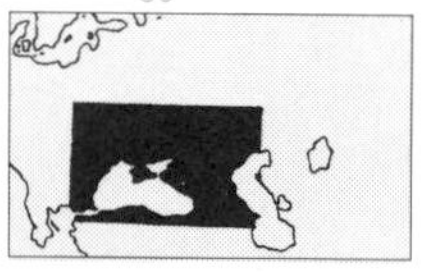

Kilometers 0 40 80 120 160 200 Km.
Statute Miles 0 40 80 120 160 200 Mi.

1:4 000 000

One centimeter represents 40 kilometers
One inch represents approximately 64 miles

Yelan-Kolenovskiy
Povorino
Peski
Samoylovka
Krasnoarmeysk
Zhirnovsk
Krasnyy Kut
Orlov Gay
Oz. Chalkar
Chalkar
Dzhambeyty
Georgiu-Dezh
Ostrogozhsk
Buturlinovka
Uryupinsk
Buzuluk
Yelan
Kamenskiy
Rovnoye
Piterka
Novouzensk
Kushum
Chapayevo
Novoannenskiy
Kukvidze
Volgogradskoye
Vdkhr.
Aleksandrov Gay
Mergenevskiy
Karsha
Ural
Pavlovsk
Kalach
Khoper
Danilovka
Pallasovka
Bol. Uzen
Furmanovo
Bazartobe
Ust Buzulukskaya
Mikhaylovka
Kamyshin
Nikolayevsk
Kazalovka
Mal. Uzen
Antonovo
Kaysatskoye
Kazanskaya
Erolovo
Olkhovka
Bykovo
Kalmykovo
Kantemirovka
Don
Veshenskaya
Serafimovich
Ilovlya
Privolzhskaya
Dzhanybek
Melovoye
Chertkovo
Kletskiy
(Kletskaya)
Ilovlya
(Iloulinskaya)
Elton
Inderborskiy
Starobelsk
Kamenskiy
Dubovka
K A Z A K H
S. S. R.
Chir
Sovetskaya
Prichalnaya
Volzhskiy
Urda
Millerovo
Volgograd
(Stalingrad)
Leninsk
Kapustin Yar
Shungay
Krasnoslobodsk
Kalach na Donu
Surovikino
Zelënyy
Voroshilovgrad
(Lugansk)
Glubokiy
Krasnoarmeysk
Volga
Vladimirovka
Topoli
Kamensk-Shakhtinskiy
Chernyshkovskiy
Verkhniy Baskunchak
Morozovsk
Akhtubinsk
(Petropavlovskiy)
Tsimlyanskoye
Vdkhr.
Makhambet
(Yamankhalinka)
Krasnodon
Krasnyy Luch
Sverdlovsk
Belaya Kalitva
Gukovo
Krasnodonetskaya
Rovenki
Sinegorskiy
Snezhnoye
Novobogatinskoye
Guryev
Tsimlyansk
Kotelnikovo
Novoshakhtinsk
Artemovskiy
Shakhty
Ust-Donetskiy
Konstantinovskiy
Volgodonsk
Obilnoye
Kopanovka
Yenotayevka
Matveyev Kurgan
Tuzlov
Novocherkassk
Dubovskoye
Zavetnoye
Bolshaya Martynovka
Zimovniki
Taganrog
Rostov
Azov
Bataysk
Manych
K A L M Y K
Krasnyy Yar
Ganyushkino
Veselovskoye
Vdkhr.
Kuberle
Mechetinskaya
Zernograd
A. S. S. R.
Astrakhan
Port Katon
Yeya
Proletarskaya
Kushchevskaya
Yegorlykskaya
Remontnoye
Kamyzyak
Gigant
Oz. Manych-
Gudilo
Krasnoye
Salsk
Elista
(Stepnoi)
Ergeni Vozyshennost
Kirovskiy
Peschanokopskoye
Yegorlyk
Leninsk
Priyutnoye
Liman
Pavlovskaya
Kanevskaya
Belaya
Glina
Krasnogvardeyskoye
Divnoye
Kalaus
Prikaspiyskaya Nizmennost
Tikhoretsk
Ipatovo
Kaspiyskiy
C A S P I A N S E A
Timashevsk
Novaleksandrovskaya
Arzgir
Kropotkin
Izobil'nyy
Svetlograd
(Petrovskoye)
O. Kulaly
Mangyshlakskiy
Zaliv
Korenovsk
Blagodarnoye
Beloye Ozero
M. Tyub Karagan
Fort Shevchenko
P-ov. Mangyshlak
Kuma
Ust-Labinsk
Stavropol
Prikumsk
Staryy Biryuzyak
Krasnodar
Armavir
Kuban
Vladimirovka
Tyuleniy
831
Nevinnomyssk
Zelenokumsk
(Vorontsovo-Aleksandrovskoye)
Kurganinsk
(Kurgannaya)
Bryanskoye
Maykop
Labinsk
Urup
Kursavka
O. Chechen
Shevchenko
Apsheronsk
Khadyzhensk
Neftegorsk
Mineralnyye Vody
Aleksandriyskaya
Cherkessk
Lopatin
Dakhovskaya
Yessentuki
Pyatigorsk
Kizlyar
Terek
Kislovodsk
Prokhladnyy
Mozdok
CHECHENO-
Karachayevsk
Mayskiy
INGUSH
Gudermes
Sochi
Teberda
Nalchik
Nartkala
Malgobek
Sulak
Matsesta
Tyrnyauz
KABARDINO-
BALKAR
A.S.S.R.
Elkhotovo
Groznyy
Khasavyurt
Kizil Yurt
Makhachkala
Adler
ABKHAZ
A.S.S.R.
Elbrus
5633
Kodori
Beslan
A.S.S.R.
Kumtorkala
Gagra
5203
N. OSSETIAN
A.S.S.R.
Ordzhonikidze
Kaspiysk
Buynaksk
Sayasan
Gudauta
Novyy Afon
Sukhumi
Inguri
Balta
Sudon
Izberbash
Tkvarcheli
Kazbek
5047
Tebulos
4492
Agvali
Khunzakh
Novokayakent
Ochamchire
Tsageri
Rioni
Oni
Gali
Dzhvari
Zugdidi
Akusha
Dagestanskiye Ogni
G E O R G I A
800
Derbent
Anaklia
Mikha-Tskhakaya
Sachkhere
Tkibuli
Chiatura
Tskhinvali
(Staliniri)
Dusheti
Kutaisi
Zestafoni
Poti
Samtredia
Khashuri
Gori
Telavi
Kvareli
Lagodekhi
Kasumkent
Mikhaylovka
Kobuleti
Makharadze
S. S. R.
Kaspi
Mtskheta
Tbilisi
Signakhi
Gurdzhaani
Zakataly
Samur
Akhty
Khachmas
Kuba
Divichi
Batumi
ADZHAR
A.S.S.R.
Khulo
Borzhomi
Akhaltsikhe
Vale
Khrami
Marneuli
Shaumyani
Rustavi
Tsiteli Tskaro
Mirzaani
Iori
Alazan
Sheki
(Nukha)
Mingechaurskoye
Vdkhr.
Kutkashen
Bazar Dyuzi
4466
Baba dag
3629
Siazan
Hopa
Borcka
Akhalkalaki
Akstafa
Pazar
Artvin
Ardahan
Cildir
Alaverdi
Tauz
Shamkhor
Kura
Mingechaur
Agdash
Geokchay
Shemakha
Sumgait
Mashtaga
O. Artem
Zhiloy
Görele
Akçaabat
Ardanuc
Kisir
3192
Kirovakan
Kirovabad
Chanlar
Yevlakh
Lyaki
Tirebolu
Trabzon
Sürmene
Rize
Kaçkar
3937
Leninakan
Dilizhan
Dashkesan
A Z E R B A I J A N
BAKU
Harsit
Artik
Aragats
4090
Sevan
Charentsavan
Ozero
Sevan
Mir-Bashir
Barda
S.S.R.
Kyurdamir
Kazi Magomed
Çakirgol
3063
Oltu
Selim
Kars
A R M E N I A N
Kamo
Terter
Alyata
Gümüşane
Çoruh
Ispir
Narman
Sarikamiş
Digor
S.S.R.
Agdzhabedi
Sabirabad
Ali-Bayramly
Alucra
Bayburt
Tortum
Aras
Kagizman
Echmiadzin
Yerevan
Martuni
Agdam
Imishly
Karachala
M. Byandovan
Bolshoy Kavkaz
Caucasus
Dogu Karadeniz Daglari
Kavkaz Mountains
-28
40
42
44
46
48
50
52

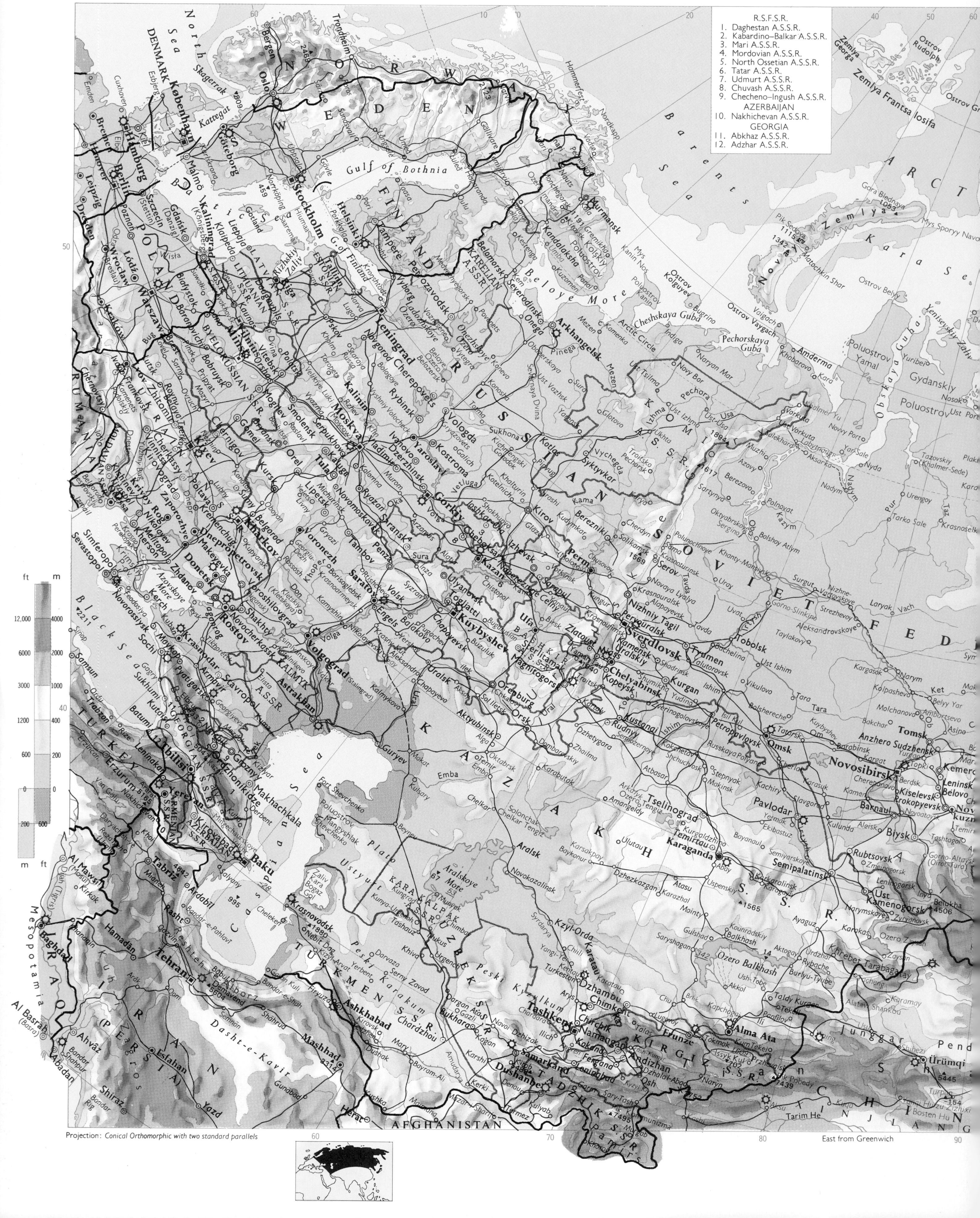
R.S.F.S.R.
1. Daghestan A.S.S.R.
2. Kabardino–Balkar A.S.S.R.
3. Mari A.S.S.R.
4. Mordovian A.S.S.R.
5. North Ossetian A.S.S.R.
6. Tatar A.S.S.R.
7. Udmurt A.S.S.R.
8. Chuvash A.S.S.R.
9. Checheno–Ingush A.S.S.R.
AZERBAIJAN
10. Nakhichevan A.S.S.R.
GEORGIA
11. Abkhaz A.S.S.R.
12. Adzhar A.S.S.R.
ft
m
12,000
4000
6000
2000
3000
1000
1200
400
600
200
0
0
200
600
m
ft
North Sea
NORWAY
SWEDEN
FINLAND
DENMARK
POLAND
Gulf of Bothnia
Barents Sea
Beloye More
Zemlya Frantsa Iosifa
Novaya Zemlya
Kara Sea
RUSSIAN S.F.S.R.
KOMI A.S.S.R.
KARELIAN A.S.S.R.
BYELORUSSIAN S.S.R.
UKRAINIAN S.S.R.
KAZAKH S.S.R.
UZBEK S.S.R.
TURKMEN S.S.R.
KIRGIZ S.S.R.
TADZHIK S.S.R.
KARA-KALPAK A.S.S.R.
BASHKIR A.S.S.R.
KALMYK A.S.S.R.
GEORGIAN S.S.R.
ARMENIAN S.S.R.
AZERBAIJAN S.S.R.
Black Sea
Caspian Sea
Aral'skoye More
TURKEY
IRAN (PERSIA)
IRAQ
AFGHANISTAN
SINKIANG
Mesopotamia
Dasht-e-Kavir
Peski Karakum
Peski Kyzylkum
Ustyurt Plato
Moskva (Moscow)
Leningrad
Kiyev
Minsk
Riga
Tallinn
Vilnius
Kishinev
Tbilisi
Yerevan
Baku
Ashkhabad
Tashkent
Dushanbe
Frunze
Alma Ata
Sverdlovsk
Novosibirsk
Omsk
Chelyabinsk
Kuybyshev
Volgograd
Gorkiy
Kazan
Perm
Arkhangelsk
Murmansk
Karaganda
Tselinograd
Stockholm
Helsinki
Warszawa
København
Tehran
Baghdad
Ürümqi
East from Greenwich
Projection: Conical Orthomorphic with two standard parallels

Kilometers 0 200 400 600 800 Km.
Statute Miles 0 200 400 600 800 Mi.

1:16 000 000

One centimeter represents 160 kilometers
One inch represents approximately 250 miles

Mys Dezhneva (East C.)
Chukotskoye More
Chukotskiy Khrebet
Anadyrskiy Zaliv
St. Lawrence I. (U.S.A.)
Ostrov Vrangelya
East Siberian Sea
Ostrov Henrietta
Ostrov Jeannette
Ostrova Delong
Novosibirskiye Ostrova
Ostrov Kotelnyy
Lyakhovskiye Ostrova
Proliv Dmitriya Lapteva
Laptev Sea
OCEAN
Ostrov Komsomolets
Ostrov Oktyabrskoy Revolyutsii
Ostrov Bolshevik
Severnaya Zemlya
Proliv Vilskitskogo
Poluostrov Taymyr
Gory Byrranga
Nordvik
Tiksi
Verkhoyansk
Verkhoyanskiy Khrebet
Khrebet Cherskogo
Srednekolymsk
Koryakskiy Khrebet
Poluostrov Kamchatka
Petropavlovsk-Kamchatskiy
Bering Sea
Magadan
Okhotsk
Sea of Okhotsk
YAKUT A.S.S.R.
Yakutsk
Vilyuysk
Olekminsk
Arctic Circle
Stanovoy Khrebet
Dzhugdzhur
Nikolayevsk-na-Amure
Sakhalin
Yuzhno-Sakhalinsk
Sovetskaya Gavan
Komsomolsk
Khabarovsk
Blagoveshchensk
Vladivostok
Nakhodka
Sikhote Alin
Kurilskiye Ostrova
Hokkaido
Sapporo
Hakodate
Honshu
Sea of Japan
JAPAN
Krasnoyarsk
Nizhneudinsk
Bratsk
Kirensk
Irkutsk
Angarsk
Ulan Ude
BURYAT A.S.S.R.
Ozero Baykal
Chita
Khrebet Yablonovyy
Vostochnyy Sayan
Ulaanbaatar (Ulan Bator)
MONGOLIA
Hangayn Nuruu
Hentiyn Nuruu
GOBI
Harbin
Qiqihar
Da Hinggan Ling
Changchun
Jilin
Shenyang
Fushun
Anshan
Dandong
Beijing
Zhangjiakou
Baotou
Yingkou
Lüda
P'yongyang
NORTH KOREA
SOUTH KOREA
Soul
Inch'on
Taejon
Pusan
Chongjin
Wonsan
Boundaries of U.S.S.R.
Boundaries of S.S.R.
Boundaries of A.S.S.R.

Kilometers 400 0 400 800 1200 1600 Km.
Statute Miles 400 0 400 800 1200 1600 Mi.

1:40 000 000

One centimeter represents 400 kilometers
One inch represents approximately 640 miles

COPYRIGHT, GEORGE PHILIP & SON, LTD.
P A C I F I C O C E A N
I N D I A N O C E A N
A R C T I C O C E A N
Aleutian Is.
Bering Sea
Bering Str.
C. Dezhneva
Kamchatka Peninsula
Klyuchevsk Vol. 4850
Sea of Okhotsk
Sredinny Ra.
Kuril Is.
Sakhalin
La Perouse Str.
Hokkaido
Honshu
Japan
Shikoku
Kyushu
Bonin Is.
Sea of Japan
Korea Str.
Korea
Yellow Sea
East China Sea
Ryukyu Is.
Formosa
Tropic of Cancer
Guam
Caroline Is.
Pelew Is.
Philippine Is.
Luzon
Mindanao
Cape Johnson Deep 10497
Halmahera
Moluccas
Ceram
Banda Sea
Arafura Sea
New Guinea
Australia
Timor
Flores
Celebes
Celebes Sea
Sulu Sea
Makasar Strait
Borneo
Kinabalu 4101
Palawan
South China Sea
Hainan
G. of Tonkin
Java Sea
Java
Bali
Sunda Str.
East Indies
Malay Peninsula
G. of Siam
Mekong
Menam
Str. of Malacca
Sumatra
Sunda Is.
Nicobar Is.
Andaman Is.
Bay of Bengal
Ceylon
Palk Strait
Equator
Chagos Arch.
Maldive Is.
Laccadive Is.
C. Comorin
Gulf of Mannar
Eastern Ghats
Western Ghats
Deccan
Godavari
Krishna
Narmada
India
Thar
Indus
Ganga
Yamuna
Sutlej
Brahmaputra
Tsangpo
Everest 8848
Himalaya
Plateau of Tibet
Kunlun Shan
Karakoram Ra.
8611
Hindu Kush
Pamirs
Communism Pk. 7495
Tien Shan
Takla Makan
Tarim Basin
Tarim
Lop Nor
Turfan Basin
Koko Nor
Nan Shan
China
Yangtze Kiang
Hwang Ho
Si-kiang
Hong (Red)
Salween
Irrawaddy
Great Plain of China
Po Hai
Gobi
Plateau of Mongolia
Great Khingan Mts.
Manchurian Plain
Sungari
Amur
Sikhote Alin Ra.
Stanovoy Ra.
Yablonovy Ra.
L. Baikal
Selenga
Sayan Mts.
Angara
Altai
Belukha 4506
Central Siberian Plateau
Lower Tunguska
Lena
Aldan
Olenek
Kotuy
Verkhoyansk Range
Indigirka
Kolyma
Gydan Ra. (Kolyma)
Wrangel I.
New Siberian Is.
Laptev Sea
Chelyuskin
Taimyr Peninsula
Severnaya Zemlya
Yenisei
Ob
Irtysh
Tobol
West Siberian Plain
Kara Sea
Novaya Zemlya
Narodnaya 1894
Ural Mountains
1640
Ural
Steppes
Turanian Plain
Syr Darya
Amu Darya
Aral Sea
L. Balkhash
Ili
Chu
Sulaiman Ra.
Helmand
Hari Rud
Plateau of Iran
Elburz Mts.
Demavend 5604
Great Salt Desert
Zagros
G. of Oman
Persian Gulf
Arabia
Ar Rub' al Khali
G. of Aden
Socotra
Ras Asir (C. Guardafui)
Arabian Sea
Seychelles
Amirantes
Somali Peninsula
Red Sea
Sinai Pen.
Suez Canal
Dead Sea
Syrian Desert
Mesopotamia
Tigris
Euphrates
Ararat 5165
Caucasus
Elbrus 5633
Caspian Sea
Volga
Don
Dnepr
Black Sea
Bosporus
Anatolia
Taurus Mts.
Cyprus
Mediterranean Sea
Nile
Libyan Desert
Lake Victoria
Adriatic Sea
Central Russian Uplands
North European Plain
Carpathians
Danube
Vistula
Oder
Elbe
Rhine
Baltic Sea
Finland
Scandinavia
White Sea
Kola Pen.
N. Dvina
Kolguyev I.
Barents Sea
Svalbard
North Cape
Arctic Circle
Greenland
Iceland
British Isles
North Sea
East from Greenwich
Projection: Bonne
m ft

Kilometers 0 400 800 1200 1600 2000 Km.
Statute Miles 0 400 800 1200 1600 2000 Mi

1:40 000 000

One centimeter represents 400 kilometers
One inch represents approximately 640 miles

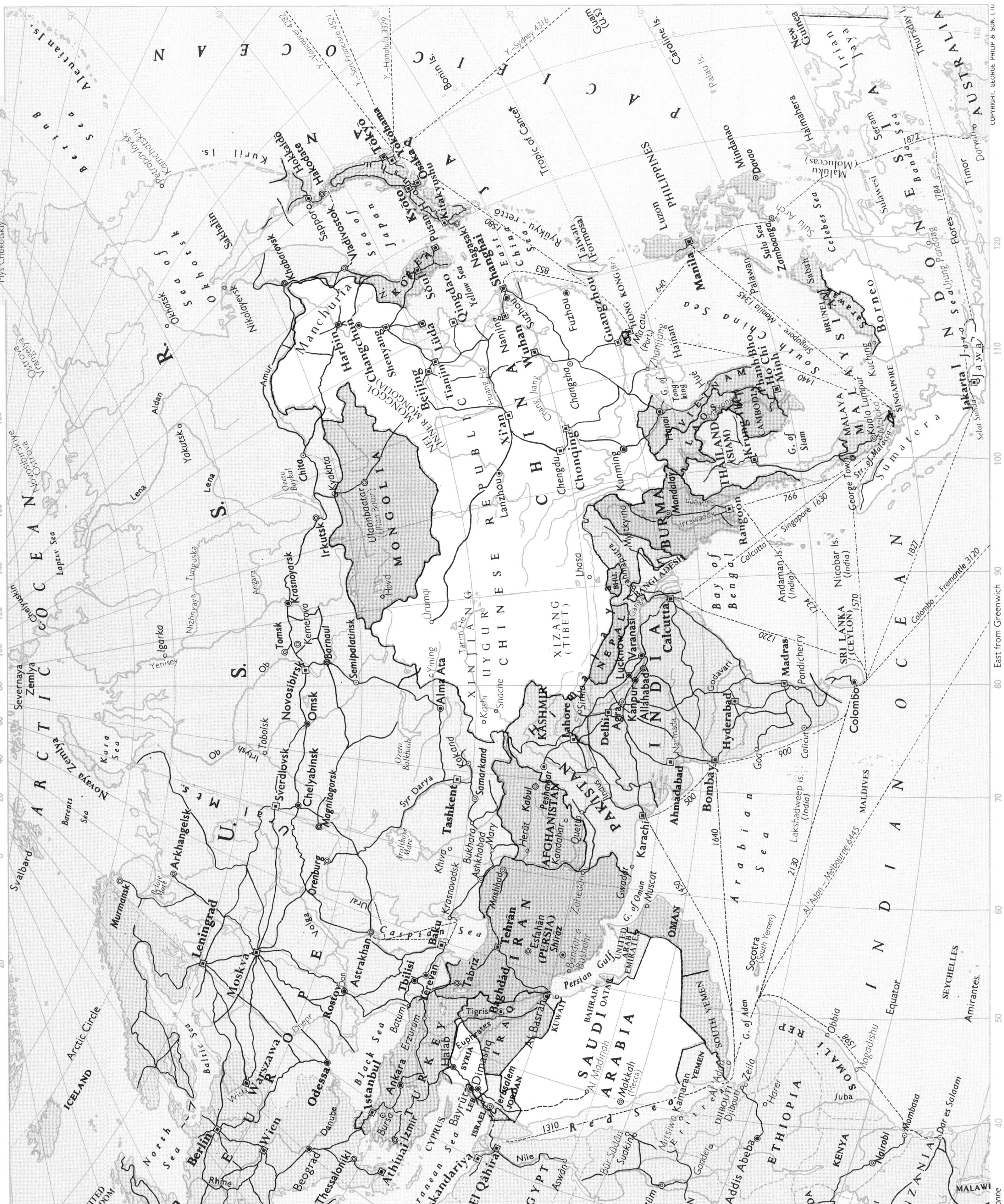

ARCTIC OCEAN
PACIFIC OCEAN
INDIAN OCEAN
U. S. S. R.
CHINESE PEOPLE'S REPUBLIC
CHINA
MONGOLIA
INDIA
PAKISTAN
AFGHANISTAN
IRAN (PERSIA)
IRAQ
SAUDI ARABIA
TURKEY
SYRIA
ISRAEL
JORDAN
KUWAIT
BAHRAIN
QATAR
UNITED ARAB EMIRATES
OMAN
YEMEN
SOUTH YEMEN
NEPAL
BHUTAN
BANGLADESH
BURMA
THAILAND (SIAM)
LAOS
CAMBODIA
VIETNAM
MALAYSIA
SINGAPORE
BRUNEI
INDONESIA
PHILIPPINES
JAPAN
KOREA
TAIWAN (FORMOSA)
SRI LANKA (CEYLON)
MALDIVES
SEYCHELLES
KASHMIR
XIZANG (TIBET)
XINJIANG UYGUR
INNER MONGOLIA (NEI MONGOL)
Manchuria
EUROPE
AFRICA
EGYPT
LIBYA
SUDAN
ETHIOPIA
SOMALI REP.
KENYA
TANZANIA
UGANDA
RWANDA
BURUNDI
ZAIRE
ZAMBIA
MALAWI
DJIBOUTI
CYPRUS
ICELAND
UNITED KINGDOM
AUSTRALIA
New Guinea
Irian Jaya
Borneo
Sumatera
Jawa
Sulawesi
Mindanao
Luzon
Hokkaido
Sakhalin
Kuril Is.
Aleutian Is.
Bonin Is.
Caroline Is.
Guam (U.S.)
Palau Is.
Andaman Is. (India)
Nicobar Is. (India)
Lakshadweep Is. (India)
Socotra (South Yemen)
Amirantes
Novaya Zemlya
Severnaya Zemlya
Svalbard
Bering Sea
Sea of Okhotsk
Sea of Japan
Yellow Sea
East China Sea
South China Sea
Sulu Sea
Celebes Sea
Banda Sea
Java Sea
Bay of Bengal
Arabian Sea
Red Sea
Persian Gulf
G. of Oman
G. of Aden
Caspian Sea
Black Sea
Mediterranean Sea
Baltic Sea
North Sea
Kara Sea
Barents Sea
Laptev Sea
Aral'skoye More
Ozero Balkhash
Ozero Baykal
G. of Siam
G. of Tongking
Str. of Malacca
Tropic of Cancer
Arctic Circle
Equator
Beijing
Shanghai
Tianjin
Wuhan
Chongqing
Guangzhou
Xi'an
Lanzhou
Chengdu
Kunming
Harbin
Changchun
Shenyang
Lüda
Qingdao
Nanjing
Suzhou
Fuzhou
Changsha
Lhasa
Ürümqi
Yining
Kashi
Shache
Ulaanbaatar (Ulan Bator)
Hovd
Tokyo
Yokohama
Osaka
Kyoto
Kitakyushu
Nagasaki
Sapporo
Hakodate
Seoul
Pusan
Vladivostok
Khabarovsk
Nikolayevsk
Okhotsk
Petropavlovsk-Kamchatskiy
Yakutsk
Chita
Irkutsk
Krasnoyarsk
Novosibirsk
Omsk
Tomsk
Barnaul
Kemerovo
Semipalatinsk
Alma Ata
Tashkent
Samarkand
Kokand
Ashkhabad
Bukhara
Khiva
Mary
Krasnovodsk
Sverdlovsk
Chelyabinsk
Magnitogorsk
Orenburg
Tobolsk
Igarka
Arkhangelsk
Murmansk
Leningrad
Moskva
Rostov
Astrakhan
Baku
Tbilisi
Yerevan
Odessa
Istanbul
Ankara
Izmir
Bursa
Erzurum
Batumi
Halab
Dimashq
Bayrut
Jerusalem
Baghdad
Al Basrah
Tabriz
Tehran
Esfahan
Shiraz
Mashhad
Bandar e Bushehr
Zahedan
Herat
Kabul
Kandahar
Peshawar
Quetta
Karachi
Lahore
Delhi
Agra
Kanpur
Lucknow
Allahabad
Varanasi
Calcutta
Ahmadabad
Bombay
Hyderabad
Madras
Pondicherry
Goa
Calicut
Colombo
Rangoon
Mandalay
Myitkyina
Hanoi
Hue
Ho Chi Minh
Krung Thep
Kuala Lumpur
George Town
Melaka
Jakarta
Manila
Davao
Zamboanga
Kuching
Ujung Pandang
Macau (Port.)
HONG KONG (Br.)
Zhanjiang
Hainan
Muscat
Gwadar
Al Madinah
Makkah (Mecca)
Aden
Kamaran
Zeila
Djibouti
Harer
Addis Abeba
Mogadishu
Obbia
Mombasa
Nairobi
Dar es Salaam
Kigoma
Kampala
Juba
El Khartum
El Obeid
Suakin
Bur Sudan
Aswan
El Qahira
El Iskandariya
Athinai
Thessaloniki
Beograd
Wien
Warszawa
Berlin
Paris
London
Roma
Amur
Lena
Yenisey
Ob
Irtysh
Angara
Tunguska
Aldan
Volga
Ural
Don
Dnepr
Danube
Rhine
Wisla
Nile
Tigris
Euphrates
Indus
Ganges
Brahmaputra
Irrawaddy
Mekong
Chang Jiang
Huang He
Tarim He
Syr Darya
Godavari
Narmada
Calcutta - Singapore 1630
Colombo - Fremantle 3120
Al 'Adan - Melbourne 6445
Singapore - Manila 1345
Y - Sydney 4316
Y - Honolulu 3379
Y - San Francisco 4521
Y - Vancouver 4282
East from Greenwich
Projection: Bonne
COPYRIGHT. GEORGE PHILIP & SON. LTD.

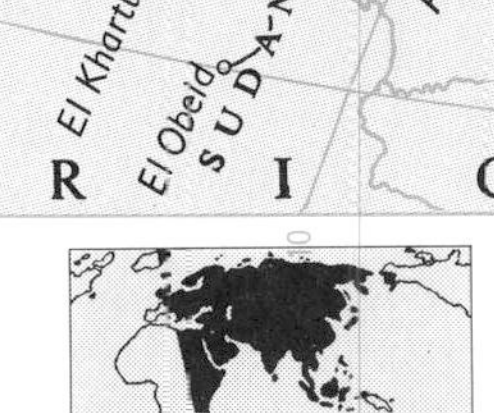

ISRAEL AND WEST JORDAN

Kilometers 0 10 20 30 40 50 Km.
Statute Miles 0 10 20 30 40 50 Mi.

1:800 000

One centimeter represents 8 kilometers
One inch represents approximately 12 miles

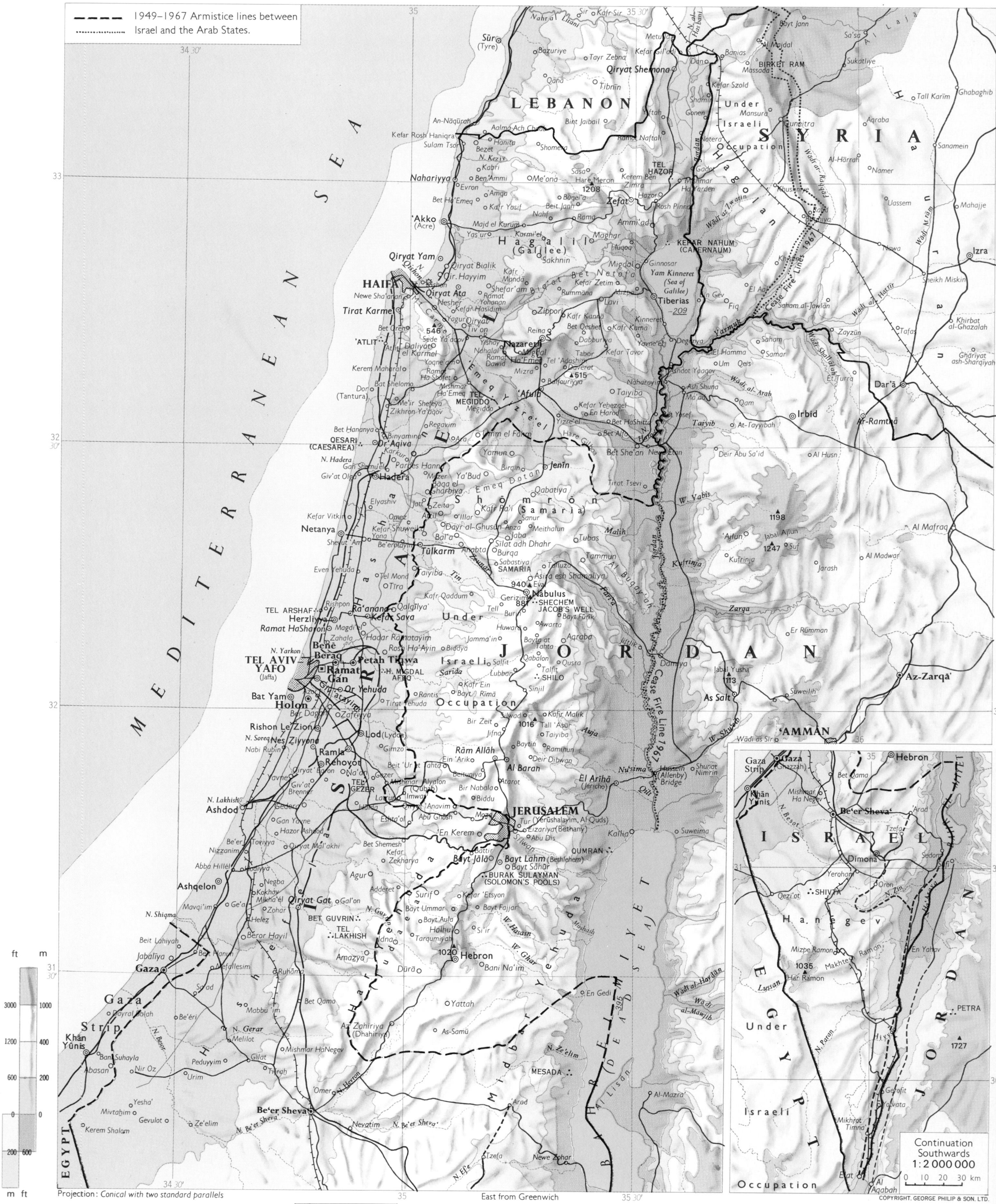
1949–1967 Armistice lines between
Israel and the Arab States.
MEDITERRANEAN SEA
LEBANON
SYRIA
JORDAN
ISRAEL
Under Israeli Occupation
Ṣūr (Tyre)
Qiryat Shemona
Nahariyya
'Akko (Acre)
HAIFA
Tiberias
Yam Kinneret (Sea of Galilee)
Nazareth
Hagalil (Galilee)
Netanya
Ṭūlkarm
Jenīn
Nablus
Shomron (Samaria)
TEL AVIV YAFO (Jaffa)
Ramat Gan
Holon
Ramla
Lod (Lydda)
Ashdod
Ashqelon
Gaza
Gaza Strip
Khān Yūnis
JERUSALEM
Bayt Lahm (Bethlehem)
Hebron
Be'er Sheva
Irbid
Dar'ā
Az-Zarqā'
'AMMAN
As Salt
Cease Fire Line 1967
BAHR LUT (DEAD SEA)
Continuation Southwards
1:2 000 000
Dimona
Elat
Al 'Aqabah
EGYPT
Hanegev
Projection: Conical with two standard parallels
East from Greenwich
COPYRIGHT, GEORGE PHILIP & SON, LTD.

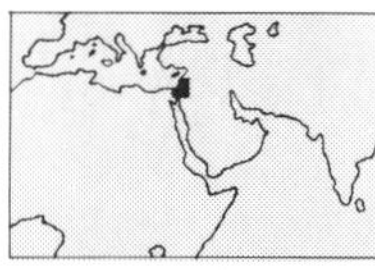

Kilometers 0 100 200 300 400 500 600 Km.
Statute Miles 0 100 200 300 400 500 600 Mi.

1:12 000 000
One centimeter represents 120 kilometers
One inch represents approximately 190 miles

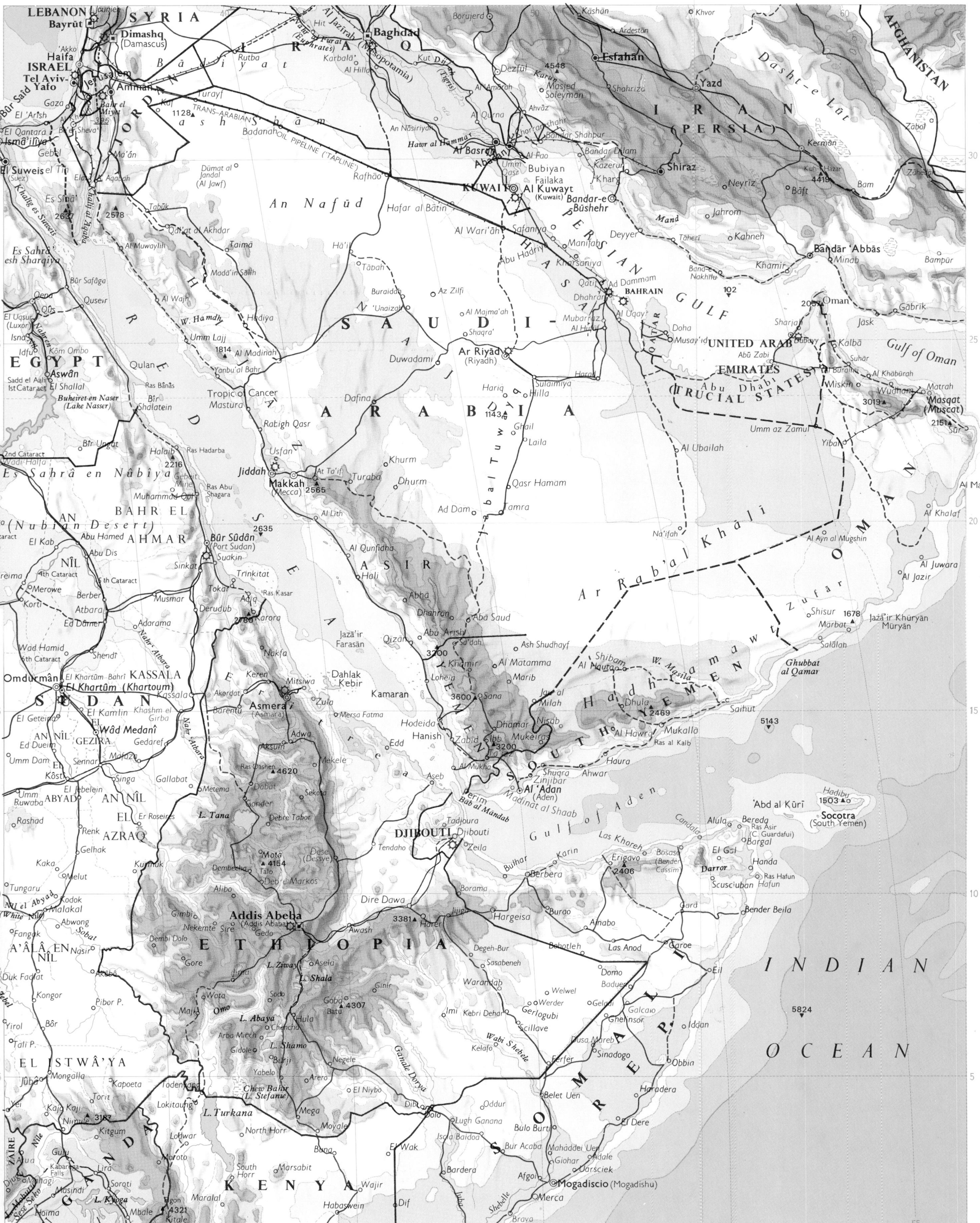

LEBANON
Bayrūt
SYRIA
Dimashq (Damascus)
ISRAEL
Haifa
Tel Aviv-Yafo
Jerusalem
'Ammān
JORDAN
IRAQ
Baghdād
Al Jazīrah (Mesopotamia)
Karbalā'
Kut
Al Hillah
Rutba
Bādiyat ash Shām
Turayf
TRANS-ARABIAN OIL PIPELINE ('TAPLINE')
Badanah
Rafhā'
An Nafūd
Dūmat al Jandal (Al Jawf)
Hafar al Bātin
Al Basrah
Abādān
KUWAIT
Al Kuwayt (Kuwait)
Bubiyan
Failaka
IRAN (PERSIA)
Esfahān
Yazd
Shīrāz
Kermān
Bandar 'Abbās
Dasht-e Lūt
AFGHANISTAN
Bandar-e Būshehr
PERSIAN GULF
BAHRAIN
Ad Dammam
QATAR
Doha
UNITED ARAB EMIRATES
Abū Zabi
Abu Dhabi
(TRUCIAL STATES)
Sharjah
Dubayy
Oman
Gulf of Oman
Masqat (Muscat)
Sūr
Al Masirah
OMAN
Rub' al Khali
Zufār
Salālah
Ghubbat al Qamar
SAUDI ARABIA
Ar Riyād (Riyadh)
Hā'il
Buraidah
'Unaizah
Az Zilfi
Al Majma'ah
Shaqra'
Duwadami
Dafina
Tabūk
Taimā
Madā'in Sālih
Al Wajh
Umm Lajj
Al Madīnah
Yanbu' al Bahr
Tropic of Cancer
Rabigh
Jiddah
Makkah (Mecca)
At Tā'if
Turaba
Al Lith
Al Qunfidha
ASIR
Abha
Abā Saud
Jazā'ir Farasān
Qizān
Sa'dah
Jabal Tuwaiq
Al Hufūf
Qasr Hamam
Tamra
Ad Dam
Khurm
Dhurm
Laila
Sulaimiya
Hilla
HEJAZ
NEJD
YEMEN
San'a
Hodeida
Marib
Al Mukha
Ta'izz
Ibb
SOUTH YEMEN
Al 'Adan (Aden)
Mukalla
Hadhramawt
Shibam
Sayhut
Gulf of Aden
Bab al Mandab
Perim
Socotra (South Yemen)
'Abd al Kūrī
RED SEA
EGYPT
Bûr Sa'îd
Ismâ'ilîya
El Suweis (Suez)
Es Sînâ'
Aswân
Buheiret en Naser (Lake Nasser)
Es Sahrâ' esh Sharqîya
Es Sahrâ' en Nûbîya
(Nubian Desert)
BAHR EL AHMAR
Bûr Sûdân (Port Sudan)
Suakin
Tokar
SUDAN
El Khartûm (Khartoum)
Omdurmân
KASSALA
Kassala
Atbara
Berber
Wad Medanî
GEZIRA
Sennar
BLUE NILE
AN NÎL EL AZRAQ
Malakal
EL ISTWÂ'YA
Jûba
ERITREA
Asmera (Asmara)
Mitsiwa
Keren
Aksum
ETHIOPIA
Addis Abeba (Addis Ababa)
L. Tana
Gonder
Dese (Dessye)
Dire Dawa
Harer
Jijiga
L. Ziway
L. Shala
L. Abaya
L. Shamo
Chew Bahir (L. Stefanie)
L. Turkana
DJIBOUTI
Djibouti
Zeila
Berbera
Hargeisa
SOMALI REPUBLIC
Mogadiscio (Mogadishu)
Obbia
Eil
Kismayu
Merca
KENYA
UGANDA
L. Kyoga
ZAIRE
INDIAN OCEAN

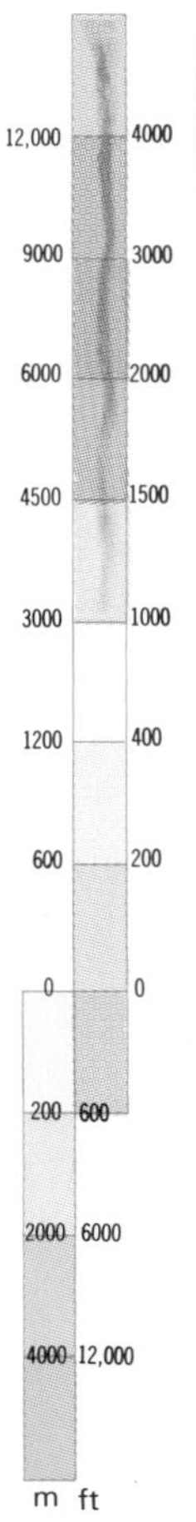

ft m
12,000 4000
9000 3000
6000 2000
4500 1500
3000 1000
1200 400
600 200
0 0
200 600
2000 6000
4000 12,000
m ft

Projection: Sanson-Flamsteed's Sinusoidal

East from Greenwich

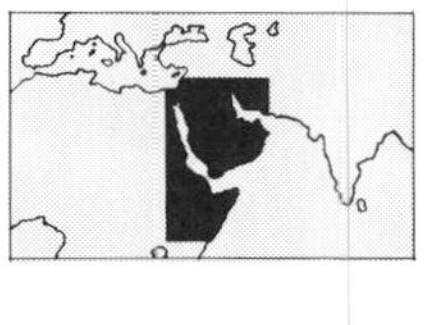

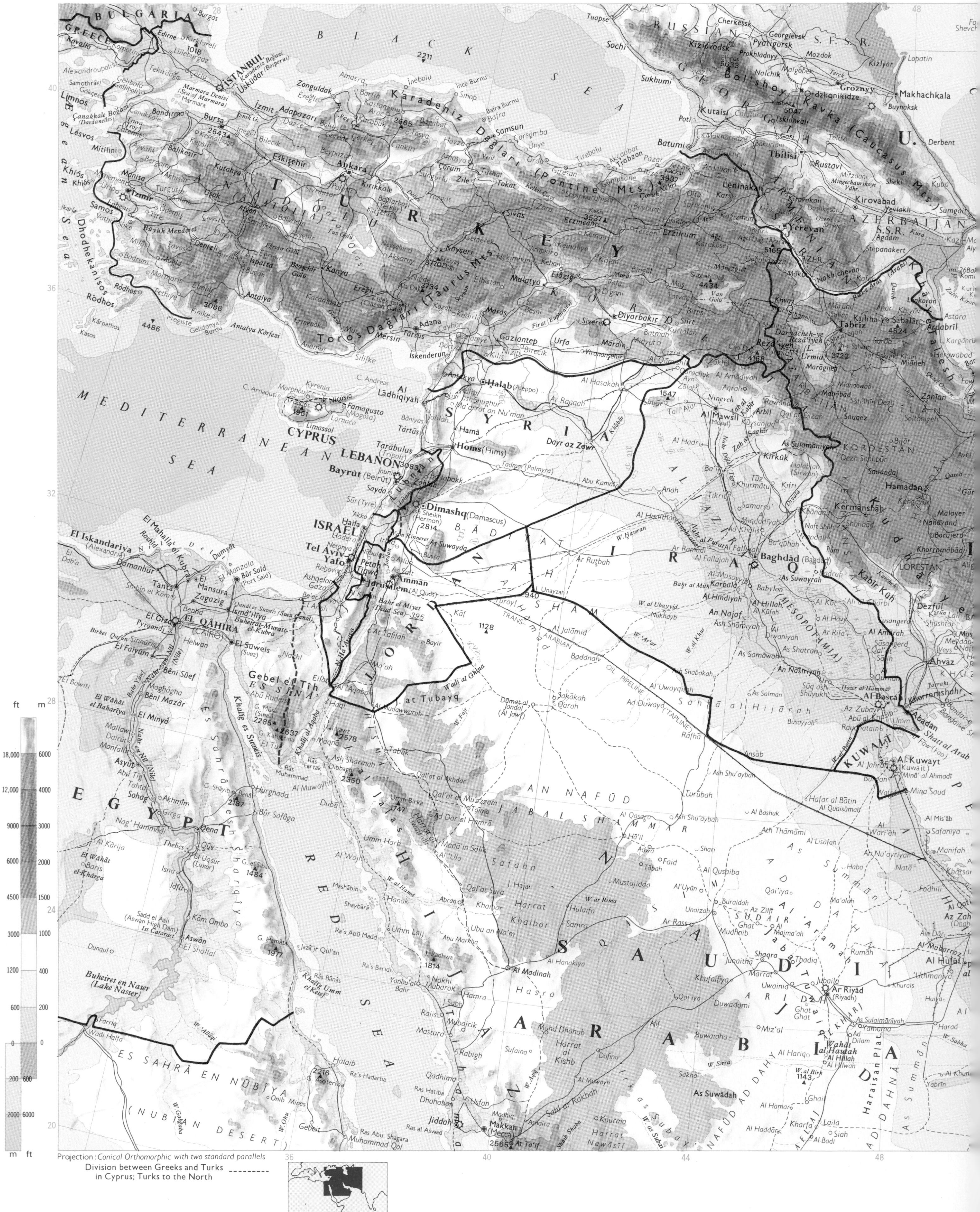
BULGARIA
GREECE
BLACK SEA
İSTANBUL
Ankara
İzmir
Bursa
Konya
Adana
Samsun
Trabzon
Erzurum
Sivas
Kayseri
Malatya
Diyarbakır
Gaziantep
TURKEY
ANATOLIA
Toros Dağları (Taurus Mts.)
Karadeniz Dağları (Pontine Mts.)
R U S S I A N S. F. S. R.
GEORGIA
Bol'shoy Kavkaz (Caucasus Mts.)
Tbilisi
Yerevan
ARMENIAN S.S.R.
AZERBAIJAN S.S.R.
Batumi
Sukhumi
Groznyy
Makhachkala
MEDITERRANEAN SEA
CYPRUS
Nicosia
LEBANON
Bayrūt (Beirūt)
SYRIA
Halab (Aleppo)
Hims (Homs)
Hamā
Dimashq (Damascus)
Dayr az Zawr
ISRAEL
Tel Aviv-Yafo
Haifa
Jerusalem (Al Quds)
'Ammān
JORDAN
Bahr el Miyet (Dead Sea) 395
IRAQ
Baghdād
Al Mawsil (Mosul)
Kirkūk
Al Başrah
(MESOPOTAMIA)
BADIYAT ASH SHAM
KUWAIT
Al Kuwayt (Kuwait)
Tabrīz
Hamadān
Kermānshāh
Ahvāz
Ābādān
Khorramshahr
Shatt al Arab
EGYPT
EL QÂHIRA (CAIRO)
El Iskandarîya (Alexandria)
Bûr Sa'îd (Port Said)
El Suweis (Suez)
Asyût
Qena
Aswân
Buheiret en Naser (Lake Nasser)
Gebel el Tîh
ES SÎNÂ
RED SEA
SAUDI ARABIA
AN NAFŪD
JABAL SHAMMAR
Al Madinah
Makkah (Mecca)
Jiddah
Ar Riyāḑ (Riyadh)
Al Hufūf
AD DAHNĀ'
ES SAHRÂ EN NÛBIYA (NUBIAN DESERT)
Wadi Halfa
TRANS-ARABIAN OIL PIPELINE ("TAPLINE")
ft m
18,000 6000
12,000 4000
9000 3000
6000 2000
4500 1500
3000 1000
1200 400
600 200
0 0
200 600
2000 6000
m ft

Projection: Conical Orthomorphic with two standard parallels

Division between Greeks and Turks in Cyprus; Turks to the North

Kilometers 0 100 200 300 400 Km.

Statute Miles 0 100 200 300 400 Mi.

1:8 000 000

One centimeter represents 80 kilometers
One inch represents approximately 130 miles

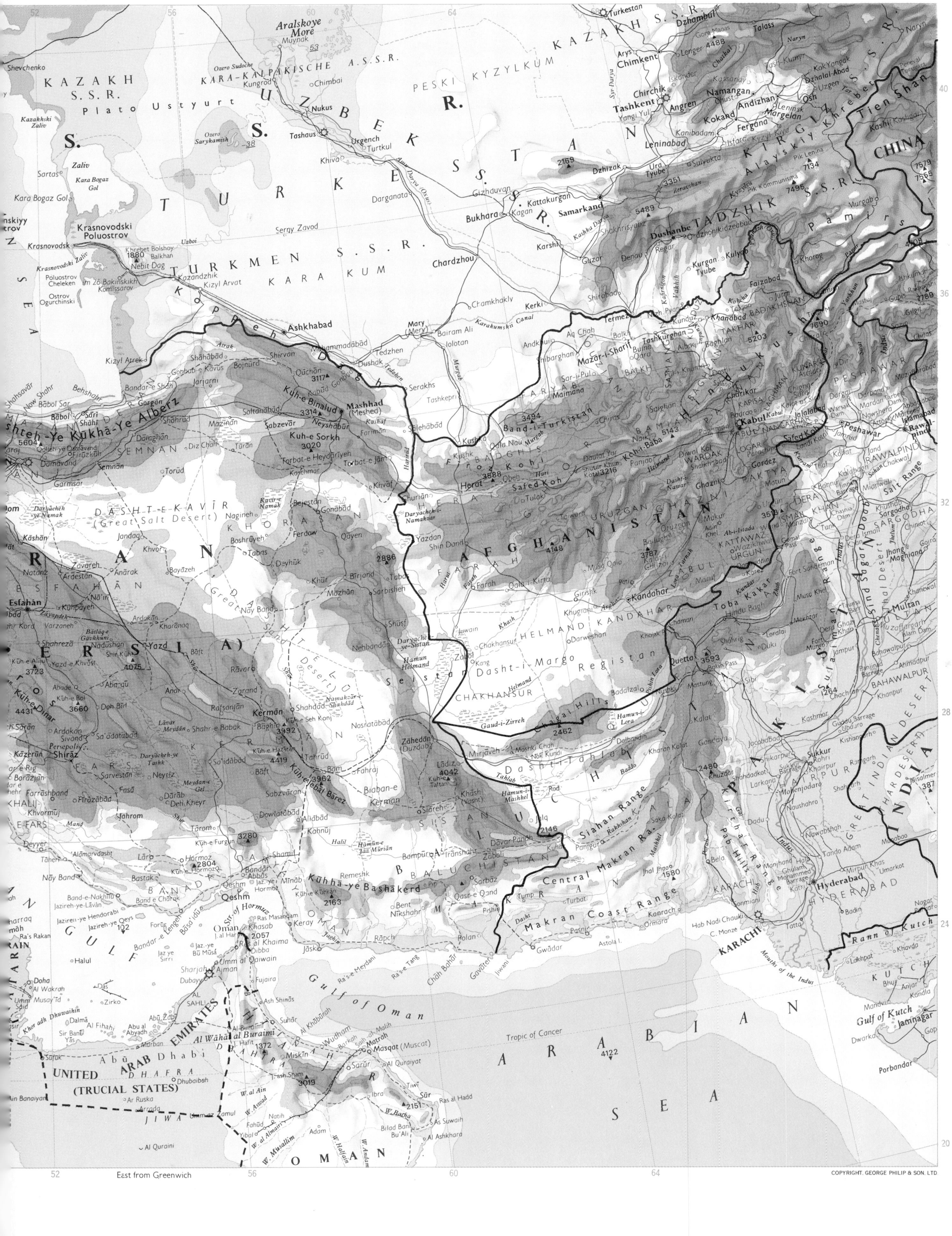

Aralskoye More
KAZAKH S.S.R.
Plato Ustyurt
KARA-KALPAKISCHE A.S.S.R.
PESKI KYZYLKUM
UZBEK S.S.R.
TURKMEN S.S.R.
KARA KUM
TADZHIK S.S.R.
KIRGIZ S.S.R.
Tien Shan
CHINA
Tashkent
Samarkand
Bukhara
Dushanbe
Ashkhabad
Krasnovodsk
Mary
Mashhad
Kabul
Peshawar
Rawalpindi
Herat
Kandahar
Quetta
Multan
Hyderabad
Karachi
AFGHANISTAN
PAKISTAN
INDIA
IRAN
PERSIA
DASHT-E-KAVĪR (Great Salt Desert)
DASHT-E-LUT (Great Sand Desert)
Dasht-i-Margo
Registan
HELMAND
BALUCHISTAN
Central Makran Range
Makran Coast Range
Esfahān
Yazd
Kermān
Shīrāz
Zāhedān
Bandar Abbās
Qeshm
Gwādar
Gulf of Oman
ARABIAN SEA
Tropic of Cancer
UNITED ARAB EMIRATES (TRUCIAL STATES)
Abu Dhabi
OMAN
Masqat (Muscat)
Sūr
Rann of Kutch
Gulf of Kutch
Mouths of the Indus
East from Greenwich

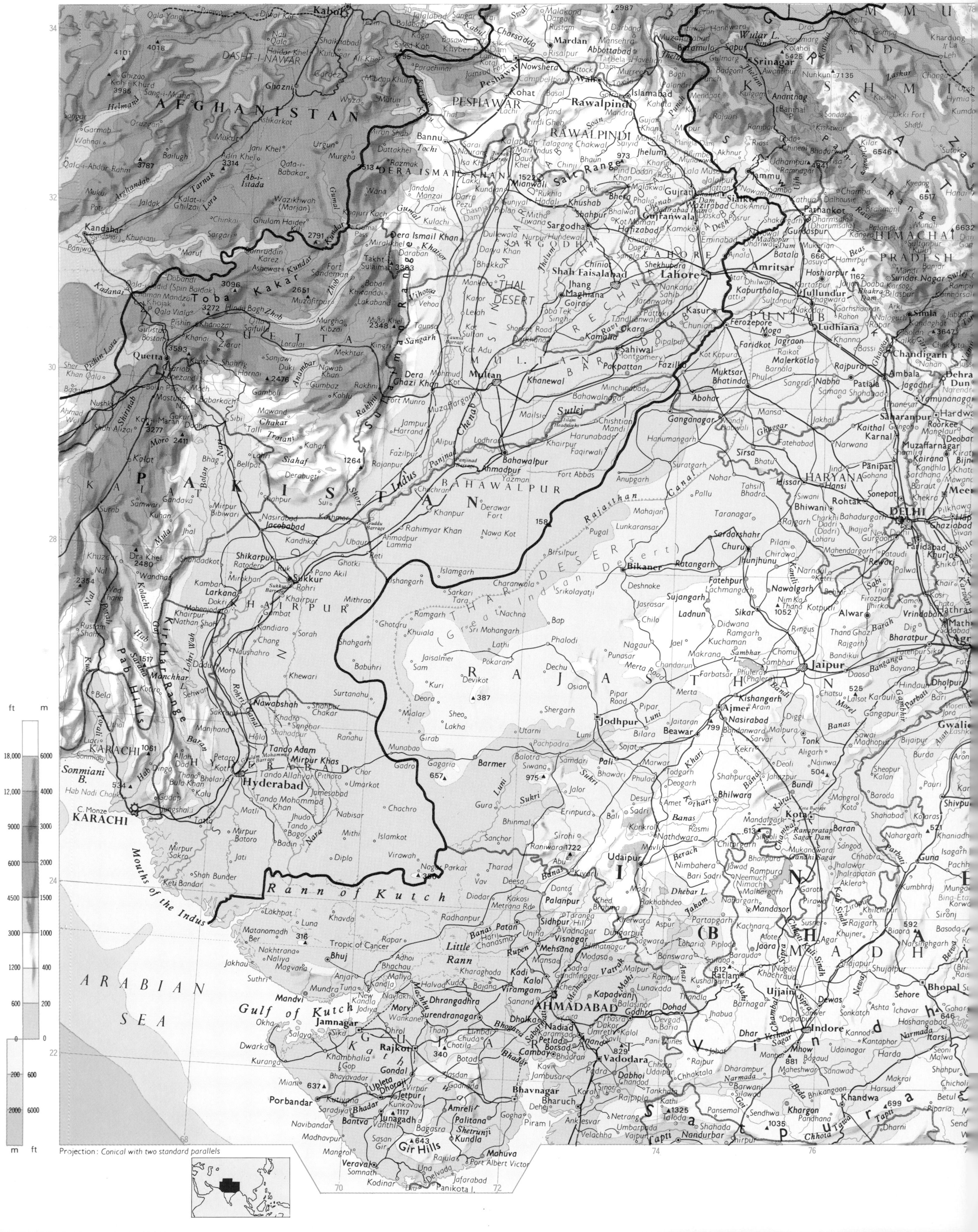
AFGHANISTAN
PAKISTAN
JAMMU AND KASHMIR
HIMACHAL PRADESH
PUNJAB
HARYANA
RAJASTHAN
MADHYA PRADESH
GUJARAT
ARABIAN SEA
Gulf of Kutch
Rann of Kutch
Little Rann
Mouths of the Indus
THAR DESERT (Great Indian Desert)
THAL DESERT
DASHT-I-NAWAR
Tropic of Cancer
Kabul
Ghazni
Kandahar
Quetta
Peshawar
Rawalpindi
Islamabad
Srinagar
Jammu
Lahore
Amritsar
Multan
Bahawalpur
Sukkur
Hyderabad
KARACHI
DELHI
Jaipur
Jodhpur
Bikaner
Ajmer
Udaipur
AHMADABAD
Vadodara
Rajkot
Jamnagar
Bhavnagar
Indore
Ujjain
Bhopal
Kota
Chandigarh
Simla
Ludhiana
Patiala
Sargodha
Gujranwala
Sialkot
Dera Ismail Khan
Dera Ghazi Khan
Shah Faisalabad
Sahiwal
Jhang Maghiana
Salt Range
Sulaiman Range
Kirthar Range
Pab Hills
Gir Hills
Toba Kakar
Indus
Chenab
Jhelum
Ravi
Sutlej
Beas
Luni
Chambal
Narmada
Tapti
Satpura
Vindhya
Sonmiani B.
C. Monze
ft
m
18,000
12,000
9000
6000
4500
3000
1200
600
200
2000
6000
6000
4000
3000
2000
1500
1000
400
200
0
600
Projection: Conical with two standard parallels

Kilometers 0 50 100 150 200 250 Km.
Statute Miles 0 50 100 150 200 250 Mi.

1:4 800 000

One centimeter represents 48 kilometers
One inch represents approximately 75 miles

JAMMU AND KASHMIR
On same scale as Main Map
U.S.S.R.
Karakoram Range
Kunlun Shan
Deosai Mountains
Zaskar Mountains
JAMMU AND KASHMIR
SODA PLAINS
HIMACHAL PRADESH
PESHAWAR
Srinagar
Rawalpindi
Islamabad
Gilgit
Leh
Jammu
Sialkot
Wazirabad
LINE OF SIMLA AGREEMENT 1972
CHINESE REPUBLIC
Gangdisê Shan
Nganglong Kangri
X I Z A N G
N E P A L
Siwalik Range
Mahabharat Range
U T T A R P R A D E S H
M A D H Y A P R A D E S H
B I H A R
W E S T B E N G A L
SIKKIM
BHUTAN
ASSAM
BANGLADESH
Mt. Everest 8848
Kanchenjunga 8598
Annapurna 8078
Dhaulagiri 8172
Nanda Devi 7817
Katmandu
Lucknow
KANPUR
Allahabad
Varanasi
Patna
Gorakhpur
Bareilly
Moradabad
Jabalpur
Ranchi
Jamshedpur
Durgapur
Asansol
Bhagalpur
Gaya
Darjeeling
Gangtok
Dhaka
Rajshahi
Khulna
Jessore
Barisal
Kharagpur
Bilaspur
Raurkela
Sambalpur
Balasore
CALCUTTA
Howrah
Garo Hills
Rajmahal Hills
Kaimur Hills
Panna Hills
Maikala Range
Sundarbans
Mouths of the Ganga
The Sandheads
80
82
84
86
88
90
East from Greenwich

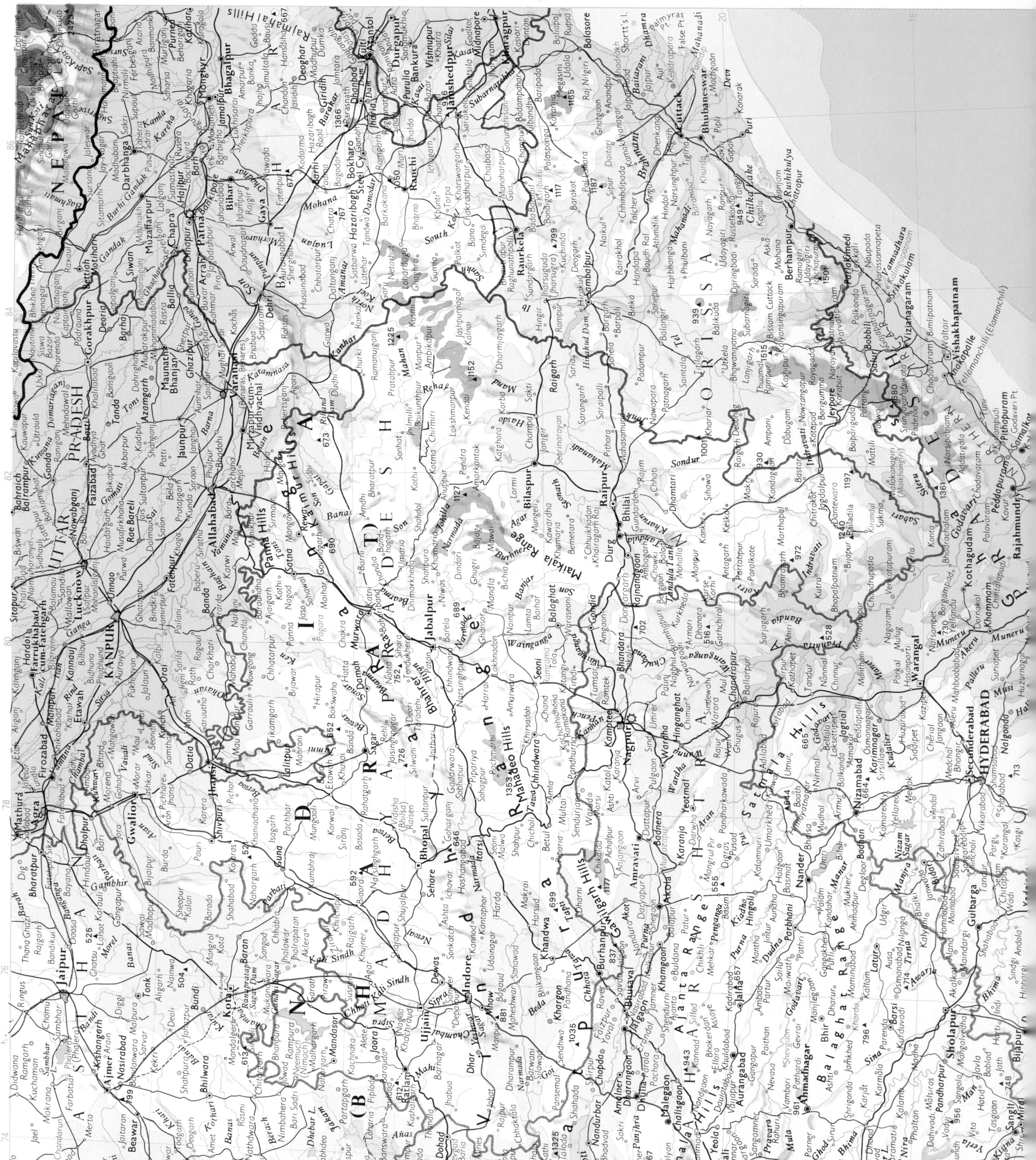
NEPAL
UTTAR PRADESH
KANPUR
Lucknow
Allahabad
Varanasi
Agra
Gwalior
Jhansi
Jaipur
Ajmer
Udaipur
Jodhpur
AHMADABAD
Vadodara
Surat
Gulf of Cambay
BOMBAY
Pune
Nasik
Aurangabad
Sholapur
HYDERABAD
Secunderabad
Nagpur
Jabalpur
Bhopal
Indore
Ujjain
Raipur
Bilaspur
Cuttack
Bhubaneswar
Puri
Berhampur
Vishakhapatnam
Rajahmundry
Warangal
Ranchi
Jamshedpur
Patna
Gaya
Bhagalpur
Gorakhpur
Asansol
Durgapur
Balasore
Sambalpur
Raurkela
Gulbarga
Bijapur
Sangli
Satara
Ratnagiri

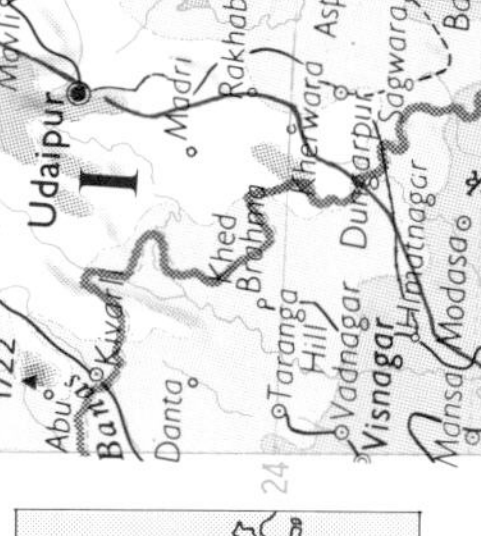

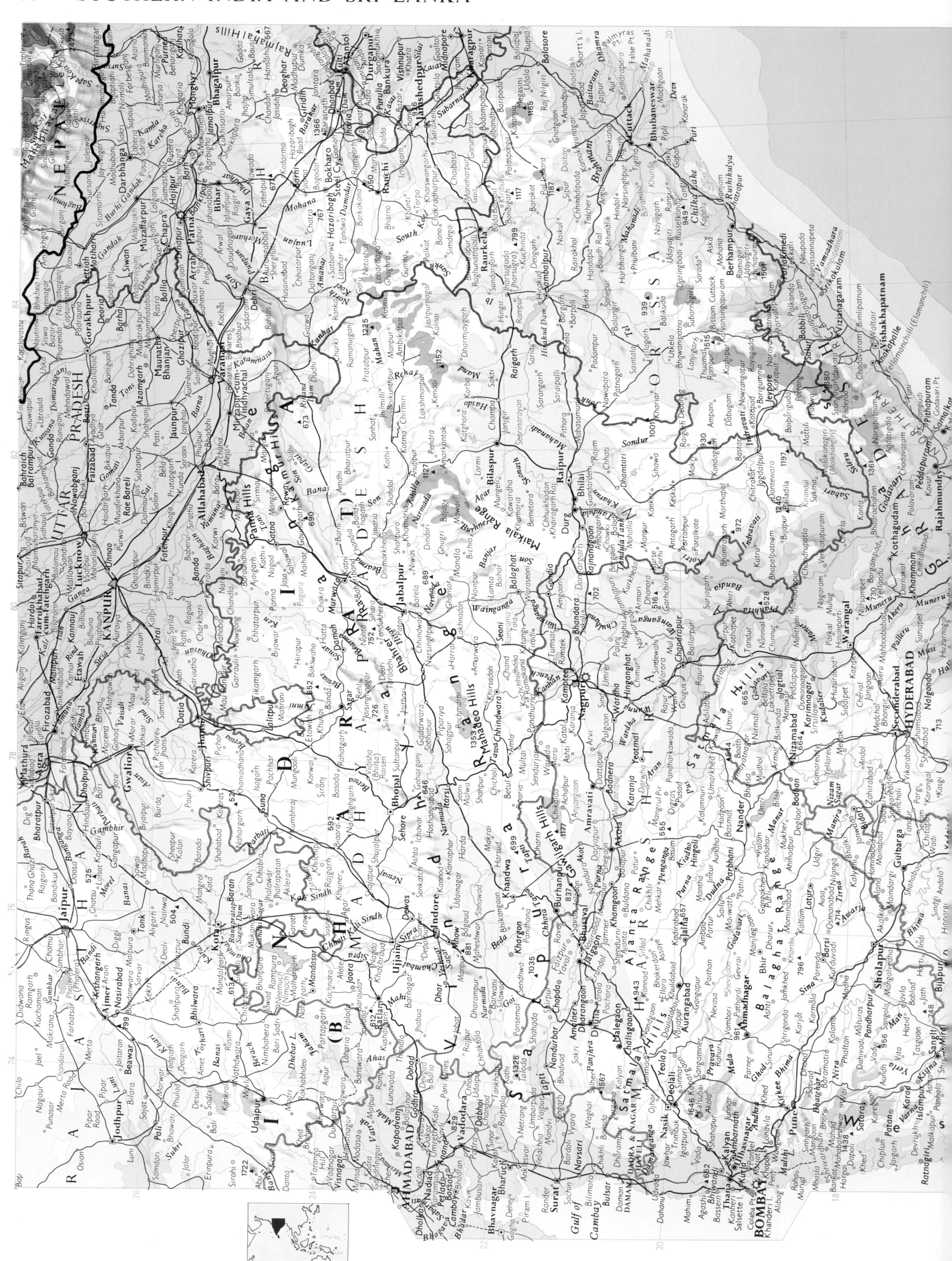

Kilometers 0 50 100 150 200 250 Km.
Statute Miles 0 50 100 150 200 250 Mi.

1:4 800 000

One centimeter represents 48 kilometers
One inch represents approximately 75 miles

B A Y   O F   B E N G A L
A R A B I A N   S E A
M a l a b a r   C o a s t
C o r o m a n d e l   C o a s t
SRI LANKA (CEYLON)
Gulf of Manaar (Mannar)
Palk Strait
Palk Bay
MADRAS
BANGALORE
Colombo
Kandy
Jaffna
Trincomalee
Pondicherry
Mysore
Madurai
Calicut
Cochin
Trivandrum
Mangalore
GOA
Nellore
Ongole
East from 80 Greenwich
Projection: Conical with two standard parallels
COPYRIGHT, GEORGE PHILIP & SON. LTD
m 3000 2000 1500 1000 400 200 0
ft 9000 6000 4500 3000 1200 600 0
200 600 2000 6000 4000 12,000

Kilometers 0 50 100 150 200 250 Km.
Statute Miles 0 50 100 150 200 250 Mi.

1:4 800 000

One centimeter represents 48 kilometers
One inch represents approximately 75 miles

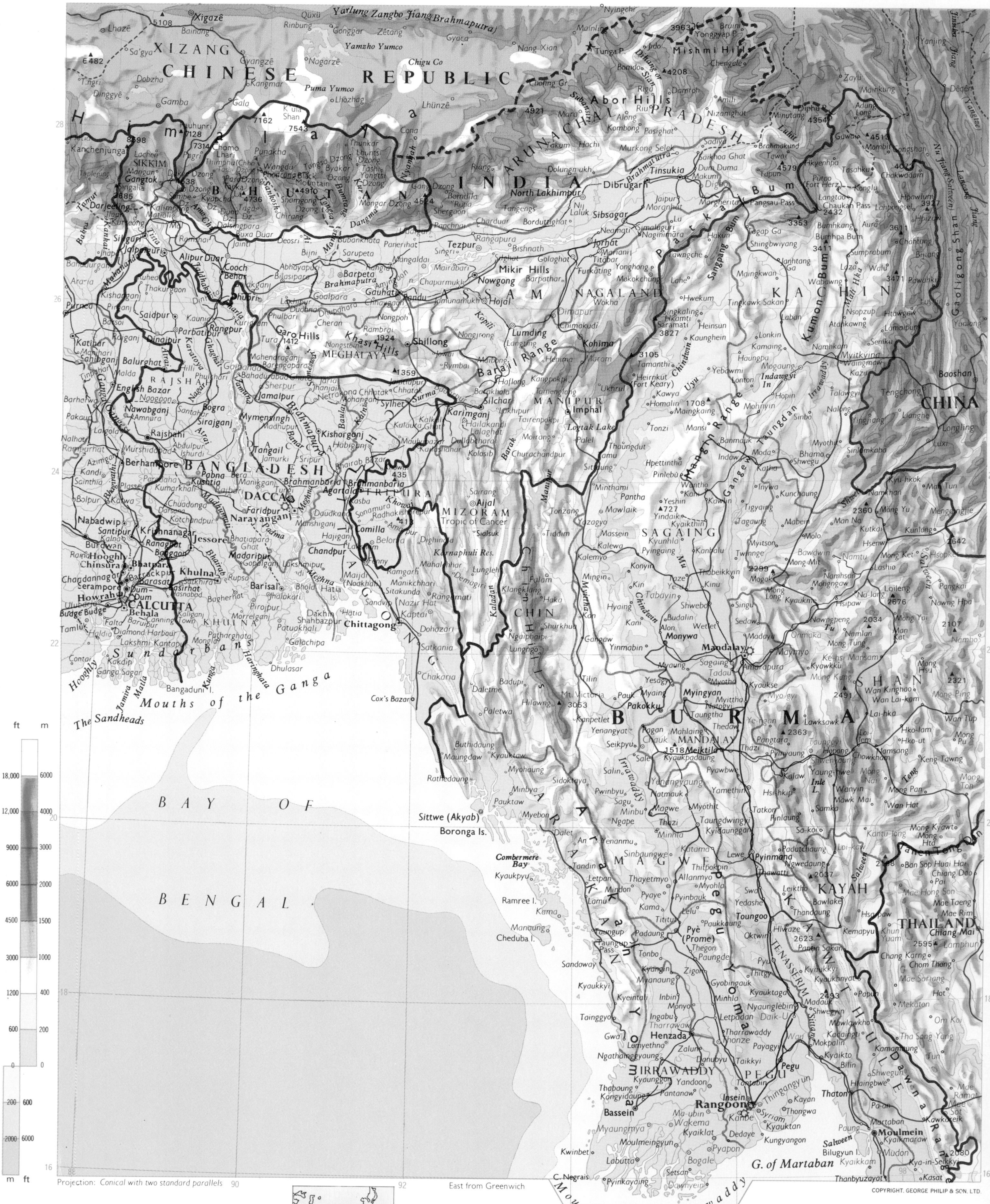
XIZANG
CHINESE REPUBLIC
Yarlung Zangbo Jiang (Brahmaputra)
Yamzho Yumco
Chigu Co
Puma Yumco
Mishmi Hills
Abor Hills
ARUNACHAL PRADESH
SIKKIM
Gangtok
BHUTAN
INDIA
Darjeeling
Kanchenjunga
Dibrugarh
Tinsukia
North Lakhimpur
Sibsagar
Jorhat
Tezpur
Mikir Hills
Nowgong
ASSAM
NAGALAND
Kohima
Gauhati
Shillong
Khasi Hills
Garo Hills
MEGHALAYA
MANIPUR
Imphal
Loktak Lake
Silchar
Sylhet
TRIPURA
Agartala
MIZORAM
Aijal
Tropic of Cancer
Karnaphuli Res.
BANGLADESH
DACCA
Narayanganj
Comilla
Chandpur
Jessore
Khulna
Barisal
Chittagong
Cox's Bazar
Rajshahi
Rangpur
Dinajpur
Mymensingh
CALCUTTA
Howrah
Hooghly
Sundarbans
Mouths of the Ganga
The Sandheads
BAY OF BENGAL
Sittwe (Akyab)
Boronga Is.
Combermere Bay
Kyaukpyu
Ramree I.
Cheduba I.
Sandoway
KACHIN
Kumon Bum
Patkai Bum
SAGAING
Chindwin
CHIN
Chin Hills
Mt. Victoria
ARAKAN
Arakan Yoma
MANDALAY
Mandalay
Monywa
Myingyan
Pakokku
Meiktila
BURMA
SHAN
Inle L.
Taunggyi
MAGWE
Pyinmana
KAYAH
Toungoo
Pegu Yoma
Pyè (Prome)
Henzada
IRRAWADDY
Bassein
PEGU
Pegu
Rangoon
Thaton
Moulmein
G. of Martaban
Salween
Sittang
TENASSERIM
Dawna Range
THAILAND
Chiang Mai
CHINA
Tengchong
Gaoligong Shan
Mouths of the Irrawaddy
C. Negrais

Projection: *Conical with two standard parallels*

East from Greenwich

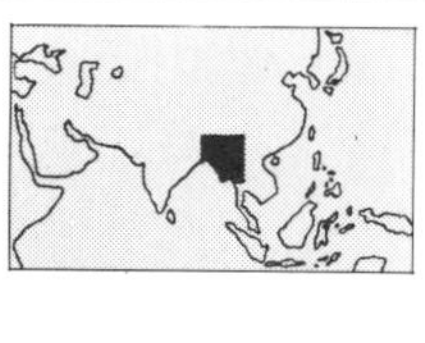

Kilometers 0 400 800 1200 1600 2000 Km.
Statute Miles 0 400 800 1200 1600 2000 Mi.

1:40 000 000

One centimeter represents 400 kilometers
One inch represents approximately 640 miles

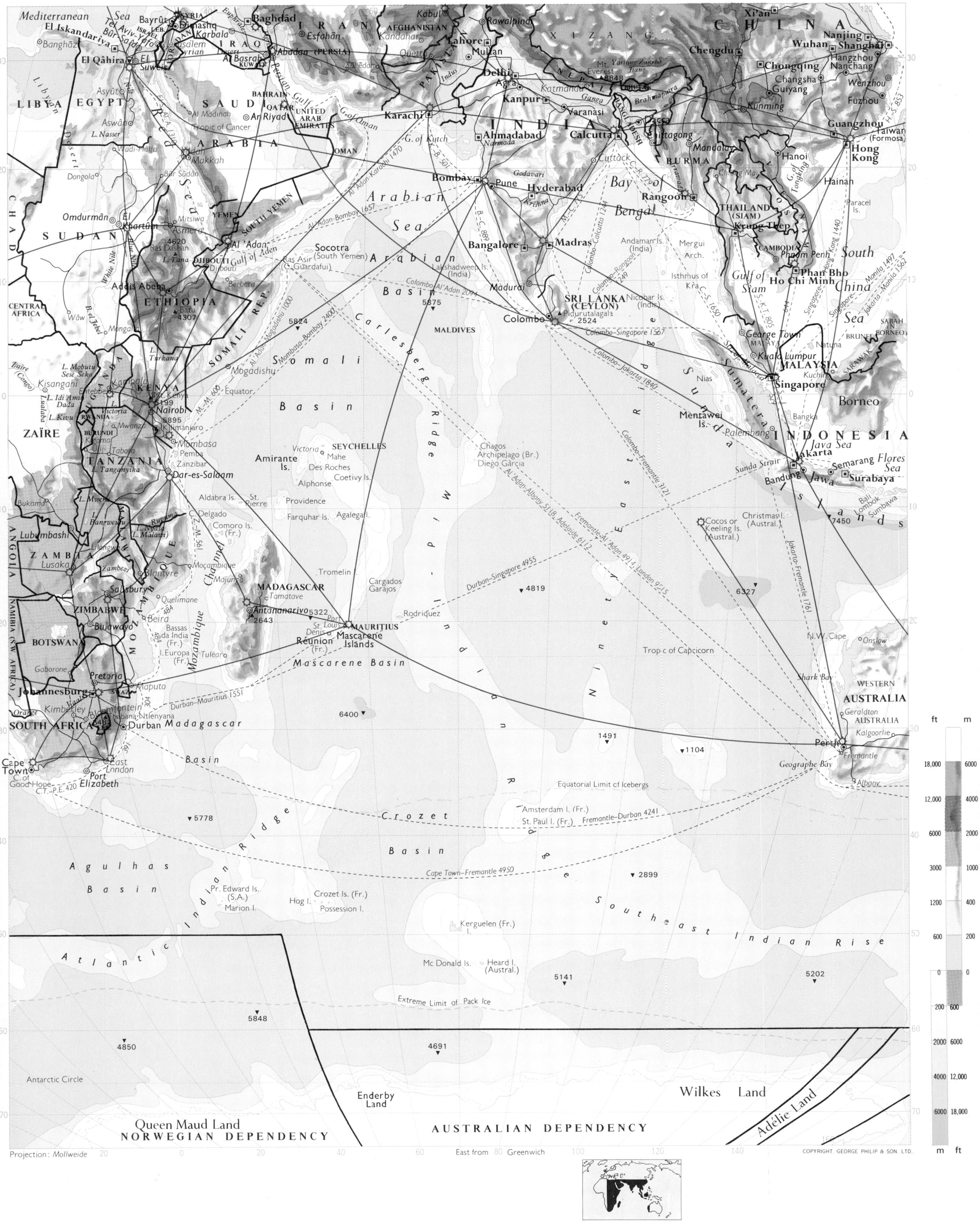
Mediterranean Sea
LIBYA
EGYPT
SUDAN
CHAD
ETHIOPIA
KENYA
TANZANIA
ZAÏRE
ZAMBIA
ANGOLA
ZIMBABWE
BOTSWANA
SOUTH AFRICA
MOZAMBIQUE
MADAGASCAR
SAUDI ARABIA
IRAQ
IRAN (PERSIA)
AFGHANISTAN
PAKISTAN
INDIA
NEPAL
BHUTAN
BANGLADESH
BURMA
THAILAND (SIAM)
CAMBODIA
MALAYSIA
INDONESIA
CHINA
XIZANG
SRI LANKA (CEYLON)
MALDIVES
SOMALI REP.
UNITED ARAB EMIRATES
OMAN
YEMEN
SOUTH YEMEN
DJIBOUTI
Arabian Sea
Bay of Bengal
Arabian Basin
Somali Basin
Carlsberg Ridge
Mid-Indian Ridge
Ninety East Ridge
Sunda Islands
Mascarene Basin
Madagascar Basin
Mozambique Channel
Agulhas Basin
Atlantic Indian Ridge
Crozet Basin
Southeast Indian Rise
South China Sea
Java Sea
Flores Sea
Borneo
Sumatera
Jawa
Tropic of Cancer
Tropic of Capricorn
Equator
Equatorial Limit of Icebergs
Extreme Limit of Pack Ice
Antarctic Circle
WESTERN AUSTRALIA
Perth
Fremantle
Geographe Bay
Shark Bay
N.W. Cape
Bombay
Karachi
Calcutta
Madras
Colombo
Singapore
Jakarta
Rangoon
Hong Kong
Durban
Cape Town
C. of Good Hope
Port Elizabeth
Mombasa
Dar-es-Salaam
Nairobi
Mogadishu
Al 'Adan
Antananarivo
Port Louis
MAURITIUS
Reunion (Fr.)
Mascarene Islands
SEYCHELLES
Amirante Is.
Chagos Archipelago (Br.)
Diego Garcia
Cocos or Keeling Is. (Austral.)
Christmas I. (Austral.)
Amsterdam I. (Fr.)
St. Paul I. (Fr.)
Kerguelen (Fr.)
Heard I. (Austral.)
Mc Donald Is.
Crozet Is. (Fr.)
Pr. Edward Is. (S.A.)
Marion I.
Queen Maud Land
NORWEGIAN DEPENDENCY
Enderby Land
AUSTRALIAN DEPENDENCY
Wilkes Land
Adélie Land
Colombo–Fremantle 3121
Cape Town–Fremantle 4950
Fremantle–Durban 4241
Durban–Singapore 4955
Colombo–Singapore 1567
Colombo–Jakarta 1840
Jakarta–Fremantle 1761
Durban–Mauritius 1551
ft m
18,000 6000
12,000 4000
6000 2000
3000 1000
1200 400
600 200
0 0
200 600
2000 6000
4000 12,000
6000 18,000
m ft
Projection: Mollweide
East from Greenwich
COPYRIGHT. GEORGE PHILIP & SON. LTD.

Gulf of Tonkin
Hainan
HANOI
Haiphong
Vientiane
Luang Prabang
KRUNG THEP (Bangkok)
Thon Buri
Rangoon
Mandalay
Moulmein
Gulf of Martaban
Da Nang
Hue
Vinh
Pakse
Ubon Ratchathani
Nakhon Ratchasima (Khorat)
Udon Thani
Chiang Mai
Phnom Dangrek
Battambang
Qui Nhon
Ban Me Thuot
Nanning
Zhanjiang
Haikou
Tavoy
Mekong
Salween
Sittang

Kilometers 0 50 100 150 200 250 Km.
Statute Miles 0 50 100 150 200 Mi.

1:4 800 000

One centimeter represents 48 kilometers
One inch represents approximately 75 miles

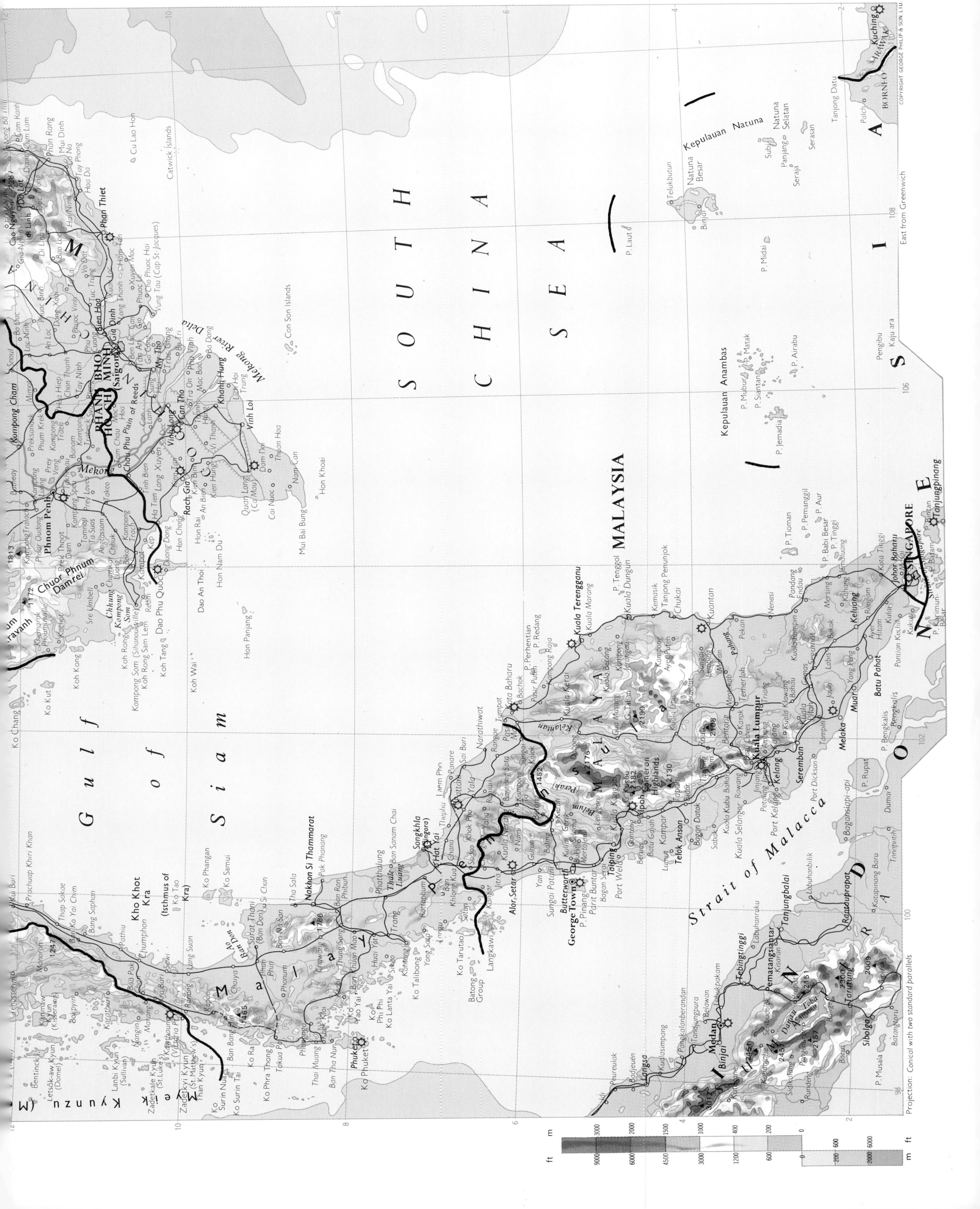
SOUTH CHINA SEA
Gulf of Siam
MALAYSIA
Strait of Malacca
SINGAPORE
Kuala Lumpur
George Town
Phnom Penh
Kuching
Medan
Kepulauan Natuna
Kepulauan Anambas
Projection: Conical with two standard parallels
East from Greenwich
COPYRIGHT GEORGE PHILIP & SON LTD.

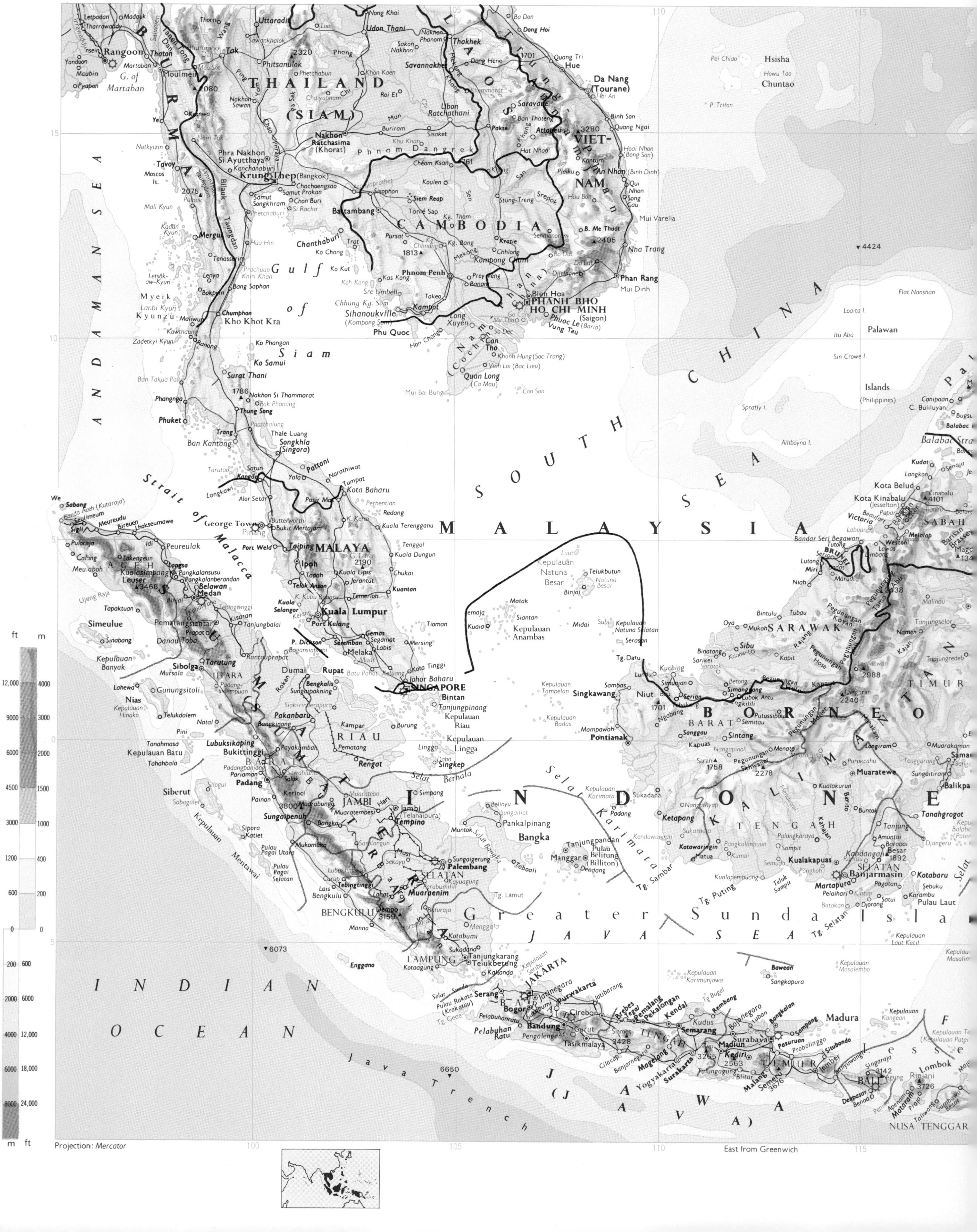
BURMA
THAILAND (SIAM)
LAOS
CAMBODIA
VIET-NAM
MALAYSIA
MALAYA
SARAWAK
SABAH
BRUNEI
INDONESIA
BORNEO
SUMATERA
JAWA (JAVA)
KALIMANTAN
ANDAMAN SEA
SOUTH CHINA SEA
Gulf of Siam
G. of Martaban
Strait of Malacca
Greater Sunda Islands
JAVA SEA
INDIAN OCEAN
Java Trench
Rangoon
Krung Thep (Bangkok)
Phnom Penh
PHANH BHO HO CHI MINH (Saigon)
Da Nang (Tourane)
Hue
Kuala Lumpur
SINGAPORE
JAKARTA
Bandung
Semarang
Surabaya
Palembang
Medan
Padang
Pontianak
Banjarmasin
Kota Kinabalu (Jesselton)
Bandar Seri Begawan
Kuching
Bangka
Belitung (Billiton)
Madura
BALI
Lombok
NUSA TENGGAR
Hsisha
Palawan
Spratly I.
Kepulauan Natuna Besar
Kepulauan Anambas
Kepulauan Riau
Kepulauan Lingga
Kepulauan Batu
Siberut
Nias
Simeulue
Enggano
ft m
12,000 4000
9000 3000
6000 2000
4500 1500
3000 1000
1200 400
600 200
0 0
200 600
2000 6000
4000 12,000
6000 18,000
8000 24,000
m ft
100
105
110
115
15
10
5
0
5
Projection: Mercator
East from Greenwich

Kilometers 0 100 200 300 400 500 Km
Statute Miles 0 100 200 300 400 500 Mi

1:10 000 000

One centimeter represents 100 kilometers
One inch represents approximately 160 miles

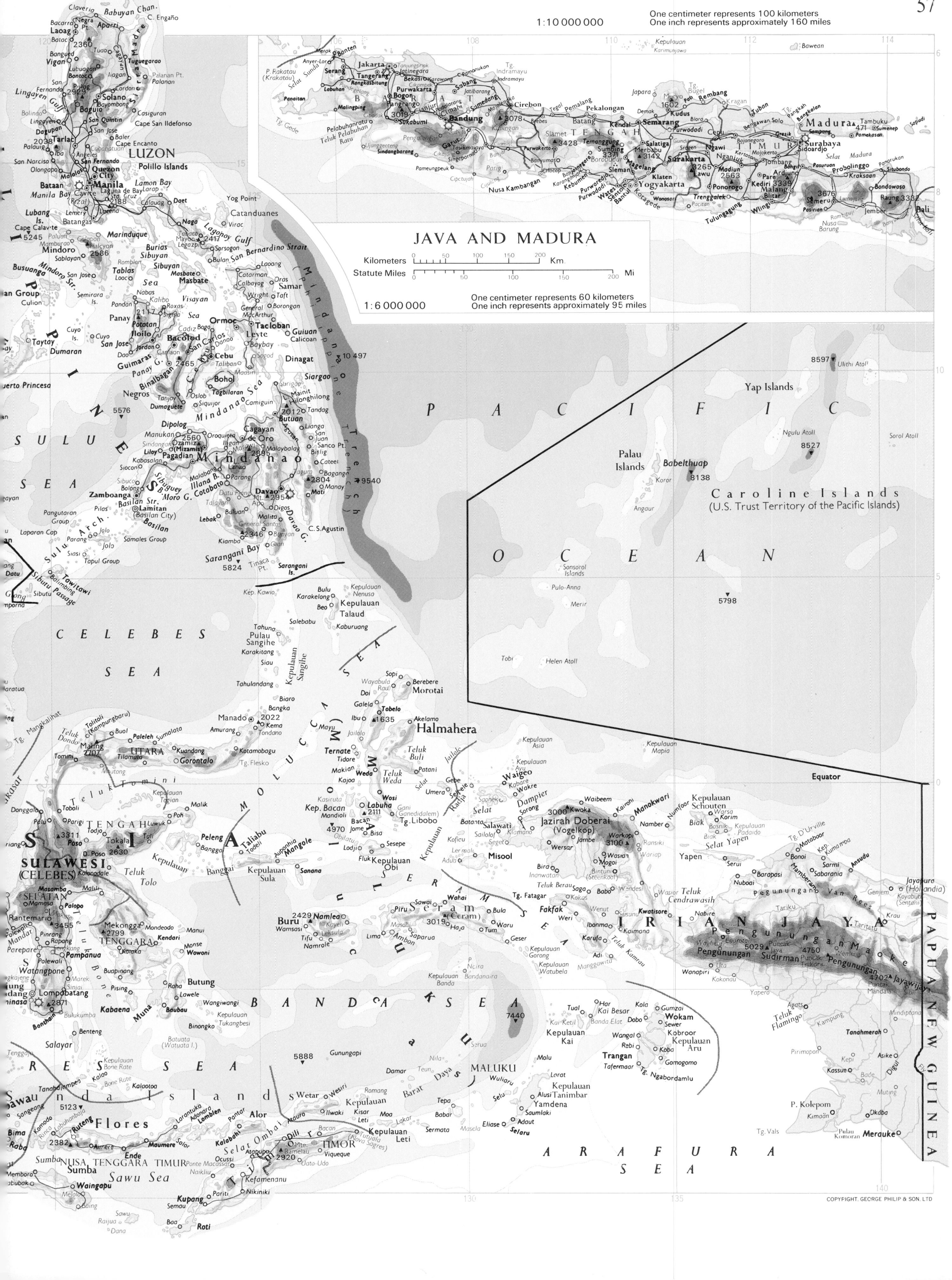

JAVA AND MADURA
Kilometers 0 50 100 150 200 Km
Statute Miles 0 50 100 150 200 Mi
1:6 000 000
One centimeter represents 60 kilometers
One inch represents approximately 95 miles
Jakarta
Bandung
Cirebon
Semarang
Surakarta
Yogyakarta
Surabaya
Madura
Malang
Kediri
Madiun
Bali
Bawean
LUZON
Manila
Quezon City
Polillo Islands
Catanduanes
Mindoro
Marinduque
Masbate
Samar
Leyte
Panay
Negros
Cebu
Bohol
Dinagat
Siargao
Mindanao
Davao
Zamboanga
Cagayan de Oro
Basilan
Sulu Arch.
SULU SEA
CELEBES SEA
Mindanao Trench (Philippine Trench)
10 497
9540
PACIFIC OCEAN
Yap Islands
Palau Islands
Babelthuap
Caroline Islands
(U.S. Trust Territory of the Pacific Islands)
Equator
Kepulauan Talaud
Pulau Sangihe
Kepulauan Sangihe
Morotai
Halmahera
Ternate
MOLUCCA SEA
Kep. Bacan
Kepulauan Obi
Kepulauan Sula
Waigeo
Misool
Salawati
Jazirah Doberai (Vogelkop)
Manokwari
Biak
Yapen
Kepulauan Schouten
SULAWESI (CELEBES)
UTARA
TENGAH
SELATAN
TENGGARA
Manado
Gorontalo
Teluk Tomini
Teluk Tolo
Teluk Bone
Peleng
Taliabu
Mangole
Buru
Seram (Ceram)
Ambon
Butung
Muna
Kabaena
BANDA SEA
MALUKU
Kepulauan Kai
Kepulauan Aru
Kepulauan Tanimbar
Yamdena
IRIAN JAYA
Pegunungan Van Rees
Pegunungan Sudirman
Pegunungan Jayawijaya
Puncak Jaya 5029
Jayapura (Hollandia)
Merauke
P. Kolepom
PAPUA NEW GUINEA
ARAFURA SEA
Flores
Sumba
Sawu Sea
Timor
Dili
Kupang
Roti
Alor
Wetar
NUSA TENGGARA TIMUR
Flores Sea
Selayar
Makassar Str.
COPYFIGHT, GEORGE PHILIP & SON, LTD

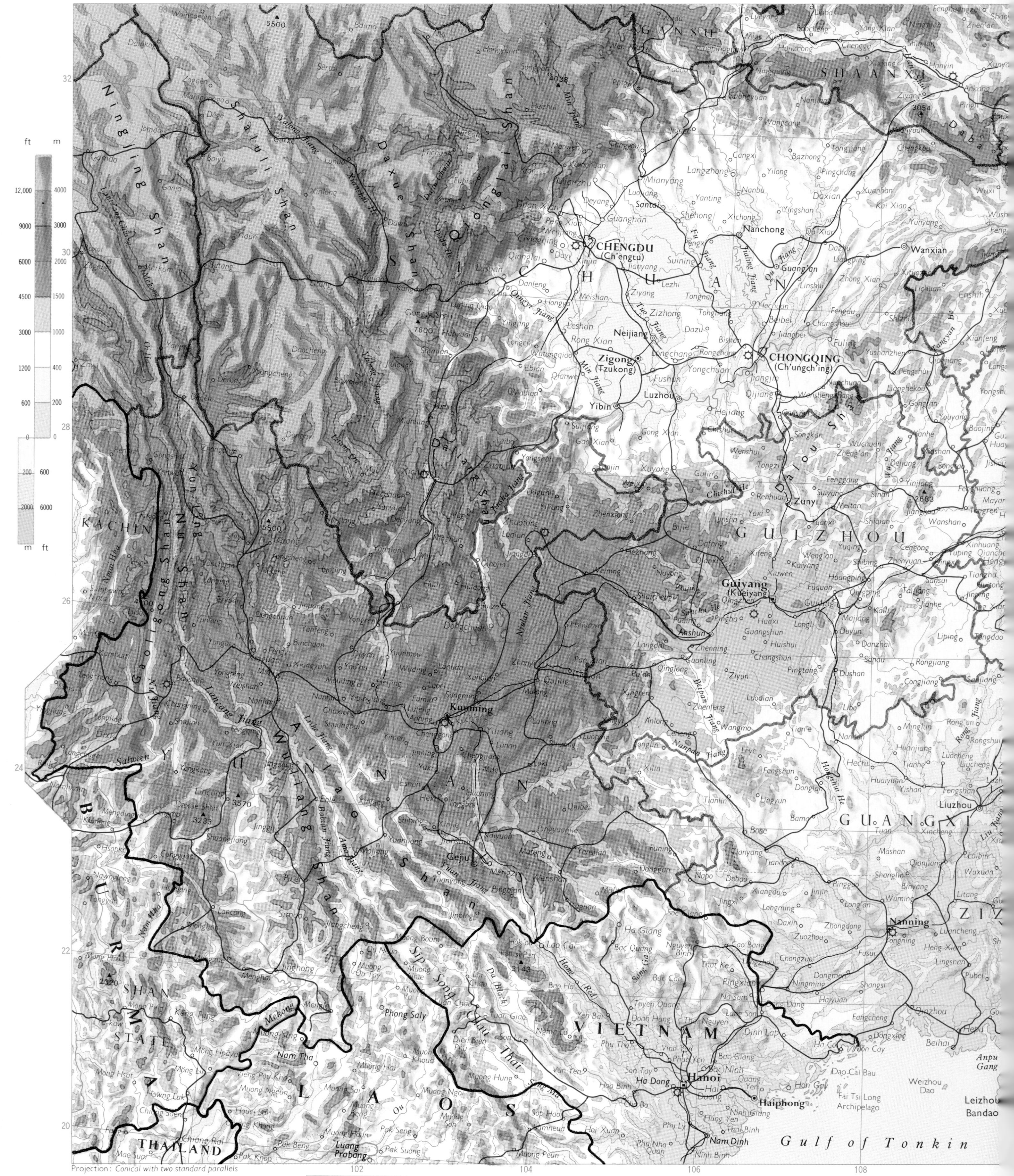
GANSU
SHAANXI
SICHUAN
GUIZHOU
YUNNAN
GUANGXI
VIETNAM
LAOS
BURMA
THAILAND
KACHIN
SHAN STATE
CHENGDU
(Ch'engtu)
CHONGQING
(Ch'ungch'ing)
Guiyang
(Kueiyang)
Kunming
Zigong
(Tzukong)
Nanning
Hanoi
Haiphong
Nam Dinh
Ha Dong
Wanxian
Nanchong
Neijiang
Luzhou
Yibin
Zunyi
Liuzhou
Anshun
Gejiu
Phong Saly
Luang Prabang
Nam Tha
Gulf of Tonkin
Leizhou Bandao
Weizhou Dao
Fai Tsi Long Archipelago
Anpu Gang
Beihai
Ningjing Shan
Shaluli Shan
Daxue Shan
Qionglai Shan
Daliang Shan
Dalou Shan
Daba Shan
Wuliang Shan
Ailao Shan
Nu Shan
Yun Ling
Gaoligong Shan
Min Jiang
Jinsha Jiang
Yalong Jiang
Dadu He
Lancang Jiang
Nu Jiang
Salween
Mekong
Jialing Jiang
Wu Jiang
Nanpan Jiang
Hongshui He
Yuan Jiang
Song Ma
Da (Black)
Hong (Red)
Gongga Shan
7600
5500
4038
3054
2583
3570
3233
3143
2320
ft
m
12,000
4000
9000
3000
6000
2000
4500
1500
3000
1000
1200
400
600
200
0
0
200
600
2000
6000
m
ft
32
30
28
26
24
22
20
98
102
104
106
108

Projection: *Conical with two standard parallels*

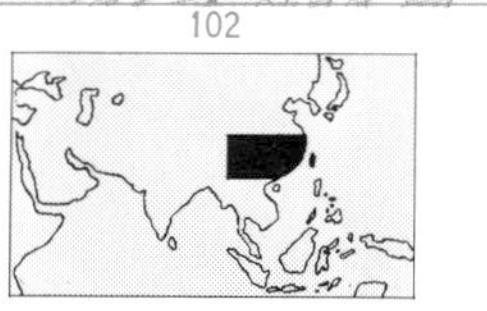

Kilometers 0 50 100 150 200 250 Km.
Statute Miles 0 50 100 150 200 250 Mi.

1:4 800 000

One centimeter represents 48 kilometers
One inch represents approximately 75 miles

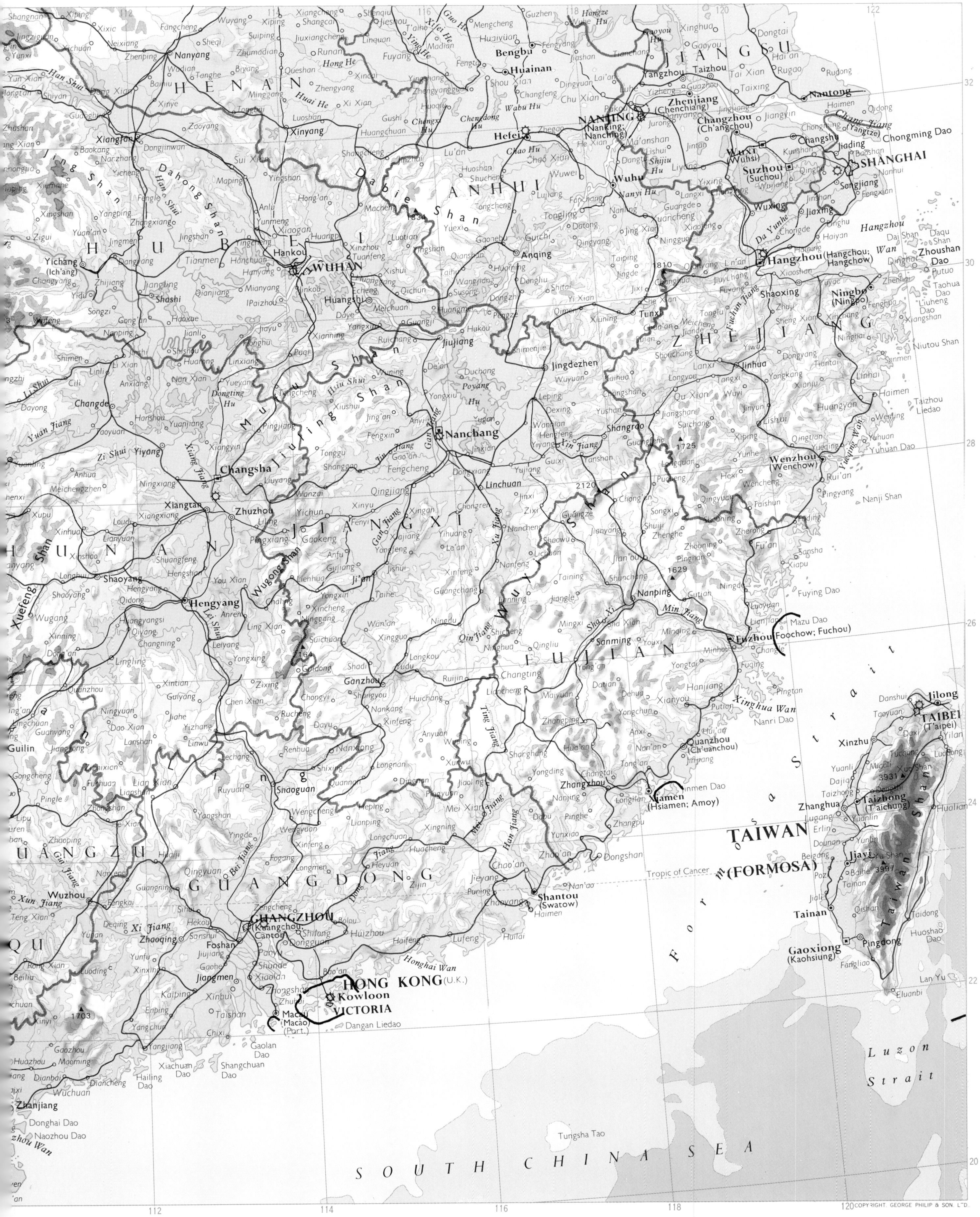
HENAN
ANHUI
JIANGSU
HUBEI
HUNAN
JIANGXI
ZHEJIANG
FUJIAN
GUANGDONG
TAIWAN
(FORMOSA)
Nanyang
Xinyang
Bengbu
Huainan
Hefei
NANJING
(Nanking; Nanching)
Zhenjiang
(Chenchiang)
Changzhou
(Ch'angchou)
Wuxi
(Wuhsi)
Suzhou
(Suchou)
SHANGHAI
Chongming Dao
Nantong
Yangzhou
Taizhou
Wuhu
Anqing
Hangzhou
(Hangchou; Hangchow)
Hangzhou Wan
Zhoushan Dao
Shaoxing
Ningbo
(Ningpo)
Jinhua
Wenzhou
(Wenchow)
Nanji Shan
Xiangfan
Yichang
(Ich'ang)
Hankou
WUHAN
Huangshi
Jiujiang
Poyang Hu
Dabie Shan
Jingdezhen
Nanchang
Changsha
Xiangtan
Zhuzhou
Changde
Dongting Hu
Hengyang
Shaoyang
Linchuan
Ganzhou
Wuyi Shan
Nanping
Fuzhou (Foochow; Fuchou)
Mazu Dao
Sanming
Quanzhou
(Ch'uanchou)
Xiamen
(Hsiamen; Amoy)
Jinmen Dao
Zhangzhou
Shantou
(Swatow)
Shaoguan
GUANGZHOU
(Kuangchou; Canton)
Foshan
Jiangmen
Huizhou
HONG KONG (U.K.)
Kowloon
VICTORIA
Macau
(Macao)
(Port.)
Dangan Liedao
Wuzhou
Zhanjiang
Donghai Dao
Naozhou Dao
Hailing Dao
Shangchuan Dao
Xiachuan Dao
Guilin
Tropic of Cancer
Formosa Strait
Jilong
TAIBEI
(T'aipei)
Xinzhu
Taizhong
(T'aichung)
Zhanghua
Jiayi
Tainan
Gaoxiong
(Kaohsiung)
Pingdong
Hualian
Taiwan Shan
Lan Yu
Luzon Strait
Tungsha Tao
SOUTH CHINA SEA
Honghai Wan
1725
1629
2120
1810
1834
1703
3931
3997
112
114
116
118
120
122
32
30
28
26
24
22
20

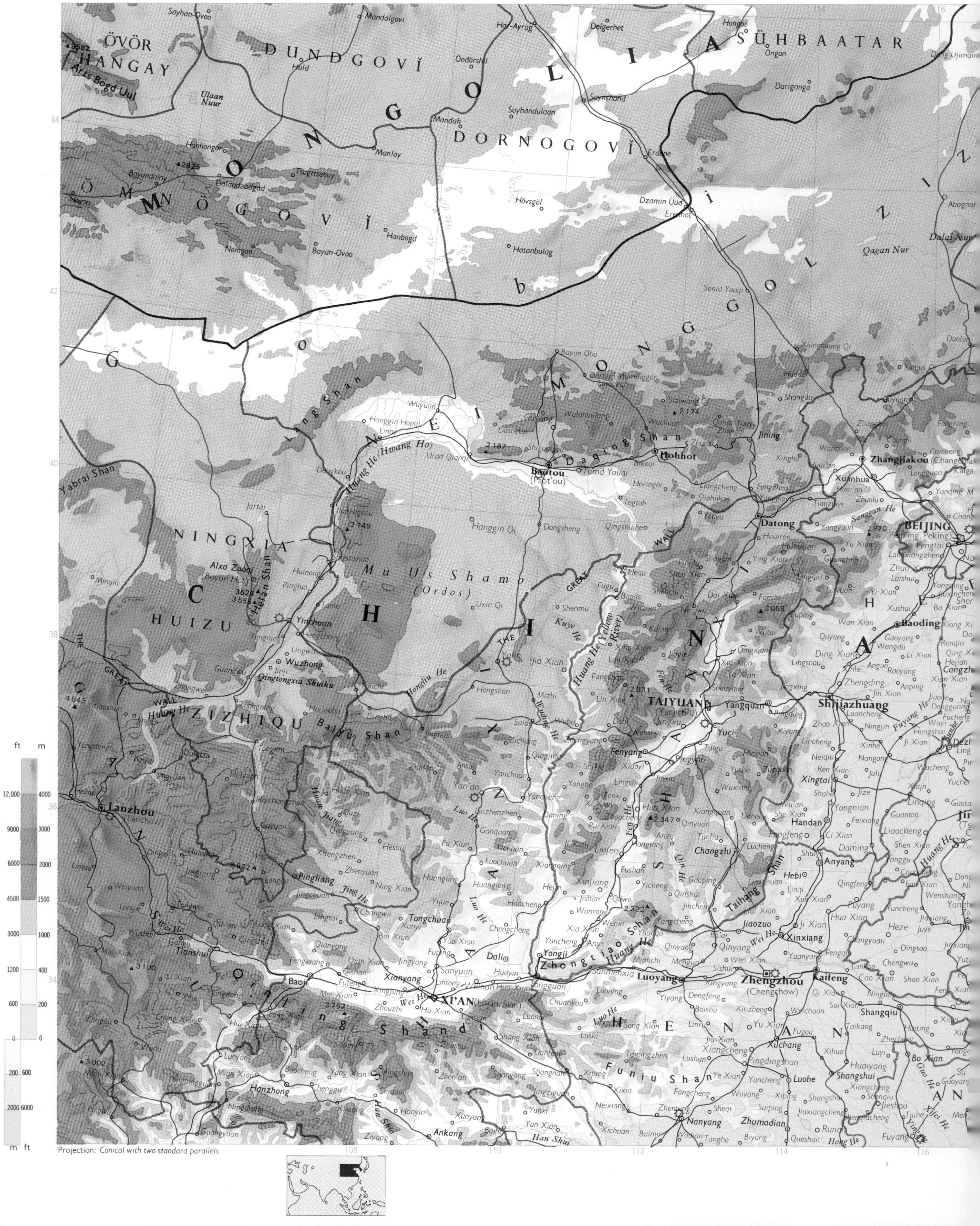
M O N G O L I A
ÖVÖR HANGAY
DUNDGOVĬ
SÜHBAATAR
DORNOGOVĬ
ÖMNÖGOVĬ
Arts Bogd Uul
Gobi
NEI MONGOL ZIZHIQU
NINGXIA HUIZU ZIZHIQU
C H I N A
SHANXI
HEBEI
HENAN
GANSU
Mu Us Shamo (Ordos)
THE GREAT WALL
Huang He (Hwang Ho)
Huang He (Yellow River)
Wei He
Han Shui
Fen He
Luo He
Jing He
Qinling Shandi
Funiu Shan
Zhongtiao Shan
Taihang Shan
Daqing Shan
Helan Shan
Baiyu Shan
Yabrai Shan
Lang Shan
Qingtongxia Shuiku
Mandalgovi
Sayhan-Ovoo
Har-Ayrag
Delgerhet
Hongor
Ongon
Dariganga
Huld
Öndörshil
Ulaan Nuur
Sayhandulaan
Sayhshand
Mandah
Manlay
Hanhongor
Bayandalay
Dalandzadgad
Tsogttsetsiy
Noyon
Nomgon
Bayan-Ovoo
Hanbogd
Hövsgöl
Hatanbulag
Erdene
Dzamin Üüd
Erenhot
Abagnar
Dalai Nur
Qagan Nur
Sonid Youqi
Xianghuang Qi
Huade
Shangdu
Bayan Obo
Darhan Muminggan Lianheqi
Siziwang Qi
Guyang
Wulanbulang
Wuchuan
Dashetai
Shiguaigou
Baotou (Pao-t'ou)
Hohhot
Tumd Youqi
Urad Qianqi
Wuyuan
Hanggin Houqi
Linhe
Dengkou
Jining
Zhangjiakou (Changchiakou)
Xuanhua
Datong
BEIJING (Pei-ching, Peking)
Fengtai
Baoding
Shijiazhuang
TAIYUAN (Yangchu)
Yuci
Yangquan
Fenyang
Linfen
Changzhi
Handan
Xingtai
Anyang
Hebi
Xinxiang
Jiaozuo
Zhengzhou (Chengchow)
Kaifeng
Luoyang
Shangqiu
Xuchang
Pingdingshan
Luohe
Nanyang
Zhumadian
Xi'AN (Hsi-an, Sian)
Xianyang
Baoji
Tongchuan
Yan'an
Tianshui
Lanzhou (Lanchow)
Pingliang
Yinchuan
Wuzhong
Alxa Zuoqi (Bayan Hot)
Hanggin Qi
Dongsheng
Hanzhong
Ankang
Shangnan
Yongji
Zhongwei
Dingxi
Guyuan
2825
3682
2174
2187
2149
3628
3556
3058
2870
2831
2347
2322
4843
3100
3767
3002
ft m
12,000 4000
9000 3000
6000 2000
4500 1500
3000 1000
1200 400
600 200
0 0
200 600
2000 6000
m ft

Projection: Conical with two standard parallels

Kilometers 0 50 100 150 200 250 Km.
Statute Miles 0 50 100 150 200 250 Mi.

1:4 800 000

One centimeter represents 48 kilometers
One inch represents approximately 75 miles

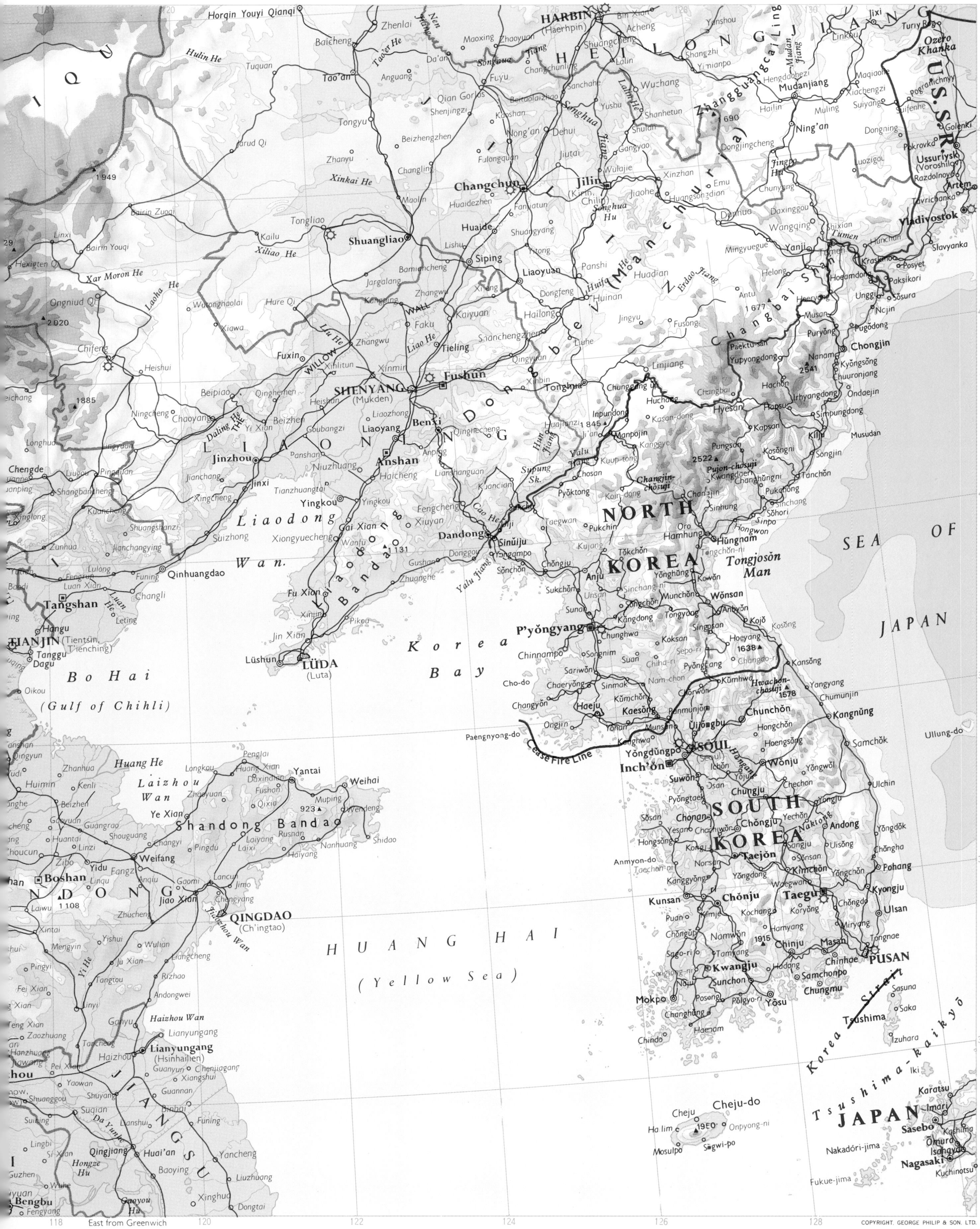

HARBIN
(Haerbin)
HEILONGJIANG
U.S.S.R.
Ozero Khanka
Ussuriysk
(Voroshilov)
Vladivostok
Mudanjiang
Changchun
Jilin
Shuangliao
Siping
Liaoyuan
JILIN
Dongbei (Manchuria)
Changbai Shan
Paektu-san
SHENYANG
(Mukden)
Fushun
Benxi
Anshan
Liaoyang
Jinzhou
Fuxin
Tonghua
Yingkou
Dandong
Sinŭiju
LIAONING
Liaodong Wan
Liaodong Bandao
LÜDA
(Luta)
Lüshun
Bo Hai
(Gulf of Chihli)
TIANJIN (Tientsin, T'ienching)
Tangshan
Qinhuangdao
Chengde
Chifeng
Tongliao
Korea Bay
NORTH KOREA
P'yŏngyang
Hamhŭng
Hŭngnam
Chongjin
Wŏnsan
Tongjosŏn Man
Kaesŏng
Cease Fire Line
SEA OF JAPAN
SOUTH KOREA
SOUL
(Seoul)
Inch'ŏn
Ch'unch'ŏn
Taejŏn
Taegu
Kwangju
Chŏnju
Kunsan
Mokpo
PUSAN
Ulsan
Pohang
Korea Strait
Tsushima
Tsushima-kaikyō
Cheju-do
Cheju
JAPAN
Sasebo
Nagasaki
HUANG HAI
(Yellow Sea)
Shandong Bandao
Laizhou Wan
Yantai
Weihai
QINGDAO
(Ch'ingtao)
Weifang
Boshan
Lianyungang
Haizhou Wan
JIANGSU
Qingjiang
Huai'an
Bengbu
118
East from Greenwich
120
122
124
126
128
34
36
38
40
42
44

Kilometers 0 200 400 600 800 Km.
Statute Miles 0 200 400 600 800 Mi.

1:16 000 000

One centimeter represents 160 kilometers
One inch represents approximately 250 miles

UNION OF SOVIET SOCIALIST REPUBLICS
MONGOLIA
CHINA
XIZANG (TIBET)
JAPAN
NORTH KOREA
SOUTH KOREA
VIETNAM
LAOS
THAILAND (SIAM)
BURMA
INDIA
NEPAL
BHUTAN
BANGLADESH
PHILIPPINES
TAIWAN (FORMOSA)
KAZAKH S.S.R.
KIRGIZ S.S.R.
JAMMU & KASHMIR
EAST CHINA SEA
SOUTH CHINA SEA
YELLOW SEA
BAY OF BENGAL
BEIJING
SHANGHAI
TIANJIN
GUANGZHOU
CHONGQING
CHENGDU
WUHAN
NANJING
SHENYANG
HARBIN
XI'AN
LANZHOU
KUNMING
Lhasa
Ürümqi
Hong Kong
Tarim Pendi
Junggar Pendi
Kunlun Shan
Altun Shan
Qilian Shan
Tanggula Shan
Hoh Xil Shan
Bayan Har Shan
Tian Shan
Altai
Gobi
Da Hinggan Ling
Xiao Hinggan Ling
Mu Us Shamo
Hainan Dao
Ryukyu-retto
Bashi Channel
Batan Is.
Tropic of Cancer
Projection: Bonne
East from Greenwich
COPYRIGHT, GEORGE PHILIP & SON, LTD.
m ft
6000 18,000
4000 12,000
3000 9000
2000 6000
1500 4500
1000 3000
400 1200
200 600
0
200 600
2000 6000
4000 12,000
6000 18,000

Kilometers 0 50 100 150 200 250 300 Km.
Statute Miles 0 50 100 150 200 250 300 Mi

1:6 000 000

One centimeter represents 60 kilometers
One inch represents approximately 95 miles

C H I N A
U. S. S. R.
NORTH KOREA
SOUTH KOREA
S E A O F J A P A N
Sea of Okhotsk
P A C I F I C O C E A N
KOREA STRAIT
Tsushima-Kaikyō
Mudanjiang
Ningan
Turii Rog
Ozero Khanka
Spassk-Dalni
Varfolomeyevka
Verkhove
Tetyukhe
Ussurysk (Voroshilov)
Vladivostok
Suchan
Nakhodka
Tumen
Hunchun
Zaliv Petra Velikogo
Najin
Chongjin
Songjin
Tanchon
Kosŏng
Ullung Do
Samchok
Pusan
Rebun-Tō
Rishiri-Tō
Wakkanai
Teshio
Otoineppu
Enbetsu
HOKKAIDŌ
Monbetsu
Yubetsu
Abashiri-Wan
Shibetsu
Kitami
Abashiri
Rumoi
Daisetsu-Zan 2290
Asahikawa
HOKKAIDO
Nemuro
Ishikari-Wan (Otaru-Wan)
Kamui-Misaki
Bibai
Iwamisawa
Obihiro
Honbetsu
Kushiro
Iwanai
Otaru
Yūbari
Sapporo
Tomakomai
Poroshiri Dake 2052
Mombetsu
Setana
Muroran
Urakawa
Samani
Okushiri-Tō
Erimo-Misaki
Esashi
Hakodate
Esan-Misaki
Tsugaru-Kaikyō
Matsumae
Shiriya-Zaki
Mutsu
Mutsu-Wan
Aomori
Hirosaki
Towada-Ko
Hachinohe
Kuji
Noshiro
Odate
Oga-Hantō
Iwate-San 2041
Akita
Morioka
Miyako
Honjō
Hanamaki
Kamaishi
Yokote
Ichinoseki
Sakata
Tsuruoka
Mogami
Shinjō
TŌHOKU
Kogota
Ishinomaki
Yamagata
Shiogama
Sendai
Iwanuma
Sado
Niigata
Shibata
Yonezawa
Fukushima
Bandai-San 1819
Suzu-Misaki
Wajima
Nagaoka
Kashiwazaki
Aizuwakamatsu
Koriyama
Naoetsu
Tajima
Toyama-Wan
Takada
Iwaki
Nanao
Himi
Takaoka
Nagano
Nikkō
Hitachi
Kanazawa
Toyama
Maebashi
Kiryū
Utsunomiya
Nakaminato
Oki-Shotō
CHŪBU
Matsumoto
Takasaki
Tochigi
Mito
Fukui
Takayama
Chichibu
Tsuchiura
KANTŌ
Kyō-ga-Saki
Wakasa-Wan
Takefu
Suwa
Kawagoe
Urawa
Kawaguchi
Sawara
Hi-no-Misaki
Tsuruga
Ontake-San 3063
Kōfu
TŌKYŌ
Ichikawa
Chōshi
Matsue
Tottori
Toyooka
Maizuru
Kawasaki
Chiba
Izumo
Yonago
Ayabe
Biwa-Ko
Gifu
Fuji-San 3776
Yokohama
Yokosuka
CHŪGOKU
Tsuyama
Kyōto
Ichinomiya
Fuji-no-miya
Fujisawa
Katsuura
Hamada
Himeji
Amagasaki
Hikone
Nagoya
Shimizu
Numazu
Atami
Tateyama
Masuda
Okayama
Kōbe
Ōsaka
Yokkaichi
Okazaki
Shizuoka
Kurashiki
Akashi
Tsu
Itō
Ō-Shima
Fukuyama
Onomichi
Nara
Matsusaka
Toyohashi
Hamamatsu
Hiroshima
Mihara
Sakai
Ise-Wan
Tsushima
Iki
Yamaguchi
Hōfu
Kure
Takamatsu
Toba
Shimonoseki
Tokuyama
Marugame
Kishiwada
Wakayama
Daiō-Misaki
Nii-Jima
Ube
Suō-Nada
Tokushima
Owase
Miyake-Jima
Fukuoka
Kitakyūshū
Niihama
Mikura-Jima
Karatsu
Nakatsu
Matsuyama
SHIKOKU
KINKI
Kurume
Beppu
Setonaikai
Kii-Suidō
Shingū
Sasebo
Saga
Ōmuta
Ōita
Yawatahama
Kōchi
Shio-no-Misaki
Nakadori-Jima
Kashima
Usuki
Uwajima
Tosa-Wan
Muroto-Misaki
Isahaya
Aso-zan 1592
Saiki
Nagasaki
Kumamoto
Bungo-Suidō
Nakamura
Shimabara
SHIKOKU
Hachijo-Jima
Fukue-Jima
Yatsushiro
Ashizuri-zaki
Shimo-Jima
Nobeoka
Minamata
Aoga-Shima
KYŪSHŪ
Sendai
Miyazaki
Kobayashi
Kagoshima
Miyakonojō
Kanoya
Makurazaki
Kagoshima-Wan
Shibushi-Wan
Ōsumi-Kaikyō
Ōsumi-Shotō
Nishinoomote
Tane-ga-Shima
Kuchinoerabu-Jima
Yaku-Jima
Tokara-Kaikyō
Naka-no-Shima
Suwanose-Jima
Nemuro-Kaikyō
Ōsumi-Shotō
Kuchinoerabu-Jima
Tokara-Kaikyō
Yaku-Jima
Naka-no-Shima
Suwanose-Jima
Satsunan-Shotō
Nansei-Shotō (Ryūkyū-Shotō)
Naze
Kikai-Jima
Amami Ō Shima
Setouchi
Tokunoshima
Okinoerabu-Jima
Okinawa-Shotō
Okinawa-Jima
Ishikawa
Ginowan
Koza
Kerama-Shotō
Naha
Nansei-Shoto Trench
7507
PACIFIC OCEAN
Miyako-Jima
Hirara
Yaeyama-Shotō
Yonaguri-Jima
Ishigaki-Jima
Ishigaki
Iriomote-Jima
RYŪKYŪ ISLANDS
Continuation southwards in same scale
ft m
4500 1500
3000 1000
1200 400
600 200
0 0
200 600
m ft

Projection: Bonne

East from Greenwich

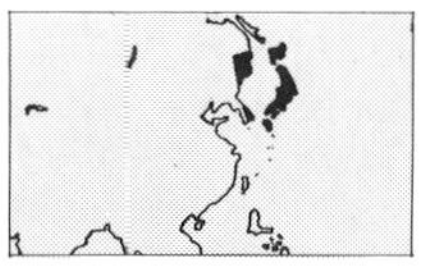

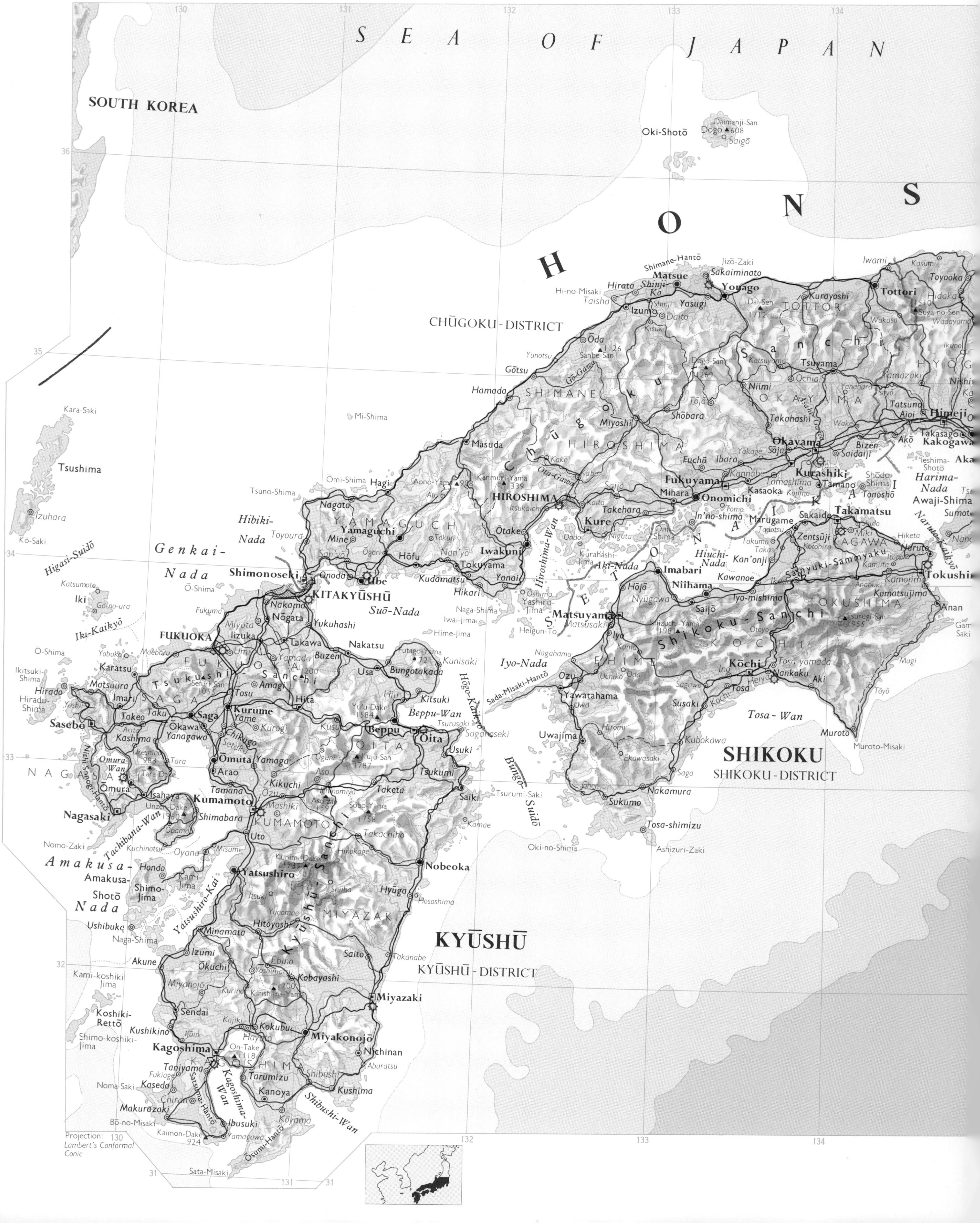
SEA OF JAPAN
SOUTH KOREA
HONSHU
CHŪGOKU - DISTRICT
SHIKOKU
SHIKOKU - DISTRICT
KYŪSHŪ
KYŪSHŪ - DISTRICT
Oki-Shotō
Dogo
Daimanji-San
608
Saigō
Shimane-Hantō
Jizō-Zaki
Sakaiminato
Matsue
Hirata
Shinji-Ko
Yonago
Yasugi
Hi-no-Misaki
Taisha
Izumo
Daito
Dai-Sen
1712
TOTTORI
Kurayoshi
Tottori
Iwami
Toyooka
Ōda
Sanbe-San
1126
Yunotsu
Gōtsu
Hamada
SHIMANE
Chūgoku-Sanchi
Niimi
OKAYAMA
Tsuyama
Tatsuno
Aioi
Himeji
Takasago
Kakogawa
Shōbara
Takahashi
Miyoshi
HIROSHIMA
Okayama
Sōja
Kurashiki
Tamano
Bizen
Saidaiji
Akō
Fuchū
Ibara
Fukuyama
Mihara
Onomichi
Kasaoka
Masuda
Mi-Shima
Kara-Saki
Tsushima
Izuhara
Kō-Saki
Ōmi-Shima
Hagi
Tsuno-Shima
Aono-Yama
Kanmuri-Yama
1339
HIROSHIMA
Kure
Takehara
Ōtake
Iwakuni
Nagato
YAMAGUCHI
Yamaguchi
Mine
Hōfu
Tokuyama
Kudamatsu
Yanai
Hikari
Hibiki-Nada
Toyoura
Genkai-Nada
Shimonoseki
Onoda
Ube
KITAKYŪSHŪ
Suō-Nada
Higasi-Suidō
Iki
Iki-Kaikyō
Katsumoto
Gōno-ura
Ō-Shima
Nakama
Nōgata
Yukuhashi
Iizuka
FUKUOKA
Nakatsu
Takawa
Buzen
Futago-Yama
721
Kunisaki
Bungotakada
Usa
Iyo-Nada
Hōgo-Kaikyō
Sada-Misaki-Hantō
Karatsu
Ikitsuki-Shima
Hirado
Hirado-Shima
Matsuura
Imari
SAGA
Tsukushi-Sanchi
Amagi
Tosu
Hita
Kurume
Saga
Takeo
Taku
Sasebo
Kashima
Ōkawa
Yanagawa
Yame
Ōmuta
Arao
Yamaga
Beppu
Beppu-Wan
Ōita
ŌITA
Yufu-Dake
1584
Kuju-San
1787
Kitsuki
Tsurusaki
Saganoseki
Usuki
Tsukumi
Saiki
Bungo-Suidō
Tsurumi-Saki
NAGASAKI
Ōmura
Ōmura-Wan
Tara-Dake
983
Isahaya
Kumamoto
Nagasaki
Unzen-Dake
1360
Shimabara
Tamana
Kikuchi
Aso-San
1592
Sobo-Yama
1758
Taketa
KUMAMOTO
Takachiho
Uto
Nishi-Sonogi-Hantō
Tachibana-Wan
Nomo-Zaki
Amakusa-Nada
Hondo
Amakusa-Shotō
Kami-Jima
Shimo-Jima
Misumi
Ōyano
Yatsushiro
Yatsushiro-Kai
Kunimi-Dake
1739
Kyūshū-Sanchi
Nobeoka
Hyūga
Hososhima
MIYAZAKI
Hitoyoshi
Ushibuka
Naga-Shima
Minamata
Izumi
Akune
Ōkuchi
Kami-koshiki-Jima
Koshiki-Rettō
Shimo-koshiki-Jima
Sendai
Kushikino
Kobayashi
Kirishima-Yama
1700
Saito
Takanabe
Miyazaki
Kokubu
Miyakonojō
Nichinan
Aburatsu
Kagoshima
KAGOSHIMA
On-Take
1118
Taniyama
Kaseda
Noma-Saki
Kagoshima-Wan
Tarumizu
Kanoya
Kushima
Shibushi
Shibushi-Wan
Makurazaki
Bō-no-Misaki
Ibusuki
Kaimon-Dake
924
Ōsumi-Hantō
Sata-Misaki
Satsuma-Hantō
SETO NAIKAI
Hiroshima-Wan
Aki-Nada
Imabari
Niihama
Saijō
Matsuyama
Hiuchi-Nada
Kan'onji
Kawanoe
Marugame
Sakaide
Takamatsu
Zentsūji
KAGAWA
Naruto
Tokushima
Sanuki-Sammyaku
TOKUSHIMA
Komatsujima
Anan
Tsurugi-San
1955
Shikoku-Sanchi
KŌCHI
Ishizuchi-Yama
1981
Iyo-mishima
Ōzu
Yawatahama
Uwajima
EHIME
Kōchi
Nankoku
Aki
Susaki
Tosa
Tosa-Wan
Muroto
Muroto-Misaki
Kubokawa
Nakamura
Sukumo
Tosa-shimizu
Ashizuri-Zaki
Oki-no-Shima
Harima-Nada
Awaji-Shima
Shōdo-Shima
Ieshima-Shotō
Projection: Lambert's Conformal Conic

Kilometers 0 20 40 60 80 100 Km.
Statute Miles 0 20 40 60 80 100 Mi.

1:2 000 000

One centimeter represents 20 kilometers
One inch represents approximately 32 miles

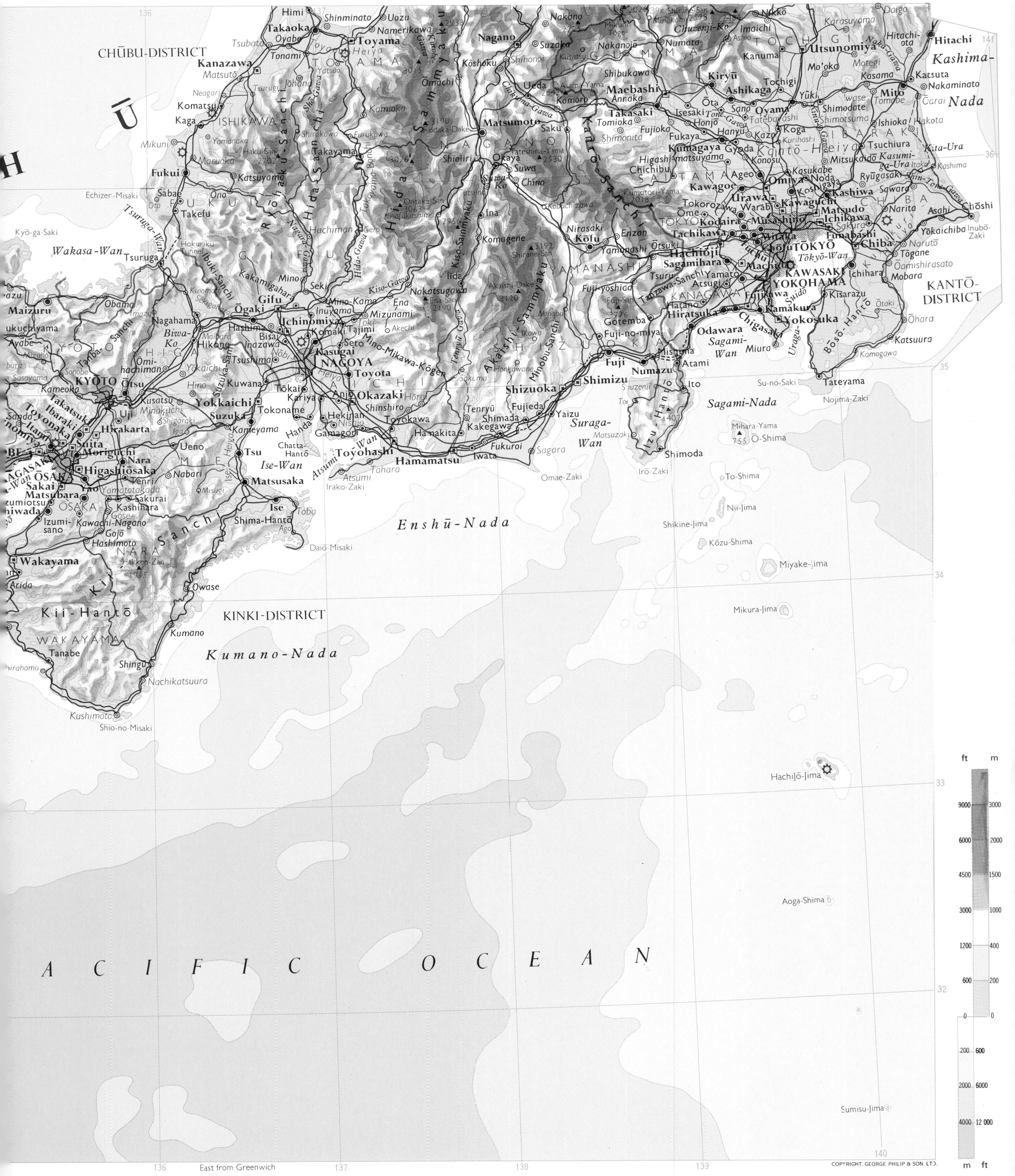
CHŪBU-DISTRICT
KINKI-DISTRICT
KANTŌ-DISTRICT
Kanazawa
Takaoka
Toyama
Himi
Uozu
Shinminato
Namerikawa
Komatsu
Kaga
Mikuni
Fukui
Sabae
Takefu
Tsuruga
Tsuruga-Wan
Wakasa-Wan
Kyō-ga-Saki
Echizen-Misaki
Maizuru
Obama
Fukuchiyama
Ayabe
Kameoka
KYŌTO
Ōtsu
Uji
Takatsuki
Ibaraki
Toyonaka
Itami
Suita
Moriguchi
Hirakarta
Higashiōsaka
Nara
Tenri
Yao
Sakai
Matsubara
Izumi-sano
Gojō
Hashimoto
Wakayama
Arida
Kii-Hantō
Tanabe
Shingu
Nachikatsuura
Kushimoto
Shio-no-Misaki
Owase
Kumano
Kumano-Nada
Ise
Toba
Shima-Hantō
Daiō-Misaki
Matsusaka
Tsu
Ise-Wan
Ueno
Nabari
Kameyama
Suzuka
Yokkaichi
Kuwana
Tōkai
NAGOYA
Kasugai
Ichinomiya
Gifu
Ōgaki
Hashima
Hikone
Nagahama
Biwa-Ko
Omi-hachiman
Seki
Mino
Inuyama
Tajimi
Seto
Toyota
Okazaki
Anjo
Kariya
Hekinan
Handa
Tokoname
Chatta-Hantō
Gamagori
Toyohashi
Toyokawa
Shinshiro
Atsumi
Irako-Zaki
Hamamatsu
Iwata
Fukuroi
Kakegawa
Shimada
Fujieda
Yaizu
Shizuoka
Shimizu
Fuji
Fuji-no-miya
Numazu
Mishima
Atami
Ito
Shimoda
Suruga-Wan
Omae-Zaki
Enshū-Nada
Sagami-Nada
Sagami-Wan
Odawara
Hiratsuka
Chigasaki
Fujisawa
Kamakura
Yokosuka
YOKOHAMA
KAWASAKI
TŌKYŌ
Tōkyō-Wan
Chiba
Funabashi
Ichikawa
Matsudo
Kashiwa
Noda
Urawa
Ōmiya
Kawaguchi
Kawagoe
Tokorozawa
Tachikawa
Hachiōji
Sagamihara
Machida
Atsugi
Yamato
Ageo
Kumagaya
Gyōda
Fukaya
Honjo
Chichibu
Kōfu
Nirasaki
Enzan
Ōtsuki
Gotemba
Fuji-yoshida
Maebashi
Takasaki
Annaka
Tomioka
Kiryū
Ashikaga
Ōta
Oyama
Koga
Tochigi
Utsunomiya
Nikkō
Imaichi
Kanuma
Mito
Katsuta
Hitachi
Hitachi-ota
Kashima-Nada
Tsuchiura
Ishioka
Kasumi-ga-Ura
Kita-Ura
Narita
Chōshi
Asahi
Yōkaichiba
Inubō-Zaki
Tōgane
Mobara
Ichihara
Kisarazu
Ōhara
Katsuura
Tateyama
Nojima-Zaki
Bōsō-Hantō
Miura
Uraga-Suidō
Nagano
Ueda
Komoro
Matsumoto
Suwa
Okaya
Chino
Ina
Komagene
Iida
Takayama
Ōmachi
Hida-Sammyaku
Kiso-Sammyaku
Akaishi-Sammyaku
Kantō-Sanchi
Kantō-Heiya
Kii-Sanchi
Ōshima
Mihara-Yama
To-Shima
Nii-Jima
Shikine-Jima
Kōzu-Shima
Miyake-Jima
Mikura-Jima
Hachijō-Jima
Aoga-Shima
Sumisu-Jima
PACIFIC OCEAN
HONSHŪ
East from Greenwich
136
137
138
139
140
141
35
34
33
32
36
ft
m
9000 3000
6000 2000
4500 1500
3000 1000
1200 400
600 200
0 0
200 600
2000 6000
4000 12 000

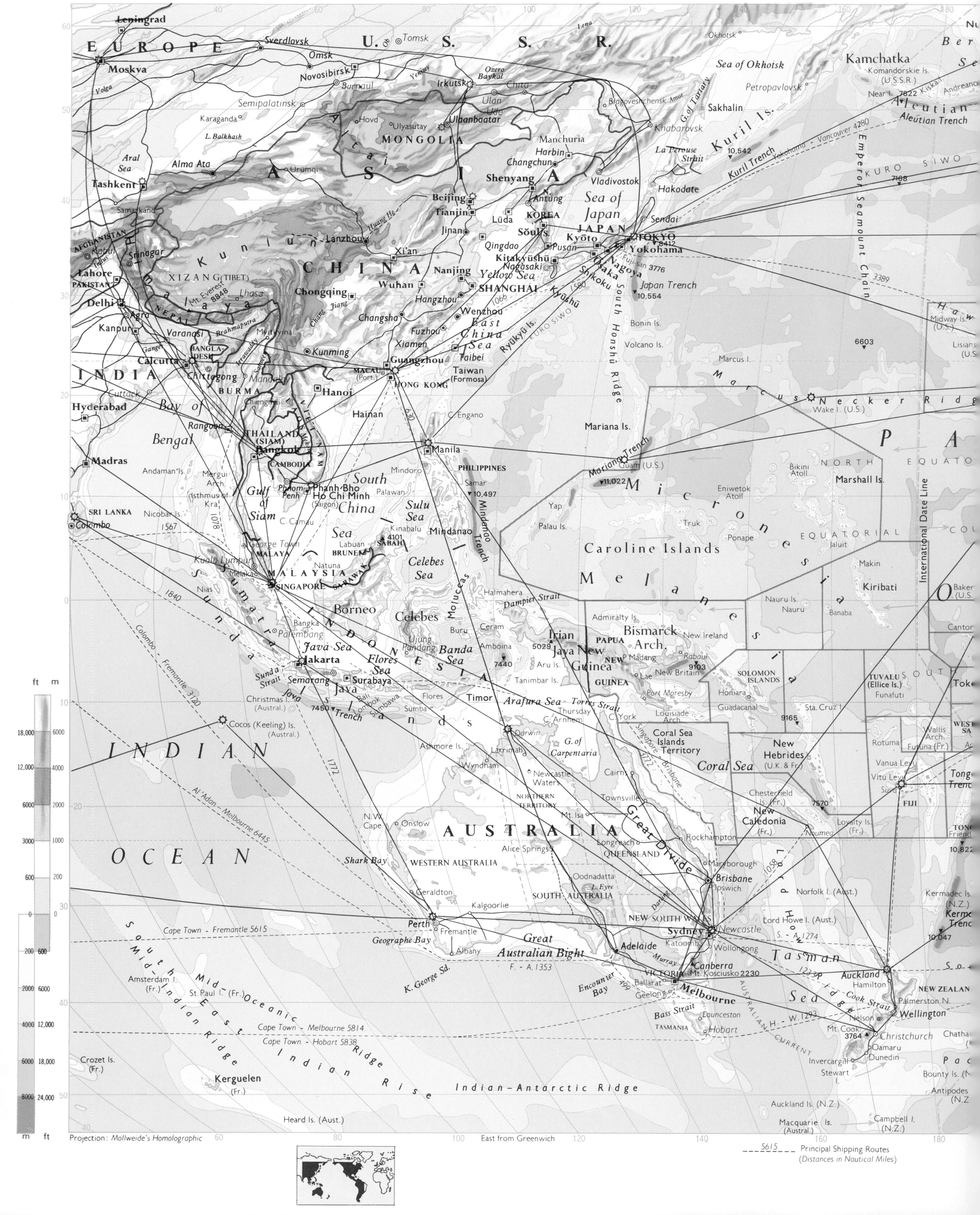
EUROPE
U. S. S. R.
Leningrad
Moskva
Volga
Sverdlovsk
Omsk
Tomsk
Novosibirsk
Barnaul
Yenisey
Irkutsk
Ozero Baykal
Chita
Lena
Okhotsk
Sea of Okhotsk
Kamchatka
Komandorskie Is. (U.S.S.R.)
Petropavlovsk
Near I.
7822
Kiska I.
Aleutian Trench
Semipalatinsk
Karaganda
L. Balkhash
Aral Sea
Alma Ata
Tashkent
Samarkand
Ürümqi
Hovd
Ulyasutay
Ulaanbaatar
Ulan Ude
MONGOLIA
Altai
ASIA
Blagoveshchensk
Amur
G. of Tartary
Sakhalin
Khabarovsk
Manchuria
Harbin
Changchun
Shenyang
La Perouse Strait
Kuril Is.
10,542
Kuril Trench
Yokohama - Vancouver 4280
Emperor Seamount Chain
KURO SIWO
7168
Vladivostok
Hakodate
Beijing
Tianjin
Antung
Sea of Japan
Lüda
KOREA
Sendai
Huang He
Lanzhou
Jinan
Sŏul
JAPAN
TOKYO
8412
Kyoto
Yokohama
AFGHANISTAN
Kabul
Indus
Srinagar
Kunlun
Xi'an
Qingdao
Pusan
Kitakyūshū
Nagasaki
Nagoya
Osaka
Fuji-san 3776
Lahore
PAKISTAN
XIZANG (TIBET)
Mt. Everest 8848
Lhasa
CHINA
Nanjing
Yellow Sea
SHANGHAI
Wuhan
Chongqing
Shikoku
Kyūshū
Japan Trench
10,554
3389
Delhi
Agra
Himalaya
NEPAL
Hangzhou
Jiang
1066
1580
Kanpur
Varanasi
Brahmaputra
Myitkyina
Changsha
Wenzhou
East China Sea
Ryūkyū Is.
KURO SIWO
South Honshū Ridge
Bonin Is.
Midway Is. (U.S.)
Ganges
BANGLA-DESH
Irrawaddy
Salween
Kunming
Fuzhou
Xiamen
Taibei
Volcano Is.
6603
Lisians (U.S.)
Calcutta
INDIA
Chittagong
Mandalay
Guangzhou
MACAU (Port.)
HONG KONG
Taiwan (Formosa)
Marcus I.
Marcus Necker Ridge
Wake I. (U.S.)
Hyderabad
Cuttack
BURMA
Chiengmai
Hanoi
Hainan
C. Engano
Bay of Bengal
Rangoon
THAILAND (SIAM)
Bangkok
VIETNAM
Mariana Is.
PACIFIC
Madras
Andaman Is.
CAMBODIA
Manila
Mariana Trench
Guam (U.S.)
11,022
NORTH EQUATORIAL
Bikini Atoll
Marshall Is.
Mergui Arch.
Isthmus of Kra
Gulf of Siam
Phnom Penh
Phanh Bho Ho Chi Minh (Saigon)
Mindoro
PHILIPPINES
Samar
10,497
South China Sea
Palawan
Micronesia
Eniwetok Atoll
SRI LANKA
Colombo
Nicobar Is.
1567
1078
C. Camau
Sulu Sea
Mindanao
Mindanao Trench
Yap
Palau Is.
Truk
Ponape
EQUATORIAL
Jaluit
International Date Line
Kinabalu 4101
SABAH
Labuan
BRUNEI
George Town
MALAYA
Kuala Lumpur
Melaka
Caroline Islands
Natuna
SARAWAK
MALAYSIA
SINGAPORE
Celebes Sea
Moluccas
Makin
Kiribati
Melanesia
Baker (U.S.)
1840
Nias
Sumatra
Halmahera
Dampier Strait
Nauru Is.
Nauru
Banaba
Borneo
Celebes
INDONESIA
Admiralty Is.
Bismarck Arch.
New Ireland
Canton
Bangka
Palembang
Buru
Ceram
Irian Jaya
New Guinea
PAPUA NEW GUINEA
Madang
Rabaul
9103
Ujung Pandang
Banda Sea
Amboina
5029
Java Sea
Jakarta
Flores Sea
7440
Aru Is.
New Britain
SOLOMON ISLANDS
TUVALU (Ellice Is.)
Funafuti
Sunda Strait
Semarang
Surabaya
Java
Bali
Lombok
Sumbawa
Tanimbar Is.
Lae
Colombo - Fremantle 3120
Christmas I. (Austral.)
Java Trench
7450
Flores
Sumba
Timor
Arafura Sea
Torres Strait
Port Moresby
Honiara
Guadacanal
Sta. Cruz I.
Thursday I.
C. Arnhem
C. York
Louisiade Arch.
9165
Cocos (Keeling) Is. (Austral.)
Sunda Islands
Darwin
Coral Sea Islands Territory
New Hebrides (U.K. & Fr.)
Wallis Arch.
Futuna (Fr.)
Rotuma
INDIAN
1772
Ashmore Is.
Larrimah
Wyndham
G. of Carpentaria
Singapore - Brisbane 1712
Coral Sea
Vanua Levu
Vitu Levu
Suva
FIJI
Newcastle Waters
Cairns
NORTHERN TERRITORY
Townsville
Mt. Isa
Chesterfield Is. (Fr.)
7570
Al' Adan - Melbourne 6445
N.W. Cape
Onslow
AUSTRALIA
Great Divide
New Caledonia (Fr.)
Noumea
Loyalty Is. (Fr.)
Rockhampton
Longreach
QUEENSLAND
Alice Springs
OCEAN
Shark Bay
WESTERN AUSTRALIA
Maryborough
Brisbane
Ipswich
1058
10,822
Oodnadatta
L. Eyre
SOUTH AUSTRALIA
Geraldton
Lord Howe Rise
Norfolk I. (Aust.)
Kermadec Is. (N.Z.)
Kermadec Trench
Darling
Kalgoorlie
NEW SOUTH WALES
Sydney
Newcastle
Lord Howe I. (Aust.)
Perth
Fremantle
Cape Town - Fremantle 5615
Katoomba
S. - A. 1274
10,047
Geographe Bay
Great Australian Bight
Adelaide
Wollongong
Murray
Canberra
Tasman Sea
Albany
F. - A. 1353
Mt. Kosciusko 2230
VICTORIA
Auckland
Hamilton
K. George Sd.
South Mid-Indian Ridge
Mid-Oceanic Ridge
Amsterdam I. (Fr.)
St. Paul I. (Fr.)
Encounter Bay
499
Ballarat
Geelong
Melbourne
1234
Lord Howe Ridge
NEW ZEALAND
Cook Strait
Palmerston N.
Wellington
Bass Strait
AUSTRALIAN CURRENT
Launceston
Hobart
TASMANIA
H. - W. 1293
Nelson
Cape Town - Melbourne 5814
Cape Town - Hobart 5838
Mt. Cook 3764
Christchurch
Oamaru
Dunedin
Chatham
South East Indian Rise
Crozet Is. (Fr.)
Invercargill
Stewart I.
Bounty Is.
Kerguelen (Fr.)
Indian-Antarctic Ridge
Antipodes
Auckland Is. (N.Z.)
Heard Is. (Aust.)
Macquarie Is. (Austral.)
Campbell I. (N.Z.)
ft m
18,000 6000
12,000 4000
6000 2000
3000 1000
600 200
0 0
200 600
2000 6000
4000 12,000
6000 18,000
8000 24,000
m ft
Projection: Mollweide's Homolographic
East from Greenwich
20 40 60 80 100 120 140 160 180
60 50 40 30 20 10 0 10 20 30 40 50
5615 Principal Shipping Routes (Distances in Nautical Miles)

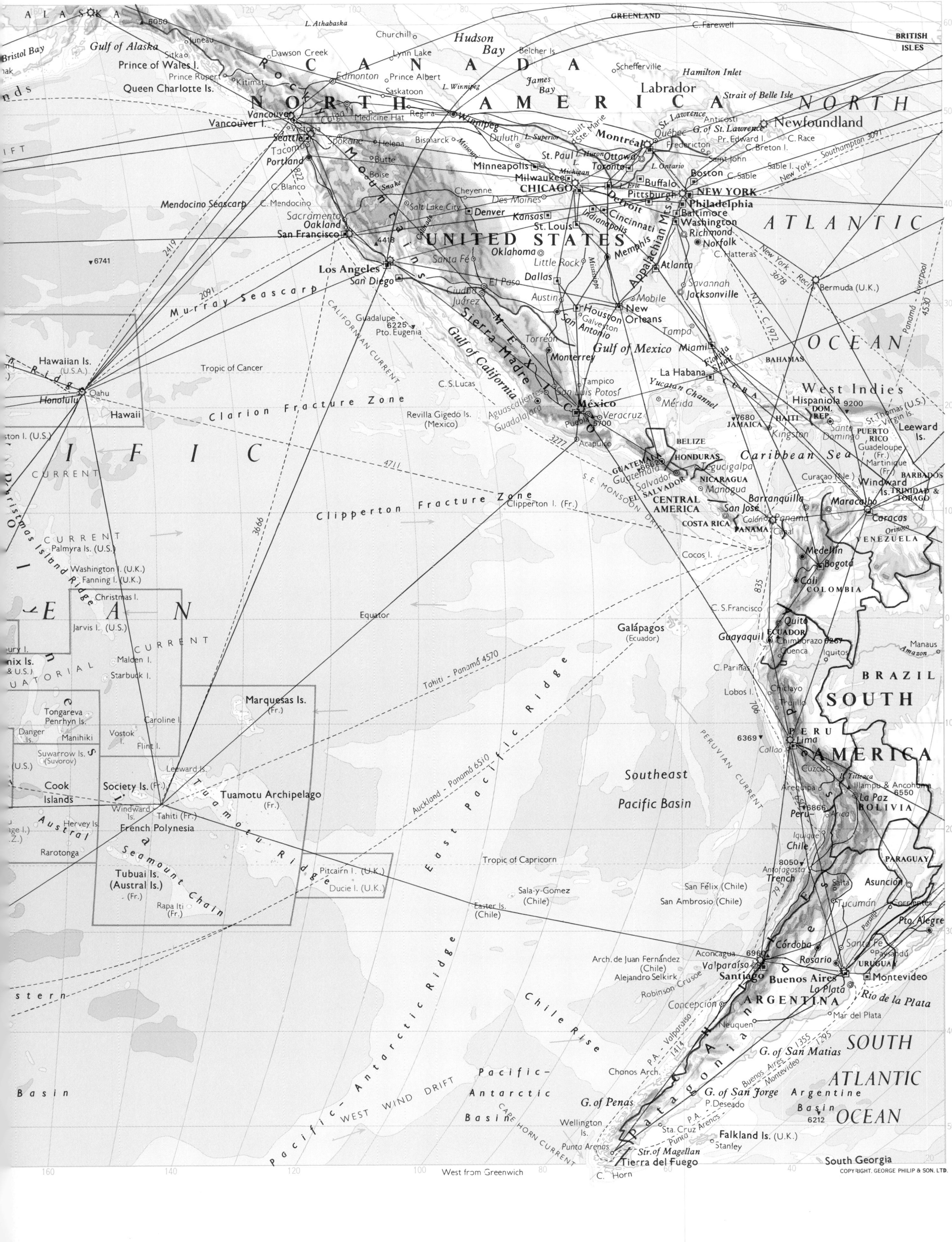

ALASKA
Gulf of Alaska
Prince of Wales I.
Queen Charlotte Is.
CANADA
NORTH AMERICA
Hudson Bay
James Bay
Labrador
Hamilton Inlet
Strait of Belle Isle
Newfoundland
GREENLAND
C. Farewell
BRITISH ISLES
Rocky Mountains
UNITED STATES
Vancouver
Seattle
Portland
San Francisco
Oakland
Sacramento
Los Angeles
San Diego
Salt Lake City
Denver
Kansas
St. Louis
CHICAGO
Milwaukee
Minneapolis
St. Paul
Detroit
Toronto
Ottawa
Montréal
Québec
Boston
NEW YORK
Philadelphia
Baltimore
Washington
Richmond
Norfolk
C. Hatteras
Pittsburgh
Buffalo
Cincinnati
Indianapolis
Memphis
Atlanta
Appalachian Mts.
New Orleans
Houston
Dallas
Austin
San Antonio
Mobile
Jacksonville
Savannah
Miami
Tampa
Oklahoma
Little Rock
El Paso
Ciudad Juárez
Santa Fé
Cheyenne
Des Moines
Bismarck
Winnipeg
Regina
Edmonton
Saskatoon
Prince Albert
Medicine Hat
Calgary
Spokane
Helena
Butte
Boise
Churchill
Lynn Lake
Dawson Creek
Juneau
Sitka
Prince Rupert
Kitimat
Schefferville
Anticosti
G. of St. Lawrence
C. Race
C. Breton I.
Sable I.
Gulf of Mexico
Monterrey
Torreón
Tampico
San Luis Potosí
México
Veracruz
Puebla
Acapulco
Guadalajara
Aguascalientes
Mérida
Yucatan Channel
Gulf of California
Sierra Madre
MEXICO
La Habana
CUBA
BAHAMAS
West Indies
Hispaniola
HAITI
DOM. REP.
JAMAICA
Kingston
Santo Domingo
PUERTO RICO
Leeward Is.
Windward Is.
BARBADOS
TRINIDAD & TOBAGO
Caribbean Sea
BELIZE
HONDURAS
Tegucigalpa
GUATEMALA
EL SALVADOR
NICARAGUA
Managua
CENTRAL AMERICA
COSTA RICA
San José
PANAMA
Panamá
Barranquilla
Maracaibo
Caracas
VENEZUELA
Medellín
Bogotá
Cali
COLOMBIA
Quito
ECUADOR
Guayaquil
Chimborazo
Cuenca
Iquitos
Manaus
Amazon
BRAZIL
SOUTH AMERICA
PERU
Lima
Callao
Chiclayo
Trujillo
Cuzco
Arequipa
Arica
La Paz
BOLIVIA
Lake Titicaca
Illampu & Ancohuma
PARAGUAY
Asunción
Iquique
Antofagasta
Salta
Tucumán
Córdoba
Rosario
Santa Fe
Corrientes
Pto. Alegre
URUGUAY
Montevideo
Buenos Aires
La Plata
Río de la Plata
Mar del Plata
ARGENTINA
Aconcagua
Valparaíso
Santiago
Concepción
Neuquén
Patagonia
Andes
G. of San Matías
G. of San Jorge
P. Deseado
G. of Penas
Chonos Arch.
Wellington I.
Punta Arenas
Str. of Magellan
Tierra del Fuego
C. Horn
Falkland Is. (U.K.)
Stanley
South Georgia
SOUTH ATLANTIC OCEAN
Argentine Basin
ATLANTIC OCEAN
Bermuda (U.K.)
Hawaiian Is. (U.S.A.)
Honolulu
Oahu
Hawaii
Tropic of Cancer
Clarion Fracture Zone
Clipperton Fracture Zone
Clipperton I. (Fr.)
Murray Seascarp
Mendocino Seascarp
C. Mendocino
C. Blanco
Guadalupe
Pto. Eugenia
C. S. Lucas
Revilla Gigedo Is. (Mexico)
CALIFORNIAN CURRENT
PACIFIC OCEAN
Palmyra Is. (U.S.)
Washington I. (U.K.)
Fanning I. (U.K.)
Christmas I.
Christmas Island Ridge
Jarvis I. (U.S.)
Malden I.
Starbuck I.
EQUATORIAL CURRENT
Equator
Galápagos (Ecuador)
Cocos I.
C. S. Francisco
C. Pariñas
Lobos I.
Marquesas Is. (Fr.)
Tongareva Penrhyn Is.
Manihiki
Danger Is.
Suwarrow Is. (Suvorov)
Vostok I.
Flint I.
Caroline I.
Cook Islands
Society Is. (Fr.)
Leeward Is.
Windward Is.
Tahiti (Fr.)
French Polynesia
Tuamotu Archipelago (Fr.)
Tuamotu Ridge
Hervey Is.
Rarotonga
Austral Seamount Chain
Tubuai Is. (Austral Is.) (Fr.)
Rapa Iti (Fr.)
Pitcairn I. (U.K.)
Ducie I. (U.K.)
Tropic of Capricorn
Easter Is. (Chile)
Sala-y-Gomez (Chile)
San Félix (Chile)
San Ambrosio (Chile)
Arch. de Juan Fernández (Chile)
Alejandro Selkirk
Robinson Crusoe
Southeast Pacific Basin
East Pacific Ridge
PERUVIAN CURRENT
Peru-Chile Trench
S.E. MONSOON DRIFT
Chile Rise
Pacific-Antarctic Ridge
Pacific-Antarctic Basin
WEST WIND DRIFT
CAPE HORN CURRENT
Tahiti - Panamá 4570
Auckland - Panamá 6510
New York - Southampton 3091
New York - Recife 3678
Panamá - Liverpool 4530
West from Greenwich

Kilometers 0 40 80 120 160 200 Km.
Statute Miles 0 40 80 120 160 200 Mi.
1:4 000 000
One centimeter represents 40 kilometers
One inch represents approximately 64 miles

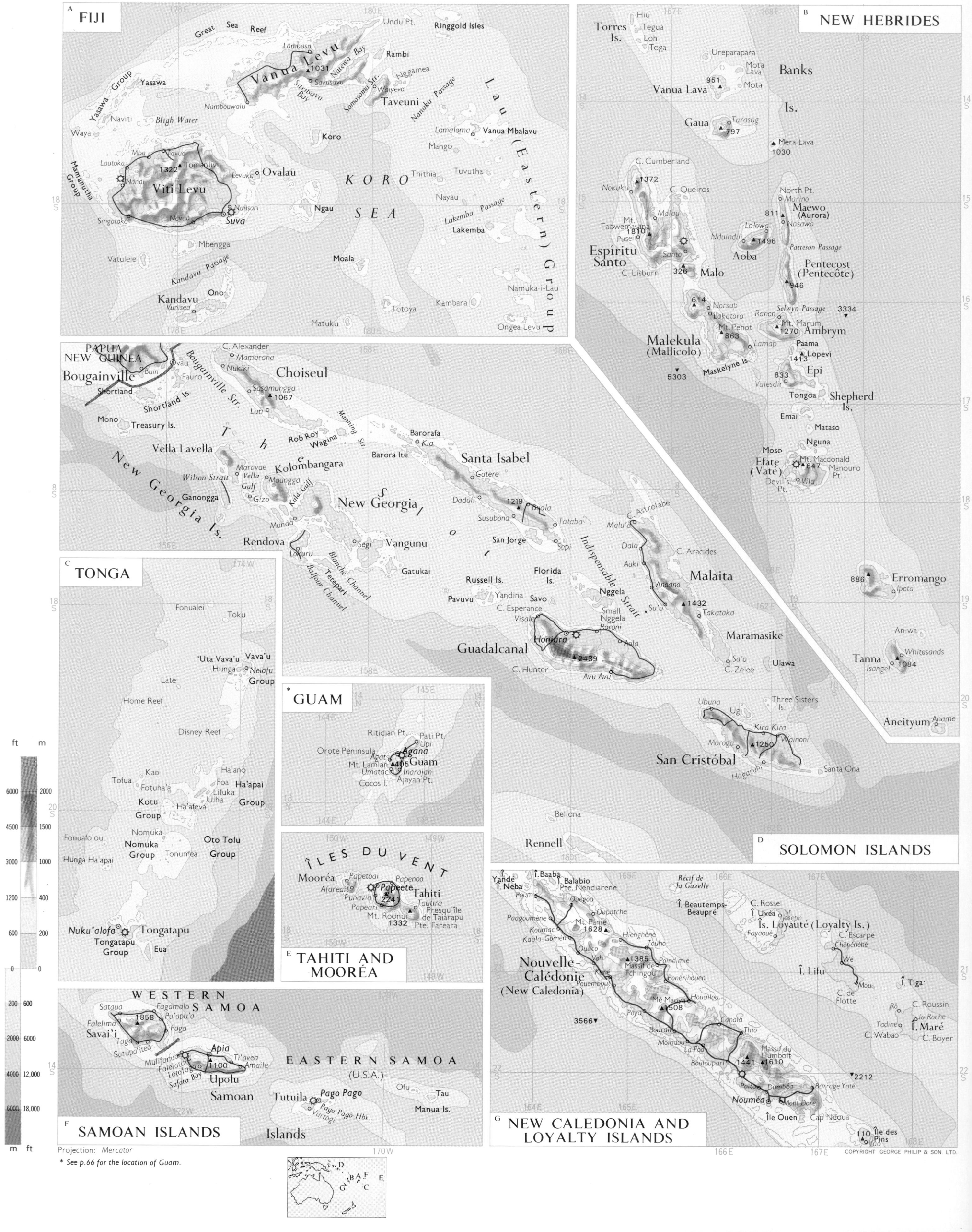
A FIJI
Great Sea Reef
Undu Pt.
Ringgold Isles
Lombasa
Vanua Levu
1031
Natewa Bay
Rambi
Yasawa Group
Yasawa
Savusavu
Savusavu Bay
Nambouwalu
Somosomo Str.
Nggamea
Waiyevo
Taveuni
Nanuku Passage
Lau (Eastern) Group
Naviti
Bligh Water
Waya
Koro
Lomaloma
Vanua Mbalavu
Mango
Mamanutha Group
Lautoka
Mba
Tavua
Tomanivi
1322
Nandi
Viti Levu
Levuka
Ovalau
KORO SEA
Thithia
Tuvutha
Nayau
Nausori
Suva
Navua
Singatoka
Ngau
Lakemba Passage
Lakemba
Mbengga
Vatulele
Kandavu Passage
Moala
Ono
Kandavu
Vunisea
Namuka-i-Lau
Kambara
Totoya
Matuku
Ongea Levu
B NEW HEBRIDES
Hiu
Torres Is.
Tegua
Loh
Toga
Ureparapara
Mota Lava
Mota
Banks Is.
951
Vanua Lava
Gaua
Tarasag
797
Mera Lava
1030
C. Cumberland
1372
Nokuku
C. Queiros
North Pt.
Marino
Maewo (Aurora)
811
Nasawa
Mt. Tabwemasana
1810
Pusei
Malau
Lolowai
1496
Nduindui
Aoba
Patteson Passage
Espiritu Santo
Santo
C. Lisburn
326
Malo
Pentecost (Pentecôte)
946
614
Norsup
Lakatoro
Mt. Penot
863
Malekula (Mallicolo)
Ranon
Selwyn Passage
3334
Mt. Marum
1270
Ambrym
Lamap
Paama
Lopevi
1413
Maskelyne Is.
Epi
5303
833
Valesdir
Tongoa
Shepherd Is.
Emai
Mataso
Nguna
Moso
Efate (Vaté)
Mt. Macdonald
647
Manouro Pt.
Devil's Pt.
Vila
886
Erromango
Ipota
Aniwa
Whitesands
Tanna
Isangel
1084
Aneityum
Aname
PAPUA NEW GUINEA
Bougainville
Buin
Ovau
Fauro
Shortland
Shortland Is.
Bougainville Str.
C. Alexander
Mamarana
Nukiki
Choiseul
Sasamungga
1067
Luti
Mono
Treasury Is.
Manning Str.
Vella Lavella
Rob Roy
Wagina
Barorafa
Kia
Barora Ite
Santa Isabel
Gatere
The Slot
Kolombangara
Maravae
Vella Gulf
Wilson Strait
Ganongga
Gizo
Munda
Kula Gulf
New Georgia Is.
New Georgia
Dadali
1219
Buala
Susubona
Tataba
San Jorge
Sepi
Segi
Vangunu
Rendova
Lokuru
Blanche Channel
Tetepari
Balfour Channel
Gatukai
Indispensable Strait
C. Astrolabe
Malu'u
Dala
Auki
C. Aracides
Malaita
Anogno
1432
Takataka
Su'u
Russell Is.
Florida Is.
Pavuvu
Yandina
Savo
Nggela
Small Nggela
C. Esperance
Visale
Honiara
Roroni
Aola
Guadalcanal
2439
C. Hunter
Avu Avu
Maramasike
Sa'a
C. Zelee
Ulawa
Three Sisters Is.
Ubuna
Ugi
Kira Kira
Moroga
1250
Wainoni
San Cristóbal
Hagaruhi
Santa Ona
Bellona
Rennell
D SOLOMON ISLANDS
C TONGA
Fonualei
Toku
'Uta Vava'u
Vava'u
Hunga
Neiafu
Group
Late
Home Reef
Disney Reef
Kao
Ha'ano
Tofua
Fotuha'a
Foa
Lifuka
Ha'apai
Kotu Group
Uiha
Ha'afeva
Group
Nomuka
Nomuka Group
Fonuafo'ou
Oto Tolu Group
Tonumea
Hunga Ha'apai
Nuku'alofa
Tongatapu
Tongatapu Group
Eua
GUAM
Ritidian Pt.
Pati Pt.
Upi
Orote Peninsula
Agat
Agana
Guam
Mt. Lamlam
405
Umatac
Inarajan
Cocos I.
Ajayan Pt.
ÎLES DU VENT
Mooréa
Papetoai
Papenoo
Afareaitu
Papeete
Tahiti
Punavia
Papeari
1224
Tautira
Presqu'île de Taiarapu
Mt. Roonui
1332
Pte. Fareara
E TAHITI AND MOORÉA
WESTERN SAMOA
Sataua
Fagamalo
Pu'apu'a
Falelima
1858
Faga
Savai'i
Taga
Satupa'itea
Apia
Mulifanua
Falelatai
Lotofaga
1100
Ti'avea
Amaile
Safata Bay
Upolu
EASTERN SAMOA (U.S.A.)
Samoan
Tutuila
Pago Pago
Pago Pago Hbr.
Vaitogi
Ofu
Tau
Manua Is.
Islands
F SAMOAN ISLANDS
Yandé
Î. Neba
Î. Baaba
Balabio
Pte. Nendiarene
Récif de la Gazelle
Poum
Ouégoa
Î. Beautemps-Beaupré
C. Rossel
Î. Uvéa
St. Joseph
Is. Loyauté (Loyalty Is.)
Fayaoué
C. Escarpé
Chépénéhé
Wé
Paagoumène
Oubatche
Koumac
Mt. Panié
1628
Kaala-Gomen
Hienghène
Touho
Ouaco
Voh
1385
Massif de Tchingou
Poindimié
Î. Lifu
Nouvelle Calédonie (New Caledonia)
Koné
Pouembout
Ponérihouen
Mou
Î. Tiga
C. de Flotte
Houaïlou
Mé Maoya
1508
C. Roussin
Poya
Rô
La Roche
3566
Canala
Tadine
Î. Maré
C. Wabao
C. Boyer
Bourail
Thio
Moindou
La Foa
Massif du Humboldt
1441
1610
Bouloupari
2212
Païta
Dumbéa
Baie de Yaté
Nouméa
Mont Dore
Île Ouen
Cap Ndoua
110
Île des Pins
Vao
G NEW CALEDONIA AND LOYALTY ISLANDS
COPYRIGHT GEORGE PHILIP & SON. LTD.
ft m
6000 2000
4500 1500
3000 1000
1200 400
600 200
0 0
200 600
2000 6000
4000 12,000
6000 18,000
m ft

Projection: Mercator

* See p.66 for the location of Guam.

Kilometers 0 50 100 150 200 250 Km.
Statute Miles 0 50 100 150 200 250 Mi.

1:5 200 000

One centimeter represents 52 kilometers
One inch represents approximately 82 miles

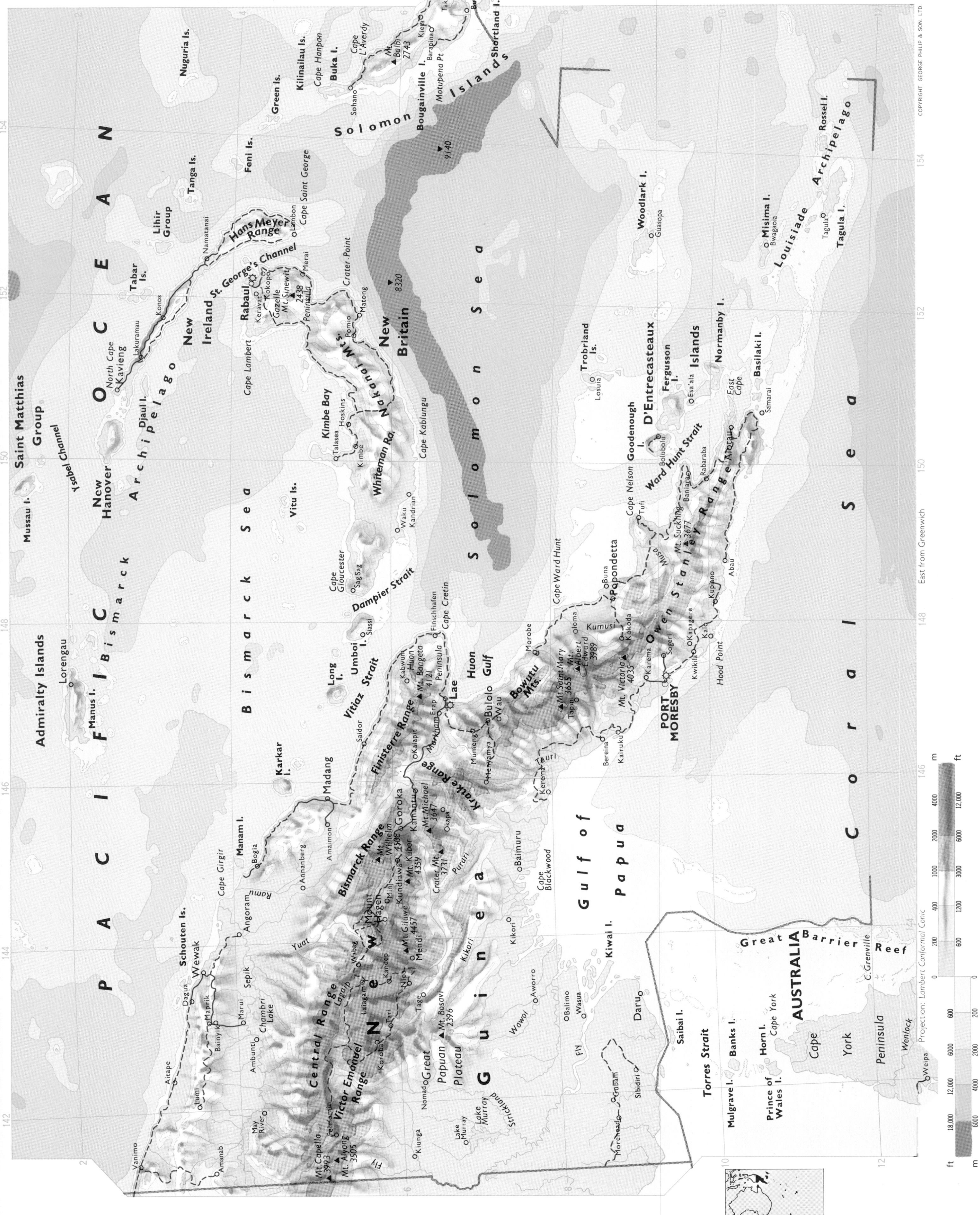
PACIFIC OCEAN
Bismarck Sea
Solomon Sea
Coral Sea
Gulf of Papua
New Guinea
New Britain
New Ireland
New Hanover
Bougainville I.
Buka I.
Solomon Islands
Bismarck Archipelago
Admiralty Islands
Manus I.
Lorengau
Saint Matthias Group
Mussau I.
Lihir Group
Tanga Is.
Feni Is.
Green Is.
Nuguria Is.
Kilinailau Is.
Tabar Is.
Shortland Is.
Woodlark I.
Trobriand Is.
D'Entrecasteaux Islands
Goodenough I.
Fergusson I.
Normanby I.
Louisiade Archipelago
Misima I.
Rossel I.
Tagula I.
Basilaki I.
Rabaul
Kavieng
Madang
Lae
Wewak
Goroka
Mount Hagen
Mendi
PORT MORESBY
Popondetta
Daru
Vanimo
Kimbe
Alotau
Samarai
St. George's Channel
Hans Meyer Range
Nakanai Mts.
Whiteman Ra.
Dampier Strait
Vitiaz Strait
Huon Gulf
Huon Peninsula
Finisterre Range
Bismarck Range
Kratke Range
Bowutu Mts.
Owen Stanley Range
Central Range
Victor Emanuel Range
Great Papuan Plateau
Mt. Wilhelm 4508
Mt. Giluwe 4457
Mt. Victoria 4035
Mt. Albert Edward 3989
Mt. Bangeta 4121
Ward Hunt Strait
Torres Strait
Cape York Peninsula
AUSTRALIA
Great Barrier Reef
Sepik
Fly
Ramu
Purari
Strickland
Projection: Lambert Conformal Conic
East from Greenwich
COPYRIGHT GEORGE PHILIP & SON, LTD.

Java Trench
TIMOR SEA
INDIAN OCEAN
WESTERN AUSTRALIA
NORTHERN TERRITORY
SOUTH AUSTRALIA
Ashmore Reef
Cartier I.
Scott Reef
Rowley Shoals
Bathurst I.
Melville I.
Croker I.
Cobourg Pen.
Dundas Str.
Van Diemen Gulf
Goulburn Is.
Clarence Str.
P. Darwin
Darwin
Castlereagh B.
Rum Jungle
Batchelor
Pt. Blaze
Anson B.
C. Ford
Arnhem Land
Pine Creek
Daly
Katherine
Roper
Mataranka
Birdum
Larrimah
Daly Waters
Victoria
Victoria River Downs
Wave Hill
Newcastle Waters
L. Woods
Powell Creek
Renner Springs
Tanami Desert
Tennant Creek
Gordon Downs
Hordern Hills
The Granites
Barrow Creek
Reynolds Ra.
Mt. Ziel 1510
Macdonnell Ras.
Alice Springs
L. Macdonald
James Ra.
Palmer
Finke
Hugh
L. Amadeus
Mt. Olga 1151
Ayers Rock 933
Charlotte Waters
Musgrave Ranges
Mt. Woodroffe 1549
Everard Ras.
L. Maurice
Maralinga
Ooldea
Tarcoola
Deakin
Forrest
Eucla Motel
Nullarbor Plain
EYRE
Hampton Tableland
Head of Bight
Penong
Ceduna
C. Adieu
Fowlers B.
Nuyts Archipelago
Streaky B.
C. Radstock
Anxious B.
Investigator Group
Coffin B.
Great Australian Bight
C. Londonderry
C. Talbot
C. Bougainville
Vansittart B.
Admiralty G.
Bonaparte Archipelago
Montague Sd.
York Sd.
Jos. Bonaparte Gulf
Cambridge G.
Queens Chan.
Drysdale
Brunswick B.
Wyndham
Kununurra
Ord
DUNCAN
Mt. Hann 776
Kimberley
Collier B.
C. Levêque
King Sd.
Yampi Sound
Lacepede Is.
King Leopold Ras.
Mt. Ord 1007
Durack Range
Meda
Derby
C. Baskerville
Carnot B.
C. Boileau
Broome
Fitzroy
Fitzroy Crossing
Hall's Creek
GREAT NORTHERN
Sturt
Roebuck B.
C. Latouche Treville
C. Bossut
La Grange
Dampier Downs
Eighty Mile Beach
Canning Basin
Gregory Lake
Great Sandy Desert
Dampier Archipelago
P. Hedland
Goldsworthy
De Grey
Hampton Har.
Port Sampson
Monte Bello Is.
Barrow I.
C. Dampier
Preston
Roebourne
Pilbara
Yule
Shaw
Marble Bar
Throssell Ra.
L. Dora
L. Mackay
L. Blanche
Fortescue
Hamersley Ra.
Mt. Enid
Wittenoom
Nullagine
Mt. Bruce 1226
Ophthalmia Range
Tom Price
Mt. Newman 1128
Mt. Whaleback
Robertson Ra.
L. Disappointment
Gibson Desert
Rawlinson Ra.
N.W. Cape
Exmouth G.
Exmouth
Learmonth
Pt. Cloates
Onslow
N.W. COASTAL
Ashburton
C. Farquhar
Barlee Ra.
Mt. Augustus 1105
Mt. Egerton 994
L. McLeod
Lyons
C. Cuvier
Geographe Chan.
Bernier I.
Dorre I.
Carnarvon
Gascoyne
Wooramel
Naturaliste Chan.
Dirk Hartog I.
Shark B.
Denham
S. Passage
Steep Pt.
Robinson Ras.
Peak Hill
L. Buchanan
Barrow Ra.
L. Carnegie
L. Wells 712
Wiluna
Meekatharra
Murchison
Nannine
Cue
Sanford
L. Yeo
Great Victoria Desert
Laverton
L. Rason
L. Austin
Sandstone
Tallering Peak 453
Mt. Magnet
Yalgoo
Gantheaume B.
P. Gregory
Houtman Abrolhos
Northampton
Champion B.
Mullewa
Geraldton
Mongers Lake
L. Barlee
Leonora
L. Raeside
Malcolm
L. Carey
L. Minigwal
L. Ballard
Menzies
Dongara
L. Moore
Kanowna
Premier Downs
Rawlinna
Zanthus
Coastal Plains
Darling Range
GERALDTON
Bonnie Rock
Bencubbin
Kalgoorlie
Coolgardie
Boulder
L. Lefroy
L. Cowan
Wedge I.
Basin
Bullfinch
EASTERN
Southern Cross
GREAT
Swan
Northam
Merredin
Kellerberrin
The Johnston Lakes
Norseman
L. Dundas
Eyre
Pt. Dover
Pt. Culver
Midland Junction
Perth
York
Fremantle
Kwinana
Beverley
Brookton
Narrogin
ALBANY
Pinjarra
Newdegate
Ravensthorpe
Hopetoun
Esperance
Rocky Pt.
Bunbury
Collie
Wagin
Nyabing
Geographe B.
Katanning
Gnowangerup
C. Naturaliste
Busselton
Bridgetown
Stirling Ra.
Doubtful B.
Pt. Hood
C. Knob
Esperance B.
C. le Grand
Arid Archipelago of the Recherche
C. Pasley
Augusta
C. Leeuwin
Manjimup
Pemberton
Mt Barker
Albany
Flinders B.
Pt.d'Entrecasteaux
Pt. Nuyts
Denmark
Tor B.
King George Sound
ft m
6000 2000
4500 1500
3000 1000
1200 400
600 200
0 0
200 600
2000 6000
4000 12,000
6000 18,000
m ft
10
15
20
25
30
35
105
110
115
120
125
130
Projection: Bonne
East from Greenwich

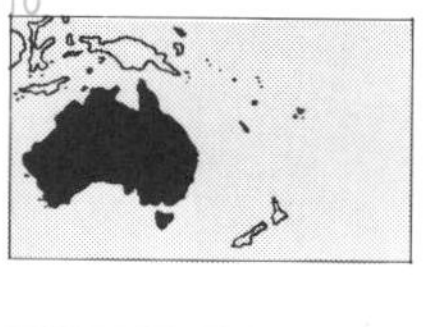

Kilometers 0 100 200 300 400 500 Km.
Statute Miles 0 100 200 300 400 500 Mi.

1:11 200 000

One centimeter represents 112 kilometers
One inch represents approximately 180 miles

CORAL SEA
CORAL SEA ISLANDS TERRITORY
PACIFIC OCEAN
TASMAN SEA
Tropic of Capricorn
QUEENSLAND
NEW SOUTH WALES
VICTORIA
TASMANIA
Gulf of Carpentaria
Great Barrier Reef
Great Dividing Range
Cape York Peninsula
Thursday I.
Banks I.
Prince of Wales I.
C. York
Newcastle B.
Endeavour Str.
Wessel Is.
English Co. Is.
C. Wilberforce
Melville B.
C. Arnhem
Gove
P. Bradshaw
Caledon B.
C. Grey
Blue Mud B.
Alyangula
Groote Eylandt
C. Beatrice
Limmen Bight
Maria I.
Sir Edward Pellew Group
Vanderlin I.
Borroloola
McArthur
Mornington I.
C. van Diemen
Wellesley Is.
Bentinck I.
P. Musgrave
Shelburne B.
C. Grenville
Temple B.
C. Weymouth
C. Direction
Duifken Pt.
Albatross B.
Weipa
Wenlock
Archer
C. Keer-Weer
Holroyd
Coen
Princess Charlotte B.
Bathurst B.
C. Melville
Osprey Rf.
Coleman
Normanby
C. Flattery
C. Bedford
Cooktown
Laura
Mitchell
C. Tribulation
Mossman
Trinity Bay
Gilbert
Chillagoe
Mareeba
Cairns
Atherton
Bartle Frere 1612
Innisfail
C. Grafton
Burketown
Normanton
Croydon
Ravenshoe
Einasleigh
Forsyth
Newcastle Ra.
Gregory Ra.
Norman
Hinchinbrook I.
Ingham
Palm Is.
Halifax B.
Townsville
C. Cleveland
C. Bowling Green
Ayr
Home Hill
Bowen
Charters Towers
Pentland
Flinders
Leichhardt
Camooweal
Dobbyn
Kajabbi
Austral Downs
Mount Isa
Mary Kathleen
Cloncurry
Julia Cr.
Richmond
Hughenden
Duchess
Dajarra
Urandangi
Georgina
Selwyn Range
Selwyn
Winton
Muttaburra
Landsborough
Boulia
Hay
Diamantina
Whitsunday I.
Cumberland Is.
Proserpine
Collinsville
Netherdale
Denham Ra.
Repulse B.
Mackay
Sarina
C. Palmerston
Broadsound Ra.
Isaac
Peak Ra.
Belyando
Blair Athol
Clermont
Aramac
Longreach
Ilfracombe
Barcaldine
Alpha
Emerald
Capricorn
Nogoa
Mackenzie
C. Townshend
Townshend I.
Swain Rfs.
Saumarez Rf.
Bird I.
Cato I.
Yeppoon
Rockhampton
Keppel B.
C. Capricorn
Curtis I.
Gladstone
P. Curtis
Bustard Head
Biloela
Mt. Morgan
Springsure
Blackall
Thomson
Bedourie
Eyre Cr.
L. Machattie
Jundah
Barcoo
Yaraka
Windorah
Birdsville
Warrego Ra.
Expedition Ra.
Dawson
Theodore
Monto
Burnett
Bundaberg
Hervey Bay
Sandy C.
Fraser I.
Childers
Maryborough
Gympie
Nambour
Bribie I.
Moreton B.
Moreton I.
Brisbane
N. Stradbroke I.
Southport
Taroom
Gayndah
Wandoan
Murgon
Kingaroy
Nanango
Miles
Roma
Mitchell
Augathella
Adavale
Charleville
Quilpie
Grey Range
Bulloo
Wyandra
Cunnamulla
Thargomindah
Balonne
Maranoa
Condamine
Dalby
Moonie
St. George
Toowoomba
Ipswich
Warwick
Stanthorpe
Goondiwindi
Dirranbandi
Mungindi
Macintyre
Warrego
Paroo
Tibooburra
Cooper Creek
Strzelecki Cr.
L. Yamma Yamma
L. Eyre (North) -52
L. Eyre (South)
L. Gregory
L. Blanche
L. Callabonna
L. Frome
Warburton
Macumba
Leigh Creek
Copley
Woomera
L. Torrens
Pimba
Flinders Ranges
St. Mary's Pk. 1089
Hawker
Mt. Brown 965
Port Augusta
Quorn
Whyalla
Iron Knob
Peterborough
P. Pirie
Jamestown
Burra
Wallaroo
Kadina
Spencer Gulf
Yorke Penin.
Gulf St. Vincent
Gawler
Elizabeth
Adelaide
Port Lincoln
Investigator Str.
Kangaroo I.
Backstairs Pass.
Victor Harbor
Encounter B.
Coorong
Mt. Lofty Ra.
Murray Bridge
Alexandrina
Pinnaroo
Renmark
Loxton
Ouyen
Mildura
Wentworth
Murray
Darling
Broken Hill
Main Barrier Ra.
Menindee
Wilcannia
Paroo Chan.
Bourke
Brewarrina
Walgett
Barwon
Gwydir
Moree
Warialda
Inverell
Glen Innes
Tenterfield
Casino
Lismore
Ballina
C. Byron
Murwillumbah
Mt. Barney 1351
Sutherland Pt.
Clarence
Grafton
Maclean
New England Range
Round Mountain 1615
Armidale
Coffs Harbour
Macleay
Kempsey
Port Macquarie
Narrabri
Coonamble
Liverpool Plains
Gunnedah
Tamworth
Liverpool Ra.
Barrington Tops 1585
Taree
Muswellbrook
Singleton
Maitland
Cessnock
Newcastle
P. Stephens
Sugarloaf Pt.
Cobar
Nyngan
Bogan
Macquarie
Castlereagh
Gilgandra
Narromine
Dubbo
Wellington
Mudgee
Orange
Bathurst
Lithgow
Katoomba
Penrith
Hawkesbury R.
SYDNEY
& Port Jackson
Wollongong
Shellharbour
Bowral
Goulburn
Nowra
Jervis B.
Canberra
Queanbeyan
Batemans B.
Cooma
Bega
Bombala
Twofold B.
Eden
Disaster B.
Mallacoota Inlet
Howe
C. Howe
C. Everard
Ivanhoe
Hillston
Lachlan
Condobolin
Parkes
Forbes
Cowra
Young
Cootamundra
Junee
Wagga Wagga
Narrandera
Leeton
Griffith
Hay
Balranald
Murrumbidgee
Riverina
Deniliquin
Tumut
Yass
Kosciusko 2230
Mt. Bogong 1986
Australian Alps
Albury
Wodonga
Hume
Benalla
Wangaratta
Echuca
Shepparton
Bendigo
Swan Hill
Kerang
Wimmera
Horsham
Stawell
Ararat
Maryborough
Castlemaine
Bordertown
Naracoorte
Kingston S.E.
Penola
Millicent
Mt. Gambier
C. Northumberland
Discovery B.
C. Bridgewater
Portland
Hamilton
Ballarat
Geelong
MELBOURNE
Port Phillip B.
Port Fairy
Warrnambool
Colac
C. Otway
Phillip I.
Wonthaggi
Yallourn
Moe
Morwell
Sale
Traralgon
Bairnsdale
Gippsland
Ninety Mile Beach
Snowy
Corner Inlet
Wilsons Promontory
Bass Strait
King I.
Hunter I.
C. Grim
Flinders I.
Furneaux Group
Cape Barren I.
C. Portland
Clarke I.
Devonport
Burnie
Ulverstone
Sandy C.
Beaconsfield
Launceston
Scottsdale
Ben Lomond 1527
Mt. Ossa 1617
Zeehan
Strahan
Queenstown
Macquarie Harb.
Great L.
St. Marys
Freycinet Penin.
New Norfolk
Hobart
Huonville
Low Rocky Pt.
P. Davey
Tasman Penin.
P. Arthur
Storm B.
Bruny I.
S.E. Cape
Misima I.
Louisiade Archipelago
Rossel I.
Tagula I.
San Cristobal
Rennell
Lihou Rfs & Cays.
Avon Is.
Chesterfield Is.
Bellona Rfs.
Lord Howe I.
140
145
150
155
160
10
15
20
25
30
35

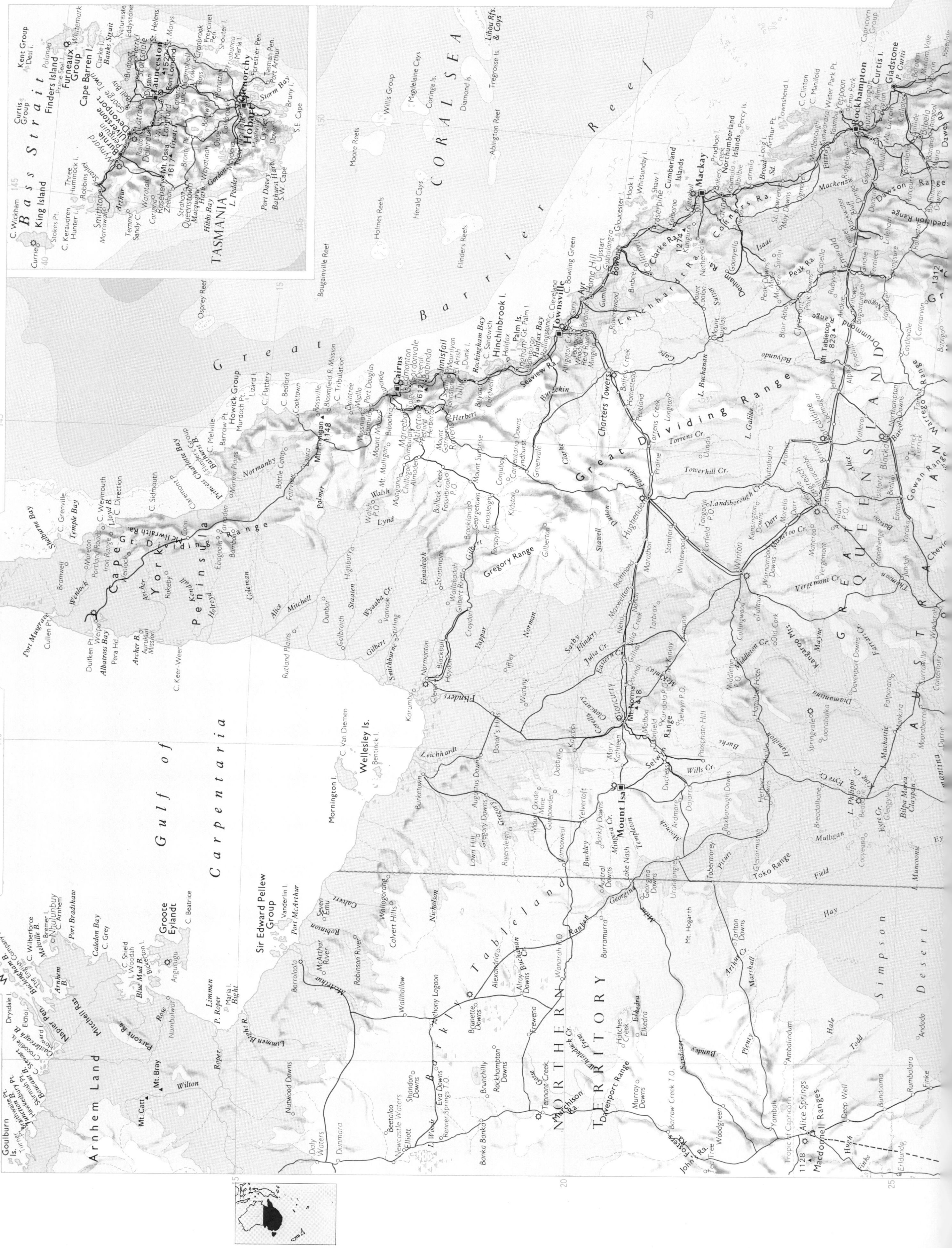
Bass Strait
King Island
Flinders Island
Furneaux Group
Cape Barren I.
Launceston
Devonport
Burnie
Hobart
Glenorchy
TASMANIA
CORAL SEA
Great Barrier Reef
Gulf of Carpentaria
Cape York Peninsula
Great Dividing Range
QUEENSLAND
NORTHERN TERRITORY
Barkly Tableland
Simpson Desert
Arnhem Land
Groote Eylandt
Sir Edward Pellew Group
Wellesley Is.
Mornington I.
Cairns
Townsville
Mackay
Rockhampton
Gladstone
Mount Isa
Cloncurry
Charters Towers
Hughenden
Winton
Longreach
Alice Springs
Tennant Creek
Macdonnell Ranges
Selwyn Range
Gregory Range
Cumberland Islands
Northumberland Islands
Hinchinbrook I.
Howick Group
Wessel Is.
Tropic of Capricorn

Kilometers 0 50 100 150 200 250 300 Km.
Statute Miles 0 50 100 150 200 Mi.
1:6 400 000
One centimeter represents 64 kilometers
One inch represents approximately 100 miles
TASMAN SEA
Bass Strait
NEW SOUTH WALES
SOUTH AUSTRALIA
SYDNEY
MELBOURNE
ADELAIDE
CANBERRA
BRISBANE
Newcastle
Broken Hill
Kangaroo I.
King Island
Flinders Island
Spencer Gulf
Lake Torrens
Lake Gairdner
Lake Eyre
COPYRIGHT GEORGE PHILIP & SON, LTD.
Projection: Bonne
East from Greenwich
m 1500 1000 400 200 0 200 600 2000 6000 12,000
ft 4500 3000 1200 600 0 600 2000 6000 4000 m ft

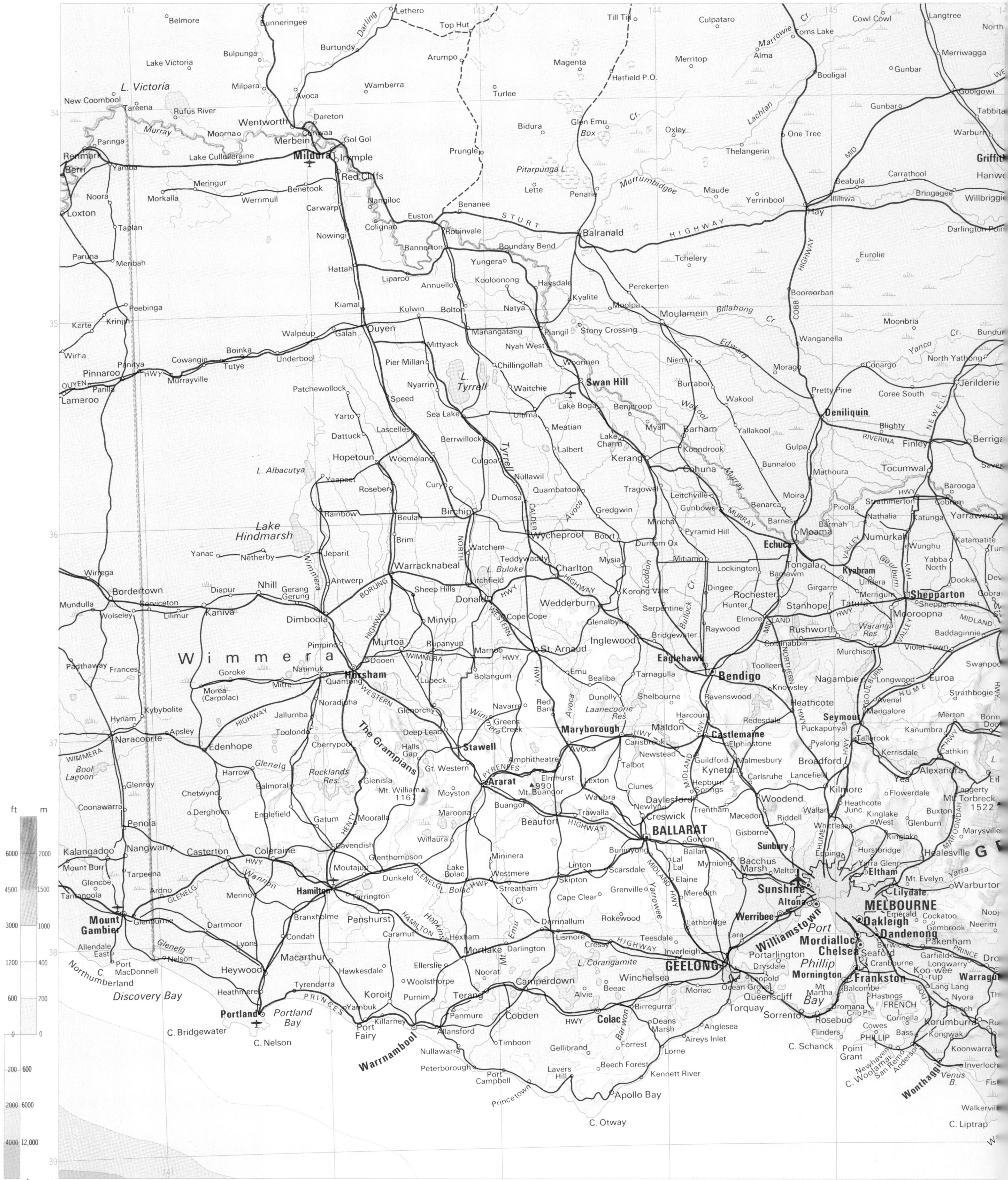
Belmore
Bunnerringee
Lethero
Top Hut
Darling
Till Till
Culpataro
Cowl Cowl
Langtree
North
Burtundy
Arumpo
Lake Victoria
Bulpunga
Magenta
Merritop
Marrowie Cr.
Toms Lake
Alma
Merriwagga
Gunbar
L. Victoria
Milparla
Wamberra
Hatfield P.O.
Booligal
New Coombool
Tareena
Rufus River
Avoca
Turlee
Goolgowi
Wentworth
Dareton
Gunbar
Tabbita
Murray
Moorna
Curlwaa
Bidura
Glen Emu
Box
Cr.
Oxley
Lachlan
One Tree
Warburn
Paringa
Merbein
Gol Gol
Renmark
Lake Cullulleraine
Mildura
Irymple
Prungle
Thelangerin
MID
Griffith
Berri
Yamba
Red Cliffs
Pitarpunga L.
Carrathool
Hanwood
Noora
Meringur
Benetook
Lette
Murrumbidgee
Maude
Beabula
Willbriggie
Morkalla
Werrimull
Penarie
Yerrinbool
Illilliwa
Bringagee
Loxton
Carwarp
Nangiloc
Benanee
Hay
Taplan
Colignan
Euston
STURT
HIGHWAY
Darlington Point
Nowingi
Robinvale
Balranald
Bannerton
Boundary Bend
Paruna
Meribah
Yungera
Tchelery
Eurolie
Hattah
Liparoo
Kooloonong
Haysdale
Annuello
Perekerten
COBB HIGHWAY
Booroorban
Kiamal
Kulwin
Bolton
Natya
Kyalite
Moolpa
Peebinga
Moulamein
Billabong
Cr.
Karte
Krinjih
Ouyen
Galah
Walpeup
Manangatang
Piangil
Stony Crossing
Moonbria
Cr.
Bunduru
Mittyack
Nyah West
Edward
Wanganella
Yanco
Wirha
Pinnaroo
Panitya
Cowangie
Boinka
Tutye
Underbool
Murrayville
HWY
Pier Millan
Chillingollah
Woorinen
Niemur
Morago
Conargo
North Yathong
L. Tyrrell
Nyarrin
Swan Hill
Burraboi
Jerilderie
OUYEN
Parilla
Lameroo
Patchewollock
Speed
Waitchie
Wakool
Pretty Pine
Coree South
Sea Lake
Ultima
Lake Boga
Benjeroop
Yarto
Meatian
Myall
Barham
Yallakool
Deniliquin
Dattuck
Lascelles
Berrwillock
Lake Charm
Koondrook
Blighty
RIVERINA
Finley
Berrigan
Hopetoun
Woomelang
Culgoa
Tyrrell
Lalbert
Kerang
Gulpa
Cohuna
Bunnaloo
Mathoura
Tocumwal
L. Albacutya
Yaapeet
Nullawil
Rosebery
Cury
Quambatook
Tragowel
Leitchville
Barooga
Dumosa
Moira
Avoca
Gunbower
Benarca
Strathmerton
Cobram
Rainbow
Beulah
Birchip
CALDER
Gredgwin
Mincha
MURRAY
Picola
Nathalia
Katunga
Yarrawonga
Barnes
Barmah
Lake Hindmarsh
Wycheproof
Boort
Pyramid Hill
Moama
Numurkah
Katamatite
Brim
NORTH
Durham Ox
Echuca
Wunghu
Yanac
Netherby
Jeparit
Watchem
Teddywaddy
Mitiamo
Tongala
Yabba North
Wimmera
L. Buloke
Charlton
Mysia
Lockington
Kyabram
Goulburn
Wirrega
Warracknabeal
Loddon
Bamawm
Undera
Dookie
Bordertown
Diapur
Nhill
Gerang Gerung
Antwerp
BORUNG
Sheep Hills
Litchfield
HIGHWAY
Korong Vale
Dingee
Girgarre
Merrigum
Shepparton
Mundulla
Serviceton
Donald
HWY
Wedderburn
Bullock Cr.
Rochester
Hunter
Stanhope
Tatura
Shepparton East
Wolseley
Lillimur
Kaniva
Dimboola
WESTERN
Cope Cope
Serpentine
Mooroopna
MIDLAND
Minyip
Glenalbyn
Elmore
Pimpinio
Rupanyup
Inglewood
Bridgewater
Raywood
Rushworth
Waranga Res.
Baddaginnie
Wimmera
Murtoa
Marnoo
St. Arnaud
Colbinabbin
Violet Town
Padthaway
Frances
Natimuk
Dooen
WIMMERA
Eaglehawk
Murchison
Horsham
Swanpool
Goroke
Quantong
Lubeck
Bolangum
Emu
Bealiba
Tarnagulla
Bendigo
Toolleen
Nagambie
Longwood
Euroa
Morea (Carpolac)
Mitre
Noradjuha
WESTERN
Glenorchy
Dunolly
Shelbourne
Knowsley
HUME
Strathbogie
Kybybolite
Navarre
Red Bank
Laanecoorie Res.
Ravenswood
Heathcote
Avenal
Mangalore
Hynam
Jallumba
Wimmera
Greens Creek
Harcourt
Redesdale
Seymour
Merton
Apsley
Toolondo
The Grampians
Deep Lead
Maryborough
Maldon
Castlemaine
Puckapunyal
Kanumbra
Naracoorte
Edenhope
Cherrypool
Halls Gap
Stawell
Carisbrook
Elphinstone
Pyalong
Tallarook
WIMMERA
Glenelg
Rocklands Res.
Amphitheatre
Avoca
Newstead
Guildford
Malmesbury
Broadford
Kerrisdale
Cathkin
Bool Lagoon
Harrow
Gt. Western
PYRENEES
Talbot
Kyneton
Carlsruhe
Lancefield
Yea
Alexandra
Glenroy
Balmoral
Glenisla
Elmhurst
Lexton
Clunes
Hepburn Springs
Kilmore
Flowerdale
Chetwynd
Mt. William 1167
Ararat
990
Mt. Buangor
Waubra
Daylesford
Trentham
Woodend
Heathcote Junc.
Taggerty
Mt. Torbreck 1522
Coonawarra
Moyston
Buangor
Newlyn
Creswick
Macedon
Wallan
Kinglake West
Buxton
Dergholm
Englefield
Maroona
Beaufort
Trawalla
HIGHWAY
BALLARAT
Riddell
Penola
Gatum
Mooralla
HENTY
Willaura
Gordon
Gisborne
Whittlesea
Glenburn
Marysville
Kalangadoo
Nangwarry
Casterton
Coleraine
Cavendish
Buninyong
Ballan
Sunbury
HUME
Kinglake
Hurstbridge
Healesville
Mount Burr
Tarpeena
HWY
Glenthompson
Mininera
Linton
Lal Lal
Myrniong
Bacchus Marsh
Melton
Epping
Yarra Glen
Eltham
Glencoe
Ardno
Wannon
Moutajup
Dunkeld
Lake Bolac
Westmere
Scarsdale
Elaine
Sunshine
Mt. Evelyn
Yarra
Warburton
Tantanoola
GLENELG
Merino
Hamilton
Tarrington
GLENELG
L. Bolac
Streatham
Cape Clear
Grenville
Yarrowee
Meredith
Altona
Lilydale
Mount Gambier
Glenburnie
Dartmoor
Branxholme
Penshurst
Caramut
HAMILTON
Hopkins
Hexham
Derrinallum
Rokewood
Werribee
Williamstown
MELBOURNE
Emerald
Cockatoo
Noojee
Oakleigh
Gembrook
Neerim
Allendale East
Lyons
Condah
Mortlake
Darlington
Lismore
Teesdale
Lethbridge
Lara
Port
Dandenong
Pakenham
Glenelg
Nelson
Macarthur
Emu
Cressy
Inverleigh
Mordialloc
Chelsea
Berwick
Garfield
PRINCE
Drouin
C. Northumberland
Port MacDonnell
Heywood
Hawkesdale
Ellerslie
Mt. Noorat
L. Corangamite
GEELONG
Portarlington
Phillip
Seaford
Cranbourne
Longwarry
Tyrendarra
Woolsthorpe
Camperdown
Winchelsea
Drysdale
Leopold
Mornington
Koo-wee-rup
Warragul
Discovery Bay
Heathmere
Koroit
Purnim
Terang
Alvie
Beeac
Moriac
Ocean Grove
Queenscliff
Mt Martha
Frankston
Balcombe
Lang Lang
Nyora
PRINCES
Yambuk
Killarney
Panmure
Cobden
Birregurra
Torquay
Sorrento
Bay
Hastings
Dromana
Crib Pt
FRENCH
Loch
Portland
Portland Bay
Port Fairy
Allansford
HWY.
Colac
Deans Marsh
Rosebud
Corinella
Korumburra
C. Bridgewater
Barwon
Anglesea
Flinders
Cowes
Bass
Kongwak
C. Nelson
Warrnambool
Nullawarre
Timboon
Gellibrand
Forrest
Aireys Inlet
C. Schanck
PHILLIP
Point Grant
Koonwarra
Lorne
Newhaven
San Remo
Anderson
Inverloch
Peterborough
Port Campbell
Lavers Hill
Beech Forest
Kennett River
C. Woolamai
Venus B.
Fish Creek
Princetown
Apollo Bay
Wonthaggi
Walkerville
C. Otway
C. Liptrap
141
142
143
144
145
34
35
36
37
38
39
ft
m
6000
2000
4500
1500
3000
1000
1200
400
600
200
0
0
200
600
2000
6000
4000
12,000
m
ft

Projection: Alber's Equal area with two standard parallels

142 143 144 145 East from Greenwich

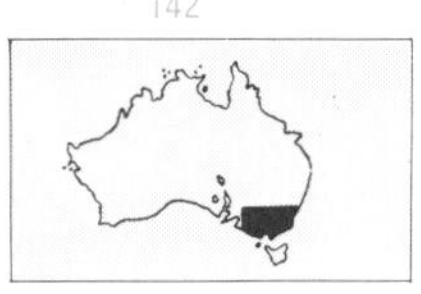

Kilometers 0 20 40 60 80 100 Km.
Statute Miles 0 20 40 60 80 100 Mi.

1:2 000 000

One centimeter represents 20 kilometers
One inch represents approximately 32 miles

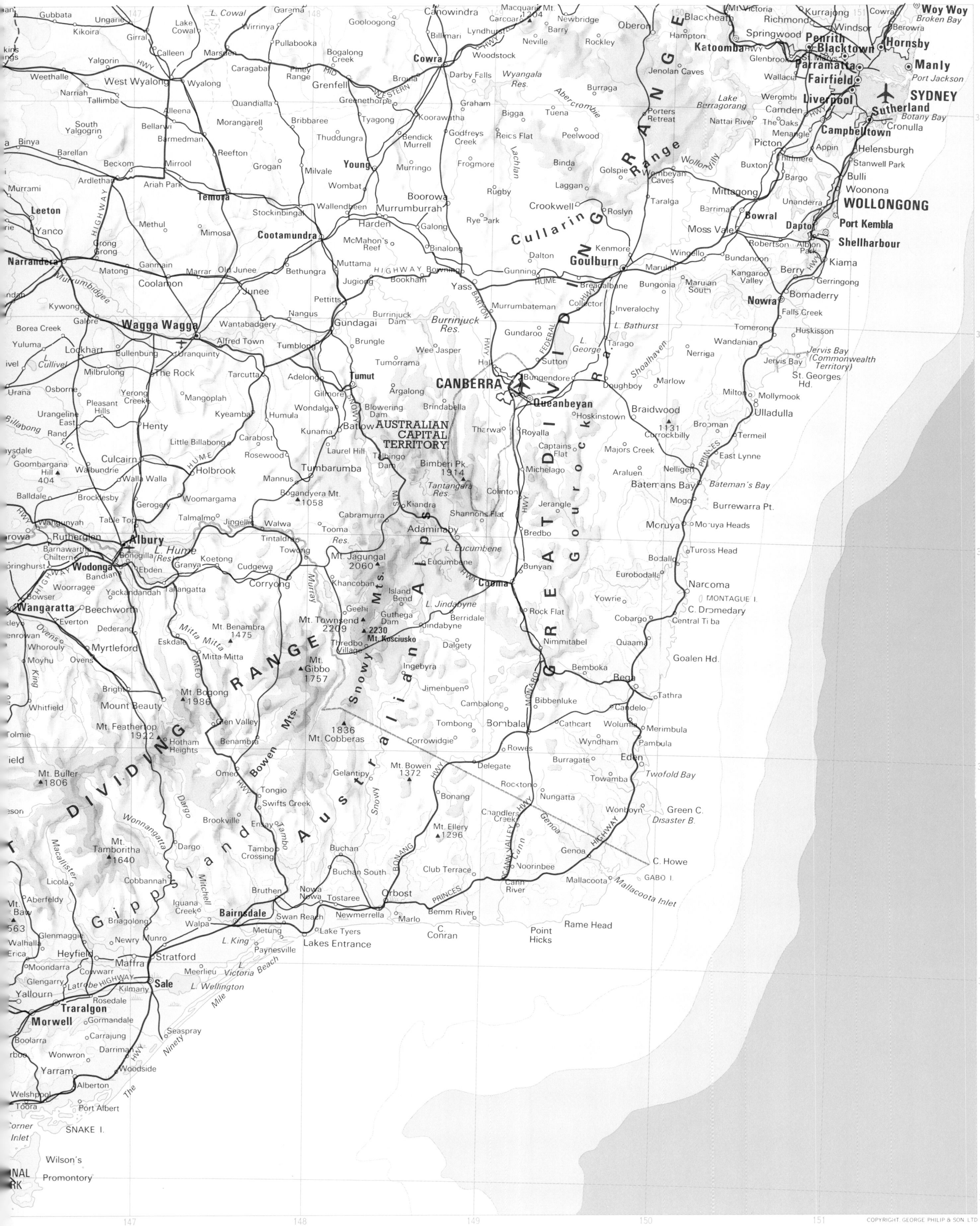

SYDNEY
CANBERRA
AUSTRALIAN CAPITAL TERRITORY
WOLLONGONG
GREAT DIVIDING RANGE
DIVIDING RANGE
Australian Alps
Snowy Mts.
Gippsland
Cullarin Range
Gourock Ra.
Bowen Mts.
Katoomba
Penrith
Blacktown
Hornsby
Manly
Parramatta
Fairfield
Liverpool
Sutherland
Campbelltown
Cronulla
Botany Bay
Port Jackson
Broken Bay
Woy Woy
Richmond
Windsor
Springwood
Blackheath
Kurrajong
Oberon
Jenolan Caves
Camden
Picton
Helensburgh
Bulli
Woonona
Port Kembla
Shellharbour
Kiama
Gerringong
Bomaderry
Nowra
Berry
Bowral
Mittagong
Moss Vale
Goulburn
Yass
Queanbeyan
Bungendore
Braidwood
Batemans Bay
Moruya
Narooma
Cooma
Bega
Eden
Merimbula
Pambula
Twofold Bay
Bombala
Delegate
Mallacoota
Mallacoota Inlet
C. Howe
GABO I.
Orbost
Lakes Entrance
Bairnsdale
Sale
Traralgon
Morwell
Yallourn
Maffra
Stratford
Heyfield
Yarram
Port Albert
SNAKE I.
Wilson's Promontory
Corner Inlet
Ninety Mile Beach
L. Wellington
L. Victoria
L. King
Albury
Wodonga
Rutherglen
Wangaratta
Beechworth
Myrtleford
Mount Beauty
Bright
Corryong
Tallangatta
L. Hume
Wagga Wagga
Junee
Coolamon
Cootamundra
Temora
Young
Cowra
Canowindra
Grenfell
West Wyalong
Narrandera
Leeton
Yanco
Lockhart
The Rock
Holbrook
Culcairn
Henty
Tumut
Gundagai
Tumbarumba
Batlow
Adelong
Burrinjuck Res.
Harden
Murrumburrah
Boorowa
Crookwell
Taralga
Mt. Kosciusko 2230
Mt. Townsend 2209
Mt. Jagungal 2060
Bimberi Pk. 1914
Mt. Bogong 1986
Mt. Feathertop 1922
Mt. Buller 1806
Mt. Gibbo 1757
Mt. Tamboritha 1640
Mt. Benambra 1475
Mt. Bowen 1372
Mt. Ellery 1296
Mt. Cobberas 1836
Thredbo Village
Jindabyne
L. Jindabyne
L. Eucumbene
Adaminaby
Khancoban
Tantangara Res.
L. George
L. Bathurst
Murray
Snowy
Murrumbidgee
Lachlan
Shoalhaven
Abercrombie
Wollondilly
Jervis Bay (Commonwealth Territory)
Ulladulla
Milton
Huskisson
St. Georges Hd.
Tathra
Green C.
Disaster B.
Point Hicks
Rame Head
C. Conran
Omeo
Swifts Creek
Buchan
Cann River
Genoa
HUME HWY
PRINCES HWY
MONARO HWY
SNOWY MTS HWY
FEDERAL HWY
BARTON HWY
MID WESTERN HWY

NEW SOUTH WALES—EAST

Kilometers 0 20 40 60 80 100 Km.

Statute Miles 0 20 40 60 80 100 Mi.

1:2 000 000

One centimeter represents 20 kilometers
One inch represents approximately 32 miles

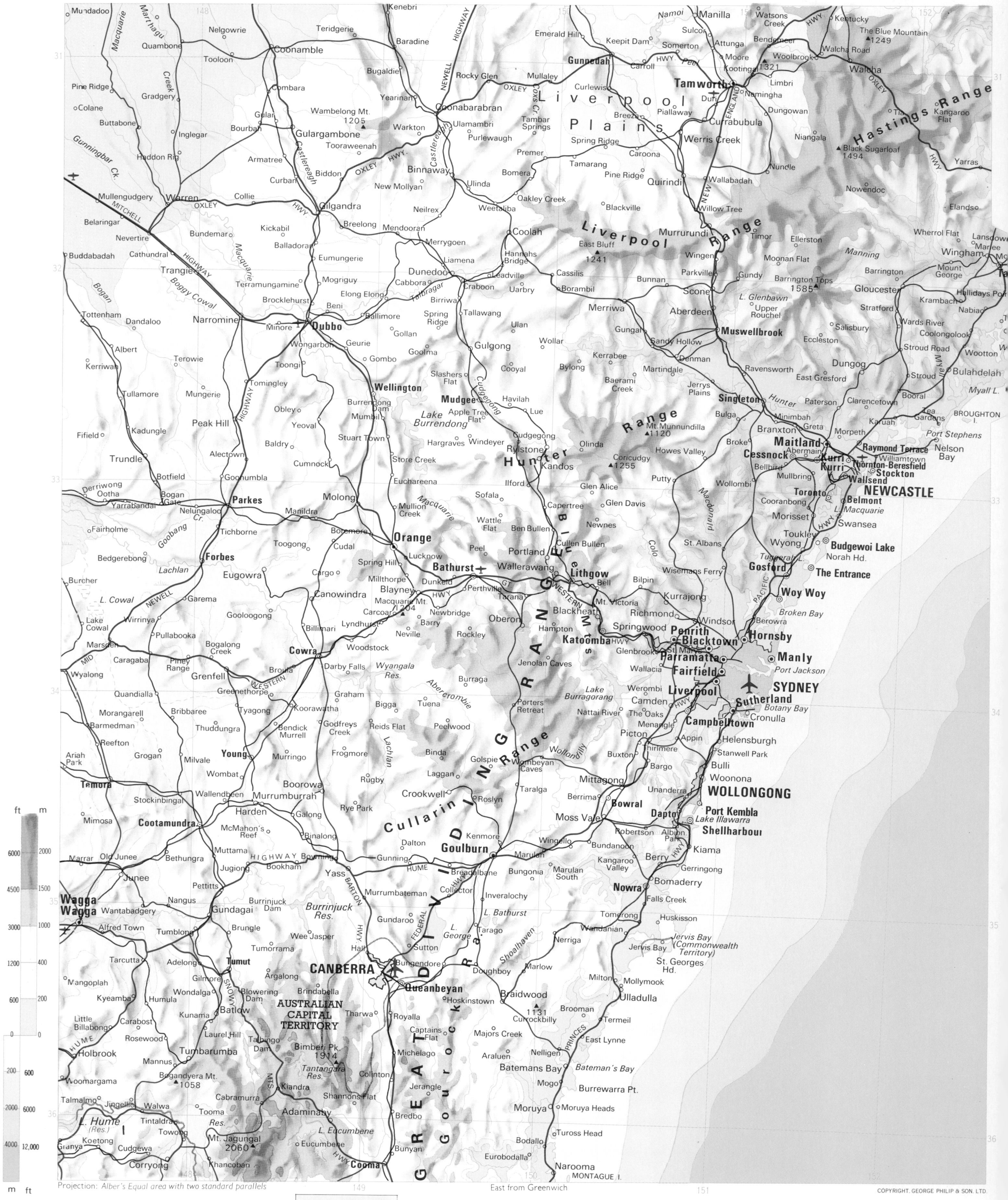

Mundadoo
Kenebri
Manilla
Watsons Creek
Kentucky
The Blue Mountain 1249
Nelgowrie
Teridgerie
Baradine
Emerald Hill
Keepit Dam
Sulcor
Attunga
Bendemeer
Walcha Road
Quambone
Coonamble
Somerton
Moore
Woolbrook
Walcha
Tooloon
Gunnedah
Carroll
Kootingal 1321
Bugaldie
Rocky Glen
Mullaley
Curlewis
Tamworth
Limbri
Pine Ridge
Combara
Yearinan
Liverpool Plains
Duri
Nemingha
Hastings Range
Gradgery
Wambelong Mt. 1205
Coonabarabran
Breeza
Piallaway
Dungowan
Kangaroo Flat
Colane
Gular
Warkton
Ulamambri
Tambar Springs
Currabubula
Buttabone
Bourbah
Gulargambone
Purlewaugh
Spring Ridge
Werris Creek
Niangala
Inglegar
Tooraweenah
Black Sugarloaf 1494
Haddon Rig
Armatree
Premer
Caroona
Yarras
Curban
Biddon
Binnaway
Bomera
Tamarang
Pine Ridge
Quirindi
Nundle
Warren
Collie
New Mollyan
Ulinda
Wallabadah
Nowendoc
Mullengudgery
Gilgandra
Neilrex
Weetaliba
Oakley Creek
Blackville
Willow Tree
Elandso
Belaringar
Breelong
Mendooran
Coolah
Murrurundi
Timor
Ellerston
Wherrol Flat
Nevertire
Kickabil
Bundemar
Balladoran
Merrygoen
East Bluff 1241
Liverpool Range
Wingen
Moonan Flat
Manning
Wingham
Buddabadah
Cathundral
Eumungerie
Liamena
Hannahs Bridge
Dunedoo
Cassilis
Parkville
Gundy
Barrington Tops 1585
Barrington
Mount George
Trangie
Terramungamine
Mogriguy
Cabbora
Leadville
Craboon
Uarbry
Borambil
Bunnan
Scone
Gloucester
Hallidays Point
Brocklehurst
Elong Elong
Birriwa
L. Glenbawn
Upper Rouchel
Krambach
Tottenham
Dandaloo
Narromine
Beni
Ballimore
Spring Ridge
Tallawang
Merriwa
Aberdeen
Stratford
Nabiac
Minore
Dubbo
Gollan
Ulan
Gungal
Muswellbrook
Salisbury
Wards River
Coolongolook
Albert
Wongarbon
Geurie
Goolma
Gulgong
Wollar
Sandy Hollow
Eccleston
Stroud Road
Kerriwah
Terowie
Toongi
Gombo
Cooyal
Bylong
Kerrabee
Denman
Martindale
Ravensworth
Dungog
Wootton
Tomingley
Wellington
Slashers Flat
Baerami Creek
Jerrys Plains
East Gresford
Stroud
Bulahdelah
Tullamore
Mungerie
Burrendong Dam
Mudgee
Havilah
Singleton
Hunter
Paterson
Clarencetown
Myall L.
Oblev
Mumbil
Apple Tree Flat
Lue
Bulga
Minimbah
Boorai
Tea Gardens
Broughton I.
Peak Hill
Yeoval
Lake Burrendong
Mt. Munnundilla 1120
Hunter Range
Branxton
Greta
Karuah
Morpeth
Port Stephens
Fifield
Kadungle
Stuart Town
Hargraves
Windeyer
Cudgegong
Olinda
Broke
Maitland
Abermain
Raymond Terrace
Nelson Bay
Baldry
Rylstone
Howes Valley
Cessnock
Kurri Kurri
Williamtown
Trundle
Alectown
Cumnock
Store Creek
Kandos
Coricudgy 1255
Bellbird
Heddon-Beresfield
Stockton
Botfield
Goonumbla
Euchareena
Ilford
Putty
Wollombi
Mulbring
Wallsend
Newcastle
Derriwong
Ootha
Bogan Gate
Parkes
Molong
Glen Alice
Toronto
Belmont
Yarrabandai
Nelungaloo
Manildra
Mullion Creek
Sofala
Capertree
Glen Davis
Cooranbong
Lake Macquarie
Fairholme
Tichborne
Wattle Flat
Ben Bullen
Newnes
Morisset
Swansea
Bowenfels
Orange
Cullen Bullen
Toukley
Budgewoi Lake
Bedgerebong
Forbes
Toogong
Cudal
Lucknow
Peel
Portland
St. Albans
Wyong
Norah Hd.
Lachlan
Eugowra
Spring Hill
Bathurst
Wallerawang
Lithgow
Tuggerah L.
Gosford
The Entrance
Burcher
Cargo
Millthorpe
Blayney
Dunkeld
Perthville
Bell
Bilpin
Wisemans Ferry
L. Cowal
Garema
Canowindra
Macquarie Mt. 1204
Tarana
Mt. Victoria
Kurrajong
Woy Woy
Broken Bay
Lake Cowal
Wirrinya
Gooloogong
Carcoar
Newbridge
Blackheath
Richmond
Berowra
Lyndhurst
Barry
Oberon
Hampton
Springwood
Penrith
Windsor
Pullabooka
Billimari
Neville
Rockley
Katoomba
Blacktown
Hornsby
Marsden
Bogalong Creek
Woodstock
Glenbrook
St. Marys
Manly
Caragabal
Piney Range
Cowra
Jenolan Caves
Parramatta
Port Jackson
Wyalong
Grenfell
Broula
Darby Falls
Wyangala Res.
Wallacia
Fairfield
Sydney
Quandialla
Greenethorpe
Abercrombie
Burraga
Wérombi
Liverpool
Camden
Sutherland
Graham
Lake Burragorang
Botany Bay
Morangarell
Bribbaree
Tyagong
Koorawatha
Bigga
Tuena
Porters Retreat
Nattai River
The Oaks
Cronulla
Barmedman
Thuddungra
Bendick Murrell
Godfreys Creek
Reids Flat
Peelwood
Menangle
Campbelltown
Reefton
Picton
Appin
Helensburgh
Ariah Park
Grogan
Milvale
Young
Murringo
Frogmore
Binda
Wollondilly
Thirlmere
Stanwell Park
Buxton
Golspie
Wombeyan Caves
Bargo
Bulli
Temora
Wombat
Rugby
Laggan
Mittagong
Woonona
Stockinbingal
Wallendbeen
Murrumburrah
Boorowa
Crookwell
Roslyn
Taralga
Berrima
Unanderra
Wollongong
Harden
Galong
Rye Park
Cullarin Range
Bowral
Mimosa
Cootamundra
Moss Vale
Dapto
Port Kembla
Lake Illawarra
McMahon's Reef
Binalong
Kenmore
Wingello
Robertson
Albion Park
Shellharbour
Muttama
Dalton
Goulburn
Bundanoon
Kiama
Marrar
Old Junee
Bethungra
Bowning
Gunning
Marulan
Kangaroo Valley
Berry
Jugiong
Bookham
Breadalbane
Bungonia
Marulan South
Gerringong
Junee
Yass
Collector
Nowra
Bomaderry
Pettitts
Murrumbateman
Inveralochy
Falls Creek
Wagga Wagga
Nangus
Wantabadgery
Gundagai
Burrinjuck Dam
Burrinjuck Res.
L. Bathurst
Tomerong
Huskisson
Alfred Town
Tumblong
Brungle
Gundaroo
Tarago
Wandandian
Wee Jasper
L. George
Jervis Bay
Jervis Bay (Commonwealth Territory)
Nerriga
Shoalhaven
Tumorrama
Hall
Sutton
St. Georges Hd.
Tarcutta
Adelong
Tumut
Argalong
Canberra
Bungendore
Doughboy
Marlow
Milton
Mollymook
Mangoplah
Gilmore
Wondalga
Brindabella
Queanbeyan
Braidwood
Ulladulla
Kyeamba
Humula
Blowering Dam
Australian Capital Territory
Hoskinstown
Brooman
Batlow
Kunama
Tharwa
Royalla
1131
Termeil
Little Billabong
Carabost
Laurel Hill
Captains Flat
Currockbilly
Rosewood
Talbingo Dam
Bimberi Pk. 1914
Majors Creek
East Lynne
Holbrook
Tumbarumba
Michelago
Araluen
Nelligen
Mannus
Tantangara Res.
Colinton
Batemans Bay
Bateman's Bay
Woomargama
Bogandyera Mt. 1058
Kiandra
Mogo
Burrewarra Pt.
Talmalmo
Jingellic
Cabramurra
Shannons Flat
Jerangle
Walwa
Tooma
Adaminaby
Moruya
Moruya Heads
L. Hume (Res.)
Tintaldra
Towong
Mt. Jagungal 2060
Bredbo
L. Eucumbene
Tuross Head
Granya
Koetong
Cudgewa
Eucumbene
Bunyan
Bodalla
Corryong
Khancoban
Cooma
Eurobodalla
Narooma
Montague I.
Great Dividing Range
Blue Mts
Gourock Ra.
Macquarie
Castlereagh
Bogan
Lachlan
Goobang
Boggy Cowal
Talbragar
Cudgegong
Macdonald
Colo
Namoi
Peel
Gunningbar Ck.
Marthagu Creek
Oxley Hwy
Newell Highway
Mitchell Highway
Mid Western Hwy
Great Western Hwy
Hume Highway
Barton Hwy
Federal Hwy
Monaro Hwy
Princes Hwy
Pacific Hwy
New England Hwy
Snowy Mts.
Hume
31
32
33
34
35
36
148
149
150
151
152
ft
m
6000
4500
3000
1200
600
0
200
2000
1500
1000
400
200
0
600
6000
12,000
ft
m
Projection: Alber's Equal area with two standard parallels
East from Greenwich

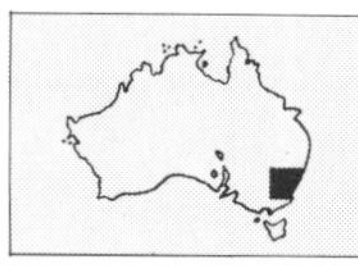

Kilometers 0 20 40 60 80 100 Km.
Statute Miles 0 20 40 60 80 100 Mi.

1:2 000 000

One centimeter represents 20 kilometers
One inch represents approximately 32 miles

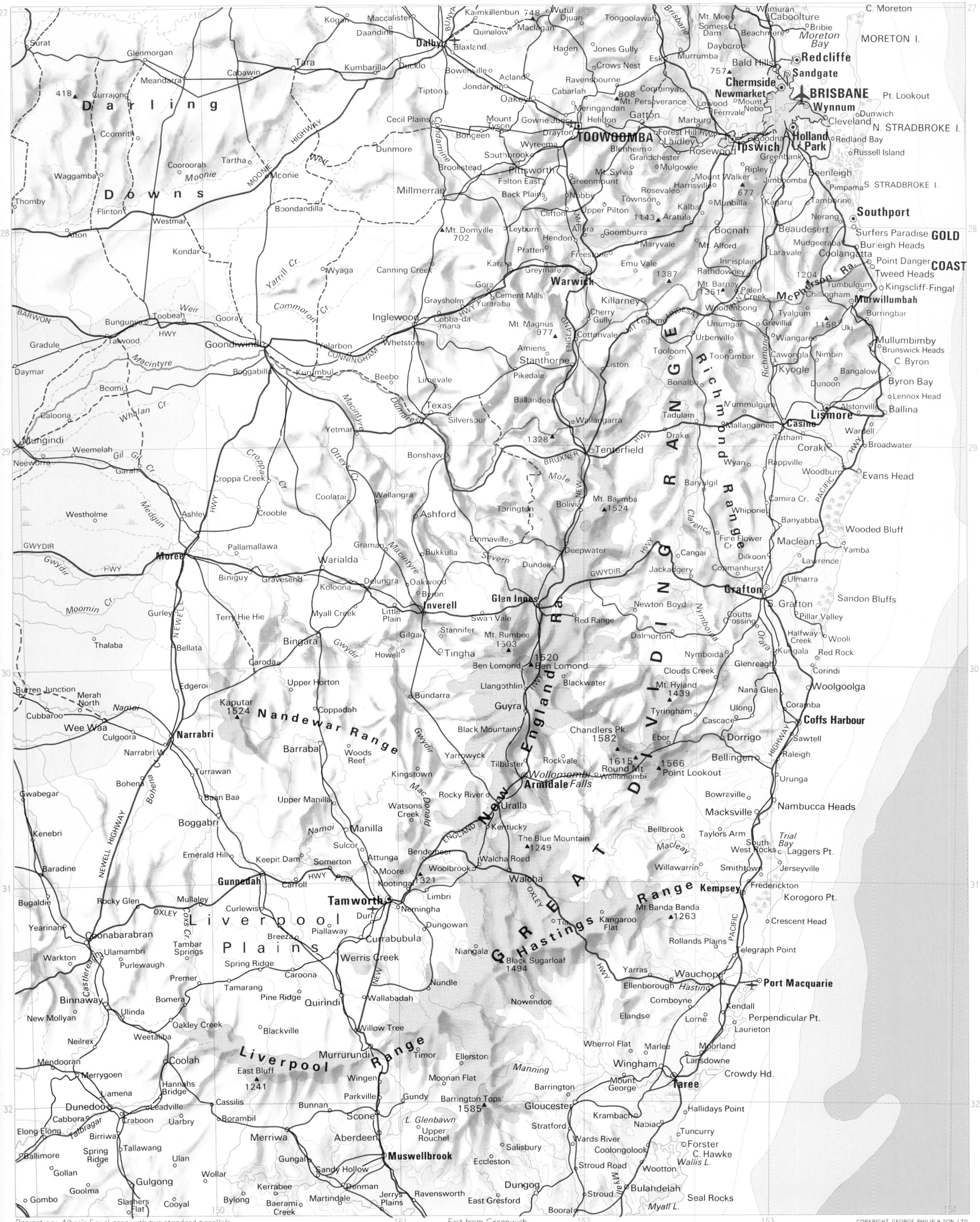

Darling Downs
Surat
Glenmorgan
Meandarra
Cabawin
Tara
Currajong
418
Kogan
Maccalister
Daandine
Dalby
Kaimkillenbun
748
Wutul
Djuan
Toogoolawah
Quinalow
Maclagan
Blaxland
Kumbarilla
Ducklo
Bowenville
Jondaryan
Acland
Haden
Jones Gully
Crows Nest
Ravensbourne
Cabarlah
Tipton
Oakey
Cecil Plains
Mount Tyson
Gowrie Jct.
Drayton
TOOWOOMBA
Bongeen
Wyreema
Southbrook
Pittsworth
Brookstead
Felton East
Back Plains
Millmerran
Nobby
Clifton
Dunmore
Ccomrith
Cooroorah
Tartha
Moonie
Waggamba
Thomby
Flinton
Westmar
Alton
Kondar
Boondandilla
Mt. Domville 702
Leyburn
Hendon
Pratten
Allora
Goomburra
Freestone
Karara
Greymare
Warwick
Canning Creek
Wyaga
Yarrill Cr.
Commoron Cr.
Gore
Cement Mills
Yuraraba
Graysholm
Inglewood
Cobba-da-mana
Whetstone
Mt. Magnus 977
Amiens
Stanthorpe
Pikedale
Ballandean
Wallangarra
Texas
Silverspur
Limevale
Beebo
Yelarbon
Kurumbul
Bungunya
Toobeah
Gooray
Goondiwindi
Boggabilla
Talwood
Gradule
Daymar
Boomi
Caloona
Whalan Cr.
Mungindi
Weemelah
Neeworra
Garah
Gil Gil Cr.
Yetman
Bonshaw
Croppa Creek
Coolatai
Ashley
Crooble
Westholme
Medgun
Pallamallawa
Moree
Biniguy
Gravesend
Warialda
Graman
Bukkulla
Ashford
Wallangra
Kaputar 1524
Nandewar Range
Narrabri
Wee Waa
Culgoora
Cubbaroo
Burren Junction
Merah North
Namoi
Gurley
Terry Hie Hie
Bellata
Thalaba
Edgeroi
Bingara
Myall Creek
Upper Horton
Coppadah
Barraba
Woods Reef
Bundarra
Inverell
Little Plain
Delungra
Koloona
Oakwood
Byron
Gilgai
Stannifer
Howell
Tingha
Swan Vale
Mt. Rumbee 1503
Glen Innes
Emmaville
Dundee
Deepwater
Torington
Bolivia
Mt. Bajimba 1524
Tenterfield
Drake
Tadulam
Liston
Bonalbo
Tooloom
Killarney
Cherry Gully
Cottonvale
Woodenbong
Unumgar
Urbenville
Toonumbar
Mt. Barney 1351
Rathdowney
Innisplain
Mt. Alford
Bocnah
Beaudesert
Laravale
Mudgeeraba
Coolangatta
Tweed Heads
Point Danger
Kingscliff-Fingal
Tumbulgum
Chillingham
Murwillumbah
Burringbar
Tyalgum
Uki
1158
McPherson Ra.
Mullumbimby
Brunswick Heads
C. Byron
Byron Bay
Lennox Head
Ballina
Bangalow
Dunoon
Nimbin
Wiangaree
Cawongla
Kyogle
Grevillia
Lismore
Alstonville
Wardell
Broadwater
Coraki
Casino
Mallanganee
Mummulgum
Tatham
Rappville
Woodburn
Evans Head
Wyan
Baryulgil
Camira Cr.
Whiporie
Banyabba
Fine Flower Cr.
Dilkoon
Maclean
Wooded Bluff
Yamba
Lawrence
Cangai
Jackadgery
Copmanhurst
Grafton
S. Grafton
Ulmarra
Sandon Bluffs
Pillar Valley
Wooli
Red Rock
Corindi
Woolgoolga
Coramba
Coffs Harbour
Sawtell
Nana Glen
Ulong
Glenreagh
Kungala
Halfway Creek
Coutts Crossing
Nymboida
Newton Boyd
Red Range
Dalmorton
Clouds Creek
Mt. Hyland 1439
Tyringham
Cascade
Dorrigo
Ebor
Bellingen
Raleigh
Urunga
Nambucca Heads
Bowraville
Macksville
Taylors Arm
South West Rocks
Trial Bay
Laggers Pt.
Jerseyville
Smithtown
Kempsey
Frederickton
Korogoro Pt.
Crescent Head
Rollands Plains
Telegraph Point
Port Macquarie
Wauchope
Hastings
Ellenborough
Comboyne
Kendall
Lorne
Perpendicular Pt.
Laurieton
Elands
Moorland
Marlee
Wherrol Flat
Lansdowne
Crowdy Hd.
Wingham
Taree
Mount George
Hallidays Point
Krambach
Nabiac
Tuncurry
Forster
C. Hawke
Wallis L.
Wootton
Bulahdelah
Seal Rocks
Myall L.
Stroud
Stroud Road
Coolongolook
Wards River
Stratford
Gloucester
Barrington
Barrington Tops 1585
Manning
Dungog
East Gresford
Booral
Eccleston
Salisbury
Moonan Flat
Ellerston
Gundy
Scone
Parkville
Aberdeen
Upper Rouchel
L. Glenbawn
Muswellbrook
Sandy Hollow
Denman
Jerrys Plains
Ravensworth
Martindale
Baerami Creek
Kerrabee
Bylong
Wollar
Gungal
Merriwa
Bunnan
Cassilis
Borambil
Uarbry
Ulan
Gulgong
Cooyal
Slashers Flat
Goolma
Gollan
Gombo
Ballimore
Spring Ridge
Tallawang
Birriwa
Talbragar
Craboon
Elong Elong
Cabbora
Dunedoo
Leadville
Hannahs Bridge
Lamena
Merrygoen
Mendooran
Neilrex
Coolah
Weetaliba
New Mollyan
Binnaway
Ulinda
Bomera
Warkton
Ulamambri
Purlewaugh
Coonabarabran
Yearinan
Bugaldie
Rocky Glen
Baradine
Kenebri
Gwabegar
Newell Highway
Castlereagh
Liverpool Plains
Liverpool Range
East Bluff 1241
Murrurundi
Blackville
Oakley Creek
Willow Tree
Wallabadah
Quirindi
Pine Ridge
Tamarang
Premer
Spring Ridge
Tambar Springs
Caroona
Werris Creek
Currabubula
Breeza
Piallaway
Curlewis
Gunnedah
Carroll
Mullaley
Emerald Hill
Keepit Dam
Somerton
Boggabri
Baan Baa
Bohena
Turrawan
Narrabri W.
Upper Manilla
Manilla
Watsons Creek
Kingstown
Sulcor
Attunga
Moore
Kootingal
Tamworth
Nemingha
Duri
Dungowan
Limbri
1321
Woolbrook
Bendemeer
Walcha
Walcha Road
Niangala
Black Sugarloaf 1494
Hastings Range
Great Dividing Range
Mt Banda Banda 1263
Kangaroo Flat
Tia
Yarras
Nowendoc
Nundle
Timor
Wingen
The Blue Mountain 1249
Kentucky
Uralla
Armidale
Wollomombi Falls
Rocky River
Tilbuster
Rockvale
Round Mt. 1615
1566 Point Lookout
Chandlers Pk. 1582
Wollomombi
Yarrowyck
Black Mountain
Guyra
Llangothlin
Blackwater
Ben Lomond 1520
New England Ra.
Macleay
Willawarrin
Bellbrook
Tamborine
Nerang
Southport
Surfers Paradise
GOLD COAST
Burleigh Heads
Pimpama
S. STRADBROKE I.
Beenleigh
Jimboomba
Ripley
Greenbank
Goodna
Ipswich
Holland Park
Redland Bay
Russell Island
Cleveland
N. STRADBROKE I.
Dunwich
Pt. Lookout
Wynnum
BRISBANE
Sandgate
Redcliffe
Chermside
Newmarket
Mount Nebo
Lowood
Fernvale
Marburg
Rosewood
Laidley
Forest Hill
Gatton
Helidon
Meringandan
Mt. Perseverance 808
Coominya
Esk
Murrumba
Bald Hills
757
Daybcro
Mt. Mee
Somerset Dam
Beachmere
Caboolture
Wamuran
Bribie
Moreton Bay
C. Moreton
MORETON I.
Blenheim
Grandchester
Mulgowie
Mt. Sylvia
Greenmount
Rosevale
Harrisville
Mount Walker 677
Townson
Kalba
Munbilla
Kagaru
1143 Aratula
Upper Pilton
Maryvale
Emu Vale
1387
1204
1328
Mt. Lindesay
Richmond Range
Clarence
Severn
Mole
Macintyre
Dumaresq
Ottleys Cr.
Croppa Cr.
Gwydir
Moomin Cr.
Peel
Oxley Hwy
Barwon
Weir
Condamine
Richmond
Orara
Nymboida
Pacific Hwy
Cunningham Hwy
Bruxner Hwy
Gwydir Hwy
New England Hwy
Newell Hwy
Moonie Highway
Myall

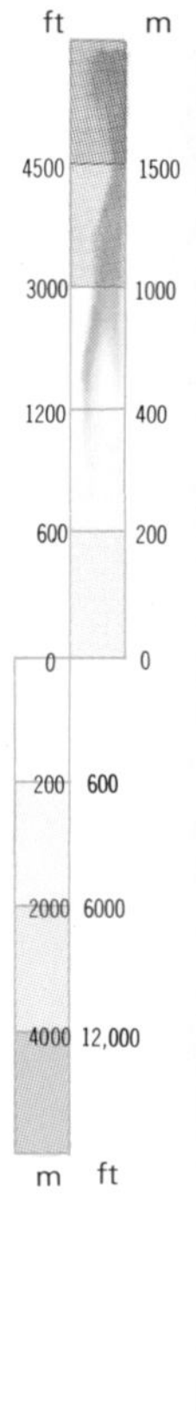

ft
m
4500
1500
3000
1000
1200
400
600
200
0
0
200
600
2000
6000
4000
12,000
m
ft

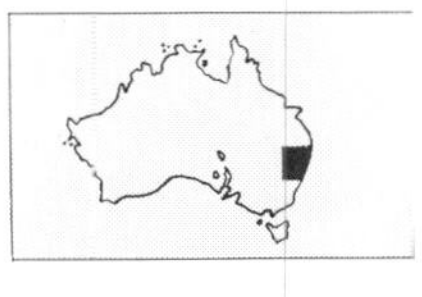

Projection: Alber's Equal area with two standard parallels

East from Greenwich

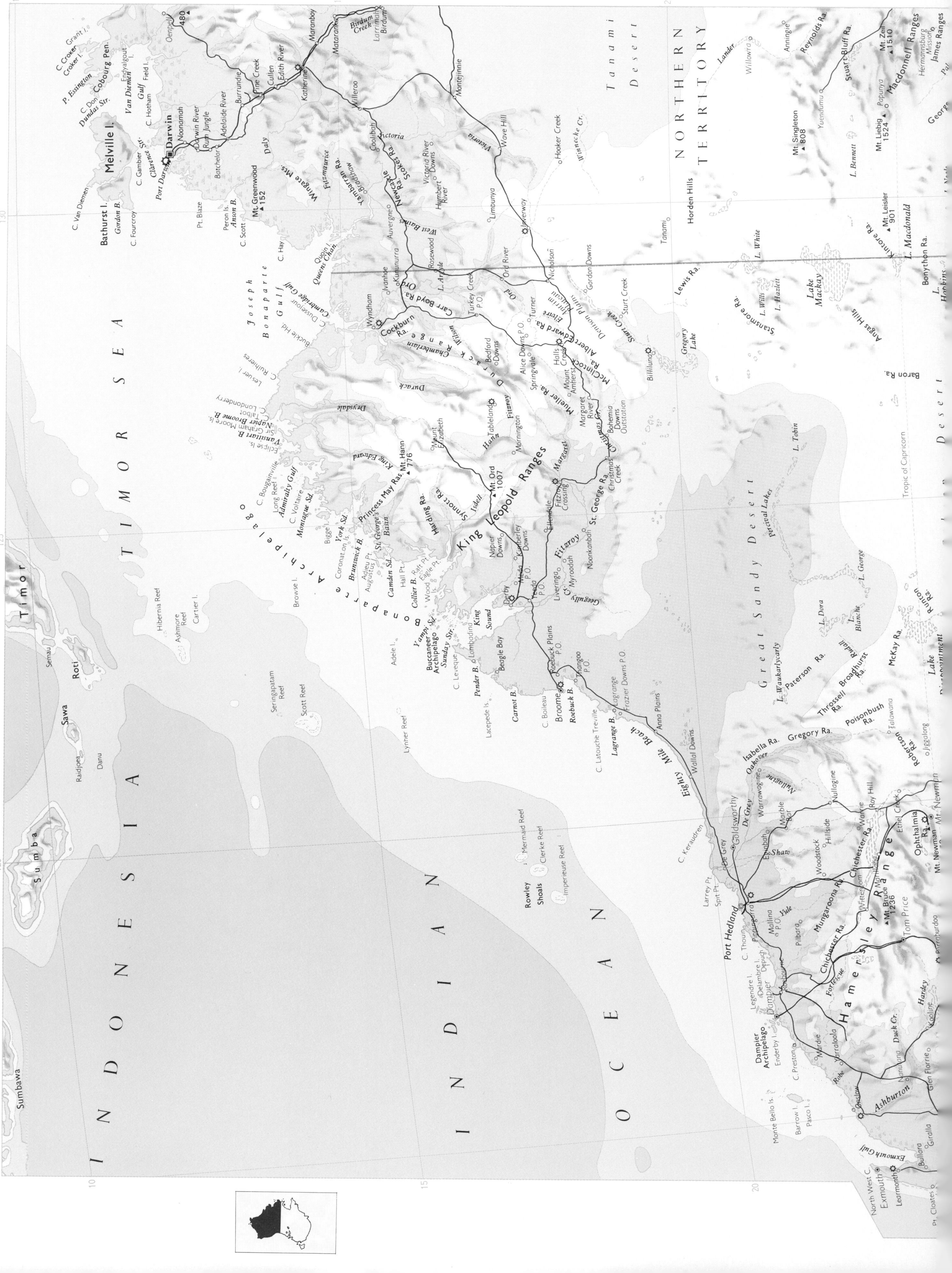

INDONESIA
TIMOR SEA
INDIAN OCEAN
NORTHERN TERRITORY
Tanami Desert
Great Sandy Desert
Timor
Roti
Sawa
Sumba
Sumbawa
Melville I.
Bathurst I.
Darwin
Katherine
Wyndham
Kununurra
Joseph Bonaparte Gulf
Cambridge Gulf
Bonaparte Archipelago
Admiralty Gulf
King Leopold Ranges
Durack Ra.
Fitzroy
Fitzroy Crossing
Halls Creek
Derby
King Sound
Broome
Roebuck B.
Eighty Mile Beach
Port Hedland
Dampier
Dampier Archipelago
Hamersley Range
Chichester Ra.
Mt. Bruce 1236
Tom Price
Mt. Newman
Onslow
Ashburton
Exmouth Gulf
Exmouth
North West C.
Rowley Shoals
Scott Reef
Ashmore Reef
Cartier I.
Lake Mackay
L. Macdonald
Macdonnell Ranges
Tropic of Capricorn
Lake Disappointment

Kilometers 0 50 100 150 200 250 300 Km.
Statute Miles 0 50 100 150 200 250 300 Mi.

1:6 400 000

One centimeter represents 64 kilometers
One inch represents approximately 100 miles

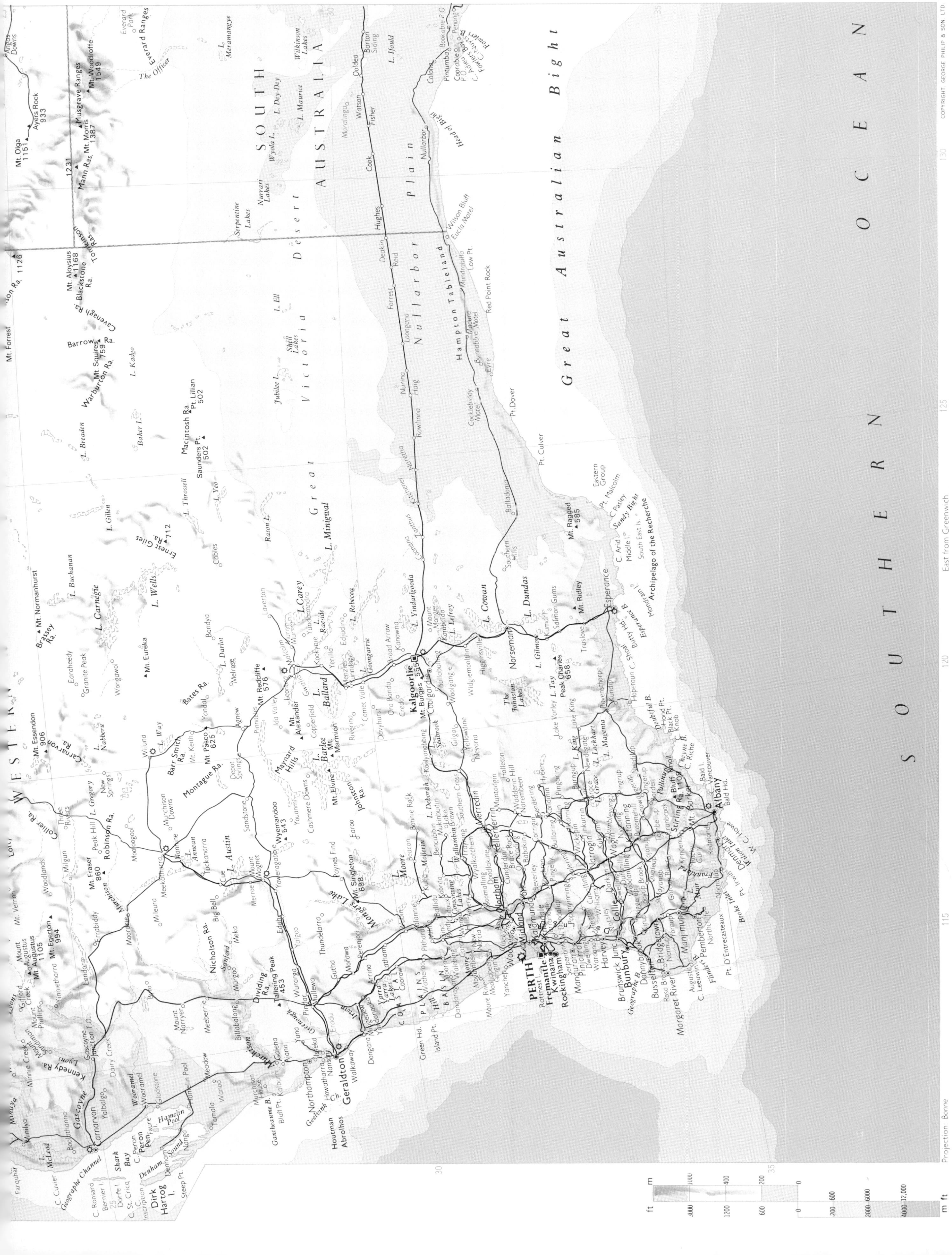
SOUTHERN OCEAN
Great Australian Bight
Nullarbor Plain
Great Victoria Desert
SOUTH AUSTRALIA
WESTERN
PERTH
Fremantle
Kwinana
Rockingham
Kalgoorlie
Coolgardie
Geraldton
Carnarvon
Albany
Esperance
Bunbury
Norseman
Archipelago of the Recherche
Hampton Tableland
Head of Bight
Shark Bay
Dirk Hartog I.
Houtman Abrolhos
Ayers Rock 933
Mt. Olga 1151
Musgrave Ranges
Everard Ranges
L. Carnegie
L. Wells
L. Moore
L. Barlee
L. Ballard
L. Lefroy
L. Cowan
L. Dundas
Projection: Bonne
East from Greenwich
COPYRIGHT GEORGE PHILIP & SON, LTD.
m ft
4000-12,000
2000-6000
200-600
0
600
1200
3000

NEW ZEALAND—NORTH ISLAND

Kilometers 0 40 80 120 160 Km.
Statute Miles 0 40 80 120 160 Mi.

1:2 800 000

One centimeter represents 28 kilometers
One inch represents approximately 45 miles

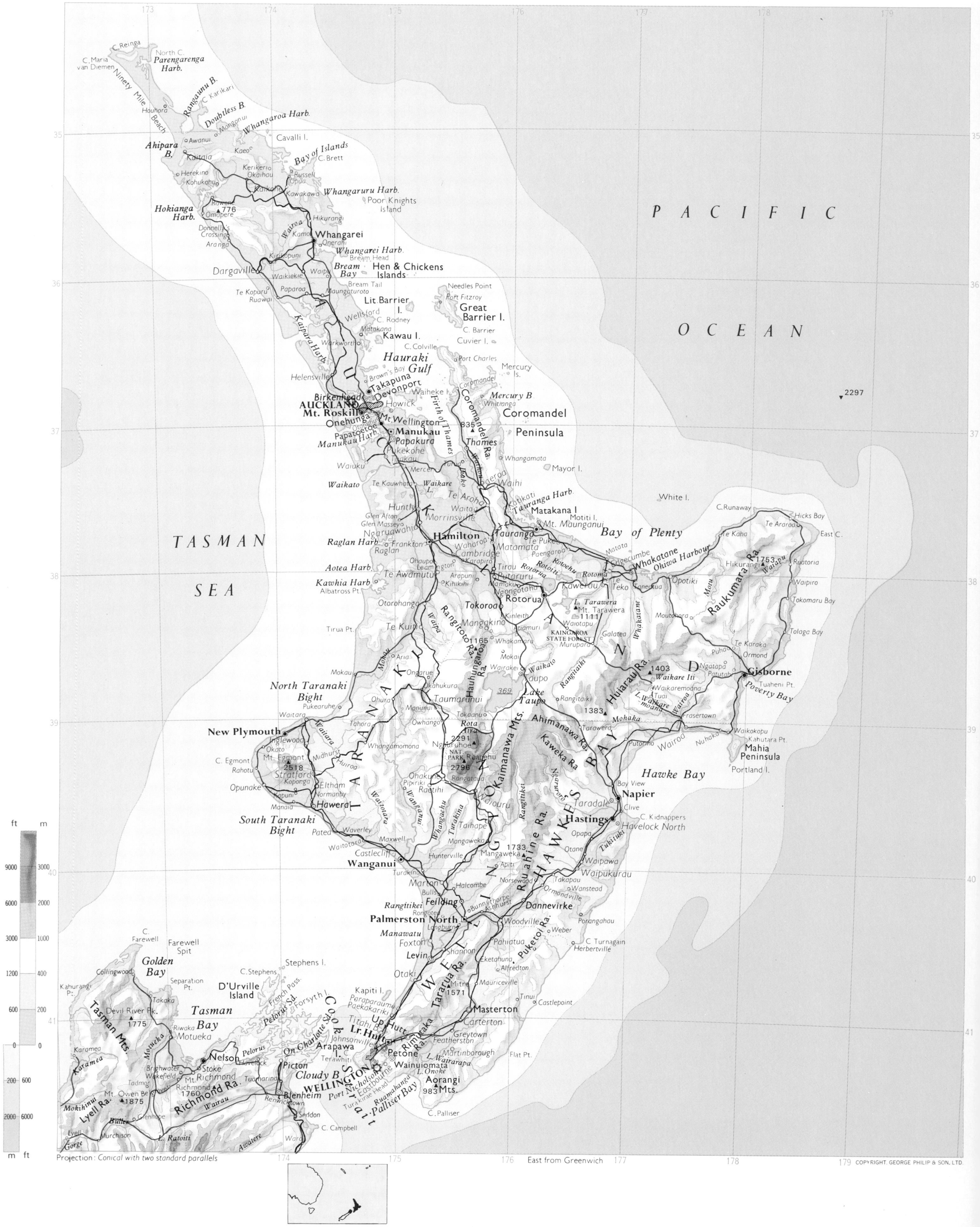
PACIFIC OCEAN
TASMAN SEA
C. Reinga
North C.
Parengarenga Harb.
C. Maria van Diemen
Ninety Mile Beach
Rangaunu B.
C. Karikari
Houhora
Doubtless B.
Whangaroa Harb.
Ahipara B.
Kaitaia
Cavalli I.
Bay of Islands
C. Brett
Kerikeri
Okaihau
Russell
Opua
Kawakawa
Whangaruru Harb.
Poor Knights Island
Hokianga Harb.
776
Dargaville
Hikurangi
Whangarei
Whangarei Harb.
Bream Head
Bream Bay
Hen & Chickens Islands
Bream Tail
Needles Point
Port Fitzroy
Lit. Barrier I.
Great Barrier I.
C. Rodney
C. Barrier
Kawau I.
Cuvier I.
Wellsford
Warkworth
Kaipara Harb.
C. Colville
Port Charles
Mercury Is.
Hauraki Gulf
Helensville
Takapuna
Devonport
Birkenhead
AUCKLAND
Mt. Roskill
Onehunga
Howick
Mt. Wellington
Waiheke I.
Mercury B.
Whitianga
Coromandel
Coromandel Peninsula
Coromandel Ra.
Firth of Thames
835
Thames
Manukau
Papakura
Papatoetoe
Manukau Harb.
Pukekohe
Waiuku
Mercer
Whangamata
Mayor I.
Waikato
Te Kauwhata
Waikare L.
Waihi
Te Aroha
Tauranga Harb.
Matakana I.
Motiti I.
White I.
C. Runaway
Hicks Bay
East C.
Huntly
Morrinsville
Glen Afton
Glen Massey
Ngaruawahia
Hamilton
Tauranga
Mt. Maunganui
Bay of Plenty
Te Araroa
Raglan Harb.
Frankton
Raglan
Cambridge
Matamata
Te Puke
Whakatane
Ohiwa Harbour
Hikurangi
1753
Ruatoria
Aotea Harb.
Te Awamutu
Tirau
Putaruru
Rotoiti
Rotoma
Te Teko
Opotiki
Raukumara Ra.
Waipiro
Kawhia Harb.
Albatross Pt.
Rotorua
Kawerau
L. Tarawera
Mt. Tarawera
1111
Tokomaru Bay
Otorohanga
Tokoroa
Tirua Pt.
Te Kuiti
Rangitoto Ra.
KAINGAROA STATE FOREST
Murupara
Tolaga Bay
1165
Mangakino
Te Karaka
Ormond
Mokau
Hauhungaroa Ra.
Taupo
1403
Waikare Iti
Huiarau Ra.
Gisborne
Tuaheni Pt.
Poverty Bay
North Taranaki Bight
Taumarunui
369
Lake Taupo
Rangitaiki
L. Waikaremoana
Waitara
Pukearuhe
1383
Frasertown
New Plymouth
Inglewood
Okato
C. Egmont
Mt. Egmont
2518
Stratford
Opunake
Eltham
Hawera
TARANAKI
Rota Aira
2291
NAT. PARK
Ruapehu
2796
Ahimanawa Ra.
Kaimanawa Mts.
Kaweka Ra.
Wairoa
Waikokopu
Mahia Peninsula
Portland I.
Hawke Bay
Bay View
Napier
Taradale
Hastings
Clive
C. Kidnappers
Havelock North
HAWKES BAY
South Taranaki Bight
Patea
Waverley
Castlecliff
Wanganui
Taihape
Mangaweka
1733
Ruahine Ra.
Waipawa
Waipukurau
Marton
Bulls
Feilding
Rangitikei
Palmerston North
Dannevirke
Woodville
Manawatu
Foxton
Levin
Shannon
Pahiatua
Puketoi Ra.
C. Turnagain
Herbertville
Otaki
WELLINGTON
Tararua Ra.
1571
Masterton
Castlepoint
Kapiti I.
Paraparaumu
Up. Hutt
Lr. Hutt
Carterton
Greytown
Featherston
Rimutaka Ra.
Petone
Wainuiomata
Martinborough
L. Wairarapa
L. Onoke
Flat Pt.
Aorangi Mts.
983
Palliser Bay
C. Palliser
Cook Strait
C. Farewell
Farewell Spit
Golden Bay
Collingwood
Separation Pt.
D'Urville Island
C. Stephens
Stephens I.
French Pass
Kahurangi Pt.
Tasman Mts.
Devil River Pk.
1775
Takaka
Tasman Bay
Pelorus Sd.
Forsyth I.
Riwaka
Motueka
Nelson
Stoke
Pelorus
Havelock
Queen Charlotte Sd.
Arapawa I.
Picton
Cloudy B.
Brightwater
Wakefield
Richmond
Mt. Richmond
1760
Richmond Ra.
Blenheim
Karamea
Mokihinui
Mt. Owen
1875
Lyell Ra.
Buller
Wairau
Seddon
C. Campbell
Murchison
Gorge
Ward
2297
173
174
175
176
177
178
179
35
36
37
38
39
40
41
ft
m
9000
3000
6000
2000
3000
1000
1200
400
600
200
0
0
200
600
2000
6000
m
ft

Projection: Conical with two standard parallels

East from Greenwich

Kilometers 0 40 80 120 160 Km.
Statute Miles 0 40 80 120 160 Mi

1:2 800 000

One centimeter represents 28 kilometers
One inch represents approximately 45 miles

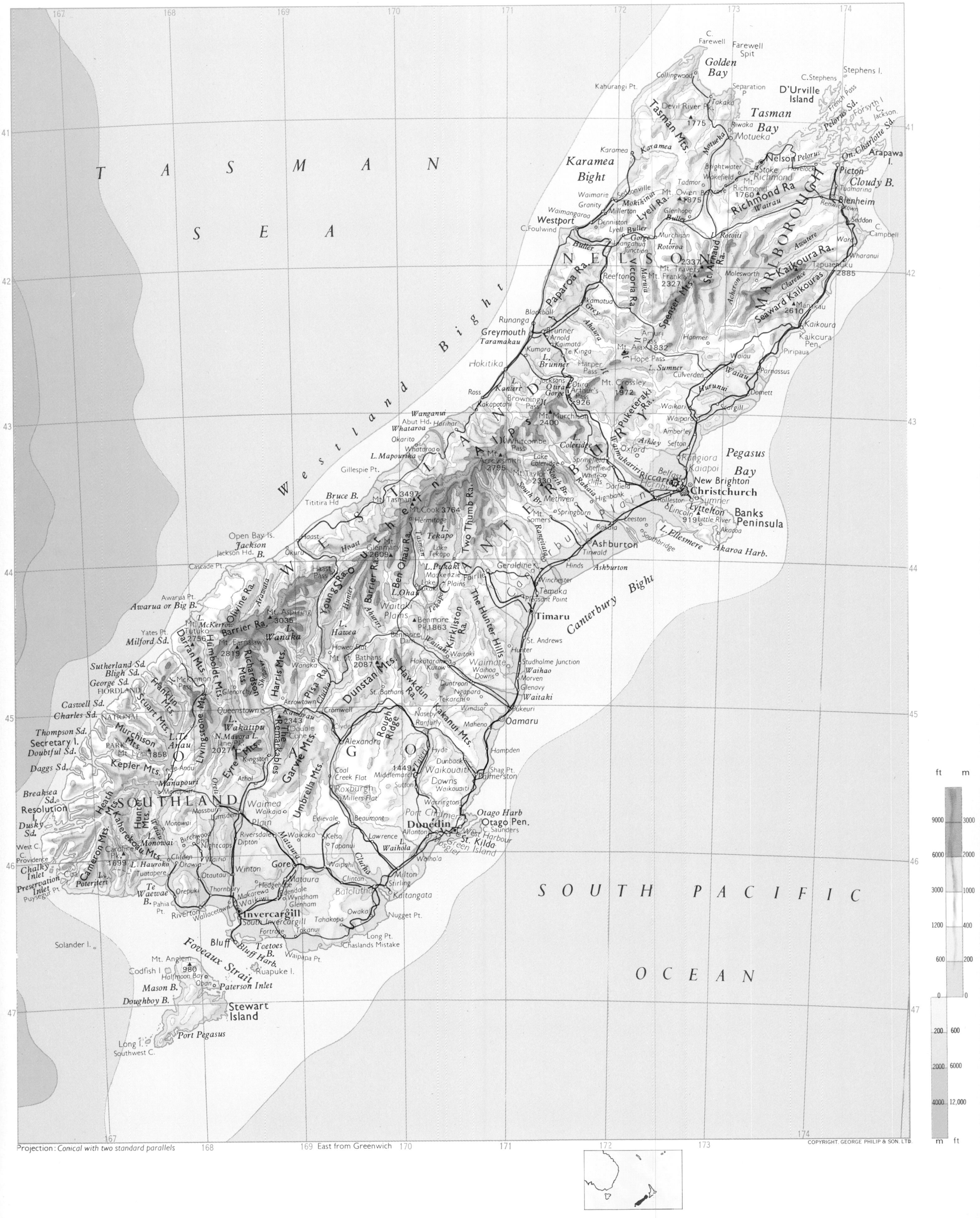
TASMAN SEA
SOUTH PACIFIC OCEAN
Westland Bight
Canterbury Bight
Karamea Bight
Golden Bay
Tasman Bay
Pegasus Bay
Cloudy B.
Foveaux Strait
NELSON
MARLBOROUGH
WESTLAND
CANTERBURY
OTAGO
SOUTHLAND
FIORDLAND NATIONAL PARK
Southern Alps
Canterbury Plains
Stewart Island
D'Urville Island
Banks Peninsula
Otago Pen.
Christchurch
Nelson
Blenheim
Picton
Westport
Greymouth
Hokitika
Timaru
Oamaru
Dunedin
Invercargill
Queenstown
Gore
Bluff
Mt. Cook 3764
Mt. Tasman 3497
Mt. Aspiring 3035
L. Wakatipu
L. Te Anau
L. Manapouri
L. Wanaka
L. Hawea
L. Pukaki
L. Tekapo
L. Ellesmere
Milford Sd.
Projection: Conical with two standard parallels
East from Greenwich
COPYRIGHT. GEORGE PHILIP & SON. LTD.
ft
m

Kilometers 0 300 600 900 1200 1500 Km.
Statute Miles 0 300 600 900 1200 1500 Mi.

1:32 000 000

One centimeter represents 320 kilometers
One inch represents approximately 500 miles

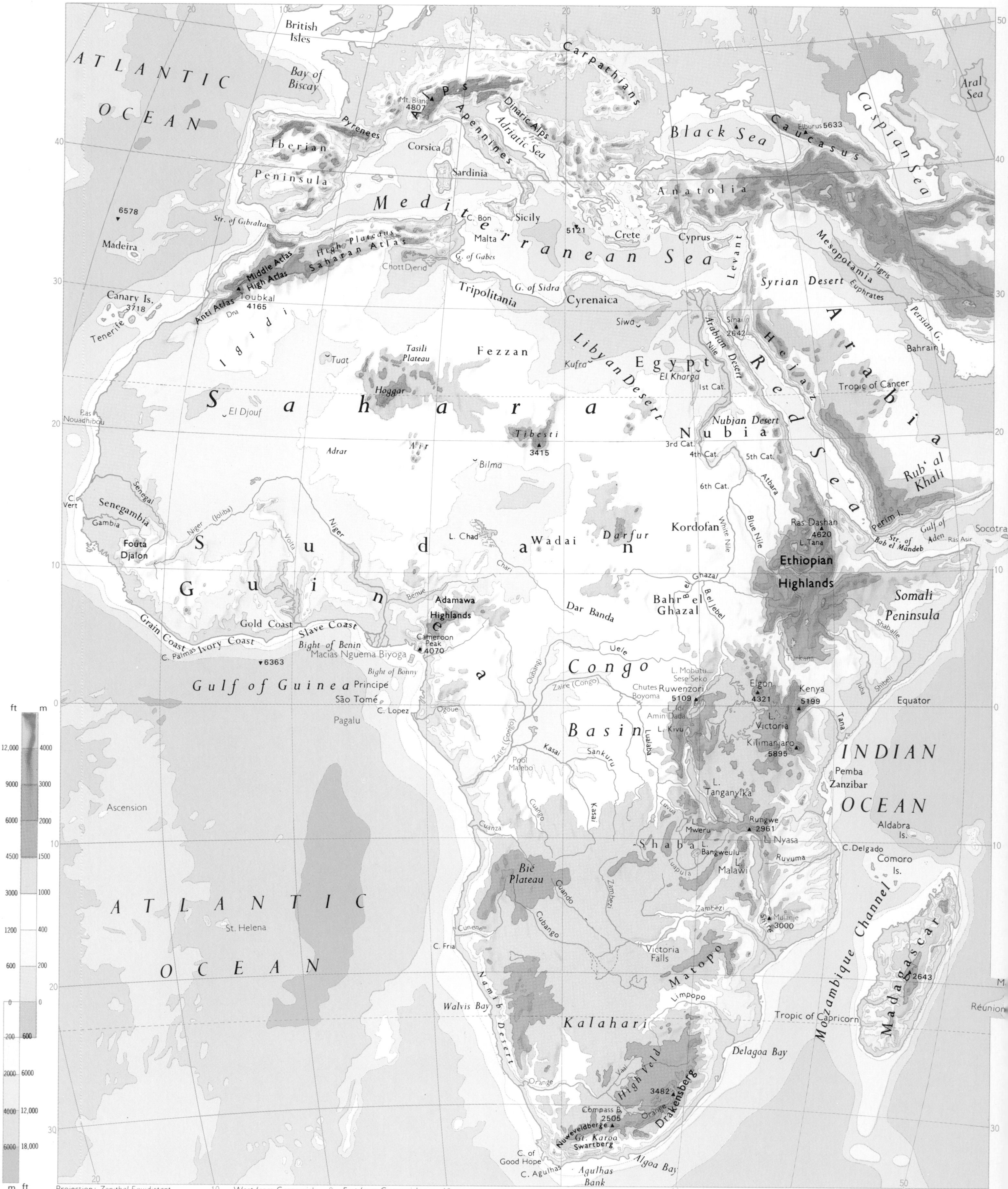
ATLANTIC OCEAN
British Isles
Bay of Biscay
Carpathians
Aral Sea
Caspian Sea
Mt. Blanc 4807
Alps
Dinaric Alps
Adriatic Sea
Apennines
Pyrenees
Corsica
Sardinia
Iberian Peninsula
Black Sea
Elburus 5633
Caucasus
Anatolia
Mediterranean Sea
6578
Madeira
Str. of Gibraltar
C. Bon
Sicily
Malta
5121
Crete
Cyprus
Levant
Mesopotamia
Tigris
Euphrates
High Plateaus
Saharan Atlas
Middle Atlas
High Atlas
Anti Atlas
G. of Gabes
Chott Djerid
Tripolitania
G. of Sidra
Cyrenaica
Syrian Desert
Canary Is.
3718
Tenerife
Toubkal 4165
Dra
Igidi
Siwa
Sinai 2642
Arabian Desert
Hejaz
Arabia
Persian G.
Bahrain I.
Tuat
Tasili Plateau
Fezzan
Libyan Desert
Kufra
Egypt
El Kharga
Nile
Red Sea
Tropic of Cancer
Hoggar
Ist Cat.
Ras Nouadhibou
Sahara
El Djouf
Tibesti 3415
Nubian Desert
Nubia
3rd Cat.
4th Cat.
5th Cat.
Adrar
Air
Bilma
Rub' al Khali
6th Cat.
Atbara
C. Vert
Senegal
Senegambia
Gambia
Niger (Joliba)
Niger
Volta
Fouta Djalon
Sudan
L. Chad
Wadai
Darfur
Kordofan
White Nile
Blue Nile
Ras Dashan 4620
L. Tana
Perim I.
Str. of Bab el Mandeb
Gulf of Aden
Socotra
Ras Asir
Ethiopian Highlands
Guinea
Chari
Benue
Adamawa Highlands
Bahr el Ghazal
Ghazal
Bel Jebel
Dar Banda
Somali Peninsula
Shaballe
Grain Coast
Gold Coast
Slave Coast
Ivory Coast
C. Palmas
Bight of Benin
Cameroon Peak 4070
Macias Nguema Biyoga
6363
Uele
Turkana
Bight of Bonny
Gulf of Guinea
Principe
São Tomé
Oubangi
Congo Basin
L. Mobutu Sese Seko
Chutes Boyoma
Zaire (Congo)
Ruwenzori 5109
Elgon 4321
Kenya 5199
Juba
Shibeli
Equator
C. Lopez
Pagalu
Ogooue
L. Idi Amin Dada
L. Victoria
L. Kivu
Lualaba
Tana
Zaire (Congo)
Kasai
Sankuru
Pool Malebo
Kilimanjaro 5895
INDIAN OCEAN
Pemba
Zanzibar
L. Tanganyika
Ascension
Cuango
Kasai
Luvua
Cuanza
L. Mweru
Rungwe 2961
Aldabra Is.
Shaba
L. Bangweulu
L. Nyasa
C. Delgado
Ruvuma
L. Malawi
Luapula
Comoro Is.
Bié Plateau
Cuando
Zambezi
Zambezi
Mulanje 3000
Shire
Mozambique Channel
ATLANTIC OCEAN
St. Helena
Cunene
Cubango
C. Fria
Victoria Falls
Matopo
Madagascar
2643
Namib Desert
Walvis Bay
Limpopo
Réunion
Kalahari
Tropic of Capricorn
Delagoa Bay
Vaal
High Veld
Orange
3482
Drakensberg
Compass B. 2505
Nuweveldberge
Orange
Gt. Karoo
Swartberg
C. of Good Hope
C. Agulhas
Agulhas Bank
Algoa Bay
Projection: Zenithal Equidistant.
West from Greenwich
East from Greenwich
ft m
12,000 4000
9000 3000
6000 2000
4500 1500
3000 1000
1200 400
600 200
0 0
200 600
2000 6000
4000 12,000
6000 18,000
m ft

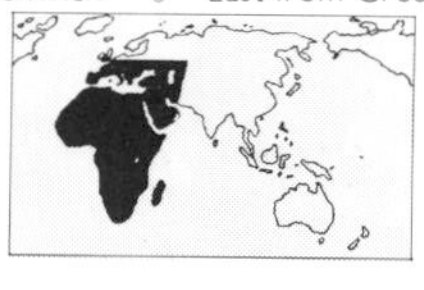

Kilometers 0 300 600 900 1200 1500 Km.
Statute Miles 0 300 600 900 1200 1500 Mi.

1:32 000 000

One centimeter represents 320 kilometers
One inch represents approximately 500 miles

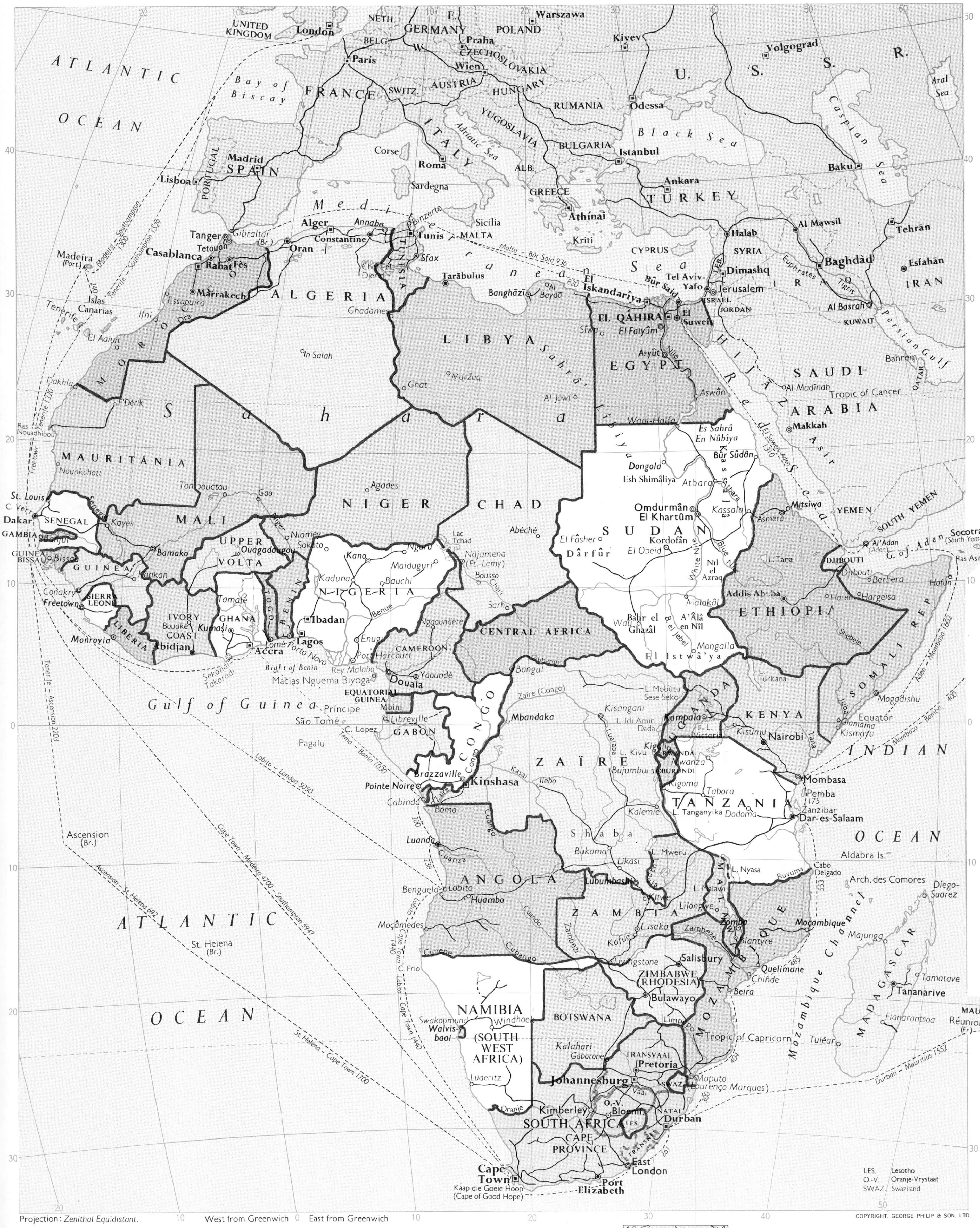

ATLANTIC OCEAN
UNITED KINGDOM
London
NETH.
BELG.
Paris
FRANCE
E. GERMANY
W.
Praha
CZECHOSLOVAKIA
Wien
AUSTRIA
SWITZ.
HUNGARY
POLAND
Warszawa
Kiyev
U. S. S. R.
Volgograd
Aral Sea
Caspian Sea
Odessa
RUMANIA
Black Sea
YUGOSLAVIA
BULGARIA
Istanbul
ALB.
ITALY
Adriatic Sea
Roma
Corse
Sardegna
Sicilia
MALTA
GREECE
Athínai
Kriti
TURKEY
Ankara
Baku
Bay of Biscay
PORTUGAL
Lisboa
Madrid
SPAIN
Gibraltar (Br.)
Tanger
Tetouan
Rabat
Fès
Casablanca
Marrakech
Essaouira
Ifni
Madeira (Port.)
Islas Canarias
Tenerife
El Aaiun
MOROCCO
Dakhla
F'Dérik
Oran
Alger
Constantine
Annaba
Bizerte
Tunis
Sfax
Djerba
TUNISIA
ALGERIA
Ghadames
In Salah
Mediterranean Sea
Malta – Bûr Saîd 936
Tarâbulus
Banghâzi
Al Baydâ
LIBYA
Ghat
Marzuq
Al Jawf
Sahara
Sahrâ' Lîbîya
El Iskandarîya
Bûr Saîd
EL QÂHIRA
El Suweis
Sîwa
El Faiyûm
Asyût
Nile
EGYPT
Aswân
Wadi-Halfa
CYPRUS
LEB.
SYRIA
Dimashq
Halab
Tel Aviv-Yafo
Jerusalem
ISRAEL
JORDAN
Al Mawsil
Baghdâd
IRAQ
Euphrates
Tigris
Tehrân
Esfahân
IRAN
Al Basrah
KUWAIT
Persian Gulf
Bahrein
QATAR
HIJAZ
SAUDI-ARABIA
Al Madînah
Makkah
Tropic of Cancer
Red Sea
El Suweis–Aden 1310
Asir
YEMEN
SOUTH YEMEN
Al 'Adan (Aden)
Socotra (South Yemen)
G. of Aden
Ras Asir
Hafun
Ras Nouadhibou
Nouakchott
MAURITANIA
Tenerife – Freetown 1320
Madeira – Southampton 1300
Tenerife – Southampton 1529
St. Louis
C. Vert
Dakar
SENEGAL
GAMBIA
Banjul
GUINEA-BISSAU
Bissau
GUINEA
Conakry
SIERRA LEONE
Freetown
LIBERIA
Monrovia
Kayes
Bamako
MALI
Tombouctou
Gao
Kankan
UPPER VOLTA
Ouagadougou
Niger
Niamey
IVORY COAST
Bouake
Abidjan
GHANA
Tamale
Kumasi
Accra
TOGO
Lomé
BENIN
Porto Novo
Sekondi Takoradi
NIGER
Agades
Sokoto
Kano
Nguru
Maiduguri
Kaduna
Bauchi
NIGERIA
Ibadan
Lagos
Benue
Enugu
Port Harcourt
Bight of Benin
Rey Malabo
Macias Nguema Biyoga
CAMEROON
Ngoundéré
Yaoundé
Douala
EQUATORIAL GUINEA
Mbini
Gulf of Guinea
Principe
São Tomé
Pagalu
Libreville
GABON
C. Lopez
CHAD
Lac Tchad
Ndjamena (Ft.-Lamy)
Bousso
Chari
Sarh
Abéché
CENTRAL AFRICA
Bangui
Ubangi
SUDAN
El Fasher
Dârfûr
El Obeid
Kordofân
Omdurmân
El Khartûm
Atbara
Kassala
Dongola
Esh Shimâliya
Es Sahrâ En Nûbiya
Bûr Sûdân
Blue Nile
White Nile
Nil el Azraq
Malakâl
Bahr el Ghazâl
Wau
A'Âlâ en Nil
Bahr el Jebel
Mongalla
El Istwâ'ya
Mitsiwa
Asmera
L. Tana
DJIBOUTI
Djibouti
Berbera
Hargeisa
Harer
Addis Ababa
ETHIOPIA
Shebele
SOMALI REP.
Mogadishu
Juba
Kismayu
Aden – Mombasa 1602
Mombasa – Bombay 400
Equator
INDIAN OCEAN
L. Turkana
KENYA
Nairobi
Tana
Kisumu
L. Victoria
UGANDA
Kampala
L. Mobutu Sese Seko
L. Idi Amin Dada
Kigali
RWANDA
BURUNDI
Bujumbura
L. Kivu
Mwanza
Tabora
Kigoma
TANZANIA
Dodoma
Dar-es-Salaam
L. Tanganyika
Zanzibar
Pemba
Mombasa
CONGO
Brazzaville
Kinshasa
Pointe Noire
Cabinda
Boma
Zaire (Congo)
Mbandaka
Kisangani
Lualaba
ZAÏRE
Kasai
Ilebo
Kalemie
Shaba
Bukama
Likasi
Lubumbashi
L. Mweru
Luanda
Cuanza
Cuango
ANGOLA
Benguela
Lobito
Huambo
Moçâmedes
Cunene
Cubango
Cuando
Lobito – London 5050
Tema – Bonny 1030
Ascension (Br.)
St. Helena (Br.)
Ascension – St. Helena 692
Tenerife – Ascension 2203
Cape Town – Madeira 4700 – Southampton 5947
St. Helena – Cape Town 1700
Lobito – Cape Town 1440
ZAMBIA
Kitwe
Lusaka
Kafue
Zambezi
Livingstone
MALAWI
L. Malawi
Lilongwe
Zomba
Blantyre
L. Nyasa
Ruvuma
Cabo Delgado
MOZAMBIQUE
Moçambique
Quelimane
Chinde
Beira
ZIMBABWE (RHODESIA)
Salisbury
Bulawayo
Limpopo
NAMIBIA (SOUTH WEST AFRICA)
Windhoek
Swakopmund
Walvis-baai
Lüderitz
Oranje
C. Frio
BOTSWANA
Kalahari
Gaborone
TRANSVAAL
Pretoria
Johannesburg
Vaal
SWAZ.
Maputo (Lourenço Marques)
O.-V.
Bloemfontein
Kimberley
LES.
NATAL
Durban
SOUTH AFRICA
CAPE PROVINCE
Transkei
East London
Port Elizabeth
Cape Town
Kaap die Goeie Hoop (Cape of Good Hope)
Tropic of Capricorn
Aldabra Is.
Arch. des Comores
Diégo-Suarez
Mozambique Channel
Majunga
MADAGASCAR
Tamatave
Tananarive
Fianarantsoa
Tuléar
MAURITIUS
Réunion (Fr.)
Durban – Mauritius 1552
ATLANTIC OCEAN

LES. Lesotho
O.-V. Oranje-Vrystaat
SWAZ. Swaziland

Projection: *Zenithal Equidistant.* West from Greenwich 0 East from Greenwich

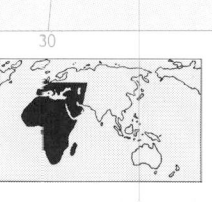

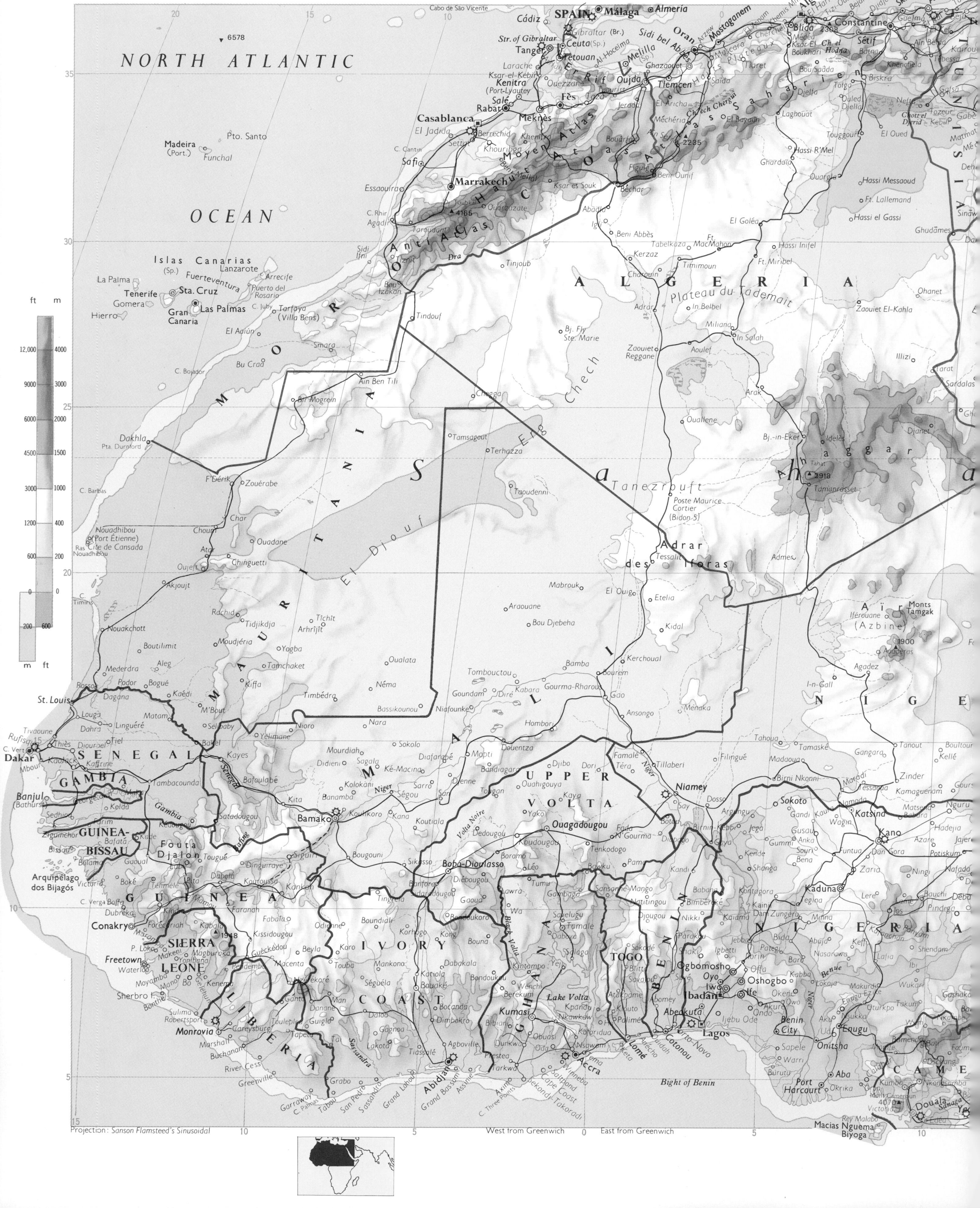
NORTH ATLANTIC
OCEAN
Madeira (Port.)
Funchal
Pto. Santo
Islas Canarias (Sp.)
Lanzarote
Fuerteventura
Tenerife
Sta. Cruz
Gomera
Hierro
La Palma
Gran Canaria
Las Palmas
SPAIN
Málaga
Almería
Cádiz
Str. of Gibraltar
Gibraltar (Br.)
Tanger
Ceuta (Sp.)
Tetouan
Melilla (Sp.)
Larache
Kenitra (Port-Lyautey)
Salé
Rabat
Fès
Meknès
Casablanca
El Jadida
Settat
Safi
Marrakech
Essaouira
Agadir
Sidi Ifni
Tarfaya (Villa Bens)
El Aaiún
Smara
Bu Craa
C. Bojador
Dakhla
C. Barbas
Nouadhibou (Port Étienne)
Oran
Mostaganem
Sidi bel Abbès
Tlemcen
Oujda
Alger (Algiers)
Blida
Constantine
Annaba
Skikda
Sétif
Biskra
Laghouat
Ghardaïa
Ouargla
Hassi R'Mel
Hassi Messaoud
Béchar
El Goléa
Tindouf
Adrar
In Salah
Plateau du Tademait
Tanezrouft
Ahaggar
Tamanrasset
2918
Ghudāmes
TUNISIA
ALGERIA
MOROCCO
Haut Atlas
Moyen Atlas
Anti Atlas
Er Rif
Atlas Saharien
4165
El Djouf
Chech
Erg
MAURITANIA
F'Dérik
Zouérate
Atar
Chinguetti
Akjoujt
Nouakchott
Tidjikdja
Kiffa
Rosso
Aleg
Néma
Oualata
St. Louis
Dakar
Thiès
Kaolack
SENEGAL
GAMBIA
Banjul (Bathurst)
Ziguinchor
GUINEA-BISSAU
Bissau
Arquipélago dos Bijagós
Fouta Djalon
GUINEA
Conakry
Kankan
Kindia
Labé
SIERRA LEONE
Freetown
LIBERIA
Monrovia
MALI
Tombouctou
Gao
Mopti
Ségou
Bamako
Kayes
Kidal
Adrar des Iforas
Niger
Niamey
NIGER
Aïr (Azbine)
Agadez
Zinder
Maradi
Tahoua
UPPER VOLTA
Ouagadougou
Bobo-Dioulasso
Koudougou
IVORY COAST
Abidjan
Bouaké
Korhogo
Man
Daloa
GHANA
Kumasi
Accra
Tamale
Lake Volta
Sekondi Takoradi
TOGO
Lomé
BENIN
Cotonou
Porto-Novo
NIGERIA
Lagos
Ibadan
Ogbomosho
Oshogbo
Kano
Kaduna
Sokoto
Katsina
Zaria
Benin City
Onitsha
Enugu
Aba
Port Harcourt
Bight of Benin
Macias Nguema Biyoga
Douala
CAMEROON
Projection: Sanson Flamsteed's Sinusoidal
West from Greenwich
East from Greenwich
ft
m
12,000
9000
6000
4500
3000
1200
600
0
200
600
4000
3000
2000
1500
1000
400
200
0

Kilometers 0 100 200 300 400 500 600 Km.
Statute Miles 0 100 200 300 400 500 600 Mi.

1:12 000 000

One centimeter represents 120 kilometers
One inch represents approximately 190 miles

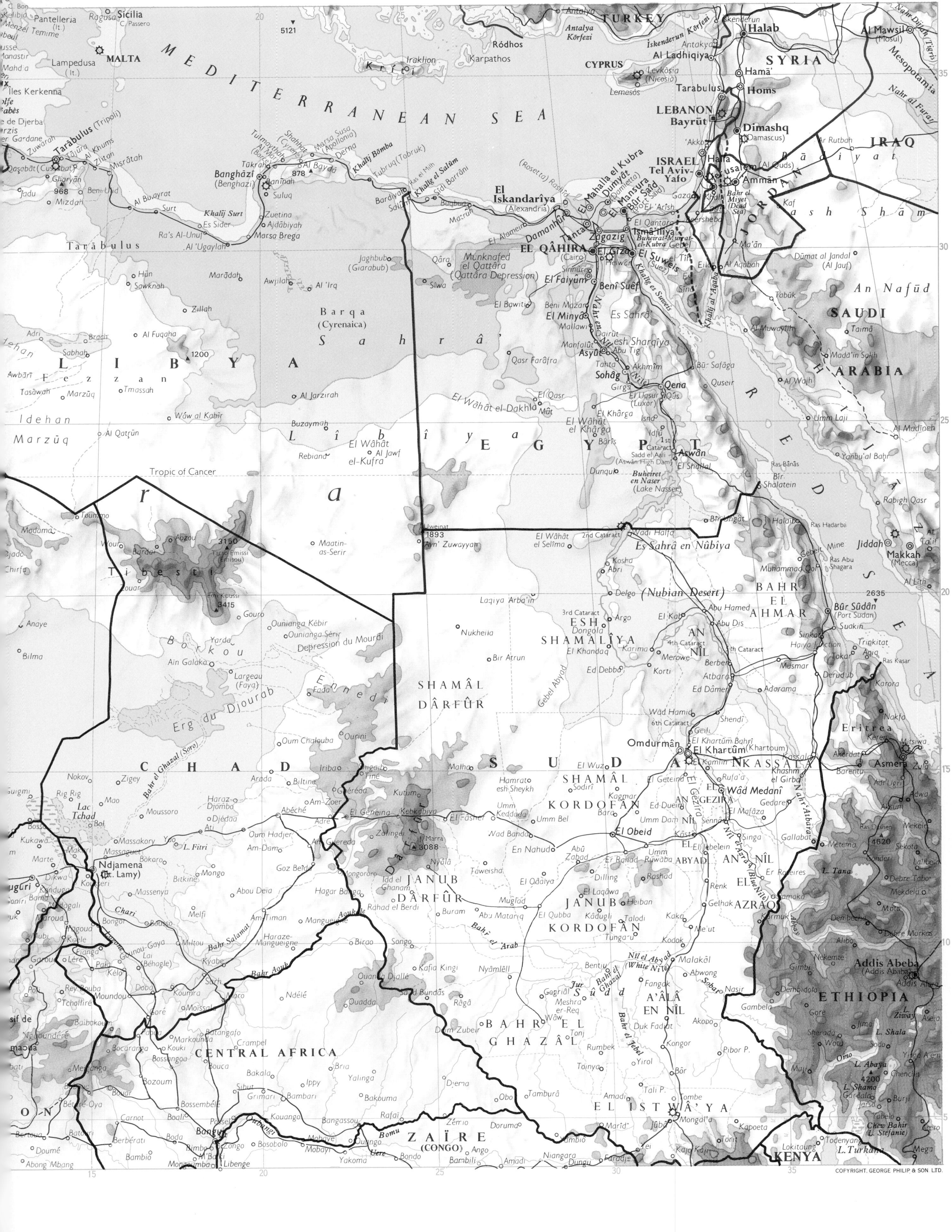

MEDITERRANEAN SEA
TURKEY
SYRIA
LEBANON
ISRAEL
JORDAN
IRAQ
SAUDI ARABIA
CYPRUS
MALTA
LIBYA
EGYPT
CHAD
SUDAN
CENTRAL AFRICA
ZAÏRE (CONGO)
ETHIOPIA
KENYA
Eritrea
RED SEA
Sicilia
Pantelleria (It.)
Lampedusa (It.)
Iles Kerkenna
Kríti
Iraklion
Ródhos
Karpathos
Antalya
Antalya Körfezi
İskenderun Körfezi
İskenderun
Antakya
Halab
Al Mawsil (Mosul)
Mesopotamia
Al Ladhiqiya
Hamā'
Homs
Tarabulus
Bayrūt
Dimashq (Damascus)
Levkôsia (Nicosia)
Lemesós
'Akko
Haifa
Tel Aviv-Yafo
Jerusalem (Al Quds)
'Ammān
Bahr el Miyet (Dead Sea)
Beersheba
Ma'ān
Al 'Aqabah
Eilat
Gaza
El 'Arîsh
Ar Rutbah
Bādiyat ash Shām
Dūmat al Jandal (Al Jauf)
An Nafūd
Tabūk
Al Muwaylih
Madā'in Salih
Taimā
Al Wajh
Umm Lajj
Al Madīnah
Yanbu'al Bahr
Rābigh
Jiddah
Makkah (Mecca)
Al Lith
Tarabulus (Tripoli)
Misrātah
Zlitan
Al Khums
Gharyān
Banghāzī (Benghazi)
Tubruq (Tobruk)
Darnah
Al Baydā
Marsa Susa (Apollonia)
Khalīj Surt
Surt
Ajdābiyah
Marsa Brega
Zuetina
Es Sider
Al Buayrat
Mizdah
Hūn
Sawknah
Zillah
Maradah
Awjilah
Jaghbub (Giarabub)
Al Fuqaha
Sabhah
Fezzan
Idehan Marzūq
Marzūq
Tmassah
Al Jarzirah
Wāw al Kabīr
Al Qatrūn
Buzaymah
Rebiana
Al Jawf
El Wâhât el-Kufra
Barqa (Cyrenaica)
Sahrâ' Lîbîya
Tropic of Cancer
El Iskandarîya (Alexandria)
El Alamein
Matrûh
Sîdi Barrâni
Salûm
Bardiyah
Sîwa
Qâra
Munkhafed el Qattâra (Qattâra Depression)
EL QÂHIRA (Cairo)
El Gîza
Helwân
Bûr Sa'îd (Port Said)
Dumyât
El Mansura
El Mahalla el Kubra
Tanta
Damanhûr
Zagazig
Ismâ'ilîya
El Suweis (Suez)
El Faiyûm
Benî Suef
El Minya
Mallawi
Manfalût
Asyût
Sohâg
Akhmîm
Qena
El Uqsur (Luxor)
Isna
Idfu
Aswân
Sadd el Aali (Aswân High Dam)
Buheiret en Naser (Lake Nasser)
El Wâhât el Khârga
El Khârga
El Wâhât el-Dakhla
Qasr Farâfra
Bûr Safâga
Quseir
Ras Bânâs
Bir Shalatein
Es Sahrâ' en Nûbîya
(Nubian Desert)
Wadi Halfa
2nd Cataract
Uweinat 1893
Ayn' Zuwayyah
Maatin-as-Serir
El Wâhât el Selîma
Abu Hamed
Bûr Sûdân (Port Sudan)
Suakin
Sinkat
Tokar
Karima
Merowe
Dongola
Berber
Atbara
ESH SHAMALÎYA
AN NÎL
BAHR EL AHMAR
SHAMÂL DÂRFÛR
SHAMÂL KORDOFÂN
JANUB DÂRFÛR
JANUB KORDOFÂN
KASSALA
Kassala
GEZIRA
AN NÎL ABYAD
AN NÎL EL AZRAQ
A'ÂLÂ EN NÎL
BAHR EL GHAZÂL
EL ISTWÂ'YA
Omdurmân
El Khartûm (Khartoum)
Wâd Medanî
El Obeid
El Fasher
Geneina
Nyala
Jebel Marra 3088
Kosti
Senna
Renk
Malakâl
Bor
Juba
Wau
Laqiya Arba'in
Nukheila
Bir Atrun
Gebel Abyad
Tibesti
Emi Koussi 3415
Tarso Emissi 3150
Bardai
Aozou
Borkou
Largeau (Faya)
Ennedi
Erg du Djourab
Fada
Dépression du Mourdi
Ounianga Kébir
Bilma
Lac Tchad
Ndjamena (Ft. Lamy)
Abéché
Moussoro
Ati
Mongo
Am-Timan
Chari
Bahr Salamat
Bahr Aouk
Sarh
Moundou
Bangui
Bambari
Berbérati
Bossangoa
Ubangi
Asmera
Massawa
Gonder
L. Tana
Addis Abeba
Gambela
L. Abaya
L. Shala
L. Ziway
L. Turkana
Chew Bahir (L. Stefanie)
4620
4200

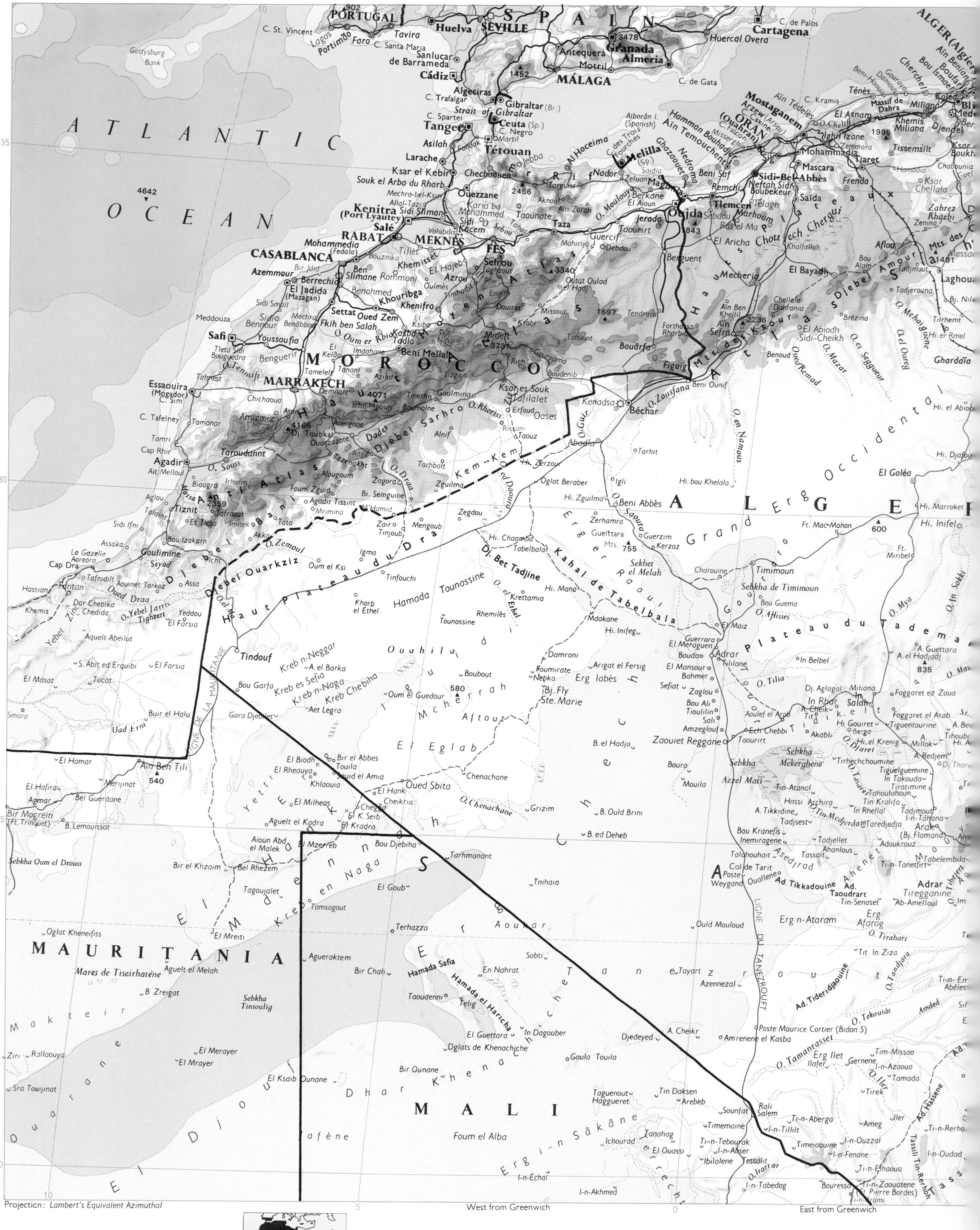

ATLANTIC OCEAN
PORTUGAL
SPAIN
MOROCCO
ALGERIA
MAURITANIA
MALI
ALGER (Alger)
Huelva
SEVILLE
Cartagena
Granada
Almeria
MÁLAGA
Cádiz
Gibraltar (Br.)
Strait of Gibraltar
Ceuta (Sp.)
Tanger
Tétouan
Melilla (Sp.)
Alborán I. (Spanish)
ORAN (Ouahran)
Mostaganem
Sidi-Bel-Abbès
Tlemcen
Oujda
Kenitra (Port Lyautey)
Salé
RABAT
MEKNÈS
FES
CASABLANCA
El Jadida (Mazagan)
Safi
Essaouira (Mogador)
MARRAKECH
Agadir
Tiznit
Goulimine
Tindouf
Béchar
Figuig
Haut Atlas
Moyen Atlas
Anti Atlas
Rif
Djebel Ouarkziz
Djebel Bani
Hamada du Dra
Haut Plateau du Dra
Hamada Tounassine
Grand Erg Occidental
Erg Iguidi
Erg Chech
El Eglab
Plateau du Tademait
Tanezrouft
Adrar
Timimoun
Reggane
El Djouf
Erg Chech
Aouker
Hamada Safia
Hamada el Haricha
Taoudenni
Ouarane
Makteir
Bir Mogrein (Ft. Trinquet)
Ain Ben Tili
Dj. Toubkal 4165
4071
3737
3340
2456
2359
4642
Gettysburg Bank
C. St. Vincent
C. Trafalgar
C. Spartel
C. de Gata
C. de Palos
C. Sim
C. Tafelney
Cap Rhir
Cap Dra
Projection: Lambert's Equivalent Azimuthal
West from Greenwich
East from Greenwich
ft
m
12,000
9000
6000
4500
3000
1200
600
0
200
2000
4000
4000
3000
2000
1500
1000
400
200
600
6000
12,000

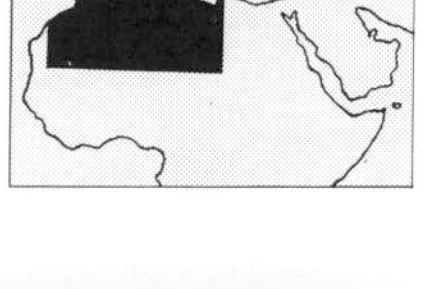

Kilometers 0 50 100 150 200 250 300 Km.
Statute Miles 0 50 100 150 200 250 300 Mi.

1:6 400 000

One centimeter represents 64 kilometers
One inch represents approximately 100 miles

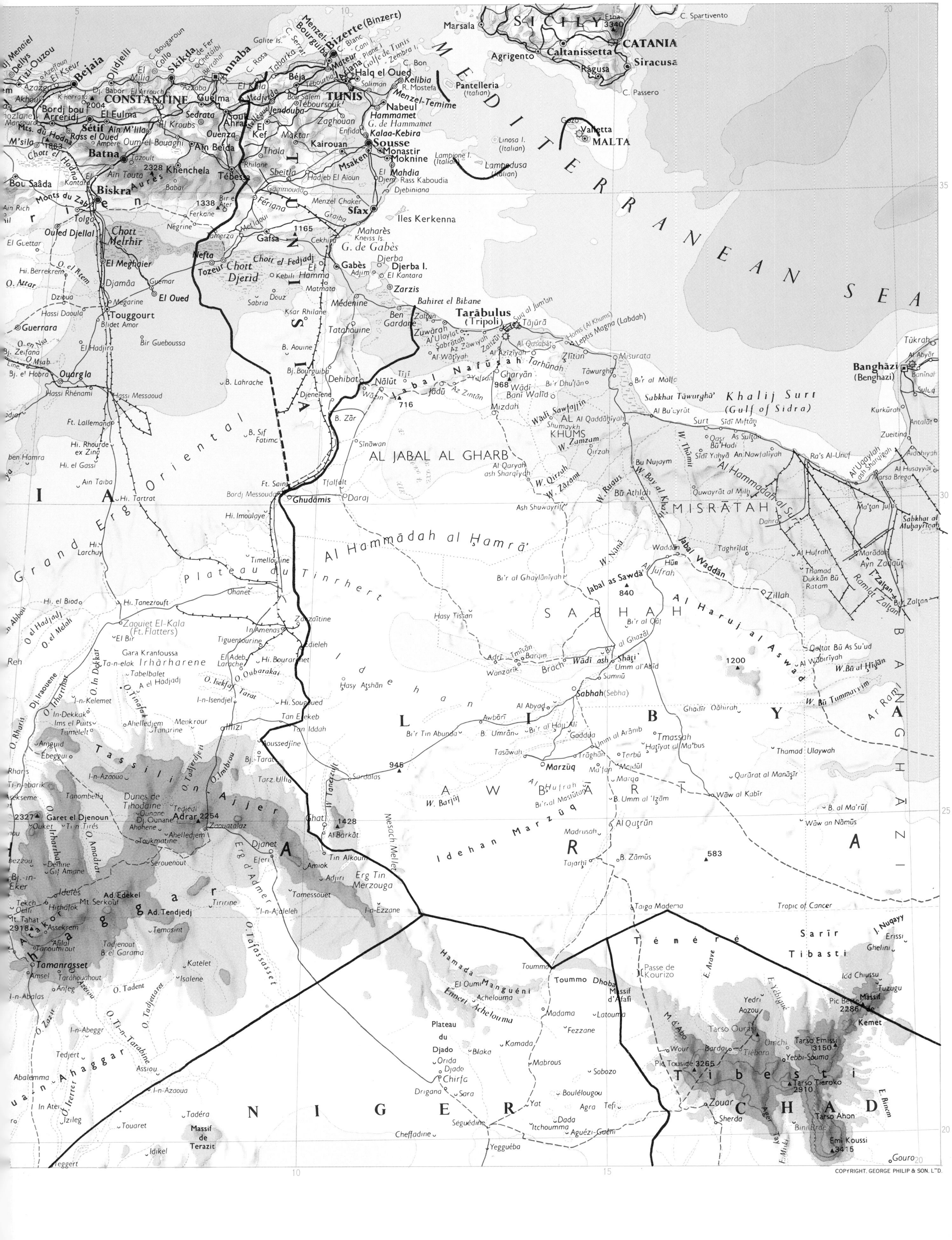
MEDITERRANEAN SEA
SICILY
Marsala
Etna 3340
CATANIA
Agrigento
Caltanissetta
Siracusa
Ragusa
C. Passero
C. Spartivento
Pantelleria (Italian)
Linosa I. (Italian)
Lampione I. (Italian)
Lampedusa (Italian)
Gozo
Valletta
MALTA
TUNISIA
Bizerte (Binzert)
Menzel-Bourguiba
Galite Is.
C. Serrat
C. Blanc
Mateur
Golfe de Tunis
Zembra I.
C. Bon
Tabarka
Béja
Halq el Oued
TUNIS
Kelibia
R. Mostefa
Menzel-Temime
Nabeul
Hammamet
G. de Hammamet
Zaghouan
Enfida
Kalaa-Kebira
Sousse
Monastir
Moknine
Mahdia
Rass Kaboudia
Djebiniana
Kairouan
Msaken
Maktar
El Kef
Jendouba
Teboursouk
Souk Ahras
Thala
Sbeitla
Hadjeb El Aioun
Menzel Chaker
Sfax
Iles Kerkenna
Maharès
Kneiss Is.
G. de Gabès
Gafsa
Cekhira
Gabès
Djerba
Djerba I.
Adjim
El Kantara
Zarzis
El Hamma
Kebili
Matmata
Chott el Fedjadj
Chott Djerid
Tozeur
Nefta
Tamerza
Métlaoui
Fériana
Kasserine
Douz
Sabria
Médenine
Ksar Rhilane
Ben Gardane
Tatahouine
Bahiret el Bibane
B. Aouine
Bj. Bourguiba
Dehibat
Remada
Tebessa
Galite Is.
C. Rosa
El Kala
Annaba
Skikda
Collo
C. Bougaroun
El Milia
Djidjelli
Bejaia
Dellys
Tizi-Ouzou
Azazga
El Kseur
Akbou
Dj. Babor
CONSTANTINE
Guelma
Sedrata
Bordj bou Arreridj
Sétif
El Eulma
Mts. du Hodna
Ain M'lila
Oum el Bouaghi
Ain Beida
Ouenza
Batna
Khenchela
Ain Touta
Aurès
Chott el Hodna
Biskra
Bou Saâda
Monts du Zab
Tolga
Ouled Djellal
Chott Melrhir
El Meghaier
Négrine
Ferkane
El Guettar
Hi. Berrekrem
O. el Rtem
Djamâa
El Oued
Guemar
Touggourt
Blidet Amor
Megarine
Hassi Daoula
Guerrara
Bir Gueboussa
El Hadjira
Ouargla
Hassi Rhénami
Hassi Messaoud
B. Lahrache
Ft. Lallemand
Hi. Rhourde ex Zina
Hi. el Gassi
Ain Taiba
Hi. Tartrat
B. Sif Fatima
Ft. Saint
Bordj Messouda
Hi. Imoulaye
Grand Erg Oriental
Plateau du Tinrhert
Timellouline
Ohanet
Hi. Tanezrouft
In Amenas
Zarzaïtine
Edjeleh
Tiguentourine
El Adeb Larache
Hi. Bourarhet
Zaouiet El-Kala (Ft. Flatters)
El Bir
Gara Kranfoussa
Ta-n-elak
Irhârharene
Tabelbalet
A el Hadjadj
O. Isekfa
O. Oubarakat
Tarat
I-n-Isendjel
Hi. Souguied
Tan Elekeb
Tan Iddah
Illizi
Menkrour
Tanarine
Ahelledjem
Ims el Puits
Tamelelt
In-Dekkak
I-n-Kelemet
Ouessedjine
Bj.-Tarat
Tarz Ulli
Tassili n Ajjer
Dunes de Tihodaine
Adrar 2254
Ahellegjem
Garet el Djenoun
2327
Ouanene
Dj. Ouanene
Zaouatallaz
Djanet
Ghat
Al Barkat
1428
Erg d'Admer
Tin Alkoum
Amiok
Adjiri
Erg Tin Merzouga
Tamessouet
I-n-Ajaleh
I-n-Ezzane
Ahaggar
Ad. Edekel
Mt. Serkout
Ad. Tendjedj
Hirhafok
Tahat
2918
Assekrem
Atakor
Tamanrasset
Tadjenout
B. el Garama
Temasint
Katelet
Isalene
O. Tafassasset
O. Tadent
O. Ti-n-Tarabine
Assiou
I-n-Abeggr
Tedjert
Abalemma
In Ater
Izileg
I-n-Azaoua
Touaret
Tadéra
Massif de Terazit
Idikel
Teggert
NIGER
Tarābulus (Tripoli)
Tājūrā
Zuwārah
Az Zāwiyah
Şabrātah
Al Ujaylat
Zaltan
Sūq al Jum'ah
Leptis Magna (Labdah)
Homs (Al Khums)
Al Qasabat
Zlīţan
Misurata
Tawurghā'
Al 'Azīzīyah
Tarhūnah
Gharyān
Yafran
Jabal Nafūsah
Nālūt
Wāzin
Jādū
Az Zintān
716
968
Wādī Banī Walīd
Bi'r Dhu'lan
Mizdah
B. Zār
Sīnāwan
Dijeneiene
AL JABAL AL GHARB
Al Qaryah ash Sharqīyah
Ghudāmis
Daraj
Tfalfalt
Wādī Sawfajjin
Al Qaddāḥiyah
AL KHUMS
Shumaykh
W. Zamzum
Qirzah
Sabkhat Tāwurghā'
Khalij Surt (Gulf of Sidra)
Al Bu'ayrat
Surt
Sidī Mītāq
Qasr Bū Hādī
As Sulţān
Sidī Yahya
An Nawfalīyah
Ra's Al-Unuf
Bu Nujaym
Al Hammādah as Sūr
Quwayrat al Mill
Bū Athlah
MISRĀTAH
Dahra
W. Qirzah
W. Zamzum
Ash Shuwayrif
Al Hammādah al Hamrā'
Bi'r al Ghaylānīyah
Jabal as Sawdā'
840
Waddān
Hūn
Al Jufrah
Jabal Waddān
Taghrīfat
Zillah
Al Hufrah
Thamad Dukkān Bū Ratam
Marādah
Ayn Zaqqūt
Ramlat Zaltan
Bi'r Zaltan
Sabkhat al Muhayrīqah
Ma'tan Jalīt
Al 'Uqaylah
Marsa Brega
Al Husayyat
Zueitina
Antalat
Kurkurah
Banghāzī (Benghazi)
Tūkrah
Al Abyār
Suluq
Ajdābiyah
Hasy Tissan
SABHAH
Bi'r al Qāf
Al Harūj al Aswad
1200
Qeltat Bū As Su'ud
Al Wābirīyah
W. Bū al Hīyān
W. Bū Tumma'im
BANGHĀZĪ
Ar Ramla
Ghadīr Qāhirah
Idehan
Adri
Tmisān
Barqin
Brach
Wādī ash Shāţi'
Umm al Abīd
Sumnū
Wanzarik
Hasy Atshān
Sabhah (Sebha)
Al Abyad
Awbārī
Bi'r Tin Abunda
B. Umrān
Bi'r al Hajj 'Alī
Ghuddua
Umm al Arānib
Tmassah
Hutiyat al Ma'bus
Thamad Ulaywah
Tasāwah
Trāghān
Tarbū
Marzūq
Majdūl
Marqa
945
Surdalas
W. Tanezzuft
Al Hufrah
Bi'r al Mastūtah
W. Barjūj
B. Umm al 'Izām
Qurārat al Manāşīr
Wāw al Kabīr
B. al Ma'rūf
Wāw an Nāmūs
LIBYA
AWBĀRĪ
Idehan Marzūq
Mesach Mellet
Al Qaţrūn
Madrusah
B. Zāmūs
Tajarhi
583
Taiga Madema
Tropic of Cancer
Ténéré
Sarīr Tibasti
J. Nuqayy
Erissi
Ghelini
Icd Chiussu
Tuzugu
Massif de Kemet
Pic Bette 2286
Hamada Manguéni
El Oumi
Acheloumа
Enneri Acheloumа
Toummo
Toummo Dhoba
Passe de Kourizo
Massif d'Afafi
E. Arave
Madama
Latouma
Fezzane
Kamada
Mabrous
Sobozo
Plateau du Djado
Orida
Djado
Chirfa
Blaka
Drigana
Sara
Yat
Boulélougou
Agra
Tefi
Dada
Itchoumma
Aguézi-Guéni
Séguédine
Cheffadine
Yegguéba
Yedri
Aozou
E. Yebigué
M. d'Abo
Tarso Ourari
Omchi
Tarso Emissi 3150
Wour
Bardai
Tiebero
Yebbi-Souma
Pic Tousidé 3265
Tibesti
Tarso Tieroko 2910
Zouar
Sherda
Tarso Ahon
Bini Erde
Emi Koussi 3415
E. Bingm
E. Miski
Gouro
CHAD
35
30
25
20
5
10
15

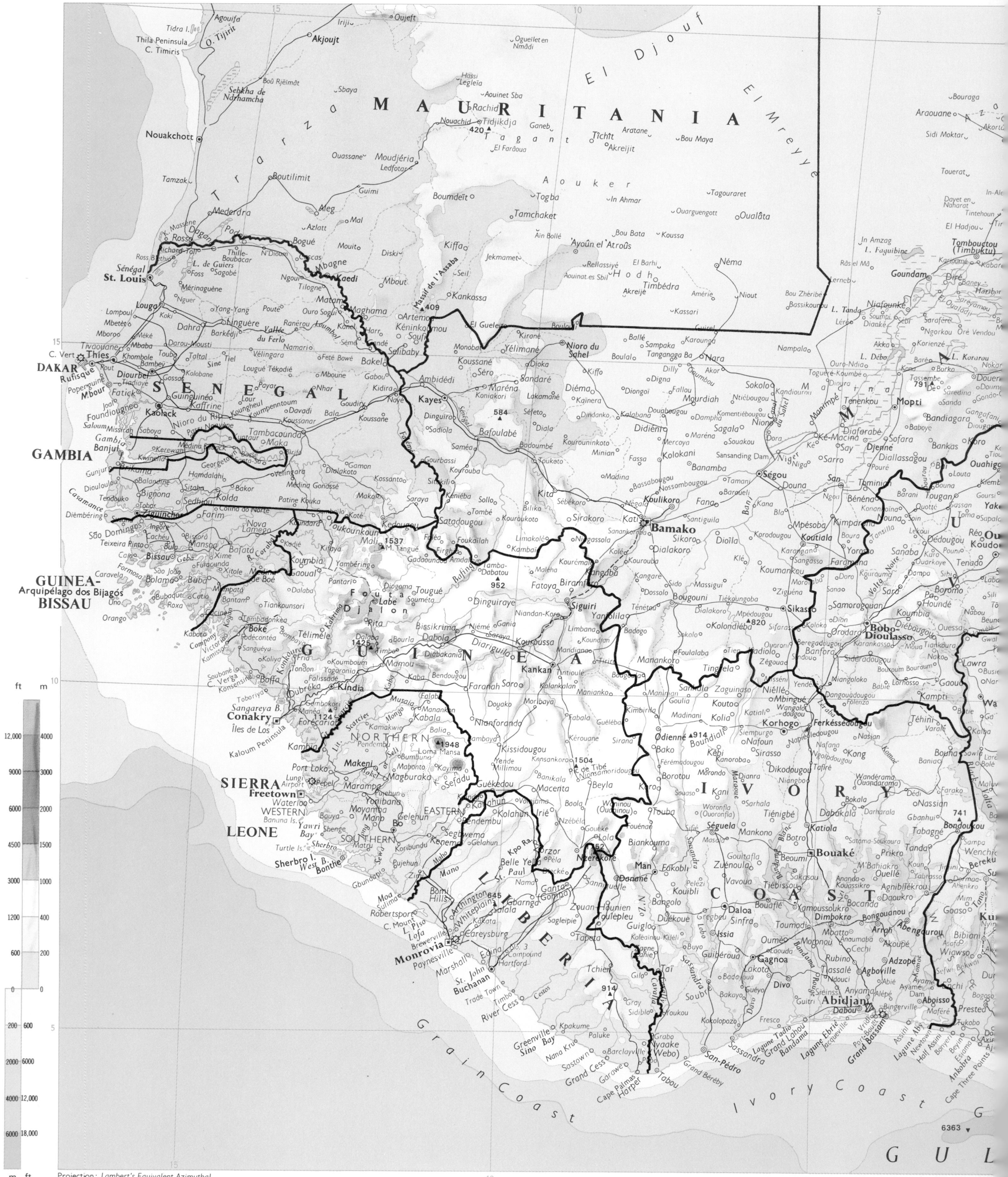
MAURITANIA
SENEGAL
GAMBIA
GUINEA-BISSAU
GUINEA
SIERRA LEONE
LIBERIA
IVORY COAST
El Djouf
Tagant
Aouker
Hodh
Fouta Djalon
Grain Coast
Ivory Coast
Nouakchott
Akjoujt
Tidjikdja
Boutilimit
Aleg
Kiffa
Néma
Oualâta
Tichit
Rosso
St. Louis
DAKAR
Thiès
Rufisque
Diourbel
Kaolack
Tambacounda
Banjul
Ziguinchor
Bissau
Kayes
Bamako
Koulikoro
Ségou
Mopti
Tombouctou (Timbuktu)
Sikasso
Bobo-Dioulasso
Conakry
Kindia
Kankan
Siguiri
Labé
Freetown
Monrovia
Buchanan
Harper
Man
Daloa
Bouaké
Korhogo
Gagnoa
Abidjan
Grand Bassam
San-Pédro
Cape Palmas
Bondoukou
Kolahun
Nzérékoré
ft m
12,000 4000
9000 3000
6000 2000
4500 1500
3000 1000
1200 400
600 200
0 0
200 600
2000 6000
4000 12,000
6000 18,000
m ft
G U L

Projection: Lambert's Equivalent Azimuthal

West from Greenwich

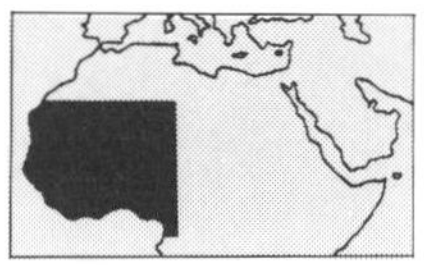

Kilometers 0 50 100 150 200 250 300 Km.
Statute Miles 0 50 100 150 200 250 300 Mi.

1:6 400 000

One centimeter represents 64 kilometers
One inch represents approximately 100 miles

ALGERIA
Adrar des Iforhas
Tassili Oua-n-Ahaggar
Massif de Terazit
Aïr (Azbine)
Monts Bagzane
Agadez
Ténéré
Talak
NIGER
Tahoua
Niamey
Zinder
Maradi
Tillabéri
Gao
Bourem
Kidal
Lac Tchad
N.E. NIGERIA on same scale as general map
CHAD
Maiduguri
Bama
Mubi
Garoua
Maroua
BORNO
NIGERIA
Sokoto
Kano
Katsina
Zaria
Kaduna
Jos
Jos Plateau
Bauchi
Gombe
Potiskum
Nguru
Gusau
Birnin Kebbi
Minna
Ilorin
Ogbomosho
Oshogbo
Ibadan
Abeokuta
LAGOS
Benin City
Onitsha
Enugu
Port-Harcourt
Calabar
Makurdi
Yola
GONGOLA
BENUE
ANAMBRA
BENDEL
CROSS RIVER
KADUNA
SOKOTO
KANO
PLATEAU
BENIN
Parakou
Djougou
Natitingou
Abomey
Porto-Novo
Cotonou
Ouidah
TOGO
Lomé
Sokodé
Palimé
GHANA
Tamale
Yendi
Bolgatanga
ACCRA
Tema
Winneba
Cape Coast
Lake Volta
UPPER VOLTA
Ouagadougou
Tenkodogo
Koupéla
Fada N'Gourma
Diapaga
CAMEROON
DOUALA
Yaoundé
Kumba
Buea
Victoria
Bamenda
Nkongsamba
Mt. Cameroun 4070
Rey Malabo
Pico Santa Isabel
MACIAS NGUEMA BIYOGA
EQUATORIAL GUINEA
Bight of Bonny
Slave Coast
Bight of Benin
Niger Delta
GULF OF GUINEA

East from Greenwich

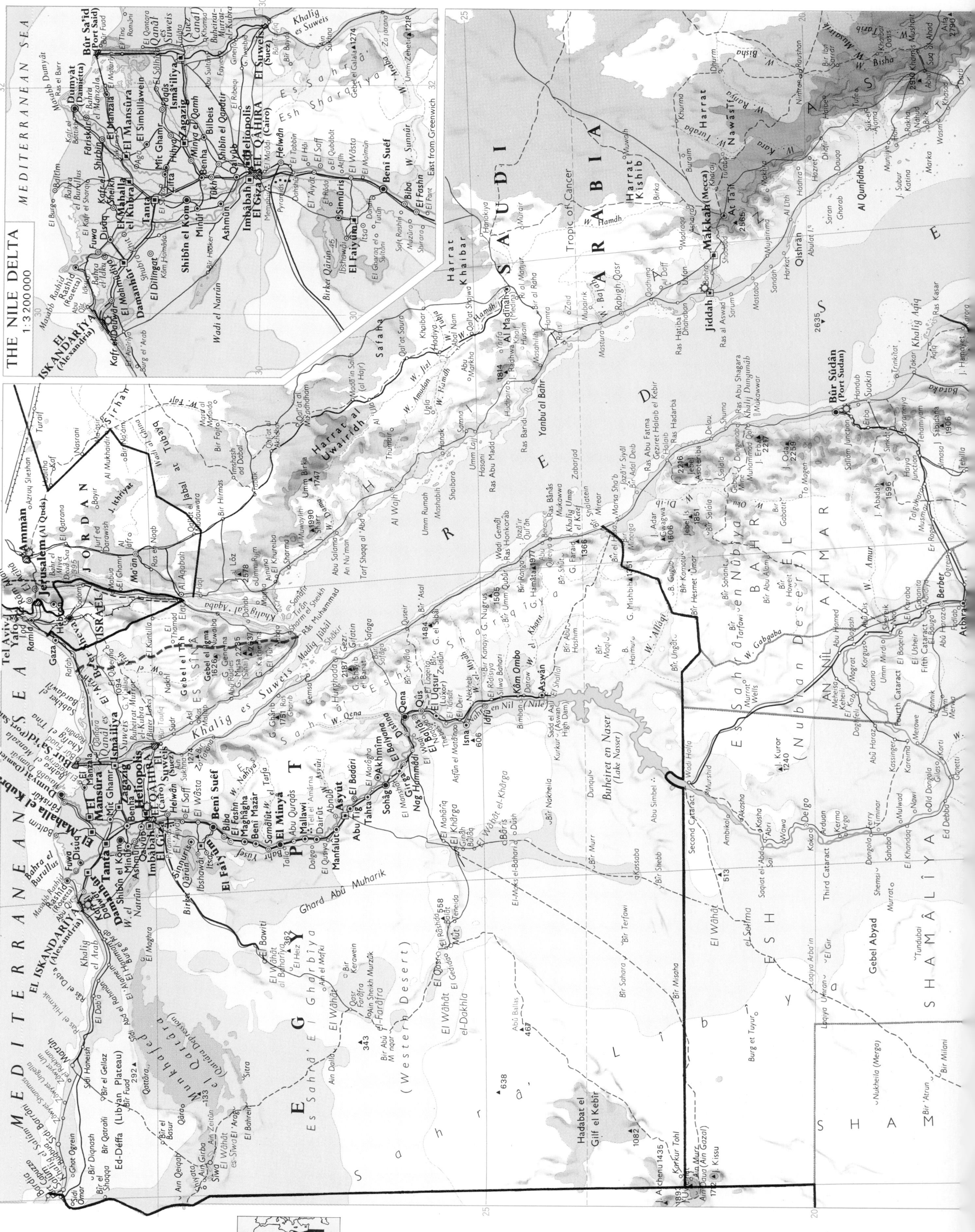
THE NILE DELTA
1:3 200 000
MEDITERRANEAN SEA
East from Greenwich
EL ISKANDARÎYA (Alexandria)
Bûr Sa'îd (Port Said)
Dumyât (Damietta)
EL QÂHIRA (Cairo)
El Mansûra
Zagazig
Tanta
El Mahalla el Kubra
Isma'ilîya
El Suweis (Suez)
El Faiyûm
Beni Suef
Wadi el Natrûn
Birket Qârûn
MEDITERRANEAN SEA
JORDAN
ISRAEL
Jerusalem (Al Quds)
Ammân
Tel Aviv-Yafo
Gaza
SAUDI ARABIA
Tropic of Cancer
Al Madinah (Medina)
Makkah (Mecca)
Jiddah
Bûr Sûdân (Port Sudan)
RED SEA
Khalîg es Suweis
E G Y P T
Es Sahrâ' el Gharbîya (Western Desert)
Munkhafad el Qattâra (Qattara Depression)
El Wâhât el Khârga
El Wâhât el Dakhla
Buheiret en Naser (Lake Nasser)
Aswân
Qena
Luxor
Asyût
El Minyâ
Wadi Halfa
Second Cataract
Third Cataract
Fourth Cataract
Fifth Cataract
Atbara
Berber
Dongola
Hadabat el Gilf el Kebir
Ghard Abû Muharik
Sahrâ' en Nûbîya (Nubian Desert)
Bahr el Nîl
Es Sahrâ' esh Shamâlîya
Matrûh
Sîdi Barrâni
Es Sallûm
Sîwa
Gebel Abyad

Kilometers 0 50 100 150 200 250 300 Km.

Statute Miles 0 50 100 150 200 250 300 Mi.

1:6 400 000

One centimeter represents 64 kilometers
One inch represents approximately 100 miles

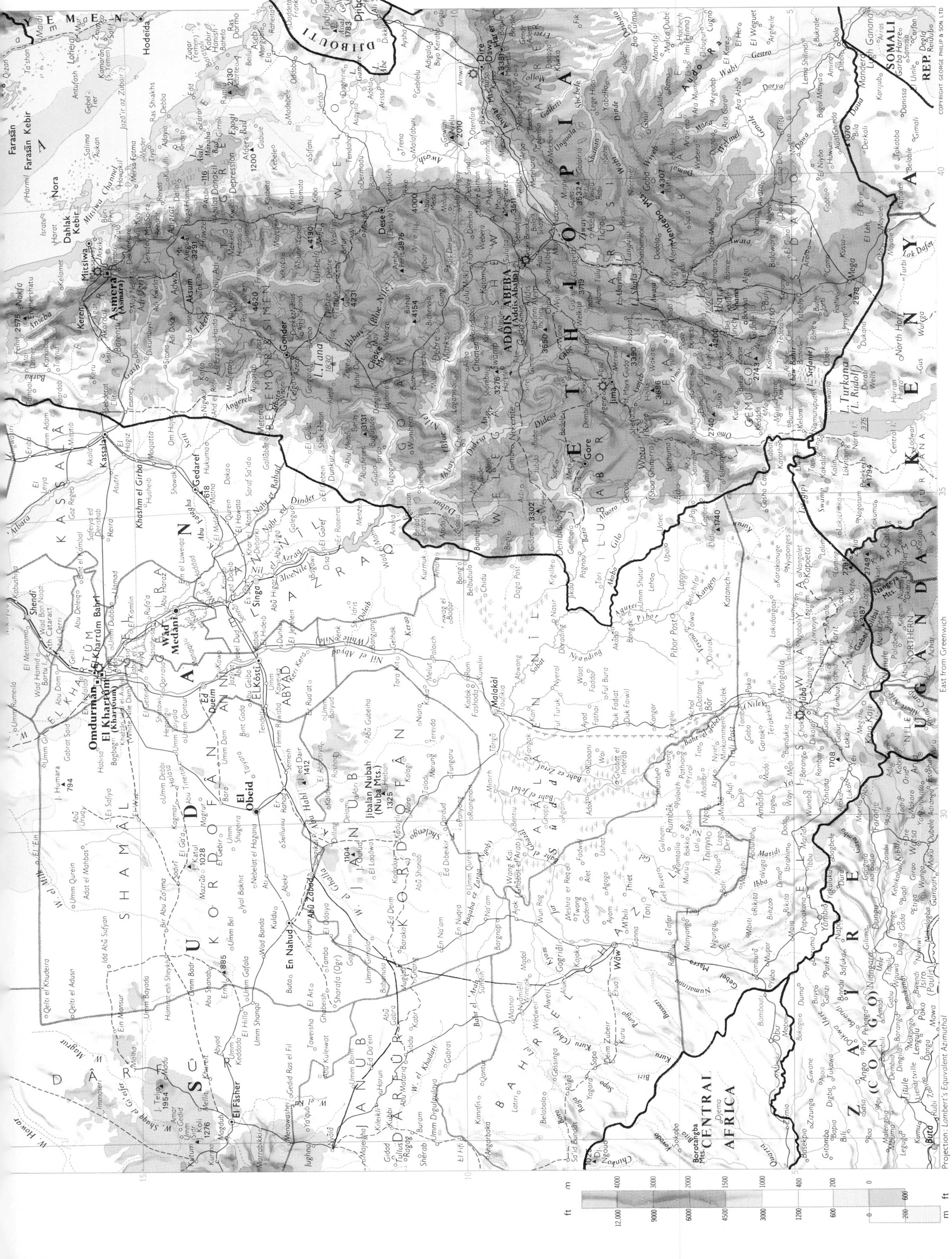
ETHIOPIA
ADDIS ABEBA (Addis Ababa)
Asmera (Asmara)
Mitsiwa
Gonder
Dese
Gore
Jima
DJIBOUTI
Djibouti
YEMEN
Hodeida
SOMALI REP.
KENYA
UGANDA
ZAIRE (CONGO)
CENTRAL AFRICA
El Khartûm (Khartoum)
Omdurman
Kassala
Gedaref
Wad Medani
El Obeid
En Nahud
El Fasher
Malakal
Wau
Juba
L. Tana
L. Turkana (L. Rudolf)
Blue Nile
White Nile
Nile
East from Greenwich
Projection: Lambert's Equivalent Azimuthal
m ft
4000 12,000
3000 9000
2000 6000
1500 4500
1000 3000
400 1200
200 600
0 0
200 600
COPYRIGHT GEORGE PHILIP & SON LTD

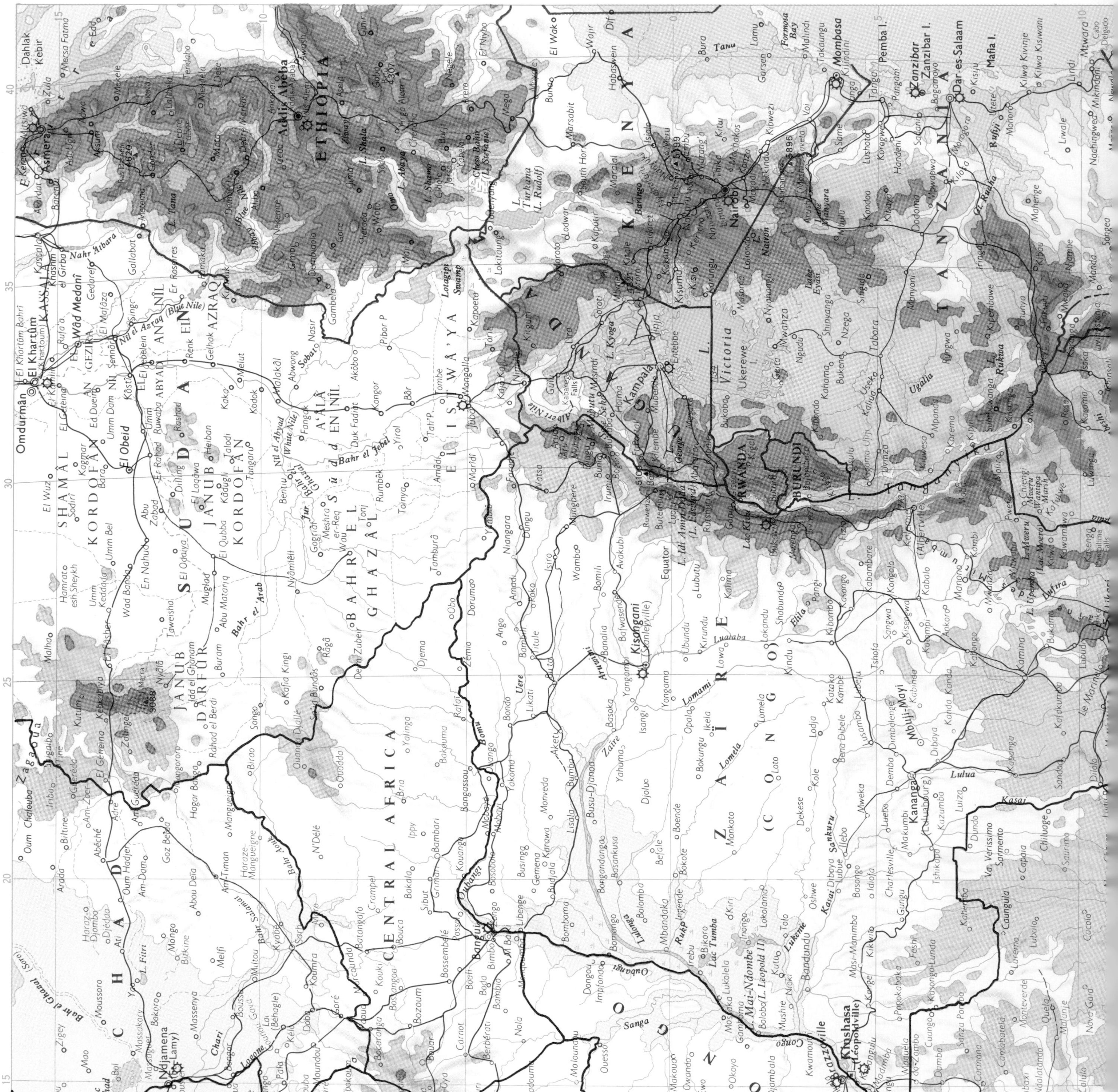
ETHIOPIA
Addis Abeba
Asmera
El Khartûm
Omdurmân
Nairobi
Mombasa
Kampala
Dar es Salaam
Zanzibar
RWANDA
BURUNDI
L. Victoria
CENTRAL AFRICA
CHAD
NIGER
NIGERIA
CAMEROON
GABON
EQUATORIAL GUINEA
CABINDA
Ndjamena
Bangui
Yaoundé
Douala
Libreville
Kinshasa
Brazzaville
Luanda
Kisangani
Kano
Lac Tchad
Pemba I.
Mafia I.

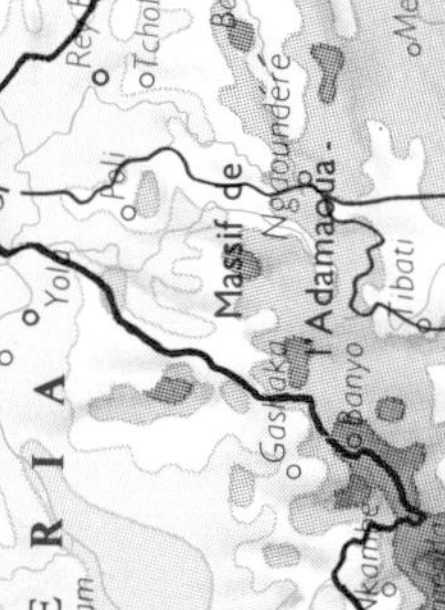

Kilometers 0 100 200 300 400 500 600 Km.
Statute Miles 0 100 200 300 400 500 600 Mi.

1:12 000 000

One centimeter represents 120 kilometers
One inch represents approximately 190 miles

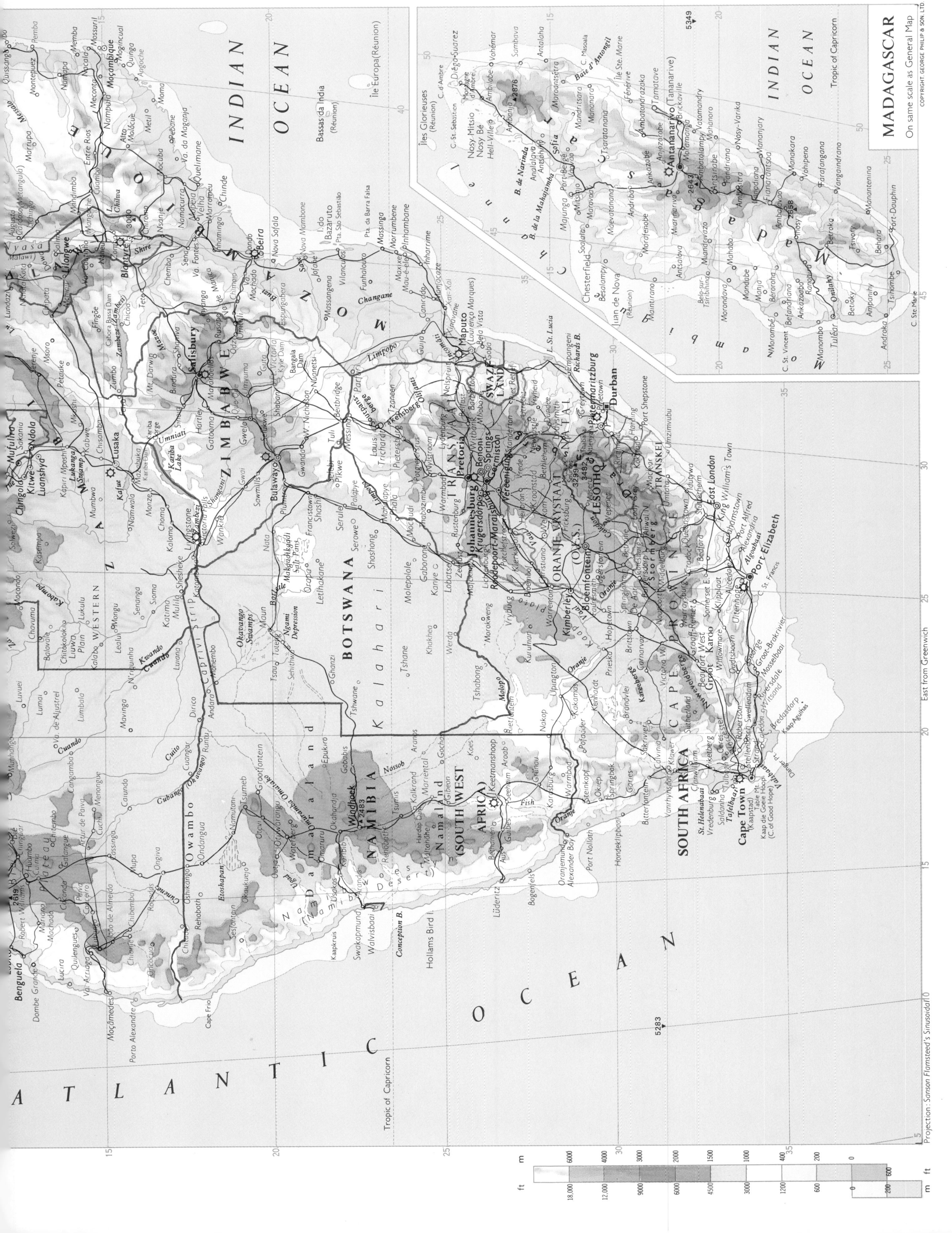

MADAGASCAR
On same scale as General Map
COPYRIGHT GEORGE PHILIP & SON, LTD
INDIAN OCEAN
ATLANTIC OCEAN
BOTSWANA
ZIMBABWE
NAMIBIA
(SOUTH WEST AFRICA)
SOUTH AFRICA
LESOTHO
SWAZILAND
ORANJE VRYSTAAT (O.V.S.)
TRANSKEI
CAPE PROVINCE
Kalahari
Tropic of Capricorn
East from Greenwich
Projection: Sanson Flamsteed's Sinusoidal
m 6000 4000 3000 2000 1500 1000 400 200 0 200
ft 18,000 12,000 9000 6000 4500 3000 1200 600 0 600

SOMALI REP.
ETHIOPIA
KENYA
UGANDA
TANZANIA
RWANDA
BURUNDI
SUDAN
CENTRAL AFRICA
NAIROBI
MOMBASA
DAR ES SALAAM
Zanzibar
Pemba I.
Kampala
Entebbe
Jinja
Kisumu
Nakuru
Arusha
Tanga
Dodoma
Tabora
Mwanza
Kigoma
Ujiji
Bujumbura
Bukavu
Goma
Kisangani (Stanleyville)
Juba
L. Turkana (L. Rudolf)
Lake Victoria
L. Kyoga
L. Natron
L. Eyasi
L. Manyara
L. Kivu
L. Tanganyika
L. Rukwa
L. Mobutu
Tana River
Lualaba
Mega
Moyale
Marsabit
Lodwar
Garissa
Lamu
Malindi
Voi
Pangani

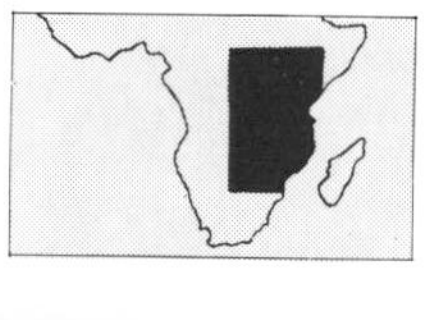

Kilometers 0 50 100 150 200 250 300 Km.

Statute Miles 0 50 100 150 200 250 300 Mi.

1:6 400 000

One centimeter represents 64 kilometers
One inch represents approximately 100 miles

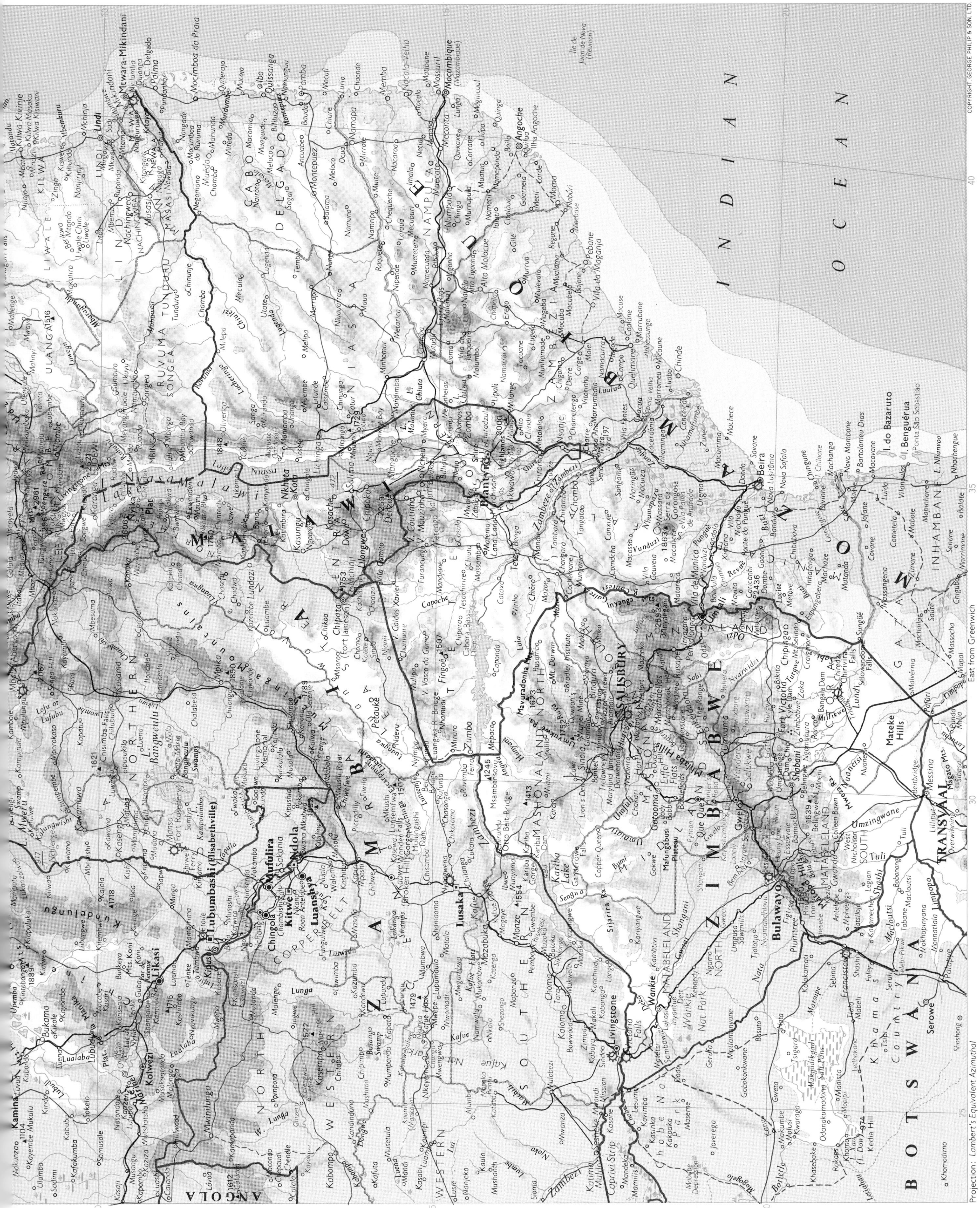

INDIAN OCEAN
MOZAMBIQUE
ZAMBIA
MALAWI
ZIMBABWE
BOTSWANA
ANGOLA
TRANSVAAL
Lake Malawi
Kariba Lake
Lusaka
Salisbury
Bulawayo
Blantyre
Lilongwe
Beira
Ndola
Kitwe
Livingstone
Lubumbashi (Elisabethville)
Moçambique
Mtwara-Mikindani
Lindi
Zambezi
East from Greenwich

Projection: Lambert's Equivalent Azimuthal

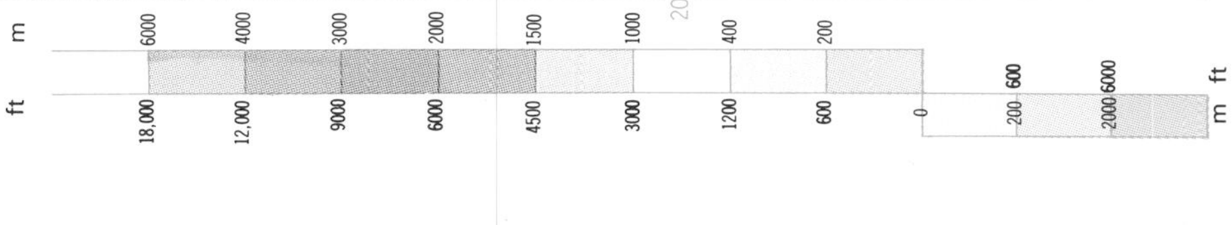

m
6000
4000
3000
2000
1500
1000
400
200
0
200 600
2000 6000
ft
18,000
12,000
9000
6000
4500
3000
1200
600
0
600
6000
m ft

ANGOLA
CUANDO-CUBANGO
ZAMBIA
NAMIBIA
(SOUTH-WEST AFRICA)
BOTSWANA
SOUTH AFRICA
CAPE PROVINCE
ORANJE (O.F.S.)
ATLANTIC OCEAN
Kalahari
Namib Desert
Damaraland
Kaokoveld
Caprivi Strip
Okavango Swamps
Ngami Depression
Kalahari Gemsbok National Park
BETSJOEANALAND (BECHUANALAND)
Little Namaqualand
Great Bushman Land
Tropic of Capricorn
Porto Alexandre
Moçâmedes
Livingstone (Maramba)
Victoria Falls
Windhoek
Walvisbaai (Walvis Bay)
Swakopmund
Lüderitz
Keetmanshoop
Mariental
Tsumeb
Grootfontein
Otjiwarongo
Okahandja
Gobabis
Rehoboth
Maun
Ghanzi
Serowe
Mahalapye
Mochudi
Molepolole
Gaberone
Kanye
Lobatse
Mafeking
Vryburg
Kimberley
Bloemfontein
Upington
Springbok
Calvinia
Beaufort West
Graaff-Reinet
Cradock
De Aar
Worcester
Paarl
Stellenbosch
CAPE TOWN (Kaapstad)
Wynberg
Simonstown
Kaap die Goeie Hoop (Cape of Good Hope)
Kaap Agulhas
Mosselbaai
George
Knysna
Oudtshoorn
Uitenhage
PORT ELIZABETH
Algoabaai
Projection: Lambert's Equivalent Azimuthal
ft m
9000 3000
6000 2000
4500 1500
3000 1000
1200 400
600 200
0 0
200 600
2000 6000
4000 12,000
m ft

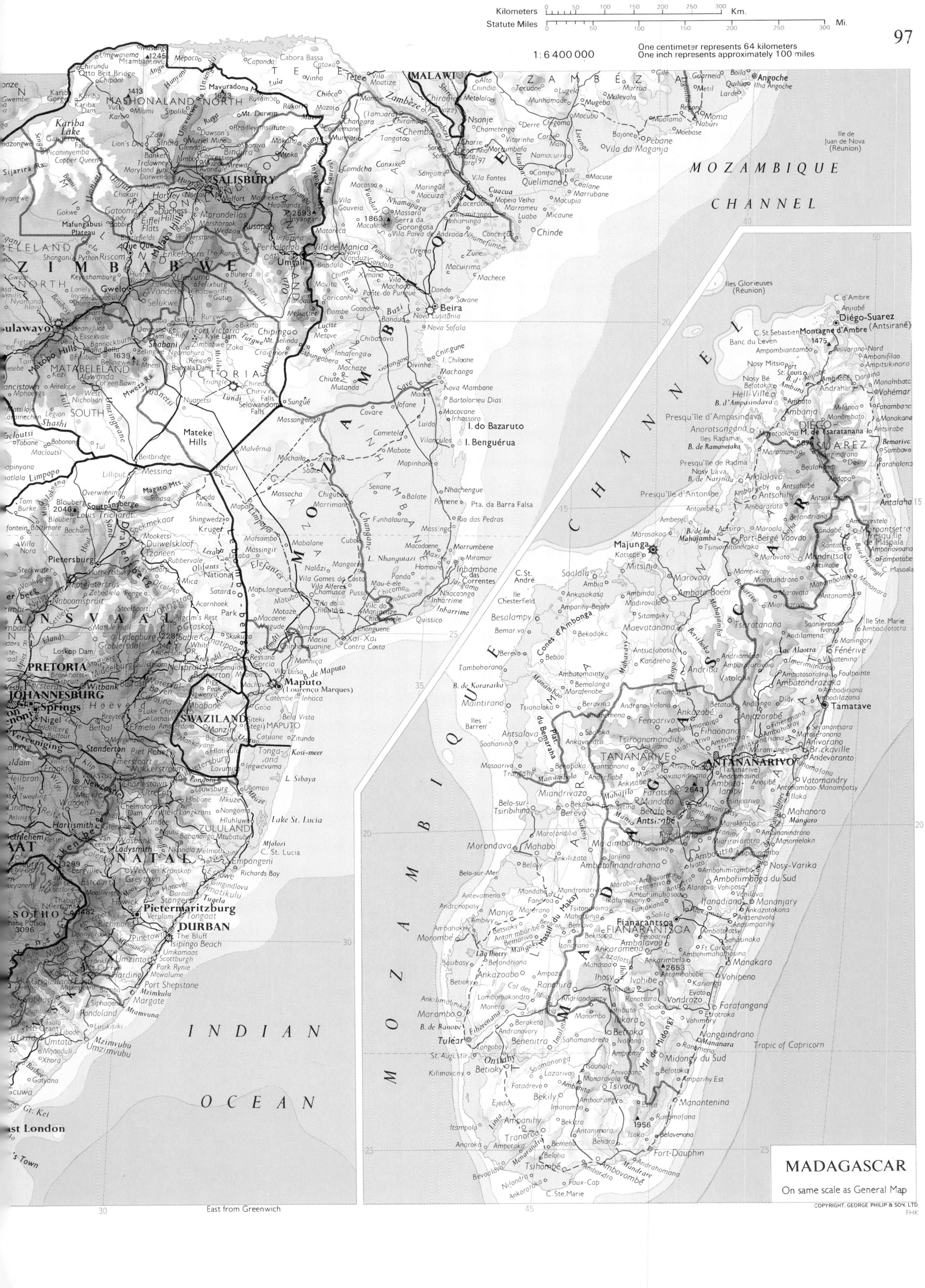
Kilometers 0 50 100 150 200 250 300 Km.
Statute Miles 0 50 100 150 200 250 300 Mi.
1:6 400 000
One centimeter represents 64 kilometers
One inch represents approximately 100 miles
ZIMBABWE
MASHONALAND NORTH
SALISBURY
MIDLANDS
MATABELELAND
VICTORIA
Bulawayo
Gwelo
Que Que
Umtali
Fort Victoria
Kariba Lake
MALAWI
TETE
ZAMBÉZIA
MOZAMBIQUE
Beira
Chinde
Quelimane
Angoche
Mozambique Channel
INHAMBANE
GAZA
MAPUTO
Maputo (Lourenço Marques)
Inhambane
I. do Bazaruto
I. Benguérua
Pta. da Barra Falsa
TRANSVAAL
PRETORIA
JOHANNESBURG
Springs
Pietersburg
SWAZILAND
Mbabane
NATAL
ZULULAND
Pietermaritzburg
DURBAN
Ladysmith
Richards Bay
Lake St. Lucia
LESOTHO
East London
INDIAN OCEAN
Ile de Juan de Nova (Réunion)
Iles Glorieuses (Réunion)
MADAGASCAR
Diégo-Suarez (Antsirané)
Montagne d'Ambre
DIEGO-SUAREZ
M. de Tsaratanana
Majunga
MAJUNGA
TANANARIVE
ANTANANARIVO (Tananarive)
Tamatave
TAMATAVE
Antsirabe
FIANARANTSOA
Fianarantsoa
Morondava
Tuléar
TULÉAR
Fort-Dauphin
Tropic of Capricorn
Ile Ste. Marie
Nosy-Varika
Manakara
Farafangana
Ambovombe
C. Ste. Marie
MADAGASCAR
On same scale as General Map
East from Greenwich
COPYRIGHT, GEORGE PHILIP & SON, LTD.
FHK

Iceland
Denmark Strait
Greenland Sea
Greenland
Gunnbjørns Fjeld 3700
Mt. Forel 3360
Petermann's Peak 2940
Julianehåb
Godthåb
Davis Strait
Disko I.
Thule
Kane Basin
Nares Str.
Baffin Bay
Bylot I.
Ellesmere I.
Axel Heiberg
Sverdrup Is.
Queen Elizabeth Islands
Devon I.
Lancaster Sound
Melville Sound
Parry Is.
Melville I.
M'Clure Strait
Banks I.
Victoria I.
Prince of Wales I.
Somerset I.
Boothia Pen.
Gulf of Boothia
Baffin Island
Cumberland Sound
Frobisher Bay
Resolution I.
Hudson Strait
Ungava Peninsula
Melville Pen.
Foxe Basin
Foxe Channel
Southampton I.
Hudson Bay
James Bay
Belcher Is.
C. Henrietta Maria
Labrador
Hamilton Inlet
Belle Isle Strait
Newfoundland
Anticosti
Gulf of St. Lawrence
Nova Scotia
Halifax
Bay of Fundy
Sable I.
C. Race
C. Cod
Nantucket I.
Laurentian Plateau
Quebec
Montreal
Ottawa
Mt. Washington 1917
Hudson
New York
Long I.
Philadelphia
Washington
Chesapeake Bay
C. Hatteras
Bermuda
ATLANTIC
Appalachian Mts.
Allegheny Mts.
Blue Ridge 2037
Cumberland Plateau
Atlanta
L. Ontario
Niagara Falls
Toronto
Hamilton
L. Erie
Detroit
L. Huron
L. Superior
L. Michigan
Chicago
Ohio
St. Louis
Memphis
Mississippi
Ozark Plateau
Kansas City
Missouri
Arkansas
Red
Dallas
Minneapolis
Lake Winnipeg
Winnipeg
Nelson
Churchill
Reindeer L.
Regina
Chesterfield Inlet
Dubawnt
Back
Arctic Circle
Athabasca L.
Great Slave L.
Great Bear L.
Mackenzie
Mackenzie Mts.
Liard
Peace
Athabasca
N. Saskatchewan
S. Saskatchewan
Edmonton
Calgary
Kicking Horse Pass
Crowsnest Pass
Yellowhead Pass
Mt. Robson 3954
Selkirk Mts.
Great Plains
N. Platte
S. Platte
Denver
Mt. Elbert 4399
Blanca Pk. 4364
Llano Estacado
Rocky Mountains
Wasatch Mountains
Great Salt Lake
Snake
Colorado Plateau
Grand Canyon
Gila
Colorado
Great Basin
Death Valley
Sierra Nevada
Mt. Whitney 4418
Los Angeles
San Joaquin
Sacramento
San Francisco
C. Mendocino
Coast Range
Cascade Range
Mt. Shasta 4317
Columbia
Portland
Mt. Rainier 4392
Seattle
Vancouver
Vancouver I.
Juan de Fuca Strait
C. Flattery
C. Blanco
Fraser
Coast Mountains
Mt. Waddington 4041
Queen Charlotte Sound
Queen Charlotte Islands
Alexander Archipelago
Finlay
Skeena
Stikine
Mt. Logan 6050
Mt. St. Elias 5489
Gulf of Alaska
Kodiak I.
Alaska Pen.
Alaska Range
Mt. McKinley 6194
Yukon
Porcupine
Brooks Range
C. Barrow
Beaufort Sea
C. Bathurst
ARCTIC OCEAN
3800
Wrangel I.
Bering Strait
C. Prince of Wales
C. Dezhnev
St. Lawrence I.
Nunivak I.
Asia
Bering Sea
Aleutian Islands
7391
PACIFIC
Mendocino Seascarp
Murray Seascarp
Tropic of Cancer

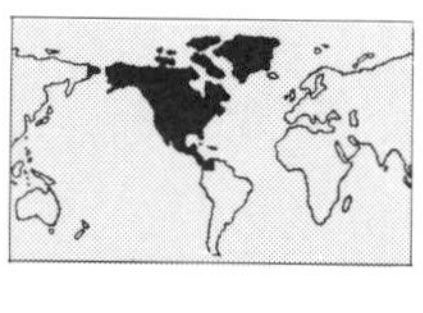

Kilometers 0 200 400 600 800 1000 Km.

Statute Miles 0 200 400 600 800 1000 Mi.

1:24 000 000

One centimeter represents 240 kilometers
One inch represents approximately 380 miles

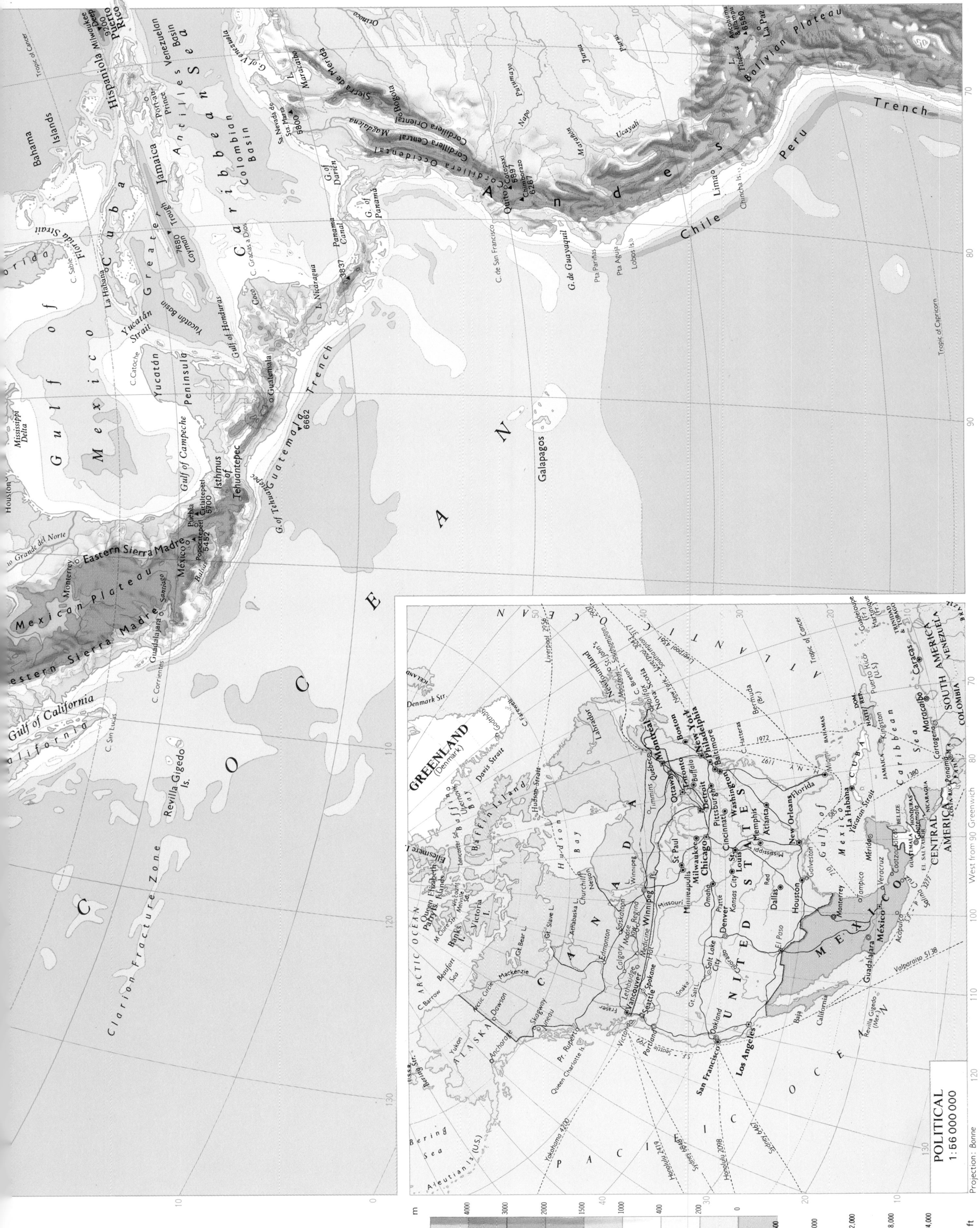

Gulf of Mexico
Caribbean Sea
Greater Antilles
Cuba
Jamaica
Hispaniola
Puerto Rico
Bahama Islands
Yucatán Peninsula
Yucatán Strait
Gulf of Honduras
Gulf of Campeche
Isthmus of Tehuantepec
Guatemala
Middle America Trench
Colombian Basin
Venezuelan Basin
Cayman Trough
Panama Canal
G. of Panama
G. of Darién
Cordillera Occidental
Cordillera Central
Cordillera Oriental
Sierra de Mérida
Andes
Bolivian Plateau
L. Titicaca
La Paz
Lima
Quito
Peru Chile Trench
G. de Guayaquil
Galapagos
PACIFIC OCEAN
Mexican Plateau
Eastern Sierra Madre
Western Sierra Madre
Gulf of California
Revilla Gigedo Is.
Clarion Fracture Zone
Tropic of Cancer
Tropic of Capricorn
POLITICAL
1:56 000 000
Projection: Bonne
West from 90 Greenwich
GREENLAND (Denmark)
CANADA
UNITED STATES
MEXICO
ALASKA
CENTRAL AMERICA
SOUTH AMERICA
ATLANTIC OCEAN
ARCTIC OCEAN
Hudson Bay
Bering Sea

PACIFIC OCEAN
ALASKA
YUKON TERRITORY
NORTHWEST TERRITORIES
MACKENZIE
KEEWATIN
BRITISH COLUMBIA
ALBERTA
SASKATCHEWAN
MANITOBA
CANADA
UNITED STATES
WASHINGTON
MONTANA
NORTH DAKOTA
SOUTH DAKOTA
MINNESOTA
NEBRASKA
WYOMING
Rocky Mountains
Mackenzie Mountains
Coast Mountains
Cassiar Mountains
Banks Island
Victoria Island
Prince of Wales Island
Amundsen Gulf
Coronation Gulf
Queen Maud Gulf
M'Clintock Channel
Viscount Melville Sound
Great Bear Lake
Great Slave L.
Lake Athabasca
Reindeer Lake
Lake Winnipeg
Queen Charlotte Is.
Vancouver I.
Anchorage
Fairbanks
Whitehorse
Dawson
Juneau
Yellowknife
Prince Rupert
Prince George
Vancouver
Victoria
Seattle
Tacoma
Spokane
Edmonton
Calgary
Saskatoon
Regina
Moose Jaw
Prince Albert
Lethbridge
Medicine Hat
Winnipeg
St. Boniface
Minneapolis
St. Paul
Omaha
Projection: Bonne
ALASKA
1:24 000 000
100 0 200 400 km
Brooks Range
Bering Sea
Gulf of Alaska
Aleutian Is.
PACIFIC OCEAN
West from Greenwich
ft m
9000 3000
6000 2000
4500 1500
3000 1000
1200 400
600 200
0 0
200 600
2000 6000
m ft

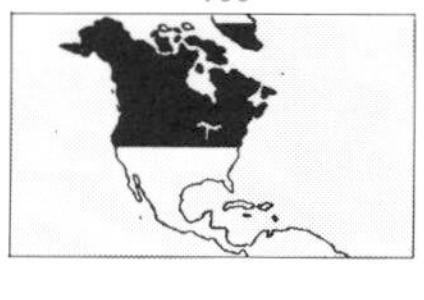

Kilometers 0 100 200 300 400 500 600 Km.
Statute Miles 0 100 200 300 400 500 600 Mi.

1:12 000 000

One centimeter represents 120 kilometers
One inch represents approximately 190 miles

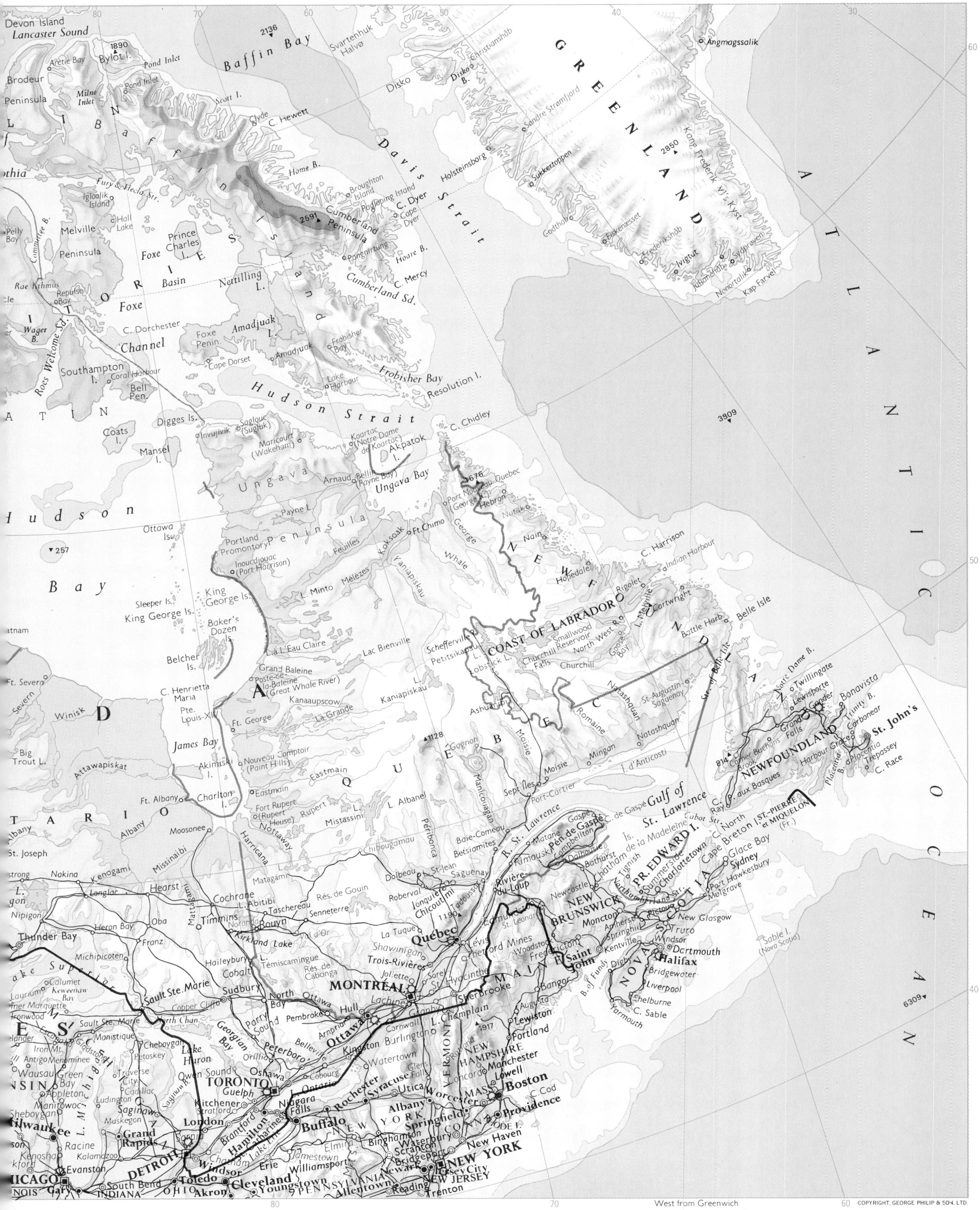

GREENLAND
ATLANTIC OCEAN
Baffin Bay
Davis Strait
Devon Island
Lancaster Sound
Bylot I.
Pond Inlet
Brodeur Peninsula
Baffin Island
Cumberland Peninsula
Cumberland Sd.
Foxe Basin
Foxe Channel
Nettilling L.
Amadjuak L.
Frobisher Bay
Resolution I.
Hudson Strait
Southampton I.
Coats I.
Mansel I.
Digges Is.
Akpatok I.
C. Chidley
Ungava Bay
Ungava Peninsula
Hudson Bay
James Bay
Belcher Is.
COAST OF LABRADOR
NEWFOUNDLAND
QUEBEC
ONTARIO
Smallwood Reservoir
Churchill Falls
Schefferville
Hopedale
Nain
Cartwright
Belle Isle
Gulf of St. Lawrence
I. d'Anticosti
PR. EDWARD I.
NOVA SCOTIA
NEW BRUNSWICK
St. John's
Cape Breton I.
Halifax
Sydney
ST.-PIERRE et MIQUELON (Fr.)
Sable I. (Nova Scotia)
Godthåb
Holsteinsborg
Sukkertoppen
Angmagssalik
Kap Farvel
Disko
Québec
MONTRÉAL
Ottawa
TORONTO
Hamilton
Buffalo
Rochester
Syracuse
Albany
Boston
Providence
NEW YORK
New Haven
DETROIT
Cleveland
Toledo
Windsor
CHICAGO
Milwaukee
Lake Superior
Lake Huron
Lake Ontario
Lake Erie
L. Michigan
Sault Ste. Marie
Sudbury
Thunder Bay
Portland
MAINE
VERMONT
NEW HAMPSHIRE
MASS.
NEW YORK
PENNSYLVANIA
NEW JERSEY
West from Greenwich

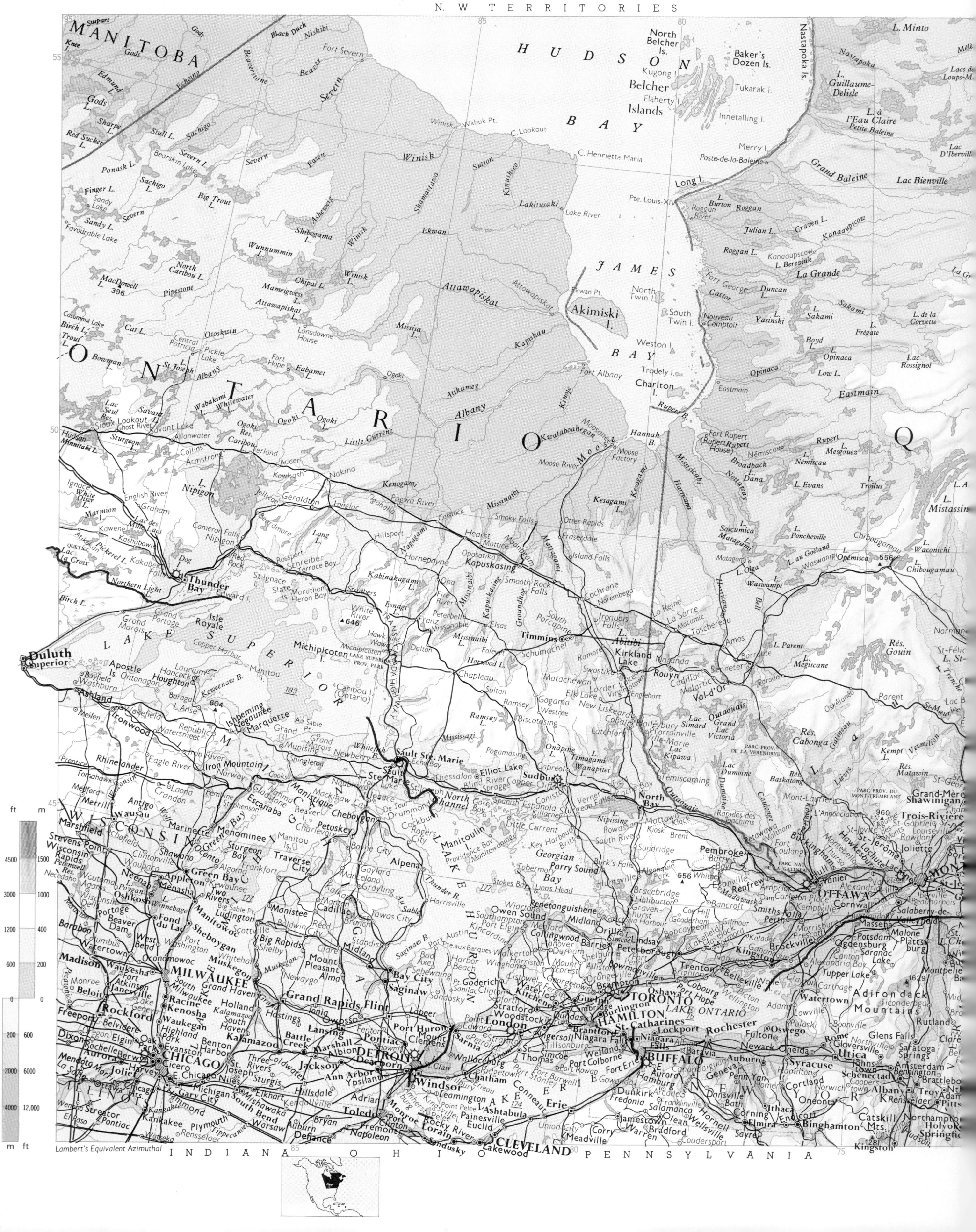
N. W TERRITORIES
MANITOBA
HUDSON BAY
ONTARIO
Q
JAMES BAY
Belcher Islands
North Belcher Is.
Baker's Dozen Is.
Akimiski I.
Nastapoka Is.
L. Minto
Guillaume-Delisle
L. à l'Eau Claire
Lac Bienville
La Grande
Eastmain
Mistassini
Rupert B.
Fort Severn
Winisk
C. Lookout
C. Henrietta Maria
Attawapiskat
Fort Albany
Moosonee
Moose Factory
Kenogami
Albany
L. Nipigon
Geraldton
Hearst
Kapuskasing
Cochrane
Timmins
Kirkland Lake
Rouyn
Val-d'Or
Amos
Chibougamau
Thunder Bay
Isle Royale
LAKE SUPERIOR
Duluth
Superior
Marquette
Sault Ste. Marie
Sudbury
North Bay
North Channel
Manitoulin I.
Georgian Bay
LAKE HURON
LAKE MICHIGAN
WISCONSIN
Green Bay
Milwaukee
Madison
Chicago
Rockford
Grand Rapids
Flint
Lansing
Saginaw
Bay City
Detroit
Windsor
Toledo
London
Kitchener
Waterloo
Guelph
Hamilton
Toronto
LAKE ONTARIO
St. Catharines
Niagara Falls
Buffalo
Rochester
Syracuse
Utica
Albany
Binghamton
Erie
Cleveland
LAKE ERIE
Ottawa
Kingston
Pembroke
Trois-Rivières
Adirondack Mountains
NEW YORK
Lambert's Equivalent Azimuthal
INDIANA
OHIO
PENNSYLVANIA
ft
m
4500
1500
3000
1000
1200
400
600
200
0
0
200
600
2000
6000
4000
12,000
m
ft

Kilometers 0 50 100 150 200 250 300 Km.
Statute Miles 0 50 100 150 200 250 300 Mi.

1:5 600 000

One centimeter represents 56 kilometers
One inch represents approximately 90 miles

COAST OF LABRADOR
NEWFOUNDLAND
QUEBEC
GULF OF ST. LAWRENCE
ATLANTIC OCEAN
NEW BRUNSWICK
NOVA SCOTIA
PRINCE EDWARD ISLAND
MAINE
SAINT-PIERRE ET MIQUELON (Fr.)
Î. d'Anticosti
Cabot Strait
Str. of Belle Isle
Bay of Fundy
Cape Breton Island
Avalon Peninsula
Smallwood Reservoir
Rés. Manicouagan
Long Range Mts.
Mealy Mts.
Mts. Chic-Chocs
Pén. de Gaspé
Îs. de la Madeleine (Quebec)
Sable I. (Nova Scotia)
Schefferville
Labrador City
Churchill Falls
Goose Bay
Happy Valley
North-West River
Hopedale
Nain
Cartwright
Battle Harbour
Sept-Îles
Port-Cartier
Havre-St-Pierre
Baie-Comeau
Rimouski
Matane
Gaspé
Chicoutimi
Arvida
Alma
Rivière-du-Loup
Lévis
Lauzon
Montmagny
Thetford Mines
Sherbrooke
Campbellton
Dalhousie
Bathurst
Edmundston
Chatham
Newcastle
Moncton
Fredericton
Saint John
Summerside
Charlottetown
Amherst
Truro
New Glasgow
Halifax
Dartmouth
Yarmouth
Sydney
Glace Bay
New Waterford
Corner Brook
Stephenville
Gander
St. John's
Grand Falls
Bangor
Augusta
Portland
Lewiston
Auburn
Manchester
Portsmouth
Lowell
Lynn
BOSTON
Brockton
Miquelon
St. Pierre
West from Greenwich

L. Obamsca
L. Paul-Sauvé
L. Montreuil
L. Soscumica
L. Poncheville
L. Opataca
L. Lemieux
Brock
L. Bouchier
Maicasagi
L. Sauvage
L. la Trêve
L. Opémisca
Kattawagami L.
L. Grasset
L. Matagami
Matagami
L. au Goéland
L. Olga
Chibougamau
Chapais
Waswanipi
Waswanipi
L. Opawica
L. Waswanipi
Desmaraisville
Island Falls
Pierre L.
Little Abitibi L.
L. Mistaouac
Bell
Miquelon
L. Surprise
Cochrane
Norembega
Normétal
Desméloizes
L. Turgeon
L. Quévillon
Lebel-sur-Quévillon
Iroquois Falls
La Reine
La Sarre
Dupuy
L. Chicobi
Frederick House L.
Lake Abitibi
Macamic
L. Obalski
Connaught
Hoyle
Val Gagné
KETTLE LAKES PROV. PK.
Palmarolle
Taschereau
Rochebaucourt
L. Parent
Timmins
Porcupine
Matheson
Villemontel
Amos
Obedjiwan
South Porcupine
Night Hawk L.
Holtyre
L. Duparquet
Duparquet
PARC AIGUEBELLE
Landrienne
Champneuf
L. Mégiscane
Ramore
Barraute
Watabeag L.
Bourkes
ESKER LAKES PROV. PARK
L. Dasserat
Évain
L. Preissac
L. la Motte
Belcourt
Senneterre
Mégiscane
Kirkland Lake
Noranda
L. Faillon
Swastika
Arntfield
Rouyn
Cadillac
L. Malartic
Larder Lake
Virginiatown
Paradis
Forsythe
Malartic
Sullivan
Val-d'Or
L. Guéguen
Matachewan
Larder L.
L. Opasatica
L. Lemoine
Soucy
Clova
Oskélanéo
L. Matchi-Manitou
Rollet
L. Sabourin
Charlton
Englehart
L. Roger
L. Villebon
L. Camachigama
Réservoir Decelles
Earlton
Rémigny
Elk Lake
Belle Vallée
Rapide-Sept
L. Granet
Gowganda
Thornloe
Notre-Dame-du-Nord
L. Simard
Grand Lac Victoria
L. Échouani
Bazin
New Liskeard
Angliers
Makobe L.
Réservoir Dozois
Capitachouane
L. des Augustines
Haileybury
Guigues
L. des Quinze
Laforce
Smoothwater L.
Cobalt
Laverlochère
Latulipe
Cawasachouane
Lorrainville
Belleterre
Réservoir Cabonga
Némiscachin
Latchford
Ville-Marie
Béarn
Burwash L.
L. Ostaboningue
L. à la Truite
Rés. Mitchinaméc
Fabre
PARC PROV DE LA VÉRENDRYE
L. Saseginaga
PARC DE KIPAWA
L. Ogascanane
Obabika L.
Timagami
Gatineau
Lièvre
Bear Island
Lac Kipawa
L. aux Foins
L. de l'Écorce
L. Timagami
L. Dumoine
L. Wanapitei
Sturgeon
Timiskaming
Marten River
Kipawa
L. Sairs
Capreol
Tee Lake
Val Caron
Hanmer
Témiscaming
Ste-Anne-du-Lac
L. Pin-Blanc
Réservoir Baskatong
Azilda
Falconbridge
River Valley
L. Beauchêne
L. du Fils
Sudbury
Field
Ferme-Neuve
Markstay
L. Bleu
Copper Cliff
Coniston
Tomiko L.
PARC PONTIAC
Montcerf
Mont-Laurier
Lac-des-Écorces
Warren
Verner
Sturgeon Falls
Cache Bay
Feronia
Val-Barrette
L. Nominingue
Burwash
Notre Dame du Lac
North Bay
Lake Nipissing
Mattawa
Ottawa
L. St-Patrice
Coulonge
Maniwaki
L. des Îles
Rutter
Noelville
Callander
Bonfield
Outaouais
Dumoine
Deux-Rivières
Nominingue
Astorville
Rapides des Joachims
Messines
Lac des Trente et un Milles
L. du Cerf
Labelle
French River
French
Powassan
Kiosk
Rolphton
Bouchette
Notre-Dame-du-Laus
PARC PROV. PAPINEAU-LABELLE
L. Gagnon
La Conception
GRUNDY L. PROV. PK
Port Loring
Commanda
Brent
Deep River
Noire
Key Harbour
Trout Creek
Cedar L.
Chalk River
Gracefield
Britt
Chapeau
Waltham Sta.
Lac-Ste-Marie
Lac Rémi
Byng Inlet
Drocourt
South River
L. Lavieille
Fort-Coulonge
L. du Poisson Blanc
Sundridge
ALGONQUIN PROV. PARK
Petawawa
Venosta
Namur
Pointe au Baril Sta.
Bernard L.
Big Trout L.
Opeongo L.
Pembroke
ÎLE DU GRAND CALUMET
Low
Chénéville
Ardbeg
Magnetawan
Bonnechère
Alice
Poltimore
Ripon
Dunchurch
Burk's Falls
Round L.
Beachburg
Bryson
Campbell's Bay
Glen Almond
St-André-Avellin
Shawanaga
McKellar
Kearney
Algonquin Park
Aylen L.
Golden Lake
Cobden
Wakefield
Papineauville
Montebello
Waubamik
Emsdale
Killaloe Sta.
Shawville
Buckingham
Thurso
Nobel
Sprucedale
Madawaska
Golden L.
Eganville
L. des Chats
Bristol
Masson
Angers
Rockland
Hawkesbury
Parry Sound
Novar
Whitney
Barry's Bay
Douglas
Quyon
Pointe-Gatineau
Gatineau
Cumberland
Vankleek Hill
Huntsville
Bark L.
Renfrew
Braeside
Arnprior
Hull
OTTAWA
Aylmer
Bourget
Rosseau
Dwight
Kawagama L.
L. Clear
Combermere
Kanata
Deschênes
Vars
Limoges
Alexandria
Georgian Bay
L. Joseph
Rosseau L.
L. of Bays
Dorset
Lake St. Peter
Madawaska
Calabogie
Pakenham
Bells Corner
Casselman
Port Carling
Baysville
Griffith
White L.
Stittsville
Moose Creek
MacTier
L. Muskoka
Bracebridge
Eagle Lake
Almonte
Manotick
Osgoode
Bala
Haliburton
Denbigh
Flower Sta.
Richmond
North Gower
Avonmore
HOPE I.
Honey Harbour
L. Muskoka
Wilberforce
Bancroft
Weslemkoon L.
Lavant Sta.
Mississippi L.
Carleton Place
Chesterville
GRIFFITH I.
CHRISTIAN I.
Gravenhurst
Minden
Plevna
Lanark
Kemptville
Winchester
Cornwall
Gooderham
Elphin
South Nation
Q U
O N T A R I O
Timiskaming
ft m
4500 1500
3000 1000
1200 400
600 200
0 0
200 600
m ft
50
49
48
47
46
45
81 80 79 78 77 76 75
Projection: Bonne

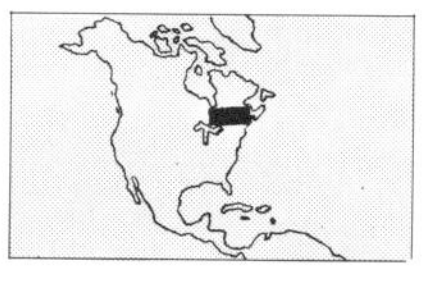

Kilometers 0 20 40 60 80 100 Km.
Statute Miles 0 20 40 60 80 100 Mi.

1:2 000 000

One centimeter represents 20 kilometers
One inch represents approximately 32 miles

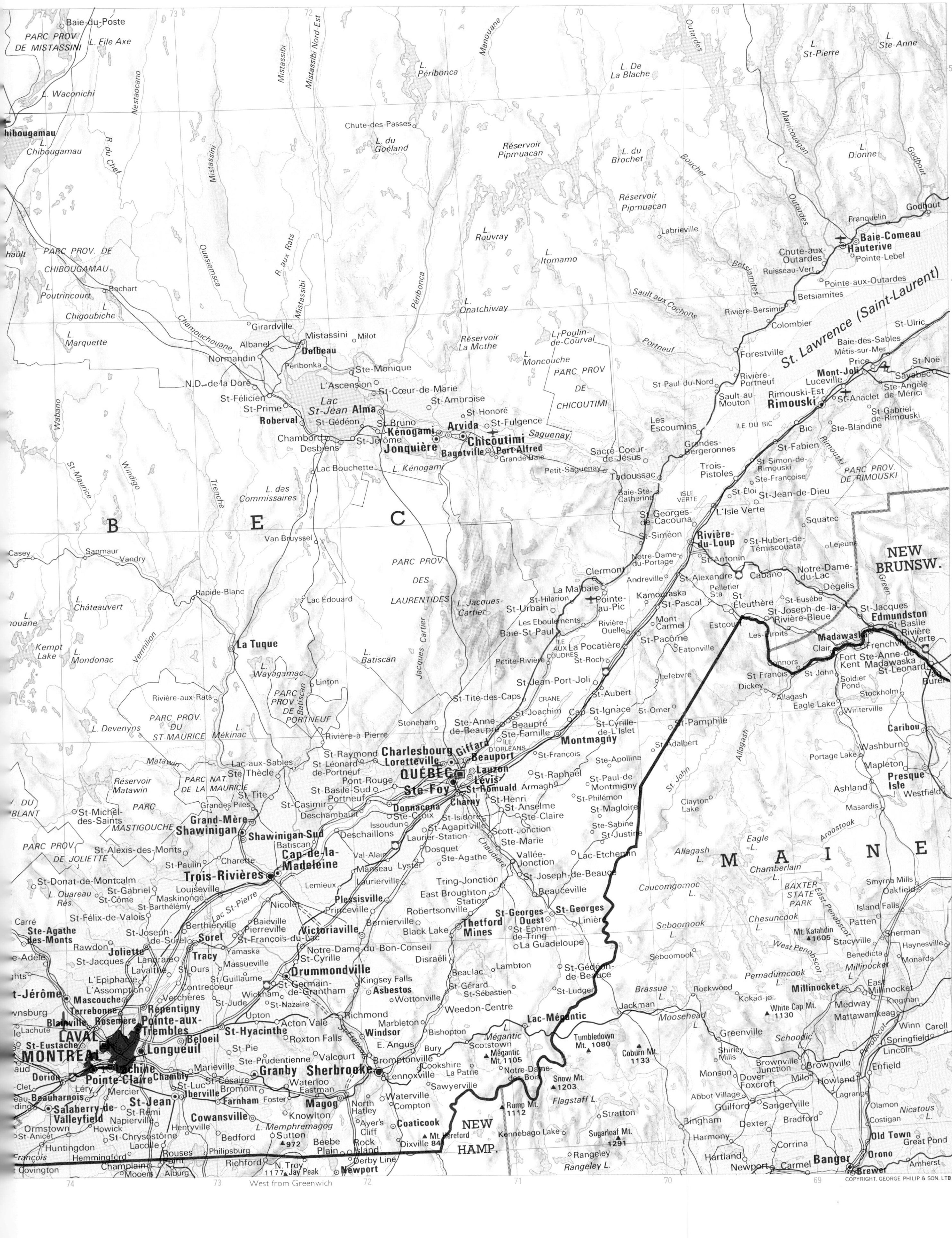

QUÉBEC
MAINE
NEW BRUNSW.
NEW HAMP.
St. Lawrence (Saint-Laurent)
PARC PROV. DE MISTASSINI
PARC PROV. DE CHIBOUGAMAU
PARC PROV. DE CHICOUTIMI
PARC PROV. DES LAURENTIDES
PARC PROV. DE PORTNEUF
PARC PROV. DU ST-MAURICE
PARC NAT. DE LA MAURICIE
PARC MASTIGOUCHE
PARC PROV. DE JOLIETTE
PARC PROV. DE RIMOUSKI
BAXTER STATE PARK
Chibougamau
L. Chibougamau
L. Waconichi
Baie-du-Poste
L. File Axe
L. Péribonca
Chute-des-Passes
L. du Goéland
Réservoir Pipmuacan
L. De La Blache
L. du Brochet
L. St-Pierre
L. Ste-Anne
L. Dionne
Baie-Comeau
Hauterive
Franquelin
Godbout
Chute-aux-Outardes
Pointe-Lebel
Pointe-aux-Outardes
Betsiamites
Labrieville
L. Rouvray
L. Itomamo
L. Onatchiway
Réservoir La Mothe
L. Poulin-de-Courval
L. Moncouche
Bochart
L. Poutrincourt
L. Chigoubiche
L. Marquette
Girardville
Albanel
Mistassini
Milot
Dolbeau
Normandin
Péribonka
Ste-Monique
N.D.-de-la Doré
St-Félicien
St-Prime
Roberval
L'Ascension
Lac St-Jean
Alma
St-Cœur-de-Marie
St-Ambroise
St-Honoré
St-Fulgence
St-Gédéon
St-Bruno
Chambord
St-Jérôme
Desbiens
Kénogami
Arvida
Chicoutimi
Saguenay
Jonquière
Bagotville
Port-Alfred
Grande Baie
Lac Bouchette
L. Kénogami
L. des Commissaires
Forestville
Colombier
Rivière-Bersimis
Rivière-Portneuf
St-Paul-du-Nord
Sault-au-Mouton
Les Escoumins
Grandes-Bergeronnes
Sacré-Coeur-de-Jésus
Petit-Saguenay
Tadoussac
Baie-Ste-Catherine
Rimouski
Rimouski-Est
Mont-Joli
Luceville
Bic
St-Fabien
Trois-Pistoles
St-Simon-de-Rimouski
St-Jean-de-Dieu
St-Ulric
Baie-des-Sables
Métis-sur-Mer
Price
Sayabec
St-Anaclet
St-Noël
St-Georges-de-Cacouna
L'Isle Verte
St-Siméon
Rivière-du-Loup
St-Hubert-de-Témiscouata
Squatec
Lejeune
Notre-Dame-du-Portage
St-Antonin
Clermont
St-Alexandre
Cabano
Notre-Dame-du-Lac
Dégelis
La Malbaie
Pointe-au-Pic
St-Hilarion
St-Urbain
Kamouraska
St-Pascal
Pelletier Sta.
St-Éleuthère
St-Joseph-de-la-Rivière-Bleue
Edmundston
St-Jacques
Baie-St-Paul
Les Éboulements
Rivière-Ouelle
La Pocatière
Mont-Carmel
Estcourt
St-Pacôme
Madawaska
Frenchville
Fort Kent
St-Basile
Rivière Verte
Ste-Anne-de-Madawaska
St-Leonard
Van Buren
Connors
St Francis
St John
Dickey
Allagash
Eagle Lake
Wintervile
Caribou
Washburn
Presque Isle
Mapleton
Ashland
Westfield
Masardis
Van Bruyssel
Casey
Sanmaur
Vandry
Rapide-Blanc
L. Châteauvert
Lac Édouard
La Tuque
L. Jacques-Cartier
L. Batiscan
L. Wayagamac
Linton
Rivière-aux-Rats
L. Devenyns
Mékinac
L. Mondonac
Kempt Lake
St-Jean-Port-Joli
St-Aubert
St-Tite-des-Caps
St-Joachim
Cap-St-Ignace
St-Omer
Stoneham
Ste-Anne-de-Beaupré
Beaupré
Ste-Famille
St-Cyrille-de-L'Islet
Montmagny
St-Pamphile
Rivière-à-Pierre
St-Raymond
Charlesbourg
Giffard
Loretteville
Beauport
St-Léonard-de-Portneuf
Québec
Lauzon
Lévis
Ste-Foy
Pont-Rouge
St-Basile-Sud
Portneuf
St-Romuald
Charny
Lac-aux-Sables
Ste-Thècle
Ste-Tite
Grandes Piles
Réservoir Matawin
St-Casimir
Deschambault
Donnacona
Grand-Mère
Shawinigan
Shawinigan-Sud
St-Michel-des-Saints
St-Alexis-des-Monts
Cap-de-la-Madeleine
Trois-Rivières
Louiseville
Maskinongé
St-Donat-de-Montcalm
St-Gabriel
St-Côme
L. Ouareau Rés.
St-Félix-de-Valois
Ste-Agathe-des-Monts
Rawdon
Joliette
St-Jacques
L'Épiphanie
L'Assomption
Mascouche
Terrebonne
St-Jérôme
Laval
Montréal
Lachine
Pointe-Claire
Dorion
Longueuil
Pointe-aux-Trembles
Repentigny
Beauharnois
Salaberry-de-Valleyfield
Ormstown
Huntingdon
Sorel
Tracy
Berthierville
Yamaska
St-Hyacinthe
Beloeil
Drummondville
Victoriaville
Nicolet
Plessisville
Princeville
Thetford Mines
Asbestos
Richmond
Windsor
Sherbrooke
Granby
Magog
Coaticook
Cowansville
Farnham
Iberville
St-Jean
Chambly
Lennoxville
Cookshire
Bromptonville
L. Memphremagog
Sutton
Rock Island
Derby Line
Newport
N. Troy
Jay Peak
Richford
Rouses Point
Alburg
Champlain
Mooers
Covington
Lac-Mégantic
Mégantic
Mt. Mégantic 1105
Notre-Dame-des-Bois
St-Georges
St-Georges-Ouest
Beauceville
St-Joseph-de-Beauce
Vallée-Jonction
Ste-Marie
Scott-Jonction
Lac-Etchemin
St-Gédéon-de-Beauce
St-Ludger
Jackman
Moosehead L.
Greenville
Tumbledown Mt. 1080
Coburn Mt. 1133
Snow Mt. 1203
Rump Mt. 1112
Mt. Hereford
Dixville
Flagstaff L.
Stratton
Kennebago Lake
Sugarloaf Mt. 1291
Rangeley
Rangeley L.
Bingham
Harmony
Hartland
Dexter
Corrina
Newport
Carmel
Bangor
Brewer
Orono
Old Town
Great Pond
Amherst
Monson
Dover-Foxcroft
Guilford
Sangerville
Abbot Village
Milo
Brownville
Brownville Junction
Howland
Lagrange
Enfield
Lincoln
Medway
Mattawamkeag
Millinocket
East Millinocket
Mt. Katahdin 1605
Patten
Sherman
Island Falls
Oakfield
Smyrna Mills
Chesuncook L.
Chamberlain L.
Allagash L.
Eagle L.
Caucomgomoc L.
Seboomook L.
Brassua L.
Pemadumcook L.
White Cap Mt. 1130
Clayton Lake
West from Greenwich
COPYRIGHT, GEORGE PHILIP & SON, LTD.

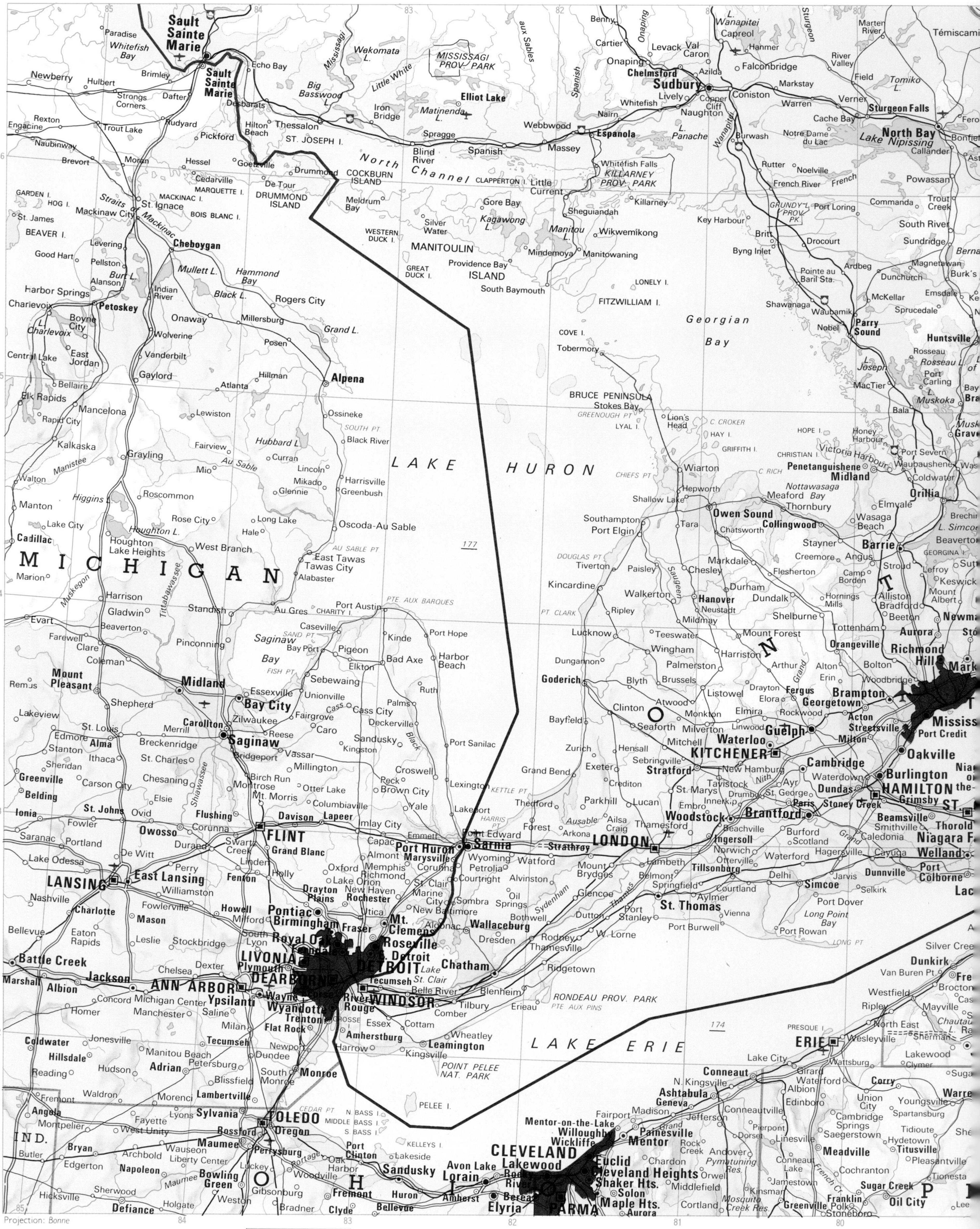
Sault Sainte Marie
Paradise
Whitefish Bay
Newberry
Hulbert
Brimley
Strongs Corners
Dafter
Rexton
Engadine
Trout Lake
Rudyard
Naubinway
Brevort
Moran
Hessel
Pickford
Echo Bay
Desbarats
Hilton Beach
Thessalon
ST. JOSEPH I.
Goetzville
Drummond
De Tour
DRUMMOND ISLAND
COCKBURN ISLAND
Mississagi
Wekomata L.
Big Basswood L.
Little White
MISSISSAGI PROV. PARK
Iron Bridge
Matinenda L.
Elliot Lake
aux Sables
Spragge
Blind River
Spanish
Massey
Webbwood
Espanola
North Channel
Spanish
Benny
Cartier
Onaping
Levack
Val Caron
Chelmsford
Sudbury
Lively
Copper Cliff
Azilda
Whitefish
Nairn
Naughton
Capreol
Hanmer
Falconbridge
Wanapitei L.
Sturgeon
Coniston
Markstay
Warren
Verner
Sturgeon Falls
Marten River
Témiscaming
River Valley
Field
Tomiko L.
Cache Bay
North Bay
Lake Nipissing
Notre Dame du Lac
Callander
Bonfield
Burwash
L. Panache
Whitefish Falls
KILLARNEY PROV. PARK
Killarney
CLAPPERTON I.
Little Current
Rutter
Noelville
French River
French
Powassan
GARDEN I.
HOG I.
MACKINAC I.
MARQUETTE I.
BOIS BLANC I.
St. Ignace
Mackinaw City
Straits of Mackinac
St. James
BEAVER I.
Levering
Cheboygan
Good Hart
Pellston
Burt L.
Alanson
Mullett L.
Hammond Bay
Indian River
Black L.
Rogers City
Harbor Springs
Charlevoix
Petoskey
Boyne City
Onaway
Millersburg
L. Charlevoix
Wolverine
Grand L.
Posen
Central Lake
East Jordan
Vanderbilt
Gaylord
Hillman
Alpena
Bellaire
Atlanta
Elk Rapids
Mancelona
Lewiston
Ossineke
Rapid City
SOUTH PT
Black River
Kalkaska
Fairview
Hubbard L.
Grayling
Curran
Manistee
Au Sable
Lincoln
Mio
Mikado
Harrisville
Walton
Glennie
Greenbush
Higgins L.
Roscommon
Manton
Lake City
Rose City
Long Lake
Oscoda-Au Sable
Hale
Cadillac
Houghton L.
Houghton Lake Heights
West Branch
AU SABLE PT
East Tawas
Tawas City
Alabaster
MICHIGAN
Marion
Muskegon
Tittabawassee
Harrison
Gladwin
Standish
Au Gres
CHARITY I.
Port Austin
PTE. AUX BARQUES
Evart
Beaverton
Farewell
Clare
Pinconning
Caseville
SAND PT
Saginaw Bay
Bay Port
Kinde
Port Hope
Pigeon
Harbor Beach
Coleman
Elkton
Bad Axe
Mount Pleasant
Midland
FISH PT
Sebewaing
Remus
Essexville
Unionville
Bay City
Ruth
Palms
Shepherd
Cass City
Lakeview
Carollton
Zilwaukee
Fairgrove
Deckerville
Merrill
Caro
St. Louis
Saginaw
Reese
Edmore
Alma
Breckenridge
Sandusky
Kingston
Port Sanilac
Stanton
Ithaca
Bridgeport
Vassar
Black
Sheridan
St. Charles
Millington
Croswell
Greenville
Chesaning
Birch Run
Belding
Carson City
Elsie
Montrose
Otter Lake
Peck
Brown City
Lexington
Mt. Morris
Columbiaville
Yale
Ionia
St. Johns
Ovid
Flushing
Davison
Lapeer
Imlay City
Lakeport
Fowler
Corunna
Flint
Saranac
Portland
Owosso
Durand
Swartz Creek
Grand Blanc
Capac
Emmett
Port Huron
Marysville
Point Edward
Sarnia
Lake Odessa
De Witt
Linden
Almont
Memphis
Perry
Lansing
East Lansing
Fenton
Holly
Oxford
Lake Orion
Richmond
Corunna
Nashville
Williamston
Drayton Plains
New Haven
Rochester
St. Clair
Marine City
Charlotte
Fowlerville
Howell
Pontiac
Birmingham
Utica
Mt. Clemens
Algonac
Bellevue
Mason
Milford
Fraser
Roseville
Eaton Rapids
Leslie
Stockbridge
South Lyon
Royal Oak
Battle Creek
Livonia
Plymouth
Detroit
Lake St. Clair
Chelsea
Dexter
Dearborn
Jackson
Marshall
Albion
Ann Arbor
Tecumseh
Belle River
Wayne
Windsor
Ypsilanti
Concord
Michigan Center
Wyandotte
River Rouge
Homer
Manchester
Saline
Trenton
Essex
Cottam
Grosse Ile
Milan
Flat Rock
Amherstburg
Coldwater
Jonesville
Tecumseh
Newport
Harrow
Kingsville
Hillsdale
Manitou Beach
Dundee
Reading
Hudson
Adrian
Petersburg
South Monroe
Monroe
Blissfield
Fremont
Waldron
Morenci
Lambertville
Angola
Lyons
Sylvania
Montpelier
Fayette
West Unity
Toledo
Oregon
Rossford
IND.
Bryan
Maumee
Perrysburg
Butler
Archbold
Wauseon
Edgerton
Napoleon
Liberty Center
Maumee
Bowling Green
Luckey
Woodville
Hicksville
Sherwood
Weston
Gibsonburg
Holgate
Defiance
Bradner
Fremont
Clyde
Bellevue
OHIO
Port Clinton
Lakeside
Sandusky
Huron
Avon Lake
Lorain
Amherst
Elyria
Lakewood
Cleveland
Parma
Euclid
Cleveland Heights
Shaker Hts.
Solon
Maple Hts.
Aurora
Mentor
Wickliffe
Willoughby
Mentor-on-the-Lake
Painesville
Fairport
Madison
Geneva
Ashtabula
N. Kingsville
Conneaut
Jefferson
Rock Creek
Chardon
Orwell
Middlefield
Andover
Pymatuning Res.
Kinsman
Mosquito Creek Res.
Cortland
Greenville
Jamestown
Conneaut Lake
Meadville
Linesville
Saegerstown
Cambridge Springs
Conneautville
Union City
Edinboro
Waterford
Albion
Girard
Lake City
Erie
Wesleyville
Wattsburg
Corry
Youngsville
Spartansburg
Tidioute
Titusville
Pleasantville
Cochranton
Sugar Creek
Franklin
Polk
Oil City
Stoneboro
Tionesta
Warren
Lakewood
Clymer
Sherman
Chautauqua L.
Mayville
North East
Westfield
Ripley
Brocton
Fredonia
Dunkirk
Van Buren Pt.
Silver Creek
PRESQUE I.
LAKE ERIE
PELEE I.
POINT PELEE NAT. PARK
N. BASS I.
MIDDLE BASS I.
S. BASS I.
KELLEYS I.
CEDAR PT
Leamington
Wheatley
Tilbury
Comber
Blenheim
Erieau
RONDEAU PROV. PARK
PTE. AUX PINS
Chatham
Ridgetown
Wallaceburg
Dresden
Thamesville
Rodney
W. Lorne
Dutton
Sombra
Courtright
Petrolia
Wyoming
Oil Springs
Bothwell
Sydenham
Alvinston
Watford
Strathroy
Mount Brydges
Glencoe
Forest
Arkona
Thedford
Kettle PT
HARRIS PT
Parkhill
Ausable
Ailsa Craig
Lucan
London
Lambeth
Belmont
Springfield
St. Thomas
Port Stanley
Aylmer
Vienna
Port Burwell
Tillsonburg
Courtland
Otterville
Norwich
Ingersoll
Beachville
Woodstock
Thamesford
Embro
Innerkip
St. Marys
Tavistock
New Hamburg
Stratford
Sebringville
Mitchell
Hensall
Exeter
Crediton
Grand Bend
Zurich
Bayfield
Clinton
Seaforth
Goderich
Blyth
Brussels
Atwood
Monkton
Milverton
Listowel
Elmira
Linwood
Waterloo
Kitchener
Guelph
Cambridge
Ayr
Paris
Brantford
Burford
Scotland
Waterford
Delhi
Simcoe
Port Dover
Long Point Bay
LONG PT
Port Rowan
Jarvis
Selkirk
Hagersville
Cayuga
Dunnville
Port Colborne
Welland
Caledonia
Smithville
Beamsville
Grimsby
Stoney Creek
Hamilton
Dundas
St. George
Drumbo
Waterdown
Burlington
Oakville
Milton
Streetsville
Acton
Georgetown
Brampton
Port Credit
Mississauga
Rockwood
Fergus
Elora
Drayton
Arthur
Alton
Erin
Orangeville
Bolton
Woodbridge
Richmond Hill
Markham
Aurora
Tottenham
Newmarket
Beeton
Bradford
Alliston
Mount Albert
Keswick
Camp Borden
Lefroy
Stroud
Angus
Barrie
GEORGINA I.
Beaverton
Brechin
L. Simcoe
Orillia
Coldwater
Elmvale
Wasaga Beach
Stayner
Creemore
Collingwood
Thornbury
Meaford
Nottawasaga Bay
Midland
Penetanguishene
Waubaushene
Port Severn
Victoria Harbour
Honey Harbour
HOPE I.
CHRISTIAN I.
GRIFFITH I.
C. RICH
Owen Sound
Chatsworth
Tara
Hepworth
Wiarton
Shallow Lake
Southampton
Port Elgin
Paisley
Chesley
Saugeen
Markdale
Flesherton
Durham
Dundalk
Hanover
Neustadt
Walkerton
Mildmay
Shelburne
Hornings Mills
Mount Forest
Harriston
Palmerston
Teeswater
Wingham
Ripley
Lucknow
Kincardine
Tiverton
DOUGLAS PT
PT. CLARK
Dungannon
CHIEFS PT
C. CROKER
HAY I.
Lion's Head
LYAL I.
GREENOUGH PT
Stokes Bay
BRUCE PENINSULA
Tobermory
COVE I.
Georgian Bay
FITZWILLIAM I.
LONELY I.
MANITOULIN ISLAND
Providence Bay
South Baymouth
GREAT DUCK I.
WESTERN DUCK I.
Silver Water
Kagawong L.
Gore Bay
Meldrum Bay
Manitou L.
Mindemoya
Manitowaning
Wikwemikong
Sheguiandah
Key Harbour
Britt
Byng Inlet
Pointe au Baril Sta.
Shawanaga
Waubamik
Nobel
Parry Sound
Drocourt
GRUNDY L. PROV. PK
Port Loring
Ardbeg
Dunchurch
Magnetawan
McKellar
Spruccdale
Emsdale
Burk's Falls
Sundridge
South River
Trout Creek
Commanda
Huntsville
Rosseau
Rosseau L.
L. Joseph
Port Carling
MacTier
L. Muskoka
Bala
Bracebridge
Gravenhurst
LAKE HURON
177
174
ONTARIO
Cheboygan
ft
m
4500
1500
3000
1000
1200
400
600
200
0
0
200
600
m
ft
85
84
83
82
81
80
46
45
44
43
42

Projection: Bonne

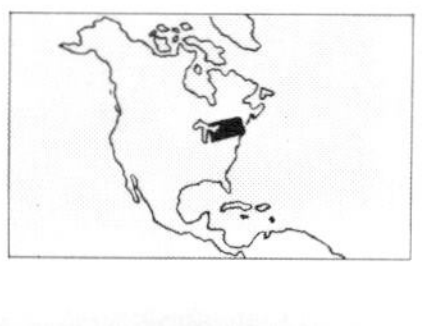

Kilometers 0 20 40 60 80 100 Km.
Statute Miles 0 20 40 60 80 100 Mi.

1:2 000 000

One centimeter represents 20 kilometers
One inch represents approximately 32 miles

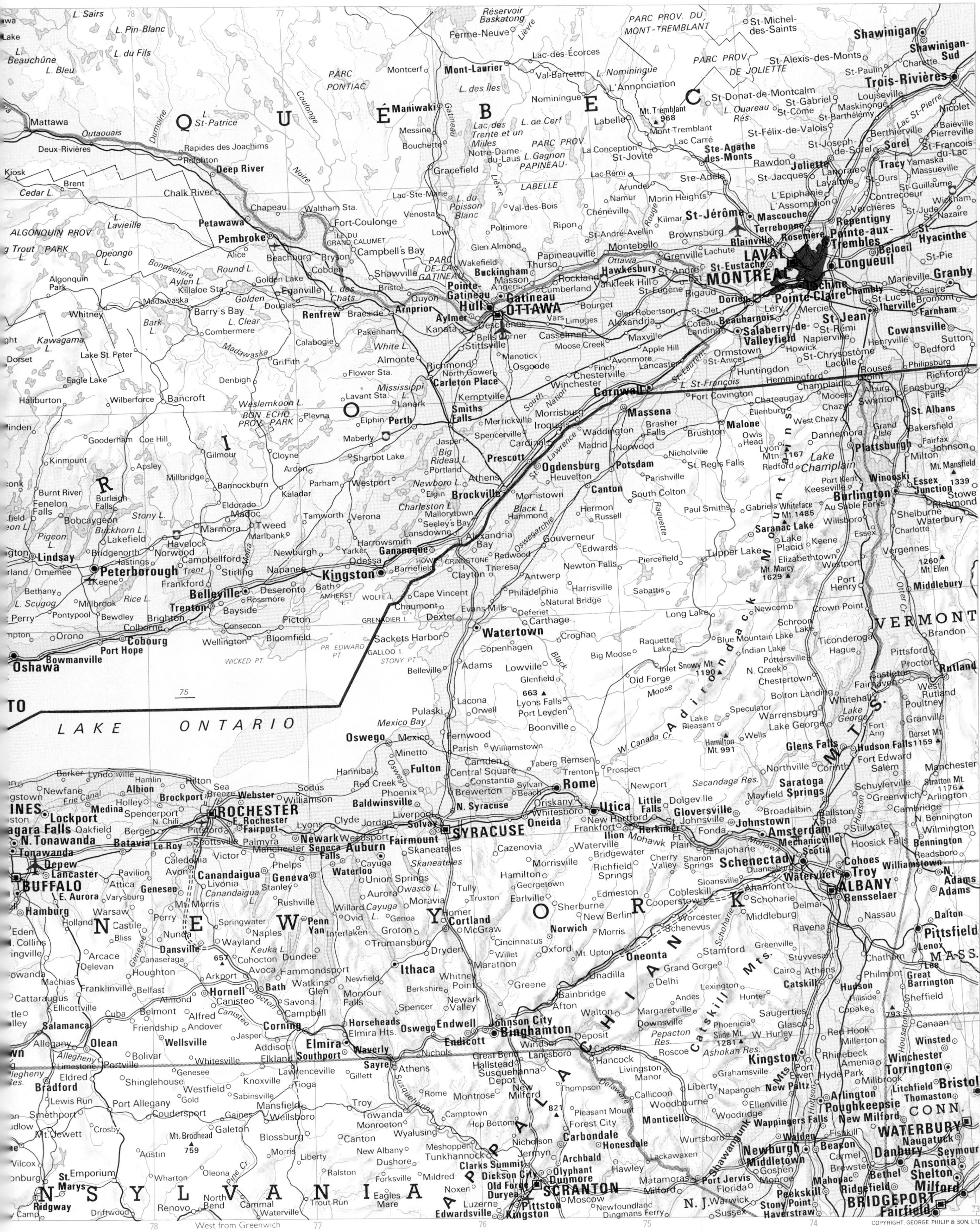
QUÉBEC
ONTARIO
NEW YORK
PENNSYLVANIA
VERMONT
MASS.
CONN.
N. J.
LAKE ONTARIO
ADIRONDACK MOUNTAINS
APPALACHIAN MTS.
GREEN MTS.
Catskill Mts.
PARC PROV. DU MONT-TREMBLANT
PARC PROV. DE JOLIETTE
PARC PONTIAC
PARC PROV. PAPINEAU-LABELLE
ALGONQUIN PROV. PARK
BON ECHO PROV. PARK
Réservoir Baskatong
Lake Champlain
Sacandaga Res.
Pepacton Res.
Ashokan Res.
Outaouais
St. Lawrence
Hudson
Mohawk
Susquehanna
Delaware
Mattawa
Deux-Rivières
Rapides des Joachims
Rolphton
Deep River
Chalk River
Petawawa
Pembroke
Renfrew
Arnprior
Hull
OTTAWA
Gatineau
Aylmer
Kanata
Maniwaki
Mont-Laurier
Ferme-Neuve
Lac-des-Écorces
Nominingue
L'Annonciation
Labelle
Mt. Tremblant 968
St-Jovite
Ste-Agathe-des-Monts
St-Jérôme
St-Donat-de-Montcalm
St-Michel-des-Saints
St-Alexis-des-Monts
Shawinigan
Shawinigan-Sud
Trois-Rivières
Louiseville
Joliette
Berthierville
Sorel
Tracy
Repentigny
Terrebonne
Mascouche
Rosemère
LAVAL
MONTRÉAL
Longueuil
Pointe-aux-Trembles
Lachine
Dorion
Pointe-Claire
Beauharnois
Salaberry-de-Valleyfield
St-Jean
Iberville
Chambly
Beloeil
Granby
St-Hyacinthe
Cowansville
Farnham
Bromont
Hawkesbury
Rockland
Buckingham
Carleton Place
Smiths Falls
Perth
Kemptville
Prescott
Brockville
Gananoque
Kingston
Napanee
Belleville
Trenton
Cobourg
Port Hope
Oshawa
Bowmanville
Peterborough
Lindsay
Bancroft
Haliburton
Cornwall
Massena
Ogdensburg
Potsdam
Canton
Malone
Plattsburgh
Burlington
Winooski
Essex Junction
St. Albans
Middlebury
Rutland
Saranac Lake
Lake Placid
Mt. Marcy 1629
Watertown
Oswego
Fulton
Rome
Utica
Syracuse
Auburn
Geneva
Canandaigua
ROCHESTER
Brockport
Lockport
Niagara Falls
N. Tonawanda
BUFFALO
Batavia
Ithaca
Cortland
Elmira
Corning
Binghamton
Johnson City
Endicott
Oneonta
Norwich
Olean
Salamanca
Bradford
Hornell
Schenectady
ALBANY
Troy
Saratoga Springs
Glens Falls
Amsterdam
Johnstown
Gloversville
Pittsfield
Bennington
Kingston
Poughkeepsie
Newburgh
Middletown
Peekskill
Monticello
Port Jervis
SCRANTON
Carbondale
Wilkes-Barre
Kingston
WATERBURY
Danbury
BRIDGEPORT
Bristol
Torrington
Milford
Fairfield
West from Greenwich
78
77
76
75
74
73
46
45
44
43
42

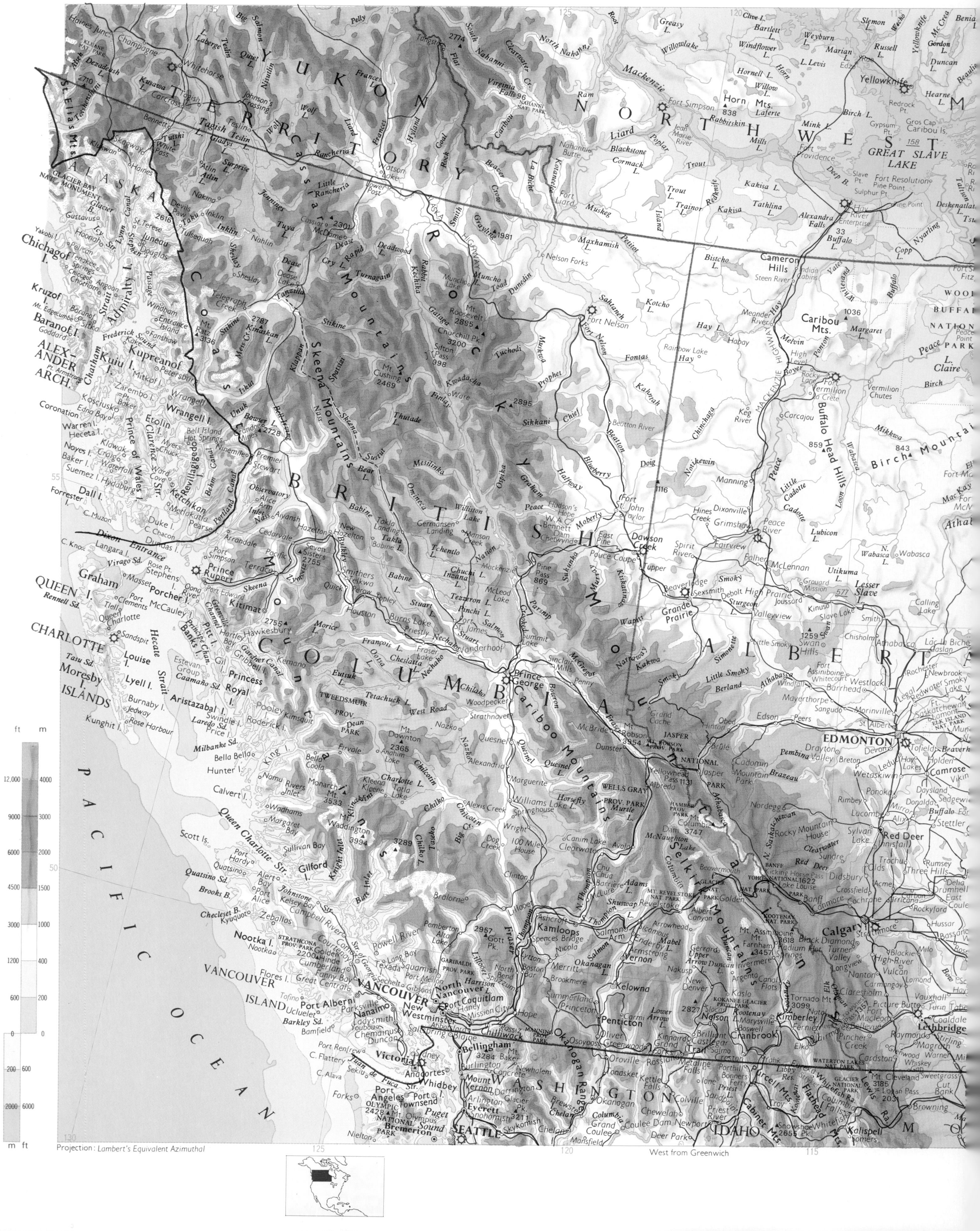
YUKON TERRITORY
NORTHWEST T
BRITISH COLUMBIA
ALBERTA
ALASKA
WASHINGTON
IDAHO
PACIFIC OCEAN
QUEEN CHARLOTTE ISLANDS
VANCOUVER ISLAND
ALEXANDER ARCH.
GREAT SLAVE LAKE
Rocky Mountains
Coast Mountains
Skeena Mountains
Cassiar Mountains
Cariboo Mountains
Selkirk Mountains
Whitehorse
Yellowknife
Fort Simpson
Fort Nelson
Dawson Creek
Prince Rupert
Kitimat
Prince George
Grande Prairie
Peace River
EDMONTON
Red Deer
Calgary
Lethbridge
Kamloops
Kelowna
Penticton
VANCOUVER
Victoria
Nanaimo
Port Alberni
Bellingham
SEATTLE
Jasper
Banff
Juneau
Skagway
Chichagof I.
Baranof I.
Prince of Wales I.
Graham I.
Moresby I.
Queen Charlotte Str.
Str. of Georgia
Juan de Fuca Str.
Dixon Entrance
Hecate Strait
Mt. Robson 3954
Horn Mts.
Caribou Mts.
Cameron Hills
Buffalo Head Hills
Birch Mountains
ft m
12,000 4000
9000 3000
6000 2000
4500 1500
3000 1000
1200 400
600 200
0 0
200 600
2000 6000
m ft
Projection: Lambert's Equivalent Azimuthal
West from Greenwich

Kilometers 0 50 100 150 200 250 300 Km.

Statute Miles 0 50 100 150 200 250 300 Mi.

1:5 600 000

One centimeter represents 56 kilometers
One inch represents approximately 90 miles

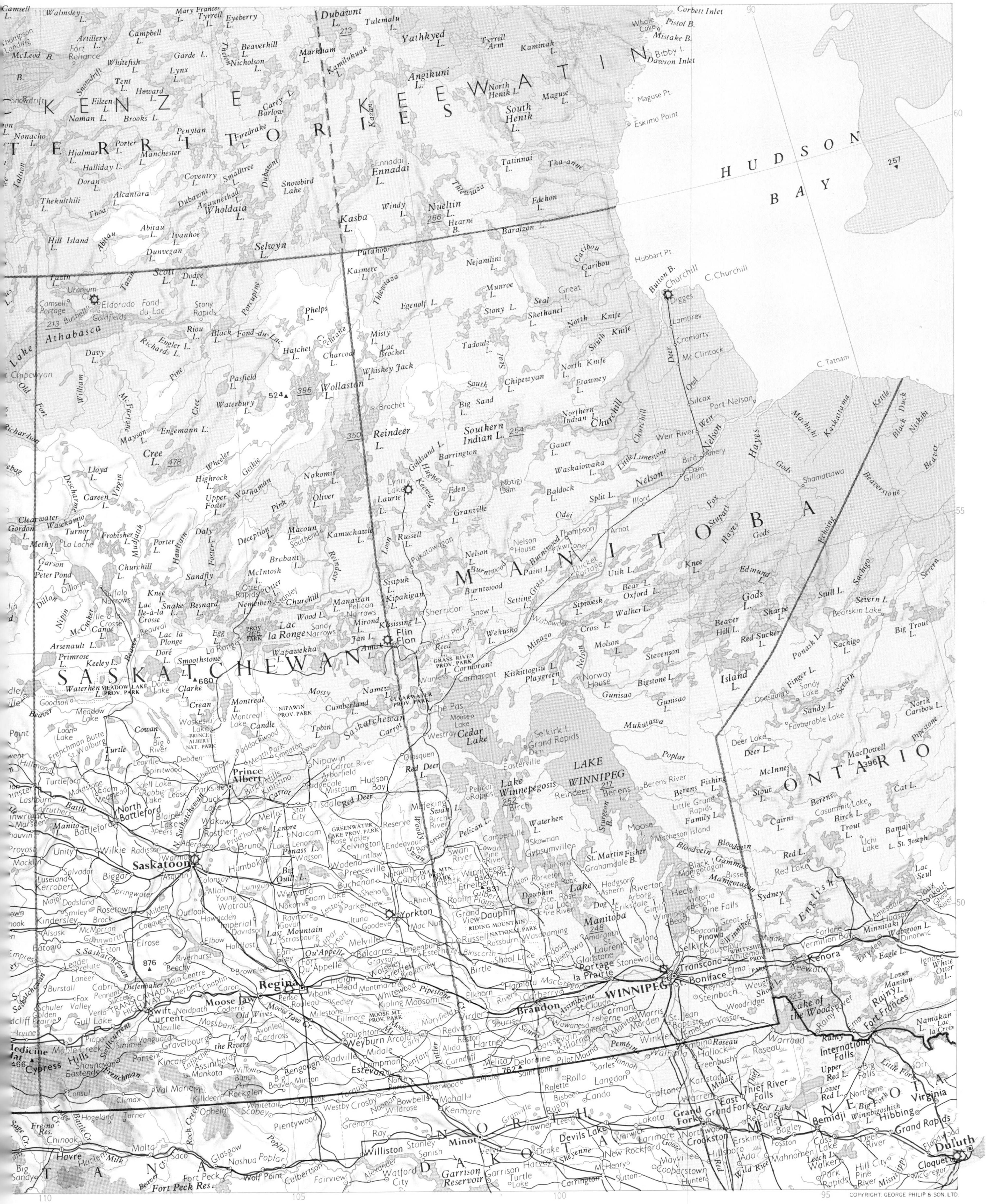

KEEWATIN
MACKENZIE
TERRITORIES
HUDSON BAY
SASKATCHEWAN
MANITOBA
ONTARIO
NORTH DAKOTA
MINNESOTA
MONTANA
Lake Athabasca
Wollaston L.
Reindeer L.
Southern Indian L.
Cree L.
Lac la Ronge
Churchill
Nelson
Hayes
Lake Winnipeg
Lake Winnipegosis
Lake Manitoba
Cedar Lake
Lake of the Woods
Saskatoon
Regina
Prince Albert
Moose Jaw
Swift Current
North Battleford
Yorkton
Brandon
WINNIPEG
Portage la Prairie
Flin Flon
The Pas
Thompson
Churchill
Kenora
Minot
Grand Forks
Duluth
Estevan
Weyburn
Medicine Hat
Cypress Hills
Kasba L.
Nueltin L.
Dubawnt L.
Yathkyed L.
Eskimo Point
C. Churchill
C. Tatnam
Port Nelson
Eldorado
Uranium City

BRITISH COLUMBIA
ALBERTA
SASKATCHEWAN
MANITOBA
CANADA
Vancouver
Vancouver I.
Victoria
Calgary
Lethbridge
Regina
Saskatoon
Moose Jaw
Medicine Hat
Swift Current
Maple Creek
Lake Winnipegosis
L. Manitoba
Brandon
WASHINGTON
Seattle
Tacoma
Spokane
Olympia
Mt. Rainier 4392
Yakima
Walla Walla
Columbia
Puget Sd.
OREGON
Portland
Salem
Eugene
Mt. Hood 3427
Blue Mountains
Medford
Klamath Falls
IDAHO
Boise
Idaho Falls
Pocatello
Twin Falls
Lewiston
MONTANA
Great Falls
Helena
Butte
Missoula
Billings
Bozeman
Glacier Nat. Park
Missouri
Yellowstone
Fort Peck Reservoir
NORTH DAKOTA
Bismarck
Minot
Williston
SOUTH DAKOTA
Pierre
Rapid City
Black Hills 2207
WYOMING
Casper
Cheyenne
Laramie
Rock Springs
Yellowstone National Park
Grand Teton Mt. 4196
Gannett Pk. 4202
Bighorn Mts.
Wind River Ra.
NEBRASKA
North Platte
Scottsbluff
CALIFORNIA
San Francisco
Oakland
Berkeley
San Jose
Sacramento
Stockton
Fresno
Bakersfield
LOS ANGELES
Long Beach
San Bernardino
Pasadena
Glendale
San Diego
Santa Barbara
Eureka
Redding
Lassen Pk. 3187
Mt. Shasta 4317
Mt. Whitney 4418
Death Valley -86
Sierra Nevada
Coast Ranges
Yosemite National Park
Sequoia Nat. Park
Monterey
NEVADA
Reno
Carson City
Las Vegas
Elko
Winnemucca
Great Basin
Lake Tahoe
UTAH
Salt Lake City
Great Salt Lake 1282
Ogden
Provo
Uinta Mts.
Wasatch Mts.
Lake Powell
COLORADO
Denver
Colorado Springs
Pueblo
Grand Junction
Rocky Mountains
Sangre de Cristo Mts.
San Juan Mts.
Pikes Pk. 4301
ARIZONA
Phoenix
Tucson
Flagstaff
Grand Canyon Nat. Park
Humphreys Pk. 3851
Yuma
NEW MEXICO
Albuquerque
Santa Fe
Las Cruces
Roswell
Rio Grande
TEXAS
El Paso
Lubbock
Amarillo
Midland
Odessa
San Angelo
Edwards Plateau
Laredo
OKLAHOMA
KANSAS
MEXICO
Tijuana
Mexicali
Ensenada
Hermosillo
Chihuahua
Ciudad Juárez
Torreón
Monterrey
Nuevo Laredo
Los Mochis
Ciudad Obregón
Guaymas
BAJA CALIFORNIA NORTE
BAJA CALIFORNIA SUR
SONORA
CHIHUAHUA
COAHUILA
DURANGO
Golfo de California
Sierra Madre Occidental
Guadalupe (Mex.)
PACIFIC OCEAN
HAWAII
1:8 000 000
0 100 200 km
Kauai
Niihau
Oahu
Honolulu
Molokai
Lanai
Maui
Kahoolawe
Hawaii
Hilo
Mauna Kea 4205
Mauna Loa 4170
Haleakala 3056
Kauai Channel
Kaiwi Channel
Alenuihaha Channel
PACIFIC OCEAN
Hawaiian Islands
ft m
12,000 4000
9000 3000
6000 2000
4500 1500
3000 1000
1200 400
600 200
0 0
200 600
2000 6000
m ft
130
120
110
105
100
156
158
45
40
35
30
22
20

Projection: Albers' Equal Area with two standard parallels

West from Greenwich

Kilometers 0 100 200 300 400 500 Km.
Statute Miles 0 100 200 300 400 500 Mi.

1:9 600 000

One centimeter represents 96 kilometers
One inch represents approximately 150 miles

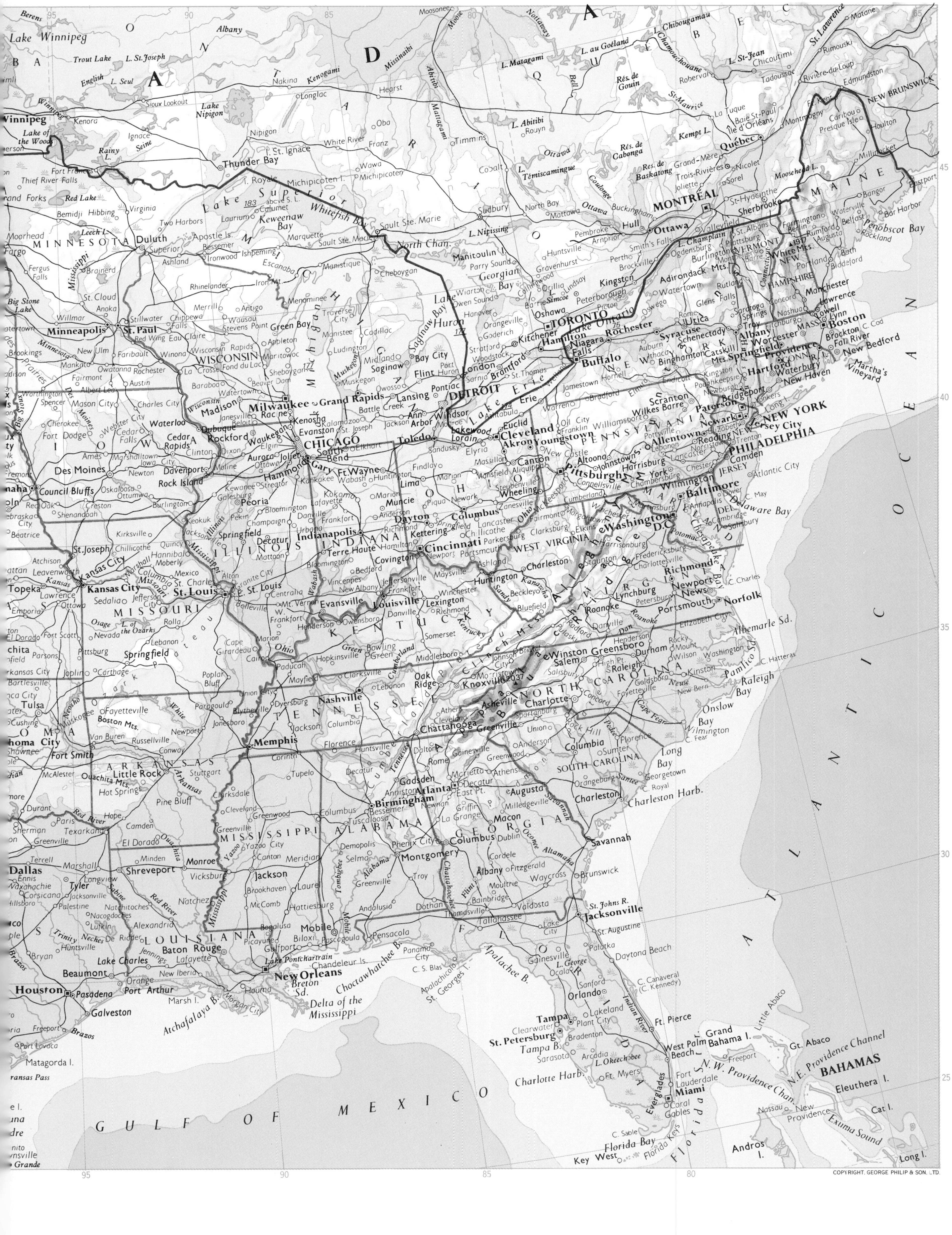
C A N A D A
O N T A R I O
Q U E B E C
NEW BRUNSWICK
Lake Winnipeg
Winnipeg
Thunder Bay
Lake Superior
Lake Nipigon
Lake Michigan
Lake Huron
Lake Erie
Lake Ontario
Georgian Bay
MONTRÉAL
Québec
Ottawa
TORONTO
MINNESOTA
WISCONSIN
MICHIGAN
IOWA
ILLINOIS
INDIANA
OHIO
PENNSYLVANIA
NEW YORK
VERMONT
NEW HAMPSHIRE
MAINE
MASS.
CONN.
R.I.
NEW JERSEY
DEL.
MARYLAND
WEST VIRGINIA
VIRGINIA
KENTUCKY
TENNESSEE
NORTH CAROLINA
SOUTH CAROLINA
GEORGIA
ALABAMA
MISSISSIPPI
LOUISIANA
ARKANSAS
MISSOURI
FLORIDA
Minneapolis
St. Paul
Duluth
Milwaukee
CHICAGO
DETROIT
Cleveland
Buffalo
Pittsburgh
PHILADELPHIA
NEW YORK
Boston
Baltimore
Washington D.C.
Richmond
Norfolk
Cincinnati
Columbus
Indianapolis
Louisville
St. Louis
Kansas City
Memphis
Nashville
Atlanta
Birmingham
New Orleans
Houston
Dallas
Jacksonville
Tampa
Miami
Savannah
Charleston
Appalachian Mts.
Delta of the Mississippi
Choctawhatchee B.
Apalachee B.
GULF OF MEXICO
ATLANTIC OCEAN
BAHAMAS
Grand Bahama I.
Gt. Abaco
Eleuthera I.
Andros I.
Cape Cod
Martha's Vineyard
C. Hatteras
Florida Keys
Key West

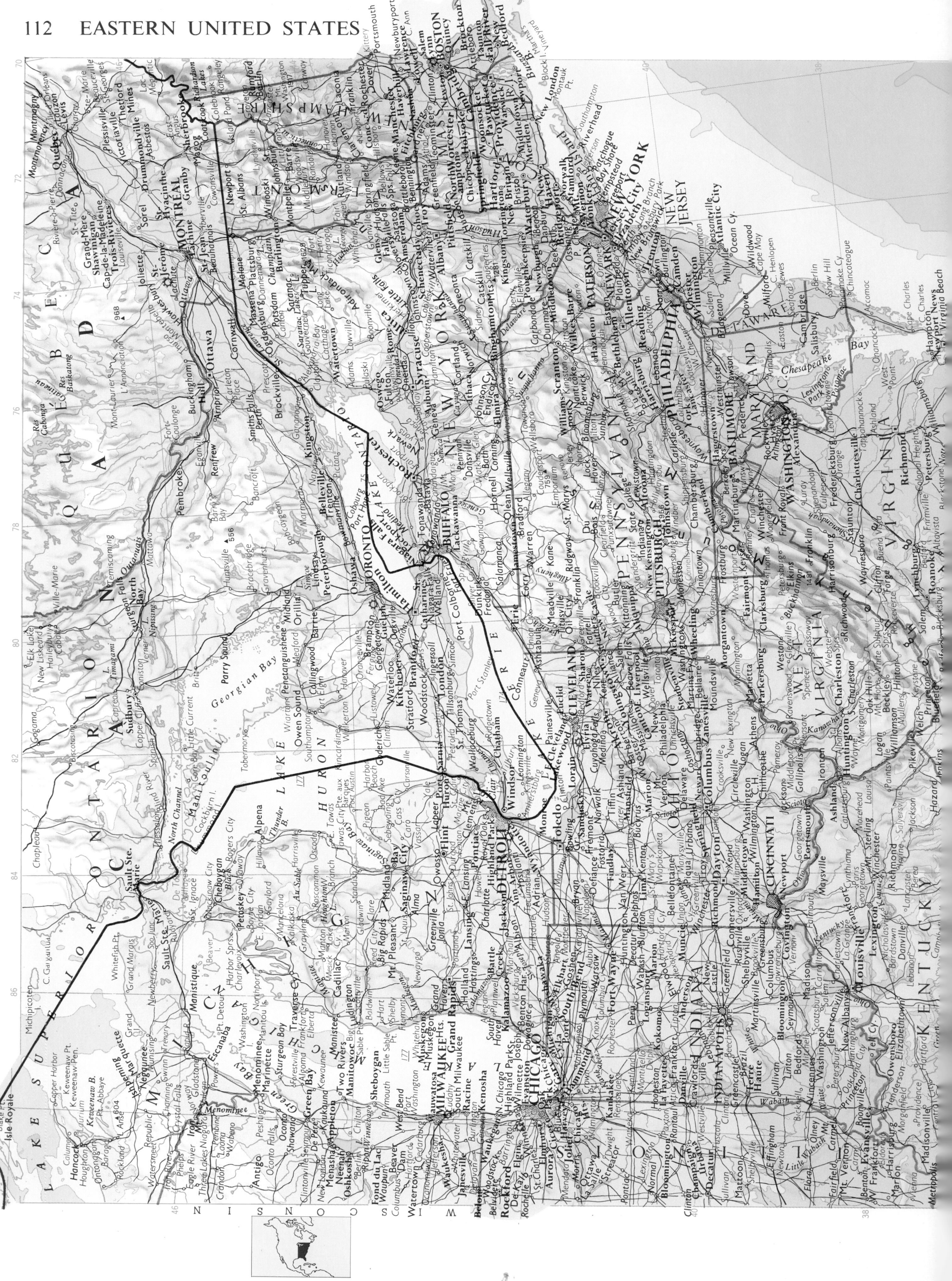
ONTARIO
QUEBEC
CANADA
LAKE SUPERIOR
LAKE HURON
LAKE ONTARIO
LAKE ERIE
MICHIGAN
WISCONSIN
ILLINOIS
INDIANA
OHIO
KENTUCKY
PENNSYLVANIA
NEW YORK
NEW JERSEY
MARYLAND
DELAWARE
WEST VIRGINIA
VIRGINIA
VERMONT
NEW HAMPSHIRE
MASSACHUSETTS
CONNECTICUT
Georgian Bay
Chesapeake Bay

Kilometers 0 50 100 150 200 250 Km.
Statute Miles 0 50 100 150 200 250 Mi.

1:4 800 000

One centimeter represents 48 kilometers
One inch represents approximately 75 miles

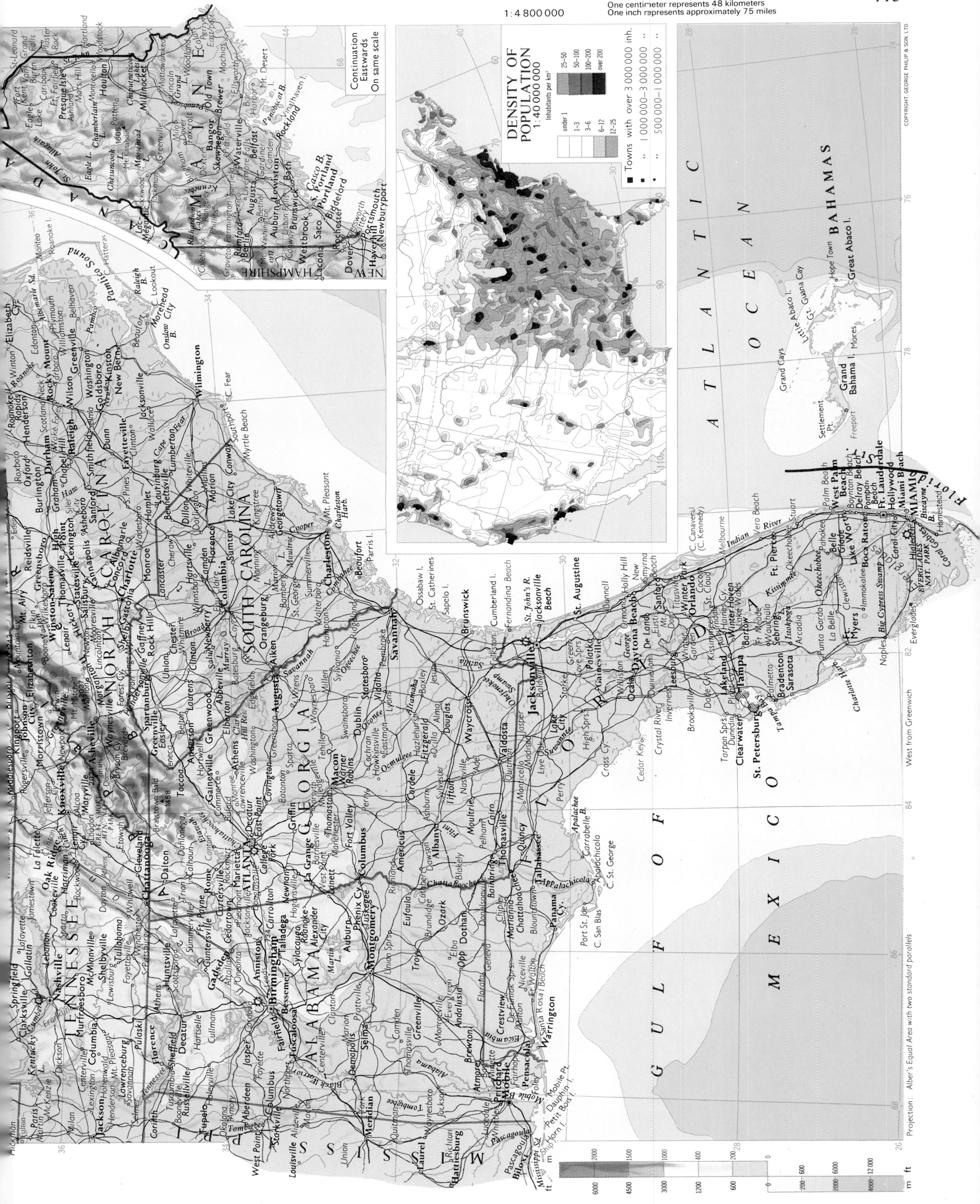

DENSITY OF POPULATION
1:40 000 000
Inhabitants per km²
under 1
1–3
3–6
6–12
12–25
25–50
50–100
100–200
over 200
■ Towns with over 3 000 000 inh.
▪ " 1 000 000–3 000 000 "
• " 500 000–1 000 000 "
Continuation Eastwards On same scale
A T L A N T I C O C E A N
G U L F O F M E X I C O
BAHAMAS
TENNESSEE
NORTH CAROLINA
SOUTH CAROLINA
GEORGIA
ALABAMA
MISSISSIPPI
FLORIDA
MAINE
NEW HAMPSHIRE
CANADA
ATLANTA
Jacksonville
Savannah
Charleston
Birmingham
Montgomery
Mobile
Tampa
St. Petersburg
Orlando
MIAMI
Charlotte
Raleigh
Wilmington
Nashville
Knoxville
Chattanooga
Macon
Augusta
Columbia
Tallahassee
Pensacola
Portland
Bangor
Projection: Alber's Equal Area with two standard parallels
West from Greenwich
m ft

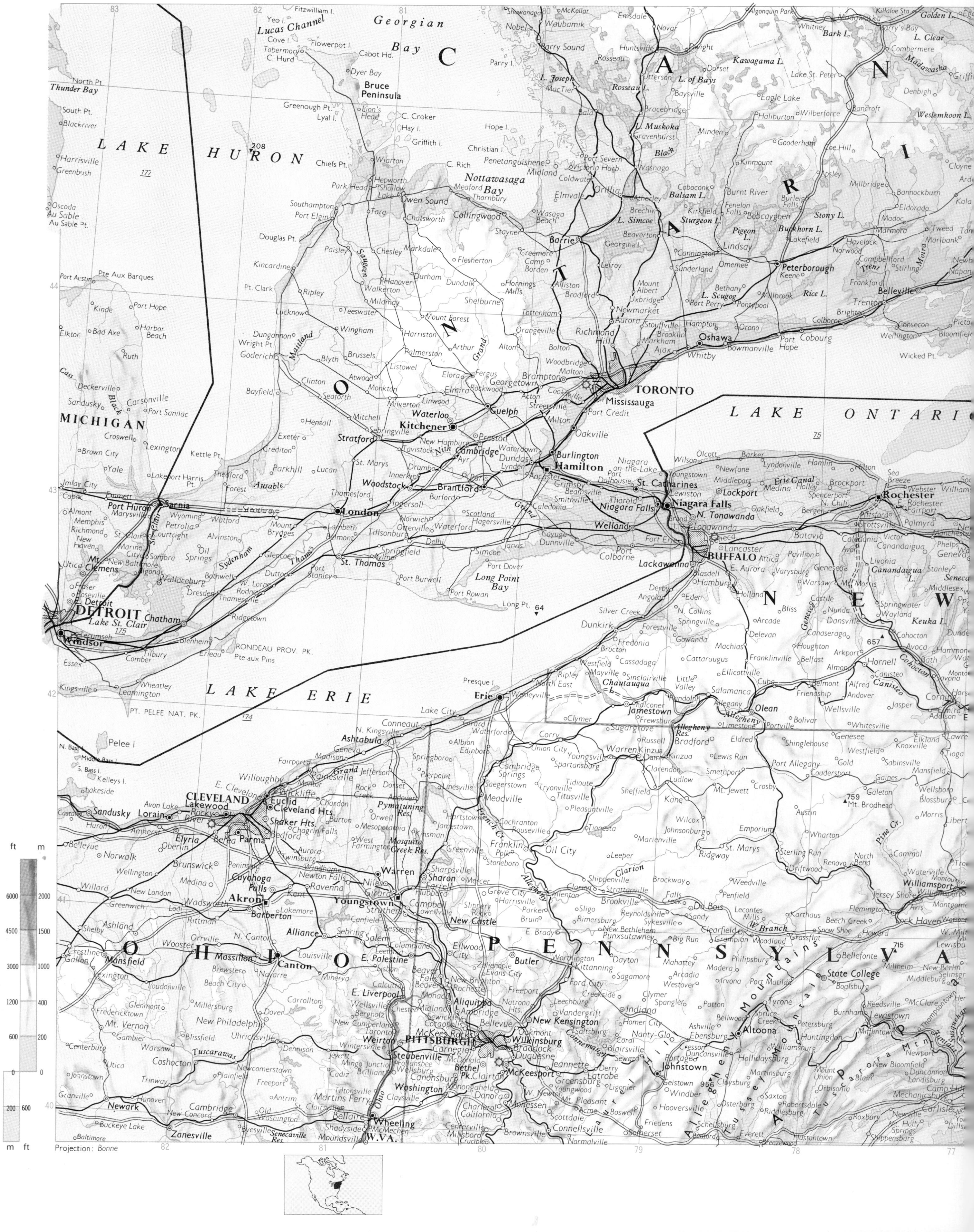

Georgian Bay
Bruce Peninsula
LAKE HURON
LAKE ONTARIO
LAKE ERIE
CANADA
ONTARIO
MICHIGAN
OHIO
PENNSYLVANIA
NEW YORK
TORONTO
Mississauga
Hamilton
Kitchener
Waterloo
Guelph
London
Brantford
Niagara Falls
St. Catharines
BUFFALO
Rochester
DETROIT
Windsor
Sarnia
Port Huron
CLEVELAND
Akron
Canton
Youngstown
Erie
PITTSBURGH
Altoona
Johnstown
Wheeling
Oshawa
Peterborough
Barrie
Lake St. Clair
L. Simcoe
Long Point Bay
Chautauqua L.
Allegheny Res.
Allegheny Mountains
Tuscarora Mtn
Projection: Bonne
ft
m
6000
2000
4500
1500
3000
1000
1200
400
600
200
0
0
200
600
m
ft

Kilometers 0 20 40 60 80 100 Km.

Statute Miles 0 20 40 60 80 100 Mi.

1:2 000 000

One centimeter represents 20 kilometers
One inch represents approximately 32 miles

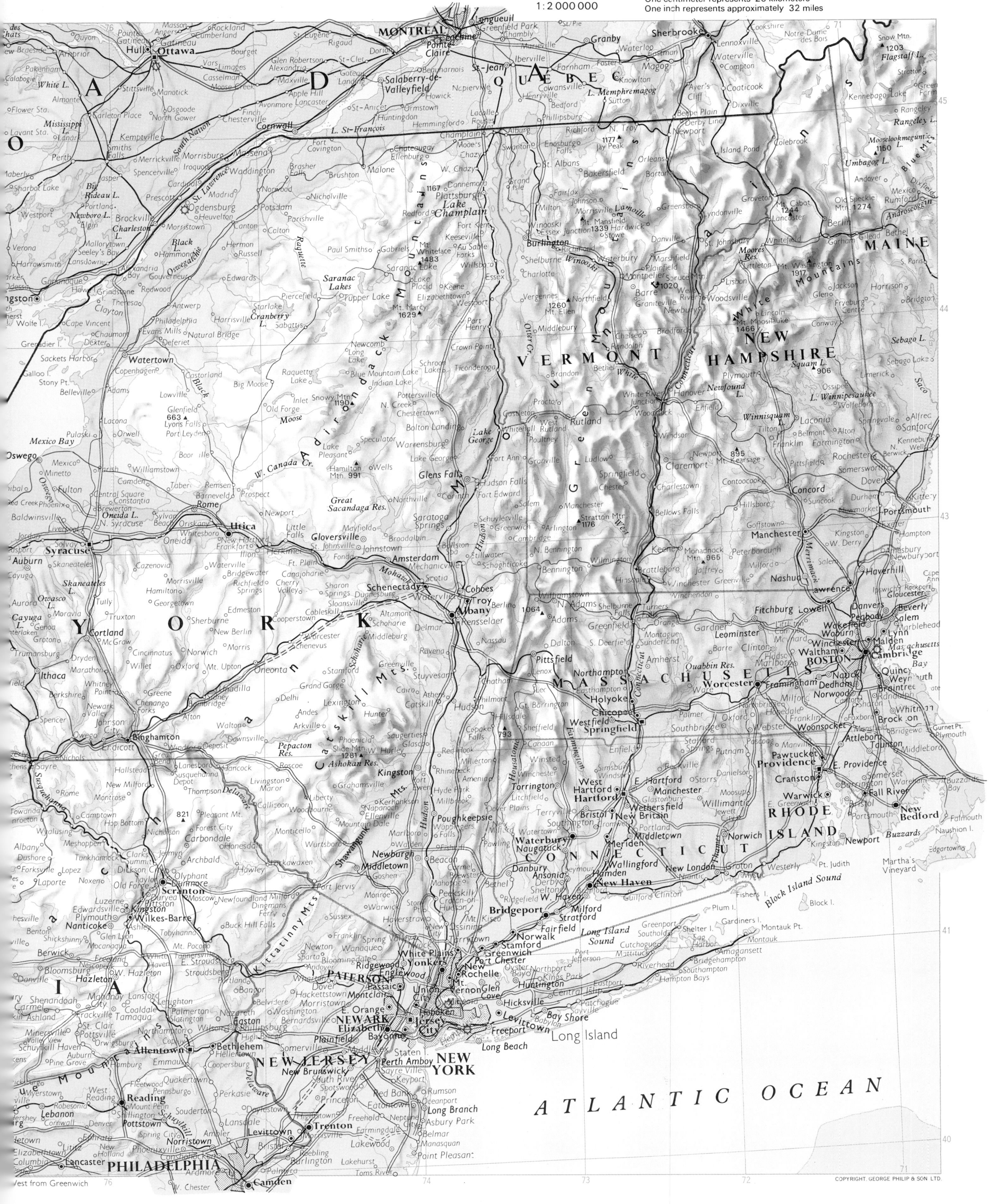

MONTREAL
Ottawa
Q U E B E C
C A N A D A
Sherbrooke
Granby
Cornwall
VERMONT
NEW HAMPSHIRE
MAINE
MASSACHUSETTS
RHODE ISLAND
CONNECTICUT
NEW JERSEY
NEW YORK
Y O R K
Albany
Schenectady
Troy
Utica
Syracuse
Binghamton
Burlington
Montpelier
Concord
Manchester
Portsmouth
BOSTON
Cambridge
Worcester
Springfield
Hartford
Providence
New Haven
Bridgeport
Stamford
PATERSON
NEWARK
Jersey City
Trenton
PHILADELPHIA
Camden
Allentown
Bethlehem
Scranton
Wilkes-Barre
Reading
Lake Champlain
Adirondack Mountains
Green Mountains
White Mountains
Catskill Mts.
Long Island
Long Island Sound
Block Island Sound
ATLANTIC OCEAN
West from Greenwich
76
74
73
72
71
45
44
43
41
40

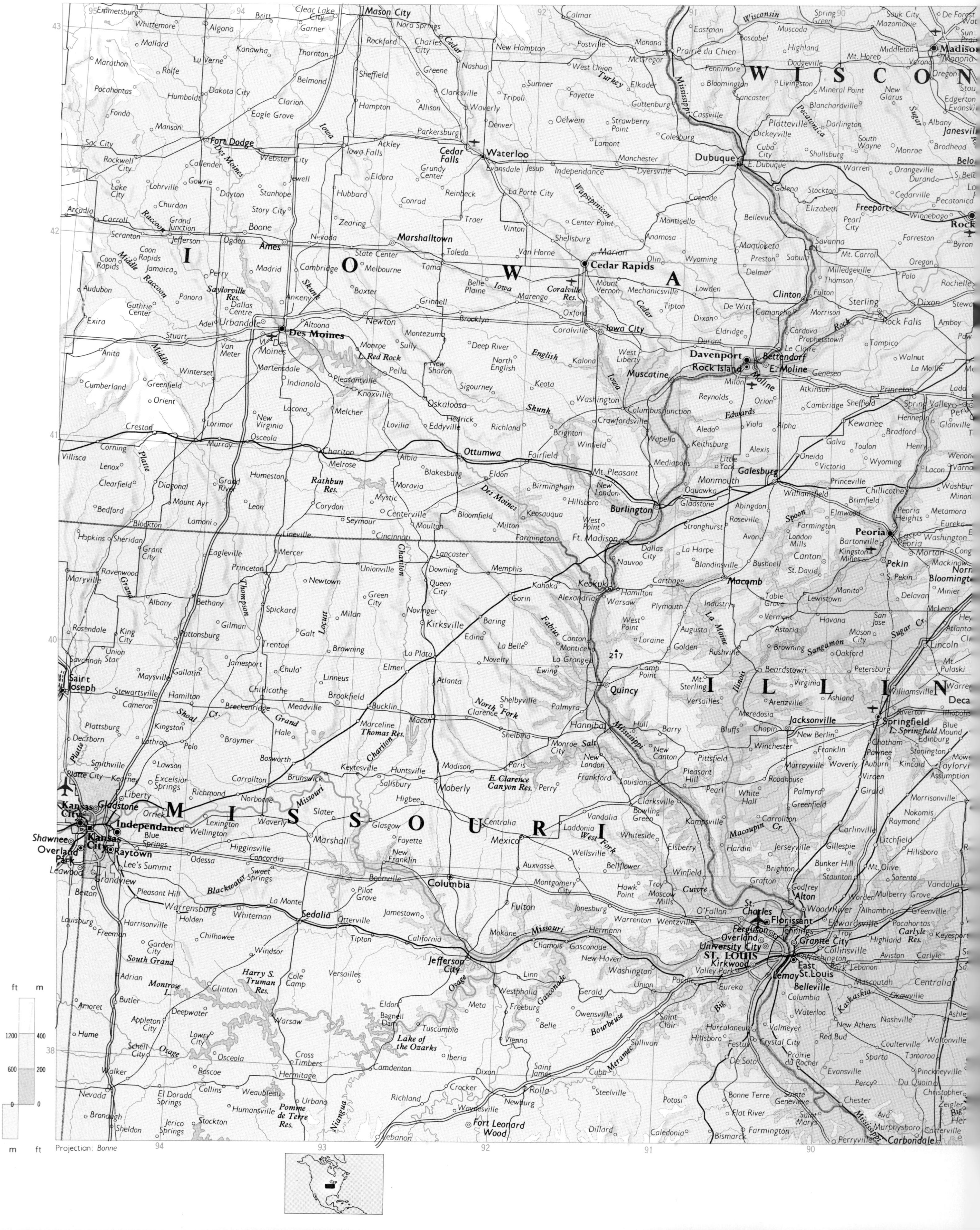
I O W A
M I S S O U R I
I L L I N
W I S C O N
Mason City
Fort Dodge
Waterloo
Cedar Falls
Dubuque
Cedar Rapids
Iowa City
Davenport
Bettendorf
Rock Island
E. Moline
Clinton
Muscatine
Des Moines
W. Des Moines
Ames
Marshalltown
Ottumwa
Burlington
Keokuk
Ft. Madison
Mt. Pleasant
Galesburg
Peoria
East Peoria
Pekin
Macomb
Quincy
Hannibal
Springfield
Jacksonville
Alton
St. Charles
Florissant
ST. LOUIS
East St. Louis
Granite City
Belleville
Kirkwood
Lemay
University City
Overland
Ferguson
Columbia
Jefferson City
Sedalia
Saint Joseph
Kansas City
Independance
Gladstone
Raytown
Shawnee
Overland Park
Leawood
Kirksville
Moberly
Mexico
Fort Leonard Wood
Rolla
Lake of the Ozarks
Harry S. Truman Res.
Saylorville Res.
L. Red Rock
Rathbun Res.
Coralville Res.
Thomas Res.
E. Clarence Canyon Res.
Pomme de Terre Res.
L. Springfield
Carlyle Res.
Mississippi
Missouri
Des Moines
Iowa
Cedar
Skunk
Wapsipinicon
Raccoon
Grand
Chariton
Osage
Gasconade
Meramec
Illinois
La Moine
Spoon
Sangamon
Kaskaskia
Rock
Wisconsin
Madison
Janesville
Freeport
Rockford
Dixon
Sterling
Projection: Bonne
ft
m
1200
400
600
200
0
0
m
ft
95
94
93
92
91
90
43
42
41
40
38

Kilometers 0 20 40 60 80 100 Km.

Statute Miles 0 20 40 60 80 100 Mi.

1:2 000 000

One centimeter represents 20 kilometers
One inch represents approximately 32 miles

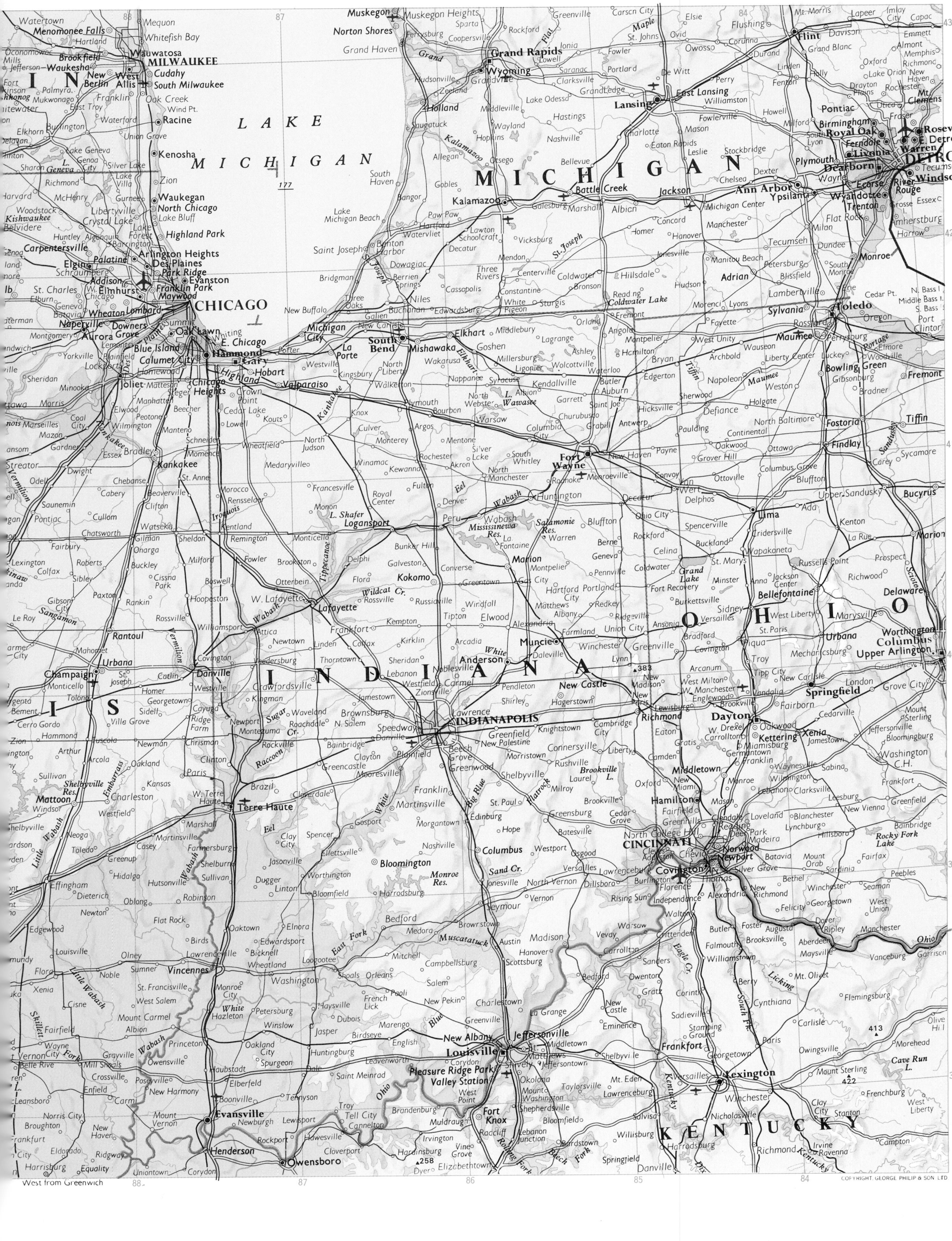
LAKE MICHIGAN
MICHIGAN
INDIANA
OHIO
KENTUCKY
CHICAGO
MILWAUKEE
DETROIT
INDIANAPOLIS
CINCINNATI
Grand Rapids
Lansing
Flint
Kalamazoo
Battle Creek
Jackson
Ann Arbor
Toledo
South Bend
Fort Wayne
Lima
Dayton
Springfield
Columbus
Kokomo
Lafayette
Muncie
Anderson
Richmond
Terre Haute
Bloomington
Evansville
Louisville
Lexington
Frankfort
Covington
Newport
Hamilton
Middletown
Champaign
Danville
Kankakee
Joliet
Elgin
Waukegan
Kenosha
Racine
Hammond
Gary
Owensboro
Henderson
Jeffersonville
New Albany
Fort Knox

West from Greenwich

Kilometers 0 50 100 150 200 Km.
Statute Miles 0 50 100 150 200

1:4 800 000

One centimeter represents 48 kilometers
One inch represents approximately 75 mi

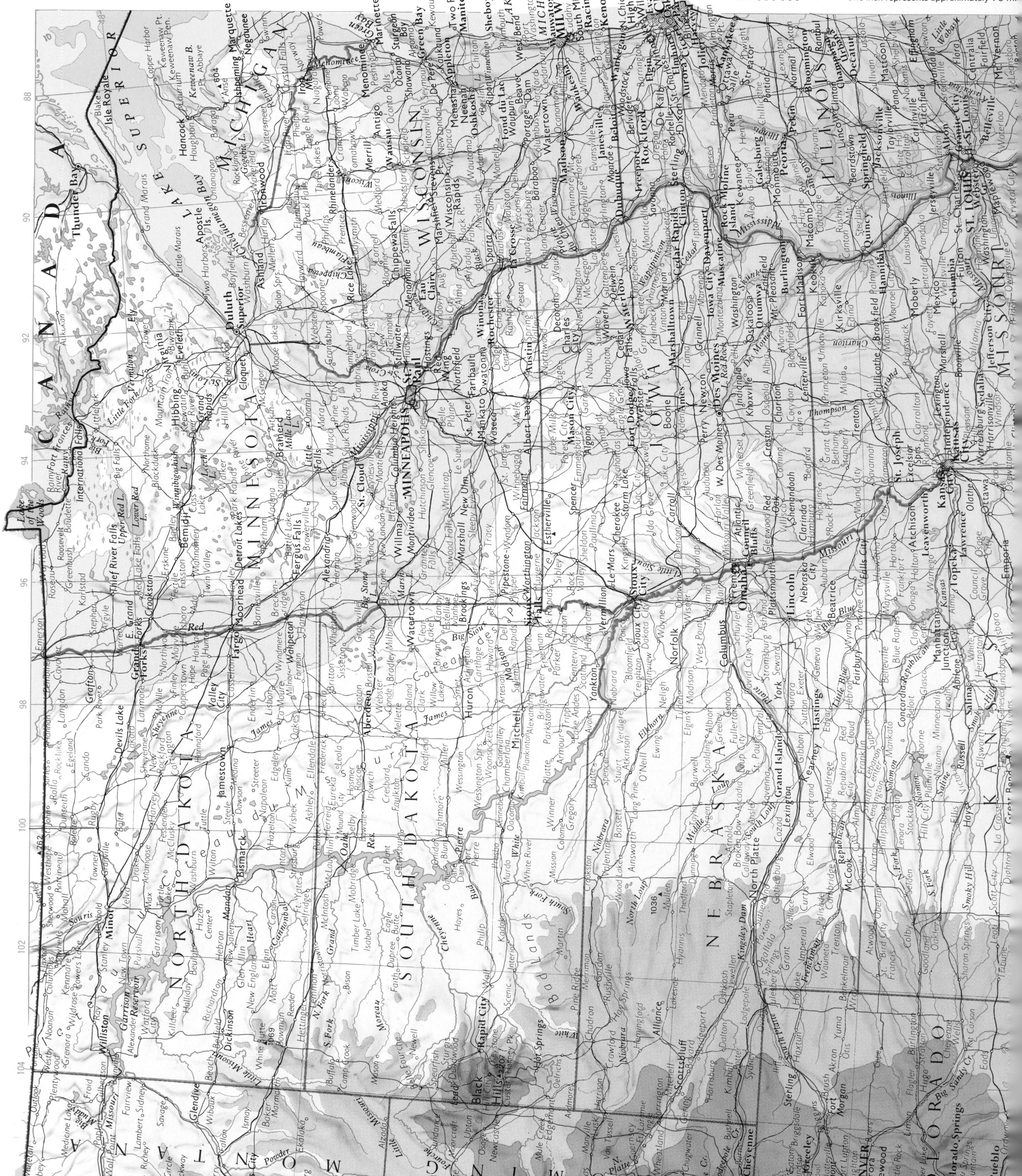

CANADA
LAKE SUPERIOR
LAKE MICHIGAN
MINNESOTA
WISCONSIN
MICHIGAN
IOWA
ILLINOIS
MISSOURI
NORTH DAKOTA
SOUTH DAKOTA
NEBRASKA
KANSAS
MONTANA
WYOMING
COLORADO
CHICAGO
MILWAUKEE
MINNEAPOLIS
St. Paul
DES MOINES
Omaha
DENVER
Kansas City
ST. LOUIS
Duluth
Bismarck
Pierre
Cheyenne
Laramie Mountains

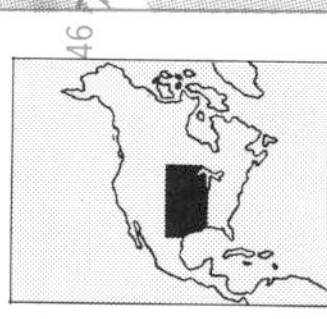

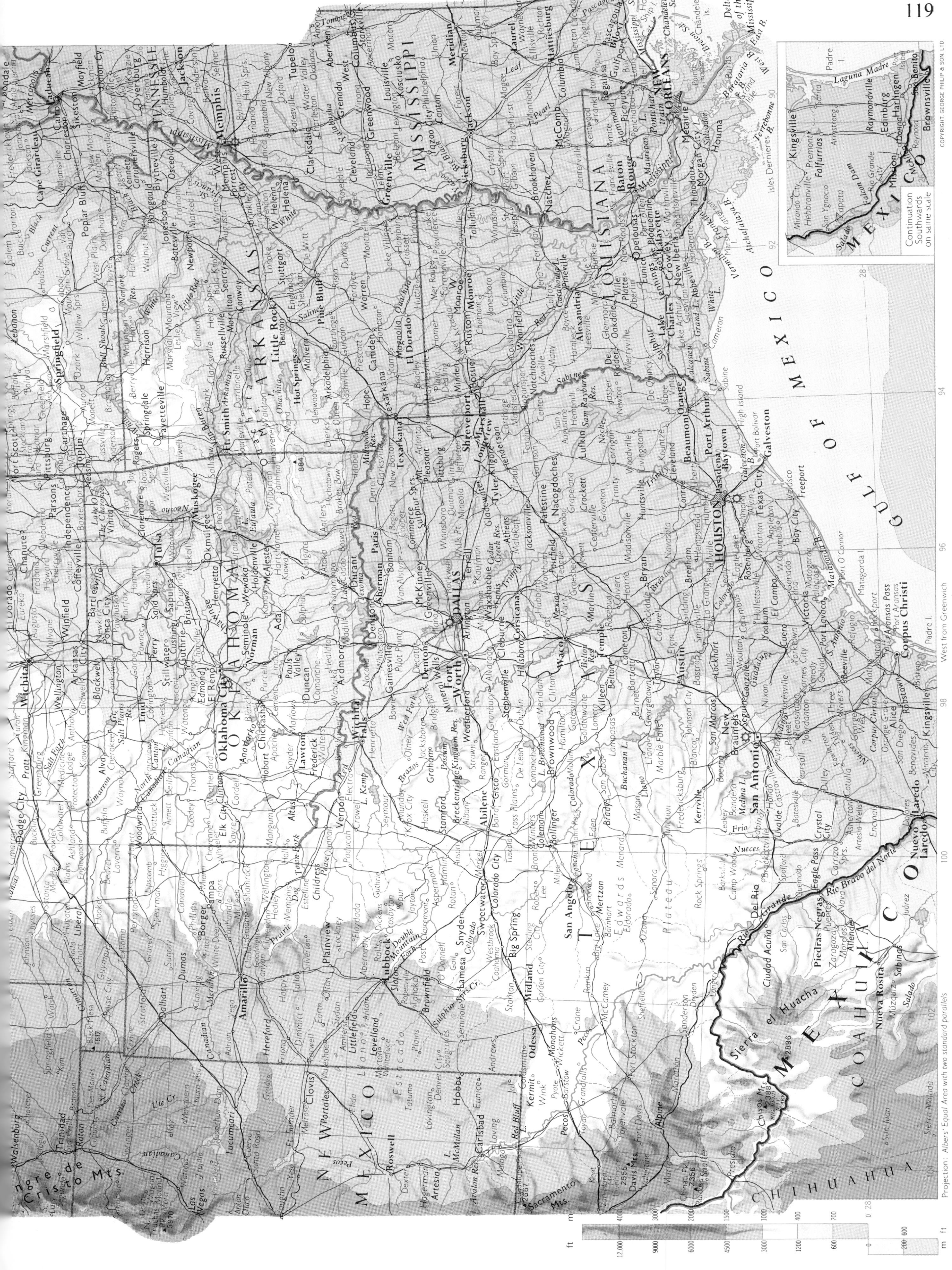
GULF OF MEXICO
MEXICO
TEXAS
OKLAHOMA
ARKANSAS
LOUISIANA
MISSISSIPPI
NEW MEXICO
COAHUILA
CHIHUAHUA
TENNESSEE
Dallas
Houston
San Antonio
Austin
Fort Worth
Oklahoma City
Tulsa
Wichita
Little Rock
Memphis
Jackson
Shreveport
Baton Rouge
New Orleans
Corpus Christi
Galveston
Beaumont
Port Arthur
Amarillo
Lubbock
El Paso
Abilene
Waco
Laredo
Brownsville
Kingsville
Delta of the Mississippi
Sierra el Huacha
Sacramento Mts.
Davis Mts.
Chisos Mts.
Sangre de Cristo Mts.
Edwards Plateau
Llano Estacado
Continuation Southwards on same scale
West from Greenwich
Projection: Albers' Equal Area with two standard parallels
COPYRIGHT GEORGE PHILIP & SON, LTD.

Kilometers 0 50 100 150 200 250 Km.

Statute Miles 0 50 100 150 200 250 Mi.

1:4 800 000

One centimeter represents 48 kilometers
One inch represents approximately 75 miles

BRITISH COLUMBIA
ALBERTA
SASKATCHEWAN
CANADA
MONTANA
WYOMING
IDAHO
WASHINGTON
OREGON
NEVADA
CALIFORNIA
Bitterroot Range
Lemhi Range
Salmon River Mountains
Blue Mountains
Cascade Range
Coast Ranges
Bighorn Mountains
Wind River Range
Uinta Mountains
Medicine Bow Range
GREAT SALT LAKE
Great Salt Lake Desert
SEATTLE
PORTLAND
Spokane
Boise
Salt Lake City
Reno
Sacramento
Helena
Butte
Billings
Great Falls
Missoula
Olympia
Salem
Eugene
Ogden
Provo
Pocatello
Idaho Falls
Twin Falls
Casper
Rock Springs
Rawlins
Laramie
Vancouver
Victoria
Juan de Fuca Strait

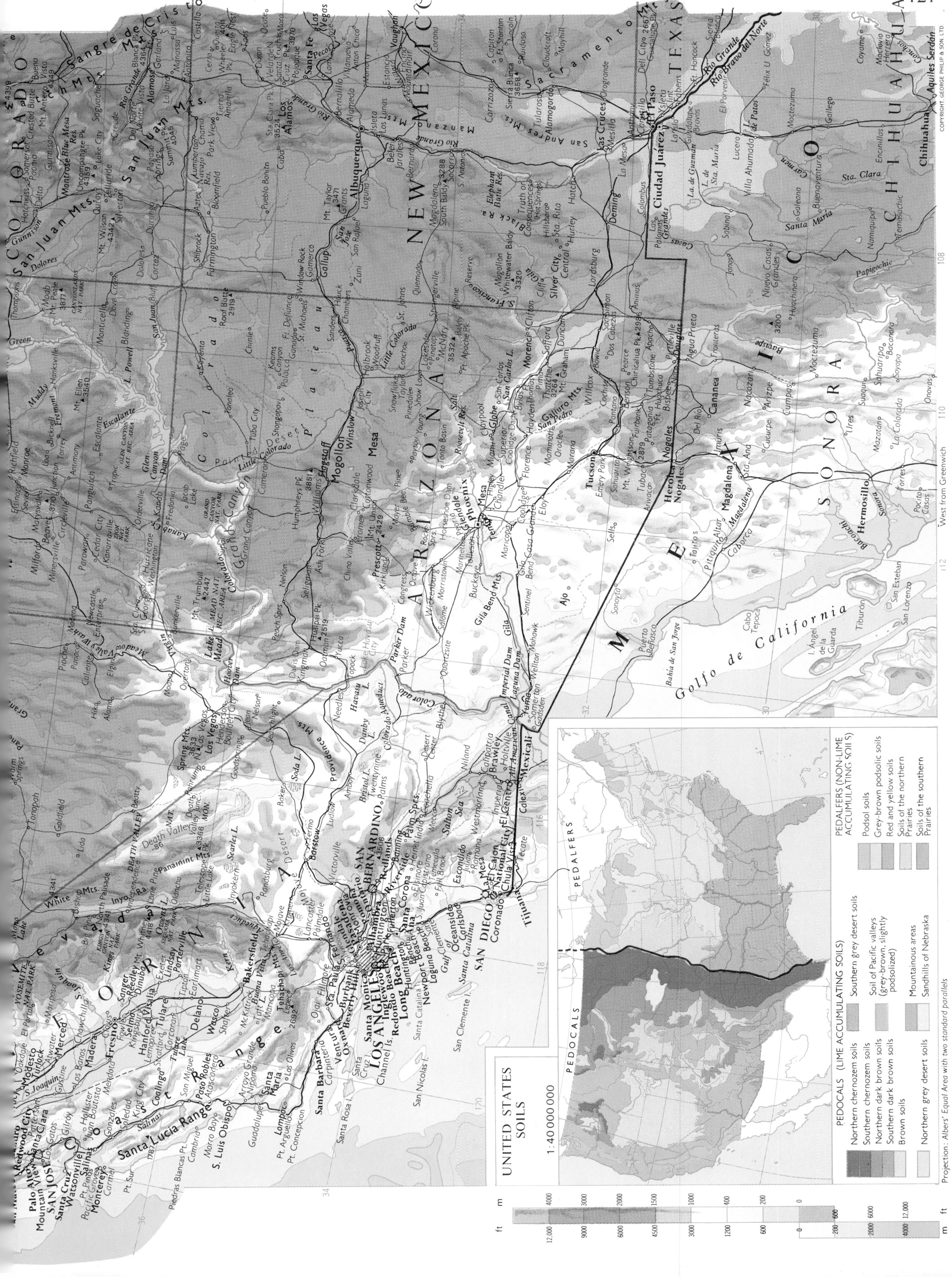
COLORADO
NEW MEXICO
ARIZONA
NEVADA
CALIFORNIA
TEXAS
MEXICO
SONORA
CHIHUAHUA
Colorado Plateau
Golfo de California
Coast Range
Santa Lucia Range
San Juan Mts.
Sangre de Cristo Mts.
Sacramento Mts.
San Andres Mts.
LOS ANGELES
SAN DIEGO
SAN BERNARDINO
Long Beach
Santa Barbara
Bakersfield
Fresno
SAN JOSE
Las Vegas
Phoenix
Tucson
Albuquerque
Santa Fe
El Paso
Ciudad Juárez
Chihuahua
Hermosillo
Mexicali
Tijuana
Yuma
Flagstaff
Grand Canyon
Death Valley
Salton Sea
Lake Mead
Hoover Dam
West from Greenwich
UNITED STATES SOILS
1: 40 000 000
PEDOCALS
PEDALFERS
PEDOCALS (LIME ACCUMULATING SOILS)
Northern chernozem soils
Southern chernozem soils
Northern dark brown soils
Southern dark brown soils
Brown soils
Northern grey desert soils
Southern grey desert soils
Soil of Pacific valleys (grey-brown, slightly podsolized)
Mountainous areas
Sandhills of Nebraska
PEDALFERS (NON-LIME ACCUMULATING SOILS)
Podsol soils
Grey-brown podsolic soils
Red and yellow soils
Soils of the northern Prairies
Soils of the southern Prairies
Projection: Albers' Equal Area with two standard parallels
COPYRIGHT GEORGE PHILIP & SON LTD
m
ft
4000
3000
2000
1500
1000
400
200
0
12 000
9000
6000
4500
3000
1200
600
0

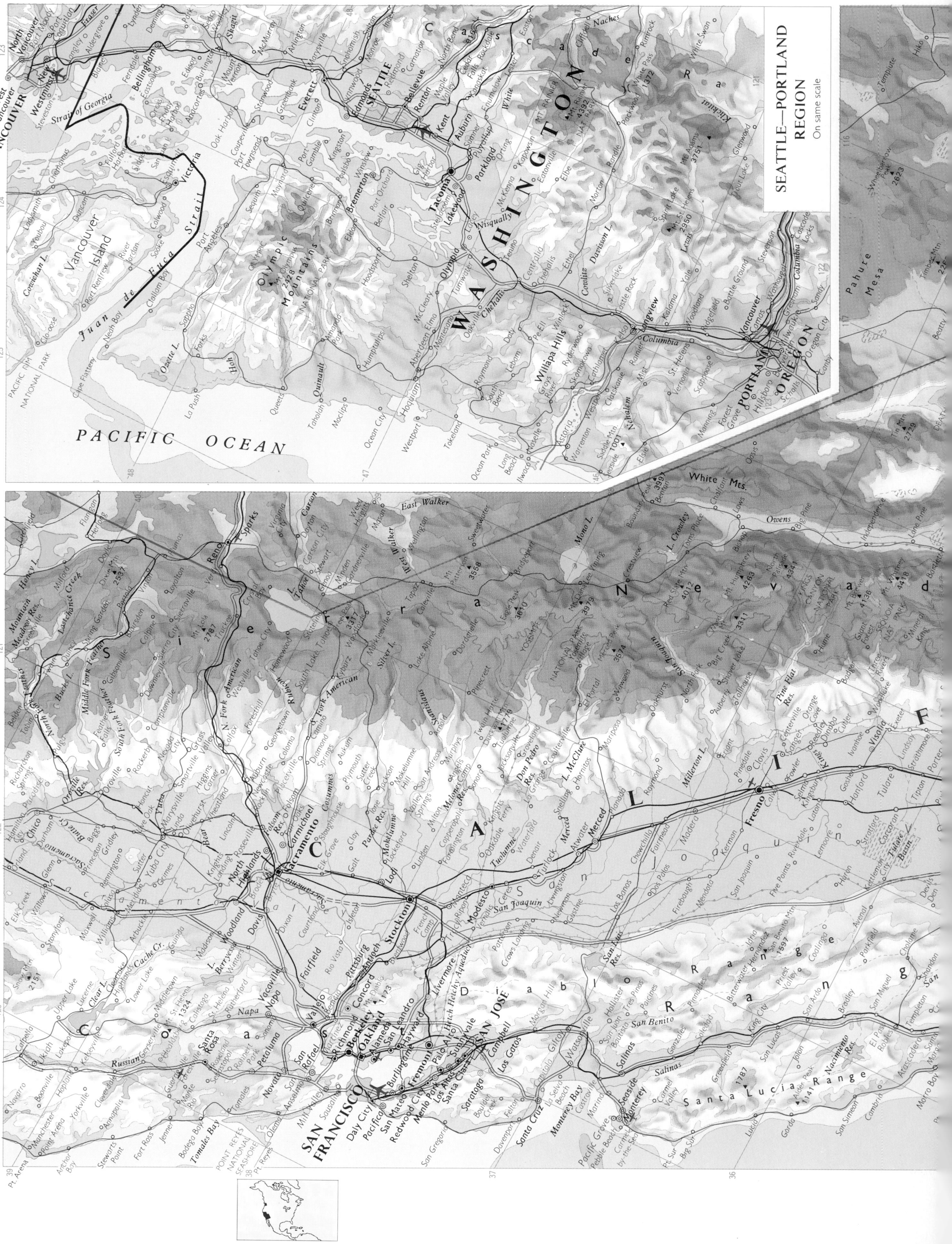
SEATTLE—PORTLAND REGION
On same scale
PACIFIC OCEAN
WASHINGTON
OREGON
Cascade Range
Vancouver Island
Strait of Georgia
Juan de Fuca Strait
Olympic Mountains
VANCOUVER
Victoria
Bellingham
Everett
SEATTLE
Bellevue
Renton
Kent
Tacoma
Bremerton
Olympia
Longview
Vancouver
PORTLAND
Willapa Hills
Mt. Rainier 4392
Mt. St. Helens 2950
Mt. Adams 3751
White Mts.
Pahute Mesa
Sierra Nevada
CALIFORNIA
Sacramento
Stockton
Modesto
Merced
Fresno
Visalia
SAN FRANCISCO
Oakland
Berkeley
SAN JOSE
Santa Rosa
Monterey
Salinas
Santa Lucia Range
Diablo Range
Coast Ranges
San Joaquin
L. Tahoe
Mono L.
Reno
Carson
Monterey Bay
Tomales Bay
Pacific Grove

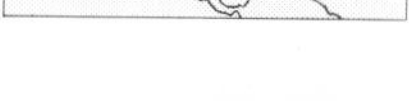

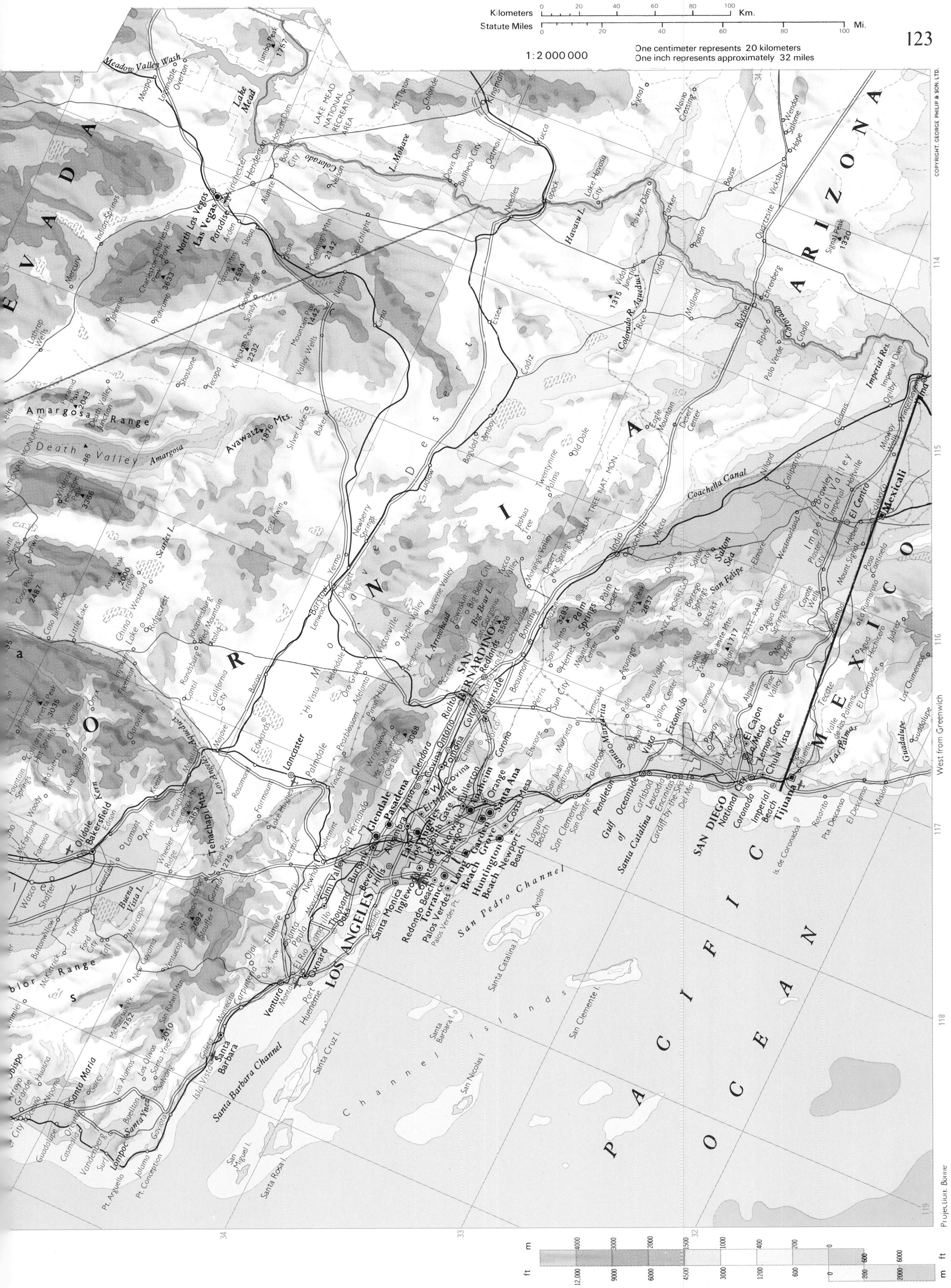
Kilometers 0 20 40 60 80 100 Km.
Statute Miles 0 20 40 60 80 100 Mi.
1:2 000 000
One centimeter represents 20 kilometers
One inch represents approximately 32 miles
COPYRIGHT, GEORGE PHILIP & SON, LTD.
NEVADA
ARIZONA
CALIFORNIA
MEXICO
PACIFIC OCEAN
Mojave Desert
Meadow Valley Wash
Lake Mead
LAKE MEAD NATIONAL RECREATION AREA
Hoover Dam
Boulder City
Henderson
Las Vegas
North Las Vegas
Paradise
Colorado
L. Mohave
Davis Dam
Bullhead City
Kingman
Needles
Topock
Havasu L.
Lake Havasu City
Parker Dam
Parker
Poston
Quartzsite
Blythe
Ehrenberg
Imperial Res.
Imperial Dam
Yuma
Signal Peak 1320
Amargosa Range
Death Valley
DEATH VALLEY NATIONAL MONUMENT
Avawatz Mts.
Searles L.
Ridgecrest
China Lake
Barstow
Victorville
Hesperia
Lancaster
Palmdale
Mojave
Tehachapi Mts.
Bakersfield
Kern
Buena Vista L.
Twentynine Palms
JOSHUA TREE NAT. MON.
Colorado R. Aqueduct
Coachella Canal
Indio
Coachella
Palm Springs
Palm Desert
Salton Sea
Imperial Valley
El Centro
Brawley
Calexico
Mexicali
SAN BERNARDINO
Redlands
Riverside
Big Bear L.
L. Arrowhead
Pomona
Ontario
Glendale
Pasadena
LOS ANGELES
Long Beach
Anaheim
Santa Ana
Orange
Huntington Beach
Newport Beach
Costa Mesa
Torrance
Inglewood
Santa Monica
Burbank
Beverly Hills
Thousand Oaks
Simi Valley
Oxnard
Ventura
Port Hueneme
Santa Barbara
Santa Barbara Channel
Santa Maria
Lompoc
Pt. Arguello
Pt. Conception
San Miguel I.
Santa Rosa I.
Santa Cruz I.
Anacapa I.
Santa Barbara I.
San Nicolas I.
Santa Catalina I.
Avalon
San Clemente I.
Channel Islands
San Pedro Channel
Gulf of Santa Catalina
San Clemente
Oceanside
Escondido
Vista
SAN DIEGO
National City
Chula Vista
Coronado
Imperial Beach
El Cajon
La Mesa
Lemon Grove
Tijuana
Tecate
Ensenada
Is. de Coronados
Rosarito
West from Greenwich
Projection: Bonne
m ft
4000 12,000
3000 9000
2000 6000
1500 4500
1000 3000
400 1200
200 600
0 0
200 600
2000 6000

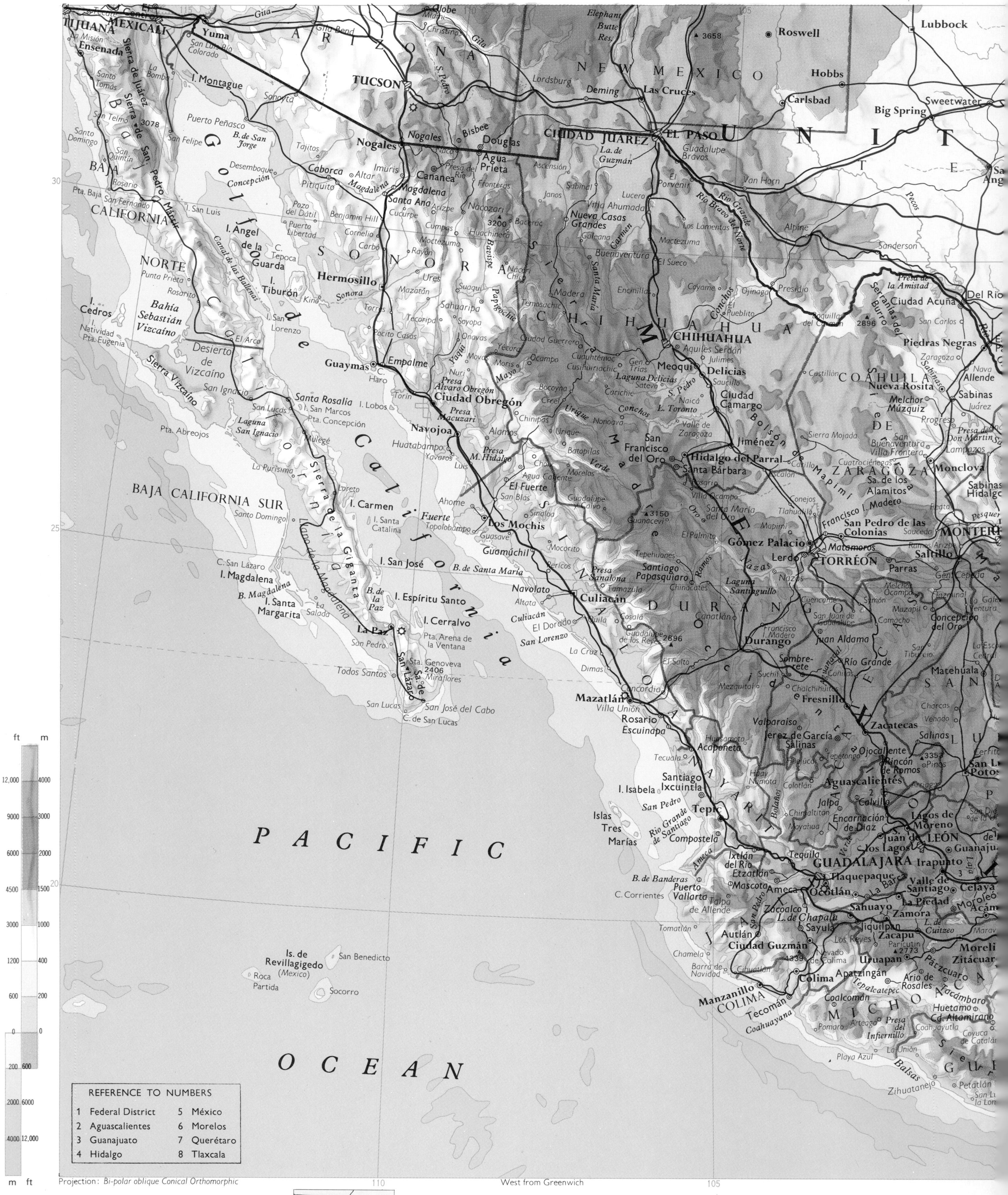
PACIFIC
OCEAN
Golfo de California
BAJA CALIFORNIA NORTE
BAJA CALIFORNIA SUR
SONORA
CHIHUAHUA
SINALOA
DURANGO
NAYARIT
JALISCO
COLIMA
MICHOACÁN
ZACATECAS
COAHUILA
ARIZONA
NEW MEXICO
Sierra Madre Occidental
Bolsón de Mapimí
Desierto de Vizcaíno
Sierra Vizcaíno
Sierra de la Giganta
Llano de la Magdalena
Sierra de San Pedro Mártir
Sierra de Juárez
Tijuana
Mexicali
Ensenada
Yuma
Tucson
Nogales
Hermosillo
Guaymas
Empalme
Ciudad Obregón
Navojoa
Los Mochis
Culiacán
Mazatlán
Chihuahua
Ciudad Juárez
El Paso
Las Cruces
Deming
Roswell
Hobbs
Carlsbad
Lubbock
Big Spring
Sweetwater
Delicias
Hidalgo del Parral
Jiménez
Torreón
Gómez Palacio
Lerdo
Durango
Fresnillo
Zacatecas
Aguascalientes
Tepic
Guadalajara
Tlaquepaque
Irapuato
Celaya
León
Colima
Manzanillo
Uruapan
Zamora
Monclova
Piedras Negras
Ciudad Acuña
Saltillo
Santa Rosalía
La Paz
San José del Cabo
C. de San Lucas
Todos Santos
I. Cedros
I. Tiburón
I. Angel de la Guarda
I. Carmen
I. Espíritu Santo
I. Cerralvo
Islas Tres Marías
Is. de Revillagigedo (Mexico)
San Benedicto
Socorro
Roca Partida
L. de Chapala
REFERENCE TO NUMBERS
1 Federal District
2 Aguascalientes
3 Guanajuato
4 Hidalgo
5 México
6 Morelos
7 Querétaro
8 Tlaxcala
ft m
12,000 4000
9000 3000
6000 2000
4500 1500
3000 1000
1200 400
600 200
0 0
200 600
2000 6000
4000 12,000
m ft
Projection: Bi-polar oblique Conical Orthomorphic
West from Greenwich
110
105

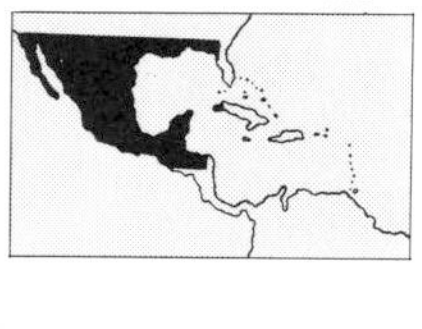

Kilometers 0 50 100 150 200 250 300 Km.
Statute Miles 0 50 100 150 200 250 300 Mi.

1:6 400 000

One centimeter represents 64 kilometers
One inch represents approximately 100 miles

GULF OF MEXICO
Golfo de Campeche
Canal de Yucatán
Golfo de Honduras
Golfo de Tehuantepec
ARKANSAS
MISSISSIPPI
ALABAMA
GEORGIA
FLORIDA
LOUISIANA
STATES
YUCATÁN
CAMPECHE
TABASCO
QUINTANA ROO
CHIAPAS
OAXACA
PUEBLA
VERACRUZ
GUATEMALA
BELIZE
HONDURAS
CUBA
Dallas
Fort Worth
Houston
San Antonio
Austin
Galveston
Corpus Christi
Brownsville
Matamoros
Shreveport
Baton Rouge
New Orleans
Mobile
Pensacola
Panama City
Tallahassee
Jackson
Montgomery
Columbus
Tampico
Tuxpan
Veracruz
Jalapa
Mexico
Puebla
Oaxaca
Acapulco
Coatzacoalcos
Villahermosa
Ciudad del Carmen
Campeche
Mérida
Progreso
Cozumel
Belize City
Guatemala
Tegucigalpa
San Pedro Sula
Puerto Barrios
Clearwater

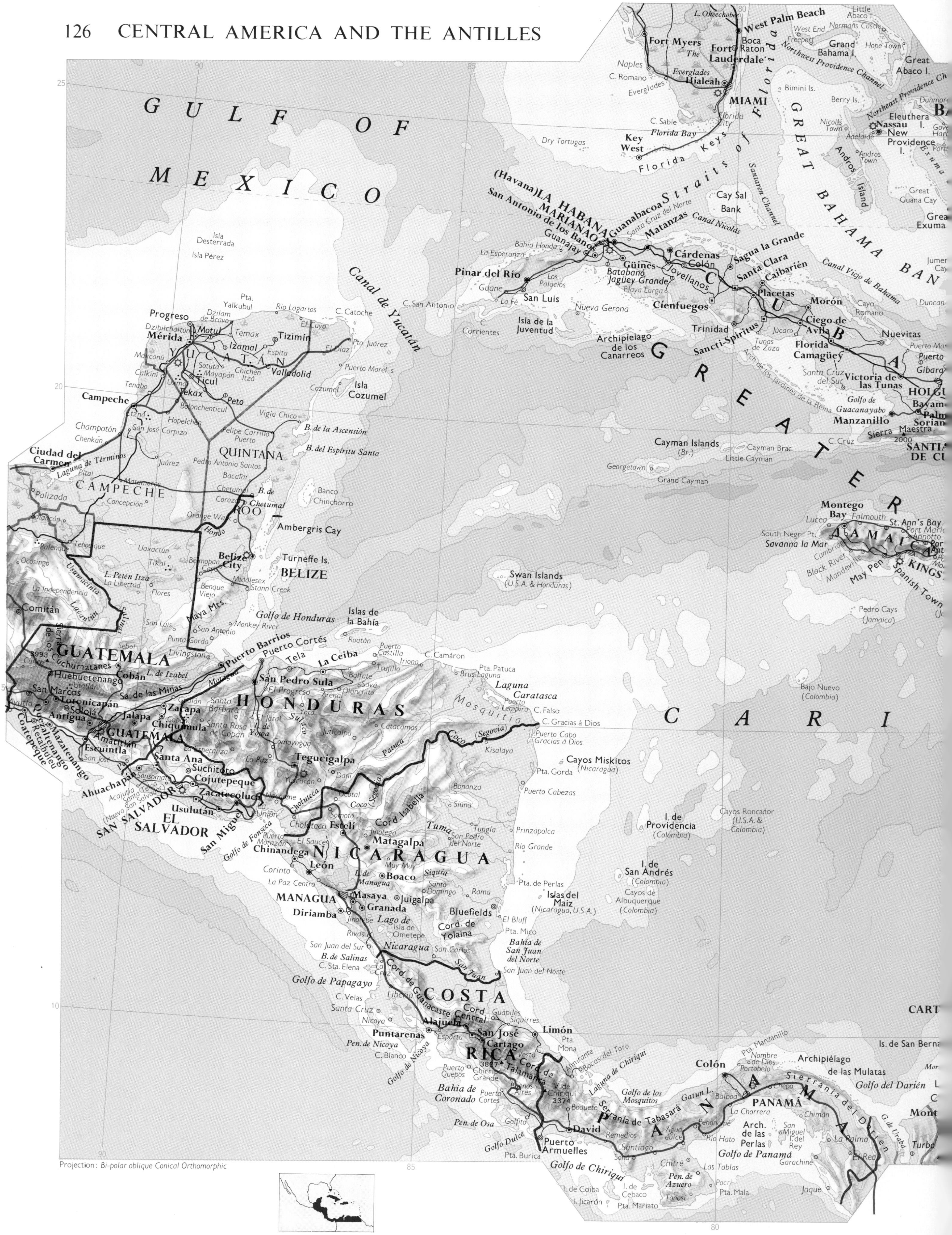
GULF OF MEXICO
Straits of Florida
Florida Keys
GREAT BAHAMA BANK
GREATER
CUBA
CARI
L. Okeechobee
West Palm Beach
Fort Myers
Boca Raton
Fort Lauderdale
Naples
C. Romano
Everglades
Hialeah
MIAMI
C. Sable
Florida Bay
Florida City
Key West
Dry Tortugas
Bimini Is.
Berry Is.
Grand Bahama I.
Freeport
West End
Northwest Providence Channel
Northeast Providence Channel
Great Abaco I.
Little Abaco I.
Eleuthera I.
Nassau
New Providence I.
Andros Island
Andros Town
Nicolls Town
Adelaide
Great Guana Cay
Great Exuma
Cay Sal Bank
Santaren Channel
Canal Nicolás
Canal Viejo de Bahama
(Havana) LA HABANA
MARIANAO
Guanabacoa
San Antonio de los Baños
Guanajay
Bahía Honda
La Esperanza
Matanzas
Santa Cruz del Norte
Cárdenas
Colón
Sagua la Grande
Güines
Batabanó
Jagüey Grande
Jovellanos
Playa Larga
Santa Clara
Caibarién
Pinar del Río
Guane
Los Palacios
La Fé
San Luis
C. San Antonio
C. Corrientes
Nueva Gerona
Isla de la Juventud
Archipiélago de los Canarreos
Cienfuegos
Trinidad
Placetas
Sancti-Spíritus
Tunas de Zaza
Morón
Ciego de Avila
Júcaro
Cayo Romano
Nuevitas
Florida
Camagüey
Arch. de los Jardines de la Reina
Santa Cruz del Sur
Victoria de las Tunas
Golfo de Guacanayabo
Manzanillo
Bayamo
Sierra Maestra
C. Cruz
Cayman Islands (Br.)
Cayman Brac
Little Cayman
Georgetown
Grand Cayman
Montego Bay
Falmouth
St. Ann's Bay
Lucea
South Negril Pt.
Savanna la Mar
Black River
Mandeville
May Pen
Spanish Town
JAMAICA
Pedro Cays (Jamaica)
Swan Islands (U.S.A. & Honduras)
Bajo Nuevo (Colombia)
Canal de Yucatán
Isla Desterrada
Isla Pérez
Progreso
Dzilam de Bravo
Pta. Yalkubul
Río Lagartos
C. Catoche
El Cuyo
Mérida
Dzibilchaltún
Motul
Temax
Tizimín
Izamal
Espita
Maxcanú
Sotuta
Mayapán
Chichén Itzá
Valladolid
Calkiní
Uxmal
Ticul
Tenabo
Tekax
Peto
YUCATÁN
Pto. Juárez
Puerto Morelos
Cozumel
Isla Cozumel
Campeche
Champotón
Chenkán
Hopelchén
Bolonchenticul
José Carpizo
Felipe Carrillo Puerto
Vigía Chico
B. de la Ascensión
B. del Espíritu Santo
Ciudad del Carmen
Laguna de Términos
QUINTANA ROO
CAMPECHE
Palizada
Juárez
Pedro Antonio Santos
Bacalar
Concepción
Chetumal
B. de Chetumal
Banco Chinchorro
Ambergris Cay
Hondo
Palenque
Tenosique
Uaxactún
Tikal
Belmopan
Belize City
Turneffe Is.
BELIZE
L. Petén Itzá
La Libertad
Flores
Benque Viejo
Middlesex
Stann Creek
Ocosingo
La Independencia
Usumacinta
Comitán
Maya Mts.
San Luis
Golfo de Honduras
Monkey River
Islas de la Bahía
Punta Gorda
San Antonio
Roatán
GUATEMALA
Cuchumatanes
Huehuetenango
Cobán
L. de Izabel
Livingston
Puerto Barrios
Puerto Cortés
Tela
La Ceiba
Puerto Castilla
Trujillo
C. Camarón
Pta. Patuca
Brus Laguna
Laguna Caratasca
Puerto Lempira
C. Falso
C. Gracias á Dios
Puerto Cabo Gracias á Dios
San Marcos
Totonicapán
Sololá
Antigua
Sa. de las Minas
Zacapa
Jalapa
Chiquimula
GUATEMALA
Amatitlán
Escuintla
San José
Quezaltenango
Mazatenango
Retalhuleu
Coatepeque
San Pedro Sula
El Progreso
HONDURAS
Santa Bárbara
Santa Rosa de Copán
Yoro
Olanchito
Catacamas
Juticalpa
Mosquitia
Coco (Segovia)
Kisalaya
Cayos Miskitos (Nicaragua)
Pta. Gorda
Puerto Cabezas
Tegucigalpa
Patuca
Yuscarán
Danlí
Comayagua
La Paz
Santa Ana
Suchitoto
Cojutepeque
Ahuachapán
Sonsonate
Acajutla
Zacatecoluca
(Nueva San Salvador)
SAN SALVADOR
EL SALVADOR
Usulután
San Miguel
La Unión
Choluteca
Estelí
Ocotal
Cord. Isabella
Bonanza
Siuna
Tuma
Tungla
Prinzapolca
Río Grande
San Pedro del Norte
Golfo de Fonseca
Puerto Morazán
El Sauce
Jinotega
Matagalpa
NICARAGUA
Chinandega
León
Corinto
La Paz Centro
Muy Muy
L. de Managua
Boaco
Siquia
Santo Domingo
Rama
Pta. de Perlas
Islas del Maíz (Nicaragua, U.S.A.)
MANAGUA
Masaya
Granada
Juigalpa
Diriamba
Jinotepe
Lago de Nicaragua
Isla de Ometepe
Bluefields
El Bluff
Cord. de Yolaina
Pta. Mico
Rivas
San Juan del Sur
B. de Salinas
C. Sta. Elena
San Carlos
Bahía de San Juan del Norte
San Juan del Norte
San Juan
Golfo de Papagayo
C. Velas
Santa Cruz
Liberia
Cord. de Guanacaste
COSTA RICA
Cord. Central
Guápiles
Siquirres
Nicoya
Alajuela
Esparta
Puntarenas
San José
Cartago
Limón
Pta. Mona
Pen. de Nicoya
C. Blanco
Golfo de Nicoya
Puerto Quepos
Chirripó Grande
Cord. de Talamanca
Almirante
Bocas del Toro
Laguna de Chiriquí
Bahía de Coronado
Puerto Cortés
Buenos Aires
V. de Chiriquí
Boquete
Pen. de Osa
Golfito
Golfo Dulce
Puerto Armuelles
Pta. Burica
David
Golfo de Chiriquí
Golfo de los Mosquitos
Serranía de Tabasará
Remedios
Santiago
Soná
Aguadulce
Penonomé
Río Hato
Chitré
Las Tablas
Pen. de Azuero
Tonosí
Pocrí
Pta. Mala
I. de Coiba
I. Jicarón
I. de Cebaco
Pta. Mariato
Colón
Nombre de Dios
Portobelo
Pta. Manzanillo
Gatun L.
Balboa
PANAMÁ
La Chorrera
Chepo
Chimán
Arch. de las Perlas
San Miguel
I. del Rey
Golfo de Panamá
Garachiné
Jaque
La Palma
El Real
Serranía del Darién
G. de Urabá
Archipiélago de las Mulatas
Golfo del Darién
Is. de San Bernardo
Turbo
I. de Providencia (Colombia)
Cayos Roncador (U.S.A. & Colombia)
I. de San Andrés (Colombia)
Cayos de Albuquerque (Colombia)
Projection: Bi-polar oblique Conical Orthomorphic

Kilometers 0 50 100 150 200 250 300 Km.
Statute Miles 0 50 100 150 200 250 300 Mi.

1:6 400 000

One centimeter represents 64 kilometers
One inch represents approximately 100 miles

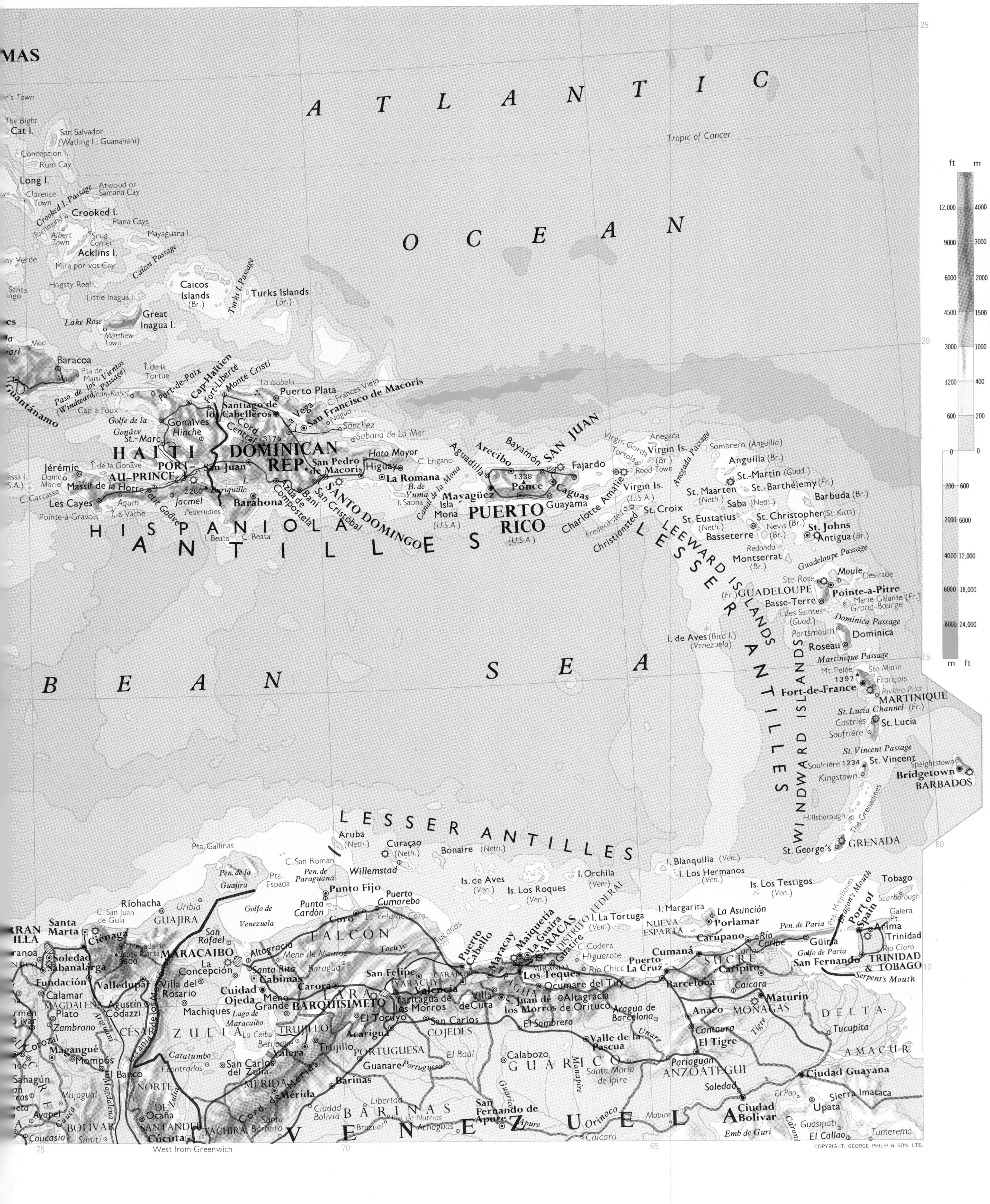

ATLANTIC OCEAN
Tropic of Cancer
CARIBBEAN SEA
HISPANIOLA
ANTILLES
LESSER ANTILLES
LEEWARD ISLANDS
WINDWARD ISLANDS
HAITI
DOMINICAN REP.
PUERTO RICO (U.S.A.)
SAN JUAN
SANTO DOMINGO
PORT-AU-PRINCE
Cat I.
San Salvador (Watling I., Guanahani)
Conception I.
Rum Cay
Long I.
Clarence Town
Atwood or Samana Cay
Crooked I. Passage
Crooked I.
Plana Cays
Mayaguana I.
Acklins I.
Mira por vos Cay
Caicos Passage
Hogsty Reef
Little Inagua I.
Caicos Islands (Br.)
Turks I. Passage
Turks Islands (Br.)
Great Inagua I.
Lake Rose
Matthew Town
Baracoa
Guantánamo
Paso de los Vientos (Windward Passage)
Cap-à-Foux
Golfe de la Gonâve
Port-de-Paix
Cap-Haïtien
Fort-Liberté
Monte Cristi
Puerto Plata
Santiago de los Cabelleros
La Vega
San Francisco de Macorís
Gonaïves
Hinche
St.-Marc
Cord. Central
3175
Sánchez
Sabana de La Mar
Hato Mayor
Jérémie
Massif de la Hotte
2280
Jacmel
Les Cayes
Barahona
Enriquillo
Azua de Compostela
Baní
San Cristóbal
San Pedro de Macorís
Higüey
La Romana
I. Saona
Canal de la Mona
Isla Mona (U.S.A.)
Aguadilla
Mayagüez
Arecibo
Bayamón
Fajardo
1338
Ponce
Caguas
Guayama
Virgin Is. (Br.)
Road Town
Virgin Is. (U.S.A.)
Charlotte Amalie
Christiansted
Frederiksted
St. Croix
Anegada
Anegada Passage
Sombrero (Anguilla)
Anguilla (Br.)
St.-Martin (Guad.)
St. Maarten (Neth.)
St.-Barthélemy (Fr.)
Barbuda (Br.)
Saba (Neth.)
St. Eustatius (Neth.)
St. Christopher (St. Kitts)
Nevis (Br.)
Basseterre
St. Johns
Antigua (Br.)
Redonda
Montserrat (Br.)
Guadeloupe Passage
GUADELOUPE (Fr.)
Pointe-a-Pitre
Basse-Terre
Marie-Galante (Fr.)
Grand-Bourg
I. des Saintes (Guad.)
Dominica Passage
Dominica
Portsmouth
Roseau
I. de Aves (Bird I.) (Venezuela)
Martinique Passage
Mt. Pelée 1397
Fort-de-France
MARTINIQUE (Fr.)
St. Lucia Channel
Castries
St. Lucia
Soufrière
St. Vincent Passage
Soufrière 1234
St. Vincent
Kingstown
Bridgetown
BARBADOS
The Grenadines
Hillsborough
St. George's
GRENADA
Aruba (Neth.)
Curaçao (Neth.)
Willemstad
Bonaire (Neth.)
Pta. Gallinas
Pen. de la Guajira
C. San Román
Pen. de Paraguaná
Punto Fijo
Puerto Cumarebo
Is. de Aves (Ven.)
Is. Los Roques (Ven.)
I. Orchila (Ven.)
I. Blanquilla (Ven.)
I. Los Hermanos (Ven.)
Is. Los Testigos (Ven.)
Tobago
Scarborough
I. Margarita
La Asunción
Porlamar
I. La Tortuga (Ven.)
NUEVA ESPARTA
Ríohacha
Santa Marta
Ciénaga
GUAJIRA
Golfo de Venezuela
Coro
FALCÓN
MARACAIBO
Cabimas
Valledupar
Barranquilla
Soledad
Sabanalarga
Puerto Cabello
Maracay
Maiquetía
La Guaira
CARACAS
DISTRITO FEDERAL
Los Teques
MIRANDA
Cumaná
SUCRE
Carúpano
Puerto La Cruz
Barcelona
Caripito
Maturín
MONAGAS
Golfo de Paria
Güiria
Port of Spain
Arima
TRINIDAD & TOBAGO
San Fernando
Serpent's Mouth
Dragon's Mouth
San Felipe
YARACUY
Valencia
BARQUISIMETO
LARA
Carora
El Tocuyo
Acarigua
PORTUGUESA
San Carlos
COJEDES
ARAGUA
Villa de Cura
Ocumare del Tuy
Altagracia de Orituco
San Juan de los Morros
Aragua de Barcelona
Anaco
Cantaura
El Tigre
ANZOÁTEGUI
DELTA AMACURO
Tucupita
El Sombrero
Valle de la Pascua
GUÁRICO
Calabozo
Santa María de Ipire
Pariaguán
Soledad
Ciudad Guayana
Ciudad Bolívar
Sierra Imataca
Upata
Guasipati
El Callao
Tumeremo
Emb de Guri
ZULIA
Lago de Maracaibo
Machiques
TRUJILLO
Valera
Trujillo
San Carlos del Zulia
MÉRIDA
Mérida
Cord. de Mérida
Barinas
BARINAS
Guanare
San Fernando de Apure
TÁCHIRA
Cúcuta
NORTE DE SANTANDER
Ocaña
El Banco
Magangué
Mompós
CÉSAR
MAGDALENA
Plato
Zambrano
Corozal
Sahagún
BOLÍVAR
Caucasia
VENEZUELA
Orinoco
Caicara
ft m
12,000 4000
9000 3000
6000 2000
4500 1500
3000 1000
1200 400
600 200
0 0
200 600
2000 6000
4000 12,000
6000 18,000
8000 24,000
m ft
75
70
65
60
25
20
15
10
West from Greenwich

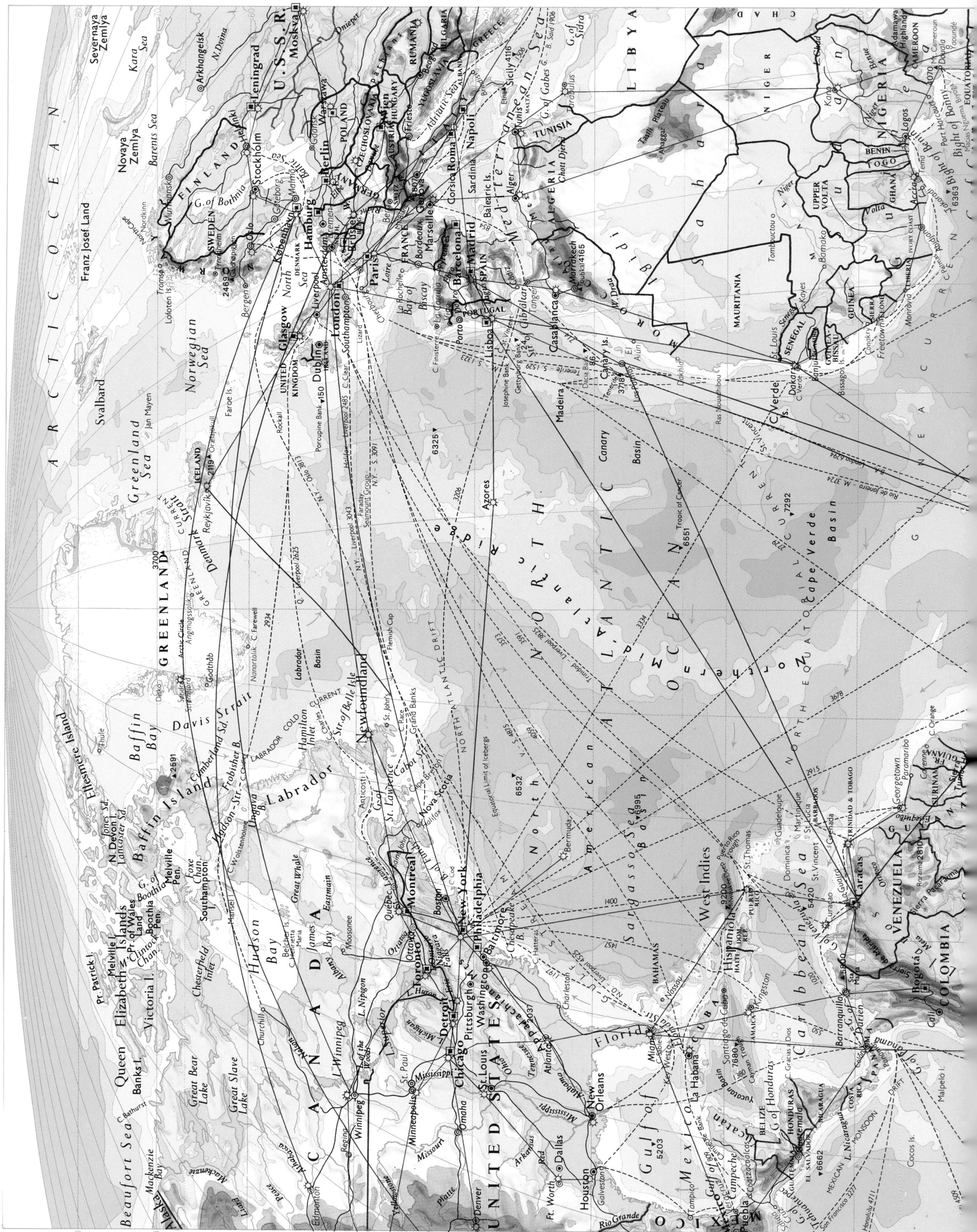
ARCTIC OCEAN
Franz Josef Land
Svalbard
Greenland Sea
Jan Mayen
Norwegian Sea
Barents Sea
Novaya Zemlya
Kara Sea
Severnaya Zemlya
Arkhangelsk
Leningrad
Moskva
U.S.S.R.
FINLAND
Helsinki
Stockholm
SWEDEN
Oslo
G. of Bothnia
Baltic Sea
København
DENMARK
North Sea
Hamburg
Berlin
POLAND
Warszawa
CZECHOSLOVAKIA
AUSTRIA
HUNGARY
RUMANIA
YUGOSLAVIA
BULGARIA
ALBANIA
GREECE
Adriatic Sea
Napoli
Roma
Corsica
Sardinia
Sicily
Mediterranean Sea
Balearic Is.
Marseille
Barcelona
Madrid
SPAIN
PORTUGAL
Lisboa
Bordeaux
Bay of Biscay
FRANCE
Paris
Bruxelles
Amsterdam
London
Southampton
UNITED KINGDOM
Glasgow
Liverpool
Dublin
IRELAND
Faroe Is.
Bergen
Lofoten Is.
ICELAND
Reykjavik
Denmark Strait
GREENLAND
Godthåb
C. Farewell
Davis Strait
Baffin Bay
Baffin Island
Ellesmere Island
Cumberland Sd.
Frobisher B.
Hudson Str.
Ungava B.
Labrador
Labrador Basin
Newfoundland
St. John's
Grand Banks
Str. of Belle Isle
G. of St. Lawrence
Nova Scotia
Cabot Str.
Hudson Bay
James Bay
Queen Elizabeth Islands
Victoria I.
Banks I.
Beaufort Sea
Great Bear Lake
Great Slave Lake
CANADA
Winnipeg
L. Winnipeg
L. Superior
L. Michigan
L. Huron
Montreal
Quebec
Ottawa
Toronto
Detroit
Chicago
Minneapolis
St. Louis
Pittsburgh
Washington
Baltimore
Philadelphia
New York
Boston
UNITED STATES
Denver
Omaha
Dallas
Houston
New Orleans
Atlanta
Miami
Florida
Gulf of Mexico
Yucatan Basin
La Habana
CUBA
BAHAMAS
Hispaniola
HAITI
DOM. REP.
PUERTO RICO
Caribbean Sea
West Indies
Bermuda
Sargasso Sea
North American Basin
NORTH ATLANTIC OCEAN
Mid-Atlantic Ridge
Azores
Madeira
Canary Is.
Canary Basin
Cape Verde Is.
Cape Verde Basin
Tropic of Cancer
NORTH ATLANTIC DRIFT
LABRADOR COLD CURRENT
NORTH EQUATORIAL CURRENT
GUATEMALA
HONDURAS
NICARAGUA
COSTA RICA
PANAMA
COLOMBIA
Bogotá
VENEZUELA
Caracas
GUYANA
SURINAM
Georgetown
Paramaribo
TRINIDAD & TOBAGO
MEXICO
Monterrey
MOROCCO
Casablanca
ALGERIA
Alger
TUNISIA
Tunis
LIBYA
Sahara
MAURITANIA
SENEGAL
Dakar
NIGER
MALI
UPPER VOLTA
GHANA
TOGO
BENIN
NIGERIA
Lagos
CAMEROON
CHAD
GUINEA
SIERRA LEONE
Freetown
LIBERIA
Monrovia
IVORY COAST
Abidjan
Accra
Bight of Benin
Bight of Bonny
GUINEA-BISSAU

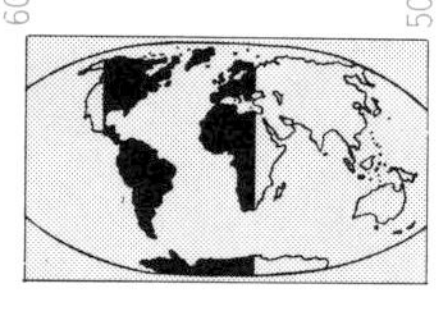

Kilometers 0 300 600 900 1200 1500 Km.
Statute Miles 0 300 600 900 1200 1500 Mi.

1:36 000 000

One centimeter represents 360 kilometers
One inch represents approximately 570 miles

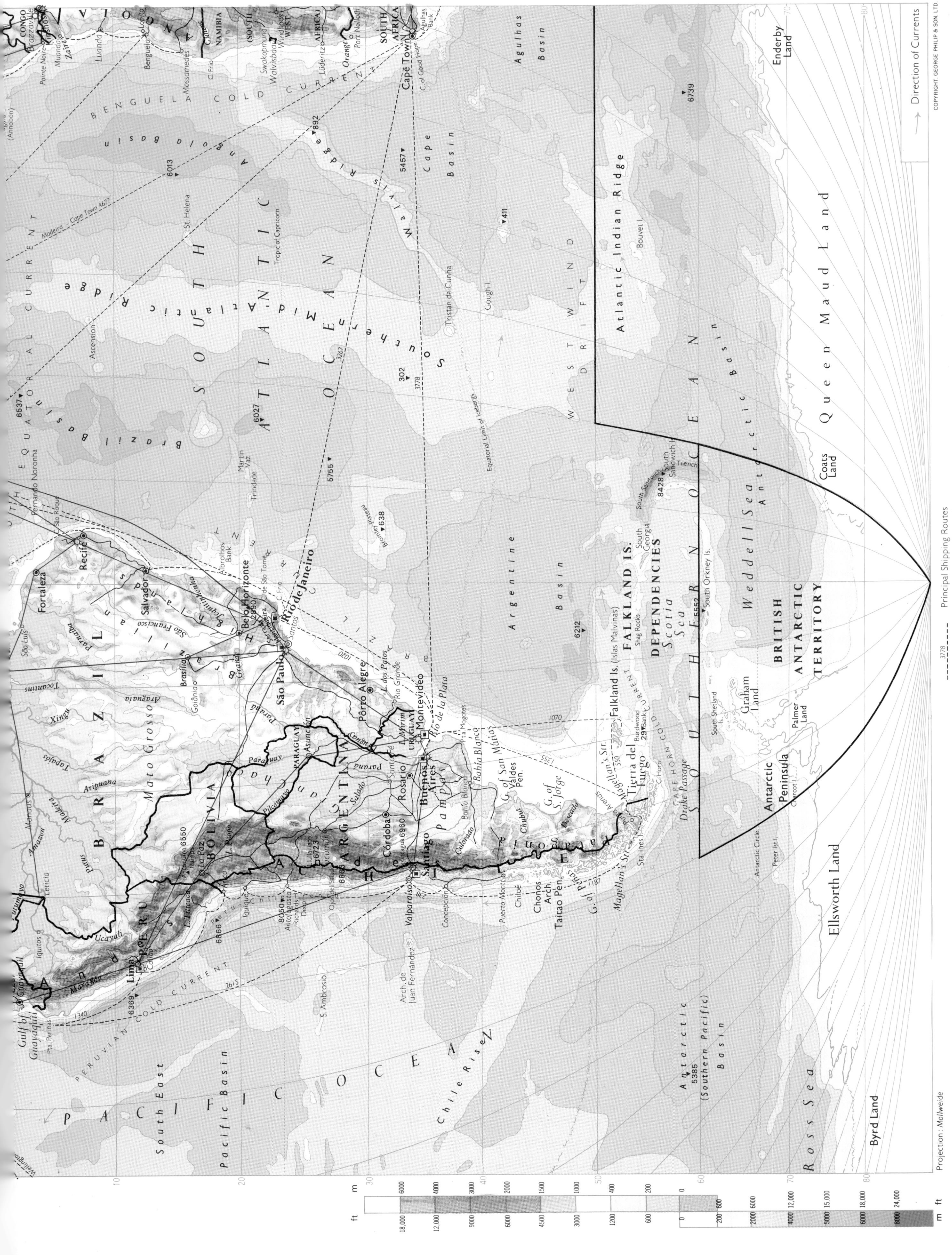

SOUTH ATLANTIC OCEAN
PACIFIC OCEAN
SOUTHERN OCEAN
BRAZIL
BOLIVIA
PERU
CHILE
ARGENTINA
PARAGUAY
URUGUAY
ANGOLA
NAMIBIA
SOUTH AFRICA
FALKLAND IS.
DEPENDENCIES
BRITISH ANTARCTIC TERRITORY
Falkland Is. (Islas Malvinas)
South Georgia
South Sandwich Is.
South Orkney Is.
South Shetland Is.
Scotia Sea
Weddell Sea
Ross Sea
Drake Passage
Antarctic Peninsula
Graham Land
Palmer Land
Ellsworth Land
Byrd Land
Queen Maud Land
Coats Land
Enderby Land
Tierra del Fuego
Magellan's Str.
Mato Grosso
Pampas
Rio de Janeiro
São Paulo
Buenos Aires
Montevideo
Santiago
Valparaiso
Córdoba
Rosario
Pôrto Alegre
Asunción
La Paz
Lima
Salvador
Recife
Fortaleza
Belo Horizonte
Brasília
Cape Town
Argentine Basin
Brazil Basin
Angola Basin
Cape Basin
Agulhas Basin
Mid-Atlantic Ridge
Walvis Ridge
Atlantic Indian Ridge
Chile Rise
South East Pacific Basin
Antarctic (Southern Pacific) Basin
WEST WIND DRIFT
BENGUELA COLD CURRENT
PERUVIAN COLD CURRENT
SOUTH EQUATORIAL CURRENT
BRAZIL CURRENT
CAPE HORN COLD CURRENT
Tristan da Cunha
Gough I.
St. Helena
Ascension
Bouvet I.
Trindade
Martin Vaz
Equatorial Limit of Icebergs
Tropic of Capricorn
Antarctic Circle
Direction of Currents
Principal Shipping Routes (Distances in Nautical Miles)
Projection: Mollweide
COPYRIGHT GEORGE PHILIP & SON. LTD.
m ft

Kilometers 0 200 400 600 800 1000 Km.
Statute Miles 0 200 400 600 800 1000 Mi.

1: 24 000 000

One centimeter represents 240 kilometers
One inch represents approximately 380 miles

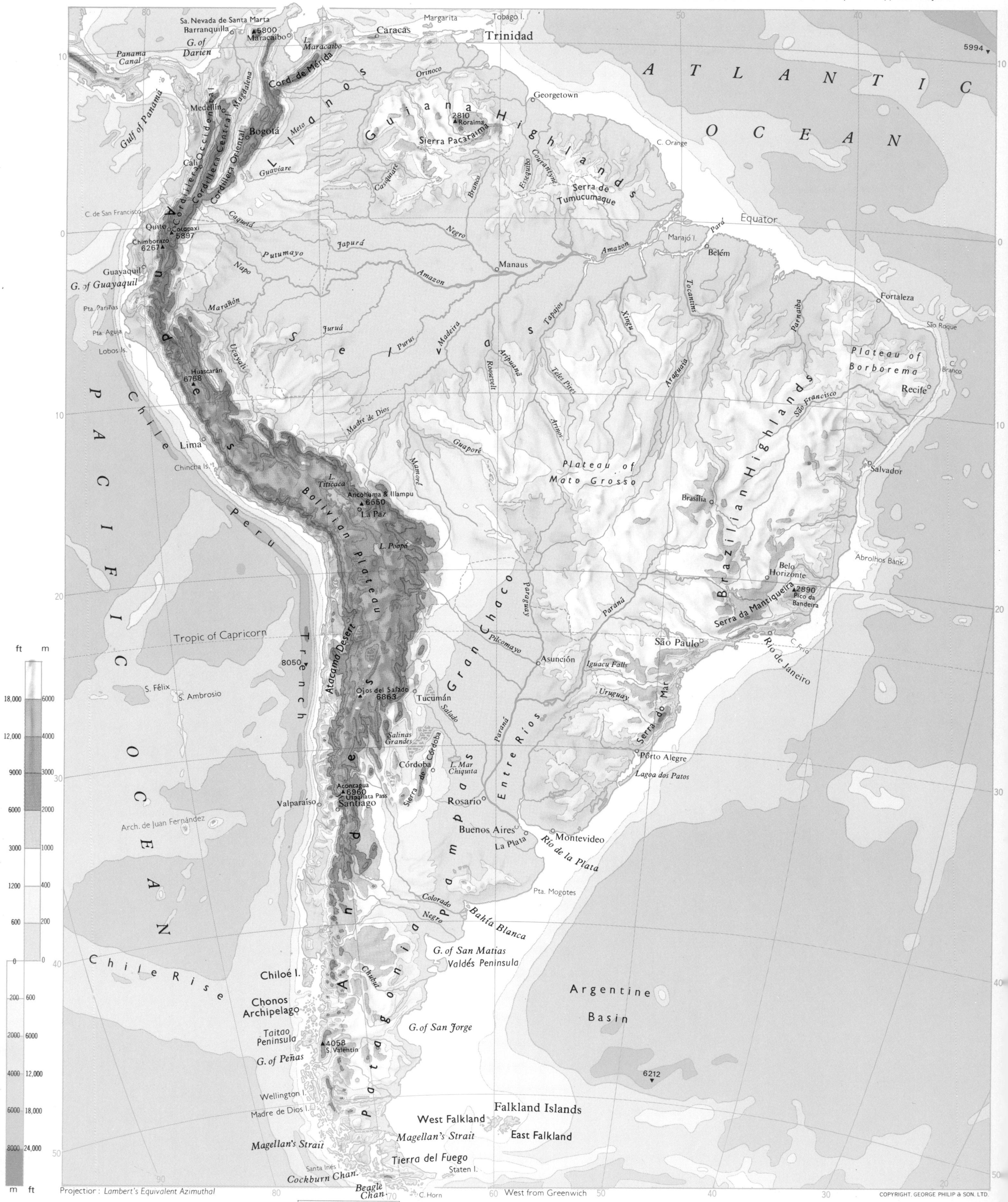
Sa. Nevada de Santa Marta
Barranquilla
5800
Maracaibo
G. of Darien
Panama Canal
L. Maracaibo
Cord. de Mérida
Caracas
Margarita
Tobago I.
Trinidad
5994
A T L A N T I C
O C E A N
Orinoco
Llanos
Guiana Highlands
2810 Roraima
Sierra Pacaraima
Georgetown
C. Orange
Medellín
Gulf of Panamá
Magdalena
Cordillera Occidental
Cordillera Central
Cordillera Oriental
Bogotá
Meta
Guaviare
Casiquiare
Branca
Essequibo
Courantyne
Serra de Tumucumaque
Cali
C. de San Francisco
Quito
Cotopaxi 5897
Chimborazo 6267
Caquetá
Negro
Equator
Pará
Marajó I.
Belém
Putumayo
Japurá
Amazon
Manaus
Guayaquil
G. of Guayaquil
Napo
Pta. Pariñas
Pta. Aguja
Marañón
Lobos Is.
Juruá
Purus
Madeira
Tapajós
Xingu
Tocantins
Parnaíba
Fortaleza
C. São Roque
Selvas
Ucayali
Aripuanã
Roosevelt
Teles Pires
Araguaia
Plateau of Borborema
C. Branco
Recife
Huascarán 6768
Andes
P A C I F I C   O C E A N
Chile Peru Trench
Madre de Dios
Guaporé
Arinos
São Francisco
Brazilian Highlands
Lima
Chincha Is.
Mamoré
Plateau of Mato Grosso
Salvador
L. Titicaca
Ancohuma & Illampu 6550
La Paz
Bolivian Plateau
Brasília
L. Poopó
Abrolhos Bank
Belo Horizonte
2890 Pico da Bandeira
Serra da Mantiqueira
Paraguay
Paraná
Gran Chaco
Tropic of Capricorn
Pilcomayo
São Paulo
C. Frio
Rio de Janeiro
Asunción
Iguaçu Falls
8050
Atacama Desert
S. Félix
S. Ambrosio
Ojos del Salado 6863
Tucumán
Salado
Uruguay
Serra do Mar
Entre Ríos
Salinas Grandes
Sierra de Córdoba
Córdoba
L. Mar Chiquita
Porto Alegre
Lagoa dos Patos
Aconcagua 6960
Uspallata Pass
Santiago
Valparaíso
Rosario
Pampas
Arch. de Juan Fernández
Buenos Aires
La Plata
Montevideo
Río de la Plata
Pta. Mogotes
Colorado
Negro
Bahía Blanca
G. of San Matías
Valdés Peninsula
Chile Rise
Chiloé I.
Chubut
Patagonia
Chonos Archipelago
Taitao Peninsula
G. of San Jorge
Argentine Basin
4058 S. Valentín
G. of Peñas
6212
Wellington I.
Madre de Dios I.
West Falkland
Falkland Islands
East Falkland
Magellan's Strait
Tierra del Fuego
Santa Inés I.
Staten I.
Cockburn Chan.
Beagle Chan.
C. Horn
West from Greenwich
ft m
18,000 6000
12,000 4000
9000 3000
6000 2000
3000 1000
1200 400
600 200
0 0
200 600
2000 6000
4000 12,000
6000 18,000
8000 24,000
m ft

Projection : Lambert's Equivalent Azimuthal

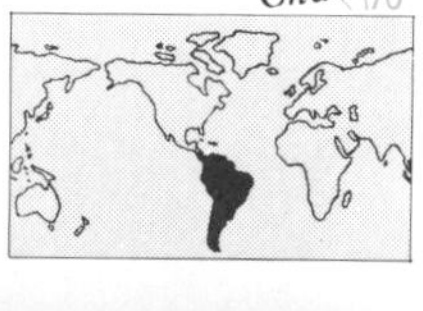

Kilometers 0 100 200 300 400 500 600 Km.
Statute Miles 0 100 200 300 400 500 600 Mi.

1:12 800 000

One centimeter represents 128 kilometers
One inch represents approximately 200 miles

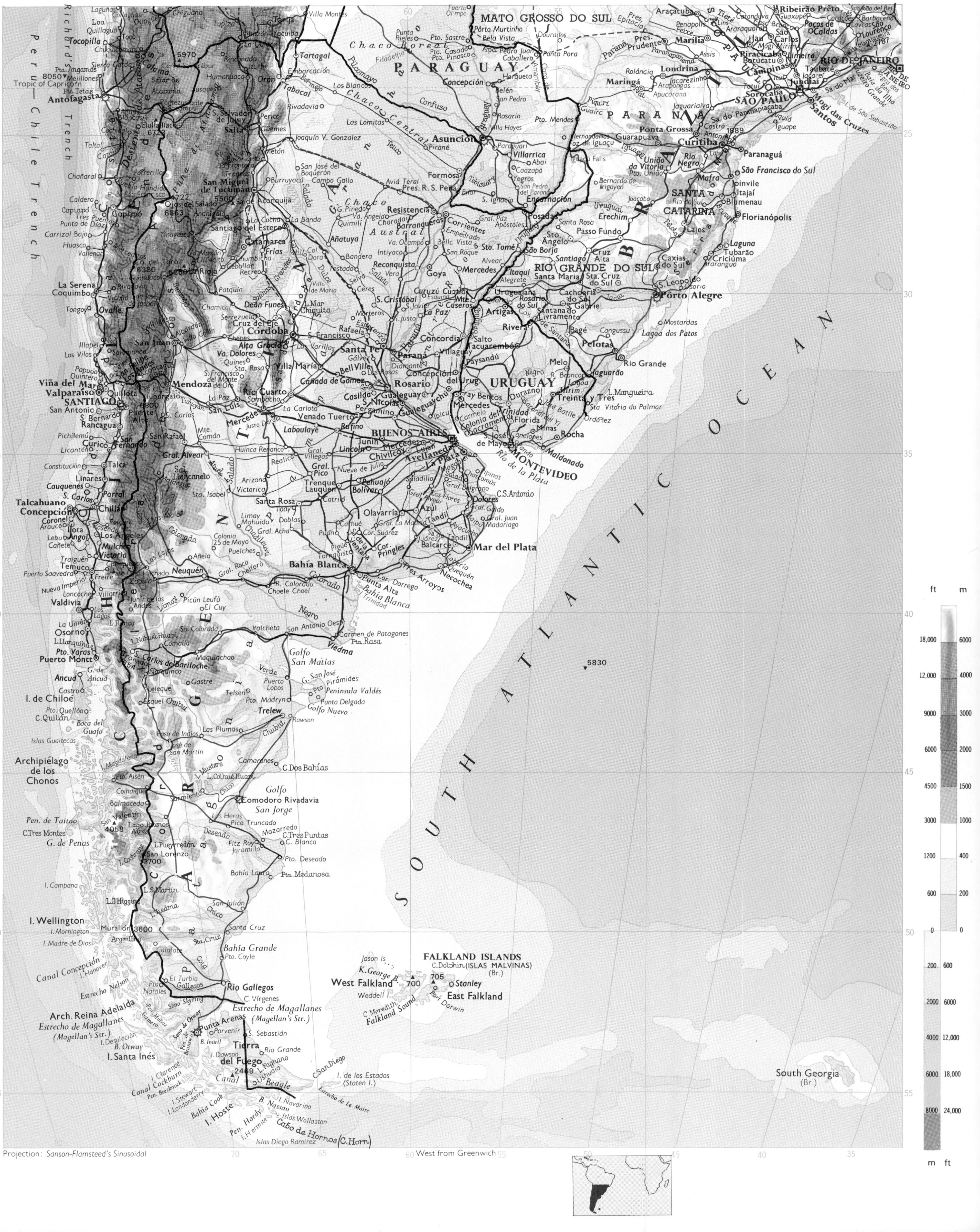

MATO GROSSO DO SUL
PARAGUAY
Asunción
Concepción
URUGUAY
MONTEVIDEO
BUENOS AIRES
SANTIAGO
Valparaíso
Viña del Mar
Mendoza
Córdoba
Rosario
Santa Fe
Tucumán
Salta
Antofagasta
Tropic of Capricorn
Peru—Chile Trench
Richard's Deep
Concepción
Talcahuano
Valdivia
Puerto Montt
Bahía Blanca
Mar del Plata
La Plata
Neuquén
Comodoro Rivadavia
Golfo San Jorge
Golfo San Matías
Península Valdés
Río Gallegos
Punta Arenas
Estrecho de Magallanes (Magellan's Str.)
Tierra del Fuego
Canal Beagle
Cabo de Hornos (C.Horn)
I. de los Estados (Staten I.)
FALKLAND ISLANDS (ISLAS MALVINAS) (Br.)
West Falkland
East Falkland
Stanley
South Georgia (Br.)
SOUTH ATLANTIC OCEAN
SÃO PAULO
RIO DE JANEIRO
Curitiba
Florianópolis
Pôrto Alegre
RIO GRANDE DO SUL
SANTA CATARINA
PARANÁ
Lagoa dos Patos
Archipiélago de los Chonos
I. de Chiloé
I. Wellington
Arch. Reina Adelaida
I. Santa Inés
I. Hoste
5830
Projection: Sanson-Flamsteed's Sinusoidal
West from Greenwich
ft m
18,000 6000
12,000 4000
9000 3000
6000 2000
4500 1500
3000 1000
1200 400
600 200
0 0
200 600
2000 6000
4000 12,000
6000 18,000
8000 24,000
m ft

NICARAGUA
Masaya
Granada
Rama
L. de Nicaragua
Bluefields
Managua
Juigalpa
Rivas
S. Juan del Sur
San Juan del Norte
Islas del Maiz (Nic., U.S.)
I. de San Andrés (Colombia)
Cayos de Albuquerque (Colombia)
COSTA RICA
N.coya
Alajuela
Siquirres
Puntarenas
San José
Cartago
C.Blanco
G. de Nicoya
Bocas del Toro
G. de los Mosquitos
Almirante
V. de Chiriqui
David
PANAMA
Colón
Pta. Manzanillo
Panamá
La Chorrera
Arch. de las Perlas
B. de Coronado
G. Dulce
Pto. Armuelles
Aguadulce
Santiago
Golfo de Chiriqui
Chitré
Isla Coiba
Golfo de Panamá
Pta. Mala
Pen. de Azuero
Cocos Ridge
El Real
La Palma
Golfo del Darién
Turbo
Jurado
Riosucio
G. de Cupica
Is. de S. Bernardo
G. de Morrosquillo
Pen. de la Guajira
Pta. Gallinas
Pen. de Paraguaná
Aruba (Neth.)
Curaçao
Willemstad
Bonaire (Neth.)
Los Roques (Ven.)
Orchila (Ven.)
Blanquilla (Ven.)
Los Hermanos
I. La Tortuga (Ven.)
I. Margarita
La Asunción
Los Testigos
St. George's
GRENADA
The Grenadines
Tobago
Scarborough
Port of Spain
TRINIDAD & TOBAGO
Rio Claro
Is. de Aves (Ven.)
Santa Marta
Riohacha
Uribia
Barranquilla
Ciénaga
Cartagena
Soledad
Sabanalarga
Calamar
Arjona
Sincelejo
Montería
Mompós
Magangué
El Banco
Maracaibo
Machiques
Coro
Punto Fijo
G. de Venezuela
La Vela
Puerto Cumarebo
Tucacas
Puerto Cabello
Maracay
Maiquetia
La Guaira
CARACAS
Cabimas
Barquisimeto
San Felipe
Valencia
Trujillo
Valera
Guanare
Mérida
Barinas
San Cristóbal
Cúcuta
Ocaña
Pamplona
Rubio
Guasdualito
Arauca
Apure
San Juan de los Morros
Calabozo
Valle de la Pascua
San Fernando de Apure
Barcelona
Puerto La Cruz
Cumaná
Carúpano
Pen. de Araya
Maturín
El Tigre
Tucupita
Ciudad Guayana
Ciudad Bolívar
Soledad
Orinoco
Caicara
Guasipati
El Callao
Tumeremo
La Paragua
La Urbana
Ayacucho
Pto. Carreño
Pto. Páez
Meta
2285
2560
Mt. Roraima
2810
Sierra Pacaraima
Matthew's Ridge
Barima
Mazaruni
Pakaraima Mts.
Bartica
VENEZUELA
Barrancabermeja
Bucaramanga
Medellín
Antioquia
Pto. Berrío
Vélez
Socorro
Tunja
Sogamoso
Chiquinquirá
Trinidad
Quibdó
Manizales
Pereira
Cartago
Armenia
Tuluá
Ibagué
Tolima 5215
Girardot
BOGOTÁ
Fusagasugá
Villavicencio
Orocué
S. José de Ocune
San Fernando de Atabapo
Vichada
Tomo
Meta
C.Corrientes
Pta. Charambira
Buenaventura
Buga
Palmira
Cali
Malpelo (Colombia)
COLOMBIA
Huila 5750
Neiva
Campoalegre
Garzón
Florencia
Popayán
Puracé
4646
I. Gorgona
Mosquera
Tumaco
Patia
Barbacoas
Pasto
Mocoa
Guaviare
San José del Guaviare
Inírida
Guainía
Vaupés
Mitú
Caquetá
Caguán
Yarí
Pto. Asís
Putumayo
La Tagua
Pto. Leguizamo
San Carlos
Cucuí
S. Gabriel
Sa. Tapirapecó
Sa. Imeri
Sierra Parima
Uraricoera
Mucajaí
Boa Vista
RORAIMA
Catrimani
Branco
Jauaperi
Esmeraldas
S. Lorenzo
Tulcán
Ibarra
Otavalo
Cayambe
Equator
Cojimies
Quito
Cotopaxi 5896
Latacunga
Bahía de Caráquez
Chone
Manta
Portoviejo
Montecristi
Jipijapa
ECUADOR
Chimborazo 6267
Riobamba
Sangay 5230
Babahoyo
Guayaquil
Salinas
Santa Elena
Milagro
Alausí
Azogues
Cuenca
Pto. Bolívar
Machala
G. de Guayaquil
Tumbes
Zorritos
Zaruma
Loja
Talara
Sullana
Paita
Piura
Catacaos
Chulucanas
Huancabamba
Jaén
Bayovar
Pta. Negra
Desierto de Sechura
Reventazón
Chiclayo
Pimentel
Cajamarca
Pacasmayo
Pto. Chicama
Trujillo
Salaverry
Chimbote
Moyobamba
Chachapoyas
Saposoa
Tarapoto
Lamas
Huallaga
Toyabamba
Huascarán 6768
Huaraz
Casma
Huánuco
Huarmey
Barranca
Huacho
Cerro de Pasco
Ambo
Pto. Bermúdez
La Oroya
Tarma
Jauja
Huancayo
Callao
LIMA
I. San Lorenzo
Cañete
Chincha Alta
Pisco
Ica
Huancavelica
Ayacucho
Abancay
Cuzco
Urcos
6384
Sicuani
Coracora
6425
Arequipa
Camaná
Mollendo
Moquegua
Ilo
Tacna
Arica
6866
6369
Milne Edwards Trench
Peru-Chile Trench
Krümmel Trench
PERU
PACIFIC OCEAN
Nuevo Rocafuerte
Cabo Pantoja
Curaray
Napo
Santa Clotilde
Tigre
Pebas
Iquitos
Nauta
Amazonas (Amazon)
Leticia
Benjamin Constant
Marañón
Barranca
Lagunas
Yurimaguas
Ucayali
Requena
Contamana
Pucallpa
Masisea
Cruzeiro do Sul
Taumaturgo
Porto Valter
Tarauacá
Feijó
Sena Madureira
Rio Branco
Xapuri
Brasiléia
Cobija
Iñapari
ACRE
Urubamba
Manu
Pto. Maldonado
Madre de Dios
Puerto Heath
Riberalta
Guajará-Mirim
Villa Bella
Abunã
Porto Velho
Humaitá
Lábrea
Purus
Juruá
Eirunepé
Jutaí
Javari
Içá
Tonantins
Santo Antônio do Içá
São Paulo de Olivença
Tefé
Fonte Boa
Coari
Codajás
Manacapuru
Manaus
Japurá
Solimões (Amazonas)
Negro
Barcelos
Carvoeiro
Moura
Uaupés
Apaporis
La Pedrera
Arica
Maraã
AMAZONAS
Madeira
Manicoré
Borba
Canutama
Tapauá
Aripuanã
Ji-Paraná
Calama
Ariquemes
Presidente Hermes
Pimenta Bueno
Vilhena
RONDÔNIA
Serra dos Parecis
Guaporé
Príncipe da Beira
Barão de Melgaço
Mato Grosso
1995
Trinidad
Magdalena
Exaltación
L. Rogoaguado
L. Rogagua
Rurrenabaque
San Borja
Sta. Ana
Ixiamas
Apolo
Mamoré
Beni
San Miguel
Concepción
San Javier
San Ignacio
San Matías
Santa Cruz
Portachuelo
L. Concepción
San José
Roboré
Puerto Suárez
BOLIVIA
La Paz
Illimani 6462
Ancohuma 6550
Coroico
Lago Titicaca
Puno
Juliaca
3812
Juli
Viacha
Corocoro
Cochabamba
Oruro
L. Poopó
Sajama 6520
Charaña
Challapata
Sucre
Potosí
Rio Mulatos
Uyuni
Salar de Uyuni
Cuzco 5950
Tupiza
Tarija
Villazón
Yacuiba
Camiri
Villa Montes
Tartagal
Chaco Boreal
Bahía Negra
Fuerto Olimpo
Pto. Sastre
Pto. Casado
Pto. Pinasco
PARAGUAY
ARGENTINA
CHILE
Pisagua
Iquique
Pozo Almonte
Pintados
Pica
Lagunas
Loa
Quillagua
Tocopilla
Calama
Chuquicamata
5970
Sol de Copasa
Sillajhuay 5995
Pta. Angamos
Cerro Sairecabur
Rinconada
ft
m
18,000
12,000
9000
6000
4500
3000
1200
600
0
6000
4000
3000
2000
1500
1000
400
200
0
200
2000
4000
6000
8000
600
6000
12,000
18,000
24,000
m
ft
10
5
0
5
10
15
20
85
80
75
70
65
60
West

Projection: Sanson-Flamsteed's Sinusoidal

Kilometers 0 100 200 300 400 500 600 Km.
Statute Miles 0 100 200 300 400 500 600 Mi.

1:12 800 000

One centimeter represents 128 kilometers
One inch represents approximately 200 miles

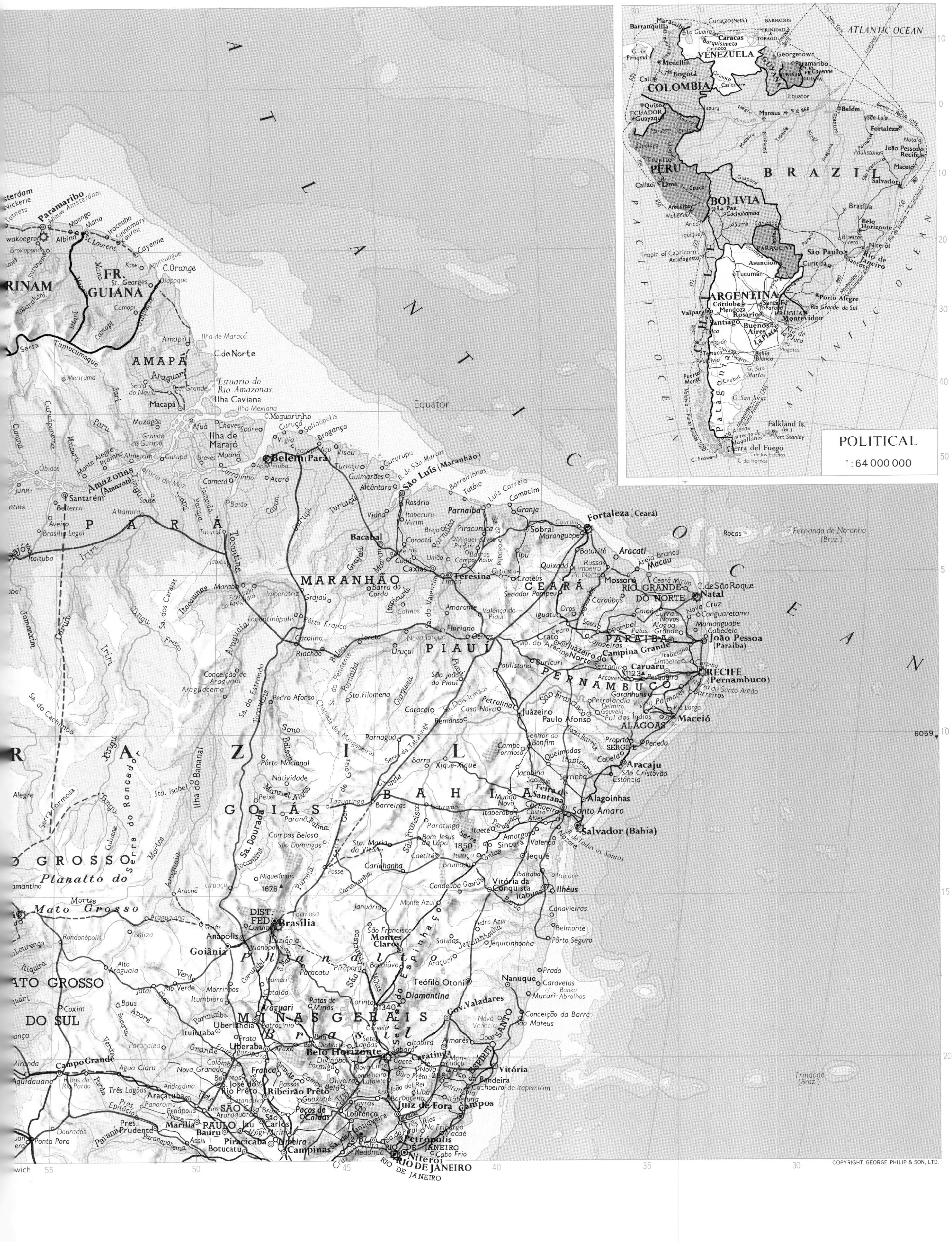
ATLANTIC OCEAN
Equator
Paramaribo
Cayenne
FR. GUIANA
SURINAM
AMAPÁ
Macapá
Ilha de Marajó
Belém (Pará)
São Luís (Maranhão)
Santarém
Amazonas (Amazon)
PARÁ
MARANHÃO
Teresina
Fortaleza (Ceará)
CEARÁ
RIO GRANDE DO NORTE
Natal
PARAIBA
João Pessoa (Paraiba)
Campina Grande
PERNAMBUCO
RECIFE (Pernambuco)
ALAGOAS
Maceió
SERGIPE
Aracaju
PIAUÍ
BAHIA
Salvador (Bahia)
Feira de Santana
Ilhéus
Vitória da Conquista
BRAZIL
GOIÁS
DIST. FED.
Brasília
Goiânia
Anápolis
MATO GROSSO
Planalto do Mato Grosso
MINAS GERAIS
Belo Horizonte
Montes Claros
Teófilo Otoni
Gov. Valadares
ESPIRITO SANTO
Vitória
Juiz de Fora
Campos
Petrópolis
Niterói
RIO DE JANEIRO
SÃO PAULO
Campinas
Ribeirão Prêto
Uberaba
Uberlândia
Campo Grande
Bauru
Marília
Fernando de Noronha (Braz.)
Trindade (Braz.)
Rocas
6059
POLITICAL
1:64 000 000
VENEZUELA
COLOMBIA
ECUADOR
PERU
BOLIVIA
BRAZIL
PARAGUAY
ARGENTINA
CHILE
URUGUAY
GUYANA
PACIFIC OCEAN
ATLANTIC OCEAN
Falkland Is.
Tierra del Fuego
Tropic of Capricorn

CARIBBEAN SEA
PACIFIC OCEAN
COLOMBIA
ECUADOR
PERU
PANAMA
VENEZUELA
LORETO
AMAZONAS
CAQUETÁ
VAUPÉS
GUAINÍA
VICHADA
META
ARAUCA
APURE
BARINAS
ZULIA
FALCÓN
LARA
GUAJIRA
ANTIOQUIA
CHOCÓ
SANTANDER
BOYACÁ
CAUCA
HUILA
NARIÑO
PUTUMAYO
NAPO
PASTAZA
MORONA-SANTIAGO
MANABÍ
GUAYAS
PICHINCHA
ESMERALDAS
AZUAY
LOJA
BOGOTÁ
MEDELLÍN
CALI
BARRANQUILLA
CARTAGENA
MARACAIBO
BARQUISIMETO
CARACAS
QUITO
GUAYAQUIL
Bucaramanga
Cúcuta
Manizales
Pereira
Ibagué
Neiva
Popayán
Pasto
Santa Marta
Valledupar
Montería
Sincelejo
Villavicencio
Tunja
Buenaventura
Tumaco
Esmeraldas
Ibarra
Latacunga
Ambato
Riobamba
Cuenca
Machala
Iquitos
Leticia
Mérida
San Cristóbal
Valencia
Maracay
Puerto Ayacucho
San Fernando de Apure
Golfo de Venezuela
Golfo del Darién
Golfo de Panamá
Golfo de Guayaquil
Golfo de Urabá
Golfo de Cupica
Golfo de Tibugá
Lago de Maracaibo
Península de la Guajira
Aruba (Neth.)
Curaçao (Neth.)
Bonaire (Neth.)
Magdalena
Cauca
Orinoco
Meta
Guaviare
Caquetá
Putumayo
Napo
Amazonas
Marañón
Japurá
ft
m
18,000
12,000
9000
6000
4500
3000
1200
600
0
200
2000
4000
6000
4000
3000
2000
1500
1000
400
200
0
600
6000
12,000
m
ft
75
70
80
10
5
0

Projection: Lambert's Equivalent Azimuthal

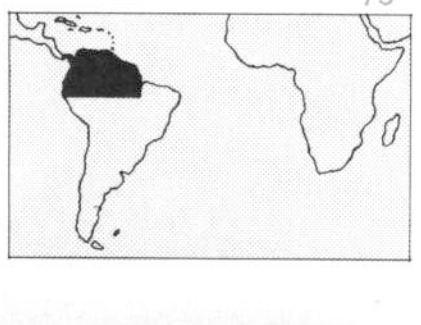

Kilometers 0 50 100 150 200 250 300 Km.
Statute Miles 0 50 100 150 200 250 300 Mi.

1:6 400 000

One centimeter represents 64 kilometers
One inch represents approximately 100 miles

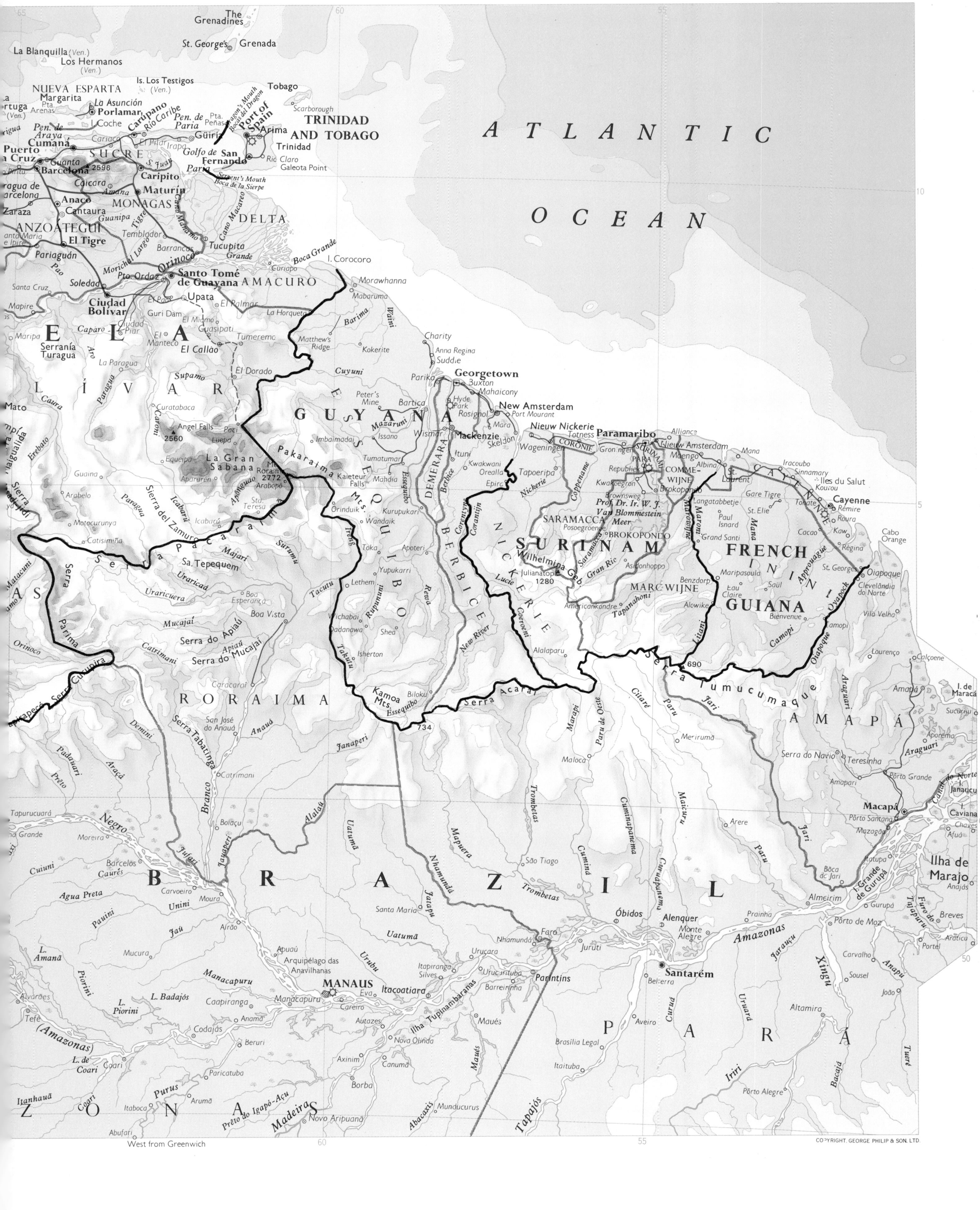

ATLANTIC
OCEAN
The Grenadines
St. George's
Grenada
La Blanquilla (Ven.)
Los Hermanos (Ven.)
Is. Los Testigos (Ven.)
Tobago
Scarborough
NUEVA ESPARTA
Margarita
La Asunción
Porlamar
Carúpano
Río Caribe
Pen. de Paria
Port of Spain
Arima
TRINIDAD AND TOBAGO
Trinidad
San Fernando
Golfo de Paria
Galeota Point
Serpent's Mouth
Boca de la Sierpe
Cumaná
SUCRE
Puerto La Cruz
Barcelona
2596
Caripito
Maturín
MONAGAS
Anaco
Cantaura
ANZOÁTEGUI
El Tigre
DELTA AMACURO
Tucupita
Boca Grande
I. Corocoro
Santo Tomé de Guayana
Pto. Ordaz
Orinoco
Soledad
Ciudad Bolívar
Upata
Guri Dam
El Callao
Tumeremo
El Dorado
Angel Falls
2560
La Gran Sabana
Roraima
2772
Pakaraima Mts.
Morawhanna
Mabaruma
Barima
Matthew's Ridge
Kokerite
Charity
Anna Regina
Suddie
Georgetown
Buxton
Mahaicony
Bartica
Cuyuni
Mazaruni
GUYANA
ESSEQUIBO
DEMERARA
BERBICE
Mackenzie
Wismar
Ituni
New Amsterdam
Port Mourant
Rosignol
Skeldon
Kaieteur Falls
Tumatumari
Kurupukari
Orinduik
Lethem
Rupununi
Takutu
Tacutu
Isherton
Kamoa Mts.
Serra Acaraí
734
Nieuw Nickerie
Totness
CORONIE
Paramaribo
Wageningen
Nieuw Amsterdam
Moengo
Albina
PARA
COMMEWIJNE
Brokopondo
Prof. Dr. Ir. W. J. Van Blommestein Meer
SARAMACCA
BROKOPONDO
SURINAM
NICKERIE
Wilhelmina Geb.
Julianatop
1280
MAROWIJNE
Benzdorp
Tapanahoni
Apetina
Lucie
Coeroeni
Alalapuru
Corantijn
Coppename
Marowijne
Maroni
Litani
FRENCH GUIANA
CAYENNE
INNINI
Mana
Iracoubo
Sinnamary
Kourou
Iles du Salut
Cayenne
Rémire
Roura
Kaw
Régina
Cabo Orange
Oiapoque
St. Georges
Maripasoula
Saül
Camopi
Oyapock
690
Serra Tumucumaque
AMAPÁ
Amapá
I. de Maracá
Serra do Navio
Teresinha
Pôrto Grande
Macapá
Pôrto Santana
Mazagão
Araguari
Jari
Canal do Norte
I. Caviana
Ilha de Marajó
Almeirim
Gurupá
Breves
Pôrto de Moz
Xingu
Altamira
RORAIMA
Boa Vista
Serra do Apiaú
Serra do Mucajaí
Sa. Tepequem
Serra Pacaraima
Serra Parima
Uraricoera
Mucajaí
Catrimani
Caracaraí
Branco
Serra Tabatinga
Serra Curupira
Negro
BRAZIL
Barcelos
Carvoeiro
Moura
Jauaperi
Jufari
Unini
Jaú
Airão
Arquipélago das Anavilhanas
MANAUS
Manacapuru
Itacoatiara
Uatumã
Nhamundá
Trombetas
Mapuera
Cuminá
Óbidos
Alenquer
Monte Alegre
Faro
Juruti
Parintins
Santarém
Amazonas
Urubu
Tapajós
Madeira
Maués
Borba
Purus
Coari
Tefé
(Amazonas)
Codajás
PARÁ
Itaituba
Aveiro
Curuá
Iriri
Curuá
Jari
Paru
Maicuru
Belterra
Brasília Legal
Nova Olinda
Novo Aripuanã
West from Greenwich
COPYRIGHT, GEORGE PHILIP & SON, LTD.

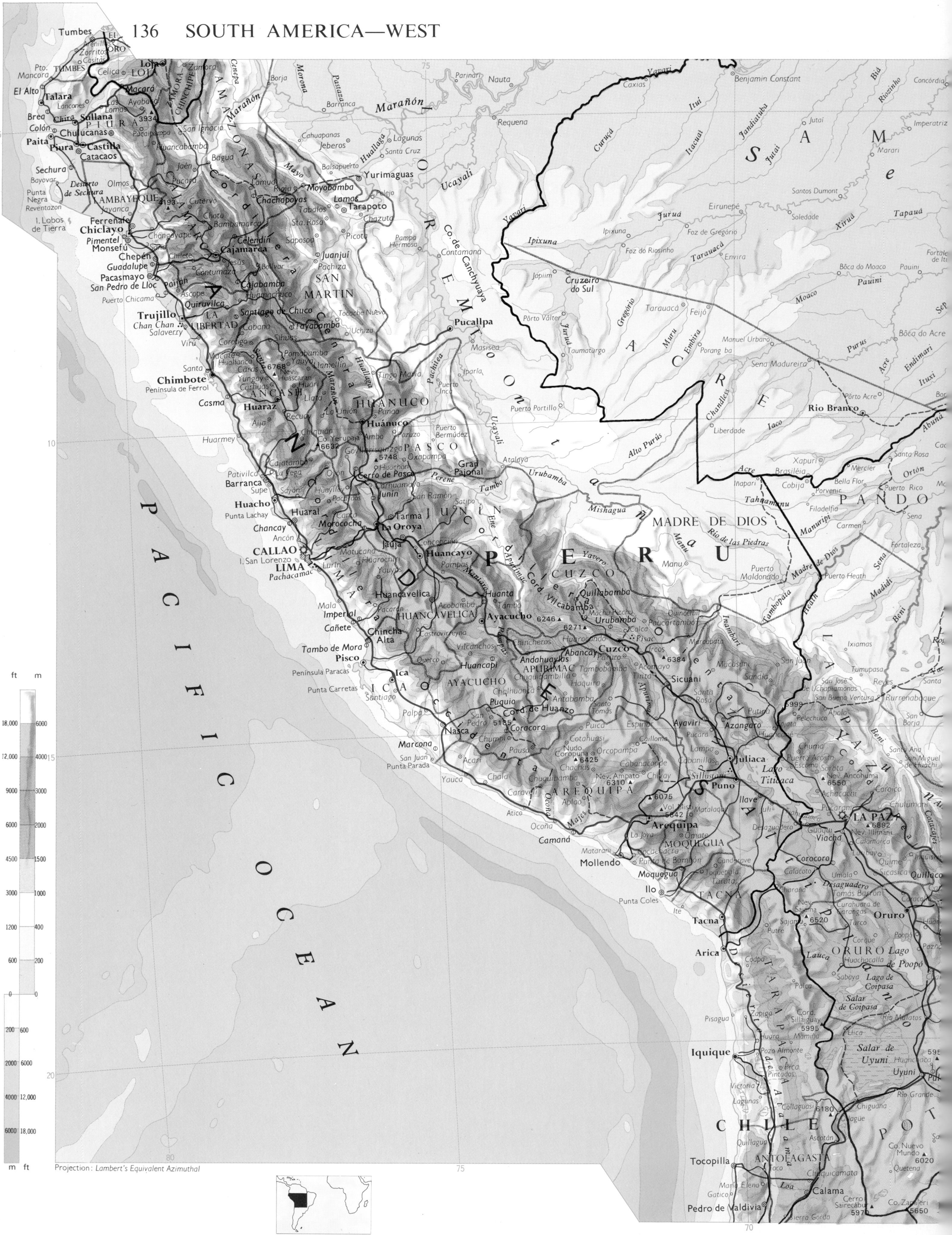
PACIFIC OCEAN
PERU
ANDES
MADRE DE DIOS
ACRE
PANDO
LA PAZ
ORURO
CHILE
TARAPACA
ANTOFAGASTA
TACNA
MOQUEGUA
AREQUIPA
PUNO
CUZCO
APURIMAC
AYACUCHO
HUANCAVELICA
ICA
LIMA
JUNIN
PASCO
HUANUCO
ANCASH
LA LIBERTAD
SAN MARTIN
CAJAMARCA
LAMBAYEQUE
PIURA
AMAZONAS
LORETO
TUMBES
Tumbes
Talara
Sullana
Paita
Piura
Chiclayo
Cajamarca
Chachapoyas
Moyobamba
Yurimaguas
Tarapoto
Trujillo
Chimbote
Huaraz
Huánuco
Pucallpa
Cerro de Pasco
La Oroya
Huancayo
CALLAO
LIMA
Huancavelica
Ayacucho
Pisco
Ica
Nasca
Cuzco
Abancay
Sicuani
Juliaca
Puno
Arequipa
Mollendo
Moquegua
Ilo
Tacna
Arica
Iquique
Tocopilla
Calama
Pedro de Valdivia
Oruro
Viacha
Rio Branco
Cruzeiro do Sul
Lago Titicaca
Lago de Poopó
Salar de Coipasa
Salar de Uyuni
Marañón
Ucayali
Huallaga
Urubamba
Purus
Juruá
Yavari
Madre de Dios
Beni
Cord. Vilcabamba
Cord. de Huanzo
Cordillera Central
Cordillera Occidental
ft
m
18,000
12,000
9000
6000
4500
3000
1200
600
0
6000
4000
3000
2000
1500
1000
400
200
Projection: Lambert's Equivalent Azimuthal

Kilometers 0 50 100 150 200 250 300 Km.
Statute Miles 0 50 100 150 200 250 300 Mi.

1:6 400 000

One centimeter represents 64 kilometers
One inch represents approximately 100 miles

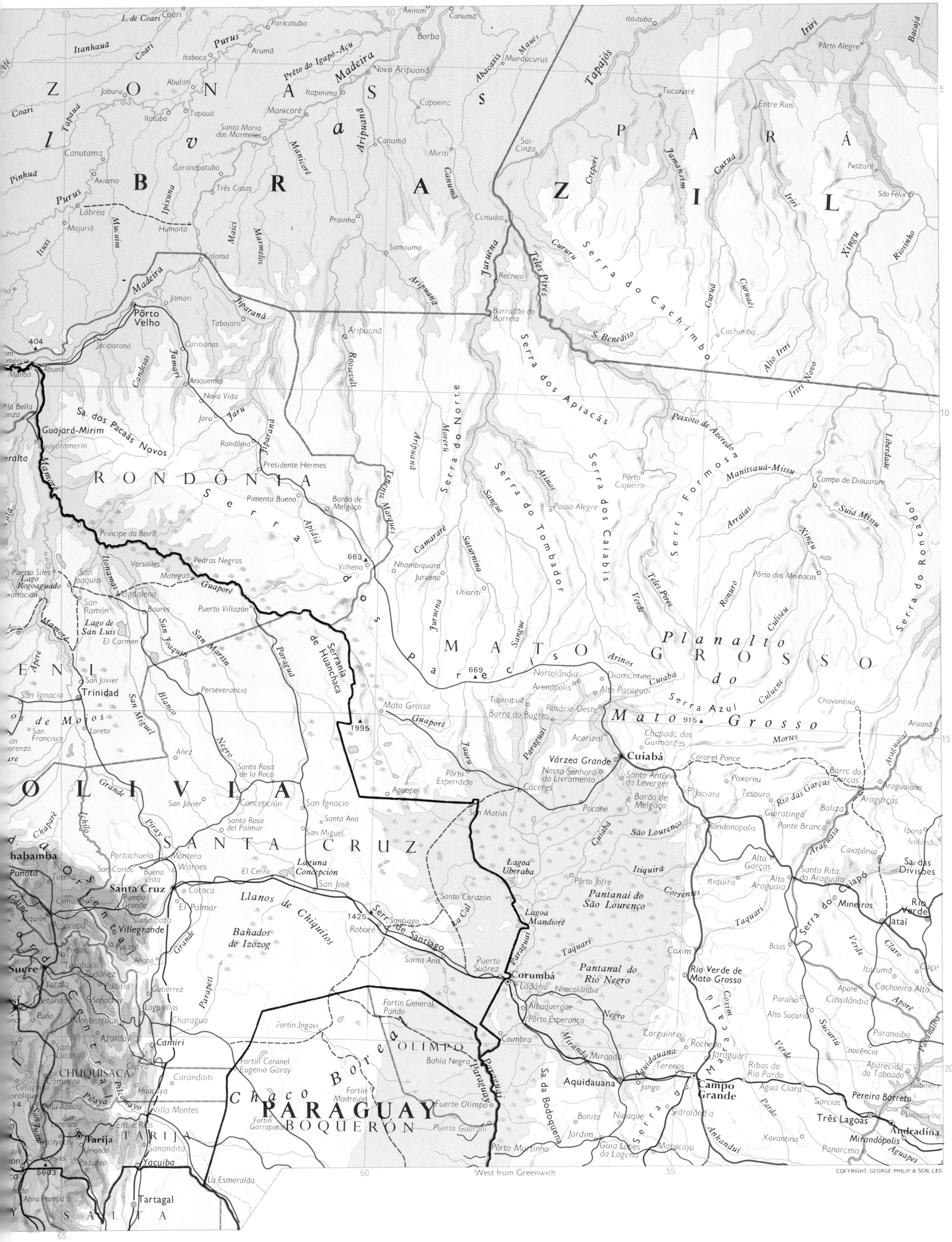

Z O N A S
A M A Z O N A S
B R A Z I L
P A R Á
R O N D Ô N I A
M A T O G R O S S O
Planalto do Mato Grosso
B O L I V I A
S A N T A C R U Z
C H U Q U I S A C A
T A R I J A
S A L T A
P A R A G U A Y
B O Q U E R Ó N
O L I M P O
Chaco Boreal
Serra dos Parecis
Serra do Cachimbo
Serra dos Apiacás
Serra do Norte
Serra do Tombador
Serra dos Caiabis
Serra Formosa
Serra do Roncador
Serra Azul
Serra do Caiapó
Serra de Maracaju
Serrania de Huanchaca
Serr. de Santiago
Sa. dos Pacaás Novos
Llanos de Chiquitos
Bañados de Izozog
Pantanal do São Lourenço
Pantanal do Rio Negro
Sa. da Bodoquena
Cordillera Central
Cordillera Oriental
L. de Coari
Coari
Paricatuba
Axinim
Canumã
Borba
Purus
Itanhauã
Itaboca
Arumã
Prêto do Igapó-Açu
Madeira
Novo Aripuanã
Abacaxis
Maués
Mundurucus
Tapajós
Itaituba
Iriri
Pôrto Alegre
Bacajá
Abufari
Jaburu
Itapinima
Tucunaré
Tapauá
Itatuba
Manicoré
Capoeira
Entre Rios
Santa Maria dos Marmelos
Aripuanã
Canumã
Miriti
Sai-Cinza
Crepori
Jamanxim
Curuá
Nazaré
Canutama
Pinhuã
Axioma
Caranapatuba
Três Casas
Ipixuna
São Félix
Lábrea
Majuriá
Mucuim
Humaitá
Maici
Marmelos
Prainha
Cenudos
Xingu
Riosinho
Ituxi
Calama
Samaúma
Juruena
Teles Pires
Cururu
Recreio
Curuaés
Jamari
Tabajara
Pôrto Velho
Jiparaná
Barracão do Barreto
Aripuanã
Cachimbo
S. Benedito
Alto Iriri
Iriri Novo
404
Jaciparaná
Caritianas
Roosevelt
Abunã
Candeias
Ariquemes
Nova Vida
Jaru
Rondônia
Guajará-Mirim
Guayaramerín
Mamoré
Presidente Hermes
Moreru
Arinos
Pôrto Cajueiro
Peixoto de Azevedo
Manitsauá-Missu
Liberdade
Campo de Diauarum
Pimenta Bueno
Barão de Melgaço
Tenente Marques
Pouso Alegre
Sangue
Arraias
Suiá Missu
Principe da Beira
Apidiá
Camararé
Saturnina
663
Vilhena
Nhambiquara
Juruena
Utiariti
Pôrto dos Meinacos
Ronuro
Puerto Siles
Lago Rogoaguado
Exaltación
San Joaquín
Ionamas
Versalles
Pedras Negras
Mategua
Guaporé
Magdalena
San Ramón
Baures
Puerto Villazón
Lago de San Luis
El Carmen
San Joaquín
San Martín
Paraguá
Culuene
Culiseu
Mamoré
Aperé
669
Arinos
Cuiabá
Nortelândia
Arenápolis
Diamantino
Alto Paraguai
San Javier
Trinidad
San Ignacio
Perseverancia
Llanos de Mojos
San Francisco
Loreto
San Miguel
Blanco
Tapirapuã
Barra do Bugres
Rosário Oeste
915
Chavantina
Aruanã
Mato Grosso
1995
Guaporé
Jauru
Paraguai
Acorizal
Chapada dos Guimarães
Mortes
Araguaia
Añez
Negro
Santa Rosa de la Roca
Pôrto Esperidião
Aguapeí
Cáceres
Várzea Grande
Cuiabá
Nossa Senhora do Livramento
Santo Antônio do Leverger
Coronel Ponce
Poxoreu
Barra do Garças
Araguaiana
Aragarças
Jaciara
Tesouro
Rio das Garças
Guiratinga
Baliza
Grande
San Javier
Concepción
San Ignacio
San Matías
Poconé
Barão de Melgaço
São Lourenço
Rondonópolis
Ponte Branca
Iporá
Ivolândia
Chaparé
Ichilo
Piray
Santa Rosa del Palmar
Santa Ana
San Miguel
Portachuelo
Montero
Warnes
San Carlos
Buena Vista
El Cerro
Laguna Concepción
Lagoa Uberaba
Itiquira
Alto Garças
Alto Araguaia
Caiapônia
Sa. das Divisões
Santa Rita do Araguaia
Santa Cruz
Cotoca
Totora
Comarapa
Pampa Grande
El Palmar
San José
Pôrto Jofre
Correntes
Itiquira
Santo Corazón
Lagoa Mandioré
Mineiros
Rio Verde
Jataí
Samaipata
Vallegrande
Grande
1425
Santiago
Roboré
La Gaiba
Taquari
Coxim
Baús
Claro
Sucre
Tarabuco
Zudáñez
Padilla
Yotala
Sopachuy
Parapetí
Puerto Suárez
Santa Ana
Corumbá
Ladário
Nhecolândia
Rio Verde de Mato Grosso
Itarumã
Caçu
Aporé
Cachoeira Alta
Cassilândia
Gutiérrez
Lagunillas
Charagua
Monteagudo
Azurduy
Fortín General Pando
Fortín Ingavi
Albuquerque
Pôrto Esperança
Negro
Paraíso
Alto Sucuriú
Sucuriú
Paranaíba
Camiri
Coimbra
Corguinho
Rochedo
Inocência
Lucas
Cuevo
Fortín Coronel Eugenio Garay
Bahía Negra
Miranda
Aquidauana
Terenos
Jaraguari
Ribas do Rio Pardo
Aparecida do Taboado
Camargo
Carandaiti
Huacaya
Pilcomayo
Pilaya
Villa Montes
Fortín Galpón
Fuerte Olimpo
Aquidauana
Jango
Campo Grande
Água Clara
Pardo
Garcias
Pereira Barreto
Rubinéia
Entre Ríos
Tarija
Sanandita
Uriondo
Padcaya
Fortín Garrapatal
Puerto Guaraní
Bonito
Nioaque
Sidrolândia
Anhanduí
Três Lagoas
Andradina
Lussanvira
Jardim
Guia Lopes da Laguna
Maracaju
Xavantina
Mirandópolis
Panorama
Aguapeí
Yacuiba
5603
Pôrto Murtinho
Tartagal
La Esmeralda
Abra Pampa
60
55
65
5
10
15
20
West from Greenwich
COPYRIGHT, GEORGE PHILIP & SON, LTD.

ATLANTIC OCEAN
AMAPÁ
PARÁ
MARANHÃO
PIAUÍ
CEARÁ
RIO GRANDE DO NORTE
PARAÍBA
PERNAMBUCO
ALAGOAS
BRAZIL
Macapá
Ilha de Marajó
BELÉM (Pará)
Abaetetuba
Bragança
Tocantins
Xingu
SÃO LUÍS
Caxias
Teresina
Parnaíba
Sobral
FORTALEZA (Ceará)
NATAL
João Pessoa (Paraíba)
RECIFE (Pernambuco)
MACEIÓ
Aracaju
Campina Grande
Juàzeiro do Norte
Crato
Petrolina
Juàzeiro
Floriano
Imperatriz
Carolina
Marabá
Serra do Gurupi
Sa. do Tiracambu
Serra dos Carajás
Serra dos Gradaús
Chapada das Mangabeiras
Serra do Estrondo
Serra do Penitente
Francisco
Parnaíba
640
1229
35
40
45
50
0
5
10

Kilometers 0 50 100 150 200 250 300 Km.
Statute Miles 0 50 100 150 200 250 300 Mi.

1: 6 400 000

One centimeter represents 64 kilometers
One inch represents approximately 100 miles

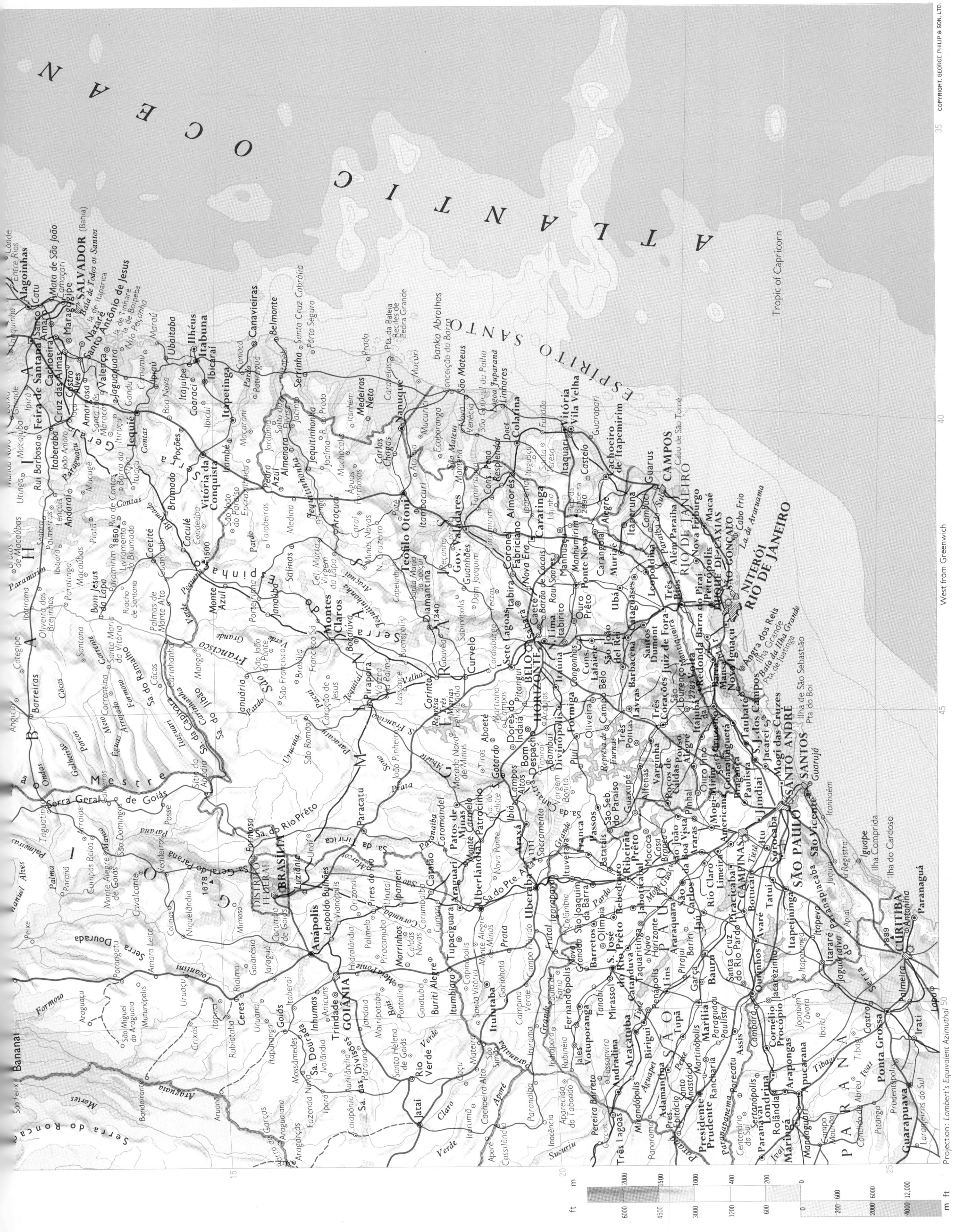

ATLANTIC OCEAN
Tropic of Capricorn
West from Greenwich
ESPIRITO SANTO
BAHIA
MINAS GERAIS
GOIÁS
SÃO PAULO
PARANÁ
RIO DE JANEIRO
SALVADOR (Bahia)
Baía de Todos os Santos
Feira de Santana
Vitória da Conquista
Ilhéus
Itabuna
Jequié
Teófilo Otoni
Montes Claros
Gov. Valadares
Vitória
Vila Velha
Campos
NITERÓI
RIO DE JANEIRO
DUQUE DE CAXIAS
SÃO GONÇALO
Petrópolis
Nova Iguaçu
Juiz de Fora
BELO HORIZONTE
Uberaba
Uberlândia
Ribeirão Prêto
CAMPINAS
SÃO PAULO
SANTO ANDRÉ
SANTOS
São Vicente
Sorocaba
Jundiaí
Bauru
Londrina
Maringá
Ponta Grossa
CURITIBA
Paranaguá
Guarapuava
DISTRITO FEDERAL
BRASÍLIA
Anápolis
GOIÂNIA
Serra Geral de Goiás
Serra do Espinhaço
Serra da Mantiqueira
Serra do Mar
Cabo Frio
Ilha de São Sebastião
Ilha Grande
Banca Abrolhos
Projection: Lambert's Equivalent Azimuthal
COPYRIGHT, GEORGE PHILIP & SON, LTD.
m 2000 1500 1000 400 200 0 200 600 2000 4000
ft 6000 4500 3000 1200 600 0 600 2000 6000 12000

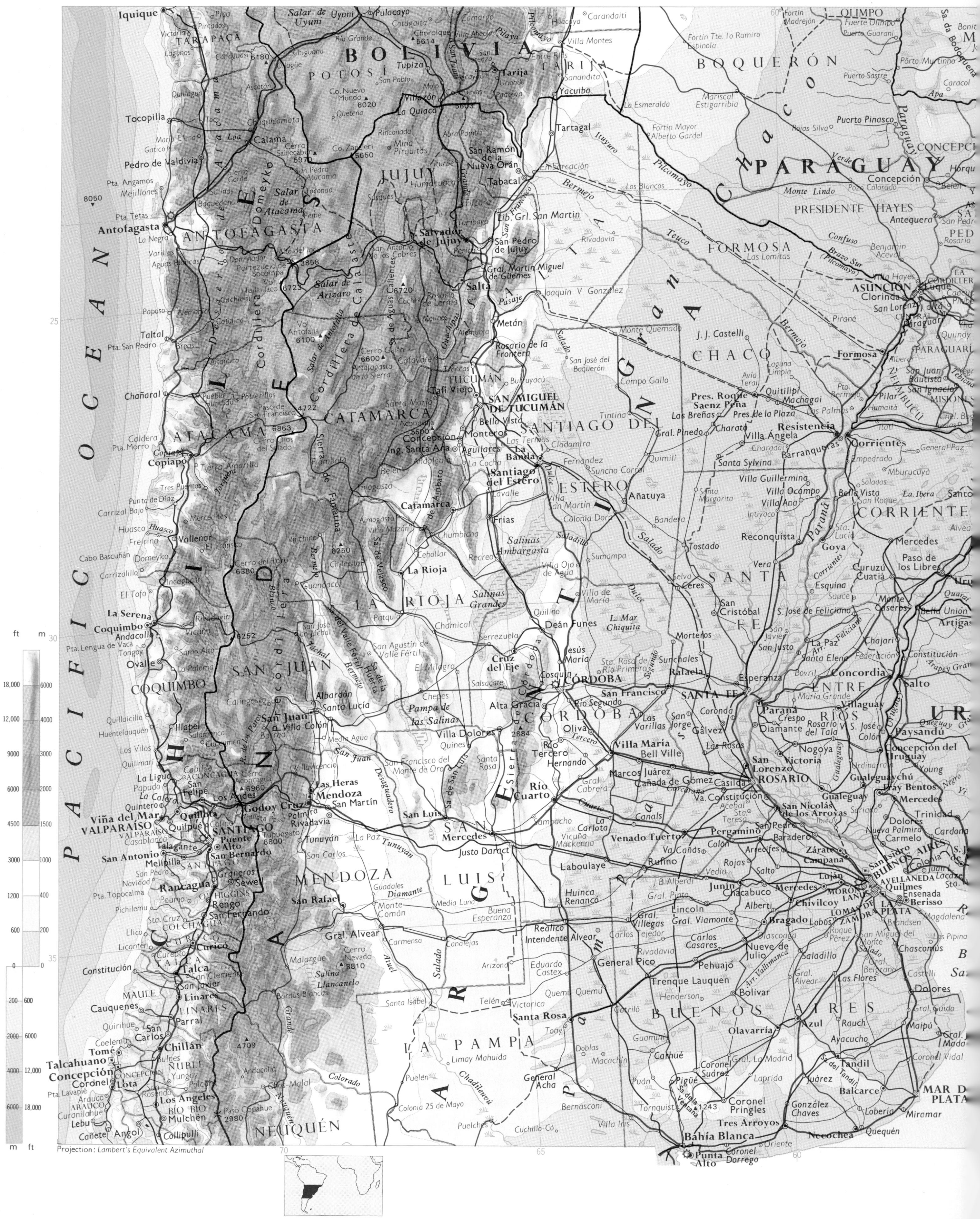
PACIFIC OCEAN
ANDES
ARGENTINA
CHILE
BOLIVIA
PARAGUAY
Gran Chaco
Cordillera Domeyko
TARAPACÁ
ANTOFAGASTA
ATACAMA
COQUIMBO
POTOSÍ
TARIJA
BOQUERÓN
PRESIDENTE HAYES
JUJUY
SALTA
FORMOSA
CHACO
CATAMARCA
TUCUMÁN
SANTIAGO DEL ESTERO
CORRIENTES
LA RIOJA
SAN JUAN
CÓRDOBA
SANTA FE
ENTRE RÍOS
MENDOZA
SAN LUIS
LA PAMPA
BUENOS AIRES
NEUQUÉN
Iquique
Tocopilla
Calama
Antofagasta
Taltal
Chañaral
Copiapó
Vallenar
La Serena
Coquimbo
Ovalle
Illapel
Viña del Mar
VALPARAÍSO
SANTIAGO
San Antonio
Rancagua
Curicó
Talca
Linares
Chillán
Talcahuano
Concepción
Los Angeles
Tarija
Tupiza
Villazón
La Quiaca
Yacuiba
San Salvador de Jujuy
Salta
Tartagal
ASUNCIÓN
Concepción
Formosa
Resistencia
Corrientes
SAN MIGUEL DE TUCUMÁN
Santiago del Estero
Catamarca
La Rioja
San Juan
Mendoza
San Luis
San Rafael
CÓRDOBA
Río Cuarto
Villa María
SANTA FE
Paraná
ROSARIO
Paysandú
Salto
BUENOS AIRES
LA PLATA
MAR DEL PLATA
Santa Rosa
Bahía Blanca
Tandil
Olavarría
Pergamino
Junín
Projection: Lambert's Equivalent Azimuthal

Kilometers 0 50 100 150 200 250 300 Km.
Statute Miles 0 50 100 150 200 250 300 Mi.

1:6 400 000

One centimeter represents 64 kilometers
One inch represents approximately 100 miles

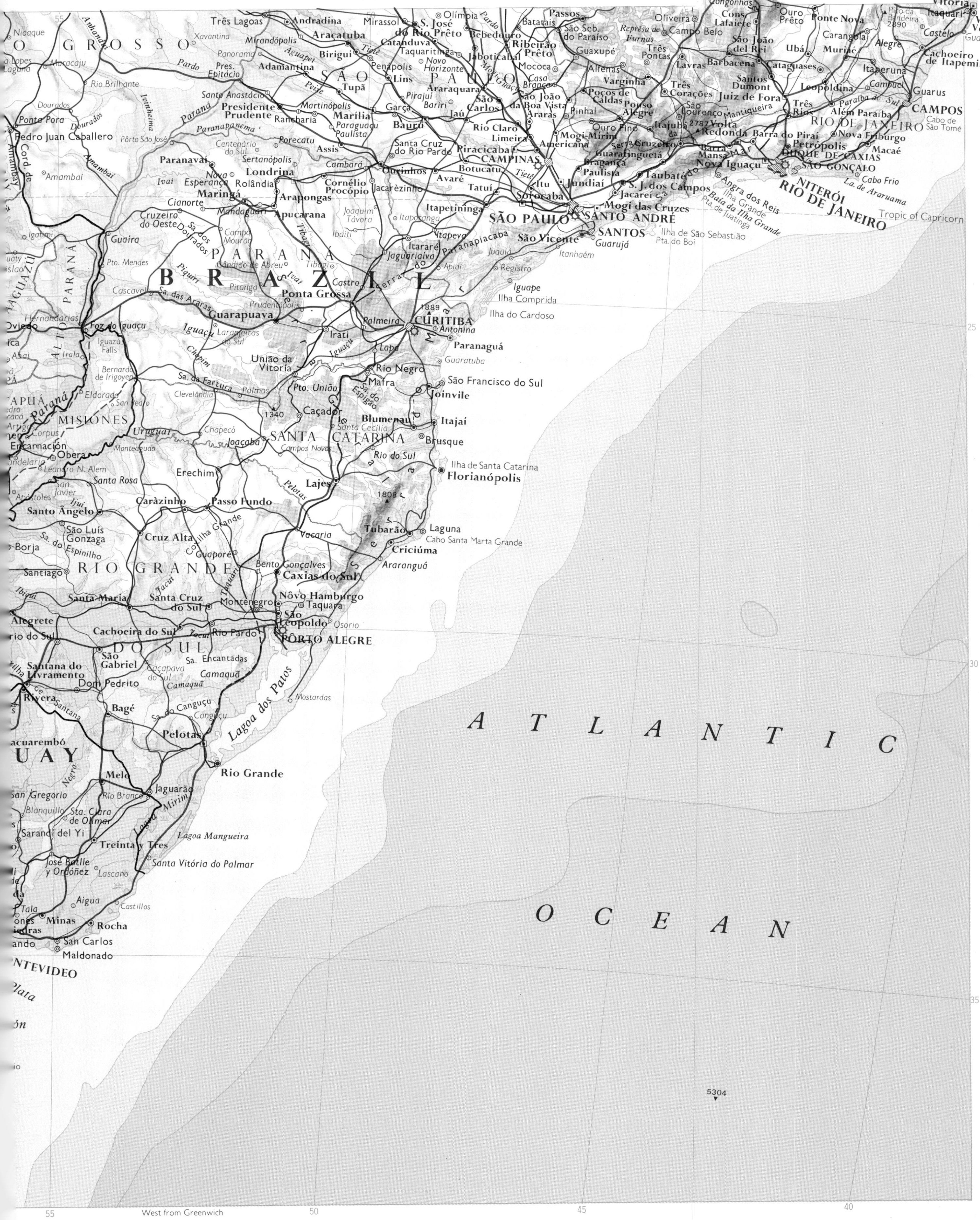
BELO HORIZONTE
N. Lima
Itabirito
Vitória
Vila Velha
Guarapari
Itaquari
Castelo
Cachoeiro de Itapemirim
Pico da Bandeira 2890
Ouro Prêto
Ponte Nova
Congonhas
Cons. Lafaiete
Oliveira
Campo Belo
São João del Rei
Ubá
Carangola
Muriaé
Alegre
Barbacena
Cataguases
Itaperuna
Santos Dumont
Juiz de Fora
Leopoldina
Cambuci
Guarus
CAMPOS
Cabo de São Tomé
Três Rios
Além Paraíba
Paraíba do Sul
RIO DE JANEIRO
Nova Friburgo
Macaé
Petrópolis
DUQUE DE CAXIAS
SÃO GONÇALO
NITERÓI
RIO DE JANEIRO
Cabo Frio
La. de Araruama
Tropic of Capricorn
Barra do Piraí
Volta Redonda
Barra Mansa
Nova Iguaçu
Mar
Mantiqueira
2787
São Lourenço
Itajubá
Cruzeiro
Guaratinguetá
Taubaté
S. J. dos Campos
Jacareí
Mogi das Cruzes
Angra dos Reis
Ilha Grande
Baía da Ilha Grande
Pta. de Juatinga
Ilha de São Sebastião
Pta. do Boi
SANTOS
Guarujá
São Vicente
SANTO ANDRÉ
SÃO PAULO
Itanhaém
Três Corações
Lavras
Varginha
Três Pontas
Alfenas
Poços de Caldas
Pouso Alegre
Ouro Fino
Bragança Paulista
Jundiaí
Sorocaba
Itu
Tietê
Represa de Furnas
Passos
Batatais
São Seb. do Paraíso
Guaxupé
Franca
Ribeirão Prêto
Bebedouro
Jaboticabal
Mococa
Casa Branca
São João da Boa Vista
Pinhal
Mogi-Mirim
Americana
CAMPINAS
Limeira
Rio Claro
Piracicaba
Araras
São Carlos
Araraquara
Jaú
Bariri
Olímpia
S. José do Rio Prêto
Mirassol
Catanduva
Taquaritinga
Novo Horizonte
Pardo
Mogi Guaçu
Três Lagoas
Andradina
Araçatuba
Birigui
Penápolis
Lins
Tietê
Mirandópolis
Aguapeí
Adamantina
SÃO PAULO
Tupã
Pirajuí
Garça
Bauru
Marília
Paraguaçu Paulista
Martinópolis
Presidente Prudente
Rancharia
Santo Anastácio
Presidente Epitácio
Pres. Epitácio
Panorama
Xavantina
Pardo
MATO GROSSO
Nioaque
Lopes
Laguna
Maracaju
Anhandui
Rio Brilhante
Ivinheima
Dourados
Ponta Porã
Pedro Juan Caballero
Cord. de Amambay
Amambai
Amambaí
Pôrto São José
Paranapanema
Paraná
Centenário do Sul
Sertanópolis
Porecatu
Assis
Cambará
Santa Cruz do Rio Pardo
Ourinhos
Botucatu
Avaré
Tatuí
Itapetininga
Itapeva
Itararé
Jaguariaíva
Paranapiacaba
Serra do Mar
Juquiá
Registro
Apiaí
Iguape
Ilha Comprida
Ilha do Cardoso
Itaporanga
Joaquim Távora
Ibaiti
Cornélio Procópio
Jacarèzinho
Londrina
Rolândia
Arapongas
Apucarana
Maringá
Mandaguari
Nova Esperança
Paranavaí
Ivaí
Cianorte
Cruzeiro do Oeste
Campo Mourão
Sa. dos Dourados
Umuarama
Igatimi
Guaíra
Pto. Mendes
PARANÁ
BRAZIL
Cândido de Abreu
Tibagi
Piquiri
Pitanga
Ivaí
Castro
Ponta Grossa
Prudentópolis
Cascavel
Sa. das Araras
Guarapuava
Serra da Esperança
1889
Palmeira
CURITIBA
Antonina
Paranaguá
Guaratuba
Irati
Lapa
Iguaçu
Laranjeiras do Sul
Foz do Iguaçu
Iguazú Falls
Irala
Hernandarias
Oviedo
ALTO PARANÁ
AGUAZÚ
Chopim
União da Vitória
Bernardo de Irigoyen
Rio Negro
Mafra
São Francisco do Sul
Joinvile
Pto. União
Sa. do Espigão
Sa. da Fartura
Palmas
Clevelândia
Eldorado
San Pedro
MISIONES
Paraná
Corpus
Encarnación
Obera
Leandro N. Alem
Uruguai
Chapecó
Joaçaba
Montecarlo
Caçador
1340
SANTA CATARINA
Campos Novos
Blumenau
Santa Cecília
Itajaí
Brusque
Rio do Sul
Ilha de Santa Catarina
Florianópolis
Serra Geral
Erechim
Santa Rosa
San Javier
Apóstoles
Ijuí
Santo Ângelo
Carazinho
Passo Fundo
Pelotas
Lajes
1808
Laguna
Tubarão
Cabo Santa Marta Grande
Criciúma
Araranguá
Vacaria
São Luís Gonzaga
Sa. do Espinilho
Borja
Cruz Alta
Guaporé
Santiago
RIO GRANDE DO SUL
Bento Gonçalves
Caxias do Sul
Nôvo Hamburgo
Taquara
Ibicuí
Santa Maria
Santa Cruz do Sul
Montenegro
Jacuí
Taquari
São Leopoldo
Osório
PÔRTO ALEGRE
Alegrete
Rio Pardo
Cachoeira do Sul
São Gabriel
Sa. Encantadas
Santana do Livramento
Caçapava do Sul
Camaquã
Dom Pedrito
Rivera
Santana
Bagé
Canguçu
Lagoa dos Patos
Mostardas
Pelotas
Rio Grande
Tacuarembó
URUGUAY
Negro
Melo
Río Branco
Jaguarão
San Gregorio
Blanquillo
Sta. Clara de Olimar
Lagoa Mirim
Lagoa Mangueira
Sarandí del Yi
Treinta y Tres
Santa Vitória do Palmar
José Batlle y Ordóñez
Lascano
Aiguá
Castillos
Minas
Rocha
San Carlos
Maldonado
MONTEVIDEO
Plata
ATLANTIC OCEAN
5304
25
30
35
55
50
45
40

55 West from Greenwich 50 45 40

Kilometers 0 50 100 150 200 250 300 Km.
Statute Miles 0 50 100 150 200 250 300 Mi.

1:6 400 000

One centimeter represents 64 kilometers
One inch represents approximately 100 miles

LA PAMPA
BUENOS AIRES
NEUQUÉN
RÍO NEGRO
CHUBUT
SANTA CRUZ
TIERRA DEL FUEGO
ARGENTINA
CHILE
Patagonia
Andes
CAUTÍN
VALDIVIA
OSORNO
LLANQUIHUE
CHILOÉ
AISÉN
MAGALLANES
SOUTH ATLANTIC OCEAN
PACIFIC OCEAN
FALKLAND ISLANDS
(ISLAS MALVINAS)
West Falkland
East Falkland
Jason Is.
Pebble I.
C. Dolphin
King George B.
Queen Charlotte B.
Mt. Adam
700
Mt. Usborne
705
Port Darwin
Stanley
Falkland Sound
Weddell I.
C. Meredith
Beauchêne I.
Golfo San Matías
Golfo San Jorge
Bahía Grande
Strait of Magellan
Isla Grande de Tierra del Fuego
Archipiélago de los Chonos
Isla de Chiloé
Golfo de Penas
Península de Taitao
Archipiélago Guayaneco
Estrecho de Magallanes
Canal Beagle
Cabo de Hornos (Cape Horn)
Islas Diego Ramírez
Is. Hermite
Islas Wollaston
I. de los Estados (Staten I.)
Est. de Le Maire
C. San Diego
Bahía Blanca
Punta Alta
Tres Arroyos
Coronel Pringles
Coronel Dorrego
Necochea
Quequén
Balcarce
Loberia
Juárez
Tornquist
Neuquén
Cipolletti
Gral. Roca
Zapala
Temuco
Valdivia
Osorno
Puerto Montt
Puerto Varas
San Carlos de Bariloche
Ancud
Castro
Esquel
Trelew
Rawson
Puerto Madryn
Comodoro Rivadavia
Caleta Olivia
Puerto Deseado
San Julián
Santa Cruz
Río Gallegos
Puerto Natales
Punta Arenas
Porvenir
Río Grande
Ushuaia
Viedma
Carmen de Patagones
San Antonio Oeste
Coihaique
Puerto Aisén
Calafate
Meseta de Somuncurá
Meseta de Montemayor
Gran Altiplanicie Central
L. Nahuel Huapi
L. Buenos Aires
L. Viedma
Lago Argentino
L. Fagnano
Mte. San Valentín 4058
Mte. Fitzroy 3375
Mte. Darwin
Projection: Lambert's Equivalent Azimuthal
West from Greenwich
COPYRIGHT, GEORGE PHILIP & SON, LTD.

Kilometers 0 300 600 900 1200 1500 Km.
Statute Miles 0 300 600 900 1200 1500 Mi.

1:28 000 000

One centimeter represents 280 kilometers
One inch represents approximately 450 miles

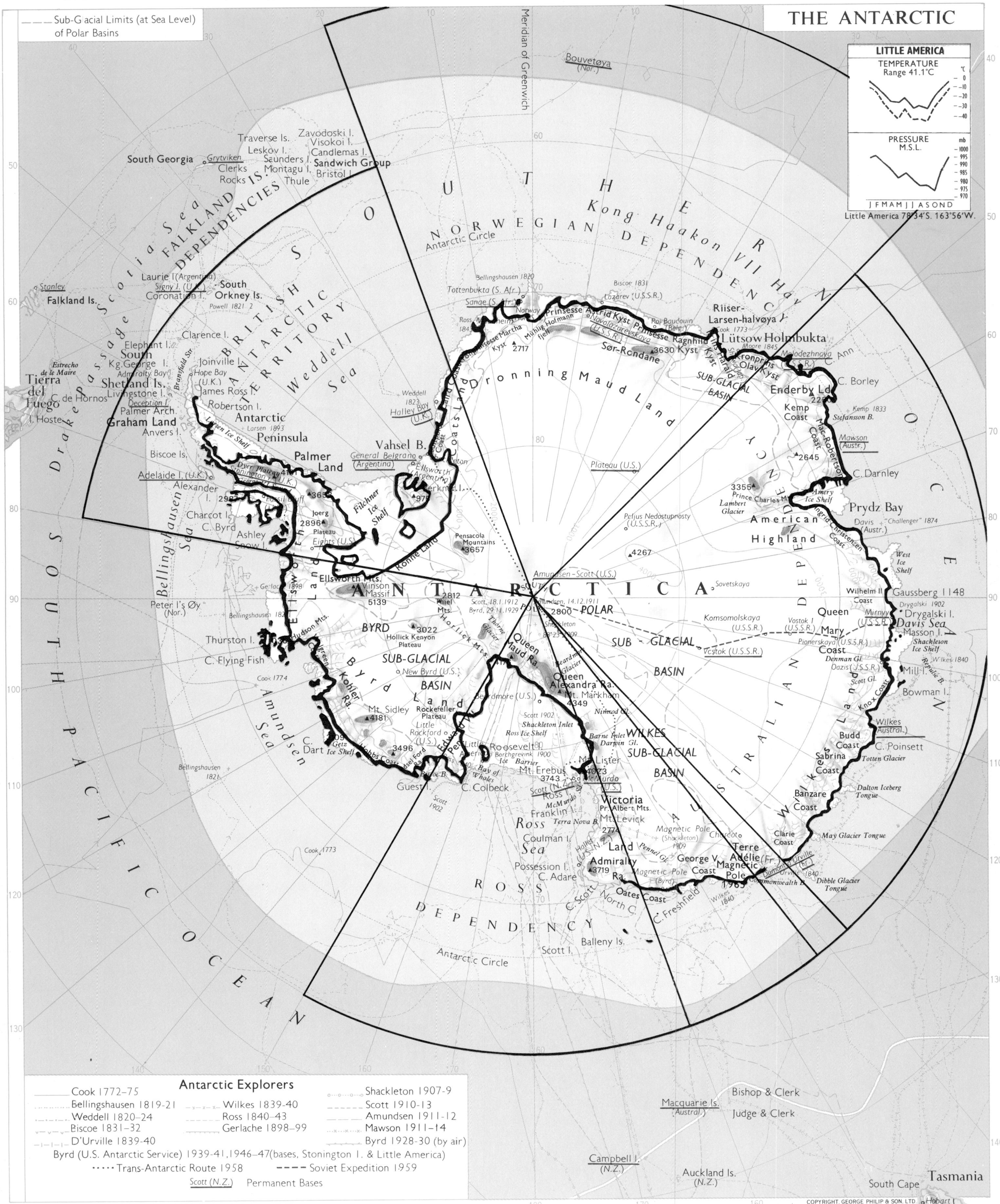
THE ANTARCTIC
Sub-Glacial Limits (at Sea Level) of Polar Basins
LITTLE AMERICA
TEMPERATURE
Range 41.1°C
PRESSURE
M.S.L.
J F M A M J J A S O N D
Little America 78°34'S. 163°56'W.
Meridian of Greenwich
Bouvetøya (Nor.)
South Georgia
Grytviken
Clerks Rocks
Traverse Is.
Leskov I.
Zavodoski I.
Visokoi I.
Candlemas I.
Saunders I.
Montagu I.
Bristol I.
Thule
Sandwich Group
Scotia Sea
FALKLAND IS. DEPENDENCIES
SOUTHERN OCEAN
Stanley
Falkland Is.
Laurie I. (Argentina)
Signy I. (U.K.)
Coronation I.
South Orkney Is.
Powell 1821
BRITISH ANTARCTIC TERRITORY
Weddell Sea
Drake Passage
Estrecho de le Maire
Tierra del Fuego
C. de Hornos
I. Hoste
Elephant I.
Clarence I.
South Shetland Is.
Kg. George I.
Admiralty Bay
Livingstone I.
Deception I.
Joinville I.
Hope Bay (U.K.)
James Ross I.
Robertson I.
Palmer Arch.
Graham Land
Anvers I.
Antarctic Peninsula
Larsen 1893
Larsen Ice Shelf
Biscoe Is.
Adelaide I. (U.K.)
Alexander I.
Charcot I.
C. Byrd
Palmer Land
Vahsel B.
General Belgrano (Argentina)
Ellsworth (Argentina)
Filchner Ice Shelf
Halley Bay (U.K.)
Weddell 1823
Coats Land
Joerg Plateau
Eights Coast
Ashley Snow I.
Bellingshausen Sea
Peter I's Øy (Nor.)
Ronne Land
Ellsworth Land
Ellsworth Mts.
Vinson Massif 5139
Thiel Mts.
Pensacola Mountains 3657
Thurston I.
C. Flying Fish
Cook 1774
Amundsen Sea
Hudson Mts.
BYRD SUB-GLACIAL BASIN
Hollick Kenyon Plateau
Horlick Mts.
New Byrd (U.S.)
Byrd Land
Kohler Ra.
Mt. Sidley 4181
Rockefeller Plateau
Little Rockford (U.S.)
Getz Ice Shelf
C. Dart
Guest I.
C. Colbeck
Bay of Whales
Little America
Ross Ice Shelf
Roosevelt I.
Mt. Erebus 3743
Scott (N.Z.)
McMurdo (U.S.)
Ross I.
Franklin I.
Ross Sea
Coulman I.
Possession I.
C. Adare
Victoria Land
Mt. Lister
Pr. Albert Mts.
Mt. Levick
Terra Nova B.
Admiralty Ra.
Queen Maud Ra.
Queen Alexandra Ra.
Mt. Markham 4349
Beardmore Glacier
Shackleton Inlet
Nimrod Gl.
Barne Inlet
Darwin Gl.
Amundsen–Scott (U.S.)
POLE
ANTARCTICA
Scott, 18.1.1912
Byrd, 29.11.1929
Amundsen, 14.12.1911
2800
POLAR SUB-GLACIAL BASIN
Vostok I (U.S.S.R.)
Vostok (U.S.S.R.)
Komsomolskaya (U.S.S.R.)
Sovetskaya
Pol'us Nedostupnosty (U.S.S.R.)
Plateau (U.S.)
Dronning Maud Land
NORWEGIAN DEPENDENCY
Kong Haakon VII Hav
Antarctic Circle
Bellingshausen 1820
Tottenbukta (S. Afr.)
Sanae (S. Afr.)
Norway
Prinsesse Martha Kyst
Mühlig-Hofmann fjell
2717
Prinsesse Astrid Kyst
Novolazarevskaya (U.S.S.R.)
Prinsesse Ragnhild Kyst
Roi Baudouin (Belg.)
Sør-Rondane 3630
Biscoe 1831
Lazarev (U.S.S.R.)
Riiser-Larsen-halvøya
Lützow Holmbukta
Kronprins Olav Kyst
Molodezhnaya
C. Ann
C. Borley
Enderby Ld
Kemp Coast
Kemp 1833
Stefansson B.
Mac Robertson Coast
Mawson (Austr.)
C. Darnley
2645
3355
Prince Charles Mts.
Lambert Glacier
Amery Ice Shelf
Prydz Bay
Davis (Austr.)
"Challenger" 1874
Ingrid Christensen Coast
American Highland
4267
West Ice Shelf
Gaussberg 1148
Wilhelm II Coast
Drygalski 1902
Drygalski I.
Mirnyy (U.S.S.R.)
Davis Sea
Masson I.
Queen Mary Coast
Pionerskaya (U.S.S.R.)
Shackleton Ice Shelf
Denman Gl.
Oazis (U.S.S.R.)
Wilkes 1840
Scott Gl.
Bowman I.
Knox Coast
Wilkes Land
AUSTRALIAN DEPENDENCY
Wilkes (Austral.)
Budd Coast
C. Poinsett
Sabrina Coast
Totten Glacier
Dalton Iceberg Tongue
Banzare Coast
Clarie Coast
May Glacier Tongue
Terre Adélie (Fr.)
Dumont d'Urville (Fr.)
Dibble Glacier Tongue
Commonwealth B.
Magnetic Pole 1965
Magnetic Pole (Shackleton) 1909
Magnetic Pole (Byrd)
George V Coast
Oates Coast
C. Freshfield
North C.
C. Scott
WILKES SUB-GLACIAL BASIN
ROSS DEPENDENCY
Balleny Is.
Scott I.
SOUTH PACIFIC OCEAN
Bellingshausen 1821
Cook 1773
Scott 1902
Macquarie Is. (Austral.)
Bishop & Clerk
Judge & Clerk
Campbell I. (N.Z.)
Auckland Is. (N.Z.)
South Cape
Tasmania
Hobart
Antarctic Explorers
Cook 1772–75
Bellingshausen 1819–21
Weddell 1820–24
Biscoe 1831–32
D'Urville 1839–40
Wilkes 1839–40
Ross 1840–43
Gerlache 1898–99
Shackleton 1907–9
Scott 1910–13
Amundsen 1911–12
Mawson 1911–14
Byrd 1928–30 (by air)
Byrd (U.S. Antarctic Service) 1939–41, 1946–47 (bases, Stonington I. & Little America)
Trans-Antarctic Route 1958
Soviet Expedition 1959
Scott (N.Z.) Permanent Bases

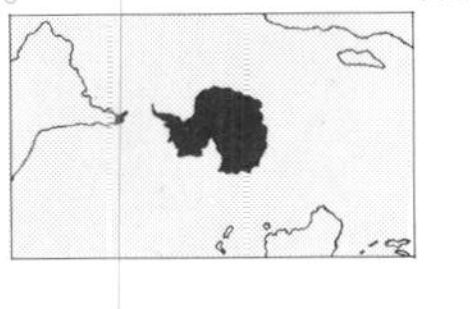

Kilometers 0 300 600 900 1200 1500 Km.
Statute Miles 0 300 600 900 1200 1500 Mi.

1:28 000 000

One centimeter represents 280 kilometers
One inch represents approximately 450 miles

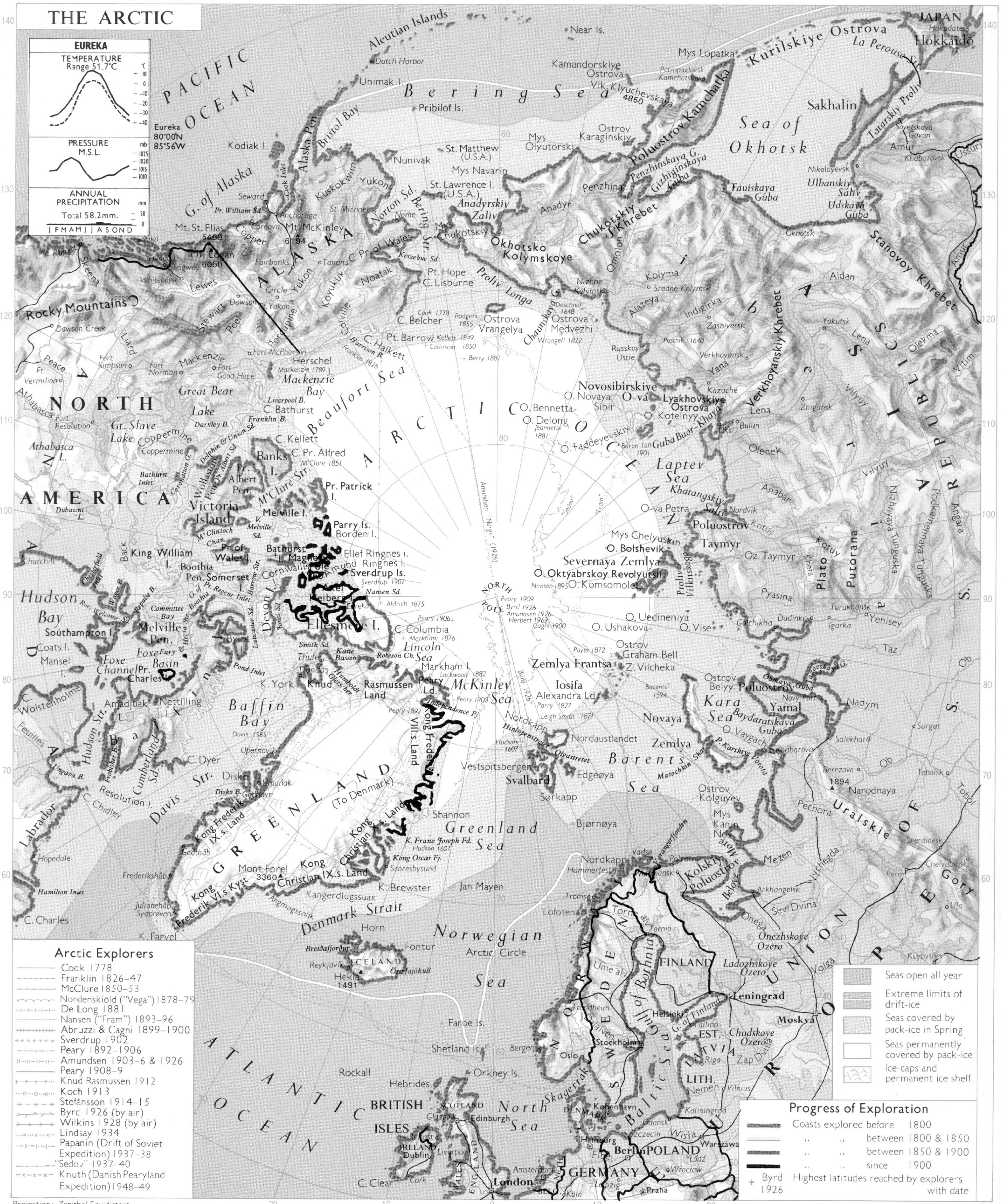
THE ARCTIC
EUREKA
TEMPERATURE Range 51.7°C
PRESSURE M.S.L.
ANNUAL PRECIPITATION
Total 58.2mm.
J F M A M J J A S O N D
Eureka 80°00'N 85°56'W
Arctic Explorers
Cock 1778
Franklin 1826–47
McClure 1850–53
Nordenskiöld ("Vega") 1878–79
De Long 1881
Nansen ("Fram") 1893–96
Abruzzi & Cagni 1899–1900
Sverdrup 1902
Peary 1892–1906
Amundsen 1903–6 & 1926
Peary 1908–9
Knud Rasmussen 1912
Koch 1913
Stefánsson 1914–15
Byrd 1926 (by air)
Wilkins 1928 (by air)
Lindsay 1934
Papanin (Drift of Soviet Expedition) 1937–38
"Sedov" 1937–40
Knuth (Danish Pearyland Expedition) 1948–49
Seas open all year
Extreme limits of drift-ice
Seas covered by pack-ice in Spring
Seas permanently covered by pack-ice
Ice-caps and permanent ice shelf
Progress of Exploration
Coasts explored before 1800
between 1800 & 1850
between 1850 & 1900
since 1900
+ Byrd 1926 Highest latitudes reached by explorers with date
PACIFIC OCEAN
ARCTIC OCEAN
ATLANTIC OCEAN
NORTH AMERICA
Bering Sea
Sea of Okhotsk
Beaufort Sea
Laptev Sea
Kara Sea
Barents Sea
Greenland Sea
Norwegian Sea
North Sea
Baffin Bay
Hudson Bay
Lincoln Sea
McKinley Sea
Denmark Strait
Davis Str.
GREENLAND (To Denmark)
ALASKA
NORTH POLE
Aleutian Islands
Kurilskiye Ostrova
JAPAN
Hokkaido
Kamchatka
Sakhalin
Novosibirskiye O-va
Severnaya Zemlya
Zemlya Frantsa Iosifa
Novaya Zemlya
Svalbard
Vestspitsbergen
Nordaustlandet
Ellesmere I.
Victoria Island
Banks I.
Melville I.
Baffin I.
Iceland
FINLAND
SWEDEN
NORWAY
BRITISH ISLES
IRELAND
GERMANY
POLAND
Leningrad
Moskva
London
Berlin
Rocky Mountains
Mt. McKinley 6194
Mt. St. Elias 5489
Mt. Logan 6050
Mont Forel 3360
Hekla 1491

Projection: Zenithal Equidistant

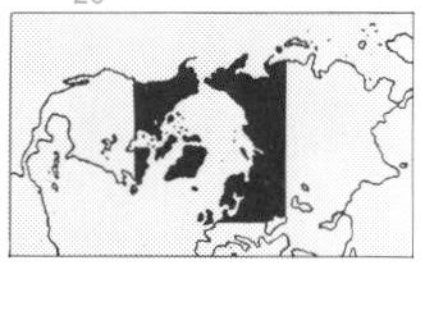

Equatorial Scale: 1:128 000 000

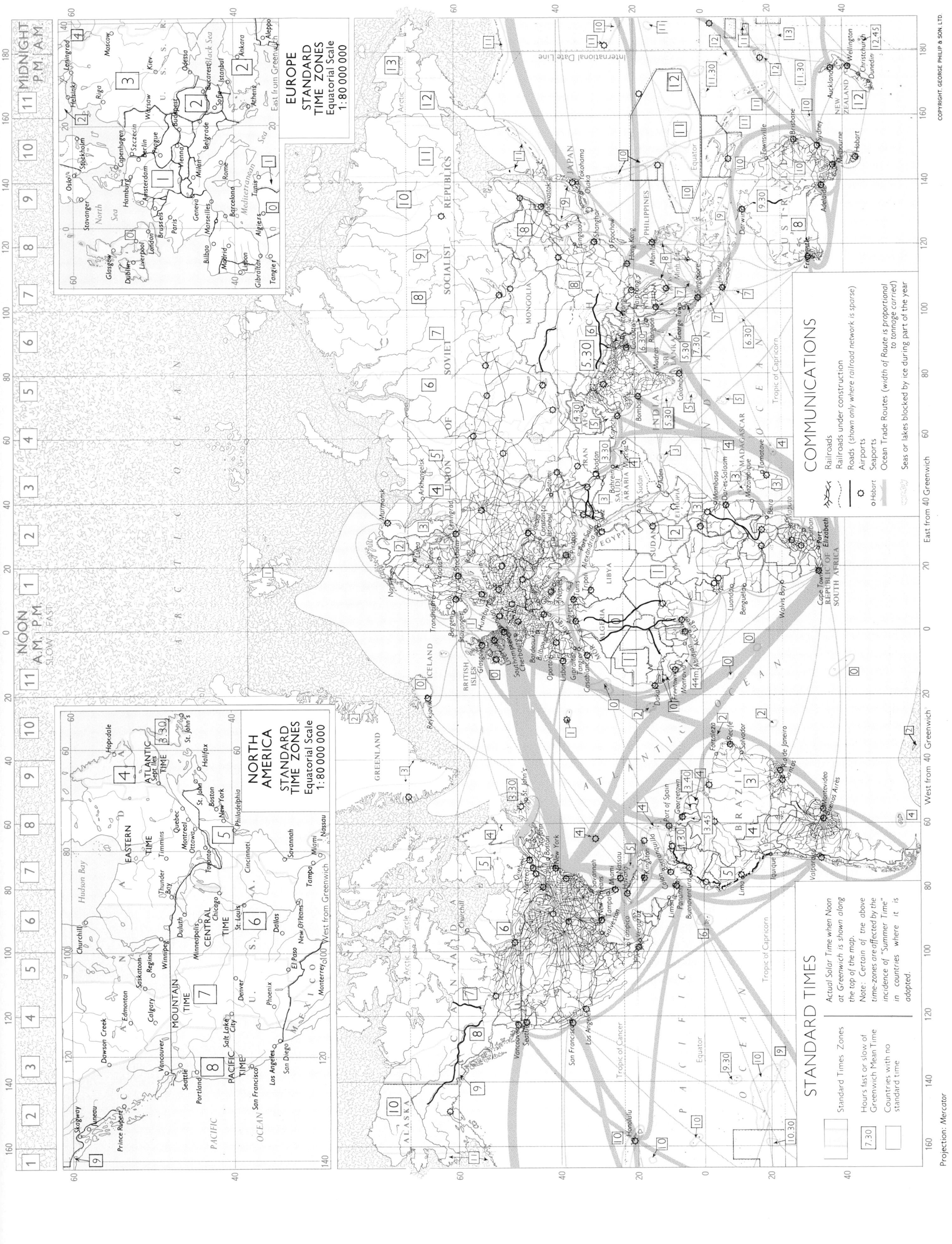
NOON
A.M. P.M.
SLOW FAST
MIDNIGHT
P.M. A.M.
EUROPE
STANDARD
TIME ZONES
Equatorial Scale
1:80 000 000
NORTH
AMERICA
STANDARD
TIME ZONES
Equatorial Scale
1:80 000 000
COMMUNICATIONS
Railroads
Railroads under construction
Roads (shown only where railroad network is sparse)
Airports
Seaports
Ocean Trade Routes (width of Route is proportional to tonnage carried)
Seas or lakes blocked by ice during part of the year
STANDARD TIMES
Standard Times Zones
Hours fast or slow of Greenwich Mean Time
Countries with no standard time
Actual Solar Time when Noon at Greenwich is shown along the top of the map.
Note: Certain of the above time-zones are affected by the incidence of "Summer Time" in countries where it is adopted.
West from 40 Greenwich
East from 40 Greenwich

Projection: Mercator

Equatorial Scale: 1:136 000 000

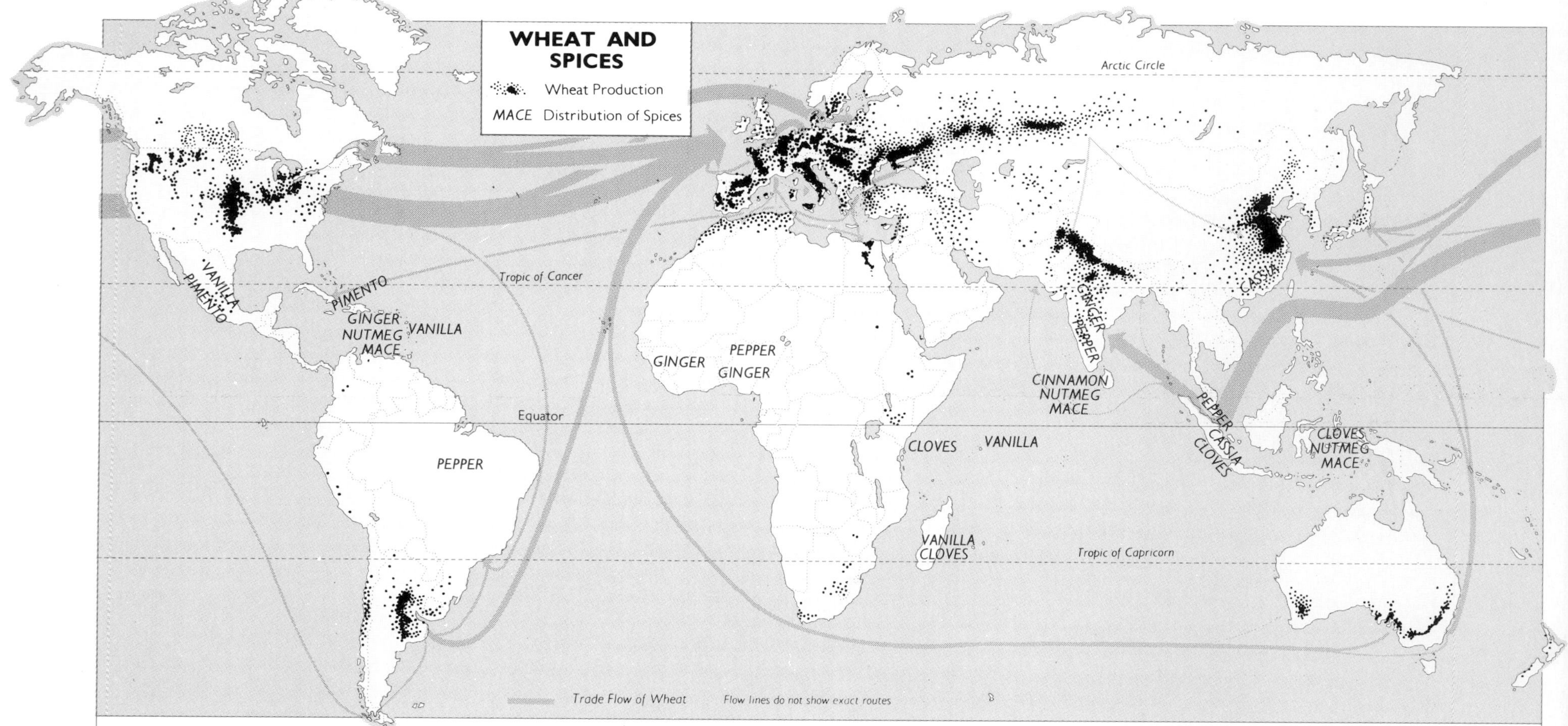
WHEAT AND SPICES
Wheat Production
MACE Distribution of Spices
Arctic Circle
Tropic of Cancer
Equator
Tropic of Capricorn
VANILLA
PIMENTO
PIMENTO
GINGER
NUTMEG
MACE
VANILLA
GINGER
PEPPER
GINGER
PEPPER
GINGER
PEPPER
CASSIA
CINNAMON
NUTMEG
MACE
CLOVES
VANILLA
VANILLA
CLOVES
PEPPER
CASSIA
CLOVES
CLOVES
NUTMEG
MACE
Trade Flow of Wheat
Flow lines do not show exact routes

WHEAT

World Production
1977-1979 average
million tonnes
422.1

Exports	th tonnes	% of world total	Imports	th tonnes	% of world total
U.S.A.	33379	43	U.S.S.R.	9250	12
Australia	11711	15	China	8951	12
Canada	11696	15	Japan	5926	8
France	7247	9	Brazil	3655	5
Argentina	4295	6	Egypt	3609	5
U.S.S.R.	2600	3	Italy	2934	4

Percentage of World Total

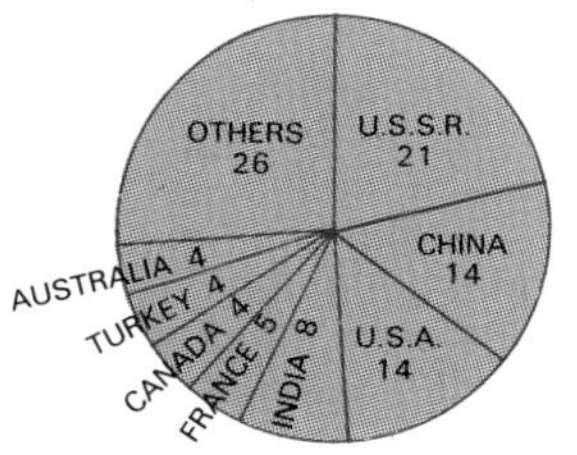
OTHERS 26
U.S.S.R. 21
CHINA 14
U.S.A. 14
INDIA 8
FRANCE 5
CANADA 4
TURKEY 4
AUSTRALIA 4

Yield	kg/ha
World average	**1782**
U.S.S.R.	1562
China	1500
U.S.A.	2301
India	1574
France	4773
Canada	1690
Turkey	1896
Australia	1390

SPICES

No reliable figures available

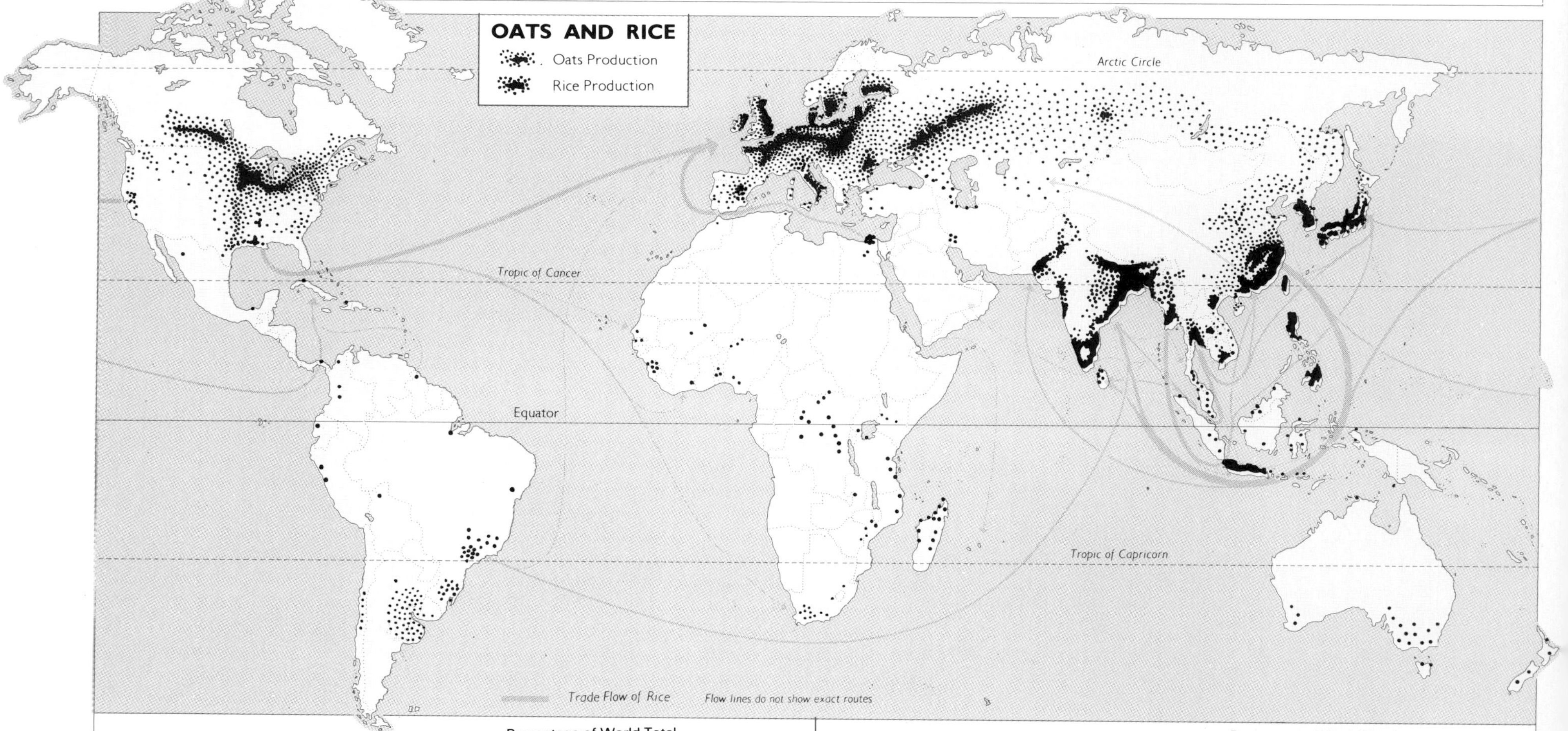
OATS AND RICE
Oats Production
Rice Production
Arctic Circle
Tropic of Cancer
Equator
Tropic of Capricorn
Trade Flow of Rice
Flow lines do not show exact routes

OATS

World Production
1977-1979 average
million tonnes
48.2

Exports	th tonnes	% of world total	Imports	th tonnes	% of world total
Australia	403	29	Japan	207	18
France	352	26	Italy	178	16
Sweden	291	21	Switzerland	145	13
Argentina	108	8	Poland	110	10
			W. Germany	109	10

Percentage of World Total

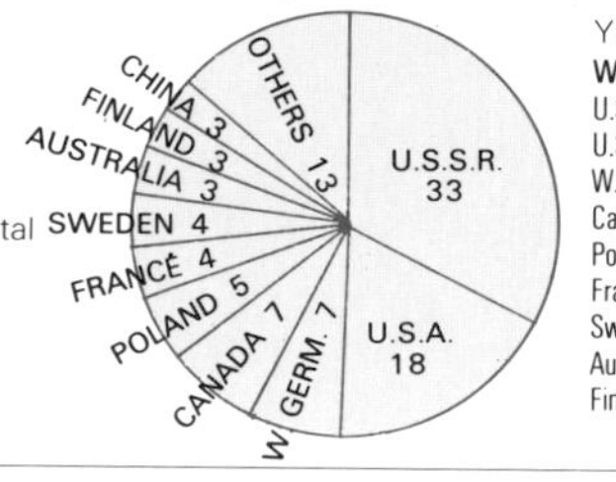
U.S.S.R. 33
U.S.A. 18
W. GERM. 7
CANADA 7
POLAND 5
FRANCE 4
SWEDEN 4
AUSTRALIA 3
FINLAND 3
CHINA 3
OTHERS 13

Yield	kg/ha
World average	**1604**
U.S.S.R.	1144
U.S.A.	1950
W. Germany	4112
Canada	1933
Poland	2010
France	3002
Sweden	3610
Australia	1122
Finland	2843

RICE

World Production
1977-1979 average
million tonnes
378.6

Exports	th tonnes	% of world total	Imports	th tonnes	% of world total
Thailand	2723	22	Indonesia	1908	18
U.S.A.	2281	19	Brazil	711	7
China	1470	12	Bangladesh	658	6
Pakistan	1367	11	U.S.S.R.	631	6
Burma	607	5			
Japan	603	5			

Percentage of World Total

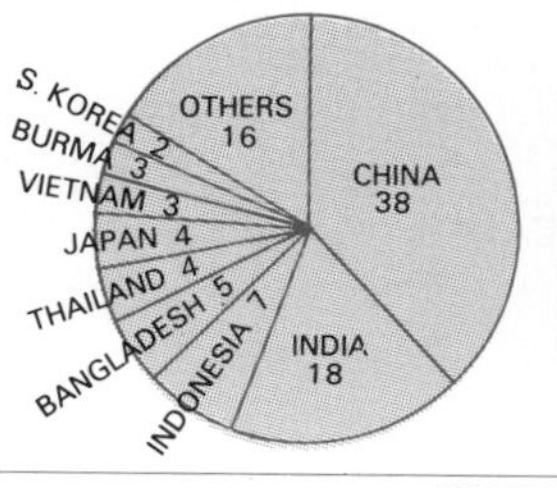
CHINA 38
INDIA 18
INDONESIA 7
BANGLADESH 5
THAILAND 4
JAPAN 4
VIETNAM 3
BURMA 3
S. KOREA 2
OTHERS 16

Yield	kg/ha
World average	**2615**
China	3717
India	1792
Indonesia	2977
Bangladesh	1936
Thailand	1884
Japan	6240
Vietnam	1869
Burma	1995
S. Korea	6556

Maps based on Modified Homolographic Projection

1 tonne (metric ton) = 0·98 tons = 2204·62 pounds
1 kg (kilogram) = 2·20 pounds
1 ha (hectare) = 2·47 acres
1 kg/ha = 0·89 pounds/acres

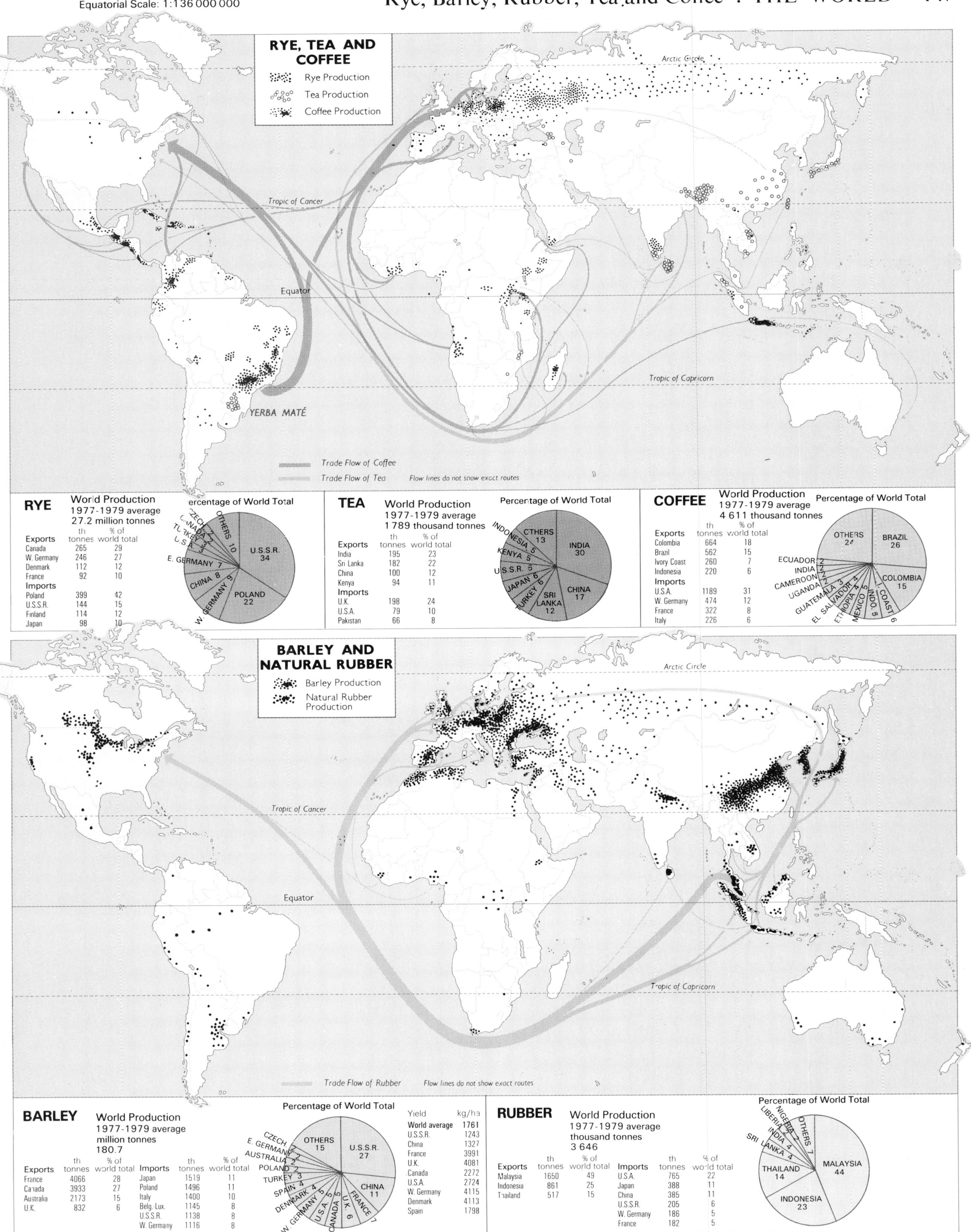

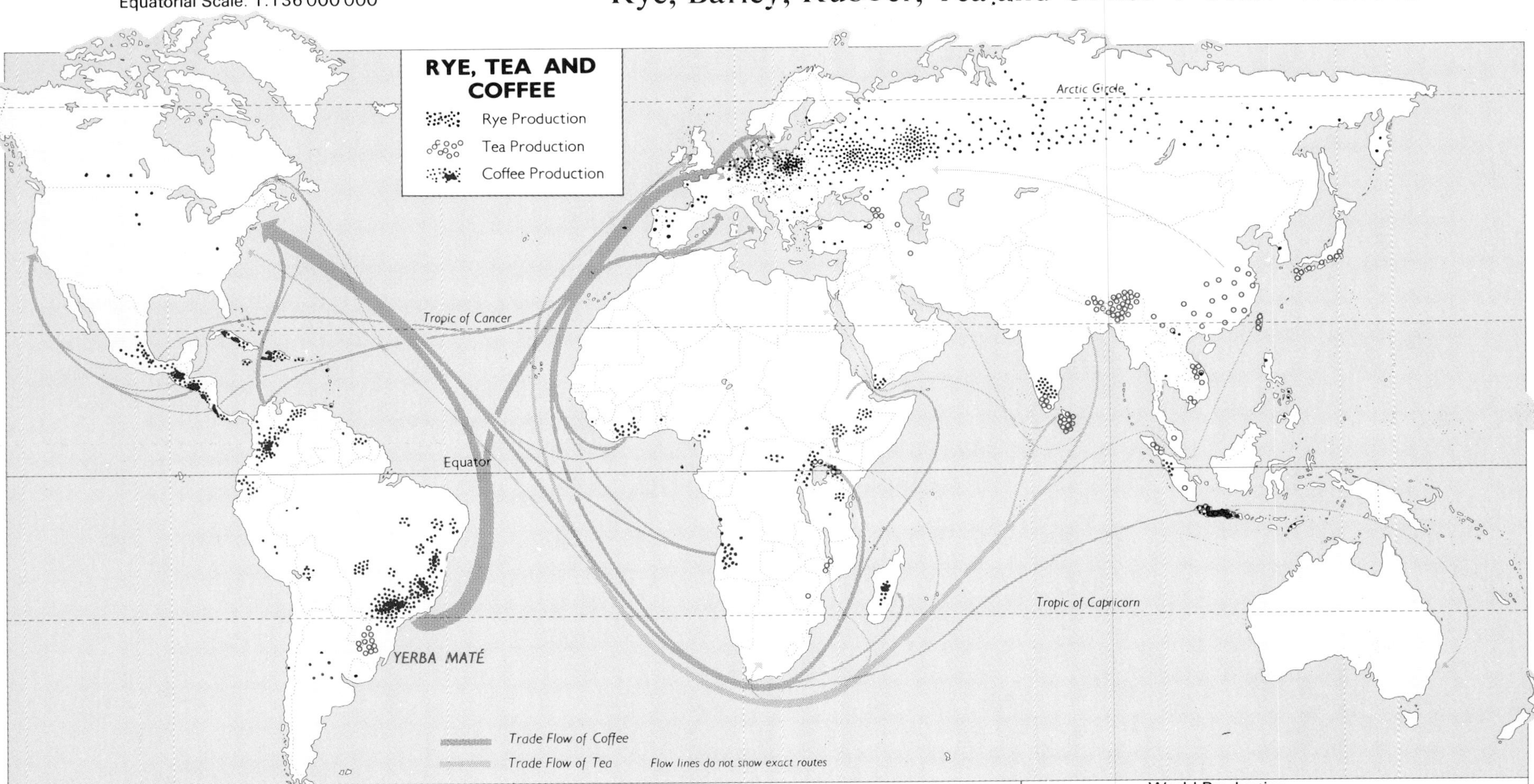
RYE, TEA AND COFFEE
Rye Production
Tea Production
Coffee Production
Arctic Circle
Tropic of Cancer
Equator
Tropic of Capricorn
YERBA MATÉ
Trade Flow of Coffee
Trade Flow of Tea
Flow lines do not show exact routes

RYE

World Production
1977-1979 average
27.2 million tonnes

Exports	th tonnes	% of world total
Canada	265	29
W. Germany	246	27
Denmark	112	12
France	92	10
Imports		
Poland	399	42
U.S.S.R.	144	15
Finland	114	12
Japan	98	10

Percentage of World Total

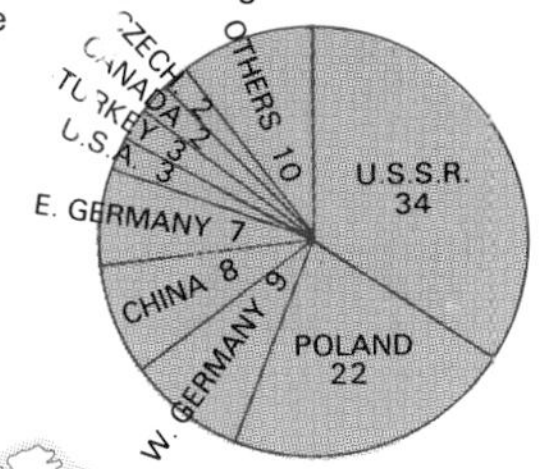
CZECH. 2
CANADA 2
TURKEY 3
U.S.A. 3
OTHERS 10
U.S.S.R. 34
E. GERMANY 7
CHINA 8
W. GERMANY 9
POLAND 22

TEA

World Production
1977-1979 average
1 789 thousand tonnes

Exports	th tonnes	% of world total
India	195	23
Sri Lanka	182	22
China	100	12
Kenya	94	11
Imports		
U.K.	198	24
U.S.A.	79	10
Pakistan	66	8

Percentage of World Total

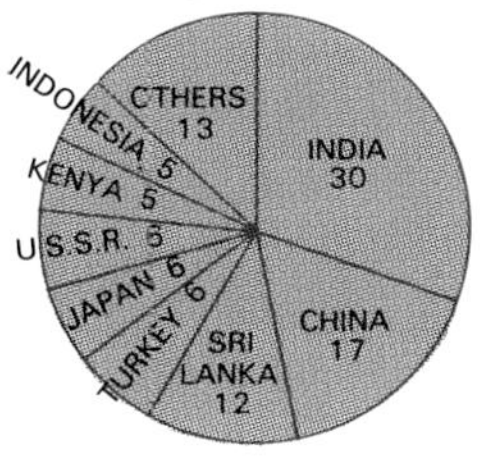
INDONESIA 5
OTHERS 13
INDIA 30
KENYA 5
U.S.S.R. 5
JAPAN 6
TURKEY 6
SRI LANKA 12
CHINA 17

COFFEE

World Production
1977-1979 average
4 611 thousand tonnes

Exports	th tonnes	% of world total
Colombia	664	18
Brazil	562	15
Ivory Coast	260	7
Indonesia	220	6
Imports		
U.S.A.	1189	31
W. Germany	474	12
France	322	8
Italy	226	6

Percentage of World Total

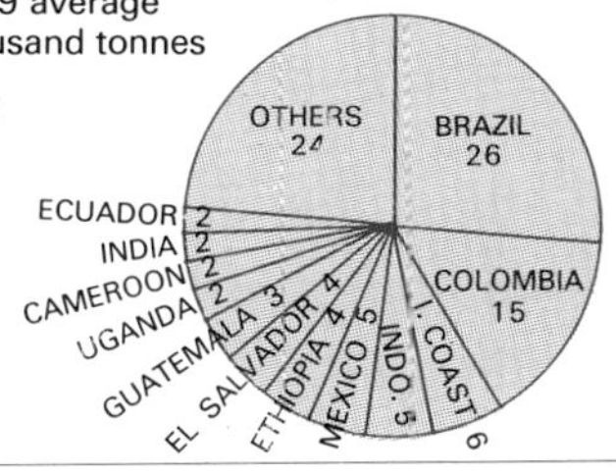
OTHERS 24
BRAZIL 26
ECUADOR 2
INDIA 2
CAMEROON 2
UGANDA 2
GUATEMALA 3
EL SALVADOR 4
ETHIOPIA 4
MEXICO 5
INDO. 5
I. COAST 6
COLOMBIA 15

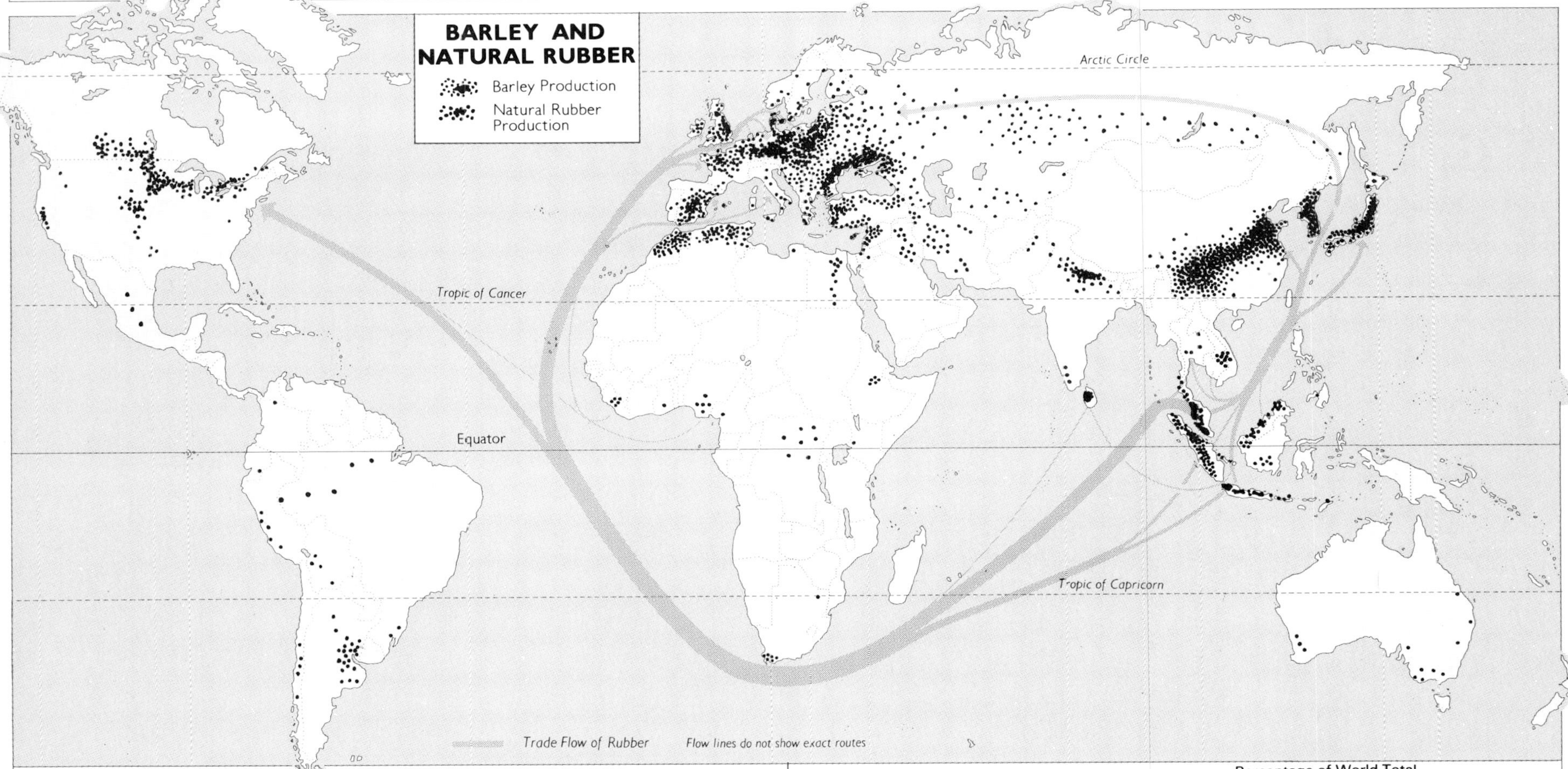
BARLEY AND NATURAL RUBBER
Barley Production
Natural Rubber Production
Arctic Circle
Tropic of Cancer
Equator
Tropic of Capricorn
Trade Flow of Rubber
Flow lines do not show exact routes

BARLEY

World Production
1977-1979 average
million tonnes
180.7

Exports	th tonnes	% of world total	Imports	th tonnes	% of world total
France	4066	28	Japan	1519	11
Canada	3933	27	Poland	1496	11
Australia	2173	15	Italy	1400	10
U.K.	832	6	Belg.-Lux.	1145	8
			U.S.S.R.	1138	8
			W. Germany	1116	8

Percentage of World Total

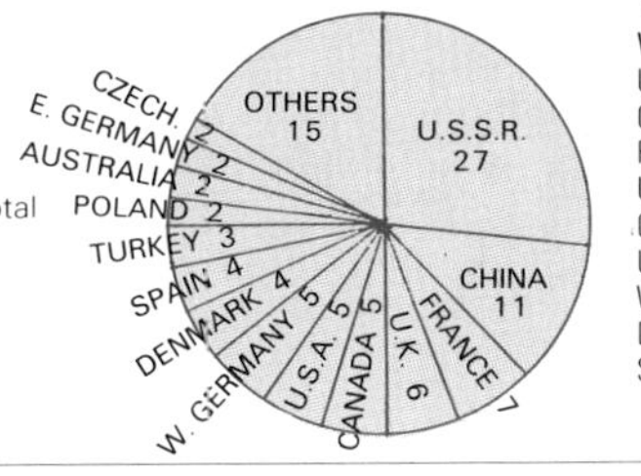
CZECH. 2
E. GERMANY 2
AUSTRALIA 2
POLAND 2
TURKEY 3
SPAIN 4
DENMARK 4
W. GERMANY 5
U.S.A. 5
CANADA 5
U.K. 6
FRANCE 7
OTHERS 15
U.S.S.R. 27
CHINA 11

Yield	kg/ha
World average	**1761**
U.S.S.R.	1243
China	1327
France	3991
U.K.	4081
Canada	2272
U.S.A.	2724
W. Germany	4115
Denmark	4113
Spain	1798

RUBBER

World Production
1977-1979 average
thousand tonnes
3 646

Exports	th tonnes	% of world total	Imports	th tonnes	% of world total
Malaysia	1650	49	U.S.A.	765	22
Indonesia	861	25	Japan	388	11
Thailand	517	15	China	385	11
			U.S.S.R.	205	6
			W. Germany	186	5
			France	182	5

Percentage of World Total

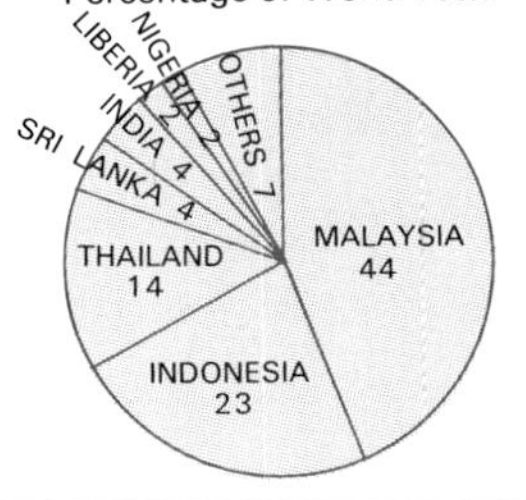
LIBERIA 2
NIGERIA 2
OTHERS 7
INDIA 4
SRI LANKA 4
MALAYSIA 44
THAILAND 14
INDONESIA 23

Maps based on Modified Homolographic Projection

1 tonne (metric ton) = 0·98 tons = 2204·62 pounds
1 kg (kilogram) = 2·20 pounds
1 ha (hectare) = 2·47 acres
1 kg/ha = 0·89 pounds/acres

Equatorial Scale: 1:136 000 000

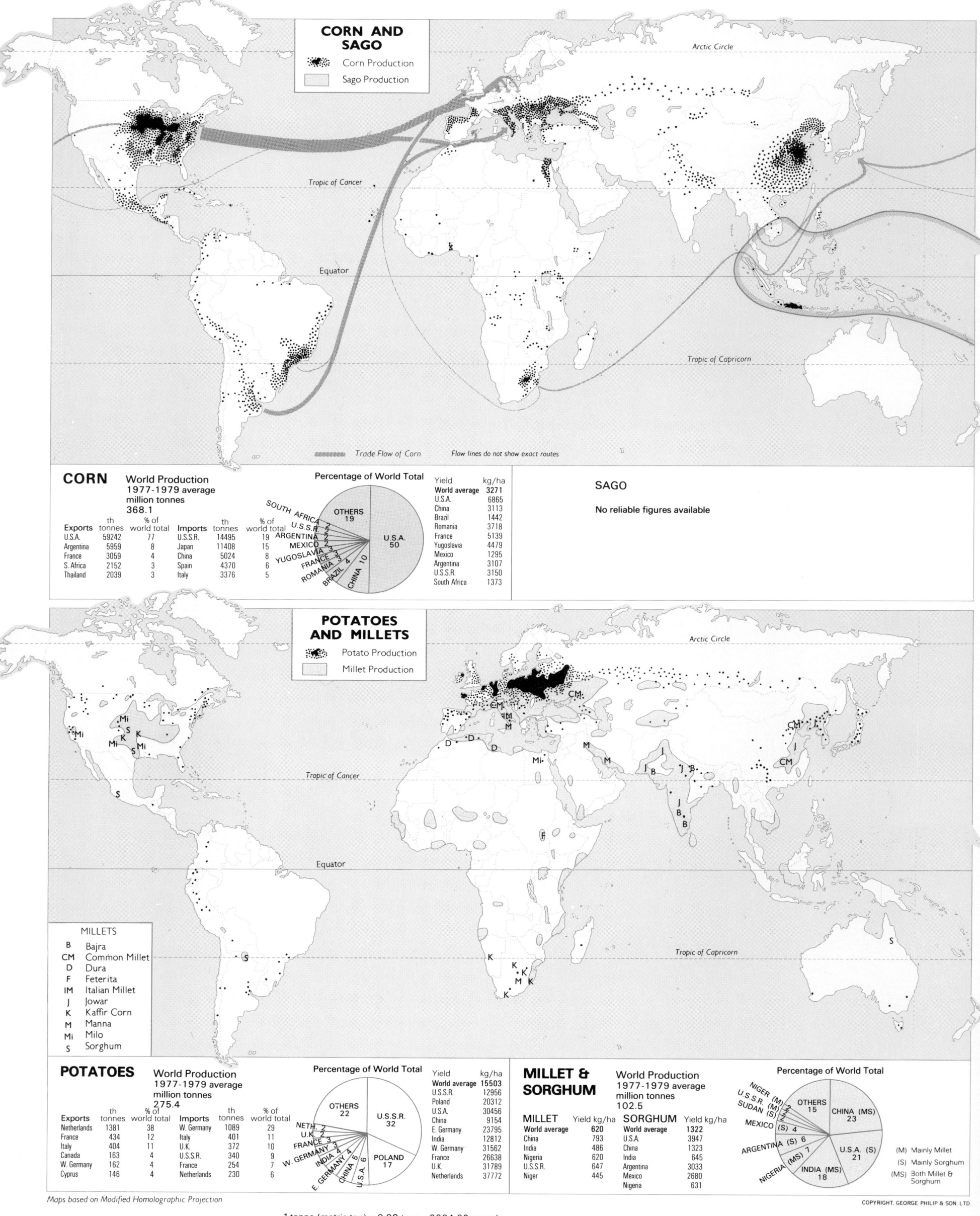

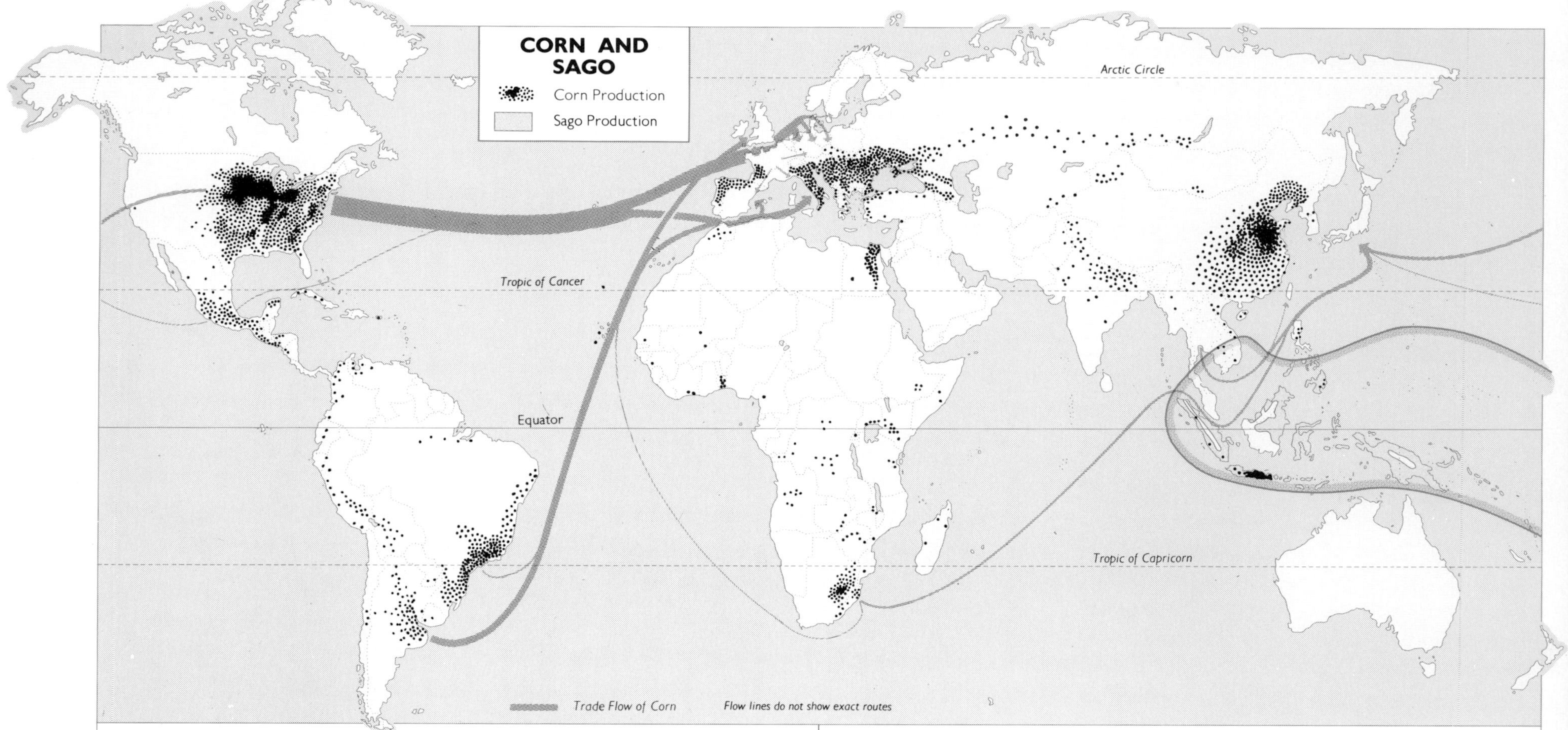
CORN AND SAGO
Corn Production
Sago Production
Arctic Circle
Tropic of Cancer
Equator
Tropic of Capricorn
Trade Flow of Corn
Flow lines do not show exact routes

CORN

World Production
1977-1979 average
million tonnes
368.1

Exports	th tonnes	% of world total	Imports	th tonnes	% of world total
U.S.A.	59242	77	U.S.S.R.	14495	19
Argentina	5959	8	Japan	11408	15
France	3059	4	China	5024	8
S. Africa	2152	3	Spain	4370	6
Thailand	2039	3	Italy	3376	5

Percentage of World Total

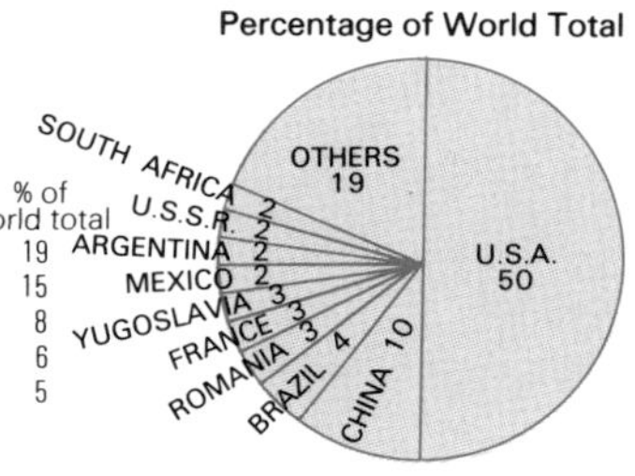
U.S.A. 50
OTHERS 19
SOUTH AFRICA 2
U.S.S.R. 2
ARGENTINA 2
MEXICO 2
YUGOSLAVIA 3
FRANCE 3
ROMANIA 3
BRAZIL 4
CHINA 10

Yield	kg/ha
World average	**3271**
U.S.A.	6865
China	3113
Brazil	1442
Romania	3718
France	5139
Yugoslavia	4479
Mexico	1295
Argentina	3107
U.S.S.R.	3150
South Africa	1373

SAGO

No reliable figures available

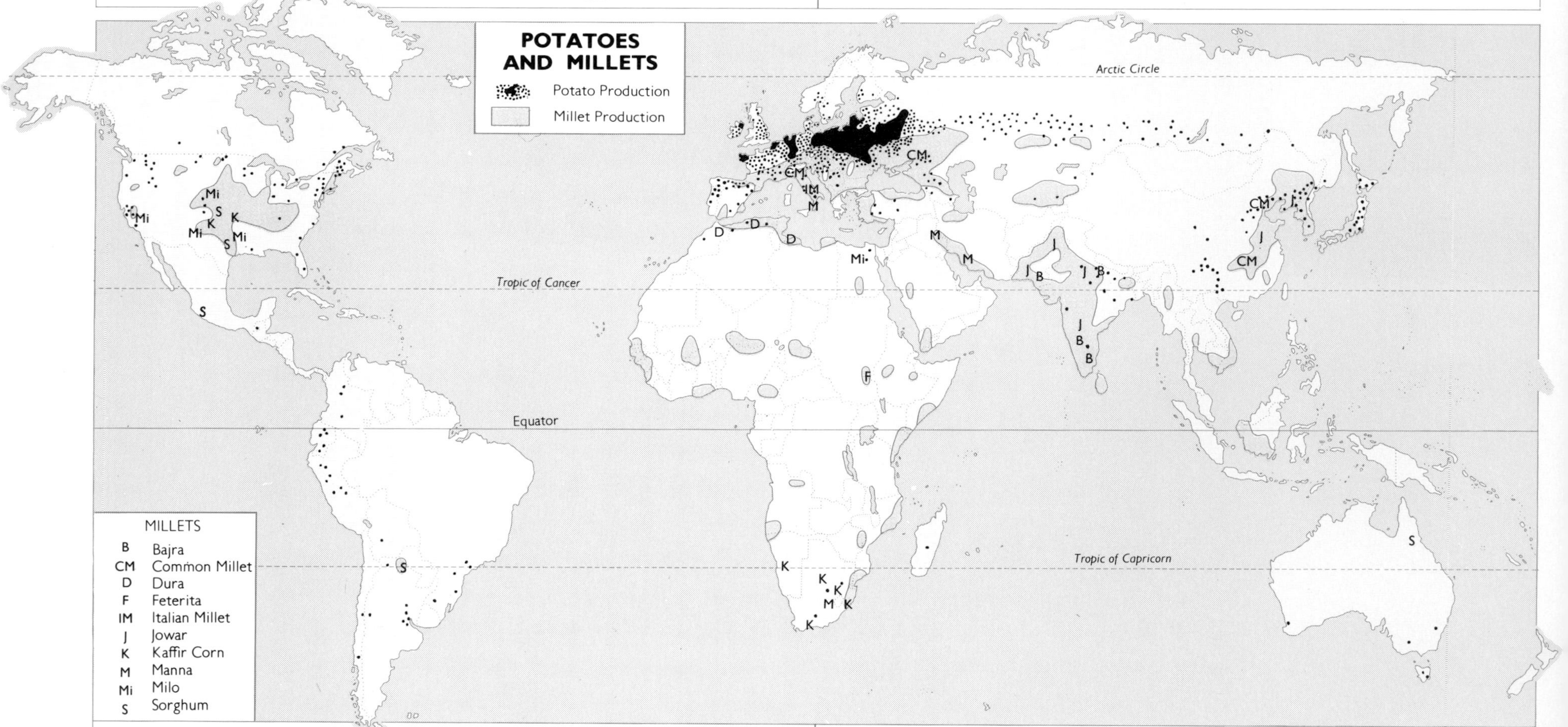
POTATOES AND MILLETS
Potato Production
Millet Production
Arctic Circle
Tropic of Cancer
Equator
Tropic of Capricorn
MILLETS
B Bajra
CM Common Millet
D Dura
F Feterita
IM Italian Millet
J Jowar
K Kaffir Corn
M Manna
Mi Milo
S Sorghum

POTATOES

World Production
1977-1979 average
million tonnes
275.4

Exports	th tonnes	% of world total	Imports	th tonnes	% of world total
Netherlands	1381	38	W. Germany	1089	29
France	434	12	Italy	401	11
Italy	404	11	U.K.	372	10
Canada	163	4	U.S.S.R.	340	9
W. Germany	162	4	France	254	7
Cyprus	146	4	Netherlands	230	6

Percentage of World Total

U.S.S.R. 32
POLAND 17
OTHERS 22
NETH. 2
U.K. 2
FRANCE 3
W. GERMANY 3
INDIA 4
E. GERMANY 4
CHINA 5
U.S.A. 6

Yield	kg/ha
World average	**15503**
U.S.S.R.	12956
Poland	20312
U.S.A.	30456
China	9154
E. Germany	23795
India	12812
W. Germany	31562
France	26638
U.K.	31789
Netherlands	37772

MILLET & SORGHUM

World Production
1977-1979 average
million tonnes
102.5

MILLET	Yield kg/ha	SORGHUM	Yield kg/ha
World average	**620**	**World average**	**1322**
China	793	U.S.A.	3947
India	486	China	1323
Nigeria	620	India	645
U.S.S.R.	647	Argentina	3033
Niger	445	Mexico	2680
		Nigeria	631

Percentage of World Total

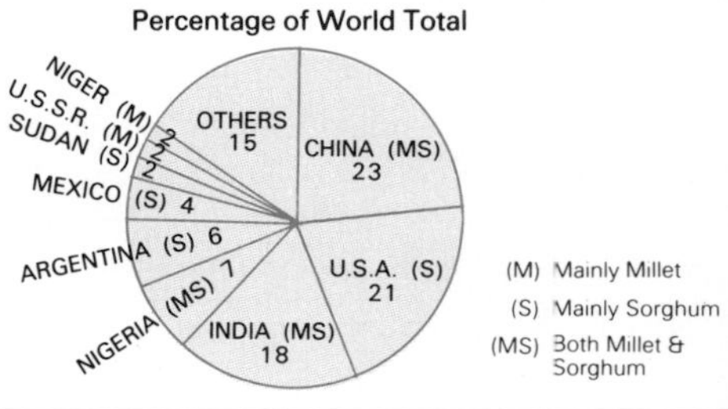
CHINA (MS) 23
U.S.A. (S) 21
INDIA (MS) 18
NIGERIA (MS) 7
ARGENTINA (S) 6
MEXICO (S) 4
SUDAN (S) 2
U.S.S.R. (M) 2
NIGER (M) 2
OTHERS 15
(M) Mainly Millet
(S) Mainly Sorghum
(MS) Both Millet & Sorghum

Maps based on Modified Homolographic Projection

1 tonne (metric ton) = 0·98 tons = 2204·62 pounds
1 kg (kilogram) = 2·20 pounds
1 ha (hectare) = 2·47 acres
1 kg/ha = 0·89 pounds/acres

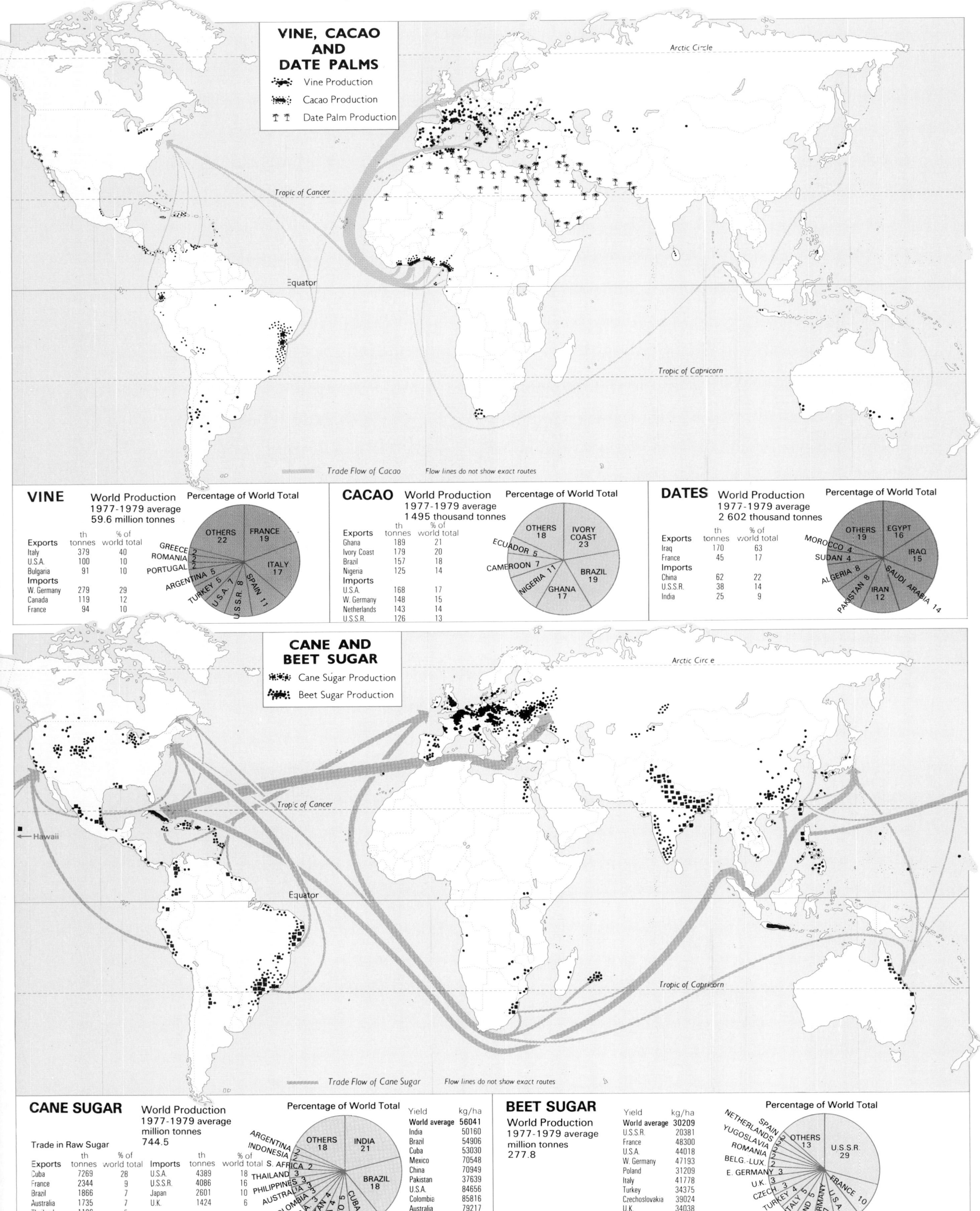

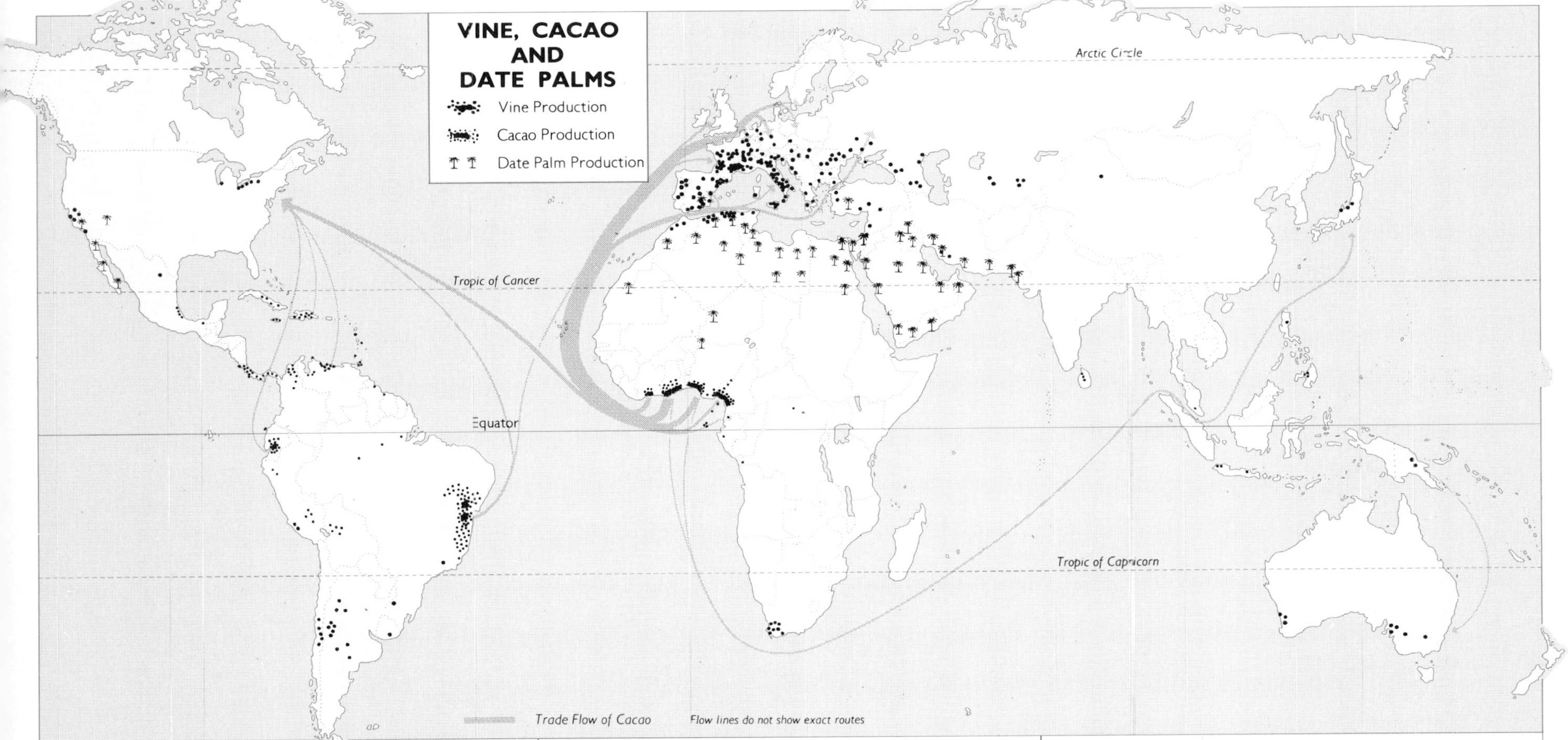
VINE, CACAO AND DATE PALMS
Vine Production
Cacao Production
Date Palm Production
Arctic Circle
Tropic of Cancer
Equator
Tropic of Capricorn
Trade Flow of Cacao
Flow lines do not show exact routes

VINE

World Production
1977-1979 average
59.6 million tonnes

Exports	th tonnes	% of world total
Italy	379	40
U.S.A.	100	10
Bulgaria	91	10
Imports		
W. Germany	279	29
Canada	119	12
France	94	10

Percentage of World Total

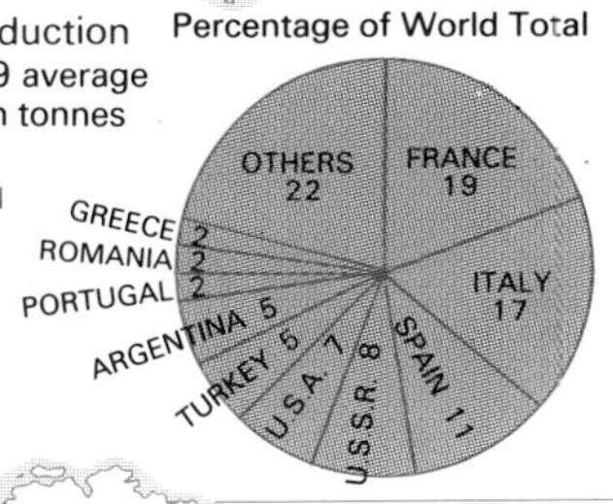
OTHERS 22
FRANCE 19
ITALY 17
SPAIN 11
U.S.S.R. 8
U.S.A. 7
TURKEY 5
ARGENTINA 5
PORTUGAL 2
ROMANIA 2
GREECE 2

CACAO

World Production
1977-1979 average
1 495 thousand tonnes

Exports	th tonnes	% of world total
Ghana	189	21
Ivory Coast	179	20
Brazil	157	18
Nigeria	125	14
Imports		
U.S.A.	168	17
W. Germany	148	15
Netherlands	143	14
U.S.S.R.	126	13

Percentage of World Total

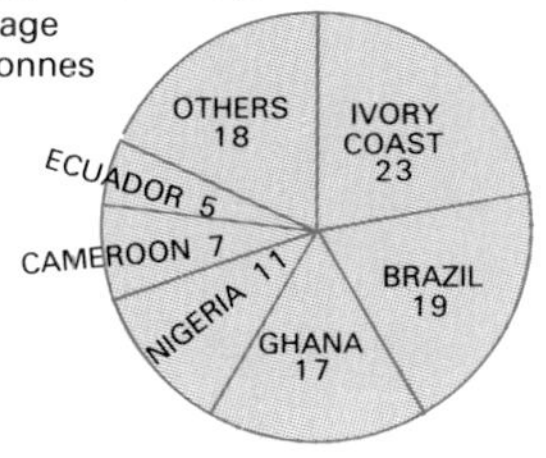
OTHERS 18
IVORY COAST 23
BRAZIL 19
GHANA 17
NIGERIA 11
CAMEROON 7
ECUADOR 5

DATES

World Production
1977-1979 average
2 602 thousand tonnes

Exports	th tonnes	% of world total
Iraq	170	63
France	45	17
Imports		
China	62	22
U.S.S.R.	38	14
India	25	9

Percentage of World Total

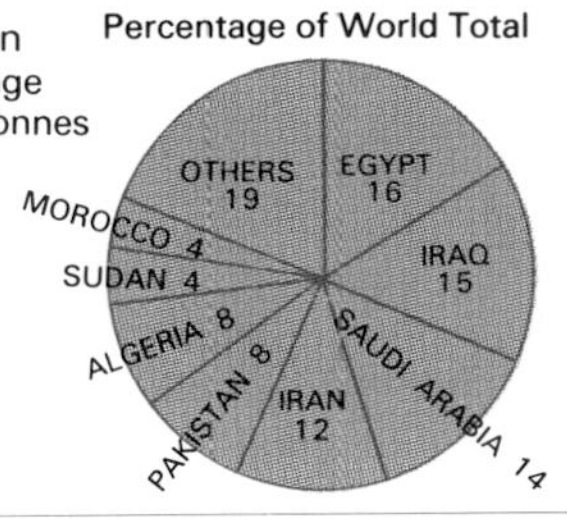
OTHERS 19
EGYPT 16
IRAQ 15
SAUDI ARABIA 14
IRAN 12
PAKISTAN 8
ALGERIA 8
SUDAN 4
MOROCCO 4

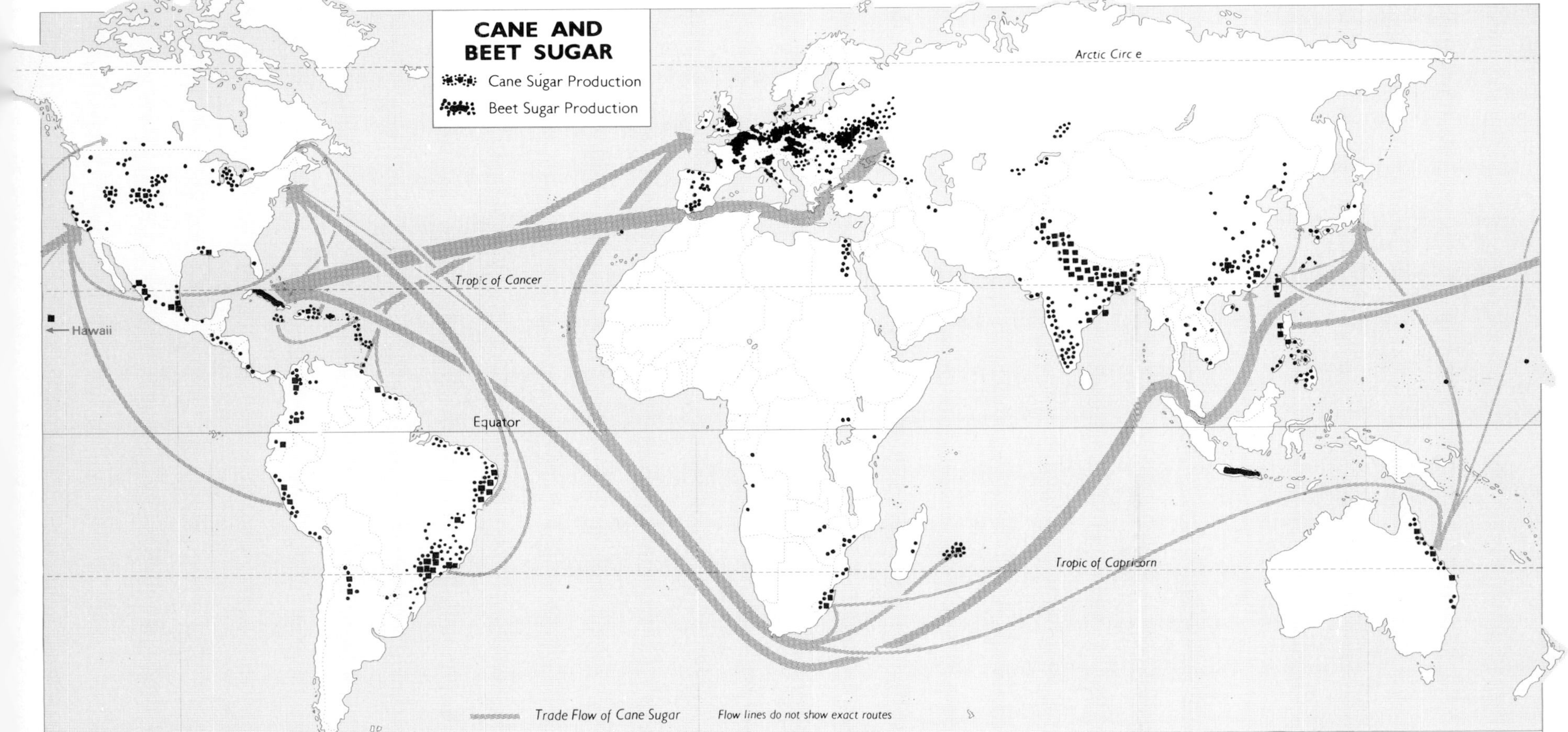
CANE AND BEET SUGAR
Cane Sugar Production
Beet Sugar Production
Arctic Circle
Tropic of Cancer
Hawaii
Equator
Tropic of Capricorn
Trade Flow of Cane Sugar
Flow lines do not show exact routes

CANE SUGAR

World Production
1977-1979 average
million tonnes
744.5

Trade in Raw Sugar

Exports	th tonnes	% of world total	Imports	th tonnes	% of world total
Cuba	7269	28	U.S.A.	4389	18
France	2344	9	U.S.S.R.	4086	16
Brazil	1866	7	Japan	2601	10
Australia	1735	7	U.K.	1424	6
Thailand	1186	5			
Philippines	1158	4			

Percentage of World Total

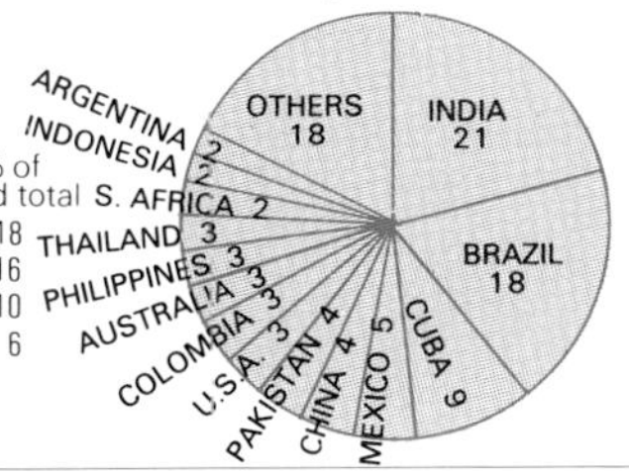
OTHERS 18
INDIA 21
BRAZIL 18
CUBA 9
MEXICO 5
CHINA 4
PAKISTAN 4
U.S.A. 3
COLOMBIA 3
AUSTRALIA 3
PHILIPPINES 3
THAILAND 3
S. AFRICA 2
INDONESIA 2
ARGENTINA 2

Yield	kg/ha
World average	**56041**
India	50160
Brazil	54906
Cuba	53030
Mexico	70548
China	70949
Pakistan	37639
U.S.A.	84656
Colombia	85816
Australia	79217
Philippines	42411

BEET SUGAR

World Production
1977-1979 average
million tonnes
277.8

Yield	kg/ha
World average	**30209**
U.S.S.R.	20381
France	48300
U.S.A.	44018
W. Germany	47193
Poland	31209
Italy	41778
Turkey	34375
Czechoslovakia	39024
U.K.	34038
E. Germany	26000

Percentage of World Total

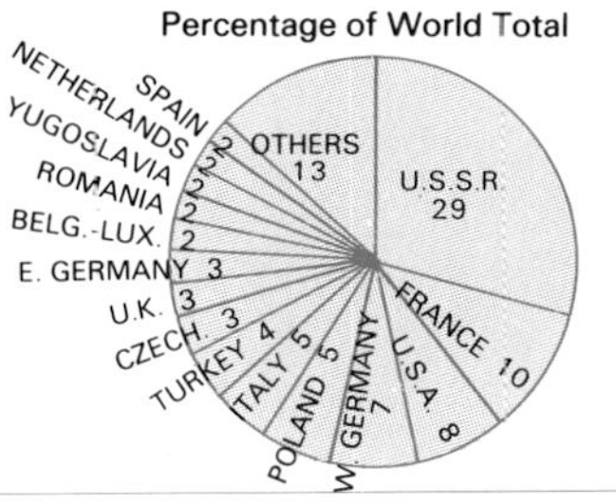
OTHERS 13
U.S.S.R. 29
FRANCE 10
U.S.A. 8
W. GERMANY 7
POLAND 5
ITALY 5
TURKEY 4
CZECH 3
U.K. 3
E. GERMANY 3
BELG.-LUX 2
ROMANIA 2
YUGOSLAVIA 2
NETHERLANDS 2
SPAIN 2

Maps based on Modified Homolographic Projection

1 tonne (metric ton) = 0·98 tons = 2204·62 pounds
1 kg (kilogram) = 2·20 pounds
1 ha (hectare) = 2·47 acres
1 kg/ha = 0·89 pounds/acres

Equatorial Scale: 1:136 000 000

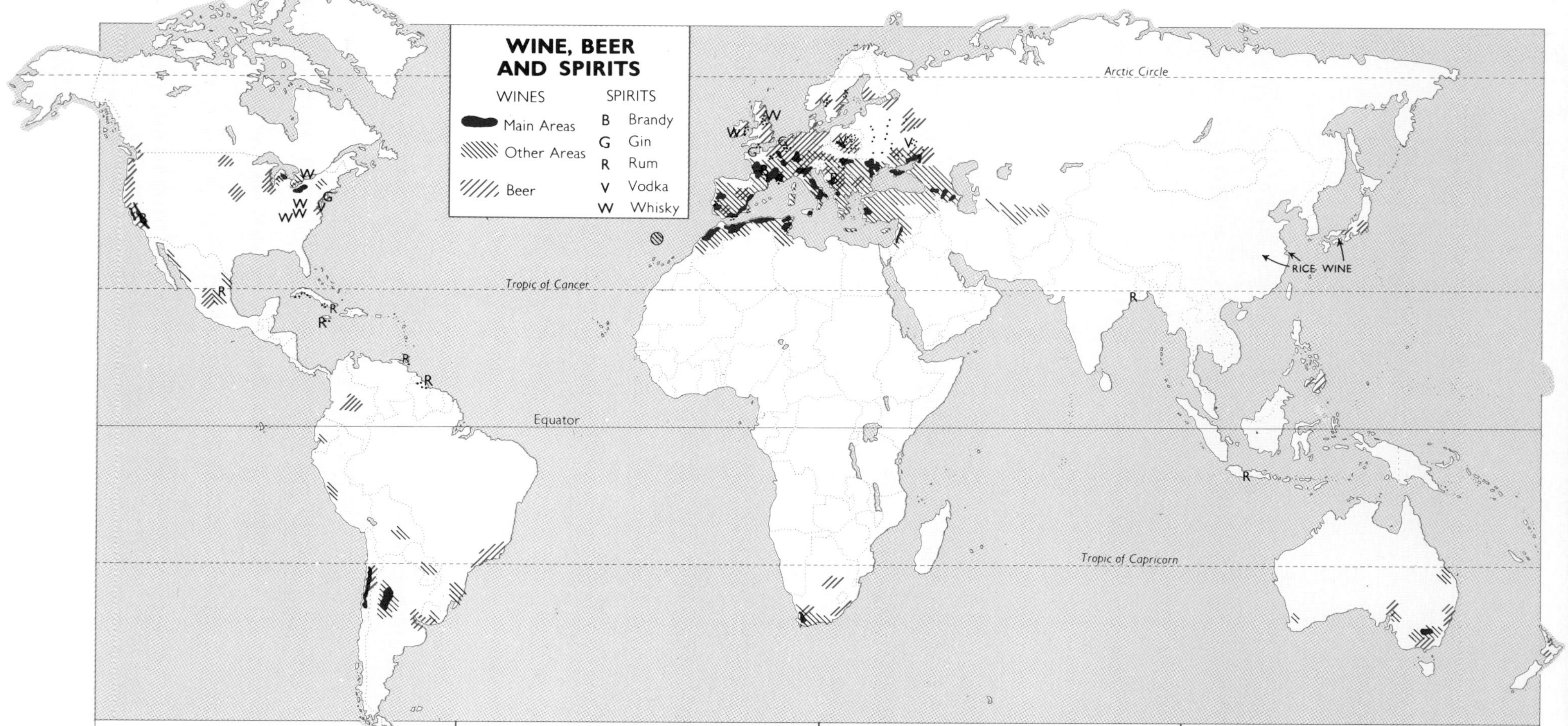
WINE, BEER AND SPIRITS
WINES
Main Areas
Other Areas
Beer
SPIRITS
B Brandy
G Gin
R Rum
V Vodka
W Whisky
Arctic Circle
Tropic of Cancer
Equator
Tropic of Capricorn
RICE WINE

WINE PRODUCTION

World Production
1977-1979 average
million tonnes
314.2

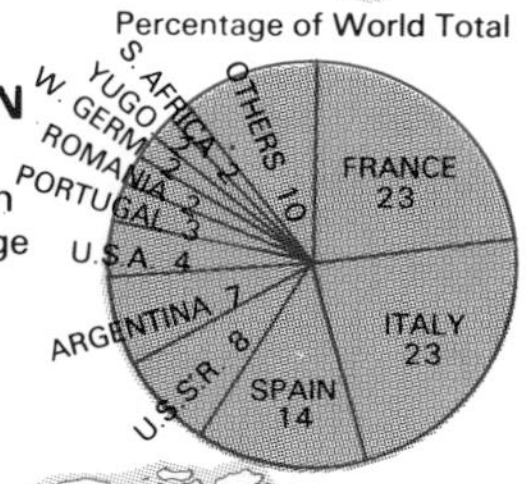
Percentage of World Total
FRANCE 23
ITALY 23
SPAIN 14
U.S.S.R. 8
ARGENTINA 7
U.S.A. 4
PORTUGAL 3
ROMANIA 3
W. GERM. 2
YUGO. 2
S. AFRICA 2
OTHERS 10

WINE EXPORTS

World Exports
1976-1978 average
million tonnes
4.29

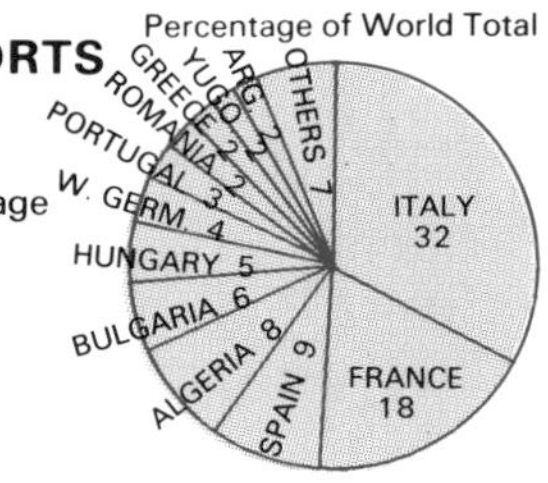
Percentage of World Total
ITALY 32
FRANCE 18
SPAIN 9
ALGERIA 8
BULGARIA 6
HUNGARY 5
W. GERM. 4
PORTUGAL 4
ROMANIA 3
GREECE 2
YUGO. 2
ARG. 2
OTHERS 7

WINE IMPORTS

World Imports
1976-1978 average
million tonnes
4.30

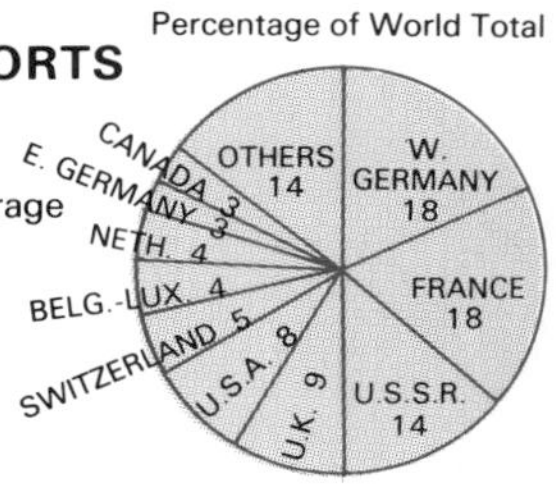
Percentage of World Total
W. GERMANY 18
FRANCE 18
U.S.S.R. 14
U.K. 9
U.S.A. 8
SWITZERLAND 5
BELG.-LUX. 4
NETH. 4
E. GERMANY 3
CANADA 3
OTHERS 14

BEER PRODUCTION

World Production
1976-1978 average
million hectolitres
809.0

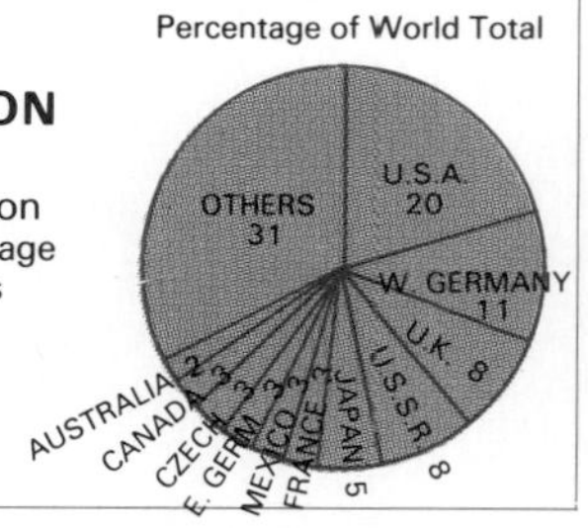
Percentage of World Total
U.S.A. 20
W. GERMANY 11
U.K. 8
U.S.S.R. 8
JAPAN 5
FRANCE
MEXICO
E. GERM.
CZECH.
CANADA
AUSTRALIA
OTHERS 31

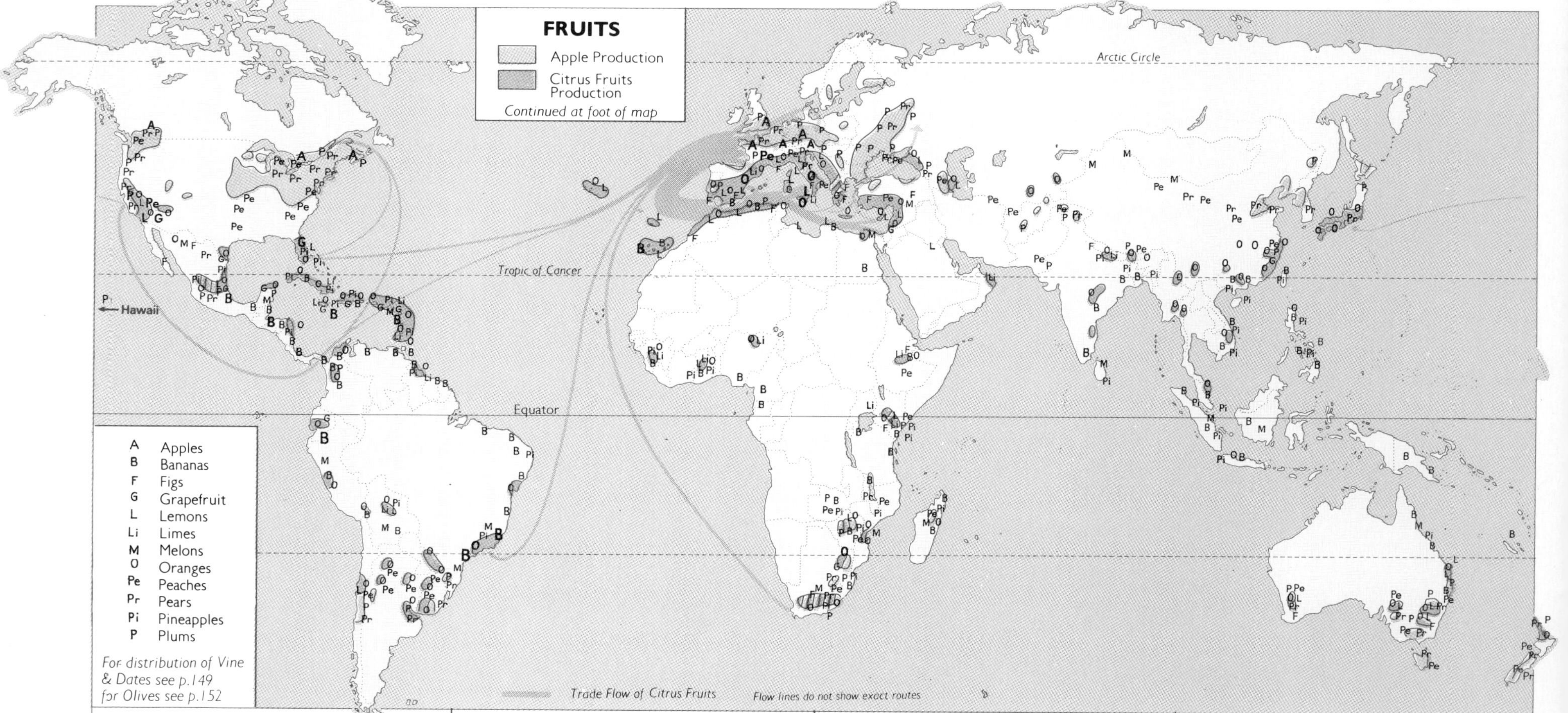
FRUITS
Apple Production
Citrus Fruits Production
Continued at foot of map
Arctic Circle
Tropic of Cancer
Equator
Hawaii
A Apples
B Bananas
F Figs
G Grapefruit
L Lemons
Li Limes
M Melons
O Oranges
Pe Peaches
Pr Pears
Pi Pineapples
P Plums
For distribution of Vine & Dates see p.149 for Olives see p.152
Trade Flow of Citrus Fruits
Flow lines do not show exact routes

CITRUS FRUITS

World Production
1977-1979 average
million tonnes
53.1

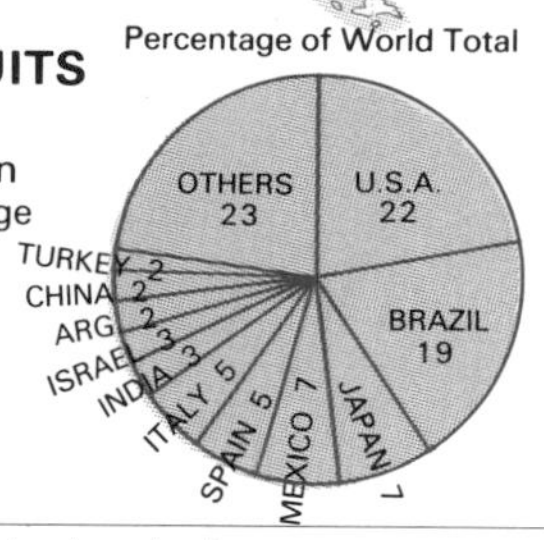
Percentage of World Total
U.S.A. 22
BRAZIL 19
JAPAN 7
MEXICO 7
SPAIN 5
ITALY 5
INDIA 3
ISRAEL 3
ARG. 2
CHINA 2
TURKEY 2
OTHERS 23

BANANAS

World Production
1977-1979 average
million tonnes
36.9

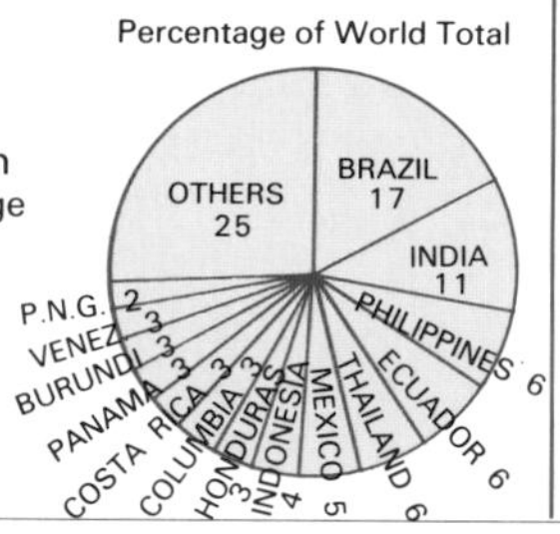
Percentage of World Total
BRAZIL 17
INDIA 11
PHILIPPINES 6
ECUADOR 6
THAILAND 6
MEXICO 5
INDONESIA 4
HONDURAS 3
COLUMBIA 3
COSTA RICA 3
PANAMA 3
BURUNDI 3
VENEZ. 3
P.N.G. 2
OTHERS 25

APPLES

World Production
1977-1979 average
million tonnes
33.0

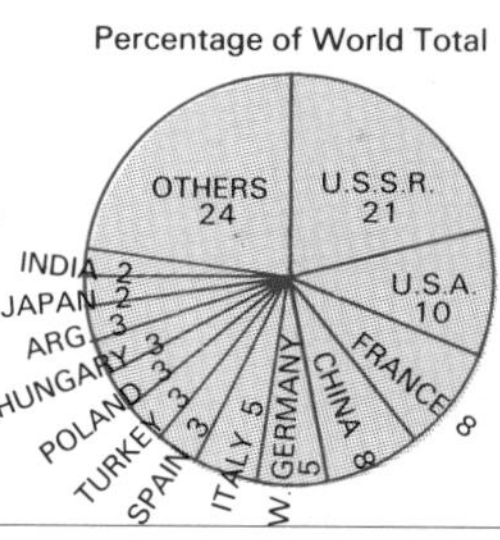
Percentage of World Total
U.S.S.R. 21
U.S.A. 10
FRANCE 8
CHINA 8
W. GERMANY 5
ITALY 5
SPAIN 3
TURKEY 3
POLAND 3
HUNGARY 3
ARG. 3
JAPAN 3
INDIA 2
OTHERS 24

PEARS

World Production
1977-1979 average
million tonnes
7.24

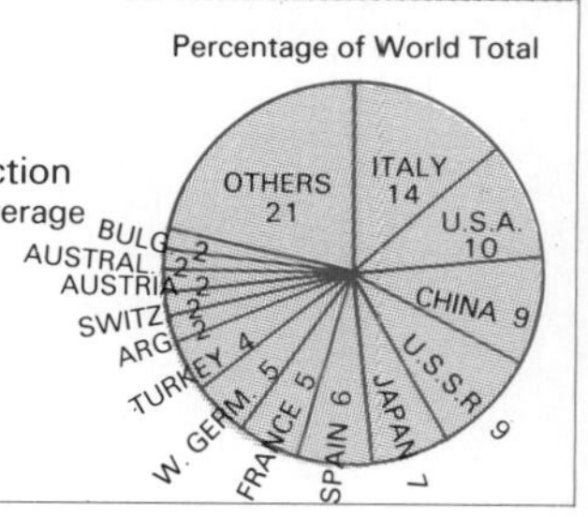
Percentage of World Total
ITALY 14
U.S.A. 10
CHINA 9
U.S.S.R. 9
JAPAN 7
SPAIN 6
FRANCE 5
W. GERM. 5
TURKEY 4
ARG.
SWITZ.
AUSTRIA
AUSTRAL.
BULG.
OTHERS 21

Maps based on Modified Homolographic Projection

1 tonne (metric ton) = 0·98 tons = 2204·62 pounds
1 kg (kilogram) = 2·20 pounds
1 ha (hectare) = 2·47 acres
1 kg/ha = 0·89 pounds/acres

Equatorial Scale: 1:136 000 000

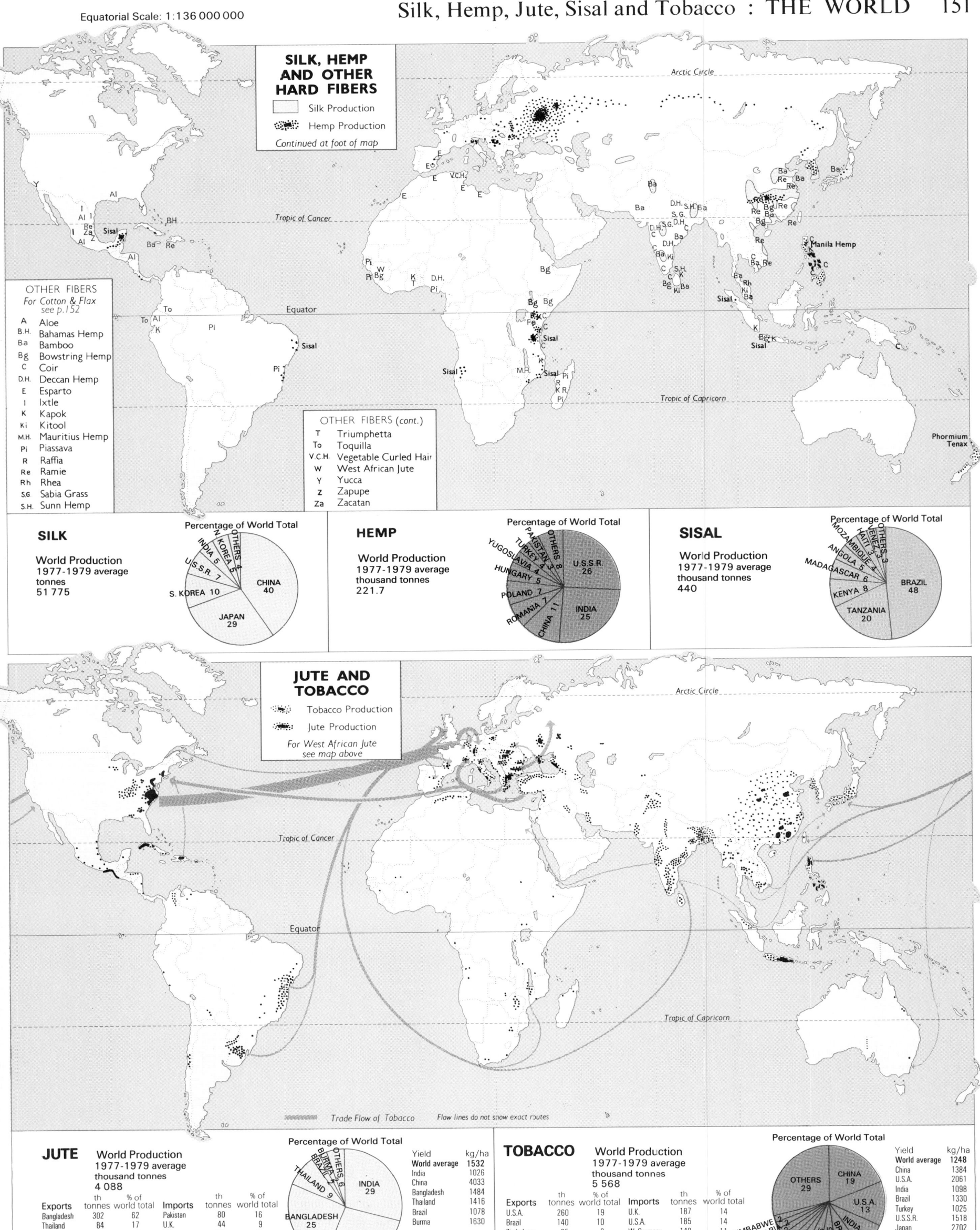

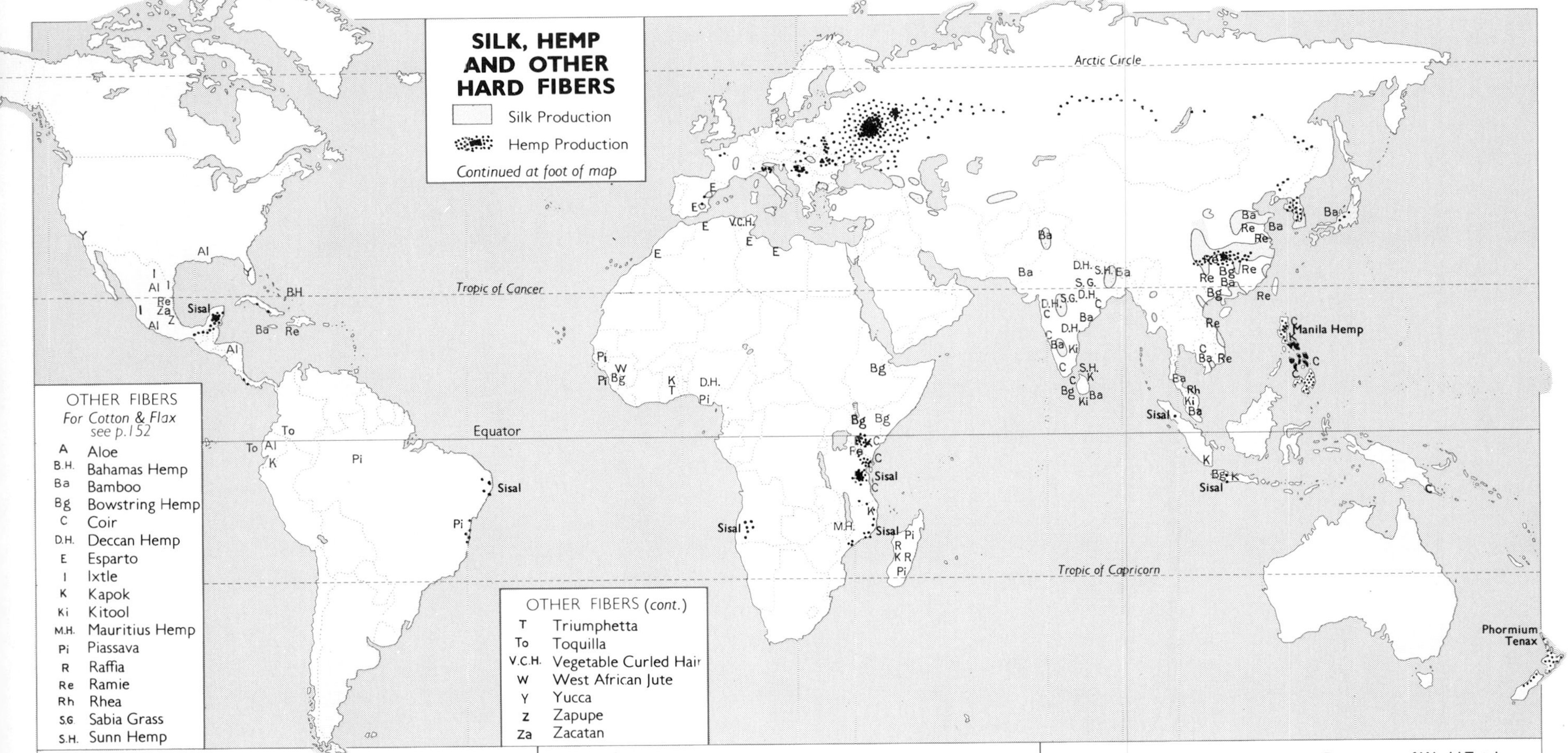
SILK, HEMP AND OTHER HARD FIBERS
Silk Production
Hemp Production
Continued at foot of map
Arctic Circle
Tropic of Cancer
Equator
Tropic of Capricorn
Manila Hemp
Sisal
Phormium Tenax
OTHER FIBERS
For Cotton & Flax see p.152
A Aloe
B.H. Bahamas Hemp
Ba Bamboo
Bg Bowstring Hemp
C Coir
D.H. Deccan Hemp
E Esparto
I Ixtle
K Kapok
Ki Kitool
M.H. Mauritius Hemp
Pi Piassava
R Raffia
Re Ramie
Rh Rhea
S.G. Sabia Grass
S.H. Sunn Hemp
OTHER FIBERS (cont.)
T Triumphetta
To Toquilla
V.C.H. Vegetable Curled Hair
W West African Jute
Y Yucca
Z Zapupe
Za Zacatan

SILK

World Production
1977-1979 average
tonnes
51 775

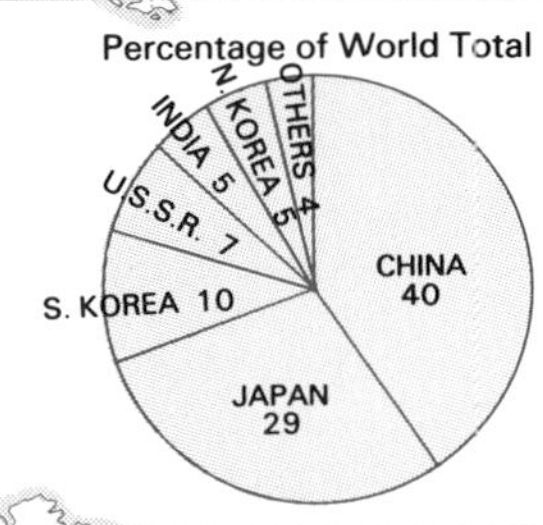
Percentage of World Total
CHINA 40
JAPAN 29
S. KOREA 10
U.S.S.R. 7
INDIA 5
N. KOREA 5
OTHERS 4

HEMP

World Production
1977-1979 average
thousand tonnes
221.7

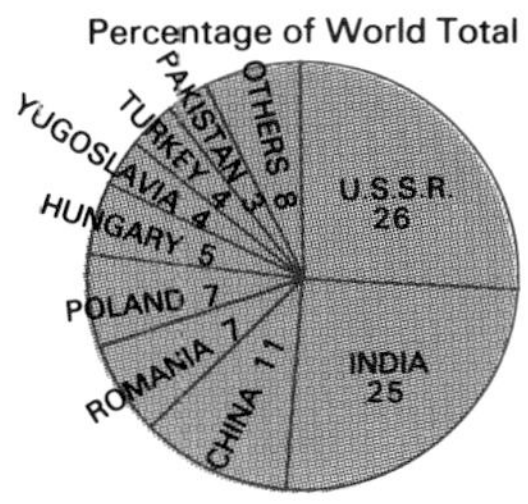
Percentage of World Total
U.S.S.R. 26
INDIA 25
CHINA 11
ROMANIA 7
POLAND 7
HUNGARY 5
YUGOSLAVIA 4
TURKEY 4
PAKISTAN 3
OTHERS 8

SISAL

World Production
1977-1979 average
thousand tonnes
440

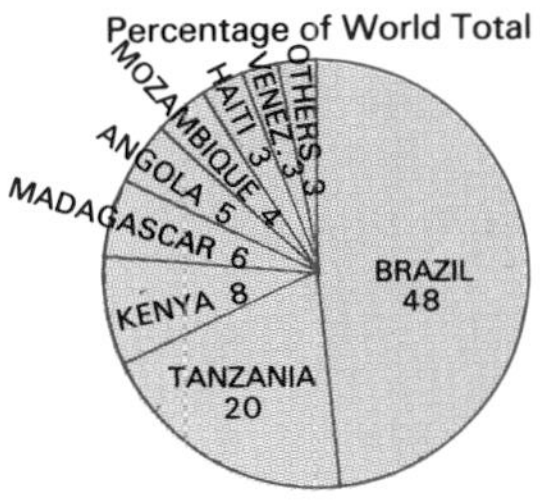
Percentage of World Total
BRAZIL 48
TANZANIA 20
KENYA 8
MADAGASCAR 6
ANGOLA 5
MOZAMBIQUE 4
HAITI 3
VENEZ. 3
OTHERS 3

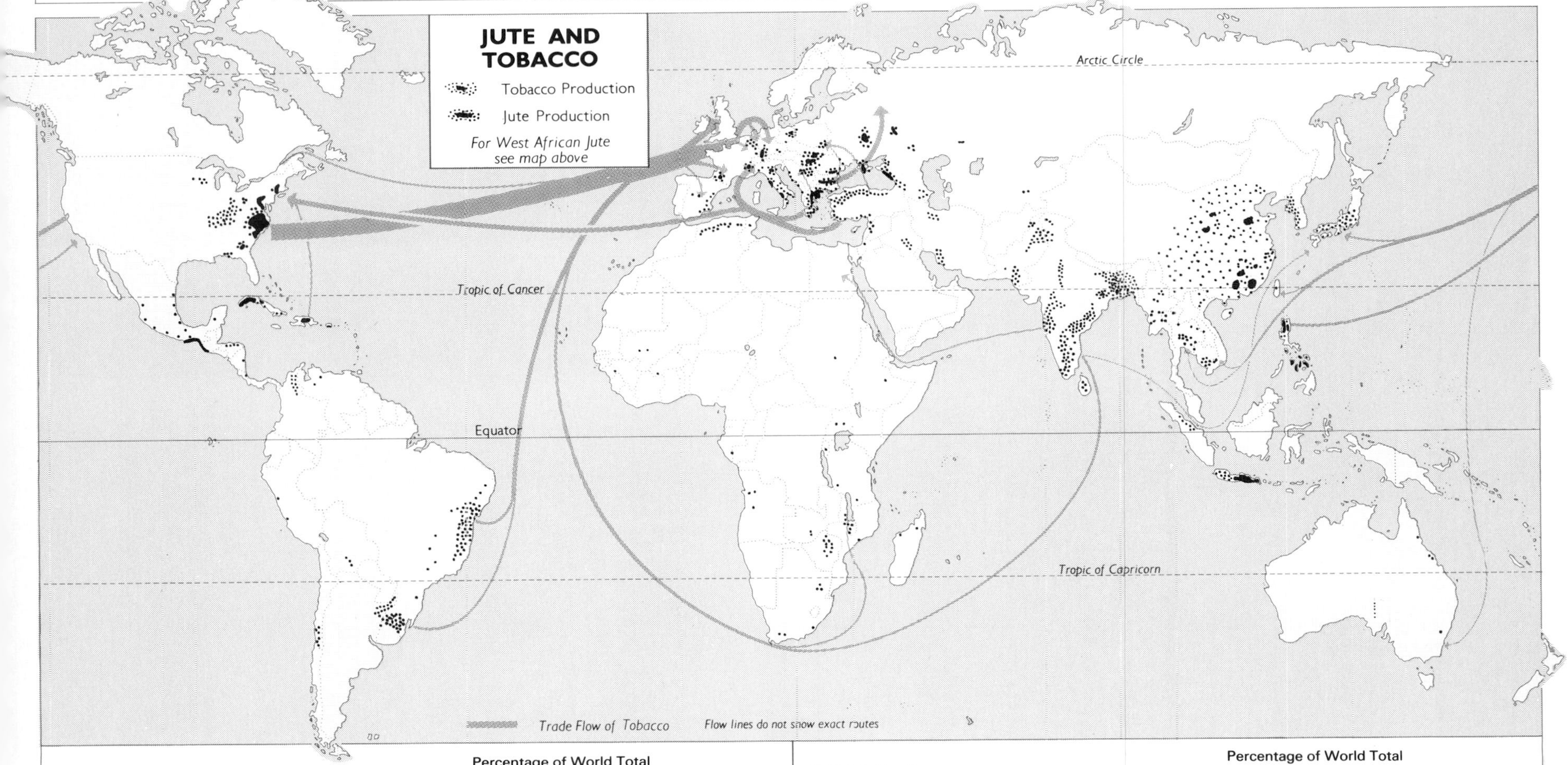
JUTE AND TOBACCO
Tobacco Production
Jute Production
For West African Jute see map above
Arctic Circle
Tropic of Cancer
Equator
Tropic of Capricorn
Trade Flow of Tobacco
Flow lines do not show exact routes

JUTE

World Production
1977-1979 average
thousand tonnes
4 088

Exports	th tonnes	% of world total
Bangladesh	302	62
Thailand	84	17
Nepal	34	7

Imports	th tonnes	% of world total
Pakistan	80	16
U.K.	44	9
China	31	6
U.S.S.R.	27	5
France	22	4
Japan	22	4

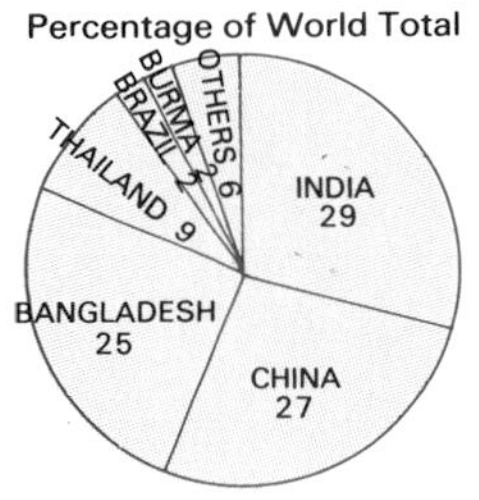
Percentage of World Total
INDIA 29
CHINA 27
BANGLADESH 25
THAILAND 9
BRAZIL 2
BURMA 2
OTHERS 6

Yield	kg/ha
World average	**1532**
India	1026
China	4033
Bangladesh	1484
Thailand	1416
Brazil	1078
Burma	1630

TOBACCO

World Production
1977-1979 average
thousand tonnes
5 568

Exports	th tonnes	% of world total
U.S.A.	260	19
Brazil	140	10
Zimbabwe	85	6
Bulgaria	72	5
Turkey	70	5

Imports	th tonnes	% of world total
U.K.	187	14
U.S.A.	185	14
W. Germany	148	11
France	84	6

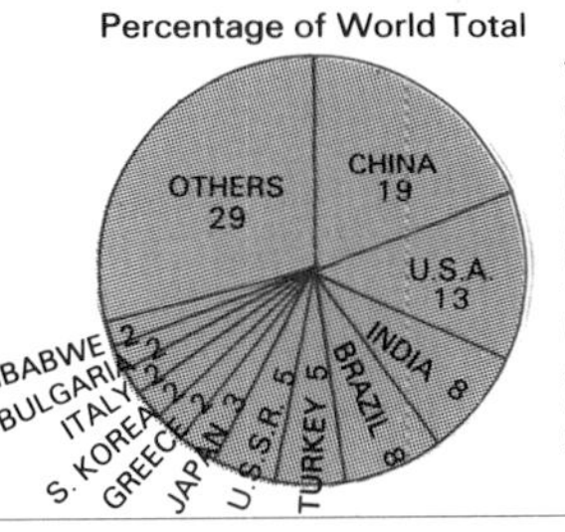
Percentage of World Total
CHINA 19
U.S.A. 13
INDIA 8
BRAZIL 8
TURKEY 5
U.S.S.R. 5
JAPAN 3
GREECE 2
S. KOREA 2
ITALY 2
BULGARIA 2
ZIMBABWE 2
OTHERS 29

Yield	kg/ha
World average	**1248**
China	1384
U.S.A.	2061
India	1098
Brazil	1330
Turkey	1025
U.S.S.R.	1518
Japan	2702
Greece	1245
S. Korea	2086

Maps based on Modified Homolographic Projection

1 tonne (metric ton) = 0·98 tons = 2204·62 pounds
1 kg (kilogram) = 2·20 pounds
1 ha (hectare) = 2·47 acres
1 kg/ha = 0·89 pounds/acres

Equatorial Scale: 1:136 000 000

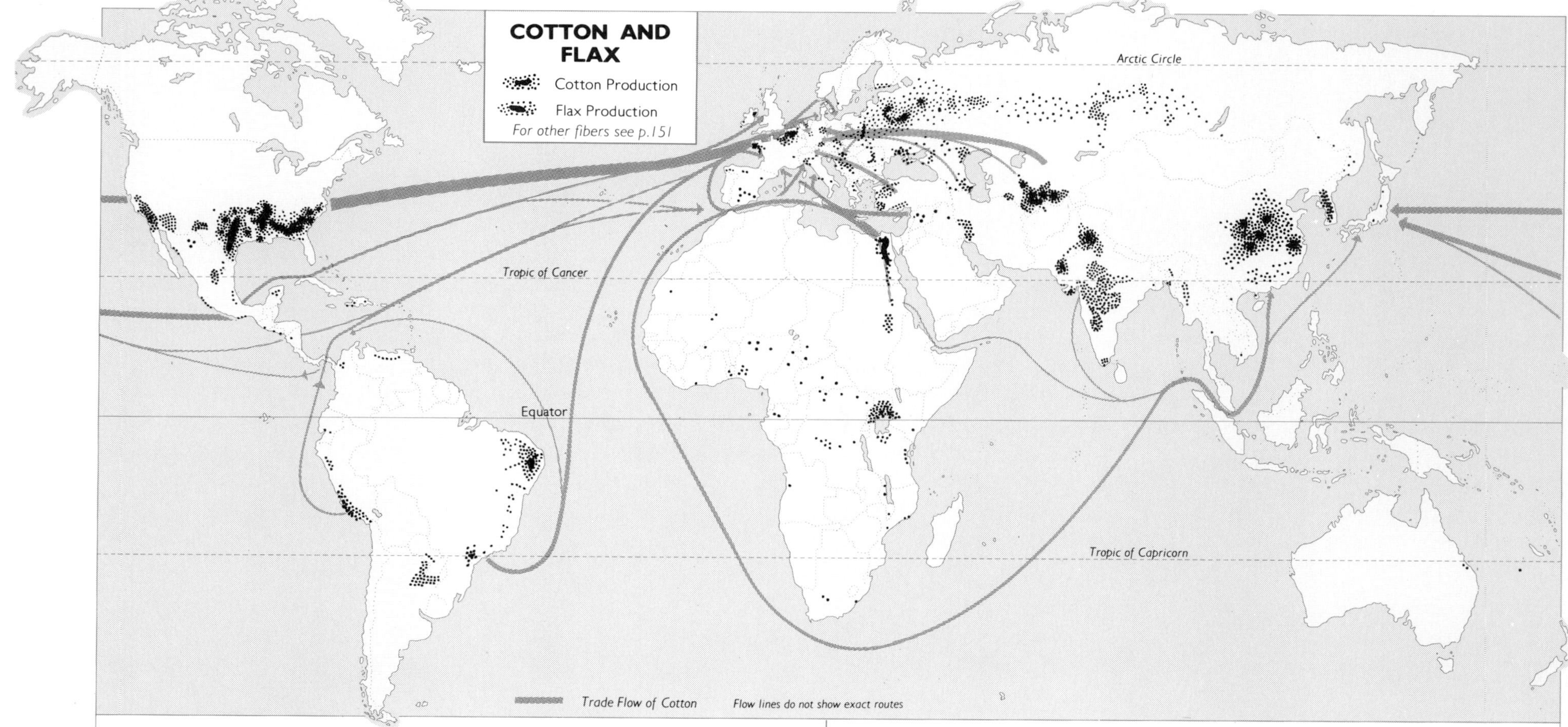
COTTON AND FLAX
Cotton Production
Flax Production
For other fibers see p.151
Arctic Circle
Tropic of Cancer
Equator
Tropic of Capricorn
Trade Flow of Cotton
Flow lines do not show exact routes

COTTON-LINT

World Production
1977-1979 average
million tonnes
13.7

Exports	th tonnes	% of world total	Imports	th tonnes	% of world total
U.S.A.	1448	34	Japan	735	17
U.S.S.R.	789	18	China	728	17
Mexico	212	5	S. Korea	308	7
Sudan	180	4	Italy	231	5
Guatemala	153	4	Hong Kong	197	4
Turkey	151	4	France	183	4

Percentage of World Total
OTHERS 14
U.S.A. 23
U.S.S.R. 20
CHINA 16
INDIA 9
PAKISTAN 5
BRAZIL 4
TURKEY 4
EGYPT 3
MEXICO 2

FLAX

World Production
1977-1979 average
thousand tonnes
672

Exports	th tonnes	% of world total	Imports	th tonnes	% of world total
France	98	36	Belgium-Lux.	131	49
Belgium-Lux.	57	21	Japan	22	8
Netherlands	32	12	Italy	22	8
U.S.S.R.	24	9	France	19	7
China	19	7	U.K.	14	5

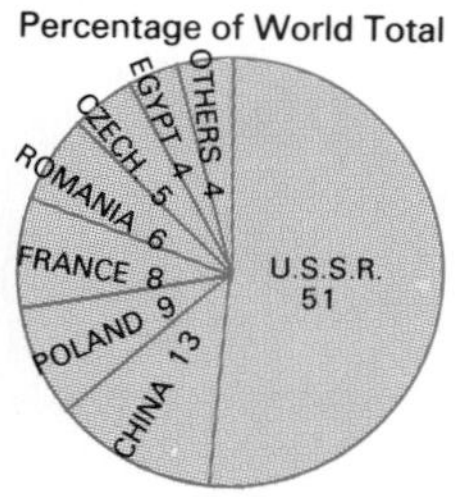
Percentage of World Total
U.S.S.R. 51
CHINA 13
POLAND 9
FRANCE 8
ROMANIA 6
CZECH. 5
EGYPT 4
OTHERS 4

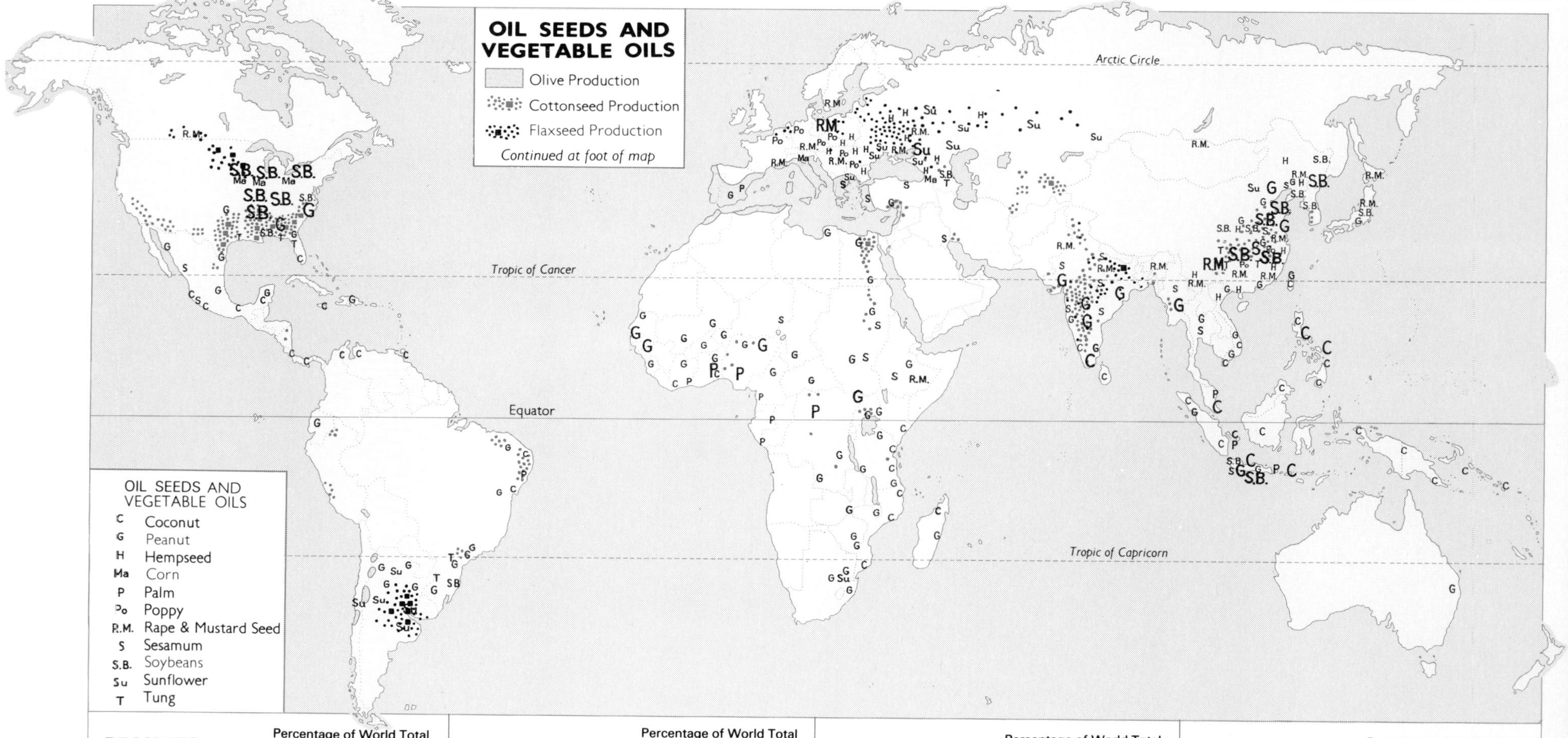
OIL SEEDS AND VEGETABLE OILS
Olive Production
Cottonseed Production
Flaxseed Production
Continued at foot of map
Arctic Circle
Tropic of Cancer
Equator
Tropic of Capricorn
OIL SEEDS AND VEGETABLE OILS
C Coconut
G Peanut
H Hempseed
Ma Corn
P Palm
Po Poppy
R.M. Rape & Mustard Seed
S Sesamum
S.B. Soybeans
Su Sunflower
T Tung

PEANUTS

World Production
1977-1979 average
million tonnes
18.6

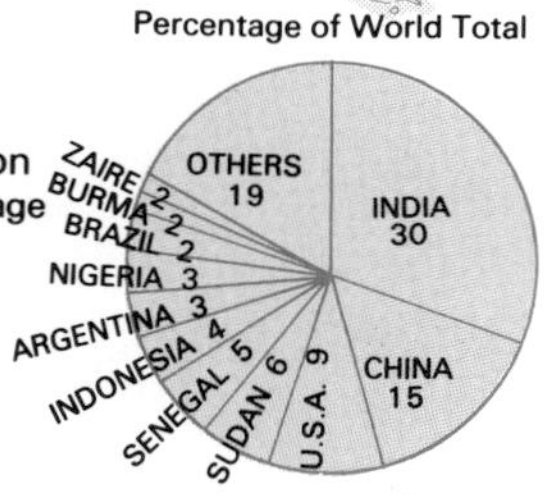
Percentage of World Total
INDIA 30
CHINA 15
U.S.A. 9
SUDAN 6
SENEGAL 5
INDONESIA 4
ARGENTINA 3
NIGERIA 3
BRAZIL 2
BURMA 2
ZAIRE 2
OTHERS 19

COTTONSEED

World Production
1977-1979 average
million tonnes
25.5

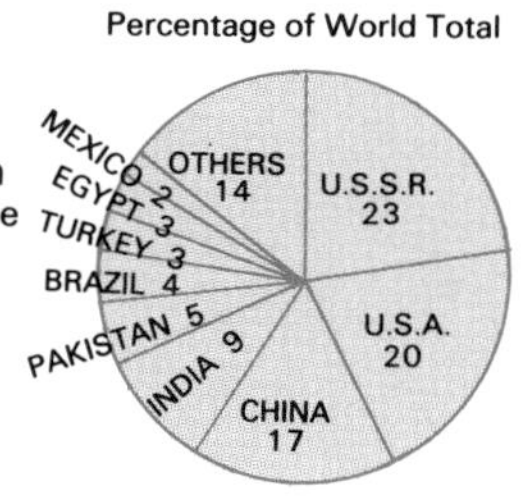
Percentage of World Total
U.S.S.R. 23
U.S.A. 20
CHINA 17
INDIA 9
PAKISTAN 5
BRAZIL 4
TURKEY 3
EGYPT 3
MEXICO 2
OTHERS 14

PALM OIL

World Production
1977-1979 average
thousand tonnes
4 114

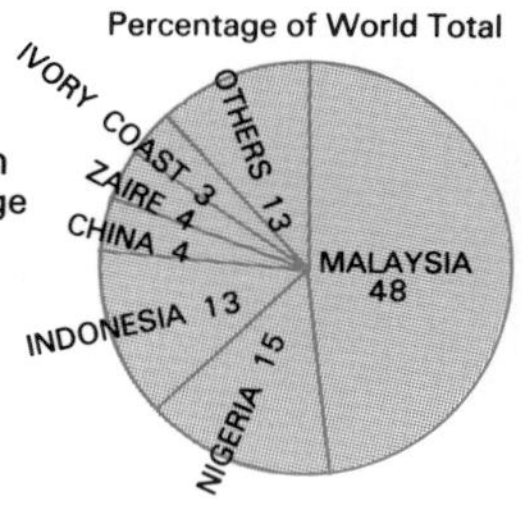
Percentage of World Total
MALAYSIA 48
NIGERIA 15
INDONESIA 13
CHINA 4
ZAIRE 4
IVORY COAST 3
OTHERS 13

OLIVE OIL

World Production
1977-1979 average
thousand tonnes
1 730

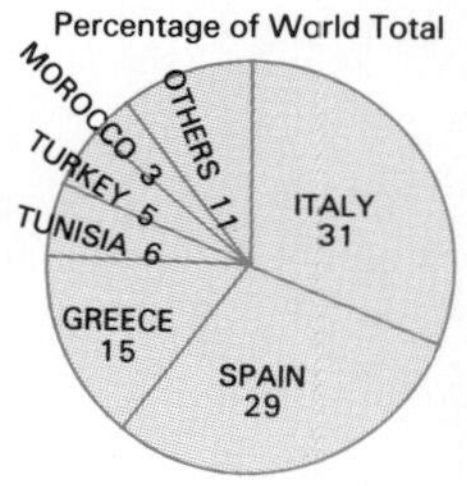
Percentage of World Total
ITALY 31
SPAIN 29
GREECE 15
TUNISIA 6
TURKEY 5
MOROCCO 3
OTHERS 11

Maps based on Modified Homolographic Projection

1 tonne (metric ton) = 0·98 tons = 2204·62 pounds
1 kg (kilogram) = 2·20 pounds
1 ha (hectare) = 2·47 acres
1 kg/ha = 0·89 pounds/acres

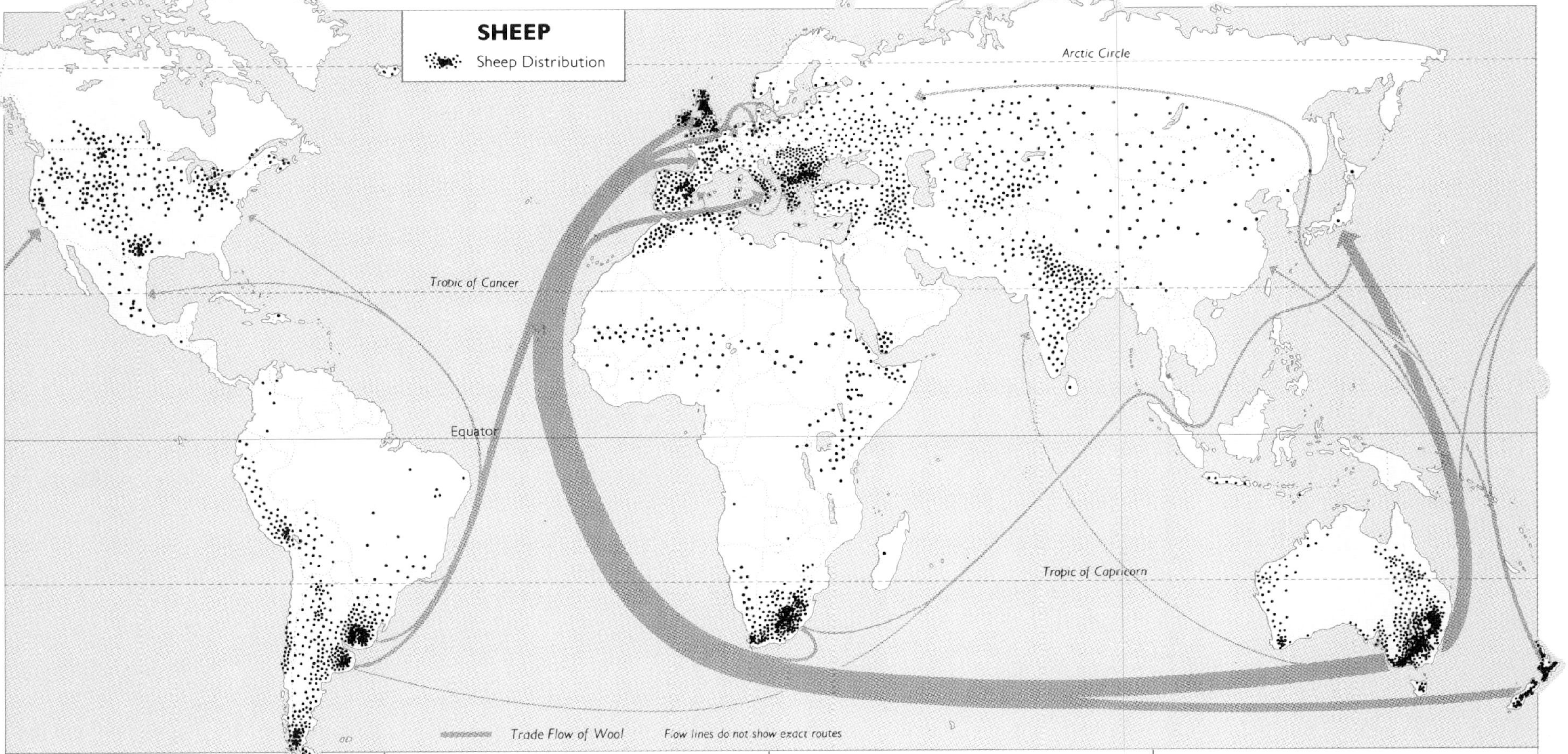
SHEEP
Sheep Distribution
Arctic Circle
Tropic of Cancer
Equator
Tropic of Capricorn
Trade Flow of Wool
Flow lines do not show exact routes

SHEEP

World Total
1977-1979 average
million head
1063.7

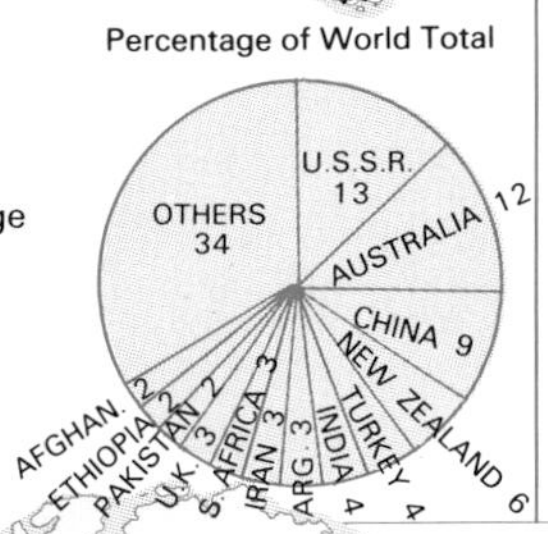
Percentage of World Total
U.S.S.R. 13
AUSTRALIA 12
CHINA 9
NEW ZEALAND 6
TURKEY 4
INDIA 4
ARG. 3
IRAN 3
S. AFRICA 3
U.K. 3
PAKISTAN 2
ETHIOPIA 2
AFGHAN. 2
OTHERS 34

MUTTON & LAMB EXPORTS

(Fresh, Chilled and Frozen)

World Exports
1976-1978 average
thousand tonnes
775.8

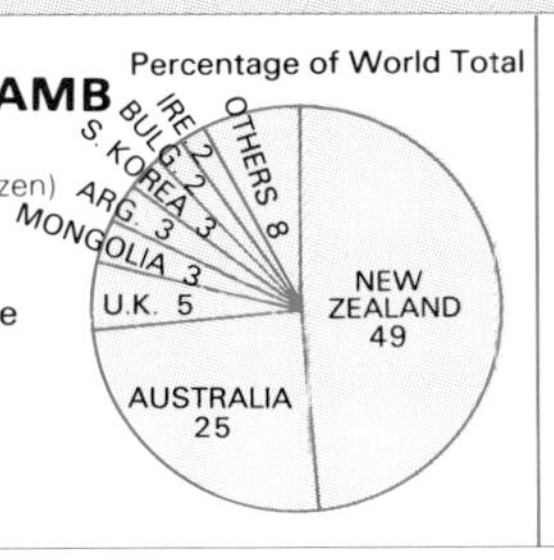
Percentage of World Total
NEW ZEALAND 49
AUSTRALIA 25
U.K. 5
MONGOLIA 3
ARG. 3
S. KOREA 3
BULG. 2
IRE. 2
OTHERS 8

MUTTON & LAMB IMPORTS

(Fresh, Chilled and Frozen)

World Imports
1976-1978 average
thousand tonnes
712.3

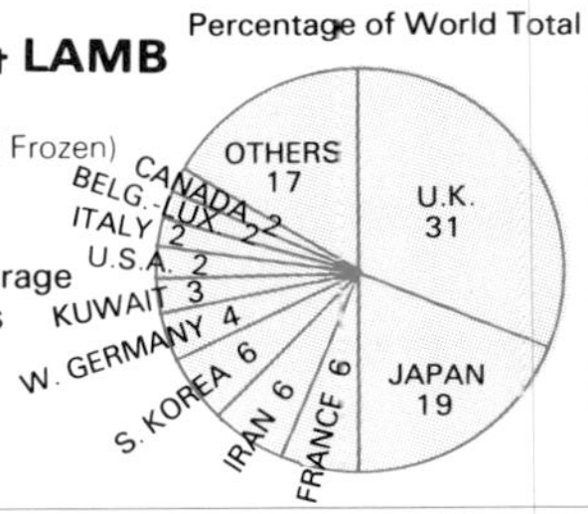
Percentage of World Total
U.K. 31
JAPAN 19
FRANCE 6
IRAN 6
S. KOREA 6
W. GERMANY 4
KUWAIT 3
U.S.A. 2
ITALY 2
BELG.-LUX. 2
CANADA 2
OTHERS 17

WOOL (Greasy)

World Production
1977-1979 average
2.62 million tonnes

	th tonnes	% of w total
Exports		
Australia	494	56
New Zealand	137	16
Imports		
Japan	159	18
U.S.S.R.	127	15
U.K.	114	13
France	102	12

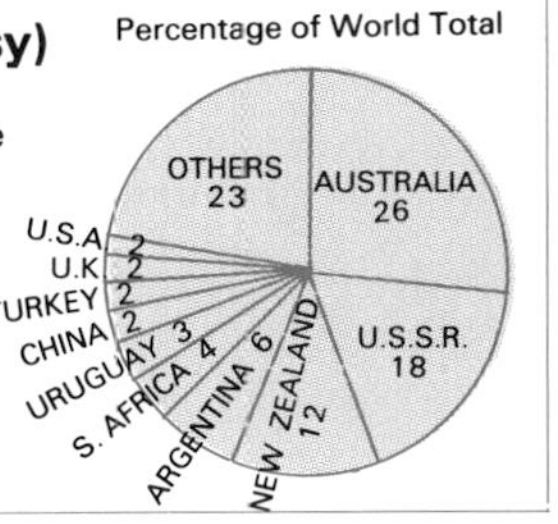
Percentage of World Total
AUSTRALIA 26
U.S.S.R. 18
NEW ZEALAND 12
ARGENTINA 4
S. AFRICA 4
URUGUAY 3
CHINA 2
TURKEY 2
U.K. 2
U.S.A. 2
OTHERS 23

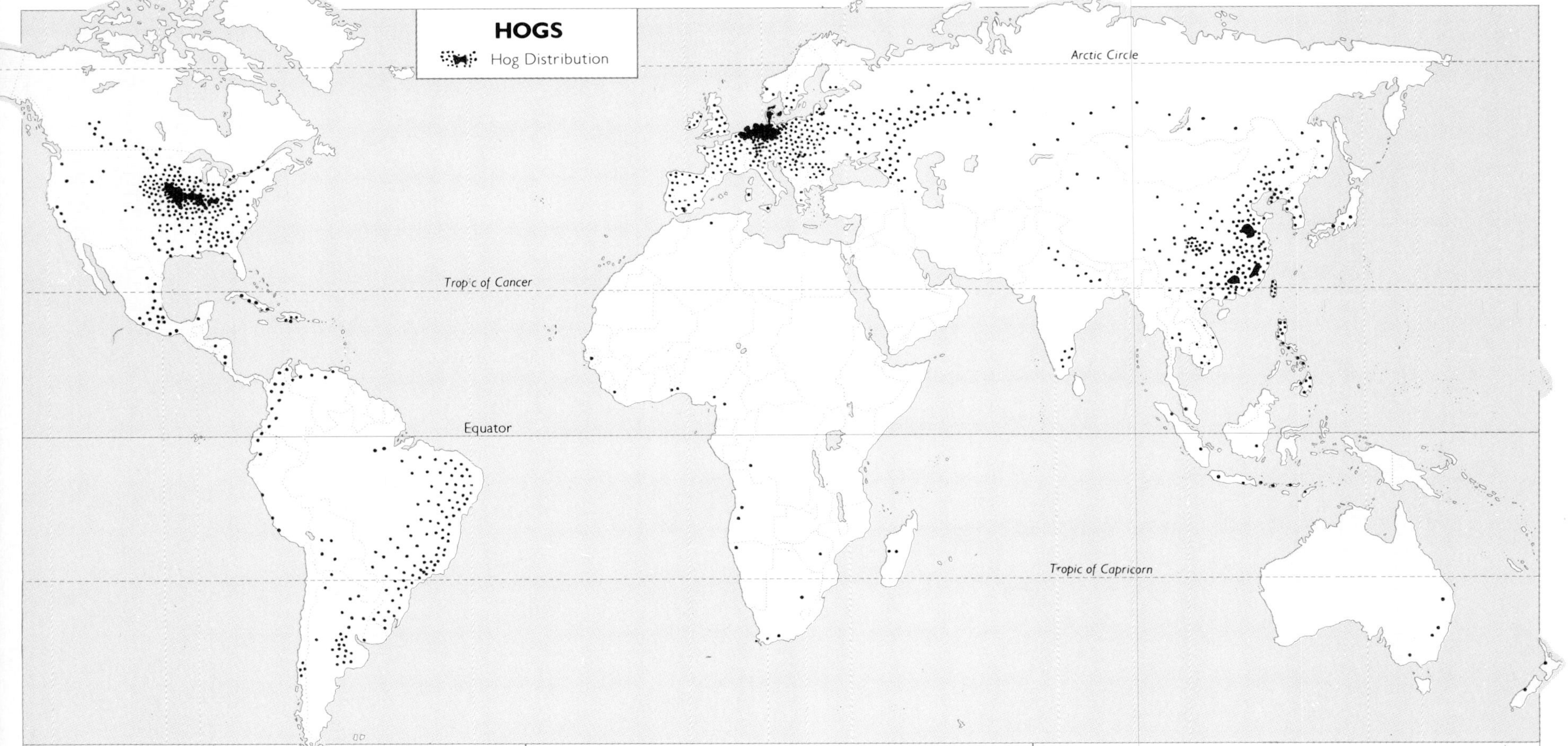
HOGS
Hog Distribution
Arctic Circle
Tropic of Cancer
Equator
Tropic of Capricorn

HOGS

World Total
1977-1979 average
735.1 million head

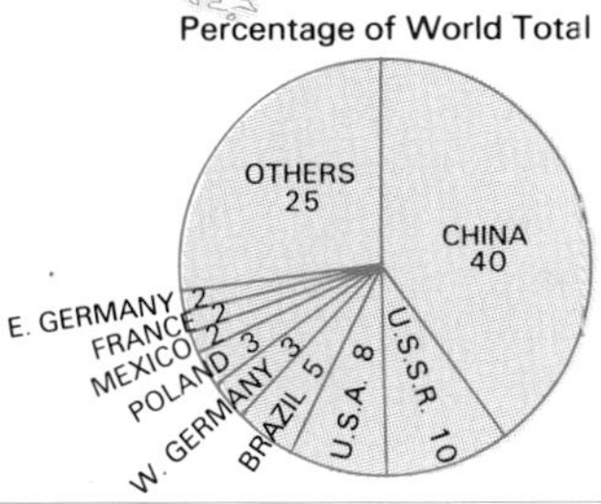
Percentage of World Total
CHINA 40
U.S.S.R. 10
U.S.A. 8
BRAZIL 5
W. GERMANY 3
POLAND 3
MEXICO 2
FRANCE 2
E. GERMANY 2
OTHERS 25

PORK EXPORTS

(Fresh, Chilled and Frozen)

World Exports
1977-1979 average
thousand tonnes
1195.9

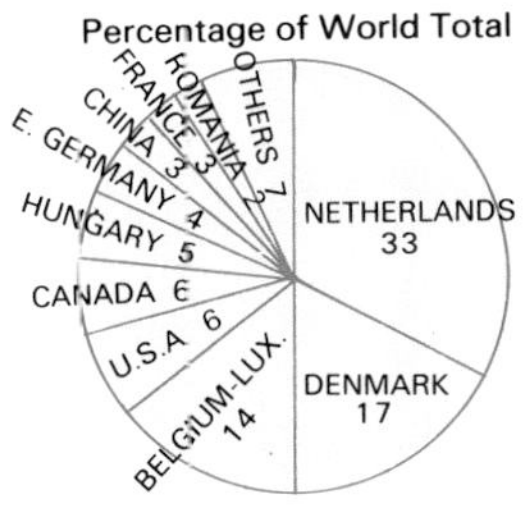
Percentage of World Total
NETHERLANDS 33
DENMARK 17
BELGIUM-LUX. 14
U.S.A. 6
CANADA 6
HUNGARY 5
E. GERMANY 4
CHINA 3
FRANCE 3
ROMANIA 2
OTHERS 7

PORK IMPORTS

(Fresh, Chilled and Frozen)

World Imports
1977-1979 average
thousand tonnes
1073.3

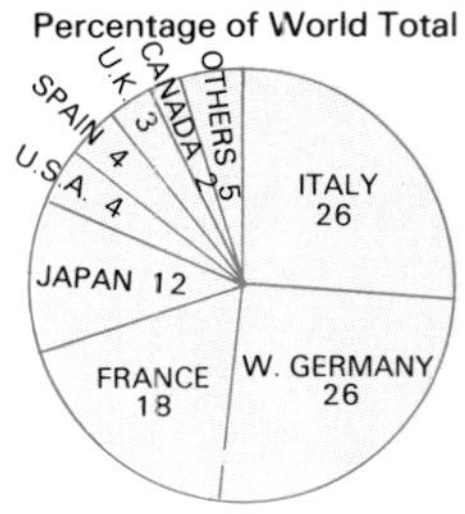
Percentage of World Total
ITALY 26
W. GERMANY 26
FRANCE 18
JAPAN 12
U.S.A. 4
SPAIN 4
U.K. 3
CANADA 2
OTHERS 5

Maps based on Modified Homolographic Projection

1 tonne (metric ton) = 0·98 tons = 2204·62 pounds
1 kg (kilogram) = 2·20 pounds
1 ha (hectare) = 2·47 acres
1 kg/ha = 0·89 pounds/acres

Equatorial Scale: 1:136 000 000

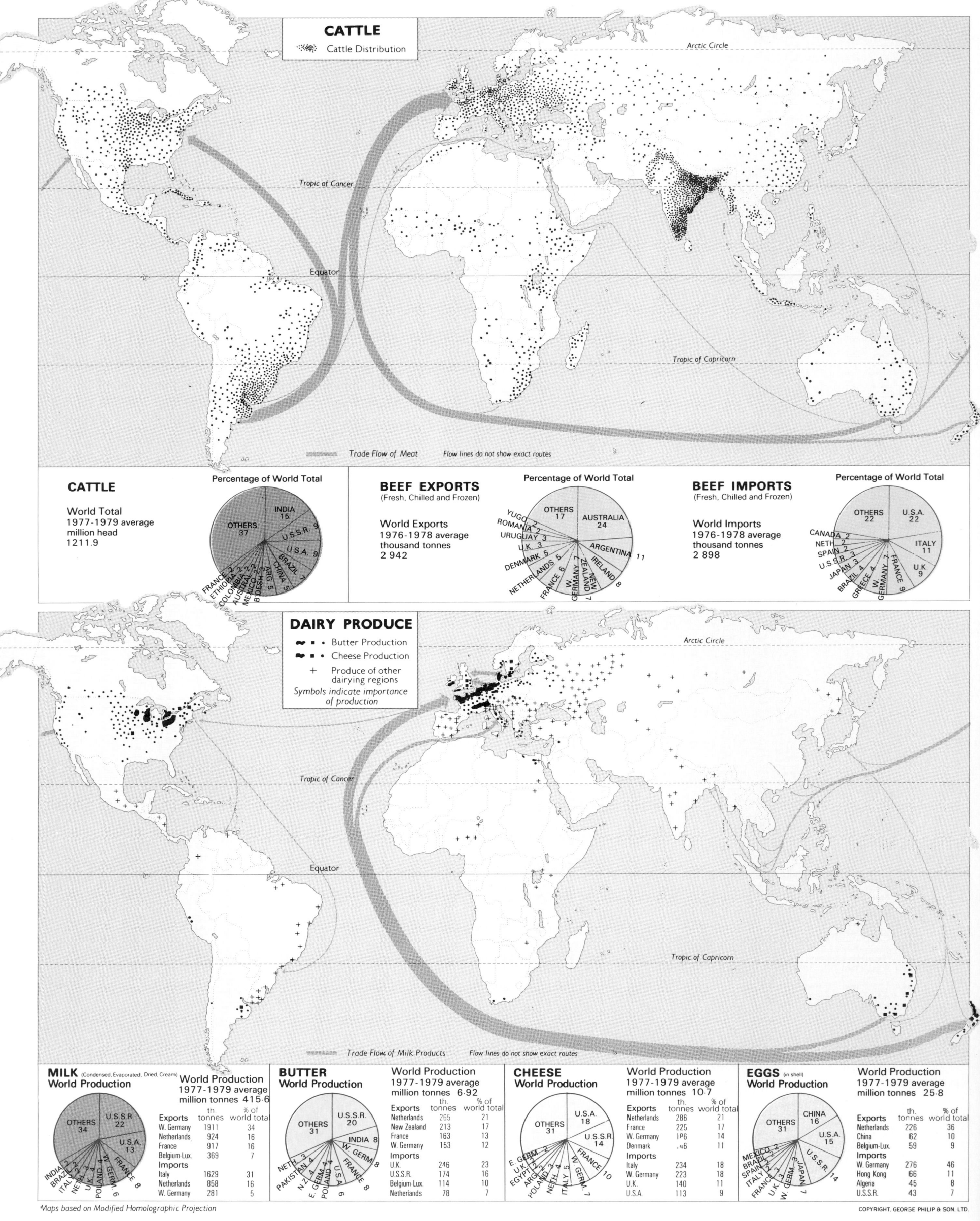

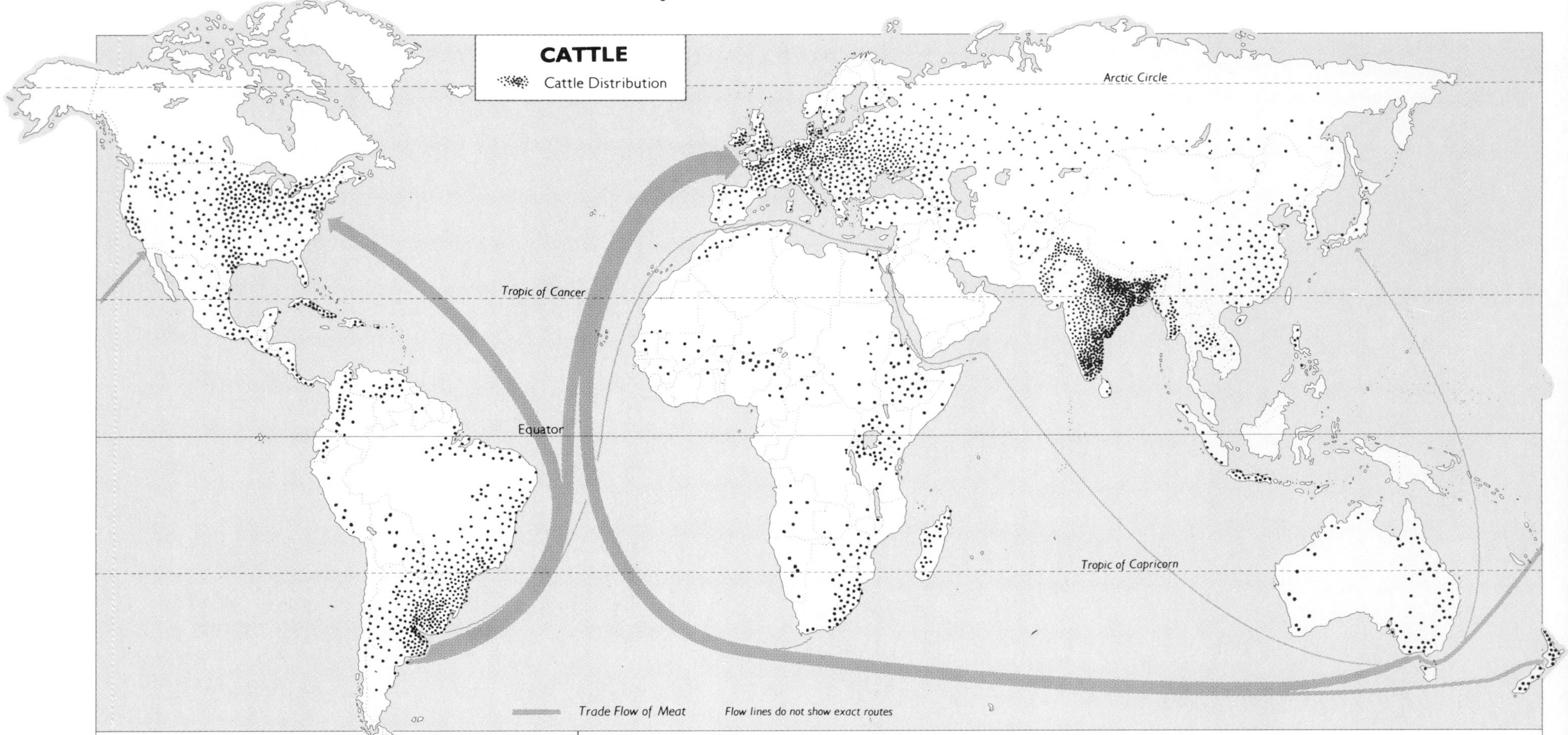
CATTLE
Cattle Distribution
Arctic Circle
Tropic of Cancer
Equator
Tropic of Capricorn
Trade Flow of Meat
Flow lines do not show exact routes

CATTLE

World Total
1977-1979 average
million head
1211.9

Percentage of World Total

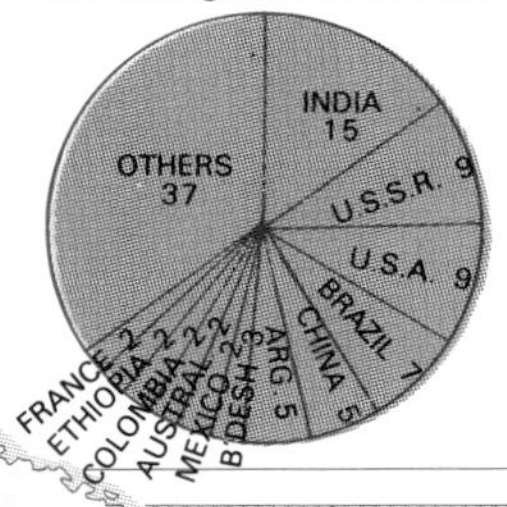
INDIA 15
U.S.S.R. 9
U.S.A. 9
BRAZIL 7
CHINA 5
ARG. 5
B'DESH 3
MEXICO 2
AUSTRAL. 2
COLOMBIA 2
ETHIOPIA 2
FRANCE 2
OTHERS 37

BEEF EXPORTS

(Fresh, Chilled and Frozen)

World Exports
1976-1978 average
thousand tonnes
2 942

Percentage of World Total

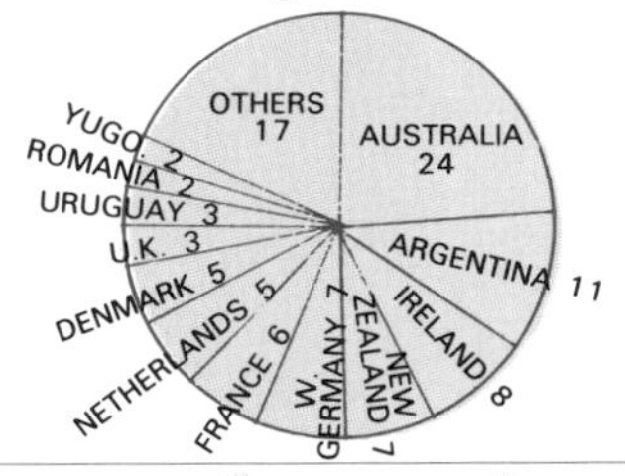
OTHERS 17
AUSTRALIA 24
ARGENTINA 11
IRELAND 8
NEW ZEALAND 7
W. GERMANY 7
FRANCE 6
NETHERLANDS 5
DENMARK 5
U.K. 3
URUGUAY 3
ROMANIA 2
YUGO. 2

BEEF IMPORTS

(Fresh, Chilled and Frozen)

World Imports
1976-1978 average
thousand tonnes
2 898

Percentage of World Total

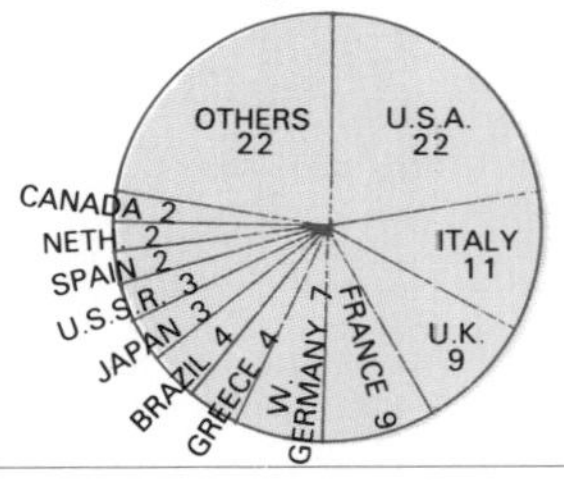
OTHERS 22
U.S.A. 22
ITALY 11
U.K. 9
FRANCE 9
W. GERMANY 7
GREECE 4
BRAZIL 4
JAPAN 3
U.S.S.R. 3
SPAIN 2
NETH. 2
CANADA 2

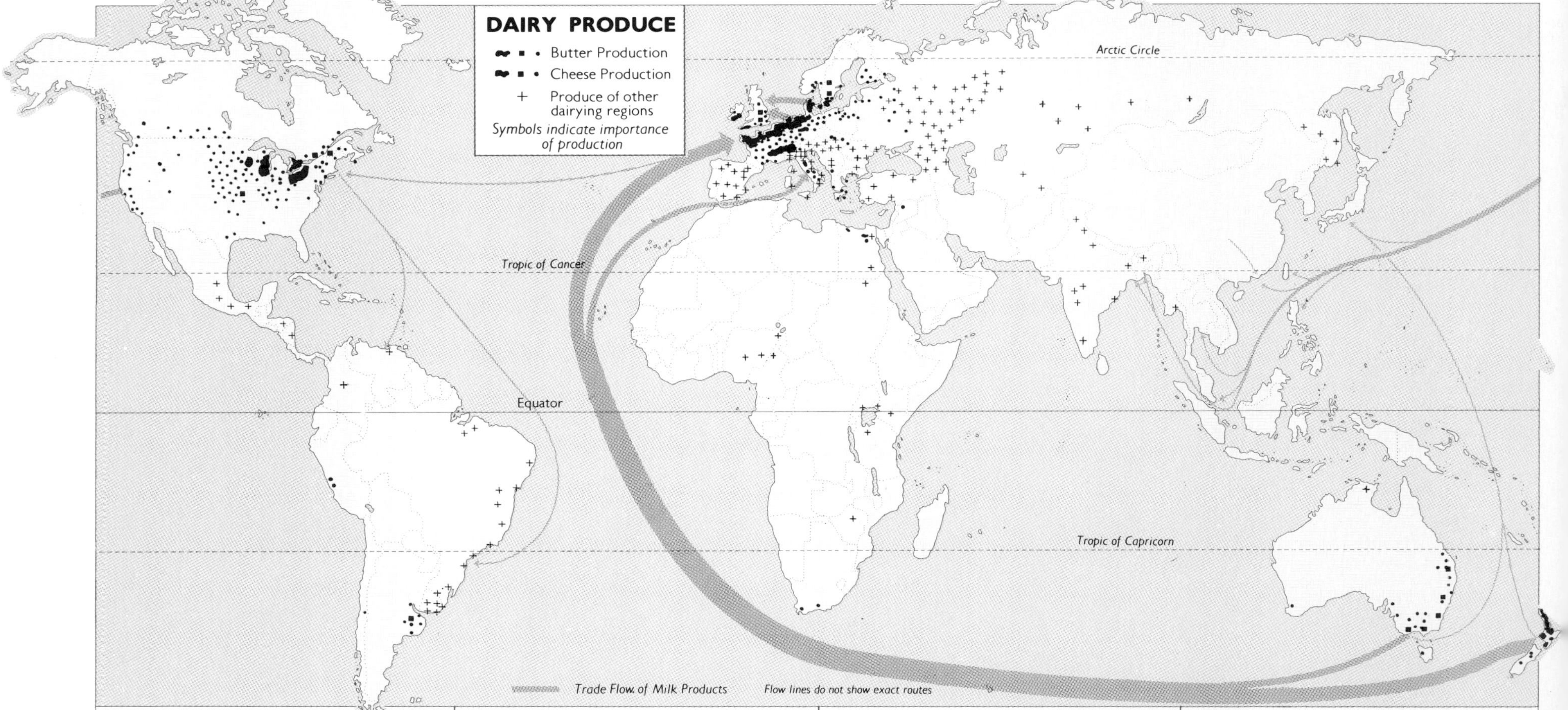
DAIRY PRODUCE
Butter Production
Cheese Production
Produce of other dairying regions
Symbols indicate importance of production
Arctic Circle
Tropic of Cancer
Equator
Tropic of Capricorn
Trade Flow of Milk Products
Flow lines do not show exact routes

MILK (Condensed, Evaporated, Dried, Cream)
World Production

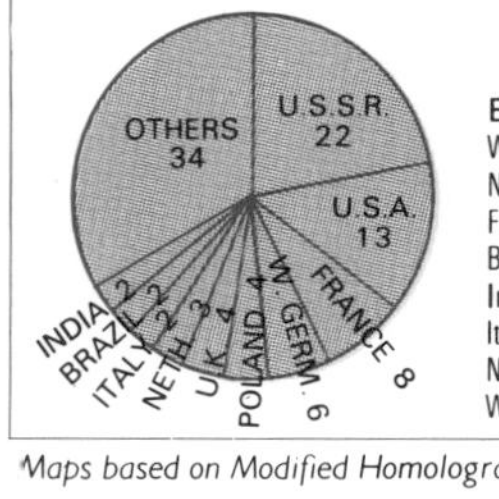
OTHERS 34
U.S.S.R. 22
U.S.A. 13
FRANCE 8
W. GERM. 6
POLAND 4
U.K. 4
NETH. 3
ITALY 2
BRAZIL 2
INDIA 2

World Production
1977-1979 average
million tonnes 415·6

	th. tonnes	% of world total
Exports		
W. Germany	1911	34
Netherlands	924	16
France	917	16
Belgium-Lux.	369	7
Imports		
Italy	1629	31
Netherlands	858	16
W. Germany	281	5

BUTTER
World Production

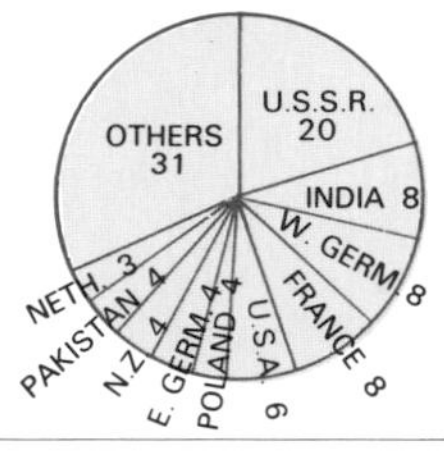
OTHERS 31
U.S.S.R. 20
INDIA 8
W. GERM. 8
FRANCE 8
U.S.A. 6
POLAND 4
E. GERM. 4
N.Z. 4
PAKISTAN 4
NETH. 3

World Production
1977-1979 average
million tonnes 6·92

	th. tonnes	% of world total
Exports		
Netherlands	265	21
New Zealand	213	17
France	163	13
W. Germany	153	12
Imports		
U.K.	246	23
U.S.S.R.	174	16
Belgium-Lux.	114	10
Netherlands	78	7

CHEESE
World Production

OTHERS 31
U.S.A. 18
U.S.S.R. 14
FRANCE 10
W. GERM. 7
ITALY 5
NETH. 4
POLAND 3
ARG. 2
EGYPT 2
U.K. 2
E. GERM. 2

World Production
1977-1979 average
million tonnes 10·7

	th. tonnes	% of world total
Exports		
Netherlands	286	21
France	225	17
W. Germany	186	14
Denmark	146	11
Imports		
Italy	234	18
W. Germany	223	18
U.K.	140	11
U.S.A.	113	9

EGGS (in shell)
World Production

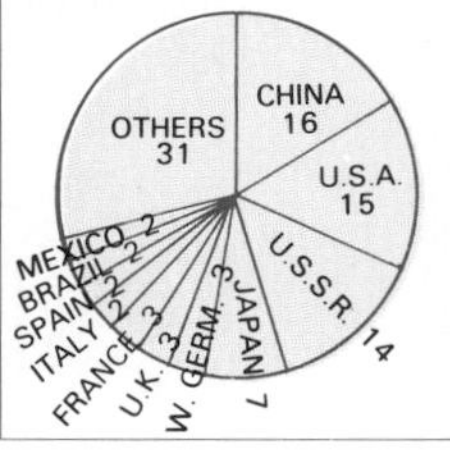
OTHERS 31
CHINA 16
U.S.A. 15
U.S.S.R. 14
JAPAN 7
W. GERM. 3
U.K. 3
FRANCE 3
ITALY 2
SPAIN 2
BRAZIL 2
MEXICO 2

World Production
1977-1979 average
million tonnes 25·8

	th. tonnes	% of world total
Exports		
Netherlands	226	36
China	62	10
Belgium-Lux.	59	9
Imports		
W. Germany	276	46
Hong Kong	66	11
Algeria	45	8
U.S.S.R.	43	7

Maps based on Modified Homolographic Projection

1 tonne (metric ton) = 0·98 tons = 2204·62 pounds
1 kg (kilogram) = 2·20 pounds
1 ha (hectare) = 2·47 acres
1 kg/ha = 0·89 pounds/acres

Equatorial Scale: 1:136 000 000

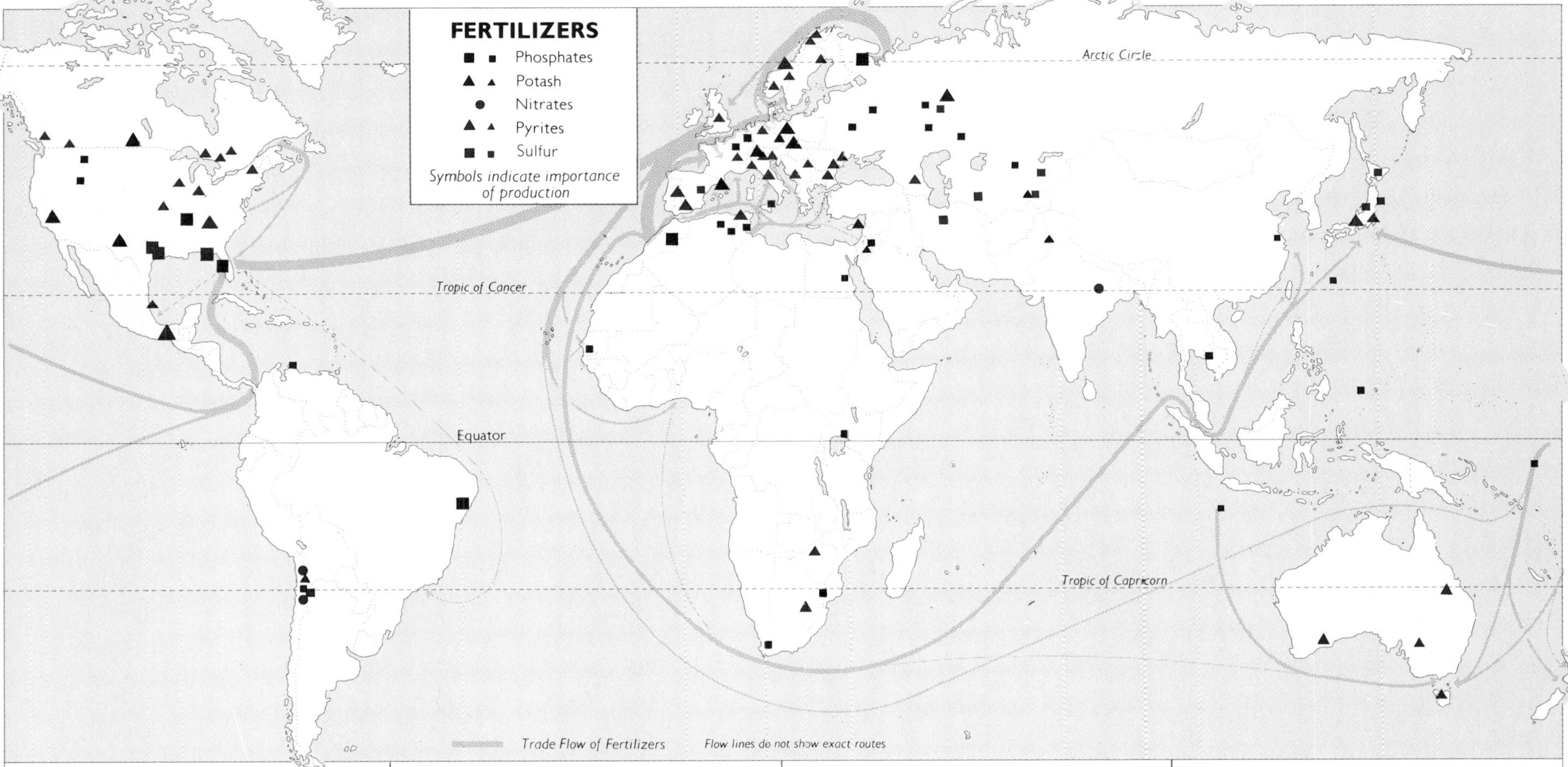
FERTILIZERS
Phosphates
Potash
Nitrates
Pyrites
Sulfur
Symbols indicate importance of production
Arctic Circle
Tropic of Cancer
Equator
Tropic of Capricorn
Trade Flow of Fertilizers
Flow lines do not show exact routes

PHOSPHATE ROCK

World Production
1976-1978 average
million tonnes
116·7

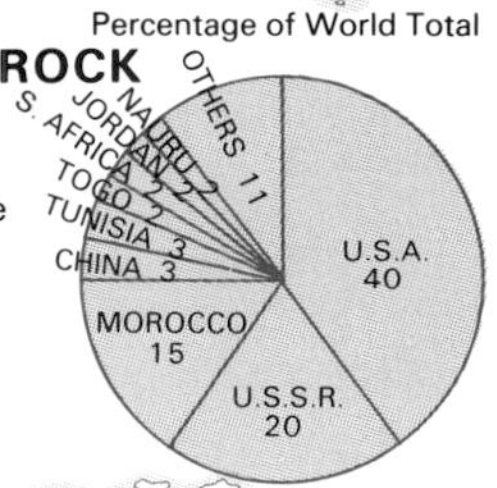
Percentage of World Total
U.S.A. 40
U.S.S.R. 20
MOROCCO 15
CHINA 3
TUNISIA 3
TOGO
S. AFRICA
JORDAN
NAURU
OTHERS 11

COMMERCIAL PHOSPHATE FERTILIZERS

World Production
1977-1979 average
million tonnes
30·2

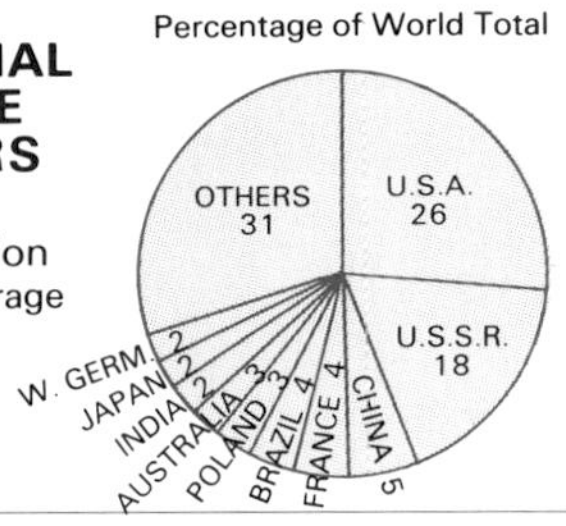
Percentage of World Total
U.S.A. 26
U.S.S.R. 18
CHINA 5
FRANCE 4
BRAZIL 4
POLAND 3
AUSTRALIA
INDIA
JAPAN
W. GERM.
OTHERS 31

COMMERCIAL POTASH FERTILIZERS

World Production
1977-1979 average
million tonnes
25·8

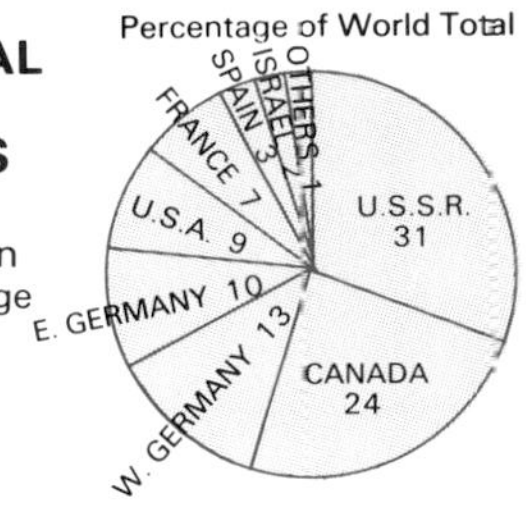
Percentage of World Total
U.S.S.R. 31
CANADA 24
W. GERMANY 13
E. GERMANY 10
U.S.A. 9
FRANCE 7
SPAIN 3
ISRAEL
OTHERS 1

COMMERCIAL NITROGENOUS FERTILIZERS

World Production
1977-1979 average
million tonnes
49·8

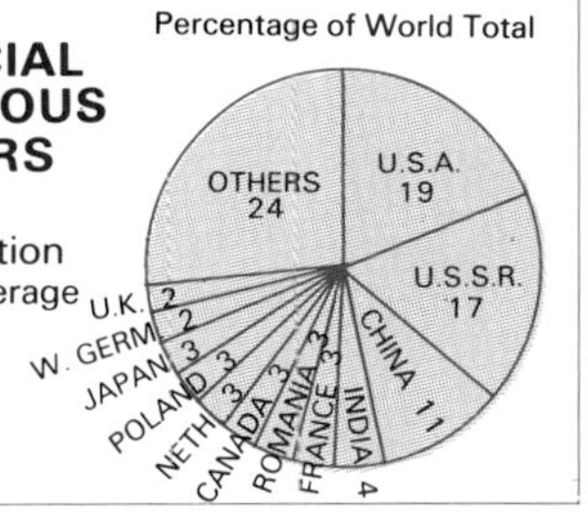
Percentage of World Total
U.S.A. 19
U.S.S.R. 17
CHINA 11
INDIA 4
FRANCE 3
ROMANIA 3
CANADA
NETH.
POLAND
JAPAN
W. GERM.
U.K.
OTHERS 24

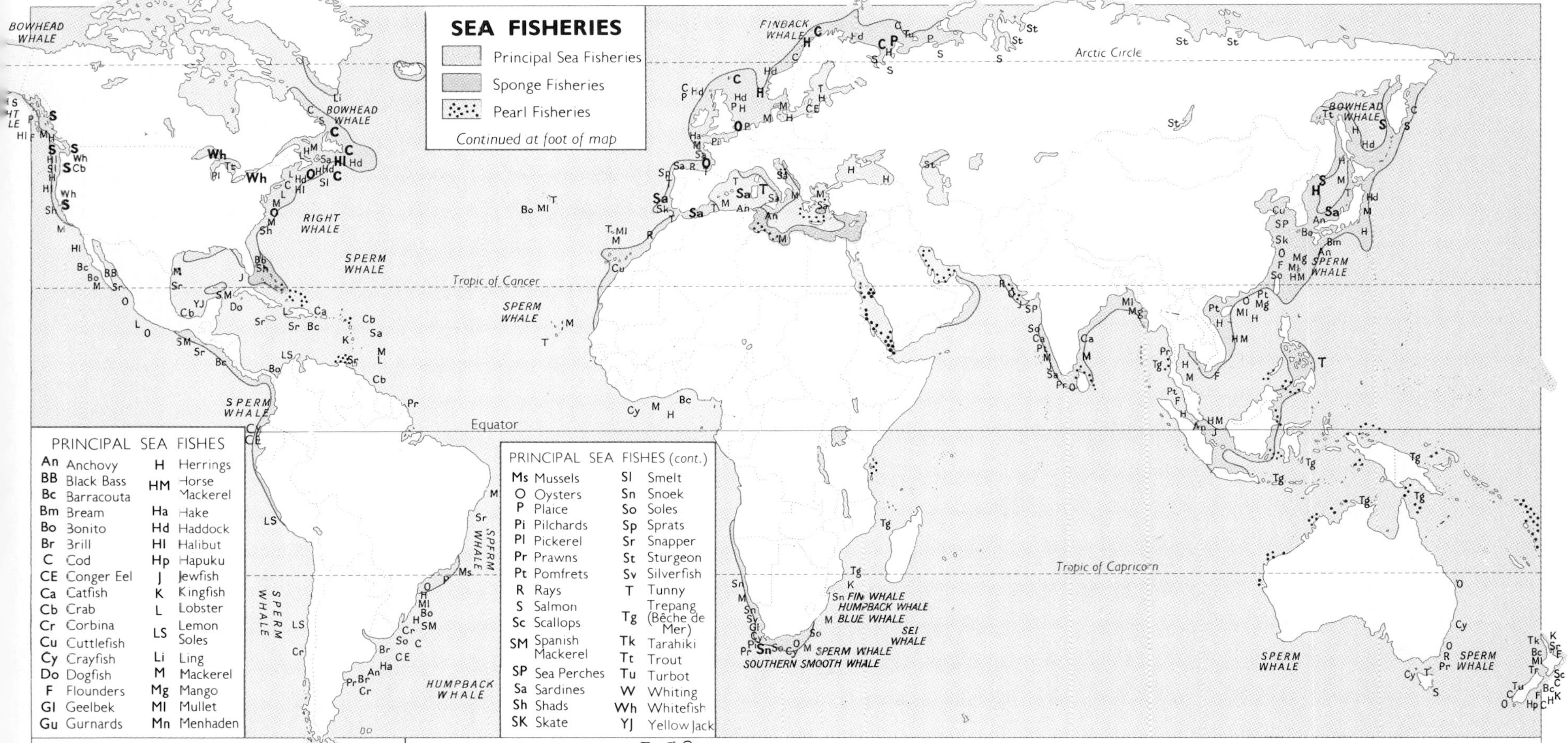
SEA FISHERIES
Principal Sea Fisheries
Sponge Fisheries
Pearl Fisheries
Continued at foot of map
Arctic Circle
Tropic of Cancer
Equator
Tropic of Capricorn
BOWHEAD WHALE
FINBACK WHALE
RIGHT WHALE
SPERM WHALE
HUMPBACK WHALE
FIN WHALE
BLUE WHALE
SEI WHALE
SOUTHERN SMOOTH WHALE

PRINCIPAL SEA FISHES

An	Anchovy	H	Herrings
BB	Black Bass	HM	Horse Mackerel
Bc	Barracouta	Ha	Hake
Bm	Bream	Hd	Haddock
Bo	Bonito	Hl	Halibut
Br	Brill	Hp	Hapuku
C	Cod	J	Jewfish
CE	Conger Eel	K	Kingfish
Ca	Catfish	L	Lobster
Cb	Crab	LS	Lemon Soles
Cr	Corbina	Li	Ling
Cu	Cuttlefish	M	Mackerel
Cy	Crayfish	Mg	Mango
Do	Dogfish	Ml	Mullet
F	Flounders	Mn	Menhaden
Gl	Geelbek		
Gu	Gurnards		

PRINCIPAL SEA FISHES (cont.)

Ms	Mussels	Sl	Smelt
O	Oysters	Sn	Snoek
P	Plaice	So	Soles
Pi	Pilchards	Sp	Sprats
Pl	Pickerel	Sr	Snapper
Pr	Prawns	St	Sturgeon
Pt	Pomfrets	Sv	Silverfish
R	Rays	T	Tunny
S	Salmon	Tg	Trepang (Bêche de Mer)
Sc	Scallops	Tk	Tarahiki
SM	Spanish Mackerel	Tt	Trout
SP	Sea Perches	Tu	Turbot
Sa	Sardines	W	Whiting
Sh	Shads	Wh	Whitefish
SK	Skate	YJ	Yellow Jack

FISH LANDINGS

World Total Caught
1976-1978 average
million tonnes
71·9

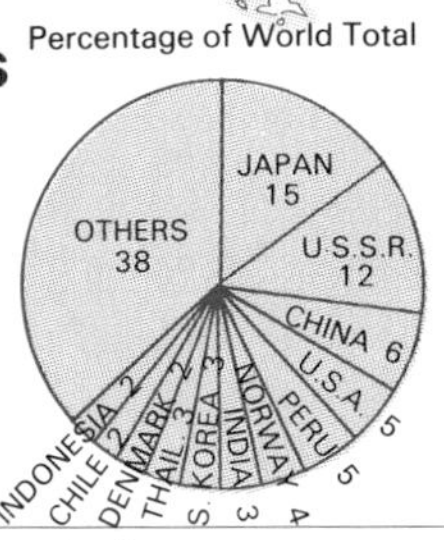
Percentage of World Total
JAPAN 15
U.S.S.R. 12
CHINA 6
U.S.A. 5
PERU 5
NORWAY 4
INDIA 3
S. KOREA
THAILAND
DENMARK
CHILE
INDONESIA 2
OTHERS 38

WHALING

World Total
1976-1978 average
number of whales caught
22 089

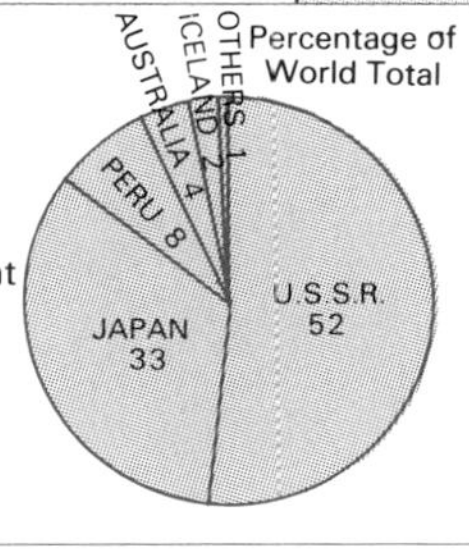
Percentage of World Total
U.S.S.R. 52
JAPAN 33
PERU 8
AUSTRALIA 4
ICELAND 2
OTHERS 1

Types caught

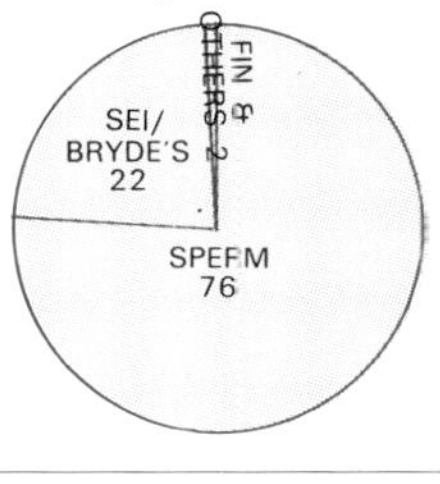
Percentage of World Total
SPERM 76
SEI/BRYDE'S 22
FIN & OTHERS 2

Regions where caught

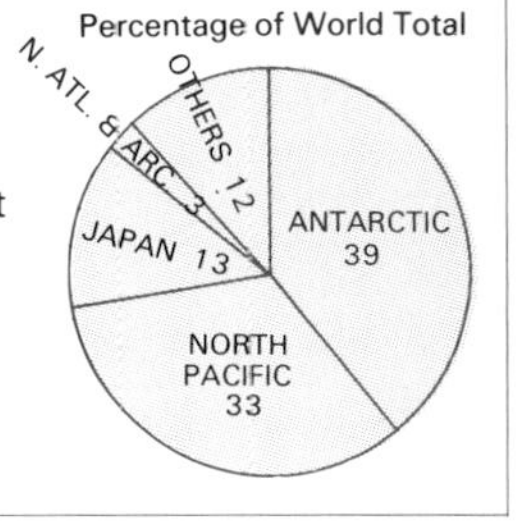
Percentage of World Total
ANTARCTIC 39
NORTH PACIFIC 33
JAPAN 13
OTHERS 12
N. ATL. & ARC. 3

Maps based on Modified Homolographic Projection

1 tonne (metric ton) = 0·98 tons = 2204·62 pounds
1 kg (kilogram) = 2·20 pounds
1 ha (hectare) = 2·47 acres
1 kg/ha = 0·89 pounds/acres

Equatorial Scale: 1:136 000 000

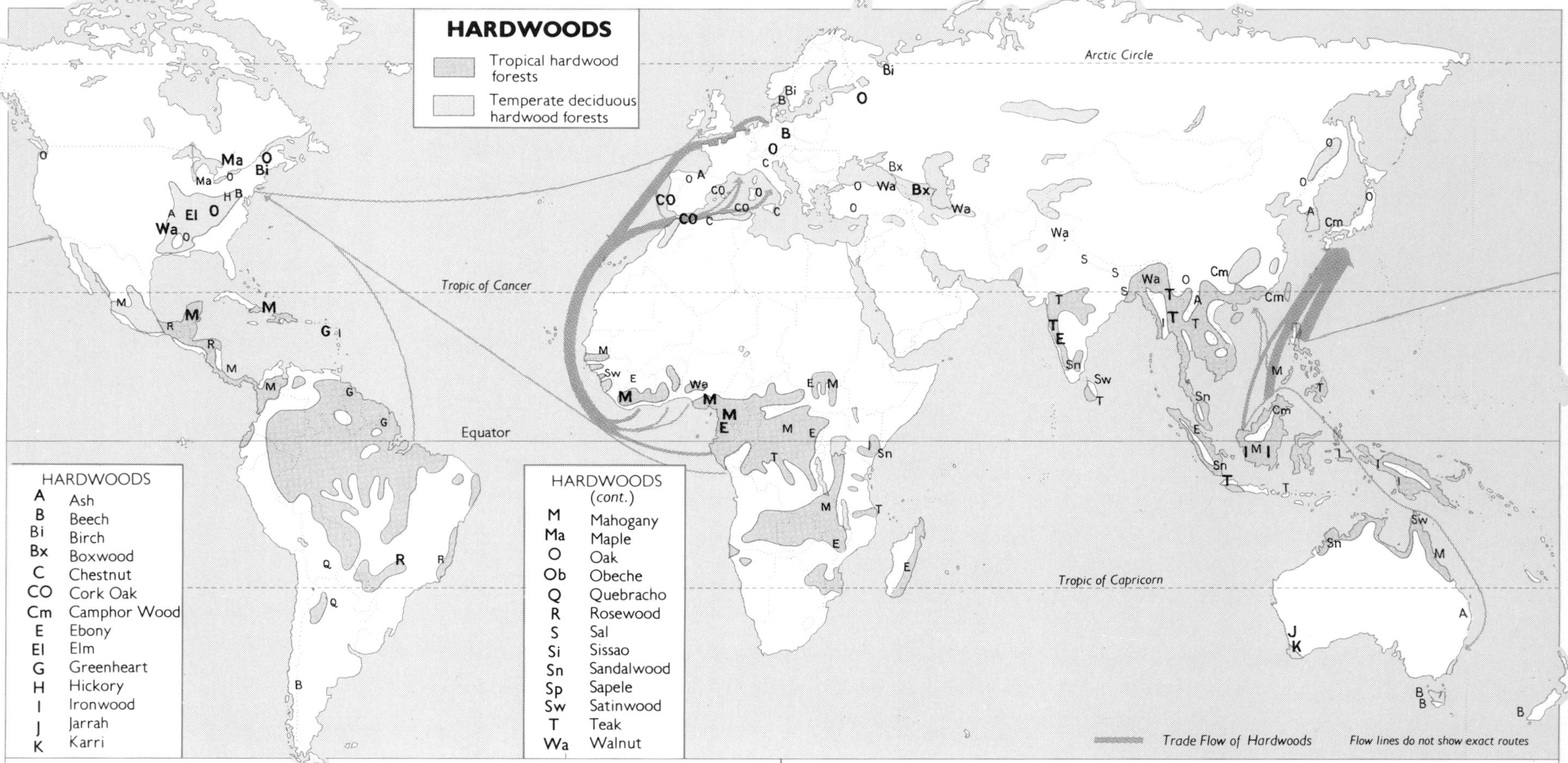
HARDWOODS
Tropical hardwood forests
Temperate deciduous hardwood forests
Arctic Circle
Tropic of Cancer
Equator
Tropic of Capricorn
HARDWOODS
A Ash
B Beech
Bi Birch
Bx Boxwood
C Chestnut
CO Cork Oak
Cm Camphor Wood
E Ebony
El Elm
G Greenheart
H Hickory
I Ironwood
J Jarrah
K Karri
HARDWOODS (cont.)
M Mahogany
Ma Maple
O Oak
Ob Obeche
Q Quebracho
R Rosewood
S Sal
Si Sissao
Sn Sandalwood
Sp Sapele
Sw Satinwood
T Teak
Wa Walnut
Trade Flow of Hardwoods
Flow lines do not show exact routes

HARDWOODS

World Removals
1976-1978 average
million cubic meters
1 443

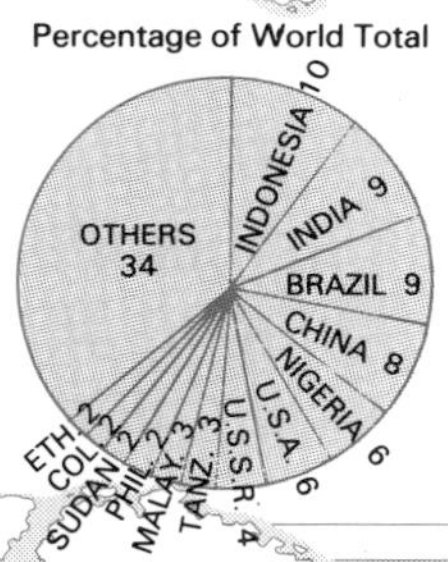
Percentage of World Total
OTHERS 34
INDONESIA 10
INDIA 9
BRAZIL 9
CHINA 8
NIGERIA 6
U.S.A. 6
U.S.S.R. 4
TANZ. 3
MALAY. 3
PHIL. 2
SUDAN 2
COL. 2
ETH.

INDUSTRIAL HARDWOODS

World Production
1976-1978 average
million cubic meters
408

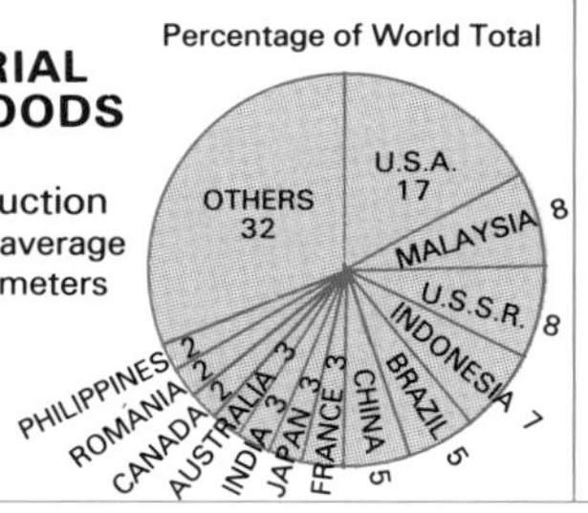
Percentage of World Total
OTHERS 32
U.S.A. 17
MALAYSIA 8
U.S.S.R. 8
INDONESIA 7
BRAZIL 5
CHINA 5
FRANCE 3
JAPAN 3
INDIA 3
AUSTRALIA 3
CANADA
ROMANIA
PHILIPPINES

SOFTWOODS

World Removals
1976-1978 average
million cubic meters
1 134

Percentage of World Total
OTHERS 12
U.S.S.R. 27
U.S.A. 23
CANADA 13
CHINA 9
SWEDEN 4
FINLAND 3
BRAZIL 3
JAPAN 2
W. GERMANY 2
POLAND 2

INDUSTRIAL SOFTWOODS

World Production
1976-1978 average
million cubic meters
963

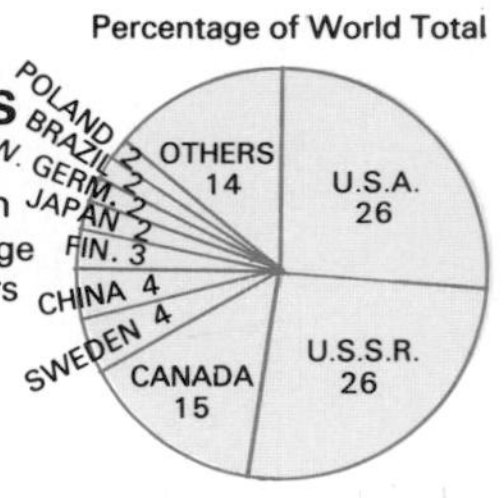
Percentage of World Total
OTHERS 14
U.S.A. 26
U.S.S.R. 26
CANADA 15
SWEDEN 4
CHINA 4
FIN. 3
JAPAN
W. GERM.
BRAZIL
POLAND

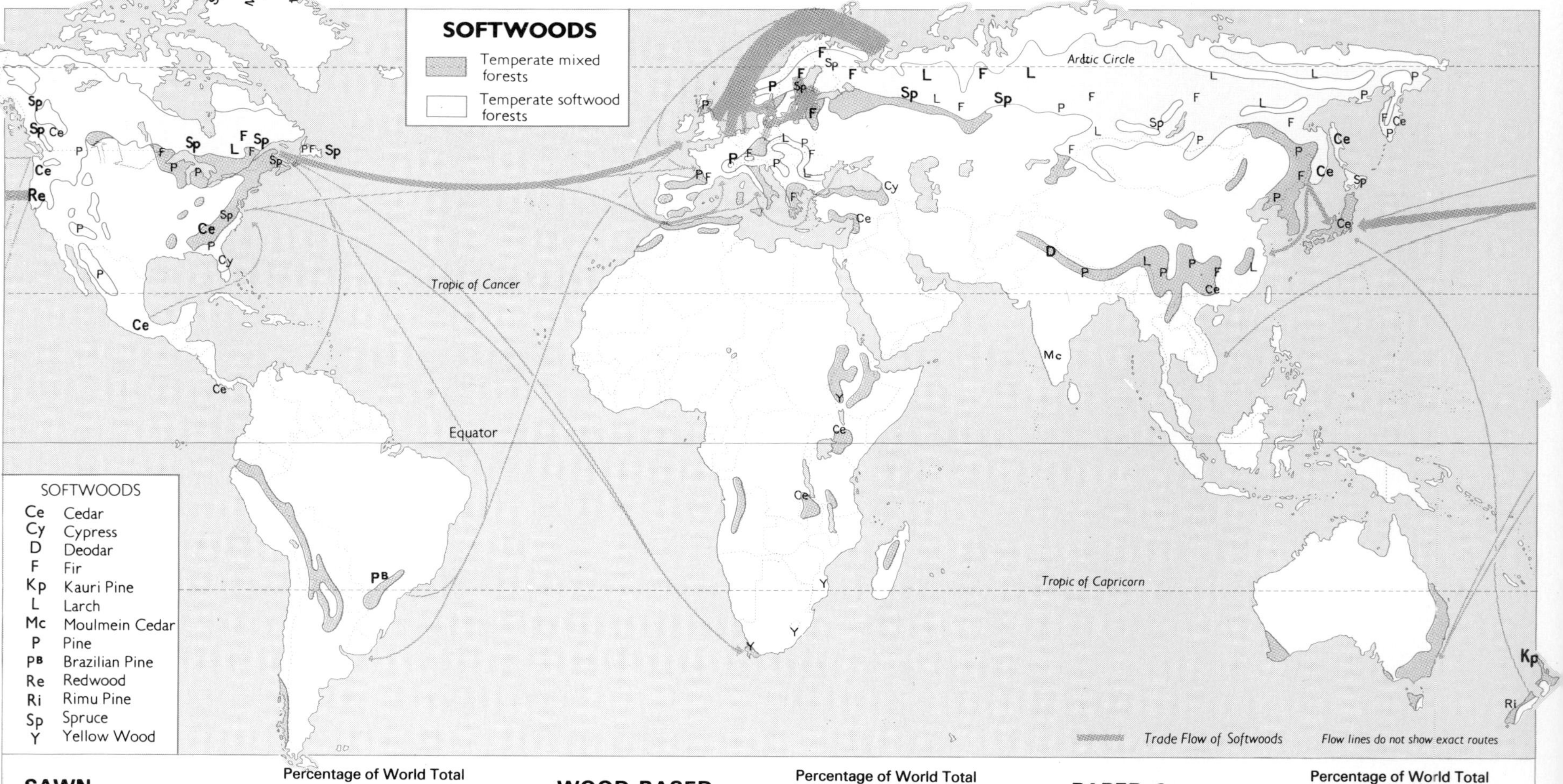
SOFTWOODS
Temperate mixed forests
Temperate softwood forests
Arctic Circle
Tropic of Cancer
Equator
Tropic of Capricorn
SOFTWOODS
Ce Cedar
Cy Cypress
D Deodar
F Fir
Kp Kauri Pine
L Larch
Mc Moulmein Cedar
P Pine
PB Brazilian Pine
Re Redwood
Ri Rimu Pine
Sp Spruce
Y Yellow Wood
Trade Flow of Softwoods
Flow lines do not show exact routes

SAWN SOFTWOOD

World Production
1976-1978 average
million cubic metres
336

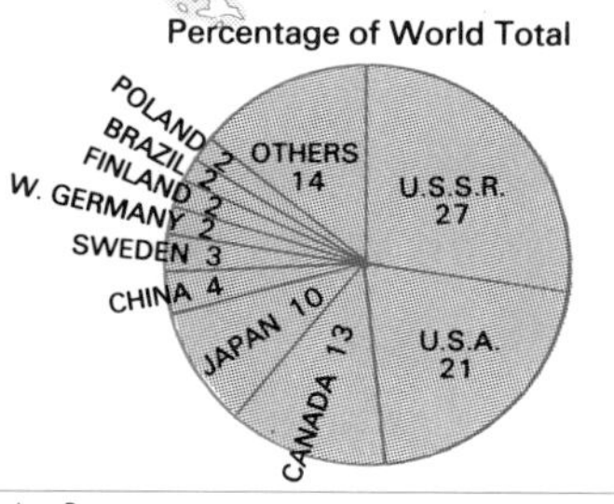
Percentage of World Total
OTHERS 14
U.S.S.R. 27
U.S.A. 21
CANADA 13
JAPAN 10
CHINA 4
SWEDEN 3
W. GERMANY 3
FINLAND
BRAZIL
POLAND

WOOD-BASED PANELS

World Production
1976-1978 average
million cubic metres
99.4

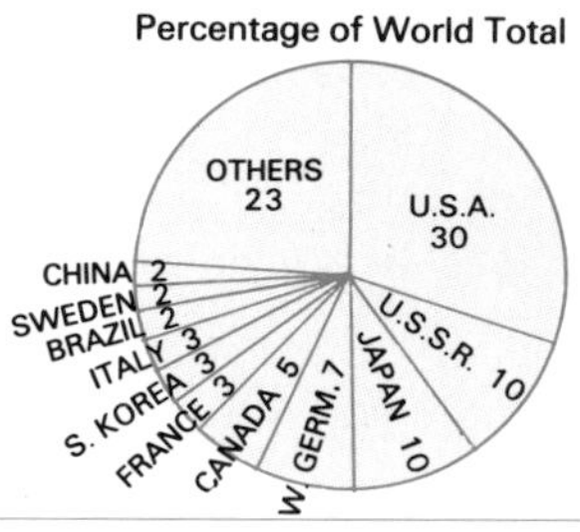
Percentage of World Total
OTHERS 23
U.S.A. 30
U.S.S.R. 10
JAPAN 10
W. GERM. 7
CANADA 5
FRANCE 3
S. KOREA 3
ITALY
BRAZIL
SWEDEN
CHINA 2

PAPER & PAPERBOARD

World Production
1976-1978 average
million tonnes
248.9

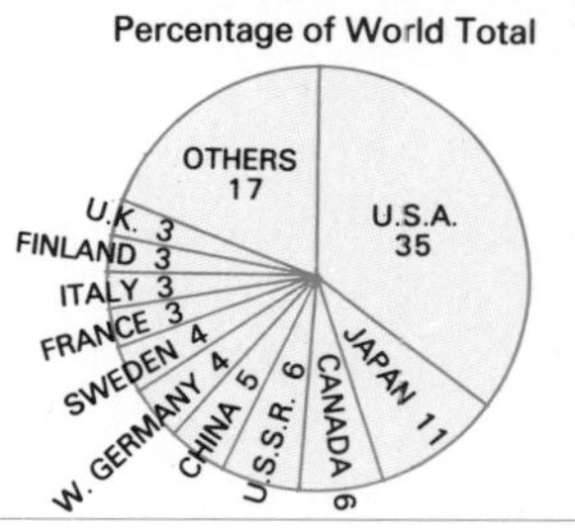
Percentage of World Total
OTHERS 17
U.S.A. 35
JAPAN 11
CANADA 6
U.S.S.R. 6
CHINA 5
W. GERMANY 4
SWEDEN 4
FRANCE 3
ITALY 3
FINLAND 3
U.K. 3

Maps based on Modified Homolographic Projection

1 tonne (metric ton) = 0·98 tons = 2204·62 pounds
1 kg (kilogram) = 2·20 pounds
1 ha (hectare) = 2·47 acres
1 kg/ha = 0·89 pounds/acres

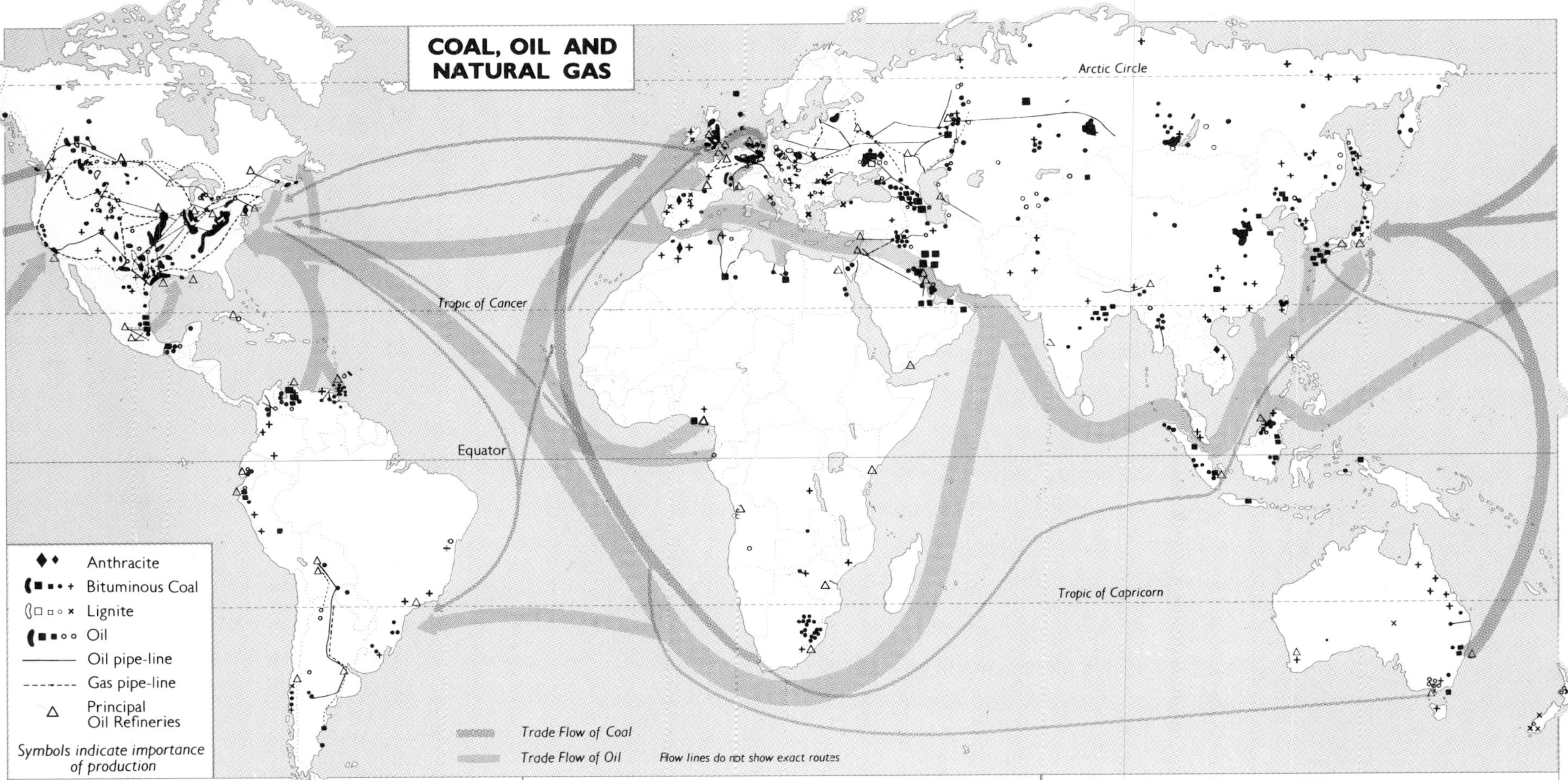
COAL, OIL AND NATURAL GAS
Arctic Circle
Tropic of Cancer
Equator
Tropic of Capricorn
Anthracite
Bituminous Coal
Lignite
Oil
Oil pipe-line
Gas pipe-line
Principal Oil Refineries
Symbols indicate importance of production
Trade Flow of Coal
Trade Flow of Oil
Flow lines do not show exact routes

COAL

World Production
1977-1979 average
million tonnes
3 452 *including lignite*

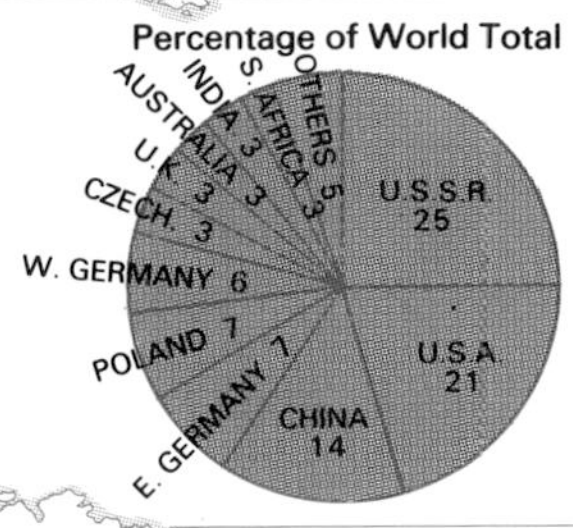
Percentage of World Total
U.S.S.R. 25
U.S.A. 21
CHINA 14
E. GERMANY 7
POLAND 7
W. GERMANY 6
CZECH. 3
U.K. 3
AUSTRALIA 3
INDIA 3
S. AFRICA 3
OTHERS 5

OIL – CRUDE PETROLEUM

World Production
1977-1979 average
million tonnes
3 053

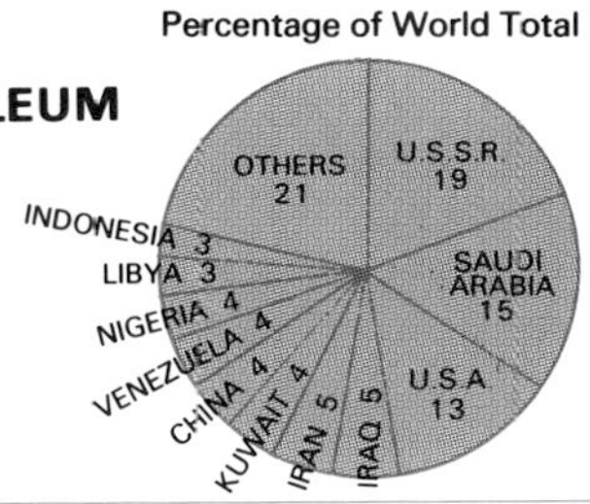
Percentage of World Total
OTHERS 21
U.S.S.R. 19
SAUDI ARABIA 15
U.S.A. 13
IRAQ 5
IRAN 5
KUWAIT 4
CHINA 4
VENEZUELA 4
NIGERIA 4
LIBYA 3
INDONESIA 3

NATURAL GAS

World Production
1977-1979 average
teracalories
12 116 335

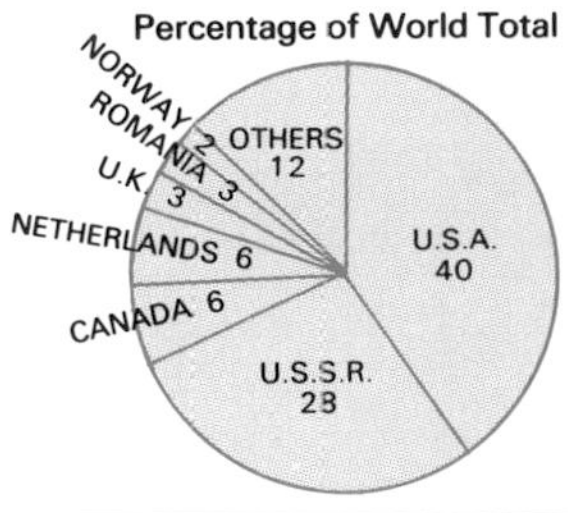
Percentage of World Total
OTHERS 12
U.S.A. 40
U.S.S.R. 23
CANADA 6
NETHERLANDS 6
U.K. 3
ROMANIA 3
NORWAY 3

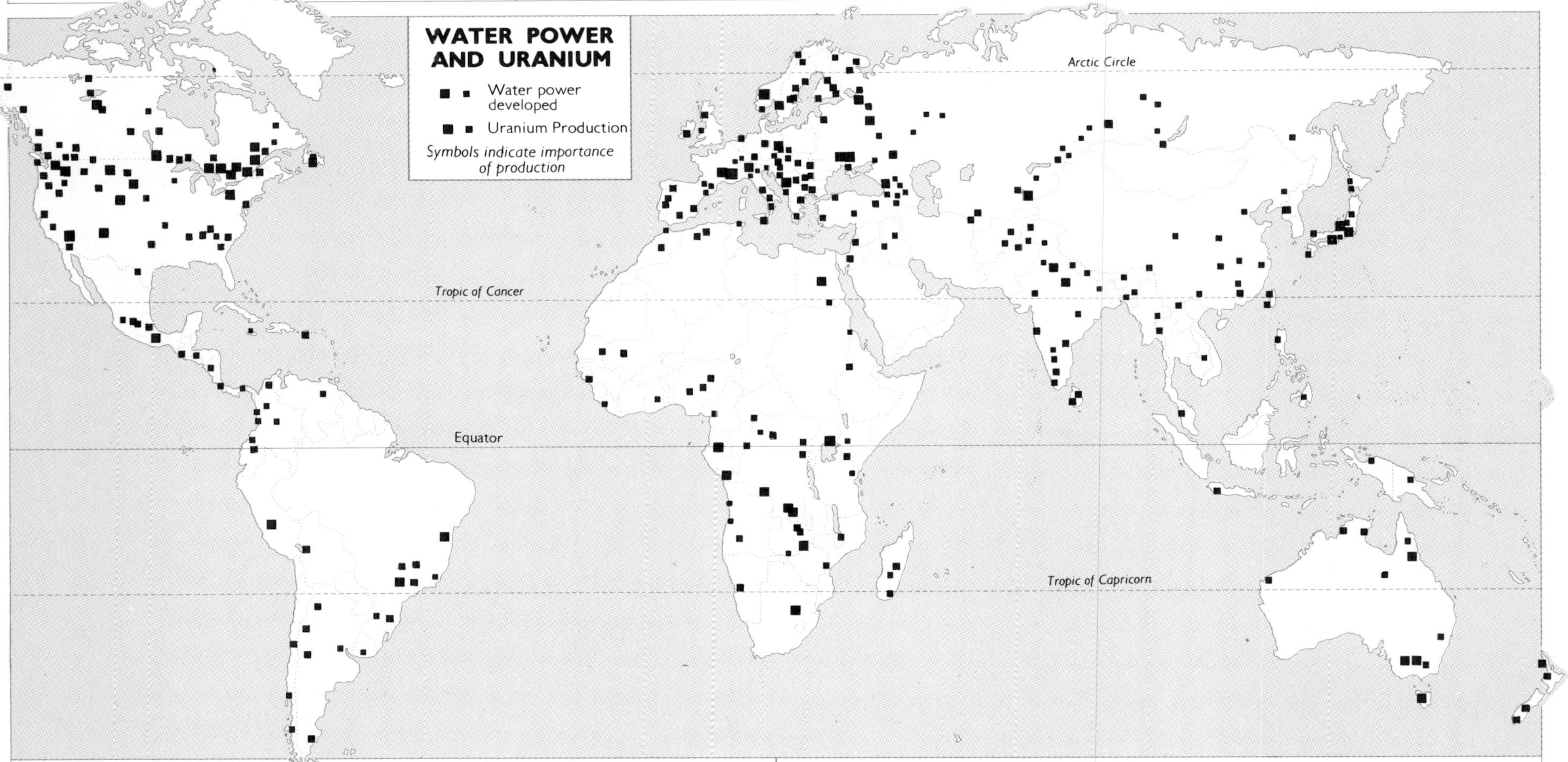
WATER POWER AND URANIUM
Water power developed
Uranium Production
Symbols indicate importance of production
Arctic Circle
Tropic of Cancer
Equator
Tropic of Capricorn

WATER POWER

World Total
1978
Installed Hydro-Electrical Capacity
megawatts
407 460

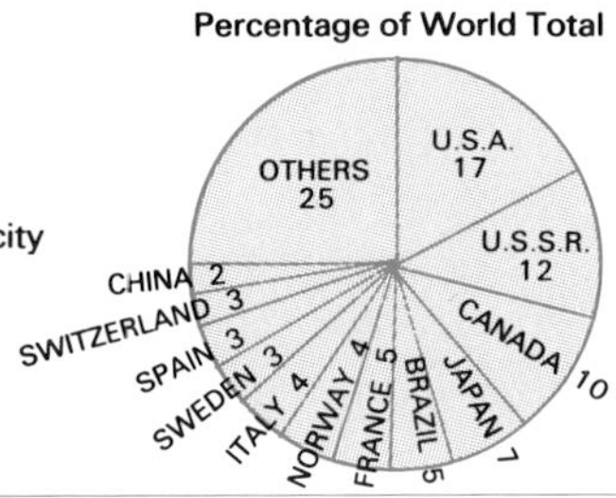
Percentage of World Total
OTHERS 25
U.S.A. 17
U.S.S.R. 12
CANADA 10
JAPAN 7
BRAZIL 5
FRANCE 5
NORWAY 4
ITALY 4
SWEDEN 3
SPAIN 3
SWITZERLAND 3
CHINA 2

URANIUM

World Production
1977-1979 average
tonnes
31 129

(excluding U.S.S.R. & China)

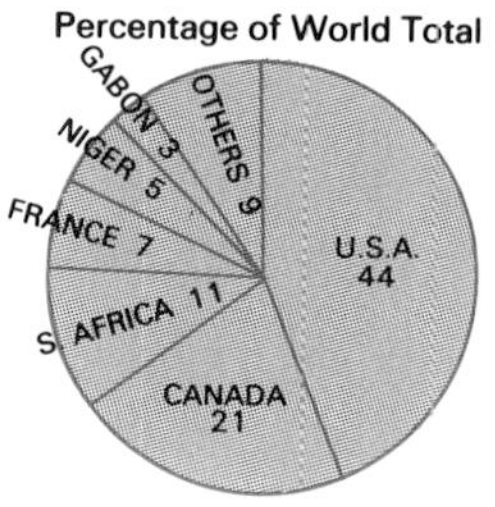
Percentage of World Total
U.S.A. 44
CANADA 21
S. AFRICA 11
FRANCE 7
NIGER 5
GABON 3
OTHERS 9

Maps based on Modified Homolographic Projection

1 tonne (metric ton) = 0·98 tons = 2204·62 pounds
1 kg (kilogram) = 2·20 pounds
1 ha (hectare) = 2·47 acres
1 kg/ha = 0·89 pounds/acres

Equatorial Scale: 1:136 000 000

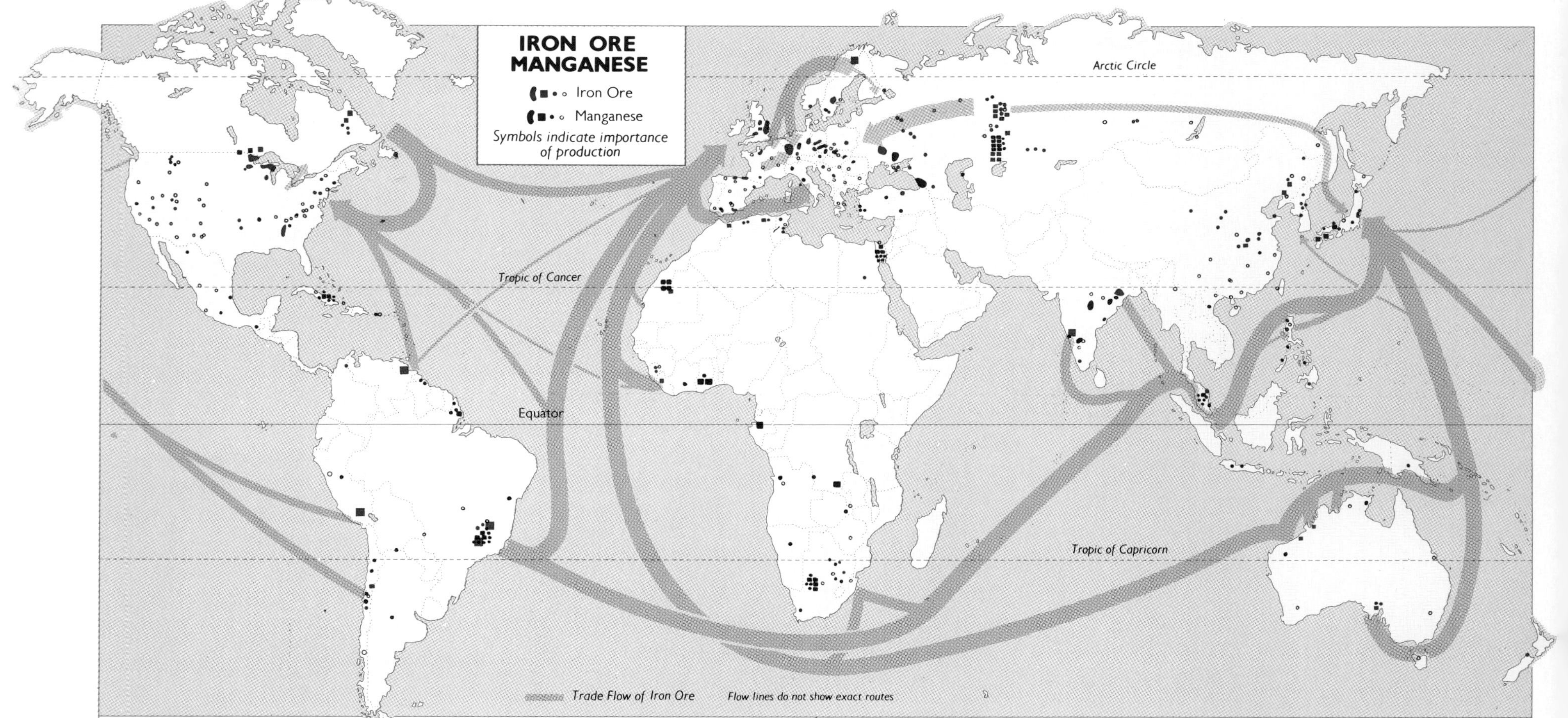
IRON ORE
MANGANESE
Iron Ore
Manganese
Symbols indicate importance of production
Arctic Circle
Tropic of Cancer
Equator
Tropic of Capricorn
Trade Flow of Iron Ore
Flow lines do not show exact routes

IRON ORE

World Production
1977-1979 average
million tonnes
525.8

Exports	m tonnes	Imports	m tonnes
Australia	75.1	Japan	114.7
Brazil	66.3	W. Germany	42.6
U.S.S.R.	40.6	U.S.A.	34.2
Canada	31.9	Belgium & Lux.	24.4
Sweden	22.5	Poland	17.2

Percentage of World Total

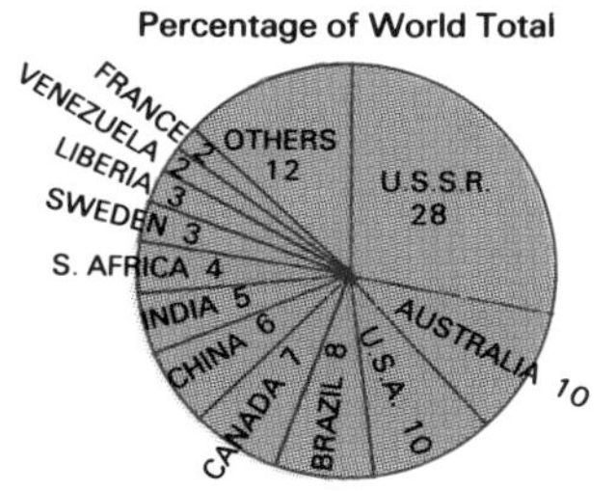
U.S.S.R. 28
AUSTRALIA 10
U.S.A. 10
BRAZIL 8
CANADA 7
CHINA 6
INDIA 5
S. AFRICA 4
SWEDEN 3
LIBERIA 3
VENEZUELA
FRANCE
OTHERS 12

MANGANESE

World Production
1977-1979 average
million tonnes
8.75

Exports	th tonnes	Imports	th tonnes
S. Africa	2500	Japan	2055
Australia	1301	France	958
U.S.S.R.	1186	Norway	803
Gabon	1142	W. Germany	673
Brazil	894	Poland	651

Percentage of World Total

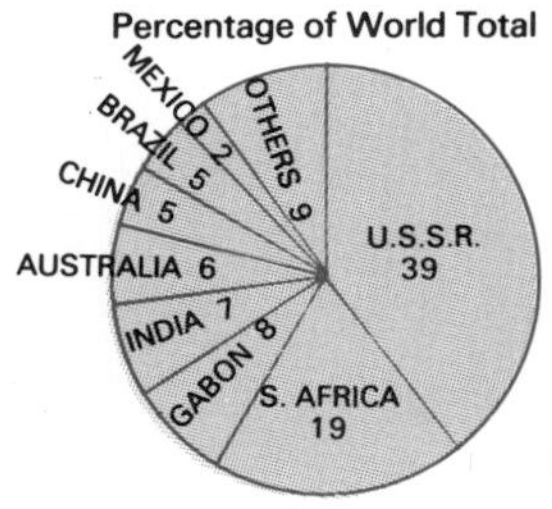
U.S.S.R. 39
S. AFRICA 19
GABON 8
INDIA 7
AUSTRALIA 6
CHINA 5
BRAZIL 5
MEXICO 2
OTHERS 9

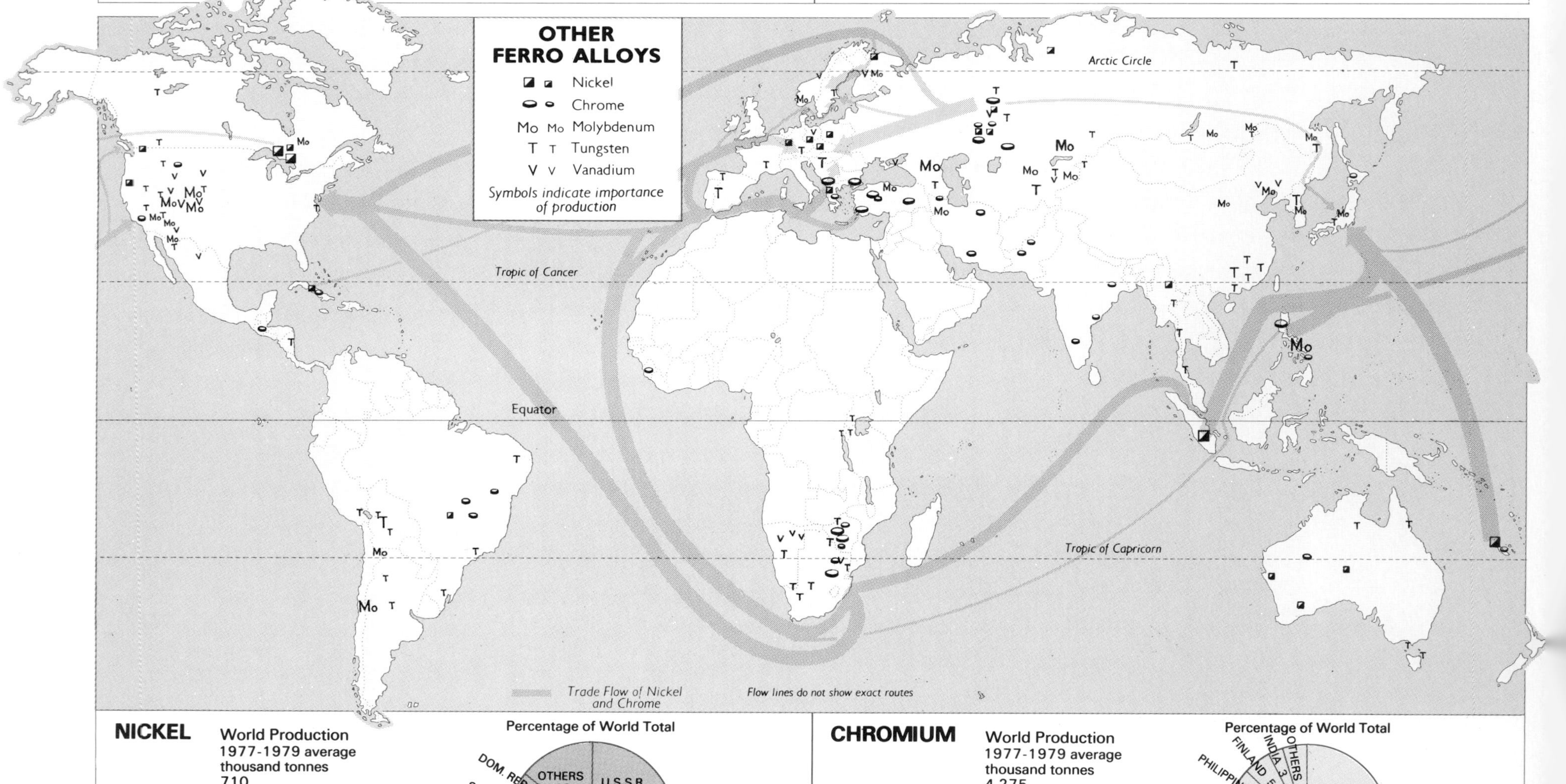
OTHER
FERRO ALLOYS
Nickel
Chrome
Mo Mo Molybdenum
T T Tungsten
V V Vanadium
Symbols indicate importance of production
Arctic Circle
Tropic of Cancer
Equator
Tropic of Capricorn
Trade Flow of Nickel and Chrome
Flow lines do not show exact routes

NICKEL

World Production
1977-1979 average
thousand tonnes
710

Exports	th tonnes	Imports	th tonnes
New Caledonia	1661	Japan	3044
Philippines	590	U.S.A.	173
Indonesia	576	W. Germany	59
Canada	175	Norway	55
Australia	61	U.K.	52

Percentage of World Total

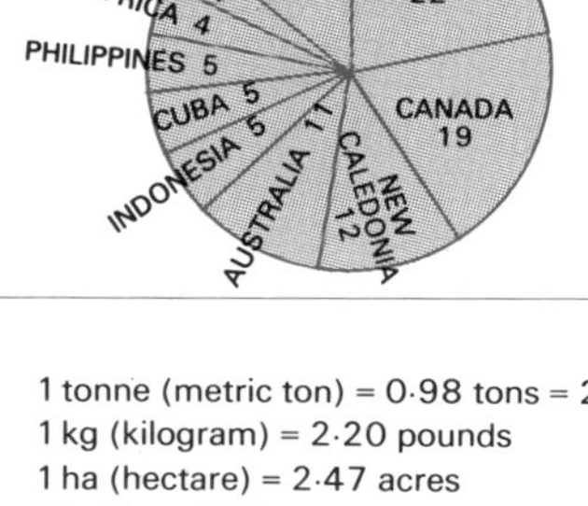
U.S.S.R. 22
CANADA 19
NEW CALEDONIA 12
AUSTRALIA 11
INDONESIA 5
CUBA 5
PHILIPPINES 5
S. AFRICA 4
DOM. REP. 4
OTHERS 13

CHROMIUM

World Production
1977-1979 average
thousand tonnes
4 275

Exports	th tonnes	Imports	th tonnes
S. Africa	1423	U.S.A.	919
Albania	800	Japan	670
U.S.S.R.	738	Sweden	558
Philippines	456	W. Germany	372
Finland	364	France	242

Percentage of World Total

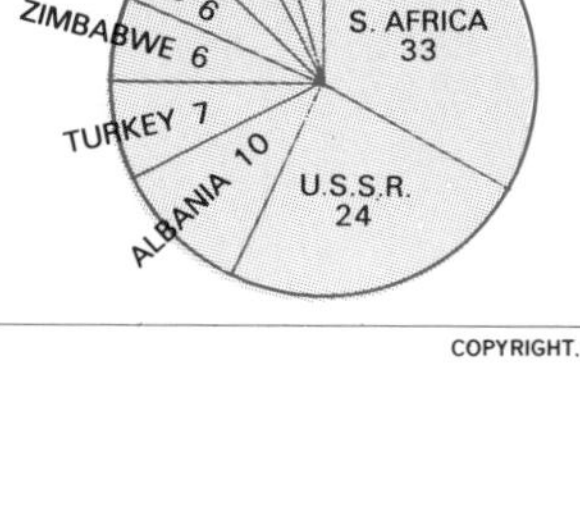
S. AFRICA 33
U.S.S.R. 24
ALBANIA 10
TURKEY 7
ZIMBABWE 6
PHILIPPINES 6
FINLAND 5
INDIA 3
OTHERS 6

Maps based on Modified Homolographic Projection

1 tonne (metric ton) = 0·98 tons = 2204·62 pounds
1 kg (kilogram) = 2·20 pounds
1 ha (hectare) = 2·47 acres
1 kg/ha = 0·89 pounds/acres

Equatorial Scale: 1:136 000 000

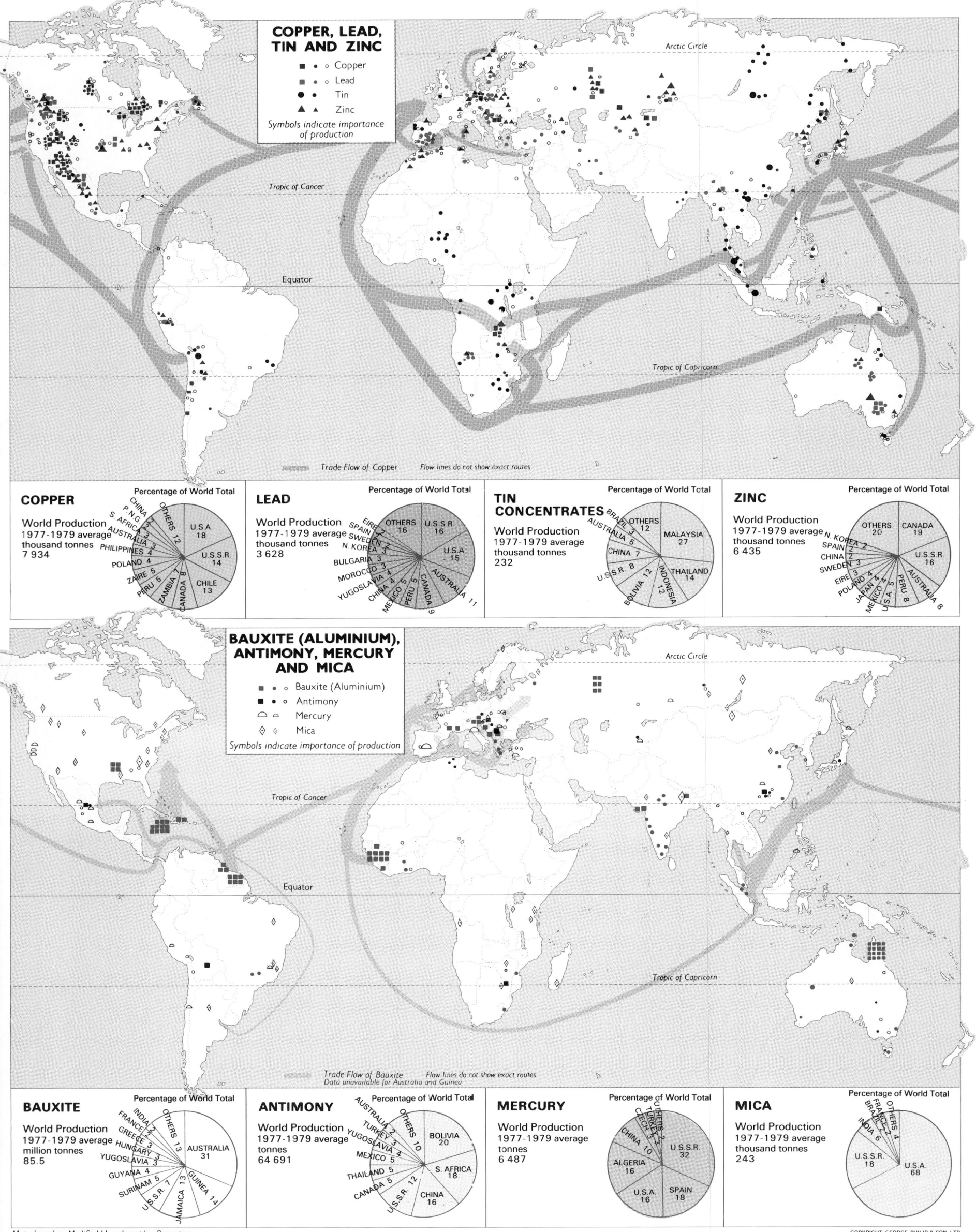

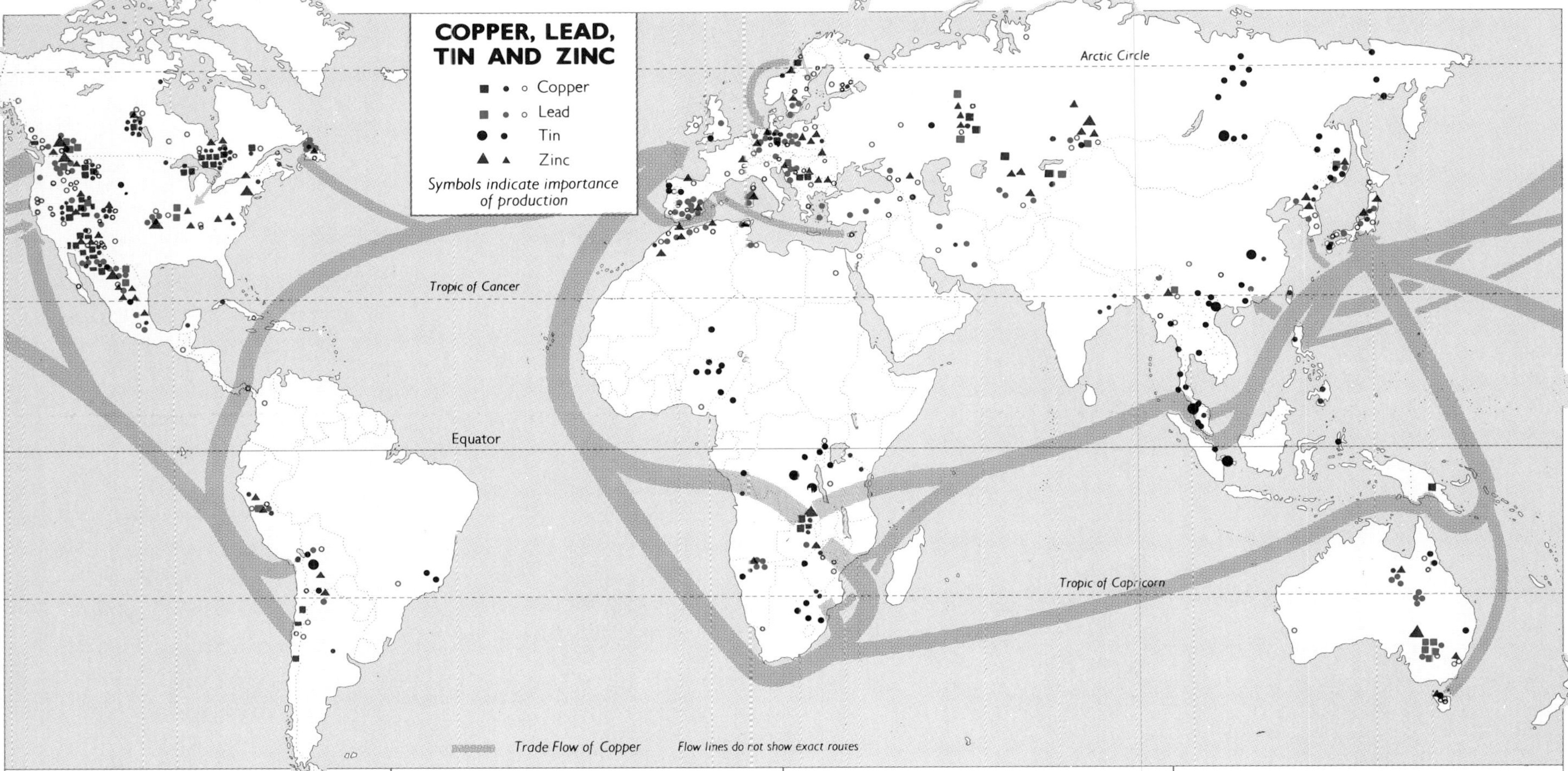
COPPER, LEAD, TIN AND ZINC
Copper
Lead
Tin
Zinc
Symbols indicate importance of production
Arctic Circle
Tropic of Cancer
Equator
Tropic of Capricorn
Trade Flow of Copper
Flow lines do not show exact routes

COPPER

World Production
1977-1979 average
thousand tonnes
7 934

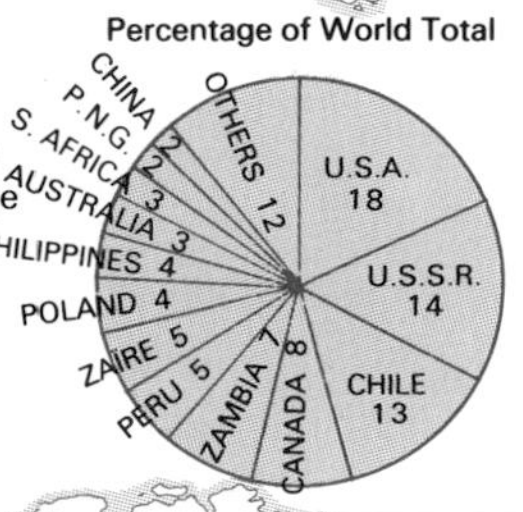
Percentage of World Total
U.S.A. 18
U.S.S.R. 14
CHILE 13
CANADA 8
ZAMBIA 7
PERU 5
ZAIRE 5
POLAND 4
PHILIPPINES 4
AUSTRALIA 3
S. AFRICA 3
P.N.G. 2
CHINA 2
OTHERS 12

LEAD

World Production
1977-1979 average
thousand tonnes
3 628

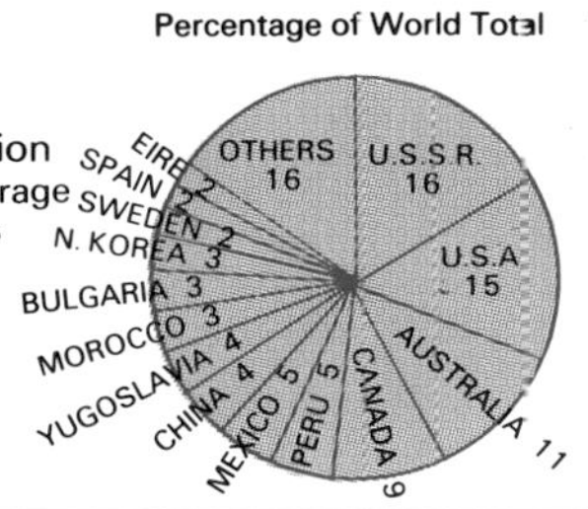
Percentage of World Total
OTHERS 16
U.S.S.R. 16
U.S.A. 15
AUSTRALIA 11
CANADA 9
PERU 5
MEXICO 5
CHINA 4
YUGOSLAVIA 4
MOROCCO 3
BULGARIA 3
N. KOREA 3
SWEDEN 2
SPAIN 2
EIRE 2

TIN CONCENTRATES

World Production
1977-1979 average
thousand tonnes
232

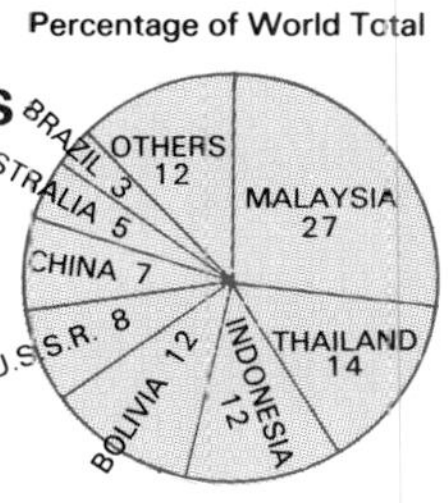
Percentage of World Total
OTHERS 12
MALAYSIA 27
THAILAND 14
INDONESIA 12
BOLIVIA 12
U.S.S.R. 8
CHINA 7
AUSTRALIA 5
BRAZIL 3

ZINC

World Production
1977-1979 average
thousand tonnes
6 435

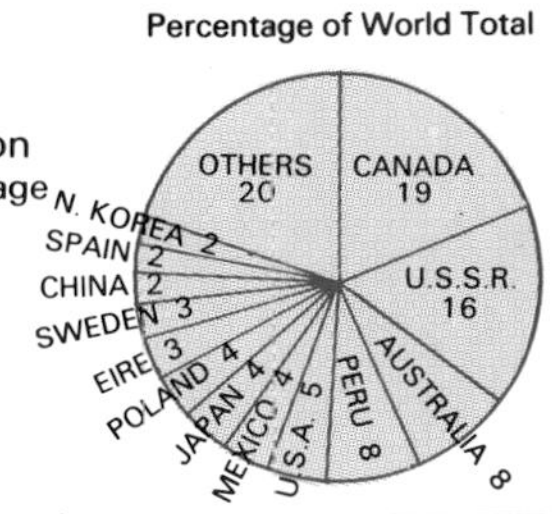
Percentage of World Total
OTHERS 20
CANADA 19
U.S.S.R. 16
AUSTRALIA 8
PERU 8
U.S.A. 5
MEXICO 4
JAPAN 4
POLAND 3
EIRE 3
SWEDEN 3
CHINA 2
SPAIN 2
N. KOREA 2

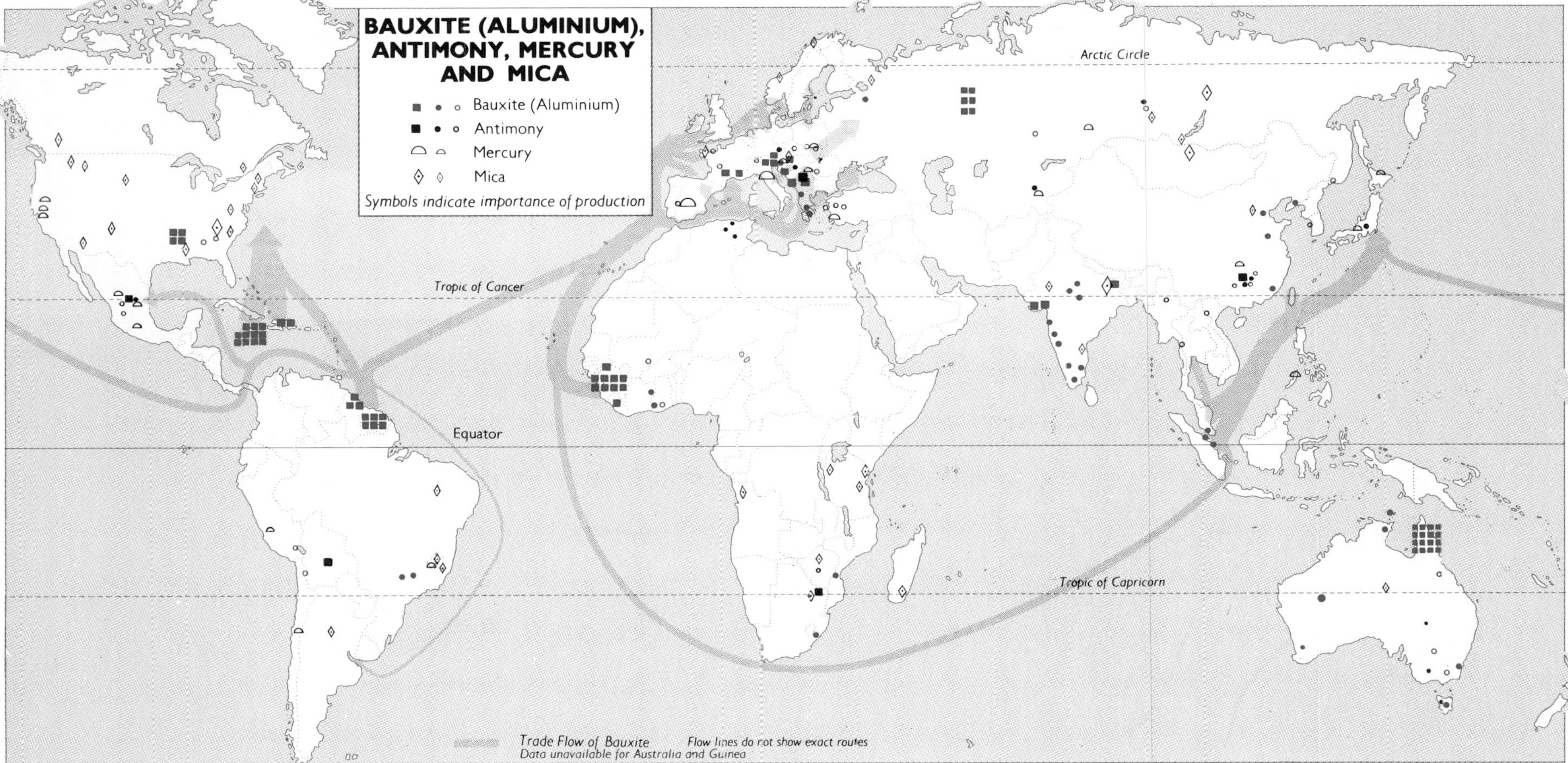
BAUXITE (ALUMINIUM), ANTIMONY, MERCURY AND MICA
Bauxite (Aluminium)
Antimony
Mercury
Mica
Symbols indicate importance of production
Arctic Circle
Tropic of Cancer
Equator
Tropic of Capricorn
Trade Flow of Bauxite
Flow lines do not show exact routes
Data unavailable for Australia and Guinea

BAUXITE

World Production
1977-1979 average
million tonnes
85.5

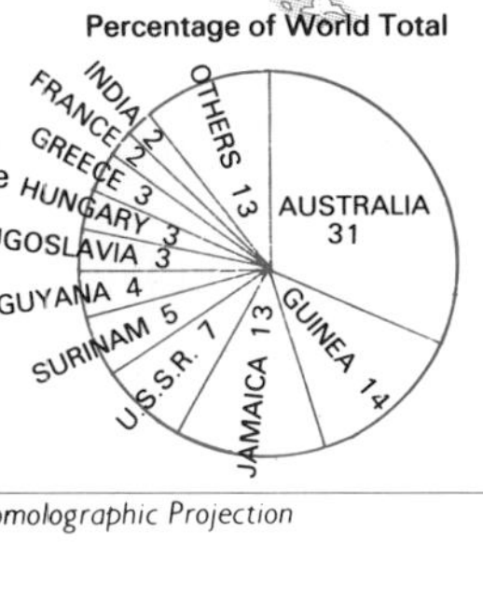
Percentage of World Total
OTHERS 13
AUSTRALIA 31
GUINEA 14
JAMAICA 13
U.S.S.R. 7
SURINAM 5
GUYANA 4
YUGOSLAVIA 3
HUNGARY 3
GREECE 3
FRANCE 2
INDIA 2

ANTIMONY

World Production
1977-1979 average
tonnes
64 691

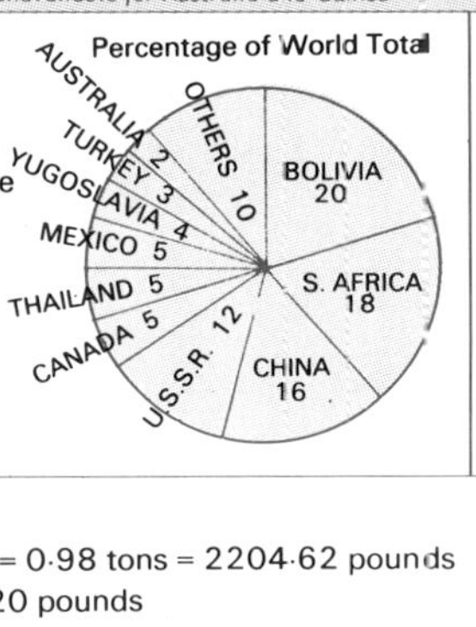
Percentage of World Total
OTHERS 10
BOLIVIA 20
S. AFRICA 18
CHINA 16
U.S.S.R. 12
CANADA 5
THAILAND 5
MEXICO 5
YUGOSLAVIA 4
TURKEY 3
AUSTRALIA 2

MERCURY

World Production
1977-1979 average
tonnes
6 487

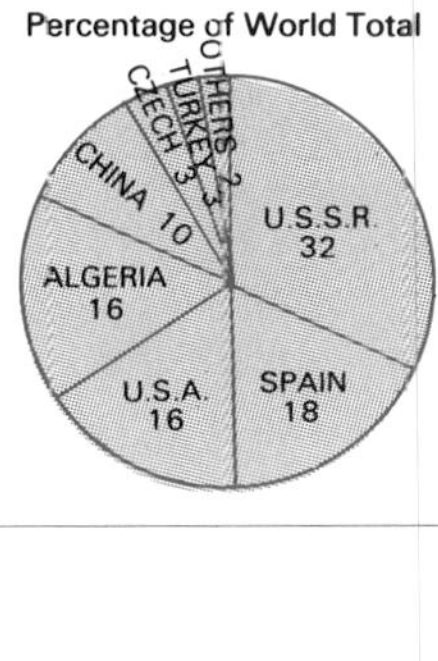
Percentage of World Total
OTHERS 2
U.S.S.R. 32
SPAIN 18
U.S.A. 16
ALGERIA 16
CHINA 10
CZECH 3
TURKEY 3

MICA

World Production
1977-1979 average
thousand tonnes
243

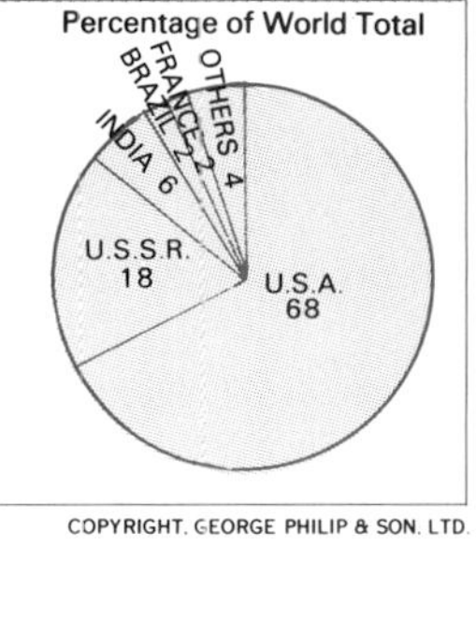
Percentage of World Total
OTHERS 4
U.S.A. 68
U.S.S.R. 18
INDIA 6
BRAZIL 2
FRANCE 2

Maps based on Modified Homolographic Projection

1 tonne (metric ton) = 0·98 tons = 2204·62 pounds
1 kg (kilogram) = 2·20 pounds
1 ha (hectare) = 2·47 acres
1 kg/ha = 0·89 pounds/acres

Equatorial Scale: 1:136 000 000

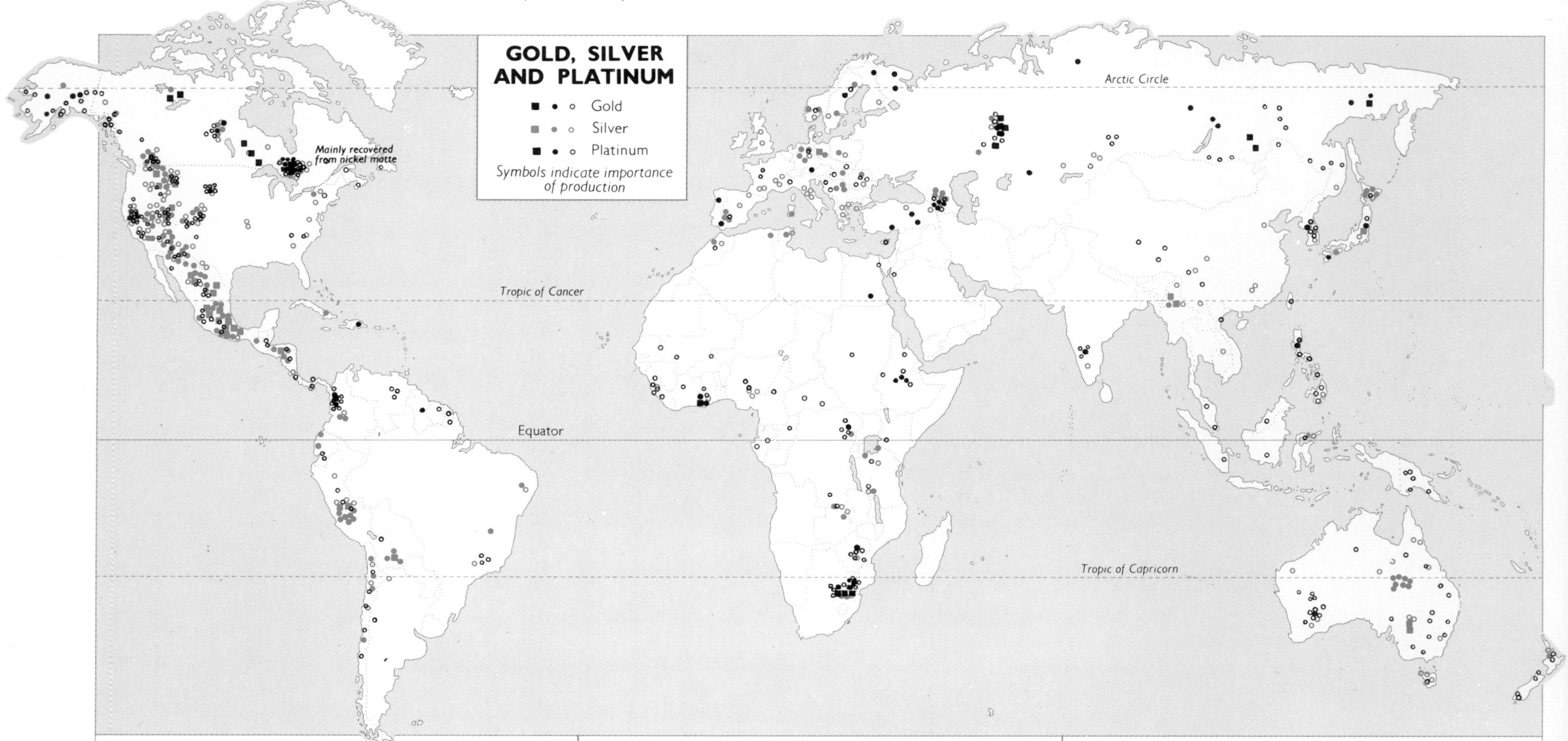
GOLD, SILVER AND PLATINUM
Gold
Silver
Platinum
Symbols indicate importance of production
Mainly recovered from nickel matte
Arctic Circle
Tropic of Cancer
Equator
Tropic of Capricorn

GOLD

World Production
1977-1979 average
kilograms
1 267

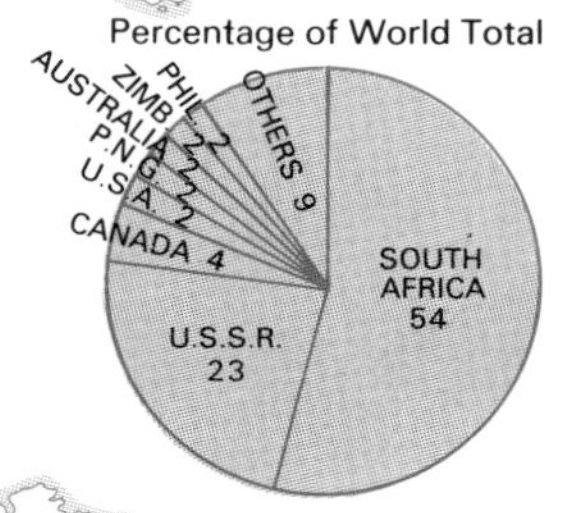
Percentage of World Total
SOUTH AFRICA 54
U.S.S.R. 23
CANADA 4
U.S.A.
P.N.G.
AUSTRALIA
ZIMB.
PHIL. 2
OTHERS 9

SILVER

World Production
1977-1979 average
tonnes
10 839

Percentage of World Total
OTHERS 20
U.S.S.R. 14
MEXICO 14
PERU 12
CANADA 11
U.S.A. 11
AUSTRALIA 8
POLAND 6
CHILE 2
JAPAN 2

PLATINUM

World Production
1977-1979 average
kilograms
201

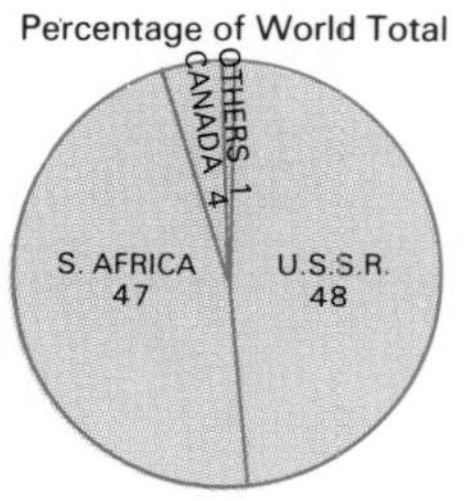
Percentage of World Total
OTHERS 1
CANADA 4
S. AFRICA 47
U.S.S.R. 48

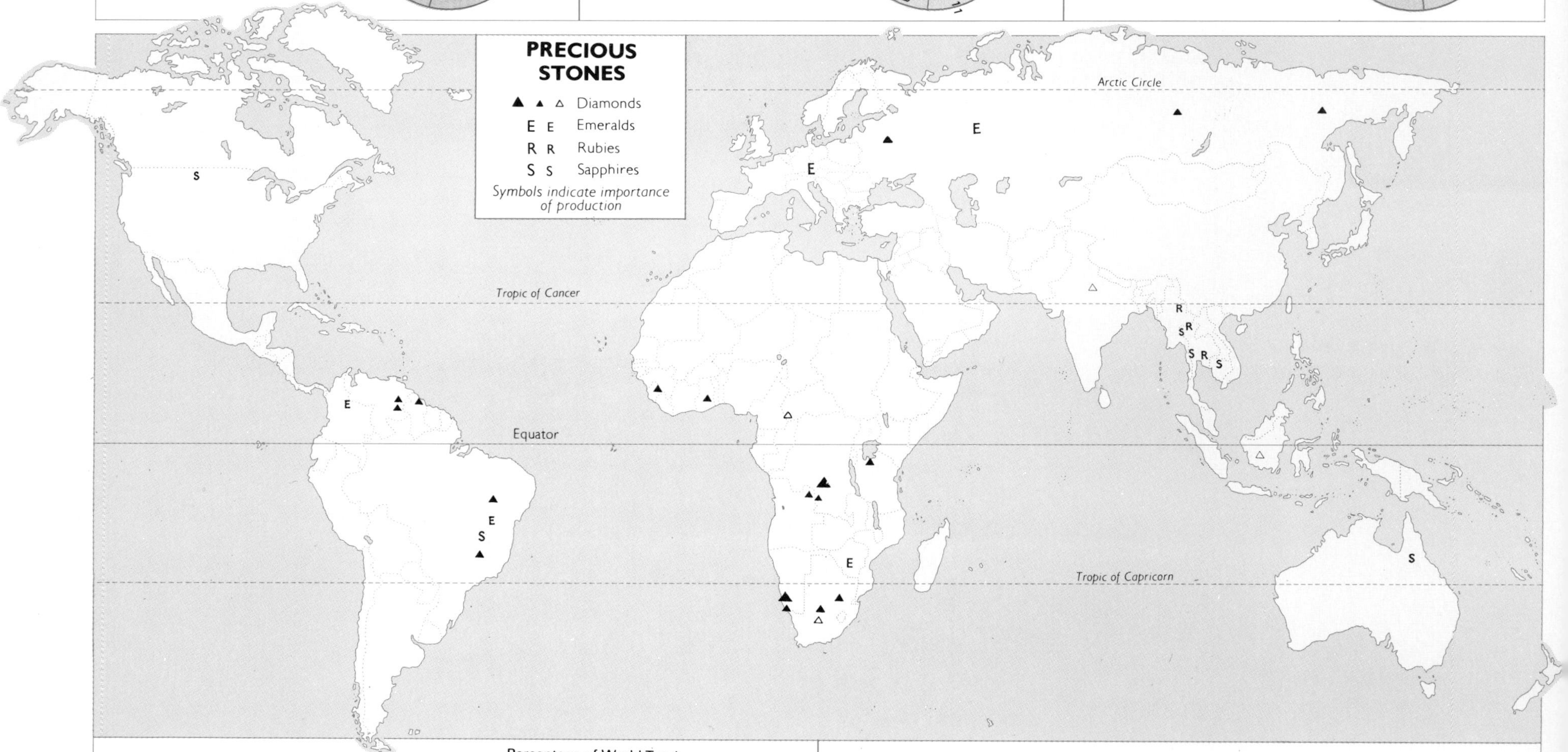
PRECIOUS STONES
Diamonds
E E Emeralds
R R Rubies
S S Sapphires
Symbols indicate importance of production
Arctic Circle
Tropic of Cancer
Equator
Tropic of Capricorn

DIAMONDS

World Production
1977-1979 average
million metric carats
38.7

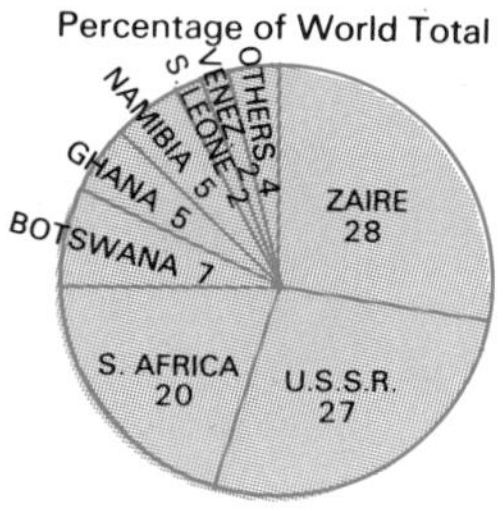
Percentage of World Total
ZAIRE 28
U.S.S.R. 27
S. AFRICA 20
BOTSWANA 7
GHANA 5
NAMIBIA 5
S. LEONE 2
VENEZ. 2
OTHERS 4

EMERALDS, RUBIES & SAPPHIRES

No reliable figures available

Maps based on Modified Homolographic Projection

1 tonne (metric ton) = 0·98 tons = 2204·62 pounds
1 kg (kilogram) = 2·20 pounds
1 ha (hectare) = 2·47 acres
1 kg/ha = 0·89 pounds/acres

ECONOMIC SECTION

INTRODUCTION

It is the aim of the statistics in this section to present for various countries a picture of their economic character and position in the world. The tabular format allows for the inclusion of a great deal of information within a compact space; the format also facilitates comparisons among countries.

The information presented includes both the elementary and the sophisticated. Throughout, the goal has been to be specific about a few items rather than general about many. Those items chosen are the most important within the general categories of area and population, production, manufactures, and trade. The arrangement of columns, as further explained below, corresponds to these four categories. Additional explanation of the terms used is contained under the appropriate part of the General Notes.

Table Arrangement

Country
1. Form of government
2. Language(s)
3. Currency
4. Average exchange rate for 1979

Area and Population
1. Area in km^2
2. Population & density estimates June 1979
3. Birth & death rates per 1,000 1970-77
4. Urban population in 1,000s & percentage of total population
5. Capital city & population in 1,000s

Production
1. GDP (million \$) for l.a. year & annual growth rate for l.a. 5 year period; GDP per capita for l.a. year & annual growth rate for l.a. 5 year period. Industrial origin of GDP, % distribution.
2. Agricultural production in 1,000s of metric tons
3. Livestock in 1,000s head
4. Fish in 1,000s metric tons 1978
5. Roundwood in million m^3 1978
6. Minerals mined in 1,000s metric tons (gas in quintillion calories)

Manufactures
1. Production/consumption of all energy in million metric tons of coal equivalent 1976; Electricity production in million kWh & % hydroelectric, nuclear, geothermal
2. Manufactures in 1,000s metric tons
   (a) Agricultural l.a. year
   (b) Industrial l.a. year
   (Sawnwood, where given, in 1,000 m^3)
3. Communications: telephones & cars in use in 1,000s l.a. year
   Railways: passenger-km & metric-ton – km (millions)
   Airlines: passenger-km & metric-ton – km (1,000s)
   Sea cargo loaded and unloaded in 1,000s metric tons

Trade
Export and import totals in \$ millions
List of major items
Main trading partners in order of importance
Invisible trade balance in \$ millions 1977
Revenue from tourism in \$ millions l.a. year
Aid given or received & source in \$ millions (average 1975-77)

GENERAL NOTES

As far as possible, figures are given for 1979. When they are for different years or periods — as in the case of the exchange rates or GDP figures — the appropriate date is mentioned in the table description above. For the urban and capital populations, the most recent estimates or figures from the latest census are given.

Country, Column 1

The exchange rates for the British £ and U.S. \$ are shown. The C.F.A. franc (Communauté Financière Africaine) is the unit of currency used throughout the African territories associated with France.

Area and Population, Column 2

The area figure is for the total area of the country, including inland water bodies.

The birth and death rates are the latest available figures. The annual rate of change in population is expressed as an average for the years 1970-77. The figure includes the net balance of births, deaths, and migration.

Production, Column 3

GDP (the first figure in line 1) is Gross Domestic Product, a measure of a country's total production of goods and services. The figures are expressed in "purchaser's values," or market cost of goods and services on delivery to the purchaser. This includes the cost of materials, production, trade and transportation charges. Imported goods and services are not included. The second figure in line 1 is GDP per capita.

In Communist countries, the best similar measure is the NMP, the Net Material Product. The NMP is not directly comparable to the GDP. It is the total net value of goods and production services, including taxes, in one year. Excluded are public administration, defense, personal and professional services. The conversion into dollars is based on the commercial import/export rate. The resulting figure should be used with great caution and treated as a general indicator.

An annual average rate of increase is given following both *GDP* and *GDP per capita*. The averages are for the latest available five-year period.

The industrial origin of the GDP is divided into three categories: agriculture, industry, and other. The percentages below the GDP figures show the part of the total GDP contributed by each category.

Roundwood refers to the forest output of wood whether for use as fuel, lumber, or other products. The volume figure is without bark.

Manufactures, Column 4

The production and consumption of various types of energy is given as a coal equivalent. The equivalent is the conversion of the total calorific content of all energy sources into terms of the calorific value of one metric ton of coal. The production figure is based on the domestic production of coal, lignite, crude petroleum, natural gas, and hydro- and nuclear electricity. Imported energy sources are not included, hence the apparent discrepancy between production and consumption of energy.

Synthetic fibres refer to non-cellulosic continuous and discontinuous fibres. They include textile, glass, and spun fibres. The filaments are either natural polymers or synthetic polymers. Familiar trade names for some of these fibres are nylon, terylene, Orlon, Saran, etc.

Petroleum products include particular products obtained from crude petroleum and shale oil, such as liquefied petroleum gas, naphtha motor fuel, aviation gasoline, kerosene, jet fuel, distillate fuel oils, residual fuel oil, lubricating oils, bitumen, and paraffin wax.

Vehicles include passenger cars, commercial vehicles, and heavy trucks, but not agricultural machinery or tractors.

Rail traffic refers to all traffic within the borders of the country; air traffic includes both domestic and international flights.

Trade, Column 5

Exports are f.o.b. and imports c.i.f.

Trade partners are listed in order of importance.

Invisible trade concerns the provision of services to people abroad and dividends from overseas assets. The invisible trade balance is the net balance of private earnings from, and expenditure on, this exchange of non-physical ("invisible") goods. The most important of source activities are international banking, insurance, shipping, and tourism. Government activity is not accounted for, although this may significantly alter the overall balance.

The revenue from tourism is the total income, not a net balance.

Aid is a general term for all planned assistance to the developing countries. Aid comes from governments (official aid) and from private organizations (private aid). In 1977, net total aid from the developed market economies to the developing countries was \$17,631,000,000 and the private equivalent was \$27,023,000,000. A second distinction can be made between bilateral and multilateral aid. Bilateral aid is set up between two governments according to their own arrangements. This method accounts for over 85% of all aid. Multilateral aid is given through institutes such as the World Bank, the European Economic Community, United Nations institutions, and such regional institutions as the Colombo plan.

Sources

The principal sources used in the preparation of these tables were the Yearbooks of the UN (Statistical, Demographic, National Accounts, and International Trade), the Monthly Bulletin of Statistics of the UN, the Yearbooks of the Food and Agricultural Organization, and the International Financial Statistics of the International Monetary Fund.

Abbreviations

... — *data not available*
c — *carats (1,000s)*
geo — *geothermal*
grt — *gross registered tons (1,000s)*
hl — *hectoliters (1,000s)*
hydr — *hydroelectric*
kg — *kilograms*
l.a. — *latest available*
km, km^2 — *kilometers, square kilometers*
kWh — *kilowatt-hours*
m^3 — *cubic meters*
M — *million*
nucl — *nuclear*
t — *metric tons*
T — *thousand*

Country	Area and Population	Production	Manufactures	Trade
AFGHANISTAN 1. Republic 2. Pashto, Persian 3. Afghani 4. £1 = 93.96 $1 = 42.25	1. 647 497 km² 2. 15 488 000; 23 per km² 3. BR 45; DR 21; AI 2.5% 4. Urb. pop.; 2 744 (15%) 5. Kabul 588	1. GDP $2 616 (. . .); $153 (. . .) Agric. 49%, Indust. 17%, Others 44% 2. Wheat 2 200 Maize 750 Cottonseed 70 Cotton lint 38 3. Sheep 23 000 Cattle 3 980 Goats 3 000 5. Roundwood 8 6. Coal 218 Natural gas 25 164 Salt 81	1. 3.62/0.81; 700 kWh (75% hydr.) 2a. Sugar 15 Sawnwood 400 Meat 216 b. Cement 126 Cotton woven 96 3. Telephones 18; Cars 37 Air; 290 pass.-km; 13.9 t-km	Exports $429 Imports $328 Cotton Food Natural gas Textiles Dried fruit Petroleum products Fresh fruit Machinery Exports to: U.S.S.R., U.K. and Pakistan Imports from: U.S.S.R., Japan and Iran Aid received (net): $63 from West, $242 from East
ALBANIA 1. Republic 2. Albanian 3. Lek 4. £1 = 15.57 $1 = 7.0	1. 28 748 km² 2. 2 671 000; 90 per km² 3. BR 33; DR 8; AI 2.9% 4. Urb. pop.; 696 (34%) 5. Tirana 192	1. NMP . . . (8.4%); . . .(5.6%) 2. Wheat 420 Maize 320 Cottonseed 13 Cotton lint 7 3. Sheep 1 163 Goats 665 5. Roundwood 2 6. Lignite 1 000 Crude petroleum 2 300 Chrome 930 Copper 13 Nickel 8	1. 4.55/2.21; 2 150 kWh (77% hydr.) 2a. Sugar 40 Beer 144 hl b. Cement 800 Copper 9 Cotton woven . . . Wool, woven . . .	Exports . . . Imports . . . Fuels and minerals Machinery Exports to: India, Czechoslovakia, Poland and E. Germany Imports from: India, Czechoslovakia, Poland and E. Germany
ALGERIA 1. Republic 2. Arabic, French 3. Algerian Dinar 4. £1 = 8.351 $1 = 3.755	1. 2 381 741 km² 2. 19 129 000; 8 per km² 3. BR 48; DR 15; AI 3.2% 4. Urb. pop.; 8 467 (52%) 5. Algiers 1 503	1. GDP $16 497 (. . .); $954 (. . .) Agric. 8%, Indust. 39%, Others 53% 2. Wheat 1 200 Barley 400 Grapes 290 Oranges 297 3. Sheep 10 900 Goats 2 600 4. Fish 34 5. Crude petroleum 50 112 Natural gas 91 704 Iron ore 1 639 Phosphates 1 083	1. 91.6/12.6; 4 650 kWh (11% hydr.) 2a. Wine 2 550 hl Meat 148 b. Cotton yarn 9 Cement 2 700 Petroleum products 5 476 3. Telephones 298; Cars 400 Rail: 1 452 pass-km; 2 016 t-km Air: 1 723 pass-km; 9.2 t-km Sea: 49 824 loaded: 13 500 unloaded	Exports $9 255 Imports $8 682 Crude petroleum Machinery Wine Iron and steel Natural gas Food Exports to: France, W. Germany, U.S.A. and Italy Imports from: France, W. Germany, Italy and U.S.A. Aid received (net): $131 from West; $186 from East
ANGOLA 1. Republic 2. Portuguese 3. Kwanza £1 = 110.7 $1 = 49.78	1. 1 246 700 km² 2. 6 901 000; 5 per km² 3. BR 48; DR 25; AI 2.4% 4. Urb. pop.; 1 035 (15%) 5. Luanda 475	1. GDP $2 701 (. . .); $434 (. . .) 2. Coffee 60 Sugar cane 500 Maize 300 Palm oil 40 3. Cattle 3 120 Goats 930 4. Fish 119 5. Roundwood 8 6. Crude petroleum 6 696 Diamonds 400 c Iron ore 5 500	1. 6.75/1.08; 1 360 kWh (70% hydr.) 2a. Sugar 50 b. Cement 600 Cotton yarn 3 3. Telephones 32; Cars 75 Rail: 418 pass-km; 5 461 t-km Sea: 10 044 loaded; 3 984 unloaded	Exports $1 227 Imports $625 Coffee Machinery Diamonds Metals Crude petroleum Exports to: U.S.A., Portugal, Canada and Japan Imports from: Portugal, W. Germany, South Africa and U.S.A. Aid received (net): $17 from West
ARGENTINA 1. Republic 2. Spanish 3. Argentinian Peso 4. £1 = 3 598 $1 = 1 618	1. 2 776 889 km² 2. 26 729 000; 10 per km² 3. BR 26; DR 9; AI 1.3% 4. Urb. pop.; 19 540 (83%) 5. Buenos Aires 8 436	1. GDP $49 088 (2.8%); $1 935 (1.5%) Agric. 12%, Indust. 36%, Others 52% 2. Wheat 7 800 Maize 8 700 Linseed 1 029 Citrus fruits 1 326 Wool 172 Grapes 3 360 3. Cattle 60 174 Sheep 35 400 4. Fish 537 5. Roundwood 7 6. Coal 732 Zinc 37 Crude petroleum 24 264 Lead 31 Natural gas 72 372 Silver 56 t	1. 41.8/46.4; 32 328 kWh (18% hydr., 5% nucl.) 2a. Meat 3 851 Wine 20 267 Sugar 1 381 b. Cotton yarn 92 Steel 2 988 Petroleum Vehicles: products 20 992 pass. 190; comm. 62 Cement 6 612 Iron 1 176 3. Telephones 2 342; Cars 2 950 Rail: 11 244 pass.-km; 10 308 t-km Air: 5 292 pass.-km 129 t-km Sea: 23 352 loaded; 8 376 unloaded	Exports $6 400 Imports $3 864 Meat Machinery Cereals Iron and steel Wool Non-ferrous metals Exports to: Italy, Netherlands, Brazil and U.S.A. Imports from: U.S.A., W. Germany, Brazil and Japan Invisible trade balance: −$565 Revenue from tourism: $213 Aid received (net): $28 from West
AUSTRALIA 1. Commonwealth 2. English 3. Australian Dollar 4. £1 = 2.013 $1 = 0.905	1. 7 686 810 km² 2. 14 418 000; 2 per km² 3. BR 16; DR 7; AI 1.5% 4. Urb. pop.; 11 650 (86%) 5. Canberra 215	1. GDP $100 765 (3.3%); $7 239 (1.6%) Agric. 5%, Indust. 25%, Others 70% 2. Wheat 16 100 Barley 3 657 Oats 1 492 Wool 706 Citrus fruits 480 Other fruits 2 000 3. Sheep 134 361 Cattle 27 107 4. Fish 123 5. Roundwood 15 6. Coal 74 796 Lead 419 Crude petroleum 21 660 Zinc 483 Manganese 1 666 Gold 18 380 kg Iron ore 53 875 Nickel 73 Bauxite 25 644 Copper 232	1. 119.9/90.8; 82 522 kWh (17% hydr.) 2a. Meat 2 975 Sugar 2 963 Sawnwood 3 404 Butter & cheese 230 b. Wool yarn 20 Cement 5 112 Steel 7 536 Radios 21 Petroleum Vehicles: products 22 749 pass. 374; comm. 58 3. Telephones 5 685; Cars 5 657 Rail: . . .; 32 028 t-km Air: 20 988 pass.-km; 501 t-km Sea: 166 332 loaded; 26 712 unloaded	Exports $18 473 Imports $16 432 Wool Machinery Cereals Vehicles Metals Textiles Meat Crude petroleum Exports to: Japan, U.S.A. and N.Z. Imports from: U.S.A., Japan, U.K. and W. Germany Invisible trade balance: −$3 039 Revenue from tourism: $343 Aid given (net): $593
AUSTRIA 1. Federal Republic 2. German 3. Austrian Schilling 4. £1 = 27.64 $1 = 12.43	1. 83 849 km² 2. 7 506 000; 89 per km² 3. BR 11; DR 12; AI 0.2% 4. Urb. pop.; 3 867 (52%) 5. Vienna 1 590	1. GDP $47 954 (4.0%); $6 377 (3.8%) Agric. 5%, Indust. 33%, Others 62% 2. Wheat 850 Barley 1 129 Potatoes 1 494 Rye 278 Pears 138 3. Pigs 4 007 Cattle 2 594 5. Roundwood 13 6. Lignite 2 736 Iron ore 993 Crude petroleum 1 728 Magnesite 982 Natural gas 20 412 Antimony 655 t Salt 381	1. 9.96/30.2; 37 684 kWh (66% hydr.) 2a. Alcoholic Sugar 397 drinks 11 371 hl Sawnwood 6 017 b. Cotton yarn 18 Wool yarn 8 Steel 5 424 Aluminium 92 Petroleum products 9 303 3. Telephones 2 443; Cars 2 139 Rail: 7 308 pass.-km; 9 624 t-km Air: 10 944 pass.-km; 14 t-km	Exports $15 483 Imports £20 254 Machinery Machinery Iron and steel Food Textiles Textiles Sawnwood Vehicles Chemical products Exports to: W. Germany, Italy, Switzerland and U.K. Imports from: W. Germany, Switzerland, Italy and France Invisible trade balance: +$1 009 Revenue from tourism: $3 322 Aid given (net): $250
BANGLADESH 1. Republic 2. Bengali 3. Taka 4. £1 = 34.78 $1 = 15.64	1. 143 998 km² 2. 86 643 000; 588 per km² 3. BR 47; DR 20; AI 2.4% 4. Urb. pop.; 6 274 (9%) 5. Dacca 1 730	1. GDP $7 663 (. . .); $93 (. . .) Agric. 54%, Indust. 8%, Others 38% 2. Rice 19 355 Bananas 600 Tea 39 Jute 996 3. Cattle 31 741 Goats 11 000 4. Fish 640 5. Roundwood 10	1. 1.14/2.63; 1 930 kWh (27% hydr.) 2a. Jute 996 Sugar 144 b. Cotton yarn 46 Cement 324 3. Telephones 98; Cars 22 Rail: 3 331 pass.-km; 639 t-km Sea 1 022 loaded; 5 216 unloaded	Exports $576 Imports $1 344 Exports to: U.S.A., Pakistan, U.S.S.R. and U.K. Imports from: Japan, U.S.A. and U.K. Aid received (net): $690 from West; $45 from East

For detailed table headings and notes see page 1 of this section

Country	Area and Population	Production	Manufactures	Trade
BELGIUM 1. Kingdom 2. French, Flemish, German 3. Belgian Franc 4. £1 = 62.38 $1 = 28.05	1. 30 513 km^2 2. 9 848 000; 317 per km^2 3. BR 13; DR 11; AI 0.4% 4. Urb. pop.; 9 286 (95%) 5. Brussels 1 042	1. GDP $79 205 (3.7%); $8 058 (3.4%) Agric. 2%, Indust. 30%, Others 68% 2. Wheat 987; Barley 850 Potatoes 1 289; Apples 266 3. Pigs 5 083; Cattle 2 823 4. Fish 51 5. Roundwood 2.7 6. Coal 6 132; Lead 125 Iron ore . . .	1. 8.81/59.8; 47 099 kWh (1% hydr., 25% nucl.) 2a. Sugar 978; Sawnwood 610 b. Cotton yarn 41; Wool yarn 76 Steel 12 601; Copper 520 Coke oven coke 5 747; Plastics 832 Petroleum products 28 784; Vehicles: pass. 1 013; comm. 67 Radios 1 313; Iron 10 128 3. Telephones 3 100; Cars 3 077 Rail: 7 140 pass.-km; 7 104 t-km Air: 4 824 pass.-km; 411 t-km Sea: 37 704 loaded; 58 692 unloaded	Exports $56 258 (incl. Luxembourg): Iron and steel, Vehicles, Machinery, Non-ferrous metals, Textiles Imports $60 410 (incl. Luxembourg): Machinery, Vehicles, Non-ferrous metals, Diamonds, Petrol Trade is principally with: W. Germany, France, Netherlands and U.K. Invisible trade balance (incl. Luxembourg): +$1 389 Revenue from tourism: $993 Aid given (net): $865
BENIN 1. Republic 2. French 3. C.F.A. Franc 4. £1 = 447.0 $1 = 201.0	1. 112 622 km^2 2. 3 469 000; 30 per km^2 3. BR 49; DR 21; AI 2.7% 4. Urb. pop.; 465 (14%) 5. Porto-Novo 104	1. GDP $604 (2.2%); $184 (−0.5%) Agric. 38%, Indust. 7%, Others 55% 2. Cassava 700; Palm oil 28 Maize 230; Cottonseed 13 Groundnuts 70 3. Goats 950; Cattle 800 4. Fish 25 5. Roundwood 3	1. —/0.12; 5 kWh 2a. Sawnwood 9 3. Telephones 10; Cars 14 Rail: 132 pass.-km; 156 t-km Air: 139 pass.-km; 13 t-km Sea: 73 loaded; 982 unloaded	Exports $26: Palm oil, Oilseeds, Cotton, Cocoa Imports $267: Manufactured products, Machinery Exports to: France, Netherlands and Japan Imports from: France, W. Germany Netherlands and U.K. Aid received (net): $54 from West
BOLIVIA 1. Republic 2. Spanish 3. Bolivian Peso 4. £1 = 54.51 $1 = 24.51	1. 1 098 581 km^2 2. 5 425 000; 5 per km^2 3. BR 47; DR 18; AI 2.7% 4. Urb. pop.; 1 595 (32%) 5. La Paz 655, Sucre 63	1. GDP $2 508 (5.8%); $445 (3.1%) Agric. 18%, Indust. 25%, Others 67% 2. Maize 331; Barley 62 Potatoes 800; Citrus fruit 127 3. Sheep 8 700; Goats 3 000 5. Roundwood 4 6. Antimony 13 019 t; Crude petroleum 1 332 Tin 31; Silver 179 t Tungsten 3 997t; Zinc 59 Natural Gas 15 096	1. 5.04/1.68; 150 kWh (77% hydr.) 2a. Sugar 282 b. Cement 257 3. Telephones 49; Cars 35 Rail: 395 pass.-km; 579 t-km Air: 696 pass.-km; 43 t-km	Exports $777: Tin ore, Crude petroleum Imports $1 011: Cars, Flour Exports to: U.K., Argentina and U.S.A. Imports from: U.S.A., Japan, Argentina and Brazil Aid received (net): $54 from West
BRAZIL 1. Federal Republic 2. Portuguese 3. New Cruzeiro 4. £1 = 94.59 $1 = 42.53	1. 8 511 965 km^2 2. 118 645 000; 14 per km^2 3. BR 37; DR 9; AI 2.8% 4. Urb. pop.; 68 663 (61%) 5. Brasilia 763	1. GDP $166 344 (9.8%); $1 482 (6.8%) Agric. 10%, Indust. 26%, Others 64% 2. Maize 16 309; Rice 7 589 Cassava 24 935; Soya beans 9 959 Bananas 6 424; Oranges 9 882 Cottonseed 1 100; Tobacco 423 3. Cattle 90 000; Pigs 36 000 4. Fish 858 5. Roundwood 160 6. Coal 4 644; Crude petroleum 8 304 Iron ore 40 580; Natural gas 10 320 Manganese 1 000; Asbestos 93 Gold 5 600 kg; Tin 7	1. 26.5/73.3; 99 869 kWh (93% hydr.) 2a. Meat 3 818; Sugar 7 000 Sawnwood 13 337 b. Cotton fabric 1 076; Iron 10 008 Steel 13 752; Aluminium 186 Cement 24 876; Radios 759 Petroleum products 45 639; Vehicles: pass. 499; comm. 575 3. Telephones 4 836; Cars 7 250 Rail: 11 699 pass.-km; 60 721 t-km Sea: 97 884 loaded; 75 324 unloaded Air: 8 724 pass.-km; 478 t-km	Exports $15 250: Coffee, Cotton, Iron ore, Machinery Imports $19 804: Machinery, Crude petroleum, Cereals, Non-ferrous metals Exports to: U.S.A., W. Germany, Netherlands, and Japan Imports from: U.S.A., W. Germany, Japan, Saudi Arabia and Iraq Invisible trade balance: −$4 894 Revenue for tourism: $55 Aid received (net): $119 from West. $293 from East
BULGARIA 1. Republic 2. Bulgar 3. Lev 4. £1 = 1.96 $1 = 0.88	1. 110 912 km^2 2. 8 951 000; 79 per km^2 3. BR 16; DR 11; AI 0.5% 4. Urb. pop.; 5 332 (61%) 5. Sofia 1 032	1. NMP $14 731 (7.8%); $1 681 (7.2%) Agric. 18%, Indust. 51%, Others 31% 2. Wheat 3 000; Maize 3 300 Tobacco 110; Grapes 1 200 3. Sheep 10 105; Pigs 3 772 4. Fish 103 5. Roundwood 4 6. Coal 276; Crude petroleum 264 Lignite 27 924; Zinc 117 Iron ore 693; Lead 116	1. 14.1/41.3; 29 710 kWh (12% hydr., 20% nucl.) 2a. Meat 646; Sawnwood 1 470 Wine 3 800 hl; Sugar 240 b. Cotton yarn 85; Iron 1 452 Steel 2 484; Cement 5 400 Petroleum products 11 449 3. Telephones 946, Cars 480 Rail: 7 140 pass.-km 17 148 t-km Air: 555 pass.-km; 7.2 t-km Sea: 2 878 loaded; 19 094 unloaded	Exports $8 869: Cigarettes, Alcoholic drinks, Clothing Imports $8 514: Machinery, Ferrous metals, Petroleum products The principal trade is with U.S.S.R. then: E. Germany Revenue from tourism: $230 Aid given (net): $8
BURMA 1. Republic 2. Burmese 3. Kyat 4. £1 = 14.5 $1 = 6.52	1. 678 033 km^2 2. 32 913 000, 48 per km^2 3. BR 39; DR 16; AI 2.2% 4. Urb. pop.; 5 137 (24%) 5. Rangoon 2 276	1. GDP $3 786 (2.6%); $120 (0.3%) Agric. 47%, Indust. 10%, Others 43% 2. Rice 10 000; Groundnuts 384 Tobacco 51; Jute 85 3. Cattle 7 560; Buffaloes 1 750 4. Fish 541 5. Roundwood 4 6. Crude petroleum 1 416; Zinc 3 Lead 7; Silver 40 t	1. 1.78/1.51; 1 056 kWh (69% hydr.) 2a. Sugar 43; Sawnwood 415 b. Lead 4; Cotton yarn 14 3. Telephones 32; Cars 35 Rail: 3 072 pass.-km; 468 t-km Air: 180 pass.-km; 1.4 t-km Sea: 732 loaded; 456 unloaded	Exports $363: Sawnwood, Rice Imports $319: Machinery, Textiles Exports to: Japan, China and U.K. Imports from: Japan, U.S.A., China, W. Germany and U.K. Aid received (net): $77 from West
CAMBODIA/KAMPUCHEA 1. Republic 2. French, Cambodian 3. Riel 4. £1 = 2 669 $1 = 1 200	1. 181 035 km^2 2. 8 718 000; 47 per km^2 3. BR 46; DR 17; AI 2.9 4. Urb. pop.; 867 (10%) 5. Phnom Penh 2 000	1. GDP $881 (. . .) $125 (. . .) Agric. 41%, Indust. 17%, Others 42% 2. Rice 1 000; Maize 50 Rubber 15; Bananas 55 3. Cattle 700; Pigs 500 4. Fish 85 5. Roundwood 5	1. —/0.13; 150 kWh 2a. Sawnwood 43 3. Telephones 71; Cars 25 Rail: 54 pass.-km; 10 t-km Air: 42 pass.-km; 0.4 t-km Sea: 50 loaded; 583 unloaded	Exports $10: Rubber, Rice, Cattle Imports $101: Machinery, Textiles, Iron and Steel Exports to: Vietnam, Hong Kong and Singapore Imports from: France, Japan, China, Thailand and U.S.A. Aid received (net): $28 from West
CAMEROON 1. Republic 2. French, English 3. C.F.A. Franc 4. £1 = 447.0 $1 = 201.0	1. 475 442 km^2 2. 8 248 000. 17 per km^2 3. BR 42; DR 21; AI 2.9% 4. Urb. pop.; 2 392 (29%) 5. Yaoundé 314	1. GDP $3 309 (3.7%); $427 (1.8%) Agric. 31%, Indust. 12%, Others 57% 2. Coffee 112; Groundnuts 285 Cocoa 115; Palm oil 80 3. Goats 1 720; Cattle 3 027 4. Fish 72 5. Roundwood 9	1. 0.16/0.64; 1 346 kWh (95% hydr.) 2a. Sawnwood 351 b. Aluminium 48 3. Telephones 22; Cars 55 Rail: 237 pass.-km; 506 t-km Air: 314 pass.-km; 5.8 t-km Sea: 886 loaded; 1 699 unloaded	Exports $1 129: Cocoa, Coffee Imports $1 271: Manufactured goods, Machinery Exports to: France, Netherlands and W. Germany Imports from: France, W. Germany and U.S.A. Aid received (net); $139 from West

For detailed table headings and notes see page 1 of this section

Country	Area and Population	Production	Manufactures	Trade
CANADA 1. Commonwealth 2. English, French 3. Canadian Dollar 4. £1 = 2.598 $1 = 1.168	1. 9 221 001 km^2 2. 23 690 000; 2 per km^2 3. BR 15; DR 7; AI 1.3% 4. Urb. pop.: 17 367 (76%) 5. Ottawa 693	1. GDP $200 149 (4.7%); $8 583 (3.4%) Agric. 4%, Indust. 25%, Others 71% 2. Wheat 17 746 — Barley 8 460 Oats 2 978 — Maize 4 963 3. Cattle 12 328 — Pigs 8 025 4. Fish 1 407 5. Roundwood 156 6. Iron ore 36 424 — Crude petroleum 73 248 Coal 28 008 — Natural gas 727 656 Copper 632 — Zinc 1 204 Nickel 132 — Asbestos 380 Gold 49 176 kg — Salt 6 452 Lead 342 — Tin 3	1. 258.8/230.3; 316 549 kWh (70% hydr., 8% nucl.) 2a. Sawnwood 44 681 — Wood pulp 19 216 Paper 13 285 — Sugar 112 b. Iron 11 076 — Steel 16 080 Aluminium 1 048 — Copper 397 Radios 819 — Vehicles: Petroleum — pass. 988; comm. 676 products 79 271 — Cement 10 473 3. Telephones 14 488; Cars 10 300 Rail: 3 072 pass.-km; 215 352 t-km Air: 31 560 pass.-km; 745 t-km Sea: 116 520 loaded; 61 788 unloaded	Exports $55 336: Vehicles, Machinery, Paper and cardboard, Non-ferrous metals, Wood pulp, Sawnwood, Crude petroleum, Wheat Imports $52 230: Machinery, Vehicles, Iron and steel, Textiles, Crude petroleum, Fruit and vegetables Trade is principally with: U.S.A., U.K. and Japan Invisible trade balance: −$7 310 Revenue from tourism: $1 616 Aid given (net): $2 219
CENTRAL AFRICAN REPUBLIC 1. Republic 2. French 3. Franc C.F.A. 4. £1 = 447.0 $1 = 201.0	1. 622 984 km^2 2. 2 370 000; 4 per km^2 3. BR 41; DR 21; AI 2.2% 4. Urb. pop.: 392 (27%) 5. Bangui 187	1. GDP $391 (. . .); $218 (. . .) Agric. 31%, Indust. 18%, Others 51% 2. Maize 40 — Cassava 940 Bananas 75 — Coffee 14 Groundnuts 126 — Cottonseed 29 3. Goats 780 — Cattle 670 5. Roundwood 3 6. Diamonds 314 c	1. 0.01/0.07; 58 kWh (98% hydr.) 2a. Meat 40 — Sawnwood 75 3. Telephones 5; Cars 10 Air: 145 pass.-km; 13.1 t-km	Exports $72: Diamonds, Cotton, Coffee Imports $57: Machinery, Vehicles Exports to: France, Belgium and Lux. Imports from: France and W. Germany Aid received (net): $47 from West
CHAD 1. Republic 2. French 3. C.F.A. Franc 4. £1 = 447.0 $1 = 201.0	1. 1 284 000 km^2 2. 4 417 000; 3 per km^2 3. BR 44; DR 23; AI 2.1% 4. Urb. pop.: 792 (18%) 5. N'Djamena 179	1. GDP $651 (3.3%); $158 (1.3%) Agric. 41%, Indust. 13%, Others 46% 2. Millet 580 — Groundnuts 85 Cottonseed 70 — Cotton 43 3. Cattle 4 070 — Goats 2 278 4. Fish 115 5. Roundwood 4	1. —/10.09; 61 kWh 2a. Meat 50 3. Telephones 7; Cars 10 Air: 162 pass.-km; 14 t-km	Exports $59: Cotton, Meat Imports $118: Petroleum products, Machinery Exports to: France, Nigeria and Congo Imports from: France, Nigeria and Netherlands Aid received (net): $66 from West, $3 from East
CHILE 1. Republic 2. Spanish 3. Chilean Peso 4. £1 = 86.73 $1 = 39.0	1. 756 945 km^2 2. 10 917 000; 14 per km^2 3. BR 21; DR 7; AI 1.9% 4. Urb. pop.: 8 661 (80%) 5. Santiago 3 692	1. GDP $9 221 (−0.1%); $865 (−1.7%) Agric. 10%, Indust. 27%, Others 63% 2. Wheat 995 — Grapes 937 Wool 20 — Tobacco 7 3. Sheep 5 952 — Cattle 3 607 4. Fish 1 698 5. Roundwood 10 6. Coal 888 — Iron ore 6 742 Crude petroleum 840 — Copper 1 067 Natural gas 14 112 — Molybdenum 11	1. 5.73/10.32; 9 776 kWh (67% hydr.) 2a. Meat 303 — Sawnwood 1 267 Sugar 104 — Wood pulp 665 Wine 5 200 hl b. Iron 540 — Steel 588 Cotton yarn 23 — Copper 673 Fertilizers 139 — Cement 1 200 3. Telephones 467; Cars 300 Rail: 2 124 pass.-km; 2 040 t-km Air: 1 548 pass.-km; 88 t-km Sea: 9 947 loaded; 6 188 unloaded	Exports $3 766: Copper, Iron ore, Fishmeal, Saltpetre Imports $4 219: Machinery, Food, Manufactured products, Chemical products Exports to: Japan, W. Germany, U.K., Argentina and U.S.A. Imports from: U.S.A., W. Germany, Argentina, Japan and Brazil Aid received (net): $48 from West
CHINA 1. Republic 2. Chinese and others 3. Yuan 4. £1 = 3.36 $1 = 1.51	1. 9 561 000 km^2 2. 945 018 000; 102 per km^2 3. BR 26; DR 9; AI 2.1% 4. Urb. pop.: 188 169 (24%) 5. Peking 7 570	1. Agric. 48%, Indust. 42%, Others 10% (1956) 2. Rice 143 400 — Wheat 60 003 Soya beans 13 050 — Groundnuts 2 917 Citrus fruits 1 385 — Other fruits 11 336 Tea 303 — Tobacco 1 023 Cottonseed 4 414 — Cotton lint 2 207 3. Pigs 305 612 — Sheep 95 440 Fish 4 660 5. Roundwood 213 6. Coal 618 000 — Manganese 1 000 Crude petroleum 104 050 — Tungsten 14 500t Iron ore 70 000 — Tin 17 Salt 19 530 — Lead 155 Bauxite 1 200 — Copper 3	1. 614.8/590.1 2a. Meat 22 145 — Sawnwood 19 252 Sugar 3 582 b. Iron 34 790 — Steel 31 780 Aluminium 300 — Cement 65 240 Cotton yarn 2 400 3. Telephones . . .; Cars 50 Rail: . . .; 301 000 t-km Air: . . .; . . . Sea: 18 200 loaded; 17 000 unloaded	Exports . . .: Agricultural prods., Textiles, Minerals, Crude petroleum Imports . . .: Grain, Cotton products, Machinery, Primary materials, Petrol Exports to: Hong Kong, U.S.S.R., Japan and Singapore Imports from: Japan, Australia, U.S.S.R. and Canada Aid given (net): $201
COLOMBIA 1. Republic 2. Spanish 3. Columbian Peso 4. £1 = 97.81 $1 = 43.98	1. 1 138 914 km^2 2. 26 360 000; 23 per km^2 3. BR 34; DR 9; AI 2.9% 4. Urb. pop.: 13 410 (60%) 5. Bogotá 2 855	1. GDP $13 574 (6.5%); $568 (3.5%) Agric. 27%, Indust. 24%, Others 49% 2. Maize 870 — Rice 1 932 Cassava 2 081 — Bananas 1 300 Coffee 762 — Cottonseed 187 Tobacco 68 — Cotton lint 108 3. Cattle 26 137 — Pigs 1 916 4. Fish 64 5. Roundwood 24 6. Coal 4 930 — Silver 3 t Natural gas 20 433 — Gold 9 000 kg Crude petroleum 6 360 — Iron ore 372	1. 18.7/15.8; 15 223 kWh (68% hydr.) 2a. Meat 830 — Paper 307 Sugar 1 113 — Sawnwood 934 b. Iron 297 — Steel 240 Petroleum products 7 311 — Cement 4 260 3. Telephones 1 396; Cars 552 Rail: 336 pass.-km; 236 t-km Air: 4 116 pass.-km; 187 t-km Sea: 2 676 loaded; 4 008 unloaded	Exports $3 381: Coffee, Crude petroleum, Cotton, Bananas, Sugar and Honey Imports $4 437: Machinery, Vehicles, Iron and Steel, Organic chemicals Exports to: U.S.A., W. Germany and Venezuela Imports from: U.S.A., W. Germany, Japan, and Venezuela Revenue from tourism: $201 Aid received (net): $71 from West, $21 from East
CONGO 1. Popular Republic 2. French 3. C.F.A. Franc 4. £1 = 447.0 $1 = 201.0	1. 342 000 km^2 2. 1 498 000; 4 per km^2 3. BR 45; DR 21; AI 2.7% 4. Urb pop.: 278 (29%) 5. Brazzaville 290	1. GDP $775 (. . .); $574 (. . .) 2. Cassava 542 — Palm oil 7 3. Goats 119 — Cattle 71 4. Fish 17 5. Roundwood 3 6. Gold 203 kg — Diamonds . . . Crude petroleum 2 604	1. 3.0/0.2; 118 kWh (58% hydr.) 2a. Sugar 15 — Sawnwood 49 3. Telephones 12; Cars 20 Rail: 300 pass.-km; 492 t-km Air: 152 pass.-km; 13.4 t-km Sea: 3 288 loaded; 636 unloaded	Exports $139: Timber Imports $261: Manufactured products, Machinery Exports to: France, Italy, U.S.A. and Spain Imports from: France, U.S.A, Gabon and W. Germany Aid received (net): $59 from West
CUBA 1. Republic 2. Spanish 3. Cuban Peso 4. £1 = 1.60 $1 = 0.72	1. 114 524 km^2 2. 9 852 000; 85 per km^2 3. BR 15; DR 6; AI 1.4% 4. Urb. pop.; 5 169 (60%) 5. Havana 1 861	1. NMP $8 943 (5.4%), $943 (4.8%) 2. Rice 500 — Cassava 320 Coffee 27 — Oranges 190 Tobacco 30 3. Cattle 5 844 — Pigs 1 846 4. Fish 213 5. Roundwood 2 6. Chrome 30 — Nickel 35 Copper 3 — Crude petroleum 120	1. 0.25/11.6; 7 700 kWh (0.95% hydr.) 2a. Meat 292 — Sawnwood 105 Sugar 7 992 b. Petroleum products 6 212 Cotton, woven 156 Mm^2 — Cement 2 712 3. Telephones 321; Cars 80 Rail: 1 572 pass.-km; 1 872 t-km Air: 773 pass.-km; 9.4 t-km Sea: 8 532 loaded; 14 448 unloaded	Exports $4 456: Sugar, Minerals, Tobacco Imports $4 687: Machinery, Cereals, Fertilizers, Petroleum products Exports to: U.S.S.R., Japan and Spain Imports from: U.S.S.R. and Japan

For detailed table headings and notes see page 1 of this section

Country	Area and Population	Production	Manufactures	Trade
CYPRUS 1. Republic 2. Greek, Turkish and English 3. Cypriot Pound 4. £1 = 0.769 $1 = 0.346	1. 9 251 km² 2. 621 000; 66 per km² 3. BR 18; DR 10; AI 0.8% 4. Urb. pop.; 270 (42%) 5. Nicosia 147	1. GDP $1 042 (−1.5%); $1 629 (−2.5%) Agric. 13%, Indust. 19%, Others 68% 2. Barley 81 Potatoes 197 Grapes 195 Oranges 100 3. Sheep 495 Goats 459 6. Copper 1 Asbestos 35 Chrome 16	1. –/0.82; 860 kWh 2a. Wine 461 hl Sawnwood 19 b. Cement 1 152 3. Telephones 83; Cars 86 Air: 684 pass.-km; 27 t-km Sea: 1 644 loaded; 2 136 unloaded	Exports $456 Imports $1 001 Vegetables Machinery Citrus fruits Textiles Copper Vehicles Exports to: U.K., Saudi Arabia and Lebanon Imports from: U.K., W. Germany, Italy and Greece Revenue from Tourism: $61
CZECHOSLOVAKIA 1. Socialist Republic 2. Czech, Slovak 3. Koruna 4. £1 = 23.22 $1 = 10.44	1. 127 869 km² 2. 15 247 000; 118 per km² 3. BR 18; DR 12; AI 0.7% 4. Urb. pop; 9 795 (67%) 5. Prague 1 176	1. NMP $68 559 (5.2%); $4 561 (4.5%) Agric. 10%, Indust. 61%, Others 29% 2. Barley 3 300 Wheat 4 400 Oats 400 Potatoes 4 000 Apples 170 Tomatoes 100 3. Pigs 7 601 Cattle 4 887 5. Roundwood 18 6. Coal 28 464 Silver 35 t Lignite 96 204 Crude petroleum 108 Iron ore 524 Antimony 300 t Natural gas 6 372	1. 83.8/110.3; 66 501 kWh (7% hydr., 0.17% nucl.) 2a. Meat 1 471 Sawnwood 4 694 Sugar 930 Butter & cheese 290 Beer 22 058 hl b. Iron 9 708 Steel 14 808 Aluminium 37 Plastics 737 Wool yarn 54 Petroleum Cotton yarn 24 products 15 913 3. Telephones 2 863; Cars 1 900 Rail: 13 636 pass.-km; 72 360 t-km Air: 1 740 pass.-km; 18 t-km	Exports $13 198 Imports $14 262 Machinery Machinery Manufactured goods Petroleum Iron and steel Non-ferrous metals Vehicles Iron and steel Main trade is with: U.S.S.R., E. Germany, Poland and Hungary Aid given: (net): $57
DENMARK 1. Kingdom 2. Danish 3. Danish Krone 4. £1 = 11.93 $1 = 5.365	1. 43 069 km² 2. 5 117 000; 119 per km² 3. BR 12; DR 11; AI 0.5% 4. Urb. pop; 3 302 (67%) 5. Copenhagen 1 251	1. GDP $46 017 (2.8%); $9 041 (2.4%) Agric. 6%, Indust. 21%, Others 73% 2. Barley 6 680 Oats 206 Wheat 573 Potatoes 852 Apples 125 Rape seed 150 3. Pigs 9 357 Cattle 3 034 4. Fish 1 745 5. Roundwood 2 6. Crude petroleum 444	1. 0.29/26.99; 22 436 kWh 2a. Pork 900 Beef 245 Butter & cheese 170 Sugar 457 b. Iron 190 Steel 804 Cotton yarn 1.5 Ships (grt.) 199 Petroleum products 7 364 3. Telephones 2 718; Cars 1 423 Rail: 3 084 pass.-km; 1 764 t-km Air: 3 060 pass.-km; 132 t-km Sea 8 244 loaded; 34 524 unloaded	Exports $14 506 Imports $18 450 Machinery Machinery Pork Manufactured products Other meat Iron and steel Fish Textiles Exports to: Sweden, U.K. and W. Germany Imports from: W. Germany, Sweden and U.K. Invisible trade balance: +$627 Aid given: (net): $357
ECUADOR 1. Republic 2. Spanish 3. Sucre 4. £1 = 55.6 $1 = 25.0	1. 283 561 km² 2. 8 146 000; 28 per km² 3. BR 42; DR 12; AI 3.4% 4. Urb. pop.; 3 343 (43%) 5. Quito 743	1. GDP $6 152 (10.5%); $814 (6.8%) Agric. 20%, Indust. 29%, Others 51% 2. Maize 217 Rice 303 Bananas 2 391 Oranges 500 Cocoa 78 Coffee 102 3. Cattle 2 532 Sheep 2 278 4. Fish 476 5. Roundwood 4 6. Crude petroleum 10 896 Gold 238 kg	1. 14.1/3.33; 2 145 kWh (29% nucl.) 2a. Meat 176 Sawnwood 852 Sugar 393 b. Petroleum products 4 227 3. Telephones 221; Cars 65 Rail: 60 pass.-km; 36 t-km Air: 551 pass.-km; 9.5 t-km Sea: 9 372 loaded; 3 828 unloaded	Exports $1 494 Imports $1 986 Bananas Machinery Coffee Vehicles Cocoa Chemical products Exports to: U.S.A., Panama, Peru and Chile Imports from: U.S.A., W. Germany and Japan Aid received (net): $67 from West
EGYPT 1. Republic 2. Arabic 3. Egyptian Pound 4. £1 = 1.56 $1 = 0.70	1. 1 001 449 km² 2. 40 983 000; 41 per km² 3. BR 41; DR 11; AI 2.2% 4. Urb. pop.; 17 070 (44%) 5. Cairo 5 084	1. GDP $18 775 (4.7%); $485 (2.4%) Agric. 24%, Indust. 23%, Others 53% 2. Maize 2 938 Wheat 1 856 Rice 2 507 Tomatoes 2 421 Oranges 868 Dates 416 Cotton lint 482 Cottonseed 785 3. Cattle 1 954 Buffaloes 2 321 4. Fish 100 6. Iron ore 768 Salt 755 Crude petroleum 26 604 Phosphates 644	1. 27.26/18.0; 13 000 kWh (96% hydr.) 2a. Meat 474 Sugar 678 b. Cotton yarn 218 Iron 300 Wool yarn 13 Steel 600 Fertilizers 282 Cement 3 036 Petroleum products 10 992 3. Telephones 503; Cars 350 Rail: 8 748 pass.-km; 2 201 t-km Air: 2 652 pass.-km; 29 t-km Sea: 7 980 loaded; 10 212 unloaded	Exports $1 840 Imports $3 837 Cotton, Rice Machinery Cotton lint Manufactured products Fruit and vegetables Wheat, Vehicles Exports to: U.S.S.R., Italy and Netherlands Imports from: U.S.A., France, Italy, U.K. and W. Germany Invisible trade balance: +$870 Revenue from tourism: $658 Aid received (net): $1 032 from West, $51 from East
EIRE (Irish republic) 1. Republic 2. Irish, English 3. Irish pound 4. £1 = 1.047 $1 = 0.471	1. 70 283 km² 2. 3 368 000; 48 per km² 3. BR 21; DR 10; AI 1.2% 4. Urb. pop.; 1 556 (52%) 5. Dublin 545	1. GDP $9 389 (3.4%); $2 943 (2.2%) Agric. 14%, Indust. 30%, Others 56% 2. Barley 1 512 Wheat 260 Potatoes 1 060 Apples 10 Wool 9 Tomatoes 27 3. Cattle 7 178 Sheep 3 376 4. Fish 108 6. Lead 71 Zinc 212 Coal 60	1. 2.41/10.02; 9 299 kWh (11% hydr.) 2a. Meat 613 Sawnwood 130 Butter & cheese 170 b. Wool yarn 11 Petroleum Cotton yarn 4 products 2 655 3. Telephones 519; Cars 682 Rail: 960 pass.-km; 636 t-km Air: 2 220 pass.-km; 99 t-km Sea: 8 466 loaded; 16 379 unloaded	Exports $7 175 Imports $9 858 Cattle Machinery Beef Textiles Dairy products Vehicles Non-ferrous metals Iron and steel Machinery Crude petroleum Main trade is with U.K. Exports to: U.S.A., France, W. Germany, Netherlands and Belgium-Lux. Imports from: U.S.A., W. Germany, France, Italy and Japan Invisible trade balance: +$33 Revenue from tourism: $308
ETHIOPIA 1. Republic 2. Amharic 3. Ethiopian Birr 4. £1 = 4.60 $1 = 2.07	1. 1 221 900 km² 2. 30 421 000; 24 per km² 3. BR 50; DR 25; AI 2.3% 4. Urb. pop.; 3 794 (13%) 5. Addis-Ababa 1 196	1. GDP $2 669 (. . .); $97 (. . .) Agric. 44%, Indust. 11%, Others 45% 2. Barley 732 Millet 191 Coffee 194 Maize 1 067 3. Cattle 25 900 Sheep 23 234 4. Fish 27 5. Roundwood 25 6. Gold 247 kg Salt 108	1. 0.04/0.76; 682 kWh (54% hydr.) 2a. Sugar 168 Sawnwood 100 b. Cotton yarn 22 Cement 103 3. Telephones 79; Cars 40 Rail: 132 pass.-km; 260 t-km Air: 552 pass.-km; 23 t-km Sea: 378 loaded; 1 250 unloaded	Exports $423 Imports $576 Coffee Machinery Hides Manufactured products Exports to: U.S.A., Djibouti and Saudi Arabia Imports from: Japan, W. Germany, U.S.A., Italy and Saudi Arabia Aid received (net): $134 from West, $8 from East
FINLAND 1. Republic 2. Finnish, Swedish 3. Markka 4. £1 = 8.253 $1 = 3.711	1. 337 009 km² 2. 4 764 000; 14 per km² 3. BR 14; DR 9; AI 0.4% 4. Urb. pop.; 2 786 (59%) 5. Helsinki 825	1. GDP $30 171 (3.4%); $6 365 (2.9%) Agric. 10%, Indust. 31%, Others 59% 2. Wheat 208 Barley 650 Oats 1 283 Potatoes 674 3. Cattle 1 736 Pigs 1 332 4. Fish 128 5. Roundwood 37 6. Iron ore 507 Chrome 150 Titanium 120 Copper 41 Zinc 54 Gold 881 kg	1. 1.41/24.5; 31 734 kWh (38% hydr.) 2a. Meat 287 Butter & cheese 137 Sawnwood 7 345 Wood pulp 6 020 b. Paper 5 130 Newsprint 1 321 Iron 2 040 Steel 2 460 Cotton yarn 10 Ships (grt) 230 Petroleum products 4 566 3. Telephones 2 032; Cars: 1 170 Rail: 2 988 pass.-km; 6 324 t-km Air: 1 980 pass.-km; 46 t-km Sea: 17 184 loaded; 30 636 unloaded	Exports $11 175 Imports $11 400 Paper and cardboard Machinery Wood pulp Crude petroleum Sawnwood Petroleum products Machinery Iron and steel Ships and boats Textiles Clothing Vehicles Exports to: U.K., Sweden, U.S.S.R. and W. Germany Imports from: Sweden, W. Germany, U.S.S.R. and U.K. Invisible trade balance: −$656

For detailed table headings and notes see page 1 of this section

Country	Area and Population	Production	Manufactures	Trade
FRANCE 1. Republic 2. French 3. French Franc 4. £1 = 8.94 $1 = 4.02	1. 547 026 km^2 2. 53 478 000; 97 per km^2 3. BR 14; DR 10; AI 0.6% 4. Urb. pop.; 38 388 (73%) 5. Paris 9 863	1. GDP $380 692 (3.8%); $7 172 (3.2%) Agric. 5%, Indust. 30%, Others 65% 2. Wheat 19 393 · Barley 11 238 Oats 1 675 · Maize 10 293 Potatoes 7 139 · Sugarbeet 26 444 Apples 2 950 · Grapes 12 696 Tomatoes 825 · Pears 405 Tobacco 52 · Wool 22 Rape seed 480 3. Cattle 23 510 · Pigs 11 745 Sheep 11 543 · Goats 1 048 Horses 380 4. Fish 796 5. Roundwood 30 6. Coal 18 612 · Iron ore 9 500 Crude petroleum 1 200 · Lead 29 Natural gas 70 584 · Zinc 36 Salt 6 255 · Potash 2 075	1. 45.1/231.9; 210 845 kWh (37% hydr., 8.5% nucl.) 2a. Meat 5 281 · Butter & cheese 1 555 Wine 58 820 hl · Beer 22 781 hl Sugar 4 240 · Sawnwood 9 296 b. Iron 20 292 · Steel 23 364 Aluminium 395 · Cement 28 161 Plastics 2 684 · Paper 4 963 Synthetic fibres 325 · Petroleum products 93 998 Cotton yarn 220 · Wool yarn 138 Ships (grt) 728 · Radios 3 019 Vehicles: pass. 3 732; comm. 468 3. Telephones 17 519; Cars 18 440 Rail: 53 508 pass.-km; 67 320 t-km Air: 32 784 pass.-km; 2 031 t-km Sea: 69 324 loaded; 246 456 unloaded	Export $98 059: Machinery, Vehicles, Iron and Steel, Textiles, Wheat, Organic chemical products, Non-ferrous metals, Petroleum products, Petrol, Wine Imports $106 994: Machinery, Petrol, Iron and steel, Non-ferrous metals, Vehicles, Textile fibres, Meat, Fruits Exports to: W. Germany, Belgium-Luxembourg, Italy and U.K. Imports from: W. Germany, Italy, Belgium-Luxembourg and U.S.A. Invisible trade balance: + $2 244 Revenue from tourism: $4 377 Aid given (net): $4 652
FRENCH GUIANA 1. French colony 2. French 3. Franc 4. £1 = 8.94 $1 = 4.02	1. 91 000 km^2 2. 69 000; 1 per km^2 3. BR 25; DR 8; AI 3.4% 4. Urb. pop.; 29 (67%) 5. Cayenne 25	2. Cassava 8 · Bananas 3 3. Pigs 6 · Cattle 3 6. Gold 100 kg	1. –/0.13; 75 kWh 2a. Sugar . . . · Sawnwood 10 3. Telephones 11; Cars 17 Sea: 14 loaded; 125 unloaded	Exports $17: Timber Imports $251: Machinery Exports to: France, U.S.A. and Venezuela Imports from: France, Trinidad and Tobago Aid received (net): $65 from West
GABON 1. Republic 2. French, Bantu 3. C.F.A. Franc 4. £1 = 447.0 $1 = 201.0	1. 267 667 km^2 2. 544 000; 2 per km^2 3. BR 31; DR 23; AI 0.9% 4. Urb. pop.; 160 (32%) 5. Libreville 186	1. GDP $3 009 (. . .); $5 677 (. . .) Agric. 9%, Indust. 47%, Others 44% 2. Cassava 110 · Bananas 8 Cocoa 4 3. Goats 90 · Sheep 100 5. Roundwood 2 6. Crude petroleum 10 788 · Gold 50 kg Manganese 1 718 · Uranium 1 000 t	1. 16.7/0.68; 443 kWh (2.3% hydr) 2a. Sawnwood 108 · Beer 510 hl b. Petroleum products 1 548 3. Telephones 7; Cars 22 Air: 129 pass.-km; 7.8 t-km Sea: 11 808 loaded; 504 unloaded	Exports $1 307: Petrol, Sawnwood, Manganese ores Imports $589: Manufactured products, Machinery, Vehicles Exports to: France, U.S.A., U.K. and Bahamas Imports from: France, U.S.A. and Netherlands Aid received (net): $33 from West
GERMANY (East) 1. Republic 2. German 3. Ostmark 4. £1 = 3.87 $1 = 1.74	1. 108 174 km^2 2. 16 745 000; 155 per km^2 3. BR 14; DR 14; AI –0.2% 4. Urb. pop.; 12 679 (76%) 5. Berlin (East) 1 111	1. NMP $77 010 (5.1%); $4 583 (5.4%) Agric. 10%, Indust. 61%, Others 29% 2. Barley 3 635 · Rye 1 720 Wheat 3 226 · Potatoes 12 540 Apples 341 · Rapeseed 232 3. Pigs 11 734 · Cattle 5 572 Sheep 1 965 4. Fish 198 5. Roundwood 9 6. Coal 48 · Natural gas 26 832 Lignite 253 272 · Potash 3 396 Iron ore 33 · Salt 2 741	1. 79.3/114; $91 996 kWh (1.4% nucl.) 2a. Meat 1 693 · Butter 281 Sugar 720 · Beer 22 297 hl Sawnwood 2 197 b. Cotton yarn 136 · Wool yarn 35 Iron 2 556 · Steel 6 972 Ships (grt) 1 540 · Petroleum products 17 660 Vehicles: pass. 170; comm. 37 · Radios 1 103 3. Telephones 2 860; Cars 2 500 Rail: 22 320 pass.-km; 58 920 t-km Air: . . .; . . . Sea: 3 504 loaded; 11 940 unloaded	Exports $15 063: Machinery, Vehicles, Consumer goods, Coal, Fuels Imports $16 214: Machinery, Crude petroleum, Iron ore The principal trade is with: U.S.S.R., Czechoslovakia, W. Germany and Poland Aid given (net): $77
GERMANY (West) 1. Federal Republic 2. German 3. Deutschmark 4. £1 = 3.85 $1 = 1.73	1. 248 343 km^2 (including W. Berlin) 2. 61 337 000; 246 per km^2 3. BR 10; DR 12; AI 0.2% 4. Urb. pop.; 47 534 (77%) 5. Bonn 284	1. GDP $516 150 (2.4%); $8 406 (2.3%) Agric. 3%, Indust. 41%, Others 56% 2. Barley 8 157 · Wheat 7 971 Rye 2 105 · Potatoes 8 747 Apples 1 951 · Grapes 993 3. Pigs 22 641 · Cattle 15 007 4. Fish 412 5. Roundwood 27 6. Coal 86 316 · Zinc 117 Lignite 130 584 · Natural gas 173 520 Iron ore 526 · Crude petroleum 4 776 Salt 15 346 · Potash 2 616	1. 165.9/364.3; 335 320 kWh (5% hydr., 11% nucl.) 2a. Meat 4 609 · Butter & cheese 1 285 Sugar 3 333 · Sawnwood 10 179 Wine 6 710 hl · Beer 87 919 hl b. Cotton yarn 161 · Wool yarn 56 Iron 35 352 · Steel 46 044 Aluminium 742 · Radios 4 611 Vehicles: pass. 3 936; comm. 324 · Petroleum products 89 035 Ships (grt) 374 · Synthetic fibres 846 3. Telephones 22 932; Cars 22 614 Rail: 38 256 pass.-km; 57 264 t-km Air: 19 848 pass.-km; 586 t-km Sea: 35 544 loaded; 121 032 unloaded	Exports $171 540: Machinery, Vehicles, Iron and steel, Textiles, Organic chemicals Imports 157 747: Machinery, Non-ferrous metals, Crude petroleum, Iron and steel, Textiles, Food Exports to: France, Netherlands, U.S.A. Belgium-Luxembourg and Italy Imports from: Netherlands, France, Belgium-Luxembourg, Italy and U.S.A. Invisible trade balance: – $7 759 Revenue from tourism: $3 827 Aid given (net): $4 536
GHANA 1. Republic 2. English 3. Cedi 4. £1 = 6.12 $1 = 2.75	1. 238 537 km^2 2. 11 317 000; 46 per km^2 3. BR 49; DR 19; AI 2.8% 4. Urb. pop.; 3 017 (31%) 5. Accra 738	1. GDP $4 912 (3.0%); $498 (0.3%) Agric. 51%, Indust. 14%, Others 35% 2. Cassava 1 900 · Cocoa 270 Groundnuts 90 · Millet 130 3. Sheep 1 650 · Goats 2 000 4. Fish 264 5. Roundwood 13 6. Bauxite 252 · Manganese 290 Gold 11 094 kg · Diamonds 1 253 c	1 0.51/1.62; 4 300 kWh (99% hydr.) 2a. Sawnwood 381 · Beer 998 hl 3. Telephones 67; Cars 64 Rail: 431 pass.-km; 305 t-km Air: 324 pass.-km; 3.3 t-km Sea: 2 280 loaded; 3 100 unloaded	Exports $965: Cocoa, Aluminium Imports $1 398: Manufactured goods, Machinery Exports to: U.K., U.S.A., W. Germany, U.S.S.R. and Netherlands Imports from: U.S.A., U.K., W. Germany, and Nigeria Aid received (net): $96 from West
GREECE 1. Republic 2. Greek 3. Drachma 4. £1 = 85.13 $1 = 38.28	1. 131 944 km^2 2. 9 440 000; 71 per km^2 3. BR 16; DR 9; AI 0.7% 4. Urb. pop.; 5 686 (65%) 5. Athens 2 101	1. GDP $26 208 (4.6%); $2 824 (3.9%) Agric. 15%, Indust. 20%, Others 65% 2. Wheat 2 411 · Potatoes 963 Olives 1 060 · Tomatoes 1 669 Grapes 1 424 · Tobacco 127 3. Sheep 8 024 · Goats 4 473 4. Fish 106 5. Roundwood 3 6. Iron ore 789 · Bauxite 2 755 Lignite 23 388 · Chrome 45 Magnesite 1 065	1. 7.68/20.6; 19 019 kWh (98% hydr.) 2a. Olive oil 239 · Wine 4 350 hl Butter & cheese 172 b. Cotton yarn 114 · Steel 1 000 Cement 12 060 3. Telephones 2 320; Cars 839 Rail: 1 572 pass.-km; 852 t-km Air: 5 136 pass.-km; 68 t-km Sea: 19 128 loaded; 34 596 unloaded	Exports $3 855: Tobacco, Iron and steel, Raisins, Aluminium, Cotton Imports $9 640: Machinery, Ships and boats, Vehicles, Iron and steel, Crude petroleum Exports to: W. Germany, Italy, France and Saudi Arabia Imports from: W. Germany, Italy and Japan Invisible trade balance: + $959 Revenue from tourism: $980

For detailed table headings and notes see page 1 of this section

Country	Area and Population	Production	Manufactures	Trade
GUINEA 1. Republic 2. French 3. Syli 4. £1 = 41.6 $1 = 18.7	1. 245 857 km^2 2. 4 887 000; 19 per km^2 3. BR 47; DR 23; AI 2.5% Urb. pop.; 437 (11%) 5. Conakry 526	1. GDP $665 (. . .); $150 (. . .) 2. Cassava 550 Rice 390 Coffee 2 Bananas 98 Sweet potatoes 73 Palm oil 40 3. Sheep 430 Goats 395 5. Roundwood 3 6. Iron ore . . . Bauxite 12 060 Diamonds 80 c	1. 0.01/0.42; 500 kWh 2a. Sawnwood 90 3. Telephones 10; Cars 10 Air: 27 pass.-km; 0.2 t-km Sea: 1 300 loaded; 550 unloaded	Exports $70 Bauxite and aluminium Iron ore Coffee Imports $100 Machinery Manufactured goods Foods Main trade is with: France and U.S.S.R. Aid received (net): $14 from West, $1 from East
HAITI 1. Republic 2. French, Creole 3. Gourde 4. £1 = 11.12 $1 = 5.00	1. 27 750 km^2 2. 4 919 000; 173 per km^2 3. BR 43; DR 17; AI 1.7% 4. Urb. pop.; 1 175 (24%) 5. Port-au-Prince 746	1. GDP $1 166 (4.6%); $250 (2.9%) Agric. 41%, Indust. 15%, Others 44% 2. Bananas 53 Sisal 13 Cocoa 3 Coffee 40 3. Pigs 1 900 Goats 1 300 5. Roundwood 4 6. Bauxite 796	1. 0.02/0.13; 215 kWh (76% hydr.) 2a. Meat 57 Sugar 65 3. Telephones 18; Cars 25 Sea: 854 loaded; 484 unloaded	Exports $155 Coffee Bauxite Sugar Sisal Imports $212 Foods Textiles Machinery Mineral oils Exports to: U.S.A., France and Belgium-Luxembourg Imports from: U.S.A., Neth. Antilles, Japan, and Canada Aid received (net): $73 from West
HONG KONG 1. British colony 2. English, Chinese 3. Hong Kong Dollar 4. £1 = 10.938 $1 = 4.918	1. 1 034 km^2 2. 4 900 000; 4 386 per km^2 3. BR 18; DR 6; AI 1.9% 4. Urb. pop.; 4 017 (96%) 5. Victoria 849	1. GDP $10 737 (8.0%); $2 381 (5.9%) Agric. 1%, Indust. 24%, Others 75% 2. Rice 1 3. Pigs 510 Cattle 9 4. Fish 162 6. Iron ore . . .	1. –/5.75; 9 451 kWh 2b. Cotton yarn 185 Wool yarn 6 Woven natural silk 506 Tm^2 3. Telephones 1 132; Cars 160 Rail: 324 pass.-km; 60 t-km Sea: 7 716 loaded; 22 596 unloaded	Exports $15 156 Clothing Textiles Toys and games Radios Imports $17 137 Textiles Machines Diamonds Cotton Exports to: U.S.A., U.K., Japan and W. Germany Imports from: Japan, China, U.S.A., U.K. and Singapore Revenue from tourism: $786
HUNGARY 1. Republic 2. Hungarian 3. Forint 4. £1 = 45.17 $1 = 20.31	1. 93 030 km^2 2. 10 699 000; 115 per km^2 3. BR 15; DR 13; AI 0.4% 4. Urb. pop.; 5 517 (52%) 5. Budapest 2 082	1. NMP $56 310 (6.2%); $5 288 (5.7%) Agric. 16%, Indust. 47%, Others 37% 2. Maize 7 400 Wheat 3 706 Potatoes 1 500 Tobacco 23 Apples 980 Grapes 850 3. Pigs 8 011 Sheep 863 4. Fish 33 5. Roundwood 6 6. Coal 3 000 Bauxite 2 976 Lignite 22 656 Manganese 126 Natural gas 58 872 Crude petroleum 2 028	1. 22.2/37.7; 23 391 kWh (0.6% hydr.) 2a. Sugar 510 Sawnwood 1 112 Wine 2 280 hl b. Iron 2 376 Steel 3 912 Aluminium 72 Cotton yarn 61 Wool yarn 12 Petroleum products 9 523 3. Telephones 1 104; Cars 839 Rail: 12 612 pass.-km; 23 916 t-km Air: 653 pass.-km; 5.5 t-km	Exports $7 938 Machinery Vehicles Fruit and vegetables Iron and steel Medicinal products Imports $8 674 Machinery Vehicles Iron and steel Crude petroleum Petroleum products Chemical products Main trade is with: U.S.S.R., W. Germany E. Germany and Czechoslovakia Revenue from tourism: $320 Aid given (net): $103
ICELAND 1. Republic 2. Icelandic 3. Icelandic Krona 4. £1 = 878.3 $1 = 394.9	1. 103 000 km^2 2. 228 000; 2 per km^2 3. BR 19; DR 6; AI 1.2% 4. Urb. pop.; 194 (87%) 5. Reykjavik 83	1. GDP $917 (4.6%); $8 715 (3.2%) 2. Potatoes 10 3. Sheep 891 4. Fish 1 579 Whaling 386	1. 0.29/1.0; 2 607 kWh (97% hydr., 0.6% geo.) 2a. Meat 24 Salt fish 42 b. Aluminium 74 3. Telephones 95; Cars 80 Air: 2 160 pass.-km; 37 t-km Sea: 496 loaded; 1 279 unloaded	Exports $781 Fish, frozen and fresh Fish, salted and smoked Fish meal Aluminium Cod liver oil Imports $824 Machinery Petroleum products Textiles Iron and Steel Paper and cardboard Exports to U.S.A., U.K. and W. Germany Imports from: W. Germany, U.K., Denmark and Sweden
INDIA 1. Federal Republic 2. Hindi, English 3. Indian Rupee 4. £1 = 17.58 $1 = 7.907	1. 3 268 090 km^2 2. 650 982 000; 194 per km^2 3. BR 33; DR 15; AI 2.2% 3. Urb. pop.; 132 924 (21%) 5. Delhi 3 647	1. GDP $86 152 (2.5%); $141 (0.4%) Agric. 36%, Indust. 18%, Others 46% 2. Wheat 34 982 Millet 8 500 Rice 69 000 Tea 550 Coffee 105 Tobacco 451 Rubber 140 Jute 1 170 Cotton lint 1 220 Cottonseed 2 440 3. Cattle 181 849 Goats 71 000 4. Fish 2 368 5. Roundwood 137 6. Coal 103 452 Manganese 1 610 Iron ore 24 426 Chrome 266 Bauxite 1 920 Crude petroleum 12 828	1. 121.1/132.9 99 096 kWh (38% hydr., 3% nucl.) 2a. Sugar 6 400 Butter & cheese 2 085 Sawnwood 4 124 b. Iron 8 940 Steel 9 996 Aluminium 211 Zinc 59 Cement 18 264 Cotton yarn 960 Radios 1 919 3. Telephones 2 096, Cars 870 Rail: 192 948 pass.-km; 152 520 t-km Air: 8 028 pass.-km; 301 t-km Sea: 36 153 loaded; 28 989 unloaded	Exports $6 702 Jute products Tea Iron ore Iron and steel Cotton goods Imports $8 427 Machinery Wheat Petrol Cotton Iron and steel Exports to: U.S.A., Japan, U.S.S.R. and U.K. Imports from: U.S.A., U.K., Japan and W. Germany Revenue from tourism: $350 Aid received (net): $1 317 from West, $124 from East
INDONESIA 1. Republic 2. Bahasa Indonesia 3. Rupiah 4. £1 = 1394.4 $1 = 627.0	1. 1 904 345 km^2 2. 148 470 00, 72 per km^2 3. BR 42; DR 17; AI 2.6% 4. Urb. pop.; 23 246 (18%) 5. Jakarta 4 576	1. GDP $45 896 (7.8%); $320 (5.0%) Agric. 31%, Indust. 30%, Others 39% 2. Cassava 13 100 Groundnuts 739 Rice 26 350 Copra 950 Coffee 267 Tea 93 Tobacco 89 Rubber 851 3. Cattle 6 453 Goats 8 051 4. Fish 1 655 5. Roundwood 148 6. Coal 276 Tin 28 Bauxite 1 051 Natural gas 102 648 Nickel 37 Crude petroleum 78 324	1. 113.8/30.4; 4 380 kWh (50% hydr.) 2a. Meat 466 Sawnwood 2 500 Sugar 1 325 b. Cement 3 648 Petroleum products 21 500 3. Telephones 347; Cars 577 Rail: 4 434 pass.-km; 984 t-km Air: 4 476 pass.-km; 66 t-km Sea: 99 972 loaded; 14 880 unloaded	Exports $15 578 Crude petroleum Petroleum products Rubber Coffee Tin Spices Imports $7 225 Machinery Textiles Iron and steel Vehicles Rice Exports to: Japan, Singapore, U.S.A., Trinidad and Tobago Imports from: U.S.A., W. Germany, Japan and Singapore Aid received (net): $615 from West, $33 from East
IRAN (PERSIA) 1. Islamic Republic 2. Persian 3. Rial 4. £1 = 156.72 $1 = 70.47	1. 1 648 000 km^2 2. 36 938 000; 21 per km^2 3. BR 43; DR 12; AI 2.8% 4. Urb. pop.; 15 715 (47%) 5. Teheran 4 496	1. GDP $66 777 (10.2%); $1 629 (7.4%) Agric. 9%, Indust. 48%, Others 43% 2. Wheat 5 000 Cottonseed 192 Rice 1 212 Cotton lint 110 Dates 300 Tea 20 Raisins 60 Tobacco 15 3. Sheep 33 700 Goats 13 500 5. Roundwood 6 6. Natural gas 136 140 Crude petroleum 148 932 Chrome 165 Zinc 25 Lead 15 Salt 700	1. 467.4/49.8; 18 000 kWh (22% hydr.) 2a. Sugar 630 b. Cotton yarn 55 Wool yarn 38 Cement 6 323 Petroleum products 34 608 3. Telephones 782; Cars 1 400 Rail: 3 511 pass.-km; 4 627 t-km Air: 4 115 pass.-km; 77.2 t-km Sea: 220 320 loaded; 14 532 unloaded	Exports $19 000 Crude petroleum Petroleum products Carpets Imports $7 261 Machinery Iron and steel Vehicles Textiles Exports to: U.S.S.R., W. Germany, U.S.A., Italy and Saudi Arabia Imports from: W. Germany, U.S.A., Japan, and U.K. Invisible trade balance: –$3 442 Revenue from tourism: $153 Aid received (net): $545 from East

For detailed table headings and notes see page 1 of this section

Country	Area and Population	Production	Manufactures	Trade
IRAQ 1. Republic 2. Arabic 3. Iraq Dinar 4. £1 = 0.656 $1 = 0.295	1. 434 924 km^2 2. 12 767 000; 28 per km^2 3. BR 47; DR 15; AI 3.4% 4. Urb. pop.; 7 846 (66%) 5. Bagdad 2 969	1. GDP $13 635 (. . .); $1 226 (. . .) Agric. 7%, Indust. 63%, Others 30% 2. Barley 872 Rice 284 Wheat 1 492 Dates 392 Cottonseed 11 Cotton lint 6 3. Sheep 11 576 6. Natural gas 14 912 Crude petroleum 168 576	1. 167.7/8.4; 5 000 kWh 2b. Cotton yarn 1 Petroleum products 5 190 3. Telephones 320; Cars 180 Rail: 797 pass.-km; 2 254 t-km Air: 1 332 pass.-km; 41 t-km Sea: 35 960 loaded; 4 103 unloaded	Exports $21 502 Imports $4 213 Crude petroleum Manufactured goods Dates Machinery, Food Exports to: India, China and Kuwait Imports from: U.K. W. Germany and Japan Revenue from tourism: $84 Aid received (net): $40 from West, $33 from East
ISRAEL 1. Republic 2. Hebrew, Arabic 3. Shekel 4. £1 = 7.862 $1 = 3.535	1. 20 700 km^2 2. 3 783 000; 176 per km^2 3. BR 25; DR 7; AI 2.8% 4. Urb. pop.; 3 152 (87%) 5. Jerusalem 376	1. GDP $14 724 (5.4%); $4 079 (2.4%) Agric. 7%, Indust. 29%, Others 64% 2. Wheat 128 Cottonseed 120 Oranges 941 Cotton lint 75 Grapefruits 503 Tomatoes 225 3. Cattle 280 Sheep 200 4. Fish 26 6. Phosphates 2 216 Potash 702 Salt 100 Crude petroleum 24	1. 0.13/9.01; 11 108 kWh 2a. Meat 230 Butter & cheese 60 Wine 209 hl b. Cotton yarn 19 Wool yarn 8 Cement 1 920 3. Telephones 993; Cars 350 Rail 216 pass.-km; 636 t-km Air: 5 436 pass.-km; 290 t-km Sea 5 652 loaded; 6 780 unloaded	Exports $4 553 Imports $7 471 Diamonds Machinery Fruit Diamonds Clothing Iron and steel Exports to: U.S.A., W. Germany, U.K. and Hong Kong Imports from: U.S.A., W. Germany, U.K., Netherlands and Switzerland Invisible trade balance: −$520 Revenue from tourism: $461 Aid received (net): $637 from West
ITALY 1. Republic 2. Italian 3. Italian Lira 4. £1 = 1788.1 $1 = 804.0	1. 301 225 km^2 2. 56 909 000; 188 per km^2 3. BR 12; DR 10; AI 0.7% 4. Urb. pop.; 28 442 (52%) 5. Rome 2 898	1. GDP $170 767 (3.0%); $3 040 (2.2%) Agric. 8%, Indust. 35%, Others 57% 2. Wheat 9 140 Maize 6 260 Tomatoes 4 294 Grapes 11 730 Olives 2 400 Tobacco 113 Oranges 1 690 Apples 1 800 Pears 1 030 3. Cattle 8 556 Sheep 8 736 4. Fish 402 5. Roundwood 6 6. Lignite 1 908 Natural gas 125 364 Zinc 101 Crude petroleum 1 668 Asbestos 144 Iron ore 95 Bauxite 26	1. 28.4/184.5; 166 545 kWh (32% hydr., 2.0% nucl., 1.5% geo.) 2a. Meat 3 267 Butter & cheese 642 Sugar 1 685 Wine 66 500 hl Olive oil 496 Sawnwood 2 045 b. Iron 11 616 Steel 24 252 Aluminium 266 Woven silk 16 Cotton yarn 170 Wool yarn 289 Radios 1 540 Ships (grt) 148 Petroleum products 103 325 Vehicles: pass. 1 476; comm. 151 Synthetic Fibres 595 3. Telephones 16 125; Cars 17 110 Rail: 39 204 pass.-km; 16 632 t-km Air: 11 508 pass.-km; 296 t-km Sea: 43 692 loaded; 223 968 unloaded	Exports $72 242 Imports $77 970 Machinery Machinery Vehicles Petroleum Textiles Non-ferrous metals Clothing Iron and steel Petroleum products Textile fibres Shoes Cereals Iron and steel Vehicles Fruit Meat Exports to: France, W. Germany, U.S.A. and U.K. Imports from: W. Germany, France and U.S.A. Invisible trade balance: +$2 892 Revenue from tourism: $4 762 Aid given (net): $1 909
IVORY COAST 1. Republic 2. French 3. C.F.A. Franc 4. £1 = 447.0 $1 = 201.0	1. 322 463 km^2 2. 7 920 000; 24 per km^2 3. BR 49; DR 20; AI 2.6% 4. Urb. pop. 2 174 (32%) 5. Abidjan 850	1. GDP $6 441 (10.3%); $1 251 (7.5%) Agric. 23%, Indust. 13%, Others 64% 2. Rice 445 Coffee 275 Cassava 780 Cocoa 350 3. Sheep 1 150 Goats 1 200 4. Fish 79 5. Roundwood 10 6. Diamonds 48 c	1. 0.05/1.91; 1 243 kWh (18% hydr.) 2a. Sawnwood 835 Petroleum products 1 080 3. Telephones 67; Cars 100 Rail: 1 272 pass.-km; 528 t-km Air: 169 pass.-km; 13.2 t-km Sea: 4 020 loaded; 5 520 unloaded	Exports $2 515 Imports $2 493 Cocoa Machinery Coffee Vehicles Exports to: France, U.S.A., Italy and Netherlands Imports from: France, W. Germany and U.S.A. Aid received (net): $106 from West
JAMAICA 1. Commonwealth 2. English 3. Jamaica Dollar 4. £1 = 3.963 $1 = 1.782	1. 10 962 km^2 2. 2 162 000; 194 per km^2 3. BR 27; DR 6; AI 1.6% 4. Urb. pop. 690 (37%) 5. Kingston 573	1. GDP $3 045 (1.4%); $1 471 (−0.3%) Agric. 8%, Indust. 30%, Others 62% 2. Bananas 152 Copra 7 Oranges 19 Sugar cane 3 000 3. Goats 370 Cattle 290 4. Fish 10 6. Bauxite 11 574	1. 0.02/3.98; 2 000 kWh (5% hydr.) 2a. Meat 49 Sugar 300 b. Petroleum products 943 3. Telephones 109; Cars 60 Rail: 83 pass.-km; 186 t-km Air: 1 167 pass.-km; 11.6 t-km Sea: 5 424 loaded; 2 628 unloaded	Exports $769 Imports $1 010 Bauxite and aluminium Machinery Sugar Textiles Bananas Petroleum Exports to: U.S.A., U.K., Canada and Norway Imports from: U.S.A., Venezuela and U.K. Revenue from tourism: $106 Aid received (net): $29 from West
JAPAN 1. Constitutional Monarchy 2. Japanese 3. Japanese Yen 4. £1 = 533.1 $1 = 239.7	1. 372 077 km^2 (incl. Ryukyu Arch.) 2. 115 870 000; 309 per km^2 3. BR 14; DR 6; AI 1.3% 4. Urb. pop.; 84 967 (76%) 5. Tokyo 11 695	1. GDP $564 041 (5.1%); $5 002 (3.8%) Agric. 5%, Indust. 32%, Others 63% 2. Rice 15 600 Potatoes 3 400 Tomatoes 960 Apples 840 Pears 502 Oranges/mandarines 3 870 Tea 106 Tobacco 169 3. Pigs 9 491 Cattle 4 120 4. Fish 10 752 5. Roundwood 33 6. Coal 17 640 Lead 47 Natural gas 25 860 Manganese 106 Crude petroleum 480 Zinc 243 Iron ore 246 Gold 4 034 kg Copper 60	1. 38.2/414.9; 532 609 kWh (14% hydr., 5.9% nucl.) 2a. Meat 2 804 Sugar 700 Beer 44 210 hl Sawnwood 39 379 Wood pulp 8 853 b. Iron 85 728 Steel 111 744 Aluminium 768 Plastics 4 978 Cotton yarn 508 Wool yarn 124 Woven silk 155 Mm^2 Newsprint 2 566 Synthetic Fibres 1 734 Petroleum products 185 282 Vehicles: Radios 18 781 pass. 6 180 comm. 3 468 T.V. Receivers 13 927 Ships (grt) 4 249 3. Telephones 48 646; Cars 22 667 Rail: 311 184 pass.-km; 40 284 t-km Air: 26 880 pass.-km; 1 569 t-km Sea 82 644 loaded; 608 448 unloaded	Exports $103 045 Imports $110 670 Iron and steel Crude petroleum Electrical machinery Machinery Textiles Sawnwood Other machinery Iron ore Vehicles Textile fibres Ships and boats Non-ferrous metals Cereals Exports to: U.S.A., S. Korea and W. Germany Imports from: U.S.A. Australia, Saudi Arabia and Indonesia Invisible trade balance: −$6 012 Revenue from tourism: $425 Aid given (net): $5 075
KENYA 1. Republic 2. Bantu, English 3. Kenyan Shilling 4. £1 = 16.30 $1 = 7.328	1. 582 645 km^2 2. 15 320 000; 26 per km^2 3. BR 51; DR 14; AI 3.6% 4. Urb. pop.; 1 080 (10%) 5. Nairobi 835	1. GDP $4 427 (4.6%); $309 (1.1%) Agric. 34%, Indust. 13%, Others 53% 2. Maize 1 800 Cottonseed 22 Coffee 80 Tea 99 3. Cattle 10 470 Goats 4 500 4. Fish 43 5. Roundwood 16 6. Salt 38 Soda ash 153	1. 0.09/2.1; 1 113 kWh (67% hydr.) 2a. Sugar 250 b. Cement 1 152 Petroleum products 1 995 3. Telephones 144; Cars 153 Rail: 8 671 pass.-km; 3 538 t-km (inc. Tanzania and Uganda) Air: 563 pass.-km; 14.2 t-km Sea: 1 800 loaded; 4 272 unloaded	Exports $1 103 Imports $1 658 Coffee Machinery Tea Vehicles Petroleum products Petroleum Pyrethrum Iron and steel Exports to: U.K., W. Germany and Uganda Imports from: U.K., Japan, W. Germany, U.S.A. and Iran Revenue from tourism: $121 Aid received (net): $152 from West
KOREA (NORTH) 1. Republic 2. Korean 3. Won 4. £1 = 2.09 $1 = 0.94	1. 120 538 km^2 2. 17 489 000; 141 per km^2 3. BR 36; DR 9; AI 2.6% 4. Urb. pop.; 5 292 (37%) 5. Pyongyang 1 500	2. Rice 4 800 Maize 1 950 Potatoes 1 500 Tobacco 43 3. Pigs 2 000 Cattle 925 4. Fish 1 600 5. Roundwood 6 6. Coal 18 204 Zinc 135 Lead 100 Tungsten 2.7 Iron ore 9 500 Copper 15	1. 48.1/49.9 2b. Cotton . . . Lead 75 Steel 3 100 Zinc 130 Iron 3 300 Fertilizers 667 Petroleum products 1 235 3. Sea: 1 300 loaded; 2 000 unloaded	Exports . . . Imports . . . Minerals Machinery Metal products Main trade is with the U.S.S.R.

For detailed table headings and notes see page 1 of this section

Country	Area and Population	Production	Manufactures	Trade
KOREA (SOUTH) 1. Republic 2. Korean 3. Won 4. £1 = 1 076.4 $1 = 484.0	1. 98 477 km² 2. 37 605 000; 378 per km² 3. BR 29; DR 9; AI 1.8% 4. Urb. pop.; 16 770 (48%) 5. Séoul 6 879	1. GDP $34 615 (9.9%); $950 (8.0%) Agric. 21%, Indust. 30%, Others 49% 2. Rice 8 051 Barley 1 508 Potatoes 356 Cottonseed 2 3. Pigs 1 719 Cattle 1 651 4. Fish 2 351 5. Roundwood 10 6. Coal 18 204 Gold 749 kg Iron ore 255 Tungsten 3.4	1. 16.7/36.6; 28 135 kWh (5% hydr.) 2a. Meat 384 Sawnwood 3 333 b. Cotton yarn 245 Steel 5 196 Radios 4 768 Petroleum products 21 355 3. Telephones 1 976, Cars 241 Rail: 20 052 pass.-km; 10 704 t-km Air: 5 475 pass.-km; 394.4 t-km Sea: 16 044 loaded; 61 848 unloaded	Exports $15 055: Clothing, Plywood, Textiles Imports $20 339: Machinery, Rice, Petrol Exports to: U.S.A., Japan and Saudi Arabia Imports from: Japan, U.S.A. and Saudi Arabia Revenue from tourism: $370 Aid received (net): $227 from West
LAOS 1. Democratic Republic 2. Laotian, French 3. Kip 4. £1 = 890 $1 = 400	1. 236 800 km² 2. 3 633 000; 15 per km² 3. BR 45; DR 23; AI 2.3% 4. Urb. pop.; 466 (15%) 5. Vientiane 177	1. GDP $203 (. . .); $69 (. . .) 2. Rice 900 Coffee 3 Cottonseed 5 Tobacco 5 3. Pigs 1 642 Buffaloes 1 372 5. Roundwood 3 6. Tin 6	1. 0.03/0.21; 250 kWh (98% hydr.) 2a. Sawnwood 18 b. Woven silk . . . 3. Telephones 7; Cars 15 Air: 10 pass.-km; 0.1 t-km	Exports $5: Sawnwood, Tin Imports $65: Agricultural products, Petroleum products, Vehicles Exports to: Thailand, Malaysia and Hong Kong Imports from: Thailand, Japan, France and W. Germany Aid received (net): $33 from West, $20 from East
LEBANON 1. Republic 2. Arabic, French 3. Lebanese Pound 4. £1 = 7.243 $1 = 3.257	1. 10 400 km² 2. 3 086 000, 301 per km² 3. BR 35; DR 10; AI 3.1% 4. Urb. pop.; 1 278 (60%) 5. Beirut 702	1. GDP $1 912 (. . .); $646 (. . .) Agric. 10%, Indust. 16%, Others 74% 2. Wheat 40 Oranges 225 Apples 135 Grapes 135 Tomatoes 80 Tobacco 5 3. Goats 340 Sheep 242 6. Salt 35	1. 0.10/1.58; 1 600 kWh (50% hydr.) 2a. Sugar 10 Sawnwood 33 b. Cotton yarn 5 Petroleum products 1 769 3. Telephones 7; Cars 315 Rail: 2 pass.-km; 42 t-km Air: 1 392 pass.-km; 594 t-km Sea: 2 004 loaded; 1 296 unloaded	Exports $497: Fruit, Machinery, Vegetables, Eggs Imports $1 224: Machinery, Textiles, Vehicles, Petroleum products Exports to: Saudi Arabia, Syria Libya and Kuwait Imports from: U.S.A., W. Germany, France, Italy and U.K. Revenue from tourism: $65 Aid received (net): $26 from West
LIBYA 1. People's Republic 2. Arabic 3. Libyan Dinar 4. £1 = 0.658 $1 = 0.296	1. 1 759 540 km² 2. 2 856 000; 2 per km² 3. BR 49; DR 15; AI 4.1% 4. Urb. pop.; 688 (30%) 5. Tripoli 551	1. GDP $19 363 (17.5%); $7 422 (12.8%) Agric. 2%, Indust. 58%, Others 40% 2. Barley 200 Tomatoes 232 Dates 83 Olives 100 Tobacco 1 Groundnuts 13 3. Sheep 4 780 Goats 2 108 6. Crude petroleum 99 276 Natural gas 46 600	1. 145.6/4.04; 1 500 kWh 2a. Olive oil 19 b. Petroleum products 5 140 3. Telephones 41; Cars 400 Air: 815 pass.-km; 6.8 t-km Sea: 92 892 loaded; 8 448 unloaded	Exports $9 907: Crude petroleum Imports $4 602: Machinery, Vehicles Exports to: W. Germany, Italy, U.S.A. France and Spain Imports from: Italy, U.K., W. Germany, France and Japan Aid received (net): $8 from West, $11 from East
LUXEMBOURG 1. Grand Duchy 2. Luxembourgeois, French, German 3. Luxembourg Franc 4. £1 = 62.38 $1 = 28.05	1. 2 586 km² 2. 363 000; 137 per km² 3. BR 11; DR 11; AI 0.7% 4. Urb. pop.; 243 (68%) 5. Luxembourg 78	1. GDP $2 778 (2.8%); $7 717 (1.4%) Agric. 3%, Indust. 37%, Others 60% 2. Barley 56 Wheat 23 Oats 24 Grapes 25 3. Cattle 215 Pigs 91 6. Iron ore 184	1. 0.06/5.56; 1 324 kWh 2a. Meat 22 Wine 72 hl Beer 682 hl Sawnwood 26 b. Iron 3 804 Steel 4 944 3. Telephones 186; Cars 164 Rail: 300 pass.-km; 648 t-km Air: 175 pass.-km; 0.3 t-km	Exports (see Belgium) Imports (see Belgium)
MADAGASCAR 1. Republic 2. Malagasy, French 3. Malagasy Franc 4. £1 = 62.38 $1 = 201.0	1. 587 041 km² 2. 8 511 000; 14 per km² 3. BR 46; DR 25; AI 3.0% 4. Urb. pop.; 950 (14%) 5. Antananarivo 378	1. GDP $1 859 (. . .); $232 (. . .) Agric. 41%, Indust. 15%, Others 44% 2. Rice 2 327 Cassava 1 348 Bananas 278 Sisal 25 Coffee 60 Groundnuts 30 3. Cattle 8 744 Goats 1 583 4. Fish 54 5. Roundwood 7 6. Graphite 13 Gold 1 kg Chrome 128 Titanium . . .	1. 0.02/0.55; 366 kWh (49% hydr.) 2a. Sugar 113 Sawnwood 44 b. Cotton yarn 6 Cement 60 3. Telephones 32; Cars 57 Rail: 300 pass.-km; 216 t-km Air: 300 pass.-km; 7.4 t-km Sea: 512 loaded; 1 230 unloaded	Exports $386: Coffee, Spices Imports $443: Manufactured goods, Machinery Exports to: France, U.S.A. and Reunion Imports from: France, W. Germany and Qatar Aid received (net): $71 from West
MALAWI 1. Republic 2. Bantu, English 3. Kwacha 4. £1 = 1.777 $1 = 0.799	1. 118 484 km² 2. 5 817 000; 48 per km² 3. BR 51; DR 27; AI 3.2% 4. Urb. pop.; 414 (10%) 5. Lilongwe 103	1. GDP $723 (. . .); $140 (. . .) Agric. 49%, Indust. 11%, Others 40% 2. Maize 1 200 Groundnuts 170 Tea 33 Tobacco 54 Cottonseed 23 Cotton lint 10 3. Goats 860 Cattle 790 4. Fish 68 5. Roundwood 5	1. 0.04/0.29; 331 kWh (90% hydr.) 2a. Sawnwood 34 Beer 479 3. Telephones 22; Cars 13 Rail: 77 pass.-km; 204 t-km Air: 144 pass.-km; 7 t-km	Exports $233: Tobacco, Tea, Groundnuts Imports $400: Machinery, Textiles, Vehicles Exports to: U.K., U.S.A., W. Germany and Netherlands Imports from: U.K., Japan and South Africa Aid received (net): $68 from West
MALAYSIA 1. Federation 2. Malay, Chinese, English and others 3. Ringgit 4. £1 = 4.87 $1 = 2.19	1. 332 623 km² 2. 13 297 000; 39 per km² 3. BR 37; DR 10; AI 2.8% 4. Urb. pop.; 2 525 (29%) 5. Kuala Lumpur 452	1. GDP $9 297 (9.3%); $781 (6.6%) Agric. 28%, Indust. 23%, Others 49% 2. Rice 2 161 Palm oil 2 180 Copra 210 Bananas 450 Pineapples 206 Rubber 1 617 3. Pigs 1 171 Cattle 430 4. Fish 686 5. Roundwood 38 6. Iron ore 195 Tin 63 Bauxite 386 Tungsten 100 Crude petroleum 10 320 Gold 197 kg	1. 12.1/7.63; 7 207 kWh (14% hydr.) 2a. Meat 167 Sawnwood 5 247 b. Cement 2 208 Petroleum products 705 Tin 73 3. Telephones 375; Cars 600 Rail: 1 272 pass.-km; 1 296 t-km (incl. Singapore) Air: 2 628 pass.-km; 73 t-km Sea: 19 572 loaded; 14 184 unloaded	Exports $8 042: Rubber, Tin, Sawnwood, Fish, Palm oil Imports $6 489: Machinery, Crude petroleum, Vehicles, Textiles, Rice, Iron and steel, Foods Exports to: Singapore, Japan, U.S.A., U.K., and Netherlands Imports from: Japan, U.K., Singapore, Australia and W. Germany Aid received (net): $73 from West

For detailed table headings and notes see page 1 of this section

Country	Area and Population	Production	Manufactures	Trade
MALI 1. Republic 2. French, Arabic 3. Mali Franc 4. £=894.0 $1=402.0	1. 1 240 000 km^2 2. 6 465 000; 5 per km^2 3. BR 49; DR 23: AI 2.5% 4. Urb. pop.; 1 048 (17%) 5. Bamako 404	1. GDP $507 (. . .); $89 (. . .) 2. Millet 744 Rice 177 Groundnuts 179 Cottonseed 80 3. Sheep 6 067 Cattle 4 459 5. Roundwood 3	1. 0.01/0.16; 98 kWh (42% hydr.) 2a. Sugar 16 Meat 91 3. Telephones 5; Cars 20 Rail: 132 pass.-km; 144 t-km Air: 84 pass.-km; 0.6 t-km	Exports $107 Imports $219 Cattle Manufactured goods Fish Machinery Cotton Vehicles Exports to: France, Ivory Coast, China and W. Germany Imports from: France, Ivory Coast, China, and Senegal Aid received (net): $101 from west, $1 from East
MALTA 1. Commonwealth 2. Maltese, English 3. Maltese Pound 4. £1=0.765 $1=0.344	1. 316 km^2 2. 347 000; 1 062 per km^2 3. BR 17; DR 9; AI 0.3% 4. Urb. pop.; 296 (94%) 5. Valetta 14	1. GDP $479 (11.1%); $1 453 (11.0%) Agric. 5%, Indust. 38%, Others 57% 2. Poatoes 20 Wheat 3 Tomatoes 16 Grapes 3 3. Pigs 27 Goats 9	1. –/0.33; 417 kWh 2a. Wine 14 hl Wheat flour 36 3. Telephones 67, Cars 67 Air 588 pass.-km; 5 t-km Sea: 162 loaded; 1 060 unloaded	Exports $424 Imports $759 Clothing Foods Textiles Manufactured goods Exports to: U.K., Libya and W. Germany Imports from: U.K., Italy, W. Germany and U.S.A. Revenue from tourism: $81
MAURITANIA 1. Republic 2. Arabic, French 3. Ouguiya 4. £1=203.4 $1=45.84	1. 1 030 700 km^2 2. 1 588 000; 2 per km^2 3. BR 50; DR 23; AI 2.0% 4. Urb. pop.; 328 (23%) 5. Nouakchott 135	1. GDP $386 (. . .); $292 (. . .) Agric. 23%, Indust. 38%, Others 39% 2. Millet 35 Dates 14 3. Sheep 5 200 Cattle 1 600 4. Fish 34 6. Iron ore 11 989 Copper 3	1. –/0.15; 96 kWh 3. Telephones . . .; Cars 8 Air: 165 pass.-km; 13.6 t-km Sea: 7 022 loaded; 294 unloaded	Exports $148 Imports $259 Iron ore Machinery Fish Foods Exports to: France, U.K., W. Germany, Spain, Italy and Belgium Imports from: France, U.S.A., U.K. and Senegal Aid received (net): $50 from West
MEXICO 1. Federal Republic 2. Spanish 3. Mexican Peso 4. £1=50.71 $1=22.80	1. 1 972 547 km^2 2. 69 381 000, 34 per km^2 3. BR 42; DR 6; AI 3.5% 4. Urb. pop.: 43 643 (65%) 5. Mexico 13 994	1. GDP $74 248 (5.5%); $1 150 (1.9%) Agric. 9%, Indust. 30%, Others 61% 2. Maize 9 255 Copra 110 Bananas 929 Wheat 2 272 Tomatoes 1 082 Oranges 3 240 Coffee 228 Pineapples 455 Cottonseed 540 Tobacco 80 3. Cattle 29 920 Pigs 12 578 4. Fish 752 5. Roundwood 15 6. Crude petroleum 74 040 Lead 173 Natural gas 182 748 Zinc 246 Coal 6 950 Silver 1 537 t Iron ore 3 996 Gold 5 911 kg Copper 107 Mercury 170 t	1. 91.4/76.4; 50 632 kWh (38% hydr., 1% geo.) 2a. Meat 1 505 Sugar 3 060 Sawnwood 2 376 b. Iron 4 932 Steel 6 948 Aluminium 43 Rodios 1 126 Cotton yarn 158 Cement 15 144 Petroleum products 41 400 Vehicles: pass. 287; comm 121 3. Telephones 3 712; Cars 3 080 Rail: 5 040 pass.-km; 36 384 t-km Air: 8 532 pass.-km; 96 t-km Sea: 22 452 loaded; 11 652 unloaded	Exports $8 768 Imports $11 829 Cotton Machinery Sugar Vehicles Tomatoes Organic chemical products Coffee Iron and steel Cattle Paper and cardboard Machinery Petroleum products Exports to: U.S.A., Japan, W. Germany and Brazil Imports from: U.S.A., W. Germany, Japan and France Invisible trade balance: –$1 503 Revenue from tourism: $781 Aid received (net): $58 from West
MONGOLIA 1. People's Republic 2. Mongol 3. Tugrik 4. £1=6.45 $1=2.90	1. 1 565 000 km^2 2. 1 622 000; 1 per km^2 3. BR 39; DR 10; AI 3.0% 4. Urb. pop.; 631 (46%) 5. Ulan-Bator 400	1. NMP $. . . (5.3%); . . . (2.4%) 2. Wheat 400 Potatoes 60 3. Sheep 14 153 Goats 4 705 5. Roundwood 2 6. Coal 3 350 Lignite 3 087 Flourine. . . Copper 12 Molybdenum. . .	1. 1.1/1.74; 990 kWh 2a. Wool. . . Meat 226 Sawnwood 470 b. Cement 166 3. Telephones 38; Cars . . . Rail: 227 pass.-km; 2 542 t-km	Exports $281 Imports $417 Livestock Consumer goods Wool Machinery Meat Raw materials
MOROCCO 1. Kingdom 2. Arabic, French, Spanish 3. Dirham 4. £1=8.315 $1=3.739	1. 446 550 km^2 2. 19 470 000; 42 per km^2 3. BR 47; DR 16; AI 3.0% 4. Urb. pop.; 6 392 (38%) 5. Rabat 596	1. GDP $8 083 (. . .); $453 (. . .) Agric. 24%, Indust. 24%, Others 52% 2. Barley 1 888 Wheat 1 796 Oranges 606 Grapes 240 Dates 102 Olives 390 3. Sheep 13 500 Goats 5 650 4. Fish 292 5. Roundwood 3 6. Coal 720 Cobalt 2 Iron ore 28 Lead 165 Antimony 888 t Phosphates 20 175	1. 0.95/4.86; 3 678 kWh (36% hydr.) 2a. Meat 210 Wine 1 140 hl Olive oil 55 Sawnwood 68 Sugar 328 b. Petroleum products 2 645 Wool yarn 2.6 Cement 3 276 3. Telephones 210; Cars 380 Rail: 876 pass.-km; 3 780 t-km Air: 1 896 pass.-km; 23 t-km Sea: 20 592 loaded; 9 888 unloaded	Exports $1 872 Imports $3 807 Phosphates Machinery Oranges Manufactured goods Vegetables Exports to: France, W. Germany, Italy and Spain Imports from: France, U.S.A., W. Germany, Italy and Spain Revenue from tourism: $375 Aid received (net): $179 from West
MOZAMBIQUE 1. People's Republic 2. Portuguese, Bantu 3. Mozambique Escudo 4. £1=110.7 $1=49.78	1. 783 030 km^2 2. 10 199 000; 15 per km^2 3. BR 46; DR 21: AI 2.3% 4. Urb. pop.; 442 (6%) 5. Maputo 384	1. GDP $2 722 (. . .); $295 (. . .) 2. Cassava 2 500 Maize 350 Copra 75 Groundnuts 80 Cottonseed 30 Sisal 18 3. Cattle 1 380 Goats 330 5. Roundwood 11 6. Coal 504	1. 0.56/1.25; 4 940 kWh (91% hydr.) 2a. Sugar 200 Sawnwood 193 Beer 655 b. Petroleum products 357 3. Telephones 52; Cars 110 Rail: 396 pass.-km; 3 400 t-km Sea: 8 988 loaded; 3 540 unloaded	Exports $129 Imports $278 Cotton Machinery Cashew nuts Vehicles Sugar Iron and steel Tea Petroleum Exports to: Portugal, S. Africa, U.K. and U.S.A. Imports from: Portugal, S. Africa, W. Germany and U.K. Aid received (net): $56 from West, $20 from East
NAMIBIA (South West Africa) 1. Mandated Territory 2. English, African dialects 3. Rand 4. £1=1.839 $1=0.827	1. 824 292 km^2 2. 852 000; 1 per km^2 3. BR 44; DR 17; AI 2.9% 4. Urb. pop.; 200 (27%) 5. Windhoek 61	1. (incl. with South Africa) 2. Maize 15 Millet 20 3. Sheep 5 150 Cattle 3 000 4. Fish 418 5. Roundwood . . . 6. Copper 42 Zinc 29 Lead 41 Diamonds 1 653 c Tin 1 Vanadium 400 t	2a. Meat 60 b. Copper 50 Lead 40 3. Telephones 46; Cars . . . Rail: see South Africa	Exports . . . Imports . . (Trade included with South Africa)
NEPAL 1. Kingdom 2. Nepalesel Hindu 3. Nepalese Rupee 4. £1=26.7 $1=12.0	1. 140 797 km^2 2. 13 713 000; 95 per km^2 3. BR 44; DR 23; AI 2.3% 4. Urb. pop.; 462 (4%) 5. Katmandu 210	1. GDP $1 340 (3.3%); $106 (0.9%) Agric. 67%, Indust. 10%, Others 23% 2. Rice 2 500 Maize 800 Wheat 415 Jute 45 3. Cattle 6 850 Goats 2 480 5. Roundwood 11	1. 0.02/0.14; 180 kWh (75% hydr.) 2a. Sugar 29 3. Telephones 6; Cars . . .	Exports $97 Imports $163 Food Grains Textiles Livestock Petroleum products Jute Iron and steel Timber Machinery, Tea The main trade is with India Aid received (net): $56 from West

For detailed table headings and notes see page 1 of this section

Country	Area and Population	Production	Manufactures	Trade
NETHERLANDS 1. Kingdom 2. Dutch 3. Guilder 4. £1 = 4.237 $1 = 1.905	1. 33 680 km^2 2. 14 030 000; 341 per km^2 3. BR 13; DR 8; AI 0.9% 4. Urb. pop.; 12 178 (88%) 5. Amsterdam 965 The Hague 671	1. GDP 106 406 (3.2%); $7 683 (2.3%) Agric. 6%, Indust. 32%, Others 62% 2. Barley 288 Wheat 836 Tomatoes 395 Apples 480 Pears 105 Potatoes 6 277 3. Pigs 9 722 Cattle 5 149 4. Fish 324 5. Roundwood 1 6. Crude petroleum 1 272 Natural gas 701 244 Salt 2 939	1. 118.1/85.7; 58 285 kWh 2a. Meat 1 834 Sugar 1630 (Pork 1100) Butter & cheese 629 Sawnwood 298 b. Iron 4 812 Steel 5 808 Wool yarn 9 Cotton yarn 19 Petroleum Vehicles: products 52 495 pass. 89; comm. 16 Plastics 1 783 Ships (grt) 183 3. Telephones 5 846; Cars 4 200 Rail: 8 124 pass.-km; 2 880 t-km Air: 14 016 pass.-km; 913 t-km Sea: 73 044 loaded; 246 456 unloaded	Exports $63 667 Imports $67 284 Machinery Machinery Textiles Crude petroleum Chemical products Textiles Petroleum Vehicles Meat Iron and steel Iron and steel Clothing Vegetables Non-ferrous metals Exports to: W. Germany, Belgium-Luxembourg, France, U.K., Italy and U.S.A. Imports from: W. Germany, Belgium-Luxembourg, U.S.A., France, U.K. and Italy Invisible trade balance: +$1 108 Revenue from tourism: $1 110 Aid given (net): $1 957
NEW ZEALAND 1. Commonwealth 2. English 3. New Zealand Dollar 4. £1 = 2.25 $1 = 1.01	1. 268 675 km^2 2. 3 096 000; 12 per km^2 3. BR 17; DR 8; AI 1.4% 4. Urb. pop.; 2 593 (83%) 5. Wellington 328	1. GDP $13 136 (. . .); $4 251 (. . .) 2. Barley 355 Wheat 327 Apples 186 Pears 13 Tomatoes 50 Wool 321 3. Sheep 62 894 Cattle 8 499 4. Fish 83 5. Roundwood 9 6. Coal 1 728 Lignite 168 Natural gas 9 636 Gold 218 kg Crude petroleum 435	1. 6.0/11.4; 21 265 kWh (69% hydr., 6% geo.) 2a. Meat 1 075 Butter & cheese 304 Sawnwood 1 902 Wood pulp 1 097 Wine 410 hl b. Petroleum Vehicles: products 2 877 pass. 63; comm. 13 Cement 1 674 Wool yarn 18 3. Telephones 1 756; Cars 1 274 Rail: 504 pass.-km; 3 408 t-km Air: 4 308 pass.-km; 152 t-km Sea: 11 088 loaded; 10 896 unloaded	Exports $4 694 Imports $4 542 Meat Machinery Wool Textiles Butter Vehicles Cheese Iron and steel Petroleum products Exports to: U.K., U.S.A., Japan and Australia Imports from: U.K., Australia, U.S.A. and Japan Revenue from tourism: $155 Aid given: (net): $67
NICARAGUA 1. Republic 2. Spanish 3. Cordoba 4. £1 = 22.24 $1 = 10.00	1. 130 000 km^2 2. 2 481 000; 18 per km^2 3. BR 48; DR 14; AI 3.4% 4. Urb. pop.; 966 (49%) 5. Managua 500	1. GDP $2 233 (5.9%); $967 (2.4%) Agric. 23%, Indust. 21%, Others 56% 2. Maize 168 Rice 21 Bananas 160 Coffee 53 Cottonseed 185 Cotton lint 109 3. Cattle 2 846 Pigs 725 5. Roundwood 3 6. Copper 100 t Gold 1 900 kg	1. 0.05/1.07; 1 180 kWh (12% hydr.) 2a. Sugar 223 Meat 111 Sawnwood 402 b. Cement 161 3. Telephones 43; Cars 40 Rail: 19 pass.-km; 11 t-km Air: 77 pass.-km; 1.9 t-km Sea: 725 loaded; 1 423 unloaded	Exports $774 Imports $848 Cotton Machinery Meat Textiles Coffee Iron and steel Exports to: U.S.A., Japan, Costa Rica and W. Germany Imports from: U.S.A., Guatemala, Costa Rica, W. Germany, Japan and Venezuela Aid received (net): $39 from West
NIGER 1. Republic 2. Arabic, French 3. C.F.A. Franc 4. £1 = 447.0 $1 = 201.0	1. 1 267 000 km^2 2. 5 150 000; 4 per km^2 3. BR 51; DR 23; AI 2.7% 4. Urb. pop.; 315 (8%) 5. Niamey 130	1. GDP $599 (. . .); $130 (. . .) Agric. 51%, Indust. 7%, Others 42% 2. Groundnuts 90 Millet 1 246 3. Goats 6 400 Cattle 2 995 5. Roundwood 3 6. Tin 96 t Uranium 3 300	1. –/0.14; 70 kWh 2a. Meat 62 3. Telephones 8; Cars 20 Air: 154 pass.-km; 13.1 t-km	Exports $134 Imports $127 Groundnuts Manufactured goods Exports to: France, Italy and Nigeria Imports from: France, Ivory Coast and W. Germany Aid received (net): $121 from West
NIGERIA 1. Federal Republic 2. English, W. African 3. Naira 4. £1 = 1.24 $1 = 0.56	1. 923 768 km^2 2. 74 595 000; 78 per km^2 3. BR 50; DR 20; AI 2.8% 4. Urb. pop.; 12 535 (19%) 5. Lagos 1 477	1. GDP $25 120 (. . .); $399 (. . .) Agric. 26%, Indust. 38%, Others 36% 2. Cassava 11 500 Millet 3 100 Rubber 60 Cocoa 180 Groundnuts 621 Cottonseed 74 3. Goats 24 500 Cattle 12 000 4. Fish 519 5. Roundwood 85 6. Coal 264 Natural gas 5 040 Tin 3 Crude petroleum 114 504	1. 153.6/6.1; 3 450 kWh (75% hydr.) 2a. Meat 657 Sugar 40 Sawnwood 949 b. Petroleum products 2 833 Cement 1 536 3. Telephones 121; Cars 400 Rail: 785 pass.-km; 972 t-km Aviation: 1 164 pass.-km; 5 t-km Sea: 101 220 loaded; 5 000 unloaded	Exports $9 865 Imports $12 763 Petroleum Machinery Cocoa Textiles Groundnuts Vehicles Tin Iron and steel Exports to: Bermuda, U.S.A. and Netherlands Imports from: U.K., W. Germany, U.S.A. and Japan Aid received (net): $58 from West
NORWAY 1. Kingdom 2. Norwegian 3. Norwegian Krone 4. £1 = 10.96 $1 = 4.93	1. 324 219 km^2 2. 4 073 000; 13 per km^2 3. BR 13; DR 10; AI 0.6% 4. Urb. pop.; 1 788 (44%) 5. Oslo 645	1. GDP $35 589 (4.8%); $8 809 (4.1%) Agric. 6%, Indust. 27%, Others 67% 2. Barley 647 Apples 37 Oats 357 Potatoes 426 3. Sheep 1 919 Cattle 971 4. Fish 2 647 5. Roundwood 8 6. Coal 312 Molybdenum . . . Iron ore 2 761 Vanadium 460 t Copper 28 Zinc 28 Titanium 820 Crude petroleum 18 288	1. 31.4/21.2; 72 520 kWh (99.6% hydr.) 2a. Butter & cheese 85 Sawnwood 2 305 Canned fish 32 Wood pulp 1 394 Fish meal 10 b. Iron 1 536 Steel 924 Magnesium 39 Aluminium 660 Paper 1 225 Wool yarn 4 Ships (grt) 260 Petroleum products 7 636 3. Telephones 1 563 Cars 1 190 Rail: 2 064 pass.-km; 2 712 t-km Air: 3 912 pass.-km; 135 t-km Sea: 39 372 loaded; 22 416 unloaded	Exports $13 271 Imports $13 818 Non-ferrous metals Machinery (mainly aluminium) Ships and boats Ships and boats Vehicles Machinery Iron and steel Paper and cardboard Textiles Fish Non-ferrous metals Iron and steel Petroleum products Exports to: U.K., Sweden, W. Germany, Denmark and U.S.A. Imports from: Sweden, W. Germany, U.K., U.S.A. and Denmark Invisible trade balance: −$580 Aid given (net): $495
PAKISTAN 1. Republic 2. Urdu, English 3. Pakistan Rupee 4. £1 = 22.02 $1 = 9.90	1. 801 408 km^2 2. 79 838 000, 95 per km^2 3. BR 36; DR 12; AI 3.2% 4. Urb. pop; 16 558 (26%) 5. Islamabad 77	1. GDP $14 510 (3.6%); $200 (0.9%) Agric. 31%, Indust. 16%, Others 53% 2. Rice 4 953 Wheat 9 944 Dates 215 Maize 846 Tobacco 72 Rapeseed 243 Cotton lint 650 Cottonseed 1 301 3. Cattle 14 992 Sheep 24 185 4. Fish 293 5. Roundwood 10 6. Coal 1 272 Salt 620 Natural gas 53 784 Crude petroleum 492 Antimony 69 t Chrome 12	1. 8.33/13.1; 11 050 kWh (45% hydr., 5%nucl.) 2a. Meat 630 Sugar 662 Sawnwood 30 Jute 1 b. Petroleum Cotton yarn 328 products 3 415 Cement 3 334 3. Telephones 259; Cars 347 Rail: 13 980 pass.-km; 7 812 t-km Air: 4 992 pass.-km; 220 t-km Sea: 3 000 loaded; 11 988 unloaded	Exports $2 036 Imports $4 061 Textiles Machinery Cotton Iron and steel Leather Fertilizer Rice Crude petroleum Vehicles Exports to: Japan, Iran and U.K. Imports from: U.S.A., U.K., Japan and W. Germany Aid received (net): $471 from West, $9 from East
PANAMA 1. Republic 2. Spanish 3. Balboa 4. £1 = 2.22 $1 = 1.0	1. 75 650 km^2 2. 1 916 000, 24 per km^2 3. BR 29; DR 7; AI 3.1% 4. Urb. pop.; 928 (51%) 5. Panamá 440	1. GDP $2 213 (3.4%); $1 250 (0.3%) Agric. 17%, Indust. 17%, Others 66% 2. Rice 200 Bananas 1 000 Coffee 6 Oranges 65 3. Cattle 1 423 Pigs 205 4. Fish 114 5. Roundwood 2	1. 0.01/1.52; 1 640 kWh (24% hydr.) 2a. Meat 77 Sugar 225 Sawnwood 44 b. Petroleum products 2 294 3. Telephones 155; Cars 90 Sea: 1 183 loaded; 3 419 unloaded	Exports $288 Imports $942 Bananas Manufactured goods Petroleum products Petroleum Machinery Imports to: U.S.A. and W. Germany Imports from: U.S.A., Ecuador, Venezuela and Saudi Arabia Invisible trade balance: +$346 Aid received (net): $37 from West

For detailed table headings and notes see page 1 of this section

Country	Area and Population	Production	Manufactures	Trade
PERU 1. Republic 2. Spanish 3. Sol 4. £1 = 556.2 $1 = 250.1	1. 1 285 216 km² 2. 17 297 000; 13 per km² 3. BR 41; DR 14; AI 3.0% 4. Urb. pop.; 9 759 (63%) 5. Lima 3 303	1. GDP $10 572 (4.6%); $646 (1.7%) Agric. 13%, Indust. 36%, Others 51% 2. Maize 600 — Rice 545 Oranges 166 — Coffee 72 Cottonseed 162 — Potatoes 1 700 3. Sheep 14 473 — Cattle 4 187 4. Fish 3 365 5. Roundwood 4 6. Iron ore 2 174 — Gold 3 500 kg Antimony 763 t — Silver 1 332 t Copper 391 — Zinc 491 Lead 184 — Tungsten 725 t Molybdenum 729 t — Crude petroleum 9 360	1. 7.1/10.3; 8 557 kWh (71% hydr.) 2a. Meat 350 — Fish Meal Sugar 695 — Sawnwood 425 b. Cotton yarn . . . 3. Telephones 403; Cars 312 Rail: 528 pass.-km; 612 t-km Air: 1 353 pass.-km; 34.8 t-km Sea: 10 284 loaded; 2 688 unloaded	Exports $3 533 — Imports $2 022 Copper — Machinery Fish Meal — Chemical products Iron ore — Wheat Cotton — Iron and steel Exports to: U.S.A., Japan and Italy Imports from: U.S.A., Ecuador and Venezuela Revenue from tourism: $113 Aid received (net): $81 from West
PHILIPPINES 1. Republic 2. Tagalog, English 3. Philippine Peso 4. £1 = 16.49 $1 = 7.415	1. 300 000 km² 2. 46 580 000; 154 per km² 3. BR 41; DR 10; AI 2.9% 4. Urb. pop.; 11 678 (32%) 5. Manila 1 438	1. GDP $20 675 (6.4%); $459 (3.4%) Agric. 28%, Indust. 27%, Others 45% 2. Maize 3 300 — Rice 7 000 Bananas 2 430 — Pineapples 479 Coffee 86 — Copra 1 890 Tobacco 57 3. Pigs 7 300 — Buffaloes 3 018 4. Fish 1 558 5. Roundwood 34 6. Iron ore 2 — Copper 264 Chrome 561 — Gold 17 450 kg Silver 56 t	1. 0.76/14.4; 15 800 kWh (31% hydr.) 2a. Meat 700 — Sawnwood 1 781 Salted fish 42 — Sugar 2 355 b. Plastics 63 — Petroleum Cotton yarn 31 — products 9 655 Cement 3 936 3. Telephones 567; Cars 400 Rail: 624 pass.-km; 36 t-km Air: 4 428 pass.-km; 127 t-km Sea: 15 048 loaded; 18 888 unloaded	Exports $4 601 — Imports $6 142 Wood — Machinery Sugar — Petroleum Copra — Vehicles Copper — Iron and steel Exports to: U.S.A., Japan and Netherlands Imports from: Japan, U.S.A. and Saudi Arabia Invisible trade balance: − $249 Revenue from tourism: $311 Aid received (net): $183 from West
POLAND 1. People's Republic 2. Polish 3. Złoty 4. £1 = 73.84 $1 = 33.20	1. 312 677 km² 2. 35 225 000; 112 per km² 3. BR 19; DR 9; AI 0.9% 4. Urb. pop.; 19 772 (57%) 5. Warsaw 1 474	1. NMP $52 292 (8.8%); $1 507 (7.8%) Agric. 16%, Indust. 52%, Others 32% 2. Barley 3 785 — Wheat 4 220 Rye 5 233 — Oats 2 199 Potatoes 49 582 — Apples 1 030 Tobacco 70 — Rapeseed 233 3. Pigs 21 224 — Cattle 13 036 4. Fish 571 5. Roundwood 22 6. Coal 201 000 — Nickel 2 Lignite 38 088 — Zinc 218 Iron ore 158 — Natural gas 60 744 Copper 318 — Salt 4 393 Lead 49	1. 200.4/180.5; 109 364 kWh (2.2% hydr.) 2a. Meat 2 996 — Sawnwood 8 107 Butter & cheese 646 — Sugar 1 581 Salted fish 18 2b. Iron 11 532 — Steel 19 224 Aluminium 100 — Plastics 583 Cotton yarn 214 — Wool yarn 107 Petroleum products 13 113 — Vehicles: Woven silk 1 400 Tm — pass. 349; comm. 64 Ships (grt) 489 3. Telephones 2 925; Cars 2 002 Rail: 46 716 pass.-km; 138 096 t-km Air: 2 088 pass.-km; 18 t-km Sea: 37 798 loaded; 23 990 unloaded	Exports $16 233 — Imports $17 488 Coal — Dairy products Ships and boats — Iron ore Meat — Crude petroleum Dairy products — Cotton, Wheat Machinery — Iron and steel Clothing — Petroleum products Machinery Main trade is with: U.S.S.R., W. Germany Czechoslovakia and E. Germany Revenue from tourism: $157 Aid given (net): $100
PORTUGAL 1. Republic 2. Portuguese 3. Escudo 4. £1 = 110.7 $1 = 49.78	1. 92 082 km² 2. 9 866 000; 107 per km² 3. BR 17; DR 10; AI 0.6% 4. Urb. pop.; 2 276 (26%) 5. Lisbon 1 612	1. GDP $14 724 (4.5%); $1 580 (2.4%) Agric. 13%, Indust. 34%, Others 53% 2. Wheat 233 — Maize 456 Grapes 1 500 — Olives 236 Tomatoes 685 — Wool 10 3. Sheep 5 200 — Pigs 2 500 4. Fish 255 5. Roundwood 8 6. Coal 180 — Tin 240 t Iron ore 24 — Tungsten 1 372 t Copper 3 — Gold 242 kg	1. 0.79/10.13; 13 324 kWh (73% hydr.) 2a. Meat 423 — Sawnwood 1 980 Canned fish 47 — Salted fish 15 Wine 5 570 hl — Olive oil 41 b. Iron 372 — Steel 420 Petroleum — Vehicles: products 9 679 — pass. 32; comm. 38 Cotton yarn 101 — Wool yarn 5 3. Telephones 1 175; Cars 912 Rail: 5 508 pass.-km; 936 t-km Air: 3 924 pass.-km; 123 t-km Sea: 4 464 loaded; 4 604 unloaded	Exports $3 468 — Imports $6 086 Textiles — Machinery Clothing — Vehicles Wine — Iron and steel Diamonds — Cotton Machinery — Diamonds Fish — Cereals Cork — Crude petroleum Exports to: U.K., France and W. Germany Imports from: W. Germany, U.K., U.S.A. and France Invisible trade balance: −$105 Revenue from tourism: $404
ROMANIA 1. Socialist republic 2. Romanian 3. Leu 4. £1 = 9.94 $1 = 4.47	1. 237 500 km² 2. 22 068 000; 92 per km² 3. BR 19; DR 10; AI 1.0% 4. Urb. pop.; 10 237 (48%) 5. Bucharest 1 934	1. NMP $. . . (10.8%); . . . (9.8%) Agric. 16%, Indust. 61%, Others 23% 2. Barley 2 037 — Wheat 4 684 Grapes 1 486 — Tomatoes 1 393 Tobacco 45 — Sunflower seed 889 3. Sheep 15 612 — Pigs 10 337 4. Fish 138 5. Roundwood 21 6. Coal 7 500 — Lead 33 Lignite 25 260 — Manganese 140 Iron ore 652 — Natural gas 311 196 Bauxite 900 — Crude petroleum 12 324	1. 83.9/86.6; 59 858 kWh (15% hydr.) 2a. Meat 1 595 — Sawnwood 4 562 Sugar 650 — Butter & cheese 203 b. Iron 8 160 — Steel 11 784 Petroleum products 21 430 — Cotton yarn 175 Woven silk 1 000 Tm² — Wool yarn 64 Fertilizers 2 383 — Aluminium 231 3. Telephones 1 196; Cars 235 Rail: 22 812 pass.-km; 73 740 t-km Air: 1 104 pass.-km; 15 t-km Sea: 4 257 loaded; 4 859 unloaded	Exports $9 724 — Imports $10 916 Machinery — Machinery Consumer goods — Iron ore Petroleum products — Coke Cereals — Vehicles Iron goods Exports to: U.S.S.R., E. Germany and W. Germany Imports from: U.S.S.R., E. Germany and W. Germany Aid given (net): $275
SAUDI ARABIA 1. Kingdom 2. Arabic 3. Rial 4. £1 = 7.47 $1 = 3.36	1. 2 149 690 km² 2. 8 112 000; 4 per km² 3. BR 50; DR 20; AI 3.0% 4. Urb. pop.; 1 829 (23%) 5. Ar Riyād 667	1. GDP $56 870 (. . .); $6 155 (. . .) Agric. 1%, Indust. 69%, Others 30% 2. Wheat 150 — Millet/Sorghum 110 Dates 357 — Tomatoes 181 3. Sheep 2 800 — Goats 1 900 6. Crude petroleum 476 304 — Natural gas 63 376	1. 644/17.6; 2 500 kWh 2b. Petroleum products 23 212 Cement 1 267 3. Telephones 160; Cars 400 Rail: 72 pass.-km; 66 t-km Air: 4 923 pass.-km; 105.8 t-km Sea: 410 000 loaded; 9 259 unloaded	Exports $59 336 — Imports $20 424 Crude petroleum — Machinery Petroleum products — Vehicles Food Exports to: Japan, Italy, France and U.S.A. Imports from: U.S.A., Japan and W. Germany Invisible trade balance: − $7 547
SENEGAL 1. Republic 2. French, West African 3. C.F.A. Franc 4. £1 = 447.0 $1 = 201.0	1. 196 192 km² 2. 5 518 000; 27 per km² 3. BR 55; DR 23; AI 2.6% 4. Urb. pop.; 1 149 (32%) 5. Dakar 799	1. GDP $1 646 (. . .); $331 (. . .) 2. Millet 500 — Rice 130 Bananas 5 — Groundnuts 1 000 3. Cattle 2 806 — Goats 1 000 4. Fish 348 5. Roundwood 3 6. Phosphates 1 491 — Salt 147 Titanium . . . — Zirconium . . .	1. –/0.79; 455 kWh 2a. Sawnwood 8 b. Petroleum products 776 — Cement 384 3. Telephones 39; Cars 65 Rail: 180 pass.-km; 168 t-km Air: 152 pass.-km; 13.1 t-km Sea: 2 904 loaded; 1 908 unloaded	Exports $623 — Imports $762 Groundnut oil — Food Groundnuts — Manufactured goods Machinery Main trade is with : France Aid received (net): $126 from West

For detailed table headings and notes see page 1 of this section

Country	Area and Population	Production	Manufactures	Trade
SINGAPORE 1. Republic 2. English, Chinese, Malay, Tamil 3. Singapore Dollar 4. £1 = 4.802 $1 = 2.159	1. 581 km² 2. 2 363 000; 4 024 per km² 3. BR 17; DR 5; AI 1.5% 4. Urb. pop.: 2 363 (100%) 5. Singapore 2 308	1. GDP $5 915 (9.0%); $2 594 (7.3%) Agric. 2%, Indust. 27%, Others 71% 2. Cassava 1 3. Pigs 1 154 Cattle 9 4. Fish 16 Granite 2 235	1. –/5.15; 5 114 kWh 2a. Meat 89 Sawnwood 320 b. Manufacturing Industries . . . 3. Telephones 395; Cars 150 Rail: see Malaysia Air: 12 048 pass.-km; 574 t-km Sea: 31 896 loaded; 49 200 unloaded	Exports $14 233 Rubber Petroleum products Machinery Imports $17 635 Machinery Textiles Rubber Exports to: Malaysia, U.S.A. and Japan Imports from: Japan, Malaysia, U.S.A. and Saudi Arabia Invisible trade balance: +$1 322 Revenue from tourism: $300 Aid received (net); $13 from West
SOUTH AFRICA 1. Republic 2. English, Afrikaans 3. Rand 4. £1 = 1.839 $1 = 0.827	1. 1 221 037 km² 2. 28 483 000, 23 per km² 3. BR 38; DR 12; AI 2.5% 4. Urb. pop.: 11 018 (48%) 5. Pretoria 562; Cape Town 1 097	1. GDP $39 793 (4.0%); $1 436 (1.4%) Agric. 8%, Indust. 38%, Others 54% 2. Maize 8 240 Wheat 2 220 Oranges 560 Pineapples 185 Grapes 1 130 Cottonseed 94 Tobacco 45 Wool 99 3. Sheep 31 500 Cattle 13 200 4. Fish 628 5. Roundwood 17 6. Coal 90 360 Manganese 5 182 Iron ore 19 725 Asbestos 249 Copper 191 Antimony 11 614 t Chrome 3 297 Nickel 30 Gold 703 473 kg Diamonds 8 384 c	1. 76.3/87.4; 80 198 kWh (2.4% hydr.) 2a. Meat 990 Sugar 2 079 Wine 6 200 hl Beer 5 951 hl Sawnwood 1 555 b. Iron 7 020 Steel 8 772 Copper 152 Cotton yarn 38 Wool yarn 19 Petroleum products 12 705 Vehicles: pass. 132, comm. 58 Cement 6 828 3. Telephones 2 191; Cars 2 331 Rail: . . .; 80 172 t-km Air: 8 280 pass.-km; 257 t-km Sea: 47 160 loaded; 1 848 unloaded	Exports $7 182 Diamonds Fruit Wool Copper Iron and steel Machinery Cereals Imports $8 352 Machinery Vehicles Textiles Crude petroleum Petroleum products Chemical products Exports to: U.K., Japan, U.S.A. and W. Germany Imports from: U.K., U.S.A., W. Germany and Japan Invisible trade balance: –$1 988 Revenue from tourism: $321
SOUTH YEMEN 1. People's Republic 2. Arabic 3. South Yemen Dinar 4. £1 = 0.767 $1 = 0.345	1. 287 683 km² 2. 1 838 000; 6 per km² 3. BR 48; DR 23; AI 1.9% 4. Urb. pop.: 529 (33%) 5. Aden 285	1. GDP $245 (. . .); $145 (. . .) Agric. 19%, Indust. 27%, Others 54% 2. Millet 70 Wheat 25 Dates 42 Cottonseed 11 3. Goats 1 300 Sheep 970 4. Fish 133	1. –/0.57; 180 kWh 2b. Petroleum products 1 845 3. Telephones 9; Cars 11 Sea: 1 426 loaded; 2 204 unloaded	Exports $221 Petroleum products Cotton Imports $544 Petroleum Cotton Fabric Cereals Exports to: U.K., Yemen and South Africa Imports from: Iran, Kuwait and Japan Aid received (net): $63 from West
SPAIN 1. Monarchy 2. Spanish 3. Spanish Peseta 4. £1 = 147.1 $1 = 66.15	1. 504 782 km² 2. 37 183 000; 74 per km² 3. BR 16; DR 8; AI 1.1% 5. Madrid 3 520	1. GDP $115 590 (6.1%); $3 152 (5.0%) Agric. 9%, Indust. 30%, Others 61% 2. Barley 6 150 Wheat 4 118 Tomatoes 2 050 Oranges 1 771 Grapes 7 748 Olives 2 270 Cottonseed 79 Cotton lint 40 Tobacco 38 Wool 29 3. Sheep 14 500 Pigs 9 943 4. Fish 1 380 5. Roundwood 13 6. Coal 11 496 Lead 71 Lignite 10 032 Tungsten 434 t Iron ore 4 242 Mercury 1 116 t Copper 18 Zinc 134	1. 19/86.3; 93 803 kWh (43% hydr., 7% nucl.) 2a. Meat 2 255 Sugar 774 Olive oil 469 Wine 29 030 hl Sawnwood 2 727 b. Cotton yarn 69 Wool yarn 20 Silk fabric 252 Mm² Copper 149 Iron 6 840 Steel 12 120 Aluminium 212 Ships (grt.) 512 Radios 363 Vehicles pass. 973; comm. 166 Petroleum products 28 859 Cement 27 996 3. Telephones 9 528; cars 7 058 Rail: 18 096 pass.-km; 11 076 t-km Air: 15 180 pass.-km; 405 t-km Sea: 23 812 loaded; 84 207 unloaded	Exports $17 903 Machinery Fruits Vegetables Footwear Petroleum products Textiles Ships and boats Olive oil Imports $25 432 Machinery Crude petroleum Iron and steel Organic chemicals Maize Soya Sawnwood Copper Exports to: U.S.A., W. Germany, France and U.K. Imports from: U.S.A., W. Germany, France and Saudi Arabia Invisible trade balance: +$3 641 Revenue from tourism: $4 003
SRI LANKA 1. Republic 2. Sinhalese, English, Tamil 3. Sri Lanka Rupee 4. £1 = 34.34 $1 = 15.44	1. 65 610 km² 2. 14 741 000; 217 per km² 3. BR 29; DR 7; AI 1.6% 4. Urb. pop.: 2 848 (22%) 5. Colombo 607	1. GDP $3 412 (4.5%); $229 (2.8%) Agric. 39%, Indust. 14%, Others 47% 2. Rice 1 806 Cassava 590 Tea 210 Copra 135 Rubber 155 Tobacco 8 3. Cattle 1 623 Buffaloes 844 4. Fish 157 5. Roundwood 5 6. Graphite 9 Salt 121 Titanium 70	1. 0.14/1.45; 1 331 kWh (94% hydr.) 2a. Meat 31 Sawnwood 25 b. Cotton yarn 8 Petroleum products 1 165 3. Telephones 72; Cars 105 Rail: 3 672 pass.-km; 252 t-km Air: 132 pass.-km; 0.5 t-km Sea: 1 320 loaded; 4 332 unloaded	Exports $890 Tea Rubber Copra Coconuts Coconut fibre Imports $1 441 Machinery Rice Sugar Flour Textiles Petroleum products Exports to: U.K., Pakistan, China and U.S.A. Imports from: Saudi Arabia, Iran and U.S.A. Aid received (net); $155 from West, $20 from East
SUDAN 1. Republic 2. Arabic, Hamitic English 3. Sudanese Pound 4. £1 = 1.11 $1 = 0.50	1. 2 505 813 km² 2. 17 865 000, 7 per km² 3. BR 46; DR 20; AI 3.2% 4. Urb. pop.: 3 288 (20%) 5. Khartoum 334	1. GDP $4 689 (. . .); $298 (. . .) Agric. 39%, Indust. 11%, Others 50% 2. Millet/sorghum 2 340 Wheat 266 Dates 110 Groundnuts 1 110 Cottonseed 230 Cotton lint 131 3. Cattle 17 300 Sheep 17 200 5. Roundwood 29 6. Chrome 24 Salt 92	1. 0.05/2.59; 810 kWh 2a. Meat 408 Sugar 130 b. Cement 140 Petroleum products 976 Cotton fabrics 103 Mm² 3. Telephones 62; Cars 55 Rail: . . .; 2 288 t-km Air: 552 pass.-km; 10 t-km Sea: 1 308 loaded; 2 220 unloaded	Exports $533 Cotton Gum Arabic Sesame Groundnuts Imports $1 198 Machinery Cotton fabrics Petroleum products Exports to: India, Japan and Italy Imports from: U.K., W. Germany, Japan and Iraq Aid received (net): $131 from West, $21 from East
SWEDEN 1. Kingdom 2. Swedish 3. Krona 4. £1 = 9.23 $1 = 4.15	1. 449 750 km² 2. 8 294 000; 18 per km² 3. BR 12; DR 11; AI 0.4% 4. Urb. pop.: 6 789 (83%) 5. Stockholm 1 375	1. GDP $78 259 (2.0%); $9 474 (1.6%) Agric. 4%, Indust. 27%, Others 69% 2. Oats 1 646 Barley 2 550 Wheat 1 113 Apples 120 Potatoes 1 182 Rapeseed 313 3. Pigs 2 711 Cattle 1 911 4. Fish 190 5. Roundwood 47 6. Iron ore 16 635 Lead 79 Copper 46 Zinc 169 Gold 2 373 kg Silver 180 t	1. 8.7/49.7; 90 018 kWh (59% hydr., 22% nucl.) 2a. Meat 522 Butter & cheese 157 Sugar 346 Sawnwood 10 906 Wood pulp 8 557 b. Iron 2 904 Steel 4 728 Aluminium 79 Copper 61 Paper 5 702 Ships (grt) 461 Petroleum products 14 645 Vehicles: pass. 310; comm. 41 3. Telephones 5 930; Cars 2 868 Rail: 5 556 pass.-km; 14 760 t-km Air: 4 404 pass.-km; 197 t-km Sea: 36 468 loaded; 56 412 unloaded	Exports $27 240 Machinery Iron and Steel Paper and cardboard Wood pulp Vehicles Sawnwood Ships and boats Iron ore Imports $28 488 Machinery Petroleum products Vehicles Textiles Iron and steel Non-ferrous metals Clothing Crude petroleum Exports to: U.K., W. Germany, Denmark and Norway Imports from: W. Germany, U.K., U.S.A. and Denmark Invisible trade balance: –$2 759 Aid given (net): $1 445

For detailed table headings and notes see page 1 of this section

Country	Area and Population	Production	Manufactures	Trade
SWITZERLAND 1. Federal Republic 2. German, French, Italian 3. Swiss Franc 4. £1 = 3.51 $1 = 1.58	1. 41 288 km^{2} 2. 6 330 000; 155 per km^{2} 3. BR 12; DR 9; AI 0.3% 4. Urb. pop.: 3 423 (55%) 5. Bern 284	1. GDP $60 578 (−0.2%); $9 570 (0.1%) Agric. 6%, Indust. 40%, Others 54% 2. Potatoes 880 Apples 430 Wheat 417 Pears 148 3. Cattle 2 038 Pigs 2 062 5. Roundwood 4 6. Salt 391	1. 4.2/21.3; 45 903 kWh (79% hydr., 17% nucl.) 2a. Meat 467 Butter & cheese 153 Wine 1 220 hl Beer 3 998 hl Sawnwood 1 540 b. Iron 35 Steel 784 Aluminium 79 Cotton yarn 42 Petroleum products 4 394 Silk fabrics 18 Mm^{2} 3. Telephones 4 145; Cars 2 154 Rail: 8 292 pass.-km; 6 960 t-km Air: 10 332 pass.-km; 434 t-km	Exports $26 507 Machinery Watches Textiles Medicines Organic chemical products Imports $29 354 Machinery Vehicles Iron and steel Textiles Petroleum products Exports to: W. Germany, France, U.S.A., Italy and U.K. Imports from: W. Germany, France, Italy U.S.A. and U.K. Invisible trade balance: +$4 300 Revenue from tourism: $1 943 Aid given (net): $3 670
SYRIA 1. Republic 2. Arabic 3. Syrian Pound 4. £1 = 8.729 $1 = 3.925	1. 185 180 km^{2} 2. 8 328 000; 44 per km^{2} 3. BR 46; DR 14; AI 3.3% 4. Urb. pop.: 3 950 (49%) 5. Damascus 1 142	1. GDP $6 581 (9.8%); $839 (6.4%) Agric. 20%, Indust. 19%, Others 61% 2. Barley 395 Wheat 1 319 Grapes 346 Olives 190 Tomatoes 510 Tobacco 13 Cottonseed 213 3. Sheep 7 563 Goats 1 094 6. Crude petroleum 8 940 Salt 62 Natural gas 1 864 Phosphates 800	1. 14.9/5.65; 2 043 kWh 2a. Meat 130 Sugar 27 Olive oil 45 b. Cement 1 536 Petroleum products 8 454 Cotton, woven 355 3. Telephones 193; Cars 55 Rail: 324 pass.-km; 468 t-km Air: 795 pass.-km; 9.4 t-km Sea: 8 760 loaded; 7 740 unloaded	Exports $1 634 Cotton Livestock Crude petroleum Vegetables Wheat Imports $3 307 Machinery Iron and steel Vehicles Textiles Crude petroleum Exports to: France, Italy, W. Germany and U.S.S.R. Imports from: W. Germany, Italy, France, Iraq and Romania Aid received (net): $62 from West, $131 from East
TAIWAN 1. Republic 2. Chinese 3. New Dollar 4. £1 = 80.1 $1 = 36.0	1. 35 981 km^{2} 2. 15 600 000; 431 per km^{2} 3. BR 26; DR 5; AI 2.1% 4. Urb. pop. 8 211 (51%) 5. Tai-pei 2 196	1. GDP $32 337 (9.7%); $1 869 (7.7%) Agric. 11%, Indust. 46%, Others 43% 2. Rice 2 450 Bananas 227 Groundnuts 86 Citrus fruits 399 Pineapples 245 Tea 27 Soya beans 32 3. Pigs 8 781 Cattle 143 4. Fish 929 5. Roundwood 0.8 6. Coal 2 720 Gold 443 kg Copper . . .	1. . . ./. . .; 37 897 kWh (12% hydr., 16% nucl.) 2a. Sugar 845 Sawnwood 654 Meat . . . b. Steel 3 402 Aluminium 56 Cotton yarn 159 Radios 8 721 Petroleum products 18 367 3. Telephones 2 566; Cars 325 Rail: 7 327 pass.-km; 2 668 t-km Air: 867 pass.-km; 3 t-km Sea: 36 887 loaded; 62 440 unloaded	Exports $16 103 Textiles Electrical goods Timber products Plastics Imports $14 774 Machinery Crude petroleum Iron and steel Chemicals Exports to: U.S.A., Japan and Hong Kong Imports from: Japan, U.S.A. and Kuwait
TANZANIA 1. Federal Republic 2. Swahili 3. Tanzanian Shilling 4. £1 = 18.28 $1 = 8.221	1. 945 087 km^{2} 2. 17 982 000; 18 per km^{2} 3. BR 47; DR 22; AI 2.8% 4. Urb. pop.: 1 051 (7%) 5. Dar-es-Salaam 757	1. GDP $3 417 (. . .); $212 (. . .) Agric. 44%, Indust. 10%, Others 46% 2. Maize 900 Cassava 4 300 Bananas 746 Coffee 49 Cottonseed 115 Cotton lint 60 Tobacco 22 Sisal 85 3. Cattle 15 300 Goats 4 700 4. Fish 287 5. Roundwood 40 6. Gold 4 kg Diamonds 402 c	1. 0.06/1.07; 695 kWh (75% hydr.) 2a. Meat 198 Sawnwood 56 Sugar 130 Beer 751 hl 3. Telephones 66; Cars 45 Rail: see Kenya Air: 37 pass.-km; 0.3 t-km Sea: 966 loaded; 3 064 unloaded	Exports $523 Coffee Cotton Diamonds Sisal Cashew nuts Imports $1 084 Machinery Vehicles Textiles Petroleum products Iron and steel Exports to: U.K., W. Germany, U.S.A. and Netherlands Imports from: U.K., Japan, Netherlands and W. Germany Aid received (net): $300 from West, $17 from East
THAILAND 1. Kingdom 2. Thai 3. Baht 4. £1 = 45.41 $1 = 20.42	1. 514 000 km^{2} 2. 46 142 000; 88 per km^{2} 3. BR 40; DR 11; AI 2.8% 4. Urb. pop. 4 553 (13%) 5. Bangkok 4 702	1. GDP $18 159 (6.7%); $412 (3.8%) Agric. 28%, Indust. 22%, Others 50% 2. Maize 3 300 Rice 15 640 Bananas 2 082 Pineapples 2 000 Jute 370 Rubber 498 Cottonseed 65 Tobacco 71 Cassava 12 500 3. Buffaloes 5 500 Cattle 4 850 4. Fish 2 264 5. Roundwood 22 6. Lignite 1 356 Tungsten 2 305 Iron ore 56 Tin 40 Antimony 2 935 Manganese 72	1. 0.68/11.9; 11 690 kWh (37% hydr.) 2a. Meat 465 Sawnwood 1 427 Sugar 1 845 b. Cotton yarn 74 Petroleum products 7 980 Cement 5 244 Tin 33 3. Telephones 367; Cars 396 Rail: 6 072 pass.-km; 2 652 t-km Air: 4 680 pass.-km; 183 t-km Sea: 12 144 loaded; 15 828 unloaded	Exports $5 308 Rice Maize Rubber Fruit and vegetables Tin Imports $7 156 Machinery Vehicles Iron and steel Crude petroleum Exports to: Japan, U.S.A., Singapore, Netherlands and Indonesia Imports from: Japan, U.S.A., W. Germany and Saudi Arabia Invisible trade balance: −$346 Revenue from tourism: $211 Aid received (net): $94 from West
TOGO 1. Republic 2. Bantu, Hamitic, French 3. C.F.A. Franc 4. £1 = 447.0 $1 = 201.0	1. 56 000 km^{2} 2. 2 472 000; 43 per km^{2} 3. BR 49; DR 21; AI 2.6% 4. Urb. pop.: 330 (15%) 5. Lomé 135	1. GDP $599 (. . .); $269 (. . .) Agric. 34%, Indust. 16%, Others 50% 2. Cassava 460 Cocoa 15 Coffee 6 Groundnuts 20 Palm oil 19 3. Goats 748 Sheep 835 5. Roundwood 1 6. Phosphates 2 916	1. –/0.19; 64 kWh (6% hydr.) 2. Food industries . . . 3. Telephones 10; Cars 20 Rail: 65 pass.-km; 22 t-km Air: 140 pass.-km; 13 t-km Sea: 2 796 loaded; 774 unloaded	Exports $241 Cocoa Phosphates Coffee Imports $448 Cotton fabric Machinery Food Vehicles Exports to: France, W. Germany and Netherlands Imports from: France, W. Germany, U.K. and U.S.A. Aid received (net): $49 from West
TRINIDAD & TOBAGO 1. Commonwealth 2. English 3. Trinidad and Tobago Dollars 4. £1 = 5.34 $1 = 2.4	1. 5 128 km^{2} 2. 1 127 000; 222 per km^{2} 3. BR 26; DR 6; AI 0.2% 4. Urb. pop.: 460 (49%) 5. Port of Spain 63	1. GDP $3 509 (. . .); $3 147 (. . .) Agric. 3%, Indust. 54%, Other 43% 2. Rice 22 Bananas 5 Oranges 2 Grapefruits 6 Cocoa 3 Coffee 4 Copra 7 3. Cattle 77 Pigs 58 6. Natural gas 22 332 Crude petroleum 11 088	1. 18.4/4.66; 576 kWh 2a. Sugar 144 Beer 247 hl b. Petroleum products 4 514 3. Telephones 70; Cars 135 Air: 12 612 pass.-km; 22 t-km Sea: 20 832 loaded; 14 856 unloaded	Exports $2 476 Petroleum products Petroleum Imports $1 946 Crude petroleum Manufactured goods Exports to: U.S.A., Netherlands and Surinam Imports from: U.S.A., U.K., Saudi Arabia and Indonesia Revenue from tourism: $87 Aid received (net): $5 from West
TUNISIA 1. Republic 2. Arabic, French 3. Dinar 4. £1 = 0.881 $1 = 0.396	1. 164 150 km^{2} 2. 6 201 000; 37 per km^{2} 3. BR 36; DR 13; AI 2.7% 4. Urb. pop.: 2 205 (43%) 5. Tunis 944	1. GDP $4 981 (9.4%); $821 (6.8%) Agric. 17%, Indust. 17%, Others 66% 2. Wheat 680 Tomatoes 300 Oranges 106 Olives 450 Grapes 90 Dates 50 3. Sheep 3 652 Cattle 910 4. Fish 55 5. Roundwood 2 6. Lead 10 Crude petroleum 5 508 Iron ore 210 Zinc 9 Phosphates 4 057 Natural gas 3 624	1. 5.8/2.61; 1 725 kWh (1.7% hydr.) 2a. Sugar 7 Wine 450 hl Meat 121 Olive oil 92 b. Petroleum products 1 327 3. Telephones 144; Cars 120 Rail: 708 pass.-km; 1 368 t-km Air: 1 344 pass.-km; 12 t-km Sea: 4 356 loaded; 7 392 unloaded	Exports $1 766 Petroleum Olive oil Phosphates Fertilizer Imports $2 830 Machinery Wheat Textiles Iron and steel Exports to: France, Italy and W. Germany Imports from: France, W. Germany and Italy Revenue from tourism: $323 Aid received (net): $175 from West, $76 from East

For detailed table headings and notes see page 1 of this section

Country	Area and Population	Production	Manufactures	Trade
TURKEY 1. Republic 2. Turkish 3. Lira 4. £1 = 78.62 $1 = 35.35	1. 780 576 km^2 2. 44 312 000; 54 per km^2 3. BR 40; DR 15; AI 2.7% 4. Urb. pop.; 18 774 (45%) 5. Ankara 1 701	1. GDP $41 051 (7.4%); $999 (4.3%) Agric. 27%, Indust. 21%, Others 52% 2. Barley 5 217; Wheat 17 631 Apples 1 150; Oranges 703 Grapes 3 485; Tomatoes 3 136 Cottonseed 810; Cotton lint 505 Wool 56; Tobacco 287 3. Sheep 43 942; Goats 18 447 4. Fish 155 5. Roundwood 22 6. Coal 4 464; Zinc 1 Lignite 14 964; Crude petroleum 2 880 Iron ore 1 573; Antimony 1 896 t Chrome 1 175; Mercury 163 t	1. 12.2/29.8; 20 565 kWh (42% hydr.) 2a. Meat 858; Sawnwood 3 191 Sugar 1 145; Wine 660 hl Olive oil 74 b. Iron 324; Steel 1 788 Cotton yarn 44; Wool yarn 4 Petroleum products 11 244; Copper 22; Cement 13 788 3. Telephones 1 131; Cars 659 Rail: 5 616 pass.-km; 5 676 t-km Air: 1 908 pass.-km; 15 t-km Sea: 6 672 loaded; 20 520 unloaded	Exports $2 261: Cotton, Nuts, Tobacco, Raisins Imports $4 946: Machinery, Vehicles, Fertilizer, Crude petroleum, Iron and steel Exports to: W. Germany, U.S.A., Italy and France Imports from: W. Germany, U.S.A., Iran, Italy and France Revenue from tourism: $205 Aid received (net): $706 from West
UGANDA 1. Republic 2. English, Bantu 3. Ugandan Shilling 4. £1 = 16.30 $1 = 7.328	1. 236 036 km^2 2. 13 225 000; 54 per km^2 3. BR 45; DR 16; AI 3.4% 4. Urb. pop.; 747 (7%) 5. Kampala 331	1. GDP $3 075 (0.1%); $266 (−3.1%) Agric. 53%, Indust. 10%, Others 37% 2. Cassava 1 250; Millet/sorghum 850 Coffee 120; Tea 6 Cottonseed 24; Groundnuts 227 3. Cattle 5 367; Goats 2 144 4. Roundwood 20 6. Tin 120 t; Tungsten 139 Copper 8	1. 0.11/0.58; 725 kWh (97% hydr.) 2a. Meat 148; Sugar 9 Sawnwood 24; Beer 221 hl 4. Telephones 46; Cars 35 Rail: see Kenya Air: 197 pass.-km; 7.4 t-km	Exports $427: Coffee, Cotton, Copper Imports $187: Manufactured goods, Machinery, Vehicles Exports to: U.K., U.S.A., Spain and France Imports from: U.K., W. Germany, Kenya and Brazil Aid received (net): $19 from West
UNITED KINGDOM 1. Kingdom 2. English 3. English Pound 4. $1 = 0.450	1. 244 796 km^2 2. 55 836 000; 228 per km^2 3. BR 12; DR 12; AI 0.1% 4. Urb. pop.; 42 716 (76%) 5. London 6 877	1. GDP $244 457 (1.8%); $4 377 (1.8%) Agric. 3%, Indust. 30%, Others 67% 2. Barley 9 550; Wheat 7 140 Oats 535; Potatoes 6 485 Apples 370; Wool 49 3. Sheep 29 967; Cattle 13 534 4. Fish 1 005 5. Roundwood 4 6. Coal 122 808; Natural gas 366 096 Iron ore 1 089; Crude petroleum 77 796 Tin 2 340 t; Salt 7 310	1. 196.2/295.3; 283 280 kWh (2% hydr., 14% nucl.) 2a. Meat 2 928; Sawnwood 1 337 Butter & cheese 371; Sugar 1 196 Beer 66 418 hl b. Iron 12 900; Steel 21 468 Aluminium 360; Lead 125 Copper 121; Plastics 2 546 Cotton yarn 86; Wool yarn 174 Synthetic fibres 552; Silk fabric 742 Mm^2 Paper 4 165; Radios 391 Petroleum products 85 151; Vehicles: pass. 1 070; comm. 408 Ships (grt) 608; Cement 16 140 3. Telephones 23 182; Cars 14 927 Rail: 30 744 pass.-km; 19 980 t-km Air: 47 004 pass.-km; 1 248 t-km Sea: 100 908 loaded; 157 236 unloaded	Exports $91 030: Machinery, Vehicles, Textiles, Diamonds, Non-ferrous metals, Iron and steel, Alcoholic drinks, Aircraft Imports $102 969: Machinery, Crude petroleum, Non-ferrous metals, Fruit and vegetables, Diamonds, Minerals, Cereals, Butter, Meat, Textiles Exports to: U.S.A., W. Germany, France, Ireland, Belgium-Luxembourg and Netherlands Imports from: U.S.A., W. Germany, France and Netherlands Invisible trade balance: +$5 252 Revenue from tourism: $3 805 Aid given (net): $5 866
UNITED STATES 1. Federal Republic 2. English 3. U.S. Dollar 4. £1 = 2.22	1. 9 363 353 km^2 2. 220 584 000, 23 per km^2 3. BR 16; DR 9; AI 0.8% 4. Urb. pop.; 149 325 (74%) 5. Washington 3 021	1. GDP $1 878 835 (2.8%); $8 665 (1.9%) Agric. 3%, Indust. 29%, Others 68% 2. Barley 8 238; Oats 7 757 Maize 197 208; Wheat 58 289 Oranges 8 306; Grapefruit 2 491 Wine 1 583; Soya Beans 61 715 Cottonseed 5 258; Tobacco 702 Rice 6 199 3. Cattle 110 864; Pigs 60 101 4. Fish 3 512 5. Roundwood 338 6. Coal 703 752; Nickel 11 Iron ore 52 777; Tungsten 4 118 t Bauxite 1 820; Vanadium 3 875 t Copper 1 441; Natural gas 4 846 116 Gold 27 278 kg; Crude petroleum 420 456 Lead 520; Potash 2 253 Molybdenum 100; Phosphates 50 037	1. 2 049.7/2 485.5; 2 211 031 kWh (10% hydr., 11% nucl., 0.2 geo.) 2a. Meat 25 908; Butter & cheese 2 404 Sugar 5 059; Wine 17 904 hl Sawnwood 89 555; Wood pulp 42 425 b. Cotton yarn 1 284; Wool yarn 222 Synthetic Fibres 3 720; Silk fabric 7 794 Mm Paper 53 396 Copper 1 514; Magnesium 127 Iron 78 960; Steel 124 272 Aluminium 4 560; Plastics 11 232 Petroleum products: 602 867; Vehicles: pass. 8 112; comm. 2 976 Radios 10 300; Ships (grt) 706 3. Telephones 162 072; Cars 120 485 Rail: 16 452 pass.-km; 1 252 800 t-km Air: 404 556 pass.-km; 10 387 t-km Sea: 274 992 loaded; 548 928 unloaded	Exports $178 578: Machinery, Vehicles, Aircraft, Cereals, Chemical products, Iron and steel, Non-ferrous metals, Soya, Metals, Coal, Textiles Imports $217 664: Vehicles, Machinery, Iron and steel, Non-ferrous metals, Crude petroleum, Petroleum products, Clothing, Paper and cardboard, Textiles, Metals Exports to: Canada, Japan U.K., W. Germany and Mexico Imports from: Canada, Japan, W. Germany, U.K. and Mexico Invisible trade balance: +$20 970 Revenue from tourism: $6 164 Aid given (net): $10 616
UPPER VOLTA 1. Republic 2. French 3. C.F.A. Franc 4. £1 = 447.0 $1 = 201.0	1. 274 200 km^2 2. 6 728 000; 24 per km^2 3. BR 48; DR 23; AI 2.3% 4. Urb. pop.; . . . (8%) 5. Ouagadougou 169	1. GDP $547 (. . .); $91 (. . .) Agric. 42%, Indust. 12%, Others 46% 2. Millet/sorghum 1 000; Maize 80 Rice 40; Groundnuts 75 3. Cattle 2 700; Goats 2 700 5. Roundwood 5 6. Gold . . .	1. –/0.11; 70 kWh 2a. Meat 61 3. Telephones 6; Cars 11 Air: 140 pass.-km; 13 t-km	Exports $42: Livestock, Cotton Imports $191: Manufactured goods, Foods Exports to: Ivory Coast, Denmark and Netherlands Imports from: France, U.S.A. and Ivory Coast Aid received (net): $92 from West
URUGUAY 1. Republic 2. Spanish 3. Uruguayan Peso 4. £1 = 18.82 $1 = 8.464	1. 177 508 km^2 2. 2 878 000; 16 per km^2 3. BR 20; DR 10; AI 1.2; 4. Urb. pop.; 2 308 (83%) 5. Montevideo 1 230	1. GDP $3 693 (1.1%); $1 319 (0.1%) Agric. 10%, Indust. 27%, Others 63% 2. Maize 71; Wheat 380 Grapes 90; Oranges 44 Linseed 31; Wool 83 3. Sheep 18 690; Cattle 10 007 4. Fish 74 5. Roundwood 2	1. 0.15/3.1; 3 040 kWh (52% hydr.) 2a. Meat 322; Sawnwood 107 Sugar 82 b. Petroleum products 1 890 3. Telephones 268; Cars 168 Rail: 389 pass.-km; 307 t-km Air: 42 pass.-km; 0.2 t-km Sea: 473 loaded; 2 437 unloaded	Exports $788: Beef, Wool, Hides and skins Imports $1 206: Machinery, Vehicles, Crude petroleum Exports to: W. Germany, Brazil and U.S.A. Imports from: Argentina, Brazil, U.S.A. and Iraq Aid received (net): $12 from West
U.S.S.R. 1. Socialist Republic 2. Russian and others 3. Rouble 4. £1 = 1.44 $1 = 0.65	1. 22 402 200 km^2 2. 264 108 000; 12 per km^2 3. BR 18; DR 10; AI 0.9% 4. Urb. pop.; 161 043 (62%) 5. Moscow 8 011	1. NMP $540 214 (5.7%); $2 234 (4.8%) Agric. 17%, Indust. 52%, Others 31% 2. Barley 46 000; Wheat 90 100 Potatoes 90 300; Grapes 5 700 Tomatoes 6 400; Cottonseed 5 954 Tobacco 258 3. Sheep 142 600; Cattle 114 086 4. Fish 8 930 5. Roundwood 361 6. Coal 495 000; Tungsten 11 000 t Iron ore 146 398; Zinc 1 020 Bauxite 4 400; Natural gas 3 390 312 Chrome 2 400; Crude petroleum 590 916 Copper 1 150; Phosphates 24 800 Lead 590; Potash 7 500 Manganese 9 500; Salt 14 700 Molybdenum 17; Asbestos 2 470 Nickel 150; Diamonds 10 700	1. 1 674.1/1 349.9; 1 150 074 kWh (13% hydr., 3% nucl.) 2a. Meat 15 500; Sawnwood 106 000 Butter & cheese 3 000; Sugar 7 600 Wine 24 700 hl b. Iron 120 000; Steel 151 775 Aluminium 2 400; Copper 1 100 Magnesium 70; Paper 9 236 Cotton yarn 1 596; Wool yarn 447 Synthetic fibres 1 089; Silk fabric 45 648 Mm Linen 870; Radios 8 728 Petroleum products 394 708; Vehicles: pass. 1 314; comm. 780 3. Telephones 19 600; Cars . . . Rail: 332 400 pass.-km; 3 429 372 t-km Air: 9 432 pass.-km; 310 t-km Sea: 154 023 loaded; 33 104 unloaded	Exports $64 762: Machinery, Iron and steel, Crude petroleum, Non-ferrous metals, Petroleum products, Sawnwood, Cotton, Vehicles Imports $57 773: Machinery, Clothing, Ships, Iron and steel, Minerals, Railway rolling stock, Shoes Main trade is with: E. Germany, Poland, Czechoslovakia, Bulgaria and Hungary Aid given (net): $2 922

For detailed table headings and notes see page 1 of this section

Country	Area and Population	Production	Manufactures	Trade
VENEZUELA 1. Republic 2. Spanish 3. Bolivar 4. £1 = 9.545 $1 = 4.292	1. 912 050 km^2 2. 13 515 000; 14 per km^2 3. BR 36; DR 7; AI 3.1% 4. Urb. pop.; 9 559 (75%) 5. Caracas 2 576	1. GDP $35 592 (5.6%); $2 794 (2.4%) Agric. 6%, Indust. 39%, Others 55% 2. Maize 848 Bananas 961 Oranges 369 Tomatoes 135 Cocoa 15 Coffee 62 Cottonseed 32 Sesame 40 3. Cattle 9 963 Pigs 1 099 4. Fish 174 5. Roundwood 9 6. Iron ore 10 460 Natural gas 121 632 Gold 440 kg Crude petroleum 123 480 Diamonds 738 c Phosphates 109 Coal 84	1. 199/35.1; 23 051 kWh (52% hydr.) 2a. Meat 600 Sawnwood 349 Sugar 350 b. Iron 689 Steel 1 500 Cotton yarn 16 Synthetic fibres 21 Cement 3 426 Vehicles: Petroleum pass. 97; comm. 66 products 46 296 3. Telephones 742; Cars 1 200 Rail: 42 pass.-km; 15 t-km Air: 3 552 pass.-km; 113 t-km Sea: 131 316 loaded; 8 568 unloaded	Exports $13 111 Imports $9 456 Crude petroleum Machinery Petroleum products Vehicles Iron ore Iron and steel Coffee Cereals Manufactured goods Exports to: U.S.A., Netherlands, Antilles and Canada Imports from: U.S.A., W. Germany and Japan Invisible trade balance: −$2 211 Aid received (net): $6 from West
VIETNAM 1. Democratic Republic 2. Vietnamese 3. Dông 4. £1 = 4.85 $1 = 2.18	1. 332 559 km^2 2. 51 082 000; 151 per km^2 3. BR 41; DR 20; AI 2.9% 4. Urb. pop.; 8 149 (18%) 5. Hanoi 2 571	1. Agric. 29%, Indust. 7%, Others 64% 2. Rice 10 500 Cassava 3 800 Groundnuts 94 Tea 21 Maize 520 Tobacco 28 3. Cattle 1 600 Buffaloes 2 350 4. Fish 1 014 5. Roundwood 21 6. Coal 5 000 Phosphates 1 600 Salt 580	1. 5.1/5.8; 1 320 kWh (1.5% hydr.) 2a. Sawnwood 520 b. Cotton yarn 10 Cement 845 3. Telephones 47; Cars 66 Rail: 170 pass.-km; 1 t-km Air: 390 pass.-km; 4.1 t-km Sea 198 loaded; 4 875 unloaded	Main trade is with U.S.S.R. and other Communist countries and Japan, France, Singapore and Hong Kong
YEMEN 1. Republic 2. Arabic 3. Riyal 4. £1 = 10.14 $1 = 4.562	1. 195 000 km^2 2. 5 785 000; 29 per km^2 3. BR 49; DR 26; AI 3.0% 4. Urb. pop.; 331 (6%) 5. Sana 448	1. GDP 1 654 (. . .); $241 (. . .) Agric. 35%, Indust. 6%, Others 59% 2. Millet 70 Wheat 100 Coffee 3 Cottonseed 3 3. Sheep 3 700 Cattle 950	1. –/0.28; 65 kWh (77% hydr.) 3. Telephones 4; Cars . . . Sea: 25 loaded; 500 unloaded	Exports $7 Imports $1 283 Exports to: China, S. Yemen, Italy and Saudi Arabia Imports from: Saudi Arabia, Japan and India Aid received (net): $26 from West
YUGOSLAVIA 1. Federal Republic 2. Croatian, Serbian 3. Yugoslavian Dinar 4. £1 = 42.61 $1 = 19.16	1. 255 804 km^2 2. 22 160 000; 86 per km^2 3. BR 17; DR 9; AI 0.9% 4. Urb. pop.; 7 914 (39%) 5. Belgrade 775	1. NMP $32 206 (5.8%); $1 569 (4.8%) Agric. 17%, Indust. 40%, Others 43% 2. Maize 10 082 Wheat 4 512 Grapes 1 313 Wool 10 Tobacco 65 3. Sheep 7 339 Pigs 7 747 4. Fish 63 5. Roundwood 16 6. Coal 432 Gold 4 000 Lignite 41 676 Lead 130 Iron ore 1 638 Silver 162 t Antimony 2 283 Zinc 102 Bauxite 3 012 Chrome 2 Copper 111 Crude petroleum 4 140 Natural gas 18 456	1. 29.4/43.46; 48 580 kWh (50% hydr.) 2a. Meat 1 294 Sawnwood 4 067 Sugar 870 Wine 5 500 hl b. Iron 2 604 Steel 2 316 Copper 137 Lead 112 Cotton yarn 120 Wool yarn 44 Synthetic fibres 97 Ships (grt) 173 Petroleum products 13 029 3. Telephones 1 556; Cars 2 285 Rail: 10 440 pass.-km; 23 376 t-km Air: 2 724 pass.-km; 29 t-km Sea: 4 596 loaded; 20 592 unloaded	Exports $6 491 Imports $12 862 Machinery Machinery Non-ferrous metals Iron and steel Ships and boats Vehicles Clothing Textile fibres Meat Textiles Textiles Non-ferrous metals Iron and steel Chemical products Shoes Crude petroleum Exports to: Italy, U.S.S.R. and W. Germany Imports from: W. Germany, Italy and U.S.S.R. Invisible trade balance: +$1 452 Revenue from tourism: $841
ZAÏRE 1. Democratic Republic 2. Kiswahili, etc. 3. Zaïre 4. £1 = 4.501 $1 = 2.024	1. 2 345 409 km^2 2. 27 869 000; 12 per km^2 3. BR 47; DR 21; AI 2.5% 4. Urb. pop.; 7 997 (30%) 5. Kinshasa 2 008	1. GDP £3 695 (. . .); $148 (. . .) Agric. 19%, Indust. 22%, Others 59% 2. Cassava 12 000 Maize 350 Coffee 87 Groundnuts 310 Palm oil 170 Rubber 27 Bananas 310 Cottonseed 35 3. Goats 2 783 Cattle 1 144 4. Fish 100 5. Roundwood 21 6. Cobalt 33 Tin 3 300 t Copper 400 Zinc 74 Manganese 21 Diamonds 8 625 c Gold 2 270 kg Tungsten 250 t Crude petroleum 1 032	1. 2.37/1.58; 14 100 kWh (98% hydr.) 2a. Sugar 54 Beer 4 984 hl Sawnwood 90 b. Copper 646 Zinc 43 Petroleum Cement 475 products 183 3. Telephones 48; Cars 40 Rail: 467 pass.-km; 2 203 t-km Air: 756 pass.-km; 37 t-km Sea 464 loaded; 715 unloaded	Exports $925 Imports $589 Copper Machinery Diamonds Vehicles Cobalt Petroleum products Coffee Cotton fabric Palm oil Cereals Exports to: Belgium-Luxembourg, Italy and U.S.A. Imports from: Belgium-Luxembourg, U.S.A., France and W. Germany Aid received (net): $215 from West
ZAMBIA 1. Republic 2. English 3. Kwacha 4. £1 = 1.730 $1 = 0.778	1. 752 614 km^2 2. 5 649 000; 8 per km^2 3. BR 50; DR 19; AI 3.6% 4. Urb. pop.; 2 153 (39%) 5. Lusaka 559	1. GDP $2 687 (4.2%); $523 (0.9%) Agric. 13%, Indust. 35%, Others 52% 2. Maize 600 Tobacco 5 Millet/sorghum 80 Groundnuts 74 3. Cattle 1 800 Goats 300 4. Fish 48 5. Roundwood 6 6. Coal 648 Tin . . . Cobalt 5 Gold 245 kg Copper 588 Silver 28 t Lead 13 Zinc 50	1. 1.62/2.69; 8 683 kWh (98% hydr.) 2a. Meat 71 Sugar 105 Sawnwood 42 b. Copper 646 Zinc 40 Lead 14 Cement 324 3. Telephones 53; Cars 105 Air: 540 pass.-km; 37 t-km	Exports $856 Imports $630 Copper Machinery Zinc Vehicles Lead Textiles Cobalt Iron and steel Tobacco Petroleum products Exports to: Japan, U.K., W. Germany and U.S.A. Imports from: U.K., Saudi Arabia and U.S.A. Aid received (net): $84 from West
ZIMBABWE 1. Republic 2. English 3. Zimbabwe Dollar 4. £1 = 1.54 $1 = 0.69	1. 390 581 km^2 2. 7 140 000; 18 per km^2 3. BR 48; DR 15; AI 3.5% 4. Urb. pop.; 1 355 (20%) 5. Salisbury 616	1. GDP $3 569 (3.5%); $530 (0.0%) Agric. 16%, Indust. 32%, Others 52% 2. Maize 1 000 Millet/sorghum 180 Groundnuts 120 Tobacco 100 3. Cattle 5 000 Goats 2 061 5. Roundwood 8 6. Coal 3 186 Gold 12 063 kg Iron ore 1 201 Nickel 15 Chrome 542 Tin 948 t Copper 30 Asbestos 260	1. 3.42/4.14; 3 916 kWh (88% hydr.) 2a. Meat 170 Sugar 230 Sawnwood 72 b. Iron 320 Steel 350 Copper 26 3. Telephones 190; Cars 215 Rail: . . .; 3 996 t-km	Exports $1 164 Imports $937 Tobacco Machinery Asbestos Textiles Copper Vehicles Gold Mineral fuels Main trade with U.K., W. Germany and U.S.A. Aid received from West

For detailed table headings and notes see page 1 of this section

INDEX

The number printed in bold type against each index entry indicates the map page where the feature will be found. The geographical coordinates which follow the name are sometimes only approximate but are close enough for the place name to be located. Rivers have been indexed to their mouth or confluence.

An open square □ signifies that the name refers to an administrative subdivision of a country while a solid square ■ follows the name of a country. An arrow → follows the name of a river.

The alphabetical order of names composed of two or more words is governed primarily by the first word and then by the second. This rule applies even if the second word is a description or its abbreviation, R.,L.,I. for example. Names composed of a proper name (Gibraltar) and a description (Strait of) are positioned alphabetically by the proper name.

If the same place name occurs twice or more times in the index and all are in the same country, each is followed by the name of the administrative subdivision in which it is located. The names are placed in the alphabetical order of the subdivisions. If the same place name occurs twice or more in the index and the places are in different countries they will be followed by their country names, the latter governing the alphabetical order. In a mixture of these situations the primary order is fixed by the alphabetical sequence of the countries and the secondary order by that of the country subdivisions.

Abbreviations used in the index:

A. R.–Autonomous Region
A. S. S. R.–Autonomous Soviet Socialist Republic
Afghan.–Afghanistan
Afr.–Africa
Ala.–Alabama
Alas.–Alaska
Alg.–Algeria
Alta.–Alberta
Amer.–America
And. P.–Andhra Pradesh
Arch.–Archipelago
Argent.–Argentina
Ariz.–Arizona
Ark.–Arkansas
Atl. Oc. – Atlantic Ocean
Austral. – Australia
B. – Baie, Bahía, Bay, Bucht, Bugt
B.A. – Buenos Aires
B.C. – British Columbia
Bangla. – Bangladesh
Barr. – Barrage
Bay. – Bayern
Belg. – Belgium
Berks. – Berkshire
Bol. – Bolshoi
Boliv. – Bolivia
Bots. – Botswana
Br. – British
Bri. – Bridge
Bt. – Bight
Bucks. – Buckinghamshire
Bulg. – Bulgaria
C. – Cabo, Cap, Cape, Coast
C. Prov. – Cape Province
Calif. – California
Camb. – Cambodia
Cambs. – Cambridgeshire
Can. – Canada
Cent. – Central
Chan. – Channel
Co. – Country
Colomb. – Colombia
Colo. – Colorado
Conn. – Connecticut
Cord. – Cordillera
Cr. – Creek
Cumb. – Cumbria
Czech. – Czechoslovakia
D.C. – District of Columbia
Del. – Delaware
Dep. – Dependency
Derby. – Derbyshire
Des. – Desert
Dist. – District
Dj. – Djebel
Dumf. & Gall. – Dumfries and Galloway
E. – East
Eng. – England
Fed. – Federal, Federation
Fla. – Florida
For. – Forest
Fr. – France, French
Fs. – Falls
Ft. – Fort
G. – Golfe, Golfo, Gulf, Guba
Ga. – Georgia
Ger. – Germany
Glam. – Glamorgan
Glos. – Gloucestershire
Gr. – Grande, Great, Greater, Group
H.K. – Hong Kong
H.P. – Himachal Pradesh
Hants. – Hampshire
Harb. – Harbor, Harbour
Hd. – Head
Here. & Worcs. – Hereford and Worcester
Herts. – Hertfordshire
Hts. – Heights
Hung. – Hungary
I.o.M. – Isle of Man
I.(s). – Île, Ilha, Insel, Isla, Island, Isle
Id. – Idaho
Ill. – Illinois
Ind. – Indiana
Ind. Oc. – Indian Ocean
Indon. – Indonesia
J. – Jabal, Jabel, Jazira
Junc. – Junction
K. – Kap, Kapp
K. – Kuala
Kal. – Kalmyk A.S.S.R.
Kans. – Kansas
Kep. – Kepulauan
Ky. – Kentucky
L. – Lac, Lacul, Lago, Lagoa, Lake, Limni, Loch, Lough
La. – Lousiana
Lancs. – Lancashire
Leb. – Lebanon
Leics. – Leicestershire
Lim. – Limerick
Lincs. – Lincolnshire
Lit. – Little
Lr. – Lower
Mad. P. – Madhya Pradesh
Madag. – Madagascar
Malay. – Malaysia
Man. – Manitoba
Manch. – Manchester
Maran. – Maranhão
Mass. – Massachusetts
Md. – Maryland
Me. – Maine
Mend. – Mendoza
Mér. – Méridionale
Mich. – Michigan
Mid. – Middle
Minn. – Minnesota
Miss. – Mississippi
Mo. – Missouri
Mong. – Mongolia
Mont. – Montana
Moroc. – Morocco
Mozam. – Mozambique
Mt.(e). – Mont, Monte, Monti, Montaña, Mountain
Mys. – Mysore
N. – Nord, Norte, North, Northern, Nouveau
N.B. – New Brunswick
N.C. – North Carolina
N.D. – North Dakota
N.H. – New Hampshire
N.I. – North Island
N.J. – New Jersey
N. Mex. – New Mexico
N.S. – Nova Scotia
N.S.W. – New South Wales
N.T. – Northern Territory
N.W.T. – North West Territory
N.Y. – New York
N.Z. – New Zealand
Nat. – National
Nat.Park. – National Park
Nebr. – Nebraska
Neth. – Netherlands
Nev. – Nevada
Newf. – Newfoundland
Nic. – Nicaragua
Northants. – Northamptonshire
Northumb. – Northumberland
Notts. – Nottinghamshire
O. – Oued, ouadi
Occ. – Occidentale
O.F.S. – Orange Free State
Okla. – Oklahoma
Ont. – Ontario
Or. – Orientale
Oreg. – Oregon
Os. – Ostrov
Oxon. – Oxfordshire
Oz. – Ozero
P. – Pass, Passo, Pasul, Pulau
P.E.I. – Prince Edward Island
P.N.G. – Papua New Guinea
P.O. – Post Office
P. Rico.–Puerto Rico
Pa. – Pennsylvania
Pac. Oc. – Pacific Ocean
Pak. – Pakistan
Parag. – Paraguay
Pass. – Passage
Pen. – Peninsula, Peninsule
Phil. – Philippines
Pk. – Park, Peak
Plat. – Plateau
P-ov. – Poluostrov
Port. – Portugal, Portuguese
Prom. – Promontory
Prov. – Province, Provincial
Pt. – Point
Pta. – Ponta, Punta
Pte. – Pointe
Qué. – Québec
Queens. – Queensland
R. – Rio, River
R.I. – Rhode Island
R.S.F.S.R. – Russian Soviet Federal Socialist Republic
Ra.(s). – Range(s)
Raj. – Rajasthan
Reg. – Region
Rep. – Republic
Res. – Reserve, Reservoir
Rhld. – Pfz. – Rheinland–Pfalz
S. – San, South
S. Afr. – South Africa
S. Austral. – South Australia
S.C. – South Carolina
S.D. – South Dakota
S.-Holst. – Schleswig-Holstein
S.I. – South Island
S. Leone–Sierra Leone
S.S.R. – Soviet Socialist Republic
Sa. – Serra, Sierra
Sard. – Sardinia
Sask. – Saskatchewan
Scot. – Scotland
Sd. – Sound
Sept. – Septentrionale
Sev. – Severnaja
Sib. – Siberia
Som. – Somerset
Span. – Spanish
Sprs. – Springs
St. – Saint
Sta. – Santa, Station
Staffs. – Staffordshire
Ste. – Sainte
Sto. – Santo
Str. – Strait, Stretto
Switz. – Switzerland
T.O. – Telegraph Office
Tas. – Tasmania
Tenn. – Tennessee
Terr. – Territory
Tex. – Texas
Tg. – Tanjung
Thai. – Thailand
Tipp. – Tipperary
Trans. – Transvaal
U.K. – United Kingdom
U.S.A. – United States of America
U.S.S.R. – Union of Soviet Socialist Republics
Ukr. – Ukraine
Ut.P. – Uttar Pradesh
Utd. – United
V. – Vorota
Va. – Virginia
Vdkhr. – Vodokhranilishche
Venez. – Venezuela
Vic. – Victoria
Viet. – Vietnam
Vol. – Volcano
Vt. – Vermont
W. – Wadi, West
W.A. – Western Australia
W. Isles–Western Isles
W. Va. – West Virginia
Wash. – Washington
Wilts. – Wiltshire
Wis. – Wisconsin
Wlkp. – Wielkopolski
Wyo. – Wyoming
Yorks. – Yorkshire
Yug. – Yugoslavia
Zap. – Zapadnaja
Zimb.-Rhod. – Zimbabwe-Rhodesia

A

Aachen 30 50 47N 6 4 E
Aâlâ en Nîl □ 91 8 50N 29 55 E
Aalen 31 48 49N 10 6 E
Aalma Ach Chaab 44 33 7N 35 9 E
Aalsmeer 16 52 17N 4 43 E
Aalst 16 50 56N 4 2 E
Aalten 16 51 56N 6 35 E
Aarau 31 47 23N 8 4 E
Aarberg 31 47 2N 7 16 E
Aare → 31 47 33N 8 14 E
Aargau □ 31 47 26N 8 10 E
Aarschot 16 50 59N 4 49 E
Aba, China 58 32 59N 101 42 E
Aba, Nigeria 89 5 10N 7 19 E
Aba, Zaïre 91 3 58N 30 17 E
Âbâ, Jazîrat 91 13 30N 32 31 E
Abacaxis → 135 3 54S 58 47W
Abadan 46 30 22N 48 20 E
Abade, Ethiopia 91 9 22N 38 3 E
Abade, Iran 47 31 8N 52 40 E
Abadin 22 43 21N 7 29W
Abadla 86 31 2N 2 45W
Abaeté 139 19 9S 45 27W
Abaeté → 139 18 2S 45 12W
Abaetetuba 138 1 40S 48 50W
Abagnar Qi 60 43 52N 116 2 E
Abai 141 25 58S 55 54W
Abak 89 4 58N 7 50 E
Abakaliki 89 6 22N 8 2 E
Abakan 41 53 40N 91 10 E
Abal Nam 90 25 20N 38 37 E
Abalemma 89 16 12N 7 50 E
Abancay 136 13 35S 72 55W
Abanilla 25 38 12N 1 3W
Abano Terme 27 45 22N 11 46 E
Abapó 137 18 48S 63 25W
Abarán 25 38 12N 1 23W
Abarqū 47 31 10N 53 20 E
Abasan 44 31 19N 34 21 E
Abasheres 91 11 33N 35 23 E
Abashiri 63 44 0N 144 15 E
Abashiri-Wan 63 44 0N 144 30 E
Abau 69 10 11S 148 46 E
Abaújszántó 33 48 16N 21 12 E
Abay 40 49 38N 72 53 E
Abaya L. 91 6 30N 37 50 E
Abaza 40 52 39N 90 6 E
Abbadia San Salvatore 27 42 53N 11 40 E
Abbay (Nîl el Azraq) → 91 15 38N 32 31 E
Abbaye, Pt. 112 46 58N 88 4W
Abbeville, France 19 50 6N 1 49 E
Abbeville, La., U.S.A. 119 30 0N 92 7W
Abbeville, S.C., U.S.A. 113 34 12N 82 21W
Abbiategrasso 26 45 23N 8 55 E
Abbieglassie 73 27 15S 147 28 E
Abbotsford, B.C., Can. 108 49 5N 122 20W
Abbotsford, Qué., Can. 115 45 25N 72 53W
Abbotsford, U.S.A. 118 44 55N 90 20W
Abbottabad 48 34 10N 73 15 E
'Abd al Kūrī 45 12 5N 52 20 E
Abe, L. 91 11 8N 41 47 E
Abéché 85 13 50N 20 35 E
Abejar 24 41 48N 2 47W
Abekr 91 12 45N 28 50 E
Abêlessa 86 22 58N 4 47 E
Abelti 91 8 10N 37 30 E
Abengourou 88 6 42N 3 27W
Åbenrå 11 55 3N 9 25 E
Abensberg 31 48 49N 11 51 E
Abeokuta 89 7 3N 3 19 E
Aber 94 2 12N 32 25 E
Aberaeron 13 52 15N 4 16W
Aberayron = Aberaeron 13 52 15N 4 16W
Abercorn 73 25 12S 151 5 E
Abercorn = Mbala 95 8 46S 31 17 E
Abercrombie → 76 33 54S 149 8 E
Aberdare 13 51 43N 3 27W
Aberdare Ra. 94 0 15S 36 50 E
Aberdeen, Austral. 77 32 9S 150 56 E
Aberdeen, Can. 109 52 20N 106 8W
Aberdeen, S. Afr. 96 32 28S 24 2 E
Aberdeen, U.K. 14 57 9N 2 6W
Aberdeen, Ala., U.S.A. 113 33 49N 88 33W
Aberdeen, Idaho, U.S.A. 120 42 57N 112 50W
Aberdeen, Ohio, U.S.A. 117 38 39N 83 46W
Aberdeen, S.D., U.S.A. 118 45 30N 98 30W
Aberdeen, Wash., U.S.A. 122 47 0N 123 50W
Aberdovey 13 52 33N 4 3W
Aberfeldy, Austral. 75 37 42S 146 22 E
Aberfeldy, U.K. 14 56 37N 3 50W
Abergaria-a-Velha 22 40 41N 8 32W
Abergavenny 13 51 49N 3 1W
Abermain 76 32 49S 151 26 E
Abernathy 119 33 49N 101 49W
Aberystwyth 13 52 25N 4 6W
Abha 90 18 0N 42 34 E
Abhayapuri 52 26 24N 90 38 E
Abidiya 90 18 18N 34 3 E
Abidjan 88 5 26N 3 58W
Abilene, Kans., U.S.A. 118 39 0N 97 16W
Abilene, Texas, U.S.A. 119 32 22N 99 40W
Abingdon, U.K. 13 51 40N 1 17W
Abingdon, Ill., U.S.A. 116 40 53N 90 23W
Abingdon, Va., U.S.A. 113 36 46N 81 56W
Abington Reef 72 18 0S 149 35 E
Abitau → 109 59 53N 109 3W
Abitau L. 109 60 27N 107 15W
Abitibi L. 102 48 40N 79 40W
Abiy Adi 91 13 39N 39 3 E
Abkhaz A.S.S.R. □ 39 43 0N 41 0 E
Abkit 41 64 10N 157 10 E
Abnûb 90 27 18N 31 4 E
Åbo 9 60 28N 22 15 E
Abo, Massif d' 87 21 41N 16 8 E
Abocho 89 7 35N 6 56 E
Abohar 48 30 10N 74 10 E
Aboisso 88 5 30N 3 5W
Abomey 89 7 10N 2 5 E
Abondance 21 46 18N 6 42 E
Abong Mbang 92 4 0N 13 8 E
Abonnema 89 4 41N 6 49 E
Abony 33 47 12N 20 3 E
Aboso 88 5 23N 1 57W
Abou Deïa 85 11 20N 19 20 E
Aboyne 14 57 4N 2 48W
Abqaiq 46 26 0N 49 45 E
Abra Pampa 140 22 43S 65 42W
Abrantes 23 39 24N 8 7W
Abraveses 22 40 41N 7 55W
Abreojos, Pta. 124 26 50N 113 40W
Abreschviller 19 48 39N 7 6 E
Abrets, Les 21 45 32N 5 35 E
Abri, Esh Shimâliya, Sudan 90 20 50N 30 27 E
Abri, Janub Kordofân, Sudan 91 11 40N 30 21 E
Abrolhos, Banka 139 18 0S 38 0W
Abruzzi □ 27 42 15N 14 0 E
Absaroka Ra. 120 44 40N 110 0W
Abū al Khasib 46 30 25N 48 0 E
Abū 'Ali 46 27 20N 49 27 E
Abu Arish 45 16 53N 42 48 E
Abû Ballas 90 24 26N 27 36 E
Abu Deleiq 91 15 57N 33 48 E
Abū Dhabī 47 24 28N 54 36 E
Abû Dis, Jordan 44 31 47N 35 16 E
Abû Dis, Sudan 90 19 12N 33 38 E
Abû Dom 91 16 18N 32 25 E
Abû Gabra 91 11 2N 26 50 E
Abū Ghōsh 44 31 48N 35 6 E
Abû Gubeiha 91 11 30N 31 15 E
Abu Habl, Khawr → 91 12 37N 31 0 E
Abu Hamed 90 19 32N 33 13 E
Abu Haraz 91 14 35N 33 30 E
Abû Haraz 90 19 8N 32 18 E
Abû Higar 91 12 50N 33 59 E
Abu Kamal 46 34 30N 41 0 E
Abū Madd, Ra's 46 24 50N 37 7 E
Abu Markha 46 25 4N 38 22 E
Abu Qir 90 31 18N 30 0 E
Abu Qireiya 90 24 5N 35 28 E
Abu Qurqâs 90 28 1N 30 44 E
Abû Rudies 90 29 0N 33 15 E
Abu Salama 90 27 10N 35 51 E
Abû Simbel 90 22 18N 31 40 E
Abu Tig 90 27 4N 31 15 E
Abu Tiga 91 12 47N 34 12 E
Abû Zabad 91 12 25N 29 10 E
Abū Zābī 47 24 28N 54 22 E
Abufari 137 5 25S 62 59W
Abuja 89 9 16N 7 2 E
Abunã 137 9 40S 65 20W
Abunã → 137 9 41S 65 20W
Aburatsu 64 31 34N 131 24 E
Aburo, Mt. 94 2 4N 30 53 E
Abut Hd. 81 43 7S 170 15 E
Abwong 91 9 2N 32 14 E
Åby 11 58 40N 16 10 E
Aby, Lagune 88 5 15N 3 14W
Acacías 134 3 59N 73 46W
Acajutla 126 13 36N 89 50W
Açallândia 138 5 0S 47 50W
Acámbaro 124 20 0N 100 40W
Acaponeta 124 22 30N 105 20W
Acapulco de Juárez 125 16 51N 99 56W
Acarai, Serra 135 1 50N 57 50W
Acaraú 138 2 53S 40 7W
Acari 138 6 31S 36 38W
Acarí 136 15 25S 74 36W
Acarigua 134 9 33N 69 12W
Acatlán 125 18 10N 98 3W
Acayucan 125 17 59N 94 58W
Accéglio 26 44 28N 6 59 E
Accomac 112 37 43N 75 40W
Accra 89 5 35N 0 6W
Accrington 12 53 46N 2 22W
Acebal 140 33 20S 60 50W
Aceh □ 56 4 15N 97 30 E
Acerenza 29 40 50N 15 58 E
Acerra 29 40 57N 14 22 E
Aceuchal 23 38 39N 6 30W
Achacachi 136 16 3S 68 43W
Achaguas 134 7 46N 68 14W
Achalpur 50 21 22N 77 32 E
Achao 142 42 28S 73 30W
Acheng 61 45 30N 126 58 E
Achenkirch 31 47 32N 11 45 E
Achensee 31 47 26N 11 45 E
Acher 48 23 10N 72 32 E
Achern 31 48 37N 8 5 E
Acheron → 81 42 16S 173 4 E
Achill 15 53 56N 9 55W
Achill Hd. 15 53 59N 10 15W
Achill I. 15 53 58N 10 5W
Achill Sound 15 53 53N 9 55W
Achim 30 53 1N 9 2 E
Achinsk 41 56 20N 90 20 E
Achol 91 6 35N 31 32 E
Acireale 29 37 37N 15 9 E
Ackerman 119 33 20N 89 8W
Ackley 116 42 33N 93 3W
Acklins I. 127 22 30N 74 0W
Acme 108 51 33N 113 30W
Acobamba 136 12 52S 74 35W
Acomayo 136 13 55S 71 38W
Aconcagua □, Argent. 140 32 50S 70 0W
Aconcagua □, Chile 140 32 15S 70 30W
Aconcagua, Cerro 140 32 39S 70 0W
Aconquija, Mt. 140 27 0S 66 0W
Acopiara 138 6 6S 39 27W
Açores, Is. dos 128 38 44N 29 0W
Acorizal 137 15 12S 56 22W
Acquapendente 27 42 45N 11 50 E
Acquasanta 27 42 46N 13 24 E
Acquaviva delle Fonti 29 40 53N 16 50 E
Acqui 26 44 40N 8 28 E
Acre = 'Akko 44 32 55N 35 4 E
Acre □ 136 9 1S 71 0W
Acre → 136 8 45S 67 22W
Acri 29 39 29N 16 23 E
Acs 33 47 42N 18 0 E
Acton 106 43 38N 80 3W
Acton Vale 105 45 39N 72 34W
Açu 138 5 34S 36 54W
Ad Dahnā 46 24 30N 48 10 E
Ad Dam 45 20 33N 44 45 E
Ad Dammam 46 26 20N 50 5 E
Ad Dar al Hamrā 46 27 20N 37 45 E
Ad Dilam 46 23 55N 47 10 E
Ada, Ethiopia 91 8 48N 38 51 E
Ada, Ghana 89 5 44N 0 40 E
Ada, Minn., U.S.A. 118 47 20N 96 30W
Ada, Ohio, U.S.A. 117 40 46N 83 49W
Ada, Okla., U.S.A. 119 34 50N 96 45W
Ada, Yugo. 33 45 49N 20 9 E
Adaja → 22 41 32N 4 52W
Adale 45 2 58N 46 27 E
Ådalslinden 10 63 27N 16 55 E
Adam 47 22 15N 57 28 E
Adam, Mt. 142 51 34S 60 4W
Adamantina 139 21 42S 51 4W
Adamaoua, Massif de l' 89 7 20N 12 20 E
Adamawa Highlands = Adamaoua, Massif de l' 89 7 20N 12 20 E
Adamello, Mt. 26 46 10N 10 34 E
Adami Tulu 91 7 53N 38 41 E
Adaminaby 75 36 0S 148 45 E
Adams, Mass., U.S.A. 115 42 38N 73 8W
Adams, N.Y., U.S.A. 115 43 50N 76 3W
Adams, Wis., U.S.A. 118 43 59N 89 50W
Adam's Bridge 51 9 15N 79 40 E
Adams Center 115 43 51N 76 1W
Adams L. 108 51 10N 119 40W
Adams, Mt. 122 46 10N 121 28W
Adam's Peak 51 6 48N 80 30 E
Adamuz 23 38 2N 4 32W
Adana 46 37 0N 35 16 E
Adanero 22 40 56N 4 36W
Adapazarı 46 40 48N 30 25 E
Adarama 91 17 10N 34 52 E
Adare, C. 143 71 0S 171 0 E
Adaut 57 8 8S 131 7 E
Adavale 73 25 52S 144 32 E
Adayio 91 14 29N 40 50 E
Adda → 26 45 8N 9 53 E
Addis Ababa = Addis Abeba 91 9 2N 38 42 E
Addis Abeba 91 9 2N 38 42 E
Addis Alem 91 9 0N 38 17 E
Addison, Ill., U.S.A. 117 41 56N 87 59W
Addison, N.Y., U.S.A. 114 42 9N 77 15W
Addyston 117 39 8N 84 43W
Adebour 89 13 17N 11 50 E
Adel, Ga., U.S.A. 113 31 10N 83 28W
Adel, Iowa, U.S.A. 116 41 37N 94 1W
Adelaide, Austral. 73 34 52S 138 30 E
Adelaide, Bahamas 126 25 0N 77 31W
Adelaide, Madag. 97 32 42S 26 20 E
Adelaide I. 143 67 15S 68 30W
Adelaide Pen. 100 68 15N 97 30W
Adelaide River 78 13 15S 131 7 E
Adelanto 123 34 35N 117 22W
Adele, I. 78 15 32S 123 9 E
Adélie, Terre 143 68 0S 140 0 E
Adelong 76 35 16S 148 4 E
Ademuz 24 40 5N 1 13W
Aden = Al 'Adan 45 12 45N 45 12 E
Aden, G. of 45 13 0N 50 0 E
Adendorp 96 32 25S 24 30 E
Adgz 86 30 47N 6 30W
Adhoi 48 23 26N 70 32 E
Adi 57 4 15S 133 30 E
Adi Daro 91 14 20N 38 14 E
Adi Keyih 91 14 51N 39 22 E
Adi Kwala 91 14 38N 38 48 E
Adi Ugri 91 14 58N 38 48 E
Adieu, C. 79 32 0S 132 10 E
Adieu Pt. 78 15 14S 124 35 E
Adigala 91 10 24N 42 15 E
Adige → 27 45 9N 12 20 E
Adigrat 91 14 20N 39 26 E
Adilabad 50 19 33N 78 20 E
Adin 120 41 10N 121 0W
Adin Khel 47 32 45N 68 5 E
Adirampattinam 51 10 28N 79 20 E
Adirondack Mts. 115 44 0N 74 15W
Adis Dera 91 10 12N 38 46 E
Adjim 87 33 47N 10 50 E
Adjohon 89 6 41N 2 32 E
Adjud 34 46 7N 27 10 E
Adjumani 94 3 20N 31 50 E
Adlavik Is. 103 55 2N 57 45W
Adler 39 43 28N 39 52 E
Admer 87 20 21N 5 27 E
Admer, Erg d' 87 24 0N 9 5 E
Admiralty B. 143 62 0S 59 0W
Admiralty G. 78 14 20S 125 55 E
Admiralty I. 100 57 40N 134 35W
Admiralty Inlet 120 48 0N 122 40W
Admiralty Is. 69 2 0S 147 0 E
Admiralty Ra. 143 72 0S 164 0 E
Ado 89 6 36N 2 56 E
Ado Ekiti 89 7 38N 5 12 E
Adok 91 8 10N 30 20 E
Adola 91 11 14N 41 44 E
Adonara 57 8 15S 123 5 E
Adoni 51 15 33N 77 18W
Adony 33 47 6N 18 52 E
Adour → 20 43 32N 1 32W
Adra, India 49 23 30N 86 42 E
Adra, Spain 25 36 43N 3 3W
Adrano 29 37 40N 14 49 E
Adrar 86 27 51N 0 11W
Adré 85 13 40N 22 20 E
Adri 87 27 32N 13 2 E
Ádria 27 45 4N 12 3 E
Adrian, Mich., U.S.A. 117 41 55N 84 0W
Adrian, Mo., U.S.A. 116 38 24N 94 21W
Adrian, Tex., U.S.A. 119 35 19N 102 37W
Adriatic Sea 6 43 0N 16 0 E
Adua 57 1 45S 129 50 E
Aduku 94 2 03N 32 45 E
Adung Long 52 28 7N 97 42 E
Adur 51 9 8N 76 40 E
Adwa, Ethiopia 91 14 15N 38 52 E
Adwa, Si. Arab. 46 27 15N 42 35 E
Adzhar A.S.S.R. □ 39 42 0N 42 0 E
Adzopé 88 6 7N 3 49W
Ægean Sea 35 37 0N 25 0 E
Æolian Is. = Eólie, I. 29 38 30N 14 50 E
Aerht'ai Shan 62 46 40N 92 45 E
Ærø 11 54 52N 10 25 E
Ærøskøbing 11 54 53N 10 24 E
Afafi, Massif d' 87 22 11N 15 10 E
Afándou 35 36 18N 28 12 E
Afarag, Erg 86 23 50N 2 47 E
Afareait 68 17 33S 149 47W
Afdera 91 13 16N 41 5 E
Affreville = Khemis Miliania 86 36 11N 2 14 E
Afghanistan ■ 47 33 0N 65 0 E
Afgoi 45 2 7N 44 59 E
Afif 46 23 53N 42 56 E
Afikpo 89 5 53N 7 54 E
Aflisses, O. → 86 28 40N 0 50 E
Aflou 86 34 7N 2 3 E
Afodo 91 10 18N 34 49 E
Afogados da Ingâzeira 138 7 45S 37 59W
Afognak I. 100 58 10N 152 50W

Afragola 29 40 54N 14 15 E
Africa 82 10 0N 20 0 E
Afton 115 42 14N 75 31W
Aftout 86 26 50N 3 45W
Afuá 138 0 15 S 50 20W
Afula 44 32 37N 35 17 E
Afyon Karahisar 46 38 45N 30 33 E
Aga 90 30 55N 31 10 E
Agadès 89 16 58N 7 59 E
Agadir 86 30 28N 9 35W
Agadir Tissint 86 29 57N 7 16W
Agana 68 13 28N 144 45 E
Agano → 63 37 57N 139 8 E
Agapa 41 71 27N 89 15 E
Agar 48 23 40N 76 2 E
Agaro 91 7 50N 36 38 E
Agartala 52 23 50N 91 23 E
Agassiz 108 49 14N 121 46W
Agat 91 15 38N 38 16 E
Agats 57 5 33 S 138 0 E
Agattu I. 100 52 25N 172 30 E
Agbélouvé 89 6 35N 1 14 E
Agboville 88 5 55N 4 15W
Agdam 39 40 0N 46 58 E
Agdash 39 40 44N 47 22 E
Agde 20 43 19N 3 28 E
Agde, C. d' 20 43 16N 3 28 E
Agen 20 44 12N 0 38 E
Ageo 65 35 58N 139 36 E
Ager Tay 87 20 0N 17 41 E
Agersø 11 55 13N 11 12 E
Agger 11 56 47N 8 13 E
Äggius 28 40 56N 9 4 E
Aghil Mts. 49 36 0N 77 0 E
Aginskoye 41 51 6N 114 32 E
Agira 29 37 40N 14 30 E
Aglou 86 29 50N 9 50W
Agly → 20 42 46N 3 3 E
Agnew 79 28 1 S 120 30 E
Agnibilékrou 88 7 10N 3 11W
Agnita 34 45 59N 24 40 E
Agnone 29 41 49N 14 20 E
Ago 65 34 20N 136 51 E
Agofie 89 8 27N 0 15 E
Agogna → 26 45 4N 8 52 E
Agogo 91 7 50N 28 45 E
Agon 18 49 2N 1 34W
Agön 10 61 34N 17 23 E
Agordo 27 46 18N 12 2 E
Agout → 20 43 47N 1 41 E
Agra 48 27 17N 77 58 E
Agramunt 24 41 48N 1 6 E
Agreda 24 41 51N 1 55W
Agri → 29 40 13N 16 44 E
Ağri Daği 46 39 50N 44 15 E
Ağri Karakose 46 39 44N 43 3 E
Agrigento 28 37 19N 13 33 E
Agrínion 35 38 37N 21 27 E
Agrópoli 29 40 23N 14 59 E
Água Branca 138 5 50 S 42 40W
Agua Caliente, Baja California, Mexico 123 32 29N 116 59W
Agua Caliente, Sinaloa, Mexico 124 26 30N 108 20W
Agua Caliente Springs 123 32 56N 116 19W
Água Clara 137 20 25 S 52 45W
Agua Hechicero 123 32 26N 116 14W
Agua Preta → 135 1 41 S 63 48W
Agua Prieta 124 31 20N 109 32W
Aguachica 134 8 19N 73 38W
Aguada Cecilio 142 40 51 S 65 51W
Aguadas 134 5 40N 75 38W
Aguadilla 127 18 27N 67 10W
Aguadulce 126 8 15N 80 32W
Aguanaval → 124 23 45N 103 10W
Aguanga 123 33 27N 116 51W
Aguanish 103 50 14N 62 2W
Aguanus → 103 50 13N 62 5W
Aguapeí 137 16 12 S 59 43W
Aguapeí → 139 21 0 S 51 0W
Aguapey → 140 29 7 S 56 36W
Aguaray Guazú → 140 24 47 S 57 19W
Aguarico → 134 0 59 S 75 11W
Aguas → 24 41 20N 0 30W
Aguas Blancas 140 24 15 S 69 55W
Aguas Calientes, Sierra de 140 25 26 S 66 40W
Águas Formosas 139 17 5 S 40 57W
Aguascalientes 124 21 53N 102 12W
Aguascalientes □ 124 22 0N 102 20W
Agudo 23 38 59N 4 52W
Águeda 22 40 34N 8 27W
Agueda → 22 41 2N 6 56W
Aguelt el Kadra 86 25 3N 7 6W
Aguié 89 13 31N 7 46 E
Aguilafuente 22 41 13N 4 7W
Aguilar 23 37 31N 4 40W
Aguilar de Campóo 22 42 47N 4 15W
Aguilares 140 27 26 S 65 35W
Aguilas 25 37 23N 1 35W
Aguja, C. de la 134 11 18N 74 12W
Agulaa 91 13 40N 39 40 E
Agulhas Basin 53 45 0 S 25 0 E
Agulhas, Kaap 96 34 52 S 20 0 E
Agung 56 8 20 S 115 28 E
Agur, Israel 44 31 42N 34 55 E
Agur, Uganda 94 2 28N 32 55 E
Agusan → 57 9 0N 125 30 E
Agustín Codazzi 134 10 2N 73 14W
Agvali 39 42 36N 46 8 E
Aha Mts. 96 19 45 S 21 0 E
Ahaggar 87 23 0N 6 30 E
Ahamansu 89 7 38N 0 35 E
Ahar 46 38 35N 47 0 E
Ahaura → 81 42 21 S 171 34 E
Ahaus 30 52 4N 7 1 E
Ahelledjem 87 26 37N 6 58 E
Ahipara B. 80 35 5 S 173 5 E
Ahiri 50 19 30N 80 0 E
Ahlen 30 51 45N 7 52 E
Ahmad Wal 48 29 18N 65 58 E
Ahmadabad (Ahmedabad) 48 23 0N 72 40 E
Ahmadnagar (Ahmednagar) 50 19 7N 74 46 E
Ahmadpur 48 29 12N 71 10 E
Ahmar Mts. 91 9 20N 41 15 E
Ahoada 89 5 8N 6 36 E
Ahome 124 25 55N 109 11W
Ahr → 30 50 33N 7 17 E
Ahrensbök 30 54 0N 10 34 E
Ahrweiler 30 50 31N 7 3 E
Ahsā, Wahāt al 46 25 50N 49 0 E
Ahuachapán 126 13 54N 89 52W
Ahuriri → 81 44 31 S 170 12 E
Åhus 11 55 56N 14 18 E
Ahvāz 46 31 20N 48 40 E
Ahvenanmaa = Åland 9 60 15N 20 0 E
Ahwar 45 13 30N 46 40 E
Ahzar 89 15 30N 3 20 E
Aiari → 134 1 22N 68 36W
Aibaq 47 36 15N 68 5 E
Aichach 31 48 28N 11 9 E
Aichi □ 65 35 0N 137 15 E
Aidone 29 37 26N 14 26 E
Aiello Cálabro 29 39 6N 16 12 E
Aigle 31 46 18N 6 58 E
Aigle, L' 18 48 46N 0 38 E
Aignay-le-Duc 19 47 40N 4 43 E
Aigre 20 45 54N 0 1 E
Aigua 141 34 13 S 54 46W
Aiguebelle, Parc 104 48 30N 78 45W
Aigueperse 20 46 3N 3 13 E
Aigues-Mortes 21 43 35N 4 12 E
Aigues-Mortes, G. d' 21 43 31N 4 3 E
Aiguilles 21 44 47N 6 51 E
Aiguillon 20 44 18N 0 21 E
Aiguillon, L' 20 46 20N 1 16W
Aigurande 20 46 27N 1 49 E
Aihui 62 50 10N 127 30 E
Aija 136 9 50 S 77 45W
Aijal 52 23 40N 92 44 E
Aiken 113 33 34N 81 50W
Ailao Shan 58 24 0N 101 20 E
Aillant-sur-Tholon 19 47 52N 3 20 E
Aillik 103 55 11N 59 18W
Ailly-sur-Noye 19 49 45N 2 20 E
Ailsa Craig 106 43 8N 81 33W
Ailsa Craig, I. 14 55 15N 5 7W
Aim 41 59 0N 133 55 E
Aimere 57 8 45 S 121 3 E
Aimogasta 140 28 33 S 66 50W
Aimorés 139 19 30 S 41 4W
Ain □ 21 46 5N 5 20 E
Ain → 21 45 45N 5 11 E
Ain Banaiyan 47 23 0N 51 0 E
Aïn-Beïda 87 35 50N 7 29 E
Ain ben Khellil 86 33 15N 0 49W
Aïn Ben Tili 86 25 59N 9 27W
Aïn Benian 86 36 48N 2 55 E
Ain Dalla 90 27 20N 27 23 E
Ain Dār 46 25 55N 49 10 E
Ain el Mafki 90 27 30N 28 15 E
Aïn Galaka 85 18 10N 18 30 E
Aïn Girba 90 29 20N 25 14 E
Aïn M'lila 87 36 2N 6 35 E
Ain Qeiqab 90 29 42N 24 55 E
Aïn-Sefra 86 32 47N 0 37W
Ain Sheikh Murzûk 90 26 47N 27 45 E
Ain Sukhna 90 29 32N 32 20 E
Aïn Tédelès 86 36 0N 0 21 E
Aïn-Témouchent 86 35 16N 1 8W
Aïn Touta 87 35 26N 5 54 E
Ain Zeitûn 90 29 10N 25 48 E
Aïn Zorah 86 34 37N 3 32W
Ainabo 45 9 0N 46 25 E
Ainaži 36 57 50N 24 24 E
Aínos Óros 35 38 10N 20 35 E
Ainsworth 118 42 33N 99 52W
Aioi 64 34 48N 134 28 E
Aipe 134 3 13N 75 15W
Aiquile 137 18 10 S 65 10W
Aïr 89 18 30N 8 0 E
Airaines 19 49 58N 1 55 E
Airão 135 1 56 S 61 22W
Airdrie 14 55 53N 3 57W
Aire 19 50 37N 2 22 E
Aire →, France 19 49 18N 4 55 E
Aire →, U.K. 12 53 42N 0 55W
Aire, Isla del 24 39 48N 4 16 E
Aire-sur-l'Adour 20 43 42N 0 15W
Aireys Inlet 74 38 29 S 144 5 E
Airvault 18 46 50N 0 8W
Aisch → 31 49 46N 11 1 E
Aisen □ 142 46 30 S 73 0W
Aisne □ 19 49 42N 3 40 E
Aisne → 19 49 26N 2 50 E
Aït Melloul 86 30 25N 9 29W
Aitana, Sierra de 25 38 35N 0 24W
Aitape 69 3 11 S 142 22 E
Aitkin 118 46 32N 93 43W
Aitolikón 35 38 26N 21 21 E
Aiuaba 138 6 38 S 40 7W
Aiud 34 46 19N 23 44 E
Aix-en-Provence 21 43 32N 5 27 E
Aix-la-Chapelle = Aachen 30 50 47N 6 4 E
Aix-les-Bains 21 45 41N 5 53 E
Aix-sur-Vienne 20 45 48N 1 8 E
Aiyang, Mt. 69 5 10 S 141 20 E
Aiyansh 108 55 17N 129 2W
Áiyina 35 37 45N 23 26 E
Aiyínion 35 40 28N 22 28 E
Aíyion 35 38 15N 22 5 E
Aizenay 18 46 44N 1 38W
Aizpute 36 56 43N 21 40 E
Aizuwakamatsu 63 37 30N 139 56 E
Ajaccio 21 41 55N 8 40 E
Ajaccio, G. d' 21 41 52N 8 40 E
Ajaju → 134 0 59N 72 20W
Ajalpan 125 18 22N 97 15W
Ajana 79 27 56 S 114 35 E
Ajanta Ra. 50 20 28N 75 50 E
Ajax 107 43 50N 79 1W
Ajax, Mt. 81 42 35 S 172 5 E
Ajayan Pt. 68 13 15N 144 43 E
Ajdabiyah 87 30 54N 20 4 E
Ajdovščina 27 45 54N 13 54 E
Ajibar 91 10 35N 38 36 E
Ajka 33 47 4N 17 31 E
'Ajlun 44 32 18N 35 47 E
Ajman 47 25 25N 55 30 E
Ajmer 48 26 28N 74 37 E
Ajo 121 32 18N 112 54W
Ajok 91 9 15N 28 28 E
Ajua 88 4 50N 1 55W
Ak Dağ 46 36 30N 30 0 E
Akaba 89 8 10N 1 2 E
Akabli 86 26 49N 1 31 E
Akaishi-Dake 65 35 27N 138 9 E
Akaishi-Sammyaku 65 35 25N 138 10 E
Akaki Beseka 91 8 55N 38 45 E
Akala 91 15 39N 36 13 E
Akaroa 81 43 49 S 172 59 E
Akasha 90 21 10N 30 32 E
Akashi 64 34 45N 135 0 E
Akbou 87 36 31N 4 31 E
Akechi 65 35 18N 137 23 E
Akelamo 57 1 35N 129 40 E
Akershus fylke □ 10 60 0N 11 10 E
Akeru → 50 17 25N 80 0 E
Aketi 92 2 38N 23 47 E
Akhalkalaki 39 41 27N 43 25 E
Akhaltsikhe 39 41 40N 43 0 E
Akharnaí 35 38 5N 23 44 E
Akhelóös → 35 38 36N 21 14 E
Akhendria 35 34 58N 25 16 E
Akhéron → 35 39 20N 20 29 E
Akhisar 46 38 56N 27 48 E
Akhladhókambos 35 37 31N 22 35 E
Akhmîm 90 26 31N 31 47 E
Akhnur 49 32 52N 74 45 E
Akhtubinsk (Petropavlovskiy) 39 48 13N 46 7 E
Akhty 39 41 30N 47 45 E
Akhtyrka 36 50 25N 35 0 E
Aki 64 33 30N 133 54 E
Aki-Nada 64 34 5N 132 40 E
Akimiski I. 102 52 50N 81 30W
Akimovka 38 46 44N 35 0 E
Åkirkeby 11 55 4N 14 55 E
Akita 63 39 45N 140 7 E
Akjoujt 88 19 45N 14 15W
Akka 86 29 22N 8 9W
'Akko 44 32 55N 35 4 E
Akkol, Kazakh, U.S.S.R. 40 43 36N 70 45 E
Akkol, Kazakh, U.S.S.R. 40 45 0N 75 39 E
Aklampa 89 8 15N 2 10 E
Aklavik 100 68 12N 135 0W
Akmonte 23 37 13N 6 38W
Aknoul 86 34 40N 3 55W
Akō 64 34 45N 134 24 E
Ako 89 10 19N 10 48 E
Akobo → 91 7 48N 33 3 E
Akola 50 20 42N 77 2 E
Akonolinga 89 3 50N 12 18 E
Akordat 91 15 30N 37 40 E
Akosombo Dam 89 6 20N 0 5 E
Akot, India 50 21 10N 77 10 E
Akot, Sudan 91 6 31N 30 9 E
Akpatok I. 101 60 25N 68 8W
Akranes 8 64 19N 21 58W
Akreïjit 88 18 19N 9 11W
Akrítas Venétiko, Ákra 35 36 43N 21 54 E
Akron, Colo., U.S.A. 118 40 13N 103 15W
Akron, Ind., U.S.A. 117 41 2N 86 1W
Akron, Ohio, U.S.A. 114 41 7N 81 31W
Akrotíri, Ákra 35 40 26N 25 27 E
Aksai Chih 49 35 15N 79 55 E
Aksaray 46 38 25N 34 2 E
Aksarka 40 66 31N 67 50 E
Aksay 40 50 41N 52 26 E
Akşehir 46 38 18N 31 30 E
Aksenovo Zilovskoye 41 53 20N 117 40 E
Aksu 62 41 5N 80 10 E
Aksum 91 14 5N 38 40 E
Aktogay, Kazakh, U.S.S.R. 40 44 25N 76 44 E
Aktogay, Kazakh, U.S.S.R. 40 46 57N 79 40 E
Aktyubinsk, U.S.S.R. 40 50 7N 57 10 E
Aktyubinsk, U.S.S.R. 40 50 17N 57 10 E
Aku 89 6 40N 7 18 E
Akune 64 32 1N 130 12 E
Akure 89 7 15N 5 5 E
Akureyri 8 65 40N 18 6W
Akusha 39 42 18N 47 30 E
Al Abyār 87 32 9N 20 29 E
Al 'Adan 45 12 45N 45 0 E
Al Amādiyah 46 37 5N 43 30 E
Al Amārah 46 31 55N 47 15 E
Al 'Aqabah 44 29 31N 35 0 E
Al Ashkhara 47 21 50N 59 30 E
Al Ayn al Mugshin 45 19 35N 54 40 E
Al 'Azīzīyah 87 32 30N 13 1 E
Al Badi 46 22 0N 46 35 E
Al Barah 44 31 55N 35 12 E
Al Barkāt 87 24 56N 10 14 E
Al Basrah 46 30 30N 47 50 E
Al Baydā 85 32 30N 21 40 E
Al Bu'ayrāt 87 31 24N 15 44 E
Al Buqay'ah 44 32 15N 35 30 E
Al Dīwaniyah 46 32 0N 45 0 E
Al Fallujah 46 33 20N 43 55 E
Al Fāw 46 30 0N 48 30 E
Al Haddār 46 21 58N 45 57 E
Al Hadithan 46 34 0N 41 13 E
Al Hāmad 46 31 30N 39 30 E
Al Hamar 46 22 23N 46 6 E
Al Hariq 46 23 29N 46 27 E
Al Hasakah 46 36 35N 40 45 E
Al Hauta 45 16 5N 48 20 E
Al Havy 46 32 5N 46 5 E
Al Hillah, Iraq 46 32 30N 44 25 E
Al Hillah, Si. Arab. 46 23 35N 46 50 E
Al Hilwah 46 23 24N 46 48 E
Al Hindiyah 46 32 30N 44 10 E
Al Hoceïma 86 35 8N 3 58W
Al Hufrah, Awbārī, Libya 87 25 32N 14 1 E
Al Hufrah, Misrātah, Libya 87 29 5N 18 3 E
Al Hūfuf 46 25 25N 49 45 E
Al Husayyāt 87 30 24N 20 37 E
Al Husn 44 32 29N 35 52 E
Al Irq 85 29 5N 21 35 E
Al Ittihad = Madinat al Shaab 45 12 50N 45 0 E
Al Jāfūrah 46 25 0N 50 15 E
Al Jahrah 46 29 25N 47 40 E
Al Jalāmid 46 31 20N 39 45 E
Al Jarzirah 85 26 10N 21 20 E
Al Jawf 85 24 10N 23 24 E
Al Jazir 45 18 30N 56 31 E
Al Jazirah 46 33 30N 44 0 E
Al Jubail 46 27 0N 49 50 E
Al Juwara 45 19 0N 57 13 E
Al Khābūrah 47 23 57N 57 5 E
Al Khalaf 45 20 30N 58 13 E
Al Khalīl = Hebron 44 31 32N 35 6 E
Al Kharj 46 24 0N 47 0 E
Al Khums (Homs) 87 32 40N 14 17 E
Al Kūt 46 32 30N 46 0 E
Al Kuwayt 46 29 20N 48 0 E
Al Lādhiqiyah 46 35 30N 35 45 E
Al Līth 90 20 9N 40 15 E
Al Madīnah 46 24 35N 39 52 E
Al-Mafraq 44 32 17N 36 14 E
Al Majma'ah 46 25 57N 45 22 E
Al Manamāh 47 26 10N 50 30 E
Al Marj 85 32 25N 20 30 E
Al Masīrah 45 20 25N 58 50 E
Al Matamma 45 16 10N 44 30 E
Al Mawsil 46 36 15N 43 5 E
Al Mazra 44 31 16N 35 31 E

Al Miqdadīyah **46** 34 0N 45 0 E
Al Mish'āb **46** 28 12N 48 36 E
Al Mubarraz **46** 25 30N 49 40 E
Al Muharraq **47** 26 15N 50 40 E
Al Mukha **45** 13 18N 43 15 E
Al Musayyib **46** 32 40N 44 25 E
Al Muwaylih **46** 27 40N 35 30 E
Al Qaddāhīyah **87** 31 15N 15 9 E
Al Qāmishli **46** 37 10N 41 10 E
Al Qaryah ash Sharqīyah **87** 30 28N 13 40 E
Al Qaşabāt **87** 32 39N 14 1 E
Al Qatif **46** 26 35N 50 0 E
Al Qaţrūn **87** 24 56N 15 3 E
Al Quaisūmah **46** 28 10N 46 20 E
Al Quds **44** 31 47N 35 10 E
Al Qunfidha **90** 19 3N 41 4 E
Al Quraiyat **47** 23 17N 58 53 E
Al Qurnah **46** 31 1N 47 25 E
Al 'Ula **46** 26 35N 38 0 E
Al Uqaylah **87** 30 12N 19 10 E
Al Uqayr **46** 25 40N 50 15 E
Al' Uwayqilah ash Sharqīgah **46** 30 30N 42 10 E
Al 'Uyūn **46** 26 30N 43 50 E
Al Wajh **90** 26 10N 36 30 E
Al Wakrah **47** 25 10N 51 40 E
Al Wari'āh **46** 27 51N 47 25 E
Al Wātīyah **87** 32 28N 11 57 E
Ala **26** 45 46N 11 0 E
Alabama □ **113** 33 0N 87 0W
Alabama → **113** 31 8N 87 57W
Alabaster **106** 44 10N 83 33W
Alaejos **22** 41 18N 5 13W
Alagna Valsésia **26** 45 51N 7 56 E
Alagoa Grande **138** 7 3S 35 35W
Alagoas □ **138** 9 0S 36 0W
Alagoinhas **139** 12 7S 38 20W
Alagón **24** 41 46N 1 12W
Alagón → **23** 39 44N 6 53W
Alajuela **126** 10 2N 84 8W
Alakamisy **97** 21 19S 47 14 E
Alalapura **135** 2 20N 56 25W
Alalaú → **135** 0 30S 61 9W
Alameda, Spain **23** 37 12N 4 39W
Alameda, Calif., U.S.A. **122** 37 46N 122 15W
Alameda, Idaho, U.S.A. **120** 43 2N 112 30W
Alameda, N. Mex., U.S.A. **121** 35 10N 106 43W
Alamitos, Sierra de los **124** 37 21N 115 10W
Alamo **123** 36 21N 115 10W
Alamo Crossing **123** 34 16N 113 33W
Alamogordo **121** 32 59N 106 0W
Alamos **124** 27 0N 109 0W
Alamosa **121** 37 30N 106 0W
Åland **9** 60 15N 20 0 E
Aland **50** 17 36N 76 35 E
Alandroal **23** 38 41N 7 24W
Alandur **51** 13 0N 80 15 E
Alange, Presa de **23** 38 45N 6 18W
Alanis **23** 38 3N 5 43W
Alanson **106** 45 27N 84 47W
Alanya **46** 36 38N 32 0 E
Alaotra, L. **97** 17 30S 48 30 E
Alapayevsk **40** 57 52N 61 42 E
Alar del Rey **22** 42 38N 4 20W
Al'Aramah **46** 25 30N 46 0 E
Alaraz **22** 40 45N 5 17W
Alaska □ **100** 65 0N 150 0W
Alaska, G. of **100** 58 0N 145 0W
Alaska Highway **108** 60 0N 130 0W
Alaska Pen. **100** 56 0N 160 0W
Alaska Range **100** 62 50N 151 0W
Alássio **26** 44 1N 8 10 E
Alataw Shankou **62** 45 5N 81 57 E
Alatri **28** 41 44N 13 21 E
Alatyr **37** 54 45N 46 35 E
Alatyr → **37** 54 52N 46 36 E
Alausi **134** 2 0S 78 50W
Álava □ **24** 42 48N 2 28W
Alava, C. **120** 48 10N 124 40W
Alaverdi **39** 41 15N 44 37 E
Alawoona **73** 34 45S 140 30 E
Alayor **24** 39 57N 4 8 E
Alazan → **39** 41 5N 46 40 E
Alba **26** 44 41N 8 1 E
Alba de Tormes **22** 40 50N 5 30W
Alba Iulia **34** 46 8N 23 39 E
Albac **34** 46 28N 23 1 E
Albacete **25** 39 0N 1 50W
Albacete □ **25** 38 50N 2 0W
Albacutya, L. **74** 35 45S 141 58 E
Ålbæk **11** 57 36N 10 25 E
Ålbæk Bucht **11** 57 35N 10 40 E
Albaida **25** 38 51N 0 31W
Albalate de las Nogueras **24** 40 22N 2 18W
Albalate del Arzobispo **24** 41 6N 0 31W
Albanel **105** 48 53N 72 27W
Albania ■ **35** 41 0N 20 0 E
Albano Laziale **28** 41 44N 12 40 E
Albany, Austral. **79** 35 1S 117 58 E
Albany, Ga., U.S.A. **113** 31 40N 84 10W
Albany, Ind., U.S.A. **117** 40 18N 85 13W
Albany, Minn., U.S.A. **118** 45 37N 94 38W
Albany, Mo., U.S.A. **116** 40 15N 94 20W
Albany, N.Y., U.S.A. **115** 42 35N 73 47W
Albany, Oreg., U.S.A. **120** 44 41N 123 0W
Albany, Tex., U.S.A. **119** 32 45N 99 20W
Albany, Wis., U.S.A. **116** 42 43N 89 26W
Albany → **102** 52 17N 81 31W
Albardón **140** 31 20S 68 30W
Albarracín **24** 40 25N 1 26W
Albarracín, Sierra de **24** 40 30N 1 30W
Albatross B. **72** 12 45S 141 30 E
Albatross Pt. **80** 38 7S 174 44 E
Albegna → **27** 42 30N 11 11 E
Albemarle **113** 35 27N 80 15W
Albemarle Sd. **113** 36 0N 76 30W
Albenga **26** 44 3N 8 12 E
Alberche → **22** 39 58N 4 46W
Alberdi **140** 26 14S 58 20W
Alberes, Mts. **24** 42 28N 2 56 E
Alberga **73** 27 12S 135 28 E
Alberique **25** 39 7N 0 31W
Albersdorf **30** 54 8N 9 19 E
Albert, Austral. **76** 32 22S 147 30 E
Albert, France **19** 50 0N 2 38 E
Albert Canyon **108** 51 8N 117 41W
Albert Edward, Mt. **69** 8 20S 147 24 E
Albert Edward Ra. **78** 18 17S 127 57 E
Albert L., Austral. **73** 35 30S 139 10 E
Albert L., U.S.A. **120** 42 40N 120 8W
Albert, L. = Mobutu Sese Seko, L. **94** 1 30N 31 0 E
Albert Lea **118** 43 32N 93 20W
Albert Nile → **94** 3 36N 32 2 E
Albert Town **127** 22 37N 74 33 E
Alberta □ **108** 54 40N 115 0W
Alberti **140** 35 1S 60 16W
Albertinia **96** 34 11S 21 34 E
Alberton, Austral. **75** 38 35S 146 40 E
Alberton, Can. **103** 46 50N 64 0W
Albertville **21** 45 40N 6 22 E
Albertville = Kalemie **94** 5 55S 29 9 E
Alberz, Reshteh-Ye Kūkhā-Ye **47** 36 0N 52 0 E
Albi **20** 43 56N 2 9 E
Albia **116** 41 0N 92 50W
Albina **135** 5 37N 54 15W
Albina, Ponta **96** 15 52S 11 44 E
Albino **26** 45 47N 9 48 E
Albion, Idaho, U.S.A. **120** 42 21N 113 37W
Albion, Ill., U.S.A. **117** 38 23N 88 4W
Albion, Ind., U.S.A. **117** 41 24N 85 25W
Albion, Mich., U.S.A. **117** 42 15N 84 45W
Albion, Nebr., U.S.A. **118** 41 47N 98 0W
Albion, Pa., U.S.A. **114** 41 53N 80 21W
Albion Park **76** 34 36S 150 45 E
Albocácer **24** 40 21N 0 1 E
Alböke **11** 56 57N 16 47 E
Alborán **23** 35 57N 3 0W
Alborea **25** 39 17N 1 24W
Ålborg **11** 57 2N 9 54 E
Ålborg B. **11** 56 50N 10 35 E
Albox **25** 37 23N 2 8W
Albreda **108** 52 35N 119 10W
Albuera, La **23** 38 45N 6 49W
Albufeira **23** 37 5N 8 15W
Albula → **31** 46 38N 9 30 E
Albuñol **25** 36 48N 3 11W
Albuquerque, Brazil **137** 19 23S 57 26W
Albuquerque, U.S.A. **121** 35 5N 106 47W
Albuquerque, Cayos de **126** 12 10N 81 50W
Alburg **115** 44 58N 73 19W
Alburno, Mte. **29** 40 32N 15 15 E
Alburquerque **23** 39 15N 6 59W
Albury **75** 36 3S 146 56 E
Alby **10** 62 30N 15 28 E
Alcácer do Sal **23** 38 22N 8 33W
Alcaçovas **23** 38 23N 8 9W
Alcalá de Chisvert **24** 40 19N 0 13 E
Alcalá de Guadaira **23** 37 20N 5 50W
Alcalá de Henares **24** 40 28N 3 22W
Alcalá de los Gazules **23** 36 29N 5 43W
Alcalá la Real **23** 37 27N 3 57W
Alcamo **28** 37 59N 12 55 E
Alcanadre **24** 42 24N 2 7W
Alcanadre → **24** 41 43N 0 12W
Alcanar **24** 40 33N 0 28 E
Alcanede **23** 39 25N 8 49W
Alcanena **23** 39 27N 8 40W
Alcañices **22** 41 41N 6 21W
Alcaníz **24** 41 2N 0 8W
Alcântara **138** 2 20S 44 30W
Alcántara **23** 39 41N 6 57W
Alcantara L. **109** 60 57N 108 9W
Alcantarilla **25** 37 59N 1 12W
Alcaracejos **23** 38 24N 4 58W
Alcaraz **25** 38 40N 2 29W
Alcaraz, Sierra de **25** 38 40N 2 20W
Alcarria, La **24** 40 31N 2 45W
Alcaudete **23** 37 35N 4 5W
Alcázar de San Juan **25** 39 24N 3 12W
Alcira **25** 39 9N 0 30W
Alcoa **113** 35 50N 84 0W
Alcobaça **23** 39 32N 9 0W
Alcobendas **24** 40 32N 3 38W
Alcolea del Pinar **24** 41 2N 2 28W
Alcora **24** 40 5N 0 14W
Alcoutim **23** 37 25N 7 28W
Alcova **120** 42 37N 106 52W
Alcoy **25** 38 43N 0 30W
Alcubierre, Sierra de **24** 41 45N 0 22W
Alcublas **24** 39 48N 0 43W
Alcudia **24** 39 51N 3 9 E
Alcudia, Bahía de **24** 39 45N 3 14 E
Alcudia, Sierra de la **23** 38 34N 4 30W
Aldabra Is. **53** 9 22S 46 28 E
Aldama **125** 23 0N 98 4W
Aldan **41** 58 40N 125 30 E
Aldan → **41** 63 28N 129 35 E
Aldeburgh **13** 52 9N 1 35 E
Aldeia Nova **23** 37 55N 7 24W
Alder **120** 45 27N 112 3W
Alder Pk. **122** 35 53N 121 22W
Alderney, I. **18** 49 42N 2 12W
Aldershot **13** 51 15N 0 43W
Aldersyde **108** 50 40N 113 53W
Alectown **76** 32 53S 148 17 E
Aledo **116** 41 10N 90 50W
Alefa **91** 11 55N 36 55 E
Aleg **88** 17 3N 13 55W
Alegre **139** 20 50S 41 30W
Alegrete **141** 29 40S 56 0W
Aleisk **40** 52 40N 83 0 E
Alejandro Selkirk, I. **67** 33 50S 80 15W
Aleksandriya **38** 48 42N 33 3 E
Aleksandriyskaya **39** 43 59N 47 0 E
Aleksandrov **37** 56 23N 38 44 E
Aleksandrovac **33** 44 28N 21 13 E
Aleksandrovka **38** 48 55N 32 20 E
Aleksandrovo **34** 43 14N 24 51 E
Aleksandrovsk-Sakhaliniskiy **41** 50 50N 142 20 E
Aleksandrovskiy Zavod **41** 50 40N 117 50 E
Aleksandrovskoye **40** 60 35N 77 50 E
Aleksandrów Kujawski **32** 52 53N 18 43 E
Aleksandrów Łódźki **32** 51 49N 19 17 E
Alekseyevka **37** 50 43N 38 40 E
Aleksin **37** 54 31N 37 9 E
Aleksinac **33** 43 31N 21 42 E
Além Paraíba **139** 21 52S 42 41W
Alemania, Argent. **140** 25 40S 65 30W
Alemania, Chile **140** 25 10S 69 55W
Ålen **10** 62 51N 11 17 E
Alençon **18** 48 27N 0 4 E
Alenuihaha Chan. **110** 20 25N 156 0W
Aleppo = Ḥalab **46** 36 10N 37 15 E
Aléria **21** 42 5N 9 26 E
Alert Bay **108** 50 30N 126 55W
Alès **21** 44 9N 4 5 E
Aleşd **34** 47 3N 22 22 E
Alessándria **26** 44 54N 8 37 E
Ålestrup **11** 56 42N 9 29 E
Ålesund **8** 62 28N 6 12 E
Alet **91** 8 14N 29 2 E
Alet-les-Bains **20** 43 0N 2 14 E
Aleutian Is. **100** 52 0N 175 0W
Aleutian Trench **66** 48 0N 180 0
Alexander **118** 47 51N 103 40W
Alexander Arch. **100** 57 0N 135 0W
Alexander B. **96** 28 36S 16 33 E
Alexander, C. **68** 6 35S 156 30 E
Alexander City **113** 32 58N 85 57W
Alexander I. **143** 69 0S 70 0W
Alexander, Mt. **79** 28 58S 120 16 E
Alexandra, Austral. **74** 37 8S 145 40 E
Alexandra, N.Z. **81** 45 14S 169 25 E
Alexandra Falls **108** 60 29N 116 18W
Alexandria, Austral. **72** 19 5S 136 40 E
Alexandria, B.C., Can. **108** 52 35N 122 27W
Alexandria, Ont., Can. **107** 45 19N 74 38W
Alexandria, Rumania **34** 43 57N 25 24 E
Alexandria, S. Afr. **96** 33 38S 26 28 E
Alexandria, Ind., U.S.A. **117** 40 18N 85 40W
Alexandria, Ky., U.S.A. **117** 38 58N 84 23W
Alexandria, La., U.S.A. **119** 31 20N 92 30W
Alexandria, Minn., U.S.A. **118** 45 50N 95 20W
Alexandria, Mo., U.S.A. **116** 40 27N 91 28W
Alexandria, S.D., U.S.A. **118** 43 40N 97 45W
Alexandria, Va., U.S.A. **112** 38 47N 77 1W
Alexandria = El Iskandarîya **90** 31 0N 30 0 E
Alexandria Bay **115** 44 20N 75 52W
Alexandrina, L. **73** 35 25S 139 10 E
Alexandroúpolis **35** 40 50N 25 54 E
Alexis **116** 41 4N 90 33W
Alexis → **103** 52 33N 56 8W
Alexis Creek **108** 52 10N 123 20W
Alfambra **24** 40 33N 1 5W
Alfândega da Fé **22** 41 20N 6 59W
Alfaro **24** 42 10N 1 50W
Alfeld **30** 52 0N 9 49 E
Alfenas **141** 21 20S 46 10W
Alfiós → **35** 37 40N 21 33 E
Alfonsine **27** 44 30N 12 1 E
Alford **14** 57 13N 2 42W
Alfred, Me., U.S.A. **115** 43 28N 70 40W
Alfred, N.Y., U.S.A. **114** 42 15N 77 45W
Alfred Town **76** 35 8S 147 30 E
Alfredton **80** 40 41S 175 54 E
Alfreton **12** 53 6N 1 22W
Alfta **10** 61 21N 16 4 E
Alga **40** 49 53N 57 20 E
Algaba, La **23** 37 27N 6 1W
Algar **23** 36 40N 5 39W
Algarinejo **23** 37 19N 4 9W
Algarve **23** 36 58N 8 20W
Algeciras **23** 36 9N 5 28W
Algemesí **25** 39 11N 0 27W
Alger **86** 36 42N 3 8 E
Algeria ■ **86** 35 10N 3 11 E
Alghero **28** 40 34N 8 20 E
Algiers = Alger **86** 36 42N 3 8 E
Algoabaai **96** 33 50S 25 45 E
Algodonales **23** 36 54N 5 24W
Algodor → **22** 39 55N 3 53W
Algoma, Oreg., U.S.A. **120** 42 25N 121 54W
Algoma, Wis., U.S.A. **112** 44 35N 87 27W
Algona **116** 43 4N 94 14W
Algonac **106** 42 37N 82 32W
Algonquin **117** 42 10N 88 18W
Algonquin Prov. Park **107** 45 50N 78 30W
Alhama de Almería **25** 36 57N 2 34W
Alhama de Aragón **24** 41 18N 1 54W
Alhama de Granada **23** 37 0N 3 59W
Alhama de Murcia **25** 37 51N 1 25W
Alhambra, Spain **25** 38 54N 3 4W
Alhambra, Calif., U.S.A. **123** 34 2N 118 10W
Alhambra, Ill., U.S.A. **116** 38 52N 89 45W
Alhaurín el Grande **23** 36 39N 4 41W
Alhucemas = Al-Hoceïma **86** 35 8N 3 58W
Ali al Gharbi **46** 32 30N 46 45 E
Ali Bayramly **39** 39 59N 48 52 E
Ali Khel **48** 33 56N 69 35 E
Ali Sabiet **91** 11 10N 42 44 E
Ália **28** 37 47N 13 42 E
Aliābād **47** 28 10N 57 35 E
Aliaga **24** 40 40N 0 42W
Aliákmon → **35** 40 30N 22 36 E
Alibag **50** 18 38N 72 56 E
Alibo **91** 9 52N 37 5 E
Alibunar **33** 45 5N 20 57 E
Alicante **25** 38 23N 0 30W
Alicante □ **25** 38 30N 0 37W
Alice, Can. **107** 45 47N 77 14W
Alice, S. Afr. **96** 32 48S 26 55 E
Alice, U.S.A. **119** 27 47N 98 1W
Alice →, Queens., Austral. **72** 24 2S 144 50 E
Alice →, Queens., Austral. **72** 15 35S 142 20 E
Alice Arm **108** 55 29N 129 31W
Alice Downs P.O. **78** 17 45S 127 56 E
Alice, Punta dell' **29** 39 23N 17 10 E
Alice Springs **72** 23 40S 133 50 E
Alicedale **96** 33 15S 26 4 E
Aliceville **113** 33 9N 88 10W
Alick Cr. → **72** 20 55S 142 20 E
Alicudi, I. **29** 38 33N 14 20 E
Alida **109** 49 25N 101 55W
Aligarh, Raj., India **48** 25 55N 76 15 E
Aligarh, Ut. P., India **48** 27 55N 78 10 E
Aligudarz **46** 33 25N 49 45 E
Alijó **22** 41 16N 7 27W
Alimena **29** 37 42N 14 4 E
Alingsås **11** 57 56N 12 31 E
Alipur **48** 29 25N 70 55 E
Alipur Duar **52** 26 30N 89 35 E
Aliquippa **114** 40 38N 80 18W
Aliste → **22** 41 34N 5 58W
Alivérion **35** 38 24N 24 2 E
Aliwal North **96** 30 45S 26 45 E
Alix **108** 52 24N 113 11W
Aljezur **23** 37 18N 8 49W
Aljustrel **23** 37 55N 8 10W
Alkamari **89** 13 27N 11 10 E
Alkmaar **16** 52 37N 4 45 E

All American Canal **121** 32 45N 115 0W
Allada **89** 6 41N 2 9 E
Allah Dad **48** 25 38N 67 34 E
Allahabad **49** 25 25N 81 58 E
Allakh-Yun **41** 60 50N 137 5 E
Allal Tazi **86** 34 30N 6 20W
Allan **109** 51 53N 106 4W
Allanche **20** 45 14N 2 57 E
Allanmyo **52** 19 30N 95 17 E
Allanridge **96** 27 45S 26 40 E
Allansford **74** 38 26S 142 39 E
Allanton **81** 45 55S 170 15 E
Allanwater **102** 50 14N 90 10W
Allaqi, Wadi → **90** 23 7N 32 47 E
Allariz **22** 42 11N 7 50W
Allassac **20** 45 15N 1 29 E
Allegan **117** 42 32N 85 52W
Allegany **114** 42 6N 78 30W
Allegheny → **114** 40 27N 80 0W
Allegheny Mts. **112** 38 0N 80 0W
Allegheny Res. **114** 42 0N 78 55W
Allègre **20** 45 12N 3 41 E
Allen **142** 38 58S 67 50W
Allen, Bog of **15** 53 15N 7 0W
Allen, L. **15** 54 12N 8 5W
Allenby (Hussein) Bridge **44** 31 53N 35 33 E
Allende **124** 28 20N 100 50W
Allentown **115** 40 36N 75 30W
Alleppey **51** 9 30N 76 28 E
Aller → **30** 52 57N 9 10 E
Allevard **21** 45 24N 6 5 E
Alliance, Surinam **135** 5 50N 54 50W
Alliance, Nebr., U.S.A. **118** 42 10N 102 50W
Alliance, Ohio, U.S.A. **114** 40 53N 81 7W
Allier □ **20** 46 25N 3 0 E
Allier → **19** 46 57N 3 4 E
Alligator Creek **72** 19 23S 146 58 E
Allingåbro **11** 56 28N 10 20 E
Allinge **11** 55 17N 14 50 E
Allison **116** 42 45N 92 48W
Alliston **106** 44 9N 79 52W
Alloa **14** 56 7N 3 49W
Allos **21** 44 15N 6 38 E
Alma, Can. **105** 48 35N 71 40W
Alma, Ga., U.S.A. **113** 31 33N 82 28W
Alma, Kans., U.S.A. **118** 39 1N 96 22W
Alma, Mich., U.S.A. **106** 43 25N 84 40W
Alma, Nebr., U.S.A. **118** 40 10N 99 25W
Alma, Wis., U.S.A. **118** 44 19N 91 54W
Alma Ata **40** 43 15N 76 57 E
Almada **23** 38 40N 9 9W
Almaden **72** 17 22S 144 40 E
Almadén **23** 38 49N 4 52W
Almagro **23** 38 50N 3 45W
Almanor, L. **120** 40 15N 121 11W
Almansa **25** 38 51N 1 5W
Almanza **22** 42 39N 5 3W
Almanzor, Pico de **22** 40 15N 5 18W
Almanzora → **25** 37 14N 1 46W
Almarcha, La **24** 39 41N 2 24W
Almas **139** 11 33S 47 9W
Almazán **24** 41 30N 2 30W
Almazora **24** 39 57N 0 3W
Almeirim, Brazil **135** 1 30S 52 34W
Almeirim, Port. **23** 39 12N 8 37W
Almelo **16** 52 22N 6 42 E
Almenar **24** 41 43N 2 12W
Almenara, Brazil **139** 16 11S 40 42W
Almenara, Spain **24** 39 46N 0 14W
Almenara, Sierra de **25** 37 34N 1 32W
Almendralejo **23** 38 41N 6 26W
Almería **25** 36 52N 2 27W
Almería □ **25** 37 20N 2 20W
Almería, G. de **25** 36 41N 2 28W
Almirante **14** 9 10N 82 30W
Almirante Montt, G. **142** 51 52S 72 50W
Almirós **35** 39 11N 22 45 E
Almodôvar **23** 37 31N 8 2W
Almodóvar del Campo **23** 38 43N 4 10W
Almogia **23** 36 50N 4 32W
Almonaster la Real **23** 37 52N 6 48W
Almont **106** 42 53N 83 2W
Almonte **107** 45 14N 76 12W
Almonte → **23** 39 41N 6 28W
Almora **49** 29 38N 79 40 E
Almoradi **25** 38 7N 0 46W
Almorox **22** 40 14N 4 24W
Almoustarat **89** 17 35N 0 8 E
Älmult **11** 56 33N 14 8 E
Almuñécar **23** 36 43N 3 41W
Almunia de Doña Godina, La **24** 41 29N 1 23W
Alnif **86** 31 10N 5 8W
Alnwick **12** 55 25N 1 42W
Aloi **94** 2 16N 33 10 E
Alon **52** 22 12N 95 5 E
Alonsa **109** 50 50N 99 0W
Alor **57** 8 15S 124 30 E
Alor Setar **55** 6 7N 100 22 E
Alora **23** 36 49N 4 46W
Alosno **23** 37 33N 7 7W
Alotau **69** 10 16S 150 30 E
Alougoum **86** 30 17N 6 56W
Aloysius Mt. **79** 26 0S 128 38 E
Alpaugh **122** 35 53N 119 29W
Alpedrinha **22** 40 6N 7 27W
Alpena **106** 45 6N 83 24W
Alpercatas → **138** 6 2S 44 19W
Alpes-de-Haute-Provence □ **21** 44 8N 6 10 E
Alpes-Maritimes □ **21** 43 55N 7 10 E
Alpha, Austral. **72** 23 39S 146 37 E
Alpha, U.S.A. **116** 41 11N 90 23W
Alphonse, I. **53** 7 0S 52 45 E
Alpi Apuane **26** 44 7N 10 14 E
Alpi Lepontine **31** 46 22N 8 27 E
Alpi Orobie **26** 46 7N 10 0 E
Alpi Retiche **31** 46 30N 10 0 E
Alpiarça **23** 39 15N 8 35W
Alpine, Ariz., U.S.A. **121** 33 57N 109 4W
Alpine, Calif., U.S.A. **123** 32 50N 116 46W
Alpine, Tex., U.S.A. **119** 30 25N 103 35W
Alps **6** 47 0N 8 0 E
Alpujarras, Las **25** 36 55N 3 20W
Alrø **11** 55 52N 10 5 E
Alroy Downs **72** 19 20S 136 5 E
Alsace **19** 48 15N 7 25 E
Alsask **109** 51 21N 109 59W
Alsásua **24** 42 54N 2 10W
Alsen **10** 63 23N 13 56 E
Alsfeld **30** 50 44N 9 19 E
Alsten **8** 65 58N 12 40 E
Alstonville **77** 28 51S 153 27 E
Alta Gracia **140** 31 40S 64 30W
Alta Lake **108** 50 10N 123 0W
Alta, Sierra **24** 40 31N 1 30W
Alta Sierra **123** 35 42N 118 33W
Altaelva → **8** 69 46N 23 45 E
Altagracia **134** 10 45N 71 30W
Altagracia de Orituco **134** 9 52N 66 23W
Altai = Aerhatai Shan **62** 46 40N 92 45 E
Altamachi → **136** 16 8S 66 50W
Altamaha → **113** 31 19N 81 17W
Altamira, Brazil **135** 3 12S 52 10W
Altamira, Chile **140** 25 47S 69 51W
Altamira, Colomb. **134** 2 3N 75 47W
Altamira, Mexico **125** 22 24N 97 55W
Altamira, Cuevas de **22** 43 20N 4 5W
Altamont, Ill., U.S.A. **117** 39 4N 88 45W
Altamont, N.Y., U.S.A. **115** 42 43N 74 3W
Altamura **29** 40 50N 16 33 E
Altanbulag **62** 50 16N 106 30 E
Altar **124** 30 40N 111 50W
Altata **124** 24 30N 108 0W
Altavista **112** 37 9N 79 22W
Altay **62** 47 48N 88 10 E
Altdorf **31** 46 52N 8 36 E
Alte Mellum **30** 53 45N 8 6 E
Altea **25** 38 38N 0 2W
Altenberg **30** 50 46N 13 47 E
Altenbruch **30** 53 48N 8 44 E
Altenburg **30** 50 59N 12 28 E
Altenkirchen, Germ., E. **30** 54 38N 13 20 E
Altenkirchen, Germ., W. **30** 50 41N 7 38 E
Altenteptow **30** 53 42N 13 15 E
Alter do Chão **23** 39 12N 7 40W
Altiplano **136** 17 0S 68 0W
Altkirch **19** 47 37N 7 15 E
Altmühl → **31** 48 54N 11 54 E
Alto Adige = Trentino-Alto Adige **26** 46 30N 11 0 E
Alto Araguaia **137** 17 15S 53 20W
Alto Chindio **95** 16 19S 35 25 E
Alto Cuchumatanes = Cuchumatanes, Sa. de los **126** 15 30N 91 10W
Alto del Inca **140** 24 10S 68 10W
Alto Garças **137** 16 56S 53 32W
Alto Iriri → **137** 8 50S 53 25W
Alto Ligonha **95** 15 30S 38 11 E
Alto Molocue **95** 15 50S 37 35 E
Alto Paraguai **137** 14 30S 56 31W
Alto Paraná □ **141** 25 0S 54 50W
Alto Parnaíba **138** 9 6S 45 57W
Alto Purús → **136** 9 12S 70 28W
Alto Río Senguerr **142** 45 2S 70 50W
Alto Santo **138** 5 31S 38 15W
Alto Sucuriú **137** 19 19S 52 47W
Alto Turi **138** 2 54S 45 38W
Alton, Austral. **77** 28 0S 149 16 E
Alton, Can. **106** 43 54N 80 5W
Alton, U.S.A. **116** 38 55N 90 5W
Alton Downs **73** 26 7S 138 57 E
Altona, Austral. **74** 37 51S 144 50 E
Altona, Ger. **30** 53 32N 9 56 E
Altoona, Iowa, U.S.A. **116** 41 39N 93 28W
Altoona, Pa., U.S.A. **114** 40 32N 78 24W
Altopáscio **26** 43 50N 10 40 E
Altos **138** 5 3S 42 28W
Altötting **31** 48 14N 12 41 E
Altstätten **31** 47 22N 9 33 E
Altun Shan **62** 38 30N 88 0 E
Alturas **120** 41 36N 120 37W
Altus **119** 34 30N 99 25W
Alucra **39** 40 22N 38 47 E
Aluksne **36** 57 24N 27 3 E
Alula **45** 11 50N 50 45 E
Alunite **123** 35 59N 114 55W
Alupka **38** 44 23N 34 2 E
Alushta **38** 44 40N 34 25 E
Alusi **57** 7 35S 131 40 E
Alustante **24** 40 36N 1 40W
Alva **119** 36 50N 98 50W
Alvaiázere **22** 39 49N 8 23W
Älvängen **11** 57 58N 12 8 E
Alvarado, Mexico **125** 18 40N 95 50W
Alvarado, U.S.A. **119** 32 25N 97 15W
Alvarães **135** 3 12S 64 50W
Alvaro Obregón, Presa **124** 27 55N 109 52W
Alvdal **10** 62 6N 10 37 E
Alvear **140** 29 5S 56 30W
Alverca **23** 38 56N 9 1W
Alvesta **11** 56 54N 14 35 E
Alvie **74** 38 14S 143 30 E
Alvin **119** 29 23N 95 12W
Alvinston **106** 42 49N 81 52W
Alvito **23** 38 15N 8 0W
Älvros **10** 62 3N 14 38 E
Älvsborgs län □ **11** 58 30N 12 30 E
Älvsbyn **8** 65 40N 21 0 E
Älvsered **11** 57 14N 12 51 E
Alwar **48** 27 38N 76 34 E
Alwaye **51** 10 8N 76 24 E
Alxa Zuoqi **60** 38 50N 105 40 E
Alyaskitovyy **41** 64 45N 141 30 E
Alyata **39** 39 58N 49 25 E
Alyth **14** 56 38N 3 15W
Alzada **118** 45 3N 104 22W
Alzano Lombardo **26** 45 44N 9 43 E
Alzey **31** 49 48N 8 4 E
Am-Dam **85** 12 40N 20 35 E
Am Guereda **85** 12 53N 21 14 E
Am Guéréda **92** 14 31N 22 5 E
Am Timan **85** 11 0N 20 10 E
Am-Zoer **92** 14 13N 21 23 E
Amacuro □ **135** 8 50N 61 5W
Amadeus, L. **79** 24 54S 131 0 E
Amâdi **91** 5 29N 30 25 E
Amadi **94** 3 40N 26 40 E
Amadjuak **101** 64 0N 72 39W
Amadjuak L. **101** 65 0N 71 8W
Amadora **23** 38 45N 9 13W
Amagasaki **65** 34 42N 135 20 E
Amager **11** 55 37N 12 35 E
Amagi **64** 33 25N 130 39 E
Amaimon **69** 5 12S 145 30 E
Amakusa-Nada **64** 32 35N 130 5 E
Amakusa-Shotō **64** 32 15N 130 10 E
Åmål **10** 59 3N 12 42 E
Amalapuram **51** 16 35N 81 55 E
Amalfi, Colomb. **134** 6 55N 75 4W
Amalfi, Italy **29** 40 39N 14 34 E
Amaliás **35** 37 47N 21 22 E
Amalner **50** 21 5N 75 5 E
Amambaí **141** 23 5S 55 13W
Amambaí → **141** 23 22S 53 56W
Amambay □ **141** 23 0S 56 0W
Amambay, Cordillera de **141** 23 0S 55 45W
Amami-Ō-Shima **63** 28 0N 129 0 E
Amana → **135** 9 45N 62 39W
Amaná, Lago **135** 2 35S 64 40W
Amanab **69** 3 40S 141 14 E
Amanda Park **122** 47 28N 123 55W
Amándola **27** 42 59N 13 21 E
Amangeldy **40** 50 10N 65 10 E
Amantea **29** 39 8N 16 3 E
Amapá **138** 2 5N 50 50W
Amapá □ **138** 1 40N 52 0W
Amapari **135** 0 37N 51 39W
Amar Gedid **91** 14 27N 25 13 E
Amara **91** 10 25N 34 10 E
Amarante, Brazil **138** 6 14S 42 50W
Amarante, Port. **22** 41 16N 8 5W
Amarante do Maranhão **138** 5 36S 46 45W
Amaranth **109** 50 36N 98 43W
Amarapura **52** 21 54N 96 3 E
Amaravati → **51** 11 0N 78 15 E
Amareleja **23** 38 12N 7 13W
Amargosa **139** 13 2S 39 36W
Amargosa → **123** 36 14N 116 51W
Amargosa Ra. **123** 36 25N 116 40W
Amarillo **119** 35 14N 101 46W
Amaro Leite **139** 13 58S 49 9W
Amaro, Mt. **27** 42 5N 14 6 E
Amarpur **49** 25 5N 87 0 E
Amasra **46** 41 45N 32 30 E
Amassama **89** 5 1N 6 2 E
Amasya **46** 40 40N 35 50 E
Amataurá **134** 3 29S 68 6W
Amatikulu **97** 29 3S 31 33 E
Amatitlán **126** 14 29N 90 38W
Amatrice **27** 42 38N 13 16 E
Amazon = Amazonas → **135** 0 5S 50 0W
Amazonas □, Brazil **136** 4 0S 62 0W
Amazonas □, Peru **136** 5 0S 78 0W
Amazonas □, Venez. **134** 3 30N 66 0W
Amazonas → **135** 0 5S 50 0W
Ambad **50** 19 38N 75 50 E
Ambahakily **97** 21 36S 43 41 E
Ambala **48** 30 23N 76 56 E
Ambalangoda **51** 6 15N 80 5 E
Ambalapuzha **51** 9 25N 76 25 E
Ambalavao **97** 21 50S 46 56 E
Ambalindum **72** 23 23S 135 0 E
Ambam **92** 2 20N 11 15 E
Ambanifilao **97** 12 48S 49 47 E
Ambanja **97** 13 40S 48 27 E
Ambarchik **41** 69 40N 162 20 E
Ambarijeby **97** 14 56S 47 41 E
Ambarnath **50** 19 12N 73 22 E
Ambaro, B. d' **97** 13 23S 48 38 E
Ambartsevo **40** 57 30N 83 52 E
Ambasamudram **51** 8 43N 77 25 E
Ambato **134** 1 5S 78 42W
Ambato-Boéni **97** 16 28S 46 43 E
Ambato, Sierra de **140** 28 25S 66 10W
Ambatofinandrahana **97** 20 33S 46 48 E
Ambatolampy **97** 19 20S 47 35 E
Ambatondrazaka **97** 17 55S 48 28 E
Ambatosoratra **97** 17 37S 48 31 E
Ambenja **97** 15 17S 46 58 E
Amberg **31** 49 25N 11 52 E
Ambergris Cay **125** 18 0N 88 0W
Ambérieu-en-Bugey **21** 45 57N 5 20 E
Amberley **81** 43 9S 172 44 E
Ambert **20** 45 33N 3 44 E
Ambia **97** 16 11S 45 33 E
Ambidédi **88** 14 35N 11 47W
Ambikapur **49** 23 15N 83 15 E
Ambikol **90** 21 20N 30 50 E
Ambinanindrano **97** 20 5S 48 23 E
Ambjörnarp **11** 57 25N 13 17 E
Ambleside **12** 54 26N 2 58W
Ambo, Begemdir & Simen, Ethiopia **91** 12 20N 37 30 E
Ambo, Shewa, Ethiopia **91** 9 0N 37 48 E
Ambo, Peru **136** 10 5S 76 10W
Ambodifototra **97** 16 59S 49 52 E
Ambodilazana **97** 18 6S 49 10 E
Ambohimahasoa **97** 21 7S 47 13 E
Ambohimanga du Sud **97** 20 52S 47 36 E
Ambon **57** 3 35S 128 20 E
Ambonga, Cones d' **97** 17 0S 45 0 E
Amboseli L. **94** 2 40S 37 10 E
Ambositra **97** 20 31S 47 25 E
Ambovombé **97** 25 11S 46 5 E
Amboy, Calif., U.S.A. **123** 34 33N 115 51W
Amboy, Ill., U.S.A. **116** 41 44N 89 20W
Amboyna I. **56** 7 50N 112 50 E
Ambre, C. d' **97** 12 40S 49 10 E
Ambridge **114** 40 36N 80 15W
Ambriz **92** 7 48S 13 8 E
Ambrizete **92** 7 10S 12 52 E
Ambrym **68** 16 15S 168 10 E
Ambunti **69** 4 13S 142 52 E
Ambur **51** 12 48N 78 43 E
Amby **73** 26 30S 148 11 E
Amchitka I. **100** 51 30N 179 0W
Amderma **40** 69 45N 61 30 E
Ameca **124** 20 30N 104 0W
Ameca → **124** 20 40N 105 15W
Amecameca **125** 19 7N 98 46W
Ameland **16** 53 27N 5 45 E
Amélia **27** 42 34N 12 25 E
Amélie-les-Bains-Palalda **20** 42 29N 2 41 E
Amen **41** 68 45N 180 0 E
Amendolaro **29** 39 58N 16 34 E
American Falls **120** 42 46N 112 56W
American Falls Res. **120** 43 0N 112 50W
American Highland **143** 73 0S 75 0 E
American Samoa **68** 14 20S 170 40W
Americana **141** 22 45S 47 20W
Americus **113** 32 0N 84 10W
Amersfoort, Neth. **16** 52 9N 5 23 E
Amersfoort, S. Afr. **97** 26 59S 29 53 E
Amery, Austral. **79** 31 9S 117 5 E
Amery, Can. **109** 56 34N 94 3W
Amery Ice Shelf **143** 69 30S 72 0 E
Ames **116** 42 0N 93 40W
Amesbury **115** 42 50N 70 52W
Amesdale **109** 50 2N 92 55W
Amfíklia **35** 38 38N 22 35 E
Amfilokhía **35** 38 52N 21 9 E
Amga **41** 60 50N 132 0 E
Amga → **41** 62 38N 134 32 E
Amgu **41** 45 45N 137 15 E
Amgun → **41** 52 56N 139 38 E

Amherst, Can.	**103**	45 48N	64 8W
Amherst, Mass., U.S.A.	**115**	42 21N	72 30W
Amherst, Ohio, U.S.A.	**114**	41 23N	82 15W
Amherst, Tex., U.S.A.	**119**	34 0N	102 24W
Amherst I.	**107**	44 8N	76 43W
Amherstburg	**106**	42 6N	83 6W
Amiata, Mte.	**27**	42 54N	11 40 E
Amiens, Austral.	**77**	28 35S	151 48 E
Amiens, France	**19**	49 54N	2 16 E
Amili	**52**	28 25N	95 52 E
Amindaion	**35**	40 42N	21 42 E
Amirante Is.	**53**	6 0S	53 0 E
Amisk L.	**109**	54 35N	102 15W
Amistad, Presa de la	**124**	29 24N	101 0W
Amite	**119**	30 47N	90 31W
Amizmiz	**86**	31 12N	8 15W
Åmli	**11**	58 45N	8 32 E
Amlwch	**12**	53 24N	4 21W
Amm Adam	**91**	16 20N	36 1 E
'Ammān	**44**	31 57N	35 52 E
Ammanford	**13**	51 48N	4 0W
Ammerån	**10**	63 9N	16 13 E
Ammerån →	**10**	63 9N	16 13 E
Ammersee	**31**	48 0N	11 7 E
Ammi'ad	**44**	32 55N	35 32 E
Amnat Charoen	**54**	15 51N	104 38 E
Amnéville	**19**	49 16N	6 9 E
Amo Jiang →	**58**	23 0N	101 50 E
Amorebieta	**24**	43 13N	2 44W
Amoret	**116**	38 15N	94 35W
Amorgós	**35**	36 50N	25 57 E
Amory	**113**	33 59N	88 29W
Amos	**104**	48 35N	78 5W
Åmot, Buskerud, Norway	**10**	59 54N	9 54 E
Åmot, Telemark, Norway	**10**	59 34N	8 0 E
Åmotsdal	**10**	59 37N	8 26 E
Amour, Djebel	**86**	33 42N	1 37 E
Amoy = Xiamen	**59**	24 25N	118 4 E
Amozoc	**125**	19 2N	98 3W
Ampang	**55**	3 8N	101 45 E
Ampanihy	**97**	24 40S	44 45 E
Ampanihy Est	**97**	23 57S	47 20 E
Ampasindava, B. d'	**97**	13 40S	48 15 E
Ampasindava, Presqu'île d'	**97**	13 42S	47 55W
Ampato, Nevado	**136**	15 40S	71 56W
Amper	**89**	9 25N	9 40 E
Amper →	**31**	48 30N	11 57 E
Ampère	**87**	35 44N	5 27 E
Ampezzo	**27**	46 25N	12 48 E
Amphitheatre	**74**	37 11S	143 22 E
Ampombiantambo	**97**	12 42S	48 57 E
Amposta	**24**	40 43N	0 34 E
Ampotaka	**97**	25 3S	44 41 E
Ampoza	**97**	22 20S	44 44 E
Amqa	**44**	32 59N	35 10 E
Amqui	**103**	48 28N	67 27W
Amraoti	**50**	20 55N	77 45 E
Amreli	**48**	21 35N	71 17 E
Amrenene el Kasba	**86**	22 10N	0 30 E
Amritsar	**48**	31 35N	74 57 E
Amroha	**49**	28 53N	78 30 E
Amrum	**30**	54 37N	8 21 E
Amsel	**87**	22 47N	5 29 E
Amsterdam, Neth.	**16**	52 23N	4 54 E
Amsterdam, U.S.A.	**115**	42 58N	74 10W
Amsterdam, Î.	**53**	37 30S	77 30 E
Amstetten	**33**	48 7N	14 51 E
Amudarya →	**40**	43 40N	59 0 E
Amund Ringnes I.	**144**	78 20N	96 25W
Amundsen Gulf	**100**	71 0N	124 0W
Amundsen Sea	**143**	72 0S	115 0W
Amungen	**10**	61 10N	15 40 E
Amuntai	**56**	2 28S	115 25 E
Amur →	**41**	52 56N	141 10 E
Amurang	**57**	1 5N	124 40 E
Amuri Pass	**81**	42 31S	172 11 E
Amurrio	**24**	43 3N	3 0W
Amursk	**41**	50 14N	136 54 E
Amurzet	**41**	47 50N	131 5 E
Amusco	**22**	42 10N	4 28W
Amvrakikós Kólpos	**35**	39 0N	20 55 E
Amvrosiyevka	**39**	47 43N	38 30 E
Amzeglouf	**86**	26 50N	0 1 E
An	**52**	19 48N	94 0W
An Bien	**55**	9 45N	105 0 E
An Hoa	**54**	15 40N	108 5 E
An Loc	**55**	11 40N	106 50 E
An Nafūd	**46**	28 15N	41 0 E
An Najaf	**46**	32 3N	44 15 E
An-Nāqūrah	**44**	33 7N	35 8 E
An Nasiriyah	**46**	31 0N	46 15 E
An Nawfaliyah	**87**	30 54N	17 58 E
An Nhon (Binh Dinh)	**54**	13 55N	109 7 E
An Nîl □	**90**	19 30N	33 0 E
An Nîl el Abyad □	**91**	14 0N	32 15 E
An Nîl el Azraq □	**91**	12 30N	34 30 E
An Nu'ayriyah	**46**	27 30N	48 30 E
An Thoi, Dao	**55**	9 58N	104 0 E
An Tuc	**54**	13 57N	108 39 E
An Uaimh	**15**	53 39N	6 40W
Anabar →	**41**	73 8N	113 36 E
Anabta	**44**	32 19N	35 7 E
Anabuki	**64**	34 2N	134 11 E
Anaco	**135**	9 27N	64 28W
Anaconda	**120**	46 7N	113 0W
Anacortes	**122**	48 30N	122 40W
Anadarko	**119**	35 4N	98 15W
Anadia, Brazil	**138**	9 42S	36 18W
Anadia, Port.	**22**	40 26N	8 27W
Anadolu	**46**	38 0N	30 0 E
Anadyr	**41**	64 35N	177 20 E
Anadyr →	**41**	64 55N	176 5 E
Anadyrskiy Zaliv	**41**	64 0N	180 0 E
Anáfi	**35**	36 22N	25 48 E
Anafópoulo	**35**	36 17N	25 50 E
Anagni	**28**	41 44N	13 8 E
Anah	**46**	34 25N	42 0 E
Anaheim	**123**	33 50N	118 0W
Anahim Lake	**108**	52 28N	125 18W
Anáhuac	**124**	27 14N	100 9W
Anai Mudi, Mt.	**51**	10 12N	77 4 E
Anaimalai Hills	**51**	10 20N	76 40 E
Anajás	**138**	0 59S	49 57W
Anajatuba	**138**	3 16S	44 37W
Anakapalle	**50**	17 42N	83 06 E
Anakie	**72**	23 32S	147 45 E
Anaklia	**39**	42 22N	41 35 E
Analalava	**97**	14 35S	48 0 E
Anamã	**135**	3 35S	61 22W
Anambar →	**48**	30 15N	68 50 E
Anambas, Kepulauan	**56**	3 20N	106 30 E
Aname	**68**	20 8S	169 47 E
Anamoose	**118**	47 55N	100 20W
Anamosa	**116**	42 7N	91 30W
Anamur	**46**	36 8N	32 58 E
Anan	**64**	33 54N	134 40 E
Anand	**48**	22 32N	72 59 E
Anandpur	**50**	21 16N	86 13 E
Anantapur	**51**	14 39N	77 42 E
Anantnag	**49**	33 45N	75 10 E
Ananyev	**38**	47 44N	29 47 E
Anapa	**38**	44 55N	37 25 E
Anápolis	**139**	16 15S	48 50W
Anapu →	**135**	1 53S	50 53W
Anar	**47**	30 55N	55 13 E
Anārak	**47**	33 25N	53 40 E
Anatolia = Anadolu	**46**	38 0N	30 0 E
Anatone	**120**	46 9N	117 4W
Añatuya	**140**	28 20S	62 50W
Anauá →	**135**	0 58N	61 21W
Anaunethad L.	**109**	60 55N	104 25W
Anavilhanas, Arquipélago das	**135**	2 42S	60 45W
Anaye	**85**	19 15N	12 50 E
Anbyŏn	**61**	39 1N	127 35 E
Ancash □	**136**	9 30S	77 45W
Ancenis	**18**	47 21N	1 10W
Ancho, C.	**142**	50 0S	74 20W
Anchor Bay	**122**	38 48N	123 34W
Anchorage	**100**	61 10N	149 50W
Anci	**60**	39 20N	116 40 E
Ancião	**22**	39 56N	8 27W
Ancohuma, Nevada	**136**	16 0S	68 50W
Ancón	**136**	11 50S	77 10W
Ancona	**27**	43 37N	13 30 E
Ancud	**142**	42 0S	73 50W
Ancud, G. de	**142**	42 0S	73 0W
Andacollo, Argent.	**140**	37 10S	70 42W
Andacollo, Chile	**140**	30 5S	71 10W
Andado	**72**	25 25S	135 15 E
Andahuaylas	**136**	13 40S	73 25W
Andalgalá	**140**	27 40S	66 30W
Åndalsnes	**10**	62 35N	7 43 E
Andalucía	**23**	37 35N	5 0W
Andalusia	**113**	31 19N	86 30W
Andalusia = Andalucía	**23**	37 35N	5 0W
Andaman Is.	**42**	12 30N	92 30 E
Andaman Sea	**56**	13 0N	96 0 E
Andara	**96**	18 2S	21 9 E
Andaraí	**139**	12 48S	41 20W
Andelot	**19**	48 15N	5 18 E
Andelys, Les	**18**	49 15N	1 25 E
Andenne	**16**	50 30N	5 5 E
Andéranboukane	**89**	15 26N	3 2 E
Andermatt	**31**	46 38N	8 35 E
Andernach	**30**	50 24N	7 25 E
Andernos-les-Bains	**20**	44 44N	1 6W
Anderslöv	**11**	55 26N	13 19 E
Anderson, Austral.	**74**	38 32S	145 27 E
Anderson, Calif., U.S.A.	**120**	40 30N	122 19W
Anderson, Ind., U.S.A.	**117**	40 5N	85 40W
Anderson, Mo., U.S.A.	**119**	36 43N	94 29W
Anderson, S.C., U.S.A.	**113**	34 32N	82 40W
Anderson →	**100**	69 42N	129 0W
Anderson, Mt.	**97**	25 5S	30 42 E
Anderstorp	**11**	57 19N	13 39 E
Andes	**136**	5 40N	75 53W
Andes, Cord de los	**136**	20 0S	68 0W
Andfjorden	**8**	69 10N	16 20 E
Andhra, L.	**50**	18 54N	73 32 E
Andhra Pradesh □	**51**	16 0N	79 0 E
Andikíthira	**35**	35 52N	23 15 E
Andímilos	**35**	36 47N	24 12 E
Andípaxoi	**35**	39 9N	20 13 E
Andizhan	**40**	41 10N	72 0 E
Andkhui	**47**	36 52N	65 8 E
Andoas	**134**	2 55S	76 25W
Andol	**50**	17 51N	78 4 E
Andong	**61**	36 40N	128 43 E
Andongwei	**61**	35 6N	119 20 E
Andorra ■	**24**	42 30N	1 30 E
Andorra La Vella	**24**	42 31N	1 32 E
Andover, U.K.	**13**	51 13N	1 29W
Andover, N.Y., U.S.A.	**114**	42 11N	77 48W
Andover, Ohio, U.S.A.	**114**	41 35N	80 35W
Andradina	**139**	20 54S	51 23W
Andrahary, Mt.	**97**	13 37S	49 17 E
Andraitx	**24**	39 35N	2 25 E
Andramasina	**97**	19 11S	47 35 E
Andrano-Velona	**97**	18 10S	46 52 E
Andranopasy	**97**	21 17S	43 44 E
Andreanof Is.	**100**	52 0N	178 0W
Andreapol	**36**	56 40N	32 17 E
Andrespol	**32**	51 45N	19 34 E
Andreville	**105**	47 41N	69 44W
Andrews, S.C., U.S.A.	**113**	33 29N	79 30W
Andrews, Tex., U.S.A.	**119**	32 18N	102 33W
Ándria	**29**	41 13N	16 17 E
Andriba	**97**	17 30S	46 58 E
Andrijevica	**33**	42 45N	19 48 E
Andrítsaina	**35**	37 29N	21 52 E
Androka	**97**	24 58S	44 2 E
Ándros	**35**	37 50N	24 57 E
Andros I.	**126**	24 30N	78 0W
Andros Town	**126**	24 43N	77 47W
Andújar	**23**	38 3N	4 5W
Aneby	**11**	57 48N	14 49 E
Anecho	**89**	6 12N	1 34 E
Anegada, Bahía	**142**	40 20S	62 20W
Anegada I.	**127**	18 45N	64 20W
Anegada Passage	**127**	18 15N	63 45W
Aneityum	**68**	20 12S	169 45 E
Añelo	**142**	38 20S	68 45W
Anergane	**86**	31 4N	7 14W
Aneto, Pico de	**24**	42 37N	0 40 E
Añez	**137**	15 40S	63 10W
Anfeg	**87**	22 29N	5 58 E
Anfu	**59**	27 21N	114 40 E
Ang Thong	**54**	14 35N	100 31 E
Angamos, Punta	**140**	23 1S	70 32W
Ang'angxi	**62**	47 10N	123 48 E
Angara →	**41**	58 30N	97 0 E
Angarab	**91**	13 11N	37 7 E
Angarsk	**41**	52 30N	104 0 E
Angas Downs	**79**	24 49S	132 14 E
Angas Hills	**78**	23 0S	127 50 E
Angaston	**73**	34 30S	139 8 E
Ånge	**10**	62 31N	15 35 E
Angel de la Guarda	**124**	29 30N	113 30W
Angel Falls	**135**	5 57N	62 30W
Angeles	**57**	15 9N	120 33 E
Ängelholm	**11**	56 15N	12 58 E
Angellala	**73**	26 24S	146 54 E
Angels Camp	**122**	38 8N	120 30W
Ängelsberg	**10**	59 58N	16 0 E
Anger →	**91**	9 37N	36 6 E
Angereb →	**91**	13 45N	36 40 E
Ångermanälven →	**10**	62 40N	18 0 E
Angermünde	**30**	53 1N	14 0 E
Angers, Can.	**104**	45 31N	75 29W
Angers, France	**18**	47 30N	0 35W
Angerville	**19**	48 19N	2 0 E
Ängesån	**8**	66 50N	22 15 E
Anghiari	**27**	43 32N	12 3 E
Angical	**139**	12 0S	44 42W
Angikuni L.	**109**	62 0N	100 0W
Angkor	**54**	13 22N	103 50 E
Anglem Mt.	**81**	46 45S	167 53 E
Anglés	**24**	41 57N	2 38 E
Anglesea	**74**	38 25S	144 12 E
Anglesey	**12**	53 17N	4 20W
Anglet	**20**	43 29N	1 31W
Angleton	**119**	29 12N	95 23W
Angliers	**104**	47 33N	79 14W
Anglin →	**20**	46 42N	0 52 E
Anglure	**19**	48 35N	3 50 E
Angmagssalik	**144**	65 40N	37 20W
Ango	**94**	4 10N	26 5 E
Angoche	**95**	16 8S	40 0 E
Angoche, I.	**95**	16 20S	39 50 E
Angol	**140**	37 56S	72 45W
Angola, Ind., U.S.A.	**117**	41 40N	85 0W
Angola, N.Y., U.S.A.	**114**	42 38N	79 2W
Angola ■	**93**	12 0S	18 0 E
Angoon	**108**	57 40N	134 40W
Angoram	**69**	4 4S	144 4 E
Angoulême	**20**	45 39N	0 10 E
Angoumois	**20**	45 50N	0 25 E
Angra dos Reis	**141**	23 0S	44 10W
Angra-Juntas	**96**	27 39S	15 31 E
Angren	**40**	41 1N	70 12 E
Angtassom	**55**	11 1N	104 41 E
Angu	**94**	3 25N	24 28 E
Anguang	**61**	45 35N	123 45 E
Anguilla	**127**	18 14N	63 5W
Anguo	**60**	38 28N	115 15 E
Angurugu	**72**	14 0S	136 25 E
Angus	**106**	44 19N	79 53W
Angus, Braes of	**14**	56 51N	3 10W
Anhanduí →	**141**	21 46S	52 9W
Anholt	**11**	56 42N	11 33 E
Anhua	**59**	28 23N	111 12 E
Anhui □	**59**	32 0N	117 0 E
Anhwei □ = Anhui □	**59**	32 0N	117 0 E
Anicuns	**139**	16 28S	49 58W
Ánidhros	**35**	36 38N	25 43 E
Anie	**89**	7 42N	1 8 E
Animas	**121**	31 58N	108 58W
Ånimskog	**11**	58 53N	12 35 E
Anina	**34**	45 6N	21 51 E
Anita	**116**	41 27N	94 46W
Anivorano	**97**	18 44S	48 58 E
Aniwa	**68**	19 17S	169 35 E
Anjangaon	**50**	21 10N	77 20 E
Anjar	**48**	23 6N	70 10 E
Anjiabé	**97**	12 7S	49 20 E
Anjidiv I.	**51**	14 40N	74 10 E
Anjō	**65**	34 57N	137 5 E
Anjou	**18**	47 20N	0 15W
Anjozorobé	**97**	18 22S	47 52 E
Anju	**61**	39 36N	125 40 E
Anka	**89**	12 13N	5 58 E
Ankang	**58**	32 40N	109 1 E
Ankara	**46**	40 0N	32 54 E
Ankaramena	**97**	21 57S	46 39 E
Ankazoabo	**97**	22 18S	44 31 E
Ankazobé	**97**	18 20S	47 10 E
Ankazotokana	**97**	21 20S	48 9 E
Ankeny	**116**	41 44N	93 36W
Ankisabe	**97**	19 17S	46 29 E
Anklam	**30**	53 48N	13 40 E
Anklesvar	**50**	21 38N	73 3 E
Ankober	**91**	9 35N	39 40 E
Ankoro	**94**	6 45S	26 55 E
Anlong	**58**	25 2N	105 27 E
Anlu	**59**	31 15N	113 45 E
Anmyŏn-do	**61**	36 25N	126 25 E
Ånn	**10**	63 19N	12 34 E
Ann Arbor	**106**	42 17N	83 45W
Ann C., Antarct.	**143**	66 30S	50 30 E
Ann C., U.S.A.	**115**	42 39N	70 37W
Anna, Ill., U.S.A.	**119**	37 28N	89 10W
Anna, Ohio, U.S.A.	**117**	40 24N	84 11W
Anna, U.S.S.R.	**37**	51 28N	40 23 E
Anna Plains	**78**	19 17S	121 37 E
Anna Regina	**135**	7 10N	58 30W
Annaba	**87**	36 50N	7 46 E
Annaberg-Buchholz	**30**	50 34N	12 58 E
Annaka	**65**	36 19N	138 54 E
Annalee →	**15**	54 3N	7 15W
Annam = Trung-Phan	**54**	16 30N	107 30 E
Annamitique, Chaîne	**54**	17 0N	106 0 E
Annan	**14**	55 0N	3 17W
Annan →	**14**	54 58N	3 18W
Annanberg	**69**	4 52S	144 42 E
Annapolis	**112**	38 95N	76 30W
Annapolis Royal	**103**	44 44N	65 32W
Annapurna	**49**	28 34N	83 50 E
Annean, L.	**79**	26 54S	118 14 E
Anneberg	**11**	57 32N	12 6 E
Annecy	**21**	45 55N	6 8 E
Annecy, L. d'	**21**	45 52N	6 10 E
Annemasse	**21**	46 12N	6 16 E
Anning	**58**	24 55N	102 26 E
Anningie	**78**	21 50S	133 7 E
Anniston	**113**	33 45N	85 50W
Annobón = Pagalu	**83**	1 25S	5 35 E
Annonay	**21**	45 15N	4 40 E
Annonciation, L'	**104**	46 25N	74 55W
Annot	**21**	43 58N	6 38 E
Annotto Bay	**126**	18 17N	77 3W
Annuello	**74**	34 53S	142 55 E
Annville	**115**	40 18N	76 32W
Annweiler	**31**	49 12N	7 58 E
Áno Viánnos	**35**	35 2N	25 21 E
Anoano	**68**	8 59S	160 46 E
Anoka	**118**	45 10N	93 26W
Anorotsangana	**97**	13 56S	47 55 E
Anping, Hebei, China	**60**	38 15N	115 30 E
Anping, Liaoning, China	**61**	41 5N	123 30 E
Anpu Gang	**58**	21 25N	109 50 E
Anqing	**59**	30 30N	117 3 E
Anqiu	**61**	36 25N	119 10 E
Anren	**59**	26 43N	113 18 E
Ansāb	**46**	29 11N	44 43 E

Ansai **60** 36 50N 109 20 E
Ansbach **31** 49 17N 10 34 E
Anse au Loup, L' **103** 51 32N 56 50W
Anse, L' **102** 46 47N 88 28W
Anseba → **91** 16 0N 38 30 E
Anserma **134** 5 13N 75 48W
Anshan **61** 41 5N 122 58 E
Anshun **58** 26 18N 105 57 E
Ansley **118** 41 19N 99 24W
Ansó **24** 42 51N 0 48W
Anson **119** 32 46N 99 54W
Anson B. **78** 13 20S 130 6 E
Ansongo **89** 15 25N 0 35 E
Ansonia, Conn., U.S.A. **115** 41 21N 73 6W
Ansonia, Ohio, U.S.A. **117** 40 13N 84 38W
Anstruther **14** 56 14N 2 40W
Ansudu **57** 2 11S 139 22 E
Antabamba **136** 14 40S 73 0W
Antakya **46** 36 14N 36 10 E
Antalaha **97** 14 57S 50 20 E
Antalya **46** 36 52N 30 45 E
Antalya Körfezi **46** 36 15N 31 30 E
Antananarivo **97** 18 55S 47 31 E
Antanimbaribé **97** 21 30S 44 48 E
Antarctic Pen. **143** 67 0S 60 0W
Antarctica **143** 90 0S 0 0
Antelope **95** 21 2S 28 31 E
Antenor Navarro **138** 6 44S 38 27W
Antequera, Parag. **140** 24 8S 57 7W
Antequera, Spain **23** 37 5N 4 33W
Antero Mt. **121** 38 45N 106 15W
Anthony, Kans., U.S.A. **119** 37 8N 98 2W
Anthony, N. Mex., U.S.A. **121** 32 1N 106 37W
Anthony Lagoon **72** 18 0S 135 30 E
Anti Atlas, Mts. **86** 30 0N 8 30W
Antibes **21** 43 34N 7 6 E
Antibes, C. d' **21** 43 31N 7 7 E
Anticosti, Î. d' **103** 49 30N 63 0W
Antifer, C. d' **18** 49 41N 0 10 E
Antigo **118** 45 8N 89 5W
Antigonish **103** 45 38N 61 58W
Antigua, Guat. **126** 14 34N 90 41W
Antigua, W. Indies **127** 17 0N 61 50W
Antilla **126** 20 40N 75 50W
Antimony **121** 38 7N 112 0W
Antioch **122** 38 7N 121 45W
Antioche, Pertuis d' **20** 46 6N 1 20W
Antioquia **134** 6 40N 75 55W
Antioquia □ **134** 7 0N 75 30W
Antipodes Is. **66** 49 45S 178 40 E
Antler **118** 48 58N 101 18W
Antler → **109** 49 8N 101 0W
Antlers **119** 34 15N 95 35W
Antofagasta **140** 23 50S 70 30W
Antofagasta □ **140** 24 0S 69 0W
Antofagasta de la Sierra **140** 26 5S 67 20W
Antofalla **140** 25 30S 68 5W
Antofalla, Salar de **140** 25 40S 67 45W
Anton **119** 33 49N 102 5W
Anton Chico **121** 35 12N 105 5W
Antongil, B. d' **97** 15 30S 49 50 E
Antonibé **97** 15 7S 47 24 E
Antonibé, Presqu'île d' **97** 14 55S 47 20 E
Antonina **141** 25 26S 48 42W
Antonito **121** 37 4N 106 1W
Antonovo **39** 49 25N 51 42 E
Antrain **18** 48 28N 1 30W
Antrim **15** 54 43N 6 13W
Antrim □ **15** 54 55N 6 20W
Antrim, Mts. of **15** 54 57N 6 8W
Antrim Plateau **78** 18 8S 128 20 E
Antrodoco **27** 42 25N 13 4 E
Antropovo **37** 58 26N 42 51 E
Antsalova **97** 18 40S 44 37 E
Antsirabé **97** 19 55S 47 2 E
Antsohihy **97** 14 50S 47 59 E
Antu **61** 42 30N 128 20 E
Antwerp, Austral. **74** 36 17S 142 4 E
Antwerp, N.Y., U.S.A. **115** 44 12N 75 36W
Antwerp, Ohio, U.S.A. **117** 41 11N 84 45W
Antwerp = Antwerpen **16** 51 13N 4 25 E
Antwerpen **16** 51 13N 4 25 E
Antwerpen □ **16** 51 15N 4 40 E
Anupgarh **48** 29 10N 73 10 E
Anuradhapura **51** 8 22N 80 28 E
Anvers = Antwerpen **16** 51 13N 4 25 E
Anvers I. **143** 64 30S 63 40W
Anvik **100** 62 37N 160 20W
Anxi, Fujian, China **59** 25 2N 118 12 E
Anxi, Gansu, China **62** 40 30N 95 43 E
Anxiang **59** 29 27N 112 11 E
Anxious B. **73** 33 24S 134 45 E
Anyama **88** 5 30N 4 3W
Anyang **60** 36 5N 114 21 E
Anyer-Lor **57** 6 6S 105 56 E
Anyi, Jiangxi, China **59** 28 49N 115 25 E
Anyi, Shanxi, China **60** 35 2N 111 2 E
Anyuan **59** 25 10N 115 24 E
Anza, Jordan **44** 32 22N 35 12 E
Anza, U.S.A. **123** 33 35N 116 39W
Anze **60** 36 10N 112 12 E
Anzhero-Sudzhensk **40** 56 10N 86 0 E
Ánzio **28** 41 28N 12 37 E
Anzoátegui □ **135** 9 0N 64 30W
Aoba **68** 15 25S 167 50 E
Aoga-Shima **65** 32 28N 139 46 E
Aoiz **24** 42 46N 1 22W
Aomori **63** 40 45N 140 45 E
Aonla **49** 28 16N 79 11 E
Aono-Yama **64** 34 28N 131 48 E
Aorangi Mts. **80** 41 28S 175 22 E
Aoreora **86** 28 51N 10 53W
Aosta **26** 45 43N 7 20 E
Aoudéras **89** 17 45N 8 20 E
Aouinet Torkoz **86** 28 31N 9 46W
Aoukar **86** 23 50N 2 45W
Aouker **88** 17 40N 10 0W
Aoulef el Arab **86** 26 55N 1 2 E
Apa → **140** 22 6S 58 2W
Apache, Ariz., U.S.A. **121** 31 46N 109 6W
Apache, Okla., U.S.A. **119** 34 53N 98 22W
Apalachee B. **113** 30 0N 84 0W
Apalachicola **113** 29 40N 85 0W
Apapa **89** 6 25N 3 25 E
Apaporis → **134** 1 23S 69 25W
Aparecida do Taboado **139** 20 5S 51 5W
Aparri **57** 18 22N 121 38 E
Apurén **135** 5 6N 62 8W
Apateu **34** 46 36N 21 47 E
Apatin **33** 45 40N 19 0 E
Apatzingán **124** 19 0N 102 20W
Apeldoorn **16** 52 13N 5 57 E
Apen **30** 53 12N 7 47 E
Apenam **56** 8 35S 116 13 E
Apennines **6** 44 20N 10 20 E
Apere → **137** 13 44S 65 18W
Apia **68** 13 50S 171 50W
Apiacás, Serra dos **137** 9 50S 57 0W
Apiaú → **135** 2 39N 61 12W
Apiaú, Serra do **135** 2 30N 62 0W
Apidiá → **137** 11 39S 61 11W
Apinajé **139** 11 31S 48 18W
Apiti **80** 39 58S 175 54 E
Apizaco **125** 19 26N 98 9W
Aplao **136** 16 0S 72 40W
Apo, Mt. **57** 6 53N 125 14 E
Apodi **138** 5 39S 37 48W
Apolda **30** 51 1N 11 30 E
Apollo Bay **74** 38 45S 143 40 E
Apollonia **35** 36 58N 24 43 E
Apollonia = Marsa Susa **85** 32 52N 21 59 E
Apolo **136** 14 30S 68 30W
Apónguao → **135** 4 48N 61 36W
Aporé **137** 18 58S 52 1W
Aporé → **139** 19 27S 50 57W
Aporema **138** 1 14N 50 49W
Apostle Is. **118** 47 0N 90 30W
Apóstoles **141** 28 0S 56 0W
Apostolovo **38** 47 39N 33 39 E
Apoteri **135** 4 2N 58 32W
Appalachian Mts. **112** 38 0N 80 0W
Appalachicola → **113** 29 40N 85 0W
Appennini **29** 41 0N 15 0 E
Appennino Ligure **26** 44 30N 9 0 E
Appenzell-Ausser Rhoden □ **31** 47 23N 9 23 E
Appenzell-Inner Rhoden □ **31** 47 20N 9 25 E
Appiano **27** 46 27N 11 17 E
Appin **76** 34 11S 150 45 E
Apple Hill **107** 45 13N 74 46W
Apple Tree Flat **76** 32 40S 149 36 E
Apple Valley **123** 34 30N 117 11W
Appleby **12** 54 35N 2 29W
Appleton **112** 44 17N 88 25W
Appleton City **116** 38 11N 94 2W
Approuague **135** 4 20N 52 0W
Approuague → **135** 4 30N 51 57W
Aprelevka **37** 55 33N 37 4 E
Apricena **29** 41 47N 15 25 E
Aprigliano **29** 39 17N 16 19 E
Aprília **28** 41 38N 12 38 E
Apsheronsk **39** 44 28N 39 42 E
Apsley, Austral. **74** 36 58S 141 5 E
Apsley, Can. **107** 44 45N 78 6W
Apt **21** 43 53N 5 24 E
Apuaú **135** 2 25S 60 53W
Apucarana **141** 23 55S 51 33W
Apulia = Púglia **29** 41 0N 16 30 E
Apure □ **134** 7 10N 68 50W
Apure → **134** 7 37N 66 25W
Apurímac □ **136** 14 0S 73 0W
Apurimac → **136** 12 17S 73 56W
Apuseni, Munţii **34** 46 30N 22 45 E
Aq Chah **47** 37 0N 66 5 E
'Aqaba, Khalīj al **46** 28 15N 33 20 E
Aqabah = Al 'Aqabah **90** 29 13N 35 0 E
Aqîq **90** 18 14N 38 12 E
Aqîq, Khalîg **90** 18 20N 38 10 E
Aqraba **44** 32 9N 35 20 E
Aqrah **46** 36 46N 43 45 E
Aquidauana **137** 20 30S 55 50W
Aquidauana → **137** 19 44S 56 50W
Áquila, L' **27** 42 21N 13 24 E
Aquiles Serdán **124** 28 37N 105 54W
Aquin **127** 18 16N 73 24W
Ar Rab 'al Khālī **45** 19 0N 50 0 E
Ar Ramadi **46** 33 25N 43 20 E
Ar-Ramthā **44** 32 34N 36 0 E
Ar Raqqah **46** 36 0N 38 55 E
Ar Rass **46** 25 50N 43 40 E
Ar Rifa'i **46** 31 50N 46 10 E
Ar Riyād **46** 24 41N 46 42 E
Ar Ruţbah **46** 33 0N 40 15 E
Arab, Bahr el → **91** 9 50N 29 0 E
Arab, Khalîg el **90** 30 55N 29 0 E
Arab, Shatt al **46** 30 0N 48 31 E
Arabatskaya Strelka **38** 45 40N 35 0 E
Arabba **27** 46 30N 11 51 E
Arabelo **135** 4 55N 64 13W
Arabia **42** 25 0N 45 0 E
Arabian Sea **42** 16 0N 65 0 E
Arac **46** 41 15N 33 21 E
Aracaju **138** 10 55S 37 4W
Aracataca **134** 10 38N 74 9W
Aracati **138** 4 30S 37 44W
Araçatuba **141** 21 10S 50 30W
Aracena **23** 37 53N 6 38W
Aracena, Sierra de **23** 37 50N 6 50W
Aracides, C. **68** 8 21S 161 0 E
Araçuaí **139** 16 52S 42 4W
Araçuaí → **139** 16 46S 42 2W
Arad **34** 46 10N 21 20 E
Arada **85** 15 0N 20 20 E
Arafura Sea **57** 9 0S 135 0 E
Aragarças **137** 15 55S 52 15W
Aragats **39** 40 30N 44 15 E
Aragón **24** 41 25N 1 0W
Aragón → **24** 42 13N 1 44W
Aragona **28** 37 24N 13 36 E
Aragua □ **134** 10 0N 67 10W
Aragua de Barcelona **135** 9 28N 64 49W
Araguacema **138** 8 50S 49 20W
Araguaçu **139** 12 49S 49 51W
Araguaia → **139** 5 21S 48 41W
Araguaiana **137** 15 43S 51 51W
Araguaína **138** 7 12S 48 12W
Araguari **139** 18 38S 48 11W
Araguari → **138** 1 15N 49 55W
Araguatins **138** 5 38S 48 7W
Araioses **138** 2 53S 41 55W
Arak **86** 25 20N 3 45 E
Arāk **46** 34 0N 49 40 E
Arakan □ **52** 19 0N 94 15 E
Arakan Yoma **52** 20 0N 94 40 E
Araks = Aras, Rud-e → **46** 39 10N 47 10 E
Aral Sea = Aralskoye More **40** 44 30N 60 0 E
Aralsk **40** 46 50N 61 20 E
Aralskoye More **40** 44 30N 60 0 E
Araluen **76** 35 36S 149 49 E
Aramac **72** 22 58S 145 14 E
Arambagh **49** 22 53N 87 48 E
Aran, I. **15** 55 0N 8 30W
Aran Is. **15** 53 5N 9 42W
Aranda de Duero **24** 41 39N 3 42W
Aranga **80** 35 44S 173 40 E
Aranjuez **22** 40 1N 3 40W
Aranos **96** 24 9S 19 7 E
Aransas Pass **119** 27 55N 97 9W
Aranzazu **134** 5 16N 75 30W
Arao **64** 32 59N 130 25 E
Araouane **88** 18 55N 3 30W
Arapahoe **118** 40 22N 99 53W
Arapari **138** 5 34S 49 15W
Arapey Grande → **140** 30 55S 57 49W
Arapiraca **138** 9 45S 36 39W
Arapkir **46** 39 5N 38 30 E
Arapongas **141** 23 29S 51 28W
Araracuara **134** 0 24S 72 17W
Araranguá **141** 29 0S 49 30W
Araraquara **139** 21 50S 48 0W
Ararás, Serra das **141** 25 0S 53 10W
Ararat **74** 37 16S 143 0 E
Ararat, Mt. = Ağri Daği **46** 39 50N 44 15 E
Arari **138** 3 28S 44 47W
Araria **49** 26 9N 87 33 E
Araripe, Chapada do **138** 7 20S 40 0W
Araripina **138** 7 33S 40 34W
Araruama, Lagoa de **139** 22 53S 42 12W
Araruna **138** 6 52S 35 44W
Aras, Rud-e → **46** 39 10N 47 10 E
Araticu **138** 1 58S 49 51W
Arauca **134** 7 0N 70 40W
Arauca □ **134** 6 40N 71 0W
Arauca → **134** 7 24N 66 35W
Arauco **140** 37 16S 73 25W
Arauco □ **140** 37 40S 73 25W
Araújos **139** 19 56S 45 14W
Arauquita **134** 7 2N 71 25W
Araure **134** 9 34N 69 13W
Arawa **91** 9 57N 41 58 E
Arawata → **81** 44 0S 168 40 E
Araxá **139** 19 35S 46 55W
Araya, Pen. de **135** 10 40N 64 0W
Arba **91** 9 0N 40 20 E
Arba Jahan **94** 2 5N 39 2 E
Arba Minch **91** 6 0N 37 30 E
Arbatax **28** 39 57N 9 42 E
Arbaza **41** 52 40N 92 30 E
Arbīl **46** 36 15N 44 5 E
Arboga **10** 59 24N 15 52 E
Arbois **19** 46 55N 5 46 E
Arboletes **134** 8 51N 76 26W
Arbore **91** 5 3N 36 50 E
Arborea **28** 39 46N 8 34 E
Arborfield **109** 53 6N 103 39W
Arborg **109** 50 54N 97 13W
Arbrå **10** 61 28N 16 22 E
Arbresie, L' **21** 45 50N 4 26 E
Arbroath **14** 56 34N 2 35W
Arbuckle **122** 39 3N 122 2W
Arbus **28** 39 30N 8 33 E
Arbuzinka **38** 47 0N 31 59 E
Arc **19** 47 28N 5 34 E
Arc → **21** 45 34N 6 12 E
Arcachon **20** 44 40N 1 10W
Arcachon, Bassin d' **20** 44 42N 1 10W
Arcade **114** 42 34N 78 25W
Arcadia, Fla., U.S.A. **113** 27 20N 81 50W
Arcadia, Ind., U.S.A. **117** 40 10N 86 1W
Arcadia, Iowa, U.S.A. **116** 42 5N 95 3W
Arcadia, La., U.S.A. **119** 32 34N 92 53W
Arcadia, Nebr., U.S.A. **118** 41 29N 99 4W
Arcadia, Pa., U.S.A. **114** 40 46N 78 54W
Arcadia, Wis., U.S.A. **118** 44 13N 91 29W
Arcanum **117** 39 59N 84 33W
Arcata **120** 40 55N 124 4W
Arcévia **27** 43 29N 12 58 E
Archangel = Arkhangelsk **40** 64 40N 41 0 E
Archar **34** 43 50N 22 54 E
Archbald **115** 41 30N 75 31W
Archbold **117** 41 31N 84 18W
Archena **25** 38 9N 1 16W
Archer → **72** 13 28S 141 41 E
Archer B. **72** 13 20S 141 30 E
Archers Post **94** 0 35N 37 35 E
Archidona **23** 37 6N 4 22W
Arci, Monte **28** 39 47N 8 44 E
Arcidosso **27** 42 51N 11 30 E
Arcila = Asilah **86** 35 29N 6 0W
Arcis-sur-Aube **19** 48 32N 4 10 E
Arckaringa **73** 27 56S 134 45 E
Arckaringa Cr. → **73** 28 10S 135 22 E
Arco, Italy **26** 45 55N 10 54 E
Arco, U.S.A. **120** 43 45N 113 16W
Arcola, Can. **109** 49 40N 102 30W
Arcola, U.S.A. **117** 39 41N 88 19W
Arcos **24** 41 12N 2 16W
Arcos de los Frontera **23** 36 45N 5 49W
Arcos de Valdevez **22** 41 55N 8 22W
Arcot **51** 12 53N 79 20 E
Arcoverde **138** 8 25S 37 4W
Arcs, Les **21** 43 27N 6 29 E
Arctic Bay **101** 73 1N 85 7W
Arctic Ocean **144** 78 0N 160 0W
Arctic Red River **100** 67 15N 134 0W
Arda →, Bulg. **35** 41 40N 26 29 E
Arda →, Italy **26** 44 53N 9 52 E
Ardabrīl **46** 38 15N 48 18 E
Ardahan **46** 41 7N 42 41 E
Ardakan **47** 30 20N 52 5 E
Ardales **23** 36 53N 4 51W
Årdalstangen **10** 61 14N 7 43 E
Ardatov **37** 54 51N 46 15 E
Ardbeg **106** 45 38N 80 5W
Ardea **35** 40 58N 22 3 E
Ardèche □ **21** 44 42N 4 16 E
Ardèche → **21** 44 16N 4 39 E
Ardee **15** 53 51N 6 32W
Arden, Can. **107** 44 43N 76 56W
Arden, U.S.A. **123** 36 1N 115 14W
Arden Stby. **11** 56 46N 9 52 E
Ardennes **16** 50 0N 5 10 E
Ardennes □ **19** 49 35N 4 40 E
Ardentes **19** 46 45N 1 50 E
Ardestān **47** 33 20N 52 25 E
Ardgour **14** 56 45N 5 25W
Árdhas → **35** 41 36N 26 25 E
Ardila → **23** 38 12N 7 28W
Ardjuno **57** 7 49S 112 34 E
Ardlethan **75** 34 22S 146 53 E
Ardmore, Austral. **72** 21 39S 139 11 E
Ardmore, Okla., U.S.A. **119** 34 10N 97 5W
Ardmore, Pa., U.S.A. **115** 39 58N 75 18W

Ardmore, S.D., U.S.A.	**118**	43 0N	103 40W
Ardnacrusha	**15**	52 43N	8 38W
Ardnamurchan, Pt. of	**14**	56 44N	6 14W
Ardno	**74**	37 49S	141 3E
Ardore Marina	**29**	38 11N	16 10E
Ardres	**19**	50 50N	2 0E
Ardrossan, Austral.	**73**	34 26S	137 53E
Ardrossan, U.K.	**14**	55 39N	4 50W
Ards □	**15**	54 35N	5 30W
Ards Pen.	**15**	54 30N	5 25W
Ardud	**34**	47 37N	22 52E
Ardunac	**39**	41 8N	42 5E
Åre	**10**	63 22N	13 15E
Arecibo	**127**	18 29N	66 42W
Areia Branca	**138**	5 0S	37 0W
Arena de la Ventana, Punta	**124**	24 4N	109 52W
Arena, Pt.	**122**	38 57N	123 44W
Arenales, Cerro	**142**	47 5S	73 40W
Arenápolis	**137**	14 26S	56 49W
Arenas	**22**	43 17N	4 50W
Arenas de San Pedro	**22**	40 12N	5 5W
Arendal	**11**	58 28N	8 46E
Arendsee	**30**	52 52N	11 27E
Arenillas	**134**	3 33S	80 10W
Arenys de Mar	**24**	41 35N	2 33E
Arenzano	**26**	44 24N	8 40E
Arenzville	**116**	39 53N	90 22W
Areópolis	**35**	36 40N	22 22E
Arequipa	**136**	16 20S	71 30W
Arequipa □	**136**	16 0S	72 50W
Arere	**135**	0 16S	53 52W
Arero	**91**	4 41N	38 50E
Arès	**20**	44 47N	1 8W
Arévalo	**22**	41 3N	4 43W
Arezzo	**27**	43 28N	11 50E
Arga →	**24**	42 18N	1 47W
Argalastí	**35**	39 13N	23 13E
Argalong	**76**	35 18S	148 27E
Argamasilla de Alba	**25**	39 8N	3 5W
Arganda	**24**	40 19N	3 26W
Arganil	**22**	40 13N	8 3W
Argelès-Gazost	**20**	43 0N	0 6W
Argelès-sur-Mer	**20**	42 34N	3 1E
Argens →	**21**	43 24N	6 44E
Argent-sur-Sauldre	**19**	47 33N	2 25E
Argenta, Can.	**108**	50 20N	116 55W
Argenta, Italy	**27**	44 37N	11 50E
Argenta, U.S.A.	**117**	39 59N	88 49W
Argentan	**18**	48 45N	0 1W
Argentário, Mte.	**27**	42 23N	11 11E
Argentat	**20**	45 6N	1 56E
Argentera	**26**	44 23N	6 58E
Argentera, Monte del	**26**	44 12N	7 5E
Argenteuil	**19**	48 57N	2 14E
Argentia	**103**	47 18N	53 58W
Argentiera, C. dell'	**28**	40 44N	8 8E
Argentière, L'	**21**	44 47N	6 33E
Argentina ■	**142**	35 0S	66 0W
Argentino, L.	**142**	50 10S	73 0W
Argenton-Château	**18**	46 59N	0 27W
Argenton-sur-Creuse	**20**	46 36N	1 30E
Argeş →	**34**	44 30N	25 50E
Arghandab →	**48**	31 30N	64 15E
Argo	**90**	19 28N	30 30E
Argolikós Kólpos	**35**	37 20N	22 52E
Argonne	**19**	49 0N	5 20E
Árgos	**35**	37 40N	22 43E
Argos	**117**	41 14N	86 15W
Argostólion	**35**	38 12N	20 33E
Arguedas	**24**	42 11N	1 36W
Arguello, Pt.	**123**	34 34N	120 40W
Argun →	**41**	53 20N	121 28E
Argungu	**89**	12 40N	4 31E
Argus Pk.	**123**	35 52N	117 26W
Argyle	**118**	48 23N	96 49W
Argyle, L.	**78**	16 20S	128 40E
Argyrádhes	**35**	39 27N	19 58E
Århus	**11**	56 8N	10 11E
Århus Amtskommune □	**11**	56 15N	10 15E
Aria	**80**	38 33S	175 0E
Ariah Park	**76**	34 22S	147 16E
Ariamsvlei	**96**	28 9S	19 51E
Ariana	**87**	36 52N	10 12E
Ariano Irpino	**29**	41 10N	15 4E
Ariano nel Polèsine	**27**	44 56N	12 5E
Ariari →	**134**	2 35N	72 47W
Aribinda	**89**	14 17N	0 52W
Arica, Chile	**136**	18 32S	70 20W
Arica, Colomb.	**134**	2 0S	71 50W
Arid, C.	**79**	34 1S	123 10E
Arida	**65**	34 5N	135 8E
Aridh	**46**	25 0N	46 0E
Ariège □	**20**	42 56N	1 30E
Ariège →	**20**	43 30N	1 25E
Arieş →	**34**	46 24N	23 20E
Arima	**127**	10 38N	61 17W
Arinos →	**137**	10 25S	58 20W
Ario de Rosales	**124**	19 12N	102 0W
Aripuanã	**137**	9 25S	60 30W
Aripuanã →	**137**	5 7S	60 25W
Ariquemes	**137**	9 55S	63 6W
Arisaig	**14**	56 55N	5 50W
Arîsh, W. el →	**90**	31 9N	33 49E
Arismendi	**134**	8 29N	68 22W
Arissa	**91**	11 10N	41 35E
Aristazabal, I.	**108**	52 40N	129 10W
Arita	**64**	33 11N	129 54E
Arivaca	**121**	31 37N	111 25W
Arivonimamo	**97**	19 1S	47 11E
Ariyalur	**51**	11 8N	79 8E
Ariza	**64**	41 19N	2 3W
Arizaro, Salar de	**140**	24 40S	67 50W
Arizona	**140**	35 45S	65 25W
Arizona □	**121**	34 20N	111 30W
Arizpe	**124**	30 20N	110 11W
Årjäng	**10**	59 24N	12 8E
Arjeplog	**8**	66 3N	18 2E
Arjona, Colomb.	**134**	10 14N	75 22W
Arjona, Spain	**23**	37 56N	4 4W
Arka	**41**	60 15N	142 0E
Arkadak	**37**	51 58N	43 19E
Arkadelphia	**119**	34 5N	93 0W
Arkaig, L.	**14**	56 58N	5 10W
Arkalyk	**40**	50 13N	66 50E
Arkansas □	**119**	35 0N	92 30W
Arkansas →	**119**	33 48N	91 4W
Arkansas City	**119**	37 4N	97 3W
Árkathos →	**35**	39 20N	21 4E
Arkhangelsk	**40**	64 40N	41 0E
Arkhangelskoye	**37**	51 32N	40 58E
Arkiko	**91**	15 33N	39 30E
Arklow	**15**	52 48N	6 10W
Arkona	**106**	43 4N	81 50W
Arkona, Kap	**30**	54 41N	13 26E
Arkonam	**51**	13 7N	79 43E
Arkösund	**11**	58 29N	16 56E
Arkticheskiy, Mys	**41**	81 10N	95 0E
Arlanc	**20**	45 25N	3 42E
Arlanza →	**22**	42 6N	4 9W
Arlanzón →	**22**	42 3N	4 17W
Arlberg Pass	**31**	47 9N	10 12E
Arlee	**120**	47 10N	114 4W
Arles	**21**	43 41N	4 40E
Arlington, S. Afr.	**97**	28 1S	27 53E
Arlington, Oreg., U.S.A.	**120**	45 48N	120 6W
Arlington, S.D., U.S.A.	**118**	44 25N	97 4W
Arlington, Va., U.S.A.	**112**	38 52N	77 5W
Arlington, Wash., U.S.A.	**122**	48 11N	122 4W
Arlington Heights	**117**	42 5N	87 59W
Arlon	**16**	49 42N	5 49E
Arlöv	**11**	55 38N	13 5E
Arly	**89**	11 35N	1 28E
Armadale	**79**	32 12S	116 0E
Armagh, Can.	**105**	46 41N	70 32W
Armagh, U.K.	**15**	54 22N	6 40W
Armagh □	**15**	54 18N	6 37W
Armagnac	**20**	43 44N	0 10E
Armançon →	**19**	47 59N	3 30E
Armavir	**39**	45 2N	41 7E
Armenia	**134**	4 35N	75 45W
Armenian S.S.R. □	**39**	40 0N	44 0E
Armentières	**19**	50 40N	2 50E
Armidale	**77**	30 30S	151 40E
Armour	**118**	43 20N	98 25W
Armstrong, B.C., Can.	**108**	50 25N	119 10W
Armstrong, Ont., Can.	**102**	50 18N	89 4W
Armstrong, U.S.A.	**119**	26 59N	97 48W
Armstrong Cr. →	**78**	16 35S	131 40E
Armur	**50**	18 48N	78 16E
Arnaouti, C.	**46**	35 0N	32 20E
Arnarfjörður	**8**	65 48N	23 40W
Arnaud →	**101**	60 0N	70 0W
Arnay-le-Duc	**19**	47 10N	4 27E
Arnedillo	**24**	42 13N	2 14W
Arnedo	**24**	42 12N	2 5W
Árnes	**8**	66 1N	21 31W
Årnes	**10**	60 7N	11 28E
Arnett	**119**	36 9N	99 44W
Arnhem	**16**	51 58N	5 55E
Arnhem B.	**72**	12 20S	136 10E
Arnhem, C.	**72**	12 20S	137 30E
Arnhem Land	**72**	13 10S	134 30E
Arni	**51**	12 43N	79 19E
Arno →	**26**	43 41N	10 17E
Arno Bay	**73**	33 54S	136 34E
Arnold, N.Z.	**81**	42 29S	171 25E
Arnold, Calif., U.S.A.	**122**	38 15N	120 20W
Arnold, Nebr., U.S.A.	**118**	41 29N	100 10W
Arnold, Pa., U.S.A.	**114**	40 36N	79 44W
Arnoldstein	**33**	46 33N	13 43E
Arnon →	**19**	47 13N	2 1E
Arnot	**109**	55 56N	96 41W
Arnøy	**8**	70 9N	20 40E
Arnprior	**107**	45 26N	76 21W
Arnsberg	**30**	51 25N	8 2E
Arnstadt	**30**	50 50N	10 56E
Arntfield	**104**	48 12N	79 15W
Aro →	**135**	8 1N	64 11W
Aroab	**96**	26 41S	19 39E
Aroche	**23**	37 56N	6 57W
Aroeiras	**138**	7 31S	35 41W
Arolsen	**30**	51 23N	9 1E
Aron →	**19**	46 50N	3 27E
Arona	**26**	45 45N	8 32E
Arosa, Ria de →	**22**	42 28N	8 57W
Arpajon, Cantal, France	**20**	44 54N	2 28E
Arpajon, Essonne, France	**19**	48 37N	2 12E
Arpino	**28**	41 40N	13 35E
Arque	**136**	17 48S	66 23W
Arrabury	**73**	26 45S	141 0E
Arrah	**49**	25 35N	84 32E
Arraias	**139**	12 56S	46 57W
Arraias →, Mato Grosso, Brazil	**137**	11 10S	53 35W
Arraias →, Pará, Brazil	**138**	7 30S	49 20W
Arraiolos	**23**	38 44N	7 59W
Arran	**14**	55 34N	5 12W
Arrandale	**108**	54 57N	130 0W
Arras	**19**	50 17N	2 46E
Arrats →	**20**	44 6N	0 52E
Arreau	**20**	42 54N	0 22E
Arrecife	**84**	28 59N	13 40W
Arrecifes	**140**	34 06S	60 9W
Arrée, Mts. d'	**18**	48 26N	3 55W
Arriaga, Chiapas, Mexico	**125**	16 15N	93 52W
Arriaga, San Luis Potosí, Mexico	**124**	21 55N	101 23W
Arrilalah P.O.	**72**	23 43S	143 54E
Arrino	**79**	29 30S	115 40E
Arrojado →	**139**	13 24S	44 20W
Arromanches-les-Bains	**18**	49 20N	0 38W
Arronches	**23**	39 8N	7 16W
Arros, R	**20**	43 40N	0 2W
Arrou	**18**	48 6N	1 8E
Arrow, L.	**15**	54 3N	8 20W
Arrow Rock Res.	**120**	43 45N	115 50W
Arrowhead	**108**	50 40N	117 55W
Arrowhead, L.	**123**	34 16N	117 10W
Arrowsmith, Mt.	**81**	43 20S	170 55E
Arrowtown	**81**	44 57S	168 50E
Arroyo de la Luz	**23**	39 30N	6 38W
Arroyo Grande	**123**	35 9N	120 32W
Års	**11**	56 48N	9 30E
Ars	**20**	46 13N	1 30W
Ars-sur-Moselle	**19**	49 5N	6 4E
Arsenault L.	**109**	55 6N	108 32W
Arsiero	**27**	45 49N	11 22E
Arsikere	**51**	13 15N	76 15E
Arsk	**37**	56 10N	49 50E
Árta	**35**	39 8N	21 2E
Artá	**24**	39 40N	3 20E
Arteaga	**124**	18 50N	102 20W
Arteijo	**22**	43 19N	8 29W
Artem,Os.	**39**	40 28N	50 20E
Artémou	**88**	15 38N	12 16W
Artemovsk, R.S.F.S.R., U.S.S.R.	**41**	54 45N	93 35E
Artemovsk, Ukr., U.S.S.R.	**38**	48 35N	38 0E
Artenay	**19**	48 5N	1 50E
Artern	**30**	51 22N	11 18E
Artesa de Segre	**24**	41 54N	1 3E
Artesia	**119**	32 55N	104 25W
Artesia Wells	**119**	28 17N	99 18W
Artesian	**118**	44 2N	97 54W
Arthez-de-Béarn	**20**	43 29N	0 38W
Arthington	**88**	6 35N	10 45W
Arthur, Can.	**106**	43 50N	80 32W
Arthur, U.S.A.	**117**	39 43N	88 28W
Arthur →	**72**	41 2S	144 40E
Arthur Cr. →	**72**	22 30S	136 25E
Arthur Pt.	**72**	22 7S	150 3E
Arthur's Pass	**81**	42 54S	171 35E
Arthur's Town	**127**	24 38N	75 42W
Artigas	**140**	30 20S	56 30W
Artik	**39**	40 38N	43 58E
Artillery L.	**109**	63 9N	107 52W
Artois	**19**	50 20N	2 30E
Artvin	**46**	41 14N	41 44E
Aru, Kepulauan	**57**	6 0S	134 30E
Aru Meru □	**94**	3 20S	36 50E
Arua	**94**	3 1N	30 58E
Aruanã	**139**	14 54S	51 10W
Aruba	**127**	12 30N	70 0W
Arudy	**20**	43 7N	0 28W
Arumã	**135**	4 44S	62 8W
Arumpo	**74**	33 48S	142 55E
Arun →	**49**	26 55N	87 10E
Arunachal Pradesh □	**52**	28 0N	95 0E
Arundel	**104**	45 58N	74 37W
Aruppukottai	**51**	9 31N	78 8E
Arusha	**94**	3 20S	36 40E
Arusha □	**94**	4 0S	36 30E
Arusha Chini	**94**	3 32S	37 20E
Arusi □	**91**	7 45N	39 00E
Aruvi →	**51**	8 48N	79 53E
Aruwimi →	**94**	1 13N	23 36E
Arvada	**120**	44 43N	106 6W
Arvakalu	**51**	8 20N	79 58E
Arvayheer	**62**	46 15N	102 48E
Arve →	**21**	46 11N	6 8E
Arvi	**50**	20 59N	78 16E
Arvida	**105**	48 25N	71 14W
Arvidsjaur	**8**	65 35N	19 10E
Arvika	**10**	59 40N	12 36E
Arvin	**123**	35 12N	118 50W
Arxan	**62**	47 11N	119 57E
Arys	**40**	42 26N	68 48E
Arzachena	**28**	41 5N	9 27E
Arzamas	**37**	55 27N	43 55E
Arzew	**86**	35 50N	0 23W
Arzgir	**39**	45 18N	44 23E
Arzignano	**27**	45 30N	11 20E
As Salt	**44**	32 2N	35 43E
As Samāwah	**46**	31 15N	45 15E
As-Samū	**44**	31 24N	35 4E
As Shatrah	**46**	31 30N	46 10E
As Sulamāniyah	**46**	35 35N	45 29E
As Sulaymānīyah	**46**	24 9N	47 18E
As Sulṭān	**87**	31 4N	17 8E
As Summān	**46**	25 0N	47 0E
As Suwaih	**47**	22 10N	59 33E
As Suwayda	**46**	32 40N	36 30E
As Suwayrah	**46**	32 55N	45 0E
Asab	**96**	25 30S	18 0E
Asaba	**89**	6 12N	6 38E
Asafo	**88**	6 20N	2 40W
Asahi	**65**	35 43N	140 39E
Asahi →	**64**	34 36N	133 58E
Asahigawa	**63**	43 46N	142 22E
Asale, L.	**91**	14 0N	40 20E
Asama-Yama	**65**	36 24N	138 31E
Asamankese	**89**	5 50N	0 40W
Asansol	**49**	23 40N	87 1E
Åsarna	**10**	62 39N	14 22E
Asbe Teferi	**91**	9 4N	40 49E
Asbesberge	**96**	29 0S	23 0E
Asbestos	**103**	45 47N	71 58W
Asbury Park	**115**	40 15N	74 1W
Ascensión	**124**	31 6N	107 59W
Ascensión, B. de la	**125**	19 50N	87 20W
Ascension, I.	**129**	8 0S	14 15W
Aschaffenburg	**31**	49 58N	9 8E
Aschendorf	**30**	53 2N	7 22E
Aschersleben	**30**	51 45N	11 28E
Asciano	**27**	43 14N	11 32E
Áscoli Piceno	**27**	42 51N	13 34E
Áscoli Satriano	**29**	41 11N	15 32E
Ascope	**136**	7 46S	79 8W
Ascotán	**140**	21 45S	68 17W
Aseb	**91**	13 0N	42 40E
Åseda	**11**	57 10N	15 20E
Asedjrad	**86**	24 51N	1 29E
Asela	**91**	8 0N	39 0E
Asenovgrad	**35**	42 1N	24 51E
Asfeld	**19**	49 27N	4 5E
Asfûn el Matâ'na	**90**	25 26N	32 30E
Åsgårdstrand	**10**	59 22N	10 27E
Ash Fork	**121**	35 14N	112 32W
Ash Grove	**119**	37 21N	93 36W
Ash Shām, Bādiyat	**46**	32 0N	40 0E
Ash Shāmiyah	**46**	31 55N	44 35E
Ash Shu'aybah	**46**	27 53N	42 43E
Ash Shu'bah	**46**	28 54N	44 44E
Ash Shuna	**44**	32 37N	35 34E
Ashaira	**90**	21 40N	40 40E
Ashanti □	**89**	7 30N	1 30W
Ashau	**54**	16 6N	107 22E
Ashburn	**113**	31 42N	83 40W
Ashburton	**81**	43 53S	171 48E
Ashburton →	**78**	21 40S	114 56E
Ashburton Downs	**78**	23 25S	117 4E
Ashburton, North Branch →	**81**	43 54S	171 44E
Ashburton, South Branch →	**81**	43 54S	171 44E
Ashby-de-la-Zouch	**12**	52 45N	1 29W
Ashcroft	**108**	50 40N	121 20W
Ashdod	**44**	31 49N	34 35E
Ashdot Yaaqov	**44**	32 39N	35 35E
Asheboro	**113**	35 43N	79 46W
Asherton	**119**	28 25N	99 43W
Asheville	**113**	35 39N	82 30W
Asheweig →	**102**	54 17N	87 12W
Ashford, Austral.	**77**	29 15S	151 3E
Ashford, U.K.	**13**	51 8N	0 53E
Ashford, U.S.A.	**120**	46 45N	122 2W
Ashikaga	**65**	36 28N	139 29E
Ashio	**65**	36 38N	139 27E
Ashizuri-Zaki	**64**	32 44N	133 0E
Ashkarkot	**48**	33 3N	67 58E
Ashkhabad	**40**	38 0N	57 50E
Ashland, Ill., U.S.A.	**116**	39 53N	90 0W
Ashland, Kans., U.S.A.	**119**	37 13N	99 43W
Ashland, Ky., U.S.A.	**112**	38 25N	82 40W

Ashland, Me., U.S.A. **103** 46 34N 68 26W
Ashland, Mont., U.S.A. **120** 45 41N 106 12W
Ashland, Nebr., U.S.A. **118** 41 5N 96 27W
Ashland, Ohio, U.S.A. **114** 40 52N 82 20W
Ashland, Oreg., U.S.A. **120** 42 10N 122 38W
Ashland, Pa., U.S.A. **115** 40 45N 76 22W
Ashland, Va., U.S.A. **112** 37 46N 77 30W
Ashland, Wis., U.S.A. **118** 46 40N 90 52W
Ashley, Austral. **77** 29 18S 149 52 E
Ashley, Ill., U.S.A. **116** 38 20N 89 11W
Ashley, Ind., U.S.A. **117** 41 32N 85 4W
Ashley, N.D., U.S.A. **118** 46 3N 99 23W
Ashley, Pa., U.S.A. **115** 41 12N 75 55W
Ashley Snow I. **143** 73 35S 77 6W
Ashmont **108** 54 7N 111 35W
Ashmore Reef **78** 12 14S 123 5 E
Ashmûn **90** 30 18N 30 55 E
Ashq'elon **44** 31 42N 34 35 E
Ashtabula **114** 41 52N 80 50W
Ashti **50** 18 50N 75 15 E
Ashton, S. Afr. **96** 33 50S 20 5 E
Ashton, U.S.A. **120** 44 6N 111 30W
Ashton-under-Lyne **12** 53 30N 2 8W
Ashuanipi, L. **103** 52 45N 66 15W
Ashurst **80** 40 16S 175 45 E
Asia **42** 45 0N 75 0 E
Asia, Kepulauan **57** 1 0N 131 13 E
Asiago **27** 45 52N 11 30 E
Asidonhoppo **135** 3 50N 55 30W
Asifabad **50** 19 20N 79 24 E
Asike **57** 6 39S 140 24 E
Asilah **86** 35 29N 6 0W
Asinara, G. dell' **28** 41 0N 8 30 E
Asinara I. **28** 41 5N 8 15 E
Asino **40** 57 0N 86 0 E
Asir □ **45** 18 40N 42 30 E
Asir, Ras **45** 11 55N 51 10 E
Aska **50** 19 2N 84 42 E
Asker **10** 59 50N 10 26 E
Askersund **11** 58 53N 14 55 E
Askim **10** 59 35N 11 10 E
Askja **8** 65 3N 16 48W
Asl **90** 29 33N 32 44 E
Asmar **47** 35 10N 71 27 E
Asmera (Asmara) **91** 15 19N 38 55 E
Asnæs **11** 55 40N 11 0 E
Asni **86** 31 17N 7 58W
Aso **64** 33 0N 131 5 E
Aso-Zan **64** 32 53N 131 6 E
Asoa **94** 4 35N 25 48 E
Asola **26** 45 12N 10 25 E
Asoteriba, Jebel **90** 21 51N 36 30 E
Asotin **120** 46 20N 117 3W
Aspe **25** 38 20N 0 40W
Aspen **121** 39 12N 106 56W
Aspermont **119** 33 11N 100 15W
Aspiring, Mt. **81** 44 23S 168 46 E
Aspres **21** 44 32N 5 44 E
Aspromonte **29** 38 10N 16 0 E
Aspur **48** 23 58N 74 7 E
Asquith **109** 52 8N 107 13W
Assa **86** 28 35N 9 6W
Assaba, Massif de l' **88** 16 10N 11 45W
Assam □ **52** 26 0N 93 0 E
Assamakka **89** 19 21N 5 38 E
Asse **16** 50 24N 4 10 E
Assekrem **87** 23 16N 5 49 E
Assémini **28** 39 18N 9 0 E
Assen **16** 53 0N 6 35 E
Assens, Fyn, Denmark **11** 55 16N 9 55 E
Assens, Fyn, Denmark **11** 56 41N 10 3 E
Assini **88** 5 9N 3 17W
Assiniboia **109** 49 40N 105 59W
Assiniboine → **109** 49 53N 97 8W
Assis **141** 22 40S 50 20W
Assisi **27** 43 4N 12 36 E
Assumption **116** 39 31N 89 3W
Assynt, L. **14** 58 25N 5 15W
Astaffort **20** 44 4N 0 40 E
Asti **26** 44 54N 8 11 E
Astipálaia **35** 36 32N 26 22 E
Astorga **22** 42 29N 6 8W
Astoria, Ill., U.S.A. **116** 40 14N 90 21W
Astoria, Oreg., U.S.A. **122** 46 16N 123 50W
Åstorp **11** 56 6N 12 55 E
Astorville **106** 46 11N 79 17W
Astrakhan **39** 46 25N 48 5 E
Astrolabe, C. **68** 8 20S 160 34 E
Astudillo **22** 42 12N 4 22W
Asturias **22** 43 15N 6 0W
Asunción **140** 25 10S 57 30W
Asunción, La **135** 11 2N 63 53W
Asutri **91** 15 25N 35 45 E
Aswa → **94** 3 43N 31 55 E
Aswad, Ras al **90** 21 20N 39 0 E
Aswân **90** 24 4N 32 57 E
Aswân High Dam = Sadd el Aali **90** 24 5N 32 54 E
Asyût **90** 27 11N 31 4 E
Asyûti, Wadi → **90** 27 11N 31 16 E
Aszód **33** 47 39N 19 28 E
At Tafilah **46** 30 45N 35 30 E
At Ta'if **90** 21 5N 40 27 E
Atacama □ **140** 27 30S 70 0W
Atacama, Desierto de **140** 24 0S 69 20W
Atacama, Salar de **140** 23 30N 68 20W
Ataco **134** 3 35N 75 23W
Atakor **87** 23 27N 5 31 E
Atakpamé **89** 7 31N 1 13 E
Atalándi **35** 38 39N 22 58 E
Atalaya **136** 10 45S 73 50W
Ataléia **139** 18 3S 41 6W
Atami **65** 35 5N 139 4 E
Atankawng **52** 25 50N 97 47 E
Atapupu **57** 9 0S 124 51 E
Atar **84** 20 30N 13 5W
Atara **41** 63 10N 129 10 E
Ataram, Erg n- **86** 23 57N 2 0 E
Atarfe **23** 37 13N 3 40W
Atascadero **121** 35 32N 120 44W
Atasu **40** 48 30N 71 0 E
Atauro **57** 8 10S 125 30 E
Atbara **90** 17 42N 33 59 E
'Atbara → **90** 17 40N 33 56 E
Atbasar **40** 51 48N 68 20 E
Atchafalaya B. **119** 29 30N 91 20W
Atchison **118** 39 40N 95 10W
Atebubu **89** 7 47N 1 0W
Ateca **24** 41 20N 1 49W
Aterno → **27** 42 11N 13 51 E
Atesine, Alpi **26** 46 55N 11 30 E
Atessa **27** 42 5N 14 27 E
Ath **16** 50 38N 3 47 E
Ath Thāmāmi **46** 27 45N 44 45 E
Athabasca **108** 54 45N 113 20W
Athabasca → **109** 58 40N 110 50W
Athabasca, L. **109** 59 15N 109 15W
Athboy **15** 53 37N 6 55W
Athenry **15** 53 18N 8 45W
Athens, Can. **107** 44 38N 75 57W
Athens, Ala., U.S.A. **113** 34 49N 86 58W
Athens, Ga., U.S.A. **113** 33 56N 83 24W
Athens, N.Y., U.S.A. **115** 42 15N 73 48W
Athens, Ohio, U.S.A. **112** 39 25N 82 6W
Athens, Pa., U.S.A. **115** 41 57N 76 36W
Athens, Tenn., U.S.A. **113** 35 45N 84 38W
Athens, Tex., U.S.A. **119** 32 11N 95 48W
Athens = Athínai **35** 37 58N 23 46 E
Atherley **106** 44 37N 79 20W
Atherton **72** 17 17S 145 30 E
Athiéme **89** 6 37N 1 40 E
Athínai **35** 37 58N 23 46 E
Athlone **15** 53 26N 7 57W
Athni **50** 16 44N 75 6 E
Athol **81** 45 30S 168 35 E
Atholl, Forest of **14** 56 51N 3 50W
Atholville **103** 47 59N 66 43W
Áthos, Mt. **35** 40 9N 24 22 E
Athy **15** 53 0N 7 0W
Ati **91** 13 5N 29 2 E
Atiak **94** 3 12N 32 2 E
Atiamuri **80** 38 24S 176 5 E
Atico **136** 16 14S 73 40W
Atienza **24** 41 12N 2 52W
Atikokan **102** 48 45N 91 37W
Atikonak L. **103** 52 40N 64 32W
Atka **41** 60 50N 151 48 E
Atkarsk **37** 51 55N 45 2 E
Atkinson, Ill., U.S.A. **116** 41 25N 90 1W
Atkinson, Nebr., U.S.A. **118** 42 35N 98 59W
Atlanta, Ga., U.S.A. **113** 33 50N 84 24W
Atlanta, Ill., U.S.A. **116** 40 16N 89 14W
Atlanta, Mich., U.S.A. **106** 45 0N 84 9W
Atlanta, Mo., U.S.A. **116** 39 54N 92 29W
Atlanta, Tex., U.S.A. **119** 33 7N 94 8W
Atlantic **118** 41 25N 95 0W
Atlantic City **112** 39 25N 74 25W
Atlantic Ocean **128** 0 0 20 0W
Atlántico □ **134** 10 45N 75 0W
Atlin **100** 59 31N 133 41W
Atlin, L. **108** 59 26N 133 45W
'Atlit **44** 32 42N 34 56 E
Atmakur **51** 14 37N 79 40 E
Atmore **113** 31 2N 87 30W
Atō **64** 34 25N 131 40 E
Atoka **119** 34 22N 96 10W
Átokos **35** 38 28N 20 49 E
Atolia **123** 35 19N 117 37W
Atouguia **23** 39 20N 9 20W
Atoyac → **125** 16 30N 97 31W
Atrak → **47** 37 50N 57 0 E
Ätran **11** 57 7N 12 57 E
Atrato → **134** 8 17N 76 58W
Atrauli **48** 28 2N 78 20 E
Atri **27** 42 35N 14 0 E
Atsbi **91** 13 52N 39 50 E
Atsugi **65** 35 25N 139 21 E
Atsumi **65** 34 35N 137 4 E
Atsumi-Wan **65** 34 44N 137 13 E
Atsuta **63** 43 24N 141 26 E
Attalla **113** 34 2N 86 5W
Attawapiskat **102** 52 56N 82 24W
Attawapiskat → **102** 52 57N 82 18W
Attawapiskat, L. **102** 52 18N 87 54W
Attendorn **30** 51 8N 7 54 E
Attica **117** 40 20N 87 15W
Attichy **19** 49 25N 3 3 E
Attigny **19** 49 28N 4 35 E
Attikamagen L. **103** 55 0N 66 30W
Attil **44** 32 23N 35 4 E
Attleboro **115** 41 56N 71 18W
Attock **48** 33 52N 72 20 E
Attopeu **54** 14 48N 106 50 E
Attunga **77** 30 55S 150 50 E
Attur **51** 11 35N 78 30 E
Atuel → **140** 36 17S 66 50W
Åtvidaberg **11** 58 12N 16 0 E
Atwater **122** 37 21N 120 37W
Atwood, Can. **106** 43 40N 81 1W
Atwood, U.S.A. **118** 39 52N 101 3W
Au Gres **106** 44 3N 83 42W
Au Sable → **106** 44 25N 83 20W
Au Sable Pt., Huron, U.S.A. **106** 44 20N 83 20W
Au Sable Pt., Superior, U.S.A. **102** 46 40N 86 10W
Aubagne **21** 43 17N 5 37 E
Aube □ **19** 48 15N 4 0 E
Aube → **19** 48 34N 3 43 E
Aubenas **21** 44 37N 4 24 E
Aubenton **19** 49 50N 4 12 E
Auberry **122** 37 7N 119 29W
Aubigny-sur-Nère **19** 47 30N 2 24 E
Aubin **20** 44 33N 2 15 E
Aubrac, Mts. d' **20** 44 38N 2 58 E
Auburn, Ala., U.S.A. **113** 32 37N 85 30W
Auburn, Calif., U.S.A. **122** 38 53N 121 4W
Auburn, Ill., U.S.A. **116** 39 36N 89 45W
Auburn, Ind., U.S.A. **117** 41 20N 85 0W
Auburn, N.Y., U.S.A. **115** 42 57N 76 39W
Auburn, Nebr., U.S.A. **118** 40 25N 95 50W
Auburn, Wash., U.S.A. **122** 47 18N 122 13W
Auburn Range **73** 25 15S 150 30 E
Auburndale **113** 28 5N 81 45W
Aubusson **20** 45 57N 2 11 E
Auch **20** 43 39N 0 36 E
Auchel **19** 50 30N 2 29 E
Auchi **89** 7 6N 6 13 E
Auckland **80** 36 52S 174 46 E
Auckland □ **80** 38 35S 177 0 E
Auckland Is. **66** 50 40S 166 5 E
Aude □ **20** 43 8N 2 28 E
Aude → **20** 43 13N 3 14 E
Auden **102** 50 14N 87 53W
Auderville **18** 49 43N 1 57W
Audierne **18** 48 1N 4 34W
Audincourt **19** 47 30N 6 50 E
Audo Ra. **91** 6 20N 41 50 E
Audubon **116** 41 43N 94 56W
Aue **30** 50 34N 12 43 E
Auerbach **30** 50 30N 12 25 E
Aueti Paraná → **134** 1 51S 65 37W
Auffay **18** 49 43N 1 07 E
Augathella **73** 25 48S 146 35 E
Augrabies Falls **96** 28 35S 20 20 E
Augsburg **31** 48 22N 10 54 E
Augusta, Italy **29** 37 14N 15 12 E
Augusta, Ark., U.S.A. **119** 35 17N 91 25W
Augusta, Ga., U.S.A. **113** 33 29N 81 59W
Augusta, Ill., U.S.A. **116** 40 14N 90 57W
Augusta, Kans., U.S.A. **119** 37 40N 97 0W
Augusta, Ky., U.S.A. **117** 38 47N 84 0W
Augusta, Me., U.S.A. **103** 44 20N 69 46W
Augusta, Mont., U.S.A. **120** 47 30N 112 29W
Augusta, Wis., U.S.A. **118** 44 41N 91 8W
Augustenborg **11** 54 57N 9 53 E
Augustines, L. des **104** 47 37N 75 56W
Augusto Cardosa **95** 12 40S 34 50 E
Augustów **32** 53 51N 23 00 E
Augustus Downs **72** 18 35S 139 55 E
Augustus I. **78** 15 20S 124 30 E
Augustus, Mt. **79** 24 20S 116 50 E
Aukan **91** 15 29N 40 50 E
Auki **68** 8 45S 160 42 E
Aukum **122** 38 34N 120 43W
Aulla **26** 44 12N 10 0 E
Aulnay **20** 46 2N 0 22W
Aulne → **18** 48 17N 4 16W
Aulnoye **19** 50 12N 3 50 E
Ault **118** 40 40N 104 42W
Ault-Onival **18** 50 5N 1 29 E
Aulus-les-Bains **20** 42 49N 1 19 E
Aumale **19** 49 46N 1 46 E
Aumont-Aubrac **20** 44 43N 3 17 E
Auna **89** 10 9N 4 42 E
Aundh **50** 17 33N 74 23 E
Aunis **20** 46 5N 0 50W
Auponhia **57** 1 58S 125 27 E
Aups **21** 43 37N 6 15 E
Aur, P. **55** 2 35N 104 10 E
Aura **52** 26 59N 97 57 E
Auraiya **49** 26 28N 79 33 E
Aurangabad, Bihar, India **49** 24 45N 84 18 E
Aurangabad, Maharashtra, India **50** 19 50N 75 23 E
Auray **18** 47 40N 3 0W
Aurès **87** 35 8N 6 30 E
Aurich **30** 53 28N 7 30 E
Aurilândia **139** 16 44S 50 28W
Aurillac **20** 44 55N 2 26 E
Auronza **27** 46 33N 12 27 E
Aurora, Can. **114** 44 0N 79 28W
Aurora, S. Afr. **96** 32 40S 18 29 E
Aurora, Colo., U.S.A. **118** 39 44N 104 55W
Aurora, Ill., U.S.A. **117** 41 42N 88 12W
Aurora, Mo., U.S.A. **119** 36 58N 93 42W
Aurora, Nebr., U.S.A. **118** 40 55N 98 0W
Aurora, Ohio, U.S.A. **114** 41 21N 81 20W
Aurora = Maewo **68** 15 10S 168 10 E
Aurskog **10** 59 55N 11 26 E
Aurukun Mission **72** 13 20S 141 45 E
Aus **96** 26 35S 16 12 E
Ausable → **106** 43 19N 81 46W
Aust-Agder fylke □ **9** 58 55N 7 40 E
Austin, Ind., U.S.A. **117** 38 45N 85 49W
Austin, Minn., U.S.A. **118** 43 37N 92 59W
Austin, Nev., U.S.A. **120** 39 30N 117 1W
Austin, Pa., U.S.A. **114** 41 40N 78 7W
Austin, Tex., U.S.A. **119** 30 20N 97 45W
Austin, L. **79** 27 40S 118 0 E
Austral Downs **72** 20 30S 137 45 E
Austral Is. = Tubuai Is. **67** 23 0S 150 0W
Austral Seamount Chain **67** 24 0S 150 0W
Australia ■ **66** 23 0S 135 0 E
Australian Alps **75** 36 30S 148 30 E
Australian Cap. Terr. □ **75** 35 30S 149 0 E
Australian Dependency □ **143** 73 0S 90 0 E
Austria ■ **33** 47 0N 14 0 E
Austvågøy **8** 68 20N 14 40 E
Autazes **135** 3 35S 59 8W
Auterive **20** 43 21N 1 29 E
Authie → **19** 50 22N 1 38 E
Authon **18** 48 12N 0 55 E
Autlán **124** 19 40N 104 30W
Autun **19** 46 58N 4 17 E
Auvergne, Austral. **78** 15 39S 130 1 E
Auvergne, France **20** 45 20N 3 15 E
Auvézère → **20** 45 12N 0 50 E
Auxerre **19** 47 48N 3 32 E
Auxi-le-Château **19** 50 15N 2 8 E
Auxonne **19** 47 10N 5 20 E
Auxvasse **116** 39 1N 91 54W
Auzances **20** 46 2N 2 30 E
Auzat **20** 45 27N 3 19 E
Ava **116** 37 53N 89 30W
Avallon **19** 47 30N 3 53 E
Avalon **123** 33 21N 118 20W
Avalon Pen. **103** 47 30N 53 20W
Avalon Res. **119** 32 30N 104 30W
Avanigadda **51** 16 0N 80 56 E
Avaré **141** 23 4S 48 58W
Ávas **35** 40 57N 25 56 E
Avawatz Mts. **123** 35 30N 116 20W
Aveiro, Brazil **135** 3 10S 55 5W
Aveiro, Port. **22** 40 37N 8 38W
Aveiro □ **22** 40 40N 8 35W
Avej **46** 35 40N 49 15 E
Avellaneda **140** 34 50S 58 10W
Avellino **29** 40 54N 14 46 E
Avenal, Austral. **74** 36 53S 145 15 E
Avenal, U.S.A. **122** 36 0N 120 8W
Averøya **10** 63 0N 7 35 E
Aversa **29** 40 58N 14 11 E
Avery **120** 47 22N 115 56W
Aves, I. de **127** 15 45N 63 55W
Aves, Is. de **127** 12 0N 67 30W
Avesnes-sur-Helpe **19** 50 8N 3 55 E
Avesta **10** 60 9N 16 10 E
Aveyron □ **20** 44 22N 2 45 E
Aveyron → **20** 44 7N 1 5 E
Avezzano **27** 42 2N 13 24 E
Aviá Terai **140** 26 45S 60 50W
Aviano **27** 46 3N 12 35 E
Avigliana **26** 45 7N 7 13 E
Avigliano **29** 40 44N 15 41 E
Avignon **21** 43 57N 4 50 E
Ávila **22** 40 39N 4 43W
Ávila □ **22** 40 30N 5 0W
Avila Beach **123** 35 11N 120 44W
Ávila, Sierra de **22** 40 40N 5 0W
Avilés **22** 43 35N 5 57W
Avisio → **27** 46 7N 11 5 E
Aviston **116** 38 36N 89 36W

Aviz	**23**	39 4N	7 53W
Avize	**19**	48 59N	4 0 E
Avoca, Austral.	**74**	37 5 S	143 26 E
Avoca, Ireland	**15**	52 52N	6 13W
Avoca, U.S.A.	**114**	42 24N	77 25W
Avoca →, Austral.	**74**	35 40 S	143 43 E
Avoca →, Ireland	**15**	52 48N	6 10W
Avola, Can.	**108**	51 45N	119 19W
Avola, Italy	**29**	36 56N	15 7 E
Avon, Ill., U.S.A.	**116**	40 40N	90 26W
Avon, N.Y., U.S.A.	**114**	43 0N	77 42W
Avon, S.D., U.S.A.	**118**	43 0N	98 3W
Avon □	**13**	51 30N	2 40W
Avon →, Austral.	**79**	31 40 S	116 7 E
Avon →, Avon, U.K.	**13**	51 30N	2 43W
Avon →, Hants., U.K.	**13**	50 44N	1 45W
Avon →, Warwick, U.K.	**13**	52 0N	2 9W
Avon Lake	**114**	41 28N	82 3W
Avondale	**95**	17 43 S	30 58 E
Avonlea	**109**	50 0N	105 0W
Avonmore	**107**	45 10N	74 58W
Avonmouth	**13**	51 30N	2 42W
Avranches	**18**	48 40N	1 20W
Avre →	**18**	48 47N	1 22 E
Avrillé	**20**	46 28N	1 28W
Avu Avu	**68**	9 50 S	160 22 E
Awag el Baqar	**91**	10 10N	33 10 E
Awaji	**65**	34 32N	135 1 E
Awaji-Shima	**64**	34 30N	134 50 E
Awali	**47**	26 0N	50 30 E
Awantipur	**49**	33 55N	75 3 E
Awanui	**80**	35 4 S	173 17 E
Awarja →	**50**	17 5N	76 15 E
Awarta	**44**	32 10N	35 17 E
Awarua Pt.	**81**	44 15 S	168 5 E
Awasa, L.	**91**	7 0N	38 30 E
Awash	**91**	9 1N	40 10 E
Awash →	**91**	11 45N	41 5 E
Awaso	**88**	6 15N	2 22W
Awatere →	**81**	41 37 S	174 10 E
Awbārī	**87**	26 46N	12 57 E
Awe, L.	**14**	56 15N	5 15W
Aweil	**91**	8 42N	27 20 E
Awgu	**89**	6 4N	7 24 E
Awjilah	**85**	29 8N	21 7 E
Aworro	**69**	7 43 S	143 11 E
Ax-les-Thermes	**20**	42 44N	1 50 E
Axarfjörður	**8**	66 15N	16 45W
Axel Heiberg I.	**144**	80 0N	90 0W
Axim	**88**	4 51N	2 15W
Axinim	**135**	4 2 S	59 22W
Axintele	**34**	44 37N	26 47 E
Axioma	**137**	6 45 S	64 31W
Axiós →	**35**	40 57N	22 35 E
Axmarsbruk	**10**	61 3N	17 10 E
Axminster	**13**	50 47N	3 1W
Axstedt	**30**	53 26N	8 43 E
Axvall	**11**	58 23N	13 34 E
Ay	**19**	49 3N	4 0 E
Ayabaca	**136**	4 40 S	79 53W
Ayabe	**65**	35 20N	135 20 E
Ayacucho, Argent.	**140**	37 5 S	58 20W
Ayacucho, Peru	**136**	13 0 S	74 0W
Ayaguz	**40**	48 10N	80 0 E
Ayakudi	**51**	10 28N	77 56 E
Ayamonte	**23**	37 12N	7 24W
Ayan	**41**	56 30N	138 16 E
Ayancık	**38**	41 57N	34 18 E
Ayapel	**134**	8 19N	75 9W
Ayas	**38**	40 10N	32 14 E
Ayaviri	**136**	14 50 S	70 35W
Ayenngré	**89**	8 40N	1 1 E
Ayer Hitam	**55**	1 55N	103 11 E
Ayer's Cliff	**105**	45 10N	72 3W
Ayers Rock	**79**	25 23 S	131 5 E
Aygues →	**21**	44 7N	4 43 E
Ayiá	**35**	39 43N	22 45 E
Ayía Marína	**35**	37 11N	26 48 E
Ayía Paraskeví	**35**	39 14N	26 16 E
Ayía Rouméli	**35**	35 14N	23 58 E
Áyios Andréas	**35**	37 21N	22 45 E
Áyios Evstrátios	**35**	39 30N	25 0 E
Áyios Ioannis, Ákra	**35**	35 20N	25 40 E
Áyios Kiríkos	**35**	37 34N	26 17 E
Áyios Mírono	**35**	35 15N	25 1 E
Áyios Nikólaos	**35**	35 11N	25 41 E
Aykathonisi	**35**	37 28N	27 0 E
Aylen L.	**107**	45 37N	77 51W
Aylesbury	**13**	51 48N	0 49W
Aylmer, Ont., Can.	**106**	42 46N	80 59W
Aylmer, Ont., Can.	**107**	45 23N	75 50W
Aylmer, Qué., Can.	**104**	45 24N	75 51W
Aylmer L.	**100**	64 0N	110 8W
Ayn Zālah	**46**	36 45N	42 35 E
ʻAyn Zaqqūţ	**87**	29 0N	19 30 E
Ayna	**25**	38 34N	2 3W
Ayolas	**140**	27 10 S	56 59W
Ayom	**91**	7 49N	28 23 E
Ayon, Ostrov	**41**	69 50N	169 0 E
Ayora	**25**	39 3N	1 3W
Ayr, Austral.	**72**	19 35 S	147 25 E
Ayr, Can.	**106**	43 17N	80 27W
Ayr, U.K.	**14**	55 28N	4 37W
Ayr →	**14**	55 29N	4 40W
Ayre, Pt. of	**12**	54 27N	4 21W
Aysha	**91**	10 50N	42 23 E
Aytos	**34**	42 42N	27 16 E
Ayu, Kepulauan	**57**	0 35N	131 5 E
Ayutla, Guat.	**126**	14 40N	92 10W
Ayutla, Mexico	**125**	16 58N	99 17W
Ayvalık	**46**	39 20N	26 46 E
Az Zahiriya	**44**	31 25N	34 58 E
Az Zahrān	**46**	26 10N	50 7 E
Az-Zarqā	**44**	32 5N	36 4 E
Az Zāwiyah	**87**	32 52N	12 56 E
Az-Zilfī	**46**	26 12N	44 52 E
Az Zintān	**87**	31 59N	12 9 E
Az Zubayr	**46**	30 20N	47 50 E
Azambuja	**23**	39 4N	8 51W
Azamgarh	**49**	26 5N	83 13 E
Azangaro	**136**	14 55 S	70 13W
Azaouak, Vallée de l'	**89**	15 50N	3 20 E
Āzārbāijān □	**46**	37 0N	44 30 E
Azare	**89**	11 55N	10 10 E
Azay-le-Rideau	**18**	47 16N	0 30 E
Azazga	**87**	36 48N	4 22 E
Azbine = Aïr	**89**	18 0N	8 0 E
Azeffoun	**87**	36 51N	4 26 E
Azemmour	**86**	33 20N	9 20W
Azerbaijan S.S.R. □	**39**	40 20N	48 0 E
Azezo	**91**	12 28N	37 15 E
Azilal,Beni Mallal	**86**	32 0N	6 30W
Azilda	**106**	46 33N	81 6W
Azimganj	**49**	24 14N	88 16 E
Aznalcóllar	**23**	37 32N	6 17W
Azogues	**134**	2 35 S	78 0W
Azor	**44**	32 2N	34 48 E
Azores, Is. = Açores, Is. dos	**128**	38 44N	29 0W
Azov	**39**	47 3N	39 25 E
Azov Sea = Azovskoye More	**38**	46 0N	36 30 E
Azovskoye More	**38**	46 0N	36 30 E
Azovy	**40**	64 55N	64 35 E
Azpeitia	**24**	43 12N	2 19W
Azrou	**86**	33 28N	5 19W
Aztec	**121**	36 54N	108 0W
Azúa de Compostela	**127**	18 25N	70 44W
Azuaga	**23**	38 16N	5 39W
Azuara	**24**	41 15N	0 53W
Azuay □	**134**	2 55 S	79 0W
Azuer →	**23**	39 8N	3 36W
Azuero, Pen. de	**126**	7 30N	80 30W
Azul	**140**	36 42 S	59 43W
Azul, Serra	**137**	14 50 S	54 50W
Azurduy	**137**	19 59 S	64 29W
Azusa	**123**	34 8N	117 52W
Azzaba	**87**	36 48N	7 6 E
Azzano Décimo	**27**	45 53N	12 46 E

B

Ba Don	**54**	17 45N	106 26 E
Ba Dong	**55**	9 40N	106 33 E
Ba Tri	**55**	10 2N	106 36 E
Ba Xian	**60**	39 8N	116 22 E
Baa	**57**	10 50 S	123 0 E
Baaba, Î.	**68**	20 3 S	164 59 E
Baamonde	**22**	43 7N	7 44W
Baan Baa	**77**	30 36 S	149 56 E
Baarle Nassau	**16**	51 27N	4 56 E
Baarn	**16**	52 12N	5 17 E
Bāb el Māndeb	**45**	12 35N	43 25 E
Baba dag	**39**	41 0N	48 19W
Babaçulândia	**138**	7 13 S	47 46W
Babadag	**34**	44 53N	28 44 E
Babahoyo	**134**	1 40 S	79 30W
Babakin	**79**	32 7 S	118 1 E
Babana	**89**	10 31N	3 46 E
Babar, Alg.	**87**	35 10N	7 6 E
Babar, Indon.	**57**	8 0 S	129 30 E
Babar, Pak.	**48**	31 7N	69 32 E
Babarkach	**48**	29 45N	68 0 E
Babayevo	**37**	59 24N	35 55 E
Babb	**120**	48 56N	113 27W
Babenhausen	**31**	49 57N	8 56 E
Babi Besar, P.	**55**	2 25N	103 59 E
Babian Jiang →	**58**	22 55N	101 47 E
Babile	**91**	9 16N	42 11 E
Babinda	**72**	17 20 S	145 56 E
Babine	**108**	55 22N	126 37W
Babine →	**108**	55 45N	127 44W
Babine L.	**108**	54 48N	126 0W
Babo	**57**	2 30 S	133 30 E
Bābol	**47**	36 40N	52 50 E
Bābol Sar	**47**	36 45N	52 45 E
Baboma	**94**	2 30N	28 10 E
Baboua	**92**	5 49N	14 58 E
Babura	**89**	12 51N	8 59 E
Babusar Pass	**49**	35 12N	73 59 E
Babušnica	**33**	43 7N	22 27 E
Babuyan Chan.	**57**	19 10N	122 0 E
Babylon, Iraq	**46**	32 40N	44 30 E
Babylon, U.S.A.	**115**	40 42N	73 20W
Bac Can	**54**	22 8N	105 49 E
Bac Giang	**54**	21 16N	106 11 E
Bac Ninh	**54**	21 13N	106 4 E
Bac Phan	**54**	22 0N	105 0 E
Bac Quang	**54**	22 30N	104 48 E
Bacabal	**138**	4 15 S	44 45W
Bacajá →	**135**	3 25 S	51 50W
Bacalar	**125**	18 50N	87 27W
Bacan, Kepulauan	**57**	0 35 S	127 30 E
Bacan,Pulau	**57**	0 50 S	127 30 E
Bacarès, Le	**20**	42 47N	3 3 E
Bacarra	**57**	18 15N	120 37 E
Bacau	**57**	8 27 S	126 27 E
Bacău	**34**	46 35N	26 55 E
Baccarat	**19**	48 28N	6 42 E
Bacchus Marsh	**74**	37 43 S	144 27 E
Bacerac	**124**	30 18N	108 50W
Băceşti	**34**	46 50N	27 11 E
Bach Long Vi, Dao	**54**	20 10N	107 40 E
Bachaquero	**134**	9 56N	71 8W
Bacharach	**31**	50 3N	7 46 E
Bachelina	**40**	57 45N	67 20 E
Bachok	**55**	6 4N	102 25 E
Bachuma	**91**	6 48N	35 53 E
Bačina	**33**	43 42N	21 23 E
Back →	**100**	65 10N	104 0W
Bačka Palanka	**33**	45 17N	19 27 E
Bačka Topola	**33**	45 49N	19 39 E
Bäckefors	**11**	58 48N	12 9 E
Backnang	**31**	48 57N	9 26 E
Backstairs Passage	**73**	35 40 S	138 5 E
Bacolod	**57**	10 40N	122 57 E
Bacqueville	**18**	49 47N	1 0 E
Bácsalmás	**33**	46 8N	19 17 E
Bad →	**118**	44 22N	100 22W
Bad Axe	**106**	43 48N	82 59W
Bad Bergzabern	**31**	49 6N	8 0 E
Bad Bramstedt	**30**	53 56N	9 53 E
Bad Doberan	**30**	54 6N	11 55 E
Bad Driburg	**30**	51 44N	9 0 E
Bad Ems	**31**	50 22N	7 44 E
Bad Frankenhausen	**30**	51 21N	11 3 E
Bad Freienwalde	**30**	52 47N	14 3 E
Bad Godesberg	**30**	50 41N	7 4 E
Bad Hersfeld	**30**	50 52N	9 42 E
Bad Hofgastein	**33**	47 17N	13 6 E
Bad Homburg	**31**	50 17N	8 33 E
Bad Honnef	**30**	50 39N	7 13 E
Bad Ischl	**33**	47 44N	13 38 E
Bad Kissingen	**31**	50 11N	10 5 E
Bad Kreuznach	**31**	49 47N	7 47 E
Bad Lands	**118**	43 40N	102 10W
Bad Langensalza	**30**	51 6N	10 40 E
Bad Lauterberg	**30**	51 38N	10 29 E
Bad Lippspringe	**30**	51 47N	8 46 E
Bad Mergentheim	**31**	49 29N	9 47 E
Bad Münstereifel	**30**	50 33N	6 46 E
Bad Muskau	**30**	51 33N	14 43 E
Bad Nauheim	**31**	50 24N	8 45 E
Bad Oeynhausen	**30**	52 16N	8 45 E
Bad Oldesloe	**30**	53 48N	10 22 E
Bad Orb	**31**	50 16N	9 21 E
Bad Pyrmont	**30**	51 59N	9 15 E
Bad Reichenhall	**31**	47 44N	12 53 E
Bad St.-Peter	**30**	54 23N	8 32 E
Bad Salzuflen	**30**	52 8N	8 44 E
Bad Segeberg	**30**	53 58N	10 16 E
Bad Tölz	**31**	47 43N	11 34 E
Bad Waldsee	**31**	47 56N	9 46 E
Bad Wildungen	**30**	51 7N	9 10 E
Bad Wimpfen	**31**	49 12N	9 10 E
Bad Windsheim	**31**	49 29N	10 25 E
Badagara	**51**	11 35N	75 40 E
Badagri	**89**	6 25N	2 55 E
Badajós, L.	**135**	3 15 S	62 50W
Badajoz	**23**	38 50N	6 59W
Badajoz □	**23**	38 40N	6 30W
Badakhshan □	**47**	36 30N	71 0 E
Badalona	**24**	41 26N	2 15 E
Badalzai	**48**	29 50N	65 35 E
Badampahar	**50**	22 10N	86 10 E
Badanah	**46**	30 58N	41 30 E
Badas	**56**	4 33N	114 25 E
Badas, Kepulauan	**56**	0 45N	107 5 E
Baddaginnie	**74**	36 34 S	145 52 E
Baddo →	**47**	28 0N	64 20 E
Bade	**57**	7 10 S	139 35 E
Baden, Austria	**33**	48 1N	16 13 E
Baden, Can.	**114**	43 14N	80 40W
Baden, Switz.	**31**	47 28N	8 18 E
Baden-Baden	**31**	48 45N	8 15 E
Baden-Württemberg □	**31**	48 40N	9 0 E
Badenoch	**14**	58 16N	4 5W
Badger, Can.	**103**	49 0N	56 4W
Badger, U.S.A.	**122**	36 38N	119 1W
Badghis □	**47**	35 0N	63 0 E
Badgom	**49**	34 1N	74 45 E
Badia Polèsine	**27**	45 6N	11 30 E
Badin	**48**	24 38N	68 54 E
Badnera	**50**	20 48N	77 44 E
Badogo	**88**	11 2N	8 13W
Badong	**59**	31 1N	110 23 E
Badrinath	**49**	30 45N	79 30 E
Baduen	**45**	7 15N	47 40 E
Badulla	**51**	7 1N	81 7 E
Badupi	**52**	21 36N	93 27 E
Baena	**23**	37 37N	4 20W
Baerami Creek	**76**	32 27 S	150 27 E
Baeza, Ecuador	**134**	0 25 S	77 53W
Baeza, Spain	**25**	37 57N	3 25W
Bafatá	**88**	12 8N	14 40W
Baffin B.	**144**	72 0N	64 0W
Baffin I.	**101**	68 0N	75 0W
Bafia	**92**	4 40N	11 10 E
Bafilo	**89**	9 22N	1 22 E
Bafing →	**88**	13 49N	10 50W
Bafoulabé	**88**	13 50N	10 55W
Bafra	**38**	41 34N	35 54 E
Bāft, Esfahān, Iran	**47**	31 40N	55 25 E
Bāft, Kermān, Iran	**47**	29 15N	56 38 E
Bafut	**89**	6 6N	10 2 E
Bafwakwandji	**94**	1 12N	26 52 E
Bafwasende	**94**	1 3N	27 5 E
Bagalkot	**51**	16 10N	75 40 E
Bagamoyo	**94**	6 28 S	38 55 E
Bagamoyo □	**94**	6 20 S	38 30 E
Bagan Datok	**55**	3 59N	100 47 E
Bagan Serai	**55**	5 1N	100 32 E
Baganga	**57**	7 34N	126 33 E
Bagansiapiapi	**56**	2 12N	100 50 E
Bagasra	**48**	21 30N	71 0 E
Bagawi	**91**	12 20N	34 18 E
Bagdad	**123**	34 35N	115 53W
Bagdarin	**41**	54 26N	113 36 E
Bagé	**141**	31 20 S	54 15W
Bagenalstown = Muine Bheag	**15**	52 42N	6 57W
Baggs	**120**	41 8N	107 46W
Bagh	**49**	33 59N	73 45 E
Baghdād	**46**	33 20N	44 30 E
Bagherhat	**52**	22 40N	89 47 E
Bagheria	**28**	38 5N	13 30 E
Bāghīn	**47**	30 12N	56 45 E
Baghlan	**47**	36 12N	69 0 E
Baghlan □	**47**	36 0N	68 30 E
Bagley	**118**	47 30N	95 22W
Bagnacavallo	**27**	44 25N	11 58 E
Bagnara Cálabra	**29**	38 16N	15 49 E
Bagnell Dam	**116**	38 14N	92 36W
Bagnères-de-Bigorre	**20**	43 5N	0 9 E
Bagnères-de-Luchon	**20**	42 47N	0 38 E
Bagni di Lucca	**26**	44 1N	10 37 E
Bagno di Romagna	**27**	43 50N	11 59 E
Bagnoles-de-l'Orne	**18**	48 32N	0 25W
Bagnoli di Sopra	**27**	45 13N	11 55 E
Bagnolo Mella	**26**	45 27N	10 14 E
Bagnols-les-Bains	**20**	44 30N	3 40 E
Bagnols-sur-Cèze	**21**	44 10N	4 36 E
Bagnorégio	**27**	42 38N	12 7 E
Bagolino	**26**	45 49N	10 28 E
Bagotville	**105**	48 22N	70 54W
Bagua	**136**	5 35 S	78 22W
Baguio	**57**	16 26N	120 34 E
Bahabón de Esgueva	**24**	41 52N	3 43W
Bahadurabad Ghat	**52**	25 11N	89 44 E
Bahadurgarh	**48**	28 40N	76 57 E
Bahama, Canal Viejo de	**126**	22 10N	77 30W
Bahamas ■	**127**	24 0N	75 0W
Baharîya,El Wâhât al	**90**	28 0N	28 50 E
Bahau	**55**	2 48N	102 26 E
Bahawalnagar	**48**	30 0N	73 15 E
Bahawalpur	**48**	29 24N	71 40 E
Bahawalpur □	**48**	29 5N	71 3 E
Baheri	**49**	28 45N	79 34 E
Baheta	**91**	13 27N	42 10 E
Bahi	**94**	5 58 S	35 21 E
Bahi Swamp	**94**	6 10 S	35 0 E
Bahía = Salvador	**139**	13 0 S	38 30W
Bahía □	**139**	12 0 S	42 0W
Bahía Blanca	**140**	38 35 S	62 13W
Bahía de Caráquez	**134**	0 40 S	80 27W
Bahía Honda	**126**	22 54N	83 10W
Bahía, Islas de la	**126**	16 45N	86 15W
Bahía Laura	**142**	48 10 S	66 30W
Bahía Negra	**137**	20 5 S	58 5W
Bahir Dar	**91**	11 37N	37 10 E
Bahmer	**86**	27 32N	0 10W
Bahönye	**33**	46 25N	17 28 E
Bahr Aouk →	**92**	8 40N	19 0 E
Bahr el Ahmar □	**90**	20 0N	35 0 E
Bahr el Ghazâl □	**91**	7 0N	28 0 E
Bahr el Jebel →	**91**	7 30N	30 30 E
Bahr Salamat →	**92**	9 20N	18 0 E
Bahr Yûsef →	**90**	28 25N	30 35 E
Bahra el Burullus	**90**	31 28N	30 48 E
Bahraich	**49**	27 38N	81 37 E
Bahrain ■	**47**	26 0N	50 35 E
Bai	**88**	13 35N	3 28W
Bai Bung, Mui	**55**	8 38N	104 44 E

Bai Duc **54** 18 3N 105 49 E
Bai Thuong **54** 19 54N 105 23 E
Baia-Mare **34** 47 40N 23 35 E
Baia-Sprie **34** 47 41N 23 43 E
Baião **138** 2 40S 49 40W
Baibokoum **85** 7 46N 15 43 E
Baicheng **61** 45 38N 122 42 E
Baie Comeau **103** 49 12N 68 10W
Baie-du-Poste **105** 50 24N 73 56W
Baie-St-Paul **105** 47 28N 70 32W
Baie-Ste-Catherine **105** 48 6N 69 44W
Baie Trinité **103** 49 25N 67 20W
Baie Verte **103** 49 55N 56 12W
Baieville **105** 46 8N 72 43W
Baignes **20** 45 23N 0 25W
Baigneux-les-Juifs **19** 47 31N 4 39 E
Baihe, China **60** 32 50N 110 5 E
Baihe, Taiwan **59** 23 24N 120 24 E
Ba'ījī **46** 35 0N 43 30 E
Baikal, L. = Baykal, Oz. **41** 53 0N 108 0 E
Bailadila, Mt. **50** 18 43N 81 15 E
Baile Atha Cliath = Dublin **15** 53 20N 6 18W
Bailei **91** 6 44N 40 18 E
Bailén **23** 38 8N 3 48W
Băileşti **34** 44 01N 23 20 E
Bailhongal **51** 15 55N 74 53 E
Bailique, Ilha **138** 1 2N 49 58W
Bailleul **19** 50 44N 2 41 E
Baima **58** 33 0N 100 26 E
Baimuru **69** 7 35S 144 51 E
Bain-de-Bretagne **18** 47 50N 1 40W
Bainbridge, Ga., U.S.A. **113** 30 53N 84 34W
Bainbridge, Ind., U.S.A. **117** 39 46N 86 49W
Bainbridge, N.Y., U.S.A. **115** 42 17N 75 29W
Bainbridge, Ohio, U.S.A. **117** 39 14N 83 16W
Baing **57** 10 14S 120 34 E
Bainiu **60** 32 50N 112 15 E
Bainville **118** 48 8N 104 10W
Bainyik **69** 3 40S 143 4 E
Baird **119** 32 25N 99 25W
Baird Mts. **100** 67 10N 160 15W
Bairin Youqi **61** 43 30N 118 35 E
Bairin Zuoqi **61** 43 58N 119 15 E
Bairnsdale **75** 37 48S 147 36 E
Baise → **20** 44 17N 0 18 E
Baisha **60** 34 20N 112 32 E
Baissa **89** 7 14N 10 38 E
Baitadi **49** 29 35N 80 25 E
Baixa Grande **139** 11 57S 40 11W
Baiyin **60** 36 45N 104 14 E
Baiyü **58** 31 16N 98 50 E
Baiyu Shan **60** 37 15N 107 30 E
Baiyuda **90** 17 35N 32 07 E
Baja **33** 46 12N 18 59 E
Baja California **124** 31 10N 115 12W
Baja, Pta. **124** 29 50N 116 0W
Bajah, Wadi → **90** 23 14N 39 20 E
Bajana **48** 23 7N 71 49 E
Bajimba, Mt. **77** 29 17S 152 6 E
Bajo Nuevo **126** 15 40N 78 50W
Bajoga **89** 10 57N 11 20 E
Bajool **72** 23 40S 150 35 E
Bakala **92** 6 15N 20 20 E
Bakar **27** 45 18N 14 32 E
Bakchav **40** 57 1N 82 5 E
Bakel **88** 14 56N 12 20W
Baker, Calif., U.S.A. **123** 35 16N 116 8W
Baker, Mont., U.S.A. **118** 46 22N 104 12W
Baker, Nev., U.S.A. **120** 38 59N 114 7W
Baker, Oreg., U.S.A. **120** 44 50N 117 55W
Baker, Canal **142** 47 45S 74 45W
Baker I. **66** 0 10N 176 35W
Baker, L., Austral. **79** 26 54S 126 5 E
Baker, L., Can. **100** 64 0N 96 0W
Baker Lake **100** 64 20N 96 3W
Baker Mt. **120** 48 50N 121 49W
Bakers Creek **72** 21 13S 149 7 E
Baker's Dozen Is. **102** 56 45N 78 45W
Bakersfield, Calif., U.S.A. **123** 35 25N 119 0W
Bakersfield, Vt., U.S.A. **115** 44 46N 72 48W
Bakhchisaray **38** 44 40N 33 45 E
Bakhmach **36** 51 10N 32 45 E
Bakhtiari □ **46** 32 0N 49 0 E
Bakinskikh Komissarov, im 26 **46** 39 20N 49 15 E
Bakırköy **35** 40 59N 28 53 E
Bakkafjörður **8** 66 2N 14 48W
Bakkagerði **8** 65 31N 13 49W
Bakony → **33** 47 35N 17 54 E
Bakony Forest = Bakony Hegység **33** 47 10N 17 30 E
Bakony Hegység **33** 47 10N 17 30 E
Bakori **89** 11 34N 7 25 E
Bakouma **92** 5 40N 22 56 E
Baku **39** 40 25N 49 45 E
Bala **106** 45 1N 79 37W
Bal'a **44** 32 20N 35 6 E
Bala, L. = Tegid, L. **12** 52 53N 3 38W
Balabac I. **56** 8 0N 117 0 E
Balabac, Str. **56** 7 53N 117 5 E
Balabagh **48** 34 25N 70 12 E
Balabakk **46** 34 0N 36 10 E
Balabalangan, Kepulauan **56** 2 20S 117 30 E
Balabio, Î. **68** 20 7S 164 11 E
Bălăciţa **34** 44 23N 23 8 E
Balaghat **50** 21 49N 80 12 E
Balaghat Ra. **50** 18 50N 76 30 E
Balaguer **24** 41 50N 0 50 E
Balakhna **37** 56 25N 43 32 E
Balaklava, Austral. **73** 34 7S 138 22 E
Balaklava, U.S.S.R. **38** 44 30N 33 30 E
Balakleya **38** 49 28N 36 55 E
Balakovo **37** 52 4N 47 55 E
Balancán **125** 17 48N 91 32W
Balanda **37** 51 30N 44 40 E
Balangir **50** 20 43N 83 35 E
Balapur **50** 20 40N 76 45 E
Balashikha **37** 55 49N 37 59 E
Balashov **37** 51 30N 43 10 E
Balasinor **48** 22 57N 73 23 E
Balasore **50** 21 35N 87 3 E
Balassagyarmat **33** 48 4N 19 15 E
Balât **90** 25 36N 29 19 E
Balaton **33** 46 50N 17 40 E
Balazote **25** 38 54N 2 09W
Balbi, Mt. **69** 5 55S 154 58 E
Balboa **126** 9 0N 79 30W
Balbriggan **15** 53 35N 6 10W
Balcarce **140** 38 0S 58 10W
Balcarres **109** 50 50N 103 35W
Balchik **34** 43 28N 28 11 E
Balclutha **81** 46 15S 169 45 E
Balcombe **74** 38 16S 145 2 E
Bald Hd. **79** 35 6S 118 1 E
Bald I. **79** 34 57S 118 27 E
Bald Knob **119** 35 20N 91 35W
Baldock L. **109** 56 33N 97 57W
Baldry **76** 32 50S 148 32 E
Baldwin, Fla., U.S.A. **113** 30 15N 82 10W
Baldwin, Mich., U.S.A. **112** 43 54N 85 53W
Baldwinsville **115** 43 10N 76 19W
Bale **27** 45 4N 13 46 E
Bale □ **91** 6 20N 41 30 E
Baleares □ **24** 39 30N 3 0 E
Baleares, Islas **24** 39 30N 3 0 E
Balearic Is. = Baleares, Islas **24** 39 30N 3 0 E
Baleia, Punta da **139** 17 40S 39 7W
Baler **57** 15 46N 121 34 E
Balfate **126** 15 48N 86 25W
Balfe's Creek **72** 20 12S 145 55 E
Balfour **97** 26 38S 28 35 E
Balfour Channel **68** 8 43S 157 27 E
Balfouriyya **44** 32 38N 35 18 E
Bali, Camer. **89** 5 54N 10 0 E
Bali, Indon. **56** 8 20S 115 0 E
Bali □ **56** 8 20S 115 0 E
Bali, Selat **57** 8 30S 114 35 E
Baligród **32** 49 20N 22 17 E
Balikesir **46** 39 35N 27 58 E
Balikpapan **56** 1 10S 116 55 E
Balimbing **57** 5 10N 120 3 E
Balimo **69** 8 6S 142 57 E
Baling **55** 5 41N 100 55 E
Baliza **137** 16 0S 52 20W
Balkan Mts. = Stara Planina **34** 43 15N 23 0 E
Balkan Pen. **6** 42 0N 22 0 E
Balkh **47** 36 44N 66 47 E
Balkh □ **47** 36 30N 67 0 E
Balkhash **40** 46 50N 74 50 E
Balkhash, Ozero **40** 46 0N 74 50 E
Ballachulish **14** 56 40N 5 10W
Balladonia **79** 32 27S 123 51 E
Balladoran **76** 31 52S 148 39 E
Ballan **74** 37 35S 144 13 E
Ballandean **77** 28 46S 151 50 E
Ballarat **74** 37 33S 143 50 E
Ballard, L. **79** 29 20S 120 10 E
Ballarpur **50** 19 50N 79 23 E
Ballater **14** 57 2N 3 2W
Ballenas, Canal de las **124** 29 10N 113 45W
Balleny Is. **143** 66 30S 163 0 E
Ballia **49** 25 46N 84 12 E
Ballidu **79** 30 35S 116 45 E
Ballimore **76** 32 12S 148 55 E
Ballina, Austral. **77** 28 50S 153 31 E
Ballina, Mayo, Ireland **15** 54 7N 9 10W
Ballina, Tipp., Ireland **15** 52 49N 8 27W
Ballinasloe **15** 53 20N 8 12W
Ballinger **119** 31 45N 99 58W
Ballinrobe **15** 53 36N 9 13W
Ballinskelligs B. **15** 51 46N 10 11W
Ballon **18** 48 10N 0 14 E
Ballycastle **15** 55 12N 6 15W
Ballymena **15** 54 53N 6 18W
Ballymena □ **15** 54 53N 6 18W
Ballymoney **15** 55 5N 6 30W
Ballymoney □ **15** 55 5N 6 23W
Ballyshannon **15** 54 30N 8 10W
Balmaceda **142** 46 0S 71 50W
Balmazújváros **33** 47 37N 21 21 E
Balmoral, Austral. **74** 37 15S 141 48 E
Balmoral, U.K. **14** 57 3N 3 13W
Balmorhea **119** 31 2N 103 41W
Balonne → **73** 28 47S 147 56 E
Balovale **93** 13 30S 23 15 E
Balrampur **49** 27 30N 82 20 E
Balranald **74** 34 38S 143 33 E
Balş **34** 44 22N 24 5 E
Balsapuerto **136** 5 48S 76 33W
Balsas **125** 18 0N 99 40W
Balsas →, Goias, Brazil **138** 9 58S 47 52W
Balsas →, Maranhão, Brazil **138** 7 15S 44 35W
Balsas →, Mexico **124** 17 55N 102 10W
Bålsta **10** 59 35N 17 30 E
Balston Spa **115** 43 0N 73 52W
Balta, Rumania **34** 44 54N 22 38 E
Balta, U.S.A. **118** 48 12N 100 7W
Balta, U.S.S.R. **38** 48 2N 29 45 E
Baltanás **22** 41 56N 4 15W
Baltic Sea **9** 56 0N 20 0 E
Baltim **90** 31 35N 31 10 E
Baltimore, Ireland **15** 51 29N 9 22W
Baltimore, U.S.A. **112** 39 18N 76 37W
Baltit **49** 36 15N 74 40 E
Baltrum **30** 53 43N 7 25 E
Baluchistan □ **47** 27 30N 65 0 E
Balurghat **49** 25 15N 88 44 E
Balygychan **41** 63 56N 154 12 E
Balzar **134** 2 2S 79 54W
Bam **47** 29 7N 58 14 E
Bama, China **58** 24 8N 107 12 E
Bama, Nigeria **89** 11 33N 13 41 E
Bamako **88** 12 34N 7 55W
Bamawn **74** 36 18S 144 40 E
Bamba **89** 17 5N 1 24W
Bambamarca **136** 6 36S 78 32W
Bambari **92** 5 40N 20 35 E
Bambaroo **72** 18 50S 146 10 E
Bamberg, Ger. **31** 49 54N 10 53 E
Bamberg, U.S.A. **113** 33 19N 81 1W
Bambesi **91** 9 45N 34 40 E
Bambey **88** 14 42N 16 28W
Bambili **94** 3 40N 26 0 E
Bamboo **72** 14 34S 143 20 E
Bambuí **139** 20 1S 45 58W
Bamenda **89** 5 57N 10 11 E
Bamfield **108** 48 45N 125 10W
Bamian □ **47** 35 0N 67 0 E
Bamiancheng **61** 43 15N 124 2 E
Bamkin **89** 6 3N 11 27 E
Bampūr **47** 27 15N 60 21 E
Ban Aranyaprathet **54** 13 41N 102 30 E
Ban Ban **54** 19 31N 103 30 E
Ban Bang Hin **55** 9 32N 98 35 E
Ban Chiang Klang **54** 19 25N 100 55 E
Ban Chik **54** 17 15N 102 22 E
Ban Choho **54** 15 2N 102 9 E
Ban Dan Lan Hoi **54** 17 0N 99 35 E
Ban Don **54** 12 53N 107 48 E
Ban Don = Surat Thani **55** 9 8N 99 20 E
Ban Don, Ao **55** 9 20N 99 25 E
Ban Dong **54** 19 30N 100 59 E
Ban Hong **54** 18 18N 98 50 E
Ban Kaeng **54** 17 29N 100 7 E
Ban Keun **54** 18 22N 102 35 E
Ban Khai **54** 12 46N 101 18 E
Ban Kheun **54** 20 13N 101 7 E
Ban Khlong Kua **55** 6 57N 100 8 E
Ban Khuan Mao **55** 7 50N 99 37 E
Ban Khun Yuam **54** 18 49N 97 57 E
Ban Ko Yai Chim **55** 11 17N 99 26 E
Ban Kok **54** 16 40N 103 40 E
Ban Laem **54** 13 13N 99 59 E
Ban Lao Ngam **54** 15 28N 106 10 E
Ban Le Kathe **54** 15 49N 98 53 E
Ban Mae Chedi **54** 19 11N 99 31 E
Ban Mae Laeng **54** 20 1N 99 17 E
Ban Mae Sariang **54** 18 10N 97 56 E
Ban Me Thuot **54** 12 40N 108 3 E
Ban Mi **54** 15 3N 100 32 E
Ban Muong Mo **54** 19 4N 103 58 E
Ban Na Mo **54** 17 7N 105 40 E
Ban Na San **55** 8 53N 99 52 E
Ban Na Tong **54** 20 56N 101 47 E
Ban Nam Bac **54** 20 38N 102 20 E
Ban Nam Ma **54** 22 2N 101 37 E
Ban Ngang **54** 15 59N 106 11 E
Ban Nong Bok **54** 17 5N 104 48 E
Ban Nong Boua **54** 15 40N 106 33 E
Ban Nong Pling **54** 15 40N 100 10 E
Ban Pak Chan **55** 10 32N 98 51 E
Ban Phai **54** 16 4N 102 44 E
Ban Pong **54** 13 50N 99 55 E
Ban Ron Phibun **55** 8 9N 99 51 E
Ban Sanam Chai **55** 7 33N 100 25 E
Ban Sangkha **54** 14 37N 103 52 E
Ban Tak **54** 17 2N 99 4 E
Ban Tako **54** 14 5N 102 40 E
Ban Tha Dua **54** 17 59N 98 39 E
Ban Tha Li **54** 17 37N 101 25 E
Ban Tha Nun **55** 8 12N 98 18 E
Ban Thahine **54** 14 12N 105 33 E
Ban Xien Kok **54** 20 54N 100 39 E
Ban Yen Nhan **54** 20 57N 106 2 E
Baña, Punta de la **24** 40 33N 0 40 E
Banaba **66** 0 45S 169 50 E
Banadar Daryay Oman □ **47** 27 30N 56 0 E
Banalia **94** 1 32N 25 5 E
Banam **55** 11 20N 105 17 E
Banamba **88** 13 29N 7 22W
Banana **72** 24 28S 150 8 E
Bananal, I. do **139** 11 30S 50 30W
Banaras = Varanasi **49** 25 22N 83 8 E
Banas →, Gujarat, India **48** 23 45N 71 25 E
Banas →, Madhya Pradesh, India **49** 24 15N 81 30 E
Bânâs, Ras. **90** 23 57N 35 50 E
Banbridge **15** 54 21N 6 17W
Banbridge □ **15** 54 21N 6 16W
Banbury **13** 52 4N 1 21W
Banchory **14** 57 3N 2 30W
Bancroft **107** 45 3N 77 51W
Band-i-Turkistan **47** 35 30N 64 0 E
Banda **49** 25 30N 80 26 E
Banda Aceh **56** 5 35N 95 20 E
Banda Banda, Mt. **77** 31 10S 152 28 E
Banda Elat **57** 5 40S 133 5 E
Banda, Kepulauan **57** 4 37S 129 50 E
Banda, La **140** 27 45S 64 10W
Banda Sea **57** 6 0S 130 0 E
Bandai-San **63** 37 36N 140 4 E
Bandama → **88** 6 32N 5 30W
Bandanaira **57** 4 32S 129 54 E
Bandanwara **48** 26 9N 74 38 E
Bandar = Machilipatnam **51** 16 12N 81 12 E
Bandār 'Abbās **47** 27 15N 56 15 E
Bandar-e Būshehr **47** 28 55N 50 55 E
Bandar-e Chārak **47** 26 45N 54 20 E
Bandar-e Deylam **46** 30 5N 50 10 E
Bandar-e Lengeh **47** 26 35N 54 58 E
Bandar-e Ma'shur **46** 30 35N 49 10 E
Bandar-e Nakhīlū **47** 26 58N 53 30 E
Bandar-e Rīg **47** 29 30N 50 45 E
Bandar-e Shāh **47** 37 0N 54 10 E
Bandar-e Shāhpūr **46** 30 30N 49 5 E
Bandar-i-Pahlavi **46** 37 30N 49 30 E
Bandar Seri Begawan **56** 4 52N 115 0 E
Bandawe **95** 11 58S 34 5 E
Bande **22** 42 3N 7 58W
Bandeira, Pico da **139** 20 26S 41 47W
Bandeirante **139** 13 41S 50 48W
Bandera, Argent. **140** 28 55S 62 20W
Bandera, U.S.A. **119** 29 45N 99 3W
Banderas, Bahía de **124** 20 40N 105 30W
Bandia → **50** 19 2N 80 28 E
Bandiagara **88** 14 12N 3 29W
Bandiana **75** 36 10S 146 55 E
Bandırma **46** 40 20N 28 0 E
Bandon **15** 51 44N 8 45W
Bandon → **15** 51 40N 8 41W
Bandula **95** 19 0S 33 7 E
Bandundu **92** 3 15S 17 22 E
Bandung **57** 6 54S 107 36 E
Bandya **79** 27 40S 122 5 E
Bañeres **25** 38 44N 0 38W
Banes **127** 21 0N 75 42W
Bañeza, La **22** 42 17N 5 54W
Banff, Can. **108** 51 10N 115 34W
Banff, U.K. **14** 57 40N 2 32W
Banff Nat. Park **108** 51 30N 116 15W
Banfora **88** 10 40N 4 40W
Bang Fai → **54** 16 57N 104 45 E
Bang Hieng → **54** 16 10N 105 10 E
Bang Krathum **54** 16 34N 100 18 E
Bang Lamung **54** 13 3N 100 56 E
Bang Mun Nak **54** 16 2N 100 23 E
Bang Pa In **54** 14 14N 100 35 E
Bang Rakam **54** 16 45N 100 7 E
Bang Saphan **55** 11 14N 99 28 E
Bangala Dam **95** 21 7S 31 25 E
Bangalore **51** 12 59N 77 40 E
Bangalow **77** 28 41S 153 30 E
Bangante **89** 5 8N 10 32 E
Bangaon **49** 23 0N 88 47 E
Bangassou **92** 4 55N 23 7 E
Bangeta, Mt. **69** 6 21S 147 3 E
Banggai **57** 1 40S 123 30 E
Banggi, P. **56** 7 17N 117 12 E
Banghāzī **87** 32 11N 20 3 E
Bangil **57** 7 36S 112 50 E

Bangjang	**91**	11 23N	32 41 E
Bangka, Pulau, Sulawesi, Indon.	**57**	1 50N	125 5 E
Bangka, Pulau, Sumatera, Indon.	**56**	2 0S	105 50 E
Bangka, Selat	**56**	2 30S	105 30 E
Bangkalan	**57**	7 2S	112 46 E
Bangkinang	**56**	0 18N	101 5 E
Bangko	**56**	2 5S	102 9 E
Bangkok = Krung Thep	**54**	13 45N	100 31 E
Bangladesh ■	**52**	24 0N	90 0 E
Bangolo	**88**	7 1N	7 29W
Bangor, N. Ireland, U.K.	**15**	54 40N	5 40W
Bangor, Wales, U.K.	**12**	53 13N	4 9W
Bangor, Me., U.S.A.	**103**	44 48N	68 42W
Bangor, Mich., U.S.A.	**117**	42 18N	86 7W
Bangor, Pa., U.S.A.	**115**	40 51N	75 13W
Bangued	**57**	17 40N	120 37 E
Bangui	**92**	4 23N	18 35 E
Banguru	**94**	0 30N	27 10 E
Bangweulu, L.	**95**	11 0S	30 0 E
Bangweulu Swamp	**95**	11 20S	30 15 E
Bani	**127**	18 16N	70 22W
Bani →	**88**	14 30N	4 12W
Bani Bangou	**89**	15 3N	2 42 E
Bani, Djebel	**86**	29 16N	8 0W
Bani Na'im	**44**	31 31N	35 10 E
Bani Suhayla	**44**	31 21N	34 19 E
Bania	**88**	9 4N	3 6W
Baniara	**69**	9 44S	149 54 E
Banihal Pass	**49**	33 30N	75 12 E
Banīnah	**87**	32 0N	20 12 E
Bāniyas	**46**	35 10N	36 0 E
Banja Luka	**33**	44 49N	17 11 E
Banjar	**57**	7 24S	108 30 E
Banjarmasin	**56**	3 20S	114 35 E
Banjarnegara	**57**	7 24S	109 42 E
Banjul	**88**	13 28N	16 40W
Banka Banka	**72**	18 50S	134 0 E
Bankeryd	**11**	57 53N	14 6 E
Banket	**95**	17 27S	30 19 E
Bankilaré	**89**	14 35N	0 44 E
Bankipore	**49**	25 35N	85 10 E
Banks I., B.C., Can.	**108**	53 20N	130 0W
Banks I., N.W.T., Can.	**144**	73 15N	121 30W
Banks I., P.N.G.	**69**	10 10S	142 15 E
Banks, Is.	**68**	13 50S	167 30 E
Banks Pen.	**81**	43 45S	173 15 E
Banks Str.	**72**	40 40S	148 10 E
Bankura	**49**	23 11N	87 18 E
Bann →, Down, U.K.	**15**	54 30N	6 31W
Bann →, Londonderry, U.K.	**15**	55 10N	6 34W
Bannalec	**18**	47 57N	3 42W
Bannang Sata	**55**	6 16N	101 16 E
Bannerton	**74**	34 42S	142 47 E
Banning	**123**	33 58N	116 52W
Banningville = Bandundu	**92**	3 15S	17 22 E
Bannockburn, Can.	**107**	44 39N	77 33W
Bannockburn, U.K.	**14**	56 5N	3 55W
Bannockburn, Zimb.-Rhod.	**95**	20 17S	29 48 E
Bañolas	**24**	42 16N	2 44 E
Banon	**21**	44 2N	5 38 E
Baños de la Encina	**23**	38 10N	3 46W
Baños de Molgas	**22**	42 15N	7 40W
Banská Bystrica	**32**	48 46N	19 14 E
Banská Štiavnica	**33**	48 25N	18 55 E
Banswara	**48**	23 32N	74 24 E
Banten	**57**	6 5S	106 8 E
Bantry	**15**	51 40N	9 28W
Bantry, B.	**15**	51 35N	9 50W
Bantul	**57**	7 55S	110 19 E
Bantva	**48**	21 29N	70 12 E
Bantval	**51**	12 55N	75 0 E
Banyabba	**77**	29 22S	153 2 E
Banyak, Kepulauan	**56**	2 10N	97 10 E
Banyo	**89**	6 52N	11 45 E
Banyuls	**20**	42 29N	3 8 E
Banyumas	**57**	7 32S	109 18 E
Banyuwangi	**57**	8 13S	114 21 E
Banzare Coast	**143**	68 0S	125 0 E
Banzyville = Mobayi	**92**	4 15N	21 8 E
Bao Ha	**54**	22 11N	104 21 E
Bao Lac	**54**	22 57N	105 40 E
Bao Loc	**55**	11 32N	107 48 E
Bao'an	**59**	22 27N	114 10 E
Baocheng	**58**	33 12N	106 56 E
Baode	**60**	39 1N	111 5 E
Baodi	**61**	39 38N	117 20 E
Baoding	**60**	38 50N	115 28 E
Baoji	**60**	34 20N	107 5 E
Baojing	**58**	28 45N	109 41 E
Baokang	**59**	31 54N	111 12 E
Baoshan, Shanghai, China	**59**	31 27N	121 26 E
Baoshan, Yunnan, China	**58**	25 10N	99 5 E
Baotou	**60**	40 32N	110 2 E
Baoying	**61**	33 17N	119 20 E
Bap	**48**	27 23N	72 18 E
Bapatla	**51**	15 55N	80 30 E
Bapaume	**19**	50 7N	2 50 E
Bāqa el Gharbiya	**44**	32 25N	35 2 E
Ba'qūbah	**46**	33 45N	44 50 E
Baquedano	**140**	23 20S	69 52W
Bar, U.S.S.R.	**38**	49 4N	27 40 E
Bar, Yugo.	**33**	42 8N	19 8 E
Bar Harbor	**103**	44 15N	68 20W
Bar-le-Duc	**19**	48 47N	5 10 E
Bar-sur-Aube	**19**	48 14N	4 40 E
Bar-sur-Seine	**19**	48 7N	4 20 E
Barabai	**56**	2 32S	115 34 E
Barabinsk	**40**	55 20N	78 20 E
Baraboo	**118**	43 28N	89 46W
Baracoa	**127**	20 20N	74 30W
Baradero	**140**	33 52S	59 29W
Baradine	**77**	30 56S	149 4 E
Baraga	**118**	46 49N	88 29W
Barahona, Dom. Rep.	**127**	18 13N	71 7W
Barahona, Spain	**24**	41 17N	2 39W
Baraka →	**90**	18 13N	37 35 E
Barakot	**49**	21 33N	84 59 E
Barakula	**73**	26 30S	150 33 E
Baralaba	**72**	24 13S	149 50 E
Baralzon L.	**109**	60 0N	98 3W
Baramati	**50**	18 11N	74 33 E
Baramba	**50**	20 25N	85 23 E
Barameiya	**90**	18 32N	36 38 E
Baramula	**49**	34 15N	74 20 E
Baran	**48**	25 9N	76 40 E
Baranoa	**134**	10 48N	74 55W
Baranof I.	**100**	57 0N	135 10W
Baranovichi	**36**	53 10N	26 0 E
Barão de Cocais	**139**	19 56S	43 28W
Barão de Grajaú	**138**	6 45S	43 1W
Barão de Melgaço, Mato Grosso, Brazil	**137**	16 14S	55 52W
Barão de Melgaço, Rondônia, Brazil	**137**	11 50S	60 45W
Baraolt	**34**	46 5N	25 34 E
Barapasi	**57**	2 15S	137 5 E
Barapina	**69**	6 21S	155 25 E
Barasat	**49**	22 46N	88 31 E
Barasoli	**91**	13 38N	42 0W
Barat Daya, Kepulauan	**57**	7 30S	128 0 E
Barataria B.	**119**	29 15N	89 45W
Baraut	**48**	29 13N	77 7 E
Baraya	**134**	3 10N	75 4W
Barbacena	**139**	21 15S	43 56W
Barbacoas, Colomb.	**134**	1 45N	78 0W
Barbacoas, Venez.	**134**	9 29N	66 58W
Barbados ■	**127**	13 0N	59 30W
Barbalha	**138**	7 19S	39 17W
Barban	**27**	45 5N	14 4 E
Barbastro	**24**	42 2N	0 5 E
Barbate	**23**	36 13N	5 56W
Barberino di Mugello	**27**	44 1N	11 15 E
Barberton, S. Afr.	**97**	25 42S	31 2 E
Barberton, U.S.A.	**114**	41 0N	81 40W
Barbezieux	**20**	45 28N	0 9W
Barbigha	**49**	25 21N	85 47 E
Barbosa	**134**	5 57N	73 37W
Barbourville	**113**	36 57N	83 52W
Barbuda I.	**127**	17 30N	61 40W
Barca, La	**124**	20 20N	102 40W
Barcaldine	**72**	23 43S	145 6 E
Barcarrota	**23**	38 31N	6 51W
Barce = Al Marj	**85**	32 25N	20 40 E
Barcellona Pozzo di Gotto	**29**	38 8N	15 15 E
Barcelona, Spain	**24**	41 21N	2 10 E
Barcelona, Venez.	**135**	10 10N	64 40W
Barcelona □	**24**	41 30N	2 0 E
Barcelonette	**21**	44 23N	6 40 E
Barcelos	**135**	1 0S	63 0W
Barcoo →	**72**	25 30S	142 50 E
Barcs	**33**	45 58N	17 28 E
Barda	**39**	40 25N	47 10 E
Barda del Medio	**142**	38 45S	68 11W
Bardai	**87**	21 25N	17 0 E
Bardas Blancas	**140**	35 49S	69 45W
Bardejov	**32**	49 18N	21 15 E
Bardera	**45**	2 20N	42 27 E
Bardi	**26**	44 38N	9 43 E
Bardi, Ra's	**46**	24 17N	37 31 E
Bardiyah	**85**	31 45N	25 0 E
Bardoli	**50**	21 12N	73 5 E
Bardolino	**26**	45 33N	10 43 E
Bardsey, I.	**12**	52 46N	4 47W
Bardstown	**117**	37 50N	85 29W
Bareilly	**49**	28 22N	79 27 E
Barengapara	**52**	25 14N	90 14 E
Barentin	**18**	49 33N	0 58 E
Barenton	**18**	48 38N	0 50W
Barents Sea	**144**	73 0N	39 0 E
Barentu	**91**	15 2N	37 35 E
Barfleur	**18**	49 40N	1 17W
Barga, China	**62**	30 40N	81 20 E
Barga, Italy	**26**	44 5N	10 30 E
Bargal	**45**	11 25N	51 0 E
Bargara	**72**	24 50S	152 25 E
Barge	**26**	44 43N	7 19 E
Barge, La	**120**	42 12N	110 4W
Bargnop	**91**	9 32N	28 25 E
Bargo	**76**	34 18S	150 35 E
Bargteheide	**30**	53 42N	10 13 E
Barguzin	**41**	53 37N	109 37 E
Barh	**49**	25 29N	85 46 E
Barhaj	**49**	26 18N	83 44 E
Barhi	**49**	24 15N	85 25 E
Bari, India	**48**	26 39N	77 39 E
Bari, Italy	**29**	41 6N	16 52 E
Bari Doab	**48**	30 20N	73 0 E
Bariadi □	**94**	2 45S	34 40 E
Barima →	**135**	8 33N	60 25W
Barinas	**134**	8 36N	70 15W
Barinas □	**134**	8 10N	69 50W
Baring	**116**	40 15N	92 12W
Baring C.	**100**	70 0N	117 30W
Baringo	**94**	0 47N	36 16 E
Baringo □	**94**	0 55N	36 0 E
Baringo, L.	**94**	0 47N	36 16 E
Barinitas	**134**	8 45N	70 25W
Baripada	**50**	21 57N	86 45 E
Bariri	**139**	22 4S	48 44W
Bârîs	**90**	24 42N	30 31 E
Barisal	**52**	22 45N	90 20 E
Barisan, Bukit	**56**	3 30S	102 15 E
Barito →	**56**	4 0S	114 50 E
Barjac	**21**	44 20N	4 22 E
Barjols	**21**	43 34N	6 2 E
Barjūj, Wadi →	**87**	25 26N	12 12 E
Bark L.	**107**	45 27N	77 51W
Barka = Baraka →	**91**	18 13N	37 35 E
Barkah	**47**	23 40N	58 0 E
Barkam	**58**	31 51N	102 28 E
Barker	**114**	43 20N	78 35W
Barkley Sound	**108**	48 50N	125 10W
Barkly Downs	**72**	20 30S	138 30 E
Barkly East	**96**	30 58S	27 33 E
Barkly Tableland	**72**	17 50S	136 40 E
Barkly West	**96**	28 5S	24 31 E
Barkol, Wadi	**90**	17 40N	32 0 E
Barksdale	**119**	29 47N	100 2W
Barlee, L.	**79**	29 15S	119 30 E
Barlee Ra.	**79**	23 30S	116 0 E
Barletta	**29**	41 20N	16 17 E
Barleur, Pointe de	**18**	49 42N	1 16W
Barlinek	**32**	53 0N	15 15 E
Barlow L.	**109**	62 00N	103 0W
Barmah	**74**	36 2S	144 58 E
Barmedman	**76**	34 9S	147 21 E
Barmer	**48**	25 45N	71 20 E
Barmera	**73**	34 15S	140 28 E
Barmouth	**12**	52 44N	4 3W
Barmstedt	**30**	53 47N	9 46 E
Barnagar	**48**	23 7N	75 19 E
Barnard Castle	**12**	54 33N	1 55W
Barnato	**73**	31 38S	145 0 E
Barnaul	**40**	53 20N	83 40 E
Barnawartha	**75**	36 6S	146 44 E
Barne Inlet	**143**	80 15S	160 0 E
Barnes	**74**	36 2S	144 47 E
Barnesville	**113**	33 6N	84 9W
Barnet	**13**	51 37N	0 15W
Barneveld, Neth.	**16**	52 7N	5 36 E
Barneveld, U.S.A.	**115**	43 16N	75 14W
Barneville	**18**	49 23N	1 46W
Barney, Mt.	**77**	28 17S	152 44 E
Barngo	**72**	25 3S	147 20 E
Barnhart	**119**	31 10N	101 8W
Barnsley	**12**	53 33N	1 29W
Barnstaple	**13**	51 5N	4 3W
Barnsville	**118**	46 43N	96 28W
Baro	**89**	8 35N	6 18 E
Baro →	**91**	8 26N	33 13 E
Baroda	**48**	25 29N	76 35 E
Baroda = Vadodara	**48**	22 20N	73 10 E
Baron Ra.	**78**	23 30S	127 45 E
Barora Ite	**68**	7 36S	158 24 E
Barorafa	**68**	7 30S	158 20 E
Barpali	**50**	21 11N	83 35 E
Barpathar	**52**	26 17N	93 53 E
Barpeta	**52**	26 20N	91 10 E
Barqa	**85**	27 0N	23 0 E
Barqin	**87**	27 33N	13 34 E
Barques, Pte. aux	**106**	44 5N	82 55W
Barquinha	**23**	39 28N	8 25W
Barquísimeto	**134**	10 4N	69 19W
Barr	**19**	48 25N	7 28 E
Barr Smith Ra.	**79**	27 10S	120 15 E
Barra, Brazil	**138**	11 5S	43 10W
Barra, U.K.	**14**	57 0N	7 30W
Barra da Estiva	**139**	13 38S	41 19W
Barra de Navidad	**124**	19 12N	104 41W
Barra do Corda	**138**	5 30S	45 10W
Barra do Mendes	**139**	11 43S	42 4W
Barra do Piraí	**139**	22 30S	43 50W
Barra Falsa, Pta. da	**97**	22 58S	35 37 E
Barra Hd.	**14**	56 47N	7 40W
Barra Mansa	**141**	22 35S	44 12W
Barra, Sd. of	**14**	57 4N	7 25W
Barraba	**77**	30 21S	150 35 E
Barracão do Barreto	**137**	8 48S	58 24W
Barrackpur	**49**	22 44N	88 30 E
Barrafranca	**29**	37 22N	14 10 E
Barranca, Lima, Peru	**136**	10 45S	77 50W
Barranca, Loreto, Peru	**134**	4 50S	76 50W
Barrancabermeja	**134**	7 0N	73 50W
Barrancas, Colomb.	**134**	10 57N	72 50W
Barrancas, Venez.	**135**	8 55N	62 5W
Barrancos	**23**	38 10N	6 58W
Barranqueras	**140**	27 30S	59 0W
Barranquilla	**134**	11 0N	74 50W
Barras, Brazil	**138**	4 15S	42 18W
Barras, Colomb.	**134**	1 45S	73 13W
Barraute	**104**	48 26N	77 38W
Barre	**115**	44 15N	72 30W
Barre do Bugres	**137**	15 0S	57 11W
Barreal	**140**	31 33S	69 28W
Barreiras	**139**	12 8S	45 0W
Barreirinha	**135**	2 30S	62 50W
Barreirinhas	**138**	2 30S	42 50W
Barreiro	**23**	38 40N	9 6W
Barreiros	**138**	8 49S	35 12W
Barrême	**21**	43 57N	6 23 E
Barren, Is.	**97**	18 25S	43 40 E
Barretos	**139**	20 30S	48 35W
Barrhead	**108**	54 10N	114 24W
Barrie	**106**	44 24N	79 40W
Barriefield	**107**	44 14N	76 28W
Barrier, C.	**80**	36 25S	175 32 E
Barrier Ra., Austral.	**73**	31 0S	141 30 E
Barrier Ra., N.Z.	**81**	44 5S	169 42 E
Barrier Reef, Gt.	**72**	19 0S	149 0 E
Barrière	**108**	51 12N	120 7W
Barrington, Austral.	**77**	31 58S	151 55 E
Barrington, Ill., U.S.A.	**117**	42 8N	88 5W
Barrington, R.I., U.S.A.	**115**	41 43N	71 20W
Barrington L.	**109**	56 55N	100 15W
Barrington Tops	**77**	32 6S	151 28 E
Barringun P.O.	**73**	29 1S	145 41 E
Barro do Garças	**137**	15 54S	52 16W
Barrow	**100**	71 16N	156 50W
Barrow →	**15**	52 10N	6 57W
Barrow Creek T.O.	**72**	21 30S	133 55 E
Barrow I.	**78**	20 45S	115 20 E
Barrow-in-Furness	**12**	54 8N	3 15W
Barrow Pt.	**72**	14 20S	144 40 E
Barrow Ra.	**79**	26 0S	127 40 E
Barrow Str.	**144**	74 20N	95 0W
Barruecopardo	**22**	41 4N	6 40W
Barruelo	**22**	42 54N	4 17W
Barry, Austral.	**76**	33 38S	149 16 E
Barry, U.K.	**13**	51 23N	3 19W
Barry, U.S.A.	**116**	39 42N	91 2W
Barry's Bay	**107**	45 29N	77 41W
Barsalogho	**89**	13 25N	1 3W
Barsat	**49**	36 10N	72 45 E
Barsi	**50**	18 10N	75 50 E
Barsø	**11**	55 7N	9 33 E
Barstow, Calif., U.S.A.	**123**	34 58N	117 2W
Barstow, Tex., U.S.A.	**119**	31 28N	103 24W
Barth	**30**	54 20N	12 36 E
Barthélemy, Col	**54**	19 26N	104 6 E
Bartica	**135**	6 25N	58 40W
Bartin	**46**	41 38N	32 21 E
Bartlesville	**119**	36 50N	95 58W
Bartlett, U.S.A.	**122**	36 29N	118 2W
Bartlett, Tex., U.S.A.	**119**	30 46N	97 30W
Bartlett, L.	**108**	63 5N	118 20W
Bartolomeu Dias	**95**	21 10S	35 8 E
Barton Siding	**79**	30 31S	132 39 E
Barton-upon-Humber	**12**	53 41N	0 27W
Bartonville	**116**	40 39N	89 39W
Bartoszyce	**32**	54 15N	20 55 E
Bartow	**113**	27 53N	81 49W
Barú, I. de	**134**	10 15N	75 35W
Baruth	**30**	52 3N	13 31 E
Barvenkovo	**38**	48 57N	37 0 E
Barwani	**48**	22 2N	74 57 E
Barwon →	**74**	38 8S	144 3 E
Baryulgil	**77**	29 12S	152 38 E
Bas-Rhin □	**19**	48 40N	7 30 E
Bašaid	**33**	45 38N	20 25 E
Bāsa'idū	**47**	26 35N	55 20 E
Basal	**48**	33 33N	72 13 E
Basankusa	**92**	1 5N	19 50 E
Basawa	**48**	34 15N	70 50 E
Bascuñán, C.	**140**	28 52S	71 35W
Basel (Basle)	**31**	47 35N	7 35 E
Basel-Landschaft □	**31**	47 26N	7 45 E
Basel-Stadt □	**31**	47 35N	7 35 E
Basento →	**29**	40 21N	16 50 E
Bashkir A.S.S.R. □	**40**	54 0N	57 0 E
Basilaki I.	**69**	10 35S	151 0 E
Basilan	**57**	6 35N	122 0 E

Basilan, Str. **57** 6 50N 122 0 E
Basildon **13** 51 34N 0 29 E
Basilicata □ **29** 40 30N 16 0 E
Basim **50** 20 3N 77 0 E
Basin **120** 44 22N 108 2W
Basingstoke **13** 51 15N 1 5W
Basirhat **52** 22 40N 88 54 E
Baška **27** 44 58N 14 45 E
Baskatong, Rés. **102** 46 46N 75 50W
Basle = Basel **31** 47 35N 7 35 E
Basmat **50** 19 15N 77 12 E
Basoda **48** 23 52N 77 54 E
Basoka **94** 1 16N 23 40 E
Basongo **92** 4 15S 20 20 E
Basque Provinces = Vascongadas **24** 42 50N 2 45W
Basra = Al Basrah **46** 30 30N 47 50 E
Bass **74** 38 29S 145 28 E
Bass Rock **14** 56 5N 2 40W
Bass Str. **72** 39 15S 146 30 E
Bassano **108** 50 48N 112 20W
Bassano del Grappa **27** 45 45N 11 45 E
Bassari **89** 9 19N 0 57 E
Basse Santa-Su **88** 13 13N 14 15W
Basse-Terre **127** 16 0N 61 40W
Bassée, La **19** 50 31N 2 49 E
Bassein, Burma **52** 16 45N 94 30 E
Bassein, India **50** 19 26N 72 48 E
Basseterre **127** 17 17N 62 43W
Bassett, Nebr., U.S.A. **118** 42 37N 99 30W
Bassett, Va., U.S.A. **113** 36 48N 79 59W
Bassi **48** 30 44N 76 21 E
Bassigny **19** 48 0N 5 10 E
Bassikounou **88** 15 55N 6 1W
Bassum **30** 52 50N 8 42 E
Båstad **11** 56 25N 12 51 E
Bastak **47** 27 15N 54 25 E
Bastar **50** 19 15N 81 40 E
Basti **49** 26 52N 82 55 E
Bastia **21** 42 40N 9 30 E
Bastia Umbra **27** 43 4N 12 34 E
Bastide-Puylaurent, La **20** 44 35N 3 55 E
Bastogne **16** 50 1N 5 43 E
Bastrop **119** 30 5N 97 22W
Basuto **96** 19 50S 26 25 E
Bat Yam **44** 32 2N 34 44 E
Bata, Eq. Guin. **92** 1 57N 9 50 E
Bata, Rumania **34** 46 1N 22 4 E
Bataan **57** 14 40N 120 25 E
Batabanó **126** 22 40N 82 20W
Batabanó, G. de **126** 22 30N 82 30W
Batac **57** 18 3N 120 34 E
Batagoy **41** 67 38N 134 38 E
Batak **35** 41 57N 24 12 E
Batakan **56** 4 5S 114 38 E
Batalha **23** 39 40N 8 50W
Batama **94** 0 58N 26 33 E
Batamay **41** 63 30N 129 15 E
Batang, China **58** 30 1N 99 0 E
Batang, Indon. **57** 6 55S 109 40 E
Batangafo **92** 7 25N 18 20 E
Batangas **57** 13 35N 121 10 E
Batanta **57** 0 55S 130 40 E
Batatais **141** 20 54S 47 37W
Batavia, Ind., U.S.A. **117** 41 55N 88 17W
Batavia, N.Y., U.S.A. **114** 43 0N 78 10W
Batavia, Ohio, U.S.A. **117** 39 5N 84 11W
Bataysk **39** 47 3N 39 45 E
Batchelor **78** 13 4S 131 1 E
Bateman's B. **76** 35 40S 150 12 E
Batemans Bay **76** 35 44S 150 11 E
Bates Ra. **79** 27 25S 121 0 E
Batesburg **113** 33 54N 81 32W
Batesville, Ark., U.S.A. **119** 35 48N 91 40W
Batesville, Ind., U.S.A. **117** 39 18N 85 13W
Batesville, Miss., U.S.A. **119** 34 17N 89 58W
Batesville, Tex., U.S.A. **119** 28 59N 99 38W
Bath, Can. **107** 44 11N 76 47W
Bath, U.K. **13** 51 22N 2 22W
Bath, Maine, U.S.A. **103** 43 50N 69 49W
Bath, N.Y., U.S.A. **114** 42 20N 77 17W
Batheay **55** 11 59N 104 57 E
Bathgate **14** 55 54N 3 38W
Bathurst, Austral. **76** 33 25S 149 31 E
Bathurst, Can. **103** 47 37N 65 43W
Bathurst = Banjul **88** 13 28N 16 40W
Bathurst B. **72** 14 16S 144 25 E
Bathurst, C. **100** 70 34N 128 0W
Bathurst Harb. **72** 43 15S 146 10 E
Bathurst I., Austral. **78** 11 30S 130 10 E
Bathurst I., Can. **144** 76 0N 100 30W
Bathurst In. **100** 68 10N 108 50W
Bathurst Inlet **100** 66 50N 108 1W
Bathurst L. **76** 35 3S 149 44 E
Batie **88** 9 53N 2 53W
Batinah **47** 24 0N 56 0 E
Batiscan **105** 46 30N 72 15W
Batiscan → **105** 46 16N 72 15W
Batiscan, L. **105** 47 22N 71 55W
Batlow **76** 35 31S 148 9 E
Batman **46** 37 55N 41 5 E
Batna **87** 35 34N 6 15 E
Batoka **95** 16 45S 27 15 E
Baton Rouge **119** 30 30N 91 5W
Batong, Ko **55** 6 32N 99 12 E
Batopilas **124** 27 0N 107 45W
Batouri **92** 4 30N 14 25 E
Battambang **54** 13 7N 103 12 E
Batticaloa **51** 7 43N 81 45 E
Battipáglia **29** 40 38N 15 0 E
Battir **44** 31 44N 35 8 E
Battle, Can. **109** 52 58N 110 52W
Battle, U.K. **13** 50 55N 0 30 E
Battle → **109** 52 43N 108 15W
Battle Camp **72** 15 20S 144 40 E
Battle Creek **117** 42 20N 85 6W
Battle Ground **122** 45 47N 122 32W
Battle Harbour **103** 52 16N 55 35W
Battle Lake **118** 46 20N 95 43W
Battle Mountain **120** 40 45N 117 0W
Battlefields **95** 18 37S 29 47 E
Battleford **109** 52 45N 108 15W
Battonya **33** 46 16N 21 3 E
Batu **91** 6 55N 39 45 E
Batu Caves **55** 3 15N 101 40 E
Batu Gajah **55** 4 28N 101 3 E
Batu, Kepulauan **56** 0 30S 98 25 E
Batu Pahat **55** 1 50N 102 56 E
Batuata **57** 6 12S 122 42 E
Batumi **39** 41 30N 41 30 E
Baturaja **56** 4 11S 104 15 E
Baturité **138** 4 28S 38 45W
Bau **56** 1 25N 110 9 E
Baubau **57** 5 25S 122 38 E
Bauchi **89** 10 22N 9 48 E
Bauchi □ **89** 10 30N 10 0 E
Baud **18** 47 52N 3 1W
Baudette **118** 48 46N 94 35W
Bauer, C. **73** 32 44S 134 4 E
Baugé **18** 47 31N 0 8W
Bauhinia Downs **72** 24 35S 149 18 E
Baule-Escoublac, La **18** 47 18N 2 23W
Baume-les-Dames **19** 47 22N 6 22 E
Baunatal **30** 51 13N 9 25 E
Baunei **28** 40 2N 9 41 E
Baures **137** 13 35S 63 35W
Bauru **141** 22 10S 49 0W
Baús **137** 18 22S 52 47W
Bauska **36** 56 24N 25 15 E
Bautzen **30** 51 11N 14 25 E
Baux, Les **21** 43 45N 4 51 E
Bavaria = Bayern **31** 49 7N 11 30 E
Båven **10** 59 0N 16 56 E
Bavi Sadri **48** 24 28N 74 30 E
Bavispe → **124** 29 30N 109 11W
Baw Baw, Mt. **75** 37 49S 146 19 E
Bawdwin **52** 23 5N 97 20 E
Bawean **56** 5 46S 112 35 E
Bawku **89** 11 3N 0 19W
Bawlake **52** 19 11N 97 21 E
Bawolung **58** 28 50N 101 16 E
Baxley **113** 31 43N 82 23W
Baxoi **58** 30 1N 96 50 E
Baxter **116** 41 49N 93 9W
Baxter Springs **119** 37 3N 94 45W
Bay Bulls **103** 47 19N 52 50W
Bay City, Mich., U.S.A. **106** 43 35N 83 51W
Bay City, Oreg., U.S.A. **120** 45 45N 123 58W
Bay City, Tex., U.S.A. **119** 28 59N 95 55W
Bay de Verde **103** 48 5N 52 54W
Bay, Laguna de **57** 14 20N 121 11 E
Bay Minette **113** 30 54N 87 43W
Bay Port **106** 43 51N 83 23W
Bay St. Louis **119** 30 18N 89 22W
Bay Shore **115** 40 44N 73 15W
Bay Springs **119** 31 58N 89 18W
Bay View **80** 39 25S 176 50 E
Baya **95** 11 53S 27 25 E
Bayamo **126** 20 20N 76 40W
Bayamón **127** 18 24N 66 10W
Bayan Har Shan **62** 34 0N 98 0 E
Bayan Hot = Alxa Zuoqi **60** 38 50N 105 40 E
Bayan Obo **60** 41 52N 109 59 E
Bayan-Ovoo **60** 42 55N 106 5 E
Bayana **48** 26 55N 77 18 E
Bayanaul **40** 50 45N 75 45 E
Bayandalay **60** 43 30N 103 29 E
Bayanhongor, Mong. **62** 46 8N 102 43 E
Bayanhongor, Mong. **62** 46 8N 100 43 E
Bayard **118** 41 48N 103 17W
Bayázeh **47** 33 30N 54 40 E
Baybay **57** 10 40N 124 55 E
Bayburt **46** 40 15N 40 20 E
Bayerischer Wald **31** 49 0N 13 0 E
Bayern □ **31** 49 7N 11 30 E
Bayeux **18** 49 17N 0 42W
Bayfield, Can. **106** 43 34N 81 42W
Bayfield, U.S.A. **118** 46 50N 90 48W
Bayir **46** 30 45N 36 55 E
Baykal, Oz. **41** 53 0N 108 0 E
Baykit **41** 61 50N 95 50 E
Baykonur **40** 47 48N 65 50 E
Baynes Mts. **96** 17 15S 13 0 E
Bayombong **57** 16 30N 121 10 E
Bayon **19** 48 30N 6 20 E
Bayona **22** 42 6N 8 52W
Bayonne, France **20** 43 30N 1 28W
Bayonne, U.S.A. **115** 40 41N 74 7W
Bayovar **136** 5 50S 81 0W
Baypore → **51** 11 10N 75 47 E
Bayram-Ali **40** 37 37N 62 10 E
Bayreuth **31** 49 56N 11 35 E
Bayrischzell **31** 47 39N 12 1 E
Bayrūt **46** 33 53N 35 31 E
Bays, L. of **106** 45 15N 79 4W
Bayside **107** 44 7N 77 30W
Baysville **106** 45 9N 79 7W
Bayt Aula **44** 31 37N 35 2 E
Bayt Fajjar **44** 31 38N 35 9 E
Bayt Fūrīk **44** 32 11N 35 20 E
Bayt Jālā **44** 31 43N 35 11 E
Bayt Lahm **44** 31 43N 35 12 E
Bayt Rīma **44** 32 2N 35 6 E
Bayt Sāhūr **44** 31 42N 35 13 E
Bayt Ummar **44** 31 38N 35 7 E
Bayta at Tahta **44** 32 9N 35 18 E
Baytin **44** 31 56N 35 14 E
Baytown **119** 29 42N 94 57W
Bayzo **89** 13 52N 4 35 E
Baza **25** 37 30N 2 47W
Bazar Dyuzi **39** 41 12N 47 50 E
Bazarny Karabulak **37** 52 15N 46 20 E
Bazarnyy Syzgan **37** 53 45N 46 40 E
Bazartobe **39** 49 26N 51 45 E
Bazaruto, I. do **97** 21 40S 35 28 E
Bazas **20** 44 27N 0 13W
Bazhong **58** 31 52N 106 46 E
Bazin → **104** 47 29N 75 22W
Bazuriye **44** 33 15N 35 16 E
Beach **118** 46 57N 103 58W
Beach City **114** 40 38N 81 35W
Beachburg **107** 45 44N 76 51W
Beachport **73** 37 29S 140 0 E
Beachville **106** 43 5N 80 49W
Beachy Head **13** 50 44N 0 16 E
Beacon, Austral. **79** 30 26S 117 52 E
Beacon, U.S.A. **115** 41 32N 73 58W
Beaconia **109** 50 25N 96 31W
Beagle Bay **78** 16 58S 122 40 E
Beagle, Canal **142** 55 0S 68 30W
Bealanana **97** 14 33N 48 44 E
Bealiba **74** 36 48S 143 34 E
Beamsville **106** 43 12N 79 28W
Bear → **122** 38 56N 121 36W
Béar, C. **20** 42 31N 3 8 E
Bear I. **15** 51 38N 9 50W
Bear L., B.C., Can. **108** 56 10N 126 52W
Bear L., Man., Can. **109** 55 8N 96 0W
Bear L., U.S.A. **120** 42 0N 111 20W
Bearcreek **120** 45 11N 109 6W
Beardmore **102** 49 36N 87 57W
Beardmore Glacier **143** 84 30S 170 0 E
Beardstown **116** 40 0N 90 25W
Béarn, Can. **104** 47 17N 79 20W
Béarn, France **20** 43 8N 0 36W
Bearpaw Mt. **120** 48 15N 109 30W
Bearskin Lake **102** 53 58N 91 2W
Beas de Segura **25** 38 15N 2 53W
Beasain **24** 43 3N 2 11W
Beata, C. **127** 17 40N 71 30W
Beata, I. **127** 17 34N 71 31W
Beatrice, U.S.A. **118** 40 20N 96 40W
Beatrice, Zimb.-Rhod. **95** 18 15S 30 55 E
Beatrice, C. **72** 14 20S 136 55 E
Beatton → **108** 56 15N 120 45W
Beatton River **108** 57 26N 121 20W
Beatty **122** 36 58N 116 46W
Beattyville **117** 37 35N 83 42W
Beaucaire **21** 43 48N 4 39 E
Beauce, Plaine de la **19** 48 10N 1 45 E
Beauceville **105** 46 13N 70 46W
Beauchêne, I. **142** 52 55S 59 15W
Beauchûne, L. **104** 46 35N 78 55W
Beaudesert **77** 27 59S 153 0 E
Beaufort, Austral. **74** 37 25S 143 25 E
Beaufort, Malay. **56** 5 30N 115 40 E
Beaufort, N.C., U.S.A. **113** 34 45N 76 40W
Beaufort, S.C., U.S.A. **113** 32 25N 80 40W
Beaufort Sea **144** 72 0N 140 0W
Beaufort West **96** 32 18S 22 36 E
Beaugency **19** 47 47N 1 38 E
Beauharnois **105** 45 20N 73 52W
Beaujeu **21** 46 10N 4 35 E
Beaulac **105** 45 50N 71 23W
Beaulieu **20** 44 59N 1 50 E
Beaulieu → **108** 62 3N 113 11W
Beauly **14** 57 29N 4 27W
Beauly → **14** 57 26N 4 28W
Beaumaris **12** 53 16N 4 7W
Beaumetz-les-Loges **19** 50 15N 2 40 E
Beaumont, Dordogne, France **20** 44 45N 0 46 E
Beaumont, Sarthe, France **18** 48 13N 0 8 E
Beaumont, N.Z. **81** 45 50S 169 33 E
Beaumont, Calif., U.S.A. **123** 33 56N 116 58W
Beaumont, Tex., U.S.A. **119** 30 5N 94 8W
Beaumont-de-Lomagne **20** 43 53N 0 59 E
Beaumont-le-Roger **18** 49 4N 0 47 E
Beaumont-sur-Oise **19** 49 9N 2 17 E
Beaune **19** 47 2N 4 50 E
Beaune-la-Rolande **19** 48 4N 2 25 E
Beauport **105** 46 52N 71 11W
Beaupré **105** 47 3N 70 54W
Beaupréau **18** 47 12N 1 00W
Beauséjour **109** 50 5N 96 35W
Beausset, Le **21** 43 10N 5 46 E
Beautemps-Beaupré, Î. **68** 20 24S 166 9 E
Beauvais **19** 49 25N 2 8 E
Beauval **109** 55 9N 107 37W
Beauvoir **18** 46 55N 2 1W
Beauvoir-sur-Niort **20** 46 12N 0 30W
Beaver, Alaska, U.S.A. **100** 66 20N 147 30W
Beaver, Okla., U.S.A. **119** 36 52N 100 31W
Beaver, Pa., U.S.A. **114** 40 40N 80 18W
Beaver, Utah, U.S.A. **121** 38 20N 112 45W
Beaver →, B.C., Can. **108** 59 52N 124 20W
Beaver →, Sask., Can. **109** 55 26N 107 45W
Beaver City **118** 40 13N 99 50W
Beaver Dam **118** 43 28N 88 50W
Beaver Falls **114** 40 44N 80 20W
Beaver I., U.S.A. **106** 45 40N 85 31W
Beaver I., U.S.A. **112** 45 40N 85 31W
Beaver, R **102** 55 55N 87 48W
Beaverhill L., Alta., Can. **108** 53 27N 112 32W
Beaverhill L., Man., Can. **109** 54 5N 94 50W
Beaverhill L., N.W.T., Can. **109** 63 2N 104 22W
Beaverlodge **108** 55 11N 119 29W
Beavermouth **108** 51 32N 117 23W
Beaverstone → **102** 54 59N 89 25W
Beaverton, Can. **106** 44 26N 79 9W
Beaverton, Mich., U.S.A. **106** 43 53N 84 29W
Beaverton, Oreg., U.S.A. **122** 45 29N 122 48W
Beaverville **117** 40 57N 87 39W
Beawar **48** 26 3N 74 18 E
Bebedouro **141** 21 0S 48 25W
Beboa **97** 17 22S 44 33 E
Bebra **30** 50 59N 9 48 E
Beccles **13** 52 27N 1 33 E
Bečej **33** 45 36N 20 3 E
Becerreá **22** 42 51N 7 10W
Béchar **86** 31 38N 2 18W
Beckley **112** 37 50N 81 8W
Beckum **30** 51 46N 8 3 E
Bécon **18** 47 30N 0 50W
Bečva → **32** 49 31N 17 40 E
Bédar **25** 37 11N 1 59W
Bédarieux **20** 43 37N 3 10 E
Bédarrides **21** 44 2N 4 54 E
Bedele **91** 8 31N 36 23 E
Bederkesa **30** 53 37N 8 50 E
Bedeso **91** 9 58N 40 52 E
Bedford, Can. **105** 45 7N 72 59W
Bedford, S. Afr. **96** 32 40S 26 10 E
Bedford, U.K. **13** 52 8N 0 29W
Bedford, Ind., U.S.A. **117** 38 50N 86 30W
Bedford, Iowa, U.S.A. **116** 40 40N 94 41W
Bedford, Ky., U.S.A. **117** 38 36N 85 19W
Bedford, Ohio, U.S.A. **114** 41 23N 81 32W
Bedford, Pa., U.S.A. **114** 40 1N 78 30W
Bedford, Va., U.S.A. **112** 37 25N 79 30W
Bedford □ **13** 52 4N 0 28W
Bedford, C. **72** 15 14S 145 21 E
Bedford Downs **78** 17 19S 127 20 E
Bedgerebong **76** 33 21S 147 43 E
Będków **32** 51 36N 19 44 E
Bednja → **27** 46 12N 16 25 E
Bednodemyanovsk **37** 53 55N 43 15 E
Bedónia **26** 44 28N 9 36 E
Bedourie **72** 24 30S 139 30 E
Bedous **20** 43 0N 0 36W
Będzin **32** 50 19N 19 7 E
Beeac **74** 38 13S 143 37 E
Beebe Plain **105** 45 1N 72 9W
Beebo **77** 28 43S 150 59 E
Beech Fork → **117** 37 55N 85 50W
Beech Grove **117** 39 40N 86 2W
Beecher **117** 41 21N 87 38W
Beechworth **75** 36 22S 146 43 E

Beechy	**109**	50 53N	107 24W
Beelitz	**30**	52 14N	12 58 E
Beenleigh	**73**	27 43 S	153 10 E
Be'er Sheva'	**44**	31 15N	34 48 E
Be'er Sheva' →	**44**	31 12N	34 40 E
Be'er Toviyya	**44**	31 44N	34 42 E
Be'eri	**44**	31 25N	34 30 E
Be'erotayim	**44**	32 19N	34 59 E
Beersheba = Be'er Sheva'	**44**	31 15N	34 48 E
Beeskow	**30**	52 9N	14 14 E
Beeston	**12**	52 55N	1 11W
Beetaloo	**72**	17 15 S	133 50 E
Beeton	**106**	44 5N	79 47W
Beetzendorf	**30**	52 42N	11 6 E
Beeville	**119**	28 27N	97 44W
Befale	**92**	0 25N	20 45 E
Befotaka	**97**	23 49 S	47 0 E
Bega	**75**	36 41 S	149 51 E
Bega, Canalul	**34**	45 37N	20 46 E
Bégard	**18**	48 38N	3 18W
Begemdir & Simen □	**91**	12 55N	37 30 E
Bègles	**20**	44 45N	0 35W
Begna →	**10**	60 41N	10 0 E
Begonte	**22**	43 10N	7 40W
Begu-Sarai	**49**	25 24N	86 9 E
Béhagle = Lai	**85**	9 25N	16 30 E
Behbehan	**46**	30 30N	50 15 E
Behror	**48**	27 51N	76 20 E
Behshahr	**47**	36 45N	53 35 E
Bei Jiang →, Guangdong, China	**59**	23 2N	112 58 E
Bei Jiang →, Guangdong, China	**59**	22 40N	113 40 E
Bei'an	**62**	48 10N	126 20 E
Beibei	**62**	29 47N	106 22 E
Beida (Al Bayda)	**85**	32 30N	21 40 E
Beigang	**59**	23 38N	120 16 E
Beihai	**58**	21 28N	109 6 E
Beijing	**60**	39 55N	116 20 E
Beijing □	**60**	39 55N	116 20 E
Beilen	**16**	52 52N	6 27 E
Beiliu	**59**	22 41N	110 21 E
Beilngries	**31**	49 1N	11 27 E
Beilpajah	**73**	32 54 S	143 52 E
Beilul	**91**	13 2N	42 20 E
Beipiao	**61**	41 52N	120 32 E
Beira	**95**	19 50 S	34 52 E
Beirut = Bayrūt	**46**	33 53N	35 31 E
Beit Hanum	**44**	31 32N	34 32 E
Beit Lahiyah	**44**	31 32N	34 30 E
Beit 'Ur et Tahta	**44**	31 54N	35 5 E
Beitaolaizhao	**61**	44 58N	125 58 E
Beitbridge	**95**	22 12 S	30 0 E
Beituniya	**44**	31 54N	35 10 E
Beiuş	**34**	46 40N	22 21 E
Beizhen, Liaoning, China	**61**	41 38N	121 54 E
Beizhen, Shandong, China	**61**	37 20N	118 2 E
Beizhengzhen	**61**	44 31N	123 15 E
Beja	**23**	38 2N	7 53W
Béja	**87**	36 43N	9 12 E
Beja □	**23**	37 55N	7 55W
Bejaia	**87**	36 42N	5 2 E
Béjar	**22**	40 23N	5 46W
Bejestān	**47**	34 30N	58 5 E
Bekasi	**57**	6 20 S	107 0 E
Békés	**33**	46 47N	21 9 E
Békéscsaba	**33**	46 40N	21 5 E
Bekily	**97**	24 13 S	45 19 E
Bekoji	**91**	7 40N	39 17 E
Bekok	**55**	2 20N	103 7 E
Bekopika	**97**	19 9 S	44 45 E
Bekwai	**89**	6 30N	1 34W
Bela, India	**49**	25 50N	82 0 E
Bela, Pak.	**48**	26 12N	66 20 E
Bela Crkva	**33**	44 55N	21 27 E
Bela Palanka	**33**	43 13N	22 17 E
Bela Vista, Brazil	**140**	22 12 S	56 20W
Bela Vista, Mozam.	**97**	26 10 S	32 44 E
Bélâbre	**20**	46 34N	1 8 E
Belalcázar	**23**	38 35N	5 10W
Belaringar	**76**	31 45 S	147 34 E
Belavenona	**97**	24 50 S	47 4 E
Belawan	**56**	3 33N	98 32 E
Belaya Glina	**39**	46 5N	40 48 E
Belaya Kalitva	**39**	48 13N	40 50 E
Belaya, Mt.	**91**	11 25N	36 8 E
Belaya Tserkov	**36**	49 45N	30 10 E
Belcher, C.	**144**	71 0N	161 0W
Belcher Is.	**102**	56 15N	78 45W
Belchite	**24**	41 18N	0 43W
Belcourt	**104**	48 24N	77 21W
Belden	**122**	40 2N	121 17W
Belém de São Francisco	**138**	8 46 S	38 58W
Belém (Pará)	**138**	1 20 S	48 30W
Belén, Argent.	**140**	27 40 S	67 5W
Belén, Colomb.	**134**	1 26N	75 56W
Belén, Parag.	**140**	23 30 S	57 6W
Belen	**121**	34 40N	106 50W
Bélesta	**20**	42 55N	1 56 E
Belet Uen	**45**	4 30N	45 5 E
Belev	**37**	53 50N	36 5 E
Belfair	**122**	47 27N	122 50W
Belfast, N.Z.	**81**	43 27 S	172 39 E
Belfast, S. Afr.	**97**	25 42 S	30 2 E
Belfast, U.K.	**15**	54 35N	5 56W
Belfast, Maine, U.S.A.	**103**	44 30N	69 0W
Belfast, N.Y., U.S.A.	**114**	42 21N	78 9W
Belfast □	**15**	54 35N	5 56W
Belfast, L.	**15**	54 40N	5 50W
Belfield	**118**	46 54N	103 11W
Belfort	**19**	47 38N	6 50 E
Belfort □	**19**	47 38N	6 52 E
Belfry	**120**	45 10N	109 2W
Belgaum	**51**	15 55N	74 35 E
Belgioioso	**26**	45 9N	9 21 E
Belgium ■	**16**	50 30N	5 0 E
Belgorod	**38**	50 35N	36 35 E
Belgorod-Dnestrovskiy	**38**	46 11N	30 23 E
Belgrade	**120**	45 50N	111 10W
Belgrade = Beograd	**33**	44 50N	20 37 E
Belgrove	**81**	41 27 S	172 59 E
Belhaven	**113**	35 34N	76 35W
Beli Drim →	**33**	42 6N	20 25 E
Beli Manastir	**33**	45 45N	18 36 E
Belice →	**28**	37 35N	12 55 E
Belin	**20**	44 30N	0 47W
Belinga	**92**	1 10N	13 2 E
Belingwe	**95**	20 29 S	29 57 E
Belingwe, N.	**95**	20 37 S	29 55 E
Belinskiy (Chembar)	**37**	53 0N	43 25 E
Belinyu	**56**	1 35 S	105 50 E
Belitung, P.	**56**	3 10 S	107 50 E
Beliu	**34**	46 30N	22 0 E
Belize ■	**125**	17 0N	88 30W
Belize City	**125**	17 25N	88 0W
Beljanica	**33**	44 08N	21 43 E
Belkovskiy, Ostrov	**41**	75 32N	135 44 E
Bell	**76**	33 28 S	150 17 E
Bell →	**104**	49 48N	77 38W
Bell Bay	**72**	41 6 S	146 53 E
Bell I.	**103**	50 46N	55 35W
Bell-Irving →	**108**	56 12N	129 5W
Bell Peninsula	**101**	63 50N	82 0W
Bell Ville	**140**	32 40 S	62 40W
Bella Bella	**108**	52 10N	128 10W
Bella Coola	**108**	52 25N	126 40W
Bella Flor	**136**	11 9 S	67 49W
Bella Unión	**140**	30 15 S	57 40W
Bella Vista, Corrientes, Argent.	**140**	28 33 S	59 0W
Bella Vista, Tucuman, Argent.	**140**	27 10 S	65 25W
Bellac	**20**	46 7N	1 3 E
Bellágio	**26**	45 59N	9 15 E
Bellaire, Mich., U.S.A.	**106**	44 59N	85 13W
Bellaire, Ohio, U.S.A.	**114**	40 1N	80 46W
Bellary	**51**	15 10N	76 56 E
Bellata	**77**	29 53 S	149 46 E
Bellbird	**76**	32 52 S	151 19 E
Bellbrook	**77**	30 47 S	152 31 E
Belle	**116**	38 17N	91 43W
Belle Fourche	**118**	44 43N	103 52W
Belle Fourche →	**118**	44 25N	102 19W
Belle Glade	**113**	26 43N	80 38W
Belle-Île	**18**	47 20N	3 10W
Belle Isle	**103**	51 57N	55 25W
Belle-Isle-en-Terre	**18**	48 33N	3 23W
Belle Isle, Str. of	**103**	51 30N	56 30W
Belle, La, Fla., U.S.A.	**113**	26 45N	81 22W
Belle, La, Mo., U.S.A.	**116**	40 7N	91 55W
Belle Plaine, Iowa, U.S.A.	**116**	41 51N	92 18W
Belle Plaine, Minn., U.S.A.	**118**	44 35N	93 48W
Belle Rive	**117**	38 14N	88 45W
Belle River	**106**	42 18N	82 43W
Belle Yella	**88**	7 24N	10 0W
Belledonne	**21**	45 30N	6 10 E
Belledune	**103**	47 55N	65 50W
Bellefontaine	**117**	40 20N	83 45W
Bellefonte	**114**	40 56N	77 45W
Bellegarde, Ain, France	**21**	46 4N	5 49 E
Bellegarde, Creuse, France	**20**	45 59N	2 18 E
Bellegarde, Loiret, France	**19**	48 0N	2 26 E
Bellême	**18**	48 22N	0 34 E
Belleoram	**103**	47 31N	55 25W
Belleterre	**104**	47 25N	78 41W
Belleville, Can.	**107**	44 10N	77 23W
Belleville, Rhône, France	**21**	46 7N	4 45 E
Belleville, Vendée, France	**18**	46 48N	1 28W
Belleville, Ill., U.S.A.	**116**	38 30N	90 0W
Belleville, Kans., U.S.A.	**118**	39 51N	97 38W
Belleville, N.Y., U.S.A.	**115**	43 46N	76 10W
Bellevue, Can.	**108**	49 35N	114 22W
Bellevue, Idaho, U.S.A.	**120**	43 25N	114 23W
Bellevue, Iowa, U.S.A.	**116**	42 16N	90 26W
Bellevue, Mich., U.S.A.	**117**	42 27N	85 1W
Bellevue, Ohio, U.S.A.	**114**	41 20N	82 48W
Bellevue, Pa., U.S.A.	**114**	40 29N	80 3W
Bellevue, Wash., U.S.A.	**122**	47 37N	122 12W
Belley	**21**	45 46N	5 41 E
Bellflower	**116**	39 0N	91 21W
Bellin (Payne Bay)	**101**	60 0N	70 0W
Bellingen	**77**	30 25 S	152 50 E
Bellingham	**122**	48 45N	122 27W
Bellingshausen Sea	**143**	66 0 S	80 0W
Bellinzona	**31**	46 11N	9 1 E
Bello	**134**	6 20N	75 33W
Bellona	**68**	11 17 S	159 47 E
Bellows Falls	**115**	43 10N	72 30W
Bellpat	**48**	29 0N	68 5 E
Bellpuig	**24**	41 37N	1 1 E
Bells Corners	**107**	45 19N	75 50W
Belluno	**27**	46 8N	12 13 E
Bellville	**119**	29 58N	96 18W
Bellwood	**114**	40 36N	78 21W
Belmar	**115**	40 10N	74 2W
Bélmez	**23**	38 17N	5 17W
Belmond	**116**	42 51N	93 37W
Belmont, Austral.	**76**	33 4 S	151 42 E
Belmont, Can.	**106**	42 53N	81 5W
Belmont, U.S.A.	**114**	42 14N	78 3W
Belmonte, Brazil	**139**	16 0 S	39 0W
Belmonte, Port.	**22**	40 21N	7 20W
Belmonte, Spain	**24**	39 34N	2 43W
Belmopan	**125**	17 18N	88 30W
Belmullet	**15**	54 13N	9 58W
Belo Horizonte	**139**	19 55 S	43 56W
Belo Jardim	**138**	8 20 S	36 26W
Belo-sur-Mer	**97**	20 42 S	44 0 E
Belo-sur-Tsiribihina	**97**	19 40 S	44 30 E
Beloeil	**105**	45 34N	73 12W
Belogorsk, R.S.F.S.R., U.S.S.R.	**41**	51 0N	128 20 E
Belogorsk, Ukraine, U.S.S.R.	**38**	45 3N	34 35 E
Belogradchik	**34**	43 53N	22 15 E
Beloha	**97**	25 10 S	45 3 E
Beloit, Kans., U.S.A.	**118**	39 32N	98 9W
Beloit, Wis., U.S.A.	**116**	42 35N	89 0W
Belomorsk	**40**	64 35N	34 30 E
Belonia	**52**	23 15N	91 30 E
Belopolye	**36**	51 14N	34 20 E
Belovo	**40**	54 30N	86 0 E
Beloye More	**40**	66 0N	38 0 E
Beloye Ozero	**39**	45 15N	46 50 E
Belozersk	**37**	60 0N	37 30 E
Belpasso	**29**	37 37N	15 0 E
Belsito	**28**	37 50N	13 47 E
Beltana	**73**	30 48 S	138 25 E
Belterra	**135**	2 45 S	55 0W
Beltinci	**27**	46 37N	16 20 E
Belton, S.C., U.S.A.	**113**	34 31N	82 39W
Belton, Tex., U.S.A.	**119**	31 4N	97 30W
Belton Res.	**119**	31 8N	97 32W
Beltsy	**38**	47 48N	28 0 E
Belturbet	**15**	54 6N	7 28W
Belukha	**40**	49 50N	86 50 E
Beluran	**56**	5 48N	117 35 E
Belvedere Maríttimo	**29**	39 37N	15 52 E
Belvès	**20**	44 46N	1 0 E
Belvidere, Ill., U.S.A.	**117**	42 15N	88 55W
Belvidere, N.J., U.S.A.	**115**	40 48N	75 5W
Belvis de la Jara	**23**	39 45N	4 57W
Belyando →	**72**	21 38 S	146 50 E
Belyy	**36**	55 48N	32 51 E
Belyy, Ostrov	**40**	73 30N	71 0 E
Belyy Yar	**40**	58 26N	84 39 E
Belzig	**30**	52 8N	12 36 E
Belzoni	**119**	33 12N	90 30W
Bemaraha, Plat. du	**97**	18 40 S	44 45 E
Bemarivo, Majunga, Madag.	**97**	17 6 S	44 31 E
Bemarivo, Tuléar, Madag.	**97**	21 45 S	44 45 E
Bemarivo →	**97**	15 27 S	47 40 E
Bemavo	**97**	21 33 S	45 25 E
Bembéréke	**89**	10 11N	2 43 E
Bembesi	**95**	20 0 S	28 58 E
Bembesi →	**95**	18 57 S	27 47 E
Bembézar →	**23**	37 45N	5 13W
Bemboka	**75**	36 38 S	149 34 E
Bement	**117**	39 55N	88 34W
Bemidji	**118**	47 30N	94 50W
Bemm River	**75**	37 47 S	148 58 E
Ben 'Ammi	**44**	33 0N	35 7 E
Ben Bullen	**76**	33 12 S	150 2 E
Ben Cruachan	**14**	56 26N	5 8W
Ben Dearg	**14**	57 47N	4 58W
Ben Gardane	**87**	33 11N	11 11 E
Ben Hope	**14**	58 24N	4 36W
Ben Lawers	**14**	56 33N	4 13W
Ben Lomond, N.S.W., Austral.	**77**	30 1 S	151 40 E
Ben Lomond, N.S.W., Austral.	**77**	30 1 S	151 43 E
Ben Lomond, Tas., Austral.	**72**	41 38 S	147 42 E
Ben Lomond, U.K.	**14**	56 12N	4 39W
Ben Luc	**55**	10 39N	106 29 E
Ben Macdhui	**14**	57 4N	3 40W
Ben Mhor	**14**	57 16N	7 21W
Ben More, Cent., U.K.	**14**	56 23N	4 31W
Ben More, Mull, U.K.	**14**	56 26N	6 2W
Ben More Assynt	**14**	58 7N	4 51W
Ben Nevis	**14**	56 48N	5 0W
Ben Ohau Ra.	**81**	44 1 S	170 4 E
Ben Quang	**54**	17 3N	106 55 E
Ben Slimane	**86**	33 38N	7 7W
Ben Vorlich	**14**	56 22N	4 15W
Ben Wyvis	**14**	57 40N	4 35W
Bena	**89**	11 20N	5 50 E
Bena Dibele	**92**	4 4 S	22 50 E
Benagalbón	**23**	36 45N	4 15W
Benagerie	**73**	31 25 S	140 22 E
Benahmed	**86**	33 4N	7 9W
Benalla	**74**	36 30 S	146 0 E
Benamejí	**23**	37 16N	4 33W
Benanee	**74**	34 31 S	142 52 E
Benares = Varanasi	**49**	25 22N	83 8 E
Bénat, C.	**21**	43 5N	6 22 E
Benavente, Port.	**23**	38 59N	8 49W
Benavente, Spain	**22**	42 2N	5 43W
Benavides, Spain	**22**	42 30N	5 54W
Benavides, U.S.A.	**119**	27 35N	98 28W
Benbecula, I.	**14**	57 26N	7 21W
Benbonyathe, Mt.	**73**	30 25 S	139 11 E
Bencubbin	**79**	30 48 S	117 52 E
Bend	**120**	44 2N	121 15W
Bendel □	**89**	6 0N	6 0 E
Bendemeer	**77**	30 53 S	151 8 E
Bender Beila	**45**	9 30N	50 48 E
Bendering	**79**	32 23 S	118 18 E
Bendery	**38**	46 50N	29 30 E
Bendick Murrell	**76**	34 8 S	148 28 E
Bendigo	**74**	36 40 S	144 15 E
Bendorf	**30**	50 26N	7 34 E
Benē Beraq	**44**	32 6N	34 51 E
Beneditinos	**138**	5 27 S	42 22W
Benedito Leite	**138**	7 13 S	44 34W
Bénéna	**88**	13 9N	4 17W
Benenitra	**97**	23 27 S	45 5 E
Benešov	**32**	49 46N	14 41 E
Bénestroff	**19**	48 54N	6 45 E
Benet	**20**	46 22N	0 35W
Benetook	**74**	34 22 S	142 0 E
Benevento	**29**	41 7N	14 45 E
Benfeld	**19**	48 22N	7 34 E
Benga	**95**	16 11 S	33 40 E
Bengal, Bay of	**42**	15 0N	90 0 E
Bengawan Solo →	**57**	7 5 S	112 35 E
Bengbu	**59**	32 58N	117 20 E
Benghazi = Banghāzī	**87**	32 11N	20 3 E
Bengkalis	**56**	1 30N	102 10 E
Bengkulu	**56**	3 50 S	102 12 E
Bengkulu □	**56**	3 48 S	102 16 E
Bengough	**109**	49 25N	105 10W
Benguela	**93**	12 37 S	13 25 E
Benguerir	**86**	32 16N	7 56W
Benguérua, I.	**97**	21 58 S	35 28 E
Benha	**90**	30 26N	31 8 E
Beni, Austral.	**76**	32 11 S	148 43 E
Beni, Zaïre	**94**	0 30N	29 27 E
Beni □	**137**	14 0 S	65 0W
Beni →	**137**	10 23 S	65 24W
Beni Abbès	**86**	30 5N	2 5W
Beni Haoua	**86**	36 30N	1 30 E
Benî Mazâr	**90**	28 32N	30 44 E
Beni Mellal	**86**	32 21N	6 21W
Beni Ounif	**86**	32 0N	1 10W
Beni Saf	**86**	35 17N	1 15W
Benî Suêf	**90**	29 5N	31 6 E
Beniah L.	**108**	63 23N	112 17W
Benicarló	**24**	40 23N	0 23 E
Benicia	**122**	38 3N	122 9W
Benidorm	**25**	38 33N	0 9W
Benidorm, Islote de	**25**	38 31N	0 9W
Benin ■	**89**	10 0N	2 0 E
Benin, Bight of	**89**	5 0N	3 0 E
Benin City	**89**	6 20N	5 31 E
Benisa	**25**	38 43N	0 03 E
Benjamin Aceval	**140**	24 58 S	57 34W
Benjamin Constant	**134**	4 40 S	70 15W
Benjamin Hill	**124**	30 10N	111 10W
Benjeroop	**74**	35 30 S	143 50 E
Benkelman	**118**	40 7N	101 32W
Benkovac	**27**	44 2N	15 37 E
Benlidi	**72**	24 35 S	144 50 E
Benmore Pk.	**81**	44 25 S	170 8 E
Bennett	**108**	59 56N	134 53W
Bennett, Ostrov	**41**	76 21N	148 56 E

Bennettsville 113 34 38N 79 39W
Bennington 115 42 52N 73 12W
Benny 106 46 47N 81 38W
Benoa 56 8 50S 115 20 E
Bénodet 18 47 53N 4 7W
Benoni 97 26 11S 28 18 E
Benoud 86 32 20N 0 16 E
Benque Viejo 125 17 5N 89 8W
Bensheim 31 49 40N 8 38 E
Benson 121 31 59N 110 19W
Bent 47 26 20N 59 31 E
Benteng 57 6 10S 120 30 E
Bentinck I. 72 17 3S 139 35 E
Bentiu 91 9 10N 29 55 E
Bento Gonçalves 141 29 10S 51 31W
Benton, Ark., U.S.A. 119 34 30N 92 35W
Benton, Calif., U.S.A. 122 37 48N 118 32W
Benton, Ill., U.S.A. 116 38 0N 88 55W
Benton Harbor 117 42 10N 86 28W
Bentong 55 3 31N 101 55 E
Bentu Liben 91 8 32N 38 21 E
Benue □ 89 7 30N 7 30 E
Benue → 89 7 48N 6 46 E
Benxi 61 41 20N 123 48 E
Benzdorp 135 3 44N 54 5W
Beo 57 4 25N 126 50 E
Beograd 33 44 50N 20 37 E
Beowawe 120 40 35N 116 30W
Bepan Jiang → 58 24 55N 106 5 E
Beppu 64 33 15N 131 30 E
Beppu-Wan 64 33 18N 131 34 E
Ber Dagan 44 32 1N 34 49 E
Bera 52 24 5N 89 37 E
Berakit 91 14 38N 39 29 E
Berati 35 40 43N 19 59 E
Berau, Teluk 57 2 30S 132 30 E
Berber 90 18 0N 34 0 E
Berbera 45 10 30N 45 2 E
Berbérati 92 4 15N 15 40 E
Berberia, Cabo 25 38 39N 1 24 E
Berbice □ 135 4 0N 58 0W
Berbice → 135 6 20N 57 32W
Berceto 26 44 30N 10 0 E
Berchtesgaden 31 47 37N 12 58 E
Berck-sur-Mer 19 50 25N 1 36 E
Berdichev 38 49 57N 28 30 E
Berdsk 40 54 47N 83 2 E
Berdyansk 38 46 45N 36 50 E
Berea, Ky., U.S.A. 112 37 35N 84 18W
Berea, Ohio, U.S.A. 114 41 21N 81 50W
Berebere 57 2 25N 128 45 E
Bereda 45 11 45N 51 0 E
Bereina 69 8 39S 146 30 E
Berekum 88 7 29N 2 34W
Berenice 90 24 2N 35 25 E
Berens → 109 52 25N 97 2W
Berens I. 109 52 18N 97 18W
Berens River 109 52 25N 97 0W
Berestechko 36 50 22N 25 5 E
Bereşti 34 46 6N 27 50 E
Beretău → 34 46 59N 21 7 E
Berettyo → 33 46 59N 21 7 E
Berettyóújfalu 33 47 13N 21 33 E
Berevo, Majunga, Madag. 97 17 14S 44 17 E
Berevo, Tuléar, Madag. 97 19 44S 44 58 E
Bereza 36 52 31N 24 51 E
Berezhany 36 49 26N 24 58 E
Berezina → 36 52 33N 30 14 E
Berezna 37 51 35N 31 46 E
Berezniki 40 59 24N 56 46 E
Berezovka 38 47 14N 30 55 E
Berezovo 40 64 0N 65 0 E
Berga, Spain 24 42 6N 1 48 E
Berga, Sweden 11 57 14N 16 3 E
Bergama 46 39 8N 27 15 E
Bérgamo 26 45 42N 9 40 E
Bergantiños 22 43 20N 8 40W
Bergedorf 30 53 28N 10 12 E
Bergen, Ger. 30 54 24N 13 26 E
Bergen, Norway 9 60 23N 5 20 E
Bergen, U.S.A. 114 43 5N 77 56W
Bergen-Binnen 16 52 40N 4 43 E
Bergen-op-Zoom 16 51 30N 4 18 E
Bergerac 20 44 51N 0 30 E
Bergheim 30 50 57N 6 38 E
Bergisch-Gladbach 30 50 59N 7 9 E
Bergkvara 11 56 23N 16 5 E
Bergsjö 10 61 59N 17 3 E
Berguent 86 34 1N 2 0W
Bergues 19 50 58N 2 24 E
Bergum 16 53 13N 5 59 E
Bergvik 10 61 16N 16 50 E
Berhala, Selat 56 1 0S 104 15 E
Berhampore 49 24 2N 88 27 E
Berhampur 50 19 15N 84 54 E
Berheci → 34 46 7N 27 19 E
Bering Sea 66 58 0N 167 0 E
Bering Str. 100 66 0N 170 0W
Beringen 16 51 3N 5 14 E
Beringovskiy 41 63 3N 179 19 E
Berislav 38 46 50N 33 30 E
Berisso 140 34 56S 57 50W
Berja 25 36 50N 2 56W
Berkane 86 34 52N 2 20W
Berkeley, U.K. 13 51 41N 2 28W
Berkeley, U.S.A. 122 37 52N 122 20W
Berkeley Springs 112 39 38N 78 12W
Berkner I. 143 79 30S 50 0W
Berkovitsa 34 43 16N 23 8 E
Berkshire □ 13 51 30N 1 20W
Berland → 108 54 0N 116 50W
Berlanga 23 38 17N 5 50W
Berleburg 30 51 3N 8 22 E
Berlenga, Ilhas 23 39 25N 9 30W
Berlin, Ger. 30 52 32N 13 24 E
Berlin, Md., U.S.A. 112 38 19N 75 12W
Berlin, N.H., U.S.A. 115 44 29N 71 10W
Berlin, Wis., U.S.A. 112 43 58N 88 55W
Berlin, E. □ 30 52 30N 13 30 E
Berlin, W. □ 30 52 30N 13 20 E
Bermeja, Sierra 23 36 30N 5 11W
Bermejo →, Formosa, Argent. 140 26 51S 58 23W
Bermejo →, San Juan, Argent. 140 32 30S 67 30W
Bermeo 24 43 25N 2 47W
Bermillo de Sayago 22 41 22N 6 8W
Bermuda ■ 128 32 45N 65 0W
Bern (Berne) 31 46 57N 7 28 E
Bern (Berne) □ 31 46 45N 7 40 E
Bernado 121 34 30N 106 53W
Bernalda 29 40 24N 16 44 E
Bernalillo 121 35 17N 106 37W
Bernard L. 106 45 45N 79 23W
Bernardo de Irigoyen 141 26 15S 53 40W
Bernasconi 140 37 55S 63 44W
Bernau, Germ., E. 30 52 40N 13 35 E
Bernau, Germ., W. 31 47 45N 12 20 E
Bernay 18 49 5N 0 35 E
Bernburg 30 51 40N 11 42 E
Berne 117 40 39N 84 57W
Berne = Bern 31 46 57N 7 28 E
Berneck 31 51 3N 11 40 E
Berner Alpen 31 46 27N 7 35 E
Bernese Oberland = Oberland 31 46 27N 7 35 E
Bernier I. 79 24 50S 113 12 E
Bernierville 105 46 6N 71 34W
Bernina, Piz 31 46 20N 9 54 E
Bernkastel-Kues 31 49 55N 7 04 E
Beror Hayil 44 31 34N 34 38 E
Béroubouay 89 10 34N 2 46 E
Beroun 32 49 57N 14 5 E
Berounka → 32 50 0N 13 47 E
Berovo 35 41 38N 22 51 E
Berrahal 87 36 54N 7 33 E
Berre, Étang de 21 43 27N 5 5 E
Berrechid 86 33 18N 7 36W
Berri 73 34 14S 140 35 E
Berriane 86 32 50N 3 46 E
Berridale 75 36 22S 148 48 E
Berrien Springs 117 41 57N 86 20W
Berrima 76 34 28S 150 20 E
Berrouaghia 86 36 10N 2 53 E
Berrwillock 74 35 36S 142 59 E
Berry, Austral. 76 34 46S 150 43 E
Berry, France 19 47 0N 2 0 E
Berry, U.S.A. 117 38 31N 84 23W
Berry Is. 126 25 40N 77 50W
Berryessa, L. 122 38 31N 122 6W
Berryville 119 36 23N 93 35W
Bersenbrück 30 52 33N 7 56 E
Berthierville 105 46 5N 73 10W
Berthold 118 48 19N 101 45W
Berthoud 118 40 21N 105 5W
Bertincourt 19 50 5N 2 58 E
Bertoua 92 4 30N 13 45 E
Bertrand 118 40 35N 99 38W
Beruas 55 4 30N 100 47 E
Berufjörður 8 64 48N 14 29W
Beruri 135 3 54S 61 22W
Berwick, Austral. 74 38 2S 145 23 E
Berwick, U.S.A. 115 41 4N 76 17W
Berwick-upon-Tweed 12 55 47N 2 0W
Berwyn Mts. 12 52 54N 3 26W
Berzasca 34 44 39N 21 58 E
Besal 49 35 4N 73 56 E
Besalampy 97 16 43S 44 29 E
Besançon 19 47 15N 6 0 E
Besar 56 2 40S 116 0 E
Beshenkovichi 36 55 2N 29 29 E
Beslan 39 43 15N 44 28 E
Besnard L. 109 55 25N 106 0W
Besni 46 37 41N 37 52 E
Bessarabka 38 46 21N 28 58 E
Bessèges 21 44 18N 4 8 E
Bessemer, Ala., U.S.A. 113 33 25N 86 57W
Bessemer, Mich., U.S.A. 118 46 27N 90 0W
Bessin 18 49 21N 1 0W
Bessines-sur-Gartempe 20 46 6N 1 22 E
Bet Alfa 44 32 31N 35 25 E
Bet Guvrin 44 31 37N 34 54 E
Bet Ha'Emeq 44 32 58N 35 8 E
Bet Hashitta 44 32 31N 35 27 E
Bet Qeshet 44 32 41N 35 21 E
Bet She'an 44 32 30N 35 30 E
Bet Tadjine, Djebel 86 29 0N 3 30W
Bet Yosef 44 32 34N 35 33 E
Betafo 97 19 50S 46 51 E
Betanzos, Boliv. 137 19 34S 65 27W
Betanzos, Spain 22 43 15N 8 12W
Bétaré-Oya 92 5 40N 14 5 E
Bétera 24 39 35N 0 28W
Bethal 97 26 27S 29 28 E
Bethanien 96 26 31S 17 8 E
Bethany, Can. 107 44 11N 78 34W
Bethany, S. Afr. 96 29 34S 25 59 E
Bethany, Ill., U.S.A. 117 39 39N 88 45W
Bethany, Mo., U.S.A. 116 40 18N 94 0W
Bethany = Eizariya 44 31 47N 35 15 E
Bethel, Alaska, U.S.A. 100 60 50N 161 50W
Bethel, Ohio, U.S.A. 117 38 58N 84 5W
Bethel, Pa., U.S.A. 114 40 20N 80 2W
Bethel, Vt., U.S.A. 115 43 50N 72 37W
Bethlehem, S. Afr. 97 28 14S 28 18 E
Bethlehem, U.S.A. 115 40 39N 75 24W
Bethlehem = Bayt Lahm 44 31 43N 35 12 E
Bethulie 96 30 30S 25 59 E
Béthune 19 50 30N 2 38 E
Béthune → 18 49 53N 1 9 E
Bethungra 76 34 45S 147 51 E
Betijoque 134 9 23N 70 44W
Betim 139 19 58S 44 7W
Betioky 97 23 48S 44 20 E
Beton Bazoches 19 48 42N 3 15 E
Betong, Malay. 56 1 24N 111 31 E
Betong, Thai. 55 5 45N 101 5 E
Betoota 72 25 40S 140 42 E
Betroka 97 23 16S 46 0 E
Betsiamites 105 48 56N 68 40W
Betsiamites → 105 48 56N 68 38W
Betsiboka → 97 16 3S 46 36 E
Betsjoeanaland 96 26 30S 22 30 E
Bettendorf 116 41 32N 90 30W
Bettiah 49 26 48N 84 33 E
Béttola 26 44 42N 9 32 E
Betul 50 21 58N 77 59 E
Betzdorf 30 50 47N 7 53 E
Beuca 34 44 14N 24 56 E
Beuil 21 44 6N 6 59 E
Beulah, Austral. 74 35 58S 142 29 E
Beulah, U.S.A. 118 47 18N 101 47W
Bevensen 30 53 5N 10 34 E
Beverley, Austral. 79 32 9S 116 56 E
Beverley, U.K. 12 53 52N 0 26W
Beverly, Mass., U.S.A. 115 42 32N 70 50W
Beverly, Wash., U.S.A. 120 46 55N 119 59W
Beverly Hills 123 34 4N 118 29W
Beverwijk 16 52 28N 4 38 E
Bewdley 107 44 5N 78 19W
Bex 31 46 15N 7 0 E
Beyin 88 5 1N 2 41W
Beykoz 35 41 8N 29 7 E
Beyla 88 8 30N 8 38W
Beynat 20 45 8N 1 44 E
Beyneu 40 45 10N 55 3 E
Beypazarı 46 40 10N 31 56 E
Beyşehir Gölü 46 37 40N 31 45 E
Bezet 44 33 4N 35 8 E
Bezhitsa 36 53 19N 34 17 E
Béziers 20 43 20N 3 12 E
Bezwada = Vijayawada 51 16 31N 80 39 E
Bhadarwah 49 32 58N 75 46 E
Bhadra → 51 14 0N 75 20 E
Bhadrakh 50 21 10N 86 30 E
Bhadravati 51 13 49N 75 40 E
Bhagalpur 49 25 10N 87 0 E
Bhairab → 52 22 51N 89 34 E
Bhairab Bazar 52 24 4N 90 58 E
Bhaisa 50 19 10N 77 58 E
Bhakkar 48 31 40N 71 5 E
Bhakra Dam 48 31 30N 76 45 E
Bhamo 52 24 15N 97 15 E
Bhamragarh 50 19 30N 80 40 E
Bhandara 50 21 5N 79 42 E
Bhanrer Ra. 48 23 40N 79 45 E
Bharatpur 48 27 15N 77 30 E
Bharuch 50 21 47N 73 0 E
Bhatghar L. 50 18 10N 73 48 E
Bhatiapara Ghat 52 23 13N 89 42 E
Bhatinda 48 30 15N 74 57 E
Bhatkal 51 13 58N 74 35 E
Bhatpara 49 22 50N 88 25 E
Bhattiprolu 51 16 7N 80 45 E
Bhaun 48 32 55N 72 40 E
Bhaunagar = Bhavnagar 48 21 45N 72 10 E
Bhavani 51 11 27N 77 43 E
Bhavani → 51 11 0N 78 15 E
Bhavnagar 48 21 45N 72 10 E
Bhawanipatna 50 19 55N 80 10 E
Bhera 48 32 29N 72 57 E
Bhilsa = Vidisha 48 23 28N 77 53 E
Bhilwara 48 25 25N 74 38 E
Bhima → 50 16 25N 77 17 E
Bhimavaram 51 16 30N 81 30 E
Bhimber 49 32 59N 74 3 E
Bhind 49 26 30N 78 46 E
Bhir 50 19 4N 75 46 E
Bhiwandi 50 19 20N 73 0 E
Bhiwani 48 28 50N 76 9 E
Bhola 52 22 45N 90 35 E
Bhongir 50 17 30N 78 56 E
Bhopal 48 23 20N 77 30 E
Bhor 50 18 12N 73 53 E
Bhubaneswar 50 20 15N 85 50 E
Bhuj 48 23 15N 69 49 E
Bhumibol Dam 54 17 15N 98 58 E
Bhusaval 50 21 3N 75 46 E
Bhutan ■ 52 27 25N 90 30 E
Biá → 134 3 28S 67 23W
Biafra, B. of = Bonny, Bight of 89 3 30N 9 20 E
Biak 57 1 10S 136 6 E
Biała → 32 50 3N 20 55 E
Biała Podlaska 32 52 4N 23 6 E
Białogard 32 54 2N 15 58 E
Białystok 32 53 10N 23 10 E
Biancavilla 29 37 39N 14 50 E
Biaro 57 2 5N 125 26 E
Biarritz 20 43 29N 1 33W
Biasca 31 46 22N 8 58 E
Biba 90 28 55N 31 0 E
Bibai 63 43 19N 141 52 E
Bibane, Bahiret el 87 33 16N 11 13 E
Bibbenluke 75 36 48S 149 17 E
Bibbiena 27 43 43N 11 50 E
Bibby I. 109 61 55N 93 0W
Biberach 31 48 5N 9 49 E
Bibey → 22 42 24N 7 13W
Bibiani 88 6 30N 2 8W
Bibile 51 7 10N 81 25 E
Biboohra 72 16 56S 145 25 E
Bibungwa 94 2 40S 28 15 E
Bic 105 48 20N 68 41W
Bic, Île du 105 48 24N 68 52W
Bicaz 34 46 53N 26 5 E
Biccari 29 41 23N 15 12 E
Biche, La → 108 59 57N 123 50W
Bichena 91 10 28N 38 10 E
Bickerton I. 72 13 45S 136 10 E
Bicknell, Ind., U.S.A. 117 38 50N 87 20W
Bicknell, Utah, U.S.A. 121 38 16N 111 35W
Bida 89 9 3N 5 58 E
Bidar 50 17 55N 77 35 E
Biddeford 103 43 30N 70 28W
Biddon 76 31 30S 148 47 E
Biddu 44 31 50N 35 8 E
Biddwara 91 5 11N 38 34 E
Biddya 44 32 7N 35 4 E
Bideford 13 51 1N 4 13W
Bidor 55 4 6N 101 15 E
Bié 93 12 22S 16 55 E
Bié Plateau 93 12 0S 16 0 E
Bieber 120 41 4N 121 6W
Biel (Bienne) 31 47 8N 7 14 E
Bielawa 32 50 43N 16 37 E
Bielé Karpaty 32 49 5N 18 0 E
Bielefeld 30 52 2N 8 31 E
Bielersee 31 47 6N 7 5 E
Biella 26 45 33N 8 3 E
Bielsk Podlaski 32 52 47N 23 12 E
Bielsko-Biała 32 49 50N 19 2 E
Bien Hoa 55 10 57N 106 49 E
Bienfait 109 49 10N 102 50W
Bienne = Biel 31 47 8N 7 14 E
Bienvenida 23 38 18N 6 12W
Bienvenue 135 3 0N 52 30W
Bienville, L. 102 55 5N 72 40W
Biescas 24 42 37N 0 20W
Biese → 30 52 53N 11 46 E
Biesiesfontein 96 30 57S 17 58 E
Bietigheim 31 48 57N 9 8 E
Biferno → 29 41 59N 15 2 E
Big →, Can. 103 54 50N 58 55W
Big →, U.S.A. 116 38 27N 90 37W
Big B. 103 55 43N 60 35W
Big Basswood L. 106 46 25N 83 23W
Big Bear City 123 34 16N 116 51W
Big Bear L. 123 34 15N 116 56W
Big Beaver 109 49 10N 105 10W
Big Bell 79 27 21S 117 40 E
Big Belt Mts. 120 46 50N 111 30W
Big Bend 97 26 50S 32 2 E
Big Bend Nat. Park 119 29 15N 103 15W
Big Black → 119 32 0N 91 5W

Big Blue →, Ind., U.S.A.	117	39 12N	85 56W
Big Blue →, Kans., U.S.A.	118	39 11N	96 40W
Big Cr. →	108	51 42N	122 41W
Big Creek	122	37 11N	119 14W
Big Cypress Swamp	113	26 12N	81 10W
Big Falls	118	48 11N	93 48W
Big Fork →	118	48 31N	93 43W
Big Horn	120	46 11N	107 25W
Big Horn Mts. = Bighorn Mts.	120	44 30N	107 30W
Big Lake	119	31 12N	101 25W
Big Moose	115	43 49N	74 58W
Big Muddy →, Ill., U.S.A.	116	38 0N	89 0W
Big Muddy →, Mont., U.S.A.	118	48 8N	104 36W
Big Pine	122	37 12N	118 17W
Big Piney	120	42 32N	110 3W
Big Quill L.	109	51 55N	104 22W
Big Rapids	112	43 42N	85 27W
Big Rideau L.	107	44 40N	76 15W
Big River	109	53 50N	107 0W
Big Run	114	40 57N	78 55W
Big Sable Pt.	112	44 5N	86 30W
Big Sand L.	109	57 45N	99 45W
Big Sandy	120	48 12N	110 9W
Big Sandy Cr. →	118	38 6N	102 29W
Big Sioux →	118	42 30N	96 25W
Big Spring	119	32 10N	101 25W
Big Springs	118	41 4N	102 3W
Big Stone City	118	45 20N	96 30W
Big Stone Gap	113	36 52N	82 45W
Big Stone L.	118	45 30N	96 35W
Big Sur	122	36 15N	121 48W
Big Trout L., Ont., Can.	102	53 40N	90 0W
Big Trout L., Ont., Can.	107	45 46N	78 37W
Biganos	20	44 39N	0 59W
Bigfork	120	48 3N	114 2W
Bigga	76	34 4S	149 9 E
Biggar, Can.	109	52 4N	108 0W
Biggar, U.K.	14	55 38N	3 31W
Bigge I.	78	14 35S	125 10 E
Biggenden	73	25 31S	152 4 E
Biggs	122	39 24N	121 43W
Bighorn →	120	46 9N	107 28W
Bighorn Mts.	120	44 30N	107 30W
Bigniba →	104	49 18N	77 20W
Bignona	88	12 52N	16 14W
Bigorre	20	43 6N	0 5 E
Bigstone L.	109	53 42N	95 44W
Bigtimber	120	45 53N	110 0W
Bigwa	94	7 10S	39 10 E
Bihać	27	44 49N	15 57 E
Bihar	49	25 5N	85 40 E
Bihar □	49	25 0N	86 0 E
Biharamulo	94	2 25S	31 25 E
Biharamulo □	94	2 30S	31 20 E
Bihor, Munţii	34	46 29N	22 47 E
Bijagós, Arquipélago dos	88	11 15N	16 10W
Bijaipur	48	26 2N	77 20 E
Bijapur, Mad. P., India	50	18 50N	80 50 E
Bijapur, Mysore, India	50	16 50N	75 55 E
Bijār	46	35 52N	47 35 E
Bijeljina	33	44 46N	19 17 E
Bijelo Polje	33	43 1N	19 45 E
Bijie	58	27 20N	105 16 E
Bijni	52	26 30N	90 40 E
Bijnor	48	29 27N	78 11 E
Bikaner	48	28 2N	73 18 E
Bikapur	49	26 30N	82 7 E
Bikeqi	60	40 43N	111 20 E
Bikin	41	46 50N	134 20 E
Bikini, atoll	66	12 0N	167 30 E
Bikoro	92	0 48S	18 15 E
Bikoué	89	3 55N	11 50 E
Bilād Banī Bū 'Ali	47	22 0N	59 20 E
Bilara	48	26 14N	73 53 E
Bilaspara	52	26 13N	90 14 E
Bilaspur, Mad. P., India	49	22 2N	82 15 E
Bilaspur, Punjab, India	48	31 19N	76 50 E
Bilauk Taung dan	54	13 0N	99 0 E
Bilbao	24	43 16N	2 56W
Bilbeis	90	30 25N	31 34 E
Bilbor	34	47 8N	25 30 E
Bíldudalur	8	65 41N	23 36W
Bileća	33	42 53N	18 27 E
Bilecik	46	40 5N	30 5 E
Biłgoraj	32	50 33N	22 42 E
Bilibino	41	68 3N	166 20 E
Bilibiza	95	12 30S	40 20 E
Bilin	52	17 14N	97 15 E
Bilir	41	65 40N	131 20 E
Bill	118	43 18N	105 18W
Billabalong	79	27 25S	115 49 E
Billiluna	78	19 37S	127 41 E
Billingham	12	54 36N	1 18W
Billings	120	45 43N	108 29W
Billingsfors	10	58 59N	12 15 E
Billiton Is. = Belitung	56	3 10S	107 50 E
Billom	20	45 43N	3 20 E
Bilma	85	18 50N	13 30 E
Bilo Gora	33	45 53N	17 15 E
Biloela	72	24 24S	150 31 E
Biloku	135	1 50N	58 25W
Biloxi	119	30 24N	88 53W
Bilpa Morea Claypan	72	25 0S	140 0 E
Bilpin	76	33 28S	150 31 E
Biltine	85	14 40N	20 50 E
Bilugyun	52	16 24N	97 32 E
Bilyana	72	18 5S	145 50 E
Bima	57	8 22S	118 49 E
Bimban	90	24 24N	32 54 E
Bimberi Peak	76	35 44S	148 51 E
Bimbila	89	8 54N	0 5 E
Bimbo	92	4 15N	18 33 E
Bimini Is.	126	25 42N	79 25W
Bin Xian, Heilongjiang, China	61	45 42N	127 22 E
Bin Xian, Shaanxi, China	60	35 2N	108 4 E
Bina-Etawah	48	24 13N	78 14 E
Binalbagan	57	10 12N	122 50 E
Binalud, Kuh-e	47	36 30N	58 30 E
Binatang	56	2 10N	111 40 E
Binbee	72	20 19S	147 56 E
Binche	16	50 26N	4 10 E
Binchuan	58	25 42N	100 38 E
Binda	73	27 52S	147 21 E
Bindi Bindi	79	30 37S	116 22 E
Bindle	73	27 40S	148 45 E
Bindura	95	17 18S	31 18 E
Bingara, N.S.W., Austral.	77	29 52S	150 36 E
Bingara, Queens., Austral.	73	28 10S	144 37 E
Bingen	31	49 57N	7 53 E
Bingerville	88	5 18N	3 49W
Bingham	103	45 5N	69 50W
Bingham Canyon	120	40 31N	112 10W
Binghamton	115	42 9N	75 54W
Bingöl	46	38 53N	40 29 E
Binh Dinh = An Nhon	54	13 55N	109 7 E
Binh Khe	54	13 57N	108 51 E
Binh Son	54	15 20N	108 40 E
Binhai	61	34 2N	119 49 E
Biniguy	77	29 34S	150 14 E
Binjai	56	3 20N	98 30 E
Binnaway	77	31 28S	149 24 E
Binongko	57	5 55S	123 55 E
Binscarth	109	50 37N	101 17W
Bint Jaibail	44	33 8N	35 25 E
Bintan	56	1 0N	104 0 E
Bintulu	56	3 10N	113 0 E
Bintuni (Steenkool)	57	2 7S	133 32 E
Binyamina	44	32 32N	34 56 E
Binyang	58	23 12N	108 47 E
Binz	30	54 23N	13 37 E
Binza	91	5 25N	28 40 E
Binzert = Bizerte	87	37 15N	9 50 E
Bío Bío □	140	37 35S	72 0W
Bio Culma	91	7 20N	42 15 E
Biograd	27	43 56N	15 29 E
Biougra	86	30 15N	9 14W
Biq'at Bet Netofa	44	32 49N	35 22 E
Bîr Abu Hashim	90	23 42N	34 6 E
Bîr Abu M'nqar	90	26 33N	27 33 E
Bîr Adal Deib	90	22 35N	36 10 E
Bi'r al Malfa	87	31 58N	15 18 E
Bir Aouine	87	32 25N	9 18 E
Bîr 'Asal	90	25 55N	34 20 E
Bir Autrun	85	18 15N	26 40 E
Bi'r Dhu'fān	87	31 59N	14 32 E
Bîr Diqnash	90	31 3N	25 23 E
Bir el Abbes	86	26 7N	6 9W
Bir el Ater	87	34 46N	8 3 E
Bîr el Basur	90	29 51N	25 49 E
Bîr el Gellaz	90	30 50N	26 40 E
Bîr el Shaqqa	90	30 54N	25 1 E
Bîr Fuad	90	30 35N	26 28 E
Bîr Haimur	90	22 45N	33 40 E
Bir Jdid	86	33 26N	8 0W
Bîr Kanayis	90	24 59N	33 15 E
Bîr Kerawein	90	27 10N	28 25 E
Bir Lahrache	87	32 1N	8 12 E
Bir Lemouissat	86	25 0N	10 32W
Bîr Maql	90	23 7N	33 40 E
Bîr Misaha	90	22 13N	27 59 E
Bir Mogrein (Fort Trinquet)	86	25 10N	11 25W
Bîr Murr	90	23 28N	30 10 E
Bir Nabala	44	31 52N	35 12 E
Bîr Nakheila	90	24 1N	30 50 E
Bîr Qatrani	90	30 55N	26 10 E
Bîr Ranga	90	24 25N	35 15 E
Bir, Ras	91	12 0N	43 20 E
Bîr Sahara	90	22 54N	28 40 E
Bîr Seiyâla	90	26 10N	33 50 E
Bir Semguine	86	30 1N	5 39W
Bîr Shalatein	90	23 5N	35 25 E
Bîr Shebb	90	22 25N	29 40 E
Bîr Shût	90	23 50N	35 15 E
Bîr Terfawi	90	22 57N	28 55 E
Bîr Umm Qubûr	90	24 35N	34 2 E
Bîr Ungât	90	22 8N	33 48 E
Bîr Za'farâna	90	29 10N	32 40 E
Bîr Zāmūs	87	24 16N	15 6 E
Bîr Zeidûn	90	25 45N	33 40 E
Bir Zeit	44	31 59N	35 11 E
Bira	57	2 3S	132 2 E
Bîra	34	47 2N	27 3 E
Biramféro	88	11 40N	9 10W
Birao	85	10 20N	22 47 E
Birawa	94	2 20S	28 48 E
Bîrca	34	43 59N	23 36 E
Birch Hills	109	52 59N	105 25W
Birch I.	109	52 26N	99 54W
Birch L., N.W.T., Can.	108	62 4N	116 33W
Birch L., Ont., Can.	102	51 23N	92 18W
Birch L., U.S.A.	102	47 48N	91 43W
Birch Mts.	108	57 30N	113 10W
Birch River	109	52 24N	101 6W
Birch Run	106	43 15N	83 48W
Birchip	74	35 56S	142 55 E
Birchwood	81	45 55S	167 53 E
Bird	109	56 30N	94 13W
Bird City	118	39 48N	101 33W
Bird I.	96	32 3S	18 17 E
Bird I. = Aves, I. de	127	12 0N	67 30W
Birdlip	13	51 50N	2 7W
Birds	117	38 50N	87 40W
Birdseye	117	38 19N	86 42W
Birdsville	72	25 51S	139 20 E
Birdum	78	15 39S	133 13 E
Birecik	46	37 0N	38 0 E
Bireuen	56	5 14N	96 39 E
Birhan	91	10 45N	37 55 E
Birifo	88	13 30N	14 0W
Birigui	141	21 18S	50 16W
Birk	90	18 8N	41 30 E
Birka	90	22 11N	40 38 E
Birkenfeld	31	49 39N	7 11 E
Birkenhead, N.Z.	80	36 49S	174 46 E
Birkenhead, U.K.	12	53 24N	3 1W
Birket Qârûn	90	29 30N	30 40 E
Birkhadem	86	36 43N	3 3 E
Bîrlad	34	46 15N	27 38 E
Birmingham, U.K.	13	52 30N	1 55W
Birmingham, Ala., U.S.A.	113	33 31N	86 50W
Birmingham, Iowa, U.S.A.	116	40 53N	91 57W
Birmingham, Mich., U.S.A.	106	42 33N	83 15W
Birmitrapur	50	22 24N	84 46 E
Birni Ngaouré	89	13 5N	2 51 E
Birni Nkonni	89	13 55N	5 15 E
Birnin Gwari	89	11 0N	6 45 E
Birnin Kebbi	89	12 32N	4 12 E
Birnin Kudu	89	11 30N	9 29 E
Birobidzhan	41	48 50N	132 50 E
Birqin	44	32 27N	35 15 E
Birr	15	53 7N	7 55W
Birregurra	74	38 20S	143 46 E
Birrie →	73	29 43S	146 37 E
Birriwa	77	32 7S	149 28 E
Birsilpur	48	28 11N	72 15 E
Birsk	40	55 25N	55 30 E
Birtin	34	46 59N	22 31 E
Birtle	109	50 30N	101 5W
Biryuchiy	38	46 10N	35 0 E
Birzai	36	56 11N	24 45 E
Bîrzava	34	46 7N	21 59 E
Bisa	57	1 15S	127 28 E
Bisáccia	29	41 0N	15 20 E
Bisacquino	28	37 42N	13 13 E
Bisai	65	35 16N	136 44 E
Bisalpur	49	28 14N	79 48 E
Bisbal, La	24	41 58N	3 2 E
Bisbee	121	31 30N	110 0W
Biscarrosse, Étang de	20	44 21N	1 10W
Biscay, B. of	128	45 0N	2 0W
Biscayne B.	113	25 40N	80 12W
Biscéglie	29	41 14N	16 30 E
Bischofshofen	33	47 26N	13 14 E
Bischofswerda	30	51 8N	14 11 E
Bischwiller	19	48 41N	7 50 E
Biscoe Bay	143	77 0S	152 0W
Biscoe I.	143	66 0S	67 0W
Biscostasing	104	47 18N	82 9W
Biscucuy	134	9 22N	69 59W
Biševo	27	42 57N	16 3 E
Bisha	91	15 30N	37 31 E
Bisha, Wadi →	90	21 24N	43 26 E
Bishan	58	29 33N	106 12 E
Bishop, Calif., U.S.A.	122	37 20N	118 26W
Bishop, Tex., U.S.A.	119	27 35N	97 49W
Bishop Auckland	12	54 40N	1 40W
Bishop's Falls	103	49 2N	55 30W
Bishop's Stortford	13	51 52N	0 11 E
Bishopton	105	45 35N	71 35W
Bisignano	29	39 30N	16 17 E
Bisina, L.	94	1 38N	33 56 E
Biskra	87	34 50N	5 44 E
Bislig	57	8 15N	126 27 E
Bismarck, Mo., U.S.A.	116	37 46N	90 38W
Bismarck, N.Dak., U.S.A.	118	46 49N	100 49W
Bismarck Arch.	69	2 30S	150 0 E
Bismarck Ra.	69	5 35S	145 0 E
Bismarck Sea	69	4 10S	146 50 E
Bismark	30	52 39N	11 31 E
Biso	94	1 44N	31 26 E
Bison	118	45 34N	102 28W
Bispgården	10	63 2N	16 40 E
Bissagos = Bijagós, Arquipélago dos	88	11 15N	16 10W
Bissau	88	11 45N	15 45W
Bissett	109	51 2N	95 41W
Bissikrima	88	10 50N	10 58W
Bistcho L.	108	59 45N	118 50W
Bistreţu	34	43 54N	23 23 E
Bistrica = Ilirska-Bistrica	27	45 34N	14 14 E
Bistriţa	34	47 9N	24 35 E
Bistriţa →	34	46 30N	26 57 E
Bistriţei, Munţii	34	47 15N	25 40 E
Biswan	49	27 29N	81 2 E
Bitam	92	2 5N	11 25 E
Bitburg	31	49 58N	6 32 E
Bitche	19	49 2N	7 25 E
Bitkine	92	11 59N	18 13 E
Bitlis	46	38 20N	42 3 E
Bitola (Bitolj)	35	41 5N	21 10 E
Bitonto	29	41 7N	16 40 E
Bitter Creek	120	41 39N	108 36W
Bitter L. = Buheirat-Murrat-el-Kubra	90	30 15N	32 40 E
Bitterfeld	30	51 36N	12 20 E
Bitterfontein	96	31 0S	18 32 E
Bitterroot →	120	46 52N	114 6W
Bitterroot Range	120	46 0N	114 20W
Bitterwater	122	36 23N	121 0W
Bitti	28	40 29N	9 20 E
Bittou	89	11 17N	0 18W
Biu	89	10 40N	12 3 E
Bivolari	34	47 31N	27 27 E
Biwa-Ko	65	35 15N	136 10 E
Biwabik	118	47 33N	92 19W
Bixad	34	47 56N	23 28 E
Biyang	59	32 38N	113 21 E
Biysk	40	52 40N	85 0 E
Bizana	97	30 50S	29 52 E
Bizen	64	34 43N	134 8 E
Bizerte (Binzert)	87	37 15N	9 50 E
Bjargtangar	8	65 30N	24 30W
Bjelasica	33	42 50N	19 40 E
Bjelovar	33	45 56N	16 49 E
Bjerringbro	11	56 23N	9 39 E
Björbo	10	60 27N	14 44 E
Björneborg	10	59 14N	14 16 E
Bjørnøya	144	74 30N	19 0 E
Bjuv	11	56 5N	12 55 E
Blace	33	43 18N	21 17 E
Blache, L. de la	105	50 5N	69 29W
Black →, Can.	106	44 42N	79 19W
Black →, Ark., U.S.A.	119	35 38N	91 19W
Black →, Mich., U.S.A.	106	43 3N	82 37W
Black →, N.Y., U.S.A.	115	43 59N	76 4W
Black →, Wis., U.S.A.	118	43 52N	91 22W
Black → = Da →	54	21 15N	105 20 E
Black Diamond	108	50 45N	114 14W
Black Forest = Schwarzwald	31	48 0N	8 0 E
Black Hills	118	44 0N	103 50W
Black I.	109	51 12N	96 30W
Black L., Can.	109	59 12N	105 15W
Black L., U.S.A.	106	45 28N	84 15W
Black Lake	105	46 1N	71 22W
Black Mesa, Mt.	119	36 57N	102 55W
Black Mt. = Mynydd Du	13	51 45N	3 45W
Black Mountain	77	30 18S	151 39 E
Black Mts.	13	51 52N	3 5W
Black Pt.	79	34 30S	119 25 E
Black Range	121	33 30N	107 55W
Black River, Jamaica	126	18 0N	77 50W
Black River, U.S.A.	106	44 53N	83 18W
Black River Falls	118	44 23N	90 52W
Black Sea	6	43 30N	35 0 E
Black Sugarloaf, Mt.	77	31 18S	151 35 E
Black Volta →	88	8 41N	1 33W
Black Warrior →	113	32 32N	87 51W
Blackall	72	24 25S	145 45 E
Blackball	81	42 22S	171 26 E
Blackbull	72	17 55S	141 45 E

Blackburn **12** 53 44N 2 30W
Blackduck **118** 47 43N 94 32W
Blackfoot **120** 43 13N 112 12W
Blackfoot → **120** 46 52N 113 53W
Blackfoot River Res. **120** 43 0N 111 35W
Blackheath **76** 33 39S 150 17 E
Blackie **108** 50 36N 113 37W
Blackpool **12** 53 48N 3 3W
Blackriver **114** 44 46N 83 17W
Blacks Harbour **103** 45 3N 66 49W
Blacksburg **112** 37 17N 80 23W
Blacksod B. **15** 54 6N 10 0W
Blackstone **112** 37 6N 78 0W
Blackstone → **108** 61 5N 122 55W
Blackstone Ra. **79** 26 00S 129 00 E
Blacktown **76** 33 48S 150 55 E
Blackville, Austral. **77** 31 40S 150 15 E
Blackville, Can. **103** 46 44N 65 50W
Blackwater, N.S.W., Austral. **77** 30 4S 151 53 E
Blackwater, Queens., Austral. **72** 23 35S 148 53 E
Blackwater →, Ireland **15** 51 55N 7 50W
Blackwater →, U.K. **15** 54 31N 6 35W
Blackwater →, U.S.A. **116** 38 59N 92 59W
Blackwater Cr. → **73** 25 56S 144 30 E
Blackwell **119** 36 55N 97 20W
Blackwells Corner **123** 35 37N 119 47W
Blackwood, C. **69** 7 49S 144 31 E
Blaenau Ffestiniog **12** 53 0N 3 57W
Blagodarnoye **39** 45 7N 43 37 E
Blagoevgrad (Gorna Dzhumayo) **35** 42 2N 23 5 E
Blagoveshchensk **41** 50 20N 127 30 E
Blain **18** 47 29N 1 45W
Blaine **122** 48 59N 122 43W
Blaine Lake **109** 52 51N 106 52W
Blainville, Can. **105** 45 40N 73 52W
Blainville, France **19** 48 33N 6 23 E
Blair **118** 41 38N 96 10W
Blair Athol **72** 22 42S 147 31 E
Blair Atholl **14** 56 46N 3 50W
Blairgowrie **14** 56 36N 3 20W
Blairmore **108** 49 40N 114 25W
Blairsden **122** 39 47N 120 37W
Blairsville **114** 40 27N 79 15W
Blaj **34** 46 10N 23 57 E
Blake Pt. **118** 48 12N 88 27W
Blakely **113** 31 22N 85 0W
Blakesburg **116** 40 58N 92 38W
Blâmont **19** 48 35N 6 50 E
Blanc, C. **87** 37 15N 9 56 E
Blanc, Le **20** 46 37N 1 3 E
Blanc, Mont **21** 45 48N 6 50 E
Blanca, Bahía **142** 39 10S 61 30W
Blanca Peak **121** 37 35N 105 29W
Blanchard **119** 35 8N 97 40W
Blanchardville **116** 42 48N 89 52W
Blanche, C. **73** 33 1S 134 9 E
Blanche Channel **68** 8 30S 157 30 E
Blanche L., S. Austral., Austral. **73** 29 15S 139 40 E
Blanche L., W. Austral., Austral. **78** 22 25S 123 17 E
Blanchester **117** 39 17N 83 59W
Blanco, S. Afr. **96** 33 55S 22 23 E
Blanco, U.S.A. **119** 30 7N 98 30W
Blanco → **140** 30 20S 68 42W
Blanco, C., C. Rica **126** 9 34N 85 8W
Blanco, C., Spain **25** 39 21N 2 51 E
Blanco, C., U.S.A. **120** 42 50N 124 40W
Blanda → **8** 65 20N 19 40W
Blandford Forum **13** 50 52N 2 10W
Blanding **121** 37 35N 109 30W
Blandinsville **116** 40 33N 90 52W
Blanes **24** 41 40N 2 48 E
Blanice → **32** 49 10N 14 5 E
Blankenberge **16** 51 20N 3 9 E
Blankenburg **30** 51 46N 10 56 E
Blanquefort **20** 44 55N 0 38W
Blanquilla, La **135** 11 51N 64 37W
Blanquillo **141** 32 53S 55 37W
Blansko **32** 49 22N 16 40 E
Blantyre **95** 15 45S 35 0 E
Blarney **15** 51 57N 8 35W
Blato **27** 42 56N 16 48 E
Blaubeuren **31** 48 24N 9 47 E
Blaydon **12** 54 56N 1 47W
Blaye **20** 45 8N 0 40W
Blaye-les-Mines **20** 44 1N 2 8 E
Blayney **76** 33 32S 149 14 E
Blaze, Pt. **78** 12 56S 130 11 E
Bleckede **30** 53 18N 10 43 E
Bled **27** 46 27N 14 7 E
Blednaya, Gora **40** 76 20N 65 0 E
Blejeşti **34** 44 19N 25 27 E
Blekinge län □ **11** 56 20N 15 20 E
Blenheim, Can. **106** 42 20N 82 0W
Blenheim, N.Z. **81** 41 38S 173 57 E
Bléone → **21** 44 5N 6 0 E
Bletchley **13** 51 59N 0 44W
Bleu, L. **104** 46 35N 78 24W
Bleymard, Le **20** 44 30N 3 42 E
Blida **86** 36 30N 2 49 E
Blidet Amor **87** 32 59N 5 58 E
Blidö **10** 59 37N 18 53 E
Blidsberg **11** 57 56N 13 30 E
Bligh Sound **81** 44 47S 167 32 E
Bligh Water **68** 17 0S 178 0 E
Blind River **106** 46 10N 82 58W
Blissfield **117** 41 50N 83 52W
Blitar **57** 8 5S 112 11 E
Blitta **89** 8 23N 1 6 E
Block I. **115** 41 11N 71 35W
Block Island Sd. **115** 41 17N 71 35W
Blockton **116** 40 37N 94 29W
Bloemfontein **96** 29 6S 26 14 E
Bloemhof **96** 27 38S 25 32 E
Blois **18** 47 35N 1 20 E
Blomskog **10** 59 16N 12 2 E
Blönduós **8** 65 40N 20 12W
Bloodvein → **109** 51 47N 96 43W
Bloody Foreland **15** 55 10N 8 18W
Bloomer **118** 45 8N 91 30W
Bloomfield, Can. **107** 43 59N 77 14W
Bloomfield, Ind., U.S.A. **117** 39 1N 86 57W
Bloomfield, Iowa, U.S.A. **116** 40 44N 92 26W
Bloomfield, Ky., U.S.A. **117** 37 55N 85 19W
Bloomfield, N. Mexico, U.S.A. **121** 36 46N 107 59W
Bloomfield, Nebr., U.S.A. **118** 42 38N 97 40W
Bloomfield River Mission **72** 15 56S 145 22 E
Bloomingburg **117** 39 36N 83 24W
Bloomington, Ill., U.S.A. **116** 40 27N 89 0W
Bloomington, Ind., U.S.A. **117** 39 10N 86 30W
Bloomington, Wis., U.S.A. **116** 42 53N 90 55W
Bloomsburg **115** 41 0N 76 30W
Blora **57** 6 57S 111 25 E
Blossburg **114** 41 40N 77 4W
Blouberg **97** 23 8S 29 0 E
Blountstown **113** 30 28N 85 5W
Blowering Dam **76** 35 26S 148 16 E
Bludenz **31** 47 10N 9 50 E
Blue → **117** 38 11N 86 18W
Blue Island **117** 41 40N 87 40W
Blue Lake **120** 40 53N 124 0W
Blue Mesa Res. **121** 38 30N 107 15W
Blue Mound **116** 39 42N 89 7W
Blue Mts., Austral. **76** 33 40S 150 0 E
Blue Mts., Ore., U.S.A. **120** 45 15N 119 0W
Blue Mts., Pa., U.S.A. **115** 40 30N 76 30W
Blue Mud B. **72** 13 30S 136 0 E
Blue Nile = An Nîl el Azraq □ **91** 12 30N 34 30 E
Blue Nile = Nîl el Azraq → **91** 15 38N 32 31 E
Blue Rapids **118** 39 41N 96 39W
Blue Ridge Mts. **113** 36 30N 80 15W
Blue Springs **116** 39 1N 94 17W
Blue Stack Mts. **15** 54 46N 8 5W
Blueberry → **108** 56 45N 120 49W
Bluefield **112** 37 18N 81 14W
Bluefields **126** 12 20N 83 50W
Blueskin B. **81** 45 44S 170 38 E
Bluff, Austral. **72** 23 35S 149 4 E
Bluff, N.Z. **81** 46 37S 168 20 E
Bluff, U.S.A. **121** 37 17N 109 33W
Bluff Harbour **81** 46 36S 168 21 E
Bluff Knoll **79** 34 24S 118 15 E
Bluff Pt. **79** 27 50S 114 5 E
Bluffs **116** 39 45N 90 32W
Bluffton, Ind., U.S.A. **117** 40 43N 85 9W
Bluffton, Ohio, U.S.A. **117** 40 54N 83 54W
Bluford **117** 38 20N 88 45W
Blumenau **141** 27 0S 49 0W
Blumenthal **30** 53 5N 8 20 E
Blunt **118** 44 32N 100 0W
Bly **120** 42 23N 121 0W
Blyberg **10** 61 9N 14 11 E
Blyth, Can. **106** 43 44N 81 26W
Blyth, U.K. **12** 55 8N 1 32W
Blythe **123** 33 40N 114 33W
Blytheswood **114** 42 8N 82 37W
Bø **10** 59 25N 9 3 E
Bo **88** 7 55N 11 50W
Bo Duc **55** 11 58N 106 50 E
Bo Hai **61** 39 0N 120 0 E
Bō-no-Misaki **64** 31 15N 130 13 E
Bo Xian **60** 33 50N 115 45 E
Boa Esperança **135** 3 21N 61 23W
Boa Nova **139** 14 22S 40 10W
Boa Viagem **138** 5 7S 39 44W
Boa Vista **135** 2 48N 60 30W
Boaco **126** 12 29N 85 35W
Bo'ai **60** 35 10N 113 3 E
Boal **22** 43 25N 6 49W
Boatman **73** 27 16S 146 55 E
Bobadah **73** 32 19S 146 41 E
Bobai **58** 22 17N 109 59 E
Bobbili **50** 18 35N 83 30 E
Bóbbio **26** 44 47N 9 22 E
Bobcaygeon **107** 44 33N 78 33W
Böblingen **31** 48 41N 9 1 E
Bobo-Dioulasso **88** 11 8N 4 13W
Boboc **34** 45 13N 26 59 E
Bobonaza → **134** 2 36S 76 38W
Bobov Dol **34** 42 20N 23 0 E
Bóbr → **32** 52 4N 15 4 E
Bobrinets **38** 48 4N 32 5 E
Bobrov **37** 51 5N 40 2 E
Bobruysk **36** 53 10N 29 15 E
Bobures **134** 9 15N 71 11W
Boca de Drago **135** 11 0N 61 50W
Boca de Uracoa **134** 9 8N 62 20W
Bôca do Acre **136** 8 50S 67 27W
Bôca do Jari **135** 1 7S 51 58W
Bôca do Moaco **136** 7 41S 68 17W
Boca Grande **135** 8 40N 60 40W
Boca Raton **113** 26 21N 80 5W
Bocaiúva **139** 17 7S 43 49W
Bocanda **88** 7 5N 4 31W
Bocaranga **92** 7 0N 15 35 E
Bocas del Toro **126** 9 15N 82 20W
Boceguillas **24** 41 20N 3 39W
Bochart **105** 49 10N 73 30W
Bochnia **32** 49 58N 20 27 E
Bocholt **30** 51 50N 6 35 E
Bochum **30** 51 28N 7 12 E
Bockenem **30** 52 1N 10 8 E
Boconó **134** 9 15N 70 16W
Boconó → **134** 8 43N 69 34W
Bocoyna **124** 27 52N 107 35W
Boda **92** 4 19N 17 26 E
Böda **11** 57 15N 17 3 E
Bodafors **11** 57 48N 14 23 E
Bodalla **76** 36 4S 150 4 E
Bodaybo **41** 57 50N 114 0 E
Boddington **79** 32 50S 116 30 E
Bodega Bay **122** 38 20N 123 3W
Boden **8** 65 50N 21 42 E
Bodensee **31** 47 35N 9 25 E
Bodenteich **30** 52 49N 10 41 E
Bodhan **50** 18 40N 77 44 E
Bodinayakkanur **51** 10 2N 77 10 E
Bodinga **89** 12 58N 5 10 E
Bodmin **13** 50 28N 4 44W
Bodmin Moor **13** 50 33N 4 36W
Bodø **8** 67 17N 14 24 E
Bodoquena, Serra da **137** 21 0S 56 50W
Bodrog → **33** 48 15N 21 35 E
Bodrum **46** 37 5N 27 30 E
Boegoebergdam **96** 29 7S 22 9 E
Boën **21** 45 44N 4 0 E
Boende **92** 0 24S 21 12 E
Boerne **119** 29 48N 98 41W
Boffa **88** 10 16N 14 3W
Bogale **52** 16 17N 95 24 E
Bogalong Creek **76** 33 50S 148 6 E
Bogalusa **119** 30 50N 89 55W
Bogan → **76** 32 45S 148 8 E
Bogan Gate **76** 33 7S 147 49 E
Bogantungan **72** 23 41S 147 17 E
Bogata **119** 33 26N 95 10W
Bogatić **33** 44 51N 19 30 E
Bogenfels **96** 27 25S 15 25 E
Bogense **11** 55 34N 10 5 E
Boggabilla **77** 28 36S 150 24 E
Boggabri **77** 30 45S 150 0 E
Boggeragh Mts. **15** 52 2N 8 55W
Boggy Cowal → **76** 32 10S 148 0 E
Bogia **69** 4 9S 145 0 E
Bognor Regis **13** 50 47N 0 40W
Bogø **11** 54 55N 12 2 E
Bogo **57** 11 3N 124 0 E
Bogodukhov **36** 50 9N 35 33 E
Bogong, Mt. **75** 36 47S 147 17 E
Bogor **57** 6 36S 106 48 E
Bogoroditsk **37** 53 47N 38 8 E
Bogorodsk **37** 56 4N 43 30 E
Bogorodskoye **41** 52 22N 140 30 E
Bogoso **88** 5 38N 2 3W
Bogota **134** 4 34N 74 0W
Bogotol **40** 56 15N 89 50 E
Bogra **52** 24 51N 89 22 E
Boguchany **41** 58 40N 97 30 E
Boguchar **39** 49 55N 40 32 E
Bogué **88** 16 45N 14 10W
Boguslav **38** 49 47N 30 53 E
Bohain **19** 49 59N 3 28 E
Bohemia Downs **78** 18 53S 126 14 E
Bohemian Forest = Böhmerwald **31** 49 30N 12 40 E
Bohena **77** 30 30S 149 42 E
Bohena Cr. → **77** 30 17S 149 42 E
Bohinjska Bistrica **27** 46 17N 14 1 E
Böhmerwald **31** 49 30N 12 40 E
Bohmte **30** 52 24N 8 20 E
Bohol **57** 9 50N 124 10 E
Bohotleh **45** 8 20N 46 25 E
Boi **89** 9 35N 9 27 E
Boi, Pta. de **141** 23 55S 45 15W
Boiaçu **135** 0 27S 61 46W
Boiano **29** 41 28N 14 29 E
Boileau, C. **78** 17 40S 122 7 E
Boinka **74** 35 11S 141 36 E
Boipeba, I. de **139** 13 39S 38 55W
Bois → **139** 18 35S 50 2W
Bois Blanc I. **106** 45 50N 84 30W
Boise **120** 43 43N 116 9W
Boise City **119** 36 45N 102 30W
Boissevain **109** 49 15N 100 5W
Boite → **27** 46 5N 12 5 E
Boitzenburg **30** 53 16N 13 36 E
Boizenburg **30** 53 22N 10 42 E
Bojador C. **84** 26 0N 14 30W
Bojnürd **47** 37 30N 57 20 E
Bojonegoro **57** 7 11S 111 54 E
Boju **89** 7 22N 7 55 E
Boka Kotorska **33** 42 23N 18 32 E
Bokala **88** 8 31N 4 33W
Boké **88** 10 56N 14 17W
Bokhara → **73** 29 55S 146 42 E
Bokkos **89** 9 17N 9 1 E
Boknafjorden **9** 59 14N 5 40 E
Bokoro **85** 12 25N 17 14 E
Bokote **92** 0 12S 21 8 E
Boksitogorsk **36** 59 32N 33 56 E
Bokungu **92** 0 35S 22 50 E
Bol, Chad **92** 13 30N 15 0 E
Bol, Yugo. **27** 43 18N 16 38 E
Bolac, L. **74** 37 43S 142 57 E
Bolama **88** 11 30N 15 30W
Bolan Pass **47** 29 50N 67 20 E
Bolangum **74** 36 42S 142 54 E
Bolaños → **124** 21 14N 104 8W
Bolbec **18** 49 30N 0 30 E
Boldeşti **34** 45 3N 26 2 E
Bole, China **62** 45 11N 81 37 E
Bole, Ethiopia **91** 6 36N 37 20 E
Bolekhov **36** 49 0N 24 0 E
Bolesławiec **32** 51 17N 15 37 E
Bolgatanga **89** 10 44N 0 53W
Bolgrad **38** 45 40N 28 32 E
Boli **91** 6 2N 28 48 E
Bolinao C. **57** 16 23N 119 55 E
Bolívar, Argent. **140** 36 15S 60 53W
Bolívar, Antioquía, Colomb. **134** 5 50N 76 1W
Bolívar, Cauca, Colomb. **134** 2 0N 77 0W
Bolívar, Peru **136** 7 18S 77 48W
Bolivar, Mo., U.S.A. **119** 37 38N 93 22W
Bolivar, Tenn., U.S.A. **119** 35 14N 89 0W
Bolívar □, Colomb. **134** 9 0N 74 40W
Bolívar □, Ecuador **134** 1 15S 79 5W
Bolívar □, Venez. **135** 6 20N 63 30W
Bolivia **77** 29 17S 151 59 E
Bolivia ■ **137** 17 6S 64 0W
Bolkhov **37** 53 25N 36 0 E
Bollène **21** 44 18N 4 45 E
Bollnäs **10** 61 21N 16 24 E
Bollon **73** 28 2S 147 29 E
Bollstabruk **10** 63 1N 17 40 E
Bollullos **23** 37 19N 6 32W
Bolmen **11** 56 55N 13 40 E
Bolo Silase **91** 8 51N 39 27 E
Bolobo **92** 2 6S 16 20 E
Bologna **27** 44 30N 11 20 E
Bologne **19** 48 10N 5 8 E
Bologoye **36** 57 55N 34 0 E
Bolomba **92** 0 35N 19 0 E
Bolonchenticul **125** 20 0N 89 49W
Bolong **57** 7 6N 122 16 E
Boloven, Cao Nguyen **54** 15 10N 106 30 E
Bolpur **49** 23 40N 87 45 E
Bolsena **27** 42 40N 11 58 E
Bolsena, L. di **27** 42 35N 11 55 E
Bolshaya Glushitsa **37** 52 24N 50 29 E
Bolshaya Martynovka **39** 47 12N 41 46 E
Bolshereche **40** 56 4N 74 45 E
Bolshevik, Ostrov **41** 78 30N 102 0 E
Bolshoi Kavkas **39** 42 50N 44 0 E
Bolshoy Anyuy → **41** 68 30N 160 49 E
Bolshoy Atlym **40** 62 25N 66 50 E
Bolshoy Begichev, Ostrov **41** 74 20N 112 30 E
Bolshoy Lyakhovskiy, Ostrov **41** 73 35N 142 0 E
Bolshoy Tokmak **38** 47 16N 35 42 E
Bol'shoy Tyuters, Ostrov **36** 59 51N 27 13 E
Bolsward **16** 53 3N 5 32 E
Boltaña **24** 42 28N 0 4 E
Boltigen **31** 46 38N 7 24 E
Bolton, Austral. **74** 34 58S 142 54 E
Bolton, Can. **106** 43 54N 79 45W
Bolton, U.K. **12** 53 35N 2 26W
Bolu **46** 40 45N 31 35 E

Bolubolu	69	9 21 S	150 20 E
Boluo	59	23 3N	114 21 E
Bolvadin	46	38 45N	31 4 E
Bolzano (Bozen)	27	46 30N	11 20 E
Bom Comércio	137	9 45 S	65 54W
Bom Conselho	138	9 10 S	36 41W
Bom Despacho	139	19 43 S	45 15W
Bom Jesus	138	9 4 S	44 22W
Bom Jesus da Gurguéia, Serra	138	9 0 S	43 0W
Bom Jesus da Lapa	139	13 15 S	43 25W
Boma	92	5 50 S	13 4 E
Bomaderry	76	34 52 S	150 37 E
Bōmba, Khalīj	85	32 20N	23 15 E
Bomba, La	124	31 53N	115 2W
Bombala	75	36 56 S	149 15 E
Bombarral	23	39 15N	9 9W
Bombay	50	18 55N	72 50 E
Bomboma	92	2 25N	18 55 E
Bombombwa	94	1 40N	25 40 E
Bomera	77	31 33 S	149 49 E
Bomi Hills	88	7 1N	10 38W
Bomili	94	1 45N	27 5 E
Bomokandi →	94	3 39N	26 8 E
Bomongo	92	1 27N	18 21 E
Bomu →	92	4 40N	23 30 E
Bon C.	87	37 1N	11 2 E
Bon Echo Prov. Park	107	45 0N	77 20W
Bon Sar Pa	54	12 24N	107 35 E
Bonaire, I.	127	12 10N	68 15W
Bonalbo	77	28 44 S	152 37 E
Bonang	75	37 11 S	148 41 E
Bonanza	126	13 54N	84 35W
Bonaparte Archipelago	78	14 0 S	124 30 E
Boñar	22	42 52N	5 19W
Bonaventure	103	48 5N	65 32W
Bonavista	103	48 40N	53 5W
Bonavista, C.	103	48 42N	53 5W
Bondeno	27	44 53N	11 22 E
Bondo	92	3 55N	23 53 E
Bondoukou	88	8 2N	2 47W
Bondowoso	57	7 56 S	113 49 E
Bone Rate	57	7 25 S	121 5 E
Bone Rate, Kepulauan	57	6 30 S	121 10 E
Bone, Teluk	57	4 10 S	120 50 E
Bonefro	29	41 42N	14 55 E
Bonegilla	75	36 8 S	146 58 E
Bo'ness	14	56 0N	3 38W
Bonfield	106	46 14N	79 9W
Bong Son = Hoai Nhon	54	14 26N	109 1 E
Bongandanga	92	1 24N	21 3 E
Bongor	85	10 35N	15 20 E
Bongouanou	88	6 42N	4 15W
Bonham	119	33 30N	96 10W
Bonifacio	21	41 24N	9 10 E
Bonifacio, Bouches de	28	41 12N	9 15 E
Bonin Is.	66	27 0N	142 0 E
Bonke	91	6 5N	37 16 E
Bonn	30	50 43N	7 6 E
Bonnat	20	46 20N	1 54 E
Bonne Terre	116	37 57N	90 33W
Bonnechere →	107	45 35N	77 50W
Bonners Ferry	120	48 38N	116 21W
Bonnétable	18	48 11N	0 25 E
Bonneuil-Matours	18	46 41N	0 34 E
Bonneval	18	48 11N	1 24 E
Bonneville	21	46 5N	6 24 E
Bonney, L.	73	37 50 S	140 20 E
Bonnie Doon	74	37 2 S	145 53 E
Bonnie Rock	79	30 29 S	118 22 E
Bonny, France	19	47 34N	2 50 E
Bonny, Nigeria	89	4 25N	7 13 E
Bonny →	89	4 20N	7 10 E
Bonny, Bight of	92	3 30N	9 20 E
Bonnyville	109	54 20N	110 45W
Bonoi	57	1 45 S	137 41 E
Bonorva	28	40 25N	8 47 E
Bonsall	123	33 16N	117 14W
Bonshaw	77	29 2 S	151 16 E
Bontang	56	0 10N	117 30 E
Bonthain	57	5 34 S	119 56 E
Bonthe	88	7 30N	12 33W
Bontoc	57	17 7N	120 58 E
Bonyeri	88	5 1N	2 46W
Bonython Ra.	78	23 40 S	128 45 E
Boogardie	79	28 2 S	117 45 E
Bookabie P.O.	79	31 50 S	132 41 E
Booker	119	36 29N	100 30W
Bookham	76	34 48 S	148 36 E
Boolaboolka, L.	73	32 38 S	143 10 E
Boolarra	75	38 20 S	146 20 E
Booligal	74	33 58 S	144 53 E
Boom	16	51 6N	4 20 E
Boomi	77	28 44 S	149 34 E
Boonah	77	27 58 S	152 41 E
Boone, Iowa, U.S.A.	116	42 5N	93 53W
Boone, N.C., U.S.A.	113	36 14N	81 43W
Booneville, Ark., U.S.A.	119	35 10N	93 54W
Booneville, Miss., U.S.A.	113	34 39N	88 34W
Boonville, Calif., U.S.A.	122	39 1N	123 22W
Boonville, Ind., U.S.A.	117	38 3N	87 13W
Boonville, Mo., U.S.A.	116	38 57N	92 45W
Boonville, N.Y., U.S.A.	115	43 31N	75 20W
Booral	76	32 30 S	151 56 E
Boorindal	73	30 22 S	146 11 E
Boorowa	76	34 28 S	148 44 E
Boort	74	36 7 S	143 46 E
Boothia, Gulf of	101	71 0N	90 0W
Boothia Pen.	100	71 0N	94 0W
Bootle, Cumb., U.K.	12	54 17N	3 24W
Bootle, Merseyside, U.K.	12	53 28N	3 1W
Booué	92	0 5 S	11 55 E
Bopeechee	73	29 36 S	137 22 E
Bophuthatswana □	96	26 0 S	26 0 E
Boppard	31	50 13N	7 36 E
Boquerón □	137	21 30 S	60 0W
Boquete, Panama	126	8 46N	82 27W
Boquete, Panama	126	8 49N	82 27W
Boquillas del Carmen	124	29 17N	102 53W
Bor	32	49 41N	12 45 E
Bôr	91	6 10N	31 40 E
Bor, Sweden	11	57 9N	14 10 E
Bor, Yugo.	33	44 8N	22 7 E
Borah, Mt.	120	44 19N	113 46W
Borama	45	9 55N	43 7 E
Borambil	77	32 4 S	150 1 E
Borang	91	4 50N	30 59 E
Borås	11	57 43N	12 56 E
Borāzjān	47	29 22N	51 10 E
Borba, Brazil	135	4 12 S	59 34W
Borba, Port.	23	38 50N	7 26W
Borborema, Planalto da	138	7 0 S	37 0W
Borçka	39	41 25N	41 41 E
Borda, C.	73	35 45 S	136 34 E
Bordeaux	20	44 50N	0 36W
Borden, Austral.	79	34 3 S	118 12 E
Borden, Can.	103	46 18N	63 47W
Borden I.	144	78 30N	111 30W
Borders □	14	55 35N	2 50W
Bordertown	73	36 19 S	140 45 E
Borðeyri	8	65 12N	21 6W
Bordighera	26	43 47N	7 40 E
Bordj bou Arridj	87	36 4N	4 45 E
Bordj Bourguiba	87	32 12N	10 2 E
Bordj el Hobra	87	32 9N	4 51 E
Bordj Fly Ste. Marie	86	27 19N	2 32W
Bordj-in-Eker	87	24 9N	5 3 E
Bordj Menaiel	87	36 46N	3 43 E
Bordj Messouda	87	30 12N	9 25 E
Bordj Nili	86	33 28N	3 2 E
Bordj Zelfana	87	32 27N	4 15 E
Boremore	76	33 15 S	149 0 E
Borensberg	11	58 34N	15 17 E
Borgarnes	8	64 32N	21 55W
Borger, Neth.	16	52 54N	6 44 E
Borger, U.S.A.	119	35 40N	101 20W
Borghamn	11	58 23N	14 41 E
Borgholm	11	56 52N	16 39 E
Bórgia	29	38 50N	16 30 E
Borgo San Dalmazzo	26	44 19N	7 29 E
Borgo San Lorenzo	27	43 57N	11 21 E
Borgo Valsugano	27	46 3N	11 27 E
Borgomanero	26	45 41N	8 28 E
Borgonovo Val Tidone	26	45 1N	9 28 E
Borgorose	27	42 12N	13 14 E
Borgosésia	26	45 43N	8 17 E
Borgvattnet	10	63 26N	15 48 E
Borikhane	54	18 33N	103 43 E
Borisoglebsk	37	51 27N	42 5 E
Borisoglebskiy	37	56 28N	43 59 E
Borisov	36	54 17N	28 28 E
Borispol	36	50 21N	30 59 E
Borja, Peru	134	4 20 S	77 40W
Borja, Spain	24	41 48N	1 34W
Borjas Blancas	24	41 31N	0 52 E
Borken	30	51 51N	6 52 E
Borkou	85	18 15N	18 50 E
Borkum	30	53 36N	6 42 E
Borlänge	10	60 29N	15 26 E
Borley, C.	143	66 15 S	52 30 E
Bormida →	26	44 23N	8 13 E
Bórmio	26	46 28N	10 22 E
Borna	30	51 8N	12 31 E
Borneo	56	1 0N	115 0 E
Bornholm	11	55 10N	15 0 E
Bornholmsgattet	11	55 15N	14 20 E
Borno □	89	12 30N	12 30 E
Bornos	23	36 48N	5 42W
Bornu Yassa	89	12 14N	12 25 E
Borobudur	57	7 36 S	110 13 E
Borodino	36	55 31N	35 40 E
Borogontsy	41	62 42N	131 8 E
Boromo	88	11 45N	2 58W
Boron	123	35 0N	117 39W
Boronga Is.	52	19 58N	93 6 E
Borongan	57	11 37N	125 26 E
Bororen	72	24 13 S	151 33 E
Borotangba Mts.	91	6 30N	25 0 E
Borovan	34	43 27N	23 45 E
Borovichi	36	58 25N	33 55 E
Borovsk	37	55 12N	36 24 E
Borrby	11	55 27N	14 10 E
Borrego Springs	123	33 15N	116 23W
Borriol	24	40 4N	0 4W
Borroloola	72	16 4 S	136 17 E
Borşa	34	47 41N	24 50 E
Bort-les-Orgues	20	45 24N	2 29 E
Borth	13	52 29N	4 3W
Borujerd	46	33 55N	48 50 E
Borzhomi	39	41 48N	43 28 E
Borzna	36	51 18N	32 26 E
Borzya	41	50 24N	116 31 E
Bosa	28	40 17N	8 32 E
Bosanska Dubica	27	45 10N	16 50 E
Bosanska Gradiška	33	45 10N	17 15 E
Bosanska Kostajnica	27	45 11N	16 33 E
Bosanska Krupa	27	44 53N	16 10 E
Bosanski Novi	27	45 2N	16 22 E
Bosanski Šamac	33	45 3N	18 29 E
Bosansko Grahovo	27	44 12N	16 26 E
Bosansko Petrovac	27	44 35N	16 21 E
Bosaso	45	11 12N	49 18 E
Bosavi, Mt.	69	6 30 S	142 49 E
Boscastle	13	50 42N	4 42W
Boscobel	116	43 8N	90 42W
Boscotrecase	29	40 46N	14 28 E
Bose	58	23 53N	106 35 E
Boshan	61	36 28N	117 49 E
Boshoek	96	25 30 S	27 9 E
Boshof	96	28 31 S	25 13 E
Boshrūyeh	47	33 50N	57 30 E
Bosilegrad	33	42 30N	22 27 E
Bosna →	33	45 4N	18 29 E
Bosna i Hercegovina □	33	44 0N	18 0 E
Bosnia = Bosna □	33	44 0N	18 0 E
Bosnik	57	1 5 S	136 10 E
Bōsō-Hantō	65	35 20N	140 20 E
Bosobolo	92	4 15N	19 50 E
Bosporus = Karadeniz Boğazı	46	41 10N	29 10 E
Bossangoa	92	6 35N	17 30 E
Bossekop	8	69 57N	23 15 E
Bossembélé	85	5 25N	17 40 E
Bossier City	119	32 28N	93 48W
Bosso	89	13 43N	13 19 E
Bosten Hu	62	41 55N	87 40 E
Boston, U.K.	12	52 59N	0 2W
Boston, U.S.A.	115	42 20N	71 0W
Boston Bar	108	49 52N	121 30W
Bosut →	33	45 20N	19 0 E
Boswell, Can.	108	49 28N	116 45W
Boswell, Ind., U.S.A.	117	40 30N	87 23W
Boswell, Okla., U.S.A.	119	34 1N	95 50W
Boswell, Pa., U.S.A.	114	40 9N	79 2W
Bosworth	116	39 28N	93 20W
Botad	48	22 15N	71 40 E
Botany Bay	76	34 0 S	151 14 E
Botene	54	17 35N	101 12 E
Botevgrad	34	42 55N	23 47 E
Botfield	76	33 1 S	147 46 E
Bothaville	96	27 23 S	26 34 E
Bothnia, G. of	8	63 0N	20 0 E
Bothwell, Austral.	72	42 20 S	147 1 E
Bothwell, Can.	106	42 38N	81 52W
Boticas	22	41 41N	7 40W
Botletle →	96	20 10 S	23 15 E
Botoşani	34	47 42N	26 41 E
Botro	88	7 51N	5 19W
Botswana ■	93	22 0 S	24 0 E
Bottineau	118	48 49N	100 25W
Bottrop	30	51 34N	6 59 E
Botucatu	141	22 55 S	48 30W
Botwood	103	49 6N	55 23W
Bou Alam	86	33 50N	1 26 E
Bou Ali	86	27 11N	0 4W
Bou Djébéha	88	18 25N	2 45W
Bou Garfa	86	27 4N	7 59W
Bou Guema	86	28 49N	0 19 E
Bou Ismael	86	36 38N	2 42 E
Bou Izakarn	86	29 12N	9 46W
Bou Saâda	87	35 11N	4 9 E
Bou Salem	87	36 45N	9 2 E
Bouaké	88	7 40N	5 2W
Bouar	92	6 0N	15 40 E
Bouârfa	86	32 32N	1 58 E
Bouca	92	6 45N	18 25 E
Boucau	20	43 32N	1 29W
Boucaut B.	72	12 0 S	134 25 E
Boucher →	105	49 10N	69 6W
Bouches-du-Rhône □	21	43 37N	5 2 E
Bouchette	104	46 12N	75 57W
Bouchier, L.	104	50 6N	77 48W
Bouda	86	27 50N	0 27W
Boudenib	86	31 59N	3 31W
Boufarik	86	36 34N	2 58 E
Bougainville C.	78	13 57 S	126 4 E
Bougainville I.	69	6 0 S	155 0 E
Bougainville Reef	72	15 30 S	147 5 E
Bougainville Str.	68	6 40 S	156 10 E
Bougaroun, C.	87	37 6N	6 30 E
Bougie = Bejaia	87	36 42N	5 2 E
Bougouni	88	11 30N	7 20W
Bouillon	16	49 44N	5 3 E
Bouïra	87	36 20N	3 59 E
Boulder, Colo., U.S.A.	118	40 3N	105 10W
Boulder, Mont., U.S.A.	120	46 14N	112 4W
Boulder City	123	36 0N	114 50W
Boulder Creek	122	37 7N	122 7W
Boulder Dam = Hoover Dam	121	36 0N	114 45W
Boulia	72	22 52 S	139 51 E
Bouligny	19	49 17N	5 45 E
Boulogne →	18	47 12N	1 47W
Boulogne-sur-Gesse	20	43 18N	0 38 E
Boulogne-sur-Mer	19	50 42N	1 36 E
Bouloire	18	47 58N	0 33 E
Bouloupari	68	21 52 S	166 4 E
Boulsa	89	12 39N	0 34W
Boultoum	89	14 45N	10 25 E
Boumalne	86	31 25N	6 0W
Boun Neua	54	21 38N	101 54 E
Boun Tai	54	21 23N	101 58 E
Bouna	88	9 10N	3 0W
Boundary Bend	74	34 43 S	143 8 E
Boundary Pk.	122	37 51N	118 21W
Boundiali	88	9 30N	6 20W
Bountiful	120	40 57N	111 58W
Bounty I.	66	48 0 S	178 30 E
Bourail	68	21 34 S	165 30 E
Bourbah	76	31 18 S	148 20 E
Bourbeuse →	116	38 24N	90 54W
Bourbon	117	41 18N	86 7W
Bourbon-Lancy	20	46 37N	3 45 E
Bourbon-l'Archambault	20	46 36N	3 4 E
Bourbonnais	20	46 28N	3 0 E
Bourbonne-les-Bains	19	47 59N	5 45 E
Bourem	89	17 0N	0 24W
Bourg	20	45 3N	0 34W
Bourg-Argental	21	45 18N	4 32 E
Bourg-de-Péage	21	45 2N	5 3 E
Bourg-en-Bresse	21	46 13N	5 12 E
Bourg-St.-Andéol	21	44 23N	4 39 E
Bourg-St.-Maurice	21	45 35N	6 46 E
Bourganeuf	20	45 57N	1 45 E
Bourges	19	47 9N	2 25 E
Bourget	107	45 26N	75 9W
Bourget, L. du	21	45 44N	5 52 E
Bourgneuf, B. de	18	47 3N	2 10W
Bourgneuf-en-Retz	18	47 2N	1 58W
Bourgneuf-la-Fôret, Le	18	48 10N	0 59W
Bourgogne	19	47 0N	4 30 E
Bourgoin-Jallieu	21	45 36N	5 17 E
Bourgueil	18	47 17N	0 10 E
Bourke	73	30 8 S	145 55 E
Bournemouth	13	50 43N	1 53W
Bourriot-Bergonce	20	44 7N	0 14W
Bouscat, Le	20	44 53N	0 32W
Bouse	123	33 55N	114 0W
Boussac	20	46 22N	2 13 E
Boussens	20	43 12N	0 58 E
Bousso	92	10 34N	16 52 E
Boutilimit	88	17 45N	14 40W
Boutonne →	20	45 55N	0 43 E
Bouvet I. = Bouvetøyo	143	54 26 S	3 24 E
Bouvetøya	143	54 26 S	3 24 E
Bouznika	86	33 46N	7 6W
Bouzonville	19	49 17N	6 32 E
Bova Marina	29	37 59N	15 56 E
Bovalino Marina	29	38 9N	16 10 E
Bovec	27	46 20N	13 33 E
Bovigny	16	50 12N	5 55 E
Bovill	120	46 58N	116 27W
Bovino	29	41 15N	15 20 E
Bow Island	108	49 50N	111 23W
Bowbells	118	48 47N	102 19W
Bowdle	118	45 30N	99 40W
Bowelling	79	33 25 S	116 30 E
Bowen	72	20 0 S	148 16 E
Bowen, Mt.	75	37 9 S	148 35 E
Bowen Mts.	75	37 0 S	148 0 E
Bowie, Ariz., U.S.A.	121	32 15N	109 30W
Bowie, Tex., U.S.A.	119	33 33N	97 50W
Bowland, Forest of	12	54 0N	2 30W
Bowling Green, Ky., U.S.A.	112	37 0N	86 25W
Bowling Green, Mo., U.S.A.	116	39 21N	91 12W
Bowling Green, Ohio, U.S.A.	117	41 22N	83 40W
Bowling Green, C.	72	19 19 S	147 25 E
Bowman	118	46 12N	103 21W
Bowman, I.	143	65 0 S	104 0 E
Bowmans	73	34 10 S	138 17 E
Bowmanville	107	43 55N	78 41W
Bowmore	14	55 45N	6 18W

Bowning	**76**	34 46 S	148 50 E
Bowral	**76**	34 26 S	150 27 E
Bowraville	**77**	30 37 S	152 52 E
Bowron →	**108**	54 3N	121 50W
Bowser	**75**	36 19 S	146 23 E
Bowser L.	**108**	56 30N	129 30W
Bowsman	**109**	52 14N	101 12W
Bowutu Mts.	**69**	7 45 S	147 10 E
Bowwood	**95**	17 5 S	26 20 E
Boxelder Creek	**120**	47 20N	108 30W
Boxholm	**11**	58 12N	15 3 E
Boxtel	**16**	51 36N	5 20 E
Boyabat	**38**	41 28N	34 42 E
Boyaca □	**134**	5 30N	72 30W
Boyce	**119**	31 25N	92 39W
Boyer →	**108**	58 27N	115 57W
Boyer, C.	**68**	21 37 S	168 6 E
Boyle	**15**	53 58N	8 19W
Boyne →	**15**	53 43N	6 15W
Boyne City	**106**	45 13N	85 1W
Boynton Beach	**113**	26 31N	80 3W
Boyup Brook	**79**	33 50 S	116 23 E
Bozeman	**120**	45 40N	111 0W
Bozen = Bolzano	**27**	46 30N	11 20 E
Bozouls	**20**	44 28N	2 43 E
Bozoum	**92**	6 25N	16 35 E
Bozovici	**34**	44 56N	22 1 E
Bra	**26**	44 41N	7 50 E
Brabant □	**16**	50 46N	4 30 E
Brabant L.	**109**	55 58N	103 43W
Brabrand	**11**	56 9N	10 7 E
Brač	**27**	43 20N	16 40 E
Bracadale, L.	**14**	57 20N	6 30W
Bracciano	**27**	42 6N	12 10 E
Bracciano, L. di	**27**	42 8N	12 11 E
Bracebridge	**106**	45 2N	79 19W
Brach	**87**	27 31N	14 20 E
Bracieux	**19**	47 30N	1 30 E
Bräcke	**10**	62 45N	15 26 E
Brackettville	**119**	29 21N	100 20W
Brački Kanal	**27**	43 24N	16 40 E
Brad	**34**	46 10N	22 50 E
Brádano →	**29**	40 23N	16 51 E
Braddock	**114**	40 24N	79 51W
Bradenton	**113**	27 25N	82 35W
Bradford, Can.	**106**	44 7N	79 34W
Bradford, U.K.	**12**	53 47N	1 45W
Bradford, Ill., U.S.A.	**116**	41 11N	89 39W
Bradford, Ohio, U.S.A.	**117**	40 8N	84 27W
Bradford, Pa., U.S.A.	**114**	41 58N	78 41W
Bradford, Vt., U.S.A.	**115**	43 59N	72 9W
Brădiceni	**34**	45 3N	23 4 E
Bradley, Ark., U.S.A.	**119**	33 7N	93 39W
Bradley, Calif., U.S.A.	**122**	35 52N	120 48W
Bradley, Ill., U.S.A.	**117**	41 9N	87 52W
Bradley, S.D., U.S.A.	**118**	45 10N	97 40W
Bradley Institute	**95**	17 7 S	31 25 E
Bradore Bay	**103**	51 27N	57 18W
Bradshaw	**78**	15 21 S	130 16 E
Brady	**119**	31 8N	99 25W
Brædstrup	**11**	55 58N	9 37 E
Braemar	**73**	33 12 S	139 35 E
Braeside	**107**	45 28N	76 24W
Braga	**22**	41 35N	8 25W
Braga □	**22**	41 30N	8 30W
Bragado	**140**	35 2 S	60 27W
Bragança, Brazil	**138**	1 0 S	47 2W
Bragança, Port.	**22**	41 48N	6 50W
Bragança □	**22**	41 30N	6 45W
Bragança Paulista	**141**	22 55 S	46 32W
Brahmanbaria	**52**	23 58N	91 15 E
Brahmani →	**50**	20 39N	86 46 E
Brahmaputra →	**52**	24 2N	90 59 E
Braich-y-pwll	**12**	52 47N	4 46W
Braidwood	**76**	35 27 S	149 49 E
Brăila	**34**	45 19N	27 59 E
Brainerd	**118**	46 20N	94 10W
Braintree, U.K.	**13**	51 53N	0 34 E
Braintree, U.S.A.	**115**	42 11N	71 0W
Braithwaite Pt.	**72**	12 5 S	133 50 E
Brak →	**96**	29 35 S	22 55 E
Brake, Ger.	**30**	53 19N	8 30 E
Brake, Ger.	**30**	51 43N	9 12 E
Bräkne-Hoby	**11**	56 14N	15 6 E
Brakwater	**96**	22 28 S	17 3 E
Brålanda	**11**	58 34N	12 21 E
Bralorne	**108**	50 50N	123 45W
Bramberg	**31**	50 6N	10 40 E
Bramminge	**11**	55 28N	8 42 E
Brämön	**10**	62 14N	17 40 E
Brampton	**106**	43 45N	79 45W
Bramsche	**30**	52 25N	7 58 E
Bramwell	**72**	12 8 S	142 37 E
Branco →	**135**	1 20 S	61 50W
Branco, Cabo	**138**	7 9 S	34 47W
Brande	**11**	55 57N	9 8 E
Brandenburg, Ger.	**30**	52 24N	12 33 E
Brandenburg, U.S.A.	**117**	38 0N	86 10W
Brandfort	**96**	28 40 S	26 30 E
Brandon, Can.	**109**	49 50N	99 57W
Brandon, U.S.A.	**115**	43 48N	73 4W
Brandon B.	**15**	52 17N	10 8W
Brandon, Mt.	**15**	52 15N	10 15W
Brandsen	**140**	35 10 S	58 15W
Brandval	**10**	60 19N	12 1 E
Brandvlei	**96**	30 25 S	20 30 E
Brandýs	**32**	50 10N	14 40 E
Branford	**115**	41 15N	72 48W
Braniewo	**32**	54 25N	19 50 E
Bransfield Str.	**143**	63 0 S	59 0W
Branson, Colo., U.S.A.	**119**	37 4N	103 53W
Branson, Mo., U.S.A.	**119**	36 40N	93 18W
Brantford	**106**	43 10N	80 15W
Brantôme	**20**	45 22N	0 39 E
Branxholme	**74**	37 52 S	141 49 E
Branxton	**76**	32 38 S	151 21 E
Branzi	**26**	46 0N	9 46 E
Bras d'or, L.	**103**	45 50N	60 50W
Brasiléia	**136**	11 0 S	68 45W
Brasília	**139**	15 47 S	47 55 E
Brasília Legal	**135**	3 49 S	55 36W
Braslav	**36**	55 38N	27 0 E
Braslovce	**27**	46 21N	15 3 E
Braşov	**34**	45 38N	25 35 E
Brass	**89**	4 35N	6 14 E
Brass →	**89**	4 15N	6 13 E
Brassac-les-Mines	**20**	45 24N	3 20 E
Brasschaat	**16**	51 19N	4 27 E
Brassey, Barisan	**56**	5 0N	117 15 E
Brassey Ra.	**79**	25 8 S	122 15 E
Brasstown Bald, Mt.	**113**	34 54N	83 45W
Bratislava	**33**	48 10N	17 7 E
Bratsk	**41**	56 10N	101 30 E
Brattleboro	**115**	42 53N	72 37W
Braţul Chilia →	**34**	45 25N	29 20 E
Bratul Sfîntu Gheorghe →	**34**	45 0N	29 20 E
Braţul Sulina →	**34**	45 10N	29 20 E
Braunau	**33**	48 15N	13 3 E
Braunschweig	**30**	52 17N	10 28 E
Braunton	**13**	51 6N	4 9W
Brava	**45**	1 20N	44 8 E
Bråviken	**10**	58 38N	16 32 E
Bravo del Norte →	**124**	25 57N	97 9W
Brawley	**123**	32 58N	115 30W
Bray	**15**	53 12N	6 6W
Bray, Mt.	**72**	14 0 S	134 30 E
Bray, Pays de	**19**	49 46N	1 26 E
Bray-sur-Seine	**19**	48 25N	3 14 E
Braymer	**116**	39 35N	93 48W
Brazeau →	**108**	52 55N	115 14W
Brazil	**117**	39 32N	87 8W
Brazil ■	**139**	10 0 S	50 0W
Brazilian Highlands = Brasil, Planalto	**130**	18 0 S	46 30W
Brazo Sur →	**140**	25 21 S	57 42W
Brazos →	**119**	28 53N	95 23W
Brazzaville	**92**	4 9 S	15 12 E
Brčko	**33**	44 54N	18 46 E
Brea	**136**	4 40 S	81 7W
Breadalbane, N.S.W., Austral.	**76**	34 48 S	149 28 E
Breadalbane, Queens., Austral.	**72**	23 50 S	139 35 E
Breadalbane, U.K.	**14**	56 30N	4 15W
Breaden, L.	**79**	25 51 S	125 28 E
Breaksea Sd.	**81**	45 35 S	166 35 E
Bream Bay	**80**	35 56 S	174 28 E
Bream Head	**80**	35 51 S	174 36 E
Bream Tail	**80**	36 3 S	174 36 E
Breas	**140**	25 29 S	70 24W
Brebes	**57**	6 52 S	109 3 E
Brechin, Can.	**106**	44 32N	79 10W
Brechin, U.K.	**14**	56 44N	2 40W
Breckenridge, Colo., U.S.A.	**120**	39 30N	106 2W
Breckenridge, Mich., U.S.A.	**106**	43 24N	84 29W
Breckenridge, Minn., U.S.A.	**118**	46 20N	96 36W
Breckenridge, Mo., U.S.A.	**116**	39 46N	93 48W
Breckenridge, Tex., U.S.A.	**119**	32 48N	98 55W
Brecknock, Pen.	**142**	54 35 S	71 30W
Břeclav	**32**	48 46N	16 53 E
Brecon	**13**	51 57N	3 23W
Brecon Beacons	**13**	51 53N	3 27W
Breda	**16**	51 35N	4 45 E
Bredaryd	**11**	57 10N	13 45 E
Bredasdorp	**96**	34 33 S	20 2 E
Bredbo	**76**	35 58 S	149 10 E
Bredstedt	**30**	54 37N	8 59 E
Breelong	**76**	31 48 S	148 47 E
Breeza	**77**	31 15 S	150 27 E
Bregalnica →	**35**	41 43N	22 9 E
Bregenz	**31**	47 30N	9 45 E
Bréhal	**18**	48 53N	1 30W
Bréhat, I. de	**18**	48 51N	3 0W
Breiðafjörður	**8**	65 15N	23 15W
Breil	**21**	43 56N	7 31 E
Breisach	**31**	48 2N	7 37 E
Brejinho de Nazaré	**138**	11 1 S	48 34W
Brejo	**138**	3 41 S	42 47W
Breloux-la-Crèche	**20**	46 23N	0 19W
Bremen	**30**	53 4N	8 47 E
Bremen □	**30**	53 6N	8 46 E
Bremer I.	**72**	12 5 S	136 45 E
Bremerhaven	**30**	53 34N	8 35 E
Bremerton	**122**	47 30N	122 38W
Bremervörde	**30**	53 28N	9 10 E
Bremsnes	**10**	63 6N	7 40 E
Brenes	**23**	37 32N	5 54W
Brenham	**119**	30 5N	96 27W
Brenner Pass	**31**	47 0N	11 30 E
Breno	**26**	45 57N	10 20 E
Brent, Can.	**107**	46 2N	78 29W
Brent, U.K.	**13**	51 33N	0 18W
Brenta →	**27**	45 11N	12 18 E
Brentwood	**13**	51 37N	0 19 E
Bréscia	**26**	45 33N	10 13 E
Breskens	**16**	51 23N	3 33 E
Breslau = Wrocław	**32**	51 5N	17 5 E
Bresle →	**18**	50 4N	1 22 E
Bresles	**19**	49 25N	2 13 E
Bressanone	**27**	46 43N	11 40 E
Bressay I.	**14**	60 10N	1 5W
Bresse, La	**19**	48 0N	6 53 E
Bresse, Plaine de	**19**	46 50N	5 10 E
Bressuire	**18**	46 51N	0 30W
Brest, France	**18**	48 24N	4 31W
Brest, U.S.S.R.	**36**	52 10N	23 40 E
Bretagne	**18**	48 0N	3 0W
Bretçu	**34**	46 7N	26 18 E
Breteuil, Eur, France	**18**	48 50N	0 53 E
Breteuil, Oise, France	**19**	49 38N	2 18 E
Breton	**108**	53 7N	114 28W
Breton, Pertuis	**20**	46 17N	1 25W
Breton Sd.	**119**	29 40N	89 12W
Brett, C.	**80**	35 10 S	174 20 E
Bretten	**31**	49 2N	8 43 E
Brevard	**113**	35 19N	82 42W
Breves	**138**	1 40 S	50 29W
Brevik	**10**	59 4N	9 42 E
Brevort	**106**	46 2N	85 2W
Brewarrina	**73**	30 0 S	146 51 E
Brewer	**103**	44 43N	68 50W
Brewer, Mt.	**122**	36 44N	118 28W
Brewster, N.Y., U.S.A.	**115**	41 23N	73 37W
Brewster, Wash., U.S.A.	**120**	48 10N	119 51W
Brewster, Kap	**144**	70 7N	22 0W
Brewton	**113**	31 9N	87 2W
Breyten	**97**	26 16 S	30 0 E
Breytovo	**37**	58 18N	37 50 E
Brežice	**27**	45 54N	15 35 E
Brézina	**86**	33 4N	1 14 E
Březnice	**32**	49 32N	13 57 E
Breznik	**34**	42 44N	22 50 E
Brezno	**32**	48 50N	19 40 E
Bria	**92**	6 30N	21 58 E
Briagolong	**75**	37 51 S	147 5 E
Briançon	**21**	44 54N	6 39 E
Briare	**19**	47 38N	2 45 E
Bribbaree	**76**	34 10 S	147 51 E
Bribie I.	**73**	27 0 S	152 58 E
Brickaville	**97**	18 49 S	49 4 E
Bricon	**19**	48 5N	5 0 E
Bricquebec	**18**	49 28N	1 38W
Bridgehampton	**115**	40 56N	72 19W
Bridgend	**13**	51 30N	3 35W
Bridgenorth	**107**	44 23N	78 23W
Bridgeport, Can.	**106**	43 29N	80 29W
Bridgeport, Calif., U.S.A.	**122**	38 14N	119 15W
Bridgeport, Conn., U.S.A.	**115**	41 12N	73 12W
Bridgeport, Mich., U.S.A.	**106**	43 22N	83 53W
Bridgeport, Nebr., U.S.A.	**118**	41 42N	103 10W
Bridgeport, Tex., U.S.A.	**119**	33 15N	97 45W
Bridger	**120**	45 20N	108 58W
Bridgeton	**112**	39 29N	75 10W
Bridgetown, Austral.	**79**	33 58 S	116 7 E
Bridgetown, Barbados	**127**	13 0N	59 30W
Bridgetown, Can.	**103**	44 55N	65 18W
Bridgewater, Austral.	**74**	36 36 S	143 59 E
Bridgewater, Can.	**103**	44 25N	64 31W
Bridgewater, Mass., U.S.A.	**115**	41 59N	70 56W
Bridgewater, S.D., U.S.A.	**118**	43 34N	97 29W
Bridgewater, C.	**74**	38 23 S	141 23 E
Bridgman	**117**	41 57N	86 33W
Bridgnorth	**13**	52 33N	2 25W
Bridgton	**115**	44 5N	70 41W
Bridgwater	**13**	51 7N	3 0W
Bridlington	**12**	54 6N	0 11W
Bridport, Austral.	**72**	40 59 S	147 23 E
Bridport, U.K.	**13**	50 43N	2 45W
Brie-Comte-Robert	**19**	48 40N	2 35 E
Brie, Plaine de la	**19**	48 35N	3 10 E
Briec	**18**	48 6N	4 0W
Brienne-le-Château	**19**	48 24N	4 30 E
Brienon	**19**	48 0N	3 35 E
Brienz	**31**	46 46N	8 2 E
Brienzersee	**31**	46 44N	7 53 E
Briey	**19**	49 14N	5 57 E
Brig	**31**	46 18N	7 59 E
Brigg	**12**	53 33N	0 30W
Briggsdale	**118**	40 40N	104 20W
Brigham City	**120**	41 30N	112 1W
Bright	**75**	36 42 S	146 56 E
Brighton, Austral.	**73**	35 5 S	138 30 E
Brighton, Can.	**107**	44 2N	77 44W
Brighton, U.K.	**13**	50 50N	0 9W
Brighton, Colo., U.S.A.	**118**	39 59N	104 50W
Brighton, Ill., U.S.A.	**116**	39 2N	90 8W
Brighton, Iowa, U.S.A.	**116**	41 10N	91 49W
Brightwater	**81**	41 22 S	173 9 E
Brignogan-Plage	**18**	48 40N	4 20W
Brignoles	**21**	43 25N	6 5 E
Brihuega	**24**	40 45N	2 52W
Brikama	**88**	13 15N	16 45W
Brilliant, Can.	**108**	49 19N	117 38W
Brilliant, U.S.A.	**114**	40 15N	80 39W
Brilon	**30**	51 23N	8 32 E
Brim	**74**	36 3 S	142 27 E
Brimfield	**116**	40 50N	89 53W
Brimley	**106**	46 25N	84 41W
Brindabella	**76**	35 22 S	148 44 E
Bríndisi	**29**	40 39N	17 55 E
Brinje	**27**	45 0N	15 9 E
Brinkley	**119**	34 55N	91 15W
Brinkworth	**73**	33 42 S	138 26 E
Brinnon	**122**	47 41N	122 54W
Brion, Î.	**103**	47 46N	61 26W
Brionne	**18**	49 11N	0 43 E
Brionski	**27**	44 55N	13 45 E
Brioude	**20**	45 18N	3 24 E
Briouze	**18**	48 42N	0 23W
Brisbane	**77**	27 25 S	153 2 E
Brisbane →	**73**	27 24 S	153 9 E
Brisighella	**27**	44 14N	11 46 E
Bristol, Can.	**104**	45 32N	76 28W
Bristol, U.K.	**13**	51 26N	2 35W
Bristol, Conn., U.S.A.	**115**	41 44N	72 57W
Bristol, Pa., U.S.A.	**115**	40 6N	74 52W
Bristol, R.I., U.S.A.	**115**	41 40N	71 15W
Bristol, S.D., U.S.A.	**118**	45 25N	97 43W
Bristol, Tenn., U.S.A.	**113**	36 36N	82 11W
Bristol B.	**100**	58 0N	160 0W
Bristol Channel	**13**	51 18N	4 30W
Bristol I.	**143**	58 45 S	28 0W
Bristol L.	**121**	34 23N	116 50W
Bristow	**119**	35 55N	96 28W
British Antarctic Territory □	**143**	66 0 S	45 0W
British Columbia □	**108**	55 0N	125 15W
British Guiana = Guyana ■	**136**	5 0N	59 0W
British Honduras = Belize	**125**	17 0N	88 30W
British Isles	**6**	55 0N	4 0W
Brits	**97**	25 37 S	27 48 E
Britstown	**96**	30 37 S	23 30 E
Britt, Can.	**106**	45 46N	80 34W
Britt, U.S.A.	**116**	43 6N	93 48W
Brittany = Bretagne	**18**	48 0N	3 0W
Britton	**118**	45 50N	97 47W
Brive-la-Gaillarde	**20**	45 10N	1 32 E
Briviesca	**24**	42 32N	3 19W
Brixton	**72**	23 32 S	144 57 E
Brlik	**40**	44 0N	74 5 E
Brno	**32**	49 10N	16 35 E
Bro	**10**	59 31N	17 38 E
Broach = Bharuch	**50**	21 47N	73 0 E
Broad →	**113**	33 59N	82 39W
Broad Arrow	**79**	30 23 S	121 15 E
Broad B.	**14**	58 14N	6 16W
Broad Haven	**15**	54 20N	9 55W
Broad Law, Mt.	**14**	55 30N	3 22W
Broad Sd.	**72**	22 0 S	149 45 E
Broadford	**74**	37 14 S	145 4 E
Broadhurst Ra.	**78**	22 30 S	122 30 E
Broads, The	**12**	52 45N	1 30 E
Broadus	**118**	45 28N	105 27W
Broadview	**109**	50 22N	102 35W
Broadwater	**77**	28 59 S	153 29 E
Broager	**11**	54 53N	9 40 E
Broaryd	**11**	57 7N	13 15 E
Brochet	**109**	57 53N	101 40W
Brochet, L.	**109**	58 36N	101 35W
Brochet, L. du	**105**	49 40N	69 37W
Brock	**109**	51 26N	108 43W
Brock →	**104**	50 0N	75 5W
Brocken	**30**	51 48N	10 40 E
Brocklehurst	**76**	32 9 S	148 38 E
Brockport	**114**	43 12N	77 56W
Brockton	**115**	42 8N	71 2W

Brockville **107** 44 35N 75 41W
Brockway, Mont., U.S.A. **118** 47 18N 105 46W
Brockway, Pa., U.S.A. **114** 41 14N 78 48W
Brocton **114** 42 25N 79 26W
Brod **35** 41 35N 21 17 E
Brodarevo **33** 43 14N 19 44 E
Brodeur Pen. **101** 72 30N 88 10W
Brodhead **116** 42 37N 89 22W
Brodick **14** 55 34N 5 9W
Brodnica **32** 53 15N 19 25 E
Brody **36** 50 5N 25 10 E
Brogan **120** 44 14N 117 32W
Broglie **18** 49 0N 0 30 E
Broke **76** 32 45 S 151 7 E
Broke Inlet **79** 34 55 S 116 25 E
Broken → **74** 36 24 S 145 24 E
Broken Bay **76** 33 30 S 151 15 E
Broken Bow, Nebr., U.S.A. **118** 41 25N 99 35W
Broken Bow, Okla., U.S.A. **119** 34 2N 94 43W
Broken Hill **73** 31 58 S 141 29 E
Broken Hill = Kabwe **95** 14 27 S 28 28 E
Brokind **11** 58 13N 15 42 E
Brokopondo **135** 5 3N 54 59W
Brokopondo □ **135** 4 30N 55 30W
Bromfield **13** 52 25N 2 45W
Bromley **13** 51 20N 0 5 E
Bromölla **11** 56 5N 14 28 E
Bromont **105** 45 17N 72 39W
Bromptonville **105** 45 28N 71 57W
Bronaugh **116** 37 41N 94 28W
Brønderslev **11** 57 16N 9 57 E
Brong-Ahafo **88** 7 50N 2 0W
Bronkhorstspruit **97** 25 46 S 28 45 E
Bronnitsy **37** 55 27N 38 10 E
Bronsby **73** 28 10 S 142 0 E
Bronson **117** 41 52N 85 12W
Bronte, Italy **29** 37 48N 14 49 E
Bronte, U.S.A. **119** 31 54N 100 18W
Bronte Park **72** 42 8 S 146 30 E
Brookfield **116** 39 50N 93 4W
Brookhaven **119** 31 40N 90 25W
Brookings, Oreg., U.S.A. **120** 42 4N 124 10W
Brookings, S.D., U.S.A. **118** 44 20N 96 45W
Brooklands **72** 18 5 S 144 0 E
Brooklin **114** 43 55N 78 55W
Brooklyn **116** 41 44N 92 27W
Brookmere **108** 49 52N 120 53W
Brooks **108** 50 35N 111 55W
Brooks B. **108** 50 15N 127 55W
Brooks L. **109** 61 55N 106 35W
Brooks Ra. **100** 68 40N 147 0W
Brookston **117** 40 36N 86 52W
Brooksville, Fla., U.S.A. **113** 28 32N 82 21W
Brooksville, Ky., U.S.A. **117** 38 41N 84 4W
Brookton **79** 32 22 S 117 1 E
Brookville **117** 39 25N 85 0W
Brooloo **73** 26 30 S 152 43 E
Broom, L. **14** 57 55N 5 15W
Brooman **76** 35 29 S 150 17 E
Broome **78** 18 0 S 122 15 E
Broomehill **79** 33 51 S 117 39 E
Broons **18** 48 20N 2 16W
Brora **14** 58 0N 3 50W
Brora → **14** 58 4N 3 52W
Brösarp **11** 55 43N 14 6 E
Brosna → **15** 53 8N 8 0W
Broşteni **34** 47 14N 25 43 E
Brotas de Macaúbas **139** 12 0 S 42 38W
Brothers **120** 43 56N 120 39W
Brøttum **10** 61 2N 10 34 E
Brou **18** 48 13N 1 11 E
Brouage **20** 45 52N 1 4W
Broughton **117** 37 56N 88 27W
Broughton I. **76** 32 37 S 152 20 E
Broughton Island **101** 67 33N 63 0W
Broughty Ferry **14** 56 29N 2 50W
Broula **76** 33 52 S 148 34 E
Brouwershaven **16** 51 45N 3 55 E
Brovary **36** 50 34N 30 48 E
Brovst **11** 57 6N 9 31 E
Browerville **118** 46 3N 94 50W
Brown City **106** 43 13N 82 59W
Brown, Pt. **73** 32 32 S 133 50 E
Brown Willy **13** 50 35N 4 34W
Brownfield **119** 33 10N 102 15W
Browning, Ill., U.S.A. **116** 40 7N 90 22W
Browning, Mo., U.S.A. **116** 40 3N 93 12W
Browning, Mont., U.S.A. **120** 48 35N 113 0W
Brownlee **109** 50 43N 106 1W
Brown's Bay **80** 36 40 S 174 40 E
Brownsburg, Can. **105** 45 41N 74 25W
Brownsburg, U.S.A. **117** 39 50N 86 26W
Brownstown **117** 38 53N 86 3W
Brownsville, Oreg., U.S.A. **120** 44 29N 123 0W
Brownsville, Tenn., U.S.A. **119** 35 35N 89 15W
Brownsville, Tex., U.S.A. **119** 25 56N 97 25W
Brownsweg **135** 5 5N 55 15W
Brownwood **119** 31 45N 99 0W
Brownwood, L. **119** 31 51N 98 35W
Browse I. **78** 14 7 S 123 33 E
Brozas **23** 39 37N 6 47W
Bruay-en-Artois **19** 50 29N 2 33 E
Bruce B. **81** 43 35 S 169 42 E
Bruce, Mt. **78** 22 37 S 118 8 E
Bruce Pen. **106** 45 0N 81 30W
Bruce Rock **79** 31 52 S 118 8 E
Bruche → **19** 48 34N 7 43 E
Bruchsal **31** 49 9N 8 39 E
Bruck an der Leitha **33** 48 1N 16 47 E
Bruck an der Mur **33** 47 24N 15 16 E
Brückenau **31** 50 17N 9 48 E
Brue → **13** 51 10N 2 59W
Bruges = Brugge **16** 51 13N 3 13 E
Brugg **31** 47 29N 8 11 E
Brugge **16** 51 13N 3 13 E
Brühl **30** 50 49N 6 51 E
Brûlé **108** 53 15N 117 58W
Brûlon **18** 47 58N 0 15W
Brumado **139** 14 14 S 41 40W
Brumado → **139** 14 13 S 41 40W
Brumath **19** 48 43N 7 40 E
Brumunddal **10** 60 53N 10 56 E
Brunchilly **72** 18 50 S 134 30 E
Brundidge **113** 31 43N 85 45W
Bruneau **120** 42 57N 115 55W
Bruneau → **120** 42 57N 115 58W
Brunei = Bandar Seri Begawan **56** 4 52N 115 0 E
Brunei ■ **56** 4 50N 115 0 E
Brunette Downs **72** 18 40 S 135 55 E
Brunflo **10** 63 5N 14 50 E
Brungle **76** 35 8 S 148 13 E
Brunico **27** 46 50N 11 55 E
Brunkeberg **10** 59 26N 8 28 E
Brunna **10** 59 52N 17 25 E
Brunnen **31** 46 59N 8 37 E
Brunner **81** 42 27 S 171 20 E
Brunner, L. **81** 42 37 S 171 27 E
Brunnsvik **10** 60 12N 15 8 E
Bruno **109** 52 20N 105 30W
Brunsbüttelkoog **30** 53 52N 9 13 E
Brunswick, Ga., U.S.A. **113** 31 10N 81 30W
Brunswick, Md., U.S.A. **112** 39 20N 77 38W
Brunswick, Me., U.S.A. **103** 43 53N 69 50W
Brunswick, Mo., U.S.A. **116** 39 26N 93 10W
Brunswick, Ohio, U.S.A. **114** 41 15N 81 50W
Brunswick = Braunschweig **30** 52 17N 10 28 E
Brunswick B. **78** 15 15 S 124 50 E
Brunswick Heads **77** 28 32 S 153 33 E
Brunswick Junction **79** 33 15 S 115 50 E
Brunswick, Pen. de **142** 53 30 S 71 30W
Bruntál **32** 50 0N 17 27 E
Bruny I. **72** 43 20 S 147 15 E
Brus Laguna **126** 15 47N 84 35W
Brusartsi **34** 43 40N 23 5 E
Brush **118** 40 17N 103 33W
Brushton **115** 44 50N 74 62W
Brusio **31** 46 14N 10 8 E
Brusque **141** 27 5 S 49 0W
Brussel **16** 50 51N 4 21 E
Brussels, Can. **114** 43 45N 81 25W
Brussels, Ont., Can. **106** 43 44N 81 15W
Brussels = Bruxelles **16** 50 51N 4 21 E
Bruthen **75** 37 42 S 147 50 E
Bruxelles **16** 50 51N 4 21 E
Bruyères **19** 48 10N 6 40 E
Bryan, Ohio, U.S.A. **117** 41 30N 84 30W
Bryan, Texas, U.S.A. **119** 30 40N 96 27W
Bryan, Mt. **73** 33 30 S 139 0 E
Bryansk **36** 53 13N 34 25 E
Bryanskoye **39** 44 20N 47 10 E
Bryant **118** 44 35N 97 28W
Bryne **9** 58 44N 5 38 E
Bryson **104** 45 41N 76 37W
Bryson City **113** 35 28N 83 25W
Bryte **122** 38 35N 121 33W
Brza Palanka **33** 44 28N 22 27 E
Brzava → **33** 45 21N 20 45 E
Brzeg **32** 50 52N 17 30 E
Brzeg Din **32** 51 16N 16 41 E
Bu Athlah **87** 30 9N 15 39 E
Bu Craa **84** 26 45N 12 50W
Bua Yai **54** 15 33N 102 26 E
Buabuq **90** 31 29N 25 29 E
Buala **68** 8 10 S 159 35 E
Buangor **74** 37 20 S 143 10 E
Buangor, Mt. **74** 37 16 S 143 13 E
Buapinang **57** 4 40 S 121 30 E
Buayan **57** 6 3N 125 6 E
Buba **88** 11 40N 14 59W
Bubanza **94** 3 6 S 29 23 E
Bucak **46** 37 28N 30 36 E
Bucaramanga **134** 7 0N 73 0W
Buccaneer Arch. **78** 16 7 S 123 20 E
Bucchiánico **27** 42 20N 14 10 E
Bucecea **34** 47 47N 26 28 E
Buchach **36** 49 5N 25 25 E
Buchan, Austral. **75** 37 30 S 148 12 E
Buchan, U.K. **14** 57 32N 2 8W
Buchan Ness **14** 57 29N 1 48W
Buchan South **75** 37 34 S 148 8 E
Buchanan, Can. **109** 51 40N 102 45W
Buchanan, Liberia **88** 5 57N 10 2W
Buchanan, U.S.A. **117** 41 50N 86 22W
Buchanan, L., Queens., Austral. **72** 21 35 S 145 52 E
Buchanan, L., W. Australia, Austral. **79** 25 33 S 123 2 E
Buchanan, L., U.S.A. **119** 30 50N 98 25W
Buchans **103** 48 50N 56 52W
Bucharest = Bucureşti **34** 44 27N 26 10 E
Buchholz **30** 53 19N 9 51 E
Buchloe **31** 48 3N 10 45 E
Buchon, Pt. **122** 35 15N 120 54W
Bückeburg **30** 52 16N 9 2 E
Buckeye **121** 33 28N 112 40W
Buckhannon **112** 39 2N 80 10W
Buckhaven **14** 56 10N 3 2W
Buckhorn L. **107** 44 29N 78 23W
Buckie **14** 57 40N 2 58W
Buckingham, Can. **104** 45 37N 75 24W
Buckingham, U.K. **13** 52 0N 0 59W
Buckingham □ **13** 51 50N 0 55W
Buckingham B. **72** 12 10 S 135 40 E
Buckingham Can. **51** 14 0N 80 5 E
Buckinguy **73** 31 3 S 147 30 E
Buckland **117** 40 37N 84 16W
Buckland Newton **13** 50 45N 2 25W
Buckle Hd. **78** 14 26 S 127 52 E
Buckleboo **73** 32 54 S 136 12 E
Buckley, Ill., U.S.A. **117** 40 35N 88 2W
Buckley, Wash., U.S.A. **120** 47 10N 122 2W
Bucklin, Kans., U.S.A. **119** 37 37N 99 40W
Bucklin, Mo., U.S.A. **116** 39 47N 92 53W
Bucks L. **122** 39 54N 121 12W
Bucquoy **19** 50 9N 2 43 E
Buctouche **103** 46 30N 64 45W
Bucureşti **34** 44 27N 26 10 E
Bucyrus **117** 40 48N 83 0W
Budafok **33** 47 26N 19 2 E
Budalin **52** 22 20N 95 10 E
Budapest **33** 47 29N 19 5 E
Budaun **49** 28 5N 79 10 E
Budd Coast **143** 68 0 S 112 0 E
Buddabadah **76** 31 56 S 147 14 E
Buddusò **28** 40 35N 9 18 E
Bude **13** 50 49N 4 33W
Budeşti **34** 44 13N 26 30 E
Budge Budge **49** 22 30N 88 5 E
Budgewoi Lake **76** 33 13 S 151 34 E
Búðareyri **8** 65 2N 14 13W
Búðir **8** 64 49N 23 23W
Budia **24** 40 38N 2 46W
Budjala **92** 2 50N 19 40 E
Búdrio **27** 44 31N 11 31 E
Buea **89** 4 10N 9 9 E
Buellton **123** 34 37N 120 12W
Buena Vista, Boliv. **137** 17 27 S 63 40W
Buena Vista, Colo., U.S.A. **121** 38 56N 106 6W
Buena Vista, Va., U.S.A. **112** 37 47N 79 23W
Buena Vista L. **123** 35 15N 119 21W
Buenaventura, Colomb. **134** 3 53N 77 4W
Buenaventura, Mexico **124** 29 50N 107 30W
Buenaventura, B. de **134** 3 48N 77 17W
Buendía, Pantano de **24** 40 25N 2 43W
Buenópolis **139** 17 54 S 44 11W
Buenos Aires, Argent. **140** 34 30 S 58 20W
Buenos Aires, Colomb. **134** 1 36N 73 18W
Buenos Aires, C. Rica **126** 9 10N 83 20W
Buenos Aires □ **140** 36 30 S 60 0W
Buenos Aires, Lago **142** 46 35 S 72 30W
Buesaco **134** 1 23N 77 9W
Buffalo, Mo., U.S.A. **116** 37 40N 93 5W
Buffalo, N.Y., U.S.A. **114** 42 55N 78 50W
Buffalo, Okla., U.S.A. **119** 36 55N 99 42W
Buffalo, S.D., U.S.A. **118** 45 39N 103 31W
Buffalo, Wyo., U.S.A. **120** 44 25N 106 50W
Buffalo → **108** 60 5N 115 5W
Buffalo Head Hills **108** 57 25N 115 55W
Buffalo L. **108** 52 27N 112 54W
Buffalo Narrows **109** 55 51N 108 29W
Buffels → **96** 29 36 S 17 15 E
Buford **113** 34 5N 84 0W
Bug →, Poland **38** 52 31N 21 5 E
Bug →, U.S.S.R. **38** 46 59N 31 58 E
Buga **134** 4 0N 76 15W
Bugaldie **77** 31 2 S 149 6 E
Buganda □ **94** 0 0N 31 30 E
Buganga **94** 0 3 S 32 0 E
Bugeat **20** 45 36N 1 55 E
Bugel, Tanjung **56** 6 26 S 111 3 E
Bugsuk **56** 8 15N 117 15 E
Bugue, Le **20** 44 55N 0 56 E
Buguma **89** 4 42N 6 55 E
Buguruslan **40** 53 39N 52 26 E
Buhăeşti **34** 46 47N 27 32 E
Buheirat-Murrat-el-Kubra **90** 30 15N 32 40 E
Buhl, Idaho, U.S.A. **120** 42 35N 114 54W
Buhl, Minn., U.S.A. **118** 47 30N 92 46W
Buick **119** 37 38N 91 2W
Builth Wells **13** 52 10N 3 26W
Buin **68** 6 48 S 155 42 E
Buina Qara **47** 36 20N 67 0 E
Buinsk **37** 55 0N 48 18 E
Buíque **138** 8 37 S 37 9W
Buir Nur **62** 47 50N 117 42 E
Buis-les-Baronnies **21** 44 17N 5 16 E
Buitrago **22** 41 0N 3 38W
Bujalance **23** 37 54N 4 23W
Buján **22** 42 59N 8 36W
Bujaraloz **24** 41 29N 0 10W
Buje **27** 45 24N 13 39 E
Buji **69** 9 8 S 142 11 E
Bujumbura (Usumbura) **94** 3 16 S 29 18 E
Buka I. **69** 5 10 S 154 35 E
Bukachacha **41** 52 55N 116 50 E
Bukama **95** 9 10 S 25 50 E
Bukandula **94** 0 13N 31 50 E
Bukavu **94** 2 20 S 28 52 E
Bukene **94** 4 15 S 32 48 E
Bukhara **40** 39 48N 64 25 E
Bukima **94** 1 50 S 33 25 E
Bukit Mertajam **55** 5 22N 100 28 E
Bukittinggi **56** 0 20 S 100 20 E
Bukkapatnam **51** 14 14N 77 46 E
Bukkulla **77** 29 30 S 151 8 E
Bukoba **94** 1 20 S 31 49 E
Bukoba □ **94** 1 30 S 32 0 E
Bukrale **91** 4 32N 42 0 E
Bukuru **89** 9 42N 8 48 E
Bukuya **94** 0 40N 31 52 E
Bula, Guin.-Biss. **88** 12 7N 15 43W
Bula, Indon. **57** 3 6 S 130 30 E
Bulahdelah **76** 32 23 S 152 13 E
Bulan **57** 12 40N 123 52 E
Bulandshahr **48** 28 28N 77 51 E
Bûlâq **90** 25 10N 30 38 E
Bulawayo **95** 20 7 S 28 32 E
Buldana **50** 20 30N 76 18 E
Bulga **76** 32 39 S 151 2 E
Bulgan **62** 48 45N 103 34 E
Bulgaria ■ **34** 42 35N 25 30 E
Bulgroo **73** 25 47 S 143 58 E
Bulgunnia **73** 30 10 S 134 53 E
Bulhar **45** 10 25N 44 30 E
Buli, Teluk **57** 1 5N 128 25 E
Buliluyan, C. **56** 8 20N 117 15 E
Bulki **91** 6 11N 36 31 E
Bulkley → **108** 55 15N 127 40W
Bull Shoals L. **119** 36 40N 93 5W
Bullabulling **79** 31 1 S 120 32 E
Bullaque → **23** 38 59N 4 17W
Bullara **78** 22 40 S 114 3 E
Bullaring **79** 32 30 S 117 45 E
Bullas **25** 38 2N 1 40W
Bulle **31** 46 37N 7 3 E
Buller → **81** 41 44 S 171 36 E
Buller Gorge **81** 41 40 S 172 10 E
Buller, Mt. **75** 37 10 S 146 28 E
Bullhead City **123** 35 11N 114 33W
Bulli **76** 34 15 S 150 57 E
Bullock Cr. → **74** 35 42 S 143 54 E
Bullock Creek **72** 17 43 S 144 31 E
Bulloo → **73** 28 43 S 142 30 E
Bulloo Downs, Queens., Austral. **73** 28 31 S 142 57 E
Bulloo Downs, W.A., Austral. **79** 24 0 S 119 32 E
Bulloo L. **73** 28 43 S 142 25 E
Bulls **80** 40 10 S 175 24 E
Bully-les-Mines **19** 50 27N 2 44 E
Bulnes **140** 36 42 S 72 19W
Bulo Burti **45** 3 50N 45 33 E
Buloke, L. **74** 36 15 S 142 58 E
Bulolo **69** 7 10 S 146 40 E
Bulsar **50** 20 40N 72 58 E
Bultfontein **96** 28 18 S 26 10 E
Bulu Karakelong **57** 4 35N 126 50 E
Bulukumba **57** 5 33 S 120 11 E
Bulun **41** 70 37N 127 30 E
Bumba **92** 2 13N 22 30 E
Bumbiri I. **94** 1 40 S 31 55 E

Bumble Bee **121** 34 8N 112 18W
Bumbum **89** 13 17N 8 10 E
Bumhkang **52** 26 51N 97 40 E
Bumhpa Bum **52** 26 51N 97 14 E
Bumi → **95** 17 0S 28 20 E
Bumtang → **52** 26 56N 90 53 E
Buna, Kenya **94** 2 58N 39 30 E
Buna, P.N.G. **69** 8 42S 148 27 E
Bunazi **94** 1 3S 31 23 E
Bunbury **79** 33 20S 115 35 E
Buncrana **15** 55 8N 7 28W
Bundaberg **73** 24 54S 152 22 E
Bundanoon **76** 34 40S 150 16 E
Bundarra **77** 30 4S 151 0W
Bünde **30** 52 11N 8 33 E
Bundemar **76** 31 50S 148 10 E
Bundey → **72** 21 46S 135 37 E
Bundi **48** 25 30N 75 35 E
Bundooma **72** 24 54S 134 16 E
Bundoran **15** 54 24N 8 17W
Bundukia **91** 5 14N 30 55 E
Bung Kan **54** 18 23N 103 37 E
Bungatakada **64** 33 35N 131 25 E
Bungil Cr. → **72** 27 5S 149 5 E
Bungo-Suidō **64** 33 0N 132 15 E
Bungoma **94** 0 34N 34 34 E
Bungonia **76** 34 51S 149 57 E
Bungu **94** 7 35S 39 0 E
Bungun Shara **62** 49 0N 104 0 E
Bungunya **77** 28 25S 149 42 E
Bunia **94** 1 35N 30 20 E
Buninyong **74** 37 36S 143 54 E
Bunji **49** 35 45N 74 40 E
Bunju **56** 3 35N 117 50 E
Bunker Hill, Ill., U.S.A. **116** 39 3N 89 57W
Bunker Hill, Ind., U.S.A. **117** 40 40N 86 6W
Bunkerville **121** 36 47N 114 6W
Bunkie **119** 31 1N 92 12W
Bunnan **77** 32 2S 150 37 E
Bunnell **113** 29 28N 81 12W
Bunnythorpe **80** 40 16S 175 39 E
Buñol **25** 39 25N 0 47W
Buntok **56** 1 40S 114 58 E
Bununu **89** 9 51N 9 32 E
Bununu Dass **89** 10 0N 9 31 E
Bunyan **76** 36 10S 149 11 E
Bunza **89** 12 8N 4 0 E
Buol **57** 1 15N 121 32 E
Buon Brieng **54** 13 9N 108 12 E
Buong Long **54** 13 44N 106 59 E
Buorkhaya, Mys **41** 71 50N 132 40 E
Buqei'a **44** 32 58N 35 20 E
Bur Acaba **45** 3 12N 44 20 E
Bûr Fuad **90** 31 15N 32 20 E
Bûr Safâga **90** 26 43N 33 57 E
Bûr Sa'îd **90** 31 16N 32 18 E
Bûr Sûdân **90** 19 32N 37 9 E
Bûr Taufiq **90** 29 54N 32 32 E
Bura **94** 1 4S 39 58 E
Buraidah **46** 26 20N 44 8 E
Buraimī, Al Wāhāt al **47** 24 10N 55 43 E
Burak Sulayman **44** 31 42N 35 7 E
Burao **45** 9 32N 45 32 E
Buras **119** 29 20N 89 33W
Burbank **123** 34 9N 118 23W
Burcher **76** 33 30S 147 16 E
Burdekin → **72** 19 38S 147 25 E
Burdett **108** 49 50N 111 32W
Burdur **46** 37 45N 30 22 E
Burdwan **49** 23 14N 87 39 E
Bure **91** 10 40N 37 4 E
Bure → **12** 52 38N 1 45 E
Bureba, La **24** 42 36N 3 24W
Büren **30** 51 33N 8 34 E
Bureya → **41** 49 27N 129 30 E
Burford **106** 43 7N 80 27W
Burg, Magdeburg, Ger. **30** 52 16N 11 50 E
Burg, Schleswig-Holstein, Ger. **30** 54 25N 11 10 E
Burg el Arab **90** 30 54N 29 32 E
Burg et Tuyur **90** 20 55N 27 56 E
Burgan **46** 29 0N 47 57 E
Burgas **34** 42 33N 27 29 E
Burgdorf, Ger. **30** 52 27N 10 0 E
Burgdorf, Switz. **31** 47 3N 7 37 E
Burgeo **103** 47 37N 57 38W
Burgersdorp **96** 31 0S 26 20 E
Burges, Mt. **79** 30 50S 121 5 E
Burghausen **31** 48 10N 12 50 E
Búrgio **28** 37 35N 13 18 E
Burglengenfeld **31** 49 11N 12 2 E
Burgo de Osma **24** 41 35N 3 4W
Burgohondo **22** 40 26N 4 47W
Burgos **24** 42 21N 3 41W
Burgos □ **24** 42 21N 3 42W
Burgstädt **30** 50 55N 12 49 E
Burgsteinfurt **30** 52 9N 7 23 E
Burgsvik **11** 57 3N 18 19 E
Burguillos del Cerro **23** 38 23N 6 35W
Burgundy = Bourgogne **19** 47 0N 4 30 E
Burhanpur **50** 21 18N 76 14 E
Burhou **18** 49 45N 2 15W
Buri Pen. **91** 15 25N 39 55 E
Burias **57** 12 55N 123 5 E
Burica, Pta. **126** 8 3N 82 51W
Burigi, L. **94** 2 2S 31 22 E
Burin, Can. **103** 47 1N 55 14W
Burin, Jordan **44** 32 11N 35 15 E
Buriram **54** 15 0N 103 0 E
Buriti Alegre **139** 18 9S 49 3W
Buriti Bravo **138** 5 50S 43 50W
Buriti dos Lopes **138** 3 10S 41 52W
Burji **91** 5 29N 37 51 E
Burkburnett **119** 34 7N 98 35W
Burke **120** 47 31N 115 56W
Burke → **72** 23 12S 139 33 E
Burketown **72** 17 45S 139 33 E
Burkettsville **117** 40 21N 84 39W
Burk's Falls **106** 45 37N 79 24W
Burleigh Falls **107** 44 33N 78 12W
Burleigh Heads **77** 28 5S 153 25 E
Burley **120** 42 37N 113 55W
Burlingame **122** 37 35N 122 21W
Burlington, Can. **106** 43 18N 79 45W
Burlington, Colo., U.S.A. **118** 39 21N 102 18W
Burlington, Ill., U.S.A. **117** 42 43N 88 33W
Burlington, Iowa, U.S.A. **116** 40 50N 91 5W
Burlington, Kans., U.S.A. **118** 38 15N 95 47W
Burlington, Ky., U.S.A. **117** 39 2N 84 43W
Burlington, N.C., U.S.A. **113** 36 7N 79 27W
Burlington, N.J., U.S.A. **115** 40 5N 74 50W
Burlington, Vt., U.S.A. **115** 44 27N 73 14W
Burlington, Wash., U.S.A. **122** 48 29N 122 19W
Burlington, Wis., U.S.A. **112** 42 41N 88 18W
Burlyu-Tyube **40** 46 30N 79 10 E
Burma ■ **52** 21 0N 96 30 E
Burnabbie **79** 32 7S 126 21 E
Burnaby I. **108** 52 25N 131 19W
Burnet **119** 30 45N 98 11W
Burney **120** 40 56N 121 41W
Burngup **79** 33 2S 118 42 E
Burnham **114** 40 37N 77 34W
Burnie **72** 41 4S 145 56 E
Burnley **12** 53 47N 2 15W
Burns, Oreg., U.S.A. **120** 43 40N 119 4W
Burns, Wyo., U.S.A. **118** 41 13N 104 18W
Burns Lake **108** 54 20N 125 45W
Burnside → **100** 66 51N 108 4W
Burnt River **107** 44 41N 78 42W
Burntwood → **109** 56 8N 96 34W
Burntwood L. **109** 55 22N 100 26W
Burqa **44** 32 18N 35 11 E
Burqin **62** 47 43N 87 0 E
Burra **73** 33 40S 138 55 E
Burraga **76** 33 57S 149 32 E
Burragate **75** 37 2S 149 38 E
Burragorang, L. **76** 33 52S 150 37 E
Burramurra **72** 20 25S 137 15 E
Burreli **35** 41 36N 20 1 E
Burren Junction **77** 30 7S 148 59 E
Burrendong Dam **76** 32 39S 149 6 E
Burrendong, L. **76** 32 45S 149 10 E
Burrewarra Pt. **76** 35 50S 150 15 E
Burriana **24** 39 50N 0 4W
Burringbar **77** 28 25S 153 29 E
Burrinjuck Dam **76** 35 0S 148 34 E
Burrinjuck Res. **76** 35 0S 148 36 E
Burro, Serranías del **124** 29 0N 102 0W
Burrundie **78** 13 32S 131 42 E
Burruyacú **140** 26 30S 64 40W
Burry Port **13** 51 41N 4 17W
Bursa **46** 40 15N 29 5 E
Burseryd **11** 57 12N 13 17 E
Burstall **109** 50 39N 109 54W
Burt L. **106** 45 27N 84 40W
Burton L. **102** 54 45N 78 20W
Burton-upon-Trent **12** 52 48N 1 39W
Burtundy **74** 33 45S 142 15 E
Buru **57** 3 30S 126 30 E
Burullus, Bahra el **90** 31 25N 31 0 E
Burundi ■ **94** 3 15S 30 0 E
Burung **56** 0 24N 103 33 E
Bururi **94** 3 57S 29 37 E
Burutu **89** 5 20N 5 29 E
Burwash **106** 46 14N 80 51W
Burwell **118** 41 49N 99 8W
Bury, Can. **105** 45 28N 71 30W
Bury, U.K. **12** 53 36N 2 19W
Bury St. Edmunds **13** 52 15N 0 42 E
Buryat A.S.S.R. □ **41** 53 0N 110 0 E
Busalla **26** 44 34N 8 58 E
Busango Swamp **95** 14 15S 25 45 E
Busayyah **46** 30 0N 46 10 E
Busca **26** 44 31N 7 29 E
Bushell **109** 59 31N 108 45W
Bushenyi **94** 0 35S 30 10 E
Bushnell, Ill., U.S.A. **118** 40 32N 90 30W
Bushnell, Nebr., U.S.A. **118** 41 18N 103 50W
Busia □ **94** 0 25N 34 6 E
Busie **88** 10 29N 2 22W
Businga **92** 3 16N 20 59 E
Buskerud fylke □ **10** 60 13N 9 0 E
Busko Zdrój **32** 50 28N 20 42 E
Busoga □ **94** 0 5N 33 30 E
Busovača **33** 44 6N 17 53 E
Busra **46** 32 30N 36 25 E
Bussang **19** 47 50N 6 50 E
Busselton **79** 33 42S 115 15 E
Busseto **26** 44 59N 10 2 E
Bussum **16** 52 16N 5 10 E
Bustamante, B. **142** 45 5S 66 18W
Busto Arsizio **26** 45 40N 8 50 E
Busto, C. **22** 43 34N 6 28W
Busu-Djanoa **92** 1 43N 21 23 E
Busuanga **57** 12 10N 120 0 E
Büsum **30** 54 7N 8 50 E
Buta **94** 2 50N 24 53 E
Butare **94** 2 31S 29 52 E
Bute, I. **14** 55 48N 5 2W
Bute Inlet **108** 50 40N 124 53W
Butemba **94** 1 9N 31 37 E
Butembo **94** 0 9N 29 18 E
Butera **29** 37 10N 14 10 E
Butha Qi **62** 48 0N 122 32 E
Buthidaung **52** 20 52N 92 32 E
Butiaba **94** 1 50N 31 20 E
Butler, Ind., U.S.A. **117** 41 26N 84 52W
Butler, Ky., U.S.A. **117** 38 47N 84 22W
Butler, Mo., U.S.A. **116** 38 17N 94 18W
Butler, Pa., U.S.A. **114** 40 52N 79 52W
Buttabone **76** 31 20S 147 39 E
Butte, Mont., U.S.A. **120** 46 0N 112 31W
Butte, Nebr., U.S.A. **118** 42 56N 98 54W
Butte Creek → **122** 39 12N 121 56W
Butterworth **55** 5 24N 100 23 E
Buttfield, Mt. **79** 24 15S 128 9 E
Button B. **109** 58 45N 94 23W
Buttonwillow **123** 35 24N 119 28W
Butty Hd. **79** 33 54S 121 39 E
Butuan **57** 8 57N 125 33 E
Butuku-Luba **89** 3 29N 8 33 E
Butung **57** 5 0S 122 45 E
Buturlinovka **37** 50 50N 40 35 E
Butzbach **30** 50 24N 8 40 E
Bützow **30** 53 51N 11 59 E
Buxar **49** 25 34N 83 58 E
Buxton, N.S.W., Austral. **76** 34 15S 150 32 E
Buxton, Vic., Austral. **74** 37 26S 145 42 E
Buxton Guyana **135** 6 48N 58 2W
Buxton, S. Afr. **96** 27 38S 24 42 E
Buxton, U.K. **12** 53 16N 1 54W
Buxy **19** 46 44N 4 40 E
Buy **37** 58 28N 41 28 E
Buyaga **41** 59 50N 127 0 E
Buynaksk **39** 42 48N 47 7 E
Büyük Çekmece **35** 41 2N 28 35 E
Büyük Menderes → **46** 37 27N 27 11 E
Buzançais **18** 46 54N 1 25 E
Buzău **34** 45 10N 26 50 E
Buzău → **34** 45 10N 27 20 E
Buzău, Pasul **34** 45 35N 26 12 E
Buzaymah, Libya **85** 24 35N 22 0 E
Buzaymah, Libya **85** 24 50N 22 2 E
Buzen **64** 33 35N 131 5 E
Buzet **27** 45 24N 13 58 E
Buzi → **95** 19 50S 34 43 E
Buziaş **34** 45 38N 21 36 E
Buzuluk **40** 52 48N 52 12 E
Buzzards Bay **115** 41 45N 70 38W
Bwagaoia **69** 10 40S 152 52 E
Bwana Mkubwe **95** 13 8S 28 38 E
Byala **34** 43 28N 25 44 E
Byala Slatina **34** 43 26N 23 55 E
Byandovan, Mys **39** 39 45N 49 28 E
Bychawa **32** 51 1N 22 36 E
Bydgoszcz **32** 53 10N 18 0 E
Byelorussian S.S.R. □ **36** 53 30N 27 0 E
Byers **118** 39 46N 104 13W
Byesville **114** 39 56N 81 32W
Byhalia **119** 34 53N 89 41W
Bykhov **36** 53 31N 30 14 E
Bykovo **39** 49 50N 45 25 E
Bylas **121** 33 11N 110 9W
Bylderup **11** 54 57N 9 6 E
Bylong **76** 32 24S 150 8 E
Bylot I. **101** 73 13N 78 34W
Byng Inlet **106** 45 46N 80 33W
Byrd, C. **143** 69 38S 76 7W
Byrd Land **143** 79 30S 125 0W
Byrd Sub-Glacial Basin **143** 82 0S 120 0W
Byro **79** 26 5S 116 11 E
Byrock **73** 30 40S 146 27 E
Byron, Austral. **77** 29 40S 151 7 E
Byron, U.S.A. **116** 42 8N 89 15W
Byron Bay **77** 28 43S 153 37 E
Byron, C. **77** 28 38S 153 40 E
Byrranga, Gory **41** 75 0N 100 0 E
Byrum **11** 57 16N 11 0 E
Bystrzyca Kłodzka **32** 50 19N 16 39 E
Byten **36** 52 50N 25 27 E
Bytom **32** 50 25N 18 54 E
Bytów **32** 54 10N 17 30 E
Byumba **94** 1 35S 30 4 E

C

Ca → **54** 18 45N 105 45 E
Ca Mau = Quan Long **55** 9 7N 105 8 E
Ca Na **55** 11 20N 108 54 E
Caacupé **140** 25 23S 57 5W
Caamano Sd. **108** 52 55N 129 25W
Caapiranga **135** 3 18S 61 13W
Caazapá **140** 26 8S 56 19W
Caazapá □ **141** 26 10S 56 0W
Caballeria, Cabo de **24** 40 5N 4 5 E
Cabana **136** 8 25S 78 5W
Cabanaconde **136** 15 38S 71 58W
Cabañaquinta **22** 43 10N 5 38W
Cabanatuan **57** 15 30N 120 58 E
Cabanes **24** 40 9N 0 2 E
Cabanillas **136** 15 36S 70 28W
Cabano **105** 47 40N 68 56W
Čabar **27** 45 36N 14 39 E
Cabazon **123** 33 55N 116 47W
Cabbora → **77** 32 2S 149 17 E
Cabedelo **138** 7 0S 34 50W
Cabery **117** 41 0N 88 12W
Cabeza del Buey **23** 38 44N 5 13W
Cabildo **140** 32 30S 71 5W
Cabimas **134** 10 23N 71 25W
Cabinda **92** 5 33S 12 11 E
Cabinda □ **92** 5 0S 12 30 E
Cabinet Mts. **120** 48 0N 115 30W
Cables **79** 27 55S 123 25 E
Cabo Blanco **142** 47 15S 65 47W
Cabo Frio **139** 22 51S 42 3W
Cabo Pantoja **134** 1 0S 75 10W
Cabo Raso **142** 44 20S 65 15W
Cabonga, Réservoir **104** 47 20N 76 40W
Cabool **119** 37 10N 92 8W
Caboolture **73** 27 5S 152 58 E
Cabora Bassa Dam **95** 15 20S 32 50 E
Caborca (Heroica) **124** 30 40N 112 10W
Cabot, Mt. **115** 44 30N 71 25W
Cabot Strait **103** 47 15N 59 40W
Cabra **23** 37 30N 4 28W
Cabra del Santo Cristo **25** 37 42N 3 16W
Cabramurra **76** 35 56S 148 26 E
Cábras **28** 39 57N 8 30 E
Cabrera, I. **25** 39 6N 2 59 E
Cabrera, Sierra **22** 42 12N 6 40W
Cabri **109** 50 35N 108 25W
Cabriel → **25** 39 14N 1 3W
Cabruta **134** 7 50N 66 10W
Cabuyaro **134** 4 18N 72 49W
Cacabelos **22** 42 36N 6 44W
Čačak **33** 43 54N 20 20 E
Cacao **135** 4 33N 52 26W
Cáceres, Brazil **137** 16 5S 57 40W
Cáceres, Colomb. **134** 7 35N 75 20W
Cáceres, Spain **23** 39 26N 6 23W
Cáceres □ **23** 39 45N 6 0W
Cache Bay **106** 46 22N 80 0W
Cache Cr. → **122** 38 45N 121 43W
Cachepo **23** 37 20N 7 49W
Cachéu **88** 12 14N 16 8W
Cachi **140** 25 5S 66 10W
Cachimbo **137** 8 57S 54 54W
Cachimbo, Serra do **137** 9 30S 55 0W
Cachoeira **139** 12 30S 39 0W
Cachoeira Alta **139** 18 48S 50 58W
Cachoeira de Itapemirim **139** 20 51S 41 7W
Cachoeira do Sul **141** 30 3S 52 53W
Cachoeiro do Arari **138** 1 1S 48 58W
Cachopo **23** 37 20N 7 49W
Cachuela Esperanza **137** 10 32S 65 38W
Cacolo **92** 10 9S 19 21 E
Caconda **93** 13 48S 15 8 E
Caçu **139** 18 37S 51 4W
Caculé **139** 14 30S 42 13W
Cadarache, Barrage de **21** 43 42N 5 47 E
Čadca **32** 49 26N 18 45 E
Caddo **119** 34 8N 96 18W
Cader Idris **12** 52 43N 3 56W
Cadí, Sierra del **24** 42 17N 1 42 E

Cadibarrawirracanna, L.	73	28 52 S	135 27 E
Cadillac, Can.	104	48 14N	78 23W
Cadillac, France	20	44 38N	0 20W
Cadillac, U.S.A.	106	44 16N	85 25W
Cadiz	57	10 57N	123 15 E
Cádiz	23	36 30N	6 20W
Cadiz	114	40 13N	81 0W
Cádiz □	23	36 36N	5 45W
Cádiz, G. de	23	36 40N	7 0W
Cadomin	108	53 2N	117 20W
Cadotte →	108	56 43N	117 10W
Cadours	20	43 44N	1 2 E
Cadoux	79	30 46 S	117 7 E
Caen	18	49 10N	0 22W
Caernarfon	12	53 8N	4 17W
Caernarfon B.	12	53 4N	4 40W
Caernarvon = Caernarfon	12	53 8N	4 17W
Caerphilly	13	51 34N	3 13W
Cæsarea = Qesari	44	32 30N	34 53 E
Caeté	139	19 55 S	43 40W
Caetité	139	13 50 S	42 32W
Cafayate	140	26 2 S	66 0W
Cafifi	134	5 13N	71 4W
Cafu	96	16 30 S	15 8 E
Cagayan	57	9 39N	121 16 E
Cagayan →	57	18 25N	121 42 E
Cagayan de Oro	57	8 30N	124 40 E
Cagli	27	43 32N	12 38 E
Cágliari	28	39 15N	9 6 E
Cágliari, G. di	28	39 8N	9 10 E
Cagnano Varano	29	41 49N	15 47 E
Cagnes-sur-Mer	21	43 40N	7 9 E
Caguán →	134	0 8 S	74 18W
Caguas	127	18 14N	66 4W
Caha Mts.	15	51 45N	9 40W
Caher	15	52 23N	7 56W
Cahersiveen	15	51 57N	10 13W
Cahore Pt.	15	52 34N	6 11W
Cahors	20	44 27N	1 27 E
Cahuapanas	136	5 15 S	77 0W
Cahuinari →	134	1 21 S	70 44W
Cai Bau, Dao	54	21 10N	107 27 E
Cai Nuoc	55	8 56N	105 1 E
Caiabis, Serra dos	137	11 30 S	56 30W
Caianda	95	11 2 S	23 31 E
Caiapó, Serra do	137	17 0 S	52 0W
Caiapônia	137	16 57 S	51 49W
Caibarién	126	22 30N	79 30W
Caicara, Bolívar, Venez.	134	7 38N	66 10W
Caicara, Monagas, Venez.	135	9 52N	63 38W
Caicó	138	6 20 S	37 0W
Caicos Is.	127	21 40N	71 40W
Caicos Passage	127	22 45N	72 45W
Cailloma	136	15 9 S	71 45W
Caine →	137	18 23 S	65 21W
Cainsville	114	43 9N	80 15W
Caird Coast	143	75 0 S	25 0W
Cairn Gorm	14	57 7N	3 40W
Cairn Toul	14	57 3N	3 44W
Cairngorm Mts.	14	57 6N	3 42W
Cairns	72	16 57 S	145 45 E
Cairo, Ga., U.S.A.	113	30 52N	84 12W
Cairo, Illinois, U.S.A.	119	37 0N	89 10W
Cairo = El Qâhira	90	30 1N	31 14 E
Cairo Montenotte	26	44 23N	8 16 E
Caithness, Ord of	14	58 9N	3 37W
Caiundo	93	15 50 S	17 28 E
Caiza	137	20 2 S	65 40W
Cajabamba	136	7 38 S	78 4W
Cajamarca	136	7 5 S	78 28W
Cajamarca □	136	6 15 S	78 50W
Cajapió	138	2 58 S	44 48W
Cajarc	20	44 29N	1 50 E
Cajatambo	136	10 30 S	77 2W
Cajàzeiras	138	6 52 S	38 30W
Čajetina	33	43 47N	19 42 E
Cakirgol	39	40 33N	39 40 E
Cakovec	27	46 23N	16 26 E
Cal, La →	137	17 27 S	58 15W
Cala	23	37 59N	6 21W
Cala →	23	37 38N	6 5W
Cala Cadolar, Punta de	25	38 38N	1 35 E
Calabar	89	4 57N	8 20 E
Calabogie	107	45 18N	76 43W
Calabozo	134	9 0N	67 28W
Calábria □	29	39 24N	16 30 E
Calaburras, Pta. de	23	36 30N	4 38W
Calaceite	24	41 1N	0 11 E
Calacota	136	17 16 S	68 38W
Calafate	142	50 19 S	72 15W
Calahorra	24	42 18N	1 59W
Calais, France	19	50 57N	1 56 E
Calais, U.S.A.	103	45 11N	67 20W
Calais, Pas de	19	50 57N	1 20 E
Calalaste, Cord. de	140	25 0 S	67 0W
Calama, Brazil	137	8 0 S	62 50W
Calama, Chile	140	22 30 S	68 55W
Calamar, Bolívar, Colomb.	134	10 15N	74 55W
Calamar, Vaupés, Colomb.	134	1 58N	72 32W
Calamarca	136	16 55 S	68 9W
Calamian Group	57	11 50N	119 55 E
Calamocha	24	40 50N	1 17W
Calañas	23	37 40N	6 53W
Calanda	24	40 56N	0 15W
Calang	56	4 37N	95 37 E
Calangiánus	28	40 56N	9 12 E
Calapan	57	13 25N	121 7 E
Călăraşi	34	44 12N	27 20 E
Calasparra	25	38 14N	1 41W
Calatafimi	28	37 56N	12 50 E
Calatayud	24	41 20N	1 40W
Calauag	57	13 55N	122 15 E
Calavà, C.	29	38 11N	14 55 E
Calavite, Cape	57	13 26N	120 20 E
Calbayog	57	12 4N	124 38 E
Calbe	30	51 57N	11 47 E
Calca	136	13 22 S	72 0W
Calcasieu L.	119	30 0N	93 17W
Calci	26	43 44N	10 31 E
Calcutta	49	22 36N	88 24 E
Caldaro	27	46 23N	11 15 E
Caldas □	134	5 15N	75 30W
Caldas da Rainha	23	39 24N	9 8W
Caldas de Reyes	22	42 36N	8 39W
Caldas Novas	139	17 45 S	48 38W
Calder →	12	53 44N	1 21W
Caldera	140	27 5 S	70 55W
Caldwell, Idaho, U.S.A.	120	43 45N	116 42W
Caldwell, Kans., U.S.A.	119	37 5N	97 37W
Caldwell, Texas, U.S.A.	119	30 30N	96 42W
Caledon	96	34 14 S	19 26 E
Caledon →	96	30 31 S	26 5 E
Caledon B.	72	12 45 S	137 0 E
Caledonia, Can.	106	43 7N	79 58W
Caledonia, Mo., U.S.A.	116	37 45N	90 46W
Caledonia, N.Y., U.S.A.	114	42 57N	77 54W
Calella	24	41 37N	2 40 E
Calemba	96	16 0 S	15 44 E
Calera, La	140	32 50 S	71 10W
Caleta Olivia	142	46 25 S	67 25W
Calexico	123	32 40N	115 33W
Calf of Man	12	54 4N	4 48W
Calgary	108	51 0N	114 10W
Calhoun	113	34 30N	84 55W
Cali	134	3 25N	76 35W
Calicoan	57	10 59N	125 50 E
Calicut (Kozhikode)	51	11 15N	75 43 E
Caliente	121	37 36N	114 34W
California, Mo., U.S.A.	116	38 37N	92 30W
California, Pa., U.S.A.	114	40 5N	79 55W
California □	121	37 25N	120 0W
California, Baja	124	32 10N	115 12W
California, Baja, T.N. □	124	30 0N	115 0W
California, Baja, T.S. □	124	25 50N	111 50W
California City	123	35 7N	117 57W
California, Golfo de	124	27 0N	111 0W
California Hot Springs	123	35 51N	118 41W
California, Lr. = California, Baja	124	25 50N	111 50W
Călimăneşti	34	45 14N	24 20 E
Călimani, Munţii	34	47 12N	25 0 E
Călineşti	34	45 21N	24 18 E
Calingasta	140	31 15 S	69 30W
Calipatria	123	33 8N	115 30W
Calistoga	122	38 36N	122 32W
Calitri	29	40 54N	15 25 E
Calkiní	125	20 21N	90 3W
Callabonna, L.	73	29 40 S	140 5 E
Callac	18	48 25N	3 27W
Callan	15	52 33N	7 25W
Callander, Can.	106	46 13N	79 22W
Callander, U.K.	14	56 15N	4 14W
Callao	136	12 0 S	77 0W
Callaway	118	41 20N	99 56W
Callender	116	42 22N	94 17W
Calles	125	23 2N	98 42W
Callide	72	24 18 S	150 28 E
Calling Lake	108	55 15N	113 12W
Calliope	72	24 0 S	151 16 E
Callosa de Ensarriá.	25	38 40N	0 8W
Callosa de Segura	25	38 7N	0 53W
Calmar	116	43 11N	91 52W
Calne	12	51 26N	2 0W
Calola	96	16 25 S	17 48 E
Caloona	77	28 52 S	149 11 E
Calore →	29	41 11N	14 28 E
Caloundra	73	26 45 S	153 10 E
Calpe	25	38 39N	0 3 E
Calpella	122	39 14N	123 12W
Calpine	122	39 40N	120 27W
Calstock	102	49 47N	84 9W
Caltabellotta	28	37 36N	13 11 E
Caltagirone	29	37 13N	14 30 E
Caltanissetta	29	37 30N	14 3 E
Caluire-et-Cuire	21	45 49N	4 51 E
Calulo	92	10 1 S	14 56 E
Calumbo	92	9 8 S	13 20 E
Calumet	112	47 14N	88 27W
Calumet City	117	41 37N	87 32W
Calunda	93	12 7 S	23 36 E
Caluso	26	45 18N	7 52 E
Calvados □	18	49 5N	0 15W
Calvert	119	30 59N	96 40W
Calvert →	72	16 17 S	137 44 E
Calvert Hills	72	17 15 S	137 20 E
Calvert I.	108	51 30N	128 0W
Calvert Ra.	78	24 0 S	122 30 E
Calvillo	124	21 51N	102 43W
Calvinia	96	31 28 S	19 45 E
Calw	31	48 43N	8 44 E
Calwa	122	36 42N	119 46W
Calzada Almuradiel	25	38 32N	3 28W
Calzada de Calatrava	23	38 42N	3 46W
Cam →	13	52 21N	0 16 E
Cam Lam	55	11 54N	109 10 E
Cam Pha	54	21 7N	107 18 E
Cam Ranh	55	11 54N	109 12 E
Cam Xuyen	54	18 15N	106 0 E
Camabatela	92	8 20 S	15 26 E
Camacã	139	15 24 S	39 30W
Camaçari	139	12 41 S	38 18W
Camachigama, L.	104	47 50N	76 19W
Camacho	124	24 25N	102 18W
Camaguán	134	8 6N	67 36W
Camagüey	126	21 20N	78 0W
Camaiore	26	43 57N	10 18 E
Camamu	139	13 57 S	39 7W
Camaná	136	16 30 S	72 50W
Camanche	116	41 47N	90 15W
Camaquã →	141	31 17 S	51 47W
Camararé →	137	12 15 S	58 55W
Camarat, C.	21	43 12N	6 41 E
Camaret	18	48 16N	4 37W
Camargo	137	20 38 S	65 15 E
Camargue	21	43 34N	4 34 E
Camarillo	123	34 13N	119 2W
Camariñas	22	43 8N	9 12W
Camarón, C.	126	16 0N	85 0W
Camarones	142	44 50 S	65 40W
Camarones, B.	142	44 45 S	65 35W
Camas	122	45 35N	122 24W
Camas Valley	120	43 0N	123 46W
Cambados	22	42 31N	8 49W
Cambalong	75	36 49 S	149 7 E
Cambará	141	23 2 S	50 5W
Cambay	48	22 23N	72 33 E
Cambay, G. of	48	20 45N	72 30 E
Cambil	25	37 40N	3 33W
Cambo-les-Bains	20	43 22N	1 23W
Cambodia ■	54	12 15N	105 0 E
Camborne	13	50 13N	5 18W
Cambrai	19	50 11N	3 14 E
Cambria	122	35 39N	121 6W
Cambrian Mts.	13	52 25N	3 52W
Cambridge, Ont., Can.	102	43 22N	80 19W
Cambridge, Ont., Can.	106	43 23N	80 15W
Cambridge, Jamaica	126	18 18N	77 54W
Cambridge, N.Z.	80	37 54 S	175 29 E
Cambridge, U.K.	13	52 13N	0 8 E
Cambridge, Idaho, U.S.A.	120	44 36N	116 40W
Cambridge, Ill., U.S.A.	116	41 18N	90 12W
Cambridge, Iowa, U.S.A.	116	41 54N	93 32W
Cambridge, Mass., U.S.A.	115	42 20N	71 8W
Cambridge, Md., U.S.A.	112	38 33N	76 2W
Cambridge, Minn., U.S.A.	118	45 34N	93 15W
Cambridge, N.Y., U.S.A.	115	43 2N	73 22W
Cambridge, Nebr., U.S.A.	118	40 20N	100 12W
Cambridge, Ohio, U.S.A.	114	40 1N	81 35W
Cambridge Bay	100	69 10N	105 0W
Cambridge City	117	39 49N	85 10W
Cambridge Gulf	78	14 55 S	128 15 E
Cambridge Springs	114	41 47N	80 4W
Cambridgeshire □	13	52 12N	0 7 E
Cambrils	24	41 8N	1 3 E
Cambuci	139	21 35 S	41 55W
Camden, Austral.	76	34 1 S	150 43 E
Camden, Ala., U.S.A.	113	31 59N	87 15W
Camden, Ark., U.S.A.	119	33 40N	92 50W
Camden, Me., U.S.A.	103	44 14N	69 6W
Camden, N.J., U.S.A.	115	39 57N	75 7W
Camden, Ohio, U.S.A.	117	39 38N	84 39W
Camden, S.C., U.S.A.	113	34 17N	80 34W
Camden Sound	78	15 27 S	124 25 E
Camdenton, U.S.A.	116	38 1N	92 45W
Camdenton, U.S.A.	119	38 0N	92 45W
Camembert	18	48 53N	0 10 E
Cámeri	26	45 30N	8 40 E
Camerino	27	43 10N	13 4 E
Cameron, Ariz., U.S.A.	121	35 55N	111 31W
Cameron, La., U.S.A.	119	29 50N	93 18W
Cameron, Mo., U.S.A.	116	39 42N	94 14W
Cameron, Tex., U.S.A.	119	30 53N	97 0W
Cameron Falls	102	49 8N	88 19W
Cameron Highlands	55	4 27N	101 22 E
Cameron Hills	108	59 48N	118 0W
Cameron Mts.	81	46 1 S	167 0 E
Cameroon ■	92	6 0N	12 30 E
Camerota	29	40 2N	15 21 E
Cameroun →	89	4 0N	9 35 E
Cameroun, Mt.	92	4 13N	9 10 E
Cametá	138	2 12 S	49 30W
Camiguin	57	8 55N	123 55 E
Caminha	22	41 50N	8 50W
Camino	122	38 47N	120 40W
Camira Creek	77	29 15 S	152 58 E
Camiranga	138	1 48 S	46 17W
Camiri	137	20 3 S	63 31W
Cammal	114	41 24N	77 28W
Camoa Mts.	135	1 30N	59 0W
Camocim	138	2 55 S	40 50W
Camogli	26	44 21N	9 9 E
Camooweal	72	19 56 S	138 7 E
Camopi	135	3 12N	52 17W
Camopi →	135	3 10N	52 20W
Camp Borden	106	44 18N	79 56W
Camp Crook	118	45 36N	103 59W
Camp Nelson	123	36 8N	118 39W
Camp Point	116	40 3N	91 4W
Camp Wood	119	29 41N	100 0W
Campagna	29	40 40N	15 5 E
Campana	140	34 10 S	58 55W
Campana, I.	142	48 20 S	75 20W
Campanario	23	38 52N	5 36W
Campania □	29	40 50N	14 45 E
Campbell, Calif., U.S.A.	122	37 17N	121 57W
Campbell, Ohio, U.S.A.	114	41 5N	80 36W
Campbell, C.	81	41 47 S	174 18 E
Campbell I.	66	52 30 S	169 0 E
Campbell L.	109	63 14N	106 55W
Campbell River	108	50 5N	125 20W
Campbell Town	72	41 52 S	147 30 E
Campbellford	107	44 18N	77 48W
Campbellpur	48	33 46N	72 26 E
Campbell's Bay	104	45 44N	76 36W
Campbellsburg	117	38 39N	86 16W
Campbellsville	112	37 23N	85 21W
Campbellton	103	47 57N	66 43W
Campbelltown	76	34 4 S	150 49 E
Campbeltown	14	55 25N	5 36W
Campeche	125	19 50N	90 32W
Campeche □	125	19 50N	90 32W
Campeche, Bahía de	125	19 30N	93 0W
Camperdown	74	38 14 S	143 9 E
Camperville	109	51 59N	100 9W
Campi Salentina	29	40 22N	18 2 E
Campidano	28	39 30N	8 40 E
Campillo de Altobuey	24	39 36N	1 49W
Campillo de Llerena	23	38 30N	5 50W
Campillos	23	37 4N	4 51W
Campina Grande	138	7 20 S	35 47W
Campiña, La	23	37 45N	4 45W
Campina Verde	139	19 31 S	49 28W
Campinas	141	22 50 S	47 0W
Campli	27	42 44N	13 40 E
Campo, Camer.	92	2 22N	9 50 E
Campo, Spain	24	42 25N	0 24 E
Campo Belo	139	20 52 S	45 16W
Campo de Criptana	25	39 24N	3 7W
Campo de Diauarum	137	11 12 S	53 14W
Campo de Gibraltar	23	36 15N	5 25W
Campo Flórido	139	19 47 S	48 35W
Campo Formoso	138	10 30 S	40 20W
Campo Grande	137	20 25 S	54 40W
Campo Maíor	138	4 50 S	42 12W
Campo Maior	23	38 59N	7 7W
Campo Mourão	139	24 3 S	52 22W
Campo Túres	27	46 53N	11 55 E
Campoalegre	134	2 41N	75 20W
Campobasso	29	41 34N	14 40 E
Campobello di Licata	28	37 16N	13 55 E
Campobello di Mazara	28	37 38N	12 45 E
Campofelice	28	37 54N	13 53 E
Camporeale	28	37 53N	13 3 E
Campos	139	21 50 S	41 20W
Campos Altos	139	19 47 S	46 10W

Campos Belos 139 13 10 S 47 3W
Campos del Puerto 25 39 26N 3 1 E
Campos Novos 141 27 21 S 51 50W
Campos Sales 138 7 4 S 40 23W
Camprodón 24 42 19N 2 23 E
Campton 117 37 44N 83 33W
Camptonville 122 39 27N 121 3W
Campuya → 134 1 40 S 73 30W
Camrose 108 53 0N 112 50W
Camsell Portage 109 59 37N 109 15W
Can Gio 55 10 25N 106 58 E
Can Tho 55 10 2N 105 46 E
Canaan 115 42 1N 73 20W
Canada ■ 100 60 0N 100 0W
Cañada de Gómez 140 32 40 S 61 30W
Canadian 119 35 56N 100 25W
Canadian → 119 35 27N 95 3W
Canakkale 46 40 8N 26 30 E
Canakkale Boğazi 46 40 0N 26 0 E
Canal Flats 108 50 10N 115 48W
Canal latéral à la Garonne 20 44 25N 0 15 E
Canala 68 21 32 S 165 57 E
Canalejas 140 35 15 S 66 34W
Canals, Argent. 140 33 35 S 62 53W
Canals, Spain 25 38 58N 0 35W
Canandaigua 114 42 55N 77 18W
Cananea 124 31 0N 110 20W
Cañar 134 2 33 S 78 56W
Cañar □ 134 2 30 S 79 0W
Canarias, Islas 84 29 30N 17 0W
Canarreos, Arch. de los 126 21 35N 81 40W
Canary Is. = Canarias, Islas 84 29 30N 17 0W
Canastra, Serra da 139 20 0 S 46 20W
Canatlán 124 24 31N 104 47W
Canaveral, C. 113 28 28N 80 31W
Cañaveras 24 40 27N 2 24W
Canavieiras 139 15 39 S 39 0W
Canbelego 73 31 32 S 146 18 E
Canberra 76 35 15 S 149 8 E
Canby, Calif., U.S.A. 120 41 26N 120 58W
Canby, Minn., U.S.A. 118 44 44N 96 15W
Canby, Ore., U.S.A. 122 45 16N 122 42W
Cancale 18 48 40N 1 50W
Canche → 19 50 31N 1 39 E
Canchyuaya, Cordillera de 136 7 30 S 74 0W
Candala 45 11 30N 49 58 E
Candarave 136 17 15 S 70 13W
Candas 22 43 35N 5 45W
Candé 18 47 34N 1 0W
Candeias → 137 8 39 S 63 31W
Candela 29 41 8N 15 31 E
Candelaria 141 27 29 S 55 44W
Candelaria, Pta. de la 22 43 45N 8 0W
Candeleda 22 40 10N 5 14W
Candelo 75 36 47 S 149 43 E
Candia = Iráklion 35 35 20N 25 12 E
Cândido de Abreu 139 24 35 S 51 20W
Cândido Mendes 138 1 27 S 45 43W
Candle L. 109 53 50N 105 18W
Candlemas I. 143 57 3 S 26 40W
Cando 118 48 30N 99 14W
Canea = Khaniá 35 35 30N 24 4 E
Canela 138 10 15 S 48 25W
Canelli 26 44 44N 8 18 E
Canelones 141 34 32 S 56 17W
Canet-Plage 20 42 41N 3 2 E
Cañete, Chile 140 37 50 S 73 30W
Cañete, Peru 136 13 8 S 76 30W
Cañete, Spain 24 40 3N 1 54W
Cañete de las Torres 23 37 53N 4 19W
Canfranc 24 42 42N 0 31W
Cangai 77 29 30 S 152 30 E
Cangamba 93 13 40 S 19 54 E
Cangas 22 42 16N 8 47W
Cangas de Narcea 22 43 10N 6 32W
Cangas de Onís 22 43 21N 5 8W
Canguaretama 138 6 20 S 35 5W
Canguçu 141 31 22 S 52 43W
Cangxi 58 31 47N 105 59 E
Cangyuan 58 23 12N 99 14 E
Cangzhou 60 38 19N 116 52 E
Cani, Is. 87 36 21N 10 5 E
Canicattì 28 37 21N 13 50 E
Canicattini 29 37 1N 15 3 E
Canim Lake 108 51 47N 120 54W
Canindé 138 4 22 S 39 19W
Canindé → 138 6 15 S 42 52W
Canipaan 56 8 33N 117 15 E
Canisteo 114 42 17N 77 37W
Canisteo → 114 42 15N 77 30W
Cañitas 124 23 36N 102 43W
Cañiza, La 22 42 13N 8 16W
Cañizal 22 41 12N 5 22W
Canjáyar 25 37 1N 2 44W
Cankırı 46 40 40N 33 37 E
Cankuzo 94 3 10 S 30 31 E
Canmore 108 51 7N 115 18W
Cann → 75 37 44 S 149 7 E
Cann River 75 37 35 S 149 7 E
Canna I. 14 57 3N 6 33W
Cannanore 51 11 53N 75 27 E
Cannelton 117 37 55N 86 45W
Cannes 21 43 32N 7 0 E
Canning Creek 77 28 10 S 151 12 E
Canning Town 49 22 23N 88 40 E
Cannington 107 44 20N 79 2W
Cannock 12 52 42N 2 2W
Cannon Ball → 118 46 20N 100 38W
Cannondale, Mt. 72 25 13 S 148 57 E
Caño Colorado 134 2 18N 68 22W
Canoe L. 109 55 10N 108 15W
Canon City 118 38 27N 105 14W
Canora 109 51 40N 102 30W
Canosa di Púglia 29 41 13N 16 4 E
Canourgue, Le 20 44 26N 3 13 E
Canowindra 76 33 35 S 148 38 E
Canso 103 45 20N 61 0W
Canta 136 11 29 S 76 37W
Cantabria, Sierra de 24 42 40N 2 30W
Cantabrian Mts. = Cantábrica 22 43 0N 5 10W
Cantábrica, Cordillera 22 43 0N 5 10W
Cantal □ 20 45 4N 2 45 E
Cantanhede 22 40 20N 8 36W
Cantaura 135 9 19N 64 21W
Cantavieja 24 40 31N 0 25W
Canterbury, Austral. 72 25 23 S 141 53 E
Canterbury, U.K. 13 51 17N 1 5 E
Canterbury □ 81 43 45 S 171 19 E
Canterbury Bight 81 44 16 S 171 55 E
Canterbury Plains 81 43 55 S 171 22 E
Cantil 123 35 18N 117 58W
Cantillana 23 37 36N 5 50W
Canto do Buriti 138 8 7 S 42 58W
Canton, Ga., U.S.A. 113 34 13N 84 29W
Canton, Ill., U.S.A. 116 40 32N 90 0W
Canton, Mass., U.S.A. 115 42 8N 71 8W
Canton, Miss., U.S.A. 119 32 40N 90 1W
Canton, Mo., U.S.A. 116 40 10N 91 33W
Canton, N.Y., U.S.A. 115 44 32N 75 3W
Canton, Ohio, U.S.A. 114 40 47N 81 22W
Canton, Okla., U.S.A. 119 36 5N 98 36W
Canton, S.D., U.S.A. 118 43 20N 96 35W
Canton = Guangzhou 59 23 5N 113 10 E
Canton I. 66 2 50 S 171 40W
Canton L. 119 36 12N 98 40W
Cantù 26 45 44N 9 8 E
Canudos 137 7 13 S 58 5W
Canumã, Amazonas, Brazil 135 4 2 S 59 4W
Canumã, Amazonas, Brazil 137 6 8 S 60 10W
Canumã → 137 3 55 S 59 10W
Canutama 137 6 30 S 64 20W
Canutillo 121 31 58N 106 36W
Canyon, Texas, U.S.A. 119 35 0N 101 57W
Canyon, Wyo., U.S.A. 120 44 43N 110 36W
Canyonlands Nat. Park 121 38 25N 109 30W
Canyonville 120 42 55N 123 14W
Canzo 26 45 54N 9 18 E
Cao Bang 54 22 40N 106 15 E
Cao He → 61 40 10N 124 32 E
Cao Lanh 55 10 27N 105 38 E
Cao Xian 60 34 50N 115 35 E
Cáorle 27 45 36N 12 51 E
Cap-aux-Meules 103 47 23N 61 52W
Cap-Chat 103 49 6N 66 40W
Cap-de-la-Madeleine 105 46 22N 72 31W
Cap-Haïtien 127 19 40N 72 20W
Cap-St-Ignace 105 47 2N 70 28W
Cap St.-Jacques = Vung Tau 55 10 21N 107 4 E
Capa 54 22 21N 103 50 E
Capa Stilo 29 38 25N 16 35 E
Capac 106 43 1N 82 56W
Capáccio 29 40 26N 15 4 E
Capaia 92 8 27 S 20 13 E
Capanaparo → 134 7 1N 67 7W
Capanema 138 1 12 S 47 11W
Caparo →, Barinas, Venez. 134 7 46N 70 23W
Caparo →, Bolívar, Venez. 135 7 30N 64 0W
Capatárida 134 11 11N 70 37W
Capbreton 20 43 39N 1 26W
Capdenac 20 44 34N 2 5 E
Cape → 72 20 49 S 146 51 E
Cape Barren I. 72 40 25 S 148 15 E
Cape Breton Highlands Nat. Park 103 46 50N 60 40W
Cape Breton I. 103 46 0N 60 30W
Cape Charles 112 37 15N 75 59W
Cape Clear 74 37 47 S 143 36 E
Cape Coast 89 5 5N 1 15W
Cape Dorset 101 64 14N 76 32W
Cape Dyer 101 66 30N 61 22W
Cape Fear → 113 34 30N 78 25W
Cape Girardeau 119 37 20N 89 30W
Cape Jervis 73 35 40 S 138 5 E
Cape May 112 39 1N 74 53W
Cape Montague 103 46 5N 62 25W
Cape Palmas 88 4 25N 7 49W
Cape Preston 78 20 51 S 116 12 E
Cape Province □ 96 32 0 S 23 0 E
Cape Tormentine 103 46 8N 63 47W
Cape Town (Kaapstad) 96 33 55 S 18 22 E
Cape Verde Is. 128 17 10N 25 20W
Cape Vincent 115 44 9N 76 21W
Cape York Peninsula 72 12 0 S 142 30 E
Capela 138 10 30 S 37 0W
Capela de Campo 138 4 40 S 41 55W
Capelinha 139 17 42 S 42 31W
Capella 72 23 2 S 148 1 E
Capella, Mt. 69 5 4 S 141 8 E
Capelle, La 19 49 59N 3 50 E
Capendu 20 43 11N 2 31 E
Capernaum = Kefar Nahum 44 32 54N 35 32 E
Capertree 76 33 6 S 149 58 E
Capestang 20 43 20N 3 2 E
Capim 138 1 41 S 47 47W
Capim → 138 1 40 S 47 47W
Capinópolis 139 18 41 S 49 35W
Capinota 136 17 43 S 66 14W
Capitachouane → 104 47 40N 76 47W
Capitan 121 33 33N 105 41W
Capitán Aracena, I. 142 54 10 S 71 20W
Capitán Pastene 142 38 13 S 73 1W
Capitola 122 36 59N 121 57W
Capivara, Serra da 139 14 35 S 45 0W
Capizzi 29 37 50N 14 26 E
Čapljina 33 43 10N 17 43 E
Capoche → 95 15 35 S 33 0 E
Capoeira 137 5 37 S 59 33W
Capraia 26 43 2N 9 50 E
Caprarola 27 42 21N 12 11 E
Capreol 106 46 43N 80 56W
Caprera 28 41 12N 9 28 E
Capri 29 40 34N 14 15 E
Capricorn Group 72 23 30 S 151 55 E
Capricorn Ra. 78 23 20 S 116 50 E
Caprino Veronese 26 45 37N 10 47 E
Caprivi Strip 96 18 0 S 23 0 E
Captainganj 49 26 55N 83 45 E
Captain's Flat 76 35 35 S 149 27 E
Captieux 20 44 18N 0 16W
Cápua 29 41 7N 14 15 E
Capulin 119 36 48N 103 59W
Caquetá □ 134 1 0N 74 0W
Caquetá → 134 1 15 S 69 15W
Carabobo 134 10 2N 68 5W
Carabobo □ 134 10 10N 68 5W
Carabost 76 35 35 S 147 43 E
Caracal 34 44 8N 24 22 E
Caracaraí 135 1 50N 61 8W
Caracas 134 10 30N 66 55W
Caracol 138 9 15 S 43 22W
Caracollo 136 17 39 S 67 10W
Caradoc 73 30 35 S 143 5 E
Caragabal 76 33 49 S 147 45 E
Caráglio 26 44 25N 7 25 E
Carahue 142 38 43 S 73 12W
Caraí 139 17 12 S 41 42W
Carajás, Serra dos 138 6 0 S 51 30W
Caramut 74 37 56 S 142 31 E
Caranapatuba 137 6 38 S 62 34W
Carandaiti 137 20 45 S 63 4W
Carangola 139 20 44 S 42 5W
Carani 79 30 57 S 116 28 E
Caransebeş 34 45 28N 22 18 E
Carantec 18 48 40N 3 55W
Caraparaná → 134 1 45 S 73 13W
Carapelle → 29 41 3N 15 55 E
Caras 136 9 3 S 77 47W
Caratasca, Laguna 126 15 20N 83 40W
Caratinga 139 19 50 S 42 10W
Caraúbas 138 5 43 S 37 33W
Caravaca 25 38 8N 1 52W
Caravággio 26 45 30N 9 39 E
Caravelas 139 17 45 S 39 15W
Caraveli 136 15 45 S 73 25W
Caràzinho 141 28 16 S 52 46W
Carballino 22 42 26N 8 5W
Carballo 22 43 13N 8 41W
Carberry 109 49 50N 99 25W
Carbia 22 42 48N 8 14W
Carbó 124 29 42N 110 58W
Carbon 108 51 30N 113 9W
Carbonara, C. 28 39 8N 9 30 E
Carbondale, Colo, U.S.A. 120 39 30N 107 10W
Carbondale, Ill., U.S.A. 116 37 45N 89 10W
Carbondale, Pa., U.S.A. 115 41 37N 75 30W
Carbonear 103 47 42N 53 13W
Carboneras 25 37 0N 1 53W
Carboneras de Guadazaón 24 39 54N 1 50W
Carbonia 28 39 10N 8 30 E
Carcabuey 23 37 27N 4 17W
Carcagente 25 39 8N 0 28W
Carcajou 108 57 47N 117 6W
Carcans, Étang d' 20 45 6N 1 7W
Carcasse, C. 127 18 30N 74 28W
Carcassonne 20 43 13N 2 20 E
Carche 25 38 26N 1 9W
Carchi □ 134 0 45N 78 0W
Carcoar 76 33 36 S 149 8 E
Carcross 100 60 13N 134 45W
Cardabia 78 23 2 S 113 48 E
Cardamom Hills 51 9 30N 77 15 E
Cárdenas, Cuba 126 23 0N 81 30W
Cárdenas, San Luis Potosí, Mexico 125 22 0N 99 41W
Cárdenas, Tabasco, Mexico 125 17 59N 93 21W
Cardenete 24 39 46N 1 41W
Cardiel, L. 142 48 55 S 71 10W
Cardiff 13 51 28N 3 11W
Cardiff-by-the-Sea 123 33 1N 117 17W
Cardigan 13 52 6N 4 41W
Cardigan B. 13 52 30N 4 30W
Cardinal 107 44 47N 75 23W
Cardón, Punta 134 11 37N 70 14W
Cardona, Spain 24 41 56N 1 40 E
Cardona, Uruguay 140 33 53 S 57 18W
Cardoner → 24 41 41N 1 51 E
Cardross 109 49 50N 105 40W
Cardston 108 49 15N 113 20W
Cardwell 72 18 14 S 146 2 E
Careen L. 109 57 0N 108 11W
Carei 34 47 40N 22 29 E
Careiro 135 3 12 S 59 45W
Careme 57 6 55 S 108 27 E
Carentan 18 49 19N 1 15W
Carey, Idaho, U.S.A. 120 43 19N 113 58W
Carey, Ohio, U.S.A. 117 40 58N 83 22W
Carey, L. 79 29 0 S 122 15 E
Carey L. 109 62 12N 102 55W
Careysburg 88 6 34N 10 30W
Cargados Garajos, Is. 53 17 0 S 59 0 E
Cargèse 21 42 7N 8 35 E
Cargo 76 33 25 S 148 48 E
Carhaix-Plouguer 18 48 18N 3 36W
Carhuamayo 136 10 51 S 76 4W
Carhuas 136 9 15 S 77 39W
Carhué 140 37 10 S 62 50W
Caribbean Sea 127 15 0N 75 0W
Cariboo Mts. 108 53 0N 121 0W
Caribou 103 46 55N 68 0W
Caribou →, Man., Can. 109 59 20N 94 44W
Caribou →, N.W.T., Can. 108 61 27N 125 45W
Caribou I. 102 47 22N 85 49W
Caribou Is. 108 61 55N 113 15W
Caribou L., Man., Can. 109 59 21N 96 10W
Caribou L., Ont., Can. 102 50 25N 89 5W
Caribou Mts. 108 59 12N 115 40W
Carichic 124 27 56N 107 3W
Carignan 19 49 38N 5 10 E
Carignano 26 44 55N 7 40 E
Carillo 124 26 50N 103 55W
Carinda 73 30 28 S 147 41 E
Cariñena 24 41 20N 1 13W
Carinhanha 139 14 15 S 44 46W
Carinhanha → 139 14 20 S 43 47W
Carini 28 38 9N 13 10 E
Carinola 28 41 11N 13 58 E
Caripito 135 10 8N 63 6W
Carisbrook 74 37 3 S 143 49 E
Caritianas 137 9 20 S 63 6W
Carlentini 29 37 15N 15 2 E
Carleton Place 107 45 8N 76 9W
Carletonville 96 26 23 S 27 22 E
Carlin 120 40 44N 116 5W
Carlingford, L. 15 54 0N 6 5W
Carlinville 116 39 20N 89 55W
Carlisle, U.K. 12 54 54N 2 55W
Carlisle, Ky., U.S.A. 117 38 18N 84 1W
Carlisle, Pa., U.S.A. 114 40 12N 77 10W
Carlitte, Pic 20 42 35N 1 55 E
Carloforte 28 39 10N 8 18 E
Carlos Casares 140 35 32 S 61 20W
Carlos Chagas 139 17 43 S 40 45W
Carlos Tejedor 140 35 25 S 62 25W
Carlota, La 140 33 30 S 63 20W
Carlow 15 52 50N 6 58W
Carlow □ 15 52 43N 6 50W
Carlsbad, Calif., U.S.A. 123 33 11N 117 25W
Carlsbad, N. Mex., U.S.A. 119 32 20N 104 14W
Carlsruhe 74 37 16 S 144 30 E
Carlyle, Can. 109 49 40N 102 20W
Carlyle, U.S.A. 118 38 38N 89 23W
Carlyle Resr. 116 38 37N 89 21W

Carmacks 100 62 5N 136 16W
Carmagnola 26 44 50N 7 42 E
Carman 109 49 30N 98 0W
Carmangay 108 50 10N 113 10W
Carmanville 103 49 23N 54 19W
Carmarthen 13 51 52N 4 20W
Carmarthen B. 13 51 40N 4 30W
Carmaux 20 44 3N 2 10 E
Carmel, Ind., U.S.A. 117 39 59N 86 8W
Carmel, N.Y., U.S.A. 115 41 25N 73 38W
Carmel-by-the-Sea 122 36 38N 121 55W
Carmel Mt. 44 32 45N 35 3 E
Carmel Valley 122 36 29N 121 43W
Carmelo 140 34 0S 58 20W
Carmen, Boliv. 136 11 40S 67 51W
Carmen, Colomb. 134 9 43N 75 8W
Carmen, Parag. 141 27 13S 56 12W
Carmen → 124 30 42N 106 29W
Carmen de Patagones 142 40 50S 63 0W
Carmen, I. 124 26 0N 111 20W
Cármenes 22 42 58N 5 34W
Carmensa 140 35 15S 67 40W
Carmi 117 38 6N 88 10W
Carmichael 122 38 38N 121 19W
Carmila 72 21 55S 149 24 E
Carmona 23 37 28N 5 42W
Carnarvon, Queens., Austral. 72 24 48S 147 45 E
Carnarvon, W. Austral., Austral. 79 24 51S 113 42 E
Carnarvon, S. Afr. 96 30 56S 22 8 E
Carnarvon Ra., Queensland, Austral. 72 25 15S 148 30 E
Carnarvon Ra., W.A., Austral. 79 25 0S 120 45 E
Carnation 122 47 39N 121 55W
Carnaxide 23 38 43N 9 14W
Carndonagh 15 55 15N 7 16W
Carnduff 109 49 10N 101 50W
Carnegie 114 40 24N 80 4W
Carnegie, L. 79 26 5S 122 30 E
Carnot 92 4 59N 15 56 E
Carnot B. 78 17 20S 121 30 E
Carnsore Pt. 15 52 10N 6 20W
Caro 106 43 29N 83 27W
Caroda 77 29 59S 150 22 E
Carol City 113 25 5N 80 16W
Carolina, Brazil 138 7 10S 47 30W
Carolina, S. Afr. 97 26 5S 30 6 E
Carolina, La 23 38 17N 3 38W
Caroline I. 67 9 15S 150 3W
Caroline Is. 66 8 0N 150 0 E
Caroline Pk. 81 45 57S 167 15 E
Caron 109 50 30N 105 50W
Caroni → 135 8 21N 62 43W
Caroona 77 31 24S 150 26 E
Carora 134 10 11N 70 5W
Carovigno 29 40 42N 17 40 E
Carpathians 32 49 50N 21 0 E
Carpaţii Meridionali 34 45 30N 25 0 E
Carpenédolo 26 45 22N 10 25 E
Carpentaria Downs 72 18 44S 144 20 E
Carpentaria, G. of 72 14 0S 139 0 E
Carpentersville 117 42 6N 88 17W
Carpentras 21 44 3N 5 2 E
Carpi 26 44 47N 10 52 E
Carpina 138 7 51S 35 15W
Carpino 29 41 50N 15 51 E
Carpinteria 123 34 25N 119 31W
Carpio 22 41 13N 5 7W
Carpolac = Morea 74 36 45S 141 18 E
Carr Boyd Ra. 78 16 15S 128 35 E
Carrabelle 113 29 52N 84 40W
Carrajung 75 38 22S 146 44 E
Carrara 26 44 5N 10 7 E
Carrascosa del Campo 24 40 2N 2 45W
Carrauntohill, Mt. 15 52 0N 9 49W
Carretas, Punta 136 14 12S 76 17W
Carrick-on-Shannon 15 53 57N 8 7W
Carrick-on-Suir 15 52 22N 7 30W
Carrickfergus 15 54 43N 5 50W
Carrickfergus □ 15 54 43N 5 49W
Carrickmacross 15 54 0N 6 43W
Carrieton 73 32 25S 138 31 E
Carrington 118 47 30N 99 7W
Carrión → 22 41 53N 4 32W
Carrión de los Condes 22 42 20N 4 37W
Carrizal Bajo 140 28 5S 71 20W
Carrizalillo 140 29 5S 71 30W
Carrizo Cr. → 119 36 30N 103 40W
Carrizo Springs 119 28 28N 99 50W
Carrizozo 121 33 40N 105 57W
Carroll, Austral. 77 30 58S 150 27 E
Carroll, U.S.A. 116 42 2N 94 55W
Carrollton, Ga., U.S.A. 113 33 36N 85 5W
Carrollton, Ill., U.S.A. 118 39 20N 90 25W
Carrollton, Ky., U.S.A. 117 38 40N 85 10W
Carrollton, Mo., U.S.A. 116 39 19N 93 24W
Carrollton, Ohio, U.S.A. 114 40 31N 81 9W
Carron → 14 57 30N 5 30W
Carron, L. 14 57 22N 5 35W
Carrot → 109 53 50N 101 17W
Carrot River 109 53 17N 103 35W
Carrouges 18 48 34N 0 10W
Carruthers 109 52 52N 109 16W
Çarşamba 46 41 15N 36 45 E
Carse of Gowrie 14 56 30N 3 10W
Carsoli 27 42 7N 13 3 E
Carson 118 46 27N 101 29W
Carson → 122 39 45N 118 40W
Carson City, Mich., U.S.A. 106 43 11N 84 51W
Carson City, Nev., U.S.A. 122 39 12N 119 46W
Carson Sink 120 39 50N 118 40W
Carsonville 112 43 25N 82 39W
Carstairs 14 55 42N 3 41W
Cartagena, Colomb. 134 10 25N 75 33W
Cartagena, Spain 25 37 38N 0 59W
Cartago, Colomb. 134 4 45N 75 55W
Cartago, C. Rica 126 9 50N 85 52W
Cartaxo 23 39 10N 8 47W
Cartaya 23 37 16N 7 9W
Carteret 18 49 23N 1 47W
Cartersville 113 34 11N 84 48W
Carterton 80 41 2S 175 31 E
Carterville 116 37 46N 89 5W
Carthage, Ark., U.S.A. 119 34 4N 92 32W
Carthage, Ill., U.S.A. 116 40 25N 91 10W
Carthage, Mo., U.S.A. 119 37 10N 94 20W
Carthage, N.Y., U.S.A. 115 43 59N 75 37W
Carthage, S.D., U.S.A. 118 44 14N 97 38W
Carthage, Texas, U.S.A. 119 32 8N 94 20W
Cartier 106 46 42N 81 33W
Cartier I. 78 12 31S 123 29 E
Cartwright 103 53 41N 56 58W
Caruaru 138 8 15S 35 55W
Carúpano 135 10 39N 63 15W
Carutapera 138 1 13S 46 1W
Caruthersville 119 36 10N 89 40W
Carvalho 135 2 16S 51 29W
Carvin 19 50 30N 2 57 E
Carvoeiro 135 1 30S 61 59W
Carvoeiro, Cabo 23 39 21N 9 24W
Carwarp 74 34 28S 142 11 E
Casa Branca, Brazil 139 21 46S 47 4W
Casa Branca, Port. 23 38 29N 8 12W
Casa Grande 121 32 53N 111 51W
Casa Nova 138 9 25S 41 5W
Casablanca, Chile 140 33 20S 71 25W
Casablanca, Moroc. 86 33 36N 7 36W
Casacalenda 29 41 45N 14 50 E
Casal di Principe 29 41 0N 14 8 E
Casalbordino 27 42 10N 14 34 E
Casale Monferrato 26 45 8N 8 28 E
Casalmaggiore 26 44 59N 10 25 E
Casalpusterlengo 26 45 10N 9 40 E
Casamance → 88 12 33N 16 46W
Casamássima 29 40 58N 16 55 E
Casanare → 134 6 2N 69 51W
Casarano 29 40 0N 18 10 E
Casares 23 36 27N 5 16W
Casas Grandes 124 30 22N 108 0W
Casas Ibañez 25 39 17N 1 30W
Casasimarro 25 39 22N 2 3W
Casatejada 22 39 54N 5 40W
Casavieja 22 40 17N 4 46W
Cascade, Idaho, U.S.A. 120 44 30N 116 2W
Cascade, Iowa, U.S.A. 116 42 18N 91 1W
Cascade, Mont., U.S.A. 120 47 16N 111 46W
Cascade → 77 30 15S 152 48 E
Cascade Locks 122 45 44N 121 54W
Cascade Pt. 81 44 1S 168 20 E
Cascade Ra. 122 47 0N 121 30W
Cascais 23 38 41N 9 25W
Cáscina 26 43 40N 10 32 E
Caselle Torinese 26 45 12N 7 39 E
Caserta 29 41 5N 14 20 E
Caseville 106 43 56N 83 16W
Casey 105 47 53N 74 11W
Cashel 15 52 31N 7 53W
Cashmere 120 47 31N 120 30W
Cashmere Downs 79 28 57S 119 35 E
Casibare → 134 3 48N 72 18W
Casiguran 57 16 22N 122 7 E
Casilda 140 33 10S 61 10W
Casino 77 28 52S 153 3 E
Casiquiare → 134 2 1N 67 7W
Casitas 136 3 54S 80 39W
Caslan 108 54 38N 112 31W
Čáslav 32 49 54N 15 22 E
Casma 136 9 30S 78 20W
Casmalia 123 34 50N 120 32W
Casola Valsenio 27 44 12N 11 40 E
Cásoli 27 42 7N 14 18 E
Caspe 24 41 14N 0 1W
Casper 120 42 52N 106 20W
Caspian Sea 40 43 0N 50 0 E
Casquets 18 49 46N 2 15W
Cass → 106 43 23N 83 59W
Cass City 106 43 34N 83 24W
Cass Lake 118 47 23N 94 38W
Cassá de la Selva 24 41 53N 2 52 E
Cassano Iónio 29 39 47N 16 20 E
Cassel 19 50 48N 2 30 E
Casselman 107 45 19N 75 5W
Casselton 118 47 0N 97 15W
Cassiar 108 59 16N 129 40W
Cassiar Mts. 108 59 30N 130 30W
Cassilândia 137 19 9S 51 45W
Cassilis 77 32 3S 149 58 E
Cassinga 93 15 5S 16 4 E
Cassino 28 41 30N 13 50 E
Cassis 21 43 14N 5 32 E
Cassopolis 117 41 55N 86 1W
Cassville, Mo., U.S.A. 119 36 45N 93 52W
Cassville, Wisc., U.S.A. 116 42 43N 90 59W
Cástagneto Carducci 26 43 9N 10 36 E
Castaic 123 34 30N 118 38W
Castanhal 138 1 18S 47 55W
Castéggio 26 45 1N 9 8 E
Castejón de Monegros 24 41 37N 0 15W
Castel di Sangro 27 41 47N 14 6 E
Castel San Giovanni 26 45 4N 9 25 E
Castel San Pietro 27 44 23N 11 30 E
Castelbuono 29 37 56N 14 4 E
Casteldelfino 26 44 35N 7 4 E
Castelfiorentino 26 43 36N 10 58 E
Castelfranco Emília 26 44 37N 11 2 E
Castelfranco Véneto 27 45 40N 11 56 E
Casteljaloux 20 44 19N 0 6 E
Castellabate 29 40 18N 14 55 E
Castellammare del Golfo 28 38 2N 12 53 E
Castellammare di Stábia 29 40 47N 14 29 E
Castellammare, G. di 28 38 5N 12 55 E
Castellamonte 26 45 23N 7 42 E
Castellana Grotte 29 40 53N 17 10 E
Castellane 21 43 50N 6 31 E
Castellaneta 29 40 40N 16 57 E
Castellar de Santisteban 25 38 16N 3 8W
Castelleone 26 45 19N 9 47 E
Castelli 140 36 7S 57 47W
Castelló de Ampurias 24 42 15N 3 4 E
Castellón □ 24 40 15N 0 5W
Castellón de la Plana 24 39 58N 0 3W
Castellote 24 40 48N 0 15W
Castelltersol 24 41 45N 2 8 E
Castelmáuro 29 41 50N 14 40 E
Castelnau-de-Médoc 20 45 2N 0 48W
Castelnaudary 20 43 20N 1 58 E
Castelnovo ne' Monti 26 44 27N 10 26 E
Castelnuovo di Val di Cécina 26 43 12N 10 54 E
Castelo 139 20 33S 41 14 E
Castelo Branco 22 39 50N 7 31W
Castelo Branco □ 22 39 52N 7 45W
Castelo de Paiva 22 41 2N 8 16W
Castelo de Vide 23 39 25N 7 27W
Castelo do Piauí 138 5 20S 41 33W
Castelsarrasin 20 44 2N 1 7 E
Casteltérmini 28 37 32N 13 38 E
Castelvetrano 28 37 40N 12 46 E
Casterton 74 37 30S 141 30 E
Castets 20 43 52N 1 6W
Castiglione del Lago 27 43 7N 12 3 E
Castiglione della Pescáia 26 42 46N 10 53 E
Castiglione della Stiviere 26 45 23N 10 30 E
Castiglione Fiorentino 27 43 20N 11 55 E
Castilblanco 23 39 17N 5 5W
Castilla 136 5 12S 80 38W
Castilla La Nueva 23 39 45N 3 20W
Castilla La Vieja 22 41 55N 4 0W
Castilla, Playa de 23 37 0N 6 33W
Castille = Castilla 22 40 0N 3 30W
Castillón 124 28 20N 103 38W
Castillon, Barrage de 21 43 53N 6 33 E
Castillon-en-Couserans 20 42 56N 1 1 E
Castillon-la-Bataille 20 44 51N 0 2W
Castillonès 20 44 39N 0 37 E
Castillos 141 34 12S 53 52W
Castle Dale 120 39 11N 111 1W
Castle Douglas 14 54 57N 3 57W
Castle Point 80 40 54S 176 15 E
Castle Rock, Colo., U.S.A. 118 39 26N 104 50W
Castle Rock, Wash., U.S.A. 122 46 20N 122 58W
Castlebar 15 53 52N 9 17W
Castleblaney 15 54 7N 6 44W
Castlecliff 80 39 57S 174 59 E
Castlegar 108 49 20N 117 40W
Castlegate 120 39 45N 110 57W
Castlemaine 74 37 2S 144 12 E
Castlereagh 15 53 47N 8 30W
Castlereagh □ 15 54 33N 5 53W
Castlereagh → 73 30 12S 147 32 E
Castlereagh B. 72 12 10S 135 10 E
Castletown 12 54 4N 4 40W
Castletown Bearhaven 15 51 40N 9 54W
Castlevale 72 24 30S 146 48 E
Castor 108 52 15N 111 50W
Castres 20 43 37N 2 13 E
Castries 127 14 0N 60 50W
Castril 25 37 48N 2 46W
Castro, Brazil 141 24 45S 50 0W
Castro, Chile 142 42 30S 73 50W
Castro Alves 139 12 46S 39 33W
Castro del Río 23 37 41N 4 29W
Castro Marim 23 37 13N 7 26W
Castro Urdiales 24 43 23N 3 11W
Castro Verde 23 37 41N 8 4W
Castrojeriz 22 42 17N 4 9W
Castropol 22 43 32N 7 0W
Castroreale 29 38 5N 15 15 E
Castrovillari 29 39 49N 16 11 E
Castroville, Calif., U.S.A. 122 36 46N 121 45W
Castroville, Tex., U.S.A. 119 29 20N 98 53W
Castrovirreyna 136 13 20S 75 18W
Castuera 23 38 43N 5 37W
Casummit Lake 102 51 29N 92 22W
Cat Ba ,Cao 54 20 50N 107 0 E
Cat I., Bahamas 127 24 30N 75 30W
Cat I., U.S.A. 119 30 15N 89 7W
Cat L. 102 51 40N 91 50W
Catacamas 126 14 54N 85 56W
Catacáos 136 5 20S 80 45W
Cataguases 139 21 23S 42 39W
Catahoula L. 119 31 30N 92 5W
Catalão 139 18 10S 47 57W
Catalina 103 48 31N 53 4W
Catalonia = Cataluña 24 41 40N 1 15 E
Cataluña 24 41 40N 1 15 E
Catamarca 140 28 30S 65 50W
Catamarca □ 140 27 0S 65 50W
Catanduanes 57 13 50N 124 20 E
Catanduva 141 21 5S 48 58W
Catánia 29 37 31N 15 4 E
Catánia, G. di 29 37 25N 15 8 E
Catanzaro 29 38 54N 16 38 E
Catarman 57 12 28N 124 35 E
Cateau, Le 19 50 6N 3 30 E
Cateel 57 7 47N 126 24 E
Catende 138 8 40S 35 43W
Cathcart, Austral. 75 36 52S 149 24 E
Cathcart, S. Afr. 96 32 18S 27 10 E
Cathkin 74 37 10S 145 38 E
Cathlamet 122 46 12N 123 23W
Cathundral 76 31 55S 147 51 E
Catio 88 11 17N 15 15W
Catismiña 135 4 5N 63 40W
Catita 138 9 31S 43 1W
Catlettsburg 112 38 23N 82 38W
Catlin 117 40 4N 87 42W
Catoche, C. 125 21 40N 87 8W
Catolé do Rocha 138 6 21S 37 45W
Catral 25 38 10N 0 47W
Catria, Mt. 27 43 28N 12 42 E
Catrimani 135 0 27N 61 41W
Catrimani → 135 0 28N 61 44W
Catskill 115 42 14N 73 52W
Catskill Mts. 115 42 15N 74 15W
Catt, Mt. 72 13 49S 134 23 E
Cattaraugus 114 42 22N 78 52W
Cattólica 27 43 58N 12 43 E
Cattólica Eraclea 28 37 27N 13 24 E
Catu 139 12 21S 38 23W
Catuala 96 16 25S 19 2 E
Catur 95 13 45S 35 30 E
Catwick Is. 55 10 0N 109 0 E
Cauca □ 134 2 30N 76 50W
Cauca → 134 8 54N 74 28W
Caucaia 138 3 40S 38 35W
Caucasia 134 8 0N 75 12W
Caucasus Mts. = Bolshoi Kavkas 39 42 50N 44 0 E
Caudebec-en-Caux 18 49 30N 0 42 E
Caudete 25 38 42N 1 2W
Caudry 19 50 7N 3 22 E
Caulnes 18 48 18N 2 10W
Caulónia 29 38 23N 16 25 E
Caungula 92 8 26S 18 38 E
Cauquenes 140 36 0S 72 22W
Caura → 135 7 38N 64 53W
Caurés → 135 1 21S 62 20W
Cauresi → 95 17 8S 33 0 E
Causapscal 103 48 19N 67 12W
Caussade 20 44 10N 1 33 E

Cauterets	20	42 52N	0 8W
Cautín □	142	39 0S	72 30W
Caux, Pays de	18	49 38N	0 35E
Cava dei Tirreni	29	40 42N	14 42E
Cávado →	22	41 32N	8 48W
Cavaillon	21	43 50N	5 2E
Cavalaire-sur-Mer	21	43 10N	6 33E
Cavalcante	139	13 48S	47 30W
Cavalerie, La	20	44 0N	3 10E
Cavalese	27	46 17N	11 29E
Cavalier	118	48 50N	97 39W
Cavalli Is.	80	35 0S	173 58E
Cavallo, Île de	21	41 22N	9 16E
Cavally →	88	4 22N	7 32W
Cavan	15	54 0N	7 22W
Cavan □	15	53 58N	7 10W
Cavárzere	27	45 8N	12 6E
Cave City	112	37 13N	85 57W
Cavenagh Range	79	26 12S	127 55E
Cavendish	74	37 31S	142 2E
Caviana, I.	138	0 10N	50 10W
Cavite	57	14 29N	120 55E
Cavour	26	44 47N	7 22E
Cavtat	33	42 35N	18 13E
Cawasachouane, L.	104	47 27N	77 45W
Cawndilla, L.	73	32 30S	142 15E
Cawnpore = Kanpur	49	26 28N	80 20E
Caxias	138	4 55S	43 20W
Caxias do Sul	141	29 10S	51 10W
Caxine, C.	86	35 56N	0 27W
Caxito	92	8 30S	13 30E
Cay Sal Bank	126	23 45N	80 0W
Cayambe	134	0 3N	78 8W
Cayambe, Vol.	134	0 2N	77 59W
Cayce	113	33 59N	81 10W
Cayenne	135	5 0N	52 18W
Cayenne □	135	4 0N	53 0W
Cayes, Les	127	18 15N	73 46W
Cayeux-sur-Mer	19	50 10N	1 30E
Caylus	20	44 15N	1 47E
Cayman Brac	126	19 43N	79 49W
Cayman Is.	126	19 40N	80 30W
Cayo	125	17 10N	89 0W
Cayo Romano	127	22 0N	78 0W
Cayuga, Can.	106	42 59N	79 50W
Cayuga, Ind., U.S.A.	117	39 57N	87 38W
Cayuga, N.Y., U.S.A.	115	42 54N	76 44W
Cayuga L.	115	42 45N	76 45W
Cazalla de la Sierra	23	37 56N	5 45W
Căzănești	34	44 36N	27 3E
Cazaux et de Sanguinet, Étang de	20	44 29N	1 10W
Cazères	20	43 13N	1 5E
Cazin	27	44 57N	15 57E
Čazma	27	45 45N	16 39E
Čazma →	27	45 35N	16 29E
Cazombo	93	11 54S	22 56E
Cazorla, Spain	25	37 55N	3 2W
Cazorla, Venez.	134	8 1N	67 0W
Cazorla, Sierra de	25	38 5N	2 55W
Cea →	22	42 0N	5 36W
Ceanannus Mor	15	53 42N	6 53W
Ceará = Fortaleza	138	3 43S	38 35W
Ceará □	138	5 0S	40 0W
Ceará Mirim	138	5 38S	35 25W
Cebaco, I. de	126	7 33N	81 9W
Cebollar	140	29 10S	66 35W
Cebollera, Sierra de	24	42 0N	2 30W
Cebreros	22	40 27N	4 28W
Cebu	57	10 18N	123 54E
Ceccano	28	41 34N	13 18E
Cechi	88	6 15N	4 25W
Cecil Plains	73	27 30S	151 11E
Cécina	26	43 19N	10 33E
Cécina →	26	43 19N	10 29E
Ceclavin	22	39 50N	6 45W
Cedar →	116	41 17N	91 21W
Cedar City	121	37 41N	113 3W
Cedar Creek Res.	119	32 4N	96 5W
Cedar Falls, Iowa, U.S.A.	116	42 39N	92 29W
Cedar Falls, Wash., U.S.A.	122	47 25N	121 45W
Cedar Grove	117	39 22N	84 56W
Cedar Key	113	29 9N	83 5W
Cedar L., Man., Can.	109	53 10N	100 0W
Cedar L., Ont., Can.	107	46 2N	78 30W
Cedar Lake	117	41 20N	87 25W
Cedar Point	117	41 44N	83 21W
Cedar Rapids	116	42 0N	91 38W
Cedarburg	112	43 18N	87 55W
Cedartown	113	34 1N	85 15W
Cedarvale	108	55 1N	128 22W
Cedarville, Calif., U.S.A.	120	41 37N	120 13W
Cedarville, Ill., U.S.A.	116	42 23N	89 38W
Cedarville, Mich., U.S.A.	106	46 0N	84 22W
Cedarville, Ohio, U.S.A.	117	39 44N	83 49W
Cedeira	22	43 39N	8 2W
Cedral	124	23 50N	100 42W
Cedrino →	28	40 23N	9 44E
Cedro	138	6 34S	39 3W
Cedros, I. de	124	28 10N	115 20W
Ceduna	73	32 7S	133 46E
Cefalù	29	38 3N	14 1E
Cega →	22	41 33N	4 46W
Cegléd	33	47 11N	19 47E
Céglie Messápico	29	40 39N	17 31E
Cehegín	25	38 6N	1 48W
Ceheng	58	24 58N	105 48E
Cehu-Silvaniei	34	47 24N	23 9E
Ceiba, La	126	15 40N	86 50W
Ceira →	22	40 13N	8 16W
Cekhira	87	34 20N	10 5E
Celano	27	42 6N	13 30E
Celanova	22	42 9N	7 58W
Celaya	124	20 31N	100 37W
Celbridge	15	53 20N	6 33W
Celebes = Sulawesi	57	2 0S	120 0E
Celebes Sea	57	3 0N	123 0E
Celendín	136	6 52S	78 10W
Celga	91	12 38N	37 3E
Čelić	33	44 43N	18 47E
Celica	134	4 7S	79 59W
Celina	117	40 32N	84 31W
Celje	27	46 16N	15 18E
Celle	30	52 37N	10 4E
Celorico da Beira	22	40 38N	7 24W
Cement	119	34 56N	98 8W
Cement Mills	77	28 20S	151 31E
Cenepa →	134	4 40S	78 10W
Cengong	58	27 13N	108 44E
Cenis, Col du Mt.	21	45 15N	6 55E
Ceno →	26	44 4N	10 5E
Cenon	20	44 50N	0 33W
Centallo	26	44 30N	7 35E
Centenário do Sul	139	22 48S	51 36W
Center, N.D., U.S.A.	118	47 9N	101 17W
Center, Texas, U.S.A.	119	31 50N	94 10W
Center Point	116	42 12N	91 46W
Centerfield	121	39 9N	111 56W
Centerville, Ala., U.S.A.	113	32 55N	87 7W
Centerville, Calif., U.S.A.	122	36 44N	119 30W
Centerville, Iowa, U.S.A.	116	40 45N	92 57W
Centerville, Mich., U.S.A.	117	41 55N	85 32W
Centerville, Miss., U.S.A.	119	31 10N	91 3W
Centerville, Pa., U.S.A.	114	40 3N	79 59W
Centerville, S.D., U.S.A.	118	43 10N	96 58W
Centerville, Tenn., U.S.A.	113	35 46N	87 29W
Centerville, Tex., U.S.A.	119	31 15N	95 56W
Cento	27	44 43N	11 16E
Central, Brazil	138	11 8S	42 8W
Central, U.S.A.	121	32 46N	108 9W
Central □, Kenya	94	0 30S	37 30E
Central □, Malawi	95	13 30S	33 30E
Central □, U.K.	14	56 10N	4 30W
Central □, Zambia	95	14 25S	28 50E
Central African Republic ■	92	7 0N	20 0E
Central City, Ky., U.S.A.	112	37 20N	87 7W
Central City, Nebr., U.S.A.	118	41 8N	98 0W
Central, Cordillera, Boliv.	137	18 30S	64 55W
Central, Cordillera, Colomb.	134	5 0N	75 0W
Central, Cordillera, C. Rica	126	10 10N	84 5W
Central, Cordillera, Dom. Rep.	127	19 15N	71 0W
Central, Cordillera, Peru	136	7 0S	77 30W
Central I.	94	3 30N	36 0E
Central Islip	115	40 49N	73 13W
Central Lake	106	45 4N	85 16W
Central Makran Range	47	26 30N	64 15E
Central Patricia	102	51 30N	90 9W
Central Ra.	69	5 0S	143 0E
Central Russian Uplands	6	54 0N	36 0E
Central Siberian Plateau	41	65 0N	105 0E
Central Tilba	75	36 20S	150 4E
Centralia, Ill., U.S.A.	116	38 32N	89 5W
Centralia, Mo., U.S.A.	116	39 12N	92 6W
Centralia, Wash., U.S.A.	122	46 46N	122 59W
Centúripe	29	37 37N	14 41E
Cephalonia = Kefallinía	35	38 15N	20 30E
Ceprano	28	41 33N	13 30E
Cepu	57	7 12S	111 31E
Ceram = Seram	57	3 10S	129 0E
Ceram Sea = Seram Sea	57	2 30S	128 30E
Cerbère	20	42 26N	3 10E
Cerbicales, Îles	21	41 33N	9 22E
Cercal	23	37 48N	8 40W
Cercemaggiore	29	41 27N	14 43E
Cerdaña	24	42 22N	1 35E
Cerdedo	22	42 33N	8 23W
Cère →	20	44 55N	1 49E
Cerea	27	45 12N	11 13E
Ceres, Argent.	140	29 55S	61 55W
Ceres, Brazil	139	15 17S	49 35W
Ceres, Italy	26	45 19N	7 22E
Ceres, S. Afr.	96	33 21S	19 18E
Ceres, U.S.A.	122	37 35N	120 57W
Céret	20	42 30N	2 42E
Cereté	134	8 53N	75 48W
Cerf, L. de	104	46 16N	75 30W
Cerignola	29	41 17N	15 53E
Cerigo = Kíthira	35	36 15N	23 0E
Cérilly	20	46 37N	2 50E
Cerisiers	19	48 8N	3 30E
Cerizay	18	46 50N	0 40W
Çerkeş	46	40 49N	32 52E
Cerknica	27	45 48N	14 21E
Cerna →	34	44 45N	24 0E
Cernavodă	34	44 22N	28 3E
Cernay	19	47 44N	7 10E
Cernik	33	45 17N	17 22E
Cerralvo	124	24 20N	109 45E
Cerreto Sannita	29	41 17N	14 34E
Cerritos	124	22 27N	100 20W
Cerro	121	36 47N	105 36W
Cerro Gordo	117	39 53N	88 44W
Cerro Sombrero	142	52 45S	69 15W
Certaldo	26	43 32N	11 2E
Cervaro →	29	41 30N	15 52E
Cervera	24	41 40N	1 16E
Cervera de Pisuerga	22	42 51N	4 30W
Cervera del Río Alhama	24	42 2N	1 58W
Cérvia	27	44 15N	12 20E
Cervignano del Friuli	27	45 49N	13 20E
Cervinara	29	41 2N	14 36E
Cervione	21	42 20N	9 29E
Cervo	22	43 40N	7 24W
César □	134	9 0N	73 30W
Cesaro	29	37 50N	14 38E
Cesena	27	44 9N	12 14E
Cesenático	27	44 12N	12 22E
Cēsis	36	57 17N	25 28E
Česká Lípa	32	50 45N	14 30E
České Budějovice	32	48 55N	14 25E
Ceskomoravská Vrchovina	32	49 20N	15 45E
Český Brod	32	50 4N	14 52E
Český Krumlov	32	48 43N	14 21E
Český Těšin	32	49 45N	18 39E
Cessnock	76	32 50S	151 21E
Cestas	20	44 44N	0 41W
Cestos →	88	5 40N	9 10W
Cétin Grad	27	45 9N	15 45E
Cetina →	27	43 26N	16 42E
Cetraro	29	39 30N	15 56E
Ceuta	86	35 52N	5 18W
Ceva	26	44 23N	8 3E
Cévennes	20	44 10N	3 50E
Ceyhan	46	37 4N	35 47E
Ceylon = Sri Lanka ■	51	7 30N	80 50E
Cèze →	21	44 13N	4 43E
Cha-am	54	12 48N	99 58E
Chabeuil	21	44 54N	5 1E
Chablais	21	46 20N	6 36E
Chablis	19	47 47N	3 48E
Chabounia	86	35 30N	2 38E
Chacabuco	140	34 40S	60 27W
Chachapoyas	136	6 15S	77 50W
Chachasp	136	15 30S	72 15W
Chachoengsao	54	13 42N	101 5E
Chachro	48	25 5N	70 15E
Chaco □	140	26 30S	61 0W
Chad ■	85	15 0N	17 15E
Chad, L. = Tchad, L.	85	13 30N	14 30E
Chadan	41	51 17N	91 35E
Chadileuvú →	140	37 46S	66 0W
Chadiza	95	14 45S	32 27E
Chadron	118	42 50N	103 0W
Chadyr-Lunga	38	46 3N	28 51E
Chae Hom	54	18 43N	99 35E
Chaem →	54	18 11N	98 38E
Chaeryŏng	61	38 24N	125 36E
Chagai Hills	47	29 30N	64 0E
Chagda	41	58 45N	130 38E
Chagny	19	46 57N	4 45E
Chagoda	36	59 10N	35 15E
Chagos Arch.	53	6 0S	72 0E
Chāh Bahār	47	25 20N	60 40E
Chahtung	52	26 41N	98 10E
Chaillé-les-Marais	20	46 25N	1 2W
Chainat	54	15 11N	100 8E
Chaise-Dieu, La	20	45 20N	3 40E
Chaitén	142	42 55S	72 43W
Châiya	55	9 23N	99 14E
Chaize-le-Vicomte, La	18	46 40N	1 18W
Chaj Doab	48	32 15N	73 0E
Chajari	140	30 42S	58 0W
Chakaria	52	21 45N	92 5E
Chake Chake	94	5 15S	39 45E
Chakhansur	47	31 10N	62 0E
Chakhansur □	47	30 0N	62 0E
Chakonipau, L.	103	56 18N	68 30W
Chakradharpur	49	22 45N	85 40E
Chakwadam	52	27 29N	98 31E
Chakwal	48	32 56N	72 53E
Chala	136	15 48S	74 20W
Chalais	20	45 16N	0 3E
Chalakudi	51	10 18N	76 20E
Chalcatongo	125	17 4N	97 34W
Chalchihuites	124	23 29N	103 53W
Chalcis = Khalkís	35	38 27N	23 42E
Chaleur B.	103	47 55N	65 30W
Chalfant	122	37 32N	118 21W
Chalhuanca	136	14 15S	73 15W
Chalindrey	19	47 48N	5 26E
Chaling	59	26 58N	113 30E
Chalisgaon	50	20 30N	75 10E
Chalk River	107	46 1N	77 27W
Chalkar	39	50 35N	51 52E
Chalkar Oz.	39	50 33N	51 45E
Chalky Inlet	81	46 3S	166 31E
Challans	18	46 50N	1 52W
Challapata	136	18 53S	66 50W
Challerange	19	49 18N	4 46E
Challis	120	44 32N	114 25W
Chalna	49	22 36N	89 35E
Chalon-sur-Saône	19	46 48N	4 50E
Chalonnes	18	47 20N	0 45W
Châlons-sur-Marne	19	48 58N	4 20E
Châlus	20	45 39N	0 58E
Chalyaphum	54	15 48N	102 2E
Cham	31	49 12N	12 40E
Cham, Cu Lao	54	15 57N	108 30E
Chama	121	36 54N	106 35W
Chaman	47	30 58N	66 25E
Chamarajnagar-Ramasamudram	51	11 52N	76 52E
Chamartín de la Rosa	24	40 28N	3 40W
Chamba	48	32 35N	76 10E
Chambal →	49	26 29N	79 15E
Chamberlain	118	43 50N	99 21W
Chamberlain →	78	15 30S	127 54E
Chambers	121	35 13N	109 30W
Chambersburg	112	39 53N	77 41W
Chambéry	21	45 34N	5 55E
Chambly	105	45 27N	73 17W
Chambois	18	48 48N	0 6E
Chambon-Feugerolles, Le	21	45 24N	4 18E
Chambord	105	48 25N	72 6W
Chambri L.	69	4 15S	143 10E
Chamela	124	19 32N	105 5W
Chamical	140	30 22S	66 27W
Chamkar Luong	55	11 0N	103 45E
Chamois	116	38 41N	91 46W
Chamonix	21	45 55N	6 51E
Chamouchouane →	105	48 37N	72 20W
Champa	49	22 2N	82 43E
Champagne, Can.	108	60 49N	136 30W
Champagne, France	19	49 0N	4 40E
Champagne, Plaine de	19	49 0N	4 30E
Champagnole	19	46 45N	5 55E
Champaign	117	40 8N	88 14W
Champassak	54	14 53N	105 52E
Champaubert	19	48 50N	3 45E
Champdeniers	20	46 29N	0 25W
Champeix	20	45 37N	3 8E
Champlain, Can.	102	46 27N	72 24W
Champlain, U.S.A.	115	44 59N	73 27W
Champlain, L.	115	44 30N	73 20W
Champneuf	104	48 35N	77 30W
Champotón	125	19 20N	90 50W
Chamusca	23	39 21N	8 29W
Chan Chan	136	8 7S	79 0W
Chana	55	6 55N	100 44E
Chañaral	140	26 23S	70 40W
Chanasma	48	23 44N	72 5E
Chancay	136	11 32S	77 25W
Chandalar	100	67 30N	148 35W
Chandannagar	49	22 52N	88 24E
Chandausi	49	28 27N	78 49E
Chandeleur Is.	119	29 48N	88 51W
Chandeleur Sd.	119	29 58N	88 40W
Chandigarh	48	30 43N	76 47E
Chandler, Can.	103	48 18N	64 46W
Chandler, Ariz., U.S.A.	121	33 20N	111 56W
Chandler, Okla., U.S.A.	119	35 43N	96 53W

Chandlers Creek	**75**	37 21 S	149 12 E
Chandlers Peak	**77**	30 24 S	152 10 E
Chandless →	**136**	9 8 S	69 51 W
Chandmani	**62**	45 22 N	98 2 E
Chandpur, Bangla.	**52**	23 8 N	90 45 E
Chandpur, India	**48**	29 8 N	78 19 E
Chandrapur	**50**	19 57 N	79 25 E
Chang	**48**	26 59 N	68 30 E
Chang Jiang →, Jiangsu, China	**59**	31 48 N	121 10 E
Chang Jiang →, Shanghai, China	**59**	31 35 N	121 15 E
Chang, Ko	**55**	12 0 N	102 23 E
Changa	**49**	33 53 N	77 35 E
Changanacheri	**51**	9 25 N	76 31 E
Changbai	**61**	41 25 N	128 5 E
Changbai Shan	**61**	42 20 N	129 0 E
Changchiak'ou = Zhangjiakou	**60**	40 48 N	114 55 E
Ch'angchou = Changzhou	**62**	31 47 N	119 58 E
Changchun	**61**	42 57 N	124 36 E
Changchunling	**61**	45 18 N	125 27 E
Changde	**59**	29 4 N	111 35 E
Changdo-ri	**61**	38 30 N	127 40 E
Changfeng	**59**	32 28 N	117 10 E
Changhai = Shanghai	**59**	31 15 N	121 26 E
Changhua	**59**	30 12 N	119 12 E
Changhŭng	**61**	34 41 N	126 52 E
Changhŭngni	**61**	40 24 N	128 19 E
Changjiang	**62**	19 20 N	108 55 E
Changjin	**61**	40 23 N	127 15 E
Changjin-chŏsuji	**61**	40 30 N	127 15 E
Changle	**59**	25 59 N	119 27 E
Changli	**61**	39 40 N	119 13 E
Changling	**61**	44 20 N	123 58 E
Changlun	**55**	6 25 N	100 26 E
Changning, Hunan, China	**59**	26 28 N	112 22 E
Changning, Yunnan, China	**58**	24 45 N	99 30 E
Changping	**60**	40 14 N	116 12 E
Changsha	**59**	28 12 N	113 0 E
Changshan	**59**	28 55 N	118 27 E
Changshou	**58**	29 51 N	107 8 E
Changshu	**59**	31 38 N	120 43 E
Changshun	**58**	26 3 N	106 25 E
Changtai	**59**	24 35 N	117 42 E
Changting	**59**	25 50 N	116 22 E
Changwu	**60**	35 10 N	107 45 E
Changxing	**59**	31 0 N	119 55 E
Changyang	**59**	30 30 N	111 10 E
Changyi	**61**	36 40 N	119 30 E
Changyŏn	**61**	38 15 N	125 6 E
Changyuan	**60**	35 15 N	114 42 E
Changzhi	**60**	36 10 N	113 6 E
Changzhou	**59**	31 47 N	119 58 E
Chanhanga	**96**	16 0 S	14 8 E
Channapatna	**51**	12 40 N	77 15 E
Channel Is., U.K.	**18**	49 30 N	2 40 W
Channel Is., U.S.A.	**123**	33 55 N	119 26 W
Channel-Port aux Basques	**103**	47 30 N	59 9 W
Channing, Mich., U.S.A.	**112**	46 9 N	88 1 W
Channing, Tex., U.S.A.	**119**	35 45 N	102 20 W
Chantada	**22**	42 36 N	7 46 W
Chanthaburi	**54**	12 38 N	102 12 E
Chantilly	**19**	49 12 N	2 29 E
Chantonnay	**18**	46 40 N	1 3 W
Chantrey Inlet	**100**	67 48 N	96 20 W
Chanute	**119**	37 45 N	95 25 W
Chanza →	**23**	37 32 N	7 30 W
Chao Hu	**59**	31 30 N	117 30 E
Chao Phraya →	**54**	13 32 N	100 36 E
Chao Phraya Lowlands	**54**	15 30 N	100 0 E
Chao Xian	**59**	31 38 N	117 50 E
Chao'an	**59**	23 42 N	116 32 E
Chaocheng	**60**	36 4 N	115 37 E
Chaoyang, Guangdong, China	**59**	23 17 N	116 30 E
Chaoyang, Liaoning, China	**61**	41 35 N	120 22 E
Chapada dos Guimarães	**137**	15 26 S	55 45 W
Chapais	**104**	49 47 N	74 51 W
Chapala	**95**	15 50 S	37 35 E
Chapala, Lago de	**124**	20 10 N	103 20 W
Chaparé →	**137**	15 58 S	64 42 W
Chaparmukh	**52**	26 12 N	92 31 E
Chaparral	**134**	3 43 N	75 28 W
Chapayevo	**39**	50 25 N	51 10 E
Chapayevsk	**37**	53 0 N	49 40 E
Chapeau	**104**	45 54 N	77 4 W
Chapecó	**141**	27 14 S	52 41 W
Chapel Hill	**113**	35 53 N	79 3 W
Chapelle-d'Angillon, La	**19**	47 21 N	2 25 E
Chapelle-Glain, La	**18**	47 38 N	1 11 W
Chapin	**116**	39 46 N	90 24 W
Chapleau	**102**	47 50 N	83 24 W
Chaplin	**109**	50 28 N	106 40 W
Chaplino	**38**	48 8 N	36 15 E
Chaplygin	**37**	53 15 N	40 0 E
Chapra	**49**	25 48 N	84 44 E
Char	**84**	21 32 N	12 45 E
Chara	**41**	56 54 N	118 20 E
Charadai	**140**	27 35 S	60 0 W
Charagua	**137**	19 45 S	63 10 W
Charalá	**134**	6 17 N	73 10 W
Charambirá, Punta	**134**	4 16 N	77 32 W
Charaña	**136**	17 30 S	69 25 W
Charapita	**134**	0 37 S	74 21 W
Charata	**140**	27 13 S	61 14 W
Charcas	**124**	23 10 N	101 20 W
Charcoal L.	**109**	58 49 N	102 22 W
Charcot I.	**143**	70 0 S	75 0 W
Chard	**13**	50 52 N	2 59 W
Chardara	**40**	41 16 N	67 59 E
Chardon	**114**	41 34 N	81 17 W
Charduar	**52**	26 51 N	92 46 E
Chardzhou	**40**	39 6 N	63 34 E
Charente	**20**	45 40 N	0 5 E
Charente □	**20**	45 50 N	0 16 E
Charente →	**20**	45 57 N	1 5 W
Charente-Maritime □	**20**	45 30 N	0 35 W
Charentsavan	**39**	40 35 N	44 41 E
Charette	**105**	46 27 N	72 56 W
Charikar	**47**	35 0 N	69 10 E
Charité, La	**19**	47 10 N	3 0 E
Chariton	**116**	41 1 N	93 19 W
Chariton →	**116**	39 19 N	92 58 W
Charity	**135**	7 24 N	58 36 W
Charity I.	**106**	44 3 N	83 27 W
Charkhari	**49**	25 24 N	79 45 E
Charkhi Dadri	**48**	28 37 N	76 17 E
Charleroi	**16**	50 24 N	4 27 E
Charlerol	**114**	40 8 N	79 54 W
Charles, C.	**112**	37 10 N	75 59 W
Charles City	**116**	43 2 N	92 41 W
Charles L.	**109**	59 50 N	110 33 W
Charles, Pk.	**79**	32 53 S	121 8 E
Charles Town	**112**	39 20 N	77 50 W
Charlesbourg	**105**	46 51 N	71 16 W
Charleston, Ill., U.S.A.	**112**	39 30 N	88 10 W
Charleston, Ill., U.S.A.	**117**	39 30 N	88 10 W
Charleston, Miss., U.S.A.	**119**	34 2 N	90 3 W
Charleston, Mo., U.S.A.	**119**	36 52 N	89 20 W
Charleston, S.C., U.S.A.	**113**	32 47 N	79 56 W
Charleston, W. Va., U.S.A.	**112**	38 24 N	81 36 W
Charleston Harb.	**113**	32 46 N	79 55 W
Charleston L.	**107**	44 32 N	76 0 W
Charleston Park	**123**	36 17 N	115 37 W
Charleston Pk.	**123**	36 16 N	115 42 W
Charlestown, S. Afr.	**97**	27 26 S	29 53 E
Charlestown, U.S.A.	**117**	38 29 N	85 40 W
Charlesville	**92**	5 27 S	20 59 E
Charleville	**73**	26 24 S	146 15 E
Charleville = Rath Luirc	**15**	52 21 N	8 40 W
Charleville-Mézières	**19**	49 44 N	4 40 E
Charlevoix	**106**	45 19 N	85 14 W
Charlevoix, L.	**106**	45 15 N	85 8 W
Charlieu	**21**	46 10 N	4 10 E
Charlotte, Mich., U.S.A.	**117**	42 36 N	84 48 W
Charlotte, N.C., U.S.A.	**113**	35 16 N	80 46 W
Charlotte Amalie	**127**	18 22 N	64 56 W
Charlotte Harbor	**113**	26 58 N	82 4 W
Charlottenberg	**10**	59 54 N	12 17 E
Charlottesville	**112**	38 1 N	78 30 W
Charlottetown	**103**	46 14 N	63 8 W
Charlton, Austral.	**74**	36 16 S	143 24 E
Charlton, U.S.A.	**118**	40 59 N	93 20 W
Charlton I.	**102**	52 0 N	79 20 W
Charmes	**19**	48 22 N	6 17 E
Charny	**105**	46 43 N	71 15 W
Charolles	**21**	46 27 N	4 16 E
Charost	**19**	47 0 N	2 7 E
Charouïne	**86**	29 0 N	0 15 W
Charre	**95**	17 13 S	35 10 E
Charroux	**20**	46 9 N	0 25 E
Charsadda	**48**	34 7 N	71 45 E
Charters Towers	**72**	20 5 S	146 13 E
Chartre, La	**18**	47 42 N	0 34 E
Chartres	**18**	48 29 N	1 30 E
Chascomús	**140**	35 30 S	58 0 W
Chasefu	**95**	11 55 S	33 8 E
Chaslands Mistake	**81**	46 38 S	169 22 E
Chasovnya-Uchurskaya	**41**	57 15 N	132 50 E
Chasseneuil-sur-Bonnieure	**20**	45 52 N	0 29 E
Chata	**48**	27 42 N	77 30 E
Châtaigneraie, La	**18**	46 38 N	0 45 W
Chatal Balkan = Udvoy Balkan	**34**	42 50 N	26 50 E
Château-Chinon	**19**	47 4 N	3 56 E
Château-du-Loir	**18**	47 40 N	0 25 E
Château-Gontier	**18**	47 50 N	0 48 W
Château-la-Vallière	**18**	47 30 N	0 20 E
Château-Landon	**19**	48 8 N	2 40 E
Château, Le	**20**	45 52 N	1 12 W
Château-Porcien	**19**	49 31 N	4 13 E
Château-Renault	**18**	47 36 N	0 56 E
Château-Salins	**19**	48 50 N	6 30 E
Château-Thierry	**19**	49 3 N	3 20 E
Châteaubourg	**18**	48 7 N	1 25 W
Châteaubriant	**18**	47 43 N	1 23 W
Châteaudun	**18**	48 3 N	1 20 E
Châteaugiron	**18**	48 3 N	1 30 W
Châteauguay	**115**	45 23 N	73 45 W
Châteaulin	**18**	48 11 N	4 8 W
Châteaumeillant	**20**	46 35 N	2 12 E
Châteauneuf	**18**	48 35 N	1 15 E
Châteauneuf-du-Faou	**18**	48 11 N	3 50 W
Châteauneuf-sur-Charente	**20**	45 36 N	0 3 W
Châteauneuf-sur-Cher	**19**	46 52 N	2 18 E
Châteauneuf-sur-Loire	**19**	47 52 N	2 13 E
Châteaurenard	**21**	43 53 N	4 51 E
Châteauroux	**19**	46 50 N	1 40 E
Châteauvert, L.	**105**	47 39 N	73 56 W
Châteaux-Arnoux	**21**	44 6 N	6 0 E
Châtelaillon-Plage	**20**	46 5 N	1 5 W
Châtelaudren	**18**	48 33 N	2 59 W
Châtelet, Le, Cher, France	**20**	46 40 N	2 20 E
Châtelet, Le, Seine-et-Marne, France	**19**	48 30 N	2 47 E
Châtelguyon	**20**	45 55 N	3 4 E
Châtellerault	**18**	46 50 N	0 30 E
Châtelus-Malvaleix	**20**	46 18 N	2 1 E
Chatfield	**118**	43 15 N	91 58 W
Chatham, N.B., Can.	**103**	47 2 N	65 28 W
Chatham, Ont., Can.	**106**	42 24 N	82 11 W
Chatham, U.K.	**13**	51 22 N	0 32 E
Chatham, Ill., U.S.A.	**116**	39 40 N	89 42 W
Chatham, La., U.S.A.	**119**	32 22 N	92 26 W
Chatham, N.Y., U.S.A.	**115**	42 21 N	73 32 W
Chatham, I.	**142**	50 40 S	74 25 W
Chatham Is.	**66**	44 0 S	176 40 W
Chatham Str.	**108**	57 0 N	134 40 W
Châtillon, Loiret, France	**19**	47 36 N	2 44 E
Châtillon, Marne, France	**19**	49 5 N	3 43 E
Chatillon	**26**	45 45 N	7 40 E
Châtillon-Coligny	**19**	47 50 N	2 51 E
Châtillon-en-Bazois	**19**	47 3 N	3 39 E
Châtillon-en-Diois	**21**	44 41 N	5 29 E
Châtillon-sur-Indre	**18**	46 59 N	1 10 E
Châtillon-sur-Seine	**19**	47 50 N	4 33 E
Châtillon-sur-Sèvre	**18**	46 56 N	0 45 W
Chatmohar	**49**	24 15 N	89 15 E
Chatra	**49**	24 12 N	84 56 E
Chatrapur	**50**	19 22 N	85 2 E
Châtre, La	**20**	46 35 N	1 59 E
Chats, L. des	**104**	45 30 N	76 20 W
Chatsworth, Can.	**106**	44 27 N	80 54 W
Chatsworth, U.S.A.	**117**	40 45 N	88 18 W
Chatsworth, Zimb.-Rhod.	**95**	19 38 S	31 13 E
Chatta-Hantō	**65**	34 45 N	136 55 E
Chattahoochee	**113**	30 43 N	84 51 W
Chattanooga	**113**	35 2 N	85 17 W
Chaturat	**54**	15 40 N	101 51 E
Chau Phu	**55**	10 42 N	105 7 E
Chaudanne, Barrage de	**21**	43 51 N	6 32 E
Chaudes-Aigues	**20**	44 51 N	3 1 E
Chaudière →	**105**	46 45 N	71 17 W
Chauffailles	**21**	46 13 N	4 20 E
Chauk	**52**	20 53 N	94 49 E
Chaukan Pass	**52**	27 8 N	97 10 E
Chaulnes	**19**	49 48 N	2 47 E
Chaumont, France	**19**	48 7 N	5 8 E
Chaumont, U.S.A.	**115**	44 4 N	76 9 W
Chaumont-en-Vexin	**19**	49 16 N	1 53 E
Chaumont-sur-Loire	**18**	47 29 N	1 11 E
Chaunay	**20**	46 13 N	0 9 E
Chauny	**19**	49 37 N	3 12 E
Chausey, Îs.	**18**	48 52 N	1 49 W
Chaussin	**19**	46 59 N	5 22 E
Chautauqua	**114**	42 17 N	79 30 W
Chauvigny	**18**	46 34 N	0 39 E
Chauvin	**109**	52 45 N	110 10 W
Chaux-de-Fonds, La	**31**	47 7 N	6 50 E
Chavantina	**137**	14 40 S	52 21 W
Chaves, Brazil	**138**	0 15 S	49 55 W
Chaves, Port.	**22**	41 45 N	7 32 W
Chavuma	**93**	13 4 S	22 40 E
Chawang	**55**	8 25 N	99 30 E
Chazelles-sur-Lyon	**21**	45 39 N	4 22 E
Chazuta	**136**	6 30 S	76 0 W
Chazy	**115**	44 52 N	73 28 W
Cheb (Eger)	**32**	50 9 N	12 28 E
Chebanse	**117**	41 0 N	87 54 W
Cheboksary	**37**	56 8 N	47 12 E
Cheboygan	**106**	45 38 N	84 29 W
Chebsara	**37**	59 10 N	38 59 E
Chech, Erg	**86**	25 0 N	2 15 W
Chechaouen	**86**	35 9 N	5 15 W
Chechen, Os.	**39**	43 59 N	47 40 E
Checheno-Ingush, A.S.S.R. □	**39**	43 30 N	45 29 E
Chechon	**61**	37 8 N	128 12 E
Chęciny	**32**	50 46 N	20 28 E
Checleset B.	**108**	50 5 N	127 35 W
Checotah	**119**	35 31 N	95 30 W
Chedabucto B.	**103**	45 25 N	61 8 W
Cheduba I.	**52**	18 45 N	93 40 E
Cheepie	**73**	26 36 S	144 59 E
Chef-Boutonne	**20**	46 7 N	0 4 W
Chef, R. du →	**105**	49 21 N	73 25 W
Chegdomyn	**41**	51 7 N	133 1 E
Chegga	**86**	25 27 N	5 40 W
Chehalis	**122**	46 44 N	122 59 W
Cheiron	**21**	43 49 N	6 58 E
Cheju	**61**	33 28 N	126 30 E
Cheju Do	**61**	33 29 N	126 34 E
Cheju-do	**61**	33 29 N	126 34 E
Chekalin	**37**	54 10 N	36 10 E
Chekiang = Zhejiang □	**59**	29 0 N	120 0 E
Chela, Sa. da	**96**	16 20 S	13 20 E
Chelan	**120**	47 49 N	120 0 W
Chelan, L.	**120**	48 5 N	120 30 W
Cheleken	**40**	39 26 N	53 7 E
Chelforó	**142**	39 0 S	66 33 W
Chéliff, O. →	**86**	36 0 N	0 8 E
Chelkar	**40**	47 48 N	59 39 E
Chelkar Tengiz, Solonchak	**40**	48 0 N	62 30 E
Chellala Dahrania	**86**	33 2 N	0 1 E
Chelles	**19**	48 52 N	2 33 E
Chełm	**32**	51 8 N	23 30 E
Chełmek	**32**	50 6 N	19 16 E
Chełmno	**32**	53 20 N	18 30 E
Chelmsford	**13**	51 44 N	0 29 E
Chelmsford Dam	**97**	27 55 S	29 59 E
Chelmźa	**32**	53 10 N	18 39 E
Chelsea, Austral.	**74**	38 5 S	145 8 E
Chelsea, Can.	**115**	45 30 N	75 47 W
Chelsea, Mich., U.S.A.	**117**	42 19 N	84 1 W
Chelsea, Okla., U.S.A.	**119**	36 35 N	95 35 W
Chelsea, Vt., U.S.A.	**115**	43 59 N	72 27 W
Cheltenham	**13**	51 55 N	2 5 W
Chelva	**24**	39 45 N	1 0 W
Chelyabinsk	**40**	55 10 N	61 24 E
Chemainus	**108**	48 55 N	123 42 W
Chemillé	**18**	47 14 N	0 45 W
Chemnitz = Karl-Marx-Stadt	**30**	50 50 N	12 55 E
Chemult	**120**	43 14 N	121 47 W
Chen, Gora	**41**	65 16 N	141 50 E
Chen Xian	**59**	25 47 N	113 1 E
Chenab →	**48**	30 23 N	71 2 E
Chenachane, O. →	**86**	25 20 N	3 20 W
Chenango Forks	**115**	42 15 N	75 51 W
Chencha	**91**	6 15 N	37 32 E
Chenchiang = Zhenjiang	**62**	32 12 N	119 24 E
Chénéville	**104**	45 53 N	75 3 W
Cheney	**120**	47 29 N	117 34 W
Cheng Xian	**60**	33 43 N	105 42 E
Chengbu	**59**	26 18 N	110 16 E
Chengcheng	**60**	35 8 N	109 56 E
Chengchou = Zhengzhou	**60**	34 45 N	113 34 E
Chengde	**61**	40 59 N	117 58 E
Chengdong Hu	**59**	32 15 N	116 20 E
Chengdu	**58**	30 38 N	104 2 E
Chengele	**52**	28 47 N	96 16 E
Chenggong	**58**	24 52 N	102 56 E
Chenggu	**58**	33 10 N	107 21 E
Chengjiang	**58**	24 39 N	103 0 E
Chengkou	**58**	31 54 N	108 31 E
Ch'engtu = Chengdu	**58**	30 38 N	104 2 E
Chengwu	**60**	34 58 N	115 50 E
Chengxi Hu	**59**	32 15 N	116 10 E
Chengyang	**61**	36 18 N	120 21 E
Chenjiagang	**61**	34 23 N	119 47 E
Chenkán	**125**	19 8 N	90 58 W
Chenoa	**117**	40 45 N	88 42 W
Chenxi	**59**	28 2 N	110 12 E
Cheom Ksan	**54**	14 13 N	104 56 E
Chepelare	**35**	41 44 N	24 40 E
Chepén	**136**	7 15 S	79 23 W
Chépénéhé	**68**	20 47 S	167 9 E
Chepes	**140**	31 20 S	66 35 W
Chepo	**126**	9 10 N	79 6 W
Cheptsa →	**37**	58 36 N	50 4 E
Cheptulil, Mt.	**94**	1 25 N	35 35 E
Chequamegon B.	**118**	46 40 N	90 30 W
Chequeche	**95**	14 13 S	38 30 E

Cher □	19	47 10N	2 30 E
Cher →	18	47 21N	0 29 E
Cheran	52	25 45N	90 44 E
Cherasco	26	44 39N	7 50 E
Cheraw	113	34 42N	79 54W
Cherbourg	18	49 39N	1 40W
Cherchell	86	36 35N	2 12 E
Cherdakly	37	54 25N	48 50 E
Cherdyn	40	60 24N	56 29 E
Cheremkhovo	41	53 8N	103 1 E
Cherepanovo	40	54 15N	83 30 E
Cherepovets	37	59 5N	37 55 E
Chergui, Chott ech	86	34 21N	0 25 E
Cherikov	36	53 32N	31 20 E
Cherkassy	40	49 30N	32 0 E
Cherkessk	39	44 15N	42 5 E
Cherlak	40	54 15N	74 55 E
Cherni	34	42 35N	23 18 E
Chernigov	36	51 28N	31 20 E
Chernobyl	36	51 13N	30 15 E
Chernogorsk	41	53 49N	91 18 E
Chernomorskoye	38	45 31N	32 40 E
Chernovskoye	37	58 48N	47 20 E
Chernovtsy	38	48 15N	25 52 E
Chernoye	41	70 30N	89 10 E
Chernyakhovsk	36	54 36N	21 48 E
Chernyshkovskiy	39	48 30N	42 13 E
Chernyshovskiy	41	63 0N	112 30 E
Cherokee, Iowa, U.S.A.	118	42 40N	95 30W
Cherokee, Okla., U.S.A.	119	36 45N	98 25W
Cherokees, L. O'The	119	36 50N	95 12W
Cherquenco	142	38 35S	72 0W
Cherry Creek	120	39 50N	114 58W
Cherry Gully	77	28 25S	152 1 E
Cherry Valley	123	33 59N	116 57W
Cherrypool	74	37 7S	142 13 E
Cherryvale	119	37 20N	95 33W
Cherskiy	41	68 45N	161 18 E
Cherskogo Khrebet	41	65 0N	143 0 E
Chertkovo	39	49 25N	40 19 E
Cherven	36	53 45N	28 28 E
Cherven-Bryag	34	43 17N	24 7 E
Cherwell →	13	51 46N	1 18W
Chesaning	106	43 11N	84 7W
Chesapeake	112	36 43N	76 15W
Chesapeake Bay	112	38 0N	76 12W
Chesha B. = Cheshskaya G.	40	67 20N	47 0 E
Cheshire □	12	53 14N	2 30W
Cheslatta L.	108	53 49N	125 20W
Chesley	106	44 17N	81 5W
Chesne, Le	19	49 30N	4 45 E
Cheste	25	39 30N	0 41W
Chester, U.K.	12	53 12N	2 53W
Chester, Calif., U.S.A.	120	40 22N	121 14W
Chester, Ill., U.S.A.	116	37 58N	89 50W
Chester, Mont., U.S.A.	120	48 31N	111 0W
Chester, N.Y., U.S.A.	115	41 22N	74 16W
Chester, Pa., U.S.A.	112	39 54N	75 20W
Chester, S.C., U.S.A.	113	34 44N	81 13W
Chesterfield	12	53 14N	1 26W
Chesterfield, Île	97	16 20S	43 58 E
Chesterfield, Îles	66	19 52S	158 15 E
Chesterfield In.	100	63 25N	90 45W
Chesterfield Inlet	100	63 30N	90 45W
Chesterton Range	73	25 30S	147 27 E
Chesterville	107	45 6N	75 14W
Chesuncook L.	103	46 0N	69 10W
Chetaibi	87	37 1N	7 20 E
Chéticamp	103	46 37N	60 59W
Chetumal	125	18 30N	88 20W
Chetumal, Bahía de	125	18 40N	88 10W
Chetwynd, Austral.	74	37 17S	141 23 E
Chetwynd, Can.	108	55 45N	121 36W
Chevanceaux	20	45 18N	0 14W
Cheviot	117	39 10N	84 37W
Cheviot Hills	12	55 20N	2 30W
Cheviot Ra.	72	25 20S	143 45 E
Cheviot, The	12	55 29N	2 8W
Chew Bahir	91	4 40N	36 50 E
Chewelah	120	48 17N	117 43W
Cheyenne, Okla., U.S.A.	119	35 35N	99 40W
Cheyenne, Wyo., U.S.A.	118	41 9N	104 49W
Cheyenne →	118	44 40N	101 15W
Cheyenne Wells	118	38 51N	102 10W
Cheylard, Le	21	44 55N	4 25 E
Cheyne B.	79	34 35S	118 50 E
Chhabra	48	24 40N	76 54 E
Chhatak	52	25 5N	91 37 E
Chhatarpur	49	24 55N	79 35 E
Chhep	54	13 45N	105 24 E
Chhindwara	49	22 2N	78 59 E
Chhlong	55	12 15N	105 58 E
Chhuk	55	10 46N	104 28 E
Chi →	54	15 11N	104 43 E
Chiamis	57	7 20S	108 21 E
Chiamussu = Jiamusi	62	46 40N	130 26 E
Chiang Dao	54	19 22N	98 58 E
Chiang Kham	54	19 32N	100 18 E
Chiang Khan	54	17 52N	101 36 E
Chiang Khong	54	20 17N	100 24 E
Chiang Mai	54	18 47N	98 59 E
Chiang Saen	54	20 16N	100 5 E
Chianie	93	15 35S	13 40 E
Chiapa →	125	16 42N	93 0W
Chiapa de Corzo	125	16 42N	93 0W
Chiapas □	125	17 0N	92 45W
Chiaramonte Gulfi	29	37 1N	14 41 E
Chiaravalle	27	43 38N	13 17 E
Chiaravalle Centrale	29	38 41N	16 25 E
Chiari	26	45 31N	9 55 E
Chiautla	125	18 18N	98 34W
Chiávari	26	44 20N	9 20 E
Chiavenna	26	46 18N	9 23 E
Chiba	65	35 30N	140 7 E
Chiba □	65	35 30N	140 20 E
Chibabava	97	20 17S	33 35 E
Chibatu	57	7 6S	107 59 E
Chibemba	93	15 48S	14 8 E
Chibougamau	105	49 56N	74 24W
Chibougamau →	104	49 42N	75 57W
Chibougamau L.	105	49 50N	74 20W
Chibougamau, Parc Prov. de	105	49 15N	73 45W
Chibuk	89	10 52N	12 50 E
Chic-Chocs, Mts.	103	48 55N	66 0W
Chicacole = Srikakulam	50	18 14N	84 4 E
Chicago	117	41 53N	87 40W
Chicago Heights	117	41 29N	87 37W
Chichagof I.	108	58 0N	136 0W
Chichaoua	86	31 32N	8 44W
Chichén Itzá	125	20 40N	88 32W
Chicheng	60	40 55N	115 55 E
Chichester	13	50 50N	0 47W
Chichester Ra.	78	21 35S	117 45 E
Chichibu	65	36 5N	139 10 E
Ch'ich'ihaerh = Qiqihar	62	47 26N	124 0 E
Chickasha	119	35 0N	98 0W
Chiclana de la Frontera	23	36 26N	6 9W
Chiclayo	136	6 42S	79 50W
Chico	122	39 45N	121 54W
Chico →, Chubut, Argent.	120	44 0S	67 0W
Chico →, Santa Cruz, Argent.	142	50 0S	68 30W
Chicobi, L.	104	48 53N	78 30W
Chicomo	97	24 31S	34 6 E
Chicontepec	125	20 58N	98 10W
Chicopee	115	42 6N	72 37W
Chicoutimi	103	48 28N	71 5W
Chicoutimi, Parc Prov. de	105	48 30N	70 20W
Chidambaram	51	11 20N	79 45 E
Chidenguele	97	24 55S	34 11 E
Chidley C.	101	60 23N	64 26W
Chiefs Pt.	106	44 41N	81 18W
Chiem Hoa	54	22 12N	105 17 E
Chiemsee	31	47 53N	12 27 E
Chiengi	95	8 45S	29 10 E
Chienti →	27	43 18N	13 45 E
Chieri	26	45 0N	7 50 E
Chiers →	19	49 39N	5 0 E
Chiese →	26	45 8N	10 25 E
Chieti	27	42 22N	14 10 E
Chifeng	61	42 18N	118 58 E
Chigasaki	65	35 19N	139 24 E
Chignecto B.	103	45 30N	64 40W
Chigorodó	134	7 41N	76 42W
Chigoubiche, L.	105	49 7N	73 30W
Chiguana	140	21 0S	67 58W
Chiha-ri	61	38 40N	126 30 E
Chihli, G. of = Bo Hai	61	39 0N	120 0 E
Chihuahua	124	28 40N	106 3W
Chihuahua □	124	28 40N	106 3W
Chiili	40	44 20N	66 15 E
Chik Bollapur	51	13 25N	77 45 E
Chikhli	50	20 20N	76 18 E
Chikmagalur	51	13 15N	75 45 E
Chikodi	51	16 26N	74 38 E
Chikonde	95	12 16S	31 38 E
Chikugo	64	33 14N	130 28 E
Chikuma-Gawa →	65	36 59N	138 35 E
Chikwawa	95	16 2S	34 50 E
Chilac	125	18 20N	97 24W
Chilako →	108	53 53N	122 57W
Chilam Chavki	49	35 5N	75 5 E
Chilanga	95	15 33S	28 16 E
Chilapa	125	17 40N	99 11W
Chilas	49	35 25N	74 5 E
Chilcotin →	108	51 44N	122 23W
Childers	73	25 15S	152 17 E
Childress	119	34 30N	100 15W
Chile ■	142	35 0S	72 0W
Chile Chico	142	46 33S	71 44W
Chile Rise	67	38 0S	92 0W
Chilecito	140	29 10S	67 30W
Chilete	136	7 10S	78 50W
Chilhowee	116	38 36N	93 51W
Chililabombwe	95	12 18S	27 43 E
Chilin = Jilin	61	43 55N	126 30 E
Chilka L.	50	19 40N	85 25 E
Chilko →	108	52 0N	123 40W
Chilko, L.	108	51 20N	124 10W
Chillagoe	72	17 7S	144 33 E
Chillán	140	36 40S	72 10W
Chillicothe, Ill., U.S.A.	116	40 55N	89 32W
Chillicothe, Mo., U.S.A.	116	39 45N	93 30W
Chillicothe, Ohio, U.S.A.	112	39 20N	82 58W
Chillingham	77	28 20S	153 17 E
Chillingollah	74	35 16S	143 3 E
Chilliwack	108	49 10N	121 54W
Chilo	48	27 25N	73 32 E
Chiloane, I.	97	20 40S	34 55 E
Chiloé □	142	43 0S	73 0W
Chiloé, I. de	142	42 30S	73 50W
Chilpancingo	125	17 30N	99 30W
Chiltern	75	36 10S	146 36 E
Chiltern Hills	13	51 44N	0 42W
Chilton	112	44 1N	88 12W
Chiluage	92	9 30S	21 50 E
Chilubula	95	10 14S	30 51 E
Chilumba	95	10 28S	34 12 E
Chilwa, L.	95	15 15S	35 40 E
Chimacum	120	48 1N	122 46W
Chimaltitán	124	21 46N	103 50W
Chimán	126	8 45N	78 40W
Chimay	16	50 3N	4 20 E
Chimbay	40	42 57N	59 47 E
Chimborazo	134	1 29S	78 55W
Chimborazo □	134	1 0S	78 40W
Chimbote	136	9 0S	78 35W
Chimkent	40	42 18N	69 36 E
Chimoio	95	19 4S	33 30 E
Chimpembe	95	9 31S	29 33 E
Chin □	52	22 0N	93 0 E
Chin Hills	52	22 30N	93 30 E
Chin Ling Shan = Qinling Shandi	60	33 50N	108 10 E
China	125	25 40N	99 20W
China ■	62	30 0N	110 0 E
China Lake	123	35 44N	117 37W
Chinacates	124	25 0N	105 14W
Chinacota	134	7 37N	72 36W
Chinan = Jinan	60	36 38N	117 1 E
Chinandega	126	12 35N	87 12W
Chinati Pk.	119	30 0N	104 25W
Chincha Alta	136	13 25S	76 7W
Chinchilla	73	26 45S	150 38 E
Chinchilla de Monte Aragón	25	38 53N	1 40W
Chinchón	24	40 9N	3 26W
Chinchorro, Banco	125	18 35N	87 20W
Chinchou = Jinzhou	61	41 5N	121 3 E
Chincoteague	112	37 58N	75 21W
Chinde	95	18 35S	36 30 E
Chindo	61	34 28N	126 15 E
Chindwin →	52	21 26N	95 15 E
Chineni	49	33 2N	75 15 E
Chinga	95	15 13S	38 35 E
Chingleput	51	12 42N	79 58 E
Chingola	95	12 31S	27 53 E
Chingole	95	13 4S	34 17 E
Ch'ingtao = Qingdao	61	36 5N	120 20 E
Chinguar	93	12 25S	16 45 E
Chinguetti	84	20 25N	12 24W
Chingune	97	20 33S	35 0 E
Chinhae	61	35 9N	128 47 E
Chinhanguanine	97	25 21S	32 30 E
Chiniot	48	31 45N	73 0 E
Chinipas	124	27 22N	108 32W
Chinju	61	35 12N	128 2 E
Chinle	121	36 14N	109 38W
Chinnamanur	51	9 50N	77 24 E
Chinnampo	61	38 52N	125 10 E
Chinnur	50	18 57N	79 49 E
Chino, Japan	65	35 59N	138 9 E
Chino, U.S.A.	123	34 1N	117 41W
Chino Valley	121	34 54N	112 28W
Chinon	18	47 10N	0 15 E
Chinook, Can.	109	51 28N	110 59W
Chinook, U.S.A.	120	48 35N	109 19W
Chinsali	95	10 30S	32 2 E
Chintamani	51	13 26N	78 3 E
Chióggia	27	45 13N	12 15 E
Chíos = Khíos	35	38 27N	26 9 E
Chipai L.	102	52 56N	87 53W
Chipata	95	13 38S	32 28 E
Chipatujah	57	7 45S	108 0 E
Chipewyan L.	109	58 0N	98 27W
Chipinga	95	20 13S	32 28 E
Chipiona	23	36 44N	6 26W
Chipley	113	30 45N	85 32W
Chiplun	50	17 31N	73 34 E
Chipman	103	46 6N	65 53W
Chipoka	95	13 57S	34 28 E
Chippawa	114	43 5N	79 2W
Chippenham	13	51 27N	2 7W
Chippewa →	118	44 25N	92 10W
Chippewa Falls	118	44 55N	91 22W
Chiquián	136	10 10S	77 0W
Chiquimula	126	14 51N	89 37W
Chiquinquira	134	5 37N	73 50W
Chiquitos, Llanos de	137	18 0S	61 30W
Chir →	39	48 30N	43 0 E
Chirala	51	15 50N	80 26 E
Chiramba	95	16 55S	34 39 E
Chiran	64	31 22N	130 27 E
Chiras	47	35 14N	65 40 E
Chirawa	48	28 14N	75 42 E
Chirayinkil	51	8 41N	76 49 E
Chirchik	40	41 29N	69 35 E
Chirfa, Niger	85	20 55N	12 22 E
Chirfa, Niger	87	20 55N	12 14 E
Chirgua →	134	8 54N	67 58W
Chiricahua Pk.	121	31 53N	109 14W
Chirikof I.	100	55 50N	155 40W
Chiriquí, Golfo de	126	8 0N	82 10W
Chiriquí, Lago de	126	9 10N	82 0W
Chiriquí, Vol. de	126	8 55N	82 35W
Chirivira Falls	95	21 10S	32 12 E
Chirpan	34	42 10N	25 19 E
Chirripó Grande, Cerro	126	9 29N	83 29W
Chisamba	95	14 55S	28 20 E
Chisholm	108	54 55N	114 10W
Chishtian Mandi	48	29 50N	72 55 E
Chishui	58	28 30N	105 42 E
Chishui He →	58	28 49N	105 50 E
Chisimba Falls	95	10 12S	30 56 E
Chisone →	26	44 49N	7 25 E
Chisos Mts.	119	29 20N	103 15W
Chistopol	37	55 25N	50 38 E
Chita, Colomb.	134	6 11N	72 28W
Chita, U.S.S.R.	41	52 0N	113 35 E
Chitapur	50	17 10N	77 5 E
Chitembo	93	13 30S	16 50 E
Chitipa	95	9 41S	33 19 E
Chitokoloki	93	13 50S	23 13 E
Chitorgarh	48	24 52N	74 38 E
Chitrakot	50	19 10N	81 40 E
Chitral	47	35 50N	71 56 E
Chitravati →	51	14 45N	78 15 E
Chitré	126	7 59N	80 27W
Chittagong	52	22 19N	91 48 E
Chittagong □	52	24 5N	91 0 E
Chittoor	51	13 15N	79 5 E
Chittur	51	10 40N	76 45 E
Chitu	91	8 38N	37 58 E
Chiusa	27	46 38N	11 34 E
Chiusi	27	43 1N	11 58 E
Chiva	25	39 27N	0 41W
Chivacoa	134	10 10N	68 54W
Chivasso	26	45 10N	7 52 E
Chivay	136	15 40S	71 35W
Chivilcoy	140	34 55S	60 0W
Chiwanda	95	11 23S	34 55 E
Chiwefwe	95	13 37S	29 31 E
Chixi	59	22 0N	112 58 E
Chizera	95	13 10S	25 0 E
Chkalov = Orenburg	40	52 0N	55 5 E
Chkolovsk	37	56 50N	43 10 E
Chloride	123	35 25N	114 12W
Cho Bo	54	20 46N	105 10 E
Cho-do	61	38 30N	124 40 E
Cho Phuoc Hai	55	10 26N	107 18 E
Choba	94	2 30N	38 5 E
Chobe National Park	96	18 0S	25 0 E
Chochiwŏn	61	36 37N	127 18 E
Chociwel	32	53 29N	15 21 E
Chocó □	134	6 0N	77 0W
Chocontá	134	5 9N	73 41W
Chodavaram	50	17 50N	82 57 E
Chodecz	32	52 24N	19 2 E
Chodziez	32	52 58N	16 58 E
Choele Choel	142	39 11S	65 40W
Chōfu	65	35 39N	139 33 E
Choiseul	68	7 0S	156 40 E
Choisy-le-Roi	19	48 45N	2 24 E
Choix	124	26 40N	108 23W
Chojnice	32	53 42N	17 32 E
Chojnów	32	51 18N	15 58 E
Choke Mts.	91	11 18N	37 15 E
Chokurdakh	41	70 38N	147 55 E
Cholame	122	35 44N	120 18W
Cholet	18	47 4N	0 52W
Choluteca	126	13 20N	87 14W
Choluteca →	126	13 0N	87 20W
Chom Bung	54	13 37N	99 36 E
Chom Thong	54	18 25N	98 41 E
Choma	95	16 48S	26 59 E
Chomen Swamp	91	9 20N	37 10 E
Chomu	48	27 15N	75 40 E
Chomutov	32	50 28N	13 23 E
Chon Buri	54	13 21N	101 1 E
Chon Thanh	55	11 24N	106 36 E
Chonan	61	36 48N	127 9 E
Chone	134	0 40S	80 0W

Chong Kai **54** 13 57N 103 35 E
Chong Mek **54** 15 10N 105 27 E
Chong'an **59** 27 45N 118 0 E
Chongde **59** 30 32N 120 26 E
Chŏngdo **61** 35 38N 128 42 E
Chŏngha **61** 36 12N 129 21 E
Chongjin **61** 41 47N 129 50 E
Chŏngju **61** 39 40N 125 5 E
Chŏngju **61** 36 39N 127 27 E
Chongli **60** 40 58N 115 15 E
Chongming **59** 31 38N 121 23 E
Chongoyape **136** 6 35 S 79 25W
Chongqing, Sichuan, China **58** 30 38N 103 40 E
Chongqing, Sichuan, China **58** 29 35N 106 25 E
Chongren **59** 27 46N 116 3 E
Chŏngŭp **61** 35 35N 126 50 E
Chongzuo **58** 22 23N 107 20 E
Chŏnju **61** 35 50N 127 4 E
Chonming Dao **59** 31 40N 121 30 E
Chonos, Arch. de los **142** 45 0 S 75 0W
Chopda **50** 21 20N 75 15 E
Chopim → **141** 25 35 S 53 5W
Chorbat La **49** 34 42N 76 37 E
Chorley **12** 53 39N 2 39W
Chorolque, Cerro **140** 20 59 S 66 5W
Chorrera, La **134** 0 44 S 73 1W
Chortkov **36** 49 2N 25 46 E
Chŏrwŏn **61** 38 15N 127 10 E
Chorzów **32** 50 18N 18 57 E
Chos-Malal **140** 37 20 S 70 15W
Chosan **61** 40 50N 125 47 E
Chōshi **65** 35 45N 140 51 E
Choszczno **32** 53 7N 15 25 E
Chota **136** 6 33 S 78 39W
Choteau **120** 47 50N 112 10W
Chotila **48** 22 23N 71 15 E
Chowchilla **122** 37 11N 120 12W
Chowkham **52** 20 52N 97 28 E
Choybalsan **62** 48 4N 114 30 E
Chrisman **117** 39 48N 87 41W
Christchurch, N.Z. **81** 43 33 S 172 47 E
Christchurch, U.K. **13** 50 44N 1 33W
Christian I. **106** 44 50N 80 12W
Christiana **96** 27 52 S 25 8 E
Christiansfeld **11** 55 21N 9 29 E
Christiansted **127** 17 45N 64 42W
Christie B. **109** 62 32N 111 10W
Christina → **109** 56 40N 111 3W
Christmas Cr. → **78** 18 29 S 125 23 E
Christmas Creek **78** 18 29 S 125 23 E
Christmas I., Ind. Oc. **66** 10 30 S 105 40 E
Christmas I., Pac. Oc. **67** 1 58N 157 27W
Christopher L. **79** 24 49 S 127 42 E
Chrudim **32** 49 58N 15 43 E
Chrzanów **32** 50 10N 19 21 E
Chtimba **95** 10 35 S 34 13 E
Chu **40** 43 36N 73 42 E
Chu → **54** 19 53N 105 45 E
Chu Chua **108** 51 22N 120 10W
Chu Lai **54** 15 28N 108 45 E
Chu Xian **59** 32 19N 118 20 E
Chuadanga **52** 23 38N 88 51 E
Ch'uanchou = Quanzhou **59** 24 55N 118 34 E
Chuankou **60** 34 20N 110 59 E
Chūbu □ **65** 36 45N 137 30 E
Chubut □ **142** 43 30 S 69 0W
Chubut → **142** 43 20 S 65 5W
Chuchi L. **108** 55 12N 124 30W
Chudovo **36** 59 10N 31 41 E
Chudskoye, Oz. **36** 58 13N 27 30 E
Chūgoku □ **64** 35 0N 133 0 E
Chūgoku-Sanchi **64** 35 0N 133 0 E
Chuguyev **38** 49 55N 36 45 E
Chugwater **118** 41 48N 104 47W
Chukai **55** 4 13N 103 25 E
Chukhloma **37** 58 45N 42 40 E
Chukotskiy Khrebet **41** 68 0N 175 0 E
Chukotskoye More **41** 68 0N 175 0W
Chula **116** 39 55N 93 29W
Chula Vista **123** 32 39N 117 8W
Chulman **41** 56 52N 124 52 E
Chulucanas **136** 5 8 S 80 10W
Chulumani **136** 16 24 S 67 31W
Chulym → **40** 57 43N 83 51 E
Chum Phae **54** 16 40N 102 6 E
Chum Saeng **54** 15 55N 100 15 E
Chuma **136** 15 24 S 68 56W
Chumar **49** 32 40N 78 35 E
Chumbicha **140** 29 0 S 66 10W
Chumerna **34** 42 45N 25 55 E
Chumikan **41** 54 40N 135 10 E
Chumphon **55** 10 35N 99 14 E
Chumpi **136** 15 4 S 73 46W
Chumuare **95** 14 31 S 31 50 E
Chumunjin **61** 37 55N 128 54 E
Chuna → **41** 57 47N 94 37 E
Chun'an **59** 29 35N 119 3 E
Chunchŏn **61** 37 58N 127 44 E
Chunga **95** 15 0 S 26 2 E
Ch'ungch'ing = Chongqing **58** 29 35N 106 25 E
Chunggang-ŭp **61** 41 48N 126 48 E
Chunghwa **61** 38 52N 125 47 E
Chungju **61** 36 58N 127 58 E
Chungmu **61** 34 50N 128 20 E
Chungt'iaoshan = Zhongtiao Shan **60** 35 0N 111 10 E
Chunian **48** 30 57N 74 0 E
Chunya **95** 8 30 S 33 27 E
Chunya □ **94** 7 48 S 33 0 E
Chunyang **61** 43 38N 129 23 E
Chuquibamba **136** 15 47 S 72 44W
Chuquibambilla **136** 14 7 S 72 41W
Chuquicamata **140** 22 15 S 69 0W
Chuquisaca □ **137** 23 30 S 63 30W
Chur **31** 46 52N 9 32 E
Churachandpur **52** 24 20N 93 40 E
Churchill **109** 58 47N 94 11W
Churchill →, Man., Can. **109** 58 47N 94 12W
Churchill →, Newf., Can. **103** 53 19N 60 10W
Churchill, C. **109** 58 46N 93 12W
Churchill Falls **103** 53 36N 64 19W
Churchill L. **109** 55 55N 108 20W
Churchill Pk. **108** 58 10N 125 10W
Churdan **116** 42 9N 94 29W
Churu **48** 28 20N 74 50 E
Churubusco **117** 41 14N 85 19W
Chushal **49** 33 40N 78 40 E
Chusovoy **40** 58 15N 57 40 E
Chute-aux-Outardes **105** 49 7N 68 24W
Chute-des-Passes **105** 49 52N 71 16W
Chuuronjang **61** 41 35N 129 40 E
Chuvash A.S.S.R.□ **37** 55 30N 47 0 E
Chuxiong **58** 25 2N 101 28 E
Ci Xian **60** 36 20N 114 25 E
Ciacova **34** 45 35N 21 10 E
Cianjur **57** 6 51 S 107 7 E
Cibadok **57** 6 53 S 106 47 E
Cibatu **57** 7 8 S 107 59 E
Cibola **123** 33 17N 114 9W
Cicero **112** 41 48N 87 48W
Cícero Dantas **138** 10 36 S 38 23W
Cidacos → **24** 42 21N 1 38W
Cide **38** 41 53N 33 1 E
Ciechanów **32** 52 52N 20 38 E
Ciego de Avila **126** 21 50N 78 50W
Ciénaga **134** 11 1N 74 15W
Ciénaga de Oro **134** 8 53N 75 37W
Cienfuegos **126** 22 10N 80 30W
Cieplice Śląskie Zdrój **32** 50 50N 15 40 E
Cierp **20** 42 55N 0 40 E
Cíes, Islas **22** 42 12N 8 55W
Cieszyn **32** 49 45N 18 35 E
Cieza **25** 38 17N 1 23W
Cifuentes **24** 40 47N 2 37W
Cihuatlán **124** 19 14N 104 35W
Cijara, Pantano de **23** 39 18N 4 52W
Cijulang **57** 7 42 S 108 27 E
Cikajang **57** 7 25 S 107 48 E
Cikampek **57** 6 23 S 107 28 E
Cilacap **57** 7 43 S 109 0 E
Çıldır **39** 41 10N 43 20 E
Cili **59** 29 30N 111 8 E
Cilician Gates P. **46** 37 20N 34 52 E
Cima **123** 35 14N 115 30W
Cimahi **57** 6 53 S 107 33 E
Cimarron, Kans., U.S.A. **119** 37 50N 100 20W
Cimarron, N. Mex., U.S.A. **119** 36 30N 104 52W
Cimarron → **119** 36 10N 96 17W
Cimone, Mte. **26** 44 10N 10 40 E
Cîmpina **34** 45 10N 25 45 E
Cîmpulung, Argeş, Rumania **34** 45 17N 25 3 E
Cîmpulung, Moldovenesc, Rumania **34** 47 32N 25 30 E
Cinca → **24** 41 26N 0 21 E
Cincinnati, Iowa, U.S.A. **116** 40 38N 92 56W
Cincinnati, Ohio, U.S.A. **117** 39 10N 84 26W
Cîndeşti **34** 45 15N 26 42 E
Ciney **16** 50 18N 5 5 E
Cíngoli **27** 43 23N 13 10 E
Cinigiano **27** 42 53N 11 23 E
Cinto, Mt. **21** 42 24N 8 54 E
Ciorani **34** 44 45N 26 25 E
Ciotat, La **21** 43 12N 5 36 E
Čiovo **27** 43 30N 16 17 E
Cipó **138** 11 6 S 38 31W
Circeo, Monte **28** 41 14N 13 3 E
Circle, Alaska, U.S.A. **100** 65 50N 144 10W
Circle, Montana, U.S.A. **118** 47 26N 105 35W
Circleville, Ohio, U.S.A. **112** 39 35N 82 57W
Circleville, Utah, U.S.A. **121** 38 12N 112 24W
Cirebon **57** 6 45 S 108 32 E
Cirencester **13** 51 43N 1 59W
Cirey-sur-Vezouze **19** 48 35N 6 57 E
Ciriè **26** 45 14N 7 35 E
Cirò **29** 39 23N 17 3 E
Cisco **119** 32 25N 99 0W
Cislău **34** 45 14N 26 20 E
Cisne **117** 38 31N 88 26W
Cisneros **134** 6 33N 75 4W
Cissna Park **117** 40 34N 87 54W
Cisterna di Latina **28** 41 35N 12 50 E
Cisternino **29** 40 45N 17 26 E
Citaré → **135** 1 11N 54 41W
Cité de Cansada **84** 20 51N 17 0W
Citeli-Ckaro **39** 41 33N 46 0 E
Citlaltépetl **125** 19 0N 97 20W
Citrusdal **96** 32 35 S 19 0 E
Città della Pieve **27** 42 57N 12 0 E
Città di Castello **27** 43 27N 12 14 E
Città Sant' Angelo **27** 42 32N 14 5 E
Cittadella **27** 45 39N 11 48 E
Cittaducale **27** 42 24N 12 58 E
Cittanova **29** 38 22N 16 5 E
Ciucaş **34** 45 31N 25 56 E
Ciudad Acuña **124** 29 20N 100 58W
Ciudad Altamirano **124** 18 20N 100 40W
Ciudad Bolívar **135** 8 5N 63 36W
Ciudad Camargo **124** 27 41N 105 10W
Ciudad de Valles **125** 22 0N 99 0W
Ciudad del Carmen **125** 18 38N 91 50W
Ciudad Delicias = Delicias **124** 28 10N 105 30W
Ciudad Guayana **135** 8 0N 62 30W
Ciudad Guerrero **124** 28 33N 107 28W
Ciudad Guzmán **124** 19 40N 103 30W
Ciudad Juárez **124** 31 40N 106 28W
Ciudad Madero **125** 22 19N 97 50W
Ciudad Mante **125** 22 50N 99 0W
Ciudad Obregón **124** 27 28N 109 59W
Ciudad Ojeda **134** 10 12N 71 19W
Ciudad Real **23** 38 59N 3 55W
Ciudad Real □ **23** 38 50N 4 0W
Ciudad Rodrigo **22** 40 35N 6 32W
Ciudad Trujillo = Sto. Domingo **127** 18 30N 70 0W
Ciudad Victoria **125** 23 41N 99 9W
Ciudadela **24** 40 0N 3 50 E
Ciulniţa **34** 44 26N 27 22 E
Cividale del Friuli **27** 46 6N 13 25 E
Cívita Castellana **27** 42 18N 12 24 E
Civitanova Marche **27** 43 18N 13 41 E
Civitavécchia **27** 42 6N 11 46 E
Civitella del Tronto **27** 42 48N 13 40 E
Civray **20** 46 10N 0 17 E
Çivril **46** 38 20N 29 43 E
Cixerri → **28** 39 20N 8 40 E
Cizre **46** 37 19N 42 10 E
Clackline **79** 31 40 S 116 32 E
Clacton-on-Sea **13** 51 47N 1 10 E
Clain → **18** 46 47N 0 33 E
Claire **105** 47 15N 68 40W
Claire, L. **108** 58 35N 112 5W
Claire, Le **116** 41 36N 90 21W
Clairemont **119** 33 9N 100 44W
Clairton **114** 40 18N 79 54W
Clairvaux-les-Lacs **21** 46 35N 5 45 E
Claise → **18** 46 56N 0 42 E
Clallam Bay **122** 48 15N 124 16W
Clamecy **19** 47 28N 3 30 E
Clanton **113** 32 48N 86 36W
Clanwilliam **96** 32 11 S 18 52 E
Clapperton I. **106** 46 0N 82 14W
Clara **15** 53 20N 7 38W
Clara → **72** 19 8 S 142 30 E
Claraville **123** 35 24N 118 20W
Clare, Austral. **73** 33 50 S 138 37 E
Clare, U.S.A. **106** 43 47N 84 45W
Clare □ **15** 52 20N 9 0W
Clare → **15** 53 22N 9 5W
Clare I. **15** 53 48N 10 0W
Claremont **115** 43 23N 72 20W
Claremont Pt. **72** 14 1 S 143 41 E
Claremore **119** 36 40N 95 37W
Claremorris **15** 53 45N 9 0W
Clarence **116** 39 45N 92 16W
Clarence →, Austral. **77** 29 25 S 153 22 E
Clarence →, N.Z. **81** 42 10 S 173 56 E
Clarence I. **143** 61 10 S 54 0W
Clarence, I. **142** 54 0 S 72 0W
Clarence Str., Austral. **78** 12 0 S 131 0 E
Clarence Str., U.S.A. **108** 55 40N 132 10W
Clarence Town **127** 23 6N 74 59W
Clarencetown **76** 32 34 S 151 46 E
Clarendon, Ark., U.S.A. **119** 34 41N 91 20W
Clarendon, Tex., U.S.A. **119** 34 58N 100 54W
Clarenville **103** 48 10N 54 1W
Claresholm **108** 50 0N 113 33W
Clarie Coast **143** 68 0 S 135 0 E
Clarinda **118** 40 45N 95 0W
Clarion, Iowa, U.S.A. **116** 42 41N 93 46W
Clarion, Pa., U.S.A. **114** 41 12N 79 22W
Clarion → **114** 41 9N 79 41W
Clarion Fracture Zone **67** 20 0N 120 0W
Clark **118** 44 55N 97 45W
Clark Fork **120** 48 9N 116 9W
Clark Fork → **120** 48 9N 116 15W
Clark Hill Res. **113** 33 45N 82 20W
Clark, Pt. **106** 44 4N 81 45W
Clarkdale **121** 34 53N 112 3W
Clarke City **103** 50 12N 66 38W
Clarke, I. **72** 40 32 S 148 10 E
Clarke L. **109** 54 24N 106 54W
Clarke Ra. **72** 20 45 S 148 20 E
Clark's Fork → **120** 45 39N 108 43W
Clark's Harbour **103** 43 25N 65 38W
Clarks Summit **115** 41 31N 75 44W
Clarksburg **112** 39 18N 80 21W
Clarksdale **119** 34 12N 90 33W
Clarkston **120** 46 28N 117 2W
Clarksville, Ark., U.S.A. **119** 35 29N 93 27W
Clarksville, Iowa, U.S.A. **116** 42 47N 92 40W
Clarksville, Mich., U.S.A. **117** 42 50N 85 15W
Clarksville, Ohio, U.S.A. **117** 39 24N 83 59W
Clarksville, Tenn., U.S.A. **113** 36 32N 87 20W
Clarksville, Tex., U.S.A. **119** 33 37N 94 59W
Claro → **139** 19 8 S 50 40W
Clatskanie **122** 46 9N 123 12W
Claude **119** 35 8N 101 22W
Claveria **57** 18 37N 121 4 E
Clay **122** 38 17N 121 10W
Clay Center **118** 39 27N 97 9W
Clay City, Ind., U.S.A. **117** 39 17N 87 7W
Clay City, Ky., U.S.A. **117** 37 52N 83 55W
Clayette, La **21** 46 17N 4 19 E
Claypool **121** 33 27N 110 55W
Claysville **114** 40 5N 80 25W
Clayton, Idaho, U.S.A. **120** 44 12N 114 31W
Clayton, Ind., U.S.A. **117** 39 41N 86 31W
Clayton, N. Mex., U.S.A. **119** 36 30N 103 10W
Cle Elum **120** 47 15N 120 57W
Clear L. **122** 39 5N 122 47W
Clear, C. **15** 51 26N 9 30W
Clear I. **15** 51 26N 9 30W
Clear, L. **107** 45 26N 77 12W
Clear Lake, S.D., U.S.A. **118** 44 48N 96 41W
Clear Lake, Wash., U.S.A. **120** 48 27N 122 15W
Clear Lake City **116** 43 8N 93 23W
Clear Lake Res. **120** 41 55N 121 10W
Clearfield, Iowa, U.S.A. **116** 40 48N 94 29W
Clearfield, Pa., U.S.A. **112** 41 0N 78 27W
Clearfield, Utah, U.S.A. **120** 41 10N 112 0W
Clearlake Highlands **122** 38 57N 122 38W
Clearmont **120** 44 43N 106 29W
Clearwater, Can. **108** 51 38N 120 2W
Clearwater, U.S.A. **113** 27 58N 82 45W
Clearwater →, Alta., Can. **108** 52 22N 114 57W
Clearwater →, Alta., Can. **109** 56 44N 111 23W
Clearwater Cr. **108** 61 36N 125 30W
Clearwater, Mts. **120** 46 20N 115 30W
Clearwater Prov. Park **109** 54 0N 101 0W
Cleburne **119** 32 18N 97 25W
Clécy **18** 48 55N 0 29W
Cleethorpes **12** 53 33N 0 2W
Cleeve Cloud **13** 51 56N 2 0W
Clelles **21** 44 50N 5 38 E
Clendale **117** 39 16N 84 28W
Clerke Reef **78** 17 22 S 119 20 E
Clerks Rocks **143** 56 0 S 34 30W
Clermont, Austral. **72** 22 49 S 147 39 E
Clermont, Can. **105** 47 41N 70 14W
Clermont, France **19** 49 23N 2 24 E
Clermont-en-Argonne **19** 49 5N 5 4 E
Clermont-Ferrand **20** 45 46N 3 4 E
Clermont-l'Hérault **20** 43 38N 3 26 E
Clerval **19** 47 25N 6 30 E
Clervaux **16** 50 4N 6 2 E
Cléry-Saint-André **19** 47 50N 1 46 E
Cles **26** 46 21N 11 4 E
Cleveland, Austral. **73** 27 30 S 153 15 E
Cleveland, Miss., U.S.A. **119** 33 43N 90 43W
Cleveland, Ohio, U.S.A. **114** 41 28N 81 43W
Cleveland, Okla., U.S.A. **119** 36 21N 96 33W

Cleveland, Tenn., U.S.A.	**113**	35 9N	84 52W
Cleveland, Tex., U.S.A.	**119**	30 18N	95 0W
Cleveland □	**12**	54 35N	1 8E
Cleveland, C.	**72**	19 11S	147 1E
Cleveland Heights	**114**	41 32N	81 30W
Clevelândia	**141**	26 24S	52 23W
Clevelândia do Norte	**135**	3 49N	51 52W
Cleves	**117**	39 10N	84 45W
Clew B.	**15**	53 54N	9 50W
Clewiston	**113**	26 44N	80 50W
Clifden, Ireland	**15**	53 30N	10 2W
Clifden, N.Z.	**81**	46 1S	167 42E
Cliff	**121**	33 0N	108 36W
Cliffdell	**122**	46 44N	120 42W
Clifton, Austral.	**77**	27 59S	151 53E
Clifton, Ariz., U.S.A.	**121**	33 8N	109 23W
Clifton, Ill., U.S.A.	**117**	40 56N	87 56W
Clifton, Tex., U.S.A.	**119**	31 46N	97 35W
Clifton Forge	**112**	37 49N	79 51W
Climax	**109**	49 10N	108 20W
Clinch →	**113**	36 0N	84 29W
Clingmans Dome	**113**	35 35N	83 30W
Clint	**121**	31 37N	106 11W
Clinton, B.C., Can.	**108**	51 6N	121 35W
Clinton, Ont., Can.	**106**	43 37N	81 32W
Clinton, N.Z.	**81**	46 12S	169 23E
Clinton, Ark., U.S.A.	**119**	35 37N	92 30W
Clinton, Ill., U.S.A.	**118**	40 8N	89 0W
Clinton, Ind., U.S.A.	**117**	39 40N	87 22W
Clinton, Iowa, U.S.A.	**116**	41 50N	90 12W
Clinton, Mass., U.S.A.	**115**	42 26N	71 40W
Clinton, Mo., U.S.A.	**116**	38 20N	93 46W
Clinton, N.C., U.S.A.	**113**	35 5N	78 15W
Clinton, Okla., U.S.A.	**119**	35 30N	99 0W
Clinton, S.C., U.S.A.	**113**	34 30N	81 54W
Clinton, Tenn., U.S.A.	**113**	36 6N	84 10W
Clinton, Wash., U.S.A.	**122**	47 59N	122 22W
Clinton, Wis., U.S.A.	**117**	42 34N	88 52W
Clinton C.	**72**	22 30S	150 45E
Clinton Colden L.	**100**	63 58N	107 27W
Clintonville	**118**	44 35N	88 46W
Clipperton Fracture Zone	**67**	19 0N	122 0W
Clipperton, I.	**67**	10 18N	109 13W
Clisson	**18**	47 5N	1 16W
Clive	**80**	39 36S	176 58E
Clive L.	**108**	63 13N	118 54W
Cliza	**137**	17 36S	65 56W
Cloates, Pt.	**78**	22 43S	113 40E
Clocolan	**97**	28 55S	27 34E
Clodomira	**140**	27 35S	64 14W
Clonakilty	**15**	51 37N	8 53W
Clonakilty B.	**15**	51 33N	8 50W
Cloncurry	**72**	20 40S	140 28E
Cloncurry →	**72**	18 37S	140 40E
Clones	**15**	54 10N	7 13W
Clonmel	**15**	52 22N	7 42W
Cloppenburg	**30**	52 50N	8 3E
Cloquet	**118**	46 40N	92 30W
Clorinda	**140**	25 16S	57 45W
Cloud Peak	**120**	44 23N	107 10W
Cloudcroft	**121**	33 0N	105 48W
Clouds Creek	**77**	30 4S	152 42E
Cloudy B.	**81**	41 25S	174 10E
Clova	**104**	48 7N	75 22W
Cloverdale, Calif., U.S.A.	**122**	38 49N	123 0W
Cloverdale, Ind., U.S.A.	**117**	39 31N	86 47W
Cloverport	**117**	37 50N	86 38W
Clovis, Calif., U.S.A.	**122**	36 47N	119 45W
Clovis, N. Mex., U.S.A.	**119**	34 20N	103 10W
Cloyes	**18**	48 0N	1 14E
Cloyne	**107**	44 49N	77 11W
Club Terrace	**75**	37 35S	148 58E
Cluj	**34**	46 47N	23 38E
Clunes	**74**	37 20S	143 45E
Cluny	**21**	46 26N	4 38E
Cluses	**21**	46 5N	6 35E
Clusone	**26**	45 54N	9 58E
Clutha →	**81**	46 20S	169 49E
Clwyd □	**12**	53 5N	3 20W
Clwyd →	**12**	53 20N	3 30W
Clyde, Can.	**101**	70 30N	68 30W
Clyde, N.Z.	**81**	45 12S	169 20E
Clyde, N.Y., U.S.A.	**114**	43 8N	76 52W
Clyde, Ohio, U.S.A.	**116**	41 18N	82 59W
Clyde →	**14**	55 56N	4 29W
Clyde, Firth of	**14**	55 20N	5 0W
Clydebank	**14**	55 54N	4 25W
Clymer	**114**	42 3N	79 39W
Côa →	**22**	41 5N	7 6W
Coachella	**123**	33 44N	116 13W
Coachella Canal	**123**	32 43N	114 57W
Coahoma	**119**	32 17N	101 20W
Coahuayana →	**124**	18 41N	103 45W
Coahuayutla	**124**	18 19N	101 42W
Coahuila de Zaragoza □	**124**	27 0N	103 0W
Coal →	**108**	59 39N	126 57W
Coal City	**117**	41 17N	88 17W
Coal Creek Flat	**81**	45 27S	169 19E
Coal I.	**81**	46 8S	166 40E
Coalane	**95**	17 48S	37 2E
Coalcomán	**124**	18 40N	103 10W
Coaldale	**108**	49 45N	112 35W
Coalgate	**119**	34 35N	96 13W
Coalinga	**122**	36 10N	120 21W
Coalville, U.K.	**12**	52 43N	1 21W
Coalville, U.S.A.	**120**	40 58N	111 24W
Coaraci	**139**	14 38S	39 32W
Coari	**135**	4 8S	63 7W
Coari →	**135**	4 30S	63 33W
Coari, L. de	**135**	4 15S	63 22W
Coast □	**94**	2 40S	39 45E
Coast Mts.	**108**	55 0N	129 0W
Coast Ranges	**122**	41 0N	123 0W
Coastal Plains Basin	**79**	30 10S	115 30E
Coatbridge	**14**	55 52N	4 2W
Coatepec	**125**	19 27N	96 58W
Coatepeque	**126**	14 46N	91 55W
Coatesville	**112**	39 59N	75 55W
Coaticook	**105**	45 10N	71 46W
Coats I.	**101**	62 30N	83 0W
Coats Land	**143**	77 0S	25 0W
Coatzacoalcos	**125**	18 7N	94 25W
Cobalt	**102**	47 25N	79 42W
Cobán	**126**	15 30N	90 21W
Cobar	**73**	31 27S	145 48E
Cobargo	**75**	36 20S	149 55E
Cobba-da-mana	**77**	28 24S	151 14E
Cobbannah	**75**	37 37S	147 12E
Cobberas, Mt.	**75**	36 53S	148 12E
Cobden, Austral.	**74**	38 20S	143 3E
Cobden, Can.	**107**	45 38N	76 53W
Cóbh	**15**	51 50N	8 18W
Cobham	**73**	30 18S	142 7E
Cobija	**136**	11 0S	68 50W
Cobleskill	**115**	42 40N	74 30W
Coboconk	**107**	44 39N	78 48W
Cobourg	**107**	43 58N	78 10W
Cobourg Pen.	**78**	11 20S	132 15E
Cobram	**74**	35 54S	145 40E
Cobre	**120**	41 6N	114 25W
Coburg	**31**	50 15N	10 58E
Coca	**22**	41 13N	4 32W
Coca →	**134**	0 29S	76 58W
Cocachacra	**136**	17 5S	71 45W
Cocal	**138**	3 28S	41 34W
Cocanada = Kakinada	**50**	16 50N	82 11E
Cocentaina	**25**	38 45N	0 27W
Cocha, La	**140**	27 50S	65 40W
Cochabamba	**137**	17 26S	66 10W
Coche, I.	**135**	10 47N	63 56W
Cochem	**31**	50 8N	7 7E
Cochemane	**95**	17 0S	32 54E
Cochin	**51**	9 59N	76 22E
Cochin China = Nam-Phan	**55**	10 30N	106 0E
Cochise	**121**	32 6N	109 58W
Cochran	**113**	32 25N	83 23W
Cochrane, Alta., Can.	**108**	51 11N	114 30W
Cochrane, Ont., Can.	**102**	49 0N	81 0W
Cochrane →	**109**	57 53N	101 34W
Cochrane, L.	**142**	47 10S	72 0W
Cockatoo	**74**	37 57S	145 32E
Cockburn	**73**	32 5S	141 0E
Cockburn, Canal	**142**	54 30S	72 0W
Cockburn I.	**106**	45 55N	83 22W
Cockburn Ra.	**78**	15 46S	128 0E
Cocklebiddy Motel	**79**	32 0S	126 3E
Coco →	**126**	15 0N	83 8W
Coco, Pta.	**134**	2 58N	77 43W
Cocoa	**113**	28 22N	80 40W
Cocobeach	**92**	0 59N	9 34E
Côcos	**139**	14 10S	44 33W
Côcos →	**139**	12 44S	44 48W
Cocos I., Guam	**68**	13 14N	144 39E
Cocos I., Pac. Oc.	**67**	5 25N	87 55W
Cocos Is.	**66**	12 10S	96 55E
Cod, C.	**111**	42 8N	70 10W
Codajás	**135**	3 55S	62 0W
Codera, C.	**134**	10 35N	66 4W
Coderre	**109**	50 11N	106 31W
Codigoro	**27**	44 50N	12 5E
Codó	**138**	4 30S	43 55W
Codogno	**26**	45 10N	9 42E
Codpa	**136**	18 50S	69 44W
Codróipo	**27**	45 57N	13 0E
Cody	**120**	44 35N	109 0W
Coe Hill	**107**	44 52N	77 50W
Coelemu	**140**	36 30S	72 48W
Coelho Neto	**138**	4 15S	43 0W
Coen	**72**	13 52S	143 12E
Coeroeni →	**135**	3 21N	57 31W
Coesfeld	**30**	51 56N	7 10E
Coetivy Is.	**53**	7 8S	56 16E
Coeur d'Alene	**120**	47 45N	116 51W
Cœur d'Alene L.	**120**	47 32N	116 48W
Coevorden	**16**	52 40N	6 44E
Coffeyville	**119**	37 0N	95 40W
Coffs Harbour	**77**	30 16S	153 5E
Cofre de Perote, Cerro	**125**	19 30N	97 10W
Cofrentes	**25**	39 13N	1 5W
Cogealac	**34**	44 36N	28 36E
Coghinas →	**28**	40 55N	8 48E
Coghinas, L. di	**28**	40 46N	9 3E
Cognac	**20**	45 41N	0 20W
Cogne	**26**	45 37N	7 21E
Cogolludo	**24**	40 59N	3 10W
Cohagen	**120**	47 2N	106 36W
Cohoes	**115**	42 47N	73 42W
Cohuna	**74**	35 45S	144 15E
Coiba, I.	**126**	7 30N	81 40W
Coig →	**142**	51 0S	69 10W
Coihaique, Chile	**142**	45 34S	72 4W
Coihaique, Chile	**142**	45 30S	71 45W
Coimbatore	**51**	11 2N	76 59E
Coimbra, Brazil	**136**	19 55S	57 48W
Coimbra, Port.	**22**	40 15N	8 27W
Coimbra □	**22**	40 12N	8 25W
Coín	**23**	36 40N	4 48W
Coipasa, L. de	**136**	19 12S	68 7W
Coipasa, Salar de	**136**	19 26S	68 9W
Cojata	**136**	15 2S	69 25W
Cojedes □	**134**	9 20N	68 20W
Cojedes →	**134**	8 34N	68 5W
Cojimies	**136**	0 20N	80 0W
Cojocna	**34**	46 45N	23 50E
Cojutepequé	**126**	13 41N	88 54W
Cokeville	**120**	42 4N	111 0W
Col di Tenda	**26**	44 7N	7 36E
Colaba Pt.	**50**	18 54N	72 47E
Colac	**74**	38 21S	143 35E
Colachel	**51**	8 10N	77 15E
Colane	**76**	31 14S	147 18E
Colares	**23**	38 48N	9 30W
Colatina	**139**	19 32S	40 37W
Colbeck, C.	**143**	77 6S	157 48W
Colbinabbin	**74**	36 38S	144 48E
Colborne	**107**	44 0N	77 53W
Colby	**118**	39 27N	101 2W
Colchagua □	**140**	34 30S	71 0W
Colchester	**13**	51 54N	0 55E
Coldstream	**14**	55 39N	2 14W
Coldwater, Can.	**106**	44 42N	79 40W
Coldwater, Kans., U.S.A.	**119**	37 18N	99 24W
Coldwater, Mich., U.S.A.	**117**	41 57N	85 0W
Coldwater, Ohio, U.S.A.	**117**	40 29N	84 38W
Coldwater, L.	**117**	41 48N	84 59W
Cole Camp	**116**	38 28N	93 12W
Colebrook, Austral.	**72**	42 31S	147 21E
Colebrook, U.S.A.	**115**	44 54N	71 29W
Coleman, Can.	**108**	49 40N	114 30W
Coleman, Mich., U.S.A.	**106**	43 46N	84 35W
Coleman, Tex., U.S.A.	**119**	31 52N	99 30W
Coleman →	**72**	15 6S	141 38E
Colenso	**97**	28 44S	29 50E
Coleraine, Austral.	**74**	37 36S	141 40E
Coleraine, U.K.	**15**	55 8N	6 40E
Coleraine □	**15**	55 8N	6 40E
Coleridge, L.	**81**	43 17S	171 30E
Coleroon →	**51**	11 25N	79 50E
Colesberg	**96**	30 45S	25 5E
Colesburg	**116**	42 38N	91 12W
Coleville	**122**	38 34N	119 30W
Colfax, Calif., U.S.A.	**122**	39 6N	120 57W
Colfax, Ill., U.S.A.	**117**	40 34N	88 37W
Colfax, Ind., U.S.A.	**117**	40 12N	86 40W
Colfax, La., U.S.A.	**119**	31 35N	92 39W
Colfax, Wash., U.S.A.	**120**	46 57N	117 28W
Colhué Huapi, L.	**142**	45 30S	69 0W
Cólico	**26**	46 8N	9 22E
Coligny	**97**	26 17S	26 15E
Colima	**124**	19 10N	103 40W
Colima □	**124**	19 10N	103 40W
Colima, Nevado de, Mexico	**124**	19 30N	103 40W
Colima, Nevado de, Mexico	**124**	19 35N	103 45W
Colina	**140**	33 13S	70 45W
Colina do Norte	**88**	12 28N	15 0W
Colinas, Goiás, Brazil	**139**	14 15S	48 2W
Colinas, Maranhão, Brazil	**138**	6 0S	44 10W
Colinton	**76**	35 50S	149 10E
Coll, I.	**14**	56 40N	6 35W
Collaguasi	**140**	21 5S	68 45W
Collarada, Peña	**24**	42 43N	0 29W
Collarenebri	**73**	29 33S	148 36E
Collbran	**121**	39 16N	107 58W
Colle di Val d'Elsa	**27**	43 25N	11 7E
Colle Salvetti	**26**	43 34N	10 27E
Colle Sannita	**29**	41 22N	14 48E
Collécchio	**26**	44 45N	10 10E
Collector	**76**	34 56S	149 29E
Colleen Bawn	**95**	21 0S	29 12E
College Park	**113**	33 42N	84 27W
Collette	**103**	46 40N	65 30W
Collie, N.S.W., Austral.	**76**	31 41S	148 18E
Collie, W. Austral., Austral.	**79**	33 22S	116 8E
Collier B.	**78**	16 10S	124 15E
Collier Ra.	**79**	24 45S	119 10E
Colline Metallifere	**26**	43 10N	11 0E
Collingwood, Austral.	**72**	22 20S	142 31E
Collingwood, Can.	**106**	44 29N	80 13W
Collingwood, N.Z.	**81**	40 41S	172 40E
Collins, Can.	**102**	50 17N	89 27W
Collins, U.S.A.	**116**	37 54N	93 37W
Collinsville, Austral.	**72**	20 30S	147 56E
Collinsville, U.S.A.	**116**	38 40N	89 59W
Collipulli	**140**	37 55S	72 30W
Collo	**87**	36 58N	6 37E
Collonges	**21**	46 9N	5 52E
Collooney	**15**	54 11N	8 28W
Colmar	**19**	48 5N	7 20E
Colmars	**21**	44 11N	6 39E
Colmenar	**23**	36 54N	4 20W
Colmenar de Oreja	**24**	40 6N	3 25W
Colmenar Viejo	**22**	40 39N	3 47W
Colne	**12**	53 51N	2 11W
Colo →	**76**	33 25S	150 52E
Cologna Véneta	**27**	45 19N	11 21E
Cologne = Köln	**30**	50 56N	9 58E
Coloma	**122**	38 49N	120 53W
Colomb-Béchar = Béchar	**86**	31 38N	2 18W
Colombey-les-Belles	**19**	48 32N	5 54E
Colombey-les-Deux-Églises	**19**	48 13N	4 50E
Colômbia	**139**	20 10S	48 40W
Colombia ■	**134**	3 45N	73 0W
Colombier	**105**	48 52N	68 51W
Colombo	**51**	6 56N	79 58E
Colombus	**121**	31 54N	107 43W
Colome	**118**	43 20N	99 44W
Colón, Argent.	**140**	32 12S	58 10W
Colón, Cuba	**126**	22 42N	80 54W
Colón, Panama	**126**	9 20N	79 54W
Colón, Peru	**136**	5 0S	81 0W
Colonella	**27**	42 52N	13 50E
Colonia	**140**	34 25S	57 50W
Colonia Dora	**140**	28 34S	62 59W
Colonial Hts.	**112**	37 19N	77 25W
Colonne, C. delle	**29**	39 2N	17 11E
Colonsay, Can.	**109**	51 59N	105 52W
Colonsay, U.K.	**14**	56 4N	6 12W
Colorado □	**110**	37 40N	106 0W
Colorado →, Argent.	**142**	39 50S	62 8W
Colorado →, Calif., U.S.A.	**121**	34 45N	114 40W
Colorado →, Tex., U.S.A.	**119**	28 36N	95 58W
Colorado City	**119**	32 25N	100 50W
Colorado Desert	**110**	34 20N	116 0W
Colorado Plateau	**121**	36 40N	110 30W
Colorado R. Aqueduct	**123**	34 17N	114 10W
Colorado Springs	**118**	38 55N	104 50W
Colorno	**26**	44 55N	10 21E
Colotlán	**124**	22 6N	103 16W
Colquechaca	**137**	18 40S	66 1W
Colton, Calif., U.S.A.	**123**	34 4N	117 20W
Colton, N.Y., U.S.A.	**115**	44 34N	74 58W
Colton, Wash., U.S.A.	**120**	46 41N	117 6W
Columbia, Ill., U.S.A.	**116**	38 26N	90 12W
Columbia, La., U.S.A.	**119**	32 7N	92 5W
Columbia, Miss., U.S.A.	**119**	31 16N	89 50W
Columbia, Mo., U.S.A.	**116**	38 58N	92 20W
Columbia, Pa., U.S.A.	**115**	40 2N	76 30W
Columbia, S.C., U.S.A.	**113**	34 0N	81 0W
Columbia, Tenn., U.S.A.	**113**	35 40N	87 0W
Columbia →	**120**	46 15N	124 5W
Columbia Basin	**120**	47 30N	118 30W
Columbia, C.	**144**	83 0N	70 0W
Columbia City	**117**	41 8N	85 30W
Columbia, District of □	**112**	38 55N	77 0W
Columbia Falls	**120**	48 25N	114 16W
Columbia Heights	**118**	45 5N	93 10W
Columbia, Mt.	**108**	52 8N	117 20W
Columbiana	**114**	40 53N	80 40W
Columbiaville	**106**	43 9N	83 25W
Columbretes, Is.	**24**	39 50N	0 50E
Columbus, Ga., U.S.A.	**113**	32 30N	84 58W
Columbus, Ind., U.S.A.	**117**	39 14N	85 55W
Columbus, Kans., U.S.A.	**119**	37 15N	94 30W
Columbus, Miss., U.S.A.	**113**	33 30N	88 26W
Columbus, Mont., U.S.A.	**120**	45 38N	109 14W

Columbus, N.D., U.S.A. **118** 48 52N 102 48W
Columbus, Nebr., U.S.A. **118** 41 30N 97 25W
Columbus, Ohio, U.S.A. **117** 39 57N 83 1W
Columbus, Tex., U.S.A. **119** 29 42N 96 33W
Columbus, Wis., U.S.A. **118** 43 20N 89 2W
Columbus Grove **117** 40 55N 84 4W
Columbus Junction **116** 41 17N 91 22W
Colunga **22** 43 29N 5 16W
Colusa **122** 39 15N 122 1W
Colville **120** 48 33N 117 54W
Colville → **100** 70 25N 151 0W
Colville, C. **80** 36 29S 175 21 E
Colwyn Bay **12** 53 17N 3 44W
Comácchio **27** 44 41N 12 10 E
Comalcalco **125** 18 16N 93 13W
Comallo **142** 41 0S 70 5W
Comanche, Okla., U.S.A. **119** 34 27N 97 58W
Comanche, Tex., U.S.A. **119** 31 55N 98 35W
Comandante Luis Piedrabuena **142** 49 59S 68 54W
Comănești **34** 46 25N 26 26 E
Comarapa **137** 17 54S 64 29W
Comayagua **126** 14 25N 87 37W
Combahee → **113** 32 30N 80 31W
Combara **76** 31 10S 148 22 E
Combeaufontaine **19** 47 38N 5 54 E
Comber **106** 42 14N 82 33W
Combermere **107** 45 22N 77 37W
Combermere Bay **52** 19 37N 93 34 E
Comblain-au-Pont **16** 50 29N 5 35 E
Combles **19** 50 0N 2 50 E
Combourg **18** 48 25N 1 46W
Comboyne **77** 31 34S 152 27 E
Combronde **20** 45 58N 3 5 E
Comeragh Mts. **15** 52 17N 7 35W
Comet **72** 23 36S 148 38 E
Comet Vale **79** 29 55S 121 4 E
Comilla **52** 23 28N 91 10 E
Comino, C. **28** 40 28N 9 47 E
Cómiso **29** 36 57N 14 35 E
Comitán **125** 16 18N 92 9W
Commanda **106** 45 57N 79 36W
Commentry **20** 46 20N 2 46 E
Commerce, Ga., U.S.A. **113** 34 10N 83 25W
Commerce, Tex., U.S.A. **119** 33 15N 95 50W
Commercy **19** 48 46N 5 34 E
Commewijne □ **135** 5 25N 54 45W
Commissaires, L. des **105** 48 10N 72 16W
Committee B. **101** 68 30N 86 30W
Commonwealth B. **143** 67 0S 144 0 E
Commoron Cr. → **77** 28 22S 150 8 E
Communism Pk. = Kommunisma, Pk. **47** 38 40N 72 0 E
Como **26** 45 48N 9 5 E
Como, L. di **26** 46 5N 9 17 E
Comodoro Rivadavia **142** 45 50S 67 40W
Comorin, C. **51** 8 3N 77 40 E
Comoro Is. **5** 12 10S 44 15 E
Comox **108** 49 42N 124 55W
Compiègne **19** 49 24N 2 50 E
Compíglia Maríttima **26** 43 4N 10 37 E
Comporta **23** 38 22N 8 46W
Compostela **124** 21 15N 104 53W
Comprida, I. **141** 24 50S 47 42W
Compton, Can. **105** 45 14N 71 49W
Compton, U.S.A. **123** 33 54N 118 13W
Compton Downs **73** 30 28S 146 30 E
Con Cuong **54** 19 2N 104 54 E
Con Son, Is. **55** 8 41N 106 37 E
Cona Niyeu **142** 41 58S 67 0W
Conakry **88** 9 29N 13 49W
Conara Junction **72** 41 50S 147 26 E
Concarneau **18** 47 52N 3 56W
Conceição, Paraíba, Brazil **138** 7 33S 38 31W
Conceição, Roraima, Brazil **135** 2 11N 60 58W
Conceição, Mozam. **95** 18 47S 36 7 E
Conceição da Barra **139** 18 35S 39 45W
Conceição do Araguaia **138** 8 0S 49 2W
Conceição do Canindé **138** 7 54S 41 34W
Concepción, Argent. **140** 27 20S 65 35W
Concepción, Boliv. **137** 16 15S 62 8W
Concepción, Chile **140** 36 50S 73 0W
Concepción, Mexico **125** 18 15N 90 5W
Concepción, Parag. **140** 23 22S 57 26W
Concepción, Peru **136** 11 54S 75 19W
Concepción □ **140** 37 0S 72 30W
Concepción → **124** 30 32N 113 2W
Concepción del Oro **124** 24 40N 101 30W
Concepción del Uruguay **140** 32 35S 58 20W
Concepción, Est. de **142** 50 30S 74 55W
Concepción, L. **137** 17 20S 61 20W
Concepción, La **134** 10 30N 71 50W
Concepción, La = Ri-Aba **89** 3 28N 8 40 E
Concepcion, Pt. **121** 34 27N 120 27W
Concepción, Punta **124** 26 55N 111 59W
Conception B. **96** 23 55S 14 22 E
Conception I. **127** 23 52N 75 9W
Conception, La **104** 46 9N 74 42W
Conception, Pt. **123** 34 30N 120 34W
Concession **95** 17 27S 30 56 E
Conchas Dam **119** 35 25N 104 10W
Conche **103** 50 55N 55 58W
Conches **18** 48 51N 2 43 E
Concho **121** 34 32N 109 43W
Concho → **119** 31 30N 99 45W
Conchos →, Chihuahua, Mexico **124** 29 32N 104 25W
Conchos →, Tamaulipas, Mexico **125** 25 9N 98 35W
Concord, Calif., U.S.A. **122** 37 59N 122 2W
Concord, Mich., U.S.A. **117** 42 11N 84 38W
Concord, N.C., U.S.A. **113** 35 28N 80 35W
Concord, N.H., U.S.A. **115** 43 12N 71 30W
Concordia **140** 31 20S 58 2W
Concórdia **134** 4 36S 66 36W
Concordia, Mexico **124** 23 18N 106 2W
Concordia, Kans., U.S.A. **118** 39 35N 97 40W
Concordia, Mo., U.S.A. **116** 38 59N 93 34W
Concordia, La **125** 16 8N 92 38W
Concots **20** 44 26N 1 40 E
Concrete **120** 48 35N 121 49W
Condah **74** 37 57S 141 44 E
Condamine **73** 26 56S 150 9 E
Condat **20** 45 21N 2 46 E
Conde **139** 11 49S 37 37W
Condé **19** 50 26N 3 34 E
Conde **118** 45 13N 98 5W
Condé-sur-Noireau **18** 48 51N 0 33W
Condeúba **139** 14 52S 42 0W
Condom **20** 43 57N 0 22 E
Condon **120** 45 15N 120 8W
Condove **26** 45 8N 7 19 E
Conegliano **27** 45 53N 12 18 E
Conejera, I. **25** 39 11N 2 58 E
Conejos **124** 26 14N 103 53W
Conflans-en-Jarnisy **19** 49 10N 5 52 E
Confolens **20** 46 2N 0 40 E
Confuso → **140** 25 9S 57 34W
Congjiang **58** 25 43N 108 52 E
Congleton **12** 53 10N 2 12W
Congo **138** 7 48S 36 40W
Congo ■ **92** 1 0S 16 0 E
Congo → = Zaïre → **92** 1 30N 28 0 E
Congo Basin **82** 0 10S 24 30 E
Congo, Democratic Rep. of = Zaïre ■ **92** 3 0S 22 0 E
Congonhas **139** 20 30S 43 52W
Congress **121** 34 11N 112 56W
Conil **23** 36 17N 6 10W
Coniston **106** 46 29N 80 51W
Conjeevaram = Kanchipuram **51** 12 52N 79 45 E
Conjuboy **72** 18 35S 144 35 E
Conklin **109** 55 38N 111 5W
Conlea **73** 30 7S 144 35 E
Conn, L. **15** 54 3N 9 15W
Connacht **15** 53 23N 8 40W
Conneaut **114** 41 55N 80 32W
Connecticut □ **115** 41 40N 72 40W
Connecticut → **115** 41 17N 72 21W
Connell **120** 46 36N 118 51W
Connellsville **114** 40 3N 79 32W
Connemara **15** 53 29N 9 45W
Connemaugh → **114** 40 38N 79 42W
Conner, La **120** 48 22N 122 27W
Connerré **18** 48 3N 0 30 E
Connersville **117** 39 40N 85 10W
Connors **105** 47 10N 68 52W
Connors Ra. **72** 21 40S 149 10 E
Conoble **73** 32 55S 144 33 E
Conon → **14** 57 33N 4 28W
Cononaco → **134** 1 32S 75 35W
Cononbridge **14** 57 32N 4 30W
Conquest **109** 51 32N 107 14W
Conquet, Le **18** 48 21N 4 46W
Conrad, Iowa, U.S.A. **116** 42 14N 92 52W
Conrad, Mont., U.S.A. **120** 48 11N 112 0W
Conran, C. **75** 37 49S 148 44 E
Conroe **119** 30 15N 95 28W
Consecon **107** 44 0N 77 31W
Conselheiro Lafaiete **139** 20 40S 43 48W
Conselheiro Pena **139** 19 10S 41 30W
Conshohocken **115** 40 5N 75 18W
Consort **109** 52 1N 110 46W
Constance = Konstanz **31** 47 39N 9 10 E
Constance, L. = Bodensee **31** 47 35N 9 25 E
Constanța **34** 44 14N 28 38 E
Constantina **23** 37 51N 5 40W
Constantine, Alg. **87** 36 25N 6 42 E
Constantine, U.S.A. **117** 41 50N 85 40W
Constitución, Chile **140** 35 20S 72 30W
Constitución, Uruguay **140** 42 0S 57 50W
Consuegra **23** 39 28N 3 36W
Consul **109** 49 20N 109 30W
Contact **120** 41 50N 114 56W
Contai **49** 21 54N 87 46 E
Contamana **136** 7 19S 74 55W
Contarina **27** 45 2N 12 13 E
Contas → **139** 14 17S 39 1W
Contes **21** 43 49N 7 19 E
Continental **117** 41 6N 84 16W
Contoocook **115** 43 13N 71 45W
Contra Costa **97** 25 9S 33 30 E
Contratación **134** 6 18N 73 29W
Contrecoeur **105** 45 51N 73 14W
Contres **18** 47 24N 1 26 E
Contrexéville **19** 48 6N 5 53 E
Contumaza **136** 7 23S 78 57W
Convención **134** 8 28N 73 21W
Conversano **29** 40 57N 17 8 E
Converse **117** 40 34N 85 52W
Convoy **117** 40 55N 84 43W
Conway, Ark., U.S.A. **119** 35 5N 92 30W
Conway, N.H., U.S.A. **115** 43 58N 71 8W
Conway, S.C., U.S.A. **113** 33 49N 79 2W
Conway = Conwy **12** 53 17N 3 50W
Conway → **12** 53 18N 3 50W
Conway, L. **73** 28 17S 135 35 E
Conwy **12** 53 17N 3 50W
Cooch Behar **52** 26 22N 89 29 E
Cook, Austral. **79** 30 37S 130 25 E
Cook, U.S.A. **118** 47 49N 92 39W
Cook, Bahía **142** 55 10S 70 0W
Cook Inlet **100** 59 0N 151 0W
Cook Is. **67** 17 0S 160 0W
Cook, Mt. **81** 43 36S 170 9 E
Cook Strait **81** 41 15S 174 29 E
Cookeville **113** 36 12N 85 30W
Cookhouse **96** 32 44S 25 47 E
Cookshire **105** 45 25N 71 38W
Cookstown **15** 54 40N 6 43W
Cookstown □ **15** 54 40N 6 43W
Cooksville **114** 43 36N 79 35W
Cooktown **72** 15 30S 145 16 E
Coolabah **73** 31 1S 146 43 E
Cooladdi **73** 26 37S 145 23 E
Coolah **77** 31 48S 149 41 E
Coolangatta **77** 28 11S 153 29 E
Coolatai **77** 29 15S 150 45 E
Coolgardie **79** 30 55S 121 8 E
Coolibah **78** 15 33S 130 56 E
Coolidge **121** 33 1N 111 35W
Coolidge Dam **121** 33 10N 110 30W
Coolongolook **77** 32 12S 152 20 E
Cooma **75** 36 12S 149 8 E
Coon Rapids **116** 41 53N 94 41W
Coonabarabran **76** 31 14S 149 18 E
Coonamble **76** 30 56S 148 27 E
Coonana **79** 31 0S 123 0 E
Coondapoor **51** 13 42N 74 40 E
Coongie **73** 27 9S 140 8 E
Coongoola **73** 27 43S 145 47 E
Cooninie, L. **73** 26 4S 139 59 E
Coonoor **51** 11 21N 76 45 E
Cooper **119** 33 20N 95 40W
Cooper → **113** 33 0N 79 55W
Coopers Cr. → **73** 28 29S 137 46 E
Cooperstown, N.D., U.S.A. **118** 47 30N 98 6W
Cooperstown, N.Y., U.S.A. **115** 42 42N 74 57W
Coopersville **117** 43 4N 85 57W
Coorabie P.O. **79** 31 54S 132 18 E
Coorabulka **72** 23 41S 140 20 E
Cooranbong **76** 33 4S 151 28 E
Coorong, The **73** 35 50S 139 20 E
Coorow **79** 29 53S 116 2 E
Cooroy **73** 26 22S 152 54 E
Coos Bay **120** 43 26N 124 7W
Cootamundra **76** 34 36S 148 1 E
Cootehill **15** 54 5N 7 5W
Cooyal **76** 32 25S 149 45 E
Cooyar **73** 26 59S 151 51 E
Cooyeana **72** 24 29S 138 45 E
Copahue Paso **140** 37 49S 71 8W
Copainalá **125** 17 8N 93 11W
Copán **126** 14 50N 89 9W
Copatana **134** 2 48S 67 4W
Cope **118** 39 44N 102 50W
Cope, Cabo **25** 37 26N 1 28W
Cope Cope **74** 36 27S 143 5 E
Copenhagen = København **11** 55 41N 12 34 E
Copertino **29** 40 17N 18 2 E
Copiapó **140** 27 30S 70 20W
Copiapó → **140** 27 19S 70 56W
Copley **73** 30 36S 138 26 E
Copmanhurst **77** 29 33S 152 49 E
Copp L. **108** 60 14N 114 40W
Coppadah **77** 30 12S 150 34 E
Copparo **27** 44 52N 11 49 E
Coppename → **135** 5 48N 55 55W
Copper Center **100** 62 10N 145 25W
Copper Cliff **106** 46 28N 81 4W
Copper Harbor **112** 47 31N 87 55W
Copper Queen **95** 17 29S 29 18 E
Copperbelt □ **95** 13 15S 27 30 E
Copperfield **79** 29 1S 120 26 E
Coppermine **100** 67 50N 115 5W
Coppermine → **100** 67 49N 116 4W
Copperopolis **122** 37 58N 120 38W
Coquet → **12** 55 18N 1 45W
Coquilhatville = Mbandaka **92** 0 1N 18 18 E
Coquille **120** 43 15N 124 12W
Coquimbo **140** 30 0S 71 20W
Coquimbo □ **140** 31 0S 71 0W
Corabia **34** 43 48N 24 30 E
Coração de Jesus **139** 16 43S 44 22W
Coracora **136** 15 5S 73 45W
Coradi, Is. **29** 40 27N 17 10 E
Coraki **77** 28 59S 153 17 E
Coral Gables **113** 25 45N 80 16W
Coral Harbour **101** 64 8N 83 10W
Coral Sea **66** 15 0S 150 0 E
Coralville **116** 41 42N 91 34W
Coralville Res. **116** 41 50N 91 40W
Coramba **77** 30 12S 153 3 E
Corangamite, L. **74** 38 0S 143 30 E
Corantijn → **135** 5 50N 57 8W
Coraopolis **114** 40 30N 80 10W
Corato **29** 41 12N 16 22 E
Corbeil-Essonnes **19** 48 36N 2 26 E
Corbie **19** 49 54N 2 30 E
Corbières **20** 42 55N 2 35 E
Corbigny **19** 47 16N 3 40 E
Corbin **112** 37 0N 84 3W
Corbones → **23** 37 36N 5 39W
Corby **13** 52 49N 0 31W
Corcoles → **25** 39 40N 3 18W
Corcoran **122** 36 6N 119 35W
Corcovado, Vol. **142** 43 10S 72 55W
Corcubión **22** 42 56N 9 12W
Cordele **113** 31 55N 83 49W
Cordell **119** 35 18N 99 0W
Cordenons **27** 45 59N 12 42 E
Cordes **20** 44 5N 1 57 E
Cordisburgo **139** 19 7S 44 21W
Córdoba, Argent. **140** 31 20S 64 10W
Córdoba, Mexico **125** 18 50N 97 0W
Córdoba, Spain **23** 37 50N 4 50W
Córdoba □, Argent. **140** 31 22S 64 15W
Córdoba □, Colomb. **134** 8 20N 75 40W
Córdoba □, Spain **23** 38 5N 5 0W
Córdoba, Sierra de **140** 31 10S 64 25W
Cordon **57** 16 42N 121 32 E
Cordova, Ala., U.S.A. **113** 33 45N 87 12W
Cordova, Alaska, U.S.A. **100** 60 36N 145 45W
Cordova, Ill., U.S.A. **116** 41 41N 90 19W
Corella **24** 42 7N 1 48W
Corella → **72** 19 34S 140 47 E
Coremas **138** 7 1S 37 58W
Corentyne → **135** 5 50N 57 8W
Corfield **72** 21 40S 143 21 E
Corfu = Kérkira **35** 39 38N 19 50 E
Corgo **22** 42 56N 7 25W
Corguinho **137** 19 53S 54 52W
Cori **28** 41 39N 12 53 E
Coria **22** 40 0N 6 33W
Coricudgy, Mt. **76** 32 51S 150 24 E
Corigliano Cálabro **29** 39 36N 16 31 E
Corindi **77** 30 1S 153 12 E
Corinella **74** 38 25S 145 25 E
Coringa Is. **72** 16 58S 149 58 E
Corinna **72** 41 35S 145 10 E
Corinth, Ky., U.S.A. **117** 38 30N 84 34W
Corinth, Miss., U.S.A. **113** 34 54N 88 30W
Corinth, N.Y., U.S.A. **115** 43 15N 73 50W
Corinth Canal **35** 37 58N 23 0 E
Corinth, G. of = Korinthiakós **35** 38 16N 22 30 E
Corinto, Brazil **139** 18 20S 44 30W
Corinto, Nic. **126** 12 30N 87 10W
Cork **15** 51 54N 8 30W
Cork □ **15** 51 50N 8 50W
Cork Harbour **15** 51 46N 8 16W
Corlay **18** 48 20N 3 5W
Corleone **28** 37 48N 13 16 E
Corleto Perticara **29** 40 23N 16 2 E
Çorlu **46** 41 11N 27 49 E
Cormack L. **108** 60 56N 121 37W
Cormóns **27** 45 58N 13 29 E

Cormorant	**109**	54 14N	100 35W
Cormorant L.	**109**	54 15N	100 50W
Corn Is. = Maiz, Is. del	**126**	12 0N	83 0W
Cornelio	**124**	29 55N	111 8W
Cornélio Procópio	**141**	23 7S	50 40W
Cornell, Ill., U.S.A.	**117**	40 58N	88 43W
Cornell, Wis., U.S.A.	**118**	45 10N	91 8W
Corner Brook	**103**	48 57N	57 58W
Corner Inlet	**75**	38 45S	146 20E
Corniglio	**26**	44 29N	10 5E
Corning, Ark., U.S.A.	**119**	36 27N	90 34W
Corning, Calif., U.S.A.	**120**	39 56N	122 9W
Corning, Iowa, U.S.A.	**116**	40 57N	94 40W
Corning, N.Y., U.S.A.	**114**	42 10N	77 3W
Corno, Monte	**27**	42 28N	13 34E
Cornwall	**107**	45 2N	74 44W
Cornwall □	**13**	50 26N	4 40W
Cornwallis I.	**144**	75 8N	95 0W
Corny Pt.	**73**	34 55S	137 0E
Coro	**134**	11 25N	69 41W
Coroaci	**139**	18 35S	42 17W
Coroatá	**138**	4 8S	44 0W
Corocoro	**136**	17 15S	68 28W
Corocoro, I.	**135**	8 30N	60 10W
Coroico	**136**	16 0S	67 50W
Coromandel, Brazil	**139**	18 28S	47 13W
Coromandel, N.Z.	**80**	36 45S	175 31E
Coromandel Coast	**51**	12 30N	81 0E
Coromandel Pen.	**80**	37 0S	175 45E
Coromandel Ra.	**80**	37 0S	175 40E
Corona, Austral.	**73**	31 16S	141 24E
Corona, Calif., U.S.A.	**123**	33 49N	117 36W
Corona, N. Mex., U.S.A.	**121**	34 15N	105 32W
Coronada	**123**	32 45N	117 9W
Coronado, Bahía de	**126**	9 0N	83 40W
Coronados, G. de los	**142**	41 40S	74 0W
Coronados, Is. de	**123**	32 25N	117 15W
Coronation	**108**	52 5N	111 27W
Coronation Gulf	**100**	68 25N	110 0W
Coronation I., Antarct.	**143**	60 45S	46 0W
Coronation I., U.S.A.	**108**	55 52N	134 20W
Coronation Is.	**78**	14 57S	124 55E
Coronda	**140**	31 58S	60 56W
Coronel	**140**	37 0S	73 10W
Coronel Bogado	**140**	27 11S	56 18W
Coronel Dorrego	**140**	38 40S	61 10W
Coronel Fabriciano	**139**	19 31S	42 38W
Coronel Murta	**139**	16 37S	42 11W
Coronel Oviedo	**140**	25 24S	56 30W
Coronel Ponce	**137**	15 34S	55 1W
Coronel Pringles	**140**	38 0S	61 30W
Coronel Suárez	**140**	37 30S	61 52W
Coronel Vidal	**140**	37 28S	57 45W
Corongo	**136**	8 30S	77 53W
Coronie □	**135**	5 55N	56 20W
Coropuna, Nevado	**136**	15 30S	72 41W
Çorovoda	**35**	40 31N	20 14E
Corowa	**75**	35 58S	146 21E
Corozal, Belize	**125**	18 23N	88 23W
Corozal, Colomb.	**134**	9 19N	75 18W
Corps	**21**	44 50N	5 56E
Corpus	**141**	27 10S	55 30W
Corpus Christi	**119**	27 50N	97 28W
Corpus Christi L.	**119**	28 5N	97 54W
Corque	**136**	18 20S	67 41W
Corral	**142**	39 52S	73 26W
Corral de Almaguer	**24**	39 45N	3 10W
Corréggio	**26**	44 46N	10 47E
Corrente	**138**	10 27S	45 10W
Corrente →	**139**	13 8S	43 28W
Correntes →	**137**	17 38S	55 8W
Correntes, C. das	**97**	24 6S	35 34E
Correntina	**139**	13 20S	44 39W
Corrèze □	**20**	45 20N	1 45E
Correze →	**20**	45 10N	1 28E
Corrib, L.	**15**	53 5N	9 10W
Corrientes	**140**	27 30S	58 45W
Corrientes □	**140**	28 0S	57 0W
Corrientes →, Argent.	**140**	30 42S	59 38W
Corrientes →, Peru	**136**	3 43S	74 35W
Corrientes, C., Colomb.	**134**	5 30N	77 34W
Corrientes, C., Cuba	**126**	21 43N	84 30W
Corrientes, C., Mexico	**124**	20 25N	105 42W
Corrigan	**119**	31 0N	94 48W
Corrigin	**79**	32 20S	117 53E
Corrowidgie	**75**	36 56S	148 50E
Corry	**114**	41 55N	79 39W
Corryong	**75**	36 12S	147 53E
Corse, C.	**21**	43 1N	9 25E
Corse-du-Sud □	**21**	41 45N	9 0E
Corse	**21**	42 0N	9 0E
Corsica = Corse	**21**	42 0N	9 0E
Corsicana	**119**	32 5N	96 30W
Corté	**21**	42 19N	9 11E
Corte do Pinto	**23**	37 42N	7 29W
Cortegana	**23**	37 52N	6 49W
Cortez	**121**	37 24N	108 35W
Cortina d'Ampezzo	**27**	46 32N	12 9E
Cortland	**115**	42 35N	76 11W
Cortona	**27**	43 16N	12 0E
Coruche	**23**	38 57N	8 30W
Çorum	**46**	40 30N	34 57E
Corumbá	**137**	19 0S	57 30W
Corumbá →	**139**	18 19S	48 55W
Corumbá de Goiás	**139**	16 0S	48 50W
Corumbaíba	**139**	18 9S	48 34W
Coruña, La	**22**	43 20N	8 25W
Coruña, La □	**22**	43 10N	8 30W
Corunna, Can.	**106**	42 53N	82 26W
Corunna, U.S.A.	**106**	42 59N	84 7W
Corunna = La Coruña	**22**	43 20N	8 25W
Corvallis	**120**	44 36N	123 15W
Corvette, L. de la	**102**	53 25N	74 3W
Corydon, Ind., U.S.A.	**117**	38 13N	86 7W
Corydon, Iowa, U.S.A.	**116**	40 42N	93 22W
Corydon, Ky., U.S.A.	**117**	37 44N	87 43W
Cosalá	**124**	24 28N	106 40W
Cosamaloapán	**125**	18 23N	95 50W
Cosenza	**29**	39 17N	16 14E
Coshocton	**114**	40 17N	81 51W
Cosne-sur-Loire	**19**	47 24N	2 54E
Coso Junction	**123**	36 3N	117 57W
Coso Pk.	**123**	36 13N	117 44W
Cospeito	**22**	43 12N	7 34W
Cosquín	**140**	31 15S	64 30W
Cossato	**26**	45 34N	8 10E
Cossé-le-Vivien	**18**	47 57N	0 54W
Cosson →	**19**	47 30N	1 15E
Costa Blanca	**25**	38 25N	0 10W
Costa Brava	**24**	41 30N	3 0E
Costa del Sol	**23**	36 30N	4 30W
Costa Dorada	**24**	40 45N	1 15E
Costa Mesa	**123**	33 39N	117 55W
Costa Rica ■	**126**	10 0N	84 0W
Costa Smeralda	**28**	41 5N	9 35E
Costigliole d'Asti	**26**	44 48N	8 11E
Costilla	**121**	37 0N	105 30W
Cosumnes →	**122**	38 14N	121 25W
Coswig	**30**	51 52N	12 31E
Cotabato	**57**	7 14N	124 15E
Cotacajes →	**136**	16 0S	67 1W
Cotagaita	**140**	20 45S	65 40W
Cotahuasi	**136**	15 12S	72 50W
Côte d'Azur	**21**	43 25N	6 50E
Côte d'Or	**19**	47 10N	4 50E
Côte-d'Or □	**19**	47 30N	4 50E
Côte-St.-André, La	**21**	45 24N	5 15E
Coteau des Prairies	**118**	44 30N	97 0W
Coteau du Missouri, Plat. du	**118**	47 0N	101 0W
Coteau Landing	**105**	45 15N	74 13W
Cotegipe	**139**	12 2S	44 15W
Cotentin	**18**	49 30N	1 30W
Côtes de Meuse	**19**	49 15N	5 22E
Côtes-du-Nord □	**18**	48 25N	2 40W
Cotiella	**24**	42 31N	0 19E
Cotina →	**33**	43 36N	18 50E
Cotoca	**137**	17 49S	63 3W
Cotonou	**89**	6 20N	2 25E
Cotopaxi □	**134**	0 5S	78 55W
Cotopaxi, Vol.	**136**	0 40S	78 30W
Cotronei	**29**	39 9N	16 45E
Cotswold Hills	**13**	51 42N	2 10W
Cottage Grove	**120**	43 48N	123 2W
Cottam	**106**	42 8N	82 45W
Cottbus	**30**	51 44N	14 20E
Cottbus □	**30**	51 43N	13 30E
Cottonvale	**77**	28 31S	151 57E
Cottonwood	**121**	34 48N	112 1W
Cotulla	**119**	28 26N	99 14W
Coubre, Pte. de la	**20**	45 42N	1 15W
Couches	**19**	46 53N	4 30E
Couço	**23**	38 59N	8 17W
Coudersport	**114**	41 45N	77 40W
Coudres, Île aux	**105**	47 24N	70 23W
Couedic, C. du	**73**	36 5S	136 40E
Couëron	**18**	47 13N	1 44W
Couesnon →	**18**	48 38N	1 32W
Couhe-Vérac	**20**	46 18N	0 12E
Coulanges	**19**	47 30N	3 30E
Coulee City	**120**	47 36N	119 18W
Coulman I.	**143**	73 35S	170 0E
Coulommiers	**19**	48 50N	3 3E
Coulon →	**21**	43 51N	5 0E
Coulonge →	**104**	45 52N	76 46W
Coulonges	**20**	46 28N	0 35W
Coulterville, Calif., U.S.A.	**122**	37 42N	120 12W
Coulterville, Ill., U.S.A.	**116**	38 11N	89 36W
Council, U.S.A.	**100**	64 55N	163 45W
Council, U.S.A.	**120**	44 44N	116 26W
Council Bluffs	**118**	41 20N	95 50W
Council Grove	**118**	38 41N	96 30W
Coupeville	**122**	48 13N	122 41W
Courantyne →	**136**	5 55N	57 5W
Courçon	**20**	46 15N	0 50W
Couronne, C.	**21**	43 19N	5 3E
Cours	**21**	46 7N	4 19E
Coursan	**20**	43 14N	3 4E
Courseulles	**18**	49 20N	0 29W
Courtenay	**108**	49 45N	125 0W
Courtine, La	**20**	45 43N	2 16E
Courtland, Can.	**106**	42 51N	80 38W
Courtland, U.S.A.	**122**	38 20N	121 34W
Courtrai = Kortrijk	**16**	50 50N	3 17E
Courtright	**106**	42 49N	82 28W
Courville	**18**	48 28N	1 15E
Coushatta	**119**	32 0N	93 21W
Coutances	**18**	49 3N	1 28W
Couterne	**18**	48 30N	0 25W
Coutras	**20**	45 3N	0 8W
Coutts	**108**	49 0N	111 57W
Coutts Crossing	**77**	29 49S	152 55E
Covarrubias	**24**	42 4N	3 31W
Cove I.	**106**	45 17N	81 44W
Coveñas	**134**	9 24N	75 44W
Coventry	**13**	52 25N	1 31W
Coventry L.	**109**	61 15N	106 15W
Covilhã	**22**	40 17N	7 31W
Covina	**123**	34 5N	117 52W
Covington, Ga., U.S.A.	**113**	33 36N	83 50W
Covington, Ind., U.S.A.	**117**	40 9N	87 24W
Covington, Ky., U.S.A.	**117**	39 5N	84 30W
Covington, Ohio, U.S.A.	**117**	40 8N	84 20W
Covington, Okla., U.S.A.	**119**	36 21N	97 36W
Covington, Tenn., U.S.A.	**119**	35 34N	89 39W
Cowal, L.	**76**	33 40S	147 25E
Cowan	**109**	52 5N	100 45W
Cowan, L.	**79**	31 45S	121 45E
Cowan L.	**109**	54 0N	107 15W
Cowangie	**74**	35 12S	141 26E
Cowansville	**105**	45 14N	72 46W
Coward Springs	**73**	29 24S	136 48E
Cowarie	**73**	27 45S	138 15E
Cowcowing Lakes	**79**	30 55S	117 20E
Cowden	**117**	39 15N	88 52W
Cowdenbeath	**14**	56 7N	3 20W
Cowell	**73**	33 39S	136 56E
Cowes, Austral.	**74**	38 28S	145 14E
Cowes, U.K.	**13**	50 45N	1 18W
Cowlitz →	**122**	46 5N	122 53W
Cowra, N.S.W., Austral.	**76**	33 49S	148 42E
Cowra, Sydney, Austral.	**76**	33 50S	148 41E
Cowwarr	**75**	38 2S	146 42E
Coxim	**137**	18 30S	54 55W
Coxim →	**137**	18 34S	54 46W
Cox's Bazar	**52**	21 26N	91 59E
Cox's Cove	**103**	49 7N	58 5W
Coyame	**124**	29 28N	105 6W
Coyote Wells	**123**	32 44N	115 58W
Coyuca de Benítez	**125**	17 1N	100 8W
Coyuca de Catalan	**124**	18 18N	100 41W
Cozad	**118**	40 55N	99 57W
Cozumel	**125**	20 31N	86 55W
Cozumel, Isla de	**125**	20 30N	86 40W
Craboon	**77**	32 3S	149 30E
Cracow	**73**	25 17S	150 17E
Cracow = Kraków	**32**	50 4N	19 57E
Cradock	**96**	32 8S	25 36E
Craig, Alaska, U.S.A.	**108**	55 30N	133 5W
Craig, Colo., U.S.A.	**120**	40 32N	107 33W
Craigavon = Lurgan	**15**	54 28N	6 20W
Craigmore	**95**	20 28S	32 50E
Crailsheim	**31**	49 7N	10 5E
Craiova	**34**	44 21N	23 48E
Crampel	**92**	7 0N	19 10E
Cramsie	**72**	23 20S	144 15E
Cranberry Portage	**109**	54 35N	101 23W
Cranbourne	**74**	38 7S	145 20E
Cranbrook, Tas., Austral.	**72**	42 0S	148 5E
Cranbrook, W. Austral., Austral.	**79**	34 18S	117 33E
Cranbrook, Can.	**108**	49 30N	115 46W
Crandon	**118**	45 32N	88 52W
Crane, Oregon, U.S.A.	**120**	43 21N	118 39W
Crane, Texas, U.S.A.	**119**	31 26N	102 27W
Crane I.	**105**	47 4N	70 33W
Cranston	**115**	41 47N	71 27W
Craon	**18**	47 50N	0 58W
Craonne	**19**	49 27N	3 46E
Craponne	**20**	45 20N	3 51E
Crasna	**34**	46 32N	27 51E
Crater, L.	**120**	42 55N	122 3W
Crater Mt.	**69**	6 37S	145 7E
Crater Pt.	**69**	5 25S	152 9E
Crateús	**138**	5 10S	40 39W
Crati →	**29**	39 41N	16 30E
Crato, Brazil	**138**	7 10S	39 25W
Crato, Port.	**23**	39 16N	7 39W
Crau	**21**	43 32N	4 40E
Cravo Norte	**134**	6 18N	70 12W
Cravo Norte →	**134**	6 18N	70 12W
Crawford	**118**	42 40N	103 25W
Crawfordsville	**117**	40 2N	86 51W
Crawley	**13**	51 7N	0 10W
Crazy Mts.	**120**	46 14N	110 30W
Crean L.	**109**	54 5N	106 9W
Crécy-en-Brie	**19**	48 50N	2 53E
Crécy-en-Ponthieu	**19**	50 15N	1 53E
Crediton	**106**	43 17N	81 33W
Credo	**79**	30 28S	120 45E
Cree →, Can.	**109**	58 57N	105 47W
Cree →, U.K.	**14**	54 51N	4 24W
Cree L.	**109**	57 30N	106 30W
Creede	**121**	37 56N	106 59W
Creel	**124**	27 45N	107 38W
Creemore	**106**	44 19N	80 6W
Creighton	**118**	42 30N	97 52W
Creil	**19**	49 15N	2 34E
Crema	**26**	45 21N	9 40E
Cremona	**26**	45 8N	10 2E
Crepori →	**137**	5 42S	57 8W
Crépy	**19**	49 37N	3 32E
Crépy-en-Valois	**19**	49 14N	2 54E
Cres	**27**	44 58N	14 25E
Cres, I.	**27**	44 40N	14 25E
Cresbard	**118**	45 13N	98 57W
Crescent, Okla., U.S.A.	**119**	35 58N	97 36W
Crescent, Oreg., U.S.A.	**120**	43 30N	121 37W
Crescent City	**120**	41 45N	124 12W
Crescent Head	**77**	31 11S	152 59E
Crescentino	**26**	45 11N	8 7E
Crespino	**27**	44 59N	11 51E
Crespo	**140**	32 2S	60 19W
Cressy	**74**	38 2S	143 40E
Crest	**21**	44 44N	5 2E
Crested Butte	**121**	38 57N	107 0W
Crestline, Calif., U.S.A.	**123**	34 14N	117 18W
Crestline, Ohio, U.S.A.	**114**	40 46N	82 45W
Creston, Can.	**108**	49 10N	116 31W
Creston, Calif., U.S.A.	**122**	35 32N	120 33W
Creston, Iowa, U.S.A.	**116**	41 0N	94 20W
Creston, Wash., U.S.A.	**120**	47 47N	118 36W
Creston, Wyo., U.S.A.	**120**	41 46N	107 50W
Crestview, Calif., U.S.A.	**122**	37 46N	118 58W
Crestview, Fla., U.S.A.	**113**	30 45N	86 35W
Creswick	**74**	37 25S	143 58E
Crete	**118**	40 38N	96 58W
Crete = Kríti	**35**	35 15N	25 0E
Crete, La	**108**	58 11N	116 24W
Crete, Sea of	**35**	36 0N	25 0E
Cretin, C.	**69**	6 40S	147 53E
Creus, C.	**24**	42 20N	3 19E
Creuse □	**20**	46 0N	2 0E
Creuse →	**20**	47 0N	0 34E
Creusot, Le	**19**	46 50N	4 24E
Creuzburg	**30**	51 3N	10 15E
Crevalcore	**27**	44 41N	11 10E
Crèvecœur-le-Grand	**19**	49 37N	2 5E
Crevillente	**25**	38 12N	0 48W
Crewe	**12**	53 6N	2 28W
Crib Point	**74**	38 22S	145 13E
Criciúma	**141**	28 40S	49 23W
Cridersville	**117**	40 39N	84 9W
Crieff	**14**	56 22N	3 50W
Crikvenica	**27**	45 11N	14 40E
Crimea = Krymskaya	**38**	45 0N	34 0E
Crimmitschau	**30**	50 48N	12 23E
Crinan	**14**	56 6N	5 34W
Cristalândia	**138**	10 36S	49 11W
Cristino Castro	**138**	8 49S	44 13W
Crişul Alb →	**34**	46 42N	21 17E
Crişul Negru →	**34**	46 38N	22 26E
Crişul Repede →	**34**	46 55N	20 59E
Crittenden	**117**	38 47N	84 36W
Crivitz	**30**	53 35N	11 39E
Crixás	**139**	14 27S	49 58W
Crna Gora □	**33**	42 40N	19 20E
Crni Drim →	**35**	41 17N	20 40E
Črnomelj	**27**	45 33N	15 10E
Croaghpatrick	**15**	53 46N	9 40W
Croatia = Hrvatska □	**27**	45 20N	16 0E
Crocker	**116**	37 57N	92 16W
Crocker, Barisan	**56**	5 40N	116 30E
Crocker I.	**79**	11 12S	132 32E
Crockett	**119**	31 20N	95 30W
Crocodile = Krokodil →	**97**	25 26S	32 0E
Crocodile Is.	**72**	12 3S	134 58E
Crocq	**20**	45 52N	2 21E
Croisette, C.	**21**	43 13N	5 20E
Croisic, Le	**18**	47 18N	2 30W
Croisic, Pte. du	**18**	47 19N	2 31W

Croix, La, L. 102 48 20N 92 15W
Croker, C., Austral. 78 10 58S 132 35E
Croker, C., Can. 106 44 58N 80 59W
Cromarty, Can. 109 58 3N 94 9W
Cromarty, U.K. 14 57 40N 4 2W
Cromer 12 52 56N 1 18E
Cromwell 81 45 3S 169 14E
Cronat 19 46 43N 3 40E
Cronulla 76 34 3S 151 8E
Crooble 77 29 16S 150 16E
Crooked →, Can. 108 54 50N 122 54W
Crooked →, U.S.A. 120 44 30N 121 16W
Crooked I. 127 22 50N 74 10W
Crooked Island Passage 127 23 0N 74 30W
Crookston, Minn., U.S.A. 118 47 50N 96 40W
Crookston, Nebr., U.S.A. 118 42 56N 100 45W
Crooksville 112 39 45N 82 8W
Crookwell 76 34 28S 149 24E
Croppa Cr. → 77 28 48S 150 4E
Croppa Creek 77 28 9S 150 20E
Crosby, Minn., U.S.A. 118 46 28N 93 57W
Crosby, N.D., U.S.A. 109 48 55N 103 18W
Crosby, Pa., U.S.A. 114 41 45N 78 23W
Crosbyton 119 33 37N 101 12W
Cross → 89 4 42N 8 21E
Cross City 113 29 35N 83 5W
Cross Fell 12 54 44N 2 29W
Cross L. 109 54 45N 97 30W
Cross Plains 119 32 8N 99 7W
Cross River □ 89 6 0N 8 0E
Cross Sound 109 58 20N 136 30W
Cross Timbers 116 38 1N 93 14W
Crosse, La, Kans., U.S.A. 118 38 33N 99 20W
Crosse, La, Wis., U.S.A. 118 43 48N 91 13W
Crossett 119 33 10N 91 57W
Crossfield 108 51 25N 114 0W
Crosshaven 15 51 48N 8 19W
Crossley, Mt. 81 42 50S 172 5E
Crossville 117 38 10N 88 4W
Croswell 106 43 16N 82 37W
Croton-on-Hudson 115 41 12N 73 55W
Crotone 29 39 5N 17 6E
Crow → 108 59 41N 124 20W
Crow Agency 120 45 40N 107 30W
Crow Hd. 15 51 34N 10 9W
Crowdy Hd. 77 31 48S 152 44E
Crowell 119 33 59N 99 45W
Crowley 119 30 15N 92 20W
Crowley, L. 122 37 33N 118 42W
Crown Point 117 41 24N 87 23W
Crows Landing 122 37 23N 121 6W
Crows Nest 73 27 16S 152 4E
Crowsnest Pass 108 49 40N 114 40W
Croydon, Austral. 72 18 13S 142 14E
Croydon, U.K. 13 51 18N 0 5W
Crozet Basin 53 46 0S 52 0E
Crozet, Île 53 46 27S 52 0E
Crozon 18 48 15N 4 30W
Cruz Alta 141 28 45S 53 40W
Cruz, C. 126 19 50N 77 50W
Cruz das Almas 139 12 0S 39 6W
Cruz de Malta 138 8 15S 40 20W
Cruz del Eje 140 30 45S 64 50W
Cruz, La, C. Rica 126 11 4N 85 39W
Cruz, La, Mexico 124 23 55N 106 54W
Cruzeiro 139 22 33S 45 0W
Cruzeiro do Oeste 141 23 46S 53 4W
Cruzeiro do Sul 136 7 35S 72 35W
Cry L. 108 58 45N 129 0W
Crystal Bay 122 39 15N 120 0W
Crystal Brook 73 33 21S 138 12E
Crystal City, Mo., U.S.A. 116 38 15N 90 23W
Crystal City, Tex., U.S.A. 119 28 40N 99 50W
Crystal Falls 112 46 9N 88 11W
Crystal Lake 117 42 14N 88 19W
Crystal River 113 28 54N 82 35W
Crystal Springs 119 31 59N 90 25W
Csongrád 33 46 43N 20 12E
Csorna 33 47 38N 17 18E
Csurgo 33 46 16N 17 9E
Cu Lao Hon 55 10 54N 108 18E
Cua Rao 54 19 16N 104 27E
Cuácua → 95 17 54S 37 0E
Cuamato 96 17 2S 15 7E
Cuamba 95 14 45S 36 22E
Cuando → 93 14 0S 19 30E
Cuando Cubango □ 96 16 25S 20 0E
Cuango 92 6 15S 16 42E
Cuarto → 140 33 25S 63 2W
Cuatrociénegas 124 26 59N 102 5W
Cuauhtémoc 124 28 25N 106 52W
Cuba, Port. 23 38 10N 7 54W
Cuba, Mo., U.S.A. 116 38 4N 91 24W
Cuba, N. Mex., U.S.A. 121 36 0N 107 0W
Cuba, N.Y., U.S.A. 114 42 12N 78 18W
Cuba ■ 126 22 0N 79 0W
Cuba City 116 42 36N 90 26W
Cuballing 79 32 50S 117 10E
Cubango → 96 18 50S 22 25E
Cubbaroo 77 30 10S 149 7E
Cuchi 93 14 37S 16 58E
Cuchillo-Có 142 38 20S 64 37W
Cuchivero → 134 7 40N 65 57W
Cuchumatanes, Sierra de los 126 15 35N 91 25W
Cucuí 134 1 12N 66 50W
Cucurpe 124 30 20N 110 43W
Cucurrupí 134 4 23N 76 56W
Cúcuta 134 7 54N 72 31W
Cudahy 117 42 54N 87 50W
Cudal 76 33 16S 148 46E
Cudalbi 34 45 46N 27 41E
Cuddalore 51 11 46N 79 45E
Cuddapah 51 14 30N 78 47E
Cuddapan, L. 72 25 45S 141 26E
Cudgegong 76 32 47S 149 48E
Cudgegong → 76 32 37S 149 43E
Cudgewa 75 36 10S 147 42E
Cudillero 22 43 33N 6 9W
Cue 79 27 25S 117 54E
Cuéllar 22 41 23N 4 21W
Cuenca, Ecuador 134 2 50S 79 9W
Cuenca, Spain 24 40 5N 2 10W
Cuenca □ 24 40 0N 2 0W
Cuenca, Serranía de 24 39 55N 1 50W
Cuencamé 124 24 53N 103 41W
Cuerda del Pozo, Pantano de la 24 41 51N 2 44W
Cuernavaca 125 18 50N 99 20W
Cuero 119 29 5N 97 17W
Cuers 21 43 14N 6 5E
Cuervo 119 35 5N 104 25W
Cuevas, Cerro 137 22 0S 65 12W
Cuevas del Almanzora 25 37 18N 1 58W
Cuevo 136 20 15S 63 30W
Cugno 91 6 14N 42 31E
Cuiabá 137 15 30S 56 0W
Cuiabá → 137 17 5S 56 36W
Cuilco 126 15 24N 91 58W
Cuillin Hills 14 57 14N 6 15W
Cuillin Sd. 14 57 4N 6 20W
Cuima 93 13 25S 15 45E
Cuiseaux 21 46 30N 5 22E
Cuité 138 6 29S 36 9W
Cuito → 96 18 1S 20 48E
Cuitzeo, L. de 124 19 55N 101 5W
Cuiuni → 135 0 45S 63 7W
Cuivre → 116 38 55N 90 44W
Cuivre, West Fork → 116 39 2N 90 58W
Culan 20 46 34N 2 20E
Culbertson 118 48 9N 104 30W
Culebra, Sierra de la 22 41 55N 6 20W
Culgoa 74 35 44S 143 6E
Culgoa → 73 29 56S 146 20E
Culgoora 77 30 18S 149 35E
Culiacán 124 24 50N 107 23W
Culiacán → 124 24 30N 107 42W
Culion 57 11 54N 120 1E
Culiseu → 137 12 14S 53 17W
Cúllar de Baza 25 37 35N 2 34W
Cullarin Range 76 34 30S 149 30E
Cullen, Austral. 78 13 58S 131 54E
Cullen, U.K. 14 57 45N 2 50W
Cullen Bullen 76 33 18S 150 2E
Cullen Pt. 72 11 57S 141 54E
Cullera 25 39 9N 0 17W
Cullman 113 34 13N 86 50W
Culloden Moor 14 57 29N 4 7W
Cullom 117 40 53N 88 16W
Culoz 21 45 47N 5 46E
Culpeper 112 38 29N 77 59W
Culuene → 137 12 56S 52 51W
Culver 117 41 13N 86 25W
Culver, Pt. 79 32 54S 124 43E
Culverden 81 42 47S 172 49E
Cumaná 135 10 30N 64 5W
Cumare, Colomb. 134 0 50N 72 34W
Cumare, Colomb. 134 0 49N 72 32W
Cumari 139 18 16S 48 11W
Cumberland, B.C., Can. 108 49 40N 125 0W
Cumberland, Ont., Can. 107 45 29N 75 24W
Cumberland, Qué., Can. 104 45 30N 75 24W
Cumberland, Iowa, U.S.A. 116 41 16N 94 52W
Cumberland, Md., U.S.A. 112 39 40N 78 43W
Cumberland, Wis., U.S.A. 118 45 32N 92 3W
Cumberland → 113 36 15N 87 0W
Cumberland, C. 68 14 39S 166 37E
Cumberland I. 113 30 52N 81 30W
Cumberland Is. 72 20 35S 149 10E
Cumberland L. 109 54 3N 102 18W
Cumberland Pen. 101 67 0N 64 0W
Cumberland Plat. 113 36 0N 84 30W
Cumberland Sd. 101 65 30N 66 0W
Cumborah 73 29 40S 147 45E
Cumbres Mayores 23 38 4N 6 39W
Cumbria □ 12 54 35N 2 55W
Cumbrian Mts. 12 54 30N 3 0W
Cumbum 51 15 40N 79 10E
Cuminá → 135 1 30S 56 0W
Cuminapanema → 135 1 9S 54 54W
Cummings Mt. 123 35 2N 118 34W
Cummins 73 34 16S 135 43E
Cumnock, Austral. 76 32 59S 148 46E
Cumnock, U.K. 14 55 27N 4 18W
Cumpas 124 30 0N 109 48W
Cuncumén 140 31 53S 70 38W
Cunderdin 79 31 37S 117 12E
Cundinamarca □ 134 5 0N 74 0W
Cunene → 96 17 20S 11 50E
Cúneo 26 44 23N 7 31E
Cunillera, I. 25 38 59N 1 13E
Cunlhat 20 45 38N 3 32E
Cunnamulla 73 28 2S 145 38E
Cuorgnè 26 45 23N 7 39E
Cupar, Can. 109 50 57N 104 10W
Cupar, U.K. 14 56 20N 3 0W
Cupica, Golfo de 134 6 25N 77 30W
Ćuprija 33 43 57N 21 26E
Curaçá 138 8 59S 39 54W
Curaçao 127 12 10N 69 0W
Curacautín 142 38 26S 71 53W
Curahuara de Carangas 136 17 52S 68 26W
Curanilahue 140 37 29S 73 28W
Curaray → 134 2 20S 74 5W
Curatabaca 135 6 19N 62 51W
Curban 76 31 33S 148 32E
Curbur 79 26 28S 115 55E
Cure → 19 47 40N 3 41E
Curepto 140 35 8S 72 1W
Curiapo 136 8 33N 61 5W
Curicó 140 34 55S 71 20W
Curicó □ 140 34 50S 71 15W
Curicuriari → 134 0 14S 66 48W
Curimatá 138 10 2S 44 17W
Curiplaya 134 0 16N 74 52W
Curitiba 141 25 20S 49 10W
Curlewis 77 31 7S 150 16E
Curoca Norte 96 16 15S 12 58E
Currabubula 77 31 16S 150 44E
Currais Novos 138 6 13S 36 30W
Curralinho 138 1 45S 49 46W
Curran 106 44 41N 83 47W
Currant 120 38 51N 115 32W
Curraweena 73 30 47S 145 54E
Currawilla 72 25 10S 141 20E
Current → 119 37 15N 91 10W
Currie, Austral. 72 39 56S 143 53E
Currie, U.S.A. 120 40 16N 114 45W
Currie, Mt. 97 30 29S 29 21E
Currituck Sd. 113 36 20N 75 50W
Currockbilly Mt. 76 35 25S 150 0E
Curtea de Argeş 34 45 12N 24 42E
Curtis, Spain 22 43 7N 8 4W
Curtis, U.S.A. 118 40 41N 100 32W
Curtis Group 72 39 30S 146 37E
Curtis I. 72 23 35S 151 10E
Curuá →, Pará, Brazil 135 2 24S 54 5W
Curuá →, Pará, Brazil 137 5 23S 54 22W
Curuá, I. 138 0 48N 50 10W
Curuaés → 137 7 30S 54 45W
Curuápanema → 135 2 25S 55 2W
Curuçá 138 0 43S 47 50W
Curuguaty 141 24 31S 55 42W
Curup 56 4 26S 102 13E
Curupira, Serra 135 1 25N 64 30W
Cururu → 137 7 12S 58 3W
Cururupu 138 1 50S 44 50W
Curuzú Cuatiá 140 29 50S 58 5W
Curvelo 139 18 45S 44 27W
Curyo 74 35 50S 142 47E
Cushing 119 35 59N 96 46W
Cushing, Mt. 108 57 35N 126 57W
Cusihuiriáchic 124 28 10N 106 50W
Cusna, Monte 26 44 13N 10 25E
Cusset 20 46 8N 3 28E
Custer 118 43 45N 103 38W
Cut Bank 120 48 40N 112 15W
Cutervo 136 6 25S 78 55W
Cuthbert 113 31 47N 84 47W
Cutler 122 36 31N 119 17W
Cutral-Có 142 38 58S 69 15W
Cutro 29 39 1N 16 58E
Cuttaburra → 73 29 43S 144 22E
Cuttack 50 20 25N 85 57E
Cuvier, C. 79 23 14S 113 22E
Cuvier I. 80 36 27S 175 50E
Cuxhaven 30 53 51N 8 41E
Cuyabeno 134 0 16S 75 53W
Cuyahoga Falls 114 41 8N 81 30W
Cuyo 57 10 50N 121 5E
Cuyuni → 135 6 23N 58 41W
Cuzco, Boliv. 136 20 0S 66 50W
Cuzco, Peru 136 13 32S 72 0W
Cuzco □ 136 13 31S 71 59W
Cwmbran 13 51 39N 3 0W
Cyangugu 94 2 29S 28 54E
Cyclades = Kikladhes 35 37 20N 24 30E
Cygnet 72 43 8S 147 1E
Cynthiana 117 38 23N 84 10W
Cypress Hills 109 49 40N 109 30W
Cyprus ■ 46 35 0N 33 0E
Cyrenaica = Barqa 85 27 0N 20 0E
Cyrene 85 32 48N 21 54E
Czar 109 52 27N 110 50W
Czarne 32 53 42N 16 58E
Czechoslovakia ■ 32 49 0N 17 0E
Czersk 32 53 46N 17 58E
Częstochowa 32 50 49N 19 7E

D

Da → 54 21 15N 105 20E
Da Hinggan Ling 62 48 0N 121 0E
Da Lat 55 11 56N 108 25E
Da Nang 54 16 4N 108 13E
Da Qaidam 62 37 50N 95 15E
Da Yunhe, Jiangsu, China 61 34 25N 120 5E
Da Yunhe, Zhejiang, China 59 30 45N 120 35E
Da'an 61 45 30N 124 7E
Dab'a, Râs el 90 31 3N 28 31E
Daba Shan 58 32 0N 109 0E
Dabai 89 11 25N 5 15E
Dabajuro 134 11 2N 70 40W
Dabakala 88 8 15N 4 20W
Dabburiya 44 32 42N 35 22E
Dabeiba 134 7 1N 76 16W
Daberas 96 25 27S 18 30E
Dabhoi 48 22 10N 73 20E
Dąbie 32 53 27N 14 45E
Dabie Shan 59 31 20N 115 20E
Dabo 56 0 30S 104 33E
Dabola 88 10 50N 11 5W
Dabong 55 5 23N 102 1E
Dabou 88 5 20N 4 23W
Daboya 89 9 30N 1 20W
Dabrowa Tarnówska 32 50 10N 20 59E
Dabu 59 24 22N 116 41E
Dabus → 91 10 48N 35 10E
Dacca 52 23 43N 90 26E
Dacca □ 52 24 25N 90 25E
Dachau 31 48 16N 11 27E
Dadali 68 8 7S 159 6E
Dadanawa 135 2 50N 59 30W
Daday 38 41 28N 33 27E
Daddeto 91 12 24N 42 45E
Dade City 113 28 20N 82 12W
Dadès, Oued → 86 30 58N 6 44W
Dadiya 89 9 35N 11 24E
Dadra and Nagar Haveli □ 50 20 5N 73 0E
Dadri = Charkhi Dadri 48 28 37N 76 17E
Dadu 48 26 45N 67 45E
Dadu He → 58 29 31N 103 46E
Dăeni 34 44 51N 28 10E
Daet 57 14 2N 122 55E
Dafang 58 27 9N 105 39E
Dafter 106 46 21N 84 27W
Dagaio 91 6 8N 40 40E
Dagana 88 16 30N 15 35W
Dagash 90 19 19N 33 25E
Dagestan, A.S.S.R. □ 39 42 30N 47 0E
Daggett 123 34 52N 116 52W
Daggs Sd. 81 45 23S 166 45E
Daghfeli 90 19 18N 32 40E
Daghirie 91 11 40N 41 50E
Dagö = Hiiumaa 36 58 50N 22 45E
Dagoreti 94 1 18S 36 42E
Dagu 61 38 59N 117 40E
Dagua 69 3 27S 143 20E
Daguan 58 27 43N 103 56E
Dagupan 57 16 3N 120 20E
Dahab 90 28 30N 34 31E
Dahlak Kebir 91 15 50N 40 10E
Dahlenburg 30 53 11N 10 43E
Dahlgren 117 38 12N 88 41W
Dahlonega 113 34 35N 83 59W
Dahme, Germ., E. 30 51 51N 13 25E
Dahme, Germ., W. 30 54 13N 11 5E
Dahomey = Benin ■ 89 8 0N 2 0E
Dahong Shan 59 31 25N 113 0E
Dahra 88 15 22N 15 30W
Dahra, Massif de 86 36 7N 1 21E
Dai Hao 54 18 1N 106 25E
Dai-Sen 64 35 22N 133 32E
Dai Shan 59 30 25N 122 10E
Dai Xian 60 39 4N 112 58E
Daicheng 60 38 42N 116 38E
Daigo 65 36 46N 140 21E

Daimanji-San 64 36 14N 133 20 E
Daimiel 25 39 5N 3 35W
Daingean 15 53 18N 7 15W
Dainkog 58 32 15N 97 58 E
Daintree 72 16 20S 145 20 E
Daiō-Misaki 65 34 15N 136 45 E
Dairût 90 27 34N 30 43 E
Daisetsu-Zan 63 43 30N 142 57 E
Daitari 50 21 10N 85 46 E
Daito 64 35 19N 132 58 E
Dajarra 72 21 42S 139 30 E
Dajia 59 24 22N 120 37 E
Dajin Chuan → 58 31 16N 101 59 E
Dak Dam 54 12 20N 107 21 E
Dak Nhe 54 15 28N 107 48 E
Dak Pek 54 15 4N 107 44 E
Dak Song 55 12 19N 107 35 E
Dak Sui 54 14 55N 107 43 E
Dakar 88 14 34N 17 29W
Dakhla 84 23 50N 15 53W
Dakhla, El Wâhât el- 90 25 30N 28 50 E
Dakhovskaya 39 44 13N 40 13 E
Dakingari 89 11 37N 4 1 E
Dakor 48 22 45N 73 11 E
Dakoro 89 14 31N 6 46 E
Dakota City, Iowa, U.S.A. 116 42 43N 94 12W
Dakota City, Nebr., U.S.A. 118 42 27N 96 28W
Đakovica 33 42 22N 20 26 E
Đakovo 33 45 19N 18 24 E
Dala 68 8 30S 160 41 E
Dalaba 88 10 42N 12 15W
Dalachi 60 36 48N 105 0 E
Dalai Nur 60 43 20N 116 45 E
Dalandzadgad 60 43 27N 104 30 E
Dalbandin 47 29 0N 64 23 E
Dalbeattie 14 54 55N 3 50W
Dalbosjön 11 58 40N 12 45 E
Dalby, Austral. 77 27 10S 151 17 E
Dalby, Sweden 11 55 40N 13 22 E
Dale 117 38 10N 86 59W
Dalen 10 59 26N 8 0 E
Dalet 52 19 59N 93 51 E
Daletme 52 21 36N 92 46 E
Daleville 117 40 7N 85 33W
Dalga 90 27 39N 30 41 E
Dalgaranger, Mt. 79 27 50S 117 5 E
Dalgety 75 36 29S 148 50 E
Dalhart 119 36 10N 102 30W
Dalhousie, Can. 103 48 5N 66 26W
Dalhousie, India 48 32 38N 76 0 E
Dali, Shaanxi, China 60 34 48N 109 58 E
Dali, Yunnan, China 58 25 40N 100 10 E
Daliang Shan 58 28 0N 102 45 E
Dalias 25 36 49N 2 52W
Daling He → 61 40 55N 121 40 E
Dalkeith 14 55 54N 3 5W
Dall I. 108 54 59N 133 25W
Dallarnil 73 25 19S 152 2 E
Dallas, Oregon, U.S.A. 120 45 0N 123 15W
Dallas, Texas, U.S.A. 119 32 50N 96 50W
Dallas Center 116 41 41N 93 58W
Dallas City 116 40 38N 91 10W
Dallol 91 14 14N 40 17 E
Dalmacija □ 33 43 20N 17 0 E
Dalmatia = Dalmacija □ 33 43 20N 17 0 E
Dalmellington 14 55 20N 4 25W
Dalmorton 77 29 50S 152 28 E
Dalneretchensk 41 45 50N 133 40 E
Daloa 88 7 0N 6 30W
Dalou Shan 58 28 15N 107 0 E
Dalsjöfors 11 57 46N 13 5 E
Dalskog 11 58 44N 12 18 E
Dalton, Austral. 76 34 43S 149 12 E
Dalton, Can. 102 48 11N 84 1W
Dalton, Ga., U.S.A. 113 34 47N 84 58W
Dalton, Mass., U.S.A. 115 42 28N 73 11W
Dalton, Nebr., U.S.A. 118 41 27N 103 0W
Dalton Iceberg Tongue 143 66 15S 121 30 E
Daltonganj 49 24 0N 84 4 E
Dalvík 8 65 58N 18 32W
Daly → 78 13 35S 130 19 E
Daly City 122 37 42N 122 28W
Daly L. 109 56 32N 105 39W
Daly Waters 72 16 15S 133 24 E
Dam Doi 55 8 50N 105 12 E
Dam Ha 54 21 21N 107 36 E
Dama, Wadi → 90 27 12N 35 50 E
Daman 50 20 25N 72 57 E
Daman □ 50 20 25N 72 58 E
Damanhûr 90 31 0N 30 30 E
Damanzhuang 60 38 5N 116 35 E
Damar 57 7 7S 128 40 E
Damaraland 96 21 0S 17 0 E
Damascus = Dimashq 46 33 30N 36 18 E
Damaturu 89 11 45N 11 55 E
Damāvand 47 35 47N 52 0 E
Damāvand, Qolleh-ye 47 35 56N 52 10 E
Damba, Angola 92 6 44S 15 20 E
Damba, Ethiopia 91 15 10N 38 47 E
Dame Marie 127 18 36N 74 26W
Dāmghān 47 36 10N 54 17 E
Dămienesti 34 46 44N 27 1 E
Damietta = Dumyât 90 31 24N 31 48 E
Daming 60 36 15N 115 6 E
Damiya 44 32 6N 35 34 E
Dammarie 19 48 20N 1 30 E
Dammartin 19 49 3N 2 41 E
Damme 30 52 32N 8 12 E
Damodar → 49 23 17N 87 35 E
Damoh 49 23 50N 79 28 E
Damous 86 36 31N 1 42 E
Dampier 78 20 41S 116 42 E
Dampier Arch. 78 20 38S 116 32 E
Dampier, Selat 57 0 40S 131 0 E
Dampier Str. 69 5 50S 148 0 E
Damrei, Chuor Phnum 55 11 30N 103 0 E
Damville 18 48 51N 1 5 E
Damvillers 19 49 20N 5 21 E
Dan Dume 89 11 28N 7 8 E
Dan-Gulbi 89 11 40N 6 15 E
Dan Sadau 89 11 25N 6 20 E
Dana 57 11 0S 122 52 E
Dana, Lac 102 50 53N 77 20W
Dana, Mt. 122 37 54N 119 12W
Danakil Depression 91 12 45N 41 0 E
Danao 57 10 31N 124 1 E
Danbury 115 41 23N 73 29W
Danby L. 121 34 17N 115 0W
Dand 48 31 28N 65 32 E
Dandaloo 76 32 16S 147 38 E
Dandaragan 79 30 40S 115 40 E
Dandeldhura 49 29 20N 80 35 E
Dandenong 74 38 0S 145 15 E
Dandong 61 40 10N 124 20 E
Danfeng 60 33 45N 110 25 E
Danforth 103 45 39N 67 57W
Dangan Liedao 59 22 2N 114 8 E
Danger Is. 67 10 53S 165 49W
Danger Pt. 96 34 40S 19 17 E
Dangla 91 11 18N 36 56 E
Dangora 89 11 30N 8 7 E
Dangrek, Phnom 54 14 15N 105 0 E
Dangshan 60 34 27N 116 22 E
Dangtu 59 31 32N 118 25 E
Dangyang 59 30 52N 111 44 E
Daniel 120 42 56N 110 2W
Daniel's Harbour 103 50 13N 57 35W
Danielskull 96 28 11S 23 33 E
Danielson 115 41 50N 71 52W
Danilov 37 58 16N 40 13 E
Danilovka 37 50 25N 44 12 E
Daning 60 36 28N 110 45 E
Danissa 94 3 15N 40 58 E
Danja 89 11 21N 7 30 E
Dankalwa 89 11 52N 12 12 E
Dankama 89 13 20N 7 44 E
Dankov 37 53 20N 39 5 E
Danleng 58 30 1N 103 31 E
Danlí 126 14 4N 86 35W
Dannemora, Sweden 10 60 12N 17 51 E
Dannemora, U.S.A. 115 44 41N 73 44W
Dannenberg 30 53 7N 11 4 E
Dannevirke 80 40 12S 176 8 E
Dannhauser 97 28 0S 30 3 E
Danshui 59 25 12N 121 25 E
Dansville 114 42 32N 77 41W
Dantan 49 21 57N 87 20 E
Danube → 33 45 20N 29 40 E
Danubyu 52 17 15N 95 35 E
Danukandi 52 23 32N 90 43 E
Danvers 115 42 34N 70 55W
Danville, Ill., U.S.A. 117 40 10N 87 40W
Danville, Ind., U.S.A. 117 39 46N 86 32W
Danville, Ky., U.S.A. 117 37 40N 84 45W
Danville, Va., U.S.A. 113 36 40N 79 20W
Danyang 59 32 0N 119 31 E
Danzhai 58 26 11N 107 48 E
Danzig = Gdańsk 32 54 22N 18 40 E
Dao 57 10 30N 121 57 E
Dão → 22 40 20N 8 11W
Dao Xian 59 25 36N 111 31 E
Daocheng 58 29 0N 100 10 E
Daosa 48 26 52N 76 20 E
Daoud = Aïn Beïda 87 35 44N 7 22 E
Daoulas 18 48 22N 4 17W
Dapango 89 10 55N 0 16 E
Dapto 76 34 30S 150 47 E
Daqing Shan 60 40 40N 111 0 E
Daqu Shan 59 30 25N 122 20 E
Dar al Hamrā, Ad 46 27 22N 37 43 E
Dar es Salaam 94 6 50S 39 12 E
Dar'ā 44 32 36N 36 7 E
Dārāb 47 28 50N 54 30 E
Daraj 87 30 10N 10 28 E
Daravica 33 42 32N 20 8 E
Daraw 90 24 22N 32 51 E
Darazo 89 11 1N 10 24 E
Darband 48 34 20N 72 50 E
Darbhanga 49 26 15N 85 55 E
Darby 120 46 2N 114 7W
Darby Falls 76 33 53S 148 52 E
Dardanelle, Ark., U.S.A. 119 35 12N 93 9W
Dardanelle, Calif., U.S.A. 122 38 15N 119 50W
Dardanelles = Çanakkale Boğazi 46 40 0N 26 0 E
Darfield 81 43 29S 172 7 E
Darfo 26 45 52N 10 11 E
Dargai 48 34 25N 71 55 E
Dargan Ata 40 40 29N 62 10 E
Dargaville 80 35 57S 173 52 E
Dargo 75 37 27S 147 15 E
Dargo → 75 37 32S 147 15 E
Darhan Muminggan Lianheqi 60 41 40N 110 28 E
Darharala 88 8 23N 4 20W
Dari 91 5 48N 30 26 E
Darién, G. del 134 9 0N 77 0W
Darién, Serranía del 134 8 30N 77 30W
Dariganga 60 45 21N 113 45 E
Darjeeling 49 27 3N 88 18 E
Dark Cove 103 48 47N 54 13W
Darkan 79 33 20S 116 43 E
Darkot Pass 49 36 45N 73 26 E
Darling → 73 34 4S 141 54 E
Darling Downs 73 27 30S 150 30 E
Darling Ra. 79 32 30S 116 0 E
Darlington, Austral. 74 38 2S 143 3 E
Darlington, U.K. 12 54 33N 1 33W
Darlington, S.C., U.S.A. 113 34 18N 79 50W
Darlington, Wis., U.S.A. 116 42 43N 90 7W
Darlot, L. 79 27 48S 121 35 E
Darłowo 32 54 25N 16 25 E
Darmstadt 31 49 51N 8 40 E
Darnall 97 29 23S 31 18 E
Darnétal 18 49 25N 1 10 E
Darney 19 48 5N 6 0 E
Darnley B. 100 69 30N 123 30W
Darnley, C. 143 68 0S 69 0 E
Daroca 24 41 9N 1 25W
Darr 72 23 13S 144 7 E
Darr → 72 23 39S 143 50 E
Darran Mts. 81 44 37S 167 59 E
Darriman 75 38 26S 146 59 E
Darrington 120 48 14N 121 37W
Darror → 45 10 30N 50 0 E
Darsana 52 23 35N 88 48 E
Darsi 51 15 46N 79 44 E
Darsser Ort 30 54 29N 12 31 E
Dart → 13 50 24N 3 36W
Dart, C. 143 73 6S 126 20W
Dartmoor, Austral. 74 37 56S 141 19 E
Dartmoor, U.K. 13 50 36N 4 0W
Dartmouth, Austral. 72 23 31S 144 44 E
Dartmouth, Can. 103 44 40N 63 30W
Dartmouth, U.K. 13 50 21N 3 35W
Dartmouth, L. 73 26 4S 145 18 E
Dartuch, C. 24 39 55N 3 49 E
Daru 69 9 3S 143 13 E
Darvaza 40 40 11N 58 24 E
Darwha 50 20 15N 77 45 E
Darwin, Austral. 78 12 25S 130 51 E
Darwin, U.S.A. 123 36 15N 117 35W
Darwin Glacier 143 79 53S 159 0 E
Darwin, Mt. 142 0 10S 69 55W
Darwin River 78 12 50S 130 58 E
Daryacheh-ye-Sistan 47 31 0N 61 0 E
Daryapur 50 20 55N 77 20 E
Das 47 25 20N 53 30 E
Dase 91 14 53N 37 15 E
Dashato → 91 7 25N 42 40 E
Dashetai 60 41 0N 109 5 E
Dashkesan 39 40 40N 46 0 E
Dasht → 47 25 10N 61 40 E
Dasht-e Kavīr 47 34 30N 55 0 E
Dasht-e Lūt 47 31 30N 58 0 E
Dasht-i-Margo 47 30 40N 62 30 E
Dasht-i-Nawar 48 33 52N 68 0 E
Daska 48 32 20N 74 20 E
Dassa-Zoume 89 7 46N 2 14 E
Dasseneiland 96 33 25S 18 3 E
Dasserat, L. 104 48 16N 79 25W
Datia 49 25 39N 78 27 E
Datian 59 25 40N 117 50 E
Datong, Anhui, China 59 30 48N 117 44 E
Datong, Shanxi, China 60 40 6N 113 18 E
Dattapur 50 20 45N 78 15 E
Dattuck 74 35 34S 142 17 E
Datu Piang 57 7 2N 124 30 E
Datu, Tanjung 56 2 5N 109 39 E
Daugava → 36 57 4N 24 3 E
Daugavpils 36 55 53N 26 32 E
Daulat Yar 47 34 30N 65 45 E
Daulatabad 50 19 57N 75 15 E
Daule 134 1 56S 79 56W
Daule → 134 2 10S 79 52W
Daun 31 50 10N 6 53 E
Dauphin 109 51 9N 100 5W
Dauphin I. 113 30 16N 88 10W
Dauphin L. 109 51 20N 99 45W
Dauphiné 21 45 15N 5 25 E
Dauqa 90 19 30N 41 0 E
Daura, Borno, Nigeria 89 11 31N 11 24 E
Daura, Kaduna, Nigeria 89 13 2N 8 21 E
Davangere 51 14 25N 75 55 E
Davao 57 7 0N 125 40 E
Davao, G. of 57 6 30N 125 48 E
Dāvar Panāh 47 27 25N 62 15 E
Davenport, Calif., U.S.A. 122 37 1N 122 12W
Davenport, Iowa, U.S.A. 116 41 30N 90 40W
Davenport, Wash., U.S.A. 120 47 40N 118 5W
Davenport Downs 72 24 8S 141 7 E
Davenport Ra. 72 20 28S 134 0 E
David 126 8 30N 82 30W
David City 118 41 18N 97 10W
David Gorodok 36 52 4N 27 8 E
Davidson 109 51 16N 105 59W
Davis, Antarct. 143 68 34S 77 55 E
Davis, U.S.A. 122 38 33N 121 44W
Davis Dam 123 35 11N 114 35W
Davis Inlet 103 55 50N 60 59W
Davis Mts. 119 30 42N 104 15W
Davis Sea 143 66 0S 92 0 E
Davis Str. 101 65 0N 58 0W
Davison 106 43 2N 83 31W
Davisson, L. 122 46 30N 122 20W
Davos 31 46 48N 9 49 E
Davy L. 109 58 53N 108 18W
Davyhurst 79 30 2S 120 40 E
Dawa → 91 4 11N 42 6 E
Dawaki, Bauchi, Nigeria 89 9 25N 9 33 E
Dawaki, Kano, Nigeria 89 12 5N 8 23 E
Dawes Ra. 72 24 40S 150 40 E
Dawna Range 52 16 30N 98 30 E
Dawnyein 52 15 54N 95 36 E
Dawson, Can. 100 64 10N 139 30W
Dawson, Ga., U.S.A. 113 31 45N 84 28W
Dawson, N.D., U.S.A. 118 46 56N 99 45W
Dawson Creek 108 55 45N 120 15W
Dawson, I. 142 53 50S 70 50W
Dawson Inlet 109 61 50N 93 25W
Dawson Range 72 24 30S 149 48 E
Dawson's 95 17 0S 30 57 E
Dawu 58 30 55N 101 10 E
Dax 20 43 44N 1 3W
Daxi 59 24 52N 121 20 E
Daxian 58 31 15N 107 23 E
Daxin 58 22 50N 107 11 E
Daxindian 61 37 30N 120 50 E
Daxinggou 61 45 25N 129 40 E
Daxue Shan, Sichuan, China 58 30 30N 101 30 E
Daxue Shan, Yunnan, China 58 23 42N 99 48 E
Dayao 58 25 43N 101 20 E
Daye 59 30 6N 114 58 E
Dayi 58 30 41N 103 29 E
Daymar 77 28 37S 148 59 E
Dayong 59 29 11N 110 30 E
Dayr al-Ghusūn 44 32 21N 35 4 E
Dayr az Zawr 46 35 20N 40 5 E
Daysland 108 52 50N 112 20W
Dayton, Iowa, U.S.A. 116 42 14N 94 6W
Dayton, Ky., U.S.A. 117 39 47N 84 28W
Dayton, Nev., U.S.A. 122 39 15N 119 34W
Dayton, Ohio, U.S.A. 112 39 45N 84 10W
Dayton, Pa., U.S.A. 114 40 54N 79 18W
Dayton, Tenn., U.S.A. 113 35 30N 85 1W
Dayton, Wash., U.S.A. 120 46 20N 118 10W
Daytona Beach 113 29 14N 81 0W
Dayville 120 44 33N 119 37W
Dazhu 58 30 41N 107 15 E
Dazu 58 29 40N 105 42 E
De Aar 96 30 39S 24 0 E
De Forest 116 43 15N 89 20W
De Funiak Springs 113 30 42N 86 10W
De Grey 78 20 12S 119 12 E
De Grey → 78 20 12S 119 13 E
De Land 113 29 1N 81 19W
De Leon 119 32 9N 98 35W
De Pere 112 44 28N 88 1W
De Queen 119 34 3N 94 24W
De Quincy 119 30 30N 93 27W
De Ridder 119 30 48N 93 15W
De Smet 118 44 25N 97 35W
De Soto 116 38 7N 90 33W
De Tour 106 45 59N 83 56W
De Witt, Ark., U.S.A. 119 34 19N 91 20W
De Witt, Iowa, U.S.A. 116 41 49N 90 33W
De Witt, Mich., U.S.A. 117 42 50N 84 33W

Dead Sea = Miyet, Bahr el 46 31 30N 35 30 E
Deadwood 118 44 23N 103 44W
Deadwood L. 108 59 10N 128 30W
Deakin 79 30 46S 128 0 E
Deal 13 51 13N 1 25 E
Deal I. 72 39 30S 147 20 E
Dealesville 96 28 41S 25 44 E
De'an 59 29 21N 115 46 E
Dean, Forest of 13 51 50N 2 35W
Deán Funes 140 30 20S 64 20W
Deans Marsh 74 38 25S 143 52 E
Dearborn, Mich., U.S.A. 106 42 18N 83 15W
Dearborn, Mo., U.S.A. 116 39 32N 94 46W
Dease → 108 59 56N 128 32W
Dease L. 108 58 40N 130 5W
Dease Lake 108 58 25N 130 6W
Death Valley 123 36 19N 116 52W
Death Valley Junc. 123 36 21N 116 30W
Death Valley Nat. Monument 123 36 30N 117 0W
Deauville 18 49 23N 0 2 E
Deba Habe 89 10 14N 11 20 E
Debaltsevo 38 48 22N 38 26 E
Debao 58 23 21N 106 46 E
Debar 35 41 31N 20 30 E
Debba 91 14 20N 41 18 E
Debden 109 53 30N 106 50W
Debdou 86 33 59N 3 0W
Dębica 32 50 2N 21 25 E
Dęblin 32 51 34N 21 50 E
Débo, L. 88 15 14N 4 15W
Debolt 108 55 12N 118 1W
Deborah, L. 79 30 45S 119 0 E
Debre Birhan 91 9 41N 39 31 E
Debre Markos 91 10 20N 37 40 E
Debre May 91 11 20N 37 25 E
Debre Sina 91 9 51N 39 50 E
Debre Tabor 91 11 50N 38 26 E
Debre Zebit 91 11 48N 38 30 E
Debrecen 33 47 33N 21 42 E
Dečani 33 42 30N 20 10 E
Decatur, Ala., U.S.A. 113 34 35N 87 0W
Decatur, Ga., U.S.A. 113 33 47N 84 17W
Decatur, Ill., U.S.A. 116 39 50N 89 0W
Decatur, Ind., U.S.A. 117 40 50N 84 56W
Decatur, Mich., U.S.A. 117 42 7N 85 58W
Decatur, Texas, U.S.A. 119 33 15N 97 35W
Decazeville 20 44 34N 2 15 E
Deccan 50 18 0N 79 0 E
Decelles, Rés 104 47 42N 78 8W
Deception I. 143 63 0S 60 15W
Deception L. 109 56 33N 104 13W
Dechang 58 27 25N 102 11 E
Děčín 32 50 47N 14 12 E
Decize 19 46 50N 3 28 E
Deckerville 106 43 33N 82 46W
Decollatura 29 39 2N 16 21 E
Decorah 118 43 20N 91 50W
Dedaye 52 16 24N 95 53 E
Dederang 75 36 28S 147 1 E
Dedham 115 42 14N 71 10W
Dedilovo 37 53 59N 37 50 E
Dédougou 88 12 30N 3 25W
Deduru Oya 51 7 32N 79 50 E
Dedza 95 14 20S 34 20 E
Dee →, Scot., U.K. 14 57 4N 2 7W
Dee →, Wales, U.K. 12 53 15N 3 7W
Deep B. 108 61 15N 116 35W
Deep Lead 74 37 0S 142 43 E
Deep River 116 41 35N 92 22W
Deep Well 72 24 20S 134 0 E
Deepwater, Austral. 77 29 25S 151 51 E
Deepwater, U.S.A. 116 38 18N 93 46W
Deer → 109 58 23N 94 13W
Deer Lake, Newf., Can. 103 49 11N 57 27W
Deer Lake, Ontario, Can. 109 52 36N 94 20W
Deer Lodge 120 46 25N 112 40W
Deer Park, Ohio, U.S.A. 117 39 13N 84 23W
Deer Park, Wash., U.S.A. 120 47 55N 117 21W
Deer River 118 47 21N 93 44W
Deeral 72 17 14S 145 55 E
Deerdepoort 96 24 37S 26 27 E
Deesa 48 24 18N 72 10 E
Deferiet 115 44 2N 75 41W
Defiance 117 41 20N 84 20W
Deganya 44 32 43N 35 34 E
Dêgê 58 31 44N 98 39 E
Degebe → 23 38 13N 7 29W
Degeh-Bur 45 8 11N 43 31 E
Dégelis 105 47 30N 68 35W
Degema 89 4 50N 6 48 E
Deggendorf 31 48 49N 12 59 E
Degloor 50 18 34N 77 33 E
Deh Bīd 47 30 39N 53 11 E
Deh Kheyr 47 28 45N 54 40 E
Dehibat 87 32 0N 10 47 E
Dehiwala 51 6 50N 79 51 E
Dehkareqan 46 37 43N 45 55 E
Dehra Dun 48 30 20N 78 4 E
Dehri 49 24 50N 84 15 E
Dehua 59 25 26N 118 14 E
Dehui 61 44 30N 125 40 E
Deinze 16 50 59N 3 32 E
Deir Abu Sa'id 44 32 30N 35 42 E
Deir Dibwan 44 31 55N 35 15 E
Dej 34 47 10N 23 52 E
Deje 10 59 35N 13 29 E
Dejiang 58 28 18N 108 7 E
Dekalb 117 41 55N 88 45W
Dekemhare 91 15 6N 39 0 E
Dekese 92 3 24S 21 24 E
Del Mar 123 32 58N 117 16W
Del Norte 121 37 40N 106 27W
Del Rio, Mexico 124 29 22N 100 54W
Del Rio, U.S.A. 119 29 23N 100 50W
Delagua 119 37 21N 104 35W
Delai 90 17 21N 36 6 E
Delambre I. 78 20 27S 117 4 E
Delano 123 35 48N 119 13W
Delareyville 96 26 41S 25 26 E
Delavan, Ill., U.S.A. 116 40 22N 89 33W
Delavan, Wis., U.S.A. 117 42 40N 88 39W
Delaware 117 40 20N 83 0W
Delaware □ 112 39 0N 75 40W
Delaware → 112 39 20N 75 25W
Delegate 75 37 4S 148 56 E
Delémont 31 47 22N 7 20 E
Delft 16 52 1N 4 22 E
Delft I. 51 9 30N 79 40 E
Delfzijl 16 53 20N 6 55 E
Delgado, C. 95 10 45S 40 40 E
Delgerhet 60 45 50N 110 30 E
Delgo 90 20 6N 30 40 E
Delhi, Can. 106 42 51N 80 30W
Delhi, India 48 28 38N 77 17 E
Delhi, U.S.A. 115 42 17N 74 56W
Delia 108 51 38N 112 23W
Delice → 46 39 45N 34 15 E
Delicias 124 28 10N 105 30W
Delicias, Laguna 124 28 7N 105 40W
Delitzsch 30 51 32N 12 22 E
Dell City 121 31 58N 105 19W
Dell Rapids 118 43 53N 96 44W
Delle 19 47 30N 7 2 E
Dellys 87 36 57N 3 57 E
Delmar, Iowa, U.S.A. 116 42 0N 90 37W
Delmar, N.Y., U.S.A. 115 42 37N 73 47W
Delmenhorst 30 53 3N 8 37 E
Delmiro Gouveia 138 9 24S 38 6W
Delnice 27 45 23N 14 50 E
Delong, Ostrova 41 76 40N 149 20 E
Deloraine, Austral. 72 41 30S 146 40 E
Deloraine, Can. 109 49 15N 100 29W
Delorme, L. 103 54 31N 69 52W
Delphi 117 40 37N 86 40W
Delphos 117 40 51N 84 17W
Delportshoop 96 28 22S 24 20 E
Delray Beach 113 26 27N 80 4W
Delsbo 10 61 48N 16 32 E
Delta, Colo., U.S.A. 121 38 44N 108 5W
Delta, Utah, U.S.A. 120 39 21N 112 29W
Delta Amacuro □ 135 8 30N 61 30W
Delungra 77 29 39S 150 51 E
Delvina 35 39 59N 20 4 E
Delvinákion 35 39 57N 20 32 E
Demanda, Sierra de la 24 42 15N 3 0W
Demba 92 5 28S 22 15 E
Dembecha 91 10 32N 37 30 E
Dembi 91 8 5N 36 25 E
Dembia 94 3 33N 25 48 E
Dembidolo 91 8 34N 34 50 E
Demer → 16 50 57N 4 42 E
Demerara □ 135 6 0N 58 30W
Demidov 36 55 16N 31 30 E
Deming, N.Mex., U.S.A. 121 32 10N 107 50W
Deming, Wash., U.S.A. 122 48 49N 122 13W
Demini → 135 0 46S 62 56W
Demmin 30 53 54N 13 2 E
Demnate 86 31 44N 6 59W
Demonte 26 44 18N 7 18 E
Demopolis 113 32 30N 87 48W
Dempo, Mt. 56 4 2S 103 15 E
Demyansk 36 57 40N 32 27 E
Den Burg 16 53 3N 4 47 E
Den Chai 54 17 59N 100 4 E
Den Helder 16 52 57N 4 45 E
Den Oever 16 52 56N 5 2 E
Denain 19 50 20N 3 22 E
Denair 122 37 32N 120 48W
Denau 40 38 16N 67 54 E
Denbigh, Can. 107 45 8N 77 15W
Denbigh, U.K. 12 53 12N 3 26W
Dendang 56 3 7S 107 56 E
Dendermonde 16 51 2N 4 5 E
Deneba 91 9 47N 39 10 E
Deng Xian 59 32 34N 112 4 E
Dengchuan 58 25 59N 100 3 E
Denge 89 12 52N 5 21 E
Dengfeng 60 34 25N 113 2 E
Dengi 89 9 25N 9 55 E
Dengkou 60 40 18N 106 55 E
Denham 79 25 56S 113 31 E
Denham Ra. 72 21 55S 147 46 E
Denham Sd. 79 25 45S 113 15 E
Denia 25 38 49N 0 8 E
Denial B. 73 32 14S 133 32 E
Deniliquin 74 35 30S 144 58 E
Denison, Iowa, U.S.A. 118 42 0N 95 18W
Denison, Texas, U.S.A. 119 33 50N 96 40W
Denison Plains 78 18 35S 128 0 E
Denizli 46 37 42N 29 2 E
Denkez Iyesus 91 12 27N 37 43 E
Denman 76 32 24S 150 42 E
Denman Glacier 143 66 45S 99 25 E
Denmark 79 34 59S 117 25 E
Denmark ■ 11 55 30N 9 0 E
Denmark Str. 128 66 0N 30 0W
Dennison 114 40 21N 81 21W
Denniston 81 41 45S 171 49 E
Denpasar 56 8 45S 115 14 E
Denton, Mont., U.S.A. 120 47 25N 109 56W
Denton, Texas, U.S.A. 119 33 12N 97 10W
D'Entrecasteaux Is. 69 9 0S 151 0 E
D'Entrecasteaux Pt. 79 34 50S 115 57 E
Denu 89 6 4N 1 8 E
Denver, Colo., U.S.A. 118 39 45N 105 0W
Denver, Ind., U.S.A. 117 40 52N 86 5W
Denver, Iowa, U.S.A. 116 42 40N 92 20W
Denver City 119 32 58N 102 48W
Deoband 48 29 42N 77 43 E
Deobhog 50 19 53N 82 44 E
Deogarh 50 21 32N 84 45 E
Deoghar 49 24 30N 86 42 E
Deolali 50 19 58N 73 50 E
Deoli 48 25 50N 75 20 E
Deoria 49 26 31N 83 48 E
Deosai, Mts. 49 35 40N 75 0 E
Depew 114 42 55N 78 43W
Deping 61 37 25N 116 58 E
Deposit 115 42 5N 75 23W
Depot Springs 79 27 55S 120 3 E
Depuch I. 78 20 35S 117 44 E
Deputatskiy 41 69 18N 139 54 E
Dêqên, Yunnan, China 58 28 34N 98 51 E
Dêqên, Yunnan, China 62 28 20N 98 50 E
Deqing 59 23 8N 111 42 E
Dera Ghazi Khan 48 30 5N 70 43 E
Dera Ismail Khan 48 31 50N 70 50 E
Dera Ismail Khan □ 48 32 30N 70 0 E
Derati Wells 94 3 52N 36 37 E
Derbent, U.S.S.R. 8 42 5N 48 15 E
Derbent, U.S.S.R. 38 42 5N 48 4 E
Derby, Austral. 78 17 18S 123 38 E
Derby, U.K. 12 52 55N 1 28W
Derby, Conn., U.S.A. 115 41 20N 73 5W
Derby, N.Y., U.S.A. 114 42 40N 78 59W
Derby □ 12 52 55N 1 28W
Derg → 15 54 42N 7 26W
Derg, L. 15 53 0N 8 20W
Dergachi 37 50 9N 36 11 E
Dergholm 74 37 24S 141 14 E
Derna 85 32 40N 22 35 E
Dernieres Isles 119 29 0N 90 45W
Dêrong 58 28 44N 99 9 E
Derrinallum 74 37 57S 143 15 E
Derriwong 76 33 6S 147 21 E
Derryveagh Mts. 15 55 0N 8 40W
Derudub 90 17 31N 36 7 E
Derval 18 47 40N 1 41W
Dervéni 35 38 8N 22 25 E
Derwent 109 53 41N 110 58W
Derwent →, Derby, U.K. 12 52 53N 1 17W
Derwent →, N. Yorks., U.K. 12 53 45N 0 57W
Derwentwater, L. 12 54 35N 3 9W
Des Moines, Iowa, U.S.A. 116 41 35N 93 37W
Des Moines, N. Mex., U.S.A. 119 36 50N 103 51W
Des Moines → 118 40 23N 91 25W
Des Plaines 117 42 3N 87 52W
Des Plaines → 117 41 23N 88 15W
Desaguadero →, Argent. 140 34 30S 66 46W
Desaguadero →, Boliv. 136 18 24S 67 5W
Desaguadero →, Peru 136 16 35S 69 5W
Desbarats 106 46 20N 83 56W
Desbiens 105 48 25N 71 57W
Descanso, Pta., Mexico 123 32 12N 116 58W
Descanso, Pta., U.S.A. 123 32 21N 117 3W
Deschaillons 105 46 32N 72 7W
Deschambault 105 46 39N 71 56W
Descharme → 109 56 51N 109 13W
Deschênes, Ont., Can. 107 45 25N 75 49W
Deschênes, Qué., Can. 104 45 23N 75 48W
Deschutes → 120 45 30N 121 0W
Dese 91 11 5N 39 40 E
Deseado, C. 142 52 45S 74 42W
Desemboque 124 30 30N 112 57W
Desenzano del Gardo 26 45 28N 10 32 E
Deseronto 107 44 12N 77 3W
Desert Center 123 33 45N 115 27W
Desert Hot Springs 123 33 58N 116 30W
Désirade, I. 127 16 18N 61 3W
Deskenatlata L. 108 60 55N 112 3W
Desmaraisville 104 49 32N 76 9W
Desméloizes 104 48 57N 79 29W
Desna → 36 50 33N 30 32 E
Desnătui → 34 44 15N 23 27 E
Desolación, I. 142 53 0S 74 0W
Despeñaperros, Paso 25 38 24N 3 30W
Despotovac 33 44 6N 21 30 E
Dessau 30 51 49N 12 15 E
Dessye = Dese 91 11 5N 39 40 E
D'Estrees B. 73 35 55S 137 45 E
Desuri 48 25 18N 73 35 E
Desvrès 19 50 40N 1 48 E
Det Udom 54 14 54N 105 5 E
Detinja → 33 43 51N 19 45 E
Detmold 30 51 55N 8 50 E
Detour Pt. 112 45 37N 86 35W
Detroit, Mich., U.S.A. 106 42 23N 83 5W
Detroit, Tex., U.S.A. 119 33 40N 95 10W
Detroit Lakes 118 46 50N 95 50W
Dett 95 18 38S 26 50 E
Deurne, Belg. 16 51 12N 4 24 E
Deurne, Neth. 16 51 27N 5 49 E
Deutsche Bucht 30 54 10N 7 51 E
Deutschlandsberg 33 46 49N 15 14 E
Deux-Sèvres □ 18 46 35N 0 20W
Deva 34 45 53N 22 55 E
Devakottai 51 9 55N 78 45 E
Devaprayag 49 30 13N 78 35 E
Dévaványa 33 47 2N 20 59 E
Deveci Daği 38 40 10N 36 0 E
Devenish 74 36 20S 145 54 E
Deventer 16 52 15N 6 10 E
Devenyns, L. 105 47 5N 73 50W
Deveron → 14 57 40N 2 31W
Devgad Baria 48 22 40N 73 55 E
Devgad, I. 51 14 48N 74 5 E
Devil River Pk. 81 40 56S 172 37 E
Devils Den 122 35 46N 119 58W
Devils Lake 118 48 5N 98 50W
Devils Paw, mt. 108 58 47N 134 0W
Devil's Pt., N. Hebr. 68 17 44S 168 11 E
Devil's Pt., Sri Lanka 51 9 26N 80 6 E
Devizes 13 51 21N 2 0W
Devnya 34 43 13N 27 33 E
Devolii → 35 40 57N 20 15 E
Devon 108 53 24N 113 44W
Devon I. 144 75 10N 85 0W
Devonport, Austral. 72 41 10S 146 22 E
Devonport, N.Z. 80 36 49S 174 49 E
Devonport, U.K. 13 50 23N 4 11W
Devonshire □ 13 50 50N 3 40W
Dewas 48 22 59N 76 3 E
Dewetsdorp 96 29 33S 26 39 E
Dewsbury 12 53 42N 1 38W
Dexing 59 28 46N 117 30 E
Dexter, Mich., U.S.A. 117 42 20N 83 53W
Dexter, Mo., U.S.A. 119 36 50N 90 0W
Dexter, N. Mex., U.S.A. 119 33 15N 104 25W
Dey-Dey, L. 79 29 12S 131 4 E
Deyang 58 31 3N 104 27 E
Deyhūk 47 33 15N 57 30 E
Deyyer 47 27 55N 51 55 E
Dezadeash L. 108 60 28N 136 58W
Dezfūl 46 32 20N 48 30 E
Dezh Shāhpūr 46 35 30N 46 25 E
Dezhneva, Mys 41 66 5N 169 40W
Dezhou 60 37 26N 116 18 E
Dhafra 47 23 20N 54 0 E
Dhahaban 90 21 58N 39 3 E
Dhahira 47 23 40N 57 0 E
Dhahiriya = Az Zahiriya 44 31 25N 34 58 E
Dhahran 46 26 18N 50 10 E
Dhamar 45 14 30N 44 20 E
Dhamási 35 39 43N 22 11 E
Dhampur 49 29 19N 78 33 E
Dhamtari 50 20 42N 81 35 E
Dhanbad 49 23 50N 86 30 E
Dhankuta 49 26 55N 87 40 E
Dhanora 50 20 20N 80 22 E
Dhar 48 22 35N 75 26 E
Dharampur, Gujarat, India 50 20 32N 73 17 E

Dharampur, Mad. P., India	**48**	22 13N	75 18 E
Dharapuram	**51**	10 45N	77 34 E
Dharmapuri	**51**	12 10N	78 10 E
Dharmavaram	**51**	14 29N	77 44 E
Dharmsala (Dharamsala)	**48**	32 16N	76 23 E
Dhaulagiri	**49**	28 39N	83 28 E
Dhebar, L.	**48**	24 10N	74 0 E
Dhenkanal	**50**	20 45N	85 35 E
Dhenoúsa	**35**	37 8N	25 48 E
Dheskáti	**35**	39 55N	21 49 E
Dhespotikó	**35**	36 57N	24 58 E
Dhestina	**35**	38 25N	22 31 E
Dhimitsána	**35**	37 36N	22 3 E
Dhírfis	**35**	38 40N	23 54 E
Dhodhekánisos	**35**	36 35N	27 0 E
Dholiana	**35**	39 54N	20 32 E
Dholka	**48**	22 44N	72 29 E
Dholpur	**48**	26 45N	77 59 E
Dhond	**50**	18 26N	74 40 E
Dhoraji	**48**	21 45N	70 37 E
Dhoxáton	**35**	41 9N	24 16 E
Dhrangadhra	**48**	22 59N	71 31 E
Dhrol	**48**	22 33N	70 25 E
Dhubaibah	**47**	23 25N	54 35 E
Dhubri	**52**	26 2N	89 59 E
Dhula	**45**	15 10N	47 30 E
Dhulasar	**52**	21 52N	90 14 E
Dhulia	**50**	20 58N	74 50 E
Dhupdhara	**52**	26 10N	91 4 E
Dhurm →	**90**	20 18N	42 53 E
Di Linh	**55**	11 35N	108 4 E
Di Linh, Cao Nguyen	**55**	11 30N	108 0 E
Día	**35**	35 26N	25 13 E
Diablo, Mt.	**122**	37 53N	121 56W
Diablo Range	**122**	37 0N	121 5W
Diafarabé	**88**	14 9N	4 57W
Diagonal	**116**	40 49N	94 20W
Diala	**88**	14 10N	10 0W
Dialakoro	**88**	12 18N	7 54W
Diallassagou	**88**	13 47N	3 41W
Diamante	**140**	32 5S	60 40W
Diamante →	**140**	34 30S	66 46W
Diamantina	**139**	18 17S	43 40W
Diamantina →	**73**	26 45S	139 10 E
Diamantino	**137**	14 30S	56 30W
Diamond Harbour	**49**	22 11N	88 14 E
Diamond Is.	**72**	17 25S	151 5 E
Diamond Mts.	**120**	40 0N	115 58W
Diamond Springs	**122**	38 42N	120 49W
Diamondville	**120**	41 51N	110 30W
Dianbai	**59**	21 33N	111 0 E
Diancheng	**59**	21 30N	111 4 E
Diano Marina	**26**	43 55N	8 3 E
Dianópolis	**139**	11 38S	46 50W
Dianra	**88**	8 45N	6 14W
Diapaga	**89**	12 5N	1 46 E
Diapangou	**89**	12 5N	0 10 E
Diapur	**74**	36 19S	141 29 E
Diariguila	**88**	10 35N	10 2W
Dibaya	**92**	6 30S	22 57 E
Dibaya Lubue	**92**	4 12S	19 54 E
Dibba	**47**	25 45N	56 16 E
Dibbi	**91**	4 10N	41 52 E
Dibble Glacier Tongue	**143**	66 8S	134 32 E
Dibete	**96**	23 45S	26 32 E
Dibrugarh	**52**	27 29N	94 55 E
Dickeyville	**116**	42 38N	90 36W
Dickinson	**118**	46 50N	102 48W
Dickson	**113**	36 5N	87 22W
Dickson City	**115**	41 29N	75 40W
Dickson (Dikson)	**40**	73 40N	80 5 E
Dicomano	**27**	43 53N	11 30 E
Didesa, W. →	**91**	10 2N	35 32 E
Didiéni	**88**	13 53N	8 6W
Didsbury	**108**	51 35N	114 10W
Didwana	**48**	27 23N	17 36 E
Die	**21**	44 47N	5 22 E
Diébougou	**88**	11 0N	3 15W
Diefenbaker L.	**109**	51 0N	106 55W
Diego Garcia	**53**	7 50S	72 50 E
Diégo-Suarez	**97**	12 25S	49 20 E
Diekirch	**16**	49 52N	6 10 E
Diélette	**18**	49 33N	1 52W
Diéma	**88**	14 32N	9 12W
Diémbéring	**88**	12 29N	16 47W
Dien Ban	**54**	15 53N	108 16 E
Dien Bien Phu	**54**	21 20N	103 0 E
Dien Khanh	**55**	12 15N	109 6 E
Diepholz	**30**	52 37N	8 22 E
Dieppe	**18**	49 54N	1 4 E
Dieren	**16**	52 3N	6 6 E
Dierks	**119**	34 9N	94 0W
Diest	**16**	50 58N	5 4 E
Dieterich	**117**	39 4N	88 23W
Dieulefit	**21**	44 32N	5 4 E
Dieuze	**19**	48 49N	6 43 E
Differdange	**16**	49 31N	5 54 E
Dig	**48**	27 28N	77 20 E
Digba	**94**	4 25N	25 48 E
Digboi	**52**	27 23N	95 38 E
Digby	**103**	44 38N	65 50W
Digges	**109**	58 40N	94 0W
Digges Is.	**101**	62 40N	77 50W
Dighinala	**52**	23 15N	92 5 E
Dighton	**118**	38 30N	100 26W
Digne	**21**	44 5N	6 12 E
Digoin	**20**	46 29N	3 58 E
Digos	**57**	6 45N	125 20 E
Digranes	**8**	66 4N	14 44 E
Digras	**50**	20 6N	77 45 E
Digul →	**57**	7 7S	138 42 E
Dijlah, Nahr →	**46**	31 0N	47 25 E
Dijon	**19**	47 20N	5 0 E
Dikala	**91**	4 45N	31 28 E
Dikkil	**91**	11 8N	42 20 E
Dikomu di Kai, Mt.	**96**	24 58S	24 36 E
Diksmuide	**16**	51 2N	2 52 E
Dikumbiya	**91**	14 45N	37 30 E
Dikwa	**89**	12 4N	13 30 E
Dila	**91**	6 21N	38 22 E
Dili	**57**	8 39S	125 34 E
Dilizhan	**39**	40 46N	44 57 E
Dilkoon	**77**	29 30S	152 59 E
Dillard	**116**	37 44N	91 13W
Dillenburg	**30**	50 44N	8 17 E
Dilley	**119**	28 40N	99 12W
Dilling	**91**	12 3N	29 35 E
Dillingen	**31**	48 32N	10 29 E
Dillon, Can.	**109**	55 56N	108 56W
Dillon, Mont., U.S.A.	**120**	45 9N	112 36W
Dillon, S.C., U.S.A.	**113**	34 26N	79 20W
Dillon →	**109**	55 56N	108 56W
Dillsboro	**117**	39 1N	85 4W
Dilston	**72**	41 22S	147 10 E
Dima	**91**	6 19N	36 15 E
Dimapur	**52**	25 54N	93 45 E
Dimas	**124**	23 43N	106 47W
Dimashq	**46**	33 30N	36 18 E
Dimbokro	**88**	6 45N	4 46W
Dimboola	**74**	36 28S	142 7 E
Dîmboviţa →	**34**	44 14N	26 13 E
Dîmbovnic →	**34**	44 28N	25 18 E
Dimbulah	**72**	17 8S	145 4 E
Dimitrovgrad, Bulg.	**35**	42 5N	25 35 E
Dimitrovgrad, U.S.S.R.	**37**	54 14N	49 39 E
Dimitrovgrad, Yugo.	**33**	43 0N	22 48 E
Dimmitt	**119**	34 36N	102 16W
Dimo	**91**	5 19N	29 10 E
Dimona	**44**	31 2N	35 1 E
Dimovo	**34**	43 43N	22 50 E
Dinagat	**57**	10 10N	125 40 E
Dinajpur	**52**	25 33N	88 43 E
Dinan	**18**	48 28N	2 2W
Dinant	**16**	50 16N	4 55 E
Dinapur	**49**	25 38N	85 5 E
Dinar	**46**	38 5N	30 15 E
Dinara Planina	**27**	43 50N	16 35 E
Dinard	**18**	48 38N	2 6W
Dinaric Alps = Dinara Planina	**6**	43 50N	16 35 E
Dinder, Nahr ed →	**91**	14 6N	33 40 E
Dindi →	**51**	16 24N	78 15 E
Dindigul	**51**	10 25N	78 0 E
Ding Xian	**60**	38 30N	114 59 E
Dingbian	**60**	37 35N	107 32 E
Dingee	**74**	36 22S	144 15 E
Dingelstädt	**30**	51 19N	10 19 E
Dinghai	**59**	30 1N	122 6 E
Dingle	**15**	52 9N	10 17W
Dingle B.	**15**	52 3N	10 20W
Dingmans Ferry	**115**	41 13N	74 55W
Dingnan	**59**	24 45N	115 0 E
Dingo	**72**	23 38S	149 19 E
Dingolfing	**31**	48 38N	12 30 E
Dingtao	**60**	35 5N	115 35 E
Dinguiraye	**88**	11 18N	10 49W
Dingwall	**14**	57 36N	4 26W
Dingxi	**60**	35 30N	104 33 E
Dingxiang	**60**	38 30N	112 58 E
Dingyuan	**59**	32 32N	117 41 E
Dinh Lap	**54**	21 33N	107 6 E
Dinh, Mui	**55**	11 22N	109 1 E
Dinhata	**52**	26 8N	89 27 E
Dinokwe (Palla Road)	**96**	23 29S	26 37 E
Dinosaur National Monument	**120**	40 30N	108 58W
Dinuba	**122**	36 31N	119 22W
Dio	**11**	56 37N	14 15 E
Diósgyör	**33**	48 7N	20 43 E
Diourbel	**88**	14 39N	16 12W
Diphu Pass	**52**	28 9N	97 20 E
Diplo	**48**	24 35N	69 35 E
Dipolog	**57**	8 36N	123 20 E
Dipşa	**34**	46 58N	24 27 E
Dipton	**81**	45 54S	168 22 E
Dir	**47**	35 08N	71 59 E
Diré	**88**	16 20N	3 25W
Dire Dawa	**91**	9 35N	41 45 E
Direction, C.	**72**	12 51S	143 32 E
Diriamba	**126**	11 51N	86 19W
Dirk Hartog I.	**79**	25 50S	113 5 E
Dirranbandi	**73**	28 33S	148 17 E
Disa	**91**	12 5N	34 15 E
Disappointment, C.	**120**	46 20N	124 0W
Disappointment L.	**78**	23 20S	122 40 E
Disaster B.	**75**	37 15S	150 0 E
Discovery B.	**74**	38 10S	140 40 E
Disentis	**31**	46 42N	8 50 E
Dishna	**90**	26 9N	32 32 E
Disina	**89**	11 35N	9 50 E
Disko	**144**	69 45N	53 30W
Disko Bugt	**144**	69 10N	52 0W
Disna	**36**	55 32N	28 11 E
Disna →	**36**	55 34N	28 12 E
Disney Reef	**68**	19 17S	174 7W
Disraëli	**105**	45 54N	71 21W
Disteghil Sar	**49**	36 20N	75 12 E
Distrito Federal □, Brazil	**139**	15 45S	47 45W
Distrito Federal □, Venez.	**134**	10 30N	66 55W
Disûq	**90**	31 8N	30 35 E
Diu	**48**	20 45N	70 58 E
Dives →	**18**	49 18N	0 7W
Dives-sur-Mer	**18**	49 18N	0 8W
Divi Pt.	**51**	15 59N	81 9 E
Divichi	**39**	41 15N	48 57 E
Divide	**120**	45 48N	112 47W
Dividing Ra.	**79**	27 45S	116 0 E
Divinópolis	**139**	20 10S	44 54W
Divisões, Serra dos	**139**	17 0S	51 0W
Divnoye	**39**	45 55N	43 21 E
Divo	**88**	5 48N	5 15W
Diwal Kol	**48**	34 23N	67 52 E
Dix →	**117**	37 49N	84 44W
Dixie	**120**	45 37N	115 27W
Dixie Mt.	**122**	39 55N	120 16W
Dixon, Calif., U.S.A.	**122**	38 27N	121 49W
Dixon, Ill., U.S.A.	**116**	41 50N	89 30W
Dixon, Iowa, U.S.A.	**116**	41 45N	90 47W
Dixon, Mo., U.S.A.	**116**	37 59N	92 6W
Dixon, Mont., U.S.A.	**120**	47 19N	114 25W
Dixon, N. Mex., U.S.A.	**121**	36 15N	105 57W
Dixon Entrance	**108**	54 30N	132 0W
Dixonville	**108**	56 32N	117 40W
Dixville	**105**	45 4N	71 46W
Diyarbakir	**46**	37 55N	40 18 E
Diz Chah	**47**	35 30N	55 30 E
Djado	**87**	21 4N	12 14 E
Djado, Plateau du	**87**	21 29N	12 21 E
Djakarta = Jakarta	**57**	6 9S	106 49 E
Djamâa	**87**	33 32N	5 59 E
Djamba	**96**	16 45S	13 58 E
Djambala	**92**	2 32S	14 30 E
Djanet	**87**	24 35N	9 32 E
Djangeru	**56**	2 20S	116 29 E
Djaul I.	**69**	2 58S	150 57 E
Djawa = Jawa	**57**	7 0S	110 0 E
Djebiniana	**87**	35 1N	11 0 E
Djelfa	**86**	34 40N	3 15 E
Djema	**94**	6 3N	25 15 E
Djendel	**86**	36 15N	2 25 E
Djeneïene	**87**	31 45N	10 9 E
Djenné	**88**	14 0N	4 30W
Djenoun, Garet el	**87**	25 4N	5 31 E
Djerba	**87**	33 52N	10 51 E
Djerba, Île de	**87**	33 56N	11 0 E
Djerid, Chott	**87**	33 42N	8 30 E
Djibo	**89**	14 9N	1 35W
Djibouti	**91**	11 30N	43 5 E
Djibouti ■	**45**	12 0N	43 0 E
Djidjelli	**87**	36 52N	5 50 E
Djolu	**92**	0 35N	22 5 E
Djorong	**56**	3 58S	114 56 E
Djougou	**89**	9 40N	1 45 E
Djoum	**92**	2 41N	12 35 E
Djourab, Erg du	**85**	16 40N	18 50 E
Djugu	**94**	1 55N	30 35 E
Djúpivogur	**8**	64 39N	14 17W
Djursholm	**10**	59 25N	18 6 E
Djursland	**11**	56 27N	10 45 E
Dmitriev-Lgovskiy	**36**	52 10N	35 0 E
Dmitriya Lapteva, Proliv	**41**	73 0N	140 0 E
Dmitrov	**37**	56 25N	37 32 E
Dmitrovsk-Orlovskiy	**36**	52 29N	35 10 E
Dneiper = Dnepr →	**38**	46 30N	32 18 E
Dnepr →	**38**	46 30N	32 18 E
Dneprodzerzhinsk	**38**	48 32N	34 37 E
Dneprodzerzhinskoye Vdkhr.	**38**	49 0N	34 0 E
Dnepropetrovsk	**38**	48 30N	35 0 E
Dneprorudnoye	**38**	47 21N	34 58 E
Dnestr →	**38**	46 18N	30 17 E
Dnestrovski = Belgorod	**38**	50 35N	36 35 E
Dniester = Dnestr →	**38**	46 18N	30 17 E
Dno	**36**	57 50N	29 58 E
Doan Hung	**54**	21 30N	105 10 E
Doba	**85**	8 40N	16 50 E
Dobané	**94**	6 20N	24 39 E
Dobbiaco	**27**	46 44N	12 13 E
Dobbyn	**72**	19 44S	139 59 E
Döbeln	**30**	51 7N	13 10 E
Doberai, Jazirah	**57**	1 25S	133 0 E
Dobiegniew	**32**	52 59N	15 45 E
Doblas	**140**	37 5S	64 0W
Dobo	**57**	5 45S	134 15 E
Doboj	**33**	44 46N	18 6 E
Dobra, Rumania	**34**	44 52N	25 40 E
Dobra, Hunedoara, Rumania	**34**	45 54N	22 36 E
Dobrinishta	**35**	41 49N	23 34 E
Dobrodzień	**32**	50 45N	18 25 E
Dobruja	**34**	44 30N	28 15 E
Dobrush	**37**	52 28N	30 19 E
Dobtong	**91**	6 25N	31 40 E
Doc, Mui	**54**	17 58N	106 30 E
Doce →	**139**	19 37S	39 49W
Doda	**49**	33 10N	75 34 E
Dodecanese = Dhodhekánisos	**35**	36 35N	27 0 E
Dodge Center	**118**	44 1N	92 50W
Dodge City	**119**	37 42N	100 0W
Dodge L.	**109**	59 50N	105 36W
Dodgeville	**116**	42 55N	90 8W
Dodo	**91**	5 10N	29 57 E
Dodola	**91**	6 59N	39 11 E
Dodoma	**94**	6 8S	35 45 E
Dodoma □	**94**	6 0S	36 0 E
Dodsland	**109**	51 50N	108 45W
Dodson	**120**	48 23N	108 16W
Doetinchem	**16**	51 59N	6 18 E
Dog Creek	**108**	51 35N	122 14W
Dog L., Man., Can.	**108**	51 2N	98 31W
Dog L., Ont., Can.	**102**	48 18N	89 30W
Dogger Bank	**6**	54 50N	2 0 E
Dogliani	**26**	44 35N	7 55 E
Dōgo	**64**	36 15N	133 16 E
Dōgo-San	**64**	35 2N	133 13 E
Dogondoutchi	**89**	13 38N	4 2 E
Dogran	**48**	31 48N	73 35 E
Doguéraoua	**89**	14 0N	5 31 E
Doha	**47**	25 15N	51 35 E
Dohad	**48**	22 50N	74 15 E
Doi	**57**	2 14N	127 49 E
Doi Luang	**54**	18 30N	101 0 E
Doi Saket	**54**	18 52N	99 9 E
Doig →	**108**	56 25N	120 40W
Dois Irmãos, Sa.	**138**	9 0S	42 30W
Dokka →	**10**	61 7N	10 0 E
Dokkum	**16**	53 20N	5 59 E
Dokri	**48**	27 25N	68 7 E
Dol-de-Bretagne	**18**	48 34N	1 47W
Doland	**118**	44 55N	98 5W
Dolbeau	**105**	48 53N	72 18W
Dole	**19**	47 7N	5 31 E
Doleib, Wadi →	**91**	12 10N	33 15 E
Dolgellau	**12**	52 44N	3 53W
Dolgelley = Dolgellau	**12**	52 44N	3 53W
Dolginovo	**36**	54 39N	27 29 E
Dolianova	**28**	39 23N	9 11 E
Dolinskaya	**38**	48 6N	32 46 E
Dolisie	**92**	4 9S	12 47 E
Dollart	**16**	53 20N	7 10 E
Dolna Banya	**34**	42 18N	23 44 E
Dolni Dŭbnik	**34**	43 24N	24 26 E
Dolo, Ethiopia	**91**	4 11N	42 3 E
Dolo, Italy	**27**	45 25N	12 4 E
Dolomites = Dolomiti	**27**	46 30N	11 40 E
Dolomiti	**27**	46 30N	11 40 E
Dolores, Argent.	**140**	36 20S	57 40W
Dolores, Uruguay	**140**	33 34S	58 15W
Dolores, Colo., U.S.A.	**121**	37 30N	108 30W
Dolores, Tex., U.S.A.	**119**	27 40N	99 38W
Dolores →	**121**	38 49N	108 17W
Dolphin and Union Str.	**100**	69 5N	114 45W
Dolphin C.	**142**	51 10S	59 0W
Dom Joaquim	**139**	18 57S	43 16W
Dom Pedrito	**141**	31 0S	54 40W
Dom Pedro	**138**	4 59S	44 27W
Doma	**89**	8 25N	8 18 E
Domasi	**95**	15 15S	35 22 E
Domazlice	**32**	49 28N	13 0 E
Dombarovskiy	**40**	50 46N	59 32 E
Dombasle	**19**	48 38N	6 21 E
Dombe Grande	**93**	12 56S	13 8 E
Dombes	**21**	46 3N	5 0 E
Dombóvár	**33**	46 21N	18 9 E
Domburg	**16**	51 34N	3 30 E
Domérat	**20**	46 21N	2 32 E
Domett	**81**	42 53S	173 12 E
Domeyko	**140**	29 0S	71 0W
Domeyko, Cordillera	**140**	24 30S	69 0W
Domfront	**18**	48 37N	0 40W
Dominador	**140**	24 21S	69 20W
Dominica ■	**127**	15 20N	61 20W
Dominica Passage	**127**	15 10N	61 20W
Dominican Rep. ■	**127**	19 0N	70 30W
Dömitz	**30**	53 9N	11 13 E
Domme	**20**	44 48N	1 12 E
Domo	**45**	7 50N	47 10 E
Domodóssola	**26**	46 6N	8 19 E

Dompaire	**19**	48 14N	6 14 E
Dompierre-sur-Besbre	**20**	46 31N	3 41 E
Dompim	**88**	5 10N	2 5W
Domrémy	**19**	48 26N	5 40 E
Domsjö	**10**	63 16N	18 41 E
Domville, Mt.	**77**	28 1S	151 15 E
Domvraína	**35**	38 15N	22 59 E
Domžale	**27**	46 9N	14 35 E
Don →, India	**51**	16 20N	76 15 E
Don →, Eng., U.K.	**12**	53 41N	0 51W
Don →, Scot., U.K.	**14**	57 14N	2 5W
Don →, U.S.S.R.	**39**	47 4N	39 18 E
Don Benito	**23**	38 53N	5 51W
Don, C.	**78**	11 18S	131 46 E
Don Duong	**55**	11 51N	108 35 E
Don Martín, Presa de	**124**	27 30N	100 50W
Don Pedro Res.	**122**	37 43N	120 24W
Dona Ana	**95**	17 25S	35 5 E
Donaghadee	**15**	54 38N	5 32W
Donald	**74**	36 23S	143 0 E
Donalda	**108**	52 35N	112 34W
Donaldsonville	**119**	30 2N	91 0W
Donalsonville	**113**	31 3N	84 52W
Donau →	**33**	48 10N	17 0 E
Donaueschingen	**31**	47 57N	8 30 E
Donauwörth	**31**	48 42N	10 47 E
Doncaster	**12**	53 31N	1 9W
Dondo, Angola	**92**	9 45S	14 25 E
Dondo, Mozam.	**95**	19 33S	34 46 E
Dondo, Teluk	**57**	0 29N	120 30 E
Dondra Head	**51**	5 55N	80 40 E
Donegal	**15**	54 39N	8 8W
Donegal □	**15**	54 53N	8 0W
Donegal B.	**15**	54 30N	8 35W
Donets →	**39**	47 33N	40 55 E
Donetsk	**38**	48 0N	37 45 E
Dong Ba Thin	**55**	12 8N	109 13 E
Dong Dang	**54**	21 54N	106 42 E
Dong Giam	**54**	19 25N	105 31 E
Dong Ha	**54**	16 55N	107 8 E
Dong Hene	**54**	16 40N	105 18 E
Dong Hoi	**54**	17 29N	106 36 E
Dong Jiang →	**59**	23 6N	114 0 E
Dong Khe	**54**	22 26N	106 27 E
Dong Ujimqin Qi	**60**	45 32N	116 55 E
Dong Van	**54**	23 16N	105 22 E
Dong Xoai	**55**	11 32N	106 55 E
Donga	**89**	7 45N	10 2 E
Dong'an	**59**	26 23N	111 12 E
Dongara	**79**	29 14S	114 57 E
Dongargarh	**50**	21 10N	80 40 E
Dongbei	**61**	42 0N	125 0 E
Dongchuan	**58**	26 8N	103 1 E
Donges	**18**	47 18N	2 4W
Dongfang	**54**	18 50N	108 33 E
Dongfeng	**61**	42 40N	125 34 E
Donggala	**57**	0 30S	119 40 E
Donggan	**58**	23 22N	105 9 E
Donggou	**61**	39 52N	124 10 E
Dongguan	**59**	22 58N	113 44 E
Dongguang	**60**	37 50N	116 30 E
Donghai Dao	**59**	21 0N	110 15 E
Dongjingcheng	**61**	44 8N	129 10 E
Donglan	**58**	24 30N	107 21 E
Dongliu	**59**	30 13N	116 55 E
Dongmen	**58**	22 20N	107 48 E
Dongning	**61**	44 2N	131 5 E
Dongnyi	**58**	28 3N	100 15 E
Dongola	**90**	19 9N	30 22 E
Dongou	**92**	2 0N	18 5 E
Dongping	**60**	35 55N	116 20 E
Dongshan	**59**	23 43N	117 30 E
Dongsheng	**60**	39 50N	110 0 E
Dongshi	**59**	24 18N	120 49 E
Dongtai	**59**	32 51N	120 21 E
Dongting Hu	**59**	29 18N	112 45 E
Dongxiang	**59**	28 11N	116 34 E
Dongxing	**58**	21 34N	108 0 E
Dongyang	**59**	29 13N	120 15 E
Dongzhi	**59**	30 9N	117 0 E
Donington, C.	**73**	34 45S	136 0 E
Doniphan	**119**	36 40N	90 50W
Donja Stubica	**27**	45 59N	16 0 E
Donji Dušnik	**33**	43 12N	22 5 E
Donji Miholjac	**33**	45 45N	18 10 E
Donji Milanovac	**33**	44 28N	22 6 E
Donji Vakuf	**33**	44 8N	17 24 E
Donjon, Le	**20**	46 22N	3 48 E
Donna	**119**	26 12N	98 2W
Donnaconna	**105**	46 41N	71 41W
Donnelly's Crossing	**80**	35 42S	173 38 E
Donnybrook	**79**	33 34S	115 48 E
Donora	**114**	40 11N	79 50W
Donor's Hills	**72**	18 42S	140 33 E
Donskoy	**37**	53 55N	38 15 E
Donya Lendava	**27**	46 35N	16 25 E
Donzère-Mondragon	**21**	44 28N	4 43 E
Donzère-Mondragon, Barrage de	**21**	44 13N	4 42 E
Donzy	**19**	47 20N	3 6 E
Doodlakine	**79**	31 41S	117 23 E
Dooen	**74**	36 39S	142 16 E
Dookie	**74**	36 20S	145 41 E
Doon →	**14**	55 26N	4 41W
Dor (Tantura)	**44**	32 37N	34 55 E
Dora Báltea →	**26**	45 11N	8 5 E
Dora, L.	**78**	22 0S	123 0 E
Dora Riparia →	**26**	45 5N	7 44 E
Dorada, La	**134**	5 30N	74 40W
Dorading	**91**	8 30N	33 5 E
Doran L.	**109**	61 13N	108 6W
Dorat, Le	**20**	46 14N	1 5 E
Dorchester	**13**	50 42N	2 28W
Dorchester, C.	**101**	65 27N	77 27W
Dordogne □	**20**	45 5N	0 40 E
Dordogne →	**20**	45 2N	0 36W
Dordrecht, Neth.	**16**	51 48N	4 39 E
Dordrecht, S. Afr.	**96**	31 20S	27 3 E
Dore →	**20**	45 50N	3 35 E
Doré L.	**109**	54 46N	107 17W
Doré Lake	**109**	54 38N	107 36W
Dore, Mt.	**20**	45 32N	2 50 E
Dores do Indaiá	**139**	19 27S	45 36W
Dorfen	**31**	48 16N	12 10 E
Dorgali	**28**	40 18N	9 35 E
Dori	**89**	14 3N	0 2W
Doring →	**96**	31 54S	18 39 E
Dorion	**105**	45 23N	74 3W
Dormaa-Ahenkro	**88**	7 15N	2 52W
Dormo, Ras	**91**	13 14N	42 35 E
Dornberg	**27**	55 45N	13 50 E
Dornbirn	**31**	47 25N	9 45 E
Dornes	**19**	46 48N	3 18 E
Dornoch	**14**	57 52N	4 0W
Dornoch Firth	**14**	57 52N	4 0W
Dornogovĭ □	**60**	44 0N	110 0 E
Doro	**89**	16 9N	0 51W
Dorogobuzh	**36**	54 50N	33 18 E
Dorohoi	**34**	47 56N	26 30 E
Döröö Nuur	**62**	48 0N	93 0 E
Dorre I.	**79**	25 13S	113 12 E
Dorrigo	**77**	30 20S	152 44 E
Dorris	**120**	41 59N	121 58W
Dorset, Can.	**107**	45 14N	78 54W
Dorset, U.S.A.	**114**	41 4N	80 40W
Dorset □	**13**	50 48N	2 25W
Dorsten	**30**	51 40N	6 55 E
Dortmund	**30**	51 32N	7 28 E
Dörtyol	**46**	36 52N	36 12 E
Dorum	**30**	53 40N	8 33 E
Doruma	**94**	4 42N	27 33 E
Dos Bahías, C.	**142**	44 58S	65 32W
Dos Cabezas	**121**	32 10N	109 37W
Dos Hermanas	**23**	37 16N	5 55W
Dos Palos	**122**	36 59N	120 37W
Doshi	**47**	35 35N	68 43 E
Dosquet	**105**	46 28N	71 32W
Dosso	**89**	13 0N	3 13 E
Dothan	**113**	31 10N	85 25W
Doty	**122**	46 38N	123 17W
Douai	**19**	50 21N	3 4 E
Douala	**92**	4 0N	9 45 E
Douarnenez	**18**	48 6N	4 21W
Double Island Pt.	**73**	25 56S	153 11 E
Doubrava →	**32**	49 40N	15 30 E
Doubs □	**19**	47 10N	6 20 E
Doubs →	**19**	46 53N	5 1 E
Doubtful B.	**79**	34 15S	119 28 E
Doubtful Sd.	**81**	45 20S	166 49 E
Doubtless B.	**80**	34 55S	173 26 E
Doudeville	**18**	49 43N	0 47 E
Doué	**18**	47 11N	0 20W
Douentza	**88**	14 58N	2 48W
Doughboy	**76**	35 15S	149 38 E
Douglas, Can.	**107**	45 31N	76 56W
Douglas, S. Afr.	**96**	29 4S	23 46 E
Douglas, U.K.	**12**	54 9N	4 29W
Douglas, Alaska, U.S.A.	**108**	58 23N	134 24W
Douglas, Ariz., U.S.A.	**121**	31 21N	109 30W
Douglas, Ga., U.S.A.	**113**	31 32N	82 52W
Douglas, Wyo., U.S.A.	**118**	42 45N	105 20W
Douglas Pt.	**106**	44 19N	81 37W
Douglastown	**103**	48 46N	64 24W
Douglasville	**113**	33 46N	84 43W
Douirat	**86**	33 2N	4 11W
Doukáton, Ákra	**35**	38 34N	20 30 E
Doulevant	**19**	48 22N	4 53 E
Doullens	**19**	50 10N	2 20 E
Doumé	**92**	4 15N	13 25 E
Douna	**88**	13 13N	6 0W
Dounan	**59**	23 41N	120 26 E
Dounreay	**14**	58 34N	3 44W
Dourada, Serra	**139**	13 10S	48 45W
Dourados	**141**	22 9S	54 50W
Dourados →	**141**	21 58S	54 18W
Dourdan	**19**	48 30N	2 0 E
Douro →	**22**	41 8N	8 40W
Douvaine	**21**	46 19N	6 16 E
Douz	**87**	33 25N	9 0 E
Douze →	**20**	43 54N	0 30W
Dove →	**12**	52 51N	1 36W
Dove Creek	**121**	37 46N	108 59W
Dover, Austral.	**72**	43 18S	147 2 E
Dover, U.K.	**13**	51 7N	1 19 E
Dover, Del., U.S.A.	**112**	39 10N	75 31W
Dover, Ky., U.S.A.	**117**	38 43N	83 52W
Dover, N.H., U.S.A.	**115**	43 12N	70 51W
Dover, N.J., U.S.A.	**115**	40 53N	74 34W
Dover, Ohio, U.S.A.	**114**	40 32N	81 30W
Dover-Foxcroft	**103**	45 14N	69 14W
Dover Plains	**115**	41 43N	73 35W
Dover, Pt.	**79**	32 32S	125 32 E
Dover, Str. of	**18**	51 0N	1 30 E
Dovey →	**13**	52 32N	4 0W
Dovrefjell	**10**	62 15N	9 33 E
Dowa	**95**	13 38S	33 58 E
Dowagiac	**117**	42 0N	86 8W
Dowlatabad	**47**	28 20N	56 40W
Down □	**15**	54 20N	6 0W
Downers Grove	**117**	41 49N	88 1W
Downey	**120**	42 29N	112 3W
Downham Market	**13**	52 36N	0 22 E
Downieville	**122**	39 34N	120 50W
Downing	**116**	40 29N	92 22W
Downpatrick	**15**	54 20N	5 43W
Downpatrick Hd.	**15**	54 20N	9 21W
Doyle	**122**	40 2N	120 6W
Doylestown	**115**	40 21N	75 10W
Dozois, Rés	**104**	47 30N	77 5W
Dra, Cap	**86**	28 47N	11 0W
Draa, Oued →	**86**	30 29N	6 1W
Drac →	**21**	45 13N	5 41 E
Drachten	**16**	53 7N	6 5 E
Drăgănești	**34**	44 9N	24 32 E
Drăgănești-Viașca	**34**	44 5N	25 33 E
Dragaš	**33**	42 5N	20 35 E
Drăgășani	**34**	44 39N	24 17 E
Dragonera, I.	**24**	39 35N	2 19 E
Draguignan	**21**	43 30N	6 27 E
Drain	**120**	43 45N	123 17W
Drake, Austral.	**77**	28 55S	152 25 E
Drake, U.S.A.	**118**	47 56N	100 21W
Drake Passage	**143**	58 0S	68 0W
Drakensberg	**97**	31 0S	28 0 E
Dráma	**35**	41 9N	24 10 E
Drammen	**10**	59 42N	10 12 E
Drangajökull	**8**	66 9N	22 15W
Drangedal	**10**	59 6N	9 3 E
Dranov, Ostrov	**34**	44 55N	29 30 E
Dras	**49**	34 25N	75 48 E
Drava →	**33**	45 33N	18 55 E
Draveil	**19**	48 41N	2 25 E
Dravograd	**27**	46 36N	15 5 E
Drawa →	**32**	52 52N	15 59 E
Drawno	**32**	53 13N	15 46 E
Drayton	**106**	43 46N	80 40W
Drayton Plains	**117**	42 42N	83 23W
Drayton Valley	**108**	53 12N	114 58W
Drenthe □	**16**	52 52N	6 40 E
Dresden, Can.	**106**	42 35N	82 11W
Dresden, Ger.	**30**	51 2N	13 45 E
Dresden □	**30**	51 12N	14 0 E
Dreux	**18**	48 44N	1 23 E
Drexel	**117**	39 45N	84 18W
Driffield	**12**	54 0N	0 25W
Driftwood	**114**	41 22N	78 9W
Drigana	**87**	20 51N	12 17 E
Driggs	**120**	43 50N	111 8W
Drin-i-zi →	**35**	41 37N	20 28 E
Drina →	**33**	44 53N	19 21 E
Drincea →	**34**	44 20N	22 55 E
Drini →	**34**	42 20N	20 0 E
Drinjača →	**33**	44 15N	19 8 E
Drivstua	**10**	62 26N	9 47 E
Drniš	**27**	43 51N	16 10 E
Drøbak	**10**	59 39N	10 39 E
Drocourt	**106**	45 46N	80 21W
Drogheda	**15**	53 45N	6 20W
Drogichin	**36**	52 15N	25 8 E
Drogobych	**36**	49 20N	23 30 E
Droichead Nua	**15**	53 11N	6 50W
Droitwich	**13**	52 16N	2 10W
Dromana	**74**	38 22S	144 57 E
Drôme □	**21**	44 38N	5 15 E
Drôme →	**21**	44 46N	4 46 E
Dromedary, C.	**75**	36 17S	150 10 E
Dronero	**26**	44 29N	7 22 E
Dronfield	**72**	21 12S	140 3 E
Dronne →	**20**	45 2N	0 9W
Dronning Maud Land	**143**	72 30S	12 0 E
Dronninglund	**11**	57 10N	10 19 E
Dropt →	**20**	44 35N	0 6W
Drouin	**74**	38 10S	145 53 E
Drumbo	**106**	43 16N	80 35W
Drumheller	**108**	51 25N	112 40W
Drummond, Mich., U.S.A.	**106**	46 1N	83 50W
Drummond, Mont., U.S.A.	**120**	46 40N	113 4W
Drummond I.	**106**	46 0N	83 40W
Drummond Pt.	**73**	34 9S	135 16 E
Drummond Ra.	**72**	23 45S	147 10 E
Drummondville	**105**	45 55N	72 25W
Drumright	**119**	35 59N	96 38W
Druskininkai	**36**	54 3N	23 58 E
Drut →	**36**	53 3N	30 42 E
Druya	**36**	55 45N	27 28 E
Druzhina	**41**	68 14N	145 18 E
Drvar	**27**	44 21N	16 23 E
Drvenik	**27**	43 27N	16 3 E
Dry Tortugas	**126**	24 38N	82 55W
Dryanovo	**34**	42 59N	25 28 E
Dryden, Can.	**109**	49 47N	92 50W
Dryden, U.S.A.	**119**	30 3N	102 3W
Drygalski I.	**143**	66 0S	92 0 E
Drysdale	**74**	38 11S	144 32 E
Drysdale →	**78**	13 59S	126 51 E
Drysdale I.	**72**	11 41S	136 0 E
Dschang	**89**	5 32N	10 3 E
Du	**89**	10 26N	0 59W
Du Bois	**114**	41 8N	78 46W
Du Quoin	**116**	38 0N	89 10W
Duanesburg	**115**	42 45N	74 11W
Duaringa	**72**	23 42S	149 42 E
Dubā	**46**	27 10N	35 40 E
Dubai = Dubayy	**47**	25 18N	55 20 E
Dubawnt →	**109**	64 33N	100 6W
Dubawnt, L.	**109**	63 4N	101 42W
Dubayy	**47**	25 18N	55 20 E
Dubbo	**76**	32 11S	148 35 E
Dubele	**94**	2 56N	29 35 E
Dubica	**27**	45 11N	16 48 E
Dublin, Ireland	**15**	53 20N	6 18W
Dublin, Ga., U.S.A.	**113**	32 30N	82 34W
Dublin, Tex., U.S.A.	**119**	32 0N	98 20W
Dublin □	**15**	53 24N	6 20W
Dublin B.	**15**	53 18N	6 5W
Dubna	**37**	54 8N	36 59 E
Dubno	**36**	50 25N	25 45 E
Dubois, Idaho, U.S.A.	**120**	44 7N	112 9W
Dubois, Ind., U.S.A.	**117**	38 26N	86 48W
Dubossary	**38**	47 15N	29 10 E
Dubossasy Vdkhr.	**38**	47 30N	29 0 E
Dubovka	**39**	49 5N	44 50 E
Dubovskoye	**39**	47 28N	42 46 E
Dubrajpur	**49**	23 48N	87 25 E
Dubréka	**88**	9 46N	13 31W
Dubrovitsa	**36**	51 31N	26 35 E
Dubrovnik	**33**	42 39N	18 6 E
Dubrovskoye	**41**	58 55N	111 10 E
Dubuque	**116**	42 30N	90 41W
Duchang	**59**	29 18N	116 12 E
Duchesne	**120**	40 14N	110 22W
Duchess	**72**	21 20S	139 50 E
Ducie I.	**67**	24 40S	124 48W
Duck Cr. →	**78**	22 37S	116 53 E
Duck Lake	**109**	52 50N	106 16W
Duck Mt. Prov. Parks	**109**	51 45N	101 0W
Duckwall ,Mt.	**122**	37 58N	120 7W
Duderstadt	**30**	51 30N	10 15 E
Dudhnai	**52**	25 59N	90 47 E
Dudinka	**41**	69 30N	86 13 E
Dudley	**13**	52 30N	2 5W
Dudna →	**50**	19 17N	76 54 E
Dueñas	**22**	41 52N	4 33W
Dueodde	**11**	54 59N	15 4 E
Dueré	**139**	11 20S	49 17W
Duero →	**22**	41 8N	8 40W
Duff Is.	**66**	9 53S	167 8 E
Dufftown	**14**	57 26N	3 9W
Dugger	**117**	39 4N	87 16W
Dugi	**27**	44 0N	15 0 E
Dugo Selo	**27**	45 51N	16 18 E
Duifken Pt.	**72**	12 33S	141 38 E
Duisburg	**30**	51 27N	6 42 E
Duitama	**134**	5 50N	73 2W
Duiwelskloof	**97**	23 42S	30 10 E
Dukana	**94**	3 59N	37 20 E
Duke I.	**108**	54 50N	131 20W
Dukhan	**47**	25 25N	50 50 E
Dukhovshchina	**36**	55 15N	32 27 E
Dukou	**58**	26 30N	101 44 E
Duku, Bauchi, Nigeria	**89**	10 43N	10 43 E
Duku, Sokoto, Nigeria	**89**	11 11N	4 55 E
Dulce →	**140**	30 32S	62 33W
Dulce, Golfo	**126**	8 40N	83 20W
Dŭlgopol	**34**	43 3N	27 22 E
Duliu	**60**	39 2N	116 55 E
Dullewala	**48**	31 50N	71 25 E
Dülmen	**30**	51 49N	7 18 E
Dulovo	**34**	43 48N	27 9 E
Dululu	**72**	23 48S	150 15 E
Duluth	**118**	46 48N	92 10W
Dum Dum	**49**	22 39N	88 33 E
Dumaguete	**57**	9 17N	123 15 E
Dumai	**56**	1 35N	101 28 E
Dumaran	**57**	10 33N	119 50 E
Dumaresq →	**77**	28 40S	150 29 E
Dumaring	**57**	1 46N	118 10 E
Dumas, Ark., U.S.A.	**119**	33 52N	91 30W
Dumas, Tex., U.S.A.	**119**	35 50N	101 58W
Dūmat al Jandal	**46**	29 55N	39 40 E
Dumbarton	**14**	55 58N	4 35W
Dumbea	**68**	22 10S	166 27 E
Dumbleyung	**79**	33 17S	117 42 E
Dumfries	**14**	55 4N	3 37W

Dumfries & Galloway □ **14** 55 0N 4 0W
Dumka **49** 24 12N 87 15 E
Dümmersee **30** 52 30N 8 21 E
Dumoine → **104** 46 13N 77 51W
Dumoine L. **104** 46 55N 77 55W
Dumosa **74** 35 54S 143 13 E
Dumraon **49** 25 33N 84 8 E
Dumyât **90** 31 24N 31 48 E
Dumyât, Masabb **90** 31 28N 31 51 E
Dun Laoghaire, (Dunleary) **15** 53 17N 6 9W
Dun-le-Palestel **20** 46 18N 1 39 E
Dun-sur-Auron **19** 46 53N 2 33 E
Duna → **33** 45 51N 18 48 E
Dunaföldvár **33** 46 50N 18 57 E
Dunaj → **33** 48 5N 17 10 E
Dunajec → **32** 50 15N 20 44 E
Dunajska Streda **33** 48 0N 17 37 E
Dunapatai **33** 46 39N 19 4 E
Dunărea → **34** 45 30N 8 15 E
Dunaújváros **33** 47 0N 18 57 E
Dunav → **33** 44 47N 21 20 E
Dunback **81** 45 23S 170 36 E
Dunbar, Austral. **72** 16 0S 142 22 E
Dunbar, U.K. **14** 56 0N 2 32W
Dunblane **14** 56 10N 3 58W
Duncan, Can. **108** 48 45N 123 40W
Duncan, Ariz., U.S.A. **121** 32 46N 109 6W
Duncan, Okla., U.S.A. **119** 34 25N 98 0W
Duncan L. **108** 62 51N 113 58W
Duncan, L. **108** 53 29N 77 58W
Duncan Town **126** 22 15N 75 45W
Duncannon **114** 40 23N 77 2W
Dunchurch **106** 45 39N 79 51W
Dundalk, Can. **106** 44 10N 80 24W
Dundalk, Ireland **15** 54 1N 6 25W
Dundalk Bay **15** 53 55N 6 15W
Dundas **106** 43 17N 79 59W
Dundas I. **108** 54 30N 130 50W
Dundas, L. **79** 32 35S 121 50 E
Dundas Str. **78** 11 15S 131 35 E
Dundee, Austral. **77** 29 33S 151 50 E
Dundee, S. Afr. **97** 28 11S 30 15 E
Dundee, U.K. **14** 56 29N 3 0W
Dundee, U.S.A. **117** 41 57N 83 40W
Dundgovĭ □ **60** 45 10N 106 0 E
Dundo **92** 7 23S 20 48 E
Dundoo **73** 27 40S 144 37 E
Dundrum **15** 54 17N 5 50W
Dundrum B. **15** 54 12N 5 40W
Dundwara **49** 27 48N 79 9 E
Dunedin, N.Z. **81** 45 50S 170 33 E
Dunedin, U.S.A. **113** 28 1N 82 45W
Dunedin → **108** 59 30N 124 5W
Dunedoo **77** 32 0S 149 25 E
Dunfermline **14** 56 5N 3 28W
Dungannon, Can. **106** 43 51N 81 36W
Dungannon, U.K. **15** 54 30N 6 47W
Dungannon □ **15** 54 30N 6 55W
Dungarpur **48** 23 52N 73 45 E
Dungarvan **15** 52 6N 7 40W
Dungarvan Bay **15** 52 5N 7 35W
Dungeness **13** 50 54N 0 59 E
Dungo, L. do **96** 17 15S 19 0 E
Dungog **76** 32 22S 151 46 E
Dungowan **77** 31 13S 151 8 E
Dungu **94** 3 40N 28 32 E
Dungunâb **90** 21 10N 37 9 E
Dungunâb, Khalij **90** 21 5N 37 12 E
Dunhinda Falls **51** 7 5N 81 6 E
Dunhua **61** 43 20N 128 14 E
Dunhuang **62** 40 8N 94 36 E
Dunières **21** 45 13N 4 20 E
Dunk I. **72** 17 59S 146 29 E
Dunkeld, Austral. **74** 37 40S 142 22 E
Dunkeld, U.K. **14** 56 34N 3 36W
Dunkerque **19** 51 2N 2 20 E
Dunkery Beacon **13** 51 15N 3 37W
Dunkirk **114** 42 30N 79 18W
Dunkirk = Dunkerque **19** 51 2N 2 20 E
Dunkuj **91** 12 50N 32 49 E
Dunkur **91** 11 58N 35 58 E
Dunkwa, Central, Ghana **88** 6 0N 1 47W
Dunkwa, Central, Ghana **89** 5 30N 1 0W
Dunlap **118** 41 50N 95 36W
Dunmanus B. **15** 51 31N 9 50W
Dunmara **72** 16 42S 133 25 E
Dunmore **115** 41 27N 75 38W
Dunmore Hd. **15** 52 10N 10 35W
Dunmore Town **126** 25 30N 76 39W
Dunn **113** 35 18N 78 36W
Dunnellon **113** 29 4N 82 28W
Dunnet Hd. **14** 58 38N 3 22W
Dunning **118** 41 52N 100 4W
Dunnville **106** 42 54N 79 36W
Dunolly **74** 36 51S 143 44 E
Dunoon, Austral. **77** 28 42S 153 20 E
Dunoon, U.K. **14** 55 57N 4 56W
Dunqul **90** 23 26N 31 37 E
Duns **14** 55 47N 2 20W
Dunseith **118** 48 49N 100 2W
Dunsmuir **120** 41 10N 122 18W
Dunstable **13** 51 53N 0 31W
Dunstan Mts. **81** 44 53S 169 35 E
Dunster **108** 53 8N 119 50W
Duntroon **81** 44 51S 170 40 E
Dunvegan L. **109** 60 8N 107 10W
Duolun **60** 42 12N 116 28 E
Duong Dong **55** 10 13N 103 58 E
Duparquet **104** 48 30N 79 14W
Duparquet, L. **104** 48 28N 79 16W
Dupree **118** 45 4N 101 35W
Dupuy **104** 48 50N 79 21W
Dupuyer **120** 48 11N 112 31W
Duque de Caxias **139** 22 45S 43 19W
Duque de York, I. **142** 50 37S 75 25W
Duquesne **114** 40 22N 79 55W
Dūrā **44** 31 31N 35 1 E
Durack → **78** 15 33S 127 52 E
Durack Range **78** 16 50S 127 40 E
Durance → **21** 43 55N 4 45 E
Durand, Ill., U.S.A. **116** 42 26N 89 20W
Durand, Mich., U.S.A. **117** 42 54N 83 58W
Durango, Mexico **124** 24 3N 104 39W
Durango, Spain **24** 43 13N 2 40W
Durango, U.S.A. **121** 37 16N 107 50W
Durango □ **124** 25 0N 105 0W
Duranillin **79** 33 30S 116 45 E
Durant, Iowa, U.S.A. **116** 41 36N 90 54W
Durant, Okla., U.S.A. **119** 34 0N 96 25W
Duratón → **22** 41 37N 4 7W
Durazno **140** 33 25S 56 31W
Durazzo = Durrësi **35** 41 19N 19 28 E
Durban, France **20** 43 0N 2 49 E
Durban, S. Afr. **97** 29 49S 31 1 E
Dúrcal **23** 37 0N 3 34W
Düren **30** 50 48N 6 30 E
Durg **50** 21 15N 81 22 E
Durgapur **49** 23 30N 87 20 E
Durham, Can. **106** 44 10N 80 49W
Durham, U.K. **12** 54 47N 1 34W
Durham, Calif., U.S.A. **122** 39 39N 121 48W
Durham, N.C., U.S.A. **113** 36 0N 78 55W
Durham □ **12** 54 42N 1 45W
Durham Downs **73** 26 6S 141 47 E
Durham Ox **74** 36 6S 143 57 E
Duri **77** 31 10S 150 51 E
Durmitor **33** 43 10N 19 0 E
Durness **14** 58 34N 4 45W
Durrësi **35** 41 19N 19 28 E
Durrie **72** 25 40S 140 15 E
Durtal **18** 47 40N 0 18W
Duru **94** 4 14N 28 50 E
D'Urville Island **81** 40 50S 173 55 E
D'Urville, Tandjung **57** 1 28S 137 54 E
Duryea **115** 41 20N 75 45W
Dusa Mareb **45** 5 30N 46 15 E
Dûsh **90** 24 35N 30 41 E
Dushak **40** 37 13N 60 1 E
Dushan **58** 25 48N 107 30 E
Dushanbe **40** 38 33N 68 48 E
Dusheti **39** 42 10N 44 42 E
Dusky Sd. **81** 45 47S 166 30 E
Dussejour, C. **78** 14 45S 128 13 E
Düsseldorf **30** 51 15N 6 46 E
Dutch Harbor **100** 53 54N 166 35W
Dutlhe **96** 23 58S 23 45 E
Dutsan Wai **89** 10 50N 8 10 E
Dutton **106** 42 39N 81 30W
Dutton → **72** 20 44S 143 10 E
Duved **10** 63 24N 12 55 E
Duvno **33** 43 42N 17 13 E
Duwadami **46** 24 35N 44 15 E
Duyun, Guizhou, China **58** 26 18N 107 29 E
Duyun, Guizhou, China **62** 26 18N 107 28 E
Duzce **46** 40 50N 31 10 E
Duzdab = Zāhedān **47** 29 30N 60 50 E
Dvina, Sev. → **40** 64 32N 30 30 E
Dvina, Zap. → **36** 57 4N 24 3 E
Dvinsk = Daugavpils **36** 55 53N 26 32 E
Dvor **27** 45 4N 16 22 E
Dwarka **48** 22 18N 69 8 E
Dwellingup **79** 32 43S 116 4 E
Dwight, Can. **107** 45 20N 79 1W
Dwight, U.S.A. **117** 41 5N 88 25W
Dyakovskoya **37** 60 5N 41 12 E
Dyatkovo **36** 53 40N 34 27 E
Dyer **117** 37 24N 86 13W
Dyer, C. **101** 66 40N 61 0W
Dyer Plateau **143** 70 45S 65 30W
Dyersburg **119** 36 2N 89 20W
Dyersville **116** 42 29N 91 8W
Dyfed □ **13** 52 0N 4 30W
Dyje → **32** 48 37N 16 56 E
Dynevor Downs **73** 28 10S 144 20 E
Dynów **32** 49 50N 22 11 E
Dysart **109** 50 57N 104 2W
Dzamin Üüd **60** 43 50N 111 58 E
Dzerzhinsk, U.S.S.R. **36** 53 40N 27 7 E
Dzerzhinsk, Byelorussian S.S.R., U.S.S.R. **36** 53 40N 27 1 E
Dzerzhinsk, R.S.F.S.R., U.S.S.R. **37** 56 14N 43 30 E
Dzhalal-Abad **40** 40 56N 73 0 E
Dzhalinda **41** 53 26N 124 0 E
Dzhambeyty **39** 50 15N 52 30 E
Dzhambul **40** 42 54N 71 22 E
Dzhankoi **38** 45 40N 34 20 E
Dzhanybek **39** 49 25N 46 50 E
Dzhardzhan **41** 68 10N 124 10 E
Dzhelinde **41** 70 0N 114 20 E
Dzhetygara **40** 52 11N 61 12 E
Dzhezkazgan **40** 47 44N 67 40 E
Dzhikimde **41** 59 1N 121 47 E
Dzhizak **40** 40 6N 67 50 E
Dzhugdzur, Khrebet **41** 57 30N 138 0 E
Dzhungarskiye Vorota **40** 45 0N 82 0 E
Dzhvari **39** 42 42N 42 4 E
Działdowo **32** 53 15N 20 15 E
Działoszyn **32** 51 6N 18 50 E
Dzibilchaltún **125** 21 5N 89 36W
Dzierzgoń **32** 53 58N 19 20 E
Dzierzoniów **32** 50 45N 16 39 E
Dzilam de Bravo **125** 21 24N 88 53W
Dzioua **87** 33 14N 5 14 E
Dzungarian Gate = Alataw Shankou **62** 45 5N 81 57 E
Dzuumod **62** 47 45N 106 58 E

E

Eabamet, L. **102** 51 30N 87 46W
Eads **118** 38 30N 102 46W
Eagle, Alaska, U.S.A. **100** 64 44N 141 7W
Eagle, Colo., U.S.A. **120** 39 39N 106 55W
Eagle → **103** 53 36N 57 26W
Eagle Butt **118** 45 1N 101 12W
Eagle Creek → **117** 38 36N 85 46W
Eagle Grove **116** 42 37N 93 53W
Eagle L., Calif., U.S.A. **120** 40 35N 120 50W
Eagle L., Me., U.S.A. **103** 46 23N 69 22W
Eagle Lake, Can. **107** 45 8N 78 29W
Eagle Lake, U.S.A. **119** 29 35N 96 21W
Eagle Mountain **123** 33 52N 115 26W
Eagle Nest **121** 36 33N 105 13W
Eagle Pass **119** 28 45N 100 35W
Eagle Pk. **122** 38 10N 119 25W
Eagle Pt. **78** 16 11S 124 23 E
Eagle River **118** 45 55N 89 17W
Eaglehawk **74** 36 39S 144 16 E
Eagleville **116** 40 28N 93 59W
Ealing **13** 51 30N 0 19W
Earaheedy **79** 25 34S 121 29 E
Earl Grey **109** 50 57N 104 43W
Earle **119** 35 18N 90 26W
Earlimart **123** 35 53N 119 16W
Earlville **117** 41 35N 88 55W
Earn → **14** 56 20N 3 19W
Earn, L. **14** 56 23N 4 14W
Earnslaw, Mt. **81** 44 32S 168 27 E
Earoo **79** 29 34S 118 22 E
Earth **119** 34 18N 102 30W
Easley **113** 34 52N 82 35W
East Angus **105** 45 30N 71 40W
East Aurora **114** 42 46N 78 38W
East B. **119** 29 2N 89 16W
East Bluff, Mt. **77** 31 53S 150 13 E
East Brady **114** 40 59N 79 36W
East Broughton Station **105** 46 14N 71 5W
East C., N.Z. **80** 37 42S 178 35 E
East C., P.N.G. **69** 10 13S 150 53 E
East Chicago **117** 41 40N 87 30W
East China Sea **62** 30 5N 126 0 E
East Coulee **108** 51 23N 112 27W
East Detroit **106** 42 28N 82 56W
East Dubuque **116** 42 29N 90 39W
East Falkland **142** 51 30S 58 30W
East Grand Forks **118** 47 55N 97 5W
East Greenwich **115** 41 39N 71 27W
East Gresford **76** 32 25S 151 31 E
East Hartford **115** 41 45N 72 39W
East Helena **120** 46 37N 111 58W
East Indies **56** 0 0 120 0 E
East Jordan **106** 45 10N 85 7W
East Kilbride **14** 55 46N 4 10W
East Lansing **117** 42 44N 84 29W
East Liverpool **114** 40 39N 80 35W
East London **97** 33 0S 27 55 E
East Los Angeles **123** 34 1N 118 9W
East Lynne **76** 35 35S 150 16 E
East Moline **116** 41 31N 90 25W
East Orange **115** 40 46N 74 13W
East Pacific Ridge **67** 15 0S 110 0W
East Palestine **114** 40 50N 80 32W
East Peoria **116** 40 40N 89 34W
East Pine **108** 55 48N 120 12W
East Pt. **103** 46 27N 61 58W
East Point **113** 33 40N 84 28W
East Providence **115** 41 48N 71 22W
East Retford **12** 53 19N 0 55W
East St. Louis **116** 38 37N 90 4W
East Schelde → **16** 51 38N 3 40 E
East Siberian Sea **41** 73 0N 160 0 E
East Stroudsburg **115** 41 1N 75 11W
East Sussex □ **13** 51 0N 0 20 E
East Tawas **106** 44 17N 83 31W
East Toorale P.O. **73** 30 27S 145 28 E
East Troy **117** 42 47N 88 24W
East Walker → **122** 38 52N 119 10W
Eastbourne, N.Z. **80** 41 19S 174 55 E
Eastbourne, U.K. **13** 50 46N 0 18 E
Eastend **109** 49 32N 108 50W
Easter I. **67** 27 8S 109 23W
Easter Islands **67** 27 0S 109 0W
Eastern □, Kenya **94** 0 0S 38 30 E
Eastern □, Uganda **94** 1 50N 33 45 E
Eastern Cr. → **72** 20 40S 141 35 E
Eastern Ghats **51** 14 0N 78 50 E
Eastern Group **79** 33 30S 124 30 E
Eastern Province □ **88** 8 15N 11 0W
Easterville **109** 53 8N 99 49W
Easthampton **115** 42 15N 72 41W
Eastland **119** 32 26N 98 45W
Eastleigh **13** 50 58N 1 21W
Eastmain → **102** 52 27N 78 26W
Eastmain (East Main) **102** 52 10N 78 30W
Eastman, Can. **105** 45 18N 72 19W
Eastman, Ga., U.S.A. **113** 32 13N 83 20W
Eastman, Wis., U.S.A. **116** 43 10N 91 1W
Easton, Md., U.S.A. **112** 38 47N 76 7W
Easton, Pa., U.S.A. **115** 40 41N 75 15W
Easton, Wash., U.S.A. **122** 47 14N 121 8W
Eastport **103** 44 57N 67 0W
Eastsound **122** 48 42N 122 55W
Eaton, Colo., U.S.A. **118** 40 35N 104 42W
Eaton, Ohio, U.S.A. **117** 39 45N 84 38W
Eaton Rapids **117** 42 31N 84 39W
Eatonia **109** 51 13N 109 25W
Eatonton **113** 33 22N 83 24W
Eatontown **115** 40 18N 74 7W
Eatonville, Can. **105** 47 20N 69 41W
Eatonville, U.S.A. **122** 46 52N 122 16W
Eau Claire, Fr. Gui. **135** 3 30N 53 40W
Eau Claire, S.C., U.S.A. **113** 34 5N 81 2W
Eau Claire, Wis., U.S.A. **118** 44 46N 91 30W
Eauze **20** 43 53N 0 7 E
Ebagoola **72** 14 15S 143 12 E
Eban **89** 9 40N 4 50 E
Ebbw Vale **13** 51 47N 3 12W
Ebden **75** 36 10S 147 1 E
Ebeggui **87** 26 2N 6 0 E
Ebensburg **114** 40 29N 78 43W
Ebensee **33** 47 48N 13 46 E
Eberbach **31** 49 27N 8 59 E
Eberswalde **30** 52 49N 13 50 E
Ebian **58** 29 11N 103 13 E
Ebingen **31** 48 13N 9 1 E
Ebino **64** 32 2N 130 48 E
Eboli **29** 40 39N 15 2 E
Ebolowa **92** 2 55N 11 10 E
Ebony **96** 22 6S 15 15 E
Ebor **77** 30 22S 152 27 E
Eboulements, Les **105** 47 28N 70 21W
Ebrach **31** 49 50N 10 30 E
Ébrié, Lagune **88** 5 12N 4 26W
Ebro → **24** 40 43N 0 54 E
Ebro, Pantano del **22** 43 0N 3 58W
Ebstorf **30** 53 2N 10 23 E
Eccleston **76** 32 14S 151 30 E
Éceuillé **18** 47 10N 1 19 E
Ech Chebbi **86** 26 41N 0 29 E
Echelles, Les **21** 45 27N 5 45 E
Echeng **59** 30 23N 114 50 E
Echizen-Misaki **65** 35 59N 135 57 E
Echmiadzin **39** 40 12N 44 19 E
Echo Bay **106** 46 29N 84 4W
Echo Bay (Port Radium) **100** 66 05N 117 55W
Echoing → **109** 55 51N 92 5W
Échouani, L. **104** 47 46N 75 42W
Echternach **16** 49 49N 6 25 E
Echuca **74** 36 10S 144 20 E
Ecija **23** 37 30N 5 10W
Eckernförde **30** 54 26N 9 50 E
Eclipse Is. **78** 13 54S 126 19 E
Écommoy **18** 47 50N 0 17 E
Ecoporanga **139** 18 23S 40 50W
Écorce, L. de l' **104** 47 5N 76 24W
Ecorse **117** 42 14N 83 10W
Écos **19** 49 9N 1 35 E
Écouché **18** 48 42N 0 10W
Ecuador ■ **134** 2 0S 78 0W

Ed	**11**	58 55N	11 55 E
Ed Dabbura	**90**	17 40N	34 15 E
Ed Dâmer	**90**	17 27N	34 0 E
Ed Debba	**90**	18 0N	30 51 E
Ed-Déffa	**90**	30 40N	26 30 E
Ed Deim	**91**	10 10N	28 20 E
Ed Dueim	**91**	14 0N	32 10 E
Edah	**79**	28 16S	117 10 E
Edam, Can.	**109**	53 11N	108 46W
Edam, Neth.	**16**	52 31N	5 3 E
Edapally	**51**	11 19N	78 3 E
Eday	**14**	59 11N	2 47W
Edd	**91**	14 0N	41 38 E
Eddrachillis B.	**14**	58 16N	5 10W
Eddystone	**13**	50 11N	4 16W
Eddystone Pt.	**72**	40 59S	148 20 E
Eddyville	**116**	41 9N	92 38W
Ede, Neth.	**16**	52 4N	5 40 E
Ede, Nigeria	**89**	7 45N	4 29 E
Édea	**92**	3 51N	10 9 E
Edehon L.	**109**	60 25N	97 15W
Edekel, Adrar	**87**	23 56N	6 47 E
Eden, Austral.	**75**	37 3S	149 55 E
Eden, N.C., U.S.A.	**113**	36 29N	79 53W
Eden, N.Y., U.S.A.	**114**	42 39N	78 55W
Eden, Tex., U.S.A.	**119**	31 16N	99 50W
Eden, Wyo., U.S.A.	**120**	42 2N	109 27W
Eden →	**12**	54 57N	3 2W
Eden L.	**109**	56 38N	100 15W
Edenburg	**96**	29 43S	25 58 E
Edendale	**81**	46 19S	168 48 E
Edenderry	**15**	53 21N	7 3W
Edenhope	**74**	37 4S	141 19 E
Edenton	**113**	36 5N	76 36W
Edenville	**97**	27 37S	27 34 E
Eder →	**30**	51 15N	9 25 E
Ederstausee	**30**	51 11N	9 0 E
Edgar	**118**	40 25N	98 0W
Edgartown	**115**	41 22N	70 28W
Edge Hill	**13**	52 7N	1 28W
Edgecumbe	**80**	37 59S	176 47 E
Edgefield	**113**	33 50N	81 59W
Edgeley	**118**	46 27N	98 41W
Edgemont	**118**	43 15N	103 53W
Edgeøya	**144**	77 45N	22 30 E
Edgeroi	**77**	30 7S	149 50 E
Edgerton, Ohio, U.S.A.	**117**	41 27N	84 45W
Edgerton, Wis., U.S.A.	**116**	42 50N	89 4W
Edgewood	**117**	38 55N	88 40W
Edhessa	**35**	40 48N	22 5 E
Edievale	**81**	45 49S	169 22 E
Edina, Liberia	**88**	6 0N	10 10W
Edina, U.S.A.	**116**	40 6N	92 10W
Edinburg, Ill., U.S.A.	**116**	39 39N	89 23W
Edinburg, Ind., U.S.A.	**117**	39 21N	85 58W
Edinburg, Tex., U.S.A.	**119**	26 22N	98 10W
Edinburgh	**14**	55 57N	3 12W
Edirne	**46**	41 40N	26 34 E
Edison, Calif., U.S.A.	**123**	35 21N	118 52W
Edison, Wash., U.S.A.	**122**	48 33N	122 27W
Edithburgh	**73**	35 5S	137 43 E
Edjeleh	**87**	28 38N	9 50 E
Edjudina	**79**	29 48S	122 23 E
Edmeston	**115**	42 42N	75 15W
Edmond	**119**	35 37N	97 30W
Edmonds	**122**	47 47N	122 22W
Edmonton, Austral.	**72**	17 2S	145 46 E
Edmonton, Can.	**108**	53 30N	113 30W
Edmore	**106**	43 25N	85 3W
Edmund L.	**109**	54 45N	93 17W
Edmundston	**103**	47 23N	68 20W
Edna	**119**	29 0N	96 40W
Edna Bay	**108**	55 55N	133 40W
Edolo	**26**	46 10N	10 21 E
Edremit	**46**	39 34N	27 0 E
Edsbyn	**10**	61 23N	15 49 E
Edsel Ford Ra.	**143**	77 0S	143 0W
Edsele	**10**	63 25N	16 32 E
Edson	**108**	53 35N	116 28W
Eduardo Castex	**140**	35 50S	64 18W
Edward →	**74**	35 0S	143 30 E
Edward I.	**102**	48 22N	88 37W
Edward, L. = Idi Amin Dada, L.	**94**	0 25S	29 40 E
Edward VII Pen.	**143**	80 0S	150 0W
Edwards	**123**	34 55N	117 51W
Edwards →	**116**	41 10N	90 59W
Edwards Plat.	**119**	30 30N	101 5W
Edwardsburg	**117**	41 48N	86 6W
Edwardsport	**117**	38 49N	87 15W
Edwardsville, Ill., U.S.A.	**116**	38 49N	89 57W
Edwardsville, Pa., U.S.A.	**115**	41 15N	75 56W
Edzo	**108**	62 49N	116 4W
Eekloo	**16**	51 11N	3 33 E
Eel →, Ind., U.S.A.	**117**	40 45N	86 22W
Eel →, Ind., U.S.A.	**117**	39 7N	86 58W
Efate, I. (Vate)	**68**	17 40S	168 25 E
Ef'e, Nahal	**44**	31 9N	35 13 E
Eferi	**87**	24 30N	9 28 E
Effingham	**117**	39 8N	88 30W
Eforie Sud	**34**	44 1N	28 37 E
Ega →	**24**	42 19N	1 55W
Égadi, Ísole	**28**	37 55N	12 16 E
Eganville	**107**	45 32N	77 5W
Egeland	**118**	48 42N	99 6W
Egenolf L.	**109**	59 3N	100 0W
Eger	**33**	47 53N	20 27 E
Eger →	**33**	47 38N	20 50 E
Egersund	**9**	58 26N	6 1 E
Egerton, Mt.	**79**	24 42S	117 44 E
Egg L.	**109**	55 5N	105 30W
Eggenburg	**32**	48 38N	15 50 E
Eggenfelden	**31**	48 24N	12 46 E
Eginbah	**78**	20 53S	119 47 E
Égletons	**20**	45 24N	2 3 E
Egmont, C.	**80**	39 16S	173 45 E
Egmont, Mt.	**80**	39 17S	174 5 E
Egogi Bad	**91**	13 10N	41 30 E
Eğridir	**46**	37 52N	30 51 E
Eğridir Gölü	**46**	37 53N	30 50 E
Egtved	**11**	55 38N	9 18 E
Éguas →	**139**	13 26S	44 14W
Egume	**89**	7 30N	7 14 E
Éguzon	**20**	46 27N	1 33 E
Egvekinot	**41**	66 19N	179 50W
Egypt ■	**90**	28 0N	31 0 E
Eha Amufu	**89**	6 30N	7 46 E
Ehime □	**64**	33 30N	132 40 E
Ehingen	**31**	48 16N	9 43 E
Ehrenberg	**123**	33 36N	114 31W
Ehrwald	**31**	47 24N	10 56 E
Eibar	**24**	43 11N	2 28W
Eichstatt	**31**	48 53N	11 12 E
Eider →	**30**	54 19N	8 58 E
Eidsvold	**73**	25 25S	151 12 E
Eifel	**31**	50 10N	6 45 E
Eiffel Flats	**95**	18 20S	30 0 E
Eigg	**14**	56 54N	6 10W
Eighty Mile Beach	**78**	19 30S	120 40 E
Eil	**45**	8 0N	49 50 E
Eil, L.	**14**	56 50N	5 15W
Eildon	**74**	37 14S	145 55 E
Eildon, L.	**74**	37 10S	146 0 E
Eileen L.	**109**	62 16N	107 37W
Eilenburg	**30**	51 28N	12 38 E
Ein 'Arik	**44**	31 54N	35 8 E
Ein el Luweiqa	**91**	14 5N	33 50 E
Einasleigh	**72**	18 32S	144 5 E
Einasleigh →	**72**	17 30S	142 17 E
Einbeck	**30**	51 48N	9 50 E
Eindhoven	**16**	51 26N	5 30 E
Einsiedeln	**31**	47 7N	8 46 E
Eiríksjökull	**8**	64 46N	20 24W
Eirunepé	**136**	6 35S	69 53W
Eisenach	**30**	50 58N	10 18 E
Eisenberg	**30**	50 59N	11 50 E
Eisenerz	**33**	47 32N	14 54 E
Eisenhüttenstadt	**30**	52 9N	14 41 E
Eisenstadt	**33**	47 51N	16 31 E
Eiserfeld	**30**	50 50N	7 59 E
Eisfeld	**30**	50 25N	10 54 E
Eisleben	**30**	51 31N	11 31 E
Eizariya (Bethany)	**44**	31 47N	35 15 E
Ejby	**11**	55 25N	9 56 E
Eje, Sierra del	**22**	42 24N	6 54W
Ejea de los Caballeros	**24**	42 7N	1 9W
Ejutla	**125**	16 34N	96 44W
Ekalaka	**118**	45 55N	104 30W
Ekawasaki	**64**	33 13N	132 46 E
Eket	**89**	4 38N	7 56 E
Eketahuna	**80**	40 38S	175 43 E
Ekhínos	**35**	41 16N	25 1 E
Ekibastuz	**40**	51 50N	75 10 E
Ekimchan	**41**	53 0N	133 0W
Ekoli	**94**	0 23S	24 13 E
Eksjö	**11**	57 40N	14 58W
Ekwan →	**102**	53 12N	82 15W
Ekwan Pt.	**102**	53 16N	82 7W
El Aaiún	**84**	27 9N	13 12W
El Aat	**44**	32 50N	35 45 E
El Abiodh-Sidi-Cheikh	**86**	32 53N	0 31 E
El Aïoun	**86**	34 33N	2 30W
El 'Aiyat	**90**	29 36N	31 15 E
El Alamein	**90**	30 48N	28 58 E
El Alto	**136**	4 15S	81 14W
El 'Arag	**90**	28 40N	26 20 E
El Arahal	**23**	37 15N	5 33W
El Arba	**86**	36 37N	3 12 E
El Aricha	**86**	34 13N	1 10W
El Arīhā	**44**	31 52N	35 27 E
El Arish	**72**	17 35S	146 1 E
El 'Arîsh	**90**	31 8N	33 50 E
El Arrouch	**87**	36 37N	6 53 E
El Asnam	**86**	36 10N	1 20 E
El Astillero	**22**	43 24N	3 49W
El Badâri	**90**	27 4N	31 25 E
El Bahrein	**90**	28 30N	26 25 E
El Ballâs	**90**	26 2N	32 43 E
El Balyana	**90**	26 10N	32 3 E
El Banco	**134**	9 0N	73 58W
El Baqeir	**90**	18 40N	33 40 E
El Barco de Ávila	**22**	40 21N	5 31W
El Barco de Valdeorras	**22**	42 23N	7 0W
El Bauga	**90**	18 18N	33 52 E
El Baúl	**134**	8 57N	68 17W
El Bawiti	**90**	28 25N	28 45 E
El Bayadh	**86**	33 40N	1 1 E
El Bierzo	**22**	42 45N	6 30W
El Biodh	**86**	26 0N	6 32W
El Bluff	**126**	11 59N	83 40W
El Bolsón	**142**	41 55S	71 30W
El Bonillo	**25**	38 57N	2 35W
El Caín	**142**	41 38S	68 19W
El Cajon	**123**	32 49N	117 0W
El Callao	**135**	7 18N	61 50W
El Camp	**24**	41 5N	1 10 E
El Campo	**119**	29 10N	96 20W
El Carmen, Boliv.	**137**	13 40S	63 55W
El Carmen, Venez.	**134**	1 16N	66 52W
El Castillo	**23**	37 41N	6 19W
El Centro	**123**	32 50N	115 40W
El Cerro, Boliv.	**137**	17 30S	61 40W
El Cerro, Spain	**23**	37 45N	6 57W
El Cocuy	**134**	6 25N	72 27W
El Compadre	**123**	32 20N	116 14W
El Corcovado	**142**	43 25S	71 35W
El Coronil	**23**	37 5N	5 38W
El Cuy	**142**	39 55S	68 25W
El Cuyo	**125**	21 30N	87 40W
El Dab'a	**90**	31 0N	28 27 E
El Deir	**90**	25 25N	32 20 E
El Dere	**45**	3 50N	47 8 E
El Días	**124**	20 40N	87 20W
El Díaz	**125**	21 1N	87 17W
El Dilingat	**90**	30 50N	30 31 E
El Diviso	**134**	1 22N	78 14W
El Djem	**87**	35 18N	10 42 E
El Djouf	**88**	20 0N	11 30 E
El Dorado, Ark., U.S.A.	**119**	33 10N	92 40W
El Dorado, Kans., U.S.A.	**119**	37 55N	96 56W
El Dorado, Venez.	**135**	6 55N	61 37W
El Dorado Springs	**116**	37 54N	93 59W
El Eglab	**86**	26 20N	4 30W
El Escorial	**22**	40 35N	4 7W
El Eulma	**87**	36 9N	5 42 E
El Faiyûm	**90**	29 19N	30 50 E
El Fâsher	**91**	13 33N	25 26 E
El Fashn	**90**	28 50N	30 54 E
El Ferrol	**22**	43 29N	8 15W
El Fifi	**91**	10 4N	25 0 E
El Fuerte	**124**	26 30N	108 40W
El Gal	**45**	10 58N	50 20 E
El Gebir	**91**	13 40N	29 40 E
El Gedida	**90**	25 40N	28 30 E
El Geneina	**85**	13 27N	22 45 E
El Geteina	**91**	14 50N	32 27 E
El Gezira □	**91**	15 0N	33 0 E
El Gîza	**90**	30 0N	31 10 E
El Goléa	**86**	30 30N	2 50 E
El Guettar	**87**	34 5N	4 38 E
El Hadjira	**87**	32 36N	5 30 E
El Hagiz	**91**	15 15N	35 50 E
El Hajeb	**86**	33 43N	5 13W
El Hammam	**90**	30 52N	29 25 E
El Hank, Alg.	**86**	25 38N	5 29W
El Hank, Maurit.	**86**	24 30N	7 0W
El Harrache	**84**	36 45N	3 5 E
El Hawata	**91**	13 25N	34 42 E
El Heiz	**90**	27 50N	28 40 E
El 'Idisât	**90**	25 30N	32 35 E
El Iskandarîya	**90**	31 0N	30 0 E
El Istwâ'ya □	**91**	5 0N	30 0 E
El Jadida, Moroc.	**84**	33 11N	8 17W
El Jadida, Moroc.	**86**	33 16N	9 31W
El Jebelein	**85**	12 40N	32 55 E
El Kab	**90**	19 27N	32 46 E
El Kala	**87**	36 50N	8 30 E
El Kamlin	**91**	15 3N	33 11 E
El Kantara, Alg.	**87**	35 14N	5 45 E
El Kantara, Tunisia	**87**	33 45N	10 58 E
El Karaba	**90**	18 32N	33 41 E
El Kef	**87**	36 12N	8 47 E
El Kelâa des Srarhna	**86**	32 4N	7 27W
El Khandaq	**90**	18 30N	30 30 E
El Khârga	**90**	25 30N	30 33 E
El Khartûm	**91**	15 31N	32 35 E
El Khartûm □	**91**	16 0N	33 0 E
El Khartûm Bahrî	**91**	15 40N	32 31 E
El-Khroubs	**87**	36 10N	6 55 E
El Khureiba	**90**	28 3N	35 10 E
El Kseur	**87**	36 46N	4 49 E
El Ksiba	**86**	32 45N	6 1W
El Kuntilla	**90**	30 1N	34 45 E
El Laqâwa	**85**	11 25N	29 1 E
El Laqeita	**90**	25 50N	33 15 E
El Leiya	**91**	16 15N	35 28 E
El Mafâza	**91**	13 38N	34 30 E
El Mahalla el Kubra	**90**	31 0N	31 0 E
El Mahârîq	**90**	25 35N	30 35 E
El Mahmûdîya	**90**	31 10N	30 32 E
El Maitén	**142**	42 3S	71 10W
El Maiz	**86**	28 19N	0 9W
El-Maks el-Bahari	**90**	24 30N	30 40 E
El Manshâh	**90**	26 26N	31 50 E
El Mansour	**86**	27 47N	0 14W
El Mansûra	**46**	31 0N	31 19 E
El Mantico	**135**	7 38N	62 45W
El Manzala	**90**	31 10N	31 50 E
El Marâgha	**90**	26 35N	31 10 E
El Masid	**91**	15 15N	33 0 E
El Matariya	**90**	31 15N	32 0 E
El Meghaier	**87**	33 55N	5 58 E
El Meraguen	**86**	28 0N	0 7W
El Metemma	**91**	16 50N	33 10 E
El Miamo	**135**	7 39N	61 46W
El Milagro	**140**	30 59S	65 59W
El Milheas	**86**	25 27N	6 57W
El Milia	**87**	36 27N	6 16 E
El Minyâ	**90**	28 7N	30 33 E
El Molar	**24**	40 42N	3 45W
El Monte	**123**	34 4N	118 2W
El Mreyye	**88**	18 0N	6 0W
El Obeid	**91**	13 8N	30 10 E
El Odaiya	**85**	12 8N	28 12 E
El Oro	**125**	19 48N	100 8W
El Oro = Sta. María del Oro	**124**	25 50N	105 20W
El Oro □	**134**	3 30S	79 50W
El Oued	**87**	33 20N	6 58 E
El Palmar, Boliv.	**137**	17 50S	63 9W
El Palmar, Venez.	**135**	7 58N	61 53W
El Palmito, Presa	**124**	25 40N	105 30W
El Panadés	**24**	41 10N	1 30 E
El Pardo	**22**	40 31N	3 47W
El Paso, Ill., U.S.A.	**116**	40 44N	89 1W
El Paso, Tex., U.S.A.	**121**	31 50N	106 30W
El Paso Robles	**122**	35 38N	120 41W
El Pedernoso	**25**	39 29N	2 45W
El Pedroso	**23**	37 51N	5 45W
El Pobo de Dueñas	**24**	40 46N	1 39W
El Portal	**122**	37 44N	119 49W
El Porvenir	**124**	31 15N	105 51W
El Prat de Llobregat	**24**	41 18N	2 3 E
El Progreso	**126**	15 26N	87 51W
El Provencío	**25**	39 23N	2 35W
El Pueblito	**124**	29 3N	105 4W
El Qâhira	**90**	30 1N	31 14 E
El Qantara	**90**	30 51N	32 20 E
El Qasr	**90**	25 44N	28 42 E
El Quseima	**90**	30 40N	34 15 E
El Qusîya	**90**	27 29N	30 44 E
El Râshda	**90**	25 36N	28 57 E
El Reno	**119**	35 30N	98 0W
El Rheauya	**86**	25 52N	6 30W
El Ribero	**22**	42 30N	8 30W
El Rîdisiya	**90**	24 56N	32 51 E
El Rio	**123**	34 14N	119 10W
El Ronquillo	**23**	37 44N	6 10W
El Rubio	**23**	37 22N	5 0W
El Saff	**90**	29 34N	31 16 E
El Salto	**124**	23 47N	105 22W
El Salvador ■	**126**	13 50N	89 0W
El Sancejo	**23**	37 4N	5 6W
El Sauce	**126**	13 0N	86 40W
El Shallal	**90**	24 0N	32 53 E
El Simbillawein	**90**	30 48N	31 13 E
El Sombrero	**134**	9 23N	67 3W
El Suweis	**90**	29 58N	32 31 E
El Thamad	**90**	29 40N	34 28 E
El Tigre	**135**	8 44N	64 15W
El Tocuyo	**134**	9 47N	69 48W
El Tofo	**140**	29 22S	71 18W
El Tránsito	**140**	28 52S	70 17W
El Tûr	**90**	28 14N	33 36 E
El Turbio	**142**	51 45S	72 5W
El Uqsur	**90**	25 41N	32 38 E
El Vado	**24**	41 2N	3 18W
El Vallés	**24**	41 35N	2 20 E
El Vigía	**134**	8 38N	71 39W
El Wak	**94**	2 49N	40 56 E
El Waqf	**90**	25 45N	32 15 E
El Wâsta	**90**	29 19N	31 12 E
El Weguet	**91**	5 28N	42 17 E
El Wuz	**85**	15 0N	30 7 E
Ela	**91**	12 50N	42 20 E
Elafónisos	**35**	36 29N	22 56 E
Elaine	**73**	37 44S	144 2 E
Elamanchili = Yellamanchilli	**50**	17 26N	82 50 E
Elands	**77**	31 37S	152 20 E
Elandsvlei	**96**	32 19S	19 31 E
Élassa	**35**	35 18N	26 21 E
Elassón	**35**	39 53N	22 12 E
Elat	**44**	29 30N	34 56 E
Elâzığ	**46**	38 37N	39 14 E
Elba, Italy	**26**	42 48N	10 15 E
Elba, U.S.A.	**113**	31 27N	86 4W
Elbasani	**35**	41 9N	20 9 E

Elbe	**122**	46 45N	122 10W
Elbe →	**30**	53 50N	9 0 E
Elberfeld	**117**	38 10N	87 27W
Elbert, Mt.	**121**	39 5N	106 27W
Elberta	**112**	44 35N	86 14W
Elberton	**113**	34 7N	82 51W
Elbeuf	**18**	49 17N	1 2 E
Elbidtan	**46**	38 13N	37 12 E
Elbląg	**32**	54 10N	19 25 E
Elbow	**109**	51 7N	106 35W
Elbrus	**39**	43 21N	42 30 E
Elburg	**16**	52 26N	5 50 E
Elburn	**117**	41 54N	88 28W
Elburz Mts. = Alborz	**47**	36 0N	52 0 E
Elche	**25**	38 15N	0 42W
Elche de la Sierra	**25**	38 27N	2 3W
Elcho I.	**72**	11 55 S	135 45 E
Elda	**25**	38 29N	0 47W
Eldon	**116**	38 20N	92 38W
Eldora	**116**	42 20N	93 5W
Eldorado, Argent.	**141**	26 28 S	54 43W
Eldorado, Ont., Can.	**107**	44 35N	77 31W
Eldorado, Sask., Can.	**109**	59 35N	108 30W
Eldorado, Mexico	**124**	24 20N	107 22W
Eldorado, Ill., U.S.A.	**117**	37 50N	88 25W
Eldorado, Tex., U.S.A.	**119**	30 52N	100 35W
Eldoret	**94**	0 30N	35 17 E
Eldred	**114**	41 57N	78 24W
Eldridge	**116**	41 39N	90 35W
Electra	**119**	34 0N	99 0W
Elefantes →	**97**	24 10 S	32 40 E
Elefantes, G.	**142**	46 28 S	73 49W
Elektrogorsk	**37**	55 56N	38 50 E
Elektrostal	**37**	55 41N	38 32 E
Elele	**89**	5 5N	6 50 E
Elephant Butte Res.	**121**	33 45N	107 30W
Elephant I.	**143**	61 0 S	55 0W
Elephant Pass	**51**	9 35N	80 25 E
Elesbão Veloso	**138**	6 13 S	42 8W
Eleuthera	**126**	25 0N	76 20W
Elgepiggen	**10**	62 10N	11 21 E
Elgeyo-Marakwet □	**94**	0 45N	35 30 E
Elgin, N.B., Can.	**103**	45 48N	65 10W
Elgin, Ont., Can.	**107**	44 36N	76 13W
Elgin, U.K.	**14**	57 39N	3 20W
Elgin, Ill., U.S.A.	**117**	42 0N	88 20W
Elgin, N.D., U.S.A.	**118**	46 24N	101 46W
Elgin, Nebr., U.S.A.	**118**	41 58N	98 3W
Elgin, Nev., U.S.A.	**121**	37 21N	114 20W
Elgin, Oreg., U.S.A.	**120**	45 37N	118 0W
Elgin, Texas, U.S.A.	**119**	30 21N	97 22W
Elgon, Mt.	**94**	1 10N	34 30 E
Eliase	**57**	8 21 S	130 48 E
Elida	**119**	33 56N	103 41W
Elikón, Mt.	**35**	38 18N	22 45 E
Elisabethville = Lubumbashi	**95**	11 40 S	27 28 E
Eliseu Martins	**138**	8 13 S	43 42W
Elista	**39**	46 16N	44 14 E
Elit	**91**	15 10N	37 0 E
Elizabeth, Austral.	**73**	34 42 S	138 41 E
Elizabeth, Ill., U.S.A.	**116**	42 19N	90 13W
Elizabeth, N.J., U.S.A.	**115**	40 37N	74 12W
Elizabeth City	**113**	36 18N	76 16W
Elizabetha	**94**	1 3N	23 37 E
Elizabethton	**113**	36 20N	82 13W
Elizabethtown, Ill., U.S.A.	**117**	37 27N	88 18W
Elizabethtown, Ky., U.S.A.	**112**	37 40N	85 54W
Elizabethtown, N.Y., U.S.A.	**115**	44 13N	73 36W
Elizabethtown, Pa., U.S.A.	**115**	40 8N	76 36W
Elizondo	**24**	43 12N	1 30W
Ełk	**32**	53 50N	22 21 E
Elk City	**119**	35 25N	99 25W
Elk Creek	**122**	39 36N	122 32W
Elk Grove	**122**	38 25N	121 22W
Elk Island Nat. Park	**108**	53 35N	112 59W
Elk Lake	**102**	47 40N	80 25W
Elk Point	**109**	53 54N	110 55W
Elk Rapids	**106**	44 54N	85 25W
Elk River, Idaho, U.S.A.	**120**	46 50N	116 8W
Elk River, Minn., U.S.A.	**118**	45 17N	93 34W
Elkader	**116**	42 51N	91 24W
Elkedra	**72**	21 9 S	135 33 E
Elkedra →	**72**	21 8 S	136 22 E
Elkhart, Ind., U.S.A.	**117**	41 42N	85 55W
Elkhart, Kans., U.S.A.	**119**	37 3N	101 54W
Elkhart →	**117**	41 41N	85 58W
Elkhorn, Can.	**109**	49 59N	101 14W
Elkhorn, U.S.A.	**117**	42 40N	88 33W
Elkhorn →	**118**	41 7N	98 15W
Elkhotovo	**39**	43 19N	44 15 E
Elkhovo	**34**	42 10N	26 40 E
Elkin	**113**	36 17N	80 50W
Elkins	**112**	38 53N	79 53W
Elko, Can.	**108**	49 20N	115 10W
Elko, U.S.A.	**120**	40 50N	115 50W
Elkton	**106**	43 49N	83 11W
Ell, L.	**79**	29 13 S	127 46 E
Ellef Ringnes I.	**144**	78 30N	102 2W
Ellen, Mt.	**121**	38 4N	110 56W
Ellenborough	**77**	31 27 S	152 28 E
Ellendale, Austral.	**78**	17 56 S	124 48 E
Ellendale, U.S.A.	**118**	46 3N	98 30W
Ellensburg	**120**	47 0N	120 30W
Ellenville	**115**	41 42N	74 23W
Ellerslie	**74**	38 10 S	142 44 E
Ellerston	**77**	31 49 S	151 20 E
Ellery, Mt.	**75**	37 28 S	148 47 E
Ellesmere I.	**144**	79 30N	80 0W
Ellesworth Land	**143**	76 0 S	89 0W
Ellettsville	**117**	39 14N	86 38W
Ellice Is.	**66**	8 0 S	176 0 E
Ellinwood	**118**	38 27N	98 37W
Elliot, Austral.	**72**	17 33 S	133 32 E
Elliot, S. Afr.	**97**	31 22 S	27 48 E
Elliot Lake	**106**	46 25N	82 35W
Ellis	**118**	39 0N	99 39W
Ellisville	**119**	31 38N	89 12W
Ellon	**14**	57 21N	2 5W
Ellore = Eluru	**50**	16 48N	81 8 E
Ells →	**108**	57 18N	111 40W
Ellsworth	**118**	38 47N	98 15W
Ellsworth Land	**143**	76 0 S	89 0W
Ellsworth Mts.	**143**	78 30 S	85 0W
Ellwangen	**31**	48 57N	10 9 E
Ellwood City	**114**	40 52N	80 19W
Elm	**31**	46 54N	9 10 E
Elma, Can.	**109**	49 52N	95 55W
Elma, U.S.A.	**122**	47 0N	123 30 E
Elmalı	**46**	36 44N	29 56 E
Elmer	**116**	39 57N	92 39W
Elmhurst, Austral.	**74**	37 13 S	143 16 E
Elmhurst, U.S.A.	**117**	41 52N	87 58W
Elmina	**89**	5 5N	1 21W
Elmira, Can.	**106**	43 36N	80 33W
Elmira, U.S.A.	**114**	42 8N	76 49W
Elmore, Austral.	**74**	36 30 S	144 37 E
Elmore, Calif., U.S.A.	**123**	33 7N	115 49W
Elmore, Minn., U.S.A.	**117**	41 29N	83 18W
Elmshorn	**30**	53 44N	9 40 E
Elmvale	**106**	44 35N	79 52W
Elmwood	**116**	40 47N	89 58W
Elne	**20**	42 36N	2 58 E
Elnora	**117**	38 53N	87 5W
Elong Elong	**77**	32 8 S	149 3 E
Elora	**106**	43 41N	80 26W
Elorza	**134**	7 3N	69 31W
Eloy	**121**	32 46N	111 33W
Éloyes	**19**	48 6N	6 36 E
Elphin	**107**	44 55N	76 37W
Elphinstone	**74**	37 5 S	144 22 E
Elrose	**109**	51 12N	108 0W
Elsas	**102**	48 32N	82 55W
Elsie, Mich., U.S.A.	**106**	43 5N	84 23W
Elsie, Oreg., U.S.A.	**122**	45 52N	123 35W
Elsinore, Cal., U.S.A.	**123**	33 40N	117 15W
Elsinore, Utah, U.S.A.	**121**	38 40N	112 2W
Elson	**122**	47 32N	123 4W
Elspe	**30**	51 10N	8 1 E
Elster →	**30**	51 25N	11 57 E
Elsterwerda	**30**	51 27N	13 32 E
Eltham, Austral.	**74**	37 43 S	145 12 E
Eltham, N.Z.	**80**	39 26 S	174 19 E
Elton	**39**	49 5N	46 52 E
Eluanbi	**59**	21 51N	120 50 E
Eluru	**50**	16 48N	81 8 E
Elvas	**23**	38 50N	7 10W
Elven	**18**	47 44N	2 36W
Elverum	**10**	60 53N	11 34 E
Elvire →	**78**	17 51 S	128 11 E
Elvire, Mt.	**78**	29 14 S	119 35 E
Elvo →	**26**	45 23N	8 21 E
Elvran	**10**	63 24N	11 3 E
Elwood, Ill., U.S.A.	**117**	41 24N	88 7W
Elwood, Ind., U.S.A.	**117**	40 20N	85 50W
Elwood, Nebr., U.S.A.	**118**	40 38N	99 51W
Ely, U.K.	**13**	52 24N	0 16 E
Ely, Minn., U.S.A.	**118**	47 54N	91 52W
Ely, Nev., U.S.A.	**120**	39 10N	114 50W
Elyashiv	**44**	32 23N	34 55 E
Elyria	**114**	41 22N	82 8W
Elz →	**31**	48 21N	7 45 E
Emådalen	**10**	61 20N	14 44 E
Emai	**68**	17 4 S	168 24 E
Emba	**40**	48 50N	58 8 E
Emba →, U.S.S.R.	**40**	45 25N	52 30 E
Emba →, U.S.S.R.	**40**	46 38N	53 14 E
Embarcación	**140**	23 10 S	64 0W
Embarras Portage	**109**	58 27N	111 28W
Embarrass →	**117**	38 39N	87 37W
Embetsu	**63**	44 44N	141 47 E
Embira →	**136**	7 19 S	70 15W
Embro	**106**	43 9N	80 54W
Embrun	**21**	44 34N	6 30 E
Embu	**94**	0 32 S	37 38 E
Embu □	**94**	0 30 S	37 35 E
Emden	**30**	53 22N	7 12 E
'Emeq Yizre'el	**44**	32 35N	35 12 E
Emerald, Queens., Austral.	**72**	23 32 S	148 10 E
Emerald, Vic., Austral.	**74**	37 56 S	145 29 E
Emerald Hill	**77**	30 52 S	150 6 E
Emerson	**109**	49 0N	97 10W
Emery	**121**	38 59N	111 17W
Emery Park	**121**	32 10N	110 59W
Emi Koussi	**85**	20 0N	18 55 E
Emilia-Romagna □	**26**	44 33N	10 40 E
Emilius, Mte.	**26**	45 41N	7 23 E
Eminabad	**48**	32 2N	74 8 E
Eminence	**117**	38 22N	85 11W
Emlenton	**114**	41 11N	79 41W
Emlichheim	**30**	52 37N	6 51 E
Emmaboda	**11**	56 37N	15 32 E
Emmaville	**77**	29 26 S	151 37 E
Emme →	**31**	47 0N	7 42 E
Emmeloord	**16**	52 44N	5 46 E
Emmen	**16**	52 48N	6 57 E
Emmendingen	**31**	48 7N	7 51 E
Emmental	**31**	47 0N	7 35 E
Emmerich	**30**	51 50N	6 12 E
Emmet	**72**	24 45 S	144 30 E
Emmetsburg	**116**	43 3N	94 40W
Emmett, Idaho, U.S.A.	**120**	43 51N	116 33W
Emmett, Mich., U.S.A.	**106**	42 59N	82 46W
Empalme	**124**	28 1N	110 49W
Empangeni	**97**	28 50 S	31 52 E
Empedrado	**140**	28 0 S	58 46W
Emperor Seamount Chain	**66**	40 0N	170 0 E
Empoli	**26**	43 43N	10 57 E
Emporia, Kans., U.S.A.	**118**	38 25N	96 10W
Emporia, Va., U.S.A.	**113**	36 41N	77 32W
Emporium	**114**	41 30N	78 17W
Empress	**109**	50 57N	110 0W
Ems →	**30**	52 37N	9 26 E
Emsdale	**106**	45 32N	79 19W
Emsdetten	**30**	52 11N	7 31 E
Emu, Austral.	**74**	36 44 S	143 26 E
Emu, China	**61**	43 40N	128 6 E
Emu Park	**72**	23 13 S	150 50 E
Emu Vale	**77**	28 11 S	152 15 E
En Gedi	**44**	31 28N	35 25 E
En Gev	**44**	32 47N	35 38 E
En Harod	**44**	32 33N	35 22 E
'En Kerem	**44**	31 47N	35 6 E
En Nahud	**91**	12 45N	28 25 E
Ena	**65**	35 25N	137 25 E
Ena-San	**65**	35 26N	137 36 E
Enafors	**10**	63 17N	12 20 E
Enambú	**134**	1 1N	70 17W
Enana	**96**	17 30 S	16 23 E
Enånger	**10**	61 30N	17 9 E
Enaratoli	**57**	3 55 S	136 21 E
Enard B.	**14**	58 5N	5 20W
Encantadas, Serra	**141**	30 40 S	53 0W
Encanto, C.	**57**	15 45N	121 38 E
Encarnación	**141**	27 15 S	55 50W
Encarnación de Diaz	**124**	21 30N	102 13W
Enchi	**88**	5 53N	2 48W
Encinal	**119**	28 3N	99 25W
Encinillas	**124**	29 14N	106 18W
Encinitas	**123**	33 3N	117 17W
Encino	**121**	34 38N	105 40W
Encontrados	**134**	9 3N	72 14W
Encounter B.	**73**	35 45 S	138 45 E
Encruzilhada	**139**	15 31 S	40 54W
Ende	**57**	8 45 S	121 40 E
Endeavour	**109**	52 10N	102 39W
Endeavour Str.	**72**	10 45 S	142 0 E
Endelave	**11**	55 46N	10 18 E
Enderbury I.	**66**	3 8 S	171 5W
Enderby	**108**	50 35N	119 10W
Enderby I.	**78**	20 35 S	116 30 E
Enderby Land	**143**	66 0 S	53 0 E
Enderlin	**118**	46 37N	97 41W
Endicott, N.Y., U.S.A.	**115**	42 6N	76 2W
Endicott, Wash., U.S.A.	**120**	47 0N	117 45W
Endimari →	**136**	8 46 S	66 7W
Endyalgout I.	**78**	11 40 S	132 35 E
Ene →	**136**	11 10 S	74 18W
Enfida	**87**	36 6N	10 28 E
Enfield, U.K.	**13**	51 39N	0 4W
Enfield, U.S.A.	**117**	38 6N	88 20W
Engadine	**106**	46 4N	85 38W
Engaño, C., Dom. Rep.	**127**	18 30N	68 20W
Engaño, C., Phil.	**57**	18 35N	122 23 E
Engelberg	**31**	46 48N	8 26 E
Engels	**37**	51 28N	46 6 E
Engemann L.	**109**	58 0N	106 55W
Enger	**10**	60 35N	10 20 E
Enggano	**56**	5 20 S	102 40 E
Enghien	**16**	50 37N	4 2 E
Engil	**86**	33 12N	4 32W
Engkilili	**56**	1 3N	111 42 E
England	**119**	34 30N	91 58W
England □	**7**	53 0N	2 0W
Englee	**103**	50 45N	56 5W
Englefield	**74**	37 21 S	141 48 E
Englehart	**102**	47 49N	79 52W
Engler L.	**109**	59 8N	106 52W
Englewood, Colo., U.S.A.	**118**	39 40N	105 0W
Englewood, Kans., U.S.A.	**119**	37 7N	99 59W
Englewood, N.J., U.S.A.	**115**	40 54N	73 59W
Englewood, Ohio, U.S.A.	**117**	39 53N	84 18W
English	**117**	38 20N	86 28W
English →, Can.	**109**	50 35N	93 30W
English →, U.S.A.	**116**	41 29N	91 32W
English Bazar	**49**	24 58N	88 10 E
English Channel	**18**	50 0N	2 0W
English River	**102**	49 14N	91 0W
Enid	**119**	36 26N	97 52W
Enipévs →	**35**	39 22N	22 17 E
Eniwetok	**66**	11 30N	162 15 E
Enkeldoorn	**95**	19 2 S	30 52 E
Enkhuizen	**16**	52 42N	5 17 E
Enköping	**10**	59 37N	17 4 E
Enle	**58**	24 0N	101 9 E
Enna	**29**	37 34N	14 15 E
Ennadai	**109**	61 8N	100 53W
Ennadai L.	**109**	61 0N	101 0W
Ennedi	**85**	17 15N	22 0 E
Enngonia	**73**	29 21 S	145 50 E
Ennis, Ireland	**15**	52 51N	8 59W
Ennis, Mont., U.S.A.	**120**	45 20N	111 42W
Ennis, Texas, U.S.A.	**119**	32 15N	96 40W
Enniscorthy	**15**	52 30N	6 35W
Enniskillen	**15**	54 20N	7 40W
Ennistimon	**15**	52 56N	9 18W
Enns →	**33**	48 14N	14 32 E
Enping	**59**	22 16N	112 21 E
Enriquillo, L.	**127**	18 20N	72 5W
Ensay	**75**	37 21 S	147 50 E
Enschede	**16**	52 13N	6 53 E
Ensenada, Argent.	**140**	34 55 S	57 55W
Ensenada, Mexico	**124**	31 50N	116 50W
Ensenada, La	**142**	41 12 S	72 33W
Enshū-Nada	**65**	34 27N	137 38 E
Ensisheim	**19**	47 50N	7 20 E
Entebbe	**94**	0 4N	32 28 E
Enterprise, Can.	**108**	60 47N	115 45W
Enterprise, Oreg., U.S.A.	**120**	45 30N	117 18W
Enterprise, Utah, U.S.A.	**121**	37 37N	113 36W
Entre Rios	**140**	21 30 S	64 25W
Entre Rios, Bahia, Brazil	**139**	11 56 S	38 5W
Entre Rios, Pará, Brazil	**137**	5 24 S	54 21W
Entre Ríos	**95**	14 57 S	37 20 E
Entre Ríos □	**140**	30 30 S	58 30W
Entrepeñas, Pantano de	**24**	40 34N	2 42W
Enugu	**89**	6 20N	7 30 E
Enugu Ezike	**89**	7 0N	7 29 E
Enumclaw	**122**	47 12N	122 0W
Envermeières	**18**	49 54N	1 16 E
Envermeu	**18**	49 53N	1 15 E
Envigado	**134**	6 10N	75 35W
Envira	**136**	7 18 S	70 13W
Enz →	**31**	49 1N	9 6 E
Enza →	**26**	44 54N	10 31 E
Enzan	**65**	35 42N	138 44 E
Éolie, I.	**29**	38 30N	14 50 E
Epanomí	**35**	40 25N	22 59 E
Epe, Neth.	**16**	52 21N	5 59 E
Epe, Nigeria	**89**	6 36N	3 59 E
Épernay	**19**	49 3N	3 56 E
Épernon	**19**	48 35N	1 40 E
Ephesus	**46**	38 0N	27 19 E
Ephraim	**120**	39 21N	111 37W
Ephrata	**120**	47 20N	119 32W
Epi	**68**	16 43 S	168 15 E
Épila	**24**	41 36N	1 17W
Épinac-les-Mines	**19**	46 59N	4 31 E
Épinal	**19**	48 10N	6 27 E
Epiphanie, L'	**105**	45 51N	73 29W
Epira	**135**	5 5N	57 20W
Epping, Austral.	**74**	37 38 S	145 3 E
Epping, U.K.	**13**	51 42N	0 8 E
Epukiro	**96**	21 40 S	19 9 E
Equality	**117**	37 44N	88 20W
Equatorial Guinea ■	**92**	2 0 S	8 0 E
Equeipa	**135**	5 22N	62 43W
Er Rahad	**91**	12 45N	30 32 E
Er Rif	**86**	35 1N	4 1W
Er Roseires	**91**	11 55N	34 30 E
Er Rumman	**44**	32 9N	35 48 E
Er Yébigué	**87**	22 30N	17 30 E

Eradu	79	28 40S	115 2E
Erandol	50	20 56N	75 20E
Erap	69	6 37S	146 51E
Erāwadī Myit = Irrawaddy →	52	15 50N	95 6E
Erba, Italy	26	45 49N	9 12E
Erba, Sudan	90	19 5N	36 51E
Ercha	41	69 45N	147 20E
Ercıyaş Dağı	46	38 30N	35 30E
Erdao Jiang →	61	43 0N	127 0E
Erdene	60	44 30N	111 10E
Erding	31	48 18N	11 55E
Erdre →	18	47 13N	1 32W
Erebato →	135	5 54N	64 16W
Erebus, Mt.	143	77 35S	167 0E
Erechim	141	27 35S	52 15W
Ereğli, Turkey	46	41 15N	31 30E
Ereğli, Turkey	46	37 31N	34 4E
Erei, Monti	29	37 20N	14 20E
Erenhot	60	43 48N	111 59E
Eresma →	22	41 26N	40 45W
Erfenis Dam	96	28 30S	26 50E
Erfoud	86	31 30N	4 15W
Erft →	30	51 11N	6 44E
Erfurt	30	50 58N	11 2E
Erfurt □	30	51 10N	10 30E
Ergani	46	38 17N	39 49E
Ergeni Vozyshennost	39	47 0N	44 0E
Eria →	22	42 3N	5 44W
Eriba	91	16 40N	36 10E
Eriboll, L.	14	58 28N	4 41W
Erica	75	37 59S	146 24E
Erice	28	38 4N	12 34E
Erie, Mich., U.S.A.	117	41 47N	83 31W
Erie, Pa., U.S.A.	114	42 10N	80 7W
Erie Canal	114	43 15N	78 0W
Erie, L.	106	42 15N	81 0W
Erieau	106	42 16N	81 57W
Erigavo	45	10 35N	47 20E
Eriksdale	109	50 52N	98 7W
Erikslund	10	62 31N	15 54E
Erímanthos	35	37 57N	21 50E
Erimo-misaki	63	41 50N	143 15E
Erin	106	43 45N	80 7W
Erithraí	35	38 13N	23 20E
Eritrea □	91	14 0N	41 0E
Erjas →	23	39 40N	7 1W
Erlangen	31	49 35N	11 0E
Erldunda	72	25 14S	133 12E
Erlin	59	23 55N	120 21E
Ermelo, Neth.	16	52 18N	5 35E
Ermelo, S. Afr.	97	26 31S	29 59E
Ermenak	46	36 38N	33 0E
Ermióni	35	37 23N	23 15E
Ernakulam = Cochin	51	9 59N	76 19E
Erne →	15	54 30N	8 16W
Erne, Lough	15	54 26N	7 46W
Ernée	18	48 18N	0 56W
Ernest Giles Ra.	79	27 0S	123 45E
Ernstberg	31	50 14N	6 46E
Erode	51	11 24N	77 45E
Eromanga	73	26 40S	143 11E
Erongo	96	21 39S	15 58E
Erquy	18	48 38N	2 29W
Erquy, Cap d'	18	48 39N	2 29W
Errabiddy	79	25 25S	117 5E
Erramala Hills	51	15 30N	78 15E
Errer →	91	7 32N	42 35E
Errigal, Mt.	15	55 2N	8 8W
Erris Hd.	15	54 19N	10 0W
Erromango	68	18 45S	169 5E
Erseka	35	40 22N	20 40E
Erskine	118	47 37N	96 0W
Erstein	19	48 25N	7 38E
Ertil	37	51 55N	40 50E
Erundu	96	20 39S	16 26E
Eruwa	89	7 33N	3 26E
Ervy-le-Châtel	19	48 2N	3 55E
Erwin	113	36 10N	82 28W
Eryuan	58	26 7N	99 57E
Erzgebirge	30	50 25N	13 0E
Erzin	41	50 15N	95 10E
Erzincan	46	39 46N	39 30E
Erzurum	46	39 57N	41 15E
Es Sahrâ' Esh Sharqîya	90	26 0N	33 30E
Es Sînâ'	90	29 0N	34 0E
Es Sûkî	91	13 20N	33 58E
Esa'ala	69	9 45S	150 49E
Esambo	94	3 48S	23 30E
Esan-misaki	63	41 40N	141 10E
Esbjerg	11	55 29N	8 29E
Escada	138	8 22S	35 8W
Escalante	121	37 47N	111 37W
Escalante →	121	37 17N	110 53W
Escalón	124	26 46N	104 20W
Escalona	22	40 9N	4 29W
Escambia →	113	30 32N	87 15W
Escanaba	112	45 44N	87 5W
Escarpé, C.	68	20 41S	167 13E
Esch-sur-Alzette	16	49 32N	6 0E
Eschallens	31	46 39N	6 38E
Eschede	30	52 44N	10 13E
Eschwege	30	51 10N	10 3E
Eschweiler	30	50 49N	6 14E
Escoma	136	15 40S	69 8W
Escondida, La	124	24 6N	99 55W
Escondido	123	33 9N	117 4W
Escoumins, Les	105	48 21N	69 24W
Escuinapa	124	22 50N	105 50W
Escuintla	126	14 20N	90 48W
Eséka	89	3 41N	10 44E
Esens	30	53 40N	7 35E
Esera →	24	42 6N	0 15E
Esfahān	47	33 0N	53 0E
Esgueva →	22	41 40N	4 43W
Esh Sham = Dimashq	46	33 30N	36 18E
Esh Shamâlîya □	90	19 0N	29 0E
Eshan	58	24 11N	102 24E
Eshowe	97	28 50S	31 30E
Eshta' ol	44	31 47N	35 0E
Esiama	88	4 56N	2 25W
Esino →	27	43 39N	13 22E
Esk →, Dumfries, U.K.	14	54 58N	3 4W
Esk →, N. Yorks., U.K.	12	54 27N	0 36W
Eskifjörður	8	65 3N	13 55W
Eskilstuna	10	59 22N	16 32E
Eskimo Pt.	109	61 10N	94 15W
Eskişehir	46	39 50N	30 35E
Esla →	22	41 29N	6 3W
Esla, Pantano del	22	41 29N	6 3W
Eslöv	11	55 50N	13 20E
Esmeralda, I.	142	48 55S	75 25W
Esmeralda, La	140	22 16S	62 33W
Esmeraldas	134	1 0N	79 40W
Esmeraldas □	134	0 40N	79 30W
Esmeraldas →	134	0 58N	79 38W
Espada, Pta.	134	12 5N	71 7W
Espalion	20	44 32N	2 47E
Espalmador, I.	25	38 48N	1 26E
Espanola	106	46 15N	81 46W
Espardell, I. del	25	38 47N	1 25E
Esparraguera	24	41 33N	1 52E
Esparta	126	9 59N	84 40W
Espejo	23	37 40N	4 34W
Esperança	138	7 1S	35 51W
Esperance	79	33 45S	121 55E
Esperance B.	79	33 48S	121 55E
Esperance, C.	68	9 15S	159 43E
Esperantinópolis	138	4 53S	44 53W
Esperanza, Santa Cruz, Argent.	142	51 1S	70 49W
Esperanza, Santa Fe, Argent.	140	31 29S	61 3W
Esperanza, La, Cuba	126	22 46N	83 44W
Esperanza, La, Hond.	126	14 15N	88 10W
Esperanza, La, Río Negro	142	40 26S	68 32W
Espéraza	20	42 56N	2 14E
Espichel, C.	23	38 22N	9 16W
Espiel	23	38 11N	5 1W
Espigão, Serra do	141	26 35S	50 30W
Espinal	134	4 9N	74 53W
Espinar	136	14 51S	71 24W
Espinazo, Sierra del = Espinhaço, Serra do	139	17 30S	43 30W
Espinhaço, Serra do	139	17 30S	43 30W
Espinho	22	41 1N	8 38W
Espinilho, Serra do	141	28 30S	55 0W
Espino	134	8 34N	66 1W
Espinosa de los Monteros	22	43 5N	3 34W
Espírito Santo □	139	20 0S	40 45W
Espíritu Santo	68	15 15S	166 50E
Espíritu Santo, B. del	125	19 15N	87 0W
Espíritu Santo, I.	124	24 30N	110 23W
Espita	125	21 1N	88 19W
Esplanada	139	11 47S	37 57W
Espluga de Francolí	24	41 24N	1 7E
Espuña, Sierra	25	37 51N	1 35W
Espungabera	97	20 29S	32 45E
Esquel	142	42 55S	71 20W
Esquina	140	30 0S	59 30W
Essaouira (Mogador)	86	31 32N	9 48W
Essarts, Les	18	46 47N	1 12W
Essebie	94	2 58N	30 40E
Essen, Belg.	16	51 28N	4 28E
Essen, Ger.	30	51 28N	6 59E
Essendon, Mt.	79	25 0S	120 30E
Essequibo □	135	7 0N	59 0W
Essequibo →	135	6 50N	58 30W
Essex, Can.	106	42 10N	82 49W
Essex, Calif., U.S.A.	123	34 44N	115 15W
Essex, Ill., U.S.A.	117	41 11N	88 11W
Essex, N.Y., U.S.A.	115	44 17N	73 21W
Essex □	13	51 48N	0 30E
Essexville	106	43 37N	83 50W
Esslingen	31	48 43N	9 19E
Essonne □	19	48 30N	2 20E
Essvik	10	62 18N	17 24E
Estaca, Pta. del	22	43 46N	7 42W
Estadilla	24	42 4N	0 16E
Estados, I. de Los	142	54 40S	64 30W
Estagel	20	42 47N	2 40E
Estância	138	11 16S	37 26W
Estancia	121	34 50N	106 1W
Estarreja	22	40 45N	8 35W
Estats, Pic d'	24	42 40N	1 24E
Estcourt, Can.	105	47 28N	69 14W
Estcourt, S. Afr.	97	28 58S	29 53E
Este	27	45 12N	11 40E
Esteban	22	43 33N	6 5W
Estelí	126	13 9N	86 22W
Estella	24	42 40N	2 0W
Estelline, S.D., U.S.A.	118	44 39N	96 52W
Estelline, Texas, U.S.A.	119	34 35N	100 27W
Estena →	23	39 23N	4 44W
Estepa	23	37 17N	4 52W
Estepona	23	36 24N	5 7W
Esterhazy	109	50 37N	102 5W
Esternay	19	48 44N	3 33E
Esterri de Aneu	24	42 38N	1 5E
Estevan	109	49 10N	102 59W
Estevan Group	108	53 3N	129 38W
Estherville	118	43 25N	94 50W
Estissac	19	48 16N	3 48E
Eston	109	51 8N	108 40W
Estonian S.S.R. □	36	58 30N	25 30E
Estoril	23	38 42N	9 23W
Estouk	89	18 14N	1 2E
Estrada, La	22	42 43N	8 27W
Estrêla, Serra da	22	40 10N	7 45W
Estrella	25	38 25N	3 35W
Estremoz	23	38 51N	7 39W
Estrondo, Serra do	138	7 20S	48 0W
Esztergom	33	47 47N	18 44E
Et Tleta	86	29 37N	9 15W
Et Turra	44	32 39N	35 59E
Étables-sur-Mer	18	48 38N	2 51W
Etah	49	27 35N	78 40E
Étain	19	49 13N	5 38E
Etamamu	103	50 18N	59 59W
Étampes	19	48 26N	2 10E
Étang	19	46 52N	4 10E
Etanga	96	17 55S	13 00E
Étaples	19	50 30N	1 39E
Etawah	49	26 48N	79 6E
Etawah →	113	34 20N	84 15W
Etawney L.	109	57 50N	96 50W
Eteh	89	7 2N	7 28E
Ethel	122	46 32N	122 46W
Ethel Creek	78	23 5S	120 11E
Ethel, Oued el →	86	28 31N	3 37W
Ethelbert	109	51 32N	100 25W
Ethiopia ■	45	8 0N	40 0E
Ethiopian Highlands	82	10 0N	37 0E
Etive, L.	14	56 30N	5 12W
Etna, Mt.	29	37 45N	15 0E
Etoile	95	11 33S	27 30E
Etolin I.	108	56 5N	132 20W
Etoshapan	96	18 40S	16 30E
Etowah	113	35 20N	84 30W
Étrépagny	18	49 18N	1 36E
Étretat	18	49 42N	0 12E
Étroits, Les	105	47 24N	68 54W
Ettlingen	31	48 58N	8 25E
Ettrick Water	14	55 31N	2 55W
Etuku	94	3 42S	25 45E
Etzatlán	124	20 48N	104 5W
Etzná	125	19 35N	90 15W
Eu	18	50 3N	1 26E
Eua	68	21 22S	174 56W
Euboea = Évvoia	35	38 40N	23 40E
Euchareena	76	32 57S	149 6E
Euclid	114	41 32N	81 31W
Euclides da Cunha	138	10 31S	39 1W
Eucumbene	75	36 8S	148 38E
Eucumbene, L.	75	36 2S	148 40E
Eudora	119	33 5N	91 17W
Eufaula, Ala., U.S.A.	113	31 55N	85 11W
Eufaula, Okla., U.S.A.	119	35 20N	95 33W
Eufaula, L.	119	35 15N	95 28W
Eugene	120	44 0N	123 8W
Eugenia, Punta	124	27 50N	115 5W
Eugowra	76	33 22S	148 24E
Eulo	73	28 10S	145 3E
Eumungerie	76	31 56S	148 36E
Eunice, La., U.S.A.	119	30 35N	92 28W
Eunice, N. Mex., U.S.A.	119	32 30N	103 10W
Eupen	16	50 37N	6 3E
Euphrates = Furat, Nahr al →	46	31 0N	47 25E
Eure □	18	49 6N	1 0E
Eure →	18	49 18N	1 12E
Eure-et-Loir □	18	48 22N	1 30E
Eureka, Can.	144	80 0N	85 56W
Eureka, Calif., U.S.A.	120	40 50N	124 0W
Eureka, Ill., U.S.A.	116	40 43N	89 16W
Eureka, Kans., U.S.A.	119	37 50N	96 20W
Eureka, Mo., U.S.A.	116	38 30N	90 38W
Eureka, Mont., U.S.A.	120	48 53N	115 6W
Eureka, Nev., U.S.A.	120	39 32N	116 2W
Eureka, S.D., U.S.A.	118	45 49N	99 38W
Eureka, Utah, U.S.A.	120	40 0N	112 9W
Eureka, Mt.	79	26 35S	121 35E
Euroa	74	36 44S	145 35E
Eurobodalla	76	36 9S	149 59E
Europa, Picos de	22	43 10N	4 49W
Europa Pt. = Europa, Pta. de	23	36 3N	5 21W
Europa, Pta. de	23	36 3N	5 21W
Europe	6	20 0N	20 0E
Europoort	16	51 57N	4 10E
Euskirchen	30	50 40N	6 45E
Eustis	113	28 54N	81 36W
Eutin	30	54 7N	10 38E
Eutsuk L.	108	53 20N	126 45W
Eva	135	3 9S	59 56W
Eva Downs	72	18 1S	134 52E
Évain	104	48 14N	79 8W
Eval	44	32 15N	35 15E
Evans	118	40 25N	104 43W
Evans Head	77	29 7S	153 27E
Evans L.	102	50 50N	77 0W
Evans Mills	115	44 6N	75 48W
Evans Pass	118	41 0N	105 35W
Evansdale	116	42 30N	92 17W
Evanston, Ill., U.S.A.	117	42 0N	87 40W
Evanston, Wyo., U.S.A.	120	41 10N	111 0W
Evansville, Ill., U.S.A.	116	38 5N	89 56W
Evansville, Ind., U.S.A.	117	38 0N	87 35W
Evansville, Wis., U.S.A.	116	42 47N	89 18W
Evart	106	43 54N	85 8W
Évaux-les-Bains	20	46 12N	2 29E
Eveleth	118	47 29N	92 46W
Even Yahuda	44	32 16N	34 53E
Evensk	41	62 12N	159 30E
Evenstad	10	61 25N	11 7E
Everard, L.	73	31 30S	135 0E
Everard Ras.	79	27 5S	132 28E
Everest, Mt.	49	28 5N	86 58E
Everett, Pa., U.S.A.	114	40 2N	78 24W
Everett, Wash., U.S.A.	122	48 0N	122 10W
Everglades, U.S.A.	113	26 0N	80 30W
Everglades, U.S.A.	113	25 52N	81 23W
Everglades Nat. Park.	113	25 27N	80 53W
Evergreen	113	31 28N	86 55W
Everson	120	48 57N	122 22W
Everton	75	36 25S	146 33E
Evesham	13	52 6N	1 57W
Evian-les-Bains	21	46 24N	6 35E
Evinayong	92	1 26N	10 35E
Évinos →	35	38 27N	21 40E
Evisa	21	42 15N	8 48E
Évora	23	38 33N	7 57W
Évora □	23	38 33N	7 50W
Évreux	18	49 0N	1 8E
Évron	18	48 10N	0 24W
Evrótas →	35	36 50N	22 40E
Évvoia	35	38 30N	24 0E
Évvoia □	35	38 40N	23 40E
Ewe, L.	14	57 49N	5 38W
Ewing, Mo., U.S.A.	116	40 6N	91 43W
Ewing, Nebr., U.S.A.	118	42 18N	98 22W
Ewo	92	0 48S	14 45E
Exaltación	137	13 10S	65 20W
Excelsior Springs	116	39 20N	94 10W
Excideuil	20	45 20N	1 4E
Exe →	13	50 38N	3 27W
Exeter, Can.	106	43 21N	81 29W
Exeter, U.K.	13	50 43N	3 31W
Exeter, Calif., U.S.A.	122	36 17N	119 9W
Exeter, N.H., U.S.A.	115	43 0N	70 58W
Exeter, Nebr., U.S.A.	118	40 43N	97 30W
Exira	116	41 35N	94 52W
Exmes	18	48 45N	0 10E
Exmoor	13	51 10N	3 59W
Exmouth, Austral.	78	21 54S	114 10E
Exmouth, U.K.	13	50 37N	3 26W
Exmouth G.	78	22 15S	114 15E
Expedition Range	72	24 30S	149 12E
Extremadura	23	39 30N	6 5W
Exuma Sound	126	24 30N	76 20W
Eyasi, L.	94	3 30S	35 0E
Eyeberry L.	109	63 8N	104 43W
Eyemouth	14	55 53N	2 5W
Eygurande	20	45 40N	2 26E
Eyjafjörður	8	66 15N	18 30W
Eymet	20	44 40N	0 25E
Eymoutiers	20	45 40N	1 45E
Eyrarbakki	8	63 52N	21 9W
Eyre	79	32 15S	126 18E
Eyre Cr. →	72	26 40S	139 0E
Eyre L., (North)	73	28 30S	137 20E
Eyre L., (South)	73	29 18S	137 25E
Eyre Mts.	81	45 25S	168 25E
Eyre Pen.	73	33 30S	137 17E
Eyzies, Les	20	44 56N	1 1E

Ez Zeidab 90 17 25N 33 55 E
Ezcaray 24 42 19N 3 0W

F

Fabens 121 31 30N 106 8W
Fåborg 11 55 6N 10 15 E
Fabre 104 47 12N 79 22W
Fabriano 27 43 20N 12 52 E
Făcăeni 34 44 32N 27 53 E
Facatativá 134 4 49N 74 22W
Facture 20 44 39N 0 58W
Fada 85 17 13N 21 34 E
Fada-n-Gourma 89 12 10N 0 30 E
Faddeyevskiy, Ostrov 41 76 0N 150 0 E
Fadhili 46 26 55N 49 10 E
Fadlab 90 17 42N 34 2 E
Faenza 27 44 17N 11 53 E
Fafa 89 15 22N 0 48 E
Fafe 22 41 27N 8 11W
Faga 68 13 39S 172 8W
Fagam 89 11 1N 10 1 E
Fagamalo 68 13 25S 172 21W
Făgăras 34 45 48N 24 58 E
Făgăras, Munţii 34 45 40N 24 40 E
Fågelsjö 10 61 50N 14 35 E
Fagerhult 11 57 8N 15 40 E
Fagersta 10 60 1N 15 46 E
Făget 34 45 52N 22 10 E
Fagnano Castello 29 39 31N 16 4 E
Fagnano, L. 142 54 30S 68 0W
Fagnières 19 48 58N 4 20 E
Fahraj 47 29 0N 59 0 E
Fahūd 47 22 18N 56 28 E
Faid 46 27 1N 42 52 E
Faillon, L. 104 48 21N 76 39W
Fair Hd. 15 55 14N 6 10W
Fair Oaks 122 38 39N 121 16W
Fairbank 121 31 44N 110 12W
Fairbanks 100 64 50N 147 50W
Fairborn 117 39 52N 84 2W
Fairbury, Ill., U.S.A. 117 40 45N 88 31W
Fairbury, Nebr., U.S.A. 118 40 5N 97 5W
Fairfax, Ohio, U.S.A. 117 39 5N 83 37W
Fairfax, Okla., U.S.A. 119 36 37N 96 45W
Fairfield, Austral. 76 33 53S 150 57 E
Fairfield, Ala., U.S.A. 113 33 30N 87 0W
Fairfield, Calif., U.S.A. 122 38 14N 122 1W
Fairfield, Conn., U.S.A. 115 41 8N 73 16W
Fairfield, Idaho, U.S.A. 120 43 21N 114 46W
Fairfield, Ill., U.S.A. 117 38 20N 88 20W
Fairfield, Iowa, U.S.A. 116 41 0N 91 58W
Fairfield, Mont., U.S.A. 120 47 40N 112 0W
Fairfield, Ohio, U.S.A. 117 39 21N 84 34W
Fairfield, Texas, U.S.A. 119 31 40N 96 0W
Fairford 109 51 37N 98 38W
Fairgrove 106 43 31N 83 33W
Fairholme 76 33 14S 147 22 E
Fairhope 113 30 35N 87 50W
Fairlie 81 44 5S 170 49 E
Fairmead 122 37 5N 120 10W
Fairmont, Minn., U.S.A. 118 43 37N 94 30W
Fairmont, W. Va., U.S.A. 112 39 29N 80 10W
Fairmont Hot Springs 108 50 20N 115 56W
Fairmount 123 34 45N 118 26W
Fairplay 121 39 9N 105 40W
Fairport, N.Y., U.S.A. 114 43 8N 77 29W
Fairport, Ohio, U.S.A. 114 41 45N 81 17W
Fairview, Austral. 72 15 31S 144 17 E
Fairview, Can. 108 56 5N 118 25W
Fairview, Mich., U.S.A. 106 44 44N 84 3W
Fairview, N. Dak., U.S.A. 118 47 49N 104 7W
Fairview, Okla., U.S.A. 119 36 19N 98 30W
Fairview, Utah, U.S.A. 120 39 50N 111 0W
Fairweather, Mt. 100 58 55N 137 45W
Faith 118 45 2N 102 4W
Faizabad, Afghan. 47 37 7N 70 33 E
Faizabad, India 49 26 45N 82 10 E
Faizpur 50 21 14N 75 49 E
Fajardo 127 18 20N 65 39W
Fakfak 57 3 0S 132 15 E
Fakobli 88 7 23N 7 23W
Fakse 11 55 15N 12 8 E
Fakse B. 11 55 11N 12 15 E
Fakse Ladeplads 11 55 11N 12 9 E
Faku 61 42 12N 123 21 E
Falaise 18 48 54N 0 12W
Falaise, Mui 54 19 6N 105 45 E
Falam 52 23 0N 93 45 E
Falces 24 42 24N 1 48W
Fălciu 34 46 17N 28 7 E
Falcón □ 134 11 0N 69 50W
Falcon, C. 86 35 50N 0 50W
Falcon Dam 119 26 50N 99 20W
Falconara Marittima 27 43 37N 13 23 E
Falconbridge 106 46 35N 80 45W
Falconer 114 42 7N 79 13W
Faléa 88 12 16N 11 17W
Falelatai 68 13 55S 171 59W
Falelima 68 13 32S 172 41W
Faleshty 38 47 32N 27 44 E
Falfurrias 119 27 14N 98 8W
Falher 108 55 44N 117 15W
Falkenberg, Ger. 30 51 34N 13 13 E
Falkenberg, Sweden 11 56 54N 12 30 E
Falkensee 30 52 35N 13 6 E
Falkenstein 30 50 27N 12 24 E
Falkirk 14 56 0N 3 47W
Falkland, East, I. 142 51 40S 58 30W
Falkland Is. 142 51 30S 59 0W
Falkland Is. Dependency □ 143 57 0S 40 0W
Falkland Sd. 142 52 0S 60 0W
Falkland, West, I. 142 51 40S 60 0W
Falköping 11 58 12N 13 33 E
Fall Brook 121 33 25N 117 12W
Fall River 115 41 45N 71 5W
Fall River Mills 120 41 1N 121 30W
Fallbrook 123 33 23N 117 15W
Fallon, Mont., U.S.A. 118 46 52N 105 8W
Fallon, Nev., U.S.A. 120 39 31N 118 51W
Falls City, Nebr., U.S.A. 118 40 0N 95 40W
Falls City, Oreg., U.S.A. 120 44 54N 123 29W
Falls Creek, Austral. 76 34 58S 150 36 E
Falls Creek, U.S.A. 114 41 8N 78 49W
Falmouth, Jamaica 126 18 30N 77 40W
Falmouth, U.K. 13 50 9N 5 5W
Falmouth, U.S.A. 117 38 40N 84 20W
False Divi Pt. 51 15 43N 80 50 E
Falset 24 41 7N 0 50 E
Falso, C. 126 15 12N 83 21W
Falster 11 54 45N 11 55 E
Falsterbo 11 55 23N 12 50 E
Fălticeni 34 47 21N 26 20 E
Falun 10 60 37N 15 37 E
Famagusta 46 35 8N 33 55 E
Famatina, Sierra, de 140 27 30S 68 0W
Family L. 109 51 54N 95 27W
Famoso 123 35 37N 119 12W
Fampotabe 97 15 56S 50 8 E
Fan Xian 60 35 55N 115 38 E
Fana 88 13 0N 6 56W
Fanambana 97 13 34S 50 0 E
Fandriana 97 20 14S 47 21 E
Fang 54 19 55N 99 13 E
Fang Xian 59 32 3N 110 40 E
Fangchang 59 31 5N 118 4 E
Fangcheng, Guangxi, China 58 21 42N 108 21 E
Fangcheng, Henan, China 59 33 18N 112 59 E
Fangliao 59 22 22N 120 38 E
Fangshan 60 38 3N 111 25 E
Fangzi 61 36 33N 119 10 E
Fani i Madh → 35 41 56N 20 16 E
Fanjiatun 61 43 40N 125 0 E
Fannich, L. 14 57 40N 5 0W
Fanning I. 67 3 51N 159 22W
Fanny Bay 108 49 27N 124 48W
Fanø 11 55 25N 8 25 E
Fano 27 43 50N 13 0 E
Fanshaw 108 57 11N 133 30W
Fanshi 60 39 12N 113 20 E
Fao (Al Fāw) 46 30 0N 48 30 E
Faqirwali 48 29 27N 73 0 E
Fara in Sabina 27 42 13N 12 44 E
Faraday Seamount Group 128 50 0N 27 0W
Faradje 94 3 50N 29 45 E
Farafangana 97 22 49S 47 50 E
Farâfra, El Wâhât el- 90 27 15N 28 20 E
Farah 47 32 20N 62 7 E
Farah □ 47 32 25N 62 10 E
Farahalana 97 14 26S 50 10 E
Faraid, Gebel 90 23 33N 35 19 E
Faramana 88 11 56N 4 45W
Faranah 88 10 3N 10 45W
Farasān, Jazā'ir 45 16 45N 41 55 E
Faratsiho 97 19 24S 46 57 E
Fardes → 25 37 35N 3 0W
Fareara, Pte. 68 17 52S 149 9W
Fareham 13 50 52N 1 11W
Farewell 106 43 52N 84 55W
Farewell, C. 81 40 29S 172 43 E
Farewell C. = Farvel, K. 144 59 48N 43 55W
Farewell Spit 81 40 35S 173 0 E
Fargo 118 46 52N 96 40W
Fari'a → 44 32 12N 35 27 E
Faribault 118 44 15N 93 19W
Faridkot 48 30 44N 74 45 E
Faridpur 52 23 15N 89 55 E
Färila 10 61 48N 15 50 E
Farim 88 12 27N 15 9W
Farimān 47 35 40N 59 49 E
Farina 73 30 3S 138 15 E
Faringe 10 59 55N 18 7 E
Farinha → 138 6 51S 47 30W
Fâriskûr 90 31 20N 31 43 E
Farmer City 117 40 15N 88 39W
Farmersburg 117 39 15N 87 23W
Farmerville 119 32 48N 92 23W
Farmington, Calif., U.S.A. 122 37 56N 121 0W
Farmington, Ill., U.S.A. 116 40 42N 90 0W
Farmington, Iowa, U.S.A. 116 40 38N 91 44W
Farmington, Mo., U.S.A. 116 37 47N 90 25W
Farmington, N. Mex., U.S.A. 121 36 45N 108 28W
Farmington, N.H., U.S.A. 115 43 25N 71 7W
Farmington, Utah, U.S.A. 120 41 0N 111 12W
Farmington → 115 41 51N 72 33W
Farmland 117 40 15N 85 5W
Farmville 112 37 19N 78 22W
Farnborough 13 51 17N 0 46W
Farne Is. 12 55 38N 1 37W
Farnham 105 45 17N 72 59W
Faro, Brazil 135 2 10S 56 39W
Faro, Port. 23 37 2N 7 55W
Faro □ 23 37 12N 8 10W
Faroe Is. 6 62 0N 7 0W
Farquhar, C. 79 23 50S 113 36 E
Farquhar Is. 53 11 0S 52 0 E
Farrar → 14 57 30N 4 30W
Farrars, Cr. → 72 25 35S 140 43 E
Farrāshband 47 28 57N 52 5 E
Farrell 114 41 13N 80 29W
Farrell Flat 73 33 48S 138 48 E
Farrukhabad 49 27 30N 79 32 E
Fars □ 47 29 30N 55 0 E
Fársala 35 39 17N 22 23 E
Farsø 11 56 46N 9 19 E
Farsund 9 58 5N 6 55 E
Fartak, Râs 46 28 5N 34 34 E
Fartura, Serra da 141 26 21S 52 52W
Faru 89 12 48N 6 12 E
Farum 11 55 49N 12 21 E
Farvel, Kap 144 59 48N 43 55W
Farwell 119 34 25N 103 0W
Faryab □ 47 36 0N 65 0 E
Fasā 47 29 0N 53 39 E
Fasano 29 40 50N 17 20 E
Fashoda 91 9 50N 32 2 E
Fastnet Rock 15 51 22N 9 37W
Fastov 36 50 7N 29 57 E
Fatagar, Tanjung 57 2 46S 131 57 E
Fatehgarh 49 27 25N 79 35 E
Fatehpur, Raj., India 48 28 0N 74 40 E
Fatehpur, Ut. P., India 49 25 56N 81 13 E
Fatick 88 14 19N 16 27W
Fatima 103 47 24N 61 53W
Fátima 23 39 37N 8 39W
Fatoya 88 11 37N 9 10W
Faucille, Col de la 21 46 22N 6 2 E
Faucilles, Monts 19 48 5N 5 50 E
Faulkton 118 45 4N 99 8W
Faulquemont 19 49 3N 6 36 E
Fauquembergues 19 50 36N 2 5 E
Faure I. 79 25 52S 113 50 E
Făurei 34 45 6N 27 19 E
Fauresmith 96 29 44S 25 17 E
Fauro 68 6 55S 156 7 E
Faux-Cap 97 25 33S 45 32 E
Favara 28 37 19N 13 39 E
Favignana 28 37 56N 12 18 E
Favignana, I. 28 37 56N 12 18 E
Favone 21 41 47N 9 26 E
Favourable Lake 102 52 50N 93 39W
Fawn → 102 52 22N 88 20W
Fawnskin 123 34 16N 116 56W
Faxaflói 8 64 29N 23 0W
Faya = Largeau 85 17 58N 19 6 E
Fayaoué 68 20 38S 166 33 E
Fayence 21 43 38N 6 42 E
Fayette, Ala., U.S.A. 113 33 40N 87 50W
Fayette, Iowa, U.S.A. 116 42 51N 91 48W
Fayette, Mo., U.S.A. 116 39 10N 92 40W
Fayette, Ohio, U.S.A. 117 41 40N 84 20W
Fayette, La 112 40 22N 86 52W
Fayetteville, Ark., U.S.A. 119 36 0N 94 5W
Fayetteville, N.C., U.S.A. 113 35 0N 78 58W
Fayetteville, Tenn., U.S.A. 113 35 8N 86 30W
Fayón 24 41 15N 0 20 E
Fazenda Nova 139 16 11S 50 48W
Fazilka 48 30 27N 74 2 E
Fazilpur 48 29 18N 70 29 E
F'Dérik 84 22 40N 12 45W
Fé, La 126 22 2N 84 15W
Feale → 15 52 26N 9 40W
Fear, C. 113 33 51N 78 0W
Feather → 120 38 47N 121 36W
Feather Falls 122 39 36N 121 16W
Featherston 80 41 6S 175 20 E
Featherstone 95 18 42S 30 55 E
Feathertop, Mt. 75 36 53S 147 7 E
Fécamp 18 49 45N 0 22 E
Fedala = Mohammedia 86 33 44N 7 21W
Federación 140 31 0S 57 55W
Fedjadj, Chott el 87 33 52N 9 14 E
Fehmarn 30 54 26N 11 10 E
Fei Xian 61 35 18N 117 59 E
Feijó 136 8 9S 70 21W
Feilding 80 40 13S 175 35 E
Feira de Santana 139 12 15S 38 57W
Feixiang 60 36 30N 114 45 E
Fejø 11 54 55N 11 30 E
Felanitx 25 39 27N 3 7 E
Feldberg, Ger. 30 53 20N 13 26 E
Feldberg, Ger. 31 47 51N 7 58 E
Feldkirch 31 47 15N 9 37 E
Felhit 91 16 40N 38 1 E
Felicity 117 38 51N 84 6W
Felipe Carrillo Puerto 125 19 38N 88 3W
Felixlândia 139 18 47S 44 55W
Felixstowe 13 51 58N 1 22 E
Felletin 20 45 53N 2 11 E
Felton 122 37 3N 122 4W
Feltre 27 46 1N 11 55 E
Femø 11 54 58N 11 53 E
Femunden 10 62 10N 11 53 E
Fenelon Falls 107 44 32N 78 45W
Fénérive 97 17 22S 49 25 E
Fenerwa 91 13 5N 39 3 E
Feng Xian, Jiangsu, China 60 34 43N 116 35 E
Feng Xian, Shaanxi, China 60 33 54N 106 40 E
Fengári 35 40 25N 25 32 E
Fengcheng, Jiangxi, China 59 28 12N 115 48 E
Fengcheng, Liaoning, China 61 40 28N 124 5 E
Fengdu 58 29 55N 107 41 E
Fengfeng 60 36 28N 114 8 E
Fenggang 58 27 57N 107 47 E
Fenghua 59 29 40N 121 25 E
Fenghuang 58 27 57N 109 29 E
Fenghuangzui 58 33 30N 109 23 E
Fengjie 58 31 5N 109 36 E
Fengkai 59 23 24N 111 30 E
Fengle 59 31 29N 112 29 E
Fengning 60 41 10N 116 33 E
Fengqing 58 24 38N 99 55 E
Fengqiu 60 35 2N 114 25 E
Fengrun 61 39 48N 118 8 E
Fengshan, Guangxi, China 58 24 31N 107 3 E
Fengshan, Guangxi, China 58 24 39N 109 15 E
Fengtai, Anhui, China 59 32 50N 116 40 E
Fengtai, Beijing, China 60 39 50N 116 18 E
Fengxian 59 30 55N 121 26 E
Fengxiang 60 34 29N 107 25 E
Fengxin 59 28 41N 115 18 E
Fengyang 59 32 51N 117 29 E
Fengyi 58 25 37N 100 20 E
Fengzhen 60 40 25N 113 2 E
Feni Is. 69 4 0S 153 40 E
Fenit 15 52 17N 9 51W
Fennimore 116 42 58N 90 41W
Fenny 52 22 55N 91 32 E
Feno, C. de 21 41 58N 8 33 E
Fenoarivo 97 18 26S 46 34 E
Fens, The 12 52 45N 0 2 E
Fenton 106 42 47N 83 44W
Fenxi 60 36 40N 111 31 E
Fenyang 60 37 18N 111 48 E
Fenyi 59 27 45N 114 47 E
Feodosiya 38 45 2N 35 28 E
Fer, C. de 87 37 3N 7 10 E
Ferdow 47 33 58N 58 2 E
Fère-Champenoise 19 48 45N 4 0 E
Fère-en-Tardenois 19 49 10N 3 30 E
Fère, La 19 49 40N 3 20 E
Ferentino 28 41 42N 13 14 E
Ferfer 45 5 4N 45 9 E
Fergana 40 40 23N 71 19 E
Fergus 106 43 43N 80 24W
Fergus Falls 118 46 18N 96 7W
Ferguson 116 38 45N 90 18W

Fergusson I.	**69**	9 30S	150 45 E
Fériana	**87**	34 59N	8 33 E
Feričanci	**33**	45 32N	18 0 E
Ferkane	**87**	34 37N	7 26 E
Ferkéssédougou	**88**	9 35N	5 6W
Ferlach	**33**	46 32N	14 18 E
Ferland	**102**	50 19N	88 27W
Ferlo, Vallée du	**88**	15 15N	14 15W
Fermanagh □	**15**	54 21N	7 40W
Ferme-Neuve	**104**	46 42N	75 27W
Fermo	**27**	43 10N	13 42 E
Fermoselle	**22**	41 19N	6 27W
Fermoy	**15**	52 4N	8 18W
Fernán Nuñéz	**23**	37 40N	4 44W
Fernández	**140**	27 55 S	63 50W
Fernandina Beach	**113**	30 40N	81 30W
Fernando de Noronha	**138**	4 0 S	33 10W
Fernando Póo = Macias Nguema Biyoga	**83**	3 30N	8 40 E
Fernandópolis	**139**	20 16 S	50 14W
Ferndale, U.S.A.	**106**	42 26N	83 6W
Ferndale, Calif., U.S.A.	**120**	40 37N	124 12W
Ferndale, Wash., U.S.A.	**122**	48 51N	122 41W
Fernie	**108**	49 30N	115 5W
Fernlees	**72**	23 51 S	148 7 E
Fernley	**120**	39 36N	119 14W
Feroke	**51**	11 9N	75 46 E
Feronia	**106**	46 22N	79 19W
Ferozepore	**48**	30 55N	74 40 E
Férrai	**35**	40 53N	26 10 E
Ferrandina	**29**	40 30N	16 28 E
Ferrara	**27**	44 50N	11 36 E
Ferrato, C.	**28**	39 18N	9 39 E
Ferreira do Alentejo	**23**	38 4N	8 6W
Ferreñafe	**136**	6 42 S	79 50W
Ferret, C.	**20**	44 38N	1 15W
Ferrette	**19**	47 30N	7 20 E
Ferriday	**119**	31 35N	91 33W
Ferrières	**19**	48 5N	2 48 E
Ferriete	**26**	44 40N	9 30 E
Ferrol, Pen. de	**136**	9 10 S	78 35W
Ferron	**121**	39 3N	111 3W
Ferros	**139**	19 14 S	43 2W
Ferryland	**103**	47 2N	52 53W
Ferrysburg	**117**	43 5N	86 13W
Ferté-Bernard, La	**18**	48 10N	0 40 E
Ferté, La	**19**	48 57N	3 6 E
Ferté-Mace, La	**18**	48 35N	0 21W
Ferté-St.-Aubin, La	**19**	47 42N	1 57 E
Ferté-Vidame, La	**18**	48 37N	0 53 E
Fertile	**118**	47 31N	96 18W
Fertília	**28**	40 37N	8 13 E
Fès	**86**	34 0N	5 0W
Feshi	**92**	6 8 S	18 10 E
Fessenden	**118**	47 42N	99 38W
Festus	**116**	38 13N	90 24W
Feteşti	**34**	44 22N	27 51 E
Fethiye	**46**	36 36N	29 10 E
Fetlar	**14**	60 36N	0 52W
Feuilles →	**101**	58 47N	70 4W
Feurs	**21**	45 45N	4 13 E
Fezzan	**85**	27 0N	15 0 E
Ffestiniog	**12**	52 58N	3 56W
Fiambalá	**140**	27 45 S	67 37W
Fianarantsoa	**97**	21 26 S	47 5 E
Fianarantsoa □	**97**	19 30 S	47 0 E
Fianga	**85**	9 55N	15 9 E
Fichtelgebirge	**31**	50 10N	12 0 E
Ficksburg	**97**	28 51 S	27 53 E
Fidenza	**26**	44 51N	10 3 E
Field	**106**	46 31N	80 1W
Field →	**72**	23 48 S	138 0 E
Field I.	**78**	12 5 S	132 23 E
Fieri	**35**	40 43N	19 33 E
Fife □	**14**	56 13N	3 2W
Fife Ness	**14**	56 17N	2 35W
Fifield	**76**	32 47 S	147 28 E
Fifth Cataract	**90**	18 22N	33 50 E
Figeac	**20**	44 37N	2 2 E
Figline Valdarno	**27**	43 37N	11 28 E
Figtree	**95**	20 22 S	28 20 E
Figueira Castelo Rodrigo	**22**	40 57N	6 58W
Figueira da Foz	**22**	40 7N	8 54W
Figueiró dos Vinhos	**22**	39 55N	8 16W
Figueras	**24**	42 18N	2 58 E
Figuig	**86**	32 5N	1 11W
Fihaonana	**97**	18 36 S	47 12 E
Fiherenana	**97**	18 29 S	48 24 E
Fiherenana →	**97**	23 19 S	43 37 E
Fiji ■	**68**	17 20 S	179 0 E
Fika	**89**	11 15N	11 13 E
Filabres, Sierra de los	**25**	37 13N	2 20W
Filadelfia	**136**	11 20 S	68 46W
Filadélfia, Brazil	**138**	7 21 S	47 30W
Filadélfia, Italy	**29**	38 47N	16 17 E
Filchner Ice Shelf	**143**	78 0 S	60 0W
File Axe, L.	**105**	50 18N	73 34W
Filer	**120**	42 30N	114 35W
Filey	**12**	54 13N	0 18W
Filiaşi	**34**	44 32N	23 31 E
Filiátes	**35**	39 38N	20 16 E
Filiatrá	**35**	37 9N	21 35 E
Filicudi	**29**	38 35N	14 33 E
Filiourí →	**35**	41 15N	25 40 E
Filipstad	**10**	59 43N	14 9 E
Filisur	**31**	46 41N	9 40 E
Fillmore, Can.	**109**	49 50N	103 25W
Fillmore, Calif., U.S.A.	**123**	34 23N	118 58W
Fillmore, Utah, U.S.A.	**121**	38 58N	112 20W
Filottrano	**27**	43 28N	13 20 E
Fils, L. du	**104**	46 37N	78 7W
Filyos	**38**	41 34N	32 4 E
Filyos →	**46**	41 35N	32 10 E
Finale Lígure	**26**	44 10N	8 21 E
Finale nell' Emília	**27**	44 50N	11 18 E
Fiñana	**25**	37 10N	2 50W
Finch	**107**	45 11N	75 7W
Findhorn →	**14**	57 38N	3 38W
Findlay	**117**	41 0N	83 41W
Fine Flower Creek	**77**	29 24 S	152 42 E
Finger L.	**109**	53 33N	124 18W
Fíngõe	**95**	15 12 S	31 50 E
Finike	**46**	36 21N	30 10 E
Finistère □	**18**	48 20N	4 0W
Finisterre	**22**	42 54N	9 16W
Finisterre, C.	**22**	42 50N	9 19W
Finisterre Ra.	**69**	6 0 S	146 30 E
Finke	**72**	25 34 S	134 35 E
Finke →	**72**	27 0 S	136 10 E
Finland ■	**40**	63 0N	27 0 E
Finland, G. of	**9**	60 0N	26 0 E
Finlay →	**108**	57 0N	125 10W
Finley, Austral.	**74**	35 38 S	145 35 E
Finley, U.S.A.	**118**	47 35N	97 50W
Finn →	**15**	54 50N	7 55W
Finnigan, Mt.	**72**	15 49 S	145 17 E
Finniss, C.	**73**	33 8 S	134 51 E
Finnmark fylke □	**8**	69 30N	25 0 E
Finschhafen	**69**	6 33 S	147 50 E
Finsteraarhorn	**31**	46 31N	8 10 E
Finsterwalde	**30**	51 37N	13 42 E
Fiora →	**27**	42 20N	11 35 E
Fiordland National Park	**81**	45 0 S	167 50 E
Fiorenzuola d'Arda	**26**	44 56N	9 54 E
Fiq	**44**	32 46N	35 41 E
Fire River	**102**	48 47N	83 21W
Firebag →	**109**	57 45N	111 21W
Firebaugh	**122**	36 52N	120 27W
Firedrake L.	**109**	61 25N	104 30W
Firenze	**27**	43 47N	11 15 E
Firminy, France	**20**	44 32N	2 19 E
Firminy, France	**21**	45 23N	4 18 E
Firoz Kohi	**47**	34 45N	63 0 E
Firozabad	**49**	27 10N	78 25 E
Fīrūzābād	**47**	28 52N	52 35 E
Fīrūzkūh	**47**	35 50N	52 50 E
Firvale	**108**	52 27N	126 13W
Fish →	**96**	28 7 S	17 45 E
Fish Creek	**74**	38 43 S	146 7 E
Fish Pt.	**106**	43 43N	83 38W
Fisher	**79**	30 30 S	131 0 E
Fisher B.	**109**	51 35N	97 13W
Fishguard	**13**	51 59N	4 59W
Fishing L.	**109**	52 10N	95 24W
Fismes	**19**	49 20N	3 40 E
Fitchburg	**115**	42 35N	71 47W
Fitero	**24**	42 4N	1 52W
Fitri, L.	**92**	12 50N	17 28 E
Fitz Roy	**142**	47 0 S	67 0W
Fitzgerald, Can.	**108**	59 51N	111 36W
Fitzgerald, U.S.A.	**113**	31 45N	83 16W
Fitzmaurice →	**78**	14 45 S	130 5 E
Fitzroy →, Queens., Austral.	**72**	23 32 S	150 52 E
Fitzroy →, W. Australia, Austral.	**78**	17 31 S	123 35 E
Fitzroy Crossing	**78**	18 9 S	125 38 E
Fitzwilliam I.	**106**	45 30N	81 45W
Fiume = Rijeka	**27**	45 20N	14 27 E
Fiumefreddo Brúzio	**29**	39 14N	16 4 E
Five Points	**122**	36 26N	120 6W
Fivizzano	**26**	44 12N	10 11 E
Fizi	**94**	4 17 S	28 55 E
Fjellerup	**11**	56 29N	10 34 E
Fjerritslev	**11**	57 5N	9 15 E
Fkih ben Salah	**86**	32 32N	6 45W
Flå	**10**	63 13N	10 18 E
Flagler	**118**	39 20N	103 4W
Flagstaff	**121**	35 10N	111 40W
Flaherty, I.	**102**	56 15N	79 15W
Flambeau →	**118**	45 18N	91 15W
Flamborough Hd.	**12**	54 8N	0 4W
Flaming Gorge Dam	**120**	40 50N	109 46W
Flaming Gorge L.	**120**	41 15N	109 30W
Flamingo, Teluk	**57**	5 30 S	138 0 E
Flanagan	**117**	40 53N	88 52W
Flanders = Flandres	**16**	51 10N	3 15 E
Flandre Occidental □	**16**	51 0N	3 0 E
Flandre Orientale □	**16**	51 0N	4 0 E
Flandreau	**118**	44 5N	96 38W
Flandres, Plaines des	**16**	51 10N	3 15 E
Flanigan	**122**	40 10N	119 53W
Flåsjön	**8**	64 5N	15 40 E
Flat →, Can.	**108**	61 51N	128 0W
Flat →, U.S.A.	**117**	42 56N	85 15W
Flat River	**119**	37 50N	90 30W
Flat Rock, Ill., U.S.A.	**117**	38 54N	87 40W
Flat Rock, Mich., U.S.A.	**106**	42 6N	83 18W
Flatey, Barðastrandarsýsla, Iceland	**8**	66 10N	17 52W
Flatey, Suður-Þingeyjarsýsla, Iceland	**8**	65 22N	22 56W
Flathead L.	**120**	47 50N	114 0W
Flatrock →	**117**	38 46N	86 10W
Flattery, C., Austral.	**72**	14 58 S	145 21 E
Flattery, C., U.S.A.	**122**	48 21N	124 43W
Flavy-le-Martel	**19**	49 43N	3 12 E
Flaxton	**118**	48 52N	102 24W
Flèche, La	**18**	47 42N	0 5W
Fleetwood	**12**	53 55N	3 1W
Flemingsburg	**117**	38 25N	83 45W
Flemington	**114**	41 7N	77 28W
Flensburg Fjord	**11**	54 50N	9 40 E
Flensburg	**30**	54 46N	9 28 E
Flers	**18**	48 47N	0 33W
Flesherton	**106**	44 16N	80 33W
Flesko, Tanjung	**57**	0 29N	124 30 E
Fletton	**13**	52 34N	0 13W
Fleurance	**20**	43 52N	0 40 E
Fleurier	**31**	46 54N	6 35 E
Flin Flon	**109**	54 46N	101 53W
Flinders	**74**	38 30 S	145 2 E
Flinders →	**72**	17 36 S	140 36 E
Flinders B.	**79**	34 19 S	115 19 E
Flinders Group	**72**	14 11 S	144 15 E
Flinders I.	**72**	40 0 S	148 0 E
Flinders Ranges	**73**	31 30 S	138 30 E
Flinders Reefs	**72**	17 37 S	148 31 E
Flint, U.K.	**12**	53 15N	3 7W
Flint, U.S.A.	**106**	43 5N	83 40W
Flint →	**113**	30 52N	84 38W
Flint, I.	**67**	11 26 S	151 48W
Flinton	**73**	27 55 S	149 32 E
Fliseryd	**11**	57 6N	16 15 E
Flix	**24**	41 14N	0 32 E
Flixecourt	**19**	50 0N	2 5 E
Flodden	**12**	55 37N	2 8W
Floodwood	**118**	46 55N	92 55W
Flora, Norway	**10**	63 27N	11 22 E
Flora, Ill., U.S.A.	**112**	38 40N	88 30W
Flora, Ind., U.S.A.	**117**	40 33N	86 31W
Florac	**20**	44 20N	3 37 E
Florala	**113**	31 0N	86 20W
Florânia	**138**	6 8 S	36 49W
Florence, Ala., U.S.A.	**113**	34 50N	87 40W
Florence, Ariz., U.S.A.	**121**	33 0N	111 25W
Florence, Colo., U.S.A.	**118**	38 26N	105 0W
Florence, Ky., U.S.A.	**117**	39 0N	84 38W
Florence, Oreg., U.S.A.	**120**	44 0N	124 3W
Florence, S.C., U.S.A.	**113**	34 12N	79 44W
Florence = Firenze	**27**	43 47N	11 15 E
Florence, L.	**73**	28 53 S	138 9 E
Florennes	**16**	50 15N	4 35 E
Florensac	**20**	43 23N	3 28 E
Florenville	**16**	49 40N	5 19 E
Flores, Brazil	**138**	7 51 S	37 59W
Flores, Guat.	**126**	16 59N	89 50W
Flores, Indon.	**57**	8 35 S	121 0 E
Flores I.	**108**	49 20N	126 10W
Flores Sea	**56**	6 30 S	124 0 E
Floresta	**138**	8 40 S	37 26W
Floresville	**119**	29 10N	98 10W
Floriano	**138**	6 50 S	43 0W
Florianópolis	**141**	27 30 S	48 30W
Florida, Cuba	**126**	21 32N	78 14W
Florida, Uruguay	**141**	34 7 S	56 10W
Florida □	**113**	28 30N	82 0W
Florida B.	**126**	25 0N	81 20W
Florida Is.	**68**	9 55 S	160 15 E
Florida Keys	**126**	25 0N	80 40W
Florida, Straits of	**126**	25 0N	80 0W
Florídia	**29**	37 6N	15 9 E
Floridsdorf	**33**	48 14N	16 22 E
Flórina	**35**	40 48N	21 26 E
Florissant	**116**	38 48N	90 20W
Florø	**9**	61 35N	5 1 E
Flower Sta.	**107**	45 10N	76 41W
Flowerdale	**74**	37 20 S	145 19 E
Flower's Cove	**103**	51 14N	56 46W
Floydada	**119**	33 58N	101 18W
Fluk	**57**	1 42 S	127 44 E
Flumen →	**24**	41 43N	0 9W
Flumendosa →	**28**	39 26N	9 38 E
Fluminimaggiore	**28**	39 25N	8 30 E
Flushing	**106**	43 4N	83 51W
Flushing = Vlissingen	**16**	51 26N	3 34 E
Fluviá →	**24**	42 12N	3 7 E
Fly →	**69**	8 25 S	143 0 E
Flying Fish, C.	**143**	72 6 S	102 29W
Foa	**68**	19 45 S	174 18W
Foa, La	**68**	21 43 S	165 50 E
Foam Lake	**109**	51 40N	103 32W
Foča	**33**	43 31N	18 47 E
Focşani	**34**	45 41N	27 15 E
Fogang	**59**	23 52N	113 30 E
Foggaret el Arab	**86**	27 13N	2 49 E
Foggaret ez Zoua	**86**	27 20N	2 53 E
Fóggia	**29**	41 28N	15 31 E
Foggo	**89**	11 21N	9 57 E
Foglia →	**27**	43 55N	12 54 E
Fogo	**103**	49 43N	54 17W
Fogo I.	**103**	49 40N	54 5W
Fohnsdorf	**33**	47 12N	14 40 E
Föhr	**30**	54 40N	8 30 E
Foia	**23**	37 19N	8 37W
Foins, L. aux	**104**	47 5N	78 11W
Foix	**20**	42 58N	1 38 E
Foix □	**20**	43 0N	1 30 E
Fokino	**36**	53 30N	34 22 E
Folda, Nord-Trøndelag, Norway	**8**	64 41N	10 50 E
Folda, Nordland, Norway	**8**	67 38N	14 50 E
Folette, La	**113**	36 23N	84 9W
Foleyet	**102**	48 15N	82 25W
Foligno	**27**	42 58N	12 40 E
Folkestone	**13**	51 5N	1 11 E
Folkston	**113**	30 55N	82 0W
Follett	**119**	36 30N	100 12W
Follónica	**26**	42 55N	10 45 E
Follónica, Golfo di	**26**	42 50N	10 40 E
Folsom	**122**	38 41N	121 7W
Folsom Res.	**122**	38 42N	121 9W
Fond-du-Lac	**109**	59 19N	107 12W
Fond du Lac	**118**	43 46N	88 26W
Fond-du-Lac →	**109**	59 17N	106 0W
Fonda, Iowa, U.S.A.	**116**	42 35N	94 51W
Fonda, N.Y., U.S.A.	**115**	42 57N	74 23W
Fondak	**86**	35 34N	5 35W
Fondi	**28**	41 21N	13 25 E
Fonfría	**22**	41 37N	6 9W
Fongen	**10**	63 11N	11 38 E
Fonni	**28**	40 5N	9 16 E
Fonsagrada	**22**	43 8N	7 4W
Fonseca, G. de	**126**	13 10N	87 40W
Fontaine-Française	**19**	47 32N	5 21 E
Fontaine, La	**117**	40 40N	85 43W
Fontainebleau	**19**	48 24N	2 40 E
Fontana, L.	**142**	44 55 S	71 30W
Fontas →	**108**	58 14N	121 48W
Fonte Boa	**134**	2 33 S	66 0W
Fontem	**89**	5 32N	9 52 E
Fontenay-le-Comte	**20**	46 28N	0 48W
Fontur	**8**	66 23N	14 32W
Fonuafo'ou	**68**	20 19 S	175 25W
Fonualei	**68**	18 1 S	174 19W
Fonyód	**33**	46 44N	17 33 E
Foochow = Fuzhou	**59**	26 5N	119 16 E
Foping	**60**	33 41N	108 0 E
Foppiano	**26**	46 21N	8 24 E
Föra	**11**	57 1N	16 51 E
Forbach	**19**	49 10N	6 52 E
Forbes	**76**	33 22 S	148 0 E
Forbesganj	**49**	26 17N	87 18 E
Forcados	**89**	5 26N	5 26 E
Forcados →	**89**	5 25N	5 19 E
Forcall →	**24**	40 51N	0 16W
Forcalquier	**21**	43 58N	5 47 E
Forchheim	**31**	49 42N	11 4 E
Ford City, Calif., U.S.A.	**123**	35 10N	119 27W
Ford City, Pa., U.S.A.	**114**	40 47N	79 31W
Ford's Bridge	**73**	29 41 S	145 29 E
Fordyce	**119**	33 50N	92 20W
Forécariah	**88**	9 28N	13 10W
Forel, Mt.	**144**	66 52N	36 55W
Foremost	**108**	49 26N	111 34W
Forenza	**29**	40 50N	15 50 E
Forest, Can.	**106**	43 6N	82 0W
Forest, U.S.A.	**119**	32 21N	89 27W
Forest City, Iowa, U.S.A.	**118**	43 12N	93 39W
Forest City, N.C., U.S.A.	**113**	35 23N	81 50W
Forest City, Pa., U.S.A.	**115**	41 39N	75 29W
Forest Grove	**122**	45 31N	123 4W
Forestburg	**108**	52 35N	112 1W
Foresthill	**122**	39 1N	120 49W
Forestier Pen.	**72**	43 0 S	148 0 E
Forestville, Can.	**105**	48 48N	69 2W
Forestville, Calif., U.S.A.	**122**	38 28N	122 54W
Forestville, Wis., U.S.A.	**112**	44 41N	87 29W

Forez, Mts. du	**20**	45 40N	3 50 E
Forfar	**14**	56 40N	2 53W
Forges-les-Eaux	**19**	49 37N	1 30 E
Forks	**122**	47 56N	124 23W
Forlì	**27**	44 14N	12 2 E
Forman	**118**	46 9N	97 43W
Formazza	**26**	46 23N	8 26 E
Formby Pt.	**12**	53 33N	3 7W
Formentera	**25**	38 40N	1 30 E
Formentor, C. de	**24**	39 58N	3 13 E
Fórmia	**28**	41 15N	13 34 E
Formiga	**139**	20 27S	45 25W
Formigine	**26**	44 37N	10 51 E
Formiguères	**20**	42 37N	2 5 E
Formosa, Argent.	**140**	26 15S	58 10W
Formosa, Brazil	**139**	15 32S	47 20W
Formosa = Taiwan ■	**62**	24 0N	121 0 E
Formosa □	**140**	25 0S	60 0W
Formosa Bay	**94**	2 40S	40 20 E
Formosa, Serra	**137**	12 0S	55 0W
Formoso →	**139**	10 34S	49 56W
Fornells	**24**	40 4N	4 4 E
Fornos de Algodres	**22**	40 38N	7 32W
Fornovo di Taro	**26**	44 42N	10 7 E
Forres	**14**	57 37N	3 38W
Forrest, Vic., Austral.	**74**	38 33S	143 47 E
Forrest, W. Australia, Austral.	**79**	30 51S	128 6 E
Forrest City	**119**	35 0N	90 50W
Forrest, Mt.	**79**	24 48S	127 45 E
Forreston	**116**	42 8N	89 35W
Fors	**10**	60 14N	16 20 E
Forsa	**10**	61 44N	16 55 E
Forsayth	**72**	18 33S	143 34 E
Forserum	**11**	57 42N	14 30 E
Forshaga	**10**	59 33N	13 29 E
Forskacka	**10**	60 39N	16 54 E
Forsmo	**10**	63 16N	17 11 E
Forst	**30**	51 43N	14 37 E
Forster	**77**	32 12S	152 31 E
Forsyth, Ga., U.S.A.	**113**	33 4N	83 55W
Forsyth, Mont., U.S.A.	**120**	46 14N	106 37W
Forsyth I.	**81**	40 58S	174 5 E
Forsythe	**104**	48 14N	76 26W
Fort Albany	**102**	52 15N	81 35W
Fort Apache	**121**	33 50N	110 0W
Fort Archambault = Sarh	**85**	9 5N	18 23 E
Fort Assiniboine	**108**	54 20N	114 45W
Fort Atkinson	**117**	42 56N	88 50W
Fort Augustus	**14**	57 9N	4 40W
Fort Beaufort	**96**	32 46S	26 40 E
Fort Benton	**120**	47 50N	110 40W
Fort Bragg	**120**	39 28N	123 50W
Fort Bretonnet = Bousso	**85**	10 34N	16 52 E
Fort Bridger	**120**	41 22N	110 20W
Fort Chimo	**101**	58 6N	68 15W
Fort Chipewyan	**109**	58 42N	111 8W
Fort Collins	**118**	40 30N	105 4W
Fort-Coulonge	**104**	45 50N	76 45W
Fort Crampel = Crampel	**85**	6 51N	19 11 E
Fort-Dauphin	**97**	25 2S	47 0 E
Fort Davis	**119**	30 38N	103 53W
Fort-de-France	**127**	14 36N	61 2W
Fort de Possel = Possel	**92**	5 5N	19 10 E
Fort Defiance	**121**	35 47N	109 4W
Fort Dodge	**118**	42 29N	94 10W
Fort Edward	**115**	43 16N	73 35W
Fort Flatters = Zaouiet El-Khala	**87**	28 4N	6 40 E
Fort Foureau = Kousseri	**85**	12 0N	14 55 E
Fort Frances	**109**	48 36N	93 24W
Fort Franklin	**100**	65 10N	123 30W
Fort Garland	**121**	37 28N	105 30W
Fort George	**102**	53 50N	79 0W
Fort Good-Hope	**100**	66 14N	128 40W
Fort Gouraud = F'Dérik	**84**	22 40N	12 45W
Fort Hancock	**121**	31 19N	105 56W
Fort Hope	**102**	51 30N	88 0W
Fort Huachuca	**121**	31 32N	110 30W
Fort Irwin	**123**	35 16N	116 34W
Fort Jameson = Chipata	**95**	13 38S	32 38 E
Fort Kent	**103**	47 12N	68 30W
Fort Klamath	**120**	42 45N	122 0W
Fort Knox	**117**	37 54N	85 57 E
Fort Lallemand	**87**	31 13N	6 17 E
Fort-Lamy = Ndjamena	**85**	12 4N	15 8 E
Fort Laramie	**118**	42 15N	104 30W
Fort Lauderdale	**113**	26 10N	80 5W
Fort Leonard Wood	**116**	37 46N	92 11W
Fort Liard	**108**	60 14N	123 30W
Fort Liberté	**127**	19 42N	71 51W
Fort Lupton	**118**	40 8N	104 48W
Fort Mackay	**108**	57 12N	111 41W
Fort McKenzie	**103**	57 20N	69 0W
Fort Macleod	**108**	49 45N	113 30W
Fort MacMahon	**86**	29 43N	1 45 E
Fort McMurray	**108**	56 44N	111 7W
Fort McPherson	**100**	67 30N	134 55W
Fort Madison	**116**	40 39N	91 20W
Fort Meade	**113**	27 45N	81 45W
Fort Miribel	**86**	29 25N	2 55 E
Fort Morgan	**118**	40 10N	103 50W
Fort Myers	**113**	26 39N	81 51W
Fort Nelson	**108**	58 50N	122 44W
Fort Nelson →	**108**	59 32N	124 0W
Fort Norman	**100**	64 57N	125 30W
Fort Payne	**113**	34 25N	85 44W
Fort Peck	**120**	48 1N	106 30W
Fort Peck Dam	**120**	48 0N	106 38W
Fort Peck L.	**120**	47 40N	107 0W
Fort Pierce	**113**	27 29N	80 19W
Fort Pierre	**118**	44 25N	100 25W
Fort Pierre Bordes = Ti-n-Zaouatene	**86**	20 0N	2 55 E
Fort Plain	**115**	42 56N	74 39W
Fort Portal	**94**	0 40N	30 20 E
Fort Providence	**108**	61 3N	117 40W
Fort Qu'Appelle	**109**	50 45N	103 50W
Fort Recovery	**117**	40 25N	84 47W
Fort Resolution	**108**	61 10N	113 40W
Fort Rixon	**95**	20 2S	29 17 E
Fort Roseberry = Mansa	**95**	11 10S	28 50 E
Fort Ross	**122**	38 32N	123 13W
Fort Rupert (Rupert House)	**102**	51 30N	78 40W
Fort Saint	**87**	30 19N	9 31 E
Fort St. James	**108**	54 30N	124 10W
Fort St. John	**108**	56 15N	120 50W
Fort Sandeman	**48**	31 20N	69 31 E
Fort Saskatchewan	**108**	53 40N	113 15W
Fort Scott	**119**	37 50N	94 40W
Fort Severn	**102**	56 0N	87 40W
Fort Shevchenko, U.S.S.R.	**39**	44 30N	50 10 E
Fort Shevchenko, U.S.S.R.	**39**	43 40N	51 20 E
Fort Sibut = Sibut	**85**	5 44N	19 10 E
Fort Simpson	**108**	61 45N	121 15W
Fort Smith, Can.	**108**	60 0N	111 51W
Fort Smith, U.S.A.	**119**	35 25N	94 25W
Fort Stanton	**121**	33 33N	105 36W
Fort Stockton	**119**	30 54N	102 54W
Fort Sumner	**119**	34 24N	104 16W
Fort Thomas, Ariz., U.S.A.	**121**	33 2N	109 59W
Fort Thomas, Ky., U.S.A.	**117**	39 5N	84 27W
Fort Trinquet = Bir Mogrein	**84**	25 10N	11 35W
Fort Valley	**113**	32 33N	83 52W
Fort Vermilion	**108**	58 24N	116 0W
Fort Victoria	**95**	20 8S	30 49 E
Fort Walton Beach	**113**	30 25N	86 40W
Fort Wayne	**117**	41 5N	85 10W
Fort William	**14**	56 48N	5 8W
Fort Worth	**119**	32 45N	97 25W
Fort Yates	**118**	46 8N	100 38W
Fort Yukon	**100**	66 35N	145 20W
Fortaleza, Boliv.	**136**	12 6S	66 49W
Fortaleza, Brazil	**138**	3 45S	38 35W
Forteau	**103**	51 28N	56 58W
Fortescue →	**78**	21 20S	116 5 E
Forth, Firth of	**14**	56 5N	2 55W
Forthassa Rharbia	**86**	32 52N	1 18W
Fortín Coronel Eugenio Garay	**137**	20 31S	62 8W
Fortín Garrapatal	**137**	21 27S	61 30W
Fortín General Pando	**137**	19 45S	59 47W
Fortín Madrejón	**137**	20 45S	59 52W
Fortín Uno	**142**	38 50S	65 18W
Fortore →	**27**	41 55N	15 17 E
Fortrose, N.Z.	**81**	46 38S	168 45 E
Fortrose, U.K.	**14**	57 35N	4 10W
Fortuna, Spain	**25**	38 11N	1 7W
Fortuna, Cal., U.S.A.	**120**	40 38N	124 8W
Fortuna, N.D., U.S.A.	**118**	48 55N	103 48W
Fortune B.	**103**	47 30N	55 22W
Forūr	**47**	26 20N	54 30 E
Fos	**21**	43 26N	4 56 E
Foshan	**59**	23 4N	113 5 E
Fossacesia	**27**	42 15N	14 30 E
Fossano	**26**	44 33N	7 40 E
Fossil	**120**	45 0N	120 9W
Fossilbrook P.O.	**72**	17 47S	144 29 E
Fossombrone	**27**	43 41N	12 49 E
Fosston	**118**	47 33N	95 39W
Foster, Austral.	**75**	38 40S	146 15 E
Foster, Can.	**105**	45 17N	72 30W
Foster, U.S.A.	**117**	38 48N	84 13W
Foster →	**109**	55 47N	105 49W
Fosters Ra.	**72**	21 35S	133 48 E
Fostoria	**117**	41 8N	83 25W
Fotuha'a	**68**	19 49S	174 44W
Fougamou	**92**	1 16S	10 30 E
Fougères	**18**	48 21N	1 14W
Foul Pt.	**51**	8 35N	81 18 E
Foulness I.	**13**	51 36N	0 55 E
Foulness Pt.	**13**	51 36N	0 59 E
Foulpointe	**97**	17 41S	49 31 E
Foum el Alba	**86**	20 45N	3 0W
Foum Zguid	**86**	30 2N	6 59W
Foumban	**89**	5 45N	10 50 E
Foundiougne	**88**	14 5N	16 32W
Fountain, Colo., U.S.A.	**118**	38 42N	104 40W
Fountain, Utah, U.S.A.	**120**	39 41N	111 37W
Fountain Springs	**123**	35 54N	118 51W
Fourchambault	**19**	47 0N	3 3 E
Fourchu	**103**	45 43N	60 17W
Fourcroy, C.	**78**	11 45S	130 2 E
Fourmies	**19**	50 1N	4 2 E
Foúrnoi	**35**	37 36N	26 32 E
Fours	**19**	46 50N	3 42 E
Fouta Djalon	**88**	11 20N	12 10W
Foux, Cap-à-	**127**	19 43N	73 27W
Foveaux Str.	**81**	46 42S	168 10 E
Fowey	**13**	50 20N	4 39W
Fowler, Calif., U.S.A.	**122**	36 41N	119 41W
Fowler, Colo., U.S.A.	**118**	38 10N	104 0W
Fowler, Ind., U.S.A.	**117**	40 37N	87 19W
Fowler, Kans., U.S.A.	**119**	37 28N	100 7W
Fowler, Mich., U.S.A.	**117**	43 0N	84 45W
Fowlers B.	**79**	31 59S	132 34 E
Fowlers Bay	**79**	32 0S	132 29 E
Fowlerton	**119**	28 26N	98 50W
Fowlerville	**117**	42 40N	84 4W
Fownhope	**13**	52 0N	2 37W
Fox →	**109**	56 3N	93 18W
Fox Valley	**109**	50 30N	109 25W
Foxe Basin	**101**	68 30N	77 0W
Foxe Channel	**101**	66 0N	80 0W
Foxe Pen.	**101**	65 0N	76 0W
Foxen, L.	**10**	59 25N	11 55 E
Foxpark	**120**	41 4N	106 6W
Foxton	**80**	40 29S	175 18 E
Foyle, Lough	**15**	55 6N	7 8W
Foynes	**15**	52 37N	9 5W
Foz	**22**	43 33N	7 20W
Foz do Cunene	**96**	17 15S	11 48 E
Foz do Gregório	**136**	6 47S	70 44W
Foz do Iguaçu	**141**	25 30S	54 30W
Foz do Riosinho	**136**	7 11S	71 50W
Frackville	**115**	40 46N	76 15W
Fraga	**24**	41 32N	0 21 E
Framingham	**115**	42 18N	71 26W
Franca	**139**	20 33S	47 30W
Francavilla al Mare	**27**	42 25N	14 16 E
Francavilla Fontana	**29**	40 32N	17 35 E
France ■	**17**	47 0N	3 0 E
Frances	**73**	36 41S	140 55 E
Frances →	**108**	60 16N	129 10W
Frances L.	**108**	61 23N	129 30W
Francés Viejo, C.	**127**	19 40N	70 0W
Francesville	**117**	40 59N	86 53W
Franceville	**92**	1 40S	13 32 E
Franche-Comté	**19**	46 30N	5 50 E
Francisco de Orellana	**134**	0 28S	76 58W
Francisco I. Madero, Coahuila, Mexico	**124**	25 48N	103 18W
Francisco I. Madero, Durango, Mexico	**124**	24 32N	104 22W
Francisco Sáo	**139**	16 28S	43 30W
Francofonte	**29**	37 13N	14 50 E
François, Can.	**103**	47 35N	56 45W
François, Mart.	**127**	14 38N	60 57W
François L.	**108**	54 0N	125 30W
Franeker	**16**	53 12N	5 33 E
Frankado	**91**	12 30N	43 12 E
Frankenberg	**30**	51 3N	8 47 E
Frankenthal	**31**	49 32N	8 21 E
Frankenwald	**31**	50 18N	11 36 E
Frankford, Can.	**107**	44 12N	77 36W
Frankford, U.S.A.	**116**	39 29N	91 19W
Frankfort, Madag.	**97**	27 17S	28 30 E
Frankfort, Ind., U.S.A.	**117**	40 20N	86 33W
Frankfort, Kans., U.S.A.	**118**	39 42N	96 26W
Frankfort, Ky., U.S.A.	**117**	38 12N	84 52W
Frankfort, Mich., U.S.A.	**112**	44 38N	86 14W
Frankfort, Ohio, U.S.A.	**117**	39 24N	83 11W
Frankfurt □	**30**	52 30N	14 0 E
Frankfurt am Main	**31**	50 7N	8 40 E
Frankfurt an der Oder	**30**	52 50N	14 31 E
Fränkische Alb	**31**	49 20N	11 30 E
Fränkische Rezal →	**31**	49 11N	11 1 E
Fränkische Saale →	**31**	50 30N	9 42 E
Fränkische Schweiz	**31**	49 45N	11 10 E
Frankland →	**79**	35 0S	116 48 E
Franklin, Ill., U.S.A.	**116**	39 37N	90 3W
Franklin, Ind., U.S.A.	**117**	39 29N	86 3W
Franklin, Ky., U.S.A.	**113**	36 40N	86 30W
Franklin, La., U.S.A.	**119**	29 45N	91 30W
Franklin, Mass., U.S.A.	**115**	42 4N	71 23W
Franklin, N.H., U.S.A.	**115**	43 28N	71 39W
Franklin, N.J., U.S.A.	**115**	41 9N	74 38W
Franklin, Nebr., U.S.A.	**118**	40 9N	98 55W
Franklin, Ohio, U.S.A.	**117**	39 34N	84 18W
Franklin, Pa., U.S.A.	**114**	41 22N	79 45W
Franklin, Tenn., U.S.A.	**113**	35 54N	86 53W
Franklin, Va., U.S.A.	**113**	36 40N	76 58W
Franklin, W. Va., U.S.A.	**112**	38 38N	79 21W
Franklin, Wis., U.S.A.	**117**	42 53N	88 1W
Franklin □	**101**	71 0N	99 0W
Franklin B.	**100**	69 45N	126 0W
Franklin D. Roosevelt L.	**120**	48 30N	118 16W
Franklin I.	**143**	76 10S	168 30 E
Franklin, L.	**120**	40 20N	115 26W
Franklin Mts., Can.	**100**	65 0N	125 0W
Franklin Mts., N.Z.	**81**	44 55S	167 45 E
Franklin Park	**117**	41 56N	87 51W
Franklin Str.	**100**	72 0N	96 0W
Franklinton	**119**	30 53N	90 10W
Franklinville	**114**	42 21N	78 28W
Franklyn Mt.	**81**	42 4S	172 42 E
Franks Peak	**120**	43 50N	109 5W
Frankston	**74**	38 8S	145 8 E
Frankton Junc.	**80**	37 47S	175 16 E
Fränsta	**10**	62 30N	16 11 E
Frantsa Josifa, Zemlya	**40**	82 0N	55 0 E
Franz	**102**	48 25N	84 30W
Franz Josef Fd.	**144**	73 20N	22 0 E
Franz Josef Land = Frantsa Josifa	**40**	82 0N	55 0 E
Franzburg	**30**	54 9N	12 52 E
Frascati	**28**	41 48N	12 41 E
Fraser	**106**	42 32N	82 57W
Fraser →, B.C., Can.	**108**	49 7N	123 11W
Fraser →, Newf., Can.	**103**	56 39N	62 10W
Fraser I.	**73**	25 15S	153 10 E
Fraser Lake	**108**	54 0N	124 50W
Fraser, Mt.	**79**	25 35S	118 20 E
Fraserburg	**96**	31 55S	21 30 E
Fraserburgh	**14**	57 41N	2 0W
Fraserdale	**102**	49 55N	81 37W
Frasertown	**80**	38 58S	177 28 E
Frasne	**19**	46 50N	6 10 E
Frauenfeld	**31**	47 34N	8 54 E
Fray Bentos	**140**	33 10S	58 15W
Frazier Downs P.O.	**78**	18 48S	121 42 E
Frechilla	**22**	42 8N	4 50W
Fredericia	**11**	55 34N	9 45 E
Frederick, Md., U.S.A.	**112**	39 25N	77 23W
Frederick, Okla., U.S.A.	**119**	34 22N	99 0W
Frederick, S.D., U.S.A.	**118**	45 55N	98 29W
Frederick Sd.	**108**	57 10N	134 0W
Fredericksburg, Tex., U.S.A.	**119**	30 17N	98 55W
Fredericksburg, Va., U.S.A.	**112**	38 16N	77 29W
Frederickstown	**119**	37 35N	90 15W
Frederickton	**77**	31 0S	152 53 E
Fredericton	**103**	45 57N	66 40W
Fredericton Junc.	**103**	45 41N	66 40W
Frederikshavn	**11**	57 28N	10 31 E
Frederikssund	**11**	55 50N	12 3 E
Frederiksted	**127**	17 43N	64 53W
Fredonia, Ariz., U.S.A.	**121**	36 59N	112 36W
Fredonia, Kans., U.S.A.	**119**	37 34N	95 50W
Fredonia, N.Y., U.S.A.	**114**	42 26N	79 20W
Fredrikstad	**10**	59 13N	10 57 E
Freeburg	**116**	38 19N	91 56W
Freehold	**115**	40 15N	74 18W
Freel Pk.	**122**	38 52N	119 53W
Freeland	**115**	41 3N	75 48W
Freels, C.	**103**	49 15N	53 30W
Freeman, Calif., U.S.A.	**123**	35 35N	117 53W
Freeman, Mo., U.S.A.	**116**	38 37N	94 30W
Freeman, S.D., U.S.A.	**118**	43 25N	97 20W
Freeport, Bahamas	**126**	26 30N	78 47W
Freeport, Can.	**103**	44 15N	66 20W
Freeport, Ill., U.S.A.	**116**	42 18N	89 40W
Freeport, N.Y., U.S.A.	**115**	40 39N	73 35W
Freeport, Tex., U.S.A.	**119**	28 55N	95 22W
Freestone	**77**	28 7S	152 8 E
Freetown	**88**	8 30N	13 17W
Frégate, L.	**102**	53 15N	74 45W
Fregenal de la Sierra	**23**	38 10N	6 39W

Fregene 28 41 50N 12 12 E
Fregeneda, La 22 40 58N 6 54W
Fréhel, C. 18 48 40N 2 20W
Freiberg 30 50 55N 13 20 E
Freibourg = Fribourg 31 46 49N 7 9 E
Freiburg, Baden, Ger. 31 48 0N 7 52 E
Freiburg, Niedersachsen, Ger. 30 53 49N 9 17 E
Freire 142 38 54S 72 38W
Freirina 140 28 30S 71 10W
Freising 31 48 24N 11 47 E
Freistadt 32 48 30N 14 30 E
Freital 30 51 0N 13 40 E
Fréjus 21 43 25N 6 44 E
Fremantle 79 32 7S 115 47 E
Fremont, Calif., U.S.A. 122 37 32N 122 1W
Fremont, Ind., U.S.A. 117 41 44N 84 56W
Fremont, Mich., U.S.A. 112 43 29N 85 59W
Fremont, Nebr., U.S.A. 118 41 30N 96 30W
Fremont, Ohio, U.S.A. 117 41 20N 83 5W
Fremont → 121 38 15N 110 20W
Fremont, L. 120 43 0N 109 50W
French →, Can. 106 46 2N 80 34W
French →, U.S.A. 114 41 30N 80 2W
French Camp 122 37 53N 121 16W
French Guiana ■ 135 4 0N 53 0W
French I. 74 38 20S 145 22 E
French Lick 117 38 33N 86 37W
French River 106 46 2N 80 34W
French Terr. of Afars & Issas = Djibouti 91 11 30N 42 15 E
Frenchburg 117 37 57N 83 38W
Frenchglen 120 42 48N 119 0W
Frenchman → 120 48 24N 107 5W
Frenchman Butte 109 53 35N 109 38W
Frenchman Creek → 118 40 13N 100 50W
Frenda 86 35 2N 1 1 E
Fresco → 137 7 15S 51 30W
Freshfield, C. 143 68 25S 151 10 E
Fresnay 18 48 17N 0 1 E
Fresnillo 124 23 10N 103 0W
Fresno 122 36 47N 119 50W
Fresno Alhandiga 22 40 42N 5 37W
Fresno Res. 120 48 40N 110 0W
Freudenstadt 31 48 27N 8 25 E
Frévent 19 50 15N 2 17 E
Frew → 72 20 0S 135 38 E
Frewena 72 19 25S 135 25 E
Freycinet Pen. 72 42 10S 148 25 E
Freyung 31 48 48N 13 33 E
Fria 88 10 27N 13 38W
Fría, La 134 8 13N 72 15W
Friant 122 36 59N 119 43W
Frías 140 28 40S 65 5W
Fribourg 31 46 49N 7 9 E
Fribourg □ 31 45 40N 7 0 E
Fridafors 11 56 25N 14 39 E
Friday Harbor 122 48 32N 123 1W
Friedberg, Bayern, Ger. 31 48 21N 10 59 E
Friedberg, Hessen, Ger. 31 50 21N 8 46 E
Friedland 30 53 40N 13 33 E
Friedrichshafen 31 47 39N 9 29 E
Friedrichskoog 30 54 1N 8 52 E
Friedrichsort 30 54 24N 10 11 E
Friedrichstadt 30 54 23N 9 6 E
Friendly (Tonga) Is. 68 22 0S 173 0W
Friesack 30 52 43N 12 35 E
Friesland □ 16 53 5N 5 50 E
Friesoythe 30 53 1N 7 51 E
Frillesås 11 57 20N 12 12 E
Frinnaryd 11 57 55N 14 50 E
Frio → 119 28 30N 98 10W
Frio, C. 96 18 0S 12 0 E
Friona 119 34 40N 102 42W
Frisian Is. 30 53 30N 6 0 E
Fristad 11 57 50N 13 0 E
Fritch 119 35 40N 101 35W
Fritsla 11 57 33N 12 47 E
Fritzlar 30 51 8N 9 19 E
Friuli-Venezia Giulia □ 27 46 0N 13 0 E
Friville-Escarbotin 19 50 5N 1 33 E
Frobisher B. 101 62 30N 66 0W
Frobisher Bay 101 63 44N 68 31W
Frobisher L. 109 56 20N 108 15W
Frogmore 76 34 15S 148 52 E
Froid 118 48 20N 104 29W
Frolovo 39 49 45N 43 40 E
Fromberg 120 42 25N 108 58W
Frome 13 51 16N 2 17W
Frome Downs 73 31 13S 139 45 E
Frome, L. 73 30 45S 139 45 E
Fromentine 18 46 53N 2 9W
Frómista 22 42 16N 4 25W
Front Range 120 40 0N 105 40W
Front Royal 112 38 55N 78 10W
Fronteira 23 39 3N 7 39W
Fronteiras 138 7 5S 40 37W
Frontera 125 18 30N 92 40W
Frontignan 20 43 27N 3 45 E
Frosinone 28 41 38N 13 20 E
Frosolone 29 41 34N 14 27 E
Frostburg 112 39 43N 78 57W
Frostisen 8 68 14N 17 10 E
Frouard 19 48 47N 6 8 E
Frövi 10 59 28N 15 24 E
Fruges 19 50 30N 2 8 E
Frumoasa 34 46 28N 25 48 E
Frunze 40 42 54N 74 46 E
Frutal 139 20 0S 49 0W
Frutigen 31 46 35N 7 38 E
Frýdek-Místek 32 49 40N 18 20 E
Frýdlant 32 50 56N 15 9 E
Fu Jiang → 58 30 0N 106 16 E
Fu Xian, Liaoning, China 61 39 38N 121 58 E
Fu Xian, Shaanxi, China 60 36 0N 109 20 E
Fu'an 59 27 11N 119 36 E
Fubian 58 31 17N 102 22 E
Fucécchio 26 43 44N 10 51 E
Fucheng 60 37 50N 116 10 E
Fuchou = Fuzhou 59 26 5N 119 16 E
Fuchū 64 34 34N 133 14 E
Fūchū 65 35 40N 139 29 E
Fuchuan 59 24 50N 111 5 E
Fuchun Jiang → 59 30 5N 120 5 E
Fúcino, Conca del 27 42 1N 13 31 E
Fuding 59 27 20N 120 12 E
Fuencaliente 23 38 25N 4 18W
Fuengirola 23 36 32N 4 41W
Fuente Alamo 25 38 44N 1 24W
Fuente Álamo 25 37 42N 1 6W
Fuente de Cantos 23 38 15N 6 18W
Fuente de San Esteban, La 22 40 49N 6 15W
Fuente del Maestre 23 38 31N 6 28W
Fuente el Fresno 23 39 14N 3 46W
Fuente Ovejuna 23 38 15N 5 25W
Fuentes de Andalucía 23 37 28N 5 20W
Fuentes de Ebro 24 41 31N 0 38W
Fuentes de León 23 38 5N 6 32W
Fuentes de Oñoro 22 40 33N 6 52W
Fuentesaúco 22 41 15N 5 30W
Fuerte → 124 25 50N 109 25W
Fuerte Olimpo 140 21 0S 57 51W
Fuerteventura 84 28 30N 14 0W
Fufeng 60 34 22N 108 0 E
Fugløysund 8 70 15N 20 20 E
Fugong 58 27 5N 98 47 E
Fugou 60 34 3N 114 25 E
Fugu 60 39 2N 111 3 E
Fuhai 62 47 2N 87 25 E
Fujaira 47 25 7N 56 18 E
Fuji 65 35 9N 138 39 E
Fuji-no-miya 65 35 10N 138 40 E
Fuji-San 65 35 22N 138 44 E
Fuji-yoshida 65 35 30N 138 46 E
Fujian □ 59 26 0N 118 0 E
Fujieda 65 34 52N 138 16 E
Fujioka 65 36 15N 139 5 E
Fujisawa 65 35 22N 139 29 E
Fukaya 65 36 12N 139 12 E
Fukien □ = Fujian □ 59 26 0N 118 0 E
Fukuchiyama 65 35 19N 135 9 E
Fukui 65 36 0N 136 10 E
Fukui □ 65 36 0N 136 12 E
Fukuma 64 33 46N 130 28 E
Fukuoka 64 33 39N 130 21 E
Fukuoka □ 64 33 30N 131 0 E
Fukuroi 65 34 45N 137 55 E
Fukushima 63 37 44N 140 28 E
Fukuyama 64 34 35N 133 20 E
Fulda 30 50 32N 9 41 E
Fulda → 30 51 27N 9 40 E
Fuling 58 29 40N 107 20 E
Fullerton, Calif., U.S.A. 123 33 52N 117 58W
Fullerton, Nebr., U.S.A. 118 41 25N 98 0W
Fulongquan 61 44 20N 124 42 E
Fulton, Ill., U.S.A. 116 41 52N 90 11W
Fulton, Ind., U.S.A. 117 40 57N 86 16W
Fulton, Mo., U.S.A. 116 38 50N 91 55W
Fulton, N.Y., U.S.A. 115 43 20N 76 22W
Fulton, Tenn., U.S.A. 113 36 31N 88 53W
Fuluälven 10 61 18N 13 4 E
Fulufjället 10 61 32N 12 41 E
Fumay 19 50 0N 4 40 E
Fumel 20 44 30N 0 58 E
Fumin 58 25 10N 102 20 E
Funabashi 65 35 45N 140 0 E
Funafuti 66 8 30S 179 0 E
Funchal 84 32 45N 16 55W
Fundación 134 10 31N 74 11W
Fundão, Brazil 139 19 55S 40 24W
Fundão, Port. 22 40 8N 7 30W
Fundu 95 14 58S 30 14 E
Fundy, B. of 103 45 0N 66 0W
Funing, Hebei, China 61 39 53N 119 12 E
Funing, Jiangsu, China 61 33 45N 119 50 E
Funing, Yunnan, China 58 23 35N 105 45 E
Funiu Shan 60 33 30N 112 20 E
Funsi 88 10 21N 1 54W
Funtua 89 11 30N 7 18 E
Fuping, Hebei, China 60 38 48N 114 12 E
Fuping, Shaanxi, China 60 34 42N 109 10 E
Fuqing 59 25 41N 119 21 E
Fuquan 58 26 40N 107 27 E
Fur 11 56 50N 9 0 E
Furat, Nahr al → 46 31 0N 47 25 E
Furbero 125 20 22N 97 31W
Furmanov 37 57 10N 41 9 E
Furmanovo 39 49 42N 49 25 E
Furnas, Reprêsa de 139 20 50S 45 0W
Furneaux Group 72 40 10S 147 50 E
Furness, Pen. 12 54 12N 3 10W
Fürstenau 30 52 32N 7 40 E
Fürstenberg 30 53 11N 13 9 E
Fürstenfeld 33 47 3N 16 3 E
Fürstenfeldbruck 31 48 10N 11 15 E
Fürstenwalde 30 52 20N 14 3 E
Fürth 31 49 29N 11 0 E
Furth im Wald 31 49 19N 12 51 E
Furtwangen 31 48 3N 8 14 E
Furudal 10 61 10N 15 11 E
Furukawa 65 36 14N 137 11 E
Furusund 10 59 40N 18 55 E
Fury and Hecla Str. 101 69 56N 84 0W
Fusagasuga 134 4 21N 74 22W
Fuscaldo 29 39 25N 16 1 E
Fushan, Shandong, China 61 37 30N 121 15 E
Fushan, Shanxi, China 60 35 58N 111 51 E
Fushun, Liaoning, China 61 41 50N 123 56 E
Fushun, Sichuan, China 58 29 13N 104 52 E
Fusong 61 42 20N 127 15 E
Füssen 31 47 35N 10 43 E
Fusui 58 22 40N 107 56 E
Futago-Yama 64 33 35N 131 36 E
Futrono 142 40 8S 72 24W
Futuna 66 14 25S 178 20 E
Fuwa 90 31 12N 30 33 E
Fuxin 61 42 5N 121 38 E
Fuyang, Anhui, China 59 33 0N 115 48 E
Fuyang, Zhejiang, China 59 30 5N 119 57 E
Fuyang He → 60 38 12N 117 0 E
Fuying Dao 59 26 34N 120 9 E
Fuyu 61 45 12N 124 43 E
Fuyuan, Heilongjiang, China 62 48 20N 134 5 E
Fuyuan, Yunnan, China 58 25 40N 104 16 E
Fuzhou, Fujian, China 59 26 5N 119 16 E
Fuzhou, Jiangxi, China 62 28 0N 116 25 E
Fylde 12 53 50N 2 58W
Fyn 11 55 20N 10 30 E
Fyne, L. 14 56 0N 5 20W
Fyns Amtskommune □ 11 55 15N 10 30 E
Fyresvatn 10 59 6N 8 10 E

G

Gaanda 89 10 10N 12 27 E
Gabarin 89 11 8N 10 27 E
Gabas → 20 43 46N 0 42W
Gabela 92 11 0S 14 24 E
Gabès 87 33 53N 10 2 E
Gabès, Golfe de 87 34 0N 10 30 E
Gabgaba, W. → 90 22 10N 33 5 E
Gabo I. 75 37 33S 149 57 E
Gabon ■ 92 0 10S 10 0 E
Gaborone 96 24 45S 25 57 E
Gabriels 115 44 26N 74 12W
Gabrovo 34 42 52N 25 19 E
Gacé 18 48 49N 0 20 E
Gach Sārān 47 30 15N 50 45 E
Gacko 33 43 10N 18 33 E
Gada 89 13 38N 5 36 E
Gadag-Batgeri 51 15 30N 75 45 E
Gadamai 91 17 11N 36 10 E
Gadap 48 25 5N 67 28 E
Gadarwara 49 22 50N 78 50 E
Gadebusch 30 53 41N 11 6 E
Gadein 91 8 10N 28 45 E
Gadhada 48 22 0N 71 35 E
Gádor, Sierra de 25 36 57N 2 45W
Gadsden, Ala., U.S.A. 113 34 1N 86 0W
Gadsden, Ariz., U.S.A. 121 32 35N 114 47W
Gadwal 51 16 10N 77 50 E
Găeşti 34 44 48N 25 19 E
Gaeta 28 41 12N 13 35 E
Gaeta, G. di 28 41 0N 13 25 E
Gaffney 113 35 3N 81 40W
Gafsa 87 32 24N 8 43 E
Gagarin (Gzhatsk) 36 55 38N 35 0 E
Gagetown 103 45 46N 66 10W
Gagino 37 55 15N 45 1 E
Gagliano del Capo 29 39 50N 18 23 E
Gagnef 10 60 36N 15 5 E
Gagnoa 88 6 56N 5 16W
Gagnon 103 51 50N 68 5W
Gagnon, L., N.W.T., Can. 109 62 3N 110 27W
Gagnon, L., Qué., Can. 104 46 7N 75 7W
Gagra 39 43 20N 40 10 E
Gahini 94 1 50S 30 30 E
Gahmar 49 25 27N 83 49 E
Gai Xian 61 40 22N 122 20 E
Gaibanda 52 25 20N 89 36 E
Gail 119 32 48N 101 25W
Gail → 33 46 36N 13 53 E
Gaillac 20 43 54N 1 54 E
Gaillon 18 49 10N 1 20 E
Gaima 69 8 20S 142 59 E
Gaimán 142 43 10S 65 25W
Gaines 114 41 46N 77 35W
Gainesville, Fla., U.S.A. 113 29 38N 82 20W
Gainesville, Ga., U.S.A. 113 34 17N 83 47W
Gainesville, Mo., U.S.A. 119 36 35N 92 26W
Gainesville, Tex., U.S.A. 119 33 40N 97 10W
Gainsborough 12 53 23N 0 46W
Gairdner L. 73 31 30S 136 0 E
Gairloch, L. 14 57 43N 5 45W
Gajiram 89 12 29N 13 9 E
Gakuch 49 36 7N 73 45 E
Gal Oya Res. 51 7 5N 81 30 E
Galachipa 52 22 8N 90 26 E
Galah 74 35 4S 142 8 E
Galán, Cerro 140 25 55S 66 52W
Galana → 94 3 9S 40 8 E
Galangue 93 13 42S 16 9 E
Galápagos, Is. 67 0 0 89 0W
Galashiels 14 55 37N 2 50W
Galatea 80 38 24S 176 45 E
Galaţi 34 45 27N 28 2 E
Galatina 29 40 10N 18 10 E
Galátone 29 40 8N 18 3 E
Galax 113 36 42N 80 57W
Galaxídhion 35 38 22N 22 23 E
Galbraith 72 16 25S 141 30 E
Galcaio 45 6 30N 47 30 E
Galdhøpiggen 10 61 38N 8 18 E
Galeana 124 24 50N 100 4W
Galela 57 1 50N 127 49 E
Galena, Austral. 79 27 48S 114 42 E
Galena, U.S.A. 116 42 25N 90 26W
Galera 25 37 45N 2 33W
Galera Point 127 10 8N 61 0W
Galera, Pta. 142 39 59S 73 43W
Galesburg, Ill., U.S.A. 116 40 57N 90 23W
Galesburg, Mich., U.S.A. 117 42 17N 85 26W
Galeton 114 41 43N 77 40W
Galheirão → 139 12 23S 45 5W
Galheiros 139 13 18S 46 25W
Galich 37 58 23N 42 12 E
Galiche 34 43 34N 23 50 E
Galicia 22 42 43N 7 45W
Galien 117 41 48N 86 30W
Galilee = Hagalil 44 32 53N 35 18 E
Galilee, L. 72 22 20S 145 50 E
Galion 114 40 43N 82 48W
Galite, Is. de la 87 37 30N 8 59 E
Galiuro Mts. 121 32 40N 110 30W
Gallabat 85 12 58N 36 11 E
Gallarate 26 45 40N 8 48 E
Gallatin, Mo., U.S.A. 116 39 55N 93 58W
Gallatin, Tenn., U.S.A. 113 36 24N 86 27W
Galle 51 6 5N 80 10 E
Gállego → 24 41 39N 0 51W
Gallegos → 142 51 35S 69 0W
Galley Hd. 15 51 32N 8 56W
Galliate 26 45 27N 8 44 E
Gallinas, Pta. 134 12 28N 71 40W
Gallípoli 29 40 8N 18 0 E
Gallipoli = Gelibolu 46 40 28N 26 43 E
Gallipolis 112 38 50N 82 10W
Gällivare 8 67 9N 20 40 E

Gallo, C. 28 38 13N 13 19 E
Gallocanta, Laguna de 24 40 58N 1 30W
Galloway 14 55 0N 4 25W
Galloway, Mull of 14 54 38N 4 50W
Gallup 121 35 30N 108 45W
Gallur 24 41 52N 1 19W
Gal'on 44 31 38N 34 51 E
Galong 76 34 37S 148 34 E
Galt, Calif., U.S.A. 122 38 15N 121 18W
Galt, Mo., U.S.A. 116 40 8N 93 23W
Galtström 10 62 10N 17 30 E
Galtür 31 46 58N 10 11 E
Galty Mts. 15 52 22N 8 10W
Galtymore 15 52 22N 8 12W
Galva 116 41 10N 90 0W
Galvarino 142 38 24S 72 47W
Galve de Sorbe 24 41 13N 3 10W
Galveston, Ind., U.S.A. 117 40 35N 86 11W
Galveston, Tex., U.S.A. 119 29 15N 94 48W
Galveston B. 119 29 30N 94 50W
Gálvez, Argent. 140 32 0S 61 14W
Gálvez, Spain 23 39 42N 4 16W
Galway 15 53 16N 9 4W
Galway □ 15 53 16N 9 3W
Galway B. 15 53 10N 9 20W
Gam → 54 21 55N 105 12 E
Gamagori 65 34 50N 137 14 E
Gamare, L. 91 11 32N 41 40 E
Gamawa 89 12 10N 10 31 E
Gambaga 89 10 30N 0 28W
Gambat 48 27 17N 68 26 E
Gambela 91 8 14N 34 38 E
Gambia ■ 88 13 25N 16 0W
Gambia → 88 13 28N 16 34W
Gambier, C. 78 11 56S 130 57 E
Gambier Is. 73 35 3S 136 30 E
Gamboli 48 29 53N 68 24 E
Gamerco 121 35 33N 108 56W
Gammon → 109 51 24N 95 44W
Gammouda 87 35 3N 9 39 E
Gamoda-Saki 64 33 50N 134 45 E
Gan 20 43 12N 0 27W
Gan Gan 142 42 30S 68 10W
Gan Jiang → 59 29 15N 116 0 E
Gan Shemu'el 44 32 28N 34 56 E
Gan Yavne 44 31 48N 34 42 E
Ganado, Ariz., U.S.A. 121 35 46N 109 41W
Ganado, Tex., U.S.A. 119 29 4N 96 31W
Gananoque 107 44 20N 76 10W
Ganaveh 47 29 35N 50 35 E
Gand = Gent 16 51 2N 3 42 E
Gandak → 49 25 39N 85 13 E
Gandava 48 28 32N 67 32 E
Gander 103 48 58N 54 35W
Gander L. 103 48 58N 54 35W
Ganderowe Falls 95 17 20S 29 10 E
Gandesa 24 41 3N 0 26 E
Gandhi Sagar 48 24 40N 75 40 E
Gandi 89 12 55N 5 49 E
Gandía 25 38 58N 0 9W
Gandino 26 45 50N 9 52 E
Gandole 89 8 28N 11 35 E
Gandu 139 13 45S 39 30W
Ganedidalem = Gani 57 0 48S 128 14 E
Ganetti 90 18 0N 31 10 E
Ganga → 49 23 20N 90 30 E
Ganga, Mouths of the 49 21 30N 90 0 E
Ganganagar 48 29 56N 73 56 E
Gangapur 48 26 32N 76 49 E
Gangara 89 14 35N 8 29 E
Gangavati 51 15 30N 76 36 E
Gangaw 52 22 5N 94 5 E
Gangdise Shan 49 31 20N 81 0 E
Ganges 20 43 56N 3 42 E
Ganges = Ganga → 49 23 20N 90 30 E
Ganges, Mouth of the 49 21 30N 90 0 E
Gangoh 48 29 46N 77 18 E
Gangtok 52 27 20N 88 37 E
Gangu 60 34 40N 105 15 E
Gangyao 61 44 12N 127 4 E
Gani 57 0 48S 128 14 E
Ganj 49 27 45N 78 57 E
Gannat 20 46 7N 3 11 E
Gannett Pk. 120 43 15N 109 38W
Gannvalley 118 44 3N 98 57W
Ganongga 68 8 5S 156 35 E
Ganquan 60 36 20N 109 20 E
Gänserdorf 33 48 20N 16 43 E
Ganshui 58 28 40N 106 40 E
Gansu □ 62 36 0N 104 0 E
Ganta (Gompa) 88 7 15N 8 59W
Gantheaume B. 79 27 40S 114 10 E
Gantheaume, C. 73 36 4S 137 32 E
Gantsevichi 36 52 49N 26 30 E
Ganyu 61 34 50N 119 8 E
Ganyushkino 39 46 35N 49 20 E
Ganzhou 59 25 51N 114 56 E
Ganzi 91 4 30N 31 15 E
Gao □ 89 18 0N 1 0 E
Gao Xian 58 28 21N 104 32 E
Gao'an 59 28 26N 115 17 E
Gaohe 59 22 46N 112 57 E
Gaohebu 59 30 43N 116 49 E
Gaokeng 59 27 40N 113 58 E
Gaolan Dao 59 21 55N 113 10 E
Gaoligong Shan 58 24 45N 98 45 E
Gaomi 61 36 20N 119 42 E
Gaoping 60 35 45N 112 55 E
Gaotang 60 36 50N 116 15 E
Gaoua 88 10 20N 3 8W
Gaoual 88 11 45N 13 25W
Gaoxiong 59 22 38N 120 18 E
Gaoyang 60 38 40N 115 45 E
Gaoyou 59 32 47N 119 26 E
Gaoyou Hu 61 32 45N 119 20 E
Gaoyuan 61 37 8N 117 58 E
Gaozhou 59 21 58N 110 50 E
Gap 21 44 33N 6 5 E
Gar 62 32 10N 79 58 E
Garachiné 126 8 0N 78 12W
Garah 77 29 5S 149 38 E
Garanhuns 138 8 50S 36 30W
Garawe 88 4 35N 8 0W
Garba Tula 94 0 30N 38 32 E
Garber 119 36 30N 97 36W
Garberville 120 40 11N 123 50W
Garça 139 22 14S 49 37W
Garças → 138 8 43S 39 41W
Garças, Rio das 137 15 54S 52 16W
Garcias 137 20 34S 52 13W
Gard 45 9 30N 49 6 E
Gard □ 21 44 2N 4 10 E
Gard → 21 43 51N 4 37 E
Garda, L. di 26 45 40N 10 40 E
Gardala 85 5 40N 37 25 E
Gardanne 21 43 27N 5 27 E
Garde L. 109 62 50N 106 13W
Gardelegen 30 52 32N 11 21 E
Garden City, Kans., U.S.A. 119 38 0N 100 45W
Garden City, Mo., U.S.A. 116 38 34N 94 12W
Garden City, Tex., U.S.A. 119 31 52N 101 28W
Garden Grove 123 33 47N 117 55W
Garden I. 106 45 49N 85 30W
Gardez 48 33 37N 69 9 E
Gardiner 120 45 3N 110 42W
Gardiners I. 115 41 4N 72 5W
Gardner, Ill., U.S.A. 117 41 12N 88 17W
Gardner, Mass., U.S.A. 115 42 35N 72 0W
Gardner Canal 108 53 27N 128 8W
Gardnerville 122 38 59N 119 47W
Gare Tigre 135 4 58N 53 9W
Garema 76 33 33S 147 56 E
Garéssio 26 44 12N 8 1 E
Garey 123 34 53N 120 19W
Garfield, Austral. 74 38 6S 145 42 E
Garfield, U.S.A. 120 47 3N 117 8W
Gargano, Mte. 29 41 43N 15 43 E
Gargans, Mt. 20 45 37N 1 39 E
Gargouna 89 15 56N 0 13 E
Garhshankar 48 31 13N 76 11 E
Garibaldi Prov. Park 108 49 50N 122 40W
Garies 96 30 32S 17 59 E
Garigliano → 28 41 13N 13 44 E
Garissa 94 0 25S 39 40 E
Garissa □ 94 0 20S 40 0 E
Garkida 89 10 27N 12 36 E
Garko 89 11 45N 8 53 E
Garland 120 41 47N 112 10W
Garlasco 26 45 11N 8 55 E
Garm 40 39 0N 70 20 E
Garmab 48 32 50N 65 12 E
Garmisch-Partenkirchen 31 47 30N 11 5 E
Garmsār 47 35 20N 52 25 E
Garner 116 43 4N 93 37W
Garnett 118 38 18N 95 12W
Garo Hills 49 25 30N 90 30 E
Garob 96 26 37S 16 0 E
Garoe 45 8 25N 48 33 E
Garonne → 20 45 2N 0 36W
Garoua (Garwa) 89 9 19N 13 21 E
Garrel 30 52 58N 7 59 E
Garrett 117 41 21N 85 8W
Garrigues 20 43 40N 3 30 E
Garrison, Ky., U.S.A. 117 38 36N 83 10W
Garrison, Mont., U.S.A. 120 46 30N 112 56W
Garrison, N.D., U.S.A. 118 47 39N 101 27W
Garrison, Tex., U.S.A. 119 31 50N 94 28W
Garrison Res. 118 47 30N 102 0W
Garrovillas 23 39 40N 6 33W
Garrucha 25 37 11N 1 49W
Garry → 14 56 47N 3 47W
Garry L. 100 65 58N 100 18W
Garsen 94 2 20S 40 5 E
Garson →. 109 56 20N 110 1W
Garson L. 109 56 19N 110 2W
Gartempe → 20 46 47N 0 49 E
Gartz 30 53 12N 14 23 E
Garu 89 10 55N 0 11W
Garut 57 7 14S 107 53 E
Garvão 23 37 42N 8 21W
Garvie Mts. 81 45 30S 168 50 E
Garwa 49 24 11N 83 47 E
Garwolin 32 51 55N 21 38 E
Gary 117 41 35N 87 20W
Garz 30 54 17N 13 21 E
Garzê 58 31 39N 99 58 E
Garzón 134 2 10N 75 40W
Gas City 117 40 29N 85 36W
Gasan Kuli 40 37 40N 54 20 E
Gascogne 20 43 45N 0 20 E
Gascogne, G. de 24 44 0N 2 0W
Gasconade 116 38 40N 91 33W
Gasconade → 116 38 41N 91 33W
Gascony = Gascogne 20 43 45N 0 20 E
Gascoyne → 79 24 52S 113 37 E
Gascoyne Junc. T.O. 79 25 2S 115 17 E
Gascueña 24 40 18N 2 31W
Gash, Wadi → 91 16 48N 35 51 E
Gashaka 89 7 20N 11 29 E
Gasherbrum 49 35 40N 76 40 E
Gashua 89 12 54N 11 0 E
Gaspé 103 48 52N 64 30W
Gaspé, C. 103 48 48N 64 7W
Gaspé, Pén de 103 48 45N 65 40W
Gaspésie, Parc Prov. de la 103 48 55N 65 50W
Gassaway 112 38 42N 80 43W
Gássino Torinese 26 45 8N 7 50 E
Gassol 89 8 34N 10 25 E
Gastonia 113 35 17N 81 10W
Gastoúni 35 37 51N 21 15 E
Gastoúri 35 39 34N 19 54 E
Gastre 142 42 20S 69 15W
Gata, C. de 25 36 41N 2 13W
Gata, Sierra de 22 40 20N 6 45W
Gataga → 108 58 35N 126 59W
Gătaia 34 45 26N 21 30 E
Gatchina 36 59 35N 30 9 E
Gatere 68 7 55S 159 0 E
Gateshead 12 54 57N 1 37W
Gatesville 119 31 29N 97 45W
Gaths 95 20 2S 30 32 E
Gatico 140 22 29S 70 20W
Gâtinais 19 48 5N 2 40 E
Gâtine, Hauteurs de 20 46 35N 0 45W
Gatineau, Ont., Can. 107 45 29N 75 39W
Gatineau, Qué., Can. 104 45 29N 75 38W
Gatineau → 104 45 27N 75 42W
Gatineau, Parc de la 104 45 40N 76 0W
Gatooma 95 18 20S 29 52 E
Gattinara 26 45 37N 8 22 E
Gatukai 68 8 45S 158 15 E
Gatum 74 37 26S 141 57 E
Gatun, L. 126 9 7N 79 56W
Gaua 68 14 15S 167 30 E
Gaucín 23 36 31N 5 19W
Gaud-i-Zirreh 47 29 45N 62 0 E
Gauer L. 109 57 0N 97 50W
Gauhati 52 26 10N 91 45 E
Gauja → 36 57 10N 24 16 E
Gaussberg 143 66 45S 89 0 E
Gausta 10 59 50N 8 37 E
Gavá 24 41 18N 2 0 E
Gavarnie 20 42 44N 0 3W
Gaväter 47 25 10N 61 31 E
Gavdhopoúla 35 34 56N 24 0 E
Gávdhos 35 34 50N 24 5 E
Gavião 23 39 28N 7 56W
Gaviota 123 34 29N 120 13W
Gävle 10 60 40N 17 9 E
Gävleborgs län □ 10 61 30N 16 15 E
Gavorrano 26 42 55N 10 49 E
Gavray 18 48 55N 1 20W
Gavrilov Yam 37 57 18N 39 49 E
Gawachab 96 27 4S 17 55 E
Gawai 52 27 56N 97 30 E
Gawilgarh Hills 50 21 15N 76 45 E
Gawler 73 34 30S 138 42 E
Gaxun Nur 62 42 22N 100 30 E
Gaya, India 49 24 47N 85 4 E
Gaya, Niger 89 11 52N 3 28 E
Gaya, Nigeria 89 11 57N 9 0 E
Gaylord 106 45 1N 84 41W
Gayndah 73 25 35S 151 32 E
Gaysin 38 48 57N 28 25 E
Gayvoron 38 48 22N 29 52 E
Gaza 44 31 30N 34 28 E
Gaza □ 97 23 10S 32 45 E
Gaza Strip 44 31 29N 34 25 E
Gazaoua 89 13 32N 7 55 E
Gazelle Pen. 69 4 40S 152 0 E
Gazi 94 1 3N 24 30 E
Gaziantep 46 37 6N 37 23 E
Gazli 40 40 14N 63 24 E
Gbarnga 88 7 19N 9 13W
Gbekebo 89 6 20N 4 56 E
Gboko 89 7 17N 9 4 E
Gbongan 89 7 28N 4 20 E
Gcuwa 97 32 20S 28 11 E
Gdańsk 32 54 22N 18 40 E
Gdańska, Zatoka 32 54 30N 19 20 E
Gdov 36 58 48N 27 55 E
Gdynia 32 54 35N 18 33 E
Ge'a 44 31 38N 34 37 E
Gebe 57 0 5N 129 25 E
Gebeit Mine 90 21 3N 36 29 E
Gecoa 91 7 30N 35 18 E
Gedaref 91 14 2N 35 28 E
Gede, Tanjung 56 6 46S 105 12 E
Gedera 44 31 49N 34 46 E
Gedo 91 9 2N 37 25 E
Gèdre 20 42 47N 0 2 E
Gedser 11 54 35N 11 55 E
Gedser Odde 11 54 30N 11 58 E
Geelong 74 38 10S 144 22 E
Geelvink Chan. 79 28 30S 114 0 E
Geestenseth 30 53 31N 8 51 E
Geesthacht 30 53 25N 10 20 E
Geidam 89 12 57N 11 57 E
Geikie → 109 57 45N 103 52W
Geili 91 16 1N 32 37 E
Geilo 10 60 32N 8 14 E
Geisingen 31 47 55N 8 37 E
Geislingen 31 48 37N 9 51 E
Geita 94 2 48S 32 12 E
Geita □ 94 2 50S 32 10 E
Gejiu 58 23 20N 103 10 E
Gel → 91 7 5N 29 10 E
Gel River 91 7 5N 29 10 E
Gela 29 37 6N 14 18 E
Gela, Golfo di 29 37 0N 14 8 E
Geladi 45 6 59N 46 30 E
Gelantipy 75 37 8S 148 22 E
Gelderland □ 16 52 5N 6 10 E
Geldermalsen 16 51 53N 5 17 E
Geldern 30 51 32N 6 18 E
Geldrop 16 51 25N 5 32 E
Geleen 16 50 57N 5 49 E
Gelehun 88 8 20N 11 40W
Gelendzhik 38 44 33N 38 10 E
Gelibolu 46 40 28N 26 43 E
Gellibrand 74 38 33S 143 30 E
Gelnhausen 31 50 12N 9 12 E
Gelsenkirchen 30 51 30N 7 5 E
Gelting 30 54 43N 9 53 E
Gemas 55 2 37N 102 36 E
Gembloux 16 50 34N 4 43 E
Gembrook 74 37 58S 145 37 E
Gemena 92 3 13N 19 48 E
Gemerek 46 39 15N 36 10 E
Gemona del Friuli 27 46 16N 13 7 E
Gemsa 90 27 39N 33 35 E
Gemu-Gofa □ 91 5 40N 36 40 E
Gemünden 31 50 3N 9 43 E
Genale 91 6 0N 39 30 E
Genale Dorya, Wabi → 91 4 20N 42 0 E
Gençay 20 46 23N 0 23 E
Gendringen 16 51 52N 6 21 E
Geneina, Gebel 90 29 2N 33 55 E
General Acha 140 37 20S 64 38W
General Alvear, Buenos Aires, Argent. 140 36 0S 60 0W
General Alvear, Mendoza, Argent. 140 35 0S 67 40W
General Artigas 140 26 52S 56 16W
General Belgrano 140 36 35S 58 47W
General Cabrera 140 32 53S 63 52W
General Carrera, L. 142 46 35S 72 0W
General Cepeda 124 25 23N 101 27W
General Conesa 142 40 6S 64 25W
General Guido 140 36 40S 57 50W
General Juan Madariaga 140 37 0S 57 0W
General La Madrid 140 37 17S 61 20W
General Lorenzo Vintter 142 40 45S 64 26W
General MacArthur 57 11 18N 125 28 E
General Martin Miguel de Güemes 140 24 35S 65 0W
General Paz 140 27 45S 57 36W
General Pico 140 35 45S 63 50W
General Pinedo 140 27 15S 61 20W
General Pinto 140 34 45S 61 50W
General Sampaio 138 4 2S 39 29W
General Santos 57 6 5N 125 14 E
General Toshevo 34 43 42N 28 6 E
General Trevino 125 26 14N 99 29W
General Trías 124 28 21N 106 22W
General Viamonte 140 35 1S 61 3W
General Villegas 140 35 0S 63 0W
General Vintter, L. 142 43 55S 71 40W
Genesee, Idaho, U.S.A. 120 46 31N 116 59W
Genesee, Pa., U.S.A. 114 42 0N 77 54W
Genesee → 114 42 35N 78 0W
Geneseo, Ill., U.S.A. 116 41 25N 90 10W

Geneseo, Kans., U.S.A. **118** 38 32N 98 8W
Geneseo, N.Y., U.S.A. **114** 42 49N 77 49W
Geneva, Ala., U.S.A. **113** 31 2N 85 52W
Geneva, Ill., U.S.A. **117** 41 53N 88 18W
Geneva, Ind., U.S.A. **117** 40 36N 84 57W
Geneva, N.Y., U.S.A. **114** 42 53N 77 0W
Geneva, Nebr., U.S.A. **118** 40 35N 97 35W
Geneva, Ohio, U.S.A. **114** 41 49N 80 58W
Geneva = Genève **31** 46 12N 6 9 E
Geneva, L. **117** 42 38N 88 30W
Geneva, L. = Léman, Lac **31** 46 26N 6 30 E
Genève **31** 46 12N 6 9 E
Genève □ **31** 46 10N 6 10 E
Gengenbach **31** 48 25N 8 0 E
Gengma **58** 23 32N 99 20 E
Genichesk **38** 46 12N 34 50 E
Genil → **23** 37 42N 5 19W
Génissiat, Barrage de **21** 46 1N 5 48 E
Genjem **57** 2 46S 140 12 E
Genk **16** 50 58N 5 32 E
Genkai-Nada **64** 34 0N 130 0 E
Genlis **19** 47 15N 5 12 E
Gennargentu, Mti. del **28** 40 0N 9 10 E
Gennep **16** 51 41N 5 59 E
Gennes **18** 47 20N 0 17W
Genoa, Austral. **75** 37 29S 149 35 E
Genoa, Ill., U.S.A. **117** 42 6N 88 42W
Genoa, N.Y., U.S.A. **115** 42 40N 76 32W
Genoa, Nebr., U.S.A. **118** 41 31N 97 44W
Genoa, Nev., U.S.A. **122** 39 2N 119 50W
Genoa = Génova **26** 44 24N 8 57 E
Genoa →, Argent. **142** 44 55S 70 5W
Genoa →, Austral. **75** 37 31S 149 41 E
Genoa City **117** 42 30N 88 20W
Génova **26** 44 24N 8 56 E
Génova, Golfo di **26** 44 0N 9 0 E
Gent **16** 51 2N 3 42 E
Genthin **30** 52 24N 12 10 E
Gentio do Ouro **138** 11 25S 42 30W
Geographe B. **79** 33 30S 115 15 E
Geographe Chan. **79** 24 30S 113 0 E
Geokchay **39** 40 42N 47 43 E
Georga, Zemlya **40** 80 30N 49 0 E
George **96** 33 58S 22 29 E
George → **103** 58 49N 66 10W
George, L., N.S.W., Austral. **76** 35 10S 149 25 E
George, L., S. Austral., Austral. **73** 37 25S 140 0 E
George, L., W. A., Austral. **78** 22 45S 123 40 E
George, L., Uganda **94** 0 5N 30 10 E
George, L., Fla., U.S.A. **113** 29 15N 81 35W
George, L., N.Y., U.S.A. **115** 43 30N 73 30W
George River = Port Nouveau **101** 58 30N 65 50W
George Sound **81** 44 52S 167 25 E
George Town, Austral. **72** 41 5S 146 49 E
George Town, Bahamas **126** 23 33N 75 47W
George Town, Malay. **55** 5 25N 100 19 E
George V Coast **143** 69 0S 148 0 E
George VI Sound **143** 71 0S 68 0W
George West **119** 28 18N 98 5W
Georgetown, Austral. **72** 18 17S 143 33 E
Georgetown, Ont., Can. **106** 43 40N 79 56W
Georgetown, P.E.I., Can. **103** 46 13N 62 24W
Georgetown, Cay. Is. **126** 19 20N 81 24W
Georgetown, Gambia **88** 13 30N 14 47W
Georgetown, Guyana **135** 6 50N 58 12W
Georgetown, Calif., U.S.A. **122** 38 54N 120 50W
Georgetown, Colo., U.S.A. **120** 39 46N 105 49W
Georgetown, Ill., U.S.A. **117** 39 59N 87 38W
Georgetown, Ky., U.S.A. **112** 38 13N 84 33W
Georgetown, Ohio, U.S.A. **117** 38 50N 83 50W
Georgetown, S.C., U.S.A. **113** 33 22N 79 15W
Georgetown, Tex., U.S.A. **119** 30 40N 97 45W
Georgia □ **113** 32 0N 82 0W
Georgia, Str. of **108** 49 25N 124 0W
Georgian B. **106** 45 15N 81 0W
Georgian S.S.R. □ **39** 42 0N 43 0 E
Georgievsk **39** 44 12N 43 28 E
Georgina → **72** 23 30S 139 47 E
Georgina Downs **72** 21 10S 137 40 E
Georgina I. **106** 44 22N 79 17W
Georgiu-Dezh **37** 51 3N 39 30 E
Gera **30** 50 53N 12 11 E
Gera □ **30** 50 45N 11 45 E
Geraardsbergen **16** 50 45N 3 53 E
Geral de Goiás, Serra **139** 12 0S 46 0W
Geral do Paraná Serra **139** 15 0S 47 30W
Geral, Serra, Bahia, Brazil **139** 14 0S 41 0W
Geral, Serra, Goiás, Brazil **138** 11 15S 46 30W
Geral, Serra, Santa Catarina, Brazil **141** 26 25S 50 0W
Gerald **116** 38 24N 91 21W
Geraldine, N.Z. **81** 44 5S 171 15 E
Geraldine, U.S.A. **120** 47 36N 110 18W
Geraldton, Austral. **79** 28 48S 114 32 E
Geraldton, Can. **102** 49 44N 86 59W
Gerang Gerung **74** 36 22S 141 52 E
Gérardmer **19** 48 3N 6 50 E
Gerede **38** 40 45N 32 10 E
Gérgal **25** 37 7N 2 31W
Gerik **55** 5 25N 101 0 E
Gering **118** 41 51N 103 30W
Gerizim **44** 32 13N 35 15 E
Gerlach **120** 40 43N 119 27W
Gerlachovka **32** 49 11N 20 7 E
Gerlogubi **45** 6 53N 45 3 E
Germansen Landing **108** 55 43N 124 40W
Germantown **117** 39 38N 84 22W
Germany, East ■ **30** 52 0N 12 0 E
Germany, West ■ **30** 52 0N 9 0 E
Germersheim **31** 49 13N 8 20 E
Germiston **97** 26 15S 28 10 E
Gernsheim **31** 49 44N 8 29 E
Gero **65** 35 48N 137 14 E
Gerolstein **31** 50 12N 6 40 E
Gerolzhofen **31** 49 54N 10 21 E
Gerona **24** 41 58N 2 46 E
Gerona □ **24** 42 11N 2 30 E
Gerrard **108** 50 30N 117 17W
Gerringong **76** 34 46S 150 47 E
Gers □ **20** 43 35N 0 38 E
Gers → **20** 44 9N 0 39 E
Gersfeld **30** 50 27N 9 57 E
Gersoppa Falls **51** 14 12N 74 46 E
Gerufa **96** 19 17S 26 0 E
Geseke **30** 51 38N 8 29 E
Geser **57** 3 50S 130 54 E
Gesso → **26** 44 24N 7 33 E
Gestro, Wabi → **91** 4 12N 42 2 E
Getafe **22** 40 18N 3 44W
Gethsémani **103** 50 13N 60 40W
Gettysburg, Pa., U.S.A. **112** 39 47N 77 18W
Gettysburg, S.D., U.S.A. **118** 45 3N 99 56W
Getz Ice Shelf **143** 75 0S 130 0W
Geurie **76** 32 22S 148 50 E
Gévaudan **20** 44 40N 3 40 E
Gevgelija **35** 41 9N 22 30 E
Gévora → **23** 38 53N 6 57W
Gex **21** 46 21N 6 3 E
Geyser **120** 47 17N 110 30W
Geyserville **122** 38 42N 122 54W
Geysir **8** 64 19N 20 18W
Ghaghara → **49** 25 45N 84 40 E
Ghail **46** 21 40N 46 20 E
Ghalla, Wadi el → **91** 10 25N 27 32 E
Ghana ■ **89** 6 0N 1 0W
Ghansor **49** 22 39N 80 1 E
Ghanzi **96** 21 50S 21 34 E
Ghanzi □ **96** 21 50S 21 45 E
Gharbîya, Es Sahrâ el **90** 27 40N 26 30 E
Ghard Abû Muharik **90** 26 50N 30 0 E
Ghardaïa **86** 32 20N 3 37 E
Ghârib, G. **90** 28 6N 32 54 E
Gharyān **87** 32 10N 13 0 E
Ghāt **87** 24 59N 10 11 E
Ghat Ghat **46** 24 40N 46 15 E
Ghatal **49** 22 40N 87 46 E
Ghatampur **49** 26 8N 80 13 E
Ghatprabha → **51** 16 15N 75 20 E
Ghazal, Bahr el **85** 15 0N 17 0 E
Ghazâl, Bahr el → **91** 9 31N 30 25 E
Ghazaouet **86** 35 8N 1 50W
Ghaziabad **48** 28 42N 77 26 E
Ghazipur **49** 25 38N 83 35 E
Ghazni **48** 33 30N 68 28 E
Ghazni □ **47** 33 0N 68 0 E
Ghedi **26** 45 24N 10 16 E
Ghelinsor **45** 6 28N 46 39 E
Ghent = Gand **16** 51 2N 3 42 E
Gheorghe Gheorghiu-Dej **34** 46 17N 26 47 E
Gheorgheni **34** 46 43N 25 41 E
Ghergani **34** 44 37N 25 37 E
Gherla **34** 47 0N 23 57 E
Ghilarza **28** 40 8N 8 50 E
Ghisonaccia **21** 42 1N 9 26 E
Ghizao **48** 33 20N 65 44 E
Ghizar → **49** 36 15N 73 43 E
Ghod → **50** 18 30N 74 35 E
Ghor □ **47** 34 0N 64 20 E
Ghot Ogrein **90** 31 10N 25 20 E
Ghotaru **48** 27 20N 70 1 E
Ghotki **48** 28 5N 69 21 E
Ghudāmis **87** 30 11N 9 29 E
Ghugri **49** 22 39N 80 41 E
Ghugus **50** 19 58N 79 12 E
Ghulam Mohammad Barrage **48** 25 30N 68 20 E
Ghuriān **47** 34 17N 61 25 E
Gia Dinh **55** 10 49N 106 42 E
Gia Nghia **55** 12 0N 107 42 E
Gia Ngoc **54** 14 50N 108 58 E
Gia Vuc **54** 14 42N 108 34 E
Gian **57** 5 45N 125 20 E
Giannutri **26** 42 16N 11 5 E
Giant Forest **122** 36 36N 118 43W
Giant's Causeway **15** 55 15N 6 30W
Giarabub = Jaghbub **85** 29 42N 24 38 E
Giarre **29** 37 44N 15 10 E
Giaveno **26** 45 3N 7 20 E
Gibara **126** 21 9N 76 11W
Gibbo, Mt. **75** 36 38S 147 58 E
Gibbon **118** 40 49N 98 45W
Gibe → **91** 7 20N 37 36 E
Gibellina **28** 37 48N 13 0 E
Gibeon **96** 25 7S 17 45 E
Gibraléon **23** 37 23N 6 58W
Gibraltar **23** 36 7N 5 22W
Gibraltar, Str. of **23** 35 55N 5 40W
Gibson City **117** 40 28N 88 22W
Gibson Des. **78** 24 0S 126 0 E
Gibsonburg **117** 41 23N 83 19W
Gibsons **108** 49 24N 123 32W
Gibsonville **122** 39 46N 120 54W
Giddalur **51** 15 20N 78 57 E
Giddings **119** 30 11N 96 58W
Gide **91** 9 40N 35 16 E
Gidole **91** 5 40N 37 25 E
Gien **19** 47 40N 2 36 E
Giessen **30** 50 34N 8 40 E
Gifatin, Geziret **90** 27 10N 33 50 E
Giffard **105** 46 51N 71 12W
Gifford Creek **79** 24 3S 116 16 E
Gifhorn **30** 52 29N 10 32 E
Gifu **65** 35 30N 136 45 E
Gifu □ **65** 36 0N 137 0 E
Gig Harbor **122** 47 20N 122 35W
Gigant **39** 46 28N 41 20 E
Giganta, Sa. de la **124** 25 30N 111 30W
Gigen **34** 43 40N 24 28 E
Gigha I. **14** 55 42N 5 45W
Giglio **26** 42 20N 10 52 E
Gignac **20** 43 39N 3 32 E
Gigüela → **25** 39 8N 3 44W
Gijón **22** 43 32N 5 42W
Gil Gil, Cr. → **77** 30 19S 148 42 E
Gil I. **108** 53 12N 129 15W
Gila → **121** 32 43N 114 33W
Gila Bend **121** 33 0N 112 46W
Gila Bend Mts. **121** 33 15N 113 0W
Gilan □ **46** 37 0N 48 0 E
Gilbedi **89** 13 40N 5 45 E
Gilbert → **72** 16 35S 141 15 E
Gilbert Is. = Kiribati ■ **66** 1 0N 176 0 E
Gilbert Plains **109** 51 9N 100 28W
Gilbert River **72** 18 9S 142 52 E
Gilberton **72** 19 16S 143 35 E
Gilbués **138** 9 50S 45 21W
Gilf el Kebîr, Hadabat el **90** 23 50N 25 50 E
Gilford I. **108** 50 40N 126 30W
Gilgai **77** 29 50S 151 9 E
Gilgai No. 1 Pumping Station **79** 31 18S 119 56 E
Gilgandra **76** 31 43S 148 39 E
Gilgil **94** 0 30S 36 20 E
Gilgit **49** 35 50N 74 15 E
Gilgit → **49** 35 44N 74 37 E
Gilima **94** 3 53N 28 15 E
Giljeva Planina **33** 43 9N 20 0 E
Gillam **109** 56 20N 94 40W
Gilleleje **11** 56 8N 12 19 E
Gillen, L. **79** 26 11S 124 38 E
Gilles, L. **73** 32 50S 136 45 E
Gillespie **116** 39 7N 89 49W
Gillespie Pt. **81** 43 24S 169 49 E
Gillette **118** 44 20N 105 30W
Gilliat **72** 20 40S 141 28 E
Gillingham **13** 51 23N 0 34 E
Gilman, Ill., U.S.A. **117** 40 46N 88 0W
Gilman, Mo., U.S.A. **116** 40 8N 93 53W
Gilmer **119** 32 44N 94 55W
Gilmore **76** 35 20S 148 12 E
Gilmore, L. **79** 32 29S 121 37 E
Gilmour **107** 44 48N 77 37W
Gilo → **91** 8 10N 33 15 E
Gilort → **34** 44 38N 23 32 E
Gilroy **122** 37 1N 121 37W
Giluwe, Mt. **69** 6 8S 143 52 E
Gimbi **91** 9 3N 35 42 E
Gimigliano **29** 38 58N 16 32 E
Gimli **109** 50 40N 97 0W
Gimmi **91** 9 0N 37 20 E
Gimo **10** 60 11N 18 12 E
Gimone → **20** 44 0N 1 6 E
Gimont **20** 43 38N 0 52 E
Gimzo **44** 31 56N 34 56 E
Gin → **51** 6 5N 80 7 E
Gin Gin **73** 25 0S 151 58 E
Ginâh **90** 25 21N 30 30 E
Gindie **72** 23 44S 148 8 E
Gineta, La **25** 39 8N 2 1W
Gingin **79** 31 22S 115 54 E
Gîngiova **34** 43 54N 23 50 E
Ginir **91** 7 6N 40 40 E
Ginosa **29** 40 35N 16 45 E
Ginowan **63** 26 15N 127 47 E
Ginzo de Limia **22** 42 3N 7 47W
Giohar **45** 2 48N 45 30 E
Gióia del Colle **29** 40 49N 16 55 E
Gióia, G. di **29** 38 30N 15 50 E
Gióia Táuro **29** 38 26N 15 53 E
Gioiosa Iónica **29** 38 20N 16 19 E
Gióna, Óros **35** 38 38N 22 14 E
Giong, Teluk **57** 4 50N 118 20 E
Giovi, Passo dei **26** 44 33N 8 57 E
Giovinazzo **29** 41 10N 16 40 E
Gir Hills **48** 21 0N 71 0 E
Girab **48** 26 2N 70 38 E
Giralla **78** 22 31S 114 25 E
Giraltovce **32** 49 7N 21 32 E
Girard, Ill., U.S.A. **116** 39 27N 89 48W
Girard, Kans., U.S.A. **119** 37 30N 94 50W
Girard, Ohio, U.S.A. **114** 41 10N 80 42W
Girard, Pa., U.S.A. **114** 42 1N 80 21W
Girardot **134** 4 18N 74 48W
Girardville **105** 49 0N 72 32W
Girdle Ness **14** 57 9N 2 2W
Giresun **46** 40 55N 38 30 E
Girga **90** 26 17N 31 55 E
Girgarre **74** 36 18S 145 2 E
Girgir, C. **69** 3 50S 144 35 E
Giridih **49** 24 10N 86 21 E
Girifalco **29** 38 49N 16 25 E
Girilambone **73** 31 16S 146 57 E
Girishk **47** 31 47N 64 35 E
Giro **89** 11 7N 4 42 E
Giromagny **19** 47 44N 6 50 E
Gironde □ **20** 44 45N 0 30W
Gironde → **20** 45 32N 1 7W
Gironella **24** 42 2N 1 53 E
Giru **72** 19 30S 147 5 E
Girvan **14** 55 15N 4 50W
Gisborne, Austral. **74** 37 29S 144 36 E
Gisborne, N.Z. **80** 38 39S 178 5 E
Gisenyi **94** 1 41S 29 15 E
Gislaved **11** 57 19N 13 32 E
Gisors **19** 49 15N 1 47 E
Gitega (Kitega) **94** 3 26S 29 56 E
Giugliano in Campania **29** 40 55N 14 12 E
Giulianova **27** 42 45N 13 58 E
Giurgeni **34** 44 45N 27 48 E
Giurgiu **34** 43 52N 25 57 E
Giv'at Brenner **44** 31 52N 34 47 E
Giv'atayim **44** 32 4N 34 49 E
Give **11** 55 51N 9 13 E
Givet **19** 50 8N 4 49 E
Givors **21** 45 35N 4 45 E
Givry **19** 46 41N 4 46 E
Giza = El Gîza **90** 30 1N 31 11 E
Gizhiga **41** 62 3N 160 30 E
Gizhiginskaya, Guba **41** 61 0N 158 0 E
Gizo **68** 8 7S 156 50 E
Giżycko **32** 54 2N 21 48 E
Gizzeria **29** 38 57N 16 10 E
Gjegjan **35** 41 58N 20 3 E
Gjerstad **10** 58 54N 9 0 E
Gjirokastra **35** 40 7N 20 10 E
Gjoa Haven **100** 68 20N 96 8W
Gjøl **11** 57 4N 9 42 E
Gjøvik **10** 60 47N 10 43 E
Glace Bay **103** 46 11N 59 58W
Glacier B. **108** 58 30N 136 10W
Glacier Nat. Park, Can. **108** 51 15N 117 30W
Glacier Nat. Park, U.S.A. **120** 48 35N 113 40W
Glacier Park **120** 48 30N 113 18W
Glacier Peak Mt. **120** 48 7N 121 7W
Gladewater **119** 32 30N 94 58W
Gladstone, S.A., Austral. **73** 33 15S 138 22 E
Gladstone, W. Australia, Austral. **79** 25 57S 114 17 E
Gladstone, Can. **109** 50 13N 98 57W
Gladstone, Mich., U.S.A. **112** 45 52N 87 1W
Gladstone, Mo., U.S.A. **116** 39 13N 94 35W
Gladwin **106** 43 59N 84 29W
Gladys L. **108** 59 50N 133 0W
Glafsfjorden **10** 59 30N 12 37 E
Glåma **8** 65 48N 23 0W
Glåma → **10** 59 12N 10 57 E

Glamis 123 33 0N 115 4W
Glamoč 27 44 3N 16 51 E
Glan 11 58 37N 16 0 E
Glanville 116 41 17N 89 15W
Glarus 31 47 3N 9 4 E
Glasco, Kans., U.S.A. 118 39 25N 97 50W
Glasco, N.Y., U.S.A. 115 42 3N 73 57W
Glasgow, U.K. 14 55 52N 4 14W
Glasgow, Ky., U.S.A. 112 37 2N 85 55W
Glasgow, Mo., U.S.A. 116 39 14N 92 51W
Glasgow, Mont., U.S.A. 120 48 12N 106 35W
Glastonbury, U.K. 13 51 9N 2 42W
Glastonbury, U.S.A. 115 41 42N 72 27W
Glauchau 30 50 50N 12 33 E
Glazov 37 58 9N 52 40 E
Glen 115 44 7N 71 10W
Glen Affric 14 57 15N 5 0W
Glen Afton 80 37 37S 175 4 E
Glen Alice 76 33 2S 150 14 E
Glen Almond 104 45 42N 75 29W
Glen Canyon Dam 121 37 0N 111 25W
Glen Canyon Nat. Recreation Area 121 37 30N 111 0W
Glen Coe 12 56 40N 5 0W
Glen Cove 115 40 51N 73 37W
Glen Davis 76 33 5S 150 18 E
Glen Florrie 78 22 55S 115 59 E
Glen Garry 14 57 3N 5 7W
Glen Innes 77 29 44S 151 44 E
Glen Lyon 115 41 10N 76 7W
Glen Massey 80 37 38S 175 2 E
Glen Mor 14 57 12N 4 37 E
Glen Moriston 14 57 10N 4 58W
Glen Orchy 14 56 27N 4 52W
Glen Spean 14 56 53N 4 40W
Glen Ullin 118 46 48N 101 46W
Glen Valley 75 36 54S 147 28 E
Glenalbyn 74 36 30S 143 48 E
Glénans, Îles. de 18 47 42N 4 0W
Glenavy 81 44 54S 171 7 E
Glenbawn, L. 77 32 5S 151 0 E
Glenbrook 76 33 45S 150 37 E
Glenburn 74 37 27S 145 26 E
Glencoe, Can. 106 42 45N 81 43W
Glencoe, S. Afr. 97 28 11S 30 11 E
Glencoe, U.S.A. 118 44 45N 94 10W
Glendale, Ariz., U.S.A. 121 33 40N 112 8W
Glendale, Calif., U.S.A. 123 34 7N 118 18W
Glendale, Oreg., U.S.A. 120 42 44N 123 29W
Glendale, Zimb.-Rhod. 95 17 22S 31 5 E
Glendive 118 47 7N 104 40W
Glendo 118 42 30N 105 0W
Glendora 123 34 8N 117 52W
Glenelg 73 34 58S 138 31 E
Glenelg → 74 38 4S 140 59 E
Glengarriff 15 51 45N 9 33W
Glengarry 75 38 7S 146 37 E
Glengyle 72 24 48S 139 37 E
Glenham 81 46 26S 168 52 E
Glenhope 81 41 40S 172 39 E
Glenisla 74 37 14S 142 12 E
Glenmaggie 75 37 54S 146 43 E
Glenmary, Mt. 81 44 0S 169 55 E
Glenmora 119 31 1N 92 34W
Glenmorgan 73 27 14S 149 42 E
Glenn 122 39 31N 122 1W
Glennie 106 44 32N 83 39W
Glenns Ferry 120 43 0N 115 15W
Glenorchy, Tas., Austral. 72 42 49S 147 18 E
Glenorchy, Vic., Austral. 74 36 55S 142 41 E
Glenore 72 17 50S 141 12 E
Glenormiston 72 22 55S 138 50 E
Glenreagh 77 30 2S 153 1 E
Glenrock 120 42 53N 105 55W
Glenrothes 14 56 12N 3 11W
Glenrowan 75 36 29S 146 13 E
Glens Falls 115 43 20N 73 40W
Glenthompson 74 37 38S 142 38 E
Glenties 15 54 48N 8 18W
Glenville 112 38 56N 80 50W
Glenwood, Alta., Can. 108 49 21N 113 31W
Glenwood, Newf., Can. 103 49 0N 54 58W
Glenwood, Ark., U.S.A. 119 34 20N 93 30W
Glenwood, Hawaii, U.S.A. 110 19 29N 155 10W
Glenwood, Iowa, U.S.A. 118 41 7N 95 41W
Glenwood, Minn., U.S.A. 118 45 38N 95 21W
Glenwood, Wash., U.S.A. 122 46 1N 121 17W
Glenwood Sprs. 120 39 39N 107 21W
Glettinganes 8 65 30N 13 37W

Glina 27 45 20N 16 6 E
Glittertind 10 61 40N 8 32 E
Gliwice 32 50 22N 18 41 E
Globe 121 33 25N 110 53W
Glödnitz 33 46 53N 14 7 E
Głogów 32 51 37N 16 5 E
Gloria, La 134 8 37N 73 48W
Glorieuses, Îles 97 11 30S 47 20 E
Glossop 12 53 27N 1 56W
Gloucester, Austral. 77 32 0S 151 59 E
Gloucester, U.K. 13 51 52N 2 15W
Gloucester, U.S.A. 115 42 38N 70 39W
Gloucester, C. 69 5 26S 148 21 E
Gloucester I. 72 20 0S 148 30 E
Gloucestershire □ 13 51 44N 2 10W
Gloversville 115 43 5N 74 18W
Glovertown 103 48 40N 54 03W
Główno 32 51 59N 19 42 E
Głubczyce 32 50 13N 17 52 E
Glubokiy 39 48 35N 40 25 E
Glubokoye 36 55 10N 27 45 E
Głuchołazy 32 50 19N 17 24 E
Glücksburg 30 54 48N 9 34 E
Glückstadt 30 53 46N 9 28 E
Glukhov 36 51 40N 33 58 E
Glussk 36 52 53N 28 41 E
Glyngøre 11 56 46N 8 52 E
Gmünd, Kärnten, Austria 33 46 54N 13 31 E
Gmünd, Niederösterreich, Austria 32 48 45N 15 0 E
Gnarp 10 62 3N 17 16 E
Gnesta 10 59 3N 17 17 E
Gniew 32 53 50N 18 50 E
Gniezno 32 52 30N 17 35 E
Gnoien 30 53 58N 12 41 E
Gnopp 91 8 47N 29 50 E
Gnosjö 11 57 22N 13 43 E
Gnowangerup 79 33 58S 117 59 E
Go Cong 55 10 22N 106 40 E
Gō-no-ura 64 33 44N 129 40 E
Goa 51 15 33N 73 59 E
Goa □ 51 15 33N 73 59 E
Goageb 96 26 49S 17 15 E
Goalen Hd. 75 36 33S 150 4 E
Goalpara 52 26 10N 90 40 E
Goalundo Ghat 49 23 50N 89 47 E
Goaso 88 6 48N 2 30W
Goat Fell 14 55 37N 5 11W
Goba 91 7 1N 39 59 E
Gobabis 96 22 30S 19 0 E
Gobernador Gregores 142 48 46S 70 15W
Gobi 62 44 0N 111 0 E
Gobichettipalayam 51 11 31N 77 21 E
Gobles 117 42 22N 85 53W
Gobō 65 33 53N 135 10 E
Gobo 91 5 40N 31 10 E
Goch 30 51 40N 6 9 E
Gochas 96 24 59S 18 55 E
Godavari → 50 16 25N 82 18 E
Godavari Point 50 17 0N 82 20 E
Godbout 103 49 20N 67 38W
Godda 49 24 50N 87 13 E
Goddua 87 26 26N 14 19 E
Godegård 11 58 43N 15 8 E
Goderich 106 43 45N 81 41W
Goderville 18 49 38N 0 22 E
Godfrey 116 38 57N 90 11W
Godfreys Creek 76 34 8S 148 43 E
Godhavn 144 69 15N 53 38W
Godhra 48 22 49N 73 40 E
Gödöllö 33 47 38N 19 25 E
Godoy Cruz 140 32 56S 68 52W
Gods → 109 56 22N 92 51W
Gods L. 109 54 40N 94 15W
Godthåb 144 64 10N 51 35W
Godwin Austen (K2) 49 36 0N 77 0 E
Goeie Hoop, Kaap die 96 34 24S 18 30 E
Goéland, L. du 105 49 47N 71 43W
Goéland, L.au 104 49 50N 76 48W
Goeree 16 51 50N 4 0 E
Goes 16 51 30N 3 55 E
Goetzville 106 46 3N 84 5W
Gogama 102 47 35N 81 43W
Gogango 72 23 40S 150 2 E
Gogebic, L. 118 46 20N 89 34W
Gogha 48 21 40N 72 20 E
Gogriâl 91 8 30N 28 8 E
Goiana 138 7 33S 34 59W
Goianésia 139 15 18S 49 7W
Goiânia 139 16 43S 49 20W
Goiás 139 15 55S 50 10W
Goiás □ 138 12 10S 48 0W
Goiatuba 139 18 1S 49 23W
Góis 22 40 10N 8 6W
Gojam □ 91 10 55N 36 30 E
Gojeb, Wabi → 91 7 12N 36 40 E
Gojō 65 34 21N 135 42 E
Gojra 48 31 10N 72 40 E
Gokak 51 16 11N 74 52 E
Gokarannath 49 27 57N 80 39 E

Gokarn 51 14 33N 74 17 E
Gökçeada 35 40 10N 25 50 E
Gokurt 48 29 40N 67 26 E
Gola 49 28 3N 80 32 E
Golaghat 52 26 30N 94 0 E
Golakganj 49 26 8N 89 52 E
Golaya Pristen 38 46 29N 32 32 E
Golchikha 144 71 45N 83 30 E
Golconda 120 40 58N 117 32W
Gold Beach 120 42 25N 124 25W
Gold Coast, Austral. 77 28 0S 153 25 E
Gold Coast, W. Afr. 89 4 0N 1 40W
Gold Hill 120 42 28N 123 2W
Gold River 108 49 46N 126 3 E
Goldberg 30 53 34N 12 6 E
Golden, Can. 108 51 20N 117 59W
Golden, Colo., U.S.A. 118 39 42N 105 15W
Golden, Ill., U.S.A. 116 40 7N 91 1W
Golden Bay 81 40 40S 172 50 E
Golden Gate 120 37 54N 122 30W
Golden Hinde 108 49 40N 125 44W
Golden Lake 107 45 34N 77 21W
Golden Prairie 109 50 13N 109 37W
Golden Rock 51 10 45N 78 48 E
Golden Vale 15 52 33N 8 17W
Goldendale 120 45 53N 120 48W
Goldfield 121 37 45N 117 13W
Goldfields 109 59 28N 108 29W
Goldsand L. 109 57 2N 101 8W
Goldsboro 113 35 24N 77 59W
Goldsmith 119 32 0N 102 40W
Goldsworthy 78 20 21S 119 30 E
Goldthwaite 119 31 25N 98 32W
Golegã 23 39 24N 8 29W
Goleniów 32 53 35N 14 50 E
Goleta 123 34 27N 119 50W
Golfito 126 8 41N 83 5W
Golfo Aranci 28 41 0N 9 35 E
Goliad 119 28 40N 97 22W
Golija 33 43 22N 20 15 E
Gollan 77 32 16S 149 5 E
Golo → 21 42 31N 9 32 E
Golovanevsk 38 48 25N 30 30 E
Golra 48 33 37N 72 56 E
Golspie, Austral. 76 34 20S 149 42 E
Golspie, U.K. 14 57 58N 3 58W
Golyama Kamchiya → 34 43 10N 27 55 E
Goma, Ethiopia 91 8 29N 36 53 E
Goma, Rwanda 94 2 11S 29 18 E
Goma, Zaïre 94 1 37S 29 10 E
Gomare 96 19 25S 22 8 E
Gomati → 49 25 32N 83 11 E
Gombari 94 2 45N 29 3 E
Gombe 89 10 19N 11 2 E
Gombe → 94 4 38S 31 40 E
Gombi 89 10 12N 12 30 E
Gombo 76 32 24S 148 56 E
Gomel 36 52 28N 31 0 E
Gomera, I. 84 28 10N 17 5W
Gómez Palacio 124 25 40N 104 0W
Gommern 30 52 5N 11 47 E
Gomogomo 57 6 39S 134 43 E
Gonābād 47 34 15N 58 45 E
Gonaïves 127 19 20N 72 42W
Gonâve, G. de la 127 19 29N 72 42W
Gonâve, Î. de la 127 18 45N 73 0W
Gonbab-e Kāvūs 47 37 20N 55 25 E
Gonda 49 27 9N 81 58 E
Gondal 48 21 58N 70 52 E
Gonder 91 12 39N 37 30 E
Gondia 50 21 23N 80 10 E
Gondola 95 19 10S 33 37 E
Gondomar, Port. 22 41 10N 8 35W
Gondomar, Spain 22 42 7N 8 45W
Gondrecourt-le-Château 19 48 26N 5 30 E
Gong Xian 58 28 23N 104 47 E
Gong'an 59 30 7N 112 12 E
Gongcheng 59 24 50N 110 49 E
Gongga Shan 58 29 40N 101 55 E
Gongguan 58 21 48N 109 36 E
Gonghe 62 36 18N 100 32 E
Gongola □ 89 8 0N 12 0 E
Gongola → 89 9 30N 12 4 E
Gongshan 58 27 43N 98 29 E
Gongtan 58 28 55N 108 20 E
Goniadz 32 53 30N 22 44 E
Goniri 89 11 30N 12 15 E
Gonjo 58 30 52N 98 17 E
Gonnesa 28 39 17N 8 27 E
Gónnos 35 39 52N 22 29 E
Gonnosfanadiga 28 39 30N 8 39 E
Gonzales, Calif., U.S.A. 122 36 35N 121 30W
Gonzales, Tex., U.S.A. 119 29 30N 97 30W
González Chaves 140 38 02S 60 05W
Goobang Creek 76 33 6S 147 10 E
Good Hart 106 45 34N 85 7W
Good Hope, C. of = Goeie Hoop, K. die 96 34 24S 18 30 E

Goode 73 31 58S 133 45 E
Goodenough I. 69 9 20S 150 15 E
Gooderham 107 44 54N 78 21W
Goodeve 109 51 4N 103 10W
Gooding 120 43 0N 114 44W
Goodland 118 39 22N 101 44W
Goodnight 119 35 4N 101 13W
Goodooga 73 29 1S 147 28 E
Goodsoil 109 54 24N 109 13W
Goodsprings 121 35 51N 115 30W
Goole 12 53 42N 0 52W
Goolgowi 74 33 58S 145 41 E
Gooloogong 76 33 36S 148 26 E
Goomalling 79 31 15S 116 49 E
Goombalie 73 29 59S 145 26 E
Goomburra 77 28 2S 152 5 E
Goonda 95 19 48S 33 57 E
Goondiwindi 77 28 30S 150 21 E
Goongarrie 79 30 2S 121 8 E
Goonumbla 76 32 59S 148 11 E
Goonyella 72 21 47S 147 58 E
Goor 16 52 13N 6 33 E
Goorambat 74 36 24S 145 56 E
Gooray 77 28 25S 150 2 E
Goose → 103 53 20N 60 35W
Goose Bay 103 53 15N 60 20W
Goose L. 120 42 0N 120 30W
Gooty 51 15 7N 77 41 E
Gopalganj, Bangla. 52 23 1N 89 50 E
Gopalganj, India 49 26 28N 84 30 E
Göppingen 31 48 42N 9 40 E
Gor 25 37 23N 2 58W
Góra 32 51 40N 16 31 E
Gorakhpur 49 26 47N 83 23 E
Gorbatov 37 56 12N 43 2 E
Gorbea, Peña 24 43 1N 2 50W
Gorda 122 35 53N 121 26W
Gorda, Punta 126 14 20N 83 10W
Gordon, S. Austral., Austral. 73 32 7S 138 20 E
Gordon, Vic., Austral. 74 37 34S 144 6 E
Gordon, U.S.A. 118 42 49N 102 12W
Gordon → 72 42 27S 145 30 E
Gordon B. 78 11 35S 130 10 E
Gordon Downs 78 18 48S 128 33 E
Gordon, I. 142 54 55S 69 30W
Gordon L., Alta., Can. 109 56 30N 110 25W
Gordon L., N.W.T., Can. 108 63 5N 113 11W
Gordon River 79 34 10S 117 15 E
Gordonia 96 28 13S 21 10 E
Gordonvale 72 17 5S 145 50 E
Gore 77 28 17S 151 30 E
Goré 85 7 59N 16 31 E
Gore, Ethiopia 91 8 12N 35 32 E
Gore, N.Z. 81 46 5S 168 58 E
Gore Bay 106 45 57N 82 28W
Gorey 15 52 41N 6 18W
Gorgān 47 36 55N 54 30 E
Gorgona 26 43 27N 9 52 E
Gorgona, I. 136 3 0N 78 10W
Gorgora 91 12 15N 37 17 E
Gorham 115 44 23N 71 10W
Gori 39 42 0N 44 7 E
Gorin 116 40 22N 92 1W
Gorinchem 16 51 50N 4 59 E
Gorinhatã 139 19 15S 49 45W
Goritsy 37 57 4N 36 43 E
Gorízia 27 45 56N 13 37 E
Gorki = Gorkiy 37 56 20N 44 0 E
Gorkiy 37 56 20N 44 0 E
Gorkovskoye Vdkhr. 37 57 2N 43 4 E
Gørlev 11 55 30N 11 15 E
Gorlice 32 49 35N 21 11 E
Görlitz 30 51 10N 14 59 E
Gorlovka 38 48 19N 38 5 E
Gorman, Calif., U.S.A. 123 34 47N 118 51W
Gorman, Tex., U.S.A. 119 32 15N 98 43W
Gormandale 75 38 18S 146 44 E
Gorna Oryakhovitsa 34 43 7N 25 40 E
Gornja Radgona 27 46 40N 16 2 E
Gornja Tuzla 33 44 35N 18 46 E
Gornji Grad 27 46 20N 14 52 E
Gornji Milanovac 33 44 00N 20 29 E
Gornji Vakuf 33 43 57N 17 34 E
Gorno-Altaysk 40 51 50N 86 5 E
Gorno Slinkino 40 60 5N 70 0 E
Gornyy 37 51 50N 48 30 E
Gorodenka 38 48 41N 25 29 E
Gorodets 37 56 38N 43 28 E
Gorodische 37 53 13N 45 40 E
Gorodnitsa 36 50 46N 27 19 E
Gorodnya 36 51 55N 31 33 E
Gorodok, Byelorussia, U.S.S.R. 36 55 30N 30 3 E
Gorodok, Ukraine, U.S.S.R. 36 49 46N 23 32 E
Goroka 69 6 7S 145 25 E
Goroke 74 36 43S 141 29 E
Gorokhov 36 50 30N 24 45 E
Gorokhovets 37 56 13N 42 39 E

Gorom Gorom	**89**	14 26N	0 14W
Goromonzi	**95**	17 52S	31 22E
Gorong, Kepulauan	**57**	4 5S	131 25E
Gorongosa, Sa. da	**95**	18 27S	34 2E
Gorongose →	**97**	20 30S	34 40E
Gorontalo	**57**	0 35N	123 5E
Goronyo	**89**	13 29N	5 39E
Gorron	**18**	48 25N	0 50W
Gort	**15**	53 4N	8 50W
Gorumahisani	**50**	22 20N	86 24E
Gorzkowice	**32**	51 13N	19 36E
Gorzów Śląski	**32**	51 3N	18 22E
Gorzów Wielkopolski	**32**	52 43N	15 15E
Gose	**65**	34 27N	135 44E
Gosford	**76**	33 23S	151 18E
Goshen, S. Afr.	**96**	25 50S	25 0E
Goshen, Calif., U.S.A.	**122**	36 21N	119 25W
Goshen, Ind., U.S.A.	**117**	41 36N	85 46W
Goshen, N.Y., U.S.A.	**115**	41 23N	74 21W
Goslar	**30**	51 55N	10 23E
Gospič	**27**	44 35N	15 23E
Gosport, U.K.	**13**	50 48N	1 8W
Gosport, U.S.A.	**117**	39 21N	86 40W
Gosse →	**72**	19 32S	134 37E
Gostivar	**35**	41 48N	20 57E
Gostyń	**32**	51 50N	17 3E
Gostynin	**32**	52 26N	19 29E
Göta älv →	**11**	57 42N	11 54E
Göteborg	**11**	57 43N	11 59E
Gotemba	**65**	35 18N	138 56E
Götene	**11**	58 32N	13 30E
Gotha	**30**	50 56N	10 42E
Gothenburg	**118**	40 58N	100 8W
Gotland	**11**	57 30N	18 33E
Gotse Delchev (Nevrokop)	**35**	41 43N	23 46E
Gōtsu	**64**	35 0N	132 14E
Göttingen	**30**	51 31N	9 55E
Gottwaldov (Zlin)	**32**	49 14N	17 40E
Goubangzi	**61**	41 20N	121 52E
Gouda	**16**	52 1N	4 42E
Goudiry	**88**	14 15N	12 45W
Gough I.	**129**	40 10S	9 45W
Gouin Rés.	**104**	48 35N	74 40W
Gouitafla	**88**	7 30N	5 53W
Goula Touila	**86**	21 50N	1 57W
Goulburn	**76**	34 44S	149 44E
Goulburn →	**74**	36 6S	144 55E
Goulburn Is.	**72**	11 40S	133 20E
Goulia	**88**	10 1N	7 11W
Goulimine	**86**	28 56N	10 0W
Goulmina	**86**	31 41N	4 57W
Gounou-Gaya	**92**	9 38N	15 31E
Goúra	**35**	37 56N	22 20E
Gourara	**86**	29 0N	0 30E
Gouraya	**86**	36 31N	1 56E
Gourdon	**20**	44 44N	1 23E
Gouré	**89**	14 0N	10 10E
Gourits →	**96**	34 21S	21 52E
Gourma Rharous	**89**	16 55N	1 50W
Gournay-en-Bray	**19**	49 29N	1 44E
Gouro	**85**	19 36N	19 36E
Gourock Ra.	**76**	36 0S	149 25E
Goursi	**88**	12 42N	2 37W
Gouvêa	**139**	18 27S	43 44W
Gouverneur	**115**	44 18N	75 30W
Gouzon	**20**	46 12N	2 14E
Govan	**109**	51 20N	105 0W
Governador Valadares	**139**	18 15S	41 57W
Governor's Harbour	**126**	25 10N	76 14W
Gowan Ra.	**72**	25 0S	145 0E
Gowanda	**114**	42 29N	78 58W
Gower, The	**13**	51 35N	4 10W
Gowna, L.	**15**	53 52N	7 35W
Gowrie	**116**	42 17N	94 17W
Gowrie, Carse of	**14**	56 30N	3 10W
Goya	**140**	29 10S	59 10W
Goyder Lagoon	**73**	27 3S	139 58E
Goyllarisquisga	**136**	10 31S	76 24W
Goz Beïda	**85**	12 10N	21 20E
Goz Regeb	**91**	16 3N	35 33E
Graaff-Reinet	**96**	32 13S	24 32E
Grabill	**117**	41 13N	84 57W
Grabow	**30**	53 17N	11 31E
Gračac	**27**	44 18N	15 57E
Gračanica	**33**	44 43N	18 18E
Graçay	**19**	47 10N	1 50E
Grace	**120**	42 38N	111 46W
Grace, L. (North)	**79**	33 10S	118 20E
Grace, L. (South)	**79**	33 15S	118 25E
Gracefield	**104**	46 6N	76 3W
Graceville	**118**	45 36N	96 23W
Gracias a Dios, C.	**126**	15 0N	83 10W
Gradaús	**138**	7 43S	51 11W
Gradaús, Serra dos	**138**	8 0S	50 45W
Gradets	**34**	42 46N	26 30E
Gradgery	**76**	31 12S	147 52E
Grado, Italy	**27**	45 40N	13 20E
Grado, Spain	**22**	43 23N	6 4W
Gradule	**77**	28 32S	149 15E
Grady	**119**	34 52N	103 15W
Graeca, Lacul	**34**	44 5N	26 10E
Graénalon, L.	**8**	64 10N	17 20W
Grafenau	**31**	48 51N	13 24E
Gräfenberg	**31**	49 39N	11 15E
Grafton, Austral.	**77**	29 38S	152 58E
Grafton, Ill., U.S.A.	**116**	38 58N	90 26W
Grafton, N.Dak., U.S.A.	**118**	48 30N	97 25W
Gragnano	**29**	40 42N	14 30E
Graham, Austral.	**76**	34 2S	148 49E
Graham, Can.	**102**	49 20N	90 30W
Graham, N.C., U.S.A.	**113**	36 5N	79 22W
Graham, Tex., U.S.A.	**119**	33 7N	98 38W
Graham →	**108**	56 31N	122 17W
Graham Bell, Os.	**40**	80 5N	70 0E
Graham I.	**108**	53 40N	132 30W
Graham Land	**143**	65 0S	64 0W
Graham Mt.	**121**	32 46N	109 58W
Grahamdale	**109**	51 23N	98 30W
Grahamstown	**96**	33 19S	26 31E
Graïba	**87**	34 30N	10 13E
Graie, Alpi	**26**	45 30N	7 10E
Grain Coast	**88**	4 20N	10 0W
Grajaú	**138**	5 50S	46 4W
Grajaú →	**138**	3 41S	44 48W
Grajewo	**32**	53 39N	22 30E
Gral. Martin Miguel de Gäemes	**140**	24 50S	65 0W
Gramada	**34**	43 49N	22 39E
Graman	**77**	29 28S	150 56E
Gramat	**20**	44 48N	1 43E
Grammichele	**29**	37 12N	14 37E
Grampian □	**14**	57 0N	3 0W
Grampian Mts.	**14**	56 50N	4 0W
Grampians, Mts.	**74**	37 0S	142 20E
Gran →	**135**	4 1N	55 30W
Gran Altiplanicie Central	**142**	49 0S	69 30W
Gran Canaria	**84**	27 55N	15 35W
Gran Chaco	**140**	25 0S	61 0W
Gran Paradiso	**26**	45 33N	7 17E
Gran Sabana, La	**135**	5 30N	61 30W
Gran Sasso d'Italia, Mt.	**27**	42 25N	13 30E
Granada, Nic.	**126**	11 58N	86 0W
Granada, Spain	**25**	37 10N	3 35W
Granada, U.S.A.	**119**	38 5N	102 20W
Granada □	**23**	37 18N	3 0W
Granard	**15**	53 47N	7 30W
Granbury	**119**	32 28N	97 48W
Granby	**105**	45 25N	72 45W
Grand →, Can.	**106**	42 51N	79 34W
Grand →, Mich., U.S.A.	**117**	43 4N	86 15W
Grand →, Mo., U.S.A.	**116**	39 23N	93 6W
Grand →, Mo., U.S.A.	**118**	39 23N	93 6W
Grand →, S.D., U.S.A.	**118**	45 40N	100 32W
Grand Bahama	**126**	26 40N	78 30W
Grand Bank	**103**	47 6N	55 48W
Grand Bassam	**88**	5 10N	3 49W
Grand Bend	**106**	43 19N	81 45W
Grand Béréby	**88**	4 38N	6 55W
Grand Blanc	**106**	42 56N	83 38W
Grand-Bourge	**127**	15 53N	61 19W
Grand Calumet, Île du	**104**	45 44N	76 41W
Grand Canyon	**121**	36 3N	112 9W
Grand Canyon National Park	**121**	36 15N	112 20W
Grand Cayman	**126**	19 20N	81 20W
Grand Cess	**88**	4 40N	8 12W
Grand-Combe, La	**21**	44 13N	4 2E
Grand Coulee	**120**	47 48N	119 1W
Grand Coulee Dam	**120**	48 0N	118 50W
Grand Erg Occidental	**86**	30 20N	1 0E
Grand Erg Oriental	**87**	30 0N	6 30E
Grand Falls	**103**	48 56N	55 40W
Grand Forks, Can.	**108**	49 0N	118 30W
Grand Forks, U.S.A.	**118**	48 0N	97 3W
Grand-Fougeray	**18**	47 44N	1 43W
Grand Haven	**117**	43 3N	86 13W
Grand I.	**102**	46 30N	86 40W
Grand Island	**118**	40 59N	98 25W
Grand Isle	**119**	29 15N	89 58W
Grand Junction, Colo., U.S.A.	**121**	39 0N	108 30W
Grand Junction, Iowa, U.S.A.	**116**	42 2N	94 14W
Grand L., N.B., Can.	**103**	45 57N	66 7W
Grand L., Newf., Can.	**103**	49 0N	57 30W
Grand L., Newf., Can.	**103**	53 40N	60 30W
Grand L., La., U.S.A.	**119**	29 55N	92 45W
Grand L., Mich., U.S.A.	**106**	45 18N	83 30W
Grand L., Ohio, U.S.A.	**117**	40 32N	84 25W
Grand Lac Victoria	**102**	47 35N	77 35W
Grand Lahou	**88**	5 10N	5 0W
Grand Lake	**120**	40 20N	105 54W
Grand Ledge	**117**	42 45N	84 45W
Grand-Lieu, Lac de	**18**	47 6N	1 40W
Grand-Luce, Le	**18**	47 52N	0 28E
Grand Manan I.	**103**	44 45N	66 52W
Grand Marais, Can.	**118**	47 45N	90 25W
Grand Marais, U.S.A.	**112**	46 39N	85 59W
Grand Mère	**105**	46 36N	72 40W
Grand Piles	**105**	46 40N	72 40W
Grand Popo	**89**	6 15N	1 57E
Grand Portage	**102**	47 58N	89 41W
Grand-Pressigny, Le	**18**	46 55N	0 48E
Grand Rapids, Can.	**109**	53 12N	99 19W
Grand Rapids, Mich., U.S.A.	**117**	42 57N	86 40W
Grand Rapids, Minn., U.S.A.	**118**	47 15N	93 29W
Grand River	**116**	40 49N	93 58W
Grand St.-Bernard, Col. du	**31**	45 53N	7 11E
Grand Santi	**135**	4 20N	54 24W
Grand Teton	**120**	43 54N	111 50W
Grand Valley	**120**	39 30N	108 2W
Grand View	**109**	51 10N	100 42W
Grandas de Salime	**22**	43 13N	6 53W
Grande →, Jujuy, Argent.	**140**	24 20S	65 2W
Grande →, Mendoza, Argent.	**140**	36 52S	69 45W
Grande →, Boliv.	**137**	15 51S	64 39W
Grande →, Bahia, Brazil	**138**	11 30S	44 30W
Grande →, Minas Gerais, Brazil	**139**	20 6S	51 4W
Grande →, Spain	**25**	39 6N	0 48W
Grande →, U.S.A.	**119**	25 57N	97 9W
Grande →, Venez.	**135**	8 36N	61 39W
Grande, B.	**142**	50 30S	68 20W
Grande Baie	**105**	48 19N	70 52W
Grande Baleine →	**102**	55 20N	77 50W
Grande Cache	**108**	53 53N	119 8W
Grande, Coxilha	**141**	28 18S	51 30W
Grande de Santiago →	**124**	21 20N	105 50W
Grande-Entrée	**103**	47 30N	61 40W
Grande, I.	**139**	23 9S	44 14W
Grande, La	**120**	45 15N	118 0W
Grande-Motte, La	**21**	43 23N	4 3E
Grande Prairie	**108**	55 10N	118 50W
Grande-Rivière	**103**	48 26N	64 30W
Grande-Saulde →	**19**	47 22N	1 55E
Grande, Serra, Goiás, Brazil	**138**	11 15S	46 30W
Grande, Serra, Piauí, Brazil	**138**	8 0S	45 0W
Grande-Vallée	**103**	49 14N	65 8W
Grandes-Bergeronnes	**105**	48 16N	69 35W
Grandfalls	**119**	31 21N	102 51W
Grandoe Mines	**108**	56 29N	129 54W
Grândola	**23**	38 12N	8 35W
Grandpré	**19**	49 20N	4 50E
Grandview, Mo., U.S.A.	**116**	38 53N	94 32W
Grandview, Wash., U.S.A.	**120**	46 13N	119 58W
Grandview Heights	**117**	39 58N	83 2W
Grandville	**117**	42 54N	85 46W
Grandvilliers	**19**	49 40N	1 57E
Graneros	**140**	34 5S	70 45W
Granet, L.	**104**	47 47N	77 31W
Grange, La, U.S.A.	**122**	37 42N	120 27W
Grange, La, Ga., U.S.A.	**113**	33 4N	85 0W
Grange, La, Ky., U.S.A.	**112**	38 20N	85 20W
Grange, La, Mo., U.S.A.	**116**	40 3N	91 35W
Grange, La, Tex., U.S.A.	**119**	29 54N	96 52W
Grangemouth	**14**	56 1N	3 43W
Granger, U.S.A.	**120**	46 25N	120 5W
Granger, Wyo., U.S.A.	**120**	41 35N	109 58W
Grängesberg	**10**	60 6N	15 1E
Grangeville	**120**	45 57N	116 4W
Granite City	**116**	38 45N	90 3W
Granite Falls	**118**	44 45N	95 35W
Granite Mtn.	**123**	33 5N	116 28W
Granite Peak	**79**	25 40S	121 20E
Granite, Pk.	**120**	45 8N	109 52W
Granity	**81**	41 39S	171 51E
Granja	**138**	3 7S	40 50W
Granja de Moreruela	**22**	41 48N	5 44W
Granja de Torrehermosa	**23**	38 19N	5 35W
Gränna	**11**	58 1N	14 28E
Granollers	**24**	41 39N	2 18E
Gransee	**30**	53 0N	13 10E
Grant	**118**	40 53N	101 42W
Grant City	**116**	40 30N	94 25W
Grant, I.	**78**	11 10S	132 52E
Grant, Mt.	**120**	38 34N	118 48W
Grant, Pt.	**74**	38 32S	145 6E
Grant Range Mts.	**121**	38 30N	115 30W
Grantham	**12**	52 55N	0 39W
Grantown-on-Spey	**14**	57 19N	3 36W
Grants	**121**	35 14N	107 51W
Grants Pass	**120**	42 30N	123 22W
Grantsburg	**118**	45 46N	92 44W
Grantsville	**120**	40 35N	112 32W
Granville, France	**18**	48 50N	1 35W
Granville, N.D., U.S.A.	**118**	48 18N	100 48W
Granville, N.Y., U.S.A.	**112**	43 24N	73 16W
Granville L.	**109**	56 18N	100 30W
Granya	**75**	36 8S	147 15E
Grao de Gandía	**25**	39 0N	0 7W
Grapeland	**119**	31 31N	95 31W
Gras, L. de	**100**	64 30N	110 30W
Graskop	**97**	24 56S	30 49E
Gräsö	**10**	60 28N	18 35E
Grass →	**109**	56 3N	96 33W
Grass Range	**120**	47 0N	109 0W
Grass River Prov. Park	**109**	54 40N	100 50W
Grass Valley, Calif., U.S.A.	**122**	39 18N	121 0W
Grass Valley, Oreg., U.S.A.	**120**	45 22N	120 48W
Grassano	**29**	40 38N	16 17E
Grasse	**21**	43 38N	6 56E
Grasset, L.	**104**	49 55N	78 10W
Grassmere	**73**	31 24S	142 38E
Gratis	**117**	39 38N	84 32W
Gratz	**117**	38 28N	84 57W
Graubünden (Grisons) □	**31**	46 45N	9 30E
Graulhet	**20**	43 45N	1 58E
Graus	**24**	42 11N	0 20E
Gravatá	**138**	8 10S	35 29W
Grave, Pte. de	**20**	45 34N	1 4W
Gravelbourg	**109**	49 50N	106 35W
Gravelines	**19**	51 0N	2 10E
's-Gravenhage	**16**	52 7N	4 17E
Gravenhurst	**106**	44 52N	79 20W
Gravesend, Austral.	**77**	29 35S	150 20E
Gravesend, U.K.	**13**	51 25N	0 22E
Gravina di Púglia	**29**	40 48N	16 25E
Gravois, Pointe-à-	**127**	16 15N	73 56W
Gravone →	**21**	41 58N	8 45E
Gray	**19**	47 27N	5 35E
Grayling	**106**	44 40N	84 42W
Grayling →	**108**	59 21N	125 0W
Grays Harbor	**120**	46 55N	124 8W
Grays L.	**120**	43 8N	111 30W
Grays River	**122**	46 21N	123 37W
Graysholm	**77**	28 22S	151 22E
Grayson	**109**	50 45N	102 40W
Grayville	**117**	38 16N	88 0W
Graz	**33**	47 4N	15 27E
Grazalema	**23**	36 46N	5 23W
Greasy L.	**108**	62 55N	122 12W
Great Abaco I.	**126**	26 25N	77 10W
Great Australia Basin	**72**	26 0S	140 0E
Great Australian Bight	**79**	33 30S	130 0E
Great Bahama Bank	**126**	23 15N	78 0W
Great Barrier I.	**80**	36 11S	175 25E
Great Barrier Reef	**72**	18 0S	146 50E
Great Barrington	**115**	42 11N	73 22W
Great Basin	**120**	40 0N	116 30W
Great Bear →	**100**	65 0N	124 0W
Great Bear L.	**100**	65 30N	120 0W
Great Bena	**115**	41 57N	75 45W
Great Bend	**118**	38 25N	98 55W
Great Blasket I.	**15**	52 5N	10 30W
Great Britain	**6**	54 0N	2 15W
Great Bushman Land	**96**	29 20S	19 20E
Great Central	**108**	49 20N	125 10W
Great Dividing Ra.	**73**	23 0S	146 0E
Great Duck I.	**106**	45 40N	82 57W
Great Exuma I.	**126**	23 30N	75 50W
Great Falls, Can.	**109**	50 27N	96 1W
Great Falls, U.S.A.	**120**	47 27N	111 12W
Great Fish →, C. Prov., S. Afr.	**96**	33 28S	27 5E
Great Fish →, C. Prov., S. Afr.	**96**	31 30S	20 16E
Great Guana Cay	**126**	24 0N	76 20W
Great Harbour Deep	**103**	50 25N	56 32W
Great I.	**109**	58 53N	96 35W
Great Inagua I.	**127**	21 0N	73 20W
Great Indian Desert = Thar Desert	**48**	28 0N	72 0E
Great Lake	**72**	41 50S	146 40E
Great Orme's Head	**12**	53 20N	3 52W
Great Ouse →	**12**	52 47N	0 22E
Great Palm I.	**72**	18 45S	146 40E
Great Papuan Plateau	**69**	6 30S	142 25E
Great Plains	**98**	47 0N	105 0W
Great Ruaha →	**94**	7 56S	37 52E
Great Salt Lake	**120**	41 0N	112 30W
Great Salt Lake Desert	**120**	40 20N	113 50W
Great Salt Plains Res.	**119**	36 40N	98 15W
Great Sandy Desert	**78**	21 0S	124 0E

Great Scarcies → 88 9 0N 13 0W
Great Sea Reef 68 16 15S 179 0E
Great Slave L. 108 61 23N 115 38W
Great Smoky Mt. Nat. Park 113 35 39N 83 30W
Great Stour → 13 51 15N 1 20E
Great Victoria Des. 79 29 30S 126 30E
Great Wall 60 38 30N 109 30E
Great Western 74 37 10S 142 50E
Great Whernside 12 54 9N 1 59W
Great Winterhoek 96 33 07S 19 10E
Great Yarmouth 12 52 40N 1 45E
Greater Antilles 127 17 40N 74 0W
Greater London □ 13 51 30N 0 5W
Greater Manchester □ 12 53 30N 2 15W
Greater Sunda Is. 56 4 30S 110 0E
Grebbestad 11 58 42N 11 15E
Grebenka 36 50 9N 32 22E
Greco, Mte. 28 41 48N 14 0E
Gredgwin 74 35 59S 143 38E
Gredos, Sierra de 22 40 20N 5 0W
Greece ■ 35 40 0N 23 0E
Greeley, Colo., U.S.A. 118 40 30N 104 40W
Greeley, Nebr., U.S.A. 118 41 36N 98 32W
Green →, Ky., U.S.A. 117 37 54N 87 30W
Green →, Utah, U.S.A. 121 38 11N 109 53W
Green B. 112 45 0N 87 30W
Green Bay 112 44 30N 88 0W
Green C. 75 37 13S 150 1E
Green City 116 40 16N 92 57W
Green Cove Springs 113 29 59N 81 40W
Green Hd. 79 30 5S 114 56E
Green Is. 69 4 35S 154 10E
Green Island 81 45 55S 170 26E
Green River 121 38 59N 110 10W
Greenbank 122 48 6N 122 34W
Greenbush, Mich., U.S.A. 106 44 35N 83 19W
Greenbush, Minn., U.S.A. 118 48 46N 96 10W
Greencastle 117 39 40N 86 48W
Greene, Iowa, U.S.A. 116 42 54N 92 48W
Greene, N.Y., U.S.A. 115 42 20N 75 45W
Greenethorpe 76 34 0S 148 26E
Greenfield, Calif., U.S.A. 122 36 19N 121 15W
Greenfield, Calif., U.S.A. 123 35 15N 119 0W
Greenfield, Ill., U.S.A. 116 39 21N 90 12W
Greenfield, Ind., U.S.A. 117 39 47N 85 51W
Greenfield, Iowa, U.S.A. 116 41 18N 94 28W
Greenfield, Mass., U.S.A. 115 42 38N 72 38W
Greenfield, Miss., U.S.A. 119 37 28N 93 50W
Greenfield, Ohio, U.S.A. 117 39 21N 83 23W
Greenfield Park 115 45 29N 73 29W
Greenhills 117 39 16N 84 32W
Greenland 144 66 0N 45 0W
Greenland Sea 144 73 0N 10 0W
Greenock 14 55 57N 4 46W
Greenore 15 54 2N 6 8W
Greenore Pt. 15 52 15N 6 20W
Greenough → 79 28 51S 114 38E
Greenough Pt. 106 44 58N 81 26W
Greenport 115 41 5N 72 23W
Greens Creek 74 36 57S 143 0E
Greensboro, Ga., U.S.A. 113 33 34N 83 12W
Greensboro, N.C., U.S.A. 113 36 7N 79 46W
Greensburg, Ind., U.S.A. 117 39 20N 85 30W
Greensburg, Kans., U.S.A. 119 37 38N 99 20W
Greensburg, Pa., U.S.A. 114 40 18N 79 31W
Greentown 117 40 29N 85 58W
Greenup 117 39 15N 88 10W
Greenville, Liberia 88 5 1N 9 6W
Greenville, Ala., U.S.A. 113 31 50N 86 37W
Greenville, Calif., U.S.A. 122 40 8N 121 0W
Greenville, Ill., U.S.A. 116 38 53N 89 22W
Greenville, Ind., U.S.A. 117 38 22N 85 59W
Greenville, Me., U.S.A. 103 45 30N 69 32W
Greenville, Mich., U.S.A. 117 43 12N 85 14W
Greenville, Miss., U.S.A. 119 33 25N 91 0W
Greenville, N.C., U.S.A. 113 35 37N 77 26W
Greenville, Ohio, U.S.A. 117 40 5N 84 38W
Greenville, Pa., U.S.A. 114 41 23N 80 22W
Greenville, S.C., U.S.A. 113 34 54N 82 24W
Greenville, Tenn., U.S.A. 113 36 13N 82 51W
Greenville, Tex., U.S.A. 119 33 5N 96 5W
Greenwater Lake Prov. Park 109 52 32N 103 30W
Greenwich, U.K. 13 51 28N 0 0
Greenwich, Conn., U.S.A. 115 41 1N 73 38W
Greenwich, N.Y., U.S.A. 115 43 2N 73 36W
Greenwich, Ohio, U.S.A. 114 41 1N 82 32W
Greenwood, Can. 108 49 10N 118 40W
Greenwood, Ind., U.S.A. 117 39 37N 86 7W
Greenwood, Miss., U.S.A. 119 33 30N 90 4W
Greenwood, S.C., U.S.A. 113 34 13N 82 13W
Greenwood, Mt. 78 13 48S 130 4E
Gregório → 136 6 50S 70 46W
Gregory 118 43 14N 99 20W
Gregory → 72 17 53S 139 17E
Gregory Downs 72 18 35S 138 45E
Gregory, L., S. Austral., Austral. 73 28 55S 139 0E
Gregory, L., W. Australia, Austral. 79 25 38S 119 58E
Gregory Ra., Queens., Austral. 72 19 30S 143 40E
Gregory Ra., W. Austral., Austral. 78 21 20S 121 12E
Greiffenberg 30 53 6N 13 57E
Greifswald 30 54 6N 13 23E
Greifswalder Bodden 30 54 12N 13 35E
Greifswalder Oie 30 54 15N 13 55E
Grein 33 48 14N 14 51E
Greiz 30 50 39N 12 12E
Gremikha 40 67 50N 39 40E
Grenå 11 56 25N 10 53E
Grenada 119 33 45N 89 50W
Grenada ■ 127 12 10N 61 40W
Grenade 20 43 47N 1 17E
Grenadines 127 12 40N 61 20W
Grenen 11 57 44N 10 40E
Grenfell, Austral. 76 33 52S 148 8E
Grenfell, Can. 109 50 30N 102 56W
Grenoble 21 45 12N 5 42E
Grenora 118 48 38N 103 54W
Grenville, Austral. 74 37 46S 143 52E
Grenville, Can. 104 45 37N 74 36W
Grenville, C. 72 12 0S 143 13E
Grenville Chan. 108 53 40N 129 46W
Gréoux-les-Bains 21 43 45N 5 52E
Gresham 122 45 30N 122 25W
Gresik 57 7 13S 112 38E
Grèssoney St. Jean 26 45 49N 7 47E
Greta 76 32 35S 151 24E
Gretna Green 14 55 0N 3 3W
Greven 30 52 7N 7 36E
Grevená 35 40 4N 21 25E
Grevenbroich 30 51 6N 6 32E
Grevenmacher 16 49 41N 6 26E
Grevesmühlen 30 53 51N 11 10E
Grevie 11 56 22N 12 46E
Grevillia 77 28 26S 152 55E
Grey → 81 42 27S 171 12E
Grey, C. 72 13 0S 136 35E
Grey Range 73 27 0S 143 30E
Grey Res. 103 48 20N 56 30W
Greybull 120 44 30N 108 3W
Greytown, N.Z. 80 41 5S 175 29E
Greytown, S. Afr. 97 29 1S 30 36E
Gribanovskiy 37 51 28N 41 50E
Gribbell I. 108 53 23N 129 0W
Gridley 122 39 27N 121 47W
Griekwastad 96 28 49S 23 15E
Griffin 113 33 17N 84 14W
Griffith, Austral. 74 34 18S 146 2E
Griffith, Can. 107 45 15N 77 10W
Griffith I. 106 44 50N 80 55W
Grillby 10 59 38N 17 15E
Grimari 92 5 43N 20 6E
Grimaylov 36 49 20N 26 5E
Grimes 122 39 4N 121 54W
Grimma 30 51 14N 12 44E
Grimmen 30 54 6N 13 2E
Grimsby, Can. 106 43 12N 79 34W
Grimsby, U.K. 12 53 35N 0 5W
Grímsey 8 66 33N 18 0W
Grimshaw 108 56 10N 117 40W
Grimstad 11 58 22N 8 35E
Grindelwald 31 46 38N 8 2E
Grindsted 11 55 46N 8 55E
Grindstone I. 107 44 43N 76 14W
Grindu 34 44 44N 26 50E
Grinnell 116 41 45N 92 43W
Griñón 22 40 13N 3 51W
Grintavec 27 46 22N 14 32E
Grip 10 63 16N 7 37E
Griqualand East 97 30 30S 29 0E
Griqualand West 96 28 40S 23 30E
Grisolles 20 43 49N 1 19E
Grisslehamn 10 60 5N 18 49E
Grita, La 134 8 8N 71 59W
Griz Nez, C. 19 50 50N 1 35E
Grmeč Planina 27 44 43N 16 16E
Groais I. 103 50 55N 55 35W
Groblersdal 97 25 15S 29 25E
Grobming 33 47 27N 13 54E
Grodno 36 53 42N 23 52E
Grodzisk Mázowiecki 32 52 7N 20 37E
Grodzisk Wielkopolski 32 52 15N 16 22E
Grodzyanka 36 53 31N 28 42E
Groesbeck 119 31 32N 96 34W
Grogan 76 34 16S 147 49E
Groix 18 47 38N 3 29W
Groix, I. de 18 47 38N 3 28W
Grójec 32 51 50N 20 58E
Gronau, Niedersachsen, Ger. 30 52 5N 9 47E
Gronau, Nordrhein-Westfalen, Ger. 30 52 13N 7 2E
Grong 8 64 25N 12 8E
Groningen, Neth. 16 53 15N 6 35E
Groningen, Surinam 135 5 48N 55 28W
Groningen □ 16 53 16N 6 40E
Grönskåra 11 57 5N 15 43E
Groom 119 35 12N 100 59W
Groot → 96 33 45S 24 36E
Groot Berg → 96 32 47S 18 8E
Groot-Brakrivier 96 34 2S 22 18E
Groot Karoo 96 32 35S 23 0E
Groote Eylandt 72 14 0S 136 40E
Grootfontein 96 19 31S 18 6E
Grootlaagte → 96 20 55S 21 27E
Gros C. 108 61 59N 113 32W
Grosa, Punta 25 39 6N 1 36E
Grósio 26 46 18N 10 17E
Grosne → 21 46 42N 4 56E
Gross Glockner 33 47 5N 12 40E
Gross Ottersleben 30 52 5N 11 33E
Grosse I. 106 42 8N 83 9W
Grossenbrode 30 54 21N 11 4E
Grossenhain 30 51 17N 13 32E
Grosseto 26 42 45N 11 7E
Groswater B. 103 54 20N 57 40W
Groton, Conn., U.S.A. 115 41 22N 72 12W
Groton, S.D., U.S.A. 118 45 27N 98 6W
Grottáglie 29 40 32N 17 25E
Grottaminarda 29 41 5N 15 4E
Grottammare 27 42 59N 13 52E
Grouard Mission 108 55 33N 116 9W
Grouin, Pointe du 18 48 43N 1 51W
Groundhog → 102 48 45N 82 58W
Grouse Creek 120 41 44N 113 57W
Grove City, Ohio, U.S.A. 117 39 53N 83 6W
Grove City, Pa., U.S.A. 114 41 10N 80 5W
Groveland 122 37 50N 120 14W
Grover City 123 35 7N 120 37W
Grover Hill 117 41 1N 84 29W
Groveton, N.H., U.S.A. 115 44 34N 71 30W
Groveton, Tex., U.S.A. 119 31 5N 95 4W
Grožnjan 27 45 22N 13 43E
Groznyy 39 43 20N 45 45E
Grudziądz 32 53 30N 18 47E
Gruissan 20 43 8N 3 7E
Grumo Áppula 29 41 2N 16 43E
Grums 10 59 22N 13 5E
Grünberg 30 50 37N 8 55E
Grundy Center 116 42 22N 92 45W
Grundy Prov. Pk. 106 45 58N 80 30W
Gruver 119 36 19N 101 20W
Gruyères 31 46 35N 7 4E
Gryazi 37 52 30N 39 58E
Gryazovets 37 58 50N 40 10E
Grycksbo 10 60 40N 15 29E
Grythyttan 10 59 41N 14 32E
Grytviken 143 53 50S 37 10W
Gstaad 31 46 28N 7 18E
Gua Musang 55 4 53N 101 58E
Guacanayabo, G. de 126 20 40N 77 20W
Guacara 134 10 14N 67 53W
Guachípas → 140 25 40S 65 30W
Guachiría → 134 5 27N 70 36W
Guadajoz → 23 37 50N 4 51W
Guadalajara, Mexico 124 20 40N 103 20W
Guadalajara, Spain 24 40 37N 3 12W
Guadalajara □ 24 40 47N 3 0W
Guadalcanal, Solomon Is. 68 9 32S 160 12E
Guadalcanal, Spain 23 38 5N 5 52W
Guadalén → 23 38 5N 3 32W
Guadales 140 34 30S 67 55W
Guadalete → 23 36 35N 6 13W
Guadalhorce → 23 36 41N 4 27W
Guadalimar → 25 38 5N 3 28W
Guadalmena → 25 38 19N 2 56W
Guadalmez → 23 38 46N 5 4W
Guadalope → 24 41 15N 0 3W
Guadalquivir → 23 36 47N 6 22W
Guadalupe, Brazil 138 6 44S 43 47W
Guadalupe, Mexico 123 32 4N 116 32W
Guadalupe, Spain 23 39 27N 5 17W
Guadalupe, U.S.A. 123 34 59N 120 33W
Guadalupe = Guadeloupe ■ 127 16 20N 61 40W
Guadalupe →, Mexico 123 32 6N 116 51W
Guadalupe →, U.S.A. 119 28 30N 96 53W
Guadalupe Bravos 124 31 20N 106 10W
Guadalupe de los Reyes 124 24 10N 106 0W
Guadalupe I. 67 21 20N 118 50W
Guadalupe Pk. 121 31 50N 105 30W
Guadalupe, Sierra de 23 39 28N 5 30W
Guadalupe y Calvo 124 26 6N 106 58W
Guadarrama, Sierra de 22 41 0N 4 0W
Guadeloupe ■ 127 16 20N 61 40W
Guadeloupe, La 105 45 57N 70 56W
Guadeloupe Passage 127 16 50N 62 15W
Guadiamar → 23 36 55N 6 24W
Guadiana → 23 37 14N 7 22W
Guadiana Menor → 25 37 56N 3 15W
Guadiaro → 23 36 17N 5 17W
Guadiato → 23 37 48N 5 5W
Guadiela → 24 40 22N 2 49W
Guadix 25 37 18N 3 11W
Guafo, Boca del 142 43 35S 74 0W
Guafo, I. 142 43 35S 74 50W
Guainía □ 134 2 30N 69 00W
Guainía → 134 2 1N 67 7W
Guaíra 141 24 5S 54 10W
Guaira, La 134 10 36N 66 56W
Guaitecas, Islas 142 44 0S 74 30W
Guajará-Mirim 137 10 50S 65 20W
Guajira □ 134 11 30N 72 30W
Guajira, La □ 134 11 30N 72 30W
Guajira, Pen. de la 134 12 0N 72 0W
Gualaceo 134 2 54S 78 47W
Gualan 126 15 8N 89 22W
Gualdo Tadino 27 43 14N 12 46E
Gualeguay 140 33 10S 59 14W
Gualeguaychú 140 33 3S 59 31W
Gualicho, Salina 142 40 25S 65 20W
Gualjaina 142 42 45S 70 30W
Guam 68 13 27N 144 45E
Guamá 138 1 37S 47 29W
Guamá → 138 1 29S 48 30W
Guamblin, I. 142 44 50S 75 0W
Guaminí 140 37 1S 62 28W
Guamote 134 1 56S 78 43W
Guampí, Sierra de 135 6 0N 65 35W
Guamúchil 124 25 25N 108 3W
Guan Xian 58 31 2N 103 38E
Guanabacoa 126 23 8N 82 18W
Guanacaste, Cordillera del 126 10 40N 85 4W
Guanaceví 124 25 40N 106 0W
Guanahani = San Salvador, I. 127 24 0N 74 40W
Guanajay 126 22 56N 82 42W
Guanajuato 124 21 0N 101 20W
Guanajuato □ 124 20 40N 101 20W
Guanambi 139 14 13S 42 47W
Guanare 134 8 42N 69 12W
Guanare → 134 8 13N 67 46W
Guandacol 140 29 30S 68 40W
Guane 126 22 10N 84 7W
Guang'an 58 30 28N 106 35E
Guangchang 59 26 50N 116 21E
Guangde 59 30 54N 119 25E
Guangdong □ 59 23 0N 113 0E
Guangfeng 59 28 20N 118 15E
Guanghan 58 30 58N 104 17E
Guanghua 59 32 22N 111 38E
Guangji 59 29 52N 115 30E
Guangling 60 39 47N 114 22E
Guangning 59 23 40N 112 22E
Guangrao 61 37 5N 118 25E
Guangshun 58 26 8N 106 21E
Guangwu 60 37 48N 105 57E
Guangxi Zhuangzu Zizhiqu □ 58 24 0N 109 0E
Guangyuan, Sichuan, China 58 32 26N 105 51E
Guangyuan, Sichuan, China 60 32 25N 105 50E
Guangze 59 27 30N 117 12E
Guangzhou 59 23 5N 113 10E
Guanhães 139 18 47S 42 57W
Guanipa → 135 9 56N 62 26W
Guanling 58 25 56N 105 35E
Guannan 61 34 8N 119 21E

Guanta	**135**	10 14N	64 36W
Guantánamo	**127**	20 10N	75 14W
Guantao	**60**	36 42N	115 25 E
Guanyang	**59**	25 30N	111 8 E
Guanyun	**61**	34 20N	119 18 E
Guapí	**134**	2 36N	77 54W
Guápiles	**126**	10 10N	83 46W
Guaporé →	**137**	11 55 S	65 4W
Guaqui	**136**	16 41 S	68 54W
Guara, Sierra de	**24**	42 19N	0 15W
Guarabira	**138**	6 51 S	35 29W
Guaranda	**134**	1 36 S	79 0W
Guarapari	**139**	20 40 S	40 30W
Guarapuava	**141**	25 20 S	51 30W
Guaratinguetá	**141**	22 49 S	45 9W
Guaratuba	**141**	25 53 S	48 38W
Guarda	**22**	40 32N	7 20W
Guarda □	**22**	40 40N	7 20W
Guardafui, C. = Asir, Ras	**45**	11 55N	51 16 E
Guardamar del Segura	**25**	38 5N	0 39W
Guardavalle	**29**	38 31N	16 30 E
Guardia, La	**22**	41 56N	8 52W
Guardiagrele	**27**	42 11N	14 11 E
Guardo	**22**	42 47N	4 50W
Guareña	**23**	38 51N	6 6W
Guareña →	**22**	41 29N	5 23W
Guaria □	**140**	25 45 S	56 30W
Guárico □	**134**	8 40N	66 35W
Guarrojo →	**134**	4 6N	70 42W
Guarujá	**141**	24 2 S	46 25W
Guarus	**139**	21 44 S	41 20W
Guasave	**124**	25 34N	108 27W
Guascama, Pta.	**134**	2 32N	8 24W
Guasdualito	**134**	7 15N	70 44W
Guasipati	**135**	7 28N	61 54W
Guasopa	**69**	9 12 S	152 56 E
Guastalla	**26**	44 55N	10 40 E
Guatemala	**126**	14 40N	90 22W
Guatemala ■	**126**	15 40N	90 30W
Guatire	**134**	10 28N	66 32W
Guaviare →	**134**	4 3N	67 44W
Guaxupé	**141**	21 10 S	47 5W
Guayabero →	**134**	2 36N	72 47W
Guayama	**127**	17 59N	66 7W
Guayaneco, Arch.	**142**	47 45 S	75 10W
Guayaquil	**134**	2 15 S	79 52W
Guayaquil, G. de	**134**	3 10 S	81 0W
Guayaramerín	**137**	10 48 S	65 23W
Guayas →	**134**	1 23N	74 50W
Guaymas	**124**	27 59N	110 54W
Guazhou	**59**	32 17N	119 21 E
Guba	**95**	10 38 S	26 27 E
Gubam	**69**	8 39 S	141 53 E
Gúbbio	**27**	43 20N	12 34 E
Gubio	**89**	12 30N	12 42 E
Gubkin	**37**	51 17N	37 32 E
Gudalur	**51**	11 30N	76 29 E
Gudata	**39**	43 7N	40 10 E
Gudenå	**11**	56 27N	9 40 E
Gudermes	**39**	43 24N	46 5 E
Gudhjem	**11**	55 12N	14 58 E
Gudiña, La	**22**	42 4N	7 8W
Gudivada	**51**	16 30N	81 3 E
Gudiyatam	**51**	12 57N	78 55 E
Gudur	**51**	14 12N	79 55 E
Guebwiller	**19**	47 55N	7 12 E
Guecho	**24**	43 21N	2 59W
Guéguen, L.	**104**	48 6N	77 13W
Guékédou	**88**	8 40N	10 5W
Guelma	**87**	36 25N	7 29 E
Guelph	**106**	43 35N	80 20W
Guelt es Stel	**86**	35 12N	3 1 E
Guelttara	**86**	29 23N	2 10W
Guemar	**87**	33 30N	6 49 E
Guéméné-Penfao	**18**	47 38N	1 50W
Guéméné-sur-Scorff	**18**	48 4N	3 13W
Guéné	**89**	11 44N	3 16 E
Güepi	**134**	0 9 S	75 10W
Guer	**18**	47 54N	2 8W
Güer Aike	**142**	51 39 S	69 35W
Guérande	**18**	47 20N	2 26W
Guerche, La	**18**	47 57N	1 16W
Guerche-sur-l'Aubois, La	**19**	46 58N	2 56 E
Guercif	**86**	34 14N	3 21W
Guéret	**20**	46 11N	1 51 E
Guérigny	**19**	47 6N	3 10 E
Guerneville	**122**	38 30N	123 0W
Guernica	**24**	43 19N	2 40W
Guernsey, Chan. Is.	**18**	49 30N	2 35W
Guernsey, U.S.A.	**118**	42 19N	104 45W
Guerrara, Oasis, Alg.	**87**	32 51N	4 22 E
Guerrara, Saoura, Alg.	**86**	28 5N	0 8W
Guerrero □	**125**	17 30N	100 0W
Guerzim	**86**	29 39N	1 40W
Guest I.	**143**	76 18 S	148 0W
Gueugnon	**21**	46 36N	4 4 E
Gueydan	**119**	30 3N	92 30W
Guglionesi	**29**	41 55N	14 54 E
Gui Jiang →	**59**	23 30N	111 15 E
Gui Xian	**58**	23 8N	109 35 E
Guia Lopes da Laguna	**141**	21 26 S	56 7W
Guibes	**96**	26 41 S	16 42 E
Guichi	**59**	30 39N	117 27 E
Guidimouni	**89**	13 42N	9 31 E
Guiding	**58**	26 34N	107 11 E
Guidong	**59**	26 7N	113 57 E
Guiglo	**88**	6 45N	7 30W
Guigues	**104**	47 28N	79 26W
Guijo de Coria	**22**	40 6N	6 28W
Guildford, Austral.	**74**	37 9 S	144 11 E
Guildford, U.K.	**13**	51 14N	0 34W
Guilford	**103**	45 12N	69 25W
Guilin	**59**	25 18N	110 15 E
Guillaumes	**21**	44 5N	6 52 E
Guillestre	**21**	44 39N	6 40 E
Guilvinec	**18**	47 48N	4 17W
Guimarães	**138**	2 9 S	44 42W
Guimarãis	**22**	41 28N	8 24W
Guimaras	**57**	10 35N	122 37 E
Guinda	**122**	38 50N	122 12W
Guinea ■	**88**	10 20N	10 0W
Guinea-Bissau ■	**88**	12 0N	15 0W
Guinea, Gulf of	**89**	3 0N	2 30 E
Güines	**126**	22 50N	82 0W
Guingamp	**18**	48 34N	3 10W
Guipavas	**18**	48 26N	4 29W
Guiping, Guangxi Zhuangzu, China	**59**	23 22N	110 4 E
Guiping, Guangxi Zhuangzu, China	**62**	23 21N	110 2 E
Guipúzcoa □	**24**	43 12N	2 15W
Guir, O. →	**86**	31 29N	2 17W
Guiratinga	**137**	16 21 S	53 45W
Güiria	**135**	10 32N	62 18W
Guiscard	**19**	49 40N	3 0 E
Guise	**19**	49 52N	3 35 E
Guitiriz	**22**	43 11N	7 50W
Guiuan	**57**	11 5N	125 55 E
Guixi	**59**	28 16N	117 15 E
Guiyang, Guizhou, China	**58**	26 32N	106 40 E
Guiyang, Hunan, China	**59**	25 46N	112 42 E
Guizhou □	**58**	27 0N	107 0 E
Gujan-Mestras	**20**	44 38N	1 4W
Gujarat □	**48**	23 20N	71 0 E
Gujiang	**59**	27 11N	114 47 E
Gujranwala	**48**	32 10N	74 12 E
Gujrat	**48**	32 40N	74 2 E
Gukovo	**39**	48 1N	39 58 E
Gular	**76**	31 19 S	148 27 E
Gulargambone	**76**	31 20 S	148 30 E
Gulbarga	**50**	17 20N	76 50 E
Gulbene	**36**	57 8N	26 52 E
Guledgud	**51**	16 3N	75 48 E
Gulfport	**119**	30 21N	89 3W
Gulgong	**76**	32 20 S	149 49 E
Gulin	**58**	28 1N	105 50 E
Gulistan	**48**	30 30N	66 35 E
Gull Lake	**109**	50 10N	108 29W
Gullringen	**11**	57 48N	15 44 E
Gulma	**89**	12 40N	4 23 E
Gulmarg	**49**	34 3N	74 25 E
Gulnam	**91**	6 55N	29 30 E
Gulshad	**40**	46 45N	74 25 E
Gulsvik	**10**	60 24N	9 38 E
Gulu	**94**	2 48N	32 17 E
Gulwe	**94**	6 30 S	36 25 E
Gulyaypole	**38**	47 45N	36 21 E
Gum Lake	**73**	32 42 S	143 9 E
Gumal →	**48**	31 40N	71 50 E
Gumbaz	**48**	30 2N	69 0 E
Gumel	**89**	12 39N	9 22 E
Gumiel de Hizán	**24**	41 46N	3 41W
Gumlu	**72**	19 53 S	147 41 E
Gumma □	**65**	36 30N	138 20 E
Gummersbach	**30**	51 2N	7 32 E
Gummi	**89**	12 4N	5 9 E
Gümüsane	**46**	40 30N	39 30 E
Gümüşhaciköy	**38**	40 50N	35 18 E
Gumzai	**57**	5 28 S	134 42 E
Guna	**48**	24 40N	77 19 E
Guna Mt.	**91**	11 50N	37 40 E
Gunbower	**74**	35 59 S	144 24 E
Gundagai	**76**	35 3 S	148 6 E
Gundaroo	**76**	35 2 S	149 16 E
Gundelfingen	**31**	48 33N	10 22 E
Gundih	**57**	7 10 S	110 56 E
Gundlakamma →	**51**	15 30N	80 15 E
Gundy	**77**	31 59 S	151 0 E
Gungal	**76**	32 17 S	150 32 E
Gungi	**91**	10 20N	38 3 E
Gungu	**92**	5 43 S	19 20 E
Gunisao →	**109**	53 56N	97 53W
Gunisao L.	**109**	53 33N	96 15W
Gunnedah	**77**	30 59 S	150 15 E
Gunning	**76**	34 47 S	149 14 E
Gunningbar Cr. →	**76**	31 14 S	147 6 E
Gunnison, Colo., U.S.A.	**121**	38 32N	106 56W
Gunnison, Utah, U.S.A.	**120**	39 11N	111 48W
Gunnison →	**121**	39 3N	108 30W
Guntakal	**51**	15 11N	77 27 E
Guntersville	**113**	34 18N	86 16W
Guntong	**55**	4 36N	101 3 E
Guntur	**51**	16 23N	80 30 E
Gunung-Sitoli	**56**	1 15N	97 30 E
Gunungapi	**57**	6 45 S	126 30 E
Gunupur	**50**	19 5N	83 50 E
Günz →	**31**	48 27N	10 16 E
Gunza	**92**	10 50 S	13 50 E
Günzburg	**31**	48 27N	10 16 E
Gunzenhausen	**31**	49 6N	10 45 E
Guo He →	**59**	32 59N	117 10 E
Guoyang	**60**	33 32N	116 12 E
Gupis	**49**	36 15N	73 20 E
Gura	**48**	25 12N	71 39 E
Gura Humorului	**34**	47 35N	25 53 E
Gurag	**91**	8 20N	38 20 E
Gürchañ	**46**	34 55N	49 25 E
Gurdaspur	**48**	32 5N	75 31 E
Gurdon	**119**	33 55N	93 10W
Gurdzhaani	**39**	41 43N	45 52 E
Gurgaon	**48**	28 27N	77 1 E
Gurguéia →	**138**	6 50 S	43 24W
Guri Dam	**135**	7 50N	62 52W
Gurk →	**33**	46 35N	14 31 E
Gurkha	**49**	28 5N	84 40 E
Gurley	**77**	29 45 S	149 48 E
Gurnee	**117**	42 22N	87 55W
Gurun	**55**	5 49N	100 27 E
Gurupá	**138**	1 25 S	51 35W
Gurupá, I. Grande de	**135**	1 25 S	51 45W
Gurupi	**139**	11 43 S	49 4W
Gurupi →	**138**	1 13 S	46 6W
Gurupi, Serra do	**138**	5 0 S	47 30W
Guryev	**39**	47 5N	52 0 E
Gus	**94**	3 2N	36 57 E
Gus-Khrustalnyy	**37**	55 42N	40 44 E
Gusau	**89**	12 12N	6 40 E
Gusev	**36**	54 35N	22 10 E
Gushan	**61**	39 50N	123 35 E
Gushi	**59**	32 11N	115 41 E
Gushiago	**89**	9 55N	0 15W
Gusinje	**33**	42 35N	19 50 E
Gúspini	**28**	39 32N	8 38 E
Gusselby	**10**	59 38N	15 14 E
Gustanj	**27**	46 36N	14 49 E
Gustine	**122**	37 14N	121 0 E
Güstrow	**30**	53 47N	12 12 E
Gusum	**11**	58 16N	16 30 E
Gütersloh	**30**	51 54N	8 25 E
Gutha	**79**	28 58 S	115 55 E
Guthalongra	**72**	19 52 S	147 50 E
Guthega Dam	**75**	36 20 S	148 27 E
Guthrie	**119**	35 55N	97 30W
Guthrie Center	**116**	41 41N	94 30W
Gutian	**59**	26 32N	118 43 E
Gutiérrez	**137**	19 25 S	63 34W
Gutta Tifi	**91**	6 12N	36 55 E
Guttenberg	**116**	42 46N	91 10W
Guyana ■	**135**	5 0N	59 0W
Guyang	**60**	41 0N	110 5 E
Guyenne	**20**	44 30N	0 40 E
Guymon	**119**	36 45N	101 30W
Guyra	**77**	30 15 S	151 40 E
Guyuan, Hebei, China	**60**	41 37N	115 40 E
Guyuan, Ningxia Huizu, China	**60**	36 0N	106 20 E
Guzhang	**58**	28 42N	109 58 E
Guzhen	**59**	33 22N	117 18 E
Guzmán, Laguna de	**124**	31 25N	107 25W
Gwa	**52**	17 36N	94 34 E
Gwaai	**95**	19 15 S	27 45 E
Gwabegar	**77**	30 31 S	149 0 E
Gwadabawa	**89**	13 28N	5 15 E
Gwädar	**47**	25 10N	62 18 E
Gwagwada	**89**	10 15N	7 15 E
Gwalia	**79**	28 54 S	121 20 E
Gwalior	**48**	26 12N	78 10 E
Gwanda	**95**	20 55 S	29 0 E
Gwandu	**89**	12 30N	4 41 E
Gwane	**94**	4 45N	25 48 E
Gwaram	**89**	10 15N	10 25 E
Gwarzo	**89**	12 20N	8 55 E
Gweebarra B.	**15**	54 52N	8 21W
Gweedore	**15**	55 4N	8 15W
Gwelo	**95**	19 28 S	29 45 E
Gwent □	**13**	51 45N	2 55W
Gweta	**96**	20 12 S	25 17 E
Gwi	**89**	9 0N	7 10 E
Gwinn	**112**	46 15N	87 29W
Gwio Kura	**89**	12 40N	11 2 E
Gwol	**88**	10 58N	1 59W
Gwoza	**89**	11 5N	13 40 E
Gwydir →	**77**	29 27 S	149 48 E
Gwynedd □	**12**	53 0N	4 0W
Gyaring Hu	**62**	34 50N	97 40 E
Gydanskiy P-ov.	**40**	70 0N	78 0 E
Gympie	**73**	26 11 S	152 38 E
Gyobingauk	**52**	18 13N	95 39 E
Gyoda	**65**	36 10N	139 30 E
Gyoma	**33**	46 56N	20 50 E
Gyöngyös	**33**	47 48N	20 0 E
Györ	**33**	47 41N	17 40 E
Gypsum Pt.	**108**	61 53N	114 35W
Gypsumville	**109**	51 45N	98 40W
Gyttorp	**10**	59 31N	14 58 E
Gyula	**33**	46 38N	21 17 E
Gzhatsk = Gagarin	**36**	55 30N	35 0 E

H

Ha' Arava	**44**	31 10N	35 20 E
Ha Coi	**54**	21 26N	107 46 E
Ha Dong	**54**	20 58N	105 46 E
Ha Giang	**54**	22 50N	104 59 E
Ha Tien	**55**	10 23N	104 29 E
Ha Tinh	**54**	18 20N	105 54 E
Ha Trung	**54**	20 0N	105 50 E
Ha'afeva	**68**	19 57 S	174 43W
Haag	**31**	48 11N	12 12 E
Ha'ano	**68**	19 41 S	174 18W
Ha'apai Group	**68**	19 47 S	174 27W
Haapamäki	**8**	62 18N	24 28 E
Haapsalu	**36**	58 56N	23 30 E
Haarlem	**16**	52 23N	4 39 E
Haast	**81**	43 51 S	169 1 E
Haast →	**81**	43 50 S	169 2 E
Haast P.	**81**	44 6 S	169 21 E
Hab Nadi Chauki	**48**	25 0N	66 50 E
Haba	**46**	27 10N	47 0 E
Habana, La	**126**	23 8N	82 22W
Habaswein	**94**	1 2N	39 30 E
Habay	**108**	58 50N	118 44W
Habiganj	**52**	24 24N	91 30 E
Hablingbo	**11**	57 12N	18 16 E
Habo	**11**	57 55N	14 6 E
Hachenburg	**30**	50 40N	7 49 E
Hachijō-Jima	**65**	33 5N	139 45 E
Hachinohe	**63**	40 30N	141 29 E
Hachiōji	**65**	35 40N	139 20 E
Hachŏn	**61**	41 29N	129 2 E
Hadali	**48**	32 16N	72 11 E
Hadarba, Ras	**90**	22 4N	36 51 E
Hadd, Ras al	**47**	22 35N	59 50 E
Haddington	**14**	55 57N	2 48W
Haddon Rig	**76**	31 27 S	147 52 E
Hadejia	**89**	12 30N	10 5 E
Hadejia →	**89**	12 50N	10 51 E
Haden	**73**	27 13 S	151 54 E
Hadera	**44**	32 27N	34 55 E
Haderslev	**11**	55 15N	9 30 E
Hadhra	**90**	20 10N	41 5 E
Hadhramaut = Hadramawt	**45**	15 30N	49 30 E
Hadibu	**45**	12 35N	54 2 E
Hadjeb el Aïoun	**87**	35 21N	9 32 E
Hadong	**61**	35 5N	127 44 E
Hadramawt	**45**	15 30N	49 30 E
Hadrians Wall	**12**	55 0N	2 30W
Hadsten	**11**	56 19N	10 3 E
Hadsund	**11**	56 44N	10 8 E
Haeju	**61**	38 3N	125 45 E
Haenam	**61**	34 34N	126 35 E
Haerhpin = Harbin	**61**	45 48N	126 40 E
Hafar al Bātin	**46**	28 25N	46 0 E
Hafizabad	**48**	32 5N	73 40 E
Haflong	**52**	25 10N	93 5 E
Hafnarfjörður	**8**	64 4N	21 57W
Haft-Gel	**46**	31 30N	49 32 E
Hafun	**45**	10 25N	51 26 E
Hafun, Ras	**45**	10 29N	51 30 E
Hagalil	**44**	32 53N	35 18 E
Hagar Banga	**85**	10 40N	22 45 E
Hagari →	**51**	15 40N	77 0 E
Hagen	**30**	51 21N	7 29 E
Hagenow	**30**	53 25N	11 10 E
Hagerman	**119**	33 5N	104 22W
Hagerstown, Ind., U.S.A.	**117**	39 55N	85 10W
Hagerstown, Md., U.S.A.	**112**	39 39N	77 46W
Hagersville	**106**	42 58N	80 3W
Hagetmau	**20**	43 39N	0 37W
Hagfors	**10**	60 3N	13 45 E
Häggenås	**10**	63 24N	14 55 E
Hagi, Iceland	**8**	65 28N	23 25W
Hagi, Japan	**64**	34 30N	131 22 E
Hagolan	**44**	33 0N	36 45 E
Hags Hd.	**15**	52 57N	9 30W
Hague, C. de la	**18**	49 44N	1 56W
Hague, The = 's-Gravenhage	**16**	52 7N	4 17 E
Haguenau	**19**	48 49N	7 47 E
Hai □	**94**	3 10 S	37 10 E
Hai Duong	**54**	20 56N	106 19 E
Hai'an, Guangdong, China	**59**	20 18N	110 11 E
Hai'an, Jiangsu, China	**59**	32 37N	120 27 E

Haicheng, Fujian, China	**59**	24 23N	117 48 E
Haicheng, Liaoning, China	**61**	40 50N	122 45 E
Haidar Khel	**48**	33 58N	68 38 E
Haifa	**44**	32 46N	35 0 E
Haifeng	**59**	22 58N	115 10 E
Haig	**79**	30 55S	126 10 E
Haiger	**30**	50 44N	8 12 E
Haikang	**59**	20 52N	110 8 E
Haikou	**62**	20 1N	110 16 E
Hā'il	**46**	27 28N	41 45 E
Hailakandi	**52**	24 42N	92 34 E
Hailar	**62**	49 10N	119 38 E
Hailey	**120**	43 30N	114 15W
Haileybury	**102**	47 30N	79 38W
Hailin	**61**	44 37N	129 30 E
Hailing Dao	**59**	21 35N	111 47 E
Hailong	**61**	42 32N	125 40 E
Hailun	**62**	47 28N	126 50 E
Haimen, Guangdong, China	**59**	23 15N	116 38 E
Haimen, Jiangsu, China	**59**	31 52N	121 10 E
Haimen, Zhejiang, China	**59**	28 40N	121 24 E
Hainan Dao	**62**	19 0N	109 30 E
Hainan	**54**	19 0N	110 0 E
Hainaut □	**16**	50 30N	4 0 E
Haines	**120**	44 51N	117 59W
Haines City	**113**	28 6N	81 35W
Haines Junction	**108**	60 45N	137 30W
Haining	**59**	30 28N	120 40 E
Haiphong	**54**	20 47N	106 41 E
Haiti ■	**127**	19 0N	72 30W
Haiya Junction	**90**	18 20N	36 21 E
Haiyan	**59**	30 28N	120 58 E
Haiyang	**61**	36 47N	121 9 E
Haiyuan, Guangxi, China	**58**	22 8N	107 35 E
Haiyuan, Ningxia Huizu, China	**60**	36 35N	105 52 E
Haizhou	**61**	34 37N	119 7 E
Haizhou Wan	**61**	34 50N	119 20 E
Haja	**57**	3 19S	129 37 E
Hajar, Jabal	**46**	26 5N	39 10 E
Hajdúböszörmény	**33**	47 40N	21 30 E
Hajdúszobaszló	**33**	47 27N	21 22 E
Hajiganj	**52**	23 15N	90 50 E
Hajipur	**49**	25 45N	85 13 E
Hajr	**47**	24 0N	56 34 E
Haka	**52**	22 39N	93 37 E
Hakansson, Mts.	**95**	8 40S	25 45 E
Håkantorp	**11**	58 18N	12 55 E
Hakataramea	**81**	44 43S	170 30 E
Hakken-Zan	**65**	34 10N	135 54 E
Hakodate	**63**	41 45N	140 44 E
Hakota	**65**	36 5N	140 30 E
Haku-San	**65**	36 9N	136 46 E
Hakun	**52**	26 46N	95 42 E
Halab = Aleppo	**46**	36 10N	37 15 E
Halabjah	**46**	35 10N	45 58 E
Halaib	**90**	22 12N	36 30 E
Halbe	**90**	19 40N	42 15 E
Halberstadt	**30**	51 53N	11 2 E
Halcombe	**80**	40 8S	175 30 E
Halcyon, Mt.	**57**	13 0N	121 30 E
Halden	**10**	59 9N	11 23 E
Haldensleben	**30**	52 17N	11 30 E
Haldwani-cum-Kathgodam	**49**	29 31N	79 30 E
Hale, Mich., U.S.A.	**106**	44 18N	83 48W
Hale, Mo., U.S.A.	**116**	39 36N	93 20W
Hale →	**72**	24 56S	135 53 E
Haleakala Crater	**110**	20 43N	156 12W
Haleyville	**113**	34 15N	87 40W
Half Assini	**88**	5 1N	2 50W
Halfmoon Bay	**81**	46 50S	168 5 E
Halfway	**120**	44 56N	117 8W
Halfway →	**108**	56 12N	121 32W
Halfway Creek	**77**	29 54S	153 5 E
Halhul	**44**	31 35N	35 7 E
Hali, Si. Arab.	**90**	18 40N	41 15 E
Hali, Yemen	**45**	18 30N	41 30 E
Haliburton	**107**	45 3N	78 30W
Halifax, Austral.	**72**	18 32S	146 22 E
Halifax, Can.	**103**	44 38N	63 35W
Halifax, U.K.	**12**	53 43N	1 51W
Halifax B.	**72**	18 50S	147 0 E
Halifax I.	**96**	26 38S	15 4 E
Halil →	**47**	27 40N	58 30 E
Hall, Austral.	**76**	35 12S	149 1 E
Hall, Austria	**31**	47 17N	11 30 E
Hall Beach	**101**	68 46N	81 12W
Hall Pt.	**78**	15 40S	124 23 E
Hallabro	**11**	56 22N	15 5 E
Hallands län □	**11**	56 50N	12 50 E
Hallands Väderö	**11**	56 27N	12 34 E
Hallandsås	**11**	56 22N	13 0 E
Halle, Belg.	**16**	50 44N	4 13 E
Halle, Halle, Ger.	**30**	51 29N	12 0 E
Halle, Nordrhein-Westfalen, Ger.	**30**	52 4N	8 20 E
Halle □	**30**	51 28N	11 58 E
Hällefors	**10**	59 47N	14 31 E
Hallefors	**11**	59 46N	14 30 E
Hallein	**33**	47 40N	13 5 E
Hällekis	**11**	58 38N	13 27 E
Hallett	**73**	33 25S	138 55 E
Hallettsville	**119**	29 28N	96 57W
Hällevadsholm	**11**	58 35N	11 33 E
Halley Bay	**143**	75 31S	26 36W
Hallia →	**50**	16 55N	79 20 E
Halliday	**118**	47 20N	102 25W
Halliday L.	**109**	61 21N	108 56W
Hallidays Point	**77**	32 2S	152 32 E
Hallim	**61**	33 24N	126 15 E
Hällnäs	**8**	64 19N	19 36 E
Hallock	**109**	48 47N	97 0W
Halls Creek	**78**	18 16S	127 38 E
Halls Gap	**74**	37 8S	142 34 E
Hallsberg	**10**	59 5N	15 7 E
Hallstahammar	**10**	59 38N	16 15 E
Hallstavik	**10**	60 5N	18 37 E
Hallstead	**115**	41 56N	75 45W
Halmahera	**57**	0 40N	128 0 E
Halmeu	**34**	47 57N	23 2 E
Halmstad	**11**	56 41N	12 52 E
Halq el Oued	**87**	36 53N	10 18 E
Hals	**11**	56 59N	10 18 E
Halsafjorden	**10**	63 5N	8 10 E
Hälsingborg = Helsingborg	**11**	56 3N	12 42 E
Halstad	**118**	47 21N	96 50W
Haltdalen	**10**	62 56N	11 8 E
Haltern	**30**	51 44N	7 10 E
Halul	**47**	25 40N	52 40 E
Ham	**19**	49 45N	3 4 E
Ham Tan	**55**	10 40N	107 45 E
Ham Yen	**54**	22 4N	105 3 E
Hamā	**46**	35 5N	36 40 E
Hamab	**96**	28 7S	19 16 E
Hamad	**91**	15 20N	33 32 E
Hamada	**64**	34 56N	132 4 E
Hamadān	**46**	34 52N	48 32 E
Hamadān □	**46**	35 0N	49 0 E
Hamadia	**86**	35 28N	1 57 E
Hamakita	**65**	34 45N	137 47 E
Hamamatsu	**65**	34 45N	137 45 E
Hamar	**10**	60 48N	11 7 E
Hamarøy	**8**	68 5N	15 38 E
Hamâta, Gebel	**90**	24 17N	35 0 E
Hamber Prov. Park	**108**	52 20N	118 0W
Hamburg, Ger.	**30**	53 32N	9 59 E
Hamburg, Ark., U.S.A.	**119**	33 15N	91 47W
Hamburg, Iowa, U.S.A.	**118**	40 37N	95 38W
Hamburg, N.Y., U.S.A.	**114**	42 44N	78 50W
Hamburg, Pa., U.S.A.	**115**	40 33N	76 0W
Hamburg □	**30**	53 30N	10 0 E
Hamden	**115**	41 21N	72 56W
Hamdh, W. →	**90**	24 55N	36 20 E
Hämeen lääni □	**9**	61 24N	24 10 E
Hämeenlinna	**8**	61 0N	24 28 E
Hamélé	**88**	10 56N	2 45W
Hamelin Pool	**79**	26 22S	114 20 E
Hamelin Pool Bay	**79**	26 10S	114 5 E
Hameln	**30**	52 7N	9 24 E
Hamer Koke	**91**	5 15N	36 45 E
Hamersley Ra.	**78**	22 0S	117 45 E
Hamhung	**61**	39 54N	127 30 E
Hami	**62**	42 55N	93 25 E
Hamilton, Austral.	**74**	37 45S	142 2 E
Hamilton, Can.	**106**	43 15N	79 50W
Hamilton, N.Z.	**80**	37 47S	175 19 E
Hamilton, U.K.	**14**	55 47N	4 2W
Hamilton, Ill., U.S.A.	**116**	40 24N	91 21W
Hamilton, Ind., U.S.A.	**117**	41 33N	84 56W
Hamilton, Mo., U.S.A.	**116**	39 45N	93 59W
Hamilton, Mo., U.S.A.	**118**	39 45N	93 59W
Hamilton, Mont., U.S.A.	**120**	46 20N	114 6W
Hamilton, N.Y., U.S.A.	**115**	42 49N	75 31W
Hamilton, Ohio, U.S.A.	**117**	39 20N	84 35W
Hamilton, Tex., U.S.A.	**119**	31 40N	98 5W
Hamilton →	**72**	23 30S	139 47 E
Hamilton City	**122**	39 45N	122 1W
Hamilton Hotel	**72**	22 45S	140 40 E
Hamilton Inlet	**103**	54 0N	57 30W
Hamiota	**109**	50 11N	100 38W
Hamlet	**113**	34 56N	79 40W
Hamley Bridge	**73**	34 17S	138 35 E
Hamlin, N.Y., U.S.A.	**114**	43 17N	77 55W
Hamlin, Tex., U.S.A.	**119**	32 58N	100 8W
Hamm	**30**	51 40N	7 49 E
Hammam bou Hadjar	**86**	35 23N	0 58W
Hammamet	**87**	36 24N	10 38 E
Hammamet, G. de	**87**	36 10N	10 48 E
Hammarstrand	**10**	63 7N	16 20 E
Hammel	**11**	56 16N	9 52 E
Hammelburg	**31**	50 7N	9 54 E
Hammeren	**11**	55 18N	14 47 E
Hammerfest	**8**	70 39N	23 41 E
Hammond, Ill., U.S.A.	**117**	39 48N	88 36W
Hammond, Ind., U.S.A.	**117**	41 40N	87 30W
Hammond, La., U.S.A.	**119**	30 32N	90 30W
Hammond B.	**106**	45 31N	84 0W
Hammonton	**112**	39 40N	74 47W
Hamneda	**11**	56 41N	13 51 E
Hamoyet, Jebel	**90**	17 33N	38 2 E
Hampden	**81**	45 18S	170 50 E
Hampshire □	**13**	51 3N	1 20W
Hampshire Downs	**13**	51 10N	1 10W
Hampton, Austral.	**76**	33 39S	150 2 E
Hampton, Can.	**107**	43 58N	78 45W
Hampton, Ark., U.S.A.	**119**	33 35N	92 29W
Hampton, Iowa, U.S.A.	**116**	42 42N	93 12W
Hampton, N.H., U.S.A.	**115**	42 56N	70 48W
Hampton, S.C., U.S.A.	**113**	32 52N	81 2W
Hampton, Va., U.S.A.	**112**	37 4N	76 18W
Hampton Tableland	**79**	32 0S	127 0 E
Hamra	**46**	24 2N	38 55 E
Hamrat esh Sheykh	**91**	14 38N	27 55 E
Hamyang	**61**	35 32N	127 42 E
Han Jiang →	**59**	23 25N	116 40 E
Han Shui →	**59**	30 35N	114 18 E
Hana	**110**	20 45N	155 59W
Hanak	**90**	25 32N	37 0 E
Hanamaki	**63**	39 23N	141 7 E
Hanang	**94**	4 30S	35 25 E
Hanau	**31**	50 8N	8 56 E
Hanbogd	**60**	43 11N	107 10 E
Hancheng	**60**	35 31N	110 25 E
Hanchuan	**59**	30 40N	113 50 E
Hancock, Mich., U.S.A.	**118**	47 10N	88 40W
Hancock, Minn., U.S.A.	**118**	45 26N	95 46W
Hancock, Pa., U.S.A.	**115**	41 57N	75 19W
Handa, Japan	**65**	34 53N	137 0 E
Handa, Somalia	**45**	10 37N	51 2 E
Handan	**60**	36 35N	114 28 E
Handen	**10**	59 12N	18 12 E
Handeni	**94**	5 25S	38 2 E
Handeni □	**94**	5 30S	38 0 E
Handub	**90**	19 15N	37 16 E
Handwara	**49**	34 21N	74 20 E
Hanegev	**44**	30 50N	35 0 E
Haney	**108**	49 12N	122 40W
Hanford	**122**	36 23N	119 39W
Hang Chat	**54**	18 20N	99 21 E
Hang Dong	**54**	18 41N	98 55 E
Hangang →	**61**	37 50N	126 30 E
Hangayn Nuruu	**62**	47 30N	100 0 E
Hangchou = Hangzhou	**59**	30 18N	120 11 E
Hanggin Houqi	**60**	40 58N	107 4 E
Hanggin Qi	**60**	39 52N	108 50 E
Hangklip, K.	**96**	34 26S	18 48 E
Hangö	**9**	59 50N	22 57 E
Hangu	**61**	39 18N	117 53 E
Hangzhou	**59**	30 18N	120 11 E
Hangzhou Wan, Zhejiang, China	**59**	30 15N	120 40 E
Hangzhou Wan, Zhejiang, China	**62**	30 15N	120 45 E
Hanhongor	**60**	43 55N	104 28 E
Hanish J.	**45**	13 45N	42 46 E
Hanita	**44**	33 5N	35 10 E
Hanjiang	**59**	25 26N	119 6 E
Hankinson	**118**	46 9N	96 58W
Hanko	**9**	59 59N	22 57 E
Hankou	**59**	30 35N	114 30 E
Hanksville	**121**	38 19N	110 45W
Hanle	**49**	32 42N	79 4 E
Hanmer, Can.	**106**	46 39N	80 56W
Hanmer, N.Z.	**81**	42 32S	172 50 E
Hann →	**78**	17 26S	126 17 E
Hann, Mt.	**78**	16 0S	126 0 E
Hanna	**108**	51 40N	111 54W
Hannaford	**118**	47 23N	98 11W
Hannah	**118**	48 58N	98 42W
Hannah B.	**102**	51 40N	80 0W
Hannahs Bridge	**77**	31 55S	149 41 E
Hannibal	**116**	39 42N	91 22W
Hannik	**90**	18 12N	32 20 E
Hannover	**30**	52 23N	9 43 E
Hanö	**11**	56 2N	14 50 E
Hanöbukten	**11**	55 35N	14 30 E
Hanoi	**54**	21 5N	105 55 E
Hanover, Can.	**106**	44 9N	81 2W
Hanover, S. Afr.	**96**	31 4S	24 29 E
Hanover, Ind., U.S.A.	**117**	38 43N	85 28W
Hanover, N.H., U.S.A.	**115**	43 43N	72 17W
Hanover, Ohio, U.S.A.	**114**	40 5N	82 17W
Hanover, Pa., U.S.A.	**112**	39 46N	76 59W
Hanover = Hannover	**30**	52 23N	9 43 E
Hanover, I.	**142**	51 0S	74 50W
Hanpan, C.	**69**	5 0S	154 35 E
Hans Meyer Ra.	**69**	4 20S	152 55 E
Hanshou	**59**	28 56N	111 50 E
Hansi	**48**	29 10N	75 57 E
Hansjö	**10**	61 10N	14 40 E
Hanson, L.	**73**	31 0S	136 15 E
Hanyang	**59**	30 35N	114 2 E
Hanyin	**58**	32 54N	108 28 E
Hanyū	**65**	36 10N	139 32 E
Hanyuan	**58**	29 21N	102 40 E
Hanzhong	**58**	33 10N	107 1 E
Hanzhuang	**61**	34 33N	117 23 E
Haoxue	**59**	30 3N	112 24 E
Haparanda	**8**	65 52N	24 8 E
Happy	**119**	34 47N	101 50W
Happy Camp	**120**	41 52N	123 22W
Happy Valley	**103**	53 15N	60 20W
Hapsu	**61**	41 13N	128 51 E
Hapur	**48**	28 45N	77 45 E
Haql	**46**	29 10N	35 0 E
Haquira	**136**	14 14S	72 12W
Har	**57**	5 16S	133 14 E
Har-Ayrag	**60**	45 47N	109 16 E
Har Hu	**62**	38 20N	97 38 E
Har Us Nuur	**62**	48 0N	92 0 E
Har Yehuda	**44**	31 35N	34 57 E
Harad	**46**	24 22N	49 0 E
Haradera	**45**	4 33N	47 38 E
Haraisan Plateau	**46**	23 0N	47 40 E
Harat	**91**	16 5N	39 26 E
Haraz-Djombo	**85**	14 20N	19 12 E
Haraze-Mangueigne	**85**	9 57N	20 48 E
Harbin	**61**	45 48N	126 40 E
Harboør	**11**	56 38N	8 10 E
Harbor Beach	**106**	43 50N	82 38W
Harbor Springs	**106**	45 28N	85 0W
Harbour Breton	**103**	47 29N	55 50W
Harbour Grace	**103**	47 40N	53 22W
Harburg	**30**	53 27N	9 58 E
Hårby	**11**	55 13N	10 7 E
Harcourt	**72**	24 17S	149 55 E
Harda	**48**	22 27N	77 5 E
Hardangerfjorden	**9**	60 15N	6 0 E
Hardap Dam	**96**	24 32S	17 50 E
Harden	**76**	34 32S	148 24 E
Hardenberg	**16**	52 34N	6 37 E
Harderwijk	**16**	52 21N	5 38 E
Hardey →	**78**	22 45S	116 8 E
Hardin, Ill., U.S.A.	**116**	39 9N	90 37W
Hardin, Mont., U.S.A.	**120**	45 44N	107 35W
Harding	**97**	30 35S	29 55 E
Harding Ra.	**78**	16 17S	124 55 E
Hardinsburg	**117**	37 47N	86 28W
Hardisty	**108**	52 40N	111 18W
Hardman	**120**	45 12N	119 40W
Hardoi	**49**	27 26N	80 6 E
Hardwar	**48**	29 58N	78 9 E
Hardwick	**115**	44 30N	72 20W
Hardy	**119**	36 20N	91 30W
Hardy, Pen.	**142**	55 30S	68 20W
Hare B.	**103**	51 15N	55 45W
Hare Gilboa	**44**	32 31N	35 25 E
Hare Meron	**44**	32 59N	35 24 E
Haren	**30**	52 47N	7 18 E
Harer	**91**	9 20N	42 8 E
Harer □	**91**	7 12N	42 0 E
Hareto	**91**	9 23N	37 6 E
Harfleur	**18**	49 30N	0 10 E
Hargeisa	**45**	9 30N	44 2 E
Hargraves	**76**	32 46S	149 28 E
Hargshamn	**10**	60 12N	18 30 E
Hari →, Afghan.	**47**	34 20N	62 30 E
Hari →, Indon.	**56**	1 16S	104 5 E
Haricha, Hamada el	**86**	22 40N	3 15W
Harihar	**51**	14 32N	75 44 E
Harima-Nada	**64**	34 30N	134 35 E
Haringhata →	**52**	22 0N	89 58 E
Haripad	**51**	9 14N	76 28 E
Harirūd	**47**	35 0N	61 0 E
Harkat	**90**	20 25N	39 40 E
Harlan, Iowa, U.S.A.	**118**	41 37N	95 20W
Harlan, Tenn., U.S.A.	**113**	36 50N	83 20W
Harlech	**12**	52 52N	4 7W
Harlem	**120**	48 29N	108 47W
Harlingen, Neth.	**16**	53 11N	5 25 E
Harlingen, U.S.A.	**119**	26 20N	97 50W
Harlowton	**120**	46 30N	109 54W
Harmånger	**10**	61 55N	17 20 E
Harmil	**91**	16 30N	40 10 E
Harney Basin	**120**	43 30N	119 0W
Harney L.	**120**	43 0N	119 0W
Harney Pk.	**118**	43 52N	103 33W

Name	Map	Lat.	Long.
Härnön	**10**	62 36N	18 0 E
Harnösand	**10**	62 38N	17 55 E
Haro	**24**	42 35N	2 55W
Haro, C.	**124**	27 50N	110 55W
Harp L.	**103**	55 5N	61 50W
Harpanahalli	**51**	14 47N	76 2 E
Harpe, La	**116**	40 30N	91 0W
Harper	**88**	4 25N	7 43W
Harplinge	**11**	56 45N	12 45 E
Harrand	**48**	29 28N	70 3 E
Harrat al Kishb	**46**	22 30N	40 15 E
Harrat al Uwairidh	**46**	26 50N	38 0 E
Harrat Khaibar	**90**	25 45N	40 0 E
Harrat Nawāṣīf	**90**	21 30N	42 0 E
Harricana →	**104**	50 56N	79 32W
Harriman	**113**	36 0N	84 35W
Harrington Harbour	**103**	50 31N	59 30W
Harris	**14**	57 50N	6 55W
Harris L.	**73**	31 10S	135 10 E
Harris Mts.	**81**	44 49S	168 49 E
Harris Pt.	**106**	43 6N	82 9W
Harris, Sd. of	**14**	57 44N	7 6W
Harrisburg, Ill., U.S.A.	**119**	37 42N	88 30W
Harrisburg, Nebr., U.S.A.	**118**	41 36N	103 46W
Harrisburg, Oreg., U.S.A.	**120**	44 16N	123 10W
Harrisburg, Pa., U.S.A.	**114**	40 18N	76 52W
Harrismith	**97**	28 15S	29 8 E
Harrison, Ark., U.S.A.	**119**	36 10N	93 4W
Harrison, Idaho, U.S.A.	**120**	47 30N	116 51W
Harrison, Mich., U.S.A.	**106**	44 1N	84 48W
Harrison, Nebr., U.S.A.	**118**	42 42N	103 52W
Harrison B.	**100**	70 25N	151 30W
Harrison, C.	**103**	54 55N	57 55W
Harrison L.	**108**	49 33N	121 50W
Harrisonburg	**112**	38 28N	78 52W
Harrisonville	**116**	38 39N	94 21W
Harriston	**106**	43 57N	80 53W
Harrisville	**106**	44 40N	83 19W
Harrodsburg, Ind., U.S.A.	**117**	39 1N	86 33W
Harrodsburg, Ky., U.S.A.	**117**	37 46N	84 51W
Harrogate	**12**	53 59N	1 32W
Harrow, Austral.	**74**	37 9S	141 35 E
Harrow, Can.	**106**	42 2N	82 55W
Harrow, U.K.	**13**	51 35N	0 15W
Harrowsmith	**107**	44 24N	76 40W
Harry S. Truman Res.	**116**	38 14N	93 30W
Harsefeld	**30**	53 26N	9 31 E
Harstad	**8**	68 48N	16 30 E
Hart	**112**	43 42N	86 21W
Hart, L.	**73**	31 10S	136 25 E
Hartbees →	**96**	28 45S	20 32 E
Hartberg	**33**	47 17N	15 58 E
Hartford, Conn., U.S.A.	**115**	41 47N	72 41W
Hartford, Ky., U.S.A.	**112**	37 26N	86 50W
Hartford, Mich., U.S.A.	**117**	42 13N	86 10W
Hartford, S.D., U.S.A.	**118**	43 40N	96 58W
Hartford, Wis., U.S.A.	**118**	43 18N	88 25W
Hartford City	**117**	40 22N	85 20W
Hartland, Can.	**103**	46 20N	67 32W
Hartland, U.S.A.	**117**	43 6N	88 21W
Hartland Pt.	**13**	51 2N	4 32W
Hartlepool	**12**	54 42N	1 11W
Hartley	**95**	18 10S	30 14 E
Hartley Bay	**108**	53 25N	129 15W
Hartmannberge	**96**	17 0S	13 0 E
Hartney	**109**	49 30N	100 35W
Hartselle	**113**	34 25N	86 55W
Hartshorne	**119**	34 51N	95 30W
Hartsville	**113**	34 23N	80 2W
Hartwell	**113**	34 21N	82 52W
Harunabad	**48**	29 35N	73 8 E
Harur	**51**	12 3N	78 29 E
Harvard	**117**	42 25N	88 37W
Harvey, Austral.	**79**	33 5S	115 54 E
Harvey, Ill., U.S.A.	**117**	41 40N	87 40W
Harvey, N.D., U.S.A.	**118**	47 50N	99 58W
Harwich	**13**	51 56N	1 18 E
Haryana □	**48**	29 0N	76 10 E
Harz	**30**	51 40N	10 40 E
Harzgerode	**30**	51 38N	11 8 E
Hasa	**46**	26 0N	49 0 E
Hasaheisa	**91**	14 44N	33 20 E
Hasani	**90**	25 0N	37 8 E
Hasanpur	**48**	28 43N	78 17 E
Haselünne	**30**	52 40N	7 30 E
Hasharon	**44**	32 12N	34 49 E
Hashefela	**44**	31 30N	34 43 E
Hashima	**65**	35 20N	136 40 E
Hashimoto	**65**	34 19N	135 37 E
Håsjö	**10**	63 1N	16 5 E
Haskell, Okla., U.S.A.	**119**	35 51N	95 40W
Haskell, Tex., U.S.A.	**119**	33 10N	99 45W
Haslach	**31**	48 16N	8 7 E
Hasle	**11**	55 11N	14 44 E
Haslev	**11**	55 18N	11 57 E
Hasparren	**20**	43 24N	1 18W
Hasselt	**16**	50 56N	5 21 E
Hassene, Ad.	**86**	21 0N	4 0 E
Hassfurt	**31**	50 2N	10 30 E
Hassi ben Hamra	**87**	30 42N	4 50 E
Hassi Berrekrem	**87**	33 45N	5 16 E
Hassi bou Khelala	**86**	30 17N	0 18W
Hassi Daoula	**87**	33 4N	5 38 E
Hassi Djafou	**86**	30 55N	3 35 E
Hassi el Abied	**86**	31 47N	3 37 E
Hassi el Biod	**87**	28 30N	6 0 E
Hassi el Gassi	**87**	30 52N	6 5 E
Hassi el Hadjar	**87**	31 28N	4 45 E
Hassi er Rmel	**86**	32 56N	3 17 E
Hassi Imoulaye	**87**	29 54N	9 10 E
Hassi Inifel	**86**	29 50N	3 41 E
Hassi Marroket	**86**	30 10N	3 0 E
Hassi Messaoud	**87**	31 43N	6 8 E
Hassi Rhénami	**87**	31 50N	5 58 E
Hassi Tartrat	**87**	30 5N	6 28 E
Hassi Zerzour	**86**	30 51N	3 56W
Hastings, Austral.	**74**	38 18S	145 12 E
Hastings, Can.	**107**	44 18N	77 57W
Hastings, N.Z.	**80**	39 39S	176 52 E
Hastings, U.K.	**13**	50 51N	0 36 E
Hastings, Mich., U.S.A.	**117**	42 40N	85 20W
Hastings, Minn., U.S.A.	**118**	44 41N	92 51W
Hastings, Nebr., U.S.A.	**118**	40 34N	98 22W
Hastings →	**77**	31 25S	152 55 E
Hastings Ra.	**77**	31 15S	152 14 E
Hästveda	**11**	56 17N	13 55 E
Hat Yai	**55**	7 1N	100 27 E
Hatanbulag	**60**	43 8N	109 5 E
Hatano	**65**	35 22N	139 14 E
Hatch	**121**	32 45N	107 8W
Hatches Creek	**72**	20 56S	135 12 E
Hatchet L.	**109**	58 36N	103 40W
Haţeg	**34**	45 36N	22 55 E
Haţeg, Mţii.	**34**	45 25N	23 0 E
Hatfield P.O.	**73**	33 54S	143 49 E
Hatgal	**62**	50 26N	100 9 E
Hathras	**48**	27 36N	78 6 E
Hato de Corozal	**134**	6 11N	71 45W
Hato Mayor	**127**	18 46N	69 15W
Hattah	**74**	34 48S	142 17 E
Hatteras, C.	**113**	35 10N	75 30W
Hattiesburg	**119**	31 20N	89 20W
Hatvan	**33**	47 40N	19 45 E
Hau Bon	**54**	13 25N	108 28 E
Hau Duc	**54**	15 20N	108 13 E
Haubstadt	**117**	38 12N	87 34W
Haug	**10**	60 23N	10 26 E
Haugastøl	**10**	60 30N	7 50 E
Haugesund	**9**	59 23N	5 13 E
Hauhungaroa Ra.	**80**	38 42S	175 40 E
Haultain →	**109**	55 51N	106 46W
Haungpa	**52**	25 29N	96 7 E
Haura	**45**	13 50N	47 35 E
Hauraki Gulf	**80**	36 35S	175 5 E
Hauran	**44**	32 50N	36 15 E
Haut Atlas	**86**	32 30N	5 0W
Haut-Rhin □	**19**	48 0N	7 15 E
Haut Zaïre □	**94**	2 20N	26 0 E
Hautah, Wahāt al	**46**	23 40N	47 0 E
Haute-Corse □	**21**	42 30N	9 30 E
Haute-Garonne □	**20**	43 28N	1 30 E
Haute-Loire □	**20**	45 5N	3 50 E
Haute-Marne □	**19**	48 10N	5 20 E
Haute-Saône □	**19**	47 45N	6 10 E
Haute-Savoie □	**21**	46 0N	6 20 E
Haute-Vienne □	**20**	45 50N	1 10 E
Hauterive	**105**	49 10N	68 16W
Hautes-Alpes □	**21**	44 42N	6 20 E
Hautes-Pyrénées □	**20**	43 0N	0 10 E
Hauteville	**21**	45 58N	5 36 E
Hautmont	**19**	50 15N	3 55 E
Hauts-de-Seine □	**19**	48 52N	2 15 E
Hauts Plateaux	**86**	34 14N	1 0 E
Hauzenberg	**31**	48 39N	13 38 E
Havana	**116**	40 19N	90 3W
Havana = La Habana	**126**	23 8N	82 22W
Havasu, L.	**123**	34 18N	114 28W
Havdhem	**11**	57 10N	18 20 E
Havelange	**16**	50 23N	5 15 E
Havelian	**48**	34 2N	73 10 E
Havelock, N.B., Can.	**103**	46 2N	65 24W
Havelock, Ont., Can.	**107**	44 26N	77 53W
Havelock, N.Z.	**81**	41 17S	173 48 E
Haverfordwest	**13**	51 48N	4 59W
Haverhill	**115**	42 50N	71 2W
Haveri	**51**	14 53N	75 24 E
Havering	**13**	51 33N	0 20 E
Haverstraw	**115**	41 12N	73 58W
Håverud	**11**	58 50N	12 28 E
Havilah	**76**	32 37S	149 45 E
Havlíčkův Brod	**32**	49 36N	15 33 E
Havneby	**11**	55 5N	8 34 E
Havre	**120**	48 34N	109 40W
Havre-St.-Pierre	**103**	50 18N	63 33W
Havre-Aubert	**103**	47 12N	61 56W
Havre, Le	**18**	49 30N	0 5 E
Havza	**46**	41 0N	35 35 E
Haw →	**113**	35 36N	79 3W
Hawaii □	**110**	20 30N	157 0W
Hawaii	**110**	20 0N	155 0W
Hawaiian Is.	**110**	20 30N	156 0W
Hawaiian Ridge	**67**	24 0N	165 0W
Hawarden, Can.	**109**	51 25N	106 36W
Hawarden, U.S.A.	**118**	43 2N	96 28W
Hawea Flat	**81**	44 40S	169 19 E
Hawea Lake	**81**	44 28S	169 19 E
Hawera	**80**	39 35S	174 19 E
Hawesville	**117**	37 54N	86 45W
Hawick	**14**	55 25N	2 48W
Hawk Junction	**102**	48 5N	84 38W
Hawk Point	**116**	38 58N	91 8W
Hawkdun Ra.	**81**	44 53S	170 5 E
Hawke B.	**80**	39 25S	177 20 E
Hawke, C.	**77**	32 13S	152 34 E
Hawke's Bay □	**80**	39 45S	176 35 E
Hawkesbury	**102**	45 37N	74 37W
Hawkesbury I.	**108**	53 37N	129 3W
Hawkesbury Pt.	**72**	11 55S	134 5 E
Hawkesdale	**74**	38 7S	142 20 E
Hawkinsville	**113**	32 17N	83 30W
Hawkwood	**73**	25 45S	150 50 E
Hawley	**118**	46 58N	96 20W
Hawthorne	**120**	38 31N	118 37W
Hawzen	**91**	13 58N	39 28 E
Haxtun	**118**	40 40N	102 39W
Hay, Austral.	**74**	34 30S	144 51 E
Hay, U.K.	**13**	52 4N	3 9W
Hay →, Austral.	**72**	25 14S	138 0 E
Hay →, Can.	**108**	60 50N	116 26W
Hay, C.	**78**	14 5S	129 29 E
Hay I.	**106**	44 53N	80 58W
Hay L.	**108**	58 50N	118 50W
Hay Lakes	**108**	53 12N	113 2W
Hay River	**108**	60 51N	115 44W
Hay Springs	**118**	42 40N	102 38W
Hayange	**19**	49 20N	6 2 E
Hayato	**64**	31 40N	130 43 E
Hayden, Ariz., U.S.A.	**121**	33 2N	110 48W
Hayden, Colo., U.S.A.	**120**	40 30N	107 22W
Haydon	**72**	18 0S	141 30 E
Haye-Descartes, La	**18**	46 58N	0 42 E
Haye-du-Puits, La	**18**	49 17N	1 33W
Hayes	**118**	44 22N	101 1W
Hayes →	**109**	57 3N	92 12W
Haynesville	**119**	33 0N	93 7W
Hays, Can.	**108**	50 6N	111 48W
Hays, U.S.A.	**118**	38 55N	99 25W
Haysdale	**74**	34 54S	143 18 E
Haysville	**117**	38 28N	86 55W
Hayward, Calif., U.S.A.	**122**	37 40N	122 5W
Hayward, Wis., U.S.A.	**118**	46 2N	91 30W
Hayward's Heath	**13**	51 0N	0 5W
Hazard	**112**	37 18N	83 10W
Hazaribagh	**49**	23 58N	85 26 E
Hazaribagh Road	**49**	24 12N	85 57 E
Hazebrouck	**19**	50 42N	2 31 E
Hazelton, Can.	**108**	55 20N	127 42W
Hazelton, U.S.A.	**118**	46 30N	100 15W
Hazen, N.D., U.S.A.	**118**	47 18N	101 38W
Hazen, Nev., U.S.A.	**120**	39 37N	119 2W
Hazlehurst, Ga., U.S.A.	**113**	31 50N	82 35W
Hazlehurst, Miss., U.S.A.	**119**	31 52N	90 24W
Hazleton, Ind., U.S.A.	**117**	38 29N	87 34W
Hazleton, Pa., U.S.A.	**115**	40 58N	76 0W
Hazlett, L.	**78**	21 30S	128 48 E
He Xian, Anhui, China	**59**	31 45N	118 20 E
He Xian, Guangxi Zhuangzu, China	**59**	24 27N	111 30 E
Head of Bight	**79**	31 30S	131 25 E
Headlands	**95**	18 15S	32 2 E
Healdsburg	**122**	38 33N	122 51W
Healdton	**119**	34 16N	97 31W
Healesville	**74**	37 35S	145 30 E
Heanor	**12**	53 1N	1 20W
Heard I.	**53**	53 0S	74 0 E
Hearne	**119**	30 54N	96 35W
Hearne B.	**109**	60 10N	99 10W
Hearne L.	**108**	62 20N	113 10W
Hearst	**102**	49 40N	83 41W
Heart →	**118**	46 40N	100 51W
Heart's Content	**103**	47 54N	53 27W
Heath →	**136**	12 31S	68 38W
Heath Mts.	**81**	45 39S	167 9 E
Heath Pt.	**103**	49 8N	61 40W
Heath Steele	**103**	47 17N	66 5W
Heathcote	**74**	36 56S	144 45 E
Heathmere	**74**	38 12S	141 35 E
Heavener	**119**	34 54N	94 36W
Hebbronville	**119**	27 20N	98 40W
Hebei □	**60**	39 0N	116 0 E
Hebel	**73**	28 58S	147 47 E
Heber	**123**	32 44N	115 32W
Heber Springs	**119**	35 29N	91 59W
Hebert	**109**	50 30N	107 10W
Hebgen, L.	**120**	44 50N	111 15W
Hebi	**60**	35 57N	114 7 E
Hebrides	**14**	57 30N	7 0W
Hebrides, Inner Is.	**14**	57 20N	6 40W
Hebrides, Outer Is.	**14**	57 30N	7 40W
Hebron, Can.	**101**	58 5N	62 30W
Hebron, Ind., U.S.A.	**117**	41 19N	87 17W
Hebron, N.D., U.S.A.	**118**	46 56N	102 2W
Hebron, Nebr., U.S.A.	**118**	40 15N	97 33W
Hebron (Al Khalil)	**44**	31 32N	35 6 E
Heby	**10**	59 56N	16 53 E
Hecate Str.	**108**	53 10N	130 30W
Hechi	**58**	24 40N	108 2 E
Hechingen	**31**	48 20N	8 58 E
Hechuan	**58**	30 2N	106 12 E
Hecla	**118**	45 56N	98 8W
Hecla I.	**109**	51 10N	96 43W
Heddal	**10**	59 36N	9 9 E
Hédé	**18**	48 18N	1 49W
Hede	**10**	62 23N	13 30 E
Hedemora	**10**	60 18N	15 58 E
Hedgehope	**81**	46 12S	168 34 E
Hedley	**119**	34 53N	100 39W
Hedmark fylke □	**10**	61 17N	11 40 E
Hedrick	**116**	41 11N	92 19W
Hedrum	**10**	59 7N	10 5 E
Heemstede	**16**	52 22N	4 37 E
Heerde	**16**	52 24N	6 2 E
Heerenveen	**16**	52 57N	5 55 E
Heerlen	**16**	50 55N	6 0 E
Hefei	**59**	31 52N	117 18 E
Hegang	**62**	47 20N	130 19 E
Hegyalja	**33**	48 25N	21 25 E
Heichengzhen	**60**	36 24N	106 3 E
Heide	**30**	54 10N	9 7 E
Heidelberg, Ger.	**31**	49 23N	8 41 E
Heidelberg, C. Prov., S. Afr.	**96**	34 6S	20 59 E
Heidelberg, Trans., S. Afr.	**97**	26 30S	28 23 E
Heidenheim	**31**	48 40N	10 10 E
Heigun-To	**64**	33 47N	132 14 E
Heijing	**58**	25 22N	101 44 E
Heilbron	**97**	27 16S	27 59 E
Heilbronn	**31**	49 8N	9 13 E
Heiligenblut	**33**	47 2N	12 51 E
Heiligenhafen	**30**	54 21N	10 58 E
Heiligenstadt	**30**	51 22N	10 9 E
Heilongjiang □	**62**	48 0N	126 0 E
Heilunkiang = Heilongjiang □	**62**	48 0N	126 0 E
Heinola	**9**	61 13N	26 2 E
Heinsun	**52**	25 52N	95 35 E
Heirnkut	**52**	25 14N	94 44 E
Heishan	**61**	41 40N	122 5 E
Heishui, Liaoning, China	**61**	42 8N	119 18 E
Heishui, Sichuan, China	**58**	32 4N	103 2 E
Hejaz = Hijāz	**46**	26 0N	37 30 E
Hejian	**60**	38 25N	116 5 E
Hejiang	**58**	28 43N	105 46 E
Hejin	**60**	35 35N	110 42 E
Hekimhan	**46**	38 50N	38 0 E
Hekinan	**65**	34 52N	137 0 E
Hekla	**8**	63 56N	19 35W
Hekou, Gansu, China	**60**	36 10N	103 28 E
Hekou, Guangdong, China	**59**	23 13N	112 45 E
Hekou, Yunnan, China	**62**	22 30N	103 59 E
Helagsfjället	**10**	62 54N	12 25 E
Helan Shan	**60**	39 0N	105 55 E
Helechosa	**23**	39 22N	4 53W
Helena, Ark., U.S.A.	**119**	34 30N	90 35W
Helena, Mont., U.S.A.	**120**	46 40N	112 0W
Helendale	**123**	34 44N	117 19W
Helensburgh, Austral.	**76**	34 11S	151 1 E
Helensburgh, U.K.	**14**	56 0N	4 44W
Helensville	**80**	36 41S	174 29 E
Helez	**44**	31 36N	34 39 E
Helgasjön	**11**	57 0N	14 50 E
Helgeroa	**10**	59 0N	9 45 E
Helgoland	**30**	54 10N	7 51 E
Heligoland = Helgoland	**30**	54 10N	7 51 E
Heliopolis	**90**	30 6N	31 17 E
Hell-Ville	**97**	13 25S	48 16 E
Hellebæk	**11**	56 4N	12 32 E
Hellendoorn	**16**	52 24N	6 27 E
Hellevoetsluis	**16**	51 50N	4 8 E

Hellín **25** 38 31N 1 40W
Helmand □ **47** 31 20N 64 0 E
Helmand → **48** 31 12N 61 34 E
Helmand, Hamun **47** 31 15N 61 15 E
Helme → **30** 51 40N 11 20 E
Helmond **16** 51 29N 5 41 E
Helmsdale **14** 58 7N 3 40W
Helmstedt **30** 52 16N 11 0 E
Helnæs **11** 55 9N 10 0 E
Helong **61** 42 40N 129 0 E
Helper **120** 39 44N 110 56W
Helsingborg **11** 56 3N 12 42 E
Helsinge **11** 56 2N 12 12 E
Helsingfors **9** 60 15N 25 3 E
Helsingør **11** 56 2N 12 35 E
Helsinki **9** 60 15N 25 3 E
Helston **13** 50 7N 5 17W
Helvellyn **12** 54 31N 3 1W
Helwân **90** 29 50N 31 20 E
Hemavati → **51** 12 30N 76 20 E
Hemet **123** 33 45N 116 59W
Hemingford **118** 42 21N 103 4W
Hemmingford **105** 45 3N 73 35W
Hemphill **119** 31 21N 93 49W
Hempstead **119** 30 5N 96 5W
Hemse **11** 57 15N 18 22 E
Hemsö **10** 62 43N 18 5 E
Hen & Chickens Is. **80** 35 58S 174 45 E
Henan □ **62** 34 0N 114 0 E
Henares → **24** 40 24N 3 30W
Hendaye **20** 43 23N 1 47W
Henderson, Argent. **140** 36 18S 61 43W
Henderson, Ky., U.S.A. **117** 37 50N 87 38W
Henderson, N.C., U.S.A. **113** 36 20N 78 25W
Henderson, Nev., U.S.A. **123** 36 2N 115 0W
Henderson, Pa., U.S.A. **113** 35 25N 88 40W
Henderson, Tex., U.S.A. **119** 32 5N 94 49W
Hendersonville **113** 35 21N 82 28W
Hendon **77** 28 5S 151 50 E
Heng Xian **58** 22 40N 109 17 E
Hengcheng **60** 38 18N 106 28 E
Hengdaohezi **61** 44 52N 129 0 E
Hengelo **16** 52 3N 6 19 E
Hengfeng **59** 28 12N 115 48 E
Hengshan, Hunan, China **59** 27 16N 112 45 E
Hengshan, Shaanxi, China **60** 37 58N 109 5 E
Hengshui **60** 37 41N 115 40 E
Hengyang, Hunan, China **59** 26 59N 112 22 E
Hengyang, Hunan, China **59** 26 52N 112 33 E
Hénin-Beaumont **19** 50 25N 2 58 E
Henlopen, C. **112** 38 48N 75 5W
Hennan, L. **10** 62 3N 55 46 E
Hennebont **18** 47 49N 3 19W
Hennenman **96** 27 59S 27 1 E
Hennepin **116** 41 15N 89 21W
Hennessy **119** 36 8N 97 53W
Hennigsdorf **30** 52 38N 13 13 E
Henrichemont **19** 47 20N 2 30 E
Henrietta **119** 33 50N 98 15W
Henrietta Maria C. **102** 55 9N 82 20W
Henrietta, Ostrov **41** 77 6N 156 30 E
Henry **116** 41 5N 89 20W
Henryetta **119** 35 30N 96 0W
Henryville **105** 45 8N 73 11W
Hensall **106** 43 26N 81 30W
Hentiyn Nuruu **62** 48 30N 108 30 E
Henzada **52** 17 38 95 26 E
Hepburn Springs **74** 37 19S 144 9 E
Heping **59** 24 29N 115 0 E
Heppner **120** 45 21N 119 34W
Hepu **58** 21 40N 109 12 E
Hepworth **106** 44 37N 81 9W
Heqing **58** 26 37N 100 11 E
Hequ **60** 39 20N 111 15 E
Héraðsflói **8** 65 42N 14 12W
Héraðsvötn → **8** 65 45N 19 25W
Herald Cays **72** 16 58S 149 9 E
Herāt **47** 34 20N 62 7 E
Herāt □ **47** 35 0N 62 0 E
Hérault □ **20** 43 34N 3 15 E
Hérault → **20** 43 17N 3 26 E
Herbault **18** 47 36N 1 8 E
Herbert → **72** 18 31S 146 17 E
Herbert Downs **72** 23 7S 139 9 E
Herberton **72** 17 20S 145 25 E
Herbiers, Les **18** 46 52N 1 0W
Herbignac **18** 47 27N 2 18W
Herborn **30** 50 40N 8 19 E
Herby **32** 50 45N 18 50 E
Hercegnovi **33** 42 30N 18 33 E
Herculaneum **116** 38 16N 90 23W
Herðubreið **8** 65 11N 16 21W
Hereford, U.K. **13** 52 4N 2 42W
Hereford, U.S.A. **119** 34 50N 102 28W
Hereford and Worcester □ **13** 52 10N 2 30W
Hereford, Mt. **105** 45 5N 71 36W
Herefoss **11** 58 32N 8 23 E
Herekino **80** 35 18S 173 11 E
Herentals **16** 51 12N 4 51 E
Herfølge **11** 55 26N 12 9 E
Herford **30** 52 7N 8 40 E
Héricourt **19** 47 32N 6 45 E
Herington **118** 38 43N 97 0W
Herisau **31** 47 22N 9 17 E
Hérisson **20** 46 32N 2 42 E
Herkimer **115** 43 0N 74 59W
Herlong **122** 40 8N 120 8W
Herm **18** 49 30N 2 28W
Hermagor-Pressegger See **33** 46 38N 13 23 E
Herman **118** 45 51N 96 8W
Hermann **118** 38 40N 91 25W
Hermannsburg **30** 52 49N 10 6 E
Hermannsburg Mission **78** 23 57S 132 45 E
Hermanus **96** 34 27S 19 12 E
Herment **20** 45 45N 2 24 E
Hermidale **73** 31 30S 146 42 E
Hermiston **120** 45 50N 119 16W
Hermitage, N.Z. **81** 43 44S 170 5 E
Hermitage, U.S.A. **116** 37 56N 93 19W
Hermite, I. **142** 55 50S 68 0W
Hermon, Mt. = Sheikh, J. ash **46** 33 20N 35 51 E
Hermosillo **124** 29 10N 111 0W
Hernad → **33** 47 56N 21 8 E
Hernandarias **141** 25 20S 54 40W
Hernandez **122** 36 24N 120 46W
Hernando, Argent. **140** 32 28S 63 40W
Hernando, U.S.A. **119** 34 50N 89 59W
Herne **30** 51 33N 7 12 E
Herne Bay **13** 51 22N 1 8 E
Herning **11** 56 8N 8 58 E
Heroica Nogales = Nogales **124** 31 20N 110 56W
Heron Bay **102** 48 40N 86 25W
Herowābād **46** 38 37N 48 32 E
Herreid **118** 45 53N 100 5W
Herrera **23** 37 26N 4 55W
Herrera de Alcántar **23** 39 39N 7 25W
Herrera de Pisuerga **22** 42 35N 4 20W
Herrera del Duque **23** 39 10N 5 3W
Herrick **72** 41 5S 147 55 E
Herrin **116** 37 50N 89 0W
Herrljunga **11** 58 5N 13 1 E
Hersbruck **31** 49 30N 11 25 E
Herstal **16** 50 40N 5 38 E
Hertford **13** 51 47N 0 4W
Hertford □ **13** 51 51N 0 5W
's-Hertogenbosch **16** 51 42N 5 17 E
Hertzogville **96** 28 9S 25 30 E
Hervás **22** 40 16N 5 52W
Hervey Is. **67** 19 30S 159 0W
Herzberg, Cottbus, Ger. **30** 51 40N 13 13 E
Herzberg, Niedersachsen, Ger. **30** 51 38N 10 20 E
Herzliyya **44** 32 10N 34 50 E
Hesdin **19** 50 21N 2 0 E
Hesel **30** 53 18N 7 36 E
Heshui **60** 36 0N 108 0 E
Heshun **60** 37 22N 113 32 E
Hespeler **114** 43 26N 80 19W
Hesperia **123** 34 25N 117 18W
Hesse = Hessen **30** 50 40N 9 20 E
Hessel **106** 46 1N 84 28W
Hessen □ **30N50** 40N 9 20 E
Hetch Hetchy Aqueduct **122** 37 36N 121 25W
Hettinger **118** 46 0N 102 38W
Hettstedt **30** 51 39N 11 30 E
Hève, C. de la **18** 49 30N 0 5 E
Hevron → **44** 31 12N 34 42 E
Hewett, C. **101** 70 16N 67 45W
Hex River **96** 33 30S 19 35 E
Hexham, Austral. **74** 38 0S 142 41 E
Hexham, U.K. **12** 54 58N 2 7W
Hexi, Yunnan, China **58** 24 9N 102 38 E
Hexi, Zhejiang, China **59** 27 58N 119 38 E
Hexigten Qi **61** 43 18N 117 30 E
Heysham **12** 54 5N 2 53W
Heyuan **59** 23 39N 114 40 E
Heywood **74** 38 8S 141 37 E
Heze **60** 35 14N 115 20 E
Hezhang **58** 27 8N 104 41 E
Hi-no-Misaki **64** 35 26N 132 38 E
Hi Vista **123** 34 45N 117 46W
Hialeach **113** 25 49N 80 17W
Hiawatha, Kans., U.S.A. **118** 39 55N 95 33W
Hiawatha, Utah, U.S.A. **120** 39 29N 111 1W
Hibbing **118** 47 30N 93 0W
Hibbs B. **72** 42 35S 145 15 E
Hibernia Reef **78** 12 0S 123 23 E
Hibiki-Nada **64** 34 0N 130 0 E
Hickman **119** 36 35N 89 8W
Hickory **113** 35 46N 81 17W
Hicks Bay **80** 37 34S 178 21 E
Hicks Pt. **75** 37 49S 149 17 E
Hicksville, N.Y., U.S.A. **115** 40 46N 73 30W
Hicksville, Ohio, U.S.A. **117** 41 18N 84 46W
Hida **34** 47 10N 23 19 E
Hida → **65** 35 26N 137 3 E
Hida-Sammyaku **65** 36 30N 137 40 E
Hida-Sanchi **65** 36 10N 137 0 E
Hidaka **64** 35 30N 134 44 E
Hidalgo, Mexico **125** 24 15N 99 26W
Hidalgo, U.S.A. **117** 39 9N 88 9W
Hidalgo □ **125** 20 30N 99 10W
Hidalgo del Parral **124** 26 58N 105 40W
Hidalgo, Presa M. **124** 26 30N 108 35W
Hiddensee **30** 54 30N 13 6 E
Hidrolândia **139** 17 0S 49 15W
Hieflau **33** 47 36N 14 46 E
Hiendelaencina **24** 41 5N 3 0W
Hienghène **68** 20 41S 164 56 E
Hierro **84** 27 45N 17 56 E
Higashi-matsuyama **65** 36 2N 139 25 E
Higashiōsaka **65** 34 40N 135 37 E
Higasi-Suidō **64** 34 0N 129 30 E
Higbee **116** 39 19N 92 31W
Higgins **119** 36 9N 100 1W
Higgins Corner **122** 39 2N 121 5W
Higgins L. **106** 44 30N 84 45W
Higginsville, Austral. **79** 31 42S 121 38 E
Higginsville, U.S.A. **116** 39 4N 93 43W
Higgs I. L. **113** 36 20N 78 30W
High Atlas = Haut Atlas **86** 32 30N 5 0W
High I. **103** 56 40N 61 10W
High Island **119** 29 32N 94 22W
High Level **108** 58 31N 117 8W
High Point **113** 35 57N 79 58W
High Prairie **108** 55 30N 116 30W
High River **108** 50 30N 113 50W
High Springs **113** 29 50N 82 40W
High Wycombe **13** 51 37N 0 45W
Highbury **72** 16 25S 143 9 E
Highland, Ill., U.S.A. **116** 38 44N 89 41W
Highland, Ind., U.S.A. **117** 41 33N 87 28W
Highland, Wis., U.S.A. **116** 43 6N 90 21W
Highland □ **14** 57 30N 5 0W
Highland Park **117** 42 10N 87 50W
Highmore **118** 44 35N 99 26W
Highrock L. **109** 57 5N 105 32W
Higley **121** 33 27N 111 46W
Higüay **127** 18 37N 68 42W
Hihya **90** 30 40N 31 36 E
Hiiumaa **36** 58 50N 22 45 E
Híjar **24** 41 10N 0 27W
Ḩijārah, Sahrā' al **46** 30 25N 44 30 E
Hiji **64** 33 22N 131 32 E
Hikari **64** 33 58N 131 58 E
Hiketa **64** 34 13N 134 24 E
Hiko **122** 37 30N 115 13W
Hikone **65** 35 15N 136 10 E
Hilawng **52** 21 23N 93 48 E
Hildburghhausen **31** 50 24N 10 43 E
Hildesheim **30** 52 9N 9 55 E
Hill → **79** 30 23S 115 3 E
Hill City, Idaho, U.S.A. **120** 43 20N 115 2W
Hill City, Kans., U.S.A. **118** 39 25N 99 51W
Hill City, Minn., U.S.A. **118** 46 57N 93 35W
Hill City, S.D., U.S.A. **118** 43 58N 103 35W
Hill End **75** 38 1S 146 9 E
Hill Island L. **109** 60 30N 109 50W
Hillared **11** 57 37N 13 10 E
Hillegom **16** 52 18N 4 35 E
Hillerød **11** 55 56N 12 19 E
Hillerstorp **11** 57 20N 13 52 E
Hilli **52** 25 17N 89 1 E
Hillingdon **13** 51 33N 0 29W
Hillman **106** 45 5N 83 52W
Hillmond **109** 53 26N 109 41W
Hillsboro, Ill., U.S.A. **116** 39 9N 89 29W
Hillsboro, Iowa, U.S.A. **116** 40 50N 91 42W
Hillsboro, Kans., U.S.A. **118** 38 22N 97 10W
Hillsboro, Mo., U.S.A. **116** 38 14N 90 34W
Hillsboro, N. Mex., U.S.A. **121** 33 0N 107 35W
Hillsboro, N.D., U.S.A. **118** 47 23N 97 9W
Hillsboro, N.H., U.S.A. **115** 43 8N 71 56W
Hillsboro, Ohio, U.S.A. **117** 39 12N 83 37W
Hillsboro, Oreg., U.S.A. **122** 45 31N 123 0W
Hillsboro, Tex., U.S.A. **119** 32 0N 97 10W
Hillsborough **127** 12 28N 61 28W
Hillsdale, Mich., U.S.A. **117** 41 55N 84 40W
Hillsdale, N.Y., U.S.A. **115** 42 11N 73 30W
Hillside **78** 21 45S 119 23 E
Hillsport **102** 49 27N 85 34W
Hillston **73** 33 30S 145 31 E
Hilo **110** 19 44N 155 5W
Hilonghilong **57** 9 10N 125 45 E
Hilton **114** 43 16N 77 48W
Hilton Beach **106** 46 15N 83 53W
Hilversum **16** 52 14N 5 10 E
Himachal Pradesh □ **48** 31 30N 77 0 E
Himara **35** 40 8N 19 43 E
Hime-Jima **64** 33 43N 131 40 E
Himeji **64** 34 50N 134 40 E
Himi **65** 36 50N 137 0 E
Himmerland **11** 56 45N 9 30 E
Hims = Homs **46** 34 40N 36 45 E
Hinako, Kepulauan **56** 0 50N 97 20 E
Hinche **127** 19 9N 72 1W
Hinchinbrook I. **72** 18 20S 146 15 E
Hinckley, U.K. **13** 52 33N 1 21W
Hinckley, U.S.A. **120** 39 18N 112 41W
Hindås **11** 57 42N 12 27 E
Hindaun **48** 26 44N 77 5 E
Hindmarsh L. **74** 36 5S 141 55 E
Hindol **50** 20 40N 85 10 E
Hinds **81** 43 59S 171 36 E
Hindsholm **11** 55 30N 10 40 E
Hindu Bagh **48** 30 56N 67 50 E
Hindu Kush **47** 36 0N 71 0 E
Hindupur **51** 13 49N 77 32 E
Hines Creek **108** 56 20N 118 40W
Hinganghat **50** 20 30N 78 52 E
Hingham **120** 48 34N 110 29W
Hingoli **50** 19 41N 77 15 E
Hinlopenstretet **144** 79 35N 18 40 E
Hinna **89** 10 25N 11 35 E
Hino **65** 35 0N 136 15 E
Hinojosa del Duque **23** 38 30N 5 9W
Hinokage **64** 32 39N 131 24 E
Hinsdale **120** 48 26N 107 2W
Hinterrhein → **31** 46 40N 9 25 E
Hinton, Can. **108** 53 26N 117 34W
Hinton, U.S.A. **112** 37 40N 80 51W
Hippolytushoef **16** 52 54N 4 58 E
Hirado **64** 33 22N 129 33 E
Hirado-Shima **64** 33 20N 129 30 E
Hirakarta **65** 34 48N 135 40 E
Hirakud **50** 21 32N 83 51 E
Hirakud Dam **50** 21 32N 83 45 E
Hirara **63** 24 48N 125 17 E
Hirata **64** 35 24N 132 49 E
Hiratsuka **65** 35 19N 139 21 E
Hirhafok **87** 23 49N 5 45 E
Hîrlău **34** 47 23N 27 0 E
Hiromi **64** 33 13N 132 36 E
Hirosaki **63** 40 34N 140 28 E
Hiroshima **64** 34 24N 132 30 E
Hiroshima □ **64** 34 50N 133 0 E
Hiroshima-Wan **64** 34 5N 132 20 E
Hirsoholmene **11** 57 30N 10 36 E
Hirson **19** 49 55N 4 4 E
Hîrşova **34** 44 40N 27 59 E
Hirtshals **11** 57 36N 9 57 E
Hispaniola **127** 19 0N 71 0W
Hissar **48** 29 12N 75 45 E
Hita **64** 33 20N 130 58 E
Hitachi **65** 36 36N 140 39 E
Hitachiota **65** 36 30N 140 30 E
Hitchin **13** 51 57N 0 16W
Hitoyoshi **64** 32 13N 130 45 E
Hitzacker **30** 53 9N 11 1 E
Hiu **68** 13 10S 166 35 E
Hiuchi-Nada **64** 34 5N 133 20 E
Hjalmar L. **109** 61 33N 109 25W
Hjälmare kanal **10** 59 20N 15 59 E
Hjälmaren **10** 59 18N 15 40 E
Hjartdal **10** 59 37N 8 41 E
Hjerkinn **10** 62 13N 9 33 E
Hjørring **11** 57 29N 9 59 E
Hjorted **11** 57 37N 16 19 E
Hjortkvarn **11** 58 54N 15 26 E
Hko-ut **52** 20 58N 98 2 E
Hkyenhpa **52** 27 43N 97 25 E
Hlaingbwe **52** 17 8N 97 50 E
Hlinsko **32** 49 45N 15 54 E
Hlwaze **52** 18 54N 96 37 E
Hňak **144** 70 40N 52 10W
Ho **89** 6 37N 0 27 E
Ho Chi Minh, Phanh Bho **55** 10 58N 106 40 E
Ho Thuong **54** 19 32N 105 48 E
Hoa Binh **54** 20 50N 105 20 E

Hoa Da (Phan Ri) 55 11 16N 108 40 E
Hoa Hiep 55 11 34N 105 51 E
Hoai Nhon (Bon Son) 54 14 28N 109 1 E
Hoare B. 101 65 17N 62 30W
Hobart, Austral. 72 42 50S 147 21 E
Hobart, Ind., U.S.A. 117 41 32N 87 15W
Hobart, Okla., U.S.A. 119 35 0N 99 5W
Hobbs 119 32 40N 103 3W
Hobbs Coast 143 74 50S 131 0W
Hobo 134 2 35N 75 30W
Hoboken, Belg. 16 51 11N 4 21 E
Hoboken, U.S.A. 115 40 45N 74 4W
Hobro 11 56 39N 9 46 E
Hoburgen 11 56 55N 18 7 E
Hochatown 119 34 11N 94 39W
Hochschwab 33 47 35N 15 0 E
Höchst 31 50 6N 8 33 E
Höchstadt 31 49 42N 10 48 E
Hockenheim 31 49 18N 8 33 E
Hodaka-Dake 65 36 17N 137 39 E
Hodeïda 45 14 50N 43 0 E
Hodgson 109 51 13N 97 36W
Hódmezövásárhely 33 46 28N 20 22 E
Hodna, Chott el 87 35 30N 5 0 E
Hodna, Monts du 87 35 52N 4 42 E
Hodonín 32 48 50N 17 10 E
Hoeamdong 61 42 30N 130 16 E
Hoëdic 18 47 21N 2 52W
Hoek van Holland 16 52 0N 4 7 E
Hoengsŏng 61 37 29N 127 59 E
Hoeryong 61 42 30N 129 45 E
Hoëveld 97 26 30S 30 0 E
Hoeyang 61 38 43N 127 36 E
Hof, Ger. 31 50 18N 11 55 E
Hof, Iceland 8 64 33N 14 40W
Höfðakaupstaður 8 65 50N 20 19W
Hofgeismar 30 51 29N 9 23 E
Hofors 10 60 31N 16 15 E
Hofsjökull 8 64 49N 18 48W
Hofsós 8 65 53N 19 26W
Hōfu 64 34 3N 131 34 E
Hog I. 106 45 49N 85 22W
Hogan Group 72 39 13S 147 1 E
Hogansville 113 33 14N 84 50W
Hogarth, Mt. 72 21 50S 137 0 E
Hogeland 120 48 51N 108 40W
Hogenakai Falls 51 12 6N 77 50 E
Högfors 10 59 58N 15 3 E
Hōgo-Kaikyō 64 33 20N 131 58 E
Högsäter 11 58 38N 12 5 E
Högsby 11 57 10N 16 1 E
Högsjö 10 59 4N 15 44 E
Hogsty Reef 127 21 41N 73 48W
Hoh → 122 47 45N 124 29W
Hoh Xil Shan 62 35 0N 89 0 E
Hohe Rhön 31 50 24N 9 58 E
Hohe Tauern 33 47 11N 12 40 E
Hohe Venn 16 50 30N 6 5 E
Hohenau 32 48 36N 16 55 E
Hohenems 31 47 22N 9 42 E
Hohenstein Ernstthal 30 50 48N 12 43 E
Hohenwald 113 35 35N 87 30W
Hohenwestedt 30 54 6N 9 30 E
Hohhot 60 40 52N 111 40 E
Hohoe 89 7 8N 0 32 E
Hoi An 54 15 30N 108 19 E
Hoi Xuan 54 20 25N 105 9 E
Hoisington 118 38 33N 98 50W
Højer 11 54 58N 8 42 E
Hōjō 64 33 58N 132 46 E
Hok 11 57 31N 14 16 E
Hökensås 11 58 0N 14 5 E
Hökerum 11 57 51N 13 16 E
Hokianga Harbour 80 35 31S 173 22 E
Hokitika 81 42 42S 171 0 E
Hokkaidō □ 63 43 30N 143 0 E
Hokksund 10 59 44N 9 59 E
Hol-Hol 91 11 20N 42 50 E
Holbæk 11 55 43N 11 43 E
Holbrook, Austral. 76 35 42S 147 18 E
Holbrook, U.S.A. 121 35 54N 110 10W
Holden, Can. 108 53 13N 112 11W
Holden, Mo., U.S.A. 116 38 43N 94 0W
Holden, Utah, U.S.A. 120 39 0N 112 26W
Holdenville 119 35 5N 96 25W
Holderness 12 53 45N 0 5W
Holdfast 109 50 58N 105 25W
Holdich 142 45 57S 68 13W
Holdrege, U.S.A. 109 40 25N 99 30W
Holdrege, U.S.A. 118 40 26N 99 22W
Hole-Narsipur 51 12 48N 76 16 E
Holgate 117 41 15N 84 8W
Holguín 126 20 50N 76 20W
Holla, Mt. 91 7 5N 36 35 E
Hollabrunn 32 48 34N 16 5 E
Hollams Bird I. 96 24 40S 14 30 E
Holland 117 42 47N 86 7W
Hollandia = Jayapura 57 2 28S 140 38 E
Holleton 79 31 55S 119 0 E
Hollfeld 31 49 56N 11 18 E
Hollick Kenyon Plateau 143 82 0S 110 0W
Hollidaysburg 114 40 26N 78 25W
Hollis 119 34 45N 99 55W
Hollister, Calif., U.S.A. 122 36 51N 121 24W
Hollister, Idaho, U.S.A. 120 42 21N 114 40W
Holly, Colo., U.S.A. 118 38 7N 102 7W
Holly, Mich., U.S.A. 106 42 48N 83 38W
Holly Hill 113 29 15N 81 3W
Holly Springs 119 34 45N 89 25W
Hollywood, Calif., U.S.A. 110 34 7N 118 25W
Hollywood, Fla., U.S.A. 113 26 0N 80 9W
Holm 10 62 40N 16 40 E
Holman Island 100 70 42N 117 41W
Hólmavík 8 65 42N 21 40W
Holmegil 10 59 10N 11 44 E
Holmes Reefs 72 16 27S 148 0 E
Holmestrand 10 59 31N 10 14 E
Holmsbu 10 59 32N 10 27 E
Holmsjön 10 62 26N 15 20 E
Holmsland Klit 11 56 0N 8 5 E
Holmsund 8 63 41N 20 20 E
Holon 44 32 2N 34 47 E
Holroyd → 72 14 10S 141 36 E
Holstebro 11 56 22N 8 37 E
Holsworthy 13 50 48N 4 21W
Holt 8 63 33N 19 48W
Holte 11 55 50N 12 29 E
Holton, Can. 103 54 31N 57 12W
Holton, U.S.A. 118 39 28N 95 44W
Holtville 123 32 50N 115 27W
Holwerd 16 53 22N 5 54 E
Holy Cross 100 62 10N 159 52W
Holy I., England, U.K. 12 55 42N 1 48W
Holy I., Wales, U.K. 12 53 17N 4 37W
Holyhead 12 53 18N 4 38W
Holyoke, Colo., U.S.A. 118 40 39N 102 18W
Holyoke, Mass., U.S.A. 115 42 14N 72 37W
Holyrood 103 47 27N 53 8W
Holzkirchen 31 47 53N 11 42 E
Holzminden 30 51 49N 9 31 E
Homa Bay 94 0 36S 34 30 E
Homa Bay □ 94 0 50S 34 30 E
Homalin 52 24 55N 95 0 E
Homberg 30 51 2N 9 20 E
Hombori 89 15 20N 1 38W
Homburg 31 49 19N 7 21 E
Home B. 101 68 40N 67 10W
Home Hill 72 19 43S 147 25 E
Home Reef 68 18 59S 174 47W
Homedale 120 43 42N 116 59W
Homer, Alaska, U.S.A. 100 59 40N 151 35W
Homer, Ill, U.S.A. 117 40 4N 87 57W
Homer, La., U.S.A. 119 32 50N 93 4W
Homer, Mich., U.S.A. 117 42 9N 84 49W
Homestead, Austral. 72 20 20S 145 40 E
Homestead, Fla., U.S.A. 113 25 29N 80 27W
Homestead, Oreg., U.S.A. 120 45 5N 116 57W
Homewood, Calif., U.S.A. 122 39 4N 120 8W
Homewood, Ill., U.S.A. 117 41 34N 87 40W
Hominy 119 36 26N 96 24W
Homnabad 50 17 45N 77 11 E
Homoine 97 23 55S 35 8 E
Homoljske Planina 33 44 10N 21 45 E
Homorod 34 46 5N 25 15 E
Homs = Al Khums 87 32 40N 14 17 E
Homs (Hims) 46 34 40N 36 45 E
Hon Chong 55 10 25N 104 30 E
Hon Me 54 19 23N 105 56 E
Honan = Henan □ 60 34 0N 114 0 E
Honbetsu 63 43 7N 143 37 E
Honcut 122 39 20N 121 32W
Honda 134 5 12N 74 45W
Hondeklipbaai 96 30 19S 17 17 E
Hondo, Japan 64 32 27N 130 12 E
Hondo, U.S.A. 119 29 22N 99 6W
Hondo → 125 18 25N 88 21W
Honduras ■ 126 14 40N 86 30W
Honduras, Golfo de 126 16 50N 87 0W
Honesdale 115 41 34N 75 17W
Honey Harbour 106 44 52N 79 49W
Honey L. 122 40 13N 120 14W
Honfleur 18 49 25N 0 13 E
Hong → 54 20 17N 106 34 E
Hong Gai 54 20 57N 107 5 E
Hong He → 59 32 25N 115 35 E
Hong Kong ■ 62 22 11N 114 14 E
Hong'an 59 31 20N 114 40 E
Hongchŏn 61 37 44N 127 53 E
Honghai Wan 59 22 40N 115 0 E
Honghu 59 29 50N 113 30 E
Hongjiang 58 27 7N 109 59 E
Hongliu He → 60 38 0N 109 50 E
Hongor 60 45 45N 112 50 E
Hongsa 54 19 43N 101 20 E
Hongshui He → 58 23 48N 109 30 E
Hongsŏng 61 36 37N 126 38 E
Hongtong 60 36 16N 111 40 E
Honguedo, Détroit d' 103 49 15N 64 0W
Hongwon 61 40 0N 127 56 E
Hongya 58 29 57N 103 22 E
Hongyuan 58 32 51N 102 40 E
Hongze Hu 59 33 15N 118 35 E
Honiara 66 9 27S 159 57 E
Honiton 13 50 48N 3 11W
Honjo 63 39 23N 140 3 E
Honjō 65 36 14N 139 11 E
Honkawane 65 35 5N 138 5 E
Honkorâb, Ras 90 24 35N 35 10 E
Honolulu 110 21 19N 157 52W
Honshū 63 36 0N 138 0 E
Hontoria del Pinar 24 41 50N 3 10W
Hood Mt. 120 45 24N 121 41W
Hood, Pt. 79 34 23S 119 34 E
Hood Pt. 69 10 4S 147 45 E
Hood River 120 45 45N 121 31W
Hoodsport 122 47 24N 123 7W
Hooge 30 54 31N 8 36 E
Hoogeveen 16 52 44N 6 30 E
Hoogezand 16 53 11N 6 45 E
Hooghly → 49 21 56N 88 4 E
Hooghly-Chinsura 49 22 53N 88 27 E
Hook Hd. 15 52 8N 6 57W
Hook I. 72 20 4S 149 0 E
Hook of Holland = Hoek van Holland 16 52 0N 4 7 E
Hooker 119 36 55N 101 10W
Hooker Creek 78 18 23S 130 38 E
Hoopeston 117 40 30N 87 40W
Hoopstad 96 27 50S 25 55 E
Hoorn 16 52 38N 5 4 E
Hoover Dam 123 36 0N 114 45W
Hooversville 114 40 8N 78 57W
Hop Bottom 115 41 41N 75 47W
Hopà 39 41 28N 41 30 E
Hope, Can. 108 49 25N 121 25 E
Hope, Ariz., U.S.A. 123 33 43N 113 42W
Hope, Ark., U.S.A. 119 33 40N 93 36W
Hope, Ind., U.S.A. 117 39 18N 85 46W
Hope, N.D., U.S.A. 118 47 21N 97 42W
Hope Bay 143 65 0S 55 0W
Hope I. 106 44 55N 80 11W
Hope, L. 73 28 24S 139 18 E
Hope Pt. 100 68 20N 166 50W
Hope Town 126 26 35N 76 57W
Hopedale 103 55 28N 60 13W
Hopefield 96 33 3S 18 22 E
Hopei = Hebei □ 60 39 0N 116 0 E
Hopelchén 125 19 46N 89 50W
Hopetoun, Vic., Austral. 74 35 42S 142 22 E
Hopetoun, W. Australia, Austral. 79 33 57S 120 7 E
Hopetown 96 29 34S 24 3 E
Hopin 52 24 58N 96 30 E
Hopkins, Mich., U.S.A. 117 42 37N 85 46W
Hopkins, Mo., U.S.A. 116 40 31N 94 45W
Hopkins → 74 38 25S 142 30 E
Hopkins, L. 78 24 15S 128 35 E
Hopkinsville 113 36 52N 87 26W
Hopland 122 39 0N 123 7W
Hoptrup 11 55 11N 9 28 E
Hoquiam 122 46 50N 123 55W
Hōrai 65 34 58N 137 32 E
Horcajo de Santiago 24 39 50N 3 1W
Hordaland fylke □ 9 60 25N 6 15 E
Horden Hills 78 20 40S 130 20 E
Horezu 34 45 6N 24 0 E
Horgen 31 47 15N 8 35 E
Horinger 60 40 28N 111 48 E
Horlick Mts. 143 84 0S 102 0W
Hormoz 47 27 35N 55 0 E
Hormoz, Jaz. ye 47 27 8N 56 28 E
Hormuz Str. 47 26 30N 56 30 E
Horn, Ísafjarðarsýsla, Iceland 8 66 28N 22 28W
Horn, Suður-Múlasýsla, Iceland 8 65 10N 13 31W
Horn → 108 61 30N 118 1W
Horn, Cape = Hornos, Cabo de 142 55 50S 67 30W
Horn Head 15 55 13N 8 0W
Horn I., Austral. 72 10 37S 142 17 E
Horn I., P.N.G. 69 10 35S 142 20 E
Horn, I. 113 30 17N 88 40W
Horn Mts. 108 62 15N 119 15W
Hornachuelos 23 37 50N 5 14W
Hornavan 8 66 15N 17 30 E
Hornbæk 11 56 5N 12 26 E
Hornbeck 119 31 22N 93 20W
Hornbrook 120 41 58N 122 37W
Hornburg 30 52 2N 10 36 E
Hornby 81 43 33S 172 33 E
Horncastle 12 53 13N 0 8W
Horndal 10 60 18N 16 23 E
Hornell 114 42 23N 77 41W
Hornell L. 108 62 20N 119 25W
Hornepayne 102 49 14N 84 48W
Hornings Mills 106 44 9N 80 12W
Hornitos 122 37 30N 120 14W
Hornos, Cabo de 142 55 50S 67 30W
Hornoy 19 49 50N 1 54 E
Hornsby 76 33 42S 151 2 E
Hornsea 12 53 55N 0 10W
Hornslandet 10 61 35N 17 37 E
Hornslet 11 56 18N 10 19 E
Hörnum 30 54 44N 8 18 E
Horqin Youyi Quanqi 61 46 5N 122 3 E
Horqueta 140 23 15S 56 55W
Horqueta, La 135 7 55N 60 20W
Horra, La 22 41 44N 3 53W
Horred 11 57 22N 12 28 E
Horse Cr. 118 41 57N 103 58W
Horse Is. 103 50 15N 55 50W
Horsefly L. 108 52 25N 121 0W
Horsens 11 55 52N 9 51 E
Horsens Fjord 11 55 50N 10 0 E
Horseshoe Dam 121 33 45N 111 35W
Horsham, Austral. 74 36 44S 142 13 E
Horsham, U.K. 13 51 4N 0 20W
Horten 10 59 25N 10 32 E
Hortobágy → 33 47 30N 21 6 E
Horton 118 39 42N 95 30W
Horton → 100 69 56N 126 52W
Hörvik 11 56 2N 14 45 E
Horwood, L. 102 48 5N 82 20W
Hosaina 91 7 30N 37 47 E
Hosdurga 51 13 49N 76 17 E
Hose, Pegunungan 56 2 5N 114 6 E
Hoshangabad 48 22 45N 77 45 E
Hoshiarpur 48 31 30N 75 58 E
Hoskins 69 5 29S 150 27 E
Hoskinstown 76 35 25S 149 28 E
Hosmer 118 45 36N 99 29W
Hososhima 64 32 26N 131 40 E
Hospet 51 15 15N 76 20 E
Hospitalet de Llobregat 24 41 21N 2 6 E
Hospitalet, L' 20 42 36N 1 47 E
Hoste, I. 142 55 0S 69 0W
Hostens 20 44 30N 0 40W
Hot 54 18 8N 98 29 E
Hot Creek Ra. 120 39 0N 116 0W
Hot Springs, Ari., U.S.A. 119 34 30N 93 0W
Hot Springs, S.D., U.S.A. 118 43 25N 103 30W
Hotan 62 37 25N 79 55 E
Hotazel 96 27 17S 23 00 E
Hotchkiss 121 38 47N 107 47W
Hotham, C. 78 12 2S 131 18 E
Hotham Heights 75 36 58S 147 11 E
Hoting 8 64 8N 16 15 E
Hotte, Massif de la 127 18 30N 73 45W
Hottentotsbaai 96 26 8S 14 59 E
Houailou 68 21 17S 165 38 E
Houat 18 47 24N 2 58W
Houck 121 35 15N 109 15W
Houdan 19 48 48N 1 35 E
Houei Sai 54 20 18N 100 26 E
Houffalize 16 50 8N 5 48 E
Houghton 118 47 9N 88 39W
Houghton L. 106 44 20N 84 40W
Houghton Lake Heights 106 44 18N 84 51W
Houghton-le-Spring 12 54 51N 1 28W
Houhora 80 34 49S 173 9 E
Houlton 103 46 5N 67 50W
Houma 119 29 35N 90 44W
Houndé 88 11 34N 3 31W
Hourtin 20 45 11N 1 4W
Hourtin, Étang d' 20 45 10N 1 6W
Houston, Can. 108 54 25N 126 39W
Houston, Mo., U.S.A. 119 37 20N 92 0W
Houston, Tex., U.S.A. 119 29 50N 95 20W
Houtman Abrolhos 79 28 43S 113 48 E
Hov 11 55 55N 10 15 E
Hova 11 58 53N 14 14 E
Høvåg 11 58 10N 8 16 E
Hovd (Jargalant) 62 48 2N 91 37 E
Hove 13 50 50N 0 10W
Hovmantorp 11 56 47N 15 7 E
Hövsgöl 60 43 37N 109 39 E
Hövsgöl Nuur 62 51 0N 100 30 E
Hovsta 10 59 22N 15 15 E
Howakil 91 15 10N 40 16 E
Howar, Wadi → 91 17 30N 27 8 E
Howard, Austral. 73 25 16S 152 32 E
Howard, Kans., U.S.A. 119 37 30N 96 16W
Howard, Pa., U.S.A. 114 41 0N 77 40W
Howard, S.D., U.S.A. 118 44 2N 97 30W
Howard I. 72 12 10S 135 24 E
Howard L. 109 62 15N 105 57W
Howatharra 79 28 29S 114 33 E
Howe 120 43 48N 113 0W

Howe, C. 75 37 30S 150 0 E
Howe I. 107 44 16N 76 17W
Howell 106 42 38N 83 56W
Howes Valley 76 32 51S 150 51 E
Howick, Can. 105 45 11N 73 51W
Howick, N.Z. 80 36 54S 174 56 E
Howick, S. Afr. 97 29 28S 30 14 E
Howick Group 72 14 20S 145 30 E
Howitt, L. 73 27 40S 138 40 E
Howley 103 49 12N 57 2W
Howrah 49 22 37N 88 20 E
Howth Hd. 15 53 21N 6 0W
Höxter 30 51 45N 9 26 E
Hoy I. 14 58 50N 3 15W
Hoya 30 52 47N 9 10 E
Hoyerswerda 30 51 26N 14 14 E
Hoyos 22 40 9N 6 45W
Hpawlum 52 27 12N 98 12 E
Hpettintha 52 24 14N 95 23 E
Hpizow 52 26 57N 98 24 E
Hrádec Králové 32 50 15N 15 50 E
Hranice 32 49 34N 17 45 E
Hron → 33 47 49N 18 45 E
Hrubieszów 32 50 49N 23 51 E
Hrvatska 27 45 20N 16 0 E
Hsenwi 52 23 22N 97 55 E
Hsiamen = Xiamen 59 24 25N 118 4 E
Hsian = Xi'an 60 34 15N 109 0 E
Hsinhailien = Lianyungang 61 34 40N 119 11 E
Hsipaw 52 22 37N 97 18 E
Hsüchou = Xuzhou 61 34 18N 117 18 E
Htawgaw 52 25 57N 98 23 E
Hu Xian 60 34 8N 108 42 E
Hua Hin 54 12 34N 99 58 E
Hua Xian, Henan, China 60 35 30N 114 30 E
Hua Xian, Shaanxi, China 60 34 30N 109 48 E
Hua'an 59 25 1N 117 32 E
Huacaya 137 20 45S 63 43W
Huacheng 59 24 4N 115 37 E
Huachinera 124 30 9N 108 55W
Huacho 136 11 10S 77 35W
Huachón 136 10 35S 76 0W
Huade 60 41 55N 113 59 E
Huadian 61 43 0N 126 40 E
Huai He → 59 33 0N 118 30 E
Huai Yot 55 7 45N 99 37 E
Huai'an, Hebei, China 60 40 30N 114 20 E
Huai'an, Jiangsu, China 61 33 30N 119 10 E
Huaide 61 43 30N 124 40 E
Huaidezhen 61 43 48N 124 50 E
Huaihua 58 27 32N 109 57 E
Huaiji 59 23 55N 112 12 E
Huainan 59 32 38N 116 58 E
Huaining 59 30 24N 116 40 E
Huairen 60 39 48N 113 20 E
Huairou 60 40 20N 116 35 E
Huaiyang 60 33 40N 114 52 E
Huaiyuan, Anhui, China 61 32 55N 117 10 E
Huaiyuan, Guangxi, China 58 24 31N 108 22 E
Huajianzi 61 41 23N 125 20 E
Huajuapan de Leon 125 17 50N 97 48W
Hualian 59 23 59N 121 37 E
Huallaga → 136 5 0S 75 30W
Huallanca 136 8 50S 77 56W
Hualpai Pk. 121 35 8N 113 58W
Huamachuco 136 7 50S 78 5W
Huambo 93 12 42S 15 54 E
Huan Jiang → 60 34 28N 109 0 E
Huan Xian 60 36 33N 107 7 E
Huancabamba 136 5 10S 79 15W
Huancane 136 15 10S 69 44W
Huancapi 136 13 40S 74 0W
Huancavelica 136 12 50S 75 5W
Huancavelica □ 136 13 0S 75 0W
Huancayo 136 12 5S 75 12W
Huanchaca 136 20 15S 66 40W
Huanchaca, Serranía de 137 14 30S 60 39W
Huang Hai 61 35 0N 123 0 E
Huang He 62 37 55N 118 50 E
Huang Xian 61 37 38N 120 30 E
Huangchuan 59 32 15N 115 10 E
Huanggang 59 30 29N 114 52 E
Huangling 60 35 34N 109 15 E
Huangliu 62 18 20N 108 50 E
Huanglong 60 35 30N 109 59 E
Huanglongtan 59 32 40N 110 33 E
Huangmei 59 30 5N 115 56 E
Huangpi 59 30 50N 114 22 E
Huangping 58 26 52N 107 54 E
Huangshi 59 30 10N 115 3 E
Huangsongdian 61 43 45N 127 25 E
Huangyan 59 28 38N 121 19 E
Huangyangsi 59 26 33N 111 39 E
Huaning 58 24 17N 102 56 E
Huanjiang 58 24 50N 108 18 E
Huanta 136 12 55S 74 20W
Huantai 61 36 58N 117 56 E
Huánuco 136 9 55S 76 15W
Huánuco □ 136 9 55S 76 14W
Huanuni 136 18 16S 66 51W
Huanzo, Cordillera de 136 14 35S 73 20W
Huaping 58 26 46N 101 25 E
Huaral 136 11 32S 77 13W
Huaraz 136 9 30S 77 32W
Huari 136 9 14S 77 14W
Huarmey 136 10 5S 78 5W
Huarochiri 136 12 9S 76 15W
Huarocondo 136 13 26S 72 14W
Huarong 59 29 29N 112 30 E
Huasamota 124 22 30N 104 30W
Huascarán 136 9 8S 77 36W
Huascarán, Nevado 136 9 7S 77 37W
Huasco 140 28 30S 71 15W
Huasco → 140 28 27S 71 13W
Huasna 123 35 6N 120 24W
Huatabampo 124 26 50N 109 50W
Huauchinango 125 20 11N 98 3W
Huautla de Jiménez 125 18 8N 96 51W
Huaxi 58 26 25N 106 40 E
Huay Namota 124 21 56N 104 30W
Huayin 60 34 35N 110 5 E
Huayllay 136 11 03S 76 21W
Huayuan 58 28 37N 109 29 E
Huazhou 59 21 33N 110 33 E
Hubbard, Iowa, U.S.A. 116 42 18N 93 18W
Hubbard, Tex., U.S.A. 119 31 50N 96 50W
Hubbard L. 106 44 49N 83 34W
Hubbart Pt. 109 59 21N 94 41W
Hubei □ 59 31 0N 112 0 E
Hubli 51 15 22N 75 15 E
Huchang 61 41 25N 127 2 E
Hückelhoven-Ratheim 30 51 6N 6 13 E
Huddersfield 12 53 38N 1 49W
Hudi 90 17 43N 34 18 E
Hudiksvall 10 61 43N 17 10 E
Hudson, Can. 109 50 6N 92 09W
Hudson, Mass., U.S.A. 115 42 23N 71 35W
Hudson, Mich., U.S.A. 117 41 50N 84 20W
Hudson, N.Y., U.S.A. 115 42 15N 73 46W
Hudson, Wis., U.S.A. 118 44 57N 92 45W
Hudson, Wyo., U.S.A. 120 42 54N 108 37W
Hudson → 115 40 42N 74 2W
Hudson Bay, Can. 101 60 0N 86 0W
Hudson Bay, Sask., Can. 109 52 51N 102 23W
Hudson Falls 115 43 18N 73 34W
Hudson Hope 108 56 0N 121 54W
Hudson Mts. 143 74 32S 99 20W
Hudson Str. 101 62 0N 70 0W
Hudsonville 117 42 52N 85 52W
Hue 54 16 30N 107 35 E
Huebra → 22 41 2N 6 48W
Huechucuicui, Pta. 142 41 48S 74 2W
Huedin 34 46 52N 23 2 E
Huehuetenango 126 15 20N 91 28W
Huejúcar 124 22 21N 103 13W
Huelgoat 18 48 22N 3 46W
Huelma 25 37 39N 3 28W
Huelva 23 37 18N 6 57W
Huelva □ 23 37 40N 7 0W
Huelva → 23 37 27N 6 0W
Huentelauquén 140 31 38S 71 33W
Huércal Overa 25 37 23N 1 57W
Huerta, Sa. de la 140 31 10S 67 30W
Huertas, C. de las 25 38 21N 0 24W
Huerva → 24 41 39N 0 52W
Huesca 24 42 8N 0 25W
Huesca □ 24 42 20N 0 1 E
Huéscar 25 37 44N 2 35W
Huetamo 124 18 36N 100 54W
Huete 24 40 10N 2 43W
Hugh → 72 25 1S 134 1 E
Hughenden 72 20 52S 144 10 E
Hughes, Austral. 79 30 42S 129 31 E
Hughes, U.S.A. 100 66 0N 154 20W
Hugo 118 39 12N 103 27W
Hugoton 119 37 11N 101 22W
Hui Xian, Gansu, China 60 33 50N 106 4 E
Hui Xian, Henan, China 60 35 27N 113 12 E
Hui'an 59 25 1N 118 43 E
Hui'anbu 60 37 28N 106 38 E
Huiarau Ra. 80 38 45S 176 55 E
Huichapán 125 20 24N 99 40W
Huidong 58 26 34N 102 35 E
Huifa He → 61 43 0N 127 50 E
Huila □, Angola 96 15 30S 15 0 E
Huila □, Colomb. 134 2 30N 75 45W
Huila, Nevado del 134 3 0N 76 0W
Huilai 59 23 0N 116 18 E
Huili 58 26 35N 102 17 E
Huimin 61 37 27N 117 28 E
Huinan 61 42 40N 126 2 E
Huinca Renancó 140 34 51S 64 22W
Huining 60 35 38N 105 0 E
Huinong 60 39 5N 106 35 E
Huiroa 80 39 15S 174 30 E
Huishui 58 26 7N 106 38 E
Huisne → 18 47 59N 0 11 E
Huiting 60 34 5N 116 5 E
Huitong 58 26 51N 109 45 E
Huixtla 125 15 9N 92 28W
Huiya 46 24 40N 49 15 E
Huize 58 26 24N 103 15 E
Huizhou 59 23 0N 114 23 E
Hukou 59 29 45N 116 21 E
Hukuma 91 14 55N 36 2 E
Hukuntsi 96 23 58S 21 45 E
Hula 91 6 33N 38 30 E
Hulaifa 46 25 58N 40 45 E
Hulan 62 46 1N 126 37 E
Hulbert 106 46 21N 85 9W
Huld 60 45 5N 105 30 E
Hülda 44 31 50N 34 51 E
Hulin He → 61 45 0N 122 10 E
Hull, Can. 104 45 25N 75 44W
Hull, U.K. 12 53 45N 0 20W
Hull, U.S.A. 116 39 43N 91 13W
Hull → 12 53 43N 0 25W
Hulst 16 51 17N 4 2 E
Hultsfred 11 57 30N 15 52 E
Hulun Nur 62 49 0N 117 30 E
Humahuaca 140 23 10S 65 25W
Humaitá, Brazil 137 7 35S 63 1W
Humaitá, Parag. 140 27 2S 58 31W
Humansdorp 96 34 2S 24 46 E
Humansville 116 37 48N 93 35W
Humber → 12 53 40N 0 10W
Humberside □ 12 53 50N 0 30W
Humbert River 78 16 30S 130 45 E
Humble 119 29 59N 93 18W
Humboldt, Can. 109 52 15N 105 9W
Humboldt, Iowa, U.S.A. 116 42 42N 94 15W
Humboldt, Tenn., U.S.A. 119 35 50N 88 55W
Humboldt → 120 40 2N 118 31W
Humboldt Gletscher 144 79 30N 62 0W
Humboldt Mts. 81 44 30S 168 15 E
Humbolt, Massif du 68 21 53S 166 25 E
Hume, Calif., U.S.A. 122 36 48N 118 54W
Hume, Kans., U.S.A. 116 38 5N 94 35W
Hume, L. 75 36 0S 147 0 E
Humenné 32 48 55N 21 50 E
Humeston 116 40 51N 93 30W
Humphreys, Mt. 122 37 17N 118 40W
Humphreys Pk. 121 35 24N 111 38W
Humpolec 32 49 31N 15 20 E
Humptulips 122 47 14N 123 57W
Humula 76 35 30S 147 46 E
Hün 87 29 2N 16 0 E
Hun Jiang → 61 40 50N 125 38 E
Húnaflói 8 65 50N 20 50W
Hunan □ 59 27 30N 112 0 E
Hunchun 61 42 52N 130 28 E
Hundested 11 55 58N 11 52 E
Hundred Mile House 108 51 38N 121 18W
Hunedoara 34 45 40N 22 50 E
Hünfeld 30 50 40N 9 47 E
Hung Yen 54 20 39N 106 4 E
Hunga 68 18 41S 174 7W
Hunga Ha'api 68 20 41S 175 7W
Hungary ■ 33 47 20N 19 20 E
Hungary, Plain of 6 47 0N 20 0 E
Hungerford 73 28 58S 144 24 E
Hŭngnam 61 39 49N 127 45 E
Huni Valley 88 5 33N 1 56W
Hunsberge 96 27 45S 17 12 E
Hunsrück 31 49 30N 7 0 E
Hunstanton 12 52 57N 0 30 E
Hunsur 51 12 16N 76 16 E
Hunte → 30 52 30N 8 19 E
Hunter, Austral. 74 36 26S 144 30 E
Hunter, N.Z. 81 44 36S 171 2 E
Hunter, N.D., U.S.A. 118 47 12N 97 17W
Hunter, N.Y., U.S.A. 115 42 13N 74 13W
Hunter →, Austral. 76 32 52S 151 46 E
Hunter →, N.Z. 81 44 21S 169 27 E
Hunter, C. 68 9 48S 159 50 E
Hunter Hills, The 81 44 26S 170 46 E
Hunter I., Austral. 72 40 30S 144 45 E
Hunter I., Can. 108 51 55N 128 0W
Hunter Mts. 81 45 43S 167 25 E
Hunter Ra. 76 32 45S 150 15 E
Hunters Road 95 19 9S 29 49 E
Hunterton 73 26 12S 148 30 E
Hunterville 80 39 56S 175 35 E
Huntingburg 117 38 20N 86 58W
Huntingdon, Can. 105 45 6N 74 10W
Huntingdon, U.K. 13 52 20N 0 11W
Huntingdon, U.S.A. 114 40 28N 78 1W
Huntington, Ind., U.S.A. 117 40 52N 85 30W
Huntington, N.Y., U.S.A. 115 40 52N 73 25W
Huntington, Oreg., U.S.A. 120 44 22N 117 21W
Huntington, Ut., U.S.A. 120 39 24N 111 1W
Huntington, W. Va., U.S.A. 112 38 20N 82 30W
Huntington Beach 123 33 40N 118 0W
Huntington Park 121 33 58N 118 15W
Huntley 117 42 10N 88 26W
Huntly, N.Z. 80 37 34S 175 11 E
Huntly, U.K. 14 57 27N 2 48W
Huntsville, Can. 106 45 20N 79 14W
Huntsville, Ala., U.S.A. 113 34 45N 86 35W
Huntsville, Mo., U.S.A. 116 39 26N 92 33W
Huntsville, Tex., U.S.A. 119 30 45N 95 35W
Hunyani → 95 15 57S 30 39 E
Hunyani Dams. 95 18 0S 31 10 E
Hunyuan 60 39 42N 113 42 E
Hunza → 49 35 54N 74 20 E
Huo Xian 60 36 36N 111 42 E
Huon, G. 69 7 0S 147 30 E
Huon Pen. 69 6 20S 147 30 E
Huong Hoa 54 16 37N 106 45 E
Huong Khe 54 18 13N 105 41 E
Huonville 72 43 0S 147 5 E
Huoqiu 59 32 20N 116 12 E
Huoshan, Anhui, China 59 31 25N 116 20 E
Huoshan, Anhui, China 59 32 28N 118 30 E
Huoshao Dao 59 22 40N 121 30 E
Hupeh □ = Hubei □ 59 31 0N 112 0 E
Hure Qi 61 42 45N 121 45 E
Hurezani 34 44 49N 23 40 E
Hurghada 90 27 15N 33 50 E
Hurley, N. Mex., U.S.A. 121 32 45N 108 7W
Hurley, Wis., U.S.A. 118 46 26N 90 10W
Huron, Calif., U.S.A. 122 36 12N 120 6W
Huron, Ohio, U.S.A. 114 41 22N 82 34W
Huron, S.D., U.S.A. 118 44 22N 98 12W
Huron, L. 106 45 0N 83 0W
Hurricane 121 37 10N 113 12W
Hurso 91 9 35N 41 33 E
Hurum 10 61 9N 8 46 E
Hurunui → 81 42 54S 173 18 E
Hurup 11 56 46N 8 25 E
Húsavík 8 66 3N 17 21W
Huşi 34 46 41N 28 7 E
Huskisson 76 35 2S 150 41 E
Huskvarna 11 57 47N 14 15 E
Hussar 108 51 3N 112 41W
Hussein (Allenby) Br. 44 31 53N 35 33 E
Husum, Ger. 30 54 27N 9 3 E
Husum, Sweden 10 63 21N 19 12 E
Hutchinson, Kans., U.S.A. 119 38 3N 97 59W
Hutchinson, Minn., U.S.A. 118 44 50N 94 22W
Hutsonville 117 39 6N 87 40W
Hüttental 30 50 52N 8 1 E
Huttig 119 33 5N 92 10W
Hutton, Mt. 73 25 51S 148 20 E
Huwarā 44 32 9N 35 15 E
Huwun 91 4 23N 40 6 E
Huy 16 50 31N 5 15 E
Hvammur 8 65 13N 21 49W
Hvar, Yugo. 27 43 11N 16 28 E
Hvar, Yugo. 27 43 10N 16 45 E
Hvarski Kanal 27 43 15N 16 35 E
Hvítá 8 64 40N 21 5W
Hvítá → 8 64 0N 20 58W
Hvítárvatn 8 64 37N 19 50W
Hwachon-chosuji 61 38 5N 127 50 E
Hwang Ho = Huang He → 61 37 50N 118 50 E
Hwekum 52 26 7N 95 22 E
Hyannis 118 42 0N 101 45W
Hyargas Nuur 62 49 0N 93 0 E
Hyatts 112 38 59N 76 55W
Hybo 10 61 49N 16 15 E
Hyde 81 45 18S 170 16 E
Hyde Park 135 6 30N 58 16W
Hyden 79 32 24S 118 53 E
Hyderabad, India 50 17 22N 78 29 E
Hyderabad, Pak. 48 25 23N 68 24 E
Hyderabad □ 48 25 3N 68 24 E
Hyères 21 43 8N 6 9 E
Hyères, Îles d' 21 43 0N 6 28 E
Hyesan 61 41 20N 128 10 E
Hyland → 108 59 52N 128 12W
Hyland, Mt. 77 30 10S 152 27 E
Hyltebruk 11 56 59N 13 15 E
Hymia 49 33 40N 78 2 E
Hyndman Pk. 120 43 50N 114 10W
Hyōgo □ 64 35 15N 135 0 E
Hyrum 120 41 35N 111 56W

Hysham 120 46 21N 107 11W
Hythe 13 51 4N 1 5E
Hyūga 64 32 25N 131 35E
Hyvinkää 9 60 38N 24 50E

I

I-n-Azaoua 87 20 45N 7 31E
I-n-Échaï 86 20 10N 2 5W
I-n-Gall 89 16 51N 7 1E
I-n-Tabedog 86 19 48N 1 11E
Iabès, Erg 86 27 30N 2 2W
Iaco → 136 9 3S 68 34W
Iaçu 139 12 45S 40 13W
Iakora 97 23 6S 46 40E
Iaşi 34 47 10N 27 40E
Iauaretê 134 0 36N 69 12W
Iba 57 15 22N 120 0E
Ibadan 89 7 22N 3 58E
Ibagué 134 4 20N 75 20W
Ibaiti 139 23 50S 50 10W
Iballja 34 42 12N 20 0E
Ibăneşti 34 46 45N 24 50E
Ibar → 33 43 43N 20 45E
Ibara 64 34 36N 133 28E
Ibaraki 65 34 49N 135 34E
Ibaraki □ 65 36 10N 140 10E
Ibarra 134 0 21N 78 7W
Ibba 91 4 49N 29 2E
Ibba, Bahr el 91 5 30N 28 55E
Ibbenbüren 30 52 16N 7 41E
Ibembo 94 2 35N 23 35E
Ibera, Laguna 140 28 30S 57 9W
Iberia 116 38 5N 92 18W
Iberian Peninsula 6 40 0N 5 0W
Iberville 105 45 19N 73 17W
Iberville, Lac d' 102 55 55N 73 15W
Ibi 89 8 15N 9 44E
Ibiá 139 19 30S 46 30W
Ibicaraí 139 14 51S 39 36W
Ibicuí 139 14 51S 39 59W
Ibicuy 140 33 55S 59 10W
Ibioapaba, Sa. da 138 4 0S 41 30W
Ibipetuba 138 11 0S 44 32W
Ibitiara 139 12 39S 42 13W
Ibiza 25 38 54N 1 26E
Ibiza, I. 25 39 0N 1 30E
Íblei, Monti 29 37 15N 14 45E
Ibo 95 12 22S 40 40E
Ibonma 57 3 29S 133 31E
Ibotirama 139 12 13S 43 12W
Ibshawâi 90 29 21N 30 40E
Ibu 57 1 35N 127 33E
Ibuki-Sanchi 65 35 25N 136 18E
Iburg 30 52 10N 8 3E
Ibusuki 64 31 12N 130 40E
Ibwe Munyama 95 16 5S 28 31E
Icá 136 14 0S 75 48W
Ica □ 136 14 20S 75 30W
Içá → 136 2 55S 67 58W
Icabarú 135 4 20N 61 45W
Icabarú → 135 4 45N 62 15W
Içana 134 0 21N 67 19W
Içana → 134 0 26N 67 19W
Icatu 138 2 46S 44 4W
Iceland ■ 8 65 0N 19 0W
Icha 41 55 30N 156 0E
Ich'ang = Yichang 59 30 40N 111 20E
Ichchapuram 50 19 10N 84 40E
Ichihara 65 35 28N 140 5E
Ichihawa 65 35 44N 139 55E
Ichilo → 137 15 57S 64 50W
Ichinomiya, Gifu, Japan 65 35 18N 136 48E
Ichinomiya, Kumamoto, Japan 64 32 58N 131 5E
Ichinoseki 63 38 55N 141 8E
Ichŏn 61 37 17N 127 27E
Icht 86 29 6N 8 54W
Icó 138 6 24S 38 51W
Icoraci 138 1 18S 48 28W
Icy Str. 108 58 20N 135 30W
Ida Grove 118 42 20N 95 25W
Ida Valley 79 28 42S 120 29E
Idabel 119 33 53N 94 50W
Idaga Hamus 91 14 13N 39 48E
Idah 89 7 5N 6 40E
Idaho □ 120 44 10N 114 0W
Idaho City 120 43 50N 115 52W
Idaho Falls 120 43 30N 112 1W
Idaho Springs 120 39 49N 105 30W
Idanha-a-Nova 22 39 50N 7 15W
Idar-Oberstein 31 49 43N 7 19E
Idd el Ghanam 85 11 30N 24 19E
Iddan 45 6 10N 48 55E
Idehan 87 27 10N 11 30E
Idehan Marzūq 87 24 50N 13 51E
Idelès 87 23 50N 5 53E
Idfû 90 25 0N 32 49E
Ídhi Óros 35 35 15N 24 45E
Ídhra 35 37 20N 23 28E
Idi 56 5 2N 97 37E
Idi Amin Dada, L. 94 0 25S 29 40E
Idiofa 92 4 55S 19 42E
Idkerberget 10 60 22N 15 15E
Idku, Bahra el 90 31 18N 30 18E
Idlip 46 35 55N 36 38E
Idna 44 31 34N 34 58E
Idria 122 36 25N 120 41W
Idrija 27 46 0N 14 5E
Idritsa 36 56 25N 28 30E
Idstein 31 50 13N 8 17E
Idutywa 97 32 8S 28 18E
Ieper 16 50 51N 2 53E
Ierápetra 35 35 0N 25 44E
Ierissós 35 40 22N 23 52E
Ierzu 28 39 48N 9 32E
Ieshima-Shotō 64 34 40N 134 32E
Iesi 27 43 32N 13 12E
Ifach, Punta 25 38 38N 0 5E
Ifanadiana 97 21 19S 47 39E
Ife 89 7 30N 4 31E
Iférouâne 89 19 5N 8 24E
Iffley 72 18 53S 141 12E
Ifon 89 6 58N 5 40E
Iforas, Adrar des 89 19 40N 1 40E
Ifrane 86 33 33N 5 7W
Iga 65 34 45N 136 10E
Iganga 94 0 37N 33 28E
Igara Paraná → 134 2 9S 71 47W
Igarapava 139 20 3S 47 47W
Igarapé Açu 138 1 4S 47 33W
Igarapé-Mirim 138 1 59S 48 58W
Igarka 41 67 30N 86 33E
Igatimi 141 24 5S 55 40W
Igatpuri 50 19 40N 73 35E
Igbetti 89 8 44N 4 8E
Igbo-Ora 89 7 29N 3 15E
Igboho 89 8 53N 3 50E
Iggesund 10 61 39N 17 10E
Ighil Izane 86 35 44N 0 31E
Iglene 86 22 57N 4 58E
Iglésias 28 39 19N 8 27E
Igli 86 30 25N 2 19W
Igloolik 101 69 20N 81 49W
Igma 86 29 9N 6 24W
Igma, Gebel el 90 28 55N 34 0E
Ignace 102 49 30N 91 40W
Igoshevo 37 59 25N 42 35E
Iguaçu → 141 25 36S 54 36W
Iguaçu, Cat. del 141 25 41S 54 26W
Iguala 125 18 20N 99 40W
Igualada 24 41 37N 1 37E
Iguana Creek 75 37 46S 147 23E
Iguape 139 24 43S 47 33W
Iguassu = Iguaçu 141 25 41N 54 26W
Iguatu 138 6 20S 39 18W
Iguéla 92 2 0S 9 16E
Igunga □ 94 4 20S 33 45E
Ihiala 89 5 51N 6 55E
Ihosy 97 22 24S 46 8E
Ihotry, L. 97 21 56S 43 41E
Iida 65 35 35N 137 50E
Iisalmi 8 63 32N 27 10E
Iizuka 64 33 38N 130 42E
Ijebu-Igbo 89 6 56N 4 1E
Ijebu-Ode 89 6 47N 3 58E
IJmuiden 16 52 28N 4 35E
IJssel → 16 52 35N 5 50E
IJsselmeer 16 52 45N 5 20E
Ijuí → 141 27 58S 55 20W
Ijüin 64 31 37N 130 24E
Ikale 89 7 40N 5 37E
Ikare 89 7 32N 5 40E
Ikaría 35 37 35N 26 10E
Ikast 11 56 8N 9 10E
Ikawa 65 35 13N 138 15E
Ikeda 64 34 1N 133 48E
Ikeja 89 6 36N 3 23E
Ikela 92 1 6S 23 6E
Ikerre-Ekiti 89 7 25N 5 19E
Ikhtiman 34 42 27N 23 48E
Iki 64 33 45N 129 42E
Iki-Kaikyō 64 33 40N 129 45E
Ikimba L. 94 1 30S 31 20E
Ikire 89 7 23N 4 15E
Ikitsuki-Shima 64 33 23N 129 26E
Ikom 89 6 0N 8 42E
Ikopa → 97 16 45S 46 40E
Ikot Ekpene 89 5 12N 7 40E
Ikungu 94 1 33S 33 42E
Ikuno 64 35 10N 134 48E
Ikurun 89 7 54N 4 40E
Ila 89 8 0N 4 39E
Ilagan 57 17 7N 121 53E
Ilam 49 26 58N 87 58E
Ilanskiy 41 56 14N 96 3E
Ilaro 89 6 53N 3 3E
Iława 32 53 36N 19 34E
Ilayangudi 51 9 34N 78 37E
Ilbilbie 72 21 45S 149 20E
Île-à-la Crosse 109 55 27N 107 53W
Île-à-la-Crosse, Lac 109 55 40N 107 45W
Île-Bouchard, L' 18 47 7N 0 26E
Île-de-France □ 19 49 0N 2 20E
Île-sur-le-Doubs, L' 19 47 26N 6 34E
Ilebo 92 4 17S 20 55E
Ileje □ 95 9 30S 33 25E
Ilek 40 51 32N 53 21E
Ilek → 40 51 30N 53 22E
Ilero 89 8 0N 3 20E
Îles, L. des 104 46 20N 75 18W
Ilesha, Oyo, Nigeria 89 7 37N 4 40E
Ilesha, Oyo, Nigeria 89 8 57N 3 28E
Ilford, Austral. 76 33 0S 149 52E
Ilford, Can. 109 56 4N 95 35W
Ilfracombe, Austral. 72 23 30S 144 30E
Ilfracombe, U.K. 13 51 13N 4 8W
Ilha Grande 135 0 27S 65 2W
Ilha Grande, Baía da 139 23 9S 44 30W
Ílhavo 22 40 33N 8 43W
Ilhéus 139 14 49S 39 2W
Ilich 40 40 50N 68 27E
Iliff 118 40 50N 103 3W
Iligan 57 8 12N 124 13E
Ilíki, L. 35 38 24N 23 15E
Iliodhrómia 35 39 12N 23 50E
Ilion 115 43 0N 75 3W
Ilirska-Bistrica 27 45 34N 14 14E
Ilkal 51 15 57N 76 8E
Ilkeston 12 52 59N 1 19W
Illana B. 57 7 35N 123 45E
Illapel 140 32 0S 71 10W
'Illar 44 32 23N 35 7E
Ille 20 42 40N 2 37E
Ille-et-Vilaine □ 18 48 10N 1 30W
Iller → 31 48 23N 9 58E
Illescas 22 40 8N 3 51W
Illiers 18 48 18N 1 15E
Illimani 136 16 30S 67 50W
Illinois □ 111 40 15N 89 30W
Illinois → 116 38 55N 90 28W
Illiopolis 116 39 51N 89 15W
Illizi 87 26 31N 8 32E
Illora 23 37 17N 3 53W
Ilm → 30 51 7N 11 45E
Ilmen, Oz. 36 58 15N 31 10E
Ilmenau 30 50 41N 10 55E
Ilo 136 17 40S 71 20W
Ilobu 89 7 45N 4 25E
Iloilo 57 10 45N 122 33E
Ilora 89 7 45N 3 50E
Ilorin 89 8 30N 4 35E
Iloulya 39 49 15N 44 2E
Ilovatka 37 50 30N 45 50E
Ilovlya → 39 49 14N 43 54E
Ilubabor □ 91 7 25N 35 0E
Ilukste 36 55 55N 26 20E
Ilva Micá 34 47 17N 24 40E
Ilwaco 122 46 19N 124 3W
Ilwaki 57 7 55S 126 30E
Ilyichevsk 38 46 10N 30 35E
Imabari 64 34 4N 133 0E
Imaichi 65 36 43N 139 46E
Imaloto → 97 23 27S 45 13E
Imandra, Oz. 40 67 45N 33 0E
Imari 64 33 15N 129 52E
Imasa 90 18 0N 36 12E
Imbâbah 90 30 5N 31 12E
Imbabura □ 134 0 30N 78 45W
Imbaimadai 135 5 44N 60 17W
Imbler 120 45 31N 118 0W
Imdahane 86 32 8N 7 0W
Imeni Poliny Osipenko 41 52 30N 136 29E
Imeri, Serra 134 0 50N 65 25W
Imerimandroso 97 17 26S 48 35E
Imi (Hinna) 91 6 28N 42 10E
Imishly 39 39 49N 48 4E
Imitek 86 29 43N 8 10W
Imlay 120 40 45N 118 9W
Imlay City 106 43 0N 83 2W
Immenstadt 31 47 34N 10 13E
Immingham 12 53 37N 0 12W
Immokalee 113 26 25N 81 26W
Imo □ 89 5 15N 7 20E
Imola 27 44 20N 11 42E
Imotski 33 43 27N 17 12E
Imperatriz, Amazonas, Brazil 136 5 18S 67 11W
Imperatriz, Maranhão, Brazil 138 5 30S 47 29W
Impéria 26 43 52N 8 0E
Imperial, Can. 109 51 21N 105 28W
Imperial, Peru 136 13 4S 76 21W
Imperial, Calif., U.S.A. 123 32 52N 115 34W
Imperial, Nebr., U.S.A. 118 40 38N 101 39W
Imperial Beach 123 32 35N 117 8W
Imperial Dam 123 32 50N 114 30W
Imperial Res. 123 32 53N 114 28W
Imperial Valley 123 32 55N 115 30W
Imperieuse Reef 78 17 36S 118 50E
Impfondo 92 1 40N 18 0E
Imphal 52 24 48N 93 56E
Imphy 19 46 56N 3 15E
Imst 31 47 15N 10 44E
Imuruan B. 57 10 40N 119 10E
In Belbel 86 27 55N 1 12E
In Delimane 89 15 52N 1 31E
In Rhar 86 27 10N 1 59E
In Salah 86 27 10N 2 32E
In Tallak 89 16 19N 3 15E
Ina 65 35 50N 138 0E
Ina-Bonchi 65 35 45N 137 58E
Inajá 138 8 54S 37 49W
Inangahua Junc. 81 41 52S 171 59E
Inanwatan 57 2 10S 132 14E
Iñapari 136 11 0S 69 40W
Inarajan 68 13 16N 144 45E
Inari 8 68 54N 27 5E
Inazawa 65 35 15N 136 47E
Inca 24 39 43N 2 54E
Incaguasi 140 29 12S 71 5W
İnce Burnu 46 42 2N 35 0E
Inchini 91 8 55N 37 37E
Inchon 61 37 27N 126 40E
Incio 22 42 39N 7 21W
Incomáti → 97 25 46S 32 43E
Incudine, L' 21 41 50N 9 12E
Inda Silase 91 14 10N 38 15E
Indalsälven → 10 62 36N 17 30E
Indaw 52 24 15N 96 5E
Indbir 91 8 7N 37 52E
Independence, Calif., U.S.A. 122 36 51N 118 14W
Independence, Iowa, U.S.A. 116 42 27N 91 52W
Independence, Kans., U.S.A. 119 37 10N 95 43W
Independence, Ky., U.S.A. 117 38 57N 84 33W
Independence, Mo., U.S.A. 116 39 3N 94 25W
Independence, Oreg., U.S.A. 120 44 53N 123 12W
Independence Fjord 144 82 10N 29 0W
Independence Mts. 120 41 30N 116 2W
Independência 138 5 23S 40 19W
Independencia, La 125 16 31N 91 47W
Independenţa 34 45 25N 27 42E
Inderborskiy 39 48 30N 51 42E
Index 122 47 50N 121 33W
India ■ 5 20 0N 78 0E
Indian → 113 27 59N 80 34W
Indian-Antarctic Ridge 66 49 0S 120 0E
Indian Cabins 108 59 52N 117 40W
Indian Harbour 103 54 27N 57 13W
Indian Head 109 50 30N 103 41W
Indian Ocean 53 5 0S 75 0E
Indian Springs 123 36 35N 115 40W
Indiana 114 40 38N 79 9W
Indiana □ 117 40 0N 86 0W
Indianapolis 117 39 42N 86 10W
Indianola, Iowa, U.S.A. 116 41 20N 93 32W
Indianola, Miss., U.S.A. 119 33 27N 90 40W
Indiapora 139 19 57S 50 17W
Indiga 40 67 50N 48 50E
Indigirka → 41 70 48N 148 54E
Inđija 33 45 6N 20 7E
Indio 123 33 46N 116 15W
Indispensable Strait 68 9 0S 160 30E
Indonesia ■ 56 5 0S 115 0E
Indore 48 22 42N 75 53E
Indramayu 57 6 21S 108 20E
Indramayu, Tg. 57 6 20S 108 20E
Indravati → 50 19 20N 80 20E
Indre □ 19 47 12N 1 39E
Indre → 18 47 16N 0 19E
Indre-et-Loire □ 18 47 12N 0 40E
Indus → 48 24 20N 67 47E
Indus, Mouth of the 48 24 00N 68 00E
Industry 116 40 20N 90 36W
İnebolu 46 41 55N 33 40E
İnegöl 46 40 5N 29 31E
Inés, Mt. 142 48 30S 69 40W
Ineu 34 46 26N 21 51E
Infante, Kaap 96 34 27S 20 51E
Infantes 25 38 43N 3 1W
Infiernillo, Presa del 124 18 9N 102 0W
Infiesto 22 43 21N 5 21W
Ingapirca 134 2 38S 78 56W
Ingebyra 75 36 39S 148 31E
Ingelgar 76 31 21S 147 50E
Ingende 92 0 12S 18 57E
Ingeniero Jacobacci 142 41 20S 69 36W
Ingenio Santa Ana 140 27 25S 65 40W
Ingersoll 106 43 4N 80 55W
Ingham 72 18 43S 146 10E
Ingleborough 12 54 11N 2 23W
Inglewood, Queensland, Austral. 77 28 25S 151 2E

Inglewood, Vic., Austral. **74** 36 29S 143 53 E
Inglewood, N.Z. **80** 39 9S 174 14 E
Inglewood, U.S.A. **123** 33 58N 118 21W
Ingólfshöfði **8** 63 48N 16 39W
Ingolstadt **31** 48 45N 11 26 E
Ingomar **120** 46 35N 107 21W
Ingonish **103** 46 42N 60 18W
Ingore **88** 12 24N 15 48W
Ingrid Christensen Coast **143** 69 30S 76 00 E
Ingul → **38** 46 50N 32 15 E
Ingulec **38** 47 42N 33 14 E
Ingulets → **38** 46 41N 32 48 E
Inguri → **39** 42 38N 41 35 E
Inhaca, I. **97** 26 1S 32 57 E
Inhafenga **97** 20 36S 33 53 E
Inhambane **97** 23 54S 35 30 E
Inhambane □ **97** 22 30S 34 20 E
Inhambupe **139** 11 47S 38 21W
Inhaminga **95** 18 26S 35 0 E
Inharrime **97** 24 30S 35 0 E
Inharrime → **97** 24 30S 35 0 E
Inhuma **138** 6 40S 41 42W
Inhumas **139** 16 22S 49 30W
Iniesta **25** 39 27N 1 45W
Ining = Yining **62** 43 58N 81 10 E
Inini □ **135** 4 0N 53 0W
Inírida → **134** 3 55N 67 52W
Inishbofin **15** 53 35N 10 12W
Inishmore **15** 53 8N 9 45W
Inishowen **15** 55 14N 7 15W
Injune **73** 25 53S 148 32 E
Inklin **108** 58 56N 133 5W
Inklin → **108** 58 50N 133 10W
Inkom **120** 42 51N 112 15W
Inle Aing **52** 20 30N 96 58 E
Inn → **31** 48 35N 13 28 E
Innamincka **73** 27 44S 140 46 E
Inner Hebrides, Is. **14** 57 0N 6 30W
Inner Mongolia = Nei Monggol Zizhiqu □ **60** 42 0N 112 0 E
Inner Sound **14** 57 30N 5 55W
Innerkip **106** 43 13N 80 42W
Innerste → **30** 52 45N 9 40 E
Innetalling I. **102** 56 0N 79 0W
Innisfail, Austral. **72** 17 33S 146 5 E
Innisfail, Can. **108** 52 0N 113 57W
Innisplain **77** 28 11S 152 54 E
In'no-shima **64** 34 19N 133 10 E
Innsbruck **31** 47 16N 11 23 E
Inny → **15** 53 30N 7 50W
Ino **64** 33 33N 133 26 E
Inocência **139** 19 47S 51 48W
Inongo **92** 1 55S 18 30 E
Inoucdjouac (Port Harrison) **101** 58 27N 78 15W
Inowrocław **32** 52 50N 18 12 E
Inpundong **61** 41 25N 126 34 E
Inquisivi **136** 16 50S 67 10W
Inscription, C. **79** 25 29S 112 59 E
Insein **52** 16 50N 96 5 E
Însurăţei **34** 44 50N 27 40 E
Intendente Alvear **140** 35 12S 63 32W
Interior **118** 43 46N 101 59W
Interlaken **31** 46 41N 7 50 E
International Falls **118** 48 36N 93 25W
Intiyaco **140** 28 43S 60 5W
Intutu **134** 3 32S 74 48W
Inubō-Zaki **65** 35 42N 140 52 E
Inútil, B. **142** 53 30S 70 15W
Inuvik **100** 68 16N 133 40W
Inuyama **65** 35 23N 136 56 E
Inveralochy **76** 34 57S 149 40 E
Inveraray **14** 56 13N 5 5W
Inverbervie **14** 56 50N 2 17W
Invercargill **81** 46 24S 168 24 E
Inverell **77** 29 45S 151 8 E
Invergordon **14** 57 41N 4 10W
Inverleigh **74** 38 6S 144 3 E
Inverloch **74** 38 38S 145 45 E
Invermere **108** 50 30N 116 2W
Inverness, Can. **103** 46 15N 61 19W
Inverness, U.K. **14** 57 29N 4 12W
Inverness, U.S.A. **113** 28 50N 82 20W
Inverurie **14** 57 15N 2 21W
Inverway **78** 17 50S 129 38 E
Investigator Group **73** 34 45S 134 20 E
Investigator Str. **73** 35 30S 137 0 E
Invona **114** 40 46N 78 35W
Inya **40** 50 28N 86 37 E
Inyanga **95** 18 12S 32 40 E
Inyangani **95** 18 5S 32 50 E
Inyantue **95** 18 30S 26 40 E
Inyazura **95** 18 40S 32 16 E
Inyo Range **121** 37 0N 118 0W
Inyokern **123** 35 38N 117 48W
Inywa **52** 23 56N 96 17 E
Inza **37** 53 55N 46 25 E
Inzhavino **37** 52 22N 42 30 E
Ioánnina **35** 39 42N 20 47 E
Iola **119** 38 0N 95 20W
Ioma **69** 8 19S 147 52 E
Ion Corvin **34** 44 7N 27 50 E
Iona **14** 56 20N 6 25W
Ione, Calif., U.S.A. **122** 38 20N 120 56W
Ione, Wash., U.S.A. **120** 48 44N 117 29W
Ionia **117** 42 59N 85 7W
Ionian Is. = Iónioi Nísoi **35** 38 40N 20 0 E
Ionian Sea **6** 37 30N 17 30 E
Iónioi Nísoi **35** 38 40N 20 8 E
Iori → **39** 41 3N 46 17 E
Íos **35** 36 41N 25 20 E
Iowa □ **118** 42 18N 93 30W
Iowa → **116** 41 10N 91 1W
Iowa City **116** 41 40N 91 35W
Iowa Falls **116** 42 30N 93 15W
Ipala **94** 4 30S 32 52 E
Ipameri **139** 17 44S 48 9W
Iparía **136** 9 17S 74 29W
Ipáti **35** 38 52N 22 14 E
Ipatovo **39** 45 45N 42 50 E
Ipel → **33** 48 10N 19 35 E
Ipiales **134** 0 50N 77 37W
Ipiaú **139** 14 8S 39 44W
Ipin = Yibin **58** 28 45N 104 32 E
Ipirá **139** 12 10S 39 44W
Ipiranga **134** 3 13S 65 57W
Ipixuna **136** 7 0S 71 40W
Ipixuna →, Amazonas, Brazil **136** 7 11S 71 51W
Ipixuna →, Amazonas, Brazil **137** 5 45S 63 2W
Ipoh **55** 4 35N 101 5 E
Iporá **139** 11 23S 50 40W
Ippy **92** 6 5N 21 7 E
Ipsárion Óros **35** 40 40N 24 40 E
Ipswich, Austral. **77** 27 35S 152 40 E
Ipswich, U.K. **13** 52 4N 1 9 E
Ipswich, Mass., U.S.A. **115** 42 40N 70 50W
Ipswich, S.D., U.S.A. **118** 45 28N 99 1W
Ipu **138** 4 23S 40 44W
Ipueiras **138** 4 33S 40 43W
Ipupiara **139** 11 49S 42 37W
Iput → **36** 52 26N 31 2 E
Iquique **136** 20 19S 70 5W
Iquitos **134** 3 45S 73 10W
Iracoubo **135** 5 30N 53 10W
Iráklia **35** 36 50N 25 28 E
Iráklion **35** 35 20N 25 12 E
Irako-Zaki **65** 34 35N 137 1 E
Irala **141** 25 55S 54 35W
Iramba □ **94** 4 30S 34 30 E
Iran ■ **47** 33 0N 53 0 E
Iran, Pegunungan **56** 2 20N 114 50 E
Iranamadu Tank **51** 9 23N 80 29 E
Irānshahr **47** 27 15N 60 40 E
Irapa **135** 10 34N 62 35W
Irapuato **124** 20 40N 101 30W
Iraq ■ **46** 33 0N 44 0 E
Irarrar, O. → **86** 20 0N 1 30 E
Irati **141** 25 25S 50 38W
Irbid **44** 32 35N 35 48 E
Irebu **92** 0 40S 17 46 E
Irecê **138** 11 18S 41 52W
Iregua → **24** 42 27N 2 24 E
Ireland ■ **15** 53 0N 8 0W
Ireland's Eye **15** 53 25N 6 4W
Irele **89** 7 40N 5 40 E
Ireng → **135** 3 33N 59 51W
Iret **41** 60 3N 154 20 E
Irgiz, Bol. **37** 52 10N 49 10 E
Irhârharene **87** 27 37N 7 30 E
Irharrhar, O. → **87** 28 3N 6 15 E
Irherm **86** 30 7N 8 18W
Irhil Mgoun **86** 31 30N 6 28W
Irhyangdong **61** 41 15N 129 30 E
Iri **61** 35 59N 127 0 E
Irian Jaya □ **57** 4 0S 137 0 E
Iriba **92** 15 7N 22 15 E
Irié **88** 8 15N 9 10W
Iringa **94** 7 48S 35 43 E
Iringa □, Tanz. **94** 7 48S 35 43 E
Iringa □, Tanz. **95** 9 0S 35 0 E
Irinjalakuda **51** 10 21N 76 14 E
Iriomote-Jima **63** 24 19N 123 48 E
Iriona **126** 15 57N 85 11W
Iriri → **135** 3 52S 52 37W
Iriri Novo → **137** 8 46S 53 22W
Irish Sea **12** 54 0N 5 0W
Irkineyeva **41** 58 30N 96 49 E
Irkutsk **41** 52 18N 104 20 E
Irma **109** 52 55N 111 14W
Irō-Zaki **65** 34 36N 138 51 E
Iroise, Mer d' **18** 48 15N 4 45W
Iron Baron **73** 32 58S 137 11 E
Iron Bridge **106** 46 17N 83 14W
Iron Gate = Portile de Fier **34** 44 42N 22 30 E
Iron Knob **73** 32 46S 137 8 E
Iron Mountain **112** 45 49N 88 4W
Iron River **118** 46 6N 88 40W
Ironbridge **13** 52 38N 2 29W
Ironstone Kopje **96** 25 17S 24 5 E
Ironton, Mo., U.S.A. **119** 37 40N 90 40W
Ironton, Ohio, U.S.A. **112** 38 35N 82 40W
Ironwood **118** 46 30N 90 10W
Iroquois **107** 44 51N 75 19W
Iroquois → **117** 41 5N 87 49W
Iroquois Falls **102** 48 46N 80 41W
Irpen **36** 50 30N 30 15 E
Irrara Cr. → **73** 29 35S 145 31 E
Irrawaddy □ **52** 17 0N 95 0 E
Irrawaddy → **52** 15 50N 95 6 E
Irsina **29** 40 45N 16 15 E
Irtysh → **40** 53 36N 75 30 E
Irumu **94** 1 32N 29 53 E
Irún **24** 43 20N 1 52W
Irurzun **24** 42 55N 1 50W
Irvine, Can. **109** 49 57N 110 16W
Irvine, U.K. **14** 55 37N 4 40W
Irvine, U.S.A. **117** 37 42N 83 58W
Irvinestown **15** 54 28N 7 38W
Irvington **117** 37 53N 86 17W
Irwin → **79** 29 15S 114 54 E
Irwin, Pt. **79** 35 5S 116 55 E
Irymple **74** 34 14S 142 8 E
Is-sur-Tille **19** 47 30N 5 10 E
Isa **89** 13 14N 6 24 E
Isaac → **72** 22 55S 149 20 E
Isabel **118** 45 27N 101 22W
Isabela, I. **124** 21 51N 105 55W
Isabela, La **127** 19 58N 71 2W
Isabella, Cord. **126** 13 30N 85 25W
Isabella Ra. **78** 21 0S 121 4 E
Ísafjarðardjúp **8** 66 10N 23 0W
Ísafjörður **8** 66 5N 23 9W
Isagarh **48** 24 48N 77 51 E
Isahaya **64** 32 52N 130 2 E
Isaka **94** 3 56S 32 59 E
Isana → **134** 0 26N 67 19W
Isangi **92** 0 52N 24 10 E
Isar → **31** 48 49N 12 58 E
Isarco → **27** 46 57N 11 18 E
Ísari **35** 37 22N 22 0 E
Isbergues **19** 50 36N 2 24 E
Iscayachi **137** 21 31S 65 3W
Íschia **28** 40 45N 13 51 E
Iscia Baidoa **45** 3 8N 43 30 E
Iscuandé **134** 2 28N 77 59W
Isdell → **78** 16 27S 124 51 E
Ise **65** 34 25N 136 45 E
Ise-Heiya **65** 34 40N 136 30 E
Ise-Wan **65** 34 43N 136 43 E
Isefjord **11** 55 53N 11 50 E
Iseo **26** 45 40N 10 3 E
Iseo, L. d' **26** 45 45N 10 3 E
Iseramagazi **94** 4 37S 32 10 E
Isère □ **21** 45 15N 5 40 E
Isère → **21** 44 59N 4 51 E
Iserlohn **30** 51 22N 7 40 E
Isérnia **29** 41 35N 14 12 E
Isesaki **65** 36 19N 139 12 E
Iseyin **89** 8 0N 3 36 E
Isherton **135** 2 20N 59 25W
Ishigaki-Shima **63** 24 20N 124 10 E
Ishikari-Wan (Otaru-Wan) **63** 43 25N 141 1 E
Ishikawa **63** 26 25N 127 48 E
Ishikawa □ **65** 36 30N 136 30 E
Ishim **40** 56 10N 69 30 E
Ishim → **40** 57 45N 71 10 E
Ishinomaki **63** 38 32N 141 20 E
Ishioka **65** 36 11N 140 16 E
Ishizuchi-Yama **64** 33 45N 133 6 E
Ishkuman **49** 36 30N 73 50 E
Ishpeming **112** 46 30N 87 40W
Ishurdi **52** 24 9N 89 3 E
Isigny-sur-Mer **18** 49 19N 1 6W
Isil Kul **40** 54 55N 71 16 E
Isiolo **94** 0 24N 37 33 E
Isiolo □ **94** 2 30N 37 30 E
Isipingo Beach **97** 30 00S 30 57 E
Isiro **94** 2 53N 27 40 E
Isisford **72** 24 15S 144 21 E
İskenderun **46** 36 32N 36 10 E
Iskilip **38** 40 50N 34 20 E
Iskŭr → **34** 43 45N 24 25 E
Iskut → **108** 56 45N 131 49W
Isla → **14** 56 32N 3 20W
Isla Cristina **23** 37 13N 7 17W
Isla Vista **123** 34 27N 119 52W
Islamabad **48** 33 40N 73 10 E
Islamkot **48** 24 42N 70 13 E
Islampur **50** 17 2N 74 20 E
Island → **108** 60 25N 121 12W
Island Bend **75** 36 19S 148 31 E
Island Falls, Can. **106** 49 35N 81 20W
Island Falls, U.S.A. **103** 46 0N 68 16W
Island L. **109** 53 47N 94 25W
Island Lagoon **73** 31 30S 136 40 E
Island Pt. **79** 30 20S 115 1 E
Island Pond **115** 44 50N 71 50W
Islands, B. of, Can. **103** 49 11N 58 15W
Islands, B. of, N.Z. **80** 35 15S 174 6 E
Islands, B. of, N.Z. **80** 35 20S 174 20 E
Islay **14** 55 46N 6 10W
Isle → **20** 44 55N 0 15W
Isle-Adam, L' **19** 49 6N 2 14 E
Isle aux Morts **103** 47 35N 59 0W
Isle-Jourdain, L', Gers, France **20** 43 36N 1 5 E
Isle-Jourdain, L', Vienne, France **20** 46 13N 0 31 E
Isle of Wight □ **13** 50 40N 1 20W
Isle Royale **118** 48 0N 88 50W
Isle Verte, L' **105** 48 1N 69 20W
Isleta **121** 34 58N 106 46W
Isleton **122** 38 10N 121 37W
Ismail **38** 45 22N 28 46 E
Ismâ'ilîya **46** 30 37N 32 18 E
Ismaning **31** 48 14N 11 41 E
Ismay **118** 46 33N 104 44W
Isna **90** 25 17N 32 30 E
Isogstalo **49** 34 15N 78 46 E
Isola del Gran Sasso d'Italia **27** 42 30N 13 40 E
Ísola del Liri **28** 41 39N 13 32 E
Ísola della Scala **26** 45 16N 11 0 E
Ísola di Capo Rizzuto **29** 38 56N 17 5 E
Isparta **46** 37 47N 30 30 E
Isperikh **34** 43 43N 26 50 E
Íspica **29** 36 47N 14 53 E
Ispir **39** 40 40N 40 50 E
Israel ■ **44** 32 0N 34 50 E
Issano **135** 5 49N 59 26W
Isseka **79** 28 30S 114 35 E
Issia **88** 6 33N 6 33W
Issoire **20** 45 32N 3 15 E
Issoudun, Can. **105** 46 35N 71 38W
Issoudun, France **19** 46 57N 2 0 E
Issyk-Kul, Ozero **40** 42 25N 77 15 E
Ist **27** 44 17N 14 47 E
İstanbul **46** 41 0N 29 0 E
Istmina **134** 5 10N 76 39W
Istok **33** 42 45N 20 24 E
Istokpoga, L. **113** 27 22N 81 14W
Istra, U.S.S.R. **37** 55 55N 36 50 E
Istra, Yugo. **27** 45 10N 14 0 E
Istranca Dağları **35** 41 48N 27 30 E
Istres **21** 43 31N 4 59 E
Istria = Istra **27** 45 10N 14 0 E
Itá **140** 25 29S 57 21W
Itabaiana, Paraíba, Brazil **138** 7 18S 35 19W
Itabaiana, Sergipe, Brazil **138** 10 41S 37 37W
Itabaianinha **138** 11 16S 37 47W
Itaberaba **139** 12 32S 40 18W
Itaberaí **139** 16 2S 49 48W
Itabira **139** 19 37S 43 13W
Itabirito **139** 20 15S 43 48W
Itaboca **135** 4 50S 62 40W
Itabuna **139** 14 48S 39 16W
Itacaiunas → **138** 5 21S 49 8W
Itacajá **138** 8 19S 47 46W
Itacoatiara **135** 3 8S 58 25W
Itacuaí → **136** 4 20S 70 12W
Itaguaçu **139** 19 48S 40 51W
Itaguari → **139** 14 11S 44 40W
Itaguatins **138** 5 47S 47 29W
Itaim → **138** 7 2S 42 2W
Itainópolis **138** 7 24S 41 31W
Itaituba **135** 4 10S 55 50W
Itajaí **141** 27 50S 48 39W
Itajubá **139** 22 24S 45 30W
Itajuípe **139** 14 41S 39 22W
Itaka **95** 8 50S 32 49 E
Itako **65** 35 56N 140 33 E
Italy ■ **7** 42 0N 13 0 E
Itamataré **138** 2 16S 46 24W
Itambacuri **139** 18 1S 41 42W
Itambé **139** 15 15S 40 37W
Itampolo **97** 24 41S 43 57 E
Itanhauã → **135** 4 45S 63 48W
Itanhém **139** 17 9S 40 20W
Itano **64** 34 7N 134 28 E
Itapaci **139** 14 57S 49 34W
Itapagé **138** 3 41S 39 34W
Itaparica, I. de **139** 12 54S 38 42W
Itapebi **139** 15 56S 39 32W
Itapecuru-Mirim **138** 3 24S 44 20W
Itaperuna **139** 21 10S 41 54W
Itapetinga **139** 15 15S 40 15W
Itapetininga **141** 23 36S 48 7W
Itapeva **141** 23 59S 48 59W
Itapicuru →, Bahia, Brazil **138** 11 47S 37 32W
Itapicuru →, Maranhão, Brazil **138** 2 52S 44 12W
Itapinima **137** 5 25S 60 44W
Itapipoca **138** 3 30S 39 35W
Itapiranga **135** 2 45S 58 1W
Itapiúna **138** 4 33S 38 57W
Itaporanga **138** 7 18S 38 0W

Itapuá □	**141**	26 40 S	55 40 W
Itapuranga	**139**	15 40 S	49 59 W
Itaquari	**139**	20 20 S	40 25 W
Itaquatiara	**136**	2 58 S	58 30 W
Itaquí	**140**	29 8 S	56 30 W
Itararé	**141**	24 6 S	49 23 W
Itarsi	**48**	22 36 N	77 51 E
Itarumã	**139**	18 42 S	51 25 W
Itatí	**140**	27 16 S	58 15 W
Itatira	**138**	4 30 S	39 37 W
Itatuba	**137**	5 46 S	63 20 W
Itatupa	**135**	0 37 S	51 12 W
Itaueira	**138**	7 36 S	43 2 W
Itaueira →	**138**	6 41 S	42 55 W
Itaúna	**139**	20 4 S	44 34 W
Itchen →	**13**	50 57 N	1 20 W
Ite	**136**	17 55 S	70 57 W
Ithaca, Mich., U.S.A.	**106**	43 18 N	84 36 W
Ithaca, N.Y., U.S.A.	**115**	42 25 N	76 30 W
Ithaca = Itháki	**35**	38 25 N	20 43 E
Itháki	**35**	38 25 N	20 40 E
Itinga	**139**	16 36 S	41 47 W
Itiquira	**137**	17 12 S	54 7 W
Itiquira →	**137**	17 18 S	56 44 W
Itiruçu	**139**	13 31 S	40 9 W
Itiúba	**138**	10 43 S	39 51 W
Ito	**65**	34 58 N	139 5 E
Itomamo, L.	**105**	49 11 N	70 28 W
Iton →	**18**	49 9 N	1 12 E
Itonamas →	**136**	12 28 S	64 24 W
Itsa	**90**	29 15 N	30 47 E
Itsukaichi	**64**	34 22 N	132 22 E
Itsuki	**64**	32 24 N	130 50 E
Íttiri	**28**	40 38 N	8 32 E
Itu, Brazil	**141**	23 17 S	47 15 W
Itu, Nigeria	**89**	5 10 N	7 58 E
Ituaçu	**139**	13 50 S	41 18 W
Ituango	**134**	7 4 N	75 45 W
Ituiutaba	**139**	19 0 S	49 25 W
Itumbiara	**139**	18 20 S	49 10 W
Ituna	**109**	51 10 N	103 24 W
Itunge Port	**95**	9 40 S	33 55 E
Ituni	**135**	5 28 N	58 15 W
Itupiranga	**138**	5 9 S	49 20 W
Iturama	**139**	19 44 S	50 11 W
Iturbe	**140**	23 0 S	65 25 W
Ituri →	**94**	1 40 N	27 1 E
Iturup, Ostrov	**41**	45 0 N	148 0 E
Ituverava	**139**	20 20 S	47 47 W
Ituxi →	**137**	7 18 S	64 51 W
Ituyuro →	**140**	22 40 S	63 50 W
Itzehoe	**30**	53 56 N	9 31 E
Iuka	**117**	38 37 N	88 47 W
Ivaí →	**141**	23 18 S	53 42 W
Ivalo	**8**	68 38 N	27 35 E
Ivalojoki →	**8**	68 40 N	27 40 E
Ivanhoe, N.S.W., Austral.	**73**	32 56 S	144 20 E
Ivanhoe, N.T., Austral.	**78**	15 41 S	128 41 E
Ivanhoe, U.S.A.	**122**	36 25 N	119 13 W
Ivanhoe L.	**109**	60 25 N	106 30 W
Ivanić Grad	**27**	45 41 N	16 25 E
Ivanjica	**33**	43 35 N	20 12 E
Ivanjšcice	**27**	46 12 N	16 13 E
Ivankoyskoye Vdkhr.	**37**	56 37 N	36 32 E
Ivano-Frankovsk	**38**	48 56 N	24 43 E
Ivano-Frankovsk (Stanislav)	**36**	48 40 N	24 40 E
Ivanovo, Byelorussia, U.S.S.R.	**36**	52 7 N	25 29 E
Ivanovo, R.S.F.S.R., U.S.S.R.	**37**	57 5 N	41 0 E
Ivato	**97**	20 37 S	47 10 E
Ivaylovgrad	**35**	41 32 N	26 8 E
Ivinheima →	**141**	23 14 S	53 42 W
Iviza = Ibiza	**25**	39 0 N	1 30 E
Ivohibe	**97**	22 31 S	46 57 E
Ivolândia	**139**	16 34 S	50 51 W
Ivory Coast ■	**88**	7 30 N	5 0 W
Ivösjön	**11**	56 8 N	14 25 E
Ivrea	**26**	45 30 N	7 52 E
Ivugivik, (N.D. d'Ivugivic)	**101**	62 24 N	77 55 W
Iwahig	**56**	8 35 N	117 32 E
Iwai-Jima	**64**	33 47 N	131 58 E
Iwaki	**63**	37 3 N	140 55 E
Iwakuni	**64**	34 15 N	132 8 E
Iwami	**64**	35 32 N	134 15 E
Iwamizawa	**63**	43 12 N	141 46 E
Iwanai	**63**	42 58 N	140 30 E
Iwanuma	**63**	38 7 N	140 51 E
Iwase	**65**	36 21 N	140 6 E
Iwata	**65**	34 42 N	137 51 E
Iwate-San	**63**	39 51 N	141 0 E
Iwo	**89**	7 39 N	4 9 E
Ixiamas	**136**	13 50 S	68 5 W
Ixopo	**97**	30 11 S	30 5 E
Ixtepec	**125**	16 32 N	95 10 W
Ixtlán de Juárez	**125**	17 23 N	96 28 W
Ixtlán del Río	**124**	21 5 N	104 21 W
Iyo	**64**	33 45 N	132 45 E
Iyo-mishima	**64**	33 58 N	133 30 E
Iyo-Nada	**64**	33 40 N	132 20 E
Izabel, L. de	**126**	15 30 N	89 10 W
Izamal	**125**	20 56 N	89 1 W
Izberbash	**39**	42 35 N	47 52 E
Izegem	**16**	50 55 N	3 12 E
Izhevsk	**40**	56 51 N	53 14 E
İzmir (Smyrna)	**46**	38 25 N	27 8 E
İzmit	**46**	40 45 N	29 50 E
Iznajar	**23**	37 15 N	4 19 W
Iznalloz	**25**	37 24 N	3 30 W
Izola	**27**	45 32 N	13 39 E
Izozog	**137**	18 48 S	62 10 W
Izra	**44**	32 51 N	36 15 E
Iztochni Rodopi	**35**	41 45 N	25 30 E
Izu-Hantō	**65**	34 45 N	139 0 E
Izuhara	**64**	34 12 N	129 17 E
Izumi	**64**	32 5 N	130 22 E
Izumiotsu	**65**	34 30 N	135 24 E
Izumisano	**65**	34 23 N	135 18 E
Izumo	**64**	35 20 N	132 46 E
Izyaslav	**36**	50 5 N	26 50 E
Izyum	**38**	49 12 N	37 19 E

J

J.F. Rodrigues	**138**	2 55 S	50 20 W
Jaba	**91**	6 20 N	35 7 E
Jaba'	**44**	32 20 N	35 13 E
Jabal el Awlîya	**91**	15 10 N	32 31 E
Jabalīya	**44**	31 32 N	34 27 E
Jabalón →	**23**	38 53 N	4 5 W
Jabalpur	**49**	23 9 N	79 58 E
Jablah	**46**	35 20 N	36 0 E
Jablanac	**27**	44 42 N	14 56 E
Jablonec	**32**	50 43 N	15 10 E
Jabłonowo	**32**	53 23 N	19 10 E
Jaboatão	**138**	8 7 S	35 1 W
Jaboticabal	**141**	21 15 S	48 17 W
Jaburu	**137**	5 30 S	64 0 W
Jaca	**24**	42 35 N	0 33 W
Jacala	**125**	21 1 N	99 11 W
Jacaré →	**138**	10 3 S	42 13 W
Jacareí	**141**	23 20 S	46 0 W
Jacarèzinho	**141**	23 5 S	50 0 W
Jaciara	**137**	15 59 S	54 57 W
Jacinto	**139**	16 10 S	40 17 W
Jaciparaná	**137**	9 15 S	64 23 W
Jackadgery	**77**	29 35 S	152 34 E
Jackman	**103**	45 35 N	70 17 W
Jacksboro	**119**	33 14 N	98 15 W
Jackson, Austral.	**73**	26 39 S	149 39 E
Jackson, Ala., U.S.A.	**113**	31 32 N	87 53 W
Jackson, Calif., U.S.A.	**122**	38 19 N	120 47 W
Jackson, Ky., U.S.A.	**112**	37 35 N	83 22 W
Jackson, Mich., U.S.A.	**117**	42 18 N	84 25 W
Jackson, Minn., U.S.A.	**118**	43 35 N	95 0 W
Jackson, Miss., U.S.A.	**119**	32 20 N	90 10 W
Jackson, Mo., U.S.A.	**119**	37 25 N	89 42 W
Jackson, Ohio, U.S.A.	**112**	39 0 N	82 40 W
Jackson, Tenn., U.S.A.	**113**	35 40 N	88 50 W
Jackson, Wyo., U.S.A.	**120**	43 30 N	110 49 W
Jackson Bay	**81**	43 58 S	168 42 E
Jackson, C.	**81**	40 59 S	174 20 E
Jackson Center	**117**	40 27 N	84 4 W
Jackson, L.	**120**	43 55 N	110 40 W
Jacksons	**81**	42 46 S	171 32 E
Jacksonville, Ala., U.S.A.	**113**	33 49 N	85 45 W
Jacksonville, Calif., U.S.A.	**122**	37 52 N	120 24 W
Jacksonville, Fla., U.S.A.	**113**	30 15 N	81 38 W
Jacksonville, Ill., U.S.A.	**116**	39 42 N	90 15 W
Jacksonville, N.C., U.S.A.	**113**	34 50 N	77 29 W
Jacksonville, Oreg., U.S.A.	**120**	42 19 N	122 56 W
Jacksonville, Tex., U.S.A.	**119**	31 58 N	95 19 W
Jacksonville Beach	**113**	30 19 N	81 26 W
Jacmel	**127**	18 14 N	72 32 W
Jacob Lake	**121**	36 45 N	112 12 W
Jacobabad	**48**	28 20 N	68 29 E
Jacobina	**138**	11 11 S	40 30 W
Jacob's Well	**44**	32 13 N	35 13 E
Jacques-Cartier	**105**	45 31 N	73 29 W
Jacques-Cartier →	**105**	46 40 N	71 45 W
Jacques-Cartier, L.	**105**	47 35 N	71 13 W
Jacques-Cartier, Mt.	**103**	48 57 N	66 0 W
Jacqueville	**88**	5 12 N	4 25 W
Jacuí →	**141**	30 2 S	51 15 W
Jacumba	**123**	32 37 N	116 11 W
Jacundá →	**138**	1 57 S	50 26 W
Jade	**30**	53 22 N	8 14 E
Jadebusen	**30**	53 30 N	8 15 E
Jadotville = Likasi	**95**	10 55 S	26 48 E
Jadraque	**24**	40 55 N	2 55 W
Jādū	**87**	32 0 N	12 0 E
Jaén, Peru	**136**	5 25 S	78 40 W
Jaén, Spain	**23**	37 44 N	3 43 W
Jaén □	**23**	37 50 N	3 30 W
Jafène	**86**	20 35 N	5 30 W
Jaffa = Tel Aviv-Yafo	**44**	32 4 N	34 48 E
Jaffa, C.	**73**	36 58 S	139 40 E
Jaffna	**51**	9 45 N	80 2 E
Jagadhri	**48**	30 10 N	77 20 E
Jagadishpur	**49**	25 30 N	84 21 E
Jagdalpur	**50**	19 3 N	82 0 E
Jagersfontein	**96**	29 44 S	25 27 E
Jaghbub	**85**	29 42 N	24 38 E
Jagst →	**31**	49 14 N	9 11 E
Jagtial	**50**	18 50 N	79 0 E
Jaguaquara	**139**	13 32 S	39 58 W
Jaguariaíva	**141**	24 10 S	49 50 W
Jaguaribe	**138**	5 53 S	38 37 W
Jaguaribe →	**138**	4 25 S	37 45 W
Jaguaruana	**138**	4 50 S	37 47 W
Jagüey Grande	**126**	22 35 N	81 7 W
Jagungal, Mt.	**76**	36 8 S	148 22 E
Jahangirabad	**48**	28 19 N	78 4 E
Jahrom	**47**	28 30 N	53 31 E
Jaicós	**138**	7 21 S	41 8 W
Jailolo	**57**	1 5 N	127 30 E
Jailolo, Selat	**57**	0 5 N	129 5 E
Jainti	**52**	26 45 N	89 40 E
Jaintiapur	**52**	25 8 N	92 7 E
Jaipur	**48**	27 0 N	75 50 E
Jajce	**33**	44 19 N	17 17 E
Jajpur	**50**	20 53 N	86 22 E
Jakarta	**57**	6 9 S	106 49 E
Jakobstad (Pietarsaari)	**8**	63 40 N	22 43 E
Jakupica	**35**	41 45 N	21 22 E
Jal	**119**	32 8 N	103 8 W
Jalalabad, Afghan.	**48**	34 30 N	70 29 E
Jalalabad, India	**49**	27 41 N	79 42 E
Jalalpur Jattan	**48**	32 38 N	74 11 E
Jalama	**123**	34 29 N	120 29 W
Jalapa, Guat.	**126**	14 39 N	89 59 W
Jalapa, Mexico	**125**	19 30 N	96 56 W
Jalas, Jabal al	**46**	27 30 N	36 30 E
Jalaun	**49**	26 8 N	79 25 E
Jales	**139**	20 10 S	50 33 W
Jaleswar	**49**	26 38 N	85 48 E
Jalgaon, Maharashtra, India	**50**	21 2 N	76 31 E
Jalgaon, Maharashtra, India	**50**	21 0 N	75 42 E
Jalingo	**89**	8 55 N	11 25 E
Jalisco □	**124**	20 0 N	104 0 W
Jalkot	**49**	35 14 N	73 24 E
Jallas →	**22**	42 54 N	9 8 W
Jallumba	**74**	36 55 S	141 57 E
Jalna	**50**	19 48 N	75 38 E
Jalón →	**24**	41 47 N	1 4 W
Jalpa	**124**	21 38 N	102 58 W
Jalpaiguri	**52**	26 32 N	88 46 E
Jalq	**47**	27 35 N	62 46 E
Jaluit I.	**66**	6 0 N	169 30 E
Jamaari	**89**	11 44 N	9 53 E
Jamaica	**116**	41 51 N	94 18 W
Jamaica ■	**126**	18 10 N	77 30 W
Jamalpur, Bangla.	**52**	24 52 N	89 56 E
Jamalpur, India	**49**	25 18 N	86 28 E
Jamalpurganj	**49**	23 2 N	88 1 E
Jamanxim →	**137**	4 43 S	56 18 W
Jamari	**137**	8 45 S	63 27 W
Jamari →	**137**	8 27 S	63 30 W
Jambe	**57**	1 15 S	132 10 E
Jambi	**56**	1 38 S	103 30 E
Jambi □	**56**	1 30 S	102 30 E
Jambusar	**48**	22 3 N	72 51 E
James →	**118**	42 52 N	97 18 W
James B.	**102**	51 30 N	80 0 W
James Range	**78**	24 10 S	132 30 E
James Ross I.	**143**	63 58 S	57 50 W
Jamesport	**116**	39 58 N	93 48 W
Jamestown, Austral.	**73**	33 10 S	138 32 E
Jamestown, S. Afr.	**96**	31 6 S	26 45 E
Jamestown, Ind., U.S.A.	**117**	39 56 N	86 38 W
Jamestown, Ky., U.S.A.	**112**	37 0 N	85 5 W
Jamestown, Mo., U.S.A.	**116**	38 48 N	92 30 W
Jamestown, N.D., U.S.A.	**118**	46 54 N	98 42 W
Jamestown, N.Y., U.S.A.	**114**	42 5 N	79 18 W
Jamestown, Ohio, U.S.A.	**117**	39 39 N	83 44 W
Jamestown, Pa., U.S.A.	**114**	41 32 N	80 27 W
Jamestown, Tenn., U.S.A.	**113**	36 25 N	85 0 W
Jamieson	**75**	37 19 S	146 9 E
Jamiltepec	**125**	16 17 N	97 49 W
Jamkhaudi	**50**	16 30 N	75 15 E
Jamma'in	**44**	32 8 N	35 12 E
Jammalamadugu	**51**	14 51 N	78 25 E
Jammerbugt	**11**	57 15 N	9 20 E
Jammu	**48**	32 43 N	74 54 E
Jammu & Kashmir □	**49**	34 25 N	77 0 E
Jamnagar	**48**	22 30 N	70 6 E
Jamner	**50**	20 45 N	75 52 E
Jampur	**48**	29 39 N	70 40 E
Jamrud Fort	**48**	33 59 N	71 24 E
Jamshedpur	**49**	22 44 N	86 12 E
Jamtara	**49**	23 59 N	86 49 E
Jämtlands län □	**10**	62 40 N	13 50 E
Jamuna →	**52**	23 51 N	89 45 E
Jamurki	**52**	24 9 N	90 2 E
Jan Kemp	**96**	27 55 S	24 51 E
Jan L.	**109**	54 56 N	102 55 W
Jan Mayen Is.	**144**	71 0 N	9 0 W
Janaúba	**139**	15 48 S	43 19 W
Janaucu, I.	**138**	0 30 N	50 10 W
Jand	**48**	33 30 N	72 6 E
Janda, Laguna de la	**23**	36 15 N	5 45 W
Jandaia	**139**	17 6 S	50 7 W
Jandaq	**47**	34 3 N	54 22 E
Jandiatuba →	**134**	3 28 S	68 42 W
Jandola	**48**	32 20 N	70 9 E
Jandowae	**73**	26 45 S	151 7 E
Jándula →	**23**	38 3 N	4 6 W
Jane Pk.	**81**	45 15 S	168 20 E
Janesville	**116**	42 39 N	89 1 W
Janga	**89**	10 5 N	1 0 W
Jangaon	**50**	17 44 N	79 5 E
Jango	**137**	20 27 S	55 29 W
Janhtang Ga	**52**	26 32 N	96 38 E
Janjina	**33**	42 58 N	17 25 E
Janos	**124**	30 45 N	108 10 W
Jánosháza	**33**	47 8 N	17 12 E
Janów Podlaski	**32**	52 11 N	23 11 E
Januária	**139**	15 25 S	44 25 W
Janub Dârfûr □	**91**	11 0 N	25 0 E
Janub Kordofân □	**91**	12 0 N	30 0 E
Janville	**19**	48 10 N	1 50 E
Janzé	**18**	47 55 N	1 28 W
Jaora	**48**	23 40 N	75 10 E
Japan ■	**63**	36 0 N	136 0 E
Japan, Sea of	**63**	40 0 N	135 0 E
Japan Trench	**66**	32 0 N	142 0 E
Japara	**57**	6 30 S	110 40 E
Japen = Yapen	**57**	1 50 S	136 0 E
Japurá →	**134**	3 8 S	64 46 W
Jaque	**134**	7 27 N	78 8 W
Jara, La	**121**	37 16 N	106 0 W
Jaraguá	**139**	15 45 S	49 20 W
Jaraguari	**137**	20 9 S	54 35 W
Jaraicejo	**23**	39 40 N	5 49 W
Jaraiz	**22**	40 4 N	5 45 W
Jarales	**121**	34 39 N	106 51 W
Jarama →	**24**	40 2 N	3 39 W
Jaramillo	**142**	47 10 S	67 7 W
Jarandilla	**22**	40 8 N	5 39 W
Jaranwala	**48**	31 15 N	73 26 E
Jarash	**44**	32 17 N	35 54 E
Jarauçu →	**135**	1 48 S	52 22 W
Jarbidge	**120**	41 56 N	115 27 W
Jardim	**140**	21 28 S	56 2 W
Jardín →	**25**	38 50 N	2 10 W
Jardines de la Reina, Is.	**126**	20 50 N	78 50 W
Jargalang	**61**	43 5 N	122 55 E
Jargalant (Kobdo)	**62**	48 2 N	91 37 E
Jargeau	**19**	47 50 N	2 1 E
Jari →	**135**	1 9 S	51 54 W
Jarjarni	**47**	37 5 N	56 20 E
Jarmen	**30**	53 56 N	13 20 E
Jarnac	**20**	45 40 N	0 11 W
Jarny	**19**	49 9 N	5 53 E
Jarocin	**32**	51 59 N	17 29 E
Jarosław	**32**	50 2 N	22 42 E
Järpås	**11**	58 23 N	12 57 E
Järpen	**10**	63 21 N	13 26 E
Jarrahdale	**79**	32 24 S	116 5 E
Jarres, Plaine des	**54**	19 27 N	103 10 E
Jarso	**91**	5 15 N	37 30 E
Jartai	**60**	39 45 N	105 48 E
Jaru	**137**	10 26 S	62 27 W
Jaru →	**137**	10 5 S	61 59 W
Jarud Qi	**61**	44 28 N	120 50 E
Jarvis	**106**	42 53 N	80 6 W
Jarvis I.	**67**	0 15 S	159 55 W
Jarwa	**49**	27 38 N	82 30 E
Jaša Tomić	**33**	45 26 N	20 50 E
Jasin	**55**	2 20 N	102 26 E
Jāsk	**47**	25 38 N	57 45 E
Jasło	**32**	49 45 N	21 30 E
Jason, Is.	**142**	51 0 S	61 0 W
Jasonville	**117**	39 10 N	87 13 W
Jasper, Alta., Can.	**108**	52 55 N	118 5 W
Jasper, Ont., Can.	**107**	44 50 N	75 56 W
Jasper, Ont., Can.	**113**	44 52 N	75 57 W
Jasper, Ala., U.S.A.	**113**	33 48 N	87 16 W
Jasper, Fla., U.S.A.	**113**	30 31 N	82 58 W

Jasper, Ind., U.S.A. **117** 38 24N 86 56W
Jasper, La., U.S.A. **119** 30 59N 93 58W
Jasper, Minn., U.S.A. **118** 43 52N 96 22W
Jasper Nat. Park **108** 52 50N 118 8W
Jastrebarsko **27** 45 41N 15 39 E
Jastrzębie Zdrój **32** 49 57N 18 35 E
Jászárokszállás **33** 47 39N 20 1 E
Jászberény **33** 47 30N 19 55 E
Jászladány **33** 47 23N 20 10 E
Jataí **139** 17 58 S 51 48W
Jatapu → **135** 2 13 S 58 17W
Jati **48** 24 20N 68 19 E
Jatibarang **57** 6 28 S 108 18 E
Jatinegara **57** 6 13 S 106 52 E
Játiva **25** 39 0N 0 32W
Jatobal **138** 4 35 S 49 33W
Jatt **44** 32 24N 35 2 E
Jaú **141** 22 10 S 48 30W
Jaú → **135** 1 54 S 61 26W
Jau al Milah **45** 15 15N 45 40 E
Jauaperí → **135** 1 26 S 61 35W
Jauja **136** 11 45 S 75 15W
Jaunjelgava **36** 56 35N 25 0 E
Jaunpur **49** 25 46N 82 44 E
Jauru → **137** 16 22 S 57 46W
Java = Jawa **57** 7 0 S 110 0 E
Java Sea **56** 4 35 S 107 15 E
Java Trench **66** 10 0 S 110 0W
Javadi Hills **51** 12 40N 78 40 E
Jávea **25** 38 48N 0 10 E
Javhlant = Ulyasutay **62** 47 56N 97 28 E
Javier, I. **142** 47 5 S 74 25W
Javla **50** 17 18N 75 9 E
Javron **18** 48 25N 0 25W
Jawa **57** 7 0 S 110 0 E
Jawor **32** 51 4N 16 11 E
Jaworzno **32** 50 13N 19 11 E
Jay **119** 36 25N 94 46W
Jaya, Puncak **57** 3 57 S 137 17 E
Jayanca **136** 6 24 S 79 50W
Jayapura **57** 2 28 S 140 38 E
Jayawijaya, Pegunungan **57** 5 0 S 139 0 E
Jayton **119** 33 17N 100 35W
Jazminal **124** 24 56N 101 25W
Jean **123** 35 47N 115 20W
Jean Marie River **100** 61 32N 120 38W
Jean Rabel **127** 19 50N 73 5W
Jeanerette **119** 29 52N 91 38W
Jeanette, Ostrov **41** 76 43N 158 0 E
Jeannette **114** 40 20N 79 36W
Jebba, Moroc. **86** 35 11N 4 43W
Jebba, Nigeria **89** 9 9N 4 48 E
Jebel, Bahr el → **85** 9 45N 30 20 E
Jebel Qerri **91** 16 16N 32 50 E
Jeberos **136** 5 15 S 76 10W
Jedburgh **14** 55 28N 2 33W
Jędrzejów **32** 50 35N 20 15 E
Jedway **108** 52 17N 131 14W
Jeetze → **30** 53 9N 11 6 E
Jefferson, Iowa, U.S.A. **116** 42 3N 94 25W
Jefferson, Ohio, U.S.A. **114** 41 40N 80 46W
Jefferson, Tex., U.S.A. **119** 32 45N 94 23W
Jefferson, Wis., U.S.A. **117** 43 0N 88 49W
Jefferson City, Mo., U.S.A. **116** 38 34N 92 10W
Jefferson City, Tenn., U.S.A. **113** 36 8N 83 30W
Jefferson, Mt., Nev., U.S.A. **120** 38 51N 117 0W
Jefferson, Mt., Oreg., U.S.A. **120** 44 45N 121 50W
Jeffersontown **117** 38 17N 85 44W
Jeffersonville, Ind., U.S.A. **117** 38 20N 85 42W
Jeffersonville, Ohio, U.S.A. **117** 39 38N 83 34W
Jega **89** 12 15N 4 23 E
Jekabpils **36** 56 29N 25 57 E
Jelenia Góra **32** 50 50N 15 45 E
Jelgava **36** 56 41N 23 49 E
Jelli **91** 5 25N 31 45 E
Jellicoe **102** 49 40N 87 30W
Jemaja **56** 3 5N 105 45 E
Jemaluang **55** 2 16N 103 52 E
Jember **57** 8 11 S 113 41 E
Jembongan **56** 6 45N 117 20 E
Jemeppe **16** 50 37N 5 30 E
Jemnice **32** 49 1N 15 34 E
Jena, Ger. **30** 50 56N 11 33 E
Jena, U.S.A. **119** 31 41N 92 7W
Jendouba **87** 36 29N 8 47 E
Jenīn **44** 32 28N 35 18 E
Jenkins **112** 37 13N 82 41W
Jenner **122** 38 27N 123 7W
Jennings, La., U.S.A. **119** 30 10N 92 45W
Jennings, Mo., U.S.A. **116** 38 43N 90 16W
Jennings → **108** 59 38N 132 5W
Jenny **11** 57 47N 16 35 E
Jenolan Caves **76** 33 49 S 150 1 E
Jeparit **74** 36 8 S 142 1 E
Jequié **139** 13 51 S 40 5W
Jequitaí → **139** 17 4 S 44 50W
Jequitinhonha **139** 16 30 S 41 0W
Jequitinhonha → **139** 15 51 S 38 53W
Jerada **86** 34 17N 2 10W
Jerangle **76** 35 52 S 149 23 E
Jerantut **55** 3 56N 102 22 E
Jérémie **127** 18 40N 74 10W
Jeremoabo **138** 10 4 S 38 21W
Jerez de García Salinas **124** 22 39N 103 0W
Jerez de la Frontera **23** 36 41N 6 7W
Jerez de los Caballeros **23** 38 20N 6 45W
Jerez, Punta **125** 22 58N 97 40W
Jericho **72** 23 38 S 146 6 E
Jericho = El Arīhā **44** 31 52N 35 27 E
Jerichow **30** 52 30N 12 2 E
Jerico Springs **116** 37 37N 94 1W
Jerilderie **74** 35 20 S 145 41 E
Jermyn **115** 41 31N 75 31W
Jerome **121** 34 50N 112 0W
Jerrobert **109** 51 56N 109 8W
Jerrys Plains **76** 32 29 S 150 53 E
Jersey City **115** 40 41N 74 8W
Jersey, I. **18** 49 13N 2 7W
Jersey Shore **114** 41 17N 77 18W
Jerseyville, Austral. **77** 30 54 S 153 3 E
Jerseyville, U.S.A. **116** 39 5N 90 20W
Jerusalem **44** 31 47N 35 10 E
Jervis B. **76** 35 8 S 150 46 E
Jervis Bay **76** 35 8 S 150 43 E
Jesenice **27** 46 28N 14 3 E
Jeseník **32** 50 0N 17 8 E
Jesenké **33** 48 20N 20 10 E
Jesselton = Kota Kinabalu **56** 6 0N 116 4 E
Jessnitz **30** 51 42N 12 19 E
Jessore **52** 23 10N 89 10 E
Jesup, U.S.A. **113** 31 36N 81 54W
Jesup, U.S.A. **116** 42 29N 92 4W
Jesús **136** 7 15 S 78 25W
Jesús Carranza **125** 17 28N 95 1W
Jesús María **140** 30 59 S 64 5W
Jetmore **119** 38 10N 99 57W
Jetpur **48** 21 45N 70 10 E
Jevnaker **10** 60 15N 10 26 E
Jewell **116** 42 20N 93 39W
Jewett, Ohio, U.S.A. **114** 40 22N 81 2W
Jewett, Tex., U.S.A. **119** 31 20N 96 8W
Jewett City **115** 41 36N 72 0W
Jeypore **50** 18 50N 82 38 E
Jeziorany **32** 53 58N 20 46 E
Jhajjar **48** 28 37N 76 42 E
Jhal Jhao **47** 26 20N 65 35 E
Jhalakati **52** 22 39N 90 12 E
Jhalawar **48** 24 40N 76 10 E
Jhang Maghiana **48** 31 15N 72 22 E
Jhansi **49** 25 30N 78 36 E
Jharia **49** 23 45N 86 26 E
Jharsuguda **50** 21 56N 84 5 E
Jhelum **48** 33 0N 73 45 E
Jhelum → **48** 31 20N 72 10 E
Jhunjhunu **48** 28 10N 75 30 E
Ji Xian, Hebei, China **60** 37 35N 115 30 E
Ji Xian, Henan, China **60** 35 22N 114 5 E
Ji Xian, Shanxi, China **60** 36 7N 110 40 E
Jia Xian, Henan, China **60** 33 59N 113 12 E
Jia Xian, Shaanxi, China **60** 38 12N 110 28 E
Jiading **59** 31 22N 121 15 E
Jiahe **59** 25 38N 112 19 E
Jiali **59** 23 12N 120 10 E
Jialing Jiang → **58** 29 30N 106 20 E
Jiamusi **62** 46 40N 130 26 E
Ji'an, Jiangxi, China **59** 27 6N 114 59 E
Ji'an, Jilin, China **61** 41 5N 126 10 E
Jianchang **61** 40 55N 120 35 E
Jianchangying **61** 40 10N 118 50 E
Jianchuan **58** 26 38N 99 55 E
Jiande **59** 29 23N 119 15 E
Jiangbei **58** 29 40N 106 34 E
Jiangcheng **58** 22 36N 101 52 E
Jiangdi **58** 26 57N 103 37 E
Jiange **58** 32 4N 105 32 E
Jiangjin **58** 29 14N 106 14 E
Jiangkou **58** 27 40N 108 49 E
Jiangle **59** 26 42N 117 23 E
Jiangling **59** 30 25N 112 12 E
Jiangmen **59** 22 32N 113 0 E
Jiangshan **59** 28 40N 118 37 E
Jiangsu □ **62** 33 0N 120 0 E
Jiangxi □ **59** 27 30N 116 0 E
Jiangyin **59** 31 54N 120 17 E
Jiangyong **59** 25 20N 111 22 E
Jiangyou **58** 31 44N 104 43 E
Jianhe **58** 26 37N 108 31 E
Jianli **59** 29 46N 112 56 E
Jianning **59** 26 50N 116 50 E
Jian'ou **59** 27 3N 118 17 E
Jianshi **59** 30 35N 109 43 E
Jianshui **58** 23 36N 102 43 E
Jianyang, Fujian, China **59** 27 20N 118 5 E
Jianyang, Sichuan, China **58** 30 24N 104 33 E
Jiao Xian **61** 36 18N 120 1 E
Jiaohe, Hebei, China **60** 38 2N 116 20 E
Jiaohe, Jilin, China **61** 43 40N 127 22 E
Jiaoling **59** 24 41N 116 12 E
Jiaozhou Wan **61** 36 5N 120 10 E
Jiaozuo **60** 35 16N 113 12 E
Jiashan **59** 32 46N 117 59 E
Jiawang **61** 34 28N 117 26 E
Jiaxiang **60** 35 25N 116 20 E
Jiaxing **59** 30 49N 120 45 E
Jiayi **59** 23 30N 120 24 E
Jiayu **59** 29 55N 113 55 E
Jibão, Serra do **139** 14 48 S 45 0W
Jibiya **89** 13 5N 7 12 E
Jibou **34** 47 15N 23 17 E
Jicarón, I. **126** 7 10N 81 50W
Jičín **32** 50 25N 15 28 E
Jiddah **46** 21 29N 39 10 E
Jieshou **59** 33 18N 115 22 E
Jiexiu **60** 37 2N 111 55 E
Jieyang **59** 23 35N 116 21 E
Jifna **44** 31 58N 35 13 E
Jiggalong **78** 23 24 S 120 47 E
Jihlava **32** 49 28N 15 35 E
Jijiga **45** 9 20N 42 50 E
Jijona **25** 38 34N 0 30W
Jikamshi **89** 12 12N 7 45 E
Jilin **61** 43 44N 126 30 E
Jilin □ **61** 44 0N 124 0 E
Jiloca → **24** 41 21N 1 39W
Jilong **59** 25 8N 121 42 E
Jima **91** 7 40N 36 47 E
Jimbolia **34** 45 47N 20 43 E
Jimena de la Frontera **23** 36 27N 5 24W
Jimenbuen **75** 36 42 S 148 53 E
Jiménez **124** 27 10N 104 54W
Jimo **61** 36 23N 120 30 E
Jin Jiang → **59** 28 24N 115 48 E
Jin Xian, Hebei, China **60** 38 2N 115 2 E
Jin Xian, Liaoning, China **61** 38 55N 121 42 E
Jinan **60** 36 38N 117 1 E
Jincheng **60** 35 29N 112 50 E
Jinchuan **58** 31 30N 102 3 E
Jind **48** 29 19N 76 22 E
Jindabyne **75** 36 25 S 148 35 E
Jindabyne L. **75** 36 20 S 148 38 E
Jindrichuv Hradeç **32** 49 10N 15 2 E
Jing He → **60** 34 27N 109 4 E
Jing Shan **59** 31 20N 111 35 E
Jing Xian, Anhui, China **59** 30 38N 118 25 E
Jing Xian, Hunan, China **58** 26 33N 109 40 E
Jing'an **59** 28 50N 115 17 E
Jingbian **60** 37 20N 108 30 E
Jingchuan **60** 35 20N 107 20 E
Jingde **59** 30 15N 118 27 E
Jingdezhen **59** 29 20N 117 11 E
Jingdong **58** 24 23N 100 47 E
Jingellic **76** 35 56 S 147 40 E
Jinggu **58** 23 35N 100 41 E
Jinghai **60** 38 55N 116 55 E
Jinghong **58** 22 0N 100 45 E
Jingjiang **59** 32 2N 120 16 E
Jingle **60** 38 20N 111 55 E
Jingmen **59** 31 0N 112 10 E
Jingning **60** 35 30N 105 43 E
Jingpo Hu **61** 43 55N 128 55 E
Jingshan **59** 31 1N 113 7 E
Jingtai **60** 37 10N 104 6 E
Jingxi **58** 23 8N 106 27 E
Jingxing **60** 38 2N 114 8 E
Jingyang **60** 34 30N 108 50 E
Jingyu **61** 42 25N 126 45 E
Jingyuan **60** 36 30N 104 40 E
Jingziguan **60** 33 15N 111 0 E
Jinhua **59** 29 8N 119 38 E
Jining, Nei Mongol Zizhiqu, China **60** 41 5N 113 0 E
Jining, Shandong, China **60** 35 22N 116 34 E
Jinja **94** 0 25N 33 12 E
Jinjang **55** 3 13N 101 39 E
Jinji **60** 37 58N 106 8 E
Jinjiang, Fujian, China **59** 24 43N 118 33 E
Jinjiang, Yunnan, China **58** 26 14N 100 34 E
Jinjie **58** 23 15N 107 18 E
Jinjini **88** 7 26N 3 42W
Jinkou **59** 30 20N 114 8 E
Jinmen Dao **59** 24 25N 118 25 E
Jinnah Barrage **47** 32 58N 71 33 E
Jinning **58** 24 38N 102 38 E
Jinotega **126** 13 6N 85 59W
Jinotepe **126** 11 50N 86 10W
Jinping, Guizhou, China **58** 26 41N 109 10 E
Jinping, Yunnan, China **58** 22 45N 103 18 E
Jinsha **58** 27 29N 106 12 E
Jinsha Jiang → **58** 28 50N 104 36 E
Jinshan **59** 30 54N 121 10 E
Jinshi **59** 29 40N 111 50 E
Jintan **59** 31 42N 119 36 E
Jinxi, Jiangxi, China **59** 27 56N 116 45 E
Jinxi, Liaoning, China **61** 40 52N 120 50 E
Jinxian **59** 28 26N 116 17 E
Jinxiang **60** 35 5N 116 22 E
Jinyun **59** 28 35N 120 5 E
Jinzhai **59** 31 40N 115 53 E
Jinzhou **61** 41 5N 121 3 E
Jiparaná (Machado) → **137** 8 3 S 62 52W
Jipijapa **134** 1 0 S 80 40W
Jiquilpan **124** 19 57N 102 42W
Jis rash Shughur **46** 35 49N 36 18 E
Jishan **60** 35 34N 110 58 E
Jishou **58** 28 21N 109 43 E
Jishui **59** 27 12N 115 8 E
Jitarning **79** 32 48 S 117 57 E
Jitra **55** 6 16N 100 25 E
Jiu → **34** 44 40N 23 25 E
Jiudengkou **60** 39 56N 106 40 E
Jiujiang, Guangdong, China **59** 22 50N 113 0 E
Jiujiang, Jiangxi, China **59** 29 42N 115 58 E
Jiuling Shan **59** 28 40N 114 40 E
Jiulong **58** 28 57N 101 31 E
Jiuquan **62** 39 50N 98 20 E
Jiutai **61** 44 10N 125 50 E
Jiuxiangcheng **59** 33 12N 114 50 E
Jiuxincheng **60** 39 17N 115 59 E
Jiuyuhang **59** 30 18N 119 56 E
Jixi, Anhui, China **59** 30 5N 118 34 E
Jixi, Heilongjiang, China **61** 45 20N 130 50 E
Jiyang **61** 37 0N 117 12 E
Jize **60** 36 54N 114 56 E
Jizera → **32** 50 10N 14 43 E
Jizl Wadi **90** 25 30N 38 30 E
Jizō-zaki **64** 35 34N 133 20 E
Joaçaba **141** 27 5 S 51 31W
Joaíma **139** 16 39 S 41 2W
João **138** 2 46 S 50 59W
João Amaro **139** 12 46 S 40 22W
João Câmara **138** 5 32 S 35 48W
João de Almeida **93** 15 10 S 13 42 E
João Pessoa **138** 7 10 S 34 52W
João Pinheiro **139** 17 45 S 46 10W
Joaquim Távora **139** 23 30 S 49 58W
Joaquín V. González **140** 25 10 S 64 0W
Jobourg, Nez de **18** 49 41N 1 57W
Jódar **25** 37 50N 3 21W
Jodhpur **48** 26 23N 73 8 E
Jœuf **19** 49 12N 6 1 E
Joggins **103** 45 42N 64 27W
Jogjakarta = Yogyakarta **57** 7 49 S 110 22 E
Jōhana **65** 36 30N 136 57 E
Johannesburg, S. Afr. **97** 26 10 S 28 2 E
Johannesburg, U.S.A. **123** 35 26N 117 38W
Johansfors **11** 56 42N 15 32 E
Jōhen **64** 32 58N 132 32 E
John Day **120** 44 25N 118 57W
John Day → **120** 45 44N 120 39W
John o' Groats **14** 58 39N 3 3W
Johnnie **123** 36 25N 116 5W
Johnson **119** 37 35N 101 48W
Johnson City, Ill., U.S.A. **116** 37 49N 88 56W
Johnson City, N.Y., U.S.A. **115** 42 9N 75 57W
Johnson City, N.Y., U.S.A. **115** 42 7N 75 57W
Johnson City, Tenn., U.S.A. **113** 36 18N 82 21W
Johnson City, Tex., U.S.A. **119** 30 15N 98 24W
Johnsonburg **114** 41 30N 78 40W
Johnsondale **123** 35 58N 118 32W
Johnson's Crossing **108** 60 29N 133 18W
Johnsonville **80** 41 13 S 174 48 E
Johnston Falls = Mambilima Falls **95** 10 31 S 28 45 E
Johnston I. **67** 17 10N 169 8W
Johnston Ra. **79** 29 40 S 119 20 E
Johnstone Str. **108** 50 28N 126 0W
Johnstown, N.Y., U.S.A. **115** 43 1N 74 20W
Johnstown, Pa., U.S.A. **114** 40 19N 78 53W
Johor Baharu **55** 1 28N 103 46 E
Joigny **19** 48 0N 3 20 E

Joinvile **141** 26 15 S 48 55 E
Joinville **19** 48 27N 5 10 E
Joinville I. **143** 65 0 S 55 30W
Jojutla **125** 18 37N 99 11W
Jokkmokk **8** 66 35N 19 50 E
Jökulsá á Brú → **8** 65 40N 14 16W
Jökulsá Fjöllum → **8** 66 10N 16 30W
Joliet **117** 41 30N 88 0W
Joliette **105** 46 3N 73 24W
Joliette, Parc. Prov. de **105** 46 30N 74 0W
Jolo **57** 6 0N 121 0 E
Jolon **122** 35 58N 121 9W
Jombang **57** 7 33 S 112 14 E
Jomda **58** 31 28N 98 12 E
Jome **57** 1 16 S 127 30 E
Jomfruland **11** 58 52N 9 36 E
Jönåker **11** 58 44N 16 40 E
Jonava **36** 55 8N 24 12 E
Jones Sound **144** 76 0N 85 0W
Jonesboro, Ark., U.S.A. **119** 35 50N 90 45W
Jonesboro, Ill., U.S.A. **119** 37 26N 89 18W
Jonesboro, La., U.S.A. **119** 32 15N 92 41W
Jonesburg **116** 38 51N 91 18W
Jonesport **103** 44 32N 67 38W
Jonesville, Ind., U.S.A. **117** 39 5N 85 54W
Jonesville, Mich, U.S.A. **117** 41 59N 84 40W
Jonglei **91** 6 25N 30 50 E
Joniskis **36** 56 13N 23 35 E
Jönköping **11** 57 45N 14 10 E
Jönköpings län □ **11** 57 30N 14 30 E
Jonquière **105** 48 27N 71 14W
Jonsberg **11** 58 30N 16 48 E
Jonsered **11** 57 45N 12 10 E
Jonzac **20** 45 27N 0 28W
Joplin **119** 37 0N 94 31W
Jordan, Phil. **57** 10 41N 122 38 E
Jordan, U.S.A. **120** 47 25N 106 58W
Jordan ■ **46** 31 0N 36 0 E
Jordan → **44** 31 48N 35 32 E
Jordan Valley **120** 43 0N 117 2W
Jordânia **139** 15 55 S 40 11W
Jorge, C. **142** 51 40 S 75 35W
Jorhat **52** 26 45N 94 12 E
Jörn **8** 65 4N 20 1 E
Jorquera → **140** 28 3 S 69 58W
Jos **89** 9 53N 8 51 E
José Batlle y Ordóñez **141** 33 20 S 55 10W
José de San Martín **142** 44 4 S 70 26W
Joseph **120** 45 27N 117 13W
Joseph Bonaparte G. **78** 14 35 S 128 50 E
Joseph City **121** 35 0N 110 16W
Joseph, L. **106** 45 10N 79 44W
Joseph, Lac **103** 52 45N 65 18W
Joshua Tree **123** 34 8N 116 19W
Joshua Tree Nat. Mon. **123** 33 56N 116 5W
Josselin **18** 47 57N 2 33W
Jostedal **9** 61 35N 7 15 E
Jotunheimen **10** 61 35N 8 25 E
Jounieh **46** 33 59N 35 38 E
Jourdanton **119** 28 54N 98 32W
Joussard **108** 55 22N 115 50W
Jouzjan □ **47** 36 10N 66 0 E
Jovellanos **126** 22 40N 81 10W
Jowai **52** 25 26N 92 12 E
Joya, La **136** 16 43 S 71 52W
Joyeuse **21** 44 29N 4 16 E
Józefów **32** 52 10N 21 11 E
Ju Xian **61** 36 35N 118 20 E
Juan Aldama **124** 24 20N 103 23W
Juan Bautista **121** 36 55N 121 33W
Juan Bautista Alberdi **140** 34 26 S 61 48W
Juan de Fuca Str. **122** 48 15N 124 0W
Juan de Nova, I. **97** 17 3 S 43 45 E
Juan Fernández, Arch. de **67** 33 50 S 80 0W
Juan José Castelli **140** 25 27 S 60 57W
Juan L. Lacaze **140** 34 26 S 57 25W
Juanjuí **136** 7 10 S 76 45W
Juárez, Argent. **140** 37 40 S 59 43W
Juárez, Mexico **123** 32 20N 115 57W
Juárez, Mexico **124** 27 37N 100 44W
Juárez, Sierra de **124** 32 0N 116 0W
Juatinga, Ponta de **139** 23 17 S 44 30W
Juàzeiro **138** 9 30 S 40 30W
Juàzeiro do Norte **138** 7 10 S 39 18W
Jûbâ **91** 4 50N 31 35 E
Juba → **45** 1 30N 42 35 E
Jubaila **46** 24 55N 46 25 E
Jûbâl, Madîq **90** 27 30N 34 0 E
Jubbulpore = Jabalpur **49** 23 9N 79 58 E
Jübek **30** 54 31N 9 24 E
Jubga **39** 44 19N 38 48 E
Jubilee L. **79** 29 0 S 126 50 E
Juby, C. **84** 28 0N 12 59W
Júcar → **25** 39 5N 0 10W
Júcaro **126** 21 37N 78 51W
Juchitán **125** 16 27N 95 5W
Judaea = Yehuda **44** 31 35N 34 57 E
Judenburg **33** 47 12N 14 38 E
Judith → **120** 47 44N 109 38W
Judith Gap **120** 46 40N 109 46W
Judith Pt. **115** 41 20N 71 30W
Jufari → **135** 1 13 S 62 0W
Jugiong **76** 34 48 S 148 19 E
Juigalpa **126** 12 6N 85 26W
Juillac **20** 45 20N 1 19 E
Juist **30** 53 40N 7 0 E
Juiz de Fora **139** 21 43 S 43 19W
Jujuy □ **140** 23 20 S 65 40W
Julesberg **118** 41 0N 102 20W
Juli **136** 16 10 S 69 25W
Julia Cr. → **72** 20 0 S 141 11 E
Julia Creek **72** 20 39 S 141 44 E
Juliaca **136** 15 25 S 70 10W
Julian **123** 33 4N 116 38W
Julian Alps = Julijske Alpe **27** 46 15N 14 1 E
Julianatop **135** 3 40N 56 30W
Julianehåb **144** 60 43N 46 0W
Jülich **30** 50 55N 6 20 E
Julijske Alpe **27** 46 15N 14 1 E
Julimes **124** 28 25N 105 27W
Jullundur **48** 31 20N 75 40 E
Julu **60** 37 15N 115 2 E
Jumbo **95** 17 30 S 30 58 E
Jumbo Pk. **123** 36 12N 114 11W
Jumentos Cays **127** 23 0N 75 40 E
Jumet **16** 50 27N 4 25 E
Jumilla **25** 38 28N 1 19W
Jumla **49** 29 15N 82 13 E
Jumna = Yamuna → **48** 25 30N 81 53 E
Junagadh **48** 21 30N 70 30 E
Junction, Tex., U.S.A. **119** 30 29N 99 48W
Junction, Utah, U.S.A. **121** 38 10N 112 15W
Junction B. **72** 11 52 S 133 55 E
Junction City, Kans., U.S.A. **118** 39 4N 96 55W
Junction City, Oreg., U.S.A. **120** 44 14N 123 12W
Jundah **72** 24 46 S 143 2 E
Jundiaí **141** 24 30 S 47 0W
Juneau **100** 58 20N 134 20W
Junee **76** 34 53 S 147 35 E
Jungfrau **31** 46 32N 7 58 E
Junggar Pendi **62** 44 30N 86 0 E
Jungshahi **48** 24 52N 67 44 E
Juniata → **114** 40 30N 77 40W
Junín, Argent. **140** 34 33 S 60 57W
Junín, Peru **136** 11 12 S 76 0W
Junín □ **136** 11 30 S 75 0W
Junín de los Andes **142** 39 45 S 71 0W
Junnar **50** 19 12N 73 58 E
Junquera, La **24** 42 25N 2 53 E
Junta, La **119** 38 0N 103 30W
Juntura **120** 43 44N 118 4W
Juparanã, Lagoa **139** 19 16 S 40 8W
Jupiter → **103** 49 29N 63 37W
Juquiá **139** 24 19 S 47 38W
Jur, Nahr el → **91** 8 45N 29 15 E
Jura, France **19** 46 35N 6 5 E
Jura, U.K. **14** 56 0N 5 50W
Jura □ **19** 46 47N 5 45 E
Jura, Sd. of **14** 55 57N 5 45W
Jura Suisse **31** 47 10N 7 0 E
Jurado **134** 7 7N 77 46W
Jurilovca **34** 44 46N 28 52 E
Jurm **47** 36 50N 70 52 E
Jurong **59** 31 57N 119 9 E
Juruá → **134** 2 37 S 65 44W
Juruena **137** 13 0 S 58 10W
Juruena → **137** 7 20 S 58 3W
Juruti **135** 2 9 S 56 4W
Jussey **19** 47 50N 5 55 E
Justo Daract **140** 33 52 S 65 12W
Jutaí **136** 5 11 S 68 54W
Jutaí → **134** 2 43 S 66 57W
Jüterbog **30** 52 0N 13 6 E
Juticalpa **126** 14 40N 86 12W
Jutland = Jylland **6** 56 25N 9 30 E
Juvigny-sous-Andaine **18** 48 32N 0 30W
Juvisy **19** 48 43N 2 23 E
Juwain **47** 31 45N 61 30 E
Juye **60** 35 22N 116 5 E
Juzennecourt **19** 48 10N 4 48 E
Jylland **6** 56 25N 9 30 E
Jyväskylä **8** 62 14N 25 50 E

K

K2 **49** 35 58N 76 32 E
Kaala-Gomén **68** 20 40 S 164 25 E
Kaap die Goeie Hoop **96** 34 24 S 18 30 E
Kaap Plato **96** 28 30 S 24 0 E
Kaapkruis **96** 21 43 S 14 0 E
Kaapstad = Cape Town **96** 33 56 S 18 27 E
Kabaena **57** 5 15 S 122 0 E
Kabala **88** 9 38N 11 37W
Kabale **94** 1 15 S 30 0 E
Kabalo **94** 6 0 S 27 0 E
Kabambare **94** 4 41 S 27 39 E
Kabango **95** 8 35 S 28 30 E
Kabanjahe **56** 3 6N 98 30 E
Kabara **88** 16 40N 2 50W
Kabardinka **38** 44 40N 37 57 E
Kabardino-Balkar, A.S.S.R. □ **39** 43 30N 43 30 E
Kabare **57** 0 4 S 130 58 E
Kabarega Falls **94** 2 15N 31 30 E
Kabasalan **57** 7 47N 122 44 E
Kabba **89** 7 50N 6 3 E
Kabe **64** 34 31N 132 31 E
Kabi **89** 13 30N 12 35 E
Kabin Buri **54** 13 57N 101 43 E
Kabinakagami L. **102** 48 54N 84 25W
Kabīr Kūh **46** 33 0N 47 30 E
Kabīr, Zab al **46** 36 0N 43 0 E
Kablungu, C. **69** 6 20 S 150 1 E
Kabna **90** 19 6N 32 40 E
Kabompo **95** 13 36 S 24 14 E
Kabompo → **93** 14 10 S 23 11 E
Kabondo **95** 8 58 S 25 40 E
Kabongo **94** 7 22 S 25 33 E
Kabou **89** 9 28N 0 55 E
Kaboudia, Rass **87** 35 13N 11 10 E
Kabra **72** 23 25 S 150 25 E
Kabūd Gonbad **47** 37 5N 59 45 E
Kabul **48** 34 28N 69 11 E
Kabul □ **47** 34 30N 69 0 E
Kabul → **48** 33 55N 72 14 E
Kabunga **94** 1 38 S 28 3 E
Kaburuang **57** 3 50N 126 30 E
Kabushiya **91** 16 54N 33 41 E
Kabwe **95** 14 30 S 28 29 E
Kabwum **69** 6 11 S 147 15 E
Kačanik **33** 42 13N 21 12 E
Kachanovo **36** 57 25N 27 38 E
Kachebera **95** 13 50 S 32 50 E
Kachin □ **52** 26 0N 97 30 E
Kachira, Lake **94** 0 40 S 31 7 E
Kachiry **40** 53 10N 75 50 E
Kachisi **91** 9 40N 37 50 E
Kachot **55** 11 30N 103 3 E
Kaçkar **39** 40 45N 41 10 E
Kadaingti **52** 17 37N 97 32 E
Kadan Kyun **56** 12 30N 98 20 E
Kadanai → **48** 31 22N 65 45 E
Kadarkút **33** 46 13N 17 39 E
Kadayanallur **51** 9 3N 77 22 E
Kade **89** 6 7N 0 56W
Kadgo, L. **79** 26 42 S 127 18 E
Kadi **48** 23 18N 72 23 E
Kadina **73** 34 0 S 137 43 E
Kadiri **51** 14 12N 78 13 E
Kadirli **46** 37 23N 36 5 E
Kadiyevka **39** 48 35N 38 40 E
Kadoka **118** 43 50N 101 31W
Kadom **37** 54 37N 42 30 E
Kâdugli **85** 11 0N 29 45 E
Kaduna **89** 10 30N 7 21 E
Kaduna □ **89** 11 0N 7 30 E
Kadungle **76** 32 45 S 147 36 E
Kaedi **88** 16 9N 13 28W
Kaelé **89** 10 7N 14 27 E
Kaeng Khoï **54** 14 35N 101 0 E
Kaeo **80** 35 6 S 173 49 E
Kaesŏng **61** 37 58N 126 35 E
Kāf **46** 31 25N 37 29 E
Kafakumba **92** 9 38 S 23 46 E
Kafanchan **89** 9 40N 8 20 E
Kafareti **89** 10 25N 11 12 E
Kaffrine **88** 14 8N 15 36W
Kafia Kingi **85** 9 20N 24 25 E
Kafinda **95** 12 32 S 30 20 E
Kafir Malik **44** 32 0N 35 18 E
Kafirévs, Ákra **35** 38 9N 24 38 E
Kafr 'Ein **44** 32 3N 35 7 E
Kafr el Dauwâr **90** 31 8N 30 8 E
Kafr el Sheikh **90** 31 15N 30 50 E
Kafr Kama **44** 32 44N 35 26 E
Kafr Kannā **44** 32 45N 35 20 E
Kafr Mandā **44** 32 49N 35 15 E
Kafr Quaddum **44** 32 14N 35 7 E
Kafr Ra'i **44** 32 23N 35 9 E
Kafr Sir **44** 33 19N 35 23 E
Kafr Yasif **44** 32 58N 35 10 E
Kafue **95** 15 46 S 28 9 E
Kafue Flats **95** 15 40 S 27 25 E
Kafue Gorge **95** 15 54 S 28 34 E
Kafue Hook **95** 14 58 S 26 0 E
Kafulwe **95** 9 0 S 29 1 E
Kaga, Afghan. **48** 34 14N 70 10 E
Kaga, Japan **65** 36 16N 136 15 E
Kagan **40** 39 43N 64 33 E
Kagawa □ **64** 34 15N 134 0 E
Kagawong L. **106** 45 54N 82 15W
Kagera → **94** 0 57 S 31 47 E
Kağizman **46** 40 5N 43 10 E
Kagoshima **64** 31 35N 130 33 E
Kagoshima □ **64** 31 30N 130 30 E
Kagoshima-Wan **64** 31 25N 130 40 E
Kagul **38** 45 50N 28 15 E
Kahajan → **56** 3 40 S 114 0 E
Kahama **94** 4 8 S 32 30 E
Kahama □ **94** 3 50 S 32 0 E
Kahang **55** 2 12N 103 32 E
Kahe **94** 3 30 S 37 25 E
Kahemba **92** 7 18 S 18 55 E
Kaherekoau Mts. **81** 45 45 S 167 15 E
Kahil, Djebel bou **87** 34 26N 4 0 E
Kahniah → **108** 58 15N 120 55W
Kahnūj **47** 27 55N 57 40 E
Kahoka **116** 40 25N 91 42W
Kahoolawe **110** 20 33N 156 35W
Kahurangi, Pt. **81** 40 50 S 172 10 E
Kahuta **48** 33 35N 73 24 E
Kai Besar **57** 5 35 S 133 0 E
Kai Kai **96** 19 52 S 21 15 E
Kai, Kepulauan **57** 5 55 S 132 45W
Kai-Ketjil **57** 5 45 S 132 40 E
Kai Xian **58** 31 11N 108 21 E
Kaiama **89** 9 36N 4 1 E
Kaiapit **69** 6 18 S 146 18 E
Kaiapoi **81** 42 24 S 172 40 E
Kaibara **65** 35 8N 135 5 E
Kaieteur Falls **135** 5 1N 59 10W
Kaifeng **60** 34 48N 114 21 E
Kaihua **59** 29 12N 118 20 E
Kaiingveld **96** 30 0 S 22 0 E
Kaikohe **80** 35 25 S 173 49 E
Kaikoura **81** 42 25 S 173 43 E
Kaikoura Pen. **81** 42 25 S 173 43 E
Kaikoura Ra. **81** 41 59 S 173 41 E
Kailahun **88** 8 18N 10 39W
Kailashahar **52** 24 19N 92 0 E
Kaili **58** 26 33N 107 59 E
Kailu **61** 43 38N 121 18 E
Kailua **110** 19 39N 156 0W
Kaimana **57** 3 39 S 133 45 E
Kaimanawa Mts. **80** 39 15 S 175 56 E
Kaimata **81** 42 34 S 171 28 E
Kaimganj **49** 27 33N 79 24 E
Kaimon-Dake **64** 31 11N 130 32 E
Kaimur Hill **49** 24 30N 82 0 E
Kainan **64** 34 9N 135 12 E
Kainantu **69** 6 18 S 145 52 E
Kaingaroa Forest **80** 38 24 S 176 30 E
Kainji Res. **89** 10 1N 4 40 E
Kaipara Harbour **80** 36 25 S 174 14 E
Kaiping **59** 22 23N 112 42 E
Kaipokok B. **103** 54 54N 59 47W
Kairana **48** 29 24N 77 15 E
Kaironi **57** 0 47 S 133 40 E
Kairouan **87** 35 45N 10 5 E
Kairuku **69** 8 51 S 146 35 E
Kaiserslautern **31** 49 30N 7 43 E
Kaitaia **80** 35 8 S 173 17 E
Kaitangata **81** 46 17 S 169 51 E
Kaithal **48** 29 48N 76 26 E
Kaitu → **48** 33 10N 70 30 E
Kaiwi Channel **110** 21 13N 157 30W
Kaiyang **58** 27 4N 106 59 E
Kaiyuan, Liaoning, China **61** 42 28N 124 1 E
Kaiyuan, Yunnan, China **58** 23 40N 103 12 E
Kajaani **8** 64 17N 27 46 E
Kajabbi **72** 20 0 S 140 1 E
Kajan → **56** 2 55N 117 35 E
Kajang **55** 2 59N 101 48 E
Kajiado **94** 1 53 S 36 48 E
Kajiado □ **94** 2 0 S 36 30 E
Kajiki **64** 31 44N 130 40 E
Kajo Kaji **91** 3 58N 31 40 E
Kajoa **57** 0 1N 127 28 E
Kaka **85** 10 38N 32 10 E
Kakabeka Falls **102** 48 24N 89 37W
Kakamega **94** 0 20N 34 46 E
Kakamega □ **94** 0 20N 34 46 E
Kakamigahara **65** 35 28N 136 48 E
Kakanj **33** 44 9N 18 7 E
Kakanui Mts. **81** 45 10 S 170 30 E
Kakapotahi **81** 43 0 S 170 45 E
Kake **64** 34 36N 132 19 E
Kakegawa **65** 34 45N 138 1 E
Kakhib **39** 42 28N 46 34 E
Kakhovka **38** 46 40N 33 15 E
Kakhovskoye Vdkhr. **38** 47 5N 34 16 E
Kakinada (Cocanada) **50** 16 57N 82 11 E
Kakisa → **108** 61 3N 118 10W
Kakisa L. **108** 60 56N 117 43W
Kakogawa **64** 34 46N 134 51 E
Kakwa → **108** 54 37N 118 28W
Kala **89** 12 2N 14 40 E
Kala Oya → **51** 8 20N 79 45 E
Kala Shank'ou **49** 35 42N 78 20 E
Kalaa-Kebira **87** 35 59N 10 32 E
Kalabagh **48** 33 0N 71 28 E
Kalabahi **57** 8 13 S 124 31 E
Kalabáka **35** 39 42N 21 39 E

Kalabo 93 14 58S 22 40E
Kalach 37 50 22N 41 0E
Kaladar 107 44 37N 77 5W
Kalahari 96 24 0S 21 30E
Kalahari Gemsbok Nat. Park 96 25 30S 20 30E
Kalahasti 51 13 45N 79 44E
Kalakamati 97 20 40S 27 25E
Kalakan 41 55 15N 116 45E
K'alak'unlun Shank'ou 49 35 33N 77 46E
Kalam 49 35 34N 72 30E
Kalama, U.S.A. 122 46 0N 122 55W
Kalama, Zaïre 94 2 52S 28 35E
Kalamariá 35 40 33N 22 55E
Kalamata 35 37 3N 22 10E
Kalamazoo 117 42 20N 85 35W
Kalamazoo → 117 42 40N 86 12W
Kalamb 50 18 3N 74 48E
Kalambo Falls 95 8 37S 31 35E
Kálamos 35 38 37N 20 55E
Kalamunda 79 31 57S 116 5E
Kalan 46 39 7N 39 32E
Kalannie 79 30 22S 117 5E
Kalao 57 7 21S 121 0E
Kalaotoa 57 7 20S 121 50E
Kälarne 10 62 59N 16 8E
Kalárovo 33 47 54N 18 0E
Kalasin 54 16 26N 103 30E
Kalat 47 29 8N 66 31E
Kalat □ 48 27 30N 66 0E
Kalat-i-Ghilzai 47 32 15N 66 58E
Kálathos (Calato) 35 36 9N 28 8E
Kalaus → 39 45 40N 44 7E
Kalávrita 35 38 3N 22 8E
Kalaw 52 20 38N 96 34E
Kalba 88 9 30N 2 42W
Kalbarri 79 27 40S 114 10E
Kalecik 38 40 4N 33 26E
Kalehe 94 2 6S 28 50E
Kalema 94 1 12S 31 55E
Kalemie 94 5 55S 29 9E
Kalemyo 52 23 11N 94 4E
Kalety 32 50 35N 18 52E
Kalewa 52 23 10N 94 15E
Kálfafellsstaður 8 64 11N 15 53W
Kalgan = Zhangjiakou 60 40 48N 114 55E
Kalgoorlie 79 30 40S 121 22E
Kaliakra, Nos 34 43 21N 28 30E
Kalianda 56 5 50S 105 45E
Kalibo 57 11 43N 122 22E
Kaliganj Town 49 22 25N 89 8E
Kalima 94 2 33S 26 32E
Kalimantan Barat □ 56 0 0 110 30E
Kalimantan Selatan □ 56 2 30S 115 30E
Kalimantan Tengah □ 56 2 0S 113 30E
Kalimantan Timur □ 56 1 30N 116 30E
Kálimnos 35 37 0N 27 0E
Kalimpong 49 27 4N 88 35E
Kalinadi → 51 14 50N 74 7E
Kalinin 37 56 55N 35 55E
Kaliningrad 36 54 42N 20 32E
Kalinkovichi 36 52 12N 29 20E
Kalinovik 33 43 31N 18 29E
Kalipetrovo (Stančevo) 34 44 5N 27 14E
Kaliro 94 0 56N 33 30E
Kalispell 120 48 10N 114 22W
Kalisz 32 51 45N 18 8E
Kaliua 94 5 5S 31 48E
Kaliveli Tank 51 12 5N 79 50E
Kalix → 8 65 50N 23 11E
Kalka 48 30 46N 76 57E
Kalkaska 106 44 44N 85 11W
Kalkfeld 96 20 57S 16 14E
Kalkfontein 96 22 4S 20 57E
Kalkrand 96 24 1S 17 35E
Kallakurichi 51 11 44N 79 1E
Kållandsö 11 58 40N 13 5E
Kallia 44 31 46N 35 30E
Kallidaikurichi 51 8 38N 77 31E
Kallinge 11 56 15N 15 18E
Kallithéa 35 37 55N 23 41E
Kallonís, Kólpos 35 39 10N 26 10E
Kalmalo 89 13 40N 5 20E
Kalmar 11 56 40N 16 20E
Kalmar län □ 11 57 25N 16 0E
Kalmar sund 11 56 40N 16 25E
Kalmyk A.S.S.R. □ 39 46 30N 45 30E
Kalmykovo 39 49 0N 51 47E
Kalna 49 23 13N 88 25E
Kalo 69 10 1S 147 48E
Kalocsa 33 46 32N 19 0E
Kalol, Gujarat, India 48 23 15N 72 33E
Kalol, Gujarat, India 48 22 37N 73 31E
Kalola 95 10 0S 28 0E
Kalolímnos 35 37 4N 27 8E
Kalomo 95 17 0S 26 30E
Kalona 116 41 29N 91 43W
Kalpi 49 26 8N 79 47E
Kalrayan Hills 51 11 45N 78 40E
Kalsubai, Mt. 50 19 35N 73 45E
Kaltungo 89 9 48N 11 19E
Kalu 48 25 5N 67 39E
Kaluga 37 54 35N 36 10E
Kalulushi 95 12 50S 28 3E
Kalundborg 11 55 41N 11 5E
Kałuszyn 32 52 13N 21 52E
Kalutara 51 6 35N 80 0E
Kalyan 50 20 30N 74 3E
Kalyazin 37 57 15N 37 55E
Kama, Burma 52 19 1N 95 4E
Kama, Zaïre 94 3 30S 27 5E
Kama → 40 55 45N 52 0E
Kamachumu 94 1 37S 31 37E
Kamae 64 32 48N 131 56E
Kamaing 52 25 26N 96 35E
Kamaishi 63 39 20N 142 0E
Kamakura 65 35 19N 139 33E
Kamalia 48 30 44N 72 42E
Kamamaung 52 17 21N 97 40E
Kamandorskiye Ostrava 41 55 0N 167 0E
Kamango 94 0 40N 29 52E
Kamapanda 95 12 5S 24 0E
Kamaran 45 15 21N 42 35E
Kamativi 95 18 15S 27 27E
Kamba 89 11 50N 3 45E
Kambalda 79 31 10S 121 37E
Kambam 51 9 45N 77 16E
Kambar 48 27 37N 68 1E
Kambia 88 9 3N 12 53W
Kambolé 95 8 47S 30 48E
Kambove 95 10 51S 26 33E
Kamchatka, P-ov. 41 57 0N 160 0E
Kamen 40 53 50N 81 30E
Kamen Kashirskiy 36 51 39N 24 56E
Kamenets-Podolskiy 40 48 45N 26 10E
Kamenjak, Rt 27 44 47N 13 55E
Kamenka 37 50 47N 39 20E
Kamenka Bugskaya 36 50 8N 24 16E
Kamenka Dneprovskaya 38 47 29N 34 14E
Kamensk-Shakhtinskiy 39 48 23N 40 20E
Kamensk Uralskiy 40 56 25N 62 2E
Kamenskiy 37 50 48N 45 25E
Kamenskoye 41 62 45N 165 30E
Kamenyak 34 43 24N 26 57E
Kamenz 30 51 17N 14 7E
Kameoka 65 35 0N 135 35E
Kameyama 65 34 51N 136 27E
Kami-Jima 64 32 27N 130 20E
Kami-koshiki-Jima 64 31 50N 129 52E
Kamiah 120 46 12N 116 2W
Kamień Pomorski 32 53 57N 14 43E
Kamiita 64 34 6N 134 22E
Kamilukuak, L. 109 62 22N 101 40W
Kamina 95 8 45S 25 0E
Kaminak L. 109 62 10N 95 0W
Kamioka 65 36 25N 137 15E
Kamituga Mungombe 94 3 2S 28 10E
Kamloops 108 50 40N 120 20W
Kamloops L. 108 50 45N 120 40W
Kamnik 27 46 14N 14 37E
Kamo 80 35 42S 174 20E
Kamogawa 65 35 5N 140 5E
Kamoke 48 32 4N 74 4E
Kamouraska 105 47 34N 69 52W
Kamp → 33 48 23N 15 42E
Kampala 94 0 20N 32 30E
Kampar 55 4 18N 101 9E
Kampar → 56 0 30N 103 8E
Kampen 16 52 33N 5 53E
Kamphaeng Phet 54 16 28N 99 30E
Kampolombo, L. 95 11 37S 29 42E
Kampong Ayer Puteh 55 4 15N 103 10E
Kampong Jerangau 55 4 50N 103 10E
Kampong Raja 55 5 45N 102 35E
Kampong To 55 6 3N 101 13E
Kampot 55 10 36N 104 10E
Kampsville 116 39 18N 90 37W
Kamptee 50 21 9N 79 19E
Kampti 88 10 7N 3 25W
Kampuchea = Cambodia ■ 54 13 0N 105 0E
Kampung → 57 5 44S 138 24E
Kampungbaru = Tolitoli 57 1 5N 120 50E
Kamrau, Teluk 57 3 30S 133 36E
Kamsack 109 51 34N 101 54W
Kamskoye Ustye 37 55 10N 49 20E
Kamuchawie L. 109 56 18N 101 59W
Kamui-Misaki 63 43 20N 140 21E
Kamyshin 37 50 10N 45 24E
Kamyzyak 39 46 4N 48 10E
Kan 52 22 25N 94 5E
Kanaaupscow 102 54 2N 76 30W
Kanab 121 37 3N 112 29W
Kanab Creek 121 37 0N 112 40W
Kanagawa □ 65 35 20N 139 20E
Kanairiktok → 103 55 2N 60 18W
Kanakapura 51 12 33N 77 28E
Kanália 35 39 30N 22 53E
Kananga 92 5 55S 22 18E
Kanarraville 121 37 34N 113 12W
Kanash 37 55 30N 47 32E
Kanaskat 122 47 19N 121 54W
Kanata 107 45 20N 75 59W
Kanawha → 112 38 50N 82 8W
Kanazawa 65 36 30N 136 38E
Kanbalu 52 23 12N 95 31E
Kanchanaburi 54 14 2N 99 31E
Kanchenjunga 49 27 50N 88 10E
Kanchipuram (Conjeeveram) 51 12 52N 79 45E
Kanda Kanda 92 6 52S 23 48E
Kandahar 47 31 32N 65 30E
Kandalaksha 40 67 9N 32 30E
Kandangan 56 2 50S 115 20E
Kandavu 68 19 0S 178 15E
Kandavu Passage 68 18 45S 178 0E
Kandé 89 9 57N 1 3E
Kandep 69 5 54S 143 32E
Kandewu 95 14 1S 26 16E
Kandhíla 35 37 46N 22 22E
Kandhkot 48 28 16N 69 8E
Kandhla 48 29 18N 77 19E
Kandi, Benin 89 11 7N 2 55E
Kandi, India 49 23 58N 88 5E
Kandinduna 95 13 58S 24 19E
Kandla 48 23 0N 70 10E
Kandos 76 32 45S 149 58E
Kandrian 69 6 14S 149 37E
Kandukur 51 15 12N 79 57E
Kandy 51 7 18N 80 43E
Kane 114 41 39N 78 53W
Kane Bassin 144 79 30N 68 0W
Kanevskaya 39 46 3N 39 3E
Kanfanar 27 45 7N 13 50E
Kang 47 30 55N 61 55E
Kangaba 88 11 56N 8 25W
Kangar 55 6 27N 100 12E
Kangaroo Flat 77 31 8S 152 5E
Kangaroo I. 73 35 45S 137 0E
Kangaroo Mts. 72 23 25S 142 0E
Kangaroo Valley 76 34 42S 150 32E
Kangavar 46 34 40N 48 0E
Kangding 58 30 2N 101 57E
Kăngdong 61 39 9N 126 5E
Kangean, Kepulauan 56 6 55S 115 23E
Kangerdlugsuak 144 68 10N 32 20W
Kanggye 61 41 0N 126 35E
Kanggyŏng 61 36 10N 127 0E
Kanghwa 61 37 45N 126 30E
Kangnŭng 61 37 45N 128 54E
Kango 92 0 11N 10 5E
Kangping 61 42 33N 123 18E
Kangpokpi 52 25 8N 93 58E
Kangyidaung 52 16 56N 94 54E
Kanhangad 51 12 21N 74 58E
Kanheri 50 19 13N 72 50E
Kani 88 8 29N 6 36W
Kaniama 94 7 30S 24 12E
Kaniapiskau → 103 56 40N 69 30W
Kaniapiskau L. 103 54 10N 69 55W
Kanin Nos, Mys 40 68 45N 43 20E
Kanin, P-ov. 40 68 0N 45 0E
Kaniva 74 36 22S 141 18E
Kanjiža 33 46 3N 20 4E
Kanjut Sar 49 36 7N 75 25E
Kankakee 117 41 6N 87 50W
Kankakee → 117 41 23N 88 16W
Kankan 88 10 23N 9 15W
Kanker 50 20 10N 81 40E
Kankunskiy 41 57 37N 126 8E
Kanmuri-Yama 64 34 30N 132 4E
Kannabe 64 34 32N 133 23E
Kannapolis 113 35 32N 80 37W
Kannauj 49 27 3N 79 56E
Kano 89 12 2N 8 30E
Kano □ 89 11 45N 9 0E
Kan'onji 64 34 7N 133 39E
Kanoroba 88 9 7N 6 8W
Kanowha 116 42 57N 93 47W
Kanowit 56 2 14N 112 20E
Kanowna 79 30 32S 121 31E
Kanoya 64 31 25N 130 50E
Kanpetlet 52 21 10N 93 59E
Kanpur 49 26 28N 80 20E
Kansas 117 39 33N 87 56W
Kansas □ 118 38 40N 98 0W
Kansas → 118 39 7N 94 36W
Kansas City, Kans., U.S.A. 116 39 0N 94 40W
Kansas City, Mo., U.S.A. 116 39 3N 94 30W
Kansenia 95 10 20S 26 0E
Kansk 41 56 20N 95 37E
Kansŏng 61 38 24N 128 30E
Kansu = Gansu □ 62 37 0N 103 0E
Kantang 55 7 25N 99 31E
Kantché 89 13 31N 8 30E
Kantemirovka 39 49 43N 39 55E
Kantharalak 54 14 39N 104 39E
Kantō □ 65 36 15N 139 30E
Kantō-Heiya 65 36 0N 139 30E
Kantō-Sanchi 65 35 59N 138 50E
Kantu-long 52 19 57N 97 36E
Kanturk 15 52 10N 8 55W
Kanuma 65 36 34N 139 42E
Kanumbra 74 37 3S 145 40E
Kanus 96 27 50S 18 39E
Kanye 96 25 0S 25 28E
Kanyu 96 20 7S 24 37E
Kanzenze 95 10 30S 25 12E
Kanzi, Ras 94 7 1S 39 33E
Kao 68 19 40S 175 1W
Kaohsiung = Gaoxiong 59 22 38N 120 18E
Kaokoveld 96 18 20S 13 37E
Kaolack 88 14 5N 16 8W
Kaoshan 61 44 38N 125 40E
Kapadvanj 48 23 5N 73 0E
Kapagere 69 9 46S 147 42E
Kapanga 92 8 30S 22 40E
Kapata 95 14 16S 26 15E
Kapchagai 40 43 50N 77 10E
Kapéllo, Ákra 35 36 9N 23 3E
Kapema 95 10 45S 28 22E
Kapfenberg 33 47 26N 15 18E
Kapiri Mposhi 95 13 59S 28 43E
Kapisa □ 47 35 0N 69 20E
Kapiskau → 102 52 47N 81 55W
Kapit 56 2 0N 112 55E
Kapiti I. 80 40 50S 174 56E
Kaplice 32 48 42N 14 30E
Kapoe 55 9 34N 98 32E
Kapoeta 91 4 50N 33 35E
Kaponga 80 39 29S 174 9E
Kapos → 33 46 44N 18 30E
Kaposvár 33 46 25N 17 47E
Kapowsin 122 46 59N 122 13W
Kappeln 30 54 37N 9 56E
Kapps 96 22 32S 17 18E
Kaprije 27 43 42N 15 43E
Kapsan 61 41 4N 128 19E
Kapsukas 36 54 33N 23 19E
Kapuas → 56 0 25S 109 20E
Kapuas Hulu, Pegunungan 56 1 30N 113 30E
Kapuka 95 10 30S 32 55E
Kapulo 95 8 18S 29 15E
Kapunda 73 34 20S 138 56E
Kapurthala 48 31 23N 75 25E
Kapuskasing 102 49 25N 82 30W
Kapuskasing → 102 49 49N 82 0W
Kapustin Yar 39 48 37N 45 40E
Kaputar, Mt. 77 30 15S 150 10E
Kaputir 94 2 5N 35 28E
Kapuvár 33 47 36N 17 1E
Kara 40 69 10N 65 0E
Kara Bogaz Gol, Zaliv 40 41 0N 53 30E
Kara Kalpak A.S.S.R. □ 40 43 0N 60 0E
Kara-Saki 64 34 41N 129 30E
Kara Sea 40 75 0N 70 0E
Kara, Wadi 90 20 0N 41 25E
Karabük 38 41 12N 32 37E
Karaburuni 35 40 25N 19 20E
Karabutak 40 49 59N 60 14E
Karachala 39 39 45N 48 53E
Karachayevsk 39 43 50N 42 0E
Karachev 36 53 10N 35 5E
Karachi 48 24 53N 67 0E
Karachi □ 48 25 30N 67 0E
Karad 50 17 15N 74 10E
Karadeniz Boğazı 46 41 10N 29 5E
Karadeniz Dağlari 46 41 30N 35 0E
Karaga 89 9 58N 0 28W
Karaganda 40 49 50N 73 10E
Karagayly 40 49 26N 76 0E
Karaginskiy, Ostrov 41 58 45N 164 0E
Karagwe □ 94 2 0S 31 0E
Karaikkudi 51 10 0N 78 45E
Karaitivu I. 51 9 45N 79 52E
Karaitivu, I. 51 8 22N 79 52E
Karaj 47 35 48N 51 0E
Karak 55 3 25N 102 2E
Karakas 40 48 20N 83 30E
Karakitang 57 3 14N 125 28E
Karakobis 96 22 3S 20 37E
Karakoram 49 35 30N 77 0E
Karakoram Pass 49 35 33N 77 50E
Karakum, Peski 40 39 30N 60 0E
Karalon 41 57 5N 115 50E
Karaman 46 37 14N 33 13E
Karamay 62 45 30N 84 58E
Karambu 56 3 53S 116 6E
Karamea 81 41 14S 172 6E
Karamea → 81 41 13S 172 26E
Karamea Bight 81 41 22S 171 40E
Karamoja □ 94 3 0N 34 15E
Karamsad 48 22 35N 72 50E
Karanganjar 57 7 38S 109 37E

Karanja	50	20 29N	77 31 E
Karapiro	80	37 53S	175 32 E
Karara	77	28 12S	151 37 E
Karasburg	96	28 0S	18 44 E
Karasino	40	66 50N	86 50 E
Karasuk	40	53 44N	78 2 E
Karasuyama	65	36 39N	140 9 E
Karatau	40	43 10N	70 28 E
Karatau, Khrebet	40	43 30N	69 30 E
Karatoya ~→	52	24 7N	89 36 E
Karauli	48	26 30N	77 4 E
Karawa	92	3 18N	20 17 E
Karawanken	33	46 30N	14 40 E
Karazhal	40	48 2N	70 49 E
Karbalā	46	32 36N	44 3 E
Kårböle	10	61 59N	15 22 E
Karcag	33	47 19N	20 57 E
Karcha ~→	49	34 45N	76 10 E
Karda	41	55 0N	103 16 E
Kardhámila	35	38 35N	26 5 E
Kardhítsa	35	39 23N	21 54 E
Kärdla	36	58 50N	22 40 E
Kareeberge	96	30 50S	22 0 E
Kareima	90	18 30N	31 49 E
Karelian A.S.S.R. □	40	65 30N	32 30 E
Karema	69	9 12S	147 18 E
Kargānrūd	46	37 55N	49 0 E
Kargasok	40	59 3N	80 53 E
Kargat	40	55 10N	80 15 E
Kargı	38	41 11N	34 30 E
Kargil	49	34 32N	76 12 E
Karguéri	89	13 27N	10 30 E
Karia ba Mohammed	86	34 22N	5 12W
Kariba	95	16 28S	28 50 E
Kariba Gorge	95	16 30S	28 50 E
Kariba Lake	95	16 40S	28 25 E
Karibib	96	21 0S	15 56 E
Karikal	51	10 59N	79 50 E
Karimata, Kepulauan	56	1 25S	109 0 E
Karimata, Selat	56	2 0S	108 40 E
Karimnagar	50	18 26N	79 10 E
Karimunjawa, Kepulauan	56	5 50S	110 30 E
Karin	45	10 50N	45 52 E
Kariya	65	34 58N	137 1 E
Karkal	51	13 15N	74 56 E
Karkar I.	69	4 40S	146 0 E
Karkaralinsk	40	49 26N	75 30 E
Karkinitskiy Zaliv	38	45 56N	33 0 E
Karkur	44	32 29N	34 57 E
Karkur Tohl	90	22 5N	25 5 E
Karl Libknekht	36	51 40N	35 35 E
Karl-Marx-Stadt	30	50 50N	12 55 E
Karl-Marx-Stadt □	30	50 45N	13 0 E
Karla, L = Voiviïs, Límni	35	39 30N	22 45 E
Karlobag	27	44 32N	15 5 E
Karlovac	27	45 31N	15 36 E
Karlovka	38	49 29N	35 8 E
Karlovy Vary	32	50 13N	12 51 E
Karlsborg	11	58 33N	14 33 E
Karlshamn	11	56 10N	14 51 E
Karlskoga	10	59 22N	14 33 E
Karlskrona	11	56 10N	15 35 E
Karlsruhe	31	49 3N	8 23 E
Karlstad, Sweden	10	59 23N	13 30 E
Karlstad, U.S.A.	118	48 38N	96 30W
Karlstadt	31	49 57N	9 46 E
Karnal	48	29 42N	77 2 E
Karnali ~→	49	29 0N	83 20 E
Karnaphuli Res.	52	22 40N	92 20 E
Karnataka □	51	14 15N	76 0 E
Karnes City	119	28 53N	97 53W
Karnische Alpen	33	46 36N	13 0 E
Karo	88	12 16N	3 18W
Karoi	95	16 48S	29 45 E
Karonga	95	9 57S	33 55 E
Karoonda	73	35 1S	139 59 E
Káros	35	36 54N	25 40 E
Karousádhes	35	39 47N	19 45 E
Kárpathos	35	35 37N	27 10 E
Karpáthos, Stenón	35	36 0N	27 30 E
Karrebæk	11	55 12N	11 39 E
Kars, Turkey	46	40 40N	43 5 E
Kars, U.S.S.R.	38	40 36N	43 5 E
Karsakpay	40	47 55N	66 40 E
Karsha	39	49 45N	51 35 E
Karshi	40	38 53N	65 48 E
Karst	27	45 35N	14 0 E
Karsun	37	54 14N	46 57 E
Kartaly	40	53 3N	60 40 E
Kartapur	48	31 27N	75 32 E
Karthaus	114	41 8N	78 9W
Kartuzy	32	54 22N	18 10 E
Karuah	76	32 37S	151 56 E
Karufa	57	3 50S	133 20 E
Karumba	72	17 31S	140 50 E
Karumo	94	2 25S	32 50 E
Karumwa	94	3 12S	32 38 E
Karungu	94	0 50S	34 10 E
Karup	11	56 19N	9 10 E
Karur	51	10 59N	78 2 E
Karviná	32	49 53N	18 25 E
Karwi	49	25 12N	80 57 E
Kasache	95	13 25S	34 20 E
Kasai	64	34 55N	134 52 E
Kasai ~→	92	3 30S	16 10 E
Kasai Oriental □	94	5 0S	24 30 E
Kasaji	95	10 25S	23 27 E
Kasama, Japan	65	36 23N	140 16 E
Kasama, Zambia	95	10 16S	31 9 E
Kasan-dong	61	41 18N	126 55 E
Kasane	96	17 34S	24 50 E
Kasanga	95	8 30S	31 10 E
Kasangulu	92	4 33S	15 15 E
Kasaoka	64	34 30N	133 30 E
Kasaragod	51	12 30N	74 58 E
Kasat	52	15 56N	98 13 E
Kasba	52	23 45N	91 2 E
Kasba L.	109	60 20N	102 10W
Kasba Tadla	86	32 36N	6 17W
Kaschmar	47	35 16N	58 26 E
Kaseda	64	31 25N	130 19 E
Kasempa	95	13 30S	25 44 E
Kasenga	95	10 20S	28 45 E
Kasese	94	0 13N	30 3 E
Kasewa	95	14 28S	28 53 E
Kasganj	49	27 48N	78 42 E
Kashabowie	102	48 40N	90 26W
Kāshān	47	34 5N	51 30 E
Kashi	62	39 30N	76 2 E
Kashihara	65	34 27N	135 46 E
Kashima, Ibaraki, Japan	65	35 58N	140 38 E
Kashima, Saga, Japan	64	33 7N	130 6 E
Kashima-Nada	65	36 0N	140 45 E
Kashimbo	95	11 12S	26 19 E
Kashin	37	57 20N	37 36 E
Kashipur, Orissa, India	50	19 16N	83 3 E
Kashipur, Ut. P., India	49	29 15N	79 0 E
Kashira	37	54 45N	38 10 E
Kashiwa	65	35 52N	139 59 E
Kashiwazaki	63	37 22N	138 33 E
Kashmir	49	34 0N	76 0 E
Kashmor	48	28 28N	69 32 E
Kashpirovka	37	53 0N	48 30 E
Kashun Noerh = Gaxun Nur	62	42 22N	100 30 E
Kasimov	37	54 55N	41 20 E
Kasinge	94	6 15S	26 58 E
Kasiruta	57	0 25S	127 12 E
Kaskaskia ~→	116	37 58N	89 57W
Kaskattama ~→	109	57 3N	90 4W
Kaskinen	8	62 22N	21 15 E
Kaskö	8	62 22N	21 15 E
Kaslo	108	49 55N	116 55W
Kasmere L.	109	59 34N	101 10W
Kasongo	94	4 30S	26 33 E
Kasongo Lunda	92	6 35S	16 49 E
Kásos	35	35 20N	26 55 E
Kasos, Stenón	35	35 30N	26 30 E
Kaspi	39	41 54N	44 17 E
Kaspiysk	39	42 52N	47 40 E
Kaspiyskiy	39	45 22N	47 23 E
Kassab ed Doleib	91	13 30N	33 35 E
Kassaba	90	22 40N	29 55 E
Kassala	91	16 0N	36 0 E
Kassalâ □	91	15 20N	36 26 E
Kassel	30	51 19N	9 32 E
Kassinger	90	18 46N	31 51 E
Kassue	57	6 58S	139 21 E
Kastamonu	46	41 25N	33 43 E
Kastav	27	45 22N	14 20 E
Kastélli	35	35 29N	23 38 E
Kastellorizon = Megiste	46	36 8N	29 34 E
Kastellou, Ákra	35	35 30N	27 15 E
Kastlösa	11	56 26N	16 25 E
Kastóri	35	37 10N	22 17 E
Kastoría	35	40 30N	21 19 E
Kastornoye	37	51 55N	38 2 E
Kástron	35	39 50N	25 2 E
Kasugai	65	35 12N	136 59 E
Kasukabe	65	35 58N	139 49 E
Kasulu	94	4 37S	30 5 E
Kasulu □	94	4 37S	30 5 E
Kasumi	64	35 38N	134 38 E
Kasumiga-Ura	65	36 0N	140 25 E
Kasumkent	39	41 47N	48 15 E
Kasungu	95	13 0S	33 29 E
Kasur	48	31 5N	74 25 E
Kata	41	58 46N	102 40 E
Kataba	95	16 5S	25 10 E
Katako Kombe	94	3 25S	24 20 E
Katákolon	35	37 38N	21 19 E
Katale	94	4 52S	31 7 E
Katama	91	9 35N	38 36 E
Katamatite	74	36 6S	145 41 E
Katanda	94	0 55S	29 21 E
Katangi	50	21 56N	79 50 E
Katangli	41	51 42N	143 14 E
Katanich	91	6 0N	33 40 E
Katavi Swamp	94	6 50S	31 10 E
Kateríni	35	40 18N	22 37 E
Katherîna, Gebel	90	28 30N	33 57 E
Katherine	78	14 27S	132 20 E
Kathiawar	48	22 20N	71 0 E
Kathua	49	32 23N	75 30 E
Kati	88	12 41N	8 4W
Katiet	56	2 21S	99 54 E
Katihar	49	25 34N	87 36 E
Katima Mulilo	96	17 28S	24 13 E
Katimbira	95	12 40S	34 0 E
Katiola	88	8 10N	5 10W
Katkopberg	96	30 0S	20 0 E
Katmandu	49	27 45N	85 20 E
Kato Akhaïa	35	38 8N	21 33 E
Káto Stavros	35	40 39N	23 43 E
Katol	50	21 17N	78 38 E
Katompi	94	6 2S	26 23 E
Katonga ~→	94	0 34N	31 50 E
Katoomba	76	33 41S	150 19 E
Katowice	32	50 17N	19 5 E
Katrine, L.	14	56 15N	4 30W
Katrineholm	10	59 9N	16 12 E
Katsepe	97	15 45S	46 15 E
Katsina Ala ~→	89	7 10N	9 20 E
Katsumoto	64	33 51N	129 42 E
Katsuta	65	36 25N	140 31 E
Katsuura	65	35 10N	140 20 E
Katsuyama	65	36 3N	136 30 E
Kattawaz-Urgun □	47	32 10N	68 20 E
Kattegatt	11	57 0N	11 20 E
Katumba	94	7 40S	25 17 E
Katunga	74	35 58S	145 28 E
Katungu	94	2 55S	40 3 E
Katwa	49	23 30N	88 5 E
Katwijk-aan-Zee	16	52 12N	4 24 E
Kauai	110	22 0N	159 30W
Kauai Chan.	110	21 45N	158 50W
Kaub	31	50 5N	7 46 E
Kaufbeuren	31	47 50N	10 37 E
Kaufman	119	32 35N	96 20W
Kaukauna	112	44 20N	88 13W
Kaukauveld	96	20 0S	20 15 E
Kauliranta	8	66 27N	23 41 E
Kaunas	36	54 54N	23 54 E
Kaunghein	52	25 41N	95 26 E
Kaura Namoda	89	12 37N	6 33 E
Kautokeino	8	69 0N	23 4 E
Kavacha	41	60 16N	169 51 E
Kavadarci	35	41 26N	22 3 E
Kavaja	35	41 11N	19 33 E
Kavali	51	14 55N	80 1 E
Kavála	35	40 57N	24 28 E
Kavarna	34	43 26N	28 22 E
Kavieng	69	2 36S	150 51 E
Kavkaz, Bolshoi	39	42 50N	44 0 E
Kaw = Caux	135	4 30N	52 15W
Kawa	91	13 42N	32 34 E
Kawachi-Nagano	65	34 28N	135 31 E
Kawagama L.	107	45 18N	78 45W
Kawagoe	65	35 55N	139 29 E
Kawaguchi	65	35 52N	139 45 E
Kawaihae	110	20 3N	155 50W
Kawakawa	80	35 23S	174 6 E
Kawama	95	9 30S	28 30 E
Kawambwa	95	9 48S	29 3 E
Kawanoe	64	34 1N	133 34 E
Kawarau	81	45 3S	168 45 E
Kawardha	49	22 0N	81 17 E
Kawasaki	65	35 35N	139 42 E
Kawau I.	80	36 25S	174 52 E
Kawene	102	48 45N	91 15W
Kawerau	80	38 7S	176 42 E
Kawhia Harbour	80	38 5S	174 51 E
Kawio, Kepulauan	57	4 30N	125 30 E
Kawkareik	52	16 33N	98 14 E
Kawlin	52	23 47N	95 41 E
Kawthoolei □ = Kawthule	52	18 0N	97 30 E
Kawthule □	52	18 0N	97 30 E
Kawya	52	24 50N	94 58 E
Kaya	89	13 4N	1 10W
Kayah □	52	19 15N	97 15 E
Kayan	52	16 54N	96 34 E
Kayangulam	51	9 10N	76 33 E
Kaycee	120	43 45N	106 46W
Kayeli	57	3 20S	127 10 E
Kayenta	121	36 46N	110 15W
Kayes	88	14 25N	11 30W
Kayima	88	8 54N	11 15W
Kayomba	95	13 11S	24 2 E
Kayoro	89	11 0N	1 28W
Kayrunnera	73	30 40S	142 30 E
Kaysatskoye	39	49 47N	46 49 E
Kayseri	46	38 45N	35 30 E
Kaysville	120	41 2N	111 58W
Kayuagung	56	3 24S	104 50 E
Kazachinskoye	41	56 16N	107 36 E
Kazachye	41	70 52N	135 58 E
Kazakh S.S.R. □	40	50 0N	70 0 E
Kazan	37	55 48N	49 3 E
Kazanlúk	34	42 38N	25 20 E
Kazanskaya	39	49 50N	41 10 E
Kazatin	38	49 45N	28 50 E
Kāzerūn	47	29 38N	51 40 E
Kazi Magomed	39	40 3N	49 0 E
Kazincbarcika	33	48 17N	20 36 E
Kazo	65	36 7N	139 36 E
Kaztalovka	39	49 47N	48 43 E
Kazu	52	25 27N	97 46 E
Kazumba	92	6 25S	22 5 E
Kazym ~→	40	63 54N	65 50 E
Kcynia	32	53 0N	17 30 E
Ké	88	13 58N	5 18W
Ke-hsi Mansam	52	21 56N	97 50 E
Ké-Macina	88	13 58N	5 22W
Kea	35	37 30N	24 22 E
Kéa	35	37 35N	24 22 E
Keams Canyon	121	35 53N	110 9W
Kearney, Can.	106	45 33N	79 13W
Kearney, Mo., U.S.A.	116	39 22N	94 22W
Kearney, Nebr., U.S.A.	118	40 45N	99 3W
Keban	46	38 50N	38 50 E
Kebele	91	12 52N	40 40 E
Kébi	88	9 18N	6 37W
Kebili	87	33 47N	9 0 E
Kebkabiya	85	13 50N	24 0 E
Kebri Dehar	45	6 45N	44 17 E
Kebumen	57	7 42S	109 40 E
Kecel	33	46 31N	19 16 E
Kechika ~→	108	59 41N	127 12W
Kecskemét	33	46 57N	19 42 E
Kedada	91	5 25N	35 58 E
Kedainiai	36	55 15N	24 2 E
Kedgwick	103	47 40N	67 20W
Kedia Hill	96	21 28S	24 37 E
Kediri	57	7 51S	112 1 E
Kédougou	88	12 35N	12 10W
Kedzierzyn	32	50 20N	18 12 E
Keefers	108	50 0N	121 40W
Keeler	122	36 29N	117 52W
Keeley L.	109	54 54N	108 8W
Keeling Is. = Cocos Is.	66	12 12S	96 54 E
Keene, Can.	107	44 15N	78 10W
Keene, Calif., U.S.A.	123	35 13N	118 33W
Keene, N.H., U.S.A.	115	42 57N	72 17W
Keeper Hill	15	52 46N	8 17W
Keepit Dam	77	30 52S	150 29 E
Keer-Weer, C.	72	14 0S	141 32 E
Keeseville	115	44 29N	73 30W
Keetmanshoop	96	26 35S	18 8 E
Keewatin	118	47 23N	93 0W
Keewatin □	109	63 20N	95 0W
Keewatin ~→	109	56 29N	100 46W
Kefa □	91	6 55N	36 30 E
Kefallinía	35	38 20N	20 30 E
Kefamenanu	57	9 28S	124 29 E
Kefar Etsyon	44	31 39N	35 7 E
Kefar Hasīdim	44	32 47N	35 5 E
Kefar Nahum	44	32 54N	35 34 E
Kefar Sava	44	32 11N	34 54 E
Kefar Szold	44	33 11N	35 39 E
Kefar Vitkin	44	32 22N	34 53 E
Kefar Yehezqel	44	32 34N	35 22 E
Kefar Yona	44	32 20N	34 54 E
Kefar Zekharya	44	31 43N	34 57 E
Kefar Zetim	44	32 48N	35 27 E
Keffi	89	8 55N	7 43 E
Keflavík	8	64 2N	22 35W
Keg River	108	57 54N	117 55W
Kegahka	103	50 9N	61 18W
Kegalla	51	7 15N	80 21 E
Kehl	31	48 34N	7 50 E
Keighley	12	53 52N	1 54W
Keimoes	96	28 41S	21 0 E
Keita	89	14 46N	5 56 E
Keith, Austral.	73	36 6S	140 20 E
Keith, U.K.	14	57 33N	2 58W
Keith Arm	100	64 20N	122 15W
Keithsburg	116	41 6N	90 56W
Kekri	48	26 0N	75 10 E
Kël	41	69 30N	124 10 E
Kelamet	91	16 0N	38 30 E
Kelan	60	38 43N	111 31 E
Kelang	55	3 2N	101 26 E
Kelani Ganga ~→	51	6 58N	79 50 E
Kelantan ~→	55	6 13N	102 14 E
Kelheim	31	48 58N	11 57 E
Kelibia	87	36 50N	11 3 E
Kellé, Congo	92	0 8S	14 38 E
Kellé, Niger	89	14 18N	10 10 E
Keller	120	48 2N	118 44W
Kellerberrin	79	31 36S	117 38 E
Kellett C.	144	72 0N	126 0W
Kelleys I.	114	41 35N	82 42W
Kellogg	120	47 30N	116 5W
Kelloselkä	8	66 56N	28 53 E
Kells = Ceanannus Mor	15	53 42N	6 53W
Kélo	92	9 10N	15 45 E
Kelowna	108	49 50N	119 25W
Kelsey Bay	108	50 25N	126 0W
Kelseyville	122	38 59N	122 50W

Kelso, N.Z.	**81**	45 54 S	169 15 E
Kelso, U.K.	**14**	55 36N	2 27W
Kelso, U.S.A.	**122**	46 10N	122 57W
Keluang	**55**	2 3N	103 18 E
Kelvington	**109**	52 10N	103 30W
Kem	**40**	65 0N	34 38 E
Kem-Kem	**86**	30 40N	4 30W
Kema	**57**	1 22N	125 8 E
Kemah	**46**	39 32N	39 5 E
Kemano	**108**	53 35N	128 0W
Kemapyu	**52**	18 49N	97 19 E
Kemasik	**55**	4 25N	103 25 E
Kembolcha	**91**	11 2N	39 42 E
Kemenets-Podolskiy	**38**	48 40N	26 40 E
Kemerovo	**40**	55 20N	86 5 E
Kemi älv = Kemijoki →	**8**	65 47N	24 32 E
Kemijärvi	**8**	66 43N	27 22 E
Kemijoki →	**8**	65 47N	24 32 E
Kemmerer	**120**	41 52N	110 30W
Kemp Coast	**143**	69 0S	55 0 E
Kemp L.	**119**	33 45N	99 15W
Kempsey	**77**	31 1S	152 50 E
Kempt, L.	**105**	47 25N	74 22W
Kempten	**31**	47 42N	10 18 E
Kempton	**117**	40 16N	86 14W
Kemptville	**107**	45 0N	75 38W
Kenadsa	**86**	31 48N	2 26W
Kendal, Indon.	**56**	6 56S	110 14 E
Kendal, U.K.	**12**	54 19N	2 44W
Kendall	**77**	31 35S	152 44 E
Kendall →	**72**	14 4S	141 35 E
Kendallville	**117**	41 25N	85 15W
Kendari	**57**	3 50S	122 30 E
Kendawangan	**56**	2 32S	110 17 E
Kende	**89**	11 30N	4 12 E
Kendenup	**79**	34 30S	117 38 E
Kendrapara	**50**	20 35N	86 30 E
Kendrick	**120**	46 43N	116 41W
Kene Thao	**54**	17 44N	101 10 E
Kenebri	**77**	30 46S	149 1 E
Kenedy	**119**	28 49N	97 51W
Kenema	**88**	7 50N	11 14W
Keng Kok	**54**	16 26N	105 12 E
Keng Tawng	**52**	20 45N	98 18 E
Kenge	**92**	4 50S	17 4 E
Kengeja	**94**	5 26S	39 45 E
Kenhardt	**96**	29 19S	21 12 E
Kéninkoumou	**88**	15 17N	12 18W
Kénitra (Port Lyautey)	**86**	34 15N	6 40W
Kenli	**61**	37 30N	118 20 E
Kenmare, Ireland	**15**	51 52N	9 35W
Kenmare, U.S.A.	**118**	48 40N	102 4W
Kenmare →	**15**	51 40N	10 0W
Kenmore	**76**	34 44S	149 45 E
Kennebec	**118**	43 56N	99 54W
Kennedy	**95**	18 52S	27 10 E
Kennedy Ra.	**79**	24 45S	115 10 E
Kennet →	**13**	51 24N	0 58W
Kenneth Ra.	**79**	23 50S	117 8 E
Kennett	**119**	36 7N	90 0W
Kennett River	**74**	38 40S	143 52 E
Kennewick	**120**	46 11N	119 2W
Kénogami	**105**	48 25N	71 15W
Kenogami →	**102**	51 6N	84 28W
Kénogami, L.	**105**	48 20N	71 23W
Kenora	**109**	49 47N	94 29W
Kenosha	**117**	42 33N	87 48W
Kensington, Can.	**103**	46 28N	63 34W
Kensington, U.S.A.	**118**	39 48N	99 2W
Kensington Downs	**72**	22 31S	144 19 E
Kent, Ohio, U.S.A.	**114**	41 8N	81 20W
Kent, Oreg., U.S.A.	**120**	45 11N	120 45W
Kent, Tex., U.S.A.	**119**	31 5N	104 12W
Kent, Wash., U.S.A.	**122**	47 23N	122 14W
Kent □	**13**	51 12N	0 40 E
Kent Gr.	**72**	39 30S	147 20 E
Kent Pen.	**100**	68 30N	107 0W
Kentau	**40**	43 32N	68 36 E
Kentdale	**79**	34 54S	117 3 E
Kentland	**117**	40 45N	87 25W
Kenton	**117**	40 40N	83 35W
Kentucky	**77**	30 45S	151 28 E
Kentucky □	**112**	37 20N	85 0W
Kentucky →	**117**	38 41N	85 11W
Kentucky Dam	**112**	37 2N	88 15W
Kentucky L.	**113**	36 25N	88 0W
Kentville	**103**	45 6N	64 29W
Kentwood	**119**	31 0N	90 30W
Kenya ■	**94**	1 0N	38 0 E
Kenya, Mt.	**94**	0 10S	37 18 E
Keo Neua, Deo	**54**	18 23N	105 10 E
Keokuk	**116**	40 25N	91 24W
Keosauqua	**116**	40 44N	91 58W
Keota	**116**	41 22N	91 57W
Kep, Camb.	**55**	10 29N	104 19 E
Kep, Viet.	**54**	21 24N	106 16 E
Kepi	**57**	6 32S	139 19 E
Kepler Mts.	**81**	45 25S	167 20 E
Kępno	**32**	51 18N	17 58 E
Kepsut	**46**	39 40N	28 9 E
Kepulauan Sunda, Ketjil Timor □	**57**	9 30S	122 0 E
Kerala □	**51**	11 0N	76 15 E
Kerama-Shotō	**63**	26 12N	127 22 E
Keran	**49**	34 35N	73 59 E
Kerang	**74**	35 40S	143 55 E
Keraudren, C.	**78**	19 58S	119 45 E
Keravat	**69**	4 17S	152 2 E
Keray	**47**	26 15N	57 30 E
Kerch	**38**	45 20N	36 20 E
Kerchenskiy Proliv	**38**	45 10N	36 30 E
Kerchoual	**89**	17 12N	0 20 E
Kerem Maharal	**44**	32 39N	34 59 E
Kerema	**69**	7 58S	145 50 E
Keren	**91**	15 45N	38 28 E
Kerewan	**88**	13 29N	16 10W
Kerguelen	**53**	48 15S	69 10 E
Keri Kera	**91**	12 21N	32 42 E
Kericho	**94**	0 22S	35 15 E
Kericho □	**94**	0 30S	35 15 E
Kerikeri	**80**	35 12S	173 59 E
Kerinci	**56**	1 40S	101 15 E
Kerkenna, Iles	**87**	34 48N	11 11 E
Kerki	**40**	37 50N	65 12 E
Kérkira	**35**	39 38N	19 50 E
Kerkrade	**16**	50 53N	6 4 E
Kerma	**90**	19 33N	30 32 E
Kermadec Is.	**66**	30 0S	178 15W
Kermadec Trench	**66**	30 30S	176 0W
Kermān	**47**	30 15N	57 1 E
Kerman	**122**	36 43N	120 4W
Kermān □	**47**	30 0N	57 0 E
Kermānshāh	**46**	34 23N	47 0 E
Kermānshāh □	**46**	34 0N	46 30 E
Kermit	**119**	31 56N	103 3W
Kern →	**123**	35 16N	119 18W
Kernville	**123**	35 45N	118 26W
Keroh	**55**	5 43N	101 1 E
Kerrabee	**76**	32 24S	150 19 E
Kerrisdale	**74**	37 10S	145 16 E
Kerriwah	**76**	32 26S	147 22 E
Kerrobert	**109**	52 0N	109 11W
Kerrville	**119**	30 1N	99 8W
Kerry □	**15**	52 7N	9 35W
Kerry Hd.	**15**	52 26N	9 56W
Kersa	**91**	9 28N	41 48 E
Kerteminde	**11**	55 28N	10 39 E
Kertosono	**57**	7 38S	112 9 E
Keru	**91**	15 40N	37 5 E
Kerulen →	**62**	48 48N	117 0 E
Kerzaz	**86**	29 29N	1 37W
Kesagami →	**102**	51 40N	79 45W
Kesagami L.	**102**	50 23N	80 15W
Kestell	**97**	28 17S	28 42 E
Kestenga	**40**	66 0N	31 50 E
Keswick, Can.	**106**	44 15N	79 28W
Keswick, U.K.	**12**	54 35N	3 9W
Keszthely	**33**	46 50N	17 15 E
Ket →	**40**	58 55N	81 32 E
Keta	**89**	5 49N	1 0 E
Ketapang	**56**	1 55S	110 0 E
Ketchikan	**100**	55 25N	131 40W
Ketchum	**120**	43 41N	114 27W
Kete Krachi	**89**	7 46N	0 1W
Ketef, Khalîg Umm el	**90**	23 40N	35 35 E
Keti Bandar	**48**	24 8N	67 27 E
Ketri	**48**	28 1N	75 50 E
Kętrzyn	**32**	54 7N	21 22 E
Kettering, U.K.	**13**	52 24N	0 44W
Kettering, U.S.A.	**117**	39 41N	84 10W
Kettle →	**109**	56 40N	89 34W
Kettle Falls	**120**	48 41N	118 2W
Kettle Pt.	**106**	43 13N	82 1W
Kettleman City	**122**	36 1N	119 58W
Kevin	**120**	48 45N	111 58W
Kewanee	**116**	41 18N	89 55W
Kewanna	**117**	41 1N	86 25W
Kewaunee	**112**	44 27N	87 30W
Keweenaw B.	**112**	46 56N	88 23W
Keweenaw Pen.	**112**	47 30N	88 0W
Keweenaw Pt.	**112**	47 26N	87 40W
Key Harbour	**106**	45 50N	80 45W
Key West	**126**	24 33N	82 0W
Keyesport	**116**	38 45N	89 17W
Keynshamburg	**95**	19 15S	29 40 E
Keyport	**115**	40 26N	74 12W
Keyser	**112**	39 26N	79 0W
Keystone, S.D., U.S.A.	**118**	43 54N	103 27W
Keystone, W. Va., U.S.A.	**112**	37 30N	81 30W
Keytesville	**116**	39 26N	92 56W
Kezhma	**41**	58 59N	101 9 E
Kežmarok	**32**	49 10N	20 28 E
Khabarovo	**40**	69 30N	60 30 E
Khabarovsk	**41**	48 30N	135 5 E
Khābūr →	**46**	35 0N	40 30 E
Khachmas	**39**	41 31N	48 42 E
Khachraud	**48**	23 25N	75 20 E
Khadari, W. el →	**91**	10 29N	27 15 E
Khadro	**48**	26 11N	68 50 E
Khadyzhensk	**39**	44 26N	39 32 E
Khadzhilyangar	**49**	35 45N	79 20 E
Khagaria	**49**	25 30N	86 32 E
Khaibar	**90**	25 49N	39 16 E
Khaibar, Harrat	**46**	25 45N	40 0 E
Khaipur, Bahawalpur, Pak.	**48**	29 34N	72 17 E
Khaipur, Hyderabad, Pak.	**48**	27 32N	68 49 E
Khair	**48**	27 57N	77 46 E
Khairabad	**49**	27 33N	80 47 E
Khairagarh Raj	**49**	21 27N	81 2 E
Khairpur □	**48**	27 20N	69 8 E
Khakhea	**93**	24 48S	23 22 E
Khalfallah	**86**	34 20N	0 16 E
Khalij-e-Fars □	**47**	28 20N	51 45 E
Khalilabad	**49**	26 48N	83 5 E
Khálki	**35**	39 36N	22 30 E
Khalkís	**35**	38 27N	23 42 E
Khalmer-Sede = Tazovskiy	**40**	67 30N	78 30 E
Khalmer Yu	**40**	67 58N	65 1 E
Khalturin	**37**	58 40N	48 50 E
Kham Keut	**54**	18 15N	104 43 E
Khamaria	**50**	23 10N	80 52 E
Khamas Country	**96**	21 45S	26 30 E
Khambhalia	**48**	22 14N	69 41 E
Khamgaon	**50**	20 42N	76 37 E
Khamilonísion	**35**	35 50N	26 15 E
Khamir	**45**	16 0N	44 0 E
Khammam	**50**	17 11N	80 6 E
Khān Yūnis	**44**	31 21N	34 18 E
Khanabad	**47**	36 45N	69 5 E
Khānaqin	**46**	34 23N	45 25 E
Khancoban	**76**	36 12S	148 7 E
Khandrá	**35**	35 3N	26 8 E
Khandwa	**50**	21 49N	76 22 E
Khandyga	**41**	62 42N	135 35 E
Khanewal	**48**	30 20N	71 55 E
Khanh Duong	**54**	12 44N	108 44 E
Khanh Hung, Viet.	**55**	9 36N	105 58 E
Khanh Hung, Viet.	**55**	9 37N	105 50 E
Khaniá	**35**	35 30N	24 4 E
Khanion Kólpos	**35**	35 33N	23 55 E
Khanka, Oz.	**41**	45 0N	132 30 E
Khanna	**48**	30 42N	76 16 E
Khanpur	**48**	28 42N	70 35 E
Khanty-Mansiysk	**40**	61 0N	69 0 E
Khapalu	**49**	35 10N	76 20 E
Khapcheranga	**41**	49 42N	112 24 E
Kharagpur	**49**	22 20N	87 25 E
Kharaij	**90**	21 25N	41 0 E
Kharan Kalat	**47**	28 34N	65 21 E
Kharānaq	**47**	32 20N	54 45 E
Kharda	**50**	18 40N	75 34 E
Khardung La	**49**	34 20N	77 43 E
Kharfa	**46**	22 0N	46 35 E
Kharg, Jazireh	**46**	29 15N	50 28 E
Khârga, El Wâhât el	**90**	25 10N	30 35 E
Khargon	**50**	21 45N	75 40 E
Kharit, Wadi el →	**90**	24 26N	33 3 E
Kharkov	**38**	49 58N	36 20 E
Kharmanli	**35**	41 55N	25 55 E
Kharovsk	**37**	59 56N	40 13 E
Kharsaniya	**46**	27 10N	49 10 E
Khartoum = El Khartûm	**91**	15 31N	32 35 E
Khasab	**47**	26 14N	56 15 E
Khasavyurt	**39**	43 16N	46 40 E
Khasebake	**96**	20 42S	24 29 E
Khāsh	**47**	28 15N	61 15 E
Khashm el Girba	**91**	14 59N	35 58 E
Khasi Hills	**52**	25 30N	91 30 E
Khaskovo	**35**	41 56N	25 30 E
Khatanga	**41**	72 0N	102 20 E
Khatanga →	**41**	72 55N	106 0 E
Khatangskiy, Saliv	**144**	66 0N	112 0 E
Khatauli	**48**	29 17N	77 43 E
Khatyrka	**41**	62 3N	175 15 E
Khavar □	**46**	37 20N	47 0 E
Khazzân Jabal el Awliyâ	**91**	15 24N	32 20 E
Khe Bo	**54**	19 8N	104 41 E
Khe Long	**54**	21 29N	104 46 E
Khed, Maharashtra, India	**50**	17 43N	73 27 E
Khed, Maharashtra, India	**50**	18 51N	73 56 E
Khekra	**48**	28 52N	77 20 E
Khemarak Phouminville	**55**	11 37N	102 59 E
Khemis Miliana	**86**	36 11N	2 14 E
Khemisset	**86**	33 50N	6 1W
Khemmarat	**54**	16 10N	105 15 E
Khenchela	**87**	35 28N	7 11 E
Khenifra	**86**	32 58N	5 46W
Kherrata	**87**	36 27N	5 13 E
Kherson	**38**	46 35N	32 35 E
Khersónisos Akrotíri	**35**	35 30N	24 10 E
Kheta →	**41**	71 54N	102 6 E
Khilok	**41**	51 30N	110 45 E
Khimki	**37**	55 50N	37 20 E
Khíos	**35**	38 27N	26 9 E
Khiuma = Hiiumaa	**36**	58 50N	22 45 E
Khiva	**40**	41 30N	60 18 E
Khiyāv	**46**	38 30N	47 45 E
Khlaouia	**86**	25 50N	6 32W
Khlong Khlung	**54**	16 12N	99 43 E
Khmelnitskiy	**38**	49 23N	27 0 E
Khmer Republic ■ = Cambodia	**54**	12 15N	105 0 E
Khoai, Hon	**55**	8 26N	104 50 E
Khojak P.	**47**	30 55N	66 30 E
Khok Kloi	**55**	8 17N	98 19 E
Khok Pho	**55**	6 43N	101 6 E
Khokholskiy	**37**	51 35N	38 40 E
Kholm	**36**	57 10N	31 15 E
Kholmsk	**41**	47 40N	142 5 E
Khomas Hochland	**96**	22 40S	16 0 E
Khomayn	**46**	33 40N	50 7 E
Khomo	**96**	21 7S	24 35 E
Khon Kaen	**54**	16 30N	102 47 E
Khong	**54**	14 7N	105 51 E
Khong Sedone	**54**	15 34N	105 49 E
Khonu	**41**	66 30N	143 12 E
Khoper →	**37**	49 30N	42 20 E
Khor el 'Atash	**91**	13 20N	34 15 E
Khóra	**35**	37 3N	21 42 E
Khóra Sfakion	**35**	35 15N	24 9 E
Khorasan □	**47**	34 0N	58 0 E
Khorat = Nakhon Ratchasima	**54**	14 59N	102 12 E
Khorat, Cao Nguyen	**54**	15 30N	102 50 E
Khorb el Ethel	**86**	28 30N	6 17W
Khorixas	**96**	20 16S	14 59 E
Khorog	**40**	37 30N	71 36 E
Khorol	**38**	49 48N	33 15 E
Khorramābād	**46**	33 30N	48 25 E
Khorromshahr	**46**	30 29N	48 15 E
Khotin	**38**	48 31N	26 27 E
Khouribga	**86**	32 58N	6 57W
Khowai	**52**	24 5N	91 40 E
Khoyniki	**36**	51 54N	29 55 E
Khrami →	**39**	41 30N	45 0 E
Khrenovoye	**37**	51 4N	40 16 E
Khristianá	**35**	36 14N	25 13 E
Khu Khan	**54**	14 42N	104 12 E
Khufaifiya	**46**	24 50N	44 35 E
Khugiani	**48**	31 28N	66 14 E
Khulna	**52**	22 45N	89 34 E
Khulna □	**52**	22 25N	89 35 E
Khulo	**39**	41 33N	42 19 E
Khunzakh	**39**	42 35N	46 42 E
Khūr	**47**	32 55N	58 18 E
Khurai	**48**	24 3N	78 23 E
Khurais	**46**	24 55N	48 5 E
Khurja	**48**	28 15N	77 58 E
Khurma	**46**	21 58N	42 3 E
Khūryān Mūryān, Jazā 'ir	**45**	17 30N	55 58 E
Khushab	**48**	32 20N	72 20 E
Khuzdar	**48**	27 52N	66 30 E
Khuzestan □	**46**	31 0N	50 0 E
Khvalynsk	**37**	52 30N	48 2 E
Khvatovka	**37**	52 24N	46 32 E
Khvor	**47**	33 45N	55 0 E
Khvormūj	**47**	28 40N	51 30 E
Khvoy	**46**	38 35N	45 0 E
Khvoynaya	**36**	58 58N	34 28 E
Khyber Pass	**48**	34 10N	71 8 E
Kia	**68**	7 32S	158 26 E
Kiabukwa	**95**	8 40S	24 48 E
Kiadho →	**50**	19 37N	77 40 E
Kiama	**76**	34 40S	150 50 E
Kiamal	**74**	34 58S	142 18 E
Kiamba	**57**	6 2N	124 46 E
Kiambi	**94**	7 15S	28 0 E
Kiambu	**94**	1 8S	36 50 E
Kiandra	**76**	35 53S	148 31 E
Kiangsi = Jiangxi	**59**	27 30N	116 0 E
Kiangsu = Jiangsu □	**62**	33 0N	120 0 E
Kiania	**97**	20 18S	47 8 E
Kibæk	**11**	56 2N	8 51 E
Kibanga Port	**94**	0 10N	32 58 E
Kibangou	**92**	3 26S	12 22 E
Kibara	**94**	2 8S	33 30 E
Kibara, Mts.	**94**	8 25S	27 10 E
Kibombo	**94**	3 57S	25 53 E
Kibondo	**94**	3 35S	30 45 E
Kibondo □	**94**	4 0S	30 55 E
Kibumbu	**94**	3 32S	29 45 E
Kibungu	**94**	2 10S	30 32 E
Kibuye, Burundi	**94**	3 39S	29 59 E
Kibuye, Rwanda	**94**	2 3S	29 21 E
Kibwesa	**94**	6 30S	29 58 E
Kibwezi	**94**	2 27S	37 57 E
Kichiga	**41**	59 50N	163 5 E
Kickabil	**76**	31 50S	148 30 E
Kicking Horse Pass	**108**	51 28N	116 16W
Kidal	**89**	18 26N	1 22 E
Kidderminster	**13**	52 24N	2 13W
Kidete	**94**	6 25S	37 17 E
Kidira	**88**	14 28N	12 13W
Kidnappers, C.	**80**	39 38S	177 5 E
Kidston	**72**	18 52S	144 8 E

Kidugallo	**94**	6 49S	38 15E
Kiel	**30**	54 16N	10 8E
Kiel Kanal = Nord-Ostee-Kanal	**30**	54 15N	9 40E
Kielce	**32**	50 52N	20 42E
Kieler Bucht	**30**	54 30N	10 30E
Kien Binh	**55**	9 55N	105 19E
Kien Hung	**55**	9 43N	105 17E
Kien Tan	**55**	10 7N	105 17E
Kienge	**95**	10 30S	27 30E
Kiessé	**89**	13 29N	4 1E
Kieta	**69**	6 12S	155 36E
Kiev = Kiyev	**36**	50 30	30 28E
Kiffa	**88**	16 37N	11 24W
Kifisiá	**35**	38 4N	23 49E
Kifissós →	**35**	38 35N	23 20E
Kifri	**46**	34 45N	45 0E
Kigali	**94**	1 59S	30 4E
Kigarama	**94**	1 1S	31 50E
Kigoma □	**94**	5 0S	30 0E
Kigoma-Ujiji	**94**	4 55S	29 36E
Kigomasha, Ras	**94**	4 58S	38 58E
Kihee	**73**	27 23S	142 37E
Kihikihi	**80**	38 2S	175 22E
Kii-Hantō	**65**	34 0N	135 45E
Kii-Sanchi	**65**	34 20N	136 0E
Kii-Suido	**64**	33 40N	135 0E
Kikai-Jima	**63**	28 19N	129 58E
Kikinda	**33**	45 50N	20 30E
Kikládhes	**35**	37 20N	24 30E
Kikori	**69**	7 25S	144 15E
Kikori →	**69**	7 38S	144 20E
Kikuchi	**64**	32 59N	130 47E
Kikwit	**92**	5 5S	18 45E
Kilafors	**10**	61 14N	16 36E
Kilakarai	**51**	9 12N	78 47E
Kílalki	**35**	36 15N	27 35E
Kilauea Crater	**110**	19 24N	155 17W
Kilcoy	**73**	26 59S	152 30E
Kildare	**15**	53 10N	6 50W
Kildare □	**15**	53 10N	6 50W
Kilembe	**94**	0 15N	30 3E
Kilgore	**119**	32 22N	94 55W
Kilifi	**94**	3 40S	39 48E
Kilifi □	**94**	3 30S	39 40E
Kilimanjaro	**94**	3 7S	37 20E
Kilimanjaro □	**94**	4 0S	38 0E
Kilinailau, Is.	**69**	4 45S	155 20E
Kilindini	**94**	4 4S	39 40E
Kilis	**46**	36 50N	37 10E
Kiliya	**38**	45 28N	29 16E
Kilju	**61**	40 57N	129 25E
Kilkee	**15**	52 41N	9 40W
Kilkenny	**15**	52 40N	7 17W
Kilkenny □	**15**	52 35N	7 15W
Kilkieran B.	**15**	53 18N	9 45W
Kilkís	**35**	40 58N	22 57E
Killala	**15**	54 13N	9 12W
Killala B.	**15**	54 20N	9 12W
Killaloe	**15**	52 48N	8 28W
Killaloe Sta.	**107**	45 33N	77 25W
Killam	**108**	52 47N	111 51W
Killarney, Queens., Austral.	**77**	28 20S	152 18E
Killarney, Vic., Austral.	**74**	38 21S	142 18E
Killarney, Can.	**109**	45 55N	81 30W
Killarney, Ireland	**15**	52 2N	9 30W
Killarney, Lakes of	**15**	52 0N	9 30W
Killarney Prov. Park	**106**	46 2N	81 35W
Killary Harbour	**15**	53 38N	9 52W
Killdeer, Can.	**109**	49 6N	106 22W
Killdeer, U.S.A.	**118**	47 26N	102 48W
Killeen	**119**	31 7N	97 45W
Killiecrankie, Pass of	**14**	56 44N	3 46W
Killin	**14**	56 28N	4 20W
Killíni, Greece	**35**	37 54N	22 25E
Killíni, Greece	**35**	37 55N	21 8E
Killybegs	**15**	54 38N	8 26W
Kilmany	**75**	38 8S	146 55E
Kilmar	**104**	45 46N	74 37W
Kilmarnock	**14**	55 36N	4 30W
Kilmore	**74**	37 25S	144 53E
Kilondo	**95**	9 45S	34 20E
Kilosa	**94**	6 48S	37 0E
Kilosa □	**94**	6 48S	37 0E
Kilrush	**15**	52 39N	9 30W
Kilsmo	**10**	59 6N	15 35E
Kilwa □	**95**	9 0S	39 0E
Kilwa Kisiwani	**95**	8 58S	39 32E
Kilwa Kivinje	**95**	8 45S	39 25E
Kilwa Masoko	**95**	8 55S	39 30E
Kim	**119**	37 18N	103 20W
Kimaam	**57**	7 58S	138 53E
Kimamba	**94**	6 45S	37 10E
Kimba	**73**	33 8S	136 23E
Kimball, Nebr., U.S.A.	**118**	41 17N	103 40W
Kimball, S.D., U.S.A.	**118**	43 47N	98 57W
Kimbe	**69**	5 33S	150 11E
Kimbe B.	**69**	5 15S	150 30E
Kimberley, Can.	**108**	49 40N	115 59W
Kimberley, S. Afr.	**96**	28 43S	24 46E
Kimberley Downs	**78**	17 24S	124 22E
Kimberly	**120**	42 33N	114 25W
Kimchŏn	**61**	36 11N	128 4E
Kími	**35**	38 38N	24 6E
Kimje	**61**	35 48N	126 45E
Kímolos	**35**	36 48N	24 37E
Kímolos, I.	**35**	36 48N	24 35E
Kimovsk	**37**	54 0N	38 29E
Kimparana	**88**	12 48N	5 0W
Kimry	**37**	56 55N	37 15E
Kimsquit	**108**	52 45N	126 57W
Kimstad	**11**	58 35N	15 58E
Kinabalu	**56**	6 0N	116 0E
Kínaros	**35**	36 59N	26 15E
Kinaskan L.	**108**	57 38N	130 8W
Kincaid, Can.	**109**	49 40N	107 0W
Kincaid, U.S.A.	**116**	39 35N	89 25W
Kincardine	**106**	44 10N	81 40W
Kinde	**106**	43 56N	83 0W
Kindersley	**109**	51 30N	109 10W
Kindia	**88**	10 0N	12 52W
Kindu	**94**	2 55S	25 50E
Kineshma	**37**	57 30N	42 5E
Kinesi	**94**	1 25S	33 50E
King →	**75**	36 24S	146 23E
King City, Calif., U.S.A.	**122**	36 11N	121 8W
King City, Mo., U.S.A.	**116**	40 3N	94 31W
King Cr. →	**72**	24 35S	139 30E
King Edward →	**78**	14 14S	126 35E
King Frederick VI Land = Kong Frederik VI.s. Kyst	**144**	63 0N	43 0W
King George B.	**142**	51 30S	60 30W
King George I.	**143**	60 0S	60 0W
King George Is.	**101**	57 20N	80 30W
King I., Austral.	**72**	39 50S	144 0E
King I., Can.	**108**	52 10N	127 40W
King, L., Vic., Austral.	**75**	37 55S	147 45E
King, L., W. Australia, Austral.	**79**	33 10S	119 35E
King Leopold Ranges	**78**	17 30S	125 45E
King, Mt.	**72**	25 10S	147 30E
King Sd.	**78**	16 50S	123 20E
King William I.	**100**	69 10N	97 25W
King William's Town	**96**	32 51S	27 22E
Kingaroy	**73**	26 32S	151 51E
Kingfisher	**119**	35 50N	97 55W
Kingisepp	**36**	59 25N	28 40E
Kingisepp (Kuressaare)	**36**	58 15N	22 30E
Kinglake	**74**	37 31S	145 19E
Kinglake West	**74**	37 31S	145 19E
Kingman, Ariz., U.S.A.	**123**	35 12N	114 2W
Kingman, Ind., U.S.A.	**117**	39 58N	87 18W
Kingman, Kans., U.S.A.	**119**	37 41N	98 9W
Kings →	**122**	36 10N	119 50W
Kings Canyon National Park	**122**	37 0N	118 35W
King's Lynn	**12**	52 45N	0 25E
Kings Mountain	**113**	35 13N	81 20W
King's Peak	**120**	40 46N	110 27W
Kingsbridge	**13**	50 17N	3 46W
Kingsburg	**122**	36 35N	119 36W
Kingsbury	**117**	41 31N	86 42W
Kingscliff-Fingal	**77**	28 16S	153 34E
Kingscote	**73**	35 40S	137 38E
Kingscourt	**15**	53 55N	6 48W
Kingsey Falls	**105**	45 51N	72 4W
Kingsley	**118**	42 37N	95 58W
Kingsley Dam	**118**	41 20N	101 40W
Kingsport	**113**	36 33N	82 36W
Kingston, Can.	**107**	44 14N	76 30W
Kingston, Jamaica	**126**	18 0N	76 50W
Kingston, N.Z.	**81**	45 20S	168 43E
Kingston, Mich., U.S.A.	**106**	43 29N	83 11W
Kingston, Mo., U.S.A.	**116**	39 38N	94 2W
Kingston, N.Y., U.S.A.	**115**	41 55N	74 0W
Kingston, Pa., U.S.A.	**115**	41 19N	75 58W
Kingston, R.I., U.S.A.	**115**	41 29N	71 30W
Kingston, Wash., U.S.A.	**122**	47 48N	122 30W
Kingston Mines	**116**	40 34N	89 47W
Kingston Pk.	**123**	35 45N	115 54W
Kingston South East	**73**	36 51S	139 55E
Kingston-upon-Thames	**13**	51 23N	0 20W
Kingstown, Austral.	**77**	30 29S	151 6E
Kingstown, St. Vinc.	**127**	13 10N	61 10W
Kingstree	**113**	33 40N	79 48W
Kingsville, Can.	**106**	42 2N	82 45W
Kingsville, U.S.A.	**119**	27 30N	97 53W
Kingussie	**14**	57 5N	4 2W
Kinistino	**109**	52 57N	105 2W
Kinkala	**92**	4 18S	14 49E
Kinki □	**65**	33 30N	136 0E
Kinleith	**80**	38 20S	175 56E
Kinmount	**107**	44 48N	78 45W
Kinmundy	**117**	38 46N	88 51W
Kinna	**11**	57 32N	12 42E
Kinnaird	**108**	49 17N	117 39W
Kinnairds Hd.	**14**	57 40N	2 0W
Kinnared	**11**	57 2N	13 7E
Kinneret	**44**	32 44N	35 34E
Kinneret, Yam	**44**	32 45N	35 35E
Kino	**124**	28 45N	111 59W
Kinoje →	**102**	52 8N	81 25W
Kinomoto	**65**	35 30N	136 13E
Kinoni	**94**	0 41S	30 28E
Kinross	**14**	56 13N	3 25W
Kinsale	**15**	51 42N	8 31W
Kinsale, Old Hd. of	**15**	51 37N	8 32W
Kinshasa	**92**	4 20S	15 15E
Kinsley	**119**	37 57N	99 30W
Kinston	**113**	35 18N	77 35W
Kintampo	**89**	8 5N	1 41W
Kintap	**56**	3 51S	115 13E
Kintore Ra.	**78**	23 15S	128 47E
Kintyre	**14**	55 30N	5 35W
Kintyre, Mull of	**14**	55 17N	5 55W
Kinu	**52**	22 46N	95 37E
Kinu-Gawa →	**65**	35 36N	139 57E
Kinushseo →	**102**	55 15N	83 45W
Kinuso	**108**	55 20N	115 25W
Kinyangiri	**94**	4 25S	34 37E
Kinzig →	**31**	48 37N	7 49E
Kinzua	**114**	41 52N	78 58W
Kinzua Dam	**114**	41 53N	79 0W
Kiosk	**107**	46 6N	78 53W
Kiowa, Kans., U.S.A.	**119**	37 3N	98 30W
Kiowa, Okla., U.S.A.	**119**	34 45N	95 50W
Kipahigan L.	**109**	55 20N	101 55W
Kipanga	**94**	6 15S	35 20E
Kiparissía	**35**	37 15N	21 40E
Kiparissiakós Kólpos	**35**	37 25N	21 25E
Kipawa	**104**	46 47N	78 59W
Kipawa L.	**104**	46 50N	79 0W
Kipawa, Parc de	**104**	47 0N	78 50W
Kipembawe	**94**	7 38S	33 27E
Kipengere Ra.	**95**	9 12S	34 15E
Kipili	**94**	7 28S	30 32E
Kipini	**94**	2 30S	40 32E
Kipling	**109**	50 6N	102 38W
Kippure	**15**	53 11N	6 23W
Kipushi	**95**	11 48S	27 12E
Kira Kira	**68**	10 27S	161 56E
Kirandul	**50**	18 33N	81 10E
Kiratpur	**48**	29 32N	78 12E
Kirchhain	**30**	50 49N	8 54E
Kirchheim	**31**	48 38N	9 20E
Kirchheim-Bolanden	**31**	49 40N	8 0E
Kirensk	**41**	57 50N	107 55E
Kirgiz S.S.R. □	**40**	42 0N	75 0E
Kiri	**92**	1 29S	19 0E
Kiribati ■	**66**	1 0N	176 0E
Kiriburu	**50**	22 0N	85 0E
Kırıkkale	**46**	39 51N	33 32E
Kirikopuni	**80**	35 50S	174 1E
Kirillov	**37**	59 51N	38 14E
Kirin = Jilin	**61**	43 55N	126 30E
Kirin = Jilin □	**61**	44 0N	126 0E
Kirindi →	**51**	6 15N	81 20E
Kirishi	**36**	59 28N	31 59E
Kirishima-Yama	**64**	31 58N	130 55E
Kirkcaldy	**14**	56 7N	3 10W
Kirkcudbright	**14**	54 50N	4 3W
Kirkee	**50**	18 34N	73 56E
Kirkenær	**10**	60 27N	12 3E
Kirkenes	**8**	69 40N	30 5E
Kirkfield	**107**	44 34N	78 59W
Kirkintilloch	**14**	55 57N	4 10W
Kirkjubæjarklaustur	**8**	63 47N	18 4W
Kirkland, Ariz., U.S.A.	**121**	34 29N	112 46W
Kirkland, Ill., U.S.A.	**117**	42 5N	88 51W
Kirkland Lake	**102**	48 9N	80 2W
Kırklareli	**46**	41 44N	27 15E
Kirklin	**117**	40 12N	86 22W
Kirkliston Ra.	**81**	44 25S	170 34E
Kirksville	**116**	40 8N	92 35W
Kirkūk	**46**	35 30N	44 21E
Kirkwall	**14**	58 59N	2 59W
Kirkwood, S. Afr.	**96**	33 22S	25 15E
Kirkwood, U.S.A.	**116**	38 35N	90 24W
Kirlampudi	**50**	17 12N	82 12E
Kirn	**31**	49 46N	7 29E
Kirov, R.S.F.S.R., U.S.S.R.	**36**	54 3N	34 20E
Kirov, R.S.F.S.R., U.S.S.R.	**40**	58 35N	49 40E
Kirov, R.S.F.S.R., U.S.S.R.	**40**	58 35N	49 40E
Kirovabad	**39**	40 45N	46 20E
Kirovakan	**39**	40 48N	44 30E
Kirovo-Chepetsk	**37**	58 28N	50 0E
Kirovograd	**38**	48 35N	32 20E
Kirovsk, R.S.F.S.R., U.S.S.R.	**40**	67 48N	33 50E
Kirovsk, Turkmen S.S.R., U.S.S.R.	**40**	37 42N	60 23E
Kirovsk, Ukraine, U.S.S.R.	**39**	48 35N	38 30E
Kirovski	**39**	45 51N	48 11E
Kirovskiy	**41**	54 27N	155 42E
Kirriemuir, Can.	**109**	51 56N	110 20W
Kirriemuir, U.K.	**14**	56 41N	3 0W
Kirsanov	**37**	52 35N	42 40E
Kırşehir	**46**	39 14N	34 5E
Kirstonia	**96**	25 30S	23 45E
Kirtachi	**89**	12 52N	2 30E
Kirthar Range	**48**	27 0N	67 0E
Kiruna	**8**	67 52N	20 15E
Kirundu	**94**	0 50S	25 35E
Kirup	**79**	33 40S	115 50E
Kirya	**37**	55 5N	46 45E
Kiryū	**65**	36 24N	139 20E
Kisa	**11**	58 0N	15 39E
Kisaga	**94**	4 30S	34 23E
Kisalaya	**126**	14 40N	84 3W
Kisanga	**94**	2 30N	26 35E
Kisangani	**94**	0 35N	25 15E
Kisar	**57**	8 5S	127 10E
Kisaran	**56**	3 0N	99 37E
Kisarawe	**94**	6 53S	39 0E
Kisarawe □	**94**	7 3S	39 0E
Kisarazu	**65**	35 23N	139 55E
Kisbér	**33**	47 30N	18 0E
Kiselevsk	**40**	54 5N	86 39E
Kishanganga →	**49**	34 18N	73 28E
Kishanganj	**49**	26 3N	88 14E
Kishangarh	**48**	27 50N	70 30E
Kishi	**89**	9 1N	3 52E
Kishinev	**38**	47 0N	28 50E
Kishiwada	**65**	34 28N	135 22E
Kishon	**44**	32 49N	35 2E
Kishorganj	**52**	24 26N	90 40E
Kishtwar	**49**	33 20N	75 48E
Kishwaukee →	**116**	42 12N	89 8W
Kisii	**94**	0 40S	34 45E
Kisii □	**94**	0 40S	34 45E
Kisiju	**94**	7 23S	39 19E
Kısır, Dağ	**39**	41 0N	43 5E
Kisizi	**94**	1 0S	29 58E
Kiska I.	**100**	52 0N	177 30E
Kiskatinaw →	**108**	56 8N	120 10W
Kiskittogisu L.	**109**	54 13N	98 20W
Kiskörös	**33**	46 37N	19 20E
Kiskundorozsma	**33**	46 16N	20 5E
Kiskunfelégyháza	**33**	46 42N	19 53E
Kiskunhalas	**33**	46 28N	19 37E
Kiskunmajsa	**33**	46 30N	19 48E
Kislovodsk	**39**	43 50N	42 45E
Kismayu	**83**	0 20S	42 30E
Kiso-Gawa →	**65**	35 20N	136 45E
Kiso-Sammyaku	**65**	35 45N	137 45E
Kisofukushima	**65**	35 52N	137 43E
Kisoro	**94**	1 17S	29 48E
Kispest	**33**	47 27N	19 9E
Kissidougou	**88**	9 5N	10 0W
Kissimmee	**113**	28 18N	81 22W
Kissimmee →	**113**	27 20N	80 55W
Kississing L.	**109**	55 10N	101 20W
Kistanje	**27**	43 58N	15 55E
Kisújszállás	**33**	47 12N	20 50E
Kisuki	**64**	35 17N	132 54E
Kisumu	**94**	0 3S	34 45E
Kisvárda	**33**	48 14N	22 4E
Kiswani	**94**	4 5S	37 57E
Kiswere	**95**	9 27S	39 30E
Kit Carson	**118**	38 48N	102 45W
Kita	**88**	13 5N	9 25W
Kita-Ura	**65**	36 0N	140 34E
Kitab	**40**	39 7N	66 52E
Kitakami-Gawa →	**63**	38 25N	141 19E
Kitakyūshū	**64**	33 50N	130 50E
Kitale	**94**	1 0N	35 0E
Kitami	**63**	43 48N	143 54E
Kitangiri, L.	**94**	4 5S	34 20E
Kitano-Kaikyō	**64**	34 17N	134 58E
Kitaya	**95**	10 38S	40 8E
Kitchener, Austral.	**79**	30 55S	124 8E
Kitchener, Can.	**106**	43 27N	80 29W
Kitega = Citega	**94**	3 30S	29 58E
Kiteto □	**94**	5 0S	37 0E
Kitgum Matidi	**94**	3 17N	32 52E
Kíthira, Greece	**35**	36 9N	23 0E
Kíthira, Greece	**35**	36 15N	23 0E
Kíthnos, Greece	**35**	37 25N	24 25E
Kíthnos, Greece	**35**	37 26N	24 27E
Kitimat	**108**	54 3N	128 38W
Kitiyab	**91**	17 13N	33 35E
Kítros	**35**	40 22N	22 34E
Kitsuki	**64**	33 25N	131 37E
Kittakittaooloo, L.	**73**	28 3S	138 14E
Kittanning	**114**	40 49N	79 30W
Kittatinny Mts.	**115**	41 0N	75 0W
Kittery	**115**	43 7N	70 42W
Kitui	**94**	1 17S	38 0E

Kitui □ 94 1 30S 38 25 E
Kitwe 95 12 54S 28 13 E
Kitzbühel 31 47 27N 12 24 E
Kitzingen 31 49 44N 10 9 E
Kivarli 48 24 33N 72 46 E
Kivu □ 94 3 10S 27 0 E
Kivu, L. 94 1 48S 29 0 E
Kiwai I. 69 8 35S 143 30 E
Kiyev 36 50 30N 30 28 E
Kiyevskoye Vdkhr. 36 51 0N 30 0 E
Kiziguru 94 1 46S 30 23 E
Kızıl Irmak → 38 39 15N 36 0 E
Kizil Jilga 49 35 26N 78 50 E
Kızılcahamam 38 40 30N 32 30 E
Kizimkazi 94 6 28S 39 30 E
Kizlyar 39 43 51N 46 40 E
Kizyl-Arvat 40 38 58N 56 15 E
Kjellerup 11 56 17N 9 25 E
Kladanj 33 44 14N 18 42 E
Kladno 32 50 10N 14 7 E
Kladovo 33 44 36N 22 33 E
Klaeng 54 12 47N 101 39 E
Klagenfurt 33 46 38N 14 20 E
Klagshamn 11 55 32N 12 53 E
Klagstorp 11 55 22N 13 23 E
Klaipeda 36 55 43N 21 10 E
Klamath → 120 41 40N 124 4W
Klamath Falls 120 42 20N 121 50W
Klamath Mts. 120 41 20N 123 0W
Klangklang 52 22 41N 93 26 E
Klanjec 27 46 3N 15 45 E
Klappan → 108 58 0N 129 43W
Klaten 57 7 43S 110 36 E
Klatovy 32 49 23N 13 18 E
Klawak 108 55 35N 133 0W
Klawer 96 31 44S 18 36 E
Kleczew 32 52 22N 18 9 E
Kleena Kleene 108 52 0N 124 59W
Klein 120 46 26N 108 31W
Klein-Karas 96 27 33S 18 7 E
Klein Karoo 96 33 45S 21 30 E
Klekovača 27 44 25N 16 32 E
Klemtu 108 52 35N 128 55W
Klenovec, Czech. 32 48 36N 19 54 E
Klenovec, Yugo. 35 41 32N 20 49 E
Klerksdorp 96 26 51S 26 38 E
Kletnya 36 53 23N 33 12 E
Kletsk 36 53 5N 26 45 E
Kletskaïa Kletskiy 40 49 20N 43 0 E
Kletskiy 39 49 20N 43 0 E
Kleve 30 51 46N 6 10 E
Klickitat 120 45 50N 121 10W
Klickitat → 122 45 42N 121 17W
Klimovichi 36 53 36N 32 0 E
Klin 37 56 20N 36 48 E
Klinaklini → 108 51 21N 125 40W
Klintsey 36 52 50N 32 10 E
Klipplaat 96 33 0S 24 22 E
Klitmøller 11 57 3N 8 30 E
Kljajićevo 33 45 45N 19 17 E
Ključ 27 44 32N 16 48 E
Kłobuck 32 50 55N 18 55 E
Kłodzko 32 50 28N 16 38 E
Klosterneuburg 33 48 18N 16 19 E
Klosters 31 46 52N 9 52 E
Klötze 30 52 38N 11 9 E
Klouto 89 6 57N 0 44 E
Kluane L. 100 61 15N 138 40W
Kluczbork 32 50 58N 18 12 E
Klyuchevskaya, Guba 41 55 50N 160 30 E
Knaresborough 12 54 1N 1 29W
Knee L., Man., Can. 109 55 3N 94 45W
Knee L., Sask., Can. 109 55 51N 107 0W
Kneïss, I. 87 34 22N 10 18 E
Knezha 34 43 30N 24 5 E
Knić 33 43 53N 20 45 E
Knight Inlet 108 50 45N 125 40W
Knighton 13 52 21N 3 2W
Knights Ferry 122 37 50N 120 40W
Knight's Landing 122 38 50N 121 43W
Knightstown 117 39 49N 85 32W
Knin 27 44 1N 16 17 E
Knittelfeld 33 47 13N 14 51 E
Knjaževac 33 43 35N 22 18 E
Knob, C. 79 34 32S 119 16 E
Knockmealdown Mts. 15 52 16N 8 0W
Knokke 16 51 20N 3 17 E
Knowlton 105 45 13N 72 31W
Knowsley 74 36 50S 144 35 E
Knox 117 41 18N 86 36W
Knox, C. 108 54 11N 133 5W
Knox City 119 33 26N 99 49W
Knox Coast 143 66 30S 108 0 E
Knoxville, Iowa, U.S.A. 116 41 20N 93 5W
Knoxville, Tenn., U.S.A. 113 35 58N 83 57W
Knutshø 10 62 18N 9 41 E
Knysna 96 34 2S 23 2 E
Knyszyn 32 53 20N 22 56 E
Ko Kha 54 18 11N 99 24 E
Kō-Saki 64 34 5N 129 13 E
Ko Tao 55 10 6N 99 48 E
Koartac (Notre Dame de Koartac) 101 60 55N 69 40W
Koba, Aru, Indon. 57 6 37S 134 37 E
Koba, Bangka, Indon. 56 2 26S 106 14 E
Kobarid 27 46 15N 13 30 E
Kobayashi 64 31 56N 130 59 E
Kobdo = Hovd 62 48 2N 91 37 E
Kōbe 65 34 45N 135 10 E
Kobelyaki 38 49 11N 34 9 E
København 11 55 41N 12 34 E
Koblenz 31 50 21N 7 36 E
Kobo 91 12 2N 39 56 E
Kobrin 36 52 15N 24 22 E
Kobroor, Kepulauan 57 6 10S 134 30 E
Kobuchizawa 65 35 52N 138 19 E
Kobuleti 39 41 55N 41 45 E
Kobyłka 32 52 21N 21 10 E
Kobylkino 37 54 8N 43 56 E
Kobylnik 36 54 58N 26 39 E
Kočani 35 41 55N 22 25 E
Koceljevo 33 44 28N 19 50 E
Kočevje 27 45 39N 14 50 E
Kochang 61 35 41N 127 55 E
Kochas 49 25 15N 83 56 E
Kocher → 31 49 14N 9 12 E
Kocheya 41 52 32N 120 42 E
Kōchi 64 33 30N 133 35 E
Kōchi □ 64 33 40N 133 30 E
Kōchi-Heiya 64 33 28N 133 30 E
Kochiu = Gejiu 62 23 20N 103 10 E
Kodaira 65 35 44N 139 29 E
Koddiyar Bay 51 8 33N 81 15 E
Kodiak 100 57 30N 152 45W
Kodiak I. 100 57 30N 152 45W
Kodinar 48 20 46N 70 46 E
Kodori → 39 42 47N 41 10 E
Koes 96 26 0S 19 15 E
Koetong 75 36 10S 147 30 E
Kofiau 57 1 11S 129 50 E
Koforidua 89 6 3N 0 17W
Kōfu 65 35 40N 138 30 E
Koga 65 36 11N 139 43 E
Kogaluk → 103 56 12N 61 44W
Kogan 73 27 2S 150 40 E
Kogin Baba 89 7 55N 11 35 E
Kogota 63 38 33N 141 3 E
Koh-i-Baba 47 34 30N 67 0 E
Koh-i-Khurd 48 33 30N 65 59 E
Kohat 48 33 40N 71 29 E
Kohima 52 25 35N 94 10 E
Kohler Ra. 143 77 0S 110 0W
Kohtla Järve 36 59 20N 27 20 E
Kohukohu 80 35 22S 173 38 E
Koin-dong 61 40 28N 126 18 E
Kojima 64 34 30N 133 50 E
Kōjo 64 34 33N 133 55 E
Kojō 61 38 58N 127 58 E
Kojonup 79 33 48S 117 10 E
Koka 90 20 5N 30 35 E
Kokand 40 40 30N 70 57 E
Kokanee Glacier Prov. Park 108 49 47N 117 10W
Kokas 57 2 42S 132 26 E
Kokchetav 40 53 20N 69 25 E
Kokemäenjoki → 9 61 32N 21 44 E
Kokerite 135 7 12N 59 35W
Kokhma 37 56 55N 41 18 E
Kokkola (Gamlakarleby) 8 63 50N 23 8 E
Koko 89 11 28N 4 29 E
Kokoda 69 8 54S 147 47 E
Kokolopozo 88 5 8N 6 5W
Kokomo 117 40 30N 86 6W
Kokonau 57 4 43S 136 26 E
Kokopo 69 4 22S 152 19 E
Kokoro 89 14 12N 0 55 E
Koksan 61 38 46N 126 40 E
Koksoak → 101 58 30N 68 10W
Kokstad 97 30 32S 29 29 E
Kokubu 64 31 44N 130 46 E
Kokuora 41 71 35N 144 50 E
Kola, Indon. 57 5 35S 134 30 E
Kola, U.S.S.R. 40 68 45N 33 8 E
Kola Pen. = Kolskiy P-ov. 40 67 30N 38 0 E
Kolahoi 49 34 12N 75 22 E
Kolahun 88 8 15N 10 4W
Kolaka 57 4 3S 121 46 E
Kolar 51 13 12N 78 15 E
Kolar Gold Fields 51 12 58N 78 16 E
Kolarovgrad 34 43 18N 26 55 E
Kolby Kås 11 55 48N 10 32 E
Kolchugino 37 56 17N 39 22 E
Kolda 88 12 55N 14 57W
Kolding 11 55 30N 9 29 E
Kole 92 3 16S 22 42 E
Koléa 86 36 38N 2 46 E
Kolepom, Pulau 57 8 0S 138 30 E
Kolguyev, Ostrov 40 69 20N 48 30 E
Kolhapur 50 16 43N 74 15 E
Kolia 88 9 46N 6 28W
Kolín 32 50 2N 15 9 E
Kolind 11 56 21N 10 34 E
Kölleda 30 51 11N 11 14 E
Kollegal 51 12 9N 77 9 E
Kolleru L. 50 16 40N 81 10 E
Kolmanskop 96 26 45S 15 14 E
Köln 30 50 56N 6 58 E
Koło 32 52 14N 18 40 E
Kołobrzeg 32 54 10N 15 35 E
Kologriv 37 58 48N 44 25 E
Kolokani 88 13 35N 7 45W
Kolombangara 68 8 0S 157 5 E
Kolomna 37 55 8N 38 45 E
Kolomyya 38 48 31N 25 2 E
Kolondiéba 88 11 5N 6 54W
Kolonodale 57 2 3S 121 25 E
Koloona 77 29 37S 150 46 E
Kolosib 52 24 15N 92 45 E
Kolpashevo 40 58 20N 83 5 E
Kolpino 36 59 44N 30 39 E
Kolpny 37 52 12N 37 10 E
Kolskiy Poluostrov 40 67 30N 38 0 E
Kolubara → 33 44 35N 20 15 E
Koluszki 32 51 45N 19 46 E
Kolwezi 95 10 40S 25 25 E
Kolyberovo 37 55 15N 38 40 E
Kolyma → 41 69 30N 161 0 E
Kolymskoye, Okhotsko 41 63 0N 157 0 E
Kôm Ombo 90 24 25N 32 52 E
Komagene 65 35 44N 137 58 E
Komaki 65 35 17N 136 55 E
Komárno 33 47 49N 18 5 E
Komárom 33 47 43N 18 7 E
Komarovo 36 58 38N 33 40 E
Komatipoort 97 25 25S 31 55 E
Komatsu 65 36 25N 136 30 E
Komatsujima 64 34 0N 134 35 E
Kombissiri 89 12 4N 1 20W
Kombori 88 13 26N 3 56W
Komen 27 45 49N 13 45 E
Komenda 89 5 4N 1 28W
Komi, A.S.S.R. □ 40 64 0N 55 0 E
Komiža 27 43 3N 16 11 E
Komló 33 46 15N 18 16 E
Kommamur Canal 51 16 0N 80 25 E
Kommunarsk 39 48 30N 38 45 E
Kommunizma, Pik 40 39 0N 72 2 E
Komodo 57 8 37S 119 20 E
Komoé 88 5 12N 3 44W
Komono 92 3 10S 13 20 E
Komoran, Pulau 57 8 18S 138 45 E
Komoro 65 36 19N 138 26 E
Komotini 35 41 9N 25 26 E
Kompong Bang 55 12 24N 104 40 E
Kompong Cham 55 12 0N 105 30 E
Kompong Chhnang 55 12 20N 104 35 E
Kompong Chikreng 54 13 5N 104 18 E
Kompong Kleang 54 13 6N 104 8 E
Kompong Luong 55 11 49N 104 48 E
Kompong Pranak 54 13 35N 104 55 E
Kompong Som = Sihanoukville 55 10 38N 103 30 E
Kompong Som, Chhung 55 10 50N 103 32 E
Kompong Speu 55 11 26N 104 32 E
Kompong Sralao 54 14 5N 105 46 E
Kompong Thom 54 12 35N 104 51 E
Kompong Trabeck, Camb. 54 13 6N 105 14 E
Kompong Trabeck, Camb. 55 11 9N 105 28 E
Kompong Trach 55 11 25N 105 48 E
Kompong Tralach 55 11 54N 104 47 E
Komrat 38 46 18N 28 40 E
Komsberge 96 32 40S 20 45 E
Komsomolets, Ostrov 41 80 30N 95 0 E
Komsomolsk 41 50 30N 137 0 E
Komsomolskaya 143 66 33S 93 1 E
Komsomolskiy 37 53 30N 49 30 E
Konakovo 37 56 52N 36 45 E
Konawa 119 34 59N 96 46W
Kondagaon 50 19 35N 81 35 E
Kondakovo 41 69 36N 152 0 E
Kondar 77 28 5S 150 0 E
Konde 94 4 57S 39 45 E
Kondinin 79 32 34S 118 8 E
Kondoa 94 4 55S 35 50 E
Kondoa □ 94 5 0S 36 0 E
Kondratyevo 41 57 22N 98 15 E
Konduga 89 11 35N 13 26 E
Koné 68 21 4S 164 52 E
Kong 88 8 54N 4 36W
Kong → 54 13 32N 105 58 E
Kong Christian IX.s Land 144 68 0N 36 0W
Kong Christian X.s Land 144 74 0N 29 0W
Kong Frederik VI.s Kyst 144 63 0N 43 0W
Kong Frederik VIII.s Land 144 78 30N 26 0W
Kong, Koh 55 11 20N 103 0 E
Kong Oscar Fjord 144 72 20N 24 0W
Konga 11 56 30N 15 6 E
Kongeå 11 55 24N 9 39 E
Kongju 61 36 30N 127 0 E
Konglu 52 27 13N 97 57 E
Kongolo 94 5 22S 27 0 E
Kongor 85 7 1N 31 27 E
Kongoussi 89 13 19N 1 32W
Kongsberg 10 59 39N 9 39 E
Kongsvinger 10 60 12N 12 2 E
Kongwa 94 6 11S 36 26 E
Kongwak 74 38 30S 145 42 E
Koni 95 10 40S 27 11 E
Koni, Mts. 95 10 36S 27 10 E
Königsberg = Kaliningrad 36 54 42N 20 32 E
Königshofen 31 50 18N 10 29 E
Königslutter 30 52 14N 10 50 E
Königswusterhausen 30 52 19N 13 38 E
Konin 32 52 12N 18 15 E
Kónitsa 35 40 5N 20 48 E
Konjice 27 46 20N 15 28 E
Konkouré → 88 9 50N 13 42W
Könnern 30 51 40N 11 45 E
Konnur 51 16 14N 74 49 E
Kono 88 8 30N 11 5W
Konongo 89 6 40N 1 15W
Konos 69 3 10S 151 44 E
Konosha 40 61 0N 40 5 E
Kōnosu 65 36 3N 139 31 E
Konotop 36 51 12N 33 7 E
Konqi He → 62 40 45N 90 10 E
Końskie 32 51 15N 20 23 E
Konstantinovka 38 48 32N 37 39 E
Konstantinovski 39 47 33N 41 10 E
Konstanz 31 47 39N 9 10 E
Kontagora 89 10 23N 5 27 E
Kontum 54 14 24N 108 0 E
Kontum, Plat. du 54 14 30N 108 0 E
Konya 46 37 52N 32 35 E
Konya Ovasi 46 38 30N 33 0 E
Konyin 52 22 58N 94 42 E
Konz 31 49 41N 6 36 E
Konza 94 1 45S 37 7 E
Koo-wee-rup 74 38 13S 145 28 E
Kookynie 79 29 17S 121 22 E
Kooline 78 22 57S 116 20 E
Kooloonong 74 34 48S 143 10 E
Koolyanobbing 79 30 48S 119 36 E
Koondrook 74 35 33S 144 8 E
Koorawatha 76 34 2S 148 33 E
Koorda 79 30 48S 117 35 E
Kooskia 120 46 9N 115 59W
Koostatak 109 51 26N 97 26W
Kootenai → 120 49 15N 117 39W
Kootenay L. 108 49 45N 116 50W
Kootenay Nat. Park 108 51 0N 116 0W
Kopanovka 39 47 28N 46 50 E
Kopaonik Planina 33 43 10N 21 50 E
Kopargaon 50 19 51N 74 28 E
Kópavogur 8 64 6N 21 55W
Koper 27 45 31N 13 44 E
Kopervik 9 59 17N 5 17 E
Kopeysk 40 55 7N 61 37 E
Kopi 73 33 24S 135 40 E
Köping 10 59 31N 16 3 E
Kopiste 27 42 48N 16 42 E
Köpmanholmen 10 63 10N 18 35 E
Koppal 51 15 23N 76 5 E
Koppang 10 61 34N 11 3 E
Koppeh Dāgh 47 38 0N 58 0 E
Kopperå 10 63 24N 11 50 E
Koppom 10 59 43N 12 10 E
Koprivnica 27 46 12N 16 45 E
Kopychintsy 36 49 7N 25 58 E
Korab 35 41 44N 20 40 E
Koraput 50 18 50N 82 40 E
Korba 49 22 20N 82 45 E
Korbach 30 51 17N 8 50 E
Korbu, G. 55 4 41N 101 18 E
Korça 35 40 37N 20 50 E
Korčula 27 42 57N 17 8 E
Korčula, I. 27 42 57N 17 0 E
Korčulanski Kanal 27 43 3N 16 40 E
Kordestan 46 35 30N 42 0 E
Kordestān □ 46 36 0N 47 0 E
Korea Bay 61 39 0N 124 0 E
Korea Strait 61 34 0N 129 30 E
Koregaon 50 17 40N 74 10 E
Korenevo 36 51 27N 34 55 E
Korenovsk 39 45 30N 39 22 E
Korets 36 50 40N 27 5 E
Korgus 90 19 16N 33 29 E
Korhogo 88 9 29N 5 28W
Koribundu 88 7 41N 11 46W
Korim 57 0 58S 136 10 E
Korinthiakós Kólpos 35 38 16N 22 30 E
Kórinthos 35 37 56N 22 55 E
Korioumé 88 16 35N 3 0W
Kōriyama 63 37 24N 140 23 E
Körmend 33 47 5N 16 35 E

Kornat	**27**	43 50N	15 20 E
Korneshty	**38**	47 21N	28 1 E
Kornsjø	**10**	58 57N	11 39 E
Kornstad	**10**	62 59N	7 27 E
Koro, Fiji	**68**	17 19 S	179 23 E
Koro, Ivory C.	**88**	8 32N	7 30W
Koro, Mali	**88**	14 1N	2 58W
Koro Sea	**68**	17 30 S	179 45W
Koroba	**69**	5 44 S	142 47 E
Korocha	**37**	50 55N	37 30 E
Korogoro Pt.	**77**	31 3 S	153 4 E
Korogwe	**94**	5 5 S	38 25 E
Korogwe □	**94**	5 0 S	38 20 E
Koroit	**74**	38 18 S	142 24 E
Korong Vale	**74**	36 22 S	143 45 E
Koronowo	**32**	53 19N	17 55 E
Koror	**57**	7 20N	134 28 E
Körös ⇝	**33**	46 43N	20 12 E
Korosten	**36**	50 57N	28 25 E
Korotoyak	**37**	51 1N	39 2 E
Korraraika, B. de	**97**	17 45 S	43 57 E
Korsakov	**41**	46 36N	142 42 E
Korshunovo	**41**	58 37N	110 10 E
Korsze	**32**	54 11N	21 9 E
Korti	**90**	18 6N	31 33 E
Kortrijk	**16**	50 50N	3 17 E
Korumburra	**74**	38 26 S	145 50 E
Korwai	**48**	24 7N	78 5 E
Koryakskiy Khrebet	**41**	61 0N	171 0 E
Koryŏng	**61**	35 44N	128 15 E
Kos, Greece	**35**	36 52N	27 19 E
Kos, Greece	**35**	36 50N	27 15 E
Kosa	**91**	7 50N	36 50 E
Kosaya Gora	**37**	54 10N	37 30 E
Kościan	**32**	52 5N	16 40 E
Kościerzyna	**32**	54 8N	17 59 E
Kosciusko	**119**	33 3N	89 34W
Kosciusko, I.	**108**	56 0N	133 40W
Kosciusko, Mt.	**75**	36 27 S	148 16 E
Kőszély ⇝	**33**	47 25N	21 5 E
Kosgi	**50**	16 58N	77 43 E
Kosha	**90**	20 50N	30 30 E
Koshigaya	**65**	35 54N	139 48 E
K'oshih = Kashi	**62**	39 30N	76 2 E
Koshiki-Rettō	**64**	31 45N	129 49 E
Koshkonog, L.	**117**	42 53N	88 58W
Kōshoku	**65**	36 38N	138 6 E
Kosi	**48**	27 48N	77 29 E
Kosi-meer	**97**	27 0 S	32 50 E
Košice	**32**	48 42N	21 15 E
Kosjerić	**33**	44 0N	19 55 E
Kosŏng	**61**	38 40N	128 22 E
Kosovska-Mitrovica	**33**	42 54N	20 52 E
Kostajnica	**27**	45 17N	16 30 E
Kostanjevica	**27**	45 51N	15 27 E
Kostelec	**32**	50 14N	16 35 E
Koster	**96**	25 52 S	26 54 E
Kôstî	**91**	13 8N	32 43 E
Kostroma	**37**	57 50N	40 58 E
Kostromskoye Vdkhr.	**37**	57 52N	40 49 E
Kostyukovichi	**36**	53 20N	32 4 E
Koszalin	**32**	53 50N	16 8 E
Kőszeg	**33**	47 23N	16 33 E
Kot Adu	**48**	30 30N	71 0 E
Kot Moman	**48**	32 13N	73 0 E
Kota	**48**	25 14N	75 49 E
Kota Baharu	**55**	6 7N	102 14 E
Kota Belud	**56**	6 21N	116 26 E
Kota Kinabalu	**56**	6 0N	116 4 E
Kota Tinggi	**55**	1 44N	103 53 E
Kotaagung	**56**	5 38 S	104 29 E
Kotabaru	**56**	3 20 S	116 20 E
Kotabumi	**56**	4 49 S	104 54 E
Kotagede	**57**	7 54 S	110 26 E
Kotamobagu	**57**	0 57N	124 31 E
Kotaneelee ⇝	**108**	60 11N	123 42W
Kotawaringin	**56**	2 28 S	111 27 E
Kotchandpur	**52**	23 24N	89 1 E
Kotcho L.	**108**	59 7N	121 12W
Kotelnich	**37**	58 20N	48 10 E
Kotelnikovo	**39**	47 38N	43 8 E
Kotelnyy, Ostrov	**41**	75 10N	139 0 E
Kothagudam	**50**	17 30N	80 40 E
Kothapet	**50**	19 21N	79 28 E
Köthen	**30**	51 44N	11 59 E
Kothi	**49**	24 45N	80 40 E
Kotiro	**48**	26 17N	67 13 E
Kotka	**9**	60 28N	26 58 E
Kotlas	**40**	61 15N	47 0 E
Kotli	**48**	33 30N	73 55 E
Kotmul	**49**	35 32N	75 10 E
Kotohira	**64**	34 11N	133 49 E
Kotonkoro	**89**	11 3N	5 58 E
Kotor	**33**	42 25N	18 47 E
Kotoriba	**27**	46 23N	16 48 E
Kotovo	**37**	50 22N	44 45 E
Kotovsk	**38**	47 45N	29 35 E
Kotputli	**48**	27 43N	76 12 E
Kotri	**48**	25 22N	68 22 E
Kotri ⇝	**50**	19 15N	80 35 E
Kótronas	**35**	36 38N	22 29 E
Kottayam	**51**	9 35N	76 33 E
Kottur	**51**	10 34N	76 56 E
Kotuy ⇝	**41**	71 54N	102 6 E
Kotzebue	**100**	66 50N	162 40W
Kouango	**92**	5 0N	20 10 E
Koudougou	**88**	12 10N	2 20W
Koufonísi	**35**	34 56N	26 8 E
Kougaberge	**96**	33 48 S	23 50 E
Kouibli	**88**	7 15N	7 14W
Kouilou ⇝	**92**	4 10 S	12 5 E
Kouki	**92**	7 22N	17 3 E
Koula Moutou	**92**	1 15 S	12 25 E
Koulen	**54**	13 50N	104 40 E
Koulikoro	**88**	12 40N	7 50W
Koumac	**68**	20 33 S	164 17 E
Koumala	**72**	21 38 S	149 15 E
Koumankou	**88**	11 58N	6 6W
Koumbia, Guin.	**88**	11 48N	13 29W
Koumbia, Upp. Vol.	**88**	11 10N	3 50W
Koumboum	**88**	10 25N	13 0W
Koumpenntoum	**88**	13 59N	14 34W
Koumra	**85**	8 50N	17 35 E
Koundara	**88**	12 29N	13 18W
Kounradskiy	**40**	46 59N	75 0 E
Kountze	**119**	30 20N	94 22W
Koupéla	**89**	12 11N	0 21W
Kourizo, Passe de	**87**	22 28N	15 27 E
Kourou	**135**	5 9N	52 39W
Kouroussa	**88**	10 45N	9 45W
Koussané	**88**	14 53N	11 14W
Kousseri	**85**	12 0N	14 55 E
Koutiala	**88**	12 25N	5 23W
Kouto	**88**	9 53N	6 25W
Kouts	**117**	41 18N	87 2W
Kouvé	**89**	6 25N	1 25 E
Kovačica	**33**	45 5N	20 38 E
Kovel	**36**	51 10N	24 20 E
Kovilpatti	**51**	9 10N	77 50 E
Kovin	**33**	44 44N	20 59 E
Kovrov	**37**	56 25N	41 25 E
Kovur, Andhra Pradesh, India	**50**	17 3N	81 39 E
Kovur, Andhra Pradesh, India	**51**	14 30N	80 1 E
Kowkash	**102**	50 20N	87 12W
Kowloon	**62**	22 20N	114 15 E
Kowŏn	**61**	39 26N	127 14 E
Koyabuti, Indon.	**57**	2 36 S	140 37 E
Koyabuti, Indon.	**57**	2 36 S	140 37 E
Kōyama	**64**	31 20N	130 56 E
Koyan, Pegunungan	**56**	3 15N	114 30 E
Koyuk	**100**	64 55N	161 20W
Koyukuk ⇝	**100**	64 56N	157 30W
Koyulhisar	**38**	40 20N	37 52 E
Koza	**63**	26 19N	127 46 E
Kozan	**46**	37 35N	35 50 E
Kozàni	**35**	40 19N	21 47 E
Kozara	**27**	45 0N	17 0 E
Kozarac	**27**	44 58N	16 48 E
Kozelsk	**36**	54 2N	35 48 E
Kozhikode = Calicut	**51**	11 15N	75 43 E
Kozje	**27**	46 5N	15 35 E
Kozlovets	**34**	43 30N	25 20 E
Koźmin	**32**	51 48N	17 27 E
Kōzu-Shima	**65**	34 13N	139 10 E
Kpabia	**89**	9 10N	0 20W
Kpandae	**89**	8 30N	0 2W
Kpessi	**89**	8 4N	1 16 E
Kra Buri	**55**	10 22N	98 46 E
Kra, Isthmus of = Kra, Kho Khot	**55**	10 15N	99 30 E
Kra, Kho Khot	**55**	10 15N	99 30 E
Krabi	**55**	8 4N	98 55 E
Kragan	**57**	6 43 S	111 38 E
Kragerø	**10**	58 52N	9 25 E
Kragujevac	**33**	44 2N	20 56 E
Krakatau = Rakata, Pulau	**56**	6 10 S	105 20 E
Krakor	**54**	12 32N	104 12 E
Kraków	**32**	50 4N	19 57 E
Kraksaan	**57**	7 43 S	113 23 E
Kråkstad	**10**	59 39N	10 55 E
Kralanh	**54**	13 35N	103 25 E
Králiky	**32**	50 6N	16 45 E
Kraljevo	**33**	43 44N	20 41 E
Kralovice	**32**	49 59N	13 29 E
Kralupy	**32**	50 13N	14 20 E
Kramatorsk	**38**	48 50N	37 30 E
Krambach	**77**	32 4 S	152 16 E
Kramer	**121**	35 0N	117 38W
Kramfors	**10**	62 55N	17 48 E
Kramis, C.	**86**	36 26N	0 45 E
Krångede	**10**	63 9N	16 10 E
Kranj	**27**	46 16N	14 22 E
Kranjska Gora	**27**	46 29N	13 48 E
Kranzberg	**96**	21 59 S	15 37 E
Krapina	**27**	46 10N	15 52 E
Krapina ⇝	**27**	45 50N	15 50 E
Krapivna	**37**	53 58N	37 10 E
Krapkowice	**32**	50 29N	17 56 E
Kraskino	**41**	42 44N	130 48 E
Kraslice	**32**	50 19N	12 31 E
Krasnaya Gorbatka	**37**	55 52N	41 45 E
Krasnaya Polyana	**39**	43 40N	40 13 E
Kraśnik	**32**	50 55N	22 5 E
Kraśnik Fabryczny	**32**	50 58N	22 11 E
Krasnoarmeisk	**38**	48 18N	37 11 E
Krasnoarmeysk, R.S.F.S.R., U.S.S.R.	**37**	51 0N	45 42 E
Krasnoarmeysk, R.S.F.S.R., U.S.S.R.	**39**	48 30N	44 25 E
Krasnodar	**39**	45 5N	39 0 E
Krasnodonetskaya	**39**	48 5N	40 50 E
Krasnogorskiy	**37**	56 10N	48 28 E
Krasnograd	**38**	49 27N	35 27 E
Krasnogvardeyskoye	**39**	45 52N	41 33 E
Krasnogvardyesk	**38**	45 32N	34 16 E
Krasnokutsk	**36**	50 10N	34 50 E
Krasnoperekopsk	**38**	46 0N	33 54 E
Krasnoselkupsk	**40**	65 20N	82 10 E
Krasnoslobodsk	**39**	48 42N	44 33 E
Krasnoturinsk	**40**	59 46N	60 12 E
Krasnoufimsk	**40**	56 57N	57 46 E
Krasnouralsk	**40**	58 21N	60 3 E
Krasnovodsk	**40**	40 0N	52 52 E
Krasnoyarsk	**41**	56 8N	93 0 E
Krasnoye, Kal., U.S.S.R.	**39**	46 16N	45 0 E
Krasnoye, R.S.F.S.R., U.S.S.R.	**37**	59 15N	47 40 E
Krasnoye = Krasnyy	**36**	54 25N	31 30 E
Krasnozavodsk	**37**	56 27N	38 25 E
Krasny Liman	**38**	48 58N	37 50 E
Krasny Sulin	**39**	47 52N	40 8 E
Krasnystaw	**32**	50 57N	23 5 E
Krasnyy	**36**	54 25N	31 30 E
Krasnyy Kholm	**37**	58 10N	37 10 E
Krasnyy Kut	**37**	50 50N	47 0 E
Krasnyy Luch	**39**	48 13N	39 0 E
Krasnyy Yar, Kal., U.S.S.R.	**39**	46 43N	48 23 E
Krasnyy Yar, R.S.F.S.R., U.S.S.R.	**37**	50 42N	44 45 E
Krasnyy Yar, R.S.F.S.R., U.S.S.R.	**37**	53 30N	50 22 E
Krasnyyoskolskoye Vdkhr.	**38**	49 30N	37 30 E
Kraszna ⇝	**33**	48 0N	22 20 E
Kratie	**54**	12 32N	106 10 E
Kratke Ra.	**69**	6 45 S	146 0 E
Krau	**57**	3 19 S	140 5 E
Kravanh, Chuor Phnum	**55**	12 0N	103 32 E
Krawang	**57**	6 19N	107 18 E
Krefeld	**30**	51 20N	6 32 E
Krémaston, Límni	**35**	38 52N	21 30 E
Kremenchug	**38**	49 5N	33 25 E
Kremenchugskoye Vdkhr.	**38**	49 20N	32 30 E
Kremenets	**38**	50 8N	25 43 E
Kremennaya	**38**	49 1N	38 10 E
Kremikovtsi	**34**	42 46N	23 28 E
Kremmen	**30**	52 45N	13 1 E
Kremmling	**120**	40 10N	106 30W
Krems	**33**	48 25N	15 36 E
Kremsmünster	**33**	48 3N	14 8 E
Kretinga	**36**	55 53N	21 15 E
Krettamia	**86**	28 47N	3 27W
Krettsy	**36**	58 15N	32 30 E
Kreuzberg	**31**	50 22N	9 58 E
Kribi	**92**	2 57N	9 56 E
Krichem	**34**	42 8N	24 28 E
Krichev	**36**	53 45N	31 50 E
Krim	**27**	45 53N	14 30 E
Krishna ⇝	**50**	15 57N	80 59 E
Krishnagiri	**51**	12 32N	78 16 E
Krishnanagar	**49**	23 24N	88 33 E
Krishnaraja Sagara	**51**	12 20N	76 30 E
Kristiansand	**9**	58 9N	8 1 E
Kristianstad	**11**	56 2N	14 9 E
Kristiansund	**10**	63 7N	7 45 E
Kristiinankaupunki	**8**	62 16N	21 21 E
Kristinehamn	**10**	59 18N	14 13 E
Kristinestad	**8**	62 16N	21 21 E
Kríti	**35**	35 15N	25 0 E
Kriva ⇝	**34**	42 5N	21 47 E
Kriva Palanka	**34**	42 11N	22 19 E
Krivaja ⇝	**33**	44 27N	18 9 E
Krivoy Rog	**38**	47 51N	33 20 E
Križevci	**27**	46 3N	16 32 E
Krk, Yugo.	**27**	45 8N	14 40 E
Krk, Yugo.	**27**	45 5N	14 36 E
Krka ⇝	**27**	45 50N	15 30 E
Krkonoše	**32**	50 50N	15 35 E
Krnov	**32**	50 5N	17 40 E
Krobia	**32**	51 47N	16 59 E
Krokeaí	**35**	36 53N	22 32 E
Krokom	**10**	63 20N	14 30 E
Krolevets	**36**	51 35N	33 20 E
Kroměříz	**32**	49 18N	17 21 E
Kromy	**36**	52 40N	35 48 E
Kronach	**31**	50 14N	11 19 E
Kronobergs län □	**11**	56 45N	14 30 E
Kronprins Olav Kyst	**143**	69 0 S	42 0 E
Kronprinsesse Märtha Kyst	**143**	73 30 S	10 0 E
Kronshtadt	**36**	60 5N	29 45 E
Kroonstad	**96**	27 43 S	27 19 E
Kröpelin	**30**	54 4N	11 48 E
Kropotkin, R.S.F.S.R., U.S.S.R.	**39**	45 28N	40 28 E
Kropotkin, R.S.F.S.R., U.S.S.R.	**41**	59 0N	115 30 E
Kropp	**30**	54 24N	9 32 E
Krościenko	**32**	49 29N	20 25 E
Krosno	**32**	49 42N	21 46 E
Krosno Odrzańskie	**32**	52 3N	15 7 E
Krotoszyn	**32**	51 42N	17 23 E
Krško	**27**	45 57N	15 30 E
Kruger Nat. Pk.	**97**	24 0 S	31 40 E
Krugersdorp	**97**	26 5 S	27 46 E
Kruis, Kaap	**96**	21 55 S	13 57 E
Kruja	**35**	41 32N	19 46 E
Krulevshchina	**36**	55 5N	27 45 E
Kruma	**34**	42 14N	20 28 E
Krumbach	**31**	48 15N	10 22 E
Krung Thep	**54**	13 45N	100 35 E
Krupanj	**33**	44 25N	19 22 E
Krupinica ⇝	**33**	48 15N	18 52 E
Kruševac	**33**	43 35N	21 28 E
Kruzof I.	**108**	57 10N	135 40W
Krylbo	**10**	60 7N	16 15 E
Krymsk Abinsk	**38**	44 50N	38 0 E
Krymskiy P.-ov.	**38**	45 0N	34 0 E
Krynica Morska	**32**	54 23N	19 28 E
Krynki	**32**	53 17N	23 43 E
Krzywiń	**32**	51 58N	16 50 E
Krzyz	**32**	52 52N	16 0 E
Ksabi	**86**	32 51N	4 13W
Ksar Chellala	**86**	35 13N	2 19 E
Ksar el Boukhari	**86**	35 51N	2 52 E
Ksar el Kebir	**86**	35 0N	6 0W
Ksar es Souk	**86**	31 58N	4 20W
Ksar Rhilane	**87**	33 0N	9 39 E
Ksiba, El	**86**	32 46N	6 0W
Ksour, Mts. des	**86**	32 45N	0 30W
Kstovo	**37**	56 12N	44 13 E
Kuala	**56**	2 55N	105 47 E
Kuala Berang	**55**	5 5N	103 1 E
Kuala Dungun	**55**	4 45N	103 25 E
Kuala Kangsar	**55**	4 46N	100 56 E
Kuala Kerai	**55**	5 30N	102 12 E
Kuala Klawang	**55**	2 56N	102 5 E
Kuala Kubu Baharu	**55**	3 34N	101 39 E
Kuala Lipis	**55**	4 10N	102 3 E
Kuala Lumpur	**55**	3 9N	101 41 E
Kuala Marang	**55**	5 12N	103 13 E
Kuala Nerang	**55**	6 16N	100 37 E
Kuala Pilah	**55**	2 45N	102 15 E
Kuala Rompin	**55**	2 49N	103 29 E
Kuala Selangor	**55**	3 20N	101 15 E
Kuala Terengganu, Malay.	**55**	5 20N	103 8 E
Kuala Terengganu, Malay.	**55**	5 20N	103 8 E
Kualakapuas	**56**	2 55 S	114 20 E
Kualakurun	**56**	1 10 S	113 50 E
Kualapembuang	**56**	3 14 S	112 38 E
Kualasimpang	**56**	4 17N	98 3 E
Kuancheng	**61**	40 37N	118 30 E
Kuandang	**57**	0 56N	123 1 E
Kuandian	**61**	40 45N	124 45 E
Kuangchou = Guangzhou	**59**	23 5N	113 10 E
Kuantan	**55**	3 49N	103 20 E
Kuba	**39**	41 21N	48 32 E
Kubak	**47**	27 10N	63 10 E
Kuban ⇝	**38**	45 20N	37 30 E
Kubenskoye, Oz.	**37**	59 40N	39 25 E
Kuberle	**39**	47 0N	42 20 E
Kubokawa	**64**	33 12N	133 8 E
Kubor, Mt.	**69**	6 10 S	144 44 E
Kubrat	**34**	43 49N	26 31 E
Kučevo	**33**	44 30N	21 40 E
Kucha Gompa	**49**	34 25N	76 56 E
Kuchaman	**48**	27 13N	74 47 E
Kuching	**56**	1 33N	110 25 E
Kuchinoerabu-Jima	**63**	30 28N	130 11 E
Kuchinotsu	**64**	32 36N	130 11 E
Kud ⇝	**48**	26 5N	66 20 E
Kudalier ⇝	**50**	18 35N	79 48 E
Kudamatsu	**64**	34 0N	131 52 E
Kudat	**56**	6 55N	116 55 E
Kudremukh, Mt.	**51**	13 15N	75 20 E
Kudus	**57**	6 48 S	110 51 E
Kudymkar	**40**	59 1N	54 39 E
Kueiyang = Guiyang	**58**	26 32N	106 40 E
Kufra, El Wâhât el	**85**	24 17N	23 15 E
Kufrinja	**44**	32 20N	35 41 E
Kufstein	**31**	47 35N	12 11 E
Kugong, I.	**102**	56 18N	79 50W

Kūh-e-Aliju	47	31 30N	51 41 E
Kūh-e-Dinar	47	30 40N	51 0 E
Kūh-e-Hazārān	47	29 35N	57 20 E
Kūh-e-Jebāl Bārez	47	29 0N	58 0 E
Kūh-e-Sorkh	47	35 30N	58 45 E
Kūh-e-Taftan	47	28 40N	61 0 E
Kūhak	47	27 12N	63 10 E
Kūhhā-ye-Bashākerd	47	26 45N	59 0 E
Kūhhā-ye Sabalān	47	38 15N	47 45 E
Kuhnsdorf	33	46 37N	14 38 E
Kūhpāyeh	47	32 44N	52 20 E
Kui Buri	55	12 3N	99 52 E
Kujang	61	39 57N	126 1 E
Kuji	63	40 11N	141 46 E
Kujū-San	64	33 5N	131 15 E
Kujukuri-Heiya	65	35 45N	140 30 E
Kukawa	89	12 58N	13 27 E
Kukerin	79	33 13S	118 0 E
Kukko	91	8 26N	41 35 E
Kukup	55	1 20N	103 27 E
Kukvidze	37	50 40N	43 15 E
Kula	33	45 37N	19 32 E
Kula Gulf	68	8 5S	157 18 E
Kulai	55	1 44N	103 35 E
Kulal, Mt.	94	2 42N	36 57 E
Kulaly, O.	39	45 0N	50 0 E
Kulasekharapattanam	51	8 20N	78 0 E
Kuldiga	36	56 58N	21 59 E
Kuldja = Yining	62	43 58N	81 10 E
Kuldu	91	12 50N	28 30 E
Kulebaki	37	55 22N	42 25 E
Kulen Vakuf	27	44 35N	16 2 E
Kulgam	49	33 36N	75 2 E
Kuli	39	42 2N	47 12 E
Kulim	55	5 22N	100 34 E
Kulin	79	32 40S	118 2 E
Kulja	79	30 28S	117 18 E
Kulm	118	46 22N	98 58W
Kulmbach	31	50 6N	11 27 E
Kulsary	40	46 59N	54 1 E
Kultay	39	45 5N	51 40 E
Kulti	49	23 43N	86 50 E
Kulunda	40	52 35N	78 57 E
Kulungar	48	34 0N	69 2 E
Kulwin	74	35 0S	142 42 E
Kulyab	40	37 55N	69 50 E
Kum Tekei	40	43 10N	79 30 E
Kuma	64	33 39N	132 54 E
Kuma →	39	44 55N	47 0 E
Kumaganum	89	13 8N	10 38 E
Kumagaya	65	36 9N	139 22 E
Kumai	56	2 44S	111 43 E
Kumamba, Kepulauan	57	1 36S	138 45 E
Kumamoto	64	32 45N	130 45 E
Kumamoto □	64	32 55N	130 55 E
Kumano	65	33 54N	136 5 E
Kumano-Nada	65	33 47N	136 20 E
Kumanovo	34	42 9N	21 42 E
Kumara	81	42 37S	171 12 E
Kumarkhali	52	23 51N	89 15 E
Kumarl	79	32 47S	121 33 E
Kumasi	88	6 41N	1 38W
Kumba	92	4 36N	9 24 E
Kumbakonam	51	10 58N	79 25 E
Kumbarilla	73	27 15S	150 55 E
Kumbo	89	6 15N	10 36 E
Kumbukkan Oya →	51	6 35N	81 40 E
Kŭmchŏn	61	38 10N	126 29 E
Kumdok	49	33 32N	78 10 E
Kumeny	37	58 10N	49 47 E
Kŭmhwa	61	38 17N	127 28 E
Kumi	94	1 30N	33 58 E
Kumla	10	59 8N	15 10 E
Kummerower See	30	53 47N	12 52 E
Kumo	89	10 1N	11 12 E
Kumon Bum	52	26 30N	97 15 E
Kumotori-Yama	65	35 51N	138 57 E
Kumta	51	14 29N	74 25 E
Kumtorkala	39	43 2N	46 50 E
Kumusi →	69	8 16S	148 13 E
Kumylzhenskaya	39	49 51N	42 38 E
Kunama	76	35 35S	148 4 E
Kunar □	47	34 30N	71 3 E
Kunashir, Ostrov	41	44 0N	146 0 E
Kunch	49	26 0N	79 10 E
Kunda	36	59 30N	26 34 E
Kundiawa	69	6 2S	145 1 E
Kundip	79	33 42S	120 10 E
Kundla	48	21 21N	71 25 E
Kunduz	47	36 50N	68 50 E
Kunduz □	47	36 50N	68 50 E
Kunene →	96	17 20S	11 50 E
Kungala	77	29 58S	153 7 E
Kungälv	11	57 53N	11 59 E
Kunghit I.	108	52 6N	131 3W
Kungrad	40	43 6N	58 54 E
Kungsbacka	11	57 30N	12 5 E
Kungur	40	57 25N	56 57 E
Kungurri	72	21 3S	148 46 E
Kungyangon	52	16 27N	96 20 E
Kunhar →	49	34 20N	73 30 E
Kunhegyes	33	47 22N	20 36 E

Kunimi-Dake	64	32 33N	131 1 E
Kuningan	57	6 59S	108 29 E
Kunisaki	64	33 33N	131 45 E
Kunlong	52	23 20N	98 50 E
Kunlun Shan	62	36 0N	85 0 E
Kunming	58	25 1N	102 41 E
Kunnamkulam	51	10 38N	76 7 E
Kunsan	61	35 59N	126 45 E
Kunshan	59	31 22N	120 58 E
Kununurra	78	15 40S	128 50 E
Kunwarara	72	22 55S	150 9 E
Kunya-Urgenoh	40	42 19N	59 10 E
Künzelsau	31	49 17N	9 41 E
Kuopio	8	62 53N	27 35 E
Kuopion lääni □	8	63 25N	27 10 E
Kupa →	27	45 28N	16 24 E
Kupang	57	10 19S	123 39 E
Kupiano	69	10 4S	148 14 E
Kupres	33	44 1N	17 15 E
Kupyansk	38	49 52N	37 35 E
Kupyansk-Uzlovoi	38	49 45N	37 34 E
Kuqa	62	41 35N	82 30 E
Kur →	52	26 50N	91 0 E
Kura →	39	39 50N	49 20 E
Kurahashi-Jima	64	34 8N	132 31 E
Kuranda	72	16 48S	145 35 E
Kurashiki	64	34 40N	133 50 E
Kurayoshi	64	35 26N	133 50 E
Kurduvadi	50	18 8N	75 29 E
Kŭrdzhali	35	41 38N	25 21 E
Kure	64	34 14N	132 32 E
Kuressaare = Kingisepp	36	58 15N	22 15 E
Kurgaldzhino	40	50 35N	70 20 E
Kurgan	40	55 26N	65 18 E
Kuria Muria I. = Khyryān Muryān J.	45	17 30N	55 58 E
Kurichchi	51	11 36N	77 35 E
Kuridala P.O	72	21 16S	140 29 E
Kurigram	52	25 49N	89 39 E
Kurihashi	65	36 8N	139 42 E
Kuril Is. = Kurilskiye Os.	41	45 0N	150 0 E
Kuril Trench	66	44 0N	153 0 E
Kurilsk	41	45 14N	147 53 E
Kurilskiye Ostrova	41	45 0N	150 0 E
Kuring Kuru	96	17 42S	18 32 E
Kurino	64	31 57N	130 43 E
Kurkur	90	23 50N	32 0 E
Kurkûrah	87	31 30N	20 1 E
Kurla	50	19 5N	72 52 E
Kurlovskiy	37	55 25N	40 40 E
Kurma	91	13 55N	24 40 E
Kurmuk	91	10 33N	34 21 E
Kurnool	51	15 45N	78 0 E
Kurobe-Gawe →	65	36 55N	137 25 E
Kurogi	64	33 12N	130 40 E
Kurovskoye	37	55 35N	38 55 E
Kurow	81	44 44S	170 29 E
Kurrajong	76	33 33S	150 42 E
Kurram →	48	32 36N	71 20 E
Kurri Kurri	76	32 50S	151 28 E
Kuršenai	36	56 1N	23 3 E
Kurseong	49	26 56N	88 18 E
Kursk	37	51 42N	36 11 E
Kuršumlija	33	43 9N	21 19 E
Kurtalan	46	37 55N	41 40 E
Kuru (Chel), Bahr el →	91	8 10N	26 50 E
Kuruktag, Xinjiang Uygar, China	62	41 0N	89 0 E
Kuruktag, Xinjiang Uygur, China	62	41 20N	90 0 E
Kuruman	96	27 28S	23 28 E
Kurumbul →	77	28 38S	150 35 E
Kurume	64	33 15N	130 30 E
Kurunegala	51	7 30N	80 23 E
Kurupukari	135	4 43N	58 37W
Kurya	41	61 15N	108 10 E
Kusatsu, Gumma, Japan	65	36 37N	138 36 E
Kusatsu, Shiga, Japan	65	34 58N	135 57 E
Kusawa L.	108	60 20N	136 13W
Kusel	31	49 31N	7 25 E
Kushchevskaya	39	46 33N	39 35 E
Kushikino	64	31 44N	130 16 E
Kushima	64	31 29N	131 14 E
Kushimoto	65	33 28N	135 47 E
Kushiro	63	43 0N	144 25 E
Kushiro →	63	42 59N	144 23 E
Kushk	47	34 55N	62 30 E
Kushka	40	35 20N	62 18 E
Kushol	49	33 40N	76 36 E
Kushtia	52	23 55N	89 5 E
Kushum →	39	49 0N	50 20 E
Kuskokwim →	100	60 17N	162 27W
Kuskokwim Bay	100	59 50N	162 56W
Kussa	91	4 9N	38 58 E
Kustanay	40	53 10N	63 35 E
Kusu	64	33 16N	131 9 E
Kut, Ko	55	11 40N	102 35 E
Kutahya	46	39 30N	30 2 E
Kutaisi	39	42 19N	42 40 E

Kutaraja = Banda Aceh	56	5 35N	95 20 E
Kutch, G. of	48	22 50N	69 15 E
Kutch, Rann of	48	24 0N	70 0 E
Kutina	27	45 29N	16 48 E
Kutiyana	48	21 36N	70 2 E
Kutkai	52	23 27N	97 56 E
Kutkashen	39	40 58N	47 47 E
Kutná Hora	32	49 57N	15 16 E
Kutno	32	52 15N	19 23 E
Kuttabul	72	21 5S	148 48 E
Kutu	92	2 40S	18 11 E
Kutum	91	14 10N	24 40 E
Kuŭp-tong	61	40 45N	126 1 E
Kuvshinovo	36	57 2N	34 11 E
Kuwait = Al Kuwayt	46	29 30N	47 30 E
Kuwait ■	46	29 30N	47 30 E
Kuwana	65	35 0N	136 43 E
Kuybyshev, U.S.S.R.	37	53 8N	50 6 E
Kuybyshev, R.S.F.S.R., U.S.S.R.	40	55 27N	78 19 E
Kuybyshevo	38	47 25N	36 40 E
Kuybyshevskoye Vdkhr.	37	55 2N	49 30 E
Kuye He →	60	38 23N	110 46 E
Küysanjaq	46	36 5N	44 38 E
Kuyumba	41	60 58N	96 59 E
Kuzhithura	51	8 18N	77 11 E
Kuznetsk	37	53 12N	46 40 E
Kvænangen	8	70 5N	21 15 E
Kvam	10	61 40N	9 42 E
Kvarner	27	44 50N	14 10 E
Kvarnerič	27	44 43N	14 37 E
Kvillsfors	11	57 24N	15 29 E
Kviteseid	10	59 24N	8 29 E
Kwabhaga	97	30 51S	29 0 E
Kwadacha →	108	57 28N	125 38W
Kwakhanai	96	21 39S	21 16 E
Kwakoegron	135	5 12N	55 25W
Kwale, Kenya	94	4 15S	39 31 E
Kwale, Nigeria	89	5 46N	6 26 E
Kwale □	94	4 15S	39 10 E
Kwamouth	92	3 9S	16 12 E
Kwando →	96	18 27S	23 32 E
Kwangdaeri	61	40 31N	127 32 E
Kwangju	61	35 9N	126 54 E
Kwangsi-Chuang □ = Guangxi Zhuangzu □	58	24 0N	109 0 E
Kwangtung □ = Guangdong □	59	23 0N	113 0 E
Kwara □	89	8 0N	5 0 E
Kwaraga	96	20 26S	24 32 E
Kwataboahegan →	102	51 9N	80 50W
Kwatisore	57	3 18S	134 50 E
Kweichow □ = Guizhou □	58	27 0N	107 0 E
Kwiguk	100	63 45N	164 35W
Kwikila	69	9 49S	147 38 E
Kwimba □	94	3 0S	33 0 E
Kwinana	79	32 15S	115 47 E
Kwitaba	94	3 56S	29 39 E
Kwoka	57	0 31S	132 27 E
Kya-in-Seikkyi	52	16 2N	98 8 E
Kyabe	85	9 30N	19 0 E
Kyabra Cr. →	73	25 36S	142 55 E
Kyabram	74	36 19S	145 4 E
Kyaiklat	52	16 25N	95 40 E
Kyaikmaraw	52	16 23N	97 44 E
Kyaikthin	52	23 32N	95 40 E
Kyaikto	54	17 20N	97 3 E
Kyakhta	41	50 30N	106 25 E
Kyangin	52	18 20N	95 20 E
Kyaukhnyat	52	18 15N	97 31 E
Kyaukse	52	21 36N	96 10 E
Kyauktaw	52	20 51N	92 59 E
Kyawkku	52	21 48N	96 56 E
Kyburz	122	38 47N	120 18W
Kyeamba	76	35 26S	147 40 E
Kyegegwa	94	0 30N	31 0 E
Kyeintali	52	18 0N	94 29 E
Kyenjojo	94	0 40N	30 37 E
Kyidaunggan	52	19 53N	96 12 E
Kyle Dam	95	20 15S	31 0 E
Kyle of Lochalsh	14	57 17N	5 43W
Kyll →	31	49 48N	6 42 E
Kyllburg	31	50 2N	6 35 E
Kyneton	74	37 10S	144 29 E
Kynuna	72	21 37S	141 55 E
Kyō-ga-Saki	65	35 45N	135 15 E
Kyoga, L.	94	1 35N	33 0 E
Kyogle	77	28 40S	153 0 E
Kyongju	61	35 51N	129 14 E
Kyŏngsŏng	61	41 35N	129 36 E
Kyōto	65	35 0N	135 45 E
Kyōto □	65	35 15N	135 45 E
Kyren	41	51 45N	101 45 E
Kyrenia	46	35 20N	33 20 E
Kyritz	30	52 57N	12 25 E
Kystatyam	41	67 20N	123 10 E
Kytalktakh	41	65 30N	123 40 E

Kyu-hkok	52	24 4N	98 4 E
Kyulyunken	41	64 10N	137 5 E
Kyunhla	52	23 25N	95 15 E
Kyuquot	108	50 3N	127 25W
Kyurdamir	39	40 25N	48 3 E
Kyūshū	64	33 0N	131 0 E
Kyūshū □	64	33 0N	131 0 E
Kyūshū-Sanchi	64	32 35N	131 17 E
Kyustendil	34	42 16N	22 41 E
Kyusyur	41	70 39N	127 15 E
Kywong	75	34 58S	146 44 E
Kyzyl	41	51 50N	94 30 E
Kyzyl-Kiya	40	40 16N	72 8 E
Kyzylkum, Peski	40	42 30N	65 0 E
Kzyl-Orda	40	44 48N	65 28 E

L

Laaber →	31	49 0N	12 3 E
Laage	30	53 55N	12 21 E
Laanecoorie Res.	74	36 52S	143 50 E
Laasphe	30	50 56N	8 23 E
Laba →	39	45 11N	39 42 E
Laban	52	25 52N	96 40 E
Labastide	20	43 28N	2 39 E
Labastide-Murat	20	44 39N	1 33 E
Labbézenga	89	15 2N	0 48 E
Labdah = Leptis Magna	87	32 40N	14 12 E
Labé	88	11 24N	12 16W
Labe = Elbe →	32	50 3N	15 20 E
Laberec →	32	48 37N	21 58 E
Laberge, L.	108	61 11N	135 12W
Labin	27	45 5N	14 8 E
Labinsk	39	44 40N	40 48 E
Labis	55	2 22N	103 2 E
Laboe	30	54 25N	10 13 E
Labouheyre	20	44 13N	0 55W
Laboulaye	140	34 10S	63 30W
Labra, Peña	22	43 3N	4 26W
Labrador City	103	52 57N	66 55W
Labrador, Coast of □	101	53 20N	61 0W
Lábrea	137	7 15S	64 51W
Labrède	20	44 41N	0 32W
Labrieville	105	49 18N	69 34W
Labuan	56	5 21N	115 13 E
Labuha	57	0 30S	127 30 E
Labuhan	57	6 26S	105 50 E
Labuhanbajo	57	8 28S	120 1 E
Labuk, Telok	56	6 10N	117 50 E
Labutta	52	16 9N	94 46 E
Labytnangi	40	66 39N	66 21 E
Lac Allard	103	50 33N	63 24W
Lac-aux-Sables	105	46 51N	72 24W
Lac Bouchette	105	48 16N	72 11W
Lac Carré	105	46 7N	74 29W
Lac-des-Écorces	104	46 34N	75 22W
Lac du Flambeau	118	46 1N	89 51W
Lac Édouard	105	47 40N	72 16W
Lac-Etchemin	105	46 24N	70 30W
Lac la Biche	108	54 45N	111 58W
Lac la Martre	100	63 8N	117 16W
Lac-Mégantic	105	45 35N	70 53W
Lac-Rémi	104	46 1N	74 46W
Lac-Ste-Marie	104	45 57N	75 57W
Lac Seul	109	50 28N	92 0W
Lac Thien	54	12 25N	108 11 E
Lacanau, Étang de	20	44 58N	1 7W
Lacanau-Médoc	20	44 59N	1 5W
Lacantúm →	125	16 36N	90 40W
Lacara →	23	38 55N	6 25W
Lacaune	20	43 43N	2 40 E
Lacaune, Mts. de	20	43 43N	2 50 E
Laccadive Is. = Lakshadweep Is.	42	10 0N	72 30 E
Lacepede B.	73	36 40S	139 40 E
Lacepede Is.	78	16 55S	122 0 E
Lacerdónia	95	18 3S	35 35 E
Lacey	122	47 7N	122 49W
Lachay, Pta.	136	11 17S	77 44W
Lachen	52	27 46N	88 36 E
Lachi	48	33 25N	71 20 E
Lachine	105	45 30N	73 40W
Lachlan →	73	34 22S	143 55 E
Lachmangarh	48	27 50N	75 4 E
Lachute	105	45 39N	74 21W
Lackawanna	114	42 49N	78 50W
Lacolle	105	45 5N	73 22W
Lacombe	108	52 30N	113 44W
Lacon	116	41 2N	89 24W
Lacona, Iowa, U.S.A.	116	41 11N	93 23W
Lacona, N.Y., U.S.A.	115	43 37N	76 5W
Láconi	28	39 54N	9 4 E
Laconia	115	43 32N	71 30W
Lacq	20	43 25N	0 35W
Lacrosse	120	46 51N	117 58W
Ladakh Ra.	49	34 0N	78 0 E
Ladário	137	19 1S	57 35W
Ladd	116	41 23N	89 13W
Laddonia	116	39 15N	91 39W

Ládhon →	35	37 40N	21 50 E
Ladik	38	40 57N	35 58 E
Ladismith	96	33 28S	21 15 E
Lādiz	47	28 55N	61 15 E
Ladnun	48	27 38N	74 25 E
Ladoga, L. = Ladozhskoye Oz.	40	61 15N	30 30 E
Ladon	19	48 0N	2 30 E
Ladozhskoye Ozero	40	61 15N	30 30 E
Ladrillero, G.	142	49 20S	75 35W
Lady Babbie	95	18 30S	29 20 E
Lady Grey	96	30 43S	27 13 E
Ladybrand	96	29 9S	27 29 E
Ladysmith, Can.	108	49 0N	123 49W
Ladysmith, S. Afr.	97	28 32S	29 46 E
Ladysmith, U.S.A.	118	45 27N	91 4W
Lae	69	6 40S	147 2 E
Laem Ngop	55	12 10N	102 26 E
Laem Pho	55	6 55N	101 19 E
Læsø	11	57 15N	10 53 E
Læsø Rende	11	57 20N	10 45 E
Lafayette, Colo., U.S.A.	118	40 0N	105 2W
Lafayette, Ga., U.S.A.	113	34 44N	85 15W
Lafayette, Ind., U.S.A.	117	40 25N	86 54W
Lafayette, La., U.S.A.	119	30 18N	92 0W
Lafayette, Tenn., U.S.A.	113	36 35N	86 0W
Laferte →	108	61 53N	117 44W
Lafia	89	8 30N	8 34 E
Lafiagi	89	8 52N	5 20 E
Laflamme →	104	49 17N	77 9W
Lafleche	109	49 45N	106 40W
Lafon	91	5 5N	32 29 E
Laforce	104	47 32N	78 44W
Laforsen	10	61 56N	15 3 E
Lagaip →	69	5 4S	142 52 E
Lagan →, Sweden	11	56 56N	13 58 E
Lagan →, U.K.	15	54 35N	5 55W
Lagarfljót →	8	65 40N	14 18W
Lagarto	138	10 54S	37 41W
Lage, Ger.	30	52 0N	8 47 E
Lage, Spain	22	43 13N	9 0W
Lägerdorf	30	53 53N	9 35 E
Laggan	76	34 23S	149 31 E
Laggers Pt.	77	30 52S	153 4 E
Laghman □	47	34 20N	70 0 E
Laghouat	86	33 50N	2 59 E
Lagnieu	21	45 55N	5 20 E
Lagny	19	48 52N	2 40 E
Lago	29	39 9N	16 8 E
Lago Posadas	142	47 30S	71 40W
Lago Ranco	142	40 19S	72 30W
Lagôa	23	37 8N	8 27W
Lagoaça	22	41 11N	6 44W
Lagodekhi	39	41 50N	46 22 E
Lagónegro	29	40 8N	15 45 E
Lagonoy Gulf	57	13 50N	123 50 E
Lagos, Nigeria	89	6 25N	3 27 E
Lagos, Port.	23	37 5N	8 41W
Lagos de Moreno	124	21 21N	101 55W
Lagrange, Austral.	78	18 45S	121 43 E
Lagrange, U.S.A.	117	41 39N	85 25W
Lagrange B.	78	18 38S	121 42 E
Laguardia	24	42 33N	2 35W
Laguépie	20	44 8N	1 57 E
Laguna, Brazil	141	28 30S	48 50W
Laguna, U.S.A.	121	35 3N	107 28W
Laguna Beach	123	33 31N	117 52W
Laguna Dam	121	32 55N	114 30W
Laguna de la Janda	23	36 15N	5 45W
Laguna Limpia	140	26 32S	59 45W
Laguna Madre	125	27 0N	97 20W
Lagunas, Chile	140	21 0S	69 45W
Lagunas, Peru	136	5 10S	75 35W
Lagunillas	137	19 38S	63 43W
Lahad Datu	57	5 0N	118 20 E
Lahan Sai	54	14 25N	102 52 E
Lahanam	54	16 16N	105 16 E
Laharpur	49	27 43N	80 56 E
Lahat	56	3 45S	103 30 E
Lahe	52	26 20N	95 26 E
Lahewa	56	1 22N	97 12 E
Lahijan	46	37 10N	50 6 E
Lahn →	31	50 52N	8 35 E
Laholm	11	56 30N	13 2 E
Laholmsbukten	11	56 30N	12 45 E
Lahontan Res.	120	39 28N	118 58W
Lahore	48	31 32N	74 22 E
Lahore □	48	31 55N	74 5 E
Lahpongsel	52	27 7N	98 25 E
Lahr	31	48 20N	7 52 E
Lahti	9	60 58N	25 40 E
Lai (Béhagle)	85	9 25N	16 18 E
Lai Chau	54	22 5N	103 3 E
Lai-hka	52	21 16N	97 40 E
Laiagam	69	5 33S	143 30 E
Lai'an	59	32 28N	118 30 E
Laibin	58	23 42N	109 14 E
Laidley	73	27 39S	152 20 E
Laifeng	59	29 27N	109 20 E
Laignes	19	47 50N	4 20 E
Laikipia □	94	0 30N	36 30 E
Laila	46	22 10N	46 40 E
Laingsburg	96	33 9S	20 52 E
Lairg	14	58 1N	4 24W
Lais	56	3 35S	102 0 E
Laishui	60	39 23N	115 45 E
Laiwu	61	36 15N	117 40 E
Laixi	61	36 50N	120 31 E
Laiyang	61	36 59N	120 45 E
Laiyuan	60	39 20N	114 40 E
Laizhou Wan	61	37 30N	119 30 E
Laja →	124	20 55N	100 46W
Lajere	89	11 58N	11 25 E
Lajes, Rio Grande d. N., Brazil	138	5 41S	36 14W
Lajes, Sta. Catarina, Brazil	141	27 48S	50 20W
Lajinha	139	20 9S	41 37W
Lajkovac	33	44 27N	20 14 E
Lajosmizse	33	47 3N	19 32 E
Lak Sao	54	18 11N	104 59 E
Lakaband	48	31 2N	69 15 E
Lakar	57	8 15S	128 17 E
Lakatoro	68	16 0S	167 0 E
Lake Alpine	122	38 29N	120 0W
Lake Andes	118	43 10N	98 32W
Lake Anse	112	46 42N	88 25W
Lake Arthur	119	30 8N	92 40W
Lake Bluff	117	42 17N	87 50W
Lake Boga	74	35 26S	143 38 E
Lake Bolac	74	37 42S	142 49 E
Lake Brown	79	30 56S	118 20 E
Lake Cargelligo	73	33 15S	146 22 E
Lake Charles	119	30 15N	93 10W
Lake Charm	74	35 36S	143 46 E
Lake City, Colo, U.S.A.	121	38 3N	107 27W
Lake City, Fla., U.S.A.	113	30 10N	82 40W
Lake City, Iowa, U.S.A.	116	42 12N	94 42W
Lake City, Mich., U.S.A.	106	44 20N	85 10W
Lake City, Minn., U.S.A.	118	44 28N	92 21W
Lake City, Pa., U.S.A.	114	42 2N	80 20W
Lake City, S.C., U.S.A.	113	33 51N	79 44W
Lake Coleridge	81	43 17S	171 30 E
Lake Cowal	76	33 41S	147 21 E
Lake Cullulleraine	74	34 15S	141 37 E
Lake Forest	117	42 15N	87 50W
Lake Geneva	117	42 36N	88 26W
Lake George	115	43 25N	73 43W
Lake Grace	79	33 7S	118 28 E
Lake Harbour	101	62 50N	69 50W
Lake Havasu City	123	34 25N	114 29W
Lake Hughes	123	34 41N	118 26W
Lake Isabella	123	35 38N	118 28W
Lake King	79	33 5S	119 45 E
Lake Lenore	109	52 24N	104 59W
Lake Louise	108	51 30N	116 10W
Lake Mead Nat. Rec. Area	123	36 0N	114 30W
Lake Michigan Beach	117	42 13N	86 25W
Lake Mills, Iowa, U.S.A.	118	43 23N	93 33W
Lake Mills, Wis., U.S.A.	117	43 5N	88 55W
Lake Murray	69	6 48S	141 29 E
Lake Nash	72	20 57S	138 0 E
Lake Odesse	117	42 47N	85 8W
Lake Orion	117	42 47N	83 14W
Lake Providence	119	32 49N	91 12W
Lake River	102	54 30N	82 31W
Lake St. Peter	107	45 18N	78 2W
Lake Superior Prov. Park	102	47 45N	84 45W
Lake Tekapo	81	44 0S	170 30 E
Lake Varley	79	32 48S	119 30 E
Lake Villa	117	42 25N	88 5W
Lake Village	119	33 20N	91 19W
Lake Wales	113	27 55N	81 32W
Lake Worth	113	26 36N	80 3W
Lakefield	107	44 25N	78 16W
Lakeland	113	28 0N	82 0W
Lakemba	68	18 13S	178 47W
Lakeport, Calif., U.S.A.	122	39 1N	122 56W
Lakeport, Mich., U.S.A.	106	43 7N	82 30W
Lakes Entrance	75	37 50S	148 0 E
Lakeside, Ariz., U.S.A.	121	34 12N	109 59W
Lakeside, Calif., U.S.A.	123	32 52N	116 55W
Lakeside, Nebr., U.S.A.	118	42 5N	102 24W
Lakeview, Mich., U.S.A.	106	43 27N	85 17W
Lakeview, Oreg., U.S.A.	120	42 15N	120 22W
Lakewood, Calif., U.S.A.	123	33 51N	118 8W
Lakewood, N.J., U.S.A.	115	40 5N	74 13W
Lakewood, Ohio, U.S.A.	114	41 28N	81 50W
Lakhaniá	35	35 58N	27 54 E
Lakhipur, Assam, India	52	26 2N	90 18 E
Lakhipur, Assam, India	52	24 48N	93 0 E
Lakhonpheng	54	15 54N	105 34 E
Lakhpat	48	23 48N	68 47 E
Laki	8	64 4N	18 14W
Lakin	119	37 58N	101 18W
Lakitusaki →	102	54 21N	82 25W
Lakonikós Kólpos	35	36 40N	22 40 E
Lakota, Ivory C.	88	5 50N	5 30W
Lakota, U.S.A.	118	48 0N	98 22W
Laksefjorden	8	70 45N	26 50 E
Lakselv	8	70 2N	24 56 E
Laksham	52	23 14N	91 8 E
Lakshmi Kantapur	49	22 5N	88 20 E
Lakshmipur	52	22 58N	90 50 E
Lakuramau	69	2 54S	151 15 E
Lal Lal	74	37 38S	144 1 E
Lala Musa	48	32 40N	73 57 E
Lalago	94	3 28S	33 58 E
Lalapanzi	95	19 20S	30 15 E
Lalbert	74	35 38S	143 20 E
Lalganj	49	25 52N	85 13 E
Lalibela	91	12 2N	39 2 E
Lalin	61	45 12N	127 0 E
Lalín	22	42 40N	8 5W
Lalin He →	61	45 32N	125 40 E
Lalinde	20	44 50N	0 44 E
Lalitpur	49	24 42N	78 28 E
Lam	54	21 21N	106 31 E
Lam Pao Res.	54	16 50N	103 15 E
Lama Kara	89	9 30N	1 15 E
Lamaipum	52	25 40N	97 57 E
Lamap	68	16 26S	167 43 E
Lamar, Colo., U.S.A.	118	38 9N	102 35W
Lamar, Mo., U.S.A.	119	37 30N	94 20W
Lamarque	142	39 24S	65 40W
Lamas	136	6 28S	76 31W
Lamastre	21	44 59N	4 35 E
Lamballe	18	48 29N	2 31W
Lambaréné	92	0 41S	10 12 E
Lambasa	68	16 30S	179 10 E
Lambay I.	15	53 30N	6 0W
Lambayeque □	136	6 45S	80 0W
Lambert	118	47 44N	104 39W
Lambert, C.	69	4 11S	151 31 E
Lambert Glacier	143	71 0S	70 0 E
Lambesc	21	43 39N	5 16 E
Lambeth	106	42 54N	81 18W
Lámbia	35	37 52N	21 53 E
Lambon	69	4 45S	152 48 E
Lambro →	26	45 8N	9 32 E
Lambton	105	45 50N	71 5W
Lame	89	45 35N	106 40W
Lame Deer	120	45 45N	106 40W
Lamego	22	41 5N	7 52W
Lamèque	103	47 45N	64 38W
Lameroo	73	35 19S	140 33 E
Lamesa	119	32 45N	101 57W
Lamía	35	38 55N	22 26 E
Lamitan	57	6 40N	122 10 E
Lammermuir Hills	14	55 50N	2 40W
Lamoille	120	40 47N	115 31W
Lamon Bay	57	14 30N	122 20 E
Lamoni	116	40 37N	93 56W
Lamont, Can.	108	53 46N	112 50W
Lamont, Calif., U.S.A.	123	35 15N	118 55W
Lamont, Iowa, U.S.A.	116	42 35N	91 40W
Lampa	136	15 22S	70 22W
Lampang	54	18 18N	99 31 E
Lampasas	119	31 5N	98 10W
Lampaul	18	48 28N	5 7W
Lampazos de Naranjo	124	27 2N	100 32W
Lampedusa, I.	87	35 36N	12 40 E
Lampeter	13	52 6N	4 6W
Lampione, I.	87	35 33N	12 20 E
Lampman	109	49 25N	102 50W
Lamprey	109	58 33N	94 8W
Lampung □	56	5 30S	104 30 E
Lamu, Burma	52	19 14N	94 10 E
Lamu, Kenya	94	2 16S	40 55 E
Lamu □	94	2 0S	40 45 E
Lamud	136	6 10S	77 57W
Lamut, Tg.	56	3 50S	105 58 E
Lamy	121	35 30N	105 58W
Lan Xian	60	38 15N	111 35 E
Lan Yu	59	22 5N	121 35 E
Lanai I.	110	20 50N	156 55W
Lanak La	49	34 27N	79 32 E
Lanak'o Shank'ou = Lanak La	49	34 27N	79 32 E
Lanao, L.	57	7 52N	124 15 E
Lanark, Can.	107	45 1N	76 22W
Lanark, U.K.	14	55 40N	3 48W
Lancang	58	22 36N	99 58 E
Lancang Jiang →	58	21 40N	101 10 E
Lancashire □	12	53 40N	2 30W
Lancaster, Can.	104	45 10N	74 30W
Lancaster, U.K.	12	54 3N	2 48W
Lancaster, Calif., U.S.A.	123	34 47N	118 8W
Lancaster, Ky., U.S.A.	112	37 40N	84 40W
Lancaster, Mo., U.S.A.	116	40 31N	92 32W
Lancaster, N.H., U.S.A.	115	44 27N	71 33W
Lancaster, N.Y., U.S.A.	114	42 53N	78 43W
Lancaster, Pa., U.S.A.	115	40 4N	76 19W
Lancaster, S.C., U.S.A.	113	34 45N	80 47W
Lancaster, Wis., U.S.A.	116	42 48N	90 43W
Lancaster Sd.	144	74 13N	84 0W
Lancefield	74	37 18S	144 45 E
Lancer	109	50 48N	108 53W
Lanchow = Lanzhou	60	36 1N	103 52 E
Lanciano	27	42 15N	14 22 E
Lanco	142	39 24S	72 46W
Lancones	136	4 30S	80 30W
Lancun	61	36 25N	120 10 E
Łancut	32	50 10N	22 13 E
Lándana	92	5 11S	12 5 E
Landau, Bayern, Ger.	31	48 41N	12 41 E
Landau, Rhld-Pfz., Ger.	31	49 12N	8 7 E
Landeck	31	47 9N	10 34 E
Landen	16	50 45N	5 5 E
Lander	120	42 50N	108 49W
Lander →	78	22 0S	132 0 E
Landerneau	18	48 28N	4 17W
Landeryd	11	57 7N	13 15 E
Landes □	20	43 57N	0 48W
Landes, Les	20	44 20N	1 0W
Landete	24	39 56N	1 25W
Landi Kotal	48	34 7N	71 6 E
Landivisiau	18	48 31N	4 6W
Landor	79	25 10S	116 54 E
Landquart	31	46 58N	9 32 E
Landrecies	19	50 7N	3 40 E
Landrienne	104	48 30N	77 50W
Land's End	13	50 4N	5 43W
Landsberg	31	48 3N	10 52 E
Landsborough Cr. →	72	22 28S	144 35 E
Landsbro	11	57 24N	14 56 E
Landshut	31	48 31N	12 10 E
Landskrona	11	55 53N	12 50 E
Landstuhl	31	49 25N	7 34 E
Landvetter	11	57 41N	12 17 E
Lanesboro	115	41 57N	75 34W
Lanett	113	33 0N	85 15W
Lang Bay	108	49 45N	124 21W
Lang Lang	74	38 15S	145 34 E
Lang Qua	54	22 16N	104 27 E
Lang Shan	60	41 0N	106 30 E
Lang Son	54	21 52N	106 42 E
Lang Suan	55	9 57N	99 4 E
La'nga Co	49	30 45N	81 15 E
Lángadhás	35	40 46N	23 2 E
Langádhia	35	37 43N	22 1 E
Långan →	10	63 19N	14 44 E
Langara I.	108	54 14N	133 1W
Langatabbetje	135	4 59N	54 28W
Langdai	58	26 6N	105 21 E
Langdon	118	48 47N	98 24W
Langeac	20	45 7N	3 29 E
Langeais	18	47 20N	0 24 E
Langeb Baraka →	90	17 28N	36 50 E
Langeberge, C. Prov., S. Afr.	96	28 15S	22 33 E
Langeberge, C. Prov., S. Afr.	96	33 55S	21 40 E
Langeland	11	54 56N	10 48 E
Langen	31	49 59N	8 40 E
Langenburg	109	50 51N	101 43W
Langeness	30	54 34N	8 35 E
Langeoog	30	53 44N	7 33 E
Langeskov	11	55 22N	10 35 E
Langesund	10	59 0N	9 45 E
Länghem	11	57 36N	13 14 E
Langhirano	26	44 39N	10 16 E
Langholm	14	55 9N	2 59W
Langjökull	8	64 39N	20 12W
Langkawi, P.	55	6 25N	99 45 E
Langkon	56	6 30N	116 40 E
Langlade	103	46 50N	56 20W
Langlois	120	42 54N	124 26W
Langnau	31	46 56N	7 47 E
Langogne	20	44 43N	3 50 E
Langon	20	44 33N	0 16W
Langøya	8	68 45N	14 50 E
Langpran, Gunong	56	1 0N	114 23 E

Langres	**19**	47 52N	5 20 E
Langres, Plateau de	**19**	47 45N	5 3 E
Langsa	**56**	4 30N	97 57 E
Långsele	**10**	63 12N	17 4 E
Långshyttan	**10**	60 27N	16 2 E
Langtao	**52**	27 15N	97 34 E
Langting	**52**	25 31N	93 7 E
Langtry	**119**	29 50N	101 33W
Langu	**55**	6 53N	99 47 E
Languedoc	**20**	43 58N	4 0 E
Langxi	**59**	31 10N	119 12 E
Langxiangzhen	**60**	39 43N	116 8 E
Langzhong	**58**	31 38N	105 58 E
Lanigan	**109**	51 51N	105 2W
Lankao	**60**	34 48N	114 50 E
Lannemezan	**20**	43 8N	0 23 E
Lannilis	**18**	48 35N	4 32W
Lannion	**18**	48 46N	3 29W
Lanoraie	**105**	45 58N	73 13W
Lanouaille	**20**	45 24N	1 9 E
Lanping	**58**	26 28N	99 15 E
Lansdale	**115**	40 14N	75 18W
Lansdowne, Austral.	**77**	31 48 S	152 30 E
Lansdowne, Can.	**107**	44 24N	76 1W
Lansdowne House	**102**	52 14N	87 53W
Lansford	**115**	40 48N	75 55W
Lanshan	**59**	25 24N	112 10 E
Lansing	**117**	42 47N	84 40W
Lanslebourg	**21**	45 17N	6 52 E
Lant, Pulau	**56**	4 10 S	116 0 E
Lanta Yai, Ko	**55**	7 35N	99 3 E
Lantian	**60**	34 11N	109 20 E
Lanus	**140**	34 44 S	58 27W
Lanusei	**28**	39 53N	9 31 E
Lanxi	**59**	29 13N	119 28 E
Lanzarote	**84**	29 0N	13 40W
Lanzhou	**60**	36 1N	103 52 E
Lanzo Torinese	**26**	45 16N	7 29 E
Lao →	**29**	39 45N	15 45 E
Lao Bao	**54**	16 35N	106 30 E
Lao Cai	**54**	22 30N	103 57 E
Laoag	**57**	18 7N	120 34 E
Laoang	**57**	12 32N	125 8 E
Laoha He →	**61**	43 25N	120 35 E
Laois □	**15**	53 0N	7 20W
Laon	**19**	49 33N	3 35 E
Laona	**112**	45 32N	88 41W
Laos ■	**54**	17 45N	105 0 E
Lapa	**141**	25 46 S	49 44W
Lapalisse	**20**	46 15N	3 38 E
Laparan Cap	**57**	6 0N	120 0 E
Lapeer	**106**	43 3N	83 20W
Lapland = Lappland	**8**	68 7N	24 0 E
Laporte	**115**	41 27N	76 30W
Lapovo	**33**	44 10N	21 2 E
Lappland	**8**	68 7N	24 0 E
Laprairie	**115**	45 20N	73 30W
Laprida	**140**	37 34 S	60 45W
Laptev Sea	**41**	76 0N	125 0 E
Lapush	**120**	47 56N	124 33W
Lăpuşul →	**34**	47 25N	23 40 E
Lār	**47**	27 40N	54 14 E
Lara	**74**	38 2 S	144 26 E
Lara □	**134**	10 10N	69 50W
Larabanga	**88**	9 16N	1 56W
Laracha	**22**	43 15N	8 35W
Larache	**86**	35 10N	6 5W
Laragne-Monteglin	**21**	44 18N	5 49 E
Laramie	**118**	41 20N	105 38W
Laramie Mts.	**118**	42 0N	105 30W
Laranjeiras	**138**	10 48 S	37 10W
Laranjeiras do Sul	**141**	25 23 S	52 23W
Larantuka	**57**	8 21 S	122 55 E
Larap	**57**	14 18N	122 39 E
Larat	**57**	7 0 S	132 0 E
Laravale	**77**	28 6 S	152 57 E
Larde	**95**	16 28 S	39 43 E
Larder Lake	**102**	48 5N	79 40W
Lárdhos, Ákra	**35**	36 4N	28 10 E
Laredo, Spain	**24**	43 26N	3 28W
Laredo, U.S.A.	**119**	27 34N	99 29W
Laredo Sd.	**108**	52 30N	128 53W
Largeau (Faya)	**85**	17 58N	19 6 E
Largentière	**21**	44 34N	4 18 E
Largs	**14**	55 48N	4 51W
Lari	**26**	43 34N	10 35 E
Lariang	**57**	1 26 S	119 17 E
Larimore	**118**	47 55N	97 35W
Larino	**29**	41 48N	14 54 E
Lárisa	**35**	39 49N	22 28 E
Larkana	**48**	27 32N	68 18 E
Larnaca	**46**	35 0N	33 35 E
Larne	**15**	54 52N	5 50W
Larned	**118**	38 15N	99 10W
Larrey, Pt.	**78**	19 55 S	119 7 E
Larrimah	**78**	15 35 S	133 12 E
Larsen Ice Shelf	**143**	67 0 S	62 0W
Laru	**94**	2 54N	24 25 E
Larvik	**10**	59 4N	10 0 E
Laryak	**40**	61 15N	80 0 E
Larzac, Causse du	**20**	44 0N	3 17 E
Las Animas	**119**	38 8N	103 18W
Las Anod	**45**	8 26N	47 19 E
Las Blancos	**25**	37 38N	0 49W
Las Brenãs	**140**	27 5 S	61 7W
Las Cabezas de San Juan	**23**	37 0N	5 58W
Las Chimeneas	**123**	32 8N	116 5W
Las Coloradas	**142**	39 34 S	70 36W
Las Cruces	**121**	32 18N	106 50W
Las Flores	**140**	36 10 S	59 7W
Las Heras	**140**	32 51 S	68 49W
Las Horquetas	**142**	48 14 S	71 11W
Las Khoreh	**45**	11 10N	48 20 E
Las Lajas	**142**	38 30 S	70 25W
Las Lomas	**136**	4 40 S	80 10W
Las Lomitas	**140**	24 43 S	60 35W
Las Marismas	**23**	37 5N	6 20W
Las Mercedes	**134**	9 7N	66 24W
Las Navas de la Concepción	**23**	37 56N	5 30W
Las Navas de Tolosa	**23**	38 18N	3 38W
Las Palmas, Argent.	**140**	27 8 S	58 45W
Las Palmas, Canary Is.	**84**	28 10N	15 28W
Las Palmas □	**84**	28 10N	15 28W
Las Palmas →	**123**	32 12N	116 33W
Las Piedras	**141**	34 44 S	56 14W
Las Pipinas	**140**	35 30 S	57 19W
Las Plumas	**142**	43 40 S	67 15W
Las Rosas	**140**	32 30 S	61 35W
Las Tablas	**126**	7 49N	80 14W
Las Termas	**140**	27 29 S	64 52W
Las Varillas	**140**	31 50 S	62 50W
Las Vegas, N. Mex., U.S.A.	**121**	35 35N	105 10W
Las Vegas, Nev., U.S.A.	**123**	36 10N	115 5W
Lascano	**141**	33 35 S	54 12W
Lascaux	**20**	45 5N	1 10 E
Lascelles	**74**	35 34 S	142 34 E
Lashburn	**109**	53 10N	109 40W
Lashio	**52**	22 56N	97 45 E
Lashkar	**48**	26 10N	78 10 E
Łasin	**32**	53 30N	19 2 E
Laško	**27**	46 10N	15 16 E
Lassance	**139**	17 54 S	44 34W
Lassay	**18**	48 27N	0 30W
Lassen, Pk.	**120**	40 29N	121 31W
Last Mountain L.	**109**	51 5N	105 14W
Lastchance Cr. →	**122**	40 2N	121 15W
Lastoursville	**92**	0 55 S	12 38 E
Lastovo	**27**	42 46N	16 55 E
Lastovo, I.	**27**	42 46N	16 55 E
Lastovski Kanal	**27**	42 50N	17 0 E
Lat Yao	**54**	15 45N	99 48 E
Latacunga	**134**	0 50 S	78 35W
Latakia = Al Lādhiqīyah	**46**	35 30N	35 45 E
Latchford	**102**	47 20N	79 50W
Late	**68**	18 48 S	174 39W
Laterza	**29**	40 38N	16 47 E
Latham	**79**	29 44 S	116 20 E
Lathen	**30**	52 51N	7 21 E
Lathrop	**116**	39 33N	94 20W
Lathrop Wells	**123**	36 39N	116 24W
Latiano	**29**	40 33N	17 43 E
Latina	**28**	41 26N	12 53 E
Latisana	**27**	45 47N	13 1 E
Latium = Lazio	**27**	42 10N	12 30 E
Laton	**122**	36 26N	119 41W
Latorica →	**33**	48 28N	21 50 E
Latouche Treville, C.	**78**	18 27 S	121 49 E
Latrobe, Tas., Austral.	**72**	41 14 S	146 30 E
Latrobe, Vic., Austral.	**75**	38 8 S	146 44 E
Latrobe, U.S.A.	**114**	40 19N	79 21W
Latrónico	**29**	40 5N	16 0 E
Latrun	**44**	31 50N	34 58 E
Latulipe	**104**	47 26N	79 2W
Latur	**50**	18 25N	76 40 E
Latvian S.S.R. □	**36**	56 50N	24 0 E
Lau (Eastern) Group	**68**	17 0 S	178 30W
Lauca →	**136**	19 9 S	68 10W
Lauchhammer	**30**	51 35N	13 48 E
Lauenburg	**30**	53 23N	10 33 E
Lauffen	**31**	49 4N	9 9 E
Laugarbakki	**8**	65 20N	20 55W
Laujar	**25**	37 0N	2 54W
Launceston, Austral.	**72**	41 24 S	147 8 E
Launceston, U.K.	**13**	50 38N	4 21W
Laune →	**15**	52 5N	9 40W
Laupheim	**31**	48 13N	9 53 E
Laura	**72**	15 32 S	144 32 E
Laureana di Borrello	**29**	38 28N	16 5 E
Laurel, Ind., U.S.A.	**117**	39 31N	85 11W
Laurel, Miss., U.S.A.	**119**	31 41N	89 9W
Laurel, Mont., U.S.A.	**120**	45 46N	108 49W
Laurel Hill	**76**	35 34 S	148 6 E
Laurencekirk	**14**	56 50N	2 30W
Laurens	**113**	34 32N	82 2W
Laurentian Plat.	**103**	52 0N	70 0W
Laurentides, Parc Prov. des	**105**	47 45N	71 15W
Lauria	**29**	40 3N	15 50 E
Laurie I.	**143**	60 44 S	44 37W
Laurie L.	**109**	56 35N	101 57W
Laurier-Station	**105**	46 32N	71 38W
Laurierville	**105**	46 18N	71 39W
Laurieton	**77**	31 39 S	152 48 E
Laurinburg	**113**	34 50N	79 25W
Laurium	**112**	47 14N	88 26W
Lausanne	**31**	46 32N	6 38 E
Laut, Kepulauan	**56**	4 45N	108 0 E
Laut Ketil, Kepulauan	**56**	4 45 S	115 40 E
Lautaro	**142**	38 31 S	72 27W
Lauterbach	**30**	50 39N	9 23 E
Lauterecken	**31**	49 38N	7 35 E
Lautoka	**68**	17 37 S	177 27 E
Lauzon	**105**	46 48N	71 10W
Lava Hot Springs	**120**	42 38N	112 1W
Lavadores	**22**	42 14N	8 41W
Lavagna	**26**	44 18N	9 22 E
Laval, Can.	**105**	45 35N	73 45W
Laval, France	**18**	48 4N	0 48W
Lavalle	**140**	28 15 S	65 15W
Lavaltrie	**105**	45 53N	73 17W
Lavandou, Le	**21**	43 8N	6 22 E
Lavant Sta.	**107**	45 3N	76 42W
Lávara	**35**	41 19N	26 22 E
Lavardac	**20**	44 12N	0 20 E
Lavaur	**20**	43 30N	1 49 E
Lavaveix	**20**	46 5N	2 8 E
Lavelanet	**20**	42 57N	1 51 E
Lavello	**29**	41 4N	15 47 E
Laverendrye Prov. Park	**102**	46 15N	17 15W
Laverlochère	**104**	47 26N	79 18W
Laverne	**119**	36 43N	99 58W
Lavers Hill	**74**	38 40 S	143 25 E
Laverton	**79**	28 44 S	122 29 E
Lavi	**44**	32 47N	35 25 E
Lavieille, L.	**107**	45 51N	78 14W
Lavos	**22**	40 6N	8 49W
Lavras	**139**	21 20 S	45 0W
Lavre	**23**	38 46N	8 22W
Lavrentiya	**41**	65 35N	171 0W
Lávrion	**35**	37 40N	24 4 E
Lavumisa	**97**	27 20 S	31 55 E
Lawas	**56**	4 55N	115 25 E
Lawele	**57**	5 16 S	123 3 E
Lawksawk	**52**	21 15N	96 52 E
Lawn Hill	**72**	18 36 S	138 33 E
Lawra	**88**	10 39N	2 51W
Lawrence, Ind., U.S.A.	**117**	39 50N	86 2W
Lawrence, Kans., U.S.A.	**118**	39 0N	95 10W
Lawrence, Mass., U.S.A.	**115**	42 40N	71 9W
Lawrenceburg, Ind., U.S.A.	**117**	39 5N	84 50W
Lawrenceburg, Ky., U.S.A.	**117**	38 2N	84 54W
Lawrenceburg, Tenn., U.S.A.	**113**	35 12N	87 19W
Lawrenceville, Ga., U.S.A.	**113**	33 55N	83 59W
Lawrenceville, Ill., U.S.A.	**117**	38 44N	87 41W
Laws	**122**	37 24N	118 20W
Lawson	**116**	39 26N	94 12W
Lawton, Mich., U.S.A.	**117**	42 10N	85 50W
Lawton, Tex., U.S.A.	**119**	34 33N	98 25W
Lawu	**57**	7 40 S	111 13 E
Laxford, L.	**14**	58 25N	5 10W
Laxmeshwar	**51**	15 9N	75 28 E
Layon →	**18**	47 20N	0 45W
Laysan I.	**67**	25 30N	167 0W
Laytonville	**120**	39 44N	123 29W
Laza	**52**	26 30N	97 38 E
Lazio □	**27**	42 10N	12 30 E
Lea →	**13**	51 30N	0 10W
Leach	**55**	12 21N	103 46 E
Lead	**118**	44 20N	103 40W
Leader	**109**	50 50N	109 30W
Leadhills	**14**	55 25N	3 47W
Leadville, Austral.	**77**	32 1 S	149 38 E
Leadville, U.S.A.	**121**	39 17N	106 23W
Leaf →	**119**	31 0N	88 45W
Leakey	**119**	29 45N	99 45W
Lealui	**93**	15 10 S	23 2 E
Leamington, Can.	**106**	42 3N	82 36W
Leamington, U.K.	**13**	52 18N	1 32W
Leamington, U.S.A.	**120**	39 37N	112 17W
Le'an	**59**	27 22N	115 48 E
Leandro Norte Alem	**141**	27 34 S	55 15W
Learmonth	**78**	22 13 S	114 10 E
Leask	**109**	53 5N	106 45W
Leavenworth, Ind., U.S.A.	**117**	38 12N	86 21W
Leavenworth, Mo., U.S.A.	**118**	39 25N	95 0W
Leavenworth, Wash., U.S.A.	**120**	47 44N	120 37W
Leawood	**116**	38 57N	94 37W
Łeba	**32**	54 45N	17 32 E
Lebak	**57**	6 32N	124 5 E
Lebam	**122**	46 34N	123 33W
Lebanon, Ill., U.S.A.	**116**	38 38N	89 49W
Lebanon, Ind., U.S.A.	**117**	40 3N	86 28W
Lebanon, Kans., U.S.A.	**118**	39 50N	98 35W
Lebanon, Ky., U.S.A.	**112**	37 35N	85 15W
Lebanon, Mo., U.S.A.	**116**	37 40N	92 40W
Lebanon, Ohio, U.S.A.	**117**	39 26N	84 13W
Lebanon, Oreg., U.S.A.	**120**	44 31N	122 57W
Lebanon, Pa., U.S.A.	**115**	40 20N	76 28W
Lebanon, Tenn., U.S.A.	**113**	36 15N	86 20W
Lebanon ■	**46**	34 0N	36 0 E
Lebanon Junction	**117**	37 50N	85 44W
Lebec	**123**	34 50N	118 59W
Lebedin	**36**	50 35N	34 30 E
Lebedyan	**37**	53 0N	39 10 E
Lebel-sur-Quévillon	**104**	49 3N	76 59W
Lebombo-berge	**97**	24 30 S	32 0 E
Lębork	**32**	54 33N	17 46 E
Lebrija	**23**	36 53N	6 5W
Lebu	**140**	37 40 S	73 47W
Lecce	**29**	40 20N	18 10 E
Lecco	**26**	45 50N	9 27 E
Lecco, L. di.	**26**	45 51N	9 22 E
Lécera	**24**	41 13N	0 43W
Lech	**31**	47 13N	10 9 E
Lech →	**31**	48 44N	10 56 E
Lechang	**59**	25 10N	113 20 E
Lechtaler Alpen	**31**	47 15N	10 30 E
Lectoure	**20**	43 56N	0 38 E
Leczyca	**32**	52 5N	19 15 E
Ledbury	**13**	52 3N	2 25W
Ledesma	**22**	41 6N	5 59W
Ledong	**54**	18 41N	109 5 E
Leduc	**108**	53 15N	113 30W
Ledyczek	**32**	53 33N	16 59 E
Lee, Mass., U.S.A.	**115**	42 17N	73 18W
Lee, Nev., U.S.A.	**120**	40 35N	115 36W
Lee →	**15**	51 50N	8 30W
Lee Vining	**122**	37 58N	119 7W
Leech L.	**118**	47 9N	94 23W
Leedey	**119**	35 53N	99 24W
Leeds, U.K.	**12**	53 48N	1 34W
Leeds, U.S.A.	**113**	33 32N	86 30W
Leek	**12**	53 7N	2 2W
Leer	**30**	53 13N	7 29 E
Lee's Summit	**116**	38 55N	94 23W
Leesburg, Fla., U.S.A.	**113**	28 47N	81 52W
Leesburg, Ohio, U.S.A.	**117**	39 21N	83 33W
Leeston	**81**	43 45 S	172 19 E
Leesville	**119**	31 12N	93 15W
Leeton	**75**	34 33 S	146 23 E
Leetonia	**114**	40 53N	80 45W
Leeuwarden	**16**	53 15N	5 48 E
Leeuwin, C.	**79**	34 20 S	115 9 E
Leeward Is., Pac. Oc.	**67**	16 0 S	147 0W
Leeward Is., W. Indies	**127**	16 30N	63 30W
Lefebvre	**105**	47 12N	69 49W
Lefors	**119**	35 30N	100 50W
Lefroy	**106**	44 16N	79 34W
Lefroy, L.	**79**	31 21 S	121 40 E
Legal	**108**	53 55N	113 35W
Legazpi	**57**	13 10N	123 45 E
Legendre I.	**78**	20 22 S	116 55 E
Leghorn = Livorno	**26**	43 32N	10 18 E
Legion	**95**	21 25 S	28 30 E
Legionowo	**32**	52 25N	20 50 E
Legnago	**27**	45 10N	11 19 E
Legnano	**26**	45 35N	8 55 E
Legnica	**32**	51 12N	16 10 E
Legrad	**27**	46 17N	16 51 E
Legume	**77**	28 20 S	152 19 E
Leh	**49**	34 9N	77 35 E
Lehi	**120**	40 20N	111 51W
Lehighton	**115**	40 50N	75 44W
Lehrte	**30**	52 22N	9 58 E
Lehututu	**96**	23 54 S	21 55 E
Lei Shui →	**59**	26 55N	112 35 E
Leiah	**48**	30 58N	70 58 E
Leibnitz	**33**	46 47N	15 34 E
Leibo	**58**	28 11N	103 34 E
Leicester	**13**	52 39N	1 9W
Leicester □	**13**	52 40N	1 10W
Leichhardt →	**72**	17 35 S	139 48 E
Leichhardt Ra.	**72**	20 46 S	147 40 E
Leiden	**16**	52 9N	4 30 E
Leie →	**16**	51 2N	3 45 E
Leigh Creek	**73**	30 28 S	138 24 E
Leikthо	**52**	19 13N	96 35 E
Leine →	**30**	52 20N	9 50 E
Leinster □	**15**	53 0N	7 10W
Leinster, Mt.	**15**	52 38N	6 47W
Leipzig	**30**	51 20N	12 23 E
Leipzig □	**30**	51 20N	12 30 E
Leiria	**23**	39 46N	8 53W
Leiria □	**23**	39 46N	8 53W

Leisler, Mt. **78** 23 23S 129 20E
Leitchville **74** 35 54S 144 18E
Leith **14** 55 59N 3 10W
Leith Hill **13** 51 10N 0 23W
Leitha → **33** 48 0N 16 35E
Leitrim **15** 54 0N 8 5W
Leitrim □ **15** 54 8N 8 0W
Leiyang **59** 26 27N 112 45E
Leiza **24** 43 5N 1 55W
Leizhou Bandao **58** 21 0N 110 0E
Leizhou Wan **59** 20 50N 110 20E
Lejeune **105** 47 46N 68 34W
Lek → **16** 52 0N 6 0E
Leksula **57** 3 46S 126 31E
Leland **119** 33 25N 90 52W
Leland Lakes **109** 60 0N 110 59W
Leleque **142** 42 28S 71 0W
Lelu **52** 19 4N 95 30E
Lelystad **16** 52 30N 5 25E
Lema **89** 12 58N 4 13E
Léman, Lac **31** 46 26N 6 30E
Lemay **116** 38 32N 90 16W
Lemera **94** 3 0S 28 55E
Lemery **57** 13 51N 120 56E
Lemgo **30** 52 2N 8 52E
Lemhi Ra. **120** 44 30N 113 30W
Lemieux **105** 46 18N 72 7W
Lemieux, L. **104** 50 19N 74 38W
Lemmer **16** 52 51N 5 43E
Lemmon **118** 45 59N 102 10W
Lemoine, L. **104** 48 0N 78 0W
Lemon Grove **123** 32 45N 117 2W
Lemont **117** 41 40N 88 0W
Lemoore **122** 36 23N 119 46W
Lempdes **20** 45 22N 3 17E
Lemvig **11** 56 33N 8 20E
Lemyethna **52** 17 36N 95 9E
Lena → **41** 72 52N 126 40E
Lencloître **18** 46 50N 0 20E
Lençóis **139** 12 35S 41 24W
Lendinara **27** 45 4N 11 37E
Lengau de Vaca, Pta. **140** 30 14S 71 38W
Lengerich **30** 52 12N 7 50E
Lenggong **55** 5 6N 100 58E
Lenggries **31** 47 41N 11 34E
Lenhovda **11** 57 0N 15 16E
Lenin **39** 48 20N 40 56E
Leninabad **40** 40 17N 69 37E
Leninakan **39** 40 47N 43 50E
Leningrad **36** 59 55N 30 20E
Leninogorsk **40** 50 20N 83 30E
Leninsk **39** 48 40N 45 15E
Leninsk-Kuznetskiy **40** 54 44N 86 10E
Leninskaya Sloboda **37** 56 7N 44 29E
Leninskoye, R.S.F.S.R., U.S.S.R. **37** 58 23N 47 3E
Leninskoye, R.S.F.S.R., U.S.S.R. **41** 47 56N 132 38E
Lenk **31** 46 27N 7 28E
Lenmalu **57** 1 45S 130 15E
Lenne → **30** 51 25N 7 30E
Lennox Head **77** 28 46S 153 37E
Lennox, I. **142** 55 18S 66 50W
Lennoxville **105** 45 22N 71 51W
Leno **26** 45 24N 10 14E
Lenoir **113** 35 55N 81 36W
Lenoir City **113** 35 40N 84 20W
Lenora **118** 39 39N 100 1W
Lenore L. **109** 52 30N 104 59W
Lenox, Iowa, U.S.A. **116** 40 53N 94 34W
Lenox, Mass., U.S.A. **115** 42 20N 73 18W
Lens **19** 50 26N 2 50E
Lensk (Mukhtuya) **41** 60 48N 114 55E
Lenskoye **38** 45 3N 34 1E
Lentini **29** 37 18N 15 0E
Lenwood **123** 34 53N 117 7W
Lenzen **30** 53 6N 11 26E
Léo **88** 11 3N 2 2W
Leoben **33** 47 22N 15 5E
Leola **118** 45 47N 98 58W
Leominster, U.K. **13** 52 15N 2 43W
Leominster, U.S.A. **115** 42 32N 71 45W
Léon **20** 43 53N 1 18W
León, Mexico **124** 21 7N 101 30W
León, Nic. **126** 12 20N 86 51W
León, Spain **22** 42 38N 5 34W
Leon **116** 40 40N 93 40W
León □ **22** 42 40N 5 55W
León, Montañas de **22** 42 30N 6 18W
Leonardtown **112** 38 19N 76 39W
Leonforte **29** 37 39N 14 22E
Leongatha **74** 38 30S 145 58E
Leonídhion **35** 37 9N 22 52E
Leonora **79** 28 49S 121 19E
Leopold **74** 38 13S 144 28E
Léopold II, Lac = Mai-Ndombe **92** 2 0S 18 20E
Leopoldina **139** 21 28S 42 40W
Leopoldo Bulhões **139** 16 37S 48 46W
Leopoldsburg **16** 51 7N 5 13E
Léopoldville = Kinshasa **92** 4 20S 15 15E
Leoti **118** 38 31N 101 19W
Leoville **109** 53 39N 107 33W
Lépa, L. do **96** 17 0S 19 0E
Lepe **23** 37 15N 7 12W
Lepel **36** 54 50N 28 40E
Lepikha **41** 64 45N 125 55E
Leping **59** 28 47N 117 7E
Lepontino, Alpi **26** 46 22N 8 27E
Leptis Magna **87** 32 40N 14 12E
Lequeitio **24** 43 20N 2 32W
Lercara Friddi **28** 37 42N 13 36E
Lerdo **124** 25 32N 103 32W
Léré **92** 9 39N 14 13E
Lere **89** 9 43N 9 18E
Leribe **97** 28 51S 28 3E
Lérici **26** 44 4N 9 58E
Lérida **24** 41 37N 0 39E
Lérida □ **24** 42 6N 1 0E
Lérins, Is. de **21** 43 31N 7 3E
Lerma **22** 42 0N 3 47W
Léros **35** 37 10N 26 50E
Lérouville **19** 48 50N 5 30E
Lerwick **14** 60 10N 1 10W
Léry **105** 45 21N 73 48W
Lesbos, I. = Lésvos **35** 39 10N 26 20E
Leshan **58** 29 33N 103 41E
Lésina, L. di **27** 41 53N 15 25E
Lesja **10** 62 7N 8 51E
Lesjaverk **10** 62 12N 8 34E
Leskov, I. **143** 56 0S 28 0W
Leskovac **33** 43 0N 21 58E
Leslie, Ark., U.S.A. **119** 35 50N 92 35W
Leslie, Mich., U.S.A. **117** 42 27N 84 26W
Lesneven **18** 48 35N 4 20W
Lešnica **33** 44 39N 19 20E
Lesnoye **36** 58 15N 35 18E
Lesotho ■ **97** 29 40S 28 0E
Lesozavodsk **41** 45 30N 133 29E
Lesparre-Médoc **20** 45 18N 0 57W
Lessay **18** 49 14N 1 30W
Lesse → **16** 50 15N 4 54E
Lesser Antilles **127** 15 0N 61 0W
Lesser Slave L. **108** 55 30N 115 25W
Lessines **16** 50 42N 3 50E
Lester **122** 47 12N 121 29W
Lestock **109** 51 19N 103 59W
Lesuer I. **78** 13 50S 127 17E
Lesuma **96** 17 58S 25 12E
Lésvos **35** 39 10N 26 20E
Leszno **32** 51 50N 16 30E
Letchworth **13** 51 58N 0 13W
Letea, Ostrov **34** 45 18N 29 20E
Lethbridge, Austral. **74** 37 58S 144 6E
Lethbridge, Can. **108** 49 45N 112 45W
Lethem **135** 3 20N 59 50W
Leti **57** 8 10S 127 40E
Leti, Kepulauan **57** 8 10S 128 0E
Letiahau → **96** 21 16S 24 0E
Leticia **134** 4 9S 70 0W
Leting **61** 39 23N 118 55E
Letlhakeng **96** 24 0S 24 59E
Letpadan **52** 17 45N 95 45E
Letpan **52** 19 28N 94 10E
Letterkenny **15** 54 57N 7 42W
Leu **34** 44 10N 24 0E
Leucadia **123** 33 4N 117 18W
Leucate **20** 42 56N 3 3E
Leucate, Étang de **20** 42 50N 3 0E
Leuk **31** 46 19N 7 37E
Leuser, G. **56** 3 46N 97 12E
Leutkirch **31** 47 49N 10 1E
Leuven (Louvain) **16** 50 52N 4 42E
Leuze, Hainaut, Belg. **16** 50 36N 3 37E
Leuze, Namur, Belg. **16** 50 33N 4 54E
Lev Tolstoy **37** 53 13N 39 29E
Levack **106** 46 38N 81 23W
Levádhia **35** 38 27N 22 54E
Levan **120** 39 37N 111 52W
Levant, I. du **21** 43 3N 6 28E
Lévanto **26** 44 10N 9 37E
Levanzo, I. **28** 38 0N 12 19E
Levelland **119** 33 38N 102 23W
Leven **14** 56 12N 3 0W
Leven, Banc du **97** 12 30S 47 45E
Leven, L. **14** 56 12N 3 22W
Levens **21** 43 50N 7 12E
Leveque C. **78** 16 20S 123 0E
Leverano **29** 40 16N 18 0E
Levering **106** 45 38N 84 47W
Leverkusen **30** 51 2N 6 59E
Levet **19** 46 56N 2 22E
Levice **33** 48 13N 18 35E
Levick, Mt. **143** 75 0S 164 0E
Levico **27** 46 0N 11 18E
Levie **21** 41 40N 9 7E
Levier **19** 46 58N 6 8E
Levin **80** 40 37S 175 18E
Lévis **105** 46 48N 71 9W
Levis, L. **108** 62 37N 117 58W
Levítha **35** 37 0N 26 28E
Levittown, N.Y., U.S.A. **115** 40 41N 73 31W
Levittown, Pa., U.S.A. **115** 40 10N 74 51W
Lévka **35** 35 18N 24 3E
Levkás **35** 38 40N 20 43E
Levkôsia = Nicosia **46** 35 10N 33 25E
Levoča **32** 49 2N 20 35E
Levroux **19** 47 0N 1 38E
Levski **34** 43 21N 25 10E
Levskigrad **34** 42 38N 24 47E
Levuka **68** 17 34S 179 0E
Lewe **52** 19 38N 96 7E
Lewellen **118** 41 22N 102 5W
Lewes, U.K. **13** 50 53N 0 2E
Lewes, U.S.A. **112** 38 45N 75 8W
Lewis → **122** 45 51N 122 48W
Lewis, Butt of **14** 58 30N 6 12W
Lewis, I. **14** 58 10N 6 40W
Lewis Ra., Austral. **78** 20 3S 128 50E
Lewis Ra., U.S.A. **120** 48 0N 113 15W
Lewisburg, Ohio, U.S.A. **117** 39 51N 84 33W
Lewisburg, Pa., U.S.A. **114** 40 57N 76 57W
Lewisburg, Tenn., U.S.A. **113** 35 29N 86 46W
Lewisport **117** 37 56N 86 54W
Lewisporte **103** 49 15N 55 3W
Lewiston, Idaho, U.S.A. **120** 46 25N 117 0W
Lewiston, Mich., U.S.A. **106** 44 53N 84 18W
Lewiston, Utah, U.S.A. **120** 41 58N 111 56W
Lewistown, Ill., U.S.A. **116** 40 24N 90 9W
Lewistown, Mont., U.S.A. **120** 47 0N 109 25W
Lewistown, Pa., U.S.A. **114** 40 37N 77 33W
Lexington, Ill., U.S.A. **117** 40 37N 88 47W
Lexington, Ky., U.S.A. **117** 38 6N 84 30W
Lexington, Mich., U.S.A. **106** 43 15N 82 30W
Lexington, Miss., U.S.A. **119** 33 8N 90 2W
Lexington, Mo., U.S.A. **116** 39 7N 93 55W
Lexington, N.C., U.S.A. **113** 35 50N 80 13W
Lexington, Nebr., U.S.A. **118** 40 48N 99 45W
Lexington, Ohio, U.S.A. **114** 40 39N 82 35W
Lexington, Oreg., U.S.A. **120** 45 29N 119 46W
Lexington, Tenn., U.S.A. **113** 35 38N 88 25W
Lexington Park **112** 38 16N 76 27W
Lexton **74** 37 16S 143 31E
Leyburn **77** 28 1S 151 35E
Leye **58** 24 48N 106 29E
Leyre → **20** 44 39N 1 1W
Leyte **57** 11 0N 125 0E
Lezay **20** 46 17N 0 0E
Lezha **35** 41 47N 19 42E
Lezhi **58** 30 19N 104 58E
Lézignan-Corbières **20** 43 13N 2 43E
Lezoux **20** 45 49N 3 21E
Lgov **36** 51 42N 35 16E
Lhasa **62** 29 25N 90 58E
Lhazê **62** 29 5N 87 38E
Lhokseumawe **56** 5 10N 97 10E
Lhuntsi Dzong **52** 27 39N 91 10E
Li **54** 17 48N 98 57E
Li Shui → **59** 29 24N 112 1E
Li Xian, Gansu, China **60** 34 10N 105 5E
Li Xian, Hebei, China **60** 38 30N 115 35E
Li Xian, Hunan, China **59** 29 36N 111 42E
Li Xian, Sichuan, China **58** 31 23N 103 13E
Liádhoi **35** 36 50N 26 11E
Liamena **77** 31 58S 149 22E
Lian Xian **59** 24 51N 112 22E
Liancheng **59** 25 42N 116 40E
Lianga **57** 8 38N 126 6E
Liangcheng, Nei Mongol Zizhiqu, China **60** 40 28N 112 25E
Liangcheng, Shandong, China **61** 35 32N 119 37E
Liangdang **60** 33 56N 106 18E
Lianghekou **58** 29 11N 108 44E
Liangping **58** 30 38N 107 47E
Lianjiang, Fujian, China **59** 26 12N 119 27E
Lianjiang, Guangdong, China **59** 21 40N 110 20E
Lianping **59** 24 26N 114 30E
Lianshan **59** 24 38N 112 8E
Lianshanguan **61** 40 53N 123 43E
Lianshui **61** 33 42N 119 20E
Lianyuan **59** 27 40N 111 38E
Lianyungang **61** 34 43N 119 28E
Liao He → **61** 41 0N 121 50E
Liaocheng **60** 36 28N 115 58E
Liaodong Bandao **61** 40 0N 122 30E
Liaodong Wan **61** 40 20N 121 10E
Liaoning □ **61** 42 0N 122 0E
Liaoyang **61** 41 15N 122 58E
Liaoyuan **61** 42 58N 125 2E
Liaozhong **61** 41 23N 122 50E
Liapádhes **35** 39 42N 19 40E
Liard → **108** 61 51N 121 18W
Liari **48** 25 37N 66 30E
Líbano **134** 4 55N 75 4W
Libau = Liepaja **36** 56 30N 21 0E
Libby **120** 48 20N 115 33W
Libenge **92** 3 40N 18 55E
Liberal, Kans., U.S.A. **119** 37 4N 101 0W
Liberal, Mo., U.S.A. **119** 37 35N 94 30W
Liberdade **136** 10 5S 70 20W
Liberdade → **137** 9 40S 52 17W
Liberec **32** 50 47N 15 7E
Liberia **126** 10 40N 85 30W
Liberia ■ **88** 6 30N 9 30W
Libertad **134** 8 20N 69 37W
Libertad, La **126** 16 47N 90 7W
Libertad, La □ **136** 8 0S 78 30W
Liberty, Ind., U.S.A. **117** 39 38N 84 56W
Liberty, Mo., U.S.A. **116** 39 15N 94 24W
Liberty, Tex., U.S.A. **119** 30 5N 94 50W
Liberty Center **117** 41 27N 84 1W
Libertyville **117** 42 18N 87 57W
Libo **58** 25 22N 107 53E
Libobo, Tanjung **57** 0 54S 128 28E
Libourne **20** 44 55N 0 14W
Libramont **16** 49 55N 5 23E
Libreville **92** 0 25N 9 26E
Libya ■ **85** 27 0N 17 0E
Libyan Plateau = Ed-Déffa **90** 30 40N 26 30E
Licantén **140** 35 55S 72 0W
Licata **28** 37 6N 13 55E
Licheng **60** 36 28N 113 20E
Lichfield **12** 52 40N 1 50W
Lichinga **95** 13 13S 35 11E
Lichtenburg **96** 26 8S 26 8E
Lichtenfels **31** 50 7N 11 4E
Lichuan, Hubei, China **58** 30 18N 108 57E
Lichuan, Jiangxi, China **59** 27 18N 116 55E
Licking, South Fork → **117** 38 40N 84 19W
Licola **75** 37 39S 146 39E
Licosa, Punta **29** 40 15N 14 53E
Lida, U.S.A. **121** 37 30N 117 30W
Lida, U.S.S.R. **36** 53 53N 25 15E
Lidhult **11** 56 50N 13 27E
Lidingö **10** 59 22N 18 8E
Lidköping **11** 58 31N 13 14E
Lido, Italy **27** 45 25N 12 23E
Lido, Niger **89** 12 54N 3 44E
Lido di Ostia **28** 41 44N 12 14E
Lidzbark Warminski **32** 54 7N 20 34E
Liebenwalde **30** 52 51N 13 23E
Lieberose **30** 51 59N 14 18E
Liechtenstein ■ **31** 47 8N 9 35E
Liège **16** 50 38N 5 35E
Liège □ **16** 50 32N 5 35E
Lienart **94** 3 3N 25 31E
Lienyünchiangshih = Lianyungang **61** 34 40N 119 11E
Lienz **33** 46 50N 12 46E
Liepaja **36** 56 30N 21 0E
Lier **16** 51 7N 4 34E
Liévin **19** 50 24N 2 47E
Lièvre → **104** 45 31N 75 26W
Liezen **33** 47 34N 14 15E
Liffey → **15** 53 21N 6 20W
Lifford **15** 54 50N 7 30W
Liffré **18** 48 12N 1 30W
Lifjell **10** 59 27N 8 45E
Lifuka **68** 19 48S 174 21W
Lightning Ridge **73** 29 22S 148 0E
Lignano **27** 45 42N 13 8E
Ligny-en-Barrois **19** 48 36N 5 20E
Ligny-le-Châtel **19** 47 54N 3 45E
Ligoúrion **35** 37 37N 23 2E
Ligua, La **140** 32 30S 71 16W
Ligueil **18** 47 2N 0 49E
Liguria □ **26** 44 30N 9 0E
Ligurian Sea **26** 43 20N 9 0E
Lihir Group **69** 3 0S 152 35E
Lihou Reefs and Cays **72** 17 25S 151 40E
Lihue **110** 21 59N 159 24W
Lijiang **58** 26 55N 100 20E
Likasi **95** 10 55S 26 48E
Likati **92** 3 20N 24 0E
Likhoslavl **36** 57 12N 35 30E
Likhovski **39** 48 10N 40 10E

Likoma I. **95** 12 3S 34 45 E
Likumburu **95** 9 43S 35 8 E
Lilimur **74** 36 23S 141 11 E
Liling **59** 27 42N 113 29 E
Lille **19** 50 38N 3 3 E
Lille Bælt **11** 55 20N 9 45 E
Lillebonne **18** 49 30N 0 32 E
Lillehammer **10** 61 8N 10 30 E
Lillers **19** 50 35N 2 28 E
Lillesand **11** 58 15N 8 23 E
Lilleshall **13** 52 45N 2 22W
Lillestrøm **10** 59 58N 11 5 E
Lillian Point, Mt. **79** 27 40S 126 6 E
Lillo **24** 39 45N 3 20W
Lillooet → **108** 49 15N 121 57W
Lilongwe **95** 14 0S 33 48 E
Liloy **57** 8 4N 122 39 E
Lilydale **74** 37 46S 145 20 E
Lim → **33** 43 0N 19 40 E
Lima, Indon. **57** 3 37S 128 4 E
Lima, Peru **136** 12 0S 77 0W
Lima, Sweden **10** 60 55N 13 20 E
Lima, Mont., U.S.A. **120** 44 41N 112 38W
Lima, Ohio, U.S.A. **117** 40 42N 84 5W
Lima □ **136** 12 3S 77 3W
Lima → **22** 41 41N 8 50W
Limages **104** 45 20N 75 16W
Limassol **46** 34 42N 33 1 E
Limavady **15** 55 3N 6 58W
Limavady □ **15** 55 0N 6 55W
Limay → **142** 39 0S 68 0W
Limay Mahuida **140** 37 10S 66 45W
Limbang **56** 4 42N 115 6 E
Limbara, Monti **28** 40 50N 9 10 E
Limbdi **48** 22 34N 71 51 E
Limbri **77** 31 3S 151 5 E
Limbunya **78** 17 14S 129 50 E
Limburg **31** 50 22N 8 4 E
Limburg □, Belg. **16** 51 2N 5 25 E
Limburg □, Neth. **16** 51 20N 5 55 E
Limedsforsen **10** 60 52N 13 25 E
Limeira **141** 22 35S 47 28W
Limerick **15** 52 40N 8 38W
Limerick □ **15** 52 30N 8 50W
Limestone **114** 42 2N 78 39W
Limestone → **109** 56 31N 94 7W
Limevale **77** 28 44S 151 12 E
Limfjorden **11** 56 55N 9 0 E
Limia → **22** 41 41N 8 50W
Limmared **11** 57 34N 13 20 E
Limmen Bight **72** 14 40S 135 35 E
Limmen Bight → **72** 15 7S 135 44 E
Límni **35** 38 43N 23 18 E
Límnos **35** 39 50N 25 5 E
Limoeiro **138** 7 52S 35 27W
Limoeiro do Norte **138** 5 5S 38 0W
Limoges, Can. **107** 45 20N 75 15W
Limoges, France **20** 45 50N 1 15 E
Limón **126** 10 0N 83 2W
Limon **118** 39 18N 103 38W
Limone Piemonte **26** 44 12N 7 32 E
Limousin **20** 46 0N 1 0 E
Limousin, Plateaux du **20** 46 0N 1 0 E
Limoux **20** 43 4N 2 12 E
Limpopo → **97** 25 15S 33 30 E
Limuru **94** 1 2S 36 35 E
Lin Xian **60** 37 57N 110 58 E
Lin'an **59** 30 15N 119 42 E
Linares, Chile **140** 35 50S 71 40W
Linares, Colomb. **134** 1 23N 77 31W
Linares, Mexico **125** 24 50N 99 40W
Linares, Spain **25** 38 10N 3 40W
Linares □ **140** 36 0S 71 0W
Linas Mte. **28** 39 25N 8 38 E
Lincang **58** 23 58N 100 1 E
Lincheng **60** 37 25N 114 30 E
Linchuan **59** 27 57N 116 15 E
Lincoln, Argent. **140** 34 55S 61 30W
Lincoln, Can. **106** 43 10N 79 29W
Lincoln, N.Z. **81** 43 38S 172 30 E
Lincoln, U.K. **12** 53 14N 0 32W
Lincoln, Calif., U.S.A. **122** 38 54N 121 17W
Lincoln, Ill., U.S.A. **116** 40 10N 89 20W
Lincoln, Kans., U.S.A. **118** 39 6N 98 9W
Lincoln, Maine, U.S.A. **103** 45 27N 68 29W
Lincoln, Mich., U.S.A. **106** 44 41N 83 25W
Lincoln, N. Mex., U.S.A. **121** 33 30N 105 26W
Lincoln, N.H., U.S.A. **115** 44 3N 71 40W
Lincoln, Nebr., U.S.A. **118** 40 50N 96 42W
Lincoln □ **12** 53 14N 0 32W
Lincoln Sea **144** 84 0N 55 0W
Lincoln Wolds **12** 53 20N 0 5W
Lincolnton **113** 35 30N 81 15W
Lind **120** 47 0N 118 33W
Linda **122** 39 6N 121 34W
Lindås **11** 56 38N 15 35 E
Lindau **31** 47 33N 9 41 E
Linden, Guyana **136** 6 0N 58 10W
Linden, Calif., U.S.A. **122** 38 1N 121 5W
Linden, Ind., U.S.A. **117** 40 11N 86 54W
Linden, Mich., U.S.A. **106** 42 49N 83 47W
Linden, Tex., U.S.A. **119** 33 0N 94 20W
Linderöd **11** 55 56N 13 47 E
Linderödsåsen **11** 55 53N 13 53 E
Lindesberg **10** 59 36N 15 15 E
Lindi **95** 9 58S 39 38 E
Lindi □ **95** 9 40S 38 30 E
Lindi → **94** 0 33N 25 5 E
Lindoso **22** 41 52N 8 11W
Lindow **30** 52 58N 12 58 E
Lindsay, Can. **107** 44 22N 78 43W
Lindsay, Calif., U.S.A. **122** 36 14N 119 6W
Lindsay, Okla., U.S.A. **119** 34 51N 97 37W
Lindsborg **118** 38 35N 97 40W
Línea de la Concepción, La **23** 36 15N 5 23W
Lineville **116** 40 35N 93 31W
Linfen **60** 36 3N 111 30 E
Ling Xian, Hunan, China **59** 26 29N 113 48 E
Ling Xian, Shandong, China **60** 37 22N 116 30 E
Lingao **54** 19 56N 109 42 E
Lingayen **57** 16 1N 120 14 E
Lingayen G. **57** 16 10N 120 15 E
Lingbi **61** 33 33N 117 33 E
Lingchuan, Guangxi Zhuangzu, China **59** 25 26N 110 21 E
Lingchuan, Shanxi, China **60** 35 45N 113 12 E
Lingen **30** 52 32N 7 21 E
Lingga **56** 0 12S 104 37 E
Lingga, Kepulauan **56** 0 10S 104 30 E
Linghed **10** 60 48N 15 55 E
Lingle **118** 42 10N 104 18W
Lingling **59** 26 17N 111 37 E
Lingqiu **60** 39 28N 114 22 E
Lingshan **58** 22 25N 109 18 E
Lingshi **60** 36 48N 111 48 E
Lingshou **60** 38 20N 114 20 E
Lingshui **54** 18 27N 110 0 E
Lingtai **60** 35 0N 107 40 E
Linguéré **88** 15 25N 15 5W
Lingwu **60** 38 6N 106 20 E
Lingyuan **61** 41 10N 119 15 E
Lingyun **58** 25 2N 106 35 E
Linh Cam **54** 18 31N 105 31 E
Linhai **59** 28 50N 121 8 E
Linhares **139** 19 25S 40 4W
Linhe **60** 40 48N 107 20 E
Linière **105** 46 4N 70 32W
Linjiang **61** 41 50N 127 0 E
Linköping **11** 58 28N 15 36 E
Linkou **61** 45 15N 130 18 E
Linli **59** 29 27N 111 30 E
Linlithgow **14** 55 58N 3 38W
Linn **116** 38 29N 91 51W
Linn, Mt. **120** 40 0N 123 0W
Linneus **116** 39 53N 93 11W
Linnhe, L. **14** 56 36N 5 25W
Linosa, I. **87** 35 51N 12 50 E
Linqi **60** 35 45N 113 52 E
Linqing **60** 36 50N 115 42 E
Linqu **61** 36 25N 118 30 E
Linru **60** 34 11N 112 52 E
Lins **141** 21 40S 49 44W
Linshui **58** 30 21N 106 57 E
Lintao **60** 35 18N 103 52 E
Linth → **31** 47 7N 9 7W
Linthal **31** 46 54N 9 0 E
Lintlaw **109** 52 4N 103 14W
Linton, Austral. **74** 37 41S 143 33 E
Linton, Can. **105** 47 15N 72 16W
Linton, Ind., U.S.A. **117** 39 0N 87 10W
Linton, N. Dak., U.S.A. **118** 46 21N 100 12W
Lintong **60** 34 20N 109 10 E
Linville **73** 26 50S 152 11 E
Linwood **106** 43 35N 80 43W
Linwu **59** 25 19N 112 31 E
Linxe **20** 43 56N 1 13W
Linxi **61** 43 36N 118 2 E
Linxia **62** 35 36N 103 10 E
Linxiang **59** 29 28N 113 23 E
Linyanti → **96** 17 50S 25 5 E
Linyi **61** 35 5N 118 21 E
Linz, Austria **33** 48 18N 14 18 E
Linz, Ger. **30** 50 33N 7 18 E
Linzhenzhen **60** 36 30N 109 59 E
Linzi **61** 36 50N 118 20 E
Lion-d'Angers, Le **18** 47 37N 0 43W
Lion, G. du **20** 43 0N 4 0 E
Lioni **29** 40 52N 15 10 E
Lion's Den **95** 17 15S 30 5 E
Lion's Head **102** 44 58N 81 15W
Liozno **36** 55 0N 30 50 E
Lipali **95** 15 50S 35 50 E
Lípari **29** 38 26N 14 58 E
Lípari, Is. **29** 38 40N 15 0 E
Liperoo **74** 34 48S 142 34 E
Lipetsk **37** 52 37N 39 35 E
Liping **58** 26 15N 109 7 E
Lipkany **38** 48 14N 26 48 E
Lipljan **33** 42 31N 21 7 E
Lipno **32** 52 49N 19 15 E
Lipova **34** 46 8N 21 42 E
Lipovets **38** 49 12N 29 1 E
Lippe → **30** 51 39N 6 38 E
Lippstadt **30** 51 40N 8 19 E
Lipscomb **119** 36 16N 100 16W
Lipsko **32** 51 9N 21 40 E
Lipsói **35** 37 19N 26 50 E
Liptovsky Svaty Milkulaš **32** 49 6N 19 35 E
Liptrap C. **74** 38 50S 145 55 E
Lipu **59** 24 30N 110 22 E
Lira **94** 2 17N 32 57 E
Liri → **28** 41 25N 13 52 E
Liria **24** 39 37N 0 35W
Lisala **92** 2 12N 21 38 E
Lisboa **23** 38 42N 9 10W
Lisboa □ **23** 39 0N 9 12W
Lisbon, N. Dak., U.S.A. **118** 46 30N 97 46W
Lisbon, N.H., U.S.A. **115** 44 13N 71 52W
Lisbon, Ohio, U.S.A. **114** 40 45N 80 42W
Lisbon = Lisboa **23** 38 42N 9 10W
Lisburn **15** 54 30N 6 9W
Lisburne, C. **100** 68 50N 166 0W
Liscannor, B. **15** 52 57N 9 24W
Liscia → **28** 41 11N 9 9 E
Lishe Jiang → **58** 24 15N 101 35 E
Lishi **60** 37 31N 111 8 E
Lishu **61** 43 20N 124 18 E
Lishui, Jiangsu, China **59** 31 38N 119 2 E
Lishui, Zhejiang, China **59** 28 28N 119 54 E
Lisianski I. **66** 26 2N 174 0W
Lisichansk **38** 48 55N 38 30 E
Lisieux **18** 49 10N 0 12 E
Lisle-sur-Tarn **20** 43 52N 1 49 E
Lismore, N.S.W., Austral. **77** 28 44S 153 21 E
Lismore, Vic., Austral. **74** 37 58S 143 21 E
Lismore, Ireland **15** 52 8N 7 58W
Lisse **16** 52 16N 4 33 E
List **30** 55 1N 8 26 E
Lista **9** 58 7N 6 39 E
Lister, Mt. **143** 78 0S 162 0 E
Liston **77** 28 39S 152 6 E
Listowel, Can. **106** 43 44N 80 58W
Listowel, Ireland **15** 52 27N 9 30W
Lit-et-Mixe **20** 44 2N 1 15W
Litang, Guangxi, China **58** 23 12N 109 8 E
Litang, Sichuan, China **58** 30 1N 100 17 E
Litang, Malay. **57** 5 27N 118 31 E
Litang Qu → **58** 28 4N 101 32 E
Litani →, Leb. **44** 33 20N 35 14 E
Litani →, Surinam **44** 3 40N 54 0W
Litchfield, Austral. **74** 36 18S 142 52 E
Litchfield, Calif., U.S.A. **122** 40 24N 120 23W
Litchfield, Conn., U.S.A. **115** 41 44N 73 12W
Litchfield, Ill., U.S.A. **116** 39 10N 89 40W
Litchfield, Minn., U.S.A. **118** 45 5N 94 31W
Lithgow **76** 33 25S 150 8 E
Líthinon, Ákra **35** 34 55N 24 44 E
Lithuanian S.S.R. □ **36** 55 30N 24 0 E
Litija **27** 46 3N 14 50 E
Litókhoron **35** 40 8N 22 34 E
Litoměřice **32** 50 33N 14 10 E
Little Abaco I. **126** 26 50N 77 30W
Little America **143** 79 0S 160 0W
Little Barrier I. **80** 36 12S 175 8 E
Little Belt Mts. **120** 46 50N 111 0W
Little Billabong **76** 35 35S 147 33 E
Little Blue → **118** 39 41N 96 40W
Little Bushman Land **96** 29 10S 18 10 E
Little Cadotte → **108** 56 41N 117 6W
Little Cayman, I. **126** 19 41N 80 3W
Little Churchill → **109** 57 30N 95 22W
Little Colorado → **121** 36 11N 111 48W
Little Current **106** 45 55N 82 0W
Little Current → **102** 50 57N 84 36W
Little Falls, Minn., U.S.A. **118** 45 58N 94 19W
Little Falls, N.Y., U.S.A. **115** 43 3N 74 50W
Little Fork → **118** 48 31N 93 35W
Little Grand Rapids **109** 52 0N 95 29W
Little Humboldt → **120** 41 0N 117 43W
Little Inagua I. **127** 21 40N 73 50W
Little Lake **123** 35 58N 117 58W
Little Marais **118** 47 24N 91 8W
Little Minch **14** 57 35N 6 45W
Little Missouri → **118** 47 30N 102 25W
Little Namaqualand **96** 29 0S 17 9 E
Little Ouse → **13** 52 25N 0 50 E
Little Plain **77** 29 43S 150 59 E
Little Rann of Kutch **48** 23 25N 71 25 E
Little Red → **119** 35 11N 91 27W
Little River **81** 43 45S 172 49 E
Little Rock **119** 34 41N 92 10W
Little Ruaha → **94** 7 57S 37 53 E
Little Sable Pt. **112** 43 40N 86 32W
Little Sioux → **118** 41 49N 96 4W
Little Smoky → **108** 54 44N 117 11W
Little Snake → **120** 40 27N 108 26W
Little Valley **114** 42 15N 78 48W
Little Wabash → **117** 37 54N 88 5W
Little White → **106** 46 23N 83 20W
Little York **116** 41 1N 90 45W
Littlefield **119** 33 57N 102 17W
Littlefork **118** 48 24N 93 35W
Littlehampton **13** 50 48N 0 32W
Littleton **115** 44 19N 71 47W
Liu He → **61** 40 55N 121 35 E
Liu Jiang → **58** 23 55N 109 30 E
Liuba, Shaanxi, China **58** 33 40N 106 55 E
Liuba, Shaanxi, China **60** 33 38N 106 55 E
Liucheng **58** 24 38N 109 14 E
Liugou **61** 40 57N 118 15 E
Liuhe **61** 42 17N 125 43 E
Liuheng Dao **59** 29 40N 122 5 E
Liukang Tenggaja **57** 6 45S 118 50 E
Liuli **95** 11 3S 34 38 E
Liuwa Plain **93** 14 20S 22 30 E
Liuyang **59** 28 10N 113 37 E
Liuzhou **58** 24 22N 109 22 E
Liuzhuang **61** 33 12N 120 18 E
Livadherón **35** 40 2N 21 57 E
Livarot **18** 49 0N 0 9 E
Live Oak, Calif., U.S.A. **122** 39 17N 121 40W
Live Oak, Fla., U.S.A. **113** 30 17N 83 0W
Lively **106** 46 26N 81 9W
Liveringa **78** 18 3S 124 10 E
Livermore **122** 37 41N 121 47W
Livermore, Mt. **119** 30 45N 104 8W
Liverpool, Austral. **76** 33 54S 150 58 E
Liverpool, Can. **103** 44 5N 64 41W
Liverpool, U.K. **12** 53 25N 3 0W
Liverpool Plains **77** 31 15S 150 15 E
Liverpool Ra. **77** 31 50S 150 30 E
Livingston, Guat. **126** 15 50N 88 50W
Livingston, Calif., U.S.A. **122** 37 23N 120 43W
Livingston, Mont., U.S.A. **120** 45 40N 110 40W
Livingston, Wis., U.S.A. **116** 42 54N 90 26W
Livingstone, U.S.A. **119** 30 44N 94 54W
Livingstone, Zambia **95** 17 46S 25 52 E
Livingstone I. **143** 63 0S 60 15W
Livingstone Memorial **95** 12 20S 30 18 E
Livingstone Mts., N.Z. **81** 45 15S 168 9 E
Livingstone Mts., Tanz. **95** 9 40S 34 20 E
Livingstonia **95** 10 38S 34 5 E
Livny **37** 52 30N 37 30 E
Livonia **106** 42 25N 83 23W
Livorno **26** 43 32N 10 18 E
Livramento **141** 30 55S 55 30W
Livramento do Brumado **139** 13 39S 41 50W
Livron-sur-Drôme **21** 44 46N 4 51 E
Liwale **95** 9 48S 37 58 E
Liwale □ **95** 9 0S 38 0 E
Liwale Chini **95** 9 40S 38 0 E
Lixi **58** 26 23N 101 59 E
Liyang **59** 31 26N 119 28 E
Lizard I. **72** 14 42S 145 30 E
Lizard Pt. **13** 49 57N 5 11W
Lizarda **138** 9 36S 46 41W
Lizzano **29** 40 23N 17 25 E
Ljubija **27** 44 55N 16 35 E
Ljubljana **27** 46 4N 14 33 E
Ljubno **27** 46 25N 14 46 E
Ljubuški **33** 43 12N 17 34 E
Ljung **11** 58 1N 13 3 E
Ljungan → **10** 62 18N 17 23 E
Ljungaverk **10** 62 30N 16 5 E
Ljungby **11** 56 49N 13 55 E
Ljusdal **10** 61 46N 16 3 E
Ljusnan → **10** 61 12N 17 8 E
Ljusne **10** 61 13N 17 7 E
Ljutomer **27** 46 31N 16 11 E
Llagostera **24** 41 50N 2 54 E
Llamellín **136** 9 0S 76 54W
Llancanelo, Salina **140** 35 40S 69 8W
Llandeilo **13** 51 53N 4 0W
Llandovery **13** 51 59N 3 49W
Llandrindod Wells **13** 52 15N 3 23W
Llandudno **12** 53 19N 3 51W
Llanelli **13** 51 41N 4 11W
Llanes **22** 43 25N 4 50W

Llangollen	**12**	52 58N	3 10W
Llangothlin	**77**	30 7S	151 41 E
Llanidloes	**13**	52 28N	3 31W
Llano	**119**	30 45N	98 41W
Llano →	**119**	30 50N	98 25W
Llano Estacado	**119**	34 0N	103 0W
Llanos	**136**	5 0N	71 35W
Llanquihue □	**142**	41 30S	73 0W
Llanquihue, L.	**142**	41 10S	75 50W
Llera	**125**	23 19N	99 1W
Llerena	**23**	38 17N	6 0W
Llica	**136**	19 52S	68 16W
Llico	**140**	34 46S	72 5W
Llobregat →	**24**	41 19N	2 9 E
Lloret de Mar	**24**	41 41N	2 53 E
Lloyd B.	**72**	12 45S	143 27 E
Lloyd L.	**109**	57 22N	108 57W
Lloydminster	**109**	53 17N	110 0W
Lluchmayor	**25**	39 29N	2 53 E
Llullaillaco, volcán	**140**	24 43S	68 30W
Lo →	**54**	21 18N	105 25 E
Loa	**121**	38 18N	111 40W
Loa →	**140**	21 26S	70 41W
Loano	**26**	44 8N	8 14 E
Lobatse	**96**	25 12S	25 40 E
Löbau	**30**	51 5N	14 42 E
Lobenstein	**30**	50 25N	11 39 E
Lobería	**140**	38 10S	58 40W
Lobito	**93**	12 18S	13 35 E
Lobón, Canal de	**23**	38 50N	6 55W
Lobos	**140**	35 10S	59 0W
Lobos de Tierra, I.	**136**	6 27S	80 52W
Lobos, I.	**124**	27 15N	110 30W
Lobos, Is.	**130**	6 57S	80 45W
Lobstick L.	**103**	54 0N	65 0W
Loc Binh	**54**	21 46N	106 54 E
Loc Ninh	**55**	11 50N	106 34 E
Locarno	**31**	46 10N	8 47 E
Loch	**74**	38 21S	145 42 E
Lochaber	**14**	56 55N	5 0W
Lochcarron	**14**	57 25N	5 30W
Loche, La	**109**	56 29N	109 26W
Lochem	**16**	52 9N	6 26 E
Loches	**18**	47 7N	1 0 E
Lochgelly	**14**	56 7N	3 18W
Lochgilphead	**14**	56 2N	5 37W
Lochinver	**14**	58 9N	5 15W
Lochnagar, Austral.	**72**	23 33S	145 38 E
Lochnagar, U.K.	**14**	56 57N	3 14W
Łochów	**32**	52 33N	21 42 E
Lochy →	**14**	56 52N	5 3W
Lock	**73**	33 34S	135 46 E
Lock Haven	**114**	41 7N	77 31W
Lockeford	**122**	38 10N	121 9W
Lockeport	**103**	43 47N	65 4W
Lockerbie	**14**	55 7N	3 21W
Lockhart	**119**	29 55N	97 40W
Lockhart, L.	**79**	33 15S	119 3 E
Lockington	**74**	36 16S	144 34 E
Lockney	**119**	34 7N	101 27W
Lockport, Ill., U.S.A.	**117**	41 35N	88 3W
Lockport, N.Y., U.S.A.	**114**	43 12N	78 42W
Locle, Le	**31**	47 3N	6 44 E
Locminé	**18**	47 54N	2 51W
Locri	**29**	38 14N	16 14 E
Locronan	**18**	48 7N	4 15W
Loctudy	**18**	47 50N	4 12W
Locust Cr. →	**116**	39 40N	93 17W
Lod	**44**	31 57N	34 54 E
Loddon →	**74**	35 31S	143 51 E
Lodève	**20**	43 44N	3 19 E
Lodge Grass	**120**	45 21N	107 20W
Lodgepole	**118**	41 12N	102 40W
Lodgepole Cr. →	**118**	41 20N	104 30W
Lodhran	**48**	29 32N	71 30 E
Lodi, Italy	**26**	45 19N	9 30 E
Lodi, U.S.A.	**122**	38 12N	121 16W
Lodja	**94**	3 30S	23 23 E
Lodosa	**24**	42 25N	2 4W
Lödöse	**11**	58 2N	12 9 E
Lodwar	**94**	3 10N	35 40 E
Łódź	**32**	51 45N	19 27 E
Loei	**54**	17 29N	101 35 E
Loengo	**94**	4 48S	26 30 E
Lofoten	**8**	68 10N	13 0 E
Lofsdalen	**10**	62 10N	13 20 E
Lofsen →	**10**	62 7N	13 57 E
Loftahammar	**11**	57 54N	16 41 E
Lofty Ra.	**79**	24 15S	119 30 E
Logan, Kans., U.S.A.	**118**	39 40N	99 35W
Logan, Ohio, U.S.A.	**112**	39 25N	82 22W
Logan, Utah, U.S.A.	**120**	41 45N	111 50W
Logan, W. Va., U.S.A.	**112**	37 51N	81 59W
Logan, Mt.	**100**	60 31N	140 22W
Logan Pass	**108**	48 41N	113 44W
Logandale	**123**	36 36N	114 29W
Logansport, Ind., U.S.A.	**117**	40 45N	86 21W
Logansport, La., U.S.A.	**119**	31 58N	93 58W
Logar □	**47**	34 0N	69 0 E
Logo	**91**	5 20N	30 18 E
Logo Dergo	**91**	6 10N	29 18 E
Logroño	**24**	42 28N	2 27W
Logroño □	**24**	42 28N	2 27W
Logrosán	**23**	39 20N	5 32W
Løgstør	**11**	56 58N	9 14 E
Loh	**68**	13 21S	166 38 E
Lohardaga	**49**	23 27N	84 45 E
Loheia	**45**	15 45N	42 40 E
Lohja	**9**	60 12N	24 5 E
Lohr	**31**	50 0N	9 35 E
Lohrville	**116**	42 17N	94 33W
Loi-kaw	**52**	19 40N	97 17 E
Loimaa	**9**	60 50N	23 5 E
Loir →	**18**	47 33N	0 32W
Loir-et-Cher □	**18**	47 40N	1 20 E
Loire □	**21**	45 40N	4 5 E
Loire →	**18**	47 16N	2 10W
Loire-Atlantique □	**18**	47 25N	1 40W
Loiret □	**19**	47 58N	2 10 E
Loitz	**30**	53 58N	13 8 E
Loja, Ecuador	**136**	3 59S	79 16W
Loja, Spain	**23**	37 10N	4 10W
Loja □	**134**	4 0S	79 13W
Loji	**57**	1 38S	127 28 E
Loka	**91**	4 13N	31 0 E
Lokandu	**94**	2 30S	25 45 E
Løken	**10**	59 48N	11 29 E
Lokerane	**96**	24 54S	24 42 E
Lokeren	**16**	51 6N	3 59 E
Lokhvitsa	**36**	50 25N	33 18 E
Lokichokio	**94**	4 19N	34 13 E
Lokitaung	**94**	4 12N	35 48 E
Lokka	**8**	67 49N	27 45 E
Løkken	**11**	57 22N	9 41 E
Løkkenverk	**10**	63 8N	9 45 E
Loknya	**36**	56 49N	30 4 E
Lokobo	**91**	4 20N	30 30 E
Lokoja	**89**	7 47N	6 45 E
Lokolama	**92**	2 35S	19 50 E
Lokuru	**68**	8 20S	157 0 E
Lokuti	**91**	4 21N	33 15 E
Lol	**91**	6 28N	29 36 E
Lol →	**91**	9 13N	26 30 E
Lola	**88**	7 52N	8 29W
Lola, Mt.	**122**	39 26N	120 22W
Lolibai, Gebel	**91**	3 50N	33 0 E
Lolimi	**91**	4 35N	34 0 E
Loliondo	**94**	2 2S	35 39 E
Lolland	**11**	54 45N	11 30 E
Lollar	**30**	50 39N	8 43 E
Lolo	**120**	46 50N	114 8W
Lolodorf	**89**	3 16N	10 49 E
Lolowai	**68**	15 18S	168 0 E
Lom	**34**	43 48N	23 12 E
Lom →	**34**	43 45N	23 15 E
Lom Kao	**54**	16 53N	101 14 E
Lom Sak	**54**	16 47N	101 15 E
Loma	**120**	47 59N	110 29W
Loma Linda	**123**	34 3N	117 16W
Lomaloma	**68**	17 17S	178 59W
Lomami →	**94**	0 46N	24 16 E
Lomas de Zamóra	**140**	34 45S	58 25W
Lombadina	**78**	16 31S	122 54 E
Lombard, Ill., U.S.A.	**117**	41 53N	88 1W
Lombard, Mont., U.S.A.	**120**	46 7N	111 28W
Lombardia □	**26**	45 35N	9 45 E
Lombardy = Lombardia	**26**	45 35N	9 45 E
Lombez	**20**	43 29N	0 55 E
Lomblen	**57**	8 30S	123 32 E
Lombok	**56**	8 45S	116 30 E
Lomé	**89**	6 9N	1 20 E
Lomela	**92**	2 19S	23 15 E
Lomela →	**92**	1 30S	22 50 E
Lomello	**26**	45 5N	8 46 E
Lometa	**119**	31 15N	98 25W
Lomié	**92**	3 13N	13 38 E
Loming	**91**	4 27N	33 40W
Lomma	**11**	55 43N	13 6 E
Lomond	**108**	50 24N	112 36W
Lomond, L.	**14**	56 8N	4 38W
Lomphat	**54**	13 30N	106 59 E
Lompobatang	**57**	5 24S	119 56 E
Lompoc	**123**	34 41N	120 32W
Lomsegga	**10**	61 49N	8 21 E
Łomza	**32**	53 10N	22 2 E
Lonavla	**50**	18 46N	73 29 E
Loncoche	**142**	39 20S	72 50W
Loncopuè	**142**	38 4S	70 37W
Londa	**51**	15 30N	74 30 E
Londe, La	**21**	43 8N	6 14 E
Londiani	**94**	0 10S	35 33 E
Londinières	**18**	49 50N	1 25 E
London, Can.	**106**	42 59N	81 15W
London, U.K.	**13**	51 30N	0 5W
London, Ky., U.S.A.	**112**	37 11N	84 5W
London, Ohio, U.S.A.	**117**	39 54N	83 28W
London, Greater □	**13**	51 30N	0 5W
London Mills	**116**	40 43N	90 11W
Londonderry	**15**	55 0N	7 20W
Londonderry □	**15**	55 0N	7 20W
Londonderry, C.	**78**	13 45S	126 55 E
Londonderry, I.	**142**	55 0S	71 0W
Londrina	**141**	23 18S	51 10W
Lone Pine	**122**	36 35N	118 2W
Lonely I.	**106**	45 34N	81 28W
Long Beach, Calif., U.S.A.	**123**	33 46N	118 12W
Long Beach, N.Y., U.S.A.	**115**	40 35N	73 40W
Long Beach, Wash., U.S.A.	**122**	46 20N	124 1W
Long Branch	**115**	40 19N	74 0W
Long Creek	**120**	44 43N	119 6W
Long Eaton	**12**	52 54N	1 16W
Long I., Austral.	**72**	22 8S	149 53 E
Long I., Bahamas	**127**	23 20N	75 10W
Long I., P.N.G.	**69**	5 20S	147 5 E
Long I., U.S.A.	**115**	40 50N	73 20W
Long I. Sd.	**115**	41 10N	73 0W
Long L.	**102**	49 30N	86 50W
Long Lake, Mich., U.S.A.	**106**	44 25N	83 52W
Long Lake, N.Y., U.S.A.	**115**	43 57N	74 25W
Long Pine	**118**	42 33N	99 41W
Long Pt., Newf., Can.	**103**	48 47N	58 46W
Long Pt., Ont., Can.	**106**	42 35N	80 2W
Long Pt., N.Z.	**81**	46 34S	169 36 E
Long Point B.	**106**	42 40N	80 10W
Long Range Mts.	**103**	49 30N	57 30W
Long Reef	**78**	13 55S	125 45 E
Long Str.	**144**	70 0N	175 0 E
Long Thanh	**55**	10 47N	106 57 E
Long Xian	**60**	34 55N	106 55 E
Long Xuyen	**55**	10 19N	105 28 E
Longá	**35**	36 53N	21 55 E
Long'an	**58**	23 10N	107 40 E
Longarone	**27**	46 15N	12 18 E
Longburn	**80**	40 23S	175 35 E
Longchang	**58**	29 18N	105 15 E
Longchi	**58**	29 25N	103 24 E
Longchuan, Guangdong, China	**59**	24 5N	115 17 E
Longchuan, Yunnan, China	**58**	24 23N	97 58 E
Longde	**60**	35 30N	106 20 E
Longeau	**19**	47 47N	5 20 E
Longford, Austral.	**72**	41 32S	147 3 E
Longford, Ireland	**15**	53 43N	7 50W
Longford □	**15**	53 42N	7 45W
Longguan	**60**	40 45N	115 30 E
Longhua	**61**	41 18N	117 45 E
Longhui	**59**	27 7N	111 2 E
Longido	**94**	2 43S	36 42 E
Longiram	**56**	0 5S	115 45 E
Longkou, Jiangxi, China	**59**	26 8N	115 10 E
Longkou, Shandong, China	**61**	37 40N	120 18 E
Longlac	**102**	49 45N	86 25W
Longli	**58**	26 25N	106 58 E
Longlin	**58**	24 47N	105 20 E
Longling	**58**	24 37N	98 39 E
Longmen	**59**	23 40N	114 18 E
Longming	**58**	22 59N	107 7 E
Longmont	**118**	40 10N	105 4W
Longnan	**59**	24 55N	114 47 E
Longnawan	**56**	1 51N	114 55 E
Longobucco	**29**	39 27N	16 37 E
Longone →	**85**	10 0N	15 40 E
Longquan	**59**	28 7N	119 10 E
Longreach	**72**	23 28S	144 14 E
Longs Peak	**120**	40 20N	105 37W
Longshan	**58**	29 29N	109 25 E
Longsheng	**58**	25 48N	110 0 E
Longton	**72**	20 58S	145 55 E
Longtown	**13**	51 58N	2 59W
Longué	**18**	47 22N	0 8W
Longueau	**19**	49 52N	2 21 E
Longueuil, Can.	**115**	45 32N	73 28W
Longueuil, Qué., Can.	**105**	45 32N	73 30W
Longuyon	**19**	49 27N	5 35 E
Longview, Can.	**108**	50 32N	114 10W
Longview, Tex., U.S.A.	**119**	32 30N	94 45W
Longview, Wash., U.S.A.	**122**	46 9N	122 58W
Longwarry	**74**	38 8S	145 48 E
Longwood	**74**	36 48S	145 26 E
Longwy	**19**	49 30N	5 45 E
Longxi	**60**	34 53N	104 40 E
Longyou	**59**	29 1N	119 8 E
Longzhou	**58**	22 22N	106 50 E
Lonigo	**27**	45 23N	11 22 E
Löningen	**30**	52 43N	7 44 E
Lonja →	**27**	45 30N	16 40 E
Lonkin	**52**	25 39N	96 22 E
Lonoke	**119**	34 48N	91 57W
Lonquimay	**142**	38 26S	71 14W
Lons-le-Saunier	**19**	46 40N	5 31 E
Lønstrup	**11**	57 29N	9 47 E
Looc	**57**	12 20N	112 5 E
Loogootee	**117**	38 41N	86 55W
Lookout, C., Can.	**102**	55 18N	83 56W
Lookout, C., U.S.A.	**113**	34 30N	76 30W
Loolmalasin	**94**	3 0S	35 53 E
Loon →, Alta., Can.	**108**	57 8N	115 3W
Loon →, Man., Can.	**109**	55 53N	101 59W
Loon Lake	**109**	54 2N	109 10W
Loongana	**79**	30 52S	127 5 E
Loop Hd.	**15**	52 34N	9 55W
Lop Buri	**54**	14 48N	100 37 E
Lop Nor = Lop Nur	**62**	40 20N	90 10 E
Lop Nur	**62**	40 20N	90 10 E
Lopare	**33**	44 39N	18 46 E
Lopatin	**39**	43 50N	47 35 E
Lopatina, G.	**41**	50 47N	143 10 E
Lopaye	**91**	6 37N	33 40 E
Lopera	**23**	37 56N	4 14W
Lopevi	**68**	16 30S	168 21 E
Lopez, C.	**92**	0 47S	8 40 E
Lopphavet	**8**	70 27N	21 15 E
Lora →	**47**	32 0N	67 15 E
Lora Cr. →	**73**	28 10S	135 22 E
Lora del Río	**23**	37 39N	5 33W
Lora, Hamun-i-	**47**	29 38N	64 58 E
Lora, La	**22**	42 45N	4 0W
Lorain	**114**	41 28N	82 55W
Loraine	**116**	40 9N	91 13W
Loralai	**48**	30 20N	68 41 E
Lorca	**25**	37 41N	1 42W
Lord Howe I.	**66**	31 33S	159 6 E
Lord Howe Ridge	**66**	30 0S	162 30 E
Lordsburg	**121**	32 22N	108 45W
Lorengau	**69**	2 1S	147 15 E
Loreto, Boliv.	**137**	15 13S	64 40W
Loreto, Brazil	**138**	7 5S	45 10W
Loreto, Italy	**27**	43 26N	13 36 E
Loreto, Mexico	**124**	26 1N	111 21W
Loreto □	**134**	5 0S	75 0W
Loreto Aprutina	**27**	42 24N	13 59 E
Loretteville	**105**	46 51N	71 21W
Lorgues	**21**	43 28N	6 22 E
Lorica	**134**	9 14N	75 49W
Lorient	**18**	47 45N	3 23W
Lorimor	**116**	41 7N	94 3W
Loristan □	**46**	33 20N	47 0 E
Lorn, Firth of	**14**	56 20N	5 40W
Lorne, N.S.W., Austral.	**77**	31 36S	152 39 E
Lorne, Vic., Austral.	**74**	38 33S	143 59 E
Lorne, U.K.	**14**	56 26N	5 10W
Lörrach	**31**	47 36N	7 38 E
Lorraine	**19**	49 0N	6 0 E
Lorrainville	**104**	47 21N	79 23W
Los Alamos, Calif., U.S.A.	**123**	34 44N	120 17W
Los Alamos, N. Mex., U.S.A.	**121**	35 57N	106 17W
Los Altos	**122**	37 23N	122 7W
Los Andes	**140**	32 50S	70 40W
Los Angeles, Chile	**140**	37 28S	72 23W
Los Angeles, U.S.A.	**123**	34 0N	118 10W
Los Angeles Aqueduct	**123**	35 25N	118 0W
Los Antiguos	**142**	46 35S	71 40W
Los Banos	**122**	37 8N	120 56W
Los Barrios	**23**	36 11N	5 30W
Los Blancos	**140**	23 40S	62 30W
Los Gatos	**122**	37 15N	121 59W
Los Hermanos	**135**	11 45N	84 25W
Los, Îles de	**88**	9 30N	13 50W
Los Lagos	**142**	39 51S	72 50W
Los Lamentos	**124**	30 36N	105 50W
Los Lomas	**136**	4 40S	80 10W
Los Lunas	**121**	34 48N	106 47W
Los Menucos	**142**	40 50S	68 10W
Los Mochis	**124**	25 45N	109 5W
Los Monegros	**24**	41 29N	0 13W
Los Monos	**142**	46 1S	69 36W
Los Olivos	**123**	34 40N	120 7W
Los Palacios	**126**	22 35N	83 15W
Los Palacios y Villafranca	**23**	37 10N	5 55W
Los Reyes	**124**	19 34N	102 30W
Los Ríos □	**134**	1 30S	79 25W
Los Roques	**134**	11 50N	66 45W
Los Santos de Maimona	**23**	38 27N	6 22W
Los Teques	**134**	10 21N	67 2W
Los Testigos	**135**	11 23N	63 6W
Los Vilos	**140**	32 10S	71 30W
Los Yébenes	**23**	39 36N	3 55W
Losada →	**134**	2 12N	73 55W
Loshkalakh	**41**	62 45N	147 20 E
Lošinj	**27**	44 30N	14 30 E
Lossiemouth	**14**	57 43N	3 17W
Losuia	**69**	8 30S	151 4 E
Lot □	**20**	44 39N	1 40 E
Lot →	**20**	44 18N	0 20 E
Lot-et-Garonne □	**20**	44 22N	0 30 E
Lota	**140**	37 5S	73 10W
Løten	**10**	60 51N	11 21 E

Lothian □ 14 55 50N 3 0W
Lothiers 19 46 42N 1 33 E
Lotofaga 68 14 1S 171 30W
Lotschbergtunnel 31 46 26N 7 43 E
Lottefors 10 61 25N 16 24 E
Loudéac 18 48 11N 2 47W
Loudi 59 27 42N 111 59 E
Loudon 113 35 35N 84 22W
Loudonville 114 40 40N 82 15W
Loudun 18 47 0N 0 5 E
Loué 18 47 59N 0 9W
Loue → 19 47 1N 5 27 E
Louga 88 15 45N 16 5W
Loughborough 12 52 46N 1 11W
Loughrea 15 53 11N 8 33W
Loughros More B. 15 54 48N 8 30W
Louhans 21 46 38N 5 12 E
Louis Trichardt 97 23 0S 29 43 E
Louis XIV, Pte. 102 54 37N 79 45W
Louisa 112 38 5N 82 40W
Louisbourg 103 45 55N 60 0W
Louisburg 116 38 37N 94 41W
Louise I. 108 52 55N 131 50W
Louiseville 105 46 20N 72 56W
Louisiade Arch. 69 11 10S 153 0 E
Louisiana 116 39 25N 91 0W
Louisiana □ 119 30 50N 92 0W
Louisville, Ky., U.S.A. 117 38 15N 85 45W
Louisville, Miss., U.S.A. 119 33 7N 89 3W
Loulay 20 46 3N 0 30W
Loulé 23 37 9N 8 0W
Lount L. 109 50 10N 94 20W
Louny 32 50 20N 13 48 E
Loup City 118 41 19N 98 57W
Loupe, La 18 48 29N 1 1 E
Lourdes 20 43 6N 0 3W
Lourdes-du-Blanc-Sablon 103 51 24N 57 12W
Lourenço 135 2 30N 51 40W
Lourenço-Marques = Maputo 97 25 58S 32 32 E
Loures 23 38 50N 9 9W
Lourinhã 23 39 14N 9 17W
Louroux-Béconnais, Le 18 47 30N 0 55W
Lousã 22 40 7N 8 14W
Louth, Austral. 73 30 30S 145 8 E
Louth, Ireland 15 53 47N 6 33W
Louth, U.K. 12 53 23N 0 0W
Louth □ 15 53 55N 6 30W
Louvière, La 16 50 27N 4 10 E
Louviers 18 49 12N 1 10 E
Lovat → 36 58 14N 30 28 E
Love 109 53 29N 104 10W
Lovech 34 43 8N 24 42 E
Loveland, Colo., U.S.A. 118 40 27N 105 4W
Loveland, Ohio, U.S.A. 117 39 16N 84 16W
Lovell 120 44 51N 108 20W
Lovelock 120 40 17N 118 25W
Lóvere 26 45 50N 10 4 E
Loves Park 116 42 19N 89 3W
Loviisa 9 60 28N 26 12 E
Lovilia 116 41 8N 92 55W
Loving 119 32 17N 104 4W
Lovington, Ill., U.S.A. 117 39 43N 88 38W
Lovington, N.Mex., U.S.A. 119 33 0N 103 20W
Lovios 22 41 55N 8 4W
Lovisa 9 60 28N 26 12 E
Lovran 27 45 18N 14 15 E
Lövstabukten 10 60 35N 17 45 E
Low 104 45 50N 76 0W
Low Pt. 79 32 25S 127 25 E
Lowa 94 1 25S 25 47 E
Lowa → 94 1 24S 25 51 E
Lowden 116 41 52N 90 56W
Lowell, Ind., U.S.A. 117 41 18N 87 25W
Lowell, Mass., U.S.A. 115 42 38N 71 19W
Lowell, Mich., U.S.A. 117 42 56N 85 20W
Lower Arrow L. 108 49 40N 118 5W
Lower Hutt 80 41 10S 174 55 E
Lower L. 120 41 17N 120 3W
Lower Lake 122 38 56N 122 36W
Lower Neguac 103 47 20N 65 10W
Lower Post 108 59 58N 128 30W
Lower Red L. 118 47 58N 95 0W
Lower Saxony = Niedersachsen 30 52 45N 9 0 E
Lowestoft 13 52 29N 1 44 E
Łowicz 32 52 6N 19 55 E
Lowry City 116 38 8N 93 44W
Lowville 115 43 48N 75 30W
Loxton 73 34 28S 140 31 E
Loyalton 122 39 41N 120 14W
Loyalty Is. = Loyauté, Is. 68 21 0S 167 30 E
Loyang = Luoyang 60 34 40N 112 26 E
Loyev 36 51 55N 30 40 E
Loyoro 94 3 22N 34 14 E
Lož 27 45 43N 30 14 E
Lozère □ 20 44 35N 3 30 E
Loznica 33 44 32N 19 14 E
Lozovaya 38 49 0N 36 20 E
Luacano 92 11 15S 21 37 E
Lualaba → 94 0 26N 25 20 E
Luampa 95 15 4S 24 20 E
Lu'an 59 31 45N 116 29 E
Luan Chau 54 21 38N 103 24 E
Luan He → 61 39 20N 119 5 E
Luan Xian 61 39 40N 118 40 E
Luancheng, Guangxi, China 58 22 48N 108 55 E
Luancheng, Hebei, China 60 37 53N 114 40 E
Luanda 92 8 50S 13 15 E
Luang Prabang 54 19 52N 102 10 E
Luang Thale 55 7 30N 100 15 E
Luangwa Val. 95 13 30S 31 30 E
Luanne 61 40 55N 117 40 E
Luanping 61 40 53N 117 23 E
Luanshya 95 13 3S 28 28 E
Luapula □ 95 11 0S 29 0 E
Luapula → 95 9 26S 28 33 E
Luarca 22 43 32N 6 32W
Luashi 95 10 50S 23 36 E
Lubalo 92 9 10S 19 15 E
Lubań 32 51 5N 15 15 E
Lubana, Ozero 36 56 45N 27 0 E
Lubang Is. 57 13 50N 120 12 E
Lubartów 32 51 28N 22 42 E
Lubawa 32 53 30N 19 48 E
Lubban 44 32 9N 35 14 E
Lübben 30 51 56N 13 54 E
Lübbenau 30 51 49N 13 59 E
Lubbock 119 33 40N 101 53W
Lubeck 74 36 45S 142 34 E
Lübeck 30 53 52N 10 41 E
Lübecker Bucht 30 54 3N 11 0 E
Lubefu 94 4 47S 24 27 E
Lubefu → 94 4 10S 23 0 E
Lubero = Luofu 94 0 1S 29 15 E
Lubicon L. 108 56 23N 115 56W
Lublin 32 51 12N 22 38 E
Lubliniec 32 50 43N 18 45 E
Lubny 36 50 3N 32 58 E
Lubok Antu 56 1 3N 111 50 E
Lubon 32 52 21N 16 51 E
Lubongola 94 2 35S 27 50 E
Lubran 46 34 0N 36 0 E
Lubsko 32 51 45N 14 57 E
Lübtheen 30 53 18N 11 4 E
Lubuagan 57 17 21N 121 10 E
Lubudi → 95 9 0S 25 35 E
Lubuklinggau 56 3 15S 102 55 E
Lubuksikaping 56 0 10N 100 15 E
Lubumbashi 95 11 40S 27 28 E
Lubunda 94 5 12S 26 41 E
Lubungu 95 14 35S 26 24 E
Lubutu 94 0 45S 26 30 E
Luc An Chau 54 22 6N 104 43 E
Luc-en-Diois 21 44 36N 5 28 E
Luc, Le 21 43 23N 6 21 E
Lucan 106 43 11N 81 24W
Lucca 26 43 50N 10 30 E
Luce Bay 14 54 45N 4 48W
Lucea 126 18 25N 78 10W
Lucedale 113 30 55N 88 34W
Lucena, Phil. 57 13 56N 121 37 E
Lucena, Spain 23 37 27N 4 31W
Lucena del Cid 24 40 9N 0 17W
Lučenec 33 48 18N 19 42 E
Lucera 29 41 30N 15 20 E
Lucerne 122 39 6N 122 48W
Lucerne = Luzern 31 47 3N 8 18 E
Lucerne Valley 123 34 27N 116 57W
Lucero 124 30 49N 106 30W
Luceville 105 48 32N 68 22W
Luchena → 25 37 44N 1 50W
Lucheng 60 36 20N 113 11 E
Lucheringo → 95 11 43S 36 17 E
Lüchow 30 52 58N 11 8 E
Luchuan 59 22 21N 110 12 E
Lucie → 135 13 51S 12 35 E
Lucira 93 14 0S 12 35 E
Luckau 30 51 50N 13 43 E
Luckenwalde 30 52 5N 13 11 E
Luckey 117 41 27N 83 29W
Lucknow, Austral. 76 33 21S 149 11 E
Lucknow, Can. 106 43 57N 81 31W
Lucknow, India 49 26 50N 81 0 E
Luçon 20 46 28N 1 10W
Lüda 61 38 50N 121 40 E
Luda Kamchiya → 34 43 3N 27 29 E
Ludbreg 27 46 15N 16 38 E
Lüdenscheid 30 51 13N 7 37 E
Lüderitz 96 26 41S 15 8 E
Ludewe □ 95 10 0S 34 50 E
Ludhiana 48 30 57N 75 56 E
Ludian 58 27 10N 103 33 E
Luding Qiao 58 29 53N 102 12 E
Lüdinghausen 30 51 46N 7 28 E
Ludington 112 43 58N 86 27W
Ludlow, U.K. 13 52 23N 2 42W
Ludlow, Calif., U.S.A. 123 34 43N 116 10W
Ludlow, Vt., U.S.A. 115 43 25N 72 40W
Luduş 34 46 29N 24 5 E
Ludvika 10 60 8N 15 14 E
Ludwigsburg 31 48 53N 9 11 E
Ludwigshafen 31 49 27N 8 27 E
Ludwigslust 30 53 19N 11 28 E
Ludza 36 56 32N 27 43 E
Lue 76 32 38S 149 50 E
Luebo 92 5 21S 21 23 E
Lueki 94 3 20S 25 48 E
Luena, Zaïre 95 9 28S 25 43 E
Luena, Zambia 95 10 40S 30 25 E
Luepa 135 5 43N 61 31W
Lüeyang 60 33 22N 106 10 E
Lufeng, Guangdong, China 59 22 57N 115 38 E
Lufeng, Yunnan, China 58 25 0N 102 5 E
Lufkin 119 31 25N 94 40W
Lufupa 95 10 37S 24 56 E
Luga 36 58 40N 29 55 E
Luga → 36 59 40N 28 18 E
Lugang 59 24 4N 120 23 E
Lugano 31 46 0N 8 57 E
Lugano, L. di 31 46 0N 9 0 E
Lugansk = Voroshilovgrad 39 48 35N 39 20 E
Lugard's Falls 94 3 6S 38 41 E
Lugela 95 16 25S 36 43 E
Lugenda → 95 11 25S 38 33 E
Lugh Ganana 45 3 48N 42 34 E
Lugnaquilla 15 52 58N 6 28W
Lugnvik 10 62 56N 17 55 E
Lugo, Italy 27 44 25N 11 53 E
Lugo, Spain 22 43 2N 7 35W
Lugo □ 22 43 0N 7 30W
Lugoj 34 45 42N 21 57 E
Lugones 22 43 26N 5 50W
Lugovoy 40 42 54N 72 45 E
Luhe 59 32 19N 118 50 E
Luhe → 30 53 18N 10 11 E
Luhuo 58 31 21N 100 48 E
Luiana 93 17 25S 22 59 E
Luino 26 46 0N 8 42 E
Luis 124 26 36N 109 11W
Luís Correia 138 3 0S 41 35W
Luís Gonçalves 138 5 37S 50 25W
Luisa 92 7 40S 22 30 E
Luitpold Coast 143 78 30S 32 0W
Luizi 94 6 0S 27 25 E
Luján 140 34 45S 59 5W
Lujiang 59 31 20N 117 15 E
Lukanga Swamps 95 14 30S 27 40 E
Lukenie → 92 3 0S 18 50 E
Lukhisaral 49 25 11N 86 5 E
Lŭki 35 41 50N 24 43 E
Lukolela 92 1 10S 17 12 E
Lukosi 95 18 30S 26 30 E
Lukovit 34 43 13N 24 11 E
Łukow 32 51 58N 22 22 E
Lukoyanov 37 55 2N 44 29 E
Lukulu 93 14 28S 23 12 E
Lula 94 0 30N 25 10 E
Lule älv → 8 65 35N 22 10 E
Luleå 8 65 35N 22 10 E
Lüleburgaz 46 41 23N 27 22 E
Luliang 58 25 0N 103 40 E
Luling 119 29 45N 97 40W
Lulong 61 39 53N 118 51 E
Lulonga → 92 1 0N 19 0 E
Lulua → 92 6 30S 22 50 E
Luluabourg = Kananga 92 5 55S 22 26 E
Lumai 93 13 13S 21 25 E
Lumajang 57 8 8S 113 16 E
Lumbala 93 14 18S 21 18 E
Lumberton, Miss., U.S.A. 119 31 4N 89 28W
Lumberton, N. Mex., U.S.A. 121 36 58N 106 57W
Lumberton, N.C., U.S.A. 113 34 37N 78 59W
Lumbres 19 50 40N 2 5 E
Lumbwa 94 0 12S 35 28 E
Lumby 108 50 10N 118 50W
Lumding 52 25 46N 93 10 E
Lumege 93 11 45S 20 50 E
Lumeyen 91 4 55N 33 28 E
Lumi 69 3 30S 142 2 E
Lumsden 81 45 44S 168 27 E
Lumut 55 4 13N 100 37 E
Lunan 58 24 40N 103 18 E
Lunavada 48 23 8N 73 37 E
Lunca 34 47 22N 25 1 E
Lund, Sweden 11 55 44N 13 12 E
Lund, U.S.A. 120 38 53N 115 0W
Lundazi 95 12 20S 33 7 E
Lunde 10 59 17N 9 5 E
Lunderskov 11 55 29N 9 19 E
Lundi → 95 21 43S 32 34 E
Lundu 56 1 40N 109 50 E
Lundy, I. 13 51 10N 4 41W
Lune → 12 54 0N 2 51W
Lüneburg 30 53 15N 10 23 E
Lüneburg Heath = Lüneburger Heide 30 53 0N 10 0 E
Lüneburger Heide 30 53 0N 10 0 E
Lunel 21 43 39N 4 9 E
Lünen 30 51 36N 7 31 E
Lunenburg 103 44 22N 64 18W
Lunéville 19 48 36N 6 30 E
Lunga → 95 14 34S 26 25 E
Lungi Airport 88 8 40N 13 17W
Lungleh 52 22 55N 92 45 E
Lungngo 52 21 57N 93 36 E
Luni 48 26 0N 73 6 E
Luni → 48 24 41N 71 14 E
Luninets 36 52 15N 26 50 E
Luning 120 38 30N 118 10W
Lunino 37 53 35N 45 6 E
Lunner 10 60 19N 10 35 E
Lunsemfwa → 95 14 54S 30 12 E
Lunsemfwa Falls 95 14 30S 29 6 E
Luo He → 60 34 35N 110 20 E
Luocheng 58 24 48N 108 53 E
Luochuan 60 35 45N 109 26 E
Luoci 58 25 19N 102 18 E
Luodian 58 25 24N 106 43 E
Luoding 59 22 45N 111 40 E
Luodong 59 24 41N 121 46 E
Luofu 94 0 10S 29 15 E
Luohe 60 33 32N 114 2 E
Luojiang 58 31 18N 104 33 E
Luonan 60 34 5N 110 10 E
Luoning 60 34 35N 111 40 E
Luoshan 59 32 13N 114 30 E
Luotian 59 30 46N 115 22 E
Luoyang 60 34 40N 112 26 E
Luoyuan 59 26 28N 119 30 E
Luozi 92 4 54S 14 0 E
Luozigou 61 43 42N 130 18 E
Lupeni 34 45 21N 23 13 E
Lupoing 58 24 53N 104 21 E
Lupundu 95 14 18S 26 45 E
Luquan 58 25 35N 102 25 E
Luque, Parag. 140 25 19S 57 25W
Luque, Spain 23 37 35N 4 16W
Luray 112 38 39N 78 26W
Lure 19 47 40N 6 30 E
Luremo 92 8 30S 17 50 E
Lurgan 15 54 28N 6 20W
Luribay 136 17 6S 67 39W
Lurin 136 12 17S 76 52W
Lusaka 95 15 28S 28 16 E
Lusambo 94 4 58S 23 28 E
Luseland 109 52 5N 109 24W
Lushan, Henan, China 60 33 45N 112 55 E
Lushan, Sichuan, China 58 30 12N 102 52 E
Lushih 60 34 3N 111 3 E
Lushnja 35 40 55N 19 41 E
Lushoto 94 4 47S 38 20 E
Lushoto □ 94 4 45S 38 20 E
Lushui 58 25 58N 98 44 E
Lüshun 61 38 45N 121 15 E
Lusignan 20 46 26N 0 8 E
Lusigny-sur-Barse 19 48 16N 4 15 E
Lusk 118 42 47N 104 27W
Lussac-les-Châteaux 20 46 24N 0 43 E
Lussanvira 139 20 42S 51 7W
Luta = Lüda 61 38 50N 121 40 E
Luti 68 7 14S 157 0 E
Luton 13 51 53N 0 24W
Lutong 56 4 30N 114 0 E
Lutsk 36 50 50N 25 15 E
Lützow Holmbukta 143 69 10S 37 30 E
Luverne 118 43 35N 96 12W
Luvua 95 8 48S 25 17 E
Luwegu → 95 8 31S 37 23 E
Luwuk 57 0 56S 122 47 E
Luxembourg 16 49 37N 6 9 E
Luxembourg ■ 16 50 0N 6 0 E
Luxembourg □ 16 49 58N 5 30 E
Luxeuil-les-Bains 19 47 49N 6 24 E
Luxi, Hunan, China 59 28 20N 110 7 E
Luxi, Yunnan, China 58 24 27N 98 36 E
Luxi, Yunnan, China 58 24 40N 103 55 E
Luxor = El Uqsur 90 25 41N 32 38 E
Luy → 20 43 39N 1 9W
Luy-de-Béarn → 20 43 39N 0 48W
Luy-de-France → 20 43 39N 0 48W
Luyi 60 33 50N 115 35 E
Luz-St-Sauveur 20 42 53N 0 1 E
Luzern 31 47 3N 8 18 E
Luzern □ 31 47 2N 7 55 E
Luzhai 58 24 29N 109 42 E
Luzhou 58 28 52N 105 20 E
Luziânia 139 16 20S 48 0W
Luzilândia 138 3 28S 42 22W
Luzon 57 16 0N 121 0 E
Luzy 19 46 47N 3 58 E

Luzzi 29 39 28N 16 17 E
Lvov 36 49 50N 24 0 E
Lyakhovichi 36 53 2N 26 32 E
Lyakhovskiye, Ostrova 41 73 40N 141 0 E
Lyaki 39 40 34N 47 22 E
Lyal I. 106 44 57N 81 24W
Lyall Mt. 81 45 16S 167 32 E
Lyallpur 48 31 30N 73 5 E
Lychen 30 53 13N 13 20 E
Lyckeby 11 56 12N 15 37 E
Lycksele 8 64 38N 18 40 E
Lydda = Lod 44 31 57N 34 54 E
Lydenburg 97 25 10S 30 29 E
Lyell 81 41 48S 172 4 E
Lyell I. 108 52 40N 131 35W
Lyell Range 81 41 38S 172 20 E
Lygnern 11 57 30N 12 15 E
Lyman 120 41 24N 110 15W
Lyme Regis 13 50 44N 2 57W
Lymington 13 50 46N 1 32W
Lynchburg, Ohio, U.S.A. 117 39 15N 83 48W
Lynchburg, Va., U.S.A. 112 37 23N 79 10W
Lynd → 72 16 28S 143 18 E
Lynd Ra. 73 25 30S 149 20 E
Lynden, Can. 114 43 14N 80 9W
Lynden, U.S.A. 122 48 56N 122 32W
Lyndhurst, N.S.W., Austral. 76 33 41S 149 2 E
Lyndhurst, Queens., Austral. 72 19 12S 144 20 E
Lyndhurst, S. Australia, Austral. 73 30 15S 138 18 E
Lyndon → 79 23 29S 114 6 E
Lyndonville, N.Y., U.S.A. 114 43 19N 78 25W
Lyndonville, Vt., U.S.A. 115 44 32N 72 1W
Lyngdal 10 59 54N 9 32 E
Lynher Reef 78 15 27S 121 55 E
Lynn, Ind., U.S.A. 117 40 3N 84 56W
Lynn, Mass., U.S.A. 115 42 28N 70 57W
Lynn Canal 108 58 50N 135 20W
Lynn Lake 109 56 51N 101 3W
Lynnwood 122 47 49N 122 19W
Lynton 13 51 14N 3 50W
Lyntupy 36 55 4N 26 23 E
Lynx L. 109 62 25N 106 15W
Lyø 11 55 3N 10 9 E
Lyon 21 45 46N 4 50 E
Lyonnais 21 45 45N 4 15 E
Lyons, Austral. 74 38 2S 141 28 E
Lyons, Colo., U.S.A. 118 40 17N 105 15W
Lyons, Ga., U.S.A. 113 32 10N 82 15W
Lyons, Kans., U.S.A. 118 38 24N 98 13W
Lyons, N.Y., U.S.A. 114 43 3N 77 0W
Lyons = Lyon 21 45 46N 4 50 E
Lyrestad 11 58 48N 14 4 E
Lys → 19 50 39N 2 24 E
Lysekil 11 58 17N 11 26 E
Lyskovo 37 56 0N 45 3 E
Lyster 105 46 22N 71 37W
Lysvik 10 60 1N 13 9 E
Lytle 119 29 14N 98 46W
Lyttelton 81 43 35S 172 44 E
Lytton 108 50 13N 121 31W
Lyuban 36 59 16N 31 18 E
Lyubim 37 58 20N 40 39 E
Lyuboml 36 51 10N 24 2 E
Lyubotin 38 50 0N 36 0 E
Lyubytino 36 58 50N 33 16 E
Lyudinovo 36 53 52N 34 28 E

M

Ma → 54 19 47N 105 56 E
Ma'ad 44 32 37N 35 36 E
Ma'alah 46 26 31N 47 20 E
Maamba 96 17 17S 26 28 E
Ma'an 46 30 12N 35 44 E
Ma'anshan, Anhui, China 59 31 44N 118 29 E
Ma'anshan, Anhui, China 62 31 9N 118 28 E
Ma'arrat un Nu'man 46 35 38N 36 40 E
Maas → 16 51 45N 4 32 E
Maaseik 16 51 6N 5 45 E
Maassluis 16 51 56N 4 16 E
Maastricht 16 50 50N 5 40 E
Maatin-as-Serir 85 21 45N 22 0 E
Maave 97 21 4S 34 47 E
Mabaruma 135 8 10N 59 50W
Mabein 52 23 29N 96 37 E
Mabel L. 108 50 35N 118 43W
Mabenge 94 4 15N 24 12 E
Maberly 107 44 50N 76 32W
Mabian 58 28 47N 103 37 E
Mablethorpe 12 53 21N 0 14 E
Mabrouk 89 19 29N 1 15W
Mabton 120 46 15N 120 12W
Mac Bac 55 9 46N 106 7 E
Mac Tier 114 45 9N 79 46W
Macachín 140 37 10S 63 43W
Macaé 139 22 20S 41 43W
Macaíba 138 5 51S 35 21W
Macajuba 139 12 9S 40 22W
McAlester 119 34 57N 95 46W
McAllen 119 26 12N 98 15W
Macallister → 75 38 2S 146 59 E
Macamic 104 48 45N 79 0W
Macão 23 39 35N 7 59W
Macao = Macau ■ 62 22 16N 113 35 E
Macapá 138 0 5N 51 4W
Macará 134 4 23S 79 57W
Macarani 139 15 33S 40 24W
Macarena, Serranía de la 134 2 45N 73 55W
Macarthur 74 38 5S 142 0 E
McArthur → 72 15 54S 136 40 E
McArthur River 72 16 27S 136 7 E
Macas 134 2 19S 78 7W
Macate 136 8 48S 78 7W
Macau 138 5 0S 36 40W
Macau ■ 62 22 16N 113 35 E
Macaúbas 139 13 2S 42 42W
Macaya → 134 0 59N 72 20W
McBride 108 53 20N 120 19W
McCall 120 44 55N 116 6W
McCamey 119 31 8N 102 15W
McCammon 120 42 41N 112 11W
McCauley I. 108 53 40N 130 15W
McCleary 122 47 3N 123 16W
Macclesfield 12 53 16N 2 9W
McClintock 109 57 50N 94 10W
McClintock Ra. 78 18 44S 127 38 E
McCloud 120 41 14N 122 5W
McClure 114 40 42N 77 20W
McClure, L. 122 37 35N 120 16W
McClure Str. 144 75 0N 119 0W
McClusky 118 47 30N 100 31W
McComb 119 31 13N 90 30W
McCook 118 40 15N 100 35W
McCullough Mtn. 123 35 35N 115 13W
McCusker → 109 55 32N 108 39W
McDame 108 59 44N 128 59W
McDermitt 120 42 0N 117 45W
Macdonald → 76 33 22S 151 0 E
MacDonald → 77 30 45S 150 45 E
McDonald I. 53 54 0S 73 0 E
Macdonald L. 78 23 30S 129 0 E
Macdonald, Mt. 68 17 36S 168 23 E
Macdonnell Ranges 78 23 40S 133 0 E
McDouall Peak 73 29 51S 134 55 E
Macdougall L. 100 66 0N 98 27W
MacDowell L. 102 52 15N 92 45W
Macduff 14 57 40N 2 30W
Maceda 22 42 16N 7 39W
Macedo da Cavaleiros 92 11 25S 16 45 E
Macedon 74 37 24S 144 35 E
Macedonia = Makedonija 35 41 53N 21 40 E
Maceió 138 9 40S 35 41W
Maceira 23 39 41N 8 55W
Macenta 88 8 35N 9 32W
Macerata 27 43 19N 13 28 E
McFarland 123 35 41N 119 14W
McFarlane → 109 59 12N 107 58W
Macfarlane, L. 73 32 0S 136 40 E
McGehee 119 33 40N 91 25W
McGill 120 39 27N 114 50W
Macgillycuddy's Reeks 15 52 2N 9 45W
MacGregor 109 49 57N 98 48W
McGregor, Iowa, U.S.A. 116 42 58N 91 15W
McGregor, Minn., U.S.A. 118 46 37N 93 17W
McGregor → 108 55 10N 122 0W
McGregor Ra. 73 27 0S 142 45 E
Mach 47 29 50N 67 20 E
Machacalis 139 17 5S 40 45W
Machado = Jiparana → 137 8 3S 62 52W
Machagai 140 26 56S 60 2W
Machakos 94 1 30S 37 15 E
Machakos □ 94 1 30S 37 15 E
Machala 134 3 20S 79 57W
Machanga 97 20 59S 35 0 E
Machattie, L. 72 24 50S 139 48 E
Machava 97 25 54S 32 28 E
Machece 95 19 15S 35 32 E
Machecoul 18 47 0N 1 49W
Macheng 59 31 12N 115 2 E
McHenry 117 42 21N 88 16W
Machevna 41 61 20N 172 20 E
Machezo 23 39 21N 4 20W
Machias 103 44 40N 67 28W
Machichaco, Cabo 24 43 28N 2 47W
Machichi → 109 57 3N 92 6W
Machida 65 35 28N 139 23 E
Machilipatnam 51 16 12N 81 8 E
Machine, La 19 46 54N 3 27 E
Machiques 134 10 4N 72 34W
Machupicchu 136 13 8S 72 30W
Machynlleth 13 52 36N 3 51W
Macias Nguema Biyoga 89 3 30N 8 40 E
McIlwraith Ra. 72 13 50S 143 20 E
Măcin 34 45 16N 28 8 E
Macina 88 14 50N 5 0W
McIntosh 118 45 57N 101 20W
McIntosh L. 109 55 45N 105 0W
Macintyre → 77 28 37S 150 47 E
Macizo Galaico 22 42 30N 7 30W
Mackay, Austral. 72 21 8S 149 11 E
Mackay, U.S.A. 120 43 58N 113 37W
Mackay → 108 57 10N 111 38W
Mackay, L. 78 22 30S 129 0 E
McKay Ra. 79 23 0S 122 30 E
McKees Rock 114 40 27N 80 3W
McKeesport 114 40 21N 79 50W
McKellar 106 45 30N 79 55W
McKenna 122 46 56N 122 33W
Mackenzie, Can. 108 55 20N 123 05W
Mackenzie, Guyana 135 6 0N 58 17W
McKenzie 113 36 10N 88 31W
Mackenzie □ 100 61 30N 115 0W
Mackenzie →, Austral. 72 23 38S 149 46 E
Mackenzie →, Can. 100 69 10N 134 20W
McKenzie → 120 44 2N 123 6W
Mackenzie City = Linden 136 6 0N 58 10W
Mackenzie Highway 108 58 0N 117 15W
Mackenzie Mts. 100 64 0N 130 0W
Mackenzie Plains 81 44 10S 170 25W
McKerrow L. 81 44 25S 168 5 E
Mackinac I. 106 45 51N 84 37W
Mackinac, Straits of 106 45 49N 84 42W
Mackinaw 116 40 32N 89 21W
Mackinaw → 116 40 33N 89 44W
Mackinaw City 106 45 47N 84 44W
McKinlay 72 21 16S 141 18 E
McKinlay → 72 20 50S 141 28 E
McKinley, Mt. 100 63 2N 151 0W
McKinley Sea 144 84 0N 10 0W
McKinney 119 33 10N 96 40W
Mackinnon Road 94 3 40S 39 1 E
Mackintosh Ra. 79 27 39S 125 32 E
McKittrick 123 35 18N 119 39W
Macksville 77 30 40S 152 56 E
McLaughlin 118 45 50N 100 50W
Maclean 77 29 26S 153 16 E
McLean, Ill., U.S.A. 116 40 19N 89 10W
McLean, Tex., U.S.A. 119 35 15N 100 35W
McLeansboro 117 38 5N 88 30W
Maclear 97 31 2S 28 23 E
Macleay → 77 30 56S 153 0 E
McLennan 108 55 42N 116 50W
MacLeod, B. 109 62 53N 110 0W
McLeod L. 79 24 9S 113 47 E
MacLeod Lake 108 54 58N 123 0W
M'Clintock Chan. 100 72 0N 102 0W
McLoughlin, Mt. 120 42 10N 122 19W
McLure 108 51 2N 120 13W
McMahon's Reef 76 34 39S 148 26 E
McMechen 114 39 57N 80 44W
McMillan L. 119 32 40N 104 20W
McMinnville, Oreg., U.S.A. 120 45 16N 123 11W
McMinnville, Tenn., U.S.A. 113 35 43N 85 45W
McMorran 109 51 19N 108 42W
McMurdo Sd. 143 77 0S 170 0 E
McMurray 122 48 19N 122 19W
McMurray = Fort McMurray 108 56 45N 111 27W
McNary 121 34 4N 109 53W
McNaughton L. 108 52 0N 118 10W
MacNutt 109 51 5N 101 36W
Macodoene 97 23 32S 35 5 E
Macomb 116 40 25N 90 40W
Macomer 28 40 16N 8 48 E
Mâcon 21 46 19N 4 50 E
Macon, Ga., U.S.A. 113 32 50N 83 37W
Macon, Ill., U.S.A. 116 39 43N 89 0W
Macon, Miss., U.S.A. 113 33 7N 88 31W
Macon, Mo., U.S.A. 116 39 40N 92 26W
Macondo 93 12 37S 23 46 E
Macossa 95 17 55S 33 56 E
Macoun L. 109 56 32N 103 40W
Macoupin Cr. → 116 39 11N 90 38W
Macovane 97 21 30S 35 0 E
McPherson 118 38 25N 97 40W
McPherson Pk. 123 34 53N 119 53W
Macpherson Ra. 77 28 15S 153 15 E
Macquarie Harbour 72 42 15S 145 23 E
Macquarie Is. 66 54 36S 158 55 E
Macquarie, L. 76 33 4S 151 36 E
Macquarie, Mt. 76 33 37S 149 10 E
MacRobertson Coast 143 68 30S 63 0 E
Macroom 15 51 54N 8 57W
MacTier 106 45 8N 79 47W
Macubela 95 16 53S 37 49 E
Macugnaga 26 45 57N 7 58 E
Mačuirima 95 19 14S 35 5 E
Macuiza 95 18 7S 34 29 E
Macujer 134 0 24N 73 10W
Macusani 136 14 4S 70 29W
Macuse 95 17 45S 37 10 E
Macuspana 125 17 46N 92 36W
Macusse 96 17 48S 20 23 E
Mácuzari, Presa 124 27 10N 109 10W
McVille 118 47 46N 98 11W
Madā 'in Salih 90 26 51N 37 58 E
Madagali 89 10 56N 13 33 E
Madagascar ■ 97 20 0S 47 0 E
Madā'in Sālih 46 26 46N 37 57 E
Madama 87 22 0N 13 40 E
Madame I. 103 45 30N 60 58W
Madanapalle 51 13 33N 78 28 E
Madang 69 5 12S 145 49 E
Madaoua 89 14 5N 6 27 E
Madara 89 11 45N 10 35 E
Madaripur 52 23 19N 90 15 E
Madauk 52 17 56N 96 52 E
Madawaska 107 45 30N 77 55W
Madawaska → 107 45 27N 76 21W
Madaya 52 22 12N 96 10 E
Madbar 91 6 17N 30 45 E
Maddalena 28 41 15N 9 23 E
Maddalena, La 28 41 13N 9 25 E
Maddaloni 29 41 4N 14 23 E
Madebele 91 12 30N 41 10 E
Madeira, Atl. Oc. 84 32 50N 17 0W
Madeira, U.S.A. 117 39 11N 84 22W
Madeira → 135 3 22S 58 45W
Madeleine, Îs. de la 103 47 30N 61 40W
Madera 122 37 0N 120 1W
Madha 50 18 0N 75 30 E
Madhubani 49 26 21N 86 7 E
Madhumati → 52 22 53N 89 52 E
Madhya Pradesh □ 48 21 50N 81 0 E
Madi Opei 94 3 47N 33 5 E
Madian 59 33 0N 116 6 E
Madidi → 136 12 32S 66 52W
Madill 119 34 5N 96 49W
Madimba 92 5 0S 15 0 E
Madinat al Shaab 45 12 50N 45 0 E
Madingou 92 4 10S 13 33 E
Madirovalo 97 16 26S 46 32 E
Madison, Calif., U.S.A. 122 38 41N 121 59W
Madison, Fla., U.S.A. 113 30 29N 83 39W
Madison, Ind., U.S.A. 117 38 42N 85 20W
Madison, Mo., U.S.A. 116 39 28N 92 13W
Madison, Nebr., U.S.A. 118 41 53N 97 25W
Madison, Ohio, U.S.A. 114 41 45N 81 4W
Madison, S.D., U.S.A. 118 44 0N 97 8W
Madison, Wis., U.S.A. 116 43 5N 89 25W
Madison → 120 45 56N 111 30W
Madison Junc. 120 44 42N 110 56W
Madisonville, Ky., U.S.A. 112 37 20N 87 30W
Madisonville, Tex., U.S.A. 119 30 57N 95 55W
Madista 96 21 15S 25 6 E
Madiun 57 7 38S 111 32 E
Madley 13 52 3N 2 51W
Madoc 107 44 30N 77 28W
Madol 91 9 3N 27 45 E
Madon → 19 48 36N 6 6 E
Madona 36 56 53N 26 5 E
Madonie, Le 28 37 50N 13 50 E
Madras, India 51 13 8N 80 19 E
Madras, U.S.A. 120 44 40N 121 10W
Madras = Tamil Nadu □ 51 11 0N 77 0 E
Madre de Dios □ 136 12 0S 70 15W
Madre de Dios → 136 10 59S 66 8W
Madre de Dios, I. 142 50 20S 75 10W
Madre del Sur, Sierra 125 17 30N 100 0W
Madre, Laguna, Mexico 125 25 0N 97 30W
Madre, Laguna, U.S.A. 119 25 0N 97 40W
Madre Occidental, Sierra 124 27 0N 107 0W
Madre Oriental, Sierra 124 25 0N 100 0W
Madre, Sierra, Mexico 125 16 0N 93 0W
Madre, Sierra, Phil. 57 17 0N 122 0 E
Madri 48 24 16N 73 32 E
Madrid, Spain 22 40 25N 3 45W
Madrid, U.S.A. 116 41 53N 93 49W
Madrid □ 22 40 30N 3 45W
Madridejos 23 39 28N 3 33W
Madrigal de las Altas Torres 22 41 5N 5 0W
Madrona, Sierra 23 38 27N 4 16W
Madroñera 23 39 26N 5 42W
Madu 91 14 37N 26 4 E

Name	Map	Lat.	Long.
Madura Motel	**79**	31 55S	127 0E
Madura, Selat	**57**	7 30S	113 20E
Madurai	**51**	9 55N	78 10E
Madurantakam	**51**	12 30N	79 50E
Madzhalis	**39**	42 9N	47 47E
Mae Chan	**54**	20 9N	99 52E
Mae Hong Son	**54**	19 16N	98 1E
Mae Khlong →	**54**	13 24N	100 0E
Mae Phrik	**54**	17 27N	99 7E
Mae Ramat	**54**	16 58N	98 31E
Mae Rim	**54**	18 54N	98 57E
Mae Sot	**54**	16 43N	98 34E
Mae Suai	**54**	19 39N	99 33E
Mae Tha	**54**	18 28N	99 8E
Maebaru	**64**	33 33N	130 12E
Maebashi	**65**	36 24N	139 4E
Maella	**24**	41 8N	0 7E
Măeruş	**34**	45 53N	25 31E
Maesteg	**13**	51 36N	3 40W
Maestra, Sierra	**126**	20 15N	77 0W
Maestrazgo, Mts. del	**24**	40 30N	0 25W
Maevatanana	**97**	16 56N	46 49E
Maewo (Aurora)	**68**	15 10S	168 10E
Ma'fan	**87**	25 56N	14 29E
Mafeking, Can.	**109**	52 40N	101 10W
Mafeking, S. Afr.	**96**	25 50S	25 38E
Maféré	**88**	5 30N	3 2W
Mafeteng	**96**	29 51S	27 15E
Maffra	**75**	37 53S	146 58E
Mafia	**94**	7 45S	39 50E
Mafra, Brazil	**141**	26 10S	50 0W
Mafra, Port.	**23**	38 55N	9 20W
Mafungabusi Plateau	**95**	18 30S	29 8E
Magadan	**41**	59 38N	150 50E
Magadi	**94**	1 54S	36 19E
Magadi, L.	**94**	1 54S	36 19E
Magaliesburg	**97**	26 1S	27 32E
Magallanes □	**142**	52 0S	72 0W
Magallanes, Estrecho de	**142**	52 30S	75 0W
Magangué	**134**	9 14N	74 45W
Magaria	**89**	13 4N	9 5E
Magburaka	**88**	8 47N	12 0W
Magdalena, Argent.	**140**	35 5S	57 30W
Magdalena, Boliv.	**137**	13 13S	63 57W
Magdalena, Malay.	**56**	4 25N	117 55E
Magdalena, Mexico	**124**	30 50N	112 0W
Magdalena, U.S.A.	**121**	34 10N	107 20W
Magdalena □	**134**	10 0N	74 0W
Magdalena →, Colomb.	**134**	11 6N	74 51W
Magdalena →, Mexico	**124**	30 40N	112 25W
Magdalena, B.	**124**	24 30N	112 10W
Magdalena, I., Chile	**142**	44 40S	73 0W
Magdalena, I., Mexico	**124**	24 40N	112 15W
Magdalena, I., Mexico	**124**	24 50N	112 15W
Magdalena, Llano de la	**124**	25 0N	111 30W
Magdeburg	**30**	52 8N	11 36E
Magdeburg □	**30**	52 20N	11 30E
Magdelaine Cays	**72**	16 33S	150 18E
Magdi'el	**44**	32 10N	34 54E
Magdub	**91**	13 42N	25 5E
Magee	**119**	31 53N	89 45W
Magee, I.	**15**	54 48N	5 44W
Magelang	**57**	7 29S	110 13E
Magellan's Str. = Magallanes, Est. de	**142**	52 30S	75 0W
Magenta	**26**	45 28N	8 53E
Magenta, L.	**79**	33 30S	119 2E
Maggia →	**31**	46 18N	8 36E
Maggiorasca, Mte.	**26**	44 33N	9 29E
Maggiore, L.	**26**	46 0N	8 35E
Maghama	**88**	15 32N	12 57W
Maghar	**44**	32 54N	35 24E
Magherafelt	**15**	54 44N	6 37W
Maghnia	**86**	34 50N	1 43W
Magione	**27**	43 10N	12 12E
Magliano in Toscana	**27**	42 36N	11 18E
Máglie	**29**	40 8N	18 17E
Magnac-Laval	**20**	46 13N	1 11E
Magnetawan	**106**	45 40N	79 39W
Magnetic Pole, 1976 (North)	**144**	76 12N	100 12W
Magnetic Pole, 1976 (South)	**143**	68 48S	139 30E
Magnitogorsk	**40**	53 27N	59 4E
Magnolia, Ark., U.S.A.	**119**	33 18N	93 12W
Magnolia, Miss., U.S.A.	**119**	31 8N	90 28W
Magnor	**10**	59 56N	12 15E
Magnus, Mt.	**77**	28 30S	151 50E
Magny-en-Vexin	**19**	49 9N	1 47E
Magog	**105**	45 18N	72 9W
Magoro	**94**	1 45N	34 12E
Magosa = Famagusta	**46**	35 8N	33 55E
Magoye	**95**	16 1S	27 30E
Magpie L.	**103**	51 0N	64 41W
Magrath	**108**	49 25N	112 50W
Magro →	**25**	39 11N	0 25W
Magrur, Wadi →	**91**	16 5N	26 30E
Magu □	**94**	2 31S	33 28E
Maguan	**58**	23 0N	104 21E
Maguarinho, C.	**138**	0 15S	48 30W
Maguse L.	**109**	61 40N	95 10W
Maguse Pt.	**109**	61 20N	93 50W
Magwe	**52**	20 10N	95 0E
Maha Sarakham	**54**	16 12N	103 16E
Mahābād	**46**	36 50N	45 45E
Mahabaleshwar	**50**	17 58N	73 43E
Mahabharat Lekh	**49**	28 30N	82 0E
Mahabo	**97**	20 23S	44 40E
Mahad	**50**	18 6N	73 29E
Mahadeo Hills	**48**	22 20N	78 30E
Mahadeopur	**50**	18 48N	80 0E
Mahagi	**94**	2 20N	31 0E
Mahaicony	**135**	6 36N	57 48W
Mahajamba →	**97**	15 33S	47 8E
Mahajamba, B. de la	**97**	15 24S	47 5E
Mahajan	**48**	28 48N	73 56E
Mahajilo →	**97**	19 42S	45 22E
Mahakam →	**56**	0 35S	117 17E
Mahalapye	**96**	23 1S	26 51E
Mahallāt	**47**	33 55N	50 30E
Mahanadi →	**50**	20 20N	86 25E
Mahanoro	**97**	19 54S	48 48E
Mahanoy City	**115**	40 48N	76 10W
Maharashtra □	**50**	20 30N	75 30E
Maharès	**87**	34 32N	10 29E
Mahari Mts.	**94**	6 20S	30 0E
Mahasolo	**97**	19 7S	46 22E
Mahaweli → Ganga	**51**	8 30N	81 15E
Mahaxay	**54**	17 22N	105 12E
Mahboobabad	**50**	17 42N	80 2E
Mahbubnagar	**50**	16 45N	77 59E
Mahdia, Guyana	**135**	5 13N	59 8W
Mahdia, Tunisia	**87**	35 28N	11 0E
Mahé	**51**	11 42N	75 34E
Mahe	**49**	33 10N	78 32E
Mahé, I.	**53**	5 0S	55 30E
Mahendra Giri	**51**	8 20N	77 30E
Mahendraganj	**52**	25 20N	89 45E
Mahenge	**95**	8 45S	36 41E
Maheno	**81**	45 10S	170 50E
Mahia Pen.	**80**	39 9S	177 55E
Mahirija	**86**	34 0N	3 16W
Mahlaing	**52**	21 6N	95 39E
Mahmiya	**91**	17 12N	33 43E
Mahmud Kot	**48**	30 16N	71 0E
Mahmudia	**34**	45 5N	29 5E
Mahnomen	**118**	47 22N	95 57W
Mahoba	**49**	25 15N	79 55E
Mahomet	**117**	40 12N	88 24W
Mahón	**24**	39 50N	4 18E
Mahone Bay	**103**	44 30N	64 20W
Mahuta	**89**	11 32N	4 58E
Mai-Ndombe, L.	**92**	2 0S	18 20E
Mai-Sai	**54**	20 20N	99 55E
Maibara	**65**	35 19N	136 17E
Maicao	**134**	11 23N	72 13W
Maicasagi →	**104**	49 58N	76 33W
Maîche	**19**	47 16N	6 48E
Maici →	**137**	6 30S	61 43W
Maicurú →	**135**	2 14S	54 17W
Màida	**29**	38 51N	16 21E
Maidan Khula	**48**	33 36N	69 50E
Maidenhead	**13**	51 31N	0 42W
Maidi	**91**	16 20N	42 45E
Maidstone, Can.	**109**	53 5N	109 20W
Maidstone, U.K.	**13**	51 16N	0 31E
Maiduguri	**89**	12 0N	13 20E
Maignelay	**19**	49 32N	2 30E
Maigualida, Sierra	**135**	5 30N	65 10W
Maijdi	**52**	22 48N	91 10E
Maikala Ra.	**50**	22 0N	81 0E
Mailly-le-Camp	**19**	48 41N	4 12E
Mailsi	**48**	29 48N	72 15E
Maimana	**47**	35 53N	64 38E
Main →, Ger.	**31**	50 0N	8 18E
Main →, U.K.	**15**	54 49N	6 20W
Main Centre	**109**	50 35N	107 21W
Mainburg	**31**	48 37N	11 49E
Maine	**18**	48 0N	0 0E
Maine □	**103**	45 20N	69 0W
Maine →	**15**	52 10N	9 40W
Maine-et-Loire □	**18**	47 31N	0 30W
Maïne-Soroa	**89**	13 13N	12 2E
Maingkwan	**52**	26 15N	96 37E
Mainit, L.	**57**	9 31N	125 30E
Mainkaing	**52**	24 48N	95 16E
Mainland, I., Orkney, U.K.	**14**	59 0N	3 10W
Mainland, I., Shetland, U.K.	**14**	60 15N	1 22W
Mainpuri	**49**	27 18N	79 4E
Maintenon	**19**	48 35N	1 35E
Maintirano	**97**	18 3S	44 1E
Mainz	**31**	50 0N	8 17E
Maipú	**140**	36 52S	57 50W
Maiquetía	**134**	10 36N	66 57W
Maira →	**26**	44 49N	7 38E
Mairabari	**52**	26 30N	92 22E
Maire, Le, Est. de	**142**	54 50S	65 0W
Mairipotaba	**139**	17 18S	49 28W
Maisí	**127**	20 17N	74 9W
Maisi, Pta. de	**127**	20 10N	74 10W
Maisse	**19**	48 24N	2 21E
Maitland, N.S.W., Austral.	**76**	32 33S	151 36E
Maitland, S. Australia, Austral.	**73**	34 23S	137 40E
Maitland →	**114**	43 45N	81 33W
Maiyema	**89**	12 5N	4 25E
Maiyuan	**59**	25 34N	117 28E
Maiz, Islas del	**126**	12 15N	83 4W
Maizuru	**65**	35 25N	135 22E
Majagual	**134**	8 33N	74 38W
Majalengka	**57**	6 55S	108 14E
Majari →	**135**	3 29N	60 58W
Majd el Kurum	**44**	32 56N	35 15E
Majene	**57**	3 38S	118 57E
Majes →	**136**	16 40S	72 44W
Maji	**91**	6 12N	35 30E
Majiang	**58**	26 28N	107 32E
Major	**109**	51 52N	109 37W
Majorca, I. = Mallorca	**24**	39 30N	3 0E
Majors Creek	**76**	35 33S	149 45E
Majunga □	**97**	17 0S	47 0E
Majuriã	**137**	7 30S	64 55W
Maka	**88**	13 40N	14 10W
Makak	**89**	3 36N	11 0E
Makale	**57**	3 6S	119 51E
Makamba	**94**	4 8S	29 49E
Makarewa	**81**	46 20S	168 21E
Makari	**92**	12 35N	14 28E
Makarikari = Makgadikgadi Salt Pans	**96**	20 40S	25 45E
Makarovo	**41**	57 40N	107 45E
Makarska	**33**	43 20N	17 2E
Makaryev	**37**	57 52N	43 50E
Makasar = Ujung Pandang	**57**	5 10S	119 20E
Makasar, Selat	**57**	1 0S	118 20E
Makat	**40**	47 39N	53 19E
Makedonija □	**35**	41 53N	21 40E
Makena	**110**	20 39N	156 27W
Makeni	**88**	8 55N	12 5W
Makeyevka	**38**	48 0N	38 0E
Makgadikgadi Salt Pans	**96**	20 40S	25 45E
Makgobistad	**96**	25 45S	25 12E
Makhachkala	**39**	43 0N	47 30E
Makhambet	**39**	47 43N	51 40E
Makharadze	**39**	41 55N	42 2E
Makian	**57**	0 20N	127 20E
Makin	**66**	3 30N	174 0E
Makindu	**94**	2 18S	37 50E
Makinsk	**40**	52 37N	70 26E
Makkah	**90**	21 30N	39 54E
Makkovik	**103**	55 10N	59 10W
Maklakovo	**41**	58 16N	92 29E
Makó	**33**	46 14N	20 33E
Makokou	**92**	0 40N	12 50E
Makongo	**94**	3 25N	26 17E
Makoro	**94**	3 10N	29 59E
Makoua	**92**	0 5S	15 50E
Makrá	**35**	36 15N	25 54E
Makran	**47**	26 13N	61 30E
Makran Coast Range	**47**	25 40N	64 0E
Makrana	**48**	27 2N	74 46E
Maksimkin Yar	**40**	58 42N	86 50E
Maktar	**87**	35 48N	9 12E
Mākū	**46**	39 15N	44 31E
Makum	**52**	27 30N	95 23E
Makumbe	**96**	20 15S	24 26E
Makumbi	**92**	5 50S	20 43E
Makunda	**96**	22 30S	20 7E
Makurazaki	**64**	31 15N	130 20E
Makurdi	**89**	7 43N	8 35E
Makwassie	**96**	27 17S	26 0E
Mal	**52**	25 51N	88 45E
Mal B.	**15**	52 50N	9 30W
Mal i Nemërçkës	**35**	40 15N	20 15E
Mal i Tomorit	**35**	40 42N	20 11E
Mala	**136**	12 40S	76 38W
Mala Kapela	**27**	44 45N	15 30E
Mala, Pta.	**126**	7 28N	80 2W
Malabang	**57**	7 36N	124 3E
Malabar Coast	**51**	11 0N	75 0E
Malacca, Str. of	**55**	3 0N	101 0E
Malacky	**33**	48 27N	17 0E
Malad City	**120**	42 10N	112 20E
Malafaburi	**91**	10 37N	40 30E
Málaga, Colomb.	**134**	6 42N	72 44W
Málaga, Spain	**23**	36 43N	4 23W
Malaga	**119**	32 12N	104 2W
Málaga □	**23**	36 38N	4 58W
Malagarasi	**94**	5 5S	30 50E
Malagarasi →	**94**	5 12S	29 47E
Malagón	**23**	39 11N	3 52W
Malagón →	**23**	37 35N	7 29W
Malaimbandy	**97**	20 20S	45 36E
Malaita	**68**	9 0S	161 0E
Malakâl	**91**	9 33N	31 40E
Malakand	**48**	34 40N	71 55E
Malakoff	**119**	32 10N	95 55W
Malamyzh	**41**	50 0N	136 50E
Malang	**57**	7 59S	112 45E
Malanje	**92**	9 36S	16 17E
Mälaren	**10**	59 30N	17 10E
Malargüe	**140**	35 32S	69 30W
Malartic	**104**	48 9N	78 9W
Malartic, L.	**104**	48 15N	78 5W
Malatya	**46**	38 25N	38 20E
Malau	**68**	15 0S	166 0E
Malawi ■	**95**	13 0S	34 0E
Malawi, L. (Lago Niassa)	**95**	12 30S	34 30E
Malay Pen.	**55**	7 25N	100 0E
Malaya □	**55**	4 0N	102 0E
Malaya Belozërka	**38**	47 12N	34 56E
Malaya Vishera	**36**	58 55N	32 25E
Malaybalay	**57**	8 5N	125 7E
Malayer	**46**	34 19N	48 51E
Malaysia ■	**56**	5 0N	110 0E
Malaysia, Western □	**55**	5 0N	102 0E
Malazgirt	**46**	39 10N	42 33E
Malbaie, La	**105**	47 40N	70 10W
Malbon	**72**	21 5S	140 17E
Malbooma	**73**	30 41S	134 11E
Malbork	**32**	54 3N	19 1E
Malca Dube	**91**	6 40N	41 52E
Malcésine	**26**	45 46N	10 48E
Malchin	**30**	53 43N	12 44E
Malchow	**30**	53 29N	12 25E
Malcolm	**79**	28 51S	121 25E
Malcolm, Pt.	**79**	33 48S	123 45E
Maldegem	**16**	51 14N	3 26E
Malden, Mass., U.S.A.	**115**	42 26N	71 5W
Malden, Mo., U.S.A.	**119**	36 35N	90 0W
Malden I.	**67**	4 3S	155 1W
Maldive Is. ■	**53**	7 0N	73 0E
Maldon	**74**	37 0S	144 6E
Maldonado	**141**	35 0S	55 0W
Maldonado, Punta	**125**	16 19N	98 35W
Malé	**26**	46 20N	10 55E
Maléa, Ákra	**35**	36 28N	23 7E
Malegaon	**50**	20 30N	74 38E
Malei	**95**	17 12S	36 58E
Malekula(Mallicolo)	**68**	16 15S	167 30E
Malela	**94**	4 22S	26 8E
Malenge	**95**	12 40S	26 42E
Målerås	**11**	56 54N	15 34E
Malerkotla	**48**	30 32N	75 58E
Malesherbes	**19**	48 15N	2 24E
Malestroit	**18**	47 49N	2 25W
Malfa	**29**	38 35N	14 50E
Malgobek	**39**	43 30N	44 34E
Malgomaj	**8**	64 40N	16 30E
Malgrat	**24**	41 39N	2 46E
Malha	**85**	15 8N	25 10E
Malheur →	**120**	44 3N	116 59W
Malheur L.	**120**	43 19N	118 42W
Mali	**88**	12 10N	12 20W
Mali ■	**89**	15 0N	2 0W
Mali Hka →	**52**	25 42N	97 30E
Mali Kanal	**33**	45 36N	19 24E
Malibu	**123**	34 2N	118 41W
Malih →	**44**	32 20N	35 34E
Malik	**57**	0 39S	123 16E
Malili	**57**	2 42S	121 6E
Malimba, Mts.	**94**	7 30S	29 30E
Malin	**36**	50 46N	29 3E
Malin Hd.	**15**	55 18N	7 24W
Malinau	**56**	3 35N	116 40E
Malindi	**94**	3 12S	40 5E
Maling	**57**	1 0N	121 0E
Malingping	**57**	6 45S	106 2E
Malinyi	**95**	8 56S	36 0E
Malipo	**58**	23 7N	104 42E
Maliqi	**35**	40 45N	20 48E
Malita	**57**	6 19N	125 39E
Malkapur, Maharashtra, India	**50**	16 57N	73 58E
Malkapur, Maharashtra, India	**50**	20 53N	73 58E
Małkinia Górna	**32**	52 42N	22 5E
Malko Tŭrnovo	**35**	41 59N	27 31E
Mallacoota Inlet	**75**	37 34S	149 40E
Mallaig	**14**	57 0N	5 50W
Mallanganee	**77**	28 54S	152 44E
Mallard	**116**	42 56N	94 41W
Mallawan	**49**	27 4N	80 12E
Mallawi	**90**	27 44N	30 44E
Malleco □	**142**	38 10S	72 20W
Mallemort	**21**	43 44N	5 11E
Málles Venosta	**26**	46 42N	10 32E
Mallina P.O.	**78**	20 53S	118 2E
Mallorca	**24**	39 30N	3 0E
Mallorytown	**115**	44 29N	75 53W
Mallow	**15**	52 8N	8 40W
Malmbäck	**11**	57 34N	14 28E
Malmberget	**8**	67 11N	20 40E

Malmédy 16 50 25N 6 2 E
Malmesbury, Austral. 74 37 9S 144 25 E
Malmesbury, S. Afr. 96 33 28S 18 41 E
Malmö 11 55 36N 12 59 E
Malmöhus län □ 11 55 45N 13 30 E
Malmslätt 11 58 27N 15 33 E
Malmyzh 37 56 35N 50 41 E
Malo 68 15 40S 167 11 E
Maloarkhangelsk 37 52 28N 36 30 E
Maloca 135 0 43N 55 57W
Malolos 57 14 50N 120 49 E
Malombe L. 95 14 40S 35 15 E
Malone 115 44 50N 74 19W
Malong 58 25 24N 103 34 E
Malorita 36 51 50N 24 3 E
Maloyaroslovets 37 55 2N 36 20 E
Malpartida 23 39 26N 6 30W
Malpelo 136 4 3N 81 35W
Malpica 22 43 19N 8 50W
Malprabha → 51 16 20N 76 5 E
Malta, Brazil 138 6 54S 37 31W
Malta, Idaho, U.S.A. 120 42 15N 113 30W
Malta, Mont., U.S.A. 120 48 20N 107 55W
Malta ■ 7 35 50N 14 30 E
Malta Channel 28 36 40N 14 0 E
Malton, Can. 114 43 42N 79 38W
Malton, U.K. 12 54 9N 0 48W
Malu'a 68 8 0S 160 0 E
Maluku 57 1 0S 127 0 E
Maluku □ 57 3 0S 128 0 E
Maluku, Kepulauan 57 3 0S 128 0 E
Malumfashi 89 11 48N 7 39 E
Malung 10 60 42N 13 44 E
Malvalli 51 12 28N 77 8 E
Malvan 51 16 2N 73 30 E
Malvern, U.K. 13 52 7N 2 19W
Malvern, U.S.A. 119 34 22N 92 50W
Malvern Hills 13 52 0N 2 19W
Malvérnia 97 22 6S 31 42 E
Malvik 10 63 25N 10 40 E
Malvinas, Is. = Falkland Is. 142 51 30S 59 0W
Malya 94 3 5S 33 38 E
Malyy Lyakhovskiy, Ostrov 41 74 7N 140 36 E
Mama 41 58 18N 112 54 E
Mamadysh 37 55 44N 51 23 E
Mamaku 80 38 5S 176 8 E
Mamanguape 138 6 50S 35 4W
Mamanutha Group 68 17 34S 177 4 E
Mamarana 68 7 0S 157 0 E
Mamasa 57 2 55S 119 20 E
Mambasa 94 1 22N 29 3 E
Mamberamo → 57 2 0S 137 50 E
Mambilima 95 10 31S 28 45 E
Mambirima 95 11 25S 27 33 E
Mambo 94 4 52S 38 22 E
Mambrui 94 3 5S 40 5 E
Mamburao 57 13 13N 120 39 E
Mameigwess L. 102 52 35N 87 50W
Mamers 18 48 21N 0 22 E
Mamfe 89 5 50N 9 15 E
Mamiña 136 20 5S 69 14W
Mámmola 29 38 23N 16 13 E
Mammoth 121 32 46N 110 43W
Mamoré → 137 10 23S 65 53W
Mamou 88 10 15N 12 0W
Mampatá 88 11 54N 14 53W
Mampawah 56 0 30N 109 5 E
Mampong 89 7 6N 1 26W
Mamuil Malal, Paso 142 39 35S 71 28W
Mamuju 57 2 41S 118 50 E
Man 88 7 30N 7 40W
Man → 50 17 31N 75 32 E
Man, I. of 12 54 15N 4 30W
Man Na 52 23 27N 97 19 E
Man Tun 52 23 52N 98 38 E
Mana 135 5 45N 53 55W
Mana →, Ethiopia 91 5 40N 40 50 E
Mana →, Fr. Gui. 135 5 45N 53 55W
Måna → 10 59 55N 8 50 E
Manaar, Gulf of 51 8 30N 79 0 E
Manabí □ 134 0 40S 80 5W
Manacacías → 134 4 23N 72 4W
Manacapuru 135 3 16S 60 37W
Manacapuru → 135 3 18S 60 37W
Manacor 24 39 32N 3 12 E
Manado 57 1 29N 124 51 E
Managua 126 12 6N 86 20W
Managua, L. 126 12 20N 86 30W
Manaia 80 39 33S 174 8 E
Manakana 97 13 45S 50 4 E
Manakara 97 22 8S 48 1 E
Manakau Mt. 81 42 15S 173 42 E
Manam I. 69 4 5S 145 0 E
Manamāh, Al 47 26 11N 50 35 E
Manambao → 97 17 35S 44 0 E
Manambato 97 13 43S 49 7 E
Manambolo → 97 19 18S 44 22 E
Manambolosy 97 16 2S 49 40 E
Mananara 97 16 10S 49 46 E
Mananara → 97 23 21S 47 42 E
Manangatang 74 35 5S 142 54 E
Mananjary 97 21 13S 48 20 E
Manantenina 97 24 17S 47 19 E
Manaos = Manaus 135 3 0S 60 0W
Manapire → 134 7 42N 66 7W
Manapouri 81 45 34S 167 39 E
Manapouri, L. 81 45 32S 167 32 E
Manar → 50 18 50N 77 20 E
Manas 62 44 17N 85 56 E
Manasir 47 24 30N 51 10 E
Manaslu, Mt. 49 28 33N 84 33 E
Manasquan 115 40 7N 74 3W
Manassa 121 37 12N 105 58W
Manaung 52 18 45N 93 40 E
Manaus 135 3 0S 60 0W
Manawan L. 109 55 24N 103 14W
Manawatu → 80 40 28S 175 12 E
Manay 57 7 17N 126 33 E
Mancelona 106 44 54N 85 5W
Mancha, La 25 39 10N 2 54W
Mancha Real 23 37 48N 3 39W
Manche □ 18 49 10N 1 20W
Manchester, U.K. 12 53 30N 2 15W
Manchester, Calif., U.S.A. 122 38 58N 123 41W
Manchester, Conn., U.S.A. 115 41 47N 72 30W
Manchester, Ga., U.S.A. 113 32 53N 84 32W
Manchester, Iowa, U.S.A. 116 42 28N 91 27W
Manchester, Ky., U.S.A. 112 37 9N 83 45W
Manchester, Mich., U.S.A. 117 42 9N 84 2W
Manchester, N.H., U.S.A. 115 42 58N 71 29W
Manchester, N.Y., U.S.A. 114 42 56N 77 16W
Manchester, Vt., U.S.A. 115 43 10N 73 5W
Manchester L. 109 61 28N 107 29W
Manchuria = Dongbei 61 42 0N 125 0 E
Manciano 27 42 35N 11 30 E
Mancifa 91 6 53N 41 50 E
Mancora, Pta. 136 4 9S 81 1W
Mand → 47 28 20N 52 30 E
Manda, Chunya, Tanz. 94 6 51S 32 29 E
Manda, Ludewe, Tanz. 95 10 30S 34 40 E
Mandaguari 141 23 32S 51 42W
Mandah 60 44 27N 108 2 E
Mandal 9 58 2N 7 25 E
Mandalay 52 22 0N 96 4 E
Mandale = Mandalay 52 22 0N 96 4 E
Mandalgovi 60 45 45N 106 10 E
Mandali 46 33 43N 45 28 E
Mandan 118 46 50N 101 0W
Mandapeta 50 16 47N 81 56 E
Mandar, Teluk 57 3 35S 119 15 E
Mandas 28 39 40N 9 8 E
Mandasaur 48 24 3N 75 8 E
Mandasor = Mandasaur 48 24 3N 75 8 E
Mandawai (Katingan) → 56 3 30S 113 0 E
Mandelieu-la-Napoule 21 43 34N 6 57 E
Mandera 94 3 55N 41 53 E
Mandera □ 94 3 30N 41 0 E
Mandi, India 48 31 39N 76 58 E
Mandi, Zambia 95 14 30S 23 45 E
Mandioli 57 0 40S 127 20 E
Mandla 49 22 39N 80 30 E
Mandø 11 55 18N 8 33 E
Mandoto 97 19 34S 46 17 E
Mandoúdhion 35 38 48N 23 29 E
Mandra 48 33 23N 73 12 E
Mandrare → 97 25 10S 46 30 E
Mandritsara 97 15 50S 48 49 E
Mandurah 79 32 36S 115 48 E
Mandúria 29 40 25N 17 38 E
Mandvi 48 22 51N 69 22 E
Mandya 51 12 30N 77 0 E
Mandzai 48 30 55N 67 6 E
Mané 89 12 59N 1 21W
Maner → 50 18 30N 79 40 E
Maneroo 72 23 22S 143 53 E
Maneroo Cr. → 72 23 21S 143 53 E
Manfalût 90 27 20N 30 52 E
Manfred 73 33 19S 143 45 E
Manfredónia 29 41 40N 15 55 E
Manfredónia, G. di 29 41 30N 16 10 E
Manga, Brazil 139 14 46S 43 56W
Manga, Upp. Vol. 89 11 40N 1 4W
Mangabeiras, Chapada das 138 10 0S 46 30W
Mangalagiri 51 16 26N 80 36 E
Mangaldai 52 26 26N 92 2 E
Mangalia 34 43 50N 28 35 E
Mangalore, Austral. 74 36 56S 145 10 E
Mangalore, India 51 12 55N 74 47 E
Manganeses 22 41 45N 5 43W
Mangaon 50 18 15N 73 20 E
Manggar 56 2 50S 108 10 E
Manggawitu 57 4 8S 133 32 E
Mangin Range 52 24 15N 95 45 E
Mangkalihat, Tanjung 57 1 2N 118 59 E
Mangla Dam 49 33 9N 73 44 E
Manglares, C. 134 1 36N 79 2W
Manglaur 48 29 44N 77 49 E
Mangnai 62 37 52N 91 43 E
Mango 68 17 27S 179 9W
Mangoky → 97 21 29S 43 41 E
Mangole 57 1 50S 125 55 E
Mangombe 94 1 20S 26 48 E
Mangonui 80 35 1S 173 32 E
Mangoplah 76 35 23S 147 17 E
Mangualde 22 40 38N 7 48W
Mangueigne 85 10 30N 21 15 E
Mangueira, Lagoa da 141 33 0S 52 50W
Manguéni, Hamada 87 22 35N 12 40 E
Mangum 119 34 50N 99 30W
Mangyshlak P-ov. 39 44 30N 52 30 E
Manhattan, Kans., U.S.A. 118 39 10N 96 40W
Manhattan, Nev., U.S.A. 121 38 31N 117 3W
Manhatten 117 41 26N 87 59W
Manhiça 97 25 23S 32 49 E
Manhuaçu 139 20 15S 42 2W
Manhumirim 139 20 22S 41 57W
Maní 134 4 49N 72 17W
Mania → 97 19 42S 45 22 E
Maniago 27 46 11N 12 40 E
Manica e Sofala □ 97 19 10S 33 45 E
Manicaland □ 95 19 0S 32 30 E
Manicoré 137 5 48S 61 16W
Manicoré → 137 5 51S 61 19W
Manicouagan → 105 49 30N 68 30W
Manicouagan L. 103 51 25N 68 15W
Manifah 46 27 44N 49 0 E
Manifold 72 22 41S 150 40 E
Manifold, C. 72 22 41S 150 50 E
Maniganggo 58 31 56N 99 10 E
Manigotagan 109 51 6N 96 18W
Manigotagan L. 109 50 52N 95 37W
Manihiki 67 10 24S 161 1W
Manika, Plat. de la 95 10 0S 25 5 E
Manikganj 52 23 52N 90 0 E
Manila, Phil. 57 14 40N 121 3 E
Manila, U.S.A. 120 41 0N 109 44W
Manila B. 57 14 0N 120 0 E
Manildra 76 33 11S 148 41 E
Manilla 77 30 45S 150 43 E
Manimpé 88 14 11N 5 28W
Maningory 97 17 9S 49 30 E
Manipur □ 52 25 0N 94 0 E
Manipur → 52 23 45N 94 20 E
Manisa 46 38 38N 27 30 E
Manistee 112 44 15N 86 20W
Manistee → 106 44 15N 86 21W
Manistique 112 45 59N 86 18W
Manito 116 40 25N 89 47W
Manito L. 109 52 43N 109 43W
Manitoba □ 109 55 30N 97 0W
Manitoba, L. 109 51 0N 98 45W
Manitou 109 49 15N 98 32W
Manitou Beach 117 41 58N 84 19W
Manitou I. 102 47 22N 87 30W
Manitou Is. 112 45 8N 86 0W
Manitou L., Ont., Can. 106 45 51N 82 0W
Manitou L., Ont., Can. 109 49 15N 93 0W
Manitou L., Qué., Can. 103 50 55N 65 17W
Manitou Springs 118 38 52N 104 55W
Manitoulin I. 106 45 40N 82 30W
Manitowaning 106 45 46N 81 49W
Manitowoc 112 44 8N 87 40W
Manitsauá-Missu → 137 10 58S 53 20W
Maniwaki 104 46 23N 75 58W
Manizales 134 5 5N 75 32W
Manja 97 21 26S 44 20 E
Manjakandriana 97 18 55S 47 47 E
Manjeri 51 11 7N 76 11 E
Manjhand 48 25 50N 68 10 E
Manjil 46 36 46N 49 30 E
Manjimup 79 34 15S 116 6 E
Manjra → 50 18 49N 77 52 E
Mankato, Kans., U.S.A. 118 39 49N 98 11W
Mankato, Minn., U.S.A. 118 44 8N 93 59W
Mankayana 97 26 38S 31 6 E
Mankono 88 8 1N 6 10W
Mankota 109 49 25N 107 5W
Manlay 60 44 9N 107 0 E
Manlleu 24 42 2N 2 17 E
Manly 76 33 48S 151 17 E
Manmad 50 20 18N 74 28 E
Mann Ranges, Mts. 79 26 6S 130 5 E
Manna 56 4 25S 102 55 E
Mannahill 73 32 25S 140 0 E
Mannar 51 9 1N 79 54 E
Mannar, G. of 51 8 30N 79 0 E
Mannar I. 51 9 5N 79 45 E
Mannargudi 51 10 45N 79 51 E
Mannheim 31 49 28N 8 29 E
Manning, Can. 108 56 53N 117 39W
Manning, Oreg., U.S.A. 122 45 45N 123 13W
Manning, S.C., U.S.A. 113 33 40N 80 9W
Manning → 77 31 52S 152 43 E
Manning Prov. Park 108 49 5N 120 45W
Manning Str. 68 7 30S 158 0 E
Mannington 112 39 35N 80 25W
Mannu → 28 39 15N 9 32 E
Mannu, C. 28 40 2N 8 24 E
Mannum 73 34 50S 139 20 E
Mannus 76 35 45S 147 55 E
Mano 88 8 3N 12 2W
Manoa 137 9 40S 65 27W
Manokwari 57 0 54S 134 0 E
Manombo 97 22 57S 43 28 E
Manono 94 7 15S 27 25 E
Manosque 21 43 49N 5 47 E
Manotick 107 45 13N 75 41W
Manouane L. 103 50 45N 70 45W
Manouane, L. 105 47 33N 74 6W
Manouro, Pt. 68 17 41S 168 36 E
Manpojin 61 41 6N 126 24 E
Manresa 24 41 48N 1 50 E
Mans, Le 18 48 0N 0 10 E
Mansa, Gujarat, India 48 23 27N 72 45 E
Mansa, Punjab, India 48 30 0N 75 27 E
Mansa, Zambia 95 11 13S 28 55 E
Manseau 105 46 22N 72 0W
Mansehra 48 34 20N 73 15 E
Mansel I. 101 62 0N 80 0W
Mansfield, Austral. 75 37 4S 146 6 E
Mansfield, U.K. 12 53 8N 1 12W
Mansfield, La., U.S.A. 119 32 2N 93 40W
Mansfield, Mass., U.S.A. 115 42 2N 71 12W
Mansfield, Ohio, U.S.A. 114 40 45N 82 30W
Mansfield, Pa., U.S.A. 114 41 48N 77 4W
Mansfield, Wash., U.S.A. 120 47 51N 119 44W
Mansi 52 24 48N 95 52 E
Mansidão 138 10 43S 44 2W
Mansilla de las Mulas 22 42 30N 5 25W
Mansle 20 45 52N 0 9 E
Manso → 139 13 50S 47 0W
Mansoa 88 12 0N 15 20W
Manson 116 42 32N 94 32W
Manson Creek 108 55 37N 124 32W
Mansoura, Djebel 87 36 1N 4 31 E
Manta 134 1 0S 80 40W
Manta, B. de 134 0 54S 80 44W
Mantalingajan, Mt. 56 8 55N 117 45 E
Mantare 94 2 42S 33 13 E
Manteca 122 37 50N 121 12W
Mantecal 134 7 34N 69 17W
Mantena 139 18 47S 40 59W
Manteno 117 41 15N 87 50W
Manteo 113 35 55N 75 41W
Mantes-la-Jolie 19 49 0N 1 41 E
Manthani 50 18 40N 79 35 E
Manthelan 18 47 9N 0 47 E
Manti 120 39 23N 111 32W
Mantiqueira, Serra da 139 22 0S 44 0W
Manton 106 44 23N 85 25W
Mantorp 11 58 21N 15 20 E
Mántova 26 45 20N 10 42 E
Mänttä 8 62 0N 24 40 E
Mantua = Mántova 26 45 20N 10 42 E
Manturovo 37 58 30N 44 30 E
Manu 136 12 10S 70 51W
Manu → 136 12 16S 70 55W
Manua Is. 68 14 13S 169 35W
Manuel Alves → 139 11 19S 48 28W
Manuel Alves Grande → 138 7 27S 47 35W
Manuel Urbano 138 8 53S 69 18W
Manui 57 3 35S 123 5 E
Manukan 57 8 14N 123 3 E
Manukau 80 37 1S 174 55 E
Manukau Harbour 80 37 3S 174 45 E
Manunui 80 38 54S 175 21 E
Manuripi → 136 11 6S 67 36W
Manus I. 69 2 0S 147 0 E
Manvi 51 15 57N 76 59 E
Manville 118 42 48N 104 36W
Manwath 50 19 19N 76 32 E
Many 119 31 36N 93 28W
Manyane 96 23 21S 21 42 E
Manyara, L. 94 3 40S 35 50 E
Manych → 39 47 15N 40 0 E
Manych-Gudilo, Oz. 39 46 24N 42 38 E
Manyonga → 94 4 10S 34 15 E
Manyoni 94 5 45S 34 55 E

Manyoni □ 94 6 30S 34 30E
Manzai 48 32 12N 70 15E
Manzala, Bahra el 90 31 10N 31 56E
Manzanares 25 39 0N 3 22W
Manzaneda, Cabeza de 22 42 12N 7 15W
Manzanillo, Cuba 126 20 20N 77 31W
Manzanillo, Mexico 124 19 0N 104 20W
Manzanillo, Pta. 126 9 30N 79 40W
Manzano Mts. 121 34 30N 106 45W
Manzhouli 62 49 35N 117 25E
Manzini 97 26 30S 31 25E
Mao 85 14 4N 15 19E
Maoke, Pegunungan 57 3 40S 137 30E
Maolin 61 43 58N 123 30E
Maoming 59 21 50N 110 54E
Maowen 58 31 41N 103 49E
Maoxing 61 45 28N 124 40E
Mapam Yumco 62 30 45N 81 28E
Mapastepec 125 15 26N 92 54W
Mapia, Kepulauan 57 0 50N 134 20E
Mapimí 124 25 50N 103 50W
Mapimí, Bolsón de 124 27 30N 104 15W
Maping 59 31 34N 113 32E
Mapinga 94 6 40S 39 12E
Mapinhane 97 22 20S 35 0E
Mapire 135 7 45N 64 42W
Maple → 117 42 58N 84 56W
Maple Creek 109 49 55N 109 29W
Maple Valley 122 47 25N 122 3W
Mapleton 120 44 4N 123 58W
Maplewood 118 38 33N 90 18W
Maprik 69 3 44S 143 3E
Mapuca 51 15 36N 73 46E
Mapuera → 135 1 5S 57 2W
Maputo 97 25 58S 32 32E
Maputo, B. de 97 25 50S 32 45E
Maqiaohe 61 44 40N 130 30E
Maqnā 46 28 25N 34 50E
Maquela do Zombo 92 6 0S 15 15E
Maquinchao 142 41 15S 68 50W
Maquoketa 116 42 4N 90 40W
Mar Chiquita, L. 140 30 40S 62 50W
Mar del Plata 140 38 0S 57 30W
Mar Menor, L. 25 37 40N 0 45W
Mar, Serra do 141 25 30S 49 0W
Mara, Guyana 135 6 0N 57 36W
Mara, India 52 28 11N 94 14E
Mara, Tanz. 94 1 30S 34 32E
Mara □ 94 1 45S 34 20E
Maraã 134 1 52S 65 25W
Marabá 138 5 20S 49 5W
Maracá, I. de 138 2 10N 50 30W
Maracaibo 134 10 40N 71 37W
Maracaibo, Lago de 134 9 40N 71 30W
Maracaju 141 21 38S 55 9W
Maracajú, Serra de 137 23 57S 55 1W
Maracanã 138 0 46S 47 27W
Maracás 139 13 26S 40 18W
Maracay 134 10 15N 67 28W
Marādah 87 29 15N 19 15E
Maradi 89 13 29N 8 10E
Maradun 89 12 35N 6 18E
Marāgheh 46 37 30N 46 12E
Maragogipe 139 12 46S 38 55W
Marajó, B. de 138 1 0S 48 30W
Marajó, Ilha de 138 1 0S 49 30W
Maralal 94 1 0N 36 38E
Maralinga 79 30 13S 131 32E
Marama 73 35 10S 140 10E
Maramasike 68 9 30S 161 25E
Marampa 88 8 45N 12 28W
Maran 55 3 35N 102 45E
Marana 121 32 30N 111 9W
Maranboy 78 14 30S 132 40E
Maranchón 24 41 6N 2 15W
Marand 46 38 30N 45 45E
Marandellas 95 18 5S 31 42E
Maranguape 138 3 55S 38 50W
Maranhão = São Luis 138 2 31S 44 16W
Maranhão □ 138 5 0S 46 0W
Marano, L. di 27 45 42N 13 13E
Maranoa → 73 27 50S 148 37E
Marañón → 136 4 30S 73 35W
Marapi → 135 0 37N 55 58W
Marari 136 5 43S 67 47W
Maraş 46 37 37N 36 53E
Mărăşeşti 34 45 52N 27 14E
Maratea 29 39 59N 15 43E
Marateca 23 38 34N 8 40W
Marathókambos 35 37 43N 26 42E
Marathon, Austral. 72 20 51S 143 32E
Marathon, Can. 102 48 44N 86 23W
Marathón 35 38 11N 23 58E
Marathon, Iowa, U.S.A. 116 42 52N 94 59W
Marathon, N.Y., U.S.A. 115 42 25N 76 3W
Marathon, Tex., U.S.A. 119 30 15N 103 15W
Maratua 57 2 10N 118 35E
Maraú 139 14 6S 39 0W
Maravae 68 7 54S 156 44E
Maravatío 124 19 51N 100 25W
Marbat 45 17 0N 54 45E
Marbella 23 36 30N 4 57W
Marble Bar 78 21 9S 119 44E
Marble Falls 119 30 30N 98 15W
Marblehead 115 42 29N 70 51W
Marbleton 105 45 37N 71 35W
Marburg 30 50 49N 8 36E
Marby 10 63 7N 14 18E
Marcal → 33 47 41N 17 32E
Marcapata 136 13 31S 70 52W
Marcaria 26 45 7N 10 34E
Marceline 116 39 43N 92 57W
March 13 52 33N 0 5E
Marchand = Rommani 86 33 20N 6 40W
Marché 20 46 0N 1 20E
Marche □ 27 43 22N 13 10E
Marche-en-Famenne 16 50 14N 5 19E
Marchena 23 37 18N 5 23W
Marches = Marche 27 43 22N 13 10E
Marciana Marina 26 42 44N 10 12E
Marcianise 29 41 3N 14 16E
Marcigny 21 46 17N 4 2E
Marcillac-Vallon 20 44 29N 2 27E
Marcillat 20 46 12N 2 38E
Marck 19 50 57N 1 57E
Marckolsheim 19 48 10N 7 30E
Marcona 136 15 10S 75 0W
Marcos Juárez 140 32 42S 62 5W
Marcus 66 24 0N 153 45E
Marcus Necker Ridge 66 20 0N 175 0E
Marcy Mt. 115 44 7N 73 55W
Mardan 48 34 20N 72 0E
Mardie 78 21 12S 115 59E
Mardin 46 37 20N 40 43E
Maré, Î. 68 21 30S 168 0E
Marechal Deodoro 138 9 43S 35 54W
Maree L. 14 57 40N 5 30W
Mareeba 72 16 59S 145 28E
Marek 57 4 41S 120 24E
Maremma 26 42 45N 11 15E
Maréna 88 14 0N 7 20W
Marenberg 27 46 38N 15 13E
Marengo 116 41 42N 92 5W
Marennes 20 45 49N 1 7W
Marenyi 94 4 22S 39 8E
Marerano 97 21 23S 44 52E
Maréttimo 28 37 58N 12 5E
Mareuil-sur-Lay 20 46 32N 1 14W
Marfa 119 30 15N 104 0W
Margable 91 12 54N 42 38E
Marganets 38 47 40N 34 40E
Margao 51 15 12N 73 58E
Margaret → 79 33 57S 115 7E
Margaret Bay 108 51 20N 126 35W
Margaret L. 108 58 56N 115 25W
Margarita, Isla de 135 11 0N 64 0W
Margarítion 35 39 22N 20 26E
Margate, S. Afr. 97 30 50S 30 20E
Margate, U.K. 13 51 23N 1 24E
Margeride, Mts. de la 20 44 43N 3 38E
Margherita 52 27 16N 95 40E
Margherita di Savola 29 41 25N 16 5E
Marguerite 108 52 30N 122 25W
Marhoum 86 34 27N 0 11W
Mari, A.S.S.R. □ 37 56 30N 48 0E
María Elena 140 22 18S 69 40W
María Grande 140 31 45S 59 55W
Maria I., N.T., Austral. 72 14 52S 135 45E
Maria I., Tas., Austral. 72 42 35S 148 0E
Maria van Diemen, C. 80 34 29S 172 40E
Mariager 11 56 40N 10 0E
Mariager Fjord 11 56 42N 10 19E
Mariakani 94 3 50S 39 27E
Marian L. 108 63 0N 116 15W
Mariana Is. 66 17 0N 145 0E
Mariana Trench 66 13 0N 145 0E
Marianao 126 23 8N 82 24W
Mariani 52 26 39N 94 19E
Marianna, Ark., U.S.A. 119 34 48N 90 48W
Marianna, Fla., U.S.A. 113 30 45N 85 15W
Mariannelund 11 57 37N 15 35E
Mariano Machado 93 13 3S 14 35E
Mariánské Lázně 32 49 48N 12 41E
Marias → 120 47 56N 110 30W
Mariato, Punta 126 7 12N 80 52W
Mariazell 33 47 47N 15 19E
Marib 45 15 25N 45 30E
Maribo 11 54 48N 11 30E
Maribor 27 46 36N 15 40E
Marico → 96 23 35S 26 57E
Maricopa, Ariz., U.S.A. 121 33 5N 112 2W
Maricopa, Calif., U.S.A. 123 35 7N 119 27W
Marîdî 91 4 55N 29 25E
Maridi, Wadi → 91 6 15N 29 21E
Marié → 134 0 27S 66 26W
Marie-Galante 127 15 56N 61 16W
Mariecourt 101 61 30N 72 0W
Mariefred 10 59 15N 17 12E
Mariehamn 9 60 5N 19 55E
Marienberg, Ger. 30 50 40N 13 10E
Marienberg, Neth. 16 52 30N 6 35E
Marienbourg 16 50 6N 4 31E
Mariental 96 24 36S 18 0E
Marienville 114 41 27N 79 8W
Mariestad 11 58 43N 13 50E
Marietta, Ga., U.S.A. 113 34 0N 84 30W
Marietta, Ohio, U.S.A. 112 39 27N 81 27W
Marieville 105 45 26N 73 10W
Marignane 21 43 25N 5 13E
Mariinsk 40 56 10N 87 20E
Mariinskiy Posad 37 56 10N 47 45E
Marília 141 22 13S 50 0W
Marillana 78 22 37S 119 16E
Marín 22 42 23N 8 42W
Marina 122 36 41N 121 48W
Marina di Cirò 29 39 22N 17 8E
Mariña, La 22 43 30N 7 40W
Marina Plains 72 14 37S 143 57E
Marinduque 57 13 25N 122 0E
Marine City 106 42 45N 82 29W
Marinel, Le 95 10 25S 25 17E
Marineo 28 37 57N 13 23E
Marinette, Ariz., U.S.A. 121 33 41N 112 16W
Marinette, Wis., U.S.A. 112 45 4N 87 40W
Maringá 141 23 26S 52 2W
Marinha Grande 23 39 45N 8 56W
Marion, Ala., U.S.A. 113 32 33N 87 20W
Marion, Ill., U.S.A. 116 37 45N 88 55W
Marion, Ind., U.S.A. 117 40 35N 85 40W
Marion, Iowa, U.S.A. 116 42 2N 91 36W
Marion, Kans., U.S.A. 118 38 25N 97 2W
Marion, Mich., U.S.A. 106 44 7N 85 8W
Marion, N.C., U.S.A. 113 35 42N 82 0W
Marion, Ohio, U.S.A. 117 40 38N 83 8W
Marion, S.C., U.S.A. 113 34 11N 79 22W
Marion, Va., U.S.A. 113 36 51N 81 29W
Marion I. 53 47 0S 38 0E
Marion, L. 113 33 30N 80 15W
Maripa 135 7 26N 65 9W
Maripasoula 135 3 40N 54 4W
Mariposa 122 37 31N 119 59W
Mariscal Estigarribia 140 22 3S 60 40W
Maritime Alps = Alpes Maritimes 26 44 10N 7 10E
Mariyampole = Kapsukas 36 54 33N 23 19E
Marka 90 18 14N 41 19E
Markam 58 29 42N 98 38E
Markapur 51 15 44N 79 19E
Markaryd 11 56 28N 13 35E
Markdale 106 44 19N 80 39W
Marked Tree 119 35 35N 90 24W
Markelsdorfer Huk 30 54 33N 11 0E
Marken 16 52 26N 5 12E
Market Drayton 12 52 55N 2 30W
Market Harborough 13 52 29N 0 55W
Markham 106 43 52N 79 16W
Markham → 69 6 41S 147 2E
Markham I. 144 84 0N 0 45W
Markham L. 109 62 30N 102 35W
Markham Mt. 143 83 0S 164 0E
Marki 32 52 20N 21 2E
Markleeville 122 38 44N 119 47W
Markoupoulon 35 37 53N 23 57E
Markovo 41 64 40N 169 40E
Markoye 89 14 39N 0 2E
Marks 37 51 45N 46 50E
Markstay 106 46 29N 80 32W
Marksville 119 31 10N 92 2W
Markt Schwaben 31 48 14N 11 49E
Marktredwitz 31 50 1N 12 2E
Marlbank 107 44 26N 77 6W
Marlboro 115 42 19N 71 33W
Marlborough 72 22 46S 149 52E
Marlborough □ 81 41 45S 173 33E
Marlborough Downs 13 51 25N 1 55W
Marle 19 49 43N 3 47E
Marlee 77 31 47S 152 20E
Marlin 119 31 25N 96 50W
Marlo 75 37 46S 148 31E
Marlow, Austral. 76 35 17S 149 55E
Marlow, Ger. 30 54 8N 12 34E
Marlow, U.S.A. 119 34 40N 97 58W
Marmagao 51 15 25N 73 56E
Marmande 20 44 30N 0 10E
Marmara 38 40 35N 27 38E
Marmara Denizi 46 40 45N 28 15E
Marmara, Sea of = Marmara Denizi 46 40 45N 28 15E
Marmaris 46 36 50N 28 14E
Marmarth 118 46 21N 103 52W
Marmelos → 137 6 6S 61 46W
Marmion L. 102 48 55N 91 20W
Marmion Mt. 79 29 16S 119 50E
Marmolada, Mte. 27 46 25N 11 55E
Marmolejo 23 38 3N 4 13W
Marmora 107 44 28N 77 41W
Marnay 19 47 20N 5 48E
Marne 30 53 57N 9 1E
Marne □ 19 49 0N 4 10E
Marne → 19 8 23N 18 36E
Maro 92 8 30N 19 0E
Maroa 134 2 43N 67 33W
Maroala 97 15 23S 47 59E
Maroantsetra 97 15 26S 49 44E
Maromandia 97 14 13S 48 5E
Maroni → 135 4 0N 52 0W
Maroochydore 73 26 29S 153 5E
Maroona 74 37 27S 142 54E
Maros → 33 46 25N 20 20E
Marosakoa 97 15 26S 46 38E
Marostica 27 45 44N 11 40E
Maroua 89 10 40N 14 20E
Marovoay 97 16 6S 46 39E
Marowijne □ 135 4 0N 55 0W
Marowijne → 135 5 45N 53 58W
Marquard 96 28 40S 27 28E
Marqueira 23 38 41N 9 9W
Marquesas Is. 67 9 30S 140 0W
Marquette 112 46 30N 87 21W
Marquette I. 106 45 58N 84 18W
Marquette, L. 105 48 54N 73 54W
Marquise 19 50 50N 1 40E
Marra, Gebel 91 7 20N 27 35E
Marradi 27 44 5N 11 37E
Marrakech 86 31 9N 8 0W
Marrar 76 34 50S 147 23E
Marrat 46 25 0N 45 35E
Marrawah 72 40 55S 144 42E
Marrecas, Serra das 138 9 0S 41 0W
Marree 73 29 39S 138 1E
Marrimane 97 22 58S 33 34E
Marronne → 20 45 4N 1 56E
Marroquí, Punta 23 36 0N 5 37W
Marrowie Creek 73 33 23S 145 40E
Marrubane 95 18 0S 37 0E
Marrupa 95 13 8S 37 30E
Mars, Le 118 43 0N 96 0W
Marsa Susa (Apollonia) 85 32 52N 21 59E
Marsabit 94 2 18N 38 0E
Marsabit □ 94 2 45N 37 45E
Marsala 28 37 48N 12 25E
Marsciano 27 42 54N 12 20E
Marsden 76 33 47S 147 32E
Marseillan 20 43 23N 3 31E
Marseille 21 43 18N 5 23E
Marseilles 117 41 20N 88 43W
Marseilles = Marseille 21 43 18N 5 23E
Marsh I. 119 29 35N 91 50W
Marsh L. 118 45 5N 96 0W
Marshall, Liberia 88 6 8N 10 22W
Marshall, Ark., U.S.A. 119 35 58N 92 40W
Marshall, Ill., U.S.A. 117 39 23N 87 42W
Marshall, Mich., U.S.A. 117 42 17N 84 59W
Marshall, Minn., U.S.A. 118 44 25N 95 45W
Marshall, Mo., U.S.A. 116 39 8N 93 15W
Marshall, Tex., U.S.A. 119 32 29N 94 20W
Marshall → 72 22 59S 136 59E
Marshall Is. 66 9 0N 171 0E
Marshalltown 116 42 5N 92 56W
Marshfield, Mo., U.S.A. 119 37 20N 92 58W
Marshfield, Wis., U.S.A. 118 44 42N 90 10W
Mársico Nuovo 29 40 26N 15 43E
Märsta 10 59 37N 17 52E
Marstal 11 54 51N 10 30E
Marstrand 11 57 53N 11 35E
Mart 119 31 34N 96 51W
Marta → 27 42 14N 11 42E
Martaban 52 16 30N 97 35E
Martaban, G. of 52 16 5N 96 30E
Martagne 18 46 59N 0 57W
Martano 29 40 14N 18 18E
Martapura, Kalimantan, Indon. 56 3 22S 114 47E
Martapura, Sumatera, Indon. 56 4 19S 104 22E
Marte 89 12 23N 13 46E
Martel 20 44 57N 1 37E
Martelange 16 49 49N 5 43E
Marten River 106 46 44N 79 49W
Martensdale 116 41 23N 93 45W
Martés, Sierra 25 39 20N 1 0W
Marthaguy Creek → 73 30 16S 147 35E
Martha's Vineyard 115 41 25N 70 35W
Martigné-Ferchaud 18 47 50N 1 20W
Martigny 31 46 6N 7 3E

Martigues 21 43 24N 5 4 E
Martil 86 35 36N 5 15W
Martin, Czech. 32 49 6N 18 48 E
Martin, S.D., U.S.A. 118 43 11N 101 45W
Martin, Tenn., U.S.A. 119 36 23N 88 51W
Martín → 24 41 18N 0 19W
Martin, L. 113 32 45N 85 50W
Martina Franca 29 40 42N 17 20 E
Martinborough 80 41 14 S 175 29 E
Martindale 76 32 27 S 150 40 E
Martinez 122 38 1N 122 8W
Martinho Campos 139 19 20 S 45 13W
Martinique 127 14 40N 61 0W
Martinique Passage 127 15 15N 61 0W
Martínon 35 38 35N 23 15 E
Martinópolis 141 22 11 S 51 12W
Martins Ferry 115 40 5N 80 46W
Martinsburg, Pa., U.S.A. 114 40 18N 78 21W
Martinsburg, W. Va., U.S.A. 112 39 30N 77 57W
Martinsville, Ill., U.S.A. 117 39 20N 87 53W
Martinsville, Ind., U.S.A. 117 39 29N 86 23W
Martinsville, Va., U.S.A. 113 36 41N 79 52W
Marton 80 40 4 S 175 23 E
Martorell 24 41 28N 1 56 E
Martos 23 37 44N 3 58W
Martuni 39 40 9N 45 10 E
Maru 89 12 22N 6 22 E
Marudi 56 4 10N 114 19 E
Maruf 47 31 30N 67 6 E
Marugame 64 34 15N 133 40 E
Marúggio 29 40 20N 17 33 E
Marui 69 4 4 S 143 2 E
Maruim 138 10 45 S 37 5W
Marulan 76 34 43 S 150 3 E
Marulan South 76 34 47 S 150 3 E
Marum, Mt. 68 16 15 S 168 7 E
Marunga 96 17 28 S 20 2 E
Marungu, Mts. 94 7 30 S 30 0 E
Maruoka 65 36 9N 136 16 E
Marvejols 20 44 33N 3 19 E
Marwar 48 25 43N 73 45 E
Mary 40 37 40N 61 50 E
Mary Frances L. 109 63 19N 106 13W
Mary Kathleen 72 20 44 S 139 48 E
Maryborough, Queens., Austral. 73 25 31 S 152 37 E
Maryborough, Vic., Austral. 74 37 0 S 143 44 E
Maryfield 109 49 50N 101 35W
Maryland □ 112 39 10N 76 40W
Maryland Jc. 95 17 45 S 30 31 E
Maryport 12 54 43N 3 30W
Mary's Harbour 103 52 18N 55 51W
Marystown 103 47 10N 55 10W
Marysvale 121 38 25N 112 17W
Marysville, Austral. 74 37 33 S 145 45 E
Marysville, Can. 108 49 35N 116 0W
Marysville, Calif., U.S.A. 122 39 14N 121 40W
Marysville, Kans., U.S.A. 118 39 50N 96 49W
Marysville, Mich., U.S.A. 106 42 55N 82 29W
Marysville, Ohio, U.S.A. 117 40 15N 83 20W
Marysville, Wash., U.S.A. 122 48 3N 122 11W
Maryvale 77 28 4 S 152 12 E
Maryville, Mo., U.S.A. 116 40 21N 94 52W
Maryville, Tenn., U.S.A. 113 35 50N 84 0W
Marzo, Punta 134 6 50N 77 42W
Marzūq 87 25 53N 13 57 E
Masada = Mesada 44 31 20N 35 19 E
Masafa 95 13 50 S 27 30 E
Masai 55 1 29N 103 55 E
Masai Steppe 94 4 30 S 36 30 E
Masaka 94 0 21 S 31 45 E
Masakali 89 13 2N 12 32 E
Masalembo, Kepulauan 56 5 35 S 114 30 E
Masalima, Kepulauan 56 5 4 S 117 5 E
Masamba 57 2 30 S 120 15 E
Masan 61 35 11N 128 32 E
Masanasa 25 39 25N 0 25W
Masandam, Ras 47 26 30N 56 30 E
Masasi 95 10 45 S 38 52 E
Masasi □ 95 10 45 S 38 50 E
Masaya 126 12 0N 86 7W
Masba 89 10 35N 13 1 E
Masbate 57 12 21N 123 36 E
Mascara 86 35 26N 0 6 E
Mascarene Is. 53 22 0 S 55 0 E
Mascota 124 20 30N 104 50W
Mascouche 105 45 45N 73 36W
Mascoutah 116 38 29N 89 48W
Masela 57 8 9 S 129 51 E
Maseru 96 29 18 S 27 30 E
Mashaba 95 20 2 S 30 29 E
Mashābih 46 25 35N 36 30 E
Mashan 58 23 40N 108 11 E
Masherbrum 49 35 38N 76 18 E
Mashhad 47 36 20N 59 35 E
Mashi 89 13 0N 7 54 E
Mashiki 64 32 51N 130 53 E
Mashkel, Hamun-i- 47 28 30N 63 0 E
Mashki Chah 47 29 5N 62 30 E
Mashonaland, North, □ 95 16 30 S 30 0 E
Mashonaland, South, □ 95 18 0 S 31 30 E
Mashtaga 39 40 35N 50 0 E
Masi 8 69 26N 23 40 E
Masi-Manimba 92 4 40 S 17 54 E
Masindi 94 1 40N 31 43 E
Masindi Port 94 1 43N 32 2 E
Masisea 136 8 35 S 74 22W
Masisi 94 1 23 S 28 49 E
Masjed Soleyman 46 31 55N 49 18 E
Mask, L. 15 53 36N 9 24W
Maskelyne Is. 68 16 32 S 167 49 E
Maski 51 15 56N 76 46 E
Maskinongé 105 46 14N 73 1W
Maslinica 27 43 24N 16 13 E
Masnou 24 41 28N 2 20 E
Masoala, C. 97 15 59 S 50 13 E
Masoarivo 97 19 3 S 44 19 E
Masohi 57 3 2 S 128 15 E
Masomeloka 97 20 17 S 48 37 E
Mason, Mich., U.S.A. 117 42 35N 84 27W
Mason, Nev., U.S.A. 122 38 56N 119 8W
Mason, Ohio, U.S.A. 117 39 22N 84 19W
Mason, S.D., U.S.A. 118 45 12N 103 27W
Mason, Tex., U.S.A. 119 30 45N 99 15W
Mason B. 81 46 55 S 167 45 E
Mason City, Ill., U.S.A. 116 40 12N 89 42W
Mason City, Iowa, U.S.A. 116 43 9N 93 12W
Mason City, Wash., U.S.A. 120 48 0N 119 0W
Masqat 47 23 37N 58 36 E
Massa 26 44 2N 10 7 E
Massa Maríttima 26 43 3N 10 52 E
Massa, O. → 86 30 2N 9 40W
Massachusetts □ 115 42 25N 72 0W
Massachusetts B. 115 42 30N 70 0W
Massada 44 33 41N 35 36 E
Massafra 29 40 35N 17 8 E
Massaguet 92 12 28N 15 26 E
Massakory 85 13 0N 15 49 E
Massangena 97 21 34 S 33 0 E
Massapê 138 3 31 S 40 19W
Massarosa 26 43 53N 10 17 E
Massat 20 42 53N 1 21 E
Massawa = Mitsiwa 91 15 35N 39 25 E
Massena 115 44 52N 74 55W
Massenya 85 11 21N 16 9 E
Masset 108 54 2N 132 10W
Massey 106 46 12N 82 5W
Massiac 20 45 15N 3 11 E
Massif Central 20 45 30N 2 21 E
Massillon 114 40 47N 81 30W
Massinga 97 23 46 S 32 4 E
Masson 104 45 32N 75 25W
Masson I. 143 66 10 S 93 20 E
Massueville 105 45 55N 72 56W
Mastaba 90 20 52N 39 30 E
Masterton 80 40 56 S 175 39 E
Mastigouche, Parc 105 46 40N 73 41W
Mástikho, Ákra 35 38 10N 26 2 E
Mastuj 49 36 20N 72 36 E
Mastung 47 29 50N 66 56 E
Mastura 90 23 7N 38 52 E
Masuda 64 34 40N 131 51 E
Maswa □ 94 3 30 S 34 0 E
Mata de São João 139 12 31 S 38 17W
Matabeleland North □ 95 19 0 S 28 0 E
Matabeleland South □ 95 21 0 S 29 0 E
Mataboor 57 1 41 S 138 3 E
Matachel → 23 38 50N 6 17W
Matachewan 102 47 56N 80 39W
Matacuni → 135 3 2N 65 16W
Matad 62 47 11N 115 27 E
Matadi 92 5 52 S 13 31 E
Matagalpa 126 13 0N 85 58W
Matagami 104 49 45N 77 34W
Matagami, L. 104 49 50N 77 40W
Matagorda 119 28 43N 96 0W
Matagorda, B. 119 28 30N 96 15W
Matagorda I. 119 28 10N 96 40W
Matak, P. 55 3 18N 106 16 E
Matakana 73 32 59 S 145 54 E
Matalaque 136 16 26 S 70 49W
Matale 51 7 30N 80 37 E
Matam 88 15 34N 13 17W
Matamata 80 37 48 S 175 47 E
Matameye 89 13 26N 8 28 E
Matamoros, Campeche, Mexico 125 18 50N 90 50W
Matamoros, Coahuila, Mexico 124 25 33N 103 15W
Matamoros, Puebla, Mexico 125 18 2N 98 17W
Matamoros, Tamaulipas, Mexico 125 25 50N 97 30W
Matandu → 95 8 45 S 34 19 E
Matane 103 48 50N 67 33W
Matang 58 23 30N 104 7 E
Matankari 89 13 46N 4 1 E
Matanuska 100 61 39N 149 19W
Matanzas 126 23 0N 81 40W
Matapan, C. = Taínaron, Akra 35 36 22N 22 27 E
Matapédia 103 48 0N 66 59W
Matara 51 5 58N 80 30 E
Mataram 56 8 41 S 116 10 E
Matarani 136 77 0 S 72 10W
Mataranka 78 14 55 S 133 4 E
Mataró 24 41 32N 2 29 E
Matarraña → 24 41 14N 0 22 E
Mataso 68 17 14 S 168 26 E
Matata 80 37 54 S 176 48 E
Matatiele 97 30 20 S 28 49 E
Mataura 81 46 11 S 168 51 E
Mataura → 81 46 34 S 168 44 E
Matawin → 105 46 54N 72 56W
Matawin, Rés. 105 46 46N 73 50W
Matchi-Manitou, L. 104 48 0N 77 4W
Mategua 137 13 1 S 62 48W
Matehuala 124 23 40N 100 40W
Mateira 139 18 54 S 50 30W
Mateke Hills 95 21 48 S 31 0 E
Matélica 27 43 15N 13 0 E
Matera 29 40 40N 16 37 E
Mátészalka 33 47 58N 22 20 E
Matetsi 95 18 12 S 26 0 E
Mateur 87 37 0N 9 40 E
Matfors 10 62 21N 17 2 E
Matha 20 45 52N 0 20W
Matheson Island 109 51 45N 96 56W
Mathis 119 28 4N 97 48W
Mathura 48 27 30N 77 40 E
Mati 57 6 55N 126 15 E
Mati → 35 41 40N 20 0 E
Matías Romero 125 16 53N 95 2W
Matibane 95 14 49 S 40 45 E
Matinenda L. 106 46 22N 82 57W
Matlock 12 53 8N 1 32W
Matmata 87 33 37N 9 59 E
Matna 91 13 49N 35 10 E
Mato → 135 7 9N 65 7W
Mato Grosso □ 137 14 0 S 55 0W
Mato Grosso, Planalto do 137 15 0 S 59 57W
Mato, Serrania de 134 6 25N 65 25W
Matochkin Shar 40 73 10N 56 40 E
Matong 69 5 36 S 151 50 E
Matopo Hills 95 20 36 S 28 20 E
Matopos 95 20 20 S 28 29 E
Matosinhos 22 41 11N 8 42W
Matour 21 46 19N 4 29 E
Matrah 47 23 37N 58 30 E
Matrûh 90 31 19N 27 9 E
Matsena 89 13 5N 10 5 E
Matsesta 39 43 34N 39 51 E
Matsubara 65 34 33N 135 34 E
Matsudo 65 35 47N 139 54 E
Matsue 64 35 25N 133 10 E
Matsumae 63 41 26N 140 7 E
Matsumoto 65 36 15N 138 0 E
Matsusaka 65 34 34N 136 32 E
Matsutō 65 36 31N 136 34 E
Matsuura 64 33 20N 129 49 E
Matsuyama 64 33 45N 132 45 E
Matsuzaki 65 34 43N 138 50 E
Mattagami → 102 50 43N 81 29W
Mattancheri 51 9 50N 76 15 E
Mattawa 102 46 20N 78 45W
Mattawamkeag 103 45 30N 68 21W
Matterhorn 31 45 58N 7 39 E
Matteson 117 41 30N 87 42W
Matthew Town 127 20 57N 73 40W
Matthews 117 40 23N 85 31W
Matthew's Ridge 135 7 37N 60 10W
Mattice 102 49 40N 83 20W
Mattituck 115 40 58N 72 32W
Mattmar 10 63 18N 13 45 E
Matua 56 2 58 S 110 46 E
Matuba 97 24 28 S 32 49 E
Matucana 136 11 55 S 76 25W
Matuku 68 19 10 S 179 44 E
Matun 48 33 22N 69 58 E
Maturín 135 9 45N 63 11W
Matveyev Kurgan 39 47 35N 38 47 E
Mau-é-ele 97 24 18 S 34 2 E
Mau Escarpment 94 0 40 S 36 0 E
Mau Ranipur 49 25 16N 79 8 E
Maubeuge 19 50 17N 3 57 E
Maubourguet 20 43 29N 0 1 E
Maud, Pt. 78 23 6 S 113 45 E
Maude 74 34 29 S 144 18 E
Maudheim 143 71 5 S 11 0W
Maués 135 3 20 S 57 45W
Maui 110 20 45N 156 20 E
Maule □ 140 36 5 S 72 30W
Mauléon-Licharre 20 43 14N 0 54W
Maullín 142 41 38 S 73 37W
Maulvibazar 52 24 29N 91 42 E
Maumee 117 41 35N 83 40W
Maumee → 117 41 42N 83 28W
Maumere 57 8 38 S 122 13 E
Maun 96 20 0 S 23 26 E
Mauna Kea 110 19 50N 155 28W
Mauna Loa 110 21 8N 157 10W
Maunath Bhanjan 49 25 56N 83 33 E
Maungaturoto 80 36 6 S 174 23 E
Maungdow 52 20 50N 92 21 E
Maupin 120 45 12N 121 9W
Maure-de-Bretagne 18 47 53N 2 0W
Maurepas L. 119 30 18N 90 35W
Maures 21 43 15N 6 15 E
Mauriac 20 45 13N 2 19 E
Maurice L. 79 29 30 S 131 0 E
Mauriceville 80 40 45 S 175 42 E
Mauricie, Parc Nat. de la 105 46 45N 73 0W
Mauritania ■ 84 20 50N 10 0W
Mauritius ■ 53 20 0 S 57 0 E
Mauron 18 48 9N 2 18W
Maurs 20 44 43N 2 12 E
Mauston 118 43 48N 90 5W
Mauterndorf 33 47 9N 13 40 E
Mauvezin 20 43 44N 0 53 E
Mauzé-sur-le-Mignon 20 46 12N 0 41W
Mavaca → 135 2 31N 65 11W
Mavelikara 51 9 14N 76 32 E
Mavinga 93 15 50 S 20 21 E
Mavli 48 24 45N 73 55 E
Mavqi'im 44 31 38N 34 32 E
Mavrova 35 40 26N 19 32 E
Mavuradonha Mts. 95 16 30 S 31 30 E
Mawa 94 2 45N 26 40 E
Mawana 48 29 6N 77 58 E
Mawand 48 29 33N 68 38 E
Mawk Mai 52 20 14N 97 37 E
Mawlaik 52 23 40N 94 26 E
Mawlawkho 52 17 50N 97 38 E
Mawson Base 143 67 30 S 62 53 E
Max 118 47 50N 101 20W
Maxcanú 125 20 40N 92 0W
Maxhamish L. 108 59 50N 123 17W
Maxixe 97 23 54 S 35 17 E
Maxville 107 45 17N 74 51W
Maxwell, N.Z. 80 39 51 S 174 49 E
Maxwell, U.S.A. 122 39 17N 122 11W
Maxwelton 72 20 43 S 142 41 E
May Downs 72 22 38 S 148 55 E
May Glacier Tongue 143 66 08 S 130 35 E
May Nefalis 91 15 0N 38 12 E
May Pen 126 17 58N 77 15W
May River 69 4 19 S 141 58 E
Maya 24 43 12N 1 29W
Maya → 41 54 31N 134 41 E
Maya Gudo, Mt. 91 7 30N 37 8 E
Maya Mts. 125 16 30N 89 0W
Mayaguana 127 22 30N 72 44W
Mayagüez 127 18 12N 67 9W
Mayahi 89 13 58N 7 40 E
Mayals 24 41 22N 0 30 E
Mayang 58 27 53N 109 49 E
Mayanup 79 33 58 S 116 25 E
Mayapán 125 20 28N 89 27W
Mayarí 127 20 40N 75 41W
Mayavaram = Mayuram 51 11 3N 79 42 E
Maybell 120 40 30N 108 4W
Maychew 91 12 50N 39 31 E
Maydena 72 42 45 S 146 30 E
Mayen 31 50 18N 7 10 E
Mayenne 18 48 20N 0 38W
Mayenne □ 18 48 10N 0 40W
Mayenne → 18 47 30N 0 32W
Mayer 121 34 28N 112 17W
Mayerthorpe 108 53 57N 115 8W
Mayfield 113 36 45N 88 40W
Mayhill 121 32 58N 105 30W
Maykop 39 44 35N 40 25 E
Maymyo 54 22 2N 96 28 E
Maynard 122 47 59N 122 55W
Maynard Hills 79 28 35 S 119 50 E
Mayne → 72 23 40 S 141 55 E
Maynooth 15 53 22N 6 38W
Mayo 100 63 38N 135 57W
Mayo □ 15 53 47N 9 7W
Mayo →, Argent. 142 45 45 S 69 45W
Mayo →, Mexico 124 26 45N 109 47W
Mayo →, Peru 136 6 38 S 76 15W
Mayo L. 100 63 45N 135 0W

Mayon, Mt. **57** 13 15N 123 42 E
Mayor I. **80** 37 16S 176 17 E
Mayorga **22** 42 10N 5 16W
Mayskiy **39** 43 47N 44 2 E
Mayson L. **109** 57 55N 107 10W
Maysville, Ky., U.S.A. **117** 38 39N 83 46W
Maysville, Mo., U.S.A. **116** 39 53N 94 21W
Mayu **57** 1 30N 126 30 E
Mayuram **51** 11 3N 79 42 E
Mayville, N.D., U.S.A. **118** 47 30N 97 23W
Mayville, N.Y., U.S.A. **114** 42 14N 79 31W
Maywood **117** 41 53N 87 51W
Mayya **41** 61 44N 130 18 E
Mazabuka **95** 15 52S 27 44 E
Mazagán = El Jadida **86** 33 11N 8 17W
Mazagão **135** 0 7S 51 16W
Mazamet **20** 43 30N 2 20 E
Mazán **134** 3 30S 73 0W
Mazan Deran □ **47** 36 30N 52 0 E
Mazapil **124** 24 38N 101 34W
Mazar-i-Sharif **47** 36 41N 67 0 E
Mazar, O. → **86** 31 50N 1 36 E
Mazara del Vallo **28** 37 40N 12 34 E
Mazarredo **142** 47 10S 66 50W
Mazarrón **25** 37 38N 1 19W
Mazarrón, Golfo de **25** 37 27N 1 19W
Mazaruni → **135** 6 25N 58 35W
Mazatán **124** 29 0N 110 8W
Mazatenango **126** 14 35N 91 30W
Mazatlán **124** 23 10N 106 30W
Mažeikiai **36** 56 20N 22 20 E
Māzhān **47** 32 30N 59 0 E
Mazinān **47** 36 19N 56 56 E
Mazoe, Mozam. **95** 16 42S 33 7 E
Mazoe, Zimb.-Rhod. **95** 17 28S 30 58 E
Mazomanie **116** 43 11N 89 48W
Mazon **117** 41 14N 88 25W
Mazrûb **91** 14 0N 29 20 E
Mazu Dao **59** 26 10N 119 55 E
Mazurian Lakes = Mazurski, Pojezierze **32** 53 50N 21 0 E
Mazurski, Pojezierze **32** 53 50N 21 0 E
Mazzarino **29** 37 19N 14 12 E
Mba **68** 17 33S 177 41 E
Mbaba **88** 14 59N 16 44W
Mbabane **97** 26 18S 31 6 E
Mbagne **88** 16 6N 14 47W
M'bahiakro **88** 7 33N 4 19W
M'Baiki **92** 3 53N 18 1 E
Mbala **95** 8 46S 31 24 E
Mbale **94** 1 8N 34 12 E
Mbalmayo **92** 3 33N 11 33 E
Mbamba Bay **95** 11 13S 34 49 E
Mbandaka **92** 0 1S 18 18 E
Mbanga **89** 4 30N 9 33 E
Mbanza Congo **92** 6 18S 14 16 E
Mbanza Ngungu **92** 5 12S 14 53 E
Mbarara **94** 0 35S 30 40 E
Mbatto **88** 6 28N 4 22W
Mbengga **68** 18 23S 178 8 E
Mbenkuru → **95** 9 25S 39 50 E
Mberubu **89** 6 10N 7 38 E
Mbesuma **95** 10 0S 32 2 E
Mbeya **95** 8 54S 33 29 E
Mbeya □ **94** 8 15S 33 30 E
Mbia **91** 6 15N 29 18 E
Mbinga **95** 10 50S 35 0 E
Mbinga □ **95** 10 50S 35 0 E
Mbini □ **92** 1 30N 10 0 E
Mbiti **91** 5 42N 28 3 E
Mboki **91** 5 19N 25 58 E
Mboro **88** 15 9N 16 54W
Mboune **88** 14 42N 13 34W
Mbour **88** 14 22N 16 54W
Mbout **88** 16 1N 12 38W
Mbozi □ **95** 9 0S 32 50 E
Mbuji-Mayi **94** 6 9S 23 40 E
Mbulu **94** 3 45S 35 30 E
Mbulu □ **94** 3 52S 35 33 E
Mbumbi **96** 18 26S 19 59 E
Mburucuyá **140** 28 1S 58 14W
Mcherrah **86** 27 0N 4 30W
Mchinja **95** 9 44S 39 45 E
Mchinji **95** 13 47S 32 58 E
Mdennah **86** 24 37N 6 0W
Mé Maoya **68** 21 22S 165 22 E
Mead, L. **123** 36 1N 114 44W
Meade **119** 37 18N 100 25W
Meadow **79** 26 35S 114 40 E
Meadow Lake **109** 54 10N 108 26W
Meadow Lake Prov. Park **109** 54 27N 109 0W
Meadow Valley Wash **123** 36 30N 114 24W
Meadow Valley Wash → **121** 36 39N 114 35W
Meadville, Mo., U.S.A. **116** 39 47N 93 18W
Meadville, Pa., U.S.A. **114** 41 39N 80 9W
Meaford **106** 44 36N 80 35W
Mealhada **22** 40 22N 8 27W
Mealy Mts. **103** 53 10N 58 0W
Meander = Menderes, Büyük → **46** 37 45N 27 40 E
Meander River **108** 59 2N 117 42W
Meares, C. **120** 45 37N 124 0W
Mearim → **138** 3 4S 44 35W
Meath □ **15** 53 32N 6 40W
Meath Park **109** 53 27N 105 22W
Meatian **74** 35 34S 143 21 E
Meaulne **20** 46 36N 2 36 E
Meaux **19** 48 58N 2 50 E
Mecanhelas **95** 15 12S 35 54 E
Mecaya → **134** 0 29N 75 11W
Mecca **123** 33 37N 116 3W
Mecca = Makkah **90** 21 30N 39 54 E
Mechanicsburg **114** 40 12N 77 0W
Mechanicsville **116** 41 54N 91 16W
Mechanicville **115** 42 54N 73 41W
Mechara **91** 8 36N 40 20 E
Mechelen **16** 51 2N 4 29 E
Méchéria **86** 33 35N 0 18W
Mechernich **30** 50 35N 6 39 E
Mechetinskaya **39** 46 45N 40 32 E
Mechra Benâbbou **86** 32 39N 7 48W
Mecitözü **38** 40 32N 35 17 E
Meconta **95** 14 59S 39 50 E
Meda **22** 40 57N 7 18W
Meda P.O. **78** 17 22S 123 59 E
Medak **50** 18 1N 78 15 E
Medan **56** 3 40N 98 38 E
Médanos **142** 38 50S 62 42W
Medanosa, Pta. **142** 48 8S 66 0W
Medaryville **117** 41 4N 86 55W
Medawachchiya **51** 8 30N 80 30 E
Meddouza, C. **86** 32 33N 9 9W
Médéa **86** 36 12N 2 50 E
Medeiros Neto **139** 17 20S 40 14W
Medellín **134** 6 15N 75 35W
Medemblik **16** 52 46N 5 8 E
Medenine **87** 33 21N 10 30 E
Meder **91** 14 42N 40 44 E
Mederdra **88** 17 0N 15 38W
Medford, Oreg., U.S.A. **120** 42 20N 122 52W
Medford, Wis., U.S.A. **118** 45 9N 90 21W
Medgidia **34** 44 15N 28 19 E
Medgun → **77** 29 3S 149 24 E
Medi **91** 5 4N 30 42 E
Media Agua **140** 31 58S 68 25W
Media Luna **140** 34 45S 66 44W
Mediapolis **116** 41 0N 91 10W
Mediaş **34** 46 9N 24 22 E
Medical Lake **120** 47 35N 117 42W
Medicina **27** 44 29N 11 38 E
Medicine Bow **120** 41 56N 106 11W
Medicine Bow Pk. **120** 41 21N 106 19W
Medicine Bow Ra. **120** 41 10N 106 25W
Medicine Hat **109** 50 0N 110 45W
Medicine Lake **118** 48 30N 104 30W
Medicine Lodge **119** 37 20N 98 37W
Medina, Brazil **139** 16 15S 41 29W
Medina, Colomb. **134** 4 30N 73 21W
Medina, N.D., U.S.A. **118** 46 57N 99 20W
Medina, N.Y., U.S.A. **114** 43 15N 78 27W
Medina, Ohio, U.S.A. **114** 41 9N 81 50W
Medina = Al Madīnah **46** 24 35N 39 35 E
Medina → **119** 29 10N 98 20W
Medina de Ríoseco **22** 41 53N 5 3W
Medina del Campo **22** 41 18N 4 55W
Medina L. **119** 29 35N 98 58W
Medina-Sidonia **23** 36 28N 5 57W
Medinaceli **24** 41 12N 2 30W
Mediterranean Sea **6** 35 0N 15 0 E
Medjerda, O. → **87** 37 7N 10 13 E
Medley **109** 54 25N 110 16W
Médoc **20** 45 10N 0 56W
Medora **117** 38 49N 86 10W
Medstead **109** 53 19N 108 5W
Medulin **27** 44 49N 13 55 E
Medveda **33** 42 50N 21 32 E
Medveditsa → **37** 49 35N 42 41 E
Medvedok **37** 57 20N 50 1 E
Medvezhi, Ostrava **41** 71 0N 161 0 E
Medvezhyegorsk **40** 63 0N 34 25 E
Medway → **13** 51 28N 0 45 E
Medyn **37** 54 59N 35 56 E
Medzilaborce **32** 49 17N 21 52 E
Meeberrie **79** 26 57S 115 51 E
Meekatharra **79** 26 32S 118 29 E
Meeker **120** 40 1N 107 58W
Meeniyan **74** 38 35S 146 0 E
Meerane **30** 50 51N 12 30 E
Meerlieu **75** 38 2S 147 24 E
Meersburg **31** 47 42N 9 16 E
Meerut **48** 29 1N 77 42 E
Meeteetse **120** 44 10N 108 56W
Mega **91** 3 57N 38 19 E
Megálo Petalí **35** 38 0N 24 15 E
Megalópolis **35** 37 25N 22 7 E
Meganísi **35** 38 39N 20 48 E
Mégantic, L. **105** 45 32N 70 53W
Mégantic, Mt. **105** 45 28N 71 9W
Mégara **35** 37 58N 23 22 E
Megarine **87** 33 14N 6 2 E
Mégève **21** 45 51N 6 37 E
Meghalaya □ **52** 25 50N 91 0 E
Meghezez, Mt. **91** 9 18N 39 26 E
Meghna → **52** 22 50N 90 50 E
Megiddo **44** 32 36N 35 11 E
Mégiscane → **104** 48 29N 75 38W
Mégiscane, L. **104** 48 35N 75 55W
Megiste **46** 36 8N 29 34 E
Mehadia **34** 44 56N 22 23 E
Mehaïguene, O. → **86** 32 15N 2 59 E
Meheisa **90** 19 38N 32 57 E
Mehndawal **49** 26 58N 83 5 E
Mehsana **48** 23 39N 72 26 E
Mehun-sur-Yèvre **19** 47 10N 2 13 E
Mei Jiang → **59** 24 25N 116 35 E
Mei Xian, Guangdong, China **59** 24 16N 116 6 E
Mei Xian, Shaanxi, China **60** 34 18N 107 55 E
Meia Ponte → **139** 18 32S 49 36W
Meicheng **59** 29 29N 119 16 E
Meichengzhen **59** 28 9N 111 40 E
Meichuan **59** 30 8N 115 31 E
Meiganga **92** 6 30N 14 25 E
Meiktila **52** 20 53N 95 54 E
Meiningen **30** 50 32N 10 25 E
Meio → **139** 13 36S 44 7W
Me'ir Shefeya **44** 32 35N 34 58 E
Meira, Sierra de **22** 43 15N 7 15W
Meiringen **31** 46 43N 8 12 E
Meishan **58** 30 3N 103 23 E
Meissen **30** 51 10N 13 29 E
Meissner **30** 51 13N 9 51 E
Meitan **58** 27 45N 107 29 E
Meithalun **44** 32 21N 35 16 E
Méjean, Causse **20** 44 15N 3 30 E
Mejillones **140** 23 10S 70 30W
Meka **79** 27 25S 116 48 E
Mekambo **92** 1 2N 13 50 E
Mekdela **91** 11 24N 39 10 E
Mekele **91** 13 33N 39 30 E
Mékinac, L. **105** 47 3N 72 41W
Meknès **86** 33 57N 5 33W
Meko **89** 7 27N 2 52 E
Mekong → **55** 9 30N 106 15 E
Mekongga **57** 3 39S 121 15 E
Melagiri Hills **51** 12 20N 77 30 E
Melah, Sebkhet el **86** 29 20N 1 30W
Melaka **55** 2 15N 102 15 E
Melalap **56** 5 10N 116 5 E
Mélambes **35** 35 8N 24 40 E
Melanesia **66** 4 0S 155 0 E
Melapalaiyam **51** 8 39N 77 44 E
Melbourne, Austral. **74** 37 50S 145 0 E
Melbourne, Fla., U.S.A. **113** 28 4N 80 35W
Melbourne, Iowa, U.S.A. **116** 41 57N 93 6W
Melcher **116** 41 13N 93 15W
Melchor Múzquiz **124** 27 50N 101 30W
Melchor Ocampo (San Pedro Ocampo) **124** 24 52N 101 40W
Méldola **27** 44 7N 12 3 E
Meldorf **30** 54 5N 9 5 E
Meldrum Bay **106** 45 56N 83 6W
Mêle-sur-Sarthe, Le **18** 48 31N 0 22 E
Melegnano **26** 45 21N 9 20 E
Melenci **33** 45 32N 20 20 E
Melenki **37** 55 20N 41 37 E
Mélèzes → **101** 57 30N 71 0W
Melfi, Chad **85** 11 0N 17 59 E
Melfi, Italy **29** 41 0N 15 33 E
Melfort, Can. **109** 52 50N 104 37W
Melfort, Zimb.-Rhod. **95** 18 0S 31 25 E
Melgaço **22** 42 7N 8 15W
Melgar de Fernamental **22** 42 27N 4 17W
Melhus **10** 63 17N 10 18 E
Meligalá **35** 37 15N 21 59 E
Melilla **86** 35 21N 2 57W
Melilot **44** 31 22N 34 37 E
Melipilla **140** 33 42S 71 15W
Melita **109** 49 15N 101 0W
Mélito di Porto Salvo **29** 37 55N 15 47 E
Melitopol **38** 46 50N 35 22 E
Melk **33** 48 13N 15 20 E
Mellan-Fryken **10** 59 45N 13 10 E
Mellansel **8** 63 25N 18 17 E
Melle, France **20** 46 14N 0 10W
Melle, Ger. **30** 52 12N 8 20 E
Mellégue, O. → **87** 36 32N 8 51 E
Mellen **118** 46 19N 90 36W
Mellerud **11** 58 41N 12 28 E
Mellette **118** 45 11N 98 29W
Mellid **22** 42 55N 8 1W
Mellit **91** 14 7N 25 34 E
Mellizo Sur, Cerro **142** 48 33S 73 10W
Mellrichstadt **31** 50 26N 10 19 E
Melnik **35** 41 30N 23 25 E
Mělník **32** 50 22N 14 23 E
Melo **141** 32 20S 54 10W
Melolo **57** 9 53S 120 40 E
Melones Res. **122** 37 57N 120 31W
Melouprey **54** 13 48N 105 16 E
Melovoye **39** 49 25N 40 5 E
Melrhir, Chott **87** 34 25N 6 24 E
Melrose, N.S.W., Austral. **73** 32 42S 146 57 E
Melrose, W. Australia, Austral. **79** 27 50S 121 15 E
Melrose, U.K. **14** 53 35N 2 44W
Melrose, Iowa, U.S.A. **116** 40 59N 93 3W
Melrose, N.Mex., U.S.A. **119** 34 27N 103 33W
Melstone **120** 46 36N 107 50W
Melsungen **30** 51 8N 9 34 E
Melton Mowbray **12** 52 46N 0 52W
Melun **19** 48 32N 2 39 E
Melunga **96** 17 15S 16 22 E
Melur **51** 10 2N 78 23 E
Melut **91** 10 30N 32 13 E
Melville **109** 50 55N 102 50W
Melville B. **72** 12 0S 136 45 E
Melville, C. **72** 14 11S 144 30 E
Melville I., Austral. **78** 11 30S 131 0 E
Melville I., Can. **144** 75 30N 112 0W
Melville, L. **103** 53 30N 60 0W
Melville Pen. **101** 68 0N 84 0W
Melvin → **108** 59 11N 117 31W
Memaliaj **35** 40 25N 19 58 E
Memba **95** 14 11S 40 30 E
Memboro **57** 9 30S 119 30 E
Membrilla **25** 38 59N 3 21W
Memel **97** 27 38S 29 36 E
Memel = Klaipeda **36** 55 43N 21 10 E
Memmingen **31** 47 59N 10 12 E
Memphis, Mich., U.S.A. **106** 42 54N 82 46W
Memphis, Mo., U.S.A. **116** 40 28N 92 10W
Memphis, Tenn., U.S.A. **119** 35 7N 90 0W
Memphis, Tex., U.S.A. **119** 34 45N 100 30W
Memphrémagog, L. **105** 45 8N 72 17W
Mena **119** 34 40N 94 15W
Menai Strait **12** 53 14N 4 10W
Ménaka **89** 15 59N 2 18 E
Menan = Chao Phraya → **54** 13 32N 100 36 E
Menangle **76** 34 6S 150 44 E
Menarandra → **97** 25 17S 44 30 E
Menard **119** 30 57N 99 48W
Menasha **112** 44 13N 88 27W
Menate **56** 0 12S 113 3 E
Mendawai → **56** 3 17S 113 21 E
Mende **20** 44 31N 3 30 E
Mendebo Mts. **91** 7 0N 39 22 E
Menderes → **46** 37 25N 28 45 E
Mendez **125** 25 7N 98 34W
Mendhar **49** 33 35N 74 10 E
Mendi, Ethiopia **91** 9 47N 35 4 E
Mendi, P.N.G. **69** 6 11S 143 39 E
Mendip Hills **13** 51 17N 2 40W
Mendocino **120** 39 26N 123 50W
Mendocino Seascarp **67** 41 0N 140 0W
Mendon **117** 42 0N 85 27W
Mendooran **77** 31 50S 149 6 E
Mendota, Calif., U.S.A. **122** 36 46N 120 24W
Mendota, Ill., U.S.A. **116** 41 35N 89 5W
Mendoza **140** 32 50S 68 52W
Mendoza □ **140** 33 0S 69 0W
Mene Grande **134** 9 49N 70 56W
Menemen **46** 38 34N 27 3 E
Menen **16** 50 47N 3 7 E
Menéndez, L. **142** 42 40S 71 51W
Menfi **28** 37 36N 12 57 E
Mengcheng, Anhui, China **59** 33 18N 116 31 E
Mengcheng, Anhui, China **60** 33 20N 116 35 E
Mengdingjie **58** 23 31N 98 58 E
Mengeš **27** 46 24N 14 35 E
Menggala **56** 4 30S 105 15 E
Menghai **58** 21 49N 100 55 E
Mengíbar **23** 37 58N 3 48W
Mengjin **60** 34 55N 112 45 E
Mengla **58** 21 20N 101 25 E
Menglian **58** 22 21N 99 27 E
Mengoub **86** 29 49N 5 26W
Mengshan **59** 24 14N 110 55 E
Mengyin **61** 35 40N 117 58 E
Mengzhe **58** 22 2N 100 15 E
Mengzi **58** 23 20N 103 22 E
Menihek L. **103** 54 0N 67 0W
Menin = Menen **16** 50 47N 3 7 E
Menindee **73** 32 20S 142 25 E
Menindee, L. **73** 32 20S 142 25 E

Meningie	**73**	35 35 S	139 0 E
Menlo Park	**122**	37 27 N	122 12 W
Menominee	**112**	45 9 N	87 39 W
Menominee →	**112**	45 5 N	87 36 W
Menomonee Falls	**117**	43 11 N	88 7 W
Menomonie	**118**	44 50 N	91 54 W
Menongue	**93**	14 48 S	17 52 E
Menorca	**24**	40 0 N	4 0 E
Mentawai, Kepulauan	**56**	2 0 S	99 0 E
Mentekab	**55**	3 29 N	102 21 E
Menton	**21**	43 50 N	7 29 E
Mentone	**117**	41 10 N	86 2 W
Mentor	**114**	41 40 N	81 21 W
Menyamya	**69**	7 10 S	145 59 E
Menzel-Bourguiba	**87**	39 9 N	9 49 E
Menzel Chaker	**87**	35 0 N	10 26 E
Menzel-Temime	**87**	36 46 N	11 0 E
Menzies	**79**	29 40 S	120 58 E
Me'ona (Tarshiha)	**44**	33 1 N	35 15 E
Meoqui	**124**	28 17 N	105 29 W
Mepaco	**95**	15 57 S	30 48 E
Meppel	**16**	52 42 N	6 12 E
Meppen	**30**	52 41 N	7 20 E
Mequinenza	**24**	41 22 N	0 17 E
Mequon	**117**	43 14 N	87 59 W
Mer Rouge	**119**	32 47 N	91 48 W
Mera Lava	**68**	14 25 S	168 3 E
Merabéllou, Kólpos	**35**	35 10 N	25 50 E
Merah North	**77**	30 11 S	149 18 E
Merai	**69**	4 52 S	152 19 E
Merak	**57**	5 56 S	106 0 E
Meramangye, L.	**79**	28 25 S	132 13 E
Meramec →	**116**	38 23 N	90 54 W
Meran = Merano	**27**	46 40 N	11 10 E
Merano	**27**	46 40 N	11 10 E
Merate	**26**	45 42 N	9 23 E
Merauke	**57**	8 29 S	140 24 E
Merbabu	**57**	7 30 S	110 40 E
Merbein	**74**	34 10 S	142 2 E
Merca	**45**	1 48 N	44 50 E
Mercadal	**24**	39 59 N	4 5 E
Mercara	**51**	12 30 N	75 45 E
Mercato Saraceno	**27**	43 57 N	12 11 E
Merced	**122**	37 18 N	120 30 W
Merced Pk.	**122**	37 36 N	119 24 W
Mercedes, Buenos Aires, Argent.	**140**	34 40 S	59 30 W
Mercedes, Corrientes, Argent.	**140**	29 10 S	58 5 W
Mercedes, San Luis, Argent.	**140**	33 40 S	65 21 W
Mercedes, Uruguay	**140**	33 12 S	58 0 W
Merceditas	**140**	28 20 S	70 35 W
Mercer, N.Z.	**80**	37 16 S	175 5 E
Mercer, Mo., U.S.A.	**116**	40 31 N	93 32 W
Mercer, Pa., U.S.A.	**114**	41 14 N	80 13 W
Mercier, Boliv.	**136**	10 42 S	68 5 W
Mercier, Can.	**105**	45 19 N	73 45 W
Mercury	**123**	36 40 N	116 0 W
Mercy C.	**101**	65 0 N	63 30 W
Merdrignac	**18**	48 11 N	2 27 W
Meredith	**74**	37 49 S	144 5 E
Meredith C.	**142**	52 15 S	60 40 W
Meredith, L.	**119**	35 30 N	101 35 W
Meredosia	**116**	39 50 N	90 34 W
Méréville	**19**	48 20 N	2 5 E
Merewa	**91**	7 40 N	37 0 E
Mergenevsky	**39**	49 59 N	51 15 E
Mergui Arch. = Myeik Kyunzu	**55**	11 30 N	97 30 E
Mérida, Mexico	**125**	20 9 N	89 40 W
Mérida, Spain	**23**	38 55 N	6 25 W
Mérida, Venez.	**134**	8 24 N	71 8 W
Mérida □	**134**	8 30 N	71 10 W
Mérida, Cord. de	**134**	9 0 N	71 0 W
Meriden	**115**	41 33 N	72 47 W
Meridian, Calif., U.S.A.	**122**	39 9 N	121 55 W
Meridian, Idaho, U.S.A.	**120**	43 41 N	116 25 W
Meridian, Miss., U.S.A.	**113**	32 20 N	88 42 W
Meridian, Tex., U.S.A.	**119**	31 55 N	97 37 W
Merimbula	**75**	36 53 S	149 54 E
Mering	**31**	48 15 N	11 0 E
Meringur	**74**	34 20 S	141 19 E
Merino	**74**	37 44 S	141 35 E
Meriruma	**135**	1 15 N	54 50 W
Merkel	**119**	32 30 N	100 0 W
Merksem	**16**	51 16 N	4 25 E
Merlebach	**19**	49 5 N	6 52 E
Merlerault, Le	**18**	48 41 N	0 16 E
Mermaid Reef	**78**	17 6 S	119 36 E
Mern	**11**	55 3 N	12 3 E
Merowe	**90**	18 29 N	31 46 E
Merredin	**79**	31 28 S	118 18 E
Merrick	**14**	55 8 N	4 30 W
Merrickville	**107**	44 55 N	75 50 W
Merrigum	**74**	36 22 S	145 8 E
Merrill, Mich., U.S.A.	**106**	43 25 N	84 20 W
Merrill, Oregon, U.S.A.	**120**	42 2 N	121 37 W
Merrill, Wis., U.S.A.	**118**	45 11 N	89 41 W
Merriman	**118**	42 55 N	101 42 W
Merritt	**108**	50 10 N	120 45 W
Merriwa	**77**	32 6 S	150 22 E
Merriwagga	**74**	33 47 S	145 43 E
Merroe	**79**	27 53 S	117 50 E
Merry I.	**102**	55 29 N	77 31 W
Merrygoen	**77**	31 51 S	149 12 E
Merryville	**119**	30 47 N	93 31 W
Mersa Fatma	**91**	14 57 N	40 17 E
Mersch	**16**	49 44 N	6 7 E
Merseburg	**30**	51 20 N	12 0 E
Mersey →	**12**	53 20 N	2 56 W
Merseyside □	**12**	53 25 N	2 55 W
Mersin	**46**	36 51 N	34 36 E
Mersing	**55**	2 25 N	103 50 E
Merta	**48**	26 39 N	74 4 E
Merthyr Tydfil	**13**	51 45 N	3 23 W
Mértola	**23**	37 40 N	7 40 E
Merton	**74**	36 59 S	145 43 E
Mertzon	**119**	31 17 N	100 48 W
Méru	**19**	49 13 N	2 8 E
Meru	**94**	0 3 N	37 40 E
Meru □	**94**	0 3 N	37 46 E
Meru, mt.	**94**	3 15 S	36 46 E
Merville	**19**	50 38 N	2 38 E
Méry-sur-Seine	**19**	48 31 N	3 54 E
Merzifon	**38**	40 53 N	35 32 E
Merzig	**31**	49 26 N	6 37 E
Merzouga, Erg Tin	**87**	24 0 N	11 4 E
Mesa	**121**	33 20 N	111 56 W
Mesa, La, Calif., U.S.A.	**123**	32 48 N	117 5 W
Mesa, La, N. Mex., U.S.A.	**121**	32 6 N	106 48 W
Mesach Mellet	**87**	24 30 N	11 30 E
Mesada	**44**	31 20 N	35 19 E
Mesagne	**29**	40 34 N	17 48 E
Mesaras, Kólpos	**35**	35 6 N	24 47 E
Meschede	**30**	51 20 N	8 17 E
Mesfinto	**91**	13 20 N	37 22 E
Mesgouez, L.	**102**	51 20 N	75 0 W
Meshchovsk	**36**	54 22 N	35 17 E
Meshed = Mashhad	**47**	36 20 N	59 35 E
Meshoppen	**115**	41 36 N	76 3 W
Meshra er Req	**85**	8 25 N	29 18 E
Mesick	**112**	44 24 N	85 42 W
Mesilinka →	**108**	56 6 N	124 30 W
Mesilla	**121**	32 20 N	106 50 W
Meslay-du-Maine	**18**	47 58 N	0 33 W
Mesocco	**31**	46 23 N	9 12 E
Mesolóngion	**35**	38 21 N	21 28 E
Mesopotamia = Al Jazirah	**46**	33 30 N	44 0 E
Mesoraca	**29**	39 5 N	16 47 E
Mess Cr.	**108**	57 55 N	131 14 W
Messac	**18**	47 49 N	1 50 W
Messad	**86**	34 8 N	3 30 E
Messalo →	**95**	12 25 S	39 15 E
Méssaména	**89**	3 48 N	12 49 E
Messeix	**20**	45 37 N	2 33 E
Messier, Canal	**142**	48 20 S	74 33 W
Messina, Italy	**29**	38 10 N	15 32 E
Messina, S. Afr.	**97**	22 20 S	30 0 E
Messina, Str. di	**29**	38 5 N	15 35 E
Messine	**104**	46 14 N	76 2 W
Messíni	**35**	37 4 N	22 1 E
Messiniakós, Kólpos	**35**	36 45 N	22 5 E
Messkirch	**31**	47 59 N	9 7 E
Mesta →	**35**	41 30 N	24 0 E
Mestanza	**23**	38 35 N	4 4 W
Mestre	**27**	45 30 N	12 13 E
Mestre, Espigão	**139**	12 30 S	46 10 W
Městys Zelezná Ruda	**32**	49 8 N	13 15 E
Meta	**116**	38 19 N	92 10 W
Meta □	**134**	3 30 N	73 0 W
Meta →	**134**	6 12 N	67 28 W
Metairie	**119**	29 59 N	90 9 W
Metaline Falls	**120**	48 52 N	117 22 W
Metamora	**116**	40 47 N	89 22 W
Metán	**140**	25 30 S	65 0 W
Metauro →	**27**	43 50 N	13 3 E
Metehara	**91**	8 58 N	39 57 E
Metema	**91**	12 56 N	36 13 E
Metengobalame	**95**	14 49 S	34 30 E
Méthana	**35**	37 35 N	23 23 E
Methven	**81**	43 38 S	171 40 E
Methy L.	**109**	56 28 N	109 30 W
Metlakatla	**108**	55 10 N	131 33 W
Metlaoui	**87**	34 24 N	8 24 E
Metlika	**27**	45 40 N	15 20 E
Metropolis	**119**	37 10 N	88 47 W
Mettuppalaiyam	**51**	11 18 N	76 59 E
Mettur	**51**	11 48 N	77 47 E
Mettur Dam	**51**	11 45 N	77 45 E
Metulla	**44**	33 17 N	35 34 E
Metung	**75**	37 54 S	147 52 E
Metz	**19**	49 8 N	6 10 E
Meulaboh	**56**	4 11 N	96 3 E
Meulan	**19**	49 0 N	1 52 E
Meung-sur-Loire	**19**	47 50 N	1 40 E
Meureudu	**56**	5 19 N	96 10 E
Meurthe →	**19**	48 47 N	6 9 E
Meurthe-et-Moselle □	**19**	48 52 N	6 0 E
Meuse □	**19**	49 8 N	5 25 E
Meuse →	**16**	50 45 N	5 41 E
Meuselwitz	**30**	51 3 N	12 18 E
Mexborough	**12**	53 29 N	1 18 W
Mexia	**119**	31 38 N	96 32 W
Mexiana, I.	**138**	0 0	49 30 W
Mexicali	**124**	32 40 N	115 30 W
México	**125**	19 20 N	99 10 W
Mexico, Me., U.S.A.	**115**	44 35 N	70 30 W
Mexico, Mo., U.S.A.	**116**	39 10 N	91 55 W
Mexico ■	**124**	20 0 N	100 0 W
México □	**124**	19 20 N	99 10 W
Mexico, G. of	**125**	25 0 N	90 0 W
Meyenburg	**30**	53 19 N	12 15 E
Meymac	**20**	45 32 N	2 10 E
Meyrargues	**21**	43 38 N	5 32 E
Meyrueis	**20**	44 12 N	3 27 E
Meyssac	**20**	45 3 N	1 40 E
Mezdra	**34**	43 12 N	23 42 E
Mèze	**20**	43 27 N	3 36 E
Mezen	**40**	65 50 N	44 20 E
Mezen →	**40**	66 11 N	43 59 E
Mézenc	**21**	44 55 N	4 11 E
Mezha →	**36**	55 50 N	31 45 E
Mézidon	**18**	49 5 N	0 1 W
Mézilhac	**21**	44 49 N	4 21 E
Mézin	**20**	44 4 N	0 16 E
Mezöberény	**33**	46 49 N	21 3 E
Mezökövácsháza	**33**	46 25 N	20 57 E
Mezökövesd	**33**	47 49 N	20 35 E
Mézos	**20**	44 5 N	1 10 W
Mezötúr	**33**	47 0 N	20 41 E
Mezquital	**124**	23 29 N	104 23 W
Mezzolombardo	**26**	46 13 N	11 5 E
Mgeta	**95**	8 22 S	36 6 E
Mglin	**36**	53 2 N	32 50 E
Mhlaba Hills	**95**	18 30 S	30 30 E
Mhow	**48**	22 33 N	75 50 E
Mi-Shima	**64**	34 46 N	131 9 E
Miahuatlán	**125**	16 21 N	96 36 W
Miajadas	**23**	39 9 N	5 54 W
Mialar	**48**	26 15 N	70 20 E
Miallo	**72**	16 28 S	145 22 E
Miami, Ariz., U.S.A.	**121**	33 25 N	110 54 W
Miami, Fla., U.S.A.	**113**	25 45 N	80 15 W
Miami, Tex., U.S.A.	**119**	35 44 N	100 38 W
Miami →	**112**	39 20 N	84 40 W
Miami Beach	**113**	25 49 N	80 6 W
Miamisburg	**117**	39 40 N	84 11 W
Mian Xian	**60**	33 10 N	106 32 E
Mianchi	**60**	34 48 N	111 48 E
Miandowāb	**46**	37 0 N	46 5 E
Miandrivazo	**97**	19 31 S	45 29 E
Mīāneh	**46**	37 30 N	47 40 E
Mianning	**58**	28 32 N	102 9 E
Mianwali	**48**	32 38 N	71 28 E
Mianyang, Hubei, China	**59**	30 25 N	113 25 E
Mianyang, Sichuan, China	**58**	31 22 N	104 47 E
Mianzhu	**58**	31 22 N	104 7 E
Miaoli	**59**	24 37 N	120 49 E
Miarinarivo	**97**	18 57 S	46 55 E
Miass	**40**	54 59 N	60 6 E
Miastko	**32**	54 0 N	16 58 E
Michael, Mt.	**69**	6 27 S	145 22 E
Michelago	**76**	35 41 S	149 11 E
Michelstadt	**31**	49 40 N	9 0 E
Michigan □	**111**	44 40 N	85 40 W
Michigan Center	**106**	42 14 N	84 20 W
Michigan City	**117**	41 42 N	86 56 W
Michigan, L.	**112**	44 0 N	87 0 W
Michipicoten	**102**	47 55 N	84 55 W
Michipicoten I.	**102**	47 40 N	85 40 W
Michoacan □	**124**	19 0 N	102 0 W
Michurin	**34**	42 9 N	27 51 E
Michurinsk	**37**	52 58 N	40 27 E
Miclere	**72**	22 34 S	147 32 E
Mico, Pta.	**126**	12 0 N	83 30 W
Micronesia	**66**	11 0 N	160 0 E
Mid Glamorgan □	**13**	51 40 N	3 25 W
Mid-Indian Ridge	**66**	40 0 S	75 0 E
Mid-Oceanic Ridge	**66**	42 0 S	90 0 E
Midai, P.	**55**	3 0 N	107 47 E
Midale	**109**	49 25 N	103 20 W
Midas	**120**	41 14 N	116 48 W
Middagsfjället	**10**	63 27 N	12 19 E
Middelburg, Neth.	**16**	51 30 N	3 36 E
Middelburg, C. Prov., S. Afr.	**96**	31 30 S	25 0 E
Middelburg, Trans., S. Afr.	**97**	25 49 S	29 28 E
Middelfart	**11**	55 30 N	9 43 E
Middle →	**116**	41 26 N	93 30 W
Middle Alkali L.	**120**	41 30 N	120 3 W
Middle Fork Feather →	**122**	39 35 N	121 25 W
Middle Loup →	**118**	41 17 N	98 23 W
Middle Raccoon →	**116**	41 35 N	93 35 W
Middleboro	**115**	41 56 N	70 52 W
Middleburg, N.Y., U.S.A.	**115**	42 36 N	74 19 W
Middleburg, Pa., U.S.A.	**114**	40 46 N	77 5 W
Middlebury, Ind., U.S.A.	**117**	41 41 N	85 42 W
Middlebury, Vt., U.S.A.	**115**	44 0 N	73 9 W
Middlemarch	**81**	45 30 S	170 9 E
Middleport	**112**	39 0 N	82 5 W
Middlesboro	**113**	36 36 N	83 43 W
Middlesbrough	**12**	54 35 N	1 14 W
Middlesex, Belize	**126**	17 2 N	88 31 W
Middlesex, U.S.A.	**115**	40 36 N	74 30 W
Middleton, Can.	**103**	44 57 N	65 4 W
Middleton, U.S.A.	**116**	43 6 N	89 30 W
Middleton Cr. →	**72**	22 35 S	141 51 E
Middleton P.O.	**72**	22 22 S	141 32 E
Middletown, Calif., U.S.A.	**122**	38 45 N	122 37 W
Middletown, Conn., U.S.A.	**115**	41 37 N	72 40 W
Middletown, N.Y., U.S.A.	**115**	41 28 N	74 28 W
Middletown, Ohio, U.S.A.	**117**	39 29 N	84 25 W
Middletown, Pa., U.S.A.	**115**	40 12 N	76 44 W
Middleville	**117**	42 43 N	85 28 W
Midelt	**86**	32 46 N	4 44 W
Midhurst	**80**	39 17 S	174 18 E
Midi, Canal du	**20**	43 45 N	1 21 E
Midi d'Ossau	**24**	42 50 N	0 25 W
Midland, Austral.	**79**	31 54 S	115 59 E
Midland, Can.	**106**	44 45 N	79 50 W
Midland, Calif., U.S.A.	**123**	33 52 N	114 48 W
Midland, Mich., U.S.A.	**106**	43 37 N	84 17 W
Midland, Pa., U.S.A.	**114**	40 39 N	80 27 W
Midland, Tex., U.S.A.	**119**	32 0 N	102 3 W
Midlands □	**95**	19 40 S	29 0 E
Midleton	**15**	51 52 N	8 12 W
Midlothian	**119**	32 30 N	97 0 W
Midnapore	**49**	22 25 N	87 21 E
Midongy du Sud	**97**	23 35 S	47 1 E
Midongy, Massif de	**97**	23 30 S	47 0 E
Midour →	**20**	43 54 N	0 30 W
Midouze →	**20**	43 48 N	0 51 W
Midu	**58**	25 18 N	100 30 E
Midvale	**120**	40 39 N	111 58 W
Midway Is.	**66**	28 13 N	177 22 W
Midway Wells	**123**	32 41 N	115 7 W
Midwest	**120**	43 27 N	106 19 W
Midyat	**46**	37 25 N	41 23 E
Mie □	**65**	34 30 N	136 10 E
Miechów	**32**	50 21 N	20 5 E
Międzychód	**32**	52 35 N	15 53 E
Międzyrzec Podlaski	**32**	51 58 N	22 45 E
Międzyrzecz	**32**	52 26 N	15 35 E
Miélan	**20**	43 27 N	0 19 E
Mielec	**32**	50 15 N	21 25 E
Mienga	**96**	17 12 S	19 48 E
Miercurea Ciuc	**34**	46 21 N	25 48 E
Mieres	**22**	43 18 N	5 48 W
Mieso	**91**	9 15 N	40 43 E
Migdal	**44**	32 51 N	35 30 E
Migdal Afeq	**44**	32 5 N	34 58 E
Migennes	**19**	47 58 N	3 31 E
Migliarino	**27**	44 45 N	11 56 E
Miguel Alemán, Presa	**125**	18 15 N	96 40 W
Miguel Alves	**138**	4 11 S	42 55 W
Miguel Calmon	**138**	11 26 S	40 36 W
Mihara	**64**	34 24 N	133 5 E
Mihara-Yama	**65**	34 43 N	139 23 E
Miiintown	**114**	40 34 N	77 24 W
Mijares →	**24**	39 55 N	0 1 W
Mijas	**23**	36 36 N	4 40 W
Mikardo	**106**	44 34 N	83 28 W
Mikese	**94**	6 48 S	37 55 E
Mikha-Tskhakaya	**39**	42 15 N	42 7 E
Mikhailovka	**38**	47 36 N	35 16 E
Mikhaylov	**37**	54 14 N	39 0 E
Mikhaylovgrad	**34**	43 27 N	23 16 E
Mikhaylovka, Azerbaijan, U.S.S.R.	**39**	41 31 N	48 52 E
Mikhaylovka, R.S.F.S.R., U.S.S.R.	**37**	50 3 N	43 5 E
Mikhnevo	**37**	55 4 N	37 59 E
Miki, Hyōgo, Japan	**64**	34 48 N	134 59 E
Miki, Kagawa, Japan	**64**	34 12 N	134 7 E
Mikinai	**35**	37 43 N	22 46 E
Mikindani	**95**	10 15 S	40 2 E
Mikkeli	**9**	61 43 N	27 15 E
Mikkelin lääni □	**8**	61 56 N	28 0 E
Mikkwa →	**108**	58 25 N	114 46 W
Mikniya	**91**	17 0 N	33 45 E

Place	Page	Lat.	Long.
Mikołajki	**32**	53 49N	21 37 E
Míkonos	**35**	37 30N	25 25 E
Mikrón Dhérion	**35**	41 19N	26 6 E
Mikulov	**32**	48 48N	16 39 E
Mikumi	**94**	7 26S	37 0 E
Mikuni	**65**	36 13N	136 9 E
Mikuni-Tōge	**65**	36 50N	138 50 E
Mikura-Jima	**65**	33 52N	139 36 E
Milaca	**118**	45 45N	93 40W
Milagro	**134**	2 11S	79 36W
Milan, Ill., U.S.A.	**116**	41 27N	90 34W
Milan, Mich., U.S.A.	**106**	42 5N	83 40W
Milan, Mo., U.S.A.	**116**	40 10N	93 5W
Milan, Tenn., U.S.A.	**113**	35 55N	88 45W
Milan = Milano	**26**	45 28N	9 10 E
Milang	**73**	32 2S	139 10 E
Milange	**95**	16 3S	35 45 E
Milano	**26**	45 28N	9 10 E
Milâs	**46**	37 20N	27 50 E
Milazzo	**29**	38 13N	15 13 E
Milbank	**118**	45 17N	96 38W
Milden	**109**	51 29N	107 32W
Mildmay	**106**	44 3N	81 7W
Mildura	**74**	34 13S	142 9 E
Mile	**58**	24 28N	103 20 E
Miléai	**35**	39 20N	23 9 E
Miles, Austral.	**73**	26 40S	150 9 E
Miles, U.S.A.	**119**	31 39N	100 11W
Miles City	**118**	46 24N	105 50W
Milestone	**109**	49 59N	104 31W
Mileto	**29**	38 37N	16 3 E
Miletto, Mte.	**29**	41 26N	14 23 E
Mileura	**79**	26 22S	117 20 E
Milford, U.S.A.	**122**	40 10N	120 22W
Milford, Conn., U.S.A.	**115**	41 13N	73 4W
Milford, Del., U.S.A.	**112**	38 52N	75 27W
Milford, Ill., U.S.A.	**117**	40 40N	87 43W
Milford, Mass., U.S.A.	**115**	42 8N	71 30W
Milford, Mich., U.S.A.	**117**	42 35N	83 36W
Milford, Pa., U.S.A.	**115**	41 20N	74 47W
Milford, Utah, U.S.A.	**121**	38 20N	113 0W
Milford Haven	**13**	51 43N	5 2W
Milford Haven, B.	**13**	51 40N	5 10W
Milford Sd.	**81**	44 41S	167 47 E
Milgun	**79**	25 6S	118 18 E
Milḥ, Baḥr al	**46**	32 40N	43 35 E
Milh, Ras el	**85**	31 54N	25 6 E
Miliana, Aïn Salah, Alg.	**86**	27 20N	2 32 E
Miliana, Médéa, Alg.	**86**	36 20N	2 15 E
Miling	**79**	30 30S	116 17 E
Militello in Val di Catánia	**29**	37 16N	14 46 E
Milk →	**120**	48 5N	106 15W
Milk River	**108**	49 10N	112 5W
Milk, W. el	**90**	17 55N	30 20 E
Mill City	**120**	44 45N	122 28W
Mill, I.	**143**	66 0S	101 30 E
Mill Shoals	**117**	38 15N	88 21W
Mill Valley	**122**	37 54N	122 32W
Millau	**20**	44 8N	3 4 E
Millbridge	**107**	44 41N	77 36W
Millbrook	**107**	44 10N	78 29W
Mille	**113**	33 7N	83 15W
Mille Lacs, L.	**118**	46 10N	93 30W
Mille Lacs, L. des	**102**	48 45N	90 35W
Milledgeville	**116**	41 58N	89 46W
Millen	**113**	32 50N	81 57W
Miller	**118**	44 35N	98 59W
Millerovo	**39**	48 57N	40 28 E
Miller's Flat	**81**	45 39S	169 23 E
Millersburg, Ind., U.S.A.	**117**	41 32N	85 42W
Millersburg, Mich., U.S.A.	**106**	45 20N	84 4W
Millersburg, Ohio, U.S.A.	**114**	40 32N	81 52W
Millersburg, Pa., U.S.A.	**114**	40 32N	76 58W
Millerton, N.Z.	**81**	41 39S	171 54 E
Millerton, U.S.A.	**115**	41 57N	73 32W
Millerton L.	**122**	37 0N	119 42W
Millevaches, Plateau de	**20**	45 45N	2 0 E
Millicent	**73**	37 34S	140 21 E
Millington	**106**	43 17N	83 32W
Millinocket	**103**	45 45N	68 45W
Millmerran	**73**	27 53S	151 16 E
Mills L.	**108**	61 30N	118 20W
Millsboro	**114**	40 0N	80 0W
Millthorpe	**76**	33 26S	149 12 E
Milltown Malbay	**15**	52 51N	9 25W
Millville	**112**	39 22N	75 0W
Millwood Res.	**119**	33 45N	94 0W
Milly	**19**	48 24N	2 28 E
Milna	**27**	43 20N	16 28 E
Milne →	**72**	21 10S	137 33 E
Milne Inlet	**101**	72 30N	80 0W
Milnor	**118**	46 19N	97 29W
Milo	**108**	50 34N	112 53W
Mílos	**35**	36 44N	24 25 E
Mílos, I.	**35**	36 44N	24 15 E
Miloševo	**33**	45 42N	20 20 E
Milot	**105**	48 54N	71 49W
Milparinka P.O.	**73**	29 46S	141 57 E
Milroy	**117**	39 30N	85 28W
Miltenberg	**31**	49 41N	9 13 E
Milton, Austral.	**76**	35 20S	150 27 E
Milton, Can.	**106**	43 33N	79 53W
Milton, Ont., Can.	**106**	43 31N	79 53W
Milton, N.Z.	**81**	46 7S	169 59 E
Milton, U.K.	**14**	57 18N	4 32W
Milton, Calif., U.S.A.	**122**	38 3N	120 51W
Milton, Fla., U.S.A.	**113**	30 38N	87 0W
Milton, Iowa, U.S.A.	**116**	40 41N	92 10W
Milton, Pa., U.S.A.	**114**	41 0N	76 53W
Milton, Wis., U.S.A.	**117**	42 47N	88 56W
Milton-Freewater	**120**	45 57N	118 24W
Milton Keynes	**13**	52 3N	0 42W
Milvale	**76**	34 18S	147 56 E
Milverton	**106**	43 34N	80 55W
Milwaukee	**117**	43 9N	87 58W
Milwaukie	**122**	45 27N	122 39W
Mim	**88**	6 57N	2 33W
Mimizan	**20**	44 12N	1 13W
Mimosa	**76**	34 34S	147 22 E
Mimoso	**139**	15 10S	48 5W
Min Jiang →, Fujian, China	**59**	26 0N	119 35 E
Min Jiang →, Sichuan, China	**58**	28 45N	104 40 E
Min Xian	**60**	34 25N	104 0 E
Mina	**121**	38 21N	118 9W
Mina Pirquitas	**140**	22 40S	66 30W
Mina Saud	**46**	28 45N	48 28 E
Minā'al Aḥmadī	**46**	29 5N	48 10 E
Mīnāb	**47**	27 10N	57 1 E
Minago →	**109**	54 33N	98 59W
Minakami	**65**	36 49N	138 59 E
Minaki	**109**	49 59N	94 40W
Minakuchi	**65**	34 58N	136 10 E
Minamata	**64**	32 10N	130 30 E
Minas	**141**	34 20S	55 10W
Minas Basin	**103**	45 20N	64 12W
Minas de Rio Tinto	**23**	37 42N	6 35W
Minas de San Quintín	**23**	38 49N	4 23W
Minas Gerais □	**139**	18 50S	46 0W
Minas Novas	**139**	17 15S	42 36W
Minas, Sierra de las	**126**	15 9N	89 31W
Minatitlán	**125**	17 58N	94 35W
Minbu	**52**	20 10N	94 52 E
Minbya	**52**	20 22N	93 16 E
Mincha	**74**	36 1S	144 6 E
Mincio →	**26**	45 4N	10 59 E
Mindanao	**57**	8 0N	125 0 E
Mindanao Sea	**57**	9 0N	124 0 E
Mindanao Trench	**57**	8 0N	128 0 E
Mindel →	**31**	48 31N	10 23 E
Mindelheim	**31**	48 4N	10 30 E
Mindemoya	**106**	45 44N	82 10W
Minden, Can.	**107**	44 55N	78 43W
Minden, Ger.	**30**	52 18N	8 45 E
Minden, La., U.S.A.	**119**	32 40N	93 20W
Minden, Nev., U.S.A.	**122**	38 57N	119 48W
Mindiptana	**57**	5 55S	140 22 E
Mindon	**52**	19 21N	94 44 E
Mindoro	**57**	13 0N	121 0 E
Mindoro Strait	**57**	12 30N	120 30 E
Mindouli	**92**	4 12S	14 28 E
Mine	**64**	34 12N	131 7 E
Minehead	**13**	51 12N	3 29W
Mineiros	**137**	17 34S	52 34W
Mineola	**119**	32 40N	95 30W
Mineral King	**122**	36 27N	118 36W
Mineral Point	**116**	42 52N	90 11W
Mineral Wells	**119**	32 50N	98 5W
Mineralnyye Vody	**39**	44 2N	43 8 E
Minersville, Pa., U.S.A.	**115**	40 11N	76 17W
Minersville, Utah, U.S.A.	**121**	38 14N	112 58W
Minerva	**114**	40 43N	81 8W
Minervino Murge	**29**	41 6N	16 4 E
Minetto	**115**	43 24N	76 28W
Mingan	**103**	50 20N	64 0W
Mingechaur	**39**	40 45N	47 0 E
Mingechaurskoye Vdkhr.	**39**	40 56N	47 20 E
Mingela	**72**	19 52S	146 38 E
Mingenew	**79**	29 12S	115 21 E
Mingera Cr. →	**72**	20 38S	138 10 E
Minggang	**59**	32 24N	114 3 E
Mingin	**52**	22 50N	94 30 E
Minglanilla	**24**	39 34N	1 38W
Minglun	**58**	25 10N	108 21 E
Mingorria	**22**	40 45N	4 40W
Mingxi	**59**	26 18N	117 12 E
Mingyuegue	**61**	43 2N	128 50 E
Minhou	**59**	26 0N	119 15 E
Miničevo	**33**	43 42N	22 18 E
Minidoka	**120**	42 47N	113 34W
Minier	**116**	40 26N	89 19W
Minigwal L.	**79**	29 31S	123 14 E
Minilya	**79**	23 55S	114 0 E
Minilya →	**79**	23 45S	114 0 E
Minimbah	**76**	32 39S	151 15 E
Mininera	**74**	37 37S	142 58 E
Minipi, L.	**103**	52 25N	60 45W
Minj	**69**	5 54S	144 37 E
Mink L.	**108**	61 54N	117 40W
Minna	**89**	9 37N	6 30 E
Minneapolis, Kans., U.S.A.	**118**	39 11N	97 40W
Minneapolis, Minn., U.S.A.	**118**	44 58N	93 20W
Minnedosa	**109**	50 14N	99 50W
Minnesota □	**118**	46 40N	94 0W
Minnesund	**10**	60 23N	11 14 E
Minnie Creek	**79**	24 3S	115 42 E
Minnitaki L.	**102**	49 57N	92 10W
Mino	**65**	35 32N	136 55 E
Miño →	**22**	41 52N	8 40W
Mino-Kamo	**65**	35 23N	137 2 E
Mino-Mikawa-Kōgen	**65**	35 10N	137 23 E
Minobu	**65**	35 22N	138 26 E
Minobu-Sanchi	**65**	35 14N	138 20 E
Minonk	**116**	40 54N	89 2W
Minooka	**117**	41 27N	88 16W
Minorca = Menorca	**24**	40 0N	4 0 E
Minore	**76**	32 14S	148 27 E
Minot	**118**	48 10N	101 15W
Minqin	**60**	38 38N	103 20 E
Minqing	**59**	26 15N	118 50 E
Minquiers, Les	**18**	48 53N	2 8W
Minsen	**30**	53 43N	7 58 E
Minsk	**36**	53 52N	27 30 E
Mińsk Mazowiecki	**32**	52 10N	21 33 E
Minster	**117**	40 24N	84 23W
Mintaka Pass	**49**	37 0N	74 58 E
Minthami	**52**	23 55N	94 16 E
Minto	**100**	64 55N	149 20W
Minton	**109**	49 10N	104 35W
Minturn	**120**	39 35N	106 25W
Minturno	**28**	41 15N	13 43 E
Minûf	**90**	30 26N	30 52 E
Minusinsk	**41**	53 50N	91 20 E
Minutang	**52**	28 15N	96 30 E
Minvoul	**92**	2 9N	12 8 E
Minya el Qamh	**90**	30 31N	31 21 E
Minyip	**74**	36 29S	142 36 E
Mio	**106**	44 39N	84 8W
Mionica	**33**	44 14N	20 6 E
Miquelon	**104**	49 25N	76 27W
Mir-Bashir	**39**	40 20N	46 58 E
Mira, Italy	**27**	45 26N	12 9 E
Mira, Port.	**22**	40 26N	8 44W
Mira →, Colomb.	**134**	1 36N	79 1W
Mira →, Port.	**23**	37 43N	8 47W
Mira por vos Cay	**127**	22 9N	74 30W
Mirabella Eclano	**29**	41 3N	14 59 E
Miracema do Norte	**138**	9 33S	48 24W
Mirador	**138**	6 22S	44 22W
Miraflores, Colomb.	**134**	1 25N	72 13W
Miraflores, Mexico	**124**	23 21N	109 45W
Miraj	**50**	16 50N	74 45 E
Miram	**72**	21 15S	148 55 E
Miramar, Argent.	**140**	38 15S	57 50W
Miramar, Mozam.	**97**	23 50S	35 35 E
Miramas	**21**	43 33N	4 59 E
Mirambeau	**20**	45 23N	0 35W
Miramichi B.	**103**	47 15N	65 0W
Miramont-de-Guyenne	**20**	44 37N	0 21 E
Miran Shah	**48**	33 0N	70 2 E
Miranda	**137**	20 10S	56 15W
Miranda □	**134**	10 15N	66 25W
Miranda →	**137**	19 25S	57 20W
Miranda de Ebro	**24**	42 41N	2 57W
Miranda do Corvo	**22**	40 6N	8 20W
Miranda do Douro	**22**	41 30N	6 16W
Mirande	**20**	43 31N	0 25 E
Mirandela	**22**	41 32N	7 10W
Mirando City	**119**	27 28N	98 59W
Mirandola	**26**	44 53N	11 2 E
Mirandópolis	**141**	21 9S	51 6W
Mirango	**95**	13 32S	34 58 E
Mirano	**27**	45 29N	12 6 E
Mirassol	**141**	20 46S	49 28W
Mirboo	**75**	38 27S	146 13 E
Mirboo North	**75**	38 24S	146 10 E
Mirear	**90**	23 15N	35 41 E
Mirebeau, Côte-d'or, France	**19**	47 25N	5 20 E
Mirebeau, Vienne, France	**18**	46 49N	0 10 E
Mirecourt	**19**	48 20N	6 10 E
Mirgorod	**36**	49 58N	33 37 E
Miri	**56**	4 18N	114 0 E
Miriam Vale	**72**	24 20S	151 33 E
Mirim, Lagoa	**141**	32 45S	52 50W
Mirimire	**134**	11 10N	68 43W
Miriti	**137**	6 15S	59 0W
Mirnyy, Antarct.	**143**	66 33S	93 1 E
Mirnyy, U.S.S.R.	**41**	62 33N	113 53 E
Mirond L.	**109**	55 6N	102 47W
Mirpur	**49**	33 32N	73 56 E
Mirpur Bibiwari	**48**	28 33N	67 44 E
Mirpur Khas	**48**	25 30N	69 0 E
Mirpur Sakro	**48**	24 33N	67 41 E
Mirror	**108**	52 30N	113 7W
Mîrşani	**34**	44 1N	23 59 E
Miryang	**61**	35 31N	128 44 E
Mirzaani	**39**	41 24N	46 5 E
Mirzapur-cum-Vindhyachal	**49**	25 10N	82 34 E
Misantla	**125**	19 56N	96 50W
Miscou I.	**103**	47 57N	64 31W
Mish'āb, Ra'as al	**46**	28 15N	48 43 E
Mishagua →	**136**	11 12S	72 58W
Mishan	**62**	45 37N	131 48 E
Mishawaka	**117**	41 40N	86 8W
Mishbih, Gebel	**90**	22 38N	34 44 E
Mishima	**65**	35 10N	138 52 E
Mishmar Aiyalon	**44**	31 52N	34 57 E
Mishmar Ha' Emeq	**44**	32 37N	35 7 E
Mishmar Ha Negev	**44**	31 22N	34 48 E
Mishmar Ha Yarden	**44**	33 0N	35 36 E
Mishmi Hills	**52**	29 0N	96 0 E
Misilmeri	**28**	38 2N	13 25 E
Misima I.	**69**	10 40S	152 45 E
Misión	**123**	32 6N	116 53W
Misión Fagnano	**142**	54 32S	67 17W
Misión, La	**124**	32 5N	116 50W
Misiones □, Argent.	**141**	27 0S	55 0W
Misiones □, Parag.	**140**	27 0S	56 0W
Miskīn	**47**	23 44N	56 52 E
Miskitos, Cayos	**126**	14 26N	82 50W
Miskolc	**33**	48 7N	20 50 E
Misoke	**94**	0 42S	28 2 E
Misool	**57**	1 52S	130 10 E
Misrātah	**87**	32 24N	15 3 E
Missanabie	**102**	48 20N	84 6W
Missão Velha	**138**	7 15S	39 10W
Missinaibi →	**102**	50 43N	81 29W
Missinaibi L.	**102**	48 23N	83 40W
Mission, S.D., U.S.A.	**118**	43 21N	100 36W
Mission, Tex., U.S.A.	**119**	26 15N	98 20W
Mission City	**108**	49 10N	122 15W
Missisa L.	**102**	52 20N	85 7W
Mississagi →	**106**	46 15N	83 9W
Mississagi Prov. Park	**106**	46 30N	82 40W
Mississauga	**106**	43 32N	79 35W
Mississinewa Res.	**117**	40 46N	86 3W
Mississippi →	**119**	29 0N	89 15W
Mississippi, Delta of the	**119**	29 15N	90 30W
Mississippi L.	**107**	45 5N	76 10W
Mississippi Sd.	**119**	30 25N	89 0W
Missoula	**120**	46 52N	114 0W
Missouri □	**118**	38 25N	92 30W
Missouri →	**118**	38 50N	90 8W
Missouri Valley	**118**	41 33N	95 53W
Mist	**122**	45 59N	123 15W
Mistake B.	**109**	62 8N	93 0W
Mistaouac, L.	**104**	49 25N	78 41W
Mistassibi →	**105**	48 53N	72 13W
Mistassibi Nord-Est. →	**105**	49 31N	71 56W
Mistassini	**105**	48 53N	72 12W
Mistassini →	**105**	48 42N	72 20W
Mistassini L.	**102**	51 0N	73 30W
Mistassini, Parc. Prov. de	**105**	50 20N	74 0W
Mistastin L.	**103**	55 57N	63 20W
Mistatim	**109**	52 52N	103 22W
Mistelbach	**32**	48 34N	16 34 E
Misterbianco	**29**	37 32N	15 0 E
Mistretta	**29**	37 56N	14 20 E
Misty L.	**109**	58 53N	101 40W
Misugi	**65**	34 31N	136 16 E
Misumi	**64**	32 37N	130 27 E
Mît Ghamr	**90**	30 42N	31 12 E
Mitaka	**65**	35 40N	139 33 E
Mitatib	**91**	15 59N	36 12 E
Mitchell, Austral.	**73**	26 29S	147 58 E
Mitchell, Can.	**106**	43 28N	81 12W
Mitchell, Ind., U.S.A.	**117**	38 42N	86 25W
Mitchell, Nebr., U.S.A.	**118**	41 58N	103 45W
Mitchell, Oreg., U.S.A.	**120**	44 31N	120 8W
Mitchell, S.D., U.S.A.	**118**	43 40N	98 0W
Mitchell →, Queens., Austral.	**72**	15 12S	141 35 E
Mitchell →, Victoria, Austral.	**75**	37 51S	147 38 E
Mitchell, Mt.	**113**	35 40N	82 20W
Mitchelstown	**15**	52 16N	8 18W
Mitchinamécus, Rés.	**104**	47 19N	75 9W
Mitha Tiwana	**48**	32 13N	72 6 E
Mitiamo	**74**	36 12S	144 15 E
Mitilíni	**35**	39 6N	26 35 E
Mitla	**125**	16 55N	96 24W
Mito	**65**	36 20N	140 30 E
Mitre	**74**	36 44S	141 46 E

Mitsinjo	**97**	16 1S	45 52 E
Mitsiwa	**91**	15 35N	39 25 E
Mitsiwa Channel	**91**	15 30N	40 0 E
Mitsukaidō	**65**	36 1N	139 59 E
Mitta Mitta	**75**	36 34S	147 22 E
Mitta Mitta →	**75**	36 14S	147 10 E
Mittagong	**76**	34 28S	150 29 E
Mittelland Kanal	**30**	52 23N	7 45 E
Mittenwalde	**30**	52 16N	13 33 E
Mitterteich	**31**	49 57N	12 15 E
Mittweida	**30**	50 59N	13 0 E
Mittyack	**74**	35 8S	142 36 E
Mitú	**134**	1 8N	70 3W
Mituas	**134**	3 52N	68 49W
Mitumba	**94**	7 8S	31 2 E
Mitumba, Chaîne des	**94**	6 0S	29 0 E
Mitwaba	**95**	8 2S	27 17 E
Mityana	**94**	0 23N	32 2 E
Mitzick	**92**	0 45N	11 40 E
Miura	**65**	35 12N	139 40 E
Mixteco →	**125**	18 11N	98 30W
Miyagi □	**63**	38 15N	140 45 E
Miyâh, W. el →	**90**	25 0N	33 23 E
Miyake-Jima	**65**	34 0N	139 30 E
Miyako	**63**	39 40N	141 59 E
Miyako-Jima	**63**	24 45N	125 20 E
Miyakonojō	**64**	31 40N	131 5 E
Miyanojō	**64**	31 54N	130 27 E
Miyata	**64**	33 49N	130 42 E
Miyazaki	**64**	31 56N	131 30 E
Miyazaki □	**64**	32 30N	131 30 E
Miyazu	**64**	35 35N	135 10 E
Miyet, Bahr el	**46**	31 30N	35 30 E
Miyi	**58**	26 47N	102 9 E
Miyoshi	**64**	34 48N	132 51 E
Miyun	**60**	40 28N	116 50 E
Miyun Sk.	**61**	40 30N	117 0 E
Mizal	**46**	23 59N	45 11 E
Mizamis = Ozamiz	**57**	8 15N	123 50 E
Mizdah	**87**	31 30N	13 0 E
Mizen Hd., Cork, Ireland	**15**	51 27N	9 50W
Mizen Hd., Wicklow, Ireland	**15**	52 52N	6 4W
Mizhi	**60**	37 47N	110 12 E
Mizil	**34**	44 59N	26 29 E
Mizoram □	**52**	23 30N	92 40 E
Mizuho	**65**	35 6N	135 17 E
Mizunami	**65**	35 22N	137 15 E
Mjöbäck	**11**	57 28N	12 53 E
Mjölby	**11**	58 20N	15 10 E
Mjörn	**11**	57 55N	12 25 E
Mjøsa	**10**	60 48N	11 0 E
Mkata	**94**	5 45S	38 20 E
Mkokotoni	**94**	5 55S	39 15 E
Mkomazi	**94**	4 40S	38 7 E
Mkulwe	**95**	8 37S	32 20 E
Mkumbi, Ras	**94**	7 38S	39 55 E
Mkushi	**95**	14 25S	29 15 E
Mkushi River	**95**	13 32S	29 45 E
Mkuze →	**97**	27 45S	32 30 E
Mladá Boleslav	**32**	50 27N	14 53 E
Mladenovac	**33**	44 28N	20 44 E
Mlala Hills	**94**	6 50S	31 40 E
Mlange	**95**	16 2S	35 33 E
Mlava →	**33**	44 45N	21 13 E
Mława	**32**	53 9N	20 25 E
Mliniště	**27**	44 15N	16 50 E
Mljet	**33**	42 43N	17 30 E
Młynąry	**32**	54 12N	19 46 E
Mme	**89**	6 18N	10 14 E
Mo i Rana	**8**	66 15N	14 7 E
Moa	**57**	8 0S	128 0 E
Moa →	**88**	6 59N	11 36 E
Moab	**121**	38 40N	109 35W
Moabi	**92**	2 24S	10 59 E
Moaco →	**136**	7 41S	68 18W
Moala	**68**	18 36S	179 53 E
Moalie Park	**73**	29 42S	143 3 E
Moaña	**22**	42 18N	8 43W
Moanda	**92**	1 28S	13 7 E
Moapa	**123**	36 45N	114 37W
Moba	**94**	7 0S	29 48 E
Mobara	**65**	35 25N	140 18 E
Mobaye	**92**	4 25N	21 5 E
Mobayi	**92**	4 15N	21 8 E
Moberley	**116**	39 25N	92 25W
Moberly →	**108**	56 12N	120 55W
Mobile	**113**	30 41N	88 3W
Mobile B.	**113**	30 30N	88 0W
Mobile, Pt.	**113**	30 15N	88 0W
Mobridge	**118**	45 31N	100 28W
Mobutu Sese Seko, L.	**94**	1 30N	31 0 E
Moc Chau	**54**	20 50N	104 38 E
Moc Hoa	**55**	10 46N	105 56 E
Mocabe Kasari	**95**	9 58S	26 12 E
Mocajuba	**138**	2 35S	49 30W
Moçambique	**95**	15 3S	40 42 E
Moçambique □	**95**	14 45S	38 30 E
Moçâmedes	**93**	15 7S	12 11 E
Moçâmedes □	**96**	16 35S	12 30 E
Mocapra →	**134**	7 56N	66 46W
Mocha, I.	**142**	38 22S	73 56W
Mochiara Grove	**96**	20 43S	21 50 E
Mochudi	**96**	24 27S	26 7 E
Mocimboa da Praia	**95**	11 25S	40 20 E
Möckeln	**11**	56 40N	14 15 E
Moclips	**122**	47 14N	124 10W
Mocoa	**134**	1 7N	76 35W
Mococa	**141**	21 28S	47 0W
Mocorito	**124**	25 30N	107 53W
Moctezuma	**124**	29 50N	109 0W
Moctezuma →	**125**	21 59N	98 34W
Mocuba	**93**	16 54S	36 57 E
Moda	**52**	24 22N	96 29 E
Modane	**21**	45 12N	6 40 E
Modasa	**48**	23 30N	73 21 E
Modder →	**96**	29 2S	24 37 E
Modderrivier	**96**	29 2S	24 38 E
Módena	**26**	44 39N	10 55 E
Modena	**121**	37 55N	113 56W
Modesto	**122**	37 43N	121 0W
Módica	**29**	36 52N	14 45 E
Modigliana	**27**	44 9N	11 48 E
Modo	**91**	5 31N	30 33 E
Modra	**33**	48 19N	17 20 E
Moe	**75**	38 12S	146 19 E
Moebase	**95**	17 3S	38 41 E
Moëlan-sur-Mer	**18**	47 49N	3 38W
Moengo	**135**	5 45N	54 20W
Moffat	**14**	55 20N	3 27W
Moga	**48**	30 48N	75 8 E
Mogadiscio = Mogadishu	**45**	2 2N	45 25 E
Mogadishu	**45**	2 2N	45 25 E
Mogador = Essaouira	**86**	31 32N	9 48W
Mogadouro	**22**	41 22N	6 47W
Mogami-gawa →	**63**	38 45N	140 0 E
Mogaung	**52**	25 20N	97 0 E
Møgeltønder	**11**	54 57N	8 48 E
Mogente	**25**	38 52N	0 45W
Mogho	**91**	4 54N	40 16 E
Mogi das Cruzes	**141**	23 31S	46 11W
Mogi-Guaçu →	**141**	20 53S	48 10W
Mogi-Mirim	**141**	22 29S	47 0W
Mogielnica	**32**	51 42N	20 41 E
Mogilev	**36**	53 55N	30 18 E
Mogilev-Podolskiy	**38**	48 20N	27 40 E
Mogilno	**32**	52 39N	17 55 E
Mogincual	**93**	15 35S	40 25 E
Mogliano Véneto	**27**	45 33N	12 15 E
Mogo	**76**	35 48S	150 10 E
Mogocha	**41**	53 40N	119 50 E
Mogoi	**57**	1 55S	133 10 E
Mogok	**52**	23 0N	96 40 E
Mogollon	**121**	33 25N	108 48W
Mogollon Mesa	**121**	35 0N	111 0W
Mogriguy	**76**	32 3S	148 40 E
Moguer	**23**	37 15N	6 52W
Mogumber	**79**	31 2S	116 3 E
Mohács	**33**	45 58N	18 41 E
Mohaka →	**80**	39 7S	177 12 E
Mohall	**118**	48 46N	101 30W
Mohammadābād	**47**	37 52N	59 5 E
Mohammadia	**86**	35 33N	0 3 E
Mohammedia	**86**	33 44N	7 21W
Mohave, L.	**123**	35 25N	114 36W
Mohawk	**121**	32 45N	113 50W
Mohawk →	**115**	42 47N	73 42W
Moheda	**11**	57 1N	14 35 E
Mohembo	**93**	18 15S	21 43 E
Möhne →	**30**	51 29N	7 57 E
Mohnyin	**52**	24 47N	96 22 E
Moholm	**11**	58 37N	14 5 E
Mohon	**19**	49 45N	4 44 E
Mohoro	**94**	8 6S	39 8 E
Moia	**91**	5 3N	28 2 E
Moidart, L.	**14**	56 47N	5 40W
Moille, La	**116**	41 32N	89 17W
Moinabad	**50**	17 44N	77 16 E
Moindou	**68**	21 42S	165 41 E
Moine, La →	**116**	39 58N	90 32W
Moineşti	**34**	46 28N	26 31 E
Mointy	**40**	47 10N	73 18 E
Moira →	**107**	44 21N	77 24W
Moirans	**21**	45 20N	5 33 E
Moirans-en-Montagne	**21**	46 26N	5 43 E
Moisakula	**36**	58 3N	25 12 E
Moisie	**103**	50 12N	66 1W
Moisie →	**103**	50 14N	66 5W
Moissac	**20**	44 7N	1 5 E
Moita	**23**	38 38N	8 58W
Mojácar	**25**	37 6N	1 55W
Mojados	**22**	41 26N	4 40W
Mojave	**123**	35 8N	118 8W
Mojave Desert	**123**	35 0N	116 30W
Mojiang	**58**	23 37N	101 35 E
Mojo, Boliv.	**140**	21 48S	65 33W
Mojo, Ethiopia	**91**	8 35N	39 5 E
Mojo, Indon.	**56**	8 10S	117 40 E
Mojokerto	**57**	7 29S	112 25 E
Mojos, Llanos de	**137**	15 0S	65 0W
Moju →	**138**	1 40S	48 25W
Mokai	**80**	38 32S	175 56 E
Mokambo	**95**	12 25S	28 20 E
Mokameh	**49**	25 24N	85 55 E
Mokane	**116**	38 41N	91 53W
Mokau →	**80**	38 35S	174 35 E
Mokelumne →	**122**	38 23N	121 25W
Mokelumne Hill	**122**	38 18N	120 43W
Mokhós	**35**	35 16N	25 27 E
Mokhotlong	**97**	29 22S	29 2 E
Mokihinui →	**81**	41 33S	171 58 E
Moknine	**87**	35 35N	10 58 E
Mokpalin	**52**	17 26N	96 53 E
Mokpo	**61**	34 50N	126 30 E
Mokra Gora	**33**	42 50N	20 30 E
Mokronog	**27**	45 57N	15 9 E
Moksha →	**37**	54 45N	41 53 E
Mokshan	**37**	53 25N	44 35 E
Mol	**16**	51 11N	5 5 E
Mola, C. de la	**24**	39 40N	4 20 E
Mola di Bari	**29**	41 3N	17 5 E
Moláoi	**35**	36 49N	22 56 E
Molat	**27**	44 15N	14 50 E
Molchanovo	**40**	57 40N	83 50 E
Mold	**12**	53 10N	3 10W
Moldavia = Moldova	**34**	46 30N	27 0 E
Moldavian S.S.R.□	**38**	47 0N	28 0 E
Molde	**8**	62 45N	7 9 E
Moldova	**34**	46 30N	27 0 E
Moldova Nouă	**34**	44 45N	21 41 E
Moldoveanu	**34**	45 36N	24 45 E
Mole →	**77**	29 0S	151 32 E
Molepolole	**96**	24 28S	25 28 E
Molesworth	**81**	42 5S	173 16 E
Molfetta	**29**	41 12N	16 35 E
Molina de Aragón	**24**	40 46N	1 52W
Moline	**116**	41 30N	90 30W
Molinella	**27**	44 38N	11 40 E
Molinos	**140**	25 28S	66 15W
Moliro	**94**	8 12S	30 30 E
Molise □	**27**	41 45N	14 30 E
Moliterno	**29**	40 14N	15 50 E
Mollahat	**49**	22 56N	89 48 E
Mölle	**11**	56 17N	12 31 E
Molledo	**22**	43 8N	4 6W
Mollendo	**136**	17 0S	72 0W
Mollerin, L.	**79**	30 30S	117 35 E
Mollerusa	**24**	41 37N	0 54 E
Mollina	**23**	37 8N	4 38W
Mölln	**30**	53 37N	10 41 E
Mölltorp	**11**	58 30N	14 26 E
Mollymook	**76**	35 21S	150 29 E
Mölndal	**11**	57 40N	12 3 E
Molo	**52**	23 22N	96 53 E
Molochansk	**38**	47 15N	35 35 E
Molochnaya →	**38**	47 0N	35 30 E
Molodechno	**36**	54 20N	26 50 E
Molokai	**110**	21 8N	157 0W
Moloma →	**37**	58 20N	48 15 E
Molong	**76**	33 5S	148 54 E
Molopo →	**96**	25 40S	24 30 E
Mólos	**35**	38 47N	22 37 E
Moloundou	**92**	2 8N	15 15 E
Molsheim	**19**	48 33N	7 29 E
Molson L.	**109**	54 22N	95 32W
Molteno	**96**	31 22S	26 22 E
Molu	**57**	6 45S	131 40 E
Molucca Sea	**57**	4 0S	124 0 E
Moluccas = Maluku	**57**	1 0S	127 0 E
Molusi	**96**	20 21S	24 29 E
Moma, Mozam.	**95**	16 47S	39 4 E
Moma, Zaïre	**94**	1 35S	23 52 E
Momanga	**96**	18 7S	21 41 E
Mombaça	**138**	5 43S	39 45W
Mombasa	**94**	4 2S	39 43 E
Mombetsu	**63**	42 27N	142 4 E
Mombuey	**22**	42 3N	6 20W
Momchilgrad	**35**	41 33N	25 23 E
Momence	**117**	41 10N	87 40W
Momi	**94**	1 42S	27 0 E
Mompós	**134**	9 14N	74 26W
Møn	**11**	54 57N	12 15 E
Mona, Canal de la	**127**	18 30N	67 45W
Mona, I.	**127**	18 5N	67 54W
Mona, Pta.	**126**	9 37N	82 36W
Mona, Punta	**23**	36 43N	3 45W
Monach Is.	**14**	57 32N	7 40W
Monaco ■	**21**	43 46N	7 23 E
Monadhliath Mts.	**14**	57 10N	4 4W
Monagas □	**135**	9 20N	63 0W
Monaghan	**15**	54 15N	6 58W
Monaghan □	**15**	54 10N	7 0W
Monahans	**119**	31 35N	102 50W
Monapo	**95**	14 56S	40 19 E
Monarch Mt.	**108**	51 55N	125 57W
Monastier-sur-Gazeille, Le	**20**	44 57N	3 59 E
Monastir	**87**	35 50N	10 49 E
Monastyriska	**36**	49 8N	25 14 E
Monbetsu	**63**	44 21N	143 22 E
Moncada	**24**	39 30N	0 24W
Moncalieri	**26**	45 0N	7 40 E
Moncalvo	**26**	45 3N	8 15 E
Moncão	**22**	42 4N	8 27W
Moncarapacho	**23**	37 5N	7 46W
Moncayo, Sierra del	**24**	41 48N	1 50W
Mönchengladbach	**30**	51 12N	6 23 E
Monchique	**23**	37 19N	8 38W
Monclova	**124**	26 50N	101 30W
Moncontour	**18**	48 22N	2 38W
Moncouche, L.	**105**	48 45N	70 42W
Moncoutant	**18**	46 43N	0 35W
Moncton	**103**	46 7N	64 51W
Mondego →	**22**	40 9N	8 52W
Mondego, Cabo	**22**	40 11N	8 54W
Mondeodo	**57**	3 34S	122 9 E
Mondolfo	**27**	43 45N	13 8 E
Mondonac, L.	**105**	47 24N	73 58W
Mondoñedo	**22**	43 25N	7 23W
Mondoví	**26**	44 23N	7 49 E
Mondovi	**118**	44 37N	91 40W
Mondragon	**21**	44 13N	4 44 E
Mondragone	**28**	41 8N	13 52 E
Mondrain I.	**79**	34 9S	122 14 E
Monduli □	**94**	3 0S	36 0 E
Monemvasía	**35**	36 41N	23 3 E
Monessen	**114**	40 9N	79 50W
Monesterio	**23**	38 6N	6 15W
Monestier-de-Clermont	**21**	44 55N	5 38 E
Monêtier-les-Bains, Le	**21**	44 58N	6 30 E
Monett	**119**	36 55N	93 56W
Monfalcone	**27**	45 49N	13 32 E
Monflanquin	**20**	44 32N	0 47 E
Monforte	**23**	39 6N	7 25W
Monforte de Lemos	**22**	42 31N	7 33W
Mong Hta	**52**	19 50N	98 35 E
Mong Ket	**52**	23 8N	98 22 E
Mong Kung	**52**	21 35N	97 35 E
Mong Kyawt	**52**	19 56N	98 45 E
Mong Nai	**52**	20 30N	97 46 E
Mong Ping	**52**	21 22N	99 2 E
Mong Pu	**52**	20 55N	98 44 E
Mong Ton	**52**	20 17N	98 45 E
Mong Tung	**52**	22 2N	97 41 E
Mong Yai	**52**	22 21N	98 3 E
Mongalla	**91**	5 8N	31 42 E
Mongers, L.	**79**	29 25S	117 5 E
Monghyr	**49**	25 23N	86 30 E
Mongla	**52**	22 8N	89 35 E
Mongngaw	**52**	22 47N	96 59 E
Mongo	**85**	12 14N	18 43 E
Mongolia ■	**62**	47 0N	103 0 E
Mongonu	**89**	12 40N	13 32 E
Mongororo	**92**	12 3N	22 26 E
Mongu	**93**	15 16S	23 12 E
Mongua	**96**	16 43S	15 20 E
Monistrol	**20**	45 57N	3 38 E
Monistrol-St-Loire	**21**	45 17N	4 11 E
Monkey Bay	**95**	14 7S	35 1 E
Monkey River	**125**	16 22N	88 29W
Monkira	**72**	24 46S	140 30 E
Monkoto	**92**	1 38S	20 35 E
Monkton	**106**	43 35N	81 5W
Monmouth, U.K.	**13**	51 48N	2 43W
Monmouth, U.S.A.	**116**	40 50N	90 40W
Mono	**68**	7 20S	155 35 E
Mono, L.	**122**	38 0N	119 9W
Monolith	**123**	35 7N	118 22W
Monon	**117**	40 52N	86 53W
Monona, Iowa, U.S.A.	**116**	43 3N	91 24W
Monona, Wis., U.S.A.	**116**	43 4N	89 20W
Monongahela	**114**	40 12N	79 56W
Monópoli	**29**	40 57N	17 18 E
Monor	**33**	47 21N	19 27 E
Monóvar	**25**	38 28N	0 53W
Monowai	**81**	45 53S	167 31 E
Monowai, L.	**81**	45 53S	167 25 E
Monqoumba	**92**	3 33N	18 40 E
Monreal del Campo	**24**	40 47N	1 20W
Monreale	**28**	38 6N	13 16 E
Monroe, Ga., U.S.A.	**113**	33 47N	83 43W
Monroe, Iowa, U.S.A.	**116**	41 31N	93 6W
Monroe, La., U.S.A.	**119**	32 32N	92 4W
Monroe, Mich., U.S.A.	**106**	41 55N	83 26W
Monroe, N.C., U.S.A.	**113**	35 2N	80 37W
Monroe, N.Y., U.S.A.	**115**	41 19N	74 11W
Monroe, Ohio, U.S.A.	**117**	39 27N	84 22W
Monroe, Utah, U.S.A.	**121**	38 45N	112 5W
Monroe, Wash., U.S.A.	**122**	47 51N	121 58W
Monroe, Wis., U.S.A.	**116**	42 38N	89 40W
Monroe City	**116**	39 40N	91 40W
Monroe, Res.	**117**	39 1N	86 31W
Monroeville, Ala., U.S.A.	**113**	31 33N	87 15W
Monroeville, Ind., U.S.A.	**117**	40 59N	84 52W
Monrovia, Liberia	**88**	6 18N	10 47W
Monrovia, U.S.A.	**121**	34 7N	118 1W
Mons	**16**	50 27N	3 58 E
Monsaraz	**23**	38 28N	7 22W
Monse	**57**	4 0S	123 10 E
Monsefú	**136**	6 52S	79 52W

Monségur	20	44 38N	0 4 E
Monsélice	27	45 16N	11 46 E
Mont-Carmel	105	47 26N	69 52W
Mont-de-Marsan	20	43 54N	0 31W
Mont d'Or, Tunnel	19	46 45N	6 18 E
Mont Dore	68	22 16S	166 34 E
Mont-Dore, Le	20	45 35N	2 50 E
Mont-Joli	105	48 37N	68 10W
Mont Laurier	104	46 35N	75 30W
Mont-sous-Vaudrey	19	46 58N	5 36 E
Mont-St-Michel, Le	18	48 40N	1 30W
Mont-Tremblant	104	46 13N	74 36W
Mont Tremblant Prov. Park	105	46 30N	74 30W
Montabaur	30	50 26N	7 49 E
Montagnac	20	43 29N	3 28 E
Montagnana	27	45 13N	11 29 E
Montagu	96	33 45S	20 8 E
Montagu I.	143	58 25S	26 20W
Montague, Can.	103	46 10N	62 39W
Montague, Calif., U.S.A.	120	41 47N	122 30W
Montague, Mass., U.S.A.	115	42 31N	72 33W
Montague I.	75	36 16S	150 13 E
Montague, I.	124	31 40N	114 56W
Montague I.	100	60 0N	147 0W
Montague Ra.	79	27 15S	119 30 E
Montague Sd.	78	14 28S	125 20 E
Montaigu	18	46 59N	1 18W
Montalbán	24	40 50N	0 45W
Montalbano di Elicona	29	38 1N	15 0 E
Montalbano Iónico	29	40 17N	16 33 E
Montalbo	24	39 53N	2 42W
Montalcino	27	43 4N	11 30 E
Montalegre	22	41 49N	7 47W
Montalto di Castro	27	42 20N	11 36 E
Montalto Uffugo	29	39 25N	16 9 E
Montalvo	123	34 15N	119 12W
Montamarta	22	41 39N	5 49W
Montaña	136	6 0S	73 0W
Montana □	110	47 0N	110 0W
Montánchez	23	39 15N	6 8W
Montañita	134	1 22N	75 28W
Montargis	19	48 0N	2 43 E
Montauban	20	44 0N	1 21 E
Montauk	115	41 3N	71 57W
Montauk Pt.	115	41 4N	71 52W
Montbard	19	47 38N	4 20 E
Montbéliard	19	47 31N	6 48 E
Montblanch	24	41 23N	1 4 E
Montbrison	21	45 36N	4 3 E
Montcalm, Pic de	20	42 40N	1 25 E
Montceau-les-Mines	19	46 40N	4 23 E
Montcerf	104	46 32N	76 3W
Montchanin	26	46 47N	4 30 E
Montclair	115	40 53N	74 13W
Montcornet	19	49 40N	4 0 E
Montcuq	20	44 21N	1 13 E
Montdidier	19	49 38N	2 35 E
Monte Albán	125	17 2N	96 45W
Monte Alegre	135	2 0S	54 0W
Monte Alegre de Goiás	139	13 14S	47 10W
Monte Alegre de Minas	139	18 52S	48 52W
Monte Azul	139	15 9S	42 53W
Monte Bello Is.	78	20 30S	115 45 E
Monte-Carlo	21	43 46N	7 23 E
Monte Carmelo	139	18 43S	47 29W
Monte Caseros	140	30 10S	57 50W
Monte Comán	140	34 40S	67 53W
Monte Cristi	127	19 52N	71 39W
Monte Dinero	142	52 18S	68 33W
Monte, La	116	38 47N	93 27W
Monte Lindo →	140	23 56S	57 12W
Monte Quemado	140	25 53S	62 41W
Monte Redondo	22	39 53N	8 50W
Monte Rio	122	38 28N	123 0W
Monte San Giovanni	28	41 39N	13 33 E
Monte San Savino	27	43 20N	11 42 E
Monte Sant' Ángelo	29	41 42N	15 59 E
Monte Santu, C. di	28	40 5N	9 42 E
Monte Vista	121	37 40N	106 8W
Monteagudo, Argent.	141	27 14S	54 8W
Monteagudo, Boliv.	137	19 49S	63 59W
Montealegre	25	38 48N	1 17W
Montebello	104	45 40N	74 55W
Montebelluna	27	45 47N	12 3 E
Montebourg	18	49 30N	1 20W
Montecastrilli	27	42 40N	12 30 E
Montecatini Terme	26	43 55N	10 48 E
Montecito	123	34 26N	119 40W
Montecristi	134	1 0S	80 40W
Montecristo	26	42 20N	10 20 E
Montefalco	27	42 53N	12 38 E
Montefiascone	27	42 31N	12 2 E
Montefrío	23	37 20N	4 0W
Montego B.	126	18 30N	78 0W
Montegranaro	27	43 13N	13 38 E
Montehanin	19	46 46N	4 44 E
Monteiro	138	7 48S	37 2W
Montejicar	25	37 33N	3 30W
Montejinnie	78	16 40S	131 38 E
Montelíbano	134	8 5N	75 29W
Montélimar	21	44 33N	4 45 E
Montella	29	40 50N	15 0 E
Montellano	23	36 59N	5 36W
Montello	118	43 49N	89 21W
Montelupo Fiorentino	26	43 44N	11 2 E
Montemor-o-Novo	23	38 40N	8 12W
Montemor-o-Velho	22	40 11N	8 40W
Montemorelos	125	25 11N	99 42W
Montendre	20	45 16N	0 26W
Montenegro	141	29 39S	51 29W
Montenegro □ = Crna Gora	33	42 40N	19 20 E
Montenero di Bisaccia	27	42 0N	14 47 E
Montepuez	95	13 8S	38 59 E
Montepuez →	95	12 32S	40 27 E
Montepulciano	27	43 5N	11 46 E
Montereale	27	42 31N	13 13 E
Montereau	19	48 22N	2 57 E
Monterey, Calif., U.S.A.	122	36 35N	121 57W
Monterey, Ind., U.S.A.	117	41 11N	86 30W
Monterey B.	122	36 50N	121 55W
Montería	134	8 46N	75 53W
Montero	137	17 20S	63 15W
Monteros	140	27 11S	65 30W
Monterotondo	27	42 3N	12 36 E
Monterrey	124	25 40N	100 30W
Montes Altos	138	5 50S	47 4W
Montes Claros	139	16 30S	43 50W
Montesano	122	47 0N	123 39W
Montesárchio	29	41 5N	14 37 E
Montescaglioso	29	40 34N	16 40 E
Montesilvano	27	42 30N	14 8 E
Montevarchi	27	43 30N	11 32 E
Monteverde	92	8 45S	16 45 E
Montevideo	141	34 50S	56 11W
Montezuma, Ind., U.S.A.	117	39 47N	87 22W
Montezuma, Iowa, U.S.A.	116	41 32N	92 35W
Montfaucon, Haute-Loire, France	21	45 11N	4 20 E
Montfaucon, Meuse, France	19	49 16N	5 8 E
Montfort-l'Amaury	19	48 47N	1 49 E
Montfort-sur-Meu	18	48 8N	1 58W
Montgenèvre	21	44 56N	6 42 E
Montgomery, U.K.	13	52 34N	3 9W
Montgomery, Ala., U.S.A.	113	32 20N	86 20W
Montgomery, Ill., U.S.A.	117	41 44N	88 21W
Montgomery, W. Va., U.S.A.	112	38 9N	81 21W
Montgomery = Sahiwal	48	30 45N	73 8 E
Montgomery City	116	38 59N	91 30W
Montguyon	20	45 12N	0 12W
Monthey	31	46 15N	6 56 E
Monticelli d'Ongina	26	45 3N	9 56 E
Monticello, Ark., U.S.A.	119	33 40N	91 48W
Monticello, Fla., U.S.A.	113	30 35N	83 50W
Monticello, Ill., U.S.A.	117	40 1N	88 34W
Monticello, Ind., U.S.A.	117	40 40N	86 45W
Monticello, Iowa, U.S.A.	116	42 18N	91 12W
Monticello, Ky., U.S.A.	113	36 52N	84 50W
Monticello, Minn., U.S.A.	118	45 17N	93 52W
Monticello, Miss., U.S.A.	119	31 35N	90 8W
Monticello, Mo., U.S.A.	116	40 7N	91 43W
Monticello, N.Y., U.S.A.	115	41 37N	74 42W
Monticello, Utah, U.S.A.	121	37 55N	109 27W
Montichiari	26	45 28N	10 29 E
Montier	19	48 30N	4 45 E
Montignac	20	45 4N	1 10 E
Montigny-les-Metz	19	49 7N	6 10 E
Montigny-sur-Aube	19	47 57N	4 45 E
Montijo	23	38 52N	6 39W
Montijo, Presa de	23	38 55N	6 26W
Montilla	23	37 36N	4 40W
Montivideo	118	44 55N	95 40W
Montlhéry	19	48 39N	2 15 E
Montluçon	20	46 22N	2 36 E
Montmagny	105	46 58N	70 34W
Montmarault	20	46 19N	2 57 E
Montmartre	109	50 14N	103 27W
Montmédy	19	49 30N	5 20 E
Montmélian	21	45 30N	6 4 E
Montmirail	19	48 51N	3 30 E
Montmoreau-St-Cybard	20	45 23N	0 8 E
Montmorency	103	46 53N	71 11W
Montmorillon	20	46 26N	0 50 E
Montmort	19	48 55N	3 49 E
Monto	72	24 52S	151 6 E
Montoire	18	47 45N	0 52 E
Montório al Vomano	27	42 35N	13 38 E
Montoro	23	38 1N	4 27W
Montour Falls	114	42 20N	76 51W
Montpelier, Idaho, U.S.A.	120	42 15N	111 20W
Montpelier, Ind., U.S.A.	117	40 33N	85 17W
Montpelier, Ohio, U.S.A.	117	41 34N	84 40W
Montpelier, Vt., U.S.A.	115	44 15N	72 38W
Montpellier	20	43 37N	3 52 E
Montpezat-de-Quercy	20	44 15N	1 30 E
Montpon	20	45 2N	0 11 E
Montréal, Can.	105	45 31N	73 34W
Montréal, France	20	43 13N	2 8 E
Montreal L.	109	54 20N	105 45W
Montreal Lake	109	54 3N	105 46W
Montredon-Labessonniè	20	43 45N	2 18 E
Montréjeau	20	43 6N	0 35 E
Montrésor	18	47 10N	1 10 E
Montreuil	19	50 27N	1 45 E
Montreuil-Bellay	18	47 8N	0 9W
Montreuil, L.	104	50 12N	77 40W
Montreux	31	46 26N	6 55 E
Montrevault	18	47 17N	1 2W
Montrevel-en-Bresse	21	46 21N	5 8 E
Montrichard	18	47 20N	1 10 E
Montrose, U.K.	14	56 43N	2 28W
Montrose, Col., U.S.A.	121	38 30N	107 52W
Montrose, Mich., U.S.A.	106	43 11N	83 54W
Montrose, Pa., U.S.A.	115	41 50N	75 55W
Montrose, L.	116	38 18N	93 50W
Monts, Pte des	103	49 20N	67 12W
Monts-sur-Guesnes	18	46 55N	0 13 E
Montsalvy	20	44 41N	2 30 E
Montsant, Sierra de	24	41 17N	1 0 E
Montsauche	19	47 13N	4 0 E
Montsech, Sierra del	24	42 0N	0 45 E
Montseny	24	41 55N	2 25W
Montserrat, Spain	24	41 36N	1 49 E
Montserrat, W. Indies	127	16 40N	62 10W
Montuenga	22	41 3N	4 38W
Montuiri	24	39 34N	2 59 E
Monveda	92	2 52N	21 30 E
Monyo	52	17 59N	95 30 E
Monywa	52	22 7N	95 11 E
Monza	26	45 35N	9 15 E
Monze	95	16 17S	27 29 E
Monze, C.	48	24 47N	66 37 E
Monzón	24	41 52N	0 10 E
Mo'oka	65	36 26N	140 1 E
Moolawatana	73	29 55S	139 45 E
Mooliabeenee	79	31 20S	116 2 E
Mooloogool	79	26 2S	119 5 E
Moomin, Cr. →	77	29 44S	149 20 E
Moonah →	72	22 3S	138 33 E
Moonan Flat	77	31 55S	151 14 E
Moonbeam	102	49 20N	82 10W
Moondarra	75	38 2S	146 30 E
Moonie	73	27 46S	150 20 E
Moonie →	77	29 19S	148 43 E
Moonta	73	34 6S	137 32 E
Moora	79	30 37S	115 58 E
Mooraberree	72	25 13S	140 54 E
Mooralla	74	37 25S	142 10 E
Moorarie	79	25 56S	117 35 E
Moorcroft	118	44 17N	104 58W
Moore	77	30 57S	150 52 E
Moore →	79	31 22S	115 30 E
Moore, L.	79	29 50S	117 35 E
Moore Reefs	72	16 0S	149 5 E
Moore River	79	31 1S	115 56 E
Moorefield	112	39 5N	78 59W
Moores Res.	115	44 45N	71 50W
Mooresville, Ind., U.S.A.	117	39 37N	86 22W
Mooresville, N.C., U.S.A.	113	35 36N	80 45W
Moorfoot Hills	14	55 44N	3 8W
Moorhead	118	46 51N	96 44W
Moorland	77	31 46S	152 38 E
Mooroopna	74	36 25S	145 22 E
Moorpark	123	34 17N	118 53W
Moorreesburg	96	33 6S	18 38 E
Moosburg	31	48 28N	11 57 E
Moose →	102	51 20N	80 25W
Moose Creek	107	45 15N	74 58W
Moose Factory	102	51 16N	80 32W
Moose I.	109	51 42N	97 10W
Moose Jaw	109	50 24N	105 30W
Moose Jaw Cr. →	109	50 34N	105 18W
Moose Lake, Can.	109	53 43N	100 20W
Moose Lake, U.S.A.	118	46 27N	92 48W
Moose Mountain Cr. →	109	49 13N	102 12W
Moose Mtn. Prov. Park	109	49 48N	102 25W
Moose River	102	50 48N	81 17W
Moosehead L.	103	45 34N	69 40W
Moosomin	109	50 9N	101 40W
Moosonee	102	51 17N	80 39W
Moosup	115	41 44N	71 52W
Mopipi	96	21 6S	24 55 E
Mopoi	91	5 6N	26 54 E
Mopti	88	14 30N	4 0W
Moqatta	91	14 38N	35 50 E
Moquegua	136	17 15S	70 46W
Moquegua □	136	16 50S	70 55W
Mór	33	47 25N	18 12 E
Móra	23	38 55N	8 10W
Mora, Sweden	10	61 2N	14 38 E
Mora, Minn., U.S.A.	118	45 52N	93 19W
Mora, N. Mex., U.S.A.	121	35 58N	105 21W
Mora de Ebro	24	41 6N	0 38 E
Mora de Rubielos	24	40 15N	0 45W
Mora la Nueva	24	41 7N	0 39 E
Morača →	33	42 20N	19 9 E
Morada Nova	138	5 7S	38 23W
Morada Nova de Minas	139	18 37S	45 22W
Moradabad	49	28 50N	78 50 E
Morafenobe	97	17 50S	44 53 E
Morąg	32	53 55N	19 56 E
Moral de Calatrava	25	38 51N	3 33W
Moraleja	22	40 6N	6 43W
Morales	134	2 45N	76 38W
Moran, Kans., U.S.A.	119	37 53N	94 35W
Moran, Mich., U.S.A.	106	46 0N	84 50W
Moran, Wyo., U.S.A.	120	43 53N	110 37W
Morangarell	76	34 8S	147 42 E
Morano Cálabro	29	39 51N	16 8 E
Morant Cays	126	17 22N	76 0W
Morant Pt.	126	17 55N	76 12W
Morar L.	14	56 57N	5 40W
Moratalla	25	38 14N	1 49W
Moratuwa	51	6 45N	79 55 E
Morava →	32	48 10N	16 59 E
Moravia	116	40 50N	92 50W
Moravian Hts. = Ceskemoravská V.	32	49 30N	15 40 E
Moravica →	33	43 52N	20 8 E
Moravice →	32	49 50N	17 43 E
Moravița	33	45 17N	21 14 E
Moravská Třebová	32	49 45N	16 40 E
Morawa	79	29 13S	116 0 E
Morawhanna	135	8 30N	59 40W
Moray Firth	14	57 50N	3 30W
Morbach	31	49 48N	7 7 E
Morbegno	26	46 8N	9 34 E
Morbihan □	18	47 55N	2 50W
Morcenx	20	44 0N	0 55W
Mordelles	18	48 5N	1 52W
Morden	109	49 15N	98 10W
Mordialloc	74	38 1S	145 6 E
Mordovian A.S.S.R. □	37	54 20N	44 30 E
Mordovo	37	52 6N	40 50 E
Møre og Romsdal fylke □	10	63 0N	9 0 E
Morea, Austral.	74	36 45S	141 18 E
Morea, Greece	6	37 45N	22 10 E
Moreau →	118	45 15N	100 43W
Morecambe	12	54 5N	2 52W
Morecambe B.	12	54 7N	3 0W
Moree	77	29 28S	149 54 E
Morehead, P.N.G.	69	8 41S	141 41 E
Morehead, U.S.A.	117	38 12N	83 22W
Morehead City	113	34 46N	76 44W
Morelia	124	19 40N	101 11W
Morella, Austral.	72	23 0S	143 52 E
Morella, Spain	24	40 35N	0 5W
Morelos	124	26 42N	107 40W
Morelos □	125	18 40N	99 10W
Morena, Sierra	23	38 20N	4 0W
Morenci, Ariz., U.S.A.	121	33 7N	109 20W
Morenci, Mich., U.S.A.	117	41 43N	84 13W
Moreni	34	44 59N	25 36 E
Morero	137	11 9S	66 15W
Moreru →	137	10 10S	59 15W
Moresby I.	108	52 30N	131 40W
Morestel	21	45 40N	5 28 E
Moret	19	48 22N	2 58 E
Moreton	72	12 22S	142 30 E
Moreton I.	77	27 10S	153 25 E
Moreuil	19	49 46N	2 30 E
Morez	21	46 31N	6 2 E
Morgan, Austral.	73	34 0S	139 35 E
Morgan, U.S.A.	120	41 3N	111 44W
Morgan City	119	29 40N	91 15W

Morgan Hill	122	37 8N	121 39W
Morganfield	112	37 40N	87 55W
Morganton	113	35 46N	81 48W
Morgantown, Ind., U.S.A.	117	39 22N	86 16W
Morgantown, W. Va., U.S.A.	112	39 39N	79 58W
Morganville	73	25 10S	151 50 E
Morgat	18	48 15N	4 32W
Morgenzon	97	26 45S	29 36 E
Morges	31	46 31N	6 29 E
Morhange	19	48 55N	6 38 E
Mori	26	45 51N	10 59 E
Moriarty	121	35 3N	106 2W
Morice L.	108	53 50N	127 40W
Morichal	134	2 10N	70 34W
Morichal Largo →	135	9 27N	62 25W
Moriguchi	65	34 44N	135 34 E
Moriki	89	12 52N	6 30 E
Morin-Heights	105	45 54N	74 15W
Morinville	108	53 49N	113 41W
Morioka	63	39 45N	141 8 E
Moris	124	28 8N	108 32W
Morisset	76	33 6S	151 30 E
Morkalla	74	34 23S	141 10 E
Morlaàs	20	43 21N	0 18W
Morlaix	18	48 36N	3 52W
Mormanno	29	39 53N	15 59 E
Mormant	19	48 37N	2 52 E
Mornington. Victoria, Austral.	74	38 15S	145 5 E
Mornington, W. Australia, Austral.	78	17 31S	126 6 E
Mornington I.	72	16 30S	139 30 E
Mornington, I.	142	49 50S	75 30W
Mórnos →	35	38 30N	22 0 E
Moro	91	10 50N	30 9 E
Moro G.	57	6 30N	123 0 E
Morobe	69	7 49S	147 38 E
Morocco	117	40 57N	87 27W
Morocco ■	86	32 0N	5 50W
Morococha	136	11 40S	76 5W
Moroga	68	10 30S	161 40 E
Morogoro	94	6 50S	37 40 E
Morogoro □	94	8 0S	37 0 E
Moroleón	124	20 8N	101 32W
Morombé	97	21 45S	43 22 E
Moron	140	34 39S	58 37W
Morón	126	22 8N	78 39W
Mörön →	62	47 14N	110 37 E
Morón de Almazán	24	41 29N	2 27W
Morón de la Frontera	23	37 6N	5 28W
Morona →	134	4 40S	77 10W
Morona-Santiago □	134	2 30S	78 0W
Morondava	97	20 17S	44 17 E
Morondo	88	8 57N	6 47W
Morongo Valley	123	34 3N	116 37W
Moronou	88	6 16N	4 59W
Morotai	57	2 10N	128 30 E
Moroto	94	2 28N	34 42 E
Moroto Summit	94	2 30N	34 43 E
Morozovsk	39	48 25N	41 50 E
Morpeth, Austral.	76	32 44S	151 39 E
Morpeth, U.K.	12	55 11N	1 41W
Morphou	46	35 12N	32 59 E
Morrelganj	52	22 28N	89 51 E
Morrilton	119	35 10N	92 45W
Morrinhos, Ceara, Brazil	138	3 14S	40 7W
Morrinhos, Minas Gerais, Brazil	139	17 45S	49 10W
Morrinsville	80	37 40S	175 32 E
Morris, Can.	109	49 25N	97 22W
Morris, Ill., U.S.A.	117	41 20N	88 20W
Morris, Minn., U.S.A.	118	45 33N	95 56W
Morris, Mt.	79	26 9S	131 4 E
Morrisburg	107	44 55N	75 7W
Morrison	116	41 47N	90 0W
Morrisonville	116	39 25N	89 27W
Morristown, Ariz., U.S.A.	121	33 54N	112 35W
Morristown, Ind., U.S.A.	117	39 40N	85 42W
Morristown, N.J., U.S.A.	115	40 48N	74 30W
Morristown, S.D., U.S.A.	118	45 57N	101 44W
Morristown, Tenn., U.S.A.	113	36 18N	83 20W
Morro Bay	122	35 27N	120 54W
Morro do Chapéu	139	11 33S	41 9W
Morro, Pta.	140	27 6S	71 0W
Morros	138	2 52S	44 3W
Morrosquillo, Golfo de	126	9 35N	75 40W
Mörrum	11	56 12N	14 45 E
Mors	11	56 50N	8 45 E
Morshansk	37	53 28N	41 50 E
Mörsil	10	63 19N	13 40 E
Mortagne	20	45 28N	0 49W
Mortagne →	19	48 33N	6 27 E
Mortagne-au-Perche	18	48 31N	0 33 E
Mortain	18	48 40N	0 57W
Mortara	26	45 15N	8 43 E
Morteau	19	47 3N	6 35 E
Morteros	140	30 50S	62 0W
Mortes, R. das →	139	11 45S	50 44W
Mortlake	74	38 5S	142 50 E
Morton, Ill., U.S.A.	116	40 37N	89 28W
Morton, Tex., U.S.A.	119	33 39N	102 49W
Morton, Wash., U.S.A.	122	46 33N	122 17W
Morundah	75	34 57S	146 19 E
Moruya	76	35 58S	150 3 E
Moruya Heads	76	35 55S	150 9 E
Morvan, Mts. du	19	47 5N	4 0 E
Morven, Austral.	73	26 22S	147 5 E
Morven, N.Z.	81	44 50S	171 6 E
Morvern	14	56 38N	5 44W
Morvi	48	22 50N	70 42 E
Morwell	75	38 10S	146 22 E
Mosalsk	36	54 30N	34 55 E
Mosbach	31	49 21N	9 9 E
Mošćenice	27	45 17N	14 16 E
Mosciano Sant' Angelo	27	42 42N	13 52 E
Moscos Is.	54	14 0N	97 30 E
Moscow	120	46 45N	116 59W
Moscow = Moskva	37	55 45N	37 35 E
Mosel →	16	50 22N	7 36 E
Moselle = Mosel →	16	50 22N	7 36 E
Moselle □	19	48 59N	6 33 E
Moses Lake	120	47 9N	119 17W
Mosgiel	81	45 53S	170 21 E
Moshi	94	3 22S	37 18 E
Moshi □	94	3 22S	37 18 E
Moshupa	96	24 46S	25 29 E
Mosjøen	8	65 51N	13 12 E
Moskenesøya	8	67 58N	13 0 E
Moskenstraumen	8	67 47N	12 45 E
Moskva	37	55 45N	37 35 E
Moskva →	37	55 5N	38 51 E
Moslavačka Gora	27	45 40N	16 37 E
Moso	68	17 30S	168 15 E
Mosomane (Artesia)	96	24 2S	26 19 E
Mosonmagyaróvár	33	47 52N	17 18 E
Mospino	38	47 52N	38 0 E
Mosquera	134	2 35N	78 24W
Mosquero	119	35 48N	103 57W
Mosqueruela	24	40 21N	0 27W
Mosquitia	126	15 20N	84 10W
Mosquitos, Golfo de los	126	9 15N	81 10W
Moss	10	59 27N	10 40 E
Moss Vale	76	34 32S	150 25 E
Mossaka	92	1 15S	16 45 E
Mossâmedes	139	16 7S	50 11W
Mossbank	109	49 56N	105 56W
Mossburn	81	45 41S	168 15 E
Mosselbaai	96	34 11S	22 8 E
Mossendjo	92	2 55S	12 42 E
Mossgiel	73	33 15S	144 5 E
Mossman	72	16 21S	145 15 E
Mossoró	138	5 10S	37 15W
Mossuril	95	14 58S	40 42 E
Mossy →	109	54 5N	102 58W
Most	32	50 31N	13 38 E
Mostaganem	86	35 54N	0 5 E
Mostar	33	43 22N	17 50 E
Mostardas	141	31 2S	50 51W
Mostefa, Rass	87	36 55N	11 3 E
Mostiska	36	49 48N	23 4 E
Mosty	36	53 27N	24 38 E
Mosul = Al Mawsil	46	36 20N	43 5 E
Mosulpo	61	33 20N	126 17 E
Mota	68	13 49S	167 42 E
Mota del Cuervo	24	39 30N	2 52W
Mota del Marqués	22	41 38N	5 11W
Mota Lava	68	13 40S	167 40 E
Motagua →	126	15 44N	88 14W
Motala	11	58 32N	15 1 E
Motegi	65	36 32N	140 11 E
Mothe-Achard, La	18	46 37N	1 40W
Mothe, La, Rés.	105	48 46N	71 9W
Motherwell	14	55 48N	4 0W
Motihari	49	26 30N	84 55 E
Motilla del Palancar	24	39 34N	1 55W
Motnik	27	46 14N	14 54 E
Motocurunya	135	4 24N	64 5W
Motovun	27	45 20N	13 50 E
Motozintla de Mendoza	125	15 21N	92 14W
Motril	25	36 31N	3 37W
Motru →	34	44 44N	22 59 E
Mott	118	46 25N	102 29W
Motte-Chalançon, La	21	44 30N	5 21 E
Motte, L. la	104	48 20N	78 2W
Motte, La	21	44 20N	6 3 E
Móttola	29	40 38N	17 0 E
Motueka	81	41 7S	173 1 E
Motul	125	21 0N	89 20W
Motupena Pt.	69	6 30S	155 10 E
Mou	68	21 5S	165 26 E
Mouchalagane →	103	50 56N	68 41W
Moucontant	18	46 43N	0 36W
Mouding	58	25 20N	101 28 E
Moudjeria	88	17 50N	12 28W
Moudon	31	46 40N	6 49 E
Mouila	92	1 50S	11 0 E
Moulamein	74	35 3S	144 1 E
Moule	127	16 20N	61 22W
Moulins	20	46 35N	3 19 E
Moulmein	52	16 30N	97 40 E
Moulmeingyun	52	16 23N	95 16 E
Moulouya, O. →	86	35 5N	2 25W
Moulton, Iowa, U.S.A.	116	40 41N	92 41W
Moulton, Tex., U.S.A.	119	29 35N	97 8W
Moultrie	113	31 11N	83 47W
Moultrie, L.	113	33 25N	80 10W
Mound City, Mo., U.S.A.	118	40 2N	95 25W
Mound City, S.D., U.S.A.	118	45 46N	100 3W
Moúnda, Ákra	35	38 5N	20 45 E
Moundou	85	8 40N	16 10 E
Moundsville	114	39 53N	80 43W
Moung	54	12 46N	103 27 E
Moungga	68	7 0S	156 0 E
Mount Airy	113	36 31N	80 37W
Mount Albert	106	44 8N	79 19W
Mount Alford	77	28 4S	152 35 E
Mount Amherst	78	18 24S	126 58 E
Mount Angel	120	45 4N	122 46W
Mount Augustus	79	24 20S	116 56 E
Mount Ayr	116	40 43N	94 14W
Mount Barker, Austral.	73	35 4S	138 55 E
Mount Barker, S.A., Austral.	73	35 5S	138 52 E
Mount Barker, W.A., Austral.	79	34 38S	117 40 E
Mount Beauty	75	36 47S	147 10 E
Mount Brydges	106	42 54N	81 29W
Mount Carmel, Ill., U.S.A.	117	38 20N	87 48W
Mount Carmel, Pa., U.S.A.	115	40 46N	76 25W
Mount Carroll	116	42 6N	89 59W
Mount Clemens	106	42 35N	82 50W
Mount Coolon	72	21 25S	147 25 E
Mount Darwin	95	16 45S	31 33 E
Mount Desert I.	103	44 15N	68 25W
Mount Dora	113	28 49N	81 32W
Mount Douglas	72	21 35S	146 50 E
Mount Eden	117	38 3N	85 9W
Mount Edgecumbe	108	57 8N	135 22W
Mount Elizabeth	78	16 0S	125 50 E
Mount Emu Creek	74	38 20S	142 40 E
Mount Evelyn	74	37 45S	145 29W
Mount Forest	106	43 59N	80 43W
Mount Gambier	73	37 50S	140 46 E
Mount Garnet	72	17 37S	145 6 E
Mount George	77	31 53S	152 12 E
Mount Hagen	69	5 52S	144 16 E
Mount Hope, N.S.W., Austral.	73	32 51S	145 51 E
Mount Hope, S.A., Austral.	73	34 7S	135 23 E
Mount Hope, U.S.A.	112	37 52N	81 9W
Mount Horeb	116	43 0N	89 42W
Mount Howitt	73	26 31S	142 16 E
Mount Isa	72	20 42S	139 26 E
Mount Keith	79	27 15S	120 30 E
Mount Laguna	123	32 52N	116 25W
Mount Larcom	72	23 48S	150 59 E
Mount Lofty Ra.	73	34 35S	139 5 E
Mount McKinley Nat. Pk.	100	64 0N	150 0W
Mount Magnet	79	28 2S	117 47 E
Mount Margaret	73	26 54S	143 21 E
Mount Martha	74	38 17S	145 1 E
Mount Maunganui	80	37 40S	176 14 E
Mount Molloy	72	16 42S	145 20 E
Mount Monger	79	31 0S	122 0 E
Mount Morgan	72	23 40S	150 25 E
Mount Morris, Mich., U.S.A.	106	43 8N	83 42W
Mount Morris, N.Y., U.S.A.	114	42 43N	77 50W
Mount Mulligan	72	16 45S	144 47 E
Mount Narryer	79	26 30S	115 55 E
Mount Olive	116	39 4N	89 44W
Mount Olivet	117	38 32N	84 2W
Mount Orab	117	39 5N	83 56W
Mount Oxide Mine	72	19 30S	139 29 E
Mount Pearl	103	47 31N	52 47W
Mount Perry	73	25 13S	151 42 E
Mount Phillips	79	24 25S	116 15 E
Mount Pleasant, Iowa, U.S.A.	116	41 0N	91 35W
Mount Pleasant, Mich., U.S.A.	106	43 35N	84 47W
Mount Pleasant, Pa., U.S.A.	114	40 9N	79 31W
Mount Pleasant, S.C., U.S.A.	113	32 45N	79 48W
Mount Pleasant, Tenn., U.S.A.	113	35 31N	87 11W
Mount Pleasant, Tex., U.S.A.	119	33 5N	95 0W
Mount Pleasant, Ut., U.S.A.	120	39 40N	111 29W
Mount Pocono	115	41 8N	75 21W
Mount Pulaski	116	40 1N	89 17W
Mount Rainier Nat. Park.	122	46 50N	121 43W
Mount Revelstoke Nat. Park	108	51 5N	118 30W
Mount Robson	108	52 56N	119 15W
Mount Robson Prov. Park	108	53 0N	119 0W
Mount Roskill	80	36 55S	174 45 E
Mount Sandiman	79	24 25S	115 30 E
Mount Shasta	120	41 20N	122 18W
Mount Signal	123	32 39N	115 37W
Mount Somers	81	43 45S	171 27 E
Mount Sterling, Ill., U.S.A.	116	40 0N	90 40W
Mount Sterling, Ky., U.S.A.	117	38 0N	84 0W
Mount Sterling, Ohio, U.S.A.	117	39 43N	83 16W
Mount Surprise	72	18 10S	144 17 E
Mount Union	114	40 22N	77 51W
Mount Vernon, Austral.	79	24 9S	118 2 E
Mount Vernon, Ill., U.S.A.	117	38 19N	88 55W
Mount Vernon, Ind., U.S.A.	117	38 17N	88 57W
Mount Vernon, Iowa, U.S.A.	116	41 55N	91 23W
Mount Vernon, N.Y., U.S.A.	115	40 57N	73 49W
Mount Vernon, Ohio, U.S.A.	114	40 20N	82 30W
Mount Vernon, Wash., U.S.A.	122	48 25N	122 20W
Mount Victoria	76	33 33S	150 16 E
Mount Washington	117	38 3N	85 33W
Mount Wellington	80	36 55S	174 52 E
Mount Willoughby	73	27 58S	134 8 E
Mount Zion	117	39 46N	88 53W
Mountain Center	123	33 42N	116 44W
Mountain City, Nev., U.S.A.	120	41 54N	116 0W
Mountain City, Tenn., U.S.A.	113	36 30N	81 50W
Mountain Grove	119	37 5N	92 20W
Mountain Home, Ark., U.S.A.	119	36 20N	92 25W
Mountain Home, Idaho, U.S.A.	120	43 11N	115 45W
Mountain Iron	118	47 30N	92 37W
Mountain Park.	108	52 50N	117 15W
Mountain Pass	123	35 29N	115 35W
Mountain View, Ark., U.S.A.	119	35 52N	92 10W
Mountain View, Calif., U.S.A.	121	37 26N	122 5W
Mountainair	121	34 35N	106 15W
Mountmellick	15	53 7N	7 20W
Moura, Austral.	72	24 35S	149 58 E
Moura, Brazil	135	1 32S	61 38W
Moura, Port.	23	38 7N	7 30W
Mourão	23	38 22N	7 22W
Mourdi, Depression du	85	18 10N	23 0 E
Mourdiah	88	14 35N	7 25W
Moure, La	118	46 27N	98 17W
Mourenx	20	43 23N	0 36W
Mouri	89	5 6N	1 14W
Mourilyan	72	17 35S	146 3 E
Mourmelon-le-Grand	19	49 8N	4 22 E
Mourne →	15	54 45N	7 39W
Mourne Mts.	15	54 10N	6 0W
Mouscron	16	50 45N	3 12 E
Moussoro	85	13 41N	16 35 E
Moutajup	74	37 40S	142 13 E
Mouthe	19	46 44N	6 12 E
Moutier	31	47 16N	7 21 E
Moûtiers	21	45 29N	6 31 E
Moutohora	80	38 18S	177 40 E
Moutong	57	0 28N	121 13 E
Mouy	19	49 18N	2 20 E
Mouzáki	35	39 25N	21 37 E
Movas	124	28 10N	109 25W
Moville	15	55 11N	7 3W
Moweaqua	116	39 37N	89 1W
Moxotó →	138	9 19S	38 14W
Moy →	15	54 5N	8 50W
Moyahua	124	21 16N	103 10W
Moyale, Ethiopia	91	3 34N	39 4 E
Moyale, Kenya	94	3 30N	39 0 E
Moyamba	88	8 4N	12 30W
Moyen Atlas	84	32 0N	5 0W
Moyhu	75	36 36S	146 15 E
Moyle □	15	55 10N	6 15W

Moyobamba	136	6 0S	77 0W
Moyston	74	37 17S	142 45E
Moyyero →	41	68 44N	103 42E
Moza	44	31 48N	35 8E
Mozambique = Moçambique	95	15 3S	40 42E
Mozambique ■	95	19 0S	35 0E
Mozambique Chan.	97	20 0S	39 0E
Mozdok	39	43 45N	44 48E
Mozhaysk	37	55 30N	36 2E
Mozirje	27	46 22N	14 58E
Mozua	94	3 57N	24 2E
Mozyr	36	52 0N	29 15E
Mpanda	94	6 23S	31 1E
Mpanda □	94	6 23S	31 40E
Mpésoba	88	12 31N	5 39W
Mpika	95	11 51S	31 25E
Mpulungu	95	8 51S	31 5E
Mpwapwa	94	6 23S	36 30E
Mpwapwa □	94	6 30S	36 20E
Mrągowo	32	53 52N	21 18E
Mramor	33	43 20N	21 45E
Mrimina	86	29 50N	7 9W
Mrkonjić Grad	33	44 26N	17 4E
Mrkopalj	27	45 21N	14 52E
Msab, Oued en →	87	32 25N	5 20E
Msaken	87	35 49N	10 33E
Msambansovu	95	15 50S	30 3E
M'sila	87	35 46N	4 30E
Msta →	36	58 25N	31 20E
Mstislavl	36	54 0N	31 50E
Mtama	95	10 17S	39 21E
Mtilikwe →	95	21 9S	31 30E
Mtsensk	37	53 25N	36 30E
Mtskheta	39	41 52N	44 45E
Mtwara-Mikindani	95	10 20S	40 20E
Mu →	52	21 56N	95 38E
Mu Gia, Deo	54	17 40N	105 47E
Mu Us Shamo	60	39 0N	109 0E
Muaná	138	1 25S	49 15W
Muanda	92	6 0S	12 20E
Muang Chiang Rai	54	19 52N	99 50E
Muang Lamphun	54	18 40N	99 2E
Muang Pak Beng	54	19 54N	101 8E
Muar	55	2 3N	102 34E
Muarabungo	56	1 28S	102 52E
Muaradjuloi	56	0 12S	114 3E
Muaraenim	56	3 40S	103 50E
Muarakaman	56	0 2S	116 45E
Muaratebo	56	1 30S	102 26E
Muaratembesi	56	1 42S	103 8E
Muaratewe	56	0 58S	114 52E
Mubairik	46	23 22N	39 8E
Mubarakpur	49	26 6N	83 18E
Mubende	94	0 33N	31 22E
Mubi	89	10 18N	13 16E
Mubur, P.	55	3 20N	106 12E
Mucajaí →	135	2 25N	60 52W
Mucajaí, Serra do	135	2 23N	61 10W
Mücheln	30	51 18N	11 49E
Muchinga Mts.	95	11 30S	31 30E
Muchkapskiy	37	51 52N	42 28E
Muck	14	56 50N	6 15W
Muckadilla	73	26 35S	148 23E
Muco →	134	4 15N	70 21W
Mucuim →	137	6 33S	64 18W
Mucura	135	2 31S	62 43W
Mucuri	139	18 0S	39 36W
Mucurici	139	18 6S	40 31W
Mudan Jiang →	61	46 20N	129 30E
Mudanjiang	61	44 38N	129 30E
Mudanya	38	40 25N	28 50E
Muddy →	121	38 0N	110 22W
Mudgee	76	32 32S	149 31E
Mudgeeraba	77	28 4S	153 21E
Mudhnib	46	25 50N	44 18E
Mudjatik →	109	56 1N	107 36W
Mudon	52	16 15N	97 44E
Muecate	95	14 55S	39 40E
Muêda	95	11 36S	39 28E
Muela, La	24	41 36N	1 7W
Mueller Ra.	78	18 18S	126 46E
Muerto, Mar	125	16 10N	94 10W
Muertos, Punta de los	25	36 57N	1 54W
Mufindi □	95	8 30S	35 20E
Mufu Shan	59	29 20N	114 30E
Mufulira	95	12 32S	28 15E
Mufumbiro Range	94	1 25S	29 30E
Mugardos	22	43 27N	8 15W
Muge	23	39 3N	8 40W
Muge →	23	39 8N	8 44W
Múggia	27	45 36N	13 47E
Mugi	64	33 40N	134 25E
Mugia	22	43 3N	9 10W
Mugila, Mts.	94	7 0S	28 50E
Muğla	46	37 15N	28 22E
Mŭglizh	34	42 37N	25 32E
Mugu	49	29 45N	82 30E
Muhammad Qol	90	20 53N	37 9E
Muhammad Râs	90	27 42N	34 13E
Muhammadabad	49	26 4N	83 25E
Muharraqa = Sa'ad	44	31 28N	34 33E
Muhesi →	94	7 0S	35 20E
Muheza □	94	5 0S	39 0E
Mühldorf	31	48 14N	12 33E
Mühlhausen	30	51 12N	10 29E
Mühlig Hofmann fjella	143	72 30S	5 0E
Muhutwe	94	1 35S	31 45E
Muine Bheag	15	52 42N	6 59W
Muiños	22	41 58N	7 59W
Muir, L.	79	34 30S	116 40E
Muja	91	12 2N	39 30E
Mukachevo	36	48 27N	22 45E
Mukah	56	2 55N	112 5E
Mukallā	45	14 33N	49 2E
Mukawwa, Geziret	90	23 55N	35 53E
Mukdahan	54	16 32N	104 43E
Mukden = Shenyang	61	41 48N	123 27E
Mukeiras	45	13 59N	45 52E
Mukhtolovo	37	55 29N	43 15E
Mukinbudin	79	30 55S	118 5E
Mukombwe	95	15 48S	26 32E
Mukomuko	56	2 30S	101 10E
Mukomwenze	94	6 49S	27 15E
Muktsar	48	30 30N	74 30E
Mukur	48	32 50N	67 42E
Mukutawa →	109	53 10N	97 24W
Mukwela	95	17 0S	26 40E
Mukwonago	117	42 52N	88 20W
Mula	25	38 3N	1 33W
Mula →	50	18 34N	74 21E
Mulange	94	3 40S	27 10E
Mulatas, Arch. de las	126	9 50N	78 31W
Mulberry Grove	116	38 55N	89 16W
Mulchén	140	37 45S	72 20W
Mulde →	30	51 10N	12 48E
Muldraugh	117	37 56N	85 59W
Mule Creek	118	43 19N	104 8W
Muleba	94	1 50S	31 37E
Muleba □	94	2 0S	31 30E
Mulegé	124	26 53N	112 1W
Muleshoe	119	34 17N	102 42W
Mulgathing	73	30 15S	134 8E
Mulgrave	103	45 38N	61 31W
Mulgrave I.	69	10 5S	142 10E
Mulhacén	25	37 4N	3 20W
Mülheim	30	51 26N	6 53E
Mulhouse	19	47 40N	7 20E
Muli	58	27 52N	101 8E
Mulifanua	68	13 50S	171 59W
Muling	61	44 35N	130 10E
Mull	14	56 27N	6 0W
Mullaittvu	51	9 15N	80 49E
Mullaley	77	31 5S	149 56E
Mullbring	76	32 54S	151 28E
Mullen	118	42 5N	101 0W
Mullengudgery	76	31 43S	147 23E
Mullens	112	37 34N	81 22W
Muller, Pegunungan	56	0 30N	113 30E
Mullet Pen.	15	54 10N	10 2W
Mullett L.	106	45 30N	84 30W
Mullewa	79	28 29S	115 30E
Müllheim	31	47 48N	7 37E
Mulligan →	72	26 40S	139 0E
Mullin	119	31 33N	98 38W
Mullingar	15	53 31N	7 20W
Mullins	113	34 12N	79 15W
Mullion Creek	76	33 7S	149 7E
Mullsjö	11	57 56N	13 55E
Mullumbimby	77	28 30S	153 30E
Mulobezi	95	16 45S	25 7E
Mulshi L.	50	18 30N	73 48E
Multai	50	21 50N	78 21E
Multan	48	30 15N	71 36E
Multan □	48	30 29N	72 29E
Multrå	10	63 10N	17 24E
Mulumbe, Mts.	95	8 40S	27 30E
Mulungushi Dam	95	14 48S	28 48E
Mulvane	119	37 30N	97 15W
Mulwad	90	18 45N	30 39E
Mumbil	76	32 41S	149 2E
Mumeng	69	7 1S	146 37E
Mummulgum	77	28 50S	152 50E
Mumra	39	45 45N	47 41E
Mun →	54	15 19N	105 30E
Muna	57	5 0S	122 30E
Munawwar	49	32 47N	74 27E
Münchberg	31	50 11N	11 48E
Müncheberg	30	52 30N	14 9E
München	31	48 8N	11 33E
Munchen-Gladbach = Mönchengladbach	30	51 12N	6 23E
Muncho Lake	108	59 0N	125 50W
Munchŏn	61	39 14N	127 19E
Muncie	117	40 10N	85 20W
Munda	68	8 20S	157 16E
Mundadoo	76	30 48S	147 14E
Mundakayam	51	9 30N	76 50E
Mundala, Puncak	57	4 30S	141 0E
Mundare	108	53 35N	112 20W
Munday	119	33 26N	99 39W
Münden	30	51 25N	9 42E
Mundiwindi	78	23 47S	120 9E
Mundo →	25	38 30N	2 15W
Mundo Novo	139	11 50S	40 29W
Mundra	48	22 54N	69 48E
Mundrabilla	79	31 52S	127 51E
Munducurus	135	4 47S	58 16W
Munera	25	39 2N	2 29W
Muneru →	51	16 45N	80 3E
Mungallala	73	26 25S	147 34E
Mungallala Cr. →	73	28 53S	147 5E
Mungana	72	17 8S	144 27E
Mungaoli	48	24 24N	78 7E
Mungari	95	17 12S	33 30E
Mungbere	94	2 36N	28 28E
Mungerie	76	32 33S	148 1E
Mungindi	77	28 58S	149 1E
Munhango	93	12 10S	18 38E
Munich = München	31	48 8N	11 33E
Munising	112	46 25N	86 39W
Munjiye	90	18 47N	41 20E
Munka-Ljungby	11	56 16N	12 58E
Munkedal	11	58 28N	11 40E
Munkfors	10	59 50N	13 30E
Munku-Sardyk	41	51 45N	100 20E
Münnerstadt	31	50 15N	10 11E
Munnundilla, Mt.	76	32 44S	150 32E
Muñoz Gamero, Pen.	142	52 30S	73 5E
Munro	75	37 56S	147 11E
Munroe L.	109	59 13N	98 35W
Munsan	61	37 51N	126 48E
Munshiganj	52	23 33N	90 32E
Munster	19	48 2N	7 8E
Münster, Niedersachsen, Ger.	30	52 59N	10 5E
Münster, Nordrhein-Westfalen, Ger.	30	51 58N	7 37E
Munster □	15	52 20N	8 40W
Muntadgin	79	31 45S	118 33E
Muntele Mare	34	46 30N	23 12E
Muntok	56	2 5S	105 10E
Munyak	40	43 30N	59 15E
Muong Beng	54	20 23N	101 46E
Muong Boum	54	22 24N	102 49E
Muong Et	54	20 49N	104 1E
Muong Hai	54	21 3N	101 49E
Muong Hiem	54	20 5N	103 22E
Muong Houn	54	20 8N	101 23E
Muong Hung	54	20 56N	103 53E
Muong Kau	54	15 6N	105 47E
Muong Khao	54	19 38N	103 32E
Muong Khoua	54	21 5N	102 31E
Muong Liep	54	18 29N	101 40E
Muong May	54	14 49N	106 56E
Muong Ngeun	54	20 36N	101 3E
Muong Ngoi	54	20 43N	102 41E
Muong Nhie	54	22 12N	102 28E
Muong Nong	54	16 22N	106 30E
Muong Ou Tay	54	22 7N	101 48E
Muong Oua	54	18 18N	101 20E
Muong Peun	54	20 13N	103 52E
Muong Phalane	54	16 39N	105 34E
Muong Phieng	54	19 6N	101 32E
Muong Phine	54	16 32N	106 2E
Muong Sai	54	20 42N	101 59E
Muong Saiapoun	54	18 24N	101 31E
Muong Sen	54	19 24N	104 8E
Muong Sing	54	21 11N	101 9E
Muong Son	54	20 27N	103 19E
Muong Soui	54	19 33N	102 52E
Muong Va	54	21 53N	102 19E
Muong Xia	54	20 19N	104 50E
Muonio	8	67 57N	23 40E
Mupa	93	16 5S	15 50E
Muping	61	37 22N	121 36E
Muqaddam, Wadi →	90	18 4N	31 30E
Mur →	33	46 18N	16 53E
Mur-de-Bretagne	18	48 12N	3 0W
Mura →	27	46 18N	16 53E
Murallón, Cuerro	142	49 48S	73 30W
Muranda	94	1 52S	29 20E
Murang'a	94	0 45S	37 9E
Murashi	37	59 30N	49 0E
Murat	20	45 7N	2 53E
Muravera	28	39 25N	9 35E
Murça	22	41 24N	7 28W
Murchison, Austral.	74	36 39S	145 14E
Murchison, N.Z.	81	41 49S	172 21E
Murchison →	79	27 45S	114 0E
Murchison Falls = Kabarega Falls	94	2 15N	31 38E
Murchison House	79	27 39S	114 14E
Murchison Mts.	81	45 13S	167 23E
Murchison Ra.	72	20 0S	134 10E
Murchison Rapids	95	15 55S	34 35E
Murcia	25	38 20N	1 10W
Murcia □	25	37 50N	1 30W
Murdo	118	43 56N	100 43W
Murdoch Pt.	72	14 37S	144 55E
Mure, La	21	44 55N	5 48E
Mures →	34	46 0N	22 0E
Mureş (Mureşul) →	34	46 15N	20 13E
Muret	20	43 30N	1 20E
Murfatlar	34	44 10N	28 26E
Murfreesboro	113	35 50N	86 21W
Murg →	31	48 55N	8 10E
Murgab	40	38 10N	74 2E
Murgon	73	26 15S	151 54E
Murgoo	79	27 24S	116 28E
Muriaé	139	21 8S	42 23W
Murias de Paredes	22	42 52N	6 11W
Murici	138	9 19S	35 56W
Muriel Mine	95	17 14S	30 40E
Müritz see	30	53 25N	12 40E
Murka	94	3 27S	38 0E
Murmansk	40	68 57N	33 10E
Murnau	31	47 40N	11 11E
Muro, France	21	42 34N	8 54E
Muro, Spain	24	39 45N	3 3E
Muro, C. de	21	41 44N	8 37E
Muro Lucano	29	40 45N	15 30E
Murom	37	55 35N	42 3E
Muroran	63	42 25N	141 0E
Muros	22	42 45N	9 5W
Muros y de Noya, Ría de	22	42 45N	9 0W
Muroto	64	33 18N	134 9E
Muroto-Misaki	64	33 15N	134 10E
Murphy	120	43 11N	116 33W
Murphys	122	38 8N	120 28W
Murphysboro	116	37 50N	89 20W
Murrat	90	18 51N	29 33E
Murray, Iowa, U.S.A.	116	41 3N	93 57W
Murray, Ky., U.S.A.	113	36 40N	88 20W
Murray, Utah, U.S.A.	120	40 41N	111 58W
Murray →, Austral.	73	35 20S	139 22E
Murray →, Can.	108	56 11N	120 45W
Murray Bridge	73	35 6S	139 14E
Murray Downs	72	21 4S	134 40E
Murray Harbour	103	46 0N	62 28W
Murray, L., P.N.G.	69	7 0S	141 35E
Murray, L., U.S.A.	113	34 8N	81 30W
Murray Seascarp	67	30 0N	135 0W
Murraysburg	96	31 58S	23 47E
Murrayville, Austral.	74	35 16S	141 11E
Murrayville, U.S.A.	116	39 35N	90 15W
Murree	48	33 56N	73 28E
Murrieta	123	33 33N	117 13W
Murrin Murrin	79	28 58S	121 33E
Murringo	76	34 16S	148 32E
Murrumbateman	76	34 58S	149 0E
Murrumbidgee →	73	34 43S	143 12E
Murrumburrah	76	34 32S	148 22E
Murrurundi	77	31 42S	150 51E
Mursala	56	1 41N	98 28E
Murshid	90	21 40N	31 10E
Murshidabad	49	24 11N	88 19E
Murska Sobota	27	46 39N	16 12E
Murtazapur	50	20 40N	77 25E
Murtle L.	108	52 8N	119 38W
Murtoa	74	36 35S	142 28E
Murtosa	22	40 44N	8 40W
Muru	91	6 36N	29 16E
Muru →	136	8 9S	70 45W
Murungu	94	4 12S	31 10E
Murupara	80	38 28S	176 42E
Murwara	49	23 46N	80 28E
Murwillumbah	77	28 18S	153 27E
Muryo	57	6 36S	110 53E
Mürz →	33	47 30N	15 25E
Mürzzuschlag	33	47 36N	15 41E
Muş	46	38 45N	41 30E
Musa →	69	9 3S	148 55E
Musa, Gebel (Sinai)	90	28 32N	33 59E
Musa Khel Bazar	48	30 59N	69 52E
Musa Qala	47	32 20N	64 50E
Musairik, Wadi →	90	19 30N	43 10E
Musala	34	42 13N	23 37E
Musan	61	42 12N	129 12E
Musangu	95	10 28S	23 55E
Musasa	94	3 25S	31 30E
Musashino	65	35 42N	139 34E
Musay'īd	47	25 0N	51 33E
Muscat = Masqat	47	23 37N	58 36E
Muscat & Oman = Oman ■	45	23 0N	58 0E
Muscatine	116	41 25N	91 5W
Muscoda	116	43 11N	90 27W
Musel	22	43 34N	5 42W
Musetula	95	14 28S	24 1E
Musgrave Ras.	79	26 0S	132 0E
Mushie	92	2 56S	16 55E
Mushin	89	6 32N	3 21E
Musi →, India	50	16 41N	79 40E
Musi →, Indon.	56	2 20S	104 56E
Muskeg →	108	60 20N	123 20W
Muskegon	106	43 15N	86 17W
Muskegon →	112	43 25N	86 0W
Muskegon Hts.	117	43 12N	86 17W
Muskogee	119	35 50N	95 25W
Muskoka, L.	106	45 0N	79 25W
Muskwa →	108	58 47N	122 48W
Musmar	90	18 13N	35 40E
Musofu	95	13 30S	29 0E

Musoma 94 1 30S 33 48 E
Musoma □ 94 1 50S 34 30 E
Musquaro, L. 103 50 38N 61 5W
Musquodoboit Harbour 103 44 50N 63 9W
Mussau I. 69 1 30S 149 40 E
Musselburgh 14 55 57N 3 3W
Musselshell → 120 47 21N 107 58W
Mussidan 20 45 2N 0 22 E
Mussomeli 28 37 35N 13 43 E
Mussooree 48 30 27N 78 6 E
Mussuco 96 17 2S 19 3 E
Mustajidda 46 26 30N 41 50 E
Mustang 49 29 10N 83 55 E
Musters, L. 142 45 20S 69 25W
Musudan 61 40 50N 129 43 E
Muswellbrook 76 32 16S 150 56 E
Mût 90 25 28N 28 58 E
Mut 46 36 40N 33 28 E
Mutanda, Mozam. 97 21 0S 33 34 E
Mutanda, Zambia 95 12 24S 26 13 E
Mutaray 41 60 56N 101 0 E
Muting 57 7 23S 140 20 E
Mutshatsha 95 10 35S 24 20 E
Mutsu-Wan 63 41 5N 140 55 E
Muttaburra 72 22 38S 144 29 E
Muttama 76 34 46S 148 8 E
Mutuáli 95 14 55S 37 0 E
Mutunópolis 139 13 40S 49 15W
Muvatupusha 51 9 53N 76 35 E
Muxima 92 9 33S 13 58 E
Muy, Le 21 43 28N 6 34 E
Muy Muy 126 12 39N 85 36W
Muya 41 56 27N 115 50 E
Muyinga 94 3 14S 30 33 E
Muzaffarabad 49 34 25N 73 30 E
Muzaffargarh 48 30 5N 71 14 E
Muzaffarnagar 48 29 26N 77 40 E
Muzaffarpur 49 26 7N 85 23 E
Muzhi 40 65 25N 64 40 E
Muzillac 18 47 35N 2 30W
Muzon C. 108 54 40N 132 40W
Muztag 62 36 20N 87 28 E
Mvôlô 91 6 2N 29 53 E
Mwadui 94 3 26S 33 32 E
Mwandi Mission 95 17 30S 24 51 E
Mwango 94 6 48S 24 12 E
Mwanza, Tanz. 94 2 30S 32 58 E
Mwanza, Zaïre 94 7 55S 26 43 E
Mwanza, Zambia 95 16 58S 24 28 E
Mwanza □ 94 2 0S 33 0 E
Mwaya 95 9 32S 33 55 E
Mweelrea 15 53 37N 9 48W
Mweka 92 4 50S 21 34 E
Mwenga 94 3 1S 28 28 E
Mwepo 95 11 50S 26 10 E
Mweru, L. 95 9 0S 28 40 E
Mweza Range 95 21 0S 30 0 E
Mwimbi 95 8 38S 31 39 E
Mwinilunga 95 11 43S 24 25 E
My Tho 55 10 29N 106 23 E
Mya, O. → 87 30 46N 4 54 E
Myall 74 35 32S 143 55 E
Myall → 76 32 30S 152 15 E
Myall Creek 77 29 44S 150 47 E
Myall, L. 76 32 30S 152 18 E
Myanaung 52 18 18N 95 22 E
Myaungmya 52 16 30N 94 40 E
Myeik Kyunzu 54 11 30N 97 30 E
Myerstown 115 40 22N 76 18W
Myingyan 52 21 30N 95 20 E
Myitkyina 52 25 24N 97 26 E
Myittha → 52 23 12N 94 17 E
Myjava 32 48 41N 17 37 E
Mymensingh 52 24 45N 90 24 E
Mynydd du 13 51 45N 3 45W
Mýrdalsjökull 8 63 40N 19 6W
Myrniong 74 37 38S 144 23 E
Myrrhee 75 36 46S 146 17 E
Myrtle Beach 113 33 43N 78 50W
Myrtle Creek 120 43 0N 123 9W
Myrtle Point 120 43 0N 124 4W
Myrtleford 75 36 34S 146 44 E
Mysen 10 59 33N 11 20 E
Mysia 74 36 13S 143 46 E
Myslenice 32 49 51N 19 57 E
Myślibórz 32 52 55N 14 50 E
Mysłowice 32 50 15N 19 12 E
Mysore 51 12 17N 76 41 E
Mysore □ = Karnataka 51 13 15N 77 0 E
Mystic, Conn., U.S.A. 115 41 21N 71 58W
Mystic, Iowa, U.S.A. 116 40 47N 92 57W
Mystishchi 37 55 50N 37 50 E
Myszków 32 50 45N 19 22 E
Myton 120 40 10N 110 2W
Mývatn 8 65 36N 17 0W
Mzimba 95 11 55S 33 39 E
Mzimvubu → 97 31 38S 29 33 E
Mzuzu 95 11 30S 33 55 E

N

N' Dioum 88 16 31N 14 39W
Na-lang 52 22 42N 97 33 E
Na Noi 54 18 19N 100 43 E
Na Phao 54 17 35N 105 44 E
Na Sam 54 22 3N 106 37 E
Na San 54 21 12N 104 2 E
Naab → 31 49 1N 12 2 E
Na'am 91 9 42N 28 27 E
Na'an 44 31 53N 34 52 E
Naantali 9 60 29N 22 2 E
Naas 15 53 12N 6 40W
Nababeep 96 29 36S 17 46 E
Nabadwip 49 23 34N 88 20 E
Nabari 65 34 37N 136 5 E
Nabas 57 11 47N 122 6 E
Nabberu, L. 79 25 30S 120 30 E
Nabburg 31 49 27N 12 11 E
Naberezhnyye Chelny = Nabereznyje Celny 40 55 42N 52 19 E
Nabeul 87 36 30N 10 44 E
Nabha 48 30 26N 76 14 E
Nabi Rubin 44 31 56N 34 44 E
Nabiac 77 32 5S 152 25 E
Nabire 57 3 15S 135 26 E
Nabisar 48 25 8N 69 40 E
Nabisipi → 103 50 14N 62 13W
Nabiswera 94 1 27N 32 15 E
Nablus = Nābulus 44 32 14N 35 15 E
Naboomspruit 97 24 32S 28 40 E
Nābulus 44 32 14N 35 15 E
Nacala-Velha 95 14 32S 40 34 E
Nacaome 126 13 31N 87 30W
Nacaroa 95 14 22S 39 56 E
Naches 120 46 48N 120 42W
Naches → 122 46 38N 120 31W
Nachikatsuura 65 33 33N 135 58 E
Nachingwea 95 10 23S 38 49 E
Nachingwea □ 95 10 30S 38 30 E
Nachna 48 27 34N 71 41 E
Náchod 32 50 25N 16 8 E
Nacimiento Res. 122 35 46N 121 0W
Nacka 10 59 17N 18 12 E
Nackara 73 32 48S 139 12 E
Naco, Mexico 124 31 20N 109 56W
Naco, U.S.A. 121 31 24N 109 58W
Nacogdoches 119 31 33N 94 39W
Nácori Chico 124 29 39N 109 1W
Nacozari 124 30 24N 109 39W
Nadi 90 18 40N 33 41 E
Nadiad 48 22 41N 72 56 E
Nădlac 34 46 10N 20 50 E
Nador 86 35 14N 2 58W
Nadūshan 47 32 2N 53 35 E
Nadvornaya 36 48 40N 24 35 E
Nadym 40 65 35N 72 42 E
Nadym → 40 66 12N 72 0 E
Næstved 11 55 13N 11 44 E
Nafada 89 11 8N 11 20 E
Naft Shāh 46 34 0N 45 30 E
Nafūd ad Dahy 46 22 0N 45 0 E
Nafūsah, Jabal 87 32 12N 12 30 E
Nag Hammâdi 90 26 2N 32 18 E
Naga 57 13 38N 123 15 E
Naga, Kreb en 86 24 12N 6 0W
Naga-Shima, Kagoshima, Japan 64 32 10N 130 9 E
Naga-Shima, Yamaguchi, Japan 64 33 49N 132 5 E
Nagagami → 102 49 40N 84 40W
Nagahama, Ehime, Japan 64 33 36N 132 29 E
Nagahama, Shiga, Japan 65 35 23N 136 16 E
Nagaland □ 52 26 0N 94 30 E
Nagambie 74 36 47S 145 10 E
Nagano 65 36 40N 138 10 E
Nagano □ 65 36 15N 138 0 E
Nagaoka 63 37 27N 138 50 E
Nagappattinam 51 10 46N 79 51 E
Nagar Parkar 48 24 28N 70 46 E
Nagara → 65 35 40N 136 43 E
Nagari Hills 51 13 3N 79 45 E
Nagarjuna Sagar 51 16 35N 79 17 E
Nagasaki 64 32 47N 129 50 E
Nagasaki □ 64 32 50N 129 40 E
Nagato 64 34 19N 131 5 E
Nagaur 48 27 15N 73 45 E
Nagbhil 50 20 34N 79 55 E
Nagercoil 51 8 12N 77 26 E
Nagiloc 74 34 30S 142 22 E
Nagina 49 29 30N 78 30 E
Nagineh 47 34 20N 57 15 E
Nagold 31 34 14N 57 2 E
Nagold → 31 48 52N 8 42 E
Nagoorin 72 24 17S 151 15 E
Nagornyy 41 55 58N 124 57 E
Nagorsk 37 59 18N 50 48 E
Nagorum 94 4 1N 34 33 E
Nagoya 65 35 10N 136 50 E
Nagpur 50 21 8N 79 10 E
Nagua 127 19 23N 69 50W
Nagykanizsa 33 46 28N 17 0 E
Nagykörös 33 47 5N 19 48 E
Nagyléta 33 47 23N 21 55 E
Naha 63 26 13N 127 42 E
Nahalal 44 32 41N 35 12 E
Nahanni Butte 108 61 2N 123 31W
Nahanni Nat. Pk. 108 61 15N 125 0W
Nahariyya 44 33 1N 35 5 E
Nahāvand 46 34 10N 48 22 E
Nahe → 31 49 58N 7 57 E
Nahf 44 32 56N 35 18 E
Nahîya, Wadi → 90 28 55N 31 0 E
Nahlin 108 58 55N 131 38W
Nahud 90 18 12N 41 40 E
Nahuel Huapi, L. 142 41 0S 71 32W
Naicá 124 27 53N 105 31W
Naicam 109 52 30N 104 30W
Na'ifah 45 19 59N 50 46 E
Naila 31 50 19N 11 43 E
Nain 103 56 34N 61 40W
Nā'in 47 32 54N 53 0 E
Naini Tal 49 29 30N 79 30 E
Naintré 18 46 46N 0 29 E
Naipu 34 44 12N 25 47 E
Naira 57 4 28S 130 0 E
Nairn, Can. 106 46 20N 81 35W
Nairn, U.K. 14 57 35N 3 54W
Nairobi 94 1 17S 36 48 E
Naivasha 94 0 40S 36 30 E
Naivasha L. 94 0 48S 36 20 E
Najac 20 44 14N 1 58 E
Najafābād 47 32 40N 51 15 E
Najd 46 26 30N 42 0 E
Nájera 24 42 26N 2 48W
Najerilla → 24 42 32N 2 48W
Najibabad 48 29 40N 78 20 E
Najin 61 42 12N 130 15 E
Naju 61 35 3N 126 43 E
Naka → 65 36 20N 140 36 E
Naka-no-Shima 63 29 51N 129 46 E
Nakalagba 94 2 50N 27 58 E
Nakama 64 33 56N 130 43 E
Nakaminato 65 36 21N 140 36 E
Nakamura 64 33 0N 133 0 E
Nakanai Mts. 69 5 40S 151 0 E
Nakano 65 36 45N 138 22 E
Nakanojō 65 36 35N 138 51 E
Nakatsu 64 33 34N 131 15 E
Nakatsugawa 65 35 29N 137 30 E
Nakfa 91 16 40N 38 32 E
Nakhi Mubarak 46 24 10N 38 10 E
Nakhichevan A.S.S.R. □ 40 39 14N 45 30 E
Nakhl 90 29 55N 33 43 E
Nakhodka 41 42 53N 132 54 E
Nakhon Nayok 54 14 12N 101 13 E
Nakhon Pathom 54 13 49N 100 3 E
Nakhon Phanom 54 17 23N 104 43 E
Nakhon Ratchasima (Khorat) 54 14 59N 102 12 E
Nakhon Sawan 54 15 35N 100 10 E
Nakhon Si Thammarat 55 8 29N 100 0 E
Nakhon Thai 54 17 5N 100 44 E
Nakina, B.C., Can. 108 59 12N 132 52W
Nakina, Ont., Can. 102 50 10N 86 40W
Nakło nad Notecią 32 53 9N 17 38 E
Nakodar 48 31 8N 75 31 E
Nakskov 11 54 50N 11 8 E
Näkten 10 62 48N 14 38 E
Naktong → 61 35 7N 128 57 E
Nakuru 94 0 15S 36 4 E
Nakuru □ 94 0 15S 35 5 E
Nakuru, L. 94 0 23S 36 5 E
Nakusp 108 50 20N 117 45W
Nal → 48 25 20N 65 30 E
Nalchik 39 43 30N 43 33 E
Nälden 10 63 21N 14 14 E
Näldsjön 10 63 25N 14 15 E
Nalerigu 89 10 35N 0 25W
Nalgonda 50 17 6N 79 15 E
Nalhati 49 24 17N 87 52 E
Nallamalai Hills 51 15 30N 78 50 E
Nalón → 22 43 32N 6 4W
Nālūt 87 31 54N 11 0 E
Nam Can 55 8 46N 104 59 E
Nam Co 62 30 30N 90 45 E
Nam Dinh 54 20 25N 106 5 E
Nam Du, Hon 55 9 41N 104 21 E
Nam Ngum Dam 54 18 35N 102 34 E
Nam-Phan 56 10 30N 106 0 E
Nam Phong 54 16 42N 102 52 E
Nam Tha 54 20 58N 101 30 E
Nam Tok 54 14 21N 99 4 E
Namak, Daryácheh-ye 47 34 30N 52 0 E
Namak, Kavir-e 47 34 30N 57 30 E
Namakkal 51 11 13N 78 13 E
Namaland 96 24 30S 17 0 E
Namangan 40 41 0N 71 40 E
Namapa 95 13 43S 39 50 E
Namaqualand 96 30 0S 18 0 E
Namasagali 94 1 2N 33 0 E
Namatanai 69 3 40S 152 29 E
Namber 57 1 2S 134 49 E
Nambour 73 26 32S 152 58 E
Nambouwalu 68 17 0S 178 45 E
Nambucca Heads 77 30 37S 153 0 E
Namche Bazar 49 27 51N 86 47 E
Namchonjŏm 61 38 15N 126 26 E
Namecunda 95 14 54S 37 37 E
Nameh 56 2 34N 116 21 E
Nameponda 95 15 50S 39 50 E
Namerikawa 65 36 46N 137 20 E
Nametil 95 15 40S 39 21 E
Namew L. 109 54 14N 101 56W
Namhsan 52 22 48N 97 2 E
Nami 55 22 58N 97 10 E
Namib Desert = Namib Woestyn 96 22 30S 15 0 E
Namib-Woestyn 96 22 30S 15 0 E
Namibia ■ 96 22 0S 18 9 E
Namkhan 52 23 50N 97 41 E
Namlea 57 3 18S 127 5 E
Namoi → 77 30 12S 149 30 E
Namous, O. en → 86 31 0N 0 15W
Nampa 120 43 34N 116 34W
Nampula 95 15 6N 39 15 E
Namrole 57 3 46S 126 46 E
Namse Shankou 49 30 0N 82 25 E
Namsen → 8 64 27N 11 42 E
Namtay 41 62 43N 129 37 E
Namtu 52 23 5N 97 28 E
Namtumbo 95 10 30S 36 4 E
Namu 108 51 52N 127 50W
Namucha Shank'ou 49 30 0N 82 28 E
Namur, Belg. 16 50 27N 4 52 E
Namur, Can. 104 45 54N 74 56W
Namur □ 16 50 17N 5 0 E
Namutoni 96 18 49S 16 55 E
Namwala 95 15 44S 26 30 E
Namwŏn 61 35 23N 127 23 E
Namysłów 32 51 6N 17 42 E
Nan 54 18 48N 100 46 E
Nan → 54 15 42N 100 9 E
Nan Xian 59 29 20N 112 22 E
Nana Glen 77 30 8S 153 2 E
Nanaimo 108 49 10N 124 0W
Nanam 61 41 44N 129 40 E
Nanan 59 24 59N 118 21 E
Nanango 73 26 40S 152 0 E
Nan'ao 59 23 28N 117 5 E
Nanao 63 37 0N 137 0 E
Nanbu 58 31 18N 106 3 E
Nanchang 59 28 42N 115 55 E
Nancheng 59 27 33N 116 35 E
Nanching = Nanjing 62 32 2N 118 47 E
Nanchong 58 30 43N 106 2 E
Nanchuan 58 29 9N 107 6 E
Nancy 19 48 42N 6 12 E
Nanda Devi 49 30 23N 79 59 E
Nandan, China 58 24 58N 107 29 E
Nandan, Japan 64 34 10N 134 42 E
Nander 50 19 10N 77 20 E
Nandewar Ra. 77 30 15S 150 35 E
Nandi 68 17 25S 177 20 E
Nandi □ 94 0 15N 35 0 E
Nandikotkur 51 15 52N 78 18 E
Nandura 50 20 52N 76 25 E
Nandurbar 50 21 20N 74 15 E
Nandyal 51 15 30N 78 30 E
Nanfeng, Guangdong, China 59 23 45N 111 47 E
Nanfeng, Jiangxi, China 59 27 12N 116 28 E
Nanga 79 26 7S 113 45 E
Nanga Eboko 92 4 41N 12 22 E
Nanga Parbat 49 35 10N 74 35 E
Nangade 95 11 5S 39 36 E
Nangapinoh 56 0 20S 11 44 E
Nangarhar □ 47 34 20N 70 0 E
Nangatayap 56 1 32S 110 34 E
Nangeya Mts. 94 3 30N 33 30 E
Nangis 19 48 33N 3 0 E
Nangong 60 37 23N 115 22 E
Nangus 76 35 0S 147 52 E
Nanhua 58 25 13N 101 21 E
Nanhuang 61 36 58N 121 48 E
Nanhui 59 31 5N 121 44 E
Nanjangud 51 12 6N 76 43 E
Nanjeko 95 15 31S 23 30 E
Nanji Shan 59 27 27N 121 4 E
Nanjian 58 25 2N 100 25 E
Nanjiang 58 32 28N 106 51 E
Nanjing, Fujian, China 59 24 25N 117 20 E
Nanjing, Jiangsu, China 62 32 2N 118 47 E
Nanjirinji 95 9 41S 39 5 E
Nankana Sahib 48 31 27N 73 38 E
Nanking = Nanjing 62 32 2N 118 47 E
Nankoku 64 33 39N 133 44 E
Nanling 59 30 55N 118 20 E

Nannine **79** 26 51S 118 18 E
Nanning **58** 22 48N 108 20 E
Nannup **79** 33 59S 115 48 E
Nanpan Jiang → **58** 25 10N 106 0 E
Nanpara **49** 27 52N 81 33 E
Nanpi **60** 38 2N 116 45 E
Nanping, Fujian, China **59** 26 38N 118 10 E
Nanping, Henan, China **59** 29 55N 112 3 E
Nanri Dao **59** 25 15N 119 25 E
Nanripe **95** 13 52S 38 52 E
Nansei-Shotō **63** 26 0N 128 0 E
Nansen Sd. **144** 81 0N 91 0W
Nansio **94** 2 3S 33 4 E
Nanson **79** 28 35S 114 45 E
Nant **20** 44 1N 3 18 E
Nantes **18** 47 12N 1 33W
Nanteuil-le-Haudouin **19** 49 9N 2 48 E
Nantiat **20** 46 1N 1 11 E
Nanticoke **115** 41 12N 76 1W
Nanton **108** 50 21N 113 46W
Nantong **59** 32 1N 120 52 E
Nantua **21** 46 10N 5 35 E
Nantucket I. **98** 41 16N 70 3W
Nanuku Passage **68** 16 45S 179 15W
Nanuque **139** 17 50S 40 21W
Nanutana **78** 22 32S 115 30 E
Nanxiong **59** 25 6N 114 15 E
Nanyang **59** 33 11N 112 30 E
Nanyi Hu **59** 31 5N 119 0 E
Nan'yō **64** 34 3N 131 49 E
Nanyuan **60** 39 44N 116 22 E
Nanyuki **94** 0 2N 37 4 E
Nanzhang **59** 31 45N 111 50 E
Náo, C. de la **25** 38 44N 0 14 E
Naococane L. **103** 52 50N 70 45W
Naoetsu **63** 37 12N 138 10 E
Naogaon **52** 24 52N 88 52 E
Náousa **35** 40 42N 22 9 E
Naozhou Dao **59** 20 55N 110 20 E
Napa **122** 38 18N 122 17W
Napa → **122** 38 10N 122 19W
Napanee **107** 44 15N 77 0W
Napanoch **115** 41 44N 74 22W
Nape **54** 18 18N 105 6 E
Nape Pass = Keo Neua, Deo **54** 18 23N 105 10 E
Naperville **117** 41 46N 88 9W
Napiéolédougou **88** 9 18N 5 35W
Napier **80** 39 30S 176 56 E
Napier Broome B. **78** 14 2S 126 37 E
Napier Downs **78** 17 11S 124 36 E
Napier Pen. **72** 12 4S 135 43 E
Napierville **105** 45 11N 73 25W
Napierville □ **105** 45 10N 73 30W
Naples **113** 26 10N 81 45W
Naples = Nápoli **29** 40 50N 14 17 E
Napo **58** 23 22N 105 50 E
Napo □ **134** 0 30S 77 0W
Napo → **134** 3 20S 72 40W
Napoleon, N. Dak., U.S.A. **118** 46 32N 99 49W
Napoleon, Ohio, U.S.A. **117** 41 24N 84 7W
Nápoli **29** 40 50N 14 17 E
Nápoli, G. di **29** 40 40N 14 10 E
Napopo **94** 4 15N 28 0 E
Nappa Merrie **73** 27 36S 141 7 E
Nappanee **117** 41 27N 86 0W
Naqâda **90** 25 53N 32 42 E
Nara, Japan **65** 34 40N 135 49 E
Nara, Mali **88** 15 10N 7 20W
Nara □ **65** 34 30N 136 0 E
Nara, Canal **48** 24 30N 69 20 E
Nara Visa **119** 35 39N 103 10W
Naracoorte **73** 36 58S 140 45 E
Naradhan **75** 33 34S 146 17 E
Narasapur **51** 16 26N 81 40 E
Narasaropet **51** 16 14N 80 4 E
Narathiwat **55** 6 30N 101 48 E
Narayanganj **52** 23 40N 90 33 E
Narayanpet **50** 16 45N 77 30 E
Narbonne **20** 43 11N 3 0 E
Narcea → **22** 43 33N 6 44W
Nardò **29** 40 10N 18 0 E
Narembeen **79** 32 7S 118 24 E
Naretha **79** 31 0S 124 45 E
Narew → **32** 52 26N 20 41 E
Nari → **48** 29 40N 68 0 E
Narinda, B. de **97** 14 55S 47 30 E
Narino □ **134** 1 30N 78 0W
Narita **65** 35 47N 140 19 E
Narmada → **48** 21 38N 72 36 E
Narnaul **48** 28 5N 76 11 E
Narni **27** 42 30N 12 30 E
Naro, Ghana **88** 10 22N 2 27W
Naro, Italy **28** 37 18N 13 48 E
Naro Fominsk **37** 55 23N 36 43 E
Narok **94** 1 55S 33 52 E
Narok □ **94** 1 20S 36 30 E
Narón **22** 43 32N 8 9W
Narooma **75** 36 14S 150 4 E
Narowal **48** 32 6N 74 52 E
Narrabri **77** 30 19S 149 46 E
Narrabri West **77** 30 21S 149 46 E
Narran → **73** 28 37S 148 12 E
Narrandera **75** 34 42S 146 31 E
Narraway → **108** 55 44N 119 55W
Narrogin **79** 32 58S 117 14 E
Narromine **76** 32 12S 148 12 E
Narsampet **50** 17 57N 79 58 E
Narsimhapur **49** 22 54N 79 14 E
Naruto **64** 34 11N 134 37 E
Narutō **65** 35 36N 140 25 E
Naruto-Kaikyō **64** 34 14N 134 39 E
Narva **36** 59 23N 28 12 E
Narva → **36** 59 27N 28 2 E
Narvik **8** 68 28N 17 26 E
Narvskoye Vdkhr. **36** 59 18N 28 14 E
Narwana **48** 29 39N 76 6 E
Naryan-Mar **40** 68 0N 53 0 E
Naryilco **73** 28 37S 141 53 E
Narym **40** 59 0N 81 30 E
Narymskoye **40** 49 10N 84 15 E
Naryn **40** 41 26N 75 58 E
Nasa **8** 66 29N 15 23 E
Nasarawa **89** 8 32N 7 41 E
Năsăud **34** 47 19N 24 29 E
Nasawa **68** 15 0S 168 0 E
Naseby **81** 45 1S 170 10 E
Naselle **122** 46 22N 123 49W
Naser, Buheirat en **90** 23 0N 32 30 E
Nashua, Iowa, U.S.A. **116** 42 55N 92 34W
Nashua, Mont., U.S.A. **120** 48 10N 106 25W
Nashua, N.H., U.S.A. **115** 42 50N 71 25W
Nashville, Ark., U.S.A. **119** 33 56N 93 50W
Nashville, Ga., U.S.A. **113** 31 3N 83 15W
Nashville, Ill., U.S.A. **116** 38 21N 89 23W
Nashville, Ind., U.S.A. **117** 39 12N 86 14W
Nashville, Mich., U.S.A. **117** 42 36N 85 5W
Nashville, Tenn., U.S.A. **113** 36 12N 86 46W
Našice **33** 45 32N 18 4 E
Nasielsk **32** 52 35N 20 50 E
Nasik **50** 19 58N 73 50 E
Nasirabad **48** 26 15N 74 45 E
Naskaupi → **103** 53 47N 60 51W
Naso **29** 38 8N 14 46 E
Nass → **108** 55 0N 129 40W
Nassau, Bahamas **126** 25 0N 77 20W
Nassau, U.S.A. **115** 42 30N 73 34W
Nassau, Bahía **142** 55 20S 68 0W
Nasser City = Kôm Ombo **90** 24 25N 32 52 E
Nasser, L. = Naser, Buheiret en **90** 23 0N 32 30 E
Nassian **88** 8 28N 3 28W
Nässjö **11** 57 39N 14 42 E
Nastopoka Is. **102** 57 0N 77 0W
Näsum **11** 56 10N 14 29 E
Näsviken **10** 61 46N 16 52 E
Nata **96** 20 12S 26 12 E
Natã **46** 27 15N 48 35 E
Natagaima **134** 3 37N 75 6W
Natal, Brazil **138** 5 47S 35 13W
Natal, Can. **108** 49 43N 114 51W
Natal, Indon. **56** 0 35N 99 7 E
Natal □ **97** 28 30S 30 30 E
Natalinci **33** 44 15N 20 49 E
Natanz **47** 33 30N 51 55 E
Natashquan **103** 50 14N 61 46W
Natashquan → **103** 50 7N 61 50W
Natchez **119** 31 35N 91 25W
Natchitoches **119** 31 47N 93 4W
Natewa B. **68** 16 35S 179 40 E
Nathalia **74** 36 1S 145 13 E
Nathdwara **48** 24 55N 73 50 E
Natick **115** 42 16N 71 19W
Natih **47** 22 25N 56 30 E
Natimuk **74** 36 42S 142 0 E
Nation → **108** 55 30N 123 32W
National City **123** 32 39N 117 7W
Natitingou **89** 10 20N 1 26 E
Natividad, I. **124** 27 50N 115 10W
Natogyi **52** 21 25N 95 39 E
Natoma **118** 39 14N 99 0W
Natron, L. **94** 2 20S 36 0 E
Natrona **114** 40 39N 79 43W
Natrûn, W. el. → **90** 30 25N 30 13 E
Nattai River **76** 34 3S 150 26 E
Natuna Besar, Kepulauan **55** 4 0N 108 15 E
Natuna Selatan, Kepulauan **55** 2 45N 109 0 E
Natural Bridge **115** 44 5N 75 30W
Naturaliste C. **72** 40 50S 148 15 E
Natya **74** 34 57S 143 13 E
Nau-Nau **96** 18 57S 21 4 E
Nau Qala **48** 34 5N 68 5 E
Naubinway **106** 46 7N 85 27W
Naucelle **20** 44 13N 2 20 E
Nauders **31** 46 54N 10 30 E
Nauen **30** 52 36N 12 52 E
Naugatuck **115** 41 28N 73 4W
Naughton **106** 46 24N 81 12W
Naujoji Vilnia **36** 54 48N 25 27 E
Naumburg **30** 51 10N 11 48 E
Nauru I. **66** 1 0S 166 0 E
Nauru Is. **66** 0 32S 166 55 E
Nausori **68** 18 2S 178 32 E
Nauta **134** 4 31S 73 35W
Nautla **125** 20 20N 96 50W
Nauvoo **116** 40 33N 91 23W
Nava **124** 28 25N 100 46W
Nava del Rey **22** 41 22N 5 6W
Navacerrada, Puerto de **22** 40 47N 4 0W
Navahermosa **23** 39 41N 4 28W
Navajo Res. **121** 36 55N 107 30W
Navalcarnero **22** 40 17N 4 5W
Navalmoral de la Mata **22** 39 52N 5 33W
Navalvillar de Pela **23** 39 9N 5 24W
Navan = An Uaimh **15** 53 39N 6 40W
Navare **20** 43 20N 1 20W
Navarino, I. **142** 55 0S 67 40W
Navarra □ **24** 42 40N 1 40W
Navarre, Austral. **74** 36 53S 143 11 E
Navarre, France **20** 43 15N 1 20W
Navarre, U.S.A. **114** 40 43N 81 31W
Navarrenx **20** 43 20N 0 45W
Navarro **122** 39 10N 123 32W
Navas del Marqués, Las **22** 40 36N 4 20W
Navasota **119** 30 20N 96 5W
Navassa **127** 18 30N 75 0W
Nave **26** 45 35N 10 17 E
Naver → **14** 58 34N 4 15W
Navia **22** 43 35N 6 42W
Navia → **22** 43 15N 6 50W
Navia de Suarna **22** 42 58N 6 59W
Navidad **140** 33 57S 71 50W
Naviti **68** 17 7S 177 15 E
Navlya **36** 52 53N 34 30 E
Navoi **40** 40 9N 65 22 E
Navojoa **124** 27 0N 109 30W
Navolato **124** 24 47N 107 42W
Návpaktos **35** 38 23N 21 50 E
Návplion **35** 37 33N 22 50 E
Navrongo **89** 10 51N 1 3W
Navsari **50** 20 57N 72 59 E
Navua **68** 18 6S 177 43 E
Nawa Kot **48** 28 21N 71 24 E
Nawabganj **52** 24 35N 88 14 E
Nawabganj, Bara Banki **49** 26 56N 81 14 E
Nawabganj, Bareilly **49** 28 32N 79 40 E
Nawabshah **48** 26 15N 68 25 E
Nawada **49** 24 50N 85 33 E
Nawakot **49** 27 55N 85 10 E
Nawalgarh **48** 27 50N 75 15 E
Nawanshahr **49** 32 33N 74 48 E
Nawapara **50** 20 46N 82 33 E
Nawāsīf, Harrat **46** 21 20N 42 10 E
Nawi **90** 18 32N 30 50 E
Nawng Hpa **52** 22 30N 98 30 E
Náxos, Greece **35** 37 8N 25 25 E
Náxos, Greece **35** 37 5N 25 30 E
Nay **20** 43 10N 0 18W
Nāy Band **47** 27 20N 52 40 E
Naya → **134** 3 13N 77 22W
Nayakhan **41** 61 56N 159 0 E
Nayarit □ **124** 22 0N 105 0W
Nayé **88** 14 28N 12 12W
Nayong **58** 26 50N 105 20 E
Nazaré, Brazil **139** 13 2S 39 0W
Nazaré, Goiás, Brazil **138** 6 23S 47 40W
Nazaré, Pará, Brazil **137** 6 25S 52 29W
Nazaré, Port. **23** 39 36N 9 4W
Nazareth **44** 32 42N 35 17 E
Nazas **124** 25 10N 104 6W
Nazas → **124** 25 35N 103 25W
Naze **63** 28 22N 129 27 E
Naze, The **13** 51 53N 1 19 E
Nazeret **91** 8 32N 39 22 E
Nazir Hat **52** 22 35N 91 49 E
Nazko **108** 53 1N 123 37W
Nazko → **108** 53 7N 123 34W
Nchanga **95** 12 30S 27 49 E
Ncheu **95** 14 50S 34 47 E
Ndala **94** 4 45S 33 15 E
Ndalatando **92** 9 12S 14 48 E
Ndali **89** 9 50N 2 46 E
Ndareda **94** 4 12S 35 30 E
N'Délé **85** 8 25N 20 36 E
Ndendé **92** 2 22S 11 23 E
Ndjamena **85** 12 10N 14 59 E
Ndjolé **92** 0 10S 10 45 E
Ndola **95** 13 0S 28 34 E
Ndoto Mts. **94** 2 0N 37 0 E
Ndoua, C. **68** 22 24S 166 56 E
Ndrhamcha, Sebkha de **88** 18 30N 15 55W
Nduguti **94** 4 18S 34 41 E
Nduindui **68** 15 24S 167 46 E
Nea → **10** 63 15N 11 0 E
Néa Flippiás **35** 39 12N 20 53 E
Neagari **65** 36 26N 136 25 E
Neagh, Lough **15** 54 35N 6 25W
Neah Bay **122** 48 25N 124 40W
Neale L. **78** 24 15S 130 0 E
Neápolis, Kozan, Greece **35** 40 20N 21 24 E
Neápolis, Lakonia, Greece **35** 36 27N 23 8 E
Near Is. **100** 53 0N 172 0 E
Neath **13** 51 39N 3 49W
Nebal, Î. **68** 20 9S 163 56 E
Nebbou **89** 11 9N 1 51W
Nebine Cr. → **73** 29 7S 146 56 E
Nebit Dag **40** 39 30N 54 22 E
Nebo **72** 59 12N 32 25 E
Nebolchy **36** 59 12N 32 58 E
Nebraska □ **118** 41 30N 100 0W
Nebraska City **118** 40 40N 95 52W
Nébrodi, Monti **28** 37 55N 14 50 E
Necedah **118** 44 2N 90 7W
Nechako → **108** 53 30N 122 44W
Neches → **119** 29 55N 93 52W
Neckar → **31** 49 31N 8 26 E
Necochea **140** 38 30S 58 50W
Nedelišće **27** 46 23N 16 22 E
Nédha → **35** 37 25N 21 45 E
Nedroma **86** 35 1N 1 45W
Needilup **79** 33 55S 118 45 E
Needles **123** 34 50N 114 35W
Needles, Pt. **80** 36 3S 175 25 E
Needles, The **13** 50 39N 1 35W
Neembucú □ **140** 27 0S 58 0W
Neemuch (Nimach) **48** 24 30N 74 56 E
Neenah **112** 44 10N 88 30W
Neepawa **109** 50 15N 99 30W
Neerim **74** 37 59S 145 57 E
Neeworra **77** 29 2S 149 3 E
Nefta **87** 33 53N 7 50 E
Neftah Sidi Boubekeur **86** 35 1N 0 4 E
Neftegorsk **39** 44 25N 39 45 E
Negapatam = Nagappattinam **51** 10 46N 79 50 E
Negaunee **112** 46 30N 87 36W
Negba **44** 31 40N 34 41 E
Negele **91** 5 20N 39 36 E
Negev = Hanegev **44** 30 50N 35 0 E
Negombo **51** 7 12N 79 50 E
Negotin **33** 44 16N 22 37 E
Negra, La **140** 23 46S 70 18W
Negra, Peña **22** 42 11N 6 30W
Negra Pt. **57** 18 40N 120 50 E
Negra, Pta. **136** 6 6S 81 10W
Negrais C. **52** 16 0N 94 12 E
Negreira **22** 42 54N 8 45W
Négrine **87** 34 30N 7 30 E
Negro →, Argent. **142** 41 2S 62 47W
Negro →, Boliv. **137** 14 11S 63 7W
Negro →, Brazil **135** 3 0S 60 0W
Negro →, Uruguay **141** 33 24S 58 22W
Negro, C. **86** 35 40N 5 11W
Negros **57** 10 0N 123 0 E
Nehalem → **122** 45 40N 123 56W
Nehbandān **47** 31 35N 60 5 E
Neheim-Hüsten **30** 51 27N 7 58 E
Nehoiaşu **34** 45 24N 26 20 E
Nei Monggol Zizhiqu □ **60** 42 0N 112 0 E
Neiafu **68** 18 39S 173 59W
Neidpath **109** 50 12N 107 20W
Neihart **120** 47 0N 110 44W
Neijiang **58** 29 35N 104 55 E
Neilrex **77** 31 44S 149 20 E
Neilton **120** 17 24N 123 52W
Neiqiu **60** 37 15N 114 30 E
Neira de Jusá **22** 42 53N 7 14W
Neisse → **30** 52 4N 14 46 E
Neiva **134** 2 56N 75 18W
Neixiang **60** 33 10N 111 52 E
Nejanilini L. **109** 59 33N 97 48W
Nejo **91** 9 30N 35 28 E
Nekemte **91** 9 4N 36 30 E
Nêkheb **90** 25 10N 32 48 E
Neksø **11** 55 4N 15 8 E
Nelas **22** 40 32N 7 52W
Nelia **72** 20 39S 142 12 E
Nelidovo **36** 56 13N 32 49 E
Neligh **118** 42 11N 98 2W
Nelkan **41** 57 40N 136 4 E
Nelligen **76** 35 39S 150 8 E
Nellikuppam **51** 11 46N 79 43 E
Nellore **51** 14 27N 79 59 E
Nelma **41** 47 39N 139 0 E
Nelson, Austral. **74** 38 3S 141 2 E
Nelson, Can. **108** 49 30N 117 20W
Nelson, N.Z. **81** 41 18S 173 16 E

Nelson, U.K. **12** 53 50N 2 14W
Nelson, Ariz., U.S.A. **121** 35 35N 113 16W
Nelson, Nev., U.S.A. **123** 35 46N 114 48W
Nelson □ **81** 42 11S 172 15E
Nelson → **109** 54 33N 98 2W
Nelson Bay **76** 32 43S 152 9E
Nelson, C., Austral. **74** 38 26S 141 32E
Nelson, C., P.N.G. **69** 9 0S 149 20E
Nelson, Estrecho **142** 51 30S 75 0W
Nelson Forks **108** 59 30N 124 0W
Nelson House **109** 55 47N 98 51W
Nelson L. **109** 55 48N 100 7W
Nelspruit **97** 25 29S 30 59E
Nelungaloo **76** 33 7S 148 0E
Néma **88** 16 40N 7 15W
Neman (Nemunas) → **36** 55 25N 21 10E
Nemeiben L. **109** 55 20N 105 20W
Nemingha **77** 31 6S 151 0E
Nemira **34** 46 17N 26 19E
Némiscachingue, L. **104** 47 25N 74 30W
Nemours **19** 48 16N 2 40E
Nemunas = Neman → **36** 55 25N 21 10E
Nemuro **63** 43 20N 145 35E
Nemuro-Kaikyō **63** 43 30N 145 30E
Nemuy **41** 55 40N 136 9E
Nen Jiang → **61** 45 28N 124 30E
Nenagh **15** 52 52N 8 11W
Nenana **100** 64 30N 149 20W
Nenasi **55** 3 9N 103 23E
Nendiarene, Pte. **68** 20 14S 164 19E
Nene → **12** 52 38N 0 13E
Nenjiang **62** 49 10N 125 10E
Neno **95** 15 25S 34 40E
Nenusa, Kepulauan **57** 4 45N 127 1E
Neodesha **119** 37 30N 95 37W
Neoga **117** 39 19N 88 27W
Neópolis **138** 10 18S 36 35W
Neosho **119** 36 56N 94 28W
Neosho → **119** 35 59N 95 10W
Nepal ■ **49** 28 0N 84 30E
Nepalganj **49** 28 5N 81 40E
Nephi **120** 39 43N 111 52W
Nephin **15** 54 1N 9 21W
Neptune City **115** 40 13N 74 4W
Néra → **34** 44 48N 21 25E
Nérac **20** 44 8N 0 21E
Nerang **77** 27 58S 153 20E
Nerchinsk **41** 52 0N 116 39E
Nerchinskiy Zavod **41** 51 20N 119 40E
Nereju **34** 45 43N 26 43E
Nerekhta **37** 57 26N 40 38E
Néret L. **103** 54 45N 70 44W
Neringa **36** 55 30N 21 5E
Nerja **23** 36 43N 3 55W
Nerl → **37** 56 11N 40 34E
Nerpio **25** 38 11N 2 16W
Nerriga **76** 35 6S 150 6E
Nerva **23** 37 42N 6 30W
Nes **8** 65 53N 17 24W
Nes Ziyyona **44** 31 56N 34 48W
Nesbyen **10** 60 34N 9 35E
Nesebŭr **34** 42 41N 27 46E
Neskaupstaður **8** 65 9N 13 42W
Nesland **10** 59 31N 7 59E
Neslandsvatn **10** 58 57N 9 10E
Nesle **19** 49 45N 2 53E
Nesodden **10** 59 48N 10 40E
Nesque → **21** 43 59N 4 59E
Ness, Loch **14** 57 15N 4 30W
Nestaocano → **105** 49 38N 73 28W
Néstos → **35** 41 20N 24 35E
Nesttun **9** 60 19N 5 21E
Nesvizh **36** 53 14N 26 38E
Netanya **44** 32 20N 34 51E
Nète → **16** 51 7N 4 14E
Nether Stowey **13** 51 0N 3 10W
Netherbury **13** 50 46N 2 45W
Netherby **74** 36 8S 141 40E
Netherdale **72** 21 10S 148 33E
Netherlands ■ **16** 52 0N 5 30E
Netherlands Guiana =Surinam ■ **135** 4 0N 56 0W
Neto → **29** 39 13N 17 8E
Netrakona **52** 24 53N 90 47E
Nettancourt **19** 48 51N 4 57E
Nettilling L. **101** 66 30N 71 0W
Nettuno **28** 41 29N 12 40E
Netzahualcoyotl, Presa **125** 17 10N 93 30W
Neu-Isenburg **31** 50 3N 8 42E
Neu-Ulm **31** 48 23N 10 2E
Neubrandenburg **30** 53 33N 13 17E
Neubrandenburg □ **30** 53 30N 13 20E
Neubukow **30** 54 1N 11 40E
Neuburg **31** 48 43N 11 11E
Neuchâtel **31** 47 0N 6 55E
Neuchâtel □ **31** 47 0N 6 55E
Neuchâtel, Lac de **31** 46 53N 6 50E
Neudau **33** 47 11N 16 6E
Neuenhaus **30** 52 30N 6 55E
Neuf-Brisach **19** 48 0N 7 30E
Neufahrn **31** 48 44N 12 11E
Neufchâteau, Belg. **16** 49 50N 5 25E
Neufchâteau, France **19** 48 21N 5 40E
Neufchâtel **19** 49 43N 1 30E
Neufchâtel-sur-Aisne **19** 49 26N 4 0E
Neuhaus **30** 53 16N 10 54E
Neuillé-Pont-Pierre **18** 47 33N 0 33E
Neuilly-St-Front **19** 49 10N 3 15E
Neukalen **30** 53 49N 12 48E
Neumarkt **31** 49 16N 11 28E
Neumarkt-Sankt Veit **31** 48 22N 12 30E
Neumünster **30** 54 4N 9 58E
Neung-sur-Beuvron **19** 47 30N 1 50E
Neunkirchen, Austria **33** 47 43N 16 4E
Neunkirchen, Ger. **31** 49 23N 7 12E
Neuquén **142** 38 55S 68 0E
Neuquén □ **140** 38 0S 69 50W
Neuquén → **142** 38 59S 68 0W
Neuruppin **30** 52 56N 12 48E
Neuse → **113** 35 5N 76 30W
Neusiedler See **33** 47 50N 16 47E
Neuss **30** 51 12N 6 39E
Neussargues-Moissac **20** 45 9N 3 1E
Neustadt, Can. **106** 44 5N 81 0W
Neustadt, Baden-W., Ger. **31** 47 54N 8 13E
Neustadt, Bayern, Ger. **31** 49 42N 12 10E
Neustadt, Bayern, Ger. **31** 48 48N 11 47E
Neustadt, Bayern, Ger. **31** 50 23N 11 0E
Neustadt, Bayern, Ger. **31** 49 34N 10 37E
Neustadt, Gera, Ger. **30** 50 45N 11 43E
Neustadt, Hessen, Ger. **30** 50 51N 9 9E
Neustadt, Niedersachsen, Ger. **30** 52 30N 9 30E
Neustadt, Potsdam, Ger. **30** 52 50N 12 27E
Neustadt, Rhld-Pfz., Ger. **31** 49 21N 8 10E
Neustadt, Schleswig-Holstein, Ger. **30** 54 6N 10 49E
Neustrelitz **30** 53 22N 13 4E
Neuvic **20** 45 23N 2 16E
Neuville, Rhône, France **21** 45 52N 4 51E
Neuville, Vienne, France **18** 46 41N 0 15E
Neuville-aux-Bois **19** 48 4N 2 3E
Neuvy-le-Roi **18** 47 36N 0 36E
Neuvy-St-Sépulchure **20** 46 35N 1 48E
Neuvy-sur-Barangeon **19** 47 20N 2 15E
Neuwerk **30** 53 55N 8 30E
Neuwied **30** 50 26N 7 29E
Nevada, Iowa, U.S.A. **116** 42 1N 93 27W
Nevada, Mo., U.S.A. **116** 37 51N 94 22W
Nevada □ **120** 39 20N 117 0W
Nevada City **122** 39 20N 121 0W
Nevada de Sta. Marta, Sa. **136** 10 55N 73 50W
Nevada, Sierra, Spain **25** 37 3N 3 15W
Nevada, Sierra, U.S.A. **120** 39 0N 120 30W
Nevado, Cerro **140** 35 30S 68 32W
Nevanka **41** 56 31N 98 55E
Nevasa **50** 19 34N 75 0E
Nevel **36** 56 0N 29 55E
Nevers **19** 47 0N 3 9E
Nevertire **76** 31 50S 147 44E
Neville, Austral. **76** 33 41S 149 12E
Neville, Can. **109** 49 58N 107 39W
Nevinnomyssk **39** 44 40N 42 0E
Nevis **127** 17 0N 62 30W
Nevoria **79** 31 25S 119 25E
Nevrokop = Gotse Delchev **35** 41 33N 23 46E
Nevşehir **46** 38 33N 34 40E
New → **135** 3 20N 57 37W
New Albany, Ind., U.S.A. **117** 38 20N 85 50W
New Albany, Miss., U.S.A. **119** 34 30N 89 0W
New Albany, Pa., U.S.A. **115** 41 35N 76 28W
New Amsterdam **135** 6 15N 57 36W
New Angledool **73** 29 10S 147 55E
New Athens **116** 38 19N 89 53W
New Baltimore **106** 42 41N 82 44W
New Bedford **115** 41 40N 70 52W
New Berlin, Ill., U.S.A. **116** 39 44N 89 55W
New Berlin, Wis., U.S.A. **117** 42 59N 88 6W
New Bern **113** 35 8N 77 3W
New Bethlehem **114** 41 0N 79 22W
New Bloomfield **114** 40 24N 77 12W
New Boston **119** 33 27N 94 21W
New Braunfels **119** 29 43N 98 9W
New Brighton, N.Z. **81** 43 29S 172 43E
New Brighton, U.S.A. **114** 40 42N 80 19W
New Britain **115** 41 41N 72 47W
New Britain, I. **69** 5 50S 150 20E
New Brunswick **115** 40 30N 74 28W
New Brunswick □ **103** 46 50N 66 30W
New Buffalo **117** 41 47N 86 45W
New Bussa **89** 9 53N 4 31E
New Byrd **143** 80 0S 120 0W
New Caledonia = Nouvelle-Calédonie **68** 21 0S 165 0E
New Canton **116** 39 37N 91 8W
New Carlisle, Ind., U.S.A. **117** 41 45N 86 32W
New Carlisle, Ohio, U.S.A. **117** 39 56N 84 2W
New Castile = Castilla La Neuva **23** 39 45N 3 20W
New Castle, Ind., U.S.A. **117** 39 55N 85 23W
New Castle, Ky., U.S.A. **117** 38 26N 85 10W
New Castle, Pa., U.S.A. **114** 41 0N 80 20W
New City **115** 41 8N 74 0W
New Cumberland **114** 40 30N 80 36W
New Cuyama **123** 34 57N 119 38W
New Delhi **48** 28 37N 77 13E
New Denver **108** 50 0N 117 25W
New England **118** 46 36N 102 47W
New England Ra. **77** 30 20S 151 45E
New Forest **13** 50 53N 1 40W
New Franklin **116** 39 1N 92 44W
New Georgia Is. **68** 8 15S 157 30E
New Glarus **116** 42 49N 89 38W
New Glasgow **103** 45 35N 62 36W
New Guinea **66** 4 0S 136 0E
New Hamburg **106** 43 23N 80 42W
New Hampshire □ **115** 43 40N 71 40W
New Hampton **116** 43 2N 92 20W
New Hanover **97** 29 22S 30 31E
New Hanover I. **69** 2 30S 150 10E
New Harmony **117** 38 7N 87 56W
New Haven, Conn., U.S.A. **115** 41 20N 72 54W
New Haven, Ill., U.S.A. **117** 37 55N 88 8W
New Haven, Ind., U.S.A. **117** 41 4N 85 1W
New Haven, Mich., U.S.A. **106** 42 44N 82 46W
New Haven, Mo., U.S.A. **116** 38 37N 91 13W
New Hazelton **108** 55 20N 127 30W
New Hebrides **68** 15 0S 168 0E
New Iberia **119** 30 2N 91 54W
New Ireland **69** 3 20S 151 50E
New Jersey □ **115** 40 30N 74 10W
New Kensington **114** 40 36N 79 43W
New Lexington **112** 39 40N 82 15W
New Liskeard **102** 47 31N 79 41W
New London, Conn., U.S.A. **115** 41 23N 72 8W
New London, Iowa, U.S.A. **116** 40 55N 91 24W
New London, Minn., U.S.A. **118** 45 17N 94 55W
New London, Mo., U.S.A. **116** 39 35N 91 24W
New London, Ohio, U.S.A. **114** 41 4N 82 25W
New London, Wis., U.S.A. **118** 44 23N 88 43W
New Madison **117** 39 58N 84 43W
New Madrid **119** 36 40N 89 30W
New Meadows **120** 45 0N 116 32W
New Mexico □ **110** 34 30N 106 0W
New Miami **117** 39 26N 84 32W
New Milford, Conn., U.S.A. **115** 41 35N 73 25W
New Milford, Pa., U.S.A. **115** 41 50N 75 45W
New Mollyan **77** 31 34S 149 14E
New Norcia **79** 30 57S 116 13E
New Norfolk **72** 42 46S 147 2E
New Orleans **119** 30 0N 90 5W
New Palestine **117** 39 45N 85 52W
New Paris **117** 39 55N 84 48W
New Pekin **117** 38 31N 86 2W
New Philadelphia **114** 40 29N 81 25W
New Plymouth, N.Z. **80** 39 4S 174 5E
New Plymouth, U.S.A. **120** 43 58N 116 49W
New Providence **126** 25 25N 78 35W
New Radnor **13** 52 15N 3 10W
New Richmond, Ohio, U.S.A. **117** 38 57N 84 17W
New Richmond, Wis., U.S.A. **118** 45 6N 92 34W
New Roads **119** 30 43N 91 30W
New Rochelle **115** 40 55N 73 46W
New Rockford **118** 47 44N 99 7W
New Ross **15** 52 24N 6 58W
New Salem **118** 46 51N 101 25W
New Sharon **116** 41 28N 92 39W
New Siberian Is. = Novosibirskiye Os. **41** 75 0N 142 0E
New Smyrna Beach **113** 29 0N 80 50W
New South Wales □ **73** 33 0S 146 0E
New Springs **79** 25 49S 120 1E
New Tamale **89** 9 10N 1 10W
New Town **118** 47 59N 102 30W
New Ulm **118** 44 15N 94 30W
New Vienna **117** 39 19N 83 42W
New Virginia **116** 41 11N 93 44W
New Waterford **103** 46 13N 60 4W
New Westminster **108** 49 13N 122 55W
New York □ **115** 42 40N 76 0W
New York City **115** 40 45N 74 0W
New Zealand ■ **66** 40 0S 176 0E
Newala **95** 10 58S 39 18E
Newala □ **95** 10 46S 39 20E
Newark, Del., U.S.A. **112** 39 42N 75 45W
Newark, N.J., U.S.A. **115** 40 41N 74 12W
Newark, N.Y., U.S.A. **114** 43 2N 77 10W
Newark, Ohio, U.S.A. **114** 40 5N 82 24W
Newark-on-Trent **12** 53 6N 0 48W
Newaygo **112** 43 25N 85 48W
Newberg, Mo., U.S.A. **116** 37 55N 91 54W
Newberg, Oreg., U.S.A. **120** 45 22N 123 0W
Newberry, Mich., U.S.A. **106** 46 20N 85 32W
Newberry, S.C., U.S.A. **113** 34 17N 81 37W
Newberry Springs **123** 34 50N 116 41W
Newboro L. **107** 44 38N 76 20W
Newbridge **76** 33 35S 149 22E
Newbrook **108** 54 24N 112 57W
Newburgh, Can. **107** 44 19N 76 52W
Newburgh, Ind., U.S.A. **117** 37 57N 87 24W
Newburgh, N.Y., U.S.A. **115** 41 30N 74 1W
Newbury, U.K. **13** 51 24N 1 19W
Newbury, U.S.A. **115** 44 7N 72 6W
Newburyport **115** 42 48N 70 50W
Newcastle, Austral. **76** 33 0S 151 46E
Newcastle, Can. **103** 47 1N 65 38W
Newcastle, S. Afr. **97** 27 45S 29 58E
Newcastle, U.K. **15** 54 13N 5 54W
Newcastle, Calif., U.S.A. **122** 38 50N 121 8W
Newcastle, Wyo., U.S.A. **118** 43 50N 104 12W
Newcastle Emlyn **13** 52 2N 4 29W
Newcastle Ra. **78** 15 45S 130 15E
Newcastle-under-Lyme **12** 53 2N 2 15W
Newcastle-upon-Tyne **12** 54 59N 1 37W
Newcastle Waters **72** 17 30S 133 28E
Newdegate **79** 33 6S 119 0E
Newe Etan **44** 32 30N 35 32E
Newe Sha'anan **44** 32 47N 34 59E
Newe Zohar **44** 31 9N 35 21E
Newell **118** 44 48N 103 25W
Newenham, C. **100** 58 40N 162 15W
Newfoundland **103** 48 30N 56 0W
Newfoundland □ **103** 53 0N 58 0W
Newhalem **108** 48 41N 121 16W
Newhall **123** 34 23N 118 32W
Newham **13** 51 31N 0 2E
Newhaven, Austral. **74** 38 32S 145 20E
Newhaven, U.K. **13** 50 47N 0 4E
Newkirk **119** 36 52N 97 3W
Newlyn **74** 37 23S 144 0E
Newman, Austral. **78** 23 18S 119 45E
Newman, Calif., U.S.A. **122** 37 19N 121 1W
Newman, Ill., U.S.A. **117** 39 48N 87 59W
Newman, Mt. **79** 23 20S 119 34E
Newmarket, Can. **106** 44 3N 79 28W
Newmarket, Ireland **15** 52 13N 9 0W
Newmarket, U.K. **13** 52 15N 0 23E
Newmarket, U.S.A. **115** 43 4N 70 57W
Newmerrella **75** 37 45S 148 25E
Newnan **113** 33 22N 84 48W
Newnes **76** 33 9S 150 16E
Newport, Gwent, U.K. **13** 51 35N 3 0W
Newport, I. of W., U.K. **13** 50 42N 1 18W
Newport, Salop, U.K. **13** 52 47N 2 22W
Newport, Ark., U.S.A. **119** 35 38N 91 15W
Newport, Ind., U.S.A. **117** 39 53N 87 26W
Newport, Ky., U.S.A. **117** 39 5N 84 23W
Newport, Mich., U.S.A. **106** 42 2N 83 22W
Newport, N.H., U.S.A. **115** 43 23N 72 8W
Newport, Oreg., U.S.A. **120** 44 41N 124 2W
Newport, Pa., U.S.A. **114** 40 28N 77 8W
Newport, R.I., U.S.A. **115** 41 13N 71 19W

Newport, Tenn., U.S.A.	**113**	35 59N	83 12W
Newport, Vt., U.S.A.	**115**	44 57N	72 17W
Newport, Wash., U.S.A.	**120**	48 11N	117 2W
Newport Beach	**123**	33 40N	117 58W
Newport News	**112**	37 2N	76 30W
Newquay	**13**	50 24N	5 6W
Newry, Austral.	**75**	37 59S	146 53 E
Newry, U.K.	**15**	54 10N	6 20W
Newry & Mourne □	**15**	54 10N	6 15W
Newstead	**74**	37 7S	144 4 E
Newton, Ill., U.S.A.	**117**	38 59N	88 10W
Newton, Iowa, U.S.A.	**116**	41 40N	93 3W
Newton, Mass., U.S.A.	**112**	42 21N	71 10W
Newton, Miss., U.S.A.	**119**	32 19N	89 10W
Newton, N.C., U.S.A.	**113**	35 42N	81 10W
Newton, N.J., U.S.A.	**115**	41 3N	74 46W
Newton, Texas, U.S.A.	**119**	30 54N	93 42W
Newton Abbot	**13**	50 32N	3 37W
Newton Boyd	**77**	29 45S	152 16 E
Newton Stewart	**14**	54 57N	4 30W
Newtonabbey □	**15**	54 45N	6 0W
Newtonmore	**14**	57 4N	4 7W
Newtown, U.K.	**13**	52 31N	3 19W
Newtown, U.S.A.	**116**	40 22N	93 20W
Newtownabbey	**15**	54 40N	5 55W
Newtownards	**15**	54 37N	5 40W
Newville	**114**	40 10N	77 24W
Nexon	**20**	45 41N	1 11 E
Neya	**37**	58 21N	43 49 E
Neyrīz	**47**	29 15N	54 19 E
Neyshābūr	**47**	36 10N	58 50 E
Neyyattinkara	**51**	8 26N	77 5 E
Nezhin	**36**	51 5N	31 55 E
Nezperce	**120**	46 13N	116 15W
Ngabang	**56**	0 23N	109 55 E
Ngabordamlu, Tanjung	**57**	6 56S	134 11 E
Ngaiphaipi	**52**	22 14N	93 15 E
Ngambé	**89**	5 48N	11 29 E
Ngami Depression	**96**	20 30S	22 46 E
Ngamo	**95**	19 3S	27 32 E
Nganglong Kangri	**49**	33 0N	81 0 E
Nganjuk	**57**	7 32S	111 55 E
Ngao	**54**	18 46N	99 59 E
Ngaoundéré	**92**	7 15N	13 35 E
Ngapara	**81**	44 57S	170 46 E
Ngara	**94**	2 29S	30 40 E
Ngara □	**94**	2 29S	30 40 E
Ngaruawahia	**80**	37 42S	175 11 E
Ngatapa	**80**	38 32S	177 45 E
Ngathainggyaung	**52**	17 24N	95 5 E
Ngau	**68**	18 2S	179 18 E
Ngauruhoe, Mt.	**80**	39 13S	175 45 E
Ngawi	**57**	7 24S	111 26 E
Nggamea	**68**	16 46S	179 46W
Nggela	**68**	9 5S	160 15 E
Nghia Lo	**54**	21 33N	104 28 E
Ngoma	**95**	13 8S	33 45 E
Ngomahura	**95**	20 26S	30 43 E
Ngomba	**95**	8 20S	32 53 E
Ngonye Falls	**96**	16 35S	23 30 E
Ngop	**91**	6 17N	30 9 E
Ngoring Hu	**62**	34 55N	97 5 E
Ngorkou	**88**	15 40N	3 41W
Ngorongoro	**94**	3 11S	35 32 E
Ngozi	**94**	2 54S	29 50 E
Ngudu	**94**	2 58S	33 25 E
N'Guigmi	**85**	14 20N	13 20 E
Ngunga	**94**	3 37S	33 37 E
Nguru	**89**	12 56N	10 29 E
Nguru Mts.	**94**	6 0S	37 30 E
Nguyen Binh	**54**	22 39N	105 56 E
Ngwenya	**97**	26 11S	31 7 E
Nha Trang	**55**	12 16N	109 10 E
Nhacoongo	**97**	24 18S	35 14 E
Nhambiquara	**137**	12 50S	59 49W
Nhamundá	**135**	2 14S	56 43W
Nhamundá →	**135**	2 12S	56 41W
Nhangutazi, L.	**97**	24 0S	34 30 E
Nhecolândia	**137**	19 17S	56 58W
Nhill	**74**	36 18S	141 40 E
Nho Quan	**54**	20 18N	105 45 E
Nhulunbuy	**72**	12 10S	137 20 E
Nia-nia	**94**	1 30N	27 40 E
Niafounké	**88**	16 0N	4 5W
Niagara	**112**	45 45N	88 0W
Niagara Falls, Can.	**106**	43 7N	79 5W
Niagara Falls, U.S.A.	**114**	43 5N	79 0W
Niagara-on-the-Lake	**106**	43 15N	79 4W
Niah	**56**	3 58N	113 46 E
Niamey	**89**	13 27N	2 6 E
Nianforando	**88**	9 37N	10 36W
Nianfors	**10**	61 36N	16 46 E
Niangala	**77**	31 18S	151 25 E
Niangara	**94**	3 42N	27 50 E
Niangua →	**116**	38 0N	92 48W
Nias	**56**	1 0N	97 30 E
Niassa □	**95**	13 30S	36 0 E
Nibbiano	**26**	44 54N	9 20 E
Nibe	**11**	56 59N	9 38 E
Nicaragua ■	**126**	11 40N	85 30W
Nicaragua, Lago de	**126**	12 0N	85 30W
Nicastro	**29**	39 0N	16 18 E
Nice	**21**	43 42N	7 14 E
Niceville	**113**	30 30N	86 30W
Nichinan	**64**	31 38N	131 23 E
Nicholás, Canal	**126**	23 30N	80 5W
Nicholasville, U.S.A.	**112**	37 54N	84 31W
Nicholasville, U.S.A.	**117**	37 53N	84 34W
Nichols	**115**	42 1N	76 22W
Nicholson, Austral.	**78**	18 2S	128 54 E
Nicholson, U.S.A.	**115**	41 37N	75 47W
Nicholson →	**72**	17 31S	139 36 E
Nicholson Ra.	**79**	27 15S	116 45 E
Nickerie □	**135**	4 0N	57 0W
Nickerie →	**135**	5 58N	57 0W
Nicobar Is.	**42**	9 0N	93 0 E
Nicoclí	**134**	8 26N	76 48W
Nicola	**108**	50 12N	120 40W
Nicolet	**105**	46 17N	72 35W
Nicolls Town	**126**	25 8N	78 0W
Nicosia, Cyprus	**46**	35 10N	33 25 E
Nicosia, Italy	**29**	37 45N	14 22 E
Nicótera	**29**	38 33N	15 57 E
Nicoya	**126**	10 9N	85 27W
Nicoya, G. de	**126**	10 0N	85 0W
Nicoya, Pen. de	**126**	9 45N	85 40W
Nidd →	**12**	54 1N	1 32W
Nidda	**30**	50 24N	9 2 E
Nidda →	**31**	50 6N	8 34 E
Nidzica	**32**	53 25N	20 28 E
Niebüll	**30**	54 47N	8 49 E
Nied →	**19**	49 23N	6 40 E
Niederaula	**30**	50 48N	9 37 E
Niederbronn	**19**	48 57N	7 39 E
Niedere Tauern	**33**	47 20N	14 0 E
Niedermarsberg	**30**	51 28N	8 52 E
Niedersachsen □	**30**	52 45N	9 0 E
Niellé	**88**	10 5N	5 38W
Niemba	**94**	5 58S	28 24 E
Nienburg	**30**	52 38N	9 15 E
Niers →	**30**	51 45N	5 58 E
Niesky	**30**	51 18N	14 48 E
Nieuw Amsterdam	**135**	5 53N	55 5W
Nieuw Nickerie	**135**	6 0N	56 59W
Nieuwpoort	**16**	51 8N	2 45 E
Nieves	**22**	42 7N	8 26W
Nièvre □	**19**	47 10N	3 40 E
Nigata	**64**	34 13N	132 39 E
Niğde	**46**	38 0N	34 40 E
Nigel	**97**	26 27S	28 25 E
Niger ■	**89**	13 30N	10 0 E
Niger □	**89**	10 0N	5 0 E
Niger →	**89**	5 33N	6 33 E
Nigeria ■	**89**	8 30N	8 0 E
Nightcaps	**81**	45 57S	168 2 E
Nigríta	**35**	40 56N	23 29 E
Nihtaur	**49**	29 20N	78 23 E
Nii-Jima	**65**	34 20N	139 15 E
Niigata	**63**	37 58N	139 0 E
Niihama	**64**	33 55N	133 16 E
Niihau	**110**	21 55N	160 10W
Niimi	**64**	34 59N	133 28 E
Níjar	**25**	36 53N	2 15W
Nijkerk	**16**	52 13N	5 30 E
Nijmegen	**16**	51 50N	5 52 E
Nijverdal	**16**	52 22N	6 28 E
Nike	**89**	6 26N	7 29 E
Nikel	**8**	69 24N	30 12 E
Nikiniki	**57**	9 49S	124 30 E
Nikki	**89**	9 58N	3 12 E
Nikkō	**65**	36 45N	139 35 E
Nikolayev	**38**	46 58N	32 0 E
Nikolayevsk	**37**	50 0N	45 35 E
Nikolayevsk-na-Amur	**41**	53 8N	140 44 E
Nikolsk	**37**	59 30N	45 28 E
Nikolskoye	**41**	55 12N	166 0 E
Nikopol, Bulg.	**34**	43 43N	24 54 E
Nikopol, U.S.S.R.	**38**	47 35N	34 25 E
Niksar	**38**	40 31N	37 2 E
Nīkshahr	**47**	26 15N	60 10 E
Nikšić	**33**	42 50N	18 57 E
Nîl el Abyad →	**91**	15 38N	32 31 E
Nîl el Azraq →	**91**	15 38N	32 31 E
Nîl, Nahr en →	**90**	30 10N	31 6 E
Niland	**123**	33 16N	115 30W
Nile □	**94**	2 0N	31 30 E
Nile Delta	**90**	31 40N	31 0 E
Nile → = Nîl, Nahr en →	**90**	30 10N	31 6 E
Niles	**114**	41 8N	80 40W
Nilgiri Hills	**51**	11 30N	76 30 E
Nilo Peçanha	**139**	13 37S	39 6W
Nimach = Neemuch	**48**	24 30N	74 56 E
Nimbahera	**48**	24 37N	74 45 E
Nimbin	**77**	28 36S	153 13 E
Nîmes	**21**	43 50N	4 23 E
Nimfaíon, Ákra-	**35**	40 5N	24 20 E
Nimmitabel	**75**	36 29S	149 15 E
Nimneryskiy	**41**	57 50N	125 10 E
Nimrod Glacier	**143**	82 27S	161 0 E
Nimule	**91**	3 32N	32 3 E
Nin	**27**	44 16N	15 12 E
Nindigully	**73**	28 21S	148 50 E
Ninemile	**108**	56 0N	130 7W
Ninety Mile Beach, The	**75**	38 15S	147 24 E
Nineveh	**46**	36 25N	43 10 E
Ning Xian	**60**	35 30N	107 58 E
Ningaloo	**78**	22 41S	113 41 E
Ning'an	**61**	44 22N	129 20 E
Ningbo	**59**	29 51N	121 28 E
Ningcheng	**61**	41 32N	119 53 E
Ningde	**59**	26 38N	119 23 E
Ningdu	**59**	26 25N	115 59 E
Ninggang	**59**	26 42N	113 55 E
Ningguo	**59**	30 35N	119 0 E
Ninghai	**59**	29 15N	121 27 E
Ninghua	**59**	26 14N	116 45 E
Ningjin	**60**	37 35N	114 57 E
Ningjing Shan	**58**	30 0N	98 20 E
Ninglang	**58**	27 20N	100 55 E
Ningling	**60**	34 25N	115 22 E
Ningming	**58**	22 8N	107 4 E
Ningnan	**58**	27 5N	102 36 E
Ningpo = Ningbo	**59**	29 51N	121 28 E
Ningqiang	**58**	32 47N	106 15 E
Ningshan	**58**	33 21N	108 21 E
Ningsia Hui A.R. = Ningxia Huizu Zizhiqu □	**60**	38 0N	106 0 E
Ningwu	**60**	39 0N	112 18 E
Ningxia Huizu Zizhiqu □	**60**	38 0N	106 0 E
Ningxiang	**59**	28 15N	112 30 E
Ningyang	**60**	35 47N	116 45 E
Ningyuan	**59**	25 37N	111 57 E
Ninh Binh	**54**	20 15N	105 55 E
Ninh Giang	**54**	20 44N	106 24 E
Ninh Hoa	**54**	12 30N	109 7 E
Ninh Ma	**54**	12 48N	109 21 E
Ninove	**16**	50 51N	4 2 E
Nioaque	**141**	21 5S	55 50W
Niobrara	**118**	42 48N	97 59W
Niobrara →	**118**	42 45N	98 0W
Nioki	**92**	2 47S	17 40 E
Niono	**88**	14 15N	6 0W
Nioro du Rip	**88**	13 40N	15 50W
Nioro du Sahel	**88**	15 15N	9 30W
Niort	**20**	46 19N	0 29W
Nipa	**69**	6 9S	143 29 E
Nipani	**51**	16 20N	74 25 E
Nipawin	**109**	53 20N	104 0W
Nipawin Prov. Park	**109**	54 0N	104 37W
Nipigon	**102**	49 0N	88 17W
Nipigon, L.	**102**	49 50N	88 30W
Nipin →	**109**	55 46N	109 2W
Nipishish L.	**103**	54 12N	60 45W
Nipissing L.	**106**	46 20N	80 0W
Nipomo	**123**	35 4N	120 29W
Nipton	**123**	35 28N	115 16W
Niquelândia	**139**	14 33S	48 23W
Nira →	**50**	17 58N	75 8 E
Nirasaki	**65**	35 42N	138 27 E
Nirmal	**50**	19 3N	78 20 E
Nirmali	**49**	26 20N	86 35 E
Niš	**33**	43 19N	21 58 E
Nisa	**23**	39 30N	7 41W
Nisab	**45**	14 25N	46 29 E
Nišava →	**33**	43 20N	21 46 E
Niscemi	**29**	37 8N	14 21 E
Nishi-Sonogi-Hantō	**64**	32 55N	129 45 E
Nishinomiya	**65**	34 45N	135 20 E
Nishinoomote	**63**	30 43N	130 59 E
Nishio	**65**	34 52N	137 3 E
Nishiwaki	**64**	34 59N	134 58 E
Nísiros	**35**	36 35N	27 12 E
Niskibi →	**102**	56 29N	88 9W
Nisqually →	**122**	47 6N	122 42W
Nissafors	**11**	57 25N	13 37 E
Nissan →	**11**	56 40N	12 51 E
Nissedal	**10**	59 10N	8 30 E
Nisser	**10**	59 7N	8 28 E
Nissum Fjord	**11**	56 20N	8 11 E
Nisutlin →	**108**	60 14N	132 34W
Nitchequon	**103**	53 10N	70 58W
Niterói	**139**	22 52S	43 0W
Nith →, Can.	**106**	43 12N	80 23W
Nith →, U.K.	**14**	55 20N	3 5W
Nitra	**33**	48 19N	18 4 E
Nittedal	**10**	60 1N	10 57 E
Nittendau	**31**	49 12N	12 16 E
Niue I. (Savage I.)	**67**	19 2S	169 54W
Niulan Jiang →	**58**	27 30N	103 5 E
Niut	**56**	0 55N	110 6 E
Niutou Shan	**59**	29 5N	121 59 E
Niuzhuang	**61**	40 58N	122 28 E
Nivelles	**16**	50 35N	4 20 E
Nivernais	**19**	47 0N	3 40 E
Nixon, Nev., U.S.A.	**120**	39 54N	119 22W
Nixon, Tex., U.S.A.	**119**	29 17N	97 45W
Nizam Sagar	**50**	18 10N	77 58 E
Nizamabad	**50**	18 45N	78 7 E
Nizamghat	**52**	28 20N	95 45 E
Nizhne Kolymsk	**41**	68 34N	160 55 E
Nizhne-Vartovskoye	**40**	60 56N	76 38 E
Nizhneangarsk	**41**	55 47N	109 30 E
Nizhnegorskiy	**38**	45 27N	34 38 E
Nizhneudinsk	**41**	54 54N	99 3 E
Nizhneyansk	**41**	71 26N	136 4 E
Nizhniy Lomov	**37**	53 34N	43 38 E
Nizhniy Novgorod = Gorkiy	**37**	56 20N	44 0 E
Nizhniy Tagil	**40**	57 55N	59 57 E
Nizhnyaya Tunguska →	**41**	64 20N	93 0 E
Nizip	**46**	37 5N	37 50 E
Nizké Tatry	**32**	48 55N	20 0 E
Nizza Monferrato	**26**	44 46N	8 22 E
Njakwa	**95**	11 1S	33 56 E
Njanji	**95**	14 25S	31 46 E
Njinjo	**95**	8 48S	38 54 E
Njombe	**95**	9 20S	34 50 E
Njombe □	**95**	9 20S	34 49 E
Njombe →	**94**	6 56S	35 6 E
Nkambe	**89**	6 35N	10 40 E
Nkana	**95**	12 50S	28 8 E
Nkawkaw	**89**	6 36N	0 49W
Nkhota Kota	**95**	12 56S	34 15 E
Nkongsamba	**92**	4 55N	9 55 E
Nkunka	**95**	14 57S	25 58 E
Nkwanta	**88**	6 10N	2 10W
Nmaushahr	**49**	33 11N	74 15 E
Noakhali = Maijdi	**52**	22 50N	91 10 E
Noatak	**100**	67 32N	162 59W
Nobel	**106**	45 25N	80 6W
Nobeoka	**64**	32 36N	131 41 E
Nōbi-Heiya	**65**	35 15N	136 45 E
Noble	**117**	38 42N	88 14W
Noblejas	**24**	39 58N	3 26W
Noblesville	**117**	40 1N	85 59W
Noce →	**26**	46 9N	11 4 E
Nocera Inferiore	**29**	40 45N	14 37 E
Nocera Terinese	**29**	39 2N	16 9 E
Nocera Umbra	**27**	43 8N	12 47 E
Nochixtlán	**125**	17 28N	97 14W
Noci	**29**	40 47N	17 7 E
Nockatunga	**73**	27 42S	142 42 E
Nocona	**119**	33 48N	97 45W
Noda	**65**	35 56N	139 52 E
Noel	**119**	36 36N	94 29W
Noelville	**106**	46 8N	80 26W
Nogales, Mexico	**124**	31 20N	110 56W
Nogales, U.S.A.	**121**	31 33N	110 56W
Nōgata	**64**	33 48N	130 44 E
Nogent-en-Bassigny	**19**	48 0N	5 20 E
Nogent-le-Rotrou	**18**	48 20N	0 50 E
Nogent-sur-Seine	**19**	48 30N	3 30 E
Noggerup	**79**	33 32S	116 5 E
Noginsk, Moskva, U.S.S.R.	**37**	55 50N	38 25 E
Noginsk, Sib., U.S.S.R.	**41**	64 30N	90 50 E
Nogoa →	**72**	23 40S	147 55 E
Nogoyá	**140**	32 24S	59 48W
Nogueira de Ramuin	**22**	42 21N	7 43W
Noguera Pallaresa →	**24**	42 15N	1 0 E
Noguera Ribagorzana →	**24**	41 40N	0 43 E
Nohar	**48**	29 11N	74 49 E
Noire →	**104**	45 54N	76 57W
Noire, Mt.	**18**	48 11N	3 40W
Noirétable	**20**	45 48N	3 46 E
Noirmoutier	**18**	47 0N	2 15W
Noirmoutier, Î. de	**18**	46 58N	2 10W
Nojane	**96**	23 15S	20 14 E
Nojima-Zaki	**65**	34 54N	139 53 E
Nok Kundi	**47**	28 50N	62 45 E
Nokaneng	**96**	19 40S	22 17 E
Nokhtuysk	**41**	60 0N	117 45 E
Nokomis, Can.	**109**	51 35N	105 0W
Nokomis, U.S.A.	**116**	39 18N	89 18W
Nokomis L.	**109**	57 0N	103 0W
Nokou	**92**	14 35N	14 47 E
Nol	**11**	57 56N	12 5 E
Nola, C. Afr. Rep.	**92**	3 35N	16 4 E
Nola, Italy	**29**	40 54N	14 29 E
Nolay	**19**	46 58N	4 35 E
Noli, C. di	**26**	44 12N	8 26 E
Noma Omuramba →	**96**	18 52S	20 53 E
Noma-Saki	**64**	31 25N	130 7 E
Nomad	**69**	6 19S	142 13 E
Noman L.	**109**	62 15N	108 55W
Nombre de Dios	**126**	9 34N	79 28W
Nome	**100**	64 30N	165 24W
Nominingue	**104**	46 24N	75 2W
Nominingue, L.	**104**	46 26N	74 59W
Nomo-Zaki	**64**	32 35N	129 44 E
Nomuka	**68**	20 17S	174 48W
Nomuka Group	**68**	20 20S	174 48W
Nonacho L.	**109**	61 42N	109 40W
Nonancourt	**18**	48 47N	1 11 E
Nonant-le-Pin	**18**	48 42N	0 12 E
Nonda	**72**	20 40S	142 28 E

Nong Chang **54** 15 23N 99 51 E
Nong Het **54** 19 29N 103 59 E
Nong Khai **54** 17 50N 102 46 E
Nong'an **61** 44 25N 125 5 E
Nonoava **124** 27 28N 106 44W
Nonthaburi **54** 13 51N 100 34 E
Nontron **20** 45 31N 0 40 E
Noojee **74** 37 57S 146 1 E
Noonamah **78** 12 40S 131 4 E
Noonan **118** 48 51N 102 59W
Noondoo **73** 28 35S 148 30 E
Noorat **74** 38 12S 142 55 E
Noord Brabant □ **16** 51 40N 5 0 E
Noord Holland □ **16** 52 30N 4 45 E
Noordbeveland **16** 51 35N 3 50 E
Noordoostpolder **16** 52 45N 5 45 E
Noordwijk aan Zee **16** 52 14N 4 26 E
Noorinbee **75** 37 32S 149 10 E
Nootka **108** 49 38N 126 38W
Nootka I. **108** 49 32N 126 42W
Noqui **92** 5 55S 13 30 E
Nora, Ethiopia **91** 16 6N 40 4 E
Nora, Sweden **10** 59 32N 15 2 E
Nora Springs **116** 43 9N 92 1W
Noradjuha **74** 36 50S 141 58 E
Norah Hd. **76** 33 18S 151 32 E
Noranda **104** 48 20N 79 0W
Norberg **10** 60 4N 15 56 E
Norborne **116** 39 18N 93 40W
Nórcia **27** 42 50N 13 5 E
Norco **123** 33 56N 117 33W
Nord □ **19** 50 15N 3 30 E
Nord-Ostee Kanal **30** 54 5N 9 15 E
Nord-Süd Kanal **30** 53 0N 10 32 E
Nord-Trøndelag fylke □ **8** 64 20N 12 0 E
Nordagutu **10** 59 25N 9 20 E
Nordaustlandet, Arctica **144** 79 14N 23 0 E
Nordaustlandet, Svalb. **144** 79 14N 23 0 E
Nordborg **11** 55 5N 9 50 E
Nordby, Århus, Denmark **11** 55 58N 10 32 E
Nordby, Ribe, Denmark **11** 55 27N 8 24 E
Norddeich **30** 53 37N 7 10 E
Nordegg **108** 52 29N 116 5W
Norden **30** 53 35N 7 12 E
Nordenham **30** 53 29N 8 28 E
Norderhov **10** 60 7N 10 17 E
Norderney **30** 53 42N 7 15 E
Nordfriesische Inseln **30** 54 40N 8 20 E
Nordhausen **30** 51 29N 10 47 E
Nordhorn **30** 52 27N 7 4 E
Nordjyllands Amtskommune □ **11** 57 0N 10 0 E
Nordkapp, Norway **8** 71 10N 25 44 E
Nordkapp, Svalb. **144** 80 31N 20 0 E
Nordkinn **6** 71 3N 27 40 E
Nordland fylke □ **8** 65 40N 13 0 E
Nördlingen **31** 48 50N 10 30 E
Nordrhein-Westfalen □ **30** 51 45N 7 30 E
Nordstrand **30** 54 27N 8 50 E
Nordvik **41** 74 2N 111 32 E
Nore **10** 60 10N 9 0 E
Nore → **15** 52 40N 7 20W
Norefjell **10** 60 16N 9 29 E
Norembega **102** 48 59N 80 43W
Noresund **10** 60 11N 9 37 E
Norfolk, Nebr., U.S.A. **118** 42 3N 97 25W
Norfolk, Va., U.S.A. **112** 36 40N 76 15W
Norfolk □ **12** 52 39N 1 0 E
Norfolk Broads **12** 52 30N 1 15 E
Norfolk I. **66** 28 58S 168 3 E
Norfork Res. **119** 36 13N 92 15W
Norilsk **41** 69 20N 88 6 E
Norley **73** 27 45S 143 48 E
Normal **116** 40 30N 89 0W
Norman **119** 35 12N 97 30W
Norman → **72** 17 28S 140 49 E
Norman Wells **100** 65 17N 126 51W
Normanby **80** 39 32S 174 18 E
Normanby → **72** 14 23S 144 10 E
Normanby I. **69** 10 55S 151 5 E
Normandie **18** 48 45N 0 10 E
Normandie, Collines de **18** 48 55N 0 45W
Normandin **105** 48 49N 72 31W
Normandy = Normandie **18** 48 45N 0 10 E
Normanhurst, Mt. **79** 25 4S 122 30 E
Normanton **72** 17 40S 141 10 E
Normétal **104** 49 0N 79 22W
Norna, Mt. **72** 20 55S 140 42 E
Nornalup **79** 35 0S 116 48 E
Norquay **109** 51 53N 102 5W
Ñorquinco **142** 41 51S 70 55W
Norrahammar **11** 57 43N 14 7 E
Norrbottens län □ **8** 66 58N 20 0 E
Nørre Åby **11** 55 27N 9 52 E
Nørre Nebel **11** 55 47N 8 17 E
Nørresundby **11** 57 5N 9 52 E
Norris **120** 45 40N 111 40W
Norris City **117** 37 59N 88 20W
Norristown **115** 40 9N 75 21W
Norrköping **11** 58 37N 16 11 E
Norrtälje **10** 59 46N 18 42 E
Norseman **79** 32 8S 121 43 E
Norsholm **11** 58 31N 15 59 E
Norsk **41** 52 30N 130 0 E
Norsup **68** 16 3S 167 24 E
Norte de Santander □ **134** 8 0N 73 0W
Norte, Pta. **142** 42 5S 63 46W
Nortelândia **137** 14 25S 56 48W
North Adams **115** 42 42N 73 6W
North America **98** 40 0N 100 0W
North Atlantic Ocean **128** 30 0N 50 0W
North Baltimore **117** 41 11N 83 41W
North Battleford **109** 52 50N 108 17W
North Bay **106** 46 20N 79 30W
North Belcher Is. **102** 56 50N 79 50W
North Bend, Can. **108** 49 50N 121 27W
North Bend, Oreg., U.S.A. **120** 43 28N 124 14W
North Bend, Pa., U.S.A. **114** 41 20N 77 42W
North Bend, Wash., U.S.A. **122** 47 30N 121 47W
North Berwick, U.K. **14** 56 4N 2 44W
North Berwick, U.S.A. **115** 43 18N 70 43W
North Buganda □ **94** 1 0N 32 0 E
North Canadian → **119** 35 17N 95 31W
North C., Antarct. **143** 71 0S 166 0 E
North C., Can. **103** 47 2N 60 20W
North C., N.Z. **80** 34 23S 173 4 E
North C., P.N.G. **69** 2 32S 150 50 E
North Caribou L. **102** 52 50N 90 40W
North Carolina □ **113** 35 30N 80 0W
North Channel, Br. Is. **14** 55 0N 5 30W
North Channel, Can. **106** 46 0N 83 0W
North Chicago **117** 42 19N 87 50W
North College Hill **117** 39 13N 84 33W
North Dakota □ **118** 47 30N 100 0W
North Dandalup **79** 32 30S 115 57 E
North Down □ **15** 54 40N 5 45W
North Downs **13** 51 17N 0 30 E
North East **114** 42 17N 79 50W
North East Frontier Agency = Arunachal Pradesh **52** 28 0N 95 0 E
North East Providence Chan. **126** 26 0N 76 0W
North Eastern □ **94** 1 30N 40 0 E
North English **116** 41 31N 92 5W
North Esk → **14** 56 44N 2 25W
North European Plain **6** 55 0N 20 0 E
North Fabius → **116** 39 54N 91 28W
North Foreland **13** 51 22N 1 28 E
North Fork **122** 37 14N 119 21W
North Fork, American → **122** 38 45N 121 8W
North Fork, Feather → **122** 39 17N 121 38W
North Fork, Salt → **116** 39 26N 91 53W
North Frisian Is. = Nordfr'sche Inseln **30** 54 50N 8 20 E
North Gower **107** 45 8N 75 43W
North Hatley **105** 45 17N 71 58W
North Henik L. **109** 61 45N 97 40W
North Highlands **122** 38 40N 121 25W
North Horr **94** 3 20N 37 8 E
North I., Kenya **94** 4 5N 36 5 E
North I., N.Z. **81** 38 0S 175 0 E
North Island **80** 38 0S 176 0 E
North Judson **117** 41 13N 86 46W
North Kansas City **116** 39 9N 94 35W
North Kingsville **114** 41 53N 80 42W
North Knife → **109** 58 53N 94 45W
North Koel → **49** 24 45N 83 50 E
North Korea ■ **61** 40 0N 127 0 E
North Lakhimpur **52** 27 14N 94 7 E
North Las Vegas **123** 36 15N 115 6W
North Liberty **117** 41 32N 86 26W
North Loup → **118** 41 17N 98 23W
North Manchester **117** 41 0N 85 46W
North Minch **14** 58 5N 5 55W
North Nahanni → **108** 62 15N 123 20W
North Ossetian A.S.S.R. □ **39** 43 30N 44 30 E
North Palisade **122** 37 6N 118 32W
North Platte **118** 41 10N 100 50W
North Platte → **118** 41 15N 100 45W
North Pt., Can. **103** 47 5N 64 0W
North Pt., N. Hebr. **68** 14 56S 168 6 E
North Pole **144** 90 0N 0 0 E
North Portal **109** 49 0N 102 33W
North Powder **120** 45 2N 117 59W
North Ronaldsay **14** 59 20N 2 30W
North Sea **6** 56 0N 4 0 E
North Sporades = Voríai Sporádhes **35** 39 15N 23 30 E
North Sydney **103** 46 12N 60 15W
North Thompson → **108** 50 40N 120 20W
North Tonawanda **114** 43 5N 78 50W
North Troy **115** 44 59N 72 24W
North Truchas Pk. **121** 36 0N 105 30W
North Twin I. **102** 53 20N 80 0W
North Tyne → **12** 54 59N 2 7W
North Uist **14** 57 40N 7 15W
North Vancouver **108** 49 25N 123 3W
North Vernon **117** 39 0N 85 35W
North Wabasca L. **108** 56 0N 113 55W
North Walsham **12** 52 49N 1 22 E
North Webster **117** 41 25N 85 48W
North West C. **78** 21 45S 114 9 E
North West Christmas I. Ridge **67** 6 30N 165 0W
North West Highlands **14** 57 35N 5 2W
North West Providence Channel **126** 26 0N 78 0W
North West River **103** 53 30N 60 10W
North Western □ **95** 13 30S 25 30 E
North York Moors **12** 54 25N 0 50W
North Yorkshire □ **12** 54 15N 1 25W
Northallerton **12** 54 20N 1 26W
Northampton, Austral. **79** 28 27S 114 33 E
Northampton, U.K. **13** 52 14N 0 54W
Northampton, Mass., U.S.A. **115** 42 22N 72 31W
Northampton, Pa., U.S.A. **115** 40 38N 75 24W
Northampton □ **13** 52 16N 0 55W
Northampton Downs **72** 24 35S 145 48 E
Northbridge **115** 42 12N 71 40W
Northcliffe **79** 34 39S 116 7 E
Northeim **30** 51 42N 10 0 E
Northern □, Malawi **95** 11 0S 34 0 E
Northern □, Uganda **94** 3 5N 32 30 E
Northern □, Zambia **95** 10 30S 31 0 E
Northern Circars **50** 17 30N 82 30 E
Northern Indian L. **109** 57 20N 97 20W
Northern Ireland □ **15** 54 45N 7 0W
Northern Light, L. **102** 48 15N 90 39W
Northern Province □ **88** 9 15N 11 30W
Northern Territory □ **78** 16 0S 133 0 E
Northfield **118** 44 30N 93 10W
Northome **118** 47 53N 94 15W
Northport, Ala., U.S.A. **113** 33 15N 87 35W
Northport, Mich., U.S.A. **112** 45 8N 85 39W
Northport, Wash., U.S.A. **120** 48 55N 117 48W
Northumberland □ **12** 55 12N 2 0W
Northumberland, C. **73** 38 5S 140 40 E
Northumberland Is. **72** 21 30S 149 50 E
Northumberland Str. **103** 46 20N 64 0W
Northwest Territories □ **100** 65 0N 100 0W
Northwich **12** 53 16N 2 30W
Northwood, Iowa, U.S.A. **118** 43 27N 93 0W
Northwood, N.D., U.S.A. **118** 47 44N 97 30W
Norton, U.S.A. **118** 39 50N 99 53W
Norton, Zimb.-Rhod. **95** 17 52S 30 40 E
Norton Sd. **100** 64 0N 164 0W
Norton Shores **117** 43 8N 86 15W
Nortorf **30** 54 14N 9 47 E
Norwalk, Calif., U.S.A. **123** 33 54N 118 5W
Norwalk, Conn., U.S.A. **115** 41 9N 73 25W
Norwalk, Ohio, U.S.A. **114** 41 13N 82 38W
Norway **112** 45 46N 87 57W
Norway ■ **8** 67 0N 11 0 E
Norway House **109** 53 59N 97 50W
Norwegian Dependency **143** 66 0S 15 0 E
Norwegian Sea **128** 66 0N 1 0 E
Norwich, Can. **106** 42 59N 80 36W
Norwich, U.K. **12** 52 38N 1 17 E
Norwich, Conn., U.S.A. **115** 41 33N 72 5W
Norwich, N.Y., U.S.A. **115** 42 32N 75 30W
Norwood, Can. **107** 44 23N 77 59W
Norwood, Mass., U.S.A. **115** 42 10N 71 10W
Norwood, Ohio, U.S.A. **117** 39 10N 84 27W
Noshiro **63** 40 12N 140 0 E
Nosok **40** 70 10N 82 20 E
Nosovka **36** 50 50N 31 37 E
Nosratābād **47** 29 55N 60 0 E
Noss Hd. **14** 58 29N 3 4W
Nossa Senhora da Glória **138** 10 14S 37 25W
Nossa Senhora das Dores **138** 10 29S 37 13W
Nossa Senhora do Livramento **137** 15 48S 56 22W
Nossebro **11** 58 12N 12 43 E
Nossob **96** 22 15S 17 48 E
Nossob → **96** 26 55S 20 37 E
Nosy Varika **97** 20 35S 48 32 E
Noteć → **32** 52 44N 15 26 E
Notigi Dam **109** 56 40N 99 10W
Notikewin → **108** 57 2N 117 38W
Notios Evvoïkos Kólpos **35** 38 20N 24 0 E
Noto **29** 36 52N 15 4 E
Noto, G. di **29** 36 50N 15 10 E
Notodden **10** 59 35N 9 17 E
Notre-Dame **103** 46 18N 64 46W
Notre Dame B. **103** 49 45N 55 30W
Notre Dame de Koartac **101** 60 55N 69 40W
Notre-Dame-de-la-Doré **105** 48 43N 72 39W
Notre-Dame-des-Bois **105** 45 24N 71 4W
Notre-Dame-du-Bon-Conseil **105** 46 0N 72 21W
Notre Dame du Lac **106** 46 18N 80 11W
Notre-Dame-du-Lac **105** 47 36N 68 48W
Notre-Dame-du-Laus **104** 46 5N 75 37W
Notre-Dame-du-Nord **104** 47 36N 79 30W
Notre-Dame-du-Portage **105** 47 46N 69 37W
Nottawasaga B. **106** 44 35N 80 15W
Nottaway → **102** 51 22N 78 55W
Nøtterøy **10** 59 14N 10 24 E
Nottingham **12** 52 57N 1 10W
Nottingham □ **12** 53 10N 1 0W
Nottoway → **112** 36 33N 76 55W
Notwani → **96** 23 35S 26 58 E
Nouadhibou **84** 20 54N 17 0W
Nouadhibou, Ras **84** 20 50N 17 0W
Nouakchott **88** 18 9N 15 58W
Noumea **68** 22 17S 166 30 E
Noupoort **96** 31 10S 24 57 E
Nouveau Comptoir (Paint Hills) **102** 53 0N 78 49W
Nouvelle Calédonie **68** 21 0S 165 0 E
Nouzonville **19** 49 48N 4 44 E
Nová Baňa **33** 48 28N 18 39 E
Nová Bystřice **32** 49 2N 15 8 E
Nova Chaves **92** 10 31S 21 15 E
Nova Cruz **138** 6 28S 35 25W
Nova Era **139** 19 45S 43 3W
Nova Esperança **141** 23 8S 52 24W
Nova Friburgo **139** 22 16S 42 30W
Nova Gaia **92** 10 10S 17 35 E
Nova Gradiška **33** 45 17N 17 28 E
Nova Granada **139** 20 30S 49 20W
Nova Iguaçu **139** 22 45S 43 28W
Nova Iorque **138** 7 0S 44 5W
Nova Lamego **88** 12 19N 14 11W
Nova Lima **141** 19 59S 43 51W
Nova Lisboa = Huambo **93** 12 42S 15 44 E
Nova Lusitânia **95** 19 50S 34 34 E
Nova Mambone **97** 21 0S 35 3 E
Nova Mesto **27** 45 47N 15 12 E
Nova Ponte **139** 19 8S 47 41W
Nova Scotia □ **103** 45 10N 63 0W
Nova Sofala **97** 20 7S 34 42 E
Nova Venécia **139** 18 45S 40 24W
Nova Vida **137** 10 11S 62 47W
Nova Zagora **34** 42 32N 25 59 E
Noval Iorque **138** 6 48S 44 0W
Novaleksandrovskaya **39** 45 29N 41 17 E
Novannenskiy **37** 50 32N 42 39 E
Novar **106** 45 27N 79 15W
Novara **26** 45 27N 8 36 E
Novata **122** 38 6N 122 35W
Novaya Kakhovka **38** 46 42N 33 27 E
Novaya Lyalya **40** 59 10N 60 35 E
Novaya Sibir, O. **41** 75 10N 150 0 E
Novaya Zemlya **40** 75 0N 56 0 E
Novelda **25** 38 24N 0 45W
Novellara **26** 44 50N 10 43 E
Novelty **116** 40 1N 92 12W
Noventa Vicentina **27** 45 18N 11 30 E
Novgorod **36** 58 30N 31 25 E
Novgorod-Severskiy **36** 52 2N 33 10 E
Novi Bečej **33** 45 36N 20 10 E
Novi Grad **27** 45 19N 13 33 E
Novi Krichim **34** 42 8N 24 31 E
Novi Lígure **26** 44 45N 8 47 E
Novi-Pazar **34** 43 25N 27 15 E
Novi Pazar **33** 43 12N 20 28 E
Novi Sad **33** 45 18N 19 52 E
Novi Vinodolski **27** 45 10N 14 48 E
Novigrad **27** 44 10N 15 32 E
Novinger **116** 40 14N 92 43W
Novo Acôrdo **138** 10 10S 46 48W
Novo Aripuanã **135** 5 8S 60 22W
Nôvo Cruzeiro **139** 17 29S 41 53W
Nôvo Hamburgo **141** 29 37S 51 7W

Novo Horizonte	139	21 25S	49 10W
Novo Redondo	92	11 10S	13 48E
Novo-Zavidovskiy	37	56 32N	36 29E
Novoakrainka	38	48 25N	31 30E
Novoaltaysk	40	53 30N	84 0E
Novoazovsk	38	47 15N	38 4E
Novobelitsa	36	52 27N	31 2E
Novobogatinskoye	39	47 20N	51 11E
Novocherkassk	39	47 27N	40 5E
Novodevichye	37	53 37N	48 50E
Novograd-Volynskiy	36	50 34N	27 35E
Novogrudok	36	53 40N	25 50E
Novokayakent	39	42 30N	47 52E
Novokazalinsk	40	45 48N	62 6E
Novokhopersk	37	51 5N	41 39E
Novokuybyshevsk	37	53 6N	49 58E
Novokuznetsk	40	53 45N	87 10E
Novomirgorod	38	48 45N	31 33E
Novomoskovsk, R.S.F.S.R., U.S.S.R.	37	54 5N	38 15E
Novomoskovsk, Ukraine, U.S.S.R.	38	48 33N	35 17E
Novopolotsk	36	55 32N	28 37E
Novorossiysk	38	44 43N	37 46E
Novorybnoye	41	72 50N	105 50E
Novorzhev	36	57 3N	29 25E
Novoselitsa	38	48 14N	26 15E
Novoshakhtinsk	39	47 46N	39 58E
Novosibirsk	40	55 0N	83 5E
Novosibirskiye Ostrava	41	75 0N	142 0E
Novosil	37	52 58N	36 58E
Novosokolniki	36	56 33N	30 5E
Novotulskiy	37	54 10N	37 43E
Novouzensk	37	50 32N	48 17E
Novovolynsk	36	50 45N	24 4E
Novozybkov	36	52 30N	32 0E
Novska	33	45 19N	17 0E
Novvy Port	40	67 40N	72 30E
Novy Bug	38	47 34N	32 29E
Nový Bydzov	32	50 14N	15 29E
Novy Dwór Mazowiecki	32	52 26N	20 44E
Novyy Oskol	37	50 44N	37 55E
Now Shahr	47	36 40N	51 30E
Nowa Deba	32	50 26N	21 41E
Nowa Nowa	75	37 44S	148 3E
Nowa Ruda	32	50 35N	16 30E
Nowa Sól	32	51 48N	15 44E
Nowe	32	53 41N	18 44E
Nowe Warpno	33	53 42N	14 18E
Nowendoc	77	31 32S	151 44E
Nowgong	52	26 20N	92 50E
Nowingi	74	34 33S	142 15E
Nowogard	32	53 41N	15 10E
Nowogród	32	53 14N	21 53E
Nowra	76	34 53S	150 35E
Nowy Korczyn	32	50 19N	20 48E
Nowy Sącz	32	49 40N	20 41E
Noxen	115	41 25N	76 4W
Noxon	120	48 0N	115 43W
Noya	22	42 48N	8 53W
Noyant	18	47 30N	0 6E
Noyers	19	47 40N	4 0E
Noyes, I.	108	55 30N	133 40W
Noyon, France	19	49 34N	3 0E
Noyon, Mong.	60	43 2N	102 4E
Nozay	18	47 34N	1 38W
Nr'iquinha	93	16 0S	21 25E
Nsa, O. en →	87	32 28N	5 24E
Nsanje	95	16 55S	35 12E
Nsawam	89	5 50N	0 24W
Nsomba	95	10 45S	29 51E
Nsopzup	52	25 51N	97 30E
Nsukka	89	6 51N	7 29E
Nu Jiang →	58	29 58N	97 25E
Nu Shan	58	26 0N	99 20E
Nuanetsi →	95	22 40S	31 50E
Nuatja	89	7 0N	1 17E
Nuba Mts. = Nubah, Jibalan	91	12 0N	31 0E
Nubah, Jibalan	91	12 0N	31 0E
Nûbîya, Es Sahrâ En	90	21 30N	33 30E
Ñuble □	140	37 0S	72 0W
Nuboai	57	2 10S	136 30E
Nubra →	49	34 35N	77 35E
Nueces →	119	27 50N	97 30W
Nueima →	44	31 54N	35 25E
Nueltin L.	109	60 30N	99 30W
Nueva Antioquia	134	6 5N	69 26W
Nueva Casas Grandes	124	30 25N	107 55W
Nueva Esparta □	135	11 0N	64 0W
Nueva Gerona	126	21 53N	82 49W
Nueva, I.	142	55 13S	66 30W
Nueva Imperial	142	38 45S	72 58W
Nueva Palmira	140	33 52S	58 20W
Nueva Rosita	124	28 0N	101 11W
Nueva San Salvador	126	13 40N	89 18W
Nuéve de Julio	140	35 30S	61 0W
Nuevitas	126	21 30N	77 20W
Nuevo, Golfo	142	43 0S	64 30W
Nuevo Guerrero	125	26 34N	99 15W
Nuevo Laredo	125	27 30N	99 30W
Nuevo León □	124	25 0N	100 0W
Nuevo Mundo, Cerro	136	21 55S	66 53W
Nuevo Rocafuerte	134	0 55S	75 27W
Nugget Pt.	81	46 27S	169 50E
Nugrus, Gebel	90	24 47N	34 35E
Nuhaka	80	39 3S	177 45E
Nuits	19	47 44N	4 12E
Nuits-St-Georges	19	47 10N	4 56E
Nukey Bluff, Mt.	73	32 26S	135 29E
Nukheila (Merga)	90	19 1N	26 21E
Nukiki	68	6 45S	156 29E
Nuku'alofa	68	21 10S	174 0W
Nukus	40	42 20N	59 7E
Nulato	100	64 40N	158 10W
Nules	24	39 51N	0 9W
Nullagine	78	21 53S	120 6E
Nullagine →	78	21 20S	120 20E
Nullarbor	79	31 28S	130 55E
Nullarbor Plain	79	30 45S	129 0E
Nullawarre	74	38 30S	142 45E
Nullawil	74	35 49S	143 10E
Numalla, L.	73	28 43S	144 20E
Numan	89	9 29N	12 3E
Numata	65	36 45N	139 4E
Numatinna →	91	7 38N	27 20E
Numazu	65	35 7N	138 51E
Numbulwar	72	14 15S	135 45E
Numfoor	57	1 0S	134 50E
Numurkah	74	36 5S	145 26E
Nunaksaluk I.	103	55 49N	60 20W
Nundle	77	31 29S	151 9E
Nuneaton	13	52 32N	1 29W
Nungatta	75	37 11S	149 20E
Nungo	95	13 23S	37 43E
Nungwe	94	2 48S	32 2E
Nunivak	100	60 0N	166 0W
Nunkun	49	33 57N	76 2E
Nunspeet	16	52 21N	5 45E
Nuoro	28	40 20N	9 20E
Nuqayy, Jabal	87	23 11N	19 30E
Nuquí	134	5 42N	77 17W
Nure →	26	45 3N	9 49E
Nuremburg = Nürnberg	31	49 26N	11 5E
Nuri	124	28 2N	109 22W
Nurina	79	30 56S	126 33E
Nuriootpa	73	34 27S	139 0E
Nürnberg	31	49 26N	11 5E
Nurran, L. = Terewah, L.	73	29 52S	147 35E
Nurrari Lakes	79	29 1S	130 5E
Nurri	28	39 43N	9 13E
Nusa Barung	57	8 22S	113 20E
Nusa Kambangan	57	7 47S	109 0E
Nusa Tenggara Barat □	56	8 50S	117 30E
Nusa Tenggara Timur	57	9 30S	122 0E
Nushki	48	29 35N	66 0E
Nutak	101	57 28N	61 59W
Nutwood Downs	72	15 49S	134 10E
Nuwaiba	90	28 58N	34 40E
Nuwakot	49	28 10N	83 55E
Nuwara Eliya	51	6 58N	80 48E
Nuwefontein	96	28 1S	19 6E
Nuweveldberge	96	32 10S	21 45E
Nuyts Arch.	73	32 35S	133 20E
Nuyts, C.	79	32 2S	132 21E
Nuzvid	50	16 47N	80 53E
Nyaake (Webo)	88	4 52N	7 37W
Nyabing	79	33 30S	118 7E
Nyack	115	41 5N	73 57W
Nyadal	10	62 48N	17 59E
Nyah	74	35 12S	143 25E
Nyah West	74	35 16S	143 21E
Nyahanga	94	2 20S	33 37E
Nyahua	94	5 25S	33 23E
Nyahururu	94	0 2N	36 27E
Nyainqentanglha Shan	62	30 0N	90 0E
Nyakanazi	94	3 2S	31 10E
Nyakasu	94	3 58S	30 6E
Nyakrom	89	5 40N	0 50W
Nyâlâ	91	12 2N	24 58E
Nyamandhlovu	95	19 55S	28 16E
Nyambiti	94	2 48S	33 27E
Nyamwaga	94	1 27S	34 33E
Nyandekwa	94	3 57S	32 32E
Nyanding →,	91	8 40N	32 41E
Nyangana	96	18 0S	20 40E
Nyanguge	94	2 30S	33 12E
Nyangwena	95	15 18S	28 45E
Nyankpala	89	9 21N	0 58W
Nyanza, Burundi	94	4 21S	29 36E
Nyanza, Rwanda	94	2 20S	29 42E
Nyanza □	94	0 10S	34 15E
Nyarling →	108	60 41N	113 23W
Nyarrin	74	35 22S	142 43E
Nyasa, L. = Malawi, L.	95	12 0S	34 30E
Nyaunglebin	52	17 52N	96 42E
Nyazwidzi →	95	20 0S	31 17E
Nyborg	11	55 18N	10 47E
Nybro	11	56 44N	15 55E
Nyda	40	66 40N	72 58E
Nyeri	94	0 23S	36 56E
Nyerol	91	8 41N	32 1E
Nyhem	10	62 54N	15 37E
Nyiel	91	6 9N	31 13E
Nyilumba	95	10 30S	40 22E
Nyinahin	88	6 43N	2 3W
Nyirbátor	33	47 49N	22 9E
Nyíregyháza	33	47 58N	21 47E
Nykarleby	8	63 22N	22 31E
Nykøbing, Sjælland, Denmark	11	55 55N	11 40E
Nykøbing, Storstrøm, Denmark	11	54 56N	11 52E
Nykøbing, Viborg, Denmark	11	56 48N	8 51E
Nyköping	11	58 45N	17 0E
Nykroppa	10	59 37N	14 18E
Nykvarn	10	59 11N	17 25E
Nyland	10	63 1N	17 45E
Nylstroom	97	24 42S	28 22E
Nymagee	73	32 7S	146 20E
Nymboida →	77	29 22S	152 32E
Nymburk	32	50 10N	15 1E
Nynäshamn	10	58 54N	17 57E
Nyon	31	46 23N	6 14E
Nyons	21	44 22N	5 10E
Nyora	74	38 20S	145 41E
Nyord	11	55 4N	12 13E
Nyou	89	12 42N	2 1W
Nysa	32	50 30N	17 22E
Nysa →	32	52 4N	14 46E
Nyssa	120	43 56N	117 2W
Nysted	11	54 40N	11 44E
Nyūgawa	64	33 56N	133 5E
Nyunzu	94	5 57S	27 58E
Nyurba	41	63 17N	118 28E
Nzega	94	4 10S	33 12E
Nzega □	94	4 10S	33 10E
N'Zérékoré	88	7 49N	8 48W
Nzilo, Chutes de	95	10 18S	25 27E
Nzubuka	94	4 45S	32 50E

O

O-Shima	64	33 54N	130 25E
Ō-Shima	64	34 29N	129 33E
Oacoma	118	43 50N	99 26W
Oahe	118	44 33N	100 29W
Oahe Dam	118	44 28N	100 25W
Oahe Res.	118	45 30N	100 25W
Oahu	110	21 30N	158 0W
Oak Creek, Colo., U.S.A.	120	40 15N	106 59W
Oak Creek, Wis., U.S.A.	117	42 52N	87 55W
Oak Harb.	122	48 20N	122 38W
Oak Hill	112	38 0N	81 7W
Oak Lawn	117	41 43N	87 44W
Oak Park	112	41 55N	87 45W
Oak Ridge	113	36 1N	84 12W
Oak View	123	34 24N	119 18W
Oakbank	73	33 4S	140 33E
Oakdale, Calif., U.S.A.	122	46 14N	98 4W
Oakdale, La., U.S.A.	119	30 50N	92 38W
Oakengates	12	52 42N	2 29W
Oakes	118	46 14N	98 4W
Oakesdale	120	47 11N	117 15W
Oakey	73	27 25S	151 43E
Oakford	116	40 6N	89 58W
Oakham	12	52 40N	0 43W
Oakhurst	122	37 19N	119 40W
Oakland, Calif., U.S.A.	122	37 50N	122 18W
Oakland, Ill., U.S.A.	117	39 39N	88 2W
Oakland, Oreg., U.S.A.	120	43 23N	123 18W
Oakland City	117	38 20N	87 20W
Oakleigh	74	37 54S	145 6E
Oakley, Id., U.S.A.	120	42 14N	113 55W
Oakley, Kans., U.S.A.	118	39 8N	100 51W
Oakley Creek	77	31 37S	149 46E
Oakover →	78	20 15S	119 10E
Oakridge	120	43 47N	122 31W
Oaktown	117	38 52N	87 27W
Oakville, Can.	106	43 27N	79 41W
Oakville, U.S.A.	122	46 50N	123 14W
Oakwood, Austral.	77	29 38S	151 4E
Oakwood, Ohio, U.S.A.	117	39 43N	84 11W
Oakwood, Ohio, U.S.A.	117	41 6N	84 23W
Oakwood, Tex., U.S.A.	119	31 35N	95 47W
Oamaru	81	45 5S	170 59E
Ōamishirasato	65	35 31N	140 18E
Oarai	65	36 21N	140 34E
Oasis, Calif., U.S.A.	123	33 28N	116 6W
Oasis, Nev., U.S.A.	122	37 29N	117 55W
Oates Coast	143	69 0S	160 0E
Oatman	123	35 1N	114 19W
Oaxaca	125	17 2N	96 40W
Oaxaca □	125	17 0N	97 0W
Ob →	40	66 45N	69 30E
Oba	102	49 4N	84 7W
Obala	89	4 9N	11 32E
Obalski, L.	104	48 43N	77 58W
Obama, Eukui, Japan	65	35 30N	135 45E
Obama, Nagasaki, Japan	64	32 43N	130 13E
Obamsca, L.	104	50 24N	78 16W
Oban, N.Z.	81	46 55S	168 10E
Oban, U.K.	14	56 25N	5 30W
Obbia	45	5 25N	48 30E
Obed	108	53 30N	117 10W
Obedjwan	104	48 40N	74 56W
Obeh	47	34 28N	63 10E
Obera	141	27 21S	55 2W
Oberammergau	31	47 35N	11 3E
Oberdrauburg	33	46 44N	12 58E
Oberengadin	31	46 35N	9 55E
Oberhausen	30	51 28N	6 50E
Oberkirch	31	48 31N	8 5E
Oberlin, Kans., U.S.A.	118	39 52N	100 31W
Oberlin, La., U.S.A.	119	30 42N	92 42W
Oberlin, Ohio, U.S.A.	114	41 15N	82 10W
Obernai	19	48 28N	7 30E
Oberndorf	31	48 17N	8 35E
Oberon	76	33 45S	149 52E
Oberpfälzer Wald	31	49 30N	12 25E
Oberstdorf	31	47 25N	10 16E
Obi, Kepulauan	57	1 23S	127 45E
Obiaruku	89	5 51N	6 9E
Óbidos, Brazil	135	1 50S	55 30W
Óbidos, Port.	23	39 19N	9 10W
Obihiro	63	42 56N	143 12E
Obilatu	57	1 25S	127 20E
Obilnoye	39	47 32N	44 30E
Obing	31	48 0N	12 25E
Öbisfelde	30	52 27N	10 57E
Objat	20	45 16N	1 24E
Obley	76	32 40S	148 34E
Oblong	117	39 0N	87 55W
Obluchye	41	49 1N	131 4E
Obninsk	37	55 8N	36 37E
Obo, C. Afr. Rep.	94	5 20N	26 32E
Obo, Ethiopia	91	3 46N	38 52E
Oboa, Mt.	94	1 45N	34 45E
Obock	91	12 0N	43 20E
Oborniki	32	52 39N	16 50E
Obot	91	4 32N	37 20E
Obout	89	3 28N	11 47E
Oboyan	37	51 13N	36 37E
Obozerskaya	40	63 20N	40 15E
Obrovac	27	44 11N	15 41E
Observatory Inlet	108	55 10N	129 54W
Obshchi Syrt	6	52 0N	53 0E
Obskaya Guba	40	69 0N	73 0E
Obuasi	89	6 17N	1 40W
Obubra	89	6 8N	8 20E
Obzor	34	42 50N	27 52E
Ocala	113	29 11N	82 5W
Ocamo →	135	2 48N	65 14W
Ocampo	124	28 9N	108 24W
Ocaña, Colomb.	134	8 15N	73 20W
Ocaña, Spain	24	39 55N	3 30W
Ocanomowoc	118	43 7N	88 30W
Ocate	119	36 12N	104 59W
Occidental, Cordillera, Colomb.	134	5 0N	76 0W
Occidental, Cordillera, Peru	136	14 0S	74 0W
Ocean City, N.J., U.S.A.	112	39 18N	74 34W
Ocean City, Wash., U.S.A.	122	47 4N	124 10W
Ocean Grove	74	38 16S	144 32E
Ocean I. = Banaba	66	0 52S	169 35E
Ocean Park	122	46 30N	124 2W
Oceanlake	120	45 0N	124 0W
Oceano	123	35 6N	120 37W
Oceanport	115	40 20N	74 3W
Oceanside	123	33 13N	117 26W
Ochagavia	24	42 55N	1 5W
Ochamchire	39	42 46N	41 32E
Ochiai	64	35 1N	133 45E
Ochil Hills	14	56 14N	3 40W
Ochre River	109	51 4N	99 47W
Ochsenfurt	31	49 38N	10 3E
Ochsenhausen	31	48 4N	9 57E
Ocilla	113	31 35N	83 12W
Ockelbo	10	60 54N	16 45E
Ocmulgee →	113	31 58N	82 32W
Ocna Sibiului	34	45 52N	24 2E
Ocoña	136	16 26S	73 8W
Ocoña →	136	16 28S	73 8W
Oconee →	113	31 58N	82 32W

Oconomowoc	**117**	43 6N	88 30W
Oconto	**112**	44 52N	87 53W
Oconto Falls	**112**	44 52N	88 10W
Ocosingo	**125**	17 10N	92 15W
Ocotal	**126**	13 41N	86 31W
Ocotlán	**124**	20 21N	102 42W
Ocreza →	**23**	39 32N	7 50W
Octave	**121**	34 10N	112 43W
Octeville	**18**	49 38N	1 40W
Octyabrskoy Revolyutsii, Os.	**41**	79 30N	97 0 E
Ocumare del Tuy	**134**	10 7N	66 46W
Ocuri	**137**	18 45S	65 50W
Ocussi	**57**	9 20S	124 23 E
Oda, Ghana	**89**	5 50N	0 51W
Oda, Japan	**64**	33 36N	132 53 E
Ōda	**64**	35 11N	132 30 E
Oda, Jebel	**90**	20 21N	36 39 E
Ódáðahraun	**8**	65 5N	17 0W
Ödåkra	**11**	56 7N	12 45 E
Odanakumadona	**96**	20 55S	24 46 E
Odate	**63**	40 16N	140 34 E
Odawara	**65**	35 20N	139 6 E
Odda	**9**	60 3N	6 35 E
Odder	**11**	55 58N	10 10 E
Oddobo	**91**	12 21N	42 6 E
Oddur	**45**	4 11N	43 52 E
Ödeborg	**11**	58 32N	11 58 E
Odei →	**109**	56 6N	96 54W
Odell	**117**	41 0N	88 31W
Odemira	**23**	37 35N	8 40W
Ödemiş	**46**	38 15N	28 0 E
Odendaalsrus	**96**	27 48S	26 45 E
Odense	**11**	55 22N	10 23 E
Odenwald	**31**	49 40N	9 0 E
Oder →	**30**	53 33N	14 38 E
Oderzo	**27**	45 47N	12 29 E
Odessa, Can.	**107**	44 17N	76 43W
Odessa, Mo., U.S.A.	**116**	39 0N	93 57W
Odessa, Tex., U.S.A.	**119**	31 51N	102 23W
Odessa, Wash., U.S.A.	**120**	47 19N	118 35W
Odessa, U.S.S.R.	**38**	46 30N	30 45 E
Odiel →	**23**	37 10N	6 55W
Odienné	**88**	9 30N	7 34W
Odobeşti	**34**	45 43N	27 4 E
O'Donnell	**119**	33 0N	101 48W
Odorheiul Secuiesc	**34**	46 21N	25 21 E
Odoyevo	**37**	53 56N	36 42 E
Odra →, Poland	**32**	53 33N	14 38 E
Odra →, Spain	**22**	42 14N	4 17W
Odžaci	**33**	45 30N	19 17 E
Oeiras, Brazil	**138**	7 0S	42 8W
Oeiras, Port.	**23**	38 41N	9 18W
Oelrichs	**118**	43 11N	103 14W
Oelsnitz	**30**	50 24N	12 11 E
Oelwein	**118**	42 41N	91 55W
Oenpelli	**78**	12 20S	133 4 E
O'Fallon	**116**	38 50N	90 43W
Ofanto →	**29**	41 22N	16 13 E
Offa	**89**	8 13N	4 42 E
Offaly □	**15**	53 15N	7 30W
Offenbach	**31**	50 6N	8 46 E
Offenburg	**31**	48 29N	7 56 E
Offerdal	**10**	63 28N	14 0 E
Offida	**27**	42 56N	13 40 E
Offranville	**18**	49 52N	1 0 E
Ofidhousa	**35**	36 33N	26 8 E
Ofotfjorden	**8**	68 27N	16 40 E
Ofu	**68**	14 11S	169 41W
Oga-Hantō	**63**	39 58N	139 47 E
Ogahalla	**102**	50 6N	85 51W
Ōgaki	**65**	35 21N	136 37 E
Ogallala	**118**	41 12N	101 40W
Ogascanane, L.	**104**	47 5N	78 25W
Ogbomosho	**89**	8 1N	4 11 E
Ogden, Iowa, U.S.A.	**116**	42 3N	94 0W
Ogden, Utah, U.S.A.	**120**	41 13N	112 1W
Ogdensburg	**115**	44 40N	75 27W
Ogeechee →	**113**	31 51N	81 6W
Ogilby	**123**	32 49N	114 50W
Oglesby	**116**	41 21N	89 3W
Oglio →	**26**	45 2N	10 39 E
Ogmore	**72**	22 37S	149 35 E
Ognon →	**19**	47 16N	5 28 E
Ogoja	**89**	6 38N	8 39 E
Ogoki →	**102**	51 38N	85 57W
Ogoki L.	**102**	50 50N	87 10W
Ogoki Res.	**102**	50 45N	88 15W
Ogooué →	**92**	1 0S	10 0 E
Ōgori	**64**	34 6N	131 24 E
Ogosta →	**34**	43 48N	23 55 E
Ogowe = Ogooué →	**92**	1 0S	10 0 E
Ogrein	**90**	17 55N	34 50 E
Ogulin	**27**	45 16N	15 16 E
Ogun □	**89**	7 0N	3 0 E
Oguni	**64**	33 11N	131 8 E
Oguta	**89**	5 44N	6 44 E
Ogwashi-Uku	**89**	6 15N	6 30 E
Ogwe	**89**	5 0N	7 14 E
Ohai	**81**	44 55S	168 0 E
Ohakune	**80**	39 24S	175 24 E
Ōhara	**65**	35 15N	140 23 E
Ohau, L.	**81**	44 15S	169 53 E
Ohaupo	**80**	37 56S	175 20 E
Oheida	**116**	41 4N	90 13W
Ohey	**16**	50 26N	5 8 E
O'Higgins □	**140**	34 15S	70 45W
Ohio □	**112**	40 20N	14 10 E
Ohio →	**112**	38 0N	86 0W
Ohio City	**117**	40 46N	84 37W
Ohiwa Harbour	**80**	37 59S	177 10 E
Ohre →, Czech.	**32**	50 30N	14 10 E
Ohre →, Ger.	**30**	52 18N	11 47 E
Ohrid	**35**	41 8N	20 52 E
Ohridsko, Jezero	**35**	41 8N	20 52 E
Ohrigstad	**97**	24 19S	30 36 E
Öhringen	**31**	49 11N	9 31 E
Oiapoque →	**135**	4 8N	51 40W
Oikou	**61**	38 35N	117 42 E
Oil City	**114**	41 26N	79 40W
Oil Springs	**106**	42 47N	82 7W
Oildale	**123**	35 25N	119 1W
Oise □	**19**	49 28N	2 30 E
Oise →	**19**	49 0N	2 4 E
Oita	**64**	33 14N	131 36 E
Oita □	**64**	33 15N	131 30 E
Oiticica	**138**	5 3S	41 5W
Ojai	**123**	34 28N	119 16W
Ojinaga	**124**	29 34N	104 25W
Ojos del Salado, Cerro	**140**	27 0S	68 40W
Oka →	**37**	56 20N	43 59 E
Okaba	**57**	8 6S	139 42 E
Okahandja	**96**	22 0S	16 59 E
Okahukura	**66**	38 48S	175 14 E
Okaihau	**80**	35 19S	173 47 E
Okanagan L.	**108**	50 0N	119 30W
Okanogan	**120**	48 6N	119 43W
Okanogan →	**120**	48 6N	119 43W
Okapa	**69**	6 38S	145 39 E
Okaputa	**96**	20 5S	17 0 E
Okara	**48**	30 50N	73 31 E
Okarito	**81**	43 15S	170 9 E
Okato	**80**	39 12S	173 53 E
Okavango Swamps	**96**	18 45S	22 45 E
Okawa	**64**	33 9N	130 21 E
Okawville	**116**	38 26N	89 33W
Okaya	**65**	36 0N	138 10 E
Okayama	**64**	34 40N	133 54 E
Okayama □	**64**	35 0N	133 50 E
Okazaki	**65**	34 57N	137 10 E
Oke-Iho	**89**	8 1N	3 18 E
Okeechobee	**113**	27 16N	80 46W
Okeechobee L.	**113**	27 0N	80 50W
Okefenokee Swamp	**113**	30 50N	82 15W
Okehampton	**13**	50 44N	4 1W
Okene	**89**	7 32N	6 11 E
Oker →	**30**	52 30N	10 22 E
Okha	**41**	53 40N	143 0 E
Ókhi Óros	**35**	38 5N	24 25 E
Okhotsk	**41**	59 20N	143 10 E
Okhotsk, Sea of	**41**	55 0N	145 0 E
Okhotskiy Perevoz	**41**	61 52N	135 35 E
Okhotsko Kolymskoye	**41**	63 0N	157 0 E
Oki-no-Shima	**64**	32 44N	132 33 E
Oki-Shotō	**64**	36 5N	133 15 E
Okiep	**96**	29 39S	17 53 E
Okigwi	**89**	5 52N	7 20 E
Okija	**89**	5 54N	6 55 E
Okinawa-Jima	**63**	26 32N	128 0 E
Okinawa-Shotō	**63**	27 0N	128 0 E
Okino-erabu-Shima	**63**	27 21N	128 33 E
Okitipupa	**89**	6 31N	4 50 E
Oklahoma □	**119**	35 20N	97 30W
Oklahoma City	**119**	35 25N	97 30W
Okmulgee	**119**	35 38N	96 0W
Oknitsa	**38**	48 25N	27 30 E
Okolo	**94**	2 37N	31 8 E
Okolona, Ky., U.S.A.	**117**	38 8N	85 41W
Okolona, Miss., U.S.A.	**119**	34 0N	88 45W
Okondeka	**96**	21 38S	15 37 E
Okondja	**92**	0 35S	13 45 E
Okrika	**89**	4 40N	7 10 E
Oktabrsk	**40**	49 28N	57 25 E
Oktyabrskoye	**40**	62 28N	66 3 E
Okulovka	**36**	58 25N	33 19 E
Okuru	**81**	43 55S	168 55 E
Okushiri-Tō	**63**	42 15N	139 30 E
Okuta	**89**	9 14N	3 12 E
Okwa →	**96**	22 30S	23 0 E
Ola	**119**	35 2N	93 10W
Ólafsfjörður	**8**	66 4N	18 39W
Ólafsvík	**8**	64 53N	23 43W
Olancha	**123**	36 15N	118 1W
Olancha Pk.	**123**	36 15N	118 7W
Olanchito	**126**	15 30N	86 30W
Öland	**11**	56 45N	16 38 E
Olargues	**20**	43 34N	2 53 E
Olary	**73**	32 18S	140 19 E
Olascoaga	**140**	35 15S	60 39W
Olathe	**118**	38 50N	94 50W
Olavarría	**140**	36 55S	60 20W
Oława	**32**	50 57N	17 20 E
Ólbia	**28**	40 55N	9 30 E
Ólbia, G. di	**28**	40 55N	9 35 E
Old Bahama Chan. = Bahama, Canal Viejo de	**126**	22 10N	77 30W
Old Baldy Pk. = San Antonio, Mt.	**123**	34 17N	117 38W
Old Castile = Castilla la Vieja □	**22**	41 55N	4 0W
Old Castle	**15**	53 46N	7 10W
Old Cork	**72**	22 57S	141 52 E
Old Crow	**100**	67 30N	140 5 E
Old Dale	**123**	34 8N	115 47W
Old Dongola	**90**	18 11N	30 44 E
Old Forge, N.Y., U.S.A.	**115**	43 43N	74 58W
Old Forge, Pa., U.S.A.	**115**	41 20N	75 46W
Old Fort →	**109**	58 36N	110 24W
Old Junee	**76**	34 49S	147 31 E
Old Serenje	**95**	13 7S	30 45 E
Old Shinyanga	**94**	3 33S	33 27 E
Old Speckle, Mt.	**115**	44 35N	70 57W
Old Town	**103**	45 0N	68 41W
Old Wives L.	**109**	50 5N	106 0W
Oldbury	**13**	51 38N	2 30W
Oldeani	**94**	3 22S	35 35 E
Oldenburg, Niedersachsen, Ger.	**30**	53 10N	8 10 E
Oldenburg, Schleswig-Holstein, Ger.	**30**	54 16N	10 53 E
Oldenzaal	**16**	52 19N	6 53 E
Oldham	**12**	53 33N	2 8W
Oldman →	**108**	49 57N	111 42W
Olds	**108**	51 50N	114 10W
Olean	**114**	42 8N	78 25W
Oléggio	**26**	45 36N	8 38 E
Oleiros	**22**	39 56N	7 56W
Olekma →	**41**	60 22N	120 42 E
Olekminsk	**41**	60 25N	120 30 E
Olema	**122**	38 3N	122 47W
Olenek	**41**	68 28N	112 18 E
Olenek →	**41**	73 0N	120 10 E
Olenino	**36**	56 15N	33 30 E
Oléron, Île d'	**20**	45 55N	1 15W
Oleśnica	**32**	51 13N	17 22 E
Olesno	**32**	50 51N	18 26 E
Olevsk	**36**	51 12N	27 39 E
Olga	**41**	43 50N	135 14 E
Olga, L.	**104**	49 47N	77 15W
Olga, Mt.	**79**	25 20S	130 50 E
Olgastretet	**144**	78 35N	25 0 E
Ølgod	**11**	55 49N	8 36 E
Olhão	**23**	37 3N	7 48W
Olib	**27**	44 23N	14 44 E
Olib, I.	**27**	44 23N	14 44 E
Oliena	**28**	40 18N	9 22 E
Oliete	**24**	41 1N	0 41W
Olifantshoek	**96**	27 57S	22 42 E
Ólimbos	**35**	35 44N	27 11 E
Ólimbos, Óros	**35**	40 6N	22 23 E
Olímpia	**141**	20 44S	48 54W
Olimpo □	**140**	20 30S	58 45W
Olin	**116**	42 0N	91 9W
Olinda, Austral.	**76**	32 50S	150 10 E
Olinda, Brazil	**138**	8 1S	34 51W
Olindiná	**138**	11 22S	38 21W
Olite	**24**	42 29N	1 40W
Oliva, Argent.	**140**	32 0S	63 38W
Oliva, Spain	**25**	38 58N	0 9W
Oliva de la Frontera	**23**	38 17N	6 54W
Oliva, Punta del	**22**	43 37N	5 28W
Olivares	**24**	39 46N	2 20W
Olive Hill	**117**	38 18N	83 13W
Olivehurst	**122**	39 6N	121 34W
Oliveira	**139**	20 39S	44 50W
Oliveira de Azemeis	**22**	40 49N	8 29W
Oliveira dos Brejinhos	**139**	12 19S	42 54W
Olivença	**95**	11 47S	35 13 E
Olivenza	**23**	38 41N	7 9W
Oliver	**108**	49 13N	119 37W
Oliver L.	**109**	56 56N	103 22W
Olivine Ra.	**81**	44 15S	168 30 E
Olkhovka	**39**	49 48N	44 32 E
Olkusz	**32**	50 18N	19 33 E
Ollagüe	**140**	21 15S	68 10W
Olmedo	**22**	41 20N	4 43W
Olmos	**136**	5 59S	79 46W
Olney, Ill., U.S.A.	**117**	38 40N	88 0W
Olney, Tex., U.S.A.	**119**	33 25N	98 45W
Olofström	**11**	56 17N	14 32 E
Oloma	**89**	3 29N	11 19 E
Olomane →	**103**	50 14N	60 37W
Olomouc	**32**	49 38N	17 12 E
Olongapo	**57**	14 50N	120 18 E
Oloron, Gave d'	**20**	43 33N	1 5W
Oloron-Ste-Marie	**20**	43 11N	0 38W
Olot	**24**	42 11N	2 30 E
Olovo	**33**	44 8N	18 35 E
Olovyannaya	**41**	50 58N	115 35 E
Oloy →	**41**	66 29N	159 29 E
Olpe	**30**	51 2N	7 50 E
Olshanka	**38**	48 16N	30 58 E
Olsztyn	**32**	53 48N	20 29 E
Olt →	**34**	43 50N	24 40 E
Olten	**31**	47 21N	7 53 E
Olteniţa	**34**	44 7N	26 42 E
Olton	**119**	34 16N	102 7W
Oltu	**46**	40 35N	41 58 E
Olvega	**24**	41 47N	2 0W
Olvera	**23**	36 55N	5 18W
Olympia, Greece	**35**	37 39N	21 39 E
Olympia, U.S.A.	**122**	47 0N	122 58W
Olympic Mts.	**122**	47 50N	123 45W
Olympic Nat. Park	**122**	47 48N	123 30W
Olympus, Mt.	**122**	47 52N	123 40W
Olympus, Mt. = Ólimbos, Óros	**35**	40 6N	22 23 E
Olyphant	**115**	41 27N	75 36W
Om →	**40**	54 59N	73 22 E
Om Hajer	**91**	14 20N	36 41 E
Om Koi	**54**	17 48N	98 22 E
Omachi	**65**	36 30N	137 50 E
Omae-Zaki	**65**	34 36N	138 14 E
Omagh	**15**	54 36N	7 20W
Omagh □	**15**	54 35N	7 15W
Omaha	**118**	41 15N	96 0W
Omak	**120**	48 24N	119 31W
Oman ■	**45**	23 0N	58 0 E
Oman, G. of	**47**	24 30N	58 30 E
Omaruru	**96**	21 26S	16 0 E
Omaruru →	**96**	22 7S	14 15 E
Omate	**136**	16 45S	71 0W
Ombai, Selat	**57**	8 30S	124 50 E
Ombombo	**96**	18 43S	13 57 E
Omboué	**92**	1 35S	9 15 E
Ombrone →	**26**	42 39N	11 0 E
Omchi	**87**	21 22N	17 53 E
Omdraai	**96**	20 5S	21 56 E
Omdurmân	**91**	15 40N	32 28 E
Ōme	**65**	35 47N	139 15 E
Omegna	**26**	45 52N	8 23 E
Omemee	**107**	44 18N	78 33W
Omeo	**75**	37 6S	147 36 E
Omeonga	**94**	3 40S	24 22 E
Ometepe, Isla de	**126**	11 32N	85 35W
Ometepec	**125**	16 39N	98 23W
Omez	**44**	32 22N	35 0 E
Omi-Shima	**64**	34 15N	133 0 E
Ōmi-Shima	**64**	34 25N	131 9 E
Omihachiman	**65**	35 7N	136 3 E
Omineca →	**108**	56 3N	124 16W
Omiš	**27**	43 28N	16 40 E
Omišalj	**27**	45 13N	14 32 E
Omitara	**96**	22 16S	18 2 E
Ōmiya	**65**	35 54N	139 38 E
Omme Å →	**11**	55 56N	8 32 E
Ommen	**16**	52 31N	6 26 E
Ömnögovi □	**60**	43 15N	104 0 E
Omo →	**85**	6 25N	36 10 E
Omolon →	**41**	68 42N	158 36 E
Omono-Gawa →	**63**	39 46N	140 3 E
Omsk	**40**	55 0N	73 12 E
Omsukchan	**41**	62 32N	155 48 E
Omul, Vf.	**34**	45 27N	25 29 E
Omura	**64**	32 56N	130 0 E
Omura-Wan	**64**	32 57N	129 52 E
Omurtag	**34**	43 8N	26 26 E
Ōmuta	**64**	33 0N	130 26 E
On-Take	**64**	31 35N	130 39 E
Oña	**24**	42 43N	3 25W
Onaga	**118**	39 32N	96 12W
Onalaska	**118**	43 53N	91 14W
Onamia	**118**	46 4N	93 38W
Onancock	**112**	37 42N	75 49W
Onang	**57**	3 2S	118 49 E
Onaping	**106**	46 37N	81 25W
Onaping →	**106**	46 37N	81 18W
Onaping L.	**102**	47 3N	81 30W
Onarga	**117**	40 43N	88 1W
Onatchiway, L.	**105**	49 3N	71 5W
Oñate	**24**	43 3N	2 25W
Onavas	**124**	28 28N	109 30W
Onawa	**118**	42 2N	96 2W
Onaway	**106**	45 21N	84 11W
Oncocua	**96**	16 30S	13 25 E
Onda	**24**	39 55N	0 17W
Ondaejin	**61**	41 34N	129 40 E
Ondangua	**96**	17 57S	16 4 E
Ondárroa	**24**	43 19N	2 25W
Ondas →	**139**	12 8S	45 0W
Ondava →	**32**	48 27N	21 48 E
Ondo, Japan	**64**	34 11N	132 32 E
Ondo, Nigeria	**89**	7 4N	4 47 E
Ondo □	**89**	7 0N	5 0 E
Ondombo	**96**	21 3S	16 5 E
Öndörhaan	**62**	47 19N	110 39 E
Öndörshil	**60**	45 13N	108 5 E
Öndverðarnes	**8**	64 52N	24 0W
Onega	**40**	64 0N	38 10 E
Onega, G. of = Onezhskaya G.	**40**	64 30N	37 0 E
Onega, L. = Onezhskoye Oz.	**40**	62 0N	35 30 E

Onehunga	**80**	36 55S	174 48 E
Oneida	**115**	43 5N	75 40W
Oneida L.	**115**	43 12N	76 0W
O'Neill	**118**	42 30N	98 38W
Onekotan, Ostrov	**41**	49 25N	154 45 E
Onema	**94**	4 35S	24 30 E
Oneonta, Ala., U.S.A.	**113**	33 58N	86 29W
Oneonta, N.Y., U.S.A.	**115**	42 26N	75 5W
Onerahi	**80**	35 45S	174 22 E
Onezhskoye Ozero	**40**	62 0N	35 30 E
Ongarue	**80**	38 42S	175 19 E
Ongea Levu	**68**	19 8S	178 24W
Ongerup	**79**	33 58S	118 28 E
Ongiva	**96**	16 48S	15 50 E
Ongjin	**61**	37 56N	125 21 E
Ongkharak	**54**	14 8N	101 1 E
Ongniud Qi	**61**	43 0N	118 38 E
Ongoka	**94**	1 20S	26 0 E
Ongole	**51**	15 33N	80 2 E
Ongon	**60**	45 41N	113 5 E
Onguren	**41**	53 38N	107 36 E
Oni	**39**	42 33N	43 26 E
Onida	**118**	44 42N	100 5W
Onilahy →	**97**	23 34S	43 45 E
Onitsha	**89**	6 6N	6 42 E
Onmaka	**52**	22 17N	96 41 E
Ono, Fiji	**68**	18 55S	178 29 E
Ono, Fukui, Japan	**65**	35 59N	136 29 E
Ono, Hyōgo, Japan	**64**	34 51N	134 56 E
Onoda	**64**	34 2N	131 25 E
Onomichi	**64**	34 25N	133 12 E
Onpyŏng-ni	**61**	33 25N	126 55 E
Ons, Islas d'	**22**	42 23N	8 55W
Onsala	**11**	57 26N	12 0 E
Onslow	**78**	21 40S	115 12 E
Onslow B.	**113**	34 20N	77 20W
Onstwedde	**16**	53 2N	7 4 E
Ontake-San	**65**	35 53N	137 29 E
Ontaneda	**22**	43 12N	3 57W
Ontario, Calif., U.S.A.	**123**	34 2N	117 40W
Ontario, Oreg., U.S.A.	**120**	44 1N	117 1W
Ontario □	**102**	52 0N	88 10W
Ontario, L.	**107**	43 40N	78 0W
Onteniente	**25**	38 50N	0 35W
Ontonagon	**118**	46 52N	89 19W
Ontur	**25**	38 38N	1 29W
Onyx	**123**	35 41N	118 14W
Oodnadatta	**73**	27 33S	135 30 E
Ooldea	**79**	30 27S	131 50 E
Oona River	**108**	53 57N	130 16W
Oorindi	**72**	20 40S	141 1 E
Oost-Vlaanderen □	**16**	51 5N	3 50 E
Oostende	**16**	51 15N	2 50 E
Oosterhout	**16**	51 39N	4 47 E
Oosterschelde	**16**	51 33N	4 0 E
Ootacamund	**51**	11 30N	76 44 E
Ootha	**76**	33 6S	147 29 E
Ootsa L.	**108**	53 50N	126 2W
Ootsi	**96**	25 2S	25 45 E
Opala, U.S.S.R.	**41**	51 58N	156 30 E
Opala, Zaïre	**92**	0 40S	24 20 E
Opanake	**51**	6 35N	80 40 E
Opapa	**80**	39 47S	176 42 E
Opasatica, L.	**104**	48 5N	79 18W
Opasatika	**102**	49 30N	82 50W
Opasquia	**109**	53 16N	93 34W
Opataca, L.	**104**	50 22N	74 55W
Opatija	**27**	45 21N	14 17 E
Opava	**32**	49 57N	17 58 E
Opawica, L.	**104**	49 35N	75 55W
Opelousas	**119**	30 35N	92 7W
Opémisca L.	**102**	50 0N	75 0W
Opémisca, L.	**104**	49 56N	74 52W
Open Bay Is.	**81**	43 51S	168 51 E
Opeongo L.	**107**	45 42N	78 23W
Opheim	**120**	48 52N	106 30W
Ophir	**100**	63 10N	156 40W
Ophthalmia Ra.	**78**	23 15S	119 30 E
Opi	**89**	6 36N	7 28 E
Opinaca →	**102**	52 15N	78 2W
Opinaca L.	**102**	52 39N	76 20W
Opiskotish, L.	**103**	53 10N	67 50W
Opobo	**89**	4 35N	7 34 E
Opochka	**36**	56 42N	28 45 E
Opoczno	**32**	51 22N	20 18 E
Opole	**32**	50 42N	17 58 E
Oporto = Porto	**22**	41 8N	8 40W
Opotiki	**80**	38 1S	177 19 E
Opp	**113**	31 19N	86 13W
Oppegård	**10**	59 48N	10 48 E
Oppenheim	**31**	49 50N	8 22 E
Óppido Mamertina	**29**	38 16N	15 59 E
Oppland fylke □	**10**	61 15N	9 40 E
Oppstad	**10**	60 17N	11 40 E
Oprtalj	**27**	45 23N	13 50 E
Opua	**80**	35 19S	174 9 E
Opunake	**80**	39 26S	173 52 E
Opuzen	**33**	43 1N	17 34 E
Oquawka	**116**	40 56N	90 57W
Or Yehuda	**44**	32 2N	34 50 E
Ora	**27**	46 20N	11 19 E
Ora Banda	**79**	30 20S	121 0 E
Oracle	**121**	32 36N	110 46W
Oradea	**34**	47 2N	21 58 E
Öræfajökull	**8**	64 2N	16 39W
Orahovac	**33**	42 24N	20 40 E
Orai	**49**	25 58N	79 30 E
Oraison	**21**	43 55N	5 55 E
Oran, Alg.	**86**	35 45N	0 39W
Oran, Argent.	**140**	23 10S	64 20W
Orange, Austral.	**76**	33 15S	149 7 E
Orange, France	**21**	44 8N	4 47 E
Orange, Calif., U.S.A.	**123**	33 47N	117 51W
Orange, Mass., U.S.A.	**115**	42 35N	72 15W
Orange, Tex., U.S.A.	**119**	30 10N	93 50W
Orange, Va., U.S.A.	**112**	38 17N	78 5W
Orange, C.	**135**	4 20N	51 30W
Orange Cove	**122**	36 38N	119 19W
Orange Free State = Oranje Vrystaat □	**96**	28 30S	27 0 E
Orange Grove	**119**	27 57N	97 57W
Orange Walk	**125**	18 6N	88 33W
Orangeburg	**113**	33 35N	80 53W
Orangeville, Can.	**106**	43 55N	80 5W
Orangeville, U.S.A.	**116**	42 28N	89 39W
Oranienburg	**30**	52 45N	13 15 E
Oranje →	**96**	28 41S	16 28 E
Oranje Vrystaat □	**96**	28 30S	27 0 E
Oranjemund	**96**	28 38S	16 29 E
Orapa	**96**	21 13S	25 25 E
Or'Aquiva	**44**	32 30N	34 54 E
Orara →	**77**	29 45S	152 49 E
Oras	**57**	12 9N	125 28 E
Orăştie	**34**	45 50N	23 10 E
Oraşul Stalin = Braşov	**34**	45 38N	25 35 E
Orava →	**32**	49 24N	19 20 E
Oravita	**34**	45 2N	21 43 E
Orawia	**81**	46 1S	167 50 E
Oraya, La	**136**	11 32S	75 54W
Orb →	**20**	43 17N	3 17 E
Orba →	**26**	44 53N	8 37 E
Ørbæk	**11**	55 17N	10 39 E
Orbe	**31**	46 43N	6 32 E
Orbec	**18**	49 1N	0 23 E
Orbetello	**27**	42 26N	11 11 E
Órbigo →	**22**	42 5N	5 42W
Orbost	**75**	37 40S	148 29 E
Örbyhus	**10**	60 15N	17 43 E
Orce	**25**	37 44N	2 28W
Orce →	**25**	37 44N	2 28W
Orchies	**19**	50 28N	3 14 E
Orchila, Isla	**134**	11 48N	66 10W
Orco →	**26**	45 10N	7 52 E
Orcopampa	**136**	15 20S	72 23W
Orcutt	**123**	34 52N	120 27W
Ord →	**78**	15 33S	138 15 E
Ord, Mt.	**78**	17 20S	125 34 E
Ord River	**78**	17 23S	128 51 E
Ordenes	**22**	43 5N	8 29W
Orderville	**121**	37 18N	112 43W
Ordos = Mu Us Shamo	**60**	39 0N	109 0 E
Ordu	**46**	40 55N	37 53 E
Orduña, Álava, Spain	**24**	42 58N	2 58 E
Orduña, Granada, Spain	**25**	37 20N	3 30W
Ordway	**118**	38 15N	103 42W
Ordzhonikidze, U.S.S.R.	**40**	43 0N	44 35 E
Ordzhonikidze, R.S.F.S.R., U.S.S.R.	**39**	43 0N	44 43 E
Ordzhonikidze, Ukraine S.S.R., U.S.S.R.	**38**	47 39N	34 3 E
Ore, Sweden	**10**	61 8N	15 10 E
Ore, Zaïre	**94**	3 17N	29 30 E
Ore Mts. = Erzgebirge	**30**	50 25N	13 0 E
Orealla	**135**	5 15N	57 23W
Orebić	**33**	43 0N	17 11 E
Örebro	**10**	59 20N	15 18 E
Örebro län □	**10**	59 27N	15 0 E
Oregon, Ill., U.S.A.	**116**	42 1N	89 20W
Oregon, Ohio, U.S.A.	**117**	41 38N	83 25W
Oregon, Wis., U.S.A.	**116**	42 56N	89 23W
Oregon □	**120**	44 0N	121 0W
Oregon City	**122**	45 21N	122 35W
Öregrund	**10**	60 21N	18 30 E
Öregrundsgrepen	**10**	60 25N	18 15 E
Orekhov	**38**	47 30N	35 48 E
Orekhovo-Zuyevo	**37**	55 50N	38 55 E
Orel	**37**	52 57N	36 3 E
Orel →	**38**	48 30N	34 54 E
Orellana, Canal de	**23**	39 2N	6 0W
Orellana la Vieja	**23**	39 1N	5 32W
Orellana, Pantano de	**23**	39 5N	5 10W
Orem	**120**	40 20N	111 45W
Orenburg	**40**	51 45N	55 6 E
Orense	**22**	42 19N	7 55W
Orense □	**22**	42 15N	7 51W
Orepuki	**81**	46 19S	167 46 E
Orestiás	**35**	41 30N	26 33 E
Øresund	**11**	55 45N	12 45 E
Oreti →	**81**	46 28S	168 14 E
Orford Ness	**13**	52 6N	1 31 E
Orgañà	**24**	42 13N	1 20 E
Orgaz	**23**	39 39N	3 53W
Orgeyev	**38**	47 24N	28 50 E
Orgon	**21**	43 47N	5 3 E
Orhon Gol →	**62**	49 30N	106 0 E
Ória	**29**	40 30N	17 38 E
Orient, Austral.	**73**	28 7S	142 50 E
Orient, U.S.A.	**116**	41 12N	94 25W
Oriental, Cordillera, Boliv.	**137**	17 0S	66 0W
Oriental, Cordillera, Colomb.	**134**	6 0N	73 0W
Oriente	**140**	38 44S	60 37W
Origny-Ste-Benoîte	**19**	49 50N	3 30 E
Orihuela	**25**	38 7N	0 55W
Orihuela del Tremedal	**24**	40 33N	1 39W
Oriku	**35**	40 20N	19 30 E
Orillia	**106**	44 40N	79 24W
Orinduik	**135**	4 40N	60 3W
Orinoco →	**135**	9 15N	61 30W
Orion	**116**	41 21N	90 23W
Orissa □	**50**	20 0N	84 0 E
Oristano	**28**	39 54N	8 35 E
Oristano, Golfo di	**28**	39 50N	8 22 E
Orituco →	**134**	8 45N	67 27W
Orizaba	**125**	18 50N	97 10W
Orizona	**139**	17 3S	48 18W
Orjen	**33**	42 35N	18 34 E
Orjiva	**25**	36 53N	3 24W
Orkanger	**10**	63 18N	9 52 E
Orkelljunga	**11**	56 17N	13 17 E
Örkény	**33**	47 9N	19 26 E
Orkla →	**10**	63 18N	9 51 E
Orkney	**96**	26 58S	26 40 E
Orkney □	**14**	59 0N	3 0W
Orkney Is.	**14**	59 0N	3 0W
Orland, Calif., U.S.A.	**122**	39 46N	122 12W
Orland, Ind., U.S.A.	**117**	41 47N	85 12W
Orlando	**113**	28 30N	81 25W
Orlando, C. d'	**29**	38 10N	14 43 E
Orléanais	**19**	48 0N	2 0 E
Orléans	**19**	47 54N	1 52 E
Orleans	**115**	44 49N	72 10W
Orléans, Î. d'	**105**	46 54N	70 58W
Orlice →	**32**	50 5N	16 10 E
Orlik	**41**	52 30N	99 55 E
Orlov	**32**	49 17N	20 51 E
Orlov Gay	**37**	50 56N	48 19 E
Ormara	**47**	25 16N	64 33 E
Ormea	**26**	44 9N	7 54 E
Ormília	**35**	40 16N	23 39 E
Ormoc	**57**	11 0N	124 37 E
Ormond, N.Z.	**80**	38 33S	177 56 E
Ormond, U.S.A.	**113**	29 13N	81 5W
Ormondville	**80**	40 5S	176 19 E
Ormož	**27**	46 25N	16 10 E
Ormstown	**105**	45 8N	74 0W
Ornans	**19**	47 7N	6 10 E
Orne □	**18**	48 40N	0 5 E
Orne →	**18**	49 18N	0 15W
Ørnhøj	**11**	56 13N	8 34 E
Ornö	**10**	59 4N	18 24 E
Örnsköldsvik	**10**	63 17N	18 40 E
Oro	**61**	40 1N	127 27 E
Oro →	**124**	25 35N	105 2W
Oro Grande	**123**	34 36N	117 20W
Orocué	**134**	4 48N	71 20W
Orodo	**89**	5 34N	7 4 E
Orogrande	**121**	32 20N	106 4W
Orol	**22**	43 34N	7 39W
Oromocto	**103**	45 54N	66 29W
Oron, Israel	**44**	30 55N	35 1 E
Oron, Nigeria	**89**	4 48N	8 14 E
Orono	**107**	43 59N	78 37W
Oropesa	**22**	39 57N	5 10W
Oroquieta	**57**	8 32N	123 44 E
Orós	**138**	6 15S	38 55W
Orosei, G. di	**28**	40 15N	9 40 E
Orosháza	**33**	46 32N	20 42 E
Orote Pen.	**68**	13 26N	144 38 E
Orotukan	**41**	62 16N	151 42 E
Oroville, Calif., U.S.A.	**122**	39 31N	121 30W
Oroville, Wash., U.S.A.	**120**	48 58N	119 30W
Oroville, Res.	**122**	39 33N	121 29W
Orrefors	**11**	56 50N	15 45 E
Orrick	**116**	39 13N	94 7W
Orroroo	**73**	32 43S	138 38 E
Orrville	**114**	40 50N	81 46W
Orsa	**10**	61 7N	14 37 E
Orsara di Púglia	**29**	41 17N	15 16 E
Orsasjön	**10**	61 7N	14 37 E
Orsha	**36**	54 30N	30 25 E
Orsk	**40**	51 12N	58 34 E
Ørslev	**11**	55 3N	11 56 E
Orsogna	**27**	42 13N	14 17 E
Orşova	**34**	44 41N	22 25 E
Ørsted	**11**	56 30N	10 20 E
Orta, L. d'	**26**	45 48N	8 21 E
Orta Nova	**29**	41 20N	15 40 E
Orte	**27**	42 28N	12 23 E
Ortegal, C.	**22**	43 43N	7 52W
Orteguaza →	**134**	0 43N	75 16W
Orthez	**20**	43 29N	0 48W
Ortigueira	**22**	43 40N	7 50W
Orting	**122**	47 6N	122 12W
Ortles	**26**	46 31N	10 33 E
Ortón →	**136**	10 50S	67 0W
Ortona	**27**	42 21N	14 24 E
Orune	**28**	40 25N	9 20 E
Oruro	**136**	18 0S	67 9W
Oruro □	**136**	18 40S	67 30W
Orust	**11**	58 10N	11 40 E
Oruzgan	**48**	33 0N	66 35 E
Orvault	**18**	47 17N	1 38W
Orvieto	**27**	42 43N	12 8 E
Orwell	**114**	41 32N	80 52W
Orwell →	**13**	52 2N	1 12 E
Oryakhovo	**34**	43 40N	23 57 E
Orzinuovi	**26**	45 24N	9 55 E
Orzysz	**32**	53 50N	21 58 E
Osa, Pen. de	**126**	8 0N	84 0W
Osage, Iowa, U.S.A.	**118**	43 15N	92 50W
Osage, Wyo., U.S.A.	**118**	43 59N	104 25W
Osage →	**116**	38 35N	91 57W
Osage City	**118**	38 43N	95 51W
Ōsaka	**65**	34 40N	135 30 E
Ōsaka □	**65**	34 30N	135 30 E
Ōsaka-Wan	**65**	34 30N	135 18 E
Osan	**61**	37 11N	127 4 E
Osawatomie	**118**	38 30N	94 55W
Osborne	**118**	39 30N	98 45W
Osby	**11**	56 23N	13 59 E
Osceola, Ark., U.S.A.	**119**	35 40N	90 0W
Osceola, Iowa, U.S.A.	**116**	41 0N	93 20W
Osceola, Mo., U.S.A.	**116**	38 3N	93 42W
Oschatz	**30**	51 17N	13 8 E
Oschersleben	**30**	52 2N	11 13 E
Öschiri	**28**	40 43N	9 7 E
Oscoda	**112**	44 26N	83 20W
Oscoda-Au-Sable	**106**	44 26N	83 20W
Ösel = Saaremaa	**36**	58 30N	22 30W
Osëry	**37**	54 52N	38 28 E
Osgood	**117**	39 8N	85 18W
Osgoode	**107**	45 8N	75 36W
Osh	**40**	40 37N	72 49 E
Oshawa	**107**	43 50N	78 50W
Oshikango	**96**	17 25S	15 55 E
Oshima	**64**	33 55N	132 14 E
ŌShima	**65**	34 44N	139 24 E
Oshkosh, Nebr., U.S.A.	**118**	41 27N	102 20W
Oshkosh, Wis., U.S.A.	**118**	44 3N	88 35W
Oshmyany	**36**	54 26N	25 52 E
Oshogbo	**89**	7 48N	4 37 E
Oshwe	**92**	3 25S	19 28 E
Osijek	**33**	45 34N	18 41 E
Ósilo	**28**	40 45N	8 41 E
Osimo	**27**	43 28N	13 30 E
Osintorf	**36**	54 40N	30 39 E
Osipenko = Berdyansk	**38**	46 45N	36 50 E
Osipovichi	**36**	53 19N	28 33 E
Oskaloosa	**116**	41 18N	92 40W
Oskarshamn	**11**	57 15N	16 27 E
Oskélanéo	**104**	48 5N	75 15W
Oskol →	**37**	49 6N	37 25 E
Oslo	**10**	59 55N	10 45 E
Oslob	**57**	9 31N	123 26 E
Oslofjorden	**10**	59 20N	10 35 E
Osmanabad	**50**	18 5N	76 10 E
Osmancık	**38**	40 45N	34 47 E
Osmaniye	**46**	37 5N	36 10 E
Ösmo	**10**	58 58N	17 55 E
Osnabrück	**30**	52 16N	8 2 E
Osona	**96**	22 3S	16 59 E
Osor	**26**	44 42N	14 24 E
Osorio	**141**	29 53S	50 17W
Osorno, Chile	**142**	40 25S	73 0W
Osorno, Spain	**22**	42 24N	4 22W
Osorno □	**142**	40 34S	73 9W
Osorno, Vol.	**142**	41 0S	72 30W
Osoyoos	**108**	49 0N	119 30W
Ospika →	**108**	56 20N	124 0W
Osprey Reef	**72**	13 52S	146 36 E
Oss	**16**	51 46N	5 32 E
Ossa de Montiel	**25**	38 58N	2 45W
Óssa, Mt.	**72**	41 52S	146 3 E
Óssa, Oros	**35**	39 47N	22 42 E
Ossabaw I.	**113**	31 45N	81 8W
Osse →	**20**	44 7N	0 17 E
Ossineke	**106**	44 55N	83 26W
Ossining	**115**	41 9N	73 50W
Ossipee	**115**	43 41N	71 9W
Ossokmanuan L.	**103**	53 25N	65 0W
Ossora	**41**	59 20N	163 13 E
Ostaboningue, L.	**104**	47 9N	78 53W

Ostashkov	**36**	57 4N	33 2 E		
Oste ⤳	**30**	53 30N	9 12 E		
Ostend = Oostende	**16**	51 15N	2 50 E		
Oster	**36**	50 57N	30 53 E		
Osterburg	**30**	52 47N	11 44 E		
Osterburken	**31**	49 26N	9 25 E		
Österbybruk	**10**	60 13N	17 55 E		
Österbymo	**11**	57 49N	15 15 E		
Östergötlands län □	**11**	58 35N	15 45 E		
Osterholz-Scharmbeck	**30**	53 14N	8 48 E		
Østerild	**11**	57 2N	8 51 E		
Österkorsberga	**11**	57 18N	15 6 E		
Östersund	**10**	63 10N	14 38 E		
Østfold fylke □	**10**	59 25N	11 25 E		
Ostfreisland	**30**	53 20N	7 30 E		
Ostfriesische Inseln	**30**	53 45N	7 15 E		
Óstia, Lido di (Lido di Roma)	**28**	41 43N	12 17 E		
Ostiglía	**27**	45 4N	11 9 E		
Ostra	**27**	43 40N	13 5 E		
Ostrava	**32**	49 51N	18 18 E		
Ostróda	**32**	53 42N	19 58 E		
Ostrog	**36**	50 20N	26 30 E		
Ostrogozhsk	**37**	50 55N	39 7 E		
Ostrogróg Sźamotuły	**32**	52 37N	16 33 E		
Ostrołeka	**32**	53 4N	21 32 E		
Ostrov, Bulg.	**34**	43 40N	24 9 E		
Ostrov, Rumania	**34**	44 6N	27 24 E		
Ostrov, U.S.S.R.	**36**	57 25N	28 20 E		
Ostrów Mazowiecka	**32**	52 50N	21 51 E		
Ostrów Wielkopolski	**32**	51 36N	17 44 E		
Ostrowiec-Świętokrzyski	**32**	50 55N	21 22 E		
Ostrzeszów	**32**	51 25N	17 52 E		
Ostseebad-Külungsborn	**30**	54 10N	11 40 E		
Ostuni	**29**	40 44N	17 34 E		
Osum ⤳	**34**	43 40N	24 50 E		
Osumi ⤳	**35**	40 40N	20 10 E		
Osumi-Hantō	**64**	31 20N	130 55 E		
Osumi-Kaikyō	**63**	30 55N	131 0 E		
Ōsumi-Shotō	**63**	30 30N	130 0 E		
Osuna	**23**	37 14N	5 8W		
Oswego	**115**	43 29N	76 30W		
Oswestry	**12**	52 52N	3 3W		
Oświecim	**32**	50 2N	19 11 E		
Ōta	**65**	36 18N	139 22 E		
Ota-Gawa ⤳	**64**	34 21N	132 18 E		
Otago □	**81**	44 44S	169 10 E		
Otago Harb.	**81**	45 47S	170 42 E		
Otago Pen.	**81**	45 48S	170 39 E		
Otahuhu	**80**	36 56S	174 51 E		
Otake	**64**	34 12N	132 13 E		
Ōtaki	**65**	35 17N	140 15 E		
Otaki	**80**	40 45S	175 10 E		
Otane	**80**	39 54S	176 39 E		
Otaru	**63**	43 10N	141 0 E		
Otautau	**81**	46 9S	168 1 E		
Otava ⤳	**32**	49 26N	14 12 E		
Otavalo	**134**	0 13N	78 20W		
Otavi	**96**	19 40S	17 24 E		
Otchinjau	**96**	16 30S	13 56 E		
Otelec	**34**	45 36N	20 50 E		
Otero de Rey	**22**	43 6N	7 36W		
Othello	**120**	46 53N	119 8W		
Othonoí	**35**	39 52N	19 22 E		
Óthris, Óros	**35**	39 4N	22 42 E		
Otira	**81**	42 49S	171 35 E		
Otira Gorge	**81**	42 53S	171 33 E		
Otis	**118**	40 12N	102 58W		
Otjiwarongo	**96**	20 30S	16 33 E		
Oto Tolu Group	**68**	20 21S	174 32W		
Otočac	**27**	44 53N	15 12 E		
Otoineppu	**63**	44 44N	142 16 E		
Otorohanga	**80**	38 12S	175 14 E		
Otoskwin ⤳	**102**	52 13N	88 6W		
Otosquen	**109**	53 17N	102 1W		
Ōtoyo	**64**	33 43N	133 45 E		
Otranto	**29**	40 9N	18 28 E		
Otranto, C. d'	**29**	40 7N	18 30 E		
Otranto, Str. of	**29**	40 15N	18 40 E		
Otsego	**117**	42 27N	85 42W		
Ōtsu	**65**	35 0N	135 50 E		
Ōtsuki	**65**	35 36N	138 57 E		
Otta	**10**	61 46N	9 32 E		
Ottapalam	**51**	10 46N	76 23 E		
Ottawa, Can.	**107**	45 27N	75 42W		
Ottawa, Ill., U.S.A.	**117**	41 20N	88 55W		
Ottawa, Kans., U.S.A.	**118**	38 40N	95 6W		
Ottawa, Ohio, U.S.A.	**117**	41 1N	84 3W		
Ottawa = Outaouais ⤳	**105**	45 27N	74 8W		
Ottawa Is.	**101**	59 35N	80 10W		
Ottélé	**89**	3 38N	11 19 E		
Ottenby	**11**	56 15N	16 24 E		
Otter L.	**109**	55 35N	104 39W		
Otter Lake	**106**	43 13N	83 28W		
Otter Rapids, Ont., Can.	**102**	50 11N	81 39W		
Otter Rapids, Sask., Can.	**109**	55 38N	104 44W		
Otterbein	**117**	40 29N	87 6W		
Otterberg	**31**	49 30N	7 46 E		
Otterndorf	**30**	53 47N	8 52 E		
Otterup	**11**	55 30N	10 22 E		
Otterville, Can.	**106**	42 55N	80 36W		
Otterville, U.S.A.	**116**	38 42N	93 0W		
Otteys Cr. ⤳	**77**	28 45S	150 33 E		
Otto Beit Bridge	**95**	15 59S	28 56 E		
Ottosdal	**96**	26 46S	25 59 E		
Ottoshoop	**96**	25 45S	25 58 E		
Ottoville	**117**	40 57N	84 22W		
Ottsjö	**10**	63 13N	13 2 E		
Ottumwa	**116**	41 0N	92 25W		
Otu	**89**	8 14N	3 22 E		
Otukpa (Al Owuho)	**89**	7 9N	7 41 E		
Oturkpo	**89**	7 16N	8 8 E		
Otway, Bahía	**142**	53 30S	74 0W		
Otway, C.	**74**	38 52S	143 30 E		
Otwock	**32**	52 5N	21 20 E		
Ötz	**31**	47 13N	10 53 E		
Ötz ⤳	**31**	47 14N	10 50 E		
Ötztaler Alpen	**31**	46 45N	11 0 E		
Ou ⤳	**54**	20 4N	102 13 E		
Ou Neua	**54**	22 18N	101 48 E		
Ouachita ⤳	**119**	31 38N	91 49W		
Ouachita, L.	**119**	34 40N	93 25W		
Ouachita Mts.	**119**	34 50N	94 30W		
Ouaco	**68**	20 50S	164 29 E		
Ouadane	**84**	20 50N	11 40W		
Ouadda	**85**	8 15N	22 20 E		
Ouagadougou	**89**	12 25N	1 30W		
Ouahigouya	**88**	13 31N	2 25W		
Ouahila	**86**	27 50N	5 0W		
Ouahran = Oran	**86**	35 49N	0 39W		
Oualâta	**88**	17 20N	6 55W		
Ouallene	**86**	24 41N	1 11 E		
Ouanda Djallé	**85**	8 55N	22 53 E		
Ouango	**92**	4 19N	22 30 E		
Ouareau, L., Rés.	**105**	46 17N	74 9W		
Ouargla	**87**	31 59N	5 16 E		
Ouarkziz, Djebel	**86**	28 50N	8 0W		
Ouarzazate	**86**	30 55N	6 50W		
Ouasiemsca ⤳	**105**	49 0N	72 30W		
Ouatagouna	**89**	15 11N	0 43 E		
Oubangi ⤳	**92**	1 0N	17 50 E		
Oubarakai, O. ⤳	**87**	27 20N	9 0 E		
Oubatche	**68**	20 26S	164 39 E		
Ouche ⤳	**19**	47 6N	5 16 E		
Ouddorp	**16**	51 50N	3 57 E		
Oude Rijn ⤳	**16**	52 12N	4 24 E		
Oudenaarde	**16**	50 50N	3 37 E		
Oudon	**18**	47 22N	1 19W		
Oudon ⤳	**18**	47 38N	1 18 E		
Oudtshoorn	**96**	33 35S	22 14 E		
Oued Sbita	**86**	25 50N	5 2W		
Oued Zem	**86**	32 52N	6 34W		
Ouégoa	**68**	20 20S	164 26 E		
Ouellé	**88**	7 26N	4 1W		
Ouen, Î.	**68**	22 26S	166 49 E		
Ouenza	**87**	35 57N	8 4 E		
Ouessa	**88**	11 4N	2 47W		
Ouessant, Île d'	**18**	48 28N	5 6W		
Ouesso	**92**	1 37N	16 5 E		
Ouest, Pte.	**103**	49 52N	64 40W		
Ouezzane	**86**	34 51N	5 35W		
Ouidah	**89**	6 25N	2 0 E		
Ouistreham	**18**	49 17N	0 18W		
Oujda	**86**	34 41N	1 55W		
Oujeft	**84**	20 2N	13 0W		
Ouled Djellal	**87**	34 28N	5 2 E		
Ouled Naïl, Mts. des	**86**	34 30N	3 30 E		
Oulmès	**86**	33 17N	6 0W		
Oulu	**8**	65 1N	25 29 E		
Oulujärvi	**8**	64 25N	27 15 E		
Oulujoki ⤳	**8**	65 1N	25 30 E		
Oulun lääni □	**8**	64 36N	27 20 E		
Oulx	**26**	45 2N	6 49 E		
Oum el Bouaghi	**87**	35 55N	7 6 E		
Oum el Ksi	**86**	29 4N	6 59W		
Oum-er-Rbia, O. ⤳	**86**	33 19N	8 21W		
Oumè	**88**	6 21N	5 27W		
Ounane, Dj.	**87**	25 4N	7 19 E		
Ounasjoki ⤳	**8**	66 31N	25 30 E		
Ounguati	**96**	21 54S	15 46 E		
Ounianga Kébir	**85**	19 4N	20 29 E		
Our ⤳	**16**	49 55N	6 5 E		
Ouray	**121**	38 3N	107 40W		
Ourcq ⤳	**19**	49 1N	3 1 E		
Oureg, Oued el ⤳	**86**	32 34N	2 10 E		
Ourém	**138**	1 33S	47 6W		
Ouricuri	**138**	7 53S	40 5W		
Ourinhos	**141**	23 0S	49 54W		
Ourini	**85**	16 7N	22 25 E		
Ourique	**23**	37 38N	8 16W		
Ouro Fino	**141**	22 16S	46 25W		
Ouro Prêto	**139**	20 20S	43 30W		
Ouro Sogui	**88**	15 36N	13 19W		
Oursi	**89**	14 41N	0 27W		
Ourthe ⤳	**16**	50 29N	5 35 E		
Ouse	**72**	42 38S	146 42 E		
Ouse ⤳, Sussex, U.K.	**13**	50 43N	0 3 E		
Ouse ⤳, Yorks., U.K.	**12**	54 3N	0 7 E		
Oust	**20**	42 52N	1 13 E		
Oust ⤳	**18**	47 35N	2 6W		
Outaouais ⤳	**105**	45 27N	74 8W		
Outardes	**105**	50 20N	69 10W		
Outardes ⤳	**105**	49 24N	69 30W		
Outat Oulad el Haj	**86**	33 22N	3 42W		
Outer Hebrides, Is.	**14**	57 30N	7 40W		
Outer I.	**103**	51 10N	58 35W		
Outes	**22**	42 52N	8 55W		
Outjo	**96**	20 5S	16 7 E		
Outlook, Can.	**109**	51 30N	107 0W		
Outlook, U.S.A.	**118**	48 53N	104 46W		
Outreau	**19**	50 40N	1 36 E		
Ouvèze ⤳	**21**	43 59N	4 51 E		
Ouyen	**74**	35 1S	142 22 E		
Ouzouer-le-Marché	**18**	47 54N	1 32 E		
Ovada	**26**	44 39N	8 40 E		
Ovalle	**140**	30 33S	71 18W		
Ovar	**22**	40 51N	8 40W		
Ovejas	**134**	9 32N	75 14W		
Ovens	**75**	36 35S	146 46 E		
Ovens ⤳	**75**	36 2S	146 12 E		
Over Flakkee	**16**	51 45N	4 5 E		
Overijssel □	**16**	52 25N	6 35 E		
Overland	**116**	38 41N	90 23W		
Overland Park	**116**	38 58N	94 40W		
Overpelt	**16**	51 12N	5 20 E		
Overton	**123**	36 32N	114 31W		
Overum	**11**	58 0N	16 20 E		
Ovid, Colo., U.S.A.	**118**	41 0N	102 17W		
Ovid, Mich., U.S.A.	**106**	43 1N	84 22W		
Ovidiopol	**38**	46 15N	30 30 E		
Oviedo	**22**	43 25N	5 50W		
Oviedo □	**22**	43 20N	6 0W		
Oviken	**10**	63 0N	14 23 E		
Oviksfjällen	**10**	63 0N	13 49 E		
Övör Hangay □	**60**	45 0N	102 30 E		
Ovoro	**89**	5 26N	7 16 E		
Ovruch	**36**	51 25N	28 45 E		
Owaka	**81**	46 27S	169 40 E		
Owambo	**96**	17 20S	16 30 E		
Owase	**65**	34 7N	136 12 E		
Owatonna	**118**	44 3N	93 10W		
Owego	**115**	42 6N	76 17W		
Owen Falls	**94**	0 30N	33 5 E		
Owen Mt.	**81**	41 35S	172 33 E		
Owen Sound	**106**	44 35N	80 55W		
Owen Stanley Range	**69**	8 30S	147 0 E		
Owendo	**92**	0 17N	9 30 E		
Owens ⤳	**122**	36 32N	117 59W		
Owens L.	**123**	36 20N	118 0W		
Owensboro	**117**	37 40N	87 5W		
Owensville, Ind., U.S.A.	**117**	38 16N	87 41W		
Owensville, Mo., U.S.A.	**116**	38 20N	91 30W		
Owenton	**117**	38 32N	84 50W		
Owerri	**89**	5 29N	7 0 E		
Owhango	**80**	39 0S	175 23 E		
Owingsville	**117**	38 9N	83 46W		
Owl ⤳	**109**	57 51N	92 44W		
Owo	**89**	7 10N	5 39 E		
Owosso	**117**	43 0N	84 10W		
Owyhee	**120**	42 0N	116 3W		
Owyhee ⤳	**120**	43 46N	117 2W		
Owyhee Res.	**120**	43 40N	117 16W		
Ox Mts.	**15**	54 6N	9 0W		
Oxapampa	**136**	10 33S	75 26W		
Oxberg	**10**	61 7N	14 11 E		
Oxelösund	**11**	58 43N	17 15 E		
Oxford, N.Z.	**81**	43 18S	172 11 E		
Oxford, U.K.	**13**	51 45N	1 15W		
Oxford, Iowa, U.S.A.	**116**	41 43N	91 47W		
Oxford, Mich., U.S.A.	**117**	42 49N	83 16W		
Oxford, Miss., U.S.A.	**119**	34 22N	89 30W		
Oxford, N.C., U.S.A.	**113**	36 19N	78 36W		
Oxford, Ohio, U.S.A.	**117**	39 30N	84 40W		
Oxford □	**13**	51 45N	1 15W		
Oxford L.	**109**	54 51N	95 37W		
Oxley, N.S.W., Austral.	**74**	34 11S	144 6 E		
Oxley, Vic., Austral.	**75**	36 25S	146 22 E		
Oxnard	**123**	34 10N	119 14W		
Oya	**56**	2 55N	111 55 E		
Oyabe	**65**	36 47N	136 56 E		
Oyama	**65**	36 18N	139 48 E		
Oyana	**64**	32 32N	130 30 E		
Oyapock ⤳	**135**	4 8N	51 40W		
Oyem	**92**	1 34N	11 31 E		
Oyen	**109**	51 22N	110 28W		
Öyeren	**10**	59 50N	11 15 E		
Oykel ⤳	**14**	57 55N	4 26W		
Oymyakon	**41**	63 25N	142 44 E		
Oyo	**89**	7 46N	3 56 E		
Oyo □	**89**	8 0N	3 30 E		
Oyón	**136**	10 37S	76 47W		
Oyonnax	**21**	46 16N	5 40 E		
Oyster B.	**115**	40 52N	73 32W		
Ozamis (Mizamis)	**57**	8 15N	123 50 E		
Ozark, Ala., U.S.A.	**113**	31 29N	85 39W		
Ozark, Ark., U.S.A.	**119**	35 30N	93 50W		
Ozark, Mo., U.S.A.	**119**	37 0N	93 15W		
Ozark Plateau	**119**	37 20N	91 40W		
Ozarks, L. of	**116**	38 10N	92 40W		
Ózd	**33**	48 14N	20 15 E		
Ozette, L.	**122**	48 6N	124 38W		
Ozieri	**28**	40 35N	9 0 E		
Ozona	**119**	30 43N	101 11W		
Ozorków	**32**	51 57N	19 16 E		
Ozu, Ehime, Japan	**64**	33 30N	132 33 E		
Ozu, Kumanoto, Japan	**64**	32 52N	130 52 E		
Ozuluama	**125**	21 40N	97 50W		

P

Pa	**88**	11 33N	3 19W
Pa-an	**52**	16 51N	97 40 E
Pa Mong Dam	**54**	18 0N	102 22 E
Paagoumène	**68**	20 29S	164 11 E
Paama	**68**	16 28S	168 14 E
Paar ⤳	**31**	48 13N	10 59 E
Paarl	**96**	33 45S	18 56 E
Paauilo	**110**	20 3N	155 22W
Pab Hills	**48**	26 30N	66 45 E
Pabianice	**32**	51 40N	19 20 E
Pabna	**52**	24 1N	89 18 E
Pabo	**94**	3 1N	32 10 E
Pacaás Novos, Serra dos	**137**	10 45S	64 15W
Pacaipampa	**136**	5 35S	79 39W
Pacaja ⤳	**138**	1 56S	50 50W
Pacajus	**138**	4 10S	38 31W
Pacaraima, Serra	**135**	4 5N	61 30W
Pacaraima, Sierra = Pacaraima Serra	**135**	4 0N	62 30W
Pacarán	**136**	12 50S	76 3W
Pacaraos	**136**	11 12S	76 42W
Pacasmayo	**136**	7 20S	79 35W
Pacaudière, La	**20**	46 11N	3 52 E
Paceco	**28**	37 59N	12 32 E
Pachacamac	**136**	12 14S	77 53W
Pachhar	**48**	24 40N	77 42 E
Pachino	**29**	36 43N	15 4 E
Pachitea ⤳	**136**	8 46S	74 33W
Pachiza	**136**	7 16S	76 46W
Pacho	**134**	5 8N	74 10W
Pachora	**50**	20 38N	75 29 E
Pachuca	**125**	20 10N	98 40W
Pacific, Can.	**108**	54 48N	128 28W
Pacific, U.S.A.	**116**	38 29N	90 45W
Pacific-Antarctic Basin	**67**	46 0S	95 0W
Pacific-Antarctic Ridge	**67**	43 0S	115 0W
Pacific Grove	**122**	36 38N	121 58W
Pacific Ocean	**66**	10 0N	140 0W
Pacifica	**122**	37 36N	122 30W
Pacitan	**57**	8 12S	111 7 E
Packenham	**107**	45 22N	76 25W
Packwood	**122**	46 36N	121 40W
Pacofi	**108**	53 0N	132 30W
Pacuí ⤳	**139**	16 46S	45 1W
Padaido, Kepulauan	**57**	1 5S	138 0 E
Padalarang	**57**	7 50S	107 30 E
Padang	**56**	1 0S	100 20 E
Padangpanjang	**56**	0 40S	100 20 E
Padangsidempuan	**56**	1 30N	99 15 E
Padatchuang	**52**	19 46N	94 48 E
Padauari ⤳	**135**	0 15S	64 5W
Padborg	**11**	54 49N	9 21 E
Padcaya	**137**	21 52S	64 48W
Paddockwood	**109**	53 30N	105 30W
Paderborn	**30**	51 42N	8 44 E
Padilla	**137**	19 19S	64 20W
Padloping Island	**101**	67 0N	62 50W
Padma ⤳	**52**	23 22N	90 32 E
Padmanabhapuram	**51**	8 16N	77 17 E
Pádova	**27**	45 24N	11 52 E
Padra	**48**	22 15N	73 7 E
Padrauna	**49**	26 54N	83 59 E
Padre I.	**119**	27 0N	97 20W
Padrón	**22**	42 41N	8 39W
Padstow	**12**	50 33N	4 57W
Padua = Pádova	**27**	45 24N	11 52 E
Paducah, Ky., U.S.A.	**112**	37 0N	88 40W
Paducah, Tex., U.S.A.	**119**	34 3N	100 16W
Padul	**23**	37 1N	3 38W
Padula	**29**	40 20N	15 40 E
Padwa	**50**	18 27N	82 47 E
Paekakariki	**80**	40 59S	174 58 E
Paengaroa	**80**	37 49S	176 29 E
Paengnyong-do	**61**	37 57N	124 40 E
Paeroa	**80**	37 23S	175 41 E
Paesana	**26**	44 40N	7 18 E
Pag, Yugo.	**27**	44 27N	15 5 E
Pag, Yugo.	**27**	44 30N	14 50 E
Paga	**89**	11 1N	1 8W
Pagadian	**57**	7 55N	123 30 E
Pagai Selatan	**56**	3 0S	100 15W
Pagai Utara	**56**	2 35S	100 0 E
Pagalu, I.	**83**	1 25S	5 36 E

Pagastikós Kólpos **35** 39 15N 23 0 E
Pagatan **56** 3 33S 115 59 E
Page, Ariz., U.S.A. **121** 36 57N 111 27W
Page, N.D., U.S.A. **118** 47 11N 97 37W
Paglieta **27** 42 10N 14 30 E
Pagnau **91** 8 15N 34 7 E
Pagny-sur-Moselle **19** 48 59N 6 2 E
Pago Pago **68** 14 16S 170 43W
Pagosa Springs **121** 37 16N 107 4W
Pagwa River **102** 50 2N 85 14W
Pahala **110** 19 12N 155 25W
Pahang → **55** 3 30N 103 9 E
Pahiatua **80** 40 27S 175 50 E
Pahokee **113** 26 50N 80 40W
Pahrump **123** 36 15N 116 0W
Pahute Mesa **122** 37 25N 116 50W
Pai **54** 19 19N 98 27 E
Paia **110** 20 54N 156 22W
Paicines **122** 36 44N 121 17W
Paide **36** 58 57N 25 31 E
Paignton **13** 50 26N 3 33W
Paiján **136** 7 42S 79 20W
Päijänne, L. **9** 61 30N 25 30 E
Paimbœuf **18** 47 17N 2 0W
Paimpol **18** 48 48N 3 4W
Painan **56** 1 21S 100 34 E
Painesville **114** 41 42N 81 18W
Paint I. **109** 55 28N 97 57W
Paint Rock **119** 31 30N 99 56W
Painted Desert **121** 36 0N 111 30W
Paintsville **112** 37 50N 82 50W
Paisley, Can. **106** 44 18N 81 16W
Paisley, U.K. **14** 55 51N 4 27W
Paisley, U.S.A. **120** 42 43N 120 40W
Paita, N. Cal. **68** 22 8S 166 22 E
Paita, Peru **136** 5 11S 81 9W
Paiva → **22** 41 4N 8 16W
Paiva Couceiro **93** 14 37S 14 40 E
Paizhou **59** 30 12N 113 55 E
Pajares **22** 43 1N 5 46W
Pajares, Puerto de **22** 43 0N 5 46W
Pak Lay **54** 18 15N 101 27 E
Pak Phanang **55** 8 21N 100 12 E
Pak Sane **54** 18 22N 103 39 E
Pak Song **54** 15 11N 106 14 E
Pak Suong **54** 19 58N 102 15 E
Pakala **51** 13 29N 79 8 E
Pakanbaru **56** 0 30N 101 15 E
Pakaraima Mts. **135** 6 0N 60 0W
Pakemba **95** 13 3S 29 58 E
Pakenham, Austral. **74** 38 6S 145 30 E
Pakenham, Can. **104** 45 18N 76 18W
Pakistan ■ **47** 30 0N 70 0 E
Pakkading **54** 18 19N 103 59 E
Pakokku **52** 21 20N 95 0 E
Pakpattan **48** 30 25N 73 27 E
Pakrac **33** 45 27N 17 12 E
Paks **33** 46 38N 18 55 E
Pakse **54** 15 5N 105 52 E
Paktya □ **47** 33 0N 69 15 E
Pakwach **94** 2 28N 31 27 E
Pala, Chad **85** 9 25N 15 5 E
Pala, U.S.A. **123** 33 22N 117 5W
Pala, Zaïre **94** 6 45S 29 30 E
Palabek **94** 3 22N 32 33 E
Palacios **119** 28 44N 96 12W
Palafrugell **24** 41 55N 3 10 E
Palagiano **29** 40 35N 17 0 E
Palagonía **29** 37 20N 14 43 E
Palagruža **27** 42 24N 16 15 E
Palaiokhóra **35** 35 16N 23 39 E
Palais, Le **18** 47 20N 3 10W
Palakol **51** 16 31N 81 46 E
Palam **50** 19 0N 77 0 E
Palamás **35** 39 26N 22 4 E
Palamós **24** 41 50N 3 10 E
Palampur **48** 32 10N 76 30 E
Palana, Austral. **72** 39 45S 147 55 E
Palana, U.S.S.R. **41** 59 10N 159 59 E
Palanan **57** 17 8N 122 29 E
Palanan Pt. **57** 17 17N 122 30 E
Palandri **49** 33 42N 73 40 E
Palangkaraya **56** 2 16S 113 56 E
Palanpur **48** 24 10N 72 25 E
Palapye **96** 22 30S 27 7 E
Palar → **51** 12 27N 80 13 E
Palas **49** 35 4N 73 14 E
Palatine **117** 42 7N 88 3W
Palatka, U.S.A. **113** 29 40N 81 40W
Palatka, U.S.S.R. **41** 60 6N 150 54 E
Palau Is. **66** 7 30N 134 30 E
Palauig **57** 15 26N 119 54 E
Palavas **20** 43 32N 3 56 E
Palawan, Is. **56** 9 30N 118 30 E
Palayancottai **51** 8 45N 77 45 E
Palazzo San Gervásio **29** 40 53N 15 58 E
Palazzolo Acreide **29** 37 4N 14 54 E
Palca **136** 19 7S 69 9W
Paldiski **36** 59 23N 24 9 E
Palel **52** 24 27N 94 2 E
Paleleh **57** 1 10N 121 50 E
Palembang **56** 3 0S 104 50 E
Palen Creek **77** 28 17S 152 48 E
Palena → **142** 43 50S 73 50W
Palena, L. **142** 43 55S 71 40W
Palencia **22** 42 1N 4 34W
Palencia □ **22** 42 31N 4 33W
Palermo, Colomb. **134** 2 54N 75 26W
Palermo, Italy **28** 38 8N 13 20 E
Palermo, U.S.A. **120** 39 30N 121 37W
Palestine, Asia **44** 32 0N 35 0 E
Palestine, U.S.A. **119** 31 42N 95 35W
Palestrina **28** 41 50N 12 52 E
Paletwa **52** 21 10N 92 50 E
Palghat **51** 10 46N 76 42 E
Palgrave, Mt. **78** 23 22S 115 58 E
Pali **48** 25 50N 73 20 E
Palimé **89** 6 57N 0 44 E
Palinuro, C. **29** 40 1N 15 14 E
Palisade **118** 40 21N 101 10W
Palitana **48** 21 32N 71 49 E
Palizada **125** 18 18N 92 8W
Palizzi **29** 37 58N 15 59 E
Palk Bay **51** 9 30N 79 15 E
Palk Strait **51** 10 0N 79 45 E
Palkonda **50** 18 36N 83 48 E
Palkonda Ra. **51** 13 50N 79 20 E
Pallamallawa **77** 29 29S 150 10 E
Pallanza = Verbánia **26** 45 50N 8 55 E
Pallasovka **37** 50 4N 47 0 E
Palleru → **50** 16 45N 80 2 E
Pallinup **79** 34 0S 117 55 E
Pallisa **94** 1 12N 33 43 E
Palliser Bay **80** 41 26S 175 5 E
Palliser, C. **80** 41 37S 175 14 E
Pallu **48** 28 59N 74 14 E
Palm Beach **113** 26 46N 80 0W
Palm Desert **123** 33 43N 116 22W
Palm Is. **72** 18 40S 146 35 E
Palm Springs **123** 33 51N 116 35W
Palma, Canary Is. **84** 28 40N 17 50W
Palma, Mozam. **95** 10 46S 40 29 E
Palma, Spain **24** 39 33N 2 39 E
Palma → **139** 12 33S 47 52W
Palma, Bahía de **25** 39 30N 2 39 E
Palma del Río **23** 37 43N 5 17W
Palma di Montechiaro **28** 37 12N 13 46 E
Palma, La, Canary Is. **84** 28 45N 17 50W
Palma, La, Panama **126** 8 15N 78 0W
Palma, La, Spain **23** 37 21N 6 38W
Palma Soriano **126** 20 15N 76 0W
Palmanova **27** 45 54N 13 18 E
Palmares **138** 8 41S 35 28W
Palmarito **134** 7 37N 70 10W
Palmarola **28** 40 57N 12 50 E
Palmarolle **104** 48 40N 79 12W
Palmas **141** 26 29S 52 0W
Palmas, C. **88** 4 27N 7 46W
Palmas de Monte Alto **139** 14 16S 43 10W
Pálmas, G. di **28** 39 0N 8 30 E
Palmdale **123** 34 36N 118 7W
Palmeira **139** 25 25S 50 0W
Palmeira dos Índios **138** 9 25S 36 37W
Palmeirais **138** 6 0S 43 0W
Palmeiras → **139** 12 22S 47 8W
Palmeirinhas, Pta. das **92** 9 2S 12 57 E
Palmela **23** 38 32N 8 57W
Palmelo **139** 17 20S 48 27W
Palmer, Alaska, U.S.A. **100** 61 35N 149 10W
Palmer, Mass., U.S.A. **115** 42 9N 72 21W
Palmer → **72** 15 34S 142 26 E
Palmer Arch **143** 64 15S 65 0W
Palmer Lake **118** 39 10N 104 52W
Palmer Land **143** 73 0S 60 0W
Palmerston **106** 43 50N 80 51W
Palmerston North **81** 40 21S 175 39 E
Palmerton **115** 40 47N 75 36W
Palmetto **113** 27 33N 82 33W
Palmi **29** 38 21N 15 51 E
Palmira, Argent. **140** 32 59S 68 34W
Palmira, Colomb. **134** 3 32N 76 16W
Palms **106** 43 37N 82 47W
Palmyra, Ill., U.S.A. **116** 39 26N 90 0W
Palmyra, Mo., U.S.A. **116** 39 45N 91 30W
Palmyra, N.Y., U.S.A. **114** 42 5N 77 18W
Palmyra, Wis., U.S.A. **117** 42 52N 88 36W
Palmyra = Tadmor **46** 34 30N 37 17 E
Palmyra Is. **67** 5 52N 162 6W
Palni **51** 10 30N 77 30 E
Palni Hills **51** 10 14N 77 33 E
Palo Alto **122** 37 25N 122 8W
Palo del Colle **29** 41 4N 16 43 E
Palo Verde **123** 33 26N 114 45W
Paloma, La **140** 30 35S 71 0W
Palombara Sabina **27** 42 4N 12 45 E
Palopo **57** 3 0S 120 16 E
Palos, Cabo de **25** 37 38N 0 40W
Palos Verdes **123** 33 48N 118 23W
Palos Verdes, Pt. **123** 33 43N 118 26W
Palouse **120** 46 59N 117 5W
Palpa **136** 14 30S 75 15W
Palparara **72** 24 47S 141 28 E
Pålsboda **11** 59 3N 15 22 E
Palu, Indon. **57** 1 0S 119 52 E
Palu, Turkey **46** 38 45N 40 0 E
Paluan **57** 13 26N 120 29 E
Palwal **48** 28 8N 77 19 E
Pama **89** 11 19N 0 44 E
Pamanukan **57** 6 16S 107 49 E
Pamban I. **51** 9 15N 79 20 E
Pambula **75** 36 55S 149 53 E
Pamekasan **57** 7 10S 113 29 E
Pameungpeuk **57** 7 38S 107 44 E
Pamiers **20** 43 7N 1 39 E
Pamirs **40** 37 40N 73 0 E
Pamlico → **113** 35 25N 76 30W
Pamlico Sd. **113** 35 20N 76 0W
Pampa **119** 35 35N 100 58W
Pampa de Agma **142** 43 45S 69 40W
Pampa de las Salinas **140** 32 1S 66 58W
Pampa Grande **137** 18 5S 64 6W
Pampa Hermosa **136** 7 7S 75 4W
Pampa, La □ **140** 36 50S 66 0W
Pampanua **57** 4 16S 120 8 E
Pamparato **26** 44 16N 7 54 E
Pampas, Argent. **140** 35 0S 63 0W
Pampas, Peru **136** 12 20S 74 50W
Pampas → **136** 13 24S 73 12W
Pamplona, Colomb. **134** 7 23N 72 39W
Pamplona, Spain **24** 42 48N 1 38W
Pampoenpoort **96** 31 3S 22 40 E
Pan Xian **58** 25 46N 104 38 E
Pana **116** 39 25N 89 10W
Panaca **121** 37 51N 114 23W
Panache, L. **106** 46 15N 81 20W
Panagyurishte **34** 42 30N 24 15 E
Panaitan **57** 6 35S 105 10 E
Panaji (Panjim) **51** 15 25N 73 50 E
Panamá **126** 9 0N 79 25W
Panama ■ **126** 8 48N 79 55W
Panama Canal **126** 9 10N 79 37W
Panama City **113** 30 10N 85 41W
Panamá, Golfo de **126** 8 4N 79 20W
Panamint Mts. **121** 36 30N 117 20W
Panamint Springs **123** 36 20N 117 28W
Panão **136** 9 55S 75 55W
Panare **55** 6 51N 101 30 E
Panarea **29** 38 38N 15 3 E
Panaro → **26** 44 55N 11 25 E
Panarukan **57** 7 40S 113 52 E
Panay **57** 11 10N 122 30 E
Panay, G. **57** 11 0N 122 30 E
Pancake Ra. **121** 38 30N 116 0W
Pančevo **33** 44 52N 20 41 E
Panco **57** 8 42S 118 40 E
Pancorbo, Paso **24** 42 32N 3 5W
Pandan **57** 11 45N 122 10 E
Pandeglang **57** 6 25S 106 0 E
Pandharpur **50** 17 41N 75 20 E
Pandhurna **50** 21 36N 78 35 E
Pandilla **24** 41 32N 3 43W
Pando **141** 34 44S 56 0W
Pando □ **136** 11 20S 67 40W
Pando, L. = Hope L. **73** 28 24S 139 18 E
Panevezys **36** 55 42N 24 25 E
Panfilov **40** 44 10N 80 0 E
Panfilovo **37** 50 25N 42 46 E
Panga **94** 1 52N 26 18 E
Pangalanes, Canal des **97** 22 48S 47 50 E
Pangani **94** 5 25S 38 58 E
Pangani □ **94** 5 25S 39 0 E
Pangani → **94** 5 26S 38 58 E
Pange Creek **76** 31 45S 147 8 E
Pangfou = Bengbu **61** 32 56N 117 20 E
Pangil **94** 3 10S 26 35 E
Pangkah, Tanjung **57** 6 51S 112 33 E
Pangkai **52** 22 40N 98 40 E
Pangkalanberandan **56** 4 1N 98 20 E
Pangkalanbuun **56** 2 41S 111 37 E
Pangkalansusu **56** 4 2N 98 13 E
Pangkoh **56** 3 5S 114 8 E
Pangnirtung **101** 66 8N 65 54W
Pangong Tso **49** 34 0N 78 20 E
Pangrango **57** 6 46S 107 1 E
Pangsau Pass **52** 27 15N 96 10 E
Pangtara **52** 20 57N 96 40 E
Panguipulli **142** 39 38S 72 20W
Panguitch **121** 37 52N 112 30W
Pangutaran Group **57** 6 18N 120 34 E
Panhandle **119** 35 23N 101 23W
Pani Mines **48** 22 29N 73 50 E
Panie, Mt. **68** 20 36S 164 46 E
Panipat **48** 29 25N 77 2 E
Panitya **74** 35 15S 141 0 E
Panjal Range **48** 32 30N 76 50 E
Panjgur **47** 27 0N 64 5 E
Panjim = Panaji **51** 15 25N 73 50 E
Panjinad Barrage **47** 29 22N 71 15 E
Panjwai **48** 31 26N 65 27 E
Pankajene **57** 4 46S 119 34 E
Pankalpinang **56** 2 0S 106 0 E
Pankshin **89** 9 16N 9 25 E
Panmunjŏm **61** 37 59N 126 38 E
Panmure **74** 38 20S 142 43 E
Panna **49** 24 40N 80 15 E
Panna Hills **49** 24 40N 81 15 E
Pannuru **51** 16 5N 80 34 E
Panora **116** 41 41N 94 22W
Panorama **141** 21 21S 51 51W
Panruti **51** 11 46N 79 35 E
Panshan **61** 41 3N 122 2 E
Panshi **61** 42 58N 126 5 E
Pantano **121** 32 0N 110 32W
Pantar **57** 8 28S 124 10 E
Pantelleria **28** 36 52N 12 0 E
Pantelleria, I. **28** 36 52N 12 0 E
Pantha **52** 23 55N 94 35 E
Pantin Sakan **52** 18 38N 97 33 E
Pantón **22** 42 31N 7 37W
Pánuco **125** 22 0N 98 15W
Panyam **89** 9 27N 9 8 E
Panyu **59** 22 51N 113 20 E
Pao →, Apure, Venez. **134** 8 33N 68 1W
Pao →, Orinoco, Venez. **135** 8 6N 64 17W
Páola **29** 39 21N 16 2 E
Paola **118** 38 36N 94 50W
Paoli **117** 38 33N 86 28W
Paonia **121** 38 56N 107 37W
Paoting = Baoding **60** 38 50N 115 28 E
Paot'ou = Baotou **60** 40 32N 110 2 E
Paoua **92** 7 9N 16 20 E
Papá **33** 47 22N 17 30 E
Papagayo → **125** 16 36N 99 43W
Papagayo, Golfo de **126** 10 30N 85 50W
Papagni → **51** 15 35N 77 45 E
Papakura **80** 37 4S 174 59 E
Papantla **125** 20 30N 97 30W
Papar **56** 5 45N 116 0 E
Paparoa **80** 36 6S 174 16 E
Paparoa Range **81** 42 5S 171 35 E
Pápas, Ákra **35** 38 13N 21 20 E
Papatoetoe **80** 36 59S 174 51 E
Papeari **68** 17 45S 149 21W
Papeete **68** 17 32S 149 34W
Papenburg **30** 53 7N 7 25 E
Papenoo **68** 17 30S 149 25W
Papetoai **68** 17 29S 149 52W
Papigochic → **124** 29 9N 109 40W
Papineau-Labelle, Parc Prov. **104** 46 10N 75 15W
Papineauville **104** 45 37N 75 1W
Paposo **140** 25 0S 70 30W
Papua, Gulf of **69** 9 0S 144 50 E
Papua New Guinea ■ **69** 8 0S 145 0 E
Papuča **27** 44 22N 15 30 E
Papudo **140** 32 29S 71 27W
Papuk **33** 45 30N 17 30 E
Papun **52** 18 0N 97 30 E
Pará = Belém **138** 1 20S 48 30W
Pará □, Brazil **137** 3 20S 52 0W
Pará □, Surinam **135** 40 0S 53 0W
Parábita **29** 40 3N 18 8 E
Paraburdoo **78** 23 14S 117 32 E
Paracas, Pen. **136** 13 53S 76 20W
Paracatu **139** 17 10S 46 50W
Paracatu → **139** 16 30S 45 4W
Parachilna **73** 31 10S 138 21 E
Parachinar **48** 33 55N 70 5 E
Paraćin **33** 43 54N 21 27 E
Paracuru **138** 3 24S 39 4W
Parada, Punta **136** 15 22S 75 11W
Paradas **23** 37 18N 5 29W
Paradela **22** 42 44N 7 37W
Paradip **50** 20 15N 86 35 E
Paradis **104** 48 15N 76 35W
Paradise, Calif., U.S.A. **122** 39 46N 121 37W
Paradise, Mich., U.S.A. **106** 46 38N 85 3W
Paradise, Mont., U.S.A. **120** 47 27N 114 17W
Paradise, Nev., U.S.A. **123** 36 4N 115 7W
Paradise → **103** 53 27N 57 19W
Paradise Valley **120** 41 30N 117 28W
Parado **57** 8 42S 118 30 E
Paragould **119** 36 5N 90 30W
Paraguá → **137** 13 34S 61 53W
Paragua → **135** 6 55N 62 55W
Paragua, La **135** 6 50N 63 20W
Paraguaçu → **139** 12 45S 38 54W
Paraguaçu Paulista **141** 22 22S 50 35W
Paraguaipoa **134** 11 21N 71 57W
Paraguaná, Pen. de **134** 12 0N 70 0W
Paraguarí **140** 25 36S 57 0W
Paraguarí □ **140** 26 0S 57 10W
Paraguay ■ **140** 23 0S 57 0W
Paraguay → **140** 27 18S 58 38W
Paraíba = João Pessoa **138** 7 10S 35 0W
Paraíba □ **138** 7 0S 36 0W
Paraíba do Sul → **139** 21 37S 41 3W
Parainen **9** 60 18N 22 18 E
Paraiso **125** 18 24N 93 14W
Parakhino Paddubye **36** 58 26N 33 10 E
Parakou **89** 9 25N 2 40 E
Paramagudi **51** 9 31N 78 39 E

Paramaribo	135	5 50N	55 10W
Parambu	138	6 13S	40 43W
Paramillo, Nudo del	134	7 4N	75 55W
Paramirim	139	13 26S	42 15W
Paramirim →	139	11 34S	43 18W
Paramithiá	35	39 30N	20 35 E
Paramushir, Ostrov	41	50 24N	156 0 E
Paran →	44	30 20N	35 10 E
Paraná	140	31 45S	60 30W
Paranã	139	12 30S	47 48W
Paraná □	141	24 30S	51 0W
Paraná →	140	33 43S	59 15W
Paranaguá	141	25 30S	48 30W
Paranaíba →	139	20 6S	51 4W
Paranapanema →	141	22 40S	53 9W
Paranapiacaba, Serra do	141	24 31S	48 35W
Paranavaí	141	23 4S	52 56W
Parang, Jolo, Phil.	57	5 55N	120 54 E
Parang, Mindanao, Phil.	57	7 23N	124 16 E
Parangaba	138	3 45S	38 33W
Paraparauma	80	40 57S	175 3 E
Parapóla	35	36 55N	23 27 E
Paraspóri, Ákra	35	35 55N	27 15 E
Paratinga	139	12 40S	43 10W
Paratoo	73	32 42S	139 40 E
Parattah	72	42 22S	147 23 E
Paraúna	139	16 55S	50 26W
Paray-le-Monial	21	46 27N	4 7 E
Parbati →	48	25 50N	76 30 E
Parbatipur	52	25 39N	88 55 E
Parbhani	50	19 8N	76 52 E
Parchim	30	53 25N	11 50 E
Parczew	32	51 40N	22 52 E
Pardee Res.	122	38 16N	120 51W
Pardes Hanna	44	32 28N	34 57 E
Pardilla	22	41 33N	3 43W
Pardo →, Bahia, Brazil	139	15 40S	39 0W
Pardo →, Mato Grosso, Brazil	141	21 46S	52 9W
Pardo →, Minas Gerais, Brazil	139	15 48S	44 48W
Pardo →, São Paulo, Brazil	139	20 10S	48 38W
Pardubice	32	50 3N	15 45 E
Pare	57	7 43S	112 12 E
Pare □	94	4 10S	38 0 E
Pare Mts.	94	4 0S	37 45 E
Parecis, Serra dos	137	13 0S	60 0W
Paredes de Nava	22	42 9N	4 42W
Parelhas	138	6 41S	36 39W
Paren	41	62 30N	163 15 E
Parengarenga Harbour	80	34 31S	173 0 E
Parent	104	47 55N	74 35W
Parent, Lac.	104	48 31N	77 1W
Parentis-en-Born	20	44 21N	1 4W
Parepare	57	4 0S	119 40 E
Parfino	36	57 59N	31 34 E
Parfuri	97	22 28S	31 17 E
Parham	107	44 39N	76 43W
Paria, Golfo de	134	10 20N	62 0W
Paria, Pen. de	135	10 50N	62 30W
Pariaguán	135	8 51N	64 34W
Pariaman	56	0 47S	100 11 E
Paricatuba	135	4 26S	61 53W
Paricutín, Cerro	124	19 28N	102 15W
Parigi, Java, Indon.	57	7 42S	108 29 E
Parigi, Sulawesi, Indon.	57	0 50S	120 5 E
Parika	135	6 50N	58 20W
Parima, Serra	135	2 30N	64 0W
Parinari	136	4 35S	74 25W
Parîng	34	45 20N	23 37 E
Parintins	135	2 40S	56 50W
Paris, Can.	106	43 12N	80 25W
Paris, France	19	48 50N	2 20 E
Paris, Idaho, U.S.A.	120	42 13N	111 30W
Paris, Ill., U.S.A.	117	39 36N	87 42W
Paris, Ky., U.S.A.	117	38 12N	84 12W
Paris, Mo., U.S.A.	116	39 29N	92 0W
Paris, Tenn., U.S.A.	113	36 20N	88 20W
Paris, Tex., U.S.A.	119	33 40N	95 30W
Paris, Ville de □	19	48 50N	2 20 E
Parish	115	43 24N	76 9W
Pariti	57	10 15S	123 45 E
Park	122	48 45N	122 18W
Park City	120	40 42N	111 35W
Park Falls	118	45 58N	90 27W
Park Range	120	40 0N	106 30W
Park Rapids	118	46 56N	95 0W
Park Ridge	117	42 2N	87 51W
Park River	118	48 25N	97 43W
Park Rynie	97	30 25S	30 45 E
Park View	121	36 45N	106 37W
Parker, Ariz., U.S.A.	123	34 8N	114 16W
Parker, S.D., U.S.A.	118	43 25N	97 7W
Parker Dam	123	34 13N	114 5W
Parkersburg, Iowa, U.S.A.	116	42 35N	92 47W
Parkersburg, W. Va., U.S.A.	112	39 18N	81 31W
Parkerview	109	51 21N	103 18W
Parkes	76	33 9S	148 11 E
Parkfield	122	35 54N	120 26W
Parkhill	106	43 15N	81 38W
Parkland	122	47 9N	122 26W
Parkside	109	53 10N	106 33W
Parkston	118	43 25N	98 0W
Parksville	108	49 20N	124 21W
Parkville	77	31 58S	150 53 E
Parlakimedi	50	18 45N	84 5 E
Parma, Italy	26	44 50N	10 20 E
Parma, Idaho, U.S.A.	120	43 49N	116 59W
Parma, Ohio, U.S.A.	114	41 25N	81 42W
Parma →	26	44 56N	10 26 E
Parnaguá	138	10 10S	44 38W
Parnaíba, Piauí, Brazil	138	2 54S	41 47W
Parnaíba, São Paulo, Brazil	137	19 34S	51 14W
Parnaíba →	138	3 0S	41 50W
Parnamirim	138	8 5S	39 34W
Parnarama	138	5 31S	43 6W
Parnassós	35	38 35N	22 30 E
Parnassus	81	42 42S	173 23 E
Párnis	35	38 14N	23 45 E
Párnon Óros	35	37 15N	22 45 E
Pärnu	36	58 28N	24 33 E
Parola	50	20 47N	75 7 E
Paroo →	73	31 28S	143 32 E
Paropamisus Range = Fī roz Kohi	47	34 45N	63 0 E
Páros, Greece	35	37 5N	25 12 E
Páros, Greece	35	37 5N	25 9 E
Parowan	121	37 54N	112 56W
Parpaillon	21	44 30N	6 40 E
Parral	140	36 10S	71 52W
Parramatta	76	33 48S	151 1 E
Parras	124	25 30N	102 20W
Parrett →	13	51 7N	2 58W
Parris I.	113	32 20N	80 30W
Parrsboro	103	45 30N	64 25W
Parry Is.	144	77 0N	110 0W
Parry Sound	106	45 20N	80 0W
Parsberg	31	49 10N	11 43 E
Parshall	118	47 56N	102 11W
Parsnip →	108	55 10N	123 2W
Parsons	119	37 20N	95 17W
Parsons Ra.	72	13 30S	135 15 E
Partabpur	50	20 0N	80 42 E
Partanna	28	37 43N	12 51 E
Partapgarh	48	24 2N	74 40 E
Parthenay	18	46 38N	0 16W
Partinico	28	38 3N	13 6 E
Partur	50	19 40N	76 14 E
Paru →	135	1 33S	52 38W
Parú →	134	4 20N	66 27W
Paru de Oeste →	135	1 30N	56 0W
Parucito →	134	5 18N	65 59W
Parur	51	10 13N	76 14 E
Paruro	136	13 45S	71 50W
Parvatipuram	50	18 50N	83 25 E
Parwan □	47	35 0N	69 0 E
Parys	96	26 52S	27 29 E
Pas-de-Calais □	19	50 30N	2 30 E
Pasadena, Calif., U.S.A.	123	34 5N	118 9W
Pasadena, Tex., U.S.A.	119	29 45N	95 14W
Pasaje	134	3 23S	79 50W
Pasaje →	140	25 39S	63 56W
Pascagoula	119	30 21N	88 30W
Pascagoula →	119	30 21N	88 35W
Paşcani	34	47 14N	26 45 E
Pasco	120	46 10N	119 0W
Pasco □	136	10 40S	76 0W
Pasco, Cerro de	136	10 45S	76 10W
Pasco, Mt.	79	27 25S	120 40 E
Pasewalk	30	53 30N	14 0 E
Pasfield L.	109	58 24N	105 20W
Pasha →	36	60 29N	32 55 E
Pashiwari	49	34 40N	75 10 E
Pashmakli = Smolyan	35	41 36N	24 38 E
Pasighat	52	28 4N	95 21 E
Pasing	31	48 9N	11 27 E
Pasirian	57	8 13S	113 8 E
Pasley, C.	79	33 52S	123 35 E
Pašman	27	43 58N	15 20 E
Pasni	47	25 15N	63 27 E
Paso Cantinela	123	32 33N	115 47W
Paso de Indios	142	43 55S	69 0W
Paso de los Libres	140	29 44S	57 10W
Paso de los Toros	140	32 45S	56 30W
Paso Flores	142	40 35S	70 38W
Paso Robles	121	35 40N	120 45W
Pasorapa	137	18 16S	64 37W
Paspébiac	103	48 3N	65 17W
Pasrur	48	32 16N	74 43 E
Passage West	15	51 52N	8 20W
Passaic	115	40 50N	74 8W
Passau	31	48 34N	13 27 E
Passero, C.	29	36 42N	15 8 E
Passo Fundo	141	28 10S	52 20W
Passos	139	20 45S	46 37W
Passow	30	53 13N	14 10 E
Passy	21	45 55N	6 41 E
Pastaza □	134	2 0S	77 0W
Pastaza →	134	4 50S	76 52W
Pastęk	32	54 3N	19 41 E
Pasto	134	1 13N	77 17W
Pasto Zootécnico do Cunene	96	16 20S	15 20 E
Pastos Bons	138	6 36S	44 5W
Pastrana	24	40 27N	2 53W
Pasuruan	57	7 40S	112 44 E
Patagonia, Argent.	142	45 0S	69 0W
Patagonia, U.S.A.	121	31 35N	110 45W
Patan, Gujarat, India	50	17 22N	73 57 E
Patan, Maharashtra, India	48	23 54N	72 14 E
Patani	57	0 20N	128 50 E
Pataudi	48	28 18N	76 48 E
Patay	19	48 2N	1 40 E
Patchewollock	74	35 22S	142 12 E
Patchogue	115	40 46N	73 1W
Patea	80	39 45S	174 30 E
Pategi	89	8 50N	5 45 E
Patensie	96	33 46S	24 49 E
Paternò	29	37 34N	14 53 E
Paternoster, Kepulauan	56	7 5S	118 15 E
Pateros	120	48 4N	119 58W
Paterson, Austral.	76	32 35S	151 36 E
Paterson, U.S.A.	115	40 55N	74 10W
Paterson Inlet	81	46 56S	168 12 E
Paterson Ra.	78	21 45S	122 10 E
Pathankot	48	32 18N	75 45 E
Patharghata	52	22 2N	89 58 E
Pathfinder Res.	120	42 30N	107 0W
Pathiu	55	10 42N	99 19 E
Pathum Thani	54	14 1N	100 32 E
Pati	57	6 45S	111 3 E
Pati Pt.	68	13 40N	144 50 E
Patía	134	2 4N	77 4W
Patía →	134	2 13N	78 40W
Patiala	48	30 23N	76 26 E
Patine Kouka	88	12 45N	13 45W
Pativilca	136	10 42S	77 48W
Patkai Bum	52	27 0N	95 30 E
Pátmos	35	37 21N	26 36 E
Patna	49	25 35N	85 12 E
Patonga	94	2 45N	33 15 E
Patos	138	6 55S	37 16W
Patos de Minas	139	18 35S	46 32W
Patos, Lag. dos	141	31 20S	51 0 E
Patquía	140	25 30N	102 11W
Pátrai	35	38 14N	21 47 E
Pátraikós, Kólpos	35	38 17N	21 30 E
Patricio Lynch, I.	142	48 35S	75 30W
Patrie, La	105	45 24N	71 15W
Patrocínio	139	18 57S	47 0W
Patta	94	2 10S	41 0 E
Pattada	28	40 35N	9 7 E
Pattanapuram	51	9 6N	76 50 E
Pattani	55	6 48N	101 15 E
Patten	103	45 59N	68 28W
Patterson, Calif., U.S.A.	122	37 30N	121 9W
Patterson, La., U.S.A.	119	29 44N	91 20W
Patterson, Mt.	122	38 29N	119 20W
Patteson, Passage	68	15 26S	168 12 E
Patti, India	48	31 17N	74 54 E
Patti, Italy	29	38 8N	14 57 E
Pattoki	48	31 5N	73 52 E
Patton	114	40 38N	78 40W
Pattonsburg	116	40 3N	94 8W
Pattukkottai	51	10 25N	79 20 E
Patu	138	6 6S	37 38W
Patuakhali	52	22 20N	90 25 E
Patuca →	126	15 50N	84 18W
Patuca, Punta	126	15 49N	84 14W
Pátzcuaro	124	19 30N	101 40W
Pau	20	43 19N	0 25W
Pau d' Arco	138	7 30S	49 22W
Pau dos Ferros	138	6 7S	38 10W
Pau, Gave de	20	43 33N	1 12W
Paucartambo	136	13 19S	71 35W
Pauillac	20	45 11N	0 46W
Pauini	136	7 40S	66 58W
Pauini →	135	1 42S	62 50W
Pauk	52	21 27N	94 30 E
Paul I.	103	56 30N	61 20W
Paul Isnard	135	4 47N	54 1W
Paul-Sauvé, L.	104	50 15N	78 20W
Paulding	117	41 8N	84 35W
Paulhan	20	43 33N	3 28 E
Paulis = Isiro	94	2 47N	27 37 E
Paulista	138	7 57S	34 53W
Paulistana	138	8 9S	41 9W
Paullina	118	42 55N	95 40W
Paulo Afonso	138	9 21S	38 15W
Paulo de Faria	139	20 2S	49 24W
Paulpietersburg	97	27 23S	30 50 E
Pauls Valley	119	34 40N	97 17W
Pauma Valley	123	33 16N	116 58W
Paungde	52	18 29N	95 30 E
Pauni	50	20 48N	79 40 E
Pausa	136	15 16S	73 22W
Pauto →	134	5 9N	70 55W
Pavelets	37	53 49N	39 14 E
Pavia	26	45 10N	9 10 E
Pavlikeni	34	43 14N	25 20 E
Pavlodar	40	52 33N	77 0 E
Pavlograd	38	48 30N	35 52 E
Pavlovo, Gorkiy, U.S.S.R.	37	55 58N	43 5 E
Pavlovo, Yakut A.S.S.R., U.S.S.R.	41	63 5N	115 25 E
Pavlovsk	37	50 26N	40 5 E
Pavlovskaya	39	46 17N	39 47 E
Pavlovskiy-Posad	37	55 47N	38 42 E
Pavullo nel Frignano	26	44 20N	10 50 E
Pavuvu	68	9 4S	159 8 E
Paw-Paw	116	41 41N	88 59W
Paw Paw	117	42 13N	85 53W
Pawahku	52	26 11N	98 40 E
Pawhuska	119	36 40N	96 25W
Pawling	115	41 35N	73 37W
Pawnee, Ill., U.S.A.	116	39 35N	89 35W
Pawnee, Okla., U.S.A.	119	36 24N	96 50W
Pawnee City	118	40 8N	96 10W
Pawtucket	115	41 51N	71 22W
Paxoí	35	39 14N	20 12 E
Paxton, Ill., U.S.A.	117	40 25N	88 7W
Paxton, Nebr., U.S.A.	118	41 12N	101 27W
Payakumbah	56	0 20S	100 35 E
Payerne	31	46 49N	6 56 E
Payette	120	44 0N	117 0W
Paymogo	23	37 44N	7 21W
Payne	117	41 5N	84 44W
Payne L.	101	59 30N	74 30W
Paynes Find	79	29 15S	117 42 E
Paynesville, Austral.	75	37 55S	147 43 E
Paynesville, Liberia	88	6 20N	10 45W
Paynesville, U.S.A.	118	45 21N	94 44W
Pays Basque	20	43 15N	1 0W
Paysandú	140	32 19S	58 8W
Payson, Ariz., U.S.A.	121	34 17N	111 15W
Payson, Utah, U.S.A.	120	40 8N	111 41W
Paz →	126	13 44N	90 10W
Paz, Bahía de la	124	24 15N	110 25W
Paz Centro, La	126	12 20N	86 41W
Paz, La, Entre Ríos, Argent.	140	30 50S	59 45W
Paz, La, San Luis, Argent.	140	33 30S	67 20W
Paz, La, Boliv.	136	16 20S	68 10W
Paz, La, Hond.	126	14 20N	87 47W
Paz, La, Mexico	124	24 10N	110 20W
Paz, La □	136	15 30S	68 0W
Pazar	46	41 10N	40 50 E
Pazardzhik	34	42 12N	24 20 E
Pazin	27	45 14N	13 56 E
Pazña	136	18 36S	66 55W
Pčinja →	35	41 50N	21 45 E
Pe Ell	122	46 30N	123 18W
Peabody	115	42 31N	70 56W
Peace →	108	59 0N	111 25W
Peace Point	108	59 7N	112 27W
Peace River	108	56 15N	117 18W
Peach Springs	121	35 36N	113 30W
Peak Downs	72	22 14S	148 0 E
Peak Downs Mine	72	22 17S	148 11 E
Peak Hill, N.S.W., Austral.	76	32 47S	148 11 E
Peak Hill, W. A., Austral.	79	25 35S	118 43 E
Peak Range	72	22 50S	148 20 E
Peak, The	12	53 24N	1 53W
Peake	73	35 25S	140 0 E
Peake Cr. →	73	28 2S	136 7 E
Peale Mt.	121	38 25N	109 12W
Pearblossom	123	34 30N	117 55W
Pearce	121	31 57N	109 56W
Pearl	116	39 28N	90 38W
Pearl →	119	30 23N	89 45W
Pearl Banks	51	8 45N	79 45 E
Pearl City, Hawaii, U.S.A.	110	21 24N	158 0W
Pearl City, Ill., U.S.A.	116	42 16N	89 50W
Pearsall	119	28 55N	99 8W
Pearse I.	108	54 52N	130 14W
Peary Land	144	82 40N	33 0W
Pease →	119	34 12N	99 7W
Pebane	95	17 10S	38 8 E
Pebas	134	3 10S	71 46W
Pebble Beach	122	36 34N	121 57W
Pebole, I.	142	51 20S	59 40W
Peč	33	42 40N	20 17 E
Peçanha	139	18 33S	42 34W
Pecatonica	116	42 19N	89 22W
Pecatonica →	116	42 26N	89 17W
Péccioli	26	43 32N	10 43 E
Pechea	34	45 36N	27 49 E
Pechenezhin	38	48 30N	24 48 E

Pechenga 40 69 30N 31 25 E
Pechnezhskoye Vdkhr. 37 50 0N 37 10 E
Pechora → 40 68 13N 54 15 E
Pechorskaya Guba 40 68 40N 54 0 E
Pechory 36 57 48N 27 40 E
Pecica 34 46 10N 21 3 E
Peck 106 43 16N 82 49W
Pečka 33 44 18N 19 33 E
Pécora, C. 28 39 28N 8 23 E
Pecos 119 31 25N 103 35W
Pecos → 119 29 42N 102 30W
Pécs 33 46 5N 18 15 E
Peddapalli 50 18 40N 79 24 E
Peddapuram 50 17 6N 8 13 E
Pedder, L. 72 42 55S 146 10 E
Pedernales 127 18 2N 71 44W
Pedirka 73 26 40S 135 14 E
Pedra Azul 139 16 2S 41 17W
Pedra Grande, Recifes de 139 17 45S 38 58W
Pedras Negras 137 12 51S 62 54W
Pedreiras 138 4 32S 44 40W
Pedrera, La 134 1 18S 69 43W
Pedro Afonso 138 9 0S 48 10W
Pedro Antonio Santos 125 18 54N 88 15W
Pedro Cays 126 17 5N 77 48W
Pedro Chico 134 1 4N 70 25W
Pedro de Valdivia 140 22 55S 69 38W
Pedro Juan Caballero 141 22 30S 55 40W
Pedro Muñoz 25 39 25N 2 56W
Pedrógão Grande 22 39 55N 8 9W
Peduyim 44 31 20N 34 37 E
Peebinga 73 34 52S 140 57 E
Peebles, U.K. 14 55 40N 3 12W
Peebles, U.S.A. 117 38 57N 83 23W
Peechelba 75 36 12S 146 15 E
Peekskill 115 41 18N 73 57W
Peel, Austral. 76 33 20S 149 38 E
Peel, I. of Man 12 54 14N 4 40W
Peel →, Austral. 77 30 50S 150 29 E
Peel →, Can. 100 67 0N 135 0W
Peelwood 76 34 7S 149 27 E
Peene → 30 54 9N 13 46 E
Peera Peera Poolanna L. 73 26 30S 138 0 E
Peers 108 53 40N 116 0W
Pegasus Bay 81 43 20S 173 10 E
Pegnitz 31 49 45N 11 33 E
Pegnitz → 31 49 29N 10 59 E
Pego 25 38 51N 0 8W
Pegu Yoma 52 19 0N 96 0 E
Pehuajó 140 35 45S 62 0W
Pei Xian 60 34 44N 116 55 E
Peine, Chile 140 23 45S 68 8W
Peine, Ger. 30 52 19N 10 12 E
Peip'ing = Beijing 60 39 55N 116 20 E
Peiss 31 47 58N 11 47 E
Peissenberg 31 47 48N 11 4 E
Peitz 30 51 50N 14 23 E
Peixe 139 12 0S 48 40W
Peixe → 139 21 31S 51 58W
Peixoto de Azeredo → 137 10 6S 55 31W
Pek → 33 44 45N 21 29 E
Pekalongan 57 6 53S 109 40 E
Pekan 55 3 30N 103 25 E
Pekin 116 40 35N 89 40W
Peking = Beijing 60 39 55N 116 20 E
Pelabuhan Ratu, Teluk 57 7 5S 106 30 E
Pelabuhanratu 57 7 0S 106 32 E
Pélagos 35 39 17N 24 4 E
Pelaihari 56 3 55S 114 45 E
Pelat, Mont 21 44 16N 6 42 E
Peleaga 34 45 22N 22 55 E
Pelechuco 136 14 48S 69 4W
Pelee I. 106 41 47N 82 40W
Pelée, Mt. 127 14 48N 61 0W
Pelee, Pt. 106 41 54N 82 31W
Pelejo 136 6 10S 75 49W
Pelekech 94 3 52N 35 8 E
Peleng 57 1 20S 123 30 E
Pelham 113 31 5N 84 6W
Pelhřimov 32 49 24N 15 12 E
Pelican L. 109 52 28N 100 20W
Pelican Narrows 109 55 10N 102 56W
Pelican Portage 108 55 51N 112 35W
Pelican Rapids 109 52 45N 100 42W
Pella 116 41 30N 93 0W
Péllaro 29 38 1N 15 40 E
Pelletier Sta. 105 47 33N 69 26W
Pellston 106 45 33N 84 47W
Pellworm 30 54 30N 8 40 E
Pelly → 100 62 47N 137 19W
Pelly Bay 101 68 38N 89 50W
Pelly L. 100 66 0N 102 0W
Peloponnese = Pelóponnisos 35 37 10N 22 0 E
Peloritani, Monti 29 38 2N 15 25 E
Peloro, C. 29 38 15N 15 40 E
Pelorus Sound 81 40 59S 173 59 E
Pelotas 141 31 42S 52 23W
Pelvoux, Massif de 21 44 52N 6 20 E
Pemalang 57 6 53S 109 23 E
Pematang 56 0 12S 102 4 E
Pematangsiantar 56 2 57N 99 5 E
Pemba, Mozam. 95 12 58S 40 30 E
Pemba, Tanz. 94 5 0S 39 45 E
Pemba, Zambia 95 16 30S 27 28 E
Pemba Channel 94 5 0S 39 37 E
Pemberton, Austral. 79 34 30S 116 0 E
Pemberton, Can. 108 50 25N 122 50W
Pembina 109 48 58N 97 15W
Pembina → 109 49 0N 98 12W
Pembine 112 45 38N 87 59W
Pembino 118 48 58N 97 15W
Pembroke, Can. 107 45 50N 77 7W
Pembroke, U.K. 13 51 41N 4 57W
Pembroke, U.S.A. 113 32 5N 81 32W
Pen-y-Ghent 12 54 10N 2 15W
Peña de Francia, Sierra de 22 40 32N 6 10W
Peña, Sierra de la 24 42 32N 0 45W
Penafiel 22 41 12N 8 17W
Peñafiel 22 41 35N 4 7W
Peñaflor 23 37 43N 5 21W
Peñalara, Pico 22 40 51N 3 57W
Penalva 138 3 18S 45 10W
Penamacôr 22 40 10N 7 10W
Penápolis 141 21 30S 50 0W
Peñaranda de Bracamonte 22 40 53N 5 13W
Peñarroya-Pueblonuevo 23 38 19N 5 16W
Peñas, C. de 22 43 42N 5 52W
Peñas de San Pedro 25 38 44N 2 0W
Penas, G. de 142 47 0S 75 0W
Peñas, Pta. 135 11 17N 62 0W
Peñausende 22 41 17N 5 52W
Pench'i = Benxi 61 41 20N 123 48 E
Pend Oreille → 120 49 4N 117 37W
Pend Oreille, L. 120 48 0N 116 30W
Pendembu 88 9 7N 12 14W
Pendências 138 5 15S 36 43W
Pender B. 78 16 45S 122 42 E
Pendleton, Calif., U.S.A. 123 33 16N 117 23W
Pendleton, Ind., U.S.A. 117 40 0N 85 45W
Pendleton, Oreg., U.S.A. 120 45 35N 118 50W
Penedo 138 10 15S 36 36W
Penetanguishene 106 44 50N 79 55W
Peng Xian 58 31 4N 103 32 E
Pengalengan 57 7 9S 107 30 E
Penge, Kasai Oriental, Congo 94 5 30S 24 33 E
Penge, Kivu, Congo 94 4 27S 28 25 E
Penglai 61 37 48N 120 42 E
Pengshui 58 29 17N 108 12 E
Penguin 72 41 8S 146 6 E
Pengxi 58 30 44N 105 45 E
Pengze 59 29 52N 116 32 E
Penhalonga 95 18 52S 32 40 E
Peniche 23 39 19N 9 22W
Penicuik 14 55 50N 3 14W
Penida 56 8 45S 115 30 E
Peñíscola 24 40 22N 0 24 E
Penitente, Serra dos 138 8 45S 46 20W
Penmarch 18 47 49N 4 21W
Penmarch, Pte. de 18 47 48N 4 22W
Pennabilli 27 43 50N 12 17 E
Pennant 109 50 32N 108 14W
Penne 27 42 28N 13 56 E
Pennel Glacier 143 69 20S 157 27 E
Penner → 51 14 35N 80 10 E
Pennine, Alpi 26 46 5N 7 50 E
Pennines 12 54 50N 2 20W
Pennington 122 39 15N 121 47W
Pennino, Mte. 27 43 6N 12 54 E
Pennsylvania □ 112 40 50N 78 0W
Pennville 117 40 30N 85 9W
Penny 108 53 51N 121 20W
Pennyan 114 42 39N 77 7W
Peno 36 57 2N 32 49 E
Penola 73 37 25S 140 21 E
Penonomé 126 8 31N 80 21W
Penot, Mt. 68 16 20S 167 31 E
Penrhyn Is. 67 9 0S 158 30W
Penrith, Austral. 76 33 43S 150 38 E
Penrith, U.K. 12 54 40N 2 45W
Pensacola 113 30 30N 87 10W
Pensacola Mts. 143 84 0S 40 0W
Pense 109 50 25N 104 59W
Penshurst 74 37 49S 142 20 E
Pentecost = Pentecôte 68 15 42S 168 10 E
Pentecoste 138 3 48S 39 17W
Pentecôte 68 15 42S 168 10 E
Penticton 108 49 30N 119 38W
Pentland 72 20 32S 145 25 E
Pentland Firth 14 58 43N 3 10W
Pentland Hills 14 55 48N 3 25W
Penukonda 51 14 5N 77 38 E
Penylan L. 109 61 50N 106 20W
Penza 37 53 15N 45 5 E
Penzance 13 50 7N 5 32W
Penzberg 31 47 46N 11 23 E
Penzhino 41 63 30N 167 55 E
Penzhinskaya Guba 41 61 30N 163 0 E
Penzlin 30 53 32N 13 6 E
Peoria, Ariz., U.S.A. 121 33 40N 112 15W
Peoria, Ill., U.S.A. 116 40 40N 89 40W
Peoria Heights 116 40 45N 89 35W
Peotone 117 41 20N 87 48W
Pepperwood 120 40 23N 124 0W
Pera Hd. 72 12 55S 141 37 E
Perabumilih 56 3 27S 104 15 E
Perakhóra 35 38 2N 22 56 E
Perales de Alfambra 24 40 38N 1 0W
Perales del Puerto 22 40 10N 6 40W
Peralta 24 42 21N 1 49W
Pérama 35 35 20N 24 40 E
Percé 103 48 31N 64 13W
Perche 18 48 31N 1 1 E
Perche, Collines du 18 48 30N 0 40 E
Percival Lakes 78 21 25S 125 0 E
Percy, France 18 48 55N 1 11W
Percy, U.S.A. 116 38 5N 89 41W
Percy Is. 72 21 39S 150 16 E
Perdido → 142 42 55S 67 0W
Pereira 134 4 49N 75 43W
Pereira Barreto 139 20 38S 51 7W
Perekerten 74 34 55S 143 40 E
Perené → 136 11 9S 74 14W
Perenjori 79 29 26S 116 16 E
Pereslavi-Zalesskiy 37 56 45N 38 50 E
Pereyaslav-Khmelnitskiy 36 50 3N 31 28 E
Pérez, I. 125 22 24N 89 42W
Pergamino 140 33 52S 60 30W
Pérgine Valsugano 27 46 4N 11 15 E
Pérgola 27 43 35N 12 50 E
Perham 118 46 36N 95 36W
Perhentian, Kepulauan 55 5 54N 102 42 E
Periam 34 46 2N 20 59 E
Péribonca → 105 48 45N 72 5W
Péribonca, L. 105 50 1N 71 10W
Peribonka 105 48 46N 72 3W
Perico 140 24 20S 65 5W
Pericos 124 25 3N 107 42W
Périers 18 49 11N 1 25W
Périgord 20 45 0N 0 40 E
Périgueux 20 45 10N 0 42 E
Perijá, Sierra de 134 9 30N 73 3W
Perim 45 12 39N 43 25 E
Peristéra 35 39 15N 23 58 E
Perito Moreno 142 46 36S 70 56W
Peritoró 138 4 20S 44 18W
Periyakulam 51 10 5N 77 30 E
Periyar → 51 10 15N 76 10 E
Periyar, L. 51 9 25N 77 10 E
Perkam, Tg. 57 1 35S 137 50 E
Perković 27 43 41N 16 10 E
Perlas, Arch. de las 126 8 41N 79 7W
Perlas, Punta de 126 12 30N 83 30W
Perleberg 30 53 5N 11 50 E
Perlevka 37 51 48N 38 57 E
Perm (Molotov) 40 58 0N 57 10 E
Pernambuco = Recife 138 8 0S 35 0W
Pernambuco □ 138 8 0S 37 0W
Pernatty Lagoon 73 31 30S 137 12 E
Pernik 34 42 35N 23 2 E
Peron, C. 79 25 30S 113 30 E
Peron Is. 78 13 9S 130 4 E
Peron Pen. 79 26 0S 113 10 E
Péronne 19 49 55N 2 57 E
Perosa Argentina 26 44 57N 7 11 E
Perow 108 54 35N 126 10W
Perpendicular Pt. 77 31 37S 152 52 E
Perpignan 20 42 42N 2 53 E
Perris 123 33 47N 117 14W
Perros-Guirec 18 48 49N 3 28W
Perry, Fla., U.S.A. 113 30 9N 83 40W
Perry, Ga., U.S.A. 113 32 25N 83 41W
Perry, Iowa, U.S.A. 116 41 48N 94 5W
Perry, Maine, U.S.A. 113 44 59N 67 20W
Perry, Mich., U.S.A. 117 42 50N 84 13W
Perry, Mo., U.S.A. 116 39 26N 91 40W
Perry, Okla., U.S.A. 119 36 20N 97 20W
Perrysburg 117 41 34N 83 38W
Perryton 119 36 28N 100 48W
Perryville 116 37 42N 89 50W
Persberg 10 59 47N 14 15 E
Persepolis 47 29 55N 52 50 E
Perseverancia 137 14 44S 62 48W
Persia = Iran ■ 47 35 0N 50 0 E
Persian Gulf 47 27 0N 50 0 E
Perstorp 11 56 10N 13 25 E
Perth, Austral. 79 31 57S 115 52 E
Perth, Can. 107 44 55N 76 15W
Perth, U.K. 14 56 24N 3 27W
Perth Amboy 115 40 31N 74 16W
Perthus, Le 20 42 30N 2 53 E
Perthville 76 33 30S 149 31 E
Pertuis 21 43 42N 5 30 E
Peru, Ill., U.S.A. 116 41 18N 89 12W
Peru, Ind., U.S.A. 117 40 42N 86 0W
Peru ■ 134 8 0S 75 0W
Peru-Chile Trench 67 20 0S 72 0W
Perúgia 27 43 6N 12 24 E
Perušić 27 44 40N 15 22 E
Pervomaysk 38 48 10N 30 46 E
Pervouralsk 40 56 55N 60 0 E
Pésaro 27 43 55N 12 53 E
Pesca, La 125 23 46N 97 47W
Pescara 27 42 28N 14 13 E
Pescara → 27 42 28N 14 13 E
Peschanokopskoye 39 46 14N 41 4 E
Péscia 26 43 54N 10 40 E
Pescina 27 42 0N 13 39 E
Peshawar 48 34 2N 71 37 E
Peshawar □ 48 33 30N 71 20 E
Peshtigo 112 45 4N 87 46W
Peski 37 51 14N 42 29 E
Peskovka 37 59 23N 52 20 E
Pêso da Régua 22 41 10N 7 47W
Pesqueira 138 8 20S 36 42W
Pesqueria → 124 25 54N 99 11W
Pessac 20 44 48N 0 37W
Pestovo 36 58 33N 35 42 E
Pestravka 37 52 28N 49 57 E
Petah Tiqwa 44 32 6N 34 53 E
Petaling Jaya 55 3 4N 101 42 E
Petaluma 122 38 13N 122 39W
Petange 16 49 33N 5 55 E
Petatlán 124 17 31N 101 16W
Petauke 95 14 14S 31 20 E
Petawawa 107 45 54N 77 17W
Petén Itzá, Lago 126 16 58N 89 50W
Peter 1st, I. 143 69 0S 91 0W
Peter Pond L. 109 55 55N 108 44W
Peterbell 102 48 36N 83 21W
Peterborough, Austral. 73 32 58S 138 51 E
Peterborough, Can. 107 44 20N 78 20W
Peterborough, U.K. 13 52 35N 0 14W
Peterborough, U.S.A. 115 42 55N 71 59W
Peterhead 14 57 30N 1 49W
Peter's Mine 135 6 14N 59 20W
Petersburg, Alas., U.S.A. 100 56 50N 133 0W
Petersburg, Ill., U.S.A. 116 40 1N 89 51W
Petersburg, Ind., U.S.A. 117 38 30N 87 15W
Petersburg, Va., U.S.A. 112 37 17N 77 26W
Petersburg, W. Va., U.S.A. 112 38 59N 79 10W
Petford 72 17 20S 144 58 E
Petília Policastro 29 39 7N 16 48 E
Petit Bois I. 113 30 16N 88 25W
Petit-Cap 103 48 3N 64 30W
Petit Goâve 127 18 27N 72 51W
Petit-Quevilly, Le 18 49 26N 1 0 E
Petit Saint Bernard, Col du 26 45 40N 6 52 E
Petitcodiac 103 45 57N 65 11W
Petite Baleine → 102 55 50N 77 0W
Petite-Rivière 105 47 20N 70 33W
Petite Saguenay 105 48 15N 70 4W
Petitsikapau, L. 103 54 37N 66 25W
Petlad 48 22 30N 72 45 E
Peto 125 20 10N 88 53W
Petone 80 41 13S 174 53 E
Petoskey 106 45 22N 84 57W
Petra, Jordan 44 30 20N 35 22 E
Petra, Spain 24 39 37N 3 6 E
Petra, Ostrova 144 76 15N 118 30 E
Petralia 29 37 49N 14 4 E
Petrel 25 38 30N 0 46W
Petrich 35 41 24N 23 13 E
Petrijanec 27 46 23N 16 17 E
Petrikov 36 52 11N 28 29 E
Petrinja 27 45 28N 16 18 E
Petrolândia 138 9 5S 38 20W
Petrolia 106 42 54N 82 9W
Petrolina 138 9 24S 40 30W
Petropavlovsk 40 54 53N 69 13 E
Petropavlovsk-Kamchatskiy 41 53 3N 158 43 E
Petrópolis 139 22 33S 43 9W
Petroşeni 34 45 28N 23 20 E
Petroskey 112 45 22N 84 57W
Petrova Gora 27 45 15N 15 45 E
Petrovac 33 42 13N 18 57 E
Petrovsk 37 52 22N 45 19 E
Petrovsk-Zabaykalskiy 41 51 20N 108 55 E
Petrovskoye = Svetlograd 39 45 25N 42 58 E
Petrozavodsk 40 61 41N 34 20 E
Petrus Steyn 97 27 38S 28 8 E
Petrusburg 96 29 4S 25 26 E
Pettitts 76 34 56S 148 10 E
Peumo 140 34 21S 71 12W
Peureulak 56 4 48N 97 45 E
Pevek 41 69 41N 171 19 E

Peveragno	**26**	44 20N	7 37 E
Peyrehorade	**20**	43 34N	1 7W
Peyruis	**21**	44 1N	5 56 E
Pézenas	**20**	43 28N	3 24 E
Pfaffenhofen	**31**	48 31N	11 31 E
Pfarrkirchen	**31**	48 25N	12 57 E
Pfeffenhausen	**31**	48 40N	11 58 E
Pforzheim	**31**	48 53N	8 43 E
Pfullendorf	**31**	47 55N	9 15 E
Pfungstadt	**31**	49 47N	8 36 E
Phala	**96**	23 45S	26 50 E
Phalodi	**48**	27 12N	72 24 E
Phalsbourg	**19**	48 46N	7 15 E
Phan	**54**	19 28N	99 43 E
Phan Rang	**55**	11 34N	109 0 E
Phan Thiet	**55**	11 1N	108 9 E
Phanat Nikhom	**54**	13 27N	101 11 E
Phangan, Ko	**55**	9 45N	100 0 E
Phangnga	**55**	8 28N	98 30 E
Phanh Bho Ho Chi Minh	**55**	10 58N	106 40 E
Phanom Sarakham	**54**	13 45N	101 21 E
Pharenda	**49**	27 5N	83 17 E
Phatthalung	**55**	7 39N	100 6 E
Phayao	**54**	19 11N	99 55 E
Phelps, N.Y., U.S.A.	**114**	42 57N	77 5W
Phelps, Wis., U.S.A.	**118**	46 2N	89 2W
Phelps L.	**109**	59 15N	103 15W
Phenix City	**113**	32 30N	85 0W
Phet Buri	**54**	13 1N	99 55 E
Phetchabun	**54**	16 25N	101 8 E
Phetchabun, Thiu Khao	**54**	16 0N	101 20 E
Phi Phi, Ko	**55**	7 45N	98 46 E
Phiafay	**54**	14 48N	106 0 E
Phibun Mangsahan	**54**	15 14N	105 14 E
Phichai	**54**	17 22N	100 10 E
Phichit	**54**	16 26N	100 22 E
Philadelphia, Miss., U.S.A.	**119**	32 47N	89 5W
Philadelphia, N.Y., U.S.A.	**115**	44 9N	75 40W
Philadelphia, Pa., U.S.A.	**115**	40 0N	75 10W
Philip	**118**	44 4N	101 42W
Philippeville	**16**	50 12N	4 33 E
Philippi L.	**72**	24 20S	138 55 E
Philippines ■	**57**	12 0N	123 0 E
Philippolis	**96**	30 15S	25 16 E
Philippopolis = Plovdiv	**34**	42 8N	24 44 E
Philipsburg, Can.	**105**	45 2N	73 5W
Philipsburg, Mont., U.S.A.	**120**	46 20N	113 21W
Philipsburg, Pa., U.S.A.	**114**	40 53N	78 10W
Philipstown	**96**	30 28S	24 30 E
Phillip	**74**	38 30S	145 12 E
Phillips, Texas, U.S.A.	**119**	35 48N	101 17W
Phillips, Wis., U.S.A.	**118**	45 41N	90 22W
Phillipsburg, Kans., U.S.A.	**118**	39 48N	99 20W
Phillipsburg, Pa., U.S.A.	**115**	40 43N	75 12W
Phillott	**73**	27 53S	145 50 E
Philmont	**115**	42 14N	73 37W
Philomath	**120**	44 28N	123 21W
Phimai	**54**	15 13N	102 30 E
Phitsanulok	**54**	16 50N	100 12 E
Phnom Dangrek	**54**	14 20N	104 0 E
Phnom Penh	**55**	11 33N	104 55 E
Phoenix, Ariz., U.S.A.	**121**	33 30N	112 10W
Phoenix, N.Y., U.S.A.	**115**	43 13N	76 18W
Phoenix Is.	**66**	3 30S	172 0W
Phoenixville	**115**	40 12N	75 29W
Phon	**54**	15 49N	102 36 E
Phon Tiou	**54**	17 53N	104 37 E
Phong →	**54**	16 23N	102 56 E
Phong Saly	**54**	21 42N	102 9 E
Phong Tho	**54**	22 32N	103 21 E
Phonhong	**54**	18 30N	102 25 E
Phonum	**55**	8 49N	98 48 E
Photharam	**54**	13 41N	99 51 E
Phra Chedi Sam Ong	**54**	15 16N	98 23 E
Phra Nakhon Si Ayutthaya	**54**	14 25N	100 30 E
Phra Thong, Ko	**55**	9 5N	98 17 E
Phrae	**54**	18 7N	100 9 E
Phrom Phiram	**54**	17 2N	100 12 E
Phu Dien	**54**	18 58N	105 31 E
Phu Loi	**54**	20 14N	103 14 E
Phu Ly	**54**	20 35N	105 50 E
Phu Qui	**54**	19 20N	105 20 E
Phu Tho	**54**	21 24N	105 13 E
Phuc Yen	**54**	21 16N	105 45 E
Phuket	**55**	7 52N	98 22 E
Phuket, Ko	**55**	8 0N	98 22 E
Phulbari	**52**	25 55N	90 2 E
Phulera (Phalera)	**48**	26 52N	75 16 E
Phun Phin	**55**	9 7N	99 12 E
Phuoc Le (Baria)	**55**	10 30N	107 10 E
Piacá	**138**	7 42S	47 18W
Piacenza	**26**	45 2N	9 42 E
Piaçubaçu	**138**	10 24S	36 25W
Piádena	**26**	45 8N	10 22 E
Pialba	**73**	25 20S	152 45 E
Piallaway	**77**	31 12S	150 38 E
Pian Cr. →	**73**	30 2S	148 12 E
Piana	**21**	42 15N	8 34 E
Pianella	**27**	42 24N	14 5 E
Piangil	**74**	35 5S	143 20 E
Pianoro	**27**	44 20N	11 20 E
Pianosa, Puglia, Italy	**27**	42 12N	15 44 E
Pianosa, Toscana, Italy	**26**	42 36N	10 4 E
Piapot	**109**	49 59N	109 8W
Piare →	**27**	45 32N	12 44 E
Pias	**23**	38 1N	7 29W
Piaseczno	**32**	52 5N	21 2 E
Piatã	**139**	13 9S	41 48W
Piatra	**34**	43 51N	25 9 E
Piatra Neamţ	**34**	46 56N	26 21 E
Piauí □	**138**	7 0S	43 0W
Piaui →	**138**	6 38S	42 42W
Piave →	**27**	45 32N	12 44 E
Piazza Ármerina	**29**	37 21N	14 20 E
Pibor →	**91**	7 35N	33 0 E
Pibor Post	**91**	6 47N	33 3 E
Pica	**136**	20 35S	69 25W
Picardie	**19**	50 0N	2 15 E
Picardie, Plaine de	**19**	50 0N	2 0 E
Picardy = Picardie	**19**	50 0N	2 15 E
Picayune	**119**	30 31N	89 40W
Piccadilly	**95**	14 0S	29 30 E
Picerno	**29**	40 40N	15 37 E
Pichilemu	**140**	34 22S	72 0W
Pichincha, □	**134**	0 10S	78 40W
Pickerel L.	**102**	48 40N	91 25W
Pickford	**106**	46 10N	84 22W
Pickle Lake	**102**	51 30N	90 12W
Pico Truncado	**142**	46 40S	68 0W
Picola	**74**	36 0S	145 3 E
Picos	**138**	7 5S	41 28W
Picos Ancares, Sierra de	**22**	42 51N	6 52W
Picota	**136**	6 54S	76 24W
Picquigny	**19**	49 56N	2 10 E
Picton, Austral.	**76**	34 12S	150 34 E
Picton, Can.	**107**	44 1N	77 9W
Picton, N.Z.	**81**	41 18S	174 3 E
Picton, I.	**142**	55 2S	66 57W
Pictou	**103**	45 41N	62 42W
Picture Butte	**108**	49 55N	112 45W
Picuí	**138**	6 31S	36 21W
Picún Leufú	**142**	39 30S	69 5W
Pidurutalagala	**51**	7 10N	80 50 E
Piedad, La	**124**	20 20N	102 1W
Piedecuesta	**134**	6 59N	73 3W
Piedicavallo	**26**	45 41N	7 57 E
Piedmont	**113**	33 55N	85 39W
Piedmont = Piemonte	**26**	45 0N	7 30 E
Piedmont Plat.	**113**	34 0N	81 30W
Piedmonte d'Alife	**29**	41 22N	14 22 E
Piedra →	**24**	41 18N	1 47W
Piedra del Anguila	**142**	40 2S	70 4W
Piedra Lais	**134**	3 10N	65 50W
Piedrabuena	**23**	39 0N	4 10W
Piedrahita	**22**	40 28N	5 23W
Piedras Blancas Pt.	**121**	35 45N	121 18W
Piedras Negras	**124**	28 35N	100 35W
Piedras, R. de las →	**136**	12 30S	69 15W
Piemonte □	**26**	45 0N	7 30 E
Pier Millan	**74**	35 14S	142 40 E
Pierce	**120**	46 29N	115 53W
Piercefield	**115**	44 13N	74 35W
Pierre, France	**19**	46 54N	5 13 E
Pierre, U.S.A.	**118**	44 23N	100 20W
Pierre Benite, Barrage	**21**	45 42N	4 49 E
Pierrefeu	**21**	43 8N	6 9 E
Pierrefonds	**19**	49 20N	3 0 E
Pierrefontaine	**19**	47 14N	6 32 E
Pierrefort	**20**	44 55N	2 50 E
Pierrelatte	**21**	44 23N	4 43 E
Pierreville	**105**	46 4N	72 49W
Piešťany	**32**	48 38N	17 55 E
Piesting →	**33**	48 6N	16 40 E
Piet Retief	**97**	27 1S	30 50 E
Pietarsaari	**8**	63 40N	22 43 E
Pietermaritzburg	**97**	29 35S	30 25 E
Pietersburg	**97**	23 54S	29 25 E
Pietraperzia	**29**	37 26N	14 8 E
Pietrasanta	**26**	43 57N	10 12 E
Pietrosu	**34**	47 12N	25 8 E
Pietrosul	**34**	47 35N	24 43 E
Pieve di Cadore	**27**	46 25N	12 22 E
Pieve di Teco	**26**	44 3N	7 54 E
Pievepélago	**26**	44 12N	10 35 E
Pigádhia	**35**	35 30N	27 12 E
Pigeon	**106**	43 50N	83 17W
Pigeon I.	**51**	14 2N	74 20 E
Pigeon L.	**107**	44 27N	78 30W
Piggott	**119**	36 20N	90 10W
Pigna	**26**	43 57N	7 40 E
Pigüe	**140**	37 36S	62 25W
Pihani	**49**	27 36N	80 15 E
Pikalevo	**36**	59 37N	34 0 E
Pikedale	**77**	28 39S	151 38 E
Pikes Peak	**118**	38 50N	105 10W
Piketberg	**96**	32 55S	18 40 E
Pikeville	**112**	37 30N	82 30W
Pikou	**61**	39 18N	122 22 E
Pikwitonei	**109**	55 35N	97 9W
Piła	**32**	53 10N	16 48 E
Pila	**25**	38 16N	1 11W
Pilani	**48**	28 22N	75 33 E
Pilão Arcado	**138**	10 9S	42 26W
Pilar, Brazil	**138**	9 36S	35 56W
Pilar, Parag.	**140**	26 50S	58 20W
Pilas	**57**	6 39N	121 37 E
Pilaya →	**137**	20 55S	64 4W
Pilbara	**78**	21 15S	118 16 E
Pilcomayo →	**140**	25 21S	57 42W
Pilibhit	**49**	28 40N	79 50 E
Pilica →	**32**	51 52N	21 17 E
Pilkhawa	**48**	28 43N	77 42 E
Pillar Valley	**77**	29 46S	153 7 E
Pillaro	**134**	1 10S	78 32W
Pílos	**35**	36 55N	21 42 E
Pilot Grove	**116**	38 53N	92 55W
Pilot Mound	**109**	49 15N	98 54W
Pilot Point	**119**	33 26N	97 0W
Pilot Rock	**120**	45 30N	118 50W
Pilsen = Plzen	**32**	49 45N	13 22 E
Pilštanj	**27**	46 8N	15 39 E
Pima	**121**	32 54N	109 50W
Pimba	**73**	31 18S	136 46 E
Pimenta Bueno	**137**	11 35S	61 10W
Pimentel	**136**	6 45S	79 55W
Pimpino	**74**	36 34S	142 7 E
Pin-Blanc, L.	**104**	46 45N	78 8W
Pina	**24**	41 29N	0 33W
Pinang	**55**	5 25N	100 15 E
Pinar del Río	**126**	22 26N	83 40W
Pinaroo	**73**	35 17S	140 53 E
Pinchang	**58**	31 36N	107 3 E
Pincher Creek	**108**	49 30N	113 57W
Pinchi L.	**108**	54 38N	124 30W
Pinckneyville	**116**	38 5N	89 20W
Pinconning	**106**	43 52N	83 57W
Pîncota	**34**	46 20N	21 45 E
Pind Dadan Khan	**48**	32 36N	73 7 E
Pindar	**79**	28 30S	115 47 E
Pindaré →	**138**	3 17S	44 47W
Pindaré Mirim	**138**	3 37S	45 21W
Pindi Gheb	**48**	33 14N	72 21 E
Pindiga	**89**	9 58N	10 53 E
Pindobal	**138**	3 16S	48 25W
Pindos Óros	**35**	40 0N	21 0 E
Pindus Mts. = Pindos Óros	**35**	40 0N	21 0 E
Pine	**121**	34 27N	111 30W
Pine →	**109**	58 50N	105 38W
Pine Bluff	**119**	34 10N	92 0W
Pine, C.	**103**	46 37N	53 32W
Pine City	**118**	45 46N	93 0W
Pine Falls	**109**	50 34N	96 11W
Pine Flat Res.	**122**	36 50N	119 20W
Pine, La	**120**	43 40N	121 30W
Pine Pass	**108**	55 25N	122 42W
Pine Point	**108**	60 50N	114 28W
Pine Ridge, N.S.W., Austral.	**76**	31 10S	147 30 E
Pine Ridge, N.S.W., Austral.	**77**	31 30S	150 28 E
Pine Ridge, U.S.A.	**118**	43 0N	102 35W
Pine River, Can.	**109**	51 45N	100 30W
Pine River, U.S.A.	**118**	46 43N	94 24W
Pine Valley	**123**	32 50N	116 32W
Pinecrest	**122**	38 12N	120 1W
Pinedale, Ariz., U.S.A.	**121**	34 23N	110 16W
Pinedale, Calif., U.S.A.	**122**	36 50N	119 48W
Pinega →	**40**	64 8N	46 54 E
Pinehill	**72**	23 38S	146 57 E
Pinerolo	**26**	44 47N	7 21 E
Pineto	**27**	42 36N	14 4 E
Pinetop	**121**	34 10N	109 57W
Pinetown	**97**	29 48S	30 54 E
Pinetree	**120**	43 42N	105 52W
Pineville, Ky., U.S.A.	**113**	36 42N	83 42W
Pineville, La., U.S.A.	**119**	31 22N	92 30W
Piney	**19**	48 22N	4 21 E
Piney Range	**76**	33 50S	147 58 E
Ping →	**54**	15 42N	100 9 E
Pingaring	**79**	32 40S	118 32 E
Pingba	**58**	26 23N	106 12 E
Pingchuan	**58**	27 35N	101 55 E
Pingding	**60**	37 47N	113 38 E
Pingdingshan	**60**	33 43N	113 27 E
Pingdong	**59**	22 39N	120 30 E
Pingdu	**61**	36 42N	119 59 E
Pingelly	**79**	32 32S	117 5 E
Pingguo	**58**	23 19N	107 36 E
Pinghe	**59**	24 17N	117 21 E
Pinghu	**59**	30 40N	121 2 E
Pingjiang	**59**	28 45N	113 36 E
Pingle	**59**	24 40N	110 40 E
Pingli	**58**	32 27N	109 22 E
Pingliang	**60**	35 35N	106 31 E
Pinglu	**60**	39 31N	112 30 E
Pingluo	**60**	38 52N	106 30 E
Pingnan, Fujian, China	**59**	26 55N	119 0 E
Pingnan, Guangxi Zhuangzu, China	**59**	23 33N	110 22 E
Pingquan	**61**	41 1N	118 37 E
Pingrup	**79**	33 32S	118 29 E
Pingtan	**59**	25 31N	119 47 E
Pingtang	**58**	25 49N	107 17 E
Pingwu	**58**	32 25N	104 30 E
Pingxiang, Guangxi Zhuangzu, China	**58**	22 6N	106 46 E
Pingxiang, Jiangxi, China	**59**	27 43N	113 48 E
Pingyao	**60**	37 12N	112 10 E
Pingyi	**61**	35 30N	117 35 E
Pingyin	**60**	36 20N	116 25 E
Pingyuan, Guangdong, China	**59**	24 37N	115 57 E
Pingyuan, Shandong, China	**60**	37 10N	116 22 E
Pingyuanjie	**58**	23 45N	103 48 E
Pinhal	**141**	22 10S	46 46W
Pinheiro	**138**	2 31S	45 5W
Pinhel	**22**	40 50N	7 1W
Pinhuá →	**137**	6 21S	65 0W
Pini	**56**	0 10N	98 40 E
Piniós →, Ilia, Greece	**35**	37 48N	21 20 E
Piniós →, Trikkala, Greece	**35**	39 55N	22 10 E
Pinjarra	**79**	32 37S	115 52 E
Pink →	**109**	56 50N	103 50W
Pinlebu	**52**	24 5N	95 22 E
Pinnacles, Austral.	**79**	28 12S	120 26 E
Pinnacles, U.S.A.	**122**	36 33N	121 19W
Pinneberg	**30**	53 39N	9 48 E
Pino Hachado, Paso	**142**	38 39S	70 54W
Pinon Hills	**123**	34 26N	117 39W
Pinos	**124**	22 20N	101 40W
Pinos, I. de	**126**	21 40N	82 40W
Pinos, Mt	**123**	34 49N	119 8W
Pinos Pt.	**121**	36 38N	121 57W
Pinos Puente	**23**	37 15N	3 45W
Pinotepa Nacional	**125**	16 19N	98 3W
Pinrang	**57**	3 46S	119 41 E
Pins, Î. des	**68**	22 37S	167 30 E
Pins, Pte. aux	**106**	42 15N	81 51W
Pinsk	**36**	52 10N	26 1 E
Pintados	**136**	20 35S	69 40W
Pintumba	**79**	31 30S	132 12 E
Pinyang	**59**	27 42N	120 31 E
Pinyug	**40**	60 5N	48 0 E
Pinzolo	**26**	46 9N	10 45 E
Pio XII	**138**	3 53S	45 17W
Pioche	**121**	38 0N	114 35W
Piombino	**26**	42 54N	10 30 E
Piombino, Canale di	**26**	42 50N	10 25 E
Pioner, I.	**41**	79 50N	92 0 E
Pionki	**32**	51 29N	21 28 E
Piorini →	**135**	3 23S	63 30W
Piorini, L.	**135**	3 15S	62 35W
Piotrków Trybunalski	**32**	51 23N	19 43 E
Piove di Sacco	**27**	45 18N	12 1 E
Pip	**47**	26 45N	60 10 E
Pipar	**48**	26 25N	73 31 E
Pipariya	**48**	22 45N	78 23 E
Pipestone	**118**	44 0N	96 20W
Pipestone →	**102**	52 53N	89 23W
Pipestone Cr. →	**109**	49 42N	100 45W
Pipiriki	**80**	39 28S	175 5 E
Pipmuacan, Rés.	**105**	49 45N	70 30W
Pippingarra	**78**	20 27S	118 42 E
Pipriac	**18**	47 49N	1 58W
Piqua	**117**	40 10N	84 10W
Piquet Carneiro	**138**	5 48S	39 25W
Piquiri →	**141**	24 3S	54 14W
Piracanjuba	**139**	17 18S	49 1W
Piracicaba	**141**	22 45S	47 40W
Piracuruca	**138**	3 50S	41 50W
Piraiévs	**35**	37 57N	23 42 E
Piráino	**29**	38 10N	14 52 E
Pirajuí	**141**	21 59S	49 29W
Piran (Pirano)	**27**	45 31N	13 33 E
Pirané	**140**	25 42S	59 6W
Piranhas	**138**	9 27S	37 46W
Pirapemas	**138**	3 43S	44 14W
Pirapora	**139**	17 20S	44 56W
Piray →	**137**	16 32S	63 45W
Pires do Rio	**139**	17 18S	48 17W
Pirganj	**52**	25 51N	88 24 E
Pírgos, Ilia, Greece	**35**	37 40N	21 27 E
Pírgos, Messinia, Greece	**35**	36 50N	22 16 E
Pirgovo	**34**	43 44N	25 43 E
Piriac-sur-Mer	**18**	47 22N	2 33W
Piribebuy	**140**	25 26S	57 2W
Pirin Planina	**35**	41 40N	23 30 E

Pirineos 24 42 40N 1 0 E
Piripiri 138 4 15S 41 46W
Piritu 134 9 23N 69 12W
Pirmasens 31 49 12N 7 30 E
Pirna 30 50 57N 13 57 E
Pirojpur 52 22 35N 90 1 E
Pirot 33 43 9N 22 39 E
Pirtleville 121 31 25N 109 35W
Piru, Indon. 57 3 4S 128 12 E
Piru, U.S.A. 123 34 25N 118 48W
Piryatin 36 50 15N 32 25 E
Pisa 26 43 43N 10 23 E
Pisa Ra. 81 44 52S 169 12 E
Pisac 136 13 25S 71 50W
Pisagua 136 19 40S 70 15W
Pisarovina 27 45 35N 15 50 E
Pisciotta 29 40 7N 15 12 E
Pisco 136 13 50S 76 12W
Písek 32 49 19N 14 10 E
Pishan 62 37 30N 78 33 E
Pishin Lora → 48 29 9N 64 55 E
Pising 57 5 8S 121 53 E
Pismo Beach 123 35 9N 120 38W
Pissos 20 44 19N 0 49W
Pisticci 29 40 24N 16 33 E
Pistóia 26 43 57N 10 53 E
Pistol B. 109 62 25N 92 37W
Pisuerga → 22 41 33N 4 52W
Pisz 32 53 38N 21 49 E
Pitalito 134 1 51N 76 2W
Pitanga 139 24 46S 51 44W
Pitangui 139 19 40S 44 54 E
Pitarpunga, L. 74 34 24S 143 30 E
Pitcairn I. 67 25 5S 130 5W
Pite älv → 8 65 44N 20 50W
Piteå 8 65 20N 21 25 E
Piteşti 34 44 52N 24 54 E
Pithapuram 50 17 10N 82 15 E
Pithara 79 30 20S 116 35 E
Píthion 35 41 24N 26 40 E
Pithiviers 19 48 10N 2 13 E
Pitigliano 27 42 38N 11 40 E
Pitiquito 124 30 42N 112 2W
Pitlochry 14 56 43N 3 43W
Pitrufquén 142 38 59S 72 39W
Pitt I. 108 53 30N 129 50W
Pittsburg, Calif., U.S.A. 122 38 1N 121 50W
Pittsburg, Kans., U.S.A. 119 37 21N 94 43W
Pittsburg, Tex., U.S.A. 119 32 59N 94 58W
Pittsburgh 114 40 25N 79 55W
Pittsfield, Ill., U.S.A. 116 39 35N 90 46W
Pittsfield, Mass., U.S.A. 115 42 28N 73 17W
Pittsfield, N.H., U.S.A. 115 43 17N 71 18W
Pittston 115 41 19N 75 50W
Pittsworth 73 27 41S 151 37 E
Pituri → 72 22 35S 138 30 E
Piuí 139 20 28S 45 58W
Pium 138 10 27S 49 11W
Piura 136 5 15S 80 38W
Piura □ 136 5 10S 80 0W
Pivijay 134 10 28N 74 37W
Pixley 122 35 58N 119 18W
Piyai 35 39 17N 21 25 E
Pizarro 134 4 58N 77 22W
Pizzo 29 38 44N 16 10 E
Placentia 103 47 20N 54 0W
Placentia B. 103 47 0N 54 40W
Placerville 122 38 47N 120 51W
Placetas 126 22 15N 79 44W
Plain Dealing 119 32 56N 93 41W
Plainfield, Ill., U.S.A. 117 41 37N 88 12W
Plainfield, N.J., U.S.A. 115 40 37N 74 28W
Plains, Kans., U.S.A. 119 37 20N 100 35W
Plains, Mont., U.S.A. 120 47 27N 114 57W
Plains, Tex., U.S.A. 119 33 11N 102 50W
Plainview, Nebr., U.S.A. 118 42 25N 97 48W
Plainview, Tex., U.S.A. 119 34 10N 101 40W
Plainville 118 39 18N 99 19W
Plainwell 112 42 28N 85 40W
Plaisance 20 43 36N 0 3 E
Pláka 35 40 0N 25 24 E
Plakhino 40 67 45N 86 5 E
Plana Cays 127 22 38N 73 30W
Planada 122 37 18N 120 19W
Plancoët 18 48 32N 2 13W
Plandište 33 45 16N 21 10 E
Planeta Rica 134 8 25N 75 36W
Planina, Slovenija, Yugo. 27 46 10N 15 20 E
Planina, Slovenija, Yugo. 27 45 47N 14 19 E
Plankinton 118 43 45N 98 27W
Plano 119 33 0N 96 45W
Plant City 113 28 0N 82 8W
Plant, La 118 45 11N 100 40W
Plaquemine 119 30 20N 91 15W
Plasencia 22 40 3N 6 8W
Plaški 27 45 4N 15 22 E
Plassen 10 61 9N 12 30 E
Plaster City 123 32 47N 115 51W
Plaster Rock 103 46 53N 67 22W
Plata, La, Argent. 140 35 0S 57 55W
Plata, La, Colomb. 134 2 23N 75 53W
Plata, La, U.S.A. 116 40 2N 92 29W
Plata, La, L. 142 44 55S 71 50W
Plata, Río de la 140 34 45S 57 30W
Platani → 28 37 23N 13 16 E
Plateau 143 79 55S 40 0 E
Plateau □ 89 8 0N 8 30 E
Plateau du Coteau du Missouri 118 47 9N 101 5W
Plato 134 9 47N 74 47W
Platte 118 43 28N 98 50W
Platte → 116 39 16N 94 50W
Platte City 116 39 22N 94 47W
Platteville, Colo., U.S.A. 118 40 18N 104 47W
Platteville, Wis., U.S.A. 116 42 44N 90 29W
Plattling 31 48 46N 12 53 E
Plattsburg, Miss., U.S.A. 116 39 34N 94 27W
Plattsburg, N.Y., U.S.A. 115 44 41N 73 30W
Plattsmouth 118 41 0N 95 50W
Plau 30 53 27N 12 16 E
Plauen 30 50 29N 12 9 E
Plavnica 33 42 20N 19 13 E
Plavsk 37 53 40N 37 18 E
Playa Azul 124 17 59N 102 24W
Playgreen L. 109 54 0N 98 15W
Pleasant Bay 103 46 51N 60 48W
Pleasant Hill, Ill., U.S.A. 116 39 27N 90 52W
Pleasant Hill, Mo., U.S.A. 116 38 48N 94 14W
Pleasant Pt. 81 44 16S 171 9 E
Pleasanton 119 29 0N 98 30W
Pleasantville, Iowa, U.S.A. 116 41 23N 93 18W
Pleasantville, N.J., U.S.A. 112 39 25N 74 30W
Pleasure Ridge Park 117 38 9N 85 50W
Pléaux 20 45 8N 2 13 E
Pleiku (Gia Lai) 54 13 57N 108 0 E
Plélan-le-Grand 18 48 0N 2 7W
Plémet 18 48 11N 2 36W
Pléneuf-Val-André 18 48 35N 2 32W
Pleniţa 34 44 14N 23 10 E
Plenty → 72 23 25S 136 31 E
Plenty, Bay of 80 37 45S 177 0 E
Plentywood 118 48 45N 104 35W
Plessisville 105 46 14N 71 47W
Plestin-les-Grèves 18 48 40N 3 39W
Pleszew 32 51 53N 17 47 E
Pleternica 33 45 17N 17 48 E
Pletipi L. 103 51 44N 70 6W
Pleven 34 43 26N 24 37 E
Plevlja 33 43 21N 19 21 E
Plevna 107 44 58N 76 59W
Płock 32 52 32N 19 40 E
Plöcken Passo 27 46 37N 12 57 E
Ploëmeur 18 47 44N 3 26W
Ploërmel 18 47 55N 2 26W
Ploieşti 34 44 57N 26 5 E
Plomb du Cantal 20 45 2N 2 48 E
Plombières 19 47 59N 6 27 E
Plomin 27 45 8N 14 10 E
Plön 30 54 8N 10 22 E
Plöner See 30 45 10N 10 22 E
Plonge, Lac La 109 55 8N 107 20W
Płońsk 32 52 37N 20 21 E
Płoty 32 53 48N 15 18 E
Plouaret 18 48 37N 3 28W
Plouay 18 47 55N 3 21W
Ploudalmézeau 18 48 34N 4 41W
Plougasnou 18 48 42N 3 49W
Plouha 18 48 41N 2 57W
Plouhinee 18 48 0N 4 29W
Plovdiv 34 42 8N 24 44 E
Plum I. 115 41 10N 72 12W
Plumas 122 39 45N 119 4W
Plummer 120 47 21N 116 59W
Plumtree 95 20 27S 27 55 E
Plunge 36 55 53N 21 59 E
Pluvigner 18 47 46N 3 1W
Plymouth, U.K. 13 50 23N 4 9W
Plymouth, Calif., U.S.A. 122 38 29N 120 51W
Plymouth, Ill., U.S.A. 116 40 15N 90 58W
Plymouth, Ind., U.S.A. 117 41 20N 86 19W
Plymouth, Mass., U.S.A. 115 41 58N 70 40W
Plymouth, Mich., U.S.A. 106 42 22N 83 28W
Plymouth, N.C., U.S.A. 113 35 54N 76 46W
Plymouth, N.H., U.S.A. 115 43 44N 71 41W
Plymouth, Pa., U.S.A. 115 41 17N 76 0W
Plymouth, Wis., U.S.A. 112 43 42N 87 58W
Plymouth Sd. 13 50 20N 4 10W
Plynlimon = Pumlumon Fawr 13 52 29N 3 47W
Plyussa → 36 58 40N 29 0 E
Plzen 32 49 45N 13 22 E
Pniewy 32 52 31N 16 16 E
Pô 89 11 14N 1 5W
Po → 26 44 57N 12 4 E
Po, Foci del 27 44 55N 12 30 E
Po Hai = Bo Hai 61 39 0N 120 0 E
Pobé 89 7 0N 2 56 E
Pobeda 41 65 12N 146 12 E
Pobedino 41 49 51N 142 49 E
Pobedy Pik 40 40 45N 79 58 E
Pobiedziska 32 52 29N 17 11 E
Pobla de Lillet, La 24 42 16N 1 59 E
Pobla de Segur 24 42 15N 0 58 E
Pobladura de Valle 22 42 6N 5 44W
Pocahontas, Arkansas, U.S.A. 119 36 18N 91 0W
Pocahontas, Ill., U.S.A. 116 38 50N 89 33W
Pocahontas, Iowa, U.S.A. 116 42 41N 94 42W
Pocatello 120 42 50N 112 25W
Pocatière, La 105 47 22N 70 2W
Pochep 36 52 58N 33 29 E
Pochinki 37 54 41N 44 59 E
Pochinok 36 54 28N 32 29 E
Pochontas 108 53 10N 117 51W
Pochutla 125 15 50N 96 31W
Poci 135 5 57N 61 29W
Pocinhos 138 7 4S 36 3W
Pocito Casas 124 28 32N 111 6W
Poções 139 14 31S 40 21W
Pocomoke City 112 38 4N 75 32W
Poconé 137 16 15S 56 37W
Poços de Caldas 141 21 50S 46 33W
Poddebice 32 51 54N 18 58 E
Poděbrady 32 50 9N 15 8 E
Podensac 20 44 40N 0 22W
Podgorica = Titograd 33 42 30N 19 19 E
Podkamennaya Tunguska → 41 61 50N 90 13 E
Podlapac 27 44 37N 15 47 E
Podolsk 37 55 25N 37 30 E
Podor 88 16 40N 15 2W
Podravska Slatina 33 45 42N 17 45 E
Podujevo 33 42 54N 21 10 E
Poel 30 54 0N 11 25 E
Pofadder 96 29 10S 19 22 E
Pogamasing 102 46 55N 81 50W
Poggiardo 29 40 3N 18 21 E
Poggibonsi 27 43 27N 11 8 E
Pogoanele 34 44 55N 27 0 E
Pogradeci 35 40 57N 20 37 E
Poh 57 0 46S 122 51 E
Pohang 61 36 1N 129 23 E
Pohorelá 32 48 50N 20 2 E
Pohorje 27 46 30N 15 20 E
Poiana Mare 34 43 57N 23 5 E
Poindimié 68 20 56S 165 20 E
Poinsett, C. 143 65 42S 113 18 E
Point Danger 77 28 9S 153 30 E
Point Edward 106 43 0N 82 30W
Point Gatineau 104 45 28N 75 42W
Point Lookout, Mt. 77 30 29S 152 24 E
Point Pedro 51 9 50N 80 15 E
Point Pelee Nat. Park 106 41 57N 82 31W
Point Pleasant, U.S.A. 115 40 5N 74 4W
Point Pleasant, W. Va., U.S.A. 112 38 50N 82 7W
Pointe-à-la Hache 119 29 35N 89 55W
Pointe-à-Pitre 127 16 10N 61 30W
Pointe au Baril Sta. 106 45 35N 80 23W
Pointe-au-Pic 105 47 38N 70 9W
Pointe-aux-Outardes 105 49 3N 68 26W
Pointe-aux-Trembles 105 45 40N 73 30W
Pointe-Claire 105 45 26N 73 50W
Pointe-Gatineau 107 45 28N 75 42W
Pointe-Lebel 105 49 10N 68 12W
Pointe-Noire 92 4 48S 11 53 E
Poirino 26 44 55N 7 50 E
Poisonbush Ra. 78 22 30S 121 30 E
Poisson-Blanc, L. du 104 46 0N 75 45W
Poissy 19 48 55N 2 0 E
Poitiers 18 46 35N 0 20 E
Poitou, Plaines et Seuil du 20 46 30N 0 1W
Poix 19 49 47N 2 0 E
Poix-Terron 19 49 38N 4 38 E
Pojoaque 121 35 55N 106 0W
Pokataroo 73 29 37S 148 44 E
Poko, Sudan 91 5 41N 31 55 E
Poko, Zaïre 94 3 7N 26 52 E
Pokrovsk 41 61 29N 126 12 E
Pol 22 43 9N 7 20W
Pola de Allande 22 43 16N 6 37W
Pola de Gordón, La 22 42 51N 5 41W
Pola de Lena 22 43 10N 5 49W
Pola de Siero 22 43 24N 5 39W
Pola de Somiedo 22 43 5N 6 15W
Polacca 121 35 52N 110 25W
Polan 47 25 30N 61 10 E
Poland ■ 32 52 0N 20 0 E
Polanów 32 54 7N 16 41 E
Polar Sub-Glacial Basin 143 85 0S 110 0 E
Polcura 140 37 17S 71 43W
Polden Hills 13 51 7N 2 50W
Polessk 36 54 50N 21 8 E
Polewali, Sulawesi, Indon. 57 3 21S 119 23 E
Polewali, Sulawesi, Indon. 57 4 8S 119 43 E
Polgar 33 47 54N 21 6 E
Pŏlgyo-ri 61 34 51N 127 21 E
Poli 92 8 34N 13 15 E
Políaigos 35 36 45N 24 38 E
Policastro, Golfo di 29 39 55N 15 35 E
Police 32 53 33N 14 33 E
Polignano a Mare 29 41 0N 17 12 E
Poligny 19 46 50N 5 42 E
Políkhnitas 35 39 4N 26 10 E
Polillo Is. 57 14 56N 122 0 E
Polístena 29 38 25N 16 4 E
Políyiros 35 40 23N 23 25 E
Polk 114 41 22N 79 57W
Polla 29 40 31N 15 27 E
Pollachi 51 10 35N 77 0 E
Pollensa 24 39 54N 3 2 E
Pollensa, B. de 24 39 55N 3 5 E
Póllica 29 40 13N 15 3 E
Pollino, Mte. 29 39 54N 16 13 E
Pollock 118 45 58N 100 18W
Polna 36 58 31N 28 0 E
Polnovat 40 63 50N 65 54 E
Polo, Ill., U.S.A. 116 42 0N 89 38W
Polo, Mo., U.S.A. 116 39 33N 94 3W
Pologi 38 47 29N 36 15 E
Polonnoye 36 50 6N 27 30 E
Polotsk 36 55 30N 28 50 E
Polson 120 47 45N 114 12W
Poltava 38 49 35N 34 35 E
Poltimore 104 45 47N 75 43W
Polunochnoye 40 60 52N 60 25 E
Polur 51 12 32N 79 11 E
Polynesia 67 10 0S 162 0W
Pomarance 26 43 18N 10 51 E
Pomarico 29 40 31N 16 33 E
Pomaro 124 18 20N 103 18W
Pombal, Brazil 138 6 45S 37 50W
Pombal, Port. 22 39 55N 8 40W
Pómbia 35 35 0N 24 51 E
Pomeroy, Ohio, U.S.A. 112 39 0N 82 0W
Pomeroy, Wash., U.S.A. 120 46 30N 117 33W
Pomio 69 5 32S 151 33 E
Pomme de Terre, Res. 116 37 54N 93 19W
Pomona 123 34 2N 117 49W
Pomorie 34 42 32N 27 41 E
Pompano Beach 113 26 12N 80 6W
Pompei 29 40 45N 14 30 E
Pompey 19 48 50N 6 2 E
Pompeys Pillar 120 46 0N 108 0W
Ponape 66 6 55N 158 10 E
Ponask, L. 102 54 0N 92 41W
Ponass L. 109 52 16N 103 58W
Ponca 118 42 38N 96 41W
Ponca City 119 36 40N 97 5W
Ponce 127 18 1N 66 37W
Ponchatoula 119 30 27N 90 25W
Poncheville, L. 104 50 10N 76 55W
Poncin 21 46 6N 5 25 E
Pond 123 35 43N 119 20W
Pond Inlet 101 72 40N 77 0W
Pondicherry 51 11 59N 79 50 E
Pondoland 97 31 10S 29 30 E
Ponds, I. of 103 53 27N 55 52W
Ponérihouen 68 21 5S 165 24 E
Ponferrada 22 42 32N 6 35W
Pongo, Wadi 91 8 42N 27 40 E
Poniatowa 32 51 11N 22 3 E
Ponikva 27 46 16N 15 26 E
Ponnaiyar → 51 11 50N 79 45 E
Ponnani 51 10 45N 75 59 E
Ponneri 51 13 20N 80 15 E
Ponoi → 40 66 59N 41 17 E
Ponoka 108 52 42N 113 40W
Ponorogo 57 7 52S 111 29 E
Pons, France 20 45 35N 0 34W
Pons, Spain 24 41 55N 1 12 E
Ponsul → 23 39 40N 7 31W
Pont-à-Mousson 19 48 54N 6 1 E
Pont-Audemer 18 49 21N 0 30 E
Pont-Aven 18 47 51N 3 47W

Pont Canavese 26 45 24N 7 33 E
Pont-de-Roide 19 47 23N 6 45 E
Pont-de-Salars 20 44 18N 2 44 E
Pont-de-Vaux 19 46 26N 4 56 E
Pont-de-Veyle 21 46 17N 4 53 E
Pont-l'Abbé 18 47 52N 4 15W
Pont-l'Évêque 18 49 18N 0 11 E
Pont-Rouge 105 46 45N 71 42W
Pont-St-Esprit 21 44 16N 4 40 E
Pont-sur-Yonne 19 48 18N 3 10 E
Ponta de Pedras 138 1 23S 48 52W
Ponta Grossa 141 25 7S 50 10W
Ponta Pora 141 22 20S 55 35W
Pontacq 20 43 11N 0 8W
Pontailler 19 47 18N 5 24 E
Pontal → 138 9 8S 40 12W
Pontalina 139 17 31S 49 27W
Pontarlier 19 46 54N 6 20 E
Pontassieve 27 43 47N 11 25 E
Pontaubault 18 48 40N 1 20W
Pontaumur 20 45 52N 2 40 E
Pontcharra 21 45 26N 6 1 E
Pontchartrain, L. 119 30 12N 90 0W
Pontchâteau 18 47 25N 2 5W
Ponte Alta do Norte 138 10 45S 47 34W
Ponte Alta, Serra do 139 19 42S 47 40W
Ponte Branca 137 16 27S 52 40W
Ponte da Barca 22 41 48N 8 25W
Ponte de Sor 23 39 17N 7 57W
Ponte dell 'Olio 26 44 52N 9 39 E
Ponte di Legno 26 46 15N 10 30 E
Ponte do Lima 22 41 46N 8 35W
Ponte do Pungué 95 19 30S 34 33 E
Ponte Leccia 21 42 28N 9 13 E
Ponte Macassar 57 9 30S 123 58 E
Ponte nell' Alpi 27 46 10N 12 18 E
Ponte Nova 139 20 25S 42 54W
Ponte Ṣan Martino 26 45 36N 7 47 E
Ponte San Pietro 26 45 42N 9 35 E
Pontebba 27 46 30N 13 17 E
Pontecorvo 28 41 28N 13 40 E
Pontedera 26 43 40N 10 37 E
Pontefract 12 53 42N 1 19W
Ponteix 109 49 46N 107 29W
Pontelandolfo 29 41 17N 14 41 E
Pontevedra 22 42 26N 8 40W
Pontevedra □ 22 42 25N 8 39W
Pontevedra, R. de → 22 42 22N 8 45W
Pontevico 26 45 16N 10 6 E
Ponthierville = Ubundi 94 0 22S 25 30 E
Pontiac, Ill., U.S.A. 117 40 50N 88 40W
Pontiac, Mich., U.S.A. 117 42 40N 83 20W
Pontiac, Parc 104 46 30N 76 30W
Pontian Kechil 55 1 29N 103 23 E
Pontianak 56 0 3S 109 15 E
Pontine Is. = Ponziane, Isole 28 40 55N 13 0 E
Pontine Mts. = Karadeniz D. 46 41 30N 35 0 E
Pontínia 28 41 25N 13 2 E
Pontivy 18 48 5N 3 0W
Pontoise 19 49 3N 2 5 E
Ponton → 108 58 27N 116 11W
Pontorson 18 48 34N 1 30W
Pontrémoli 26 44 22N 9 52 E
Pontrieux 18 48 42N 3 10W
Ponts-de-Cé, Les 18 47 25N 0 30W
Pontypool, Can. 107 44 6N 78 38W
Pontypool, U.K. 13 51 42N 3 1W
Pontypridd 13 51 36N 3 21W
Ponza, I. 28 40 55N 12 57 E
Ponziane, Isole 28 40 55N 13 0 E
Poochera 73 32 43S 134 51 E
Poole 13 50 42N 1 58W
Pooley I. 108 52 45N 128 15W
Poona = Pune 50 18 29N 73 57 E
Poonamallee 51 13 3N 80 10 E
Pooncarie 73 33 22S 142 31 E
Poopelloe, L. 73 31 40S 144 0 E
Poopó 136 18 23S 66 59W
Poopó, Lago de 136 18 30S 67 35W
Poor Knights Is. 80 35 29S 174 43 E
Popanyinning 79 32 40S 117 2 E
Popayán 134 2 27N 76 36W
Poperinge 16 50 51N 2 42 E
Popigay 41 72 1N 110 39 E
Popilta, L. 73 33 10S 141 42 E
Popio, L. 73 33 10S 141 52 E
Poplar 118 48 3N 105 9W
Poplar →, Man., Can. 109 53 0N 97 19W
Poplar →, N.W.T., Can. 108 61 22N 121 52W
Poplar Bluff 119 36 45N 90 22W
Poplarville 119 30 55N 89 30W
Popocatepetl 125 19 10N 98 40W
Popokabaka 92 5 41S 16 40 E
Pópoli 27 42 12N 13 50 E
Popondetta 69 8 48S 148 17 E
Popovača 27 45 30N 16 41 E
Popovo 34 43 21N 26 18 E
Poprád 32 49 3N 20 18 E
Poprád → 32 49 38N 20 42 E
Poradaha 52 23 51N 89 1 E
Porali → 48 25 35N 66 26 E
Porangaba 136 8 48S 70 36W
Porangahau 80 40 17S 176 37 E
Porangatu 139 13 26S 49 10W
Porbandar 48 21 44N 69 43 E
Porce → 134 7 28N 74 53W
Porcher I. 108 53 50N 130 30W
Porco 137 19 50S 65 59W
Porcos → 139 12 42S 45 7W
Porcuna 23 37 52N 4 11W
Porcupine 106 48 30N 81 11W
Porcupine →, Can. 109 59 11N 104 46W
Porcupine →, U.S.A. 100 66 35N 145 15W
Pordenone 27 45 58N 12 40 E
Poreč 27 45 14N 13 36 E
Porecatu 139 22 43S 51 24W
Poretskoye 37 55 9N 46 21 E
Pori 9 61 29N 21 48 E
Porjus 8 66 57N 19 50 E
Porkhov 36 57 45N 29 38 E
Porkkala 9 59 59N 24 26 E
Porlamar 135 10 57N 63 51W
Porlezza 26 46 2N 9 8 E
Porma → 22 42 49N 5 28W
Pornic 18 47 7N 2 5W
Poronaysk 41 49 13N 143 0 E
Póros 35 37 30N 23 30 E
Poroshiri Dake 63 42 41N 142 52 E
Poroto Mts. 95 9 0S 33 30 E
Porquerolles, Îles de 21 43 0N 6 13 E
Porrentruy 31 47 25N 7 6 E
Porreras 24 39 29N 3 2 E
Porretta, Passo di 26 44 2N 10 56 E
Porsangen 8 70 40N 25 40 E
Porsgrunn 10 59 10N 9 40 E
Port 19 47 43N 6 4 E
Port Adelaide 73 34 46S 138 30 E
Port Alberni 108 49 40N 124 50W
Port Albert 75 38 42S 146 42 E
Port Albert Victor 48 21 0N 71 30 E
Port Alfred, Can. 105 48 18N 70 53W
Port Alfred, S. Afr. 96 33 36S 26 55 E
Port Alice 108 50 20N 127 25W
Port Allegany 114 41 49N 78 17W
Port Allen 119 30 30N 91 15W
Port Alma 72 23 38S 150 53 E
Port Angeles 122 48 7N 123 30W
Port Antonio 126 18 10N 76 30W
Port Aransas 119 27 49N 97 4W
Port Arthur, Austral. 72 43 7S 147 50 E
Port Arthur, U.S.A. 119 30 0N 94 0W
Port au Port B. 103 48 40N 58 50W
Port-au-Prince 127 18 40N 72 20W
Port Augusta 73 32 30S 137 50 E
Port Augusta West 73 32 29S 137 29 E
Port Austin 106 44 3N 82 59W
Port Bell 94 0 18N 32 35 E
Port Bergé Vaovao 97 15 33S 47 40 E
Port Blandford 103 48 20N 54 10W
Port Bolivar 119 29 20N 94 40W
Port Bou 24 42 25N 3 9 E
Port Bouët 88 5 16N 3 57W
Port Bradshaw 72 12 30S 137 20 E
Port Broughton 73 33 37S 137 56 E
Port Burwell 106 42 40N 80 48W
Port Campbell 74 38 37S 143 1 E
Port Carling 106 45 7N 79 35W
Port-Cartier 103 50 2N 66 50W
Port Chalmers 81 45 49S 170 30 E
Port Chester 115 41 0N 73 41W
Port Clements 108 53 40N 132 10W
Port Clinton 117 41 30N 82 58W
Port Colborne 106 42 50N 79 10W
Port Coquitlam 108 49 15N 122 45W
Port Credit 106 43 33N 79 35W
Port Curtis 72 23 57S 151 20 E
Port Dalhousie 114 43 13N 79 16W
Port Darwin, Austral. 78 12 24S 130 45 E
Port Darwin, Falk. Is. 142 51 50S 59 0W
Port Davey 72 43 16S 145 55 E
Port-de-Bouc 21 43 24N 4 59 E
Port-de-Paix 127 19 50N 72 50W
Port Dickson 55 2 30N 101 49 E
Port Douglas 72 16 30S 145 30 E
Port Dover 106 42 47N 80 12W
Port Edward 108 54 12N 130 10W
Port Elgin 102 44 25N 81 25W
Port Elizabeth 96 33 58S 25 40 E
Port Ellen 14 55 38N 6 10W
Port-en-Bessin 18 49 21N 0 45W
Port Erin 12 54 5N 4 45W
Port Essington 78 11 15S 132 10 E
Port Étienne = Nouadhibou 84 20 54N 17 0W
Port Fairy 74 38 22S 142 12 E
Port Fitzroy 80 36 8S 175 20 E
Port Fouâd = Bûr Fuad 90 31 15N 32 20 E
Port Gamble 122 47 51N 122 35W
Port-Gentil 92 0 40S 8 50 E
Port Gibson 119 31 57N 91 0W
Port Glasgow 14 55 57N 4 40W
Port Harcourt 89 4 40N 7 10 E
Port Hardy 108 50 41N 127 30W
Port Harrison 101 58 25N 78 15W
Port Hawkesbury 103 45 36N 61 22W
Port Hedland 78 20 25S 118 35 E
Port Henry 115 44 0N 73 30W
Port Hood 103 46 0N 61 32W
Port Hope, Can. 107 43 56N 78 20W
Port Hope, U.S.A. 106 43 57N 82 43W
Port Hueneme 123 34 7N 119 12W
Port Huron 106 43 0N 82 28W
Port Isabel 119 26 4N 97 9W
Port Jackson 76 33 50S 151 18 E
Port Jefferson 115 40 58N 73 5W
Port Jervis 115 41 22N 74 42W
Port-Joinville 18 46 45N 2 23W
Port Katon 39 46 52N 38 46 E
Port Kelang 55 3 0N 101 23 E
Port Kembla 76 34 52S 150 49 E
Port-la-Nouvelle 20 43 1N 3 3 E
Port Laoise 15 53 2N 7 20W
Port Lavaca 119 28 38N 96 38W
Port-Leucate-Barcarès 20 42 53N 3 3 E
Port Lincoln 73 34 42S 135 52 E
Port Loko 88 8 48N 12 46W
Port Loring 106 45 55N 80 0W
Port Louis, France 18 47 42N 3 22W
Port Louis, Maur. 53 20 10S 57 30 E
Port Lyautey = Kenitra 86 34 15N 6 40W
Port Macdonnell 73 38 0S 140 48 E
Port Macquarie 77 31 25S 152 25 E
Port Maria 126 18 25N 77 5W
Port Mellon 108 49 32N 123 31W
Port-Menier 103 49 51N 64 15W
Port Morant 126 17 54N 76 19W
Port Moresby 69 9 24S 147 8 E
Port Mourant 135 6 15N 57 20W
Port Mouton 103 43 58N 64 50W
Port Musgrave 72 11 55S 141 50 E
Port-Navalo 18 47 34N 2 54W
Port Nelson 109 57 3N 92 36W
Port Nicholson 80 41 20S 174 52 E
Port Nolloth 96 29 17S 16 52 E
Port Nouveau-Québec (George River) 101 58 30N 65 59W
Port O'Connor 119 28 26N 96 24W
Port of Spain 127 10 40N 61 31W
Port Orchard 122 47 31N 122 38W
Port Oxford 120 42 45N 124 28W
Port Pegasus 81 47 12S 167 41 E
Port Perry 107 44 6N 78 56W
Port Phillip B. 74 38 10S 144 50 E
Port Pirie 73 33 10S 138 1 E
Port Radium = Echo Bay 100 66 10N 117 40W
Port Renfrew 108 48 30N 124 20W
Port Roper 72 14 45S 135 47 E
Port Rowan 106 42 40N 80 30W
Port Safaga = Bûr Safâga 90 26 43N 33 57 E
Port Said = Bûr Sa'îd 90 31 16N 32 18 E
Port St. Joe 113 29 49N 85 20W
Port St. Louis 97 13 7S 48 48 E
Port-St-Louis-du-Rhône 21 43 23N 4 49 E
Port Sanilac 106 43 26N 82 33W
Port Saunders 103 50 40N 57 18W
Port Severn 106 44 48N 79 43W
Port Shepstone 97 30 44S 30 28 E
Port Simpson 108 54 30N 130 20W
Port Stanley 106 42 40N 81 10W
Port Stephens 76 32 38S 152 12 E
Port Sudan = Bûr Sûdân 90 19 32N 37 9 E
Port Talbot 13 51 35N 3 48W
Port Taufîq = Bûr Taufiq 90 29 54N 32 32 E
Port Townsend 122 48 7N 122 50W
Port-Vendres 20 42 32N 3 8 E
Port Wakefield 73 34 12S 138 10 E
Port Washington 112 43 25N 87 52W
Port Weld 55 4 50N 100 38 E
Portachuelo 137 17 10S 63 20W
Portadown 15 54 27N 6 26W
Portage 118 43 31N 89 25W
Portage → 117 41 32N 82 58W
Portage La Prairie 109 49 58N 98 18W
Portageville 119 36 25N 89 40W
Portalegre 23 39 19N 7 25W
Portalegre □ 23 39 20N 7 40W
Portales 119 34 12N 103 25W
Portarlington, Austral. 74 38 7S 144 40 E
Portarlington, Ireland 15 53 10N 7 10W
Porte City, La 116 42 19N 92 12W
Porte, La 117 41 36N 86 43W
Porteirinha 139 15 44S 43 2W
Portel, Brazil 138 1 57S 50 49W
Portel, Port. 23 38 19N 7 41W
Porter 117 41 36N 87 4W
Porter L., N.W.T., Can. 109 61 41N 108 5W
Porter L., Sask., Can. 109 56 20N 107 20W
Porters Retreat 76 34 2S 149 49 E
Porterville, S. Afr. 96 33 0S 18 57 E
Porterville, U.S.A. 122 36 5N 119 0W
Porthcawl 13 51 28N 3 42W
Porthill 120 49 0N 116 30W
Portile de Fier 34 44 42N 22 30 E
Portimão 23 37 8N 8 32W
Portland, N.S.W., Austral. 76 33 20S 150 0 E
Portland, Victoria, Austral. 74 38 20S 141 35 E
Portland, Can. 107 44 42N 76 12W
Portland, Conn., U.S.A. 115 41 34N 72 39W
Portland, Ind., U.S.A. 117 40 26N 84 59W
Portland, Me., U.S.A. 103 43 40N 70 15W
Portland, Mich., U.S.A. 117 42 52N 84 58W
Portland, Oreg., U.S.A. 122 45 35N 122 40W
Portland B. 74 38 15S 141 45 E
Portland, Bill of 13 50 31N 2 27W
Portland I. 80 39 20S 177 51 E
Portland, I. of 13 50 32N 2 25W
Portland Prom. 101 58 40N 78 33W
Portneuf 105 46 43N 71 55W
Portneuf → 105 48 38N 69 5W
Portneuf, Parc Prov. de 105 47 10N 72 25W
Pôrto 138 3 54S 42 42W
Porto 22 41 8N 8 40W
Porto □ 22 41 8N 8 20W
Pôrto Acre 136 9 34S 67 31W
Pôrto Alegre, Pará, Brazil 135 4 22S 52 44W
Pôrto Alegre, Rio Grande do Sul, Brazil 141 30 5S 51 10W
Porto Alexandre 96 15 55S 11 55 E
Porto Amboim = Gunza 92 10 50S 13 50 E
Porto Argentera 26 44 15N 7 27 E
Porto Azzurro 26 42 46N 10 24 E
Porto Botte 28 39 3N 8 33 E
Pôrto Cajueiro 137 11 3S 55 53W
Porto Civitanova 27 43 19N 13 44 E
Pôrto da Fôlha 138 9 55S 37 17W
Pôrto de Móz 138 1 41S 52 13W
Pôrto de Pedras 138 9 10S 35 17W
Pôrto des Meinacos 137 12 33S 53 7W
Porto Empédocle 28 37 18N 13 30 E
Pôrto Esperança 137 19 37S 57 29W
Pôrto Esperidão 137 15 51S 58 28W
Pôrto Franco 138 6 20S 47 24W
Porto Garibaldi 27 44 41N 12 14 E
Pôrto Grande 135 0 42N 51 24W
Porto, G. de 21 42 17N 8 34 E
Pôrto Jofre 137 17 20S 56 48W
Pórto Lágo 35 40 58N 25 6 E
Porto Mendes 141 24 30S 54 15W
Pôrto Murtinho 137 21 45S 57 55W
Pôrto Nacional 138 10 40S 48 30W
Porto Novo, Benin 89 6 23N 2 42 E
Porto Novo, India 51 11 30N 79 38 E
Porto Recanati 27 43 26N 13 40 E
Porto San Giórgio 27 43 11N 13 49 E
Pôrto Santana 135 0 3S 51 11W
Porto Santo 84 33 45N 16 25W
Porto Santo Stefano 26 42 26N 11 7 E
Pôrto São José 141 22 43S 53 10W
Pôrto Seguro 139 16 26S 39 5W
Porto Tolle 27 44 57N 12 20 E
Porto Tórres 28 40 50N 8 23 E
Pôrto União 141 26 10S 51 10W
Pôrto Válter 136 8 15S 72 40W
Porto-Vecchio 21 41 35N 9 16 E
Pôrto Velho 137 8 46S 63 54W
Portobelo 126 9 35N 79 42W
Portoferráio 26 42 50N 10 20 E
Portogruaro 27 45 47N 12 50 E
Portola 122 39 49N 120 28W
Portomaggiore 27 44 41N 11 47 E
Portoscuso 28 39 12N 8 22 E
Portovénere 26 44 2N 9 50 E
Portoviejo 134 1 7S 80 28W
Portpatrick 14 54 50N 5 7W
Portree 14 57 25N 6 11W
Portrush 15 55 13N 6 40W
Portsall 18 48 37N 4 45W
Portsmouth, Domin. 127 15 34N 61 27W
Portsmouth, U.K. 13 50 48N 1 6W
Portsmouth, N.H., U.S.A. 115 43 5N 70 45W
Portsmouth, Ohio, U.S.A. 112 38 45N 83 0W
Portsmouth, R.I., U.S.A. 115 41 35N 71 15W

Portsmouth, Va., U.S.A.	**112**	36 50N	76 20W
Portsoy	**14**	57 41N	2 41W
Porttipahta	**8**	68 5N	26 40 E
Portugal ■	**22**	40 0N	7 0W
Portugalete	**24**	43 19N	3 4W
Portuguesa □	**134**	9 10N	69 15W
Portuguese-Guinea = Guinea-Bissau ■	**88**	12 0N	15 0W
Portuguese Timor = Timor	**57**	8 0S	126 30 E
Portumna	**15**	53 5N	8 12W
Portville	**114**	42 3N	78 21W
Porvenir, Boliv.	**136**	11 10S	68 50W
Porvenir, Chile	**142**	53 10S	70 16W
Porvoo	**9**	60 24N	25 40 E
Porzuna	**23**	39 9N	4 9W
Posada →	**28**	40 40N	9 45 E
Posadas, Argent.	**141**	27 30S	55 50W
Posadas, Spain	**23**	37 47N	5 11W
Poschiavo	**31**	46 19N	10 4 E
Posen	**106**	45 16N	83 42W
Posets	**24**	42 39N	0 25 E
Poseyville	**117**	38 10N	87 47W
Poshan = Boshan	**61**	36 28N	117 49 E
Posídhion, Ákra	**35**	39 57N	23 30 E
Poso	**57**	1 20S	120 55 E
Posoegroenoe	**135**	4 23N	55 43W
Posong	**61**	34 46N	127 5 E
Posse	**139**	14 4S	46 18W
Possel	**92**	5 5N	19 10 E
Possession I.	**143**	72 4S	172 0 E
Pössneck	**30**	50 42N	11 34 E
Post	**119**	33 13N	101 21W
Post Falls	**120**	47 46N	116 59W
Postavy	**36**	55 4N	26 50 E
Poste Maurice Cortier (Bidon 5)	**86**	22 14N	1 2 E
Postmasburg	**96**	28 18S	23 5 E
Postojna	**27**	45 46N	14 12 E
Poston	**123**	34 0N	114 24W
Postville	**116**	43 5N	91 34W
Potchefstroom	**96**	26 41S	27 7 E
Poté	**139**	17 49S	41 49W
Poteau	**119**	35 5N	94 37W
Poteet	**119**	29 4N	98 35W
Potelu, Lacul	**34**	43 44N	24 20 E
Potenza	**29**	40 40N	15 50 E
Potenza →	**27**	43 27N	13 38 E
Potenza Picena	**27**	43 22N	13 37 E
Poteriteri, L.	**81**	46 5S	167 10 E
Potes	**22**	43 15N	4 42W
Potgietersrus	**97**	24 10S	28 55 E
Poti	**39**	42 10N	41 38 E
Potiraguá	**139**	15 36S	39 53W
Potiskum	**89**	11 39N	11 2 E
Potomac →	**112**	38 0N	76 23W
Potosí	**137**	19 38S	65 50W
Potosi	**116**	37 56N	90 47W
Potosí □	**136**	20 31S	67 0W
Potosi Mt.	**123**	35 57N	115 29W
Pototan	**57**	10 54N	122 38 E
Potrerillos	**140**	26 30S	69 30W
Potsdam, Ger.	**30**	52 23N	13 4 E
Potsdam, U.S.A.	**115**	44 40N	74 59W
Potsdam □	**30**	52 40N	12 50 E
Pottenstein	**31**	49 46N	11 25 E
Potter	**118**	41 15N	103 20W
Pottery Hill = Abu Ballas	**90**	24 26N	27 36 E
Pottstown	**115**	40 17N	75 40W
Pottsville	**115**	40 39N	76 12W
Pouancé	**18**	47 44N	1 10W
Pouce Coupé	**108**	55 40N	120 10W
Pouembout	**68**	21 8S	164 53 E
Poughkeepsie	**115**	41 40N	73 57W
Pouilly	**19**	47 18N	2 57 E
Poulaphouca Res.	**15**	53 8N	6 30W
Pouldu, Le	**18**	47 41N	3 36W
Poulin-de-Courval, L.	**105**	48 52N	70 27W
Poulsbo	**122**	47 45N	122 39W
Poum	**68**	20 14S	164 2 E
Pourri, Mont	**21**	45 32N	6 52 E
Pouso Alegre, Mato Grosso, Brazil	**137**	11 46S	57 16W
Pouso Alegre, Minas Gerais, Brazil	**141**	22 14S	45 57W
Poutrincourt, L.	**105**	49 11N	74 7W
Pouzages	**20**	46 40N	0 50W
Pouzauges	**18**	46 47N	0 50W
Povenets	**40**	62 50N	34 50 E
Poverty Bay	**80**	38 43S	178 2 E
Póvoa de Lanhosa	**22**	41 33N	8 15W
Póvoa de Varzim	**22**	41 25N	8 46W
Povorino	**37**	51 12N	42 5 E
Powassan	**106**	46 5N	79 25W
Poway	**123**	32 58N	117 2W
Powder →	**118**	46 47N	105 12W
Powder River	**120**	43 5N	107 0W
Powell	**120**	44 45N	108 45W
Powell, L.	**121**	37 25N	110 45W
Powell River	**108**	49 50N	124 35W
Powers, Mich., U.S.A.	**112**	45 40N	87 32W
Powers, Oreg., U.S.A.	**120**	42 53N	124 2W
Powers Lake	**118**	48 37N	102 38W
Powys □	**13**	52 20N	3 20W
Poxoreu	**137**	15 50S	54 23W
Poya	**68**	21 19S	165 7 E
Poyang Hu	**59**	29 5N	116 20 E
Poyarkovo	**41**	49 36N	128 41 E
Poza de la Sal	**24**	42 35N	3 31W
Poza Rica	**125**	20 33N	97 27W
Požarevac	**33**	44 35N	21 18 E
Pozi	**59**	23 30N	120 13 E
Poznań	**32**	52 25N	16 55 E
Pozo	**123**	35 20N	120 24W
Pozo Alcón	**25**	37 42N	2 56W
Pozo Almonte	**136**	20 10S	69 50W
Pozo Colorado	**140**	23 30S	58 45W
Pozo del Dátil	**124**	30 0N	112 15W
Pozoblanco	**23**	38 23N	4 51W
Pozuzo	**136**	10 5S	75 35W
Pozzallo	**29**	36 44N	14 52 E
Pozzuoli	**29**	40 46N	14 6 E
Pra →	**89**	5 1N	1 37W
Prachin Buri	**54**	14 0N	101 25 E
Prachuap Khiri Khan	**55**	11 49N	99 48 E
Pradelles	**20**	44 46N	3 52 E
Pradera	**134**	3 25N	76 15W
Prades	**20**	42 38N	2 23 E
Prado	**139**	17 20S	39 13W
Prado del Rey	**23**	36 48N	5 33W
Præstø	**11**	55 8N	12 2 E
Pragersko	**27**	46 27N	15 42 E
Prague = Praha	**32**	50 5N	14 22 E
Praha	**32**	50 5N	14 22 E
Prahecq	**20**	46 19N	0 26W
Prahita →	**50**	19 0N	79 55 E
Prahova →	**34**	44 50N	25 50 E
Prahovo	**33**	44 18N	22 39 E
Praid	**34**	46 32N	25 10 E
Prainha, Amazonas, Brazil	**137**	7 10S	60 30W
Prainha, Pará, Brazil	**135**	1 45S	53 30W
Prairie	**72**	20 50S	144 35 E
Prairie →	**119**	34 30N	99 23W
Prairie City	**120**	44 27N	118 44W
Prairie du Chien	**116**	43 1N	91 9W
Prairie du Rocher	**116**	38 5N	90 6W
Praja	**56**	8 39S	116 17 E
Pramánda	**35**	39 32N	21 8 E
Pran Buri	**54**	12 23N	99 55 E
Prang	**89**	8 1N	0 56W
Prapat	**56**	2 41N	98 58 E
Prata	**139**	19 25S	48 54W
Prática di Mare	**28**	41 40N	12 26 E
Prato	**26**	43 53N	11 5 E
Prátola Peligna	**27**	42 7N	13 51 E
Pratovécchio	**27**	43 44N	11 43 E
Prats-de-Mollo	**20**	42 25N	2 27 E
Pratt	**119**	37 40N	98 45W
Pratten	**77**	28 6S	151 48 E
Prattville	**113**	32 30N	86 28W
Pravara →	**50**	19 35N	74 45 E
Pravdinsk	**37**	56 29N	43 28 E
Pravia	**22**	43 30N	6 12W
Pré-en-Pail	**18**	48 28N	0 12W
Pré St. Didier	**26**	45 45N	7 0 E
Precordillera	**140**	30 0S	69 1W
Predáppio	**27**	44 7N	11 58 E
Predazzo	**27**	46 19N	11 37 E
Predejane	**33**	42 51N	22 9 E
Preeceville	**109**	51 57N	102 40W
Préfailles	**18**	47 9N	2 11W
Pregonero	**134**	8 1N	71 46W
Pregrada	**27**	46 11N	15 45 E
Preissac, L.	**104**	48 20N	78 20W
Preko	**27**	44 7N	15 14 E
Prelate	**109**	50 51N	109 24W
Prelog	**27**	46 18N	16 32 E
Premer	**77**	31 29S	149 56 E
Premier	**108**	56 4N	129 56W
Premont	**119**	27 19N	98 8W
Premuda	**27**	44 20N	14 36 E
Prenjasi	**35**	41 6N	20 32 E
Prentice	**118**	45 31N	90 19W
Prenzlau	**30**	53 19N	13 51 E
Prepansko Jezero	**35**	40 55N	21 0 E
Přerov	**32**	49 28N	17 27 E
Presanella	**26**	46 13N	10 40 E
Prescott, Can.	**107**	44 45N	75 30W
Prescott, Ariz., U.S.A.	**121**	34 35N	112 30W
Prescott, Ark., U.S.A.	**119**	33 49N	93 22W
Preservation Inlet	**81**	46 8S	166 35 E
Preševo	**33**	42 19N	21 39 E
Presho	**118**	43 56N	100 4W
Presicce	**29**	39 53N	18 13 E
Presidencia de la Plaza	**140**	27 0S	29 50W
Presidencia Roque Saenz Peña	**140**	26 45S	60 30W
Presidente Epitácio	**139**	21 56S	52 6W
Presidente Hayes □	**140**	24 0S	59 0W
Presidente Hermes	**137**	11 17S	61 55W
Presidente Prudente	**141**	22 5S	51 25W
Presidio, Mexico	**124**	29 29N	104 23W
Presidio, U.S.A.	**119**	29 30N	104 20W
Preslav	**34**	43 10N	26 52 E
Prešov	**32**	49 0N	21 15 E
Prespa, L. = Prepansko Jezero	**35**	40 55N	21 0 E
Presque Isle	**103**	46 40N	68 0W
Prestbury	**13**	51 54N	2 2W
Prestea	**88**	5 22N	2 7W
Presteigne	**13**	52 17N	3 0W
Presto	**137**	18 55S	64 56W
Preston, Can.	**114**	43 23N	80 21W
Preston, U.K.	**12**	53 46N	2 42W
Preston, Idaho, U.S.A.	**120**	42 10N	111 55W
Preston, Iowa, U.S.A.	**116**	42 6N	90 24W
Preston, Minn., U.S.A.	**118**	43 39N	92 3W
Preston, Nev., U.S.A.	**120**	38 59N	115 2W
Preston, C.	**78**	20 51S	116 12 E
Prestonpans	**14**	55 58N	3 0W
Prestwick	**14**	55 30N	4 38W
Prêto →, Amazonas, Brazil	**135**	0 8S	64 6W
Prêto →, Bahia, Brazil	**138**	11 21S	43 52W
Prêto do Igapó-Açu →	**135**	4 26S	59 48W
Pretoria	**97**	25 44S	28 12 E
Preuilly-sur-Claise	**18**	46 51N	0 56 E
Préveza	**35**	38 57N	20 47 E
Priazovskoye	**38**	46 44N	35 40 E
Pribilov Is.	**144**	56 0N	170 0W
Priboj	**33**	43 35N	19 32 E
Pribram	**32**	49 41N	14 2 E
Price	**120**	39 40N	110 48W
Price I.	**108**	52 23N	128 41W
Prichalnaya	**39**	48 57N	44 33 E
Priego	**24**	40 26N	2 21W
Priego de Córdoba	**23**	37 27N	4 12W
Priekule	**36**	57 27N	21 45 E
Prien	**31**	47 52N	12 20 E
Prieska	**96**	29 40S	22 42 E
Priest L.	**120**	48 30N	116 55W
Priest River	**120**	48 11N	116 55W
Priest Valley	**122**	36 10N	120 39W
Priestly	**108**	54 8N	125 20W
Prievidza	**32**	48 46N	18 36 E
Prijedor	**27**	44 58N	16 41 E
Prikaspiyskaya Nizmennost	**39**	47 0N	48 0 E
Prikumsk	**38**	44 50N	44 10 E
Prilep	**35**	41 21N	21 37 E
Priluki	**36**	50 30N	32 24 E
Prime Seal I.	**72**	40 3S	147 43 E
Primeira Cruz	**138**	2 30S	43 26W
Primorsko-Akhtarsk	**38**	46 2N	38 10 E
Primrose L.	**109**	54 55N	109 45W
Prince Albert	**109**	53 15N	105 50W
Prince Albert Mts.	**143**	76 0S	161 30 E
Prince Albert Nat. Park	**109**	54 0N	106 25W
Prince Albert Pen.	**100**	72 30N	116 0W
Prince Albert Sd.	**100**	70 25N	115 0W
Prince Alfred C.	**144**	74 20N	124 40W
Prince Charles I.	**101**	67 47N	76 12W
Prince Charles Mts.	**143**	72 0S	67 0 E
Prince Edward I. □	**103**	46 20N	63 20W
Prince Edward Is.	**53**	45 15S	39 0 E
Prince Edward Pt.	**107**	43 56N	76 52W
Prince George	**108**	53 55N	122 50W
Prince of Wales I., Can.	**100**	73 0N	99 0W
Prince of Wales I., U.S.A.	**100**	53 30N	131 30W
Prince of Wales Is.	**69**	10 40S	142 10 E
Prince Patrick I.	**144**	77 0N	120 0W
Prince Regent Inlet	**144**	73 0N	90 0W
Prince Rupert	**108**	54 20N	130 20W
Princesa Isabel	**138**	7 44S	38 0W
Princess Charlotte B.	**72**	14 25S	144 0 E
Princess May Ranges	**78**	15 30S	125 30 E
Princess Royal I.	**108**	53 0N	128 40W
Princeton, Can.	**108**	49 27N	120 30W
Princeton, Calif., U.S.A.	**122**	39 24N	122 1W
Princeton, Ill., U.S.A.	**116**	41 25N	89 25W
Princeton, Ind., U.S.A.	**117**	38 20N	87 35W
Princeton, Ky., U.S.A.	**112**	37 6N	87 55W
Princeton, Mo., U.S.A.	**116**	40 23N	93 35W
Princeton, N.J., U.S.A.	**115**	40 18N	74 40W
Princeton, W. Va., U.S.A.	**112**	37 21N	81 8W
Princetown	**74**	38 41S	143 10 E
Princeville, Can.	**105**	46 10N	71 53W
Princeville, U.S.A.	**116**	40 56N	89 46W
Principe Chan.	**108**	53 28N	130 0W
Principe da Beira	**137**	12 20S	64 30W
Principe, I. de	**83**	1 37N	7 27 E
Prineville	**120**	44 17N	120 50W
Prins Albert	**96**	33 12S	22 2 E
Prins Harald Kyst	**143**	70 0S	35 1 E
Prinsesse Astrid Kyst	**143**	70 45S	12 30 E
Prinsesse Ragnhild Kyst	**143**	70 15S	27 30 E
Prinzapolca	**126**	13 20N	83 35W
Prior, C.	**22**	43 34N	8 17W
Pripet = Pripyat →	**36**	51 20N	30 9 E
Pripet Marshes = Polesye	**36**	52 0N	28 10 E
Pripyat →	**36**	51 20N	30 9 E
Prislop, Pasul	**34**	47 37N	25 15 E
Priština	**33**	42 40N	21 13 E
Pritchard	**113**	30 47N	88 5W
Pritzwalk	**30**	53 10N	12 11 E
Privas	**21**	44 45N	4 37 E
Priverno	**28**	41 29N	13 10 E
Privolzhsk	**37**	57 23N	41 17 E
Privolzhskaya Vozvyshennost	**37**	51 0N	46 0 E
Privolzhskiy	**37**	51 25N	46 3 E
Privolzhye	**37**	52 52N	48 33 E
Priyutnoye	**39**	46 12N	43 40 E
Prizren	**33**	42 13N	20 45 E
Prizzi	**28**	37 44N	13 24 E
Prnjavor	**33**	44 52N	17 43 E
Probolinggo	**57**	7 46S	113 13 E
Procida	**28**	40 46N	14 0 E
Proddatur	**51**	14 45N	78 30 E
Proença-a-Nova	**23**	39 45N	7 54W
Prof. Van Blommestein Meer	**135**	4 45N	55 5W
Progreso	**125**	21 20N	89 40W
Prokhladnyy	**39**	43 50N	44 2 E
Prokletije	**34**	42 30N	19 45 E
Prokopyevsk	**40**	54 0N	86 45 E
Prokuplje	**33**	43 16N	21 36 E
Proletarskaya	**39**	46 42N	41 50 E
Prophet →	**108**	58 48N	122 40W
Prophetstown	**116**	41 40N	89 56W
Propriá	**138**	10 13S	36 51W
Propriano	**21**	41 41N	8 52 E
Proserpine	**72**	20 21S	148 36 E
Prosser	**120**	46 11N	119 52W
Prostějov	**32**	49 30N	17 9 E
Proston	**73**	26 8S	151 32 E
Protection	**119**	37 16N	99 30W
Próti	**35**	37 5N	21 32 E
Provadiya	**34**	43 12N	27 30 E
Provence	**21**	43 40N	5 46 E
Providence, Ky., U.S.A.	**112**	37 25N	87 46W
Providence, R.I., U.S.A.	**115**	41 50N	71 28W
Providence Bay	**106**	45 41N	82 15W
Providence C.	**81**	45 59S	166 29 E
Providence Mts.	**121**	35 0N	115 30W
Providencia	**134**	0 28S	76 28W
Providencia, I. de	**126**	13 25N	81 26W
Provideniya	**41**	64 23N	173 18W
Provins	**19**	48 33N	3 15 E
Provo	**120**	40 16N	111 37W
Provost	**109**	52 25N	110 20W
Prozor	**33**	43 50N	17 34 E
Prudentópolis	**139**	25 12S	50 57W
Prud'homme	**109**	52 20N	105 54W
Prudnik	**32**	50 20N	17 38 E
Prüm	**31**	50 14N	6 22 E
Pruszcz Gd.	**32**	54 17N	18 40 E
Pruszków	**32**	52 9N	20 49 E
Prut →	**34**	46 3N	28 10 E
Prvič	**27**	44 55N	14 47 E
Prydz B.	**143**	69 0S	74 0 E
Pryor	**119**	36 17N	95 20W
Przasnysz	**32**	53 2N	20 45 E
Przedbórz	**32**	51 6N	19 53 E
Przemyśl	**32**	49 50N	22 45 E
Przeworsk	**32**	50 6N	22 32 E
Przewóz	**32**	51 28N	14 57 E
Przhevalsk	**40**	42 30N	78 20 E
Przysucha	**32**	51 22N	20 38 E
Psakhná	**35**	38 34N	23 35 E
Psará	**35**	38 37N	25 38 E
Psel →	**38**	49 5N	33 20 E
Pserimos	**35**	36 56N	27 12 E
Pskov	**36**	57 50N	28 25 E
Psunj	**33**	45 25N	17 19 E
Pszczyna	**32**	49 59N	18 58 E
Pteleón	**35**	39 3N	22 57 E
Ptich →	**36**	52 9N	28 52 E
Ptolemaís	**35**	40 30N	21 43 E
Ptuj	**27**	46 28N	15 50 E
Ptujska Gora	**27**	46 23N	15 47 E
Pu Xian	**60**	36 24N	111 6 E
Pua	**54**	19 11N	100 55 E
Puán	**140**	37 30S	62 45W
Pu'an	**58**	25 46N	104 57 E
Puan	**61**	35 44N	126 44 E
Pu'apu'a	**68**	13 34S	172 9W
Pubei	**58**	22 16N	109 31 E
Pucacuro →	**134**	3 20S	74 58W
Pucallpa	**136**	8 25S	74 30W
Pucará, Boliv.	**137**	18 43S	64 11W

Place	Map	Lat.	Long.
Pucará, Peru	**136**	15 5 S	70 24 W
Pucarani	**136**	16 23 S	68 30 W
Pucheng	**59**	27 59 N	118 31 E
Pučišće	**27**	43 22 N	16 43 E
Pucka, Zatoka	**32**	54 30 N	18 40 E
Puckapunyal	**74**	37 0 S	145 3 E
Puding	**58**	26 18 N	105 44 E
Pudukkottai	**51**	10 28 N	78 47 E
Puebla	**125**	19 0 N	98 10 W
Puebla □	**125**	18 30 N	98 0 W
Puebla de Alcocer	**23**	38 59 N	5 14 W
Puebla de Cazalla, La	**23**	37 10 N	5 20 W
Puebla de Don Fadrique	**25**	37 58 N	2 25 W
Puebla de Don Rodrigo	**23**	39 5 N	4 37 W
Puebla de Guzmán	**23**	37 37 N	7 15 W
Puebla de los Infantes, La	**23**	37 47 N	5 24 W
Puebla de Montalbán, La	**22**	39 52 N	4 22 W
Puebla de Sanabria	**22**	42 4 N	6 38 W
Puebla de Trives	**22**	42 20 N	7 10 W
Puebla del Caramiñal	**22**	42 37 N	8 56 W
Puebla, La	**24**	39 50 N	3 0 E
Pueblo	**118**	38 20 N	104 40 W
Pueblo Bonito	**121**	36 4 N	107 57 W
Pueblo Hundido	**140**	26 20 S	70 5 W
Pueblo Nuevo	**134**	8 26 N	71 26 W
Puelches	**140**	38 5 S	65 51 W
Puelén	**140**	37 32 S	67 38 W
Puente Alto	**140**	33 32 S	70 35 W
Puente del Arzobispo	**22**	39 48 N	5 10 W
Puente-Genil	**23**	37 22 N	4 47 W
Puente la Reina	**24**	42 40 N	1 49 W
Puenteareas	**22**	42 10 N	8 28 W
Puentedeume	**22**	43 24 N	8 10 W
Puentes de Garcia Rodriguez	**22**	43 27 N	7 50 W
Pu'er	**58**	23 0 N	101 15 E
Puerco →	**121**	34 22 N	107 50 W
Puerta, La	**25**	38 22 N	2 45 W
Puerto Acosta	**136**	15 32 S	69 15 W
Puerto Aisén	**142**	45 27 S	73 0 W
Puerto Ángel	**125**	15 40 N	96 29 W
Puerto Arista	**125**	15 56 N	93 48 W
Puerto Armuelles	**126**	8 20 N	82 51 W
Puerto Ayacucho	**134**	5 40 N	67 35 W
Puerto Barrios	**126**	15 40 N	88 32 W
Puerto Bermejo	**140**	26 55 S	58 34 W
Puerto Bermúdez	**136**	10 20 S	75 0 W
Puerto Bolívar	**134**	3 19 S	79 55 W
Puerto Cabello	**134**	10 28 N	68 1 W
Puerto Cabezas	**126**	14 0 N	83 30 W
Puerto Cabo Gracias á Dios	**126**	15 0 N	83 10 W
Puerto Capaz = Jebba	**86**	35 11 N	4 43 W
Puerto Carreño	**134**	6 12 N	67 22 W
Puerto Castilla	**126**	16 0 N	86 0 W
Puerto Chicama	**136**	7 45 S	79 20 W
Puerto Coig	**142**	50 54 S	69 15 W
Puerto Cortes	**126**	8 55 N	84 0 W
Puerto Cortés	**126**	15 51 N	88 0 W
Puerto Cumarebo	**134**	11 29 N	69 30 W
Puerto de Santa María	**23**	36 36 N	6 13 W
Puerto Deseado	**142**	47 55 S	66 0 W
Puerto Guaraní	**137**	21 18 S	57 55 W
Puerto Heath	**136**	12 34 S	68 39 W
Puerto Huitoto	**134**	0 18 N	74 3 W
Puerto Inca	**136**	9 22 S	74 54 W
Puerto Juárez	**125**	21 11 N	86 49 W
Puerto La Cruz	**135**	10 13 N	64 38 W
Puerto Leguízamo	**134**	0 12 S	74 46 W
Puerto Libertad	**124**	29 55 N	112 41 W
Puerto Limón	**134**	3 23 N	73 30 W
Puerto Lobos	**142**	42 0 S	65 3 W
Puerto López	**134**	4 5 N	72 58 W
Puerto Lumbreras	**25**	37 34 N	1 48 W
Puerto Madryn	**142**	42 48 S	65 4 W
Puerto Maldonado	**136**	12 30 S	69 10 W
Puerto Manotí	**126**	21 22 N	76 50 W
Puerto Mazarrón	**25**	37 34 N	1 15 W
Puerto Mercedes	**134**	1 11 N	72 53 W
Puerto Miraña	**134**	1 20 S	70 19 W
Puerto Montt	**142**	41 28 S	73 0 W
Puerto Morelos	**125**	20 49 N	86 52 W
Puerto Nariño	**134**	4 56 N	67 48 W
Puerto Natales	**142**	51 45 S	72 15 W
Puerto Nuevo	**134**	5 53 N	69 56 W
Puerto Nutrias	**134**	8 5 N	69 18 W
Puerto Ordaz	**135**	8 16 N	62 44 W
Puerto Padre	**126**	21 13 N	76 35 W
Puerto Páez	**134**	6 13 N	67 28 W
Puerto Peñasco	**124**	31 20 N	113 33 W
Puerto Pinasco	**140**	22 36 S	57 50 W
Puerto Pirámides	**142**	42 35 S	64 20 W
Puerto Plata	**127**	19 48 N	70 45 W
Puerto Portillo	**136**	9 45 S	72 42 W
Puerto Princesa	**57**	9 46 N	118 45 E
Puerto Quellón	**142**	43 7 S	73 37 W
Puerto Quepos	**126**	9 29 N	84 6 W
Puerto Real	**23**	36 33 N	6 12 W
Puerto Rico	**136**	11 5 S	67 38 W
Puerto Rico ■	**127**	18 15 N	66 45 W
Puerto Rico Trough	**128**	20 0 N	63 0 W
Puerto Saavedra	**142**	38 47 S	73 24 W
Puerto Sastre	**140**	22 2 S	57 55 W
Puerto Siles	**137**	12 48 S	65 5 W
Puerto Suárez	**137**	18 58 S	57 52 W
Puerto Tejada	**134**	3 14 N	76 24 W
Puerto Umbría	**134**	0 52 N	76 33 W
Puerto Vallarta	**124**	20 36 N	105 15 W
Puerto Varas	**142**	41 19 S	72 59 W
Puerto Villazón	**137**	13 32 S	61 57 W
Puerto Wilches	**134**	7 21 N	73 54 W
Puertollano	**23**	38 43 N	4 7 W
Puertomarin	**22**	42 48 N	7 36 W
Puesto Cunambo	**134**	2 10 S	76 0 W
Pueyrredón, L.	**142**	47 20 S	72 0 W
Pugachev	**37**	52 0 N	48 49 E
Puge, China	**58**	27 20 N	102 31 E
Puge, Tanz.	**94**	4 45 S	33 11 E
Puget Sd.	**120**	47 15 N	122 30 W
Puget-Théniers	**21**	43 58 N	6 53 E
Púglia □	**29**	41 0 N	16 30 E
Pugŏdong	**61**	42 5 N	130 0 E
Pugu	**94**	6 55 S	39 4 E
Puha	**80**	38 30 S	177 50 E
Pui	**34**	45 30 N	23 4 E
Puica	**136**	15 0 S	72 33 W
Puig Mayor, Mte.	**24**	39 49 N	2 47 E
Puigcerdá	**24**	42 24 N	1 50 E
Puigmal	**24**	42 23 N	2 7 E
Puisaye, Collines de	**19**	47 34 N	3 18 E
Puiseaux	**19**	48 11 N	2 30 E
Pujilí	**134**	0 57 S	78 41 W
Pujon-chosuji	**61**	40 35 N	127 35 E
Puka	**34**	42 2 N	19 53 E
Pukaki L.	**81**	44 4 S	170 1 E
Pukatawagan	**109**	55 45 N	101 20 W
Pukchin	**61**	40 12 N	125 45 E
Pukchŏng	**61**	40 14 N	128 10 E
Pukearuhe	**80**	38 55 S	174 31 E
Pukekohe	**80**	37 12 S	174 55 E
Puketeraki Ra.	**81**	42 58 S	172 13 E
Pukeuri	**81**	45 4 S	171 2 E
Pukou	**59**	32 7 N	118 38 E
Pula	**28**	39 0 N	9 0 E
Pula (Pola)	**27**	44 54 N	13 57 E
Pulacayo	**136**	20 25 S	66 41 W
Pulaski, N.Y., U.S.A.	**115**	43 32 N	76 9 W
Pulaski, Tenn., U.S.A.	**113**	35 10 N	87 0 W
Pulaski, Va., U.S.A.	**112**	37 4 N	80 49 W
Pulawy	**32**	51 23 N	21 59 E
Pulga	**122**	39 48 N	121 29 W
Pulgaon	**50**	20 44 N	78 21 E
Pulicat, L.	**51**	13 40 N	80 15 E
Puliyangudi	**51**	9 11 N	77 24 E
Pullabooka	**76**	33 44 S	147 46 E
Pullman	**120**	46 49 N	117 10 W
Pulog, Mt.	**57**	16 40 N	120 50 E
Puloraja	**56**	4 55 N	95 24 E
Pultusk	**32**	52 43 N	21 6 E
Pumlumon Fawr	**13**	52 29 N	3 47 W
Puna	**137**	19 45 S	65 28 W
Puná, I.	**134**	2 55 S	80 5 W
Punakha	**52**	27 42 N	89 52 E
Punalur	**51**	9 0 N	76 56 E
Punasar	**48**	27 6 N	73 6 E
Punata	**137**	17 32 S	65 50 W
Punavia	**68**	17 38 S	149 36 W
Punch	**49**	33 48 N	74 4 E
Pune	**50**	18 29 N	73 57 E
Pungsan	**61**	40 50 N	128 9 E
Pungue, Ponte de	**95**	19 0 S	34 0 E
Puning	**59**	23 20 N	116 12 E
Punjab □	**48**	31 0 N	76 0 E
Puno	**136**	15 55 S	70 3 W
Punta Alta	**142**	38 53 S	62 4 W
Punta Arenas	**142**	53 10 S	71 0 W
Punta Cardón	**134**	11 38 N	70 14 W
Punta Coles	**136**	17 43 S	71 23 W
Punta de Bombón	**136**	17 10 S	71 48 W
Punta de Díaz	**140**	28 0 S	70 45 W
Punta de Piedras	**134**	10 54 N	64 6 W
Punta Delgado	**142**	42 43 S	63 38 W
Punta Gorda, Belize	**125**	16 10 N	88 45 W
Punta Gorda, U.S.A.	**113**	26 55 N	82 0 W
Punta Prieta	**124**	28 58 N	114 17 W
Puntabie	**73**	32 12 S	134 13 E
Puntarenas	**126**	10 0 N	84 50 W
Punto Fijo	**134**	11 50 N	70 13 W
Punxsutawney	**114**	40 56 N	79 0 W
Puqi	**59**	29 40 N	113 50 E
Puquio	**136**	14 45 S	74 10 W
Pur →	**40**	67 31 N	77 55 E
Purace, Vol.	**134**	2 21 N	76 23 W
Purari →	**69**	7 49 S	145 0 E
Purbeck, Isle of	**13**	50 40 N	2 5 W
Purcell	**119**	35 0 N	97 25 W
Purchena Tetica	**25**	37 21 N	2 21 W
Puri	**50**	19 50 N	85 58 E
Purificación	**134**	3 51 N	74 55 W
Purísima, La	**124**	26 10 N	112 4 W
Purlewaugh	**77**	31 20 S	149 30 E
Purli	**50**	18 50 N	76 35 E
Purmerend	**16**	52 30 N	4 58 E
Purna →	**50**	19 6 N	77 2 E
Purnea	**49**	25 45 N	87 31 E
Purnim	**74**	38 16 S	142 36 E
Purukcahu	**56**	0 35 S	114 35 E
Purulia	**49**	23 17 N	86 24 E
Purus →	**135**	3 42 S	61 28 W
Pŭrvomay	**34**	42 8 N	25 17 E
Purwakarta	**57**	6 35 S	107 29 E
Purwodadi, Jawa, Indon.	**57**	7 7 S	110 55 E
Purwodadi, Jawa, Indon.	**57**	7 51 S	110 0 E
Purwokerto	**57**	7 25 S	109 14 E
Purworedjo	**57**	7 43 S	110 2 E
Puryŏng	**61**	42 0 N	129 43 E
Pus →	**50**	19 55 N	77 55 E
Pusad	**50**	19 56 N	77 36 E
Pusan	**61**	35 5 N	129 0 E
Push, La	**122**	47 55 N	124 38 W
Pushchino	**41**	54 10 N	158 0 E
Pushkin	**36**	59 45 N	30 25 E
Pushkino	**37**	51 16 N	47 0 E
Püspökladány	**33**	47 19 N	21 6 E
Pussa	**97**	24 30 S	33 55 E
Pustoshka	**36**	56 20 N	29 30 E
Putahow L.	**109**	59 54 N	100 40 W
Putao	**52**	27 28 N	97 30 E
Putaruru	**80**	38 2 S	175 50 E
Putbus	**30**	54 19 N	13 29 E
Putian	**59**	25 23 N	119 0 E
Putignano	**29**	40 50 N	17 5 E
Putina	**136**	14 55 S	69 55 W
Puting, Tanjung	**56**	3 31 S	111 46 E
Putlitz	**30**	53 15 N	12 3 E
Putna →	**34**	45 42 N	27 26 E
Putnam	**115**	41 55 N	71 55 W
Putorana, Gory	**41**	69 0 N	95 0 E
Putorino	**80**	39 4 S	177 0 E
Putre	**136**	18 12 S	69 35 W
Puttalam Lagoon	**51**	8 15 N	79 45 E
Putten	**16**	52 16 N	5 36 E
Puttgarden	**30**	54 28 N	11 15 E
Puttur	**51**	12 46 N	75 12 E
Putty	**76**	32 57 S	150 42 E
Putumayo →, Colomb.	**134**	3 0 S	67 0 W
Putumayo →, Colomb.	**134**	3 7 S	67 58 W
Putuo	**59**	29 56 N	122 20 E
Putussibau	**56**	0 50 N	112 56 E
Puy-de-Dôme	**20**	45 46 N	2 57 E
Puy-de-Dôme □	**20**	45 47 N	3 0 E
Puy-de-Sancy	**20**	45 32 N	2 48 E
Puy-Guillaume	**20**	45 57 N	3 29 E
Puy, Le	**20**	45 3 N	3 52 E
Puy l'Évêque	**20**	44 31 N	1 9 E
Puyallup	**122**	47 10 N	122 22 W
Puyang	**60**	35 40 N	115 1 E
Puyehue	**142**	40 40 S	72 37 W
Puylaurens	**20**	43 35 N	2 0 E
Puyo	**134**	1 28 S	77 59 W
Puyôo	**20**	43 33 N	0 56 W
Pwani □	**94**	7 0 S	39 0 E
Pweto	**95**	8 25 S	28 51 E
Pwinbyu	**52**	20 23 N	94 40 E
Pwllheli	**12**	52 54 N	4 26 W
Pyalong	**74**	37 7 S	144 51 E
Pyana →	**37**	55 30 N	46 0 E
Pyapon	**52**	16 20 N	95 40 E
Pyasina →	**41**	73 30 N	87 0 E
Pyatigorsk	**39**	44 2 N	43 6 E
Pyatikhatki	**38**	48 28 N	33 38 E
Pyaye	**52**	19 12 N	95 10 E
Pyè	**52**	18 49 N	95 13 E
Pyinbauk	**52**	19 10 N	95 12 E
Pyinmana	**52**	19 45 N	96 12 E
Pyŏktong	**61**	40 50 N	125 50 E
Pyŏnggang	**61**	38 24 N	127 17 E
Pyŏngtaek	**61**	37 1 N	127 4 E
P'yŏngyang	**61**	39 0 N	125 45 E
Pyote	**119**	31 34 N	103 5 W
Pyramid Hill	**74**	36 2 S	144 6 E
Pyramid L.	**120**	40 0 N	119 30 W
Pyramid Pk.	**123**	36 25 N	116 37 W
Pyramids	**90**	29 58 N	31 9 E
Pyrénées	**20**	42 45 N	0 18 E
Pyrenees = Pyrénées	**20**	42 45 N	0 18 E
Pyrénées-Atlantiques □	**20**	43 15 N	1 0 W
Pyrénées-Orientales □	**20**	42 35 N	2 26 E
Pyrzyce	**32**	53 10 N	14 55 E
Pyshchug	**37**	58 57 N	45 47 E
Pytalovo	**36**	57 5 N	27 55 E
Pyttegga	**10**	62 13 N	7 42 E
Pyu	**52**	18 30 N	96 28 E

Q

Place	Map	Lat.	Long.
Qabalon	**44**	32 8 N	35 17 E
Qabatiya	**44**	32 25 N	35 16 E
Qadhima	**46**	22 20 N	39 13 E
Qagan Nur	**60**	43 30 N	114 55 E
Qahar Youyi Zhongqi	**60**	41 12 N	112 40 E
Qaidam Pendi	**62**	37 0 N	95 0 E
Qa'iya	**46**	24 33 N	43 15 E
Qal' at Shajwa	**90**	25 2 N	38 57 E
Qala-i-Jadid (Spin Baldak)	**48**	31 1 N	66 25 E
Qala-i-Kirta	**47**	32 15 N	63 0 E
Qala Nau	**47**	35 0 N	63 5 E
Qala Yangi	**48**	34 20 N	66 30 E
Qal'at al Akhdar	**46**	28 0 N	37 10 E
Qal'at al Mu'azzam	**46**	27 45 N	37 31 E
Qal'at Saura	**90**	26 10 N	38 40 E
Qalqīlya	**44**	32 12 N	34 58 E
Qalyûb	**90**	30 12 N	31 11 E
Qam	**44**	32 36 N	35 43 E
Qamar, Ghubbat al	**45**	16 20 N	52 30 E
Qamdo	**58**	31 15 N	97 6 E
Qamruddin Karez	**48**	31 45 N	68 20 E
Qāna	**44**	33 12 N	35 17 E
Qâra	**90**	29 38 N	26 30 E
Qara Qash →	**49**	35 0 N	78 30 E
Qara Tagh La = Kala Shank'ou	**49**	35 42 N	78 20 E
Qarachuk	**46**	37 0 N	42 2 E
Qarah	**46**	29 55 N	40 3 E
Qardud	**91**	10 20 N	29 56 E
Qarqan	**62**	38 5 N	85 20 E
Qarqan He →	**62**	39 30 N	88 30 E
Qarrasa	**91**	14 38 N	32 5 E
Qasim	**46**	26 0 N	43 0 E
Qaşr Bū Hadi	**87**	31 1 N	16 45 E
Qasr-e Qand	**47**	26 15 N	60 45 E
Qasr Farâfra	**90**	27 0 N	28 1 E
Qatar ■	**47**	25 30 N	51 15 E
Qattâra	**90**	30 12 N	27 3 E
Qattâra Depression = Qattâra, Munkhafed el	**90**	29 30 N	27 30 E
Qattâra, Munkhafed el	**90**	29 30 N	27 30 E
Qāyen	**47**	33 40 N	59 10 E
Qazvin	**46**	36 15 N	50 0 E
Qena	**90**	26 10 N	32 43 E
Qena, Wadi →	**90**	26 12 N	32 44 E
Qesari	**44**	32 30 N	34 53 E
Qeshm	**47**	26 55 N	56 10 E
Qi Xian	**60**	34 40 N	114 48 E
Qian Gorlos	**61**	45 5 N	124 42 E
Qian Xian	**60**	34 31 N	108 15 E
Qiancheng	**58**	27 12 N	109 50 E
Qianjiang, Guangxi, China	**58**	23 38 N	108 58 E
Qianjiang, Hubei, China	**59**	30 24 N	112 55 E
Qianjiang, Sichuan, China	**58**	29 33 N	108 47 E
Qianshan	**59**	30 37 N	116 35 E
Qianwei	**58**	29 13 N	103 56 E
Qianxi	**58**	27 3 N	106 3 E
Qianyang, Hunan, China	**59**	27 18 N	110 10 E
Qianyang, Shaanxi, China	**60**	34 40 N	107 8 E
Qianyang, Zhejiang, China	**59**	30 11 N	119 25 E
Qiaojia	**58**	26 56 N	102 58 E
Qichun	**59**	30 18 N	115 25 E
Qidong, Hunan, China	**59**	26 49 N	112 7 E
Qidong, Jiangsu, China	**59**	31 48 N	121 38 E
Qijiang	**58**	28 57 N	106 35 E
Qila Safed	**47**	29 0 N	61 30 E
Qila Saifulla	**48**	30 45 N	68 17 E
Qilian Shan	**62**	38 30 N	96 0 E
Qimen	**59**	29 50 N	117 42 E
Qin He →	**60**	35 1 N	113 22 E
Qin Jiang →	**59**	26 15 N	115 55 E
Qin'an	**60**	34 48 N	105 40 E
Qing Xian	**60**	38 35 N	116 45 E
Qingcheng	**61**	37 15 N	117 40 E
Qingdao	**61**	36 5 N	120 20 E
Qingfeng	**60**	35 52 N	115 8 E
Qinghai □	**62**	36 0 N	98 0 E
Qinghai Hu	**62**	36 40 N	100 10 E
Qinghecheng	**61**	41 15 N	124 30 E
Qinghemen	**61**	41 48 N	121 25 E
Qingjian	**60**	37 8 N	110 8 E
Qingjiang, Jiangsu, China	**61**	33 30 N	119 2 E
Qingjiang, Jiangxi, China	**59**	28 4 N	115 29 E
Qingliu	**59**	26 11 N	116 48 E
Qinglong	**58**	25 49 N	105 12 E
Qingping	**58**	26 39 N	107 47 E
Qingpu	**59**	31 10 N	121 6 E

Qingshui **60** 34 48N 106 8 E
Qingshuihe **60** 39 55N 111 35 E
Qingtian **59** 28 12N 120 15 E
Qingtongxia Shuiku **60** 37 50N 105 58 E
Qingxi **58** 27 8N 108 43 E
Qingxu **60** 37 34N 112 22 E
Qingyang, Anhui, China **59** 30 38N 117 50 E
Qingyang, Gansu, China **60** 36 2N 107 55 E
Qingyi Jiang → **58** 29 32N 103 44 E
Qingyuan, Guangdong, China **59** 23 40N 112 59 E
Qingyuan, Liaoning, China **61** 42 10N 124 55 E
Qingyuan, Zhejiang, China **59** 27 36N 119 3 E
Qingyun **61** 37 45N 117 20 E
Qingzhen **58** 26 31N 106 25 E
Qinhuangdao **61** 39 56N 119 30 E
Qinling Shandi **60** 33 50N 108 10 E
Qinshui **60** 35 40N 112 8 E
Qinyang **60** 35 7N 112 57 E
Qinyuan **60** 36 29N 112 20 E
Qinzhou **58** 21 58N 108 38 E
Qionghai **54** 19 15N 110 26 E
Qionglai **58** 30 25N 103 31 E
Qionglai Shan **58** 31 0N 102 30 E
Qiongshan **54** 19 51N 110 26 E
Qiongzhou Haixia **54** 20 10N 110 15 E
Qiqihar **62** 47 26N 124 0 E
Qiryat 'Anavim **44** 31 49N 35 7 E
Qiryat Ata **44** 32 49N 35 6 E
Qiryat Bialik **44** 32 50N 35 5 E
Qiryat 'Eqron **44** 31 52N 34 49 E
Qiryat Gat **44** 31 36N 35 47 E
Qiryat Hayyim **44** 32 49N 35 4 E
Qiryat Shemona **44** 33 13N 35 35 E
Qiryat Yam **44** 32 51N 35 4 E
Qishan, China **60** 34 25N 107 38 E
Qishan, Taiwan **59** 22 52N 120 25 E
Qishon → **44** 32 49N 35 2 E
Qishrān **90** 20 14N 40 2 E
Qitai **62** 44 2N 89 35 E
Qiubei **58** 24 2N 104 12 E
Qixia **61** 37 17N 120 52 E
Qiyang **59** 26 35N 111 50 E
Qizan **91** 16 57N 42 34 E
Qizān **45** 17 0N 42 20 E
Qom **47** 34 40N 51 0 E
Qomolangma Feng (Mt. Everest) **62** 28 0N 86 45 E
Qu Jiang → **58** 30 0N 106 10 E
Qu Xian, Sichuan, China **58** 30 48N 106 58 E
Qu Xian, Zhejiang, China **59** 28 57N 118 54 E
Quaama **75** 36 27S 149 55 E
Quackenbrück **30** 52 40N 7 59 E
Quairading **79** 32 0S 117 21 E
Quakertown **115** 40 27N 75 20W
Qualeup **79** 33 48S 116 48 E
Quambatook **74** 35 49S 143 34 E
Quambone **76** 30 57S 147 53 E
Quan Long **55** 9 7N 105 8 E
Quanan **119** 34 20N 99 45W
Quandialla **76** 34 1S 147 47 E
Quang Ngai **54** 15 13N 108 58 E
Quang Yen **54** 20 56N 106 52 E
Quannan **59** 24 45N 114 33 E
Quantock Hills **13** 51 8N 3 10W
Quantong **74** 36 43S 142 3 E
Quanzhou, Fujian, China **59** 24 55N 113 34 E
Quanzhou, Guangxi Zhuangzu, China **59** 25 57N 111 5 E
Quaraí **140** 30 15S 56 20W
Quarré-les-Tombes **19** 47 21N 4 0 E
Quartu Sant' Elena **28** 39 15N 9 10 E
Quartzsite **123** 33 44N 114 16W
Quatsino **108** 50 30N 127 40W
Quatsino Sd. **108** 50 25N 127 58W
Qubab = Mishmar Aiyalon **44** 31 52N 34 57 E
Qūchān **47** 37 10N 58 27 E
Que Que **95** 18 58S 29 48 E
Queanbeyan **76** 35 17S 149 14 E
Québec **105** 46 52N 71 13W
Québec □ **103** 50 0N 70 0W
Quedlinburg **30** 51 47N 11 9 E
Queen Alexandra Ra. **143** 85 0S 170 0 E
Queen Charlotte **108** 53 15N 132 2W
Queen Charlotte Bay **142** 51 50S 60 40W
Queen Charlotte Is. **108** 53 20N 132 10W
Queen Charlotte Sd. **81** 41 10S 174 15 E
Queen Charlotte Str. **108** 51 0N 128 0W
Queen City **116** 40 25N 92 34W
Queen Elizabeth Is. **4** 76 0N 95 0W
Queen Elizabeth Nat. Park **94** 0 0S 30 0 E
Queen Mary Coast **143** 70 0S 95 0 E
Queen Maud G. **100** 68 15N 102 30W
Queen Maud Ra. **143** 86 0S 160 0W
Queens Chan. **78** 15 0S 129 30 E
Queenscliff **74** 38 16S 144 39 E
Queensland □ **72** 22 0S 142 0 E
Queenstown, Austral. **72** 42 4S 145 35 E
Queenstown, N.Z. **81** 45 1S 168 40 E
Queenstown, S. Afr. **96** 31 52S 26 52 E
Queets **122** 47 32N 124 20W
Queguay Grande → **140** 32 9S 58 9W
Queimadas **138** 11 0S 39 38W
Queiros, C. **68** 14 55S 167 1 E
Quela **92** 9 10S 16 56 E
Quelimane **95** 17 53S 36 58 E
Quemado, N. Mex., U.S.A. **121** 34 17N 108 28W
Quemado, Tex., U.S.A. **119** 28 58N 100 35W
Quemú-Quemú **140** 36 3S 63 36W
Quequén **140** 38 30S 58 30W
Querco **136** 13 50S 74 52W
Querétaro **124** 20 40N 100 23W
Querétaro □ **124** 20 30N 100 0W
Querfurt **30** 51 22N 11 33 E
Querqueville **18** 49 40N 1 42W
Quesada **25** 37 51N 3 4W
Queshan **60** 32 55N 114 2 E
Quesnel **108** 53 0N 122 30W
Quesnel → **108** 52 58N 122 29W
Quesnel L. **108** 52 30N 121 20W
Quesnoy, Le **19** 50 15N 3 38 E
Questa **121** 36 45N 105 35W
Questembert **18** 47 40N 2 28W
Quetena **136** 22 10S 67 25W
Quetico Prov. Park **102** 48 30N 91 45W
Quetrequile **142** 41 33S 69 22W
Quetta **47** 30 15N 66 55 E
Quetta □ **47** 30 15N 66 55 E
Quevedo **134** 1 2S 79 29W
Quévillon, L. **104** 49 4N 76 57W
Quezaltenango **126** 14 50N 91 30W
Quezon City **57** 14 38N 121 0 E
Qui Nhon **54** 13 40N 109 13 E
Quiaca, La **140** 22 5S 65 35W
Quibaxi **92** 8 24S 14 27 E
Quibdo **134** 5 42N 76 40W
Quiberon **18** 47 29N 3 9W
Quíbor **134** 9 56N 69 37W
Quick **108** 54 36N 126 54W
Quickborn **30** 53 42N 9 52 E
Quiet L. **108** 61 5N 133 5W
Quiindy **140** 25 58S 57 14W
Quila **124** 24 23N 107 13W
Quilán, C. **142** 43 15S 74 30W
Quilcene **122** 47 49N 122 53W
Quilengues **93** 14 12S 14 12 E
Quilimarí **140** 32 5S 71 30W
Quilino **140** 30 14S 64 29W
Quillabamba **136** 12 50S 72 50W
Quillacollo **136** 17 26S 66 17W
Quillagua **140** 21 40S 69 40W
Quillaicillo **140** 31 17S 71 40W
Quillan **20** 42 53N 2 10 E
Quillebeuf **18** 49 28N 0 30 E
Quillota **140** 32 54S 71 16W
Quilmes **140** 34 43S 58 15W
Quilon **51** 8 50N 76 38 E
Quilpie **73** 26 35S 144 11 E
Quilpué **140** 33 5S 71 33W
Quilua **95** 16 17S 39 54 E
Quime **136** 17 2S 67 15W
Quimilí **140** 27 40S 62 30W
Quimper **18** 48 0N 4 9W
Quimperlé **18** 47 53N 3 33W
Quinault → **122** 47 23N 124 18W
Quincemil **136** 13 15S 70 40W
Quincy, Calif., U.S.A. **122** 39 56N 121 0W
Quincy, Fla., U.S.A. **113** 30 34N 84 34W
Quincy, Ill., U.S.A. **118** 39 55N 91 20W
Quincy, Mass., U.S.A. **115** 42 14N 71 0W
Quincy, Wash., U.S.A. **120** 47 22N 119 56W
Quines **140** 32 13S 65 48W
Quinga **95** 15 49S 40 15 E
Quingey **19** 47 7N 5 52 E
Quintana de la Serena **23** 38 45N 5 40W
Quintana Roo □ **125** 19 0N 88 0W
Quintanar de la Orden **24** 39 36N 3 5W
Quintanar de la Sierra **24** 41 57N 2 55W
Quintanar del Rey **25** 39 21N 1 56W
Quintero **140** 32 45S 71 30W
Quintin **18** 48 26N 2 56W
Quinto **24** 41 25N 0 32W
Quinyambie **73** 30 15S 141 0 E
Quinze, L. des **104** 47 35N 79 5W
Quípar → **25** 38 15N 1 40W
Quirihue **140** 36 15S 72 35W
Quirindi **77** 31 28S 150 40 E
Quiriquire **134** 9 59N 63 13W
Quiroga **22** 42 28N 7 18W
Quiruvilca **136** 8 1S 78 19W
Quissac **21** 43 55N 4 0 E
Quissanga **95** 12 24S 40 28 E
Quitilipi **140** 26 50S 60 13W
Quitman, Ga., U.S.A. **113** 30 49N 83 35W
Quitman, Miss., U.S.A. **113** 32 2N 88 42W
Quitman, Tex., U.S.A. **119** 32 48N 95 25W
Quito **134** 0 15S 78 35W
Quixadá **138** 4 55S 39 0W
Quixaxe **95** 15 17S 40 4 E
Quixeramobim **138** 5 12S 39 17W
Qujing **58** 25 32N 103 41 E
Qul'ân, Jazâ'ir **90** 24 22N 35 31 E
Qumran **44** 31 43N 35 27 E
Quneitra **44** 33 7N 35 48 E
Quoin I. **78** 14 54S 129 32 E
Quoin Pt. **96** 34 46S 19 37 E
Quondong **73** 33 6S 140 18 E
Quorn **73** 32 25S 138 0 E
Qurein **91** 13 30N 34 50 E
Qûs **90** 25 55N 32 50 E
Quseir **90** 26 7N 34 16 E
Qusra **44** 32 5N 35 20 E
Quthing **97** 30 25S 27 36 E
Quwo **60** 35 38N 111 25 E
Quyang **60** 38 35N 114 40 E
Quynh Nhai **54** 21 49N 103 33 E
Quyon **104** 45 31N 76 14W
Quzi **60** 36 20N 107 20 E
Qytet Stalin (Kuçove) **35** 40 47N 19 57 E

R

Ra, Ko **55** 9 13N 98 16 E
Råå **11** 56 0N 12 45 E
Raahe **8** 64 40N 24 28 E
Ra'anana **44** 32 12N 34 52 E
Raasay I. **14** 57 25N 6 4W
Raasay, Sd. of **14** 57 30N 6 8W
Rab **27** 44 45N 14 45 E
Rab, I. **27** 44 45N 14 45 E
Raba **57** 8 36S 118 55 E
Rába → **33** 47 38N 17 38 E
Rabaçal → **22** 41 30N 7 12W
Rabah **89** 13 5N 5 30 E
Rabai **94** 3 50S 39 31 E
Rabaraba **69** 9 58S 149 49 E
Rabastens, Hautes-Pyrénées, France **20** 43 25N 0 10 E
Rabastens, Tarn, France **20** 43 50N 1 43 E
Rabat **86** 34 2N 6 48W
Rabaul **69** 4 24S 152 18 E
Rabbit → **108** 59 41N 127 12W
Rabbit Lake **109** 53 8N 107 46W
Rabbitskin → **108** 61 47N 120 42W
Rabigh **46** 22 50N 39 5 E
Rabka **32** 49 37N 19 59 E
Rácale **29** 39 57N 18 6 E
Racalmuto **28** 37 25N 13 41 E
Racconigi **26** 44 47N 7 41 E
Raccoon → **116** 41 35N 93 37W
Raccoon Cr. → **117** 39 47N 87 23W
Race, C. **103** 46 40N 53 5W
Rach Gia **55** 10 5N 105 5 E
Raciąż **32** 52 46N 20 10 E
Racibórz **32** 50 7N 18 18 E
Racine **117** 42 41N 87 51W
Rackerby **122** 39 26N 121 22W
Radama, Îs. **97** 14 0S 47 47 E
Rădăuţi **34** 47 50N 25 59 E
Radbuza → **32** 49 35N 13 5 E
Radcliff **117** 37 51N 85 57W
Radeburg **30** 51 6N 13 55 E
Radeče **27** 46 5N 15 14 E
Radekhov **36** 50 25N 24 32 E
Radford **112** 37 8N 80 32W
Radhanpur **48** 23 50N 71 38 E
Radhwa, Jabal **46** 24 34N 38 18 E
Radiska → **35** 41 38N 20 37 E
Radisson **109** 52 30N 107 20W
Radium Hot Springs **108** 50 35N 116 2W
Radja, Kepulauan **57** 0 30S 130 00 E
Radma, Presqu'île d' **97** 14 16S 47 53 E
Radna **34** 46 7N 21 41 E
Radnor Forest **13** 52 17N 3 10W
Radolfzell **31** 47 44N 8 58 E
Radom **32** 51 23N 21 12 E
Radomir **34** 42 37N 23 4 E
Radomsko **32** 51 5N 19 28 E
Radomyshl **36** 50 30N 29 12 E
Radoviš **35** 41 38N 22 28 E
Radovljica **27** 46 22N 14 12 E
Radstock **13** 51 17N 2 25W
Răducăneni **34** 46 58N 27 54 E
Radviliškis **36** 55 49N 23 33 E
Radville **109** 49 30N 104 15W
Rae **108** 62 50N 116 3W
Rae Bareli **49** 26 18N 81 20 E
Rae Isthmus **101** 66 40N 87 30W
Raeren **16** 50 41N 6 7 E
Raeside, L. **79** 29 20S 122 0 E
Raetihi **80** 39 25S 175 17 E
Rafaela **140** 31 10S 61 30W
Rafah **90** 31 18N 34 14 E
Rafai **94** 4 59N 23 58 E
Raffadali **28** 37 23N 13 29 E
Rafhā **46** 29 35N 43 35 E
Rafid **44** 32 57N 35 52 E
Rafsanjān **47** 30 30N 56 5 E
Raft Pt. **78** 16 4S 124 26 E
Ragag **91** 10 59N 24 40 E
Ragged Mt. **79** 33 27S 123 25 E
Raglan, Austral. **72** 23 42S 150 49 E
Raglan, N.Z. **80** 37 55S 174 55 E
Ragunda **10** 63 6N 16 23 E
Ragusa **29** 36 56N 14 42 E
Raha **57** 4 55S 123 0 E
Rahad el Berdi **85** 11 20N 23 40 E
Rahad, Nahr ed → **91** 14 28N 33 31 E
Rahaeng = Tak **54** 16 55N 99 10 E
Rahden **30** 52 26N 8 36 E
Raheita **91** 12 46N 43 4 E
Rahimyar Khan **48** 28 30N 70 25 E
Rahotu **80** 39 20S 173 49 E
Raichur **51** 16 10N 77 20 E
Raiganj **49** 25 37N 88 10 E
Raigarh, Madhya Pradesh, India **50** 21 56N 83 25 E
Raigarh, Orissa, India **50** 19 51N 82 6 E
Raiis **46** 23 33N 38 43 E
Raijua **57** 10 37S 121 36 E
Railton **72** 41 25S 146 28 E
Rainbow **74** 35 55S 142 0 E
Rainbow Lake **108** 58 30N 119 23W
Rainier **122** 46 4N 123 0W
Rainier, Mt. **122** 46 50N 121 50W
Rainy L. **109** 48 42N 93 10W
Rainy River **109** 48 43N 94 29W
Raipur **50** 21 17N 81 45 E
Raja, Kepulauan **57** 0 30S 129 40 E
Raja, Ujung **56** 3 40N 96 25 E
Rajahmundry **50** 17 1N 81 48 E
Rajajooseppi **8** 68 28N 28 29 E
Rajang → **56** 2 30N 112 0 E
Rajapalaiyam **51** 9 25N 77 35 E
Rajasthan □ **48** 26 45N 73 30 E
Rajasthan Canal **48** 28 0N 72 0 E
Rajauri **49** 33 25N 74 21 E
Rajbari **52** 23 47N 89 41 E
Rajgarh, Mad. P., India **48** 24 2N 76 45 E
Rajgarh, Raj., India **48** 28 40N 75 25 E
Rajhenburg **27** 46 1N 15 29 E
Rajkot **48** 22 15N 70 56 E
Rajmahal Hills **49** 24 30N 87 30 E
Rajnandgaon **50** 21 5N 81 5 E
Rajpipla **50** 21 50N 73 30 E
Rajpura **48** 30 25N 76 32 E
Rajshahi **52** 24 22N 88 39 E
Rajshahi □ **49** 25 0N 89 0 E
Rakaia **81** 43 45S 172 1 E
Rakaia → **81** 43 36S 172 15 E
Rakan, Ra's **47** 26 10N 51 20 E
Rakaposhi **49** 36 10N 74 25 E
Rakha **90** 18 25N 41 30 E
Rakhni **48** 30 4N 69 56 E
Rakkestad **10** 59 25N 11 21 E
Rakops **96** 21 1S 24 28 E
Rákospalota **33** 47 30N 19 5 E
Rakovica **27** 44 59N 15 38 E
Rakovník **32** 50 6N 13 42 E
Rakovski **34** 42 21N 24 57 E
Raleigh, Austral. **77** 30 27S 153 2 E
Raleigh, U.S.A. **113** 35 47N 78 39W
Raleigh B. **113** 34 50N 76 15W
Ralja **33** 44 33N 20 34 E
Ralls **119** 33 40N 101 20W
Ram → **108** 62 1N 123 41W
Rām Allāh **44** 31 55N 35 10 E
Rama, Israel **44** 32 56N 35 21 E
Rama, Nic. **126** 12 9N 84 15W
Ramacca **29** 37 24N 14 40 E
Ramachandrapuram **50** 16 50N 82 4 E
Ramales de la Victoria **24** 43 15N 3 28W
Ramalho, Serra do **139** 13 45S 44 0W
Raman **55** 6 29N 101 18 E
Ramanathapuram **51** 9 25N 78 55 E
Ramanetaka, B. de **97** 14 13S 47 52 E
Ramas C. **51** 15 5N 73 55 E
Ramat Gan **44** 32 4N 34 48 E
Ramat HaSharon **44** 32 7N 34 50 E
Ramatlhabama **96** 25 37S 25 33 E
Ramban **49** 33 14N 75 12 E
Rambervillers **19** 48 20N 6 38 E
Rambi **68** 16 30S 179 59W
Rambipuji **57** 8 12S 113 37 E
Rambla, La **23** 37 37N 4 45W
Rambouillet **19** 48 40N 1 48 E
Ramdurg **51** 15 58N 75 22 E
Rame Hd. **75** 37 47S 149 30 E
Ramea **103** 47 28N 57 4W
Ramechhap **49** 27 25N 86 10 E
Ramelau **57** 8 55S 126 22 E

Ramenskoye 37 55 32N 38 15 E
Ramgarh, Bihar, India 49 23 40N 85 35 E
Ramgarh, Rajasthan, India 48 27 16N 75 14 E
Ramgarh, Rajasthan, India 48 27 30N 70 36 E
Rāmhormoz 46 31 15N 49 35 E
Ramla 44 31 55N 34 52 E
Ramlat Zalṭan 87 28 30N 19 30 E
Ramlu 91 13 32N 41 40 E
Ramme 11 56 30N 8 11 E
Rammun 44 31 55N 35 17 E
Ramnad = Ramanathapuram 51 9 25N 78 55 E
Ramnagar 49 32 47N 75 18 E
Ramnäs 10 59 46N 16 12 E
Ramon 37 51 55N 39 21 E
Ramon, Har 44 30 30N 34 38 E
Ramona 123 33 1N 116 56W
Ramore 102 48 30N 80 25W
Ramos → 124 25 35N 105 3W
Ramoutsa 96 24 50S 25 52 E
Rampart 100 65 0N 150 15W
Rampur, H.P., India 48 31 26N 77 43 E
Rampur, Mad. P., India 48 23 25N 73 53 E
Rampur, Orissa, India 50 21 48N 83 58 E
Rampur, U.P., India 49 28 50N 79 5 E
Rampura 48 24 30N 75 27 E
Rampurhat 49 24 10N 87 50 E
Ramsey, Can. 102 47 25N 82 20W
Ramsey, U.K. 12 54 20N 4 21W
Ramsey, U.S.A. 116 39 8N 89 7W
Ramsgate 13 51 20N 1 25 E
Ramshai 52 26 44N 88 51 E
Ramsjö 10 62 11N 15 37 E
Ramtek 50 21 20N 79 15 E
Ramu → 69 4 0S 144 41 E
Ramvik 10 62 49N 17 51 E
Ranaghat 49 23 15N 88 35 E
Ranahu 48 25 55N 69 45 E
Ranau 56 6 2N 116 40 E
Rancagua 140 34 10S 70 50W
Rance → 18 48 34N 1 59W
Rance, Barrage de la 18 48 30N 2 3W
Rancharia 139 22 15S 50 55W
Rancheria → 108 60 13N 129 7W
Ranchester 120 44 57N 107 12W
Ranchi 49 23 19N 85 27 E
Ranco, L. 142 40 15S 72 25W
Randan 20 46 2N 3 21 E
Randazzo 29 37 53N 14 56 E
Randers 11 56 29N 10 1 E
Randers Fjord 11 56 37N 10 20 E
Randfontein 97 26 8S 27 45 E
Randle 122 46 32N 121 57W
Randolph, Mass., U.S.A. 115 42 10N 71 3W
Randolph, N.Y., U.S.A. 114 42 10N 78 59W
Randolph, Utah, U.S.A. 120 41 43N 111 10W
Randolph, Vt., U.S.A. 115 43 55N 72 39W
Randsburg 123 35 22N 117 44W
Randsfjorden 10 60 15N 10 25 E
Råne älv → 8 65 50N 22 20 E
Ranfurly 81 45 7S 170 6 E
Rangae 55 6 19N 101 44 E
Rangamati 52 22 38N 92 12 E
Rangataua 80 39 26S 175 28 E
Rangaunu B. 80 34 51S 173 15 E
Rångedala 11 57 47N 13 9 E
Rangeley 115 44 58N 70 33W
Rangely 120 40 3N 108 53W
Ranger 119 32 30N 98 42W
Rangia 52 26 28N 91 38 E
Rangiora 81 43 19S 172 36 E
Rangitaiki → 80 37 54S 176 49 E
Rangitata → 81 43 45S 171 15 E
Rangitikei → 80 40 17S 175 15 E
Rangitoto Range 80 38 25S 175 35 E
Rangkasbitung 57 6 22S 106 16 E
Rangoon 52 16 45N 96 20 E
Rangpur 52 25 42N 89 22 E
Rangsit 54 13 59N 100 37 E
Ranibennur 51 14 35N 75 30 E
Raniganj 49 23 40N 87 5 E
Ranipet 51 12 56N 79 23 E
Ranken → 72 20 31S 137 36 E
Rankin, Ill., U.S.A. 117 40 28N 87 54W
Rankin, Tex., U.S.A. 119 31 16N 101 56W
Rankin Inlet 100 62 30N 93 0W
Rankins Springs 75 33 49S 146 14 E
Rannoch, L. 14 56 41N 4 20W
Rannoch Moor 14 56 38N 4 48W
Ranobe, B. de 97 23 3S 43 33 E
Ranohira 97 22 29S 45 24 E
Ranomafana, Tamatave, Madag. 97 18 57S 48 50 E
Ranomafana, Tuléar, Madag. 97 24 34S 47 0 E
Ranon 68 16 10S 168 7 E
Ranong 55 9 56N 98 40 E
Ransiki 57 1 30S 134 10 E
Ransom 117 41 9N 88 39W
Rantau 56 2 56S 115 9 E
Rantauprapat 56 2 15N 99 50 E
Rantemario 57 3 15S 119 57 E
Rantis 44 32 4N 35 3 E
Rantoul 117 40 18N 88 10W
Ranum 11 56 54N 9 14 E
Ranwanlenau 96 19 37S 22 49 E
Raon l'Étape 19 48 24N 6 50 E
Raoui, Erg er 86 29 0N 2 0W
Raoyang 60 38 15N 115 45 E
Rapa Iti 67 27 35S 144 20W
Rapallo 26 44 21N 9 12 E
Rapang 57 3 45S 119 55 E
Rāpch 47 25 40N 59 15 E
Rapid → 108 59 15N 129 5W
Rapid City, Mich., U.S.A. 106 44 50N 85 17W
Rapid City, S.D., U.S.A. 118 44 0N 103 0W
Rapid River 112 45 55N 87 0W
Rapide-Blanc 105 47 48N 73 2W
Rapide-Sept 104 47 46N 78 19W
Rapides des Joachims 104 46 13N 77 43W
Rapla 36 59 1N 24 52 E
Rappville 77 29 6S 152 57 E
Raquete 95 14 8S 38 13 E
Rarotonga 67 21 30S 160 0W
Ras al Khaima 47 25 50N 56 5 E
Ra's al-Unuf 87 30 25N 18 15 E
Ra's at Tannūrah 46 26 40N 50 10 E
Ras Bânâs 85 23 57N 35 59 E
Ras Dashen 91 13 8N 38 26 E
Ras el Ma 86 34 26N 0 50W
Ras Gharib 90 28 6N 33 18 E
Ras Mallap 90 29 18N 32 50 E
Rasa, Punta 142 40 50S 62 15W
Raseiniai 36 55 25N 23 5 E
Rashad 91 11 55N 31 0 E
Rashîd 90 31 21N 30 22 E
Rashîd, Masabb 90 31 22N 30 17 E
Rasht 46 37 20N 49 40 E
Rasi Salai 54 15 20N 104 9 E
Rasipuram 51 11 30N 78 15 E
Raška 33 43 19N 20 39 E
Rason, L. 79 28 45S 124 25 E
Raşova 34 44 15N 27 55 E
Rasra 49 25 50N 83 50 E
Rass el Oued 87 35 57N 5 2 E
Rasskazovo 37 52 35N 41 50 E
Rastatt 31 48 50N 8 12 E
Rat Buri 54 13 30N 99 54 E
Rat Is. 100 51 50N 178 15 E
Rat River 108 61 7N 112 36W
Ratangarh 48 28 5N 74 35 E
Rath 49 25 36N 79 37 E
Rath Luirc (Charleville) 15 52 21N 8 40W
Rathbun Res. 116 40 49N 93 53W
Rathdowney 77 28 13S 152 52 E
Rathdrum, Ireland 15 52 57N 6 13W
Rathdrum, U.S.A. 120 47 50N 116 58W
Rathedaung 52 20 29N 92 45 E
Rathenow 30 52 38N 12 23 E
Rathkeale 15 52 32N 8 57W
Rathlin I. 15 55 18N 6 14W
Rathlin O'Birne I. 15 54 40N 8 50W
Ratlam 48 23 20N 75 0 E
Ratnagiri 50 16 57N 73 18 E
Ratnapura 51 6 40N 80 20 E
Raton 119 37 0N 104 30W
Rats, R. aux → 105 48 53N 72 14W
Rattaphum 55 7 8N 100 16 E
Rattray Hd. 14 57 38N 1 50W
Rättvik 10 60 52N 15 7 E
Ratz, Mt. 108 57 23N 132 12W
Ratzeburg 30 53 41N 10 46 E
Raub 55 3 47N 101 52 E
Rauch 140 36 45S 59 5W
Raufarhöfn 8 66 27N 15 57W
Raufoss 10 60 44N 10 37 E
Raukumara Ra. 80 38 5S 177 55 E
Raul Soares 139 20 5S 42 22W
Rauland 10 59 43N 8 0 E
Rauma 9 61 10N 21 30 E
Rauma → 10 62 34N 7 43 E
Raung 57 8 8S 114 4 E
Raurkela, India 49 22 14N 84 50 E
Raurkela, India 50 22 14N 84 50 E
Rava Russkaya 36 50 15N 23 42 E
Ravanusa 28 37 16N 13 58 E
Rāvar 47 31 20N 56 51 E
Ravena 115 42 28N 73 49W
Ravenna, Italy 27 44 28N 12 15 E
Ravenna, Ky., U.S.A. 117 37 42N 83 55W
Ravenna, Nebr., U.S.A. 118 41 3N 98 58W
Ravenna, Ohio, U.S.A. 114 41 11N 81 15W
Ravensburg 31 47 48N 9 38 E
Ravenshoe 72 17 37S 145 29 E
Ravensthorpe 79 33 35S 120 2 E
Ravenswood, Queens., Austral. 72 20 6S 146 54 E
Ravenswood, Vic., Austral. 74 36 53S 144 15 E
Ravenswood, U.S.A. 112 38 58N 81 47W
Ravensworth 76 32 26S 151 4 E
Ravenwood 116 40 23N 94 41W
Ravi → 48 30 35N 71 49 E
Ravna Gora 27 45 24N 14 50 E
Rawa Mazowiecka 32 51 46N 20 12 E
Rawalpindi 48 33 38N 73 8 E
Rawāndūz 46 36 40N 44 30 E
Rawang 55 3 20N 101 35 E
Rawdon 105 46 3N 73 40W
Rawene 80 35 25S 173 32 E
Rawicz 32 51 36N 16 52 E
Rawlinna 79 30 58S 125 28 E
Rawlins 120 41 50N 107 20W
Rawlinson Range 79 24 40S 128 30 E
Rawson 142 43 15S 65 0W
Ray 118 48 21N 103 6W
Ray, C. 103 47 33N 59 15W
Rayachoti 51 14 4N 78 50 E
Rayadrug 51 14 40N 76 50 E
Rayagada 50 19 15N 83 20 E
Raychikhinsk 41 49 46N 129 25 E
Raymond, Can. 108 49 30N 112 35W
Raymond, Calif., U.S.A. 122 37 13N 119 54W
Raymond, Ill., U.S.A. 116 39 19N 89 34W
Raymond, Wash., U.S.A. 122 46 45N 123 48W
Raymond Terrace 76 32 45S 151 44 E
Raymondville 119 26 30N 97 50W
Raymore 109 51 25N 104 31W
Rayne 119 30 16N 92 16W
Rayón 124 29 43N 110 35W
Rayong 54 12 40N 101 20 E
Raytown 116 39 1N 94 28W
Rayville 119 32 30N 91 45W
Raywood 74 36 30S 144 15 E
Raz, Pte. du 18 48 2N 4 47W
Ražana 33 44 6N 19 55 E
Ražanj 33 43 40N 21 31 E
Razelm, Lacul 34 44 50N 29 0 E
Razgrad 34 43 33N 26 34 E
Razmak 48 32 45N 69 50 E
Razole 51 16 36N 81 48 E
Ré, Île de 20 46 12N 1 30W
Reading, U.K. 13 51 27N 0 57W
Reading, Mich., U.S.A. 117 41 50N 84 45W
Reading, Ohio, U.S.A. 117 39 13N 84 26W
Reading, Pa., U.S.A. 115 40 20N 75 53W
Real, Cordillera 136 17 0S 67 10W
Realicó 140 35 0S 64 15W
Réalmont 20 43 48N 2 10 E
Reata 124 26 8N 101 5W
Rebais 19 48 50N 3 10 E
Rebecca L. 79 30 0S 122 15 E
Rebi 57 6 23S 134 7 E
Rebiana 85 24 12N 22 10 E
Rebun-Tō 63 45 20N 142 45 E
Recanati 27 43 24N 13 32 E
Recaş 34 45 46N 21 30 E
Recherche, Arch. of the 79 34 15S 122 50 E
Rechitsa 36 52 13N 30 15 E
Recife 138 8 0S 35 0W
Recklinghausen 30 51 36N 7 10 E
Reconquista 140 29 10S 59 45W
Recreio 137 8 0S 58 25W
Recreo 140 29 25S 65 10W
Recuay 136 9 43S 77 28W
Red →, Can. 109 50 24N 96 48W
Red →, Minn., U.S.A. 118 48 10N 97 0W
Red →, Tex., U.S.A. 119 31 0N 91 40W
Red → = Hong → 54 20 17N 106 34 E
Red Bank, Austral. 74 36 56S 143 21 E
Red Bank, U.S.A. 115 40 21N 74 4W
Red Bay 103 51 44N 56 25W
Red Bluff 120 40 11N 122 11W
Red Bluff L. 119 31 59N 103 58W
Red Bud 116 38 13N 90 0W
Red Cliffs 74 34 19S 142 11 E
Red Cloud 118 40 8N 98 33W
Red Deer 108 52 20N 113 50W
Red Deer →, Alta., Can. 109 50 58N 110 0W
Red Deer →, Man., Can. 109 52 53N 101 1W
Red Deer L. 109 52 55N 101 20W
Red Indian L. 103 48 35N 57 0W
Red Lake 109 51 3N 93 49W
Red Lake Falls 118 47 54N 96 15W
Red Lodge 120 45 10N 109 10W
Red Mountain 123 35 22N 117 38W
Red Oak 118 41 0N 95 10W
Red Point Rock 79 32 13S 127 32 E
Red Range 77 29 46S 151 57 E
Red Rock, Austral. 77 29 59S 153 14 E
Red Rock, Can. 102 48 55N 88 15W
Red Rock, L. 116 41 30N 93 15W
Red Sea 45 25 0N 36 0 E
Red Slate Mt. 122 37 31N 118 52W
Red Sucker L 109 54 9N 93 40W
Red Wing 118 44 32N 92 35W
Redbridge 13 51 35N 0 7 E
Redcar 12 54 37N 1 4W
Redcliff 109 50 10N 110 50W
Redcliffe 73 27 12S 153 0 E
Redcliffe, Mt. 79 28 30S 121 30 E
Reddersburg 96 29 41S 26 10 E
Redding 120 40 30N 122 25W
Redditch 13 52 18N 1 57W
Redenção 138 4 13S 38 43W
Redesdale 74 37 2S 144 31 E
Redfield 118 45 0N 98 30W
Redkey 117 40 21N 85 9W
Redknife → 108 61 14N 119 22W
Redlands 123 34 0N 117 11W
Redmond, Austral. 79 34 55S 117 40 E
Redmond, Oreg., U.S.A. 120 44 19N 121 11W
Redmond, Wash., U.S.A. 122 47 40N 122 7W
Redon 18 47 40N 2 6W
Redonda, I. 127 16 58N 62 19W
Redondela 22 42 15N 8 38W
Redondo 23 38 39N 7 37W
Redondo Beach 123 33 52N 118 26W
Redrock Pt. 108 62 11N 115 2W
Redruth 13 50 14N 5 14W
Redvers 109 49 35N 101 40W
Redwater 108 53 55N 113 6W
Redwood 115 44 18N 75 48W
Redwood City 122 37 30N 122 15W
Redwood Falls 118 44 30N 95 2W
Ree, L. 15 53 35N 8 0W
Reed City 112 43 52N 85 30W
Reed, L 109 54 38N 100 30W
Reeder 118 46 7N 102 52W
Reedley 122 36 36N 119 27W
Reedsburg 118 43 34N 90 5W
Reedsport 120 43 45N 124 4W
Reefton, Austral. 76 34 15S 147 27 E
Reefton, N.Z. 81 42 6S 171 51 E
Reese 106 43 27N 83 42W
Reftele 11 57 11N 13 35 E
Refugio 119 28 18N 97 17W
Rega → 32 54 10N 15 18 E
Regalbuto 29 37 40N 14 38 E
Regavim 44 32 32N 35 2 E
Regen 31 48 58N 13 9 E
Regen → 31 49 2N 12 6 E
Regeneração 138 6 15S 42 41W
Regensburg 31 49 1N 12 7 E
Réggio di Calábria 29 38 7N 15 38 E
Réggio nell' Emilia 26 44 42N 10 38 E
Regina 109 50 27N 104 35W
Régina 135 4 19N 52 8W
Registan □ 47 30 15N 65 0 E
Registro 141 24 29S 47 49W
Reguengos de Monsaraz 23 38 25N 7 32W
Rehar → 49 23 55N 82 40 E
Rehoboth, Damaraland, Namibia 96 23 15S 17 4 E
Rehoboth, Owambo, Namibia 96 17 55S 15 5 E
Rehovot 44 31 54N 34 48 E
Reichenbach 30 50 36N 12 19 E
Reid 79 30 49S 128 26 E
Reid River 72 19 40S 146 48 E
Reids Flat 76 34 7S 149 0 E
Reidsville 113 36 21N 79 40W
Reigate 13 51 14N 0 11W
Reillo 24 39 54N 1 53W
Reims 19 49 15N 4 0 E
Reina 44 32 43N 35 18 E
Reina Adelaida, Arch. 142 52 20S 74 0W
Reinbeck 116 42 18N 92 0W
Reindeer → 109 55 36N 103 11W
Reindeer I. 109 52 30N 98 0W
Reindeer L. 109 57 15N 102 15W
Reine, La 104 48 50N 79 30W
Reinga, C. 80 34 25S 172 43 E
Reinosa 22 43 2N 4 15W
Reinosa, Paso 22 42 56N 4 10W
Reira 91 15 25N 34 50 E
Reitz 97 27 48S 28 29 E
Reivilo 96 27 36S 24 8 E
Rejmyra 11 58 50N 15 55 E
Reka → 27 45 40N 14 0 E
Rekinniki 41 60 51N 163 40 E
Reliance 109 63 0N 109 20W
Remad, Oued → 86 33 28N 1 20W
Rémalard 18 48 26N 0 47 E
Remanso 138 9 41S 42 4W
Remarkable, Mt. 73 32 48S 138 10 E
Rembang 57 6 42S 111 21 E

Remchi	**86**	35 2N	1 26W
Remedios, Colomb.	**134**	7 2N	74 41W
Remedios, Panama	**126**	8 15N	81 50W
Remeshk	**47**	26 55N	58 50 E
Remich	**16**	49 32N	6 22 E
Rémigny	**104**	47 46N	79 12W
Remington	**117**	40 45N	87 8W
Rémire	**135**	4 53N	52 17W
Remiremont	**19**	48 0N	6 36 E
Remo	**91**	6 48N	41 20 E
Remontnoye	**39**	46 34N	43 37 E
Remoulins	**21**	43 55N	4 35 E
Remscheid	**30**	51 11N	7 12 E
Remus	**106**	43 36N	85 9W
Ren Xian	**60**	37 8N	114 40 E
Renascença	**134**	3 50S	66 21W
Rend L.	**116**	38 2N	88 58W
Renda	**91**	14 30N	40 0 E
Rende	**29**	39 19N	16 11 E
Rendína	**35**	39 4N	21 58 E
Rendova	**68**	8 33S	157 17 E
Rendsburg	**30**	54 18N	9 41 E
Rene	**41**	66 2N	179 25W
Renfrew, Can.	**107**	45 30N	76 40W
Renfrew, U.K.	**14**	55 52N	4 24W
Rengat	**56**	0 30S	102 45 E
Rengo	**140**	34 24S	70 50W
Renhua	**59**	25 5N	113 40 E
Renhuai	**58**	27 48N	106 24 E
Reni	**38**	45 28N	28 15 E
Renigunta	**51**	13 38N	79 30 E
Renk	**85**	11 50N	32 50 E
Renkum	**16**	51 58N	5 43 E
Renmark	**73**	34 11S	140 43 E
Rennell	**68**	11 40S	160 10 E
Rennell Sd.	**108**	53 23N	132 35W
Renner Springs T.O.	**72**	18 20S	133 47 E
Rennes	**18**	48 7N	1 41W
Rennes, Bassin de	**18**	48 12N	1 33W
Reno	**122**	39 30N	119 50W
Reno →	**27**	44 37N	12 17 E
Renovo	**114**	41 20N	77 47W
Renqiu	**60**	38 43N	116 5 E
Rensselaer, Ind., U.S.A.	**117**	40 57N	87 10W
Rensselaer, N.Y., U.S.A.	**115**	42 38N	73 41W
Rentería	**24**	43 19N	1 54W
Renton	**122**	47 30N	122 9W
Renwicktown	**81**	41 30S	173 51 E
Réo	**88**	12 28N	2 35W
Réole, La	**20**	44 35N	0 1W
Reotipur	**49**	25 33N	83 45 E
Repalle	**51**	16 2N	80 45 E
Repentigny	**105**	45 44N	73 28W
Republic, Mich., U.S.A.	**112**	46 25N	87 59W
Republic, Wash., U.S.A.	**120**	48 38N	118 42W
Republican →	**118**	39 3N	96 48W
Republican City	**118**	40 9N	99 20W
Republiek	**135**	5 30N	55 13W
Repulse B.	**143**	64 30S	99 30 E
Repulse Bay	**101**	66 30N	86 30W
Requena, Peru	**136**	5 5S	73 52W
Requena, Spain	**25**	39 30N	1 4W
Resele	**10**	63 20N	17 5 E
Reserve, Can.	**109**	52 28N	102 39W
Reserve, U.S.A.	**121**	33 50N	108 54W
Resht = Rasht	**46**	37 20N	49 40 E
Resistencia	**140**	27 30S	59 0W
Reşiţa	**34**	45 18N	21 53 E
Resolution I., Can.	**101**	61 30N	65 0W
Resolution I., N.Z.	**81**	45 40S	166 40 E
Resplandes	**138**	6 17S	45 13W
Resplendor	**139**	19 20S	41 15W
Ressano Garcia	**97**	25 25S	32 0 E
Reston	**109**	49 33N	101 6W
Retalhuleu	**126**	14 33N	91 46W
Reteag	**34**	47 10N	24 0 E
Retenue, Lac de	**95**	11 0S	27 0 E
Rethel	**19**	49 30N	4 20 E
Rethem	**30**	52 47N	9 25 E
Réthimnon	**35**	35 18N	24 30 E
Rétiers	**18**	47 55N	1 25W
Retortillo	**22**	40 48N	6 21W
Réunion, Î.	**53**	22 0S	56 0 E
Reus	**24**	41 10N	1 5 E
Reuss →	**31**	47 16N	8 24 E
Reuterstadt Stavenhagen	**30**	53 41N	12 54 E
Reutlingen	**31**	48 28N	9 13 E
Reutte	**31**	47 29N	10 42 E
Reval = Tallinn	**36**	59 29N	24 58 E
Revel	**20**	43 28N	2 0 E
Revelganj	**49**	25 50N	84 40 E
Revelstoke	**108**	51 0N	118 10W
Reventazón, Peru	**136**	6 10S	81 0W
Reventazón, Peru	**136**	6 10S	80 58W
Revigny	**19**	48 50N	5 0 E
Revilla Gigedo, Is.	**67**	18 40N	112 0W
Revillagigedo I.	**108**	55 50N	131 20W
Revin	**19**	49 55N	4 39 E
Revuè →	**95**	19 50S	34 0 E
Rewa	**49**	24 33N	81 25 E
Rewa →	**135**	3 19N	58 42W
Rewari	**48**	28 15N	76 40 E
Rexburg	**120**	43 55N	111 50W
Rexton	**106**	46 10N	85 14W
Rey Bouba	**85**	8 40N	14 15 E
Rey Malabo	**92**	3 45N	8 50 E
Rey, Rio del →	**89**	4 30N	8 48 E
Reyes	**136**	14 19S	67 23W
Reyes, Pt.	**122**	37 59N	123 2W
Reykjahlið	**8**	65 40N	16 55W
Reykjanes	**8**	63 48N	22 40W
Reykjavík	**8**	64 10N	21 57 E
Reynolds, Can.	**109**	49 40N	95 55W
Reynolds, U.S.A.	**116**	41 20N	90 40W
Reynolds Ra.	**78**	22 30S	133 0 E
Reynoldsville	**114**	41 5N	78 58W
Reynosa	**125**	26 5N	98 18W
Reza'iyeh	**46**	37 40N	45 0 E
Rezā'īyeh, Daryācheh-ye	**46**	37 50N	45 30 E
Rezekne	**36**	56 30N	27 17 E
Rharis, O. →	**87**	26 0N	5 4 E
Rhayader	**13**	52 19N	3 30W
Rheden	**16**	52 0N	6 3 E
Rhein	**109**	51 25N	102 15W
Rhein →	**30**	51 52N	6 20 E
Rhein-Main-Donau-Kanal	**31**	49 1N	11 27 E
Rheinbach	**30**	50 38N	6 54 E
Rheine	**30**	52 17N	7 25 E
Rheinland-Pfalz □	**31**	50 0N	7 0 E
Rheinsberg	**30**	53 6N	12 52 E
Rheriss, Oued →	**86**	30 50N	4 34W
Rheydt	**30**	51 10N	6 24 E
Rhin = Rhein →	**30**	51 52N	6 20 E
Rhinau	**19**	48 19N	7 43 E
Rhine = Rhein →	**16**	51 52N	6 20 E
Rhinelander	**118**	45 38N	89 29W
Rhino Camp	**94**	3 0N	31 22 E
Rhir, Cap	**86**	30 38N	9 54W
Rho	**26**	45 31N	9 2 E
Rhode Island □	**115**	41 38N	71 37W
Rhodes = Ródhos	**35**	36 15N	28 10 E
Rhodes' Tomb	**95**	20 30S	28 30 E
Rhodesia = Zimbabwe-Rhodesia ■	**95**	20 0S	30 0 E
Rhodope Mts. = Rhodopi Planina	**35**	41 40N	24 20 E
Rhodopi Planina	**35**	41 40N	24 20 E
Rhondda	**13**	51 39N	3 30W
Rhône □	**21**	45 54N	4 35 E
Rhône →	**21**	43 28N	4 42 E
Rhum	**14**	57 0N	6 20W
Rhumney	**13**	51 32N	3 7W
Rhyl	**12**	53 19N	3 29W
Ri-Aba	**89**	3 28N	8 40 E
Riachão	**138**	7 20S	46 37W
Riacho de Santana	**139**	13 37S	42 57W
Rialma	**139**	15 18S	49 34W
Rialto	**123**	34 6N	117 22W
Riang	**52**	27 31N	92 56 E
Riaño	**22**	42 59N	5 0W
Rians	**21**	43 37N	5 44 E
Riansares →	**24**	39 32N	3 18W
Riasi	**49**	33 10N	74 50 E
Riau □	**56**	0 0	102 35 E
Riau, Kepulauan	**56**	0 30N	104 20 E
Riaza	**24**	41 18N	3 30W
Riaza →	**24**	41 42N	3 55W
Riba de Saelices	**24**	40 55N	2 17W
Ribadavia	**22**	42 17N	8 8W
Ribadeo	**22**	43 35N	7 5W
Ribadesella	**22**	43 30N	5 7W
Ribamar	**138**	2 33S	44 3W
Ribas	**24**	42 19N	2 15 E
Ribas do Rio Pardo	**137**	20 27S	53 46W
Ribble →	**12**	54 13N	2 20W
Ribe	**11**	55 19N	8 44 E
Ribeauvillé	**19**	48 10N	7 20 E
Ribécourt	**19**	49 30N	2 55 E
Ribeira	**22**	42 36N	8 58W
Ribeira do Pombal	**138**	10 50S	38 32W
Ribeirão Prêto	**141**	21 10S	47 50W
Ribeiro Gonçalves	**138**	7 32S	45 14W
Ribemont	**19**	49 47N	3 27 E
Ribera	**28**	37 30N	13 13 E
Ribérac	**20**	45 15N	0 20 E
Riberalta	**137**	11 0S	66 0W
Ribnica	**27**	45 45N	14 45 E
Ribnitz-Damgarten	**30**	54 14N	12 24 E
Riccarton	**81**	43 32S	172 37 E
Riccia	**29**	41 30N	14 50 E
Riccione	**27**	44 0N	12 39 E
Rice	**123**	34 5N	114 51W
Rice L.	**107**	44 12N	78 10W
Rice Lake	**118**	45 30N	91 42W
Riceys, Les	**19**	47 59N	4 22 E
Rich	**86**	32 16N	4 30W
Rich, C.	**106**	44 43N	80 38W
Rich Hill	**119**	38 5N	94 22W
Richards Bay	**97**	28 48S	32 6 E
Richards Deep	**129**	25 0S	73 0W
Richards L.	**109**	59 10N	107 10W
Richardson →	**109**	58 25N	111 14W
Richardson Mts.	**81**	44 49S	168 34 E
Richardson Springs	**122**	39 51N	121 46W
Richardton	**118**	46 56N	102 22W
Riche, C.	**79**	34 36S	118 47 E
Richelieu	**18**	47 0N	0 20 E
Richey	**118**	47 42N	105 5W
Richfield, Idaho, U.S.A.	**120**	43 2N	114 5W
Richfield, Utah, U.S.A.	**121**	38 50N	112 0W
Richford	**115**	45 0N	72 40W
Richibucto	**103**	46 42N	64 54W
Richland, Ga., U.S.A.	**113**	32 7N	84 40W
Richland, Iowa, U.S.A.	**116**	41 13N	91 58W
Richland, Mo., U.S.A.	**116**	37 51N	92 26W
Richland, Oreg., U.S.A.	**120**	44 49N	117 9W
Richland, Wash., U.S.A.	**120**	46 15N	119 15W
Richland Center	**118**	43 21N	90 22W
Richlands	**112**	37 7N	81 49W
Richmond, N.S.W., Austral.	**76**	33 35S	150 42 E
Richmond, Queens., Austral.	**72**	20 43S	143 8 E
Richmond, Ont., Can.	**107**	45 11N	75 50W
Richmond, Qué., Can.	**105**	45 40N	72 9W
Richmond, N.Z.	**81**	41 20S	173 12 E
Richmond, S. Afr.	**97**	29 51S	30 18 E
Richmond, N. Yorks., U.K.	**12**	54 24N	1 43W
Richmond, Surrey, U.K.	**13**	51 28N	0 18W
Richmond, Calif., U.S.A.	**122**	37 58N	122 21W
Richmond, Ind., U.S.A.	**117**	39 50N	84 50W
Richmond, Ky., U.S.A.	**117**	37 40N	84 20W
Richmond, Mich., U.S.A.	**106**	42 47N	82 45W
Richmond, Mo., U.S.A.	**118**	39 15N	93 58W
Richmond, Tex., U.S.A.	**119**	29 32N	95 42W
Richmond, Utah, U.S.A.	**120**	41 55N	111 48W
Richmond, Va., U.S.A.	**112**	37 33N	77 27W
Richmond →	**77**	28 52S	153 35 E
Richmond Hill	**106**	43 52N	79 27W
Richmond, Mt.	**81**	41 32S	173 22 E
Richmond, Ra.	**77**	29 0S	152 45 E
Richmond Ra.	**81**	41 32S	173 22 E
Richton	**113**	31 23N	88 58W
Richwood, Ohio, U.S.A.	**117**	40 26N	83 18W
Richwood, W. Va., U.S.A.	**112**	38 17N	80 32W
Ricla	**24**	41 31N	1 24W
Riddarhyttan	**10**	59 49N	15 33 E
Riddell	**74**	37 28S	144 42 E
Ridge Farm	**117**	39 54N	87 39W
Ridgecrest	**123**	35 37N	117 40W
Ridgedale	**109**	53 0N	104 10W
Ridgefield	**122**	45 49N	122 45W
Ridgeland	**113**	32 30N	80 58W
Ridgelands	**72**	23 16S	150 17 E
Ridgetown	**106**	42 26N	81 52W
Ridgeville	**117**	40 18N	85 2W
Ridgewood	**115**	40 59N	74 7W
Ridgway, Ill., U.S.A.	**117**	37 48N	88 16W
Ridgway, Pa., U.S.A.	**114**	41 25N	78 43W
Riding Mt. Nat. Park	**109**	50 50N	100 0W
Ridley Mt.	**79**	33 12S	122 7 E
Ried	**33**	48 14N	13 30 E
Riedlingen	**31**	48 9N	9 28 E
Rienza →	**27**	46 49N	11 47 E
Riesa	**30**	51 19N	13 19 E
Riesco, I.	**142**	52 55S	72 40W
Riesi	**29**	37 16N	14 4 E
Rietfontein	**96**	26 44S	20 1 E
Rieti	**27**	42 23N	12 50 E
Rieupeyroux	**20**	44 19N	2 12 E
Riez	**21**	43 49N	6 6 E
Rifle	**120**	39 40N	107 50W
Rifstangi	**8**	66 32N	16 12W
Rift Valley □	**94**	0 20N	36 0 E
Rig Rig	**85**	14 13N	14 25 E
Riga	**36**	56 53N	24 8 E
Riga, G. of = Rīgas Jūras Līcis	**36**	57 40N	23 45 E
Rīgas Jūras Līcis	**36**	57 40N	23 45 E
Rigaud	**105**	45 29N	74 18W
Rigby	**120**	43 41N	111 58W
Riggins	**120**	45 29N	116 26W
Rignac	**20**	44 25N	2 16 E
Rigolet	**103**	54 10N	58 23W
Riihimäki	**9**	60 45N	24 48 E
Riiser-Larsen-halvøya	**143**	68 0S	35 0 E
Rijau	**89**	11 8N	5 17 E
Rijeka	**27**	45 20N	14 21 E
Rijn →	**16**	52 12N	4 21 E
Rijssen	**16**	52 19N	6 30 E
Rijswijk	**16**	52 4N	4 22 E
Rike	**91**	10 50N	39 53 E
Rikita	**91**	5 5N	28 29 E
Rila Planina	**34**	42 10N	23 0 E
Riley	**120**	43 35N	119 33W
Rilly	**19**	49 11N	4 3 E
Rima →	**89**	13 4N	5 10 E
Rima, Wadi ar →	**46**	26 5N	41 30 E
Rimavská Sobota	**33**	48 22N	20 2 E
Rimbey	**108**	52 35N	114 15W
Rimbo	**10**	59 44N	18 21 E
Rimforsa	**11**	58 6N	15 43 E
Rimi	**89**	12 58N	7 43 E
Rímini	**27**	44 3N	12 33 E
Rîmnicu Sărat	**34**	45 26N	27 3 E
Rîmnicu Vîlcea	**34**	45 9N	24 21 E
Rimouski	**105**	48 27N	68 30W
Rimouski →	**105**	48 27N	68 32W
Rimouski-Est	**105**	48 28N	68 31W
Rimouski, Parc Prov. de	**105**	48 0N	68 15W
Rimrock	**122**	46 38N	121 10W
Rinca	**57**	8 45S	119 35 E
Rincón de Romos	**124**	22 14N	102 18W
Rinconada	**140**	22 26S	66 10W
Rineanna	**15**	52 42N	85 7W
Ringarum	**11**	58 21N	16 26 E
Ringe	**11**	55 13N	10 28 E
Ringgold Is.	**68**	16 15S	179 25W
Ringim	**89**	12 13N	9 10 E
Ringkøbing	**11**	56 5N	8 15 E
Ringling	**120**	46 16N	110 56W
Ringsaker	**10**	60 54N	10 45 E
Ringsjön	**11**	55 55N	13 30 E
Ringsted	**11**	55 25N	11 46 E
Ringvassøy	**8**	69 56N	19 15 E
Rinjani	**56**	8 24S	116 28 E
Rinteln	**30**	52 11N	9 3 E
Rio Branco	**136**	9 58S	67 49W
Río Branco	**141**	32 40S	53 40W
Rio Brilhante	**141**	21 48S	54 33W
Río Bueno	**142**	40 19S	72 58W
Río Chico	**134**	10 19N	65 59W
Rio Claro, Brazil	**141**	22 19S	47 35W
Rio Claro, Trin.	**127**	10 20N	61 25W
Río Colorado	**142**	39 0S	64 0W
Río Cuarto	**140**	33 10S	64 25W
Rio das Pedras	**97**	23 8S	35 28 E
Rio de Contas	**139**	13 36S	41 48W
Rio de Janeiro	**139**	23 0S	43 12W
Rio de Janeiro □	**139**	22 50S	43 0W
Rio do Prado	**139**	16 35S	40 34W
Rio do Sul	**141**	27 13S	49 37W
Río Gallegos	**142**	51 35S	69 15W
Río Grande, Argent.	**142**	53 50S	67 45W
Río Grande, Boliv.	**136**	20 51S	67 17W
Rio Grande	**141**	32 0S	52 20W
Río Grande, Mexico	**124**	23 50N	103 2W
Río Grande, Nic.	**126**	12 54N	83 33W
Rio Grande →	**119**	25 57N	97 9W
Rio Grande City	**119**	26 23N	98 49W
Río Grande del Norte →	**110**	26 0N	97 0W
Rio Grande do Norte □	**138**	5 40S	36 0W
Rio Grande do Sul □	**141**	30 0S	53 0W
Río Hato	**126**	8 22N	80 10W
Rio Lagartos	**125**	21 36N	88 10W
Rio Largo	**138**	9 28S	35 50W
Rio Maior	**23**	39 19N	8 57W
Rio Marina	**26**	42 48N	10 25 E
Río Mayo	**142**	45 40S	70 15W
Río Mulatos	**136**	19 40S	66 50W
Río Muni = Mbini □	**92**	1 30N	10 0 E
Rio Negro, Brazil	**141**	26 0S	50 0W
Rio Negro, Pantanal do, Brazil	**137**	19 0S	56 0W
Río Negro	**142**	40 47S	73 14W
Rio Pardo	**141**	30 0S	52 30W
Río Pico	**142**	44 0S	70 22W
Río, Punta del	**25**	36 49N	2 24W
Rio Real	**139**	11 28S	37 56W
Río Segundo	**140**	31 40S	63 59W
Río Tercero	**140**	32 15S	64 8W
Rio Tinto, Brazil	**138**	6 48S	35 5W
Rio Tinto, Port.	**22**	41 11N	8 34W
Rio Verde	**139**	17 50S	51 0W
Río Verde	**125**	21 56N	99 59W
Rio Verde de Mato Grosso	**137**	18 56S	54 52W
Rio Vista	**122**	38 11N	121 44W
Ríobamba	**134**	1 50S	78 45W
Ríohacha	**134**	11 33N	72 55W

Rioja **136** 6 11 S 77 5 W
Rioja, La, Argent. **140** 29 20 S 67 0 W
Rioja, La, Spain **24** 42 20 N 2 20 W
Rioja, La □ **140** 29 30 S 67 0 W
Riom **20** 45 54 N 3 7 E
Riom-ès-Montagnes **20** 45 17 N 2 39 E
Rion-des-Landes **20** 43 55 N 0 56 W
Rionegro **134** 6 9 N 75 22 W
Rionero in Vúlture **29** 40 55 N 15 40 E
Rios **22** 41 58 N 7 16 W
Riosucio **134** 5 30 N 75 40 W
Ríosucio **134** 7 27 N 77 7 W
Riou L. **109** 59 7 N 106 25 W
Rioz **19** 47 25 N 6 04 E
Riozinho → **134** 2 55 S 67 7 W
Riparia, Dora → **26** 45 7 N 7 24 E
Ripatransone **27** 43 0 N 13 45 E
Ripley, Can. **106** 44 4 N 81 35 W
Ripley, Calif., U.S.A. **123** 33 32 N 114 39 W
Ripley, N.Y., U.S.A. **114** 42 16 N 79 44 W
Ripley, Ohio, U.S.A. **117** 38 45 N 83 51 W
Ripley, Tenn., U.S.A. **119** 35 43 N 89 34 W
Ripoll **24** 42 15 N 2 13 E
Ripon, Can. **104** 45 45 N 75 10 W
Ripon, U.K. **12** 54 8 N 1 31 W
Ripon, Calif., U.S.A. **122** 37 44 N 121 7 W
Ripon, Wis., U.S.A. **112** 43 51 N 88 50 W
Riposto **29** 37 44 N 15 12 E
Risalpur **48** 34 3 N 71 59 E
Risan **33** 42 32 N 18 42 E
Risaralda □ **134** 5 0 N 76 10 W
Riscle **20** 43 39 N 0 5 W
Rishiri-Tō **63** 45 11 N 141 15 E
Rishon Le Zion **44** 31 58 N 34 48 E
Rishpon **44** 32 12 N 34 49 E
Rising Sun **117** 38 57 N 84 51 W
Risle → **18** 49 26 N 0 23 E
Rison **119** 33 57 N 92 11 W
Risør **11** 58 43 N 9 13 E
Riti **89** 7 57 N 9 41 E
Ritidian Pt. **68** 13 39 N 144 51 E
Rittman **114** 40 57 N 81 48 W
Ritzville **120** 47 10 N 118 21 W
Riu **52** 28 19 N 95 3 E
Riva Bella **18** 49 17 N 0 18 W
Riva del Garda **26** 45 53 N 10 50 E
Rivadavia, Buenos Aires, Argent. **140** 35 29 S 62 59 W
Rivadavia, Mendoza, Argent. **140** 33 13 S 68 30 W
Rivadavia, Salta, Argent. **140** 24 5 S 62 54 W
Rivadavia, Chile **140** 29 57 S 70 35 W
Rivarolo Canavese **26** 45 20 N 7 42 E
Rivas **126** 11 30 N 85 50 W
Rive-de-Gier **21** 45 32 N 4 37 E
River Cess **88** 5 30 N 9 32 W
River Rouge **117** 42 16 N 83 9 W
River Valley **106** 46 35 N 80 11 W
Rivera **141** 31 0 S 55 50 W
Riverdale **122** 36 26 N 119 52 W
Riverdsale **96** 34 7 S 21 15 E
Riverhead **115** 40 53 N 72 40 W
Riverhurst **109** 50 55 N 106 50 W
Riverina **79** 29 45 S 120 40 E
Rivers **109** 50 2 N 100 14 W
Rivers □ **89** 5 0 N 6 30 E
Rivers Inl. **108** 51 40 N 127 20 W
Rivers, L. of the **109** 49 49 N 105 44 W
Riverside, Calif., U.S.A. **123** 34 0 N 117 22 W
Riverside, Wyo., U.S.A. **120** 41 12 N 106 57 W
Riversleigh **72** 19 5 S 138 40 E
Riverton, Austral. **73** 34 10 S 138 46 E
Riverton, Can. **109** 51 1 N 97 0 W
Riverton, N.Z. **81** 46 21 S 168 0 E
Riverton, Ill., U.S.A. **116** 39 51 N 89 33 W
Riverton, Wyo., U.S.A. **120** 43 1 N 108 27 W
Rives **21** 45 21 N 5 31 E
Rivesaltes **20** 42 47 N 2 50 E
Riviera **26** 44 0 N 8 30 E
Rivière-à-Pierre **105** 46 59 N 72 11 W
Rivière-au-Renard **103** 48 59 N 64 23 W
Rivière-aux-Rats **105** 47 13 N 72 53 W
Rivière-Bersimis **105** 48 56 N 68 42 W
Rivière-du-Loup **105** 47 50 N 69 30 W
Rivière-Ouelle **105** 47 26 N 70 1 W
Rivière-Pentecôte **103** 49 57 N 67 1 W
Rivière-Pilot **127** 14 26 N 60 53 W
Rivière-Portneuf **105** 48 38 N 69 6 W
Rívoli **26** 45 3 N 7 31 E
Rivoli B. **73** 37 32 S 140 3 E
Rivungo **96** 16 9 S 21 51 E
Riwaka **81** 41 5 S 172 59 E
Riyadh = Ar Riyāḍ **46** 24 41 N 46 42 E
Rize **46** 41 0 N 40 30 E
Rizhao **61** 35 25 N 119 30 E
Rizzuto, C. **29** 38 54 N 17 5 E
Rjukan **10** 59 54 N 8 33 E
Rô **68** 21 22 S 167 50 E
Roa, Norway **10** 60 17 N 10 37 E
Roa, Spain **22** 41 41 N 3 56 W
Roachdale **117** 39 51 N 86 48 W
Road Town **127** 18 27 N 64 37 W
Roag, L. **14** 58 10 N 6 55 W
Roan Antelope **95** 13 2 S 28 19 E
Roanne **21** 46 3 N 4 4 E
Roanoke, Ala., U.S.A. **113** 33 9 N 85 23 W
Roanoke, Ind., U.S.A. **117** 40 58 N 85 22 W
Roanoke, Va., U.S.A. **112** 37 19 N 79 55 W
Roanoke → **113** 35 56 N 76 43 W
Roanoke I. **113** 35 55 N 75 40 W
Roanoke Rapids **113** 36 28 N 77 42 W
Roatán **126** 16 18 N 86 35 W
Rob Roy **68** 7 23 S 157 36 E
Robbins I. **72** 40 42 S 145 0 E
Robe → **78** 21 42 S 116 15 E
Röbel **30** 53 24 N 12 37 E
Robert Lee **119** 31 55 N 100 26 W
Robert Williams **93** 12 46 S 15 30 E
Roberts, Idaho, U.S.A. **120** 43 44 N 112 8 W
Roberts, Ill., U.S.A. **117** 40 37 N 88 11 W
Robertsganj **49** 24 44 N 83 4 E
Robertson, Austral. **76** 34 37 S 150 36 E
Robertson, S. Afr. **96** 33 46 S 19 50 E
Robertson I. **143** 65 15 S 59 30 W
Robertson Ra. **78** 23 15 S 121 0 E
Robertsonville **105** 46 9 N 71 13 W
Robertsport **88** 6 45 N 11 26 W
Robertstown **73** 33 58 S 139 5 E
Roberval **105** 48 32 N 72 15 W
Robeson Ch. **144** 82 0 N 61 30 W
Robinson **117** 39 0 N 87 44 W
Robinson → **72** 16 3 S 137 16 E
Robinson Crusoe I. **67** 33 38 S 78 52 W
Robinson Ranges **79** 25 40 S 119 0 E
Robinson River **72** 16 45 S 136 58 E
Robinvale **74** 34 40 S 142 45 E
Robla, La **22** 42 50 N 5 41 W
Roblin **109** 51 14 N 101 21 W
Roboré **137** 18 10 S 59 45 W
Robson, Mt. **108** 53 10 N 119 10 W
Robstown **119** 27 47 N 97 40 W
Roc, Pointe du **18** 48 50 N 1 37 W
Roca, C. da **23** 38 40 N 9 31 W
Roca Partida, I. **124** 19 1 N 112 2 W
Roçadas **96** 16 45 S 15 0 E
Rocas, I. **138** 4 0 S 34 1 W
Rocca d'Aspidé **29** 40 27 N 15 10 E
Rocca San Casciano **27** 44 3 N 11 45 E
Roccalbegna **27** 42 47 N 11 30 E
Roccastrada **27** 43 0 N 11 10 E
Roccella Iónica **29** 38 20 N 16 24 E
Rocha **141** 34 30 S 54 25 W
Rochdale **12** 53 36 N 2 10 W
Roche-Bernard, La **18** 47 31 N 2 19 W
Roche-Canillac, La **20** 45 12 N 1 57 E
Roche, La, France **21** 46 4 N 6 19 E
Roche, La, N. Cal. **68** 21 26 S 168 2 E
Roche-sur-Yon, La **18** 46 40 N 1 25 W
Rochebaucourt **104** 48 41 N 77 30 W
Rochechouart **20** 45 50 N 0 49 E
Rochedo **137** 19 57 S 54 52 W
Rochefort, Belg. **16** 50 9 N 5 12 E
Rochefort, France **20** 45 56 N 0 57 W
Rochefort-en-Terre **18** 47 42 N 2 22 W
Rochefoucauld, La **20** 45 44 N 0 24 E
Rochelle **116** 41 55 N 89 5 W
Rochelle, La **20** 46 10 N 1 9 W
Rocher River **108** 61 23 N 112 44 W
Rocheservière **18** 46 57 N 1 30 W
Rochester, Austral. **74** 36 22 S 144 41 E
Rochester, Can. **108** 54 22 N 113 27 W
Rochester, U.K. **13** 51 22 N 0 30 E
Rochester, Ind., U.S.A. **117** 41 5 N 86 15 W
Rochester, Mich., U.S.A. **117** 42 41 N 83 8 W
Rochester, Minn., U.S.A. **118** 44 1 N 92 28 W
Rochester, N.H., U.S.A. **115** 43 19 N 70 57 W
Rochester, N.Y., U.S.A. **114** 43 10 N 77 40 W
Rochester, Pa., U.S.A. **114** 40 41 N 80 17 W
Rociana **23** 37 19 N 6 35 W
Rociu **34** 44 43 N 25 2 E
Rock → **108** 60 7 N 127 7 W
Rock Falls **116** 41 47 N 89 41 W
Rock Flat **75** 36 21 S 149 13 E
Rock Hill **113** 34 55 N 81 2 W
Rock Island, Can. **105** 45 26 N 73 34 W
Rock Island, U.S.A. **116** 41 30 N 90 35 W
Rock Port **118** 40 26 N 95 30 W
Rock Rapids **118** 43 25 N 96 10 W
Rock River **120** 41 49 N 106 0 W
Rock Sound **126** 24 54 N 76 12 W
Rock Sprs., Ariz., U.S.A. **121** 34 2 N 112 11 W
Rock Sprs., Mont., U.S.A. **120** 46 55 N 106 11 W
Rock Sprs., Tex., U.S.A. **119** 30 2 N 100 11 W
Rock Sprs., Wyo., U.S.A. **120** 41 40 N 109 10 W
Rock Valley **118** 43 10 N 96 17 W
Rockall **6** 57 37 N 13 42 W
Rockdale, Tex., U.S.A. **119** 30 40 N 97 0 W
Rockdale, Wash., U.S.A. **122** 47 22 N 121 28 W
Rockefeller Plat. **143** 80 0 S 140 0 W
Rockford, Ill., U.S.A. **116** 42 20 N 89 0 W
Rockford, Iowa, U.S.A. **116** 43 3 N 92 57 W
Rockford, Mich., U.S.A. **117** 43 7 N 85 34 W
Rockford, Ohio, U.S.A. **117** 40 41 N 84 39 W
Rockglen **109** 49 11 N 105 57 W
Rockhampton **72** 23 22 S 150 32 E
Rockhampton Downs **72** 18 57 S 135 10 E
Rockingham **79** 32 15 S 115 38 E
Rockingham B. **72** 18 5 S 146 10 E
Rockingham Forest **13** 52 28 N 0 42 W
Rocklake **118** 48 50 N 99 13 W
Rockland, Can. **107** 45 33 N 75 17 W
Rockland, Idaho, U.S.A. **120** 42 37 N 112 57 W
Rockland, Me., U.S.A. **103** 44 6 N 69 6 W
Rockland, Mich., U.S.A. **118** 46 40 N 89 10 W
Rocklands Reservoir **74** 37 15 S 142 5 E
Rockley **76** 33 41 S 149 33 E
Rocklin **122** 38 48 N 121 14 W
Rockmart **113** 34 1 N 85 2 W
Rockport, Ky., U.S.A. **117** 37 53 N 87 3 W
Rockport, Tex., U.S.A. **119** 28 2 N 97 3 W
Rockton **75** 37 10 S 149 18 E
Rockvale **77** 30 25 S 151 53 E
Rockville, Conn., U.S.A. **115** 41 51 N 72 27 W
Rockville, Ind., U.S.A. **117** 39 46 N 87 14 W
Rockville, Md., U.S.A. **112** 39 7 N 77 10 W
Rockwall **119** 32 55 N 96 30 W
Rockwell City **116** 42 20 N 94 35 W
Rockwood, Can. **106** 43 37 N 80 8 W
Rockwood, Mich., U.S.A. **117** 42 4 N 83 15 W
Rockwood, Tenn., U.S.A. **113** 35 52 N 84 40 W
Rocky Ford **118** 38 7 N 103 45 W
Rocky Fork Lake **117** 39 12 N 83 23 W
Rocky Glen **77** 31 6 S 149 35 E
Rocky Gully **79** 34 30 S 116 57 E
Rocky Lane **108** 58 31 N 116 22 W
Rocky Mount **113** 35 55 N 77 48 W
Rocky Mountain House **108** 52 22 N 114 55 W
Rocky Mts. **108** 55 0 N 121 0 W
Rocky River, Austral. **77** 30 36 S 151 29 E
Rocky River, U.S.A. **114** 41 30 N 81 40 W
Rockyford **108** 51 14 N 113 10 W
Rocroi **19** 49 55 N 4 30 E
Rod **47** 28 10 N 63 5 E
Roda, La, Albacete, Spain **25** 39 13 N 2 15 W
Roda, La, Sevilla, Spain **23** 37 12 N 4 46 W
Rødberg **10** 60 17 N 8 56 E
Rødby **11** 54 41 N 11 23 E
Rødbyhavn **11** 54 39 N 11 22 E
Roddickton **103** 50 51 N 56 8 W
Rødding **11** 55 23 N 9 3 E
Rødekro **11** 55 4 N 9 20 E
Rødenes **10** 59 35 N 11 34 E
Rodenkirchen **30** 53 24 N 8 26 E
Roderick I. **108** 52 38 N 128 22 W
Rodez **20** 44 21 N 2 33 E
Rodholívas **35** 40 55 N 24 0 E
Ródhos, Greece **35** 36 15 N 28 10 E
Ródhos, Greece **35** 36 30 N 28 0 E
Rodi Garganico **29** 41 55 N 15 53 E
Rodna **34** 47 25 N 24 50 E
Rodney **106** 42 34 N 81 41 W
Rodney, C. **80** 36 17 S 174 50 E
Rodniki **37** 57 7 N 41 47 E
Rodriguez **53** 19 45 S 63 20 E
Rodstock, C. **73** 33 12 S 134 20 E
Roe → **15** 55 10 N 6 59 W
Roebling **115** 40 7 N 74 45 W
Roebourne **78** 20 44 S 117 9 E
Roebuck B. **78** 18 5 S 122 20 E
Roebuck Plains P.O. **78** 17 56 S 122 28 E
Roermond **16** 51 12 N 6 0 E
Roes Welcome Sd. **101** 65 0 N 87 0 W
Roeselare **16** 50 57 N 3 7 E
Rogachev **36** 53 8 N 30 5 E
Rogagua, L. **136** 13 43 S 66 50 W
Rogaland fylke □ **9** 59 12 N 6 20 E
Rogaška Slatina **27** 46 15 N 15 42 E
Rogatec **27** 46 15 N 15 46 E
Roger, L. **104** 47 50 N 78 59 W
Rogers **119** 36 20 N 94 5 W
Rogers City **106** 45 25 N 83 49 W
Rogerson **120** 42 10 N 114 40 W
Rogersville **113** 36 27 N 83 1 W
Roggan **102** 54 25 N 79 32 W
Roggeveldberge **96** 32 10 S 20 10 E
Roggiano Gravina **29** 39 37 N 16 9 E
Rogliano, France **21** 42 57 N 9 30 E
Rogliano, Italy **29** 39 11 N 16 20 E
Rogoaguado, L. **137** 13 0 S 65 30 W
Rogue → **120** 42 30 N 124 0 W
Rohan **18** 48 4 N 2 45 W
Rohault, L. **105** 49 23 N 74 20 W
Rohnert Park **122** 38 16 N 122 40 W
Rohrbach **19** 49 3 N 7 15 E
Rohri **48** 27 45 N 68 51 E
Rohri Canal **48** 26 15 N 68 27 E
Rohtak **48** 28 55 N 76 43 E
Roi Et **54** 16 4 N 103 40 E
Roisel **19** 49 58 N 3 6 E
Rojas **140** 34 10 S 60 45 W
Rojo, C. **125** 21 33 N 97 20 W
Rokan → **56** 2 0 N 100 50 E
Rokeby **72** 13 39 S 142 40 E
Rokewood **74** 37 54 S 143 44 E
Rokiskis **36** 55 55 N 25 35 E
Rokitno **36** 50 57 N 35 56 E
Rolândia **141** 23 18 S 51 23 W
Rolette **118** 48 42 N 99 50 W
Rolfe **116** 42 49 N 94 31 W
Rolla, Kansas, U.S.A. **119** 37 10 N 101 40 W
Rolla, Mo., U.S.A. **116** 37 56 N 91 42 W
Rolla, N. Dak., U.S.A. **118** 48 50 N 99 36 W
Rollag **10** 60 2 N 9 18 E
Rollands Plains **77** 31 17 S 152 42 E
Rolleston, Austral. **72** 24 28 S 148 35 E
Rolleston, N.Z. **81** 43 35 S 172 24 E
Rollet **104** 47 55 N 79 15 W
Rolling → **117** 38 0 N 85 56 W
Rollingstone **72** 19 2 S 146 24 E
Rom **91** 9 54 N 32 16 E
Roma, Austral. **73** 26 32 S 148 49 E
Roma, Italy **28** 41 54 N 12 30 E
Roman, Rumania **34** 46 57 N 26 55 E
Roman, U.S.S.R. **41** 66 4 N 112 14 E
Romana, La **127** 18 27 N 68 57 W
Romanche → **21** 45 5 N 5 43 E
Romang **57** 7 30 S 127 20 E
Romàni **90** 30 59 N 32 38 E
Romano, Cayo **126** 22 0 N 77 30 W
Romano di Lombardía **26** 45 32 N 9 45 E
Romanovka = Bessarabka **38** 46 21 N 28 58 E
Romans **21** 45 3 N 5 3 E
Romanshorn **31** 47 33 N 9 22 E
Romblon **57** 12 33 N 122 17 E
Rombo □ **94** 3 10 S 37 30 E
Rome, Ga., U.S.A. **113** 34 20 N 85 0 W
Rome, N.Y., U.S.A. **115** 43 14 N 75 29 W
Rome = Roma **28** 41 54 N 12 30 E
Romeleåsen **11** 55 34 N 13 33 E
Romenay **21** 46 30 N 5 1 E
Romerike **10** 60 7 N 11 10 E
Romilly **19** 48 31 N 3 44 E
Romîni **34** 44 59 N 24 11 E
Rommani **86** 33 31 N 6 40 W
Romney **112** 39 21 N 78 45 W
Romney Marsh **13** 51 0 N 1 0 E
Romny **36** 50 48 N 33 28 E
Rømø **11** 55 10 N 8 30 E
Romodan **36** 50 0 N 33 15 E
Romodanovo **37** 54 26 N 45 23 E
Romont **31** 46 42 N 6 54 E
Romorantin-Lanthenay **19** 47 21 N 1 45 E
Romsdalen **10** 62 25 N 8 0 E
Ron **54** 17 53 N 106 27 E
Rona **14** 57 33 N 6 0 W
Ronan **120** 47 30 N 114 6 W
Roncador, Cayos **126** 13 32 N 80 4 W
Roncador, Serra do **139** 12 30 S 52 30 W
Roncesvalles, Paso **24** 43 1 N 1 19 W
Ronceverte **112** 37 45 N 80 28 W
Ronciglione **27** 42 18 N 12 12 E
Ronco → **27** 44 24 N 12 12 E
Ronda **23** 36 46 N 5 12 W
Ronda, Serranía de **23** 36 44 N 5 3 W
Rondane **10** 61 57 N 9 50 E
Rondeau Prov. Park **106** 42 19 N 81 51 W
Rondón **134** 6 17 N 71 6 W
Rondônia **137** 10 52 S 61 57 W
Rondônia □ **137** 11 0 S 63 0 W
Rondonópolis **137** 16 26 S 54 38 W
Rong Jiang → **58** 24 35 N 109 20 E
Rong Xian, Guangxi Zhuangzu, China **59** 22 50 N 110 31 E

Rong Xian, Sichuan, China 58 29 23N 104 22 E
Rong'an 58 25 14N 109 22 E
Rongchang 58 29 20N 105 32 E
Ronge, La 109 55 5N 105 20W
Ronge,Lac La 109 55 6N 105 17W
Rongjiang 58 25 57N 108 28 E
Rongotea 80 40 19S 175 25 E
Rongshui 58 25 5N 109 12 E
Ronne Land 143 83 0S 70 0W
Ronneby 11 56 12N 15 17 E
Ronsard, C. 79 24 46S 113 10 E
Ronse 16 50 45N 3 35 E
Ronuro → 137 11 56S 53 33W
Roodhouse 116 39 29N 90 24W
Roof Butte 121 36 29N 109 5W
Roonui, Mt. 68 17 49S 149 12W
Roorkee 48 29 52N 77 59 E
Roosendaal 16 51 32N 4 29 E
Roosevelt, Minn., U.S.A. 118 48 51N 95 2W
Roosevelt, Utah, U.S.A. 120 40 19N 110 1W
Roosevelt → 137 7 35S 60 20W
Roosevelt I. 143 79 30S 162 0W
Roosevelt, Mt. 108 58 26N 125 20W
Roosevelt Res. 121 33 46N 111 0W
Roper → 72 14 43S 135 27 E
Ropesville 119 33 25N 102 10W
Roque Pérez 140 35 25S 59 24W
Roquebrou, La 20 44 58N 2 12 E
Roquefort 20 44 2N 0 20W
Roquefort-sur-Soulzon 20 43 58N 2 59 E
Roquemaure 21 44 3N 4 48 E
Roquetas 24 40 50N 0 30 E
Roquevaire 21 43 20N 5 36 E
Roraima □ 135 2 0N 61 30W
Roraima, Mt. 135 5 10N 60 40W
Rorketon 109 51 24N 99 35W
Røros 10 62 35N 11 23 E
Rorschach 31 47 28N 9 30 E
Rørvik 8 64 54N 11 15 E
Rosa 95 9 33S 31 15 E
Rosa Brook 79 33 57S 115 10 E
Rosa, C. 87 37 0N 8 16 E
Rosa, Monte 31 45 57N 7 53 E
Rosal 22 41 57N 8 51W
Rosal de la Frontera 23 37 59N 7 13W
Rosalia 120 47 14N 117 25W
Rosamond 123 34 52N 118 10W
Rosans 21 44 24N 5 29 E
Rosario 140 33 0S 60 40W
Rosário 138 3 0S 44 15W
Rosario, Baja Calif. N., Mexico 124 30 0N 115 50W
Rosario, Durango, Mexico 124 26 30N 105 35W
Rosario, Sinaloa, Mexico 124 23 0N 105 52W
Rosario, Parag. 140 24 30S 57 35W
Rosario de la Frontera 140 25 50S 65 0W
Rosario de Lerma 140 24 59S 65 35W
Rosario del Tala 140 32 20S 59 10W
Rosário do Sul 141 30 15S 54 55W
Rosário Oeste 137 14 50S 56 25W
Rosario, Villa del 134 10 19N 72 19W
Rosarito, Mexico 124 28 38N 114 4W
Rosarito, U.S.A. 123 32 18N 117 4W
Rosarno 29 38 29N 15 59 E
Rosas 24 42 19N 3 10 E
Roscoe, Miss., U.S.A. 116 37 58N 93 48W
Roscoe, S.D., U.S.A. 118 45 27N 99 20W
Roscoff 18 48 44N 4 0W
Roscommon, Ireland 15 53 38N 8 11W
Roscommon, U.S.A. 106 44 27N 84 35W
Roscommon □ 15 53 40N 8 15W
Roscrea 15 52 58N 7 50W
Rose → 72 14 16S 135 45 E
Rose Blanche 103 47 38N 58 45W
Rose City 106 44 25N 84 7W
Rose Harbour 108 52 15N 131 10W
Rose Pt. 108 54 11N 131 39W
Rose Valley 109 52 19N 103 49W
Roseau, Domin. 127 15 20N 61 24W
Roseau, U.S.A. 118 48 51N 95 46W
Rosebery, Tas., Austral. 72 41 46S 145 33 E
Rosebery, Vic., Austral. 74 35 48S 142 27 E
Rosebud, Austral. 74 38 21S 144 54 E
Rosebud, U.S.A. 119 31 5N 97 0W
Roseburg 120 43 10N 123 20W
Rosedale, Queens., Austral. 72 24 38S 151 53 E
Rosedale, Vic., Austral. 75 38 11S 146 48 E
Rosedale, Ind., U.S.A. 117 39 38N 87 17W
Rosedale, Miss., U.S.A. 119 33 51N 91 0W
Roseland 122 38 25N 122 43W
Rosemary 108 50 46N 112 5W
Rosemère 105 45 38N 73 48W
Rosenberg 119 29 30N 95 48W
Rosendaël 19 51 3N 2 24 E
Rosendale 116 40 4N 94 51W
Rosenheim 31 47 51N 12 9 E
Roseto degli Abruzzi 27 42 40N 14 2 E
Rosetown 109 51 35N 107 59W
Rosetta = Rashîd 90 31 21N 30 22 E
Roseville, Calif., U.S.A. 122 38 46N 121 17W
Roseville, Ill., U.S.A. 116 40 44N 90 40W
Roseville, Mich., U.S.A. 106 42 30N 82 56W
Rosewood, N.S.W., Austral. 76 35 38S 147 52 E
Rosewood, N.T., Austral. 78 16 28S 128 58 E
Rosewood, Queens., Austral. 73 27 38S 152 36 E
Rosh Haniqra, Kefar 44 33 5N 35 5 E
Rosh Pinna 44 32 58N 35 32 E
Rosières 19 49 49N 2 43 E
Rosignano Marittimo 26 43 23N 10 28 E
Rosignol 135 6 15N 57 30W
Roşiori de Vede 34 44 9N 25 0 E
Rositsa 34 43 57N 27 57 E
Rositsa → 34 43 10N 25 30 E
Roskilde 11 55 38N 12 3 E
Roskilde Amtskommune □ 11 55 35N 12 5 E
Roskilde Fjord 11 55 50N 12 2 E
Roslavl 36 53 57N 32 55 E
Roslyn 76 34 29S 149 37 E
Rosmaninhal 23 39 44N 7 5W
Røsnæs 11 55 44N 10 55 E
Rosolini 29 36 49N 14 58 E
Rosporden 18 47 57N 3 50W
Ross, Austral. 72 42 2S 147 30 E
Ross, N.Z. 81 42 53S 170 49 E
Ross Dependency □ 143 70 0S 170 5W
Ross I. 143 77 30S 168 0 E
Ross Ice Shelf 143 80 0S 180 0W
Ross L. 120 48 50N 121 5W
Ross on Wye 13 51 55N 2 34W
Ross Sea 143 74 0S 178 0 E
Rossan Pt. 15 54 42N 8 47W
Rossano Cálabro 29 39 36N 16 39 E
Rossburn 109 50 40N 100 49W
Rosseau 106 45 16N 79 39W
Rosseau L. 106 45 10N 79 35W
Rossel, C. 68 20 23S 166 36 E
Rossford 117 41 36N 83 34W
Rossignol, L., N.S., Can. 103 44 12N 65 10W
Rossignol, L., Qué., Can. 102 52 43N 73 40W
Rössing 96 22 30S 14 50 E
Rossland 108 49 6N 117 50W
Rosslare 15 52 17N 6 23W
Rosslau 30 51 52N 12 15 E
Rossmore 107 44 8N 77 23W
Rosso 88 16 40N 15 45W
Rossosh 39 50 15N 39 28 E
Rossport 102 48 50N 87 30W
Røssvatnet 8 65 45N 14 5 E
Rossville, Austral. 72 15 48S 145 15 E
Rossville, U.S.A. 117 40 25N 86 35W
Rosthern 109 52 40N 106 20W
Rostock 30 54 4N 12 9 E
Rostock □ 30 54 10N 12 30 E
Rostov, Don, U.S.S.R. 39 47 15N 39 45 E
Rostov, Moskva, U.S.S.R. 37 57 14N 39 25 E
Rostrenen 18 48 14N 3 21W
Roswell 119 33 26N 104 32W
Rosyth 14 56 2N 3 26W
Rota 23 36 37N 6 20W
Rotälven → 10 61 15N 14 3 E
Rotan 119 32 52N 100 30W
Rotenburg 30 53 6N 9 24 E
Roth 31 49 15N 11 6 E
Rothenburg ob der Tauber 31 49 21N 10 11 E
Rother → 13 50 59N 0 40 E
Rotherham 12 53 26N 1 21W
Rothes 14 57 31N 3 12W
Rothesay, Can. 103 45 23N 66 0W
Rothesay, U.K. 14 55 50N 5 3W
Roti 57 10 50S 123 0 E
Rotkop 96 26 44S 15 27 E
Roto 73 33 0S 145 30 E
Roto Aira L. 80 39 3S 175 45 E
Rotoehu L. 80 38 1S 176 32 E
Rotoiti L. 81 41 51S 172 49 E
Rotoma L. 80 38 2S 176 35 E
Rotondella 29 40 10N 16 30 E
Rotoroa, L. 81 41 55S 172 39 E
Rotorua 80 38 9S 176 16 E
Rotorua, L. 80 38 5S 176 18 E
Rott → 31 48 26N 13 26 E
Rottenburg 31 48 28N 8 56 E
Rotterdam 16 51 55N 4 30 E
Rottnest I. 79 32 0S 115 27 E
Rottumeroog 16 53 33N 6 34 E
Rottweil 31 48 9N 8 38 E
Rotuma 66 12 25S 177 5 E
Roubaix 19 50 40N 3 10 E
Rouen 18 49 27N 1 4 E
Rouge → 104 45 17N 74 10W
Rough Ridge 81 45 10S 169 55 E
Rouillac 20 45 47N 0 4W
Rouleau 109 50 10N 104 56W
Round L. 107 45 38N 77 30W
Round Mt. 77 30 26S 152 16 E
Round Mountain 120 38 46N 117 3W
Roundup 120 46 25N 108 35W
Roura 135 4 44N 52 20W
Rousay 14 59 10N 3 2W
Rouses Point 115 44 58N 73 22W
Rousse, L'Île 21 42 37N 8 57 E
Roussillon, Isère, France 21 45 24N 4 49 E
Roussillon, Pyrénées-Or., France 20 42 30N 2 35 E
Roussin, C. 68 21 20S 167 59 E
Rouvray, L. 105 49 18N 70 49W
Rouxville 96 30 25S 26 50 E
Rouyn 104 48 20N 79 0W
Rovaniemi 8 66 29N 25 41 E
Rovato 26 45 34N 10 0 E
Rovenki 39 48 5N 39 21 E
Rovereto 26 45 53N 11 3 E
Rovigo 27 45 4N 11 48 E
Rovinari 34 44 56N 23 10 E
Rovinj 27 45 5N 13 40 E
Rovira 134 4 15N 75 20W
Rovno 36 50 40N 26 10 E
Rovnoye 37 50 52N 46 3 E
Rovuma → 95 10 29S 40 28 E
Rowena 73 29 48S 148 55 E
Rowes 75 37 0S 149 6 E
Rowley Shoals 78 17 30S 119 0 E
Roxa 88 11 15N 15 45W
Roxas 57 11 36N 122 49 E
Roxboro 113 36 24N 78 59W
Roxborough Downs 72 22 30S 138 45 E
Roxburgh 81 45 33S 169 19 E
Roxen 11 58 30N 15 40 E
Roxton Falls 105 45 34N 72 31W
Roy, Mont., U.S.A. 120 47 17N 109 0W
Roy, N. Mex., U.S.A. 119 35 57N 104 8W
Roy Hill 78 22 37S 119 58 E
Roy, Le, Ill., U.S.A. 117 40 21N 88 46W
Roy, Le, Kans., U.S.A. 119 38 8N 95 35W
Roya, Peña 24 40 25N 0 40W
Royal Center 117 40 52N 86 30W
Royal Oak 117 42 30N 83 5W
Royalla 76 35 30S 149 9 E
Royan 20 45 37N 1 2W
Roye 19 49 42N 2 48 E
Røyken 10 59 45N 10 23 E
Rožaj 33 42 50N 20 15 E
Rozay 19 48 40N 2 56 E
Rozier, Le 20 44 13N 3 12 E
Rožnava 32 48 37N 20 35 E
Rozoy-sur-Serre 19 49 40N 4 8 E
Rtishchevo 37 55 16N 43 50 E
Rúa 22 42 24N 7 6W
Ruacaná 96 17 20S 14 12 E
Ruahine Ra. 80 39 55S 176 2 E
Ruamahanga → 80 41 24S 175 8 E
Ruapehu 80 39 17S 175 35 E
Ruapuke I. 81 46 46S 168 31 E
Ruatoria 80 37 55S 178 20 E
Ruãus, W. → 87 30 26N 15 24 E
Ruawai 80 36 8S 173 59 E
Rubeho, Mts. 94 6 50S 36 25 E
Rubezhnoye 38 49 6N 38 25 E
Rubh a' Mhail 14 55 55N 6 10W
Rubha Hunish, C. 14 57 42N 6 20W
Rubiataba 139 15 8S 49 48W
Rubicon → 122 38 53N 121 4W
Rubicone → 27 44 8N 12 28 E
Rubinéia 139 20 13S 51 2W
Rubino 88 6 4N 4 18W
Rubio 134 7 43N 72 22W
Rubono 94 0 29N 30 9 E
Rubtsovsk 40 51 30N 81 10 E
Ruby, Austral. 74 38 27S 145 55 E
Ruby, U.S.A. 100 64 40N 155 35W
Ruby L. 120 40 10N 115 28W
Ruby Mts. 120 40 30N 115 30W
Rubyvale 72 23 25S 147 45 E
Rucava 36 56 9N 21 12 E
Rucheng 59 25 33N 113 38 E
Rud 10 60 1N 10 1 E
Ruda 11 57 6N 16 7 E
Ruda Śląska 32 50 16N 18 50 E
Rudall 73 33 43S 136 17 E
Ruden 30 54 13N 13 47 E
Rüdersdorf 30 52 28N 13 48 E
Rudewa 95 10 7S 34 40 E
Rudkøbing 11 54 56N 10 41 E
Rudnik 33 44 7N 20 35 E
Rudnogorsk 41 57 15N 103 42 E
Rudnya 36 54 55N 31 7 E
Rudnyy 40 52 57N 63 7 E
Rudolf, Ostrov 40 81 45N 58 30 E
Rudolstadt 30 50 44N 11 20 E
Rudong 59 32 20N 121 12 E
Rudozem 35 41 29N 24 51 E
Rudyard 106 46 14N 84 35W
Rue 19 50 15N 1 40 E
Rue, La 117 40 35N 83 23W
Ruelle 20 45 41N 0 14 E
Rufa'a 91 14 44N 33 22 E
Ruffec-Charente 20 46 2N 0 12 E
Rufi 91 5 58N 30 18 E
Rufiji □ 94 8 0S 38 30 E
Rufiji → 94 7 50S 39 15 E
Rufino 140 34 20S 62 50W
Rufisque 88 14 40N 17 15W
Rufunsa 95 15 4S 29 34 E
Rugao 59 32 23N 120 31 E
Rugby, Austral. 76 34 23S 149 0 E
Rugby, U.K. 13 52 23N 1 16W
Rugby, U.S.A. 118 48 21N 100 0W
Rügen 30 54 22N 13 25 E
Rugezi 94 2 6S 33 18 E
Rugles 18 48 50N 0 40 E
Ruhāma 44 31 31N 34 43 E
Ruhea 52 26 10N 88 25 E
Ruhengeri 94 1 30S 29 36 E
Ruhla 30 50 53N 10 21 E
Ruhland 30 51 27N 13 52 E
Ruhr → 30 51 25N 6 44 E
Ruhuhu → 95 10 31S 34 34 E
Rui Barbosa 139 12 18S 40 27W
Rui'an 59 27 47N 120 40 E
Ruichang 59 29 40N 115 39 E
Ruidosa 119 29 59N 104 39W
Ruidoso 121 33 19N 105 39W
Ruili 58 24 1N 97 43 E
Ruisseau-Vert 105 49 4N 68 28W
Ruk 48 27 50N 68 42 E
Rukwa □ 94 7 0S 31 30 E
Rukwa L. 94 8 0S 32 20 E
Rulhieres, C. 78 13 56S 127 22 E
Rum Cay 126 23 40N 74 58W
Rum Jungle 78 13 0S 130 59 E
Ruma 33 45 0N 19 50 E
Rumāh 46 25 29N 47 10 E
Rumania ■ 34 46 0N 25 0 E
Rumbalara 72 25 20S 134 29 E
Rumbee, Mt. 77 29 55S 151 35 E
Rumbêk 91 6 54N 29 37 E
Rumford 115 44 30N 70 30W
Rumilly 21 45 53N 5 56 E
Rumoi 63 43 56N 141 39W
Rumonge 94 3 59S 29 26 E
Rumorosa, La 123 32 33N 116 4W
Rumsey 108 51 51N 112 48W
Rumula 72 16 35S 145 20 E
Rumuruti 94 0 17N 36 32 E
Runan 60 33 0N 114 30 E
Runanga 81 42 25S 171 15 E
Runaway, C. 80 37 32S 178 2 E
Runcorn 12 53 20N 2 44W
Rungwa 94 6 55S 33 32 E
Rungwa → 94 7 36S 31 50 E
Rungwe 95 9 11S 33 32 E
Rungwe □ 95 9 25S 33 32 E
Runka 89 12 28N 7 20 E
Runn 10 60 30N 15 40 E
Ruoqiang 62 38 55N 88 10 E
Rupa 52 27 15N 92 21 E
Rupanyup 74 36 36S 142 40 E
Rupar 48 31 2N 76 38 E
Rupat 56 1 45N 101 40 E
Rupert → 102 51 29N 78 45W
Rupert House = Fort Rupert 102 51 30N 78 40W
Rupsa 52 21 44N 89 30 E
Rupununi → 135 4 3N 58 35W
Rur → 30 51 20N 6 0 E
Rurrenabaque 136 14 30S 67 32W
Rus → 25 39 30N 2 30W
Rusambo 95 16 30S 32 4 E
Rusape 95 18 35S 32 8 E
Ruschuk = Ruse 34 43 48N 25 59 E
Ruse 34 43 48N 25 59 E
Ruşeţu 34 44 57N 27 14 E
Rushan 61 36 56N 121 30 E
Rushden 13 52 17N 0 37W
Rushford 118 43 48N 91 46W
Rushville, Ill., U.S.A. 116 40 6N 90 35W
Rushville, Ind., U.S.A. 117 39 38N 85 22W
Rushville, Nebr., U.S.A. 118 42 43N 102 28W
Rushworth 74 36 32S 145 1 E
Rusken 11 57 15N 14 20 E
Russas 138 4 55S 37 50W
Russell, Can. 109 50 50N 101 20W
Russell, N.Z. 80 35 16S 174 10 E

Russell, U.S.A. 118 38 56N 98 55W
Russell Is. 68 9 4S 159 12 E
Russell L., Man., Can. 109 56 15N 101 30W
Russell L., N.W.T., Can. 108 63 5N 115 44W
Russellkonda 50 19 57N 84 42 E
Russellville, Ala., U.S.A. 113 34 30N 87 44W
Russellville, Ark., U.S.A. 119 35 15N 93 8W
Russellville, Ky., U.S.A. 113 36 50N 86 50W
Russi 27 44 21N 12 1 E
Russian → 122 38 27N 123 8W
Russian S.F.S.R. □ 41 62 0N 105 0 E
Russiaville 117 40 25N 86 16W
Russkaya Polyana 40 53 47N 73 53 E
Russkoye Ustie 144 71 0N 149 0 E
Rustam 48 34 25N 72 13 E
Rustam Shahr 48 26 58N 66 6 E
Rustavi 39 41 30N 45 0 E
Rustenburg 96 25 41S 27 14 E
Ruston 119 32 30N 92 58W
Rutana 94 3 55S 30 0 E
Rute 23 37 19N 4 23W
Ruteng 57 8 35S 120 30 E
Ruth, Mich., U.S.A. 106 43 42N 82 45W
Ruth, Nev., U.S.A. 120 39 15N 115 1W
Rutherford 122 38 26N 122 24W
Rutherglen, Austral. 75 36 5S 146 29 E
Rutherglen, U.K. 14 55 50N 4 11W
Rutigliano 29 41 1N 17 0 E
Rutland Plains 72 15 38S 141 43 E
Rutledge → 109 61 4N 112 0W
Rutledge L. 109 61 33N 110 47W
Rutshuru 94 1 13S 29 25 E
Rutter 106 46 6N 80 40W
Ruurlo 16 52 5N 6 24 E
Ruvo di Púglia 29 41 7N 16 27 E
Ruvu 94 6 49S 38 43 E
Ruvu → 94 6 23S 38 52 E
Ruvuma □ 95 10 20S 36 0 E
Ruwaidha 46 23 40N 44 40 E
Ruwenzori 94 0 30N 29 55 E
Ruyigi 94 3 29S 30 15 E
Ruyuan 59 24 46N 113 16 E
Ruzayevka 37 54 4N 45 0 E
Ružomberok 32 49 3N 19 17 E
Rwanda ■ 94 2 0S 30 0 E
Ry 11 56 5N 9 45 E
Ryakhovo 34 44 0N 26 18 E
Ryan, L. 14 55 0N 5 2W
Ryazan 37 54 40N 39 40 E
Ryazhsk 37 53 45N 40 3 E
Rybache 40 46 40N 81 20 E
Rybinsk 37 58 5N 38 50 E
Rybinskoye Vdkhr. 37 58 30N 38 25 E
Rybnik 32 50 6N 18 32 E
Rybnitsa 38 47 45N 29 0 E
Rychwał 32 52 4N 18 10 E
Ryd 11 56 27N 14 42 E
Ryde 13 50 44N 1 9W
Ryderwood 122 46 23N 123 3W
Rydöbruk 11 56 58N 13 7 E
Rydsnäs 11 57 47N 15 9 E
Rydułtowy 32 50 4N 18 23 E
Rye 13 50 57N 0 46 E
Rye → 12 54 12N 0 53W
Rye Park 76 34 31S 148 56 E
Rye Patch Res. 120 40 38N 118 20W
Ryegate 120 46 21N 109 15W
Rylsk 36 51 36N 34 43 E
Rylstone 76 32 46S 149 58 E
Ryōhaku-Sanchi 65 36 9N 136 49 E
Rypin 32 53 3N 19 25 E
Ryūgasaki 65 35 54N 140 11 E
Ryūkyū Is. = Nansei-Shotō 63 26 30N 128 0 E
Rzeszów 32 50 5N 21 58 E
Rzhev 36 56 20N 34 20 E

S

Sa 54 18 34N 100 45 E
Sa Dec 55 10 20N 105 46 E
Sa-koi 52 19 54N 97 3 E
Sa'ad (Muharraqa) 44 31 28N 34 33 E
Sa'ādatābād 47 30 10N 53 5 E
Saale → 30 51 57N 11 56 E
Saaler Bodden 30 54 20N 12 25 E
Saalfeld 30 50 39N 11 21 E
Saane → 31 46 23N 7 18 E
Saar (Sarre) → 19 49 42N 6 34 E
Saarbrücken 31 49 15N 6 58 E
Saarburg 31 49 36N 6 32 E
Saaremaa 36 58 30N 22 30 E
Saarland □ 31 49 15N 7 0 E
Saarlouis 31 49 19N 6 45 E
Saba 127 17 42N 63 26W
Šabac 33 44 48N 19 42 E
Sabadell 24 41 28N 2 7 E
Sabae 65 35 57N 136 11 E
Sabagalet 56 1 36S 98 40 E
Sabah □ 56 6 0N 117 0 E
Sabak 55 3 46N 100 58 E
Sábana de la Mar 127 19 7N 69 24W
Sábanalarga 134 10 38N 74 55W
Sabang 56 5 50N 95 15 E
Sabará 139 19 55S 43 46W
Sabarania 57 2 5S 138 18 E
Sabari → 50 17 35N 81 16 E
Sabastiya 44 32 17N 35 12 E
Sabattis 115 44 6N 74 40W
Sabáudia 28 41 17N 13 2 E
Sabaya 136 19 1S 68 23W
Sabhah 87 27 9N 14 29 E
Sabie 97 25 10S 30 48 E
Sabina 117 39 29N 83 38W
Sabinal, Mexico 124 30 58N 107 25W
Sabinal, U.S.A. 119 29 20N 99 27W
Sabinal, Punta del 25 36 43N 2 44W
Sabinas 124 27 50N 101 10W
Sabinas → 124 27 37N 100 42W
Sabinas Hidalgo 124 26 33N 100 10W
Sabine 119 29 42N 93 54W
Sabine → 119 30 0N 93 35W
Sabine L. 119 29 50N 93 50W
Sabinópolis 139 18 40S 43 6W
Sabinov 32 49 6N 21 5 E
Sabirabad 39 40 5N 48 30 E
Sabkhat Tawurgha 87 31 48N 15 30 E
Sablayan 57 12 50N 120 50 E
Sable, C., Can. 103 43 29N 65 38W
Sable, C., U.S.A. 126 25 13N 81 0W
Sable I. 103 44 0N 60 0W
Sablé-sur-Sarthe 18 47 50N 0 20W
Sables-d'Olonne, Les 20 46 30N 1 45W
Sables, R. aux → 106 46 13N 82 3W
Saboeiro 138 6 32S 39 54W
Sabolev 41 54 20N 155 30 E
Sabor → 22 41 10N 7 7W
Sabou 88 12 1N 2 15W
Sabourin, L. 104 47 58N 77 41W
Sabrātah 87 32 47N 12 29 E
Sabria 87 33 22N 8 45 E
Sabrina Coast 143 68 0S 120 0 E
Sabugal 22 40 20N 7 5W
Sabula 116 42 5N 90 23W
Sabzevār 47 36 15N 57 40 E
Sabzvāran 47 28 45N 57 50 E
Sac City 116 42 26N 95 0W
Sacedón 24 40 29N 2 41W
Sachigo → 102 55 6N 88 58W
Sachigo, L. 102 53 50N 92 12W
Sachkhere 39 42 25N 43 28 E
Sacile 27 45 58N 12 30 E
Sackets Harbor 115 43 56N 76 7W
Säckingen 31 47 34N 7 56 E
Saco, Me., U.S.A. 113 43 30N 70 27W
Saco, Mont., U.S.A. 120 48 28N 107 19W
Sacramento, Brazil 139 19 53S 47 27W
Sacramento, U.S.A. 122 38 33N 121 30 E
Sacramento → 122 38 3N 121 56W
Sacramento Mts. 121 32 30N 105 30W
Sacramento Valley 122 39 0N 122 0W
Sacratif, Cabo 25 36 42N 3 28W
Sacré-Coeur-de-Jésus 105 48 14N 69 48W
Săcueni 34 47 20N 22 5 E
Sada 22 43 22N 8 15W
Sada-Misaki-Hantō 64 33 22N 132 1 E
Sádaba 24 42 19N 1 12W
Sadani 94 5 58S 38 35 E
Sadao 55 6 38N 100 26 E
Sadasivpet 50 17 38N 77 59 E
Sadd el Aali 90 23 54N 32 54 E
Saddle Mt. 122 45 58N 123 41W
Sade 89 11 22N 10 45 E
Sadiba 96 18 53S 23 1 E
Sadieville 117 38 23N 84 32W
Sadimi 95 9 25S 23 32 E
Sadiya 52 27 50N 95 40 E
Sado 63 38 0N 138 25 E
Sado → 23 38 29N 8 55W
Sado, Shima 63 38 15N 138 30 E
Sadon 39 42 52N 43 58 E
Sæby 11 57 21N 10 30 E
Saegerstown 114 41 42N 80 10W
Saelices 24 39 55N 2 49W
Safaga 90 26 42N 34 0 E
Safaha 90 26 25N 39 0 E
Safaniya 46 28 5N 48 50 E
Safata B. 68 14 0S 171 50W
Säffle 10 59 8N 12 55 E
Safford 121 32 50N 109 43W
Saffron Walden 13 52 2N 0 15 E
Safi, Jordan 44 31 2N 35 28 E
Safi, Moroc. 86 32 18N 9 20W
Safonovo 36 55 4N 33 16 E
Safranbolu 38 41 15N 32 41 E
Sag Harbor 115 40 59N 72 17W
Sag Sag 69 5 32S 148 23 E
Saga, Indon. 57 2 40S 132 55 E
Saga, Kōchi, Japan 64 33 5N 133 6 E
Saga, Saga, Japan 64 33 15N 130 16 E
Saga □ 64 33 15N 130 20 E
Sagaing □ 52 23 55N 95 56 E
Sagala 88 14 9N 6 38W
Sagami-Nada 65 34 58N 139 30 E
Sagami-Wan 65 35 15N 139 25 E
Sagamihara 65 35 33N 139 25 E
Saganoseki 64 33 15N 131 53 E
Sagara, India 51 14 14N 75 6 E
Sagara, Japan 65 34 41N 138 12 E
Sagara, L. 94 5 20S 31 0 E
Sagawa 64 33 28N 133 11 E
Saghīr, Zab al 46 35 10N 43 20 E
Sagil 62 50 15N 91 15 E
Saginaw 106 43 26N 83 55W
Saginaw B. 106 43 50N 83 40W
Sagleipie 88 7 0N 8 52W
Saglouc (Sugluk) 101 62 10N 74 40W
Sagŏ-ri 61 35 25N 126 49 E
Sagone 21 42 7N 8 42 E
Sagone, G. de 21 42 4N 8 40 E
Sagra, La 25 37 57N 2 35W
Sagres 23 37 0N 8 58W
Sagu 52 20 13N 94 46 E
Sagua la Grande 126 22 50N 80 10W
Saguache 121 38 10N 106 10W
Saguenay → 105 48 22N 71 0W
Sagunto 24 39 42N 0 18W
Sahaba 90 18 57N 30 25 E
Sahagún, Colomb. 134 8 57N 75 27W
Sahagún, Spain 22 42 18N 5 2W
Saham 44 32 42N 35 46 E
Sahand, Kūh-e 46 37 44N 46 27 E
Sahara 86 23 0N 5 0 E
Saharanpur 48 29 58N 77 33 E
Saharien Atlas 86 34 9N 3 29 E
Sahasinaka 97 21 49S 47 49 E
Sahaswan 49 28 5N 78 45 E
Sahel, Canal du 88 14 20N 6 0W
Sahibganj 49 25 12N 87 40 E
Sahiwal 48 30 45N 73 8 E
Sahtaneh → 108 59 2N 122 28W
Sahuaripa 124 29 0N 109 13W
Sahuarita 121 31 58N 110 59W
Sahuayo 124 20 4N 102 43W
Sahy 33 48 4N 18 55 E
Sai Buri 55 6 43N 101 39 E
Sai-Cinza 137 6 17S 57 42W
Saibai I. 69 9 25S 142 40 E
Sa'id Bundas 85 8 24N 24 48 E
Saïda 86 34 50N 0 11 E
Sa'īdabad 47 29 30N 55 45 E
Saïdia 86 35 5N 2 14W
Saidor 69 5 40S 146 29 E
Saidu 49 34 43N 72 24 E
Saighan 47 35 10N 67 55 E
Saignes 20 45 20N 2 31 E
Saigō 64 36 12N 133 20 E
Saigon = Phanh Bho Ho Chi Minh 55 10 46N 106 40 E
Saih-al-Malih 47 23 37N 58 31 E
Saihut 45 15 12N 51 10 E
Saijō, Ehime, Japan 64 33 55N 133 11 E
Saijō, Hiroshima, Japan 64 34 25N 132 45 E
Saiki 64 32 58N 131 51 E
Saillans 21 44 42N 5 12 E
Sailolof 57 1 7S 130 46 E
St. Abb's Head 14 55 55N 2 10W
St-Adalbert 105 46 51N 69 53W
St. Aegyd 33 47 52N 15 33 E
St-Affrique 20 43 57N 2 53 E
St-Agapitville 105 46 34N 71 26W
St-Agrève 21 45 0N 4 23 E
St-Aignan 18 47 16N 1 22 E
St. Albans 76 33 16S 150 59 E
St. Alban's 103 47 51N 55 50W
St. Albans, U.K. 13 51 44N 0 19W
St. Albans, Vt., U.S.A. 115 44 49N 73 7W
St. Albans, W. Va., U.S.A. 112 38 21N 81 50W
St. Alban's Head 13 50 34N 2 3W
St. Albert 108 53 37N 113 32W
St-Alexandre 105 47 41N 69 38W
St-Alexis-des-Monts 105 46 28N 73 8W
St-Amand 19 50 25N 3 26 E
St-Amand-en-Puisaye 19 47 32N 3 5 E
St-Amand-Mont-Rond 20 46 43N 2 30 E
St-Amarin 19 47 54N 7 0 E
St-Ambroise 105 48 33N 71 20W
St-Amour 21 46 26N 5 21 E
St-Anaclet 105 48 29N 68 26W
St-André-Avellin 104 45 43N 75 3W
St. André, C. 97 16 11S 44 27 E
St-André-de-Cubzac 20 44 59N 0 26W
St-André-de-l'Eure 18 48 54N 1 16 E
St-André-Est 105 45 34N 74 20W
St-André-les-Alpes 21 43 58N 6 30 E
St. Andrew's 103 47 45N 59 15W
St. Andrews, N.Z. 81 44 33S 171 10 E
St. Andrews, U.K. 14 56 20N 2 48W
St-Anicet 105 45 8N 74 22W
St. Ann B. 103 46 22N 60 25W
St. Anne, U.K. 18 49 43N 2 11W
St. Anne, U.S.A. 117 41 1N 87 43W
St. Ann's Bay 126 18 26N 77 15W
St-Anselme 105 46 37N 70 58W
St. Anthony, Can. 103 51 22N 55 35W
St. Anthony, U.S.A. 120 44 0N 111 40W
St-Antonin 105 47 46N 69 29W
St-Antonin-Noble-Val 20 44 10N 1 45 E
St-Apolline 105 46 48N 70 12W
St. Arnaud 74 36 40S 143 16 E
St. Arnaud Ra. 81 42 1S 172 53 E
St. Arthur 103 47 33N 67 46W
St. Asaph 12 53 15N 3 27W
St-Astier 20 45 8N 0 31 E
St-Aubert 105 47 11N 70 13W
St-Aubin-du-Cormier 18 48 15N 1 26W
St. Augustin 97 23 33S 43 46 E
St-Augustin-Saguenay 103 51 13N 58 38W
St. Augustine 113 29 52N 81 20W
St. Austell 13 50 20N 4 48W
St-Avold 19 49 6N 6 43 E
St-Barthélémy 105 46 11N 73 8W
St.-Barthélemy, I. 127 17 50N 62 50W
St-Basile-Sud 105 46 45N 71 49W
St. Bathans 81 44 53S 169 50 E
St. Bathan's Mt. 81 44 45S 169 45 E
St. Bee's Hd. 12 54 30N 3 38 E
St-Benoît-du-Sault 20 46 26N 1 24 E
St. Bernard, Col du Grand 31 45 53N 7 11 E
St. Boniface 109 49 53N 97 5W
St-Bonnet 21 44 40N 6 5 E
St-Brévin-les-Pins 18 47 14N 2 10W
St-Brice-en-Coglès 18 48 25N 1 22W
St. Bride's 103 46 56N 54 10W
St. Bride's B. 13 51 48N 5 15W
St-Brieuc 18 48 30N 2 46W
St-Bruno 105 48 28N 71 39W
St-Calais 18 47 55N 0 45 E
St-Casimir 105 46 40N 72 8W
St-Cast 18 48 37N 2 18W
St. Catharines 106 43 10N 79 15W
St. Catherines I. 113 31 35N 81 10W
St. Catherine's Pt. 13 50 34N 1 18W
St-Céré 20 44 51N 1 54 E
St.-Cergue 31 46 27N 6 10 E
St-Cernin 20 45 5N 2 25 E
St-Césaire 105 45 25N 73 0W
St-Chamond 21 45 28N 4 31 E
St. Charles, Ill., U.S.A. 117 41 55N 88 21W
St. Charles, Mich., U.S.A. 106 43 18N 84 9W
St. Charles, Mo., U.S.A. 116 38 46N 90 30W
St-Chély-d'Apcher 20 44 48N 3 17 E
St-Chinian 20 43 25N 2 56 E
St. Christopher (St. Kitts) 127 17 20N 62 40W
St-Chrysostôme 105 45 6N 73 46W
St-Ciers-sur-Gironde 20 45 17N 0 37W
St. Clair, Mich, U.S.A. 106 42 47N 82 27W
St. Clair, Mo., U.S.A. 116 38 21N 90 59W
St. Clair, Pa., U.S.A. 115 40 42N 76 12W
St. Clair, L. 106 42 30N 82 45W
St. Clairsville 114 40 5N 80 53W
St-Claud 20 45 54N 0 28 E
St. Claude 109 49 40N 98 20W
St-Claude 21 46 22N 5 52 E
St-Clet 105 45 21N 74 13W
St-Cloud 18 48 51N 2 12 E
St. Cloud, Fla., U.S.A. 113 28 15N 81 15W
St. Cloud, Minn., U.S.A. 118 45 30N 94 11W
St-Coeur de Marie 105 48 39N 71 43W
St-Côme 105 46 16N 73 47W
St. Cricq, C. 79 25 17S 113 6 E
St. Croix 127 17 45N 64 45W
St. Croix → 118 44 45N 92 50W
St. Croix Falls 118 45 18N 92 22W
St-Cyprien 20 42 37N 3 0 E
St-Cyr 21 43 11N 5 43 E
St-Cyrille-de-L'Islet 105 47 2N 70 17W
St. David 116 40 30N 90 3W
St. David's, Can. 103 48 12N 58 52W
St. David's, U.K. 13 51 54N 5 16W
St. David's Head 13 51 55N 5 16W
St-Denis 19 48 56N 2 22 E
St.-Denis 53 20 52S 55 27 E
St-Denis-d'Orques 18 48 2N 0 17W
St-Dié 19 48 17N 6 56 E
St-Dizier 19 48 40N 5 0 E
St-Donat-de-Montcalm 105 46 19N 74 13W
St-Egrève 21 45 14N 5 41 E
St. Elias, Mt. 100 60 14N 140 50W
St.Elias Mts. 108 60 33N 139 28W

Place	Page	Lat.	Long.
St.-Elie	**135**	4 49N	53 17W
St. Elmo	**117**	39 2N	88 51W
St-Éloi	**105**	48 2N	69 14W
St-Élouthère	**105**	47 30N	69 15W
St-Éloy-les-Mines	**20**	46 10N	2 51 E
St-Émilion	**20**	44 53N	0 9W
St-Éphrem-de-Tring	**105**	46 2N	70 59W
St-Étienne	**21**	45 27N	4 22 E
St-Étienne-de-Tinée	**21**	44 16N	6 56 E
St. Eugène	**107**	45 30N	74 28W
St-Eusèbe	**105**	47 33N	68 55W
St-Eustache	**105**	45 33N	73 54W
St. Eustatius	**127**	17 20N	63 0W
St-Fabien	**105**	48 18N	68 52W
St-Félicien	**105**	48 40N	72 25W
St-Félix-de-Valois	**105**	46 10N	73 26W
St-Florent	**21**	42 41N	9 18 E
St-Florent-sur-Cher	**19**	46 59N	2 15 E
St-Florentin	**19**	48 0N	3 45 E
St-Flour	**20**	45 2N	3 6 E
St-Fons	**21**	45 42N	4 52 E
St. Francis	**118**	39 48N	101 47W
St. Francis →	**119**	34 38N	90 36W
St. Francis, C.	**96**	34 14S	24 49 E
St-Francis, L.	**105**	45 10N	74 22W
St. Francisville, U.S.A.	**117**	38 36N	87 39W
St. Francisville, U.S.A.	**119**	30 48N	91 22W
St-François	**105**	46 48N	70 49W
St-François →	**105**	46 7N	72 55W
St-François-du-Lac	**105**	46 5N	72 50W
St-François, L.	**105**	45 10N	74 22W
St-Fulgence	**105**	48 27N	70 54W
St-Fulgent	**18**	46 50N	1 10W
St-Gabriel-de-Brandon	**105**	46 17N	73 24W
St-Gabriel-de-Rimouski	**105**	48 25N	68 10W
St-Gaudens	**20**	43 6N	0 44 E
St-Gédéon	**105**	48 30N	71 46W
St-Gédéon-de-Beauce	**105**	45 45N	70 40W
St-Gengoux-le-National	**21**	46 37N	4 40 E
St-Geniez-d'Olt	**20**	44 27N	2 58 E
St. George, Austral.	**73**	28 1S	148 30 E
St. George, N.B., Can.	**103**	45 11N	66 50W
St. George, Ont., Can.	**106**	43 15N	80 15W
St. George, S.C., U.S.A.	**113**	33 13N	80 37W
St. George, Utah, U.S.A.	**121**	37 10N	113 35W
St. George, C., Can.	**103**	48 30N	59 16W
St. George, C., P.N.G.	**69**	4 49S	152 53 E
St. George, C., U.S.A.	**113**	29 36N	85 2W
St. George Ra.	**78**	18 40S	125 0 E
St-Georges	**16**	50 37N	5 20 E
St. George's	**103**	48 26N	58 31W
St. Georges	**102**	46 42N	72 35W
St-Georges	**105**	46 8N	70 40W
St. Georges	**135**	4 0N	52 0W
St. George's	**127**	12 5N	61 43W
St. George's B.	**103**	48 24N	58 53W
Saint George's Channel	**69**	4 10S	152 20 E
St-Georges-de-Didonne	**20**	45 36N	1 0W
St-Georges-de-Cacouna	**105**	47 55N	69 30W
St. Georges Head	**76**	35 12S	150 42 E
St-Georges-Ouest	**105**	46 7N	70 40W
St-Gérard	**105**	45 46N	71 25W
St-Germain	**19**	48 53N	2 5 E
St-Germain-Lembron	**20**	45 27N	3 14 E
St-Germain-de-Calberte	**20**	44 13N	3 48 E
St-Germain-de-Grantham	**105**	45 50N	72 34W
St-Germain-des-Fossés	**20**	46 12N	3 26 E
St-Germain-du-Plain	**19**	46 42N	4 58 E
St-Germain-Laval	**21**	45 50N	4 1 E
St-Gers	**20**	45 18N	0 37W
St-Gervais, Haute Savoie, France	**21**	45 53N	6 42 E
St-Gervais, Puy de Dôme, France	**20**	46 4N	2 50 E
St-Gildas, Pte. de	**18**	47 8N	2 14W
St-Gilles-Croix-de-Vie	**18**	46 41N	1 55W
St-Gilles-du-Gard	**21**	43 40N	4 26 E
St-Girons	**20**	42 59N	1 8 E
St. Goar	**31**	50 12N	7 43 E
St-Gualtier	**18**	46 39N	1 26 E
St-Guénolé	**18**	47 49N	4 23W
St-Guillaume-d'Upton	**105**	45 53N	72 46W
St. Helena	**120**	38 29N	122 30W
St. Helena, I.	**129**	15 55S	5 44W
St Helena, Mt.	**122**	38 40N	122 36W
St. Helenabaai	**96**	32 40S	18 10 E
St. Helens, Austral.	**72**	41 20S	148 15 E
St. Helens, U.K.	**12**	53 28N	2 44W
St. Helens, U.S.A.	**122**	45 55N	122 50W
St. Helens, Mt.	**122**	46 12N	122 11W
St. Helier	**18**	49 11N	2 6W
St-Henri	**105**	46 42N	71 4W
St-Hilaire	**18**	48 35N	1 7W
St-Hilarion	**105**	47 34N	70 24W
St-Hippolyte	**19**	47 20N	6 50 E
St-Hippolyte-du-Fort	**20**	43 58N	3 52 E
St-Honoré, Can.	**105**	48 32N	71 5W
St-Honoré, France	**19**	46 54N	3 50 E
St-Hubert	**16**	50 2N	5 23 E
St-Hubert-de-Témiscouata	**105**	47 49N	69 9W
St-Hyacinthe	**105**	45 40N	72 58W
St. Ignace	**106**	45 53N	84 43W
St. Ignace I.	**102**	48 45N	88 0W
St. Ignatius	**120**	47 19N	114 8W
St-Imier	**31**	47 9N	6 58 E
St-Isidore	**105**	45 20N	73 42W
St. Ives, Cambs., U.K.	**13**	52 20N	0 5W
St. Ives, Cornwall, U.K.	**13**	50 13N	5 29W
St-Jacques	**105**	45 57N	73 34W
St-James	**18**	48 31N	1 20W
St. James, Mich., U.S.A.	**106**	45 45N	85 31W
St. James, Minn., U.S.A.	**118**	43 57N	94 40W
St. James, Mo., U.S.A.	**116**	38 0N	91 37W
St. Jean	**105**	45 20N	73 20W
St-Jean	**21**	45 30N	5 10 E
St-Jean →	**103**	50 17N	64 20W
St. Jean Baptiste	**109**	49 15N	97 20W
St-Jean-d'Angély	**20**	45 57N	0 31W
St-Jean-de-Maurienne	**21**	45 16N	6 21 E
St-Jean-de-Dieu	**105**	48 0N	69 3W
St-Jean-de-Luz	**20**	43 23N	1 39W
St-Jean-de-Monts	**18**	46 47N	2 4W
St-Jean-du-Gard	**20**	44 7N	3 52 E
St-Jean-en-Royans	**21**	45 1N	5 18 E
St-Jean, L.	**105**	48 40N	72 0W
St-Jean-Port-Joli	**105**	47 15N	70 13W
St-Jérôme, Qué., Can.	**105**	45 47N	74 0W
St-Jérôme, Qué., Can.	**105**	48 26N	71 53W
St-Joachim	**105**	47 4N	70 50W
St. Joe	**117**	41 19N	84 54W
St. John, Can.	**103**	45 20N	66 8W
St. John, Kans., U.S.A.	**119**	37 59N	98 45W
St. John, N.D., U.S.A.	**118**	48 58N	99 40W
St. John →	**103**	45 15N	66 4W
St. John, C.	**103**	50 0N	55 32W
St. John's, Antigua	**127**	17 6N	61 51W
St. John's, Can.	**103**	47 35N	52 40W
St. Johns, Ariz., U.S.A.	**121**	34 31N	109 26W
St. Johns, Mich., U.S.A.	**117**	43 0N	84 31W
St. John's →	**113**	30 20N	81 30W
St. Johnsbury	**115**	44 25N	72 1W
St. Johnsville	**115**	43 0N	74 43W
St.-Joseph	**68**	20 27S	166 36 E
St. Joseph, Ill, U.S.A.	**117**	40 7N	88 2W
St. Joseph, La., U.S.A.	**119**	31 55N	91 15W
St. Joseph, Mich., U.S.A.	**117**	42 5N	86 30W
St. Joseph, Mo., U.S.A.	**116**	39 46N	94 50W
St. Joseph →	**117**	42 7N	86 30W
St-Joseph-de-Beauce	**105**	46 18N	70 53W
St-Joseph-de-la-Rivière-Bleue	**105**	47 26N	69 3W
St-Joseph-de-Sorel	**105**	46 2N	73 7W
St. Joseph, I.	**106**	46 12N	83 58W
St. Joseph, L.	**102**	51 10N	90 35W
St-Jovite	**104**	46 8N	74 38W
St-Jude	**105**	45 46N	72 59W
St-Juéry	**20**	43 55N	2 12 E
St-Julien	**21**	46 8N	6 5 E
St-Julien-Chapteuil	**21**	45 2N	4 4 E
St-Julien-du-Sault	**19**	48 1N	3 17 E
St-Junien	**20**	45 53N	0 55 E
St-Just-en-Chaussée	**19**	49 30N	2 25 E
St-Just-en-Chevalet	**20**	45 55N	3 50 E
St-Justin	**20**	43 59N	0 14W
St-Justine	**105**	46 24N	70 21W
St. Kilda	**81**	45 53S	170 31 E
St. Kilda	**6**	57 9N	8 34W
St. Kitts	**127**	17 20N	62 40W
St. Laurent	**109**	50 25N	97 58W
St-Laurent	**135**	5 29N	54 3W
St-Laurent-du-Pont	**21**	45 23N	5 45 E
St-Laurent-en-Grandvaux	**21**	46 35N	5 58 E
St. Lawrence, Austral.	**72**	22 16S	149 31 E
St. Lawrence, Can.	**103**	46 54N	55 23W
St. Lawrence →	**103**	49 30N	66 0W
St. Lawrence, Gulf of	**103**	48 25N	62 0W
St. Lawrence, I.	**100**	63 0N	170 0W
St. Leonard	**103**	47 12N	67 58W
St-Léonard-de-Noblat	**20**	45 49N	1 29 E
St-Léonard-de-Portneuf	**105**	46 53N	71 55W
St. Lewis →	**103**	52 26N	56 11W
St-Lô	**18**	49 7N	1 5W
St-Louis	**88**	16 8N	16 27W
St. Louis, Mich., U.S.A.	**106**	43 27N	84 38W
St. Louis, Mo., U.S.A.	**116**	38 40N	90 12W
St. Louis →	**118**	47 15N	92 45W
St-Loup-sur-Semouse	**19**	47 53N	6 16 E
St-Luc	**105**	45 22N	73 18W
St. Lucia ■	**127**	14 0N	60 50W
St. Lucia, C.	**97**	28 32S	32 29 E
St. Lucia Channel	**127**	14 15N	61 0W
St. Lucia, Lake	**97**	28 5S	32 30 E
St-Ludger	**105**	45 45N	70 42W
St. Lunaire-Griquet	**103**	51 31N	55 28W
St. Maarten	**127**	18 0N	63 5W
St-Magloire	**105**	46 35N	70 17W
St-Maixent-l'École	**20**	46 24N	0 12W
St-Malo	**18**	48 39N	2 1W
St-Malo, G. de	**18**	48 50N	2 30W
St-Mandrier	**21**	43 4N	5 56 E
St-Marc	**127**	19 10N	72 41W
St-Marcellin	**21**	45 9N	5 20 E
St-Marcouf, Îs.	**18**	49 30N	1 10W
St. Maries	**120**	47 17N	116 34W
St-Martin, Charente-M., France	**20**	46 12N	1 22W
St-Martin, Pas-de-Calais, France	**19**	50 42N	1 38 E
St-Martin, I.	**127**	18 0N	63 0W
St. Martin L.	**109**	51 40N	98 30W
St-Martin-Vésubie	**21**	44 4N	7 15 E
St. Martins	**103**	45 22N	65 34W
St. Martinsville	**119**	30 10N	91 50W
St-Martory	**20**	43 9N	0 56 E
St. Mary B.	**103**	46 50N	53 50W
St. Mary Is.	**51**	13 20N	74 35 E
St. Mary, Mt.	**69**	8 8S	147 2 E
St. Mary Pk.	**73**	31 32S	138 34 E
St. Marys, N.S.W., Austral.	**76**	33 44S	150 49 E
St. Marys, Tas., Austral.	**72**	41 35S	148 11 E
St. Marys, Can.	**106**	43 20N	81 10W
St. Mary's	**13**	49 55N	6 17W
St. Marys	**116**	37 53N	89 57W
St. Mary's	**117**	40 33N	84 20W
St. Marys	**114**	41 27N	78 33W
St. Marys Bay	**103**	44 25N	66 10W
St. Mary's, C.	**103**	46 50N	54 12W
St-Mathieu, Pte. de	**18**	48 20N	4 45W
St. Matthews	**117**	38 15N	85 39W
St. Matthias Grp.	**69**	1 30S	150 0 E
St-Maur-des-Fossés	**19**	48 48N	2 30 E
St-Maurice →	**105**	46 21N	72 31W
St-Maurice, Parc Prov. du	**105**	47 5N	73 15W
St-Médard-de-Guizières	**20**	45 1N	0 4W
St-Méen-le-Grand	**18**	48 11N	2 12W
St. Meinrad	**117**	38 10N	86 49W
St. Michaels	**121**	35 38N	109 5W
St. Michael's Mt.	**13**	50 7N	5 30W
St-Michel	**21**	45 15N	6 29 E
St-Michel-des-Saints	**105**	46 41N	73 55W
St-Mihiel	**19**	48 54N	5 30 E
St-Nazaire, Can.	**105**	45 44N	72 37W
St-Nazaire, France	**18**	47 17N	2 12W
St. Neots	**13**	52 14N	0 16W
St-Nicolas-de-Port	**19**	48 38N	6 18 E
St-Omer, Can.	**105**	47 3N	69 43W
St-Omer, France	**19**	50 45N	2 15 E
St. Ouen	**19**	48 50N	2 20 E
St-Ouen	**19**	50 2N	2 7 E
St-Ours	**105**	45 53N	73 9W
St-Pacome	**105**	47 24N	69 58W
St-Palais	**20**	45 40N	1 8W
St-Pamphile	**105**	46 58N	69 48W
St-Pardoux-la-Rivière	**20**	45 29N	0 45 E
St. Paris	**117**	40 8N	83 58W
St. Pascal	**105**	47 32N	69 48W
St-Patrice, L.	**104**	46 22N	77 20W
St. Paul, Can.	**108**	54 0N	111 17W
St. Paul, Ind. Oc.	**53**	30 40S	77 34 E
St. Paul, Ind., U.S.A.	**117**	39 33N	85 38W
St. Paul, Minn., U.S.A.	**118**	44 54N	93 5W
St. Paul, Nebr., U.S.A.	**118**	41 15N	98 30W
St-Paul-de-Fenouillet	**20**	42 50N	2 28 E
St-Paul-de-Montmigny	**105**	46 44N	70 22W
St-Paul-du-Nord	**105**	48 34N	69 14W
St. Paul, I.	**103**	47 12N	60 9W
St-Paulin	**105**	46 25N	73 1W
St-Péray	**21**	44 57N	4 50 E
St-Père-en-Retz	**18**	47 11N	2 2W
St. Peter	**118**	44 21N	93 57W
St. Peter Port	**18**	49 27N	2 31W
St. Peters, N.S., Can.	**103**	45 40N	60 53W
St. Peters, P.E.I., Can.	**103**	46 25N	62 35W
St. Petersburg	**113**	27 45N	82 40W
St-Philbert-de-Grand-Lieu	**18**	47 2N	1 39W
St-Philemon	**105**	46 41N	70 27W
St-Pie	**105**	45 30N	72 54W
St Pierre	**103**	46 46N	56 12W
St-Pierre-d'Oléron	**20**	45 57N	1 19W
St-Pierre-Église	**18**	49 40N	1 24W
St-Pierre-en-Port	**18**	49 48N	0 30 E
St-Pierre et Miquelon □	**103**	46 55N	56 10W
St. Pierre, I.	**53**	9 20S	46 0 E
St-Pierre, L., Qué., Can.	**105**	50 8N	68 26W
St-Pierre, L., Qué., Can.	**105**	46 12N	72 52W
St-Pierre-le-Moûtier	**19**	46 47N	3 7 E
St.-Pierre-sur-Dives	**18**	49 2N	0 1W
St.-Pol	**19**	50 21N	2 20 E
St-Pol-de-Léon	**18**	48 41N	4 0W
St-Pol-sur-Mer	**19**	51 1N	2 20 E
St-Pons	**20**	43 30N	2 45 E
St-Pourçain-sur-Sioule	**20**	46 18N	3 18 E
St-Prime	**105**	48 35N	72 20W
St-Quay-Portrieux	**18**	48 39N	2 51W
St-Quentin	**19**	49 50N	3 16 E
St-Rambert-d'Albon	**21**	45 17N	4 49 E
St-Raphaël, Can.	**105**	46 48N	70 45W
St-Raphaël, France	**21**	43 25N	6 46 E
St-Raymond	**105**	46 54N	71 50W
St. Regis, Mont., U.S.A.	**120**	47 20N	115 3W
St. Regis, N.Y., U.S.A.	**115**	44 39N	74 34W
St-Rémi	**105**	45 16N	73 37W
St-Rémy-de-Provence	**21**	43 48N	4 50 E
St-Renan	**18**	48 26N	4 37W
St-Roch	**105**	47 18N	70 12W
St-Romuald	**105**	46 46N	71 20W
St-Saëns	**18**	49 41N	1 16 E
St-Sauveur-en-Puisaye	**19**	47 37N	3 12 E
St-Sauveur-le-Vicomte	**18**	49 23N	1 32W
St-Savin	**20**	46 34N	0 50 E
St-Savinien	**20**	45 53N	0 42W
St-Sébastien	**105**	45 47N	70 58W
St. Sébastien, C.	**97**	12 26S	48 44 E
St-Seine-l'Abbaye	**19**	47 26N	4 47 E
St-Sernin	**20**	43 54N	2 35 E
St-Servan-sur-Mer	**18**	48 38N	2 0W
St-Sever	**20**	43 46N	0 34W
St-Sever-Calvados	**18**	48 50N	1 3W
St-Siméon	**105**	47 51N	69 54W
St-Simon-de-Rimouski	**105**	48 12N	69 3W
St. Stephen	**103**	45 16N	67 17W
St-Sulpice-Laurière	**20**	46 3N	1 29 E
St-Sulpice-la-Pointe	**20**	43 46N	1 41 E
St-Thégonnec	**18**	48 31N	3 57W
St. Thomas, Can.	**106**	42 45N	81 10W
St. Thomas, W. Indies	**127**	18 21N	64 55W
St-Tite	**105**	46 45N	72 34W
St-Tite-des-Caps	**105**	47 8N	70 47W
St-Tropez	**21**	43 17N	6 38 E
St. Troud = Sint Truiden	**16**	50 48N	5 10 E
St-Urbain	**105**	47 33N	70 32W
St-Vaast-la-Hougue	**18**	49 35N	1 17W
St-Valéry	**19**	50 10N	1 38 E
St-Valéry-en-Caux	**18**	49 52N	0 43 E
St-Vallier	**21**	45 11N	4 50 E
St-Vallier-de-Thiey	**21**	43 42N	6 51 E
St-Varent	**18**	46 53N	0 13W
St. Vincent	**128**	18 0N	26 1W
St. Vincent ■	**127**	13 10N	61 10W
St-Vincent C.	**93**	21 58S	43 20 E
St-Vincent-de-Tyrosse	**20**	43 39N	1 18W
St. Vincent, G.	**73**	35 0S	138 0 E
St. Vincent Passage	**127**	13 30N	61 0W
St-Vith	**16**	50 17N	6 9 E
St-Yrieux-la-Perche	**20**	45 31N	1 12 E
Ste-Adèle	**105**	45 57N	74 7W
Ste-Adresse	**18**	49 31N	0 5 E
Ste-Agathe	**105**	46 23N	71 25W
Ste-Agathe-des-Monts	**105**	46 3N	74 17W
Ste Anne de Beaupré	**105**	47 2N	70 58W
Ste-Anne-des-Monts	**103**	49 8N	66 30W
Ste-Anne-du-Lac	**104**	46 48N	75 25W
Ste-Blandine	**105**	48 22N	68 28W
Ste-Claire	**105**	46 36N	70 51W
Ste-Croix, Can.	**105**	46 38N	71 44W
Ste-Croix, Switz.	**19**	46 49N	6 34W
Ste-Énimie	**20**	44 22N	3 26 E
Ste-Famille	**105**	46 58N	70 58W
Ste-Foy	**105**	46 47N	71 17W
Ste-Foy-la-Grande	**20**	44 50N	0 13 E
Ste-Françoise	**105**	48 6N	69 4W
Ste. Genevieve	**116**	37 59N	90 2W
Ste-Hermine	**20**	46 32N	1 4W

Ste-Livrade-sur-Lot	**20**	44 24N	0 36 E
Ste-Marguerite →	**103**	50 9N	66 36W
Ste Marie	**127**	14 48N	61 1W
Ste-Marie-aux-Mines	**19**	48 10N	7 12 E
Ste. Marie, C.	**97**	25 36S	45 8 E
Ste-Marie de la Madeleine	**105**	46 26N	71 0W
Ste. Marie, Î.	**97**	16 50S	49 55 E
Ste-Maure-de-Touraine	**18**	47 7N	0 37 E
Ste-Maxime	**21**	43 19N	6 39 E
Ste-Menehould	**19**	49 5N	4 54 E
Ste-Mère-Église	**18**	49 24N	1 19W
Ste-Monique	**105**	48 44N	71 51W
Ste-Pudentienne	**105**	45 28N	72 40W
Ste-Rose	**127**	16 20N	61 45W
Ste.-Rose du lac	**109**	51 4N	99 30W
Ste-Sabine	**105**	45 15N	73 2W
Ste-Thècle	**105**	46 49N	72 31W
Saintes	**20**	45 45N	0 37W
Saintes, Île des	**127**	15 50N	61 35W
Saintes-Maries-de-la-Mer	**21**	43 26N	4 26 E
Saintonge	**20**	45 40N	0 50W
Sairecábur, Cerro	**140**	22 43S	67 54W
Sairs, L.	**104**	46 49N	78 26W
Saitama □	**65**	36 0N	139 0 E
Saito	**64**	32 3N	131 24 E
Sajama	**136**	18 7S	69 0W
Sajum	**49**	33 20N	79 0 E
Sakai	**65**	34 30N	135 30 E
Sakaide	**64**	34 15N	133 50 E
Sakaiminato	**64**	35 38N	133 11 E
Sakākah	**46**	30 0N	40 8 E
Sakami, L.	**102**	53 15N	77 0W
Sâkâne, 'Erg i-n	**86**	20 30N	1 30W
Sakania	**95**	12 43S	28 30 E
Sakarya →	**38**	41 7N	30 39 E
Sakchu	**61**	40 23N	125 2 E
Sakeny →	**97**	20 0S	45 25 E
Sakété	**89**	6 40N	2 45 E
Sakhalin, Ostrov	**41**	51 0N	143 0 E
Sakhi Gopal	**50**	19 58N	85 50 E
Sakhnin	**44**	32 52N	35 12 E
Saki	**38**	45 9N	33 34 E
Sakiai	**36**	54 59N	23 0 E
Sakołow Małopolski	**32**	50 10N	22 9 E
Sakon Nakhon	**54**	17 10N	104 9 E
Sakrand	**48**	26 10N	68 15 E
Sakri	**50**	21 2N	74 20 E
Sakskøbing	**11**	54 49N	11 39 E
Saku	**65**	36 17N	138 31 E
Sakuma	**65**	35 3N	137 49 E
Sakura	**65**	35 43N	140 14 E
Sakurai	**65**	34 30N	135 51 E
Sal →	**39**	47 31N	40 45 E
Sala	**10**	59 58N	16 35 E
Sala Consilina	**29**	40 23N	15 35 E
Sala-y-Gómez	**67**	26 28S	105 28W
Salaberry-de-Valleyfield	**105**	45 15N	74 8W
Salada, La	**124**	24 30N	111 30W
Saladas	**140**	28 15S	58 40W
Saladillo	**140**	35 40S	59 55W
Salado →, Buenos Aires, Argent.	**140**	35 44S	57 22W
Salado →, La Pampa, Argent.	**142**	37 30S	67 0W
Salado →, Río Negro, Argent.	**142**	41 34S	65 3W
Salado →, Santa Fe, Argent.	**140**	31 40S	60 41W
Salado →, Mexico	**124**	26 52N	99 19W
Salaga	**89**	8 31N	0 31W
Salala, Liberia	**88**	6 42N	10 7W
Salala, Sudan	**90**	21 17N	36 16 E
Salālah	**45**	16 56N	53 59 E
Salamanca, Chile	**140**	31 46S	70 59W
Salamanca, Spain	**22**	40 58N	5 39W
Salamanca, U.S.A.	**114**	42 10N	78 42W
Salamanca □	**22**	40 57N	5 40W
Salamina	**134**	5 25N	75 29W
Salamis	**35**	37 56N	23 30 E
Salamonie, Res.	**117**	40 45N	85 35W
Salar de Atacama	**140**	23 30S	68 25W
Salar de Uyuni	**136**	20 30S	67 45W
Sălard	**34**	47 12N	22 3 E
Salas	**22**	43 25N	6 15W
Salas de los Infantes	**24**	42 2N	3 17W
Salatiga	**57**	7 19S	110 30 E
Salaverry	**136**	8 15S	79 0W
Salawati	**57**	1 7S	130 52 E
Salawe	**94**	3 17S	32 56 E
Salayar	**57**	6 7S	120 30 E
Salazar →	**24**	42 40N	1 20W
Salbris	**19**	47 25N	2 3 E
Salcombe	**13**	50 14N	3 47W
Saldaña	**22**	42 32N	4 48W
Saldanha	**96**	33 0S	17 58 E
Saldanhabaai	**96**	33 6S	18 0 E
Saldus	**36**	56 38N	22 30 E
Sale	**75**	38 6S	147 6 E
Salé	**86**	34 3N	6 48W
Sale	**12**	53 26N	2 19W
Salebabu	**57**	3 55N	126 40 E
Sālehābād	**47**	35 40N	61 2 E
Salekhard	**40**	66 30N	66 35 E
Salem, India	**51**	11 40N	78 11 E
Salem, Ill., U.S.A.	**116**	38 38N	88 57W
Salem, Ind., U.S.A.	**117**	38 38N	86 6W
Salem, Mass., U.S.A.	**115**	42 29N	70 53W
Salem, Mo., U.S.A.	**119**	37 40N	91 30W
Salem, N.J., U.S.A.	**112**	39 34N	75 29W
Salem, Ohio, U.S.A.	**114**	40 52N	80 50W
Salem, Oreg., U.S.A.	**120**	45 0N	123 0W
Salem, S.D., U.S.A.	**118**	43 44N	97 23W
Salem, Va., U.S.A.	**112**	37 19N	80 8W
Salemi	**28**	37 49N	12 47 E
Salernes	**21**	43 34N	6 15 E
Salerno	**29**	40 40N	14 44 E
Salerno, G. di	**29**	40 35N	14 45 E
Salfit	**44**	32 5N	35 11 E
Salford	**12**	53 30N	2 17W
Salgir →	**38**	45 38N	35 1 E
Salgótarján	**33**	48 5N	19 47 E
Salgueiro	**138**	8 4S	39 6W
Salies-de-Béarn	**20**	43 28N	0 56W
Salin	**52**	20 35N	94 40 E
Salina, Italy	**29**	38 35N	14 50 E
Salina, U.S.A.	**118**	38 50N	97 40W
Salina Cruz	**125**	16 10N	95 10W
Salinas, Brazil	**139**	16 10S	42 10W
Salinas, Chile	**140**	23 31S	69 29W
Salinas, Ecuador	**134**	2 10S	80 58W
Salinas, U.S.A.	**122**	36 40N	121 41W
Salinas →, Mexico	**125**	16 28N	90 31W
Salinas →, U.S.A.	**122**	36 45N	121 48W
Salinas Ambargasta	**140**	29 0S	65 0W
Salinas, B. de	**126**	11 4N	85 45W
Salinas, Cabo de	**25**	39 16N	3 4 E
Salinas (de Hidalgo)	**124**	22 30N	101 40W
Salinas Grandes	**140**	30 0S	65 0W
Salinas, Pampa de las	**140**	31 58S	66 42W
Saline	**106**	42 12N	83 49W
Saline →, U.S.A.	**118**	38 51N	97 30W
Saline →, U.S.A.	**119**	33 10N	92 8W
Salinópolis	**138**	0 40S	47 20W
Salins	**19**	46 57N	5 53 E
Salins-les-Bains	**19**	46 58N	5 52 E
Salir	**23**	37 14N	8 2W
Salisbury, N.S.W., Austral.	**77**	32 11S	151 33 E
Salisbury, S. Australia, Austral.	**73**	34 46S	138 40 E
Salisbury, U.K.	**13**	51 4N	1 48W
Salisbury, Md., U.S.A.	**112**	38 20N	75 38W
Salisbury, Mo., U.S.A.	**116**	39 25N	92 48W
Salisbury, N.C., U.S.A.	**113**	35 20N	80 29W
Salisbury, Zimb.-Rhod.	**95**	17 43S	31 2 E
Salisbury Plain	**13**	51 13N	1 50W
Săliște	**34**	45 45N	23 56 E
Salitre →	**138**	9 29S	40 39W
Salka	**89**	10 20N	4 58 E
Salle, La	**116**	41 20N	89 6W
Sallent	**24**	41 49N	1 54 E
Salles-Curan	**20**	44 11N	2 48 E
Salling	**11**	56 40N	8 55 E
Sallisaw	**119**	35 26N	94 45W
Sallom Junction	**90**	19 17N	37 6 E
Salmerón	**24**	40 33N	2 29W
Salmo	**108**	49 10N	117 20W
Salmon	**120**	45 12N	113 56W
Salmon →, Can.	**108**	54 3N	122 40W
Salmon →, U.S.A.	**120**	45 51N	116 46W
Salmon Arm	**108**	50 40N	119 15W
Salmon Falls	**120**	42 48N	114 59W
Salmon Gums	**79**	32 59S	121 38 E
Salmon Res.	**103**	48 05N	56 00W
Salmon River Mts.	**120**	45 0N	114 30W
Salo	**9**	60 22N	23 10 E
Salò	**26**	45 37N	10 32 E
Salobreña	**23**	36 44N	3 35W
Salome	**123**	33 51N	113 37W
Salon-de-Provence	**21**	43 39N	5 6 E
Salonica = Thessaloníki	**35**	40 38N	23 0 E
Salonta	**34**	46 49N	21 42 E
Salop □	**13**	52 36N	2 45W
Salor →	**23**	39 39N	7 3W
Salou, Cabo	**24**	41 3N	1 10 E
Salsacate	**140**	31 20S	65 5W
Salses	**20**	42 50N	2 55 E
Salsette I.	**50**	19 5N	72 50 E
Salsk	**39**	46 28N	41 30 E
Salso →	**29**	37 6N	13 55 E
Salsomaggiore	**26**	44 48N	9 59 E
Salt →, Can.	**108**	60 0N	112 25W
Salt →, Ariz., U.S.A.	**121**	33 23N	112 18W
Salt →, Mo., U.S.A.	**116**	39 29N	91 5W
Salt Creek	**73**	36 8S	139 38 E
Salt Fork →	**119**	36 37N	97 7W
Salt Lake City	**120**	40 45N	111 58W
Salt Range	**48**	32 30N	72 25 E
Salta	**140**	24 57S	65 25W
Salta □	**140**	24 48S	65 30W
Saltcoats	**14**	55 38N	4 47W
Saltee Is.	**15**	52 7N	6 37W
Saltfjorden	**8**	67 15N	14 10 E
Saltholm	**11**	55 38N	12 43 E
Salthólmavík	**8**	65 24N	21 57W
Saltillo	**124**	25 30N	100 57W
Salto, Argent.	**140**	34 20S	60 15W
Salto, Uruguay	**140**	31 27S	57 50W
Salto da Divisa	**139**	16 0S	39 57W
Salton City	**123**	33 29N	115 51W
Salton Sea	**123**	33 20N	115 50W
Saltpond	**89**	5 15N	1 3W
Saltsjöbaden	**11**	59 15N	18 20 E
Saltspring	**108**	48 54N	123 37W
Saltville	**112**	36 53N	81 46W
Saluda →	**113**	34 0N	81 4W
Salûm	**90**	31 31N	25 7 E
Salûm, Khâlig el	**90**	31 30N	25 9 E
Salur	**50**	18 27N	83 18 E
Salut, Îs. du	**135**	5 15N	52 35W
Saluzzo	**26**	44 39N	7 29 E
Salvación, B.	**142**	50 50S	75 10W
Salvador, Brazil	**139**	13 0S	38 30W
Salvador, Can.	**109**	52 10N	109 32W
Salvador, L.	**119**	29 46N	90 16W
Salvaterra	**138**	0 46S	48 31W
Salvaterra de Magos	**23**	39 1N	8 47W
Salvisa	**117**	37 54N	84 51W
Sálvora, Isla	**22**	42 30N	8 58W
Salwa	**47**	24 45N	50 55 E
Salween →	**52**	16 31N	97 37 E
Salyersville	**112**	37 45N	83 4W
Salza →	**33**	47 40N	14 43 E
Salzach →	**33**	48 12N	12 56 E
Salzburg	**33**	47 48N	13 2 E
Salzgitter	**30**	52 13N	10 22 E
Salzwedel	**30**	52 50N	11 11 E
Sam Neua	**54**	20 29N	104 0 E
Sam Ngao	**54**	17 18N	99 0 E
Sam Rayburn Res.	**119**	31 15N	94 20W
Sam Son	**54**	19 44N	105 54 E
Sam Teu	**54**	19 59N	104 38 E
Sama	**40**	60 12N	60 22 E
Sama de Langreo	**22**	43 18N	5 40W
Samagaltai	**41**	50 36N	95 3 E
Samaipata	**137**	18 9S	63 52W
Samales Group	**57**	6 0N	122 0 E
Samalkot	**50**	17 3N	82 13 E
Samâlût	**90**	28 20N	30 42 E
Samana	**48**	30 10N	76 13 E
Samana Cay	**127**	23 3N	73 45W
Samanga	**95**	8 20S	39 13 E
Samangan □	**47**	36 15N	68 3 E
Samangwa	**94**	4 23S	24 10 E
Samani	**63**	42 7N	142 56 E
Samar	**57**	12 0N	125 0 E
Samarai	**69**	10 39S	150 41 E
Samaria = Shōmrōn	**44**	32 15N	35 13 E
Samarinda	**56**	0 30S	117 9 E
Samarkand	**40**	39 40N	66 55 E
Samarra'	**46**	34 16N	43 55 E
Samastipur	**49**	25 50N	85 50 E
Samatan	**20**	43 29N	0 55 E
Samaúma	**137**	7 50S	60 2W
Samba, Kashmir	**49**	32 32N	75 10 E
Samba, Zaïre	**94**	4 38S	26 22 E
Sambaíba	**138**	7 8S	45 21W
Sambaina	**97**	19 37S	47 8 E
Sambalpur	**50**	21 28N	84 4 E
Sambar, Tanjung	**56**	2 59S	110 19 E
Sambas	**56**	1 20N	109 20 E
Sambava	**97**	14 16S	50 10 E
Sambawizi	**95**	18 24S	26 13 E
Sambhal	**49**	28 35N	78 37 E
Sambhar	**48**	26 52N	75 6 E
Sambiase	**29**	38 58N	16 16 E
Sambonifacio	**26**	45 24N	11 16 E
Sambor, Camb.	**54**	12 46N	106 0 E
Sambor, U.S.S.R.	**36**	49 30N	23 10 E
Sambre →	**16**	50 27N	4 52 E
Sambuca di Sicilia	**28**	37 39N	13 6 E
Samburu □	**94**	1 10N	37 0 E
Sambusu	**96**	17 55S	19 21 E
Samchŏk	**61**	37 30N	129 10 E
Samchonpo	**61**	35 0N	128 6 E
Same	**94**	4 2S	37 38 E
Samer	**19**	50 38N	1 44 E
Samfya	**95**	11 22S	29 31 E
Sámi	**35**	38 15N	20 39 E
Samna	**90**	25 12N	37 17 E
Samnū	**87**	27 15N	14 55 E
Samo Alto	**140**	30 22S	71 0W
Samoan Is.	**68**	14 0S	171 0W
Samobor	**27**	45 47N	15 44 E
Samoëns	**21**	46 5N	6 45 E
Samokov	**34**	42 18N	23 35 E
Samoorombón, Bahía	**140**	36 5S	57 20W
Samorogouan	**88**	11 21N	4 57W
Sámos	**35**	37 45N	26 50 E
Samos	**22**	42 44N	7 20W
Samoš	**33**	45 13N	20 49 E
Samothráki	**35**	40 28N	25 28 E
Samothráki, I.	**35**	40 25N	25 40 E
Sampa	**88**	8 0N	2 36W
Sampacho	**140**	33 20S	64 50W
Sampang	**57**	7 11S	113 13 E
Samper de Calanda	**24**	41 11N	0 28W
Sampit	**56**	2 34S	113 0 E
Sampit, Teluk	**56**	3 5S	113 3 E
Samra	**46**	25 35N	41 0 E
Samrong, Camb.	**54**	14 15N	103 30 E
Samrong, Thai.	**54**	15 10N	100 40 E
Samsø	**11**	55 50N	10 35 E
Samsø Bælt	**11**	55 45N	10 45 E
Samsun	**46**	41 15N	36 22 E
Samtredia	**39**	42 7N	42 24 E
Samui, Ko	**55**	9 30N	100 0 E
Samur →	**39**	41 53N	48 32 E
Samusole	**95**	10 2S	24 0 E
Samut Prakan	**54**	13 32N	100 40 E
Samut Sakhon	**54**	13 31N	100 13 E
Samut Songkhram (Mekong)	**54**	13 24N	100 1 E
Samwari	**48**	28 30N	66 46 E
San	**88**	13 15N	4 57W
San →, Camb.	**54**	13 32N	105 57 E
San →, Poland	**32**	50 45N	21 51 E
San Adrián, C. de	**22**	43 21N	8 50W
San Agustín	**134**	1 53N	76 16W
San Agustin, C.	**57**	6 20N	126 13 E
San Agustín de Valle Fértil	**140**	30 35S	67 30W
San Ambrosio	**67**	26 28S	79 53W
San Andreas	**122**	38 0N	120 39W
San Andrés, I. de	**126**	12 42N	81 46W
San Andres Mts.	**121**	33 0N	106 45W
San Andrés Tuxtla	**125**	18 30N	95 20W
San Angelo	**119**	31 30N	100 30W
San Anselmo	**122**	37 59N	122 34W
San Antonio, Belize	**125**	16 15N	89 2W
San Antonio, Chile	**140**	33 40S	71 40W
San Antonio, N. Mex., U.S.A.	**121**	33 58N	106 57W
San Antonio, Tex., U.S.A.	**119**	29 30N	98 30W
San Antonio, Venez.	**134**	3 30N	66 44W
San Antonio →	**119**	28 30N	96 50W
San Antonio Abad	**25**	38 59N	1 19 E
San Antonio, C., Argent.	**140**	36 15S	56 40W
San Antonio, C., Cuba	**126**	21 50N	84 57W
San Antonio, C. de	**25**	38 48N	0 12 E
San Antonio de los Baños	**126**	22 54N	82 31W
San Antonio de los Cobres	**140**	24 10S	66 17W
San Antonio, Mt. (Old Baldy Pk.)	**123**	34 17N	117 38W
San Antonio Oeste	**142**	40 40S	65 0W
San Ardo	**122**	36 1N	120 54W
San Augustine	**119**	31 30N	94 7W
San Bartolomeo in Galdo	**29**	41 23N	15 2 E
San Benedetto	**26**	45 2N	10 57 E
San Benedetto del Tronto	**27**	42 57N	13 52 E
San Benedicto, I.	**124**	19 18N	110 49W
San Benito	**119**	26 5N	97 39W
San Benito →	**122**	36 53N	121 50W
San Benito Mt.	**122**	36 22N	120 37W
San Bernardino	**123**	34 7N	117 18W
San Bernardino Str.	**57**	13 0N	125 0 E
San Bernardo	**140**	33 40S	70 50W
San Bernardo, I. de	**134**	9 45N	75 50W
San Blas	**124**	26 4N	108 46W
San Blas, C.	**113**	29 40N	85 12W
San Borja	**136**	14 50S	66 52W
San Buenaventura, Boliv.	**136**	14 28S	67 35W
San Buenaventura, Mexico	**124**	27 5N	101 32W
San Carlos, Argent.	**140**	33 50S	69 0W
San Carlos, Boliv.	**137**	17 24S	63 45W
San Carlos, Chile	**140**	36 10S	72 0W
San Carlos, Mexico	**124**	29 0N	100 54W
San Carlos, Nic.	**126**	11 12N	84 50W
San Carlos, Phil.	**57**	10 29N	123 25 E
San Carlos, Uruguay	**141**	34 46S	54 58W
San Carlos, U.S.A.	**121**	33 24N	110 27W
San Carlos, Amazonas, Venez.	**134**	1 55N	67 4W
San Carlos, Cojedes, Venez.	**134**	9 40N	68 36W
San Carlos = Butuku-Luba	**89**	3 29N	8 33 E
San Carlos de Bariloche	**142**	41 10S	71 25W
San Carlos de la Rápita	**24**	40 37N	0 35 E

San Carlos del Zulia 134 9 1N 71 55W
San Carlos L. 121 33 15N 110 25W
San Cataldo 28 37 30N 13 58 E
San Celoni 24 41 42N 2 30 E
San Clemente, Chile 140 35 30S 71 29W
San Clemente, Spain 25 39 24N 2 25W
San Clemente, U.S.A. 123 32 53N 118 30W
San Clemente, U.S.A. 123 33 29N 117 36W
San Constanzo 27 43 46N 13 5 E
San Cristóbal, Argent. 140 30 20S 61 10W
San Cristóbal, Colomb. 134 2 18S 73 2W
San Cristóbal, Dom. Rep. 127 18 25N 70 6W
San Cristóbal, Pac. Oc. 68 10 30S 161 0 E
San Cristóbal, Venez. 134 16 50N 92 40W
San Cristóbal de las Casas 125 16 50N 92 33W
San Damiano d'Asti 26 44 51N 8 4 E
San Daniele del Friuli 27 46 10N 13 0 E
San Demétrio Corone 29 39 34N 16 22 E
San Diego, Calif., U.S.A. 123 32 43N 117 10W
San Diego, Tex., U.S.A. 119 27 47N 98 15W
San Diego, C. 142 54 40S 65 10W
San Diego de la Unión 124 21 28N 100 52W
San Donà di Piave 27 45 38N 12 34 E
San Elpídio a Mare 27 43 16N 13 41 E
San Estanislao 140 24 39S 56 26W
San Esteban de Gormaz 24 41 34N 3 13W
San Felice sul Panaro 26 44 51N 11 9 E
San Felipe, Chile 140 32 43S 70 42W
San Felipe, Colomb. 134 1 55N 67 6W
San Felipe, Mexico 124 31 0N 114 52W
San Felipe, Venez. 134 10 20N 68 44W
San Felipe → 123 33 12N 115 49W
San Felíu de Guixols 24 41 45N 3 1 E
San Felíu de Llobregat 24 41 23N 2 2 E
San Félix 67 26 23S 80 0W
San Fernando, Chile 140 34 30S 71 0W
San Fernando, Mexico 124 30 0N 115 10W
San Fernando, Luzon, Phil. 57 15 5N 120 37 E
San Fernando, Luzon, Phil. 57 16 40N 120 23 E
San Fernando, Spain 23 36 28N 6 17W
San Fernando, Trin. 127 10 20N 61 30W
San Fernando, U.S.A. 123 34 15N 118 29W
San Fernando → 124 24 55N 98 10W
San Fernando de Apure 134 7 54N 67 15W
San Fernando de Atabapo 134 4 3N 67 42W
San Fernando di Púglia 29 41 18N 16 5 E
San Francisco, Argent. 140 31 30S 62 5W
San Francisco, Boliv. 137 15 16S 65 31W
San Francisco, U.S.A. 122 37 47N 122 30W
San Francisco → 121 32 59N 109 22W
San Francisco de Macorîs 127 19 19N 70 15W
San Francisco del Monte de Oro 140 32 36S 66 8W
San Francisco del Oro 124 26 52N 105 50W
San Francisco Javier 25 38 40N 1 25 E
San Francisco, Paso de 140 27 0S 68 0W
San Francisco Solano, Pta. 134 6 18N 77 29W
San Fratello 29 38 1N 14 33 E
San Gabriel 134 0 36N 77 49W
San Gavino Monreale 28 39 33N 8 47 E
San Gil 134 6 33N 73 8W
San Gimignano 26 43 28N 11 3 E
San Giórgio di Nogaro 27 45 50N 13 13 E
San Giórgio Iónico 29 40 27N 17 23 E
San Giovanni Bianco 26 45 52N 9 40 E
San Giovanni in Fiore 29 39 16N 16 42 E
San Giovanni in Persiceto 27 44 39N 11 12 E
San Giovanni Rotondo 29 41 41N 15 42 E
San Giovanni Valdarno 27 43 32N 11 30 E
San Giuliano Terme 26 43 45N 10 26 E
San Gorgonio Mt. 123 34 7N 116 51W
San Gottardo, Paso del 31 46 33N 8 33 E
San Grcángelo 28 40 14N 16 14 E
San Gregorio, Uruguay 141 32 37S 55 40W
San Gregorio, U.S.A. 122 37 20N 122 23W
San Guiseppe Iato 28 37 57N 13 11 E
San Ignacio, Boliv. 137 16 20S 60 55W
San Ignacio, Mexico 124 27 27N 113 0W
San Ignacio, Parag. 140 26 52S 57 3W
San Ignacio, Laguna 124 26 50N 113 11W
San Ildefonso, C. 57 16 0N 122 1 E
San Isidro 140 34 29S 58 31W
San Jacinto, Colomb. 134 9 50N 75 8W
San Jacinto, U.S.A. 123 33 47N 116 57W
San Javier, Misiones, Argent. 141 27 55S 55 5W
San Javier, Santa Fe, Argent. 140 30 40S 59 55W
San Javier, Beni, Boliv. 137 14 34S 64 42W
San Javier, Santa Cruz, Boliv. 137 16 18S 62 30W
San Javier, Chile 140 35 40S 71 45W
San Javier, Spain 25 37 49N 0 50W
San Jerónimo, Sa. de 134 8 0N 75 50W
San Joaquín 137 13 4S 64 49W
San Joaquin 122 36 36N 120 11W
San Joaquin 134 10 16N 67 47W
San Joaquin → 137 13 8S 63 41W
San Joaquin → 122 37 4N 121 51W
San Joaquin Valley 122 37 0N 120 30W
San Jorge 140 31 54S 61 50W
San Jorge, Bahía de 124 31 20N 113 20W
San Jorge, Golfo 142 46 0S 66 0W
San Jorge, G. de 24 40 50N 0 55W
San José, Boliv. 137 17 53S 60 50W
San José, C. Rica 126 10 0N 84 2W
San José, Guat. 126 14 0N 90 50W
San José, Mexico 124 25 0N 110 50W
San Jose, Luzon, Phil. 57 15 45N 120 55 E
San Jose, Mindoro, Phil. 57 12 27N 121 4 E
San Jose, Panay, Phil. 57 10 50N 122 5 E
San José 25 38 55N 1 18 E
San Jose, Calif., U.S.A. 122 37 20N 121 53W
San Jose, Ill., U.S.A. 116 40 18N 89 36W
San Jose, N. Mex., U.S.A. 121 35 26N 105 30W
san Jose → 121 34 58N 106 7W
San José Carpizo 125 19 26N 90 32W
San José de Feliciano 140 30 26S 58 46W
San José de Jáchal 140 30 15S 68 46W
San José de Mayo 140 34 27S 56 40W
San José de Ocune 134 4 15N 70 20W
San José de Uchapiamonas 136 14 13S 68 5W
San José del Cabo 124 23 0N 109 40W
San José del Guaviare 134 2 35N 72 38W
San José do Anauá 135 0 58N 61 22W
San Juan, Argent. 140 31 30S 68 30W
San Juan, Colomb. 134 8 46N 76 32W
San Juan, Dom. Rep. 127 18 45N 72 45W
San Juan, Mexico 124 21 20N 102 50W
San Juan, Ica, Peru 136 15 22S 75 7W
San Juan, Puno, Peru 136 14 2S 69 19W
San Juan, Phil. 57 8 25N 126 20 E
San Juan, Pto. Rico 127 18 28N 66 8W
San Juan □ 140 31 9S 69 0W
San Juan →, Argent. 140 32 20S 67 25W
San Juan →, Boliv. 137 21 2S 65 19W
San Juan →, Colomb. 134 4 3N 77 27W
San Juan →, Nic. 126 10 56N 83 42W
San Juan →, Calif., U.S.A. 122 36 14N 121 9W
San Juan →, Utah, U.S.A. 121 37 20N 110 20W
San Juan →, Venez. 135 10 14N 62 38W
San Juan Bautista, Parag. 140 26 37S 57 6W
San Juan Bautista, Spain 25 39 5N 1 31 E
San Juan Bautista, U.S.A. 122 36 51N 121 32W
San Juan, C. 92 1 5N 9 20 E
San Juan Capistrano 123 33 29N 117 40W
San Juan de Guadalupe 124 24 38N 102 44W
San Juan de los Morros 134 9 55N 67 21W
San Juan del César 134 10 46N 73 1W
San Juan del Norte 126 10 58N 83 40W
San Juan del Norte, B. de 126 11 0N 83 40W
San Juan del Puerto 23 37 20N 6 50W
San Juan del Río 125 20 25N 100 0W
San Juan del Sur 126 11 20N 85 51W
San Juan I. 122 48 32N 123 5W
San Juan Mts. 121 38 30N 108 30W
San Julián 142 49 15S 67 45W
San Just, Sierra de 24 40 45N 0 49W
San Justo 140 30 47S 60 30W
San Kamphaeng 54 18 45N 99 8 E
San Lázaro, C. 124 24 50N 112 18W
San Lázaro, Sa. de 124 23 25N 110 0W
San Leandro 122 37 40N 122 6W
San Leonardo 24 41 51N 3 5W
San Lorenzo, Argent. 140 32 45S 60 45W
San Lorenzo, Beni, Boliv. 137 15 22S 65 48W
San Lorenzo, Tarija, Boliv. 137 21 26S 64 47W
San Lorenzo, Ecuador 134 1 15N 78 50W
San Lorenzo, Parag. 140 25 20S 57 32W
San Lorenzo, Venez. 134 9 47N 71 4W
San Lorenzo → 124 24 15N 107 24W
San Lorenzo de la Parrilla 24 39 51N 2 22W
San Lorenzo de Morunys 24 42 8N 1 35 E
San Lorenzo, I., Mexico 124 28 35N 112 50W
San Lorenzo, I., Peru 136 12 7S 77 15W
San Lorenzo, Mt. 142 47 40S 72 20W
San Lucas, Boliv. 137 20 5S 65 7W
San Lucas, Baja California S., Mexico 124 27 10N 112 14W
San Lucas, Baja California S., Mexico 124 22 53N 109 54W
San Lucas, U.S.A. 122 36 8N 121 1W
San Lucas, C. de 124 22 50N 110 0W
San Lúcido 29 39 18N 16 3 E
San Luis, Argent. 140 33 20S 66 20W
San Luis, Cuba 126 22 17N 83 46W
San Luis, Guat. 126 16 14N 89 27W
San Luis, U.S.A. 121 37 3N 105 26W
San Luis □ 140 34 0S 66 0W
San Luís de la Loma 124 17 18N 100 55W
San Luis de la Paz 124 21 19N 100 32W
San Luis, I. 124 29 58N 114 26W
San Luis, L. de 137 13 45S 64 0W
San Luis Obispo 121 35 21N 120 38W
San Luis Potosí 124 22 9N 100 59W
San Luis Potosí □ 124 22 10N 101 0W
San Luis Res. 122 37 4N 121 5W
San Luis Río Colorado 124 32 29N 114 58W
San Luis, Sierra de 140 32 30S 66 10W
San Marco Argentano 29 39 34N 16 8 E
San Marco dei Cavoti 29 41 20N 14 50 E
San Marco in Lámis 29 41 43N 15 38 E
San Marcos, Colomb. 134 8 39N 75 8W
San Marcos, Guat. 126 14 59N 91 52W
San Marcos, Mexico 124 27 13N 112 6W
San Marcos, U.S.A. 119 29 53N 98 0W
San Marino 27 43 56N 12 25 E
San Marino ■ 27 43 56N 12 25 E
San Martín, Argent. 140 33 5S 68 28W
San Martín, Colomb. 134 3 42N 73 42W
San Martin → 137 13 8S 63 43W
San Martin de los Andes 142 40 10S 71 20W
San Martín de Valdeiglesias 22 40 21N 4 24W
San Martín, L. 142 48 50S 72 50W
San Martino de Calvi 26 45 57N 9 4 E
San Mateo, Spain 24 40 28N 0 10 E
San Mateo, U.S.A. 122 37 32N 122 19W
San Matías 137 16 25S 58 20W
San Matías, Golfo 142 41 30S 64 0W
San Miguel, El Sal. 126 13 30N 88 12W
San Miguel, Panama 126 8 27N 78 55W
San Miguel, Spain 25 39 3N 1 26 E
San Miguel, U.S.A. 122 35 45N 120 42W
San Miguel, Venez. 134 9 40N 65 11W
San Miguel →, Boliv. 137 13 52S 63 56W
San Miguel →, Ecuador 134 0 25N 76 30W
San Miguel de Huachi 136 15 40S 67 15W
San Miguel de Salinas 25 37 59N 0 47W
San Miguel de Tucumán 140 26 50S 65 20W
San Miguel del Monte 140 35 23S 58 50W
San Miguel I. 123 34 2N 120 23W
San Miniato 26 43 40N 10 50 E
San Narciso 57 15 2N 120 3 E
San Nicolás de los Arroyas 140 33 25S 60 10W
San Nicolas I. 123 33 16N 119 30W
San Onafre 123 33 22N 117 34W
San Onofre 134 9 44N 75 32W
San Pablo 140 21 43S 66 38W
San Paolo di Civitate 29 41 44N 15 16 E
San Pedro, Buenos Aires, Argent. 141 26 30S 54 10W
San Pedro, Jujuy, Argent. 140 24 12S 64 55W
San Pedro, Colomb. 134 4 56N 71 53W
San-Pédro 88 4 50N 6 33W
San Pedro, Mexico 124 23 55N 110 17W
San Pedro, Peru 136 14 49S 74 5W
San Pedro □ 140 24 0S 57 0W
San Pedro →, Chihuahua, Mexico 124 28 20N 106 10W
San Pedro →, Michoacan, Mexico 124 19 23N 103 51W
San Pedro →, Nayarit, Mexico 124 21 45N 105 30W
San Pedro →, U.S.A. 121 33 0N 110 50W
San Pedro Channel 123 33 35N 118 25W
San Pedro de Arimena 134 4 37N 71 42W
San Pedro de Atacama 140 22 55S 68 15W
San Pedro de Jujuy 140 24 12S 64 55W
San Pedro de las Colonias 124 25 50N 102 59W
San Pedro de Lloc 136 7 15S 79 28W
San Pedro de Macorís 127 18 30N 69 18W
San Pedro del Norte 126 13 4N 84 33W
San Pedro del Paraná 140 26 43S 56 13W
San Pedro del Pinatar 25 37 50N 0 50W
San Pedro Mártir, Sierra 124 31 0N 115 30W
San Pedro Mixtepec 125 16 2N 97 7W
San Pedro Ocampo = Melchor Ocampo 124 24 52N 101 40W
San Pedro, Pta. 140 25 30S 70 38W
San Pedro, Sierra de 23 39 18N 6 40W
San Pedro Sula 126 15 30N 88 0W
San Pedro,Pta. 140 25 30S 70 38W
San Pietro, I. 28 39 9N 8 17 E
San Pietro Vernótico 29 40 28N 18 0 E
San Quintín 124 30 29N 115 57W
San Quintin 57 16 1N 120 56 E
San Rafael, Argent. 140 34 40S 68 21W
San Rafael, Calif., U.S.A. 122 37 59N 122 32W
San Rafael, N. Mex., U.S.A. 121 35 6N 107 58W
San Rafael, Venez. 134 10 58N 71 46W
San Rafael Mt. 123 34 41N 119 52W
San Ramón, Boliv. 137 13 17S 64 43W
San Ramón, Peru 136 11 8S 75 20W
San Ramón de la Nueva Orán 140 23 10S 64 20W
San Remo, Austral. 74 38 33S 145 22 E
San Remo, Italy 26 43 48N 7 47 E
San Román, C. 134 12 12N 70 0W
San Roque, Argent. 140 28 25S 58 45W
San Roque, Spain 23 36 17N 5 21W
San Rosendo 140 37 16S 72 43W
San Saba 119 31 12N 98 45W
San Salvador 126 13 40N 89 10W
San Salvador de Jujuy 140 24 10S 64 48W
San Salvador I. 127 24 0N 74 32W
San Sebastián, Argent. 142 53 10S 68 30W
San Sebastián, Spain 24 43 17N 1 58W
San Sebastián, Venez. 134 9 57N 67 11W
San Serverino Marche 27 43 13N 13 10 E
San Simeon 122 35 44N 121 11W
San Simon 121 32 14N 109 16W
San Stéfano di Cadore 27 46 34N 12 33 E
San Telmo 124 30 58N 116 6W
San Tiburcio 124 24 8N 101 32W
San Valentin, Mte. 142 46 30S 73 30W
San Vicente de Alcántara 23 39 22N 7 8W
San Vicente de la Barquera 22 43 23N 4 29W
San Vicente del Caguán 134 2 7N 74 46W
San Vincenzo 26 43 6N 10 29 E
San Vito 28 39 26N 9 32 E
San Vito al Tagliamento 27 45 55N 12 50 E
San Vito, C. 28 38 11N 12 41 E
San Vito Chietino 27 42 19N 14 27 E
San Vito dei Normanni 29 40 40N 17 40 E
San Yanaro 134 2 47N 69 42W
San Ygnacio 119 27 6N 99 24W
Saña 136 6 54S 79 36W
San'a 45 15 27N 44 12 E
Sana → 27 45 3N 16 23 E
Sanaba 88 12 25N 3 47W
Sanabria, La 22 42 0N 6 30W
Sanâfir 90 27 55N 34 37 E
Sanaga → 92 3 35N 9 38 E
Sanak I. 100 53 30N 162 30W
Sanaloa, Presa 124 24 50N 107 20W
Sanana 57 2 5S 125 59 E
Sanand 48 22 59N 72 25 E
Sanandaj 46 35 18N 47 1 E
Sanandita 140 21 40S 63 45W
Sanary 21 43 7N 5 48 E
Sanawad 48 22 11N 76 5 E
Sanbe-San 64 35 6N 132 38 E
Sancergues 19 47 10N 2 54 E
Sancerre 19 47 20N 2 50 E
Sancerrois, Coll. du 19 47 20N 2 40 E
Sancha He → 58 26 48N 106 7 E
Sanchahe 61 44 50N 126 2 E
Sánchez 127 19 15N 69 36W
Sanchor 48 24 45N 71 55 E
Sanco, Pt. 57 8 15N 126 24 E
Sancoins 19 46 47N 2 55 E
Sancti-Spíritus 126 21 52N 79 33W
Sand → 97 22 25S 30 5 E
Sand Creek → 117 39 5N 85 52W
Sand Pt. 106 43 54N 83 27W
Sand Springs 119 36 12N 96 5W
Sanda 65 34 53N 135 14 E
Sandah 90 20 35N 39 32 E
Sandakan 56 5 53N 118 4 E

Sandanski 35 41 35N 23 16 E
Sandaré 88 14 40N 10 15W
Sanday 14 59 15N 2 30W
Sandefjord 10 59 10N 10 15 E
Sanders, Ariz., U.S.A. 121 35 12N 109 25W
Sanders, Ky., U.S.A. 117 38 40N 84 56W
Sanderson 119 30 5N 102 30W
Sandfly L. 109 55 43N 106 6W
Sandgate 73 27 18S 153 3 E
Sandía 136 14 10S 69 30W
Sandıklı 46 38 30N 30 20 E
Sandnes 9 58 50N 5 45 E
Sandness 14 60 18N 1 38W
Sandoa 92 9 41S 23 0 E
Sandon Bluffs 77 29 41S 153 20 E
Sandona 134 1 17N 77 28W
Sandoval 116 38 37N 89 7W
Sandover → 72 21 43S 136 32 E
Sandpoint 120 48 20N 116 34W
Sandringham 12 52 50N 0 30 E
Sandslån 10 63 2N 17 49 E
Sandspit 108 53 14N 131 49W
Sandstone 79 27 59S 119 16 E
Sandu 58 26 0N 107 52 E
Sandusky, Mich., U.S.A. 106 43 26N 82 50W
Sandusky, Ohio, U.S.A. 114 41 25N 82 40W
Sandusky → 117 41 27N 83 0W
Sandvig 11 55 18N 14 48 E
Sandviken 10 60 38N 16 46 E
Sandwich 117 41 39N 88 37W
Sandwich B., Can. 103 53 40N 57 15W
Sandwich B., S. Afr. 96 23 25S 14 20 E
Sandwich, C. 72 18 14S 146 18 E
Sandwich Group 143 57 0S 27 0W
Sandy, Nev., U.S.A. 123 35 49N 115 36W
Sandy, Oreg., U.S.A. 122 45 24N 122 16W
Sandy Bight 79 33 50S 123 20 E
Sandy C., Queens., Austral. 73 24 42S 153 15 E
Sandy C., Tas., Austral. 72 41 25S 144 45 E
Sandy Cay 127 23 13N 75 18W
Sandy Cr. → 120 41 15N 109 47W
Sandy Hollow 76 32 20S 150 32 E
Sandy L. 102 53 2N 93 0W
Sandy Lake 102 53 0N 93 15W
Sandy Narrows 109 55 5N 103 4W
Sandy Point 74 38 50S 146 6 E
Sanford, Fla., U.S.A. 113 28 45N 81 20W
Sanford, Me., U.S.A. 115 43 28N 70 47W
Sanford, N.C., U.S.A. 113 35 30N 79 10W
Sanford → 79 27 22S 115 53 E
Sanford Mt. 100 62 30N 143 0W
Sang-i-Masha 48 33 8N 67 27 E
Sanga 95 12 22S 35 21 E
Sanga → 92 1 5S 17 0 E
Sanga-Tolon 41 61 50N 149 40 E
Sangamner 50 19 37N 74 15 E
Sangamon → 116 40 2N 90 21W
Sangar, Afghan. 48 32 56N 65 30 E
Sangar, U.S.S.R. 41 64 2N 127 31 E
Sangar Sarai 48 34 27N 70 35 E
Sangasanga 56 0 36S 117 13 E
Sangay, vol. 134 2 0S 78 20W
Sange 94 6 58S 28 21 E
Sangeang 57 8 12S 119 6 E
Sanger 122 36 41N 119 35W
Sangerhausen 30 51 28N 11 18 E
Sanggan He → 60 38 12N 117 15 E
Sanggau 56 0 5N 110 30 E
Sangihe, Kepulauan 57 3 0N 126 0 E
Sangihe, P. 57 3 45N 125 30 E
Sangju 61 36 25N 128 10 E
Sangkapura 56 5 52S 112 40 E
Sangkhla 54 14 57N 98 28 E
Sangli 50 16 55N 74 33 E
Sangmélina 92 2 57N 12 1 E
Sangonera → 25 37 59N 1 4W
Sangpang Bum 52 26 30N 95 50 E
Sangre de Cristo Mts. 119 37 0N 105 0W
Sangro → 27 42 14N 14 32 E
Sangudo 108 53 50N 114 54W
Sangue → 137 11 1S 58 39W
Sangüesa 24 42 37N 1 17W
Sanguinaires, Îs. 21 41 51N 8 36 E
Sangzhi 59 29 25N 110 12 E
Sanhala 88 10 3N 6 51W
Sanish 118 48 0N 102 30W
Sanje 94 0 49S 31 30 E
Sanjiang 58 25 48N 109 37 E
Sankaranayinarkovil 51 9 10N 77 35 E
Sankeshwar 51 16 23N 74 32 E
Sankosh → 52 26 24N 89 47 E
Sankt Blasien 31 47 47N 8 7 E
Sankt Gallen 31 47 26N 9 22 E
Sankt Gallen □ 31 47 25N 9 22 E
Sankt Gotthard P. = San Gottardo, Paso del 31 46 33N 8 33 E
Sankt Ingbert 31 49 16N 7 6 E
Sankt Moritz 31 46 30N 9 50 E
Sankt Olof 11 55 37N 14 8 E
Sankt Pölten 33 48 12N 15 38 E
Sankt Valentin 33 48 11N 14 33 E
Sankt Veit 33 46 54N 14 22 E
Sankt Wendel 31 49 27N 7 9 E
Sankuru → 92 4 17S 20 25 E
Sanlúcar de Barrameda 23 36 46N 6 21W
Sanlúcar la Mayor 23 37 26N 6 18W
Sanluri 28 39 35N 8 55 E
Sanmaur 105 47 54N 73 47W
Sanmenxia 60 34 47N 111 12 E
Sanming 59 26 15N 117 40 E
Sannan 65 35 2N 135 1 E
Sannaspos 96 29 6S 26 34 E
Sannicandro Gargánico 29 41 50N 15 34 E
Sannidal 10 58 55N 9 15 E
Sannieshof 96 26 30S 25 47 E
Sano 65 36 19N 139 35 E
Sanok 32 49 35N 22 10 E
Sanquhar 14 55 21N 3 56W
Sansanding Dam 88 13 48N 6 0W
Sansanné-Mango 89 10 20N 0 30 E
Sansepolcro 27 43 34N 12 8 E
Sansha 59 26 58N 120 12 E
Sanshui 59 23 10N 112 56 E
Sanski Most 27 44 46N 16 40 E
Sansui 58 26 58N 108 39 E
Santa 136 8 59S 78 40W
Sant' Ágata de Goti 29 41 6N 14 30 E
Sant' Ágata di Militello 29 38 2N 14 8 E
Santa Ana, Boliv. 137 13 50S 65 40W
Santa Ana, Santa Cruz, Boliv. 137 16 37S 60 43W
Santa Ana, Santa Cruz, Boliv. 137 18 43S 58 44W
Santa Ana, Ecuador 134 1 16S 80 20W
Santa Ana, El Sal. 126 14 0N 89 31W
Santa Ana, Mexico 124 30 31N 111 8W
Santa Ana, U.S.A. 123 33 48N 117 55W
Santa Ana → 134 9 30N 71 57W
Sant' Ángelo Lodigiano 26 45 14N 9 25 E
Sant' Antíoco 28 39 2N 8 30 E
Sant' Arcángelo di Romagna 27 44 4N 12 26 E
Santa Bárbara 134 5 53N 75 35W
Santa Barbara 126 14 53N 88 14W
Santa Bárbara, Mexico 124 26 48N 105 50W
Santa Bárbara, Spain 24 40 42N 0 29 E
Santa Barbara 123 34 25N 119 40W
Santa Bárbara 134 7 47N 71 10W
Santa Barbara Channel 123 34 20N 120 0W
Santa Barbara I. 123 33 29N 119 2W
Santa Bárbara, Mt. 25 37 23N 2 50W
Santa Catalina, Colomb. 134 10 36N 75 17W
Santa Catalina, Mexico 124 25 40N 110 50W
Santa Catalina, G. of 123 33 0N 118 0W
Santa Catalina I. 123 33 20N 118 30W
Santa Catarina □ 141 27 25S 48 30W
Santa Catarina, I. de 141 27 30S 48 40W
Santa Caterina Villarmosa 29 37 37N 14 1 E
Santa Cecília 141 26 56S 50 18W
Santa Clara, Cuba 126 22 20N 80 0W
Santa Clara, Calif., U.S.A. 122 37 21N 122 0W
Santa Clara, Utah, U.S.A. 121 37 10N 113 38W
Santa Clara de Olimar 141 32 50S 54 54W
Santa Clara Pk. 121 35 58N 106 45W
Santa Clotilde 134 2 33S 73 45W
Santa Coloma de Farnés 24 41 50N 2 39 E
Santa Coloma de Gramanet 24 41 27N 2 13 E
Santa Comba 22 43 2N 8 49W
Santa Croce Camerina 29 36 50N 14 30 E
Santa Croce di Magliano 29 41 43N 14 59 E
Santa Cruz, Argent. 142 50 0S 68 32W
Santa Cruz, Boliv. 137 17 43S 63 10W
Santa Cruz, Brazil 138 6 13S 36 1W
Santa Cruz, Canary Is. 84 28 29N 16 15W
Santa Cruz, Chile 140 34 38S 71 27W
Santa Cruz, C. Rica 126 10 15N 85 35W
Santa Cruz, Peru 136 5 40S 75 56W
Santa Cruz, Phil. 57 14 20N 121 24 E
Santa Cruz, Calif., U.S.A. 122 36 55N 122 1W
Santa Cruz, N. Mexico, U.S.A. 121 35 59N 106 1W
Santa Cruz, Venez. 135 8 3N 64 27W
Santa Cruz □, Argent. 142 49 0S 70 0W
Santa Cruz □, Boliv. 137 17 43S 63 10W
Santa Cruz → 142 50 10S 68 20W
Santa Cruz Cabrália 139 16 17S 39 2W
Santa Cruz de Mudela 25 38 39N 3 28W
Santa Cruz del Norte 126 23 9N 81 55W
Santa Cruz del Retamar 22 40 8N 4 14W
Santa Cruz del Sur 126 20 44N 78 0W
Santa Cruz do Rio Pardo 141 22 54S 49 37W
Santa Cruz do Sul 141 29 42S 52 25W
Santa Cruz I. 123 34 0N 119 45W
Santa Cruz, Is. 66 10 30S 166 0 E
Santa Domingo, Cay 126 21 25N 75 15W
Santa Elena, Argent. 140 30 58S 59 47W
Santa Elena, Ecuador 134 2 16S 80 52W
Santa Elena, C. 126 10 54N 85 56W
Sant' Eufémia, Golfo di 29 38 50N 16 10 E
Santa Fe, Argent. 140 31 35S 60 41W
Santa Fe, Spain 23 37 11N 3 43W
Santa Fe, U.S.A. 121 35 40N 106 0W
Santa Fé □ 140 31 50S 60 55W
Santa Filomena 138 9 6S 45 50W
Santa Genoveva 124 23 18N 109 52W
Santa Helena 138 2 14S 45 18W
Santa Helena de Goiás 139 17 53S 50 35W
Santa Inês 139 13 17S 39 48W
Santa Inés 23 38 32N 5 37W
Santa Inés, I. 142 54 0S 73 0W
Santa Isabel, Argent. 140 36 10S 66 54W
Santa Isabel, Brazil 139 11 45S 51 30W
Santa Isabel, Solomon Is. 68 8 0S 159 0 E
Santa Isabel = Rey Malabo 89 3 45N 8 50 E
Santa Isabel do Araguaia 138 6 7S 48 19W
Santa Isabel do Morro 139 11 34S 50 40W
Santa Isabel, Pico 89 3 36N 8 49 E
Santa Lucía, Corrientes, Argent. 140 28 58S 59 5W
Santa Lucía, San Juan, Argent. 140 31 30S 68 30W
Santa Lucía, Spain 25 37 35N 0 58W
Santa Lucia 140 34 27S 56 24W
Santa Lucia Range 122 36 0N 121 20W
Santa Margarita, Argent. 140 38 28S 61 35W
Santa Margarita, Mexico 124 24 30N 111 50W
Santa Margarita, U.S.A. 122 35 23N 120 37W
Santa Margarita → 123 33 13N 117 23W
Santa Margherita 26 44 20N 9 11 E
Santa María 140 26 40S 66 0W
Santa Maria, Brazil 141 29 40S 53 48W
Santa Maria, Spain 24 39 39N 2 45 E
Santa Maria, U.S.A. 123 34 58N 120 29W
Santa Maria, Zambia 95 11 5S 29 58 E
Santa María → 124 31 0N 107 14W
Santa María, Bahía de 124 25 10N 108 40W
Santa Maria, Cabo de 23 36 58N 7 53W
Santa Maria Capua Vetere 29 41 3N 14 15 E
Santa Maria da Vitória 139 13 24S 44 12W
Santa María de Ipire 135 8 49N 65 19W
Santa María del Oro 124 25 58N 105 20W
Santa Maria di Leuca, C. 29 39 48N 18 20 E
Santa Maria do Suaçuí 139 18 12S 42 25W
Santa Maria dos Marmelos 137 6 7S 61 51W
Santa María la Real de Nieva 22 41 4N 4 24W
Santa Marta, Colomb. 134 11 15N 74 13W
Santa Marta, Spain 23 38 37N 6 39W
Santa Marta Grande, C. 141 28 43S 48 50W
Santa Marta, Ría de 22 43 44N 7 45W
Santa Marta, Sierra Nevada de 134 10 55N 73 50W
Santa Monica 123 34 0N 118 30W
Santa Olalla, Huelva, Spain 23 37 54N 6 14W
Santa Olalla, Toledo, Spain 22 40 2N 4 25W
Santa Ona 68 10 0S 162 0 E
Sant' Onofrio 29 38 42N 16 10 E
Santa Paula 123 34 20N 119 2W
Santa Pola 25 38 13N 0 35W
Santa Quitéria 138 4 20S 40 10W
Santa Rita, U.S.A. 121 32 50N 108 0W
Santa Rita, Guarico, Venez. 134 8 8N 66 16W
Santa Rita, Zulia, Venez. 134 10 32N 71 32W
Santa Rita do Araquaia 137 17 20S 53 12W
Santa Rosa, La Pampa, Argent. 140 36 40S 64 17W
Santa Rosa, San Luis, Argent. 140 32 21S 65 10W
Santa Rosa, Boliv. 136 10 36S 67 20W
Santa Rosa, Brazil 141 27 52S 54 29W
Santa Rosa, Colomb. 134 3 32N 69 48W
Santa Rosa, Ecuador 134 3 27S 79 58W
Santa Rosa, Peru 136 14 30S 70 50W
Santa Rosa, Calif., U.S.A. 122 38 26N 122 43W
Santa Rosa, N. Mexico, U.S.A. 119 34 58N 104 40W
Santa Rosa, Venez. 134 1 29N 66 55W
Santa Rosa de Cabal 134 4 52N 75 38W
Santa Rosa de Copán 126 14 47N 88 46W
Santa Rosa de Osos 134 6 39N 75 28W
Santa Rosa de Río Primero 140 31 8S 63 20W
Santa Rosa de Viterbo 134 5 53N 72 59W
Santa Rosa del Palmar 137 16 54S 62 24W
Santa Rosa I., Calif., U.S.A. 123 34 0N 120 6W
Santa Rosa I., Fla., U.S.A. 113 30 23N 87 0W
Santa Rosa Mts. 120 41 45N 117 30W
Santa Rosalía 124 27 20N 112 20W
Santa Sofia 27 43 57N 11 55 E
Santa Sylvina 140 27 50S 61 10W
Santa Tecla = Nueva San Salvador 126 13 40N 89 25W
Santa Teresa, Argent. 140 33 25S 60 47W
Santa Teresa, Brazil 139 19 55S 40 36W
Santa Teresa, Mexico 125 25 17N 97 51W
Santa Teresa, Venez. 135 4 43N 61 4W
Santa Teresa di Riva 29 37 58N 15 21 E
Santa Teresa Gallura 28 41 14N 9 12 E
Santa Vitória 139 18 50S 50 8W
Santa Vitória do Palmar 141 33 32S 53 25W
Santa Ynez 123 34 37N 120 5W
Santa Ynez → 123 34 37N 120 41W
Santa Ysabel 123 33 7N 116 40W
Santadi 28 39 5N 8 42 E
Santahar 52 24 48N 88 59 E
Santai 58 31 5N 104 58 E
Santaluz 138 11 15S 39 22W
Santana 139 13 2S 44 5W
Santana, Coxilha de 141 30 50S 55 35W
Santana do Ipanema 138 9 22S 37 14W
Santana do Livramento 141 30 55S 55 30W
Santander, Colomb. 134 3 1N 76 28W
Santander, Spain 22 43 27N 3 51W
Santander □ 22 43 25N 4 0W
Santander Jiménez 125 24 11N 98 29W
Santañy 25 39 20N 3 5 E
Santaquin 120 40 0N 111 51W
Santarém, Brazil 135 2 25S 54 42W
Santarém, Port. 23 39 12N 8 42W
Santarém □ 23 39 10N 8 40W
Santaren Channel 126 24 0N 79 30W
Santéramo in Colle 29 40 48N 16 45 E
Santerno → 27 44 10N 11 38 E
Santhia 26 45 20N 8 10 E
Santiago, Boliv. 137 18 19S 59 34W
Santiago, Brazil 141 29 11S 54 52W
Santiago, Chile 140 33 24S 70 40W
Santiago, Panama 126 8 0N 81 0W
Santiago, Peru 136 14 11S 75 43W
Santiago □ 140 33 30S 70 50W
Santiago → 134 4 27S 77 38W
Santiago, C. 142 50 46S 75 27W
Santiago de Chuco 136 8 9S 78 11W
Santiago de Compostela 22 42 52N 8 37W
Santiago de Cuba 126 20 0N 75 49W
Santiago de los Cabelleros 127 19 30N 70 40W
Santiago del Estero 140 27 50S 64 15W
Santiago del Estero □ 140 27 40S 63 15W
Santiago do Cacém 23 38 1N 8 42W
Santiago Ixcuintla 124 21 50N 105 11W
Santiago Papasquiaro 124 25 0N 105 20W
Santiago, Punta de 89 3 12N 8 40 E
Santiago, Serranía de 137 18 25S 59 25W
Santiaguillo, L. de 124 24 50N 104 50W
Santillana del Mar 22 43 24N 4 6W
Santipur 49 23 17N 88 25 E
Santisteban del Puerto 25 38 17N 3 15W
Santo 68 15 27S 167 10 E
Santo → 136 8 56S 78 37W
Santo Amaro 139 12 30S 38 43W
Santo Anastácio 141 21 58S 51 39W
Santo André 141 23 39S 46 29W
Santo Ângelo 141 28 15S 54 15W
Santo Antonio 137 15 50S 56 0W
Santo Antônio de Jesus 139 12 58S 39 16W

Santo Antônio do Içá	**134**	3 5 S	67 57W
Santo Antônio do Leverger	**137**	15 52 S	56 5W
Santo Antonio do Zaire	**92**	6 13 S	12 20 E
Santo Corazón	**137**	18 0 S	58 45W
Santo Domingo, Dom. Rep.	**127**	18 30N	64 54W
Santo Domingo, Baja Calif. N., Mexico	**124**	30 43N	116 2W
Santo Domingo, Baja Calif. S., Mexico	**124**	25 32N	112 2W
Santo Domingo, Nic.	**126**	12 14N	84 59W
Santo Domingo de la Calzada	**24**	42 26N	2 57W
Santo Domingo de los Colorados	**134**	0 15 S	79 9W
Santo Stéfano di Camastro	**29**	38 1N	14 22 E
Santo Stino di Livenza	**27**	45 45N	12 40 E
Santo Tirso	**22**	41 21N	8 28W
Santo Tomás, Mexico	**124**	31 33N	116 24W
Santo Tomás, Peru	**136**	14 26 S	72 8W
Santo Tomé	**141**	28 40 S	56 5W
Santo Tomé de Guayana	**135**	8 22N	62 40W
Santoña	**22**	43 29N	3 27W
Santos	**141**	24 0 S	46 20W
Santos Dumont	**141**	22 55 S	43 10W
Santos, Sierra de los	**23**	38 7N	5 12W
Sanur	**44**	32 22N	35 15 E
Sanvignes-les-Mines	**19**	46 40N	4 18 E
San'yō	**64**	34 2N	131 5 E
Sanyuan	**60**	34 35N	108 58 E
Sanyuki-Sammyaku	**64**	34 5N	133 0 E
Sanza Pombo	**92**	7 18 S	15 56 E
São Anastácio	**141**	22 0 S	51 40W
São Bartolomeu de Messines	**23**	37 15N	8 17W
São Benedito	**138**	4 3 S	40 53W
São Bento	**138**	2 42 S	44 50W
São Bento do Norte	**138**	5 4 S	36 2W
São Borja	**141**	28 39 S	56 0W
São Bras d'Alportel	**23**	37 8N	7 37W
São Caitano	**138**	8 21 S	36 6W
São Carlos	**141**	22 0 S	47 50W
São Cristóvão	**138**	11 1 S	37 15W
São Domingos	**139**	13 25 S	46 19W
São Domingos do Maranhão	**138**	5 42 S	44 22W
São Félix	**139**	11 36 S	50 39W
São Francisco	**139**	16 0 S	44 50W
São Francisco →	**138**	10 30 S	36 24W
São Francisco do Maranhão	**138**	6 15 S	42 52W
São Francisco do Sul	**141**	26 15 S	48 36W
São Gabriel	**141**	30 20 S	54 20W
São Gabriel da Palha	**139**	18 47 S	40 39W
São Gonçalo	**139**	22 48 S	43 5W
São Gotardo	**139**	19 19 S	46 3W
Sao Hill	**95**	8 20 S	35 12 E
São João da Boa Vista	**141**	22 0 S	46 52W
São João da Pesqueira	**22**	41 8N	7 24W
São João da Ponte	**139**	15 56 S	44 1W
São João del Rei	**139**	21 8 S	44 15W
São João do Araguaia	**138**	5 23 S	48 46W
São João do Paraíso	**139**	15 19 S	42 1W
São João do Piauí	**138**	8 21 S	42 15W
São João dos Patos	**138**	6 30 S	43 42W
São José, B. de	**138**	2 38 S	44 4W
São José da Laje	**138**	9 1 S	36 3W
São José de Mipibu	**138**	6 5 S	35 15W
São José do Peixe	**138**	7 24 S	42 34W
São José do Rio Prêto	**141**	20 50 S	49 20W
São José dos Campos	**141**	23 7 S	45 52W
São Leopoldo	**141**	29 50 S	51 10W
São Lourenço, Minas Gerais, Brazil	**139**	22 7 S	45 3W
São Lourenço, Pantanal do, Brazil	**137**	17 30 S	56 20W
São Lourenço →	**137**	17 53 S	57 27W
São Luís do Curu	**138**	3 40 S	39 14W
São Luís Gonzaga	**141**	28 25 S	55 0W
São Luís (Maranhão)	**138**	2 39 S	44 15W
São Marcos →	**139**	18 15 S	47 37W
São Marcos, B. de	**138**	2 0 S	44 0W
São Martinho	**22**	40 18N	8 8W
São Mateus	**139**	18 44 S	39 50W
São Mateus →	**139**	18 35 S	39 44W
São Miguel do Araguaia	**139**	13 19 S	50 13W
São Miguel dos Campos	**138**	9 47 S	36 5W
São Nicolau →	**138**	5 45 S	42 2W
São Paulo	**141**	23 32 S	46 37W
São Paulo □	**141**	22 0 S	49 0W
São Paulo de Olivença	**134**	3 27 S	68 48W
Sao Paulo, I.	**128**	0 50N	31 40W
São Pedro do Sul	**22**	40 46N	8 4W
São Rafael	**138**	5 47 S	36 55W
São Raimundo das Mangabeiras	**138**	7 1 S	45 29W
São Raimundo Nonato	**138**	9 1 S	42 42W
São Romão	**139**	16 22 S	45 4W
São Roque, C. de	**138**	5 30 S	35 16W
São Sebastião do Paraíso	**141**	20 54 S	46 59W
São Sebastião, I. de	**141**	23 50 S	45 18W
São Simão	**139**	18 56 S	50 30W
São Teotónio	**23**	37 30N	8 42W
São Tomé	**138**	5 58 S	36 4W
São Tomé, C. de	**139**	22 0 S	40 59W
São Tomé, I.	**83**	0 10N	6 39 E
São Vicente	**141**	23 57 S	46 23W
São Vicente, Cabo de	**23**	37 0N	9 0W
Saona, I.	**127**	18 10N	68 40W
Saône →	**19**	45 44N	4 50 E
Saône-et-Loire □	**19**	46 25N	4 50 E
Saonek	**57**	0 22 S	130 55 E
Sãoo Joaquim da Barra	**139**	20 35 S	47 53W
Saoura, O. →	**86**	29 0N	0 55W
Sapão →	**138**	11 1 S	45 32W
Saparua	**57**	3 33 S	128 40 E
Sapé	**138**	7 6 S	35 13W
Sapele	**89**	5 50N	5 40 E
Sapelo I.	**113**	31 28N	81 15W
Sapiéntza	**35**	36 45N	21 43 E
Sapone	**89**	12 3N	1 35W
Saposoa	**136**	6 55 S	76 45W
Sapozhok	**37**	53 59N	40 41 E
Sapphire Mts.	**120**	46 20N	113 45W
Sappho	**122**	48 4N	124 16W
Sapporo	**63**	43 0N	141 21 E
Sapri	**29**	40 5N	15 37 E
Sapudi	**57**	7 2 S	114 17 E
Sapulpa	**119**	36 0N	96 0W
Sapur	**49**	34 18N	74 27 E
Saqqez	**46**	36 15N	46 20 E
Sar-i-Pul	**47**	36 10N	66 0 E
Sar Planina	**34**	42 10N	21 0 E
Sara	**88**	11 40N	3 53W
Sara Buri	**54**	14 30N	100 55 E
Sarāb	**46**	38 0N	47 30 E
Saragossa = Zaragoza	**24**	41 39N	0 53W
Saraguro	**134**	3 35 S	79 16W
Saraipalli	**50**	21 20N	82 59 E
Sarajevo	**33**	43 52N	18 26 E
Saramacca □	**135**	5 0N	56 0W
Saramacca →	**135**	5 50N	55 55W
Saramati	**52**	25 44N	95 2 E
Saran	**90**	19 35N	40 30 E
Saran, G.	**56**	0 30 S	111 25 E
Saranac	**117**	42 56N	85 13W
Saranac Lake	**115**	44 20N	74 10W
Saranda	**94**	5 45 S	34 59 E
Sarandí del Yi	**141**	33 18 S	55 38W
Sarandí Grande	**140**	33 44 S	56 20W
Sarangani B.	**57**	6 0N	125 13 E
Sarangani Is.	**57**	5 25N	125 25 E
Sarangarh	**50**	21 30N	83 5 E
Saransk	**37**	54 10N	45 10 E
Sarapul	**40**	56 28N	53 48 E
Sarasota	**113**	27 20N	82 30W
Saratoga, Calif., U.S.A.	**122**	37 16N	122 2W
Saratoga, Wyo., U.S.A.	**120**	41 30N	106 48W
Saratoga Springs	**115**	43 5N	73 47W
Saratov	**37**	51 30N	46 2 E
Saravane	**54**	15 43N	106 25 E
Sarawak □	**56**	2 0N	113 0 E
Saraya	**88**	12 50N	11 45W
Sarbāz	**47**	26 38N	61 19 E
Sarbisheh	**47**	32 30N	59 40 E
Sarca →	**26**	45 52N	10 52 E
Sardalas	**87**	25 50N	10 34 E
Sardarshahr	**48**	28 30N	74 29 E
Sardegna	**28**	39 57N	9 0 E
Sardhana	**48**	29 9N	77 39 E
Sardinata	**134**	8 5N	72 48W
Sardinia	**117**	39 0N	83 49W
Sardinia = Sardegna	**28**	39 57N	9 0 E
Saréyamou	**88**	16 7N	3 10W
Sargasso Sea	**128**	27 0N	72 0W
Sargent	**118**	41 42N	99 24W
Sargodha	**48**	32 10N	72 40 E
Sargodha □	**48**	31 50N	72 0 E
Sarh	**85**	9 5N	18 23 E
Sarhro, Jebel	**86**	31 6N	5 0W
Sārī	**47**	36 30N	53 4 E
Sária	**35**	35 54N	27 17 E
Sarida →	**44**	32 4N	34 45 E
Sarikamiş	**46**	40 22N	42 35 E
Sarikei	**56**	2 8N	111 30 E
Sarina	**72**	21 22 S	149 13 E
Sariñena	**24**	41 47N	0 10W
Sarír Tibasti	**87**	22 50N	18 30 E
Sarita	**119**	27 14N	97 49W
Sariwŏn	**61**	38 31N	125 46 E
Sariyer	**35**	41 10N	29 3 E
Sark	**18**	49 25N	2 20W
Sarkad	**33**	46 47N	21 23 E
Sarlat-la-Canéda	**20**	44 54N	1 13 E
Sarles	**118**	48 58N	99 0W
Sărmaşu	**34**	46 45N	24 13 E
Sarmi	**57**	1 49 S	138 44 E
Sarmiento	**142**	45 35 S	69 5W
Särna	**10**	61 41N	13 8 E
Sarnano	**27**	43 2N	13 17 E
Sarnen	**31**	46 53N	8 13 E
Sarnia	**106**	42 58N	82 23W
Sarno	**29**	40 48N	14 35 E
Sarny	**36**	51 17N	26 40 E
Särö	**11**	57 31N	11 57 E
Sarolangun	**56**	2 19 S	102 42 E
Saronikós Kólpos	**35**	37 45N	23 45 E
Saronno	**26**	45 38N	9 2 E
Sárospatak	**33**	48 18N	21 33 E
Sarpsborg	**10**	59 16N	11 2 E
Sarracín	**24**	42 15N	3 45W
Sarralbe	**19**	48 55N	7 1 E
Sarre = Saar →	**19**	49 42N	6 34 E
Sarre, La	**104**	48 45N	79 5W
Sarre-Union	**19**	48 55N	7 4 E
Sarrebourg	**19**	48 43N	7 3 E
Sarreguemines	**19**	49 1N	7 4 E
Sarriá	**22**	42 49N	7 29W
Sarrión	**24**	40 9N	0 49W
Sarro	**88**	13 40N	5 15W
Sarstedt	**30**	52 13N	9 50 E
Sartène	**21**	41 38N	8 58 E
Sarthe □	**18**	47 58N	0 10 E
Sarthe →	**18**	47 33N	0 31W
Sartilly	**18**	48 45N	1 28W
Sartynya	**40**	63 22N	63 11 E
Sarum	**90**	21 11N	39 10 E
Sarūr	**47**	23 17N	58 4 E
Sárvár	**33**	47 15N	16 56 E
Sarvestān	**47**	29 20N	53 10 E
Särvfjället	**10**	62 42N	13 30 E
Sárviz →	**33**	46 24N	18 41 E
Sary-Tash	**40**	39 44N	73 15 E
Sarych, Mys.	**38**	44 25N	33 45 E
Saryshagan	**40**	46 12N	73 38 E
Sarzana	**26**	44 5N	9 59 E
Sarzeau	**18**	47 31N	2 48W
Sasa	**44**	33 2N	35 23 E
Sasabeneh	**45**	7 59N	44 43 E
Sasamungga	**68**	7 0 S	156 50 E
Sasaram	**49**	24 57N	84 5 E
Sasayama	**65**	35 4N	135 13 E
Sasebo	**64**	33 10N	129 43 E
Saseginaga, L.	**104**	47 6N	78 35W
Saser Mt.	**49**	34 50N	77 50 E
Saskatchewan □	**109**	54 40N	106 0W
Saskatchewan →	**109**	53 12N	99 15W
Saskatoon	**109**	52 10N	106 38W
Saskylakh	**41**	71 55N	114 1 E
Sasolburg	**97**	26 46 S	27 49 E
Sasovo	**37**	54 25N	41 55 E
Sassandra	**88**	5 0N	6 8W
Sassandra →	**88**	4 58N	6 5W
Sássari	**28**	40 44N	8 33 E
Sassnitz	**30**	54 29N	13 39 E
Sasso Marconi	**27**	44 22N	11 12 E
Sassocorvaro	**27**	43 47N	12 30 E
Sassoferrato	**27**	43 26N	12 51 E
Sassuolo	**26**	44 31N	10 47 E
Sástago	**24**	41 19N	0 21W
Sastown	**88**	4 45N	8 27W
Sasumua Dam	**94**	0 45 S	36 40 E
Sata-Misaki	**64**	30 59N	130 40 E
Satadougou	**88**	12 25N	11 25W
Satanta	**119**	37 30N	101 [illegible]W
Satara	**50**	17 44N	73 5[illegible] E
Sataua	**68**	13 28 S	172 4[illegible]W
Satilla →	**113**	30 59N	81 2[illegible]W
Satipo	**136**	11 15 S	74 2[illegible]W
Satkania	**52**	22 4N	92 [illegible] E
Satkhira	**52**	22 43N	89 [illegible] E
Satmala Hills	**50**	20 15N	74 40 E
Satna	**49**	24 35N	80 50 E
Sator	**27**	44 11N	16 37 E
Sátoraljaújhely	**33**	48 25N	21 41 E
Satpura Ra.	**48**	21 25N	76 10 E
Satrup	**30**	54 39N	9 38 E
Satsuma-Hantō	**64**	31 25N	130 25 E
Satsuna-Shotō	**63**	30 0N	130 0 E
Sattahip	**54**	12 41N	100 54 E
Sattenapalle	**51**	16 25N	80 6 E
Satu Mare	**34**	47 46N	22 55 E
Satui	**56**	3 50 S	115 27 E
Satun	**55**	6 43N	100 2 E
Satupe'itea	**68**	13 45 S	172 18W
Saturnina →	**137**	12 15 S	58 10W
Sauce	**140**	30 5 S	58 46W
Sauceda	**124**	25 55N	101 18W
Saucillo	**124**	28 1N	105 17W
Saúde	**138**	10 56 S	40 24W
Sauðarkrókur	**8**	65 45N	19 40W
Saudi Arabia ■	**46**	26 0N	44 0 E
Sauerland	**30**	51 0N	8 0 E
Saugatuck	**117**	42 40N	86 12W
Saugeen →	**106**	44 30N	81 22W
Saugerties	**115**	42 4N	73 58W
Saugues	**20**	44 58N	3 32 E
Sauherad	**10**	59 25N	9 15 E
Sauid el Amia	**86**	25 57N	6 8W
Saujon	**20**	45 41N	0 55W
Sauk Center	**118**	45 42N	94 56W
Sauk City	**116**	43 17N	89 43W
Sauk Rapids	**118**	45 35N	94 10W
Saül	**135**	3 37N	53 12W
Saulgau	**31**	48 4N	9 32 E
Saulieu	**19**	47 17N	4 14 E
Sault	**21**	44 6N	5 24 E
Sault-au-Moulton	**105**	48 33N	69 15W
Sault aux Cochons →	**105**	48 44N	69 4W
Sault Ste. Marie, Can.	**106**	46 30N	84 20W
Sault Ste. Marie, U.S.A.	**106**	46 27N	84 22W
Saumlaki	**57**	7 55 S	131 20 E
Saumur	**18**	47 15N	0 5W
Saunders C.	**81**	45 53 S	170 45 E
Saunders I.	**143**	57 48 S	26 28W
Saunders Point, Mt.	**79**	27 52 S	125 38 E
Saunemin	**117**	40 54N	88 24W
Saurbær, Borgarfjarðarsýsla, Iceland	**8**	64 24N	21 35W
Saurbær, Eyjafjarðarsýsla, Iceland	**8**	65 27N	18 13W
Sauri	**89**	11 42N	6 44 E
Saurimo	**92**	9 40 S	20 12 E
Sausalito	**122**	37 51N	122 29W
Sautatá	**134**	7 50N	77 4W
Sauvage, L.	**104**	50 6N	74 30W
Sauveterre	**20**	43 25N	0 57W
Sauzé-Vaussais	**20**	46 8N	0 8 E
Savá	**126**	15 32N	86 15W
Sava	**27**	40 28N	17 32 E
Sava →	**27**	44 50N	20 26 E
Savage	**118**	47 27N	104 20W
Savai'i	**68**	13 28 S	172 24W
Savalou	**89**	7 57N	1 58 E
Savane	**95**	19 37 S	35 8 E
Savanna	**116**	42 5N	90 10W
Savanna la Mar	**126**	18 10N	78 10W
Savannah, Ga., U.S.A.	**113**	32 4N	81 4W
Savannah, Mo., U.S.A.	**116**	39 55N	94 46W
Savannah, Tenn., U.S.A.	**113**	35 12N	88 18W
Savannah →	**113**	32 2N	80 53W
Savannakhet	**54**	16 30N	104 49 E
Savant L.	**102**	50 16N	90 44W
Savant Lake	**102**	50 14N	90 40W
Savantvadi	**51**	15 55N	73 54 E
Savanur	**51**	14 59N	75 21 E
Savda	**50**	21 9N	75 56 E
Savé	**89**	8 2N	2 29 E
Save →	**20**	43 47N	1 17 E
Sāveh	**46**	35 2N	50 20 E
Savelugu	**89**	9 38N	0 54W
Savenay	**18**	47 20N	1 55W
Saverdun	**20**	43 14N	1 34 E
Saverne	**19**	48 39N	7 20 E
Savigliano	**26**	44 39N	7 40 E
Savigny-sur-Braye	**18**	47 53N	0 49 E
Saviñao	**22**	42 35N	7 38W
Savio →	**27**	44 19N	12 20 E
Savo	**68**	9 8 S	159 48 E
Savoie □	**21**	45 26N	6 35 E
Savona	**26**	44 19N	8 29 E
Sävsjö	**11**	57 20N	14 40 E
Sävsjøström	**11**	57 1N	15 25 E
Savusavu	**68**	17 34 S	178 15 E
Savusavu B.	**68**	16 45 S	179 15 E
Sawahlunto	**56**	0 40 S	100 52 E
Sawai	**57**	3 0 S	129 5 E
Sawai Madhopur	**48**	26 0N	76 25 E
Sawang Daen Din	**54**	17 28N	103 28 E
Sawankhalok	**54**	17 19N	99 50 E
Sawara	**65**	35 55N	140 30 E
Sawatch Mts.	**121**	38 30N	106 30W
Sawdā, Jabal as	**87**	28 51N	15 12 E
Sawel, Mt.	**15**	54 48N	7 5W
Sawfajjin, W. →	**87**	31 46N	14 30 E
Sawi	**55**	10 14N	99 5 E
Sawknah	**85**	29 4N	15 47 E
Sawmills	**95**	19 30 S	28 2 E
Sawtell	**77**	30 19 S	153 6 E
Sawu	**57**	10 35 S	121 50 E
Sawu Sea	**57**	9 30 S	121 50 E
Sawyerville	**105**	45 20N	71 34W
Saxby →	**72**	18 25 S	140 53 E
Saxony, Lower = Niedersachsen	**30**	52 45N	9 0 E
Saxton	**114**	40 12N	78 18W
Say	**89**	13 8N	2 22 E
Saya	**89**	9 30N	3 18 E
Sayabec	**103**	48 35N	67 41W
Sayaboury	**54**	19 15N	101 45 E
Sayán	**136**	11 8 S	77 12W

Place	Page	Lat.	Long.
Sayan, Vostochnyy	41	54 0N	96 0 E
Sayan, Zapadnyy	41	52 30N	94 0 E
Sayasan	39	42 56N	46 15 E
Sayda	46	33 35N	35 25 E
Sayhan-Ovoo	60	45 27N	103 54 E
Sayhandulaan	60	44 40N	109 1 E
Saylorville Res.	116	41 43N	93 41W
Saynshand	60	44 55N	110 11 E
Sayō	64	34 59N	134 22 E
Sayre, Okla., U.S.A.	119	35 20N	99 40W
Sayre, Pa., U.S.A.	115	42 0N	76 30W
Sayula	124	19 50N	103 40W
Sayville	115	40 45N	73 7W
Sazin	49	35 35N	73 30 E
Sazlika →	35	41 59N	25 50 E
Sbeïtla	87	35 12N	9 7 E
Scaër	18	48 2N	3 42W
Scafell Pikes	12	54 26N	3 14W
Scalea	29	39 49N	15 47 E
Scalpay	14	57 51N	6 40W
Scandia	108	50 20N	112 0W
Scandiano	26	44 36N	10 40 E
Scandinavia	6	64 0N	12 0 E
Scansano	27	42 40N	11 20 E
Scapa Flow	14	58 52N	3 6W
Scappoose	122	45 45N	122 53W
Scarborough, Trin.	127	11 11N	60 42W
Scarborough, U.K.	12	54 17N	0 24W
Scargill	81	42 56S	172 58 E
Scarpe →	19	50 31N	3 27 E
Scarsdale	74	37 41S	143 39 E
Scédro	27	43 6N	16 43 E
Scenic	118	43 49N	102 32W
Schaal See	30	53 40N	10 57 E
Schaffhausen □	31	47 42N	8 36 E
Schagen	16	52 49N	4 48 E
Schanck, C.	74	38 30S	144 55 E
Schärding	32	48 27N	13 27 E
Scharhörn	30	53 58N	8 24 E
Scharnitz	31	47 23N	11 15 E
Scheessel	30	53 10N	9 33 E
Schefferville	103	54 48N	66 50W
Schelde →	16	51 15N	4 16 E
Schell City	116	38 1N	94 7W
Schenectady	115	42 50N	73 58W
Scherfede	30	51 32N	9 2 E
Schesslitz	31	49 59N	11 2 E
Scheveningen	16	52 6N	4 16 E
Schiedam	16	51 55N	4 25 E
Schiermonnikoog	16	53 30N	6 15 E
Schifferstadt	31	49 22N	8 23 E
Schiltigheim	19	48 35N	7 45 E
Schio	27	45 42N	11 21 E
Schirmeck	19	48 29N	7 12 E
Schlei →	30	54 45N	9 52 E
Schleiden	30	50 32N	6 26 E
Schleiz	30	50 35N	11 49 E
Schleswig	30	54 32N	9 34 E
Schleswig-Holstein □	30	54 10N	9 40 E
Schlüchtern	31	50 20N	9 32 E
Schmalkalden	30	50 43N	10 28 E
Schmölin	30	50 54N	12 22 E
Schmölln	30	53 15N	14 6 E
Schneeberg, Austria	33	47 47N	15 48 E
Schneeberg, Ger.	30	50 35N	12 39 E
Schneider	117	41 13N	87 28W
Schofield	118	44 54N	89 39W
Scholls	122	45 24N	122 56W
Schönberg, Rostock, Ger.	30	53 50N	10 55 E
Schönberg, Schleswig-Holstein, Ger.	30	54 23N	10 20 E
Schönebeck	30	52 2N	11 42 E
Schongau	31	47 49N	10 54 E
Schöningen	30	52 8N	10 57 E
Schoolcraft	117	42 7N	85 38W
Schortens	30	53 37N	7 51 E
Schouten I.	72	42 20S	148 20 E
Schouten, Kepulauan	57	1 0S	136 0 E
Schouwen	16	51 43N	3 45 E
Schramberg	31	48 12N	8 24 E
Schrankogl	31	47 3N	11 7 E
Schraumberg	117	42 0N	88 15W
Schreiber	102	48 45N	87 20W
Schrobenhausen	31	48 33N	11 16 E
Schruns	31	47 5N	9 56 E
Schuler	109	50 20N	110 6W
Schumacher	102	48 30N	81 16W
Schurz	120	38 57N	118 48W
Schuyler	118	41 30N	97 3W
Schuylkill Haven	115	40 37N	76 11W
Schwabach	31	49 19N	11 3 E
Schwäbisch Gmünd	31	48 49N	9 48 E
Schwäbisch Hall	31	49 7N	9 45 E
Schwäbische Alb	31	48 30N	9 30 E
Schwabmünchen	31	48 11N	10 45 E
Schwandorf	31	49 20N	12 7 E
Schwarmstedt	30	52 41N	9 37 E
Schwärze	30	52 50N	13 49 E
Schwarzenberg	30	50 31N	12 49 E
Schwarzwald	31	48 0N	8 0 E
Schwaz	31	47 20N	11 44 E
Schwedt	30	53 4N	14 18 E
Schweinfurt	31	50 3N	10 12 E
Schweizer Reneke	96	27 11S	25 18 E
Schwerin	30	53 37N	11 22 E
Schwerin □	30	53 35N	11 20 E
Schweriner See	30	53 45N	11 26 E
Schwetzingen	31	49 22N	8 35 E
Schwyz	31	47 2N	8 39 E
Schwyz □	31	47 2N	8 39 E
Sciacca	28	37 30N	13 3 E
Scicli	29	36 48N	14 41 E
Scie, La	103	49 57N	55 36W
Scilla	29	38 18N	15 44 E
Scillave	45	6 22N	44 32 E
Scilly, Isles of	13	49 55N	6 15W
Scinawa	32	51 25N	16 26 E
Scioto →	112	38 44N	83 0W
Scobey	118	48 47N	105 30W
Scone, Austral.	77	32 5S	150 52 E
Scone, U.K.	14	56 25N	3 26W
Scórdia	29	37 19N	14 50 E
Scoresby Sund	144	70 20N	23 0W
Scorno, Punta dello	28	41 7N	8 23 E
Scotia, Calif., U.S.A.	120	40 36N	124 4W
Scotia, N.Y., U.S.A.	115	42 50N	73 58W
Scotia Sea	143	56 5S	56 0W
Scotland, Can.	106	43 1N	80 22W
Scotland, U.S.A.	118	43 10N	97 45W
Scotland □	14	57 0N	4 0W
Scotland Neck	113	36 6N	77 32W
Scotstown	105	45 32N	71 17W
Scott	143	77 0S	165 0 E
Scott, C., Antarct.	143	71 30S	168 0 E
Scott, C., Austral.	78	13 30S	129 49 E
Scott City	118	38 30N	100 52W
Scott Glacier	143	66 15S	100 5 E
Scott, I.	143	67 0S	179 0 E
Scott Inlet	101	71 0N	71 0W
Scott Is.	108	50 48N	128 40W
Scott-Jonction	105	46 30N	71 4W
Scott L.	109	59 55N	106 18W
Scott Reef	78	14 0S	121 50 E
Scottburgh	97	30 15S	30 47 E
Scottdale	114	40 8N	79 35W
Scottsbluff	118	41 55N	103 35W
Scottsboro	113	34 40N	86 0W
Scottsburg	117	38 40N	85 46W
Scottsdale	72	41 9S	147 31 E
Scottsville, Ky., U.S.A.	113	36 48N	86 10W
Scottsville, N.Y., U.S.A.	114	43 2N	77 47W
Scottville	112	43 57N	86 18W
Scranton, Iowa, U.S.A.	116	42 1N	94 33W
Scranton, Pa., U.S.A.	115	41 22N	75 41W
Scugog, L.	107	44 10N	78 55W
Scunthorpe	12	53 35N	0 38W
Scusciuban	45	10 18N	50 12 E
Sea Breeze	114	43 12N	77 32W
Sea Lake	74	35 28S	142 55 E
Seabra	139	12 25S	41 46W
Seabrook, L.	79	30 55S	119 40 E
Seaford, Austral.	74	38 10S	145 11 E
Seaford, U.S.A.	112	38 37N	75 36W
Seaforth	106	43 35N	81 25W
Seagraves	119	32 56N	102 30W
Seal →	109	58 50N	97 30W
Seal Cove	103	49 57N	56 22W
Seal L.	103	54 20N	61 30W
Seal Rocks	76	32 26S	152 32 E
Sealy	119	29 46N	96 9W
Seaman	117	38 57N	83 34W
Searchlight	123	35 31N	114 55W
Searcy	119	35 15N	91 45W
Searles L.	123	35 47N	117 17W
Seaside, Calif., U.S.A.	122	36 37N	121 50W
Seaside, Oreg., U.S.A.	122	45 59N	123 55W
Seaspray	75	38 25S	147 15 E
Seattle	122	47 41N	122 15W
Seaview Ra.	72	18 40S	145 45 E
Seaward Kaikouras, Mts.	81	42 10S	173 44 E
Sebastián Vizcaíno, Bahía	124	28 0N	114 30W
Sebastopol	122	38 24N	122 49W
Sebastopol = Sevastopol	38	44 35N	33 30 E
Sebderat	91	15 26N	36 42 E
Sebdou	86	34 38N	1 19W
Sebewaing	106	43 45N	83 27W
Sebezh	36	56 14N	28 22 E
Sébi	88	15 50N	4 12W
Sebinkarahisar	38	40 22N	38 28 E
Sebiş	34	46 23N	22 13 E
Sebkra Azzel Mati	86	26 10N	0 43 E
Sebkra Mekerghene	86	26 21N	1 30 E
Sebnitz	30	50 58N	14 17 E
Sebou, Oued →	86	34 16N	6 40W
Sebring, Fla., U.S.A.	113	27 30N	81 26W
Sebring, Ohio, U.S.A.	114	40 55N	81 2W
Sebringville	106	43 24N	81 4W
Sebta = Ceuta	86	35 52N	5 19W
Sebuku	56	3 30S	116 25 E
Sebuku, Teluk	56	4 0N	118 10 E
Secchia →	26	44 4N	11 0 E
Sechelt	108	49 25N	123 42W
Sechura	136	5 39S	80 50W
Sechura, Desierto de	136	6 0S	80 30W
Seclin	19	50 33N	3 2 E
Secondigny	18	46 37N	0 26W
Secretary I.	81	45 15S	166 56 E
Secunderabad	50	17 28N	78 30 E
Sécure →	137	15 10S	64 52W
Sedalia	116	38 40N	93 18W
Sedan, Austral.	73	34 34S	139 19 E
Sedan, France	19	49 43N	4 57 E
Sedan, U.S.A.	119	37 10N	96 11W
Sedano	24	42 43N	3 49W
Seddon	81	41 40S	174 7 E
Seddonville	81	41 33S	172 1 E
Sede Ya'aqov	44	32 43N	35 7 E
Sedgewick	108	52 48N	111 41W
Sedhiou	88	12 44N	15 30W
Sedičany	32	49 40N	14 25 E
Sedico	27	46 8N	12 6 E
Sedley	109	50 10N	104 0W
Sedom	44	31 5N	35 20 E
Sedova, Pik	40	73 29N	54 58 E
Sédrata	87	36 7N	7 31 E
Sedro Woolley	122	48 30N	122 15W
Seduva	36	55 45N	23 45 E
Seebad Ahlbeck	30	53 56N	14 10 E
Seehausen	30	52 52N	11 43 E
Seeheim	96	26 50S	17 45 E
Seekoe →	96	30 18S	25 1 E
Seelaw	30	52 32N	14 22 E
Seeley's Bay	107	44 29N	76 14W
Se'elim, Nahal	44	31 21N	35 24 E
Sées	18	48 38N	0 10 E
Seesen	30	51 53N	10 10 E
Sefadu	88	8 35N	10 58W
Séfeto	88	14 8N	9 49W
Sefrou	86	33 52N	4 52W
Sefton	81	43 15S	172 41 E
Sefuri-San	64	33 28N	130 18 E
Sefwi Bekwai	88	6 10N	2 25W
Seg-ozero	36	63 0N	33 10 E
Segamat	55	2 30N	102 50 E
Segarcea	34	44 6N	23 43 E
Segbwema	88	8 0N	11 0W
Seget	57	1 24S	130 58 E
Seggueur, O. →	86	32 4N	2 4 E
Segid	91	16 55N	42 0 E
Segonzac	20	45 36N	0 14W
Segorbe	24	39 50N	0 30W
Ségou	88	13 30N	6 16W
Segovia, Colomb.	134	7 7N	74 42W
Segovia, Spain	22	40 57N	4 10W
Segovia = Coco →	126	15 0N	83 8W
Segovia □	22	40 55N	4 10W
Segré	18	47 40N	0 52W
Segre →	24	41 40N	0 43 E
Séguéla	88	7 55N	6 40W
Seguin	119	29 34N	97 58W
Segundo	119	37 12N	104 50W
Segundo →	140	30 53S	62 44W
Segura →	25	38 6N	0 54W
Segura, Sierra de	25	38 5N	2 45W
Sehore	48	23 10N	77 5 E
Sehwan	48	26 28N	67 53 E
Seica Mare	34	46 1N	24 7 E
Seikpyu	52	20 54N	94 48 E
Seiling	119	36 10N	98 56W
Seille →, Moselle, France	19	49 7N	6 11 E
Seille →, Saône-et-Loire, France	21	46 31N	4 57 E
Sein, Î. de	18	48 2N	4 52W
Seine →	18	49 26N	0 26 E
Seine, B. de la	18	49 40N	0 40W
Seine-et-Marne □	19	48 45N	3 0 E
Seine-Maritime □	18	49 40N	1 0 E
Seine-Saint-Denis □	19	48 58N	2 24 E
Seistan	47	30 50N	61 0 E
Sejerø	11	55 54N	11 9 E
Sejerø Bugt	11	55 53N	11 15 E
Seka	91	8 10N	36 52 E
Sekayu	56	2 51S	103 51 E
Seke	94	3 20S	33 31 E
Sekenke	94	4 18S	34 11 E
Seki	65	35 29N	136 55 E
Sekigahara	65	35 22N	136 28 E
Sekiu	120	48 16N	124 18W
Sekken Veøy	10	62 45N	7 30 E
Sekondi-Takoradi	88	5 0N	1 48W
Sekuma	96	24 36S	23 50 E
Sela Dingay	91	9 58N	39 32 E
Selah	120	46 44N	120 30W
Selama	55	5 12N	100 42 E
Selárgius	28	39 14N	9 14 E
Selaru	57	8 9S	131 0 E
Selb	31	50 9N	12 9 E
Selby, U.K.	12	53 47N	1 5W
Selby, U.S.A.	118	45 34N	100 2W
Selca	27	43 20N	16 50 E
Selden	118	39 33N	100 39W
Seldovia	100	59 30N	151 45W
Sele →	29	40 27N	14 58 E
Selemdzha →	41	51 42N	128 53 E
Selenge →	62	49 25N	103 59 E
Selenica	35	40 33N	19 39 E
Selenter See	30	54 19N	10 26 E
Sélestat	19	48 16N	7 26 E
Seletan, Tg.	56	4 10S	114 40 E
Seletin	34	47 50N	25 12 E
Selfridge	118	46 3N	100 57W
Sélibaby	88	15 10N	12 15W
Seliger, Oz.	36	57 15N	33 0 E
Seligman	121	35 17N	112 56W
Selim	94	5 31N	23 41 E
Şelim	39	40 30N	42 46 E
Selîma, El Wâhât el	90	21 22N	29 19 E
Selinda Spillway	96	18 35S	23 10 E
Selinoús	35	37 35N	21 37 E
Selizharovo	36	56 51N	33 27 E
Seljord	10	59 30N	8 40 E
Selkirk, Man., Can.	109	50 10N	96 55W
Selkirk, Ont., Can.	106	42 49N	79 56W
Selkirk, U.K.	14	55 33N	2 50W
Selkirk I.	109	53 20N	99 6W
Selkirk Mts.	108	51 15N	117 40W
Selles-sur-Cher	19	47 16N	1 33 E
Sellières	19	46 50N	5 32 E
Sells	121	31 57N	111 57W
Sellye	33	45 52N	17 51 E
Selma, Ala., U.S.A.	113	32 30N	87 0W
Selma, Calif., U.S.A.	122	36 39N	119 39W
Selma, N.C., U.S.A.	113	35 32N	78 15W
Selmer	113	35 9N	88 36W
Selongey	19	47 36N	5 10 E
Selowandoma Falls	95	21 15S	31 50 E
Selpele	57	0 1S	130 5 E
Selsey Bill	13	50 44N	0 47W
Seltz	19	48 48N	8 4 E
Selu	57	7 32S	130 55 E
Selukwe	95	19 40S	30 0 E
Sélune →	18	48 38N	1 22W
Selva, Argent.	140	29 50S	62 0W
Selva, Italy	27	46 33N	11 46 E
Selva, Spain	24	41 13N	1 8 E
Selva Beach, La	122	36 56N	121 51W
Selva, La	24	42 0N	2 45 E
Selvas	136	6 30S	67 0W
Selwyn L.	109	60 0N	104 30W
Selwyn P.O.	72	21 32S	140 30 E
Selwyn Passage	68	16 3S	168 12 E
Selwyn Ra.	72	21 10S	140 0 E
Seman →	35	40 45N	19 50 E
Semarang	57	7 0S	110 26 E
Semau	57	10 13S	123 22 E
Sembabule	94	0 4S	31 25 E
Sémé	88	15 4N	13 41W
Semeih	91	12 43N	30 53 E
Semenov	37	56 43N	44 30 E
Semenovka	38	49 37N	33 10 E
Semeru	57	8 4S	112 55 E
Semiluki	37	51 41N	39 2 E
Seminoe Res.	120	42 0N	107 0W
Seminole, Okla., U.S.A.	119	35 15N	96 45W
Seminole, Tex., U.S.A.	119	32 41N	102 38W
Semiozernoye	40	52 22N	64 8 E
Semipalatinsk	40	50 30N	80 10 E
Semirara Is.	57	12 0N	121 20 E
Semisopochnoi	100	52 0N	179 40W
Semitau	56	0 29N	111 57 E
Semiyarskoye	40	50 55N	78 23 E
Semmering Pass	33	47 41N	15 45 E
Semnān	47	35 55N	53 25 E
Semnān □	47	36 0N	54 0 E
Semois →	16	49 53N	4 44 E
Semporna	57	4 30N	118 33 E
Semuda	56	2 51S	112 58 E
Semur-en-Auxois	19	47 30N	4 20 E
Sena, Boliv.	136	11 32S	67 11W
Sena, Mozam.	95	17 25S	35 0 E
Sena →	136	11 31S	67 11W
Sena Madureira	136	9 5S	68 45W
Senador Pompeu	138	5 40S	39 20W
Senaja	56	6 45N	117 3 E
Senanga	96	16 2S	23 14 E
Senatobia	119	34 38N	89 57W
Sendafa	91	9 11N	39 3 E
Sendai, Kagoshima, Japan	64	31 50N	130 20 E
Sendai, Miyagi, Japan	63	38 15N	140 53 E
Sendamangalam	51	11 17N	78 17 E
Sendeling's Drift	96	28 12S	16 52 E
Sendenhorst	30	51 50N	7 49 E
Sendurjana	50	21 32N	78 17 E
Seneca, Oreg., U.S.A.	120	44 10N	119 2W
Seneca, S.C., U.S.A.	113	34 43N	82 59W
Seneca Falls	115	42 55N	76 50W
Seneca L.	114	42 40N	76 58W

Senegal ■ 88 14 30N 14 30W
Senegal → 88 15 48N 16 32W
Senekal 97 28 30S 27 36 E
Senftenberg 30 51 30N 14 1 E
Senga Hill 95 9 19S 31 11 E
Senge Khambab (Indus) → 48 28 40N 70 10 E
Sengerema □ 94 2 10S 32 20 E
Sengiley 37 53 58N 48 46 E
Sengkang 57 4 8S 120 1 E
Sengua → 95 17 7S 28 5 E
Senguerr → 142 45 35S 68 50W
Senhor-do-Bonfim 138 10 30S 40 10W
Senica 32 48 41N 17 25 E
Senigállia 27 43 42N 13 12 E
Seniku 52 25 32N 97 48 E
Senio → 27 44 35N 12 15 E
Senise 28 40 6N 16 15 E
Senj 27 45 0N 14 58 E
Senja 8 69 25N 17 30 E
Senlis 19 49 13N 2 35 E
Senmonorom 54 12 27N 107 12 E
Sennâr 91 13 30N 33 35 E
Senneterre 104 48 25N 77 15W
Senniquelle 88 7 19N 8 38W
Senno 36 54 45N 29 43 E
Sennori 28 40 49N 8 36 E
Seno 54 16 35N 104 50 E
Senonches 18 48 34N 1 2 E
Senorbì 28 39 33N 9 8 E
Senožeče 27 45 43N 14 3 E
Sens 19 48 11N 3 15 E
Senta 33 45 55N 20 3 E
Sentein 20 42 53N 0 58 E
Sentery 94 5 17S 25 42 E
Sentinel 121 32 45N 113 13W
Sento Sé 138 9 40S 41 18W
Sentolo 57 7 55S 110 13 E
Senya Beraku 89 5 28N 0 31W
Seo de Urgel 24 42 22N 1 23 E
Seohara 49 29 15N 78 33 E
Seoni 49 22 5N 79 30 E
Seoriuarayan 50 21 45N 82 34 E
Seoul = Sŏul 61 37 31N 127 6 E
Separation Point 103 53 37N 57 25W
Sepik → 69 3 49S 144 30 E
Sepo-ri 61 38 57N 127 25 E
Sepone 54 16 45N 106 13 E
Sepopa 96 18 49S 22 12 E
Sept-Îles 103 50 13N 66 22W
Septemvri 34 42 13N 24 6 E
Sepúlveda 22 41 18N 3 45W
Sequeros 22 40 31N 6 2W
Sequim 122 48 3N 123 9W
Sequoia Nat. Park 122 36 30N 118 30W
Serafimovich 39 49 36N 42 43 E
Seraing 16 50 35N 5 32 E
Seraja 55 2 41N 108 35 E
Seram 57 3 10S 129 0 E
Seram Sea 57 2 30S 128 30 E
Serampore 49 22 44N 88 21 E
Serang 57 6 8S 106 10 E
Serasan 55 2 29N 109 4 E
Seravezza 26 43 59N 10 13 E
Serbia = Srbija 33 43 30N 21 0 E
Serdo 91 11 56N 41 14 E
Serdobsk 37 52 28N 44 10 E
Seredka 36 58 12N 28 10 E
Seregno 26 45 40N 9 12 E
Seremban 55 2 43N 101 53 E
Serena, La, Chile 140 29 55S 71 10W
Serena, La, Spain 23 38 45N 5 40W
Serengeti □ 94 2 0S 34 30 E
Serengeti Plain 94 2 40S 35 0 E
Sergach 37 55 30N 45 30 E
Serge → 24 41 54N 0 50 E
Sergino 40 62 30N 65 38 E
Sergipe □ 138 10 30S 37 30W
Seria 56 4 37N 114 23 E
Serian 56 1 10N 110 31 E
Seriate 26 45 42N 9 43 E
Seribu, Kepulauan 56 5 36S 106 33 E
Sérifontaine 19 49 20N 1 45 E
Sérifos 35 37 9N 24 30 E
Sérignan 20 43 17N 3 17 E
Seringapatam Reef 78 13 38S 122 5 E
Sermaize-les-Bains 19 48 47N 4 54 E
Sermata 57 8 15S 128 50 E
Sérmide 27 45 0N 11 17 E
Serny Zavod 40 39 59N 58 50 E
Séro 88 14 48N 10 59W
Serón 25 37 20N 2 29W
Serós 24 41 27N 0 24 E
Serov 40 59 29N 60 35 E
Serowe 96 22 25S 26 43 E
Serpa 23 37 57N 7 38 E
Serpeddi, Punta 28 39 19N 9 18 E
Serpentara 28 39 8N 9 38 E
Serpentine, Vic., Austral. 74 36 25S 144 0 E
Serpentine, W.A., Austral. 79 32 23S 115 58 E
Serpentine Lakes 79 28 30S 129 10 E
Serpis → 25 38 59N 0 9W
Serpukhov 37 54 55N 37 28 E
Serra do Navio 135 0 59N 52 3W
Serra San Bruno 29 38 31N 16 23 E
Serra Talhada 138 7 59S 38 18W
Serracapriola 29 41 47N 15 12 E
Serradilla 22 39 50N 6 9W
Sérrai 35 41 5N 23 31 E
Serramanna 28 39 26N 8 56 E
Serrat, C. 87 37 14N 9 10 E
Serre-Poncon, Barrage de 21 44 22N 6 20 E
Serres 21 44 26N 5 43 E
Serrezuela 140 30 40S 65 20W
Serrinha 139 11 39S 39 0W
Serrita 138 7 56S 39 19W
Sersale 29 39 1N 16 44 E
Sertã 22 39 48N 8 6W
Sertânia 138 8 5S 37 20W
Sertanópolis 141 23 4S 51 2W
Sêrtar 58 32 20N 100 41 E
Serua 57 6 18S 130 1 E
Serui 57 1 53S 136 10 E
Serule 96 21 57S 27 20 E
Sérvia 35 40 9N 21 58 E
Serviceton 74 36 22S 141 0 E
Sese Is. 94 0 20S 32 20 E
Sesepe 57 1 30S 127 59 E
Sesfontein 96 19 7S 13 39 E
Sesheke 96 17 29S 24 13 E
Sesia → 26 45 5N 8 37 E
Sesimbra 23 38 28N 9 6W
Sessa Aurunca 28 41 14N 13 55 E
Sesser 116 38 7N 89 3W
Sestao 24 43 18N 3 0W
Sesto S. Giovanni 26 45 32N 9 14 E
Sestri Levante 26 44 17N 9 22 E
Sestrières 26 44 58N 6 56 E
Sestrunj 27 44 10N 15 0 E
Sestu 28 39 18N 9 6 E
Setaka 64 33 9N 130 28 E
Setana 63 42 26N 139 51 E
Sète 20 43 25N 3 42 E
Sete Lagôas 139 19 27S 44 16W
Sétif 87 36 9N 5 26 E
Seto 65 35 14N 137 6 E
Seto Naikai 64 34 20N 133 30 E
Setouchi 63 28 8N 129 19 E
Setsan 52 16 3N 95 23 E
Settat 86 33 0N 7 40W
Setté Cama 92 2 32S 9 45 E
Séttimo Tor 26 45 9N 7 46 E
Setting L. 109 55 0N 98 38W
Settle 12 54 5N 2 18W
Settlement Pt. 113 26 40N 79 0W
Setto Calende 26 45 44N 8 37 E
Setúbal 23 38 30N 8 58W
Setúbal □ 23 38 25N 8 35W
Setúbal, B. de 23 38 40N 8 56W
Seugne → 20 45 42N 0 32W
Seul Réservoir, Lac 102 50 25N 92 30W
Seulimeum 56 5 27N 95 15 E
Sevan, Oz. 38 40 20N 45 20 E
Sevastopol 38 44 35N 33 30 E
Seven Emu 72 16 20S 137 8 E
Seven Sisters 108 54 56N 128 10W
Sever → 23 39 40N 7 32W
Sévérac-le-Château 20 44 20N 3 5 E
Severn →, Austral. 77 29 8S 150 59 E
Severn →, Can. 102 56 2N 87 36W
Severn →, U.K. 13 51 35N 2 38W
Severn L. 102 53 54N 90 48W
Severnaya Zemlya 41 79 0N 100 0 E
Severo-Kurilsk 41 50 40N 156 8 E
Severo-Yeniseyskiy 41 60 22N 93 1 E
Severodonetsk 39 48 58N 38 30 E
Severodvinsk 40 64 27N 39 58 E
Sevier 121 38 39N 112 11W
Sevier → 121 39 10N 113 6W
Sevier L. 120 39 0N 113 20W
Sevilla, Colomb. 134 4 16N 75 57W
Sevilla, Spain 23 37 23N 6 0W
Sevilla □ 23 37 25N 5 30W
Seville = Sevilla 23 37 23N 6 0W
Sevnica 27 46 2N 15 19 E
Sèvre-Nantaise → 18 47 12N 1 33W
Sèvre Niortaise → 20 46 18N 1 8W
Sevsk 36 52 10N 34 30 E
Seward, Alaska, U.S.A. 100 60 6N 149 26W
Seward, Nebr., U.S.A. 118 40 55N 97 6W
Seward Pen. 100 65 0N 164 0W
Sewell 140 34 10S 70 23W
Sewer 57 5 53S 134 40 E
Sewickley 114 40 33N 80 12W
Sexsmith 108 55 21N 118 47W
Seychelles 53 5 0S 56 0 E
Seyðisfjörður 8 65 16N 14 0W
Seym → 36 51 27N 32 34 E
Seymchan 41 62 54N 152 30 E
Seymour, Austral. 74 37 0S 145 10 E
Seymour, Conn., U.S.A. 115 41 23N 73 5W
Seymour, Ind., U.S.A. 117 39 0N 85 50W
Seymour, Iowa, U.S.A. 116 40 45N 93 7W
Seymour, Tex., U.S.A. 119 33 35N 99 18W
Seymour, Wis., U.S.A. 112 44 30N 88 20W
Seyne 21 44 21N 6 22 E
Seyne-sur-Mer, La 21 43 7N 5 52 E
Seyssel 21 45 57N 5 50 E
Sežana 27 45 43N 13 41 E
Sézanne 19 48 40N 3 40 E
Sezze 28 41 30N 13 3 E
Sfax 87 34 49N 10 48 E
Sfîntu Gheorghe 34 45 52N 25 48 E
Sha Xi → 59 26 35N 118 0 E
Sha Xian 59 26 23N 117 45 E
Shaanxi □ 60 35 0N 109 0 E
Shaba 94 8 0S 25 0 E
Shabani 95 20 17S 30 2 E
Shabunda 94 2 40S 27 16 E
Shache 62 38 20N 77 10 E
Shackleton 143 78 30S 36 1W
Shackleton Ice Shelf 143 66 0S 100 0 E
Shackleton Inlet 143 83 0S 160 0 E
Shaddad 90 21 25N 40 2 E
Shadi, China 59 26 7N 114 47 E
Shadi, Kashmir 49 33 24N 77 4 E
Shadrinsk 40 56 5N 63 32 E
Shafer, L. 117 40 46N 86 46W
Shaffa 89 10 30N 12 6 E
Shafter, Calif., U.S.A. 123 35 32N 119 14W
Shafter, Tex., U.S.A. 119 29 49N 104 18W
Shaftesbury 13 51 0N 2 12W
Shag Pt. 81 45 29S 170 52 E
Shagamu 89 6 51N 3 39 E
Shagram 49 36 24N 72 20 E
Shah Bunder 48 24 13N 67 56 E
Shahabad, Andhra Pradesh, India 50 17 10N 76 54 E
Shahabad, Punjab, India 48 30 10N 76 55 E
Shahabad, Raj., India 48 25 15N 77 11 E
Shahabad, Ut. P., India 49 27 36N 79 55 E
Shāhābād 47 37 40N 56 50 E
Shahada 50 21 33N 74 30 E
Shahadpur 48 25 55N 68 35 E
Shahapur 51 15 50N 74 34 E
Shāhbād 46 34 10N 46 30 E
Shahdād 47 30 30N 57 40 E
Shahdadkot 48 27 50N 67 55 E
Shahe 60 37 0N 114 32 E
Shahganj 49 26 3N 82 44 E
Shahhat (Cyrene) 85 32 48N 21 54 E
Shāhī 47 36 30N 52 55 E
Shahjahanpur 49 27 54N 79 57 E
Shahpur, Mad. P., India 48 22 12N 77 58 E
Shahpur, Mysore, India 50 16 40N 76 48 E
Shahpūr 46 38 12N 44 45 E
Shahpur 48 28 46N 68 27 E
Shahpura 49 23 10N 80 45 E
Shahr Kord 47 32 15N 50 55 E
Shahrezā 47 32 0N 51 55 E
Shahrig 48 30 15N 67 40 E
Shāhrūd 47 36 30N 55 0 E
Shahsād, Namakzār-e 47 30 20N 58 20 E
Shahsavār 47 36 45N 51 12 E
Shahukou 60 40 20N 112 18 E
Shaibara 90 25 26N 36 47 E
Shaikhabad 48 34 2N 68 45 E
Shajapur 48 23 27N 76 21 E
Shakargarh 48 32 17N 75 10 E
Shakawe 96 18 28S 21 49 E
Shaker Heights 114 41 29N 81 36W
Shakhty 39 47 40N 40 16 E
Shakhunya 37 57 40N 46 46 E
Shaki 89 8 41N 3 21 E
Shakopee 118 44 45N 93 30W
Shala, L. 91 7 30N 38 30 E
Shallow Lake 106 44 36N 81 5W
Shaluli Shan 58 30 40N 99 55 E
Sham, J. ash 47 23 10N 57 5 E
Shama 89 5 1N 1 35W
Shamâl Dârfûr □ 91 15 0N 25 0 E
Shamâl Kordofân □ 91 15 0N 30 0 E
Shamattawa 109 55 51N 92 5W
Shamattawa → 102 55 1N 85 23W
Shambe 91 7 8N 30 46 E
Shambu 91 9 32N 37 3 E
Shamgong Dzong 52 27 13N 90 35 E
Shamil 47 27 30N 56 55 E
Shamkhor 39 40 50N 46 0 E
Shamli 48 29 32N 77 18 E
Shammar, Jabal 46 27 40N 41 0 E
Shamo, L. 91 5 45N 37 30 E
Shamokin 115 40 47N 76 33W
Shamrock 119 35 15N 100 15W
Shan □ 52 21 30N 98 30 E
Shan Xian 60 34 50N 116 5 E
Shanan → 91 8 0N 40 20 E
Shanchengzhen 61 42 20N 125 20 E
Shandon 122 35 39N 120 23W
Shandon Downs 72 17 45S 134 50 E
Shandong □ 61 36 0N 118 0 E
Shandong Bandao 61 37 0N 121 0 E
Shang Xian 60 33 50N 109 58 E
Shangalowe 95 10 50S 26 30 E
Shangani 95 19 41S 29 20 E
Shangani → 95 18 41S 27 10 E
Shangbancheng 61 40 50N 118 1 E
Shangcai 59 33 18N 114 14 E
Shangcheng 59 31 47N 115 26 E
Shangchuan Dao 59 21 40N 112 50 E
Shangdu 60 41 30N 113 30 E
Shanggao 59 28 17N 114 55 E
Shanghai 59 31 15N 121 26 E
Shanghang 59 25 2N 116 23 E
Shanghe 61 37 20N 117 10 E
Shangjin 59 33 7N 110 3 E
Shanglin 58 23 27N 108 33 E
Shangnan 60 33 32N 110 50 E
Shangqiu 60 34 26N 115 36 E
Shangrao 59 28 25N 117 59 E
Shangshui 60 33 42N 114 35 E
Shangsi 58 22 8N 107 58 E
Shangzhi 61 45 22N 127 56 E
Shanhetun 61 44 33N 127 15 E
Shani 89 10 14N 12 2 E
Shaniko 120 45 0N 120 50W
Shannon, Greenl. 144 75 10N 18 30W
Shannon, N.Z. 80 40 33S 175 25 E
Shannon → 15 52 35N 9 30W
Shannons Flat 76 35 55S 148 58 E
Shansi = Shanxi □ 60 37 0N 112 0 E
Shantar, Ostrov Bolshoy 41 55 9N 137 40 E
Shantou 59 23 18N 116 40 E
Shantung = Shandong □ 61 36 0N 118 0 E
Shanxi □ 60 37 0N 112 0 E
Shanyang 60 33 31N 109 55 E
Shanyin 60 39 25N 112 56 E
Shaoguan 59 24 48N 113 35 E
Shaowu 59 27 22N 117 28 E
Shaoxing 59 30 0N 120 35 E
Shaoyang, Hunan, China 59 27 14N 111 25 E
Shaoyang, Hunan, China 59 26 59N 111 20 E
Shapinsay 14 59 2N 2 50W
Shaqra 46 25 15N 45 16 E
Sharafa (Ogr) 91 11 59N 27 7 E
Sharavati → 51 14 20N 74 25 E
Sharbot Lake 107 44 46N 76 41W
Shari 46 27 14N 43 29 E
Sharjah 47 25 23N 55 26 E
Shark B. 79 25 55S 113 32 E
Sharm el Sheikh 90 27 53N 34 15 E
Sharon, Mass., U.S.A. 115 42 5N 71 11W
Sharon, Pa., U.S.A. 114 41 18N 80 30W
Sharon, Wis., U.S.A. 117 42 30N 88 44W
Sharon, Plain of = Hasharon 44 32 12N 34 49 E
Sharon Springs 118 38 54N 101 45W
Sharp Pt. 72 10 58S 142 43 E
Sharpe L. 109 54 5N 93 40W
Sharpsville 114 41 15N 80 28W
Sharya 37 58 22N 45 20 E
Shasha 91 6 29N 35 59 E
Shashemene 91 7 13N 38 33 E
Shashi 59 30 25N 112 14 E
Shashi → 95 21 14S 29 20 E
Shasta, Mt. 120 41 30N 122 12W
Shasta Res. 120 40 50N 122 15W
Shatsk 37 54 0N 41 45 E
Shattuck 119 36 17N 99 55W
Shaumyani 39 41 22N 41 45 E
Shaunavon 109 49 35N 108 25W
Shaver Lake 122 37 9N 119 18W
Shaw → 78 20 21S 119 17 E
Shaw I. 72 20 30S 149 2 E
Shawan 62 44 34N 85 50 E
Shawanaga 106 45 31N 80 17W
Shawano 112 44 45N 88 38W
Shawinigan 105 46 35N 72 50W
Shawinigan Sud 105 46 31N 72 45W
Shawnee, Kans., U.S.A. 116 39 1N 94 43W
Shawnee, Okla., U.S.A. 119 35 15N 97 0W
Shawville 104 45 36N 76 30W
Shayib el Banat, Bebel 90 26 59N 33 29 E
Shchekino 37 54 1N 37 34 E
Shcherbakov = Rybinsk 37 58 5N 38 50 E
Shchigri 37 51 55N 36 58 E
Shchors 36 51 48N 31 56 E
Shchuchiosk 40 52 56N 70 12 E
She Xian, Anhui, China 59 29 50N 118 25 E

She Xian, Hebei, China **60** 36 30N 113 40 E
Shea **135** 2 48N 59 4W
Shebekino **37** 50 28N 36 54 E
Shebele, Wabi → **91** 2 0N 44 0 E
Sheboygan **112** 43 46N 87 45W
Shechem **44** 32 13N 35 21 E
Shediac **103** 46 14N 64 32W
Sheelin, Lough **15** 53 48N 7 20W
Sheep Haven **15** 55 12N 7 55W
Sheep Hills **74** 36 20S 142 33 E
Sheerness **13** 51 26N 0 47 E
Sheet Harbour **103** 44 56N 62 31W
Shefar'am **44** 32 48N 35 10 E
Sheffield, U.K. **12** 53 23N 1 28W
Sheffield, Ala., U.S.A. **113** 34 45N 87 42W
Sheffield, Ill., U.S.A. **116** 41 21N 89 44W
Sheffield, Iowa, U.S.A. **116** 42 54N 93 13W
Sheffield, Mass., U.S.A. **115** 42 6N 73 23W
Sheffield, Pa., U.S.A. **114** 41 42N 79 3W
Sheffield, Tex., U.S.A. **119** 30 42N 101 49W
Shegaon **50** 20 48N 76 47 E
Sheguiandah **106** 45 54N 81 55W
Sheho **109** 51 35N 103 13W
Shehojele **91** 10 40N 35 9 E
Shehong **58** 30 54N 105 18 E
Shehuen → **142** 49 35S 69 34W
Sheikhpura **49** 25 9N 85 53 E
Shek Hasan **91** 12 5N 35 58 E
Shekhupura **48** 31 42N 73 58 E
Sheki **39** 41 10N 47 5 E
Sheksna → **37** 59 0N 38 30 E
Shelbina **116** 39 47N 92 2W
Shelbourne **74** 36 53S 144 2 E
Shelburn **117** 39 10N 87 24W
Shelburne, N.S., Can. **103** 43 47N 65 20W
Shelburne, Ont., Can. **106** 44 4N 80 15W
Shelburne, U.S.A. **115** 44 23N 73 15W
Shelburne B. **72** 11 50S 142 50 E
Shelburne Falls **115** 42 36N 72 45W
Shelby, Mich., U.S.A. **112** 43 34N 86 27W
Shelby, Mont., U.S.A. **120** 48 30N 111 52W
Shelby, N.C., U.S.A. **113** 35 18N 81 34W
Shelby, Ohio, U.S.A. **114** 40 52N 82 40W
Shelbyville, Ill., U.S.A. **117** 39 25N 88 45W
Shelbyville, Ind., U.S.A. **117** 39 30N 85 42W
Shelbyville, Ky., U.S.A. **117** 38 13N 85 14W
Shelbyville, Mo., U.S.A. **116** 39 48N 92 2W
Shelbyville, Tenn., U.S.A. **113** 35 30N 86 25W
Shelbyville, Res. **117** 39 26N 88 46W
Sheldon, Iowa, U.S.A. **118** 43 6N 95 40W
Sheldon, Mo., U.S.A. **116** 37 40N 94 18W
Sheldrake **103** 50 20N 64 51W
Shelikhova, Zaliv **41** 59 30N 157 0 E
Shell Creek Ra. **120** 39 15N 114 30W
Shell Lake **109** 53 19N 107 2W
Shell Lakes **79** 29 20S 127 30 E
Shellbrook **109** 53 13N 106 24W
Shellharbour **76** 34 31S 150 51 E
Shelling Rocks **15** 51 45N 10 35W
Shellsburg **116** 42 6N 91 52W
Shelon → **36** 58 10N 30 30 E
Shelton, Conn., U.S.A. **115** 41 18N 73 7W
Shelton, Wash., U.S.A. **122** 47 15N 123 6W
Shemakha **39** 40 38N 48 37 E
Shen Xian **60** 36 15N 115 40 E
Shenandoah, Iowa, U.S.A. **118** 40 50N 95 25W
Shenandoah, Pa., U.S.A. **115** 40 49N 76 13W
Shenandoah, Va., U.S.A. **112** 38 30N 78 38W
Shenandoah → **112** 39 19N 77 44W
Shenchi **60** 39 8N 112 10 E
Shencottah **51** 8 59N 77 18 E
Shendam **89** 8 49N 9 30 E
Shendî **91** 16 46N 33 22 E
Shendurni **50** 20 39N 75 36 E
Sheng Xian **59** 29 35N 120 50 E
Shengfang **60** 39 3N 116 42 E
Shëngjergji **35** 41 17N 20 10 E
Shëngjini **35** 41 50N 19 35 E
Shenjingzi **61** 44 40N 124 30 E
Shenmu **60** 38 50N 110 29 E
Shennongjia **59** 31 43N 110 44 E
Shenqiu **60** 33 25N 115 5 E
Shensi = Shaanxi □ **60** 35 0N 109 0 E
Shenyang **61** 41 48N 123 27 E
Shepetovka **36** 50 10N 27 10 E
Shephelah = Hashefela **44** 31 30N 34 43 E
Shepherd **106** 43 32N 84 41W
Shepherd Is. **68** 16 55S 168 36 E
Shepherdsville **117** 37 59N 85 43W
Shepparton **74** 36 23S 145 26 E
Shepparton East **74** 36 25S 145 30 E
Sheqi **60** 33 12N 112 57 E
Sher Khan Qala **48** 29 55N 66 20 E
Sher Qila **49** 36 7N 74 2 E
Sherada **91** 7 18N 36 30 E
Sherborne **13** 50 56N 2 31W
Sherbro I. **88** 7 30N 12 40W
Sherbrooke **105** 45 28N 71 57W
Sherda **87** 20 7N 16 46 E
Shereik **90** 18 44N 33 47 E
Sheridan, Ark., U.S.A. **119** 34 20N 92 25W
Sheridan, Col., U.S.A. **118** 39 44N 105 3W
Sheridan, Ill., U.S.A. **117** 41 32N 88 41W
Sheridan, Ind., U.S.A. **117** 40 8N 86 13W
Sheridan, Iowa, U.S.A. **116** 40 31N 94 37W
Sheridan, Wyo., U.S.A. **120** 44 50N 107 0W
Sherkot **49** 29 22N 78 35 E
Sherman **119** 33 40N 96 35W
Sherpur **52** 25 0N 90 0 E
Sherridon **109** 55 8N 101 5W
Sherwood, N.D., U.S.A. **118** 48 59N 101 36W
Sherwood, Ohio, U.S.A. **117** 41 17N 84 33W
Sherwood, Tex., U.S.A. **119** 31 18N 100 45W
Sherwood Forest **12** 53 5N 1 5W
Sheslay **108** 58 17N 131 52W
Sheslay → **108** 58 48N 132 5W
Shethanei L. **109** 58 48N 97 50W
Shetland □ **14** 60 30N 1 30W
Shetland Is. **14** 60 30N 1 30W
Shevaroy Hills **51** 11 58N 78 12 E
Shewa □ **91** 9 33N 38 10 E
Sheyenne **118** 47 52N 99 8W
Sheyenne → **118** 47 5N 96 50W
Shiawassee → **106** 43 38N 83 50W
Shibam **45** 16 0N 48 36 E
Shibata **63** 37 57N 139 20 E
Shibetsu **63** 44 10N 142 23 E
Shibîn El Kôm **90** 30 31N 30 55 E
Shibîn el Qanâtir **90** 30 19N 31 19 E
Shibing **58** 27 2N 108 7 E
Shibogama L. **102** 53 35N 88 15W
Shibukawa **65** 36 29N 139 0 E
Shibushi **64** 31 25N 131 8 E
Shibushi-Wan **64** 31 24N 131 8 E
Shicheng **59** 26 22N 116 20 E
Shidao **61** 36 50N 122 25 E
Shidian **58** 24 40N 99 5 E
Shido **64** 34 19N 134 10 E
Shiel, L. **14** 56 48N 5 32W
Shield, C. **72** 13 20S 136 20 E
Shiga □ **65** 35 20N 136 0 E
Shigaib **85** 15 5N 23 35 E
Shigaraki **65** 34 57N 136 2 E
Shigu **58** 26 51N 99 56 E
Shiguaigou **60** 40 52N 110 15 E
Shihchiachuangi = Shijiazhuang **60** 38 2N 114 28 E
Shiiba **64** 32 29N 131 4 E
Shijiazhuang **60** 38 2N 114 28 E
Shijiu Hu **59** 31 25N 118 50 E
Shikarpur, India **48** 28 17N 78 7 E
Shikarpur, Pak. **48** 27 57N 68 39 E
Shikine-Jima **65** 34 19N 139 13 E
Shikoku **64** 33 30N 133 30 E
Shikoku □ **64** 33 30N 133 30 E
Shikoku-Sanchi **64** 33 30N 133 30 E
Shilka **41** 52 0N 115 55 E
Shilka → **41** 53 20N 121 26 E
Shillelagh **15** 52 46N 6 32W
Shillong **52** 25 35N 91 53 E
Shilo **44** 32 4N 35 18 E
Shilong **59** 23 5N 113 52 E
Shilou **60** 37 0N 110 48 E
Shilovo **37** 54 25N 40 57 E
Shima-Hantō **65** 34 22N 136 45 E
Shimabara **64** 32 48N 130 20 E
Shimada **65** 34 49N 138 10 E
Shimane □ **64** 35 0N 132 30 E
Shimane-Hantō **64** 35 30N 133 0 E
Shimanovsk **41** 52 15N 127 30 E
Shimen **59** 29 35N 111 20 E
Shimenjie **59** 29 29N 116 48 E
Shimian **58** 29 17N 102 23 E
Shimizu **65** 35 0N 138 30 E
Shimo-Jima **64** 32 15N 130 7 E
Shimo-Koshiki-Jima **64** 31 40N 129 43 E
Shimoda **65** 34 40N 138 57 E
Shimodate **65** 36 20N 139 55 E
Shimoga **51** 13 57N 75 32 E
Shimoni **94** 4 38S 39 20 E
Shimonita **65** 36 13N 138 47 E
Shimonoseki **64** 33 58N 131 0 E
Shimotsuma **65** 36 11N 139 58 E
Shimpuru Rapids **96** 17 45S 19 55 E
Shimsha → **51** 13 15N 77 10 E
Shimsk **36** 58 15N 30 50 E
Shin, L. **14** 58 7N 4 30W
Shin-Tone → **65** 35 44N 140 51 E
Shinan **58** 22 44N 109 53 E
Shinano-Gawa → **63** 36 50N 138 30 E
Shindand **47** 33 12N 62 8 E
Shingbwiyang **52** 26 41N 96 13 E
Shingleton **102** 46 25N 86 33W
Shingū **65** 33 40N 135 55 E
Shinji **64** 35 24N 132 54 E
Shinji Ko **64** 35 26N 132 57 E
Shinjō **63** 38 46N 140 18 E
Shinkafe **89** 13 8N 6 29 E
Shinminato **65** 36 47N 137 4 E
Shinonoi **65** 36 35N 138 9 E
Shinshiro **65** 34 54N 137 30 E
Shinyanga **94** 3 45S 33 27 E
Shinyanga □, Tanz. **94** 3 30S 33 30 E
Shinyanga □, Tanz. **94** 3 50S 34 0 E
Shio-no-Misaki **65** 33 25N 135 45 E
Shiogama **63** 38 19N 141 1 E
Shiojiri **65** 36 6N 137 58 E
Ship I. **119** 30 16N 88 55W
Shipehenski Prokhod **34** 42 45N 25 15 E
Shiping **58** 23 45N 102 23 E
Shippegan **103** 47 45N 64 45W
Shippensburg **114** 40 4N 77 32W
Shiprock **121** 36 51N 108 45W
Shiqian **58** 27 32N 108 13 E
Shiquan **60** 33 5N 108 15 E
Shir Kūh **47** 31 39N 54 3 E
Shirahama **65** 33 41N 135 20 E
Shirakawa **65** 36 17N 136 56 E
Shirane-San, Gumma, Japan **65** 36 48N 139 22 E
Shirane-San, Yamanashi, Japan **65** 35 42N 138 9 E
Shiraoi **63** 42 33N 141 21 E
Shirāz **47** 29 42N 52 30 E
Shirbin **90** 31 11N 31 32 E
Shire → **95** 17 42S 35 19 E
Shirinab → **48** 30 15N 66 28 E
Shiriya-Zaki **63** 41 25N 141 30 E
Shirley **117** 39 53N 85 35W
Shirol **50** 16 47N 74 41 E
Shirpur **50** 21 21N 74 57 E
Shirvan **47** 37 30N 57 50 E
Shishou **59** 29 38N 112 22 E
Shisur **45** 17 30N 54 0 E
Shitai **59** 30 12N 117 25 E
Shivali (Sirkali) **51** 11 15N 79 41 E
Shively **117** 38 12N 85 49W
Shivpuri **48** 25 26N 77 42 E
Shivta **44** 30 53N 34 40 E
Shiwele Ferry **95** 11 25S 28 31 E
Shixian **61** 43 5N 129 50 E
Shixing **59** 24 46N 114 5 E
Shiyan **59** 32 35N 110 45 E
Shiyata **90** 29 25N 25 7 E
Shizhu **58** 29 58N 108 7 E
Shizong **58** 24 50N 104 0 E
Shizuishan **60** 39 15N 106 50 E
Shizuoka **65** 35 0N 138 24 E
Shizuoka □ **65** 35 15N 138 40 E
Shklov **36** 54 16N 30 15 E
Shkoder = Shkodra **34** 42 6N 19 1 E
Shkodra **34** 42 6N 19 20 E
Shkumbini → **35** 41 5N 19 50 E
Shmidt, O. **41** 81 0N 91 0 E
Shō Gawa → **65** 36 47N 137 4 E
Shoa Ghimirra = Wota **91** 7 4N 35 51 E
Shoal, C. **79** 33 52S 121 10 E
Shoal Cr. → **116** 39 39N 93 35W
Shoal Lake **109** 50 30N 100 35W
Shoalhaven → **76** 34 54S 150 42 E
Shoals **117** 38 40N 86 47W
Shōbara **64** 34 51N 133 1 E
Shōdo-Shima **64** 34 30N 134 15 E
Shoeburyness **13** 51 31N 0 49 E
Sholapur **50** 17 43N 75 56 E
Shologontsy **41** 66 13N 114 0 E
Shomera **44** 33 4N 35 17 E
Shōmrōn **44** 32 15N 35 13 E
Shongopovi **121** 35 49N 110 37W
Shoranur **51** 10 46N 76 19 E
Shorapur **51** 16 31N 76 48 E
Shortland I. **69** 7 0S 155 45 E
Shoshone, Calif., U.S.A. **123** 35 58N 116 16W
Shoshone, Idaho, U.S.A. **120** 43 0N 114 27W
Shoshone L. **120** 44 30N 110 40W
Shoshone Mts. **120** 39 30N 117 30W
Shoshong **96** 22 56S 26 31 E
Shoshoni **120** 43 13N 108 5W
Shostka **36** 51 57N 33 32 E
Shou Xian **59** 32 37N 116 42 E
Shouchang **59** 29 18N 119 12 E
Shouguang **61** 37 52N 118 45 E
Shouning **59** 27 27N 119 31 E
Shouyang **60** 37 54N 113 8 E
Show Low **121** 34 16N 110 0W
Shpola **38** 49 1N 31 30 E
Shreveport **119** 32 30N 93 50W
Shrewsbury **12** 52 42N 2 45W
Shrivardhan **50** 18 4N 73 3 E
Shropshire □ = Salop **13** 52 36N 2 45W
Shuangbai **58** 24 42N 101 38 E
Shuangcheng **61** 45 20N 126 15 E
Shuangfeng **59** 27 29N 112 11 E
Shuanggou **61** 34 2N 117 30 E
Shuangjiang **58** 23 26N 99 58 E
Shuangliao **61** 43 29N 123 30 E
Shuangshanzi **61** 40 20N 119 8 E
Shuangyang **61** 43 28N 125 40 E
Shuangyashan **62** 46 28N 131 5 E
Shucheng **59** 31 28N 116 57 E
Shu'eib, Wadi **44** 31 54N 35 38 E
Shuguri Falls **95** 8 33S 37 22 E
Shuicheng **58** 26 38N 104 48 E
Shuiji **59** 27 13N 118 20 E
Shuiye **60** 36 7N 114 8 E
Shujalpur **48** 23 18N 76 46 E
Shukpa Kunzang **49** 34 22N 78 22 E
Shulan **61** 44 28N 127 0 E
Shule **62** 39 25N 76 3 E
Shullsburg **116** 42 35N 90 15W
Shumagin Is. **100** 55 0N 159 0W
Shumerlya **37** 55 30N 46 25 E
Shumikha **40** 55 10N 63 15 E
Shunchang **59** 26 54N 117 48 E
Shunde **59** 22 42N 113 14 E
Shungay **39** 48 30N 46 45 E
Shungnak **100** 66 55N 157 10W
Shuo Xian **60** 39 20N 112 33 E
Shuqra **45** 13 22N 45 44 E
Shur → **47** 28 30N 55 0 E
Shurkhua **52** 22 15N 93 38 E
Shūsf **47** 31 50N 60 5 E
Shūshtar **46** 32 0N 48 50 E
Shuswap L. **108** 50 55N 119 3W
Shuweika **44** 32 20N 35 1 E
Shuya **37** 56 50N 41 28 E
Shuyang **61** 34 10N 118 42 E
Shuzenji **65** 34 58N 138 56 E
Shwebo **52** 22 30N 95 45 E
Shwegu **52** 24 15N 96 26 E
Shwegun **52** 17 9N 97 39 E
Shwenyaung **52** 20 46N 96 57 E
Shyok **49** 34 15N 78 12 E
Shyok → **49** 35 13N 75 53 E
Si Chon **55** 9 0N 99 54 E
Si Kiang = Xi Jiang → **59** 22 5N 113 20 E
Si Prachan **54** 14 37N 100 9 E
Si Racha **54** 13 10N 100 48 E
Si Xian **61** 33 30N 117 50 E
Siah **46** 22 0N 47 0 E
Siahan Range **47** 27 30N 64 40 E
Siaksrinderapura **56** 0 51N 102 0 E
Sialkot **48** 32 32N 74 30 E
Sialsuk **52** 23 24N 92 45 E
Siam = Thailand ■ **54** 16 0N 102 0 E
Siam, G. of **55** 11 30N 101 0 E
Sian = Xi'an **60** 34 15N 109 0 E
Siantan, P. **55** 3 10N 106 15 E
Siàpo → **134** 2 7N 66 28W
Siāreh **47** 28 5N 60 14 E
Siargao **57** 9 52N 126 3 E
Siari **49** 34 55N 76 40 E
Siasi **57** 5 34N 120 50 E
Siassi **69** 5 40S 147 51 E
Siátista **35** 40 15N 21 33 E
Siau **57** 2 50N 125 25 E
Siauliai **36** 55 56N 23 15 E
Siaya □ **94** 0 0N 34 20 E
Siazan **39** 41 3N 49 10 E
Sibâi, Gebel el **90** 25 45N 34 10 E
Sibari **29** 39 47N 16 27 E
Sibaya, L. **97** 27 20S 32 45 E
Šibenik **27** 43 48N 15 54 E
Siberia **42** 60 0N 100 0 E
Siberut **56** 1 30S 99 0 E
Sibi **48** 29 30N 67 54 E
Sibil **57** 4 59S 140 35 E
Sibiti **92** 3 38S 13 19 E
Sibiu **34** 45 45N 24 9 E
Sibley, Ill., U.S.A. **117** 40 35N 88 23W
Sibley, Iowa, U.S.A. **118** 43 21N 95 43W
Sibley, La., U.S.A. **119** 32 34N 93 16W
Sibolga **56** 1 42N 98 45 E
Sibsagar **52** 27 0N 94 36 E
Sibu **56** 2 18N 111 49 E
Sibuco **57** 7 20N 122 10 E
Sibuguey B. **57** 7 50N 122 45 E
Sibut **92** 5 46N 19 10 E
Sibutu **57** 4 45N 119 30 E
Sibutu Passage **57** 4 50N 120 0 E
Sibuyan **57** 12 25N 122 40 E
Sibuyan Sea **57** 12 30N 122 20 E

Sicamous	108	50 49N	119 0W
Siccus →	73	31 42S	139 25E
Sichuan □	58	31 0N	104 0E
Sicilia, Canale di	28	37 25N	12 30E
Sicilia, I.	29	37 30N	14 30E
Sicilian Channel = Sicilia, Canale di	28	37 25N	12 30E
Sicily = Sicilia	29	37 30N	14 30E
Sicuani	136	14 21S	71 10W
Siculiana	28	37 20N	13 23E
Sidamo □	91	5 0N	37 50E
Sidaouet	89	18 34N	8 3E
Siddipet	50	18 0N	78 51E
Sidell	117	39 55N	87 49W
Sidéradougou	88	10 42N	4 12W
Siderno Marina	29	38 16N	16 17E
Sidheros, Ákra	35	35 19N	26 19E
Sidhirókastron	35	41 13N	23 24E
Sidhpur	48	23 56N	72 25E
Sîdi Abd el Rahmân	90	30 55N	29 44E
Sîdi Barrâni	90	31 38N	25 58E
Sidi-bel-Abbès	86	35 13N	0 39W
Sidi Bennour	86	32 40N	8 25W
Sidi Haneish	90	31 10N	27 35E
Sidi Ifni	86	29 29N	10 12W
Sidi Kacem	86	34 11N	5 49W
Sīdī Miftāh	87	31 8N	16 58E
Sidi Moussa, O. →	86	26 58N	3 54E
Sidi Omar	90	31 24N	24 57E
Sidi Slimane	86	34 16N	5 56W
Sidi Smaïl	86	32 50N	8 31W
Sīdī Yaḩyā	87	30 55N	16 30E
Sidlaw Hills	14	56 32N	3 10W
Sidley, Mt.	143	77 2S	126 2W
Sidmouth	13	50 40N	3 13W
Sidmouth, C.	72	13 25S	143 36E
Sidney, Can.	108	48 39N	123 24W
Sidney, Mont., U.S.A.	118	47 42N	104 7W
Sidney, N.Y., U.S.A.	115	42 18N	75 20W
Sidney, Ohio, U.S.A.	117	40 18N	84 6W
Sidoarjo	57	7 30S	112 46E
Sidoktaya	52	20 27N	94 15E
Sidra, G. of = Khalīj Surt	87	31 40N	18 30E
Siedlce	32	52 10N	22 20E
Sieg →	30	50 46N	7 7E
Siegburg	30	50 48N	7 12E
Siegen	30	50 52N	8 2E
Siem Pang	54	14 7N	106 23E
Siem Reap	54	13 20N	103 52E
Siena	27	43 20N	11 20E
Sieradź	32	51 37N	18 41E
Sierck-les-Bains	19	49 26N	6 20E
Sierpc	32	52 55N	19 43E
Sierpe, Bocas de la	134	10 0N	61 30W
Sierra Blanca, N. Mex., U.S.A.	121	33 20N	105 54W
Sierra Blanca, Tex., U.S.A.	121	31 11N	105 17W
Sierra City	122	39 34N	120 42W
Sierra Colorada	142	40 35S	67 50W
Sierra de Yeguas	23	37 7N	4 52W
Sierra Gorda	140	22 50S	69 15W
Sierra Grande	142	41 36S	65 22W
Sierra Leone ■	88	9 0N	12 0W
Sierra Mojada	124	27 19N	103 42W
Sierraville	122	39 36N	120 22W
Sierre	31	46 17N	7 31E
Sif Fatima	87	31 6N	8 41E
Sífnos	35	37 0N	24 45E
Sifton	109	51 21N	100 8W
Sifton Pass	108	57 52N	126 15W
Sig	86	35 32N	0 12W
Sigdal	10	60 4N	9 38E
Sigean	20	43 2N	2 58E
Sighetul Marmatiei	34	47 57N	23 52E
Sighişoara	34	46 12N	24 50E
Sigli	56	5 25N	96 0E
Siglufjörður	8	66 12N	18 55W
Sigma	57	11 29N	122 40E
Sigmaringen	31	48 5N	9 13E
Signakhi	39	41 40N	45 57E
Signal	123	34 30N	113 38W
Signal Pk.	123	33 25N	114 4W
Signy I.	143	60 45S	45 56W
Signy-l'Abbaye	19	49 40N	4 25E
Sigourney	116	41 20N	92 12W
Sigsig	134	3 0S	78 50W
Sigtuna	10	59 36N	17 44E
Sigüenza	24	41 3N	2 40W
Siguiri	88	11 31N	9 10W
Sigulda	36	57 10N	24 55E
Sigurd	121	38 49N	112 0W
Sihanoukville = Kompong Som	55	10 40N	103 30E
Sihaus	136	8 40S	77 40W
Sihui	59	23 20N	112 40E
Si'ir	44	31 35N	35 9E
Siirt	46	37 57N	41 55E
Sijarira Ra.	95	17 36S	27 45E
Sikao	55	7 34N	99 21E
Sikar	48	27 33N	75 10E
Sikasso	88	11 18N	5 35W
Sikerete	96	19 0S	20 48E
Sikeston	119	36 52N	89 35W
Sikhote Alin, Khrebet	41	46 0N	136 0E
Sikiá.	35	40 2N	23 56E
Síkinos	35	36 40N	25 8E
Sikkani Chief →	108	57 47N	122 15W
Sikkim □	52	27 50N	88 30E
Sikoro	88	12 19N	7 8W
Sil →	22	42 27N	7 43W
Sila, La	29	39 15N	16 35E
Silacayoapan	125	17 30N	98 9W
Silandro	26	46 38N	10 48E
Sīlat adh Dhahr	44	32 19N	35 11E
Silba	27	44 24N	14 41E
Silba, I.	27	44 24N	14 41E
Silchar	52	24 49N	92 48E
Silcox	109	57 12N	94 10W
Siler City	113	35 44N	79 30W
Sileru →	50	17 49N	81 24E
Silesia = Slask	32	51 0N	16 30E
Silet	86	22 44N	4 37E
Silgarhi Doti	49	29 15N	81 0E
Silghat	52	26 35N	93 0E
Silifke	46	36 22N	33 58E
Siliguri	52	26 45N	88 25E
Siling Co	62	31 50N	89 20E
Siliqua	28	39 20N	8 49E
Silistra	34	44 6N	27 19E
Siljan, L.	10	60 55N	14 45E
Silkeborg	11	56 10N	9 32E
Sillajhuay, Cordillera	136	19 46S	68 40W
Sillé-le-Guillaume	18	48 10N	0 8W
Sillustani	136	15 50S	70 7W
Siloam Springs	119	36 15N	94 31W
Silogui	56	1 10S	9 0E
Silsbee	119	30 20N	94 8W
Silute	36	55 21N	21 33E
Silva Porto = Bié	93	12 22S	16 55E
Silver City, N. Mex., U.S.A.	121	32 50N	108 18W
Silver City, Nev., U.S.A.	120	39 15N	119 48W
Silver Cr. →	120	43 16N	119 13W
Silver Creek	114	42 33N	79 9W
Silver Grove	117	39 2N	84 24W
Silver L.	122	38 39N	120 6W
Silver Lake, Calif., U.S.A.	123	35 21N	116 7W
Silver Lake, Ind., U.S.A.	117	41 4N	85 53W
Silver Lake, Oreg., U.S.A.	120	43 9N	121 4W
Silver Lake, Wis., U.S.A.	117	42 33N	88 13W
Silver Water	106	45 52N	82 52W
Silverspur	77	28 52S	151 17E
Silverton, Colo., U.S.A.	121	37 51N	107 45W
Silverton, Tex., U.S.A.	119	34 30N	101 16W
Silves	23	37 11N	8 26W
Silvi	27	42 32N	14 5E
Silvia	134	2 37N	76 21W
Silvies →	120	43 22N	118 48W
Silvretta Gruppe	31	46 50N	10 6E
Silwa Bahari	90	24 45N	32 55E
Silwad	44	31 59N	35 15E
Silz	31	47 16N	10 56E
Sim, C.	86	31 26N	9 51W
Simanggang	56	1 15N	111 32E
Simao	58	22 47N	101 5E
Simão Dias	138	10 44S	37 49W
Simard, L.	104	47 40N	78 40W
Simba	94	2 10S	37 36E
Simbach	31	48 16N	13 3E
Simbo	94	4 51S	29 41E
Simcoe	106	42 50N	80 20W
Simcoe, L.	106	44 25N	79 20W
Simenga	41	62 42N	108 25E
Simeto →	29	37 25N	15 10E
Simeulue	56	2 45N	95 45E
Simferopol	38	44 55N	34 3E
Sími	35	36 35N	27 50E
Simi Valley	123	34 16N	118 47W
Simikot	49	30 0N	81 50E
Simití	134	7 58N	73 57W
Simla	48	31 2N	77 9E
Şimleu-Silvaniei	34	47 17N	22 50E
Simmern	31	49 59N	7 32E
Simmie	109	49 56N	108 6W
Simmler	123	35 21N	119 59W
Simões	138	7 36S	40 49W
Simojärvi	8	66 5N	27 3E
Simojoki →	8	65 35N	25 1E
Simojovel	125	17 12N	92 38W
Simonette →	108	55 9N	118 15W
Simonstown	96	34 14S	18 26E
Simpang	56	1 16S	104 5E
Simplício Mendes	138	7 51S	41 54W
Simplon Pass	31	46 15N	8 0E
Simplon Tunnel	31	46 15N	8 7E
Simpson Des.	72	25 0S	137 0E
Simpungdong	61	40 56N	129 29E
Simrishamn	11	55 33N	14 22E
Simunjan	56	1 25N	110 45E
Simushir, Ostrov	41	46 50N	152 30E
Sina →	50	17 30N	75 55E
Sinabang	56	2 30N	96 24E
Sinadogo	45	5 50N	47 0E
Sinai = Es Sînâ'	90	29 0N	34 0E
Sinai, Mt. = Musa, G.	90	28 32N	33 59E
Sinaia	34	45 21N	25 38E
Sinaloa	124	25 50N	108 20W
Sinaloa □	124	25 0N	107 30W
Sinalunga	27	43 12N	11 43E
Sinan	58	27 56N	108 13E
Sīnāwan	87	31 0N	10 37E
Sinbaungwe	52	19 43N	95 10E
Sinbo	52	24 46N	97 3E
Sincé	134	9 15N	75 9W
Sincelejo	134	9 18N	75 24W
Sinchang	61	40 7N	128 28E
Sinchang-ni	61	39 24N	126 8E
Sinclair	120	41 47N	107 10W
Sinclair Mills	108	54 5N	121 40W
Sincorá, Serra do	139	13 30S	41 0W
Sind	48	26 0N	68 30E
Sind →	49	34 18N	74 45E
Sind Sagar Doab	48	32 0N	71 30E
Sindal	11	57 28N	10 10E
Sindangan	57	8 10N	123 5E
Sindangbarang	57	7 27S	107 1E
Sinde	95	17 28S	25 51E
Sinelnikovo	38	48 25N	35 30E
Sines	23	37 56N	8 51W
Sines, Cabo de	23	37 58N	8 53W
Sineu	24	39 39N	3 0E
Sinewit, Mt.	69	4 44S	152 2E
Sinfra	88	6 35N	5 56W
Sing Buri	54	14 53N	100 25E
Singa	91	13 10N	33 57E
Singanallur	51	11 2N	77 1E
Singaparna	57	7 23S	108 4E
Singapore ■	55	1 17N	103 51E
Singapore, Straits of	55	1 15N	104 0E
Singaraja	56	8 6S	115 10E
Singatoka	68	18 8S	177 30E
Singen	31	47 45N	8 50E
Singida	94	4 49S	34 48E
Singida □	94	6 0S	34 30E
Singitikós Kólpos	35	40 6N	24 0E
Singkaling Hkamti	52	26 0N	95 39E
Singkawang	56	1 0N	108 57E
Singkep	56	0 30S	104 20E
Singleton	76	32 33S	151 0E
Singleton, Mt.	79	29 27S	117 15E
Singö	10	60 12N	18 45E
Singoli	48	25 0N	75 22E
Singora = Songkhla	55	7 12N	100 36E
Singosan	61	38 52N	127 25E
Sinhung	61	40 11N	127 34E
Siniscóla	28	40 35N	9 40E
Sinj	27	43 42N	16 39E
Sinjai	57	5 7S	120 20E
Sinjār	46	36 19N	41 52E
Sinjil	44	32 3N	35 15E
Sinkat	90	18 55N	36 49E
Sinking-Uighur □ = Xinjiang Uygur □	62	42 0N	86 0E
Sinmak	61	38 25N	126 14E
Sinnai	28	39 18N	9 13E
Sinnar	50	19 48N	74 0E
Sinni →	29	40 9N	16 42E
Sinnuris	90	29 26N	30 31E
Sinoe, L.	34	44 35N	28 50E
Sinoia	95	17 20S	30 8E
Sinop	38	42 1N	35 11E
Sinpo	61	40 0N	128 13E
Sinskoye	41	61 8N	126 48E
Sint Eustatius, I.	127	17 30N	62 59W
Sint Maarten	127	18 0N	63 5W
Sint Maarten, I.	127	18 4N	63 4W
Sint Niklaas	16	51 10N	4 9E
Sint Truiden	16	50 48N	5 10E
Sîntana	34	46 20N	21 30E
Sintang	56	0 5N	111 35E
Sinton	119	28 1N	97 30W
Sintra	23	38 47N	9 25W
Sinŭiju	61	40 5N	124 24E
Sinyukha →	38	48 3N	30 51E
Siocon	57	7 40N	122 10E
Siófok	33	16 39S	23 36E
Sioma	96	16 25S	23 28E
Sion	31	46 14N	7 20E
Sioux City	118	42 32N	96 25W
Sioux Falls	118	43 35N	96 40W
Sioux Lookout	102	50 10N	91 50W
Sip Song Chau Thai	54	21 30N	103 30E
Siping	61	43 8N	124 21E
Sipiwesk L.	109	55 5N	97 35W
Sipora	56	2 18S	99 40E
Siquia →	126	12 10N	84 20W
Siquijor	57	9 12N	123 35E
Siquirres	126	10 6N	83 30W
Siquisique	134	10 34N	69 42W
Sir Edward Pellew Group	72	15 40S	137 10E
Sir Graham Moore Is.	78	13 53S	126 34E
Sira	51	13 41N	76 49E
Siracusa	29	37 4N	15 17E
Sirajganj	49	24 25N	89 47E
Sirakoro	88	12 41N	9 14W
Sirasso	88	9 16N	6 6W
Siret	34	47 55N	26 5E
Siret →	34	47 58N	26 5E
Şiria	34	46 16N	21 38E
Sirino, Monte	29	40 7N	15 50E
Sirkali (Shivali)	51	11 15N	79 41E
Sírna.	35	36 22N	26 42E
Sirohi	48	24 52N	72 53E
Sironj	48	24 5N	77 39E
Síros	35	37 28N	24 57E
Sirretta Pk.	123	35 56N	118 19W
Sirsa	48	29 33N	75 4E
Sirsi	51	14 40N	74 49E
Siruela	23	38 58N	5 3W
Sisak	27	45 30N	16 21E
Sisaket	54	15 8N	104 23E
Sisante	25	39 25N	2 12W
Sisargas, Islas	22	43 21N	8 50W
Sishen	96	27 47S	22 59E
Sishui, Henan, China	60	34 48N	113 15E
Sishui, Shandong, China	61	35 42N	117 18E
Sisipuk L.	109	55 45N	101 50W
Sisophon	54	13 38N	102 59E
Sisseton	118	45 43N	97 3W
Sissonne	19	49 34N	3 51E
Sistan-Baluchistan □	47	27 0N	62 0E
Sistema Central	22	40 40N	5 55W
Sistema Ibérico	24	41 0N	2 10W
Sisteron	21	44 12N	5 57E
Sisters	120	44 21N	121 32W
Sitamarhi	49	26 37N	85 30E
Sitapur	49	27 38N	80 45E
Siteki	97	26 32S	31 58E
Sitges	24	41 17N	1 47E
Sitía	35	35 13N	26 6E
Sítio da Abadia	139	14 48S	46 16W
Sitka	100	57 9N	135 20W
Sitona	91	14 25N	37 23E
Sitoti	96	23 15S	23 40E
Sitra	90	28 40N	26 53E
Sittang →	52	17 10N	96 58E
Sittard	16	51 0N	5 52E
Sittaung	52	24 10N	94 35E
Sittensen	30	53 17N	9 32E
Situbondo	57	7 45S	114 0E
Siuna	126	13 37N	84 45W
Sivaganga	51	9 50N	78 28E
Sivagiri	51	9 16N	77 26E
Sivakasi	51	9 24N	77 47E
Sivana	48	28 37N	78 6E
Sivand	47	30 5N	52 55E
Sivas	46	39 43N	36 58E
Siverek	46	37 50N	39 19E
Sivrihisar	46	39 30N	31 35E
Sîwa	90	29 11N	25 31E
Sîwa, El Wâhât es	90	29 10N	25 30E
Siwalik Range	49	28 0N	83 0E
Siwan	49	26 13N	84 21E
Siyâl, Jazâ'ir	90	22 49N	36 12E
Sizewell	13	52 13N	1 38E
Siziwang Qi	60	41 25N	111 40E
Sjælland	11	55 30N	11 30E
Sjællands Odde	11	56 0N	11 15E
Själevad	10	63 18N	18 36E
Sjenica	33	43 16N	20 0E
Sjoa	10	61 41N	9 33E
Sjöbo	11	55 37N	13 45E
Sjösa	11	58 47N	17 4E
Skadovsk	38	46 17N	32 52E
Skagafjörður	8	65 54N	19 35W
Skagen	11	57 43N	10 35E
Skagern	10	59 0N	14 20E
Skagerrak	11	57 30N	9 0E
Skagit →	122	48 20N	122 25W
Skagway	100	59 23N	135 20W
Skala Podolskaya	38	48 50N	26 15E
Skalat	36	49 23N	25 55E
Skals	11	56 34N	9 24E
Skanderborg	11	56 2N	9 55E
Skänninge	11	58 24N	15 5E
Skanör	11	55 24N	12 50E
Skara	11	58 25N	13 30E
Skaraborgs län □	11	58 20N	13 30E
Skardu	49	35 20N	75 44E
Skarrild	11	55 58N	8 53E
Skarzysko Kamienna	32	51 7N	20 52E
Skattungbyn	10	61 10N	14 56E
Skebokvarn	10	59 7N	16 45E
Skeena →	108	54 9N	130 5W
Skeena Mts.	108	56 40N	128 30W
Skegness	12	53 9N	0 20E
Skeldon	135	5 55N	57 20W

Skellefte älv →	**8**	64 45N	21 10 E
Skellefteå	**8**	64 45N	20 58 E
Skelleftehamn	**8**	64 47N	20 59 E
Skellig Rocks	**15**	51 47N	10 32W
Skender Vakuf	**33**	44 29N	17 22 E
Skene	**11**	57 30N	12 37 E
Skerries, The	**12**	53 27N	4 40W
Skhoinoúsa	**35**	36 53N	25 31 E
Skhwaner, Pegunungan	**56**	1 0S	112 30 E
Ski	**10**	59 43N	10 52 E
Skíathos	**35**	39 12N	23 30 E
Skibbereen	**15**	51 33N	9 16W
Skiddaw	**12**	54 39N	3 9W
Skien	**10**	59 12N	9 35 E
Skierniewice	**32**	51 58N	20 10 E
Skikda	**87**	36 50N	6 58 E
Skillett Fork, Little Wabash →	**117**	38 6N	88 9W
Skillingaryd	**11**	57 27N	14 5 E
Skillinge	**11**	55 30N	14 16 E
Skillingmark	**10**	59 48N	12 1 E
Skinári, Ákra	**35**	37 56N	20 40 E
Skipton, Austral.	**74**	37 39S	143 40 E
Skipton, U.K.	**12**	53 57N	2 1W
Skirmish Pt.	**72**	11 59S	134 17 E
Skíros	**35**	38 55N	24 34 E
Skivarp	**11**	55 26N	13 34 E
Skive	**11**	56 33N	9 2 E
Skjálfandafljót	**8**	65 15N	17 25W
Skjálfandi	**8**	66 5N	17 30W
Skjeberg	**10**	59 12N	11 12 E
Skjern	**11**	55 57N	8 30 E
Škofja Loka	**27**	46 9N	14 19 E
Skoghall	**10**	59 20N	13 30 E
Skole	**36**	49 3N	23 30 E
Skópelos	**35**	39 9N	23 47 E
Skopin	**37**	53 55N	39 32 E
Skopje	**35**	42 1N	21 32 E
Skórcz	**32**	53 47N	18 30 E
Skovorodino	**41**	54 0N	125 0 E
Skowhegan	**103**	44 49N	69 40W
Skownan	**109**	51 58N	99 35W
Skradin	**27**	43 52N	15 53 E
Skreanäs	**11**	56 52N	12 35 E
Skull	**15**	51 32N	9 40W
Skultorp	**11**	58 24N	13 51 E
Skunk →	**116**	40 42N	91 7W
Skuodas	**36**	56 21N	21 45 E
Skurup	**11**	55 28N	13 30 E
Skutskär	**11**	60 37N	17 25 E
Skvira	**38**	49 44N	29 40 E
Skwierzyna	**32**	52 33N	15 30 E
Skye	**14**	57 15N	6 10W
Skykomish	**120**	47 43N	121 16W
Slagelse	**11**	55 23N	11 19 E
Slamet, G.	**56**	7 16S	109 8 E
Slaney →	**15**	52 52N	6 45W
Slangerup	**11**	55 50N	12 11 E
Slano	**33**	42 48N	17 53 E
Slantsy	**36**	59 7N	28 5 E
Slashers Flat	**76**	32 29S	149 30 E
Slate Is.	**102**	48 40N	87 0W
Slater	**116**	39 13N	93 4W
Slatina	**34**	44 28N	24 22 E
Slaton	**119**	33 27N	101 38W
Slave →	**108**	61 18N	113 39W
Slave Coast	**89**	6 0N	2 30 E
Slave Lake	**108**	55 17N	114 43W
Slave Pt.	**108**	61 11N	115 56W
Slavgorod	**40**	53 1N	78 37 E
Slavnoye	**36**	54 24N	29 15 E
Slavonska Požega	**33**	45 20N	17 40 E
Slavonski Brod	**33**	45 11N	18 0 E
Slavuta	**36**	50 15N	27 2 E
Slavyansk	**38**	48 55N	37 36 E
Slavyansk-na-Kubani	**38**	45 15N	38 11 E
Sławno	**32**	54 20N	16 41 E
Sławoborze	**32**	53 55N	15 42 E
Sleaford	**12**	53 0N	0 22W
Sleaford B.	**73**	34 55S	135 45 E
Sleat, Sd. of	**14**	57 5N	5 47W
Sleeper, Is.	**101**	58 30N	81 0W
Sleepy Eye	**118**	44 15N	94 45W
Sleman	**57**	7 40S	110 20 E
Slemon L.	**108**	63 13N	116 4W
Slidell	**119**	30 20N	89 48W
Sliedrecht	**16**	51 50N	4 45 E
Slieve Aughty	**15**	53 4N	8 30W
Slieve Bloom	**15**	53 4N	7 40W
Slieve Donard	**15**	54 10N	5 57W
Slieve Gullion	**15**	54 8N	6 26W
Slieve Mish	**15**	52 12N	9 50W
Slievenamon	**15**	52 25N	7 37W
Sligo	**15**	54 17N	8 28W
Sligo □	**15**	54 10N	8 35W
Sligo B.	**15**	54 20N	8 40W
Slite	**9**	57 42N	18 48 E
Sliven	**34**	42 42N	26 19 E
Slivnitsa	**34**	42 50N	23 0 E
Sljeme	**27**	45 57N	15 58 E
Sloan	**123**	35 57N	115 13W
Sloansville	**115**	42 45N	74 22W
Slobozia	**34**	44 34N	27 23 E
Slocan	**108**	49 48N	117 28W
Slochteren	**16**	53 12N	6 48 E
Slöinge	**11**	56 51N	12 42 E
Slonim	**36**	53 4N	25 19 E
Slough	**13**	51 30N	0 35W
Sloughhouse	**122**	38 26N	121 12W
Slovenia = Slovenija	**27**	45 58N	14 30 E
Slovenija □	**27**	45 58N	14 30 E
Slovenj Gradec	**27**	46 31N	15 5 E
Slovenska Bistrica	**27**	46 24N	15 35 E
Slovenské Rudohorie	**32**	48 45N	20 0 E
Slovensko □	**32**	48 30N	19 0 E
Słubice	**32**	52 22N	14 35 E
Sluis	**16**	51 18N	3 23 E
Slunj	**27**	45 6N	15 33 E
Słupca	**32**	52 15N	17 52 E
Słupsk	**32**	54 30N	17 3 E
Slurry	**96**	25 49S	25 42 E
Slyne Hd.	**15**	53 25N	10 10W
Slyudyanka	**41**	51 40N	103 40 E
Smålandsfarvandet	**11**	55 10N	11 20 E
Smalandsstenar	**11**	57 9N	13 24 E
Small Nggela	**68**	9 0S	160 0 E
Smalltree L.	**109**	61 0N	105 0W
Smallwood Reservoir	**103**	54 20N	63 10W
Smara	**86**	26 48N	11 41W
Smarje	**27**	46 15N	15 34 E
Smart Syndicate Dam	**96**	30 45S	23 10 E
Smartville	**122**	39 13N	121 18W
Smeaton	**109**	53 30N	104 49W
Smederevo	**33**	44 40N	20 57 E
Smederevska Palanka	**33**	44 22N	20 58 E
Smela	**38**	49 15N	31 58 E
Smethport	**114**	41 50N	78 28W
Smidovich	**41**	48 36N	133 49 E
Smiley	**109**	51 38N	109 29W
Smith	**108**	55 10N	114 0W
Smith →	**108**	59 34N	126 30W
Smith Arm	**108**	66 15N	123 0W
Smith Center	**118**	39 50N	98 50W
Smith Sund	**144**	78 30N	74 0W
Smithburne →	**72**	17 3S	140 57 E
Smithers	**108**	54 45N	127 10W
Smithfield, Madag.	**97**	30 9S	26 30 E
Smithfield, N.C., U.S.A.	**113**	35 31N	78 16W
Smithfield, Utah, U.S.A.	**120**	41 50N	111 50W
Smiths Falls	**107**	44 55N	76 0W
Smithton	**72**	40 53S	145 6 E
Smithtown	**77**	30 58S	152 48 E
Smithville, Can.	**106**	43 6N	79 33W
Smithville, Mo., U.S.A.	**116**	39 23N	94 35W
Smithville, Tex., U.S.A.	**119**	30 2N	97 12W
Smoky →	**108**	56 10N	117 21W
Smoky Bay	**73**	32 22S	134 13 E
Smoky Falls	**102**	50 4N	82 10W
Smoky Hill →	**118**	39 3N	96 48W
Smoky Lake	**108**	54 10N	112 30W
Smøla	**10**	63 23N	8 3 E
Smolensk	**36**	54 45N	32 0 E
Smolikas, Óros	**35**	40 9N	20 58 E
Smolník	**32**	48 43N	20 44 E
Smolyan	**35**	41 36N	24 38 E
Smooth Rock Falls	**102**	49 17N	81 37W
Smoothstone L.	**109**	54 40N	106 50W
Smorgon	**36**	54 20N	26 24 E
Smyadovo	**34**	43 2N	27 1 E
Smyrna = İzmir	**46**	38 25N	27 8 E
Snaefell	**12**	54 18N	4 26W
Snaefellsjkull	**8**	64 45N	23 46W
Snake →	**120**	46 12N	119 2W
Snake I.	**75**	38 47S	146 33 E
Snake L.	**109**	55 32N	106 35W
Snake Ra.	**120**	39 0N	114 30W
Snake River	**120**	44 10N	110 42W
Snake River Plain	**120**	43 13N	113 0W
Snarum	**10**	60 1N	9 54 E
Snedsted	**11**	56 55N	8 32 E
Sneek	**16**	53 2N	5 40 E
Snejbjerg	**11**	56 8N	8 54 E
Snelling	**122**	37 31N	120 26W
Snezhnoye	**39**	48 0N	38 58 E
Snežnik	**27**	45 36N	14 35 E
Snigirevka	**38**	47 2N	32 49 E
Snizort, L.	**14**	57 33N	6 28W
Snøhetta	**10**	62 19N	9 16 E
Snohomish	**122**	47 53N	122 6W
Snoul	**55**	12 4N	106 26 E
Snow Hill	**112**	38 10N	75 21W
Snow Lake	**109**	54 52N	100 3W
Snow Mt.	**122**	39 22N	122 44W
Snowbird L.	**109**	60 45N	103 0W
Snowdon	**12**	53 4N	4 8W
Snowdrift	**109**	62 24N	110 44W
Snowdrift →	**109**	62 24N	110 44W
Snowflake	**121**	34 30N	110 4W
Snowshoe Pk.	**120**	48 13N	115 41W
Snowtown	**73**	33 46S	138 14 E
Snowville	**120**	41 59N	112 47W
Snowy →	**75**	37 46S	148 30 E
Snowy Mts.	**75**	36 30S	148 20 E
Snug Corner	**127**	22 33N	73 52W
Snyder, Okla., U.S.A.	**119**	34 40N	99 0W
Snyder, Tex., U.S.A.	**119**	32 45N	100 57W
Soacha	**134**	4 35N	74 13W
Soahanina	**97**	18 42S	44 13 E
Soalala	**97**	16 6S	45 20 E
Soan →	**48**	33 1N	71 44 E
Soanierana-Ivongo	**97**	16 55S	49 35 E
Soap Lake	**120**	47 23N	119 31W
Sobat, Nahr →	**91**	9 22N	31 33 E
Sobhapur	**48**	22 47N	78 17 E
Sobinka	**37**	56 0N	40 0 E
Sobo-Yama	**64**	32 51N	131 22 E
Sobótka	**32**	50 54N	16 44 E
Sobrado	**22**	43 2N	8 2W
Sobral	**138**	3 50S	40 20W
Sobreira Formosa	**23**	39 46N	7 51W
Soc Giang	**54**	22 54N	106 1 E
Soča →	**27**	46 20N	13 40 E
Sochaczew	**32**	52 15N	20 13 E
Soch'e = Shache	**62**	38 20N	77 10 E
Sochi	**39**	43 35N	39 40 E
Society Is.	**67**	17 0S	151 0W
Society Is. = Société, Is. de la	**67**	17 0S	151 0W
Socompa, Portezuelo de	**140**	24 27S	68 18W
Socorro, Colomb.	**134**	6 29N	73 16W
Socorro, U.S.A.	**121**	34 4N	106 54W
Socorro, I.	**124**	18 45N	110 58W
Socotra, I.	**45**	12 30N	54 0 E
Socúellmos	**25**	39 16N	2 47W
Soda L.	**121**	35 7N	116 2W
Soda Plains	**49**	35 30N	79 0 E
Soda Springs	**120**	42 40N	111 40W
Sodankylä	**8**	67 29N	26 40 E
Söderfors	**10**	60 23N	17 25 E
Söderhamn	**10**	61 18N	17 10 E
Söderköping	**10**	58 31N	16 20 E
Södermanlands län □	**10**	59 10N	16 30 E
Södertälje	**10**	59 12N	17 39 E
Sodiri	**85**	14 27N	29 0 E
Sodo	**91**	7 0N	37 41 E
Södra Vi	**11**	57 45N	15 45 E
Sodražica	**27**	45 45N	14 39 E
Sodus	**114**	43 13N	77 5W
Soekmekaar	**97**	23 30S	29 55 E
Soest, Ger.	**30**	51 34N	8 7 E
Soest, Neth.	**16**	52 9N	5 19 E
Sofádhes	**35**	39 20N	22 4 E
Sofala	**76**	33 4S	149 43 E
Sofara	**88**	13 59N	4 9W
Sofia = Sofiya	**34**	42 45N	23 20 E
Sofia →	**97**	15 27S	47 23 E
Sofievka	**38**	48 6N	33 55 E
Sofiiski	**41**	52 15N	133 59 E
Sofikón	**35**	37 47N	23 3 E
Sofiya	**34**	42 45N	23 20 E
Sogad	**57**	10 30N	125 0 E
Sogakofe	**89**	6 2N	0 39 E
Sogamoso	**134**	5 43N	72 56W
Sögel	**30**	52 50N	7 32 E
Sogeri	**69**	9 26S	147 35 E
Sognefjorden	**9**	61 10N	5 50 E
Sŏgwi-po	**61**	33 13N	126 34 E
Sohâg	**90**	26 33N	31 43 E
Sohano	**69**	5 22S	154 37 E
Sŏhori	**61**	40 7N	128 23 E
Soignies	**16**	50 35N	4 5 E
Soira, Mt.	**91**	14 45N	39 30 E
Soissons	**19**	49 25N	3 19 E
Sōja	**64**	34 40N	133 45 E
Sojat	**48**	25 55N	73 45 E
Sokal	**36**	50 31N	24 15 E
Söke	**46**	37 48N	27 28 E
Sokki, Oued In →	**86**	29 30N	3 42 E
Sokna	**10**	60 16N	9 50 E
Soknedal	**10**	62 57N	10 13 E
Soko Banja	**33**	43 40N	21 51 E
Sokodé	**89**	9 0N	1 11 E
Sokol	**37**	59 30N	40 5 E
Sokółka	**32**	53 25N	23 30 E
Sokolo	**88**	14 53N	6 8W
Sokołów Małpolski	**32**	50 12N	22 7 E
Sokołów Podlaski	**32**	52 25N	22 15 E
Sokoto	**89**	13 2N	5 16 E
Sokoto □	**89**	12 30N	5 0 E
Sokoto →	**89**	11 20N	4 10 E
Sol Iletsk	**40**	51 10N	55 0 E
Solai	**94**	0 2N	36 12 E
Solana, La	**25**	38 59N	3 14W
Solano	**57**	16 31N	121 15 E
Solares	**22**	43 23N	3 43W
Solberga	**11**	57 45N	14 43 E
Solec Kujawski	**32**	53 5N	18 14 E
Soledad, Colomb.	**134**	10 55N	74 46W
Soledad, U.S.A.	**122**	36 27N	121 16W
Soledad, Venez.	**135**	8 10N	63 34W
Solemint	**123**	34 25N	118 27W
Solent, The	**13**	50 45N	1 25W
Solenzara	**21**	41 53N	9 23 E
Solesmes	**19**	50 10N	3 30 E
Solfonn	**9**	60 2N	6 57 E
Soligalich	**37**	59 5N	42 10 E
Solikamsk	**40**	59 38N	56 50 E
Solila	**97**	21 25S	46 37 E
Solimões →	**135**	2 15S	66 30W
Solingen	**30**	51 10N	7 4 E
Sollebrunn	**11**	58 8N	12 32 E
Sollefteå	**10**	63 12N	17 20 E
Sollentuna	**10**	59 26N	17 56 E
Soller	**24**	39 43N	2 45 E
Solling	**30**	51 44N	9 36 E
Solna	**10**	59 22N	18 1 E
Solnechnogorsk	**37**	56 10N	36 57 E
Sologne	**19**	47 40N	2 0 E
Solok	**56**	0 45S	100 40 E
Sololá	**126**	14 49N	91 10 E
Solomon Is. ■	**68**	6 0S	155 0 E
Solomon, N. Fork →	**118**	39 29N	98 26W
Solomon Sea	**69**	7 0S	150 0 E
Solomon, S. Fork →	**118**	39 25N	99 12W
Solomon's Pools = Burak Sulayman	**44**	31 42N	35 7 E
Solon	**62**	46 32N	121 10 E
Solon Springs	**118**	46 19N	91 47W
Solonópole	**138**	5 44S	39 1W
Solor	**57**	8 27S	123 0 E
Solotcha	**37**	54 48N	39 53 E
Solothurn	**31**	47 13N	7 32 E
Solothurn □	**31**	47 18N	7 40 E
Solsona	**24**	42 0N	1 31 E
Solta	**27**	43 24N	16 15 E
Soltanābād	**47**	36 29N	58 5 E
Soltāniyeh	**46**	36 20N	48 55 E
Soltau	**30**	52 59N	9 50 E
Soltsy	**36**	58 10N	30 30 E
Solunska Glava	**35**	41 44N	21 31 E
Solvang	**123**	34 36N	120 8W
Solvay	**115**	43 5N	76 17W
Sölvesborg	**11**	56 5N	14 35 E
Solway Firth	**12**	54 45N	3 38W
Solwezi	**95**	12 11S	26 21 E
Somali Rep. ■	**45**	7 0N	47 0 E
Sombe Dzong	**52**	27 13N	89 8 E
Sombernon	**19**	47 20N	4 40 E
Sombor	**33**	45 46N	19 9 E
Sombra	**106**	42 43N	82 29W
Sombrerete	**124**	23 40N	103 40W
Sombrero	**127**	18 37N	63 30W
Somers	**120**	48 4N	114 18W
Somerset, Can.	**109**	49 25N	98 39W
Somerset, Colo., U.S.A.	**121**	38 55N	107 30W
Somerset, Ky., U.S.A.	**112**	37 5N	84 40W
Somerset, Mass., U.S.A.	**115**	41 45N	71 10W
Somerset, Pa., U.S.A.	**114**	40 1N	79 4W
Somerset □	**13**	51 9N	3 0W
Somerset East	**96**	32 42S	25 35 E
Somerset I.	**100**	73 30N	93 0W
Somerset West	**96**	34 8S	18 50 E
Somersworth	**115**	43 15N	70 51W
Somerton, Austral.	**77**	30 55S	150 38 E
Somerton, U.S.A.	**121**	32 35N	114 47W
Somerville	**115**	40 34N	74 36W
Someş →	**34**	47 15N	23 45 E
Someşul Mare →	**34**	47 18N	24 30 E
Somma Lombardo	**26**	45 41N	8 42 E
Somma Vesuviana	**29**	40 52N	14 23 E
Sommariva	**73**	26 24S	146 36 E
Sommatino	**28**	37 20N	14 0 E
Somme □	**19**	50 0N	2 20 E
Somme, B. de la	**18**	50 14N	1 33 E
Sommen	**11**	58 12N	15 0 E
Sommen, L.	**11**	58 0N	15 15 E
Sommepy-Tahure	**19**	49 15N	4 31 E
Sömmerda	**30**	51 10N	11 8 E
Sommesous	**19**	48 44N	4 12 E
Sommières	**21**	43 47N	4 6 E
Somosomo Str.	**68**	16 0S	180 0 E
Somoto	**126**	13 28N	86 37W
Sompolno	**32**	52 26N	18 30 E
Somport, Paso	**24**	42 48N	0 31W
Somport, Puerto de	**24**	42 48N	0 31W
Somuncurá	**142**	41 30S	67 0W
Son, Norway	**10**	59 32N	10 42 E
Son, Spain	**22**	42 43N	8 58W
Son Ha	**54**	15 3N	108 34 E
Son Hoa	**54**	13 2N	108 58 E
Son La	**54**	21 20N	103 50 E
Son Tay	**54**	21 8N	105 30 E
Soná	**126**	8 0N	81 20W
Sonamarg	**49**	34 18N	75 21 E
Sonamukhi	**49**	23 18N	87 27 E
Sonamura	**52**	23 29N	91 15 E
Sŏnchŏn	**61**	39 48N	124 55 E
Soncino	**26**	45 24N	9 52 E
Sondags →	**96**	33 44S	25 51 E
Sóndalo	**26**	46 20N	10 20 E

Sondar 49 33 28N 75 56 E
Sønder Omme 11 55 50N 8 54 E
Sønder Ternby 11 57 31N 9 58 E
Sønderborg 11 54 55N 9 49 E
Sønderjyllands Amtskommune □ 11 55 10N 9 10 E
Sondershausen 30 51 22N 10 50 E
Sóndrio 26 46 10N 9 53 E
Sone 95 17 23 S 34 55 E
Sonepat 48 29 0N 77 5 E
Sonepur 50 20 55N 83 50 E
Song 54 18 28N 100 11 E
Song Cau 54 13 27N 109 18 E
Song Xian 60 34 12N 112 8 E
Songchŏn 61 39 12N 126 15 E
Songea 95 10 40 S 35 40 E
Songea □ 95 10 30 S 36 0 E
Songeons 19 49 32N 1 50 E
Songhua Hu 61 43 35N 126 50 E
Songhua Jiang → 62 47 45N 132 30 E
Songjiang 59 31 1N 121 12 E
Songjin 61 40 40N 129 10 E
Songjŏng-ni 61 35 8N 126 47 E
Songkan 58 28 35N 106 52 E
Songkhla 55 7 13N 100 37 E
Songming 58 25 12N 103 2 E
Songnim 61 38 45N 125 39 E
Songpan 58 32 40N 103 30 E
Songtao 58 28 11N 109 10 E
Songwe, Malawi 95 9 44 S 33 58 E
Songwe, Zaïre 94 3 20 S 26 16 E
Songxi 59 27 31N 118 44 E
Songzi 59 30 12N 111 45 E
Sonid Youqi 60 42 45N 112 48 E
Sonkovo 37 57 50N 37 5 E
Sonmiani 48 25 25N 66 40 E
Sonnino 28 41 25N 13 13 E
Sono →, Goias, Brazil 138 9 58 S 48 11W
Sono →, Minas Gerais, Brazil 139 17 2 S 45 32W
Sonobe 65 35 6N 135 28 E
Sonora, Calif., U.S.A. 122 37 59N 120 27W
Sonora, Texas, U.S.A. 119 30 33N 100 37W
Sonora □ 124 29 0N 111 0W
Sonora → 124 28 50N 111 33W
Sonora P. 120 38 17N 119 35W
Sonoyta 124 31 51N 112 50W
Sŏnsan 61 36 14N 128 17 E
Sonsomate 126 13 43N 89 44W
Sonsón 134 5 42N 75 18W
Sonthofen 31 47 31N 10 16 E
Soo Junction 112 46 20N 85 14W
Sop Hao 54 20 33N 104 27 E
Sop Prap 54 17 53N 99 20 E
Sopachuy 137 19 29 S 64 31W
Sopi 57 2 34N 128 28 E
Sopo, Nahr → 91 8 40N 26 30 E
Sopot 32 54 27N 18 31 E
Sopotnica 35 41 23N 21 13 E
Sopron 33 47 45N 16 32 E
Sop's Arm 103 49 46N 56 56W
Sør-Rondane 143 72 0 S 25 0 E
Sør Trøndelag fylke □ 10 63 0N 11 0 E
Sora 28 41 45N 13 36 E
Sorada 50 19 45N 84 26 E
Sorah 48 27 13N 68 56 E
Söråker 10 62 30N 17 32 E
Sorano 27 42 40N 11 42 E
Sorata 136 15 50 S 68 40W
Sorbas 25 37 6N 2 7W
Sorel 105 46 0N 73 10W
Sorento, Austral. 74 38 22 S 144 47 E
Sorento, U.S.A. 116 39 0N 89 34W
Soresina 26 45 17N 9 51 E
Sorgono 28 40 01N 9 06 E
Sorgues 21 44 1N 4 53 E
Soria 24 41 43N 2 32W
Soria □ 24 41 46N 2 28W
Soriano 140 33 24 S 58 19W
Soriano nel Cimino 27 42 25N 12 14 E
Sorkh, Kuh-e 47 35 40N 58 30 E
Sorø 11 55 26N 11 32 E
Soro 88 10 9N 9 48W
Sorocaba 141 23 31 S 47 27W
Soroki 38 48 8N 28 12 E
Soron 49 27 55N 78 45 E
Sorong 57 0 55 S 131 15 E
Soroti 94 1 43N 33 35 E
Sørøya 8 70 40N 22 30 E
Sørøysundet 8 70 25N 23 0 E
Sorraia → 23 38 55N 8 53W
Sorrento 29 40 38N 14 23 E
Sorris Sorris 96 21 0 S 14 46 E
Sorsele 8 65 31N 17 30 E
Sorso 28 40 50N 8 34 E
Sorsogon 57 13 0N 124 0 E
Sortino 29 37 9N 15 1 E
Sos 24 42 30N 1 13W
Sŏsan 61 36 47N 126 27 E
Soscumica, L. 104 50 15N 77 27W
Sosna → 37 52 42N 38 55 E
Sosnovka 41 54 9N 109 35 E
Sosnowiec 32 50 20N 19 10 E
Sospel 21 43 52N 7 27 E
Sostanj 27 46 23N 15 4 E
Sõsura 61 42 16N 130 36 E
Soto la Marina → 125 23 40N 97 40W
Soto y Amío 22 42 46N 5 53W
Sotteville-lès-Rouen 18 49 24N 1 5 E
Sotuta 125 20 29N 89 43W
Souanké 92 2 10N 14 3 E
Soucy 104 48 10N 75 30W
Soufi 88 15 13N 12 17W
Souillac 20 44 53N 1 29 E
Souk-Ahras 87 36 23N 7 57 E
Souk el Arba du Rharb 86 34 43N 5 59W
Soukhouma 54 14 38N 105 48 E
Sŏul 61 37 31N 126 58 E
Soulac-sur-Mer 20 45 30N 1 7W
Soultz 19 48 57N 7 52 E
Soúnion, Ákra 35 37 37N 24 1 E
Sour el Ghozlane 87 36 10N 3 45 E
Sources, Mt. aux 97 28 45 S 28 50 E
Sourdeval 18 48 43N 0 55W
Soure, Brazil 138 0 35 S 48 30W
Soure, Port. 22 40 4N 8 38W
Souris, Man., Can. 109 49 40N 100 20W
Souris, P.E.I., Can. 103 46 21N 62 15W
Souris → 118 49 40N 99 34W
Sousa 138 6 45 S 38 10W
Sousel, Brazil 138 2 38 S 52 29W
Sousel, Port. 23 38 57N 7 40W
Souss, O. → 86 30 27N 9 31W
Sousse 87 35 50N 10 38 E
Soustons 20 43 45N 1 19W
Souterraine, La 20 46 15N 1 30 E
South Africa, Rep. of, ■ 93 30 0 S 25 0 E
South America 130 10 0 S 60 0W
South Aulatsivik I. 103 56 45N 61 30W
South Australia □ 73 32 0 S 139 0 E
South Baldy, Mt. 121 34 6N 107 27W
South Baymouth 106 45 33N 82 1W
South Beloit 116 42 29N 89 2W
South Bend, Ind., U.S.A. 117 41 38N 86 20W
South Bend, Wash., U.S.A. 122 46 44N 123 52W
South Boston 113 36 42N 78 58W
South Branch 103 47 55N 59 2W
South Brook 103 49 26N 56 5W
South Buganda □ 94 0 15 S 31 30 E
South Carolina □ 113 33 45N 81 0W
South Charleston 112 38 20N 81 40W
South China Sea 55 10 0N 113 0 E
South Dakota □ 118 45 0N 100 0W
South Downs 13 50 53N 0 10W
South East C. 72 43 40 S 146 50 E
South-East Indian Rise 66 43 0 S 80 0 E
South East Is. 79 34 17 S 123 30 E
South Esk → 14 56 44N 3 3W
South Foreland 13 51 7N 1 23 E
South Fork → 120 47 54N 113 15W
South Fork, American → 122 38 45N 121 5W
South Fork, Feather → 122 39 17N 121 36W
South Gate 123 33 57N 118 12W
South Georgia 143 54 30 S 37 0W
South Glamorgan □ 13 51 30N 3 20W
South Grafton 77 29 41 S 152 57 E
South Grand → 116 38 17N 93 55W
South Haven 117 42 22N 86 20W
South Henik, L. 109 61 30N 97 30W
South Honshu Ridge 66 23 0N 143 0 E
South Horr 94 2 12N 36 56 E
South I., Kenya 94 2 35N 36 35 E
South I., N.Z. 81 43 0 S 170 0 E
South Invercargill 81 46 26 S 168 23 E
South Island 81 44 0 S 170 0 E
South Knife → 109 58 55N 94 37W
South Korea ■ 61 36 0N 128 0 E
South Lake Tahoe 122 38 57N 119 59W
South Loup → 118 41 4N 98 40W
South Lyon 106 42 28N 83 39W
South Milwaukee 117 42 50N 87 52W
South Molton 13 51 1N 3 50W
South Monroe 106 41 54N 83 25W
South Nahanni → 108 61 3N 123 21W
South Nation → 107 45 34N 75 6W
South Negril Pt. 126 18 14N 78 30W
South Orkney Is. 143 63 0 S 45 0W
South Pass 120 42 20N 108 58W
South Pekin 116 40 30N 89 39W
South Pines 113 35 10N 79 25W
South Pittsburg 113 35 1N 85 42W
South Platte → 118 41 7N 100 42W
South Pt. 106 44 54N 83 19W
South Pole 143 90 0 S 0 0 E
South Porcupine 106 48 30N 81 12W
South River, Can. 106 45 52N 79 23W
South River, U.S.A. 115 40 27N 74 23W
South Ronaldsay 14 58 46N 2 58W
South Sandwich Is. 143 57 0 S 27 0W
South Saskatchewan → 109 53 15N 105 5W
South Seal → 109 58 48N 98 8W
South Shetland Is. 143 62 0 S 59 0W
South Shields 12 54 59N 1 26W
South Sioux City 118 42 30N 96 24W
South Taranaki Bight 80 39 40 S 174 5 E
South Thompson → 108 50 40N 120 20W
South Twin I. 102 53 7N 79 52W
South Tyne → 12 54 46N 2 25W
South Uist 14 57 20N 7 15W
South Wayne 116 42 34N 89 53W
South West Africa ■ = Namibia 96 22 0 S 18 9 E
South West C. 72 43 34 S 146 3 E
South West Rocks 77 30 52 S 153 3 E
South Whitley 117 41 5N 85 38W
South Yemen ■ 45 15 0N 48 0 E
South Yorkshire □ 12 53 30N 1 20W
Southampton, Can. 106 44 30N 81 25W
Southampton, U.K. 13 50 54N 1 23W
Southampton, U.S.A. 115 40 54N 72 22W
Southampton I. 101 64 30N 84 0W
Southbridge, N.Z. 81 43 48 S 172 16 E
Southbridge, U.S.A. 115 42 4N 72 2W
Southeast Pacific Basin 67 16 30 S 92 0W
Southend 109 56 19N 103 22W
Southend-on-Sea 13 51 32N 0 42 E
Southern □, Malawi 95 15 0 S 35 0 E
Southern □, S. Leone 88 8 0N 12 30W
Southern □, Zambia 95 16 20 S 26 20 E
Southern Alps 81 43 41 S 170 11 E
Southern Cross 79 31 12 S 119 15 E
Southern Hills 79 32 15 S 122 40 E
Southern Indian L. 109 57 10N 98 30W
Southern Ocean 143 62 0 S 60 0 E
Southern Uplands 14 55 30N 3 3W
Southington 115 41 37N 72 53W
Southland □ 81 45 51 S 168 13 E
Southold 115 41 4N 72 26W
Southport, Austral. 77 27 58 S 153 25 E
Southport, U.K. 12 53 38N 3 1W
Southport, U.S.A. 113 33 55N 78 0W
Southwestern Pacific Basin 66 42 0 S 170 0W
Southwold 13 52 19N 1 41 E
Soutpansberge 97 23 0 S 29 30 E
Souvigny 20 46 33N 3 10 E
Sovetsk, Lithuania, U.S.S.R. 36 55 6N 21 50 E
Sovetsk, R.S.F.S.R., U.S.S.R. 37 57 38N 48 53 E
Sovetskaya Gavan 41 48 50N 140 0 E
Sovicille 27 43 16N 11 12 E
Sovra 33 42 44N 17 34 E
Sōya-Misaki 63 45 30N 142 0 E
Soyopa 124 28 41N 109 37W
Sozh → 36 51 57N 30 48 E
Sozopol 34 42 23N 27 42 E
Spa 16 50 29N 5 53 E
Spain ■ 7 40 0N 5 0W
Spalding, Austral. 73 33 30 S 138 37 E
Spalding, U.K. 12 52 47N 0 9W
Spalding, U.S.A. 118 41 45N 98 27W
Spånga 10 59 23N 17 55 E
Spangler 114 40 39N 78 48W
Spaniard's Bay 103 47 38N 53 20W
Spanish 106 46 12N 82 20W
Spanish → 106 46 11N 82 19W
Spanish Fork 120 40 10N 111 37W
Spanish Town 126 18 0N 76 57W
Sparks 122 39 30N 119 45W
Sparta, Ga., U.S.A. 113 33 18N 82 59W
Sparta, Ill., U.S.A. 116 38 7N 89 42W
Sparta, Mich., U.S.A. 117 43 10N 85 42W
Sparta, Wis., U.S.A. 118 43 55N 90 47W
Sparta = Spárti 35 37 5N 22 25 E
Spartanburg 113 35 0N 82 0W
Spartansburg 114 41 48N 79 43W
Spartel, C. 86 35 47N 5 56W
Spárti 35 37 5N 22 25 E
Spartivento, C., Calabria, Italy 29 37 56N 16 4 E
Spartivento, C., Sard., Italy 28 38 52N 8 50 E
Spas-Demensk 36 54 20N 34 0 E
Spas-Klepiki 37 55 10N 40 10 E
Spassk-Dalniy 41 44 40N 132 48 E
Spassk-Ryazanskiy 37 54 24N 40 25 E
Spátha, Akra 35 35 42N 23 43 E
Spatsizi → 108 57 42N 128 7W
Spearfish 118 44 32N 103 52W
Spearman 119 36 15N 101 10W
Speed 74 35 21 S 142 27 E
Speedway 117 39 47N 86 15W
Speers 109 52 43N 107 34W
Speightstown 127 13 15N 59 39W
Speke Gulf 94 2 20 S 32 50 E
Spenard 100 61 11N 149 50W
Spence Bay 100 69 32N 93 32W
Spencer, Idaho, U.S.A. 120 44 18N 112 8W
Spencer, Ind., U.S.A. 117 39 17N 86 46W
Spencer, Iowa, U.S.A. 118 43 5N 95 19W
Spencer, N.Y., U.S.A. 115 42 14N 76 30W
Spencer, Nebr., U.S.A. 118 42 52N 98 43W
Spencer, W. Va., U.S.A. 112 38 47N 81 24W
Spencer B. 96 25 30 S 14 47 E
Spencer, C. 73 35 20 S 136 53 E
Spencer G. 73 34 0 S 137 20 E
Spencerville, Can. 107 44 51N 75 33W
Spencerville, U.S.A. 117 40 43N 84 21W
Spences Bridge 108 50 25N 121 20W
Spenser Mts. 81 42 15 S 172 45 E
Sperkhiós → 35 38 57N 22 3 E
Sperrin Mts. 15 54 50N 7 0W
Spessart 31 50 10N 9 20 E
Spétsai 35 37 15N 23 10 E
Spey → 14 57 26N 3 25W
Speyer 31 49 19N 8 26 E
Speyer → 31 49 19N 8 27 E
Spezia = La Spézia 26 44 7N 9 49 E
Spézia, La 26 44 8N 9 50 E
Spezzano Albanese 29 39 41N 16 19 E
Spickard 116 40 14N 93 36W
Spiekeroog 30 53 45N 7 42 E
Spielfeld 27 46 43N 15 38 E
Spiez 31 46 40N 7 40 E
Spilimbergo 27 46 7N 12 53 E
Spinazzola 29 40 58N 16 5 E
Spirit Lake, Idaho, U.S.A. 120 47 56N 116 56W
Spirit Lake, Wash., U.S.A. 122 46 15N 122 9W
Spirit River 108 55 45N 118 50W
Spiritwood 109 53 24N 107 33W
Spišská Nová Ves 32 48 58N 20 34 E
Spit Pt. 78 20 4 S 118 59 E
Spithead 13 50 43N 1 5W
Spittal 33 46 48N 13 31 E
Spitzbergen = Svalbard 144 78 0N 17 0 E
Split 27 43 31N 16 26 E
Split L. 109 56 8N 96 15W
Splitski Kanal 27 43 31N 16 20 E
Splügenpass 31 46 30N 9 20 E
Spofford 119 29 10N 100 27W
Spokane 120 47 45N 117 25W
Spoleto 27 42 46N 12 47 E
Spoon → 116 40 19N 90 4W
Spooner 118 45 49N 91 51W
Sporyy Navolok, Mys 40 75 50N 68 40 E
Spragge 106 46 15N 82 40W
Sprague 120 47 18N 117 59W
Sprague River 120 42 28N 121 31W
Spratly, I. 56 8 20N 112 0 E
Spray 120 44 50N 119 46W
Spree → 30 52 32N 13 13 E
Spremberg 30 51 33N 14 21 E
Spring City 120 39 31N 111 28W
Spring Garden 122 39 52N 120 47W
Spring Green 116 43 11N 90 4W
Spring Hill 76 33 23 S 149 9 E
Spring Mts. 121 36 20N 115 43W
Spring Ridge 77 32 15 S 149 21 E
Spring Valley, Ill., U.S.A. 116 41 20N 89 14W
Spring Valley, Minn., U.S.A. 118 43 40N 92 23W
Spring Valley, N.Y., U.S.A. 115 41 7N 74 4W
Springbok 96 29 42 S 17 54 E
Springburn 81 43 40 S 171 32 E
Springdale, Can. 103 49 30N 56 6W
Springdale, Ark., U.S.A. 119 36 10N 94 5W
Springdale, Wash., U.S.A. 120 48 1N 117 50W
Springe 30 52 12N 9 35 E
Springer 119 36 22N 104 36W
Springerville 121 34 10N 109 16W
Springfield, Can. 106 42 50N 80 56W
Springfield, N.Z. 81 43 19 S 171 56 E
Springfield, Colo., U.S.A. 119 37 26N 102 40W
Springfield, Ill., U.S.A. 116 39 48N 89 40W
Springfield, Ky., U.S.A. 117 37 41N 85 13W
Springfield, Mass., U.S.A. 115 42 8N 72 37W
Springfield, Mo., U.S.A. 119 37 15N 93 20W
Springfield, Ohio, U.S.A. 117 39 58N 83 48W
Springfield, Oreg., U.S.A. 120 44 2N 123 0W

Springfield, Tenn., U.S.A.	113	36 35N	86 55W
Springfield, Vt., U.S.A.	115	43 20N	72 30W
Springfield, L.	116	39 46N	89 36W
Springfontein	96	30 15S	25 40 E
Springhill	103	45 40N	64 4W
Springhouse	108	51 56N	122 7W
Springhurst	75	36 10S	146 31 E
Springs	97	26 13S	28 25 E
Springsure	72	24 8S	148 6 E
Springvale, Queens., Austral.	72	23 33S	140 42 E
Springvale, W. Australia, Austral.	78	17 48S	127 41 E
Springvale, U.S.A.	115	43 28N	70 48W
Springville, Calif., U.S.A.	122	36 8N	118 49W
Springville, N.Y., U.S.A.	114	42 31N	78 41W
Springville, Utah, U.S.A.	120	40 14N	111 35W
Springwater	109	51 58N	108 23W
Springwood	76	33 41S	150 33 E
Spruce-Creek	114	40 36N	78 9W
Sprucedale	106	45 29N	79 28W
Spur	119	33 28N	100 50W
Spurgeon	117	38 14N	87 15W
Spurn Hd.	12	53 34N	0 8 E
Spuž	33	42 32N	19 10 E
Spuzzum	108	49 37N	121 23W
Squam L.	115	43 45N	71 32W
Squamish	108	49 45N	123 10W
Square Islands	103	52 47N	55 47W
Squatec	105	47 53N	68 43W
Squillace, Golfo di	29	38 43N	16 35 E
Squinzano	29	40 27N	18 1 E
Squires, Mt.	79	26 14S	127 28 E
Sragen	57	7 28S	110 59 E
Srbac	33	45 7N	17 30 E
Srbija □	33	43 30N	21 0 E
Srbobran	33	45 32N	19 48 E
Sre Khtum	55	12 10N	106 52 E
Sre Umbell	55	11 8N	103 46 E
Srebrnica	33	44 10N	19 18 E
Sredinnyy Khrebet	41	57 0N	160 0 E
Središče	27	46 24N	16 17 E
Sredna Gora	34	42 40N	24 20 E
Sredne Tambovskoye	41	50 55N	137 45 E
Srednekolymsk	41	67 27N	153 40 E
Srednevilyuysk	41	63 50N	123 5 E
Šrem	32	52 6N	17 2 E
Sremska Mitrovica	33	44 59N	19 33 E
Srepok →	54	13 33N	106 16 E
Sretensk	41	52 10N	117 40 E
Sri Lanka ■	51	7 30N	80 50 E
Sriharikota, I.	51	13 40N	80 20 E
Srikakulam	50	18 14N	83 58 E
Srinagar	49	34 5N	74 50 E
Sripur	52	24 14N	90 30 E
Srirangam	51	10 54N	78 42 E
Srirangapatnam	51	12 26N	76 43 E
Śrivilliputtur	51	9 31N	77 40 E
Środa Wielkopolski	32	52 15N	17 19 E
Srpska Itabej	33	45 35N	20 44 E
Staaten →	72	16 24S	141 17 E
Staberhuk	30	54 23N	11 18 E
Stade	30	53 35N	9 31 E
Staðarhólskirkja	8	65 23N	21 58W
Städjan	10	61 56N	12 52 E
Stadlandet	8	62 10N	5 10 E
Stadskanaal	16	53 4N	6 55 E
Stadthagen	30	52 20N	9 14 E
Stadtlohn	30	52 0N	6 52 E
Stadtroda	30	50 51N	11 44 E
Stafafell	8	64 25N	14 52W
Staffa	14	56 26N	6 21W
Stafford, U.K.	12	52 49N	2 9W
Stafford, U.S.A.	119	38 0N	98 35W
Stafford □	12	52 53N	2 10W
Stafford Springs	115	41 58N	72 20W
Stagnone	28	37 50N	12 28 E
Staines	13	51 26N	0 30W
Stalingrad = Volgograd	39	48 40N	44 25 E
Staliniri = Tskhinvali	39	42 14N	44 1 E
Stalino = Donetsk	38	48 0N	37 45 E
Stalinogorsk = Novomoskovsk	37	54 5N	38 15 E
Stalowa Wola	32	50 34N	22 3 E
Stalybridge	12	53 29N	2 4W
Stamford, Austral.	72	21 15S	143 46 E
Stamford, U.K.	13	52 39N	0 29W
Stamford, Conn., U.S.A.	115	41 5N	73 30W
Stamford, Tex., U.S.A.	119	32 58N	99 50W
Stamping Ground	117	38 16N	84 41W
Stamps	119	33 22N	93 30W
Stanberry	118	40 12N	94 32W
Standerton	97	26 55S	29 7 E
Standish	112	43 58N	83 57W
Stanford	120	47 11N	110 10W
Stange	10	60 43N	11 5 E
Stanger	97	29 27S	31 14 E
Stanhope, Austral.	74	36 27S	144 59 E
Stanhope, U.S.A.	116	42 17N	93 48W
Stanislaus →	122	37 40N	121 15W
Stanislav = Ivano-Frankovsk	36	49 0N	24 40 E
Stanke Dimitrov	34	42 17N	23 9 E
Stanley, Austral.	72	40 46S	145 19 E
Stanley, N.B., Can.	103	46 20N	66 44W
Stanley, Sask., Can.	109	55 24N	104 22W
Stanley, Falk. Is.	142	51 40S	59 51W
Stanley, Idaho, U.S.A.	120	44 10N	114 59W
Stanley, N.D., U.S.A.	118	48 20N	102 23W
Stanley, N.Y., U.S.A.	114	42 48N	77 6W
Stanley, Wis., U.S.A.	118	44 57N	91 0W
Stanley Res.	51	11 50N	77 40 E
Stanleyville = Kisangani	94	0 35N	25 15 E
Stann Creek	125	17 0N	88 13W
Stannifer	77	29 52S	151 14 E
Stanovoy Khrebet	41	55 0N	130 0 E
Stansmore Ra.	78	21 23S	128 33 E
Stanthorpe	77	28 36S	151 59 E
Stanton, Mich., U.S.A.	106	43 18N	85 5W
Stanton, Tex., U.S.A.	119	32 8N	101 45W
Stanwell Park	76	34 13S	150 58 E
Stanwood	122	48 15N	122 23W
Staples	118	46 21N	94 48W
Stapleton	118	41 30N	100 31W
Star City	109	52 50N	104 20W
Stara-minskaya	39	46 33N	39 0 E
Stara Moravica	33	45 50N	19 30 E
Stara Planina	34	43 15N	23 0 E
Stara Zagora	34	42 26N	25 39 E
Starachowice	32	51 3N	21 2 E
Staraya Russa	36	57 58N	31 23 E
Starbuck I.	67	5 37S	155 55W
Stargard	30	53 29N	13 19 E
Stargard Szczeciński	32	53 20N	15 0 E
Stari Trg	27	45 29N	15 7 E
Staritsa	36	56 33N	35 0 E
Starke	113	30 0N	82 10W
Starkville, Colo., U.S.A.	119	37 10N	104 31W
Starkville, Miss., U.S.A.	113	33 26N	88 48W
Starnberg	31	48 0N	11 20 E
Starnberger See	31	47 55N	11 20 E
Starobelsk	39	49 16N	39 0 E
Starodub	36	52 30N	32 50 E
Starogard	32	53 59N	18 30 E
Start Pt.	13	50 13N	3 38W
Staryy Biryuzyak	39	44 46N	46 50 E
Staryy Kheydzhan	41	60 0N	144 50 E
Staryy Krym	38	45 3N	35 8 E
Staryy Oskol	37	51 19N	37 55 E
Stassfurt	30	51 51N	11 34 E
State Center	116	42 1N	93 10W
State College	114	40 47N	77 49W
Stateline	122	38 57N	119 56W
Staten, I.	115	40 35N	74 10W
Staten, I. = Los Estados, I. de	142	54 40S	64 20W
Statesboro	113	32 26N	81 46W
Statesville	113	35 48N	80 51W
Stauffer	123	34 45N	119 3W
Staunton, Ill., U.S.A.	116	39 0N	89 49W
Staunton, Va., U.S.A.	112	38 7N	79 4W
Stavanger	9	58 57N	5 40 E
Stavelot	16	50 23N	5 55 E
Staveren	16	52 53N	5 22 E
Stavern	10	59 0N	10 1 E
Stavre	10	62 51N	15 19 E
Stavropol	39	45 5N	42 0 E
Stavroúpolis	35	41 12N	24 45 E
Stawell	74	37 5S	142 47 E
Stawell →	72	20 20S	142 55 E
Stawiszyn	32	51 56N	18 4 E
Stayner	106	44 25N	80 5W
Steamboat Springs	120	40 30N	106 50W
Steele	118	46 56N	99 52W
Steelton	114	40 17N	76 50W
Steelville	116	37 57N	91 21W
Steen River	108	59 40N	117 12W
Steenvoorde	19	50 48N	2 33 E
Steenwijk	16	52 47N	6 7 E
Steep Pt.	79	26 08S	113 8 E
Steep Rock	109	51 30N	98 48W
Ştefăneşti	34	47 44N	27 15 E
Stefanie L. = Chew Bahir	91	4 40N	36 50 E
Stefansson Bay	143	67 20S	59 8 E
Stege	11	55 0N	12 18 E
Steger	117	41 28N	87 38W
Steigerwald	31	49 45N	10 30 E
Steilacoom	122	47 10N	122 36W
Steinbach	109	49 32N	96 40W
Steinfort	16	49 39N	5 55 E
Steinheim	30	51 50N	9 6 E
Steinhuder Meer	30	52 48N	9 20 E
Steinkjer	8	63 59N	11 31 E
Stellaland	96	26 45S	24 50 E
Stellarton	103	45 32N	62 30W
Stellenbosch	96	33 58S	18 50 E
Stemshaug	10	63 19N	8 44 E
Stendal	30	52 36N	11 50 E
Stensele	8	65 3N	17 8 E
Stenstorp	11	58 17N	13 45 E
Stephan	118	48 30N	96 53W
Stephens Creek	73	31 50S	141 30 E
Stephens I., Can.	108	54 10N	130 45W
Stephens I., N.Z.	81	40 40S	174 1 E
Stephenville, Can.	103	48 31N	58 35W
Stephenville, U.S.A.	119	32 12N	98 12W
Stepnica	32	53 38N	14 36 E
Stepnoi = Elista	39	46 16N	44 14 E
Stepnyak	40	52 50N	70 50 E
Steppe	42	50 0N	50 0 E
Sterkstroom	96	31 32S	26 32 E
Sterling, Colo., U.S.A.	118	40 40N	103 15W
Sterling, Ill., U.S.A.	116	41 45N	89 45W
Sterling, Kans., U.S.A.	118	38 17N	98 13W
Sterling City	119	31 50N	100 59W
Sterling Run	114	41 25N	78 12W
Sterlitamak	40	53 40N	56 0 E
Sternberg	30	53 42N	11 48 E
Šternberk	32	49 45N	17 15 E
Stettin = Szczecin	32	53 27N	14 27 E
Stettiner Haff	30	53 50N	14 25 E
Stettler	108	52 19N	112 40W
Steubenville	114	40 21N	80 39W
Stevens Port	118	44 32N	89 34W
Stevenson	122	45 42N	121 53W
Stevenson L.	109	53 55N	96 0W
Stevns Klint	11	55 17N	12 28 E
Steward	116	41 51N	89 1W
Stewardson	117	39 16N	88 38W
Stewart, B.C., Can.	108	55 56N	129 57W
Stewart, N.W.T., Can.	100	63 19N	139 26W
Stewart, U.S.A.	122	39 5N	119 46W
Stewart, C.	72	11 57S	134 56 E
Stewart, I.	142	54 50S	71 15W
Stewart I.	81	46 58S	167 54 E
Stewarts Point	122	38 39N	123 20W
Stewartsville	116	39 45N	94 30W
Stewiacke	103	45 9N	63 22W
Steynsburg	96	31 15S	25 49 E
Steyr	33	48 3N	14 25 E
Steytlerville	96	33 17S	24 19 E
Stia	27	43 48N	11 41 E
Stigler	119	35 19N	95 6W
Stigliano	29	40 24N	16 13 E
Stigsnæs	11	55 13N	11 18 E
Stigtomta	11	58 47N	16 48 E
Stikine →	100	56 40N	132 30W
Stilfontein	96	26 50S	26 50 E
Stilís	35	38 55N	22 47 E
Stillwater, Minn., U.S.A.	118	45 3N	92 47W
Stillwater, N.Y., U.S.A.	115	42 55N	73 41W
Stillwater, Okla., U.S.A.	119	36 5N	97 3W
Stillwater Mts.	120	39 45N	118 6W
Stilwell	119	35 52N	94 36W
Štip	35	41 42N	22 10 E
Stíra	35	38 9N	24 14 E
Stiring-Wendel	19	49 12N	6 57 E
Stirling, Austral.	72	17 12S	141 35 E
Stirling, Alta., Can.	108	49 30N	112 30W
Stirling, Ont., Can.	107	44 18N	77 33W
Stirling, N.Z.	81	46 14S	169 49 E
Stirling, U.K.	14	56 7N	3 57W
Stirling Ra.	79	34 23S	118 0 E
Stittsville	107	45 15N	75 55W
Stockach	31	47 51N	9 01 E
Stockaryd	11	57 19N	14 36 E
Stockbridge	106	42 27N	84 11W
Stockerau	33	48 24N	16 12 E
Stockett	120	47 23N	111 7W
Stockholm	10	59 20N	18 3 E
Stockholms län □	10	59 30N	18 20 E
Stockinbingal	76	34 30S	147 53 E
Stockport	12	53 25N	2 11W
Stockton, Austral.	76	32 50S	151 47 E
Stockton, Calif., U.S.A.	122	38 0N	121 20W
Stockton, Ill., U.S.A.	116	42 21N	90 1W
Stockton, Kans., U.S.A.	118	39 30N	99 20W
Stockton, Mo., U.S.A.	116	37 40N	93 48W
Stockton-on-Tees	12	54 34N	1 20W
Stockvik	10	62 17N	17 23 E
Stöde	10	62 28N	16 35 E
Stogovo	35	41 31N	20 38 E
Stoke	81	41 19S	173 14 E
Stoke-on-Trent	12	53 1N	2 11W
Stokes Bay	106	45 0N	81 28W
Stokes Pt.	72	40 10S	143 56 E
Stokes Ra.	78	15 50S	130 50 E
Stokkseyri	8	63 50N	21 2W
Stokksnes	8	64 14N	14 58W
Stolac	33	43 8N	17 59 E
Stolberg	30	50 48N	6 13 E
Stolbovaya, R.S.F.S.R., U.S.S.R.	37	55 10N	37 32 E
Stolbovaya, R.S.F.S.R., U.S.S.R.	41	64 50N	153 50 E
Stolbovoy, Ostrov	41	56 44N	163 14 E
Stolbtsy	36	53 30N	26 43 E
Stolin	36	51 53N	26 50 E
Ston	33	42 51N	17 43 E
Stoneham	105	47 0N	71 22W
Stonehaven	14	56 58N	2 11W
Stonehenge	72	24 22S	143 17 E
Stonewall	109	50 10N	97 19W
Stoney Creek	106	43 14N	79 45W
Stonington	116	39 44N	89 12W
Stonington I.	143	68 11S	67 0W
Stony L., Man., Can.	109	58 51N	98 40W
Stony L., Ont., Can.	107	44 30N	78 0W
Stony Rapids	109	59 16N	105 50W
Stony Tunguska = Tunguska, Nizhnyaya	41	65 48N	88 4 E
Stonyford	122	39 23N	122 33W
Stopnica	32	50 27N	20 57 E
Stora Gla	10	59 30N	12 30 E
Stora Karlsö	11	57 17N	17 59 E
Stora Lulevatten	8	67 10N	19 30 E
Stora Sjöfallet	8	67 29N	18 40 E
Storavan	8	65 45N	18 10 E
Store Bælt	11	55 20N	11 0 E
Store Creek	76	32 54S	149 6 E
Store Heddinge	11	55 18N	12 23 E
Støren	10	63 3N	10 18 E
Storm B.	72	43 10S	147 30 E
Storm Lake	118	42 35N	95 11W
Stormberg	96	31 16S	26 17 E
Stormsrivier	96	33 59S	23 52 E
Stornoway	14	58 12N	6 23W
Storozhinets	38	48 14N	25 45 E
Storsjö	10	62 49N	13 5 E
Storsjöen, Hedmark, Norway	10	60 20N	11 40 E
Storsjöen, Hedmark, Norway	10	61 30N	11 14 E
Storsjön, Gävleborg, Sweden	10	60 35N	16 45 E
Storsjön, Jämtland, Sweden	10	62 50N	13 8 E
Storstrøms Amt. □	11	54 50N	11 45 E
Storuman	8	65 5N	17 10 E
Storvik	10	60 35N	16 33 E
Story City	116	42 11N	93 36W
Stouffville	106	43 58N	79 15W
Stoughton, Can.	109	49 40N	103 0W
Stoughton, U.S.A.	116	42 55N	88 59W
Stour →, Dorset, U.K.	13	50 48N	2 7W
Stour →, Suffolk, U.K.	13	51 55N	1 5 E
Stour (Gt. Stour) →	13	51 15N	1 20 E
Stourbridge	13	52 28N	2 8W
Stout, L.	109	52 0N	94 40W
Stove Pipe Wells Village	123	36 35N	117 11W
Stowmarket	13	52 11N	1 0 E
Strabane	15	54 50N	7 28W
Strabane □	15	54 45N	7 25W
Stracin	34	42 13N	22 2 E
Stradella	26	45 4N	9 20 E
Strahan	72	42 9S	145 20 E
Strakonice	32	49 15N	13 53 E
Straldzha	34	42 35N	26 40 E
Stralsund	30	54 17N	13 5 E
Strand	96	34 9S	18 48 E
Strangford, L.	15	54 30N	5 37W
Strängnäs	10	59 23N	17 2 E
Stranraer	14	54 54N	5 0W
Strasbourg, Can.	109	51 4N	104 55W
Strasbourg, France	19	48 35N	7 42 E
Strasburg, Ger.	30	53 30N	13 44 E
Strasburg, U.S.A.	118	46 12N	100 9W
Stratford, N.S.W., Austral.	77	32 7S	151 55 E
Stratford, Vic., Austral.	75	37 59S	147 7 E
Stratford, Can.	106	43 23N	81 0W
Stratford, N.Z.	80	39 20S	174 19 E
Stratford, Calif., U.S.A.	122	36 10N	119 49W
Stratford, Conn., U.S.A.	115	41 13N	73 8W
Stratford, Tex., U.S.A.	119	36 20N	102 3W
Stratford-on-Avon	13	52 12N	1 42W
Strath Spey	14	57 15N	3 40W
Strathalbyn	73	35 13S	138 53 E
Strathbogie	74	36 53S	145 43 E

Strathclyde □ 14 56 0N 4 50W
Strathcona Prov. Park 108 49 38N 125 40W
Strathmerton 74 35 54S 145 30E
Strathmore, Austral. 72 17 50S 142 35E
Strathmore, Can. 108 51 5N 113 18W
Strathmore, U.K. 14 56 40N 3 4W
Strathmore, U.S.A. 122 36 9N 119 4W
Strathnaver 108 53 20N 122 33W
Strathpeffer 14 57 35N 4 32W
Strathroy 106 42 58N 81 38W
Strathy Pt. 14 58 35N 4 0W
Stratton, U.K. 12 51 41N 1 45W
Stratton, U.S.A. 118 39 20N 102 36W
Straubing 31 48 53N 12 35E
Straumnes 8 66 26N 23 8W
Strausberg 30 52 40N 13 52E
Strawberry Point 116 42 41N 91 32W
Strawberry Res. 120 40 10N 111 7W
Strawn 119 32 36N 98 30W
Strážnice 32 48 54N 17 19E
Streaky B. 73 32 51S 134 18E
Streaky Bay 73 32 48S 134 13E
Streatham 74 37 43S 143 5E
Streator 117 41 9N 88 52W
Streeter 118 46 39N 99 21W
Streetsville 106 43 35N 79 42W
Strehaia 34 44 37N 23 10E
Strelcha 34 42 25N 24 19E
Strelka 41 58 5N 93 3E
Streng → 54 13 12N 103 37E
Strésa 26 45 52N 8 28E
Strezhevoy 40 60 42N 77 34E
Stříbro 32 49 44N 13 0E
Strickland → 69 7 35S 141 36E
Strimón → 35 40 46N 23 51E
Strimonikós Kólpos 35 40 33N 24 0E
Stroeder 142 40 12S 62 37W
Strofádhes 35 37 15N 21 0E
Strombacka 10 61 58N 16 44E
Strómboli 29 38 48N 15 12E
Stromeferry 14 57 20N 5 33W
Stromness 14 58 58N 3 18W
Strömsnäsbruk 11 56 35N 13 45E
Strömstad 10 58 55N 11 15E
Strömsund 8 63 51N 15 35E
Stronghurst 116 40 45N 90 55W
Stróngoli 29 39 16N 17 2E
Strongs Corners 106 46 18N 84 55W
Stronsay 14 59 8N 2 38W
Stronsburg 118 41 7N 97 36W
Stroud, Austral. 76 32 25S 152 0E
Stroud, Can. 106 44 19N 79 37W
Stroud, U.K. 13 51 44N 2 12W
Stroud Road 77 32 18S 151 57E
Stroudsberg 115 40 59N 75 15W
Struer 11 56 30N 8 35E
Struga 35 41 13N 20 44E
Strugi Krasnyye 36 58 21N 29 1E
Strumica 35 41 28N 22 41E
Strumica → 35 41 20N 22 22E
Struthers, Can. 102 48 41N 85 51W
Struthers, U.S.A. 114 41 6N 80 38W
Stryi 36 49 16N 23 48E
Stryker, U.S.A. 108 48 40N 114 44W
Stryker, U.S.A. 120 48 40N 114 54W
Strzegom 32 50 58N 16 20E
Strzelce Krajeńskie 32 52 52N 15 33E
Strzelecki Cr. → 73 29 37S 139 59E
Strzelin 32 50 46N 17 2E
Strzelno 32 52 35N 18 9E
Strzyzów 32 49 52N 21 47E
Stuart, Fla., U.S.A. 113 27 11N 80 12W
Stuart, Iowa, U.S.A. 116 41 30N 94 19W
Stuart, Nebr., U.S.A. 118 42 39N 99 8W
Stuart → 108 54 0N 123 35W
Stuart L. 108 54 30N 124 30W
Stuart Mts. 81 45 2S 167 39E
Stuart Range 73 29 10S 134 56E
Stuart Town 76 32 44S 149 4E
Stubbekøbing 11 54 53N 12 9E
Studholme Junc. 81 44 42S 171 9E
Stugun 10 63 10N 15 40E
Stühlingen 31 47 44N 8 26E
Stull, L. 109 54 24N 92 34W
Stung Treng 54 13 31N 105 58E
Stupart → 109 56 0N 93 25W
Stupino 37 54 57N 38 2E
Sturgeon → 106 46 35N 80 11W
Sturgeon B. 109 52 0N 97 50W
Sturgeon Bay 112 44 52N 87 20W
Sturgeon Falls 106 46 25N 79 57W
Sturgeon L., Alta., Can. 108 55 6N 117 32W
Sturgeon L., Ont., Can. 102 50 0N 90 45W
Sturgeon L., Ont., Can. 107 44 28N 78 43W
Sturgis, Mich., U.S.A. 117 41 50N 85 25W
Sturgis, S.D., U.S.A. 118 44 25N 103 30W
Sturkö 11 56 5N 15 42E
Sturt Cr. → 78 20 8S 127 24E
Sturt Creek 78 19 12S 128 8E
Stutterheim 96 32 33S 27 28E
Stuttgart, Ger. 31 48 46N 9 10E
Stuttgart, U.S.A. 119 34 30N 91 33W
Stuyvesant 115 42 23N 73 45W
Stykkishólmur 8 65 2N 22 40W
Styr → 36 52 7N 26 35E
Styria = Steiermark □ 33 47 26N 15 0E
Su-no-Saki 65 34 58N 139 45E
Su Xian 60 33 41N 116 59E
Suakin 90 19 8N 37 20E
Suan 61 38 42N 126 22E
Suapure → 134 6 48N 67 1W
Suaqui 124 29 12N 109 41W
Suatá → 135 7 52N 65 22W
Subang 57 6 34S 107 45E
Subansiri → 52 26 48N 93 50E
Subi, Indon. 55 2 55N 108 50E
Subi, Indon. 56 2 58N 108 50E
Subiaco 27 41 56N 13 5E
Subotica 33 46 6N 19 49E
Success 109 50 28N 108 6W
Suceava 34 47 38N 26 16E
Suceava → 34 47 38N 26 16E
Sucha-Beskidzka 32 49 44N 19 35E
Suchan 32 53 18N 15 18E
Suchil 124 23 38N 103 55W
Suchitoto 126 13 56N 89 0W
Suchou = Suzhou 62 31 18N 120 36E
Süchow = Xuzhou 61 34 18N 117 10E
Suchowola 32 53 33N 23 3E
Sucio → 134 7 27N 77 7W
Suck → 15 53 17N 8 18W
Suckling, Mt. 69 9 49S 148 53E
Sucre, Boliv. 137 19 0S 65 15W
Sucre, Colomb. 134 8 49N 74 44W
Sucre □, Colomb. 134 8 50N 75 40W
Sucre □, Venez. 135 10 25N 63 30W
Sucuaro 134 4 34N 68 50W
Sućuraj 27 43 10N 17 8E
Sucuriju 138 1 39N 49 57W
Sucuriú → 137 20 47S 51 38W
Sud-Ouest, Pte. du 103 49 23N 63 36W
Sud, Pte. 103 49 3N 62 14W
Suda → 37 59 0N 37 40E
Sudair 46 26 0N 45 0E
Sudak 38 44 51N 34 57E
Sudan 119 34 4N 102 32W
Sudan ■ 85 15 0N 30 0E
Suday 37 59 0N 43 0E
Sudbury 106 46 30N 81 0W
Sûdd 91 8 20N 30 0E
Suddie 135 7 8N 58 29W
Süderbrarup 30 54 38N 9 47E
Süderlügum 30 54 50N 8 55E
Süderoog-Sand 30 54 27N 8 30E
Sudetan Mts. = Sudety 32 50 20N 16 45E
Sudety 32 50 20N 16 45E
Sudi 95 10 11S 39 57E
Sudirman, Pegunungan 57 4 30S 137 0E
Sudogda 37 55 55N 40 50E
Sudr 90 29 40N 32 42E
Sudzha 36 51 14N 35 17E
Sueca 25 39 12N 0 21W
Suedala 11 55 30N 13 15E
Sueur, Le 118 44 25N 93 52W
Suez = El Suweis 90 28 40N 33 0E
Suez Canal = Suweis, Qanâl es 90 31 0N 33 20E
Suf 44 32 19N 35 49E
Sufaina 46 23 6N 40 33E
Suffield 109 50 12N 111 10W
Suffolk 112 36 47N 76 33W
Suffolk □ 13 52 16N 1 0E
Sufuk 47 23 50N 51 50E
Suga no-Sen 64 35 25N 134 25E
Sugar →, Ill., U.S.A. 116 42 25N 89 15W
Sugar →, Ind., U.S.A. 117 39 50N 87 23W
Sugar City 118 38 18N 103 38W
Sugar Cr. → 116 40 12N 89 41W
Sugluk = Sagloue 101 62 30N 74 15W
Suhaia, L. 34 43 45N 25 15E
Suhār 47 24 20N 56 40E
Suhbaatar 62 50 17N 106 10E
Sühbaatar □ 60 46 54N 113 25E
Suhl 30 50 35N 10 40E
Suhl □ 30 50 37N 10 43E
Sui Xian, Henan, China 59 31 42N 113 24E
Sui Xian, Henan, China 60 34 25N 115 2E
Suiá Missu → 137 11 13S 53 15W
Suichang 59 28 29N 119 15E
Suichuan 59 26 20N 114 32E
Suide 60 37 30N 110 12E
Suifenhe 61 44 25N 131 10E
Suihua 62 46 32N 126 55E
Suijiang 58 28 40N 103 59E
Suining, Hunan, China 59 26 35N 110 10E
Suining, Jiangsu, China 61 33 56N 117 58E
Suining, Sichuan, China 58 30 26N 105 35E
Suiping 60 33 10N 113 59E
Suippes 19 49 8N 4 30E
Suir → 15 52 15N 7 10W
Suita 65 34 45N 135 32E
Suixi 59 21 19N 110 18E
Suiyang, Guizhou, China 58 27 58N 107 18E
Suiyang, Heilongjiang, China 61 44 30N 130 56E
Suizhong 61 40 21N 120 20E
Sujangarh 48 27 42N 74 31E
Sukabumi 57 6 56S 106 50E
Sukadana, Kalimantan, Indon. 56 1 10S 110 0E
Sukadana, Sumatera, Indon. 56 5 5S 105 33E
Sukaradja 56 2 28S 110 25E
Sukarnapura = Jayapura 57 2 37S 140 38E
Sukchŏn 61 39 22N 125 35E
Sukhinichi 36 54 8N 35 10E
Sukhona → 40 60 30N 45 0E
Sukhothai 54 17 1N 99 49E
Sukhumi 39 43 0N 41 0E
Sukkur 48 27 42N 68 54E
Sukkur Barrage 48 27 40N 68 50E
Sukma 50 18 24N 81 45E
Sukumo 64 32 56N 132 44E
Sukunka → 108 55 45N 121 15W
Sul, Canal do 138 0 10S 48 30W
Sula → 36 49 40N 32 41E
Sula, Kepulauan 57 1 45S 125 0E
Sulaco → 126 15 2N 87 44W
Sulaiman Range 48 30 30N 69 50E
Sulak → 39 43 20N 47 34E
Sulam Tsor 44 33 4N 35 6E
Sulawesi □ 57 2 0S 120 0E
Sulcor 77 30 51S 150 48E
Sulechów 32 52 5N 15 40E
Sulejów 32 51 26N 19 53E
Sulima 88 6 58N 11 32W
Sulina 34 45 10N 29 40E
Sulingen 30 52 41N 8 47E
Sulitälma 8 67 17N 17 28E
Sullana 136 4 52S 80 39W
Sullivan, Can. 104 48 7N 77 50W
Sullivan, Ill., U.S.A. 117 39 40N 88 40W
Sullivan, Ind., U.S.A. 117 39 5N 87 26W
Sullivan, Mo., U.S.A. 116 38 10N 91 10W
Sullivan Bay 108 50 55N 126 50W
Sully 116 41 34N 92 50W
Sully-sur-Loire 19 47 45N 2 20E
Sulmona 27 42 3N 13 55E
Sulphur, La., U.S.A. 119 30 13N 93 22W
Sulphur, Okla., U.S.A. 119 34 35N 97 0W
Sulphur Pt. 108 60 56N 114 48W
Sulphur Springs 119 33 5N 95 36W
Sulphur Springs, Cr. → 119 32 12N 101 36W
Sultan, Can. 102 47 36N 82 47W
Sultan, U.S.A. 122 47 51N 121 49W
Sultanpur 49 26 18N 82 4E
Sulu Arch. 57 6 0N 121 0E
Sulu Sea 57 8 0N 120 0E
Sululta 91 9 10N 38 43E
Suluq 87 31 44N 20 14E
Sulzbach 31 49 18N 7 4E
Sulzbach-Rosenberg 31 49 30N 11 46E
Sumalata 57 1 0N 122 31E
Sumampa 140 29 25S 63 29W
Sumatera □ 56 0 40N 100 20E
Sumatera Barat □ 56 1 0S 100 0E
Sumatera Selatan □ 56 3 30S 104 0E
Sumatera Utara □ 56 2 0N 99 0E
Sumatra 120 46 38N 107 31W
Sumatra = Sumatera □ 56 0 40N 100 20E
Sumba 57 9 45S 119 35E
Sumba, Selat 57 9 0S 118 40E
Sumbawa 56 8 26S 117 30E
Sumbawa Besar 56 8 30S 117 26E
Sumbawanga □ 94 8 0S 31 30E
Sumbing 57 7 19S 110 3E
Sumburgh Hd. 14 59 52N 1 17W
Sumdo 49 35 6N 78 41E
Sumé 138 7 39S 36 55W
Sumedang 57 6 49S 107 56E
Sumenep 57 7 3S 113 51E
Sumgait 39 40 34N 49 38E
Sumisu-Jima 65 31 27N 140 3E
Summer L. 120 42 50N 120 50W
Summerland 108 49 32N 119 41W
Summerside 103 46 24N 63 47W
Summerville, Ga., U.S.A. 113 34 30N 85 20W
Summerville, S.C., U.S.A. 113 33 2N 80 11W
Summit Lake 108 54 20N 122 40W
Summit Pk. 121 37 20N 106 48W
Summitt 117 41 48N 87 48W
Sumner, N.Z. 81 43 35S 172 48E
Sumner, Ill., U.S.A. 117 38 42N 87 53W
Sumner, Iowa, U.S.A. 116 42 49N 92 7W
Sumner, Wash., U.S.A. 122 47 12N 122 14W
Sumner L. 81 42 42S 172 15E
Sumoto 64 34 21N 134 54E
Sumprabum 52 26 33N 97 36E
Sumter 113 33 55N 80 22W
Sumy 36 50 57N 34 50E
Sun City 123 33 41N 117 11W
Sun Prairie 116 43 11N 89 13W
Suna 94 5 23S 34 48E
Sunan 61 39 15N 125 40E
Sunart, L. 14 56 42N 5 43W
Sunburst 120 48 56N 111 59W
Sunbury, Austral. 74 37 35S 144 44E
Sunbury, U.S.A. 115 40 50N 76 46W
Sunchales 140 30 58S 61 35W
Suncho Corral 140 27 55S 63 27W
Sunchon 61 34 52N 127 31E
Suncook 115 43 8N 71 27W
Sunda Is. 66 5 0S 105 0E
Sunda Kecil, Kepulauan 56 7 30S 117 0E
Sunda, Selat 56 6 20S 105 30E
Sundance 118 44 27N 104 27W
Sundarbans, The 52 22 0N 89 0E
Sundargarh 50 22 4N 84 5E
Sunday Str. 78 16 25S 123 18E
Sundays = Sondags → 96 33 44S 25 51E
Sundbyberg 10 59 22N 17 58E
Sunderland, Can. 107 44 16N 79 4W
Sunderland, U.K. 12 54 54N 1 22W
Sunderland, U.S.A. 115 42 27N 72 36W
Sundre 108 51 49N 114 38W
Sundridge 106 45 45N 79 25W
Sunds 11 56 13N 9 1E
Sundsjö 10 62 59N 15 9E
Sundsvall 10 62 23N 17 17E
Sung Hei 55 10 20N 106 2E
Sungai Kolok 55 6 2N 101 58E
Sungai Lembing 55 3 55N 103 3E
Sungai Patani 55 5 37N 100 30E
Sungaigerong 56 2 59S 104 52E
Sungailiat 56 1 51S 106 8E
Sungaipakning 56 1 19N 102 0E
Sungaipenuh 56 2 1S 101 20E
Sungaitiram 56 0 45S 117 8E
Sungari = Songhua Jiang → 61 47 45N 132 30E
Sungguminasa 57 5 17S 119 30E
Sunghua Chiang = Songhua Jiang → 61 47 45N 132 30E
Sungikai 91 12 20N 29 51E
Sungüé 97 21 18S 32 28E
Sungurlu 38 40 12N 34 21E
Sunja 27 45 21N 16 35E
Sunne 10 59 52N 13 5E
Sunnyside, Utah, U.S.A. 120 39 34N 110 24W
Sunnyside, Wash., U.S.A. 120 46 24N 120 2W
Sunnyvale 122 37 23N 122 2W
Sunray 119 36 1N 101 47W
Sunshine 74 37 48S 144 52E
Suntar 41 62 15N 117 30E
Sunyani 88 7 21N 2 22W
Suō-Nada 64 33 50N 131 30E
Supai 121 36 14N 112 44W
Supamo → 135 6 48N 61 50W
Supaul 49 26 10N 86 40E
Supe, Ethiopia 91 8 34N 35 35E
Supe, Peru 136 11 0S 77 30W
Superior, Ariz., U.S.A. 121 33 19N 111 9W
Superior, Mont., U.S.A. 120 47 15N 114 57W
Superior, Nebr., U.S.A. 118 40 3N 98 2W
Superior, Wis., U.S.A. 118 46 45N 92 5W
Superior, L. 111 47 40N 87 0W
Supetar 27 43 25N 16 32E
Suphan Buri 54 14 14N 100 10E
Suphan Daği 46 38 54N 42 48E
Supung Sk. 61 40 35N 124 50E
Suq al Jum'ah 87 32 58N 13 12E
Sūq ash Shūyukh 46 30 53N 46 28E
Suqian 61 33 54N 118 8E
Sūr, Leb. 44 33 19N 35 16E
Sūr, Oman 47 22 34N 59 32E
Sur, Pt. 122 36 18N 121 54W
Sura → 37 56 6N 46 0E
Surab 48 28 25N 66 15E
Surabaja = Surabaya 57 7 17S 112 45E
Surabaya 57 7 17S 112 45E

Suraga-Wan **65** 34 45N 138 30 E
Surahammar **10** 59 43N 16 13 E
Suraia **34** 45 40N 27 25 E
Surakarta **57** 7 35S 110 48 E
Surakhany **39** 40 25N 50 1 E
Surandai **51** 8 58N 77 26 E
Surat, Austral. **73** 27 10S 149 6 E
Surat, India **50** 21 12N 72 55 E
Surat Thani **55** 9 6N 99 20 E
Suratgarh **48** 29 18N 73 55 E
Surazh **36** 53 5N 32 27 E
Surduc Pasul **34** 45 21N 23 23 E
Surdulica **33** 42 41N 22 11 E
Sûre ~→ **16** 49 44N 6 31 E
Surendranagar **48** 22 45N 71 40 E
Surf **123** 34 41N 120 36W
Surfers Paradise **77** 28 0S 153 25 E
Surgères **20** 46 7N 0 47W
Surgut **40** 61 14N 73 20 E
Suri **49** 23 50N 87 34 E
Suriapet **50** 17 10N 79 40 E
Surif **44** 31 40N 35 4 E
Surigao **57** 9 47N 125 29 E
Surin **54** 14 50N 103 34 E
Surin Nua, Ko **55** 9 30N 97 55 E
Surinam ■ **135** 4 0N 56 0W
Suriname □ **135** 5 30N 55 0W
Suriname ~→ **135** 5 50N 55 15W
Surmene **39** 41 0N 40 1 E
Surovikino **39** 48 32N 42 55 E
Surprise L. **108** 59 40N 133 15W
Surprise, L. **104** 49 20N 74 55W
Surrey □ **13** 51 16N 0 30W
Sursee **31** 47 11N 8 6 E
Sursk **37** 53 3N 45 40 E
Surt **87** 31 11N 16 39 E
Surt, Al Hammādah al **87** 30 0N 17 50 E
Surt, Khalīj **87** 31 40N 18 30 E
Surtsey **8** 63 20N 20 30W
Surubim **138** 7 50S 35 45W
Surumu ~→ **135** 3 22N 60 19W
Susa **26** 45 8N 7 3 E
Suså ~→ **11** 55 20N 11 42 E
Sušac **27** 42 46N 16 30 E
Susak **27** 44 30N 14 18 E
Susaki **64** 33 22N 133 17 E
Sūsangerd **46** 31 35N 48 6 E
Susanino **41** 52 50N 140 14 E
Susanville **120** 40 28N 120 40W
Susong **59** 30 10N 116 5 E
Susquehanna ~→ **115** 39 33N 76 5W
Susquehanna Depot **115** 41 55N 75 36W
Susques **140** 23 35S 66 25W
Sussex, Can. **103** 45 45N 65 37W
Sussex, U.S.A. **115** 41 12N 74 38W
Sussex, E. □ **13** 51 0N 0 20 E
Sussex, W. □ **13** 51 0N 0 30W
Sustut ~→ **108** 56 20N 127 30W
Susubona **68** 8 19S 159 27 E
Susuman **41** 62 47N 148 10 E
Susunu **57** 3 20S 133 25 E
Sutherland, Austral. **76** 34 2S 151 4 E
Sutherland, S. Afr. **96** 32 33S 20 40 E
Sutherland, U.S.A. **118** 41 12N 101 11W
Sutherland Falls **81** 44 48S 167 46 E
Sutherlin **120** 43 28N 123 16W
Sutivan **27** 43 23N 16 30 E
Sutlej ~→ **48** 29 23N 71 3 E
Sutter **122** 39 10N 121 45W
Sutter Creek **122** 38 24N 120 48W
Sutton, Austral. **76** 35 10S 149 15 E
Sutton, Ont., Can. **106** 44 18N 79 22W
Sutton, Qué., Can. **105** 45 6N 72 37W
Sutton, N.Z. **81** 45 34S 170 8 E
Sutton, U.S.A. **118** 40 40N 97 50W
Sutton ~→ **102** 55 15N 83 45W
Sutton-in-Ashfield **12** 53 7N 1 20W
Suttor ~→ **72** 21 36S 147 2 E
Su'u **68** 9 11S 160 56 E
Suva **68** 18 6S 178 30 E
Suva Reka **33** 42 21N 20 50 E
Suvo Rudište **33** 43 17N 20 49 E
Suvorov Is. = Suwarrow Is. **67** 13 15S 163 30W
Suwa **65** 36 2N 138 8 E
Suwa-Ko **65** 36 3N 138 5 E
Suwałki **32** 54 8N 22 59 E
Suwannaphum **54** 15 33N 103 47 E
Suwannee ~→ **113** 29 18N 83 9W
Suwanose-Jima **63** 29 38N 129 44 E
Suwanose Jima **63** 29 26N 129 30 E
Suwarrow Is. **67** 15 0S 163 0W
Suweis, Khalîg es **90** 28 40N 33 0 E
Suweis, Qanâl es **90** 31 0N 32 20 E
Suwŏn **61** 37 17N 127 1 E
Suzaka **65** 36 39N 138 19 E
Suzdal **37** 56 29N 40 26 E
Suze, La **18** 47 54N 0 2 E
Suzhou **59** 31 19N 120 38 E
Suzuka **65** 34 55N 136 36 E
Suzuka-Sam **65** 35 5N 136 30 E

Suzzara **26** 45 0N 10 45 E
Svalbard **144** 78 0N 17 0 E
Svalbarð **8** 66 12N 15 43W
Svalöv **11** 55 57N 13 8 E
Svanvik **8** 69 25N 30 3 E
Svappavaara **8** 67 40N 21 03 E
Svarstad **10** 59 27N 9 56 E
Svartisen **8** 66 40N 13 56 E
Svartvik **10** 62 19N 17 24 E
Svatovo **38** 49 35N 38 11 E
Svay Chek **54** 13 48N 102 58 E
Svay Rieng **55** 11 5N 105 48 E
Svendborg **11** 55 4N 10 35 E
Svene **10** 59 45N 9 31 E
Svenljunga **11** 57 29N 13 5 E
Svenstrup **11** 56 58N 9 50 E
Sverdlovsk **40** 56 50N 60 30 E
Sverdrup Is. **144** 79 0N 97 0W
Svetac **27** 43 3N 15 43 E
Sveti Ivan Zelina **27** 45 57N 16 16 E
Sveti Jurij **27** 46 14N 15 24 E
Sveti Lenart **27** 46 36N 15 48 E
Sveti Nikole **35** 41 51N 21 56 E
Sveti Rok **27** 40 1N 9 6 E
Sveti Trojica **27** 46 37N 15 50 E
Svetlogorsk **36** 52 38N 29 46 E
Svetlograd **39** 45 25N 42 58 E
Svetlovodsk **36** 49 2N 33 13 E
Svetozarevo **33** 44 5N 21 15 E
Svidník **32** 49 20N 21 37 E
Svilaja Pl. **27** 43 49N 16 31 E
Svilengrad **35** 41 49N 26 12 E
Svishtov **34** 43 36N 25 23 E
Svisloch **36** 53 3N 24 2 E
Svitava ~→ **32** 49 30N 16 37 E
Svitavy **32** 49 47N 16 28 E
Svobodnyy **41** 51 20N 128 0 E
Svolvær **8** 68 15N 14 34 E
Svratka ~→ **32** 49 11N 16 38 E
Svrljig **33** 43 25N 22 6 E
Swa **52** 19 15N 96 17 E
Swabian Alps = Schäbischer Alb **31** 48 30N 9 30 E
Swainsboro **113** 32 38N 82 22W
Swakopmund **96** 22 37S 14 30 E
Swale ~→ **12** 54 5N 1 20W
Swan Hill **74** 35 20S 143 33 E
Swan Hills **108** 54 42N 115 24W
Swan Islands **126** 17 22N 83 57W
Swan L. **109** 52 30N 100 40W
Swan Reach **75** 37 49S 147 53 E
Swan River **109** 52 10N 101 16W
Swan Vale **77** 29 45S 151 27 E
Swanage **13** 50 36N 1 59W
Swanpool **74** 36 44S 146 2 E
Swansea, Austral. **76** 33 3S 151 35 E
Swansea, U.K. **13** 51 37N 3 57W
Swar ~→ **49** 34 40N 72 5 E
Swartberge **96** 33 20S 22 0 E
Swartruggens **96** 25 39S 26 42 E
Swartz Creek **106** 42 58N 83 50W
Swarzędz **32** 52 25N 17 4 E
Swastika **102** 48 7N 80 6W
Swatow = Shantou **59** 23 18N 116 40 E
Swaziland ■ **97** 26 30S 31 30 E
Sweden ■ **8** 67 0N 15 0 E
Swedru **89** 5 32N 0 41W
Sweet Home **120** 44 26N 122 25W
Sweet Springs **116** 38 58N 93 25W
Sweetwater, Nev., U.S.A. **122** 38 27N 119 9W
Sweetwater, Tex., U.S.A. **119** 32 30N 100 28W
Sweetwater ~→ **120** 42 31N 107 2W
Swellendam **96** 34 1S 20 26 E
Świdnica **32** 50 50N 16 30 E
Świdnik **32** 51 13N 22 39 E
Świdwin **32** 53 47N 15 49 E
Świebodzin **32** 52 15N 15 31 E
Świecie **32** 53 25N 18 30 E
Świętokrzyskie, Góry **32** 51 0N 20 30 E
Swift Current **109** 50 20N 107 45W
Swiftcurrent ~→ **109** 50 38N 107 44W
Swifts Creek **75** 37 17S 147 44 E
Swilly, L. **15** 55 12N 7 35W
Swindle, I. **108** 52 30N 128 35W
Swindon **13** 51 33N 1 47W
Świnoujście **32** 53 54N 14 16 E
Switzerland ■ **31** 46 30N 8 0 E
Swords **15** 53 27N 6 15W
Syasstroy **36** 60 5N 32 15 E
Sychevka **36** 55 59N 34 16 E
Sydenham ~→ **106** 42 33N 82 25W
Sydney, Austral. **76** 33 53S 151 10 E
Sydney, Can. **103** 46 7N 60 7W
Sydney, U.S.A. **118** 41 12N 103 0W
Sydney Mines **103** 46 18N 60 15W
Sydprøven **144** 60 30N 45 35W
Sydra, G. of = Surt **85** 31 40N 18 30 E
Syke **30** 52 55N 8 50 E
Syktyvkar **40** 61 45N 50 40 E
Sylacauga **113** 33 10N 86 15W

Sylhet **52** 24 54N 91 52 E
Sylt **30** 54 50N 8 20 E
Sylvan Lake **108** 52 20N 114 03W
Sylvania, Ga., U.S.A. **113** 32 45N 81 37W
Sylvania, Ohio., U.S.A. **117** 41 43N 83 42W
Sylvester **113** 31 31N 83 50W
Sym **40** 60 20N 88 18 E
Symón **124** 24 42N 102 35W
Synnott Ra. **78** 16 30S 125 20 E
Syracuse, Ind., U.S.A. **117** 41 28N 85 47W
Syracuse, Kans., U.S.A. **119** 38 0N 101 46W
Syracuse, N.Y., U.S.A. **115** 43 4N 76 11W
Syrdarya ~→ **40** 45 0N 65 0 E
Syria ■ **46** 35 0N 38 0 E
Syriam **52** 16 44N 96 19 E
Syul'dzhyukyor **41** 63 14N 113 32 E
Syzran **37** 53 12N 48 30 E
Szaraz ~→ **33** 46 28N 20 44 E
Szarvas **33** 46 50N 20 38 E
Szczebrzeszyn **32** 50 42N 22 59 E
Szczecin **32** 53 27N 14 27 E
Szczecinek **32** 53 43N 16 41 E
Szczekocimy **32** 50 38N 19 48 E
Szczytno **32** 53 33N 21 0 E
Szechwan □ = Sichuan □ **58** 31 0N 104 0 E
Szeged **33** 46 16N 20 10 E
Szeghalom **33** 47 1N 21 10 E
Székesfehérvár **33** 47 15N 18 25 E
Szekszárd **33** 46 22N 18 42 E
Szendrö **33** 48 24N 20 41 E
Szentendre **33** 47 39N 19 4 E
Szentes **33** 46 39N 20 21 E
Szentgotthárd **33** 46 58N 16 19 E
Szentlörinc **33** 46 3N 18 1 E
Szigetvár **33** 46 3N 17 46 E
Szolnok **33** 47 10N 20 15 E
Szombathely **33** 47 14N 16 38 E
Szprotawa **32** 51 33N 15 35 E
Szydłowiec **32** 51 15N 20 51 E
Szypliszki **32** 54 17N 23 2 E

T

Ta Khli Khok **54** 15 18N 100 20 E
Ta Lai **55** 11 24N 107 23 E
Tabacal **140** 23 15S 64 15W
Tabaco **57** 13 22N 123 44 E
Tabagné **88** 7 59N 3 4W
Tābah **46** 26 55N 42 38 E
Tabajara **137** 8 56S 62 8W
Tabalos **136** 6 26S 76 37W
Tabar Is. **69** 2 50S 152 0 E
Tabarca, Isla de **25** 38 17N 0 30W
Tabarka **87** 36 56N 8 46 E
Tabas, Khorasan, Iran **47** 33 35N 56 55 E
Tabas, Khorasan, Iran **47** 32 48N 60 12 E
Tabasará, Serranía de **126** 8 35N 81 40W
Tabasco □ **125** 17 45N 93 30W
Tabatinga, Serra da **138** 10 30S 44 0W
Tabayin **52** 22 42N 95 20 E
Tabelbala, Kahal de **86** 28 47N 2 0W
Tabelkaza **84** 29 50N 0 55 E
Taber **108** 49 47N 112 8W
Tabernas **25** 37 4N 2 26W
Tabernes de Valldigna **25** 39 5N 0 13W
Tabira **138** 7 35S 37 33W
Tablas **57** 12 25N 122 2 E
Table B. **103** 53 40N 56 25W
Table Grove **116** 40 20N 90 27W
Table Mt. **96** 34 0S 18 22 E
Table Top, Mt. **72** 23 24S 147 11 E
Tableland **78** 17 16S 126 51 E
Tábor **32** 49 25N 14 39 E
Tabor **44** 32 42N 35 24 E
Tabora **94** 5 2S 32 50 E
Tabora □ **94** 5 0S 33 0 E
Tabou **88** 4 30N 7 20W
Tabrīz **46** 38 7N 46 20 E
Tabuenca **24** 41 42N 1 33W
Tabūk **46** 28 23N 36 36 E
Tabwemasana, Mt. **68** 15 20S 166 44 E
Tacámbaro de Codallos **124** 19 14N 101 28W
Tacheng **62** 46 40N 82 58 E
Tachibana-Wan **62** 32 45N 130 7 E
Tachikawa **65** 35 42N 139 25 E
Tach'ing Shan = Daqing Shan **60** 40 40N 111 0 E
Tachira **134** 8 7N 72 15 E
Táchira □ **134** 8 7N 72 15W
Tácina ~→ **29** 38 57N 16 55 E
Tacloban **57** 11 15N 124 58 E
Tacna **136** 18 0S 70 20W
Tacna □ **136** 17 40S 70 20W
Tacoma **122** 47 15N 122 30W
Tacuarembó **141** 31 45S 56 0W

Tacutu ~→ **135** 3 1N 60 29W
Tademaït, Plateau du **86** 28 30N 2 30 E
Tadent, O. ~→ **87** 22 25N 6 40 E
Tadine **68** 21 33S 167 52 E
Tadjerdjeri, O. ~→ **87** 26 0N 8 0W
Tadjerouna **86** 33 31N 2 3 E
Tadjettaret, O. ~→ **87** 21 20N 7 22 E
Tadjmout, Atlas, Alg. **86** 33 52N 2 30 E
Tadjmout, Sahara, Alg. **86** 25 37N 3 48 E
Tadjoura **91** 11 50N 42 55 E
Tadjoura, Golfe de **91** 11 50N 43 0 E
Tadmor, N.Z. **81** 41 27S 172 45 E
Tadmor, Syria **46** 34 36N 38 15 E
Tadotsu **64** 34 16N 133 45 E
Tadoule, L. **109** 58 36N 98 20W
Tadoussac **105** 48 11N 69 42W
Tadulam **77** 28 53S 152 35 E
Tadzhik S.S.R. □ **40** 35 30N 70 0 E
Taechŏn-ni **61** 36 21N 126 36 E
Taegu **61** 35 50N 128 37 E
Taegwan **61** 40 13N 125 12 E
Taejŏn **61** 36 20N 127 28 E
Tafalla **24** 42 30N 1 41W
Tafar **91** 6 52N 28 15 E
Tafas **44** 32 44N 36 5 E
Tafassasset, O. ~→ **87** 22 0N 9 57 E
Tafelbaai **96** 33 35S 18 25 E
Tafelney, C. **86** 31 3N 9 51W
Tafermaar **57** 6 47S 134 10 E
Tafí Viejo **140** 26 43S 65 17W
Tafiré **88** 9 4N 5 4W
Tafnidilt **86** 28 47N 10 58W
Tafraoute **86** 29 50N 8 58W
Taft, Phil. **57** 11 57N 125 30 E
Taft, Calif., U.S.A. **123** 35 9N 119 28W
Taft, Tex., U.S.A. **119** 27 58N 97 23W
Taga **68** 13 46S 172 28W
Taga Dzong **52** 27 5N 89 55 E
Taganrog **39** 47 12N 38 50 E
Taganrogskiy Zaliv **38** 47 0N 38 30 E
Tagant **88** 18 20N 11 0W
Tagap Ga **52** 26 56N 96 13 E
Tagbilaran **57** 9 39N 123 51 E
Tage **69** 6 19S 143 20 E
Taggerty **74** 37 21S 145 43 E
Tággia **26** 43 52N 7 50 E
Taghrīfat **87** 29 5N 17 26 E
Taghzout **86** 33 30N 4 49W
Tagish **108** 60 19N 134 16W
Tagish L. **100** 60 10N 134 20W
Tagliacozzo **27** 42 4N 13 13 E
Tagliamento ~→ **27** 45 38N 13 5 E
Táglio di Po **27** 45 0N 12 12 E
Tagna **134** 2 24S 70 37W
Tagomago, Isla de **25** 39 2N 1 39 E
Tagua, La **134** 0 3N 74 40W
Taguatinga **139** 12 16S 42 26W
Tagula **69** 11 22S 153 15 E
Tagula I. **69** 11 30S 153 30 E
Tagum (Hijo) **57** 7 33N 125 53 E
Tahakopa **81** 46 30S 169 23 E
Tahala **86** 34 0N 4 28W
Tahan, Gunong **55** 4 34N 102 17 E
Tahara **65** 34 40N 137 16 E
Tahat **87** 23 18N 5 33 E
Tāherī **47** 27 43N 52 20 E
Tahiti **68** 17 37S 149 27W
Tahoe City **122** 39 12N 120 9W
Tahoe, L. **122** 39 0N 120 9W
Taholah **122** 47 21N 124 17W
Tahora **80** 39 2S 174 49 E
Tahoua **89** 14 57N 5 16 E
Tahta **90** 26 44N 31 32 E
Tahuamanu ~→ **136** 11 6N 67 36W
Tahulandang **57** 2 27N 125 23 E
Tahuna **57** 3 38N 125 30 E
Taï **88** 5 55N 7 30W
Tai Hu **62** 31 5N 120 10 E
Tai Shan **61** 36 25N 117 20 E
Tai Xian **59** 32 30N 120 7 E
Tai'an **61** 36 12N 117 8 E
Taiarapu, Presq. de **68** 17 47S 149 14W
Taibei **59** 25 4N 121 29 E
Taibus Qi **60** 41 54N 115 22 E
T'aichung = Taizhong **59** 24 10N 120 38 E
Taidong **59** 22 43N 121 9 E
Taieri ~→ **81** 46 3S 170 12 E
Taiga Madema **87** 23 46N 15 25 E
Taigu **60** 37 28N 112 30 E
Taihang Shan **60** 36 0N 113 30 E
Taihape **80** 39 41S 175 48 E
Taihe, Anhui, China **60** 33 20N 115 42 E
Taihe, Jiangxi, China **59** 26 47N 114 52 E
Taihu **59** 30 22N 116 20 E
Taijiang **58** 26 39N 108 21 E
Taikang **60** 34 5N 114 50 E
Taikkyi **52** 17 20N 96 0 E
Tailem Bend **73** 35 12S 139 29 E
Tailfingen **31** 48 15N 9 1 E
Taīma **46** 27 35N 38 45 E
Taimyr = Taymyr **41** 75 0N 100 0 E

Taimyr, Oz. 41 74 20N 102 0 E
Tain 14 57 49N 4 4W
Tainan, Taiwan 59 23 17N 120 18 E
Tainan, Taiwan 59 23 0N 120 11 E
Taínaron, Ákra 35 36 22N 22 27 E
Tainggyo 52 17 49N 94 29 E
Taining 59 26 54N 117 9 E
Taiobeiras 139 15 49S 42 14W
T'aipei = Taibei 59 25 4N 121 29 E
Taiping, China 59 30 15N 118 6 E
Taiping, Malay. 55 4 51N 100 44 E
Taipingzhen 60 33 35N 111 42 E
Taipu 138 5 37S 35 36W
Taisha 64 35 24N 132 40 E
Taishan 59 22 14N 112 41 E
Taishun 59 27 30N 119 42 E
Taita □ 94 4 0S 38 30 E
Taita Hills 94 3 25S 38 15 E
Taitao, C. 142 45 53S 75 5W
Taitao, Pen. de 142 46 30S 75 0W
Taiwan ■ 59 24 0N 121 0 E
Taiwan Shan 59 23 40N 121 20 E
Taiwara 47 33 30N 64 24 E
Taixing 59 32 11N 120 0 E
Taïyetos Óros 35 37 0N 22 23 E
Taiyib → 44 31 55N 35 17 E
Taiyiba 44 32 36N 35 27 E
Taiyuan 60 37 52N 112 33 E
Taizhong, Taiwan 59 24 12N 120 35 E
Taizhong, Taiwan 59 24 18N 120 40 E
Taizhou 59 32 28N 119 55 E
Taizhou Liedao 59 28 30N 121 55 E
Ta'izz 45 13 35N 44 2 E
Tajapuru, Furo do 138 1 50S 50 25W
Tajarḥī 87 24 21N 14 28 E
Tajima 63 37 19N 139 8 E
Tajimi 65 35 19N 137 8 E
Tajitos 124 30 58N 112 18W
Tajo → 23 38 40N 9 24W
Tajumulco, Volcán de 125 15 2N 91 50W
Tājūrā 87 32 51N 13 21 E
Tak 54 16 52N 99 8 E
Takachiho 64 32 42N 131 18 E
Takada 63 37 7N 138 15 E
Takahashi 64 34 51N 133 39 E
Takaka 81 40 51S 172 50 E
Takamatsu 64 34 20N 134 5 E
Takanabe 64 32 8N 131 30 E
Takaoka 65 36 47N 137 0 E
Takapau 80 40 2S 176 21 E
Takapuna 80 36 47S 174 47 E
Takasago 64 34 45N 134 48 E
Takasaki 65 36 20N 139 0 E
Takase 64 34 7N 133 48 E
Takataka 68 9 17S 161 14 E
Takatsuki 65 34 51N 135 37 E
Takaungu 94 3 38S 39 52 E
Takawa 64 33 38N 130 51 E
Takayama 65 36 18N 137 11 E
Takayama-Bonchi 65 36 0N 137 18 E
Takefu 65 35 50N 136 10 E
Takehara 64 34 21N 132 55 E
Takengeun 56 4 45N 96 50 E
Takeo, Camb. 55 10 59N 104 47 E
Takeo, Japan 64 33 12N 130 1 E
Tåkern 11 58 22N 14 45 E
Tākestān 46 36 0N 49 40 E
Taketa 64 32 58N 131 24 E
Takh 49 33 6N 77 32 E
Takhar □ 47 36 40N 70 0 E
Takhman 55 11 29N 104 57 E
Taki 69 6 29S 155 52 E
Takla L. 108 55 15N 125 45W
Takla Landing 108 55 30N 125 50W
Takla Makan 42 39 0N 83 0 E
Takla Makan = Taklimakan Shamo 62 38 0N 83 0 E
Taklimakan Shamo 62 38 0N 83 0 E
Takoradi 88 4 58N 1 45W
Taku 64 33 18N 130 3 E
Taku → 108 58 30N 133 50W
Takua Pa 55 7 18N 9 59 E
Takum 89 7 18N 9 36 E
Takuma 64 34 13N 133 40 E
Takutu → 135 3 1N 60 29W
Tala 141 34 21S 55 46W
Talagante 140 33 40S 70 50W
Talaint 86 29 41N 9 40W
Talak 89 18 0N 5 0 E
Talamanca, Cordillera de 126 9 20N 83 20W
Talara 136 4 38S 81 18 E
Talas 40 42 30N 72 13 E
Talasea 69 5 20S 150 2 E
Talata Mafara 89 12 38N 6 4 E
Talaud, Kepulauan 57 4 30N 127 10 E
Talavera de la Reina 22 39 55N 4 46W
Talawana 78 22 51S 121 9 E
Talawgyi 52 25 4N 97 19 E
Talayan 57 6 52N 124 24 E
Talbert, Sillon de 18 48 53N 3 5W
Talbingo Dam 76 35 40S 148 20 E
Talbor 74 37 10S 143 44 E
Talbot, C. 78 13 48S 126 43 E
Talbragar → 76 32 12S 148 37 E
Talca 140 35 28S 71 40W
Talca □ 140 35 20S 71 46W
Talcahuano 140 36 40S 73 10W
Talcher 50 21 0N 85 18 E
Talcho 89 14 44N 3 28 E
Taldy Kurgan 40 45 10N 78 45 E
Talesh, Kūhā-Ye 46 39 0N 48 30 E
Talfit 44 32 5N 35 17 E
Talguharai 90 18 19N 35 56 E
Tali Post 91 5 55N 30 44 E
Taliabu 57 1 45S 125 0 E
Talibon 57 10 9N 124 20 E
Talibong, Ko 55 7 15N 99 23 E
Talihina 119 34 45N 95 1W
Talikoti 51 16 29N 76 17 E
Taliwang 56 8 50S 116 55 E
Talkeetna 100 62 20N 150 9W
Tall 'Afar 46 36 22N 42 27 E
Tall 'Asūr 44 31 59N 35 77 E
Talla 90 28 5N 30 43 E
Talladega 113 33 28N 86 2W
Tallahassee 113 30 25N 84 15W
Tallangatta 75 36 15S 147 19 E
Tallarook 74 37 5S 145 6 E
Tallawang 77 32 12S 149 28 E
Tällberg 10 60 51N 15 2 E
Tallering Pk. 79 28 6S 115 37 E
Tallinn 36 59 22N 24 48 E
Tallulah 119 32 25N 91 12W
Talluza 44 32 17N 35 18 E
Talmalmo 76 35 55S 147 29 E
Talmest 86 31 48N 9 21W
Talmont 20 46 27N 1 37W
Talnoye 38 48 50N 30 44 E
Taloda 50 21 34N 74 11 E
Talodi 91 10 35N 30 22 E
Talovaya 37 51 6N 40 45 E
Talpa de Allende 124 20 23N 104 51W
Talsinnt 86 32 33N 3 27W
Taltal 140 25 23S 70 33W
Taltson → 108 61 24N 112 46W
Taltson L. 109 61 30N 110 15W
Talwood 77 28 29S 149 29 E
Talyawalka Cr. → 73 32 28S 142 22 E
Tam Chau 55 10 48N 105 12 E
Tam Ky 54 15 34N 108 29 E
Tam Quan 54 14 35N 109 3 E
Tama 116 41 56N 92 37W
Tamala 79 26 42S 113 47 E
Tamalameque 134 8 52N 73 49W
Tamale 89 9 22N 0 50W
Taman 38 45 14N 36 41 E
Tamana 64 32 58N 130 32 E
Tamanar 86 31 1N 9 46W
Tamano 64 34 29N 133 59 E
Tamanrasset 87 22 50N 5 30 E
Tamanrasset, O. → 86 22 0N 2 0 E
Tamanthi 52 25 19N 95 17 E
Tamaqua 115 40 46N 75 58W
Tamar → 13 50 33N 4 15W
Támara 134 5 50N 72 10W
Tamarang 77 31 27S 150 5 E
Tamarite de Litera 24 41 52N 0 25 E
Tamaroa 116 38 8N 89 14W
Tamashima 64 34 32N 133 40 E
Tamaské 89 14 49N 5 43 E
Tamatave 97 18 10S 49 25 E
Tamatave □ 97 18 0S 49 0 E
Tamaulipas □ 125 24 0N 99 0W
Tamaulipas, Sierra de 125 23 30N 98 20W
Tamazula 124 24 55N 106 58W
Tamazunchale 125 21 16N 98 47W
Tamba-Dabatou 88 11 50N 10 40W
Tambacounda 88 13 45N 13 40W
Tambai 91 16 32N 37 13 E
Tambar Springs 77 31 20S 149 51 E
Tambelan, Kepulauan 56 1 0N 107 30 E
Tambellup 79 34 4S 117 37 E
Tambo, Austral. 72 24 54S 146 14 E
Tambo, Peru 136 12 57S 74 1W
Tambo →, Austral. 75 37 50S 147 50 E
Tambo →, Peru 136 10 42S 73 47W
Tambo Crossing 75 37 29S 147 50 E
Tambo de Mora 136 13 30S 76 8W
Tambobamba 136 13 54S 72 8W
Tambohorano 97 17 30S 43 58 E
Tambopata → 136 13 21S 69 36W
Tambora 56 8 12S 118 5 E
Tamboritha, Mt. 75 37 31S 146 40 E
Tambov 37 52 45N 41 28 E
Tambre → 22 42 49N 8 53W
Tambuku 57 7 8S 113 40 E
Tamburâ 91 5 40N 27 25 E
Tamchaket 88 17 25N 10 40W
Tame 134 6 28N 71 44W
Tamega → 22 41 5N 8 21W
Tamelelt, Alg. 87 26 30N 6 14 E
Tamelelt, Moroc. 86 31 50N 7 32W
Tamenglong 52 25 0N 93 35 E
Tamerza 87 34 23N 7 58 E
Tamgak, Mts. 84 19 12N 8 35 E
Tamiahua, Laguna de 125 21 30N 97 30W
Tamil Nadu □ 51 11 0N 77 0 E
Tamluk 49 22 18N 87 58 E
Tammerfors = Tampere 9 61 30N 23 50 E
Tammisaari 9 60 0N 23 26 E
Tammun' 44 32 18N 35 23 E
Tämnaren 10 60 10N 17 25 E
Tamo Abu, Pegunungan 56 3 10N 115 0 E
Tampa 113 27 57N 82 38W
Tampa B. 113 27 40N 82 40W
Tampe Downs 78 24 22S 132 24 E
Tampere 9 61 30N 23 50 E
Tampico, Mexico 125 22 20N 97 50W
Tampico, U.S.A. 116 41 38N 89 47W
Tampin 55 2 28N 102 13 E
Tamri 86 30 49N 9 50W
Tamrida = Hadibu 45 12 35N 54 2 E
Tamsagbulag 62 47 14N 117 21 E
Tamsagout 86 24 5N 6 23W
Tamsalu 36 59 11N 26 8 E
Tamuja → 23 39 38N 6 29W
Tamworth, Austral. 77 31 7S 150 58 E
Tamworth, Can. 107 44 29N 77 0W
Tamworth, U.K. 13 52 38N 1 41W
Tamyang 61 35 19N 126 59 E
Tan An 55 10 32N 106 25 E
Tana 8 70 26N 28 14 E
Tana → 94 2 32S 40 31 E
Tana, L. 91 13 5N 37 30 E
Tana River 94 2 0S 39 30 E
Tanabe 65 33 44N 135 22 E
Tanabi 139 20 37S 49 37W
Tanafjorden 8 70 35N 28 30 E
Tanagro → 29 40 35N 15 25 E
Tanahbala 56 0 30S 98 30 E
Tanahgrogot 56 1 55S 116 15 E
Tanahjampea 57 7 10S 120 35 E
Tanahmasa 56 0 12S 98 39 E
Tanahmerah 57 6 5S 140 16 E
Tanami 78 19 59S 129 43 E
Tanami Des. 78 18 50S 132 0 E
Tanana 100 65 10N 152 15W
Tanana → 100 65 9N 151 55W
Tananarive = Antananarivo 97 18 55S 47 31 E
Tananarive □ 97 19 0S 47 0 E
Tanant 86 31 54N 6 56W
Tánaro → 26 45 1N 8 47 E
Tanaunella 28 40 42N 9 45 E
Tanba-Sanchi 65 35 7N 135 48 E
Tancarville 18 49 29N 0 28 E
Tancheng 61 34 25N 118 20 E
Tanchŏn 61 40 27N 128 54 E
Tanda, U.P., India 49 28 57N 78 56 E
Tanda, U.P., India 49 26 33N 82 35 E
Tanda, Ivory C. 88 7 48N 3 10W
Tandag 57 9 4N 126 9 E
Tandaia 95 9 25S 34 15 E
Tăndărei 34 44 39N 27 40 E
Tandil 140 37 15S 59 6W
Tandil, Sa. del 140 37 30S 59 0W
Tandlianwala 48 31 3N 73 9 E
Tando Adam 48 25 45N 68 40 E
Tandou L. 73 32 40S 142 5 E
Tandsbyn 10 63 0N 14 45 E
Tandur 50 19 11N 79 30 E
Tane-ga-Shima 63 30 30N 131 0 E
Taneatua 80 38 4S 177 1 E
Tanen Tong Dan 54 19 43N 98 30 E
Tanezrouft 86 23 9N 0 11 E
Tang, Koh 55 10 16N 103 7 E
Tang Krasang 54 12 34N 105 3 E
Tanga □ 94 5 20S 38 0 E
Tanga Is. 69 3 20S 153 15 E
Tangail 52 24 15N 89 55 E
Tanganyika, L. 94 6 40S 30 0 E
Tanger 86 35 50N 5 49W
Tangerang 57 6 12S 106 39 E
Tangerhütte 30 52 26N 11 50 E
Tangermünde 30 52 32N 11 57 E
Tanggu 61 39 2N 117 40 E
Tanggula Shan 62 32 40N 92 10 E
Tanghe 60 32 47N 112 50 E
Tangier = Tanger 86 35 50N 5 49W
Tangorin P.O. 72 21 47S 144 12 E
Tangshan 61 39 38N 118 10 E
Tangtou 61 35 28N 118 30 E
Tanguiéta 89 10 35N 1 21 E
Tangxi 59 29 3N 119 25 E
Tangyan He → 58 28 54N 108 19 E
Tanimbar, Kepulauan 57 7 30S 131 30 E
Taninges 21 46 7N 6 36 E
Taniyama 64 31 31N 130 31 E
Tanjay 57 9 30N 123 5 E
Tanjong Malim 55 3 42N 101 31 E
Tanjore = Thanjavur 51 10 48N 79 12 E
Tanjung 56 2 10S 115 25 E
Tanjungbalai 56 2 55N 99 44 E
Tanjungbatu 56 2 23N 118 3 E
Tanjungkarang 56 5 20S 105 10 E
Tanjungpandan 56 2 43S 107 38 E
Tanjungpinang 56 1 5N 104 30 E
Tanjungpriok 57 6 8S 106 55 E
Tanjungredeb 56 2 9N 117 29 E
Tanjungselor 56 2 55N 117 25 E
Tank 48 32 14N 70 25 E
Tanna 68 19 30S 169 20 E
Tänndalen 10 62 33N 12 18 E
Tannis Bugt 11 57 40N 10 15 E
Tannu-Ola 41 51 0N 94 0 E
Tano → 88 5 7N 2 56W
Tanoumrout 87 23 2N 5 31 E
Tanout 89 14 50N 8 55 E
Tanquinho 139 11 58S 39 6W
Tanta 90 30 45N 30 57 E
Tantan 86 28 29N 11 1W
Tantangara Res. 76 35 45S 148 38 E
Tantoyuca 125 21 21N 98 10W
Tantung = Dandong 61 40 10N 124 20 E
Tantura = Dor 44 32 37N 34 55 E
Tanuku 50 16 45N 81 44 E
Tanumshede 11 58 42N 11 20 E
Tanunda 73 34 30S 139 0 E
Tanur 51 11 1N 75 52 E
Tanus 20 44 8N 2 19 E
Tanzania ■ 94 6 40S 34 0 E
Tanzawa-Sanchi 65 35 27N 139 0 E
Tanzilla → 108 58 8N 130 43W
Tao Ko 55 10 5N 99 52 E
Tao'an 61 45 22N 122 40 E
Tao'er He → 61 45 45N 124 5 E
Taohua Dao 59 29 50N 122 20 E
Taole 60 38 48N 106 40 E
Taormina 29 37 52N 15 16 E
Taos 121 36 28N 105 35W
Taoudenni 86 22 40N 3 55W
Taoudrart, Adrar 86 24 25N 2 24 E
Taounate 86 34 25N 4 41W
Taourirt, Alg. 86 26 37N 0 20 E
Taourirt, Moroc. 86 34 25N 2 53W
Taouz, Moroc. 86 30 53N 4 0W
Taouz, Moroc. 86 31 52N 4 20W
Taoyuan, China 59 28 55N 111 16 E
Taoyuan, Taiwan 59 25 0N 121 13 E
Tapa 36 59 15N 25 50 E
Tapa Shan = Daba Shan 58 31 50N 109 20 E
Tapachula 125 14 54N 92 17W
Tapah 55 4 12N 101 15 E
Tapajós → 135 2 24S 54 41W
Tapaktuan 56 3 15N 97 10 E
Tapanahoni → 135 4 20N 54 25W
Tapanui 81 45 56S 169 18 E
Tapauá 137 5 40S 64 20W
Tapauá → 137 5 40S 64 21W
Tapeta 88 6 29N 8 52W
Taphan Hin 54 16 13N 100 26 E
Tapia 22 43 34N 6 56W
Tapini 69 8 19S 147 0 E
Tápiószele 33 47 25N 19 55 E
Tapiraí 139 19 52S 46 1W
Tapirapé → 138 10 41S 50 38W
Tapirapecó, Serra 135 1 10N 65 0W
Tapirapuã 137 14 51S 57 45W
Tapoeripa 135 5 22N 56 34W
Tapolca 33 46 53N 17 29 E
Tappahannock 112 37 56N 76 50W
Tapti → 50 21 8N 72 41 E
Tapuaenuku, Mt. 81 42 0S 173 39 E
Tapul Group 57 5 35N 120 50 E
Tapun 52 27 35N 96 22 E
Tapurucuará 135 0 24S 65 2W
Taquara 141 29 36S 50 46W
Taquari → 137 19 15S 57 17W
Taquaritinga 139 21 24S 48 30W
Tar Island 108 57 03N 111 40W
Tara, Austral. 73 27 17S 150 31 E
Tara, Can. 106 44 28N 81 9W
Tara, Japan 64 33 2N 130 11 E
Tara, U.S.S.R. 40 56 55N 74 24 E
Tara, Zambia 95 16 58S 26 45 E
Tara → 40 56 42N 74 36 E
Tara-Dake 64 32 58N 130 6 E
Tarabagatay, Khrebet 40 48 0N 83 0 E
Tarabuco 137 19 10S 64 57W
Tarābulus, Leb. 46 34 31N 35 50 E
Tarābulus, Libya 87 32 49N 13 7 E
Taradale 80 39 33S 176 53 E
Tarago 76 35 6S 149 39 E
Tarahouahout 87 22 41N 5 59 E
Tarakan 56 3 20N 117 35 E
Tarakit, Mt. 94 2 2N 35 10 E
Taralga 76 34 26S 149 52 E
Taramakau → 81 42 34S 171 8 E
Tarana 76 33 31S 149 52 E
Taranagar 48 28 43N 74 50 E
Taranaki □ 80 39 5S 174 51 E
Tarancón 24 40 1N 3 1W
Taranga 48 23 56N 72 43 E
Taranga Hill 48 24 0N 72 40 E

Táranto **29** 40 30N 17 11 E
Táranto, G. di **29** 40 0N 17 15 E
Tarapacá **134** 2 56S 69 46W
Tarapacá □ **140** 20 45S 69 30W
Tarapoto **136** 6 30S 76 20W
Taraquá **134** 0 6N 68 28W
Tarare **21** 45 54N 4 26 E
Tararua Range **80** 40 45S 175 25 E
Tarasag **68** 14 13S 167 35 E
Tarascon, Ariège, France **20** 42 50N 1 37 E
Tarascon, Bouches-du-Rhône, France **21** 43 48N 4 39 E
Tarashcha **38** 49 30N 30 31 E
Tarat **84** 25 55N 9 3 E
Tarat, Bj. **87** 26 13N 9 18 E
Tarata **136** 17 27S 70 2W
Tarauacá **136** 8 6S 70 48W
Tarauacá → **136** 6 42S 69 48W
Taravo → **21** 41 42N 8 49 E
Tarawera **80** 39 2S 176 36 E
Tarawera L. **80** 38 13S 176 27 E
Tarawera Mt. **80** 38 14S 176 32 E
Tarazona **24** 41 55N 1 43W
Tarazona de la Mancha **25** 39 16N 1 55W
Tarbat Ness **14** 57 52N 3 48W
Tarbela Dam **48** 34 8N 72 52 E
Tarbert, Strathclyde, U.K. **14** 55 55N 5 25W
Tarbert, W. Isles, U.K. **14** 57 54N 6 49W
Tarbes **20** 43 15N 0 3 E
Tarboro **113** 35 55N 77 30W
Tarbrax **72** 21 7S 142 26 E
Tarbū **87** 26 0N 15 5 E
Tarcento **27** 46 12N 13 12 E
Tarcoola **73** 30 44S 134 36 E
Tarcoon **73** 30 15S 146 43 E
Tarcutta **76** 35 16S 147 44 E
Tardets-Sorholus **20** 43 8N 0 52W
Tardoire → **20** 45 52N 0 14 E
Taree **77** 31 50S 152 30 E
Tarentaise **21** 45 30N 6 35 E
Tarf Shaqq al Abd **90** 26 50N 36 6 E
Tarfa, Wadi el → **90** 28 25N 30 50 E
Tarfaya **84** 27 55N 12 55W
Targon **20** 44 44N 0 16W
Targuist **86** 34 59N 4 14W
Tarhbalt **86** 30 39N 5 20W
Tarhit **86** 30 58N 2 0W
Tarhūnah **87** 32 27N 13 36 E
Tari **69** 5 54S 142 59 E
Tarib, Wadi → **90** 18 30N 43 23 E
Táriba **134** 7 49N 72 13W
Tarifa **23** 36 1N 5 36W
Tarija **140** 21 30S 64 40W
Tarija □ **140** 21 30S 63 30W
Tariku → **57** 2 55S 138 26 E
Tarim He → **62** 39 30N 88 30 E
Tarim Pendi **62** 40 0N 84 0 E
Tarime □ **94** 1 15S 34 0 E
Taritatu → **57** 2 54S 138 27 E
Tarka → **96** 32 10S 26 0 E
Tarkastad **96** 32 0S 26 16 E
Tarkhankut, Mys **38** 45 25N 32 30 E
Tarko Sale **40** 64 55N 77 50 E
Tarkwa **88** 5 20N 2 0W
Tarlac **57** 15 29N 120 35 E
Tarlton Downs **72** 22 40S 136 45 E
Tarm **11** 55 56N 8 31 E
Tarma **136** 11 25S 75 45W
Tarn □ **20** 43 49N 2 8 E
Tarn → **20** 44 5N 1 6 E
Tarn-et-Garonne □ **20** 44 8N 1 20 E
Tarna → **33** 47 31N 19 59 E
Tarnagulla **74** 36 45S 143 49 E
Tårnby **11** 55 37N 12 36 E
Tarnobrzeg **32** 50 35N 21 41 E
Tarnów **32** 50 3N 21 0 E
Táro → **26** 45 0N 10 15 E
Tarong **73** 26 47S 151 51 E
Taroom **73** 25 36S 149 48 E
Taroudannt **86** 30 30N 8 52W
Tarp **30** 54 40N 9 25 E
Tarpon Springs **113** 28 8N 82 42W
Tarquinia **27** 42 15N 11 45 E
Tarqumiyah **44** 31 35N 35 1 E
Tarragona **24** 41 5N 1 17 E
Tarragona □ **24** 41 0N 1 0 E
Tarrasa **24** 41 34N 2 1 E
Tárrega **24** 41 39N 1 9 E
Tarrington **74** 37 46S 142 7 E
Tarrytown **115** 41 5N 73 52W
Tarshiha = Me'ona **44** 33 1N 35 15 E
Tarso Emissi **87** 21 27N 18 36 E
Tarso Ourari **87** 21 27N 17 27 E
Tarsus **46** 36 58N 34 55 E
Tartagal **140** 22 30S 63 50W
Tartas **20** 43 50N 0 49W
Tartna Point **73** 32 54S 142 24 E
Tartu **36** 58 20N 26 44 E
Tartūs **46** 34 55N 35 55 E
Tarumirim **139** 19 16S 41 59W
Tarumizu **64** 31 29N 130 42 E
Tarussa **37** 54 44N 37 10 E
Tarutao, Ko **55** 6 33N 99 40 E
Tarutung **56** 2 0N 98 54 E
Tarvisio **27** 46 31N 13 35 E
Tarz Ulli **87** 25 32N 10 8 E
Tasahku **52** 27 33N 97 52 E
Tasāwah **87** 26 0N 13 30 E
Taschereau **104** 48 40N 78 40W
Taseko → **108** 52 4N 123 9W
Tasgaon **50** 17 2N 74 39 E
Tash-Kumyr **40** 41 40N 72 10 E
Ta'shan **91** 16 31N 42 33 E
Tashauz **40** 41 49N 59 58 E
Tashi Chho Dzong = Thimphu **52** 27 31N 89 45 E
Tashkent **40** 41 20N 69 10 E
Tashkurghan **47** 36 45N 67 40 E
Tashtagol **40** 52 47N 87 53 E
Tasikmalaya **57** 7 18S 108 12 E
Tasjön **8** 64 15N 16 0 E
Taskan **41** 62 59N 150 20 E
Taşköpru **38** 41 30N 34 15 E
Tasman → **81** 43 48S 170 8 E
Tasman B. **81** 40 59S 173 25 E
Tasman, Mt. **81** 43 34S 170 12 E
Tasman Mts. **81** 41 3S 172 25 E
Tasman Pen. **72** 43 10S 148 0 E
Tasman Sea **66** 36 0S 160 0 E
Tasmania, □ **72** 42 0S 146 30 E
Tăşnad **34** 47 30N 22 33 E
Tassil Tin-Rerhoh **86** 20 5N 3 55 E
Tassili n-Ajjer **87** 25 47N 8 1 E
Tassili-Oua-n-Ahaggar **87** 20 41N 5 30 E
Tasu Sd. **108** 52 47N 132 2W
Tata **86** 29 46N 7 56W
Tatabánya **33** 47 32N 18 25 E
Tatahouine **87** 32 57N 10 29 E
Tatar A.S.S.R. □ **40** 55 30N 51 30 E
Tatarsk **40** 55 14N 76 0 E
Tatarskiy Proliv **41** 54 0N 141 0 E
Tatebayashi **65** 36 15N 139 32 E
Tateshina-Yama **65** 36 8N 138 11 E
Tateyama **65** 35 0N 139 50 E
Tatham **77** 28 56S 153 9 E
Tathlina L. **108** 60 33N 117 39W
Tathra **75** 36 44S 149 59 E
Tatinnai L. **109** 60 55N 97 40W
Tatnam, C. **109** 57 16N 91 0W
Tatong **75** 36 43S 146 9 E
Tatra = Tatry **32** 49 20N 20 0 E
Tatry **32** 49 20N 20 0 E
Tatsuno **64** 34 52N 134 33 E
Tatta **48** 24 42N 67 55 E
Tatuī **141** 23 25S 47 53W
Tatum **119** 33 16N 103 16W
Tat'ung = Datong **60** 40 6N 113 12 E
Tatura **74** 36 29S 145 16 E
Tatvan **46** 38 31N 42 15 E
Tau **68** 14 15S 169 30W
Tauá **138** 6 1S 40 26W
Taubaté **141** 23 0S 45 36W
Tauberbischofsheim **31** 49 37N 9 40 E
Taucha **30** 51 22N 12 31 E
Taufikia **91** 9 24N 31 37 E
Taumarunui **80** 38 53S 175 15 E
Taumaturgo **136** 8 54S 72 51W
Taung **96** 27 33S 24 47 E
Taungdwingyi **52** 20 1N 95 40 E
Taunggyi **52** 20 50N 97 0 E
Taungtha **52** 21 12N 95 25 E
Taungup **52** 18 51N 94 14 E
Taungup Pass **52** 18 40N 94 45 E
Taunsa Barrage **48** 30 42N 70 50 E
Taunton, U.K. **13** 51 1N 3 7W
Taunton, U.S.A. **115** 41 54N 71 6W
Taunus **31** 50 15N 8 20 E
Taupo **80** 38 41S 176 7 E
Taupo, L. **80** 38 46S 175 55 E
Taurage **36** 55 14N 22 16 E
Tauranga **80** 37 42S 176 11 E
Tauranga Harb. **80** 37 30S 176 5 E
Tauri → **69** 8 8S 146 8 E
Taurianova **29** 38 22N 16 1 E
Taurus Mts. = Toros Dağlari **46** 37 0N 35 0 E
Tauste **24** 41 58N 1 18W
Tautira **68** 17 44S 149 9W
Tauz **39** 41 0N 45 40 E
Tavas **46** 37 35N 29 8 E
Tavda **40** 58 7N 65 8 E
Tavda → **40** 59 20N 63 28 E
Taverny **19** 49 2N 2 13 E
Taveta **94** 3 23S 37 37 E
Taveuni **68** 16 51S 179 58W
Taviche **125** 16 38N 96 32W
Tavignano → **21** 42 7N 9 33 E
Tavira **23** 37 8N 7 40W
Tavistock, Can. **106** 43 19N 80 50W
Tavistock, U.K. **13** 50 33N 4 9W
Tavolara **28** 40 55N 9 40 E
Távora → **22** 41 8N 7 35W
Tavoy **54** 14 2N 98 12 E
Tavua **68** 17 37S 177 5 E
Taw → **13** 17 37S 177 55 E
Tawas City **106** 44 16N 83 31W
Tawau **56** 4 20N 117 55 E
Tawitawi **57** 5 10N 120 0 E
Tawngche **52** 26 34N 95 38 E
Tāwurghā **87** 32 1N 15 2 E
Taxila **48** 33 42N 72 52 E
Tay → **14** 56 37N 3 38W
Tay, Firth of **14** 56 25N 3 8W
Tay, L., Austral. **79** 32 55S 120 48 E
Tay, L., U.K. **14** 56 30N 4 10W
Tay Ninh **55** 11 20N 106 5 E
Tayabamba **136** 8 15S 77 16W
Taylakovy **40** 59 13N 74 0 E
Taylor, Can. **108** 56 13N 120 40W
Taylor, Ariz., U.S.A. **121** 34 28N 110 5W
Taylor, Nebr., U.S.A. **118** 41 46N 99 23W
Taylor, Pa., U.S.A. **115** 41 23N 75 43W
Taylor, Tex., U.S.A. **119** 30 30N 97 30W
Taylor, Mt. **81** 43 30S 171 20 E
Taylor Mt. **121** 35 16N 107 36W
Taylors Arm **77** 30 45S 152 45 E
Taylorsville **117** 38 2N 85 21W
Taylorville **116** 39 32N 89 20W
Taymyr, P-ov. **41** 75 0N 100 0 E
Tayport **14** 56 27N 2 52W
Tayr Zebna **44** 33 14N 35 23 E
Tayshet **41** 55 58N 98 1 E
Tayside □ **14** 56 25N 3 30W
Taytay **57** 10 45N 119 30 E
Taz → **40** 67 32N 78 40 E
Taza **86** 34 16N 4 6W
Taze **52** 22 57N 95 24 E
Tazenakht **86** 30 35N 7 12W
Tazin → **109** 60 26N 110 45W
Tazin L. **109** 59 44N 108 42W
Tazoult **87** 35 29N 6 11 E
Tazovskiy **40** 67 30N 78 44 E
Tbilisi (Tiflis) **39** 41 43N 44 50 E
Tchad (Chad) ■ **85** 12 30N 17 15 E
Tchad, L. **85** 13 30N 14 30 E
Tch'ang-k'ing = Changqing **58** 29 35N 106 35 E
Tchaourou **89** 8 58N 2 40 E
Tch'eng-tou = Chengdu **58** 30 38N 104 2 E
Tchentlo L. **108** 55 15N 125 0W
Tchibanga **92** 2 45S 11 0 E
Tchin Tabaraden **89** 15 58N 5 56 E
Tchingou, Massif de **68** 20 54S 165 0 E
Tczew **32** 54 8N 18 50 E
Te Anau, L. **81** 45 15S 167 45 E
Te Araroa **80** 37 39S 178 25 E
Te Aroha **80** 37 32S 175 44 E
Te Awamutu **80** 38 1S 175 20 E
Te Kaha **80** 37 44S 177 52 E
Te Karaka **80** 38 26S 177 53 E
Te Kauwhata **80** 37 25S 175 9 E
Te Kinga **81** 42 35S 171 31 E
Te Kopuru **80** 36 2S 173 56 E
Te Kuiti **80** 38 20S 175 11 E
Te Puke **80** 37 46S 176 22 E
Te Waewae B. **81** 46 13S 167 33 E
Tea → **134** 0 30S 65 9W
Tea Gardens **76** 32 38S 152 10 E
Tea Tree **72** 22 5S 133 22 E
Teague **119** 31 40N 96 20W
Teano **29** 41 15N 14 1 E
Teapa **125** 18 35N 92 56W
Teba **23** 36 59N 4 55W
Tebakang **56** 1 6N 110 30 E
Teberda **39** 43 30N 41 46 E
Tébessa **87** 35 22N 8 8 E
Tebicuary → **140** 26 36S 58 16W
Tebingtinggi, Bengkulu, Indon. **56** 3 38S 103 9 E
Tebingtinggi, Sumatera Utara, Indon. **56** 3 20N 99 9 E
Tébourba **87** 36 49N 9 51 E
Téboursouk **87** 36 29N 9 10 E
Tebulos **39** 42 36N 45 17 E
Tecate **124** 32 34N 116 38W
Tech → **20** 42 36N 3 3 E
Techiman **88** 7 35N 1 58W
Tecka **142** 7 35N 1 43W
Tecomán **124** 18 55N 103 53W
Tecopa **123** 35 51N 116 14W
Tecoripa **124** 28 37N 109 57W
Tecuala **124** 22 23N 105 27W
Tecuci **34** 45 51N 27 27 E
Tecumseh, Can. **106** 42 19N 82 54W
Tecumseh, U.S.A. **117** 42 1N 83 59W
Teddywaddy **74** 36 12S 143 21 E
Tedesa **91** 5 10N 37 40 E
Tedzhen **40** 37 23N 60 31 E
Tee Lake **104** 46 40N 79 0W
Tees → **12** 54 36N 1 25W
Teesdale **74** 38 2S 144 2 E
Teesside **12** 54 37N 1 13W
Teeswater **106** 43 59N 81 17W
Tefé **135** 3 25S 64 50W
Tefé → **135** 3 35S 64 47W
Tegal **57** 6 52S 109 8 E
Tegelen **16** 51 20N 6 9 E
Tegernsee **31** 47 43N 11 46 E
Teggiano **29** 40 24N 15 32 E
Teghra **49** 25 30N 85 34 E
Tegid, L. **12** 52 53N 3 38W
Tegina **89** 10 5N 6 11 E
Tegua **68** 13 15S 166 37 E
Tegucigalpa **126** 14 5N 87 14W
Tehachapi **123** 35 11N 118 29W
Tehachapi Mts. **123** 35 0N 118 40W
Tehamiyam **90** 18 20N 36 32 E
Tehilla **90** 17 42N 36 6 E
Têhini **88** 9 39N 3 40W
Tehrān **47** 35 44N 51 30 E
Tehrān □ **47** 35 0N 49 30 E
Tehuacán **125** 18 30N 97 30W
Tehuantepec **125** 16 21N 95 13W
Tehuantepec, Golfo de **125** 15 50N 95 0W
Tehuantepec, Istmo de **125** 17 0N 94 30W
Teich, Le **20** 44 38N 0 59W
Teifi → **13** 52 4N 4 14W
Teign → **13** 50 41N 3 42W
Teignmouth **13** 50 33N 3 30W
Teil, Le **21** 44 33N 4 40 E
Teilleul, Le **18** 48 32N 0 53W
Teixeira **138** 7 13S 37 15W
Teixeira da Silva **93** 12 10S 15 50 E
Teixeira de Sousa = Luau **92** 10 40S 22 10 E
Teixeira Pinto **88** 12 3N 16 0W
Tejo → **23** 38 40N 9 24W
Tejon Pass **123** 34 49N 118 53W
Tekamah **118** 41 48N 96 22W
Tekapo, L. **81** 43 53S 170 33 E
Tekax **125** 20 11N 89 18W
Tekeli **40** 44 50N 79 0 E
Tekeze → **91** 14 20N 35 50 E
Tekija **33** 44 42N 22 26 E
Tekirdağ **46** 40 58N 27 30 E
Tekkali **50** 18 37N 84 15 E
Tekoa **120** 47 19N 117 4W
Tekouiât, O. → **86** 22 25N 2 35 E
Tel Adashim **44** 32 30N 35 17 E
Tel Aviv-Yafo **44** 32 4N 34 48 E
Tel Hazor **44** 33 2N 35 32 E
Tel Lakhish **44** 31 34N 34 51 E
Tel Megiddo **44** 32 35N 35 11 E
Tel Mond **44** 32 15N 34 56 E
Tela **126** 15 40N 87 28W
Télagh **86** 34 51N 0 32W
Telanaipura = Jambi **56** 1 38S 103 37 E
Telavi **39** 42 0N 45 30 E
Telefomin **69** 5 10S 141 31 E
Telegraph Cr. **108** 58 0N 131 10W
Telegraph Point **77** 31 20S 152 49 E
Telekhany **36** 52 30N 25 46 E
Telemark fylke □ **10** 59 25N 8 30 E
Telén **140** 36 15S 65 31W
Teleño **22** 42 23N 6 22W
Teleorman → **34** 44 15N 25 20 E
Teles Pires → **137** 7 21S 58 3W
Telescope Peak **123** 36 6N 117 7W
Teletaye **89** 16 31N 1 30 E
Telford **12** 52 42N 2 31W
Telfs **31** 47 19N 11 4 E
Telgte **30** 51 59N 7 46 E
Télimélé **88** 10 54N 13 2W
Telkwa **108** 54 41N 127 5W
Tell **44** 33 0N 35 6 E
Tell City **117** 38 0N 86 44W
Tellicherry **51** 11 45N 75 30 E
Telluride **121** 37 58N 107 48W
Telok Anson **55** 4 3N 101 0 E
Teloloapán **125** 18 21N 99 51W
Telsen **142** 42 30S 66 50W
Telšiai **36** 55 59N 22 14 E
Teltow **30** 52 24N 13 15 E
Telukbetung **56** 5 29S 105 17 E
Telukbutun **55** 4 13N 108 12 E
Telukdalem **56** 0 33N 97 50 E
Tema **89** 5 41N 0 0 E
Temanggung **57** 7 18S 110 10 E
Temapache **125** 21 4N 97 38W
Temax **125** 21 10N 88 50W
Tembe **94** 0 16S 28 14 E
Temblador, Venez. **135** 8 59N 62 44W
Temblador, Venez. **135** 8 59N 62 44W
Tembleque **24** 39 41N 3 30W
Temblor Ra. **123** 35 30N 120 0W
Tembuland **97** 31 35S 28 0 E
Teme → **13** 52 23N 2 15W
Temecula **123** 33 26N 117 6W
Temerloh **55** 3 27N 102 25 E
Temir **40** 49 21N 57 3 E

Temirtau, Kazakh, U.S.S.R. 40 50 5N 72 56 E
Temirtau, R.S.F.S.R., U.S.S.R. 40 53 10N 87 30 E
Témiscaming 104 46 44N 79 5W
Témiscamingue, L. 104 47 10N 79 25W
Temma 72 41 12S 144 48 E
Temnikov 37 54 40N 43 11 E
Temo → 28 40 20N 8 30 E
Temora 76 34 30S 147 30 E
Temosachic 124 28 58N 107 50W
Tempe 121 33 26N 111 59W
Tempino 56 1 42S 103 30 E
Témpio Pausania 28 40 53N 9 6 E
Tempiute 122 37 39N 115 38W
Temple 119 31 5N 97 22W
Temple B. 72 12 15S 143 3 E
Templemore 15 52 48N 7 50W
Templeton 122 35 33N 120 42W
Templeton → 72 21 0S 138 40 E
Templin 30 53 8N 13 31 E
Tempoal 125 21 31N 98 23W
Temryuk 38 45 15N 37 24 E
Temska → 33 43 17N 22 33 E
Temuco 142 38 45S 72 40W
Temuka 81 44 14S 171 17 E
Tena 134 0 59S 77 49W
Tenabo 125 20 2N 90 12W
Tenaha 119 31 57N 94 25W
Tenali 51 16 15N 80 35 E
Tenancingo 125 19 0N 99 33W
Tenango 125 19 7N 99 33W
Tenasserim 55 12 6N 99 3 E
Tenasserim □ 54 14 0N 98 30 E
Tenay 21 45 55N 5 30 E
Tenby 13 51 40N 4 42W
Tendaho 91 11 48N 40 54 E
Tende 21 44 5N 7 35 E
Tende, Col de 21 44 9N 7 32 E
Tendelti 91 13 1N 31 55 E
Tendjedi, Adrar 87 23 41N 7 32 E
Tendrara 86 33 3N 1 58W
Teneida 90 25 30N 29 19 E
Tenente Marques → 137 11 10S 59 56W
Ténéré 87 23 2N 16 0 E
Tenerife, I. 84 28 20N 16 40W
Ténès 86 36 31N 1 14 E
Teng Xian, Guangxi Zhuangzu, China 59 23 21N 110 56 E
Teng Xian, Shandong, China 61 35 5N 117 10 E
Tengah □ 57 2 0S 122 0 E
Tengah Kepulauan 56 7 5S 118 15 E
Tengchong 58 25 0N 98 28 E
Tenggara □ 57 3 0S 122 0 E
Tenggarong 56 0 24S 116 58 E
Tenggol, P. 55 4 48N 103 41 E
Tengiz, Ozero 40 50 30N 69 0 E
Tenille 113 32 58N 82 50W
Tenino 122 46 51N 122 51W
Tenkasi 51 8 55N 77 20 E
Tenke, Congo 95 11 22S 26 40 E
Tenke, Zaïre 95 10 32S 26 7 E
Tenkodogo 89 11 54N 0 19W
Tenna → 27 43 12N 13 47 E
Tennant Creek 72 19 30S 134 15 E
Tennessee □ 111 36 0N 86 30W
Tennessee → 112 34 30N 86 20W
Tennsift, Oued → 86 32 3N 9 28W
Tennyson 117 38 5N 87 7W
Tenom 56 5 4N 115 57 E
Tenosique 125 17 30N 91 24W
Tenri 65 34 39N 135 49 E
Tenryū 65 34 52N 137 49 E
Tenryū-gawa → 65 35 39N 137 48 E
Tent L. 109 62 25N 107 54W
Tenterfield 77 29 0S 152 0 E
Teófilo Otoni 139 17 50S 41 30W
Teotihuacán 125 19 44N 98 50W
Tepa 57 7 52S 129 31 E
Tepalcatepec → 124 18 35N 101 59W
Tepehuanes 124 25 21N 105 44W
Tepequem, Serra 135 3 45N 61 45W
Tepetongo 124 22 28N 103 9W
Tepic 124 21 30N 104 54W
Tepoca, C. 124 30 20N 112 25W
Tequila 124 20 54N 103 47W
Ter → 24 42 0N 3 12 E
Ter Apel 16 52 53N 7 5 E
Téra 89 14 0N 0 45 E
Tera → 22 41 54N 5 44W
Téramo 27 42 40N 13 40 E
Terang 74 38 15S 142 55 E
Terawhiti, C. 80 41 16S 174 38 E
Terazit, Massif de 87 20 2N 8 30 E
Tercan 46 39 50N 40 23 E
Tercero → 140 32 58S 61 47W
Terdal 50 16 33N 75 3 E
Terebovlya 36 49 18N 25 44 E
Terek → 38 43 55N 47 30 E
Terembone Cr. → 73 30 25S 148 50 E
Terenos 137 20 26S 54 50W
Tereshka → 37 51 48N 46 26 E
Teresina 138 5 9S 42 45W
Teresinha 135 0 58N 52 2W
Terewah L. 73 29 52S 147 35 E
Terges → 23 37 49N 7 41W
Tergnier 19 49 40N 3 17 E
Terhazza 86 23 38N 5 22W
Teridgerie 76 30 53S 148 50 E
Terlizzi 29 41 8N 16 32 E
Terme 38 41 11N 37 0 E
Termeil 76 35 30S 150 22 E
Termez 40 37 15N 67 15 E
Términi Imerese 28 37 58N 13 42 E
Términos, Laguna de 125 18 35N 91 30W
Térmoli 27 42 0N 15 0 E
Ternate 57 0 45N 127 25 E
Terneuzen 16 51 20N 3 50 E
Terney 41 45 3N 136 37 E
Terni 27 42 34N 12 38 E
Ternitz 33 47 43N 16 2 E
Ternopol 36 49 30N 25 40 E
Terowie 76 32 27S 147 52 E
Terra Bella 123 35 58N 119 3W
Terra Nova B. 143 74 50S 164 40 E
Terrace 108 54 30N 128 35W
Terrace Bay 102 48 47N 87 5W
Terracina 28 41 17N 13 12 E
Terralba 28 39 42N 8 38 E
Terramungamine 76 32 2S 148 32 E
Terranuova Bracciolini 27 43 31N 11 35 E
Terrasini Favarotta 28 38 10N 13 4 E
Terrasson 20 45 7N 1 19 E
Terre Haute 117 39 28N 87 24W
Terrebonne 105 45 42N 73 38W
Terrebonne B. 119 29 15N 90 28W
Terrecht 86 20 10N 0 10W
Terrell 119 32 44N 96 19W
Terrenceville 103 47 40N 54 44W
Terrick Terrick 72 24 44S 145 5 E
Terry 118 46 47N 105 20W
Terry Hie Hie 77 29 47S 150 10 E
Terschelling 16 53 25N 5 20 E
Terter → 39 40 35N 47 22 E
Teruel 24 40 22N 1 8W
Teruel □ 24 40 48N 1 0W
Tervel 34 43 45N 27 28 E
Tervola 8 66 6N 24 49 E
Teryaweyna L. 73 32 18S 143 22 E
Tešanj 33 44 38N 17 59 E
Teseney 91 15 5N 36 42 E
Tesha → 37 55 38N 42 9 E
Teshio 63 44 53N 141 44 E
Teshio-Gawa → 63 44 53N 141 45 E
Tesiyn Gol → 62 50 40N 93 20 E
Teslin 100 60 10N 132 43W
Teslin → 108 61 34N 134 35W
Teslin L. 108 60 15N 132 57W
Tesouro 137 16 4S 53 34W
Tessalit 89 20 12N 1 0 E
Tessaoua 89 13 47N 7 56 E
Tessin 30 54 2N 12 28 E
Tessit 89 15 13N 0 18 E
Test → 13 51 7N 1 30W
Testa del Gargano 29 41 50N 16 10 E
Teste, La 20 44 37N 1 8W
Têt → 20 42 44N 3 2 E
Tetachuck L. 108 53 18N 125 55W
Tetas, Pta. 140 23 31S 70 38W
Tete 95 16 13S 33 33 E
Tete □ 95 15 15S 32 40 E
Tetepari, I. 68 8 45S 157 35 E
Teterev → 36 51 1N 30 5 E
Teterow 30 53 45N 12 34 E
Teteven 34 42 58N 24 17 E
Tethul → 108 60 35N 112 12W
Tetiyev 38 49 22N 29 38 E
Teton → 120 47 58N 111 0W
Tétouan 86 35 35N 5 21W
Tetovo 34 42 1N 21 2 E
Tetuán = Tétouan 86 35 30N 5 25W
Teuco → 140 25 35S 60 11W
Teulada 28 38 59N 8 47 E
Teulon 109 50 23N 97 16W
Teun 57 6 59S 129 8 E
Tevere → 27 41 44N 12 14 E
Teviot → 14 55 21N 2 51W
Tewantin 73 26 27S 153 3 E
Tewkesbury 13 51 59N 2 8W
Texada I. 108 49 40N 124 25W
Texarkana, Ark., U.S.A. 119 33 25N 94 0W
Texarkana, Tex., U.S.A. 119 33 25N 94 3W
Texas 77 28 49S 151 9 E
Texas □ 119 31 40N 98 30W
Texas City 119 29 20N 94 55W
Texel 16 53 5N 4 50 E
Texhoma 119 36 32N 101 47W
Texline 119 36 26N 103 0W
Texoma L. 119 34 0N 96 38W
Teykovo 37 56 55N 40 30 E
Teza → 37 56 32N 41 53 E
Tezin 48 34 24N 69 30 E
Teziutlán 125 19 50N 97 22W
Tezpur 52 26 40N 92 45 E
Tezzeron L. 108 54 43N 124 30W
Tha-anne → 109 60 31N 94 37W
Tha Deua, Laos 54 19 26N 101 50 E
Tha Deua, Laos 54 17 57N 102 53 E
Tha Pla 54 17 48N 100 32 E
Tha Rua 54 14 34N 100 44 E
Tha Sala 55 8 40N 99 56 E
Tha Song Yang 54 17 34N 97 55 E
Thaba Putsoa 97 29 45S 28 0 E
Thabana Ntlenyana 97 29 30S 29 16 E
Thabazimbi 97 24 40S 27 21 E
Thabeikkyin 52 22 53N 95 59 E
Thabor, Mt. 21 45 7N 6 34 E
Thai Binh 54 20 35N 106 1 E
Thai Muang 55 8 24N 98 16 E
Thai Nguyen 54 21 35N 105 55 E
Thailand (Siam) ■ 54 16 0N 102 0 E
Thakhek 54 17 25N 104 45 E
Thakurgaon 52 26 2N 88 34 E
Thal 48 33 28N 70 33 E
Thal Desert 48 31 10N 71 30 E
Thala 87 35 35N 8 40 E
Thalaba 77 29 51S 149 23 E
Thalabarivat 54 13 33N 105 57 E
Thallon 73 28 39S 148 49 E
Thalwil 31 47 17N 8 35 E
Thame → 13 51 35N 1 8W
Thames 80 37 7S 175 34 E
Thames →, Can. 106 42 20N 82 25W
Thames →, U.K. 13 51 30N 0 35 E
Thames →, U.S.A. 115 41 18N 72 9W
Thames, Firth of 80 37 0S 175 25 E
Thamesford 106 43 4N 81 0W
Thamesville 106 42 33N 81 59W
Thāmit, W. 87 30 51N 16 14 E
Than Uyen 54 22 0N 103 54 E
Thana 50 19 12N 72 59 E
Thanbyuzayat 52 15 58N 97 44 E
Thanesar 48 30 1N 76 52 E
Thanet, I. of 13 51 21N 1 20 E
Thangoo P.O. 78 18 10S 122 22 E
Thangool 72 24 38S 150 42 E
Thanh Hoa 54 19 48N 105 46 E
Thanh Hung 55 9 55N 105 43 E
Thanh Thuy 54 22 55N 104 51 E
Thanjavur (Tanjore) 51 10 48N 79 12 E
Thann 19 47 48N 7 5 E
Thaon 19 48 15N 6 25 E
Thap Sakae 55 11 30N 99 37 E
Thap Than 54 15 27N 99 54 E
Thar (Great Indian) Desert 48 28 0N 72 0 E
Tharad 48 24 30N 71 44 E
Thargomindah 73 27 58S 143 46 E
Tharrawaddy 52 17 38N 95 48 E
Tharrawaw 52 17 41N 95 28 E
Tharwa 76 35 31S 149 4 E
Thásos 35 40 50N 24 42 E
That Khe 54 22 16N 106 28 E
Thatcher, Ariz., U.S.A. 121 32 54N 109 46W
Thatcher, Colo., U.S.A. 119 37 38N 104 6W
Thaton 52 16 55N 97 22 E
Thau, Étang de 20 43 23N 3 36 E
Thaungdut 52 24 30N 94 40 E
Thayer 119 36 34N 91 34W
Thayetmyo 52 19 20N 95 10 E
The Alberga → 73 27 6S 135 33 E
The Bight 127 24 19N 75 24W
The Blue Mt. 77 30 50S 151 41 E
The Dalles 120 45 40N 121 11W
The English Company's Is. 72 11 50S 136 32 E
The Entrance 76 33 21S 151 30 E
The Frome → 73 29 8S 137 54 E
The Grenadines, Is. 127 12 30N 61 30W
The Hague = s'-Gravenhage 16 52 7N 4 14 E
The Hamilton → 73 26 40S 135 19 E
The Johnston Lakes 79 32 25S 120 30 E
The Macumba → 73 27 52S 137 12 E
The Neales → 73 28 8S 136 47 E
The Oaks 76 34 3S 150 34 E
The Officer → 79 27 46S 132 30 E
The Pas 109 53 45N 101 15W
The Range 95 19 2S 31 2 E
The Salt Lake 73 30 6S 142 8 E
The Stevenson → 73 27 6S 135 33 E
The Warburton → 73 28 4S 137 28 E
Thebes 90 25 40N 32 35 E
Thedford, Can. 106 43 9N 81 51W
Thedford, U.S.A. 118 41 59N 100 31W
Theebine 73 25 57S 152 34 E
Theil, Le 18 48 16N 0 42 E
Thekulthili L. 109 61 3N 110 0W
Thelon → 109 62 35N 104 3W
Thénezay 18 46 44N 0 2W
Thenia 87 36 44N 3 33 E
Thenon 20 45 9N 1 4 E
Theodore 72 24 55S 150 3 E
Thepha 55 6 52N 100 58 E
Thérain → 19 49 15N 2 27 E
Theresa 115 44 13N 75 50W
Thermaïkos Kólpos 35 40 15N 22 45 E
Thermopolis 120 43 35N 108 10W
Thermopylae P. 35 38 48N 22 35 E
Thessalon 106 46 20N 83 30W
Thessaloníki 35 40 38N 22 58 E
Thessaly = Thessalía 35 39 30N 22 0 E
Thetford 13 52 25N 0 44 E
Thetford Mines 105 46 8N 71 18W
Theun → 54 18 19N 104 0 E
Theunissen 96 28 26S 26 43 E
Thevenard 73 32 9S 133 38 E
Thiámis → 35 39 15N 20 6 E
Thiberville 18 49 8N 0 27 E
Thibodaux 119 29 48N 90 49W
Thicket Portage 109 55 19N 97 42W
Thief River Falls 118 48 15N 96 48W
Thiel Mts. 143 85 15S 91 0W
Thiene 27 45 42N 11 29 E
Thiérache 19 49 51N 3 45 E
Thiers 20 45 52N 3 33 E
Thies 88 14 50N 16 51W
Thiet 91 7 37N 28 49 E
Thika 94 1 1S 37 5 E
Thille-Boubacar 88 16 31N 15 5W
Thillot, Le 19 47 53N 6 46 E
Thimphu (Tashi Chho Dzong) 52 27 31N 89 45 E
Þingvallavatn 8 64 11N 21 9W
Thio 68 21 37S 166 14 E
Thionville 19 49 20N 6 10 E
Thíra 35 36 23N 25 27 E
Thirasía 35 36 26N 25 21 E
Thirlmere 76 34 11S 150 35 E
Thirsk 12 54 15N 1 20W
Thistle I. 73 35 0S 136 8 E
Thitgy 52 18 15N 96 13 E
Thithia 68 17 45S 179 18W
Thitpokpin 52 19 24N 95 58 E
Thívai 35 38 19N 23 19 E
Thiviers 20 45 25N 0 54 E
Thizy 21 46 2N 4 18 E
Þjórsá → 8 63 47N 20 48W
Thlewiaza →, Man., Can. 109 59 43N 100 5W
Thlewiaza →, N.W.T., Can. 109 60 29N 94 40W
Thmar Puok 54 13 57N 103 4 E
Tho Vinh 54 19 16N 105 42 E
Thoa → 109 60 31N 109 47W
Thoen 54 17 43N 99 12 E
Thoeng 54 19 41N 100 12 E
Thoissey 21 46 12N 4 48 E
Tholdi 49 35 5N 76 6 E
Thomas, Okla., U.S.A. 119 35 48N 98 48W
Thomas, W. Va., U.S.A. 112 39 10N 79 30W
Thomas, L. 73 26 4S 137 58 E
Thomas Res. 116 39 34N 92 39W
Thomaston 113 32 54N 84 20W
Thomasville, Ala., U.S.A. 113 31 55N 87 42W
Thomasville, Ga., U.S.A. 113 30 50N 84 0W
Thomasville, N.C., U.S.A. 113 35 55N 80 4W
Thompson 109 55 45N 97 52W
Thompson →, Can. 108 50 15N 121 24W
Thompson →, U.S.A. 118 39 46N 93 37W
Thompson Falls 120 47 37N 115 20W
Thompson Landing 109 62 56N 110 40W
Thompson Pk. 120 41 0N 123 3W
Thompsons 121 39 0N 109 50W
Thompsonville 115 42 0N 72 37W
Thomson 116 41 58N 90 6W
Thomson → 72 25 11S 142 53 E
Thomson's Falls = Nyahururu 94 0 2N 36 27 E
Thon Buri 55 13 43N 100 29 E
Thônes 21 45 54N 6 18 E
Thongwa 52 16 45N 96 33 E
Thonon-les-Bains 21 46 22N 6 29 E
Thonze 52 17 38N 95 47 E
Thorez 39 48 4N 38 34 E
Þórisvatn 8 64 20N 18 55W
Þorlákshöfn 8 63 51N 21 22W
Thornaby on Tees 12 54 36N 1 19W
Thornbury, Can. 106 44 34N 80 26W
Thornbury, N.Z. 81 46 17S 168 9 E
Thorne Glacier 143 87 30S 150 0W
Thornton 116 42 57N 93 23W
Thornton-Beresfield 76 32 50S 151 40 E
Thorntown 117 40 8N 86 36W
Thorold 106 43 7N 79 12W
Thorpedale 75 38 19S 146 13 E
Þórshöfn 8 66 12N 15 20W

Thouarcé **18** 47 17N 0 30W
Thouars **18** 46 58N 0 15W
Thouin, C. **78** 20 20S 118 10 E
Thousand Oaks **123** 34 10N 118 50W
Thrakikón Pélagos **35** 40 30N 25 0 E
Thredbo Village **75** 36 31S 148 20 E
Three Forks **120** 45 55N 111 32W
Three Hills **108** 51 43N 113 15W
Three Hummock I. **72** 40 25S 144 55 E
Three Lakes **118** 45 48N 89 10W
Three Oaks **117** 41 48N 86 36W
Three Points, C. **88** 4 42N 2 6W
Three Rivers, Austral. **79** 25 10S 119 5 E
Three Rivers, Calif., U.S.A. **122** 36 26N 118 54W
Three Rivers, Mich., U.S.A. **117** 41 57N 85 38W
Three Rivers, Tex., U.S.A. **119** 28 30N 98 10W
Three Sisters Is. **68** 10 10S 161 57 E
Three Sisters, Mt. **120** 44 10N 121 46W
Throssell, L. **79** 27 33S 124 10 E
Throssell Ra. **78** 22 3S 121 43 E
Thuan Hoa **55** 8 58N 105 30 E
Thubun Lakes **109** 61 30N 112 0W
Thuddungra **76** 34 8S 148 8 E
Thueyts **21** 44 41N 4 9 E
Thuin **16** 50 20N 4 17 E
Thuir **20** 42 38N 2 45 E
Thule, Antarct. **143** 59 27S 27 19W
Thule, Greenl. **144** 77 40N 69 0W
Thun **31** 46 45N 7 38 E
Thundelarra **79** 28 53S 117 7 E
Thunder B. **114** 45 0N 83 20W
Thunder Bay **102** 48 20N 89 15W
Thunersee **31** 46 43N 7 39 E
Thung Song **55** 8 10N 99 40 E
Thunkar **52** 27 55N 91 0 E
Thuong Tra **54** 16 2N 107 42 E
Thur → **31** 47 32N 9 10 E
Thurgau □ **31** 47 34N 9 10 E
Thüringer Wald **30** 50 35N 11 0 E
Thurles **15** 52 40N 7 53W
Thurloo Downs **73** 29 15S 143 30 E
Thurn P. **31** 47 20N 12 25 E
Thursday I. **72** 10 30S 142 3 E
Thurso, Can. **104** 45 36N 75 15W
Thurso, U.K. **14** 58 34N 3 31W
Thurston I. **143** 72 0S 100 0W
Thury-Harcourt **18** 49 0N 0 30W
Thutade L. **108** 57 0N 126 55W
Thuy, Le **54** 17 14N 106 49 E
Thyborøn **11** 56 42N 8 12 E
Thylungra **73** 26 4S 143 28 E
Thyolo **95** 16 7S 35 5 E
Thysville = Mbanza Ngungu **92** 5 12S 14 53 E
Ti-n-Barraouene, O. → **89** 18 40N 4 5 E
Ti-n-Emensan **86** 22 59N 4 45 E
Ti-n-Geloulet **86** 25 58N 4 2 E
Ti-n-Medjerdam, O. → **86** 25 45N 1 30 E
Ti-n-Tarabine, O. → **87** 21 0N 7 25 E
Ti-n-Zaouaténe **86** 20 0N 2 55 E
Tia **77** 31 10S 150 34 E
Tiahuanacu **136** 16 33S 68 42W
Tian Shan **62** 43 0N 84 0 E
Tianchang **59** 32 40N 119 0 E
Tiandong **58** 23 36N 107 8 E
Tian'e **58** 25 1N 107 9 E
Tianguá **138** 3 44S 40 59W
Tianhe **58** 24 48N 108 40 E
Tianjin **61** 39 8N 117 10 E
Tiankoura **88** 10 47N 3 17W
Tianlin **58** 24 21N 106 12 E
Tianmen **59** 30 39N 113 9 E
Tianquan **58** 30 7N 102 43 E
Tianshui **60** 34 32N 105 40 E
Tiantai **59** 29 10N 121 2 E
Tianyang **58** 23 42N 106 53 E
Tianzhen **60** 40 24N 114 5 E
Tianzhu **58** 26 54N 109 11 E
Tianzhuangtai **61** 40 43N 122 5 E
Tiaret **86** 35 20N 1 21 E
Tiassalé **88** 5 58N 4 57W
Ti'avea **68** 13 57S 171 24W
Tibagi **141** 24 30S 50 24W
Tibagi → **141** 22 47S 51 1W
Tibari **91** 5 2N 31 48 E
Tibati **89** 6 22N 12 30 E
Tiber = Tevere → **27** 41 44N 12 14 E
Tiber Res. **120** 48 20N 111 15W
Tiberias **44** 32 47N 35 32 E
Tiberias, L. = Kinneret, Yam **44** 32 49N 35 36 E
Tibesti **87** 21 0N 17 30 E
Tibet □ = Xizang □ **62** 32 0N 88 0 E
Tibiri **89** 13 34N 7 4 E
Ţibleş **34** 47 32N 24 15 E
Tibnīn **44** 33 12N 35 24 E
Tibooburra **73** 29 26S 142 1 E
Tibro **11** 58 28N 14 10 E
Tibugá, Golfo de **134** 5 45N 77 20W
Tiburón **124** 29 0N 112 30W
Tichborne **76** 33 12S 148 8 E
Tîchît **88** 18 21N 9 29W
Ticho **91** 7 50N 39 32 E
Ticino □ **31** 46 20N 8 45 E
Ticino → **26** 45 9N 9 14 E
Ticonderoga **115** 43 50N 73 28W
Ticul **125** 20 20N 89 31W
Tidaholm **11** 58 12N 13 55 E
Tiddim **52** 23 28N 93 45 E
Tideridjaouine, Adrar **86** 23 0N 2 15 E
Tidikelt **86** 26 58N 1 30 E
Tidjikdja **88** 18 29N 11 35W
Tidore **57** 0 40N 127 25 E
Tidra, I. **88** 19 45N 16 20W
Tiébissou **88** 7 9N 5 10W
Tiéboro **87** 21 20N 17 7 E
Tiel, Neth. **16** 51 53N 5 26 E
Tiel, Senegal **88** 14 55N 15 5W
Tieling **61** 42 20N 123 55 E
Tielt **16** 51 0N 3 20 E
Tien Shan = Tian Shan **47** 42 0N 80 0 E
Tien-tsin = Tianjin **62** 39 8N 117 10 E
Tien Yen **54** 21 20N 107 24 E
T'ienching = Tianjin **61** 39 8N 117 10 E
Tienen **16** 50 48N 4 57 E
Tiénigbé **88** 8 11N 5 43W
Tientsin = Tianjin **61** 39 8N 117 10 E
Tierp **10** 60 20N 17 30 E
Tierra Amarilla, Chile **140** 27 28S 70 18W
Tierra Amarilla, U.S.A. **121** 36 42N 106 33W
Tierra Colorada **125** 17 10N 99 35W
Tierra de Barros **23** 38 40N 6 30W
Tierra de Campos **22** 42 10N 4 50W
Tierra del Fuego □ **142** 54 0S 67 45W
Tierra del Fuego, I. Gr. de **142** 54 0S 69 0W
Tierralta **134** 8 11N 76 4W
Tiétar → **22** 39 50N 6 1W
Tieté → **141** 20 40S 51 35W
Tieyon **73** 26 12S 133 52 E
Tiffin **117** 41 8N 83 10W
Tiffin → **117** 41 20N 84 24W
Tiflèt **86** 33 54N 6 20W
Tiflis = Tbilisi **39** 41 43N 44 50 E
Tifrah **44** 31 19N 34 42 E
Tifton **113** 31 28N 83 32W
Tifu **57** 3 39S 126 24 E
Tiga, Î. **68** 21 7S 167 49 E
Tigil **41** 57 49N 158 40 E
Tignish **103** 46 58N 64 2W
Tigre □ **91** 13 35N 39 15 E
Tigre →, Peru **136** 4 30S 74 10W
Tigre →, Venez. **135** 9 20N 62 30W
Tigris = Dijlah, Nahr → **46** 31 0N 47 25 E
Tiguentourine **87** 27 52N 9 8 E
Tigyaing **52** 23 45N 96 10 E
Tîh, Gebel el **90** 29 32N 33 26 E
Tihama **46** 22 0N 39 0 E
Tihodaine, Dunes de **87** 25 15N 7 15 E
Tijesno **27** 43 48N 15 39 E
Tîjî **87** 32 0N 11 18 E
Tijirit, O. → **88** 20 1N 15 29W
Tijuana **123** 32 30N 117 10W
Tikal **126** 17 13N 89 24W
Tikamgarh **49** 24 44N 78 50 E
Tikhoretsk **39** 45 56N 40 5 E
Tikhvin **36** 59 35N 33 30 E
Tikkadouine, Adrar **86** 24 28N 1 30 E
Tiko **89** 4 4N 9 20 E
Tikrit **46** 34 35N 43 37 E
Tiksi **41** 71 40N 128 45 E
Tilamuta **57** 0 32N 122 23 E
Tilburg **16** 51 31N 5 6 E
Tilbury, Can. **106** 42 17N 82 23W
Tilbury, U.K. **13** 51 27N 0 24 E
Tilbuster **77** 30 27S 151 41 E
Tilcara **140** 23 36S 65 23W
Tilden, U.S.A. **118** 42 3N 97 45W
Tilden, U.S.A. **119** 28 28N 98 33W
Tilemses **89** 15 37N 4 44 E
Tilemsi, Vallée du **89** 17 42N 0 15 E
Tilhar **49** 28 0N 79 45 E
Tilia, O. → **86** 27 32N 0 55 E
Tilichiki **41** 60 27N 166 5 E
Tiligul → **38** 47 4N 30 57 E
Tililane **86** 27 49N 0 6W
Tilin **52** 21 41N 94 6 E
Till → **12** 55 35N 2 3W
Tillabéri **89** 14 28N 1 28 E
Tillamook **120** 45 29N 123 55W
Tillberga **10** 59 52N 16 39 E
Tillia **89** 16 8N 4 47 E
Tillsonburg **106** 42 53N 80 44W
Tílos **35** 36 27N 27 27 E
Tilpa **73** 30 57S 144 24 E
Tilrhemt **86** 33 9N 3 22 E
Tilsit = Sovetsk **36** 55 6N 21 50 E
Tilt → **14** 56 50N 3 50W
Tilton **115** 43 25N 71 36W
Timagami L. **104** 47 0N 80 10W
Timaru **81** 44 23S 171 14 E
Timashevsk **39** 45 35N 39 0 E
Timau, Italy **27** 46 35N 13 0 E
Timau, Kenya **94** 0 4N 37 15 E
Timbaúba **138** 7 31S 35 19W
Timbédra **88** 16 17N 8 16W
Timber Lake **118** 45 29N 101 6W
Timber Mt. **122** 37 6N 116 28W
Timbío **134** 2 20N 76 40W
Timbiqui **134** 2 46N 77 42W
Timboon **74** 38 30S 142 58 E
Timbuktu = Tombouctou **88** 16 50N 3 0W
Timdjaouine **86** 21 37N 4 30 E
Timellouline **87** 29 22N 8 55 E
Timétrine Montagnes **89** 19 25N 1 0W
Timfristós, Óros **35** 38 57N 21 50 E
Timhadit **86** 33 15N 5 4W
Timimoun **86** 29 14N 0 16 E
Timimoun, Sebkha de **86** 28 50N 0 46 E
Timiris, C. **88** 19 21N 16 30W
Timiş → **34** 45 30N 21 0 E
Timişoara **34** 45 43N 21 15 E
Timmins **106** 48 28N 81 25W
Timok → **33** 44 10N 22 40 E
Timon **138** 5 8S 42 52W
Timor, Austral. **77** 31 46S 151 5 E
Timor, Indon. **57** 9 0S 125 0 E
Timor □ **57** 9 0S 125 0 E
Timor Sea **78** 10 0S 127 0 E
Tin Alkoum **87** 24 42N 10 17 E
Tin Gornai **89** 16 38N 0 38W
Tin Gornaï → **89** 20 30N 4 35 E
Tin Mt. **122** 36 54N 117 28W
Tîna, Khalîg el **90** 31 20N 32 42 E
Tinaca Pt. **57** 5 30N 125 25 E
Tinaco **134** 9 42N 68 26W
Tinafak, O. → **87** 27 10N 7 0 E
Tinaquillo **134** 9 55N 68 18W
Tinca **34** 46 46N 21 58 E
Tinchebray **18** 48 47N 0 45W
Tindivanam **51** 12 15N 79 41 E
Tindouf **86** 27 42N 8 10W
Tinee → **21** 43 55N 7 11 E
Tineo **22** 43 21N 6 27W
Tinerhir **86** 31 29N 5 31W
Tinfouchi **86** 28 52N 5 49W
Ting Jiang → **59** 24 45N 116 35 E
Tinggi, Pulau **55** 2 18N 104 7 E
Tingha **77** 29 56S 151 14 E
Tingkawk Sakan **52** 26 4N 96 44 E
Tinglev **11** 54 57N 9 13 E
Tingo Maria **136** 9 10S 75 54W
Tingsryd **11** 56 31N 15 0 E
Tinh Bien **55** 10 36N 104 57 E
Tinharé, I. de **139** 13 30S 38 58W
Tinié **89** 14 17N 1 30W
Tinioulig, Sebkra **86** 22 30N 6 45W
Tinjoub **86** 29 45N 5 40W
Tinkurrin **79** 32 59S 117 46 E
Tinnoset **10** 59 55N 9 3 E
Tinnsjø **10** 59 55N 8 54 E
Tinogasta **140** 28 5S 67 32W
Tínos **35** 37 33N 25 8 E
Tiñoso, C. **25** 37 32N 1 6W
Tinsukia **52** 27 29N 95 20 E
Tinta **136** 14 3S 71 20W
Tintaldra **75** 36 2S 147 55 E
Tintina **140** 27 2S 62 45W
Tintinara **73** 35 48S 140 2 E
Tinto → **23** 37 12N 6 55W
Tinui **80** 40 52S 176 5 E
Tinwald **81** 43 55S 171 43 E
Tioga **114** 41 54N 77 9W
Tioman, Pulau **55** 2 50N 104 10 E
Tione di Trento **26** 46 3N 10 44 E
Tionesta **114** 41 29N 79 28W
Tior **91** 6 26N 31 11 E
Tioulilin **86** 27 1N 0 2W
Tipp City **117** 39 58N 84 11W
Tippecanoe → **117** 40 31N 86 47W
Tipperary **15** 52 28N 8 10W
Tipperary □ **15** 52 37N 7 55W
Tipton, U.K. **13** 52 32N 2 4W
Tipton, Calif., U.S.A. **122** 36 3N 119 19W
Tipton, Ind., U.S.A. **117** 40 17N 86 0W
Tipton, Iowa, U.S.A. **116** 41 45N 91 12W
Tipton, Mo., U.S.A. **116** 38 41N 92 48W
Tipton, Mt. **123** 35 32N 114 16W
Tiptonville **119** 36 22N 89 30W
Tiptur **51** 13 15N 76 26 E
Tiquié → **134** 0 5N 68 25W
Tīra **44** 32 14N 34 56 E
Tiracambu, Serra do **138** 3 15S 46 30W
Tirahart, O. **86** 23 45N 3 10 E
Tīrān **47** 32 45N 51 8 E
Tirân **90** 27 56N 34 45 E
Tirana **35** 41 18N 19 49 E
Tirano **26** 46 13N 10 11 E
Tiraspol **38** 46 55N 29 35 E
Tirat Karmel **44** 32 46N 34 58 E
Tirat Tsevi **44** 32 26N 35 31 E
Tirat Yehuda **44** 32 1N 34 56 E
Tiratimine **86** 25 56N 3 37 E
Tirdout **89** 16 7N 1 5W
Tire **46** 38 5N 27 50 E
Tirebolu **46** 40 58N 38 45 E
Tiree I. **14** 56 31N 6 55W
Tîrgovişte **34** 44 55N 25 27 E
Tîrgu Frumos **34** 47 12N 27 2 E
Tîrgu-Jiu **34** 45 5N 23 19 E
Tîrgu Mureş **34** 46 31N 24 38 E
Tîrgu Neamţ **34** 47 12N 26 25 E
Tîrgu Ocna **34** 46 16N 26 39 E
Tîrgu Secuiesc **34** 46 0N 26 10 E
Tirich Mir **47** 36 15N 71 55 E
Tiriola **29** 38 57N 16 32 E
Tiririca, Serra da **139** 17 6S 47 6W
Tirna → **50** 18 4N 76 57 E
Tîrnava Mare → **34** 46 15N 24 30 E
Tîrnava Mică → **34** 46 17N 24 30 E
Tîrnăveni **34** 46 19N 24 13 E
Tírnavos **35** 39 45N 22 18 E
Tirodi **50** 21 40N 79 44 E
Tiros **139** 19 0S 45 58W
Tirschenreuth **31** 49 51N 12 20 E
Tirso → **28** 39 52N 8 33 E
Tirso, L. del **28** 40 8N 8 56 E
Tirua, Pt. **80** 38 25S 174 40 E
Tiruchchirappalli **51** 10 45N 78 45 E
Tiruchendur **51** 8 30N 78 11 E
Tiruchengodu **51** 11 23N 77 56 E
Tirumangalam **51** 9 49N 77 58 E
Tirunelveli (Tinnevelly) **51** 8 45N 77 45 E
Tirupati **51** 13 39N 79 25 E
Tiruppattur **51** 12 30N 78 30 E
Tiruppur **51** 11 5N 77 22 E
Tiruturaipundi **51** 10 32N 79 41 E
Tiruvadaimarudur **51** 11 2N 79 27 E
Tiruvallar **51** 13 9N 79 57 E
Tiruvannamalai **51** 12 15N 79 5 E
Tiruvarur **51** 10 46N 79 38 E
Tiruvatipuram **51** 12 39N 79 33 E
Tiruvottiyur **51** 13 10N 80 22 E
Tisa → **33** 45 15N 20 17 E
Tisdale **109** 52 50N 104 0W
Tiseirhatène, Mares de **86** 22 51N 9 30W
Tishomingo **119** 34 14N 96 38W
Tisjön **10** 60 56N 13 0 E
Tisnaren **10** 58 58N 15 56 E
Tisovec **32** 48 41N 19 56 E
Tissemsilt **86** 35 35N 1 50 E
Tissø **11** 55 35N 11 18 E
Tista → **52** 25 23N 89 43 E
Tisza → **33** 45 15N 20 17 E
Tiszafüred **33** 47 38N 20 50 E
Tiszavasvári **33** 47 58N 21 18 E
Tit, Ahaggar, Alg. **87** 23 0N 5 10 E
Tit, Tademait, Alg. **86** 27 0N 1 29 E
Tit-Ary **41** 71 55N 127 2 E
Titaguas **24** 39 53N 1 6W
Titahi Bay **80** 41 6S 174 50 E
Titai Damer **91** 16 43N 37 25 E
Titel **33** 45 10N 20 18 E
Tithwal **49** 34 21N 73 50 E
Titicaca, L. **136** 15 30S 69 30W
Titilagarh **50** 20 15N 83 11 E
Titiwa **89** 12 14N 12 53 E
Titograd **33** 42 30N 19 19 E
Titov Veles **35** 41 46N 21 47 E
Titova Korenica **27** 44 45N 15 41 E
Titovo Užice **33** 43 55N 19 50 E
Tittabawassee → **106** 43 23N 83 59W
Titule **94** 3 15N 25 31 E
Titumate **134** 8 19N 77 5W
Titusville, Fla., U.S.A. **113** 28 37N 80 49W
Titusville, Pa., U.S.A. **114** 41 35N 79 39W
Tivaouane **88** 14 56N 16 45W
Tiveden **11** 58 50N 14 30 E
Tiverton, Can. **106** 44 16N 81 32W
Tiverton, U.K. **13** 50 54N 3 30W
Tívoli **27** 41 58N 12 45 E
Tiwī **47** 22 45N 59 12 E
Tiyo **91** 14 41N 40 15 E
Tizga **86** 32 1N 5 9W
Ti'zi N'Isli **86** 32 28N 5 47W
Tizi Ouzou **87** 36 42N 4 3 E
Tizimín **125** 21 0N 88 1W
Tiznados → **134** 8 16N 67 47W
Tiznit **86** 29 48N 9 45W
Tjeggelvas **8** 66 37N 17 45 E
Tjirebon = Cirebon **57** 6 45S 108 32 E
Tjöme **10** 59 8N 10 26 E
Tjörn **11** 58 0N 11 35 E
Tkibuli **39** 42 26N 43 0 E
Tkvarcheli **39** 42 47N 41 42 E
Tlacolula **125** 16 57N 96 23W
Tlacotalpan **125** 18 37N 95 40W

Tlahualilo 124 26 20N 103 30W
Tlaquepaque 124 20 39N 103 19W
Tlaxcala 125 19 20N 98 14W
Tlaxcala □ 125 19 30N 98 20W
Tlaxiaco 125 17 18N 97 40W
Tlell 108 53 34N 131 56W
Tlemcen 86 34 52N 1 21W
Tleta Sidi Bouguedra 86 32 16N 9 59W
Tlumach 36 48 46N 25 0 E
Tlyarata 39 42 9N 46 26 E
Tmassah 87 26 19N 15 51 E
Tmisan 87 27 32N 13 19 E
To Bong 54 12 45N 109 16 E
To-Shima 65 34 31N 139 17 E
Toad → 108 59 25N 124 57W
Toala 57 1 30S 121 40 E
Toay 140 36 43S 64 38W
Toba 65 34 30N 136 51 E
Toba, Danau 56 2 40N 98 50 E
Toba Kakar 48 31 30N 69 0 E
Toba Tek Singh 48 30 55N 72 25 E
Tobago 127 11 10N 60 30W
Tobarra, Spain 25 38 35N 1 41W
Tobarra, Spain 25 38 37N 1 44W
Tobelo 57 1 45N 127 56 E
Tobermorey 72 22 12S 137 51 E
Tobermory, Can. 106 45 12N 81 40W
Tobermory, U.K. 14 56 37N 6 4W
Tobin 122 39 55N 121 19W
Tobin, L. 78 21 45S 125 49 E
Tobin L. 109 53 35N 103 30W
Toboali 56 3 0S 106 25 E
Tobol 40 52 40N 62 39 E
Toboli 57 0 38S 120 5 E
Tobolsk 40 58 15N 68 10 E
Tobruk = Tubruq 85 32 7N 23 55 E
Tobyhanna 115 41 10N 75 25W
Tocache Nuevo 136 8 9S 76 26W
Tocantínia 138 9 33S 48 22W
Tocantinópolis 138 6 20S 47 25W
Tocantins → 138 1 45S 49 10W
Toccoa 113 34 32N 83 17W
Toce → 26 45 56N 8 29 E
Tochigi 65 36 25N 139 45 E
Tochigi □ 65 36 45N 139 45 E
Tocina 23 37 37N 5 44W
Tocopilla 140 22 5S 70 10W
Tocumwal 74 35 51S 145 31 E
Tocuyo → 134 11 3N 68 23W
Tocuyo de la Costa 134 11 2N 68 23W
Todd → 72 24 52S 135 48 E
Todeli 57 1 38S 124 34 E
Todenyang 94 4 35N 35 56 E
Todi 27 42 47N 12 24 E
Todos os Santos, Baía de 139 12 48S 38 38W
Todos Santos 124 23 27N 110 13W
Todtnau 31 47 50N 7 56 E
Toecé 89 11 50N 1 16W
Toetoes B. 81 46 42S 168 41 E
Tofield 108 53 25N 112 40W
Tofino 108 49 11N 125 55W
Töfsingdalens nationalpark 10 62 15N 12 44 E
Toftlund 11 55 11N 9 2 E
Tofua 68 19 45S 175 05W
Toga 68 13 26S 166 42 E
Tōgane 65 35 33N 140 22 E
Togba 88 17 26N 10 12W
Togian, Kepulauan 57 0 20S 121 50 E
Togliatti 37 53 32N 49 24 E
Togo ■ 89 6 15N 1 35 E
Togtoh 60 40 15N 111 10 E
Toi 65 34 54N 138 47 E
Toinya 91 6 17N 29 46 E
Tojo 57 1 20S 121 15 E
Tōjō 64 34 53N 133 16 E
Toka 135 3 58N 59 17W
Tokaanu 80 38 58S 175 46 E
Tokachi → 63 42 44N 143 42 E
Tokai 65 35 2N 136 55 E
Tokaj 33 48 8N 21 27 E
Tokanui 81 46 34S 168 56 E
Tokar 85 18 27N 37 56 E
Tokara Kaikyō 63 30 0N 130 0 E
Tokarahi 81 44 56S 170 39 E
Tokat 46 40 22N 36 35 E
Tŏkchŏn 61 39 45N 126 18 E
Tokeland 122 46 42N 123 59W
Tokelau Is. 66 9 0S 171 45W
Toki 65 35 18N 137 8 E
Tokmak 40 42 49N 75 15 E
Toko Ra. 72 23 5S 138 20 E
Tokomaru Bay 80 38 8S 178 22 E
Tokoname 65 34 53N 136 51 E
Tokoroa 80 38 13S 175 50 E
Tokorozawa 65 35 47N 139 28 E
Toku 68 18 10S 174 11W
Tokuji 64 34 11N 131 42 E
Tokuno-Shima 63 27 56N 128 55 E
Tokushima 64 34 4N 134 34 E
Tokuyama 64 34 3N 131 50 E
Tōkyō 65 35 45N 139 45 E
Tōkyō □ 65 35 40N 139 30 E
Tōkyō-Wan 65 35 25N 139 47 E
Tolbukhin 34 43 37N 27 49 E
Toledo, Spain 22 39 50N 4 2W
Toledo, Ill., U.S.A. 117 39 16N 88 15W
Toledo, Iowa, U.S.A. 116 42 0N 92 35W
Toledo, Ohio, U.S.A. 117 41 37N 83 33W
Toledo, Oreg., U.S.A. 120 44 40N 123 59W
Toledo, Wash., U.S.A. 120 46 29N 122 51W
Toledo, Montes de 23 39 33N 4 20W
Tolentino 27 43 12N 13 17 E
Tolga, Alg. 87 34 40N 5 22 E
Tolga, Norway 10 62 26N 11 1 E
Tolima □ 134 3 45N 75 15W
Tolima, Vol. 134 4 40N 75 19W
Tolitoli 57 1 5N 120 50 E
Tollarp 11 55 55N 13 58 E
Tolleson 121 33 29N 112 10W
Tollhouse 122 37 1N 119 24W
Tolmachevo 36 58 56N 29 51 E
Tolmezzo 27 46 23N 13 0 E
Tolmin 27 46 11N 13 45 E
Tolo 92 2 55S 18 34 E
Tolo, Teluk 57 2 20S 122 10 E
Tolono 117 39 59N 88 16W
Tolosa 24 43 8N 2 5W
Tolox 23 36 41N 4 54W
Toltén 142 39 13S 74 14W
Toluca 125 19 20N 99 40W
Tom Burke 97 23 5S 28 4 E
Tom Price 78 22 40S 117 48 E
Tomah 118 43 59N 90 30W
Tomahawk 118 45 28N 89 40W
Tomakomai 63 42 38N 141 36 E
Tomales 122 38 15N 122 53W
Tomales B. 122 38 15N 123 58W
Tomanlivi 68 17 37S 178 1 E
Tomar 23 39 36N 8 25W
Tomás Barrón 136 17 35S 67 31W
Tomaszów Mazowiecki 32 51 30N 19 57 E
Tomatlán 124 19 56N 105 15W
Tombador, Serra do 137 12 0S 58 0W
Tombé 91 5 53N 31 40 E
Tombigbee → 113 31 4N 87 58W
Tombong 75 36 54S 148 56 E
Tombouctou 88 16 50N 3 0W
Tombstone 121 31 40N 110 4W
Tomé 140 36 36S 72 57W
Tomé-Açu 138 2 25S 48 9W
Tomelilla 11 55 33N 13 58 E
Tomelloso 25 39 10N 3 2W
Tomerong 76 35 3S 150 35 E
Tomiko L. 106 46 32N 79 49W
Tomingley 76 32 6S 148 16 E
Tomini 57 0 30N 120 30 E
Tomini, Teluk 57 0 10S 122 0 E
Tominian 88 13 17N 4 35W
Tomiño 22 41 59N 8 46W
Tomioka 65 37 20N 141 0 E
Tomkinson Ranges 79 26 11S 129 5 E
Tommot 41 59 4N 126 20 E
Tomnavoulin 14 57 19N 3 18W
Tomnop Ta Suos 55 11 20N 104 15 E
Tomo, Colomb. 134 2 38N 67 32W
Tomo, Japan 64 34 23N 133 23 E
Tomo → 134 5 20N 67 48W
Tomobe 65 36 20N 140 20 E
Toms Place 122 37 34N 118 41W
Toms River 115 39 59N 74 12W
Tomsk 40 56 30N 85 5 E
Tomtabacken 11 57 30N 14 30 E
Tonalá 125 16 8N 93 41W
Tonale, Passo del 26 46 15N 10 34 E
Tonalea 121 36 17N 110 58W
Tonami 65 36 40N 136 58 E
Tonantins 134 2 45S 67 45W
Tonasket 120 48 45N 119 30W
Tonate 135 5 0N 52 28W
Tonawanda 114 43 0N 78 54W
Tonbridge 13 51 12N 0 18 E
Tondano 57 1 35N 124 54 E
Tondela 22 40 31N 8 5W
Tønder 11 54 58N 8 50 E
Tondi 51 9 45N 79 4 E
Tondi Kiwindi 89 14 28N 2 02 E
Tondibi 89 16 39N 0 14W
Tone → 79 34 23S 116 25 E
Tong Xian 60 39 55N 116 35 E
Tonga ■ 68 20 0S 173 0W
Tonga Trench 66 18 0S 175 0W
Tongaat 97 29 33S 31 9 E
Tongala 74 36 14S 144 56 E
Tongaland 97 27 0S 32 0 E
Tong'an 59 24 37N 118 8 E
Tongareva 67 9 0S 158 0W
Tongatapu 68 21 10S 174 0W
Tongatapu Group 68 21 0S 175 0W
Tongbai 59 32 20N 113 23 E
Tongcheng, Anhui, China 59 31 4N 116 56 E
Tongcheng, Hubei, China 59 29 15N 113 50 E
Tongchŏn-ni 61 39 50N 127 25 E
Tongchuan 60 35 6N 109 3 E
Tongdao 58 26 10N 109 42 E
Tongeren 16 50 47N 5 28 E
Tonggu 59 28 31N 114 20 E
Tongguan 60 34 40N 110 25 E
Tonghai 58 24 10N 102 53 E
Tonghua 61 41 42N 125 58 E
Tongio 75 37 14S 147 44 E
Tongjiang, Heilongjiang, China 62 47 40N 132 27 E
Tongjiang, Sichuan, China 58 31 58N 107 11 E
Tongjosŏn Man 61 39 30N 128 0 E
Tongking = Tonkin, G. of 54 20 0N 108 0 E
Tongliang 58 29 50N 106 3 E
Tongliao 61 43 38N 122 18 E
Tongling 59 30 55N 117 48 E
Tonglu 59 29 45N 119 37 E
Tongnae 61 35 12N 129 5 E
Tongnan 58 30 9N 105 50 E
Tongoa 68 16 54S 168 34 E
Tongobory 97 23 32S 44 20 E
Tongoy 140 30 16S 71 31W
Tongren 58 27 43N 109 11 E
Tongres = Tongeren 16 50 47N 5 28 E
Tongsa Dzong 52 27 31N 90 31 E
Tongue 14 58 29N 4 25W
Tongue → 118 46 24N 105 52W
Tongwei 60 35 0N 105 5 E
Tongxin 60 36 59N 105 58 E
Tongyang 61 39 9N 126 53 E
Tongyu 61 44 45N 123 4 E
Tongzi 58 28 9N 106 49 E
Tonica 116 41 13N 89 4W
Tonj 91 7 20N 28 44 E
Tonk 48 26 6N 75 54 E
Tonkawa 119 36 44N 97 22W
Tonkin = Bac-Phan 54 22 0N 105 0 E
Tonkin, G. of 54 20 0N 108 0 E
Tonlé Sap 54 13 0N 104 0 E
Tonnay-Charente 20 45 56N 0 55W
Tonneins 20 44 23N 0 19 E
Tonnerre 19 47 51N 3 59 E
Tönning 30 54 18N 8 57 E
Tonopah 121 38 4N 117 12W
Tonoshō 64 34 29N 134 11 E
Tonosí 126 7 20N 80 20W
Tønsberg 10 59 19N 10 25 E
Tonto Basin 121 33 56N 111 27W
Tonumea 68 20 30S 174 30W
Tonzang 52 23 36N 93 42 E
Tonzi 52 24 39N 94 57 E
Toobeah 77 28 25S 149 54 E
Tooele 120 40 30N 112 20W
Toogong 76 33 19S 148 38 E
Toolleen 74 36 45S 144 42 E
Toolondo 74 36 58S 141 58 E
Tooloom 77 28 36S 152 27 E
Tooloon 76 30 59S 148 10 E
Tooma 76 35 57S 148 3 E
Toompine 73 27 15S 144 19 E
Toongi 76 32 28S 148 30 E
Toonpan 72 19 28S 146 48 E
Toonumbar 77 28 34S 152 46 E
Toora 75 38 39S 146 23 E
Toora-Khem 41 52 28N 96 17 E
Tooraweenah 76 31 26S 148 52 E
Toowoomba 77 27 32S 151 56 E
Topalu 34 44 31N 28 3 E
Topaz 122 38 41N 119 30W
Topeka 118 39 3N 95 40W
Topki 40 55 20N 85 35 E
Topl'a → 32 48 45N 21 45 E
Topley 108 54 49N 126 18W
Toplica → 33 43 15N 21 49 E
Toplița 34 46 55N 25 20 E
Topocalma, Pta. 140 34 10S 72 2W
Topock 123 34 46N 114 29W
Topola 33 44 17N 20 41 E
Topoľčany 32 48 35N 18 12 E
Topoli 39 47 59N 51 38 E
Topolnitsa → 34 42 11N 24 18 E
Topolobampo 124 25 40N 109 4W
Topolovgrad 34 42 5N 26 20 E
Toppenish 120 46 27N 120 16W
Topusko 27 45 18N 15 59 E
Toquepala 136 17 24S 70 25W
Torá 24 41 49N 1 25 E
Tora Kit 91 11 2N 32 36 E
Torata 136 17 23S 70 1W
Torbat-e Heydārīyeh 47 35 15N 59 12 E
Torbat-e Jām 47 35 16N 60 35 E
Torbay, Can. 103 47 40N 52 42W
Torbay, U.K. 13 50 26N 3 31W
Torbreck, Mt. 74 37 23S 145 58 E
Tørdal 10 59 10N 8 45 E
Tordesillas 22 41 30N 5 0W
Tordoya 22 43 6N 8 36W
Töreboda 11 58 41N 14 7 E
Torey 41 50 33N 104 50 E
Torfajökull 8 63 54N 19 0W
Torgau 30 51 32N 13 0 E
Torgelow 30 53 40N 13 59 E
Torhout 16 51 5N 3 7 E
Tori 91 7 53N 33 35 E
Torigni-sur-Vire 18 49 3N 0 58W
Torija 24 40 44N 3 2W
Torin 124 27 33N 110 15W
Toriñana, C. 22 43 3N 9 17W
Torington 77 29 19S 151 44 E
Torino 26 45 4N 7 40 E
Torit 91 4 27N 32 31 E
Torkovichi 36 58 51N 30 21 E
Tormentine 103 46 6N 63 46W
Tormes → 22 41 18N 6 29W
Tornado Mt. 108 49 55N 114 40W
Torne älv → 8 65 50N 24 12 E
Torneå = Tornio 8 65 50N 24 12 E
Torneträsk 8 68 24N 19 15 E
Tornio 8 65 50N 24 12 E
Tornionjoki → 8 65 50N 24 12 E
Tornquist 140 38 8S 62 15W
Toro 22 41 35N 5 24W
Torö 11 58 48N 17 50 E
Toro, Cerro del 140 29 10S 69 50W
Toro Pk. 123 33 34N 116 24W
Törökszentmiklós 33 47 11N 20 27 E
Toroníios Kólpos 35 40 5N 23 30 E
Toronto, Austral. 76 33 0S 151 30 E
Toronto, Can. 106 43 39N 79 20W
Toronto, U.S.A. 114 40 27N 80 36W
Toronto, L. 124 27 40N 105 30W
Toropets 36 56 30N 31 40 E
Tororo 94 0 45N 34 12 E
Toros Dağlari 46 37 0N 35 0 E
Torotoro 137 18 7S 65 46W
Torowie 73 33 8S 138 55 E
Torpshammar 10 62 29N 16 20 E
Torquay, Austral. 74 38 20S 144 19 E
Torquay, Can. 109 49 9N 103 30W
Torquay, U.K. 13 50 27N 3 31W
Torquemada 22 42 2N 4 19W
Torralba de Calatrava 23 39 1N 3 44W
Torrance 123 33 50N 118 19W
Torrão 23 38 16N 8 11W
Torre Annunziata 29 40 45N 14 26 E
Tôrre de Moncorvo 22 41 12N 7 8W
Torre del Greco 29 40 47N 14 22 E
Torre del Mar 23 36 44N 4 6W
Torre-Pacheco 25 37 44N 0 57W
Torre Pellice 26 44 49N 7 13 E
Torreblanca 24 40 14N 0 12 E
Torrecampo 23 38 29N 4 41W
Torrecilla en Cameros 24 42 15N 2 38W
Torredembarra 24 41 9N 1 24 E
Torredonjimeno 23 37 46N 3 57W
Torrejoncillo 22 39 54N 6 28W
Torrelaguna 24 40 50N 3 38W
Torrelavega 22 43 20N 4 5W
Torremaggiore 29 41 42N 15 17 E
Torremolinos 23 36 38N 4 30W
Torrens Cr. → 72 22 23S 145 9 E
Torrens Creek 72 20 48S 145 3 E
Torrens, L. 73 31 0S 137 50 E
Torrente 25 39 27N 0 28W
Torrenueva 25 38 38N 3 22W
Torreón 124 25 33N 103 25W
Torreperogil 25 38 2N 3 17W
Torres 124 28 46N 110 47W
Torres, Is. 68 13 15S 166 37 E
Torres Novas 23 39 27N 8 33W
Torres Strait 69 9 50S 142 20 E
Torres Vedras 23 39 5N 9 15W
Torrevieja 25 37 59N 0 42W
Torrey 121 38 18N 111 25W
Torridge → 13 50 51N 4 10W
Torridon, L. 14 57 35N 5 50W
Torrijos 22 39 59N 4 18W
Torrington, Conn., U.S.A. 115 41 50N 73 9W
Torrington, Wyo., U.S.A. 118 42 5N 104 8W
Torroella de Montgri 24 42 2N 3 8 E
Torrox 23 36 46N 3 57W
Torsås 11 56 24N 16 0 E
Torsby 10 60 7N 13 0 E
Torsö 11 58 48N 13 45 E
Tortola 127 18 19N 65 0W
Tórtoles de Esgueva 22 41 49N 4 2W
Tortona 26 44 53N 8 54 E
Tortoreto 27 42 50N 13 55 E
Tortorici 29 38 2N 14 48 E
Tortosa 24 40 49N 0 31 E
Tortosa, C. 24 40 41N 0 52 E
Tortosendo 22 40 15N 7 31W
Tortue, Î. de la 127 20 5N 72 57W
Tortuga, La 135 11 0N 65 22W
Torūd 47 35 25N 55 5 E
Toruń 32 53 0N 18 39 E

Torup, Denmark	**11**	57 5N	9 5 E
Torup, Sweden	**11**	56 57N	13 5 E
Tory I.	**15**	55 17N	8 12W
Torysa →	**32**	48 39N	21 21 E
Torzhok	**36**	57 5N	34 55 E
Tosa	**64**	33 24N	133 23 E
Tosa-shimizu	**64**	32 52N	132 58 E
Tosa-Wan	**64**	33 15N	133 30 E
Tosa-yamada	**64**	33 36N	133 38 E
Toscana	**26**	43 30N	11 5 E
Toscano, Arcipelago	**26**	42 30N	10 30 E
Tosno	**36**	59 38N	30 46 E
Tossa	**24**	41 43N	2 56 E
Tostado	**140**	29 15 S	61 50W
Tostaree	**75**	37 44 S	148 10 E
Tostedt	**30**	53 17N	9 42 E
Tosu	**64**	33 22N	130 31 E
Tosya	**46**	41 1N	34 2 E
Totana	**25**	37 45N	1 30W
Toten	**10**	60 37N	10 53 E
Toteng	**96**	20 22 S	22 58 E
Tôtes	**18**	49 41N	1 3 E
Tótkomlós	**33**	46 24N	20 45 E
Totma	**37**	60 0N	42 40 E
Totnes	**13**	50 26N	3 41W
Totness	**135**	5 53N	56 19W
Totonicapán	**126**	14 58N	91 12W
Totora	**137**	17 42 S	65 9W
Totoya, I.	**68**	18 57 S	179 50W
Totten Glacier	**143**	66 45 S	116 10 E
Tottenham, Austral.	**76**	32 14 S	147 21 E
Tottenham, Can.	**106**	44 1N	79 49W
Tottori	**64**	35 30N	134 15 E
Tottori □	**64**	35 30N	134 12 E
Touat	**86**	27 27N	0 30 E
Touba	**88**	8 22N	7 40W
Toubkal, Djebel	**86**	31 0N	8 0W
Toucy	**19**	47 44N	3 15 E
Tougan	**88**	13 11N	2 58W
Touggourt	**87**	33 10N	6 0 E
Tougué	**88**	11 25N	11 50W
Touho	**68**	20 47 S	165 14 E
Toukley	**76**	33 14 S	151 31 E
Toukmatine	**87**	24 49N	7 11 E
Toul	**19**	48 40N	5 53 E
Toulepleu	**88**	6 32N	8 24W
Toulon, France	**21**	43 10N	5 55 E
Toulon, U.S.A.	**116**	41 6N	89 52W
Toulouse	**20**	43 37N	1 27 E
Toummo	**87**	22 45N	14 8 E
Toummo Dhoba	**87**	22 30N	14 31 E
Toumodi	**88**	6 32N	5 4W
Tounassine, Hamada	**86**	28 48N	5 0W
Toungoo	**52**	19 0N	96 30 E
Touques →	**18**	49 22N	0 8 E
Touquet-Paris-Plage, Le	**19**	50 30N	1 36 E
Tour-du-Pin, La	**21**	45 33N	5 27 E
Touraine	**18**	47 20N	0 30 E
Tourane = Da Nang	**54**	16 4N	108 13 E
Tourcoing	**19**	50 42N	3 10 E
Tournai	**16**	50 35N	3 25 E
Tournan-en-Brie	**19**	48 44N	2 46 E
Tournay	**20**	43 13N	0 13 E
Tournon	**21**	45 4N	4 50 E
Tournon-St-Martin	**18**	46 45N	0 58 E
Tournus	**21**	46 35N	4 54 E
Touros	**138**	5 12 S	35 28W
Tours	**18**	47 22N	0 40 E
Touside, Pic	**87**	21 1N	16 29 E
Touwsrivier	**96**	33 20 S	20 0 E
Tovar	**134**	8 20N	71 46W
Tovarkovskiy	**37**	53 40N	38 14 E
Tovdal	**11**	58 47N	8 10 E
Tovdalselva →	**11**	58 15N	8 5 E
Towamba	**75**	37 6 S	149 43 E
Towanda, Ill., U.S.A.	**117**	40 36N	88 53W
Towanda, N.Y., U.S.A.	**115**	41 46N	76 30W
Tower	**118**	47 49N	92 17W
Towerhill Cr. →	**72**	22 28 S	144 35 E
Towner	**118**	48 25N	100 26W
Townsend	**120**	46 25N	111 32W
Townsend Mt.	**75**	36 25 S	148 16 E
Townshend I.	**72**	22 10 S	150 31 E
Townsville	**72**	19 15 S	146 45 E
Towong	**75**	36 8 S	147 59 E
Towson	**112**	39 26N	76 34W
Towyn	**13**	52 36N	4 5W
Toyah	**119**	31 20N	103 48W
Toyahvale	**119**	30 58N	103 45W
Toyama	**65**	36 40N	137 15 E
Toyama □	**65**	36 45N	137 30 E
Toyama-Wan	**63**	37 0N	137 30 E
Tōyō	**64**	33 26N	134 16 E
Toyohashi	**65**	34 45N	137 25 E
Toyokawa	**65**	34 48N	137 27 E
Toyonaka	**65**	34 50N	135 28 E
Toyooka	**64**	35 35N	134 48 E
Toyota	**65**	35 3N	137 7 E
Toyoura	**64**	34 6N	130 57 E
Tozeur	**87**	33 56N	8 8 E

Tra On	**55**	9 58N	105 55 E
Trabancos →	**22**	41 36N	5 15W
Traben Trarbach	**31**	49 57N	7 7 E
Trabzon	**46**	41 0N	39 45 E
Tracadie	**103**	47 30N	64 55W
Tracy, Can.	**105**	46 1N	73 9W
Tracy, Calif., U.S.A.	**122**	37 46N	121 27W
Tracy, Minn., U.S.A.	**118**	44 12N	95 38W
Tradate	**26**	45 43N	8 54 E
Traer	**116**	42 12N	92 28W
Trafalgar	**75**	38 14 S	146 12 E
Trafalgar, C.	**23**	36 10N	6 2W
Trāghān	**87**	26 0N	14 30 E
Tragowel	**74**	35 50 S	144 0 E
Traiguén	**142**	38 15 S	72 41W
Trail	**108**	49 5N	117 40W
Trainor L.	**108**	60 24N	120 17W
Traíra →	**134**	1 4 S	69 26W
Tralee	**15**	52 16N	9 42W
Tralee B.	**15**	52 17N	9 55W
Tramore	**15**	52 10N	7 10W
Tran Ninh, Cao Nguyen	**54**	19 30N	103 10 E
Tranås	**11**	58 3N	14 59 E
Trancas	**140**	26 11 S	65 20W
Tranche, La	**20**	46 20N	1 26W
Tranche-sur-Mer, La	**18**	46 20N	1 27W
Trancoso	**22**	40 49N	7 21W
Tranebjerg	**11**	55 51N	10 36 E
Tranemo	**11**	57 30N	13 20 E
Trang	**55**	7 33N	99 38 E
Trangahy	**97**	19 7 S	44 31 E
Trangan	**57**	6 40 S	134 20 E
Trangie	**76**	32 4 S	148 0 E
Trångsviken	**10**	63 19N	14 0 E
Trani	**29**	41 17N	16 24 E
Tranoroa	**97**	24 42 S	45 4 E
Tranquebar	**51**	11 1N	79 54 E
Tranqueras	**141**	31 13 S	55 45W
Trans Nzoia □	**94**	1 0N	35 0 E
Transcona	**109**	49 55N	97 0W
Transilvania	**34**	46 19N	25 0 E
Transkei □	**97**	32 15 S	28 15 E
Transtrand	**10**	61 6N	13 20 E
Transvaal □	**96**	25 0 S	29 0 E
Transylvania = Transilvania	**34**	46 19N	25 0 E
Trápani	**28**	38 1N	12 30 E
Trapper Peak	**120**	45 56N	114 29W
Traralgon	**75**	38 12 S	146 34 E
Traryd	**11**	56 35N	13 45 E
Trarza □	**88**	17 30N	15 0W
Trasacco	**27**	41 58N	13 30 E
Trăscău, Munţii	**34**	46 14N	23 14 E
Trasimeno, L.	**27**	43 10N	12 5 E
Trat	**55**	12 14N	102 33 E
Traun	**33**	48 14N	14 15 E
Traunstein	**31**	47 52N	12 40 E
Tråvad	**11**	58 15N	13 5 E
Traveller's L.	**73**	33 20 S	142 0 E
Travemünde	**30**	53 58N	10 52 E
Travers, Mt.	**81**	42 1 S	172 45 E
Traverse City	**112**	44 45N	85 39W
Traverse Is.	**143**	57 0 S	28 0W
Travnik	**33**	44 17N	17 39 E
Trawalla	**74**	37 25 S	143 28 E
Trayning	**79**	31 7 S	117 16 E
Trazo	**22**	43 0N	8 30W
Trbovlje	**27**	46 12N	15 5 E
Treasury Is.	**68**	7 22 S	155 37 E
Trébbia →	**26**	45 4N	9 41 E
Trebel →	**30**	53 55N	13 1 E
Trebinje	**33**	42 44N	18 22 E
Trebisacce	**29**	39 52N	16 32 E
Trebišnica →	**33**	42 47N	18 8 E
Trebišov	**32**	48 38N	21 41 E
Trebižat →	**33**	43 15N	17 30 E
Trebnje	**27**	45 54N	15 1 E
Třeboň	**32**	48 59N	14 48 E
Trebujena	**23**	36 52N	6 11W
Trecate	**26**	45 26N	8 42 E
Tredegar	**13**	51 47N	3 16W
Tregaron	**13**	52 14N	3 56W
Trégastel-Plage	**18**	48 49N	3 31W
Tregnago	**27**	45 31N	11 10 E
Tregrosse Is.	**72**	17 41 S	150 43 E
Tréguier	**18**	48 47N	3 16W
Trégune	**18**	47 51N	3 51W
Treherne	**109**	49 38N	98 42W
Tréia	**27**	43 20N	13 20 E
Treignac	**20**	45 32N	1 48 E
Treinta y Tres	**141**	33 16 S	54 17W
Treis	**31**	50 9N	7 19 E
Trekveld	**96**	30 35 S	19 45 E
Trelde Næs	**11**	55 38N	9 53 E
Trelew	**142**	43 10 S	65 20W
Trelissac	**20**	45 11N	0 47 E
Trelleborg	**11**	55 20N	13 10 E
Trélon	**19**	50 5N	4 6 E
Tremblade, La	**20**	45 46N	1 8W
Tremblant, Mt.	**104**	46 16N	74 35W
Tremiti	**27**	42 8N	15 30 E

Tremonton	**120**	41 45N	112 10W
Tremp	**24**	42 10N	0 52 E
Trenary	**112**	46 12N	86 59W
Trenche →	**105**	47 46N	72 53W
Trenčín	**32**	48 52N	18 4 E
Trenggalek	**57**	8 5 S	111 38 E
Trenque Lauquen	**140**	36 5 S	62 45W
Trent →, Can.	**107**	44 6N	77 34W
Trent →, U.K.	**12**	53 33N	0 44W
Trente et un Milles, L. des	**104**	46 12N	75 49W
Trentham	**74**	37 23 S	144 21 E
Trentino-Alto Adige □	**26**	46 30N	11 0 E
Trento	**26**	46 5N	11 8 E
Trenton, Can.	**107**	44 10N	77 34W
Trenton, Mich., U.S.A.	**117**	42 8N	83 11W
Trenton, Mo., U.S.A.	**116**	40 5N	93 37W
Trenton, N.J., U.S.A.	**115**	40 15N	74 41W
Trenton, Nebr., U.S.A.	**118**	40 14N	101 4W
Trenton, Tenn., U.S.A.	**119**	35 58N	88 57W
Trepassey	**103**	46 43N	53 25W
Tréport, Le	**18**	50 3N	1 20 E
Trepuzzi	**29**	40 26N	18 4 E
Tres Arroyos	**140**	38 26 S	60 20W
Três Corações	**139**	21 44 S	45 15W
Três Lagoas	**139**	20 50 S	51 43W
Tres Lagos →	**142**	49 35 S	71 25W
Tres Marías	**124**	21 25N	106 28W
Três Marias, Reprêsa	**139**	18 12 S	45 15W
Tres Montes, C.	**142**	46 50 S	75 30W
Tres Pinos	**122**	36 48N	121 19W
Três Pontas	**139**	21 23 S	45 29W
Tres Puentes	**140**	27 50 S	70 15W
Tres Puntas, C.	**142**	47 0 S	66 0W
Três Rios	**139**	22 6 S	43 15W
Tres Valles	**125**	18 15N	96 8W
Treska →	**35**	42 0N	21 20 E
Trespaderne	**24**	42 47N	3 24W
Trets	**21**	43 27N	5 41 E
Treuchtlingen	**31**	48 58N	10 55 E
Treuenbrietzen	**30**	52 6N	12 51 E
Trêve, L. la	**104**	49 56N	75 30W
Treviglio	**26**	45 31N	9 35 E
Trevínca, Peña	**22**	42 15N	6 46W
Treviso	**27**	45 40N	12 15 E
Trévoux	**21**	45 57N	4 47 E
Treysa	**30**	50 55N	9 12 E
Trgovište	**33**	42 20N	22 10 E
Triabunna	**72**	42 30 S	147 55 E
Trial B.	**77**	30 48 S	153 2 E
Triang	**55**	3 15N	102 26 E
Triaucourt-en-Argonne	**19**	48 59N	5 2 E
Tribsees	**30**	54 4N	12 46 E
Tribulation, C.	**72**	16 5 S	145 29 E
Tribune	**118**	38 30N	101 45W
Tricárico	**29**	40 37N	16 9 E
Tricase	**29**	39 56N	18 20 E
Trichinopoly = Tiruchchirappalli	**51**	10 45N	78 45 E
Trichur	**51**	10 30N	76 18 E
Trida	**73**	33 1 S	145 1 E
Trier	**31**	49 45N	6 37 E
Trieste	**27**	45 39N	13 45 E
Trieste, G. di	**27**	45 37N	13 40 E
Trieux →	**18**	48 50N	3 3W
Triggiano	**29**	41 4N	16 58 E
Triglav	**27**	46 21N	13 50 E
Trigno →	**27**	42 4N	14 48 E
Trigueros	**23**	37 24N	6 50W
Tríkhonis, Límni	**35**	38 34N	21 30 E
Tríkkala	**35**	39 34N	21 47 E
Trikora, Puncak	**57**	4 15 S	138 45 E
Trilj	**27**	43 38N	16 42 E
Trillo	**24**	40 42N	2 35W
Trim	**15**	53 34N	6 48W
Trincomalee	**51**	8 38N	81 15 E
Trindade	**139**	16 40 S	49 30W
Trindade, I.	**129**	20 20 S	29 50W
Tring-Jonction	**105**	46 16N	70 59W
Trinidad, Boliv.	**137**	14 46 S	64 50W
Trinidad, Colomb.	**134**	5 25N	71 40W
Trinidad, Cuba	**126**	21 48N	80 0W
Trinidad, Uruguay	**140**	33 30 S	56 50W
Trinidad, U.S.A.	**119**	37 15N	104 30W
Trinidad, W. Indies	**127**	10 30N	61 15W
Trinidad & Tobago ■	**127**	10 30N	61 20W
Trinidad →	**125**	17 49N	95 9W
Trinidad, G.	**142**	49 55 S	75 25W
Trinidad, I.	**142**	39 10 S	62 0W
Trinitápoli	**29**	41 22N	16 5 E
Trinity, Can.	**103**	48 59N	53 55W
Trinity, U.S.A.	**119**	30 59N	95 25W
Trinity →, Calif., U.S.A.	**120**	41 11N	123 42W
Trinity →, Tex., U.S.A.	**119**	30 30N	95 0W
Trinity B.	**103**	48 20N	53 10W

Trinity Mts.	**120**	40 20N	118 50W
Trinkitat	**85**	18 45N	37 51 E
Trino	**26**	45 10N	8 18 E
Trion	**113**	34 35N	85 18W
Trionto C.	**29**	39 38N	16 47 E
Triora	**26**	44 0N	7 46 E
Tripoli	**116**	42 49N	92 16W
Tripoli = Tarābulus, Leb.	**46**	34 31N	35 50 E
Tripoli = Tarābulus, Libya	**87**	32 58N	13 12 E
Tripp	**118**	43 16N	97 58W
Tripura □	**52**	24 0N	92 0 E
Trischen	**30**	54 3N	8 32 E
Tristan da Cunha, I.	**129**	37 6 S	12 20W
Trivandrum	**51**	8 41N	77 0 E
Trivento	**29**	41 48N	14 31 E
Trnava	**33**	48 23N	17 35 E
Trobriand Is.	**69**	8 30 S	151 0 E
Trochu	**108**	51 50N	113 13W
Trodely I.	**102**	52 15N	79 26W
Trogir	**27**	43 32N	16 15 E
Troglav	**27**	43 56N	16 36 E
Trøgstad	**10**	59 37N	11 16 E
Tróia	**29**	41 22N	15 19 E
Troilus, L.	**102**	50 50N	74 35W
Troina	**29**	37 47N	14 34 E
Trois Fourches, Cap des	**86**	35 26N	2 58W
Trois-Pistoles	**105**	48 5N	69 10W
Trois-Riviéres	**105**	46 25N	72 34W
Troitsk	**40**	54 10N	61 35 E
Troitsko-Pechorsk	**40**	62 40N	56 10 E
Trölladyngja	**8**	64 54N	17 16W
Trollhättan	**11**	58 17N	12 20 E
Trollheimen	**10**	62 46N	9 1 E
Trombetas →	**135**	1 55 S	55 35W
Tromelin I.	**53**	15 52 S	54 25 E
Troms fylke □	**8**	68 56N	19 0 E
Tromsø	**8**	69 40N	18 56 E
Trona	**123**	35 46N	117 23W
Tronador	**142**	41 10 S	71 50W
Trøndelag, N. □	**8**	65 0N	12 0 E
Trondheim	**10**	63 36N	10 25 E
Trönninge	**11**	56 37N	12 51 E
Trönö	**10**	61 22N	16 54 E
Tronto →	**27**	42 54N	13 55 E
Troon	**14**	55 33N	4 40W
Tropea	**29**	38 40N	15 53 E
Tropic	**121**	37 36N	112 4W
Tropoja	**34**	42 23N	20 10 E
Trossachs, The	**14**	56 14N	4 24W
Trostan	**15**	55 4N	6 10W
Trostberg	**31**	48 2N	12 33 E
Trotternish	**14**	57 32N	6 15W
Troup	**119**	32 10N	95 3W
Trout →	**108**	61 19N	119 51W
Trout Creek	**106**	45 59N	79 22W
Trout L., N.W.T., Can.	**108**	60 40N	121 40W
Trout L., Ont., Can.	**109**	51 20N	93 15W
Trout Lake, Mich., U.S.A.	**106**	46 10N	85 2W
Trout Lake, Wash., U.S.A.	**122**	46 0N	121 32W
Trout River	**103**	49 29N	58 8W
Trouville	**18**	49 21N	0 5 E
Trowbridge	**13**	51 18N	2 12W
Troy, Turkey	**46**	39 55N	26 20 E
Troy, Ala., U.S.A.	**113**	31 50N	85 58W
Troy, Idaho, U.S.A.	**120**	46 44N	116 46W
Troy, Ill., U.S.A.	**116**	38 44N	89 54W
Troy, Ind., U.S.A.	**117**	38 0N	86 48W
Troy, Kans., U.S.A.	**118**	39 47N	95 2W
Troy, Mo., U.S.A.	**116**	38 56N	90 59W
Troy, Montana, U.S.A.	**120**	48 30N	115 58W
Troy, N.Y., U.S.A.	**115**	42 45N	73 39W
Troy, Ohio, U.S.A.	**117**	40 0N	84 10W
Troyan	**34**	42 57N	24 43 E
Troyes	**19**	48 19N	4 3 E
Trpanj	**33**	43 1N	17 15 E
Trstena	**32**	49 21N	19 37 E
Trstenik	**33**	43 36N	21 0 E
Trubchevsk	**36**	52 33N	33 47 E
Truc Giang	**55**	10 3N	106 36 E
Trucial States = Utd. Arab Emirates	**47**	24 0N	54 30 E
Truckee	**122**	39 20N	120 11W
Truite, L. à la	**104**	47 20N	78 20W
Trujillo, Colomb.	**134**	4 10N	76 19W
Trujillo, Hond.	**126**	16 0N	86 0W
Trujillo, Peru	**136**	8 6 S	79 0W
Trujillo, Spain	**23**	39 28N	5 55W
Trujillo, U.S.A.	**119**	35 34N	104 44W
Trujillo, Venez.	**134**	9 22N	70 38W
Trujillo □	**134**	9 25N	70 30W
Truk	**66**	7 25N	151 46 E
Trumann	**119**	35 42N	90 32W
Trumbull, Mt.	**121**	36 25N	113 8W
Trun	**18**	48 50N	0 2 E
Trundle	**76**	32 53 S	147 35 E

Trung-Phan **56** 16 0N 108 0 E
Truro, Can. **103** 45 21N 63 14W
Truro, U.K. **13** 50 17N 5 2W
Truslove **79** 33 20S 121 45 E
Trustrup **11** 56 20N 10 46 E
Truth or Consequences **121** 33 9N 107 16W
Trutnov **32** 50 37N 15 54 E
Truyère → **20** 44 38N 2 34 E
Tryavna **34** 42 54N 25 25 E
Tryon **113** 35 15N 82 16W
Tryonville **114** 41 42N 79 48W
Trzcianka **32** 53 3N 16 25 E
Trzebiatów **32** 54 3N 15 18 E
Trzebiez **32** 53 38N 14 31 E
Trzebinia-Siersza **32** 50 11N 19 18 E
Trzebnica **32** 51 20N 17 1 E
Tržič **27** 46 22N 14 18 E
Tsaratanana **97** 16 47S 47 39 E
Tsaratanana, Mt. de **97** 14 0S 49 0 E
Tsarevo = Michurin **34** 42 9N 27 51 E
Tsau **96** 20 8S 22 22 E
Tsaukaib **96** 26 37S 15 31 E
Tsebrikovo **38** 47 9N 30 10 E
Tselinograd **40** 51 10N 71 30 E
Tsetserleg **62** 47 36N 101 32 E
Tshabong **96** 26 2S 22 29 E
Tshane **96** 24 5S 21 54 E
Tshela **92** 4 57S 13 4 E
Tshesebe **97** 21 51S 27 32 E
Tshibeke **94** 2 40S 28 35 E
Tshibinda **94** 2 23S 28 43 E
Tshikapa **92** 6 28S 20 48 E
Tshilenge **94** 6 17S 23 48 E
Tshinsenda **95** 12 20S 28 0 E
Tshofa **94** 5 13S 25 16 E
Tshwane **96** 22 24S 22 1 E
Tsigara **96** 20 22S 25 54 E
Tsihombé **97** 25 18S 45 29 E
Tsilmamo **91** 6 1N 35 17 E
Tsimlyansk **39** 47 40N 42 6 E
Tsimlyanskoye Vdkhr. **39** 48 0N 43 0 E
Tsinan = Jinan **60** 36 38N 117 1 E
Tsineng **96** 27 05S 23 05 E
Tsinghai □ = Qinghai □ **62** 36 0N 98 0 E
Tsingtao = Qingdao **61** 36 5N 120 20 E
Tsinjomitondraka **97** 15 40S 47 8 E
Tsiroanomandidy **97** 18 46S 46 2 E
Tsivilsk **37** 55 50N 47 25 E
Tsivory **97** 24 4S 46 5 E
Tskhinvali **39** 42 14N 44 1 E
Tsna → **37** 54 55N 41 58 E
Tso Morari, L. **49** 32 50N 78 20 E
Tsodilo Hill **96** 18 49S 21 43 E
Tsogttsetsiy **60** 43 43N 105 35 E
Tsu **65** 34 45N 136 25 E
Tsu L. **108** 60 40N 111 52W
Tsuchiura **65** 36 5N 140 15 E
Tsugaru-Kaikyō **63** 41 35N 141 0 E
Tsukumi **64** 33 4N 131 52 E
Tsukushi-Sanchi **64** 33 25N 130 30 E
Tsumeb **96** 19 9S 17 44 E
Tsumis **96** 23 39S 17 29 E
Tsuna **64** 34 28N 134 56 E
Tsuno-Shima **64** 34 21N 130 52 E
Tsuru **65** 35 31N 138 57 E
Tsuruga **65** 35 45N 136 2 E
Tsuruga-Wan **65** 35 50N 136 3 E
Tsurugi **65** 36 29N 136 37 E
Tsurugi-San **64** 33 51N 134 6 E
Tsurumi-Saki **64** 32 56N 132 5 E
Tsuruoka **63** 38 44N 139 50 E
Tsurusaki **64** 33 14N 131 41 E
Tsushima, Japan **64** 34 20N 129 20 E
Tsushima, Japan **65** 35 10N 136 43 E
Tsvetkovo **38** 49 8N 31 33 E
Tu → **52** 21 50N 96 15 E
Tua → **22** 41 13N 7 26W
Tuai **80** 38 47S 177 10 E
Tuakau **80** 37 16S 174 59 E
Tual **57** 5 38S 132 44 E
Tuam **15** 53 30N 8 50W
Tuamarina **81** 41 25S 173 59 E
Tuamotu Arch. **67** 17 0S 144 0W
Tuamotu Ridge **67** 20 0S 138 0W
Tuanfeng **59** 30 38N 114 52 E
Tuanxi **58** 27 28N 107 8 E
Tuao **57** 17 55N 122 22 E
Tuapse **39** 44 5N 39 10 E
Tuatapere **81** 46 8S 167 41 E
Tuba City **121** 36 8N 111 18W
Tubac **121** 31 37N 111 20W
Tuban **57** 6 54S 112 3 E
Tubarão **141** 28 30S 49 0W
Tubas **44** 32 20N 35 22 E
Tubau **56** 3 10N 113 40 E
Tübingen **31** 48 31N 9 4 E
Tubja, W. → **90** 25 27N 38 45 E
Tubruq (Tobruk) **85** 32 7N 23 55 E
Tubuai Is. **67** 25 0S 150 0W
Tuc Trung **55** 11 1N 107 12 E
Tucacas **134** 10 48N 68 19W
Tucano **138** 10 58S 38 48W
Tuchang **59** 24 59N 121 30 E
Tuchodi → **108** 58 17N 123 42W
Tuchola **32** 53 33N 17 52 E
Tuckanarra **79** 27 8S 118 1 E
Tucson **121** 32 14N 110 59W
Tucumán □ **140** 26 48S 66 2W
Tucumcari **119** 35 12N 103 45W
Tucunaré **137** 5 18S 55 51W
Tucupido **134** 9 17N 65 47W
Tucupita **135** 9 2N 62 3W
Tucuruí **138** 3 42S 49 44W
Tudela **24** 42 4N 1 39W
Tudela de Duero **22** 41 37N 4 39W
Tudor, Lac **103** 55 50N 65 25W
Tudora **34** 47 31N 26 45 E
Tuella → **22** 41 30N 7 12W
Tuen P.O. **73** 28 33S 145 37 E
Tuena **76** 34 1S 149 19 E
Tueré → **138** 2 48S 50 59W
Tufi **69** 9 8S 149 19 E
Tuggerah, L. **76** 33 18S 151 30 E
Tuguegarao **57** 17 35N 121 42 E
Tugur **41** 53 44N 136 45 E
Tugwa **96** 17 27S 18 25 E
Tukangbesi, Kepulauan **57** 6 0S 124 0 E
Tukarak I. **102** 56 15N 78 45W
Tûkh **90** 30 21N 31 12 E
Tukobo **88** 5 1N 2 47W
Tūkrah **87** 32 30N 20 37 E
Tuktoyaktuk **100** 69 27N 133 2W
Tukums **36** 57 2N 23 10 E
Tukuyu **95** 9 17S 33 35 E
Tula, Hidalgo, Mexico **125** 20 0N 99 20W
Tula, Tamaulipas, Mexico **125** 23 0N 99 40W
Tula, Nigeria **89** 9 51N 11 27 E
Tula, U.S.S.R. **37** 54 13N 37 38 E
Tulak **47** 33 55N 63 40 E
Tulancingo **125** 20 5N 99 22W
Tulare **122** 36 15N 119 26W
Tulare Basin **122** 36 0N 119 48W
Tulare Lake **121** 36 0N 119 53W
Tularosa **121** 33 4N 106 1W
Tulbagh **96** 33 16S 19 6 E
Tulcán **134** 0 48N 77 43W
Tulcea **34** 45 13N 28 46 E
Tulchin **38** 48 41N 28 49 E
Tuléar **97** 23 21S 43 40 E
Tuléar □ **97** 21 0S 45 0 E
Tulemalu L. **109** 62 58N 99 25W
Tuli, Indon. **57** 1 24S 122 26 E
Tuli, Zimb.-Rhod. **95** 21 58S 29 13 E
Tülkarm **44** 32 19N 35 2 E
Tulla **119** 34 35N 101 44W
Tullahoma **113** 35 23N 86 12W
Tullamore, Austral. **76** 32 39S 147 36 E
Tullamore, Ireland **15** 53 17N 7 30W
Tulle **20** 45 16N 1 46 E
Tullibigeal **73** 33 25S 146 44 E
Tullins **21** 45 18N 5 29 E
Tulln **33** 48 20N 16 4 E
Tullow **15** 52 48N 6 45W
Tullus **91** 11 7N 24 31 E
Tully **72** 17 56S 145 55 E
Tulmaythah **85** 32 40N 20 55 E
Tulmur **72** 22 40S 142 20 E
Tulnici **34** 45 51N 26 38 E
Tulovo **34** 42 33N 25 32 E
Tulsa **119** 36 10N 96 0W
Tulsequah **108** 58 39N 133 35W
Tulu Milki **91** 9 55N 38 20 E
Tulu Welel **91** 8 56N 34 47 E
Tulua **134** 4 6N 76 11W
Tulun **41** 54 32N 100 35 E
Tulungagung **56** 8 5S 111 54 E
Tum **57** 3 36S 130 21 E
Tuma **37** 55 10N 40 30 E
Tuma → **126** 13 6N 84 35W
Tumaco, Colomb. **134** 1 50N 78 45W
Tumaco, Ensenada, Colomb. **134** 1 55N 78 45W
Tumatumari **135** 5 20N 58 55W
Tumba **10** 59 12N 17 48 E
Tumba, L. **92** 0 50S 18 0 E
Tumbarumba **76** 35 44S 148 0 E
Tumbaya **140** 23 50S 65 26W
Túmbes **136** 3 37S 80 27W
Tumbes □ **136** 3 50S 80 30W
Tumblong **76** 35 6S 148 1 E
Tumbulgum **77** 28 17S 153 27 E
Tumbwe **95** 11 25S 27 15 E
Tumby Bay **73** 34 21S 136 8 E
Tumd Youqi **60** 40 30N 110 30 E
Tumen **61** 43 0N 129 50 E
T'umen **61** 42 55N 129 50 E
Tumen Jiang → **61** 42 20N 130 35 E
Tumeremo **135** 7 18N 61 30W
Tumiritinga **139** 18 58S 41 38W
Tumkur **51** 13 18N 77 6 E
Tummel, L. **14** 56 43N 3 55W
Tumorrama **76** 35 11S 148 28 E
Tump **47** 26 7N 62 16 E
Tumpat **55** 6 11N 102 10 E
Tumsar **50** 21 26N 79 45 E
Tumu **88** 10 56N 1 56W
Tumucumaque, Serra **135** 2 0N 55 0W
Tumupasa **136** 14 9S 67 55W
Tumut **76** 35 16S 148 13 E
Tumwater **120** 47 0N 122 58W
Tunas de Zaza **126** 21 39N 79 34W
Tunbridge Wells **13** 51 7N 0 16 E
Tuncurry **77** 32 17S 152 29 E
Tunduru **95** 11 8S 37 25 E
Tunduru □ **95** 11 5S 37 22 E
Tundzha → **35** 41 40N 26 35 E
Tunga → **51** 15 0N 75 50 E
Tunga Pass **52** 29 0N 94 14 E
Tungabhadra → **51** 15 57N 78 15 E
Tungabhadra Dam **51** 15 0N 75 50 E
Tungamah **74** 36 10S 145 54 E
Tungaru **85** 10 9N 30 52 E
Tungi **52** 23 53N 90 24 E
Tungla **126** 13 24N 84 21W
Tungnafellsjökull **8** 64 45N 17 55W
Tungsten, Can. **108** 61 57N 128 16W
Tungsten, U.S.A. **120** 40 50N 118 10W
Tungurahua □ **134** 1 15S 78 35W
Tunguska, Nizhnyaya → **41** 65 48N 88 4 E
Tunguska, Podkamennaya → **41** 61 36N 90 18 E
Tuni **50** 17 22N 82 36 E
Tunia **134** 2 41N 76 31W
Tunica **119** 34 43N 90 23W
Tunis **87** 36 50N 10 11 E
Tunis, Golfe de **87** 37 0N 10 30 E
Tunisia ■ **87** 33 30N 9 10 E
Tunja **134** 5 33N 73 25W
Tunkhannock **115** 41 32N 75 46W
Tunliu **60** 36 13N 112 52 E
Tunnsjøen **8** 64 45N 13 25 E
Tunungayualok I. **103** 56 0N 61 0W
Tunuyán **140** 33 35S 69 0W
Tunuyán → **140** 33 33S 67 30W
Tunxi **59** 29 42N 118 25 E
Tuo Jiang → **58** 28 50N 105 35 E
Tuolumne **122** 37 59N 120 16W
Tuolumne → **122** 37 36N 121 13W
Tuoy-Khaya **41** 62 32N 111 25 E
Tupã **141** 21 57S 50 28W
Tupaciguara **139** 18 35S 48 42W
Tupelo **113** 34 15N 88 42W
Tupik **41** 54 26N 119 57 E
Tupinambaranas **135** 3 0S 58 0W
Tupirama **138** 8 58S 48 12W
Tupiratins **138** 8 23S 48 8W
Tupiza **140** 21 30S 65 40W
Tupman **123** 35 18N 119 21W
Tupper **108** 55 32N 120 1W
Tupper L. **115** 44 18N 74 30W
Tupungato, Cerro **140** 33 15S 69 50W
Tuquan **61** 45 18N 121 38 E
Tuque, La **105** 47 30N 72 50W
Túquerres **134** 1 5N 77 37W
Tur **44** 31 47N 35 14 E
Tura, India **52** 25 30N 90 16 E
Tura, U.S.S.R. **41** 64 20N 100 17 E
Turaba, Wadi → **90** 21 15N 41 32 E
Turagua, Serranía **135** 7 20N 64 35W
Turaiyur **51** 11 9N 78 38 E
Turakina **80** 40 3S 175 16 E
Turakirae Hd. **80** 41 26S 174 56 E
Tūrān **47** 35 39N 56 42 E
Turan **41** 51 55N 95 0 E
Turayf **46** 31 41N 38 39 E
Turégano **22** 41 9N 4 1W
Turek **32** 52 3N 18 30 E
Turen **134** 9 17N 69 6W
Turfan = Turpan **62** 43 58N 89 10 E
Turfan Depression = Turpan Hami **62** 42 40N 89 25 E
Turgeon → **104** 50 0N 78 56W
Turgeon, L. **104** 49 2N 79 4W
Tŭrgovishte **34** 43 17N 26 38 E
Turgutlu **46** 38 30N 27 48 E
Turhal **38** 40 24N 36 5 E
Turia → **25** 39 27N 0 19W
Turiaçu **138** 1 40S 45 19W
Turiaçu → **138** 1 36S 45 19W
Turin **108** 49 47N 112 24W
Turin = Torino **26** 45 3N 7 40 E
Turkana □ **94** 3 0N 35 30 E
Turkana, L. **94** 3 30N 36 5 E
Turkestan **40** 43 17N 68 16 E
Túrkeve **33** 47 6N 20 44 E
Turkey ■ **46** 39 0N 36 0 E
Turkey → **116** 42 43N 91 2W
Turkey Creek P.O. **78** 17 2S 128 12 E
Turki **37** 52 0N 43 15 E
Turkmen S.S.R. □ **40** 39 0N 59 0 E
Turks Is. **127** 21 20N 71 20W
Turks Island Passage **127** 21 30N 71 30W
Turku **9** 60 30N 22 19 E
Turkwe → **94** 3 6N 36 6 E
Turlock **122** 37 30N 120 55W
Turnagain → **108** 59 12N 127 35W
Turnagain, C. **80** 40 28S 176 38 E
Turneffe Is. **125** 17 20N 87 50W
Turner, Austral. **78** 17 52S 128 16 E
Turner, U.S.A. **120** 48 52N 108 25W
Turner Pt. **72** 11 47S 133 32 E
Turner Valley **108** 50 40N 114 17W
Turners Falls **115** 42 36N 72 34W
Turnhout **16** 51 19N 4 57 E
Turnor L. **109** 56 35N 108 35W
Turnovo **34** 43 5N 25 41 E
Turnu Măgurele **34** 43 46N 24 56 E
Turnu Rosu Pasul **34** 45 33N 24 17 E
Turnu-Severin **34** 44 39N 22 41 E
Turon **119** 37 48N 98 27W
Tuross Head **76** 36 3S 150 8 E
Turpan **62** 43 58N 89 10 E
Turpan Hami, Xinjiang Uygur, China **62** 42 40N 89 25 E
Turpan Hami, Xinjiang Uygur, China **62** 42 20N 88 0 E
Turriff **14** 57 32N 2 28W
Tursha **37** 56 55N 47 36 E
Tursi **29** 40 15N 16 27 E
Turtle Hd. I. **72** 10 56S 142 37 E
Turtle L., Can. **109** 53 36N 108 38W
Turtle L., U.S.A. **118** 45 22N 92 10W
Turtle Lake **118** 47 30N 100 55W
Turtleford **109** 53 23N 108 57W
Turua **80** 37 14S 175 35 E
Turūbah **46** 28 20N 43 15 E
Turukhansk **41** 65 21N 88 5 E
Turun ja Porin lääni □ **9** 60 27N 22 15 E
Turzovka **32** 49 25N 18 35 E
Tuscaloosa **113** 33 13N 87 31W
Tuscánia **27** 42 25N 11 53 E
Tuscany = Toscana **26** 43 28N 11 15 E
Tuscola, Ill., U.S.A. **117** 39 48N 88 15W
Tuscola, Tex., U.S.A. **119** 32 15N 99 48W
Tuscumbia, Ala., U.S.A. **113** 34 42N 87 42W
Tuscumbia, Mo., U.S.A. **116** 38 14N 92 28W
Tuskar Rock **15** 52 12N 6 10W
Tuskegee **113** 32 24N 85 39W
Tustna **10** 63 10N 8 5 E
Tuticorin **51** 8 50N 78 12 E
Tutin **33** 43 0N 20 20 E
Tutóia **138** 2 45S 42 20W
Tutong **56** 4 47N 114 40 E
Tutova → **34** 46 20N 27 30 E
Tutrakan **34** 44 2N 26 40 E
Tutshi L. **108** 59 56N 134 30W
Tuttle **118** 47 9N 100 00W
Tuttlingen **31** 47 59N 8 50 E
Tutuala **57** 8 25S 127 15 E
Tutuila, Amer. Sam. **68** 14 19S 170 50W
Tutuila, Pac. Oc. **66** 14 18S 170 42W
Tutuko Mt. **81** 44 35S 168 1 E
Tututepec **125** 16 9N 97 38W
Tutye **74** 35 12S 141 29 E
Tuva, A.S.S.R. □ **41** 51 30N 95 0 E
Tuvalu ■ **66** 8 0S 178 0 E
Tuvutha **68** 17 40S 178 48W
Tuxpan **125** 20 58N 97 23W
Tuxtla Gutiérrez **125** 16 50N 93 10W
Tuy **22** 42 3N 8 39W
Tuy An **54** 13 17N 109 16 E
Tuy Duc **55** 12 15N 107 27 E
Tuy Hoa **54** 13 5N 109 10 E
Tuy Phong **55** 11 14N 108 43 E
Tuya L. **108** 59 7N 130 35W
Tuyen Hoa **54** 17 50N 106 10 E
Tuyen Quang **54** 21 50N 105 10 E
Tuz Gölü **46** 38 45N 33 30 E
Tūz Khurmātu **46** 34 56N 44 38 E
Tuzla **33** 44 34N 18 41 E
Tuzlov → **39** 47 28N 39 45 E
Tvååker **11** 57 4N 12 25 E
Tvedestrand **11** 58 38N 8 58 E
Tvŭrditsa **34** 42 42N 25 53 E
Twain **122** 40 1N 121 3W
Twain Harte **122** 38 2N 120 14W
Tweed **107** 44 29N 77 19W
Tweed → **14** 55 42N 2 10W
Tweed Heads **77** 28 10S 153 31 E
Tweedsmuir Prov. Park **108** 53 0N 126 20W
Twentynine Palms **123** 34 10N 116 4W
Twillingate **103** 49 42N 54 45W
Twin Bridges **120** 45 33N 112 23W
Twin Falls **120** 42 30N 114 30W
Twin Valley **118** 47 15N 96 15W
Twinnge **52** 23 10N 96 2 E
Twisp **120** 48 21N 120 5W

Twistringen 30 52 48N 8 38 E
Two Harbors 118 47 1N 91 40W
Two Hills 108 53 43N 111 52W
Two Rivers 112 44 10N 87 31W
Two Thumbs Ra. 81 43 45S 170 44 E
Twofold B. 75 37 8S 149 59 E
Tyagong 76 34 4S 148 15 E
Tyalgum 77 28 22S 153 10 E
Tykocin 32 53 13N 22 46 E
Tyldal 10 62 8N 10 48 E
Tyler, Minn., U.S.A. 118 44 18N 96 8W
Tyler, Tex., U.S.A. 119 32 18N 95 18W
Týn nad Vltavou 32 49 13N 14 26 E
Tynda 41 55 10N 124 43 E
Tyne & Wear □ 12 54 55N 1 35W
Tyne → 12 54 58N 1 28W
Tynemouth 12 55 1N 1 27W
Tynset 10 62 17N 10 47 E
Tyre = Sūr 44 33 12N 35 11 E
Tyrendarra 74 38 12S 141 50 E
Tyrifjorden 10 60 2N 10 8 E
Tyringe 11 56 9N 13 35 E
Tyringham 77 30 15S 152 35 E
Tyristrand 10 60 5N 10 5 E
Tyrnyauz 39 43 21N 42 45 E
Tyrone 114 40 39N 78 10W
Tyrrell → 74 35 26S 142 51 E
Tyrrell Arm 109 62 27N 97 30W
Tyrrell, L. 74 35 20S 142 50 E
Tyrrell L. 109 63 7N 105 27W
Tyrrhenian Sea 28 40 0N 12 30 E
Tysfjorden 8 68 7N 16 25 E
Tystberga 11 58 51N 17 15 E
Tyumen 40 57 11N 65 29 E
Tywi → 13 51 48N 4 20W
Tzaneen 97 23 47S 30 9 E
Tzefa 44 31 7N 35 12 E
Tzermíadhes Neápolis 35 35 11N 25 29 E
Tzoumérka, Óros 35 39 30N 21 26 E
Tzukong = Zigong 58 29 15N 104 48 E

U

U Taphao 54 12 35N 101 0 E
Uachadi, Sierra 135 4 54N 65 18W
Uad Erni, O. → 86 26 45N 10 47W
Uainambi 134 1 43N 69 51W
Uanda 72 21 37S 144 55 E
Uarbry 77 32 3S 149 49 E
Uarsciek 45 2 28N 45 55 E
Uasin □ 94 0 30N 35 20 E
Uassem 44 32 59N 36 2 E
Uato-Udo 57 9 7S 125 36 E
Uatumã → 135 2 26S 57 37W
Uauá 138 9 50S 39 28W
Uaupés 134 0 8S 67 5W
Uaxactún 126 17 25N 89 29W
Ubá 141 21 8S 43 0W
Ubaitaba 139 14 18S 39 20W
Ubangi = Oubangi → 92 1 0N 17 50 E
Ubaté 134 5 19N 73 49W
Ubauro 48 28 15N 69 45 E
Ubaye → 21 44 28N 6 18 E
Ube 64 33 56N 131 15 E
Úbeda 25 38 3N 3 23W
Uberaba 139 19 50S 47 55W
Uberaba, L. 137 17 30S 57 50W
Uberlândia 139 19 0S 48 20W
Überlingen 31 47 46N 9 10 E
Ubiaja 89 6 41N 6 22 E
Ubolratna Phong, L. 54 16 45N 102 30 E
Ubombo 97 27 31S 32 4 E
Ubon Ratchathani 54 15 15N 104 50 E
Ubondo 94 0 55S 25 42 E
Ubort → 36 52 6N 28 30 E
Ubrique 23 36 41N 5 27W
Ubuna 68 10 11S 161 21 E
Ubundi 94 0 22S 25 30 E
Ucayali → 136 4 30S 73 30W
Uchi Lake 109 51 5N 92 35W
Uchiko 64 33 33N 132 39 E
Uchiura-Wan 63 42 25N 140 40 E
Uchiza 136 8 25S 76 20W
Uchte 30 52 29N 8 52 E
Uchur → 41 58 48N 130 35 E
Ucluelet 108 48 57N 125 32W
Ucuriş 34 46 41N 21 58 E
Uda → 41 54 42N 135 14 E
Udaipur 48 24 36N 73 44 E
Udaipur Garhi 49 27 0N 86 35 E
Udamalpet 51 10 35N 77 15 E
Udbina 27 44 31N 15 47 E
Uddeholm 10 60 1N 13 38 E
Uddevalla 11 58 21N 11 55 E
Uddjaur 8 65 25N 21 15 E
Udgir 50 18 25N 77 5 E
Udhampur 49 33 0N 75 5 E
Udi 89 6 23N 7 21 E
Údine 27 46 5N 13 10 E
Udipi 51 13 25N 74 42 E
Udmurt, A.S.S.R. □ 40 57 30N 52 30 E
Udon Thani 54 17 29N 102 46 E
Udubo 89 11 52N 10 35 E
Udvoy Balkan 34 42 50N 26 50 E
Udzungwa Range 95 9 30S 35 10 E
Ueckermünde 30 53 45N 14 1 E
Ueda 65 36 24N 138 16 E
Uedineniya, Os. 144 78 0N 85 0 E
Uelen 41 66 10N 170 0W
Uelzen 30 53 0N 10 33 E
Ueno 65 34 45N 136 8 E
Uere → 92 3 45N 24 45 E
Ufa 40 54 45N 55 55 E
Uffenheim 31 49 32N 10 15 E
Ugalla → 94 5 8S 30 42 E
Ugamas 96 28 0S 19 41 E
Uganda ■ 94 2 0N 32 0 E
Ugento 29 39 55N 18 10 E
Ugep 89 5 53N 8 2 E
Ugi 68 10 14S 161 44 E
Ugie 97 31 10S 28 13 E
Ugijar 25 36 58N 3 7W
Ugine 21 45 45N 6 25 E
Ugla 90 25 40N 37 42 E
Uglegorsk 41 49 5N 142 2 E
Uglich 37 57 33N 38 20 E
Ugljane 27 43 35N 16 46 E
Ugolyak 41 64 33N 120 30 E
Ugra → 36 54 30N 36 7 E
Ugŭrchin 34 43 6N 24 26 E
Uh → 33 48 7N 21 25 E
Uherske Hradiště 32 49 4N 17 30 E
Uhrichsville 114 40 23N 81 22W
Uiha 68 19 54S 174 25W
Uiju 61 40 15N 124 35 E
Uinta Mts. 120 40 45N 110 30W
Uitenhage 96 33 40S 25 28 E
Uithuizen 16 53 24N 6 41 E
Ujfehértó 33 47 49N 21 41 E
Ujh → 49 32 40N 75 30 E
Ujhani 49 28 0N 79 6 E
Uji 65 34 53N 135 48 E
Ujjain 48 23 9N 75 43 E
Ujpest 33 47 32N 19 6 E
Ujszász 33 47 19N 20 7 E
Ujung Pandang 57 5 10S 119 20 E
Uka 41 57 50N 162 0 E
Ukara I. 94 1 50S 33 0 E
Ukbek 40 41 30N 65 0 E
Ukerewe □ 94 2 0S 32 30 E
Ukerewe I. 94 2 0S 33 0 E
Ukholovo 37 53 47N 40 30 E
Ukhrul 52 25 10N 94 25 E
Ukhta 40 63 55N 54 0 E
Uki 77 28 26S 153 20 E
Ukiah 122 39 10N 123 9W
Ukki Fort 49 33 28N 76 54 E
Ukmerge 36 55 15N 24 45 E
Ukrainian S.S.R. □ 38 49 0N 32 0 E
Ukwi 96 23 29S 20 30 E
Ulaanbaatar 62 47 54N 106 52 E
Ulaangom 62 50 0N 92 10 E
Ulamambri 77 31 19S 149 23 E
Ulamba 95 9 3S 23 38 E
Ulan 77 32 16S 149 46 E
Ulan Bator = Ulaanbaatar 62 47 54N 106 52 E
Ulan Ude 41 51 45N 107 40 E
Ulanga □ 95 8 40S 36 50 E
Ulanów 32 50 30N 22 16 E
Ulawa 68 9 46S 161 57 E
Ulaya, Morogoro, Tanz. 94 7 3S 36 55 E
Ulaya, Tabora, Tanz. 94 4 25S 33 30 E
Ulcinj 35 41 58N 19 10 E
Ulco 96 28 21S 24 15 E
Ulfborg 11 56 16N 8 20 E
Ulhasnagar 50 19 15N 73 10 E
Ulinda 77 31 35S 149 30 E
Uljma 33 45 2N 21 10 E
Ulla → 22 42 39N 8 44W
Ulladulla 76 35 21S 150 29 E
Ullånger 10 62 58N 18 10 E
Ullapool 14 57 54N 5 10W
Ullared 11 57 8N 12 42 E
Ulldecona 24 40 36N 0 20 E
Ullswater 12 54 35N 2 52W
Ullung-do 61 37 30N 130 30 E
Ulm 31 48 23N 10 0 E
Ulmarra 77 29 37S 153 4 E
Ulmeni 34 45 4N 26 40 E
Ulong 77 30 14S 152 54 E
Ulricehamn 11 57 46N 13 26 E
Ulsan 61 35 20N 129 15 E
Ulsberg 10 62 45N 9 59 E
Ulster □ 15 54 35N 6 30W
Ultima 74 35 30S 143 18 E
Ulubaria 49 22 31N 88 4 E
Uluguru Mts. 94 7 15S 37 40 E
Ulungur He 62 47 1N 87 24 E
Ulutau 40 48 39N 67 1 E
Ulverston 12 54 13N 3 7W
Ulverstone 72 41 11S 146 11 E
Ulya 41 59 10N 142 0 E
Ulyanovsk 37 54 20N 48 25 E
Ulyasutay (Javhlant) 62 47 56N 97 28 E
Ulysses 119 37 39N 101 25W
Um Qeis 44 32 40N 35 41 E
Umag 27 45 26N 13 31 E
Umala 136 17 25S 68 5W
Uman 38 48 40N 30 12 E
Umarkhed 50 19 37N 77 46 E
Umatac 68 13 18N 144 39 E
Umatilla 120 45 58N 119 17W
Umba 40 66 50N 34 20 E
Umbertide 27 43 18N 12 20 E
Umboi I. 69 5 40S 148 0 E
Umbrella Mts. 81 45 35S 169 5 E
Umbria □ 27 42 53N 12 30 E
Ume älv → 8 63 45N 20 20 E
Umeå 8 63 45N 20 20 E
Umera 57 0 12S 129 37 E
Umfuli → 95 17 30S 29 23 E
Umgusa 95 19 29S 27 52 E
Umi 64 33 34N 130 30 E
Umka 33 44 40N 20 19 E
Umkomaas 97 30 13S 30 48 E
Umm al Aranib 87 26 10N 14 43 E
Umm al Qaiwain 47 25 30N 55 35 E
Umm Arda 91 15 17N 32 31 E
Umm az Zamul 47 22 42N 55 18 E
Umm Bel 91 13 35N 28 0 E
Umm Digulgulaya 91 10 28N 24 58 E
Umm Dubban 91 15 23N 32 52 E
Umm el Fahm 44 32 31N 35 9 E
Umm Koweika 91 13 10N 32 16 E
Umm Lajj 46 25 0N 37 23 E
Umm Merwa 90 18 4N 32 30 E
Umm Qurein 91 16 3N 28 49 E
Umm Rumah 90 25 50N 36 30 E
Umm Ruwaba 91 12 50N 31 20 E
Umm Said 47 25 0N 51 40 E
Umm Sidr 91 14 29N 25 10 E
Ummanz 30 54 29N 13 9 E
Umnak 100 53 20N 168 20W
Umniati → 95 16 49S 28 45 E
Umpqua → 120 43 42N 124 3W
Umrer 50 20 51N 79 18 E
Umreth 48 22 41N 73 4 E
Umshandige Dam 95 20 10S 30 40 E
Umtali 95 18 58S 32 38 E
Umtata 97 31 36S 28 49 E
Umuahia 89 5 33N 7 29 E
Umvukwe Ra. 95 16 45S 30 45 E
Umvuma 95 19 16S 30 30 E
Umzimvubu 97 31 38S 29 33 E
Umzingwane → 95 22 12S 29 56 E
Umzinto 97 30 15S 30 45 E
Una 48 20 46N 71 8 E
Una → 27 45 16N 16 55 E
Unac → 27 44 30N 16 9 E
Unadilla 115 42 20N 75 17W
Unalaska 100 53 40N 166 40W
Unanderra 76 34 27S 150 49 E
Uncastillo 24 42 21N 1 8W
Uncía 136 18 25S 66 40W
Uncompahgre Pk. 121 38 5N 107 32W
Unden 11 58 45N 14 25 E
Undera 74 36 18S 145 13 E
Underbool 74 35 10S 141 51 E
Undersaker 10 63 19N 13 21 E
Undersvik 10 61 36N 16 20 E
Undu Pt. 68 16 8S 179 57W
Unecha 36 52 50N 32 37 E
Uneiuxi → 134 0 37S 65 34W
Ungarie 75 33 38S 146 56 E
Ungarra 73 34 12S 136 2 E
Ungava B. 101 59 30N 67 30W
Ungeny 38 47 11N 27 51 E
Ungwatiri 91 16 52N 36 10 E
União da Vitória 141 26 13S 51 5W
União dos Palmares 138 9 10S 36 2W
Unije 27 44 40N 14 15 E
Unimak 100 55 0N 164 0W
Unimak Pass. 100 53 30N 165 15W
Unini → 135 1 41S 61 31W
Union, Miss., U.S.A. 119 32 34N 89 14W
Union, Mo., U.S.A. 116 38 25N 91 0W
Union, S.C., U.S.A. 113 34 43N 81 39W
Union City, N.J., U.S.A. 115 40 47N 74 5W
Union City, Ohio, U.S.A. 117 40 11N 84 49W
Union City, Pa., U.S.A. 114 41 53N 79 50W
Union City, Tenn., U.S.A. 119 36 25N 89 0W
Union Gap 120 46 38N 120 29W
Union Grove 117 42 41N 88 3W
Unión, La, Chile 142 40 10S 73 0W
Unión, La, Colomb. 134 1 35N 77 5W
Unión, La, El Sal. 126 13 20N 87 50W
Unión, La 124 17 58N 101 49W
Unión, La, Peru 136 9 43S 76 45W
Unión, La, Spain 25 37 38N 0 53W
Union, Mt. 121 34 34N 112 21W
Union of Soviet Soc. Rep. ■ 41 60 0N 100 0 E
Union Springs 113 32 9N 85 44W
Union Star 116 39 59N 94 36W
Uniondale 96 33 39S 23 7 E
Uniontown, Ky., U.S.A. 117 37 47N 87 56W
Uniontown, Pa., U.S.A. 112 39 54N 79 45W
Unionville, Mich., U.S.A. 106 43 39N 83 28W
Unionville, Miss., U.S.A. 116 40 29N 93 1W
United Arab Emirates ■ 47 23 50N 54 0 E
United Kingdom ■ 7 55 0N 3 0W
United States of America ■ 111 37 0N 96 0W
U. S. Trust Terr. of the Pacific Is. 66 10 0N 160 0 E
Unity 109 52 30N 109 5W
Universales, Mtes. 24 40 18N 1 33W
University City 116 38 40N 90 20W
Unjha 48 23 46N 72 24 E
Unnao 49 26 35N 80 30 E
Uno, Ilha 88 11 15N 16 13W
Unst 14 60 50N 0 55W
Unstrut → 30 51 10N 11 48 E
Unuk → 108 56 5N 131 3W
Unumgar 77 28 25S 152 47 E
Ünye 38 41 5N 37 15 E
Unzen-Dake 64 32 45N 130 17 E
Unzha 37 58 0N 44 0 E
Unzha → 37 57 30N 43 40 E
Uozu 65 36 48N 137 24 E
Upa → 32 50 35N 16 15 E
Upal 91 6 56N 34 12 E
Upata 135 8 1N 62 24W
Upemba, L. 95 8 30S 26 20 E
Upernavik 144 72 49N 56 20W
Upington 96 28 25S 21 15 E
Upleta 48 21 46N 70 16 E
Upolu 68 13 58S 172 0W
Upper Alkali Lake 120 41 47N 120 8W
Upper Arlington 117 40 0N 83 4W
Upper Arrow L. 108 50 30N 117 50W
Upper Foster L. 109 56 47N 105 20W
Upper Horton 77 30 6S 150 26 E
Upper Hutt 80 41 8S 175 5 E
Upper Klamath L. 120 42 16N 121 55W
Upper L. Erne 15 54 14N 7 22W
Upper Lake 122 39 10N 122 55W
Upper Manilla 77 30 38S 150 40 E
Upper Musquodoboit 103 45 10N 62 58W
Upper Red L. 118 48 0N 95 0W
Upper Rouchel 77 32 6S 151 5 E
Upper Sandusky 117 40 50N 83 17W
Upper Taimyr → 41 74 15N 99 48 E
Upper Volta ■ 88 12 0N 1 0W
Upphärad 11 58 9N 12 19 E
Uppsala 10 59 53N 17 38 E
Uppsala län □ 10 60 0N 17 30 E
Upshi 49 33 48N 77 52 E
Upstart, C. 72 19 41S 147 45 E
Upton, Can. 105 45 39N 72 41W
Upton, U.S.A. 118 44 8N 104 35W
Ur 46 30 55N 46 25 E
Urabá, Golfo de 134 8 25N 76 53W
Uracara 136 2 20S 57 50W
Urach 31 48 29N 9 25 E
Urad Qianqi 60 40 40N 108 30 E
Uraga-Suidō 65 35 13N 139 45 E
Urakawa 63 42 9N 142 47 E
Ural → 40 47 0N 51 48 E
Ural, Mt. 73 33 21S 146 12 E
Ural Mts. = Uralskie Gory 40 60 0N 59 0 E
Uralla 77 30 37S 151 29 E
Uralsk 40 51 20N 51 20 E
Uralskie Gory 40 60 0N 59 0 E
Urambo 94 5 4S 32 0 E
Urambo □ 94 5 0S 32 0 E
Urandangie 72 21 32S 138 14 E
Uranium City 109 59 34N 108 37W
Uranquinty 76 35 10S 147 12 E
Uraricaá → 135 3 20N 61 56W
Uraricuera → 135 3 2N 60 30W
Uravakonda 51 14 57N 77 12 E
Urawa 65 35 50N 139 40 E
Uray 40 60 5N 65 15 E
Urbana, Ill., U.S.A. 117 40 7N 88 12W
Urbana, Mo., U.S.A. 116 37 51N 93 10W
Urbana, Ohio, U.S.A. 117 40 9N 83 44W
Urbana, La 134 7 8N 66 56W
Urbandale 116 41 38N 93 43W
Urbánia 27 43 40N 12 31 E
Urbano Santos 138 3 12S 43 23W
Urbel → 24 42 21N 3 40W
Urbenville 77 28 29S 152 34 E
Urbino 27 43 43N 12 38 E

Urbión, Picos de **24** 42 1N 2 52W
Urcos **136** 13 40S 71 38W
Urda, Spain **23** 39 25N 3 43W
Urda, U.S.S.R. **39** 48 52N 47 23 E
Urdinarrain **140** 32 37S 58 52W
Urdos **20** 42 51N 0 35W
Urdzhar **40** 47 5N 81 38 E
Ure → **12** 54 20N 1 25W
Uren **37** 57 35N 45 55 E
Urengoy **40** 65 58N 28 25 E
Ureparapara **68** 13 32S 167 20 E
Ures **124** 29 30N 110 30W
Ureshino **64** 33 6N 129 59 E
Urfa **46** 37 12N 38 50 E
Urfahr **33** 48 19N 14 17 E
Urgench **40** 41 40N 60 41 E
Urgun **47** 32 55N 69 12 E
Uri **49** 34 8N 74 2 E
Uri □ **31** 46 43N 8 35 E
Uribante → **134** 7 25N 71 50W
Uribe **134** 3 13N 74 24W
Uribia **134** 11 43N 72 16W
Urim **44** 31 18N 34 32 E
Uriondo **140** 21 41S 64 41W
Urique **124** 27 13N 107 55W
Urique → **124** 26 29N 107 58W
Urk **16** 52 39N 5 36 E
Urla **46** 38 20N 26 47 E
Urlati **34** 44 59N 26 15 E
Urmia = Rezā'īyeh **46** 37 40N 45 0 E
Urmia, L. = Rezā'īyeh, Daryācheh-ye **46** 37 30N 45 30 E
Uroševac **33** 42 23N 21 10 E
Urrao **134** 6 20N 76 11W
Urshult **11** 56 31N 14 50 E
Ursus **32** 52 12N 20 53 E
Uruaçu **139** 14 30S 49 10W
Uruana **139** 15 30S 49 41W
Uruapan **124** 19 30N 102 0W
Uruará → **135** 2 6S 53 38W
Urubamba **136** 13 20S 72 10W
Urubamba → **136** 10 43S 73 48W
Urubaxi → **135** 0 31S 64 50W
Urubu → **135** 2 55S 58 25W
Uruçara **135** 2 32S 57 45W
Uruçui **138** 7 20S 44 28W
Uruçui Prêto → **138** 7 20S 44 38W
Uruçuí, Serra do **138** 9 0S 44 45W
Urucuia → **139** 16 8S 45 5W
Urucurituba **135** 2 41S 57 40W
Uruguai → **141** 26 0S 53 30W
Uruguaiana **140** 29 50S 57 0W
Uruguay ■ **140** 32 30S 56 30W
Uruguay → **140** 34 12S 58 18W
Urumchi = Ürümqi **62** 43 45N 87 45 E
Ürümqi **62** 43 45N 87 45 E
Urunga **77** 30 31S 153 1 E
Urup → **39** 46 0N 41 10 E
Urup, Os. **41** 46 0N 151 0 E
Urutaí **139** 17 28S 48 12W
Uruzgan □ **47** 33 30N 66 0 E
Uryung-Khaya **41** 72 48N 113 23 E
Uryupinsk **37** 50 45N 41 58 E
Urzhum **37** 57 10N 49 56 E
Urziceni **34** 44 40N 26 42 E
Usa, Japan **64** 33 31N 131 21 E
Usa, Tanz. **40** 2 23S 36 52 E
Uşak **46** 38 43N 29 28 E
Usakos **96** 22 0S 15 31 E
Usborne, Mt. **142** 51 42S 58 50W
Ušče **33** 43 30N 20 39 E
Usedom **30** 53 50N 13 55 E
Usfan **90** 21 58N 39 27 E
Ush-Tobe **40** 45 16N 78 0 E
Ushakova, O. **144** 82 0N 80 0 E
Ushant = Ouessant, Île d' **18** 48 25N 5 5W
Ushashi **94** 1 59S 33 57 E
Ushat **91** 7 59N 29 28 E
Ushibuka **64** 32 11N 130 1 E
Ushuaia **142** 54 50S 68 23W
Ushumun **41** 52 47N 126 32 E
Usk → **13** 51 37N 2 56W
Üsküdar **46** 41 0N 29 5 E
Uslar **30** 51 39N 9 39 E
Usman **37** 52 5N 39 48 E
Usoke **94** 5 7S 32 19 E
Usolye Sibirskoye **41** 52 48N 103 40 E
Usoro **89** 5 33N 6 11 E
Uspallata, P. de **140** 32 37S 69 22W
Uspenskiy **40** 48 41N 72 43 E
Ussel **20** 45 32N 2 18 E
Ussuriysk **41** 43 48N 131 59 E
Ust-Aldan = Batamay **41** 63 30N 129 15 E
Ust Amginskoye = Khandyga **41** 62 42N 135 0 E
Ust-Bolsheretsk **41** 52 50N 156 15 E
Ust Buzulukskaya **37** 50 8N 42 11 E
Ust chaun **41** 68 47N 170 30 E
Ust-Donetskiy **39** 47 35N 40 55 E
Ust'-Ilga **41** 55 5N 104 55 E
Ust Ilimpeya = Yukti **41** 63 20N 105 0 E
Ust-Ilimsk **41** 58 3N 102 39 E
Ust Ishim **40** 57 45N 71 10 E
Ust-Kamchatsk **41** 56 10N 162 28 E
Ust-Kamenogorsk **40** 50 0N 82 36 E
Ust-Karenga **41** 54 25N 116 30 E
Ust Khayryuzova **41** 57 15N 156 45 E
Ust-Kut **41** 56 50N 105 42 E
Ust Kuyga **41** 70 1N 135 43 E
Ust-Labinsk **39** 45 15N 39 41 E
Ust Luga **36** 59 35N 28 20 E
Ust Maya **41** 60 30N 134 28 E
Ust-Mil **41** 59 40N 133 11 E
Ust-Nera **41** 64 35N 143 15 E
Ust-Nyukzha **41** 56 34N 121 37 E
Ust Olenek **41** 73 0N 119 48 E
Ust-Omchug **41** 61 9N 149 38 E
Ust Port **40** 69 40N 84 26 E
Ust Tsilma **40** 65 25N 52 0 E
Ust-Tungir **41** 55 25N 120 36 E
Ust Urt = Ustyurt **40** 44 0N 55 0 E
Ust Vorkuta **40** 67 24N 64 0 E
Ustaoset **10** 60 30N 8 2 E
Ustaritz **20** 43 24N 1 27W
Uste **37** 59 35N 39 40 E
Ústí nad Labem **32** 50 41N 14 3 E
Ústí nad Orlicí **32** 49 58N 16 24 E
Ustica **28** 38 42N 13 10 E
Ustka **32** 54 35N 16 55 E
Ustrzyki Dolne **32** 49 27N 22 40 E
Ustye **41** 57 46N 94 37 E
Ustyurt, Plato **40** 44 0N 55 0 E
Ustyuzhna **37** 58 50N 36 32 E
Usu **62** 44 27N 84 40 E
Usuki **64** 33 8N 131 49 E
Usulután **126** 13 25N 88 28W
Usumacinta → **125** 17 0N 91 0W
Usure **94** 4 40S 34 22 E
Uta **57** 4 33S 136 0 E
'Uta Vava'u **68** 18 36S 174 0W
Utah □ **120** 39 30N 111 30W
Utah, L. **120** 40 10N 111 58W
Ute Cr. **119** 35 21N 103 45W
Utena **36** 55 27N 25 40 E
Ütersen **30** 53 40N 9 40 E
Utete **94** 8 0S 38 45 E
Uthai Thani **54** 15 22N 100 3 E
Uthal **48** 25 44N 66 40 E
Uthmaniyah **46** 25 5N 49 22 E
Utiariti **137** 13 0S 58 10W
Utica, Mich., U.S.A. **106** 42 38N 83 2W
Utica, N.Y., U.S.A. **115** 43 5N 75 18W
Utica, Ohio, U.S.A. **114** 40 13N 82 26W
Utiel **24** 39 37N 1 11W
Utik L. **109** 55 15N 96 0W
Utikuma L. **108** 55 50N 115 30W
Utinga **139** 12 6S 41 5W
Uto **64** 32 41N 130 40 E
Utrecht, Neth. **16** 52 5N 5 8 E
Utrecht, S. Afr. **97** 27 38S 30 20 E
Utrecht □ **16** 52 6N 5 7 E
Utrera **23** 37 12N 5 48W
Utsjoki **8** 69 51N 26 59 E
Utsunomiya **65** 36 30N 139 50 E
Uttar Pradesh □ **49** 27 0N 80 0 E
Uttaradit **54** 17 36N 100 5 E
Uttoxeter **12** 52 53N 1 50W
Ütze **30** 52 28N 10 11 E
Uusikaupunki **9** 60 47N 21 25 E
Uvá → **134** 3 41N 70 3W
Uvalde **119** 29 15N 99 48W
Uvarovo **37** 51 59N 42 14 E
Uvat **40** 59 5N 68 50 E
Uvéa, Î. **68** 20 30S 166 35 E
Uvinza **94** 5 5S 30 24 E
Uvira **94** 3 22S 29 3 E
Uvs Nuur **62** 50 20N 92 30 E
Uwa **64** 33 22N 132 31 E
Uwainid **46** 24 50N 46 0 E
Uwajima **64** 33 10N 132 35 E
Uweinat, Jebel **90** 21 54N 24 58 E
Uxbridge **106** 44 6N 79 7W
Uxin Qi **60** 38 50N 109 5 E
Uxmal **125** 20 22N 89 46W
Uyandi **41** 69 19N 141 0 E
Uyo **89** 5 1N 7 53 E
Uyu → **52** 24 51N 94 57 E
Uyuni **136** 20 28S 66 47W
Uzbek S.S.R. □ **40** 41 30N 65 0 E
Uzen, Bol. → **37** 50 0N 49 30 E
Uzen, Mal. → **37** 50 0N 48 30 E
Uzerche **20** 45 25N 1 34 E
Uzès **21** 44 1N 4 26 E
Uzh → **36** 51 15N 30 12 E
Uzhgorod **36** 48 36N 22 18 E
Uzlovaya **37** 54 0N 38 5 E
Uzunköprü **35** 41 16N 26 43 E

V

Vaal → **96** 29 4S 23 38 E
Vaaldam **97** 27 0S 28 14 E
Vaalwater **97** 24 15S 28 8 E
Vaasa **8** 63 6N 21 38 E
Vaasan lääni □ **8** 63 2N 22 50 E
Vabre **20** 43 42N 2 24 E
Vác **33** 47 49N 19 10 E
Vacaria **141** 28 31S 50 52W
Vacaville **122** 38 21N 122 0W
Vaccarès, Étang de **21** 43 32N 4 34 E
Vach → **40** 60 45N 76 38 E
Vache, Î.-à- **127** 18 2N 73 35W
Väddö **10** 59 55N 18 50 E
Vadnagar **48** 23 47N 72 40 E
Vado Lígure **26** 44 16N 8 26 E
Vadodara **48** 22 20N 73 10 E
Vadsø **8** 70 3N 29 50 E
Vadstena **11** 58 28N 14 54 E
Vaduz **31** 47 8N 9 31 E
Værøy **8** 67 40N 12 40 E
Vagney **19** 48 1N 6 43 E
Vagnhärad **10** 58 57N 17 33 E
Vagos **22** 40 33N 8 42W
Váh → **33** 47 55N 18 0 E
Vahsel B. **143** 75 0S 35 0W
Vaigach **40** 70 10N 59 0 E
Vaigai → **51** 9 15N 79 10 E
Vaiges **18** 48 2N 0 30W
Vaihingen **31** 48 55N 8 58 E
Vaijapur **50** 19 58N 74 45 E
Vaikam **51** 9 45N 76 25 E
Vailly Aisne **19** 49 25N 3 30 E
Vaippar → **51** 9 0N 78 25 E
Vaison **21** 44 14N 5 4 E
Vaitogi **68** 14 21S 170 44W
Vajpur **50** 21 24N 73 17 E
Val-Alain **105** 46 24N 71 45W
Val-Barrette **104** 46 30N 75 2[illegible]W
Val Caron **106** 46 37N 81 1W
Val-d'Ajol, Le **19** 47 55N 6 30 E
Val-de-Marne □ **19** 48 45N 2 28 E
Val-des-Bois **104** 45 54N 75 35W
Val-d'Oise □ **19** 49 5N 2 10 E
Val d'Or **104** 48 7N 77 47W
Val Marie **109** 49 15N 107 45W
Valadares **22** 41 5N 8 38W
Valahia **34** 44 35N 25 0 E
Valais □ **31** 46 12N 7 45 E
Valandovo **35** 41 19N 22 34 E
Valcheta **142** 40 40S 66 8W
Valcourt **105** 45 29N 72 18W
Valdagno **27** 45 38N 11 18 E
Valdahon, Le **19** 47 8N 6 20 E
Valday **36** 57 58N 33 9 E
Valdayskaya Vozvyshennost **36** 57 0N 33 30 E
Valdeazogues → **23** 38 45N 4 55W
Valdemarsvik **11** 58 14N 16 40 E
Valdepeñas, Ciudad Real, Spain **23** 38 43N 3 25W
Valdepeñas, Jaén, Spain **23** 37 33N 3 47W
Valderaduey → **22** 41 31N 5 42W
Valderrobres **24** 40 53N 0 9 E
Valdés, Pen. **142** 42 30S 63 45W
Valdez, Ecuador **134** 1 15N 79 0W
Valdez, U.S.A. **100** 61 14N 76 17W
Valdivia, Chile **142** 39 50S 73 14W
Valdivia, Colomb. **134** 7 11N 75 27W
Valdivia □ **142** 40 0S 73 0W
Valdobbiádene **27** 45 53N 12 0 E
Valdosta **113** 30 50N 83 20W
Valdoviño **22** 43 36N 8 8W
Valdres **10** 60 55N 9 28 E
Vale, U.S.A. **120** 44 0N 117 15W
Vale, U.S.S.R. **39** 41 30N 42 58 E
Valea lui Mihai **34** 47 32N 22 11 E
Valença, Brazil **139** 13 20S 39 5W
Valença, Port. **22** 42 1N 8 34W
Valença do Piauí **138** 6 20S 41 45W
Valençay **19** 47 9N 1 34 E
Valence **21** 44 57N 4 54 E
Valence-d'Agen **20** 44 8N 0 54 E
Valencia, Spain **25** 39 27N 0 23W
Valencia, Venez. **134** 10 11N 68 0W
Valencia □ **25** 39 20N 0 40W
Valencia, Albufera de **25** 39 20N 0 27W
Valencia de Alcántara **23** 39 25N 7 14W
Valencia de Don Juan **22** 42 17N 5 31W
Valencia del Ventoso **23** 38 15N 6 29W
Valencia, G. de **25** 39 30N 0 20 E
Valenciennes **19** 50 20N 3 34 E
Valensole **21** 43 50N 5 59 E
Valentia Hr. **15** 51 56N 10 17W
Valentia I. **15** 51 54N 10 22W
Valentim, Sa. do **138** 6 0S 43 30W
Valentine, Nebr., U.S.A. **118** 42 50N 100 35W
Valentine, Tex., U.S.A. **119** 30 36N 104 28W
Valenza **26** 45 2N 8 39 E
Valera **134** 9 19N 70 37W
Valguarnera Caropepe **29** 37 30N 14 22 E
Valier **120** 48 25N 112 9W
Valinco, G. de **21** 41 40N 8 52 E
Valjevo **33** 44 18N 19 53 E
Valkenswaard **16** 51 21N 5 29 E
Vall de Uxó **24** 39 49N 0 15W
Valla **10** 59 2N 16 20 E
Valladolid, Mexico **125** 20 40N 88 11W
Valladolid, Spain **22** 41 38N 4 43W
Valladolid □ **22** 41 38N 4 43W
Vallata **29** 41 3N 15 16 E
Valldemosa **24** 39 43N 2 37 E
Valle d'Aosta □ **26** 45 45N 7 22 E
Valle de Arán **24** 42 50N 0 55 E
Valle de Cabuérniga **22** 43 14N 4 18W
Valle de la Pascua **134** 9 13N 66 0W
Valle de las Palmas **123** 32 20N 116 43W
Valle de Santiago **124** 20 25N 101 15W
Valle de Zaragoza **124** 27 28N 105 49W
Valle del Cauca □ **134** 3 45N 76 30W
Valle Fértil, Sierra del **140** 30 20S 68 0W
Valle Hermoso **125** 25 35N 97 40W
Valle Nacional **125** 17 47N 96 19W
Vallecas **22** 40 23N 3 41W
Valledupar **134** 10 29N 73 15W
Vallée-Jonction **105** 46 22N 70 55W
Vallejo **122** 38 12N 122 15W
Vallenar **140** 28 30S 70 50W
Valleraugue **20** 44 6N 3 39 E
Vallet **18** 47 10N 1 15W
Valletta **87** 35 54N 14 30 E
Valley Center **123** 33 13N 117 2W
Valley City **118** 46 57N 98 0W
Valley Falls **120** 42 33N 120 16W
Valley Park **116** 38 33N 90 29W
Valley Springs **122** 38 11N 120 50W
Valley Station **117** 38 25N 85 50W
Valley Wells **123** 35 27N 115 46W
Valleyview **108** 55 5N 117 17W
Valli di Comácchio **27** 44 40N 12 15 E
Vallimanca, Arroyo **140** 35 40S 59 10W
Vallo della Lucánia **29** 40 14N 15 16 E
Vallon **21** 44 25N 4 23 E
Vallorbe **31** 46 42N 6 20 E
Valls **24** 41 18N 1 15 E
Vallsta **10** 61 31N 16 22 E
Valmaseda **24** 43 11N 3 12W
Valmeyer **116** 38 18N 90 19W
Valmiera **36** 57 37N 25 29 E
Valmont **18** 49 45N 0 30 E
Valmontone **28** 41 48N 12 55 E
Valmy **19** 49 5N 4 45 E
Valnera, Mte. **24** 43 9N 3 40W
Valognes **18** 49 30N 1 28W
Valona = Vlóra **35** 40 32N 19 28 E
Valongo **22** 41 8N 8 30W
Valpaços **22** 41 36N 7 17W
Valparaíso, Chile **140** 33 2S 71 40W
Valparaíso, Mexico **124** 22 50N 103 32W
Valparaiso **117** 41 27N 87 2W
Valparaíso □ **140** 33 2S 71 40W
Valpovo **33** 45 39N 18 25 E
Valréas **21** 44 24N 5 0 E
Vals **31** 46 39N 9 11 E
Vals → **96** 27 23S 26 30 E
Vals-les-Bains **21** 44 42N 4 24 E
Vals, Tanjung **57** 8 26S 137 25 E
Valsbaai **96** 34 15S 18 40 E
Valskog **10** 59 27N 15 57 E
Válta **35** 40 3N 23 25 E
Valtellina **26** 46 9N 9 55 E
Valuyki **37** 50 10N 38 5 E
Valverde del Camino **23** 37 35N 6 47W
Valverde del Fresno **22** 40 15N 6 51W
Vama **34** 47 34N 25 42 E
Vámos **35** 35 24N 24 13 E
Vamsadhara → **50** 18 21N 84 8 E
Van **46** 38 30N 43 20 E
Van Alstyne **119** 33 25N 96 36W
Van Bruyssel **105** 47 56N 72 9W
Van Buren, Can. **103** 47 10N 67 55W
Van Buren, Ark., U.S.A. **119** 35 28N 94 18W
Van Buren, Me., U.S.A. **113** 47 10N 68 1W
Van Buren, Mo., U.S.A. **119** 37 0N 91 0W
Van Canh **54** 13 37N 109 0 E
Van der Kloof Dam **96** 30 04S 24 40 E
Van Diemen, C., N.T., Austral. **78** 11 9S 130 24 E
Van Diemen, C., Queens., Austral. **72** 16 30S 139 46 E
Van Diemen G. **78** 11 45S 132 0 E
Van Gölü **46** 38 30N 43 0 E
Van Horn **119** 31 3N 104 55W
Van Horne **116** 42 1N 92 4W
Van Ninh **54** 12 42N 109 14 E

Van Reenen P. **97** 28 22S 29 27 E
Van Rees, Pegunungan **57** 2 35S 138 15 E
Van Tassell **118** 42 40N 104 3W
Van Tivu, I. **51** 8 51N 78 15 E
Van Wert **117** 40 52N 84 31W
Van Yen **54** 21 4N 104 42 E
Vanavara **41** 60 22N 102 16 E
Vanceburg **117** 38 36N 83 19W
Vancouver, Can. **108** 49 15N 123 10W
Vancouver, U.S.A. **122** 45 44N 122 41W
Vancouver, C. **79** 35 2S 118 11 E
Vancouver I. **108** 49 50N 126 0W
Vandalia, Ill., U.S.A. **116** 38 57N 89 4W
Vandalia, Mo., U.S.A. **116** 39 18N 91 30W
Vandalia, Ohio, U.S.A. **117** 39 54N 84 12W
Vandeloos Bay **51** 8 0N 81 45 E
Vandenburg **123** 34 35N 120 33W
Vanderbijlpark **97** 26 42S 27 54 E
Vanderbilt **106** 45 9N 84 40W
Vandergrift **114** 40 36N 79 33W
Vanderhoof **108** 54 0N 124 0W
Vanderlin I. **72** 15 44S 137 2 E
Vandry **105** 47 52N 73 34W
Vandyke **72** 24 10S 147 51 E
Vänern **11** 58 47N 13 30 E
Vänersborg **11** 58 26N 12 19 E
Vang Vieng **54** 18 58N 102 32 E
Vanga **94** 4 35S 39 12 E
Vangaindrano **97** 23 21S 47 36 E
Vanguard **109** 49 55N 107 20W
Vangunu **68** 8 40S 158 5 E
Vanier **107** 45 27N 75 40W
Vanimo **69** 2 42S 141 21 E
Vanivilasa Sagara **51** 13 45N 76 30 E
Vaniyambadi **51** 12 46N 78 44 E
Vankarem **41** 67 51N 175 50 E
Vankleek Hill **107** 45 32N 74 40W
Vanna **8** 70 6N 19 50 E
Vännäs **8** 63 58N 19 48 E
Vannes **18** 47 40N 2 47W
Vanoise, Massif de la **21** 45 25N 6 40 E
Vanrhynsdorp **96** 31 36S 18 44 E
Vanrook **72** 16 57S 141 57 E
Vans, Les **21** 44 25N 4 7 E
Vansbro **10** 60 32N 14 15 E
Vansittart B. **78** 14 3S 126 17 E
Vanthli **48** 21 28N 70 25 E
Vanua Levu **68** 16 33S 179 15 E
Vanua Mbalavu **68** 17 40S 178 57W
Vanwyksvlei **96** 30 18S 21 49 E
Vapnyarka **38** 48 32N 28 45 E
Var □ **21** 43 27N 6 18 E
Var → **21** 43 39N 7 12 E
Vara **11** 58 16N 12 55 E
Varada → **51** 15 0N 75 40 E
Varades **18** 47 25N 1 1W
Varaita → **26** 44 49N 7 36 E
Varallo **26** 45 50N 8 13 E
Varanasi (Benares) **49** 25 22N 83 0 E
Varangerfjorden **8** 70 3N 29 25 E
Varazdin **27** 46 20N 16 20 E
Varazze **26** 44 21N 8 36 E
Varberg **11** 57 6N 12 20 E
Varde **11** 55 38N 8 29 E
Varde Å **11** 55 35N 8 19 E
Varel **30** 53 23N 8 9 E
Varella, Mui **54** 12 54N 109 26 E
Varena **36** 54 12N 24 30 E
Varennes-sur-Allier **20** 46 19N 3 24 E
Vareš **33** 44 12N 18 23 E
Varese **26** 45 49N 8 50 E
Varese Lígure **26** 44 22N 9 33 E
Vårgårda **11** 58 2N 12 49 E
Vargem Bonita **139** 20 20S 46 22W
Vargem Grande **138** 3 33S 43 56W
Varginha **141** 21 33S 45 25W
Vargön **11** 58 22N 12 20 E
Variadero **119** 35 43N 104 17W
Varillas **140** 24 0S 70 10W
Väring **11** 58 30N 14 0 E
Värmeln **10** 59 35N 12 54 E
Värmlands län □ **10** 60 0N 13 20 E
Varna, Bulg. **34** 43 13N 27 56 E
Varna, U.S.A. **116** 41 2N 89 14W
Varna → **50** 16 48N 74 32 E
Värnamo **11** 57 10N 14 3 E
Värö **11** 57 16N 12 11 E
Vars **107** 45 21N 75 21W
Varvarin **33** 43 43N 21 20 E
Varzaneh **47** 32 25N 52 40 E
Várzea Alegre **138** 6 47S 39 17W
Várzea da Palma **139** 17 36S 44 44W
Várzea Grande **137** 15 39S 56 8W
Varzi **26** 44 50N 9 12 E
Varzo **26** 46 12N 8 15 E
Varzy **19** 47 22N 3 20 E
Vasa **8** 63 6N 21 38 E
Vasa Barris → **138** 11 10S 37 10W
Vascâo → **23** 37 31N 7 31W
Vaşcău **34** 46 28N 22 30 E
Vascongadas **24** 42 50N 2 45W
Väse **10** 59 23N 13 52 E
Vasht = Khāsh **47** 28 14N 61 14 E
Vasilevichi **36** 52 15N 29 50 E
Vasilikón **35** 38 25N 23 40 E
Vasilkov **36** 50 7N 30 15 E
Vaslui **34** 46 38N 27 42 E
Väsman **10** 60 9N 15 5 E
Vassar, Can. **109** 49 10N 95 55W
Vassar, U.S.A. **106** 43 23N 83 33W
Västeräs **11** 59 37N 16 38 E
Västerbottens län □ **8** 64 58N 18 0 E
Västernorrlands län □ **10** 63 30N 17 30 E
Västervik **11** 57 43N 16 43 E
Västmanlands län □ **10** 59 45N 16 20 E
Vasto **27** 42 8N 14 40 E
Vasvár **33** 47 3N 16 47 E
Vatan **19** 47 4N 1 50 E
Vaté = Efate, I. **68** 17 40S 168 25 E
Vathí **35** 37 46N 27 1 E
Váthia **35** 36 29N 22 29 E
Vatican City ■ **27** 41 54N 12 27 E
Vaticano, C. **28** 38 40N 15 48 E
Vatnajökull **8** 64 30N 16 48W
Vatnås **10** 59 58N 9 37 E
Vatneyri **8** 65 35N 24 0W
Vatoloha, Mt. **97** 17 52S 47 48 E
Vatomandry **97** 19 20S 48 59 E
Vatra-Dornei **34** 47 22N 25 22 E
Vättern **11** 58 25N 14 30 E
Vatulele **68** 18 33S 177 37 E
Vaucluse □ **21** 44 3N 5 10 E
Vaucouleurs **19** 48 37N 5 40 E
Vaud □ **31** 46 35N 6 30 E
Vaughan **121** 34 37N 105 12W
Vaughn **120** 47 37N 111 36W
Vaupe □ **134** 1 0N 71 0W
Vaupés → **134** 0 2N 67 16W
Vauvert **21** 43 42N 4 17 E
Vauxhall **108** 50 5N 112 9W
Vavincourt **19** 48 49N 5 12 E
Vavoua **88** 7 23N 6 29W
Vaxholm **10** 59 25N 18 20 E
Växjö **11** 56 52N 14 50 E
Vaygach, Ostrov **40** 70 0N 60 0 E
Veadeiros **139** 14 7S 47 31W
Vechta **30** 52 47N 8 18 E
Vechte → **16** 52 34N 6 6 E
Vecilla, La **22** 42 51N 5 27W
Vecsés **33** 47 26N 19 19 E
Vedaraniam **51** 10 25N 79 50 E
Veddige **11** 57 17N 12 20 E
Vedea → **34** 44 0N 25 20 E
Vedia **140** 34 30S 61 31W
Vedra, Isla del **25** 38 52N 1 12 E
Veendam **16** 53 5N 6 52 E
Veenendaal **16** 52 2N 5 34 E
Vefsna → **8** 65 48N 13 10 E
Vega, Norway **8** 65 40N 11 55 E
Vega, U.S.A. **119** 35 18N 102 26W
Vega, La, Dom. Rep. **127** 19 20N 70 30W
Vega, La, Peru **136** 10 41S 77 44W
Vegadeo **22** 43 27N 7 4W
Vegafjorden **8** 65 37N 12 0 E
Vegesack **30** 53 10N 8 38 E
Veghel **16** 51 37N 5 32 E
Vegorritis, Límni **35** 40 45N 21 45 E
Vegreville **108** 53 30N 112 5W
Vegusdal **11** 58 32N 8 10 E
Veii **27** 42 0N 12 24 E
Vejen **11** 55 30N 9 9 E
Vejer de la Frontera **23** 36 15N 5 59W
Vejle **11** 55 43N 9 30 E
Vejle Fjord **11** 55 40N 9 50 E
Vela, La **134** 11 27N 69 34W
Vela Luka **27** 42 59N 16 44 E
Velanai I. **51** 9 45N 79 45 E
Velarde **121** 36 11N 106 1W
Velas, C. **126** 10 21N 85 52W
Velasco **119** 29 0N 95 20W
Velasco, Sierra de. **140** 29 20S 67 10W
Velay, Mts. du **20** 45 0N 3 40 E
Velddrif **96** 32 42S 18 11 E
Velebit Planina **27** 44 50N 15 20 E
Velebitski Kanal **27** 44 45N 14 55 E
Veleka → **34** 42 4N 27 58 E
Velenje **27** 46 23N 15 8 E
Velestínon **35** 39 23N 22 43 E
Veleta, La **23** 37 1N 3 22W
Vélez **134** 6 1N 73 41W
Vélez Blanco **25** 37 41N 2 5W
Vélez Málaga **23** 36 48N 4 5W
Vélez Rubio **25** 37 41N 2 5W
Velhas → **139** 17 13S 44 49W
Velika **33** 45 27N 17 40 E
Velika Gorica **27** 45 44N 16 5 E
Velika Kapela **27** 45 10N 15 5 E
Velika Kladuša **27** 45 11N 15 48 E
Velika Morava → **33** 44 43N 21 3 E
Velikaya → **36** 57 48N 28 20 E
Velike Lašče **27** 45 49N 14 45 E
Velikiye Luki **36** 56 25N 30 32 E
Velikonda Range **51** 14 45N 79 10 E
Velikoye, Oz. **37** 55 15N 40 10 E
Velingrad **35** 42 4N 23 58 E
Velino, Mte. **27** 42 10N 13 20 E
Velizh **36** 55 36N 31 11 E
Velke Meziřici **32** 49 21N 16 1 E
Vella G. **68** 8 0S 156 50 E
Vella Lavella **68** 7 45S 156 40 E
Vellar → **51** 11 30N 79 36 E
Velletri **28** 41 43N 12 43 E
Vellinge **11** 55 29N 13 0 E
Vellore **51** 12 57N 79 10 E
Velsen-Noord **16** 52 27N 4 40 E
Velten **30** 52 40N 13 11 E
Velva **118** 48 6N 100 56W
Vembanad Lake **51** 9 36N 76 15 E
Veme **10** 60 14N 10 7 E
Ven **11** 55 55N 12 45 E
Vena **11** 57 31N 16 0 E
Venado **124** 22 56N 101 10W
Venado Tuerto **140** 33 50S 62 0W
Venafro **29** 41 28N 14 3 E
Venarey-les-Laumes **19** 47 32N 4 26 E
Venaria **26** 45 6N 7 39 E
Venčane **33** 44 24N 20 28 E
Vence **21** 43 43N 7 6 E
Vendas Novas **23** 38 39N 8 27W
Vendée □ **18** 46 50N 1 35W
Vendée → **18** 46 20N 1 10W
Vendée, Collines de **18** 46 35N 0 45W
Vendeuvre-sur-Barse **19** 48 14N 4 28 E
Vendôme **18** 47 47N 1 3 E
Vendrell **24** 41 10N 1 30 E
Vendsyssel **11** 57 22N 10 0 E
Véneta, Laguna **27** 45 23N 12 25 E
Véneto □ **27** 45 40N 12 0 E
Venev **37** 54 22N 38 17 E
Venézia **27** 45 27N 12 20 E
Venézia, Golfo di **27** 45 20N 13 0 E
Venezuela ■ **134** 8 0N 65 0W
Venezuela, Golfo de **134** 11 30N 71 0W
Vengurla **51** 15 53N 73 45 E
Vengurla Rocks **51** 15 55N 73 22 E
Venice = Venézia **27** 45 27N 12 20 E
Vénissieux **21** 45 43N 4 53 E
Venkatagiri **51** 14 0N 79 35 E
Venkatapuram **50** 18 20N 80 30 E
Venlo **16** 51 22N 6 11 E
Venosta **104** 45 52N 76 1W
Venraij **16** 51 31N 6 0 E
Vent, Is. du **68** 17 30S 149 30W
Venta de Cardeña **23** 38 16N 4 20W
Venta de San Rafael **22** 40 42N 4 12W
Venta, La **125** 18 8N 94 3W
Ventana, Punta de la **124** 24 4N 109 48W
Ventana, Sa. de la **140** 38 0S 62 30W
Ventersburg **96** 28 7S 27 9 E
Ventimíglia **26** 43 50N 7 39 E
Ventnor **13** 50 35N 1 12W
Ventotene **28** 40 48N 13 25 E
Ventoux **21** 44 10N 5 17 E
Ventspils **36** 57 25N 21 32 E
Ventuarí → **134** 3 58N 67 2W
Ventucopa **123** 34 50N 119 29W
Ventura **123** 34 16N 119 18W
Ventura, La **124** 24 38N 100 54W
Venturosa, La **134** 6 8N 68 48W
Venus B. **74** 38 40S 145 42 E
Vera, Argent. **140** 29 30S 60 20W
Vera, Spain **25** 37 15N 1 51W
Veracruz **125** 19 10N 96 10W
Veracruz □ **125** 19 0N 96 15W
Veraval **48** 20 53N 70 27 E
Verbánia **26** 45 56N 8 43 E
Verbicaro **29** 39 46N 15 54 E
Vercelli **26** 45 19N 8 25 E
Verchères **105** 45 47N 73 21W
Verde →, Argent. **142** 41 56S 65 5W
Verde →, Goiás, Brazil **139** 19 11S 50 44W
Verde →, Goiás, Brazil **139** 18 1S 50 14W
Verde →, Mato Grosso, Brazil **137** 11 54S 55 48W
Verde →, Mato Grosso, Brazil **137** 21 25S 56 20W
Verde →, Chihuahua, Mexico **124** 26 29N 107 58W
Verde →, Oaxaca, Mexico **125** 15 59N 97 50W
Verde →, Veracruz, Mexico **124** 21 10N 102 50W
Verde →, Parag. **140** 23 9S 57 37W
Verde, Cay **126** 23 0N 75 5W
Verde Grande → **139** 16 13S 43 49W
Verde Pequeno → **139** 14 48S 43 31W
Verden **30** 52 58N 9 18 E
Verdi **122** 39 31N 119 59W
Verdigre **118** 42 38N 98 0W
Verdon → **21** 43 43N 5 46 E
Verdon-sur-Mer, Le **20** 45 33N 1 4W
Verdun **19** 49 12N 5 24 E
Verdun-sur-le Doubs **19** 46 54N 5 0 E
Vereeniging **97** 26 38S 27 57 E
Vérendrye, Parc Prov. de la **104** 47 20N 76 40W
Verga, C. **88** 10 30N 14 10W
Vergara **24** 43 9N 2 28W
Vergato **26** 44 18N 11 8 E
Vergemont **72** 23 33S 143 1 E
Vergemont Cr. → **72** 24 16S 143 16 E
Vergennes **115** 44 9N 73 15W
Vergt **20** 45 2N 0 43 E
Verín **22** 41 57N 7 27W
Veriña **22** 43 32N 5 43W
Verkhnedvinsk **36** 55 45N 27 58 E
Verkhnevilyuysk **41** 63 27N 120 18 E
Verkhneye Kalinino **41** 59 54N 108 8 E
Verkhniy Baskunchak **39** 48 14N 46 44 E
Verkhovye **37** 52 55N 37 15 E
Verkhoyansk **41** 67 35N 133 25 E
Verkhoyanskiy Khrebet **41** 66 0N 129 0 E
Verlo **109** 50 19N 108 35W
Verma **10** 62 21N 8 3 E
Vermenton **19** 47 40N 3 42 E
Vermilion **109** 53 20N 110 50W
Vermilion →, Alta., Can. **109** 53 22N 110 51W
Vermilion →, Qué., Can. **105** 47 38N 72 56W
Vermilion →, Ill., U.S.A. **116** 41 19N 89 5W
Vermilion →, Ind., U.S.A. **117** 39 57N 87 27W
Vermilion, B. **119** 29 45N 91 55W
Vermilion Bay **109** 49 51N 93 34W
Vermilion Chutes **108** 58 22N 114 51W
Vermilion L. **118** 47 53N 92 25W
Vermillion **118** 42 50N 96 56W
Vermont **116** 40 18N 90 26W
Vermont □ **115** 43 40N 72 50W
Vernal **120** 40 28N 109 35W
Vernalis **122** 37 36N 121 17W
Verner **106** 46 25N 80 8W
Verneuil-sur-Avre **18** 48 45N 0 55 E
Vernon, Can. **108** 50 20N 119 15W
Vernon, France **18** 49 5N 1 30 E
Vernon, Ill., U.S.A. **116** 38 48N 89 5W
Vernon, Ind., U.S.A. **117** 38 59N 85 36W
Vernon, Tex., U.S.A. **119** 34 10N 99 20W
Vernonia **122** 45 52N 123 11W
Vero Beach **113** 27 39N 80 23W
Véroia **35** 40 34N 22 12 E
Verolanuova **26** 45 20N 10 5 E
Véroli **28** 41 43N 13 24 E
Verona, Can. **107** 44 29N 76 42W
Verona, Italy **26** 45 27N 11 0 E
Verona, U.S.A. **116** 42 59N 89 32W
Veropol **41** 65 15N 168 40 E
Versailles, France **19** 48 48N 2 8 E
Versailles, Ill., U.S.A. **116** 39 53N 90 39W
Versailles, Ind., U.S.A. **117** 39 4N 85 15W
Versailles, Ky., U.S.A. **117** 38 3N 84 44W
Versailles, Mo., U.S.A. **116** 38 26N 92 51W
Versailles, Ohio, U.S.A. **117** 40 13N 84 29W
Versalles **137** 12 44S 63 18W
Vert, C. **88** 14 45N 17 30W
Verte, I. **105** 48 2N 69 26W
Vertou **18** 47 10N 1 28W
Vertus **19** 48 54N 4 0 E
Verulam **97** 29 38S 31 2 E
Verviers **16** 50 37N 5 52 E
Vervins **19** 49 50N 3 53 E
Verwood **109** 49 30N 105 40W
Verzej **27** 46 34N 16 13 E
Veselí nad Lužnicí **32** 49 12N 14 43 E
Veselovskoye Vdkhr. **39** 47 0N 41 0 E
Veshenskaya **39** 49 35N 41 44 E
Vesle → **19** 49 23N 3 38 E
Vesoul **19** 47 40N 6 11 E
Vessigebro **11** 56 58N 12 40 E
Vest-Agder fylke □ **9** 58 30N 7 15 E
Vesta **126** 9 43N 83 3W
Vestfjorden **8** 67 55N 14 0 E
Vestmannaeyjar **8** 63 27N 20 15W
Vestmarka **10** 59 56N 11 59 E
Vestone **26** 45 43N 10 25 E
Vestsjællands Amtskommune □ **11** 55 30N 11 20 E
Vestspitsbergen **144** 78 40N 17 0 E
Vestvågøy **8** 68 18N 13 50 E
Vesuvio **29** 40 50N 14 22 E
Vesuvius, Mt. = Vesuvio **29** 40 50N 14 22 E
Veszprém **33** 47 8N 17 57 E
Vésztö **33** 46 55N 21 16 E
Vetapalem **51** 15 47N 80 18 E
Vetlanda **11** 57 24N 15 3 E
Vetluga **37** 57 53N 45 45 E
Vetlugu → **40** 56 18N 46 24 E

Name	Map	Lat.	Long.
Vetluzhskiy	**37**	57 17N	45 12 E
Vetovo	**34**	43 42N	26 16 E
Vetralia	**27**	42 20N	12 2 E
Vettore, Monte	**27**	42 49N	13 16 E
Veurne	**16**	51 5N	2 40 E
Vevay	**117**	38 45N	85 4W
Vevey	**31**	46 28N	6 51 E
Veynes	**21**	44 32N	5 49 E
Veys	**46**	31 30N	49 0 E
Vézelise	**19**	48 30N	6 5 E
Vézère ⤳	**20**	44 53N	0 53 E
Vi Thanh	**55**	9 42N	105 26 E
Viacha	**136**	16 39S	68 18W
Viadana	**26**	44 55N	10 30 E
Viana, Brazil	**138**	3 13S	45 0W
Viana, Spain	**24**	42 31N	2 22W
Viana del Bollo	**22**	42 11N	7 6W
Viana do Alentejo	**23**	38 17N	7 59W
Viana do Castelo	**22**	41 42N	8 50W
Vianna do Castelo □	**22**	41 50N	8 30W
Vianópolis	**139**	16 40S	48 35W
Viar ⤳	**23**	37 36N	5 50W
Viaréggio	**26**	43 52N	10 13 E
Viaur ⤳	**20**	44 8N	1 58 E
Vibank	**109**	50 20N	103 56W
Vibo Valéntia	**29**	38 40N	16 5 E
Viborg	**11**	56 27N	9 23 E
Vibraye	**18**	48 3N	0 44 E
Vic-en-Bigorre	**20**	43 24N	0 3 E
Vic-Fézensac	**20**	43 47N	0 19 E
Vic-sur-Cère	**20**	44 59N	2 38 E
Vic-sur-Seille	**19**	48 45N	6 33 E
Vicenza	**27**	45 32N	11 31 E
Vich	**24**	41 58N	2 19 E
Vichada □	**134**	5 0N	69 30W
Vichada ⤳	**134**	4 55N	67 50W
Vichuga	**37**	57 12N	41 55 E
Vichy	**20**	46 9N	3 26 E
Vicksburg, Ariz., U.S.A.	**123**	33 45N	113 45W
Vicksburg, Mich., U.S.A.	**117**	42 10N	85 30W
Vicksburg, Miss., U.S.A.	**119**	32 22N	90 56W
Vico del Gargaro	**29**	41 54N	15 57 E
Vico, L. di	**27**	42 20N	12 10 E
Viçosa	**138**	9 28S	36 14W
Viçosa do Ceará	**138**	3 34S	41 5W
Victor, Colo., U.S.A.	**118**	38 43N	105 7W
Victor, N.Y., U.S.A.	**114**	42 58N	77 24W
Victor Emanuel Ra.	**69**	5 20S	142 15 E
Victor Harbour	**73**	35 30S	138 37 E
Victoria, Argent.	**140**	32 40S	60 10W
Victoria, Camer.	**92**	4 1N	9 10 E
Victoria, Can.	**108**	48 30N	123 25W
Victoria, Chile	**142**	38 13S	72 20W
Victoria, Guin.	**88**	10 50N	14 32W
Victoria, H. K.	**62**	22 16N	114 15 E
Victoria, Malay.	**56**	5 20N	115 14 E
Victoria, Seychelles	**53**	5 0S	55 40 E
Victoria, Ill., U.S.A.	**116**	41 2N	90 6W
Victoria, Kans., U.S.A.	**118**	38 52N	99 8W
Victoria, Tex., U.S.A.	**119**	28 50N	97 0W
Victoria □	**95**	21 0S	31 30 E
Victoria ⤳	**78**	15 10S	129 40 E
Victoria Beach	**109**	50 40N	96 35W
Victoria de las Tunas	**126**	20 58N	76 59W
Victoria Falls	**95**	17 58S	25 52 E
Victoria, Grand L.	**104**	47 31N	77 30W
Victoria Harbour	**106**	44 45N	79 45W
Victoria I.	**100**	71 0N	111 0W
Victoria, L., N.S.W., Austral.	**73**	33 57S	141 15 E
Victoria, L., Vic., Austral.	**75**	38 2S	147 34 E
Victoria, L., E. Afr.	**94**	1 0S	33 0 E
Victoria, La	**134**	10 14N	67 20W
Victoria Ld.	**143**	75 0S	160 0 E
Victoria, Mt., Burma	**52**	21 15N	93 55 E
Victoria, Mt., P.N.G.	**69**	8 55S	147 32 E
Victoria Nile ⤳	**94**	2 14N	31 26 E
Victoria Ra.	**81**	42 12S	172 7 E
Victoria Res.	**103**	48 20N	57 27W
Victoria River Downs	**78**	16 25S	131 0 E
Victoria West	**96**	31 25S	23 4 E
Victoriaville	**105**	46 4N	71 56W
Victorica	**140**	36 20S	65 30W
Victorville	**123**	34 32N	117 18W
Vicuña	**140**	30 0S	70 50W
Vicuña Mackenna	**140**	33 53S	64 25W
Vidal	**123**	34 7N	114 31W
Vidal Junction	**123**	34 11N	114 34W
Vidalia	**113**	32 13N	82 25W
Vidauban	**21**	43 25N	6 27 E
Vidigueira	**23**	38 12N	7 48W
Vidin	**34**	43 59N	22 50 E
Vidio, Cabo	**22**	43 35N	6 14W
Vidisha (Bhilsa)	**48**	23 28N	77 53 E
Vidöstern	**11**	57 5N	14 0 E
Vidzy	**36**	55 23N	26 37 E
Viechtach	**31**	49 5N	12 53 E
Viedma	**142**	40 50S	63 0W
Viedma, L.	**142**	49 30S	72 30W
Vieira	**22**	41 38N	8 8W
Viella	**24**	42 43N	0 44 E
Vienenburg	**30**	51 57N	10 35 E
Vieng Pou Kha	**54**	20 41N	101 4 E
Vienna, Can.	**106**	42 41N	80 48W
Vienna, Illinois, U.S.A.	**119**	37 29N	88 54W
Vienna, Mo., U.S.A.	**116**	38 11N	91 57W
Vienna = Wien	**33**	48 12N	16 22 E
Vienne	**21**	45 31N	4 53 E
Vienne □	**20**	46 30N	0 42 E
Vienne ⤳	**18**	47 13N	0 5 E
Vientiane	**54**	17 58N	102 36 E
Vientos, Paso de los	**127**	20 0N	74 0W
Viersen	**30**	51 15N	6 23 E
Vierwaldstättersee	**31**	47 0N	8 30 E
Vierzon	**19**	47 13N	2 5 E
Vieste	**28**	41 52N	16 14 E
Vietnam ■	**54**	19 0N	106 0 E
Vieux-Boucau-les-Bains	**20**	43 48N	1 23W
Vif	**21**	45 5N	5 41 E
Vigan	**57**	17 35N	120 28 E
Vigan, Le	**20**	44 0N	3 36 E
Vigevano	**26**	45 18N	8 50 E
Vigia	**138**	0 50S	48 5W
Vigía Chico	**125**	19 46N	87 35W
Vignacourt	**19**	50 1N	2 15 E
Vignemale, Pic du	**20**	42 47N	0 10W
Vigneulles	**19**	48 59N	5 40 E
Vignola	**26**	44 29N	11 0 E
Vigo	**22**	42 12N	8 41W
Vigo, Ría de	**22**	42 15N	8 45W
Vihiers	**18**	47 10N	0 30W
Vijayadurg	**50**	16 30N	73 25 E
Vijayawada (Bezwada)	**51**	16 31N	80 39 E
Viken	**11**	58 39N	14 20 E
Viking	**108**	53 7N	111 50W
Vikna	**8**	64 52N	10 57 E
Vikramasingapuram	**51**	8 40N	76 47 E
Viksjö	**10**	62 45N	17 26 E
Vikulovo	**40**	56 50N	70 40 E
Vila	**68**	17 44S	168 19 E
Vila Alferes Chamusca	**97**	24 27S	33 0 E
Vila Arriaga	**93**	14 44S	13 24 E
Vila Caldas Xavier	**95**	14 28S	33 0 E
Vila Coutinho	**95**	14 37S	34 19 E
Vila da Maganja	**95**	17 18S	37 30 E
Vila de Aljustrel	**93**	13 30S	19 45 E
Vila de João Belo = Xai-Xai	**97**	25 6S	33 31 E
Vila de Junqueiro	**95**	15 25S	36 58 E
Vila de Manica	**95**	18 58S	32 59 E
Vila de Rei	**23**	39 41N	8 9W
Vila do Bispo	**23**	37 5N	8 53W
Vila do Chibuto	**97**	24 40S	33 33 E
Vila do Conde	**22**	41 21N	8 45W
Vila Fontes	**95**	17 51S	35 24 E
Vila Franca de Xira	**23**	38 57N	8 59W
Vila Gamito	**95**	14 12S	33 0 E
Vila General Machado	**93**	11 58S	17 22 E
Vila Gomes da Costa	**97**	24 20S	33 37 E
Vila Luisa	**97**	25 45S	32 35 E
Vila Machado	**95**	19 15S	34 14 E
Vila Marechal Carmona	**92**	7 30S	14 40 E
Vila Mouzinho	**95**	14 48S	34 25 E
Vila Nova de Foscôa	**22**	41 5N	7 9W
Vila Nova de Ourém	**23**	39 40N	8 35W
Vila Nova do Seles	**93**	11 24S	14 22 E
Vila Novo de Gaia	**22**	41 4N	8 40W
Vila Paiva de Andrada	**95**	18 44S	34 2 E
Vila Pouca de Aguiar	**22**	41 30N	7 38W
Vila Real	**22**	41 17N	7 48W
Vila Real de Santo António	**23**	37 10N	7 28W
Vila Vasco da Gama	**95**	14 54S	32 14 E
Vila Velha, Amapá, Brazil	**135**	3 13N	51 13W
Vila Velha, Espirito Santo, Brazil	**139**	20 20S	40 17W
Vila Verissimo Sarmento	**92**	8 7S	20 38 E
Vila Viçosa	**23**	38 45N	7 27W
Vilaboa	**22**	42 21N	8 39W
Vilaine ⤳	**18**	47 30N	2 27W
Vilanculos	**97**	22 1S	35 17 E
Vilar Formosa	**22**	40 38N	6 45W
Vilareal □	**22**	41 36N	7 35W
Vilaseca-Salou	**24**	41 7N	1 9'E
Vilcabamba, Cordillera	**136**	13 0S	73 0W
Vilcanchos	**136**	13 40S	74 25W
Vileyka	**36**	54 30N	26 53 E
Vilhelmina	**8**	64 35N	16 39 E
Vilhena	**137**	12 40S	60 5W
Viliga	**41**	61 36N	156 56 E
Viliya ⤳	**36**	55 54N	23 53 E
Viljandi	**36**	58 28N	25 30 E
Villa Abecia	**140**	21 0S	68 18W
Villa Ahumada	**124**	30 38N	106 30W
Villa Ana	**140**	28 28S	59 40W
Villa Ángela	**140**	27 34S	60 45W
Villa Bella	**137**	10 25S	65 22W
Villa Bens = Tarfaya	**84**	27 55N	12 55W
Villa Cañás	**140**	34 0S	61 35W
Villa Cisneros = Dakhla	**84**	23 50N	15 53W
Villa Colón	**140**	31 38S	68 20W
Villa Constitución	**140**	33 15S	60 20W
Villa de Cura	**134**	10 2N	67 29W
Villa de María	**140**	29 55S	63 43W
Villa del Rosario	**134**	10 19N	72 19W
Villa Dolores	**140**	31 58S	65 15W
Villa Frontera	**124**	26 56N	101 27W
Villa Grove	**117**	39 52N	88 10W
Villa Guillermina	**140**	28 15S	59 29W
Villa Hayes	**140**	25 0S	57 20W
Villa Iris	**140**	38 12S	63 12W
Villa María	**140**	32 20S	63 10W
Villa Mazán	**140**	28 40S	66 30W
Villa Minozzo	**26**	44 21N	10 30 E
Villa Montes	**140**	21 10S	63 30W
Villa Ocampo, Argent.	**140**	28 30S	59 20W
Villa Ocampo, Mexico	**124**	26 29N	105 30W
Villa Ojo de Agua	**140**	29 30S	63 44W
Villa San Giovanni	**29**	38 13N	15 38 E
Villa San José	**140**	32 12S	58 15W
Villa San Martín	**140**	28 15S	64 9W
Villa Santina	**27**	46 25N	12 55 E
Villa Unión	**124**	23 12N	106 14W
Villablino	**22**	42 57N	6 19W
Villacañas	**24**	39 38N	3 20W
Villacarlos	**24**	39 53N	4 17 E
Villacarriedo	**24**	43 14N	3 48W
Villacarrillo	**25**	38 7N	3 3W
Villacastín	**22**	40 46N	4 25W
Villach	**33**	46 37N	13 51 E
Villaciado	**28**	39 27N	8 45 E
Villada	**22**	42 15N	4 59W
Villadiego	**22**	42 31N	4 1W
Villadóssola	**26**	46 4N	8 16 E
Villafeliche	**24**	41 10N	1 30W
Villafranca	**24**	42 17N	1 46W
Villafranca de los Barros	**23**	38 35N	6 18W
Villafranca de los Caballeros	**25**	39 26N	3 21W
Villafranca del Bierzo	**22**	42 38N	6 50W
Villafranca del Cid	**24**	40 26N	0 16W
Villafranca del Panadés	**24**	41 21N	1 40 E
Villafranca di Verona	**26**	45 20N	10 51 E
Villagarcía de Arosa	**22**	42 34N	8 46W
Villagrán	**125**	24 29N	99 29W
Villaguay	**140**	32 0S	59 0W
Villaharta	**23**	38 9N	4 54W
Villahermosa, Mexico	**125**	18 0N	92 50W
Villahermosa, Spain	**25**	38 46N	2 52W
Villaines-la-Juhel	**18**	48 21N	0 20W
Villajoyosa	**25**	38 30N	0 12W
Villalba	**22**	43 26N	7 40W
Villalba de Guardo	**22**	42 42N	4 49W
Villalcampo, Pantano de	**22**	41 31N	6 0W
Villalón de Campos	**22**	42 5N	5 4W
Villalpando	**22**	41 51N	5 25W
Villaluenga	**22**	40 2N	3 54W
Villamanán	**22**	42 19N	5 35W
Villamartín	**23**	36 52N	5 38W
Villamayor	**24**	39 50N	2 59W
Villamblard	**20**	45 2N	0 32 E
Villanova Monteleone	**28**	40 30N	8 28 E
Villanueva, Colomb.	**134**	10 37N	72 59W
Villanueva, U.S.A.	**121**	35 16N	105 23W
Villanueva de Castellón	**25**	39 5N	0 31W
Villanueva de Córdoba	**23**	38 20N	4 38W
Villanueva de la Fuente	**25**	38 42N	2 42W
Villanueva de la Serena	**23**	38 59N	5 50W
Villanueva de la Sierra	**22**	40 12N	6 24W
Villanueva de los Castillejos	**23**	37 30N	7 15W
Villanueva del Arzobispo	**25**	38 10N	3 0W
Villanueva del Duque	**23**	38 20N	5 0W
Villanueva del Fresno	**23**	38 23N	7 10W
Villanueva y Geltrú	**24**	41 13N	1 40 E
Villaodrid	**22**	43 20N	7 11W
Villaputzu	**28**	39 28N	9 33 E
Villar del Arzobispo	**24**	39 44N	0 50W
Villar del Rey	**23**	39 7N	6 50W
Villarcayo	**24**	42 56N	3 34W
Villard-Bonnet	**21**	45 14N	5 53 E
Villard-de-Lans	**21**	45 3N	5 33 E
Villarino de los Aires	**22**	41 18N	6 23W
Villarosa	**29**	37 36N	14 9 E
Villarramiel	**22**	42 2N	4 55W
Villarreal	**24**	39 55N	0 3W
Villarrica, Chile	**142**	39 15S	72 15W
Villarrica, Parag.	**140**	25 40S	56 30W
Villarrobledo	**25**	39 18N	2 36W
Villarroya de la Sierra	**24**	41 27N	1 46W
Villarrubia de los Ojos	**25**	39 14N	3 36W
Villars	**21**	46 0N	5 2 E
Villarta de San Juan	**25**	39 15N	3 25W
Villasayas	**24**	41 24N	2 39W
Villaseca de los Gamitos	**22**	41 2N	6 7W
Villastar	**24**	40 17N	1 9W
Villatobas	**24**	39 54N	3 20W
Villavicencio, Argent.	**140**	32 28S	69 0W
Villavicencio, Colomb.	**134**	4 9N	73 37W
Villaviciosa	**22**	43 32N	5 27W
Villazón	**140**	22 0S	65 35W
Ville-Marie	**104**	47 20N	79 30W
Ville Platte	**119**	30 45N	92 17W
Villebon, L.	**104**	47 58N	77 17W
Villedieu	**18**	48 50N	1 12W
Villefort	**20**	44 28N	3 56 E
Villefranche	**19**	47 19N	1 46 E
Villefranche-de-Lauragais	**20**	43 25N	1 44 E
Villefranche-de-Rouergue	**20**	44 21N	2 2 E
Villefranche-du-Périgord	**20**	44 38N	1 5 E
Villefranche-sur-Saône	**21**	45 59N	4 43 E
Villegrande	**137**	18 30S	64 10W
Villel	**24**	40 14N	1 12W
Villemaur	**19**	48 14N	3 40 E
Villemontel	**104**	48 38N	78 22W
Villemur-sur-Tarn	**20**	43 51N	1 31 E
Villena	**25**	38 39N	0 52W
Villenauxe	**19**	48 36N	3 30 E
Villenave	**20**	44 46N	0 33W
Villeneuve, France	**19**	48 42N	2 25 E
Villeneuve, Italy	**26**	45 40N	7 10 E
Villeneuve-l'Archevêque	**19**	48 14N	3 32 E
Villeneuve-lès-Avignon	**21**	43 57N	4 49 E
Villeneuve-sur-Allier	**20**	46 40N	3 13 E
Villeneuve-sur-Lot	**20**	44 24N	0 42 E
Villeréal	**20**	44 38N	0 45 E
Villers-Bocage	**18**	49 3N	0 40W
Villers-Bretonneux	**19**	49 50N	2 30 E
Villers-Cotterêts	**19**	49 15N	3 4 E
Villers-Outreaux	**19**	50 2N	3 18 E
Villers-sur-Mer	**18**	49 21N	0 2W
Villersexel	**19**	47 33N	6 26 E
Villerupt	**19**	49 28N	5 55 E
Villerville	**18**	49 26N	0 5 E
Villiers	**97**	27 2S	28 36 E
Villingen	**31**	48 4N	8 28 E
Villingen-Schwenningen	**31**	48 3N	8 29 E
Villisca	**116**	40 55N	94 59W
Villupuram	**51**	11 59N	79 31 E
Vilna	**108**	54 7N	111 55W
Vilnius	**36**	54 38N	25 19 E
Vils	**31**	47 33N	10 37 E
Vils ⤳	**31**	48 38N	13 11 E
Vilsbiburg	**31**	48 27N	12 23 E
Vilshofen	**31**	48 38N	13 11 E
Vilskutskogo, Proliv	**41**	78 0N	103 0 E
Vilusi	**33**	42 44N	18 34 E
Vilvoorde	**16**	50 56N	4 26 E
Vilyuy ⤳	**41**	64 24N	126 26 E
Vilyuysk	**41**	63 40N	121 35 E
Vimercate	**26**	45 38N	9 25 E
Vimiosa	**22**	41 35N	6 31W
Vimmerby	**11**	57 40N	15 55 E
Vimoutiers	**18**	48 57N	0 10 E
Vimperk	**32**	49 3N	13 46 E
Viña del Mar	**140**	33 0S	71 30W
Vinaroz	**24**	40 30N	0 27 E
Vincennes	**117**	38 42N	87 29W
Vincent	**123**	34 33N	118 11W
Vinces	**134**	1 32S	79 45W
Vinchina	**140**	28 45S	68 15W
Vindel älven ⤳	**8**	63 55N	19 50 E
Vindeln	**8**	64 12N	19 43 E
Vinderup	**11**	56 29N	8 45 E
Vindhya Ra.	**48**	22 50N	77 0 E
Vine Grove	**117**	37 49N	85 59W
Vineland	**112**	39 30N	75 0W
Vinga	**34**	46 0N	21 14 E
Vingnes	**10**	61 7N	10 26 E
Vinh	**54**	18 45N	105 38 E
Vinh Linh	**54**	17 4N	107 2 E
Vinh Long	**55**	10 16N	105 57 E
Vinh Yen	**54**	21 21N	105 35 E
Vinhais	**22**	41 50N	7 0W
Vinica, Hrvatska, Yugo.	**27**	46 20N	16 9 E
Vinica, Slovenija, Yugo.	**27**	45 28N	15 16 E

Vinita 119 36 40N 95 12W
Vinkovci 33 45 19N 18 48 E
Vinnitsa 38 49 15N 28 30 E
Vinson Massif 143 78 35S 85 25W
Vinstra 10 61 37N 9 44 E
Vinton, Calif., U.S.A. 122 39 48N 120 10W
Vinton, Iowa, U.S.A. 116 42 8N 92 1W
Vinton, La., U.S.A. 119 30 13N 93 35W
Vinţu de Jos 34 46 0N 23 30 E
Viöl 30 54 32N 9 12 E
Viola 116 41 12N 90 35W
Violet Town 74 36 38S 145 42 E
Vipava 27 45 51N 13 58 E
Vipiteno 27 46 55N 11 25 E
Viqueque 57 8 52S 126 23 E
Vir 27 44 17N 15 3 E
Virac 57 13 30N 124 20 E
Virachei 54 13 59N 106 49 E
Virago Sd. 108 54 0N 132 30W
Virajpet 51 12 10N 75 50 E
Viramgam 48 23 5N 72 0 E
Viranaņşehir 46 37 13N 39 45 E
Virarajendrapet = Virajpet 51 12 10N 75 50 E
Viravanallur 51 8 40N 77 30 E
Virden, Can. 109 49 50N 100 56W
Virden, U.S.A. 116 39 30N 89 46W
Vire 18 48 50N 0 53W
Vire → 18 49 20N 1 7W
Virgem da Lapa 139 16 49S 42 21W
Vírgenes, C. 142 52 19S 68 21W
Virgin →, Can. 109 57 2N 108 17W
Virgin →, U.S.A. 121 36 50N 114 10W
Virgin Gorda 127 18 30N 64 26W
Virgin Is. 127 18 40N 64 30W
Virginia, S. Afr. 96 28 8S 26 55 E
Virginia, Ill., U.S.A. 116 39 57N 90 13W
Virginia, Minn., U.S.A. 118 47 30N 92 32W
Virginia □ 112 37 45N 78 0W
Virginia Beach 112 36 54N 75 58W
Virginia City, Mont., U.S.A. 120 45 18N 111 58W
Virginia City, Nev., U.S.A. 122 39 19N 119 39W
Virginia Falls 108 61 38N 125 42W
Virginiatown 102 48 9N 79 36W
Virieu-le-Grand 21 45 51N 5 39 E
Viroqua 118 43 33N 90 57W
Virovitica 33 45 51N 17 21 E
Virserum 11 57 20N 15 35 E
Virton 16 49 35N 5 32 E
Virtsu 36 58 32N 23 33 E
Virú 136 8 25S 78 45W
Virudunagar 51 9 30N 78 0 E
Vis 27 43 0N 16 10 E
Vis Kanal 27 43 4N 16 5 E
Visale 68 9 15S 159 42 E
Visalia 122 36 25N 119 18W
Visayan Sea 57 11 30N 123 30 E
Visby 11 57 37N 18 18 E
Viscount Melville Sd. 144 74 10N 108 0W
Visé 16 50 44N 5 41 E
Višegrad 33 43 47N 19 17 E
Viseu, Brazil 138 1 10S 46 5W
Viseu, Port. 22 40 40N 7 55W
Vişeu 34 47 45N 24 25 E
Viseu □ 22 40 40N 7 55W
Vishakhapatnam 50 17 45N 83 20 E
Vishnupur 49 23 8N 87 20 E
Visikoi I. 143 56 43S 27 15W
Visingsö 11 58 2N 14 20 E
Viskafors 11 57 37N 12 50 E
Vislanda 11 56 46N 14 30 E
Visnagar 48 23 45N 72 32 E
Višnja Gora 27 45 58N 14 45 E
Viso del Marqués 25 38 32N 3 34W
Viso, Mte. 26 44 38N 7 5 E
Visoko 33 43 58N 18 10 E
Visp 31 46 17N 7 52 E
Visselhövede 30 52 59N 9 36 E
Vista 123 33 12N 117 14W
Vistula = Wisła → 32 54 22N 18 55 E
Vit → 34 43 30N 24 30 E
Vitanje 27 46 25N 15 18 E
Vitebsk 36 55 10N 30 15 E
Viterbo 27 42 25N 12 8 E
Viti Levu 68 17 30S 177 30 E
Vitiaz Str. 69 5 40S 147 10 E
Vitigudino 22 41 1N 6 26W
Vitim 41 59 28N 112 35 E
Vitim → 41 59 26N 112 34 E
Vitória 139 20 20S 40 22W
Vitoria 24 42 50N 2 41W
Vitória da Conquista 139 14 51S 40 51W
Vitória de São Antão 138 8 10S 35 20W
Vitorino Friere 138 4 4S 45 10W
Vitré 18 48 8N 1 12W
Vitry-le-François 19 48 43N 4 33 E
Vitsi, Óros 35 40 40N 21 25 E
Vitteaux 19 47 24N 4 30 E
Vittel 19 48 12N 5 57 E
Vittória 29 36 58N 14 30 E
Vittório Véneto 27 45 59N 12 18 E
Vitu Is. 69 4 50S 149 25 E
Viver 24 39 55N 0 36W
Vivero 22 43 39N 7 38W
Viviers 21 44 30N 4 40 E
Vivonne 20 46 25N 0 15 E
Vizcaíno, Desierto de 124 27 40N 113 50W
Vizcaíno, Sierra 124 27 30N 114 0W
Vizcaya □ 24 43 15N 2 45W
Vizianagaram 50 18 6N 83 30 E
Vizille 21 45 5N 5 46 E
Vizinada 27 45 20N 13 46 E
Viziru 34 45 0N 27 43 E
Vizovice 32 49 12N 17 56 E
Vizzini 29 37 9N 14 43 E
Vlaardingen 16 51 55N 4 21 E
Vlădeasa 34 46 47N 22 50 E
Vladimir 37 56 15N 40 30 E
Vladimir Volynskiy 36 50 50N 24 18 E
Vladimirovac 33 45 1N 20 53 E
Vladimirovka, U.S.S.R. 39 44 45N 44 41 E
Vladimirovka, U.S.S.R. 39 48 27N 46 10 E
Vladislavovka 38 45 15N 35 15 E
Vladivostok 41 43 10N 131 53 E
Vlasenica 33 44 11N 18 59 E
Vlasinsko Jezero 33 42 44N 22 22 E
Vlieland 16 53 16N 4 55 E
Vlissingen 16 51 26N 3 34 E
Vlóra 35 40 32N 19 28 E
Vlorës, Gjiri i 35 40 29N 19 27 E
Vltava → 32 50 21N 14 30 E
Vo Dat 55 11 9N 107 31 E
Vobarno 26 45 38N 10 30 E
Voćin 33 45 37N 17 33 E
Vodice 27 43 47N 15 47 E
Vodnjan 27 44 59N 13 52 E
Vogelkop = Doberai, Jazirah 57 1 25S 133 0 E
Vogelsberg 30 50 37N 9 15 E
Voghera 26 44 59N 9 1 E
Voh 68 20 58S 164 42 E
Vohémar 97 13 25S 50 0 E
Vohipeno 97 22 22S 47 51 E
Voi 94 3 25S 38 32 E
Void 19 48 40N 5 36 E
Voiron 21 45 22N 5 35 E
Voisey B. 103 56 15N 61 50W
Voitsberg 33 47 3N 15 9 E
Voiviïs Límni 35 39 30N 22 45 E
Vojens 11 55 16N 9 18 E
Vojmsjön 8 64 55N 16 40 E
Vojnik 26 46 18N 15 19 E
Vojnió 27 45 19N 15 43 E
Vokhma 37 59 0N 46 45 E
Vokhma → 37 56 20N 46 20 E
Vokhtoga 37 58 46N 41 8 E
Volborg 118 45 50N 105 44W
Volcano Is. 66 25 0N 141 0 E
Volchansk 37 50 17N 36 58 E
Volchayevka 41 48 40N 134 30 E
Volchya → 38 48 0N 37 0 E
Volda 8 62 9N 6 5 E
Volga 37 57 58N 38 16 E
Volga → 39 48 30N 46 0 E
Volga Hts. = Privolzhskaya V.S. 82 51 0N 46 0 E
Volgodonsk 39 47 33N 42 5 E
Volgograd 39 48 40N 44 25 E
Volgogradskoye Vdkhr. 37 50 0N 45 20 E
Volgorechensk 37 57 28N 41 14 E
Volkach 31 49 52N 10 14 E
Volkhov 36 59 55N 32 15 E
Volkhov → 36 60 8N 32 20 E
Völklingen 31 49 15N 6 50 E
Volkovysk 36 53 9N 24 30 E
Volksrust 97 27 24S 29 53 E
Vollenhove 16 52 40N 5 58 E
Volnovakha 38 47 35N 37 30 E
Volochanka 41 71 0N 94 28 E
Volodarsk 37 56 12N 43 15 E
Vologda 37 59 10N 40 0 E
Volokolamsk 37 56 5N 35 57 E
Volokonovka 37 50 33N 37 52 E
Vólos 35 39 24N 22 59 E
Volosovo 36 59 27N 29 32 E
Volozhin 36 54 3N 26 30 E
Volsk 37 52 5N 47 22 E
Volta → 89 5 46N 0 41 E
Volta, L. 89 7 30N 0 15 E
Volta Redonda 139 22 31S 44 5W
Voltaire, C. 78 14 16S 125 35 E
Volterra 26 43 24N 10 50 E
Voltri 26 44 25N 8 43 E
Volturara Áppula 29 41 30N 15 2 E
Volturno → 29 41 1N 13 55 E
Volubilis 86 34 2N 5 33W
Volvo 73 31 41S 143 57 E
Volzhsk 37 55 57N 48 23 E
Volzhskiy 39 48 56N 44 46 E
Vondrozo 97 22 49S 47 20 E
Voorburg 16 52 5N 4 24 E
Vopnafjörður 8 65 45N 14 40W
Vóras Óros 35 40 57N 21 45 E
Vorbasse 11 55 39N 9 6 E
Vorderrhein → 31 46 49N 9 25 E
Vordingborg 11 55 0N 11 54 E
Voreppe 21 45 18N 5 39 E
Voríai Sporádhes 35 39 15N 23 30 E
Vórios Evvoïkos Kólpos 35 38 45N 23 15 E
Vorkuta 40 67 48N 64 20 E
Vorma → 10 60 9N 11 27 E
Vorona → 37 51 22N 42 3 E
Voronezh, R.S.F.S.R., U.S.S.R. 37 51 40N 39 10 E
Voronezh, Ukraine, U.S.S.R. 36 51 47N 33 28 E
Voronezh → 37 51 56N 37 17 E
Vorontsovo-Zelenokumsk 39 44 30N 44 1 E
Voroshilovgrad 39 48 38N 39 15 E
Vorovskoye 41 54 30N 155 50 E
Vorskla → 38 48 50N 34 10 E
Vorupør 11 56 58N 8 22 E
Vosges 19 48 20N 7 10 E
Vosges □ 19 48 12N 6 20 E
Voskopoja 35 40 40N 20 33 E
Voskresensk 37 55 19N 38 43 E
Voskresenskoye 37 56 51N 45 30 E
Voss 9 60 38N 6 26 E
Vostochnyy Sayan 41 54 0N 96 0 E
Vostok I. 67 10 5S 152 23W
Vouga → 22 40 41N 8 40W
Vouillé 18 46 38N 0 10 E
Voulte-sur-Rhône, La 21 44 48N 4 46 E
Vouvray 18 47 25N 0 48 E
Voúxa, Ákra 35 35 37N 23 32 E
Vouzela 22 40 43N 8 7W
Vouziers 19 49 22N 4 40 E
Voves 19 48 15N 1 38 E
Voxna 10 61 20N 15 40 E
Vozhgaly 37 58 9N 50 11 E
Voznesenka 41 56 40N 95 3 E
Voznesensk 38 47 35N 31 21 E
Voznesenye 40 61 0N 35 45 E
Vrådal 10 59 20N 8 25 E
Vrakhnéïka 35 38 10N 21 40 E
Vrancei, Munţii 34 46 0N 26 30 E
Vrangelya, Ostrov 41 71 0N 180 0 E
Vranica 33 43 55N 17 50 E
Vranje 33 42 34N 21 54 E
Vransko 27 46 17N 14 58 E
Vratsa 34 43 13N 23 30 E
Vrbas 33 45 40N 19 40 E
Vrbas → 33 45 8N 17 29 E
Vrbnik 27 45 4N 14 40 E
Vrbovec 27 45 53N 16 28 E
Vrbovsko 27 45 24N 15 5 E
Vrchlabí 32 50 38N 15 37 E
Vrede 97 27 24S 29 6 E
Vredefort 96 27 0S 26 22 E
Vredenburg 96 32 51S 18 0 E
Vredendal 96 31 41S 18 35 E
Vrena 11 58 54N 16 41 E
Vrgorac 33 43 12N 17 20 E
Vrhnika 27 45 58N 14 15 E
Vriddhachalam 51 11 30N 79 20 E
Vrïdi 88 5 15N 4 3W
Vrindaban 48 27 37N 77 40 E
Vrnograč 27 45 10N 15 57 E
Vršac 33 45 8N 21 18 E
Vrsacki Kanal 33 45 15N 21 0 E
Vryburg 96 26 55S 24 45 E
Vryheid 97 27 45S 30 47 E
Vsetín 32 49 20N 18 0 E
Vu Liet 54 18 43N 105 23 E
Vŭcha → 35 42 10N 24 26 E
Vught 16 51 38N 5 20 E
Vukovar 33 45 21N 18 59 E
Vulcan, Can. 108 50 25N 113 15W
Vulcan, U.S.A. 112 45 46N 87 51W
Vulcano 29 38 25N 14 58 E
Vŭlchedruma 34 43 42N 23 27 E
Vulci 27 42 23N 11 37 E
Vulkaneshty 38 45 35N 28 30 E
Vunduzi → 95 18 56S 34 1 E
Vung Tau 55 10 21N 107 4 E
Vunisea 68 18 3S 178 33 E
Vûrbitsa 34 42 59N 26 40 E
Vuyyuru 51 16 28N 80 50 E
Vyara 50 21 8N 73 28 E
Vyasniki 37 56 10N 42 10 E
Vyazemskiy 41 47 32N 134 45 E
Vyazma 36 55 10N 34 15 E
Vyborg 40 60 43N 28 47 E
Vychegda → 40 61 18N 46 36 E
Vychodné Beskydy 32 49 30N 22 0 E
Vypin, I. 51 10 10N 76 15 E
Vyrnwy, L. 12 52 48N 3 30W
Vyshniy Volochek 36 57 30N 34 30 E
Vyškov 32 49 17N 17 0 E
Vysoké Mýto 32 49 58N 16 10 E
Vysokovsk 37 56 22N 36 30 E
Vysotsk 36 51 43N 26 32 E

W

W.A.C. Bennett Dam 108 56 2N 122 6W
Wa 88 10 7N 2 25W
Waal → 16 51 59N 4 30 E
Wabag 69 5 32S 143 40 E
Wabakimi L. 102 50 38N 89 45W
Wabana 103 47 40N 53 0W
Wabano → 105 48 20N 74 3W
Wabao, C. 68 21 35S 167 53 E
Wabasca 108 55 57N 113 56W
Wabash 117 40 48N 85 46W
Wabash → 112 37 46N 88 2W
Wabawng 52 26 20N 97 25 E
Wabeno 112 45 25N 88 40W
Wabi → 91 7 45N 40 50 E
Wabigoon L. 109 49 44N 92 44W
Wabowden 109 54 55N 98 38W
Wąbrzeźno 32 53 16N 18 57 E
Wabu Hu 59 32 20N 116 50 E
Wabuk Pt. 102 55 20N 85 5W
Wabush 103 52 55N 66 52W
Wabuska 120 39 9N 119 13W
Wächtersbach 31 50 16N 9 18 E
Waco 119 31 33N 97 5W
Waconichi, L. 105 50 8N 74 0W
Wad Ban Naqa 91 16 32N 33 9 E
Wad Banda 91 13 10N 27 56 E
Wad el Haddad 91 13 50N 33 30 E
Wad en Nau 91 14 10N 33 34 E
Wad Hamid 91 16 30N 32 45 E
Wâd Medanî 91 14 28N 33 30 E
Wad Thana 48 27 22N 66 23 E
Wadayama 64 35 19N 134 52 E
Waddān 87 29 9N 16 10 E
Waddān, Jabal 87 29 0N 16 15 E
Waddeneilanden 16 53 25N 5 10 E
Waddenzee 16 53 6N 5 10 E
Wadderin Hill 79 32 0S 118 25 E
Waddington 115 44 51N 75 12W
Waddington, Mt. 108 51 23N 125 15W
Waddy Pt. 73 24 58S 153 21 E
Wadena, Can. 109 51 57N 103 47W
Wadena, U.S.A. 118 46 25N 95 8W
Wädenswil 31 47 14N 8 40 E
Wadesboro 113 35 2N 80 2W
Wadhams 108 51 30N 127 30W
Wādī ash Shāţi' 87 27 30N 15 0 E
Wādī Banī Walīd 87 31 49N 14 0 E
Wadi Gemâl 90 24 35N 35 10 E
Wadi Halfa 90 21 53N 31 19 E
Wadi Masila 45 16 30N 49 0 E
Wadi Sabha 46 23 50N 48 30 E
Wadian 59 32 42N 112 29 E
Wadowice 32 49 52N 19 30 E
Wadsworth 120 39 38N 119 22W
Waegwan 61 35 59N 128 23 E
Wafra 46 28 33N 47 56 E
Wageningen, Neth. 16 51 58N 5 40 E
Wageningen, Surinam 135 5 50N 56 50W
Wager B. 101 65 26N 88 40W
Wager Bay 101 65 56N 90 49W
Wagga Wagga 76 35 7S 147 24 E
Waghete 57 4 10S 135 50 E
Wagin 79 33 17S 117 25 E
Wagina 68 7 25S 157 47 E
Wagon Mound 119 36 1N 104 44W
Wagoner 119 36 0N 95 20W
Wagrowiec 32 52 48N 17 11 E
Wah 48 33 45N 72 40 E
Wahai 57 2 48S 129 35 E
Wahgunyah 75 35 57S 146 25 E
Wahiawa 110 21 30N 158 2W
Wahnai 48 32 40N 65 50 E
Wahoo 118 41 15N 96 35W
Wahpeton 118 46 20N 96 35W
Wai 50 17 56N 73 57 E
Wai, Koh 55 9 55N 102 55 E
Waiai → 81 46 12S 167 38 E
Waiau 81 42 39S 173 5 E
Waiau → 81 42 47S 173 22 E
Waiawe Ganga → 51 6 15N 81 0 E
Waibeem 57 0 30S 132 59 E
Waiblingen 31 48 49N 9 20 E
Waidhofen, Niederösterreich, Austria 32 48 49N 15 17 E
Waidhofen, Niederösterreich, Austria 33 47 57N 14 46 E
Waigeo 57 0 20S 130 40 E
Waihao → 81 44 52S 171 11 E
Waihao Downs 81 44 48S 170 55 E
Waiheke Islands 80 36 48S 175 6 E

Name	Page	Lat.	Long.
Waihi	**80**	37 23S	175 52E
Waihola	**81**	46 1S	170 8E
Waihola L.	**81**	45 59S	170 8E
Waihou →	**81**	37 15S	175 40E
Waika	**94**	2 22S	25 42E
Waikabubak	**57**	9 45S	119 25E
Waikaia	**81**	45 44S	168 51E
Waikaka	**81**	45 55S	169 1E
Waikare, L.	**80**	37 26S	175 13E
Waikaremoana	**80**	38 42S	177 12E
Waikaremoana L.	**80**	38 49S	177 9E
Waikari	**81**	42 58S	172 41E
Waikato →	**80**	37 23S	174 43E
Waikerie	**73**	34 9S	140 0E
Waikiekie	**80**	35 57S	174 16E
Waikokopu	**80**	39 3S	177 52E
Waikouaiti	**81**	45 36S	170 41E
Waimangaroa	**81**	41 43S	171 46E
Waimarie	**81**	41 35S	171 58E
Waimate	**81**	44 45S	171 3E
Waimea Plain	**81**	45 55S	168 35E
Wainganga →	**50**	18 50N	79 55E
Waingapu	**57**	9 35S	120 11E
Waingmaw	**52**	25 21N	97 26E
Waini →	**135**	8 20N	59 50W
Wainuiomata	**80**	41 17S	174 56E
Wainwright, Can.	**109**	52 50N	110 50W
Wainwright, U.S.A.	**100**	70 39N	160 1W
Waiotapu	**80**	38 21S	176 25E
Waiouru	**80**	39 28S	175 41E
Waipahi	**81**	46 6S	169 15E
Waipapa Pt.	**81**	46 40S	168 51E
Waipara	**81**	43 3S	172 46E
Waipawa	**80**	39 56S	176 38E
Waipiro	**80**	38 2S	178 22E
Waipu	**80**	35 59S	174 29E
Waipukurau	**80**	40 1S	176 33E
Wairakei	**80**	38 37S	176 6E
Wairarapa, L.	**80**	41 14S	175 15E
Wairau →	**81**	41 32S	174 7E
Wairio	**81**	45 59S	168 3E
Wairoa	**80**	39 3S	177 25E
Wairoa →	**80**	36 5S	173 59E
Waitaki →	**81**	44 56S	171 7E
Waitaki Plains	**81**	44 22S	170 0E
Waitara	**80**	38 59S	174 15E
Waitchie	**74**	35 22S	143 8E
Waitoa	**80**	37 37S	175 35E
Waitotara	**80**	39 49S	174 44E
Waitsburg	**120**	46 15N	118 0W
Waiuku	**80**	37 15S	174 45E
Waiyevo	**68**	16 48S	179 59W
Wajima	**63**	37 30N	137 0E
Wajir	**94**	1 42N	40 5E
Wajir □	**94**	1 42N	40 20E
Wakarusa	**117**	41 32N	86 1W
Wakasa	**64**	35 20N	134 24E
Wakasa-Wan	**65**	35 40N	135 30E
Wakatipu, L.	**81**	45 5S	168 33E
Wakaw	**109**	52 39N	105 44W
Wakayama	**65**	34 15N	135 15E
Wakayama-ken □	**65**	33 50N	135 30E
Wake	**64**	34 48N	134 8E
Wake Forest	**113**	35 58N	78 30W
Wake I.	**66**	19 18N	166 36E
Wakefield, Can.	**104**	45 38N	75 56W
Wakefield, N.Z.	**81**	41 24S	173 5E
Wakefield, U.K.	**12**	53 41N	1 31W
Wakefield, Mass., U.S.A.	**115**	42 30N	71 3W
Wakefield, Mich., U.S.A.	**118**	46 28N	89 53W
Wakema	**52**	16 30N	95 11E
Wakkanai	**63**	45 28N	141 35E
Wakkerstroom	**97**	27 24S	30 10E
Wakomata L.	**106**	46 34N	83 22W
Wakool	**74**	35 28S	144 23E
Wakool →	**74**	35 5S	143 33E
Wakre	**57**	0 19S	131 5E
Waku	**69**	6 5S	149 9E
Wakuach L.	**103**	55 34N	67 32W
Walamba	**95**	13 30S	28 42E
Wałbrzych	**32**	50 45N	16 18E
Walbury Hill	**13**	51 22N	1 28W
Walcha	**77**	30 55S	151 31E
Walcha Road	**77**	30 55S	151 24E
Walcheren	**16**	51 30N	3 35E
Walcott	**120**	41 50N	106 55W
Wałcz	**32**	53 17N	16 27E
Wald	**31**	47 17N	8 56E
Waldbröl	**30**	50 52N	7 36E
Waldeck	**30**	51 12N	9 4E
Walden, Colo., U.S.A.	**120**	40 47N	106 20W
Walden, N.Y., U.S.A.	**115**	41 32N	74 13W
Waldport	**120**	44 30N	124 2W
Waldron, Can.	**109**	50 53N	102 35W
Waldron, U.S.A.	**119**	34 52N	94 4W
Waldshut	**31**	47 37N	8 12E
Walebing	**79**	30 40S	116 15E
Walembele	**88**	10 30N	1 58W
Wales □	**13**	52 30N	3 30W
Walewale	**89**	10 21N	0 50W
Walgett	**73**	30 0S	148 5E
Walgreen Coast	**143**	75 15S	105 0W
Walhalla, Austral.	**75**	37 56S	146 29E
Walhalla, U.S.A.	**109**	48 55N	97 55W
Waliso	**91**	8 33N	38 1E
Walkaway	**79**	28 59S	114 48E
Walker, Minn., U.S.A.	**118**	47 4N	94 35W
Walker, Mo., U.S.A.	**116**	37 54N	94 14W
Walker L., Man., Can.	**109**	54 42N	95 57W
Walker L., Qué., Can.	**103**	50 20N	67 11W
Walker L., U.S.A.	**120**	38 56N	118 46W
Walkerston	**72**	21 11S	149 8E
Walkerton, Can.	**106**	44 10N	81 10W
Walkerton, U.S.A.	**117**	41 28N	86 29W
Walkerville	**74**	38 52S	146 0E
Wall	**118**	44 0N	102 14W
Walla Walla	**120**	46 3N	118 25W
Wallabadah, N.S.W., Austral.	**77**	31 31S	150 49E
Wallabadah, Queens., Austral.	**72**	17 57S	142 15E
Wallace, Idaho, U.S.A.	**120**	47 30N	116 0W
Wallace, N.C., U.S.A.	**113**	34 44N	77 59W
Wallace, Nebr., U.S.A.	**118**	40 51N	101 12W
Wallaceburg	**106**	42 34N	82 23W
Wallacetown	**81**	46 21S	168 19E
Wallachia = Valahia	**34**	44 35N	25 0E
Wallacia	**76**	33 50S	150 39E
Wallal	**73**	26 32S	146 7E
Wallal Downs	**78**	19 47S	120 40E
Wallambin, L.	**79**	30 57S	117 35E
Wallan	**74**	37 26S	144 59E
Wallangarra	**77**	28 56S	151 58E
Wallangra	**77**	29 15S	150 54E
Wallaroo	**73**	33 56S	137 39E
Wallasey	**12**	53 26N	3 2W
Walldürn	**31**	49 34N	9 23E
Wallendbeen	**76**	34 31S	148 11E
Wallerawang	**76**	33 25S	150 4E
Wallhallow	**72**	17 50S	135 50E
Wallingford, U.K.	**12**	51 40N	1 15W
Wallingford, U.S.A.	**115**	41 27N	72 50W
Wallis Arch.	**66**	13 18S	176 10W
Wallis, L.	**77**	32 15S	152 28E
Wallowa	**120**	45 40N	117 35W
Wallowa, Mts.	**120**	45 20N	117 30W
Wallsend, Austral.	**76**	32 55S	151 40E
Wallsend, U.K.	**12**	54 59N	1 30W
Wallula	**120**	46 3N	118 59W
Wallumbilla	**73**	26 33S	149 9E
Walmer	**96**	33 57S	25 35E
Walmsley, L.	**109**	63 25N	108 36W
Walney, Isle of	**12**	54 5N	3 15W
Walnut	**116**	41 33N	89 36W
Walnut Ridge	**119**	36 7N	90 58W
Walpa	**75**	37 48S	147 27E
Walpeup	**74**	35 7S	142 2E
Walsall	**13**	52 36N	1 59W
Walsenburg	**119**	37 42N	104 45W
Walsh	**119**	37 28N	102 15W
Walsh →	**72**	16 31S	143 42E
Walsh P.O.	**72**	16 40S	144 0E
Walsrode	**30**	52 51N	9 37E
Waltair	**50**	17 44N	83 23E
Walterboro	**113**	32 53N	80 40W
Walters	**119**	34 25N	98 20W
Waltershausen	**30**	50 53N	10 33E
Waltham	**115**	42 22N	71 12W
Waltham Sta.	**104**	45 57N	76 57W
Waltman	**120**	43 8N	107 15W
Walton, Ky., U.S.A.	**117**	38 52N	84 37W
Walton, Mich., U.S.A.	**116**	44 30N	85 14W
Walton, N.Y., U.S.A.	**115**	42 12N	75 9W
Waltonville	**116**	38 13N	89 2W
Walu	**52**	26 28N	98 2E
Walvis Ridge	**129**	30 0S	3 0E
Walvisbaai	**96**	23 0S	14 28E
Walwa	**75**	35 59S	147 44E
Wamba, Kenya	**94**	0 58N	37 19E
Wamba, Zaïre	**94**	2 10N	27 57E
Wambelong, Mt.	**76**	31 19S	148 54E
Wamego	**118**	39 14N	96 22W
Wamena	**57**	4 4S	138 57E
Wampsville	**115**	43 4N	75 42W
Wamsasi	**57**	3 27S	126 7E
Wan Hat	**52**	20 14N	97 53E
Wan Kinghao	**52**	21 34N	98 17E
Wan Lai-kam	**52**	21 21N	98 22E
Wan Tup	**52**	21 13N	98 42E
Wan Xian	**60**	38 47N	115 7E
Wana	**48**	32 20N	69 32E
Wanaaring	**73**	29 38S	144 9E
Wanaka L.	**81**	44 33S	169 7E
Wan'an	**59**	26 26N	114 49E
Wanapiri	**57**	4 30S	135 59E
Wanapitei →	**106**	46 2N	80 51W
Wanapitei L.	**106**	46 45N	80 40W
Wanbi	**73**	34 46S	140 17E
Wandaik	**135**	4 27N	59 35W
Wandanian	**76**	35 6S	150 30E
Wanderer	**95**	19 36S	30 1E
Wandiwash	**51**	12 30N	79 30E
Wandoan	**73**	26 5S	149 55E
Wanfu	**61**	40 8N	122 38E
Wang →	**54**	17 8N	99 2E
Wang Kai (Ghâbat el Arab)	**91**	9 3N	29 23E
Wang Noi	**54**	14 13N	100 44E
Wang Saphung	**54**	17 18N	101 46E
Wang Thong	**54**	16 50N	100 26E
Wanga	**94**	2 58N	29 12E
Wangal	**57**	6 8S	134 9E
Wanganella	**74**	35 6S	144 49E
Wanganui	**80**	39 56S	175 3E
Wanganui →, N.I., N.Z.	**80**	39 55S	175 4E
Wanganui →, S.I., N.Z.	**81**	43 3S	170 26E
Wangaratta	**75**	36 21S	146 19E
Wangcang	**58**	32 18N	106 20E
Wangdu	**60**	38 40N	115 7E
Wangdu Phodrang	**52**	27 28N	89 54E
Wangerooge	**30**	53 47N	7 52E
Wangi	**94**	1 58S	40 58E
Wangiwangi	**57**	5 22S	123 37E
Wangjiang	**59**	30 10N	116 42E
Wangmo	**58**	25 11N	106 5E
Wangqing	**61**	43 12N	129 42E
Wankaner	**48**	22 35N	71 0E
Wankie	**95**	18 18S	26 30E
Wankie Nat. Park	**96**	19 0S	26 30E
Wanless	**109**	54 11N	101 21W
Wannian	**59**	28 42N	117 4E
Wannon →	**74**	37 38S	141 25E
Wanon Niwat	**54**	17 38N	103 46E
Wanquan	**60**	40 50N	114 40E
Wanrong	**60**	35 25N	110 50E
Wanshan	**58**	27 30N	109 12E
Wanshengchang	**58**	28 57N	106 53E
Wanstead	**80**	40 8S	176 30E
Wantabadgery	**76**	35 0S	147 43E
Wanxian	**58**	30 42N	108 20E
Wanyin	**52**	20 23N	97 15E
Wanyuan	**58**	32 4N	108 3E
Wanzai	**59**	28 7N	114 30E
Wanzarīk	**87**	27 31N	13 30E
Wapakoneta	**117**	40 35N	84 10W
Wapato	**120**	46 30N	120 25W
Wapawekka L.	**109**	54 55N	104 40W
Wapello	**116**	41 11N	91 11W
Wappingers Falls	**115**	41 35N	73 56W
Wapsipinicon →	**116**	41 44N	90 19W
Warabi	**65**	35 49N	139 41E
Warandab	**45**	7 20N	44 2E
Waranga Res.	**74**	36 32S	145 5E
Warangal	**50**	17 58N	79 35E
Waratah	**72**	41 30S	145 30E
Waratah B.	**74**	38 54S	146 5E
Warburg	**30**	51 29N	9 10E
Warburton	**74**	37 47S	145 42E
Warburton →	**73**	28 4S	137 28E
Warburton Ra.	**79**	25 55S	126 28E
Ward	**81**	41 49S	174 11E
Ward →	**73**	26 32S	146 6E
Ward Cove	**108**	55 25N	132 43W
Ward Hunt, C.	**69**	8 2S	148 10E
Ward Hunt Str.	**69**	9 30S	150 0E
Ward Mt.	**122**	37 12N	118 54W
Wardak □	**47**	34 0N	68 0E
Wardell	**77**	28 54S	153 31E
Warden	**97**	27 50S	29 0E
Wardha	**50**	20 45N	78 39E
Wardlow	**108**	50 56N	111 31W
Wards River	**77**	32 11S	151 56E
Ware, Can.	**108**	57 26N	125 41W
Ware, U.S.A.	**115**	42 16N	72 15W
Wareham	**115**	41 45N	70 44W
Waren	**30**	53 30N	12 41E
Warendorf	**30**	51 57N	8 0E
Warialda	**77**	29 29S	150 33E
Wariap	**57**	1 30S	134 5E
Warin Chamrap	**54**	15 12N	104 53E
Warkopi	**57**	1 12S	134 9E
Warkton	**77**	31 21S	149 13E
Warkworth	**80**	36 24S	174 41E
Warley	**13**	52 30N	2 0W
Warm Springs, Mont., U.S.A.	**120**	46 11N	112 48W
Warm Springs, Nev., U.S.A.	**121**	38 16N	116 32W
Warman	**109**	52 19N	106 30W
Warmbad, North, Namibia	**96**	19 14S	13 51E
Warmbad, South, Namibia	**96**	28 25S	18 42E
Warmbad, S. Afr.	**97**	24 51S	28 19E
Warmeriville	**19**	49 20N	4 13E
Warnambool Downs	**72**	22 48S	142 52E
Warnemünde	**30**	54 9N	12 5E
Warner	**108**	49 17N	112 12W
Warner Range, Mts.	**120**	41 30S	120 20W
Warner Robins	**113**	32 41N	83 36W
Warnes	**137**	17 30S	63 10W
Warnow →	**30**	54 6N	12 9E
Waroona	**79**	32 50S	115 58E
Warora	**50**	20 14N	79 1E
Warragul	**74**	38 10S	145 58E
Warrawagine	**78**	20 51S	120 42E
Warrego →	**73**	30 24S	145 21E
Warrego Ra.	**72**	25 15S	146 0E
Warren, Austral.	**76**	31 42S	147 51E
Warren, Can.	**106**	46 27N	80 18W
Warren, Ark., U.S.A.	**119**	33 35N	92 3W
Warren, Ill., U.S.A.	**116**	42 30N	89 59W
Warren, Mich., U.S.A.	**117**	42 31N	83 2W
Warren, Minn., U.S.A.	**118**	48 12N	96 46W
Warren, Ohio, U.S.A.	**114**	41 18N	80 52W
Warren, Pa., U.S.A.	**114**	41 52N	79 10W
Warrenpoint	**15**	54 7N	6 15W
Warrensburg, Ill., U.S.A.	**116**	39 56N	89 4W
Warrensburg, Mo., U.S.A.	**118**	38 45N	93 45W
Warrenton, S. Afr.	**96**	28 9S	24 47E
Warrenton, Mo., U.S.A.	**116**	38 49N	91 9W
Warrenton, Oreg., U.S.A.	**122**	46 11N	123 59W
Warrenville	**73**	25 48S	147 22E
Warri	**89**	5 30N	5 41E
Warrie	**78**	22 12S	119 40E
Warrina	**73**	28 12S	135 50E
Warrington, N.Z.	**81**	45 43S	170 35E
Warrington, U.K.	**12**	53 25N	2 38W
Warrington, U.S.A.	**113**	30 22N	87 16W
Warrnambool	**74**	38 25S	142 30E
Warroad	**118**	48 54N	95 19W
Warsa	**57**	0 47S	135 55E
Warsaw, Ill., U.S.A.	**116**	40 22N	91 26W
Warsaw, Ind., U.S.A.	**117**	41 14N	85 50W
Warsaw, Ky., U.S.A.	**117**	38 47N	84 54W
Warsaw, Mo., U.S.A.	**116**	38 15N	93 23W
Warsaw, N.Y., U.S.A.	**114**	42 46N	78 10W
Warsaw, Ohio, U.S.A.	**114**	40 20N	82 0W
Warstein	**30**	51 26N	8 20E
Warszawa	**32**	52 13N	21 0E
Warta →	**32**	52 35N	14 39E
Waru	**57**	3 30S	130 36E
Warud	**50**	21 30N	78 16E
Warwick, Austral.	**77**	28 10S	152 1E
Warwick, U.K.	**13**	52 17N	1 36W
Warwick, U.S.A.	**115**	41 43N	71 25W
Warwick □	**13**	52 20N	1 30W
Wasa	**108**	49 45N	115 50W
Wasaga Beach	**106**	44 31N	80 1W
Wasatch, Ra.	**120**	40 30N	111 15W
Wasbank	**97**	28 15S	30 9E
Wasco, Calif., U.S.A.	**123**	35 37N	119 16W
Wasco, Oreg., U.S.A.	**120**	45 36N	120 46W
Waseca	**118**	44 3N	93 31W
Wasekamio L.	**109**	56 45N	108 45W
Wash, The	**12**	52 58N	0 20E
Washago	**106**	44 45N	79 20W
Washburn, Ill., U.S.A.	**116**	40 55N	89 17W
Washburn, N.D., U.S.A.	**118**	47 17N	101 0W
Washburn, Wis., U.S.A.	**118**	46 38N	90 55W
Washington, D.C., U.S.A.	**112**	38 52N	77 0W
Washington, Ga., U.S.A.	**113**	33 45N	82 45W
Washington, Ind., U.S.A.	**117**	38 40N	87 8W
Washington, Iowa, U.S.A.	**116**	41 20N	91 45W
Washington, Mo, U.S.A.	**116**	38 35N	91 1W
Washington, N.C., U.S.A.	**113**	35 35N	77 1W
Washington, N.J., U.S.A.	**115**	40 45N	74 59W
Washington, Pa., U.S.A.	**114**	40 10N	80 20W
Washington, Utah, U.S.A.	**121**	37 10N	113 30W
Washington □	**120**	47 45N	120 30W
Washington Court House	**117**	39 34N	83 26W
Washington I., Pac. Oc.	**67**	4 43N	160 25W
Washington I., U.S.A.	**112**	45 24N	86 54W
Washington Mt.	**115**	44 15N	71 18W
Washougal	**122**	45 35N	122 21W
Wasian	**57**	1 47S	133 19E
Wasior	**57**	2 43S	134 30E
Waskaiowaka, L.	**109**	56 33N	96 23W
Waskesiu Lake	**109**	53 55N	106 5W
Wasm	**90**	18 2N	41 32E
Wassenaar	**16**	52 8N	4 24E
Wasserburg	**31**	48 4N	12 15E

Wasserkuppe **30** 50 30N 9 56 E
Wassy **19** 48 30N 4 58 E
Waswanipi **104** 49 40N 76 29W
Waswanipi → **104** 49 40N 76 25W
Waswanipi, L. **104** 49 35N 76 40W
Watangpone **57** 4 29S 120 25 E
Watchem **74** 36 9S 142 52 E
Water Park Pt. **72** 22 56S 150 47 E
Water Valley **119** 34 9N 89 38W
Waterberg, Namibia **96** 20 30S 17 18 E
Waterberg, S. Afr. **97** 24 14S 28 0 E
Waterbury, Conn., U.S.A. **115** 41 32N 73 0W
Waterbury, Vt., U.S.A. **115** 44 22N 72 44W
Waterbury L. **109** 58 10N 104 22W
Waterdown **106** 43 20N 79 53W
Waterford, Can. **106** 42 56N 80 17W
Waterford, Ireland **15** 52 16N 7 8W
Waterford, Calif., U.S.A. **122** 37 38N 120 46W
Waterford, Wis., U.S.A. **117** 42 46N 88 13W
Waterford □ **15** 52 10N 7 40W
Waterford Harb. **15** 52 10N 6 58W
Waterhen L., Man., Can. **109** 52 10N 99 40W
Waterhen L., Sask., Can. **109** 54 28N 108 25W
Waterloo, Belg. **16** 50 43N 4 25 E
Waterloo, Ont., Can. **106** 43 30N 80 32W
Waterloo, Qué., Can. **105** 45 22N 72 32W
Waterloo, S. Leone **88** 8 26N 13 8W
Waterloo, Ill., U.S.A. **116** 38 22N 90 6W
Waterloo, Ind., U.S.A. **117** 41 24N 85 2W
Waterloo, Iowa, U.S.A. **116** 42 27N 92 20W
Waterloo, N.Y., U.S.A. **114** 42 54N 76 53W
Waterloo, Wis., U.S.A. **116** 43 11N 88 59W
Waterman **117** 41 46N 88 47W
Watersmeet **118** 46 15N 89 12W
Waterton Lakes Nat. Park **108** 49 5N 114 15W
Watertown, Conn., U.S.A. **115** 41 36N 73 7W
Watertown, N.Y., U.S.A. **115** 43 58N 75 57W
Watertown, S.D., U.S.A. **118** 44 57N 97 5W
Watertown, Wis., U.S.A. **117** 43 15N 88 45W
Waterval-Boven **97** 25 40S 30 18 E
Waterville, Can. **105** 45 16N 71 54W
Waterville, Me., U.S.A. **103** 44 35N 69 40W
Waterville, N.Y., U.S.A. **115** 42 56N 75 23W
Waterville, Pa., U.S.A. **114** 41 19N 77 21W
Waterville, Wash., U.S.A. **120** 47 38N 120 1W
Watervliet, Mich., U.S.A. **117** 42 11N 86 18W
Watervliet, N.Y., U.S.A. **115** 42 46N 73 43W
Wates **57** 7 53S 110 6 E
Watford, Can. **106** 42 57N 81 53W
Watford, U.K. **13** 51 38N 0 23W
Watford City **118** 47 50N 103 23W
Wathaman → **109** 57 16N 102 59W
Watheroo **79** 30 15S 116 0W
Wating **60** 35 40N 106 38 E
Watkins Glen **114** 42 25N 76 55W
Watling I. = San Salvador **127** 24 0N 74 35W
Watonga **119** 35 51N 98 24W
Watraba **73** 31 58S 133 13 E
Watrous, Can. **109** 51 40N 105 25W
Watrous, U.S.A. **119** 35 50N 104 55W
Watsa **94** 3 4N 29 30 E
Watseka **117** 40 45N 87 45W
Watson, Austral. **79** 30 29S 131 31 E
Watson, Can. **109** 52 10N 104 30W
Watson Lake **100** 60 6N 128 49W
Watsonville **122** 36 55N 121 49W
Wattiwarriganna Cr. → **73** 28 57S 136 10 E
Wattle Flat **76** 33 8S 149 43 E
Wattwil **31** 47 18N 9 6 E
Watuata = Batuata **57** 6 12S 122 42 E
Watubela, Kepulauan **57** 4 28S 131 35 E
Wau **69** 7 21S 146 47 E
Waubamik **106** 45 27N 80 1W
Waubaushene **106** 44 45N 79 42W
Waubay **118** 45 22N 97 17W
Waubra **74** 37 21S 143 39 E
Wauchope **77** 31 28S 152 45 E
Wauchula **113** 27 35N 81 50W
Waugh **109** 49 40N 95 11W
Waukegan **117** 42 22N 87 54W
Waukesha **117** 43 0N 88 15W
Waukon **118** 43 14N 91 33W
Wauneta **118** 40 27N 101 25W
Waupaca **118** 44 22N 89 8W
Waupun **118** 43 38N 88 44W
Waurika **119** 34 12N 98 0W
Wausau **118** 44 57N 89 40W
Wauseon **117** 41 33N 84 8W
Wautoma **118** 44 3N 89 20W
Wauwatosa **117** 43 6N 87 59W
Wave Hill **78** 17 32S 131 0 E
Waveland **117** 39 53N 87 3W
Waveney → **13** 52 24N 1 20 E
Waverley **80** 39 46S 174 37 E
Waverly, Ill., U.S.A. **116** 39 36N 89 57W
Waverly, Iowa, U.S.A. **116** 42 40N 92 30W
Waverly, Mo., U.S.A. **116** 39 13N 93 31W
Waverly, N.Y., U.S.A. **115** 42 0N 76 33W
Wavre **16** 50 43N 4 38 E
Wâw **91** 7 45N 28 1 E
Waw al Kabir **85** 25 20N 17 20 E
Wāw an Nāmūs **87** 24 55N 17 46 E
Wawa, Can. **102** 47 59N 84 47W
Wawa, Nigeria **89** 9 54N 4 27 E
Wawa, Sudan **90** 20 30N 30 22 E
Wawagosic → **104** 49 58N 79 6W
Wawanesa **109** 49 36N 99 40W
Wawasee, L. **117** 41 24N 85 42W
Wawoi → **69** 7 48S 143 16 E
Wawona **122** 37 32N 119 39W
Waxahachie **119** 32 22N 96 53W
Waxweiler **31** 50 6N 6 22 E
Way, L. **79** 26 45S 120 16 E
Wayabula Rau **57** 2 29N 128 17 E
Wayagamac, L. **105** 47 21N 72 39W
Wayatinah **72** 42 19S 146 27 E
Waycross **113** 31 12N 82 25W
Wayi **91** 5 8N 30 10 E
Wayland **117** 42 40N 85 39W
Wayne, Mich., U.S.A. **106** 42 17N 83 23W
Wayne, Nebr., U.S.A. **118** 42 16N 97 0W
Wayne, W. Va., U.S.A. **112** 38 15N 82 27W
Wayne City **117** 38 21N 88 35W
Waynesboro, Ga., U.S.A. **113** 33 6N 82 1W
Waynesboro, Miss., U.S.A. **113** 31 40N 88 39W
Waynesboro, Pa., U.S.A. **112** 39 46N 77 32W
Waynesboro, Va., U.S.A. **112** 38 4N 78 57W
Waynesburg **112** 39 54N 80 12W
Waynesville, Kans., U.S.A. **116** 37 50N 92 12W
Waynesville, N.C., U.S.A. **113** 35 31N 83 0W
Waynesville, Ohio, U.S.A. **117** 39 32N 84 5W
Waynoka **119** 36 38N 98 53W
Waza **48** 33 22N 69 22 E
Wāzin **87** 31 58N 10 40 E
Wazirabad **48** 32 30N 74 8 E
We **56** 5 51N 95 18 E
Wé **68** 20 55S 167 16 E
Weald, The **13** 51 7N 0 9 E
Wear → **12** 54 55N 1 22W
Weatherford, Okla., U.S.A. **119** 35 30N 98 45W
Weatherford, Tex., U.S.A. **119** 32 45N 97 48W
Weaubleau **116** 37 54N 93 32W
Weaverville **120** 40 44N 122 56W
Webb City **119** 37 9N 94 30W
Webbwood **106** 46 16N 81 52W
Weber **80** 40 24S 176 20 E
Webera, Basel, Ethiopia **91** 6 29N 40 33 E
Webera, Shewa, Ethiopia **91** 9 40N 39 0 E
Webster, Mass., U.S.A. **115** 42 4N 71 54W
Webster, N.Y., U.S.A. **114** 43 11N 77 27W
Webster, S.D., U.S.A. **118** 45 24N 97 33W
Webster, Wis., U.S.A. **118** 45 53N 92 25W
Webster City **116** 42 30N 93 50W
Webster Green **118** 38 38N 90 20W
Webster Springs **112** 38 30N 80 25W
Weda **57** 0 21N 127 50 E
Weda, Teluk **57** 0 30N 127 50 E
Weddell I. **142** 51 50S 61 0W
Weddell Sea **143** 72 30S 40 0W
Wedderburn **74** 36 26S 143 33 E
Wedgeport **103** 43 44N 65 59W
Wedza **95** 18 40S 31 33 E
Wee Jasper **76** 35 8S 148 40 E
Wee Waa **77** 30 11S 149 26 E
Weed **120** 41 29N 122 22W
Weed Heights **122** 38 59N 119 13W
Weedon-Centre **105** 45 42N 71 27W
Weedsport **115** 43 3N 76 35W
Weedville **114** 41 17N 78 28W
Weemelah **77** 29 2S 149 15 E
Weenen **97** 28 48S 30 7 E
Weener **30** 53 10N 7 23 E
Weert **16** 51 15N 5 43 E
Weetaliba **77** 31 35S 149 39 E
Wegliniec **32** 51 18N 15 10 E
Węgorzewo **32** 54 13N 21 43 E
Węgrów **32** 52 24N 22 0 E
Wei He →, Hebei, China **60** 36 10N 115 45 E
Wei He →, Shaanxi, China **60** 34 38N 110 15 E
Weichang **61** 41 58N 117 49 E
Weichuan **60** 34 20N 113 59 E
Weida **30** 50 47N 12 3 E
Weiden **31** 49 40N 12 10 E
Weifang **61** 36 44N 119 7 E
Weilburg **30** 50 28N 8 17 E
Weilheim **31** 47 50N 11 9 E
Weimar **30** 51 0N 11 20 E
Weinan **60** 34 31N 109 29 E
Weingarten **31** 47 49N 9 39 E
Weinheim **31** 49 33N 8 40 E
Weining **58** 26 50N 104 17 E
Weipa **72** 12 40S 141 50 E
Weir →, Austral. **77** 28 20S 149 50 E
Weir →, Can. **109** 56 54N 93 21W
Weir River **109** 56 49N 94 6W
Weirton **114** 40 23N 80 35W
Weiser **120** 44 10N 117 0W
Weishan, Shandong, China **61** 34 47N 117 5 E
Weishan, Yunnan, China **58** 25 12N 100 20 E
Weissenburg **31** 49 2N 10 58 E
Weissenfels **30** 51 11N 12 0 E
Weisswasser **30** 51 30N 14 36 E
Weixi **58** 27 10N 99 10 E
Weixin **58** 27 48N 105 3 E
Weiyuan **60** 35 7N 104 10 E
Weiz **33** 47 13N 15 39 E
Weizhou Dao **58** 21 0N 109 5 E
Wejherowo **32** 54 35N 18 12 E
Wekusko **109** 54 30N 99 45W
Wekusko L. **109** 54 40N 99 50W
Welbourn Hill **73** 27 21S 134 6 E
Welby **109** 50 33N 101 29W
Welch **112** 37 29N 81 36W
Weldya **91** 11 50N 39 34 E
Welega □ **91** 9 25N 34 20 E
Welkite **91** 8 15N 37 42 E
Welkom **96** 28 0S 26 50 E
Welland **106** 43 0N 79 15W
Welland → **12** 52 43N 0 10W
Wellesley Is. **72** 16 42S 139 30 E
Wellin **16** 50 5N 5 6 E
Wellingborough **13** 52 18N 0 41W
Wellington, Austral. **76** 32 35S 148 59 E
Wellington, Can. **107** 43 57N 77 20W
Wellington, N.Z. **80** 41 19S 174 46 E
Wellington, S. Afr. **96** 33 38S 18 57 E
Wellington, U.K. **13** 50 58N 3 13W
Wellington, Col., U.S.A. **118** 40 43N 105 0W
Wellington, Kans., U.S.A. **119** 37 15N 97 25W
Wellington, Mo., U.S.A. **116** 39 8N 93 59W
Wellington, Nev., U.S.A. **122** 38 47N 119 28W
Wellington, Ohio, U.S.A. **114** 41 9N 82 12W
Wellington, Tex., U.S.A. **119** 34 55N 100 13W
Wellington □ **81** 40 8S 175 36 E
Wellington, I. **142** 49 30S 75 0W
Wellington, L. **75** 38 6S 147 20 E
Wellington (Telford) **12** 52 42N 2 31W
Wells, Norfolk, U.K. **12** 52 57N 0 51 E
Wells, Somerset, U.K. **13** 51 12N 2 39W
Wells, Me., U.S.A. **115** 43 18N 70 35W
Wells, Minn., U.S.A. **118** 43 44N 93 45W
Wells, Nev., U.S.A. **120** 41 8N 115 0W
Wells Gray Prov. Park **108** 52 30N 120 15W
Wells L. **79** 26 44S 123 15 E
Wells River **115** 44 9N 72 4W
Wellsboro **114** 41 45N 77 20W
Wellsburg **114** 40 15N 80 36W
Wellsford **80** 36 16S 174 32 E
Wellsville, Mo., U.S.A. **116** 39 4N 91 30W
Wellsville, N.Y., U.S.A. **114** 42 9N 77 53W
Wellsville, Ohio, U.S.A. **114** 40 36N 80 40W
Wellsville, Utah, U.S.A. **120** 41 35N 111 59W
Wellton **121** 32 39N 114 6W
Welmel, Wabi → **91** 5 38N 40 47 E
Welo □ **91** 11 50N 39 48 E
Wels **33** 48 9N 14 1 E
Welshpool, Austral. **75** 38 42S 146 26 E
Welshpool, U.K. **13** 52 40N 3 9W
Welwel **45** 7 5N 45 25 E
Welwyn **109** 50 20N 101 30W
Wem **12** 52 52N 2 45W
Wembere → **94** 4 10S 34 15 E
Wen Xian, Gansu, China **60** 32 43N 104 36 E
Wen Xian, Henan, China **60** 34 55N 113 5 E
Wenatchee **120** 47 30N 120 17W
Wenchang **54** 19 38N 110 42 E
Wencheng **59** 27 46N 120 4 E
Wenchi **88** 7 46N 2 8W
Wenchow = Wenzhou **59** 28 0N 120 38 E
Wenchuan **58** 31 22N 103 35 E
Wendell **120** 42 50N 114 42W
Wendeng **61** 37 15N 122 5 E
Wendesi **57** 2 30S 134 17 E
Wendo **91** 6 40N 38 27 E
Wendon **123** 33 49N 113 33W
Wendover **120** 40 49N 114 1W
Weng'an **58** 27 5N 107 25 E
Wengcheng **59** 24 22N 113 50 E
Wenge **94** 0 3N 24 0 E
Wengyuan **59** 24 20N 114 9 E
Wenjiang **58** 30 44N 103 55 E
Wenling **59** 28 21N 121 20 E
Wenlock **72** 13 6S 142 58 E
Wenlock → **72** 12 2S 141 55 E
Wenona **116** 41 3N 89 3W
Wenshan **58** 23 20N 104 18 E
Wenshang **60** 35 45N 116 30 E
Wenshui, Guizhou, China **58** 28 27N 106 28 E
Wenshui, Shanxi, China **60** 37 26N 112 1 E
Wensu **62** 41 15N 80 10 E
Wentworth **74** 34 2S 141 54 E
Wentzville **116** 38 49N 90 51W
Wenut **57** 3 11S 133 19 E
Wenxi **60** 35 20N 111 10 E
Wenzhou **59** 28 0N 120 38 E
Weott **120** 40 19N 123 56W
Wepener **96** 29 42S 27 3 E
Werda **96** 25 24S 23 15 E
Werdau **30** 50 45N 12 20 E
Werder, Ethiopia **45** 6 58N 45 1 E
Werder, Ger. **30** 52 23N 12 56 E
Werdohl **30** 51 15N 7 47 E
Wereilu **91** 10 40N 39 28 E
Weri **57** 3 10S 132 38 E
Werne **30** 51 38N 7 38 E
Werneck **31** 49 59N 10 6 E
Wernigerode **30** 51 49N 10 45 E
Werombi **76** 33 58S 150 34 E
Werra → **30** 51 26N 9 39 E
Werribee **74** 37 54S 144 40 E
Werrimull **74** 34 25S 141 38 E
Werris Creek **77** 31 18S 150 38 E
Wersar **57** 1 30S 131 55 E
Wertach → **31** 48 24N 10 53 E
Wertheim **31** 49 44N 9 32 E
Wertingen **31** 48 33N 10 41 E
Wesel **30** 51 39N 6 34 E
Weser → **30** 53 33N 8 30 E
Wesiri **57** 7 30S 126 30 E
Weslemkoon L. **107** 45 2N 77 25W
Wesleyville, Can. **103** 49 8N 53 36W
Wesleyville, U.S.A. **114** 42 9N 80 1W
Wessel, C. **72** 10 59S 136 46 E
Wessel Is. **72** 11 10S 136 45 E
Wesselburen **30** 54 11N 8 53 E
Wessington **118** 44 30N 98 40W
Wessington Springs **118** 44 10N 98 35W
West **119** 31 50N 97 5W
West Allis **117** 43 1N 87 0W
West B. **119** 29 5N 89 27W
West Baines → **78** 15 38S 129 59 E
West Bend **112** 43 25N 88 10W
West Bengal □ **49** 23 0N 88 0 E
West Branch **106** 44 16N 84 13W
West Bromwich **13** 52 32N 2 1W
West Cape Howe **79** 35 8S 117 36 E
West Carrollton **117** 39 40N 84 17W
West Chazy **115** 44 49N 73 28W
West Chester **112** 39 58N 75 36W
West Chicago **117** 41 53N 88 12W
West Columbia **119** 29 10N 95 38W
West Covina **123** 34 4N 117 54W
West Des Moines **116** 41 30N 93 45W
West End **126** 26 41N 78 58W
West Falkland **142** 51 40S 60 0W
West Frankfurt **116** 37 56N 89 0W
West Germany ■ **30** 50 0N 8 0 E
West Glamorgan □ **13** 51 40N 3 55W
West Hartford **115** 41 45N 72 45W
West Haven **115** 41 18N 72 57W
West Helena **119** 34 30N 90 40W
West Ice Shelf **143** 67 0S 85 0 E

West Indies 127 15 0N 70 0W
West Lafayette 117 40 27N 86 55W
West Liberty, Iowa, U.S.A. 116 41 34N 91 16W
West Liberty, Ky., U.S.A. 117 37 55N 83 16W
West Liberty, Ohio, U.S.A. 117 40 15N 83 45W
West Looe 13 50 21N 4 29W
West Lorne 106 42 36N 81 36W
West Lunga → 95 13 6S 24 39 E
West Magpie → 103 51 2N 64 42W
West Manchester 117 39 55N 84 38W
West Memphis 119 35 5N 90 11W
West Midlands □ 13 52 30N 1 55W
West Milton 117 39 58N 84 20W
West Monroe 119 32 32N 92 7W
West Moors 12 50 49N 1 50W
West Newton 114 40 14N 79 46W
West Nicholson 95 21 2S 29 20 E
West Palm Beach 113 26 44N 80 3W
West Pittston 115 41 19N 75 49W
West Plains 119 36 45N 91 50W
West Pt. 73 35 1S 135 56 E
West Point, Ga., U.S.A. 113 32 54N 85 10W
West Point, Ill., U.S.A. 116 40 15N 91 11W
West Point, Iowa, U.S.A. 116 40 43N 91 27W
West Point, Ky., U.S.A. 117 37 59N 85 57W
West Point, Miss., U.S.A. 113 33 36N 88 38W
West Point, Nebr., U.S.A. 118 41 50N 96 43W
West Point, Va., U.S.A. 112 37 35N 76 47W
West Pokot □ 94 1 30N 35 15 E
West Road → 108 53 18N 122 53W
West Rutland 115 43 38N 73 0W
West Salem 117 38 31N 88 1W
West Schelde = Westerschelde 16 51 25N 3 25 E
West Siberian Plain 42 62 0N 75 0 E
West Sussex □ 13 50 55N 0 30W
West Terre Haute 117 39 27N 87 27W
West-Terschelling 16 53 22N 5 13 E
West Union, Iowa, U.S.A. 116 42 57N 91 49W
West Union, Ohio, U.S.A. 117 38 48N 83 33W
West Unity 117 41 35N 84 26W
West Virginia □ 112 39 0N 81 0W
West-Vlaanderen □ 16 51 0N 3 0 E
West Walker → 122 38 54N 119 9W
West Wyalong 73 33 56S 147 10 E
West Yellowstone 120 44 47N 111 4W
West Yorkshire □ 12 53 45N 1 40W
Westall Pt. 73 32 55S 134 4 E
Westbrook, Maine, U.S.A. 113 43 40N 70 22W
Westbrook, Tex., U.S.A. 119 32 25N 101 0W
Westbury 72 41 30S 146 51 E
Westby 118 48 52N 104 3W
Westend 123 35 42N 117 24W
Westerland 30 54 51N 8 20 E
Western □, Kenya 94 0 30N 34 30 E
Western □, Uganda 94 1 45N 31 30 E
Western □, Zambia 95 15 15S 24 30 E
Western Australia □ 79 25 0S 118 0 E
Western Duck I. 106 45 45N 83 0W
Western Ghats 51 14 0N 75 0 E
Western Isles □ 14 57 30N 7 10W
Western Samoa ■ 68 14 0S 172 0W
Westernport 112 39 30N 79 5W
Westerschelde → 16 51 25N 3 25 E
Westerstede 30 53 15N 7 55 E
Westerwald 30 50 39N 8 0 E
Westfield, Ill., U.S.A. 117 39 27N 88 0W
Westfield, Ind., U.S.A. 117 40 2N 86 8W
Westfield, Mass., U.S.A. 115 42 9N 72 49W
Westfield, N.Y., U.S.A. 114 42 20N 79 38W
Westfield, Pa., U.S.A. 114 41 54N 77 32W
Westholme 77 29 19S 149 25 E
Westhope 118 48 55N 101 0W
Westland □ 81 43 33S 169 59 E
Westland Bight 81 42 55S 170 5 E
Westlock 108 54 9N 113 55W
Westmeath □ 15 53 30N 7 30W
Westmere 74 37 42S 142 58 E
Westminster 112 39 34N 77 1W
Westmorland 121 33 2N 115 42W
Weston, Malay. 56 5 10N 115 35 E
Weston, Ohio, U.S.A. 117 41 21N 83 47W
Weston, Oreg., U.S.A. 120 45 50N 118 30W
Weston, W. Va., U.S.A. 112 39 3N 80 29W
Weston I. 102 52 33N 79 36W
Weston-super-Mare 13 51 20N 2 59W
Westphalia 116 38 26N 92 0W
Westport, Can. 107 44 40N 76 25W
Westport, Ireland 15 53 44N 9 31W
Westport, N.Z. 81 41 46S 171 37 E
Westport, Ind., U.S.A. 117 39 11N 85 34W
Westport, Ore., U.S.A. 122 46 10N 123 23W
Westport, Wash., U.S.A. 120 46 48N 124 4W
Westray 109 53 36N 101 24W
Westray, I. 14 59 18N 3 0W
Westree 102 47 26N 81 34W
Westview 108 49 50N 124 31W
Westville, Calif., U.S.A. 122 39 8N 120 42W
Westville, Ill., U.S.A. 117 40 3N 87 36W
Westville, Ind., U.S.A. 117 41 35N 86 55W
Westville, Okla., U.S.A. 119 36 0N 94 33W
Westwood 120 40 26N 121 0W
Wetar 57 7 30S 126 30 E
Wetaskiwin 108 52 55N 113 24W
Wethersfield 115 41 43N 72 40W
Wetlet 52 22 20N 95 53 E
Wetteren 16 51 0N 3 53 E
Wetzlar 30 50 33N 8 30 E
Wewak 69 3 38S 143 41 E
Wewaka 119 35 10N 96 35W
Wexford 15 52 20N 6 28W
Wexford □ 15 52 20N 6 25W
Wexford Harb. 15 52 20N 6 25W
Weyburn 109 49 40N 103 50W
Weyburn L. 108 63 0N 117 59W
Weyer 33 47 51N 14 40 E
Weymouth, Can. 103 44 30N 66 1W
Weymouth, U.K. 13 50 36N 2 28W
Weymouth, U.S.A. 115 42 13N 70 53W
Weymouth, C. 72 12 37S 143 27 E
Whakamaru 80 38 23S 175 50 E
Whakatane 80 37 57S 177 1 E
Whalan Cr. → 77 29 5S 149 1 E
Whale → 103 58 15N 67 40W
Whale Cove 100 62 11N 92 36W
Whales, B. of 143 78 0S 165 0W
Whalsay 14 60 22N 1 0W
Whangamata 80 37 12S 175 53 E
Whangamomona 80 39 8S 174 44 E
Whangarei 80 35 43S 174 21 E
Whangarei Harbour 80 35 45S 174 28 E
Whangaroa Harb. 80 35 4S 173 46 E
Wharanui 81 41 55S 174 6 E
Wharfe → 12 53 55N 1 30W
Wharfedale 12 54 7N 2 4W
Wharton, N.J., U.S.A. 115 40 53N 74 36W
Wharton, Pa., U.S.A. 114 41 31N 78 1W
Wharton, Tex., U.S.A. 119 29 20N 96 6W
Whataroa 81 43 18S 170 24 E
Whataroa → 81 43 7S 170 16 E
Wheatfield 117 41 13N 87 4W
Wheatland, Calif., U.S.A. 122 39 1N 121 25W
Wheatland, Ind., U.S.A. 117 38 40N 87 19W
Wheatland, Wyo., U.S.A. 118 42 4N 104 58W
Wheatley 106 42 6N 82 27W
Wheaton, Ill., U.S.A. 117 41 52N 88 6W
Wheaton, Minn., U.S.A. 118 45 50N 96 29W
Wheelbarrow Pk. 122 37 26N 116 5W
Wheeler, Oreg., U.S.A. 120 45 50N 123 57W
Wheeler, Tex., U.S.A. 119 35 29N 100 15W
Wheeler → 109 57 25N 105 30W
Wheeler Peak 121 38 57N 114 15W
Wheeler Pk. 121 36 34N 105 25W
Wheeler Ridge 123 35 0N 118 57W
Wheeling 114 40 2N 80 41W
Whernside 12 54 14N 2 24W
Wherrol Flat 77 31 46S 152 15 E
Whetstone 77 28 30S 150 56 E
Whidbey I. 108 48 15N 122 40W
Whiporie 77 29 18S 152 58 E
Whiskey Gap 108 49 0N 113 3W
Whiskey Jack L. 109 58 23N 101 55W
Whistleduck Cr. → 72 20 15S 135 18 E
Whistler 113 30 50N 88 10W
Whitby, Can. 107 43 52N 78 56W
Whitby, U.K. 12 54 29N 0 37W
White →, Ark., U.S.A. 119 33 53N 91 3W
White →, Colo., U.S.A. 120 40 8N 109 41W
White →, Ind., U.S.A. 112 38 25N 87 44W
White →, Ind., U.S.A. 117 38 25N 87 45W
White →, S.D., U.S.A. 118 43 45N 99 30W
White →, Wash., U.S.A. 122 47 12N 122 15W
White B. 103 50 0N 56 35W
White Bear Res. 103 48 10N 57 5W
White Bird 120 45 46N 116 21W
White Butte 118 46 23N 103 19W
White City 118 38 50N 96 45W
White Cliffs, Austral. 73 30 50S 143 10 E
White Cliffs, N.Z. 81 43 26S 171 55 E
White Deer 119 35 30N 101 8W
White, East Fork → 117 38 33N 87 14W
White Hall 116 39 25N 90 27W
White Haven 115 41 3N 75 47W
White I. 80 37 30S 177 13 E
White L., Can. 107 45 18N 76 31W
White L., U.S.A. 119 29 45N 92 30W
White Mts., Calif., U.S.A. 122 37 30N 118 15W
White Mts., N.H., U.S.A. 115 44 15N 71 15W
White Nile = Nîl el Abyad → 91 15 38N 32 31 E
White Nile Dam 91 15 24N 32 30 E
White Otter L. 102 49 5N 91 55W
White Pass, Can. 100 59 40N 135 3W
White Pass, U.S.A. 122 46 38N 121 24W
White Pigeon 117 41 48N 85 39W
White Plains 115 41 2N 73 44W
White River, Can. 102 48 35N 85 20W
White River, S. Afr. 97 25 20S 31 00 E
White River, U.S.A. 118 43 34N 100 45W
White River Junc. 115 43 38N 72 20W
White Russia = Byelorussian SSR 36 53 30N 27 0 E
White Sea = Beloye More 40 66 30N 38 0 E
White Sulphur Springs, Mont., U.S.A. 120 46 35N 110 54W
White Sulphur Springs, W. Va., U.S.A. 112 37 50N 80 16W
White Swan 122 46 23N 120 44W
White Volta (Volta Blanche) → 89 9 10N 1 15W
Whitecourt 108 54 10N 115 45W
Whiteface 119 33 35N 102 40W
Whitefield 115 44 23N 71 37W
Whitefish, Can. 106 46 23N 81 19W
Whitefish, U.S.A. 120 48 25N 114 22W
Whitefish Bay 117 43 23N 87 54W
Whitefish Falls 106 46 7N 81 44W
Whitefish L. 109 62 41N 106 48W
Whitefish Pt. 112 46 45N 85 0W
Whitegull, L. 103 55 27N 64 17W
Whitehall, Mich., U.S.A. 112 43 21N 86 20W
Whitehall, Mont., U.S.A. 120 45 52N 112 4W
Whitehall, N.Y., U.S.A. 115 43 32N 73 28W
Whitehall, Wis., U.S.A. 118 44 20N 91 19W
Whitehaven 12 54 33N 3 35W
Whitehorse 100 60 43N 135 3W
Whitehorse, Vale of 13 51 37N 1 30W
Whiteman 116 38 45N 93 40W
Whiteman Ra. 69 5 55S 150 0 E
Whitemark 72 40 7S 148 3 E
Whitemouth 109 49 57N 95 58W
Whiteplains 88 6 28N 10 40W
Whitesail, L. 108 53 35N 127 45W
Whitesands 68 19 28S 169 25 E
Whitesboro, N.Y., U.S.A. 115 43 8N 75 20W
Whitesboro, Tex., U.S.A. 119 33 40N 96 58W
Whiteshell Prov. Park 109 50 0N 95 40W
Whiteside 116 39 12N 91 2W
Whiteside, Canal 142 53 55S 70 15W
Whitetail 118 48 54N 105 15W
Whiteville 113 34 20N 78 40W
Whitewater 117 42 50N 88 45W
Whitewater Baldy, Mt. 121 33 20N 108 44W
Whitewater L. 102 50 50N 89 10W
Whitewood, Austral. 72 21 28S 143 30 E
Whitewood, Can. 109 50 20N 102 20W
Whitfield 75 36 42S 146 24 E
Whithorn 14 54 44N 4 25W
Whitianga 80 36 47S 175 41 E
Whiting 117 41 41N 87 29W
Whitman 115 42 4N 70 55W
Whitmire 113 34 33N 81 40W
Whitney 107 45 31N 78 14W
Whitney, Mt. 122 36 35N 118 14W
Whitney Pt. 115 42 19N 75 59W
Whitstable 13 51 21N 1 2 E
Whitsunday I. 72 20 15S 149 4 E
Whittemore 116 43 4N 94 26W
Whittier 100 60 46N 148 48W
Whittlesea 74 37 27S 145 9 E
Whitwell 113 35 15N 85 30W
Wholdaia L. 109 60 43N 104 20W
Whorouly 75 36 31S 146 35 E
Whyalla 73 33 2S 137 30 E
Whyjonta 73 29 41S 142 28 E
Wiangaree 77 28 30S 152 59 E
Wiarton 106 44 40N 81 10W
Wiawso 88 6 10N 2 25W
Wibaux 118 47 0N 104 13W
Wichabai 135 2 57N 59 35W
Wichian Buri 54 15 39N 101 7 E
Wichita 119 37 40N 97 20W
Wichita Falls 119 33 57N 98 30W
Wick 14 58 26N 3 5W
Wicked Pt. 107 43 52N 77 15W
Wickenburg 121 33 58N 112 45W
Wickepin 79 32 50S 117 30 E
Wickett 119 31 37N 102 58W
Wickham 105 45 45N 72 30W
Wickham, C. 72 39 35S 143 57 E
Wickliffe 114 41 36N 81 29W
Wicklow 15 53 0N 6 2W
Wicklow □ 15 52 59N 6 25W
Wicklow Hd. 15 52 59N 6 3W
Wicklow Mts. 15 53 0N 6 30W
Widgiemooltha 79 31 30S 121 34 E
Widnes 12 53 22N 2 44W
Wiedenbrück 30 51 52N 8 15 E
Wiek 30 54 37N 13 17 E
Wielbark 32 53 24N 20 55 E
Wieliczka 32 50 0N 20 5 E
Wieluń 32 51 15N 18 34 E
Wien 33 48 12N 16 22 E
Wiener Neustadt 33 47 49N 16 16 E
Wieprz →, Koszalin, Poland 32 54 26N 16 35 E
Wieprz →, Lublin, Poland 32 51 34N 21 49 E
Wierden 16 52 22N 6 35 E
Wiesbaden 31 50 7N 8 17 E
Wiesental 31 49 15N 8 30 E
Wigan 12 53 33N 2 38W
Wiggins, Colo., U.S.A. 118 40 16N 104 3W
Wiggins, Miss., U.S.A. 119 30 53N 89 9W
Wight, I. of 13 50 40N 1 20W
Wigtown 14 54 52N 4 27W
Wigtown B. 14 54 46N 4 15W
Wikwemikong 106 45 48N 81 43W
Wil 31 47 28N 9 3 E
Wilber 118 40 34N 96 59W
Wilberforce 107 45 2N 78 13W
Wilberforce, C. 72 11 54S 136 35 E
Wilburton 119 34 55N 95 15W
Wilcannia 73 31 30S 143 26 E
Wilcox 114 41 34N 78 43W
Wildbad 31 48 44N 8 32 E
Wildcat Creek → 117 40 28N 86 48W
Wildeshausen 30 52 54N 8 25 E
Wildrose, Calif., U.S.A. 123 36 14N 117 11W
Wildrose, N. Dak., U.S.A. 118 48 36N 103 11W
Wildspitze 31 46 53N 10 53 E
Wildwood 112 38 59N 74 46W
Wilhelm II Coast 143 68 0S 90 0 E
Wilhelm Mt. 69 5 50S 145 1 E
Wilhelm-Pieck-Stadt Guben 30 51 59N 14 48 E
Wilhelmina, Geb. 135 3 50N 56 30W
Wilhelmsburg, Austria 33 48 6N 15 36 E
Wilhelmsburg, Ger. 30 53 28N 10 1 E
Wilhelmshaven 30 53 30N 8 9 E
Wilhelmstal 96 21 58S 16 21 E
Wilkes Barre 115 41 15N 75 52W
Wilkes Land 143 69 0S 120 0 E
Wilkes Sub-Glacial Basin 143 75 0S 130 0 E
Wilkesboro 113 36 10N 81 9W
Wilkie 109 52 27N 108 42W
Wilkinsburg 114 40 26N 79 50W
Wilkinson Lakes 79 29 40S 132 39 E
Willamina 120 45 9N 123 32W
Willandra Billabong Creek → 73 33 22S 145 52 E
Willapa, B. 120 46 44N 124 0W
Willapa Hills 122 46 35N 123 25W
Willard, N. Mex., U.S.A. 121 34 35N 106 1W
Willard, Utah, U.S.A. 120 41 28N 112 1W
Willaura 74 37 31S 142 45 E
Willcox 121 32 13N 109 53W
Willemstad 127 12 5N 69 0W
Willeroo 78 15 14S 131 37 E
William → 109 59 8N 109 19W
William Creek 73 28 58S 136 22 E
William, Mt. 74 37 17S 142 35 E
Williambury 79 23 45S 115 12 E
Williams, Austral. 79 33 2S 116 52 E
Williams, Ariz., U.S.A. 121 35 16N 112 11W

Williams, Calif., U.S.A.	**122**	39 9N	122 9W
Williams Lake	**108**	52 10N	122 10W
Williamsburg, Ky., U.S.A.	**113**	36 45N	84 10W
Williamsburg, Pa., U.S.A.	**114**	40 27N	78 14W
Williamsburg, Va., U.S.A.	**112**	37 17N	76 44W
Williamsfield	**116**	40 55N	90 1W
Williamson, N.Y., U.S.A.	**114**	43 14N	77 15W
Williamson, W. Va., U.S.A.	**112**	37 46N	82 17W
Williamsport, Ind., U.S.A.	**117**	40 17N	87 17W
Williamsport, Pa., U.S.A.	**114**	41 18N	77 1W
Williamston, Mich., U.S.A.	**117**	42 41N	84 17W
Williamston, S.C., U.S.A.	**113**	35 50N	77 5W
Williamstown, Austral.	**74**	37 51S	144 52E
Williamstown, Ky., U.S.A.	**117**	38 38N	84 34W
Williamstown, Mass., U.S.A.	**115**	42 41N	73 12W
Williamstown, N.Y., U.S.A.	**115**	43 25N	75 54W
Williamsville, Ill., U.S.A.	**116**	39 57N	89 33W
Williamsville, Mo., U.S.A.	**119**	37 0N	90 33W
Williamtown	**76**	32 48S	151 50E
Willimantic	**115**	41 45N	72 12W
Willis Group	**72**	16 18S	150 0E
Willisburg	**117**	37 49N	85 8W
Williston, S. Afr.	**96**	31 20S	20 53E
Williston, Fla., U.S.A.	**113**	29 25N	82 28W
Williston, N.D., U.S.A.	**118**	48 10N	103 35W
Williston L.	**108**	56 0N	124 0W
Willits	**120**	39 28N	123 17W
Willmar	**118**	45 5N	95 0W
Willoughby	**114**	41 38N	81 26W
Willow Bunch	**109**	49 20N	105 35W
Willow L.	**108**	62 10N	119 8W
Willow Lake	**118**	44 40N	97 40W
Willow River	**108**	54 6N	122 28W
Willow Springs	**119**	37 0N	92 0W
Willow Tree	**77**	31 40S	150 45E
Willow Wall, The	**61**	42 10N	122 0E
Willowlake →	**108**	62 42N	123 8W
Willowmore	**96**	33 15S	23 30E
Willows, Austral.	**72**	23 39S	147 25E
Willows, U.S.A.	**122**	39 30N	122 10W
Wills Cr. →	**72**	22 43S	140 2E
Wills, L.	**78**	21 25S	128 51E
Wills Pt.	**119**	32 42N	95 57W
Willunga	**73**	35 15S	138 30E
Wilmette	**112**	42 6N	87 44W
Wilmington, Austral.	**73**	32 39S	138 7E
Wilmington, Del., U.S.A.	**112**	39 45N	75 32W
Wilmington, Ill., U.S.A.	**117**	41 19N	88 10W
Wilmington, N.C., U.S.A.	**113**	34 14N	77 54W
Wilmington, Ohio, U.S.A.	**117**	39 27N	83 50W
Wilpena Cr. →	**73**	31 25S	139 29E
Wilsall	**120**	45 59N	110 40W
Wilson	**113**	35 44N	77 54W
Wilson →, Queens., Austral.	**73**	27 38S	141 24E
Wilson →, W. Australia, Austral.	**78**	16 48S	128 16E
Wilson Bluff	**79**	31 41S	129 0E
Wilson Inlet	**79**	35 0S	117 20E
Wilson, Mt.	**121**	37 55N	108 3W
Wilson Str.	**68**	8 0S	156 39E
Wilson's Promontory	**75**	38 55S	146 25E
Wilster	**30**	53 55N	9 23E
Wilton, U.K.	**13**	51 5N	1 52W
Wilton, U.S.A.	**118**	47 12N	100 47W
Wilton →	**72**	14 45S	134 33E
Wiltshire □	**13**	51 20N	2 0W
Wiltz	**16**	49 57N	5 55E
Wiluna	**79**	26 36S	120 14E
Wimereux	**19**	50 45N	1 37E
Wimmera →	**74**	36 8S	141 56E
Winam G.	**94**	0 20S	34 15E
Winamac	**117**	41 3N	86 36W
Winburg	**96**	28 30S	27 2E
Winchelsea	**74**	38 10S	144 1E
Winchendon	**115**	42 40N	72 3W
Winchester, Can.	**107**	45 6N	75 21W
Winchester, N.Z.	**81**	44 11S	171 17E
Winchester, U.K.	**13**	51 4N	1 19W
Winchester, Conn., U.S.A.	**115**	41 53N	73 9W
Winchester, Idaho, U.S.A.	**120**	46 11N	116 32W
Winchester, Ill., U.S.A.	**116**	39 38N	90 27W
Winchester, Ind., U.S.A.	**117**	40 10N	84 56W
Winchester, Ky., U.S.A.	**117**	38 0N	84 8W
Winchester, Mass., U.S.A.	**115**	42 28N	71 10W
Winchester, N.H., U.S.A.	**115**	42 47N	72 22W
Winchester, Nev., U.S.A.	**123**	36 6N	115 10W
Winchester, Ohio, U.S.A.	**117**	38 57N	83 40W
Winchester, Tenn., U.S.A.	**113**	35 11N	86 8W
Winchester, Va., U.S.A.	**112**	39 14N	78 8W
Wind →	**120**	43 8N	108 12W
Wind Pt.	**117**	42 47N	87 46W
Wind River Range	**120**	43 0N	109 30W
Windber	**114**	40 14N	78 50W
Windermere, L.	**12**	54 20N	2 57W
Windeyer	**76**	32 46S	149 32E
Windfall, Can.	**108**	54 12N	116 13W
Windfall, U.S.A.	**117**	40 22N	85 57W
Windflower L.	**108**	62 52N	118 30W
Windhoek	**96**	22 35S	17 4E
Windigo →	**105**	47 46N	73 19W
Windom	**118**	43 48N	95 3W
Windorah	**72**	25 24S	142 36E
Window Rock	**121**	35 47N	109 4W
Windrush →	**13**	51 48N	1 35W
Windsor, Austral.	**76**	33 37S	150 50E
Windsor, N.S., Can.	**103**	44 59N	64 5W
Windsor, Newf., Can.	**103**	48 57N	55 40W
Windsor, Ont., Can.	**106**	42 18N	83 0W
Windsor, Qué., Can.	**105**	45 34N	72 0W
Windsor, N.Z.	**81**	44 59S	170 49E
Windsor, U.K.	**13**	51 28N	0 36W
Windsor, Col., U.S.A.	**118**	40 33N	104 45W
Windsor, Conn., U.S.A.	**115**	41 50N	72 40W
Windsor, Ill., U.S.A.	**117**	39 26N	88 36W
Windsor, Mo., U.S.A.	**116**	38 32N	93 31W
Windsor, N.Y., U.S.A.	**115**	42 5N	75 37W
Windsor, Vt., U.S.A.	**115**	43 30N	72 25W
Windsorton	**96**	28 16S	24 44E
Windward Is., Atl. Oc.	**127**	13 0N	63 0W
Windward Is., Pac. Oc.	**67**	18 0S	149 0W
Windward Passage = Vientos, Paso de los	**127**	20 0N	74 0W
Windy L.	**109**	60 20N	100 2W
Winefred L.	**109**	55 30N	110 30W
Winejok	**91**	9 1N	27 30E
Winfield, Ill., U.S.A.	**116**	41 5N	91 30W
Winfield, Kans., U.S.A.	**119**	37 15N	97 0W
Winfield, Mo., U.S.A.	**116**	39 0N	90 44W
Wingate Mts.	**78**	14 25S	130 40E
Wingello	**76**	34 42S	150 10E
Wingen	**77**	31 54S	150 54E
Wingham, Austral.	**77**	31 48S	152 22E
Wingham, Can.	**106**	43 55N	81 20W
Winifred	**120**	47 30N	109 28W
Winisk	**102**	55 20N	85 15W
Winisk →	**102**	55 17N	85 5W
Winisk L.	**102**	52 55N	87 22W
Wink	**119**	31 49N	103 9W
Winkler	**109**	49 10N	97 56W
Winlock	**122**	46 29N	122 56W
Winneba	**89**	5 25N	0 36W
Winnebago, Ill., U.S.A.	**116**	42 15N	89 18W
Winnebago, Minn., U.S.A.	**118**	43 43N	94 8W
Winnebago L.	**112**	44 0N	88 20W
Winnecke Cr. →	**78**	18 35S	131 34E
Winnemucca	**120**	41 0N	117 45W
Winnemucca, L.	**120**	40 25N	119 21W
Winner	**118**	43 23N	99 52W
Winnetka	**112**	42 8N	87 46W
Winnett	**120**	47 2N	108 21W
Winnfield	**119**	31 57N	92 38W
Winnibigoshish L.	**118**	47 25N	94 12W
Winning	**78**	23 9S	114 30E
Winnipeg	**109**	49 54N	97 9W
Winnipeg →	**109**	50 38N	96 19W
Winnipeg Beach	**109**	50 30N	96 58W
Winnipeg, L.	**109**	52 0N	97 0W
Winnipegosis	**109**	51 39N	99 55W
Winnipegosis L.	**109**	52 30N	100 0W
Winnipesaukee, L.	**115**	43 38N	71 21W
Winnsboro, La., U.S.A.	**119**	32 10N	91 41W
Winnsboro, S.C., U.S.A.	**113**	34 23N	81 5W
Winnsboro, Tex., U.S.A.	**119**	32 56N	95 15W
Winokapau, L.	**103**	53 15N	62 50W
Winona, Miss., U.S.A.	**119**	33 30N	89 42W
Winona, Wis., U.S.A.	**118**	44 2N	91 39W
Winooski	**115**	44 31N	73 11W
Winschoten	**16**	53 9N	7 3E
Winsen	**30**	53 21N	10 11E
Winslow, Ariz., U.S.A.	**121**	35 2N	110 41W
Winslow, Ind., U.S.A.	**117**	38 23N	87 13W
Winslow, Wash., U.S.A.	**122**	47 37N	122 31W
Winsted	**115**	41 55N	73 5W
Winston-Salem	**113**	36 7N	80 15W
Winter Garden	**113**	28 33N	81 35W
Winter Haven	**113**	28 0N	81 42W
Winter Park	**113**	28 34N	81 19W
Winterberg	**30**	51 12N	8 30E
Winterhaven	**123**	32 47N	114 39W
Winters, Calif., U.S.A.	**122**	38 32N	121 58W
Winters, Tex., U.S.A.	**119**	31 58N	99 58W
Winterset	**116**	41 18N	94 0W
Wintersville	**114**	40 22N	80 38W
Winterswijk	**16**	51 58N	6 43E
Winterthur	**31**	47 30N	8 44E
Winthrop, Minn., U.S.A.	**118**	44 31N	94 25W
Winthrop, Wash., U.S.A.	**120**	48 27N	120 6W
Winton, Queens., Austral.	**72**	22 24S	143 3E
Winton, Vic., Austral.	**74**	36 32S	146 7E
Winton, N.Z.	**81**	46 8S	168 20E
Winton, N.C., U.S.A.	**113**	36 25N	76 58W
Winton, Pa., U.S.A.	**115**	41 27N	75 33W
Winton Swamp	**74**	36 27S	146 5E
Wintzenheim	**19**	48 4N	7 17E
Wipper →	**30**	51 17N	11 10E
Wirral	**12**	53 25N	3 0W
Wirrinya	**76**	33 39S	147 48E
Wirrulla	**73**	32 24S	134 31E
Wisbech	**12**	52 39N	0 10E
Wisconsin □	**118**	44 30N	90 0W
Wisconsin →	**118**	43 0N	91 15W
Wisconsin Dells	**118**	43 38N	89 45W
Wisconsin Rapids	**118**	44 25N	89 50W
Wisdom	**120**	45 37N	113 27W
Wisemans Ferry	**76**	33 22S	150 59E
Wishaw	**14**	55 46N	3 55W
Wishek	**118**	46 20N	99 35W
Wisła	**32**	49 38N	18 53E
Wisła →	**32**	54 22N	18 55E
Wisłok →	**32**	50 13N	22 32E
Wisłoka →	**32**	50 27N	21 23E
Wismar, Ger.	**30**	53 53N	11 23E
Wismar, Guyana	**135**	5 59N	58 18W
Wisner	**118**	42 0N	96 46W
Wissant	**19**	50 52N	1 40E
Wissembourg	**19**	49 2N	7 57E
Witbank	**97**	25 51S	29 14E
Witdraai	**96**	26 58S	20 48E
Witham →	**12**	53 3N	0 8W
Withernsea	**12**	53 43N	0 2E
Witney	**13**	51 47N	1 29W
Witnossob →	**96**	26 55S	20 37E
Wittdün	**30**	54 38N	8 23E
Witten	**30**	51 26N	7 19E
Wittenberg	**30**	51 51N	12 39E
Wittenberge	**30**	53 0N	11 44E
Wittenburg	**30**	53 30N	11 4E
Wittenoom	**78**	22 15S	118 20E
Wittingen	**30**	52 43N	10 43E
Wittlich	**31**	50 0N	6 54E
Wittmund	**30**	53 39N	7 45E
Wittow	**30**	54 37N	13 21E
Wittstock	**30**	53 10N	12 30E
Witzenhausen	**30**	51 20N	9 50E
Wiyeb, Wabi →	**91**	7 15N	40 15E
Wlingi	**57**	8 5S	112 25E
Włocławek	**32**	52 40N	19 3E
Włodawa	**32**	51 33N	23 31E
Włoszczowa	**32**	50 50N	19 55E
Woburn	**115**	42 31N	71 7W
Wodian	**60**	32 50N	112 35E
Wodonga	**75**	36 5S	146 50E
Woerth	**19**	48 57N	7 45E
Woëvre, Plaine de la	**19**	49 15N	5 45E
Woinbogoin	**58**	32 51N	98 39E
Wokam	**57**	5 45S	134 28E
Wokha	**52**	26 6N	94 16E
Woking	**108**	55 35N	118 50W
Wolbrom	**32**	50 24N	19 45E
Wolcottville	**117**	41 32N	85 22W
Woldegk	**30**	53 27N	13 35E
Wolf →	**108**	60 17N	132 33W
Wolf Creek	**120**	47 1N	112 2W
Wolf L.	**108**	60 24N	131 40W
Wolf Point	**118**	48 6N	105 40W
Wolfe I.	**107**	44 7N	76 20W
Wolfenbüttel	**30**	52 10N	10 33E
Wolfenden	**108**	52 0N	119 25W
Wolfsberg	**33**	46 50N	14 52E
Wolfsburg	**30**	52 27N	10 49E
Wolgast	**30**	54 3N	13 46E
Wolhusen	**31**	47 4N	8 4E
Wolin	**32**	53 50N	14 37E
Wollar	**76**	32 20S	149 56E
Wollaston, Islas	**142**	55 40S	67 30W
Wollaston L.	**109**	58 7N	103 10W
Wollaston Pen.	**100**	69 30N	115 0W
Wollogorang	**72**	17 13S	137 57E
Wollombi	**76**	32 56S	151 8E
Wollomombi	**77**	30 30S	152 4E
Wollondilly →	**76**	34 12S	150 18E
Wollongong	**76**	34 25S	150 54E
Wolmaransstad	**96**	27 12S	26 13E
Wolmirstedt	**30**	52 15N	11 35E
Wolseley, Austral.	**73**	36 23S	140 54E
Wolseley, Can.	**109**	50 25N	103 15W
Wolseley, S. Afr.	**96**	33 26S	19 7E
Wolstenholme Fjord	**144**	76 0N	70 0W
Wolsztyn	**32**	52 8N	16 5E
Wolumla	**75**	36 51S	149 50E
Wolvega	**16**	52 52N	6 0E
Wolverhampton	**13**	52 35N	2 6W
Wolverine	**106**	45 16N	84 36W
Wombat	**76**	34 24S	148 16E
Wombera	**91**	10 45N	35 49E
Wombeyan Caves	**76**	34 17S	149 59E
Wonarah P.O.	**72**	19 55S	136 20E
Wonboyn	**75**	37 15S	149 55E
Wondai	**73**	26 20S	151 49E
Wondalga	**76**	35 24S	148 8E
Wonder Gorge	**95**	14 40S	29 0E
Wongalarroo L.	**73**	31 32S	144 0E
Wongan Hills	**79**	30 51S	116 37E
Wongarbon	**76**	32 20S	148 45E
Wongawol	**79**	26 5S	121 55E
Wŏnju	**61**	37 22N	127 58E
Wonnangatta →	**75**	37 32S	147 15E
Wonosari	**57**	7 58S	110 36E
Wŏnsan	**61**	39 11N	127 27E
Wonthaggi	**74**	38 37S	145 37E
Wonwron	**75**	38 27S	146 45E
Woocalla	**73**	31 42S	137 12E
Wood Buffalo Nat. Park	**108**	59 0N	113 41W
Wood Is.	**78**	16 24S	123 19E
Wood L.	**109**	55 17N	103 17W
Wood Lake	**118**	42 38N	100 14W
Wood River	**116**	38 52N	90 5W
Woodah I.	**72**	13 27S	136 10E
Woodanilling	**79**	33 31S	117 24E
Woodbridge	**106**	43 47N	79 36W
Woodburn	**77**	29 6S	153 23E
Wooded Bluff	**77**	29 24S	153 23E
Woodenbong	**77**	28 24S	152 39E
Woodend	**74**	37 20S	144 33E
Woodfords	**122**	38 47N	119 50W
Woodgreen	**72**	22 26S	134 12E
Woodlake	**122**	36 25N	119 6W
Woodland	**122**	38 40N	121 50W
Woodlands	**79**	24 46S	118 8E
Woodlark I.	**69**	9 10S	152 50E
Woodpecker	**108**	53 30N	122 40W
Woodridge	**109**	49 20N	96 9W
Woodroffe, Mt.	**79**	26 20S	131 45E
Woodruff, Ariz., U.S.A.	**121**	34 51N	110 1W
Woodruff, Utah, U.S.A.	**120**	41 30N	111 4W
Woods, L., Austral.	**72**	17 50S	133 30E
Woods, L., Can.	**103**	54 30N	65 13W
Woods, L. of the	**109**	49 15N	94 45W
Woods Point	**75**	37 32S	146 16E
Woods Reef	**77**	30 22S	150 45E
Woodside	**73**	38 31S	146 52E
Woodstock, N.S.W., Austral.	**76**	33 45S	148 53E
Woodstock, Queens., Austral.	**72**	19 35S	146 50E
Woodstock, W.A., Austral.	**78**	21 41S	118 57E
Woodstock, N.B., Can.	**103**	46 11N	67 37W
Woodstock, Ont., Can.	**106**	43 10N	80 45W
Woodstock, U.K.	**13**	51 51N	1 20W
Woodstock, Ill., U.S.A.	**117**	42 17N	88 30W
Woodstock, Vt., U.S.A.	**115**	43 37N	72 31W
Woodsville	**115**	44 10N	72 0W
Woodville, N.Z.	**80**	40 20S	175 53E
Woodville, Ohio, U.S.A.	**117**	41 27N	83 22W
Woodville, Tex., U.S.A.	**119**	30 45N	94 25W
Woodward	**119**	36 24N	99 28W
Woody	**123**	35 42N	118 50W
Woolamai, C.	**74**	38 30S	145 23E
Woolbrook	**77**	30 56S	151 25E

Woolgangie 79 31 12S 120 35 E
Woolgoolga 77 30 6S 153 11 E
Wooli 77 29 52S 153 17 E
Woolsthorpe 74 38 11S 142 26 E
Woomargama 76 35 50S 147 15 E
Woombye 73 26 40S 152 55 E
Woomelang 74 35 37S 142 40 E
Woomera 73 31 30S 137 10 E
Woonona 76 34 21S 150 54 E
Woonsocket 115 42 0N 71 30W
Woonsockett 118 44 5N 98 15W
Wooramel 79 25 45S 114 17 E
Wooramel → 79 25 47S 114 10 E
Woorinen 74 35 14S 143 27 E
Wooroloo 79 31 48S 116 18 E
Woorragee 75 36 16S 146 44 E
Wooster 114 40 48N 81 55W
Wootton 77 32 17S 152 18 E
Worcester, S. Afr. 96 33 39S 19 27 E
Worcester, U.K. 13 52 12N 2 12W
Worcester, Mass., U.S.A. 115 42 14N 71 49W
Worcester, N.Y., U.S.A. 115 42 35N 74 45W
Worden 116 38 56N 89 50W
Wörgl 31 47 29N 12 3 E
Workington 12 54 39N 3 34W
Worksop 12 53 19N 1 9W
Workum 16 52 59N 5 26 E
Worland 120 44 0N 107 59W
Wormhoudt 19 50 52N 2 28 E
Worms 31 49 37N 8 21 E
Worsley 79 33 15S 116 2 E
Wörth 31 49 1N 12 24 E
Wortham 119 31 48N 96 27W
Wörther See 33 46 37N 14 10 E
Worthing 13 50 49N 0 21W
Worthington, Ind., U.S.A. 117 39 7N 86 59W
Worthington, Minn., U.S.A. 118 43 35N 95 36W
Worthington, Ohio, U.S.A. 117 40 5N 83 1W
Wosi 57 0 15S 128 0 E
Wota (Shoa Ghimirra) 91 7 4N 35 51 E
Wottonville 105 45 44N 71 48W
Wou-han = Wuhan 59 30 31N 114 18 E
Wour 87 21 14N 16 0 E
Wowoni 57 4 5S 123 5 E
Woy Woy 76 33 30S 151 19 E
Wrangell 100 56 30N 132 25W
Wrangell, I. 108 56 20N 132 10W
Wrangell Mts. 100 61 40N 143 30W
Wrath, C. 14 58 38N 5 0W
Wray 118 40 8N 102 18W
Wrekin, The 12 52 41N 2 35W
Wrens 113 33 13N 82 23W
Wrexham 12 53 5N 3 0W
Wriezen 30 52 43N 14 9 E
Wright, Can. 108 51 52N 121 40W
Wright, Phil. 57 11 42N 125 2 E
Wrightson, Mt. 121 31 43N 110 56W
Wrightwood 123 34 21N 117 38W
Wrigley 100 63 16N 123 37W
Wrocław 32 51 5N 17 5 E
Września 32 52 21N 17 36 E
Wschowa 32 51 48N 16 20 E
Wu Jiang → 58 29 40N 107 20 E
Wu'an 60 36 40N 114 15 E
Wubin 79 30 6S 116 37 E
Wubu 60 37 28N 110 42 E
Wuchang 61 44 55N 127 5 E
Wucheng 60 37 12N 116 20 E
Wuchuan, Guangdong, China 59 21 33N 110 43 E
Wuchuan, Guizhou, China 58 28 25N 108 3 E
Wuchuan, Nei Mongol Zizhiqu, China 60 41 5N 111 28 E
Wudi 61 37 40N 117 35 E
Wuding 58 25 24N 102 21 E
Wuding He → 60 37 2N 110 23 E
Wudu 58 33 22N 104 54 E
Wufeng 59 30 12N 110 42 E
Wugang 59 26 44N 110 35 E
Wugong Shan 59 27 30N 114 0 E
Wuhan 59 30 31N 114 18 E
Wuhe 61 33 10N 117 50 E
Wuhsi = Wuxi 62 31 33N 120 18 E
Wuhu 59 31 22N 118 21 E
Wujiang 59 31 10N 120 38 E
Wukari 89 7 51N 9 42 E
Wulajie 61 44 6N 126 33 E
Wulanbulang 60 41 5N 110 55 E
Wulehe 89 8 39N 0 0
Wulian 61 35 40N 119 12 E
Wuliang Shan 58 24 30N 100 40 E
Wuliaru 57 7 27S 131 0 E
Wulumuchi = Ürümqi 62 43 45N 87 45 E
Wum 89 6 24N 10 2 E
Wuming 58 23 12N 108 18 E
Wuneba 91 4 49N 30 22 E
Wunghu 74 36 9S 145 27 E
Wuning 59 29 17N 115 5 E
Wunnummin L. 102 52 55N 89 10W
Wunsiedel 31 50 2N 12 0 E
Wunstorf 30 52 26N 9 29 E
Wuntho 52 23 54N 95 41 E
Wuping 59 25 5N 116 5 E
Wuppertal, Ger. 30 51 15N 7 8 E
Wuppertal, S. Afr. 96 32 13S 19 12 E
Wuqing 61 39 23N 117 4 E
Wurarga 79 28 25S 116 15 E
Wurung 72 19 13S 140 38 E
Würzburg 31 49 46N 9 55 E
Wurzen 30 51 21N 12 45 E
Wushan, Gansu, China 60 34 43N 104 53 E
Wushan, Sichuan, China 58 31 7N 109 54 E
Wustrow 30 54 4N 11 33 E
Wutach → 31 47 37N 8 15 E
Wutai 60 38 40N 113 12 E
Wutong 59 25 24N 110 4 E
Wutonghaolai 61 42 50N 120 5 E
Wutongqiao 58 29 22N 103 50 E
Wuwei, Anhui, China 59 31 18N 117 54 E
Wuwei, Gansu, China 62 37 57N 102 34 E
Wuxi, Jiangsu, China 59 31 33N 120 18 E
Wuxi, Sichuan, China 58 31 23N 109 35 E
Wuxiang 60 36 49N 112 50 E
Wuxing 59 30 51N 120 8 E
Wuxuan 58 23 34N 109 38 E
Wuyang 60 33 25N 113 35 E
Wuyi, Hebei, China 60 37 46N 115 56 E
Wuyi, Zhejiang, China 59 28 52N 119 50 E
Wuyi Shan 59 27 0N 117 0 E
Wuyo 89 10 23N 11 50 E
Wuyuan, Jiangxi, China 59 29 15N 117 50 E
Wuyuan, Nei Mongol Zizhiqu, China 60 41 2N 108 20 E
Wuzhai 60 38 54N 111 48 E
Wuzhi Shan 62 18 45N 109 45 E
Wuzhong 60 38 2N 106 12 E
Wuzhou 59 23 30N 111 18 E
Wyaaba Cr. → 72 16 27S 141 35 E
Wyaga 77 28 11S 150 37 E
Wyalkatchem 79 31 8S 117 22 E
Wyalusing 115 41 40N 76 16W
Wyan 77 29 5S 152 52 E
Wyandotte 117 42 14N 83 13W
Wyandra 73 27 12S 145 56 E
Wyangala Res. 76 33 54S 149 0 E
Wyara, L. 73 28 42S 144 14 E
Wycheproof 74 36 0S 143 17 E
Wye → 13 51 36N 2 40W
Wyemandoo, Mt. 79 28 28S 118 29 E
Wyk 30 54 41N 8 33 E
Wymondham 13 52 45N 0 42W
Wymore 118 40 10N 96 40W
Wynadotte 106 42 11N 83 14W
Wynberg 96 34 2S 18 28 E
Wynbring 73 30 33S 133 32 E
Wyndham, N.S.W., Austral. 75 36 55S 149 39 E
Wyndham, W. Australia, Austral. 78 15 33S 128 3 E
Wyndham, N.Z. 81 46 20S 168 51 E
Wyndmere 118 46 23N 97 7W
Wynne 119 35 15N 90 50W
Wynnum 73 27 27S 153 9 E
Wynyard, Austral. 72 40 59S 145 45 E
Wynyard, Can. 109 51 45N 104 10W
Wyola, L. 79 29 8S 130 17 E
Wyoming, Can. 106 42 57N 82 7W
Wyoming, Ill., U.S.A. 116 41 4N 89 47W
Wyoming, Iowa, U.S.A. 116 42 4N 91 3W
Wyoming, Mich., U.S.A. 117 42 53N 85 42W
Wyoming □ 110 42 48N 109 0W
Wyong 76 33 14S 151 24 E
Wyszków 32 52 36N 21 25 E
Wyszogród 32 52 23N 20 9 E
Wytheville 112 37 0N 81 3W

X

Xai-Xai 97 25 6S 33 31 E
Xainza 62 30 58N 88 35 E
Xambioá 138 6 25S 48 40W
Xanten 30 51 40N 6 27 E
Xánthi 35 41 10N 24 58 E
Xapuri 136 10 35S 68 35W
Xar Moron He → 61 43 25N 120 35 E
Xau, L. 96 21 15S 24 44 E
Xavantina 141 21 15S 52 48W
Xenia, Ill., U.S.A. 117 38 38N 88 38W
Xenia, Ohio, U.S.A. 117 39 42N 83 57W
Xi Jiang → 59 22 5N 113 20 E
Xi Xian, Henan, China 59 32 20N 114 43 E
Xi Xian, Shanxi, China 60 36 41N 110 58 E
Xia Xian 60 35 8N 111 12 E
Xiachengzi 61 44 40N 130 18 E
Xiachuan Dao 59 21 40N 112 40 E
Xiaguan 58 25 32N 100 16 E
Xiajiang 59 27 30N 115 10 E
Xiajin 60 36 56N 116 0 E
Xiamen 59 24 25N 118 4 E
Xi'an 60 34 15N 109 0 E
Xian Xian 60 38 12N 116 6 E
Xianfeng 59 29 40N 109 8 E
Xiang Jiang → 59 28 55N 112 50 E
Xiangcheng, Henan, China 60 33 50N 113 27 E
Xiangcheng, Henan, China 60 33 29N 114 52 E
Xiangcheng, Sichuan, China 58 28 53N 99 47 E
Xiangdu 58 23 13N 106 58 E
Xiangfan 59 32 2N 112 8 E
Xianghuang Qi 60 42 2N 113 50 E
Xiangning 60 35 58N 110 50 E
Xiangquan 60 36 30N 113 1 E
Xiangshan 59 29 29N 121 51 E
Xiangshui 61 34 12N 119 33 E
Xiangtan 59 27 51N 112 54 E
Xiangxiang 59 27 43N 112 28 E
Xiangyin 59 28 38N 112 54 E
Xiangyun 58 25 34N 100 35 E
Xiangzhou 58 23 58N 109 40 E
Xianju 59 28 51N 120 44 E
Xianning 59 29 51N 114 16 E
Xianshui He → 58 30 10N 100 59 E
Xianyang 60 34 20N 108 40 E
Xianyou 59 25 22N 118 38 E
Xiao Hinggan Ling 62 49 0N 127 0 E
Xiao Xian 60 34 15N 116 55 E
Xiaofeng 59 30 35N 119 32 E
Xiaogan 59 30 52N 113 55 E
Xiaojin 58 30 59N 102 21 E
Xiaolan 59 22 38N 113 13 E
Xiaoshan 59 30 12N 120 18 E
Xiaoyi 60 37 8N 111 48 E
Xiapu 59 26 54N 119 59 E
Xiawa 61 42 35N 120 38 E
Xiayi 60 34 15N 116 10 E
Xichang 58 27 51N 102 19 E
Xichong 58 30 57N 105 54 E
Xichuan 60 33 0N 111 30 E
Xiemahe 59 31 38N 111 12 E
Xieng Khouang 54 19 17N 103 25 E
Xifei He → 60 32 45N 116 40 E
Xifeng, Guizhou, China 58 27 7N 106 42 E
Xifeng, Liaoning, China 61 42 42N 124 45 E
Xifengzhen 60 35 40N 107 40 E
Xigazê 62 29 5N 88 45 E
Xihe 60 34 2N 105 20 E
Xihua 60 33 45N 114 30 E
Xiliao He → 61 43 32N 123 35 E
Xilin 58 24 30N 105 6 E
Xilókastron 35 38 4N 22 43 E
Xin Jiang → 59 28 45N 116 35 E
Xin Xian 60 38 22N 112 46 E
Xinavane 97 25 2S 32 47 E
Xinbin 61 41 40N 125 2 E
Xincai 59 32 43N 114 58 E
Xinchang 59 29 28N 120 52 E
Xincheng, Guangxi, China 58 24 5N 108 39 E
Xincheng, Jiangxi, China 59 26 48N 114 6 E
Xinfeng, Guangdong, China 59 24 5N 114 16 E
Xinfeng, Jiangxi, China 59 27 7N 116 11 E
Xing Xian 60 38 27N 111 7 E
Xing'an 59 25 38N 110 40 E
Xingan 59 27 46N 115 20 E
Xingcheng 61 40 40N 120 45 E
Xingguo 59 26 21N 115 21 E
Xinghe 60 40 55N 113 55 E
Xinghua 61 32 58N 119 48 E
Xinghua Wan 59 25 15N 119 20 E
Xinglong 61 40 25N 117 30 E
Xingning 59 24 3N 115 42 E
Xingping 60 34 20N 108 28 E
Xingren 58 25 24N 105 11 E
Xingshan 59 31 15N 110 45 E
Xingtai 60 37 3N 114 32 E
Xingu → 135 1 30S 51 53W
Xingyang 60 34 45N 112 52 E
Xinhe 60 37 30N 115 15 E
Xinhua 59 27 42N 111 13 E
Xinhuang 58 27 21N 109 12 E
Xinhui 59 22 25N 113 0 E
Xining 62 36 34N 101 40 E
Xinjiang 60 35 34N 111 11 E
Xinjiang Uygur Zizhiqu □ 62 42 0N 86 0 E
Xinjie 58 26 48N 101 15 E
Xinjin, Liaoning, China 61 39 25N 121 58 E
Xinjin, Sichuan, China 58 30 24N 103 47 E
Xinkai He → 61 43 32N 123 35 E
Xinle 60 38 25N 114 40 E
Xinlitun 61 42 0N 122 8 E
Xinlong 58 30 57N 100 12 E
Xinmin 61 41 59N 122 50 E
Xinning 59 26 28N 110 50 E
Xinping 58 24 5N 101 59 E
Xinshao 59 27 21N 111 26 E
Xintai 61 35 55N 117 45 E
Xintian 59 25 55N 112 13 E
Xinxiang 60 35 18N 113 50 E
Xinxing 59 22 35N 112 15 E
Xinyang 59 32 6N 114 3 E
Xinye 59 32 30N 112 21 E
Xinyi 59 22 25N 111 0 E
Xinyu 59 27 49N 114 58 E
Xinzhan 61 43 50N 127 18 E
Xinzheng 60 34 20N 113 45 E
Xinzhou 59 30 50N 114 48 E
Xinzhu 59 24 49N 120 57 E
Xiong Xian 60 38 59N 116 8 E
Xiongyuecheng 61 40 12N 122 5 E
Xiping, Henan, China 60 33 25N 111 8 E
Xiping, Henan, China 60 33 22N 114 0 E
Xiping, Zhejiang, China 59 28 16N 119 29 E
Xique-Xique 138 10 50S 42 40W
Xiruá → 136 6 3S 67 50W
Xishui 59 30 30N 115 15 E
Xituozhen 58 30 22N 108 11 E
Xiuning 59 29 45N 118 10 E
Xiuren 59 24 27N 110 12 E
Xiushan 58 28 25N 108 57 E
Xiushui 59 29 2N 114 33 E
Xiuwen 58 26 49N 106 32 E
Xiuyan 61 40 18N 123 11 E
Xixabangma Feng 49 28 20N 85 40 E
Xixia 59 33 25N 111 29 E
Xixiang 58 33 0N 107 44 E
Xiyang 60 37 38N 113 38 E
Xizang □ 62 32 0N 88 0 E
Xu Jiang → 59 28 0N 116 25 E
Xuan Loc 55 10 56N 107 14 E
Xuancheng 59 30 56N 118 43 E
Xuan'en 59 30 0N 109 30 E
Xuanhan 58 31 18N 107 38 E
Xuanhua 60 40 40N 115 2 E
Xuchang 60 34 2N 113 48 E
Xuefeng Shan 59 27 5N 110 35 E
Xuejiaping 59 31 39N 110 16 E
Xun Jiang → 59 23 35N 111 30 E
Xun Xian 60 35 42N 114 33 E
Xundian 58 25 36N 103 15 E
Xunwu 59 24 54N 115 37 E
Xunyang 60 32 48N 109 22 E
Xunyi 60 35 8N 108 20 E
Xupu 59 27 53N 110 32 E
Xushui 60 39 2N 115 40 E
Xuwen 59 20 20N 110 10 E
Xuyen Moc 55 10 34N 107 25 E
Xuyong 58 28 10N 105 22 E
Xuzhou 61 34 18N 117 10 E

Y

Ya 'Bud 44 32 27N 35 10 E
Ya Xian 54 18 14N 109 29 E
Yaamba 72 23 8S 150 22 E
Ya'an 58 29 58N 103 5 E
Yaapeet 74 35 45S 142 3 E
Yabassi 89 4 30N 9 57 E
Yabba North 74 36 13S 145 42 E
Yabelo 91 4 50N 38 8 E
Yablonovy Khrebet 41 53 0N 114 0 E
Yabrai Shan 60 39 40N 103 0 E
Yabrīn 46 23 17N 48 58 E
Yackandandah 75 36 18S 146 52 E
Yacuiba 140 22 0S 63 43W
Yacuma → 137 13 38S 65 23W
Yadgir 50 16 45N 77 5 E
Yadkin → 113 35 23N 80 3W
Yadrin 37 55 57N 46 12 E
Yaeyama-Shotō 63 24 25N 124 0 E
Yagaba 89 10 14N 1 20W
Yagodnoye 41 62 33N 149 40 E
Yagoua 92 10 20N 15 13 E
Yaguas → 134 2 45S 70 10W
Yagur 44 32 45N 35 4 E
Yaha 55 6 29N 101 8 E
Yahk 108 49 6N 116 10W
Yahuma 92 1 0N 23 10 E

Yaizu	**65**	34 52N	138 20 E
Yajiang	**58**	30 2N	100 57 E
Yajua	**89**	11 27N	12 49 E
Yakage	**64**	34 37N	133 35 E
Yakima	**120**	46 42N	120 30W
Yakima →	**120**	47 0N	120 30W
Yako	**88**	12 59N	2 15W
Yakoruda	**35**	42 1N	23 39 E
Yaku-Jima	**63**	30 20N	130 30 E
Yakut A.S.S.R. □	**41**	62 0N	130 0 E
Yakutat	**100**	59 29N	139 44W
Yakutsk	**41**	62 5N	129 50 E
Yala	**55**	6 33N	101 18 E
Yalabusha →	**119**	33 30N	90 12W
Yalbalgo	**79**	25 10S	114 45 E
Yalboroo	**72**	20 50S	148 40 E
Yale, Can.	**122**	49 34N	121 25W
Yale, U.S.A.	**106**	43 9N	82 47W
Yalgoo	**79**	28 16S	116 39 E
Yalinga	**92**	6 33N	23 10 E
Yalkubul, Punta	**125**	21 32N	88 37W
Yalleroi	**72**	24 3S	145 42 E
Yallourn	**75**	38 10S	146 18 E
Yalong Jiang →	**58**	26 40N	101 55 E
Yalpukh, Oz.	**34**	45 30N	28 41 E
Yalta	**38**	44 30N	34 10 E
Yalu Jiang →	**61**	40 0N	124 20 E
Yalutorovsk	**40**	56 41N	66 12 E
Yam Kinneret	**44**	32 49N	35 36 E
Yamada	**64**	33 33N	130 49 E
Yamaga	**64**	33 1N	130 41 E
Yamagata	**63**	38 15N	140 15 E
Yamagawa	**64**	31 12N	130 39 E
Yamaguchi	**64**	34 10N	131 32 E
Yamaguchi □	**64**	34 20N	131 40 E
Yamal, Poluostrov	**40**	71 0N	70 0 E
Yamama	**46**	24 5N	47 30 E
Yamanaka	**65**	36 15N	136 22 E
Yamanashi □	**65**	35 40N	138 40 E
Yamantau	**40**	54 20N	57 40 E
Yamaska	**105**	46 0N	72 55W
Yamato	**65**	35 27N	139 25 E
Yamatotakada	**65**	34 31N	135 45 E
Yamazaki	**64**	35 0N	134 32 E
Yamba, N.S.W., Austral.	**77**	29 26S	153 23 E
Yamba, S. Australia, Austral.	**73**	34 10S	140 52 E
Yambah	**72**	23 10S	133 50 E
Yambarran Ra.	**78**	15 10S	130 25 E
Yâmbiô	**91**	4 35N	28 16 E
Yambol	**34**	42 30N	26 36 E
Yambuk	**74**	38 18S	142 5 E
Yamdena	**57**	7 45S	131 20 E
Yame	**64**	33 13N	130 35 E
Yamethin	**52**	20 29N	96 18 E
Yamil	**89**	12 53N	8 4 E
Yamma-Yamma, L.	**73**	26 16S	141 20 E
Yampa →	**120**	40 37N	108 59W
Yampi Sd.	**78**	16 8S	123 38 E
Yampol	**38**	48 15N	28 15 E
Yamrat	**89**	10 11N	9 55 E
Yamrukchal	**34**	42 44N	24 52 E
Yamun	**44**	32 29N	35 14 E
Yamuna (Jumna) →	**48**	25 30N	81 53 E
Yamzho Yumco	**62**	28 48N	90 35 E
Yan	**89**	10 5N	12 11 E
Yan →	**51**	9 0N	81 10 E
Yana →	**41**	71 30N	136 0 E
Yanac	**74**	36 8S	141 25 E
Yanagawa	**64**	33 10N	130 24 E
Yanahara	**64**	34 58N	134 2 E
Yanai	**64**	33 58N	132 7 E
Yanam	**50**	16 47N	82 15 E
Yan'an	**60**	36 35N	109 26 E
Yanbian	**58**	26 47N	101 31 E
Yanbu 'al Bahr	**46**	24 0N	38 5 E
Yancannia	**73**	30 12S	142 35 E
Yanchang	**60**	36 43N	110 1 E
Yancheng, Henan, China	**60**	33 35N	114 0 E
Yancheng, Jiangsu, China	**61**	33 23N	120 18 E
Yanchep	**79**	31 30S	115 33 E
Yanchi	**60**	37 48N	107 20 E
Yanchuan	**60**	36 51N	110 10 E
Yanco Cr. →	**73**	35 14S	145 35 E
Yandal	**79**	27 35S	121 10 E
Yandanooka	**79**	29 18S	115 29 E
Yandaran	**72**	24 43S	152 6 E
Yandé, Î.	**68**	20 3S	163 49 E
Yandina	**68**	9 7S	159 13 E
Yandoon	**52**	17 0N	95 40 E
Yanfeng	**58**	25 52N	101 8 E
Yanfolila	**88**	11 11N	8 9W
Yang Xian	**60**	33 15N	107 30 E
Yangambi	**94**	0 47N	24 20 E
Yangbi	**58**	25 41N	99 58 E
Yangcheng	**60**	35 28N	112 22 E
Yangch'ü = Taiyuan	**60**	37 52N	112 33 E
Yangchun	**59**	22 11N	111 48 E
Yanggao	**60**	40 21N	113 55 E
Yanggu	**60**	36 8N	115 43 E
Yangi-Yer	**40**	40 17N	68 48 E
Yangjiang	**59**	21 50N	110 59 E
Yangliuqing	**61**	39 2N	117 5 E
Yangping	**59**	31 12N	111 25 E
Yangpingguan	**60**	32 58N	106 5 E
Yangquan	**60**	37 58N	113 31 E
Yangshan	**59**	24 30N	112 40 E
Yangshuo	**59**	24 48N	110 29 E
Yangtze Kiang = Chang Jiang →	**62**	31 20N	121 52 E
Yangxin	**59**	29 50N	115 12 E
Yangyang	**61**	38 4N	128 38 E
Yangyuan	**60**	40 1N	114 10 E
Yangzhou	**59**	32 21N	119 26 E
Yanhe	**58**	28 31N	108 29 E
Yanji	**61**	42 59N	129 30 E
Yanjin	**58**	28 5N	104 18 E
Yanjing	**58**	29 7N	98 33 E
Yankton	**118**	42 55N	97 25W
Yanna	**73**	26 58S	146 0 E
Yanonge	**94**	0 35N	24 38 E
Yanqi	**62**	42 5N	86 35 E
Yanqing	**60**	40 30N	115 58 E
Yanshan, Hebei, China	**61**	38 4N	117 22 E
Yanshan, Jiangxi, China	**59**	28 15N	117 41 E
Yanshan, Yunnan, China	**58**	23 35N	104 20 E
Yanshou	**61**	45 28N	128 22 E
Yantabulla	**73**	29 21S	145 0 E
Yantai	**61**	37 34N	121 22 E
Yanting	**58**	31 11N	105 24 E
Yantra →	**34**	43 40N	25 37 E
Yanwa	**58**	27 35N	98 55 E
Yanyuan	**58**	27 25N	101 30 E
Yanzhou	**60**	35 35N	116 49 E
Yao, Chad	**85**	12 56N	17 33 E
Yao, Japan	**65**	34 32N	135 36 E
Yao Xian	**60**	34 55N	108 59 E
Yao Yai, Ko	**55**	8 0N	98 35 E
Yao'an	**58**	25 31N	101 18 E
Yaodu	**58**	32 45N	105 22 E
Yaoundé	**92**	3 50N	11 35 E
Yaowan	**61**	34 15N	118 3 E
Yap	**66**	9 31N	138 6 E
Yapen	**57**	1 50S	136 0 E
Yapen, Selat	**57**	1 20S	136 10 E
Yappar →	**72**	18 22S	141 16 E
Yaqui →	**124**	27 37N	110 39W
Yar-Sale	**40**	66 50N	70 50 E
Yaracuy □	**134**	10 20N	68 45W
Yaracuy →	**134**	10 33N	68 15W
Yaraka	**72**	24 53S	144 3 E
Yaransk	**37**	57 22N	47 49 E
Yaratishky	**36**	54 3N	26 0 E
Yarda	**85**	18 35N	19 0 E
Yardea P.O.	**73**	32 23S	135 32 E
Yare →	**13**	52 36N	1 28 E
Yarensk	**40**	61 10N	49 8 E
Yarfa	**90**	24 40N	38 35 E
Yarí →	**134**	0 20S	72 20W
Yaritagua	**134**	10 5N	69 8W
Yarkand = Shache	**62**	38 20N	77 10 E
Yarker	**107**	44 23N	76 46W
Yarkhun →	**49**	36 17N	72 30 E
Yarmouth	**103**	43 50N	66 7W
Yarmuk →	**44**	32 38N	35 34 E
Yaroslavl	**37**	57 35N	39 55 E
Yarra →	**74**	37 50S	144 53 E
Yarra Glen	**74**	37 40S	145 22 E
Yarra Yarra Lakes	**79**	29 40S	115 45 E
Yarrabandai	**76**	33 6S	147 36 E
Yarraden	**72**	14 17S	143 15 E
Yarraloola	**78**	21 33S	115 52 E
Yarram	**75**	38 29S	146 9 E
Yarraman	**73**	26 50S	152 0 E
Yarranvale	**73**	26 50S	145 20 E
Yarras	**77**	31 25S	152 20 E
Yarrawonga	**74**	36 0S	146 0 E
Yarrill Cr. →	**77**	28 20S	150 8 E
Yarrowee →	**74**	38 18S	144 30 E
Yarrowyck	**77**	30 27S	151 20 E
Yarto	**74**	35 28S	142 16 E
Yartsevo	**41**	60 20N	90 0 E
Yarumal	**134**	6 58N	75 24W
Yasawa	**68**	16 47S	177 31 E
Yasawa Group	**68**	17 00S	177 23 E
Yaselda →	**36**	52 7N	26 28 E
Yashi	**89**	12 23N	7 54 E
Yashiro-Jima	**64**	33 55N	132 15 E
Yasin	**49**	36 24N	73 23 E
Yasinovataya	**38**	48 7N	37 57 E
Yasinski, L.	**102**	53 16N	77 35W
Yasothon	**54**	15 50N	104 10 E
Yass	**76**	34 49S	148 54 E
Yasugi	**64**	35 26N	133 15 E
Yas'ur	**44**	32 54N	35 10 E
Yata →	**137**	10 29S	65 26W
Yates Center	**119**	37 53N	95 45W
Yates Pt.	**81**	44 29S	167 49 E
Yathkyed L.	**109**	62 40N	98 0W
Yatsuo	**65**	36 34N	137 8 E
Yatsushiro	**64**	32 30N	130 40 E
Yatsushiro-Kai	**64**	32 30N	130 25 E
Yatta Plateau	**94**	2 0S	38 0 E
Yattah	**44**	31 27N	35 6 E
Yauca	**136**	15 39S	74 35W
Yauya	**136**	8 59S	77 17W
Yauyos	**136**	12 19S	75 50W
Yaval	**50**	21 10N	75 42 E
Yavari →	**136**	4 21S	70 2W
Yavorov	**36**	49 55N	23 20 E
Yawatahama	**64**	33 27N	132 24 E
Yawri B.	**88**	8 22N	13 0W
Yaxi	**58**	27 33N	106 41 E
Yazagyo	**52**	23 30N	94 6 E
Yazd (Yezd)	**47**	31 55N	54 27 E
Yazdan	**47**	33 30N	60 50 E
Yazoo →	**119**	32 35N	90 50W
Yazoo City	**119**	32 48N	90 28W
Ye Xian, Henan, China	**60**	33 35N	113 25 E
Ye Xian, Shandong, China	**61**	37 8N	119 57 E
Yea	**74**	37 14S	145 26 E
Yealering	**79**	32 36S	117 36 E
Yearinan	**77**	31 10S	149 11 E
Yebbi-Souma	**87**	21 7N	17 54 E
Yebel Jarris Tighzert, O. →	**86**	28 10N	9 37W
Yechŏn	**61**	36 39N	128 27 E
Yecla	**25**	38 35N	1 5W
Yécora	**124**	28 20N	108 58W
Yedashe	**52**	19 10N	96 20 E
Yeddou	**86**	28 5N	9 2W
Yeeda P.O.	**78**	17 31S	123 38 E
Yeelanna	**73**	34 9S	135 45 E
Yefremov	**37**	53 8N	38 3 E
Yegorlyk →	**39**	46 33N	41 40 E
Yegorlykskaya	**39**	46 35N	40 35 E
Yegoryevsk	**37**	55 27N	38 55 E
Yegros	**140**	26 20S	56 25W
Yehuda, Midbar	**44**	31 35N	35 15 E
Yei	**91**	4 9N	30 40 E
Yei, Nahr →	**91**	6 15N	30 13 E
Yelan	**37**	50 55N	43 43 E
Yelan-Kolenovski	**37**	51 16N	41 4 E
Yelandur	**51**	12 6N	77 0 E
Yelanskoye	**41**	61 25N	128 0 E
Yelarbon	**77**	28 33S	150 38 E
Yelatma	**37**	55 0N	41 45 E
Yelcho, L.	**142**	43 18S	72 18W
Yelets	**37**	52 40N	38 30 E
Yélimané	**88**	15 9N	10 34W
Yell	**14**	60 35N	1 5W
Yell Sd.	**14**	60 33N	1 15W
Yellamanchilli (Elamanchili)	**50**	17 33N	82 50 E
Yellow Sea = Huang Hai	**61**	35 0N	123 0 E
Yellowdine	**79**	31 17S	119 40 E
Yellowhead P.	**108**	52 53N	118 25W
Yellowknife	**108**	62 27N	114 29W
Yellowknife →	**100**	62 31N	114 19W
Yellowstone →	**118**	47 58N	103 59W
Yellowstone L.	**120**	44 30N	110 20W
Yellowstone National Park	**120**	44 35N	110 0W
Yellowtail Res.	**120**	45 6N	108 8W
Yelnya	**36**	54 35N	33 15 E
Yelsk	**36**	51 50N	29 10 E
Yelvertoft	**72**	20 13S	138 45 E
Yelwa	**89**	10 49N	4 41 E
Yemen ■	**45**	15 0N	44 0 E
Yen Bai	**54**	21 42N	104 52 E
Yenakiyevo	**38**	48 15N	38 15 E
Yenangyaung	**52**	20 30N	95 0 E
Yenanma	**52**	19 46N	94 49 E
Yenda	**75**	34 13S	146 14 E
Yendéré	**88**	10 12N	4 59W
Yendi	**89**	9 29N	0 1W
Yenisaía	**35**	41 1N	24 57 E
Yenisey →	**40**	71 50N	82 40 E
Yeniseysk	**41**	58 27N	92 13 E
Yeniseyskiy Zaliv	**40**	72 20N	81 0 E
Yenne	**21**	45 43N	5 44 E
Yenotayevka	**39**	47 15N	47 0 E
Yenyuka	**41**	57 57N	121 15 E
Yeo, L.	**79**	28 0S	124 30 E
Yeola	**50**	20 0N	74 30 E
Yeotmal	**50**	20 20N	78 15 E
Yeoval	**76**	32 47S	148 9 E
Yeovil	**13**	50 57N	2 38W
Yepes	**24**	39 55N	3 39W
Yeppoon	**72**	23 5S	150 47 E
Yeráki	**35**	37 0N	22 42 E
Yerbent	**40**	39 30N	58 50 E
Yerbogachen	**41**	61 16N	108 0 E
Yerevan	**39**	40 10N	44 31 E
Yerilla	**79**	29 24S	121 47 E
Yerla →	**50**	16 50N	74 30 E
Yermak	**40**	52 2N	76 55 E
Yermakovo	**41**	52 25N	126 20 E
Yermo	**123**	34 58N	116 50W
Yerofey Pavlovich	**41**	54 0N	122 0 E
Yershov	**37**	51 22N	48 16 E
Yerunaja, Cerro	**136**	10 16S	76 55W
Yerūshalayim	**44**	31 47N	35 10 E
Yerville	**18**	49 40N	0 53 E
Yes Tor	**13**	50 41N	3 59W
Yesagyo	**52**	21 38N	95 14 E
Yesan	**61**	36 41N	126 51 E
Yesnogorsk	**37**	54 32N	37 38 E
Yeso	**119**	34 29N	104 37W
Yessentuki	**39**	44 0N	42 53 E
Yessey	**41**	68 29N	102 10 E
Yeste	**25**	38 22N	2 19W
Yetman	**77**	28 56S	150 48 E
Yeu, I. d'	**18**	46 42N	2 20W
Yevlakh	**39**	40 39N	47 7 E
Yevpatoriya	**38**	45 15N	33 20 E
Yevstratovskiy	**37**	50 11N	39 45 E
Yeya →	**39**	46 40N	38 40 E
Yeysk	**38**	46 40N	38 12 E
Yhati	**140**	25 45S	56 35W
Yhú	**141**	25 0S	56 0W
Yi →	**140**	33 7S	57 8W
Yi He →	**61**	34 10N	118 8 E
Yi Xian, Anhui, China	**59**	29 55N	117 57 E
Yi Xian, Hebei, China	**60**	39 20N	115 30 E
Yi Xian, Liaoning, China	**61**	41 30N	121 22 E
Yialí	**35**	36 41N	27 11 E
Yi'allaq, G.	**90**	30 21N	33 31 E
Yiáltra	**35**	38 51N	22 59 E
Yiannitsa	**35**	40 46N	22 24 E
Yibal	**45**	22 10N	56 8 E
Yibin	**58**	28 45N	104 32 E
Yichang	**59**	30 40N	111 20 E
Yicheng, Henan, China	**59**	31 41N	112 12 E
Yicheng, Shanxi, China	**60**	35 42N	111 40 E
Yichuan	**60**	36 2N	110 10 E
Yichun, Heilongjiang, China	**62**	47 44N	128 52 E
Yichun, Jiangxi, China	**59**	27 48N	114 22 E
Yidu, Hubei, China	**59**	30 25N	111 27 E
Yidu, Shandong, China	**61**	36 43N	118 28 E
Yidun	**58**	30 22N	99 21 E
Yihuang	**59**	27 30N	116 12 E
Yijun	**60**	35 28N	109 8 E
Yilan	**59**	24 51N	121 44 E
Yiliang, Yunnan, China	**58**	27 38N	104 2 E
Yiliang, Yunnan, China	**58**	24 56N	103 11 E
Yilong	**58**	31 34N	106 23 E
Yimen	**58**	24 40N	102 10 E
Yimianpo	**61**	45 7N	128 2 E
Yinchuan	**60**	38 30N	106 15 E
Yindarlgooda, L.	**79**	30 40S	121 52 E
Ying He →	**59**	32 30N	116 30 E
Ying Xian	**60**	39 32N	113 10 E
Yingcheng	**59**	30 56N	113 35 E
Yingde	**59**	24 10N	113 25 E
Yingjiang	**58**	24 41N	97 55 E
Yingjing	**58**	29 41N	102 52 E
Yingkou, Liaoning, China	**61**	40 37N	122 18 E
Yingkou, Liaoning, China	**61**	40 33N	122 33 E
Yingshan, Henan, China	**59**	31 35N	113 50 E
Yingshan, Hubei, China	**59**	30 41N	115 32 E
Yingshan, Sichuan, China	**58**	31 4N	106 35 E
Yingshang	**59**	32 38N	116 12 E
Yingtan	**62**	28 12N	117 0 E
Yining	**62**	43 58N	81 10 E
Yinjiang	**58**	28 1N	108 21 E
Yinkanie	**73**	34 22S	140 17 E
Yinnietharra	**79**	24 39S	116 12 E
Yioúra	**35**	39 23N	24 10 E
Yipinglang	**58**	25 10N	101 52 E
Yirga Alem	**92**	6 48N	38 22 E
Yishan	**58**	24 28N	108 38 E
Yishui	**61**	35 47N	118 30 E
Yíthion	**35**	36 46N	22 34 E
Yitiaoshan	**60**	37 5N	104 2 E
Yitong	**61**	43 13N	125 20 E
Yiwu	**59**	29 20N	120 3 E
Yixing	**59**	31 21N	119 48 E
Yiyang, Henan, China	**60**	34 27N	112 10 E
Yiyang, Hunan, China	**59**	28 35N	112 18 E
Yiyang, Jiangxi, China	**59**	28 22N	117 20 E
Yizhang	**59**	25 27N	112 57 E
Yizheng	**59**	32 18N	119 10 E
Yizre'el	**44**	32 34N	35 19 E
Ylitornio	**8**	66 19N	23 39 E

Ylivieska **8** 64 4N 24 28 E
Yngaren **11** 58 50N 16 35 E
Ynykchanskiy **41** 60 15N 137 35 E
Yoakum **119** 29 20N 97 20W
Yobuko **64** 33 32N 129 54 E
Yog Pt. **57** 14 6N 124 12 E
Yogan **89** 6 23N 1 30 E
Yogyakarta **57** 7 49S 110 22 E
Yoho Nat. Park **108** 51 25N 116 30W
Yojoa, L. de **126** 14 53N 88 0W
Yŏju **61** 37 20N 127 35 E
Yokadouma **92** 3 26N 15 6 E
Yōkaichi **65** 35 6N 136 12 E
Yōkaichiba **65** 35 42N 140 33 E
Yokkaichi **65** 35 0N 136 38 E
Yoko **89** 5 32N 12 20 E
Yokohama **65** 35 27N 139 28 E
Yokosuka **65** 35 20N 139 40 E
Yokote **63** 39 20N 140 30 E
Yola **89** 9 10N 12 29 E
Yolaina, Cordillera de **126** 11 30N 84 0W
Yonago **64** 35 25N 133 19 E
Yŏnan **61** 37 55N 126 11 E
Yoneshiro → **63** 40 15N 140 15 E
Yonezawa **63** 37 57N 140 4 E
Yong Peng **55** 2 0N 103 3 E
Yong Sata **55** 7 8N 99 41 E
Yongampo **61** 39 56N 124 23 E
Yong'an **59** 25 59N 117 25 E
Yongcheng **60** 33 55N 116 20 E
Yŏngchŏn **61** 35 58N 128 56 E
Yongchuan **58** 29 17N 105 55 E
Yongchun **59** 25 16N 118 20 E
Yongdeng **60** 36 38N 103 25 E
Yongding **59** 24 43N 116 45 E
Yŏngdŏk **61** 36 24N 129 22 E
Yŏngdŭngpo **61** 37 31N 126 54 E
Yongfeng **59** 27 20N 115 22 E
Yongfu **58** 24 59N 109 59 E
Yonghe **60** 36 46N 110 38 E
Yŏnghŭng **61** 39 31N 127 18 E
Yongji **60** 34 52N 110 28 E
Yŏngju **61** 36 50N 128 40 E
Yongkang, Yunnan, China **58** 24 9N 99 20 E
Yongkang, Zhejiang, China **59** 28 55N 120 2 E
Yongnian **60** 36 47N 114 29 E
Yongning, Guangxi, China **58** 22 44N 108 28 E
Yongning, Ningxia Huizu, China **60** 38 15N 106 14 E
Yongping **58** 25 27N 99 38 E
Yongqing **60** 39 25N 116 28 E
Yongren **58** 26 4N 101 40 E
Yongshan **58** 28 11N 103 35 E
Yongsheng **58** 26 38N 100 46 E
Yongshun **58** 29 2N 109 51 E
Yongtai **59** 25 49N 118 58 E
Yŏngwŏl **61** 37 11N 128 28 E
Yongxin **59** 26 58N 114 15 E
Yongxing **59** 26 9N 113 8 E
Yongxiu **59** 29 2N 115 42 E
Yonibana **88** 8 30N 12 19W
Yonkers **115** 40 57N 73 51W
Yonne □ **19** 47 50N 3 40 E
Yonne → **19** 48 23N 2 58 E
Yoqne'am **44** 32 40N 35 6 E
York, Austral. **79** 31 52S 116 47 E
York, U.K. **12** 53 58N 1 7W
York, Ala., U.S.A. **113** 32 30N 88 18W
York, Nebr., U.S.A. **118** 40 55N 97 35W
York, Pa., U.S.A. **112** 39 57N 76 43W
York, C. **72** 10 42S 142 31 E
York, Kap **144** 75 55N 66 25W
York Sd. **78** 14 50S 125 5 E
Yorke Pen. **73** 34 50S 137 40 E
Yorkshire Wolds **12** 54 0N 0 30W
Yorkton **109** 51 11N 102 28W
Yorktown **119** 29 0N 97 29W
Yorkville, Calif., U.S.A. **122** 38 52N 123 13W
Yorkville, Ill., U.S.A. **117** 41 38N 88 27W
Yornup **79** 34 2S 116 10 E
Yoro **126** 15 9N 87 7W
Yosemite National Park **122** 38 0N 119 30W
Yosemite Village **122** 37 45N 119 35W
Yoshii **64** 33 16N 129 46 E
Yoshimatsu **64** 32 0N 130 47 E
Yoshkar Ola **37** 56 38N 47 55 E
Yŏsu **61** 34 47N 127 45 E
Yotala **137** 19 10S 65 17W
You Jiang → **62** 23 22N 110 3 E
You Xian **59** 27 1N 113 17 E
Youanmi **79** 28 37S 118 49 E
Youbou **108** 48 53N 124 13W
Youghal **15** 51 58N 7 51W
Youghal B. **15** 51 55N 7 50W
Youkounkoun **88** 12 35N 13 11W
Young, Austral. **76** 34 19S 148 18 E
Young, Can. **109** 51 47N 105 45W
Young, Uruguay **140** 32 44S 57 36W
Young, U.S.A. **121** 34 9N 110 56W
Young Ra. **81** 44 10S 169 30 E
Younghusband, L. **73** 30 50S 136 5 E
Younghusband Pen. **73** 36 0S 139 25 E
Youngstown, Can. **109** 51 35N 111 10W
Youngstown, N.Y., U.S.A. **114** 43 16N 79 2W
Youngstown, Ohio, U.S.A. **114** 41 7N 80 41W
Youngsville **114** 41 51N 79 21W
Youssoufia **86** 32 16N 8 31W
Youxi **59** 26 10N 118 13 E
Youyang **58** 28 47N 108 42 E
Youyu **60** 40 10N 112 20 E
Yoweragabbie **79** 28 14S 117 39 E
Yowrie **75** 36 17S 149 46 E
Yozgat **46** 39 51N 34 47 E
Ypané → **140** 23 29S 57 19W
Yport **18** 49 45N 0 15 E
Ypres = Ieper **16** 50 51N 2 53 E
Ypsilanti **117** 42 18N 83 40W
Yreka **120** 41 44N 122 40W
Ysabel Chan. **69** 2 0S 150 0 E
Ysleta **121** 31 45N 106 24W
Yssingeaux **21** 45 9N 4 8 E
Ystad **11** 55 26N 13 50 E
Ythan → **14** 57 26N 2 12W
Ytterhogdal **10** 62 12N 14 56 E
Ytyk-Kel **41** 62 30N 133 45 E
Yu Shan **59** 23 30N 120 58 E
Yu Xian, Hebei, China **60** 39 50N 114 35 E
Yu Xian, Henan, China **60** 34 10N 113 28 E
Yu Xian, Shanxi, China **60** 38 5N 113 20 E
Yuan 'an **59** 31 3N 111 34 E
Yuan Jiang →, Hunan, China **59** 28 55N 111 50 E
Yuan Jiang →, Yunnan, China **58** 22 20N 103 59 E
Yuanjiang, Hunan, China **59** 28 47N 112 21 E
Yuanjiang, Yunnan, China **58** 23 32N 102 0 E
Yuanli **59** 24 29N 120 39 E
Yuanlin **59** 23 58N 120 30 E
Yuanling **59** 28 29N 110 22 E
Yuanmou **58** 25 42N 101 53 E
Yuanqu **60** 35 18N 111 40 E
Yuanyang, Henan, China **60** 35 3N 113 58 E
Yuanyang, Yunnan, China **58** 23 10N 102 43 E
Yuat → **69** 4 10S 143 52 E
Yuba → **122** 39 8N 121 36W
Yuba City **122** 39 12N 121 37W
Yūbari **63** 43 4N 141 59 E
Yūbetsu **63** 43 13N 144 5 E
Yucatán □ **125** 21 30N 86 30W
Yucatán Basin **128** 20 0N 84 0W
Yucatán, Canal de **126** 22 0N 86 30W
Yucatán Channel = Canal de Yucatán = Yucatán, Canal de **126** 22 0N 86 30W
Yucca **123** 34 56N 114 6W
Yucca Valley **123** 34 8N 116 30W
Yucheng **60** 36 55N 116 32 E
Yuci **60** 37 42N 112 46 E
Yudino **40** 55 10N 67 55 E
Yudu **59** 25 59N 115 30 E
Yuendumu **78** 22 16S 131 49 E
Yueqing **59** 28 9N 120 59 E
Yueqing Wan **59** 28 5N 121 20 E
Yuexi, Anhui, China **59** 30 50N 116 20 E
Yuexi, Sichuan, China **58** 28 37N 102 26 E
Yueyang **59** 29 21N 113 5 E
Yufu-Dake **64** 33 17N 131 33 E
Yugan **59** 28 43N 116 37 E
Yugoslavia ■ **33** 44 0N 20 0 E
Yuhuan **59** 28 9N 121 12 E
Yujiang **59** 28 10N 116 43 E
Yukhnov **36** 54 44N 35 15 E
Yūki **65** 36 18N 139 53 E
Yukon Territory □ **100** 63 0N 135 0W
Yukti **41** 63 26N 105 42 E
Yukuhashi **64** 33 44N 130 59 E
Yule → **78** 20 41S 118 17 E
Yuli **89** 9 44N 10 12 E
Yulin, Guangxi Zhuangzu, China **59** 22 40N 110 8 E
Yulin, Shaanxi, China **60** 38 20N 109 30 E
Yuma, Ariz., U.S.A. **123** 32 45N 114 37W
Yuma, Colo., U.S.A. **118** 40 10N 102 43W
Yuma, B. de **127** 18 20N 68 35W
Yumbe **94** 3 28N 31 15 E
Yumbi **94** 1 12S 26 15 E
Yumbo **134** 1 20S 26 15 E
Yumen **62** 39 50N 97 30 E
Yun Ho **61** 35 0N 117 0 E
Yun Xian, Hubei, China **59** 32 50N 110 46 E
Yun Xian, Hubei, China **60** 32 50N 110 50 E
Yun Xian, Yunnan, China **58** 24 27N 100 8 E
Yuna **79** 28 20S 115 0 E
Yunan **59** 23 12N 111 30 E
Yuncheng, Henan, China **60** 35 36N 115 57 E
Yuncheng, Shanxi, China **60** 35 2N 111 0 E
Yunfu **59** 22 50N 112 0 E
Yungas **137** 17 0S 66 0W
Yungay, Chile **140** 37 10S 72 5W
Yungay, Peru **136** 9 2S 77 45W
Yungera **74** 34 45S 143 3 E
Yunhe **59** 28 8N 119 33 E
Yunlin **59** 23 42N 120 30 E
Yunling **58** 27 0N 99 20 E
Yunlong **58** 25 57N 99 13 E
Yunmeng **59** 31 2N 113 43 E
Yunnan □ **58** 25 0N 102 0 E
Yunndaga **79** 29 45S 121 0 E
Yunomae **64** 32 12N 130 59 E
Yunotso **64** 35 5N 132 21 E
Yunquera de Henares **24** 40 47N 3 11W
Yunta **73** 32 34S 139 36 E
Yunxi **60** 33 0N 110 22 E
Yunxiao **59** 23 59N 117 18 E
Yunyang **58** 30 58N 108 54 E
Yuping **58** 27 13N 108 56 E
Yupukarri **135** 3 45N 59 20W
Yupyongdong **61** 41 49N 128 53 E
Yuqing **58** 27 13N 107 53 E
Yur **41** 59 52N 137 41 E
Yuraraba **77** 28 20S 151 25 E
Yurgao **40** 55 42N 84 51 E
Yuribei **40** 71 8N 76 58 E
Yurimaguas **136** 5 55S 76 7W
Yurya **37** 59 1N 49 13 E
Yuryevets **37** 57 25N 43 2 E
Yuscarán **126** 13 58N 86 45W
Yusha, Jabal **44** 32 4N 35 41 E
Yushanzhen **58** 29 28N 108 22 E
Yushe **60** 37 4N 112 58 E
Yushu, Jilin, China **61** 44 43N 126 38 E
Yushu, Qinghai, China **62** 33 5N 96 55 E
Yutai **60** 35 0N 116 45 E
Yutian **61** 39 53N 117 45 E
Yuxi **58** 24 30N 102 35 E
Yuyao **59** 30 3N 121 10 E
Yuzha **37** 56 34N 42 1 E
Yuzhno-Sakhalinsk **41** 46 58N 142 45 E
Yvelines □ **19** 48 40N 1 45 E
Yverdon **31** 46 47N 6 39 E
Yvetot **18** 49 37N 0 44 E

Z

Zaandam **16** 52 26N 4 49 E
Zab, Monts du **87** 34 55N 5 0 E
Žabalj **33** 45 21N 20 5 E
Žabari **33** 44 22N 21 15 E
Zabarjad **90** 23 40N 36 12 E
Zabaykalskiy **41** 49 40N 117 25 E
Zabid **45** 14 0N 43 10 E
Ząbkowice Śląskie **32** 50 35N 16 50 E
Zabłudów **32** 53 0N 23 19 E
Zābol **47** 31 0N 61 32 E
Zābolī **47** 27 10N 61 35 E
Zabré **89** 11 12N 0 36W
Zabrze **32** 50 18N 18 50 E
Zabul □ **47** 32 0N 67 0 E
Zacapa **126** 14 59N 89 31W
Zacapu **124** 19 50N 101 43W
Zacatecas **124** 22 49N 102 34W
Zacatecas □ **124** 23 30N 103 0W
Zacatecoluca **126** 13 29N 88 51W
Zacoalco **124** 20 14N 103 33W
Zacualtipán **125** 20 39N 98 36W
Zadar **27** 44 8N 15 14 E
Zadawa **89** 11 33N 10 19 E
Zadetkyi Kyun **56** 10 0N 98 25 E
Zadonsk **37** 52 25N 38 56 E
Zafra **23** 38 26N 6 30W
Zafriya **44** 31 59N 34 51 E
Żagań **32** 51 39N 15 22 E
Zagazig **90** 30 40N 31 30 E
Zaghouan **87** 36 23N 10 10 E
Zaglivérion **35** 40 36N 23 15 E
Zaglou **86** 27 17N 0 3W
Zagnanado **89** 7 18N 2 28 E
Zagorá **35** 39 27N 23 6 E
Zagora **86** 30 22N 5 51W
Zagorsk **37** 56 20N 38 10 E
Zagreb **27** 45 50N 16 0 E
Zāgros, Kudhā-ye **47** 33 45N 47 0 E
Zaguinaso **88** 10 1N 6 14W
Zāhedān **47** 29 30N 60 50 E
Zahirabad **50** 17 43N 77 37 E
Zahlah **46** 33 52N 35 50 E
Zahna **30** 51 54N 12 47 E
Zahrez Chergui **86** 35 0N 3 30 E
Zahrez Rharbi **86** 34 50N 2 55 E
Zaïr **86** 29 47N 5 51W
Zaïre → **92** 6 4S 12 24 E
Zaïre, Rep. of ■ **92** 3 0S 23 0 E
Zaječar **33** 43 53N 22 18 E
Zakamensk **41** 50 23N 103 17 E
Zakataly **39** 41 38N 46 35 E
Zakavkazye **39** 42 0N 44 0 E
Zākhū **46** 37 10N 42 50 E
Zákinthos **35** 37 47N 20 57 E
Zakopane **32** 49 18N 19 57 E
Zala → **33** 46 43N 17 16 E
Zalaegerszeg **33** 46 53N 16 47 E
Zalalövö **33** 46 51N 16 35 E
Zalamea de la Serena **23** 38 40N 5 38W
Zalamea la Real **23** 37 41N 6 38W
Zalau **89** 10 20N 8 58 E
Žalec **27** 46 16N 15 10 E
Zaleshchiki **38** 48 45N 25 45 E
Zalingei **85** 12 51N 23 29 E
Zalţan, Jabal **87** 28 46N 19 45 E
Zambeke **94** 2 8N 25 17 E
Zambeze → **95** 18 55S 36 4 E
Zambezi → = Zambeze → **95** 18 55S 36 4 E
Zambezia □ **95** 16 15S 37 30 E
Zambia ■ **93** 15 0S 28 0 E
Zamboanga **57** 6 59N 122 3 E
Zambrano **134** 9 45N 74 49W
Zambrów **32** 52 59N 22 14 E
Zametchino **37** 53 30N 42 30 E
Zamora, Ecuador **134** 4 4S 78 58W
Zamora, Mexico **124** 20 0N 102 21W
Zamora, Spain **22** 41 30N 5 45W
Zamora □ **22** 41 30N 5 46W
Zamora-Chinchipe □ **134** 4 15S 78 50W
Zamość **32** 50 43N 23 15 E
Zamuro, Sierra del **135** 4 0N 62 30W
Zamzam, W. → **87** 31 0N 14 30 E
Zan **89** 9 26N 0 17W
Zanaga **92** 2 48S 13 48 E
Záncara → **25** 39 18N 3 18W
Zandvoort **16** 52 22N 4 32 E
Zanesville **114** 39 56N 82 2W
Zangue → **95** 17 50S 35 21 E
Zanjan **46** 36 40N 48 35 E
Zannone **28** 40 58N 13 2 E
Zanthus **79** 31 2S 123 34 E
Zanzibar **94** 6 12S 39 12 E
Zanzibar I. **94** 6 12S 39 12 E
Zanzūr **87** 32 55N 13 1 E
Zaouatalaz **87** 24 57N 8 16 E
Zaouiet El Kahla **87** 28 10N 6 40 E
Zaouiet Reggane **86** 26 32N 0 3 E
Zaoyang **59** 32 10N 112 45 E
Zaozhuang **61** 34 50N 117 35 E
Zapadna Morava → **33** 43 50N 20 30 E
Zapadnaya Dvina → **36** 57 4N 24 3 E
Západné Beskydy **32** 49 30N 19 0 E
Zapala **142** 39 0S 70 5W
Zapaleri, Cerro **140** 22 49S 67 11W
Zapata **119** 26 56N 99 17W
Zapatón → **23** 39 0N 6 49W
Zapiga **136** 19 40S 79 0W
Zapodnyy Sayan **41** 52 30N 94 0 E
Zaporozhye **38** 47 50N 35 10 E
Zapponeta **29** 41 27N 15 57 E
Zara **46** 39 58N 37 43 E
Zaragoza, Colomb. **134** 7 30N 74 52W
Zaragoza, Coahuila, Mexico **124** 28 30N 101 0W
Zaragoza, Nuevo León, Mexico **125** 24 0N 99 46W
Zaragoza, Spain **24** 41 39N 0 53W
Zaragoza □ **24** 41 35N 1 0W
Zarand **47** 30 46N 56 34 E
Zărandului, Munţii **34** 46 14N 22 7 E
Zarasai **36** 55 40N 26 20 E
Zarate **140** 34 7S 59 0W
Zaraysk **37** 54 48N 38 53 E
Zaraza **135** 9 21N 65 19W
Zarembo I. **108** 56 20N 132 50W
Zaria **89** 11 0N 7 40 E
Zarisberge **96** 24 30S 16 15 E
Zarqa → **44** 32 10N 35 37 E
Zaruma **134** 3 40S 79 38W
Żary **32** 51 37N 15 10 E
Zarza de Alange **23** 38 49N 6 13W
Zarza de Granadilla **22** 40 14N 6 3W
Zarza, La **23** 37 42N 6 51W
Zarzaïtine **87** 28 15N 9 34 E
Zarzal **134** 4 24N 76 4W
Zarzis **87** 33 31N 11 2 E
Zas **22** 43 4N 8 53W
Zashiversk **41** 67 25N 142 40 E
Zaskar → **49** 34 13N 77 20 E
Zaskar Mountains **49** 33 15N 77 30 E

Zastron **96** 30 18S 27 7 E
Zavareh **47** 33 29N 52 28 E
Zavetnoye **39** 47 13N 43 50 E
Zavidovići **33** 44 27N 18 13 E
Zavitinsk **41** 50 10N 129 20 E
Zavodoski, I. **143** 56 0S 27 45W
Zavolzhye **37** 56 37N 43 26 E
Zawiercie **32** 50 30N 19 24 E
Zawyet Shammâs **90** 31 30N 26 37 E
Zâwyet Um el Rakham **90** 31 18N 27 1 E
Zâwyet Ungeîla **90** 31 23N 26 42 E
Zāyandeh → **47** 32 35N 52 0 E
Zayarsk **41** 56 12N 102 55 E
Zaysan **40** 47 28N 84 52 E
Zaysan, Oz. **40** 48 0N 83 0 E
Zayü **58** 28 48N 97 27 E
Zāzamt, W. **87** 30 29N 14 30 E
Zazir, O. → **87** 22 0N 5 40 E
Zbarazh **36** 49 43N 25 44 E
Zbąszyń **32** 52 14N 15 56 E
Zblewo **32** 53 56N 18 19 E
Zdolbunov **36** 50 30N 26 15 E
Zdrelo **33** 44 16N 21 28 E
Zduńska Wola **32** 51 37N 18 59 E
Zearing **116** 42 10N 93 20W
Zeballos **108** 49 59N 126 50W
Zebediela **97** 24 20S 19 7 E
Zeebrugge **16** 51 19N 3 12 E
Zeehan **72** 41 52S 145 25 E
Zeeland **117** 42 49N 86 1W
Zeeland □ **16** 51 30N 3 50 E
Ze'elim **44** 31 13N 34 32 E
Zeerust **96** 25 31S 26 4 E
Zefat **44** 32 58N 35 29 E
Zegdou **86** 29 51N 4 45W
Zege **91** 11 43N 37 18 E
Zégoua **88** 10 32N 5 35W
Zehdenick **30** 52 59N 13 20 E
Zeigler **116** 37 55N 89 5W
Zeil, Mt. **78** 23 30S 132 23 E
Zeila **45** 11 21N 43 30 E
Zeist **16** 52 5N 5 15 E
Zeita **44** 32 23N 35 2 E
Zeitz **30** 51 3N 12 9 E
Zelee, C. **68** 9 44S 161 34 E
Zelenodolsk **37** 55 55N 48 30 E
Zelenogradsk **36** 54 53N 20 29 E
Zelenokumsk **39** 44 24N 43 53 E
Zelënyy **39** 48 6N 50 45 E
Zell, Baden, Ger. **31** 47 42N 7 50 E
Zell, Rhld-Pfz., Ger. **31** 50 2N 7 11 E
Zell am See **33** 47 19N 12 47 E
Zella Mehlis **30** 50 40N 10 41 E
Zelzate **16** 51 13N 3 47 E
Zembra, I. **87** 37 5N 10 56 E
Zémio **94** 5 2N 25 5 E
Zemlya Frantsa Iosifa **144** 81 0N 55 0 E
Zemmora **86** 35 44N 0 51 E
Zemoul, O. → **86** 29 15N 7 0W
Zemun **33** 44 51N 20 25 E
Zengcheng **59** 23 13N 113 52 E
Zenica **33** 44 10N 17 57 E
Zenina **86** 34 30N 2 37 E
Zentsūji **64** 34 14N 133 47 E
Žepče **33** 44 28N 18 2 E
Zeraf, Bahr ez → **91** 9 42N 30 52 E
Zerbst **30** 51 59N 12 8 E
Zerhamra **86** 29 58N 2 30W
Zermatt **31** 46 2N 7 46 E
Zernez **31** 46 42N 10 7 E
Zernograd **39** 46 52N 40 19 E
Zerqani **35** 41 30N 20 20 E
Zestafoni **39** 42 6N 43 0 E
Zetel **30** 53 25N 7 57 E
Zeulenroda **30** 50 39N 12 0 E
Zeven **30** 53 17N 9 19 E
Zévio **26** 45 23N 11 10 E
Zeya **41** 53 48N 127 14 E
Zeya → **41** 53 13N 127 35 E
Zeyse **91** 5 44N 37 23W
Zêzere → **23** 39 28N 8 20W
Zgierz **32** 51 50N 19 27 E
Zgorzelec **32** 51 10N 15 0 E
Zhabinka **36** 52 13N 24 2 E
Zhailma **40** 51 37N 61 33 E
Zhangbei **60** 41 10N 114 45 E
Zhangguangcai Ling **61** 45 0N 129 0 E
Zhanghua **59** 24 6N 120 29 E
Zhangjiakou **60** 40 48N 114 55 E
Zhangping **59** 25 17N 117 23 E
Zhangpu **59** 24 8N 117 35 E
Zhangwu, Liaoning, China **61** 42 23N 123 52 E
Zhangwu, Liaoning, China **61** 42 25N 122 35 E
Zhangye **62** 38 50N 100 23 E
Zhangzhou **59** 24 30N 117 35 E
Zhanhua **61** 37 40N 118 8 E
Zhanjiang **59** 21 15N 110 20 E
Zhanyi **58** 25 38N 103 48 E
Zhanyu **61** 44 30N 122 30 E
Zhao Xian **60** 37 43N 114 45 E
Zhao'an **59** 23 41N 117 10 E
Zhaocheng **60** 36 22N 111 38 E
Zhaojue **58** 28 1N 102 49 E
Zhaoping **59** 24 11N 110 48 E
Zhaoqing **59** 23 0N 112 20 E
Zhaotong **58** 27 20N 103 44 E
Zhaoyuan, Heilongjiang, China **61** 45 27N 125 0 E
Zhaoyuan, Shandong, China **61** 37 20N 120 23 E
Zharkovskiy **36** 55 56N 32 19 E
Zhashkov **38** 49 15N 30 5 E
Zhashui **60** 33 40N 109 8 E
Zhdanov **38** 47 5N 37 31 E
Zhecheng **60** 34 7N 115 20 E
Zhegao **59** 31 46N 117 45 E
Zhejiang □ **59** 29 0N 120 0 E
Zheleznogorsk-Ilimskiy **41** 56 34N 104 8 E
Zhen'an **58** 33 27N 109 9 E
Zhenfeng **58** 25 22N 105 40 E
Zheng'an **58** 28 32N 107 27 E
Zhengding **60** 38 8N 114 32 E
Zhenghe **59** 27 20N 118 50 E
Zhengyang **59** 32 37N 114 22 E
Zhengyangguan **59** 32 30N 116 29 E
Zhengzhou **60** 34 45N 113 34 E
Zhenhai **59** 29 59N 121 42 E
Zhenjiang **59** 32 11N 119 26 E
Zhenlai **61** 45 50N 123 5 E
Zhenning **58** 26 4N 105 45 E
Zhenping, Henan, China **59** 33 10N 112 16 E
Zhenping, Shaanxi, China **58** 31 59N 109 31 E
Zhenxiong **58** 27 27N 104 50 E
Zhenyuan, Gansu, China **60** 35 35N 107 30 E
Zhenyuan, Guizhou, China **58** 27 4N 108 21 E
Zherdevka **37** 51 56N 41 29 E
Zherong **59** 27 15N 119 52 E
Zhidan **60** 36 48N 108 48 E
Zhigansk **41** 66 48N 123 27 E
Zhigulevsk **37** 53 28N 49 30 E
Zhijiang, Hubei, China **59** 30 28N 111 45 E
Zhijiang, Hunan, China **58** 27 27N 109 42 E
Zhijin **58** 26 37N 105 45 E
Zhirnovsk **37** 50 57N 44 49 E
Zhitomir **36** 50 20N 28 40 E
Zhizdra **36** 53 45N 34 40 E
Zhlobin **36** 52 55N 30 0 E
Zhmerinka **38** 49 2N 28 2 E
Zhodino **36** 54 5N 28 17 E
Zhokhova, Ostrov **41** 76 4N 152 40 E
Zhong Xian **58** 30 21N 108 1 E
Zhongdian **58** 27 48N 99 42 E
Zhongdong **58** 22 48N 107 47 E
Zhongdu **58** 24 40N 109 40 E
Zhongning **60** 37 29N 105 40 E
Zhongshan, Guangdong, China **59** 22 26N 113 20 E
Zhongshan, Guangxi Zhuangzu, China **59** 24 29N 111 18 E
Zhongtiao Shan **60** 35 0N 111 10 E
Zhongwei **60** 37 30N 105 12 E
Zhongxiang **59** 31 12N 112 34 E
Zhongyang **60** 37 20N 111 11 E
Zhoucun **61** 36 47N 117 48 E
Zhouning **59** 27 12N 119 20 E
Zhoushan Dao **59** 28 5N 122 10 E
Zhouzhi **60** 34 10N 108 12 E
Zhovtnevoye **38** 46 54N 32 3 E
Zhuanghe **61** 39 40N 123 0 E
Zhucheng **61** 36 0N 119 27 E
Zhugqu **60** 33 40N 104 30 E
Zhuhai **59** 22 15N 113 30 E
Zhuji **59** 29 40N 120 10 E
Zhukovka **36** 53 35N 33 50 E
Zhumadian **59** 32 59N 114 2 E
Zhuo Xian **60** 39 28N 115 58 E
Zhuolu **60** 40 20N 115 12 E
Zhuozi **60** 41 0N 112 25 E
Zhupanovo **41** 53 40N 159 52 E
Zhushan **59** 32 15N 110 13 E
Zhuxi **59** 32 25N 109 40 E
Zhuzhou **59** 27 49N 113 12 E
Zi Shui → **59** 28 40N 112 40 E
Ziarat **48** 30 25N 67 49 E
Zibo **61** 36 47N 118 3 E
Zichang **60** 37 18N 109 40 E
Zielona Góra **32** 51 57N 15 31 E
Zierikzee **16** 51 40N 3 55 E
Ziesar **30** 52 16N 12 19 E
Zifta **90** 30 43N 31 14 E
Zigey **85** 14 43N 15 50 E
Zigong **58** 29 15N 104 48 E
Zigui **59** 31 0N 110 40 E
Ziguinchor **88** 12 35N 16 20W
Zihuatanejo **124** 17 38N 101 33W
Zijin **59** 23 33N 115 8 E
Zikhron Ya'Aqov **44** 32 34N 34 56 E
Zile **46** 40 15N 35 52 E
Žilina **32** 49 12N 18 42 E
Zillah **87** 28 30N 17 33 E
Zillertaler Alpen **31** 47 6N 11 45 E
Zilwaukee **106** 43 28N 83 55W
Zima **41** 54 0N 102 5 E
Zimane, Adrar in **86** 22 10N 4 30 E
Zimapán **125** 20 54N 99 20W
Zimba **95** 17 20S 26 11 E
Zimbabwe **95** 20 16S 30 54 E
Zimbabwe-Rhodesia ■ **95** 20 0S 30 0 E
Zimovniki **39** 47 10N 42 25 E
Zinder **89** 13 48N 9 0 E
Zinga **95** 9 16S 38 49 E
Zingst **30** 54 24N 12 45 E
Zini, Yebel **86** 28 0N 11 0W
Ziniaré **89** 12 35N 1 18W
Zinjibar **45** 13 5N 45 23 E
Zinkgruvan **11** 58 50N 15 6 E
Zinnowitz **30** 54 5N 13 54 E
Zion **117** 42 27N 87 50W
Zion Nat. Park **121** 37 25N 112 50W
Zionsville **117** 39 57N 86 16W
Zipaquirá **134** 5 0N 74 0W
Zippori **44** 32 45N 35 16 E
Zirc **33** 47 17N 17 42 E
Žiri **27** 46 5N 14 5 E
Žirje **27** 43 39N 15 42 E
Zirko **47** 25 0N 53 40 E
Zirl **31** 47 17N 11 14 E
Zitácuaro **124** 19 28N 100 21W
Zitava → **33** 48 14N 18 21 E
Zittau **30** 50 54N 14 47 E
Zitundo **97** 26 48S 32 47 E
Živinice **33** 44 27N 18 36 E
Ziway, L. **91** 8 0N 38 50 E
Zixi **59** 27 45N 117 4 E
Zixing **59** 25 59N 113 21 E
Ziyang, Shaanxi, China **58** 32 32N 108 31 E
Ziyang, Sichuan, China **58** 30 6N 104 40 E
Ziyun **58** 25 45N 106 5 E
Ziz, Oued → **86** 31 40N 4 15W
Zizhixian **59** 25 0N 111 47 E
Zizhong **58** 29 48N 104 47 E
Zlarin **27** 43 42N 15 49 E
Zlatar **27** 46 5N 16 3 E
Zlataritsa **34** 43 2N 25 55 E
Zlatitsa **34** 42 41N 24 7 E
Zlatograd **35** 41 22N 25 7 E
Zlatoust **40** 55 10N 59 40 E
Zletovo **35** 41 59N 22 17 E
Zlītun **87** 32 32N 14 35 E
Złocieniec **32** 53 30N 16 1 E
Złoczew **32** 51 24N 18 35 E
Złotoryja **32** 51 8N 15 55 E
Złotów **32** 53 22N 17 2 E
Zmeinogorsk **40** 51 10N 82 13 E
Żmigród **32** 51 28N 16 53 E
Zmiyev **38** 49 39N 36 27 E
Znamenka **38** 48 45N 32 30 E
Znamensk **36** 54 37N 21 17 E
Żnin **32** 52 51N 17 44 E
Znojmo **32** 48 50N 16 2 E
Zoar **96** 33 30S 21 26 E
Zobia **94** 3 0N 25 59 E
Zogang **58** 29 55N 97 42 E
Zogno **26** 45 49N 9 41 E
Zogqên **58** 32 13N 98 47 E
Zolochev **36** 49 45N 24 51 E
Zolotonosha **38** 49 39N 32 5 E
Zomba **95** 15 22S 35 19 E
Zombi **94** 3 35N 29 10 E
Zongo **92** 4 20N 18 35 E
Zonguldak **38** 41 28N 31 50 E
Zorgo **89** 12 15N 0 35W
Zorita **23** 39 17N 5 39W
Zorritos **136** 3 43S 80 40W
Zorzor **88** 7 46N 9 28W
Zossen **30** 52 13N 13 28 E
Zou Xiang **60** 35 30N 116 58 E
Zouar **87** 20 30N 16 32 E
Zouérabe **84** 22 44N 12 21W
Zousfana, O. → **86** 31 28N 2 17W
Zoushan Dao **59** 30 5N 122 10 E
Zoutkamp **16** 53 20N 6 18 E
Zrenjanin **33** 45 22N 20 23 E
Zuarungu **89** 10 49N 0 46W
Zuba **89** 9 11N 7 12 E
Zubair, Jazāir **91** 15 0N 42 10 E
Zubia **23** 37 8N 3 33W
Zubtsov **36** 56 10N 34 34 E
Zudáñez **137** 19 6S 64 44W
Zuénoula **88** 7 34N 6 3W
Zuera **24** 41 51N 0 49W
Zuetina **87** 30 58N 20 7 E
Zufar **45** 17 40N 54 0 E
Zug **31** 47 10N 8 31 E
Zugdidi **39** 42 30N 41 55 E
Zugersee **31** 47 7N 8 35 E
Zugspitze **31** 47 25N 10 59 E
Zuid-Holland □ **16** 52 0N 4 35 E
Zuidhorn **16** 53 15N 6 23 E
Zújar **25** 37 34N 2 50W
Zújar → **23** 39 1N 5 47W
Zújar, Pantano del **23** 38 55N 5 35W
Zula **91** 15 17N 39 40 E
Zulia □ **134** 10 0N 72 10W
Zulpich **30** 50 41N 6 38 E
Zululand **97** 43 19N 2 15 E
Zumaya **24** 43 19N 2 15W
Zumbo **95** 15 35S 30 26 E
Zummo **89** 9 51N 12 59 E
Zumpango **125** 19 48N 99 6W
Zungeru **89** 9 48N 6 8 E
Zunhua **61** 40 18N 117 58 E
Zuni **121** 35 7N 108 57W
Zunyi **58** 27 42N 106 53 E
Zuoquan **60** 37 5N 113 22 E
Zuozhou **58** 22 42N 107 27 E
Županja **33** 45 4N 18 43 E
Zuqar **91** 14 0N 42 40 E
Zurich **106** 43 26N 81 37W
Zürich **31** 47 22N 8 32 E
Zürich □ **31** 47 26N 8 40 E
Zürichsee **31** 47 18N 8 40 E
Zuromin **32** 53 4N 19 51 E
Zuru **89** 11 20N 5 11 E
Žut **27** 43 52N 15 17 E
Zutphen **16** 52 9N 6 12 E
Zuwārah **87** 32 58N 12 1 E
Žužemberk **27** 45 52N 14 56 E
Zvenigorodka **38** 49 4N 30 56 E
Zverinogolovskoye **40** 54 23N 64 40 E
Zvezdets **34** 42 6N 27 26 E
Zvolen **32** 48 33N 19 10 E
Zvonce **33** 42 57N 22 34 E
Zvornik **33** 44 26N 19 7 E
Zwedru (Tchien) **88** 5 59N 8 15W
Zweibrücken **31** 49 15N 7 20 E
Zwenkau **30** 51 13N 12 19 E
Zwickau **30** 50 43N 12 30 E
Zwiesel **31** 49 1N 13 14 E
Zwischenahn **30** 53 12N 8 1 E
Zwolle, Neth. **16** 52 31N 6 6 E
Zwolle, U.S.A. **119** 31 38N 93 38W
Zymoetz → **108** 54 33N 128 31W
Żyrardów **32** 52 3N 20 28 E
Zyryanka **41** 65 45N 150 51 E

GEOGRAPHICAL TERMS

This is a list of some of the geographical words from foreign languages which are found in the place names on the maps and in the index. Each is followed by the language and the English meaning.

Afr. afrikaans	*Chin.* chinese	*Gae.* gaelic	*It.* italian	*Nor.* norwegian	*Ser.-Cr.* serbo-croat	
Alb. albanian	*Cz.* czechoslovakian	*Ger.* german	*Jap.* japanese	*Pash.* pashto	*Siam.* siamese	
Amh. amharic	*Dan.* danish	*Gr.* greek	*Kor.* korean	*Pers.* persian	*Sin.* sinhalese	
Ar. arabic	*Dut.* dutch	*Heb.* hebrew	*Lapp.* lappish	*Pol.* polish	*Som.* somali	
Ber. berber	*Fin.* finnish	*Hin.* hindi	*Lith.* lithuanian	*Port.* portuguese	*Span.* spanish	
Bulg. bulgarian	*Flem.* flemish	*I.-C.* indo-chinese	*Mal.* malay	*Rum.* rumanian	*Swed.* swedish	
Bur. burmese	*Fr.* french	*Ice.* icelandic	*Mong.* mongolian	*Russ.* russian	*Tib.* tibetan	
					Turk. turkish	

A. (Ain) *Ar.* spring
–á *Ice.* river
a *Dan., Nor., Swed.* stream
–abad *Pers., Russ.* town
Abyad *Ar.* white
Ad. (Adrar) *Ar., Ber.* mountain
Ada, Adasi *Tur.* island
Addis *Amh.* new
Adrar *Ar., Ber.* mountain
Aïn *Ar.* spring
Ākra *Gr.* cape
Akrotíri *Gr.* cape
Alb *Ger.* mountains
Albufera *Span.* lagoon
–ålen *Nor.* islands
Alpen *Ger.* mountain pastures
Alpes *Fr.* mountains
Alpi *It.* mountains
Alto *Port.* high
–älv, –älven *Swed.* stream, river
Amt *Dan.* first-order administrative division
Appennino *It.* mountain range
Arch. (Archipiélago) *Span.* archipelago
Arcipélago *It.* archipelago
Arq. (Arquipélago) *Port.* archipelago
Arr. (Arroyo) *Span.* stream
–Ås, –åsen *Nor., Swed.* hill
Autonomna Oblast *Ser.-Cr.* autonomous region
Ayios *Gr.* island
Ayn *Ar.* well, waterhole

B(a). (Baía) *Port.* bay
B. (Baie) *Fr.* bay
B. (Bahía) *Span.* bay
B. (Ben) *Gae.* mountain
B. (Bir) *Ar.* well
B. (Bucht) *Ger.* bay
B. (Bugt.) *Dan.* bay
Baai, –baai *Afr.* bay
Bāb *Ar.* gate
Bäck, –bäcken *Swed.* stream
Back, backen, *Swed.* hill
Bad, –baden *Ger.* spa
Bādiya,-t *Ar.* desert
Baek *Dan.* stream
Baelt *Dan.* strait
Bahía *Span.* bay
Bahr *Ar.* sea, river
Bahra *Ar.* lake
Baía *Port.* bay
Baie *Fr.* bay
Bajo, –a, *Span.* lower
Bakke *Nor.* hill
Bala *Pers.* upper
Baltă *Rum.* marsh, lake
Banc *Fr.* bank
Bander *Ar., Mal.* port
Bandar *Pers.* bay
Banja *Ser. Cr.* spa. resort
Barat *Mal.* western
Barr. (Barrage) *Fr.* dam
Barracão *Port.* dam, waterfall
Bassin *Fr.* bay
Bayt *Heb.* house, village
Bazar *Hin.* market, bazaar
Be'er *Heb.* well
Beit *Heb.* village
Belo-, Belyy, Belaya,
Beloye, *Russ.* white
Ben *Gae.* mountain
Bender *Somal.* harbour
Berg,(e) –berg(e) *Afr.* mountain(s)
Berg, –berg *Ger.* mountain
–berg, –et *Nor., Swed.* hill, mountain, rock
Bet *Heb.* house, village
Bir, Bîr *Ar.* well
Birket *Ar.* lake, bay, marsh
Bj. (Bordj) *Ar.* port
–bjerg *Dan.* hill, point
Boca *Span.* river mouth
Bodden *Ger.* bay, inlet
Bogaz, Boğaz, –ı *Tur.* strait
Boka *Ser.-Cr.* gulf, inlet
Bol. (Bolshoi) *Russ.* great, large
Bordj *Ar.* fort
–borg *Dan., Nor., Swed.* castle, fort
–botn *Nor.* valley floor
bouche(s) *Fr.* mouth
Br. (Burnu) *Tur.* cape
Braţul *Rum.* distributary stream
–breen *Nor.* glacier
–bruck *Ger.* bridge
–brunn *Swed.* well, spring
Bucht *Ger.* bay
Bugt, –bugt *Dan.* bay
Buheirat *Ar.* lake
Bukit *Mal.* hill
Bukten *Swed.* bay
–bulag *Mong.* spring
Bûr *Ar.* port
Burg. *Ar.* fort
Burg, –burg *Ger.* castle
Burnu *Tur.* cape
Burun *Tur.* cape
Butt *Gae.* promontory
–by *Dan., Nor., Swed.* town
–byen *Nor., Swed.* town

C. (Cabo) *Port., Span.* headland, cape
C. (Cap) *Fr.* cape
C. (Capo) *It.* cape
Cabeza *Span.* peak, hill
Camp *Port., Span.* land, field
Campo *Span.* plain
Campos *Span.* upland
Can. (Canal) *Fr., Span.* canal
Canale *It.* canal
Canalul *Ser.-Cr.* canal
Cao Nguyên *Thai.* plateau, tableland
Cap *Fr.* cape
Capo *It.* cape
Cataracta *Sp.* cataract
Cauce *Span.* intermittent stream
Causse *Fr.* upland (limestone)
Cayi *Tur.* river
Cayo(s) *Span.* rock(s), islet(s)
Cerro *Span.* hill, peak
Ch. (Chaîne(s)) *Fr.* mountain range(s)
Ch. (Chott) *Ar.* salt lake
Chaco *Span.* jungle
Chaîne(s) *Fr.* mountain range(s)
Chap. (Chapada) *Port.* hills, upland
Chapa *Span.* hills, upland
Chapada *Port.* hills, upland
Chaung *Bur.* stream, river
Chen *Chin.* market town
Ch'eng *Chin.* town
Chiang *Chin.* river
Ch'ih *Chin.* pool
Ch'ŏn *Kor.* river
–chŏsuji *Kor.* reservoir
Chott *Ar.* salt lake, swamp
Chou *Chin.* district
Chu *Tib.* river
Chung *Chin.* middle
Chute *Fr.* waterfall
Co. (Cerro) *Span.* hill, peak
Coch. (Cochilla) *Port.* hills
Col *Fr., It.* Pass
Colline(s) *Fr.* hill(s)
Conca *It.* plain, basin
Cord. (Cordillera) *Span.* mountain chain
Costa *It., Span.* coast
Côte *Fr.* coast, slope, hill
Cuchillas *Spain* hills
Cu-Lao *I.-C.* island

D. (Dolok) *Mal.* mountain
Dágh *Pers.* mountain
Dağ(ı) *Tur.* mountain(s)
Dağları *Tur.* mountain range
Dake *Jap.* mountain
–dal *Nor.* valley
–dal, –e *Dan., Nor.* valley
–dal, –en *Swed.* valley, stream
Dalay *Mong.* sea, large lake
–dalir *Ice.* valley
–dalur *Ice.* valley
–damm, –en *Swed.* lake
Danau *Mal.* lake
Dao *I.-O.* island
Dar *Ar.* region
Darya *Russ.* river
Daryācheh *Pers.* marshy lake, lake
Dasht *Pers.* desert, steppe
Daung *Bur.* mountain, hill
Dayr *Ar.* depression, hill
Debre *Amh.* hill
Deli *Ser.-Cr.* mountain(s)
Denizi *Tur.* sea
Dépt. (Département) *Fr.* first-order administrative division
Desierto *Span.* desert
Dhar *Ar.* region, mountain chain
Dj. (Djebel) *Ar.* mountain
Dō *Jap., Kor.* island
Dong *Kor.* village, town
Dong *Thai.* jungle region
–dorf *Ger.* village
–dorp *Afr.* village
–drif *Afr.* ford
–dybet *Dan.* marine channel
Dzong *Tib.* town, settlement

Eil.-eiland(en) *Afr., Dut.* island(s)
–elv *Nor.* river
–'emeq *Heb.* plain, valley
'erg *Ar.* desert with dunes
Estrecho *Span.* strait
Estuario *Span.* estuary
Étang *Fr.* lagoon
–ey(jar) *Ice.* island(s)

F. (Fiume) *It.* river
F. Folyó *Hung.* river
Fd. (Fjord) *Nor.* Inlet of sea
–feld *Ger.* field
–fell *Ice.* mountain, hill
–feng *Chin.* mountain
Fiume *It.* river
Fj. (–fjell) *Nor.* mountain
–fjall *Ice.* mountain(s), hill(s)
–fjäll(et) *Swed.* hill(s), mountain(s), ridge
–fjällen *Swed.* mountains
–fjard(en) *Swed.* fjord, bay, lake
Fjeld *Dan.* mountain
–fjell *Nor.* mountain, rock
–fjord(en) *Nor.* inlet of sea
–fjorden *Dan.* bay, marine channel
–fjörður *Ice.* fjord
Fl. (Fleuve) *Fr.* river
Fl. (Fluss) *Ger.* river
–flói *Ice.* bay, marshy country
Fluss *Ger.* river
foce, –i *It.* mouth(s)
Folyó *Hung.* river
–fontein *Afr.* fountain, spring
–fors, –en, *Swed.* rapids, waterfall
Foss *Ice., Nor.* waterfall
–furt *Ger.* ford
Fylke *Nor.* first-order administrative division

G. (Gebel) *Ar.* mountain
G. (Gebirge) *Ger.* hills, mountains
G. (Golfe) *Fr.* gulf
G. (Golfo) *It.* gulf
G. (Gora) *Bulg., Russ., Ser-Cr.* mountain
G. (Gunong) *Mal.* mountain
–gang *Kor.* river
Ganga *Hin., Sin.* river
–gat *Dan.* sound
–gau *Ger.* district
Gave *Fr.* stream
–gawa *Jap.* river
Geb. (Gebirge) *Ger.* hills, mountains
Gebel *Ar.* mountain
Geziret *Ar.* island
Ghat *Hin.* range of hills
Ghiol *Rum.* lake
Ghubbat *Ar.* bay, inlet
Gji *Alb.* bay
Gjol *Alb.* lagoon, lake
Gl. (Glava) *Ser.-Cr.* mountain, peak
Glen. *Gae.* valley
Gletscher *Ger.* glacier
Gobi *Mong.* desert
Gol *Mong.* river
Golfe *Fr.* gulf
Golfo *It., Span.* gulf
Gomba *Tib.* settlement
Gora *Bulg., Russ., Ser.-Cr.* mountain(s)
Góry *Po* *Russ.* mountain
Gölü *Tur.* lake
–gorod *Russ.* small town
Grad *Bulg., Russ., Ser-Cr.* town, city
Grada *Russ.* mountain range
Guba *Russ.* bay
–Guntō *Jap.* island group
Gunong *Mal.* mountain
Gură *Rum.* passage

H. Hadabat *Ar.* plateau
–hafen *Ger.* harbour, port
Haff *Ger.* bay
Hai *Chin.* sea
Haihsia *Chin.* strait
–hale *Dan.* spit, peninsula
Hals *Dan., Nor.* peninsula, isthmus
Halvø *Dan.* peninsula
Halvøya *Nor.* peninsula
Hāmad, Hamada, Hammādah *Ar.* stony desert, plain
–hamn *Swed., Nor.* harbour, anchorage
Hāmūn *Ar.* plain
Hāmūn *Pers.* low-lying marshy area
–Hantō *Jap.* peninsula
Harju *Fin.* hill
Hassi *Ar.* well
–haug *Nor.* hill
Hav *Swed.* gulf
Havet *Nor.* sea
–havn *Dan., Nor.* harbour
Hegyseg *Hung.* forest
Heide *Ger.* heath
Hi. (hassi) *Ar.* well
Ho *Chin.* river
–hø *Nor.* peak
Hochland *Afr.* highland
Hoek, –hoek *Afr., Dut.* cape
Höfn *Ice.* harbour, port
–hög, –en, –högar, –högarna *Swed.* hill(s), peak, mountain
Höhe *Ger.* hills
Holm *Dan.* island
–holm, –holme, –holzen, *Swed.* island
Hon *I.-C.* island
Hora *Cz.* mountain
–horn *Nor.* peak
Hory *Cz.* mountain range, forest
–hoved *Dan.* point, headland, peninsula
Hráun *Ice.* lava
–hsi *Chin.* mountain, stream
–hsiang *Chin.* village
–hsien *Chin.* district
Hu *Chin.* lake
Huk *Dan., Ger.* point
Huken *Nor.* head

I. (Île) *Fr.* island
I. (Ilha) *Port.* island
I. (Insel) *Ger.* island
I. (Isla) *Span.* island
I. (Isola) *It.* island
Idehan *Ar., Ber.* sandy plain
Île(s) *Fr.* island(s)
Ilha *Port.* island
Insel(n) *Ger.* island(s)
Irmak *Tur.* river
Is. (Inseln) *Ger.* islands
Is. (Islas) *Span.* islands
Is. (Isola) *It.* island
Isola, –e *It.* island(s)
Istmo *Span.* isthmus

J. (Jabal) *Ar.* mountain
J. (Jazīra) *Ar.* island
J. (Jebel) *Ar.* mountain
J. (Jezioro) *Pol.* lake
Jabal *Ar.* mountain, range
–jaur *Swed.* lake
–järvi *Fin.* lake, bay, pond
Jasovir *Bulg.* reservoir
Jazā'ir *Ar.* islands
Jazīra *Ar.* island
Jazireh *Pers.* island
Jebel *Ar.* mountain
Jezero *Ser.-Cr.* lake
Jezioro *Pol.* lake
–Jima *Jap.* island
Jøkelen *Nor.* glacier
–joki *Fin.* stream
–jökull *Ice.* glacier
Jūras Līcis *Lat.* bay, gulf

K. (Kap) *Dan.* cape
K (Khalīg) *Ar.* gulf
K. (Kiang) *Chin.* river
K. (Kuala) *Mal.* confluence, estuary
Kaap *Afr.* cape
Kai *Jap.* sea
Kaikyō *Jap.* strait
Kamennyy *Russ.* stony
Kampong *Mal.* village
Kan. (Kanal) *Ser.-Cr.* channel, canal
Kanaal *Dut., Flem.* canal
Kanal *Dan.* channel, gulf
Kanal *Ger., Swed.* canal, stream
kanal *Ser.-Cr.* channel, canal
Kang *Kor.* river, bay
Kangri *Tib.* mountain glacier
Kap *Dan., Ger.* cape
Kapp *Nor.* cape
Kas *I.-C.* island
–kaupstaður *Ice.* market town
–kaupunki *Fin.* town
Kavīr *Pers.* salt desert
Kébir *Ar.* great
Kéfar *Heb.* village, hamlet
–ken *Jap.* first-order administrative division
Kep *Alb.* cape
Kepulauan *Mal.* archipelago
Ketjil *Mal.* lesser, little
Khalīg, Khalīj *Ar.* gulf
khamba, –idg *Tib.* source, spring
Khawr *Ar.* wadi
Khirbat *Ar.* ruins
Kho Khot *Thai.* isthmus
Khōr *Pers.* creek, estuary
Khrebet *Russ.* mountain range
Kiang *Chin.* river
–klint *Dan.* cliff
–Klintar *Swed.* hills
Kloof *Afr.* gorge
Knude *Dan.* point
Ko *Jap.* lake
Ko *Thai.* island
Kohi *Pash.* mountains
Kol *Russ.* lake
Kolymskoye *Russ.* mountain range
Kólpos *Gr., Tur.* gulf, bay
Kompong *Mal.* landing place
–kop *Afr.* hill

–köping *Swed.* market town
Körfezi *Tur.* gulf
Kosa *Russ.* spit
–koski *Fin.* cataract, rapids
–kraal *Afr.* native village
Krasnyy *Russ.* red
Kryash *Russ.* ridge, hills
Kuala *Mal.* confluence, estuary
kuan *Chin.* pass
Kuh –hha *Pers.* mountains
Kul *Russ.* lake
Kulle *Swed.* hill, shoal
Kum *Russ.* sandy desert
Kumpu *Fin.* hill
Kurgan *Russ.* mound
Kwe *Bur.* bay, gulf
Kyst *Dan.* coast
Kyun, –zu, –umya *Bur.* island(s)

L. (Lac) *Fr.* lake
L. (Lacul) *Rum.* lake
L. (Lago) *It., Span.* lake, lagoon
L. (Lagoa) *Port.* lagoon
L. (Límni) *Gr.* lake
L. (Loch) *Gae.* (lake, inlet)
L. (Lough) *Gae.* (lake, inlet)
La *Tib.* pass
La (Lagoa) *Port.* lagoon
–laagte *Afr.* watercourse
Läani *Fin.* first-order administrative division
Län *Swed.* first-order administrative division
Lac *Fr.* lake
Lacul *Rum.* lake, lagoon
Lago *It., Span.* lake, lagoon
Lagoa *Port.* lagoon
Laguna *It., Span.* lagoon, intermittent lake
Lagune *Fr.* lake
Lahti *Fin.* bay, gulf, cove
Lakhti *Russ.* bay, gulf
Lampi *Fin.* lake
Land *Ger.* first-order administrative division
–land *Dan.* region
–land *Afr., Nor.* land, province
Lido *It.* beach, shore
Liehtao *Chin.* islands
Lilla *Swed.* small
Límni *Gr.* lake
Ling *Chin.* mountain range, ice
Linna *Fin.* historical fort
Llano *Span.* prairie, plain
Loch *Gae.* (lake)
Lough *Gae.* (lake)
Lum *Alb.* river
Lund *Dan.* forest
–lund, –en *Swed.* wood(s)

M. (Maj, Mai) *Alb.* mountain, peak
M. (Mont) *Fr.* mountain peak
M. (Mys) *Russ.* cape
Madīna(h) *Ar.* town, city
Madiq *Ar.* strait
Maj *Alb.* peak
Mäki *Fin.* hill, hillside
Mal *Alb.* mountain
Mal *Russ.* little, small
Mal/a, –i, –o *Ser.-Cr.* small, little
Man *Kor.* bay
Mar *Span.* lagoon, sea
Mare *Rum.* great
Marisma *Span.* marsh
–mark *Dan., Nor.* land
Marsâ *Ar.* anchorage, bay, inlet
Masabb *Ar.* river mouth
Massif *Fr.* upland, plateau
Mato *Port.* forest
Mazar *Pers.* shrine, tomb
Meer *Afr., Dut., Ger.* lake sea
Mi., Mti. (Monti) *It.* mountains
Miao *Chin.* temple, shrine
Midbar *Heb.* wilderness
Mif. (Massif) *Fr.* upland, plateau
Misaki *Jap.* cape, point
–mo *Nor., Swed.* heath, island
–mon *Swed.* heath
Mong *Bur.* town
Mont *Fr.* hill, mountain
Montagna *It.* mountain
Montagne *Fr.* hill, mountain
Montaña *Span.* mountain
Monte *It., Port., Span.* mountain
Monti *It.* mountains
More *Russ.* sea
Mörön *Hung.* river
Mt. (Mont) *Fr.* mountain
Mt. (Monti) *It.* mountain
Mt. (Montaña) *Span.* mountain range
Mte. (Monte) *It., Port., Span.* mountain
Mţi. (Munţi) *Rum.* mountain
Mts. (Monts) *Fr.* mountains
Muang *Mal.* town
Mui *Ar., I.-C.* cape
Mull *Gae.* (promontory)
Mund, –mund *Afr.* mouth
Munkhafed *Ar.* depression
Munte *Rum.* mount
Munţi(i) *Rum.* mountain(s)
Muong *Mal.* village
Myit *Bur.* river
Myitwanya *Bur.* mouths of river
–mýri *Ice.* bog
Mys *Russ.* cape

N. (Nahal) *Heb.* river
Naes *Dan.* point, cape
Nafūd *Ar.* sandy desert
Nahal *Heb.* river
Nahr *Ar.* river, stream
Najd *Ar.* plateau, pass
Nakhon *Thai.* town
Nam *I.-C.* river
–nam *Kor.* south
–näs *Swed.* cape
–nes *Ice., Nor.* cape
Ness, –ness *Gae.* promontory, cape
Nez *Fr.* cape
–niemi *Fin.* cape, point, peninsula, island
Nizhne, –iy *Russ.* lower
Nizmennost *Russ.* plain, lowland
Nísos, Nísoi *Gr.* island(s)
Nor *Chin.* lake
Nor *Tib.* peak
Nos *Bulg., Russ.* cape, point
Nudo *Span.* mountain
Nuruu *Mong.* mountain range
Nuur *Mong.* lake

O. (Ostrov) *Russ.* island
O (Ouâdî, Oued) *Ar.* wadi
–ö *Swed.* island, peninsula, point
–öar, (–na) *Swed.* islands
Oblast *Russ.* administrative division
Öbor *Mong.* inner
Occidental *Fr., Span.* western
Odde *Dan., Nor.* point, peninsula, cape
Oji *Alb.* bay
Ojo *Span.* spring
Oki *Jap.* bay
–ön *Swed.* island peninsula
Ondör *Mong.* high, tall
–ör *Swed.* island, peninsula, point
Oraşul *Rum.* city
Ord *Gae.* point
Óri *Gr.* mountains
Oriental *Span.* eastern
Órmos *Gr.* bay
Óros *Gr.* mountain
Ort *Ger.* point, cape
Ostrov(a) *Russ.* island(s)
Otok(–i) *Ser.-Cr.* island(s)
Ouadi, –edi *Ar.* dry watercourse, wadi
Ouzan *Pers.* river
Ova (–si) *Tur.* plains, lowlands
–øy, (–a) *Nor.* island(s)
Oya *Hin.* point
Oya *Sin.* river
Oz. (Ozero, a) *Russ.* lake(s)

P. (Passo) *It.* pass
P. (Pasul) *Rum.* pass
P. (Pico) *Span.* peak
P. (Prokhod) *Bulg.* pass
–pää *Fin.* hill(s), mountain
Pahta *Lapp.* hill
Pampa, –s *Span.* plain(s) salt flat(s)
Pan. (Pantano) *Span.* Reservoir
Pantao *Chin.* peninsula
Parbat *Urdu* mountain
Pas *Fr.* gap
Paso *Span.* pass, marine channel
Pass *Ger.* pass
Passo *It.* pass
Pasul *Rum.* pass
Patam *Hin.* small village
Patna, –patnam *Hin.* small village
Pegunungan *Mal.* mountain, range
Pei, –pei *Chin.* north
Pélagos *Gr.* sea
Pen. (Península) *Span.* peninsula
Peña *Span.* rock, peak
Península *Span.* peninsula
Per. (Pereval) *Russ.* pass
Pertuis *Fr.* channel
Peski *Russ.* desert, sands
Phanom *I.-C., Thai.* mountain
Phnom *I.-C.* mountain
Phu *I.-C.* mountain
Pic *Fr.* peak
Pico(s) *Span.* peak(s)
Pik *Russ.* peak
Piz., pizzo *It.* peak
Pl. (Planina) *Ser.-Cr.* mountain, range
Plage *Fr.* beach
Plaine *Fr.* plain
Planalto *Span.* plateau
Planina *Bulg., Ser.-Cr.* mountain, range
Plat. (Plateau) *Fr.* level upland
Plato *Russ.* plateau
Playa *Span.* beach
P-ov. (Poluostrov) *Russ.* peninsula
Pointe *Fr.* point, cape
Pojezierze *Pol.* lakes plateau
Polder *Dut.* reclaimed farmland
–pólis *Gr.* city, town
Poluostrov *Russ.* peninsula
Połwysep *Pol.* peninsula
Pont *Fr.* bridge
Ponta *Port.* point, cape
Ponte *It.* bridge
Poort *Afr.* passage, gate
–poort *Dut.* port
Porta *Port.* pass
Porţil, –e *Rum.* gate
Portillo *Span.* pass
Porto *It.* port
Porto *Port., Span.* port
Pot. (Potámi, Potamós) *Gr.* river
Poulo *I.-C.* island
Pr. (Průsmyk) *Cz.* pass
Pradesh *Hin.* state
Presa *Span.* reservoir
Presqu'île *Fr.* peninsula
Prokhod *Bulg.* pass
Proliv *Russ.* strait
Prusmyk *Cz.* pass
Pso. (Passo) *It.* pass
Pta. (Ponta) *Port.* point, cape
Pta. (Punta) *It., Span.* point, cape, peak
Pte. (Pointe) *Fr.* point cape
Puerto *Span.* port, pass
Puig *Cat.* peak
Pulau *Mal.* island
Puna *Span.* desert plateau
Punta *It., Span.* point, peak
Puy *Fr.* hill

Qal'at *Ar.* fort
Qanal *Ar.* canal
Qasr *Ar.* fort
Qiryat *Heb.* town
Qolleh *Pers.* mountain

Ramla *Ar.* sand
Rann *Hin.* swampy region
Rao *I.-C.* river
Ras *Amh.* cape, headland
Rās *Ar.* cape, headland
Recife(s) *Port.* reef(s)
Reka *Bulg., Cz., Russ.* river
Repede *Rum.* rapids
Represa *Port.* dam
Reshteh *Pers.* mountain range
–Rettō *Jap.* group of islands
Ría *Span.* estuary, bay
Ribeirão *Port.* river
Rijeka *Ser.-Cr.* river
Rio *Port.* river
Río *Span.* river
Riv. (Riviera) *It.* coastal plain, coast, river
Rivier *Afr.* river
Riviera *It.* coast
Rivière *Fr.* river
Roche *Fr.* rock
Rog *Russ.* horn
–rück *Ger.* ridge
Rūd *Pers.* stream, river
Rudohorie *Cz.* ore mountains
Rzeka *Pol.* river

S. (Sungei) *Mal.* river
Sa. (Serra) *It., Port.* range of hills
Sa. (Sierra) *Span.* range of hills
–saari *Fin.* island
Sadd *Ar.* dam
Sagar, –ara *Hin., Urdu* lake
Saharā *Ar.* desert
Sahrâ *Ar.* desert
Sa'id *Ar.* highland
Sakar *Fin.* mountain
–Saki *Jap.* point
Sal. (Salar) *Span.* salt pan
Salina(s) *Span.* salt flat(s)
–salmi *Fin.* strait, sound, lake, channel
Saltsjöbad *Swed.* resort
Sammyaku *Jap.* mountain, range
Samut *Thai.* gulf
–San *Jap.* hill, mountain
Sap. (Sapadno) *Russ.* west
Sasso *It.* mountain
Se, Sé *I.-C.* river
Sebkha, –kra *Ar.* salt flats
See *Ger.* lake
–see *Ger.* sea
–şehir *Turk.* town
Selat *Mal.* strait
–selkä *Fin.* bay, lake, sound, ridge, hills
Selva *Span.* forest, wood
Seno *Span.* bay, sound
Serír *Ar.* desert of small stones
Serra *It., Port.* range of hills
Serranía *Span.* mountains
Sev. (Severo) *Russ.* north
–shahr *Pers.* city, town
Shan *Chin.* hills, mountains, pass
Shan-mo *Chin.* mountain range
Shatt *Ar.* river
–Shima *Jap.* island
Shimāli *Ar.* northern
–Shotō *Jap.* group of islands
Shuik'u *Chin.* reservoir
Sierra *Span.* hill, range
Sjö, sjön *Swed.* lake, bay, sea
Sjøen *Dan.* sea
Skär *Swed.* island, rock, cape
Skog *Nor.* forest
–skog, –skogen *Swed.* wood(s)
–skov *Dan.* forest
Slieve *Gae.* range of hills
–sø *Dan., Nor.* lake
Sør *Nor.* south, southern
Solonchak *Russ.* salt lake, marsh
Souk *Ar.* market
Spitze *Ger.* peak, mountain
–spruit *Afr.* stream
–stad *Afr., Nor., Swed.* town
–stadt *Ger.* town
Staður *Ice.* town
Stausee *Ger.* reservoir
Stenón *Gr.* strait, pass
Step *Russ.* plain
Str. (Stretto) *It.* strait
–strand *Dan., Nor.* beach
–strede *Nor.* straits
Strelka *Russ.* spit
–strete *Nor.* straits
Stretto *It.* strait
Stroedet *Dan.* strait
–ström, –strömmen *Swed.* stream(s)
–stroom *Afr.* large river
Suidō *Jap.* strait, channel
Sûn *Bur.* cape
Sund *Dan.* sound
–sund, –sundet *Swed.* sound, estuary, inlet
–sund(et) *Nor.* sound
Sungai, –ei *Mal.* river
Sungei *Mal.* river
Sur *Span.* south, southern
Sveti *Bulg.* pass
Syd *Dan., Swed.* south

Tai –tai *Chin.* tower
Tal *Mong.* plain, steppe
–tal *Ger.* valley
Tall *Ar.* hills, hummocks
Tandjung *Mal.* cape, headland
Tao *Chin.* island
Tassili *Ar.* rocky plateau
Tau *Russ.* mountain, range
Taung *Bur.* mountain, south
Taunggya *Bur.* pass
Tĕlok *I.-C., Mal.* bay bight
Teluk *Mal.* bay, gulf
Tg. (Tandjung) *Mal.* cape, headland
–thal *Ger.* valley
Thok *Tib.* town
Tierra *Span.* land, country
–tind *Nor.* peak
Tjärn, –en, –et *Swed.* lake
Tong *Nor.* village, town
Tong *Bur., Thai.* mountain range
Tonle *I.-C.* large river, lake
–träsk *Swed.* bog, swamp
Tsangpo *Tib.* large river
Tso *Tib.* lake
Tsu *Jap.* entrance, bay
Tulur *Ar.* hill
T'un *Chin.* village
Tung *Chin.* east
Tunnel *Fr.* tunnel
Tunturi *Fin.* hill(s), mountain(s), ridge

Uad *Ar.* dry watercourse, wadi
Udjung *Mal.* cape
Udd, udde, udden *Swed.* point, peninsula
Uebi *Somal.* river
Us *Mong.* water
Ust *Russ.* river mouth
Uul *Mong., Russ.* mountain, range

V. (Volcán) *Span.* volcano
–vaara *Fin.* hill, mountain, ridge, peak
–våg *Nor.* bay
Val *Fr., It.* valley
Valea *Rum.* valley
–vall, –vallen *Swed.* mountain
Valle *Span.* valley
Vallée *Fr.* valley
Valli *It.* lake, lagoon
Väst *Swed.* west
–vatn *Ice., Nor.* lake
Vatten *Swed.* lake
Vdkhr. (Vodokhranilishche) *Russ.* reservoir
–ved, –veden *Swed.* range, hills
Veld, –veld *Afr.* field
Velik/a, –e, –i, –o *Ser.Cr.* large
–vesi *Fin.* water, lake, bay sound, strait
Vest *Dan., Nor.* west
Vf. (vîrful) *Rum.* peak, mountain
–vidda *Nor.* plateau
Vig *Dan.* bay, inlet, cove, lagoon, lake, bight
–vik, –vika, –viken *Nor., Swed.* bay, cove, gulf, inlet, lake
Vila *Port.* small town
Villa *Span.* town
Ville *Fr.* town
Vinh *I.-C.* bay
Vîrful *Rum.* peak, mountain
–vlei *Afr.* pond, pool
Vodokhranilishche *Russ.* reservoir
Vol. (Volcán) *Span.* volcano, mountain
Vorota *Russ.* gate
Vostochnyy *Russ.* eastern
Vozyshennost *Russ.* heights, uplands
Vrata *Bulg.* gate, pass
Vrchovina *Cz.* mountainous country
Vrchy *Cz.* mountain range
Vung *I.-C.* gulf
–vuori *Fin.* mountain, hill

W. (Wādī) *Ar.* dry watercourse
Wâhât *Ar.* oasis
Wald *Ger.* wood, forest
Wan *Chin., Jap.* bay
Webi *Amh.* river
Woestyn *Afr.* desert

Yam *Heb.* sea
Yang *Chin.* ocean
Yazovir *Bulg.* reservoir
Yoma *Bur.* mountain range
–yüan *Chin.* spring

–**Z**aki *Jap.* peninsula
Zalew *Pol.* lagoon, swamp
Zaliv *Russ.* bay
Zan *Jap.* mountain
Zatoka *Pol.* bay
Zee *Dut.* sea
Zemlya *Russ.* land, island(s)